The 1991 Business One Irwin Business and Investment Almanac

The **1991** BUSINESS ONE IRWIN
Business and Investment Almanac

Edited by

Sumner N. Levine
State University of New York
at Stony Brook
and Editor
Financial Analyst's Handbook
and
The Investment Manager's Handbook

Executive Editor
Caroline Levine

BUSINESS ONE IRWIN
Homewood, Illinois 60430

Acquisitions editor: Amy Hollands
Project editor: Jean Roberts
Production manager: Carma W. Fazio
Compositor: Arcata Graphics/Kingsport
Typeface: 8/9 Caledonia
Printer: Arcata Graphics/Kingsport

The Library of Congress has catalogued this serial
publication as follows:

The . . . Business One Irwin business and investment almanac. —
1982-   — Homewood, Ill. : Business One Irwin, c1982-

  v. : ill. ; 24 cm.

Annual.
Editor: Sumner N. Levine.
Continues: Business One Irwin business almanac.
ISSN 0733-2610 = The Business One Irwin business and investment
almanac

  1. Business—Periodicals. 2. Investments—United States—Periodicals.
3. Corporations—United   States—Finance—Periodicals.   4. United
States—Economic conditions—1971-   —Periodicals. I. Levine, Sumner N. II. Business One Irwin. III. Title: Business One Irwin business
and investment almanac. IV. Title: Business and investment almanac.
HF5003.D68a   330.9'005   82–643830
                                               AACR 2 MARC-S

Library of Congress   [8711]

Printed in the United States of America
1 2 3 4 5 6 7 8 9 AGK 0 7 6 5 4 3 2 1 0

Preface

This 15th edition of the annual *Business One Irwin Business and Investment Almanac,* formerly the *Dow Jones-Irwin Business and Investment Almanac,* contains a number of new features in response to the rapidly changing business and investment scene as well as updates on our standard features.

The editor and publisher are, of course, pleased with the acceptance of the *Business One Irwin Business and Investment Almanac* as a standard and unique reference for the business and investment community. As always, we continue to invite suggestions from our readers. All suggestions should be sent to: *Business One Irwin Business and Investment Almanac,* P.O. Box D, Setauket, New York 11733.

Copies of the *Business One Business and Investment Almanac* may be ordered by calling: 1-800-634-3966 or by writing the order department: Business One Irwin, 1818 Ridge Road, Homewood, Illinois 60430.

Sumner N. Levine
Editor

Contents

The 1991 Business One Irwin Business and Investment Almanac

Business in Review

September 1989*

5 A UAL group is favored to win the bidding war for United Air's parent after unveiling a buy-out proposal Friday of $300 a share, or $6.75 billion. But the labor-management group, which is led by UAL's chairman and backed by British Airways, didn't get a quick agreement. UAL's board said it would study the bid, and rival suitor Marvin Davis indicated he may top $300 a share.

The economy remains healthy although manufacturing is still sluggish, latest reports indicate. The jobless rate stayed at a low 5.2% in August, but consumer confidence and a purchasing managers' index fell.

The Fed isn't likely to push interest rates down further unless there are major signs of economic weakness, policy makers suggested.

6 The dollar climbed to its highest level in 2½ months despite concerted intervention by at least a dozen central banks. The currency is being propelled by an unexpectedly strong U.S. economy and by growing speculation the Fed won't lower U.S. interest rates anytime soon, traders and analysts said.

Stocks and bonds edged lower as trading activity remained sluggish. The Dow Jones Industrial Average slipped 7.41 points to 2744.68.

United Airlines' largest union, the machinists, attacked a proposed $6.75 billion buy-out by management and the rival pilots union, but didn't rule out participating. The machinists union said piling extra debt on the carrier could threaten its survival.

7 RJR Nabisco has agreed to sell the fresh-fruit business of its Del Monte foods unit for about $875 million to Polly Peck, a London-based concern, sources said. The sale would be the

second in RJR's plan to divest about $6 billion in food operations.

The new S&L bail-out law is worded so confusingly that thrift and banking officials can't agree on such critical issues as the amount of capital that an S&L must maintain. The contradictory language stems from Congress's rush to finish the bill last month.

U.S. auto sales surged 21.4% in late August, buoyed partly by incentives that already are spreading to some 1990 models. Analysts and officials also cite buyer concerns about the price increases being planned for many models in the coming year.

8 United Air's machinists union said it has been contacted by Texas investor Robert Bass, the buy-out firm Kohlberg Kravis and "other investors" about a possible bid for parent UAL. The overtures suggest a $6.75 billion offer by UAL's pilots union and management may face unexpected competition. UAL's stock fell $5.125, to $281.75, on rumors Marvin Davis is selling his shares.

The stock-loan inquiry is looking into possible theft, money laundering and kickbacks in the stock-loan departments of major brokerage firms during the 1980s, sources said.

U.S. businesses have boosted plans for spending on new plant and equipment this year, signaling optimism about the economy. Capital outlays are now expected to rise 7.7%.

11 Plessey was acquired by GEC and Siemens after a nearly 10-month fight. The $3.1 billion acquisition is the latest in what is expected to be a wave of mergers in European electronics.

Campeau will submit a restructuring proposal to directors tomorrow that includes plans to sell the Bloomingdale's chain. Campeau confirmed that Bloomingdale's chief may lead a management buy-out of the unit.

12 Two options-brokerage firms were accused by the CFTC of using fraudulent, high-pressure sales tactics to bilk customers out of hundreds of millions of dollars. It is the biggest such case in the agency's history.

The generic-drug scandal continued to grow. FDA officials reported finding

---

* The cut-off date for Business in Review is usually Labor Day because of our production schedule. Since the last entry in the previous *Almanac* was September 1, 1989, the current entry commences September 5, 1989.

manufacturing and record-keeping problems at all but two of the 12 companies being investigated.

Drexel formally pleaded guilty to six felony counts and paid the government over $500 million, capping a three-year federal investigation stemming from the Ivan Boesky scandal.

13 A United Air group plans to present a financing plan for its $300-a-share, $6.75 billion, bid to UAL's board tomorrow in hopes of gaining approval over rival suitor Marvin Davis. UAL shares surged $4.625, to $281, amid signs the group is close to wrapping up financing from banks.

The U.S. current account gap widened further in the second quarter despite improving merchandise trade. There was a rare deficit in services trade, which one economist blamed on the high cost of U.S. foreign debt.

Bush officials will try to help U.S. exporters by seeking talks with trading partners to limit their use of export-related foreign assistance.

14 Campeau disclosed a severe cash crunch, sparking jitters throughout financial markets. The Toronto-based retail and real estate company said its largest holder, Olympia & York, may gain control under a complex accord that would inject $250 million into Campeau. Sources said Olympia & York is likely to break up Campeau and sell additional assets besides Bloomingdale's.

Junk-bond prices plunged in reaction to Campeau's woes, causing a sell-off in stocks, bonds and the dollar. The Dow Jones industrials closed off 27.74 points, at 2679.52.

U.S. auto sales softened in early September following a 13.1% jump in August. Analysts, surprised by the extent of the weakness, cited shortages of some popular models and continued caution among consumers.

15 Junk-bond prices plunged again as the market became caught in its worst shakeout ever. Buying has temporarily dried up for hundreds of issues, particularly those of Campeau.

Stock prices fell further, hurt by the turmoil in junk-bonds and a modest gain in August retail sales. The Dow Jones industrials fell 14.63, to 2664.89. Bonds and the dollar rose.

Campeau's retail suppliers were told to stop shipping merchandise to the company's Federated and Allied department-store chains because of Campeau's severe cash crunch.

Retail sales rose 0.7% in August, mainly due to a 2.6% surge in auto buying that is expected to stall this month. July sales rose 0.5% rather than 0.9% reported initially.

United Air's machinists union said it won't join a $6.75 billion pilot-management bid for UAL and urged directors to reject the offer. One machinist union leader also raised the specter of a strike to try to disrupt the bid.

18 Campeau agreed to terms of a $250 million loan from Olympia & York that would give the Reichmann-controlled company greater influence over the cash-starved Toronto concern. Campeau Chairman Robert Campeau "is no longer calling the shots on his own," an executive said. Meanwhile, more factoring firms told manufacturers to stop shipping goods to Federated and Allied stores.

Economic growth and inflation remain moderate, latest statistics show. Producer prices fell 0.4% in August, led by a 7.3% drop in energy costs. Industrial output climbed 0.3%, the fastest pace since April, though mainly due to special factors.

The U.S. trade deficit shrank further in July, to $7.58 billion, the smallest level in 4½ years. Imports declined 2.5%, reflecting the slowing economy, though exports fell 1.8%.

U.S. auto makers plan to build fewer cars in the fourth quarter than in any three-month period since the recessionary final quarter of 1982. Their caution contrasts with the aggressive output earlier this year.

UAL suitor Marvin Davis said he won't fight the company's agreement to be acquired by a pilot-management group for $6.75 billion. But the investor offered to buy the carrier at the same price if the buy-out collapses.

19 Manufacturers Hanover unveiled a major recapitalization under which it will sell a 4.9% stake to Dai-Ichi Kangyo Bank of Japan. The plan also includes a $950 million addition to reserves, an equity issue of up to $500 million and the sale of control of its CIT Group to Dai-Ichi Kangyo for $1.28 billion. Manufacturers hope to ease worries about its huge Third World loan portfolio and comparatively weak capital base.

20 Campeau reached a definitive accord in which it will cede substantial control to Olympia & York in return for a $250 million loan. Olympia & York also will supervise a major restructuring of the

Toronto-based retail and real estate concern. Apparel makers, many of which halted shipments to Campeau stores last week, had mixed reactions.

Junk-bond prices staged a partial recovery following news of the Campeau bail-out. The market was thrown into turmoil last week by disclosures about the company's financial woes.

Consumer prices held steady in August, the first time in over three years they didn't rise. A drop in energy costs kept prices in check, though economists remain wary about inflation. Housing starts fell 5%, the biggest slide in six months.

21 Chase Manhattan raised its reserves for troubled Third World loans by $1.15 billion, which will result in a $1.11 billion quarterly loss. The move, which other banks are likely to follow, could hurt Mexico's chances of getting enough new bank loans to bolster its economy and meet interest payments. Meanwhile, Chase plans a $500 million new-share issue to shore up its capital.

The dollar tumbled amid worries of stepped-up intervention, helping push bonds lower. Stocks also eased after waffling all day. The Dow Jones industrials lost 3.42, to 2683.89

France's biggest chemical and drug concern, Rhone-Poulenc, continued its U.S. expansion, agreeing to buy chemical units of GAF and RTZ for a total of about $1.3 billion.

22 J. P. Morgan became the latest major bank to boost Third World loan-loss reserves with a $2 billion addition, the biggest so far. The move will result in a $1.8 billion quarterly loss for Morgan, parent of Morgan Guaranty Trust. It also increases the likelihood that the recently announced pact to reduce Mexico's foreign bank debt may fail.

Several major airlines moved to match the fare increases proposed recently by American Airlines, making it more likely that some ticket prices will rise sharply next week.

Second-quarter GNP was revised to a 2.5% growth rate, slightly below last month's estimate but well above the initial calculation. The final report supported the view that the economy was fairly healthy but slowing down.

Campeau's agreement with Olympia & York this week for a $250 million loan has set the stage for what could become a nasty battle between Campeau and its bondholders.

25 The dollar's recent rise was criticized by the Group of Seven industrial nations as "inconsistent with longer run economic fundamentals." The statement, following a Saturday meeting in Washington, was the group's strongest sign yet of concern about the currency. But it wasn't clear what steps officials might take to combat the dollar's advance.

Chrysler sold nearly half of its 21.8% stake in Mitsubishi Motors for an after-tax profit of $310 million. Chrysler, which is planning major capital outlays, said it was cashing in on Mitsubishi's soaring value.

Michelin Group agreed to buy Uniroyal for $690 million, making the French company the world's largest tiremaker. The pact also marks the latest inroad by a foreign firm in the North American tire market.

26 The dollar plunged on concerted central-bank intervention, hurting stock and bond prices. The dollar sell-off was planned by the Group of Seven at its meeting Saturday, where officials agreed that the currency was too high, sources said. The Dow Jones industrials closed off 22.42 points, at 2659.19, while 30-year Treasury bonds lost over a point.

UAL's stock tumbled $7.125, to $274, amid concerns the Transportation Department may force a change in the $6.79 billion labor-management buyout of United Air's parent.

U.S. vehicle sales surged 12.6% in mid-September, boosted by strong truck sales at GM and a rush by consumers to beat price increases on 1990-model vehicles. But auto makers are still facing a sluggish market.

27 Two accounting giants ended merger talks that would have created the world's biggest accounting firm. Arthur Andersen and Price Waterhouse cited differences that would have taken too long to resolve.

Durable-goods orders jumped 3.8% in August, led by a sharp rise in automobile orders. The increase, the largest since December, was a boost for the manufacturing sector, which has been a drag on the economy.

28 IBM said its profit for the third quarter and full year will be well below analysts' expectations. The computer giant blamed delayed introduction of a new disk drive, a shift toward leasing and the strong dollar. Many analysts said IBM didn't lower its sights enough and that the problems might continue into 1990.

Sony signed a definitive agreement to buy Columbia Pictures for $3.4 billion, or $27 a share. Sony acknowledged it is discussing putting Hollywood executives Peter Guber and Jon Peters in top posts at Columbia.

Toyota is raising prices on its most popular car lines for 1990 by 2.5% or less in an aggressive attempt to increase its U.S. market share.

The dollar fell sharply as central banks continued to sell the U.S. currency. Stock prices moved higher but long-term bond prices slipped.

Paul Bilzerian was sentenced to four years in prison and fined $1.5 million on nine felony counts related to his takeover activities.

29 Auto makers plan to idle at least nine car and truck assembly plants next week due to slow sales, a sign that the car makers may face rough going for the rest of the year.

October 1989

2 Leading economic indicators rose 0.3% in August, their best showing since April, indicating the economy's slow growth is likely to continue. But some economists believe the threat of a recession still exists.

3 USX Corp. put on the block the oil and gas reserves of its recently acquired Texas Oil & Gas unit, valued at more than $1 billion. The steel and energy giant said proceeds will go to trim its debt load and repurchase stock. But some analysts speculated that a cash-flush USX might seek another acquisition.

The economy continued to show signs of weakness in September for the fifth consecutive month, a survey of purchasing managers showed.

New-construction spending rose 1.8% in August after slipping for two months, but spending for private residential projects eased slightly.

Coca-Cola's board approved the sale of its 49% stake in Columbia Pictures to Sony and said it expects to report an after-tax gain of $530 million as a result of the move. Directors also approved the buy-back of up to 20 million of Coke's common shares.

The Supreme Court decided that the states are free, at least for now, to prosecute corporate officials for workplace hazards that are also regulated by federal job safety laws.

4 Stock prices soared in a flurry of buying that pushed the Dow Jones industrials up 40.84 points to a record 2754.56. The surge caught some analysts by surprise, many of whom had been looking for a market correction. The dollar rallied sharply as central bank intervention ebbed, and bond prices also rose.

New factory orders surged 2.9% in August, fueled by strong auto bookings, more than making up for July's 2% decline. New-home sales remained strong in August, although running 0.4% below July's pace.

Oil prices are being propped up by developing countries, whose appetite for fuel is growing 60% faster than total world demand this year.

5 Auto makers ended the 1989-model year with the fifth-highest sales ever. But the results reflected unprecedented rebates and cut-rate financing to lure consumers into showrooms.

The Senate Finance panel filled its tax-and-spending bill with billions of dollars of breaks for wealthy people and narrow business interests. A capital-gains tax cut was defeated.

The fierce political battle over cutting capital-gains taxes has left Bush's budget strategy in shambles.

6 American Air received an informal $7.54 billion takeover offer from developer Donald Trump, fueling the airline takeover frenzy. AMR's stock rose $16.875, to $99.875, well below Trump's $120-a-share bid, reflecting doubts about Trump's intent and the possibility of a takeover. American is expected to resist any potential suitor, and Congress may crack down on airline takeovers.

GM and Chrysler reached an unprecedented accord to jointly manufacture key auto parts in the U.S. Previously, the Big Three makers have only cooperated in research.

BMW and Mercedes-Benz became the latest luxury-car makers to attempt to hold the line on 1990 model prices amid growing competition.

The dollar strengthened despite interest rate increases in Europe and continued dollar-selling by central banks. The dollar's resilience raised questions about the Group of Seven's intervention effort. Bonds soared, while the stock rally slowed.

Thrifts rescued in 1988 by the government are losing money at an unexpectedly fast rate, driving up the potential costs of the S&L bail-out plan and adding over $2 billion to thrift losses for the first half of 1989.

9 The Fed is resisting pressure to cut interest rates, though analysts say a reduction is likely in coming weeks because of the economy's unexpected sluggishness and the dollar's continued strength. The dollar gained Friday, as did bond and stock prices.

The jobless rate rose to 5.3% in September from 5.2% as factory jobs fell sharply. The report signaled a severe weakening in manufacturing and softness in the overall economy.

Some AMR shareholders said they wouldn't necessarily back Chairman Robert Crandall's "just-say-no" defense against a $7.54 billion takeover bid by developer Donald Trump.

10 The Big Three car makers may each report a quarterly loss in core North American auto operations, the first time that has happened since the recession year 1982. GM, Ford and Chrysler are still likely to post an overall profit for the period due to other businesses, but earnings may be down as much as 50%. The drop indicates the industry's vulnerability to excess production capacity.

Corporate profits are slipping after thriving for two years. The recent spate of disappointing earnings reports could signal turbulence ahead for the country's economy.

Jaguar confirmed it is holding talks with General Motors about selling a minority stake and setting up joint ventures. Such an alliance could be used against Ford, which Jaguar considers an unwelcome suitor.

11 Saatchi & Saatchi said it had been approached by "one or more" parties interested in "possible restructuring transactions." A Memphis firm that owns 10.24% of the ad giant also may hold talks with third parties.

12 Ford is taking advantage of a special tax loophole to save what experts predict will be millions of dollars. The auto maker has quietly formed a new holding company for some of its major financial units, including the newly acquired Associates, and is selling a 25% stake in it privately for $800 million. The innovative transaction could be imitated by other multinational corporations.

Renault and Volvo are exploring a merger amid mounting global competition. But a combination of the French and Swedish firms, which would create the world's fourth-largest auto maker and biggest truck maker, faces major obstacles.

Toyota Motor plans to more than double its North American car and truck-manufacturing capacity by 1995. The move will put more pressure on the Big Three U.S. auto makers in an already glutted American market.

13 Saatchi & Saatchi announced a major management reorganization that appears to remove co-founder Maurice Saatchi from day-to-day operations. Meanwhile, a top Saatchi unit executive, Carl Spielvogel, said he has offered to lead a management buy-out of the troubled British advertising and communication giant, but the company rebuffed him.

Japan's trade surplus shrank in September for the fifth month in a row, helped by a stronger dollar. But the surplus with the U.S. widened, and analysts caution that the weaker yen is spurring Japanese exports.

A top Chrysler official said the auto maker barely broke even on operations in the third quarter. The assessment was worse than analysts expected, though not a total surprise in the competitive auto market.

16 U.S. officials moved to head off any repeat of Black Monday today following Friday's plunge in stock prices. Fed Chairman Greenspan signaled that the central bank was prepared to inject massive amounts of money into the banking system to prevent a financial crisis. Other officials in the U.S. and other countries also mapped out plans, but kept their moves quiet to avoid making financial markets more jittery.

Friday's sell-off was triggered by the collapse of UAL's buy-out plan and a big rise in producer prices. The Dow Jones industrials skidded 190.58, to 2569.26. The junk-bond market came to a standstill, while Treasury bonds soared and the dollar fell.

Prospects for a new UAL buy-out proposal appear bleak. Many banks refused to back the $6.79 billion transaction, but bankers said it was not from any unwillingness to finance takeovers. The decision was based solely on problems with the UAL management-pilot plan, they said.

The surge in producer prices in September followed three months of declines, but analysts were divided on whether the 0.9% jump signaled a severe worsening of inflation. Also, retail sales grew 0.5% last month.

General Motors signaled that up to five North American assembly plants may close by the mid-1990s as it tries to cut excess capacity.

U.S. car and truck sales fell 12.6% in early October, the first sales period of the 1990-model year, dragged down by a sharp decline in GM sales.

The Boeing strike is starting to affect airlines. America West said Friday it will postpone its new service out of Houston because of delays in receiving aircraft from Boeing.

Warner and Sony are entangled in a legal battle over movie producers Peter Gruber and Jon Peters. The fight could set back Sony's plans to enter the U.S. movie business.

Hooker's U.S. unit received a $409 million bid for most of its real-estate and shopping-center assets from an investor group. The offer doesn't include Bonwit Teller or B. Altman.

17 The stock market avoided a repeat of Black Monday as prices rallied from an early slide, spurred by bargain-hunting institutions and program traders. The Dow Jones industrials closed up 88.12 points, at 2657.38, the fourth-biggest gain ever, after being down as much as 63 points in the morning. The rally erased about half of Friday's 190.58-point plunge, but analysts are cautious about the market's outlook.

The dollar also rebounded, while bond prices plummeted and Treasury bill rates soared. Junk-bonds also recovered somewhat, though trading remained stalled. Gold also rose.

The Fed eased some jitters by allowing the key federal funds rate to drift lower. The central bank also didn't have to inject huge amounts of money into the banking system.

Donald Trump withdrew his $7.54 billion offer for American Air, citing the "recent change in market conditions." Also, a UAL group tried to get financing for a lower bid, possibly $250 a share. AMR fell 22.125, to 76.50, while UAL slid 56.875, to 222.875.

Leveraged buy-outs of airlines would be subject to approval by the transportation secretary under a bill passed by a House subcommittee.

IBM's earnings tumbled 30% in the third quarter, slightly more than expected. The computer giant partly cited a stronger dollar and a delay in shipping a new high-end disk drive. Analysts are downbeat about IBM's outlook for the next few quarters.

U.S. auto makers plan to decrease car production 10.4% in the fourth quarter, with virtually all the decline coming from the Big Three. Output at Japanese-owned and managed plants in the U.S. is due to rise 42%.

The Supreme Court agreed to decide whether a federal court may dismantle a merger that has won regulatory approval but been ruled anticompetitive in a private antitrust suit.

18 UAL's stock skidded a further $24.875, to $198, as British Airways indicated it may balk at any hastily revised version of the aborted $6.79 billion buyout of United Air. British Air, a partner in the buy-out group, hinted it would prefer starting any new deal from scratch. UAL has fallen $81.75, or 29%, in the two trading days since disclosure of the buy-out's collapse jolted the stock market into its second-worst plunge.

Stock prices fell broadly in heavy trading, dominated by futures-related program selling and further declines by UAL and other airline stocks. The Dow Jones industrials closed off 18.65 points, at 2638.73, after plunging over 60.25 points in the morning. Bond prices ended lower after an early rally, while the dollar was mixed.

The U.S. trade deficit swelled to $10.77 billion in August, prompting worries that the nation's export drive had stalled. Exports declined for the second month in a row, while imports rose to a record. An analyst called it one of the worst trade reports since the dollar bottomed out in 1987.

Industrial output fell 0.1% in September, the latest sign manufacturing is slowing. An analyst cited weaker capital spending and exports.

19 Insurers are facing billions of dollars in damage claims from the California quake. But most businesses in the Bay area, including Silicon Valley, weren't greatly affected. Computer and software companies in the region are expecting virtually no long-term disruption in shipments. Meanwhile, investors quickly singled out stocks of companies expected to profit or suffer from the disaster.

Leveraged buy-outs may be curbed by two rules in pending congressional legislation. The provisions, in deficit-reduction bills recently passed by the House and Senate, could raise the price tags of such deals by up to 10% and cool the takeover boom.

A bill giving the Transportation Department the power to block airline leveraged buy-outs cleared a House panel. But Secretary Skinner said he would urge Bush to veto the bill.

Housing starts sank 5.2% in September to the lowest level since October 1982, when there was a recession. The report suggests housing is still being hurt by the Fed's inflation battle, which pushed up rates.

British Airways said it is seeking improved terms and a sharply lower price in any revised bid for United Air's parent. The British carrier also confirmed it isn't committed to going forward with any new bid. UAL's stock fell $6.25, to $191.75.

Stock prices rose slightly as trading slowed, while bonds ended little changed despite a slumping dollar. The Dow Jones industrials gained 4.92, to 2643.65. But investors remain wary about stocks, partly because of turmoil in the junk-bond market.

20 Stocks and bonds surged on the second anniversary of Black Monday as a favorable inflation report prompted speculation of lower interest rates. The Dow Jones industrials closed up 39.55, at 2683.20, after rising over 60 points in mid-afternoon. The rally brought the gain so far this week to about 114 points. The dollar finished mixed, while gold declined.

Consumer prices climbed a moderate 0.2% in September, mostly due to higher clothing costs. Energy prices continued to fall at the retail level, but economists worried about a big rise in wholesale energy costs.

23 A revised bid for UAL is being prepared by a labor-management group, sources said. The new proposal, which would transfer majority ownership of United Air's parent to employees and leave some stock in public hands, would be valued at $225 to $240 a share, or as much as $5.42 billion. But UAL's board isn't expected to give quick approval to any offer substantially below the $300-a-share bid that collapsed recently.

Takeover stock speculators have incurred paper losses of over $700 million from the failed UAL offer, their worst loss ever on a single deal.

Stock prices edged up in quiet trading Friday. The Dow Jones industrials rose 5.94, to 2689.14, making the gain for the week a record 119.88 points, or 4.7%. Most bond prices fell, but junk-bonds and the dollar rose.

New York City bonds were sold off by many investors last week amid political and economic uncertainty.

OPEC's ability to produce more oil than it can sell is starting to cast a shadow over world oil markets. OPEC officials worry that prices could collapse a few months from now if the group doesn't adopt new quotas.

24 United Air's parent quashed any immediate prospects of a buy-out, saying UAL should remain independent for now. Directors didn't specifically address an informal bid by a UAL management labor group, though the group lacked firm financing for its revised proposal. UAL said it wanted to focus again on running the airline, but it signaled willingness to consider future proposals.

About 200,000 East Germans marched in Leipzig and thousands more staged protests in three other cities in a fresh challenge to the Communist leadership to introduce democratic freedoms. In an East Berlin suburb, meanwhile, employees at an electronics plant formed an independent trade union called Reform, a worker spokesman said.

Hungary declared itself a democracy and for the first time openly commemorated the anniversary of the 1956 anti-Stalinist uprising that was crushed by the Soviet Union. A crowd estimated at 100,000 held a torch-lit march through Budapest as Acting President Szuros delivered a nationally televised address rejecting communist dominance.

25 Car and truck sales slid 20.5% in mid-October as U.S. manufacturers paid the price for heavy incentives earlier in the year. GM continued to be hardest hit, with car sales slumping 24.8% and truck sales 26%.

Durable goods orders slipped 0.1% in September, reflecting weakening auto demand after a spurt of orders for new 1990 models. Excluding transportation items, orders rose 1.8%, a positive sign for manufacturing.

Stock prices swung wildly as the market reacted to an initial plunge by UAL shares, followed by a sharp rebound in the afternoon. The Dow Jones industrials, down 85 points in the morning, closed off 3.69, at 2659.22. Bond prices surged in reaction to the sell-off in stocks, then eased slightly during the afternoon recovery. The dollar finished lower.

UAL's stock regained most of an early loss amid speculation that one or more investors may challenge the decision by United Air's parent to remain independent. The stock closed down $8.375, at $170, after plunging $33 in the morning, to $145.

26 The Big Board will launch its own vehicle for program trading today amid growing controversy over the practice. The new "baskets" of stocks will allow big investors to buy or sell all 500 S&P index stocks in a single trade. The exchange says the product, which the SEC cleared yesterday, will ease instead of worsen market volatility.

SEC Chairman Breeden said he would consider imposing "circuit breakers" to halt program trading during sharp swings in the market.

Kemper Financial Services has stopped executing its stock trades through four big securities firms because of their involvement in program trading, which Kemper and others say is ruining the market.

Bethlehem Steel's profit plunged 54% in the third quarter, hurt by higher costs and lower shipments to key clients. Also, Armco and National Intergroup had lower operating profit in steel, marking what may be the end of a two-year industry boom.

27 The U.S. economy grew at a moderate 2.5% annual rate in the third quarter despite the worst trade performance in six years. The expansion, matching the second quarter's pace, was fueled by strong consumer spending, especially for autos. But analysts expect GNP growth to slow in the current quarter. An inflation gauge slowed to a 2.9% growth rate from 5% the previous quarter.

The Big Three car makers all posted quarterly losses in core U.S. auto operations for the first time since 1982. A sharp decline in third-quarter vehicle sales at General Motors, Ford and Chrysler also dimmed the outlook for the remainder of the year.

GM is seeking to buy up to 15% of Jaguar, marking its first salvo in a looming battle with Ford for control of the British luxury car maker.

Stock prices tumbled amid growing concern about corporate earnings. The Dow Jones industrials closed off 39.55 points, at 2613.73. Most bonds eased, but long-term Treasury issues edged up. The dollar also gained, especially against the British pound.

Treasury Secretary Brady said the SEC should be given the authority to close the stock markets in a crisis. Earlier, SEC Chairman Breeden said he doesn't want such power because it could end up disrupting the markets.

30 Program trading is being curbed by more securities firms, but big institutional investors are expected to continue the practice, further roiling the stock market. Bowing to criticism, Bear Stearns, Morgan Stanley and Oppenheimer joined PaineWebber in suspending stock-index arbitrage trading for their own accounts. Still, stock-index funds are expected to continue launching big programs in the market.

Several Big Board firms are organizing to complain about program trading and the exchange's role in it. The effort is being led by Contel.

Personal spending rose 0.2% in September, the smallest gain in a year. The slowdown raises questions about the economy's strength because spending fueled much of the third-quarter GNP growth. Meanwhile, personal income edged up 0.3%.

Factory owners are buying new machinery at a healthy rate this fall, machine-tool makers say. But weak car sales raise questions about future demand from the auto sector.

RJR Nabisco agreed to sell three candy businesses to Nestle for $370 million. The accord helps RJR pay off debt and boosts Nestle's 7% share of the U.S. candy market to 12%.

31 More securities firms are bowing to the public outcry over program trading. GE's Kidder Peabody unit said it would stop doing stock-index arbitrage for its own account, while Merrill Lynch said it was halting such trading for itself as well as for clients. Also, Big Board Chairman Phelan met with stock specialists who are angry over his recent remarks that computer-driven trading strategies were "here to stay."

A big pension-insurance case will be reviewed by the Supreme Court. The justices agreed to decide whether federal insurers can require LTV to take back responsibility for funding its $2.3 billion pension shortfall.

Drug companies lost a major liability case. The Supreme Court let stand a New York ruling that all manufacturers of an anti-miscarriage drug are liable for injuries or deaths if the actual maker isn't known.

November 1989

1 A new minimum-wage plan has been worked out by Congress and Bush, opening the way for the first increase in over nine years. The compromise proposal, ending a long impasse between Democrats and the president, would boost the minimum wage to $4.25 an hour by April 1991 from $3.35

now. The legislation also includes a lower "training wage" for new workers who are teenagers.

The Big Board is considering reviving a curb on program trading when the market is volatile. The exchange, which abandoned such a "collar" last year because it didn't prevent sharp price swings, has been under attack recently for not taking action against program trading.

Leading indicators rose a slight 0.2% in September, a further indication the economy is slowing but without any clear sign of whether a recession looms. Meanwhile, new-home sales plunged 14% in the month.

Labor costs climbed 1.2% in private industry during the third quarter, matching the second-quarter rise. Health-insurance costs soared.

2 Economic growth appears to be leveling off, latest reports suggest. Factory orders and construction outlays were largely flat in September, while purchasing agents said manufacturing shrank further in October. Still, many economists aren't predicting a recession anytime soon.

The Fed is coming under pressure to cut short-term interest rates due to the apparent slowing of the economy. But it isn't clear yet whether the central bank will make such a move.

The Chicago Merc plans an additional "circuit breaker" to stem sharp drops in the market. Also, Big Board Chairman Phelan said he would support SEC halts of program trading during market crises but not any revival of a "collar" on trading.

3 A capital-gains tax cut appears unlikely this year. Republicans effectively ended their fight to enact a reduction, conceding that Democrats had enough votes to block it. Lawmakers in both parties have long said that they are more likely to approve a reduction in the capital-gains tax rate next year as part of a big deficit-reduction package.

Ford agreed to pay $2.5 billion for Jaguar, thwarting efforts by arch-rival General Motors to acquire the British luxury car maker. But Ford's victory comes at a high price.

Non-farm productivity grew at a 2.1% annual rate in the third quarter, up from 1.1% in the second quarter and a 1.3% drop in the first period.

6 U.S. car and light truck sales fell 2.8% in late October, ending the industry's slowest month since the October 1987 stock crash. The Big Three had trouble

persuading consumers to buy higher-priced 1990 models.

Corporate profits tumbled 21% in the third quarter, pulled down by major banks boosting loan-loss reserves. Auto makers and oil firms also had declines. Gainers included communications and forest products.

The jobless rate stayed at 5.3% in October as new hiring by government and the service sector offset continued layoffs in manufacturing. Friday's report showed the economy is continuing to expand modestly.

Stock and bond prices fell as the unemployment news cooled speculation that the Fed would push interest rates lower soon. The Dow Jones industrials closed down 2.05 points, at 2629.51. The dollar was mixed.

7 The Dalkon Shield case has cleared what may be the final hurdle. The Supreme Court refused to hear challenges to A. H. Robins's settlement plan, clearing the way for thousands of women claimants to receive payments for injuries from the birth-control device. The court's decision also clears the way for Robins to emerge from Chapter 11 and to be acquired by American Home Products.

A Wisconsin takeover law that limits hostile bids won't be reviewed by the Supreme Court. The justices' refusal to hear a challenge to the law indicates states have substantial authority to regulate hostile offers.

Saudi Arabia reported a significant find of high-quality, low-sulfur oil that is relatively scarce in the Mideast. The discovery should help the kingdom's revenue base because lighter crudes draw premium prices.

8 The Fed began easing credit yesterday in the face of a continued slowdown of the economy, according to government officials. The move should push the key federal funds rate to 8½% from 8¾% and allow other interest rates to drop. Though most analysts don't foresee a recession soon, they do predict economic growth will slow to a rate of slightly over 1% in coming months.

Bond prices rallied on indications of the Fed easing, while the stock market's response was more muted. The Dow Jones industrials closed up 14.96, at 2597.13. The dollar fell.

United Air's parent has given UAL Chairman Stephen Wolf permission to explore new efforts for a buy-out or recapitalization of the carrier. Also, the United pilots union has tried to contact outside investors such as Robert Bass to help fund a buy-out.

The Big Board has teamed up with two Chicago futures exchanges to investigate possible manipulative program trading during July. The inquiry was started prior to the stock market's steep slide on October 13.

Institutional investors that use program trading haven't pulled back despite the Big Board's call last week for a voluntary retreat. Also, some portfolio managers say they have few alternatives to program trading.

Braniff shut down its operations shortly after midnight Monday, saying it hopes to survive its second bankruptcy filing by becoming a charter airline. Braniff will lay off most of its remaining 2,000 employees, keeping about 150 to operate charters.

9 Bear Stearns quietly imposed a $2.50 "handling" charge on all individual investors' stock and bond trades. The brokerage firm is among the last to charge an added fee for such transactions as Wall Street struggles to shore up revenues.

More program trading is being done outside the Big Board through "off-exchange" electronic systems. Big institutional investors have been trading as many as six million shares a day in such "third markets."

A minimum-wage bill cleared the Senate and was sent to the White House for Bush's expected signature. The bill raises the minimum wage for the first time in over nine years.

10 Producer prices rose 0.4% in October, led by the steepest gain in food costs in almost two years. Though the increase was somewhat higher than expected, many analysts saw signs that inflation is moderating. Excluding the volatile food and energy sectors, prices rose only 0.1%. Also, prices for raw and intermediate products were flat last month.

A major financial scandal was reported in London. British police charged 11 people and the securities units of two big European banks in connection with alleged irregularities in a 1987 rights issue for Blue Arrow.

Lloyds Bank and NatWest sharply boosted loss reserves for troubled Third World loans. Other big British banks are expected to follow.

NBC agreed to pay $600 million for the rights to broadcast four years of National Basketball Association games, a move likely to accelerate the surge in sports-rights fees.

13 Ford Motor Chairman Donald Petersen is taking an early retirement after nearly a decade in the top job. He will be succeeded by Vice Chairman Harold Poling, who is delaying his own retirement for three years. Petersen led the No. 2 auto maker to record earnings, a renaissance of styling and one of the most successful cultural revolutions in corporate America. But Poling is facing some major challenges ahead.

The junk-bond market appears to have bottomed out after a long slide. Last week's advance of actively traded issues was the longest sustained rally in over two months.

14 Nynex reached a tentative settlement with its two striking unions after the company dropped its demand that employees pay part of their health-care premiums. In return, the unions agreed to a lower wage package. The health-care dispute has been the most contentious issue in the three-month-old strike.

Merck said near-term earnings growth will be slowed somewhat by heavy research and sales costs. Profit had risen about 25% a quarter.

Japan's trade surplus slid 39% in October, led by an unexpected drop in exports, the first in over four years.

15 Industrial and retail sectors weakened sharply in October. Output at factories, mines and utilities tumbled 0.7%, causing U.S. industry to operate at 82.8% of capacity, the lowest in 1½ years. Retail sales sank 1% last month, the steepest drop in over 2½ years, as auto sales plunged. Also, car and truck sales slid 20.2% in early November, portending more plant shutdowns that would further slow the nation's economy.

Stock prices slumped in reaction to the slowing economy, particularly the drop in auto sales. The Dow Jones industrials lost 16.18 points, to 2610.25. The dollar and bond prices also fell.

The Chicago Board Options Exchange is investigating possible manipulation of stock-index options as part of program trading-activity. The CBOE is the fourth exchange searching for program-trading abuses.

Efforts to give the SEC the power to halt program trading appear to have become stymied in Congress.

16 General Electric agreed to buy a majority stake in Hungary's state-owned lighting manufacturer. The $150 million deal is one of the biggest investments yet by a U.S. company in liberalized Eastern Europe.

U.S. aid for HDTV research will be cut off in next year's budget proposal by Bush, officials said. The administration also may curb federal support for several other research programs.

Two more computer makers refused to join U.S. Memories, the venture that hopes to challenge Japan's dominance of the semiconductor memory chip market.

Merrill Lynch said that it is ceasing all business connected with South Africa, including the trading or research of South African stocks.

Business inventories edged up 0.2% in September as sales eased 0.3%, the latest sign the economy is slowing. A buildup in retail stocks offset declines at manufacturers and wholesalers.

17 The trade deficit narrowed sharply in September, to $7.94 billion, the lowest level in five years. Imports tumbled 3.9% from a record high the previous month, while exports climbed 1.9%. Still, analysts were cautious, saying the improvement in trade mainly reflected the slowdown in the nation's economy, which reduces demand for imports.

Financial markets had mixed reactions to the trade report. Stocks and the dollar edged up, while long-term bond prices eased. The Dow Jones industrials closed up 3.08, at 2635.66.

Continental Airlines agreed to buy up to 40 medium and long-range aircraft from Airbus Industrie, the European consortium, in a transaction valued at as much as $4.5 billion. It is the second major plane order by the Texas Air unit in recent months.

20 General Electric plans to buy back up to $10 billion of its stock over five years, reflecting optimistic earnings forecasts and a change in direction after a decade of expansion. The company also boosted its dividend 15%. GE stock rose $2 to $59.50.

U.S. auto makers plan to reduce fourth-quarter car production to a seven-year low, reflecting the recent slowdown in sales and an uncertain outlook for early 1990. But Japanese-owned plants are boosting output.

Boeing reached a tentative settlement with the striking Machinists union, apparently ending a six-week old walkout. The three-year contract proposal, which was devised by a federal mediator, is due to be voted on by the rank and file tonight. A settlement would be good news for Boeing and its customers, which are anxiously awaiting planes from the company's $85 billion backlog.

Dual trading doesn't significantly add liquidity to commodities markets, a long-awaited CFTC study said. The regulatory agency plans to press ahead with curbs on the practice.

Housing starts rebounded 12% in October after two months of declines. Analysts said the rise reflected falling mortgage rates and doesn't signal a general economic resurgence.

21 Stock prices tumbled as expectations of a major cut in U.S. military spending prompted investors to dump defense shares. The Dow Jones industrials slid 20.62, to 2632.04. Bonds rose modestly and the dollar was mixed.

Most big securities firms are planning more layoffs as the industry continues to retrench. Many are being battered by renewed investor skittishness toward Wall Street following the October 13 plunge in stock prices.

22 A $6 billion tax-rise plan was worked out by congressional leaders and received Bush's support. The package, part of a broader deficit-reduction measure, contains mostly obscure tax-law changes that include increases in some excise taxes and modest restriction of tax benefits for corporate leveraged buy-outs. But the Social Security payroll tax also would rise.

A plan to cut the deficit by at least $14.7 billion in fiscal 1990 also was embraced by Bush. The bipartisan measure, which includes $4.6 billion in across-the-board spending cuts, is expected to pass Congress easily.

General Motors hopes to cut its U.S. white collar work force up to 25% in the next four to five years. The auto maker is making a renewed effort to streamline amid slumping sales and growing competition.

Merrill Lynch has begun a restructuring that will include lower bonuses, at least hundreds of layoffs, and the closing of unprofitable lines. The securities firm is the latest to cut costs amid Wall Street's continued slump.

Consumer prices rose 0.5% in October, or at a 5.9% annual rate, a sign inflation remains stubborn despite a slowing economy. The increase, the biggest since May, was led by sharp rise in the cost of gasoline, new cars and apparel. But some analysts don't expect the higher prices to stick.

Thrift regulator Danny Wall told Congress that politics played no part in his decisions regarding Lincoln S&L. The defunct thrift's chief owner,

Charles Keating, cited the Fifth Amendment and declined to testify.

OPEC ministers begin meeting in Vienna tomorrow without any framework for revamping their oil-production quota system. Meanwhile, members have been racing to boost production capacity, which may prevent an oil-price surge in the 1990s.

24 The Fed eased credit for the second time in two weeks amid further signs of economic weakness. The move is expected to push down the closely watched federal funds rate and other short-term interest rates. The prime rate, which has remained at 10½% despite the earlier Fed easing, could begin falling today.

Durable goods orders slid 0.6% in October, the latest evidence that U.S. manufacturing is stagnating. Also, September orders plunged 1.1% instead of rising 0.2%, new data show.

Stocks and bonds rallied modestly Wednesday on speculation of a Fed easing. The Dow Jones industrials rose 17.49, to 2656.78. The dollar fell, while gold neared a 1989 high.

27 The Fed is expected to continue driving down short-term interest rates in an effort to reverse the slump in manufacturing. The reductions could even include a cut in the discount rate. Some economists say the Fed is now more worried about a recession than inflation.

Stock prices climbed Friday on speculation about further rate cuts, though bonds closed little changed. The Dow Jones industrials rose 18.77 points, to 2675.55. The dollar weakened, while gold continued to rise.

Machine-tool orders fell 22% in October from a year earlier, mainly due to a downturn in the auto and truck industry. But manufacturers of factory machinery said they aren't dismayed because orders from other sectors have been holding up.

Morgan Grenfell is expected to receive a friendly takeover bid this week from Deutsche Bank that would value the British investment bank at $1.25 billion. Morgan has been trying to prevent Banque Indosuez of France from boosting its stake to 24.8%.

28 The Fed propped up the closely watched federal-funds rate, sending a strong signal to financial markets that it hasn't eased credit. The move surprised analysts, who had concluded last week that the central bank was pushing interest rates lower because of the sagging economy. Still, many believe the Fed will ease credit in coming weeks.

Bond prices declined in reaction to the Fed move, though stocks posted gains. The Dow Jones industrials closed up 19.42 points, at 2694.97. The dollar continued to slump, while gold fell back on profit-taking.

Most OPEC ministers endorsed a new plan aimed at controlling the group's oil output, though as many as three members may not participate. Still, the agreement is viewed as a breakthrough for the organization.

Deutsche Bank will offer about $1.41 billion for Morgan Grenfell, a record price for an investment bank. Morgan Grenfell is backing the bid, which could thwart Banque Indosuez's plan to boost its stake to 24.8%.

U.S. car and truck sales fell 4.4% in mid-November, improving from the 20.2% plunge earlier in the month. But the main factor was strong sales by Japanese auto makers, which contrasted sharply with the continued sales slump at the Big Three.

29 OPEC ministers settled on a new production plan that they hope will control surging oil output and head off an expected price slump. But the effectiveness of the accord, approved unanimously at OPEC's Vienna conference, depends on whether some major Persian Gulf members abide by the new quotas. U.S. traders were bearish about the agreement.

The securities industry's leading trade group may drop its longstanding opposition to banks entering the securities business. Such a policy reversal could help break a logjam in Congress over the issue.

30 The economy grew at a 2.7% rate in the third quarter, slightly faster than the government had estimated. But corporate profits fell for the third straight quarter, slumping 7.2%.

RJR Nabisco is discussing selling its 20% interest in the ESPN cable sports channel to a foreign buyer, executives close to the talks said. RJR reportedly wants up to $250 million.

December 1989

1 Personal spending fell 0.2% in October, the first decline in more than a year. Flagging car sales were responsible for nearly all of the drop, although many economists expect the weakness to

spread to other types of buying. Separately, the government said personal income jumped 0.9% in October.

Many big retailers posted weak sales for November, a sign that aggressive discounting to attract holiday shoppers is likely to continue.

Sears Roebuck's sales fell 1.6% in November, as sharp markdowns underscored the firm's problems in implementing its new pricing strategy.

The corporate takeover pace is slowing down. Securities Data Corp. said that through mid-November the dollar volume of deals announced this year had fallen 28% from 1988.

4 The economy remains sluggish, mostly due to a sharp slowing in manufacturing, new data show. Leading indicators fell 0.4% in October, while purchasing agents said manufacturing contracted in November for the seventh month in a row. But many economists say the softness is confined to manufacturing, so the overall economy isn't likely to slide into a recession. Also, construction spending rebounded 1% in October.

More signs of economic weakness are expected to emerge this week, likely prompting the Fed to lower interest rates, bankers and investment strategists say. Bonds rose slightly Friday on such speculation. Stocks rallied, and the dollar gained.

UAL told employees that United Air executives are working on a revised buyout proposal and that they plan to open talks shortly with the unions. UAL's stock soared $12.50 Friday, to $174. After the market closed, Coniston said it had boosted its UAL stake to 11.8% from 9.7%.

5 Toyota is recalling all of its Lexus 400 cars because of quality and safety problems. The move will hurt the image of the new luxury models, which Toyota introduced with much fanfare and success just four months ago.

Gold's price plunged along with other precious metals in widespread selling, mostly profit-taking. Stocks inched higher, while bonds were unchanged and the dollar was mixed.

Factory orders fell 0.2% in October after sliding a revised 1% the previous month. The decline, the latest sign of the weak economy, was concentrated in durable goods orders. Nondurable items climbed 1.1%.

Danny Wall resigned as the nation's thrift regulator, the first casualty within the government of the savings and loan scandal. Wall had been under fire recently, particularly for his reluctance to seize Lincoln S&L of California despite warnings from regional examiners that the thrift was operating recklessly.

6 IBM announced a major restructuring, as expected, to combat lackluster sales and earnings. The cost-cutting move, which includes the elimination of 10,000 jobs, will result in a $2.3 billion fourth-quarter charge. IBM also said it will buy back an additional $4 billion of its stock. The revamping reflects stiff price competition in much of the computer industry, which is expected to intensify.

Trading in IBM's stock was delayed for 1½ hours because of the announcement, prompting criticism of the company and the Big Board. IBM closed at $99.625, up 37.5 cents.

U.S. car and truck sales fell 9.3% in late November, led by a slide at GM. The auto maker's market share slipped to 31.8%, the smallest in recent history and well below Chairman Smith's pledge of 37% in 1990.

Cities and counties may be sued under federal civil rights law if their policies conflict with federal labor law, the Supreme Court ruled. But the scope of the decision was limited.

7 Chrysler is abandoning a much-touted diversification program to focus on its struggling car and truck business. The move to sell the Chrysler Technologies unit comes as the auto maker tries to cut over $1 billion in fixed costs and prepares to revamp most of its vehicle line.

Worker productivity rose sharply in nonfinancial businesses during the third quarter after showing almost no improvement in the second quarter.

A new Fed survey shows continued economic weakness, but no recession is forecast. Consumer confidence fell to the lowest level in a year.

Many thrifts won't be able to meet the tougher capital requirements that go into effect today. The result is likely to be a faster consolidation of the industry and, ultimately, a higher price tag for the S&L bail-out.

8 Pennzoil said it has acquired nearly 9% of Chevron for $2.1 billion but has "no interest in attempting to take over" the nation's fourth-biggest oil company. Chevron's stock, which has surged 20% on takeover speculation since early October, reacted by skidding $5.25, to $66.75. Still, Chevron may be ripe for some major changes, including a takeover.

The drop in Chevron's stock sent the Dow Jones industrials down 15.99, to 2720.78. Bond prices eased, while the dollar gained against the mark. Gold futures prices closed higher.

Exxon is expected to be indicted soon on criminal charges related to the March 23 oil spill near Valdez, Alaska, attorneys said. Any charges would likely include alleged violations of federal anti-pollution laws.

11 A close associate of Michael Milken has been granted immunity and ordered to testify against Drexel's former junk-bond chief, sources said. Gary Winnick, the former head of Drexel's convertible bond operations, was issued the order after prosecutors became convinced that he probably had information useful to the insider-trading inquiry. Some believe Winnick could be a key witness.

AT&T said 1989 job cuts will total about 25,000 and that it has firm plans to eliminate another 8,500 next year. Sources said even bigger reductions may be in store next year as the company steps up its cost-cutting.

The jobless rate edged up to 5.4% in November, the highest level in 10 months, from 5.3% in October. Unemployment is expected to continue rising in the coming months as the growth in new jobs slows further.

U.S. machine tool exports surged 33% in the third quarter, though they continued to be outpaced by imports, particularly from Japanese makers.

12 Bush officials are sticking to their forecast that the economy will avoid a recession for another year and grow an inflation-adjusted 2.6% through the end of 1990. Many private economists expect a much slower growth rate.

Drexel may only break even or be marginally profitable this year after being one of Wall Street's most profitable securities firms. Drexel's problems include heavy legal costs from its securities-fraud settlement and the collapse of the junk-bond market.

Amgen and Genetics Institute were unable to get a clear-cut victory in their dispute over patent rights to the anti-anemia drug EPO. A ruling by a U.S. magistrate may have set the stage for a settlement in which the firms would cross-license the rights.

13 Steel-import quotas were reached with the European Community and 16 other major foreign suppliers to limit the amount of steel allowed into the U.S. through March 31, 1992.

Shearson received $48.5 million in fees for its role in helping create the $14 billion merger of Time Inc. and Warner Communications. A half-dozen investment banking firms shared more than $125 million in fees.

14 Campeau acknowledged for the first time that its retail units may have to seek Chapter 11 protection to resolve their financial woes. The disclosure indicates Campeau's troubles are worsening despite a cash infusion from Olympia & York. Federated Department Stores may run out of cash by next month. Allied's situation is almost as uncertain.

U.S. car and truck sales plunged 23.7% in early December, darkening the industry's already gloomy outlook. The results make it likely that auto makers will have to close more plants and offer costly incentives.

GM's slide in U.S. market share is accelerating, and the company is scrambling to avoid a debacle.

Retail sales rose an unexpected 0.8% in November after falling 1.3% the month before. All major sectors except drug and proprietary stores had gains. Still, analysts were divided on the significance of the results.

Several major airlines are being investigated by the Justice Department for possible collusion on a fare increase earlier this year. The antitrust inquiry comes amid mounting concern about rising air fares.

15 A tax-free savings plan is being considered by Bush officials that would encourage people to save without tying up their money until retirement. The current proposal would let Americans contribute up to $5,000 per family each year to a special savings account in which the interest would be tax-free if the account wasn't touched for 10 years.

The Big Three auto makers are expected to lay off as many as 100,000 workers at over 35 plants next month in an effort to cut inventories. In addition, the companies are planning to beef up incentives to spur sales.

Business inventories expanded moderately in October while sales slipped, raising some concern among economists about growing stockpiles.

Merrill Lynch plans to slash year-end bonuses for its highly paid investment bankers by 15% to 25%. The bonuses could shrink further if Merrill's earnings don't improve, a sign of the firm's desperation to cut costs and of the overall slump on Wall Street.

Campeau received another blow as a big factoring firm, Heller Financial, told clients to stop shipping merchandise to Campeau's retail units. Heller made its decision after reviewing Campeau's quarterly results.

18 Inflation eased further in November as the economy remained sluggish. Producer prices fell 0.1%, the third decline in five months, mainly due to lower energy prices. Industrial output inched up 0.1% after falling the previous two months, while the operating rate slipped to 82.7% of capacity, the lowest in 1½ years.

The U.S. trade deficit widened to $10.20 billion in October, the biggest in 10 months, as a surge in imports eclipsed a small gain in exports.

General Motors agreed to buy 50% of Saab-Scania's troubled car operations for $500 million. The accord, which includes several joint ventures, will give GM a chance to build on its recent European successes.

19 Ford Motor plans to close most of its assembly plants for at least part of January because of the deepening slump in car sales. GM has already announced similar plant closings.

Ford and VW confirmed they are discussing a European joint venture, but neither would offer details about what vehicle would be made.

Stock prices sank as investors worried about the growing slump in real estate. The Dow Jones industrials skidded 42.02, to 2697.53, the first close below 2700 since late November. The Nasdaq OTC Composite index slid 1.8%, the second-biggest sell-off of the year after October 13. Treasury bond prices rose, while the dollar was mixed.

Heating oil prices surged as traders scrambled to stock up on the fuel in the face of record cold weather and tight supplies.

20 Consumer prices rose 0.4% in November, a sign that inflation persists in the services sector, particularly medical care. Food prices also surged, but energy costs declined and the increase in transportation and clothing prices slowed. Also, housing starts fell 4.7% last month, but many analysts believe the industry is rebounding.

Stocks were damped partly by the two economic reports. The Dow Jones industrials, down sharply in the morning, closed off 1.92 points, at 2695.61.

Bond prices eased, while the dollar had modest gains.

Kohl and Modrow met and agreed to open the Brandenburg Gate.

The West German chancellor and East German's Communist premier held talks in Dresden and unveiled moves aimed at smoothing ties between the two states. Besides completing economic pacts, the East Germans vowed to free political prisoners and open a passageway in the Berlin Wall at the Brandenburg Gate—long a symbol of German unity—before Christmas. In Czechoslovakia, the Communist premier endorsed dissident Vaclav Havel for president and urged lawmakers to elect the head of state by month's end.

Clashes were reported in Romania during protests calling for the ouster of Ceausescu. Witnesses said hundreds of people may have been killed in a crackdown that began over the weekend.

Shevardnadze paid an unprecedented visit to NATO headquarters in Brussels, saying the Western alliance and the Warsaw Pact should remain in place to help ensure stability at a time of change in Europe. The Soviet foreign minister met with NATO's secretary-general to discuss prospects for treaties cutting conventional forces.

Ford sees greater growth opportunities in Europe than in the U.S. during the next few years, according to Vice Chairman Harold Poling.

21 The Fed began easing credit another notch in response to continued weakness in the economy. The decline in the key federal-funds rate is expected to push other rates lower. Banks may cut their prime lending rates, now at 10½%, in the next few days. Meanwhile, third-quarter GNP growth was revised upward to a 3% annual rate from 2.7%. But analysts believe the economy is slowing sharply in the current quarter.

Financial markets had a muted response to the Fed move. The dollar rallied on the Panama invasion, then fell back to close mixed. The Dow Jones industrials ended down 7.68, at 2687.93. Treasury bond prices eased.

22 Bechtel said it became the first U.S. contractor to win a major share of a big public-works project in Japan. The award may help lessen trade tensions over the alleged exclusion of foreigners from such projects.

The severe cold that has swept over

much of the U.S. has caused some shortages of natural gas, skyrocketing heating-oil prices, and greater demand for utilities.

Consumer spending rose 0.7% in November, the first increase in two months, aided by early holiday sales and special promotions on automobiles. Personal income also climbed an unexpectedly sharp 0.8%, while personal savings gained 6.1%.

Stocks were bolstered by the economic data, which showed that consumer confidence was stronger than investors expected. The Dow Jones industrials edged up 3.20, to 2691.13. Bond prices and the dollar eased.

26 Retailers rang up respectable sales gains for the holiday shopping season, but profits are expected to be weak. Receipts for the month-long period are estimated to have risen an average 4% to 5% from 1988, when sales jumped 7%. Much of this year's business was done at deep discounts, which will cut into profits. Also, the turmoil that swept the retailing industry this fall, bringing the discounts, is likely to continue.

Florida's $3.5 billion citrus crop suffered substantial damage from the severe cold over the weekend, the third major freeze in six years, an industry group said. The weekend weather also is likely to drive up prices for winter vegetables.

Durable goods orders surged 5.1% in November, but most economists viewed the gain as an aberration. Most believe economic growth will remain slow. Meanwhile, machine-tool orders tumbled 34% in November and remain weak in December.

The Fed decided in mid-November to leave credit unchanged, but to lean toward easing if the economy weakened. The central bank nudged interest rates lower last week.

27 The cold weather is starting to crimp energy supplies at the same time it is boosting demand. Several Gulf Coast refineries have been forced to curb output because the cold has caused equipment problems and other delays. The weather also has hurt farm crops in Florida and Texas.

Heating oil, crude oil and orange juice prices continued to surge in futures trading. But some potential traders were locked out when prices reached their one-day ceiling.

The auto industry's woes deepened as

GM confirmed plans to indefinitely lay off another 2,000 U.S. assembly workers. Also, Chrysler predicted U.S. sales of cars and trucks in 1989 will be down 9% from a year ago.

Banks are under growing pressure to lower their prime rates in response to the Fed's latest credit-easing last week. But some analysts say banks may keep the prime at its current level at least through year-end.

Treasury bond prices plunged amid worries that the spurt in food and energy prices will worsen inflation. Stocks and the dollar also lost ground. The Dow Jones industrials finished off 2.13 points, at 2709.26.

Tokyo is stepping up pressure on Japanese firms to boost imports. MITI officials believe urgent action is needed because trade tensions with the U.S. are higher than ever.

28 GM plans to cut 3,200 more production jobs and slash output of some of its newest car lines. The latest cutbacks indicate the company may be giving up hope of a quick recovery in its slumping U.S. auto business.

Research and development spending in the U.S. is expected to rise 4.8% next year, a study says. The longer-term outlook is uncertain because of a likely drop in defense research.

The inflation rate is expected to surge soon because the cold weather is pushing up prices of citrus fruit, fresh vegetables and heating oil. But the increase may be short-lived.

Sears's long-term debt ratings were cut by Duff & Phelps, which cited "increased risks" from efforts to revive the firm's retail business.

Venture-capital funds are losing favor among big institutional investors, putting a further squeeze on money for start-up companies.

29 Kohlberg Kravis Roberts placed one of its companies in Chapter 11 proceedings, the latest sign of problems in the leveraged buy-out business. The filing by Hillsborough Holdings was the first-ever bankruptcy-law action by a Kohlberg company.

The economy will remain sluggish in the coming year, though high technology, health and services industries will show strong growth, the Commerce Department predicted.

Construction contracts fell 7% in November, reflecting a sharp drop in commercial and industrial building, according to F. W. Dodge Group.

January 1990

2 The economy is expected to continue expanding this year, helped by lower interest rates, a *Wall Street Journal* survey of 40 economists says. But the forecasters also say growth will be so sluggish that many industries will feel as if they're in a recession.

Leading indicators rose 0.1% in November after falling a revised 0.3% in October. The gain supports the view that the economy is slowing but not falling into a recession.

Takeover deals plunged 33% in dollar terms in 1989 as bond-market jitters put the brakes on many mergers and buy-outs. The slowdown shook up the rankings of Wall Street's top dealmakers. Goldman Sachs and Drexel were especially hurt.

Stocks ended the year on a bullish note, while bonds faltered. The Dow Jones industrials closed up 20.91 Friday, December 29, 1989, at 2753.20, within 40 points of the record high. The dollar also strengthened, though its outlook is bearish.

The OTC stock market gained more companies than it lost in 1989, as fewer defected to the exchanges. But the number of new stocks fell.

3 Stock prices rallied on bargain-hunting and optimism about the economy, pushing the Dow Jones industrials up 56.95 points, to a record 2810.15. The advance was led by technology, auto and retail stocks, all of which had languished recently. Bond prices eased in sluggish trading.

The dollar surged, prompting the New York Fed to intervene in the market several times to slow the currency's rise against the yen.

The manufacturing sector continued to weaken in December, though it was at its strongest level since June, purchasing agents said. Separately, construction spending rose 1.5% in November from the previous month.

The U.S. auto industry recovered slightly in mid-December from a slump at the beginning of the month. But car-and-truck sales were still down 18.6% from year-earlier levels.

4 Oil prices surged as much as $1.50 a barrel on world markets, but analysts suggested prices may peak soon and begin sliding sharply. Bond prices fell in response to higher oil prices and inflation worries, while stocks ended lower on profit-taking. The Dow Jones industrials closed off 0.42, at 2809.73. The dollar was mixed.

New-home sales jumped 9.6% in November, with nearly every region posting gains. Analysts said the rebound in home sales, which have been weak for over a year, reflects the recent decline in interest rates.

Consumer confidence softened a bit during December, though the outlook generally remains strong, according to the Conference Board.

Thrift withdrawals exceeded deposits by $4.5 billion in October, a smaller outflow than in September. Also, S&L regulators were told to resist the freewheeling practices used to sell sick thrifts in years past.

5 Robert Campeau lost control of his troubled retail and real-estate empire after a Canadian bank seized about half of his voting shares. The move by National Bank, following a loan default, adds pressure on Campeau to proceed quickly with a planned restructuring of the Federated and Allied retail units.

The dollar plunged as a surprise intervention by West Germany set off panic selling of the U.S. currency. In late New York trading; the dollar was down 2.6% against the mark. Stock prices eased further on profit-taking, while bonds were little changed.

Petroleum futures fell, reversing a recent rally. The slide was triggered by a collapse in heating-oil prices.

Major retailers posted an average 5% increase in sales for December, but widespread discounting made the profit outlook uncertain. The biggest gainers were apparel-based retailers such as Gap, J.C. Penney, Dayton Hudson and May Department Stores.

U.S. auto sales fell 10.5% in late December, but the pace was the strongest since late September. The Big Three posted big declines, while Japanese makers had strong gains.

Federal regulators proposed rules to increase safety standards for light trucks and minivans and to sharply reduce pollution from all vehicles.

8 The Treasury plans to sell zero-coupon bonds to Mexico at below-market prices, costing U.S. taxpayers as much as $500 million, sources said. The cut-rate bonds would provide a back-door rescue for the faltering debt accord pending between Mexico and a group of foreign banks. The proposal is certain to ignite controversy on Capitol Hill.

Some fuel-oil deliveries to the Northeast were blocked by a federal agency recently despite shortages and surging prices. The agency refused to waive a law that limits shipments on foreign tankers.

Campeau's bankers are expected to urge the company today not to pay apparel makers whose bills come due Wednesday, sources said. The banks believe Chapter 11 filings by Campeau's retail units are inevitable.

Bank of New England is negotiating to sell some operations to Fleet/Norstar, and a pact may come within days, a source said. Any accord is unlikely to include any of the Boston or large Massachusetts businesses.

The jobless rate remained at 5.3% in December amid further signs of a sluggish economy, particularly in manufacturing. However, factory orders jumped 2.4% in November.

Stock prices fell Friday as the jobless data damped expectations of lower interest rates. The Dow Jones industrials closed off 22.83, at 2773.25. The dollar rose, bonds were mixed.

9 The prime rate was cut by most banks to 10% from 10½%, the first reduction in six months. The long-awaited move should soon result in lower borrowing costs for consumers and small and medium-sized businesses. Banks have been under pressure for weeks to reduce the prime after the Fed moved in late November to ease short-term credit.

Stocks rose sharply in late trading, boosted by program buying, but bonds fell on inflation worries. The Dow Jones industrials closed up 21.12, at 2794.37. The prime-rate cut had little impact on either market, though it helped cause the dollar to weaken.

Petroleum futures tumbled in Europe and the U.S., reflecting warmer weather and technical factors.

Chicago futures traders routinely conspired to make illegal trades and boasted about stealing from the public, according to conversations secretly taped by federal agents.

Japan's big memory-chip makers are cutting production in a bid to ease a glut and boost prices. The move comes as U.S. chip makers expand.

10 Bristol-Myers Squibb will take an estimated $690 million charge against fourth-quarter profit to cover costs from last fall's merger of the two firms. Most of the charge will be for combining and trimming duplicate operations. Several analysts said the merger, creating the second largest drug and health-care products company after Merck, appears to be proceeding smoothly.

UAL's stock jumped $7.375, to $164, following the company's decision late Monday to explore a recapitalization. There was speculation that the board's move was aimed at pressuring United Air pilots and Chairman Stephen Wolf into working out a new buy-out bid for the company.

U.S. farmers planted 7.5% more acres of winter wheat last fall than they did a year earlier, prompted by high wheat prices, analysts estimate. The increase is expected to help rebuild stockpiles that have been depleted by two years of drought.

Suzuki Motor reached an accord to build cars in Hungary, the first Japanese auto maker to gain a production foothold in Eastern Europe.

11 Campeau said its Federated and Allied retail units are in the process of paying various apparel suppliers. But an attorney said the action doesn't affect whether the companies file for Chapter 11 protection.

May Department Stores said it may be interested in acquiring certain department store chains from Campeau and B.A.T's Marshall Field's unit. May is flush with cash from selling its discount stores.

General Motors appears poised to become the first U.S. auto maker to produce cars in Eastern Europe. The company is likely to announce soon a $150 million joint venture to build cars and engines in Hungary.

PaineWebber Group is revamping the way it charges institutional investors for stock trading and research. The securities firm will no longer provide a variety of free services to less-active institutions that don't generate enough commission revenue.

World oil prices surged amid further signs of tightening U.S. gasoline supplies. Petroleum analysts said there could be further price runups in oil markets unless refineries begin rebuilding gasoline inventories.

A huge oil-storage terminal in Alaska has closed indefinitely due to fears that eruptions from a nearby volcano could damage the facility.

12 The unemployment rate remained at 5.3% in February for the ninth consecutive month. Job growth outside the farm sector posted the biggest rise in 1½ years, though some analysts said the rise doesn't signal much buoyancy in the economy.

Bond prices fell sharply and the dollar strengthened as Friday's jobless report fueled speculation that the U.S. economy is stronger than expected, which could lead to higher interest rates. Stocks ended lower.

The Fed has lost much of its control over U.S. interest rates due to the growing influence of foreign financial markets, particularly in Japan and West Germany. And as the Fed loses leverage, the U.S. loses some of its control over its economic destiny.

Central banks appear to be waging a futile battle to prevent the dollar from rising, currency analysts say.

U.S. auto makers plan to boost car and truck production by 18.6% in the second quarter from the depressed first quarter, signaling a more optimistic outlook. Output would still be down 11.3% from the year-ago level.

Several major Western suppliers have halted shipments to the Soviet Union because of unpaid bills that could total as much as $500 million.

15 Stocks and bonds may decline further this week following Friday's big sell-off, some analysts say. The Dow Jones industrials slid 71.46 points, or 2.6%, to 2689.21, after two economic reports sparked worries about rising inflation and the sluggish economy. Weak earnings reports are also expected to hurt stocks.

The 0.7% surge in producer prices for December pushed wholesale inflation for the year up to 4.8%, the worst since 1981. Retail sales edged up 0.2% last month and 5% for all of 1989, the smallest gain in seven years.

Thrift regulators rescinded special accounting breaks for buyers of troubled S&Ls. The move, going further than the tougher accounting standards of the thrift bail-out law, is likely to cause more S&L failures.

Many thrifts worsened their own problems by going on a junk-bond buying spree just before a new law prohibited such purchases, and just before the junk bond market tanked.

Campeau's bank lenders delayed until Friday a decision on whether to demand payment of $2.34 billion owed by the retail units. Also, Campeau director G. William Miller may be named head of U.S. operations.

U.S. Memories will drop efforts to form an alliance of U.S. computer makers to challenge Japan's dominance in memory chips. The plan failed to get enough backers.

16 Campeau's retail units filed for Chapter 11 protection, ending weeks of speculation. Though Campeau executives were upbeat about the Federated and Allied filing, one of the largest bankruptcy-court actions in U.S. history, the move is fraught with risks. In a business dependent on image, few retailers have emerged successfully from Chapter 11.

An overhaul of corporate taxes is being prepared by the Treasury. The primary aim is to eliminate double taxation of dividends, though other corporate taxes might be increased to offset the loss of revenue.

17 Japanese takeovers of U.S. corporations climbed 8% last year, to a record $13.7 billion. This year, the Japanese may surpass the British in U.S. acquisitions for the first time.

Aristech Chemical received an $845 million bid from a manager group backed by Mitsubishi. The strategy could set a pattern for Japanese investment in the U.S.

U.S. vehicle sales jumped 27% in early January from unusually low levels a year earlier. The surge was aided by new buyer incentives, which analysts indicated may be needed to continue propping up sales.

Major brokerage firms are expected to report significant declines in fourth-quarter earnings, reflecting the continued slump on Wall Street.

18 The Fed appears unlikely to cut interest rates anytime soon. Two key Fed policy-makers, Vice Chairman Manuel Johnson and Governor Wayne Angell, indicated in interviews that they probably wouldn't be in favor of easing credit for now. Without their support, the Fed's policy committee likely wouldn't have a majority to back lowering rates.

The trade deficit widened to $10.5 billion in November, the worst showing in 11 months. Exports fell 2.7% as the Boeing strike cut jet shipments to foreign buyers. Imports slipped 1.7%. Most economists don't expect the trade gap to shrink much this year.

Manufacturing remained weak in December. Industrial output rose 0.4%, but most of the gain came from special factors. The factory operating rate edged up to 83.3% of capacity.

IBM's profit skidded 75% in the fourth quarter and 35% for the year, mostly due to a $2.42 billion charge for layoffs and consolidating operations. The computer giant was vague about prospects for the coming year.

Stock prices sank as disappointment over earnings reports sparked a sell-off in some big blue chips. The Dow Jones industrials closed off 33.49 points, at 2659.13. Bonds were little changed, while the dollar was mixed.

World oil prices declined on signs of an increase in U.S. petroleum inventories and continued mild winter weather in the U.S. and Europe.

14 Rorer Group agreed to a $3.23 billion merger with Rhone-Poulenc's pharmaceutical unit, creating one of the world's biggest drug concerns. Rhone-Poulenc would acquire 68% of Rorer, but the merged firm would remain publicly traded and based in the U.S. In addition, Rorer Chairman Robert Cawthorn would head the merged concern.

Consumer prices rose 0.4% in December, bringing the 1989 inflation rate to 4.6%, only slightly above the previous two years but still the highest since 1981. Also, housing starts plunged 8% last month, bringing the 1989 total to a seven-year low.

The White House publicly urged the Fed for the first time to cut rates. Spokesman Fitzwater cited the modest inflation report and weak housing starts in calling for easier credit.

Digital Equipment's profit declined 44% in the latest quarter, reflecting the weakness in much of the nation's computer industry. Digital's stock tumbled $5.875, to $82.

Apple Computer posted an 11% drop in earnings for the latest quarter. The company also may cut up to 800 jobs to reduce costs.

Japan's big banks are likely to cut back on lending for U.S. leveraged buy-outs following the Chapter 11 filings by two Campeau units.

22 R. J. Reynolds dropped plans to begin test marketing a new cigarette, Uptown, after protests that it was targeted at blacks. The pullout may make it harder for tobacco or liquor makers to target certain consumers.

Campeau's bankers and top retail executives believe financial data released Friday by the Federated and Allied units will persuade vendors to resume shipments to the store chains.

Japan's trade surplus shrank 36% in December and 17% for the year. But officials said the improvement was exaggerated by temporary factors and may reverse itself by midyear, worsening trade tensions.

Many states are under pressure to raise taxes this year, particularly in the hard-pressed Northeast. Still, election-year politics could make major tax increases unlikely.

23 Stock prices plunged as higher interest rates and poor corporate earnings prompted many investors to stay out of the market, allowing program selling to dominate. The Dow Jones industrials skidded 77.45 points, to 2600.45, the biggest decline since the 190.58-point slide on October 13. Bond prices eased slightly, while the dollar posted modest gains.

Merrill Lynch took a $470 million charge to pay for a major restructuring, giving the nation's biggest securities concern a record $213.4 million loss for 1989. The results were much worse than analysts had expected.

The Big Three auto makers are expected to post a 60% drop in combined fourth-quarter operating earnings. Chrysler may have its first net loss since 1982. Ford's four years of record profits are expected to end.

Chrysler will begin European vehicle production next year for the first time since 1978 with an Austrian joint venture to manufacture minivans.

Intel formed a joint venture with a Japanese chip maker that will market all the Japanese company's chips worldwide. The move follows the collapse last week of a U.S. effort to compete with Japanese chip makers.

24 A Social Security tax cut will be studied by the Senate Finance Committee amid signs of growing support for Senator Moynihan's plan. The proposed cut is becoming the focus of this year's fiscal debate, partly because it also suggests removing Social Security from the federal budget accounting, which would sharply increase the deficit.

25 United Air's three unions have formed an alliance to bid for the company, though a formal offer isn't expected when UAL's board meets today. Several issues are unresolved, including the price, financing and participation of UAL's chairman.

New York's two big futures exchanges agreed to a tentative merger. The move by the Merc and Comex reflects a desire to become a bigger player in the commodity industry, which is dominated by Chicago.

26 Stocks and bonds sank again amid worries that rising interest rates will further weaken the nation's economy. The Dow Jones industrials closed off 43.46 points, at 2561.04. Treasury bond prices also tumbled, forcing interest rates higher. The dollar fell as investors switched funds out of dollar-denominated investments to those in Japan or Europe.

Fed Chairman Greenspan said rising interest rates in Europe and Japan are causing significant amounts of capital to be diverted away from the U.S. The trend is pushing up long-term U.S. interest rates.

Most economists don't expect a recession in 1990 despite the slump in many sectors. A recent poll showed most expect inflation-adjusted GNP to rise 1.7% this year after edging up only 0.7% in the 1989 fourth quarter. The government will release its fourth-quarter GNP estimate today.

Labor costs rose 4.8% in private industry last year, down slightly from the year before. But the size of union wage settlements grew substantially.

UAL's board held off approving a recapitalization plan because of the prospect of a new employee buy-out proposal. But the airline's worsening earnings could complicate labor's efforts to raise financing for a bid.

29 Bush's budget calls for $1.23 trillion in spending for fiscal 1991 with some tax increases and a long-sought cut in capital-gains taxes. The budget, to be formally unveiled today, also estimates a deficit just under the Gramm-Rudman target of $64 billion. Bush's proposal, however, contains no "peace dividend."

The slowing economy may allow Congress to opt out of the Gramm-Rudman law this year. Such a move could wipe out what limited fiscal discipline the law has imposed.

Friday's GNP report left analysts divided over the possibility of a recession this year. The 0.5% growth in the economy during the fourth quarter was the weakest in 3½ years. For all of 1989, GNP increased at a 2.9% rate. However, orders for durable goods surged 2.5% in December.

Machine-tool orders slid 34% in December from a year earlier but were up 14% from the month before.

RJR Nabisco received lower-than-expected ratings on planned and future debt securities, causing a short-term plunge Friday in both the junk-bond and stock markets. It was the first major setback in the company's efforts to pare its huge debt.

OPEC has stopped cutting production because oil markets are stronger than anticipated. World oil demand is expected to grow about 1% this year, and recent unrest in the Soviet Union could curtail its crude exports.

30 The junk-bond market plunged in reaction to a continued slide in RJR Nabisco bonds. The sell-off helped push stock prices lower. The Dow Jones industrials closed off 5.85, at 2553.38. Treasury bonds weakened and the dollar was mostly lower.

World oil prices moved higher as gasoline and heating oil prices rallied in U.S. futures trading.

Cheney unveiled a defense plan calling for cuts in spending and personnel.

The defense secretary, providing the first details of Bush's overall strategy to reshape the U.S. military, announced a blueprint calling for a 10% cut in military spending and personnel by 1995. The proposal includes the possible closing of more than 50 bases around the world. Cheney's comments are almost certain to result in a prolonged test of wills between the administration and Congress, where there is strong sentiment for significantly deeper long-term reductions in defense spending.

Cheney, who cited "phenomenal change" in the East bloc, said the plan assumes the completion of U.S.-Soviet arms pacts in the next few years.

Personal spending surged 1% in December, mainly because of higher energy costs, while income edged up 0.5%. For all of 1989, spending rose 7.3% and income jumped 9%.

Construction spending rose 1% in December but was mainly flat for the year, forecaster F. W. Dodge said.

31 Fed Chairman Greenspan said the risk of recession has diminished in recent months and the current economic slowdown is "temporary." The comments indicate he doesn't favor a further cut in interest rates now.

The dollar soared following a TV report that Gorbachev may resign as Communist party chief. Bonds also rose, though stocks fell further and gold eased. The Dow Jones industrials closed off 10.14 points, at 2543.24.

February 1990

1 Leading indicators surged 0.8% in December, the strongest showing since April. The jump bolstered the view that the economy will rebound without a recession, though some analysts are still cautious. New-home sales skidded 9.6% in December.
   Consumer confidence fell in January to its lowest level since just after the October 1987 stock market crash.

2 Big Board Chairman John Phelan plans to resign at the end of 1990 after nearly six years in the post. He denied rumors he is considering a government job in Washington. Phelan is credited with deftly handling the exchange's warring factions and upgrading the Big Board's trading and communications systems. No successor has been named.
   Chrysler plans to close a car plant in St. Louis this fall, the third U.S. plant it has shut since 1987. The Big Three have ordered seven U.S. factories closed in that time, while Japanese makers have opened five.
   Manufacturing weakened further in January, a survey of purchasing managers said. Also, construction spending fell 0.6% in December, resulting in a 1.2% rise for 1989, the worst performance in seven years.
   Major retailers posted modest sales gains averaging 5.5% to 6% for January, a sign of possible difficulty ahead. For the fiscal year, sales grew 5.5%, with specialty retailers continuing to outpace department stores.

5 Genentech agreed to sell a controlling 60% stake to Roche Holding of Switzerland for $2.1 billion. The move allows the U.S. biotechnology giant to finance drug development without pressure from Wall Street for immediate financial gains. Investors have cooled on biotech stocks recently, though the Genentech pact sent many shares higher Friday. Genentech surged $8.125, to $29.875.
   The jobless rate remained at 5.3% in January for the eighth month in a row. There was a surprising growth in new jobs, though the figure was bolstered by weather and statistical factors. Manufacturing payrolls continued to fall.

Meanwhile, factory orders jumped 1.9% in December.
   Interest rates may rise, at least temporarily, as a flood of new government securities hits the bond market this week. Bond prices tumbled Friday in anticipation, while stocks rose in reaction to the jobless report.

6 The dollar skidded against the mark as Gorbachev's push for a multiparty state reassured investors the Soviet leader is in control. The U.S. currency had soared a week ago amid uncertainty about his hold on power. Meanwhile, stocks rose in a late rally, pushing the Dow Jones industrials up 19.82, to 2622.52. Bonds sank amid worries about this week's $30 billion Treasury auction.
   RJR Nabisco posted losses of $144 million for the fourth quarter and $1.15 billion for the year, though it had higher operating profits in core food and tobacco businesses. Most of the losses resulted from interest and debt costs tied to the firm's 1989 buy-out.
   The U.S. takeover market faces another blow: a slowdown in British acquisitions because of a proposed change in U.K. accounting rules.
   U.S. car sales fell 6.6% in late January from a strong year-earlier period, while vehicle sales for the month were up 3.4%. Chrysler reported record sales for January, but other makers remained in a slump.
   Chrysler is seeking a tie-up with Honda Motor to help sell some Chrysler models in Japan.

7 The Treasury's auction of $10 billion in three-year notes was a hit with investors, though the markets remain jittery about the rest of the $30 billion refunding, which takes place today and tomorrow. Analysts said the success of the note sale was mainly due to the relatively high yield, which averaged 8.43%. The Japanese were heavy buyers of the notes.
   Stock and bond prices fell amid worries about the remainder of the Treasury auction. The Dow Jones industrials closed off 16.21 points, at 2606.31. The dollar was mixed, while gold futures finished lower.
   Bush and his economic aides called for new policies to increase the number of skilled immigrants to help ease an impending U.S. labor shortage.

8 Stocks and bonds rose amid signs that long-term interest rates may be nearing a peak. The Dow Jones industrials closed up 33.78, at 2640.09. Analysts

cited surprisingly robust demand for the Treasury's offering of 10-year notes, which they said made it likely that interest rates are leveling off. The dollar was up slightly, while gold futures declined.

U.S. trade with the Soviets may grow to as much as $10 billion to $15 billion annually over the next two to three years from $1 billion to $3 billion now, a senior Bush official said. The U.S. is set to begin negotiating a trade agreement with Moscow on Monday.

9 U.S. auto makers are keeping a cautious eye on first-quarter production schedules because of continued uncertainty about the market. The Big Three recently shaved output plans, and more cuts may be needed.

Walt Disney surprised the movie industry by announcing it will no longer allow theaters to run commercials before its films. The ban is a major blow to the fledgling business of advertising in movie theaters.

12 RJR Nabisco has decided to delay a $1.25 billion junk-bond offering, citing poor conditions in the market. The decision is a temporary setback in the company's efforts to reduce interest payments on its huge buy-out debt.

Producer prices shot up 1.8% in January, driven by a 13.6% surge in energy costs. But financial markets and economists dismissed the report as a temporary spike caused by unusually cold December weather.

The Fed confirmed its policy-making panel voted in mid-December to ease credit slightly amid signs the economy was continuing to weaken.

13 Drexel put itself up for sale as it scrambled to avert a financial collapse. The embattled securities firm, once the nation's most profitable, said it is seeking "a major investor or a merger partner" and that talks have already begun. Still, many Wall Street executives say an outright sale will be difficult. Meanwhile, banks tried to assemble a short-term credit line for Drexel.

Stock and bond prices slumped as Drexel's woes sent junk-bond prices tumbling. Bonds also were hurt by higher overseas interest rates. The Dow Jones industrials closed off 29.06, at 2619.14. The dollar was mixed.

Safeway Stores plans to go public again in a share offering that seems to portend a financial windfall for Kohlberg Kravis, the investment bank that took Safeway private four years ago.

Time Warner posted a loss of $222 mil-lion for the fourth quarter. Huge interest payments on the Warner purchase all but wiped out record-high results at most major businesses.

14 Drexel collapsed as its parent announced plans to file for Chapter 11 and liquidate the securities firm's assets. Most of its work force is expected to be laid off this week. The U.S. government and the Big Board made no effort to save Drexel, which was hurt by a cash squeeze and inability to get short-term credit. But the firm's demise isn't expected to affect the health of the financial system.

Junk-bond prices rebounded after Drexel's financial problems triggered an early sell-off. Still, portfolio managers say the market's recovery from its months-long slide will be slow.

Stock prices rose modestly as investors shrugged off Drexel's woes, while Treasury bonds rebounded. The Dow Jones industrials closed up 4.96, at 2624.10. The dollar edged higher.

Chrysler posted a $644 million loss for the fourth quarter, its largest ever, mainly due to a $577 million charge for cutting operations. Chairman Iacocca wouldn't make any forecast for the current quarter.

Retail sales surged 1.6% in January, led by a 5.4% jump in auto sales. But the increase, the biggest in nearly 1½ years, wasn't viewed as a sign that consumer spending is rebounding.

IBM said it built the first 16-megabit memory chips to be fabricated on an existing production line. The chips can store about four times as much as the previous state-of-the-art chips.

Chips & Technology unveiled a set of computer chips that could be used to build fast, multiprocessing computers using regular software.

15 Drexel's rivals began wooing its clients less than a day after the securities firm filed for Chapter 11 protection. Many are trying to bolster their own market share in high-risk junk-bonds and other lucrative businesses long dominated by Drexel. Meanwhile, Drexel is trying to "transfer" some important businesses to its Wall Street competitors, possibly for virtually nothing.

Junk-bond prices continued to rise even as Drexel, the market's cash-strapped leader, put its junk-bond portfolio up for sale. Stocks, Treasury bonds and the dollar were flat.

A new deficit-cutting plan is being negotiated by Bush officials and key Republican senators. The revised proposal would remove the Social Security surplus from deficit calculations while still reaching Bush's goal of a budget surplus after fiscal 1993.

Bush's capital-gains tax cut would reduce federal revenue $11.4 billion over six years and would overwhelmingly favor the rich over the middle class, congressional analysts said.

U.S. car and truck sales rose 8.2% in early February as the auto market continued to rebound from a late 1989 slump. Dealers said the latest results indicate that consumers are willing to buy if the discounts are big enough.

Business inventories fell 0.2% in December, the first drop in over a year and a sign that companies may be avoiding a buildup of unsold goods. But sales were flat during the month.

Japan's trade surplus plunged 89% in January from a year earlier, the biggest decline in nearly 11 years. But the drop mainly reflected seasonal and temporary factors. The trade surplus with the U.S. fell 26%.

16 GM and Ford posted sharply lower fourth-quarter earnings, though strong overseas and financial operations helped shore up sagging U.S. auto results. GM's profit plunged 50% for the quarter and 13% for the year. Ford's skidded 73% for the quarter and 28% for the year. Both companies are likely to report lower results for the current quarter due to costly incentives and lower output.

The Big Board is taking the first steps toward an after-hours trading system, a major departure from the specialist-based trading it has used for nearly 200 years. The move, which reflects growing competition, is certain to set off a firestorm among market makers, traders and brokers.

Drexel Burnham's collapse has put in limbo more than $4 billion in planned junk-bond offerings by nearly two dozen companies. However, other Wall Street securities firms are racing to take over the junk issues.

Shearson is expected to acquire an estimated 28,000 brokerage accounts from Drexel with assets totaling as much as $5 billion. The transfer was still being negotiated last night.

U.S. oil imports surged to a 12-year high in January and accounted for nearly 54% of the nation's petroleum consumption, a record. Industry officials caution that U.S. reliance on foreign oil will continue to grow.

20 Corporate profits fell 14% in the 1989 fourth quarter, a Journal survey shows,

despite expectations by many firms of a rebound. Sharp declines were posted by the auto, aerospace, computer, oil and steel industries. Analysts expect more unpleasant earnings surprises before profits, and the economy, start to recover in the second half of 1990.

Industrial output slid 1.2% in January, mainly due to temporary layoffs in the auto sector and low demand for energy. The drop sharply reduced the industrial operating rate, to 81.9% of capacity from 83.1% in December.

The U.S. trade deficit shrank to $7.17 billion in December, the smallest gap in five years. But the improvement largely reflects a jump in aircraft orders and a slowing economy.

Brokerage commissions rose a surprising 16% last year despite a relatively sluggish stock market. Many in the industry aren't expecting much, if any, improvement this year.

21 Nekoosa agreed to be acquired by Georgia-Pacific for a sweetened $3.74 billion, ending a four-month battle and creating the nation's largest forest-products concern. The accord came after most of Nekoosa's defenses were toppled, including its search for a friendly suitor. Analysts generally applauded the merger, saying it will lead to a further consolidation of the pulp and paper business.

Stocks and bonds tumbled as a surge in Japanese and German interest rates pushed U.S. rates higher. The 30-year Treasury bond plunged 2⅛ points, pushing the yield to 8.66%, the highest since May. The Dow Jones industrials closed down 38.74 points, at 2596.85. The dollar was mixed.

Fed Chairman Greenspan signaled the central bank isn't likely to ease interest rates soon. Greenspan told Congress the economy appears to have bottomed out but will remain slow, helping curb inflation.

Puerto Rico plans to sell the government-owned phone system to raise $2 billion for various programs. The sale would surpass Conrail as the largest privatization in the U.S.

Drexel paid hefty year-end bonuses to employees shortly before its collapse last week. The move has raised eyebrows on Wall Street and caught the interest of creditors.

22 Consumer prices soared 1.1% in January, the biggest jump in over seven years, as food and energy costs surged after December's cold wave. But even excluding those two categories, prices still rose 0.6%. Analysts said the figures show inflationary pressures persist, though price increases are expected to moderate.

Many economists disagree with Fed Chairman Greenspan's assertion that the economy may have hit bottom and is starting to recover.

Stocks fell further as a major sell-off in Tokyo's market sent a chill through Wall Street. The Dow Jones industrials closed off 13.29, at 2583.56, a 2% drop for the week so far. Bond prices and the dollar edged higher.

23 Fed Chairman Greenspan said finding capital to modernize Eastern Europe is "the most important financial issue of the decade." He added that the region's capital needs are forcing up long-term interest rates.

Treasury Secretary Brady criticized pension funds for their short-term trading strategies. He suggested the Treasury may propose measures to encourage long-term investments instead of short-term profits.

26 Renault and Volvo announced an "alliance" in which they will hold major stakes in each other and coordinate operations but remain legally independent. The tie-up of the French and Swedish auto makers, which may lead to a formal merger, is the latest sign that Europe's industry is consolidating amid growing Japanese competition and rising product-development costs.

Tokyo stocks opened sharply lower Monday after posting the worst week since the October 1987 crash. Jitters about the Tokyo market sent U.S. stocks lower Friday. The Dow Jones industrials fell 10.58, to 2564.19. Bonds ended little changed.

U.S. car and truck sales fell 12.1% in mid-February, ending a rally that began in early January. Still, industry officials are heartened that sales this year have been slightly above expectations. Chrysler has scrapped plans to curb production at two plants.

GM is trying to get some U.S. plants to adopt a production strategy that has proved profitable in Europe. But the UAW is resisting.

Machine-tool orders fell 14% in January, reflecting the general slowdown in manufacturing and the more acute problems in auto and defense.

The Soviet Union's oil output is continuing to fall, but the effect on world petroleum markets is diminishing. The most likely beneficiary of the lower Soviet output will be OPEC.

28 Durable goods orders skidded a record 10.5% in January, led by a sharp decline in transportation equipment. But many economists, as well as Fed Chairman Greenspan, don't believe orders will continue to slide steeply. Last month's bigger than-expected drop followed December and November increases.

Bond prices were buoyed by the durables report, while stocks gained despite the gloomy economic news. The Dow Jones industrials closed up 14.64, at 2617.12. The dollar's rise was slowed by further intervention.

Exxon was indicted on five felony and criminal misdemeanor charges stemming from last year's Alaskan oil spill. Attorney General Thornburgh said talks on a possible plea bargain had broken down after Exxon rejected the government's terms.

The power of corporate boards to reject hostile takeover offers and pursue long-term business strategies was broadly affirmed by the Delaware Supreme Court. The court released an opinion explaining its decision last July that allowed Time Inc. to escape a hostile takeover.

The Tokyo stock market's jitters are expected to curb fund raising by many Japanese corporations. Some smaller firms also may reconsider foreign acquisitions. Tuesday's partial recovery by Tokyo stocks was driven by heavy institutional buying.

Major securities firms are paying more of their bonuses with stock rather than cash. The move, which gives employees a bigger stake in the firm's success, is a throwback to the days of Wall Street partnerships.

March 1990

1 Shearson plans to lay off about 2,000 of its 35,000 employees soon and indicated it would pull back from non-core businesses. Shearson, under pressure from parent American Express and credit-rating agencies, expects the retrenchment to result in a big quarterly charge against earnings. Shearson also confirmed it held talks with Primerica Chief Sanford Weill about possible joint ventures.

Fourth-quarter GNP growth was revised upward to a 0.9% rate from 0.5% estimated earlier. Though the revision still shows a sluggish economy at year's end, it strengthens the arguments of many analysts that the country will avoid a recession.

Bond prices slumped in reaction to

the stronger GNP figure, slowing the stock market's gain. The Dow Jones industrials closed up 10.13 at 2627.25. The dollar also continued to rise.

Dart Group was charged by the SEC with violating securities laws relating to its investment activities. But the Haft family-controlled company agreed to a relatively lenient settlement, avoiding a requirement to register as an investment firm.

Employers' use of overfunded pension plans would be sharply restricted under a bill approved by the Senate Labor panel. The measure would prohibit firms from taking excess money out of the plans unless it was in the interest of workers and retirees.

Nervous banks are tightening credit for small companies. Many banks are already reeling from bad loans, especially in real estate, and are worried that the slowing economy will cause even more loan defaults.

Fraud is common and tied to company supervision, studies find.

Some 87% of managers in a National Association of Accountants study were willing to commit fraud in one or more of the cases presented to them. More than half were willing to overstate assets, while 48% said they would establish insufficient return reserves for defective products and 38% said they would pad a government contract. "I was just so surprised that that many people would operate in a fraudulent way," says Paul Brown of New York University, co-author of the study. Those most likely to commit fraud valued pleasure and a comfortable life rather than self-respect, he says.

Company structure also affects ethical behavior, says a University of Pennsylvania Wharton School study. A survey of 443 industrial salespeople found highly supervised employees at bureaucratic firms more likely to act ethically than those at entrepreneurial laissez-faire ones. "There is evidence people think through" the risk of getting caught, says co-author Erin Anderson.

2 Several big retailers posted better-than-expected sales gains for February, aided by stronger apparel sales. Analysts estimate that last month's increases averaged 5% to 6%.

Personal income rose 0.8% in January, bolstered by a federal pay raise and increases for Social Security recipients. Spending grew almost as fast,

0.6%. Also, purchasing managers said new orders rose in February for the first time since June.

The Seabrook nuclear plant won a full-power license from the Nuclear Regulatory Commission. Lawsuits are expected to be filed soon to block the plant's start-up, but analysts predict only temporary delays.

Stock prices edged higher despite a slumping bond market and a 2.2% plunge by Tokyo shares. The Dow Jones industrials closed up 8.34, at 2635.59. The dollar climbed further.

Canada's economy grew at a 0.5% rate in the fourth quarter, damping hopes for lower interest rates.

7 Postal rates would rise an average 19% next February under a proposal by the Postal Service. The increase, which would push first-class mail up to 30 cents from 25 cents and third-class mail up by an average of 17%, reflects rising costs and the slow pace of automation, the Postal Service said. Service also is being cut just as the Post Office faces growing competition from private firms.

Business mailers say they will intensify efforts to switch to other carriers because of rising postal rates.

Factory orders plunged 5.4% in January, the steepest decline in over 15 years, mainly due to a record 10.5% drop in durable goods orders. Economists said the figures reflect continued weakness in manufacturing.

Aging Boeing jets will have to undergo extensive repairs and may face a corrosion-control program, the FAA said. Both actions could cost airlines billions of dollars.

De Beers said it will transfer control of its foreign holdings to Switzerland. But the diamond giant denied it intends to withdraw from South Africa and said the move isn't based on fears of possible nationalization by a future black government.

8 The dollar withstood a major intervention effort, finishing mixed in New York trading. Despite large, repeated dollar sales by major central banks, the currency rose for most of the day before weakening on a Japanese news report of yet more intervention to come. Stock and bond prices eased as investors waited to see which way the dollar would go.

Hilton Hotels' board decided unanimously to take the company off the market. Hilton received two takeover bids valued at $75 to $80 a share but found them inadequate. The board's decision caps a long auction period.

Bank earnings plunged 56% in the fourth quarter, mainly due to a record $8.4 billion increase in loss reserves for U.S. loans. Profits tumbled 34% for the year as banks wrote off a record $22.2 billion in bad assets.

9 USX agreed to hold a shareholder vote May 7 on whether to remain in the steel business. The unprecedented decision follows pressure from USX's biggest shareholder, Carl Icahn, who wants to shed the steel operations. The outcome of the vote may signal the future of the U.S. steel industry and provide an indication of whether investors still favor the quick-buck strategy of the 1980s.

Regulation of AT&T would ease under changes proposed by the FCC. The agency, in agreeing to a study of the long-distance industry, said there already is substantial competition in the market for big business clients.

The dollar strengthened despite continued intervention, sparking more gains by stocks and some bonds. The Dow Jones industrials closed up 26.58 points, at 2696.17, though the broader market didn't rise as much.

The Group of Seven's finance ministers and central bankers plan to meet in Paris April 7 amid worries about the weak Japanese yen and Germany's planned monetary union.

Campeau said it defaulted deliberately on $705 million of loans by refusing to make interest payments last week to two big creditors. The move appeared aimed at persuading one creditor, Edward DeBartolo, to discuss a debt restructuring.

12 The unemployment rate remained at 5.3% in February for the ninth consecutive month. Job growth outside the farm sector posted the biggest rise in 1½ years, though some analysts said the rise doesn't signal much buoyancy in the economy.

Bond prices fell sharply and the dollar strengthened as Friday's jobless report fueled speculation that the U.S. economy is stronger than expected, which could lead to higher interest rates. Stocks ended lower.

The Fed has lost much of its control over U.S. interest rates due to the growing influence of foreign financial markets, particularly in Japan and West Germany. And as the Fed loses leverage, the U.S. loses some of its control over its economic destiny.

Central banks appear to be waging a futile battle to prevent the dollar from rising, currency analysts say.

U.S. auto makers plan to boost car and truck production by 18.6% in the second quarter from the depressed first quarter, signaling a more optimistic outlook. Output would still be down 11.3% from the year-ago level.

Several major Western suppliers have halted shipments to the Soviet Union because of unpaid bills that could total as much as $500 million.

13 The dollar continued to climb, reaching a three-year high against the yen. Stocks and bonds languished as investors sat back to assess what appears to be a budding economic rebound. The Dow Jones industrials closed up 3.38 points, at 2686.71.

Heating oil and gasoline futures fell amid signs of weak demand, sending crude lower as well.

Rhone-Poulenc and Rorer reached a definitive agreement to create one of the drug industry's 10 biggest companies in a transaction they valued at about $3.15 billion. Rhone-Poulenc will control 68% of the new company.

Japanese investment in U.S. real estate fell 11% last year from 1988's record level, a major new study says. In addition, the dominant type of investment shifted to hotel/resort properties from office buildings.

14 Nomura Securities is jumping into program trading with plans to elevate it to a global scale. The move by the Japanese giant could shake up international stock markets and challenge the dominance of U.S. brokers that developed program trading strategies. Nomura's effort will be headed by Joseph Schmuckler, who resigned late yesterday as a top program trader at Kidder Peabody.

A bill giving the SEC the clout to curb program trading was approved unanimously by a House committee.

Retail sales fell 0.9% in February, reflecting a 6% plunge in auto sales. But most other retailers—including department and clothing stores and building-supply dealers—had healthy gains. Also, January sales growth was revised upward to 2.8% from 1.6%.

Bond prices tumbled as the retail sales report indicated the economy is stronger than expected. The yield on the benchmark 30-year Treasury bond rose to 8.71% for the first time since May. Stocks and the dollar fell.

Bush tried to quash speculation he

won't reappoint Fed Chairman Green-span next year but said he wants to see interest rates lower.

Bush indicated he might consider a tax increase, saying he doesn't "want to appear totally inflexible." The president's new stance was spurred by Rostenkowski's deficit plan.

Six of the biggest accounting firms won't be allowed to work on federal thrift bail-outs because they are being sued by the government for allegedly shoddy work. The firms estimate lost business could total $100 million.

Tokyo is moving quickly to try to ease trade barriers due to growing concern about U.S. retaliation. The rush was prompted by Prime Minister Kaifu's recent summit with Bush.

Japan's trade surplus continued to shrink in February, but economists say it may grow again soon.

The U.S. current account gap narrowed to $20.57 billion in the fourth quarter, the smallest in nearly six years. For all of last year, the deficit shrank to $105.88 billion.

15 The junk-bond holdings of insolvent thrifts won't be unloaded by S&L regulators, defusing worries in the market about a massive fire sale. Instead, the thrift-bail-out agency plans to become a long-term player in the junk-bond market with the estimated $4 billion to $6 billion in securities it currently holds.

Columbia S&L reversed its earlier plan and said it will sell its entire junk-bond portfolio, which it valued at about $3.5 billion. The news pushed junk prices lower in late trading.

AT&T is drawing up an early-retirement program for non-management employees that could result in another big work-force reduction this year. A similar offer last year led 12,500 managers to retire early.

U.S. auto sales fell 3.8% in early March, casting a shadow over the start of the spring selling season. Weaker sales by the Big Three more than offset gains by Japanese-brand cars built in the U.S. The sales pace was the slowest since December.

Bond prices rebounded as the drop in auto sales damped speculation that the economy was reviving. The bond rally helped boost stocks. The Dow Jones industrials closed up 13.29, at 2687.84. The dollar ended mixed.

The economy is still growing slowly in most parts of the country, a Fed survey found. The auto industry continues to be the weakest sector.

Business inventories edged up 0.2% in January after falling the month before. But the increase was offset by a 0.3% rise in sales.

16 Citicorp plans to cut back on lending to major commercial real-estate projects. The move by the nation's largest commercial real-estate lender reflects lower profit margins and a surge in problem real-estate loans. Citicorp will focus instead on fee-generating activities, such as finding investors for projects and arranging interest-rate hedges.

Drexel said it has stopped quoting prices on 3,000 to 4,000 junk-bond issues, adding more confusion to the already battered market. The move will particularly affect junk-bond mutual funds that have to calculate the value of their portfolios daily.

Wall Street is facing further cutbacks as the securities industry completes one of its slowest quarters in years. Stock trading is still sluggish and most areas of investment banking are expected to remain weak.

19 Japanese leaders endorsed a set of domestic policy changes targeting "structural" causes of Japan's trade surpluses. But the tentative package apparently is less than the U.S. is seeking and could yet be beefed up.

Producer prices were unchanged in February after soaring 1.8% the month before. Energy costs, which skyrocketed 13.6% in January, fell 5% last month. Reports on housing starts and industrial production also helped ease concerns about inflation.

Consumer prices are expected to show a rise in February of only 0.3% after a 1.1% January surge.

Norton could face a proxy fight by BTR PLC if the maker of abrasives doesn't accept the British conglomerate's $1.64 billion hostile takeover bid. But sources said the U.S. concern intends to put up a struggle.

20 United Air's unions renewed efforts to buy UAL with a $185-a-share, or $4.03 billion, bid that would give employees 75% and likely mean the ouster of Chairman Wolf. The unions put pressure on UAL's board to accept the offer by joining forces with Coniston Partners in a proxy fight to oust directors at the April 26 annual meeting. Though the union's latest proposal has several drawbacks, UAL's stock surged $12, to $154.50.

Tokyo stocks plunged 4.1% amid concern that Japanese policy makers are running out of ways to shore up the crumbling market. The Nikkei index skidded 1353.20 points, to 31263.24, the third-biggest drop ever.

U.S. stocks rebounded from an early slide as investors shook off the big decline in Tokyo. The Dow Jones industrials finished up 14.41 points, at 2755.63. Bonds were little changed and the dollar was mixed.

First Boston is said to have sold to its Swiss parent more than half of a troubled $450 million loan to Ohio Mattress. The move underscores the concern of Wall Street securities firms to remove bad loans from their books to prevent lower debt ratings.

Crude-oil prices tumbled due to apparently abundant short-term supplies and OPEC's inability to curb overproduction. The spot contract in New York fell below $20 a barrel for the first time since December.

21 Consumer prices rose 0.5% last month, a marked slowdown from January's 1.1% surge but still disturbingly high to economists. A record 18.7% drop in fuel-oil prices helped hold down the increase, but a 3.3% jump in clothing costs kept inflation higher than analysts hoped.

The U.S. trade deficit grew $1.57 billion in January, swollen by record oil imports. The report fueled concern that the recent improvement in U.S. trade will stall or worsen this year due to dependence on foreign oil.

Tokyo stocks fell a further 1.5% after Japan's central bank raised its discount rate to 5.25% from 4.25%. Speculation is mixed on how much lower Japanese stocks will go before they start to recover. The market is closed today for a Japanese holiday.

Brazil said it will continue to suspend interest payments on most of its $114 billion foreign debt. Venezuela reached an innovative accord on most of its $28 billion foreign debt.

23 Stock prices tumbled as U.S. investors began to show concern about the Tokyo stock market's continued slide. The Dow Jones industrials closed down 32.21 points, at 2695.72. Long-term bond prices edged slightly higher, while the dollar was mixed.

Tokyo shares finished the Thursday session with a 3.1% loss after plunging 6% earlier in the day. The partial recovery was helped by program trading, which was blamed for much of the Tokyo market's sharp decline earlier this year.

Thrift regulators issued an interim regulation that sharply curbs the amount

S&Ls may lend to any single borrower. The new rule, aimed at limiting risk, is one of the many provisions of the thrift-bail-out law that are being contested by S&Ls.

The Soviet Union agreed to significantly boost purchases of U.S. grain over the next five years. The accord strengthens economic ties between the two nations and secures an important market for U.S. farmers.

26 Japan's trade barriers may be starting to ease somewhat due to high-level U.S. political pressure. Both nations reached an understanding Friday that would make it easier for U.S. makers of supercomputers to sell to the Japanese government. There also have been signs of progress in two other areas targeted by the U.S.—satellites and lumber.

Treasury Secretary Brady held talks with Japanese Finance Minister Hashimoto to try to reassure financial markets, particularly after the recent slide in Tokyo stocks and the yen.

Durable-goods orders surged 3.3% in February, but the gain doesn't signal a rebound in manufacturing. Most of the increase came from an 11.2% jump in transportation orders, reflecting the reopening of auto factories that were closed in January.

Machine-tool orders skidded 31% in February, reflecting uncertainty among manufacturers about the direction of the nation's economy.

U.S. car and truck sales fell 9.5% in mid-March, the latest in a string of disappointing results. Chrysler took the hardest hit among major U.S. makers, as sales plunged 28.6%. But most Japanese models built in North America registered sales gains.

27 The U.S. and Mexico have agreed to negotiate a free-trade accord that effectively would create a unified North American market, Bush officials said. Such a pact would have enormous implications for both countries by giving each better access to the other's markets, labor, technology and expertise. But negotiating an agreement, which is likely to take over a year, could prove difficult.

The dollar surged 1.5% to a 38-month high against the yen as traders continued to batter the Japanese currency. But the dollar fell against most other major currencies. U.S. stocks and bonds closed up slightly despite a big rally on the Tokyo stock market.

Gold prices plunged over $20 an ounce, almost wiping out a rally that began last September. A big sell-off in London, apparently by the Saudi Arabian government, sparked the drop.

Thrift losses grew to a record $6.49 billion in the 1989 fourth quarter, reflecting huge non-operating losses. The red ink, which widened to a record $19.17 billion for all of last year, also illustrates the cost of delay in the S&L industry's restructuring.

28 Lockheed rejected a compromise plan that would have given Dallas investor Harold Simmons three of the company's 14 board seats and resolved a long proxy battle. Lockheed's move has apparently driven some big institutional holders to support Simmons, who is seeking control of the defense contractor. The proxy vote at tomorrow's annual meeting is likely to be close.

Eastern Airlines said it can't meet terms of a previously negotiated settlement that would have repaid unsecured creditors about 50 cents on the dollar. The carrier said it plans to slash costs and raise money by shrinking further than intended.

New York state's municipal bonds could see more trouble following a major downgrading of the state's credit rating, bond experts said.

29 Fourth-quarter GNP growth was revised upward, to a 1.1% rate from 0.9%. Still, the gain was the smallest in more than three years, partly reflecting the Fed's tighter-credit policy. Corporate earnings grew 2.8%.

New-home sales rose 3.1% in February after tumbling 6.8% the month before. But the housing industry is expected to remain weak the rest of the year due to rising interest rates and declining consumer demand.

Fidelity Investments faces a difficult period following the surprise resignation of its star mutual-fund manager, Peter Lynch. The nation's largest mutual fund group will have to find a new magnet to attract small investors. There also are questions whether the flagship Magellan Fund, which Lynch managed, can continue its rapid growth.

30 Kidder Peabody became the latest big securities firm to recapitalize amid Wall Street's slump. Parent company General Electric will pump about $550 million into Kidder, primarily by buying the unit's investment portfolio of junk-bonds, temporary "bridge" loans and related merchant banking holdings.

First Chicago said first-quarter profit would be about half the year-ago level of $124.7 million, reflecting an increase in problem real-estate loans. The banking concern is the latest to be hit by the worsening commercial real-estate sector.

April 1990

2 Wall Street's profits in underwriting stocks and bonds teetered near six-year lows in the first quarter. And the recent collapse of the junk-bond market promises even leaner times ahead. The sluggishness in underwriting fees comes at a time when securities firms are struggling with a slowdown in other businesses.

Merrill Lynch continued to be the world's biggest underwriter of stocks and bonds in the quarter, but its lead shrank as financing volume eased.

McDonnell Douglas confirmed it won a $2 billion jet order from Japan Air Lines that includes options for a stretched version of the MD-11 jet.

Chrysler is asking its top 100 executives to own stock equal to a certain percentage of their salaries. The unusual program is aimed at having the officials bet more of their pay on Chrysler's long-term financial health.

Factory orders rebounded 1.8% in February, helped by gains in the auto sector. The increase followed a revised 5.5% plunge the month before, the biggest in 15 years. Also, the February rise in durable-goods orders was revised to 2.6% from 3.3%.

Fed policy makers voted in February to leave credit unchanged. But for the first time in months, some officials talked of raising rates.

3 U.S. stocks declined in reaction to the 6.6% plunge in Tokyo shares, the second-worst ever. The dollar, whose recent strength is partly to blame for the drop in Tokyo, continued to post gains. U.S. Treasury bonds eased.

Japanese stocks may fall further if the most-recent slide prompts margin calls, some analysts said.

Manufacturing remained sluggish in March for the 11th consecutive month, purchasing managers said. Still, there were some signs of firming in the sector. Meanwhile, construction spending climbed 2.6% in February as all sectors showed gains.

Shearson expects a first-quarter loss of

$897 million to $917 million, a securities industry record, to pay for its revamping and cost-cutting plan. The firm announced several new cutbacks as part of the effort.

4 General Motors named President Robert Stempel chairman and chief executive, succeeding Roger Smith, who will retire August 1. Stempel, 56, isn't expected to make any major changes at the auto giant. Some GM officials say Stempel, considered an innovative manager, has turned cautious in recent years.

The first major clean-air bill since 1977 neared Senate approval last night. But the legislation faces an uncertain course in the House, where environmentalists are pressing for measures that are even tougher on industry than the Senate bill.

Big brokerage firms are shedding their junk-bond holdings and other illiquid investments, partly due to pressure from credit-rating agencies and regulators, including the Big Board. The sell-off also has been spurred by Drexel's recent collapse.

Xerox said it will take a $400 million pre-tax write-off for the first quarter, effectively abandoning its investment in VMS Realty Partners, the ailing Chicago real estate firm. The write-off is Xerox's biggest ever.

Leading indicators slid 1% in February, mainly due to an unusual drop in building permits. Excluding permits, the government's main economic forecasting gauge eased 0.1%.

Stocks surged due to the rebound in Tokyo shares and computer buy programs. The Dow Jones industrials closed up 36.26, at 2736.71. Bonds edged higher. The dollar was mixed.

Tokyo stocks rose sharply the day after the second-biggest decline ever. The Nikkei index climbed 2.7%.

Oil prices may fall soon unless OPEC starts curbing output, which reached an eight-year high in March, according to new estimates.

5 Timothy Ryan won Senate approval to be the nation's top savings and loan regulator, effectively nullifying a court decision that had derailed the overhaul of the S&L industry. The surprisingly wide margin of 62–37 in favor of Ryan followed a six-hour debate about whether the labor lawyer is qualified for the job.

6 A landmark trade pact was reached by the U.S. and Japan aimed at opening Japanese markets to more foreign business. The interim accord addresses U.S. complaints about Japan's clubby business practices, cautious attitude to foreign investment, restrictive land use, lack of patent protection and other barriers. The U.S., in turn, will take steps to improve its competitiveness.

Bankruptcy-law filings jumped 34% in the fourth quarter of last year, reflecting the soft economy and heavy debt burdens at many companies. The growth appears likely to continue.

Japan's securities industry is expected to undergo a major shake-up following the collapse in Tokyo share prices this year. The changes may mean stiffer competition for U.S. and European brokerages in Japan.

Petroleum prices tumbled on worries about a possible supply glut. OPEC production is now at an eight-year high, while U.S. crude inventories are the biggest in two years.

U.S. stocks and bonds were little changed amid wariness about the Tokyo stock market, the U.S. economy and the dollar's outlook.

9 UAL's outlook remains uncertain despite Friday's agreement to be acquired by United Air's unions for $4.38 billion. The buy-out itself may take several more months to complete, and much will depend on how well the unions get along among themselves and management. Moreover, the carrier has been so preoccupied with possible buy-outs that it has steadily lost ground to competitors.

The Group of Seven industrial nations voiced concern about the weak yen and hinted it might continue intervening to bolster the currency. But the group, which met Saturday in Paris, brushed aside Japanese calls for coordinated interest-rate moves.

The dollar is expected to continue its climb against the yen despite any profit-taking or central bank intervention ahead, analysts said.

The U.S.-Japan trade pact reached last week is being viewed skeptically by U.S. executives and analysts. Many note that a key question—how the accord will be monitored and enforced—has been put off until July.

The unemployment rate fell to 5.2% in March from 5.3% the month before. Still, many analysts were disappointed by the meager growth in new jobs, a sign that the economy remains sluggish. Manufacturing jobs declined during the month.

Another surge of layoffs has begun

in all sectors of the economy. The cutbacks reflect the junk-bond market's slide, retailers' troubles and further corporate retrenchments.

A tax increase will be needed to pay for the S&L bail-out, the head of the GAO said. The cost is now put at $325 billion instead of $257 billion.

10 Insurers were dealt a blow as a New Jersey judge ruled that Owens-Illinois's insurance companies will have to pay as much as $960 million to cover asbestos-related claims.

Ames Department Stores plans to close 74 stores and will post a loss of $228 million for its fiscal year.

Oil prices plunged again on new fears of a glut. Crude futures fell to the lowest levels since the summer.

An East Europe development bank will be set up by major industrial nations with $12 billion of capital. A pact was reached after the U.S. won a strict limit on Soviet borrowing.

11 The S&L Bailout Agency had another flop in its second attempt to sell 40-year bonds, a sign that demand for securities with an extra-long maturity isn't very strong. The $3.5 billion auction of "bailout bonds" went poorly despite a higher-than-expected yield of 8.89%.

Treasury-bond prices tumbled in reaction to the S&L bond auction. Stocks edged higher, while the dollar fell against the mark and yen.

The Big Three auto makers are expected to post a 70% drop in first-quarter earnings, reflecting efforts to clear bloated inventories. The strategy included a 26.5% reduction in quarterly production and sales incentives averaging $1,000 a vehicle.

Only 20% of Drexel's employees have found jobs in the securities industry since the firm collapsed two months ago, executives estimate. Those that have found work are mainly Drexel's top professionals.

OPEC is growing nervous about the continued slide in oil prices. But the group is unlikely to take any action before late May, when it holds its regular midyear conference.

Time Warner's long-term public debt was placed on S&P's Credit-Watch with negative implications due to its financing pact with Pathe.

12 Oil prices swung sharply in one of the wildest trading days ever on world markets. After plunging initially on a report of a growing supply glut, petroleum prices rebounded on rumors

OPEC may call an emergency meeting. The trading left analysts divided on where oil was headed. Meanwhile, stocks eased and bonds rose. The dollar was mixed.

Saudi Arabia made another discovery of high-quality crude oil, which is likely to strengthen the kingdom's position as the world's largest exporter of petroleum.

U.S. businesses plan to boost capital spending 7.8% this year, showing unexpected optimism about the economy. The growth in outlays for plant and equipment could help keep the eight-year economic expansion alive.

13 Gorbachev's economic proposals could free 70% of the Soviet economy from state control, slash central planning and raise most prices an average 100%, according to a key adviser, Pavel Bunich. But he cautioned that the plan still has many murky areas and isn't final.

The economic reforms may face strong opposition from the Soviet public, especially if there is mass unemployment and big price increases for basic goods, as economists expect.

Retail sales fell 0.6% in March, the first two-month decline in over three years. Still, economists said retailers are better off than the figures imply. Auto sales remained weak, but most other sectors had minor declines.

Several mall retailers reported better-than-expected sales last month, even though the Easter holiday season is in April this year.

The SEC is expected next week to waive disclosure rules for stock and bond offerings that are sold privately to big institutions. The change could swell the $165 billion U.S. market for privately placed securities.

16 Inflation moderated in March as lower food and energy costs helped cause a 0.2% drop in producer prices. Excluding the volatile food and energy sectors, prices rose a modest 0.3% for the month. Despite the improvement, some economists warned that inflation remains a threat.

Boeing said it will largely fund development of the 767-X jet itself, giving three Japanese firms a far smaller role in the $3 billion project. The announcement, ending months of speculation, also means more U.S. companies could become involved.

Workers can take age discrimination complaints to federal court even if a state agency rules that no discrimination occurred, a federal appeals court said. The decision is likely to influence other cases around the U.S.

17 IBM's profit surged 0.2% in the first quarter, a surprisingly strong performance that included the company's best U.S. results in years. The report sent IBM's stock up $3.75, to $110.875. But some analysts cautioned that the computer giant's outlook for all of 1990 remains uncertain.

Stocks finished mixed after a blue-chip rally, triggered by IBM's earnings report, was choked off by slumping bond prices. The Dow Jones industrials closed up 11.26 points, at 2763.06. The dollar also ended higher.

18 Consumer prices rose 0.5% in March, pushing the first-quarter inflation rate to 8.5%, the highest in eight years. Though economists don't expect that pace to continue, the figures suggest inflation remains a problem. There also were signs of continued weakness in the economy.

Treasury bond prices slid following the inflation report, pushing the yield to 8.72%, the highest in almost a year. Stocks recovered from an initial decline, while the dollar was mixed.

Employers were dealt a blow by the Supreme Court. The justices upheld a federal labor policy that companies can't oust a striking union by hiring new workers and asserting the employees don't support the union.

The SEC is considering tighter restrictions on investments by money-market mutual funds. The move follows defaults on some securities that were held by funds.

19 Treasury bonds sank for the second day in a row, sending stock prices and the dollar lower. Continued worries about inflation and reports of a big sell-off by Japanese investors caused the benchmark 30-year Treasury issue to decline 1⅛ points, pushing the yield up to 8.83%, the highest in nearly a year. The Dow Jones industrials slid 32.89, to 2732.88.

Oil prices skidded as much as 70 cents a barrel on world markets, reflecting disappointment that a meeting of three key OPEC members failed to result in any action.

The U.S. trade deficit shrank sharply in February, to $6.49 billion, the smallest since December 1983. Imports slid 7.6%, led by a plunge in oil buying. Analysts said the smaller deficit reflected the weak economy.

Brazil plans to resume negotiations on its $115 billion foreign debt and to begin efforts to sell off state companies. The actions reflect the government's belief that its new anti-inflation program is working.

20 Citicorp's debt faces a possible downgrade by Moody's, a move that could have a major negative impact on the banking system. Moody's cited growth in Citicorp's nonperforming real-estate loans, highly leveraged deals and Third World debt. A downgrade would boost the banking giant's short-term cost of funds and hurt its prestige.

OPEC's excess oil production is starting to slow, apparently because buyers are refusing to absorb any more. OPEC also called an emergency meeting for May 2. World oil prices surged in reaction.

Control of Eastern Air was wrested from parent Texas Air and its chairman, Frank Lorenzo. A bankruptcy judge named a trustee to run the financially troubled carrier.

The SEC eased rules for selling and trading privately placed securities, a move that could transform the way many companies raise capital.

Nissan Motor has begun construction on a new vehicle assembly plant in Mexico that is part of a $1 billion expansion in the country.

23 Michael Milken agreed to plead guilty to six felony counts and to pay $600 million in fines and restitution, the largest criminal settlement ever. Friday's decision by Drexel's former junk-bond chief came just before a grand jury was to indict him on insider trading, bribery and other charges. It's unclear how much Milken will cooperate with federal investigators in implicating others.

24 Sir James Goldsmith dropped his hostile pursuit of B.A.T amid growing anti-takeover sentiment, particularly in the U.S. The financier, whose $21.13 billion bid for B.A.T was the second-largest in history, faced obstacles in several U.S. states where the British firm operated. The final blow apparently was California's decision to bar a change in control of B.A.T's Farmers Insurance unit.

General Motors said it will shut a Michigan assembly plant in 1993, the latest in a series of closings due to slowing sales. The UAW union has vowed to make job security a top issue in coming contract talks with GM.

The Supreme Court refused to hear an appeal by GM over a warranty-related suit that may become a class action for nearly 600,000 clients.

25 Sears Roebuck's profit plunged 59% in the first quarter due to "unsatisfactory" results in its core retail business and hefty claims at its Allstate insurance unit. Sears stock slid $1.125, to $35.375, a 52-week low.

Durable goods orders surged 6.7% in March, prompting some analysts to suggest manufacturing may be rebounding. The rise, reflecting a jump in transportation-equipment orders, was the biggest in more than a year.

Sales of U.S.-built cars and trucks plunged 17.7% in mid-April, a poor performance in what is usually the heart of the spring selling season.

26 Norton agreed to be acquired for $90 a share, or about $1.9 billion, by French glassmaker Saint-Gobain, a surprising rescue of the Massachusetts abrasives maker from hostile suitor BTR of Britain. BTR, which offered $75 a share, ended its proxy fight against Norton and said it wouldn't top Saint-Gobain's bid. Norton's stock surged $13.50, to $88.75.

More foreigners are buying up U.S. companies, in part because American buyers are having problems getting bank loans or junk-bond financing.

Bush won't designate Japan as an unfair trading partner, aides said, a shift from the tough U.S. stance of a year ago. Trade Representative Carla Hills said that "Japan has moved further this year than any other country" in lowering trade barriers.

B.A.T agreed to sell its Saks Fifth Avenue chain for about $1.5 billion to Investcorp, a low-profile partnership of Arab investors. The group is taking a big gamble on an industry that has bankrupted other foreign investors.

A Safeway stock offering was slashed in price as trading was set to begin today. The supermarket chain, which went private in 1986, is one of the crown jewels of Kohlberg Kravis.

27 Citicorp's debt rating was cut by Standard & Poor's, the latest blow to the banking industry. The downgrading affects $30 billion of long-term and short-term debt as well as preferred securities. S&P said Citicorp maintains levels of capital and loan-loss reserves well below those of rivals. Citicorp is now under more pressure to boost capital and reserves by selling assets and common stock.

Treasury bond and note yields surged above 9% to the highest level in a year

as dealers slashed prices to attract buyers. One analyst called it a "fire sale." Stock prices were mixed, while the dollar strengthened.

Ames Department Stores filed for Chapter 11 protection, ending efforts to become a giant discount retailer. The filing came as talks with lenders stalled and many unpaid vendors had stopped deliveries to Ames's stores. Ames was hurt by its $800 million purchase of Zayre two years ago.

30 The economy appears to have rebounded mildly in the first quarter. GNP grew at a 2.1% rate, a slow but healthy pace and nearly twice the fourth quarter's 1.1% rate. But a GNP inflation index rose 6.5%, the sharpest gain in over eight years. Most analysts expect the Fed to keep credit unchanged, though some believe the worsening of inflation could prompt some tightening.

Machine-tool orders surged 37% in March from the month before, aided by a large order from a Soviet auto plant. But demand from U.S. durable goods makers remained sluggish.

The U.S. dropped Japan from its list of unfair traders, as expected, signaling Bush's preference for cooperation rather than confrontation in trade issues. The U.S. also said its top priority is successfully completing global trade-liberalization talks.

The toughest anti-takeover law in the nation was adopted in Pennsylvania Friday, but legal challenges may not end for months or even years.

May 1990

1 Mergers can be dismantled by federal courts as a result of antitrust suits by states or private citizens, the Supreme Court ruled. The decision, clearing the way for California to challenge the merger of two supermarket chains, raises the risks for firms involved in mergers and is likely to prompt them to cooperate more with state attorneys general.

Personal spending rose 0.4% in March, mainly because consumers paid higher prices to keep up with inflation. Personal income jumped 0.8%, but much of that stemmed from a boost in farmer subsidies.

Inflation worries are rising among economists, in part because the Fed is under pressure to avoid moves that might hurt the economic expansion.

GM was dealt a blow in the Supreme Court, which let stand a ruling allowing ex-workers to sue GM for refusing to consider rehiring them.

2 Manufacturing grew in April for the first time in 11 months, purchasing managers said. But construction spending fell 1.4% in March, the first decline this year. Both manufacturing and construction have been hurt by the Fed's efforts to battle inflation with high rates.

Stocks edged higher in reaction to the purchasing managers' report, while bond prices weakened. The Dow Jones industrials closed up 12.16, at 2668.92. The dollar drifted lower.

Mitsubishi Motors agreed to buy a majority stake in Value Rent-a-Car, becoming the first Japanese maker to align itself with a U.S. car-rental firm. Terms weren't disclosed.

3 Leading economic indicators rose 0.9% in March, the biggest increase since June 1988, suggesting the economy will continue to grow moderately. Factory orders rose 3.8% in March, as aircraft orders spurted.

The Fed hasn't found much evidence of a large-scale credit crunch, despite reports that banks were reluctant to make loans to businesses.

Stock prices advanced after the report, which also cited modest economic growth. The Dow Jones industrials rose 20.72 points to 2689.64.

4 OPEC pledged to cut oil production by nearly 1.5 million barrels a day in an urgent effort to shore up sagging petroleum prices. But oil futures prices skidded as the pact was announced. The June contract for the U.S. benchmark crude fell 69 cents to $17.99 a barrel.

GM profit skidded 54% in the first quarter, while Ford reported a 69% decline. Separately, industry car and truck sales rose 2.8% in late April.

GM is launching a marketing blitz aimed at attracting millions of Americans turned off by its lackluster cars and poor customer relations.

7 Company profits fell 18% in the first quarter, a *Wall Street Journal* survey shows, hurt by increased labor costs, higher interest payments and unusually big write-offs. Many analysts expect earnings to remain soft in the current quarter but to pick up in the second half.

The jobless rate rose to 5.4% in April from 5.2% the previous month, indicating continued weakness in the economy. The increase surprised many analysts because of recent signs the economy was picking up.

Stock and bond prices rallied Friday as the jobless report eased speculation that the Fed may tighten credit soon. The dollar finished mixed.

Drexel paid creditors over $600 million in the three months before it filed for Chapter 11 protection, which means the payments may be recoverable under federal bankruptcy law, according to bankruptcy lawyers.

Brazil began opening its market to more imports, including telephone equipment, as promised. But high import duties were imposed on most items to protect domestic firms.

8 Carl Icahn appeared to have lost his proxy fight to force USX to spin off its steel operations. But the battle, which culminated with yesterday's vote by USX shareholders, ultimately may prod the company to sell at least part of the core business. Many holders expressed dissatisfaction with the value of USX shares.

Manufacturing productivity rose at a 4.1% rate in the first quarter, but that wasn't enough to offset big declines in other sectors. Overall business productivity fell at a 0.5% rate. Wage increases appeared to slow, suggesting inflation may be easing.

The Soviets are buying U.S. corn at a near-record pace, but there are nagging concerns about Moscow's ability to pay its bills. Grain experts speculate the Soviets have had to use Japanese credit to purchase corn.

9 The Treasury told Congress it will offer a plan this week to shift regulation of stock-index futures to the SEC, ending months of uncertainty. But the move is likely to reignite the debate over regulation of the products.

The thrift-bailout agency hopes to speed the sale of real estate amassed from ailing S&Ls by cutting prices on hard-to-sell properties by up to 20%. The agency also plans to sell about $300 million in properties through a televised auction this summer.

10 The dollar skidded on speculation that Washington's effort to cut the budget deficit may push U.S. interest rates lower. The currency fell to a 28-month low against the mark. Bond prices also dropped despite a good response to the Treasury's $10 billion auction of 10-year notes. Stock prices closed mixed.

Competition is heating up again in international express delivery. JAL, Lufthansa and Nissho Iwai are seeking equity ties with DHL Worldwide Express, putting more pressure on Federal Express and UPS, which are pushing hard to expand overseas.

Inflation may be worse than recent statistics indicate, economists say. They cite hard-to-measure, extra-inflationary forces such as higher property and local taxes, soaring health costs and increasing tuition fees.

Bank failures have slowed considerably this year, according to FDIC Chairman William Seidman. As of Tuesday, 52 banks had failed in 1990, compared with 73 that failed or got FDIC aid at this time last year.

11 The Treasury sold $10 billion of 30-year bonds at an unexpectedly low yield of 8.84%, strengthening the belief among investors that U.S. interest rates are heading lower. Stock and bond prices closed higher, while the dollar finished mixed.

Fed Chairman Greenspan urged banks not to curb lending in an effort to play down fears of a credit crunch. Greenspan and other regulators met privately with bank officials.

The U.S. winter wheat harvest is expected to surge 44% this year. The surprise government forecast is likely to send wheat futures plunging today.

14 Stocks and bonds surged on Friday as reports of moderate inflation and a slowing economy damped speculation that the Fed would soon boost interest rates. Producer prices fell 0.3% in April, the second decline in two months, while retail sales slid 0.6%, mainly due to a continued slump in auto sales. Both declines surprised the markets.

The Dow Jones industrials closed up 63.07, at 2801.58, near its record, in the heaviest Big Board trading this year. Long-term Treasury bonds jumped over two points, the biggest rally of the year. The dollar was mixed but slid 2.6% against the yen.

Some top bankers said they see clear signs of a credit pinch in real estate, mainly due to tougher regulatory supervision. But the bankers suggested that last week's meeting with top regulators could help prevent a broader pullback in lending.

Kidder Peabody may dismiss up to 10% of its staff as part of a new cost-cutting drive, sources said. One target of the layoffs is likely to be the investment banking division, which the GE unit recently beefed up.

N. V. Philips is expected to announce a big management shake-up today, which is likely to include the resignation of its president. The changes are aimed at restoring investor confidence in the Dutch electronics giant's sagging stock price.

15 Stocks surged again, pushing the Dow Jones industrials to a record close of 2821.53, up 19.95, in heavy trading. But there were signs that the rally, sparked Friday by speculation of lower interest rates, was quickly losing steam. Bond prices also posted solid gains, pushing long-term interest rates lower, but their advance also weakened in late trading. The dollar continued to decline.

A new antitrust ruling by the Supreme Court made it tougher for manufacturers or distributors to be sued for putting a cap on retail prices. Experts said the decision is a victory for consumers because it allows manufacturers to cut retail prices largely without fear of a competitor suing.

The Treasury urged Congress to require that Fannie Mae and six other federally sponsored financing agencies qualify for and obtain triple-A credit ratings, without factoring in the government's implicit guarantee.

Business inventories were virtually unchanged in March, a sign that managers are avoiding any buildup in stockpiles that could lead to a recession. Sales climbed 0.6%.

16 The budget deficit is now expected to reach $128 billion to $140 billion for fiscal 1991, even if the cost of the thrift bail-out is excluded, the White House said. The latest increase in the administration's forecast came as Bush opened deficit-cutting talks with congressional leaders.

Blue-chip stocks edged higher, pushing the Dow Jones industrials up 0.92, to a record 2822.45. But the broader market declined due to profit-taking. Bonds fell modestly, while the dollar was mixed.

Industrial output fell 0.4% in April, reflecting a sharp drop in the auto industry and declines in most other sectors. Factories, utilities and mines operated at 83% of capacity, off from 83.5% in March. The reports were a further sign the economy is weak.

Car and truck sales fell 8.4% in early May, damping hopes the industry's year-long slump will end soon. Many dealers have cut new-car orders amid uncertainty that sales will start to rebound anytime soon.

Manville's trust fund for asbestos victims came under fire as two judges ordered the trust to account for a huge shortfall in funds. The judges also indicated they may order the fund to pay damages more quickly.

17 Consumer prices rose 0.2% in April, indicating retail inflation has slowed from its rapid pace at the beginning of the year. But many analysts said the figures suggest little progress is being made in reducing the nation's core inflation rate. Meanwhile, housing starts tumbled 5.8% last month, another sign that the economy remains sluggish.

Bush said he won't give details of his position on federal budget issues until a bipartisan agreement has been completed. The president said he was concerned about "frightening" the financial markets by exaggerating the extent of the budget problem.

18 The U.S. trade deficit grew by more than $2 billion in March, to $8.45 billion, as a 10% jump in imports offset record exports. Despite the wider gap, analysts were encouraged by the 4.6% rise in exports, which was broad-based. Analysts also predicted that import demand will ease with the slowing U.S. economy.

Stock prices rallied in reaction to the stronger American exports, pushing the Dow Jones industrials up 12.03, to a record 2831.71. But bonds weakened and the dollar was mixed.

The Fed apparently decided to leave credit unchanged at Tuesday's policy meeting, faced with conflicting signals on the economy. One member said the Fed hasn't changed its credit policy since just before Christmas.

21 Many banks have tightened lending standards for midsized and small firms amid worries about the economy and their own loan portfolios, a Fed survey says. Also, the Fed disclosed that complaints about a credit crunch contributed to its decision in March not to raise interest rates.

A bill to let banks underwrite and sell insurance was approved by Delaware's Legislature late Thursday. The measure, which the governor has pledged to sign, could make the state a springboard for national insurance-marketing efforts by banks.

Treasury bond investors aren't getting enough government protection, the GAO says. The agency, which cites questionable dealer sales tactics and the lack of timely price data, says the Treasury should have more control over the market.

Junk-bond prices staged the biggest rally in weeks Friday as buyers flooded the market. But investors said market liquidity remains a problem. Stocks and Treasury bonds declined, while the dollar was mixed.

Pan Am's Northeast shuttle was put up for sale just weeks after its only competitor in the market, the Trump Shuttle, went on the block. But financial and regulatory hurdles may prevent a quick sale of either service.

22 Stocks resumed climbing, pushing the Dow Jones industrials up 24.77 points, to a record 2844.68, in active trading. The rally was led by expectations that inflation and interest rates have moderated for now. Bond prices edged up slightly, while the dollar ended mixed after profit-taking trimmed earlier gains.

Technology shares have surged in recent weeks amid better-than-expected quarterly earnings reports. Computer issues such as Compaq, Digital Equipment and IBM have been particularly strong.

The United Auto Workers union plans to seek Japanese-style job guarantees in contract talks with the Big Three U.S. car makers this summer. The union also said it will push to give auto workers more say in product design and factory operations.

The U.S. had a record budget surplus for April due to a surge in individual income-tax receipts. But even the $42.52 billion surplus won't be enough to bring the fiscal 1990 deficit down to the Gramm-Rudman target of $100 million, analysts say.

Raytheon won a $414 million contract from the Army, which awarded the job to prevent layoffs at the firm's missile-making operations.

Japan is becoming less defensive about its huge trade surpluses. Amid fears of a global credit crunch, Japanese officials say their big reservoir of cash could actually help the world economy by helping fund Germany's unification or U.S. budget deficits.

23 The Treasury plans to seek massive new borrowing authority for the S&L bailout because it significantly underestimated the cost, officials said. Treasury Secretary Brady is expected to ask Congress today for authority to borrow about $80 billion to $140 billion and acknowledge his department's poor cost estimate. The total taxpayer cost of the thrift rescue, including interest, may now reach $300 billion over 10 years.

Thrift regulators' new tactic of selling partial S&Ls rather than whole ones has sharply increased the short-term cost of the bail-out.

The U.S. criticized Japan for the slow pace of financial deregulation. Tokyo also was warned it may face trade sanctions unless it agrees soon to decontrol bank deposit rates.

Bond prices rallied on heavy foreign buying, which helped lift stocks hurt by profit-taking. The Dow Jones industrials closed up 7.55 points, at a record 2852.23. The dollar was mixed.

24 Gold prices plunged for the second time in two months, sparking a volatile bond rally that also boosted stocks. The decline by gold, which closed down $11.80 an ounce on the Comex, at $364.60, was attributed again to heavy selling by Saudi Arabia. The Dow Jones industrials closed up 4.03, at a record 2856.26. The dollar edged higher.

Oil prices skidded following a report that U.S. inventories had risen to the highest level since 1982.

Taxpayers will bear most of the added costs of the S&L bail-out, which is now expected to total $90 billion to $130 billion, not including interest, Treasury Secretary Brady said.

The budget summit may find that raising taxes is easy compared with finding cuts in spending, which is more politically treacherous.

Opposition to higher taxes has softened among Americans, but they remain divided on the issue, a *Wall Street Journal*/NBC News poll says.

25 The economy grew at a 1.3% rate in the first quarter, far slower than the 2.1% reported earlier. But the change reflected a downward revision in business inventories, particularly autos, which analysts said was a healthy sign in a flat economy. Real final sales, a gauge of economic demand, increased a revised 4.1%, up from 4% estimated previously.

R. H. Macy bonds plunged as much as 8% amid growing concern in credit markets and the retailing industry about the chain's financial health. Macy still has over $5 billion in debt from its 1986 management buy-out.

29 GM holders approved a big increase in executive pensions. But criticism of the plan led GM Chairman Roger Smith and his successor, Robert Stempel, to say they may not put such an issue to a vote again.

Personal income rose 0.3% in April, the smallest gain since September. Personal spending climbed 0.6% and is expected to continue growing, particularly in the service sector.

Machine-tool orders increased 19% in April, mainly because of stronger demand from U.S. factories.

30 Stock prices surged as the earnings worries that jolted the market Friday vanished. The Dow Jones Industrial Average soared 49.57 points to 2870.49, a record close. The S&P 500 index also set a new high, its first since October. Bond prices rose steadily, while the dollar was mixed.

31 Leading economic indicators fell 0.2% in April, tempering the optimistic outlook suggested by a 1% rise in March. Also, new-home sales slid 1.6% in April, the fifth drop in a row.

New construction contracts fell 6% in April to a four-year low, F. W. Dodge said. The decline reflects the recent regulatory clampdown on high-risk real-estate lending.

Stock prices climbed further in heavier volume, pushing the Dow Jones industrials up 8.07, to 2878.56, another record. The S&P 500 index also set a record. Many investors remained puzzled by the market's advance amid weak economic data. Bonds and the dollar also rose.

Portfolio insurance has returned in a new guise, "portfolio puts," which threatens to turn market drops into huge declines. The SEC is taking a hard look at the new version of the trading strategy, which helped exacerbate the 1987 stock-market crash.

June 1990

1 Factory orders plunged 2.3% in April, another sign that manufacturing remains weak. The decline, led by a 4.3% drop in durable-goods orders, follows two months of increases.

Corporate buy-backs of junk-bonds hit a record $2.5 billion in the first quarter and are expected to set highs for the year. The trend helped spur the junk market's modest rally.

4 Donald Trump is in intense talks with bank creditors that could force him to give up big chunks of his empire. The bankers, concerned about the developer's critical cash shortage, are likely to see asset sales, new management and a much more conservative operating style.

The Dow Jones industrials closed above 2900 for the first time Friday as stocks and bonds surged in anticipation of falling interest rates. The stock average rose 24.31 to 2900.97. Last week's record-setting equity prices also reflect rising expectations for 1990 and 1991 corporate earnings.

Private-sector payrolls barely grew in May after shrinking in April, the Labor Department said. But temporary census hiring lowered the civilian unemployment rate to 5.3% from 5.4%. Meanwhile, the purchasing managers' index of manufacturing health rose in May to its highest level since April 1989.

The soft jobs picture is leading economists to prune forecasts of second-quarter gross national product.

The Soviet Union is depositing large amounts of gold with Western banks as collateral for loans. Trade creditors owed hundreds of millions of dollars have been hounding the cash-poor Soviets for overdue payments.

Chevron and the Soviets agreed to study the feasibility of jointly developing the 25-billion-barrel Tengiz oil field. Such a project could be the biggest U.S.-Soviet venture yet.

5 Non-farm productivity plunged 2.7% in the first quarter, the biggest decline since 1981 and much greater than the 1% drop first estimated.

States must provide relief to those who paid taxes later found to be unconstitutional, the Supreme Court ruled. The decision could result in billions of dollars in state liability.

Junk-bonds issued by the Trump Taj Mahal and two other casinos operated by Donald Trump sank as much as nine points on news of a cash crunch that could force the developer to give up chunks of his empire.

6 Fed officials appear to have no intention of cutting short-term interest rates, despite signs of a stagnant economy. The officials seem convinced that last week's weak employment report doesn't presage a recession. Furthermore, they are concerned that their tight-money policies have so far failed to head off an acceleration of inflation.

Sales of U.S.-built cars and light trucks fell 3.3% in late May. Despite the lagging sales, auto makers dismissed the possibility of huge discounts at the end of the model year in September, because stocks of unsold vehicles are relatively modest.

7 Shearson split itself into two divisions in the brokerage firm's latest attempt to revive its sagging fortunes. One unit, responsible for investment banking and trading, will resurrect the Lehman Brothers name. The other half will handle individual investors and money management. The regrouping in effect recognizes that Shearson's two big takeovers in the 1980s never really worked.

The credit squeeze facing some businesses isn't affecting consumers so far. Any slowdown in borrowing by consumers seems to reflect their caution more than tighter bank lending policies. Some banks are even soliciting new consumer-loan business.

The federal fund that insures single-family home mortgages with low down payments will be broke by the end of the decade, Housing Secretary Kemp said. He called for higher fees on such mortgages, a prospect bankers said would make it harder for low-income people to buy homes.

Small-business earnings rose 6.2% last year, less than the 9.2% and 6.7% increases in 1987 and 1988. The profit-growth slowdown may prompt more belt-tightening, including layoffs.

8 ConAgra agreed to acquire Beatrice's food operations from Kohlberg Kravis Roberts for $1.34 billion in cash and stock. The scaled-back price reflects a huge amount of debt on Beatrice's balance sheet. If approved by regulators, the deal will sharply tighten acquisitive ConAgra's grip on the nation's food supply.

The group seeking to buy UAL promised to pay $9 million to Gerald Greenwald, the former Chrysler Vice Chairman spearheading the buy-out, even if the takeover fails.

GM won a nearly $1 billion pact to supply pollution-control and engine-control parts to the Soviets' biggest auto maker. The five-year accord comes as GM is waging an aggressive expansion into Eastern Europe.

The U.S. and its Western allies agreed to ease their embargo on high-technology sales to the East bloc.

Retail sales rose a disappointing 3.5% in May from a year earlier as cold, wet weather held down results, especially for summer clothes, outdoor products and air conditioners.

Capital spending is expected to rise 6.7% in 1990, less than the 7.8% increase projected earlier in the year. The latest survey of businesses reflects uncertainty about the economy.

11 The Fed is looking into possible irregularities and improprieties in the handling and trading of U.S. bank loans to Latin America. Improprieties may include the use of privileged information while trading in the unregulated and volatile secondary market for developing-country debt. Mexico has complained to the U.S. about suspected wrongdoing in the trading of Mexican obligations.

Real estate seized from failed thrifts could be sold by the government in scores of $500 million chunks under a plan S&L bail-out officials are developing to speed the sale process. Critics of the idea say the government would be forced to offer huge price discounts to attract purchasers.

12 Trump's major bankers tentatively agreed to lend him $60 million more and to let him suspend interest payments on existing debt. The developer would pledge more property as collateral and possibly forfeit equity in other holdings. The pact would give Trump time to improve operations and wait out a real estate slump.

EC ministers agreed to remove several tax barriers facing companies that operate in several EC states. U.S. firms doing business in Europe had lobbied hard for the changes.

EC central bankers revamped their committee in the first real steps to form a common central bank.

Mexico and the U.S. agreed to hold talks aimed at reaching a broad free-trade agreement. Formal negotiations are expected to begin after Bush and Salinas meet again in December.

Southwestern states are expected to lead the nation in economic growth through the end of the century, the Census Department projected.

13 An appeals court struck down the SEC's "one share, one vote" rule, a move that could reshape the way some companies protect themselves from takeovers. The federal panel said the SEC had overstepped its authority and entered corporate governance, an area traditionally determined by state law.

Kohlberg Kravis has raised about $1.7 billion from investors to inject into RJR Nabisco to bolster RJR's sagging bonds, according to people close to the proposed transaction.

The FDIC isn't likely to permit banks to underwrite insurance despite a new Delaware law that permits such activity, Chairman Seidman said.

Bank earnings fell 14% in the first quarter from a year earlier. Seidman warned of growing problems in Midwest and Northwest real-estate loans.

14 Chrysler's debt is being reviewed by Moody's for possible downgrading. The agency cited a string of departures by Chrysler executives in recent weeks. The review, covering $22.28 billion in debt, will focus on the car company's prospects for improving operating performance and market share. The auto maker called the move "inappropriate."

U.S.-Japanese trade talks are stalled, top Bush officials say, and the president and Kaifu may have to meet soon to defuse tensions. U.S. aides say Japan is foot-dragging.

The thrift-bailout agency sold 13,200 foreclosed S&L properties since August, but its real estate inventory still grew 14% to 35,908 properties, valued at $14.92 billion when seized.

Retail sales fell 0.7% in April. It was the first time they dropped three consecutive months since 1981.

The retail data drove bond prices higher but helped push stocks slightly lower. The Dow Jones Industrial Average fell 3.47 points to 2929.95.

15 S&P lowered its ratings on debt issued by Chrysler and Ford, and affirmed ratings for GM. The agency, which cited growing competition and soft auto demand, downgraded Ford's senior debt to double-A-minus and Chrysler's to triple-B-minus, one notch above speculative grade.

A serious credit crunch extends well beyond the real estate industry and appears to be worsening, Commerce Secretary Mosbacher said.

Reebok said its biggest shareholder, Pentland Group of London, plans to sell its 31.5% stake. The sneaker company promptly adopted a "poison pill" takeover defense.

Gold prices tumbled on Saudi sales of the metal and the prospect of sales by the Soviets to raise cash. Central banks swooped into the market with big buy orders to halt the decline.

Stock prices eased amid growing concern about corporate earnings, while bonds gained. The Dow Jones industrials fell 1.48 to 2928.22.

The Soviet Union's economic uncertainty is hindering the country's efforts to secure new Western loans as wary British, Swiss and German bankers demand much higher rates.

18 Donald Trump has personally guaranteed more than $500 million in bank loans made to him over the past two years, bankers say. His lenders are increasingly seeking the liquidation of most of his properties, and demanding that he relinquish day-to-day control of his operations. The assets' market value is believed to fall well short of the amount the developer has borrowed.

An after-hours system for trading stocks and stock options is to be announced today by the American and Cincinnati exchanges, the Chicago Board Options Exchange and Reuters. The alliance is a response to the Big Board's night-time trading plans.

Factory output rose 0.6% in May as auto production rebounded. Consumer prices increased a modest 0.2% during the same month. Economists say the figures depict continued slow growth with steady inflation.

The U.S. merchandise trade gap narrowed to $6.94 billion in April as a 6.2% plunge in imports more than offset a 3.5% decrease in exports.

Bond prices fell sharply Friday on a stronger-than-expected industrial-production report, while stocks were mixed. Broad stock-market measures ended little changed, but the Dow Jones Industrial Average gained 7.67 points to 2935.89, a new high.

19 The U.S. pension-insurance agency can force LTV Corp. to reassume liability for more than $2 billion in pension benefits that the company stopped funding in 1987, the Supreme Court ruled. The decision could save the troubled agency billions of dollars and hinder LTV's exit from Chapter 11 proceedings.

The SEC received its third court setback in recent weeks as the Supreme Court let stand a ruling that the CFTC, and not the SEC, has the authority to regulate stock "baskets." The CFTC repeated its offer to expedite approval of the products.

An exception in patent law for drugs also applies to medical devices, the Supreme Court ruled. The decision is a defeat for medical-technology developers with long-held patents and a victory for newer companies.

Donald Trump moved closer to an accord with lenders under which he would borrow an additional $60 million and suspend interest payments on other loans. Three New Jersey banks tentatively agreed to participate.

The Trump Shuttle plans to scrap more than 25% of its Saturday flights plus four Sunday round trips.

20 RJR Nabisco is launching a $6.5 billion refinancing plan that will drastically reshape its balance sheet. The proposal, backed by main shareholder KKR, reportedly would retire more than $4 billion of the food and tobacco company's junk-bonds.

Housing starts sank 1.4% in May to their lowest level since 1982, in a further sign of a sluggish economy.

Japan's economy grew at a 10.4% annual rate in the quarter that ended in March, as its exports rose sharply.

21 Economic activity continues to be weak in most regions of the U.S., with new signs of constraints on credit, especially in real estate, the Fed reported. It cited the construction industry as particularly frail.

Bond prices fell on the Fed report, as investors concluded the agency won't soon ease on interest rates. Stocks edged higher, nudging the Dow Jones industrials up 1.74 points.

UAL's unions are asking Boeing and GE to invest in the proposed buy-out of the United Air parent. The move seeks to reduce the bid's dependence on bank loans, and may mean GE and Boeing are in line to win a huge jet and engine order.

The NASD wants to impose a "one-share, one-vote" rule on the companies whose stocks it lists. The move comes after an appeals court struck down a similar SEC regulation.

RJR Nabisco's junk-bonds soared as the company confirmed it is considering ways to retire a significant amount of its high-yield debt.

22 Coniston partners plans to disband and won't make any new investments. One of the best-known corporate raiders of the 1980s, the firm will keep its holdings in TW Services and UAL and return the rest of its cash to investors next month. The move stems from the limited availability of takeover financing.

The economy grew at a 1.9% annual rate in the first quarter, the government said, boosting its estimate from the 1.3% pace initially reported. The revision reflects export growth that was stronger than first thought.

Greenspan discounted anecdotal evidence of a credit crunch due to tighter bank lending practices. The Fed chief, saying enough credit appears to be available, predicted "continued modest economic growth."

Four defense firms face a review by Moody's for a possible downgrading of their debt. The four are Litton, Lockheed, McDonnell and Raytheon.

The FCC ordered local phone companies

to cut by $1.1 billion the annual access rates charged to long-distance concerns. Previous such reductions have been passed on to customers.

Jacobs Suchard suspended trading in its stock amid reports that Philip Morris intends to acquire all or part of the giant Swiss chocolate and coffee company. The whole firm would cost about $4.5 billion, analysts say.

Pathe Communications reached a new, $1.34 billion accord to acquire MGM/UA, but holders won't get most of their money until October.

The federal budget deficit widened to $42.55 billion in May from $25.43 billion a year earlier. The latest figure reflects sizable thrift-bailout spending and declining tax revenue.

Democrats continued to grouse about the Bush deficit-reduction plan, but didn't abandon the budget talks.

25 Philip Morris agreed to acquire 80% of Swiss coffee and chocolate maker Jacobs Suchard for $3.8 billion. Suchard's trove of brands, including Toblerone chocolate, will significantly strengthen the U.S. firm's European presence before trade barriers fall in 1992 and will help lessen the company's dependence on tobacco sales in the U.S.

Orders for durable goods leaped 3.9% in May, suggesting to some that the manufacturing sector is stabilizing. But other parts of the economy may be softening; personal income rose only 0.3% in the month, while personal spending was flat.

Machine tool orders dropped 29% in May from a high April rate but were above a year earlier.

26 U.S. auto sales fell 3.6% in mid-June from a year ago, as the Big Three's slippage more than offset gains by Japanese makers. But analysts said the figures suggest that the current sales slump may be over.

RJR Nabisco has budgeted $250 million in fees for bankers and advisers in its giant debt refinancing, suggesting that patching up leveraged companies may be the next big moneymaker for Wall Street firms.

27 Bush declared that tax increases are needed to shrink the federal deficit. In discarding his "no new taxes" pledge, the president gave new life to moribund budget talks. Though Bush didn't elaborate, the likely targets for higher levies are alcohol, tobacco, gasoline and the incomes of very wealthy people.

Trump's bankers lent him $20 million just in time to enable him to make a $43 million bond payment. The developer also reached a long-term bail-out accord that will let him suspend payments on some bank debt.

Dai-Ichi Mutual Life agreed to pay $312 million for a nearly 10% stake in Lincoln National. It is the largest Japanese investment in a U.S. insurer.

Brazil plans to lower tariffs, ease import restrictions and cut subsidies for inefficient industries. It may also unfreeze $1.8 billion in foreign funds.

28 Bush proposed major trade, investment and debt initiatives for Latin America. The plan envisions substantial relief on the nearly $12 billion in the region's debt held by the U.S. government, and would set aside $300 million in grants to foster private investment. The policy foresees an eventual free-trade zone made up of the entire Western Hemisphere.

Leading economic indicators rose 0.8% in May after a 0.1% decline in April. The index's second reversal in four months lends support to the belief that a recession is unlikely, but some worrisome signals persist.

Suspected price-fixing by airlines is the focus of a new Justice Department inquiry. United, Delta and America West have been asked for information on their ties to the industry's clearinghouse on fares.

29 Japan and the U.S. completed a broad economic pact designed to reduce their $49 billion trade imbalance. Japan promised to spend more on public works, toughen its antitrust policies and streamline its distribution system. The U.S. pledged to balance its budget, improve worker training and increase research spending. But the agreement got a cool reaction from some legislators, economists and business executives.

Polaroid is letting Minolta sell a Polaroid instant camera to U.S. customers under a Minolta brand name. The highly unusual marketing move reflects Polaroid's sluggish sales.

Crude oil inventories are at an eight-year high, raising the prospect of tumbling petroleum prices if OPEC doesn't rein in production soon. Persian Gulf producers have been cutting their third-quarter contract prices.

The SEC is moving to allow more than one exchange to list options on a single stock. An electronically linked system could be in place next year.

July 1990

2 Chrysler and GM raised prices on most cars and some trucks, following Ford's lead. The unusual midyear action reflects Detroit's desire to increase revenues amid weak sales. The Big Three also hope an increase now will soften the appearance of further price rises when 1991 models come out this fall.

Farm prices fell 1.3% in June from the previous month as prices of hogs, wheat and soybeans slipped. Despite the decline, hog prices remain far higher than a year ago.

Sales of new homes edged up 0.4% in May after a five-month decline, but failed to spark any optimism about the strength of the housing industry.

Junk-bonds posted a total return of 4.31% in the second quarter, indicating the high-risk bonds could be climbing out of their deep hole.

3 Philips plans to eliminate 10,000 jobs, about 3.5% of its work force, and expects a loss this year of about $1 billion. But newly installed Chairman Jan Timmer said the Dutch electronics giant won't give up on its troubled computer and semiconductor operations. Philips's share price sank on the announcement. Analysts criticized the job cuts as too small.

Manufacturers showed more signs of emerging from their long slump, according to purchasing managers, whose index of indicators rose in June. Separately, construction spending slipped 0.4% in May, its second drop in a row, the government said.

Foreign holdings in the U.S. exceeded U.S. holdings abroad last year by $663.75 billion, nearly 25% more than in 1988, but the government said the number was inaccurate.

5 Falling interest rates will help avert a recession for at least a year, according to a *Wall Street Journal* survey of 40 economists. But most forecasters warn of painfully slow growth, increasing unemployment and tough times for many industries.

Factory orders increased 2.1% in May, making up for most of April's decline. Durable goods, especially transportation equipment, accounted for May's strength. Orders for nondurable goods increased slightly.

The dollar declined against most currencies in European dealings yesterday, largely on technical selling. On Tuesday, the U.S. stock market gained for the fifth day in a row, while bonds rose modestly and gold rallied. The Dow Jones Industrial Average went up 12.37 points to 2911.63.

6 Japanese auto makers grabbed a record 28% share of U.S. car sales in the first half of 1990. Sales of North American-made autos, meanwhile, surged 11.9% in late June to their highest rate in six months.

9 UAL's unions said they are working with five big banks to get financing for their proposed $4.38 billion acquisition of United Airlines. The labor group, which faces an August 9 deadline, said the banks insist part of the financing come from non-banking sources, such as suppliers.

The jobless rate fell to 5.2% in June although only 40,000 new jobs were created during the month. Many economists believe unemployment can't go any lower without rekindling inflation. The figures aren't likely to prompt the Fed to ease credit.

Stock prices gained despite a rise in interest rates following the employment report. The Dow industrials advanced 25.74 points to 2904.95.

A tax increase passed by the Massachusetts Legislature will put a 5% levy on fees charged by lawyers, accountants, engineers and architects. Business leaders said it would further cripple the state's sluggish economy.

RJR Nabisco has been deluged with $7 billion of loan commitments from banks for its debt refinancing plan, more than triple what it needs. The influx suggests that big money is once again becoming available for leveraged-company transactions.

10 The pound soared against major currencies, reaching an 18-month high vs. the dollar. Signals from the Thatcher government that it favors speedy entry into the European exchange-rate system were credited for the rise. Reports that Britain plans no interest-rate cuts soon also triggered the rally. Currency traders in London forecast further gains.

OPEC heads of state are stepping in, where their ministers have failed, to try to stop the fall in oil prices. Saudi King Fahd appears to be leading the strategy to curb production.

Bond prices sagged further on Friday's strong employment report and on concerns about a heavy load of government offerings this week. Stock prices drifted higher in thin trading. The

Dow Jones industrials advanced 9.16 points to 2914.11.

Junk-bond mutual funds yielded a total return of 4.1% in the second quarter, more than any other category of domestic bond fund. Investors meanwhile pumped a net of $57.2 million into junk funds during May.

11 The dollar fell against major currencies amid expectations of higher Japanese interest rates and a stronger yen. The U.S. currency's weakness helped kill an early rise in bond prices. Stock prices sagged.

12 The U.S. won assurances from other participants at the economic summit that they will agree to reduce farm subsidies. But some Europeans claimed victory because the new understanding doesn't call for the elimination of export subsidies, and U.S. aides said tough negotiations lie ahead. Meanwhile, the summit leaders agreed to take different approaches on aid to the Soviet Union.

U.S. banks were ordered to write off 20% of their $11.1 billion in loans to Brazil and an additional 20% of their $2.9 billion in Argentine portfolios. The action could hurt profits at banks with low reserves, such as Citicorp.

Most U.S. voters believe Bush is breaking his no-tax pledge, but they don't much blame him for it and are resigned to a tax increase, according to a *Wall Street Journal*/NBC poll.

Japanese banks remain wary about making new loans to China, despite clearance from the Tokyo government to resume such lending.

13 The Fed is poised to ease interest rates modestly in response to growing evidence of a credit crunch, Greenspan said. But he said he doesn't see significant economic weakness. The Fed chief also said the agency is working to boost capital rules for banks and to toughen their enforcement. He expressed doubt about cutting deposit insurance.

Stocks and bonds rallied on Greenspan's interest-rate remarks. The Dow Jones industrials jumped 37.13 points in heavy trading to 2969.80, a record high. The dollar declined.

Big retailers reported a 5.8% average sales gain in June, as sunny weather boosted buying of apparel.

Double hulls would be required for new oil tankers, and phased in for most existing ones, under legislation approved by legislative conferees.

Japan's trade surplus surged 28% in June, despite a 10% decrease in the surplus in trade with the U.S.

16 The Fed eased interest rates modestly, but signaled that further reductions shouldn't be expected soon. The central bank pushed down the federal funds rate, which banks charge each other for loans. That could cause other short-term interest rates to decline as well.

Stock prices surged, with the Dow industrials closing at a record 2980.20, up 10.40 points, after trading above the 3000 level briefly. The dollar rose, but analysts said the credit easing could hurt the weak U.S. currency.

Producer prices rose 0.2% in June and retail sales increased 0.5%, suggesting that inflation is somewhat under control and that consumer spending may be in a modest upturn.

U.S. auto makers plan to boost third-quarter domestic output 11.6%, despite recent cutbacks by Ford and weak sales. However, sales of U.S.-built cars rose a surprisingly strong 2.5% in the first 10 days of July.

17 Stocks soared again with the Dow industrials rising 19.55 points to a record 2999.75, just shy of the 3000 level. Much of the impetus for the advance came from strong second-quarter earnings at some big companies. Bonds were little changed and the dollar ended mixed.

The budget deficit for fiscal 1991 will reach $231.4 billion, the administration projected, warning that $100 billion in across-the-board spending cuts will be triggered this fall unless a deficit-reduction accord is reached.

RJR's junk-bonds soared after the company said it would retire many of the issues as part of a refinancing.

18 IBM may sell low-tech businesses such as electric typewriters and keyboards in a buy-out that could total $3 billion, Wall Street and industry executives said. The plan is the latest sign of a new urgency among IBM executives to make each business stand on its own.

Industrial production rose 0.4% in June, bolstered by higher utility output due to a late-June heat wave.

The trade deficit widened to $7.73 billion in May from a revised $7.31 billion in April. The Senate, meantime, voted to subject imported textiles, apparel and footwear to a highly restrictive system of global quotas.

Iraq's Hussein threatened to use force against other Persian Gulf nations if they keep driving down oil prices by exceeding output quotas. Oil prices held firm despite expectations they might fall after recent runups.

19 Greenspan signaled that no further credit easing is imminent, saying that last week's move was in response to a lending crunch. But the Fed chairman held out the prospect of additional easing if agreement is reached on "substantive" cuts in the budget deficit.

Housing starts skidded 2.3% in June to the lowest annual rate since the 1982 recession. The government also said consumer prices jumped 0.5% last month, signaling that inflation continues to be a problem.

Bond prices sagged after the consumer price report and Greenspan's remarks to a Senate panel. Stocks were hit by profit-taking and earnings disappointments, and the Dow Jones industrials fell 18.07 points to 2981.68.

20 Budget negotiators are considering proposals to curb itemized tax deductions, including those for mortgage-interest payments, charitable giving and state and local tax payments. The idea of restricting itemized deductions has emerged because of Democratic demands that any tax package hit the wealthy harder than others.

An S&L consultant said only a small part of the $130 billion in thrift losses was due to fraud. He said most of the losses stemmed from falling real-estate values and high interest rates paid to attract depositors.

23 A major guarantor of loans in the student-aid program, the Higher Education Assistance Foundation, is facing possible financial collapse, raising doubts about the soundness of its $9.6 billion in loan guarantees.

Chrysler offered union employees part ownership of the company and incentive payments in return for helping the auto maker slash costs.

24 Stocks plunged in a broad sell-off that left the Dow industrials down 56.44 points at 2904.70. The industrials were off more than 105 points at one stage, triggering "circuit breakers" that helped stanch the selling pressure. Earnings disappointments sparked the slide, as investors dumped growth stocks.

Bonds closed lower, although the rout in stocks lifted prices sporadically throughout the day as investors sought the safety of Treasury issues. The dollar tumbled to a 31-month low against the mark during the session.

Loral said Ford accepted its bid for the auto maker's aerospace unit, beating out a Westinghouse group and a coalition of GM's Hughes Aircraft division and Alcatel of Belgium.

Merger talks were ended between Higher Education Assistance Foundation and another student-loan guarantor, leaving open the possibility of bank losses unless the government agrees to a full rescue.

RJR Nabisco posted a $108 million loss for the second quarter but reported strong gains in operating profit and cash flow. The solid operating figures are expected to help the firm in its $6.9 billion refinancing plan.

Ford Motor told dealers it plans to raise prices on most 1991 models by 4% to 5%, with some models jumping as much as 9%. Some dealers and analysts predicted Ford will have trouble making the increases stick.

25 Eastern Airlines expects to be indicted by a federal grand jury on charges that some employees falsified aircraft maintenance records at New York airports a few years ago.

Chrysler plans to raise prices on its restyled 1991 minivans by as much as 12%, but lower prices on some of its less popular car lines. That differs from the approach employed by Ford, which plans boosts on most models.

The administration is trying to negotiate a takeover of Higher Education Assistance Foundation, a financially troubled student-loan guarantor, by another big guarantee agency.

26 Columbia S&L agreed to sell its portfolio of junk-bonds and preferred stock to a Canadian investor group for an unexpectedly high $3 billion. But the thrift's plan carries considerable risk for the U.S. government, which would inherit the portfolio if the market turns sour again.

Trump plans to propose that holders of all or part of his $1.3 billion in debt accept equity in his casinos in exchange for letting him cancel some interest payments, according to people close to the situation.

The Soviets are selling diamonds worth $5 billion to a Swiss arm of De Beers and will borrow $1 billion from the company to ease their need for cash. De Beers hopes to strengthen its control of the diamond market.

Merck and Du Pont plan to form a firm that will combine Du Pont's experimental drugs and research operations with foreign marketing rights to certain Merck products.

Durable goods orders dropped 3.2% in June after a 4.2% rise in May, indicating lingering weakness in the nation's manufacturing sector.

Bush may ask Congress to delay its August recess in an effort to get the deficit-reduction talks moving. But congressional leaders suggested they continue talks with the administration while Congress is away.

Chrysler and GM plan further retrenchments in the face of falling North American sales. Chrysler will close a Canadian Jeep plant in 1992, while GM said it will trim output of its year-old plastic-bodied minivans.

OPEC ministers moved toward raising their target oil price by at least $1 to $2 a barrel from the current $18. To achieve such an increase, OPEC members would effectively cut back on the total oil they pump.

27 GM and Ford posted sharply lower second-quarter earnings, reflecting hard times in the U.S. market and economic unrest in Brazil. Ford's profit tumbled 45% while GM reported a 38% decline. The remainder of the year could be difficult, too, amid weak demand in the U.S. and competition from Japan.

30 OPEC approved an increase in its minimum reference price to $21 from $18 a barrel, the first rise in four years. The figure isn't a set selling price, but a goal OPEC hopes to achieve through production controls. OPEC's move reflects an unusual display of resolve, although it could be months before the group starts getting the price it wants.

Chemical Banking withdrew as one of five lead banks for the proposed $4.38 billion buy-out of UAL Corp., according to people familiar with the plan. Although described as subject to change, the move is a potentially serious blow to the buy-out group.

Economic growth slowed to a slim 1.2% in the second quarter, one of the weakest performances in the past 7½ years. Only rising business inventories and higher government spending kept the economy from contracting.

The Senate adopted a $54 billion farm bill, agreeing to halt the steady decline in farm-income supports. The measure also gives farmers a freer hand to grow crops they want without losing their subsidy eligibility.

Many banks are cutting back borrowing in the commercial paper market, as investors grow more nervous about the banking industry's health.

31 The S&L bail-out will require $100 billion over the next 12 months, Bush officials disclosed. The new plan leaves the bail-out's overall cost projections unchanged, but requires more cash sooner than previously forecast. Even Republicans balked at the figure, which includes $60 billion in spending intended to be recouped through thrift asset sales.

Consumer spending rose a strong 1% in June, the biggest increase since January. But personal income continued to grow only modestly, edging up 0.4% after gains of 0.3% each in April and May, suggesting that spending is unlikely to gain much vigor.

The dollar slumped to its lowest level against the mark in nearly 31 months. The U.S. unit, hurt by rising interest rates overseas and signs of a slowing economy at home, also fell against the yen and the pound.

Stock prices gained, boosted by rising bond prices, strong oil issues and program buying. The Dow Jones industrials rose 18.82 points to 2917.33.

Fujitsu formally agreed to acquire control of Britain's International Computers for $1.37 billion, and the Japanese firm's chairman said he favors investing in Siemens of West Germany. His remarks underscore the pursuit of the European market by Japanese computer concerns.

France's Groupe Bull posted a sharply widened first-half loss of $350 million, in a sign of woes besetting European computer makers.

GM will find it "very difficult" to maintain its European sales and market share because of factory shutdowns required for retooling, the company's chief in Europe said.

August 1990

1 UAL's stock plunged $16.875 a share to $140 after two more banks, Citicorp and Chase Manhattan, indicated they had withdrawn for now from efforts to finance a $4.38 billion buy-out of UAL. The moves, following Chemical Bank's withdrawal, leave the bid in doubt nine days before a financing deadline.

Chrysler's profit skidded 47% in the second quarter. Aggressive cost-cutting and surging results from financial services prevented a loss.

The dollar slid to its lowest level against the mark in more than 2½ years, stalling a bond rally and contributing to a mild retreat in blue-chip stocks. The Dow Jones industrials fell 12.13 points to close at 2905.20. Broader stock indexes advanced.

Ford agreed to sell its farm-equipment unit to a new joint venture 80%-owned by Fiat. The deal virtually completes Ford's exit from all businesses except autos and finance.

2   The economy remains stagnant, three monthly reports suggest. The leading indicators index and construction spending were unchanged in June, and the purchasers' index of manufacturing health fell in July. The data fueled speculation among some economists that the economy is headed for a downturn.

Bond prices rose on the gloomy economic reports, as did utility stocks and gold. Stocks in general slumped, while the dollar reversed its slide.

Oil prices soared as much as 85 cents a barrel on reports of renewed tension between Iraq and Kuwait.

3   Oil prices soared and stock and bond markets tumbled world-wide in response to Iraq's invasion of Kuwait. Crude prices surged as much as $3.50 a barrel, or 15%, and some analysts forecast a $30 price. Oil and defense stocks rallied but most issues sank on fears that costly petroleum will drag down the economy. The Dow Jones industrials fell 34.66 points, and Tokyo stocks plunged. The dollar gained against the yen, but rose little against the mark. Gold shot up, then fell back.

The jump so far in oil prices could boost consumer prices 1% over the next year, add a dime a gallon to the cost of gasoline, and cut the U.S. growth rate almost in half.

Factory orders fell a sharp 1.5% in June, providing more evidence of a weakening manufacturing sector. Durable goods were especially hurt.

6   Corporate profits fell 11% in the second quarter, a *Wall Street Journal* survey finds, the fourth decline in a row. The U.S., meantime, said the jobless rate rose to 5.5% in July, the highest in two years. Those developments, coupled with a sharp rise in oil prices following Iraq's invasion of Kuwait, suggest the economy could be heading

into a recession. Faced with a weakening economy, the Fed may move as soon as this week to lower interest rates.

Gasoline prices leaped as much as 15 cents a gallon and are likely to go higher despite outcries from motorists. Other petroleum prices may rise sharply, as many countries said they won't buy oil from Iraq or Kuwait.

Stock prices plunged in a wave of selling. The Dow Jones industrials finished at 2809.65, down 54.95 points, after being down more than 120 points during Friday's trading. Long-term U.S. bonds again fell sharply.

The Texas economy may get a boost from higher oil prices, but it appears unlikely the upturn will shrink the cost of the S&L bail-out. Nearly half of the S&L real estate seized by the government is in Texas.

7   Stocks and bonds plunged world-wide on fears of a wider Mideast conflict that would seriously disrupt oil supplies. The Dow Jones industrials plummeted 93.31 points in heavy trading to 2716.34, their biggest drop since October. More than a dozen major stocks didn't open for trading at the morning bell. Investors seeking shelter turned to short-term Treasury bills and to gold, which jumped $7.30 an ounce to $384.70.

The current stock sell-off, unlike the 1987 and '89 plunges, is rooted in real economics: fear of the twin scourges of recession and inflation.

Petroleum prices exploded, surging $3 to $4 a barrel, as Iraqi troops in Kuwait appeared to dig in on the Saudi border. Crude futures in the U.S. topped $28 a barrel, their highest level in more than four years. But some analysts, turning cautious, said prices may be nearing their peak.

A growing arsenal of financial market "circuit breakers" helped rein in program trading in recent days and ward off the possibility of an uncontrolled crash, traders say.

Productivity increased at a 1.9% annual rate in the second quarter after falling at a 1.5% rate in the first quarter. Real wages rose at a 2.2% rate in the latest quarter, indicating that inflation pressures remain.

8   Bond prices fell sharply and stocks swung wildly as oil-related news shook the financial markets throughout the day. Long-term Treasury bonds dropped half a point. The Dow Jones

industrials closed down 5.70 points at 2710.64 for their sixth consecutive loss. Broader stock indexes rose slightly. Signs of escalating tension buoyed the dollar.

Many pension funds and other big stock investors intend to hold on to their equity portfolios despite growing gloom about the market.

Oil prices jumped late yesterday on news of multinational troops going to Saudi Arabia. Global sanctions against Iraq, meanwhile, began to cut deeply into its petroleum exports.

U.S. oil drillers are ill prepared to boost output in response to a world petroleum shortage because of a lack of equipment and experienced staff.

Tokyo stock prices tumbled Tuesday on concerns about the Mideast. The Nikkei Index declined 3.4%, stunning some investors. But some analysts see a turnaround ahead.

9 Oil prices sank as much as $3 a barrel on news that Saudi Arabia and other exporters are prepared to boost production. But it will be weeks before the increases completely take effect, and they are unlikely to fully offset the petroleum shortages expected because of the Mideast crisis. A few nations are quietly beginning to lift their output.

Several oil companies cut or froze their gasoline prices in response to public outcries over alleged gouging.

Frank Lorenzo will sell most of his stake in Continental Airlines to SAS and will step down as chairman and chief executive, according to people familiar with his plans. Delta Air President Hollis Harris is expected to succeed Lorenzo as chief executive.

Tokyo stock prices rebounded sharply, buoyed by reports that Saudi Arabia had agreed to increase oil output. The Nikkei gained 856.07 points.

Iraq annexed Kuwait and the first U.S. troops landed in Saudi Arabia.

Baghdad declared that the emirate it overran a week ago was now "part of Iraq." Bush said the U.S. intends to defend the Saudi kingdom, but he expressed hopes that Kuwait can be freed through economic pressure on Iraq. Egypt's Mubarak called for an Arab meeting in Cairo today to discuss joining a multinational army in Saudi Arabia. King Hussein of Jordan said he would refuse to recognize Baghdad's "annexation." Diplomats worked to arrange the evacuation of foreigners stranded in Kuwait and Iraq, including thousands of Americans.

10 The strategic oil reserve won't be drawn down for now, the White House said, surprising some petroleum experts. World crude prices fell about 25 cents a barrel, and several more companies said they were cutting gasoline prices. The stock and bond markets, meanwhile, rallied as bargain hunters stepped in to buy. Bond prices rose about ¾ point. The Dow Jones industrials advanced 24.01 points to close at 2758.91.

Retailers reported lackluster sales gains for July as consumer demand continued to soften. The rises largely fell in the range of 2% to 8%.

U.S. agriculture officials forecast robust corn and wheat production this year but lagging soybean output.

13 Rising oil prices will cut the nation's already sluggish economic growth by half but won't cause a recession, Treasury Secretary Brady said. He again called on the Fed to ease credit, and said those in Congress who view the current problems as reasons to put off cutting the budget deficit are "dead wrong."

The likelihood of a rebound in corporate profits in the second half all but evaporated with Iraq's invasion of Kuwait. The oil crisis makes it more likely that profits will continue to decline until sometime in 1991.

Producer prices fell 1% in July, suggesting that inflationary pressures were easing before the recent jump in oil prices. The report will make it easier for the Fed to push down interest rates, but higher oil prices might prevent it from lowering rates enough to avoid a recession.

14 The economy appears headed for significantly higher unemployment and little or no economic growth in the next year, according to a survey of economists by the *Wall Street Journal* conducted since the Mideast crisis began. The consensus represents a startlingly swift mood swing from a similar survey less than two months ago, when most economists projected a continuing expansion. The economists still disagree, however, about whether a recession lies ahead.

Iraq has slashed its oil production to as little as 600,000 barrels a day, in response to the tightening world embargo. The current level, about one-sixth the country's pre-embargo output, is enough to meet the nation's internal needs plus a trickle of exports bypassing the blockade, mainly via trucks through Jordan.

Tokyo stocks nosedived in shallow trading on selling by arbitragers. The Nikkei closed with its fourth-largest single daily loss in terms of percentage, and the seventh-largest plunge in terms of points. The 225-stock index plunged 1153.12 points to 26176.43.

15 Venezuela backed off from a reported promise to Quayle to increase oil exports, shocking U.S. petroleum industry officials. Saudi Arabia still hasn't substantially boosted its output, but said it remains committed to do so. The U.S. had been counting on both nations to shelter world petroleum markets from a supply crunch caused by the loss of crude oil from Iraq and Kuwait.

The price of gold for immediate delivery has risen 7% in the past three days, to $411.50 an ounce, and further tension in the Mideast could push the metal's price even higher.

16 Industrial output leveled off in July, indicating that the economy continues to stumble. Factory production slipped 0.1% and utility output fell 0.4%, but mining posted a 1% gain. The nation's industrial operating rate fell to 83.4% of capacity, down from 83.6% in June, which could temper some of the inflation pressure stemming from higher oil prices.

Cutting U.S. dependence on foreign oil by up to 550,000 barrels a day is envisioned under a Bush strategy calling for voluntary conservation and increased domestic production. The plan would offset much of the loss of crude from Iraq and Kuwait.

Sun Microsystems and IBM signed a patent-licensing accord under which Sun will pay royalties to IBM. The pact comes in the wake of IBM's tough patent-enforcement policy.

Tokyo stock prices soared Wednesday, giving the Nikkei its third-largest single-day advance. The index jumped 1439.59 points, or 5.4%.

17 Stocks and bonds sank on rising Mideast tension and more signs of recession and inflation. The Dow Jones industrials fell 66.83 points to close at 2681.44. Long-term Treasury bonds dropped 1⅝ points. The bad economic news pushed the dollar to a new low against the mark. Gold futures prices surged $6.60 an ounce.

Consumer prices rose 0.4% in July, putting inflation at a 5.8% annual rate for 1990's first seven months, before oil prices soared. Meanwhile, housing starts fell for the sixth straight month, dropping 2.6% to their lowest level since 1982. The data show non-energy inflation persisting despite economic weakness.

Saudi Arabia and Venezuela intend to gradually boost their oil output, by as much as 2.5 million barrels a day, whether or not they win OPEC's approval at an emergency meeting the two nations are seeking.

20 Oil prices may level off this week following Saudi Arabia's pledge to boost output as much as two million barrels a day, making up about half the amount lost from the Iraq-Kuwait embargo. The Saudis plan to take the action with or without OPEC's approval. Some other oil exporters, including Venezuela and the United Arab Emirates, also are expected to increase output. Last week, the price of benchmark U.S. crude topped $28 a barrel, up about $8 since the Iraqi invasion of Kuwait August 2.

Interest rates are expected to continue climbing around the world, which could spell more trouble for the U.S. bond market. Bonds were mixed Friday, August 17, while stocks tumbled on growing Mideast tensions. The dollar hit a new low against the mark.

Junk-bond investors are running for cover again amid fears of a recession. But the sell-off this time is focused on issues that have the most to lose in an economic downturn.

21 Budget gap projections for next year are widening by tens of billions of dollars because of higher defense spending and an economic slowdown resulting from the Mideast crisis, U.S. officials say. A record deficit of $250 billion to $300 billion is likely, which could force severe Gramm-Rudman spending cuts. Bush, meanwhile, said he will "oppose the defense budget slashers."

OPEC rejected a call by Saudi Arabia and Venezuela for an emergency meeting, leaving them free to pump more oil on their own. The group may still meet immediately.

22 Stock prices plunged in a broad sell-off that began in European markets. The Dow Jones industrials fell 52.48 points to 2603.96 in hectic trading. Bonds closed slightly lower after falling sharply early in the day. The dollar

rose against the yen but fell against the mark.

European stock prices sank on rumors of Mideast fighting. Germany's blue-chip DAX Index plunged 5.2%. London's FT-SE 100 retreated 2.2%.

23 Crude oil prices passed the $30-a-barrel mark, their highest level since the early 1980s. The Mideast turmoil also pushed up prices of refined petroleum in frantic trading. Gasoline futures rose nearly three cents a gallon. Oil officials reported tightening supplies of some products in some countries.

Stocks and bonds fell sharply on the surge in oil prices. The Treasury's 30-year bond fell more than a point, pushing its yield above 9%. The Dow Jones industrials fell 43.81 points. Broad stock indexes hit their lowest points in more than a year.

Gold prices climbed further on the Mideast crisis. The December futures contract gained $3.30 an ounce.

Tokyo stock prices plunged on anxiety about the Mideast as well as world-wide sell-offs Tuesday, August 21. The Nikkei index marked a post-1987 low during trading before closing at 25210.91, off 1086.93 points.

Japanese market sentiment is turning bearish also because of a liquidity squeeze, according to analysts.

24 The mark soared to a record against the dollar. Germany's relative insulation from oil shocks is making its currency the safer haven.

Durable goods orders rose 2.9% in July after a 3.2% drop in June, but analysts say manufacturing hasn't recovered from a year's stagnation.

Sales of U.S.-made vehicles fell 4.7% in mid-August, a smaller drop than some had expected, but still a discouraging sign for auto makers. Dealers cited consumers' concerns about the economy and the Mideast.

27 Fed policy makers are increasingly worried about a U.S. recession and lean toward a modest credit easing. But officials of the central bank suggest that they won't cut interest rates until the financial markets stabilize. The bias toward easing may surprise those analysts who expected the bank to maintain its policies in the face of rising oil prices.

Real GNP rose at a 1.2% yearly rate in the second period, showing a continued weakness in the economy.

Machine-tool orders dropped 11.9% in July as exports fell sharply.

28 Stocks and bonds soared and oil prices plummeted on the prospect of a peaceful solution to the Mideast crisis. The Dow Jones industrials leaped 78.71 points, this year's biggest gain, to 2611.63. Long-term Treasury bonds jumped more than 1½ points, bringing their yield under 9%. Crude prices sank as much as $4 a barrel, their sharpest drop on record. Early Tuesday in Vienna, OPEC officials tentatively endorsed some members' moves to boost output.

Gold prices plunged about $27 an ounce, their greatest one-day decline in more than seven years. Silver and platinum also sank. The Gulf turmoil has generated only a modest rise in U.S. investor interest in gold.

Tokyo stocks posted strong gains amid a firmer yen, a healthier bond market and an absence of bad Mideast news. The Nikkei jumped 976 points Monday, August 27, to 25141.76, then rose a further 518.52 Tuesday morning.

Many banks tightened their lending standards further in recent months, largely out of concern over the economy and the state of certain industries, a Fed survey found.

Consumer spending grew 0.5% in July, as personal income rose 0.6%. But fears about the economy may limit purchases in the months ahead.

Investors seeking arbitration of disputes with brokers will have to pay higher fees to launch their claims. The NASD has already imposed the increases, and the Big Board is expected to follow suit within weeks.

29 The UAW named General Motors as its target company for negotiating a pattern-setting national labor contract to replace a three-year accord that expires September 14. A union priority in the talks is job security, while the Big Three auto makers want more management flexibility.

Retailers are trimming their plans for Christmas to avoid getting stuck with merchandise if consumers pull back. Many stores are ordering late, and some are canceling orders.

30 Oil prices fell sharply as OPEC freed its members to pump to capacity during the Mideast crisis. Stocks and bonds rallied on the falling crude prices. Oil for October delivery fell $1.96 a barrel to $25.92, its lowest price in three weeks. The Dow Jones Industrial Average gained 17.58 points to close at 2632.43. Long-term Treasury bonds rose about 1¼ points. The dollar ended mixed.

The index of leading indicators was unchanged in July, suggesting that the economy was precarious even before the Persian Gulf crisis. Private surveys indicate consumer confidence tumbled this month.

Computer-chip makers could be compelled to pay hundreds of millions of dollars to a little-known inventor if he can enforce a new patent.

The venture-capital program of the Small Business Administration faces a period of retrenchment. The weakening economy is expected to worsen the program's financial woes.

31 Oil prices rose on renewed worry that the Persian Gulf crisis might not be resolved soon enough to prevent tight supplies. Prices of refined petroleum rose faster than crude. Gasoline futures gained 4.35 cents a gallon, while crude jumped 85 cents a barrel to $26.77. Despite OPEC's promise to boost output, world markets will be short one million barrels a day.

Tokyo stock prices rose sharply Thursday as investors took in stride a 0.75-point increase in the Bank of Japan's discount rate. The Nikkei index jumped 775.17 points, or 3.1%.

Japan's discount-rate boost could sour the world economy by forcing higher rates elsewhere, analysts say.

Mideast investors moved as much as $8 billion in capital to the West after Iraq invaded Kuwait. Big U.S. banks are the main beneficiaries.

Factory orders rose 1.6% in July, nearly making up for a 1.9% drop in June. Aircraft orders were particularly strong, while autos were weak. Economists caution that the latest figures predate the Mideast crisis.

Investment Outlays by Industry of U.S. Business Enterprise and by Country of Ultimate Beneficial Owner, 1983–89

[Millions of dollars]

	1983	1984	1985	1986	1987	1988ʳ	1989ᵖ
Total	**8,091**	**15,197**	**23,106**	**39,177**	**40,310**	**72,692**	**64,565**
By industry:							
Petroleum	394	3,263	2,970	1,035	1,107	4,740	1,069
Manufacturing	3,113	3,106	12,140	16,772	19,751	36,136	28,323
Food and kindred products	691	340	3,556	1,007	4,177	3,287	678
Chemicals and allied products	653	378	3,280	7,063	4,041	2,918	11,005
Primary and fabricated metals	177	558	1,015	776	1,091	3,394	3,433
Machinery	470	535	1,556	2,426	2,834	7,737	3,948
Other manufacturing	1,121	1,295	2,733	5,500	7,608	18,800	9,258
Wholesale trade	198	840	804	1,640	1,271	2,454	2,366
Retail trade	95	1,154	1,217	5,249	1,212	8,022	7,274
Banking	173	910	257	288	924	1,800	436
Finance, except banking	457	802	489	1,781	1,604	972	3,422
Insurance	121	152	908	1,668	165	5,855	1,751
Real estate	2,659	2,227	1,921	5,171	4,765	3,518	4,653
Services	585	1,008	1,350	4,276	7,630	5,597	9,008
Other industries	298	1,735	1,050	1,298	1,881	3,597	6,263
By country [1]:							
Canada	1,072	2,587	2,914	6,503	1,276	11,360	3,927
Europe	4,908	6,463	15,382	21,126	25,517	37,173	38,124
France	295	330	754	2,491	2,044	4,199	3,125
Germany, Federal Republic of	584	685	2,270	1,351	4,664	2,090	2,452
Netherlands	492	562	771	4,700	391	2,214	3,278
United Kingdom	2,366	3,714	6,732	8,572	15,142	22,559	21,968
Other Europe	1,171	1,172	4,855	4,012	3,276	6,111	7,301
Latin America and Other Western Hemisphere	437	(ᴰ)	589	771	1,483	(ᴰ)	1,013
South and Central America	291	196	88	397	355	(ᴰ)	639
Other Western Hemisphere	147	(ᴰ)	501	375	1,128	187	374
Africa	180	(ᴰ)	57	(ᴰ)	(ᴰ)	296	(ᴰ)
Middle East	715	919	986	680	925	1,613	117
Asia and Pacific	765	(ᴰ)	3,138	9,450	10,928	21,819	21,252
Australia	54	(ᴰ)	1,630	3,194	2,691	4,556	4,472
Japan	392	1,806	1,152	5,416	7,006	16,188	14,896
Other Asia and Pacific	319	251	356	840	1,231	1,075	1,884
United States [2]	14	(ᴰ)	40	(ᴰ)	(ᴰ)	(ᴰ)	(ᴰ)
Addenda:							
European Communities (12) [3]				19,034	22,895	33,737	31,859
OPEC [4]	723	855	910	878	1,077	1,919	299

ʳ Revised.

ᵖ Preliminary.

ᴰ Suppressed to avoid disclosure of data of individual companies.

1. Where more than one investor participated in a given investment, each investor and each investor's outlays are classified by country of each ultimate beneficial owner.

2. Investment outlays can be classified by country of foreign parent as well as by country of UBO. The foreign parent is the first foreign person in the ownership chain of the acquired or established U.S. business; the UBO is the person in the ownership chain, beginning with the foreign parent, that is not owned more than 50 percent by another person. The country of UBO is often the same as that of the foreign parent, but it may be a different foreign country or the United States. Data classified by country of foreign parent are available in a set of supplementary tables.

3. European Communities (12) comprises Belgium, Denmark, France, Germany (Federal Republic of), Greece, Ireland, Italy, Luxembourg, Netherlands, United Kingdom, Portugal, and Spain.

4. OPEC is the Organization of Petroleum Exporting Countries. Its members are Algeria, Ecuador, Gabon, Indonesia, Iran, Iraq, Kuwait, Libya, Nigeria, Qatar, Saudi Arabia, the United Arab Emirates, and Venezuela.

Source: *Survey of Current Business*, Bureau of Economic Analysis, May 1990.

Highlights of the 1990 U.S. Industrial Outlook

by Jonathan C. Menes*

For 1990, the outlook is for an eighth straight year of growth for U.S. industries, but at a lower rate than 1989. For manufacturing industries the forecasts show only a modest decline. For service industries consistent and comparable data are not available, but in general, service industry growth is faster than for manufacturing.

Table 1: Growth Rate For Manufacturers Shipments For All Industries Covered

(based on constant dollars)

Item	1988	1989	1990
Median Average Rate	2.5	2.2	2.0
Mean Average Rate	2.6	2.0	1.8

Source: *U.S. Industrial Outlook datafiles*

The decline in the rate of growth of manufacturing industries follows the slowing of the economy closely. However, not all industries are affected to the same degree. Developments in certain key industries will extend through the economy with both positive and negative effects.

Table 2: Growth Rate Estimates and Projections For Selected Industry Groups

(based on constant dollar shipments)

Industry Group	1988	1989	1990
Food & Beverages	2.7	2.0	2.3
Construction*	-1.4	-1.0	0.0
Steel Mill Products	9.9	2.2	-4.1
Chemicals	2.1	3.2	1.7
Lumber & Wood Products	1.2	-3.3	1.3
Paper Industries	3.4	1.3	2.2
Rubber Plastic Products	3.5	3.5	2.8
Construction Materials	0.2	-0.3	-0.4
Industrial Machinery	4.4	3.4	2.7
Machine Tools	3.3	28.6	1.2
Household Cons. Durables	2.4	0.3	-2.5
Computers**	14.0	6.2	4.3
Electrical Equipment	3.9	1.9	1.8
Telephone Equipment	-1.0	1.8	2.1
Electronic Components**	18.6	6.3	0.0
Motor Vehicles	2.0	-7.1	-2.2
Auto Parts & Access.	1.2	1.6	1.4
Aerospace	3.2	2.4	3.5
Measuring & Controlling Devices	8.5	4.0	4.2
Medical and Dental Equip.	9.1	7.7	8.2

Source: *U.S. Industrial Outlook datafiles*
*Value of Construction put in place
**In current dollars

Two industries with major impacts are construction and motor vehicles, both cyclical industries. Lack of growth in construction affects a number of industries, especially steel, construction materials, wood products, and household consumer durables.

The motor vehicle industry continues to have a major influence on U.S. industries. With sales expected to drop below 10 million units in 1990, constant dollar shipments by this industry are expected to decline again, but not as sharply as in 1989. Again steel is affected as are glass and a variety of other basic materials. The auto parts and accessories industry is less affected because of its sales to the aftermarket and to growing export markets.

Other industries such as health-related industries, continue to benefit from strong growth trends. In 1990 overall health-care expenditures are expected to grow by more than 10 percent. In addition to stimulating the health and medical services industries, this growth continues to boost demand for medical equipment and drugs.

Another important trend detectable in the industry reviews is the emergence of an "information" economy. Services industries tied to information are some of the fastest growing. Manufacturing industries related to information also tend to do better than average. Computer equipment, for example, while growing slower than its historical rate, nevertheless outperforms the overall economy. This is also true of radio and television communications equipment.

Trade has played a very important role in the growth of a number of industries during the past several years. In 1988 manufactures exports were up almost 28 percent. In 1989, export growth through the first 10 months slowed to an annual rate of 13 percent. However a number of industries continue to benefit from strong export growth including aircraft, machine tools, certain wood products, pharmaceuticals, paper industries equipment, paper mills, and refrigeration equipment. Many of the industries that have benefited have been producers of capital goods, the same industries which were severely impacted in the earlier part of 1980s by the high dollar.

In 1990 growth in merchandise exports, including manufactures, will continue to slow, acting as a depressant on export-oriented industries. Nevertheless, a number of

* Director, Office of Industry Assessment, Trade Development, U.S. Department of Commerce.

Source: *U.S. Industrial Outlook 1990*, U.S. Department of Commerce.

industries, many but not all in the high technology fields, will continue to experience significant export growth. These include medical and scientific equipment, commercial aircraft, machine tools, and paper making machinery.

Manufacturing Industry Performance

Especially noteworthy is the relative uniformity of growth rates, with few growing very fast or very slow. More than 72 percent of the industries are forecast to grow between 0 and 5 percent in 1990.

Table 3: Distribution of 1990 Forecast Growth Rates for Manufacturing Industries

Rate of Growth	10 to 5	4.9 to 2.5	2.5 to 0	−.01 to −2.4	−2.5 to −5
Number of industries	17	53	87	24	13
Percent of total	8.8	27.3	44.8	12.4	6.7

The estimates and forecasts show remarkably consistent trends both in the past and into the future. In 1990, 153 of the 194 industries covered are expected to have positive rates of growth, measured in constant dollars, and 123 industries should have positive growth for each year from 1987 to 1990.

Fastest Growing Industries: Looking at growth rates for individual industries can provide a more detailed perspective on industry performance: A ranking of 4-digit SIC industries forecast to grow fastest in 1990 is generally consistent with the rationale earlier outlined—high tech or health related.

Table 4: 10 Fastest Growing Four Digit Industries in 1990

(based on constant dollar shipments)

SIC Code	Industry	Percent Change
3841	Surgical and medical instruments	10.0
3842	Surgical appliances and supplies	9.0
3149	Footwear, except rubber, nec	8.0
2835	Diagnostic substances	7.0
2891	Adhesives and sealants	7.0
3548	Welding apparatus	6.8
2015	Poultry slaughtering and processing	6.7
3843	Dental equipment and supplies	6.1
2439	Structural wood members, nec	5.9
3142	House slippers	5.9

Source: *U.S. Industrial Outlook datafiles*

Adhesives and sealants, while not usually considered high technology products, are utilized in the fabrication of advanced composite materials. The growth of the poultry processing industry (SIC 2015) comes as no surprise as Americans' eating preferences shift from red meat to chicken.

The growth forecast for the two footwear industries appears inconsistent with trends, but reflects some special factors. First, they are both specialty categories of footwear with

annual sales of less than $1 billion. Footwear, nec, includes infant's and children's and sports shoes which are benefiting from growing demand. Stabilization appears to be taking place in the footwear industry with imports leveling off and the domestic industry having undergone a rationalization, leaving only the most competitive companies in the business.

The performance of structural wood members appears to run counter to trend in the construction industry. However, this industry produces a specialized product that remains in demand and which is also benefiting from a lower dollar which has helped increase exports, particularly to Japan.

Table 5: 10 Fastest Growing Four Digit Industries: 1988 to 1990

(based on constant dollar shipments)

SIC Code	Industry	Percent Change
3541	Machine tools, metal cutting types	41.6
3149	Footwear, except rubber, nec	20.4
3842	Surgical appliances and supplies	18.5
3841	Surgical and medical instruments	18.0
2439	Structural wood members, nec	15.2
3843	Dental equipment and supplies	14.8
3142	House slippers	14.5
3548	Welding apparatus	14.3
3845	Electromedical equipment	13.6
2835	Diagnostic substances	13.4

Source: *U.S. Industrial Outlook datafiles*

Taking a two-year perspective on growth has relatively little effect on which industries are fastest growing. High tech and health industries continue to predominate but there are exceptions. Machine tools are one exception to the pattern. The more favorable exchange rates, leading to large export gains, the voluntary restraint agreements, and a surge in orders in 1987 and 1988 led to an outstanding year in 1989. Even though orders slowed in 1989, this very cyclical industry will remain at a high level of output in 1990.

Ranking based on changes in rate of growth can sometimes be misleading. Looking at changes in the volume of shipments gives a different perspective.

Table 6: 10 Fastest Growing Four Digit Industries in 1990

Ranked by Change in Value of Shipments

SIC Code	Industry	Billions $1987
357A*	Computers & Peripherals (SIC 3571,72,75,77)	3.0
366A	Radio Commun Eq (SIC 3663,3669,3812)	2.2
308A	Misc. Plastics Products, except Bottles	1.9
275	Commercial Printing	1.5
3724	Aircraft engines and engine parts	1.3
2834	Pharmaceutical preparations	1.2
2015	Poultry slaughtering and processing	1.1
3721	Aircraft	1.1
3842	Surgical appliances and supplies	0.9
3841	Surgical and medical instruments	0.9

Source: *U.S. Industrial Outlook datafiles*
*Current dollars

While some industries that are growing quickly on a percentage basis are also ranked high in change in dollar volume, the rankings are dominated by larger but somewhat slower growing industries.

Slowest Growing Industries: Looking at the negative side, industries that are affected by construction and, especially, residential housing, and industries tied to motor vehicles, are expected to do poorly. The poor performance of cigars and chewing tobacco is also not surprising. Rankings such as these need to be interpreted cautiously. For example, the low rate of growth of real shipments of the Carburetor, pistons, rings, valves industry (SIC 3592) is due in part to the shift in the composition of output from carburetors to fuel injectors, which have a higher unit cost.

Table 7: 10 Slowest Growing Four Digit Industries in 1990

(based on constant dollar shipments)

SIC Code	Industry	Percent Change
3633	Household laundry equipment	-5.0
3211	Flat glass	-4.9
3674*	Semiconductors & Related Devices	-4.8
2121	Cigars	-4.7
3639	Household appliances, nec	-4.4
3632	Household refrigerators and freezers	-4.2
331A	Steel Mill Products (SIC 3312,15-17	-4.1
2131	Chewing and smoking tobacco	-4.0
3441	Fabricated structural metal	-3.8
3592	Carburetors, pistons, rings, valves	-3.7
3021	Rubber and plastics footwear	-3.6

Source: *U.S. Industrial Outlook datafiles*
*Current dollars

The one industry that appears out of place on the list of slowest growing is semiconductors. The problem for semiconductors is that prices are forecast to decline more rapidly than physical output grows leading to a drop in the value of shipments.

Service Industries

Services, as already noted, will continue to perform well and for the most part outper-

form manufacturing industries. This occurs in part because service industries are typically less cyclical than manufacturing and are thus less affected by the slowing economy. Nevertheless, slower growth in demand for manufactured goods also reduces demand for services used by business.

Table 8: Growth Rates for Selected Service Industries in 1990

Industry	Unit of Measure	Rate of Growth (percent)
Space Commerce	Revenues	20.0
Elect. Info. Serv.	Revenues	20.0
Computer Software	Receipts	18.0
Computer Prof. Serv.	Revenues	17.6
Data Processing	Revenues	16.0
Mgmt. Consult. & P.R	Receipts	15.0
Oper. & Maintenance		
Airlines	Expenditures	15.0
Security	Receipts	15.0
Buildings	Expenditures	10.0
Electric Power	Expenditures	7.5
Prerecorded Music	Manuf. value	14.0
Health & Med. Serv.	Expenditures	10.4
Cable Television	Revenues	10.0
Home Entertainment	Revenues	10.0
Hotels & Motels	Receipts	8.5
Electric Power	Expenditures	7.5
Equipment Leasing	Equip. Cost Added	7.5
Food Retailing	Sales	7.5
Airlines	Revenues	7.0
Trucking	Revenues	6.5

Source: *U.S. Industrial Outlook datafiles*

Despite the downward pressures, strong positive trends will continue to spur demand for services. One such trend is the continuing evolution of the U.S. economy to an "information" economy. As a result information industries such as electronic information services, data processing, space commerce and others will all continue to grow strongly. Another strong trend also already mentioned is in health care services, with expenditures expected to reach 11.5 percent of GNP in 1989.

Travel services will continue to grow due in part to the low dollar. In 1989 for the first time travel receipts from foreign visitors to the United States exceeded travel payments by U.S. residents traveling abroad.

Table 9: Forecast Growth Rates for 194 Manufacturing Industries

SIC Code	Industry Title	Shipments (1987 dollars)				Growth 1987 to 1990	
		Outlook Chapter[1]	1990 (bill.)	Growth Rate 89-90	Rank	Compound Annual Rate	Rank
2015	Poultry slaughtering and processing	34	17.622	6.73	7	5.79	18
2021	Creamery butter	34	1.312	1.16	128	-2.60	181
2022	Cheese, natural and processed	34	14.387	2.99	57	3.63	49
2023	Dry, condensed, evaporated products	34	5.857	2.31	81	0.14	149
2024	Ice cream and frozen desserts	34	3.883	2.48	73	-0.27	157
2026	Fluid milk	34	21.692	2.58	66	1.59	119
2032	Canned specialties	34	5.69	1.97	113	1.98	115
2033	Canned fruits and vegetables	34	12.316	0.00	154	1.24	126
2034	Dehydrated fruits, vegetables, soups	34	2.036	1.29	126	3.62	50
2035	Pickles, sauces, and salad dressings	34	5.305	2.12	90	2.56	87
2037	Frozen fruits and vegetables	34	7.305	3.71	33	3.44	51
2038	Frozen specialties, nec	34	6.015	2.84	60	2.75	80
2043	Cereal breakfast foods	34	7.636	5.46	14	5.16	28
2051	Bread, cake, and related products	34	18.385	4.54	24	4.31	33
2052	Cookies and crackers	34	7.078	4.66	22	3.96	40
2053	Frozen bakery products, except bread	34	1.173	1.03	130	0.23	147
2064	Candy & other confectionery products	34	8.062	3.24	46	3.24	61
2082	Malt beverages	34	14.022	1.69	119	1.02	131

Table 9: Forecast Growth Rates for 194 Manufacturing Industries—Continued

SIC Code	Industry Title	Outlook Chapter[1]	Shipments (1987 dollars) 1990 (bill.)	Growth Rate 89–90	Rank	Growth 1987 to 1990 Compound Annual Rate	Rank
2084	Wines, brandy, and brandy spirits	34	3.221	0.88	139	0.57	140
2085	Distilled and blended liquors	34	3.121	-1.17	170	-3.00	186
2086	Bottled and canned soft drinks	34	24.588	3.28	45	3.75	43
2111	Cigarettes	34	17.05	-1.45	172	-0.61	159
2121	Cigars	34	0.161	-4.73	191	-5.70	193
2131	Chewing and smoking tobacco	34	1.017	-3.97	187	-2.99	185
2141	Tobacco stemming and redrying	34	2.071	-0.91	163	-0.19	156
2386	Leather and sheep-lined clothing	36	0.215	3.37	42	2.78	78
2411	Logging	6	10.537	-1.60	173	-1.50	173
2421	Sawmills and planing mills, general	6	16.891	2.51	67	-0.56	158
2426	Hardwood dimension & flooring mills	6	1.83	2.01	97	2.27	102
2431	Millwork	6	9.735	2.00	102	2.08	109
2435	Hardwood veneer and plywood	6	1.887	-2.02	177	-2.63	182
2436	Softwood veneer and plywood	6	4.432	-1.01	166	-3.14	187
2439	Structural wood members, nec	6	2.45	5.88	10	8.35	7
2448	Wood pallets and skids	6	1.602	1.97	112	2.33	96
2491	Wood preserving	6	2.017	5.00	17	-1.66	174
2493	Reconstituted wood products	6	2.969	0.85	140	1.02	129
251	Household Furniture	39	18.158	-1.67	174	-0.67	160
2611	Pulp mills	10	4.627	3.01	53	3.17	65
2621	Paper mills	10	31.072	2.27	84	2.46	89
2631	Paperboard mills	10	14.59	2.30	82	1.49	121
2652	Setup paperboard boxes	10	0.451	0.89	138	1.29	125
2653	Corrugated and solid fiber boxes	10	17.41	2.00	99	2.70	82
2655	Fiber cans, drums & similar products	10	1.555	0.97	134	0.83	136
2656	Sanitary food containers	10	2.282	1.02	131	1.33	124
2657	Folding paperboard boxes	10	5.965	1.02	132	1.60	118
2671	Paper coated & laminated, packaging	10	2.672	3.01	52	3.17	64
2672	Paper coated and laminated, nec	10	5.355	4.61	23	3.00	72
2673	Bags: plastics, laminated, & coated	10	5.215	2.96	58	3.64	48
2674	Bags: uncoated paper & multiwall	10	2.235	-3.04	182	-2.87	184
2675	Die-cut paper and board	10	1.877	2.23	88	2.58	85
2676	Sanitary paper products	10	12.58	2.48	72	2.76	79
2677	Envelopes	10	2.795	2.49	71	2.17	106
2678	Stationery products	10	1.317	2.25	85	2.33	95
2679	Converted paper products, nec	10	3.938	2.29	83	2.36	94
2711	Newspapers	48	32.042	0.20	148	0.27	145
2721	Periodicals	48	18.707	1.90	115	2.13	107
2731	Book publishing	48	12.966	3.55	35	3.66	47
2732	Book printing	48	3.526	2.62	65	2.71	81
2741	Miscellaneous publishing	48	7.814	2.68	63	2.68	83
275	Commercial Printing	48	49.41	3.10	50	3.42	55
2761	Manifold business forms	48	7.762	1.60	120	1.93	116
2771	Greeting cards	48	3.082	1.99	108	2.32	98
2782	Blankbooks and looseleaf binders	48	3.076	2.40	76	2.01	111
2789	Bookbinding and related work	48	1.201	0.33	146	1.02	130
2791	Typesetting	48	1.982	2.38	77	3.19	63
2796	Platemaking services	48	2.753	4.88	20	5.33	24
2812	Alkalies and chlorine	13	1.627	2.01	98	2.00	112
2813	Industrial gases	13	2.888	3.00	56	3.00	70
2819	Industrial inorganic chemicals, nec	13	13.776	2.00	105	2.00	113
2821	Plastics materials and resins	14	28.73	2.00	101	3.19	62
2822	Synthetic rubber	14	3.406	1.98	111	0.96	132
2823	Cellulosic manmade fibers	9	1.437	3.38	40	2.61	84
2824	Organic fibers, noncellulosic	9	10.859	2.25	86	2.40	91
2833	Medicinals and botanicals	50	3.575	2.11	91	2.21	104
2834	Pharmaceutical preparations	50	35.5	3.35	43	3.45	53
2835	Diagnostic substances	50	2.48	6.99	4	5.99	17
2836	Biological products exc. diagnostic	50	1.783	3.78	31	3.91	42
2841	Soap and other detergents	37	12.423	1.98	110	2.58	86
2842	Polishes and sanitation goods	37	5.897	2.33	80	2.26	103
2843	Surface active agents	37	3.43	4.99	19	4.80	30
2844	Toilet preparations	37	15.975	3.71	32	3.46	52
2851	Paints and allied products	15	14.658	4.00	28	5.17	27
2865	Cyclic crudes and intermediates	13	9.466	1.50	122	2.38	92
2869	Industrial organic chemicals, nec	13	42.481	1.53	121	0.26	146
2873	Nitrogenous fertilizers	13	2.833	-0.25	160	5.32	25
2874	Phosphatic fertilizers	13	4.506	3.99	30	5.65	21
2879	Agricultural chemicals, nec	13	6.335	0.05	151	0.01	152
2891	Adhesives and sealants	15	5.462	6.97	5	5.25	26
2895	Carbon black	12	0.65	0.00	155	4.48	32
2911	Petroleum refining	4	121.429	-0.31	161	0.95	133
3011	Tires and inner tubes	14	10.903	1.50	123	1.50	120
3021	Rubber and plastics footwear	14	0.505	-3.63	184	-4.78	190
3052	Rubber & plastics hose & belting	14	2.412	1.99	107	2.00	114
3069	Fabricated rubber products, nec	14	5.908	3.00	54	3.00	71
3085	Plastics bottles	11	3.057	3.59	34	3.39	57
308A	Misc. Plastics Products, except Bottles	14	64.263	3.10	49	3.70	45
3111	Leather tanning and finishing	36	2.222	5.01	16	0.11	151
3142	House slippers	36	0.252	5.88	9	7.30	12
3143	Men's footwear, except athletic	36	1.752	1.98	109	-5.42	192

Table 9: Forecast Growth Rates for 194 Manufacturing Industries—Continued

SIC Code	Industry Title	Outlook Chapter¹	Shipments (1987 dollars)			Growth 1987 to 1990	
			1990 (bill.)	Growth Rate 89-90	Rank	Compound Annual Rate	Rank
3111	Women's footwear, except athletic	36	1.167	2.01	95	-3.93	189
3149	Footwear, except rubber, nec	36	0.524	8.04	3	9.97	0
3151	Leather gloves and mittens	36	0.166	-0.60	162	-1.18	167
3161	Luggage	36	0.88	1.85	116	1.20	128
3171	Women's handbags and purses	36	0.432	-2.04	179	-7.68	194
3172	Personal leather goods, nec	36	0.311	-1.89	175	-4.94	191
3211	Flat glass	7	2.403	-4.91	193	-1.68	175
3221	Glass containers	11	4.597	0.79	141	0.56	141
3241	Cement, hydraulic	7	4.318	0.47	145	-0.01	155
3251	Brick and structural clay tile	7	1.182	0.77	142	-1.79	177
3253	Ceramic wall and floor tile	7	0.804	3.47	36	3.94	41
3271	Concrete block and brick	7	2.135	0.23	147	-1.08	164
3272	Concrete products, nec	7	5.549	0.20	149	-1.30	169
3273	Ready-mixed concrete	7	12.865	0.69	143	0.20	148
3275	Gypsum products	7	2.845	2.37	78	2.19	105
3296	Mineral wool	7	3.328	1.49	124	0.68	137
331A	Steel Mill Products (SIC 3312,15-17)	16	52.5	-4.14	188	0.65	138
3411	Metal cans	11	12.032	3.10	48	4.06	36
3441	Fabricated structural metal	7	8.338	-3.76	186	-1.01	163
3448	Prefabricated metal buildings	7	3.723	-0.98	165	3.33	59
3451	Screw machine products	18	3.468	2.00	103	7.39	11
3452	Bolts, nuts, rivets, and washers	18	5.636	2.01	96	3.66	46
3465	Automotive stampings	38	16.225	2.02	93	2.02	110
349A	Valves & Pipe Fittings	18	12.626	2.00	100	3.99	39
3523	Farm machinery and equipment	23	7.535	3.40	39	3.12	66
3524	Lawn and garden equipment	40	4.404	-0.23	159	-1.49	171
3531	Construction machinery	22	13.686	2.50	68	2.43	90
3532	Mining machinery	23	1.642	2.50	70	2.79	77
3533	Oil and gas field machinery	23	3.533	4.99	18	9.96	4
3541	Machine tools, metal cutting types	21	4.521	1.01	133	11.71	1
3542	Machine tools, metal forming types	21	1.741	1.81	117	7.16	13
3544	Special dies, tools, jigs & fixtures	21	7.633	-0.04	158	0.32	144
3546	Power-driven handtools	21	2.108	-1.40	171	-0.76	161
3548	Welding apparatus	21	2.555	6.81	6	6.93	15
3552	Textile machinery	23	1.406	4.38	25	4.53	31
3554	Paper industries machinery	23	2.228	4.36	26	5.43	23
3555	Printing trades machinery	23	3.386	1.20	127	5.58	22
3556	Food products machinery	23	2.214	2.41	75	3.29	60
3561	Pumps and pumping equipment	22	4.514	2.80	62	2.97	73
3562	Ball and roller bearings	18	4.122	3.00	55	3.06	67
3563	Air and gas compressors	22	3.28	2.50	69	2.81	76
3565	Packaging machinery	23	2.329	2.46	74	3.35	58
357A*	Computers & Peripherals (SIC 3571,72,75,77)	30	72.5	4.32	27	8.09	8
3585	Refrigeration and heating equipment	22	19.241	2.24	87	3.05	68
3592	Carburetors, pistons, rings, valves	38	2.041	-3.68	185	-3.72	188
3612	Transformers, except electronic	24	3.5	0.03	152	2.29	100
3613	Switchgear and switchboard apparatus	24	5.288	1.97	114	2.13	108
3621	Motors and generators	24	7.547	3.04	51	2.94	74
3625	Relays and industrial controls	24	6.585	1.14	129	2.50	88
3631	Household cooking equipment	39	3.285	-2.03	178	-1.12	166
3632	Household refrigerators and freezers	39	3.39	-4.24	189	-1.24	168
3633	Household laundry equipment	39	2.91	-4.96	194	-1.38	170
3634	Electric housewares and fans	39	2.85	-2.40	181	0.48	143
3635	Household vacuum cleaners	39	1.58	-3.07	183	0.53	142
3639	Household appliances, nec	39	2.25	-4.38	190	-2.14	179
3643	Current-carrying wiring devices	8	4.121	2.23	89	0.94	135
3644	Noncurrent-carrying wiring devices	8	2.501	0.00	156	-1.68	176
3647	Vehicular lighting equipment	38	2.179	3.47	37	3.42	56
364A	Lighting Fixtures (SIC 3645,46,48)	8	6.223	2.00	104	0.12	150
3651	Household audio and video equipment	39	6.708	-2.00	176	4.86	29
3661	Telephone and telegraph apparatus	32	17.955	2.10	92	0.94	134
366A	Radio Commun & Detection Eq (SIC 3663,3669,3812)	33	59.356	4.00	29	4.00	38
3672	Printed Circuit Boards	19	5.151	5.77	11	6.98	14
3674*	Semiconductors and related devices	19	26.686	-4.76	192	10.88	2
367B	Discrete Electronic Parts (SIC 3671,75-79)	19	34.599	1.72	118	4.12	34
3691	Storage batteries	38	3.593	2.89	59	2.87	75
3694	Engine electrical equipment	38	7.471	0.00	157	0.00	153
3714	Motor vehicle parts and accessories	38	63.304	1.42	125	1.41	122
371A	Motor Vehicles, Bodies,(SIC 3711,13,15,16)	38	133.221	-2.19	180	-2.51	180
3721	Aircraft	25	41.52	2.65	64	1.22	127
3724	Aircraft engines and engine parts	25	24.2	5.58	12	6.17	16
3728	Aircraft parts and equipment, nec	25	20.16	3.44	38	4.12	35
3731	Ship building and repairing	26	8.249	-1.03	168	-1.11	165
3732	Boat building and repairing	40	5.09	0.67	144	-1.49	172
3751	Motorcycles, bicycles, and parts	40	0.98	-0.91	164	-1.90	178
3761	Guided missiles and space vehicles	25	23.13	3.17	47	2.36	93
3764	Space propulsion units and parts	25	3.98	3.38	41	4.01	37
3769	Space vehicle equipment, nec	25	1.25	3.31	44	3.03	69
3825	Instruments to measure electricity	27	9.545	4.80	21	7.41	10
382A	Laboratory Instruments (SIC 3821,26,27,29)	27	12.698	5.12	15	5.70	20
382B	Measuring & Controlling Inst. (SIC 3822-24)	27	8.792	2.35	79	3.53	51

*Current dollars

Source: U.S. Industrial Outlook datafiles

¹ For further information consult the chapter referred to in the *U.S. Industrial Outlook 1990*, U.S. Department of Commerce.

Table 9: Forecast Growth Rates for 194 Manufacturing Industries—Continued

SIC Code	Industry Title	Shipments (1987 dollars)				Growth 1987 to 1990	
		Outlook Chapter[1]	1990 (bill.)	Growth Rate 89–90	Rank	Compound Annual Rate	Rank
3841	Surgical and medical instruments	51	9.811	9.96	1	9.07	6
3842	Surgical appliances and supplies	51	11.094	9.00	2	9.40	5
3843	Dental equipment and supplies	51	1.637	6.09	8	5.76	19
3844	X-ray apparatus and tubes	51	1.772	2.01	94	2.28	101
3845	Electromedical equipment	51	4.314	5.50	13	7.70	9
3861	Photographic equipment and supplies	28	21.661	2.82	61	3.74	44
3911	Jewelry, precious metal	40	4.57	0.97	136	2.32	97
3931	Musical instruments	40	0.837	0.97	137	0.00	154
3942	Dolls and stuffed toys	40	0.263 –1.13	169	–2.64	183	
3944	Games, toys, and children's vehicles	40	3.327	–1.01	167	–1.00	162
3949	Sporting and athletic goods, nec	40	5.315	2.00	106	1.67	117
3961	Costume jewelry	40	1.349	0.97	135	1.34	123

Industry Surveys*

The following provides information about a number of industries as well as financial data on companies in each industry. Financial Ratios are defined in the section *Investment and Financial Terms* (page 429).

EXPLANATIONS OF FINANCIAL AND STOCK MARKET INFORMATION

Revenue and Earnings

It should be noted that 12-month figures are trailing ones, calculated from figures shown in the latest interim reports and latest fiscal year reports, when appropriate. Fiscal figures are as reported by the company. Interim figures are based on cumulative data. All earnings per share figures are primary, and are reflected in all calculations. Earnings per share and total earnings figures show earnings from total operations. Earnings are before extraordinary items, but when this is not possible, special earnings footnotes are shown immediately to the right of the company name in the stock tables and these special footnotes are explained as follows:

◇—includes extraordinary gains
◆—includes extraordinary losses
□—excludes extraordinary gains
■—excludes extraordinary losses

5-Year Earnings Growth Rate The annual compound growth rate in primary earnings per share over the last five years computed by the least squares method using logarithms of the earnings per share data, brought up to date through the latest 12 months' earning per share by weighting the first and last points. The five-year earnings growth rate is calculated only for those companies which have all positive earnings per share data for each of the periods used in the calculation. An NC footnote will appear for all companies which do not have a positive earnings per share record for the five-year period. An NC footnote will appear for all companies which have an incomplete record of earnings per share for the five-year period.

Par Growth Rate Retained latest 12 months' earnings per share multiplied by latest 12 months return on common equity, as a percent of latest 12 months' earnings per share.

Extra growth rate in EPS can be derived by subtracting par growth rate from 5-year EPS growth rate.

Dividends

Dividends are the latest indicated rate, and the yield is based on that amount and the latest close.

5-Year Growth Rate The figure is arrived at by the least squares method, using dividends actually paid for the first five years and the indicated rate for the sixth point.

Ratios

Profit Margin The profit margin of the company based on latest 12 months' revenue and earnings.

Asset Turnover The latest 12 months' return on total assets divided by the latest 12 months' profit margin.

Return on Common Equity The latest 12 months' earnings divided by stockholder equity from the latest balance sheet.

Return on Total Assets Based on the latest 12 months total earnings and the total asset as reported in the company's latest fiscal year balance sheet.

Leverage Ratio The latest 12 months' return on common equity divided by the latest 12 months' return on total assets.

Debt to Equity The total long-term debt of the company as a percentage of the total common equity of the company, both from the latest annual balance sheet.

Shareholdings

Market Value Latest reported shares outstanding times latest closing price per share of the common stock.

Latest Shares Outstanding Latest reported shares outstanding, adjusted for any subsequent stock splits or dividends.

Held by Banks-Funds The single figure here represents shares held by institutions with equity assets exceeding $100 million—banks, insurance companies, investment companies and managers, independent investment advisors and others. Shares held are adjusted for any stock splits or stock dividends that occur subsequent to the quarterly reporting date of the institutions covered. The data is furnished by Computer Directions Advisers, Inc.

Insider Net Trading Net change in insider holdings—purchases vs. sales—based on the latest SEC report in thousands of shares. 0 means there were no transactions or transac-

* The financial data on companies in each industry come from Media General Financial Services, 301 East Grace Street, Richmond, VA 23219; June 30, 1990.

tions netted to 0; +0 means transactions netted to purchases of fewer than 500 shares, and −0 means transactions netted to sales of fewer than 500 shares.

The most recent monthly period for insider transactions is December 11, 1989, to January 10, 1990.

Short Interest Ratio Short interest for the latest month reported, divided by average daily volume for the month corresponding to the report. The figure shows the number of days it would take to cover the short interest if the trading rate continued at the rate of the month covered by the report.

Short interest for the current issue is for the period November 15, 1990, through June 15, 1990.

GENERAL FOOTNOTES

    *—As applied to beta figures, an asterisk denotes a co-efficient at least as large as its probable error (i.e., .6745 times the standard error of its mean).
    G—Value calculated greater than allowed range.
    L—Value calculated less than allowed range.

    a—Under current dividend yield, an "a" indicates a stock dividend.
    b—Indicates cash plus stock dividend when applied to dividend yield column.
    NA—Item not applicable to this stock.
    NE—Negative earnings invalidate calculation.
    NC—Data required for calculation not available.
    NS—Negative stockholder equity invalidates calculations.
    NM—No meaningful figure
    q—Based on first quarter information.
    s—Based on second quarter information.
    n—Based on third quarter information.
    f—Based on fiscal year information.
    *—When applied to 12-month earnings, an asterisk indicates an actual amount for an interim period, other than a quarterly multiple, resulting from a fiscal year change.

All information in this publication is based on sources believed to be reliable, but its accuracy is not guaranteed. Every effort will be made to correct errors, when discovered, in future editions.

Trends and Forecasts: Aerospace (SIC 372,376)
(in millions of dollars except as noted)

Item	1987[1]	1988[2]	1989[3]	1990[4]	Percent Change		
					1987–88	1988–89	1989–90
Industry Data							
Value of shipments[5]	104,366	105,928	112,524	121,217	1.5	6.2	7.7
Value of shipments (1987$)	104,366	107,722	110,340	114,240	3.2	2.4	3.5
Total employment (000)	816	828	846	868	1.5	2.2	2.6
Production workers (000)	411	414	424	440	0.7	2.4	3.8
Average hourly earnings ($)	14.89	15.36	16.10	–	3.2	4.8	–
Product Data							
Value of shipments[6]	97,872	99,446	105,745	114,175	1.6	6.3	8.0
Value of shipments (1987$)	97,872	100,997	103,555	107,500	3.2	2.5	3.8
Trade Data							
Value of imports	5,842	6,555	–	–	12.2	–	–
Value of exports	22,429	25,696	–	–	14.6	–	–

[1] Industry and product data are preliminary. Trade data are adjusted to conform to the 1987 SIC.
[2] Estimated, except for exports and imports.
[3] Estimated.
[4] Forecast.
[5] Value of all products and services sold by establishments in the aerospace industry.
[6] Value of products classified in the aerospace industry produced by all industries.
SOURCE: U.S. Department of Commerce: Bureau of the Census; International Trade Administration (ITA). Estimates and forecasts by ITA.

Source: *U.S. Industrial Outlook 1990*, U.S. Department of Commerce.

MEDIA GENERAL FINANCIAL SERVICES

STOCKS by INDUSTRY

Aerospace Industries

Company	Rev % Last Qtr	Rev % FY to Date	Rev % Last 12 Mos	Earn Last 12 Mos $Mil	EPS Last 12 Mos $	EPS Chg Last Qtr %	EPS Chg FY to Date %	EPS Chg Last 12 Mos %	5-Yr Growth Rate %	Par Growth Rate %	Date of Report	Div Current Rate Amt $	Div Yield %	Div 5-Yr Growth Rate %	Payout Last FY %	Payout Last 5 Yrs %	Last X-Dvd Date	Profit Margin %	Asset Turnover	Return on Total Assets	Leverage Ratio	Return on Equity	Debt to Equity %	Current Ratio	Market Value $Mil	Latest Shares Outstndg 000	Held by Banks-Funds 000	Insider Net Trading 000	Short Interest Ratio Days	Fiscal Year Ends Mo
Ind. Group ··············	5.0	9.3	5.4	2,879.8	2.44	-1.6	9.8	-24.4	1	6	---	1.13	2.8	1	39	31	---	2.8	1.39	3.9	2.85	11.1	41	1.5	46,767	1,161,473	601,989	+968	6.9	--
Boeing Co ·············	-.5	19.5	19.5	675.0f	1.96	-54.9	9.5	9.5	-3	5	12-89	1.00	1.7b	14	40	35	08-13-90	3.3	1.55	5.1	2.16	11.0	4	1.3	20,221	345,681	190,213	+4	1.8	12
Crane s ··············	1.2	1.2	5.3	58.7q	1.81	27.3	27.3	-6.7	NC	12	03-90	.75	2.9	0	41	44	05-30-90	4.0	2.25	9.0	2.30	20.7	42	2.2	836	32,300	16,684	-67	0.6	12
Curtiss-Wright ◻ ····	14.7	14.7	10.8	19.0q	3.78	-53.5	-53.5	-34.4	NC	4	03-90	1.60	2.5	3	26	62	07-06-90	9.8	.55	5.4	1.31	7.1	11	6.6	319	4,892	3,745	-31	0.0	12
Gen Dynamics ········	5.5	5.5	6.9	341.4q	8.17	64.1	64.1	-1.8	NC	14	03-90	1.00	3.1	0	14	15	07-11-90	3.4	1.53	5.2	3.10	16.1	43	1.9	1,331	41,579	21,426	-1	1.1	12
Gen Motors H ········	NA	NA	NA	NA	NA	NA	NA	NA	NA	NC	00-00	.72	3.3	NA	NA	NA	05-11-90	NA	NC	NC	NC	NC	NA	NA	2,822	130,496	69,517	-40	NA	NA
Grumman Corp ···· ◆	-4.3	-4.3	-3.3	67.8q	1.92	2.2	2.2	-18.3	NC	4	03-90	1.00	5.3	1	52	54	05-02-90	2.0	1.30	2.6	3.19	8.3	104	2.4	626	32,960	11,586	0	3.0	12
Lockheed Corp ······	13.0	13.0	1.2	9.0q	.08	4.8	4.8	-99.2	-64	-9	03-90	1.80	5.4	30	5833	22	05-16-90	.1	1.00	.1	4.00	.4	89	1.2	2,117	63,193	29,827	+1	2.3	12
Martin Marietta ·····	7.8	7.8	2.6	314.8q	6.02	17.9	17.9	-2.6	-27	18	03-90	1.35	3.1	6	21	22	05-29-90	5.3	1.70	9.0	2.58	23.2	35	1.6	2,179	50,814	28,425	-2	1.2	12
McDonnel Doug ·····	14.5	14.5	-.7	52.0q	1.35	NE	NE	-82.1	NC	-2	03-90	2.82	7.7	12	264	34	05-29-90	.3	1.33	.4	4.00	1.6	93	2.3	1,397	38,272	14,102	+167	6.3	12
Northrop Corp ···· ◇	-.3	-.3	-8.1	5.8q	.12	871.4	871.4	NE	NC	-6	03-90	1.20	5.5	4	NE	116	05-22-90	.1	2.00	.2	3.50	.7	67	1.1	869	46,553	25,307	+27	12.2	12
Rockwell Intl ········	-.3	.1	2.1	623.4s	2.49	-33.3	-22.8	-21.9	10	11	03-90	.78	2.8	9	26	24	05-08-90	5.0	1.40	7.0	2.24	15.7	14	1.3	6,758	246,867	111,145	+901	2.4	09
Utd Technol ········	6.5	6.5	7.9	712.9s	5.44	10.5	10.5	7.5	24	10	03-90	1.80	3.1	3	30	42	05-21-90	3.6	1.36	4.9	3.06	15.0	41	1.3	7,293	127,386	80,092	+9	1.3	12

Ratio note: r/t × t/a = r/a × a/e = r/e

Source: Media General Financial Services, Richmond, VA.

Trends and Forecasts: Airlines (SIC[1] 451, 452)

Item	1987	1988[1]	1989[2]	1990[3]	Percent Change		
					1987–88	1988–89	1989–90
Total operating revenues (billions $)	56.8	63.7	69.1	73.9	12.1	8.5	6.9
Revenue passenger miles (billions)	418	437	451	467	4.5	3.2	3.5
Freight revenue ton miles (billions)	12.3	12.7	15.5	18.3	3.3	22.0	18.1
Employment (000)	529	557	586	609	5.3	5.2	3.9

[1] 1987 SIC numbers remain unchanged.
[2] Estimate.
[3] Forecast.

SOURCE: U.S. Department of Commerce, International Trade Administration (ITA); U.S. Department of Transportation, Federal Aviation Administration; U.S. Department of Labor, Bureau of Labor Statistics. Estimates and forecasts by ITA.

Source: *U.S. Industrial Outlook 1990*, U.S. Department of Commerce.

Evolution of Major U.S. Passenger Carriers Since Deregulation

Parent	Antecedents
Texas Air	New York Air, Continental, Eastern, People Express (Frontier-Provincetown-Britt) Rocky Mountain
United	United
American	American, Air Cal
Delta	Delta, Atlantic Southeast, Comair, Western
Northwest	Northwest, Republic (Southern-North Central) Hughes Air West
TWA	TWA, Ozark
Pan Am	Pan Am, National, Ransome
USAir	USAir, Suburban, PSA, Piedmont (Empire, Jet Stream)

SOURCE: Federal Aviation Administration.

Source: *U.S. Industrial Outlook 1990*, U.S. Department of Commerce.

STOCKS by INDUSTRY

MEDIA GENERAL FINANCIAL SERVICES

Regional Airlines

Company	Rev. Last Qtr %	Rev. FY to Date %	Rev. Last 12 Mos %	Earn. Last 12 Mos $Mil	Earn. Last 12 Mos $	Last Qtr $	P/S Last Qtr %	P/S FY to Date %	P/S Last 12 Mos %	5-Yr Growth %	Par Growth %	Date of Report	Div Amt $	Yield %	Div 5-Yr Growth %	Payout Last FY %	Payout Last 5 Yrs %	Last X-Dvd Date	Profit Margin	Asset Turnover	Return Total Assets	Leverage Ratio	Return on Equity	Debt to Equity %	Current Ratio	Mkt Value $Mil	Latest Shares Outstndg 000	Held by Banks-Funds 000	Insider Net Trading 000	Short Int Ratio Days	Fiscal Year Ends Mo
Ind. Group	22.0	22.1	18.1	7.7	-.07	-100.0	-100.0	-100.0	-100.0	NC	1	----	.11	.8	0	9	8	----	.1	1.00	.1	5.00	.5	119	1.1	2,195	149,425	50,098	+694	2.0	--
Air Midwest Inc	21	2.1	7.8	-.2q	-.06	NE	NE	NE	NE	NC	-1	03-90	.00	.0	0	0	NE	12-10-85	-.2	1.50	-.3	4.33	-1.3	158	.8	20	3,912	947	0	0.0	12
Air Wisc	7.5	7.5	-.0	1.3q	.14	140.0	140.0	140.0	-87.3	-12	1	03-90	.08	.0	0	0	0	05-23-89	.7	.86	.6	2.33	1.4	70	1.7	91	9,010	3,373	+1	0.0	03
Airtran Cp	59.6	98.0	97.2	2.4f	.60	-100.0	250.0	25.0	25.0	NC	17	03-90	.16	2.6	0	25	19	05-21-90	3.4	2.53	8.6	2.63	22.6	81	1.7	23	3,631	510	0	0.0	03
Alaska Air Group	16.7	16.7	13.2	34.4q	2.10	-100.0	-100.0	-26.3	-26.3	4	9	03-90	.20	.9	0	7	9	07-09-90	3.6	1.08	3.9	2.59	10.1	66	1.0	324	14,389	8,842	+2	5.0	12
Am West Airline	30.8	30.8	27.0	3.8q	.08	-100.0	-100.0	-100.0	-86.4	NC	8	03-90	.00	.0	0	4	9	00-00-00	.4	1.25	.5	8.80	4.4	545	.9	156	17,581	1,831	+6945	0.0	12
Atlantic SE Air	14.4	14.4	28.2	28.9q	2.40	31.6	31.6	31.6	98.3	24	22	03-90	.40	2.1	0	11	4	05-25-90	15.5	.65	10.0	2.67	26.7	103	2.5	224	11,779	5,279	0	0.0	12
CCAIR Inc	13.1	4.7	12.7	-6.3n	-1.07	NE	-100.0	NC	NC	NC	0	03-90	.00	.0	0	0	0	00-00-00	-10.2	2.43	-24.8	.00	NM	96	1.0	12	5,782	230	0	0.0	06
HAL Inc	-3.1	-3.1	-2.2	-54.3q	-26.99	NE	NE	NE	NE	NC	0	03-90	.00	.0	0	0	NE	03-01-87	-15.7	1.60	-25.1	.00	NM	702	.5	38	2,163	208	0	5.6	12
Metro Airlines	39.3	23.4	16.0	-24.0n	-3.99	NE	NE	NE	NE	NC	0	01-90	.00	.0	0	0	0	00-00-00	-13.8	1.56	-21.5	3.38	NM	350	.8	38	6,095	480	0	0.0	04
Midway Arlns	34.0	34.0	21.1	-45.4q	-4.71	-100.0	-100.0	-100.0	-100.0	NC	-55	03-90	.00	.0	0	0	0	00-00-00	-8.5	1.92	-16.3	3.38	-55.1	87	.8	85	9,998	1,704	-4	16.8	12
PS Group	41.2	41.2	19.5	4.7q	.77	516.7	516.7	516.7	-87.2	NC	0	03-90	.60	1.6	0	130	19	04-17-90	1.8	.39	.7	2.71	1.9	104	1.7	248	6,607	3,804	0	2.3	12
SkyWest Inc	24.4	18.4	19.0	4.7f	.91	61.1	24.7	24.7	24.7	NC	15	03-90	.06	.7	1	16	15	06-25-90	4.7	1.55	7.3	2.26	16.5	56	2.2	42	5,213	1,318	0	0.0	03
SW Airlines	13.6	13.6	14.8	57.1q	1.91	-71.9	-71.9	-71.9	-22.7	5	9	03-90	.14	.5	6	6	8	06-07-90	5.5	.73	4.0	2.43	9.7	60	1.0	739	28,708	19,499	0	1.6	12
Statewest Arlns	42.9	17.9	-.8	-3.0s	-.84	NE	NE	NE	-48.4	NC	-68	03-90	.00	.0	0	0	0	00-00-00	-50.0	.32	-15.8	4.32	-68.2	285	2.9	15	4,352	8	0	0.0	09
Westair Hldg	46.7	46.7	41.7	2.3q	.32	-40.0	-40.0	-40.0	-48.4	NC	11	03-90	.00	.0	0	0	0	00-00-00	1.1	2.36	2.6	4.12	10.7	91	1.4	42	6,234	374	0	0.0	12
WorldCorp	17.2	17.2	29.6	1.3q	.00	-100.0	-100.0	-100.0	-100.0	NC	NC	03-90	.00	.0	0	0	0	00-00-00	.6	1.00	.6	.00	NS	-387	1.3	105	12,911	1,691	0	0.6	12

s/r × r/a = s/a × a/e = s/e

Source: Media General Financial Services, Richmond, VA.

Apparel

Trends and Forecasts: Apparel and Other Finished Textile Products (SIC 23)

(in millions of dollars except as noted)

Item	1987[1]	1988[2]	1989[3]	Percent Change 1987–88	Percent Change 1988–89
Industry Data					
Value of shipments	65,102	67,655	72,192	3.9	6.7
Value of shipments (1987$)	65,102	65,623	67,723	.8	3.2
Total employment (000)	1,080	1,069	1,090	−1.0	2.0
Production workers (000)	908.9	901.6	919.6	− .8	2.0
Average hourly earnings ($)	6.12	6.30	6.51	2.9	3.3
Product Data					
Value of shipments	63,056	65,263	69,505	3.5	6.5
Value of shipments (1987$)	63,056	63,497	65,402	.7	3.0
Trade Data					
Value of imports	21,503	22,170	23,722	3.1	7.0
Value of exports	1,491	1,955	2,602	31.1	33.1

[1]Industry and product data are preliminary. Trade data are adjusted to conform to the 1987 SIC.
[2]Estimated, except for exports and imports.
[3]Estimated.
SOURCE: U.S. Department of Commerce: Bureau of the Census and International Trade Administration (ITA). Estimates and forecasts by ITA.

Source: *U.S. Industrial Outlook 1990*, U.S. Department of Commerce.

Trends and Forecasts: Selected Men's and Boys' Apparel (SIC 231, 2321,–3, –5, –6)

(in millions of dollars except as noted)

Item	1987[1]	1988[2]	1989[3]	Percent Change 1987–88	Percent Change 1988–89
Industry Data					
Value of shipments[4]	15,205	15,925	16,852	4.7	5.8
2311 Men/boys' suits/coats	3,192	3,305	3,388	3.5	2.5
2321 Men's and boys' shirts	4,028	4,174	4,442	3.6	6.4
2323 Men's & boys' neckwear	476	518	556	8.8	7.3
2325 Men/boys' trousers	5,843	6,161	6,694	5.4	8.7
2326 Men/boys' work clothing	1,667	1,767	1,772	6.0	0.3
Value of shipments (1987$)	15,205	15,404	15,776	1.3	2.4
2311 Men/boys' suits/coats	3,192	3,211	3,302	0.6	2.8
2321 Men's and boys' shirts	4,028	4,090	4,173	1.5	2.0
2323 Men's & boys' neckwear	476	481	499	1.1	3.7
2325 Men/boys' trousers	5,843	5,984	6,162	2.4	3.0
2326 Men/boys' work clothing	1,667	1,638	1,640	−1.7	0.1
Total employment (000)	270	266	266	−1.5	0.0
2311 Men/boys' suits/coats	56.4	59.4	59.0	5.3	−0.7
2321 Men's and boys' shirts	78.9	71.6	70.4	−9.3	−1.7
2323 Men's & boys' neckwear	7.4	7.5	7.3	1.4	−2.7
2325 Men/boys' trousers	93.0	94.5	95.6	1.6	1.2
2326 Men/boys' work clothing	34.1	33.3	33.4	−2.3	0.3

(continued)

Trends and Forecasts: Selected Men's and Boys' Apparel (SIC 231, 2321, -3, -5, -6) *(continued)*

(in millions of dollars except as noted)

Item	1987[1]	1988[2]	1989[3]	Percent Change 1987–88	Percent Change 1988–89
Production workers (000)	236	230	226	-2.5	-1.7
2311 Men/boys' suits/coats	49.2	49.9	47.3	1.4	-5.2
2321 Men's and boys' shirts	68.3	61.8	60.8	-9.5	-1.6
2323 Men's & boys' neckwear	6.2	6.3	6.2	1.6	-1.6
2325 Men/boys' trousers	82.2	82.8	83.2	0.7	0.5
2326 Men/boys' work clothing	29.9	29.3	28.9	-2.0	-1.4
Average hourly earnings ($)	5.94	6.28	6.47	5.7	3.0
2311 Men/boys' suits/coats	6.99	7.16	7.38	2.4	3.1
2321 Men's and boys' shirts	5.50	5.72	5.96	4.0	4.2
2323 Men's & boys' neckwear	6.98	7.19	7.43	3.0	3.3
2325 Men/boys' trousers	5.87	5.99	6.16	2.0	2.8
2326 Men/boys' work clothing	5.26	5.33	5.44	1.3	2.1
Product Data					
Value of shipments[5]	14,069	14,692	15,605	4.4	6.2
2311 Men/boys' suits/coats	2,900	3,008	3,083	3.7	2.5
2321 Men's and boys' shirts	3,795	3,923	4,176	3.4	6.4
2323 Men's & boys' neckwear	421	450	473	6.9	5.1
2325 Men/boys' trousers	5,397	5,668	6,225	5.0	9.8
2326 Men/boys' work clothing	1,556	1,643	1,648	5.6	0.3
Value of shipments (1987$)	14,069	14,267	14,624	1.4	2.5
2311 Men/boys' suits/coats	2,900	2,935	2,956	1.2	0.7
2321 Men's and boys' shirts	3,795	3,830	3,891	0.9	1.6
2323 Men's & boys' neckwear	421	429	440	1.9	2.6
2325 Men/boys' trousers	5,397	5,494	5,755	1.8	4.8
2326 Men/boys' work clothing	1,556	1,579	1,592	1.5	0.2
Trade Data					
Value of imports	8,421	8,633	9,263	2.5	7.3
2311 Men/boys' suits/coats	1,057	1,188	1,509	12.4	27.0
2321 Men's and boys' shirts	5,880	5,790	5,952	-1.5	2.8
2323 Men's & boys' neckwear	85.7	114	131	33.0	14.9
2325 Men/boys' trousers	1,377	1,515	1,636	10.0	8.0
2326 Men/boys' work clothing	20.5	27.1	35.7	32.2	31.7
Value of exports	348	481	619	38.2	28.7
2311 Men/boys' suits/coats	91.5	113	97.1	23.5	-14.1
2321 Men's and boys' shirts	119	146	99.4	22.7	-31.9
2323 Men's & boys' neckwear	5.2	6.0	8.4	15.4	40.0
2325 Men/boys' trousers	130	209	405	60.8	93.8
2326 Men/boys' work clothing	2.7	6.7	9.1	148.1	35.8

[1]Industry and product data are preliminary. Trade data are adjusted to conform to the 1987 SIC.
[2]Estimated, except for exports and imports.
[3]Estimated.
[4]Value of all products and services sold by establishments in the selected men's & boys' apparel industry.
[5]Value of products classified in the selected men's & boys' apparel industry produced by all industries.
SOURCE: U.S. Department of Commerce: Bureau of the Census; International Trade Administration (ITA). Estimates and forecasts by ITA.

Source: *U.S. Industrial Outlook 1990,* U.S. Department of Commerce.

Trends and Forecasts: Girls', Children's, and Infants' Outerwear (SIC 236)

(in millions of dollars except as noted)

Item	1987[1]	1988[2]	1989[3]	Percent Change 1987–88	Percent Change 1988–89
Industry Data					
Value of shipments[4]	3,678	3,699	3,958	0.6	7.0
2361 Child's dresses/blouses	1,408	1,427	1,527	1.3	7.0
2369 Childrens outerwear nec	2,270	2,272	2,431	0.1	7.0
Value of shipments (1987$)	3,678	3,579	3,676	-2.7	2.7
2361 Child's dresses/blouses	1,408	1,350	1,392	-4.1	3.1
2369 Childrens outerwear nec	2,270	2,229	2,284	-1.8	2.5
Total employment (000)	71.3	67.5	65.9	-5.3	-2.4
2361 Child's dresses/blouses	27.9	25.4	24.9	-9.0	-2.0
2369 Childrens outerwear nec	43.4	42.1	41.0	-3.0	-2.6
Production workers (000)	60.3	57.2	55.9	-5.1	-2.3
2361 Child's dresses/blouses	23.2	21.0	20.5	-9.5	-2.4
2369 Childrens outerwear nec	37.1	36.2	35.4	-2.4	-2.2
Average hourly earnings ($)	5.65	5.90	6.09	4.4	3.2
2361 Child's dresses/blouses	5.51	5.95	6.11	8.0	2.7
2369 Childrens outerwear nec	5.74	5.94	6.06	3.5	2.0
Product Data					
Value of shipments[5]	3,509	3,520	3,901	0.3	10.8
2361 Child's dresses/blouses	1,571	1,589	1,707	1.1	7.4
2369 Childrens outerwear nec	1,938	1,931	2,194	-0.4	13.6
Value of shipments (1987$)	3,509	3,383	3,525	-3.6	4.2
2361 Child's dresses/blouses	1,571	1,502	1,548	-4.4	3.1
2369 Childrens outerwear nec	1,938	1,881	1,977	-2.9	5.1
Trade Data					
Value of imports	-	-	-	-	-
2361 Child's dresses/blouses	0.0	0.0	0.0	-	-
2369 Childrens outerwear nec	5,871	5,779	5,688	-1.6	-1.6
Value of exports	-	-	-	-	-
2361 Child's dresses/blouses	0.0	0.0	0.0	-	-
2369 Childrens outerwear nec	193	271	420	40.4	55.0

[1]Industry and product data are preliminary. Trade data are adjusted to conform to the 1987 SIC.
[2]Estimated, except for exports and imports.
[3]Estimated.
[4]Value of all products and services sold by establishments in the girls', children's, and infants' outerwear industry.
[5]Value of products classified in the girls', children's, and infants' outerwear industry produced by all industries.
SOURCE: U.S. Department of Commerce: Bureau of the Census; International Trade Administration (ITA). Estimates and forecasts by ITA.

Source: *U.S. Industrial Outlook 1990*, U.S. Department of Commerce.

Trends and Forecasts: Selected Women's Outerwear (SIC 2331, 2335, 2337)

(in millions of dollars except as noted)

Item	1987[1]	1988[2]	1989[3]	Percent Change 1987–88	Percent Change 1988–89
Industry Data					
Value of shipments[4]	14,755	14,921	16,173	1.1	8.4
2331 Women's/misses' blouses	3,871	3,980	4,431	2.8	11.3
2335 Women's/misses' dresses	6,431	6,369	6,845	–1.0	7.5
2337 Women's suits & coats	4,453	4,572	4,897	2.7	7.1
Value of shipments (1987$)	14,755	14,624	15,075	–0.9	3.1
2331 Women's/misses' blouses	3,871	3,900	4,087	0.7	4.8
2335 Women's/misses' dresses	6,431	6,254	6,398	–2.8	2.3
2337 Women's suits & coats	4,453	4,470	4,590	0.4	2.7
Total employment (000)	242	229	229	–5.4	0.0
2331 Women's/misses' blouses	74.2	70.6	68.3	–4.9	–3.3
2335 Women's/misses' dresses	113	107	107	–5.3	0.0
2337 Women's suits & coats	54.5	51.6	53.8	–5.3	4.3
Production workers (000)	199	187	188	–6.0	0.5
2331 Women's/misses' blouses	63.7	60.2	58.3	–5.5	–3.2
2335 Women's/misses' dresses	91.9	86.1	87.5	–6.3	1.6
2337 Women's suits & coats	43.7	40.6	41.9	–7.1	3.2
Average hourly earnings ($)	5.94	6.10	6.27	2.7	2.8
2331 Women's/misses' blouses	5.37	5.48	5.62	2.0	2.6
2335 Women's/misses' dresses	6.07	6.25	6.51	3.0	4.2
2337 Women's suits & coats	6.51	6.57	6.68	0.9	1.7
Product Data					
Value of shipments[5]	14,550	14,659	15,780	0.7	7.6
2331 Women's/misses' blouses	4,183	4,258	4,687	1.8	10.1
2335 Women's/misses' dresses	6,323	6,241	6,660	–1.3	6.7
2337 Women's suits & coats	4,044	4,160	4,433	2.9	6.6
Value of shipments (1987$)	14,550	14,399	14,931	–1.0	3.7
2331 Women's/misses' blouses	4,183	4,149	4,358	–0.8	5.0
2335 Women's/misses' dresses	6,323	6,153	6,380	–2.7	3.7
2337 Women's suits & coats	4,044	4,097	4,193	1.3	2.3
Trade Data					
Value of imports	–	–	–	–	–
2331 Women's/misses' blouses	–	–	–	–	–
2335 Women's/misses' dresses	778	830	877	6.7	5.7
2337 Women's suits & coats	2,027	1,939	2,253	–4.3	16.2
Value of exports	131	169	202	29.0	19.5
2331 Women's/misses' blouses	53.9	57.7	77.9	7.1	35.0
2335 Women's/misses' dresses	34.3	50.6	65.1	47.5	28.7
2337 Women's suits & coats	42.8	60.3	59.1	40.9	–2.0

[1]Industry and product data are preliminary. Trade data are adjusted to conform to the 1987 SIC.
[2]Estimated, except for exports and imports.
[3]Estimated.
[4]Value of all products and services sold by establishments in the selected women's outerwear industry.
[5]Value of products classified in the selected women's outerwear industry produced by all industries.

SOURCE: U.S. Department of Commerce: Bureau of the Census; International Trade Administration (ITA). Estimates and forecasts by ITA.

Source: *U.S. Industrial Outlook 1990,* U.S. Department of Commerce.

MEDIA GENERAL FINANCIAL SERVICES

STOCKS by INDUSTRY

Textiles - Apparel

Company	Rev LQ %	Rev FY-to-Date %	Rev 12 Mos %	$Mil (Last 12 Mos)	EPS Last 12 $	EPS LQ %	EPS FY %	EPS 12 Mos %	5-Yr Grw %	Par Grw %	Rpt Date	Div Amt	Yield %	Div 5-Yr %	Payout FY %	Payout 5 Yrs %	Last X-Dvd Date	Profit Mar %	Asset Turn	Ret on Tot Assets	Lever Ratio	Ret on Equity	Debt to Eq %	Curr Ratio	Mkt Val $Mil	Latest Shares Outstndng 000	Held by Banks-Funds 000	Insider Net Trad 000	Short Int Ratio Days	Fiscal Yr Ends Mo
Ind. Group	-4.0	4.5	4.1	429.3	1.08	2.0	-23.6	-.9	9	10	----	.34	1.9	2	25	23	----	4.6	1.48	6.8	2.12	14.4	49	2.7	6,452	374,647	152,536	-13	1.3	--
Angelica Cp	12.4	12.4	12.7	20.2q	2.16	15.2	19.2	18.0	3	8	04-90	.80	2.4	8	37	36	06-11-90	5.3	1.36	7.2	1.74	12.5	31	3.4	307	9,279	4,855	0	0.0	01
Benetton Grp	NA	NA	NA	NA	NA	NA	NA	NA	NA	NC	00-00	.97	5.6	NA	NA	NA	05-11-90	NA	NC	NA	NC	NC	NA	NA	79	4,500	170	0	NA	NA
Bobbie Brooks	2.4	2.4	43.8	4.0q	NA	NE	NE	-65.7	NC	9	03-90	.00	.0	0	0	0	00-00-00	3.1	1.58	4.9	1.76	8.6	19	2.1	10	12,833	838	0	0.0	12
Chaus Bernard	-10.1	3.9	3.7	1.5n	.12	NE	NE	NE	NC	3	03-90	.00	.0	0	0	0	00-00-00	.5	3.60	3.0	1.67	3.0	30	4.2	86	18,695	2,012	+10	1.7	06
Easto Indust	-3.6	4.5	9.0	-1.4n	.08	-100.0	-100.0	-100.0	NC	-31	07-13-89	.00	.0	0	0	0	07-13-89	-2.9	2.55	-7.4	4.20	-31.1	7	1.2	4	3,797	-3	0	0.0	06
Farah Inc	-63.0	-60.7	-56.1	-13.8e	-.36	-100.0	-100.0	NE	NC	-22	04-90	.00	.0	0	0	NE	10-28-86	-9.4	1.12	-10.5	2.11	-22.2	17	2.4	20	6,265	2,015	0	10.2	10
Garan Inc	-7.4	4.4	6.8	9.3s	3.71	-5.7	21.2	26.2	13	13	03-90	1.00	3.3	-5	36	47	05-14-90	6.6	1.55	10.2	1.41	14.4	7	3.8	75	2,507	1,318	0	0.0	09
Genesco Inc	4.8	4.8	6.6	17.6q	.76	NC	NC	-19.1	NC	13	04-90	.00	.0	0	0	0	00-00-00	3.5	1.80	6.3	2.06	13.0	37	4.0	124	22,618	9,418	0	2.2	01
Hampton Ind	-13.7	-13.7	-1.1	1.5q	.37	-100.0	-100.0	-70.9	-4	3	03-90	.00	.0	0	0	0	06-19-88	.9	1.67	1.5	1.87	2.8	45	4.1	30	3,959	635	0	0.0	03
Johnston Ind	19.9	-1.2	-2.5	2.0n	.56	-56.8	-94.5	-70.7	-3	5	03-90	.00	.0	0	21	4	05-31-89	2.4	1.25	3.0	1.57	4.7	22	3.5	37	5,042	1,284	0	0.0	06
Kellwood Co	-3.9	3.5	3.4	14.0f	1.20	-100.0	-8.3	-58.6	-1	2	04-90	.80	5.4	18	67	29	06-05-90	3.2	1.72	7.3	2.35	7.3	49	2.0	174	11,765	7,228	-3	2.5	04
Lakeland Ind	7.4	7.4	22.5	1.2q	.46	-8.3	-8.3	130.0	NC	15	04-89	.00	.0	0	0	0	00-00-00	1.8	2.25	3.1	2.01	14.5	36	3.0	8	2,550	391	0	0.1	01
Littlefield Adam	-11.8	-11.8	.0	-.3q	-.26	-100.0	-100.0	NE	NC	-21	03-90	.00	.0	0	0	0	00-00-00	-5.0	1.46	-7.3	2.93	-21.4	29	1.2	1	1,074	53	0	0.1	12
Liz Claiborne	19.3	19.3	22.2	172.9q	1.97	20.0	20.0	43.8	26	25	05-07-90	.25	.8	32	11	12	05-07-90	11.7	1.74	20.4	1.39	28.3	3	3.6	2,866	88,179	54,469	-203	0.0	12
Munsingwear	-2.0	-2.0	-30.1	-15.3q	-3.18	-68.8	-68.8	NE	NC	0	09-01-86	.00	.0	0	0	0	09-01-86	-13.8	1.53	-21.1	.00	NS	-5500	1.4	54	4,889	1,068	0	0.0	12
Nutmeg Inds	2.2	2.2	13.3	-.4q	-.08	-100.0	-68.8	-100.0	NC	4	04-90	.00	.0	0	0	0	09-27-88	-.8	1.50	-1.2	3.25	-3.9	105	2.3	9	6,775	1,708	0	0.0	01
Oak Hill Sportswre	-.8	-.8	.8	-1.3q	-.64	-100.0	-100.0	-100.0	NC	-8	03-90	.00	.0	0	0	0	00-00-00	-1.1	3.00	-3.3	2.30	-7.6	14	1.7	37	2,054	126	0	0.0	12
Oneita Ind	14.7	28.1	42.2	5.3s	1.24	29.0	54.3	67.6	NC	10	03-90	.00	.0	0	0	0	02-16-90	3.8	1.55	5.9	1.76	10.4	48	4.3	37	4,590	1,183	0	9.3	09

(continued)

Textiles - Apparel (Continued)

	Revenue			Earnings								Dividends						Ratio Analysis								Shareholdings				
	Pct Change			Last 12 Mos	Per Share Last 12 Mos	Pct Change			5-Year Growth	Par Growth	Date of	Current Rate		5-Year Growth	Payout		Last X-Dvd	Pro-ft Mar-gin	Asset Turn-over	Return on Total Assets	Lever-age Ratio	Return on Equity	Debt to Eq-uity	Curr-ent Ratio	Mar-ket Value	Latest Shares Out-strndng	Held by Banks-Funds	Insider Net Trad-ing	Short Int-erest Ratio	Fiscal Year Ends
Company	Last Qtr	FY to Date	Last 12 Mos	$Mil	Last Qtr $	Last Qtr	FY to Date	12 Mos	Rate	Rate	Report	Amt	Yield	Rate	Last FY	Last 5 Yrs	Date	gin	over	Assets	Ratio	Equity	%	Ratio	$Mil	000	000	000	Days	Mo
Oxford Inds	-5.9	-4.8	-6.5	10.0n	1.02	-45.5	4.1	537.5	NC	5	02-90	.50	5.4	6	49	90	05-09-90	1.8	2.61	4.7	1.98	9.3	34	2.6	89	9,663	5,474	0	0.0	05
Phil-Van Heu	4.9	4.9	11.1	21.8q	1.42	-100.0	-100.0	-2.7	10	54	04-90	.28	1.3	15	17	15	08-13-90	2.9	2.31	6.7	10.01	67.1	358	3.0	198	9,096	3,112	+290	0.4	01
Private Brands	4.1	4.1	50.0	.7q	.05	-33.3	-33.3	66.7	NC	6	12-89	.00	.0	0	0	0	00-00-00	1.9	1.74	3.3	1.94	6.4	0	2.8	4	8,365	68	0	0.0	09
Quiksilver Inc	29.6	34.9	40.6	8.5s	1.33	32.6	38.6	58.3	93	40	04-90	.00	.0	0	0	0	11-20-87	10.2	3.15	32.1	1.23	39.5	0	4.4	144	6,045	1,943	-95	0.0	10
Riss Togs	-12.3	-12.3	-10.1	-9.8q	-1.37	-100.0	-100.0	-100.0	NC	-11	04-90	.20	2.1	-3	NE	68	06-25-90	-4.3	1.51	-6.5	1.51	-9.8	4	2.9	70	7,342	3,840	-95	1.3	01
Salant Cp	41.4	-7.8	.0	.0*	-2.72	NE	NE	-100.0	NC	0	03-90	.00	.0	0	0	0	07-30-84	NC	NC	NC	NC	.0	1024	1.5	12	3,457	1,275	0	3.4	12
Samark Star ♦	-2.0	1.1	.0	.0*	.38	-100.0	-69.0	NE	NC	0	03-90	.00	.0	0	0	14	02-01-90	NC	NC	NC	NC	.0	167	1.9	34	15,971	1,880	0	0.0	06
Signal Apparel	-5.3	-5.3	12.6	-2.2q	-.76	-100.0	-100.0	NE	NC	-10	03-90	.00	.0	0	0	NE	12-15-87	-2.5	1.92	-4.8	2.00	-9.6	55	3.7	24	3,111	564	0	0.0	12
State O Maine	22.8	27.1	26.6	5.8f	1.15	-18.8	-5.7	-5.7	25	15	02-90	.00	.0	0	0	0	12-15-89	6.1	1.79	10.9	1.38	15.0	2	2.9	31	3,095	1,576	0	0.0	02
Superior Surg	4.0	4.0	.8	7.4q	3.31	25.0	25.0	11.1	18	13	03-90	.72	1.8	13	19	21	05-11-90	6.4	1.72	11.0	1.52	16.7	21	4.4	90	2,212	1,048	0	0.0	12
Thackeray Cp	1.9	1.9	-40.7	1.1q	.23	NE	NE	NE	NC	7	03-90	.00	.0	0	0	0	00-00-00	2.3	1.91	4.4	1.61	7.1	18	2.0	35	5,107	758	0	2.1	12
Thomaston A	3.8	14.0	14.6	6.8n	2.13	56.5	6450.0	213.2	NC	8	03-90	.44	2.3	26	36	35	06-12-90	3.3	2.03	6.7	1.49	10.0	27	4.7	61	3,138	344	0	0.0	06
Tultex Corp	-5.5	23.4	.0	.0*	.18	NE	NE	-76.6	-5	0	03-90	.36	4.6	26	200	.0	06-04-90	NC	NC	NC	NC	.0	55	2.0	218	27,632	4,438	-6	7.9	12
V.F. Corp	.8	.8	2.1	160.9q	2.55	-30.4	-30.4	-.8	6	12	03-90	1.00	3.8	12	33	31	06-04-90	6.3	1.35	8.5	2.31	19.6	78	2.7	1,515	57,986	36,572	-7	0.4	12
Wolf Howard	-8.0	8.8	11.1	.5n	.52	-60.0	4.8	116.7	NC	9	02-90	.05	1.7	0	29	NE	01-09-89	5.0	1.50	7.5	1.36	10.2	8	4.4	3	1,056	23	0	0.3	05

$r/t \times r/a = r/a \times a/e = r/e$

Source: Media General Financial Services, Richmond, VA.

Trends and Forecasts: Savings Institutions (SIC 603)
(in billions of dollars except as noted)

Item	1987	1988	1989[1]	1990[2]	Percent Change		
					1987-88	1988-89	1989-90
Assets	1,461	1,581	1,550	1,519	8.2	-2.0	-2.0
Mortgages held	996	1,076	1,065	1,097	8.0	-1.0	3.0
Mortgage-backed securities	225	238	226	235	5.8	-5.0	4.0
Deposits	1,101	1,154	1,142	1,200	4.8	-1.0	5.0
Net worth[3]	62	72	83	95	16.1	15.3	11.5
Net new savings	51	54	0	50	—	—	—
Mortgages made	308	280	235	254	-9.1	-16.1	8.1
Number of institutions	3,517	3,325	3,159	3,001	-5.5	-5.0	-5.0
Number of offices	25,500	25,946	25,427	24,918	1.7	-2.0	-2.0
Employment (000)	481	482	486	476	0.2	0.8	-2.1

SOURCE: Office of Thrift Supervision, National Council of Savings Institutions and Bureau of Labor Statistics.

[1]Estimated.
[2]Forecast.
[3]This series is highly variable, making percent changes unmeaningful.

Source: *U.S. Industrial Outlook 1990*, U.S. Department of Commerce.

Trends and Forecasts: Commercial Banking (SIC 602)
(in billions of dollars except as noted)

Item	1987	1988	1989[1]	1990[2]	Percent Change		
					1987-88	1988-89	1989-90
Assets	2,847	3,036	3,249	3,444	6.6	7.0	6.0
Loans	1,899	2,040	2,160	2,333	7.4	6.0	8.0
Investments	514	533	549	565	3.7	3.0	3.0
Deposits	2,009	2,143	2,229	2,340	6.7	4.0	5.0
Employment	1,562	1,557	1,565	1,573	—	0.5	0.5

SOURCE: Board of Governors of the Federal Reserve System and Bureau of Labor Statistics. Estimates and forecasts by U.S. Department of Commerce, International Trade Administration.

[1]Estimated.
[2]Forecast.

Source: *U.S. Industrial Outlook 1990*, U.S. Department of Commerce.

STOCKS by INDUSTRY

MEDIA GENERAL FINANCIAL SERVICES

Middle Atlantic Banks

Company	Rev %Last Qtr	Rev %FY to Date	Rev %12 Mos	Last 12 Mos $Mil	EPS Last 12 Mos $	EPS %Last Qtr	EPS %FY to Date	EPS %Last 12 Mos	EPS 5-Yr Growth	EPS Per Growth	Date of Report	Div Current Rate Amt	Div Yield	Div 5-Yr Growth	Payout Last FY	Payout Last 5 Yrs	Last X-Dvd Date	Profit Margin	Asset Turnover	Return on Assets	Leverage Ratio	Return on Equity	Debt to Equity	Current Ratio	Mkt Value $Mil	Shares Outstndg 000	Held by Banks/Funds 000	Insider Net Trad'g 000	Short Int Ratio Days	Fiscal Yr Ends Mo
Ind. Group	-8.6	-5.9	10.2	119.0	-.95	-33.3	-62.7	-100.0	NC	—	---	1.64	6.4	1	101	42	---	.1	.00	.0	NC	.2	91	NC	63,425	2,475,561	923,409	-2091	1.6	--
Abraham Linc FSB	42.6	42.6	27.7	1.0q	1.68	110.3	110.3	71.4	NC	8	06-89	.00	.0	0	0	0	08-14-89	4.3	.09	.4	19.25	7.7	160	NA	4	595	31	0	0.0	03
Anchor Svgs Bk	6.7	8.8	10.8	-218.1n	-13.24	-14.4	-14.4	-16.7	NC	-78	03-90	.00	.0	0	0	NE	00-00-00	-25.4	.09	-2.4	32.38	-77.7	320	NA	28	17,476	835	0	0.0	06
Apple Bank Sav	15.5	15.5	19.5	20.3q	4.43	5.1	5.1	4.5	NC	7	03-90	.70	1.6	0	0	0	06-08-90	5.4	.09	.5	16.00	8.0	0	NA	198	4,597	1,308	0	1.7	12
Arrow Bk	4.2	4.2	16.6	5.7q	2.33	5.1	5.1	4.5	15	11	03-90	.68	4.9	13	27	28	04-17-90	11.6	.09	1.2	12.50	15.0	15	NA	32	2,291	167	0	0.0	12
Atlantied Bancorp	7.3	2.9	21.0	1.0n	1.22	-17.1	-34.1	-3.9	NC	4	12-89	.40	3.8b	3	6	3	06-25-90	4.3	.09	.4	15.25	6.1	12	NA	9	857		0	0.0	03
Balt Bancorp	4.5	4.5	22.3	16.7q	1.37	2.6	2.6	NE	NA	4	03-90	.60	4.5	0	40	33	06-11-90	4.8	.10	.5	14.00	7.0	41	NA	169	12,750	6,028	+0	16.2	12
Banco Bilboa	NA	NA	NA	NA	NA	NA	NA	NA	NA	5	00-00	1.18	3.5	NA	NA	NA	04-09-90	NA	.10	NA	NA	NA	NA	NA	153	4,500	1,231	0	NA	12
Banco de Sant	1.8	1.8	1.8	346.8f	3.33	16.7	16.7	16.8	NC	-5	12-88	1.44	2.9	0	29	21	04-24-90	9.8	.12	1.2	15.25	18.3	47	NA	5,112	104,060	146	0	0.0	12
Bank Md	34.1	34.1	71.4	-1.4q	-.80	-100.0	-100.0	-100.0	-38	10	03-90	.00	.0	0	0	0	00-00-00	-5.8	.10	-.6	7.50	-4.5	19	NA	17	2,028	0	+2	0.0	12
Bank of NY Co	1.0	1.0	63.1	51.9q	.17	-4.8	-4.8	-96.9	NC	-25	03-90	2.12	6.7	9	821	47	04-16-90	.9	.11	.1	22.00	2.2	37	NA	2,164	67,896	47,455	0	6.4	12
Bankers Tr NY	16.0	16.0	20.8	-946.2q	-11.76	16.8	16.8	-100.0	NC	-48	03-90	2.33	5.6	11	NE	114	06-27-90	-12.6	.13	-1.7	23.35	-39.7	102	NA	3,430	81,915	55,278	+22	1.5	12
Barclays PLC	11.3	11.3	11.3	1604.1f	1.14	-17.1	-18.0	-18.0	-9	-9	12-88	1.82	6.6	0	117	27	03-16-90	8.2	.12	.8	19.38	15.5	60	NA	10,843	390,756	3,573	0	0.5	12
Bel Savgs Hdg	21.5	29.0	28.5	-11.7n	-4.69	-100.0	-100.0	-100.0	NC	-21	03-90	.00	.0	0	0	0	00-00-00	-11.8	.12	-1.4	14.73	-20.7	115	NA	4	2,501	724	0	0.0	06
Broad Natl Bncp	17.0	23.1	25.0	5.8f	2.12	0	11.6	11.6	NC	16	12-89	.58	4.0b	0	26	15	05-25-90	12.9	.10	1.3	16.62	21.6	17	NA	39	2,688	0	0	0.0	12
Bryn Mawr Bank	3.8	3.8	10.0	4.0q	3.69	-7.1	-7.1	3.9	NC	16	03-90	1.52	4.9	0	37	39	06-29-90	12.1	.13	1.3	12.54	16.3		NA	38	1,084	140	0	0.0	12
BT Fncl Cp	1.1	1.1	6.8	6.0q	1.98	27.3	27.3	8.8	1	6	03-90	.80	5.1	5	41	38	05-01-90	7.7	.09	.7	15.00	10.5	21	NA	48	3,050	642	+0	0.0	12
Cent Jersey Bcp	8.1	8.1	14.8	17.5q	2.05	-32.1	-32.1	-9.3	10	8	03-90	.90	6.2	10	40	39	06-07-90	11.9	.10	1.2	11.67	14.0	18	NA	125	8,550	642	0	0.0	12
Charter Fed SBk	-3.0	-3.0	285.7	3.1q	2.19	9.4	9.4	NC	NC	8	12-89	.60	4.7	0	18	18	04-19-90	11.5	.10	1.1	9.82	10.8	0	NA	32	1,390	329	0	0.0	09
Chase Manhtm	15.4	15.4	12.9	-752.9q	-9.01	-84.3	-84.3	-100.0	NC	-23	03-90	2.48	10.4	5	NE	210	04-25-90	-5.2	.10	-.7	26.29	-18.4	105	NA	2,980	124,814	76,138	+34	1.6	12
Chem Bkg	7.6	7.6	7.6	-448.4q	-8.23	4.0	4.0	-100.0	NC	-21	03-90	2.72	10.7	3	NE	674	06-11-90	-5.4	.11	-.6	26.67	-16.0	11	NA	2,937	115,177	53,584	0	6.5	12
Chem Bkg B	NA	NA	NA						NA								06-11-90	NA	NC	NA	NC	NA	NA	NA				0	NA	12
Citicorp	-59.7	-59.7	-1.5	200.0q	.24	-60.5	-60.5	-95.5	NA	-15	03-90	.76	30.4	9	NA	75	04-23-90	.6	.17	.1	24.00	2.4	238	NA	7,344	324,577	217,087	+11	3.0	12
Ctzns Bcp Md	15.3	20.4	20.4	32.9f	2.27	9.6	9.6	-3.0	9	7	12-89	1.78	7.9	9	137	40	06-04-90	15.4	.14	1.4	9.50	13.3	0	NA	261	14,496	459	+1	0.0	12
Ctzns Fst Bcp	5.0	5.0	17.6	34.4q	1.60	-30.2	-30.2	1.3	7	10	03-90	1.08	6.0	22	46	25	07-16-90	11.7	.09	1.1	16.27	17.9	11	NA	218	21,484	4,933	+2	66.6	12
Cmwlth Boshs	9.4	9.4	10.9	13.4q	2.14	24.4	24.4	32.9	-7	-8	03-90	.72	7.1b	2	33	42	06-25-90	9.4	.11	1.0	12.80	12.8	21	NA	98	6,230	222	+0	0.0	12
Community Bcp	11.4	8.4	121.4	1.1s	.69	-10.0	5.1	NC	NC	5	03-90	.88	5.6	-5	40	42	04-04-90	3.5	.09	.3	17.67	5.3	158	NA	31	1,495	58	0	0.0	09
Commun Bank	5.5	5.5	10.5	4.3q	1.58	-15.4	-15.4	12.1	-3	3	03-90	.20	2.7	0	15	15	06-11-90	6.8	.10	.7	13.29	9.3	3	NA	31	2,703	474	0	0.0	12
Commu Natl Bcp	14.0	14.0	50.0	2.8q	1.01	-76.7	-76.7	74.1	37	15	03-90	.76	6.6	7	46	43	07-31-89	6.2	.11	.7	22.00	15.4	0	NA	21	3,182	1	+10	16.9	12
Constellation Bcp	37.2	37.2	66.8	21.9q	2.39	-92.1	-92.1	-32.5	11	4	03-90	1.44	10.3	16	42	35	05-24-90	6.1	.11	.7	13.14	9.2	8	NA	112	8,034	2,409	+3	0.0	12
CoreStates Fnl	88.6	88.6	34.5	212.4q	4.91	-9.8	-9.8	5.4	11	10	03-90	1.92	4.8	12	33	35	05-29-90	9.3	.11	1.3	13.08	17.0	48	NA	2,192	54,800	19,994	+3	0.0	12

Dauphin Dep
Dime Svg NY
Eastchester Fincl
Elmwood Fed S Bk
Equimark Corp
Evergreen Bcp
FB&T
Fini Trust
Fst Eastern
Fst Empire St
Fst Fd Bcp
Fst Inter-Bcp
Fst Natl Penn
Fst Peo Fincl
Fst Western Bcp
Flagship Fincl
FMS Fincl
FNB Rochester
Frankford Cp
Fulton Fincl
Germantown S Bk
Glendale Bancp
Hamptons Bancshrs
Harleysville Natl
Home City S Bk
Home Savings Bk
Home Unity S Bk
HUBCO Inc
Independence Bcp
Integra Financial
Interchg Fincl
Iroquois Bcp
Jefferson Natl Bk
Johnstown Sav Bk
KeyCorp
Keystone Fincl
Keystone Heritage
Linc Sav Bank
LSB Bancshrs
Mfrs Hanover
Mellon Bank
Merchants Bk NY
Meridian Bcp
Meritor Svgs Bk

(continued)

Middle Atlantic Banks (Continued)

Company	Rev %Chg Last Qtr	Rev %Chg FY to Date	Rev %Chg Last 12 Mos	Rev Last 12 Mos $Mil	EPS Per Share Last 12 Mos $	Earn %Chg Last 12 Mos	Earn %Chg Last Qtr	Earn %Chg FY to Date	Earn %Chg Last 12 Mos	5-Yr Growth Rate	Par Growth Rate	Date of Report	Div Current Amt	Div Yield	Div 5-Yr Growth	Payout Last FY	Payout Last 5 Yrs	Last X-Div Date	Profit Margin	Asset Turnover	Return on Total Assets	Leverage Ratio	Return on Equity	Debt to Equity	Current Ratio	Mkt Value $Mil	Latest Shares Outstndng 000	Held by Banks-Funds 000	Insider Net Trading 000	Short Int Ratio Days	FY Ends Mo
Metrobank Fincl	-31.2	1.1	.0	-20.5t	-11.08	-100.0	-100.0	-100.0	-100.0	NC	0	12-89	.00	.0		NE	NE	10-31-89	-37.3	.10	-3.7	.00	NM	657	NA	3	1,850	160	0	0.0	12
Midlantic Cp	16.0	16.0	22.6	148.2q	2.49	-99.4	-99.4	-36.8	4	NC	5	03-90	1.88	13.0	10	33	28	06-26-90	6.2	.10	.6	16.83	10.1	31	NA	552	38,100	15,623	0	0.0	12
Miners Natl Bcp	48.8	48.8	25.0	2.3q	2.30	-3.5	-3.5	23.9	41	7	03-90	.92	3.5	0	37	41	03-13-89	11.5	.10	1.2	8.92	10.7	0	NA	24	921	42	+0	0.0	12
Montclair Bancorp	26.5	26.7	28.2	4.2t	1.68	10.5	9.8	.60	18	6	10-89	.60	4.8	0	33	18	05-25-90	8.4	.10	.7	8.25	6.6	8	NA	31	2,473	832	0	0.0	10
Morgan, J.P.	.9	.9	22.7	1,055.6q	-5.91	117.7	117.7	-100.0	94	-35	03-90	1.82	5.1	11	NE	94	05-19-90	-10.1	.12	-1.2	22.00	-26.4	117	NA	6,570	183,775	119,403	-72	1.2	12
Natl Comty Banks	5.8	5.8	15.0	38.8q	3.72	-53.6	-53.6	-12.5	30	11	03-90	1.40	7.4	17	32	30	06-11-90	9.9	.10	1.0	17.20	17.2	0	NA	199	10,452	643	0	0.0	12
Natl Merc Bancp	16.7	16.7	29.6	2.9q	1.08	-25.8	-25.8	-5.3	7	11	03-90	.10	1.06		9	7	07-12-90	8.3	.08	.7	17.00	11.9	6	NA	25	2,382	78	0	0.0	12
Natl Penn Bnshr	12.9	12.9	18.8	8.8q	3.32	12.2	12.2	8.1	32	12	03-90	1.16	2.7b	24	32	28	07-25-90	14.0	.11	1.5	12.07	18.1	36	NA	115	2,667	165	+6	0.0	12
Natl Sav Bk Alb	3.2	3.2	15.9	3.6q	2.99	20.0	9.0	-.7	17	6	03-90	1.20	4.4	0	17	8	06-26-90	7.1	.11	.7	13.43	9.4	36	NA	32	1,181	171	0	0.0	12
New York Bcp	-7.9	-.9	8.9	3.5q	.99	46.2	3.2	-6.6	0	6	03-90	.00	.0	0	0	0	00-00-90	3.2	.09	.3	21.00	6.3	0	NA	35	3,079	624	0	0.0	08
North Fork Bcp	10.3	10.3	38.8	19.2q	2.08	-29.8	-32.7	-67	27	8	06-26-90	.85	7.0	27	36	26	06-26-90	10.3	.11	1.1	12.27	13.5	30	NA	112	9,239	3,455	+2	3.5	12
N Side Sav Bk	-3.5	7.1	53.0	2.4s	.61	-4.7	-4.7	-63.5	0	10	03-90	.40	4.0	0	0	0	02-14-90	1.9	.10	.2	12.00	2.4	26	NA	41	4,050	2,086	0	0.0	09
Onbancorp Inc	17.9	17.9	16.5	10.9q	1.69	4.7	4.7	16.6	7	10	03-90	.15	1.4	0	7	4	06-26-90	7.0	.10	.7	15.43	10.8	0	183	80	7,621	1,498	0	0.0	09
Parkvale Fincl ■	44.9	26.1	22.0	2.9m	1.68	-4.5	-4.5	-9.7	5	7	03-90	.40	3.5	0	5	2	06-26-90	4.8	.10	.5	18.00	9.0	183	NA	20	1,706	623	0	0.0	06
Pennview Savs	8.8	7.4	7.1	1.0t	2.03	-1.9	-1.9	-1.9	9	47	09-89	.00	1.0	0	9	0	04-24-90	6.7	.10	.7	15.57	10.9	54	NA	11	497	57	0	0.0	09
People's Svg Fncl	8.5	8.5	8.3	2.8q	1.22	22.2	22.2	1.7	18	3	06-27-90	.64	7.0	14	14	18	06-27-90	10.8	.10	1.1	6.64	7.3	30	NA	20	2,200	0	0	0.0	12
Piedmont BkGrp	12.0	12.0	20.6	5.0q	1.74	4.0	4.0	-20.9	37	7	06-11-90	.72	4.4	15	37	26	06-11-90	7.1	.11	.8	14.75	11.8	24	NA	47	2,883	69	0	0.0	06
Pioneer Am Hld	10.0	10.0	15.7	1.9q	2.68	-12.7	-12.7	-6.3	43	4	06-27-90	1.00	2.2	43	43	12	06-27-90	8.6	.10	.9	11.44	10.3	0	NA	32	686	0	0	0.0	12
PNC Fincl	6.2	6.2	16.0	328.3q	3.44	-40.9	-40.9	-33.3	50	2	03-26-90	2.12	7.1	13	50	6	05-25-90	7.0	.10	.7	16.57	11.6	25	NA	2,834	94,466	47,054	+0	0.0	12
Polify Fincl	36.2	53.1	59.4	-22.6n	-10.29	-100.0	-100.0	-100.0	6	-47	01-25-90	.00	.0	0	6	5	01-25-90	-38.3	.10	-3.7	12.65	-46.8	60	NA	5	2,185	579	0	0.0	06
Poughkeepsie S B	-20.8	-5.2	-5.7	-28.6q	-8.12	-100.0	83.1	67.5	48	-34	04-06-90	.00	.0	0	NE	48	04-06-90	-17.5	.10	-1.8	18.83	-33.9	224	NA	19	3,833	1,128	0	0.0	12
Prime Bancorp	4.8	6.0	6.0	3.3n	2.16	49.2	49.2	83.1	6	9	06-26-90	.56	4.9	6	6	6	06-26-90	9.4	.11	1.0	9.40	9.4	11	NA	16	1,380	449	-1	0.0	06
Progress Fncl	-5.2	-5.2	17.1	1.9q	2.68	-75.3	-75.3	473.0	43	9	06-27-90	.24	2.3b	9	9	5	06-27-90	4.9	.12	.5	17.50	10.5	18	NA	10	962	35	0	0.0	12
Progressive Bk	-.6	-.6	6.0	-1.7q	-.59	-51.9	-51.9	-100.0	50	-3	03-26-90	.00	.0	0	NE	21	03-26-90	-2.4	.13	-.3	8.67	-2.6	0	48	17	2,920	1,301	-2141	0.0	12
Ramapo Fincl	5.6	5.6	18.7	2.2n	1.67	-58.7	-58.7	8.4	5	-9	01-25-90	.00	28.8	0	34	39	01-25-90	5.8	.10	-3.7	19.83	11.9	60	NA	5	1,306	93	0	0.0	12
Raritan Bcp	6.8	6.8	18.7	1.4q	1.22	-21.4	-21.4	-11.6	6	-21	05-09-90	.38	3.1	3	23	6	05-09-90	7.4	.10	.7	10.00	7.0	2	NA	14	1,150	7	0	0.0	12
Rep NY	8.1	8.1	20.5	26.6q	.14	8.3	8.3	-97.3	40	-16	06-11-90	1.32	2.7	4	3150	40	06-11-90	1.0	.10	.1	25.00	2.5	223	NA	1,481	30,221	13,060	-1	0.0	12
RyBPA	22.1	27.7	24.1	8.0t	1.29	-47.1	-47.1	-8	0	16	04-10-89	.00	.0	0	NE	0	04-10-89	22.2	.11	2.5	6.44	16.1	3	NA	48	6,048	82	0	0.0	12
Seabord S&L	-3.7	-3.7	10.0	-2.0q	-2.34	-100.0	-100.0	-8	29	-3	07-26-89	.20	6.2	0	NE	29	07-26-89	-18.2	.11	-1.8	16.61	-29.9	63	NA	3	891	0	0	0.0	12
Sellersville S&L	375.0	375.0	171.4	.8s	.93	-12.3	0	-100.0	123	-5	03-90	.16	.8	0	17	123	12-89	4.2	.12	.2	11.20	5.6	73	NA	16	828	37	0	0.0	06
SW National	7.9	12.8	17.0	3.9q	1.44	2.3	2.3	-21.7	43	4	03-90	.84	4.4	3	57	43	05-04-90	7.1	.10	.7	11.00	7.7	0	NA	52	2,735	192	0	0.0	12
Star States	12.8	12.8	12.5	-10.1q	-2.16	-100.0	-100.0	-100.0	36	-11	03-05-90	.00	.0	9	NE	36	03-05-90	-6.3	.11	-.7	16.00	-11.2	225	NA	15	4,736	1,294	0	0.0	12
Statewide Bcp NJ	-8.3	6.7	6.8	9.3t	.86	-55.4	-55.4	-55.4	43	-8	03-14-90	.20	2.6	9	93	43	03-14-90	4.6	.11	.5	12.60	6.3	84	NA	68	9,513	2,152	+24	0.0	12
Sterling Bncp	-25.1	-3.7	6.0	-7.9t	-1.24	-100.0	-100.0	-100.0	123	-17	06-11-90	.20	2.6	0	98	2	06-11-90	-9.2	.15	-1.4	10.43	-14.6	4	NA	49	6,322	1,037	+28	19.0	12
Suburban Bcp	9.6	9.6	18.0	5.7q	1.45	-23.3	-23.3	-23.3	6	-24	03-90	.31	1.9	0	14	6	06-04-90	6.7	.09	.6	12.33	7.4	0	NA	64	3,793	380	0	0.0	12

Summit Bancp	8.9	8.9	21.9	52.7q	2.59	4.3	4.3	35.6	14	13		12	29	35	05-25-90	12.2	.11	1.4	14.07	19.7	46	NA	293	19,834	3,71⁵	+1	0.0	12
Trustco Bcp	25.2	25.3	25.1	19.5l	3.89	19.0	19.0	19.0	12	33	0	19	8	8	08-06-90	10.9	.10	1.1	15.91	17.5	9	NA	151	4,325	3-	0	0.0	12
Trustco Bk	11.2	11.2	13.8	9.8q	3.27	18.3	18.3	23.4	12	18	21	32	35	04-04-90	12.0	.10	1.2	15.33	18.4	9	NA	89	3,008	36-	+1	0.0	12
US Trust	9.8	9.8	9.9	30.7f	3.08	2.3	2.3	2.3	6	6	8	46	35	07-03-90	7.7	.16	1.2	14.42	17.3	42	NA	352	9,512	3.34-	+7	0.0	12
UJB Financial	7.7	7.7	15.5	111.3q	2.46	-22.5	-22.5	-7.2	6	7	11	42	38	06-28-90	8.9	.09	.9	15.00	13.5	10	NA	716	44,07	13.24⁻		9.3	12
Utd Fed Bcp	-318.9	-72.6	.0	.0*	.85	-10.0	-65.2	-4.5	0	NC	NC	14	6	6	06-09-90	NC	NC	.7	NC	.0	0	NA	54	5,177	3,21⁴	0	0.0	12
Utd Natl Bk NJ	2.1	2.1	7.4	4.0q	1.90	-10.2	-10.2	-28.0	4	4	0	41	26	07-09-90	6.9	.07	.7	12.00	8.4	0	NA	46	2,030	55-	+0	0.0	12
Umnsty Bk Natl	34.2	34.6	34.1	.0f	.00	NE	-10.0	-100.0	0	NC	NC	NE	33	11	12-22-89	.0	.00	.0	.00	.0	1	NA	5	6,559	12⁴	0	0.0	12
Umnsty Natl B&T	15.8	15.8	19.0	3.1q	2.46	-15.2	-15.2	-5.4	14	22	0	12	11	02-07-90	12.4	.10	1.2	13.25	15.9	0	NA	35	1,195	⁻	0	0.0	12
Valley Natl Bcp	9.7	9.7	15.4	33.9q	2.67	.0	-0	3.5	11	11	20	49	42	03-12-90	18.9	.11	1.2	10.95	21.9	0	NA	285	12,676	55⁷	0	0.0	12
Village Fincl	29.3	29.3	24.1	2.7q	1.15	32.1	32.1	NC	6	NC		NE	14	6	00-00-00	7.5	.09	.7	9.00	6.3	0	NA	21	2,325	3₆	0	0.0	12
Wash Bancp NJ	.0	.0	.0	-4.0q	-1.73	-14.3	-14.3	NE	-13	NC		NE	22	83	03-26-90	-11.8	-.11	-1.1	11.82	-13.0	131	NA	12	2,307	10⁴	+0	0.0	12
Wash Bancp DC	-7.5	-7.5	5.4	9.1l	1.30	-66.7	-30.1	-30.1	0	NC		-2	22	0	01-04-90	3.9	.10	.4	20.75	8.3	26	NA	18	7,052	71⁴	+0	0.0	12
Wash FSB DC	5.4	5.4	8.2	3.4n	1.11	833.3	1250.0	640.0	7	NC		0	24	9	00-00-00	2.9	.10	.3	23.67	7.1	301	NA	8	3,088	11⁴	0	0.0	06
West Mass Bkshrs	17.9	17.9	23.6	.6n	.54	-15.8	-16.3	-27.0	2	NC		0	0	9	05-01-90	3.5	.09	.3	11.33	3.4	10	NA	8	1,289	10⁴	+1	0.0	12
Wolf Fincl Grp	-28.9	-13.2	55.5	.9s	.14	-100.0	-100.0	NE	12	NC		0	0	0	00-00-00	3.2	1.38	4.4	2.66	11.7	62	NA	39	6,190	27	0	0.0	08

Pacific States Banks

Ind. Group																											
	10.7	13.3	14.9	4,448.5	1.78	-35.9	10.2	2.7	4			1	27	36		6.0	.08	.5	26.40	13.2	75	1.1	44,708	1,836,799	357,⁴76	+48	1.3	
Bancorp Hawaii	10.5	10.5	14.1	82.5q	5.42	.7	.7	4.2	12	19	18	27	31	05-16-90	10.6	.09	1.0	17.10	17.1	10	NA	843	16,604	9,50	0	0.0	12
Bank of S F	41.2	41.9	40.7	2.8f	1.31	73.7	77.0	77.0	16	NC		0	27		00-00-00	7.4	.11	.8	19.63	15.7	7	NA	16	1,835	50	0	2.4	12
BankAmerica	7.5	7.5	9.6	830.0q	3.71	-7.8	-7.8	10.4	12	NC		0	16	NE	05-16-90	7.2	.11	.8	21.13	16.9	76	NA	6,269	211,596	102,395	+0	4.2	12
BSD Bancorp	28.4	28.4	22.2	3.8n	1.07	30.4	65.9	72.6	15	NC		0	0	0	04-30-90	6.9	.16	1.1	15.45	17.0	17	NA	33	3,496	67	+1	3.2	12
Cal Rep Bancorp	32.2	27.1	26.0	7.11	2.55	1.6	4.5	4.5	17	NC		15	12	12	05-30-99	12.2	.11	1.4	14.36	20.1	0	NA	66	2,771	40	0	0.0	12
Calf State Bk	1.5	1.5	2.7	3.8q	1.89	-12.2	-12.2	22	14	NC		0	0	0	03-16-89	14.1	.11	1.5	9.00	13.5	0	NA	34	2,152	209	0	0.0	12
Centennial Bancorp	17.4	16.7	22.2	1.3f	.70	61.5	16.7	16.7	16	NC		0	0	9	03-12-89	11.8	.11	1.8	12.31	16.0	9	NA	10	1,534	57	+1	0.0	12
Central Bkg Syst	-17.9	-17.9	-19.8	-29.8l	-6.9l	NE	NE	NE	14	NC		20	29	NE	06-25-84	-25.5	5.76	-46.8	.00	NS	-275	NA	6	4,288	⁻168	0	0.0	12
City Natl	6.8	6.8	21.0	59.0q	1.84	-4.3	-4.3	5.7	23	NC		20	29	29	06-26-90	12.2	.11	1.4	16.15	21.0	0	NA	590	31,047	⁻764	+1	4.0	12
CommerceBancorp	11.7	11.7	22.7	3.8f	1.92	.0	.0	20.8	15	NC		0	5	4	02-13-90	13.3	.13	1.4	11.64	16.3	13	NA	25	2,003	-405	+1	0.0	12
County Serv Bk	27.2	23.0	18.4	-2.9n	-.37	50.0	50.0	-100.0	-15	NC		0	0	0	03-09-88	-2.1	-.10	-.2	38.00	-7.6	155	NA	8	7,024	-093	0	0.0	12
CPB Inc	15.9	21.8	20.5	9.4f	2.02	2.0	2.0	11.0	0	NA		22	15	15	06-25-90	11.5	.09	1.0	13.40	13.4	1	NA	110	5,009	482	0	0.0	12
Eldorado Bcp	-12	16.2	15.3	3.8f	1.39	8.8	8.8	13.0	14	NC		0	8	12	06-04-90	12.7	.11	.9	11.57	16.2	0	NA	32	2,514	498	0	3.2	12
First Commercial Bcp	24.3	31.0	26.9	5.2f	1.10	40.9	39.2	39.2	37	NC		0	9	NE	07-10-90	15.8	.09	1.5	12.00	18.0	0	NA	47	4,651	878	+10	5.6	12
Fst Hawaiian	14.1	14.1	20.1	60.1q	2.24	20.4	20.4	28.0	13	NC		16	33	35	05-25-90	12.3	.12	1.2	17.83	21.4	22	NA	673	26,909	1,84	+2	0.3	12
Fst Intst Bcp	-1.8	10.2	10.1	-151.9f	-3.89	-100.0	-100.0	-100.0	-15	NA		5	NE	7622	06-04-90	-2.3	.13	-.3	28.33	-8.5	207	NA	1,970	48,792	3,881	+1.7	NA	12
Fst Intst Bcp A	NA	NA	NA	NA	NA	NA	NA	NA	8	NA		0	NA	NA	09-01-90	NA	NC	NC	NC	NA	NA	NA	54	43,500	3,710	0	0.0	12
Fst Mutl Svg Bk	2.0	8.8	10.5	1.5f	1.07	-23.1	.9	9	8	NC		0	6	3	06-25-90	7.1	.11	.8	12.88	10.3	73	NA	14	1,390	48	0	5.6	12
Fst Natl Cal	18.1	18.1	25.0	5.6q	1.71	17.6	17.6	24.8	14	NC		12	12	NE	02-05-90	9.3	.11	1.0	15.40	15.4	0	NA	53	3,159	248	+0	0.3	12
Estfed Fincl	-83.4	-83.4	-7.9	17.0q	2.38	4.3	4.3	9.7	13	NC		16	35	168	11-30-88	8.6	.08	1.0	18.00	12.6	361	NA	191	8,213	-3,120	+2	0.0	12
Foothill Indpt	4.8	4.8	13.6	3.3q	1.06	16.0	16.0	39.5	20	NC		16	7	7	06-04-90	13.2	.11	1.5	15.47	23.2	3	NA	16	3,020	40	+1.7	0.0	12
GBC Bcp Calif	33.1	33.1	41.8	11.4q	2.13	27.9	27.9	25.3	20	NA		19	12	6	06-25-90	18.7	.11	2.1	12.48	26.2	0	NA	101	5,377	648	0	0.0	12
GNW Fincl	7.6	7.6	8.7	3.5q	1.80	10.8	10.8	26.8	7	NC		6	6	3	04-24-90	5.6	.11	.6	13.00	7.8	73	NA	29	1,955	124	0	8.4	12
Grt Am Bank	-4.7	-4.7	-4.9	-275.7q	-11.51	-100.0	-100.0	-100.0	-74	NC		-18	NE	168	10-30-89	-17.9	.09	-1.7	43.41	-73.8	28	NA	75	23,970	6,889	+10	15.8	12
Guardian Bcp	22.7	22.7	50.0	5.7o	1.53	-20.4	-20.4	-11.6	24	NC		0	0	0	05-25-89	15.8	.09	1.4	17.21	24.1	13	NA	46	3,473	108	+2	0.0	12
Imperial Bcp	13.9	13.9	19.2	24.3q	2.29	16.7	16.7	21.2	13	NC		18	7	7	04-19-90	8.9	.09	.8	19.13	15.3	9	NA	216	10,539	640	-13	0.0	12
La Jolla Bcp	12.7	12.7	28.9	2.9q	.48	50.0	50.0	17.1	-1	NC		23	12	12	02-26-90	5.9	.12	.7	12.86	9.0	0	NA	96	6,846	318	0	0.0	12
Lincoln Bancorp	24.1	24.1	32.2	6.5q	1.25	12.5	12.5	28.2	7	NC		20	9	9	06-11-90	15.9	.11	1.3	16.00	20.8	0	NA	56	4,012	517	0	0.0	12
Metrobank	13.9	13.9	15.5	5.7q	1.32	-3.8	-3.8	4.8	10	NC		20	10	9	06-28-90	8.5	.07	.6	18.33	11.0	0	NA	54	4,746	197	0	2.2	12
Mission Valley	48.5	48.5	84.2	4.1q	1.35	-6.1	-6.1	19.5	13	NC		0	13	0	06-07-90	11.7	.11	1.3	11.69	15.2	45	NA	45	2,794	19		0.0	12

(continued)

Source: Media General Financial Services, Richmond, VA.

Pacific States Banks (Continued)

Company	Revenue Last Qtr %	FY to Date %	Last 12 Mos %	Last 12 Mos $Mil	Earnings Per Share Last 12 Mos $Mil	Last 12 Mos $	Last Qtr $	FY to Date %	Last 12 Mos %	5-Yr Growth Rate %	Par Growth %	Date of Report	Current Rate Amt $	Yield %	Div 5-Yr Growth Rate %	Payout Last FY %	Last 5 Yrs %	Last X-Dvd Date	Profit Margin %	Rtn on Total Assets	Asset Turn-over	Rtn on Assets	Lever-age	Rtn on Equity	Debt to Eq %	Curr-ent Ratio	Mar-ket Value $Mil	Latest Shares Outstdng 000	Held by Banks-Funds 000	Insider Net Trading 000	Short Int Ratio Days	Fiscal Year Ends Mo
Mitsubishi Bank	16.2	16.2	16.2	1357.6	.48	50.0	41.2	41.2	NC	12	03-88	.05	.3	0	88	96	03-23-90	6.4	.06	.4	34.00	13.6	24	NA	4,181	263,395	2	0	0.0	03
Napa Valley Bcp	28.3	28.3	31.8	3.6q	1.12	-34.5	6.7	-34.5	8	9	03-90	.32	2.6b	NA	23	15	04-06-90	6.2	.11	.7	17.14	12.0	17	NA	39	3,155	356	-0	0.0	12
Natl Austra Bk	NA	NA	NA	3.6q	NA	NA	NA	NA	NC	NC	00-00	1.21	4.7	NA	NA	16	06-18-90	NA	NC	NC	NC	NA	NA	NA	12,464	488,788	1,777	0	0.0	12
Natl Bancp Al	51.1	43.0	43.0	22.77	2.85	310.5	265.4	265.4	-7	10	12-89	.38	1.3b	10	13	16	05-07-90	10.5	.10	1.1	10.55	11.6	0	NA	231	7,969	420	+1	0.0	12
Northbay Fincl	NA	NA	NA	NA	NA	NA	NA	NA	NA	NC	00-00	.00	.0	NA	NA	NA	00-00-00	NA	NC	NC	NC	NA	0	NA	16	1,093	168	0	NA	NA
Northern Cal Comm	6.2	6.2	6.4	3.9q	1.36	8.8	7.9	8.8	6	6	03-90	.65	3.4	0	49	50	05-23-90	11.8	.10	1.2	9.33	11.2	24	NA	55	2,885	11	-3	0.0	12
Olympic Sav Bk	33.3	33.3	50.0	-1.2q	-.92	-34.5	NE	NE	-23	8	03-90	.00	.0	0	0	0	00-00-00	-4.4	.11	-.5	45.20	-22.6	655	NA	4	1,332	0	0	0.0	12
Organogenisis	.0	.0	.0	-5.0q	-.79	NE	NE	NE	-91	NC	03-90	.00	.0	0	0	0	09-14-87	NM	NC	.0	NC	-90.9	4	5.9	73	6,899	449	+0	16.7	12
Pac Bancorp	7.4	7.9	4.5	.6	.32	-27.3	-27.3	-27.3	7	13	03-90	.00	.0	0	0	0	00-00-00	2.6	.12	.3	22.33	6.7	0	NA	6	1,204	0	+0	0.0	12
Pacific Bank	10.8	10.8	31.0	7.6q	2.20	-7.1	NC	-7.1	13	03-90	.00	.0	0	0	0	00-00-00	10.0	.11	.3	13.2	13.2	0	NA	90	3,586	0	0.0	12
Pacific Inland Bcp	3.1	.0	.0	-.5q	-.38	NC	NE	NE	-6	12-89	.00	.0	0	0	0	00-00-00	-4.2	.12	-.5	11.40	-5.7	0	NA	7	1,290	0	0	0.0	12
Pac Wstrn Bcshr	15.6	12.9	13.6	13.4f	1.08	135.7	103.8	103.8	13	13	12-89	.24	2.0	8	14	24	06-12-90	10.7	.13	1.3	13.00	16.9	0	NA	147	12,257	1,482	+3	3.1	12
Plaza Comm Bcp	11.5	11.5	25.0	8.9q	1.27	11.1	25.7	11.1	23	10	03-90	.10	.9	8	8	7	07-26-89	17.8	.10	1.8	11.83	21.3	0	NA	78	6,643	163	+35	0.0	12
Puget Sound Bcp	8.8	8.8	13.6	29.1q	1.77	11.1	-31.7	11.1	-2	5	03-90	.96	4.3	12	54	38	05-30-90	6.2	.11	.7	14.14	9.9	113	NA	370	16,446	5,876	+7	0.0	12
Santa Monica Bk	15.8	15.8	23.8	12.7q	2.16	-3.8	18.0	-3.8	14	13	03-90	.60	2.3b	0	23	14	06-07-90	15.3	.10	1.6	12.38	19.8	0	NA	150	5,689	139	0	1.0	12
Santa Mon N V	NA	NA	NA	NA	NA	NA	NA	NA	NC	NC	00-00	.00	.0	NA	NA	NA	00-00-00	NA	NC	NC	NC	NA	NA	NA	89	3,482	0	0	NA	NA
SDNB Financl	20.5	20.5	11.7	1.3q	.85	12.5	19.7	12.5	10	12-89	.23	2.1b	13	23	18	04-16-90	6.8	.07	.7	12.57	8.8	89	NA	15	1,385	50	0	0.0	12
Sec Pacific	6.1	6.1	14.4	749.7q	6.26	NE	7.4	7.4	3	10	03-90	2.52	6.8	35	36	43	04-25-90	7.4	.12	.9	18.00	16.2	173	NA	4,185	113,096	66,335	0	1.6	12
Silicon Valley Bcsh	49.4	49.4	60.7	7.9q	1.38	42.9	53.3	42.9	26	26	03-90	.03	.2b	2	1	05-16-90	17.6	.10	1.8	14.83	26.7	0	NA	78	5,384	1,312	0	0.0	12
Sumitomo Bk	18.2	18.2	27.3	36.1q	4.47	9.1	18.6	9.1	20	6	03-90	1.60	5.6	6	28	33	06-25-90	7.9	.10	.8	19.38	15.5	13	NA	236	8,212	812	0	1.0	12
Transwrld Bncp	8.8	8.8	9.0	2.2q	2.01	22.2	21.8	22.2	14	03-90	.00	.0	0	0	0	03-19-90	9.2	.10	1.0	14.40	14.4	6	NA	16	1,119	4	0	0.0	12
US Bcp	19.2	19.2	21.3	157.8q	3.19	19.7	20.4	19.7	12	10	06-04-90	1.00	3.6	12	29	30	06-04-90	9.0	.10	.9	16.67	15.0	51	NA	1,383	49,609	25,351	+2	0.0	12
Union Bank	103.3	109.6	109.6	138.9f	4.10	16.8	16.8	16.8	18	15	12-89	1.32	6.0	4	29	35	06-04-90	8.4	.11	.9	19.73	17.8	29	NA	695	31,601	25,460	0	0.0	12
Valicorp Hldgs	71.2	71.2	73.3	1.5q	.57	-17.6	-31.7	-17.6	15	6	12-89	.00	.0	0	0	0	12-01-89	5.8	.07	.8	13.25	5.3	8	NA	23	4,065	10	0	0.0	12
Varifed Bcp	.0	.0	10.3	.8q	.73	40.0	-29.8	40.0	6	03-90	.00	.0	0	0	0	00-00-00	2.5	.12	.3	19.00	5.7	204	NA	23	1,156	183	0	0.0	12
Ventura C N Bcp	45.8	36.5	33.3	2.8q	.71	-27.8	22.4	-27.8	12	12-89	.00	.0	0	0	0	00-00-00	10.0	.09	.9	13.22	11.9	17	NA	33	4,366	0	0	0.0	12
Wash FSBK Ore	.0	.0	18.1	1.3q	.81	20.0	-19.8	20.0	4	6	03-90	.00	.0	0	38	24	05-09-90	3.3	.12	.4	14.50	5.8	42	NA	17	1,575	54	0	0.0	12
Wells Fargo	3.7	3.7	12.3	619.4q	11.50	18.8	19.7	18.8	22	16	03-90	4.00	5.1	25	29	33	06-26-90	10.9	.13	1.3	19.38	25.2	103	NA	4,035	51,075	32,522	0	6.2	12
West Coast Bancp	11.3	11.3	11.3	1.9q	.21	-20.0	5.0	-20.0	6	5	03-90	.00	.0	0	0	0	00-00-00	3.4	.12	.4	13.50	5.4	11	NA	22	9,169	5	0	0.0	12
WestAmer Bcp	4.3	4.3	8.2	8.2q	1.57	50.0	70.7	50.0	8	8	07-16-90	.44	1.9	3	28	33	07-16-90	5.7	.11	.6	19.33	11.6	26	NA	121	5,209	564	0	0.7	12
Westcorp	21.3	21.3	31.1	9.0q	.55	-5.3	-30.4	-5.3	-3	14	03-90	.06	.7	0	18	4	05-08-90	2.7	.11	.8	23.00	6.9	886	NA	139	16,337	3,438	0	0.2	12
Wstn Bank	16.5	16.5	12.8	3.3q	1.54	-8.3	-5.5	-8.3	97	6	03-90	.00	.0	0	0	0	06-07-90	7.5	.11	.8	17.25	13.8	5	NA	25	2,142	47	0	0.0	12
Westpac Banking	16.1	16.1	16.0	542.7f	3.68	76.9	77.8	77.8	6	14	09-88	2.00	10.8	0	0	0	06-07-90	7.3	.11	.8	15.75	12.6	38	NA	3,781	204,394	2,332	+0	0.3	09
Yankee Energy Sys	-2.5	-2.5	-5.5	6.7q	1.25	-25.1	-57.8	-57.8	-1	03-90	1.52	7.8	0	0	6	06-04-90	3.0	.67	2.0	3.45	6.9	127	1.0	106	5,433	2,407	+0	1.0	12

Source: Media General Financial Services, Richmond, VA.

Building Materials and Supplies

Trends and Forecasts: Construction Materials

(industry shipments in millions of 1987 dollars)

Item	1987	1988	1989	1990	Compound Annual 1987–90	Percent Change Annual 1987–88	1988–89	1989–90
TOTAL	47,477	47,554	47,648	47,364	-0.08	0.2	0.2	-0.6
3211 Flat Glass	2,528	2,478	2,527	2,403	-1.68	-2.0	-2.0	-4.9
3241 Hydraulic Cement	4,319	4,298	4,264	4,281	0.29	-0.5	-0.8	.5
3251 Brick & Structural Tile	1,248	1,283	1,173	1,177	-1.93	2.8	-8.6	0.3
3253 Ceramic Wall/Floor Tile	716	731	757	772	2.54	2.1	3.6	2.1
3271 Concrete Block and Brick	2,206	2,175	2,130	2,135	-1.08	-1.4	-2.1	0.2
3272 Concrete Products NEC	5,772	5,668	5,538	5,549	-1.30	-1.8	-2.3	0.2
3273 Ready Mix Concrete	12,789	12,763	12,777	12,865	0.20	-0.2	0.1	0.7
3275 Gypsum Products	2,666	2,673	2,779	2,793	1.56	0.3	4.0	0.5
3296 Mineral Wool	3,261	3,346	3,279	3,328	0.68	2.6	-2.0	1.5
3441 Fabr. Struct'l Metal	8,597	8,595	8,664	8,338	-1.01	*	0.8	-3.8
3448 Prefab Metal Buildings	3,375	3,544	3,760	3,723	3.33	5.0	6.1	-1.0

*Less than .5 percent.

Source: *U.S. Industrial Outlook 1990*, U.S. Department of Commerce.

Trends and Forecasts: Cement, Hydraulic (SIC 3241)

(in millions of dollars except as noted)

Item	1987[1]	1988[2]	1989[3]	1990[4]	Percent Change		
					1987-88	1988-89	1989-90
Industry Data							
Value of shipments[5]	4,319	4,302	4,255	—	-0.4	-1.1	—
Value of shipments (1987$)	4,319	4,298	4,264	4,281	-0.5	-0.8	0.4
Total employment (000)	19.2	19.1	19.2	—	-0.5	0.5	—
Production workers (000)	14.5	14.4	14.5	—	-0.7	0.7	—
Average hourly earnings ($)	14.08	14.28	14.41	—	1.4	0.9	—
Product Data							
Value of shipments[6]	4,100	4,078	4,038	—	-0.5	-1.0	—
Value of shipments (1987$)	4,100	4,074	4,046	4,062	-0.6	-0.7	0.4
Trade Data							
Value of imports	494	516	525	—	4.5	1.7	—
Import/new supply ratio[7]	0.108	0.112	0.115	—	3.7	2.7	—
Value of exports	21.5	24.9	26.4	—	15.8	6.0	—
Export/shipments ratio	0.005	0.006	0.007	—	20.0	16.7	—

[1] Industry and product data are preliminary. Trade data are adjusted to conform to the 1987 SIC.

[2] Estimated, except for exports and imports.

[3] Estimated.

[4] Forecast.

[5] Value of all products and services sold by establishments in the cement, hydraulic industry.

[6] Value of products classified in the cement, hydraulic industry produced by all industries.

[7] New supply is imports plus corresponding product shipments.

SOURCE: U.S. Department of Commerce: Bureau of the Census; International Trade Administration (ITA). Estimates and forecasts by ITA.

Source: *U.S. Industrial Outlook 1990*, U.S. Department of Commerce.

MEDIA GENERAL FINANCIAL SERVICES

STOCKS by INDUSTRY

Company	Rev Last Qtr %	Rev FY to Date %	Rev Last 12 Mos %	Earn Last 12 Mos $Mil	Per Share Last 12 Mos $	Earn Last Qtr %	Earn FY to Date %	Earn Last 12 Mos %	5-Yr Growth %	Par Growth %	Date of Report	Div Amt $	Yield %	5-Yr Growth %	Payout Last FY %	Payout 5 Yrs %	Last X-Div Date	Profit Margin	Asset Turnover	Return on Total Assets	Leverage Ratio	Return on Equity	Debt to Eq %	Curr Ratio	Mar-ket Value $Mil	Latest Shares Outstng 000	Held by Banks/Funds 000	Insider Net Trading 000	Short Int Ratio Days	Fiscal Year Ends Mo
Ind. Group	2.4	5.0	2.9	-24.1	-.89	-100.0	-100.0	-100.0	NG	-1	---	.24	1.6	1	33	29	---	-.4	.75	-.3	2.67	-.8	69	2.0	3,957	262,350	50,283	+59	8.8	--

Cement

Company	Rev Last Qtr %	Rev FY to Date %	Rev Last 12 Mos %	Earn Last 12 Mos $Mil	Per Share Last 12 Mos $	Earn Last Qtr %	Earn FY to Date %	Earn Last 12 Mos %	5-Yr Growth %	Par Growth %	Date of Report	Div Amt $	Yield %	5-Yr Growth %	Payout Last FY %	Payout 5 Yrs %	Last X-Div Date	Profit Margin	Asset Turnover	Return on Total Assets	Leverage Ratio	Return on Equity	Debt to Eq %	Curr Ratio	Mar-ket Value $Mil	Latest Shares Outstng 000	Held by Banks/Funds 000	Insider Net Trading 000	Short Int Ratio Days	Fiscal Year Ends Mo
Am Tech Ceramics ♦•	-11.3	-11.8	-12.0	.3n	.07	0	-18.6	-56.3	NC	2	03-90	.00	.0	0	0	0	00-00-00	1.4	.79	1.1	1.55	1.7	22	3.9	8	4,059	28	0	16.1	06
Calmat Co ♦	4.3	4.3	8.0	75.3q	2.44	-18.6	-18.6	36.3	28	11	03-90	.64	1.9	15	21	21	06-04-90	11.2	.83	9.3	1.54	14.3	16	2.1	1,046	30,761	9,331	+13	0.4	12
Conti Materials	-6.0	20.3	20.0	-1.11	-.99	-94.0	-100.0	-100.0	NC	-4	12-89	.00	.0	0	0	0	00-00-00	-1.3	1.38	-1.8	2.33	-4.2	81	2.8	14	1,162	159	0	0.0	12
Devcon Intl	-15.3	-15.3	1.3	11.9q	2.79	-2.5	-12.5	-2.8	NC	19	03-90	.10	.4	0	0	0	06-18-90	16.2	.86	13.9	1.41	19.6	9	2.3	98	4,270	159	+0	0.0	12
Fla Rock Ind	3.4	-5.8	-8.3	20.2s	2.19	-6.1	-30.6	-28.0	1	10	03-90	.50	1.7	21	30	30	06-13-90	5.0	1.26	6.3	2.02	12.7	38	1.4	278	9,214	3,309	+0	3.4	09
For Better Liv	-4.7	-4.7	-3.3	1.0q	.45	NE	NE	NE	NC	5	03-90	.10	1.3	0	0	0	05-09-90	1.2	1.75	2.1	2.90	6.1	92	2.3	7	901	0	0	0.0	12
Giant Grp	1.5	1.5	50.0	6.6q	1.65	NE	NE	NE	NC	13	03-90	.00	.0	0	0	0	00-00-00	4.5	.76	3.4	3.79	12.9	213	2.7	66	3,806	2,336	0	33.9	12
Holnam Inc	9.7	9.7	2.4	5.0q	-1.88	NE	NE	-100.0	NC	1	03-90	.00	.0	0	0	0	00-00-00	-.5	.80	-.4	3.25	1.3	111	2.1	433	101,939	7,334	0	27.6	12
Lafarge Cp	15.4	15.4	14.8	79.2q	1.60	NE	NE	-19.6	NC	7	03-90	.40	2.4	15	20	21	05-07-90	5.2	.98	5.1	1.94	9.9	49	2.0	858	50,821	9,945	+0	0.6	12
Lone Star Ind	-11.1	-9.1	-8.8	-270.7f	-16.68	-100.0	-100.0	-100.0	NC	-80	12-89	.00	.0	0	NE	NE	12-21-89	-80.1	.29	-23.6	3.37	-79.5	115	1.5	176	16,556	4,477	+0	2.1	12
Medusa Cp	13.5	13.5	0	12.7q	1.20	NE	NE	-15.5	NC	75	03-90	.80	.0	0	0	15	07-13-90	6.8	1.87	12.7	5.88	74.7	289	1.7	205	10,645	518	+46	5.2	12
Puerto Rican C	4.1	4.1	0	13.0q	6.71	-7.0	-7.0	-18.1	44	13	03-90	.80	1.6	0	8	8	07-13-90	16.3	.52	8.5	1.79	15.2	42	4.7	94	1,936	518	0	0.0	12
Southdown Ind	-.8	-.8	-10.5	34.0q	1.63	-15.2	-15.2	-29.4	NC	7	03-90	.50	1.9	10	33	33	05-14-90	5.8	.55	3.2	3.09	9.9	74	1.8	448	16,939	7,699	0	2.0	12
Texas Inds	-11.0	-6.5	-3.5	-11.4n	-1.39	NE	-100.0	-100.0	NC	-7	02-90	.40	3.4	0	292	56	05-07-90	-1.7	.94	-1.6	2.81	-4.5	103	2.6	227	9,691	6,014	0	31.8	05

Other Building Materials

Company	Rev Last Qtr %	Rev FY to Date %	Rev Last 12 Mos %	Earn Last 12 Mos $Mil	Per Share Last 12 Mos $	Earn Last Qtr %	Earn FY to Date %	Earn Last 12 Mos %	5-Yr Growth %	Par Growth %	Date of Report	Div Amt $	Yield %	5-Yr Growth %	Payout Last FY %	Payout 5 Yrs %	Last X-Div Date	Profit Margin	Asset Turnover	Return on Total Assets	Leverage Ratio	Return on Equity	Debt to Eq %	Curr Ratio	Mar-ket Value $Mil	Latest Shares Outstng 000	Held by Banks/Funds 000	Insider Net Trading 000	Short Int Ratio Days	Fiscal Year Ends Mo
Ind. Group	.6	2.2	-.4	749.7	1.48	15.8	8.2	5.8	18	69	---	.31	2.2	1	38	33	---	5.4	1.24	6.7	13.10	87.8	582	1.5	5,832	400,986	126,730	+162	2.0	--
Am Woodmark	-3.0	-2.6	-2.5	.6f	.09	-100.0	-91.0	-91.0	-17	2	04-90	.00	.0	0	0	0	05-24-88	.4	1.75	.7	2.14	1.5	67	2.3	39	7,012	120	0	0.0	04
Ameron Inc	11.8	7.9	14.8	12.6s	3.22	1.8	-26.2	13.4	7	6	05-90	1.28	2.8	0	25	29	07-20-90	2.9	1.31	3.8	2.53	9.6	50	1.7	184	4,001	954	0	0.0	11
Armstrng Wrld	-9.8	-9.8	-11.5	185.7q	3.89	55.6	55.6	11.8	14	18	03-90	1.16	3.2	13	31	45	05-07-90	7.6	1.20	9.1	2.09	26.3	26	1.8	1,511	42,257	25,520	-24	0.7	12
Bairnco Cp	.6	.6	-12.8	-4.0q	-1.22	-63.3	-63.3	-100.0	NC	-4	03-90	1.00	15.4	15	45	NE	02-27-90	-2.0	.60	-1.2	1.67	-2.0	2	2.5	68	10,442	209	+3	1.5	12
Bird Cp	-41.6	-41.6	-45.4	10.5s	2.24	NE	NE	339.2	NC	20	03-90	.00	.0	0	0	0	00-00-00	9.8	1.40	13.7	1.45	19.8	3	2.5	45	3,688	324	+14	0.0	12
Butler Mfg	-2.3	-2.3	-10.1	7.2q	1.57	-100.0	-100.0	-55.1	24	2	03-90	1.40	8.8	49	979	295	06-13-89	1.2	2.50	3.0	5.70	17.1	249	1.9	97	6,071	1,088	+140	0.0	12
Ceradyne	.0	.0	-8.0	-1.6q	-.29	NE	NE	NE	NC	-9	03-90	.00	.0	0	0	0	00-00-00	-7.0	.94	-6.6	1.33	-8.8	5	2.0	27	6,076	906	0	0.0	12
Chem Fabrics	21.9	24.9	27.0	4.9n	.96	33.3	40.4	45.5	NC	31	03-90	.00	.0	5	0	0	00-00-00	10.4	1.81	18.8	1.64	30.8	16	2.5	101	4,500	1,247	-27	0.0	06
Elcor Cp ▫■	-7.7	3.9	4.8	-3.6n	-.51	NE	580.0	-100.0	NC	-20	03-90	.22	2.3	0	NE	NE	07-09-90	-2.4	1.67	-4.0	3.50	-14.0	155	1.8	68	7,099	2,403	+21	3.2	06
Industrl Acoustics	-9.9	-9.9	-1.0	3.3q	1.13	-7.7	-7.7	-8.1	13	8	03-90	.25	2.8	0	22	29	03-14-89	3.6	1.36	4.9	2.12	10.4	9	1.6	26	2,889	98	0	0.0	12

(continued)

Other Building Materials (Continued)

Company	Revenue Pct Change Last Qtr %	Revenue FY to Date %	Revenue Last 12 Mos %	Earnings Last 12 Mos $Mil	Earnings Last 12 Mos $	EPS Pct Change Last Qtr %	EPS Pct Change FY to Date %	EPS Pct Change Last 12 Mos %	5-Year Growth Rate %	Par Growth Rate %	Date of Report	Div Current Rate Amt $	Div Yield %	Div 5-Year Growth Rate %	Payout Last FY %	Payout Last 5 Yrs %	Last X-Dvd Date	Profit Margin %	Asset Turnover	Return on Total Assets	Leverage Ratio	Return on Equity %	Debt to Equity %	Current Ratio	Market Value $Mil	Latest Shares Outstdng 000	Held by Banks-Funds 000	Insider Net Trading 000	Short Interest Ratio Days	Fiscal Year Ends Mo
Instrum Grp	95.7	145.2	137.5	1.7l	.16	NE	700.0	700.0	NC	9	12-89	.00	.0	0	0	0	09-02-86	4.5	.87	3.9	2.38	9.3	13	1.6	68	9,740	1,491	0	0.0	12
Instrum Gulf	-25.7	-11.2	.0	-.1n	.08	-100.0	-100.0	-100.0	NC	NC	03-90	.00	.0	0	0	0	00-00-00	-.8	1.38	-1.1	1.27	-1.4	0	3.8	7	2,980	57	0	0.0	06
Instrum NA	6.3	6.3	5.0	3.6q	.45	-16.7	-16.7	-10.0	NC	16	03-90	.00	.0	0	0	0	00-00-00	17.1	.60	10.2	1.52	15.5	33	4.1	47	7,805	1,476	0	0.0	12
Instrument Sys	-7.2	1.3	.9	-10.9s	-.40	NE	NE	NE	NC	-22	03-90	.00	.0	0	0	0	00-00-00	-2.7	1.48	-4.0	5.55	-22.2	247	2.6	52	27,820	4,327	0	0.0	09
Kerkhoff Inds	72.4	8.0	-10.5	-.2n	.05	-100.0	-100.0	-100.0	NC	6	02-90	.00	.0	0	0	0	00-00-00	1.2	1.58	1.9	3.11	5.9	106	1.8	6	3,175	19	0	0.0	05
Knape & Vogt Mfg	6.4	7.9	9.9	5.2n	1.33	5.1	21	19.8	0	6	03-90	.56	3.9	9	50	46	05-14-90	4.3	1.40	6.0	1.83	11.0	49	4.4	57	3,918	743	0	0.0	06
Manville Cp	1.9	1.9	6.4	187.3q	1.40	-30.8	-30.8	NE	NC	40	03-90	.00	.0	0	50	0	00-00-00	8.5	.84	7.1	5.59	39.7	170	1.5	329	47,830	11,022	0	1.7	12
Mark Controls	4.1	4.1	8.3	2.7q	.55	-11.8	-11.8	-23.6	NC	10	03-90	.00	.0	0	0	0	00-00-00	3.5	1.66	5.8	1.78	10.3	42	4.2	33	4,906	0	+16	0.0	12
Miller Bldg Sys	-5.4	.0	7.3	1.9n	.50	-25.0	.0	16.3	NC	14	03-90	.06	1.2	0	0	0	05-09-90	4.3	2.79	12.0	1.34	16.1	4	2.8	20	3,906	639	0	0.0	06
Owens Corn	12.5	12.5	7.6	171.0q	4.05	-3.7	-3.7	-16.8	NC	0	03-90	.00	.0	0	0	0	00-00-00	5.5	1.62	8.9	.00	NS	-276	1.0	937	42,090	26,116	0	123	12
Rep Gypsum	9.2	-2.1	-6.0	1.3n	.13	-25.0	-62.5	-43.5	-32	4	03-90	.00	.0	0	100	58	05-24-90	2.8	.89	2.5	1.60	4.0	28	3.6	40	10,623	2,757	+18	0.0	06
Southwal Tech	.0	.0	.0	.3n	.05	.0	.0	NE	NC	NC	03-90	.00	.0	0	0	0	00-00-00	2.1	.75	.7	1.14	.8	7	4.2	59	6,750	1,682	0	0.0	12
Supradur Cos	-1.6	-1.6	4.0	-.2n	-.30	-100.0	-100.0	-100.0	-1	-1	03-90	.00	.0	0	0	0	00-00-00	-.8	.50	-.6	2.17	-1.3	78	3.0	7	934	127	0	0.0	12
Thermal Profile	-16.7	-26.1	-28.5	-4.9l	-1.51	NE	NE	NE	NC	0	03-89	.00	.0	0	0	0	00-00-00	-49.0	NC	-24.6	.00	NM	11	.8	2	3,090	20	0	0.0	03
Trifing Med Tech	140.0	120.0	200.0	.08	-.02	NC	NC	NE	NC	0	02-90	.00	.0	0	0	0	00-00-00	.0	NC	NC	NC	NC	0	2.4	17	26,421	11	0	0.0	08
US Intec	21.8	21.8	3.3	.0q	-.02	NE	NE	NE	NC	0	03-90	.00	.0	0	0	0	00-00-00	.0	NC	NC	NC	.0	51	5.1	15	2,969	698	+1	0.0	12
USG	-1.5	-1.5	-2.0	33.4q	.60	180.0	180.0	-63.9	NC	0	03-90	.00	.0	0	0	26	00-00-00	1.5	1.40	2.1	.00	NS	-157	.9	217	54,156	10,374	0	38.5	12
Vesper Cp	-6.2	.1	3.0	9.3n	.79	8.7	-16.4	11.3	NC	38	01-90	.00	.0	0	0	0	00-00-00	6.8	2.12	14.4	2.05	38.1	45	2.2	21	8,077	0	+1	0.0	04
Vulcan Matls	6.7	6.7	2.1	132.3q	3.29	23.7	23.7	196.4	7	13	03-90	1.20	2.8b	13	35	42	08-21-90	12.1	1.09	13.2	1.51	19.9	8	2.4	1,734	39,751	22,302	0	1.0	12

Source: Media General Financial Services, Richmond, VA.

Chemicals, Plastics and Rubber

Trends and Forecasts: Chemicals and Allied Products (SIC 28)

(in millions of dollars except as noted)

Item	1987[1]	1988[2]	1989[3]	1990[4]	Percent Change		
					1987–88	1988–89	1989–90
Industry Data							
Value of shipments[5]	229,015	258,924	274,459	—	13.1	6.0	—
Value of shipments (1987$)	229,015	233,877	241,350	245,458	2.1	3.2	1.7
Total employment (000)	811	—	—	—	—	—	—
Production workers (000)	462	—	—	—	—	—	—
Average hourly earnings ($)	12.91	—	—	—	—	—	—
Product Data							
Value of shipments[6]	213,595	—	—	—	—	—	—
Value of shipments (1987$)	213,595	—	—	—	—	—	—
Trade Data							
Value of imports	17,122	20,504	23,219	23,808	19.8	13.2	2.5
Import/new supply ratio[7]	0.071	—	—	—	—	—	—
Value of exports	26,701	32,551	38,035	39,440	21.9	16.8	3.7
Export/shipments ratio	0.124	—	—	—	—	—	—

[1]Industry and product data are preliminary. Trade data are adjusted to conform to the 1987 SIC.
[2]Estimated, except for exports and imports.
[3]Estimated.
[4]Forecast.
[5]Value of all products and services sold by establishments in the chemicals and allied products industry.
[6]Value of products classified in the chemicals and allied products industry produced by all industries.
[7]New supply is imports plus corresponding product shipments.

SOURCE: U.S. Department of Commerce: Bureau of the Census; International Trade Administration (ITA). Estimates and forecasts by ITA.

Source: *U.S. Industrial Outlook 1990*, U.S. Department of Commerce.

Trends and Forecasts: Petrochemicals (SIC 2821, 2822, 2824, 2843, 2865, 2869, 2873, 2895)

(in millions of dollars except as noted)

Item	1987[1]	1988[2]	1989[3]	1990[4]	Percent Change		
					1987–88	1988–89	1989–90
Industry Data							
Value of shipments[5]	96,514	111,748	123,578	—	15.8	10.6	—
Value of shipments (1987$)	96,514	97,316	100,049	101,855	0.8	2.8	1.8
Total employment (000)	253	—	—	—	—	—	—
Production workers (000)	158	—	—	—	—	—	—
Average hourly earnings ($)	14.92	—	—	—	—	—	—
Product Data							
Value of shipments[6]	92,631	—	—	—	—	—	—
Value of shipments (1987$)	92,631	—	—	—	—	—	—
Trade Data							
Value of imports	9,693	11,441	12,641	13,557	18.0	10.5	7.2
Import/new supply ratio[7]	0.087	—	—	—	—	—	—
Value of exports	13,833	17,607	18,517	19,817	27.3	5.2	7.0
Export/shipments ratio	0.148	—	—	—	—	—	—

[1]Industry and product data are preliminary. Trade data are adjusted to conform to the 1987 SIC.

[2]Estimated, except for exports and imports.

[3]Estimated.

[4]Forecast.

[5]Value of all products and services sold by establishments in the petrochemicals industry.

[6]Value of products classified in the petrochemicals industry produced by all industries.

[7]New supply is imports plus corresponding product shipments.

SOURCE: U.S. Department of Commerce: Bureau of the Census; International Trade Administration (ITA). Estimates and forecasts by ITA.

Source: *U.S. Industrial Outlook 1990*, U.S. Department of Commerce.

Trends and Forecasts: Plastics Materials and Resins (SIC 2821)

(in millions of dollars except as noted)

Item	1987[1]	1988[2]	1989[3]	1990[4]	Percent Change		
					1987-88	1988-89	1989-90
Industry Data							
Value of shipments[5]	26,144	33,800	36,616	38,096	29.3	8.3	4.0
Value of shipments (1987$)	26,144	27,614	28,166	28,730	5.6	2.0	2.0
Total employment (000)	55.9	55.5	55.5	55.5	-0.7	0.0	0.0
Production workers (000)	34.7	-	-	-	-	-	-
Average hourly earnings ($)	15.24	-	-	-	-	-	-
Product Data							
Value of shipments[6]	27,698	-	-	-	-	-	-
Value of shipments (1987$)	27,698	-	-	-	-	-	-
Trade Data							
Value of imports	927	1,158	1,273	1,400	24.9	9.9	10.0
Import/new supply ratio[7]	0.032	-	-	-	-	-	-
Value of exports	3,688	5,034	5,437	5,763	36.5	8.0	6.0
Export/shipments ratio	0.133	-	-	-	-	-	-

[1]Industry and product data are preliminary. Trade data are adjusted to conform to the 1987 SIC.
[2]Estimated, except for exports and imports.
[3]Estimated.
[4]Forecast.
[5]Value of all products and services sold by establishments in the plastics materials and resins industry.
[6]Value of products classified in the plastics materials and resins industry produced by all industries.
[7]New supply is imports plus corresponding product shipments.

SOURCE: U.S. Department of Commerce: Bureau of the Census International Trade Administration (ITA). Estimates and forecasts by ITA.

Source: U.S. Industrial Outlook 1990, U.S. Department of Commerce.

Trends and Forecasts: Synthetic Rubber (SIC 2822)
(in millions of dollars except as noted)

Item	1987[1]	1988[2]	1989[3]	1990[4]	Percent Change		
					1987-88	1988-89	1989-90
Industry Data							
Value of shipments[5]	3,310	3,339	3,390	—	0.9	1.5	—
Value of shipments (1987$)	3,310	3,274	3,340	3,406	-1.1	2.0	2.0
Total employment (000)	10.8	10.6	—	—	-1.9	—	—
Production workers (000)	7.0	6.9	—	—	-1.4	—	—
Average hourly earnings ($)	15.22	15.41	—	—	1.2	—	—
Product Data							
Value of shipments[6]	3,452	—	3,548	3,619	—	—	—
Value of shipments (1987$)	3,452	3,478	3,548	3,619	0.8	2.0	2.0
Trade Data							
Value of imports	393	461	605	620	17.3	31.2	2.5
Import/new supply ratio[7]	0.102	—	—	—	—	—	—
Value of exports	858	985	899	905	14.8	-8.7	0.7
Export/shipments ratio	0.249	—	—	—	—	—	—

[1]Industry and product data are preliminary. Trade data are adjusted to conform to the 1987 SIC.
[2]Estimated, except for exports and imports.
[3]Estimated.
[4]Forecast.
[5]Value of all products and services sold by establishments in the synthetic rubber industry.
[6]Value of products classified in the synthetic rubber industry produced by all industries.
[7]New supply is imports plus corresponding product shipments.
SOURCE: U.S. Department of Commerce: Bureau of the Census; International Trade Administration (ITA). Estimates and forecasts by ITA.

Source: U.S. Industrial Outlook 1990, U.S. Department of Commerce.

Trends and Forecasts: Tires and Inner Tubes (SIC 3011)
(in millions of dollars except as noted)

Item	1987[1]	1988[2]	1989[3]	1990[4]	Percent Change		
					1987–88	1988–89	1989–90
Industry Data							
Value of shipments[5]	10,427	10,953	–	–	5.0	–	–
Value of shipments (1987$)	10,427	10,583	10,742	10,903	1.5	1.5	1.5
Total employment (000)	65.4	66.1	66.5	–	1.1	0.6	–
Production workers (000)	52.6	53.2	53.5	–	1.1	0.6	–
Average hourly earnings ($)	15.40	15.90	–	–	3.2	–	–
Product Data							
Value of shipments[6]	10,034	10,515	11,045	–	4.8	5.0	–
Value of shipments (1987$)	10,034	10,189	10,338	10,492	1.5	1.5	1.5
Trade Data							
Value of imports	2,227	2,405	2,711	–	8.0	12.7	–
Import/new supply ratio[7]	0.189	–	–	–	–	–	–
Value of exports	541	799	899	–	47.7	12.5	–
Export/shipments ratio	0.054	0.076	–	–	40.7	–	–

[1] Industry and product data are preliminary. Trade data are adjusted to conform to the 1987 SIC.
[2] Estimated, except for exports and imports.
[3] Estimated.
[4] Forecast.
[5] Value of all products and services sold by establishments in the tires and inner tubes industry.
[6] Value of products classified in the tires and inner tubes industry produced by all industries.
[7] New supply is imports plus corresponding product shipments.
SOURCE: U.S. Department of Commerce: Bureau of the Census; International Trade Administration (ITA). Estimates and forecasts by ITA.

Source: *U.S. Industrial Outlook 1990*, U.S. Department of Commerce.

MEDIA GENERAL FINANCIAL SERVICES

STOCKS by INDUSTRY

Chemicals, Synthetics

Revenue

Company	Pct. Change Last Qtr %	FY to Date %	Last 12 Mos %	Last 12 Mos $Mil
Ind. Group	5.8	6.6	4.7	8,620.3
Aceto Cp	-5.6	12.1	15.0	5.0
Advanced Polymer	20.0	20.0	50.0	-3.9
Air Prods & Chem	6.6	4.3	6.3	214.3
American Cyanamid	3.3	3.3	4.0	293.9
Aquanautics Cp	50.0	66.7	100.0	-.4
Borden Chem	-27.3	-27.3	-24.0	40.9
Cabot Corp	-17.7	-16.6	-4.1	-13.7
Calgon Carbon	6.7	6.7	7.0	35.8
Concap Inc	-16.2	-16.2	-10.6	-6.0
Dow Chemical	9.3	9.3	4.8	2,206.0
Dupont	8.4	8.4	7.9	2,359.0
Electrochem Ind	NA	NA	NA	NA
Ethyl Corp	-16.4	-16.4	25.0	227.4
Genex Cp	.0	.0	16.2	-5.8
Georgia Bonded	2.9	12.7	-12.7	-.4
Ga Gulf	NA	NA	NA	NA
Grace W R	7.9	7.9	5.7	256.4
Hercules Inc	13.2	13.2	12.7	-105.9
Immucor Inc	24.0	25.7	33.3	1.9
Imperial Chem	13.7	13.7	5.4	1,508.0
Monsanto Co	9.2	.9	.9	651.0
Oil Dri Cp	13.6	14.2	15.1	6.3
Pacer Tech	15.8	1.6	8.0	.0
Portage Ind	.0	15.8	.0	.1
Publicker Ind	-16.2	.0	-12.5	-3.5
Quantum Chemical	-21.2	-16.2	-35.7	177.9
Regal Intl Inc	2.2	-21.2	3.1	-1.9
Rohm & Haas	6.7	2.2	3.1	177.0
Stepan Co	6.7	6.7	3.1	8.4
Sterling Chemicals	-27.7	-37.4	-34.7	40.5

Earnings

Company	Per Share Last 12 Mos $	Pct. Change Last Qtr %	FY to Date %	Last 12 Mos %	5-Year Growth Rate %	Par Growth Rate %	Date of Report
Ind. Group	3.83	-21.6	-22.4	-14.2	27	10	--
Aceto Cp	1.22	-8.7	.0	6.1	3	5	03-90
Advanced Polymer	-.42	NE	NE	-100.0	NC	-41	03-90
Air Prods & Chem	3.88	4.8	-7.4	-3.5	35	9	03-90
American Cyanamid	3.08	-4.0	-4.0	-12.5	15	7	03-90
Aquanautics Cp	-.03	NE	NE	NC	NC	0	03-90
Borden Chem	1.13	-87.1	-87.1	-67.8	NC	-45	03-90
Cabot Corp	-.52	-1.9	-1.9	-100.0	NC	-10	03-90
Calgon Carbon	1.77	7.7	7.7	14.9	NC	18	03-90
Concap Inc	-2.18	NE	NE	NE	NC	-44	03-90
Dow Chemical	8.19	-37.1	-37.1	-13.7	75	19	03-90
Dupont	3.40	-12.6	-12.6	4.9	16	8	00-00
Electrochem Ind	NA	NA	NA	NA	NA	NC	00-00
Ethyl Corp	1.90	-6.4	-6.4	-2.1	18	17	03-90
Genex Cp	-.29	NE	NE	NE	NC	0	02-90
Georgia Bonded	.32	NE	NE	255.6	-19	3	03-90
Ga Gulf	NA	NA	NA	NA	NC	NC	00-00
Grace W R	3.01	11.8	11.8	14.0	NC	8	03-90
Hercules Inc	-2.29	-21.7	-21.7	-100.0	NC	-11	03-90
Immucor Inc	.48	60.9	60.9	65.5	12	12	02-90
Imperial Chem	8.71	2.9	2.9	-7.7	12	10	03-90
Monsanto Co	4.88	-8.6	15.9	12.7	16	16	03-90
Oil Dri Cp	.91	46.7	46.7	4.6	17	11	04-90
Pacer Tech	.00	NE	NE	-100.0	NC	NC	03-90
Portage Ind	.09	NE	NE	NE	NC	1	03-90
Publicker Ind	-.20	-100.0	-100.0	-100.0	-17	-17	03-90
Quantum Chemical	6.93	-92.5	-92.5	-49.7	NC	0	03-90
Regal Intl Inc	-.12	NE	NE	NE	8	7	03-90
Rohm & Haas	2.66	1.3	1.3	-20.1	15	8	03-90
Stepan Co	1.54	23.5	23.5	-31.6	NC	15	03-90
Sterling Chemicals	.74	-62.3	-78.6	-77.3	NC	-13	03-90

Dividends

Company	Current Rate Amt $	Yield %	5-Year Growth Rate %	Payout Last FY %	Last 5 Yrs %	Last X-Dvd Date
Ind. Group	1.60	4.1	1	33	39	-----
Aceto Cp	.64	4.9		47	36	06-05-90
Advanced Polymer	.00	.0				00-00-00
Air Prods & Chem	1.44	2.5	20	30	34	06-28-90
American Cyanamid	1.35	2.4	7	42	42	05-23-90
Aquanautics Cp	.00	.0				00-00-00
Borden Chem	1.99	20.9	1	161	107	04-23-90
Cabot Corp	1.04	3.2		NE	61	05-21-90
Calgon Carbon	.32	.7		11	7	06-11-90
Concap Inc	.00	.0				00-00-00
Dow Chemical	2.60	4.5b	12	24	31	06-25-90
Dupont	1.60	4.2	8	41	46	05-09-90
Electrochem Ind	.00	.0	NA	NA	NA	00-00-00
Ethyl Corp	.60	2.0	18	26	25	06-11-90
Genex Cp	.00	.0				00-00-00
Georgia Bonded	.10	2.5				10-02-89
Ga Gulf	.00	.0	NA	NA	10	00-00-00
Grace W R	1.40	4.7	8	47	206	04-27-90
Hercules Inc	2.24	6.7	8	NE	43	05-25-90
Immucor Inc	.00	.0				04-16-87
Imperial Chem	4.77	6.0	19	51	38	03-16-90
Monsanto Co	.25	.9	7	33	50	05-09-90
Oil Dri Cp	.20	.9	16	10	15	05-16-90
Pacer Tech	.00	.0				00-00-00
Portage Ind	.00	.0				00-00-00
Publicker Ind	.00	.0				00-00-00
Quantum Chemical	.00	.0		153	17	05-04-90
Regal Intl Inc	.00	.0				00-00-00
Rohm & Haas	1.20	3.5	14	44	35	05-14-90
Stepan Co	.56	2.3	10	37	27	05-24-90
Sterling Chemicals	1.00	14.3		0	0	04-09-90

Ratio Analysis

Company	Profit Margin %	Asset Turnover	Return on Total Assets	Leverage Ratio	Return on Equity	Debt to Equity %	Current Ratio
Ind. Group	7.0	.99	6.9	2.59	17.9	47	1.4
Aceto Cp	4.1	1.83	7.5	1.53	11.5	12	3.5
Advanced Polymer	NM	NC	NC	NC	-41.1	32	12.6
Air Prods & Chem	7.9	.81	6.4	2.31	14.8	59	1.5
American Cyanamid	6.0	.98	5.9	2.15	12.7	20	1.4
Aquanautics Cp	-20.0	1.18	-23.5	.00	NM	0	1.5
Borden Chem	9.5	.78	7.4	7.96	58.9	216	2.0
Cabot Corp	-.8	1.25	-1.0	3.30	-3.3	33	1.4
Calgon Carbon	13.9	1.10	15.3	1.44	22.1	11	3.3
Concap Inc	-7.1	1.54	-10.9	3.99	-43.5	46	1.0
Dow Chemical		.82	10.0	2.77	27.7	48	1.1
Dupont	6.5	1.05	6.8	2.24	15.2	27	1.2
Electrochem Ind	NA	NC	NA	NC	NA	NA	NA
Ethyl Corp	9.8	.41	4.0	6.30	25.2	55	2.3
Genex Cp	NM	NM	NM	NM	NM	0	3.2
Georgia Bonded	.9	2.11	1.9	2.37	4.5	5	1.5
Ga Gulf	NA	NC	NA	NC	NA	NA	NA
Grace W R	4.1	1.12	4.6	3.24	14.9	95	1.4
Hercules Inc	-3.3	.88	-2.9	1.93	-5.6	0	1.7
Immucor Inc	15.8	.71	11.2	1.04	11.7	0	19.8
Imperial Chem	6.9	1.29	8.9	2.38	21.2	41	1.6
Monsanto Co	6.9	1.01	7.4	2.17	16.5	37	1.7
Oil Dri Cp	.4	1.36	9.4	1.54	14.5	33	2.7
Pacer Tech	NM	NC	NC	NC	.0	77	1.3
Portage Ind		1.50	.6	2.33	1.4	77	1.1
Publicker Ind	-25.0	.25	-6.2	.00	-17.3		15.2
Quantum Chemical	7.0	.84	5.9	2.79	NS	-1371	1.7
Regal Intl Inc	-21.1	.69	-14.6	NM	NM	12	.7
Rohm & Haas	6.6	1.09	7.2	1.88	13.5	27	1.8
Stepan Co	2.4	1.63	3.9	3.05	11.9	97	1.8
Sterling Chemicals	8.8	1.40	12.3	2.98	36.7	60	1.5

Shareholdings

Company	Market Value $Mil	Latest Shares Outstanding 000	Held by Banks-Funds 000	Insider Net Trading 000	Short Interest Ratio Days	Fiscal Year Ends Mo
Ind. Group	88,439	2,239,637	915,373	+146	1.1	--
Aceto Cp	51	3,909	771	-3	.0	06
Advanced Polymer	59	9,469	3,119	0	.0	12
Air Prods & Chem	3,129	55,388	38,749	0	1.2	09
American Cyanamid	5,482	95,550	51,936	-1	.5	12
Aquanautics Cp	53	16,308	210	0	.0	06
Borden Chem	349	36,750	122	+0	.0	12
Cabot Corp	800	24,617	15,808	+0	.3	09
Calgon Carbon	932	20,035	8,555	0	.3	12
Concap Inc	4	2,729	712	+8	.0	12
Dow Chemical	15,429	269,500	133,626	+8	.0	12
Dupont	26,446	666,898	270,550	+112	2.9	12
Electrochem Ind	15	7,500	0	0	NA	12
Ethyl Corp	3,533	119,273	45,629	+21	1.5	12
Genex Cp	5	19,801	537	0	.0	12
Georgia Bonded	6	1,573	39	0	.0	06
Ga Gulf	233	24,523	0	0	NA	12
Grace W R	2,520	85,058	46,156	0	.7	12
Hercules Inc	1,553	46,539	33,335	-1	3.4	12
Immucor Inc	60	3,576	394	0	.0	05
Imperial Chem	13,553	170,750	18,138	0	.6	12
Monsanto Co	6,361	133,572	85,876	+3	1.0	12
Oil Dri Cp	159	6,980	1,390	0	.0	07
Pacer Tech	6	9,371	120	0	.0	06
Portage Ind	7	2,184	255	-1	.0	12
Publicker Ind	24	14,491	2,328	0	.0	12
Quantum Chemical	425	25,540	10,162	0	8.0	12
Regal Intl Inc	5	14,495	534	0	.0	12
Rohm & Haas	2,290	66,604	39,721	-1	2.5	12
Stepan Co	145	2,328	895	0	.0	12
Sterling Chemicals	385	55,055	11,630	0	.6	09

Ind. Group																												
Syntro Cp	20.0	44.4	50.0	6	-3.0s	466.0q	59.0q	3.29	NE	NE	NE	NC	-36	03-90	.00	.0	5.2	0	0	25	319	00-00-00	5.4	1.02	5.5	36.1	19.6	14	12	9,480	12	8.5	0	0	0.0	09
Union Carbide	-3.0	-3.0	.6	466.0q	59.0q	29.20	3.29	-54.2	-54.2	-40.9	NC	14	03-90	1.00	.0	4	-10	7	319	05-03-90	10.6	.65	6.9	18.5	124	1.8	2,725	141,578	1,742	11	6.5	+7	1.1	12
Wellman	127.2	127.2	69.2	59.0q	29.20	1.93	19.6	19.6	31.3	NC	17	03-90	.12	4	12	101	3	05-25-90	1.8	1.44	2.6	5.1	41	3.5	871	31,969	20,813	12	1.9	+0	6.5	12
Witco Cp	-1.1	-1.1	-5	29.20	1.37	-26.7	-26.7	-61.1	9	-1	03-90	1.72	4.8	48	811	22,527	13,827	12

Ind. Group																												
(Ind. Group)	-15.5	-10.0	-6.9	2,251.7	1.54	1.2	.8	12.1	23	14	03-90	.69	22	1	40	41	00-00-00	9.1	.88	8.0	24.9	71	1.5	24,366	793,246	256,605	+14	7.8	—
Airgas Inc	6.7	32.6	32.7	6.0f	1.00	-19.4	-39.4	-39.4	NC	12	03-90	.00	.0	0	0	0	00-00-00	2.0	1.10	2.2	12.0	350	2.5	108	5,610	1,895	+1	3.0	03
Am Cyanid	-1.0	-1.0	5.9	4.4q	.84	-73.3	-6.7	-6.7	NC	4	03-90	.44	4.3	0	46	31	05-21-90	3.5	1.03	3.6	8.6	85	3.2	53	5,166	1,041	+2	0.0	12
Balchem Cp	8.7	8.7	11.1	.30	.29	60.0	60.0	-14.7	NC	9	03-90	.03	.6	0	0	0	12-11-89	3.0	1.83	5.5	9.7	26	1.8	6	1,199	0	+0	0.0	12
Betz Laboratories	15.2	15.2	15.0	58.1q	3.67	16.5	16.5	12.2	10	13	03-90	2.16	2.9	10	50	54	07-20-90	4.2	1.45	15.7	31.8	54	2.6	1,070	14,214	9,930	+1	0.0	12
Bio Rad Lab A	21.0	21.0	20.9	10.5q	1.38	11.9	11.9	9.5	29	15	03-90	.00	.0	0	0	0	00-00-00	1.36	5.7	15.2	51	1.7	131	5,785	1,306	+1	0.0	12
Bio Rad Labs	NA	NA	NA	NA	NA	NA	NA	NA	NA	NC	NC	00-00	.00	.0	NA	NA	NA	NA	NA	NA	NA	NA	NA	NA	40	1,925	53	+12	NA	NA
Cambrex	11.6	11.6	10.6	3.8q	.71	48.5	48.5	-40.8	3	3	03-90	.15	1.8	8	0	0	06-11-86	2.8	1.47	3.0	4.4	26	4.6	43	5,321	4,511	+8	0.0	12
Chemdesign Cp	6.1	6.1	11.1	7.0q	.81	38.5	38.5	58.8	17	17	03-90	.00	.0	0	0	0	05-04-90	17.5	1.33	7.5	16.8	6	3.3	90	8,590	2,619	-0	0.0	12
Chemed Cp	1.4	1.4	9.3	2.5q	2.45	-28.1	-28.1	1.2	-1	4	03-90	1.96	6.8	4	70	59	05-25-90	4.2	2.77	12.6	20.8	71	1.7	297	10,273	6,301	-0	0.0	12
Crompt & Knwl	7.5	7.5	12.4	26.1q	2.11	24.4	24.4	45.5	46	16	03-90	.84	2.0	14	29	40	04-30-90	7.2	2.20	12.0	26.4	42	1.8	495	11,714	5,698	-2	0.0	12
Detrex Chemical	-7.6	-7.6	-4.6	-.70	-.42	3.6	3.6	-100.0	NC	-7	03-90	1.20	5.6	NE	NE	22	06-08-90	-.7	1.64	-1.1	-1.8	15	2.2	34	1,580	669	0	0.0	11
Dexter Cp	5.6	5.6	2.9	41.6q	1.68	-10.9	-10.9	20.0	7	6	03-90	.88	3.7	11	46	44	06-11-90	4.8	2.13	6.0	12.8	40	2.3	582	24,761	13,322	+0	2.0	12
Ecogen Inc	.0	.0	-250.0	-8.3q	-1.23	NE	NE	NE	NC	10	03-90	.00	.0	0	0	0	00-00-00	NM	NC	NC	NM	6	5.2	18	6,823	1,740	-0	0.0	12
Ferro Corp	3.0	3.0	5.1	43.3q	1.91	-56.7	-56.7	-17.7	32	10	03-90	.64	2.5q	8	27	30	05-09-90	4.0	2.25	6.5	14.6	43	1.9	498	19,546	7,973	+0	1.6	12
Flamemaster Cp	60.0	35.0	-20.0	-.56	.24	120.0	166.7	-4.0	NC	-7	03-90	.10	2.0	0	43	6	04-04-90	12.5	1.07	11.4	12.2	14	9.3	19	1,912	13	0	0.0	09
Fuller H B Co	4.3	3.3	4.6	16.8q	1.78	33.3	19.7	-2.2	4	-6	05-90	.60	2.2	15	35	22	04-24-90	2.2	2.43	3.7	9.0	54	1.8	255	9,265	3,960	0	0.0	11
Grt Lakes Ch	67.2	67.2	55.8	128.6q	3.65	12.6	12.6	15.2	32	19	06-90	.44	.7	16	11	15	06-25-90	14.3	1.86	11.7	21.8	19	2.1	2,207	34,826	23,876	+0	2.0	12
Hawkins Chem	51.9	35.0	18.1	3.1s	.41	42.9	12.5	64.0	21	14	03-90	.08	1.8p	0	28	23	03-26-90	6.0	2.13	12.8	17.9	0	2.5	34	7,548	314	-6	0.0	09
Huntingdon Intl	37.2	29.9	31.8	21.6q	.26	150.0	42.9	52.9	16	-1	03-90	.27	.8p	11	74	50	06-11-90	14.5	1.12	16.2	32.5	41	1.6	579	17,762	7,398	0	2.0	09
Intl Flav Frag	6.3	6.3	4.8	141.7q	3.73	7.9	7.9	7.8	8	8	06-20-90	2.16	3.1	12	53	0	06-29-90	16.0	2.01	14.6	18.5	0	5.2	2,635	38,054	7,615	+0	2.1	12
Ivax Cp	6.4	6.4	3.2	-7.6q	-.45	NE	NE	NE	NC	8	05-08-87	.00	.0	0	0	0	06-04-90	-11.9	.91	-10.2	-13.8	16	3.1	213	17,378	700	-4	20.7	12
Kinark Cp	20.3	20.3	17.8	-4.4q	-1.23	125.0	125.0	-100.0	-51	-14	00-00-00	.00	.0	0	0	0	00-00-00	-13.3	2.96	-17.1	-50.6	141	1.5	20	3,543	370	+1	0.0	12
Lawter Int	12.7	12.7	8.5	20.3q	.84	14.3	14.3	-4.5	9	9	05-09-90	.52	3.7	5	64	84	05-09-90	14.5	1.53	15.1	23.1	6	4.0	341	24,156	7,130	0	2.6	12
LeaRonal Inc	-2.6	-10.4	-10.1	10.2f	1.15	-30.6	-30.6	-6.5	13	8	05-21-90	.48	3.1	17	42	42	05-21-90	7.2	1.61	11.6	14.4	3	5.7	134	8,809	3,909	+0	5.5	02
Loctite Cp	15.1	10.4	10.0	59.9n	3.31	10.1	10.1	15.7	25	17	06-04-90	1.20	2.0	11	17	25	06-04-90	12.2	1.57	16.6	26.1	16	2.9	1,086	18,211	7,231	+0	0.0	06
Lubrizol Corp	3.5	3.5	5.5	92.4q	2.50	-2.4	-2.4	-30.7	13	6	06-11-90	1.44	3.5	8	55	55	06-11-90	7.5	1.45	9.6	13.9	8	3.0	1,531	37,008	23,544	-4	1.6	06
MacDermid Inc	-1.5	3.6	4.1	5.3f	1.49	75.8	-19.5	-19.5	3	7	06-11-90	.60	2.9	-1	30	34	06-11-90	11.3	2.13	11.3	11.3	13	1.3	75	3,565	1,455	0	0.0	03
Melamine Chem	-11.4	-6.7	-2.5	7.4n	1.34	53.1	16.9	4.7	20	9	05-14-90	.24	1.7	5	194	0	05-14-90	19.0	1.11	21.1	24.5	0	3.2	3,523	210,351	1,286	0	0.0	12
Montedison	-56.7	-56.7	-31.1	987.9s	.09	-100.0	-100.0	-35.7	-106	8	11-18-88	.33	2.0	17	0	114	11-18-88	13.4	5.96	6.7	39.9	155	1.1	2,103	47,927	85	+274.2	12
Morton Intl	25.3	13.0	11.7	121.9n	2.54	57.7	33.1	NC	11	9	05-24-90	.88	1.9	11	45	56	06-14-90	11.3	1.52	13.3	13.5	9	1.9	2,044	36,100	22,427	+0	0.0	06
Nalco Chem	14.1	14.1	9.7	124.5q	3.11	15.4	15.4	14.3	15	15	06-14-90	1.48	2.6	2	18	26	05-25-90	6.3	1.18	10.7	28.1	48	2.3	465	8,488	23,483	-0	1.1	12
NCH Corp	6.1	11.2	11.1	39.8f	4.69	1.9	1.9	15.5	16	1	04-90	.88	1.6	0	0	0	04-16-90	6.3	1.83	10.7	19.6	9	2.7	220	6,428	938	-0	0.0	04
Novellus Systs	44.8	44.8	86.6	12.3q	1.85	30.6	30.6	13.3	31	31	03-90	.00	.0	0	0	0	00-00-00	22.0	1.27	24.4	31.1	37	4.5	16	2,524	876	0	0.0	12
Nuclear Metals	-17.0	-13.2	2	1.6q	.63	-65.7	-65.7	-21.3	-19	3	02-23-90	.10	1.5	0	0	4	02-23-90	3.4	1.76	3.3	3.7	1	4.1	272	11,335	319	0	0.9	09
Petrolite Corp	1.0	.0	-6	9.1s	.80	60.0	60.0	-9.1	-2	-88	11-89	1.12	4.7	0	0	90	06-29-90	3.1	1.50	3.8	5.7	0	2.1	2	11,515	1,935	-0	0.0	10
Probex Intl	.0	.0	.0	-.7s	-.06	NE	NE	NE	15	10	03-90	.00	.0	1	178	0	11-89	NC	NC	-87.5	543	NC	3.0	169	543	05	12
Quaker Chemical	8.6	8.6	8.7	13.1q	2.08	11.8	11.8	11.2	15	10	03-90	.68	2.5	12	30	31	04-16-90	7.0	1.43	10.0	14.5	6	2.7	169	6,315	798	0	0.0	12

(continued)

Company	Rev Last Qtr %	Rev FY to Date %	Rev Last 12 Mos %	Earn Last 12 Mos $Mil	EPS Last 12 Mos $	EPS Last Qtr %	EPS FY to Date %	EPS Last 12 Mos %	Earn 5-Yr Growth %	Par Growth %	Date of Report	Div Amt $	Div Yield %	Div 5-Yr Growth %	Payout Last FY %	Payout Last 5 Yrs %	Last X-Dvd Date	Profit Margin %	Asset Turnover	Return on Total Assets %	Leverage Ratio	Return on Equity %	Debt to Equity %	Current Ratio	Mkt Value $Mil	Latest Shares Outstanding 000	Held by Banks-Funds 000	Insider Net Trading 000	Short Int Ratio Days	Fiscal Yr Ends Mo
Specialty Chemicals (Continued)																														
Scott's Liq Gld	2.9	2.9	12.0	.2q	.02	NE	NE	-66.7	NC	6	03-90	.00	.0	0	0	0	00-00-00	.7	1.86	1.3	4.54	5.9	147	1.1	6	9,063	145	0	0.0	12
Sigma-Aldrich	28.7	26.7	21.1	66.4q	2.68	14.1	14.1	13.1	23	19	03-90	.40	.6	16	14	15	05-25-90	14.2	.99	14.1	1.57	22.2	21	2.9	1,677	24,759	10,802	0	0.0	12
Stake Tech Ltd	.0	166.7	.0	-1.1f	-.13	NE	NE	NE	NC	-36	12-89	.00	.0	0	0	0	00-00-00	NM	NC	NC	NC	-35.5	23	3.2	5	6,346	296	0	0.0	06
Thiokol Inc	-2.1	-3.8	29.4	33.7n	1.74	134.8	118.8	NC	NC	12	03-90	.80	2.6	0	245	245	05-24-90	3.0	1.53	4.6	3.09	14.2	93	3.2	223	19,178	9,512	0	0.3	06
Univar Co	.7	.7	2.7	22.5q	1.27	18.5	18.5	7.6	12	15	05-90	.30	2.1b	-8	25	29	08-07-90	1.6	3.25	5.2	3.77	19.6	90	1.3	245	17,515	3,787	0	0.0	02
Vista Chem	-7.4	-9.3	-4.3	86.6s	7.17	-30.1	-32.7	-10.6	NC	0	03-90	1.80	4.6	0	21	12	05-23-90	11.7	1.31	15.3	.00	NS	-340	1.5	418	10,581	6,346	+1	31.8	09
WD Forty Co	9.8	4.1	6.1	14.8n	1.95	-17.5	-9.4	1.0	10	5	05-90	1.72	5.5	16	77	79	07-03-90	17.2	1.94	33.3	1.18	39.2	0	6.1	238	7,554	1,912	0	0.0	08
Whittaker Cp	3.4	-8.9	-44.6	6.1s	.74	-100.0	-100.0	-83.7	NC	0	04-90	.00	.0	6	6	22	00-00-00	3.0	.50	1.5	.00	NS	-423	.9	79	7,273	2,552	0	0.0	10
Ind. Group	-.2	-.3	.7	410.8	2.48	-68.5	-63.4	-41.0	12	9	---	.88	3.2	0	23	23	---	2.7	1.37	3.7	3.65	13.5	121	1.5	4,534	165,406	72,547	+189	2.9	--
Tires and Inner Tubes																														
Bandag Inc	11.7	11.7	7.8	76.1q	5.24	1.9	9.2	9.2	18	29	03-90	1.00	1.2	11	17	19	06-14-90	14.1	1.55	21.9	1.63	35.8	4	2.1	1,227	14,474	7,163	0	2.0	12
Big O Tires	6.1	6.1	14.5	1.4q	.09	NC	-10.0	-10.0	NC	5	03-90	.00	.0	0	0	0	00-00-00	1.3	1.69	2.2	2.14	4.7	47	2.1	19	17,556	387	+201	0.0	12
Cooper Tire	6.7	6.7	12.3	61.6q	3.01	34.0	38.7	38.7	23	18	03-90	.36	1.0	13	12	15	05-25-90	7.0	1.69	11.8	1.69	19.9	21	2.5	727	20,565	9,588	0	0.2	12
Danaher	-7.4	-7.4	-.6	60.3q	2.56	-2.1	51.5	51.5	84	32	03-90	.00	.0	0	0	0	09-09-87	8.2	1.45	11.9	2.65	31.5	75	1.2	463	23,273	4,145	0	9.6	12
GenCorp	-13.3	-17.8	-8.6	100.0s	3.14	-79.6	-88.8	-47.1	39	52	05-90	.60	5.3	1	7	12	04-25-90	5.7	1.39	7.9	8.16	64.5	320	1.3	357	31,731	17,089	-14	2.6	11
Goodyear Tire	1.8	1.8	1.0	111.4q	1.93	-79.6	-82.3	-68.3	5	0	03-90	1.80	6.1	7	55	31	05-10-90	1.0	1.30	1.3	4.00	5.2	138	1.5	1,741	57,807	34,196	+2	3.2	12
Ind. Group	-3.4	-.2	-.6	590.1	1.34	-30.2	-33.0	-29.6	29	9	---	.71	3.1	0	41	24	---	6.1	1.21	7.4	2.54	18.8	80	2.1	9,960	432,603	91,768	+255	3.4	--
Rubber and Plastic Products																														
Action Inds	-4.5	-.1	.0	.0q	.00	-100.0	-100.0	-100.0	NC	NC	03-90	.00	.0	0	0	0	05-26-87	NC	NC	NC	NC	.0	65	1.8	18	5,531	1,134	0	0.1	06
AEP Inds	-14.1	-10.2	.0	5.6s	1.19	3.7	8.3	25.3	17	17	04-90	.00	.0	0	0	0	12-08-89	4.9	1.73	8.5	2.05	17.4	52	3.0	67	4,731	1,067	0	0.0	10
Agristar Inc	.0	.0	.0	-1.4f	-.13	NC	NC	NC	12	-45	12-89	.00	.0	0	0	0	00-00-00	NC	NC	NC	NC	-45.2	0	26.0	14	12,418	0	0	0.0	12
Alpine Group Inc	10.0	30.3	9.0	-10.7n	-2.38	NE	NE	NE	NC	NC	01-90	.00	.0	0	0	0	00-00-00	-44.6	.44	-19.6	.00	NS	-580	1.3	12	5,800	1,044	0	23.8	04
Am Biltrite	-.5	-.5	-.6	.1q	.04	-33.3	-33.3	-98.4	-27	-1	03-90	.15	1.0	94	11	11	06-18-90	.1	1.00	.1	3.00	.3	60	1.9	30	1,921	426	0	0.0	12
Arco Chem	-2.0	-2.0	-5.9	371.0q	3.86	-29.8	-29.8	-24.8	NC	8	03-90	2.50	6.1	0	50	18	04-30-90	14.0	1.00	14.0	1.66	23.3	25	2.1	3,907	95,882	9,526	-1	1.3	12
Atlantis Grp	-10.4	-10.4	13.0	.0s	.05	NE	-88.1	-88.1	NC	2	03-90	.00	.0	0	0	0	03-05-90	.1	1.00	.1	22.00	2.2	996	1.9	19	6,860	59	+31	6.9	12
Bailey Corp	-35.2	-25.0	-7.8	.0s	-.01	-100.0	-100.0	-100.0	NC	0	01-90	.00	.0	0	0	0	01-00-00	.6	NC	NC	NC	NC	147	1.2	4	3,744	150	0	0.0	07
Bamberger Poly	-14.1	-14.1	-17.6	1.0q	.30	NE	NE	-45.5	NC	7	03-90	.00	.0	0	0	0	08-04-88	.6	2.50	1.5	4.33	6.5	129	1.8	9	3,046	266	0	0.0	12
Buffton Co	-19.9	-14.5	1.9	-6.3s	-1.59	-100.0	-100.0	-100.0	NC	-33	03-90	.00	.0	0	0	0	10-03-85	-6.1	1.54	-9.4	3.51	-33.0	135	2.1	6	3,912	206	0	0.0	06

Caltetics Cp	266.7	207.4	125.0	.5n	.16	200.0	133.3	128.6	NC	22	03-90	.00	.0	0	0	0	00-00-00	21.7	1.13	19.2	3.43	5.6	.3	11	2,714	0	0	.00	06
Carlisle Cos	5.3	5.3	-1.7	25.0q	3.09	-32.9	-32.9	33.8	0	7	03-90	1.20	3.3	3	35	44	05-14-90	12.0	1.82	7.4	1.64	4.5	NA	232	8,063	-531	-3	.00	12
Chariot Grp	-39.2	-39.2	-36.8	-.7q	-.26	-100.0	-100.0	-100.0	NC	-7	03-90	.00	.0	0	NE	32	07-11-89	-6.9	1.60	-4.3	.74	-5.8	NA	4	2,501	39	0	.00	12
Costar Cp	60.3	32.1	33.3	2.11	.76	70.0	15.2	15.2	NC	7	11-89	.00	.0	0	0	0	09-19-88	6.5	1.48	4.4	.76	5.8	NA	57	2,554	76	0	.00	11
CPC Rexcel	8.3	8.3	3.4	-1.6i	-.36	NC	NC	-100.0	NC	-11	03-90	.00	.0	0	0	0	00-00-00	-11.1	3.17	-3.5	1.30	-2.7	NA	12	4,400	529	0	.00	12
ESSEF Cp	18.4	39.5	29.7	.4s	.08	-100.0	NE	NE	NC	1	03-90	.00	.0	0	NA	0	00-00-00	1.2	3.00	.4	1.33	.3	13	4,859	-231	-28	NA	09
Fel Brands	NA	NA	NA	NA	NA	NA	NA	NA	NC	0	00-00	.04	.1	12	NA	0	06-25-90	NA	NC	NA	NA	NA	621	21,616	1,525	-330	NA	NA
Furon Co	30.2	37.1	35.3	8.3n	1.22	-15.8	-21.3	-3.2	9	12	10-89	.24	1.3	0	13	17	06-11-90	14.8	2.96	5.0	1.92	2.6	120	6,528	0	0	.00	12
Intek Diversified	-8.0	-8.0	10.0	.6q	.19	-100.0	-100.0	-20.8	NC	10	03-90	.00	.0	0	0	0	00-00-00	9.7	1.31	7.4	1.35	5.5	2	2,895	32	0	.00	12
Jasun Grp	-26.2	-28.5	-38.1	-27.8	-.05	NE	NE	NE	NC	0	03-90	.00	.0	0	0	0	03-01-89	NS	.00	-9.4	.85	-11.0	20	3,049	312	0	.00	09
Kleer-Vu Ind	-2.2	-2.2	5.8	-1.3q	-.14	NE	-99.9	-99.9	NC	-54	03-90	.00	.0	0	NE	NE	12-16-85	-54.2	6.63	-8.3	1.15	-7.2	3	7,836	463	-94	NA	12
Lexington Prec	-217.8	-67.9	.0	.0*	-.37	NE	NE	33.8	0	0	03-90	.00	.0	0	0	0	00-00-00	.0	NC	.0	NC	.0	7	4,049	425	0	.00	08
Mark IV	3.4	3.4	-1.1	62.2q	4.08	24.3	24.3	226.4	61	37	05-90	.03	.28	11	26	0	06-15-90	37.7	5.16	7.3	.99	7.4	190	14,076	243	+678	30.6	02
O'Sullivan	-17.4	-17.4	-2.8	14.1q	.86	-41.4	-41.4	-21.1	10	11	03-90	.28	2.8b	11	0	26	06-11-90	15.6	1.56	10.0	1.47	6.8	167	16,486	827	0	.00	12
Plymouth Rubb A	5.6	5.6	11.6	.50	.32	175.0	175.0	NE	-6	0	02-90	.00	.0	3	0	0	00-00-00	NS	.00	2.3	2.30	1.0	4	1,659	0	+3	.00	12
Plymouth Rubber B	NA	NA	NA	NA	NA	NA	NA	NA	NC	NC	02-90	.00	.0	NA	NA	NA	00-00-00	NA	NC	NA	NC	NC	2	839	0	0	NA	03
Polymerix Inc	.0	100.0	.0	-3.4n	-.77	NE	NE	-100.0	0	0	12-89	.00	.0	0	0	0	00-00-06	.7	NC	.0	NC	NC	10	4,392	3	0	.00	08
PVC Container	-3.9	-4.6	-3.3	.4f	.07	-36.4	-36.4	-36.4	6	6	06-89	.03	.0	0	0	0	00-00-00	6.0	3.00	2.0	1.43	1.4	3	6,245	0	0	.00	06
Rexene Cp	-25.0	-25.0	-4.0	-14.6q	-.46	-98.7	-98.7	-21.1	10	0	03-90	.28	.0	11	2438	26	09-29-89	NS	.00	-2.6	1.00	-2.6	85	31,000	810	0	68.8	12
Rogak Corp	-.5	-.5	2.1	.8q	.22	-16.7	-16.7	-71.8	-6	3	02-90	.00	.0	0	0	0	06-09-89	3.4	3.09	1.1	1.22	.9	27	3,409	497	0	.00	12
Rospatch Cp	-10.2	-10.2	21.4	-16.1q	-6.36	-81.8	-81.8	-100.0	NC	-51	03-90	.00	.0	NA	NA	NE	01-09-87	-51.4	1.67	-30.7	1.30	-23.7	16	2,527	665	0	.00	12
Rubbermaid	3.0	3.0	9.1	120.2q	1.63	12.5	12.5	16.4	18	14	03-90	.52	1.3	18	29	28	04-13-90	20.1	1.53	13.1	1.47	8.9	2,993	73,664	34,222	-4	5.6	12
Schulman, A Inc	6.0	1.2	-.1	22.3t	2.42	11.5	11.5	9.5	24	16	02-90	.44	1.0	20	17	16	04-18-90	19.5	1.56	12.5	2.45	5.1	570	13,403	246	+2	4.5	08
Sealed Air	6.0	6.0	9.2	2.9q	.32	-63.6	-63.6	-90.0	NC	0	02-90	.00	.0	0	2884	0	00-00-00	NS	.00	1.3	1.86	.7	241	8,327	825	+1	.00	12
Selfix Inc	21.4	14.2	19.2	2.3h	2.30	125.0	-3.6	-8.6	NC	-15	02-90	.00	.0	27	18	219	09-25-89	14.5	1.59	9.1	1.23	7.4	29	3,432	710	0	.00	05
San Coast Plastics	.0	9.6	10.7	.2r	.00	-100.0	NE	NE	NC	NC	03-90	.00	.0	0	0	0	00-00-00	3.2	6.40	.5	1.67	14.6	6	15,059	372	0	.00	06
Synetic Inc	-5.1	2.9	9.0	3.5n	.55	10.5	8.1	NC	11	11	03-90	.00	.0	0	0	0	00-00-00	10.8	1.24	8.7	.60	5.8	118	7,070	534	0	.00	06
Tuscarora Plastics	11.4	15.3	17.8	5.0n	1.64	10.5	13.9	18.0	15	15	05-90	.26	1.1	0	15	11	06-18-90	18.2	1.94	9.4	1.62	7.0	74	3,010	169	0	.00	08
Velcro Industries	8.6	6.8	6.3	7.1s	2.38	328.6	69.8	87.4	12	12	05-90	.00	.0	0	0	44	06-16-88	12.3	2.05	6.0	.86	7.0	63	3,004	198	0	.00	08
Versa Technol	5.5	10.9	10.4	6.0f	1.02	.0	-4.7	-4.7	-3	20	03-90	.15	1.0b	27	18	20	04-24-90	22.9	1.29	17.8	1.58	11.3	87	5,918	2,579	0	.00	03
Voplex Cp	-10.6	-10.6	-9.2	-.5q	-.18	NE	NE	-100.0	NC	-11	03-90	.40	7.4	3	NE	NE	04-27-90	-3.3	2.20	-1.5	2.14	-.7	14	2,668	515	0	.00	12
Vulcan Corp	-13.8	-13.8	8.2	2.0q	1.38	-96.7	-96.7	318.2	NC	5	03-90	.80	3.8b	5	63	100	05-21-90	11.2	1.27	8.8	1.01	8.7	32	1,506	313	0	.00	12

Source: Media General Financial Services, Richmond, VA.

Trends and Forecasts: Telephone and Telegraph Apparatus (SIC 3661)
(in millions of dollars except as noted)

Item	1987[1]	1988[2]	1989[3]	1990[4]	Percent Change		
					1987–88	1988–89	1989–90
Industry Data							
Value of shipments[5]	17,456	17,329	17,989	—	-0.7	3.8	—
Value of shipments (1987$)	17,456	17,277	17,585	17,955	-1.0	1.8	2.1
Total employment (000)	111	106	100	96.0	-4.5	-5.7	-4.0
Production workers (000)	57.9	56.8	54.0	52.1	-1.9	-4.9	-3.5
Average hourly earnings ($)	12.25	12.62	12.69	—	3.0	0.6	—
Product Data							
Value of shipments[6]	16,349	16,177	16,466	—	-1.1	1.8	—
Value of shipments (1987$)	16,349	16,129	16,096	16,812	-1.3	-0.2	4.4
Trade Data							
Value of imports	2,689	3,076	3,476	—	14.4	13.0	—
Import/new supply ratio[7]	0.141	0.159	0.171	—	12.8	7.5	—
Value of exports	946	1,312	1,666	—	38.7	27.0	—
Export/shipments ratio	0.058	0.081	0.099	—	39.7	22.2	—

[1]Industry and product data are preliminary. Trade data are adjusted to conform to the 1987 SIC.

[2]Estimated, except for exports and imports.

[3]Estimated.

[4]Forecast.

[5]Value of all products and services sold by establishments in the telephone and telegraph apparatus industry.

[6]Value of products classified in the telephone and telegraph apparatus industry produced by all industries.

[7]New supply is imports plus corresponding product shipments.

SOURCE: U.S. Department of Commerce: Bureau of the Census; International Trade Administration (ITA). Estimates and forecasts by ITA.

Source: *U.S. Industrial Outlook 1990*, U.S. Department of Commerce.

STOCKS by INDUSTRY

MEDIA GENERAL FINANCIAL SERVICES

Communications

Company	Rev Last Qtr %	Rev FY to Date %	Rev Last 12 Mos %	Rev Last 12 Mos $Mil	EPS Last 12 Mos $	EPS Pct Chg Last Qtr %	EPS Pct Chg FY to Date %	EPS Pct Chg Last 12 Mos %	EPS 5-Yr Growth %	Par Growth %	Date of Report	Div Amt $	Div Yield %	Div 5-Yr Growth %	Payout Last FY %	Payout Last 5 Yrs %	Last X-Dvd Date	Profit Margin %	Asset Turn	Return Total Assets	Leverage Ratio	Return on Equity	Debt/Eq %	Curr Ratio	Market Value $Mil	Latest Shares Out 000	Held by Funds 000	Insider Net Trad 000	Short Int Ratio Days	FY Ends Mo
Ind. Group	10.1	8.6	9.7	18,899.7	2.11	-5.2	-2.0	39.0	15	5	---	1.41	3.7	1	51	64	---	8.7	.56	4.9	2.84	13.9	75	.9	358,546	9,396,395	G	+8808	1.3	---
ACC Cp	-11.9	-11.9	-5.0	1.6q	.49	75.0	75.0	96.0	8	11	03-90	.16	1.2	0	28	9	06-28-90	4.2	1.69	7.1	2.35	16.7	30	.8	43	3,191	125	+5	0.0	12
ACS Enterprise	14.3	14.3	.0	-1.2q	-.35	NE	NE	NE	NC	-48	03-90	.00	.0	0	0	0	00-00-00	-4.0	.40	-15.8	3.04	-48.0	156	1.6	6	3,299	21	0	0.0	12
ADC Telecommun	31.7	40.0	31.2	19.9s	1.51	20.0	48.1	25.8	27	18	04-90	.00	.0	0	0	0	10-28-87	6.6	1.60	13.8	1.30	18.0	4	3.2	305	13,278	6,099	+3	0.0	10
Advanced Telecom	67.8	87.0	87.0	25.3t	1.12	0	15.5	15.5	11	22	03-90	.00	.0	0	0	0	00-00-00	7.6	1.51	11.5	1.94	22.3	61	1.5	444	22,638	4,225	0	0.0	03
AIM Telephone Inc	-20.8	.4	.0	-6.2t	-1.14	-100.0	-100.0	-100.0	NC	-63	02-90	.00	.0	0	0	0	00-00-00	-12.9	.95	-12.3	5.09	-52.6	161	1.5	9	5,504	208	0	1.4	02
ALC Commun	-10.2	-10.2	-15.3	-25.6q	-2.32	NE	NE	NE	NC	0	03-90	.00	.0	0	0	0	00-00-00	-7.9	2.01	-15.9	.00	NS	-27	.3	9	13,735	3,731	0	0.0	12
ALLTEL Cp	17.3	17.3	17.8	157.2q	2.35	5.0	5.0	16.9	13	8	03-90	1.28	3.9	7	50	54	06-04-90	12.3	.54	6.6	2.70	17.8	90	1.0	2,192	66,426	9,886	0	0.9	06
American Film Tech	66.7	70.7	112.5	2.7h	.23	500.0	500.0	NC	82	80	03-90	.00	.0	0	0	0	00-00-00	15.9	2.21	35.1	2.33	81.8	0	NA	127	9,772	312	-30	0.0	06
Am Mobile Systs	.0	.0	.0	-7.0t	-1.13	NC	NC	NC	NC	0	06-89	.00	.0	0	0	0	00-00-00	NM	.95	NS	.00	NS	-850	.3	10	4,987	415	0	0.0	06
Am Tele & Telegr	2.7	2.7	2.4	2771.0q	2.57	12.7	12.7	NE	NC	11	03-90	1.32	3.4	-9	48	136	06-25-90	7.6	.97	7.4	2.95	21.8	64	1.2	41,925	1,088,962	249,209	+4	2.6	12
Ameritech Cp	4.7	4.7	3.4	1240.9q	4.60	.9	.9	.2	6	5	03-90	3.16	5.2	0	0	46	03-26-90	12.0	.53	6.3	2.56	16.1	66	.9	16,549	270,191	3,177	-0	3.2	12
Artel Comm Cp	-31.3	-31.3	37.5	.7q	.19	-90.0	-90.0	375.0	NC	14	12-88	.2	.0	0	0	0	00-00-00	6.4	1.55	9.9	1.36	13.5	19	3.5	19	3,677	1,205	0	0.0	12
BCE Inc	9.6	12.7	12.6	657.2h	2.10	-100.0	-18.9	-18.9	-6	-2	03-90	2.52	7.5	11	122	86	06-11-90	4.6	.41	1.9	4.21	8.0	73	.9	10,194	302,052	28,249	0	8.4	12
Bell Atlantic	2.2	2.2	4.4	1099.0q	2.76	7.1	7.1	-16.8	2	2	03-90	2.36	4.8b	11	79	64	07-03-90	9.5	.44	4.2	3.05	12.8	90	.7	19,824	399,476	8,546	0	4.5	12
BellSouth	4.7	4.7	3.6	1737.0q	3.61	7.3	7.3	5.2	4	3	03-90	2.68	5.2	12	70	63	07-05-90	11.3	.47	5.8	2.29	13.3	54	.9	25,058	481,879	1,867	+0	2.3	12
British Telecom	39.7	8.2	8.1	2476.3t	4.10	-31.6	-6.2	-6.2	18	6	00-00	2.61	4.9	0	46	44	07-27-90	12.3	.64	7.9	2.08	16.4	47	.7	31,990	605,020	3,958	0	0.0	03
C TEC	NA	NA	NA	4.1c	NA	NA	NA	NA	NC	NC	00-00	.27	1.2h	NA	NA	NA	05-26-89	NA	NA	NA	NC	NA	NA	NA	210	9,345	728	-15	NA	NA
CTEC Cp	34.6	34.6	20.6	1.1q	.06	-100.0	-100.0	-93.5	-16	-5	03-90	.31	1.5o	-6	56	44	05-26-89	.6	.33	.2	6.00	1.2	290	.6	350	17,061	2,524	0	0.0	12
Cable&Wireless	NA	NA	NA	NA	NA	NA	NA	NA	NA	NC	00-00	.18	.6	NA	NA	NA	12-15-89	NA	NA	NA	NC	NM	906	1.2	31,329	1,061,996	7,545	0	NA	NA
Cellcom Cp	98.8	104.2	127.0	-5.0s	-.42	-100.0	-100.0	NA	NC	NC	00-00	.00	.0	0	0	0	06-08-89	-4.6	-2.65	-12.2	.00	NM	54	.7	41	10,466	479	0	0.0	09
Cellular Commun ---◊	51.3	49.1	50.0	-17.4t	-.45	NE	NE	NE	NC	-6	12-89	.00	.0	0	0	0	07-07-88	-20.7	.22	-4.5	1.36	-6.1	21	1.4	1,354	40,717	3,994	0	0.0	12
Celrin	100.0	100.0	.0	-4.8s	-1.08	NE	NE	NE	NA	-37	03-90	.00	.0	NA	NA	NA	00-00-00	NM	NC	NC	NC	-36.9	658	6.2	78	4,546	2,001	0	0.0	09
Celutel Inc Cl A	NA	NA	NA	NA	NA	NA	NA	NA	NA	-6	00-00	.00	.0	NA	NA	NA	00-00-00	NM	NC	NC	NC	NA	NA	NA	646	46,950	4,229	-0	0.0	12
Centel Cp	12.3	12.3	9.2	19.4q	.20	NE	NE	-68.8	-46	-6	03-90	.85	2.5	19	1200	104	07-02-90	1.6	.38	.6	3.00	1.8	127	.9	2,902	83,804	6,815	-1	6.0	12
Centex Telemgmt	36.6	36.6	40.6	7.0q	.78	40.0	40.0	32.2	NC	23	03-90	.00	.0	0	0	0	00-00-00	8.6	1.97	16.9	1.36	23.0	0	3.5	232	9,454	479	0	0.0	12

(continued)

Communications (Continued)

Company	Rev % Last Qtr	Rev % FY to Date	Rev % Last 12 Mos	Rev Last 12 Mos $Mill	Earn Last 12 Mos $Mill	EPS Last 12 Mos $	EPS % Last Qtr	EPS % FY to Date	EPS % Last 12 Mos	Par Growth Rate	5-Yr Growth Rate	Date of Report	Div Amt	Div Yield	Div 5-Yr Growth	Payout Last FY	Payout Last 5 Yrs	Last X-Dvd Date	Profit Margin	Asset Turnover	Return Total Assets	Leverage Ratio	Return on Equity	p/e	Debt to Equity %	Current Ratio	Market Value $Mill	Latest Shares Outstndng	Held by Banks Funds	Insider Net Trading	Short Int Ratio	Fiscal Yr End Mo
Century Tel	27.2	27.2	20.2	23.9q	.78	22.2	22.2	-8.2	4	NC	03-90	.42	1.5		55	55	05-29-90	10.6	.33	3.5	2.66	9.3		100	1.1	848	30,575	15,781	-36	3.2	12	
Checkpoint Sys	41.5	41.5	13.9	6.70	.73	NE	NE	284.2	21	-7	03-90	.00	.00		0	0	05-28-86	12.4	1.22	15.1	1.36	20.6		4	2.8	123	9,175	3,678	+10	0.0	12	
Cin Bell	-5	-5	68.2	88.1q	1.40	-25.6	-25.6	.7	8	16	03-90	.76	3.2	12	43	46	06-27-90	9.8	.65	6.4	2.67	17.1		70	.8	1,428	59,810	16,608	0	1.7	12	
Con Syst	42.3	42.3	68.2	-11.7q	-2.54	-100.0	-100.0	-100.0	16	NE	03-90	.00	.00		0	0	00-00-00	-11.0	3.35	-36.9	.00	NS		-92	.8	24	5,420	272	0	0.1	01	
Comcoa Inc	44.7	44.7	70.0	2.50	.49	171.4	171.4	390.0	81	NE	04-90	.00	.00		0	0	00-00-00	-4.9	2.51	12.3	6.55	80.6		342	.3	61	4,978	121	+3	0.0	01	
Commun Transmsn	-7.9	-9.8	16.1	-47.5n	-4.84	NE	NE	NE	0	NC	02-90	.00	.0		0	0	00-00-00	-12.0	.79	-9.5	.00	NM		5258	.6	13	10,402	3,286	0	0.0	05	
COMSAT	13.8	13.8	14.2	65.0q	3.47	13.5	13.5	.0	7	NC	05-08-90	1.32	4.0	0	39	122	05-08-90	15.3	.34	5.2	2.10	10.9		62	1.3	619	18,831	11,947	0	1.4	12	
Contel Cellular	96.1	96.1	65.9	-10.4q	-.11	-100.0	-100.0	.0	-8	NC	03-90	.00	.0		0	0	06-16-89	-13.3	.38	-5.0	1.60	-8.0		11	.4	1,849	99,944	7,870	-3	1.2	12	
Contel Cp	6.6	6.6	4.0	277.0q	1.74	-15.0	-15.0	-2.2	6	2	03-90	1.10	4.3b	5	61	71	06-09-90	8.8	.53	4.7	3.57	16.8		120	.6	4,050	157,264	89,120	0	1.0	12	
Digital Microwave	70.6	70.6	68.1	13.2q	1.07	-53.6	-53.6	12.6	25	NE	03-90	.00	.00		0	0	00-00-00	11.9	1.60	19.0	1.34	25.4			3.6	201	11,627	7,740	-86	0.0	06	
Eagle Telephonics	18.4	18.4	-13.6	.4n	-.37	NE	NE	NE	0	NC	01-90	.00	.00		0	0	00-00-00	-30.5	1.51	-46.0	.00	NM		3850	2.5	7	15,244	239	0	0.0	10	
Eicotel Inc	41.2	-13.6	-27.2	.4n	.10	NE	NE	NE	4	NC	12-89	.00	.0		0	24	05-15-87	2.5	.88	4.2	1.91	16.7		60	4.0	10	5,442	168	0	0.0	08	
Ericsson LM Tel	22.7	22.7	22.7	296.7n	9.39	78.0	78.5	78.5	13	0	05-07-90	1.97	.9		14	0	05-07-90	4.7	.96	4.5	3.71	16.7		19	1.8	9,148	40,975	2,507	0	0.0	12	
FamTel	-15.4	-12.2	-20.0	-2.4f	-.30	NE	NE	NE	7	NC	00-00-00	.00	.0		0	0	00-00-00	-60.0	1.43	-85.7	.00	NM		83	.1	2	7,980	0	0	0.0	12	
Gett Comm A	34.5	34.5	27.2	1.30	.88	.0	.0	-88.7	14	NE	03-90	.00	.0		0	0	00-00-00	2.3	1.17	2.7	5.19	14.0		251	1.1	35	12,612	1,348	0	0.0	12	
Graphic Scanning	129.9	6.6	-2.0	5.1q	.09	NE	NE	NE	3	NC	03-90	.00	.0		0	0	00-00-00	-50.9	.68	-34.4	.00	NM		105	1.1	303	32,337	20,272	-305	0.0	06	
GTE Cp	9.2	9.2	6.9	1443.3q	2.12	8.2	8.2	14.0	6	6	03-90	1.46	4.5	6	67	94	05-16-90	8.1	.56	4.5	4.04	18.2		137	1.0	21,387	660,603	353,348	-2	1.6	12	
Hong Kong Telec	15.8	15.8	17.4	466.3s	.64	-100.0	-100.0	-44.3	-33	NC	09-89	1.13	4.8		33	18	07-05-89	29.7	1.00	29.8	1.44	42.8		0	1.1	8,773	371,355	10,720	0	2.2	03	
IDB Comm Grp	43.5	43.5	127.5	1.4q	.30	-85.7	-85.7	1400.0	7	NC	03-90	.00	.0		0	0	00-00-00	2.1	.48	1.0	6.80	6.8		490	1.1	53	4,961	1,000	0	0.0	12	
Intellicall	159.0	159.0	170.2	5.1q	.88	60.0	60.0	51.7	10	NC	03-90	.00	.0		0	0	06-25-90	4.0	1.38	5.5	1.89	10.4		29	2.5	97	6,596	2,328	0	0.0	12	
Inter Tel	11.3	11.3	1.6	.7q	.09	NE	NE	NE	3	NC	12-89	.00	.0		0	0	00-00-00	1.1	1.36	1.5	2.27	3.4		42	1.5	11	8,017	329	0	0.0	12	
Intl Mobile Mach	433.3	433.3	75.0	-17.9q	-1.43	NE	NE	42.9	0	NC	05-15-90	.05	.1		0	0	05-15-90	NM	NC	9.8	3.17	31.1		9	1.0	85	14,535	1,159	+2	0.0	12	
Intl Telechrg	1.6	1.6	29.1	-6.5q	-.42	-100.0	-100.0	-60.0	-33	NC	03-90	.00	.0		0	0	00-00-00	-2.4	1.92	-4.6	7.13	-32.8		199	.6	30	14,947	3,107	-830	27.2	12	
LDDS s	43.2	43.2	69.0	5.1q	1.03	61.1	61.1	102.0	18	NC	03-90	.00	.0		0	0	08-14-89	4.3	.93	4.0	4.40	17.6		265	.8	123	4,904	210	0	0.0	12	
Linc Telecom	21.9	21.9	62.0	25.5q	1.52	9.1	9.1	4.1	9	31	03-90	.74	3.1	16	88	59	06-25-90	14.4	.58	8.4	1.98	16.6		36	1.3	396	16,490	4,997	0	0.0	12	
McCaw Cellular	66.6	66.6	62.0	-288.5f	-1.95	NE	NE	NE	-29	NC	12-89	.00	.0		0	0	00-00-00	-57.2	.17	-9.5	3.02	-28.7		173	4.5	3,961	163,328	43,637	0	0.0	12	
MCI Commun	20.5	20.5	23.1	621.0q	2.33	12.7	12.7	42.9	30	NC	05-15-90	.05	.1		0	16	05-15-90	9.2	1.07	9.8	3.17	31.1		112	.8	10,407	248,528	165,513	+2	0.0	12	
Metro-Tel Cp	-11.6	-11.6	-16.6	-.1n	.01	100.0	100.0	-50.0	4	NC	03-90	.00	.0		0	0	08-29-86	-48.0	1.00	2.0	1.90	3.8		42	3.7	2	2,004	25	0	0.0	06	
Millicom Inc ◆	95.9	95.9	98.5	-63.8q	-4.40	-100.0	-100.0	-100.0	0	NC	07-11-89	.00	.0		0	0	07-11-89	-48.0	.80	-38.2	1.46	16.2		183	1.5	297	15,213	4,482	0	0.0	12	
Network Equip	2.8	2.8	32.6	13.5f	.93	-19.1	-19.1	-19.1	16	NC	00-00-00	.00	.0		0	0	00-00-00	7.5	1.48	11.1	1.46	16.2		10	2.6	133	13,832	11,003	-19	1.3	03	
NW Telecom	16.0	16.0	32.1	6.5q	1.14	40.0	40.0	-30.1	24	11	03-90	.53	1.2b	11	45	43	07-06-90	10.8	.46	5.0	2.66	13.3		95	1.7	246	5,666	1,413	0	0.0	12	
NYNEX Cp	2.0	2.0	15.3	815.4q	4.12	1.4	1.4	-36.8	7	-3	03-90	4.56	5.5	12	106	65	06-25-90	6.1	.51	3.1	2.81	8.7		69	.8	16,206	197,028	72,654	0	1.5	12	
Ontelecom	-28.6	-28.6	3.5	-.4q	.00	-100.0	-100.0	-100.0	NC	NC	00-00-00	.00	.0		0	0	00-00-00	.8	2.50	-20.0	1.67	-33.3			2.0	2	3,290	33	0	0.0	12	
Pac Telecom	1.4	1.4	13.0	87.4q	2.27	97.3	97.3	47.4	21	6	03-90	1.16	3.9	6	53	67	05-14-90	13.3	.53	7.1	2.51	17.8		60	.7	1,152	38,395	2,371	+0	0.0	12	
Pac Teless	1.3	1.3	1.1	1187.0q	2.91	-14.5	-14.5	1.7	9	11	03-90	2.02	4.5	11	61	63	07-03-90	12.3	.46	5.6	2.68	15.0		68	.7	18,242	409,934	153,968	0	2.1	12	
Philip LD Tel	21.1	21.1	15.5	94.6f	1.93	13.6	13.6	-13.5	40	54	12-11-89	3.20	23.1	54	8	8	12-11-89	21.8	.39	8.5	2.79	23.7		133	1.5	616	44,400	4,924	0	0.5	12	
Racal Telecom	55.4	55.4	55.1	104.8n	1.05	75.0	75.0	75.0	-16	16	07-13-90	.56			0	0	07-13-90	25.9	.82	21.3	1.62	34.4		1	.8	5,020	80,000	12,369	0	7.4	03	
Reuters Hldg	9.0	9.0	7.3	296.4f	2.38	35.2	35.2	35.2	31	41	03-12-90	.73	1.1		23	34	03-12-90	15.2	1.22	18.5	2.39	44.2		5	.9	10,145	151,422	55,671	0	0.0	12	

Roch Tele	5.6	5.6	13.0	50.7q	1.90	-18.9	-18.9	-13.6	1	3	03-90	1.46	4.5	4	71	70	07-09-90	8.9	.54	2.69	12.9	86	1.2	771	24,002	8,233	0	0.3	12
Sothm N E Telcom	-1.4	-1.4	3.0	186.8q	3.00	-6.1	-6.1	16.7	9	6	03-90	1.76	5.3	7	66	65	06-19-90	11.2	.53	2.63	15.5	73	.9	2,061	61,520	19,226	0	5.4	12
Swm Bel	3.5	3.5	89.7	1101.8q	3.67	3.8	3.8	2.2	3	4	03-90	2.64	4.9	15	71	91	04-04-90	12.5	.42	2.54	13.2	65	.9	16,174	300,215	111,479	0	1.2	12
Synoptics Commun	106.2	106.2	89.7	11.7q	1.39	65.4	65.4	39.0	17	NC	03-90	.00	.0		0	0	00-00-00	12.6	1.09	1.25	17.1	5	5.8	466	8,814	4,331	-90	0.0	12
TEL EI	16.7	16.7	200.0	.0q	.00	NC	NC	NC	NC	NC	03-90	.00	.0		0	0	00-00-00	3.3	1.70	1.38	7.7	15	6.0	2	66,500	11	0	0.0	12
Telecom USA	29.6	29.6	34.2	35.7q	1.23	-6.3	-6.3	-3.1	NC	17	03-90	.00	.0	4	16	0	00-00-00	4.7	1.55	2.29	16.7	61	1.2	1,170	28,530	10,270	0	2.5	12
Telefonica	25.0	25.0	24.5	636.8q	6.54	-16.8	-16.8	144.9	NC	5	07-24-89	1.08	4.3	7	16	21	07-24-89	9.4	.33	1.94	6.0	62	.7	7,725	308,986	56,822	0	0.8	12
Telemundo Grp	10.2	10.2	14.4	-45.1q	-1.94	NE	NE	NE	-60	NC	03-90	.00	.0		0	0	00-00-00	-37.9	.30	5.34	-59.8	342	1.5	122	19,185	28,-17	0	4.8	12
Telephone Data	26.5	26.5	23.9	15.1q	.48	290.0	260.0	20.0	0	2	06-11-90	.28	.80	8	74	49	06-11-90	5.9	.34	2.15	4.3	72	1.6	1,068	29,257	18,176	+8198	4.8	09
Telephone Spec	33.3	36.4	50.0	.0s	.00	NE	NE	NE	NC	NC	03-90	.00	.0	8	0	0	00-00-00	3.3	NC	NC	.0	1	4.5	1	1,440	0	0	0.0	12
Telesphere Com	90.2	90.2	60.0	4.2q	.24	NE	NE	NE	0	0	03-90	.00	.0		0	0	00-00-00	1.9	2.74	.00	NS	-662	.7	89	17,808	3,-11	0	5.9	12
TIE Comm	-25.4	-25.4	-18.8	-69.8q	-2.16	NE	NE	NE	0	0	03-90	.00	.0		0	0	00-00-00	-33.7	1.14	.00	NM	17	1.4	28	34,625	2,-62	0	1.3	12
TVX Broadcast Grp	8.0	-13.5	-13.2	-29.4f	-4.03	NE	NE	NE	0	0	12-89	.00	.0		0	0	00-00-00	-22.4	.58	.00	NS	-91	1.4	37	7,311	1,-59	0	0.0	12
US West	1.4	1.4	2.7	1133.0q	2.69	-46.4	-46.4	-14.1	6	4	03-90	2.00	.0	11	61	60	07-16-90	11.7	.38	3.11	14.0	90	.7	13,406	373,682	147,00	-1	1.0	12
US West Nwwec	54.4	54.4	44.8	-12.8q	-.26	NE	NE	NE	-8	NC	03-90	5.6b	.0		0	0	00-00-00	-6.1	.89	2.31	-3.3	81	.9	1,715	50,810	7,200	0	0.0	12
Utd Artists A	51.5	51.5	22.1	-52.5q	-.53	NE	NE	NE	-7	NC	03-90	.00	.0		0	0	00-00-00	-3.9	.33	5.31	-6.9	0	NA	2,124	139,284	19,-53	0	0.0	12
Utd St Cell	63.4	63.4	114.2	-18.5q	-.66	NE	NE	NE	-23	NC	03-90	.00	.0		0	0	00-00-00	-41.1	.26	2.11	-22.6	11	.8	716	28,369	2574	0	1.0	12
Utd Telcom	14.6	14.6	4.0	394.1q	1.86	37.8	37.8	-30.6	9	1	06-04-90	1.00	.0		58	99	03-16-89	5.0	.80	4.75	4.0	180	.7	8,206	207,101	116,340	0	2.8	12
Vanguard Cellular	65.5	65.5	85.7	-6.7q	-.32	NE	NE	NE	-19	NC	03-90	.00	.0		0	0	00-00-00	-12.9	.26	5.70	-18.8	410	1.7	507	20,495	5580	0	0.0	12
Vertex Comm	51.7	55.8	42.8	1.8s	.52	16.7	22.7	6.1	13	NC	03-90	.00	.0		0	0	00-00-00	6.0	1.45	1.52	13.2	11	2.9	20	3,194	760	0	0.0	09
Viacom Inc	-21.1	-6.3		-.6f	-.28	NE	NE	NE	-30	NC	12-89	.00	.0		0	0	00-00-00	-10.0	.85	3.53	-30.0	0	NA	0	2,103	0	0	0.0	12
Video Jukebox	550.0	550.0	500.0	-1.9q	-.19	100.0	16.7	275.0	-54	NC	03-90	.00	.0		0	0	00-00-00	-31.7	.87	1.97	-54.3	0	1.2	59	9,385	1956	0	0.0	12
VTX Electronics	7.1	13.2	10.0	.3f	.15	100.0	100.0	275.0	6	NC	04-1087	2.00	.0		0	0	04-1087	.7	2.00	4.00	5.6	183	3.2	7	2,438	28	0	0.2	06
Westcott Comm	40.5	40.5	21.4	-.9q	-.14	-66.7	-66.7	-100.0	-5	NC	03-90	.00	.0		0	0	00-00-00	-5.3	.66	1.34	-4.7	18	4.1	89	7,772	1375	0	0.0	12
Wstn Union Co	-8.5	-8.5	-23.0	-50.2q	-1.90	NC	NC	NE	0	-8	09-10-84	.00	.0		0	0	09-10-84	-8.2	1.12	.00	NS	-107	.8	34	67,058	6398	0	7.5	12

Broadcasting

Ind. Group																												
Assoc Comm A	63.7	76.8	30.3	1,220.4	1.45	13.1	11.7	50.7	41	14	---	.19	.4	1	9	12	---	7.8	.65	3.08	15.7	114	2.2	33,941	774,391	135,693	+2427	3.1	--
Assoc Comm B	7.5	53.4	56.2	-8.2f	-.44	-100.0	NE	NE	NC	-46	02-01-89	.00	.0	NA	NA	NA	02-01-89	-32.8	.46	3.01	-45.8	134	1.4	289	9,101	2,566	+1	0.0	12
BHC Comm	NA	NA	NA	NA	NA	NA	NA	NA	NC	NC	02-01-89	.00	.0	NA	NA	NA	00-00-00	NA	NC	NC	NM	134	NA	286	9,303	2,600	-5	NA	12
Cap Cities/ABC	NA	NA	NA	NA	NA	NA	NA	NA	23	15	06-29-90	.00	.0	NA	NA	1	06-29-90	10.0	.80	NC	NC	51	3.2	1,392	29,300	568	0	NA	12
Carlton Comm	45.9	45.9	94.3	509.2a	1.59	-14.0	32.5	29.3	25	26	07-23-90	.44	.24	0	17	15	07-23-90	13.4	1.09	1.94	34.4	51	1.5	10,926	17,538	1,999	+0	3.1	09
CBS Inc	16.4	16.4	9.6	326.1q	12.66	51.1	51.1	10.4	38	9	05-17-90	4.40	2.2	7	38	29	05-17-90	10.6	.66	1.94	13.6	33	2.3	4,756	23,647	1,076	0	1.0	12
Chris-Craft	1822.1	525.6	525.0	473.3f	19.28	9763.2	2090.9	2090.9	NC	66	03-26-90	.00	.0	NE	NE	NE	03-26-90	30.2	.97	2.24	65.5	16	5.2	742	23,841	1,675	+125	10.1	12
Clear Channel	30.0	30.0	28.9	-.9q	-.15	NC	NC	-100.0	NC	-39	06-26-89	.00	.0	161	0	0	06-26-89	-1.8	.56	39.10	-39.1	3000	1.1	67	5,852	.178	+172	1.6	12
Fist News Net	125.2	84.1	102.7	5.9n	.31	100.0	116.7	NC	NC	16	00-00-00	.00	.0	0	0	0	00-00-00	.7	1.26	1.53	15.6	10	1.4	154	18,091	2,767	+172	0.0	06
Fst AmeriCable	100.0	100.0	200.0	-5.1q	-.09	NC	NC	NC	NC	NC	11-88	.00	.0	0	0	0	04-01-87	NM	NC	NC	NM	390	.6	6	50,517	67	0	0.0	08
Heritage Media	130.8	130.8	236.8	-30.1q	-.87	NE	NE	NE	-33	0	03-90	.00	.0	0	0	0	00-00-00	-15.7	.41	5.03	-32.7	310	.9	240	44,608	3,623	-5	0.1	12
Jacor Comm	4.3	4.3	6.8	1.10	1.10	NE	NE	NE	0	0	03-90	.00	.0	0	0	0	00-00-00	-15.4	.49	NC	NS	-1588	1.3	40	9,946	1,710	0	0.0	12
Jones Spacelink A	315.5	54.8	-7.1	-5.7n	-.09	NC	NC	NC	-21	-29	02-90	.00	.0	0	0	0	00-00-00	-4.9	.27	15.77	-20.5	1251	NA	84	61,173	168	0	0.0	05
Lin Broadcasting	16.6	16.6	19.2	-143.6q	-2.81	-100.0	-100.0	-100.0	NC	-29	03-90	.00	.0	0	0	0	04-01-87	-55.2	.39	1.36	-28.9	0	3.8	3,814	51,544	524	0	0.0	12
Midwest Comm	8.4	24.4	30.3	.6f	.25	NC	-40.0	-13.8	NC	5	03-90	.00	.0	NC	0	0	00-00-00	.3	3.00	5.67	5.1	5	1.1	9	3,013	237	0	0.0	06

(continued)

Source: Media General Financial Services, Richmond, VA.

Broadcasting (Continued)

Company	Revenue Pct. Change Last Qtr %	FY to Date %	Last 12 Mos %	Last 12 Mos $Mil	EPS Last 12 Mos $	EPS Pct Chg Last Qtr %	FY to Date %	Last 12 Mos %	5-Year Growth Rate %	Par Growth Rate %	Date of Report	Div Current Rate Amt $	Yield %	5-Year Growth Rate %	Payout Last FY %	Last 5 Yrs %	Last X-Dvd Date	Profit Margin %	Asset Turnover	Return on Total Assets	Leverage Ratio	Return on Equity	Debt to Equity %	Current Ratio	Market Value $Mil	Latest Shares Outstdng 000	Held by Banks-Funds 000	Insider Net Trading 000	Short Interest Ratio Days	Fiscal Year Ends Mo
Non-Invasive Mnt	500.0	200.0	.0	-.6	-.04	NE	NE	NC	NC	-46	04-90	.00	.0	0	0	0	00-00-00	-60.0	.57	-40.0	1.16	-46.2	0	7.0	29	20,457	89	0	0.0	07
Nostalgia Network	57.1	42.9	100.0	-2.5	-.44	NE	NE	NC	NC	0	09-89	.00	.0	0	0	0	00-00-00	-62.5	.80	-50.0	.00	NM	0	.3	7	5,763	2	+1244	0.0	12
Osborn Comm	3.9	-11.4	-13.6	-.9	-.16	-100.0	-100.0	-100.0	NC	-7	12-89	.00	.0	0	0	0	09-16-87	-4.7	.32	-1.5	4.47	-6.7	307	2.1	77	6,977	2,463	0	0.0	12
Outlet Comm	-16.0	-16.0	-13.5	-.7	-.10	-70.8	-70.8	-100.0	NC	-12	03-90	.00	.0	0	0	0	00-00-00	-.7	.43	-.3	40.33	-12.1	3067	.9	116	6,553	1,443	+4	0.0	12
Park Commun	-1.4	-1.4	1.2	18.7	.91	.0	.0	.0	6	10	03-90	.00	.0	0	0	0	09-18-89	11.5	.57	6.5	1.54	10.0	31	3.5	430	20,700	2,382	0	0.0	12
Pop Radio	276.9	238.5	260.0	1.2	.44	NE	NE	NE	NC	19	06-89	.00	.0	0	0	0	00-00-00	6.7	1.34	9.0	2.06	18.5	35	1.2	63	3,284	177	+190	0.0	06
Price Comm	-54.1	-33.4	-33.6	-50.1	-5.46	-100.0	-100.0	NE	NC	0	12-89	.00	.0	0	57	NE	06-27-89	-74.8	.34	-25.2	.00	NS	-200	2.7	32	9,230	2,555	0	56.1	12
QVC Network	207.2	207.2	170.1	-.7	-.07	-100.0	-100.0	-100.0	NC	0	04-90	.00	.0	0	0	0	12-23-89	-.1	1.00	-.1	3.00	-.3	191	1.3	187	15,106	2,098	+704	0.0	01
Sage Broadcasting	5.3	-4.8	12.5	-3.7	-.91	NE	NE	NE	NC	7	09-89	.00	.0	0	0	0	00-00-00	-41.1	.33	-13.6	.00	NM	1206	.8	7	4,001	36	0	0.0	12
Scripps Howard	5.3	5.3	7.4	22.4	2.18	77.8	77.8	29.0	NC	1	03-90	1.00	1.8	3	49	50	05-21-90	7.4	.53	3.9	3.51	13.7	146	1.6	589	10,328	1,129	0	0.0	12
Turner Bdct B	NA	NA	NA	NA	NA	NA	NA	NA	NA	NA	00-00	.00	.0	NA	NA	NA	00-00-00	NA	NA	NA	NC	NC	NA	NA	1,094	21,775	3,663	-1	NA	NA
Turner Bdct A	25.3	25.3	31.4	28.4	-.36	NE	NE	NC	NC	0	03-90	.00	.0	0	0	0	00-00-00	2.5	.52	1.3	.00	NS	-244	1.5	2,553	49,578	2,168	-1	2.0	12
Utd Television	10.7	10.7	5.8	63.5	5.80	663.8	663.8	663.8	NC	56	03-90	.00	.0	0	0	0	00-00-00	58.3	.53	31.1	1.80	56.1	0	2.3	373	10,902	3,891	+1	0.0	12
Viacom Inc	15.3	15.3	13.8	-102.6	-.96	-100.0	-100.0	-100.0	NC	-23	03-90	.00	.0	0	0	0	00-00-00	-6.9	.39	-2.7	8.33	-22.5	501	.8	2,895	106,732	14,404	0	4.9	12
Viacom Non-Vot B	NA	NA	NA	NA	NA	NA	NA	NA	NA	NC	00-00	.00	.0	NA	NA	NA	00-00-00	NA	NC	NA	NC	NA	NA	NA	1,348	53,400	0	0	NA	NA

Source: Media General Financial Services, Richmond, VA.

Computer Software and Data Processing

STOCKS by INDUSTRY

Computer Software, Data Processing

Company	Rev %Chg Last Qtr	Rev %Chg FY to Date	Rev %Chg Last 12 Mos	Rev Last 12 Mos $Mil	EPS Last 12 Mos $	EPS Last Qtr / %Chg	EPS %Chg FY to Date	EPS %Chg Last 12 Mos	EPS 5-Yr Growth	EPS Par Growth	Date of Report	Div Amt $	Div Yield %	Div 5-Yr Growth	Payout Last FY	Payout 5 Yrs	Last X-Dvd Date	Profit Margin %	Asset Turnover	Return on Total Assets %	Leverage Ratio	Return on Equity %	Debt to Equity %	Current Ratio	Market Value $Mil	Shares Outstndg 000	Held by Banks/Funds 000	Insider Net Trading 000	Short Int Ratio Days	Fiscal Yr Ends Mo
Ind. Group	17.6	24.4	22.4	1,808.8	.78	42.1	15.4	7.3	36	14	03-90	.13	.6	0	0	12	----	7.0	1.04	7.3	2.33	17.0	31	1.7	46,887	2,195,164	703,922	+330	2.1	--
Acxiom Cp	23.6	20.7	21.6	5.6	1.16	-4.8	36.5	36.5	23	17	03-90	.00	.0	0	0	15	03-24-90	6.2	1.45	9.0	1.88	16.9	40	1.8	89	4,695	1,305	0	0.0	03
Adobe Systems Inc	25.6	35.3	34.6	37.1s	1.71	-.0	23.9	34.6	NC	54	05-90	.24	.7	0	12	9	07-02-90	26.5	1.49	39.4	1.60	63.1	1	2.3	802	21,812	10,742	0	0.0	11
Advanced Cptr	-9.1	-31.0	-28.5	-1.8	-.94	NE	NE	NE	NC	NC	12-89	.00	.0	0	0	0	00-00-00	-36.0	1.14	-40.9	.00	NM	60	.8	5	1,854	20	0	0.0	12
Aldus Cp	6.7	6.7	3.4	15.0q	1.15	-18.2	-18.2	-7.3	NC	24	03-90	.00	.0	0	0	0	00-00-00	16.7	1.23	20.6	1.17	24.0	0	6.8	384	14,223	3,796	0	0.0	12
Algorex Cp	-52.4	-46.9	-44.4	-1.9	-.66	-100.0	-100.0	-100.0	NC	-51	03-90	.00	.0	0	0	0	00-00-00	-38.0	1.06	-40.4	1.27	-51.4	0	3.9	1	2,794	332	0	0.0	06
Altai Inc	63.6	47.1	20.0	-.2n	-.13	NE	NE	-100.0	NC	-4	04-90	.00	.0	0	0	0	00-00-00	-3.3	1.00	-3.3	1.30	-4.3	0	4.4	8	1,898	18	0	0.0	07
Altos Cptr Syst	.3	-2.3	-8.6	-6.7n	-.59	NE	NE	-100.0	NC	-6	03-90	.00	.0	0	0	0	00-00-00	-4.9	.88	-4.3	1.44	-6.2	19	4.9	82	10,869	3,354	0	0.0	06
Am Mgmt Syst	14.3	14.3	8.8	8.3q	.72	33.3	NE	33.3	16	17	03-90	.00	.0	0	0	18	06-11-87	3.6	1.86	6.7	2.58	17.3	29	2.2	176	9,995	3,314	0	0.0	12
American Software	22.1	27.2	26.3	18.6f	1.23	33.3	28.1	28.1	28	21	04-90	.32	1.2	24	24	0	06-04-90	20.4	.96	19.6	1.45	28.4	0	2.7	391	15,125	7,089	-243	0.0	04
Anacomp Inc	15.2	13.1	30.9	7.4s	.13	12.5	66.7	-68.3	NC	0	03-90	.00	.0	0	0	25	00-00-00	1.1	.82	.9	.00	NS	-10	.4	107	37,061	6,987	+2	15.2	09
Analysts Intl	20.9	21.3	23.8	5.7n	1.23	13.3	18.4	29.5	28	23	03-90	.48	2.4	0	38	0	00-00-00	5.5	4.09	22.5	1.66	37.3	0	2.5	90	4,577	2,392	0	0.0	09
Analytical Sur	.0	-5.0	14.2	.0s	-.04	-100.0	-100.0	-100.0	NC	NC	03-90	.00	.0	0	0	0	07-25-90						0	1.5	5	2,482	110	+1	0.0	06
ASA Int'l Ltd	-18.6	-18.6	283.3	-.9q	.00	NE	NC	NC	NC	NC	03-90	.00	.0	0	0	0	05-07-90	3.9	1.62	6.3	1.94	12.2	3	NA	21	3,921	23	0	0.0	12
Ashton Tate	-4.2	-36.5	.0	.0*	-1.09	NE	-100.0	-100.0	NC	7	03-90	.00	.0	0	0	22	01-13-87	NC	NC	NC	NC	—	1	3.0	323	26,614	11,826	0	2.0	12
ASK Cptr Systs	13.1	7.1	10.1	7.2n	.53	-66.7	-72.3	-44.2	6	26	03-90	.00	.0	0	0	0	00-00-00	12.0	1.30	4.8	1.42	6.8	1	2.4	117	13,417	6,821	+20	0.0	06
Autodesk Inc	42.3	42.3	50.0	49.0q	2.01	22.2	22.2	34.0	66	26	04-90	.30	.5	84	13	32	06-18-90	25.1	1.00	25.2	1.22	30.8	2	4.7	1,345	24,242	16,878	-15	0.0	01
Autoinfo Inc	29.4	36.7	33.3	1.7	.25	75.0	150.0	150.0	NC	17	04-90	.00	.0	0	0	0	00-00-00	21.3	.60	16.5	1.29	16.5	0	3.9	40	6,733	1,414	-15	0.0	05
Automated Systs	20.6	25.5	20.0	-1.1n	-.35	NE	NE	NE	NC	-13	03-90	.00	.0	0	0	0	00-00-00	-6.1	1.52	-9.3	1.41	-13.1	14	3.7	26	3,248	315	0	0.0	06
Automatic Data	3.7	2.3	3.2	205.0m	2.80	15.8	15.0	15.2	19	16	03-90	.70	1.3	13	21	22	06-14-90	12.0	1.76	21.6	1.77	21.6	7	1.9	4,061	73,494	45,288	+3	2.0	06
AW Cptr Systs	-14.3	-14.3	.0	-.3q	-.08	NE	NE	NE	NC	-50	04-90	.00	.0	0	0	0	00-00-00	-10.0	2.78	-17.6	2.04	-50.0	27	1.0	2	3,467	46	-1	0.0	12
Babbage's Inc	37.5	37.5	52.2	1.8q	.36	-88.9	-88.9	-41.9	NC	22	04-90	.00	.0	0	0	0	00-00-00	1.8	1.00	5.0	1.16	5.8	0	4.6	44	5,255	2,145	0	0.0	01
BGS Systs	13.6	13.6	10.5	4.50	1.47	68.2	68.2	36.1	32	NC	02-90	.40	1.7	0	102	100	05-25-90	21.4	.88	17.1	1.75	30.0	0	2.3	75	3,215	762	0	0.0	02
Bio Logic Syst	13.0	7.6	11.1	.4f	.13	-100.0	-38.1	-38.1	48	5	02-90	.00	.0	0	0	0	00-00-00	4.0	1.66	3.5	1.37	22.2	16	5.1	12	2,922	1,371	0	0.0	02
Boole & Babbage	18.4	20.7	22.0	4.9s	1.24	-32.7	-11.3	-46.1	NC	22	03-90	.00	.0	0	0	0	00-00-00	5.9	.47	9.8	2.27	-25.6	13	1.4	79	3,849	153	+20	0.0	09
CIS Technologies	214.3	214.3	200.0	-3.0q	-.11	NE	NE	NE	NC	36	03-90	.00	.0	0	0	0	00-00-00	-50.0	1.35	-23.6	1.08	-25.6	2	12.1	137	25,817	1,539	-194	0.0	12
Cabletron Systems	57.1	57.1	76.1	24.5q	.93	28.6	28.6	57.6	NC	26	05-90	.00	.0	0	0	0	00-00-00	20.8	1.35	28.1	1.21	36.4	3	3.7	497	26,317	1,539	-194	0.1	02
Cadence Design	85.9	85.9	107.5	31.4q	.99	26.1	26.1	41.4	NC	30	03-90	.00	.0	0	0	0	00-00-00	19.1	1.04	19.8	1.53	30.3	9	2.7	641	23,520	11,249	0	0.0	12

(continued)

Computer Software, Data Processing (Continued)

$r/f \times f/a = s/a \times a/e = s/e$

Company	Rev % Last Qtr	Rev % FY to Date	Rev % Last 12 Mos	Earn Last 12 Mos $Mil	Earn PS Last 12 $	Earn % FY to Date	Earn % Last 12 Mos	Earn 5-Yr Gr	Earn Par Gr	Rpt Date	Div Amt	Div Yield	Payout Last FY	Payout 5 Yrs	Last X-Dvd Date	Profit %	Asset Turn	ROA %	Lev Ratio	ROE %	Debt/Eq	Cur Ratio	Mkt Val $Mil	Shares Out 000	Held Banks/Funds 000	Insider Net Trad 000	Short Int Ratio Days	FY Mo
Carner Cp	-31.6	-31.6	26.1	2.7q	.72	-100.0	-8.9	NC	10	03-90	.00	.0	0	0	00-00-00	5.1	.96	4.9	1.96	9.6	6	1.9	43	3,824	1,498	0	0.0	12
Cheyenne Sftware	66.5	111.2	119.4	-1.4n	-.16	NE	NE	NE	-11	03-90	.00	.0	0	0	00-00-00	-.8	3.13	-2.5	4.32	-10.8	3	1.1	57	9,685	767	0	23.3	06
Cimflex Tekndg	-1141.9	4.6	.0	.0*	-.37	.0	.0	NC		03-90	.00	.0	0	0	02-13-89	NC	1.55	NC	NC	.0	5	2.0	19	22,247	1,408	0	0.0	12
Cognos Inc ◆	-7.6	4.9	4.4	-14.3f	.63	70.0	152.0	NC	-39	03-90	.00	.0	0	0	00-00-00	-15.2	2.29	-23.6	1.67	-33.3	12	2.1	91	10,424	1,660	0	0.0	02
Comptek Rsch	18.3	2.7	4.1	1.4f		131.3	106.3	NC	8	03-90	.20	3.3	25	37	05-07-90	2.8	2.29	6.4	1.72	11.0	36	4.9	13	2,191	727	0	0.0	03
Compumat Inc	18.5	52.8	52.6	.3f	.13	-16.7	-72.9	NC	NC	11-89	.00	.0	0	0	00-00-00	.3	4.00	1.2	4.67	5.6	7	1.2	5	1,909		0	0.0	11
Comp Assoc	16.8	25.8	25.8	157.8f	.85	1171.4	246.9	NC	48	03-90	.05	.30	41	13	06-12-90	12.2	1.11	13.5	1.56	21.1	6	1.9	2,946	185,570	90,598	0	2.5	03
Comp Data Syst ◆	6.2	25.0	36.2	3.2n	1.11	866.7	-16.7	NC	20	03-90	.14	1.2	41		01-25-90	2.6	2.19	5.7	2.88	16.4	56	1.5	34	2,827	908	0	0.0	06
Comp Factory	-7.0	8.5	13.1	-6.4s	-.73	-100.0	-100.0	NC	14	03-90	.00	.0	0	0	10-03-88	-1.7	2.00	-3.4	2.15	-7.3	17	2.1	26	8,658	4,095	+13	1.1	06
Comp Horizons	22.3	22.3	11.2	-1.0q	-.43	75.0	-100.0	NC	-7	03-90	.00	.0	0	0	00-00-00	-1.1	2.64	-2.9	2.64	-6.6	68	2.6	32	2,398	920	-2	0.0	12
Comp Language	.5	.5	5.8	.2q	.01	41.9	-8.9	NE	-6	03-90	.12	2.5	240	375	06-11-90	.2	2.09	.2	2.50	.5	58	1.6	65	13,736	861	0	0.0	12
Comp Sciences	16.0	15.0	15.0	65.5f	4.07	-100.0	24.1	NC	17	03-90	.00	.0	0	0	00-00-00	4.4	.64	9.2	1.84	16.9	21	1.7	765	16,114	9,756	-7	0.3	03
Computrac	-42.9	-42.9	-14.2	1.1q	.17	14.3	-51.4	NC	NC	04-90	.05	2.2	0	6	12-29-88	9.2	1.59	14.6	1.27	7.5	8	5.2	13	5,879	2,067	+0	0.0	09
Comshare Inc	16.6	15.6	15.2	6.5n	1.18	41.8	47.5	NC	24	03-90	.00	.0	0	0	00-00-00	6.6	1.59	10.5	2.29	24.0	0	1.3	126	5,240	1,060	0	0.0	06
Comver Peripherals	79.6	79.6	134.4	51.0q	1.30	131.3	106.3	NC	25	03-90	.00	.0	0	0	00-00-00	6.3	1.73	10.9	2.33	25.4	61	3.0	1,109	39,609	13,923	-34	0.0	12
Consilium Inc	41.4	41.5	47.3	4.9s	.71	353.6	65.1	NC	21	04-90	.00	.0	0	0	00-00-00	17.5	.99	17.3	1.21	21.0	0	6.5	170	6,882	1,596	0	0.0	10
Continuum Co	30.5	21.2	21.2	5.5f	1.27	1833.3	353.6	NC	25	03-90	.00	.0	0	4	03-24-86	6.9	1.84	12.7	1.31	24.8	0	1.9	164	4,374	1,008	0	24.5	03
Convergent Sol	36.4	33.3	-54.5	.36	.07	-75.0	-88.5	NC	20	03-90	.00	.0	0	0	00-00-00	6.0	.27	1.6	1.31	21	4	7.3	10	5,379	362	0	0.0	09
Corporate Sftware	52.4	52.4	46.1	3.3q	.65	4.3	-9.7	NC	11	03-90	.00	.0	0	0	11-04-87	2.2	2.64	5.8	1.83	10.6	0	2.2	69	5,007	2,077	0	0.0	12
Cybertek Cp	1.5	10.6	9.0	1.9f	.50	5.9	400.0	NC	15	03-90	.00	.0	0	0	00-00-00	7.9	.78	6.2	2.42	15.0	14	2.2	28	3,741	374	0	0.0	03
Cycare Systs	-9.6	-9.6	-2.3	3.1q	.54	NE	NE	NE	-14	03-90	.00	.0	0	0	04-30-86	3.8	.92	3.5	1.86	6.5	33	1.7	45	5,875	2,094	0	0.0	12
Daisy System Cp	-30.1	-17.9		-103.5s	-5.59	NE	NE	NE	NC	03-90	.00	.0	0	0	00-00-00	-73.9	.86	-63.8	.00	NM	1033	.9	3	18,861	2,808	0	0.0	09
Data I O	-5.5	-5.5	-7.6	1.2q	.19	-72.9	NE	NE	NC	03-90	.00	.0	0	2184	00-00-00	-10.0	1.40	-23.1	1.93	5.4	11	1.4	22	6,638	2,019	+11	0.0	12
Datatab Inc	-22.2	-18.2	.0	-.3f	-.36	-100.0	-100.0	NC	-43	12-89	.00	.0	0	0	00-00-00	-28.0	2.31	-21.9	1.86	-42.9	0	1.7		706	325	0	0.0	06
DBA Systs	-32.4	-32.8	-29.3	-11.5n	-4.26	-100.0	-100.0	NC	-55	03-90	.00	.0	0	335	00-00-00		.78		2.51	-55.0	84	1.7	8	2,685		+1	0.0	06
Decision Sys ◆	-25.0	-17.2	-16.6	-.11	-.04	NE	NE	NE	-25	04-89	.00	.0	0	0	00-00-00	-2.0	2.95	-5.9	4.24	-25.0	0	.9	3	2,331	18	0	0.0	04
Delphi Info Systs	18.0	2.9	.0	.11	.02	33.3	-27.5	NE	NC	03-90	.16	1.0	0	50	06-12-90	.5	1.60	.7	2.00	1.6	0	1.3	28	4,175	290	-3	0.0	03
DST Syst Inc	10.2	10.2	-5.1	6.9d	.71	0	-10.1	NC	4	03-90	.00	.0	0	0	00-00-00	5.3	.70	3.7	2.22	8.2	49	1.1	300	19,043	1,337	0	0.0	12
Dynamics Research	2.5	2.5	-3.2	3.6q	.71	0	0	NC	20	03-90	.00	.0	0	0	00-00-00	4.0	2.25	9.0	1.69	15.2	0	2.2	25	5,044	1,696	0	0.0	12
Eqghead Inc	33.3	33.3	33.3	-7.7f	-.47	NE	NE	NE	-7	03-90	.00	.0	0	0	00-00-00	-1.7	2.82	-4.8	1.52	-7.3	0	2.5	232	16,249	3,597	+36	0.0	03
Epsilon Data	-1.5	-10.4	-11.3	-.5n	-.19	1366.7	900.0	NE	NC	02-90	.00	.0	0	0	02-90	-1.1	2.27	-2.5	1.64	-4.1	2	3.0	56	2,902	755	0	0.0	02
Evans & Suthlnd	48.8	48.8	18.8	3.7q	.40	NE	NE	NE	4	03-90	.00	.0	0	0	00-00-00	2.5	.89	1.8	2.06	3.7	51	8.7	256	8,596	6,488	+7	0.0	01
FDP Cp	28.8	28.8	21.4	.3a	.10	4100.0	493.8	NE	2	02-90	.00	.0	0	0	00-00-00	1.8	.89	1.6	1.13	1.8	9	.3	14	3,378	577	0	0.0	12
Fnl Inds	1600.0	800.0	200.0	1.9n	1.90	1590.9	27.9	NE	18	09-89	.00	.0	0	0	00-00-00	63.3	.19	15.4	1.19	18.4	243	NA	11	974		0	0.0	11
Fst Fncl Mgt	58.0	58.0	111.6	61.5q	2.34	11.9	19.7	NC	45	03-90	.10	.50	0	1	05-25-90	6.4	.19	1.2	10.25	12.3		NA	558	26,116	12,510	+859	12.4	12
Fiserv Inc	13.6	13.6	20.7	11.9q	1.40	19.4	19.4	NC	14	03-90	.00	.0	0	0	00-00-00	7.0	.39	2.7	5.22	14.1	30	1.1	203	8,296	4,513	+1	0.0	12
Gen Computer	-16.7	3.5	13.3	-2.2n	-1.32	NE	14.6	NC	-33	03-90	.00	.0	0	27	05-11-90	-18.3	.87	-15.9	2.09	-33.3	0	1.0	6	1,574	116	-6	0.0	05
Gen Motors E EDS	10.3	13.3	13.2	435.3f	1.81	16.3	14.6	NC	17	12-89	.56	1.6	0	23	02-28-90	8.1	1.37	11.1	2.23	24.7	12	9.9	8,235	238,700	35,548	+38	1.4	12
Gen Parametrics	-61.3	-52.8	-30.7	1.1s	.14	28.6	-68.2	NC	1	04-90	.12	6.9	0		00-00-00	6.1	.57	3.5	1.11	3.9	0	1.8	14	7,850	1,089	0	0.0	10
Group 1 Sftwre	36.0	14.7	11.1	3.0f	.70	38.1	61	NC	31	03-90	.00	.0	0	0	11-06-88	15.0	1.29	19.4	1.58	30.6	3	1.8	38	4,191	301	0	0.0	03

Company																																				
Hadron Inc	9.0	-32.2	0	.0*	.01	-100.0	-100.0	-75.0	16	0	12.89	.88	.0	.0	.0	.0	00:00:00	NC	NC	NC	NC	0	39.1	76	2.1	3	14,292	-20	0	0.0	08
HBO Co ◆	-13.0	-13.0	3.6	12.70	.81	-100.0	-100.0	-2.4	NC	.25	03-90	.30	.27	34	20	30	06:25:90	6.4	1.75	11.2	3.49	39.1	21	.9	166	14,911	8,37	-3	0.0	12
Henry Jack Assoc ◆	-12.5	-12.5	-35.7	-1.2n	-34	.71	.71	-100.0	NC	-13	03-90	.88	.0	.0	.0	.0	00:00:00	-13.3	.71	-94	1.37	-12.9	3	1.9	10	3,617	786	0	0.0	06
Hogan Systs	-25.8	-9.4	-8.3	2.1f	.15	200.0	200.0	200.0	NC	7	03-90	.88	.0	.0	.0	.0	00:00:00	4.8	.90	4.3	1.51	6.5	0	2.9	47	13,369	3,335	0	0.0	08
Index Technology	38.3	38.3	32.2	2.2n	.47	-23.1	-23.1	-27.7	NC	8	03-90	.88	.0	.0	.0	.0	00:00:00	5.4	.96	52	1.46	7.6	0	3.5	37	4.68	57	+6	0.0	12
Indust'l Training	16.7	7.2	.0	.3l	.40	125.0	33.3	33.3	NC	9	12.89	.88	.0	.0	.0	.0	00:00:00	4.3	.98	4.2	2.17	9.1	39	1.5	3	776	21	+0	0.0	12
Infodata Systs	10.7	10.7	.0	-.4q	-.28	NE	NE	NE	NC	-9	03-90	.88	.0	.0	.0	.0	00:00:00	-3.3	1.58	-5.2	1.67	-8.7	11	1.9	2	1,718	240	-1	0.0	04
Info Science	-5.6	6.5	8.3	.1l	.01	-84.6	-84.6	NE	NC	2	04-89	.88	.0	.0	.0	.0	00:00:00	.9	1.13	.9	1.78	1.6	4	1.4	188	11,187	872	+409	0.0	04
Infomix Cp	33.9	33.9	43.1	8.1q	.63	325.0	325.0	81.8	NE	11	03-90	.88	.0	.0	.0	.0	00:00:00	5.2	1.10	5.7	1.91	10.9	41	2.9	51	12,249	6,57	0	0.0	12
IntelliCorp	18.2	15.0	14.2	1.8n	.20	500.0	240.0	81.8	NC	6	03-90	.88	.0	.0	.0	.0	00:00:00	6.7	.69	4.6	1.24	5.7	0	4.7	51	7,523	1,81	0	0.0	06
Interleaf Inc ◆	-11.9	7.2	7.2	-16.0f	-1.37	-100.0	-100.0	-8.3	-26	-36	03-90	.88	.0	.0	.0	.0	00:00:00	-18.0	1.20	-26.6	1.64	-35.5	29	3.1	90	11,745	5,521	0	0.0	03
Intermetrics Inc	6.0	6.0	-2.0	1.4q	.40	-17.6	-17.6	38.0	39	4	05-90	.88	.64	.0	.0	.0	04-24-90	3.0	1.83	5.5	1.60	8.8	2	2.6	11	3,574	64	0	0.0	02
Interphase	57.8	40.9	26.3	-1.4s	-.44	-100.0	-100.0	NE	NC	-8	04-90	.88	.0	.0	.0	.0	00:00:00	-5.8	1.09	-6.3	1.24	-7.8	3	4.9	19	3,330	411	+1	0.0	10
Keane Inc	42.8	42.8	35.4	3.9q	.96	22.7	22.7	17.1	40	30	03-90	.88	.0	.0	.0	.0	02-15-90	4.6	3.41	15.7	1.92	30.2	36	2.2	64	3,738	236	0	5.6	06
Landmark Graphics	23.9	23.9	32.4	5.2n	.63	-41.2	-6.1	23.5	18	17	03-90	.88	.0	.0	.5	.0	00:00:00	10.6	1.31	13.9	1.21	16.8	0	5.0	128	8,318	2,58	-22	0.0	08
LCS Ind	11.3	14.1	13.3	-.1s	.11	100.0	-8.3	-8.3	-26	1	03-90	.88	.0	.0	.0	.0	00:00:00	.3	2.00	.6	2.33	1.4	7	1.6	5	1,510	190	+4	0.0	09
LEGENT Cp	-14.1	30.3	62.5	29.0s	1.38	133.3	47.9	38.0	39	24	03-90	.88	.0	.0	.0	.0	03-02-87	20.3	.97	19.7	1.21	23.9	0	6.0	594	21,421	7,461	0	24.7	09
Logistix	60.7	15.2	20.0	-1.2n	-.19	NE	NE	NE	NC	-23	05-90	.20	.0	.0	.0	.0	00:00:00	-6.7	1.37	-9.2	2.46	-22.6	2	1.0	5	5,870	1,13	0	0.0	10
Logicon Inc	8.6	11.7	12.1	8.6f	1.90	-10.8	-10.8	-10.8	2	10	06-21-90	.88	.0	.5	5	-8	06-21-90	3.3	2.61	15.7	1.45	12.5	0	3.0	81	4,546	2,112	0	13.5	03
Lotus Development	37.9	43.9	27.8	85.9q	.63	307.7	307.7	97.1	18	31	03-90	.36	2.0	.0	12	04-24-87	14.2	3.31	14.1	2.18	30.7	73	3.7	1,440	41,432	30,0:5	-5	0.0	12
MacNeal Sch	19.6	19.6	14.6	10.1q	.84	10.5	10.5	13.5	29	12	04-90	.40	4.2	.0	38	08-20-90	21.5	.79	16.9	1.38	23.4	7	2.6	114	11,983	6,87	+4	0.0	09
Mai Basic Four	-9.3	-11.9	-16.0	-43.2s	-3.07	-64.7	-73.6	-100.0	NC	-86	03-90	.88	.0	.0	.0	12-18-88	-11.6	.95	-11.0	7.85	-86.4	312	1.3	34	15,015	2,15	0	24.7	09
Management Tech	-8.3	-8.3	11.1	1.4q	.07	-77.8	-77.8	-65.0	NC	33	07-89	.88	.0	.0	.0	00:00:00	14.0	1.03	14.4	2.26	32.6	2	.9	8	9,184	49	0	0.0	04
Marietron Inc	33.3	14.0	12.5	.2n	.09	NC	133.3	13.5	NC	4	03-90	.88	.0	.0	.0	00:00:00	2.2	1.14	2.5	1.52	3.8	0	2.6	6	2,118	4	0	0.0	04
Medstat Sys	40.9	34.1	37.5	1.4s	.50	18.2	25.0	28.2	NC	23	03-90	.88	.0	.0	.0	05-07-90	12.7	1.11	14.1	1.60	22.6	10	2.1	40	2,635	225	0	0.0	09
Mentor Graphics	28.0	29.0	25.3	46.0q	1.19	-10.3	-10.3	13.3	NC	14	05-90	.88	.0	.0	12	03-90	11.3	1.12	12.7	1.32	16.8	3	3.4	759	34,882	24,042	-20	0.0	08
Micro Syst	52.6	44.6	50.0	2.4n	.38	200.0	266.7	442.9	36	26	03-90	.88	.0	.20	6	03-90	7.3	1.95	14.2	1.82	25.8	2	2.2	38	7,312	5	0	0.0	06
Microsoft	57.8	45.1	41.5	244.5n	2.09	67.6	50.9	50.4	54	44	04-16-90	.88	.0	.0	.0	04-16-90	22.9	1.48	33.9	1.28	43.5	0	3.0	8,408	110,630	29,0:5	-20	0.0	06
MPS Systs	23.2	12.4	17.0	1.1s	.12	NE	NE	NE	NC	9	02-27-84	.88	.0	.0	.0	00:00:00	2.0	1.30	2.6	3.27	8.5	13	.9	23	8,458	2,38	0	0.0	05
Multi Solutions	-50.0	-56.7	-33.3	-.5n	-.05	-100.0	-100.0	-100.0	NC	-28	10-89	.88	.0	25	.0	00:00:00	-25.0	.83	-27.8	1.34	-27.8	0	4.0	4	14,860	0	-29	0.0	01
Nat'l Data Cp	25.0	35.1	37.3	24.8n	2.10	-4.4	28.7	30.4	18	18	05-15-90	.44	3.0	.0	34	05-01-87	8.8	1.19	10.5	2.14	22.5	11	1.2	170	11,729	8,45	0	0.0	05
Netword Inc	.0	.0	.0	-.2t	-.39	NE	NE	NE	NC	-20	01-89	.88	.0	.0	.0	05-01-87	NC	NC	NC	NC	-20.0	NC	NA	0	537	-	0	0.0	01
On Line Shwre	12.7	9.4	9.7	3.3l	.56	50.0	50.0	NE	NC	-15	05-90	.88	.0	.0	.0	05-28-87	NC	1.00	3.7	3.97	14.7	182	2.1	52	5,954	2.27	0	21.0	05
Oracle Systs	54.2	73.1	80.5	98.1n	.72	0	30.6	44.0	108	43	07-03-89	.88	.0	NE	.0	07-03-89	11.5	1.85	16.9	2.00	42.5	15	1.9	2,993	129,406	55,91x	0	0.0	05
Oscom Techs	-41.5	-41.5	-32.1	-5.4q	-1.73	NE	NE	NE	NC	-69	03-90	.88	.0	.0	.0	00:00:00	-7.3	2.00	-14.6	4.74	-69.2	0	1.2	5	3,110	63-	0	0.0	01
Pansophic Sys ◆	-26.2	14.8	14.7	-12.8f	-.69	-100.0	-100.0	-100.0	NC	-12	06-25-90	.20	.0	18	4	04-23-90	-5.9	1.19	-7.0	1.29	-9.0	1	3.4	268	18,454	11,55	+7	0.3	04
Paydex Inc	20.2	19.3	20.8	8.9n	.69	-37.5	-7.1	1.5	28	17	02-90	.16	1.4	12	4	02-90	7.7	2.10	16.2	1.36	22.1	5	3.4	209	13,041	6,96	0	0.0	05
PC Quote Inc	25.0	25.0	25.0	-.6q	-.9l	NC	NC	NC	NC	-10	03-90	.88	1.0	.0	.0	00:00:00	-6.0	.92	-5.5	1.78	-9.8	0	1.4	13	6,865	5	0	0.0	02
PDA Engineering	9.0	12.5	15.3	1.9n	.43	7.7	13.3	22.9	4	13	03-90	.88	.0	.0	.0	00:00:00	6.3	1.22	7.7	1.62	12.5	0	2.5	30	4,046	1,10	0	0.0	06
Penta Sys Intl	2.3	4.5	-18.1	-1.2s	-.21	NE	NE	NE	NC	0	06-89	.88	.0	.0	.0	00:00:00	-6.7	1.78	-11.9	.00	NM	56	.8	1	5,273	63-	0	0.0	12
Perception Tech	-22.4	-17.9	5.8	-1.7s	-.50	-100.0	-100.0	NE	NC	-9	03-90	.88	.0	.0	.0	00:00:00	-9.4	.82	-9.3	1.21	-3.8	2	5.5	13	3,298	1,21:	+7	0.0	09
Perfectdata Tech	.0	11.1	.0	.1l	.04	NC	NC	NC	NC	4	03-90	.88	.0	.0	.0	00:00:00	2.5	1.52	3.8	1.13	4.3	0	8.3	1	3,307	5	0	0.0	03
Phoenix Technology	-50.8	-46.9	-36.2	-22.4s	-2.20	-100.0	-100.0	-100.0	NC	-49	03-90	.88	.0	.0	.0	00:00:00	-60.5	.51	-31.0	1.58	-49.0	1	2.1	46	9,986	2,06	+14	0.0	09

(continued)

Source: Media General Financial Services, Richmond, VA.

Computer Software, Data Processing (Continued)

Ratio Analysis formula: $s/l \times r/a = s/l \times r/a \times a/e = s/e$

Company	Rev Last Qtr %	Rev FY to Date %	Rev Last 12 Mos %	Earn 12 Mos $Mil	Per Share $	EPS %chg Last Qtr	EPS %chg FY	EPS %chg 12 Mos	5-Yr Gro %	Par Gro %	Date of Report	Div Amt $	Yield %	Div 5-Yr %	Payout FY %	Payout 5 Yr %	Last X-Dvd	Profit Mgn %	Asset T/O	ROA %	Lev Ratio	ROE %	Debt/Eq %	Curr Ratio	Mkt Val $Mil	Shares Out 000	Banks-Funds 000	Insider Net 000	Short Days	FY End Mo
Picturetel Cp	72.1	72.1	144.4	-4.1q	-1.55	NE	NE	NE	NC	-32	03-90	.00	0	0	0	0	11-15-89	-18.6	1.03	-19.2	1.68	-32.3	7	2.4	32	2,849	0	0	0.0	12
Policy Mgmt	33.6	33.6	25.9	29.6q	1.68	21.6	21.6	22.6	10	14	03-90	.00	0	0	0	0	00-00-00	10.3	.62	6.4	1.63	10.4	36	5.6	797	19,313	13,268	0	0.0	12
Profit Tech ◆	-16.7	-21.3	-20.0	-8.2q	-.85	NE	NE	NE	NC	0	08-89	.00	0	0	0	0	00-00-00	NM	NC	NC	NC	NM	85	1.0	32	9,448	141	0	0.0	08
Quality Syst	25.0	9.1	11.1	-.8	-.20	NE	NE	NE	NC	-11	03-90	.00	0	0	0	0	00-00-00	-8.0	1.01	-8.1	1.36	-11.0	0	3.8	7	4,291	314	0	0.0	03
Rabbit Software Cp	46.7	46.7	-33.3	-11.50	-.62	NE	NE	NE	NC	-8	03-90	.00	0	0	0	0	00-00-00	NM	NC	NC	NC	NM	2700	1.1	22	19,687	602	0	0.0	12
Renaissance GRX	-31.7	48.4	72.7	-1.5n	-.20	NE	NE	NE	NC	-71	03-90	.00	0	0	0	0	00-00-00	-7.9	2.75	-21.7	3.29	-71.4	5	1.3	4	6,487	79	0	0.0	06
Sage Software	48.1	25.6	28.5	3.5f	.55	450.0	98.4	96.4	61	14	03-90	.00	0	0	0	0	00-00-00	13.0	.88	11.5	1.23	14.2	0	4.3	89	6,213	2,614	-28	0.0	04
Samna Cp	3.4	3.4	-21.4	-3.0q	-1.12	-100.0	NE	NE	NC	-36	04-90	.00	0	0	0	0	00-00-00	-27.3	.94	-25.6	1.41	-36.1	2	3.0	46	2,566	235	0	0.0	12
Sandata Inc	-3.3	2.4	9.0	.3n	.15	200.0	85.7	66.7	0	-16	03-90	.00	0	0	0	0	00-00-00	2.5	1.76	4.4	2.20	9.7	0	1.2	3	2,470	5	0	0.0	05
Satellite Info	-45.5	-51.5	-25.0	-.4n	-.16	-100.0	-100.0	-100.0	NC	-22	03-90	.00	0	0	0	0	00-00-00	-13.3	1.08	-14.3	1.55	-22.2	6	1.3	3	2,678	92	0	0.0	06
Sactec Intl	-48.0	-10.2	11.7	.7n	.16	-100.0	-93.3	60.0	NC	20	03-90	.00	0	0	0	0	00-00-00	3.7	2.32	8.6	2.33	20.0	37	1.4	13	3,501	58	0	0.0	06
Sei Software	-21.9	-21.9	-24.0	-.2q	-.05	-100.0	-100.0	NE	NC	-1	03-90	.00	0	0	0	0	00-00-00	-1.1	.85	-.6	1.50	-.9	3	1.9	17	3,756	1,328	0	0.0	12
Sofax Cp	35.1	35.1	23.0	43.7q	2.43	300.0	122.9	76.1	NC	26	03-90	.00	0	0	0	0	00-00-00	17.1	.82	14.0	1.84	25.8	23	2.6	663	17,693	1,337	0	0.0	12
Scott Instru	.0	.0	.0	-.7q	-.03	NE	NE	NE	NC	0	01-90	.00	0	0	0	0	00-00-00	-70.0	1.11	-77.8	.00	NM	75	1.0	7	26,255	166	0	0.0	12
SCS Compute	43.3	27.3	20.6	.2f	.38	220.0	NE	-2.6	NC	0	03-90	.00	0	0	0	0	00-00-00	3.3	2.08	3.3	2.39	7.9	100	3.8	11	2,827	470	0	0.0	04
SEI Corp	27.1	27.1	20.6	11.8q	1.05	300.0	0	0	17	29	03-90	.10	.5	0	6	0	06-12-90	7.5	2.08	15.6	2.07	32.3	11	.8	219	10,551	5,262	-25	0.0	12
Shared Med Syst	1.7	1.7	3.4	22.1q	.97	-9	NE	NE	17	2	03-90	.84	6.5	0	106	51	06-25-90	5.6	1.43	8.0	1.65	13.2	3	1.8	298	22,894	16,290	+1	0.0	12
Sharedata Inc.	-52.2	-6.7	12.5	.3n	.04	NE	NE	NE	NC	43	12-89	.00	0	0	0	0	00-00-00	3.3	2.76	9.1	4.71	42.9	114	1.1	8	4,094	124	-4	0.0	06
Sierra On Line	118.8	44.8	45.0	5.1	1.38	68.4	26.6	26.6	NC	33	03-90	.00	0	0	0	0	00-00-00	17.6	1.43	25.2	1.32	33.3	0	4.1	94	3,504	1,602	0	0.0	03
Silvar Lisco	-16.2	-30.9	-31.5	2.0f	.27	NE	NE	NE	NC	0	01-90	.00	0	0	0	0	00-00-00	15.4	.99	15.3	.00	NM	2800		7	7,574	1,014	0	0.0	03
Softech Inc	-23.9	-10.2	-6.2	1.2n	.31	-90.0	-45.5	-20.5	NC	5	03-90	.00	0	0	0	0	00-00-00	2.7	1.48	4.0	1.30	5.2	0	4.6	13	3,659	1,269	0	0.0	05
Software Dvlprs	137.5	102.8	100.0	.6f	.30	100.0	30.4	30.4	NC	29	03-90	.00	0	0	0	0	00-00-00	2.7	5.56	15.0	2.11	31.6	5	1.6	18	2,092	0	0	0.0	09
Software Pub	27.7	28.7	28.5	19.6q	1.59	14.7	29.2	19.5	41	32	03-90	.00	0	0	0	0	11-21-89	16.8	1.40	23.6	1.25	29.4	0	4.4	292	11,804	6,923	+1	0.0	09
Software Svcs	.0	-66.7	-50.0	-.8n	-.35	NE	NE	NE	NC	-32	02-90	.00	0	0	0	0	00-00-00	-26.7	.79	-21.1	1.52	-32.0	0	2.0	4	5,797	47	+11	0.0	05
Spinmaker Sftware	50.0	50.0	.0	-2.7q	-1.12	NE	NE	NE	NC	-87	03-90	.00	0	0	0	0	00-00-00	-54.0	.78	-42.2	2.06	-87.1	0	4.1	6	2,465	1,436	0	0.0	12
Sports-Tech Intl	63.6	.0	66.6	.4n	.28	185.7	10.5	NC	NC	13	05-90	.00	0	0	0	0	00-00-00	8.0	1.09	8.7	1.44	12.5	0	2.9	63	1,300	142	0	0.0	08
Sterling Sftwr	6.0	8.1	3.4	9.9q	.83	38.9	31.3	NE	11	12	03-90	.00	0	0	0	0	06-12-85	5.3	1.02	5.4	2.54	13.7	92	2.2	66	6,174	2,290	0	10.5	03
Stockholder Systs	18.3	10.6	14.2	3.2n	.79	12.9	-22.0	-6.0	11	12	12-89	.00	0	0	0	0	12-28-89	13.3	.85	11.3	1.42	16.1	0	3.8	61	4,051	861	0	0.0	03
Structural Dyn	20.6	20.6	18.0	10.7q	.80	50.0	50.0	50.9	12	20	05-90	.18	1.2	0	17	12	05-14-90	10.9	1.15	12.5	1.63	20.4	5	2.5	332	12,426	7,990	-347	0.0	12
Summagraphics	4.5	6.6	9.5	6.3n	1.64	-8.5	-8.5	-20.8	NC	20	02-90	.00	0	0	0	0	00-00-00	13.7	1.36	18.6	1.19	22.2	0	5.9	45	3,676	1,634	+1	0.0	05
SunGard Data	18.8	18.8	48.9	17.7q	.44	10.7	10.7	14.7	25	15	03-90	.00	0	0	0	0	00-00-00	8.4	1.10	9.2	1.65	15.2	15	1.6	330	13,610	8,547	0	0.0	12
Symantec Cp	29.6	25.3	25.0	6.7f	.83	NE	NC	NC	NC	0	03-90	.00	0	0	0	0	00-00-00	13.4	2.78	37.2	.00	NM	33	2.2	153	5,951	2,954	+3	0.0	03
Symbolics	-34.3	-18.2	-12.1	-5.7n	-.22	-100.0	-100.0	-100.0	NC	-25	04-90	.00	0	0	0	0	00-00-00	-9.8	1.15	-11.3	2.21	-25.0	3	2.0	12	27,639	4,552	-9	0.0	06
System Software	30.2	23.9	34.6	13.3q	1.13	52.4	50.0	59.2	23	21	04-90	.00	0	0	0	0	01-16-90	12.7	1.35	17.2	2.04	35.1	4	1.7	311	11,583	5,612	0	0.0	10
Systems Center	5.9	5.9	17.5	10.0q	1.24	-8.3	-8.3	31.9	23	20	03-90	.00	0	0	0	0	12-22-88	14.9	1.04	15.5	1.34	20.7	1	4.1	170	7,596	4,137	0	3.6	12

Company																													
Systems&Cptr Tech	-1.9	-.5	15.7	1.3s	.11	-100.0	-92.9	NE	NC	3	03-90	.08	.0	0	0	0	3.0	.97	29	1.14	3.3	6	8.4	51	11,876	-5,807	-6	.00	09
Technalysis Cp	8.3	8.3	16.6	2.1q	.89	21.1	21.1	18.7	15	20	03-90	.46	3.5	0	47	30	10.0	2.31	23.1	1.75	40.4	0	2.3	28	2,144	350	-29	.00	88
Technology Mktg	-28.0	-29.7	-27.2	-1.1f	-.35	-100.0	-100.0	-100.0	NC	-52	02-90	.00	.0	0	0	0	-13.8	1.66	22.9	2.29	-52.4	5	1.6	1	3,069	127	0	.00	12
Tempest Tech	11.1	5.2	.0	-1.3f	-.17	-100.0	-100.0	-100.0	NC	-7	03-90	.00	.0	0	0	0	-16.3	.39	-6.3	1.13	-7.1	0	9.4	4	8,013	913	0	.00	02
Tenera	8.7	8.7	26.4	6.0n	.65	18.2	18.2	20.4	NC	-17	03-90	.80	12.3	127	52		14.0	2.56	35.9	2.09	75.0	0	1.8	60	9,156	653	0	.12	12
Three Cl Inc	33.3	28.6	.0	-3.1n	-1.36	NE	NE	NE	NC	-74	12-89	.08	.0	0	0	0	NM	NC	NC	NC	-73.8	7	3.7	0	2,357	22	0	.00	08
Timberline Sftw	30.8	30.8	33.3	1.0q	.37	100.0	100.0	85.0	NC	33	03-90	.08	.0	0	0	0	8.3	2.31	19.2	1.73	33.3	0	1.9	32	2,407	194	-3	.00	12
Total Systs	10.4	10.4	17.2	11.6q	.73	13.3	13.3	15.9	27	16	06-19-90	.21	.6	0	0	0	17.1	1.19	20.4	1.12	22.8	0	6.7	514	15,875	486	+0	71.0	12
Triad Systems	4.5	7.1	9.1	.68	-.02	-90.0	-92.9	-100.0	NC	0	03-90	.00	.0	0	0	0	.4	1.00	.4	.00	NS	-340	1.4	37	9,780	3,334	+16	.00	09
Tseng Labs	-7.8	-7.8	20.0	4.7q	.26	-22.2	-22.2	13.0	NC	-39	03-90	.80	.0	0	0	0	15.7	2.05	3.2	1.22	39.2	0	5.1	95	17,810	647	-185	.00	12
TSR Inc	-5.9	-7.6	-4.7	-.2n	-.10	-100.0	-45.5	-100.0	NC	-2	04-01-85	.08	.0	0	0	0	-1.0	1.60	-1.6	1.25	-2.0	0	5.0	4	2,130	202	0	.00	05
202 Data Sys	.0	.0	.0	.3q	.06	-100.0	-100.0	NE	NC	25	01-90	.08	.0	0	0	0	30.0	.45	13.6	1.84	25.0	0	2.9	1	3,388	59	+100	.00	10
Utd Software Sec	50.0	.0	.0	.0l	.00	NE	NE	NE	NC	NC	12-89	.08	.0	0	0	0	.0	NC	NC	NC	.0	0	1.8	0	6,039	1	0	.00	12
Utd Systs Tech	14.3	24.0	.0	.2t	.01	NE	NE	NE	4	13	12-89	.08	.0	0	0	0	6.7	1.06	7.1	1.76	12.5	6	1.4	4	12,607	169	0	.00	12
Utd Tote	148.6	108.1	91.6	1.0s	.55	NE	NE	57.1	4	-5	05-23-89	.08	.0	0	127	22	2.2	1.23	27	2.00	5.4	59	2.0	21	3,060	624	0	.00	12
Warner Cptr	105.2	91.4	60.8	1.1s	.17	.0	-21.4	-32.0	31	10	06-28-89	.08	.0	0	0	0	3.0	1.60	4.8	1.98	9.5	1	1.5	28	6,608	442	0	.00	10
Weitek Cp	42.1	42.1	45.9	7.5q	.88	38.9	38.9	54.4	NC	25	03-90	.08	.0	0	0	0	13.9	1.48	20.6	1.21	25.0	0	5.6	172	7,908	3,114	-18	.00	12
Wiland Services	17.0	17.0	30.0	1.3q	.37	-80.0	-80.0	208.3	NC	9	03-90	.08	.0	0	0	0	5.0	1.58	7.9	2.38	18.8	64	1.6	10	3,564	283	0	.00	12
Wordstar Intl	-16.1	-13.8	-11.3	-4.9n	-.35	.0	NE	NE	NC	-18	05-90	.08	.0	0	0	0	-12.6	1.15	-14.5	1.27	-18.4	0	4.1	14	13,735	2,216	0	.00	08
Worlco Data	-10.3	-6.9	8.3	-.4n	-.11	NE	NE	NE	NC	0	03-90	.08	.0	0	0	0	-3.1	2.23	-6.9	.00	NS	-1000	.8	3	2,833	75	0	.00	03
World Wide Tech	366.7	381.1	511.1	.0s	-.17	NE	NE	NC	NC	0	12-89	.08	.0	0	0	0	.0	NC	NC	NC	.0	43	1.4	9	5,595	42	0	.00	08
Worldwide Cptr	-2.2	-2.2	.0	-.4q	.01	-16.7	-16.7	-95.0	NC	0	03-90	.08	.0	0	0	0	.0	NC	NC	1.38	.0	0	2.3	3	1,551	0	0	.00	12
Xicor Cp	66.7	66.7	.0	.1q	.11	NE	NE	NE	NC	8	03-90	.08	.0	0	0	0	5.0	1.12	5.6	2.40	7.7	0	5.0	1	1,051	0	0	.00	12
Xscribe Cp	-11.4	-26.0	-27.2	-2.3l	-.36	NE	NE	NE	NC	-32	03-90	.08	.0	0	0	0	-14.4	.92	-13.3	.00	-31.9	0	1.3	5	6,470	462	0	.00	02
Xytronics Inc	1.2	11.0	32.1	1.8s	.67	-47.4	-41.2	28.8	NC	8	04-90	.08	12.3	0	0	0	4.9	1.22	6.0	1.35	8.1	3	3.7	19	2,595	924	0	.00	10

Source: Media General Financial Services, Richmond, VA.

Trends and Forecasts: Computers and Peripherals (SIC 3571, 3572, 3575, 3577)
(in millions of dollars except as noted)

Item	1987[1]	1988[2]	1989[3]	1990[4]	Percent Change		
					1987–88	1988–89	1989–90
Industry Data							
Value of shipments[5]	57,415	65,450	69,500	72,500	14.0	6.2	4.3
Total employment (000)	292	290	281	276	-0.7	-3.1	-1.8
Production workers (000)	104	101	96.0	93.0	-2.9	-5.0	-3.1
Average hourly earnings ($)	10.51	10.92	11.38	–	3.9	4.2	–
Product Data							
Value of shipments[6]	52,355	58,650	61,600	63,300	12.0	5.0	2.8
Trade Data							
Value of imports (ITA)[7]	15,123	18,631	20,500	21,400	23.2	10.0	4.4
Value of exports (ITA)[8]	18,170	22,561	22,600	21,500	24.2	0.2	-4.9

[1]Industry and product data are preliminary. Trade data are adjusted to conform to the 1987 SIC.
[2]Estimated, except for exports and imports.
[3]Estimated.
[4]Forecast.
[5]Value of all products and services sold by establishments in the computers & peripherals industry.

[6]Value of products classified in the computers & peripherals industry produced by all industries.
[7]Import data are developed by the chapter author.
[8]Export data are developed by the chapter author.
SOURCE: U.S. Department of Commerce: Bureau of the Census; International Trade Administration (ITA). Estimates and forecasts by ITA.

Source: *U.S. Industrial Outlook 1990*, U.S. Department of Commerce.

STOCKS by INDUSTRY

MEDIA GENERAL FINANCIAL SERVICES

Computers, Subsystems and Peripherals

Company	Revenue Pct. Change Last Qtr	FY to Date	Last 12 Mos	Earnings Per Share Last 12 Mos	Last Qtr	FY to Date	Pct. Change Last Qtr	FY to Date	Last 12 Mos	5-Year Growth Rate	Par Growth Rate	Date of Report	Dividends Current Rate Amt	Yield	5-Year Growth Rate	Payout FY	Last 5 Yrs	Last X-Div Date	Ratio Analysis Profit Margin	Asset Turnover	Return on Total Assets	Leverage Ratio	Return on Equity	Debt to Equity	Current Ratio	Market Value $Mil	Latest Shares Out-stndng 000	Held by Banks/funds 000	Insider Net Trading 000	Short Interest Ratio Days	Fiscal Year Ends Mo
Ind. Group	10.7	13.6	9.0	5,682.9	3.8	-7.8	-42.8	-3	3	—	—	—	.84	2.5	0	12	14	——	3.5	1.03	3.6	2.11	7.6	29	1.8	139,011	4,092,200		G + 132	.6	——
Adaptec Inc	56.9	68.9	67.6	13.21	1.50	3.8	689.5	689.5	NC	35	03-90		.00	.0	0	0	0	00-00-00	12.1	2.28	27.6	1.26	34.9	5	5.4	183	8,730	3,496	0	0.0	03
AFP Imaging Cp	7.0	2.3	2.2	.0n	.01	NE	.0	NE	NC	7	03-90		.00	.0	0	0	0	00-00-00	.0	NC	NC	NC	.0	135	1.5	7	4,692	40	0	0.0	06
Allant Cptr Syst	29.3	29.3	8.9	3.1q	.23	600.0	600.0	NE	10	03-90		.00	.0	0	0	0	00-00-00	4.2	.79	3.3	3.03	10.0	127	3.5	101	12,986	3,090	0	0.0	12
Alloy Cptr Prods	-18.8	-18.8	-25.0	-6.0q	-1.25	NE	NE	NE	-57	03-90		.00	.0	0	0	0	00-00-00	-20.0	2.06	-41.1	1.38	-56.6	0	4.1	4	4,040	580	0	0.0	12
Alpha Microsystems	11.0	8.3	7.6	.8	.25	-94.1	-69.9	-69.9	NC	4	02-90		.00	.0	0	0	0	00-00-00	1.4	1.64	2.3	1.52	3.5	7	2.7	10	3,051	452	0	0.0	02
Alpharel Inc	-8.3	-8.3	-33.3	-10.4q	-.12	NE	NE	NE	0	03-90		.00	.0	0	0	0	05-08-90	NM	NC	NC	1.92	NM	12	1.3	3	9,209	885	0	0.0	12
Amdahl Cp	7.8	7.8	12.2	137.3q	1.24	-35.7	-38.0	44	11	03-90		.10	.6	0	7	9	05-08-90	6.4	.95	6.1	1.92	11.7	7	2.0	1,788	110,013	#,333	+6	0.4	12
Am Business Cptr	.0	-3.3	33.3	-.9n	-.08	-100.0	-100.0	NC	-22	01-90		.00	.0	0	0	0	00-00-00	-22.5	.70	-15.8	1.39	-22.0	5	3.4	74	11,763	3,759	0	0.0	04
Analogic Cp	14.1	11.1	14.2	11.7n	.80	23.5	-21.3	15.9	0	8	04-90		.00	.0	0	0	0	00-00-00	8.1	.80	6.5	1.23	8.0	8	7.3	138	14,730	1,391	0	0.0	07
Acopae Robotics	-25.0	10.0	66.6	.4n	.10	NC	NC	NC	29	12-89		.00	.0	0	0	0	00-00-00	8.0	1.61	12.9	2.22	28.6	0	1.6	9	3,550	0	0	0.0	06
Apple Cptr	8.0	7.1	13.6	513.9s	3.99	136.4	29.9	29.1	51	31	03-90		.44	1.0	0	11	8	05-21-90	9.4	1.99	18.7	1.85	34.6	0	2.6	5,600	125,144	73,071	0	0.0	09
Applied Magnet	16.1	5.3	-.3	-20.2s	-1.26	30.0	-100.0	-100.0	NC	-12	03-90		.00	.0	0	0	0	03-06-89	-6.3	1.08	-6.8	1.71	-11.6	37	3.0	210	15,997	8,387	0	1.3	03
Archive Cp	15.3	22.0	32.6	15.9s	1.17	3.6	3.8	24.5	63	19	03-90		.00	.0	0	0	0	00-00-00	8.0	1.53	12.2	1.55	18.9	1	2.4	145	13,765	8,946	0	0.0	03
Ast Corp	-22.9	41.0	41.6	5.2t	.72	-61.0	1.4	1.4	12	21	06-89		.00	.0	0	0	0	00-00-00	6.1	1.61	9.8	1.24	12.2	2	4.9	16	7,613	575	0	0.0	09
AST Research	20.5	14.7	7.6	22.4n	1.87	NE	NE	NE	NE	NC	21	03-90		.00	.0	0	0	0	00-00-00	4.4	1.95	8.6	2.40	20.6	74	3.4	281	11,783	8,111	0	0.0	06
Astrotech Intl	.0	652.9	550.0	-.5r	-.83	NE	NE	NE	-3	09-89		.00	.0	0	0	0	00-00-00	-3.8	.58	-2.2	1.55	-3.4	18	2.7	5	2,579	11	0	3.7	09
Atari Cp	-3.7	-3.7	-1.8	2.2q	.04	-50.0	-50.0	NC	82	09-90		.00	.0	0	0	NE	06-22-87	.5	1.40	.7	3.71	2.6	90	2.1	346	57,713	8,408	0	11.1	12
BancTec Inc	5.0	50.4	50.0	10.5f	1.59	51.3	28.2	28.2	18	03-90		.00	.0	0	0	0	05-21-66	5.6	1.25	7.0	2.59	18.1	76	2.1	127	6,220	5,764	0	0.0	03
Barrister Info	-20.4	-8.8	-9.3	-6.5f	-2.13	NE	NE	NE	-61	03-90		.00	.0	0	0	0	05-21-66	-22.4	1.12	-25.0	2.43	-60.7	7	1.2	1	3,055	733	+2	0.0	03
BMC Software	6.1	54.2	55.0	20.3f	.83	44.4	56.6	56.6	65	03-90		.00	.0	0	0	0	03-08-90	21.8	1.99	43.4	1.50	65.1	0	3.3	590	22,703	8,679	0	0.0	03
C COR Electronics	27.1	13.2	15.6	5.2n	1.19	46.2	-2.4	14.4	27	03-90		.00	.0	0	0	0	03-31-69	8.8	2.17	19.1	1.42	27.2	3	3.1	47	4,283	8157	0	0.0	06
Cambex Cp	37.8	39.0	33.3	2.2f	.78	81.8	81.4	NC	82	08-89		.00	.0	0	0	0	00-00-00	11.0	2.08	22.9	3.55	81.5	30	1.5	39	2,008	10	0	0.0	09
Check Tech	20.9	5.7	20.0	2.0s	.42	1200.0	175.0	NE	71	03-90		.00	.0	0	0	0	00-00-00	11.1	1.95	21.7	3.29	71.4	50	1.6	14	3,735	106	+1	0.0	09
Chips&Technologies	15.7	35.9	37.6	33.0n	2.12	-50.0	-7.0	5.5	31	03-90		.00	.0	0	0	0	00-00-00	12.0	1.95	23.4	1.34	31.3	6	4.1	313	14,720	6229	0	0.0	06
Ciprico Inc	-17.9	-10.9	-16.6	-.3n	-.18	-100.0	-100.0	-100.0	-7	03-90		.20	7.3	0	NE	20	01-08-90	-3.0	.97	-2.9	1.10	-3.2	0	10.0	5	1,999	516	0	0.0	06

(continued)

Computers, Subsystems and Peripherals (Continued)

Company	Rev Last Qtr %	Rev FY to Date %	Rev Last 12 Mos %	Rev Last 12 Mos $Mil	EPS Last 12 Mos $	EPS Last Qtr %	EPS FY to Date %	EPS Last 12 Mos %	EPS 5-Yr Growth Rate %	EPS Par Growth Rate %	Date of Report	Div Current Rate Amt $	Div Current Yield %	Div 5-Yr Growth Rate %	Payout Last FY %	Payout Last 5 Yrs %	Last X-Dvd Date	Profit Margin %	Asset Turnover	Return Total Assets	Return on Equity	Leverage Ratio	Debt to Equity %	Current Ratio	Market Value $Mil	Latest Shares Outstndg 000	Held by Banks-Funds 000	Insider Net Trading 000	Short Interest Ratio Days	Fiscal Year Ends Mo
CMS Enhancements	-12.3	-2.2	-1.5	3.4n	1.04	-70.5	-55.3	-43.5	NC	13	03-90	.00		0	0	9	12-06-89	1.7	4.00	6.8	13.2	1.94	4	2.0	19	3,163	152	-7	0.0	06
Comdisco Inc	7.8	14.5	21.1	104.0s	2.47	-25.0	-8.7	7.4	9	17	03-90	.28	1.5	15	9	11	05-21-90	5.8	.45	2.6	19.0	7.31	187	NA	758	41,534	17,079	-6	0.7	09
Comnet Cp	140.0	-19.5	-41.9	-.2n	-.27	NE	NE	NE	NC	-2	12-89	.00		0	0	0	00-00-00	-.11	.82	-.9	-2.0	2.22	39	1.5	29	2,528	703	+2	0.0	03
Compaq Cptr	27.7	27.7	32.7	342.3q	7.94	8.7	8.7	12.6	73	29	03-90	.00		0	0	0	00-00-00	11.2	1.46	16.4	29.2	1.78	23	2.3	4,888	39,097	26,396	0	1.8	12
Comnucom Systs	23.5	23.5	48.6	1.80	.07	100.0	100.0	40.0	NC	8	03-90	.00		0	0	0	00-00-00	-.6	2.50	1.5	7.9	5.27	197	2.4	46	28,574	637	0	0.0	12
Comp & Commun	-3.9	-3.9	-37.7	-18.1q	-1.60	-100.0	-100.0	NE	NC	-73	03-90	.00		0	0	0	00-00-00	-29.7	.76	-22.5	-73.0	3.24	4	1.4	13	11,314	2,348	0	0.0	12
Comp Automation	-43.8	-29.2	-44.4	.0n	.0n	NE	NE	NE	NC	0	03-90	.00		0	0	0	00-00-00	.0	NC	NC	.0	NC	0	1.0	4	2,410	79	0	0.0	06
Comp Identics	-4.4	-4.4	6.6	.8q	.09	-100.0	-100.0	NE	NC	18	03-90	.00		0	0	0	00-00-00	5.0	2.20	11.0	17.8	1.62	0	2.2	14	9,463	1,497	0	0.0	12
Comp Memories	50.0	50.0		.3q	.02	100.0	100.0	NE	NC	1	03-90	.00		0	0	0	00-00-00	15.0	.09	1.4	1.4	1.00	0	4.2	14	10,683	1,067	0	0.0	12
Comp Prods	-8.2	-8.2	-8.5	4.5q	.22	50.0	50.0	NE	NC	14	03-90	.00		0	0	0	04-01-85	3.8	1.05	4.0	13.7	3.43	185	3.4	58	19,800	4,733	0	0.0	12
Concurrent Cptr	3.3	36.0	64.4	-4.4n	-.22	NE	NE	NE	NC	-12	03-90	.00		0	0	0	00-00-00	-1.3	1.00	-1.3	-11.7	9.00	469	1.5	29	18,147	4,064	-7	0.0	06
Control Data	-50.0	-50.0	-29.6	-677.1q	-16.03	100.0	100.0	NE	NC	0	03-90	.00		0	0	NE	09-09-85	-26.9	1.35	-36.4	NM	.00	88	1.5	813	42,494	27,935	-4	1.9	12
Convex Cptrs	45.9	45.9	48.7	13.2q	.68	66.7	66.7	74.4	NC	17	03-90	.00		0	0	0	00-00-00	7.6	1.00	7.6	16.6	2.18	77	4.3	339	18,175	6,002	0	3.8	12
Copytele Inc	.0	.0	.0	-1.11	-.10	NE	NE	NE	NC	-27	10-89	.00		0	0	0	09-16-87	NC	NC	NC	-26.8	NC	0	40.0	98	11,342	1,195	-115	0.0	10
Cray Cptr	.0	.0	.0	-44.5q	-2.69	NE	NE	NE	NC	-80	03-90	.00		0	0	0	00-00-00	NC	NC	NC	-80.0	NC	0	3.1	64	17,995	7,222	0	0.0	12
Cray Research	17.1	17.1	10.7	97.0q	3.30	560.0	560.0	-21.2	13	16	03-90	.00		0	0	0	08-19-85	12.0	.84	10.1	16.3	1.61	24	2.1	1,284	28,152	20,330	+0	4.2	12
CSP Inc	-16.1	-2.3	9.0	1.0n	.36	-87.5	19.0	33.3	-15	5	06-90	.00		0	0	NE	00-00-00	8.3	.58	4.8	5.3	1.10	0	14.5	15	2,720	646	0	0.0	08
Damon Group Inc	894.3	388.7	282.3	-1.7n	-.36	-100.0	-100.0	-100.0	NC	-8	09-89	.00		0	0	0	00-00-00	-2.6	1.88	-4.9	-7.6	1.55	42	2.9	22	4,970	1,529	0	0.0	12
Data General	-8.1	-7.0	-4.1	-136.3q	-4.65	-100.0	-100.0	NE	NC	-26	03-90	.00		0	0	0	00-00-00	-10.7	1.22	-13.1	-26.1	1.99	14	1.6	340	29,528	19,552	+15	0.7	09
Data Switch Cp	16.9	16.9	-.9	1.6q	.15	NE	150.0	150.0	NC	3	03-90	.00		0	0	0	00-00-00	1.5	.87	1.3	3.3	2.54	115	2.9	41	11,209	3,565	+6	0.0	12
Dataflex	48.3	69.6	70.2	2.5f	1.00	12.5	44.9	44.9	NC	42	04-90	.00		0	0	0	06-15-89	3.1	5.29	16.4	42.4	2.59	8	1.5	20	2,437	353	+46	0.0	03
Datametrics	2.8	7.7	6.8	.08	-.07	NE	NE	NE	NC	0	04-90	.00		0	0	0	00-00-00	.0	NC	NC	.0	NC	127	1.3	4	3,619	218	0	0.0	10
Dataphaz	-20.3	-20.3	-4.6	-4.0q	-.08	NE	NE	NE	NC	-80	04-90	.00		0	0	0	00-00-00	-3.9	4.79	-18.7	-80.0	4.28	0	1.1	7	3,750	100	0	0.0	01
Datapoint Cp	-11.1	-16.7	-14.9	-44.6n	-4.41	NE	NE	NE	NC	-34	04-90	.00		0	0	0	08-12-85	-16.3	.83	-13.5	-33.5	2.48	61	1.5	27	10,119	2,470	+4	29.8	07
Dataram Cp	65.0	40.3	42.8	2.5f	1.41	100.0	76.3	76.3	NC	16	04-90	.00		0	0	34	06-15-90	12.5	1.15	14.4	16.4	1.14	0	12.3	32	1,791	194	+1	0.0	04
Datasouth Cmptr	.0	.0	6.2	-.1q	.00	-100.0	-100.0	NE	NC	NC	03-90	.00		0	0	0	00-00-00	-.6	.83	-.5	-.6	1.20	0	10.4	11	5,691	282	+6	0.0	12
Datum Inc	-8.2	-8.2	5.8	1.3q	.45	-62.5	-62.5	32.4	3	7	04-90	.00		0	0	0	00-00-00	.83	1.19	7.0	7.0	1.63	19	2.5	10	2,714	776	+20	0.0	12
Davox Corp	3.1	3.1		-2.2q	-.44	-80.0	-80.0	NE	NC	-11	04-90	.00		0	0	0	00-00-00	-5.9	1.22	-7.2	-11.4	1.58	9	2.1	24	5,194	548	+4	0.0	12
Dell Computer	37.5	37.5	41.2	8.3q	.44	154.5	154.5	-38.9	NC	10	03-90	.00		0	0	0	00-00-00	2.0	2.40	4.8	10.4	2.17	8	1.7	236	18,694	1,730	+1	0.0	01
DH Tech Inc	21.1	21.1	22.2	6.4q	1.27	36.0	36.0	47.7	51	29	04-90	.00		0	0	0	00-00-00	14.5	1.35	19.6	28.8	1.47	2	4.1	71	5,044	1,235	-11	0.0	12
Digital Equip	4.3	3.6	3.8	644.3n	5.16	-89.7	-55.4	-42.7	15	8	03-90	.00		0	0	0	05-12-86	4.9	1.22	6.0	8.0	1.33	8	2.9	10,353	121,861	83,557	+10	2.1	06
Distributed Log	-6.2	-10.4	-1.7s	-.69	-.69	NE	NE	NE	NC	-26	04-90	.00		0	0	NE	00-00-00	-3.5	1.69	-5.9	-25.8	4.37	109	1.5	3	2,507	462	0	0.0	10
ECC Intl Cp	234.9	63.4	31.5	.2n	.03	NE	-66.7	-66.7	32	-5	03-90	.20	4.3b	32	NE	20	06-15-90	.4	.75	.3	6.0	2.67	69	2.0	27	5,738	2,234	0	0.0	06
Elxsi Grp	-1.3	-1.3	16.9	.7q	-.01	-100.0	-100.0	-100.0	NC	1	03-90	.00		0	0	0	00-00-00	.0	.75	.0	1.1	3.67	122	1.0	38	16,046	2,633	0	0.0	12
Elbit Cptr	52.7	14.2	13.9	13.3f	.95	83.3	25.0	25.0	NC	10	12-89	.24	1.9	0	20	22	05-24-90	7.4	1.04	7.7	13.2	1.71	11	2.2	179	14,020	149	0	0.0	12

(continued)

Company													
Electron Assoc	-5.3	-5.3	4.7	1.4q	.48	NC	15	03-90	.00	3.2	14.6	20	2.2
Elron Electronic	134.2	134.2	51.3	12.6q	1.03	NE	17	03-90	.00	5.5	17.0	34	1.9
ELXSI Inc	-64.2	-53.9	-55.0	-14.11	-.14	NE	0	12-89	.00	NM	NM	33	3.1
EMC Cp	68.0	68.0	35.4	-10.1q	-.42	NE	-10	03-90	.00	-6.8	-10.3	16	6.3
Emulex Cp	-19.7	-21.3	-14.3	1.1q	.01	-99.2	-9	02-29-84	.00		-.3	3	3.4
Encore Cptr	284.0	577.3	5.0	.0*	-1.03	-100.0	0	03-90	.00	NC	.0	1159	.9
Esprit Systems	30.6	6.6	16.4	-3.4n	-.31	NE	21	02-90	.00	-16.2	NS	0	.7
Everex Systs	15.7	14.4	73.6	23.7n	.99	32.0	-1	04-90	.00	5.7	20.8	10	2.2
FAComputer	72.7	73.0	73.6	-.1f	-.03	NE	6	06-89	.00	-.1	-.7	3	1.1
Fleent Co	36.0	36.0	36.9	3.9n	.37	825.0	6	03-90	.00	4.4	6.2	1	3.4
Fingermatrix	.0	.0	-6.0f	-.55		NE	-94	05-89	.00	-30.0	-93.8	0	10.0
Ffcat PI Sys	-20.3	-23.2	-15.3s	-1.59		NE	-52	04-90	.00	-6.6	-52.0	48	1.8
Franklin Elec Pub	3.7	3.2	-2.9f	-.46		-100.0	-13	04-90	.00	-4.1	-12.9	31	2.6
Gandalf Tech	-26.2	-2.3	-10.2n	-.85		-66.7	-12	04-90	.00	-6.2	-11.8	7	2.0
Gateway Comm	-11.1	-11.1	1.1q	.24		60.0	-16	03-90	.00	4.4	15.7	6	3.3
Gen Automation	5.3	-6.1	-.2n	.01		NE	-29	06-14-90	.00	-.5	-26.6	414	1.1
Genee 5	.0	.0	-.1f	-.06		NC	-25	04-90	.00	-5.0	-25.0	25	1.3
Genicom Cp	3.9	3.9	-23.9q	-2.24		-100.0	-68	03-90	.00	-9.2	-69.3	289	2.4
Genisco Tech	-1.2	-4.2	1.2s	.46		233.3	40	03-90	.00	3.5	40.0	307	2.3
Genus Inc	14.0	14.0	8.1q	.74		64.4	12	07-10-90	.00	9.0	11.5	0	5.4
Griffin Tech	10.0	6.1	.7n	.27		NC	26	03-90	.00	5.0	25.9	193	1.8
Hewlett-Pack	15.5	16.1	792.0s	3.33		-5.4	13	04-90	.00	6.2	14.5	9	1.5
Hutchinson Tech	54.8	24.0	.9q	.23		NE	4	03-90	.00	.9	3.8	88	2.7
Inacomp Computers	44.7	45.7	6.9n	.94		20.5	16	04-90	.00	1.5	15.8	46	1.7
Info International	-6.8	5.8	.3f	-.15		-75.0	-18	07-10-90	.00	-.8	1.1	0	2.3
Infotron Syst	-14.5	-14.5	-5.4q	-1.05		-100.0	NC	03-90	.00	-5.9	-9.6	4	1.7
Ingres Cp	35.3	22.8	1.8s	.15		-80.8	-3	12-89	.00	1.3	2.6	6	1.6
Inmac	15.9	14.4	-6.4n	-.68		-100.0	-20	03-28-89	.00	-2.3	-17.7	60	1.5
Intelligent Electrns	119.5	178.5	20.1s	3.18		119.3	26	04-90	.00	1.7	25.7	8	1.3
Intelligent Sys	-23.8	-23.8	-.4q	-.46		-100.0	-11	08-25-89	.00	-7.6	-9.1	17	3.1
Interface Sys	3.1	21.3	2.4s	.56		-24.3	11	05-11-87	.00	6.7	11.3	13	3.5
Intergraph Cp	23.9	23.9	75.0q	1.43		-10.6	12	06-17-85	.00	8.3	11.9	1	3.6
Intermec Cp	1.5	28.5	11.5f	1.51		31.3	21	03-90	.00	6.8	21.0	9	1.9
Intl Bus Mach	11.4	11.4	3845.0q	6.67		-28.7	3	05-04-90	4.84	6.0	10.0	28	1.7
Intl Totalizator	78.4	78.4	4.50	.58		NE	47	03-24-86	.00	12.5	46.9	32	2.1
Iomega Cp	17.3	17.3	12.1q	.73		78.0	NC	03-90	.00	10.7	30.0	1	2.2
IPL Systems	119.0	119.0	2.8q	.56		75.0	30	03-90	.00	16.5	30.1	0	5.4
Iverson Tech	-50.0	-50.0	.1q	-1.00		33.3	-11	03-10-87	.00	.5	.5	86	2.7
JonesPI	7.9	7.9	1.8q	.34		-15.0	29	09-08-86	.00	4.6	28.6	116	2.5
KCR Technology	100.0	66.7	-6.3f	-.76		NE	0	03-90	.00	NM	NM	0	1.2

Source: Media General Financial Services, Richmond, VA.

Computers, Subsystems and Peripherals (Continued)

Company	Rev Pct Chg Last Qtr %	Rev Pct Chg FY to Date %	Rev Pct Chg Last 12 Mo %	Rev Last 12 Mos $Mil	EPS Last 12 Mos $	EPS Last Qtr $	EPS %Chg Last Qtr	EPS %Chg FY	EPS %Chg to Date	EPS %Chg Last 12 Mos	5-Yr Growth %	Par Growth %	Date of Report	Div Amt $	Div Yield %	Div 5-Yr Growth %	Payout Last FY %	Payout Last 5 Yrs %	Last X-Dvd Date	Profit Margin %	Asset Turnover	Return on Total Assets	Leverage Ratio	Return on Equity	Debt to Equity %	Current Ratio	Mkt Value $Mil	Latest Shares Outstndg 000	Held by Banks Funds 000	Insider Net Trading 000	Short Int Ratio Days	Fiscal Year Ends Mo
Key Tronic	-10.9	-.9	2.1	.9n	.12		-100.0	-100.0	-100.0	NE	NE	2	03-90	.00		0	0	0	00-00-00	.6	1.83	1.1	1.45	1.6	2	2.9	39	8,819	2,863	0	0.0	06
Komag	116.5	116.5	27.8	1.8q	.18		NE	NE	NE	NE	NC	2	03-90	.00		0	0	0	00-00-00	1.8	.83	1.5	1.53	2.3	28	3.3	185	13,132	2,010	-48	0.0	12
LDI Cp	32.6	32.6	31.0	9.3q	1.51	18.5	18.5	18.5	17.1	NC	14	04-90	.00		0	0	0	10-17-89	2.5	.60	1.5	9.00	13.5	283	NA	103	6,453	1,673	-266	0.0	01
Lee Data	-35.8	-31.2	-31.5	-50.0f	-4.05	NE	NE	NE	NE	NC	2	03-90	.00		0	0	0	00-00-00	-79.4	1.13	-88.8	1.90	NM	35	2.3	16	12,329	3,185	+10	0.0	03
Lexcom Co	-53.2	-46.2	-21.0	-3.1s	-.40	NE	NE	NE	NE	NC	-34	02-90	.00		0	0	0	02-10-86	-20.7	.87	-18.1	1.90	-34.4		1.7	2	7,763	1,265		0.0	08
Logic Devices	-13.2	-13.2	40.0	.2q	.07	-41.2	-41.2	-41.2	-86.0	NC	4	03-90	.00		0	0	0	00-00-00	1.4	1.21	1.7	2.41	4.1	61	2.6	22	4,499	167	-21	0.0	12
LTX Cp	49.2	-10.5	-20.2	-25.5n	-2.59	NE	NE	NE	NE	NC	-82	04-90	.00		0	0	0	00-00-00	-19.6	1.02	-19.9	4.12	-82.0	242	4.3	34	9,947	2,537	0	0.0	07
Mess Microsysts	13.0	13.0	66.6	.9q	.22	-57.1	-57.1	-57.1	NE	NC	13	03-90	.00		0	0	0	00-00-00	4.5	1.78	8.0	1.56	12.5	4	2.8	17	3,145	266	0	0.0	07
Maxstor Sys	-17.2	-17.2	39.4	-.7q	-.03	-100.0	-100.0	-100.0	NE	NC	-5	03-90	.00		0	0	0	00-00-00	-1.3	1.46	-1.9	2.63	-5.0	4	1.7	24	18,829	4,022	0	0.0	12
Maxtor Cp	44.9	39.9	39.8	18.9f	.90	328.6	328.6	246.2	246.2	75	15	06-90	.00		0	0	0	06-13-86	3.8	1.61	6.1	2.41	14.7	91	4.0	306	20,427	7,947	0	0.0	03
Memory Sciences	-50.0	-50.0	.0	-.8q	-.39	NE	NE	NE	NE	NC	-67	02-90	.00		0	0	0	00-00-00	NC	NC	NC	NC	-66.7	0	11.0	1	1,950	0	0	0.0	11
MicroAge Inc	73.2	74.4	65.7	5.6s	1.25	50.0	50.0	55.8	33.0	NC	21	03-90	.00		0	0	0	00-00-00	1.1	5.55	6.1	3.39	20.7	24	1.4	75	4,300	1,153	0	0.0	09
Micropolis Cp	-5.8	-5.8	-14.1	-37.6o	-3.24	NE	NE	NE	NE	NC	-52	03-90	.00		0	0	0	00-00-00	-12.4	1.40	-17.3	3.02	-52.3	104	2.2	91	11,578	5,124	+1	0.0	12
Miltope Grp	36.7	36.7	44.2	-2.1q	-.35	200.0	200.0	200.0	-100.0	NC	-11	03-90	.00		0	0	0	00-00-00	-2.1	1.57	-3.3	3.30	-10.9	93	2.0	34	5,863	822	+18	0.0	12
Mips Cptr Systs	.0	-6.7	28.5	2.9t	.17	NC	NC	NC	NC	NC	-21	12-89	.00		0	0	0	00-00-00	2.8	.61	1.7	1.35	2.3	1	6.9	371	20,875	3,912	0	0.0	09
Mitek Systems	-2.2	-6.7	-15.1	.5s	.08	100.0	100.0	100.0	NE	NC	42	03-90	.00		0	0	0	00-00-00	2.8	2.21	6.2	6.73	41.7	300	2.1	5	3,468	15	0	0.0	12
Moniterm	1.4	1.4	-15.1	-.5q	-.12	NE	NE	NE	NE	NC	-8	03-90	.00		0	0	0	00-00-00	-1.8	2.00	-3.6	2.28	-8.2	3	1.6	5	4,653	364	0	0.0	12
Moscom Cp	9.1	9.1	16.6	2.7o	.39	71.4	71.4	71.4	18.2	75	20	03-90	.02	.3		0	0	05-25-90	19.3	.93	17.9	1.16	20.8	2	5.7	50	6,420	351	0	0.0	12
Hall Compt Sys	2.2	2.2	12.1	6.2q	.39	-53.8	-53.8	-53.8	-55.7	-7	2	04-90	.28	3.1	23	61	26	06-04-90	2.2	1.36	3.0	1.97	5.9	45	2.4	144	15,739	7,661	+6	0.0	01
Natl Micronetics	17.8	-1.9	-6.8	-3.9n	-.39	-100.0	-100.0	-100.0	-100.0	NC	-34	03-90	.00		0	0	0	00-00-00	-9.5	1.57	-14.9	2.28	-33.9	38	1.5	5	9,680	756	-33	0.0	06
NTeam	.0	.0	.0	-.5f	-.09	NC	NC	NC	NC	NC	0	12-89	.00		0	0	0	00-00-00	-7.1	2.14	-15.2	.00	NM	513	.9	3	6,035	0	0	0.0	08
NBI Inc	-59.8	-53.2	-48.2	-52.0n	-6.11	NE	NE	NE	NE	NC	0	12-89	.00		0	0	0	00-00-00	-89.7	.89	-61.0	.00	NM	12	1.5	3	8,794	1,825	-2	2.3	06
NCR	1.2	1.2	.2	402.9o	5.34	-5.2	-5.2	-5.2	2.3	13	15	03-90	1.40	2.2	11	25	24	07-09-90	6.7	1.34	9.0	2.26	20.3	12	1.5	4,527	70,596	42,955	-3	0.0	12
Netwk Systems	18.2	18.2	13.6	19.5q	.66	116.7	116.7	116.7	88.6	-2	9	03-90	.00		0	0	0	04-16-85	13.0	.57	7.4	1.20	8.9	1	6.7	399	29,289	20,150	0	0.0	12
Norst Data	-16.3	-16.2	-16.2	-41.0t	-1.77	NE	NE	NE	NE	NC	-113	12-89	.37	4.9	NE			05-23-88	-10.9	.75	-8.2	11.41	-33.6	281	1.4	124	16,204	3,628	0	0.0	12
Novell Inc	34.4	33.9	46.0	63.2s	1.76	40.0	50.0	40.0	31.3	71	27	04-90	.00		0	0	0	00-00-00	13.2	1.38	18.2	1.47	26.8	24	5.0	1,857	33,912	19,865	0	0.0	10
Optrotech Ltd	18.2	18.1	17.7	4.5f	.85	50.0	50.0	41.7	41.7	NC	22	12-89	.00		0	0	0	00-00-00	6.2	1.40	8.7	2.51	21.8	13	1.6	41	5,315	179	0	0.0	12
Par Tech	9.5	9.5	16.0	1.8o	.27	-100.0	-100.0	-100.0	107.7	NC	4	03-90	.00		0	0	0	00-00-00	1.9	1.32	2.5	1.52	3.8	8	3.1	37	7,549	1,116	+11	0.0	12
Perceptronics	35.6	1.8	3.5	.6f	.19	NE	NE	NE	NE	NC	60	11-14-85	.00		0	0	0	11-14-85	2.1	1.62	3.4	17.65	60.0	1000	2.0	3	3,462	588	0	0.0	03
Personal Cmptr	58.3	53.2	33.3	-.4s	-.18	NE	NE	NE	NE	NC	0	01-14-88	.00		0	0	0	01-14-88	-3.3	1.21	-4.0	.00	NS	-225	3.1	15	3,887	64	0	0.0	06
Primages	-25.0	21.9	33.3	-1.1q	-.18	NE	NE	NE	NE	NC	0	12-89	.00		0	0	0	00-00-00	-13.8	1.07	-14.7	.00	NS	-450	.9	1	3,184	0	-2	0.0	12
Printronix	5.8	-7.3	-7.4	3.6f	.86	NE	NE	NE	NE	NC	6	12-89	.00		0	0	0	00-00-00	2.9	1.66	4.8	1.33	6.4	0	4.2	48	3,678	1,339	0	0.0	03
Pyramid Tech	64.9	53.9	41.3	10.5s	1.17	58.3	58.3	40.4	8.3	NC	15	03-90	.00		0	0	0	00-00-00	8.1	1.46	11.8	1.28	15.1	0	3.4	295	10,543	4,287	0	0.0	09

Ratio Analysis identity: $r/f \times f/a = r/a \times a/e = r/e$

Company											
Cantel Cp	-37.4	-38.6	-37.8	-2.8	-.17	NE	NE	NE	NC	0	04-90
CMS Inc.	33.4	31.1	20.4	12.9s	1.16	312.5	215.0	NC	19	03-90	
Quantum Cp	67.1	114.6	114.4	47.2t	1.71	-33.3	90.0	NC	47	03-90	
Recognition Equip	-7.5	-9.5	-5.4	-51.3s	-5.00	NE	90.0	NC	-71	04-90	
Penon Inc	15.9	-5.1	-16.3	7.3s	.73	-9.1	-32.7	NC	11	03-90	
Robec	21.6	21.6	21.2	4.8q	1.24	-22.9	-22.9	NC	22	03-90	
Rodime PLC	-43.1	53.9	46.2	-88.9n	-6.40	NE	NE	NC	6	06-88	
Scan Optics	3.8	3.8	-12.5	-13.5q	-2.13	NE	NE	NC	-75	03-90	
Seagate Tech	89.1	74.3	54.5	111.5n	1.94	-4.4	NE	NC	25	03-90	
Selectern Inc	-22.4	0	0	.9	.33	-54.5	-50.7	-16	0	12-89	
Sequent Cptr Systs	94.3	94.3	93.1	16.4q	.80	83.3	83.3	NC	15	03-90	
Sequoia Systs	NA	NA	NA	NA	NA	NA	NA	NA	NC	00-00	
Sharebase Cp	-45.7	-45.7	-13.7	-7.7o	-.86	NE	NE	NC	-71	03-90	
Sigma Designs	-60.8	-60.8	-28.5	6.8q	1.13	-75.5	-75.5	52	13	04-90	
Softsel	38.3	38.3	38.0	10.1q	.81	0	-11.0	-16	28	03-90	
Star Technologies	-28.9	-9.1	-2.7	-3.7n	-.23	NE	NE	NC	-74	12-89	
Storage Techml	87.1	87.1	34.6	42.5s	1.73	3300.0	3300.0	NC	15	03-90	
Stratus Cptr	14.3	14.3	22.6	34.3q	1.65	7.1	-15.8	45	6	04-90	
Sun Microsysts	27.1	32.4	29.2	41.8n	.46	-30.0	-65.4	37	9	03-90	
Supercomput Sol	0	0	0	-4.7o	-.88	NE	NE	NC	-76	03-90	
Symbol Tech	-7.9	-7.9	336.0	13.9q	.64	-96.4	-96.4	60	6	06-01-88	
Symtech Intl	73.7	73.7	40.0	-16.3q	-3.03	-100.0	NE	NC	15	12-89	
System Inds	-6.8	-6.9	-15.7	-1.7n	-.34	NE	NE	NC	-24	04-90	
Tab Products	5.0	8.2	6.1	4.9n	.75	1.4	23.4	-5	6	02-90	
Tandem Cotr	24.2	17.5	19.3	127.8s	1.22	25.8	10.4	21	13	03-90	
Tandon	13.4	13.4	21.1	12.6q	.20	NE	NE	NC	17	03-90	
Tech Data	31.9	31.9	40.7	2.4q	.38	-35.5	-35.5	30	6	04-90	
Telematics Intl	42.1	42.1	27.7	-5.4q	-.33	-69.8	NE	NC	-10	03-90	
TeleVideo Sys	-17.4	-30.4	-53.1	-20.0s	-.44	NE	-100.0	NC	-41	04-90	
Teltron	-25.2	-10.2	-10.6	-14.4t	-1.09	-100.0	-100.0	NC	-15	03-99	
Teradata Cp	128.5	83.3	79.4	17.8n	1.24	NC	200.0	NC	18	03-90	
Terminal Data	-17.5	-13.4	-16.0	-2.9s	-.64	NE	NE	NC	-26	01-22-85	
Three Com	4.5	8.6	8.5	20.5t	.71	-3.7	-39.8	22	10	03-90	
Tigera Grp	600.0	525.0	0	-.9t	-.04	NE	NE	NC	-5	05-90	
Titan Cp	13.8	13.8	3.0	2.6q	.17	300.0	300.0	NC	11	12-88	
TRW Inc	11.5	11.5	8.2	251.0q	4.11	-7.7	-17.7	NC	8	05-07-90	
Ultimate Cp	5.6	4.9	5.0	.1f	.01	-73.7	NE	NC	0	04-90	
Unisys Cp	4.7	4.7	4.7	-563.8q	-4.24	NE	NE	NC	-28	06-19-90	
Unitronix Cp	-15.5	-6.3	-5.0	-.6n	-.24	-100.0	-100.0	NC	-12	03-90	
Valcom Inc	25.1	25.1	41.2	6.6q	1.47	23.3	24.6	NC	19	03-90	

(continued)

Source: Media General Financial Services, Richmond, VA.

Computers, Subsystems and Peripherals (Continued)

Company	Revenue Pct. Change Last Qtr %	FY to Date %	Last 12 Mos %	Earnings Per Share Last 12 Mos $Mil	Last 12 Mos $	Pct. Change Last Qtr %	FY to Date %	Last 12 Mos %	5-Year Growth Rate %	Par Growth Rate %	Date of Report	Dividends Current Rate Amt $	Yield %	5-Year Growth Rate %	Payout Last FY %	Last 5 Yrs %	Last X-Dvd Date	Ratio Analysis Profit Margin %	Asset Turnover	Return on Total Assets	Leverage Ratio	Return on Equity	Debt to Equity %	Curr. ent Ratio	Shareholdings Market Value $Mil	Latest Shares Outstndg 000	Held by Banks-Funds 000	Insider Net Trading 000	Short Interest Ratio Days	Fiscal Year Ends Mo
																		w/I x r/a = w/a x a/e = w/e												
Valid Logic Syst	-15.3	-15.3	30.2	1.8q	.05	-100.0	-100.0	-83.9	NC	2	03-90	.00	0	0	0	0	00-00-00	1.1	1.18	1.3	1.69	2.2	22	2.3	96	31,913	11,756	0	0.0	12
Verdix Cp	33.3	20.0	10.0	1.8	.15	25.0	15.4	15.4	NC	26	03-90	.00	0	0	0	0	00-00-00	16.4	.99	16.2	1.59	25.7	14	2.3	20	11,753	1,415	0	0.0	08
Vermont Resch	-30.8	-40.7	-40.0	-.2s	-.11	-100.0	-100.0	-100.0	NC	-6	03-90	.00	0	0	0	0	00-00-00	-6.7	.72	-4.8	1.31	-6.3	0	3.0	3	2,059	164	+5	0.0	09
Vertex Ind	.0	3.7	33.3	-.1n	-.07	NE	NE	NE	NC	-11	04-90	.00	0	0	0	0	00-00-00	-2.5	1.48	-3.7	3.00	-11.1	44	1.9	2	1,695	0	0	0.0	07
Vitalink Commun	40.9	51.2	59.0	16.3s	1.20	29.2	44.2	64.4	NC	20	03-90	.00	0	0	0	0	00-00-00	23.3	.70	16.2	1.22	19.7	1	5.6	133	13,123	9,325	0	0.0	09
Wang Labs B	-23.2	NA	-20.3	-489.9m	-3.62	NE	NE	NE	NC	-46	03-90	.16	3.8	6	NE	NE	06-26-89	-20.5	.89	-18.3	2.42	-44.2	55	1.4	700	164,671	56,788	-3	0.4	06
Wang Labs C	NA	NA	NA	NA	NA	NA	NA	NA	NC	NC	00-00	1.10	17.3	NA	NA	NA	06-26-89	NC	NC	NA	NC	NA	NA	NA	324	50,776	35	NA	NA	06
Wells American	4.5	.0	.0	-.7s	-.13	NE	NE	NE	NC	-10	09-89	.00	0	0	0	0	00-00-00	-5.4	1.11	-6.0	1.65	-9.9	6	1.9	2	5,071	318	0	3.1	03
Wicat Systs	20.8	12.6	14.6	2.4f	.11	NE	NE	NE	NC	10	03-90	.00	0	0	0	0	00-00-00	5.1	1.43	7.3	1.38	10.1	2	2.4	101	21,050	2,751	0	0.0	03
Xeta Cp	-16.7	-4.2	.0	-1.2s	-.60	NE	NE	NE	NC	-50	04-90	.00	0	0	0	0	00-00-00	-24.0	1.11	-26.7	1.87	-50.0	13	1.5	1	1,965	2	-5	0.0	10
XL Datacomp	39.1	36.4	39.7	21.3s	1.79	-43.2	58.5	50.4	NC	27	03-90	.00	0	0	0	0	03-27-89	5.4	1.56	8.4	3.18	26.7	17	1.8	168	11,402	4,020	0	0.0	09
Zentec Corp	-33.3	-15.3	NA	-3.3q	-1.03	NE	NE	NE	NC	0	03-90	.00	0	0	0	0	00-00-00	-30.0	1.02	-30.6	.00	NM	1	3.4	1	3,556	227	0	0.0	12
Ztel Cp	-11.3	-4.5	6.8	2.5s	.45	-35.3	-45.5	-8.2	NC	18	03-90	.00	0	0	0	0	00-00-00	8.1	1.75	14.2	1.27	18.1	1	5.0	32	5,180	1,072	0	0.0	09
Zycad Cp	7.0	7.0	-7.8	-2.7q	-.19	-100.0	-100.0	-100.0	NC	-8	03-90	.00	0	0	0	0	00-00-00	-7.7	.84	-6.5	1.22	-7.9	0	4.3	13	15,103	3,545	0	0.0	12

Source: Media General Financial Services, Richmond, VA.

Construction

Value of New Construction Put in Place, 1982–94
(in billions of 1982 dollars)

Type of Construction	1982	1986	1987	1988	1989[1]	1990[2]	Percent Change 1988-89	Percent Change 1989-90	Percent Change 1989-94[3]
Total New Construction	246.6	345.3	347.6	352.4	351.0	350.8	-1	0	1
Residential	84.6	168.6	171.2	174.8	173.2	176.8	-1	2	1
Single-family	41.5	92.0	100.7	102.9	100.8	102.9	-2	2	1
Multifamily	15.5	28.0	22.4	19.7	19.1	19.1	-3	0	0
Home improvement	27.7	48.6	48.1	52.2	53.2	54.8	2	3	3
Private Nonresidential	108.1	113.1	108.3	109.5	109.3	105.9	0	-3	-2
Manufacturing facilities	17.3	12.0	11.6	12.5	13.1	14.2	5	8	5
Office	23.0	25.0	22.5	23.4	22.9	20.6	-2	-10	-5
Hotels & Motels	4.1	6.5	6.3	5.7	6.0	5.4	5	-10	-7
Other Commercial	14.2	24.7	24.7	25.1	23.8	22.7	-3	-5	-2
Religious	1.5	2.4	2.3	2.4	2.3	2.3	6	0	*
Educational	1.5	2.0	2.9	2.4	2.5	2.7	0	5	*
Hospital & Institutional	5.9	4.7	5.1	6.0	6.0	6.3	-8	5	3
Misc. buildings	1.7	2.4	2.8	3.6	3.3	3.4	-6	2	*
Telecommunications	7.1	7.7	7.9	7.2	6.8	6.7	4	-2	3
Railroads	2.6	2.6	2.2	2.3	2.4	2.5	0	2	3
Electric utilities	18.3	14.2	10.8	10.1	10.1	10.2	6	1	0
Gas utilities	5.5	4.6	4.7	5.0	5.3	5.0	0	-4	*
Petroleum pipelines	0.4	0.3	0.3	0.3	0.3	0.3	0	0	*
Farm structures	3.7	1.8	1.8	1.7	1.7	1.7	0	2	*
Misc. structures	1.3	2.1	2.4	1.7	2.4	2.0	45	-25	*
Public Works	53.8	63.6	68.1	68.1	68.4	68.0	1	-1	1
Housing & redevelopment	1.7	1.3	1.3	1.3	1.4	1.4	10	0	*
Federal industrial	1.6	1.4	1.2	1.2	1.1	1.1	-10	0	*
Educational	5.9	7.4	7.5	9.2	10.3	10.8	12	5	3
Hospital	2.0	1.8	1.9	1.9	1.8	1.9	-5	5	*
Other public buildings	5.8	8.7	9.6	9.4	9.6	9.8	2	2	*
Highways	16.3	19.6	22.1	23.2	22.0	21.4	-5	-3	0
Military facilities	2.2	3.4	3.7	3.0	2.9	2.6	-5	-10	-2
Conservation & development	5.0	4.4	4.8	4.0	4.0	3.9	0	-3	*
Sewer systems	5.5	7.7	8.3	7.5	7.7	7.3	3	-5	-2
Water supplies	2.9	3.2	3.2	3.2	3.3	3.5	3	5	3
Misc. public structures	4.9	4.8	4.7	4.4	4.2	4.4	5	0	*

Note: Detail may not add to totals because of rounding.
[1]Estimated.
[2]Forecast.
[3]Average annual rate.

*Long-term forecast not made separately for this category.
SOURCE: U.S. Department of Commerce; Bureau of the Census and International Trade Administration (ITA). Estimates and forecasts by ITA.

Source: *U.S. Industrial Outlook 1990*, U.S. Department of Commerce.

STOCKS by INDUSTRY

MEDIA GENERAL FINANCIAL SERVICES

Company	Rev Pct Chg Last Qtr %	Rev Pct Chg FY to Date %	Rev Pct Chg Last 12 Mos %	Rev Last 12 Mos $Mil	EPS Last 12 Mos $	EPS Pct Chg Last Qtr %	EPS Pct Chg FY to Date %	EPS Pct Chg Last 12 Mos %	EPS 5-Yr Growth Rate %	Par Growth Rate %	Date of Report	Div Cur Rate Amt $	Div Cur Rate Yield %	Div 5-Yr Growth Rate %	Payout Last FY %	Payout Last 5 Yrs %	Last X-Dvd Date	Pft Margin %	Return on Total Assets	Asset Turnover	Leverage Ratio	Return on Equity	Debt to Equity %	Current Ratio	Mkt Value $Mil	Latest Shares Outstndg 000	Held by Banks/Funds 000	Insider Net Trading 000	Short Interest Ratio Days	Fiscal Year Ends Mo
Contractors – General																														
Ind. Group	14.1	20.2	15.8	429.1	.96	23.6	24.0	-17.3	NC	7	---	.52	2.6	0	56	36	---	2.6	1.81	NC	3.06	14.4	32	1.3	9,541	475,622	95,428	-30	2.0	--
Am Med Bldg	-53.6	-53.6	-30.4	.0q	.01	NC	NC	NE	NC	0	03-90	.00	.0	0	0	0	00-00	.0	NC	NC	NC	NS	NC	.7	2	12,737	665	0	2.0	12
Beazer PLC ADR	46.3	46.3	46.9	148.6s	.69	20.0	21.5	-59.2	NC	2	12-89	.61	5.2	0	102	22	03-30-90	4.0	1.70	6.8	3.10	21.1	70	1.5	3,111	287,608	686	0	1.4	06
Black Ind	.0	.0	8.3	1.0q	1.29	140.9	14.9	51.8	7	2	12-89	.30	2.9	6	31	25	12-22-89	7.7	1.31	10.1	1.10	11.1	0	10.0	9	831	134	0	.0	09
Blount A	-12.3	-12.3	-37.0	14.2q	1.17	.0	.0	-76.4	21	9	05-90	.45	4.0	17	72	40	06-11-90	2.2	1.23	2.7	3.33	9.0	63	1.3	84	7,471	3,431	0	.1	02
Blount B	NA	NA	NA	NA	NA	NA	NA	NA	NA	NC	05-90	.40	3.5	NA	NA	NA	06-11-90	NA	NC	NA	NC	NA	NA	NA	54	4,766	105	0	NA	02
Fluor Corp	12.1	21.4	15.5	129.2s	1.60	56.7	43.9	53.8	NC	15	04-90	.24	.5	-40	10	NE	06-20-90	1.9	3.16	6.0	2.98	17.9	9	1.3	3,571	79,793	50,049	-17	1.3	10
Foster Wheeler	18.3	18.3	20.5	35.0q	.99	20.0	20.0	32.0	-2	4	03-90	.50	1.9	0	46	64	05-09-90	2.7	1.11	3.0	2.50	7.5	52	1.7	946	35,356	20,878	0	2.2	12
Geodynamics Cp	10.8	7.4	4.0	3.5n	1.17	-3.1	-.8	-.8	NC	9	02-90	.50	5.6	0	13	3	05-25-90	6.9	1.51	10.4	1.44	15.0	0	3.2	26	2,930	1,100	-11	.0	05
Harding Assocs	33.9	34.5	34.6	4.3n	.92	45.5	33.3	46.0	21	21	03-90	.00	.0	0	0	0	07-19-89	6.5	1.92	12.5	1.64	20.5	0	2.4	103	4,423	2,007	0	.0	05
Jacobs Eng	14.7	20.9	21.7	12.5s	1.14	40.9	45.2	50.0	NC	21	03-90	.00	.0	0	0	0	04-03-90	1.4	4.21	5.9	3.61	21.3	11	1.2	253	10,760	2,400	-3	.0	09
Morrison Knuds	-13.4	-13.4	10.0	33.1q	2.87	10.7	10.7	NE	NC	6	03-90	1.48	2.7	1	53	NE	05-10-90	1.6	2.88	4.6	2.87	13.2	1	1.2	623	11,371	8,556	0	2.1	12
Peters JM	20.3	20.3	-8.9	21.9q	1.56	-69.4	-69.4	-40.9	19	19	05-90	.00	.0	0	0	0	00-00	6.7	.75	5.0	3.82	19.1	0	NA	91	13,990	735	0	9.6	02
Stone & Web	-2.6	-2.6	-12.0	19.4q	1.29	-18.6	-18.6	-51.0	-8	0	03-90	1.20	3.1	10	88	41	06-26-90	8.1	.42	3.4	1.50	5.1	6	2.6	533	15,153	3,776	0	3.9	12
Turner Cp	67.3	67.3	30.0	7.7q	1.56	NE	NE	NE	NC	5	03-90	1.00	6.7	11	200	471	05-21-90	9.9	.09	.9	17.00	15.3	0	.9	73	4,883	736	+1	.0	12
Union Valley	-53.0	-53.0	-16.4	-1.3q	-.36	-100.0	-100.0	-100.0	NC	-8	03-90	.00	.0	0	0	0	00-00	-1.7	.47	-.8	9.38	-7.5	115	NA	4	3,560	170	0	5.2	12
Contractors – Special																														
Ind. Group	8.8	22.2	13.0	32.6	-.76	NE	NE	NE	NC	3	---	.26	1.9	-1	51	120	---	.5	1.00	.5	4.40	2.2	107	1.2	2,722	202,228	62,515	-878	1.7	--
ACMAT Cp	74.2	74.2	100.0	4.0q	.85	100.0	100.0	174.2	NC	14	03-90	.00	.0	NA	0	NE	00-00	8.7	.39	3.4	4.15	14.1	114	.6	59	4,752	49	-25	.0	12
ACMAT Cp Cl A	NA	NA	NA	NA	NA	NA	NA	NA	NC	NC	03-90	.00	.0	NA	0	NA	00-00	NA	NC	NC	NC	NA	NA	NA	32	2,938	256	0	NA	NA
Am Ship Bldg	11.8	11.8	-10.5	-9.3q	-1.45	NE	NE	NE	-50	-7	12-89	.00	.0	NA	0	NE	05-04-87	-13.7	1.03	-14.1	3.57	-50.3	86	.6	32	6,059	1,100	-112	.0	09
Avondale Inds	21.6	21.6	24.2	.7q	.04	-88.9	-88.9	-84.6	NC	-7	03-90	.92	9.8	0	767	NE	05-21-90	.1	1.00	.1	3.00	.3	21	2.1	146	15,524	7,351	-8	2.1	12
Banister Inc	89.0	89.0	95.5	-5.7q	-.98	-100.0	-100.0	-100.0	NC	-10	03-90	.00	.0	0	0	0	00-00	-.9	2.89	-2.6	3.96	-10.3	40	1.2	51	5,948	604	-933	1.2	12

Bonneville Pac	300.0	134.5	125.0	4.2h	34	NE	NE	-100.0	78.9	NC	5	01-90	.00		0	0	0	0	00-00-00	0	9.3	.16	1.5	3.47	5.2	203	1.3	81	12,909	5,120	0	0.0	04
Brand Cos	101.4	101.4	90.2	12.5q	1.31	136.7	136.7	70.1	NC	15	03-90	.00		0	0	4	00-00-00	4	3.8	2.16	8.2	1.77	14.5	1	1.5	349	9,249	2,716	0	0.0	12
Burnup & Sims Inc	9.2	2.3	-3.1	4.4n	.47	-100.0	-60.6	-44.7	NC	8	01-90	.00		0	0	NE	00-00-00	NE	2.4	1.21	2.9	2.59	7.5	85	2.6	168	12,598	79	0	0.0	04
Dravo Corp ◦□	4.8	4.8	1.7	16.5q	.94	1200.0	1200.0	NE	17	03-90	.00		0	0	NE	04-28-87	NE	5.8	1.09	5.8	2.93	17.0	49	1.4	222	14,776	9,132	+123	123	12
Dycom Ind	89.5	33.5	21.7	8.1n	1.50	57.7	29.5	19.0	26	04-90	.00		0	0	NE	12-01-87	3	5.4	3.37	18.2	1.44	26.2	7	2.6	102	4,925	1,271	+43	0.0	07
Fischbach Cp ◆	2.6	-3.8	-11.4	-45.6s	-11.65	NE	NE	NE	NC	0	03-90	.00		0	0	NE	08-19-85	NE	-6.1	2.07	-12.6	.00	NM	68	1.1	43	3,912	184	0	15.0	09
Gen Magnaplate	12.0	4.2	.0	1.2n	.36	-28.6	-26.6	-23.4	25	17	03-90	.01	.26	15	0	14	01-23-89	0	13.3	.96	12.8	1.36	17.4	19	4.9	15	3,119	98	+152	0.0	06
Goldfield Cp	15.6	15.6	.0	2.4q	.08	-25.0	-25.0	-38.5	NC	21	03-90	.00		0	0	0	00-00-00	0	12.6	1.20	15.1	1.40	21.2	19	3.2	13	30,162	4,122	0	0.1	12
Indfrlg	61.0	61.0	437.5	5.7q	.95	40.0	40.0	NC	14	02-90	.00		0	0	0	00-00-00	0	13.3	.14	1.8	7.83	14.1	367	NA	58	5,625	312	0	0.0	11
Insituform East	-22.6	NA	-9.5	1.8n	.40	-25.0	-17.5	-20.0	18	13	03-90	.05	1.2	11	0	3	06-25-90	9.5	1.16	11.0	1.31	14.4	0	2.7	19	4,557	307	0	0.0	08
Kasler Cp	32.8	32.1	20.9	2.1s	.40	1200.0	1200.0	108.3	NC	10	04-90	.10	.8	37	-9	NE	06-05-90	1.6	2.00	3.2	4.00	12.8	113	2.0	69	5,255	1198	+5	0.0	10
McDermott Intl ◆	-7.9	9.2	9.1	-10.2t	-5.09	NE	NE	NE	NC	-2	03-90	1.00	3.3	NE	NE	06-11-90	-.4	.75	-.3	5.67	-1.7	156	.9	1,124	37,458	23896	0	1.1	03
Myers LE Grp	-3.5	-3.5	1.7	2.5q	.89	-88.9	-88.9	NC	25	03-90	.09	.5	0	0	NE	05-24-90	4.2	2.86	12.0	2.29	27.5	9	1.8	45	2,390	132	0	1.1	12
Nichols Rsch	40.8	39.5	38.0	3.4n	.97	25.4	22.7	26.0	19	06-90	.00		0	0	0	00-00-00	4.9	2.73	13.4	1.39	18.6	0	3.3	35	3,374	538	+0	0.0	08
Tacoma Boatbuilding	NA	NA	NA	NA	NA	NA	NA	NA	NC	NC	00-00	.00		NA	NA	NA	00-00-00	NA	NC	NA	NC	NA	NA	NA	26	7,449	0	0	0.0	NA
Todd Shipyards ◦□	-27.6	-35.6	-35.4	32.8t	6.97	NE	NE	NE	NC	0	03-90	.00		0	0	NE	01-09-97	13.6	.71	9.6	.00	NS	0	2.8	23	4,194	587	0	8.9	03
Transatl Inds	-16.0	-16.0	-6.6	-.3q	-.18	-100.0	-100.0	-100.0	-6	03-90	.00		0	0	0	00-00-00	-1.1	.82	-.9	6.33	-5.7	238	1.4	2	2,646	482	0	0.0	01
Williams Ind	15.9	21.7	19.1	1.4n	.63	NE	800.0	800.0	-7	7	04-90	.00		0	NA	0	08-06-84	1.2	1.50	1.8	3.72	6.7	160	NA	23	2,409	982	0	0.0	07

Materials and Components Manufacturers

Ind. Group																																
	10.1	12.1	8.8	210.0	1.46	19.4	9.6	24.0	19	7	---	.52	1.3	1	29	33	-----	3.3	1.42	4.7	2.32	10.9	36	1.5	5,274	137,761	62392	-.5	2.4	--
Atkinson Guy F ◦	-2.0	-2.0	-11.4	-38.3q	-4.38	NE	NE	NE	-31	19	04-25-90	.48	3.2	NE	-18	NE	04-25-90	-4.8	2.31	-11.1	2.53	-28.1	4	1.5	132	8,777	1450	-20	0.0	12
CBI Inds ◦	7.6	7.6	7.4	42.9q	1.85	157.1	157.1	88.8	NC	8	05-07-90	.60	1.5	298	13	13	05-07-90	2.8	1.14	3.2	3.59	11.5	124	1.5	776	19,110	12722	+8	8.7	12
Dover Corp	7.9	8.5	8.4	144.0q	2.28	3.5	2.7	2.7	13	12	12-89	.72	1.8	31	13	31	06-25-90	6.8	1.50	10.2	1.89	19.3	4	1.4	2,444	62,575	30,544	+8	1.8	12
Nucor Corp	12.4	12.4	16.0	56.8q	2.66	-6.7	-6.7	-18.9	5	8	03-90	.48	.7	16	13	13	06-25-90	4.3	1.28	5.5	1.76	9.7	27	1.4	1,491	21,378	13,317	+7	4.0	12
Robertson, HH	-1.4	-1.4	25.0	2.7q	.41	NE	NE	NE	NC	3	03-90	.00		0	0	0	08-26-85	.5	1.80	.9	3.67	3.3	58	1.4	70	6,337	-977	0	0.0	12
Software Toolworks	1154.8	482.2	475.0	1.9t	.10	-100.0	-41.2	-41.2	NC	29	03-90	.00		0	0	0	04-06-90	2.8	7.29	20.4	1.43	29.2	0	2.6	360	19,484	1,382	0	0.0	08

Source: Media General Financial Services, Richmond, VA.

Trends and Forecasts: Soap, Cleaners, and Toilet Goods (SIC 284)
(in millions of dollars except as noted)

Item	1987¹	1988²	1989³	1990⁴	Percent Change 1987-88	1988-89	1989-90
Industry Data							
Value of shipments⁵	34,427	37,180	39,675	—	8.0	6.7	—
2841 Soap & other detergents	11,510	12,645	13,303	—	9.9	5.2	—
2842 Polishes/sanitation goods	5,514	5,849	6,339	—	6.1	8.4	—
2843 Surface active agents	2,980	3,376	3,829	—	13.3	13.4	—
2844 Toilet preparations	14,424	15,310	16,204	—	6.1	5.8	—
Value of shipments (1987$)	34,427	35,376	36,615	37,725	2.8	3.5	3.0
2841 Soap & other detergents	11,510	11,796	12,182	12,423	2.5	3.3	2.0
2842 Polishes/sanitation goods	5,514	5,624	5,763	5,897	2.0	2.5	2.3
2843 Surface active agents	2,980	3,120	3,267	3,430	4.7	4.7	5.0
2844 Toilet preparations	14,424	14,835	15,403	15,975	2.8	3.8	3.7
Total employment (000)	119	125	125	126	5.0	0.0	0.8
2841 Soap & other detergents	31.4	31.8	30.9	31.1	1.3	-2.8	0.6
2842 Polishes/sanitation goods	20.3	21.4	22.1	22.8	5.4	3.3	3.2
2843 Surface active agents	8.9	9.4	9.7	10.0	5.6	3.2	3.1
2844 Toilet preparations	58.4	62.6	61.9	62.0	7.2	-1.1	0.2
Production workers (000)	72.2	75.7	76.1	77.4	4.8	0.5	1.7
2841 Soap & other detergents	19.2	19.5	19.0	19.2	1.6	-2.6	1.1
2842 Polishes/sanitation goods	13.0	13.8	14.4	15.0	6.2	4.3	4.2
2843 Surface active agents	4.6	4.9	5.1	5.4	6.5	4.1	5.9
2844 Toilet preparations	35.4	37.5	37.6	37.8	5.9	0.3	0.5
Average hourly earnings ($)	10.67	10.92	10.91	—	2.3	-0.1	—
2841 Soap & other detergents	13.80	14.31	14.35	—	3.7	0.3	—
2842 Polishes/sanitation goods	9.88	10.02	9.99	—	1.4	-0.3	—
2843 Surface active agents	13.40	13.60	13.57	—	1.5	-0.2	—
2844 Toilet preparations	8.87	9.02	9.00	—	1.7	-0.2	—

Product Data

Value of shipments[6]	32,228	34,915	37,190	—	8.3	6.5	—
2841 Soap & other detergents	9,572	10,516	10,980	—	9.9	4.4	—
2842 Polishes/sanitation goods	5,090	5,400	5,852	—	6.1	8.4	—
2843 Surface active agents	2,836	3,214	3,651	—	13.3	13.6	—
2844 Toilet preparations	14,730	15,785	16,707	—	7.2	5.8	—
Value of shipments (1987$)	32,228	33,267	34,365	35,490	3.2	3.3	3.3
2841 Soap & other detergents	9,572	9,810	10,055	10,310	2.5	2.5	2.5
2842 Polishes/sanitation goods	5,090	5,192	5,320	5,450	2.0	2.5	2.4
2843 Surface active agents	2,836	2,970	3,110	3,260	4.7	4.7	4.8
2844 Toilet preparations	14,730	15,295	15,880	16,470	3.8	3.8	3.7

Trade Data

Value of imports	734	863	1,076	1,231	17.6	24.7	14.4
2841 Soap & other detergents	82.5	84.2	86.0	88.0	2.1	2.1	2.3
2842 Polishes/sanitation goods	34.4	35.9	40.0	43.0	4.4	11.4	7.5
2843 Surface active agents	171	225	300	350	31.6	33.3	16.7
2844 Toilet preparations	446	518	650	750	16.1	25.4	15.4
Import/new supply ratio[7]	0.023	—	—	—	—	—	—
2841 Soap & other detergents	0.006	—	—	—	—	—	—
2842 Polishes/sanitation goods	0.035	—	—	—	—	—	—
2843 Surface active agents	0.057	0.065	0.076	—	14.0	16.9	—
2844 Toilet preparations	0.029	0.032	0.037	—	10.3	15.6	—
Value of exports	819	993	1,170	1,345	21.2	17.8	14.6
2841 Soap & other detergents	144	134	140	145	-6.9	4.5	3.6
2842 Polishes/sanitation goods	89.3	113	140	160	26.5	23.9	14.3
2843 Surface active agents	202	244	290	350	20.8	18.9	20.7
2844 Toilet preparations	384	502	600	690	30.7	19.5	15.0
Export/shipments ratio	0.025	0.028	0.031	—	12.0	10.7	—
2841 Soap & other detergents	0.015	0.013	0.013	—	-13.3	0.0	—
2842 Polishes/sanitation goods	0.018	0.021	0.024	—	16.7	14.3	—
2843 Surface active agents	0.071	0.076	0.079	—	7.0	3.9	—
2844 Toilet preparations	0.026	0.032	0.036	—	23.1	12.5	—

[1] Industry and product data are preliminary. Trade data are adjusted to conform to the 1987 SIC.
[2] Estimated, except for exports and imports.
[3] Estimated.
[4] Forecast.
[5] Value of all products and services sold by establishments in the soap, cleaners, and toilet goods industry.
[6] Value of products classified in the soap, cleaners, and toilet goods industry produced by all industries.
[7] New supply is imports plus corresponding product shipments.

SOURCE: U.S. Department of Commerce: Bureau of the Census; International Trade Administration (ITA). Estimates and forecasts by ITA.

Source: *U.S. Industrial Outlook 1990*, U.S. Department of Commerce.

STOCKS by INDUSTRY

MEDIA GENERAL FINANCIAL SERVICES

Cosmetics and Grooming Aids

Company	Rev %Last Qtr	Rev %FY to Date	Rev %Last 12 Mos	Earn Last 12 Mos $Mil	EPS Last 12 Mos $	Earn %Last Qtr	Earn %FY to Date	Earn %Last 12 Mos	Earn 5-Yr Gr	Par Gr	Rpt Date	Div Amt	Yield	Div 5-Yr Gr	Payout Last FY	Payout 5 Yrs	Last X-Dvd Date	Profit Margin	Asset Turn	Ret Tot Assets	Lever Ratio	Ret Equity	Debt/Eq	Curr Ratio	Mkt Val $Mil	Shares Out 000	Held by Banks Funds 000	Insider Net Trad 000	Short Int Ratio Days	Fiscal Yr Ends Mo
Ind. Group	7.2	7.3	7.8	372.0	.96	-26.9	-25.9	-23.4	NA	5	00-00	.58	1.8	NA	47	57	--	3.8	1.53	5.8	6.50	37.7	190	NA	9,476	296,929	108,455	-106	1.2	--
Alberto-Culver Cl A	NA	NA	NA	NA	NA	NA	NA	NA	NC	15	00-00	.20	1.1	8	NA	20	04-30-90	NA	NA	NA	NC	NC	NA	NA	196	10,234	4,864	+4	.0	09
Alberto-Culver Cl B	7.9	8.2	12.3	31.6	1.21	16.7	17.8	17.5	NC	16	03-90	.20	.8	8	16	20	04-30-90	4.2	2.07	8.7	2.26	19.7	43	2.0	427	16,636	4,138	+9	14.8	09
Affin Inc	67.6	-8.6	-14.2	-.4	-.06	NE	-84.6	-100.0	NC	-3	04-90	.08		0	0	9	02-20-86	-2.2	1.14	-2.5	1.36	-3.4	7	4.4	47	6,688	519	0	.1	07
Aloette Cosmetics	15.2	15.2	11.1	3.9	1.31	16.0	16.0	31.0	NC	14	03-90	.32	1.7	24	24	9	04-23-90	19.0	.88	16.7	1.14	19.1	3	10.7	56	2,936	512	0	.0	12
Avon Products	-.2	-.2	4.8	63.6	.53	NE	NE	-51.8	-26	-27	03-90	1.00	2.7	-12	270	100	05-14-90	1.9	1.79	3.4	8.88	30.2	271	1.1	2,074	56,442	21,247	0	5.8	12
Beauticontrol Cos	32.5	25.5	28.2	5.7	1.09	17.9	18.2	34.6	NC	28	05-90	.28	1.3b	0	10	3	06-25-90	11.4	2.47	28.2	1.33	37.5	0	2.9	102	4,867	913	0	.0	11
Beauty Labs	-36.7	-28.6	-15.7	-1.9	-.75	-100.0	NE	NE	NC	-33	12-89	.00		0	0	0	00-00-00	-11.9	1.44	-17.1	1.95	-33.3	9	1.9	3	2,435	106	0	.0	03
Cascade Intl	76.8	87.8	70.8	6.6	.39	-33.3	16.0	18.2	NC	14	03-90	.00		0	0	0	12-11-89	16.1	1.66	26.7	1.09	29.2	0	7.2	57	18,220	433	0	.0	06
CCA Inds	82.8	82.8	100.0	.6	.07	10.2	-33.3	NE	NC	14	02-90	.00		0	0	25	00-00-00	3.0	2.47	7.4	1.84	13.6	23	2.4	10	7,656	490	0	.0	06
Del Labs	3.1	3.1	5.1	-1.8	-1.07	-28.6	10.2	-100.0	NC	-9	03-90	.40	1.5	1	NE	25	05-07-90	-1.5	1.27	-1.9	3.53	-6.7	143	2.2	30	1,145	199	0	2.5	11
DEP Cp	6.5	14.9	16.6	-.8	.08	-28.6	-37.1	-85.2	-16	-40	04-90	.00		0	0	0	05-02-88	.8	1.38	1.1	3.18	3.5	120	1.8	24	5,883	1,089	0	.0	07
Genzyme	24.7	24.7	29.6	-36.3	-2.84	-100.0	-100.0	-100.0	NC	0	03-90	.00		0	0	0	00-00-00	NM	NC	NC	NC	-39.9	6	7.2	261	14,275	7,294	0	.0	12
Gillette Co	11.3	11.3	8.4	294.1	2.65	-6.3	-6.3	1.9	30	0	03-90	1.08	1.8	10	36	45	04-25-90	7.5	1.25	9.4	.00	NM	1487	1.7	5,745	96,758	57,030	-6	1.0	12
Goody Products	-8.4	-8.4	-5.7	-5.5	-.85	-4.7	-6.3	-100.0	NC	-9	03-90	.00		18	NE	49	00-00-00	-2.6	1.42	-3.7	2.11	-7.8	66	3.7	95	6,525	1,143	+2	.0	12
Guest Supply	12.8	11.3	10.6	-2.2	-.58	NE	NE	NE	NE	8	03-90	.00		0	0	0	12-11-89	-3.0	1.57	-4.7	1.87	-8.8	44	2.5	21	3,822	681	0	.0	09
Helene Curtis	21.8	21.8	18.2	12.8	1.37	-100.0	-100.0	-21.3	20	8	05-90	.20	.8b	0	14	9	05-08-90	1.7	2.29	3.9	2.49	9.7	39	1.7	246	9,289	4,260	+9	.2	02
Jean Philippe Frag	20.0	20.0	20.0	.5	.07	.0	.0	.0	NC	14	03-90	.00		0	0	0	00-00-00	10.0	1.19	11.9	1.20	14.3	0	5.7	6	7,499	29	0	.0	12
Johnson Prdts	13.9	8.3	6.8	.5	.11	200.0	-66.7	.0	NC	5	02-90	.00		0	0	0	02-90-90	1.6	1.56	2.5	1.88	4.7	0	1.5	8	3,998	283	0	1.9	08
Lee Pharm	-25.7	-28.6	-16.6	-1.0	-.25	-100.0	-100.0	-100.0	NC	-12	03-90	.00		0	0	0	10-27-86	-4.0	1.60	-6.4	1.40	-11.5	10	1.7	10	4,135	404	+1	.0	09
MEM Co	-31.1	-31.1	0	-2.1	-1.11	NE	NE	-100.0	NC	-7	03-90	.20	2.4	-2	NE	134	06-25-90	-2.9	1.38	-4.0	1.40	-5.6	0	2.6	22	2,651	768	0	2.2	12
Ross Cosmetics	26.5	19.3	12.5	.4	.11	NE	450.0	37.5	NC	7	02-90	.00		0	0	0	00-00-00	2.2	1.82	4.0	1.78	7.1	9	2.3	24	2,144	6	0	.0	08
Saint Ives Labs	-17.9	-17.9	-8.2	2.5	.37	-78.3	-78.3	-46.4	NC	8	03-90	.00		0	0	0	00-00-00	2.5	2.48	6.2	1.26	7.8	0	4.2	53	6,928	1,228	-125	.0	12
Speciality Retail	11.3	11.3	0	-.3	-.08	NC	NC	NC	NC	NC	03-90	.00		0	0	0	00-00-00	-1.0	2.60	-2.6	NM	NM	7600	2.9	7	5,513	19	0	.0	12

Soaps and Cleansers

Company	Revenue Pct Change Last Qtr %	Revenue Pct Change FY to Date %	Revenue Last 12 Mos %	Revenue Last 12 Mos $Mil	Earnings Per Share Last 12 Mos $	Earnings Last Qtr $	Earnings Pct Change Last FY Qtr %	Earnings Pct Change FY to Date %	Earnings Last 12 Mos %	Earnings 5-Year Growth Rate %	Earnings Par Growth Rate %	Earnings Date of Report	Dividends Current Rate Amt $	Dividends Current Rate Yield %	Dividends 5-Year Growth Rate %	Dividends Payout Last FY %	Dividends Payout Last 5 Yrs %	Dividends Last X-Dvd Date	Profit Margin %	Asset Turnover	Return on Total Assets	Leverage Ratio	Return on Equity	Debt to Equity %	Current Ratio	Market Value $Mil	Latest Shares Outstanding 000	Held by Banks-Funds 000	Insider Net Trading 000	Short Interest Ratio Days	Fiscal Year Ends Mo
				$Mil	$	$	%	%	%	%	%		$	%	%	%	%		π/f ×	f/a = π/a ×	a/e =	π/e	π/e	%		$Mil	000	000	000	Days	Mo
Ind. Group	-9.5	10.2	9.7	3,702.9	3.32	-57.3	-9.4	-6.7	19	16	- - -	1.66	2.5	1	44	43	- - -	5.5	1.55	8.5	3.71	31.5	63	1.4	63,094	931,568	257,437	+18	1.7	- -
Church & Dwight	7.7	7.7	11.2	124.9	.60	180.0	180.0	-4.8	8	6	03-90	.28	1.5	7	82	42	05-11-90	3.1	1.65	5.1	2.18	11.1	47	2.2	398	20,677	9,468	+2	0.0	12
Clorox Co	13.8	11.3	9.9	130.3n	2.36	1.4	6.3	-8.5	8	6	03-90	1.44	3.4	15	49	41	04-23-90	8.9	1.20	10.7	1.55	16.6	1	1.9	2,322	55,130	3,918	+11	3.0	06
Colgate Palmol	8.1	8.1	7.0	294.0q	4.15	18.4	18.4	46.6	22	24	03-90	1.80	2.6	5	39	59	04-19-90	5.7	1.46	8.3	5.06	42.0	151	1.9	4,728	69,145	29,960	+1	0.7	12
Ecolab Inc	14.2	14.2	9.7	8.5q	.20	NE	NE	-87.0	-33	-5	03-90	.66	2.5	3	60	25	06-13-90	.6	1.33	.8	2.63	21	55	1.6	671	25,565	6,723	-7	0.5	12
Neutrogena Cp	-7.5	1.5	7.8	22.1s	.83	-79.2	-30.9	-11.7	40	21	04-90	.20	1.0	26	16	15	12-18-89	10.8	1.64	17.7	1.59	28.2	0	1.8	541	26,095	4,288	0	0.0	10
Omnitec Inc	.0	.0	200.0	-.4q	-.04	NC	NC	NC	NC	-40	12-88	.00	.0	0	0	0	00-00-00	-13.3	.74	-9.8	4.08	-40.0	270	2.0	3	10,815	15	0	0.0	09
Proct & Gambl	12.8	11.9	11.2	1489.0m	4.20	22.6	20.8	20.7	16	15	03-90	1.80	2.1b	4	42	60	04-16-90	6.4	1.42	9.1	3.14	28.6	71	1.4	30,166	346,239	47,132	+11	4.0	06
Stanhome	26.7	26.7	24.8	46.1q	2.31	19.0	19.0	14.9	25	13	03-90	.80	2.4	20	30	30	06-12-90	7.6	1.82	13.8	1.96	27.1	1	1.5	656	19,365	3,414	0	2.4	12
Unilever NV	-243.2	11.8	11.8	1106.9m	6.02	-30.3	2.0	2.0	29	30	12-89	2.41	2.8	24	30	30	05-03-90	4.9	1.69	8.3	5.94	49.3	78	1.2	13,684	160,041	23,912	0	2.8	12
Unilever PLC	-576.2	3.6	3.6	594.0m	.90	-100.0	-75.0	-75.0	3	-18	12-89	1.46	2.9	31	133	34	04-16-90	5.0	1.60	8.0	3.61	28.9	32	1.3	9,925	198,696	1,607	0	3.4	12

Source: Media General Financial Services, Richmond, VA.

Trends and Forecasts: Drugs (SIC 283)

(in millions of dollars except as noted)

Item	1987¹	1988²	1989³	1990⁴	Percent Change		
					1987–88	1988–89	1989–90
Industry Data							
Value of shipments⁵	39,090	43,091	46,774	—	10.2	8.5	—
2833 Medicinals & botanicals	3,348	3,721	3,928	—	11.1	5.6	—
2834 Pharmaceutical preps	32,070	35,500	38,781	—	10.7	9.2	—
2835 Diagnostic substances	2,083	2,196	2,318	—	5.4	5.6	—
2836 Bio prod ex diagnostic	1,589	1,674	1,747	—	5.3	4.4	—
Value of shipments (1987$)	39,090	40,503	41,887	43,338	3.6	3.4	3.5
2833 Medicinals & botanicals	3,348	3,423	3,501	3,575	2.2	2.3	2.1
2834 Pharmaceutical preps	32,070	33,240	34,350	35,500	3.6	3.3	3.3
2835 Diagnostic substances	2,083	2,187	2,318	2,480	5.0	6.0	7.0
2836 Bio prod ex diagnostic	1,589	1,653	1,718	1,783	4.0	3.9	3.8
Total employment (000)	170	172	176	179	1.2	2.3	1.7
2833 Medicinals & botanicals	11.6	12.4	13.2	14.0	6.9	6.5	6.1
2834 Pharmaceutical preps	132	133	134	135	0.8	0.8	0.7
2835 Diagnostic substances	14.1	14.4	15.2	15.8	2.1	5.6	3.9
2836 Bio prod ex diagnostic	12.8	13.1	13.4	13.7	2.3	2.3	2.2
Production workers (000)	79.1	80.7	82.0	83.1	2.0	1.6	1.3
2833 Medicinals & botanicals	6.1	6.5	6.9	7.2	6.6	6.2	4.3
2834 Pharmaceutical preps	59.8	60.5	61.1	61.6	1.2	1.0	0.8
2835 Diagnostic substances	6.7	7.0	7.3	7.5	4.5	4.3	2.7
2836 Bio prod ex diagnostic	6.5	6.7	6.7	6.8	3.1	0.0	1.5
Average hourly earnings ($)	12.25	12.55	12.88	—	2.4	2.6	—
2833 Medicinals & botanicals	15.48	15.90	16.30	—	2.7	2.5	—
2834 Pharmaceutical preps	12.41	12.72	13.06	—	2.5	2.7	—
2835 Diagnostic substances	10.78	11.05	11.34	—	2.5	2.6	—
2836 Bio prod ex diagnostic	9.03	9.30	9.60	—	3.0	3.2	—

Product Data

Item	1986	1987	1988	1989	% chg 1986–87	% chg 1987–88	% chg 1988–89
Value of shipments[5]	35,054	38,344	41,516	—	9.4	8.3	—
2833 Medicinals & botanicals	4,222	4,698	5,116	—	11.3	8.9	—
2834 Pharmaceutical preps	26,475	29,066	31,584	—	9.8	8.7	—
2835 Diagnostic substances	2,621	2,757	2,910	—	5.2	5.5	—
2836 Bio prod ex diagnostic	1,736	1,823	1,906	—	5.0	4.6	—
Value of shipments (1987$)	35,054	36,083	37,185	38,254	2.9	3.1	2.9
2833 Medicinals & botanicals	4,222	4,322	4,426	4,537	2.4	2.4	2.5
2834 Pharmaceutical preps	26,475	27,215	27,975	28,702	2.8	2.8	2.6
2835 Diagnostic substances	2,621	2,746	2,910	3,070	4.8	6.0	5.5
2836 Bio prod ex diagnostic	1,736	1,800	1,874	1,945	3.7	4.1	3.8

Trade Data

Item	1986	1987	1988	1989	% chg 1986–87	% chg 1987–88	% chg 1988–89
Value of imports	2,795	3,485	4,454	5,321	24.7	27.8	15.5
2833 Medicinals & botanicals	2,468	3,056	3,849	4,620	23.8	25.9	20.0
2834 Pharmaceutical preps	164	199	250	300	21.3	25.6	20.0
2835 Diagnostic substances	0.0	0.0	—	—	—	—	—
2836 Bio prod ex diagnostic	164	230	300	340	40.2	30.4	13.3
Import/new supply ratio[7]	0.074	0.083	0.097	—	12.2	16.9	—
2833 Medicinals & botanicals	0.369	0.394	0.429	—	6.8	8.9	—
2834 Pharmaceutical preps	0.006	0.007	0.008	—	16.7	14.3	—
2835 Diagnostic substances	0.000	0.000	—	—	—	—	—
2836 Bio prod ex diagnostic	0.036	—	—	—	—	—	—
Value of exports	3,229	3,934	4,681	5,553	21.8	19.0	18.6
2833 Medicinals & botanicals	1,982	2,463	2,963	3,570	24.3	20.3	20.5
2834 Pharmaceutical preps	676	858	1,000	1,200	26.9	16.6	20.0
2835 Diagnostic substances	0.0	0.0	—	—	—	—	—
2836 Bio prod ex diagnostic	571	614	660	720	7.5	7.5	9.1
Export/shipments ratio	0.092	0.103	0.113	—	12.0	9.7	—
2833 Medicinals & botanicals	0.469	0.524	0.579	—	11.7	10.5	—
2834 Pharmaceutical preps	0.026	0.030	0.032	—	15.4	6.7	—
2835 Diagnostic substances	0.000	0.000	—	—	—	—	—
2836 Bio prod ex diagnostic	0.131	—	—	—	—	—	—

[1]Industry and product data are preliminary. Trade data are adjusted to conform to the 1987 SIC.

[2]Estimated, except for exports and imports.

[3]Estimated.

[4]Forecast.

[5]Value of all products and services sold by establishments in the drugs industry.

[6]Value of products classified in the drugs industry produced by all industries.

[7]New supply is imports plus corresponding product shipments.

SOURCE: U.S. Department of Commerce: Bureau of the Census; International Trade Administration (ITA). Estimates and forecasts by ITA.

Source: *U.S. Industrial Outlook 1990*, U.S. Department of Commerce.

MEDIA GENERAL
FINANCIAL SERVICES

STOCKS by INDUSTRY

Drug Manufacturers

Company	Rev Last Qtr %	Rev FY-to-Date %	Rev Last 12 Mos %	Rev Last 12 Mos $Mil	EPS Last 12 Mos $	EPS Last Qtr %	EPS FY-to-Date %	EPS Last 12 Mos %	EPS 5-Yr Gr %	Par Gr %	Date of Report	Div Rate $	Div Yield %	Div 5-Yr Gr %	Payout Last FY %	Payout Last 5 Yrs %	Last X-Dvd Date	Profit Margin %	Asset Turnover	Return Total Assets	Leverage Ratio	Return on Equity	Debt/Eq %	Current Ratio	Mkt Value $Mil	Shares Outstndng 000	Held by Banks/Funds 000	Insider Net Trading 000	Short Int Ratio Days	Fiscal Yr Ends Mo
Ind. Group	-48.3	11.3	10.2	9,055.4	1.89	-5.9	4.3	1.2	24	10	—	1.11	2.4	1	45	44	—	14.2	.86	122	2.07	25.3	18	1.8	219,140	4,844,526	G	-1805	4.2	--
A L Labs	-1.1	-1.1	6.4	12.5q	1.12	24.0	24.0	21.7	15	11	03-90	.16	.7	33	11	14	06-06-90	4.7	.91	4.3	3.12	13.4	109	1.6	257	11,179	3,989	0	14.6	12
Abbott Labs	11.0	11.0	9.4	866.8q	2.00	15.9	15.9	15.6	18	19	03-90	.84	2.0	19	35	35	07-09-90	16.1	1.14	18.3	1.78	32.5	5	1.5	18,441	444,360	226,204	+4	1.3	12
Advanced Mag	33.3	36.4	14.2	.8s	.26	-80.0	-53.3	-36.6	1	5	03-90	.08	.0	0	18	0	00-00-00	10.0	.47	4.7	1.11	5.2	0	9.3	45	3,303	130	0	0.0	09
Advanced Med	NA	NA	NA	NA	NA	NE	NA	NA	NA	NC	00-00	.00	.0	NA	NA	NA	00-00-00	NA	NC	NA	NC	NA	NA	NA	118	10,639	919	+98	NA	09
Alcide Cp	12.5	-22.7	.0	-2.2n	-.10	NE	NE	NE	NC	NC	02-90	.00	.0	0	0	0	00-00-00	-73.3	1.31	-96.7	.00	NM	NA	2.0	20	23,383	3,503	0	NA	05
Allergan Inc	NA	NA	NA	NA	NA	NE	NE	NE	NE	NC	00-00	.19	1.0	NA	NA	NA	05-21-90	NM	NM	NM	NC	-44.0	23	11.5	1,218	66,732	43,389	0	0.0	12
Alliance Pharma	-50.0	-11.8	.0	-16.5n	-1.68	NE	NE	NE	NC	44	03-90	.00	.0	0	0	0	00-00-00	NM	NM	NM	NC	NM	NA	1.8	155	13,335	2,597	+66	0.0	06
Alpha 1 Bio Med	0	100.0	-100.0	-1.1n	-.33	NE	NE	NE	NC	NC	12-89	.00	.0	0	0	0	00-00-00	NC	.20	NM	NC	NM	40	1.8	16	3,423	273	0	2.6	03
Alza Cp Cl A	9.2	9.2	3.5	19.9q	.58	23.1	23.1	11.5	34	11	03-90	.00	.0	0	0	0	00-00-00	34.3	.20	6.9	1.55	10.7	40	9.0	1,302	27,851	17,379	-150	0.0	12
Am Biodynamics	66.7	50.0	100.0	-.8f	-.14	NE	NE	NE	NE	0	11-89	.00	.0	0	0	0	07-09-86	-40.0	1.82	-72.7	.00	NM	0	1.2	2	5,998	10	0	0.0	11
Am Home Prods	19.3	19.3	25.5	1152.9q	3.66	13.3	13.3	11.6	10	24	03-90	2.15	4.1b	8	55	58	05-07-90	16.4	1.24	20.3	2.88	58.5	5	3.2	16,465	313,612	187,470	0	4.3	12
Amgen	437.7	184.2	182.4	19.1f	1.11	NE	NE	NE	NC	12	03-90	.00	.0	0	0	0	00-00-00	9.6	.96	9.2	1.28	11.8	19	6.5	1,332	17,137	6,416	-8	0.0	03
Appld Bioscience	20.9	20.9	22.4	5.2q	1.54	20.6	20.6	24.2	NC	16	03-90	.00	.0	0	0	0	00-00-00	8.7	.85	7.4	2.14	15.8	7	1.0	115	3,275	2,217	0	0.0	12
Bar Labs	-5.1	3.7	9.2	.9n	.10	NE	NE	NE	NC	3	03-90	.00	.0	0	0	0	00-00-00	1.1	1.18	1.3	2.08	2.7	35	2.0	60	7,595	705	0	1.2	06
Biocraft Labs	22.0	33.8	34.1	3.2f	.23	-100.0	-61.0	-61.0	-4	2	03-90	.10	.6	0	43	3	09-14-89	2.8	1.04	2.9	1.24	3.6	6	5.2	236	14,013	2,858	+2	0.8	03
Bionerica Inc	.0	.0	.0	-.8q	-.14	NE	NE	NE	NC	-24	08-89	.00	.0	0	0	0	00-00-00	-80.0	.26	-21.1	1.15	-24.2	206	3.2	2	6,154	320	0	0.0	05
Biotechnica Intl	-20.0	-20.0	28.5	-15.3q	-1.73	-100.0	-100.0	-100.0	-24	-76	03-90	.00	.0	0	0	0	00-00-00	-56.7	.38	-21.4	3.54	-75.7	4	2.2	60	16,463	2,019	+4	0.0	12
Block Drugs Co	6.1	5.9	6.1	46.1f	2.62	4.7	5.6	5.6	12	11	03-90	.70	2.0	7	25	24	06-12-90	10.6	1.04	11.0	1.35	14.8	0	2.1	611	17,588	3,792	0	0.0	03
Bolar Pharm	-77.2	-77.2	-34.8	8.0q	.36	-100.0	-100.0	-76.6	23	11	03-90	.04	.6	14	5	4	02-12-90	9.3	.47	4.4	1.23	5.4	0	3.4	133	21,319	5,124	-2743	30.1	12
Bristol Myers Sq	8.5	8.5	7.7	812.0n	1.55	18.2	18.2	-37.5	NC	-6	03-90	2.12	3.3	14	140	88	06-29-90	9.1	1.10	9.6	1.67	.1	5	2.1	33,345	526,159	283,511	+113	3.5	12
Calif Biotech	-20.0	-20.0	50.0	-8.0q	-.71	NE	NE	NE	-13	-13	03-90	.00	.0	0	0	0	00-00-00	-66.7	.18	-11.9	1.06	-12.6	0	5.9	107	11,371	1,883	0	0.0	12
Camb Bio Sci	.0	6.6	125.0	-9.7q	-.91	NE	NE	NE	-33	-33	11-89	.00	.0	0	0	0	00-00-00	NM	NC	NC	NC	-33.2	0	6.8	43	10,634	750	-2	0.0	12
Carrington Labs	-75.0	7.7	7.7	-1.7f	-.32	NE	NE	NE	-32	-32	03-90	.00	.0	0	24	21	00-00-00	-21.3	.86	-18.3	1.75	-32.1	47	3.3	122	6,087	1,491	+19	0.0	11
Carter-Wallace	11.8	7.7	50.3	50.3f	3.30	5.0	11.1	11.1	19	13	03-90	.82	1.5	27	24	0	05-02-90	9.1	1.20	10.9	1.53	16.7	7	2.5	834	15,231	4,542	0	0.1	03
Centocor Inc	9.9	9.9	34.5	.1q	.01	NC	NC	-94.7	NC	0	03-90	.00	.0	0	0	0	00-00-00	.1	1.00	.1	1.00	.1	17	4.9	515	11,679	5,237	+0	0.0	12

Chantal Pharm	-100.0	-80.0	-100.0	-5.5f	-.32	NE	NE	NE	NE	NC	NE	NC	0	0	.00	06-88	0	0	0	NC	NC	NM	NC	NC	NM	0:00:00	31	17,322	2,525	0	0.0	06
Chattem Inc	-17.7	-58.5	.0	0*	-5.26	1432.4	NE	310.0	NE	NC	0	.56	1.8	-7	.00	02-90	0	NE	-7	NC	NC	NC	NC	NC	NC	05-11-90	39	1,260	283	-7	0.0	11
Collaborative Rsh	-33.3	-36.8	-43.7	-3.1s	-.30	NE	NE	NE	NE	NC	-24	.59	.0	0	.00	03-90	0	0	0	NC	NC	-20.4	1.16	NC	-23.7	00:00:00	20	10,656	914	0	0.0	08
Columbia Labs	200.0	250.0	250.0	-8.7q	-.92	NE	NE	NE	NE	NC	-87	.00	.0	0	.00	03-90	0	0	0	NC	NM	NC	NC	NM	-87.0	06-12-89	106	9,849	523	0	18.4	12
Cooper Develop	-20.0	-14.3	-23.5	-21.5s	-6.60	NE	NE	NE	NE	NC	0	.00	.0	0	.00	04-90	0	0	0	NC	NM	NC	NC	NM	NM	07-28-87	3	3,258	273	0	0.0	10
Cytogen	.0	.0	.0	-13.7q	-1.18	NE	NE	NE	NE	NC	-50	.00	.0	0	.00	03-90	0	0	0	NC	NM	NC	NC	NM	-49.6	00:00:00	117	12,125	966	0	0.0	12
CytRxC	200.0	200.0	200.0	-4.9q	-.29	NE	NE	NE	NE	NC	0	.92	.0	0	.00	09-89	0	0	0	NC	NM	NC	NC	NM	NM	00:00:00	32	18,421	203	0	0.0	12
Diagnostic Prd	20.1	29.1	28.0	16.0q	1.25	17.2	17.2	17.9	34	.76	18	.76	.7	17	.00	03-90	8	17	18	34	19.1	.90	1.18	22.5	25.0	05-03-90	424	11,942	3,111	+1	9.3	12
Duramed Pharm	-36.6	-36.6	-10.7	-7.3q	-1.49	-100.0	-100.0	NE	5	.90	-61	.30	.0	0	.24	03-90	0	0	0	NC	-23.3	1.14	2.63	-61.3	-23.2	00:00:00	19	6,177	1,515	+4	0.0	12
E Z EM Inc	-7.2	5.8	12.5	6.5q	.81	-75.0	-75.0	-15.6	5	.14	12	.82	.0	0	.75	02-90	0	0	-5	NC	9.1	.82	1.26	11.5	8.0	05-16-88	76	8,050	1,665	-3	0.0	05
Elan Cp	20.6	93.5	95.6	5.2q	.33	.0	106.3	106.3	NC	.47	9	.47	.0	0	.00	03-90	0	0	0	NC	5.5	.80	1.64	9.0	11.6	06-15-87	307	15,530	2,897	-30	0.1	03
Evergood Prods	16.3	20.2	21.0	-1.4f	-.85	NE	NE	NE	NC	1.80	-34	.00	.0	0	.00	12-89	0	0	0	NC	-11.0	.47	3.10	-34.1	-6.1	00:00:00	72	1,597	45	0	0.0	03
Forest Labs	100.0	60.9	60.2	29.7q	1.45	27.3	20.8	20.8	32	.77	16	.77	.0	0	.00	03-90	0	0	0	NC	15.3	.77	1.05	16.1	19.9	05-16-86	867	19,214	10,577	0	7.0	03
Genentech Inc	31.9	31.9	21.1	49.9q	.57	66.7	28.0	28.0	NC	.58	11	.58	.0	0	.00	03-90	0	0	0	NC	7.0	.58	1.51	10.6	12.1	03-02-87	2,329	83,991	22,817	+6	1.1	12
Glaxo Hldgs	19.3	19.3	14.8	1161.4s	1.54	15.4	14.1	9.2	5	.82	17	.82	2.6	20	.75	12-89	20	31	29	31	26.6	.82	1.51	32.6	26.5	03-30-90	21,601	744,864	43,260	0	2.0	06
Greenwich Pharm	.0	.0	.0	-8.6q	-.41	NE	NE	NE	NC	NC	0	NC	.0	0	.00	03-90	0	0	0	NC	NC	NC	NC	NM	NM	00:00:00	165	21,960	1,419	0	0.0	12
Halsey Drug	7.5	7.5	15.7	.4q	.06	-62.5	-62.5	-76.9	NC	2.22	6	.60	.0	0	.00	11-09-99	0	0	0	NC	4.0	.60	1.45	5.8	1.8	00:00:00	25	5,530	171	0	11.7	12
Hickam Dow	3.4	.0	.0	.6f	.20	-100.0	-100.0	-66.5	NC	.60	4	.52	.0	0	.00	12-89	0	0	0	NC	3.0	.62	1.43	4.3	5.0	05-16-86	20	2,108	720	+5	0.0	03
Hycor Biomed	13.0	13.0	11.1	1.1q	.19	NE	NE	NE	NC	1.82	22	1.67	.0	0	.00	03-90	0	0	0	NC	16.7	.58	1.32	22.0	11.0	00:00:00	39	5,333	127	0	0.0	12
ICN Biomed	148.6	152.0	94.3	8.2s	.74	84.6	110.0	124.2	15	.58	15	.58	.14	31	.00	04-99	29	31	-5	NC	4.6	.58	3.93	18.1	8.0	04-09-90	103	11,146	312	0	41.6	11
ICN Pharm	56.9	56.9	20.6	-95.2q	-7.06	-100.0	-100.0	-100.0	NC	.48	0	.48	.0	0	.00	03-90	0	0	0	NC	-21.8	.48	.00	NM	-45.3	00:00:00	43	12,207	2,405	0	24.9	11
IGI	8.7	8.7	11.7	.0q	.01	.0	.0	.0	NC	.36	0	.36	.0	0	.00	02-90	0	0	0	NC	.0	.36	.00	.0	.0	00:00:00	72	7,613	1,048	+8	85.5	12
Immunex Cp	121.7	121.7	68.4	-8.0q	-1.31	NE	NE	NE	NC	NC	-53	-.81	.0	0	.00	03-90	0	.3	-53	NC	-9.1	NC	5.86	-53.3	-25.0	00:00:00	233	7,763	3,051	-73	0.0	08
Instar Cp	NA	NA	NA	NA	NA	NE	NE	NE	NA	NC	NC	.62	.0	0	.00	00-00	NA	NA	NC	NA	NC	NC	NC	NA	NA	00:00:00	67	14,000	127	0	NA	NA
Invitron Cp	-73.5	-73.5	-52.9	-20.2q	-1.31	NE	NE	NE	NC	NC	-72	.00	2.6	0	.00	03-90	0	0	-72	NC	NC	NC	NC	NM	NM	00:00:00	15	15,421	83	+1564	0.0	12
Iroquois Brands	-33.1	-20.4	-23.8	-16.0n	-11.35	NE	87.5	NE	NC	.97	-59	.00	.0	0	.00	09-89	0	0	-59	NC	-32.3	.97	.00	NS	-33.3	00:00:00	6	2,218	99	-180	0.0	07
Jones Med Ind	63.0	63.0	36.3	1.8q	3.95	87.5	87.5	51.4	NC	.92	18	1.00	.68	17	.00	03-90	5	10	18	NC	11.0	.92	1.97	21.7	12.0	06-18-90	47	3,455	145	0	3.5	12
KV Pharma	14.5	14.1	6.8	1.2s	-.02	NE	-100.0	-100.0	NC	NC	5	.90	.0	0	.00	03-90	0	5	NC	.0	3.5	.90	1.43	5.0	3.9	07-29-86	38	4,850	1,359	+4	52.4	03
Leiner P Nutri	6.3	19.3	19.3	4.7f	.90	100.0	100.0	46.2	NC	.60	16	1.13	.0	0	.24	03-90	0	16	11	NC	6.4	.60	2.44	15.6	3.2	00:00:00	82	5,227	782	-450	0.0	03
Lifecore Biomed	41.7	5.6	.0	-.4n	-.08	-100.0	-100.0	-100.0	NC	.60	-5	.00	.0	0	.10	05-90	0	0	-5	NC	-4.8	.60	1.13	-5.4	-8.0	00:00:00	29	5,146	315	0	0.0	06
Lilly Eli Co	1.3	1.3	-.7	995.6q	3.37	17.2	17.2	18.2	13	.71	14	1.56	2.0	44	1.64	05-90	44	13	14	NC	17.0	.71	1.56	26.5	23.8	05-09-90	23,177	278,816	192,847	-180	20.4	12
Liposome Co	-88.9	-88.9	-25.0	-7.5q	-.53	NE	NE	NE	NC	.92	-62	NC	.0	0	.00	03-90	0	-62	NC	NC	NC	.92	1.82	-62.0	NM	05-14-90	16	14,194	274	0	0.0	12
Marion Merrill	14.7	14.7	21.9	78.5q	.48	-100.0	NE	-54.3	47	1.22	56	1.00	2.4	22	.60	06-14-90	24	47	56	NC	10.0	1.22	1.38	13.8	8.2	06-14-90	3,822	149,897	32,192	-16	0.8	06
Marsam Pharm	188.9	188.9	70.0	.1q	.01	NE	NE	NE	NC	.62	3	.62	.0	0	.00	07-21-90	0	0	3	NC	.0	.62	1.13	.9	1.3	07-21-90	94	4,981	270	0	0.0	12
Medchem Prods	45.1	22.1	13.6	4.5s	.99	33.3	27.3	26.9	10	.67	22	1.85	.0	0	.00	03-90	0	22	NC	12.0	.67	1.85	22.2	18.0	03-14-88	17	4,478	230	0	20.6	08
Medi Mal	.0	.0	.0	-1.0f	-.31	NE	NE	NE	NC	1.00	-59	.00	.0	0	.00	07-89	0	0	-59	NC	NC	1.00	.00	NM	NM	00:00:00	6	5,599	5	0	0.0	07
Merck & Co	11.9	11.9	10.9	1558.8q	3.95	19.8	19.8	22.7	29	.92	24	1.82	2.1	41	1.80	05-29-90	41	29	24	NC	23.1	.92	1.92	44.3	23.1	05-29-90	34,302	395,408	210,783	0	3.5	12
MGI Pharma Inc	-17.6	-17.6	.0	.0f	-.02	-100.0	-100.0	NE	NC	NC	0	NC	.0	0	.00	03-90	0	0	NC	NC	NC	NC	NC	.0	.0	00:00:00	41	8,105	1,047	+4	0.0	12
Molecular Biosyst	21.4	118.0	111.1	4.2f	.43	-100.0	-100.0	79.2	12	.49	15	1.43	.0	0	.00	03-90	0	0	15	NC	10.8	.49	1.43	15.4	22.1	06-25-90	175	9,410	2,176	0	0.0	03
Mylan Labs	26.0	8.5	7.9	26.2f	.72	160.0	44.0	44.0	10	.57	14	1.08	.4	0	.10	03-90	14	10	4	NC	19.1	.57	1.08	20.6	27.6	00:00:00	873	36,204	11,370	0	3.5	03
Natural Alternatives	38.1	61.5	120.0	1.0n	.24	NC	NC	NE	NC	3.55	59	.00	.0	0	.00	03-90	0	0	59	NC	32.3	3.55	1.82	58.8	9.1	01-05-90	18	3,847	5	0	0.0	06
Natures Sunshine	19.7	19.7	19.5	3.9q	.75	-15.0	-15.0	13.6	52	2.73	18	1.40	1.96	31	.24	03-90	12	18	52	NC	19.4	2.73	1.40	27.1	7.1	05-14-90	63	5,062	824	-58	0.0	12
Natures Bounty	23.8	30.9	31.4	.4s	.48	73.7	92.3	200.0	NC	1.83	4	1.08	.0	0	.00	03-90	0	4	NC	NC	1.1	1.83	3.18	3.5	.6	07-12-88	9	983	35	+0	0.0	09

(continued)

Drug Manufacturers (Continued)

Company	Rev Last Qtr %	Rev FY to Date %	Rev Last 12 Mos %	Rev Last 12 Mos $Mil	EPS Last 12 Mos $	EPS Chg Last Qtr %	EPS Chg FY to Date %	EPS Chg Last 12 Mos %	EPS 5-Yr Growth %	Par Growth %	Date of Report	Div Current Amt $	Div Yield %	Div 5-Yr Growth %	Payout Last FY %	Payout Last 5 Yrs %	Last X-Dvd Date	Profit Margin %	Asset Turn	Return on Total Assets %	Leverage Ratio	Return on Equity %	Debt to Equity %	Current Ratio	Mkt Value $Mil	Latest Shares Out 000	Held by Banks/Funds 000	Insider Net Trading 000	Short Int Ratio Days	Fiscal Yr Ends Mo
Newport Pharm	40.0	40.0	34.3	-2.0q	-.20	-100.0	-100.0	NE	NC	-15	03-90	.00	.0	0	0	0	00-00-00	-4.7	1.40	-6.6	2.32	-15.3	69	2.2	33	11,384	1,722	0	0.0	12
Nix O Tine Pharm	.0	100.0	NA	-1.4s	-.31	NA	NA	NC	NC	-88	11-89	.00	.0	0	0	0	00-00-00	NA	NC	NA	NC	-87.5	NA	4.2	1	5,228	1,249	0	0.0	05
North Am Vaccine	NA	NA	NA	NA	NA	NA	NA	NA	NC	NC	00-00	.00	.0	NA	NA	NA	00-00-00	NA	NA	NA	NA	NA	NA	NA	32	9,034		0	NA	NA
Novo Nordisk	12.0	12.0	31.3	108.1q	2.65	-13.2	-13.2	-31.5	4	9	03-90	.62	1.3	14	16	13	04-23-90	9.1	.67	6.1	1.87	11.4	25	1.8	1,563	31,572	1,817	+10	4.3	12
Par Pharm	-54.2	-44.4	-30.6	-7.0s	-.64	-100.0	-100.0	-100.0	NC	-13	03-90	.04	.5	0	0	0	05-26-89	9.1	.75	-6.8	1.78	-12.1	25	2.9	88	11,153	1,463	+1	8.3	09
Pfizer Inc	3.2	3.2	3.4	69.2q	4.11	4.9	4.9	-14.7	6	6	03-90	2.40	3.7	11	54	45	08-06-90	12.1	.69	8.3	1.84	15.3	51	1.5	10,601	165,313	101,603	+1	1.3	12
Pharmacia AB	28.7	3.9	3.8	122.7t	.75	-67.4	-56.1	-56.1	NC	22	12-89	.21	.8	0	27	14	05-09-90	10.1	.95	9.6	3.17	30.4	335	2.7	1,733	65,400	1,949	0	0.0	12
Pharmacontrol	14.1	18.1	13.6	-5.6s	-.58	NE	NE	NE	NC	NC	12-89	.00	.	0	0	0	00-00-00	-22.4	.99	-22.1	.00	NM	1.2		4	10,173	391	0	0.0	06
Procyte Cp	-33.3	-33.3	.	-10.7n	-.24	NE	NE	NC	NC	-10	12-89	.00	.	0	0	0	00-00-00	NM	NC	NC	NC	-9.8	47	25.8	43	5,918	423	0	0.0	12
Quadra Logic Tech	25.0	30.0	100.0		-1.08	NE	NE	NE	NC	0	10-89	.00	.	0	0	0	00-00-00	NM	NC	NC	NC	NM		7.1	113	9,392	259	0	0.0	01
Ribi Immuno	50.0	50.0	14.5	-2.8q	-.32	NE	NE	NE	NC	-28	03-90	.00	.	0	0	0	05-01-85	NM	NC	NC	4.38	-27.7	219	19.3	31	8,636	1,062	+3	0.0	12
Rorer Group	15.1	15.1	4.6	69.0q	2.13	-100.0	-100.0	6.5	11	10	03-90	.34	1.2	2	30	32	05-09-90	5.7	.68	3.9	1.85	17.1	9	2.4	2,208	32,171	22,687	0	1.0	12
Schering-Plough Cp	4.0	4.0	.	496.0q	2.20	19.6	19.6	19.6	20	12	03-90	1.12	2.4	17	43	41	04-30-90	15.5	.88	13.7	NC	25.4	-347	1.7	10,692	226,280	140,132	+32	2.3	12
SmithBc	-542.5	-100.0	.	.0*	5.99	-100.0	-92.2	160.4	NC	NC	03-90	.94	2.0	0	0	0	06-01-90	NC	NC	NC	NC	NS	81	.9	2,538	53,006	257	0	11.7	12
Summa Med	-100.0	.0	.	-4.2n	-.33	NE	NE	-100.0	NC	NC	12-89	.00	.	0	0	0	00-00-00	NM	NC	NC	NC	NM		1.9	53	14,266	978	0	0.0	03
Synbiotics	-11.1	-16.4	-14.2	-4.0t	-.83	NE	NE	NE	NC	-21	03-90	.00	.	0	0	0	00-00-00	-66.7	.29	-19.6	1.09	-21.3		14.1	18	5,003	726	-8	0.0	03
Synergen	200.0	200.0	100.0	-.8q	-.08	NE	NE	NE	NC	-2	03-90	.00	.	0	0	0	00-00-00	-5.7	.30	-1.7	1.18	-2.0	15	21.1	136	10,642	1,622	+5	0.0	12
Syntex Corp	12.3	9.3	6.3	316.8n	2.84	20.9	7.7	2.2	20	24	04-90	1.60	2.7	30	51	43	05-14-90	21.9	1.00	22.0	2.45	54.0	37	1.2	6,561	111,918	49,953	0	1.4	07
Synthetech	200.0	300.0	300.0	.0n	.00	NE	NE	NE	NC	NC	12-89	.00	.	0	0	0	00-00-00	.0	NC	.0	NC	.0	200	.7	9	10,543	415	0	0.0	03
T Cell Sciences	89.5	47.3	66.6	-1.2n	-.15	NE	NE	NE	NC	-14	01-90	.00	.	0	0	0	00-00-00	-12.0	.76	-9.1	1.57	-14.3		4.3	32	8,224	770	0	0.0	04
Tago Inc	16.7	16.7	50.0	-.1n	-.01	NC	NC	-100.0	NC	-8	10-89	.00	.	0	0	7	12-07-89	-3.3	1.79	-5.9	1.31	-7.7	0	3.8	7	9,028		0	0.0	01
Taro Vit	105.6	33.7	33.3	-.2t	-.04	-100.0	-100.0	-100.0	NC	-13	12-89	.00	.	0	0	0	00-00-00	-1.7	1.47	-2.5	5.32	-13.3	180	1.6	7	5,902	0	0	0.0	12
Teva Pharma	-3.7	-3.7	21.8	16.5q	.75	-8.7	-8.7	21.0	30	11	03-90	.15	1.3	0	19	0	03-06-90	5.9	.98	5.8	2.38	13.8	56	1.9	265	22,765	1,089	0	0.1	12
U S Bioscience	200.0	200.0	.	-6.0q	-.50	-100.0	NE	NE	NC	-88	03-90	.00	.	0	0	0	00-00-00	NM	NC	NC	1.48	-88.2	10	6.8	249	16,606	1,249	0	0.0	12
Unimed Inc	.0	5.0	16.6	-1.98	-.58	NE	NE	NE	NC	-40	03-90	.00	.	0	0	0	00-00-00	-47.5	.56	-26.8	1.48	-39.6		4.9	8	3,227	143	0	0.0	09
Utd Guardian	6.3	16.4	16.6	.0t	.00	NE	NE	NE	3	0	02-89	1.00	2.4	19	96	49	09-12-85	6.4	.91	5.8	NC	NC	44	2.4	36	4,796	340	0	25.0	02
Upjohn Co	3.4	3.4	3.4	187.3q	.99	7.0	7.0	-49.5	0	0	03-90	.00	.	0	0	0	00-00-00	15.8	1.59	25.2	1.86	10.8	15	1.8	7,602	185,418	97,598	-16	0.7	12
Utah Medical	31.6	31.6	26.6	3.0q	.39	100.0	100.0	85.7	43	43	03-90	.00	.	0	0	0	00-00-00	-2.1	.86	-1.8	1.70	42.9	1	2.1	89	7,399	1,230	-11	0.0	12
Ventrex Labs	14.7	11.9	7.6	-.3s	-.03	-100.0	-100.0	-100.0	3	-3	03-90	.00	.	0	0	0	00-00-00	NM	NC	NC	1.39	-2.5	18	4.2	10	10,745	1,887	-5	0.0	09
Viratek Inc	71.4	71.4	71.4	-17.3q	-1.88	-60.0	-60.0	NE	NC	NC	02-90	.00	.	0	0	0	08-19-86	NM	NC	NC	NC	NS		3.0	42	9,233	676	+5	0.0	11
Warner-Lambert	7.9	7.9	6.9	431.9q	3.20	20.0	20.0	21.2	20	20	03-90	1.52	2.3b	12	42	62	05-23-90	10.1	1.50	15.1	2.53	38.2	27	1.3	8,890	134,946	85,464	0	0.0	12
XOMA Cp	971.4	971.4	240.0	-18.3q	-1.32	NE	NE	NE	NC	-88	03-90	.00	.	0	0	0	00-00-00	NM	NC	NC	NC	-67.5	283	14.7	303	13,193	6,883	0	0.0	12
Xtronyx Inc	.0	100.0	.	-1.5f	-.71	NE	NE	NE	NC	NC	03-90	.00	.	0	0	0	00-00-00	NM	NC	NC	NC	NS	-50	1.6	38	2,135	15	0	0.0	03

Source: Media General Financial Services, Richmond, VA.

Electronic Components and Equipment

Trends and Forecasts: Electronic Components and Accessories (SIC 367)

(in millions of dollars except as noted)

Item	1987[1]	1988[2]	1989[2]	1990[3]	Percent Change		
					1987–88	1988–89	1989–90
Industry Data							
Value of shipments[4]	50,228	59,582	63,347	63,354	18.6	6.3	0.0
Value of shipments (1987$)	50,228	59,482	65,007	70,625	18.4	9.3	8.6
Total employment (000)	550	581	577	565	5.6	-0.7	-2.1
Production workers (000)	332	352	349	345	6.0	-0.9	-1.1
Average hourly earnings ($)	9.34	-	-	-	-	-	-
Product Data							
Value of shipments[5]	46,368	55,244	59,617	60,351	19.1	7.9	1.2
Value of shipments (1987$)	46,368	55,337	61,292	68,892	19.3	10.8	12.4
Trade Data							
Value of imports (ITA)[6]	12,566	16,842	17,744	17,273	34.0	5.4	-2.7
Value of exports (ITA)[7]	9,022	11,576	12,208	11,285	28.3	5.5	-7.6

[1]Data are preliminary.
[2]Estimated.
[3]Forecast.
[4]Value of all products and services sold by establishments in the electronic components and accessories industry.
[5]Value of products classified in the electronic components and accessories industry produced by all industries.
[6]Import data are developed by the chapter authors.
[7]Export data are developed by the chapter authors.
SOURCE: U.S. Department of Commerce: Bureau of the Census; International Trade Administration (ITA). Estimates and forecasts by ITA.

Source: *U.S. Industrial Outlook 1990*, U.S. Department of Commerce.

Trends and Forecasts: Radio and TV Communications Equipment (SIC 3663)
(in millions of dollars except as noted)

Item	1987[1]	1988[2]	1989[3]	1990[4]	Percent Change 1987-88	1988-89	1989-90
Industry Data							
Value of shipments[5]	14,294	-	-	-	-	-	-
Value of shipments (1987$)	14,294	-	-	-	-	-	-
Total employment (000)	125	-	-	-	-	-	-
Production workers (000)	57.8	-	-	-	-	-	-
Average hourly earnings ($)	11.16	-	-	-	-	-	-
Product Data							
Value of shipments[6]	13,305	14,570	16,027	-	9.5	10.0	-
Value of shipments (1987$)	13,305	-	-	-	-	-	-
Trade Data							
Value of imports (ITA)[7]	2,955	3,371	3,664	4,000	14.1	8.7	9.2
Value of exports (ITA)[8]	2,127	2,541	2,799	3,100	19.5	10.2	10.8

[1]Industry and product data are preliminary. Trade data are adjusted to conform to the 1987 SIC.
[2]Estimated, except for exports and imports.
[3]Estimated.
[4]Forecast.
[5]Value of all products and services sold by establishments in the radio & tv communications equipment industry.
[6]Value of products classified in the radio & tv communications equipment industry produced by all industries.
[7]Import data are developed by the chapter author.
[8]Export data are developed by the chapter author.
SOURCE: U.S. Department of Commerce: Bureau of the Census; International Trade Administration (ITA). Estimates and forecasts by ITA.

Source: U.S. Industrial Outlook 1990, U.S. Department of Commerce.

MEDIA GENERAL FINANCIAL SERVICES

STOCKS by INDUSTRY

Electronic Equipment Manufacturers

Company	Revenue Pct. Change Last Qtr %	FY to Date %	Last 12 Mos %	Earnings Last 12 Mos $MM	Last 12 Mos $	Per Share Last Qtr $	Last Qtr %	to Date %	Last 12 Mos %	5-Yr Growth Rate %	Par Growth Rate %	Date of Report	Dividends Current Rate Amt $	Yield %	5-Year Growth Rate %	Payout Last FY %	Last 5 Yrs %	Last X-Dvd Date	Pro-fit Mar-gin %	Asset Turn-over	Return on Total Assets	Lever-age Ratio	Return on Equity	Debt to Eq-uity %	Cur-rent Ratio	p/e	Mar-ket Value $Mil	Latest Shares Out-strdng 000	Held by Banks-funds 000	Insider Net Trad-ing 000	Short Int-erest Ratio Days	Fiscal Year Ends Mo
Ind. Group	-1.9	4.6	.7	5,327.3	1.19	-15.5	-15.5	-13.2	15.9	20	7	--	.22	.7	1	15	17	--	3.8	.97	3.7	2.30	8.5	29	1.7	121,163	3,844,861	G + 176	1.1	--	--
Acme Electric Cp	2.6	-.1	4.5	3.9n	.81	23.5	23.5	12.2	131.4	5	9	03-90	.32	3.8	4	43	71	05-03-90	4.3	1.72	7.4	2.09	15.5	65	3.8	40	4,688	1,264	+6	0.2	06
Adage Inc	-45.5	-35.5	-42.4	-10.9q	-1.27	NE	NE	NE	NC	NC	-75	06-89	.00	.0	0	0	0	00-00-00	-57.4	.75	-42.9	1.75	-75.2	2	2.5	9	8,688	1,517	0	0.0	08
Advance Circuits	30.4	31.0	18.3	9.0n	1.57	90.5	90.5	152.3	NE	NC	65	06-90	.00	.0	0	0	0	01-22-90	10.7	3.26	34.9	1.85	64.7	10	1.8	54	5,672	1,305	-13	0.0	08
Advanced Micro	.7	.7	-.3	49.1q	.48	44.4	44.4	44.4	NE	NC	7	03-90	.00	.0	0	0	0	00-00-00	4.4	1.00	4.4	1.61	7.1	18	2.2	771	81,155	3,378	+0	0.6	12
Advd Semicon	3.8	14.5	14.7	5.0r	.70	-90.1	-90.1	-32.7	-32.7	NC	12	12-89	.00	.0	0	0	0	00-00-00	2.3	1.09	2.5	4.68	11.7	116	1.4	40	7,185	683	0	0.0	12
AEL Inds Inc Cl A	9.4	9.4	-6.7	-8.5q	-2.19	400.0	400.0	400.0	NE	NC	-20	05-90	.00	.0	0	0	0	08-09-88	-6.9	.96	-6.6	3.08	-20.3	85	1.4	22	3,892	1,350	0	0.0	02
All Am Semicond	9.6	9.6	5.5	-.4q	-.12	-100.0	-100.0	-100.0	NE	NC	-9	03-90	.00	.0	0	0	0	03-14-89	-1.1	1.82	-2.0	4.45	-8.9	16	3.4	6	3,809	39	0	0.0	02
Alpha Indus	-7.2	5.0	7.9	-.1n	-.02	-100.0	-100.0	NE	NE	NC	0	12-89	.00	.0	0	0	NE	07-16-85	-.1	1.00	-.1	2.00	-.2	12	3.4	21	7,162	2,666	0	0.4	03
Altera Cp	38.4	38.4	48.8	11.6q	.58	25.0	25.0	34.9	34.9	NC	25	03-90	.00	.0	0	0	0	00-00-00	18.1	1.15	20.9	1.19	24.9	0	5.2	239	18,945	1,444	-45	0.0	12
Am Power Conv	85.2	85.2	95.2	6.5q	1.83	48.1	48.1	48.1	43.0	NC	12	03-90	.00	.0	0	0	0	06-02-89	15.9	1.65	26.3	1.65	43.0	23	3.5	137	3,471	443	0	0.0	12
Am Precision	-3.1	-3.1	2.0	4.5q	.58	-28.6	-28.6	-28.6	9.4	20	12	03-90	.18	1.1	13	24	37	06-28-90	8.3	1.38	12.1	1.45	17.5	22	4.0	151	9,165	473	+0	2.6	12
American Telecom Cp	.0	2.2	44.4	-.5n	-.08	NE	NE	NE	NC	NC	-56	03-90	.00	.0	0	0	0	00-00-00	-3.3	2.39	-9.1	6.11	-55.6	0	.9	3	7,099	209	0	0.0	06
Amtech Cp	66.7	66.7	250.0	-7.2q	-1.76	NE	NE	NE	NC	-26	03-90	.00	.0	0	0	0	00-00-00	NM	NC	NC	1.57	-28.2	0	13.4	126	6,427	616	0	0.0	12
Amtech Systs	41.9	46.0	85.7	.7s	.43	-71.4	-71.4	-33.3	79.2	NC	8	03-90	.00	.0	0	0	0	00-00-00	2.7	3.44	9.3	1.46	14.6	0	2.5	5	1,935	0	0	0.0	09
Analog Devices	1.2	-1.3	-1.7	13.7s	.29	-52.4	-52.4	-70.7	-67.0	-7	4	04-90	.00	.0	0	0	1	04-15-86	3.0	1.00	3.0	1.27	3.8	3	3.5	357	47,627	2,003	-6	1.0	10
Anaren Microwave	3.1	3.8	9.5	-1.4n	-.31	NE	NE	NE	NC	-5	03-90	.00	.0	0	0	0	00-00-00	-6.1	.70	-4.3	1.26	-5.4	14	11.5	10	4,336	748	+1	0.0	06
Andersen Grp	-12.7	-40.9	-43.4	1.1n	.66	-98.1	-98.1	-93.4	NE	NC	12	11-89	.00	.0	0	0	0	03-16-84	4.2	.90	3.8	3.18	12.1	137	3.6	14	1,781	192	0	0.0	09
Andrew Cp	22.4	25.0	21.7	18.0s	1.79	24.1	24.1	31.5	26.1	2	20	07-90	.00	.0	0	0	0	07-16-87	5.4	1.26	6.8	1.46	9.9	9	2.5	193	10,137	560	-31	0.0	09
Anthem Elects	42.9	42.9	28.7	18.5q	1.60	77.8	77.8	77.8	55.3	28	20	01-90	.00	.0	0	0	0	05-16-86	5.3	2.94	15.6	1.27	19.8	0	4.0	339	11,341	703	0	0.4	12
Appld Materials	30.1	30.1	31.5	49.1q	2.92	-18.5	-18.5	-18.5	1.4	37	19	01-90	.00	.0	0	0	0	05-16-86	9.2	1.23	11.3	1.71	19.3	12	2.4	615	16,175	406	+18	0.0	10
Astro Med	-100.0	-46.5	.0	.0*	.50	-100.0	-100.0	-61.5	-21.9	14	5	04-90	.00	.0	0	0	0	08-16-88	NC	NC	NC	2.27	-81.8	18	3.5	28	3,293	742	-3	0.0	01
Astrocom Cp	15.4	15.4	-45.4	-1.8q	-.69	NE	NE	NE	NC	-82	03-90	.00	.0	0	0	0	03-16-84	-30.0	1.20	-36.0	2.27	8.2	36	2.0	2	2,609	23	-9	0.0	12
Augat Inc	-10.7	-10.7	-7.1	15.3q	.85	NE	NE	11.8	11.8	NC	4	07-03-90	.40	2.9	4	48	508	07-03-90	5.1	1.20	6.1	1.34	8.2	9	3.5	252	18,010	974	-1	0.4	12
Avantek Inc	-1.1	-1.1	24.4	-20.9q	-1.17	NE	NE	11.8	41.8	NC	6	03-90	.00	.0	0	0	0	00-00-00	-13.2	1.17	-15.5	1.43	-22.2	0	5.5	49	17,703	7,287	0	0.2	12
Amel Inc	-8.7	-10.8	-9.3	68.8n	1.90	46.7	46.7	40.6	NC	8	03-90	.60	2.1	4	33	44	06-11-90	3.9	1.56	6.1	1.54	9.4	29	5.5	1,110	38,617	27792	-1	0.2	06
Aydin Cp	-13.6	-13.6	-11.1	9.3q	1.83	5.6	5.6	5.6	6.4	17	5	03-90	1.00	6.9b	0	0	0	12-27-89	6.1	1.05	6.4	1.81	11.6	12	3.4	71	4,895	2121	+2	0.0	12
Bishop Inc	-13.8	-3.9	.0	-.7s	-.27	NE	NE	NE	NC	-28	03-90	.00	.0	0	0	0	03-26-85	-7.0	1.44	-17.1	1.64	-28.0	0	2.3	9	2,370	262	-24	0.0	09
BMC Ind Inc	3.3	3.3	1.2	5.7q	1.03	37.5	37.5	87.5	8.4	NC	22	03-90	.00	.0	0	0	NE	02-05-85	3.4	1.44	4.9	6.49	31.8	345	2.4	238	22,703	2912	0	0.5	12
Boston Acoustics	34.5	25.0	28.5	3.4f	1.70	31.6	31.6	30.8	30.8	31	30	03-90	.00	.0	0	0	0	00-00-00	12.6	2.10	26.4	1.12	29.6	0	8.3	52	2,024	263	0	0.0	03
Brite Voice Systs	-41.9	-41.9	55.5	2.4q	.60	-70.0	-70.0	-70.0	42.9	NC	12	03-90	.00	.0	0	0	0	00-00-00	17.1	.63	10.7	1.13	12.1	0	8.3	22	4,595	152	0	0.0	12

(continued)

Electronic Equipment Manufacturers (Continued)

Company	Rev % Last Qtr	Rev % FY to Date	Rev % Last 12 Mos	Earn Last 12 Mos $Mil	EPS Last 12 Mos $	EPS % Last Qtr	EPS % FY to Date	EPS % Last 12 Mos	5-Yr Grw	Par Grw	Report Date	Div Amt $	Div Yld %	Div 5-Yr Grw	Payout FY	Payout 5 Yrs	Last X-Dvd Date	Prof Mgn	Asset Turn	Ret Tot Assets	Lev Ratio	Ret Equity	Debt/Eq	Mkt Val $Mil	Shares Out (000)	Held Banks-Funds (000)	Insider Net Trad (000)	Short Int (Days)	FY End Mo
Burr-Brown	-4.8	-4.8	-5.1	7.3n	.75	-48.4	-48.4	-40.0	13	13	03-90	.00	.0	0	0	0	12-15-86	4.4	1.02	4.5	1.91	8.6	29	96	9,560	3,548	0	.00	12
Bytex Cp	28.6	15.1	14.2	3.8f	.65	78.6	47.7	47.7	NC	13	12-89	.00	.0	0	0	0	00-00-00	9.5	1.17	11.1	1.19	13.2	1	65	6,072	1,536	0	.00	12
Calif Amp	.0	19.8	22.2	.2f	.05	NE	NE	NE	NC	10	02-90	.00	.0	0	0	0	00-00-00	1.8	1.89	3.4	2.94	10.0	10	7	4,205	61	0	.00	03
Calif Micro Dev	-68.8	-13.3	-7.1	-1.3n	-.38	NE	NE	-100.0	NC	-15	12-89	.00	.0	0	0	0	00-00-00	-5.0	.90	-4.0	3.65	-14.6	147	9	4,355	430	+5	.00	03
Calif Microwv	17.1	22.4	26.0	6.4n	.77	26.7	31.8	35.1	NC	13	03-90	.00	.0	0	0	0	00-00-00	4.4	1.70	7.5	1.77	13.3	13	73	8,416	2,588	0	.00	06
Cermetek Micro	-10.0	-33.9	-33.3	-1.9f	-.53	NE	NE	NE	14	0	06-89	.00	.0	0	NE	0	00-00-00	-47.5	2.11	.0	.00	NM	50	1	3,579	51	0	.00	06
Chyron Cp	-35.3	-9.5	-4.6	-4.1n	-.37	-100.0	-100.0	-100.0	NC	-13	03-90	.00	.0	0	NE	82	10-27-89	-10.0	.57	-5.7	2.35	-13.4	0	22	11,567	2,464	+1	.00	06
Cimn Microwave	42.0	42.0	-7.8	-6.7q	-.64	NE	-100.0	-100.0	NC	-18	03-90	.00	.0	14	0	6	11-25-86	-11.4	1.14	-13.0	1.38	-17.9	0	27	10,382	1,743	0	.00	12
Circon Inc	7.4	7.4	13.6	.09	.02	400.0	400.0	400.0	NC	17	03-90	.00	.0	0	0	0	00-00-00	.0	.14	NC	NC	NC	69	41	5,561	1,257	+2	.00	12
Circuit Resch	.0	.0	.0	.3n	.05	NC	NC	NC	NC	17	03-90	.00	.0	0	0	0	00-00-00	15.0	.95	14.3	1.17	16.7	6	1	4,772	0	0	.00	12
Cirrus Logic	152.1	127.8	155.5	12.0n	.84	250.0	305.9	-7	NC	—	12-89	.00	.0	0	0	0	00-00-00	17.4	3.27	56.9	.00	NS	-14	297	14,768	3,567	0	.00	03
Cognitronics	.0	1.9	6.2	-.5q	.21	-36.4	-36.4	75.0	NC	6	03-90	.00	.0	6	0	0	00-00-00	2.9	1.83	5.3	1.19	6.3	0	13	2,187	163	0	.3	12
Cohu Inc	6.8	5.8	.0	2.7n	1.39	-13.5	-3.8	-.7	15	11	09-89	.32	2.6	6	16	23	06-04-90	7.9	1.54	12.2	1.18	14.4	0	24	1,943	481	0	1.5	12
Comdial Cp	5.8	1.8	-3.4	-.40	-.02	NE	NE	NE	NC	-7	03-90	.00	.0	0	0	0	00-00-00	-.5	1.60	-.8	8.38	-6.7	267	13	17,975	1,436	0	.00	12
Commun Cable	1.8	1.8	22.2	.81	.81	5.0	5.0	26.6	NC	10	01-90	.00	.0	0	16	0	03-26-90	5.5	1.38	7.6	1.37	10.4	0	20	1,816	222	0	.00	12
Comptronix Cp	-10.6	-10.6	13.8	1.4q	.16	-42.9	-42.9	-20.0	NC	7	03-90	.00	.0	0	0	0	00-00-00	3.4	1.29	4.4	1.66	7.3	39	33	8,358	31	0	.00	12
Corcom	-11.6	-11.6	-6.0	-5.2q	-1.46	-100.0	-100.0	-100.0	NC	-34	03-90	.00	.0	0	0	0	00-00-00	-16.8	1.34	-22.5	1.51	-34.0	7	9	3,560	926	0	.00	12
Cosmo Commun	-46.3	-46.3	-26.6	-9.4q	-1.85	NE	NE	NE	NC	-70	03-90	.00	.0	0	0	0	00-00-00	-28.5	1.33	-37.8	1.84	-69.6	4	112	5,060	550	0	.00	12
CTS Corp	-7.1	-7.1	-5.1	2.21	2.21	-57.1	-57.1	-51.1	21	6	03-90	.75	3.7	21	21	391	06-25-90	6.8	1.47	9.9	1.41	9.7	0	112	5,464	2,616	+2	.00	12
Cubic Corp	11.6	5.0	.2	24.3s	3.45	14.7	42.4	47.4	26	16	03-90	.48	2.2	13	13	26	08-06-90	6.8	1.29	8.8	2.14	18.8	48	148	6,945	1,975	+0	.4	09
CXR Cp	16.2	37.8	50.0	-.8h	-.09	-90.9	-100.0	-100.0	NC	-6	03-90	.00	.0	0	0	0	00-00-00	-2.4	1.63	-3.9	1.49	-5.8	4	25	7,753	779	0	.1	06
Cypress Semi	14.3	14.3	39.0	31.9q	.83	15.8	15.8	31.7	15	15	03-90	.00	.0	0	0	0	00-00-00	15.5	.72	11.2	1.29	14.5	11	537	37,049	21,811	0	.4	12
Dallas Semicon	39.8	39.8	39.0	12.3q	.49	44.4	44.4	48.5	15	15	03-90	.00	.0	0	0	0	00-00-00	13.8	.84	11.6	1.28	14.8	5	194	23,527	4,666	-98	.2	12
Datamarine	-28.6	-22.6	-14.2	-.3h	-.26	-100.0	-100.0	-100.0	NC	-4	03-90	.00	.0	0	0	0	00-00-00	-1.7	1.47	-2.5	1.76	-4.4	19	6	1,127	26	+14	.00	09
Datron Systs	5.1	21.5	21.6	4.2l	1.45	23.5	26.1	26.1	19	17	03-90	.00	.0	0	0	0	00-00-00	9.3	1.08	10.0	1.57	16.7	17	25	2,675	1,420	0	.00	03
Decom Sys	39.1	7.5	14.2	.1s	.04	-100.0	NE	-100.0	NC	8	03-90	.00	.0	0	0	0	00-00-00	1.3	1.38	1.8	4.61	8.3	133	2	2,713	119	0	.00	09
Designatronics	.0	30.1	15.3	.0s	.00	75.0	83.3	164.5	NC	0	12-89	.00	.0	0	0	0	09-22-87	.0	NC	NC	NC	.0	35	10	2,920	270	0	.4	06
D-A-n-Controls	.0	.0	.0	-.8h	-.95	NE	NE	NE	NC	0	03-90	.00	.0	0	0	0	00-00-00	NC	NC	NC	NC	NC	0	1	826	0	0	.00	12
Diceon Electrns	10.5	-1.3	-9.9	-3.9s	-.67	NE	NE	-80.0	NC	-10	03-90	.00	.0	0	0	0	12-89	-3.3	1.15	-3.8	1.97	-7.5	63	27	5,379	3,149	+2	.00	09
Diodes Inc	9.7	-7.2	-7.1	-.4f	.04	NE	-100.0	-100.0	NC	-10	04-90	.00	.0	0	0	0	00-00-00	-3.1	1.48	-4.6	2.13	-9.8	39	6	3,732	127	0	.00	04
Dotronix Inc	-32.9	-37.1	-34.2	-2.1n	-.64	NE	NE	-83.8	NC	-17	03-90	.00	.0	0	0	0	07-16-86	-9.1	.93	-8.5	1.96	-16.7	17	7	3,230	302	0	.00	06
Drexler Techlgy	-97.1	-98.5	-87.5	-6.9f	-1.01	-100.0	-100.0	-100.0	NC	-45	03-90	.00	.0	0	0	0	06-04-90	NM	NC	NC	NC	-44.5	10	9	6,901	892	0	14.1	03
DSC Commun	27.3	27.3	29.7	35.1q	.82	23.1	23.1	164.5	NC	14	03-90	.00	.0	0	0	0	00-00-00	7.7	.81	6.2	2.23	13.8	137	512	40,169	23,287	-120	1.1	12
Dyersen Cp	2.2	2.2	12.1	-1.2q	-1.24	-80.0	-80.0	-100.0	NC	-17	03-90	.00	.0	0	0	0	07-16-90	-3.2	1.41	-4.5	3.80	-17.1	114	9	5,613	408	0	.00	03
Dynascan Cp	-16.0	-16.0	9.0	1.3q	.17	31.0	4.1	4.1	NC	3	02-90	.00	.0	0	0	0	00-00-00	.5	1.80	.9	1.52	2.5	0	33	6,374	2,251	0	.00	12
E Systems	15.9	15.9	10.6	85.8q	2.74	14.8	14.8	9.2	11	11	03-90	.75	3.0	19	24	24	06-11-90	5.1	1.98	10.1	1.51	15.3	16	789	31,247	15,994	-28	.7	12
EDO Cp	.0	.0	9.4	5.8q	.79	-10.5	-10.5	14.5	NC	8	03-90	.28	4.5	35	32	32	06-04-90	3.8	1.08	4.1	2.90	NC	116	34	5,417	2,048	+2	.7	12
EG & G Inc	43.5	43.5	24.2	67.9q	2.35	-8.9	-8.9	2.2	13	13	03-90	.76	2.0	28	27	20	07-16-90	3.7	2.86	10.6	1.84	19.5	3	1,097	28,967	16,040	-120	1.1	12
Eldec Cp	10.8	13.1	12.2	5.7f	1.02	4.1	4.1	4.1	9	9	03-90	.00	.0	0	20	0	06-22-87	5.2	1.17	6.1	1.52	9.3	8	68	5,454	768	+0	.00	03
Electro Sci	-28.4	-3.0	1.2	-1.0n	-.15	-100.0	-100.0	-100.0	NC	-2	02-90	.00	.0	0	0	0	00-00-00	-1.2	1.00	-1.2	1.67	-2.0	17	39	6,073	2,536	+0	.00	05

Electronic Missles
Electron Missiles
Eng Measure
Espey Mfg El
Exar Cp
Fastcomm Comm
Federated Purch
Fibronics
Flextronics Inc
Fluke, John
Gen Datacomm
Gen Instrument
Gen Kinetics
GenRad
Gentex Cp
GeoTek
Giga Tronics
Graham Field
GTI Corp
Hadco Cp
Hamilton Digital
Harris Cp
HEI Inc
Harler Microwave
Honeywell Inc
Hytek Microsysts
ICOT Corp
IEH Cp
IFR Systs
ILC Technology
Intech Inc
Integ Device
Intel Cp
Intermagnetics Genl
Intl Microelctrn
Intl Rectifier
Interpoint Cp
Intertan Inc
Jetronic Ind
Keptel
Kevlin Micro
Koss Cp
Kyocera Cp
Lasermetrics Inc
Lifeline Sys
Linear Tech
Logimetrics A
Logitek
Loral Corp

(continued)

Source: Media General Financial Services, Richmond, VA.

Electronic Equipment Manufacturers (Continued)

Company	Revenue Pct Change Last Qtr %	Rev FY to Date %	Rev Last 12 Mos %	Rev Last 12 Mos $Mil	EPS Last 12 Mos $	EPS Last Qtr $	EPS FY to Date %	EPS Last 12 Mos %	5-Yr Growth Rate %	Par Growth Rate %	Date of Report	Curr Rate Amt	Yield %	Div 5-Yr Growth Rate %	Payout Last FY %	Payout Last 5 Yrs %	Last X-Div Date	Profit Margin	Asset Turn over	Return on Total Assets	Leverage Ratio	Return on Equity	Debt to Equity	Current Ratio	Market Value $Mil	Latest Shares Outstanding 000	Held by Banks-Funds 000	Insider Net Trading 000	Short Interest Ratio Days	Fiscal Year Ends Mo
Lowrance Elect	9.0	22.6	34.0	1.5n	.44	18.2	NE	NE	NC	16	04-90	.00	.0	0	0	0	00-00-00	2.4	2.33	5.6	2.77	15.5	102	3.2	12	3,416	439	0	0.0	07
LSI Logic	3.9	3.9	25.4	-31.8q	-.76	-84.2	-84.2	-100.0	NC	-11	03-90	.00	.0	0	0	0	03-17-86	-5.8	.72	-4.2	2.55	-10.7	69	2.6	462	41,066	17,586	0	1.5	12
M/A - Com	-7.6	-11.0	2.6	-120.0s	-4.89	.0	.0	-100.0	NC	-59	03-90	.00	.0	2	2400	148	09-12-89	-28.6	.81	-23.2	2.54	-58.9	49	1.7	132	24,527	11,502	+1	0.3	09
Margaux Inc	-48.3	-48.3	-37.5	-5.6q	-.83	300.0	300.0	NE	NC	-12	06-89	.00	.0	0	0	0	00-00-00	-37.3	2.00	-74.7	.00	NM	11	.8	2	6,719	548	0	0.0	08
Marlton Tech	.0	.0	-100.0	-.7n	-.20	NE	NE	NE	NC	-12	09-88	.00	.0	0	0	0	00-00-00	NC	NC	NC	.00	-12.3	NM	2.9	3	3,338	1,077	0	0.0	12
Marshall Ind	-.9	-2.0	1.1	18.5n	2.03	-8.6	-15.5	-15.4	30	14	02-90	.00	.0	0	0	0	07-08-86	3.5	2.37	8.3	1.65	13.7	30	3.7	275	9,079	5,907	0	3.2	05
Matsushita Elec	-20.7	-6.3	-7.3	1547.5n	7.20	-12.0	-6.3	-5.3	8	7	12-89	.58	.4	14	8	8	03-23-90	3.9	.82	3.2	2.25	7.2	22	1.6	27,085	195,563	2,731	0	2.6	03
Maxim Integrated	35.8	30.9	30.9	7.0n	.55	25.0	35.5	44.7	NC	25	03-90	.00	.0	0	0	0	00-00-00	13.5	1.11	15.0	1.64	24.6	16	1.9	139	11,431	2,631	0	0.0	06
Measurement Spec	-47.5	-58.8	-30.7	-.9n	-.29	-100.0	-100.0	-100.0	NC	-47	01-90	.00	.0	0	0	0	00-00-00	-8.9	2.00	-17.8	2.65	-47.1	24	1.6	3	2,884	16	0	0.0	03
Megadata Co	-7.7	-46.8	-50.0	-1.5f	-.91	NE	NE	NE	NC	-25	10-89	.00	.0	0	0	0	12-07-84	-37.5	.62	-23.1	1.08	-25.0	0	8.8	1	1,612	81	+10	0.0	10
Merimac	-6.3	-6.3	-6.2	1.1q	.48	50.0	50.0	-15.8	-6	-6	03-90	.20	3.1	NA	33	9	05-25-90	7.3	.92	6.7	1.13	7.6	0	8.9	14	2,227	766	0	0.0	12
Methode Elec A	NA	NA	NA	NA	NA	NA	NA	NA	-9	9	04-90	.07	1.0	NA	NA	NA	04-09-90	.92	NC	NA	NA	NA	0	NA	66	9,361	3,859	0	NA	04
Methode Elec B	10.3	8.7	9.0	5.11	.46	142.9	130.0	130.0	-9	9	04-90	.07	.9	1	11	16	04-09-90	3.8	1.82	6.9	1.48	10.2	8	2.6	75	11,051	57	-6	0.0	04
Microcom	21.8	26.6	27.1	11.7f	1.22	23.1	32.6	32.6	NC	31	04-90	.06	.0	1	1	0	05-02-89	15.6	1.22	19.1	1.63	31.2	18	2.1	85	9,141	6,460	0	0.0	03
Microlog Cp	14.8	43.4	63.6	1.5s	.62	NE	NE	NE	NC	19	04-90	.00	.0	0	0	0	00-00-00	8.3	1.33	11.0	1.73	3.0	24	3.0	17	2,925	818	0	0.0	10
Micron Tech	-29.5	-33.6	-27.5	17.9n	.48	-33.5	-87.3	-87.3	NC	4	05-90	.00	.0	0	0	0	00-00-00	5.4	.54	2.9	1.31	3.8	8	4.0	466	36,715	8,099	-10	0.0	08
Microsemi	-21.7	-19.5	-7.0	-9.7s	-1.39	-83.3	-100.0	-100.0	NC	-46	03-90	.00	.0	0	0	0	07-09-85	-10.4	.86	-8.9	5.15	-45.8	225	1.8	13	7,506	2,881	0	0.0	09
Microwave Filter	6.7	6.7	6.7	.5q	.16	-50.0	-50.0	-27.3	2	9	12-89	.07	6.2	7	7	0	11-04-88	8.3	1.37	11.4	1.46	16.7	0	2.9	1	2,497	43	0	0.0	04
Microwave Labs	-70.0	-43.9	-40.0	-4.6n	-.74	-38.7	NE	-100.0	NC	0	01-90	.00	.0	0	1	0	00-00-00	NM	NC	NC	NC	NC	0	1.3	1	2,708	134	0	0.0	04
Milgray Electors	-2.8	-2.8	-1.9	1.2q	1.56	-38.7	-47.5	-47.5	NC	8	03-90	.00	.0	0	0	0	00-00-00	1.2	2.58	3.1	2.52	7.8	78	3.3	11	779	174	0	0.0	12
Missouri Rsch Labs	-24.5	-24.5	-5.8	-2.6q	-1.16	NE	NE	NE	NC	4	04-90	.03	.0	NE	NE	NE	04-10-89	-16.3	1.85	-30.2	.00	NM	139	1.3	7	2,251	49	+3	0.0	01
Mitel Cp	.7	1.3	18.1	9.2n	-.07	-86.7	-63.6	NA	NC	4	12-89	.00	.0	0	0	0	00-00-00	2.1	1.90	4.0	1.90	4.0	4	2.5	168	79,016	6,479	0	4.3	03
Mobile Telecom	93.1	93.1	75.0	-18.1n	-.69	NE	NE	NE	NC	-23	12-89	.00	.0	0	0	0	00-00-00	-43.1	.36	-15.7	1.43	-22.5	28	2.9	295	28,131	10,292	0	0.0	12
Molex Inc	3.0	2.7	3.3	64.4n	2.57	15.5	19.0	14.2	16	15	03-90	.04	.1	7	1	1	06-25-90	11.0	1.08	11.9	1.26	15.0	1	3.2	1,148	25,653	9,240	+0	0.0	06
Motorola Inc	16.5	16.5	17.7	502.0q	3.86	3.2	3.2	10.3	24	11	03-90	.76	.9	20	20	28	06-11-90	5.0	1.30	6.5	2.03	13.2	20	1.4	10,888	130,205	87,611	+5	2.3	12
Myles Cp	-1.9	-1.9	29.0	1.7q	.16	.0	NC	-48.4	NC	24	03-90	.00	.0	0	0	0	00-00-00	4.3	2.42	10.4	2.27	23.6	24	2.1	34	10,191	78	0	0.0	12
Nanometrics Inc	-4.0	-4.0	-7.0	.0q	-.01	NC	NC	-100.0	NC	0	03-90	.00	.0	0	0	0	00-00-00	.0	NC	NC	NC	4.4	12	4.6	9	7,670	1,055	0	0.0	12
Napco Sec	4.5	-7.0	-7.8	.9n	.20	-35.3	-47.8	-78.5	-9	-4	05-90	.00	.0	0	0	0	08-21-85	2.6	1.08	2.8	1.57	4.4	15	2.3	16	4,387	879	0	0.0	06
Natl Semicon	211.3	1.6	-19.6	-19.6f	-.42	-100.0	NE	NE	NC	-2	05-90	.00	.0	0	0	0	05-09-90	-1.2	1.17	-1.4	1.64	-2.3	6	1.5	757	102,700	47,982	+0	0.7	05
Nationwide Cell	66.4	66.4	57.6	-8.4q	-1.89	NE	NE	NE	NC	0	03-90	.00	.0	0	0	0	00-00-00	-10.2	3.42	-34.9	.00	NM	922	1.4	61	6,267	428	0	0.0	12
NEC Cp	6.1	6.1	-.7	403.5s	.28	16.7	16.7	33.3	-25	1	09-89	.26	.4	69	115	37	09-25-88	1.7	.94	1.6	4.88	7.8	86	1.2	19,263	298,648	444	0	0.0	03
Nellcor	35.6	15.1	14.7	11.8n	.80	1300.0	54.5	27.0	NC	16	03-90	.00	.0	0	0	0	00-00-00	8.9	1.46	13.0	1.20	15.6	0	5.0	298	14,296	8,205	-40	0.0	06
Netwks Electr	22.2	-7.9	-12.5	.2s	.16	155.6	-52.6	-59.0	NC	8	12-89	.00	.0	0	0	0	06-24-88	2.9	3.27	3.7	2.96	8.0	84	2.0	5	1,454	77	0	1.2	06
New Image Ind	100.0	69.6	71.4	1.4n	.49	16.7	35.7	35.7	NC	0	03-90	.00	.0	0	0	0	00-00-00	11.7	3.99	46.7	3.65	8.0	10	1.3	23	2,657	255	0	0.0	05
N Atlantic Ind	20.0	20.0	2.9	-1.3q	-.40	NE	NE	-100.0	-37	-11	03-90	.00	.0	0	0	0	04-04-84	-3.7	1.54	-5.7	1.95	-11.1	26	1.8	15	3,486	413	0	0.0	12
N Hills Elec	20.7	20.7	8.3	.44	.15	200.0	200.0	66.7	NC	8	04-90	.00	.0	0	0	0	00-00-00	3.1	.94	2.9	2.59	7.5	121	4.5	5	2,692	281	0	0.0	01
Northn Telecom	13.8	13.8	14.7	403.0q	1.57	50.0	50.0	134.3	4	8	03-90	.28	1.0	6	19	15	06-04-90	6.4	.98	6.3	2.38	15.0	30	1.4	6,688	241,376	33,552	+408	1.2	12
Nuclear Support	-23.0	-7.3	3.2	-.8n	-.36	-100.0	-100.0	-100.0	NC	-12	03-90	.05	.6	0	0	0	08-24-88	-1.3	1.77	-2.3	3.65	-8.4	83	.9	21	2,476	163	-4	0.0	06
Oak Inds	-14.2	-14.2	-22.7	-24.5q	-.29	NE	NE	NE	NC	-37	03-90	.00	.0	0	0	0	00-00-00	-16.0	1.18	-18.8	1.95	-36.7	26	2.5	93	82,523	16,523	0	0.1	12
Odetics A	NA	NA	NA	NA	.0	NE	NE	NE	NC	0	03-90	.00	.0	NA	NA	NA	00-00-00	NC	NC	NC	NC	NA	NA	NA	14	2,661	100	0	NA	NA

Odetics B
Orbit Instru
Ovonic Imaging
Park Electro
Parlex Cp
Pen Central
Penril Corp
Peripheral Syst
PhotoSci
Photon Tech Intl
Pico Prods
Plasma Therm
Plexus Cp
Porta Syst
Quantronic Cp
QuesTech
Qume
Radiation Syst
Radyne Cp
Ragen Cp
Relac Tech Dev
Reliability Inc
RELM Commun
Richardson Elctrns
Ripley Co Inc
RMS Intl
Robinson Nugent
Robotic Vision
Rogers Corp
Sage Labs
SBE Inc
Scan-Graphics
Science Dynamics
Sci-Atlanta
SEEQ Tech
Semtech Cp
Sensomatic Elec
SFE Tech
Sheldahl Inc
SHL Systemhouse
Silicon Gen
Siliconix Inc
Selectron Cp
Solitec Inc
Solitron Device
Spectrum Control
Sprague Tech
Std Microsystems

(continued)

Electronic Equipment Manufacturers (Continued)

Company	Rev Last Qtr %	Rev FY to Date %	Rev Last 12 Mos %	Earn Last 12 Mos $Mil	EPS Last 12 Mos $	EPS Last Qtr $	EPS FY to Date %	EPS Last 12 Mos %	EPS 5-Yr Growth %	Par Growth %	Date of Report	Div Amt $	Div Yield %	Div 5-Yr Growth %	Payout Last FY %	Payout Last 5 Yrs %	Last X-Dvd Date	Profit Margin %	Asset Turnover	Return on Total Assets %	Leverage Ratio	Return on Equity %	Debt to Equity %	Current Ratio	Market Value $Mil	Latest Shares Out 000	Held by Banks-Funds 000	Insider Net Trading 000	Short Int Ratio Days	Fiscal Year Ends Mo
Stanford Telec	-11.5	4.3	3.4	-.77	-.16	-100.0	-100.0	-100.0	NC	-2	03-90	.00	.0		0	0	06-17-86	-.8	1.50	-1.2	1.92	-2.3	3	1.8	29	4,838	1,322	-19	0.0	03
Sulcus	80.0	73.7	50.0	-1.11	-.43	NE	NE	NE	NC	-6	12-89	.00	.0		0	0	00-00-00	-36.7	1.43	-52.4	.00	NM	0	.9	6	2,662	0	0	0.0	12
Sun Electric	16.6	16.6	.5	-4.44	-.56	NE	NE	-41.2	-26	-6	03-90	.00	.0		NE	0	00-00-00	-2.3	1.30	-3.0	1.90	-5.7	27	2.4	169	8,102	3,996	+1	0.2	12
Sunair Electrns	33.3	-8.7	-20.0	.38	.10	.0	-16.7	-16.7	3	3	03-90	.00	.0		0	0	00-00-00	7.5	1.04	2.4	1.04	2.5	0	15.3	7	3,931	437	0	0.0	09
Supertex Inc	8.9	-.5	.0	2.41	.20	-16.7	-16.7	-33.1	17	17	03-90	.00	.0		162	0	00-00-00	10.9	1.23	13.4	1.27	17.0	0	4.1	29	12,180	1,670	+10	0.0	03
TCI Intl	11.3	4.4	6.1	1.55	.46	266.7	-25.0	-62.0	6	5	09-09-88	.00	.0		0	0	09-09-88	2.2	1.05	2.3	2.00	4.6	21	1.2	20	3,385	693	0	0.0	09
TDK Cp	13.2	5.6	4.2	188.2	1.24	118.8	102.0	129.6	-4	5	03-26-90	.00	.5	17	36	0	03-26-90	5.3	.87	4.6	1.78	8.2	2	2.3	5,842	120,462	1,533	0	19.6	11
Tech Ops Land		-16.7	6.3s	2.5	1.47	-5.1	7.3	7.3	21	0	06-11-90	.60	2.5		0	0	06-11-90	26.3	.96	25.2	1.41	35.6	0	2.1	102	4,236	1,943	0	9.7	09
Tech Ops Sev	10.5	1.3	-6.6	1.58	.77	25.7	20.3	137.8	15	0	06-11-90	.23	2.7		0	0	06-11-90	10.7	1.37	14.7	1.44	21.1	0	2.7	14	1,692	307	0	0.2	09
Tech Sym	10.0	10.0	2.5	7.00	1.07	47.4	47.4	47.4	8	8	03-90	.00	.0		0	0	00-00-00	5.7	.91	5.2	1.54	8.0	29	6.2	59	6,476	2,460	0	0.0	12
Teldyn	11.4	11.4	25.0	-2.0n	-1.07	-100.0	-100.0	-58.0	NE	0	00-00-00	.00	.0		0	0	00-00-00	-10.0	1.96	-19.6	.00	NM	10	1.2	2	1,826	12	0	0.0	12
Technic Commun	-29.4	-47.9	-41.1	1.1s	.92	-100.0	-73.7	-58.0	19	19	07-03-90	.00	.0		23	0	07-03-90	11.0	.91	18.6	1.86	18.6	21	2.1	15	1,223	39	0	0.0	09
Technitrol	-3.3	-3.3	12.3	7.4q	3.76	-9.8	-9.8	20.5	15	15	03-90	1.12	3.1	31	23	0	00-00-00	8.1	1.74	14.1	1.50	21.1	21	3.5	71	1,970	651	0	0.5	12
Technology Dev	-26.2	1.4	.0	.0t	.01	-100.0	-97.0	-97.0	0	0	12-89	.00	.0		0	0	00-00-00	.0	NC	NC	NC	.0	0	5.7	4	2,045	683	0	0.0	12
Teletec	5.5	5.5	.0	3.5q	.85	-6.5	-6.5	-33.1	14	14	03-90	.00	.0		0	0	00-00-00	-10.0	1.25	12.5	1.14	14.3	0	6.5	57	3,881	522	+26	0.0	12
Tektronix Inc	-2.8	-2.4	-1.7	-29.0n	-1.01	-100.0	-100.0	-100.0	NC	-9	02-90	.60	3.9		91	56	07-09-90	-2.1	1.33	-2.8	2.07	-5.8	23	1.5	451	29,085	21,488	0	0.9	05
Telco Systs	25.9	21.5	16.9	6.1n	.66	118.2	165.0	175.0	NC	15	05-90	.00	.0		0	0	00-00-00	7.3	1.36	9.9	1.49	14.8	28	4.9	110	8,333	4,639	+82	0.0	06
TeleConcepts	-8.3	-8.3	.0	-2.8q	-.41	NE	NE	NE	-85	-85	03-90	.00	.0		0	0	00-00-00	-25.5	1.48	-37.8	2.24	-84.8	52	2.3	4	6,639	207	0	1.6	12
Tellabs Inc	22.0	22.0	17.2	7.1q	.56	.0	.0	-45.6	-1	6	03-90	.00	.0		0	0	00-00-00	3.7	1.22	4.5	1.31	5.9	4	3.9	161	12,625	6,111	0	0.0	12
Temiflex	33.3	26.4	28.5	.2n	.15	NE	-66.7	NC	-6	5	03-90	.00	.0		31	NE	06-18-90	2.2	1.32	2.9	1.83	5.3	39	2.7	3	1,320	122	+0	0.0	06
Texas Inst	-3.8	-3.8	.5	220.1q	.5	-94.4	-94.4	-45.3	NC	8	06-20-90	.72	1.8		24	0	06-20-90	3.4	1.35	4.6	2.43	11.2	31	1.9	3,231	81,536	54,219	+3	0.6	12
TII Ind	32.8	-17.3	-20.5	-5.9n	-1.66	-100.0	-100.0	-100.0	NC	-57	00-00-00	.00	.0		0	0	00-00-00	-21.9	.93	-20.3	2.79	-56.7	2	1.0	2	3,545	310	+2	0.0	06
TLM Cp	-100.0	-97.9	-50.0	2.0s	.40	NE	NE	NE	32	32	10-27-86	.00	.0		0	0	10-27-86	40.0	.47	18.9	1.68	31.7	30	3.1	11	4,679	58	0	0.0	12
Torotel Inc	-52.0	-13.0	-11.1	-.4n	-.14	-100.0	-100.0	-45.6	-29	-29	01-90	.00	.0		0	0	04-24-85	-5.0	1.40	-7.0	4.09	-28.6	164	2.4	4	2,593	139	0	2.6	04
Trans-Lux Cp	.0	.0	16.6	-2.9n	.22	-66.7	-66.7	NC	1	1	03-90	.12	2.3b		31	0	06-18-90	-11.2	.43	4.3	2.33	1.4	67	2.3	8	1,487	367	0	23.2	12
Transmation Inc	8.9	11.8	14.2	1.1f	.45	23.1	21.6	21.6	21	21	03-90	.00	.0		0	0	00-00-00	4.6	2.39	11.0	1.93	21.2	12	2.2	9	2,359	159	0	0.0	03
Tridex Cp	-47.1	-34.9	-34.6	8.6f	4.33	-100.0	-100.0	-100.0	0	0	04-90	.00	.0		0	NE	09-04-87	50.6	1.01	51.2	.00	NS	-9900	1.8	9	1,908	132	0	9.6	09
Unitrode Cp	-22.4	-22.4	-20.2	-24.2a	-1.75	-100.0	-100.0	-100.0	-28	-28	04-90	.00	.0		NE	0	09-04-87	-18.6	1.10	-20.4	1.37	-28.0	11	2.0	68	13,896	7,310	0	0.6	01
Univ Sec Inst		2.3	9.0	-.5n	-.15	.0	-5.1	-6.3	-6	-6	12-89	.00	.0		0	0	00-00-00	-3.9	1.52	-6.3	1.97	-6.3	0	2.1	6	3,446	517	0	0.0	01
UTL Cp	128.6	9.8	52.9	-2.9n	-.70	-100.0	-66.7	NC	-27	-27	03-90	.00	.0		31	0	09-01-87	-11.2	.54	-6.1	4.49	-27.4	291	5.3	16	4,224	812	0	0.0	06
Varian Assoc	-7.6	.5	7.5	25.5s	1.30	-31.0	-22.5	-51.3	5	5	07-17-90	.26	.9		17	29	07-17-90	1.9	1.42	2.7	2.22	6.0	13	1.6	535	19,034	11,835	+18	0.5	09
Vaughn	-11.9	-11.9		-.40	-.14	NE	NE	NE	-15	-15	04-90	.00	.0		0	0	00-00-00	-1.5	2.60	-3.9	3.79	-14.8	152	2.5	2	2,459	122	0	0.0	01
Vicon Ind	1.8	7.1	6.9	-1.8e	-.67	-100.0	-100.0	NE	-11	-11	04-90	.00	.0		0	0	00-00-00	-3.9	1.23	-4.8	2.29	-11.0	53	3.3	9	2,758	706	0	0.0	09
Video Communications &	-25.0	-25.0	.0	-.3q	-.10	NE	NE	NE	-75	-75	03-90	.00	.0		0	0	00-00-00	-30.0	.33	-10.0	7.50	-75.0	99	.3	3	2,096		0	0.0	12
Video Display	31.0	34.2	34.1	.7f	.17	-100.0	-73.0	-73.0	6	6	02-90	.00	.0		0	0	02-90	1.3	1.82	.21	2.71	5.7	0	2.7	17	4,090	550	0	0.0	02
Vishay Inter	9.3	9.3	106.7	19.9q	1.60	50.0	50.0	146.2	11	17	05-22-90	.00	.0		1	0	05-22-90	4.7	1.00	4.7	3.60	16.9	158	2.4	261	12,371	3,167	-15	3.1	12
VLSI Tech	31.3	31.3	29.5	9.0q	.39	NE	387.5	387.5	6	6	00-00-00	.00	.0		0	0	00-00-00	1.0	.97	.97	2.07	5.8	55	1.9	245	24,175	10,908	0	0.0	12
VMX Inc	14.8	28.9	31.7	.7n	.03	NE	NE	NE	3	3	03-90	.00	.0		0	0	00-00-00	1.3	1.62	2.1	1.29	2.7	1	3.8	39	23,182	5,385	-200	0.0	06

Wavetek	14.2	9.5	5.9	2.2s	25	266.7	300.0	NE	NC	4	03-90	.00	0	0	0	00-00-00	2.5	1.16	2.9	1.28	3.7	5	38	8,220	5,654	0	09	0.0	09
Wstn Digital	17.9	3.7	-.4	19.0n	.64	100.0	-51.9	-58.7	NC	6	03-90	.00	0	0	0	00-00-00	1.9	1.68	3.2	1.97	6.3	51	387	29,184	12,665	0	06	2.4	06
Wstn Microwave	-8.0	-1.9	-9.0	-1.0s	-.69	NE	NE	NE	NC	-26	03-90	.00	0	0	0	07-10-90	-10.0	2.00	-30.0	1.32	-26.3	0	1	1,405	13	+2	09	0.0	09
Wyle Labs	5.9	5.9	2.6	9.4i	.95	200.0	200.0	41.8	NC	7	04-90	.28	2	37	61	00-00-00	.22	2.32	5.1	1.96	10.0	35	130	9,517	5,668	0	01	7.2	01
Xicor Inc	-10.0	-10.0	-5.3	-9.5q	-.53	-100.0	-100.0	-100.0	NC	-10	03-90	.00	0	0	0	00-00-00	-10.8	.71	-7.7	1.26	-9.7	2	56	17,963	7,112	0	12	0.0	12
Xyvision Inc	-37.2	-34.8	-34.7	-20.5f	-3.53	-100.0	-100.0	-100.0	NC	-62	03-90	.00	0	0	0	00-00-00	-68.3	.45	-30.8	2.01	-61.9	68	11	5,738	1,441	0	03	0.0	03
Zeus Components ... □	-2.7	-4.4	-1.0	.08	.00	-50.0	-100.0	-100.0	NC	NC	03-90	.00	0	0	0	00-00-00	.00	NC	NC	NC	0	96	6	2,715	691	0	09	0.0	09
Zmos Cp	82.1	82.1	61.5	-1.9q	-.66	NE	NE	NE	NC	-37	03-90	.00	0	0	0	00-00-00	-4.5	2.00	-9.0	4.06	-36.5	63	25	33,228	384	0	12	0.0	12

Radio, TV, Phonograph, Stereo

Ind. Group																														
Ind. Group	81.3	13.0	8.1	645.3	1.21	26.1	29.5	-8.6	9	6	- - - -	.21	2	22	18	- - - -	3.0	1.00	3.0	2.40	7.2	22	24,190	479,802	27,956	+28	12	4.4	12
Andrea Radio Cp	-30.0	-9.8	.0	.21	.30	-100.0	-48.3	-48.3	-11	-4	12-20-89	.52	-9	120	121	12-20-89	5.0	1.12	5.6	1.09	6.1	61	3	50	3	0	12	0.0	12
Amatron Intl	-14.7	-11.1	.0	.78	.27	33.3	-25.0	-25.0	NC	12	00-00-00	.00	0	0	0	00-00-00	1.8	2.22	4.0	3.08	12.3	0	6	254	210	0	09	8.0	09
Carver Cp	44.0	44.0	23.8	-2.1q	-.59	NE	NE	NE	NC	-11	03-90	.00	0	0	0	00-00-00	-8.1	1.15	-9.3	1.13	-10.5	18	16	3,611	1,050	0	12	0.0	12
Craig Corp	71.4	45.2	-15.3	6.7s	1.48	-39.5	-25.9	-24.5	NC	17	10-02-89	.00	0	0	0	00-00-00	60.9	.19	11.5	1.51	17.4	39	88	4,584	1,737	0	09	0.2	09
Elexis Cp	15.4	15.4	16.6	-.9q	-.42	NE	NE	NE	NC	0	03-90	.00	0	0	0	00-00-00	-12.9	1.01	-13.0	.00	NS	-100	0	2,245	620	0	12	0.0	12
Emerson Radio	4.3	17.0	16.9	10.4f	.29	-100.0	11.5	11.5	NC	12	03-90	.00	6	42	43	10-17-86	1.2	3.75	4.5	2.58	11.6	61	148	36,810	8,955	0	03	0.0	03
Esquire Radio	8.1	8.1	-14.8	1.0q	2.27	38.2	38.2	-22.0	NC	3	03-90	.81	0	0	0	03-27-90	2.2	1.68	3.7	1.08	4.0	0	13	482	178	0	12	0.0	12
Imrad Inc	20.0	20.0	25.0	-.1q	-.05	NE	NE	NE	NC	-2	03-90	.00	0	0	0	00-00-00	.65	.66	-1.3	1.15	-1.5	0	4	1,338	74	0	12	0.0	12
Johnson Elec	-21.4	-21.4	-20.0	-2.6q	-1.58	NE	NE	NE	NC	0	03-90	.00	0	0	0	00-00-00	-65.0	.59	-38.2	.00	NM	314	2	1,621	150	0	12	0.0	12
Kustom Elect	54.8	36.5	15.3	-.5e	-.28	-25.0	-42.1	-20.0	NC	-8	11-13-85	.00	0	0	0	11-13-85	3.3	1.76	5.8	1.31	7.6	0	8	1,906	15	+8	09	0.0	09
Microdyne □	29.4	16.8	10.5	.4s	.07	133.3	-25.0	-25.0	NC	2	04-90	.00	0	0	NE	11-06-87	1.9	.79	1.5	1.13	1.7	3	16	4,083	662	0	10	0.0	10
Pattern Proc Tech	33.3	50.0	100.0	-.8f	-.90	NE	NE	-44.0	NC	0	10-88	.00	0	0	0	07-03-89	-40.0	1.67	-66.7	.00	NM	100	1	964	21	0	03	0.0	03
Pioneer Elec	-149.1	171.8	.0	.0f	.42	NE	NE	-44.0	NC	0	12-88	.23	18	83	48	03-29-90	NC	NC	NC	NC	.0	6	6,988	83,194	96	0	03	43.6	03
Polk Audio	6.0	8.3	12.0	1.9f	1.05	28.0	209.7	47.3	23	23	03-90	.23	30	0	0	01-14-87	6.8	2.31	15.7	1.48	23.2	0	18	1,740	302	-7	03	0.0	03
Power Spectra	37.5	37.5	100.0	-.1q	-.01	-100.0	-100.0	NE	NC	-9	03-90	.00	0	0	0	00-00-00	-2.5	1.72	-4.3	2.12	-9.1	0	26	9,318	115	0	12	0.0	12
Recoton Corp	11.5	11.5	7.5	-.2q	-.09	-100.0	-100.0	-100.0	NC	-2	03-90	.00	0	0	0	00-00-00	-.5	1.20	-.6	3.00	-1.8	103	6	1,981	272	0	12	0.0	12
Sony Corp	4.9	13.6	14.5	716.8n	2.19	23.1	23.1	11.2	NC	9	03-90	.28	18	19	17	03-29-90	3.9	1.03	4.0	2.60	10.4	24	16,603	282,603	1,304	+10	03	17.4	03
Television Tech	-34.8	-19.5	-10.0	-1.3n	-.24	NC	NE	NE	NC	0	03-90	.00	0	0	0	00-00-00	-14.4	1.97	-28.3	.00	NM	22	1	5,396	49	+10	06	0.0	06
Wall To Wall Snd	4.6	12.8	13.1	-3.6f	-.69	-100.0	NE	NE	NC	-15	02-90	.00	0	0	0	00-00-00	-2.1	2.10	-4.4	3.34	-14.7	32	6	5,300	188	+17	02	0.0	02
Wells Gard El □	-5.9	-5.9	-17.5	-2.2q	-.59	-60.0	-100.0	-100.0	NC	-20	03-90	.07	2	0	0	12-06-88	-6.7	2.03	-13.6	1.30	-17.7	0	12	3,766	576	0	12	15.5	12
Zenith Eltrns □	3.5	3.5	-36.4	-79.4q	-2.97	NE	NE	-100.0	NC	-20	03-90	.00	0	0	0	00-00-00	-5.1	1.69	-8.6	2.31	-19.9	38	224	26,751	11,379	0	12	8.6	12

Source: Media General Financial Services, Richmond, VA.

Trends and Forecasts: Measuring and Controlling Instruments (SIC 3822–4)
(in millions of dollars except as noted)

Item	1987[1]	1988[2]	1989[2]	1990[3]	Percent Change		
					1987–88	1988–89	1989–90
Industry Data							
Value of shipments[4]	7,922	8,544	9,054	9,495	7.9	6.0	4.9
Value of shipments (1987$)	7,922	8,327	8,590	8,792	5.1	3.2	2.4
Total employment (000)	90.0	98.1	102	–	9.0	4.0	–
Production workers (000)	51.8	58.3	61.2	–	12.5	5.0	–
Average hourly earnings ($)	10.13	10.26	10.31	–	1.3	0.5	–
Product Data							
Value of shipments[5]	7,628	8,211	8,690	9,106	7.6	5.8	4.8
Value of shipments (1987$)	7,628	8,003	8,245	8,431	4.9	3.0	2.3
Trade Data							
Value of imports (ITA)[6]	941	1,028	1,229	–	9.2	19.6	–
Import/new supply ratio[7]	0.110	0.111	0.124	–	0.9	11.7	–
Value of exports (ITA)[8]	1,271	1,531	1,377	–	20.5	–10.1	–
Export/shipments ratio	0.167	0.186	0.158	–	11.4	–15.1	–

[1]Data are preliminary.
[2]Estimated.
[3]Forecast.
[4]Value of all products and services sold by establishments in the measuring and controlling instruments industry.
[5]Value of products classified in the measuring and controlling instruments industry produced by all industries.
[6]Import data are developed by the chapter author.
[7]New supply is imports plus corresponding product shipments.
[8]Export data are developed by the chapter author.

SOURCE: U.S. Department of Commerce: Bureau of the Census; International Trade Administration (ITA). Estimates and forecasts by ITA.

Source: *U.S. Industrial Outlook 1990*, U.S. Department of Commerce.

Trends and Forecasts: Measuring and Controlling Devices (SIC 382)
(in millions of dollars except as noted)

Item	1987[1]	1988[2]	1989[2]	1990[3]	Percent Change		
					1987–88	1988–89	1989–90
Industry Data							
Value of shipments[4]	26,377	29,136	31,030	33,009	10.5	6.5	6.4
Value of shipments (1987$)	26,377	28,625	29,778	31,035	8.5	4.0	4.2
Total employment (000)	286	304	313	—	6.3	3.0	—
Production workers (000)	151	164	171	—	8.6	4.3	—
Average hourly earnings ($)	10.64	—	—	—	—	—	—
Product Data							
Value of shipments[5]	25,643	28,258	29,997	31,841	10.2	6.2	6.1
Value of shipments (1987$)	25,643	27,763	28,788	29,939	8.3	3.7	4.0
Trade Data							
Value of imports	4,496	4,938	—	—	9.8	—	—
Import/new supply ratio[6]	0.070	—	—	—	—	—	—
Value of exports	5,630	6,742	—	—	19.8	—	—
Export/shipments ratio	0.220	—	—	—	—	—	—

[1]Data are preliminary.
[2]Estimated.
[3]Forecast.
[4]Value of all products and services sold by establishments in the measuring and controlling devices industry.
[5]Value of products classified in the measuring and controlling devices industry produced by all industries.
[6]New supply is imports plus corresponding product shipments.
SOURCE: U.S. Department of Commerce: Bureau of the Census; International Trade Administration (ITA). Estimates and forecasts by ITA.

Source: U.S. Industrial Outlook 1990, U.S. Department of Commerce.

MEDIA GENERAL FINANCIAL SERVICES

STOCKS by INDUSTRY

Electronic Controls and Instruments

Ratio formula note: r/l × r/a = r/l/a × a/e = r/e

Company	Rev %Chg Last Qtr	Rev %Chg FY-to-Date	Rev %Chg Last 12 Mos	Rev Last 12 Mos $Mil	EPS Last 12 Mos $	EPS %Chg Last Qtr	EPS %Chg FY-to-Date	EPS %Chg Last 12 Mos	5-Yr Growth %	Par Growth %	Date of Report	Div Amt $	Div Yield %	Div 5-Yr Growth %	Payout Last FY %	Payout Last 5 Yrs %	Last X-Dvd Date	Profit Margin %	Asset Turnover	Return on Total Assets %	Leverage Ratio	Return on Equity %	Debt to Equity %	Current Ratio	Mkt Value $Mil	Shares Out 000	Held by Banks-Funds 000	Insider Net Trading 000	Short Int Ratio Days	Fiscal Yr End Mo
Ind. Group	.3	4.1	-.9	587.0	.98	-21.4	-16.6	-17.5	32	7	---	.35	2.8	0	14	19	---	3.9	.59	2.3	4.48	10.3	64	1.3	7,197	576,301	142,904	-594	1.0	--
Ametek Inc	17.2	17.2	14.3	36.8	.83	-15.4	-15.4	15.3	-2	4	03-90	.64	4.9	10	71	65	06-11-90	6.0	1.08	6.5	2.91	18.9	113	3.1	581	44,268	18,769	0	2.1	12
Andros Analyz	52.1	30.4	27.7	1.2	.34	300.0	122.2	78.9	-5	5	04-90	.00	.0	0	0	0	00-00-00	5.2	.85	4.4	1.18	5.2	3	5.7	44	3,413	1,755	0	0.0	07
Amtech	-47.5	-47.5	-25.8	2.5	.84	-100.0	-100.0	16.7	NC	6	04-90	.00	.0	0	0	0	00-00-00	2.2	1.14	2.5	2.24	5.6	63	2.6	34	3,056	1,818	0	0.0	12
Amada	.0	.0	.0	.1	-1.12	NC	-100.0	NE	NC	-13	12-89	.00	.0	0	0	0	00-00-00	-1.5	1.53	-2.3	5.43	-12.5	319	2.8	7	842	87	-6	0.0	12
Aura Systs	110.0	225.0	200.0	3.4	-.16	NE	NE	NE	NC	-49	02-90	.00	.0	0	0	0	00-00-00	-37.8	.51	-19.4	2.51	-48.6	80	1.2	60	20,587	299	0	0.0	02
Base Ten A	NA	NA	NA	NA	NA	NA	NA	NA	NC	NC	00-00	.00	.0	NA	NA	NA	01-16-84	3.9	NC	NC	NC	NA	NA	NA	8	2,798	412	0	NA	10
Base Ten B	-15.3	13.9	42.8	1.3	.35	-65.7	-26.3	1066.7	NC	12	00-00	.00	.0	0	0	0	01-16-84	2.6	1.35	3.5	3.46	12.1	119	2.2	2	635	20	0	0.0	10
Boonton Electr	6.7	8.9	-7.6	.3	.15	100.0	550.0	-57.1	-17	4	03-90	.00	.0	0	0	0	00-00-00	2.5	.84	2.1	1.81	3.8	9	2.0	4	1,297	40	0	0.0	09
Bowmar Instr	-26.7	-25.1	-7.5	3.7	-.60	-100.0	NE	NE	NC	0	03-90	.00	.0	0	0	0	00-00-00	-10.0	1.62	-16.2	.00	NM	513	1.3	4	6,098	359	0	1.7	09
Brajtes	-15.9	-7.0	-6.3	2.2	-.80	NE	-100.0	-100.0	NC	-48	03-90	.00	.0	0	0	0	00-00-00	-3.7	2.35	-8.7	5.49	-47.8	NC	1.1	8	2,816	28	-469	0.0	02
Chronar Cp	-62.5	-62.5	-56.6	51.5	-4.04	NE	NE	NE	NC	0	10-04-88	.00	.0	0	0	0	10-04-88	NM	NM	-13.9	NC	NM	479	1.3	9	13,875	975	0	0.0	12
CompuDyne	-19.2	-19.2	2.2	4.4	-5.05	NE	NE	NE	NE	0	03-90	.00	.0	0	0	0	00-00-00	-9.6	1.45	5.1	.00	NS	-3	1.0	1	1,027	147	0	0.0	12
Daniel Inds	-1.4	-.4	6.2	7.3	.70	70.0	43.5	45.8	6	6	03-90	.18	1.1	2	30	0	06-04-90	4.3	1.19	5.1	1.69	8.6	31	3.1	169	10,349	4,178	0	0.0	09
Data Measurement	NA	.0	.0	1.9	-1.65	25.0	25.0	-100.0	NC	-37	03-90	.00	.0	0	0	0	00-00-00	-10.0	.92	-9.2	4.05	-37.3	2	1.2	4	1,208	38	0	0.0	12
Data Translation	-17.5	-17.3	-13.6	.8	-.26	-100.0	-89.7	-77.0	-4	4	01-09-87	.00	.0	0	0	0	01-09-87	2.1	1.33	2.8	1.29	3.6	0	3.9	12	3,080	1,158	0	0.0	11
Datakey	.0	.0	11.1	3.0	.84	20.0	20.0	33.3	NC	33	03-90	.00	.0	0	0	0	00-00-00	30.0	.93	27.8	1.17	32.6	0	9.2	34	3,120	437	-14	0.0	12
Diagnostic Rt A	-18.3	-18.3	-17.1	8.4	-1.49	-100.0	-100.0	-100.0	NA	-24	03-90	.00	.0	0	0	0	00-00-00	-14.5	.74	-10.7	2.20	-23.5	77	3.3	12	5,617	969	0	0.0	03
Diagnostic Rt B	NA	NA	NA	NA	NA	NA	NA	NA	NA	NC	03-90	.00	.0	NA	NA	NA	00-00-00	NA	NA	NA	NC	NA	NA	NA	4	2,033	615	0	NA	03
ECI Telecom	40.7	40.7	34.8	7.9	1.39	189.5	189.5	127.9	NA	43	03-90	.00	.0	0	0	0	00-00-00	13.6	.96	13.1	3.30	43.2	52	1.5	197	6,905	74	0	0.0	12
Edison Control	33.3	-8.3	.0	.1	-.05	NC	NE	NE	NC	-2	12-89	.00	.0	0	0	0	00-00-00	-10.0	.15	-1.5	1.00	-1.5	0	33.0	7	2,100	439	0	0.0	12
EIP Microwave	-17.6	-4.6	7.6	.9	-1.00	-100.0	12.0	12.0	NC	13	03-90	.12	4.0	3	1200	NE	06-11-90	6.4	2.13	13.6	1.35	18.4	0	3.1	7	2,177	126	0	0.0	09
Electro Sensors ◄	-7.7	-7.7	-7.7	.5	.43	NE	0	NE	NC	-2	04-26-90	.10	3.8	0	36	21	04-26-90	10.0	.94	9.4	1.06	10.0	0	17.0	5	1,818	118	0	0.0	12
Energy Conv Dev	-20.6	-38.1	-23.8	.5	-.56	-100.0	-100.0	-100.0	NC	-83	03-90	.00	.0	0	0	0	00-00-00	-3.1	.87	-2.7	30.85	-83.3	1067	1.1	59	6,177	1,105	0	0.0	08
Emtronics Cp	176.5	169.0	140.0	.6	-.13	NE	NE	NE	NC	-11	02-90	.00	.0	0	0	0	12-23-85	-5.0	2.04	-10.2	1.07	-10.9	0	17.0	16	5,051	127	0	0.0	06
Environ Tectonics	-16.4	-7.8	-5.0	.9	.33	133.3	230.0	230.0	NC	20	02-90	.00	.0	0	0	0	12-23-85	4.7	1.34	6.3	3.17	20.0	44	1.6	12	2,848	1	0	0.0	02

Company		
Fischer & Port	5,209	2,527
Frequency Elec	5,600	3,115
Galileo Elec	6,267	3,221
Harman Intl	8,728	4,181
Hitech Engineering	5,414	
Humphrey Inc	1,000	121
Imo Inds Inc	18,273	7,183
Impact Systs	9,333	1,388
Instron Corp	6,090	1,732
Johnson Contr	39,387	9,779
KLA Instruments	17,876	8,729
Kongo Cp	5,230	1,400
Kollmorgen Cp	10,711	4,285
Measurex Corp	17,968	-2,514
Medal Inc	5,595	948
Metrol Circuits	2,525	133
Micron Prods	2,440	52
MTS Systems Cp	4,605	2,021
Neurotech Corp	9,854	19
Newport Electrnc	1,182	93
Nicolet Instr	6,690	3,035
OI Cp	3,274	127
Pac Scientific	5,560	2,969
Panatech R&D	4,332	45
Rheometrics NC	3,085	417
See Tag Sys	14,464	703
Sym Tek Systs	1,469	164
Technology Rsch	8,809	101
Tenney Engr	3,621	619
Teradne Inc	29,235	10,966
Thomson-CSF	111,182	61
Ultrak	30,113	0
Vanzetti Sys	2,571	94
Versus Tech	2,247	0
Vixonics Inc	2,129	27
Wash Scientific	2,374	524
Whitehall Cp	3,427	1,045
X Rite	5,197	481

Source: Media General Financial Services, Richmond, VA.

Energy: Coal, Oil, and Gas

CONSUMPTION BY FUEL TYPE AND SECTOR 1973–1989 [Quadrillon (10^{15}) BTU]

	Residential and Commercial*				Transportation*		
Total	Coal	Natural Gas[1]	Petroleum	Total	Coal	Natural Gas[4]	Petroleum
1973	0.254	7.626	4.391	1973	0.003	0.743	17.831
1974	0.257	7.518	3.996	1974	0.002	0.685	17.399
1975	0.209	7.581	3.805	1975	0.001	0.595	17.614
1976	0.203	7.866	4.181	1976	[2]	0.559	18.506
1977	0.205	7.461	4.206	1977	[2]	0.543	19.241
1978	0.214	7.624	4.070	1978	[3]	0.539	20.041
1979	0.187	7.891	3.448	1979	[3]	0.612	19.825
1980	0.145	7.540	3.035	1980	[3]	0.650	19.008
1981	0.167	7.243	2.634	1981	[3]	0.658	18.811
1982	0.187	7.427	2.449	1982	[3]	0.612	18.420
1983	0.192	7.025	2.498	1983	[3]	0.505	18.593
1984	0.209	7.291	2.585	1984	[3]	0.545	19.286
1985	0.176	7.078	2.573	1985	[3]	0.519	19.534
1986	0.176	6.824	2.576	1986	[3]	0.499	20.215
1987	0.162	6.954	6.618	1987	[3]	0.535	20.780
1988	0.168	7.512	R2.693	1988	[3]	0.632	R21.510
1989	0.142	7.791	2.658	1989	[3]	0.606	21.499

* Geographic coverage: the 50 United States and District of Columbia.
The Residential and Commercial Sector consists of housing units, non-manufacturing business establishments (e.g., wholesale and retail businesses), health, social and educational institutions, and government office buildings.
R = Revised data.
˙ Totals may not equal sum of components due to independent rounding.
The Transportation Sector consists of both private and public passenger and freight transportation, as well as government transportation, including military operations.
[1] Includes supplemental gaseous fuels.
[2] Less than 0.5 trillion BTU.
[3] Since 1978, the small amounts of coal consumed for transportation have been reported as industrial sector consumption.
[4] Pipeline fuel only, including supplemental gaseous fuels.

	Industrial*				Electric Utilities*		
Total	Coal	Natural Gas[1]	Petroleum	Total	Coal	Natural Gas[1]	Petroleum[2]
1973	4.057	10.388	9.104	1973	8.658	3.748	3.515
1974	3.870	10.003	8.694	1974	8.534	3.519	3.365
1975	3.667	8.532	8.147	1975	8.786	3.240	3.166
1976	3.661	8.761	9.010	1976	9.720	3.152	3.477
1977	3.454	8.636	9.774	1977	10.262	3.284	4.901
1978	3.314	8.539	9.867	1978	10.238	3.297	3.987
1979	3.593	8.549	10.568	1979	11.260	3.613	3.283
1980	3.155	8.394	9.525	1980	12.123	3.810	2.634
1981	3.157	8.257	8.285	1981	12.583	3.768	2.202
1982	2.552	7.116	7.794	1982	12.582	3.342	1.568
1983	2.490	6.821	7.420	1983	13.213	2.998	1.544
1984	2.842	7.449	7.894	1984	14.020	3.220	1.286
1985	2.760	7.080	7.725	1985	14.542	3.160	1.090
1986	2.643	6.693	7.953	1986	14.444	2.691	1.452
1987	2.673	7.325	8.210	1987	15.173	2.935	1.257
1988	2.828	7.793	R8.463	1988	15.850	2.709	1.563
1989	2.864	8.255	8.187	1989	15.953	2.845	1.682

* Geographic coverage: the 50 United States and District of Columbia.
The Industrial Sector is made up of construction, manufacturing, agriculture, and mining establishments.
˙ Totals may not equal sum of components due to independent rounding.
[1] Includes supplemental gaseous fuels.
[2] Includes petroleum products reported as "oil consumed at steam units" through 1979 and "heavy oil" from 1980 forward, which are assumed to be residual fuel oil; petroleum products reported as "oil consumed by gas turbine and internal combustion units" through 1979 and "light oil" from 1980 forward, which are assumed to be distillate fuel oil and kerosene; and petroleum coke.

Source: *Monthly Energy Review*, U.S. Department of Energy, Energy Information Administration, 1989 Annual Summary.

PETROLEUM—CRUDE OIL[1] SUPPLY AND DISPOSITION (Thousand Barrels per Day)*

| | | Field Production | | Supply | | |
| | | | | Imports | | |
		Total Domestic	Alaskan	Total	SPR[2]	Other
		Thousand barrels per day				
1973	AVERAGE	9,208	198	3,244		3,244
1974	AVERAGE	8,774	193	3,477		3,477
1975	AVERAGE	8,375	191	4,105		4,105
1976	AVERAGE	8,132	173	5,287		5,287
1977	AVERAGE	8,245	464	6,615	21	6,594
1978	AVERAGE	8,707	1,229	6,356	162	6,195
1979	AVERAGE	8,552	1,401	6,519	67	6,452
1980	AVERAGE	8,597	1,617	5,263	44	5,219
1981	AVERAGE	8,572	1,609	4,396	256	4,141
1982	AVERAGE	8,649	1,696	3,488	165	3,323
1983	AVERAGE	8,688	1,714	3,329	234	3,096
1984	AVERAGE	8,879	1,722	3,426	197	3,229
1985	AVERAGE	8,971	1,825	3,201	118	3,083
1986	AVERAGE	8,680	1,867	4,178	48	4,130
1987	AVERAGE	8,349	1,962	4,674	73	4,601
1988	AVERAGE	8,140	2,017	5,107	51	5,055
1989	AVERAGE	7,631	1,874	5,808	56	5,752

* Geographic coverage: the 50 United States and the District of Columbia.
᾿ Totals may not equal sum of components due to independent rounding.
[1] Includes lease condensate.
[2] Strategic Petroleum Reserve.

Source: *Monthly Energy Review*, U.S. Department of Energy, Energy Information Administration, 1989 Annual Summary.

MEDIA GENERAL FINANCIAL SERVICES

STOCKS by INDUSTRY

Oil, Natural Gas Production

Company	Revenue Pct. Change Last Qtr %	FY to Date %	Last 12 Mos %	Last 12 Mos $Mil	Earnings Per Share Last 12 Mos $Mil	Last 12 $	Last Qtr %	FY to Date %	Last 12 Mos %	5-Year Growth Rate %	Par Growth Rate %	Date of Report	Current Rate Amt $	Yield %	5-Year Growth Rate %	Payout Last FY %	Last 5 Yrs. %	Last X-Dvd Date	Pro-fit Mar-gin	Asset Turn-over	Return on Total Assets	Lever-age Ratio	Return on Equity	Debt to Eq-uity %	Curr-ent Ratio	Mar-ket Value $Mil	Latest Shares Out-stndg. 000	Held by Banks-Funds 000	Insider Net Trad-ing 000	Short Int-erest Ratio Days	Fiscal Year Ends Mo
Ind. Group	8.8	11.6	15.8	1,942.8	.69	31.8	58.6	157.2	25	-3	---	.99	5.8		130	134	---	3.6	.83	3.0	2.67	8.0	84	1.3	35,168	2,058,389	297,262	+3548	6.4	---
Allegheny & West	2.3	12.7	12.2	3.6n	.45	10.3	9.3	4.7	-26	4	03-90	.00	.0		20	13	06-09-88	1.9	1.11	.21	1.90	4.0	47	2.2	63	8,109	2,658	0	0.0	06
Amarican Resources	-100.0	-50.0	200.0	.0n	-.01	NC	NC	NC	NC	0	01-90	.00	.0		0	0	00-00-00	NC	NC	NC	NC	.0	.0		1	2,724	0	0	0.0	04
Barnwell Indus	43.3	238.1		9.7s	6.70	62.9	456.1	386.5	NC	0	03-90	.00	.8		0	8	05-30-90	24.9	1.43	35.5	.00	NS	-741	4.0	40	1,416	69	0	3.0	09
Barod Cp	61.7	61.7	14.7	19.3q	.31	200.0	200.0	82.4	NC	2	03-90	.20	1.8		0	0	06-11-90	3.4	.91	3.1	1.87	5.8	32	4.0	679	61,010	16,139	0	0.3	12
Baruch-Foster	-8.7	-8.7		-.20	-.06	80.0	80.0	NE	NE	-2	03-90	.00	.0		0	0	07-08-85	-2.5	.44	-1.1	1.91	-2.1	67	2.3	15	2,718	278	0	0.0	12
Basic Petrol	45.8	44.8	40.0	2.41	1.30	NE	NE	NE	NC	2	12-89	.00	.0		0	0	08-07-89	17.1	.11	1.8	1.00	1.8	1	6.7	13	1,018	158	0	0.0	12
Berry Petro A	61.2	61.2	17.5	15.2q	.74	53.8	53.8	32.1	NC	4	03-90	.55	3.8b		100	62	06-13-90	32.3	.41	13.3	1.18	15.5	1	9.2	309	21,524	5,391	0	0.0	12
Callon Consol pfs	-17.6	2.3	7.6	1.5f	.25	-100.0	47.1	47.1	NC	-13	12-89	.70	35.0		320	136	05-04-90	10.7	.52	5.6	1.29	7.2	0	.5	12	5,932	23	0	0.0	12
Cdn Occid Pet	-1.8	-1.8	1.2	35.4d	.53	.0	.0	15.2	-15	1	03-90	.40	2.7		75	53	05-30-90	7.5	.39	2.9	2.03	5.9	37	1.3	966	66,849	1,028	+8	165.4	12
Caspen Oil	147.6	65.0	65.0	-1.2s	-.16	NE	.0	.0	-16	-16	01-90	.00	.0		0	0	00-00-00	-13.3	.45	-6.0	2.70	-16.2	111	.3	4	14,870	192	0	0.0	07
Comstock Resrcs	-10.0	-10.0	16.6	1.1q	.53	150.0	150.0	NE	NC	6	03-90	.00	.0		0	0	03-15-90	15.7	.22	3.4	1.68	5.7	38	.3	12	2,305	106	0	0.0	12
Dekalb Energy	6.5	6.5	15.4	31.4q	2.99	141.7	141.7	187.5	NC	12	03-90	.32	1.3		8	14	06-25-90	38.3	.20	7.5	1.73	13.0	21	1.2	258	10,312	3,919	-32	52.6	12
Devon Energy	-5.6	-5.6	18.1	1.4q	-.01	NE	NE	NE	NC	2	03-90	.00	.0		0	0	00-00-00	5.4	.26	1.4	1.43	2.0	16	1.5	114	8,629	1,648	0	0.0	12
Dorchester Hugoton	13.3	13.3	20.0	3.1q	.27	12.5	12.5	.0	45	7	03-90	.20	2.2b		73	65	06-25-90	51.7	.47	24.4	1.16	28.4	0	1.0	99	10,744	1,582	0	0.0	12
Equity Oil	32.4	32.4	25.0	2.3q	.19	300.0	300.0	216.7	NC	3	03-90	.10	1.6		38	58	03-12-90	15.3	.26	4.0	1.38	5.5	0	4.3	77	12,243	3,974	+180	0.0	12
Hal Financing Grp •	-8.3	-8.3	-14.2	-7.5q	-.18	-100.0	-100.0	NE	NE	-14	03-90	.00	.0		0	0	00-00-00	-25.0	.23	-5.8	2.40	-13.9	36	.9	13	41,653	1,043	0	0.0	12
Hamilton Oil	6.7	6.7	41.3	15.3q	.51	7.5	7.5	-28.2	-2	4	06-11-90	.10	.3		21	12	06-11-90	7.2	.28	2.0	2.55	5.1	72	1.3	930	26,013	6,457	0	0.0	12
Harken Energy	9.9	9.9	30.2	-6.6q	-.31	NC	NC	-100.0	-17	-10	03-90	.00	.0		0	0	00-00-00	-.6	4.00	-2.4	6.96	-16.7	230	1.1	111	29,480	1,142	+246	0.0	12
Hershey Oil	-12.5	-12.5	20.0	-1.2q	-.20	-100.0	-100.0	NE	NC	-10	03-90	.00	.0		0	0	00-00-00	-20.0	.30	-5.9	1.75	-10.3	25	.9	37	6,623	2,056	0	0.0	12
Hondo Oil&Gas	NA	NA	NA	NA	NA	NA	NA	NA	NC	NC	00-00	.00	.0		NA	NA	00-00-00	NA	NC	NA	NC	NC	NA	NA	131	12,928	0	0	NA	NA
Imperial Oil	35.3	35.3	70.1	489.4q	2.65	19.3	19.3	6.9	0	2	03-90	1.80	3.8		71	60	05-25-90	4.6	.67	3.1	2.19	6.8	61	1.4	8,916	189,694	7,245	0	0.0	12
KeyOil	90.2	90.2	437.5	.7q	.05	NC	NC	NC	NC	16	03-90	.00	.0		0	0	00-00-00	1.6	1.44	2.3	6.78	15.6	156	1.2	124	10,900	152	-2	0.0	12
La Land / Expl	13.9	13.9	7.2	39.6q	1.39	-30.9	-30.9	NE	NC	3	03-90	1.00	2.3		63	33	05-25-90	5.4	.61	3.3	2.88	9.5	88	.9	1,203	28,067	18,737	0	1.5	12
MAPCO	35.9	35.9	24.5	117.5q	3.25	23.6	23.6	9.8	7	20	03-90	1.00	2.2b		33	27	06-06-90	5.2	1.52	7.9	3.65	28.8	124	1.1	1,617	35,546	24,418	0	1.2	12
Maxus Enrgy	5.1	5.1	8.1	-17.7q	-.84	NE	NE	NE	NC	NC	03-90	.05	.5		0	NE	09-29-88	-2.9	.41	-1.2	.00	NS	-1225	1.2	895	90,679	48,391	0	6.1	12

Maxxam Inc	.0	41.5	124.7	143.6q	1570	332.9	332.9	435.8	NC	62	03-90	.00	.00	0	0	0	5.9	.76	4.5	13.71	61.7	666	1.5	332	8,616	908	0	2.7	12
Maynard Oil	41.5	33.3	2.5q	47	300.0	300.0	80.8	8	03-90	.00	.00	0	0	0	12.5	.51	6.4	1.27	8.1	NA	2.7	32	5,354	536	0	2.7	12
MGF Oil	NA	NA	NA	NA	.66	NA	NA	NA	NC	NC	00:00	1.18	14.8	0	NA	NA	NA	.32	1.5	NC	NA	NA	NA	761	95,110	260	0	NA	NA
Mitchell Energy	1.5	13.2	13.2	31.0q	.07	7.7	7.7	1220.0	-22	3	06-06-90	.32	1.8	55	69	9	4.7	.32	1.5	3.53	5.3	145	1.0	827	46,900	10,050	-4	0.6	01
Numac O & G	31.9	24.2	1.8q	.07	50.0	50.0	-53.3	-33	1	03-90	.00	.0	NA	68	18	4.4	.14	.6	2.00	.12	18	.4	141	25,575	800	+274	NA	12
Occid Petrol □	1.1	1.1	290.00q	1.03	40.7	40.7	1.0	-16	-7	06-06-90	2.50	9.7	273	215	7,561	1.1	1.00	1.4	3.50	4.9	139	1.1	332	293,250	84,052	+4	1.8	12
Omni Exploration	.0	5.3	.2	-.01	NE	NE	NE	NC	-4	09-99	.00	.0	0	0	5	-10.0	.27	-2.7	1.56	-4.2	21	.8	5	26,308	7	0	0.0	09
Parker Parsley	26.7	26.7	40.4	9.6q	1.58	-57.6	-57.6	NE	-2	-2	04-24-90	2.10	12.4	119	NE	31	16.3	.34	5.6	1.55	8.7	31	1.5	98	5,759	1	0	0.1	12
ParOil	100.0	100.0	.0	-.6q	-.25	NE	NE	NE	NC	-26	03-90	.00	.0	0	0	0	-50.0	.17	-10.3	2.53	-26.1	0	.7	9	2,177	1	0	0.0	12
Petrl Ind Inc	.0	.0	.0	.1q	.04	200.0	200.0	172.7	6	03-90	.00	.0	0	0	0	10.0	.56	5.6	1.05	5.9	0	12.0	4	1,776	18	0	0.0	12
Petro Devlp	3.2	3.2	-1.0q	.01	50.0	50.0	-80.0	0	-9	03-89	.00	.00	0	0	5	-11.1	.32	-3.6	2.58	-9.3	98	1.0	4	7,525	107	0	0.0	12
Petrominerl	28.6	28.6	.1q	1.65	20.0	20.0	19.6	2	03-90	.00	.0	0	NE	11	1.4	.86	1.2	1.42	1.7	7	2.3	8	7,861	59	0	2.6	12
Plains Petrol	13.2	13.2	12.8	17.1q	.38	20.8	20.8	57.0	31	06-06-90	.16	.5	6	7	18	38.9	.72	28.1	1.21	33.9	18	1.9	298	9,521	5,166	-2	1.0	12
Prairie Oil Roy	54.1	54.1	46.1	4.3q	.55	66.7	66.7	31.0	7	01-0-85	.00	.0	0	0	39	22.6	.20	4.5	1.64	7.4	0	.7	68	7,846	443	+20	0.0	12
Ranger Oil LTD	21.5	21.5	55.8	26.2q	.30	50.0	50.0	172.7	NC	6	03-90	.06	1.0	0	0	26	21.8	.21	4.6	1.83	8.4	0	3.8	518	84,636	4,468	0	34.5	12
Red Eagle Res	-121.7	2.9	0*	.01	50.0	50.0	-80.0	0	0	03-89	.00	.0	0	0	5	-11.1	NC	NC	2.21	.0	5	.7	16	19,659	15	0	0.0	09
Repsol SA	-1.3	-1.3	-1.2	493.8t	1.65	19.6	19.6	19.6	8	12-88	.84	3.3	0	NE	11	5.9	1.31	7.7	2.21	17.0	11	1.3	251	10,000	20,753	+0	2.6	12
Samson Energy	7.5	7.5	14.2	1.7q	.38	.0	.0	NE	-13	03-90	1.60	10.6	6	NE	18	10.6	.26	2.8	1.50	4.2	18	3.4	66	4,369	39	+0	0.0	12
Santa Fe Engy	4.8	4.8	3.2	-8.7q	-.22	-84.6	-84.6	NE	44	03-90	1.84	35.0	73	67	39	-6.7	.38	-2.4	1.96	-4.7	39	.5	198	37,242	13	0	0.1	12
Santa Fe Engy	NA	NA	NA	NA	.01	NA	NA	NA	NC	NC	06-25-90	.04	.2	31	2	NA	21.8	NC	NC	NC	NC	NA	NA	1,149	63,830	0	0	34.5	12
Sceptre Rscs	-.5	-.5	59.8	-19.3q	-.32	NC	NC	-100.0	-12	03-90	.00	.0	0	0	5	-11.3	.26	-2.9	4.28	-12.4	257	1.0	217	69,596	3,071	+865	30.2	12
Scurry Rainbow	46.8	46.8	24.0	18.6q	1.39	70.8	70.8	56.2	6	05-30-90	.50	2.3	41	33	60	27.8	.22	6.2	1.60	9.9	0	1.2	283	13,462	301	0	40.0	12
SolvEx Cp	.0	.0	.0	-.9t	-.06	NE	NE	NE	-84	03-90	.00	.0	0	0	7	-.0	.84	-64.3	NC	-64.3	7	6.0	28	14,777	199	0	0.0	06
SEstn Mich Gas	-4.7	-4.7	3.7	6.9q	.89	-14.6	-14.6	-11.9	7	07-30-90	.79	5.7b	73	67	150	3.1	.84	2.6	4.27	11.1	1.1	104	7,548	327	+0	0.0	12
Standard O&E	400.0	400.0	.0q	.14	20.0	20.0	7.7	-1	0	08-14-89	.16	2.8	31	2	.0	NC	NC	NC	.0	4	1.0	4	755	0	0	0.0	12
Sun Engy Prt	12.9	12.9	9.8	112.0q	.31	87.5	87.5	NE	-16	05-14-90	1.35	12.6	483	0	43	9.6	.31	3.0	1.63	4.9	60	1.0	4,072	378,755	282	0	0.0	12
Texas Am Engy □	-72.7	-75.0	-77.7	11.8q	1.39	-70.4	-70.4	117.2	58	09-28-85	.00	.0	0	0	60	NM	NC	NC	NC	58.1	60	11.1	10	7,501	584	0	0.0	12
Texas Meridian	28.0	28.0	62.5	-1.5q	-.13	NE	NE	NE	NC	03-90	.00	.0	0	0	3425	-11.5	NC	-3.3	.00	NM	5	1.0	5	15,321	132	0	8.2	12
Total Petro NA	24.6	24.6	22.3	34.1q	1.04	-100.0	-100.0	-69.0	1	05-21-90	.80	2.9	48	29	35	1.5	1.93	2.9	2.21	6.4	35	1.1	829	30,140	2,759	0	0.0	12
Valero Nat Gas	-1.4	-1.4	-9.6	12.9q	.70	12.5	12.5	-58.3	-20	05-04-90	2.50	17.5	373	67	356	1.0	1.00	1.2	6.42	7.7	356	1.0	258	18,087	1,223	0	0.2	12
Wainoco Oil	16.7	16.7	8.5	-5.9q	-.29	-100.0	-100.0	-100.0	-7	03-90	.00	.0	0	0	NE	-15.5	.23	-3.5	2.11	-7.4	87	2.2	178	19,826	9,748	0	7.2	12
Whiting Petro	162.5	162.5	100.0	1.6q	.19	250.0	250.0	137.5	20	03-90	.00	.0	0	0	0	26.7	.50	13.3	1.47	19.5	0	1.7	17	8,288	51	0	0.0	12
Wiser Oil	8.5	8.5	44.4	6.9q	.76	5.6	5.6	137.5	-8	4	03-90	.40	4.0	67	112	0	17.7	.37	6.5	1.15	7.5	0	3.5	164	9,033	4,086	-9	0.0	12

Oil Refining and Marketing

Ind. Group	-13.9	13.6	9.1	14,395.0	2.85	-14.0	-16.9	-28.5	3	---	2.17	4.4	1	23	29	3.6	1.08	3.9	2.87	11.2	57	1.0	243,642	4,927,195	G	+4277	1.8	--
Adams Res Energy	21.7	21.7	28.7	2.0q	.25	300.0	300.0	31.6	87	03-90	.60	1.4	0	23	157	2.1	5.19	10.9	7.98	87.0	157	1.1	12	7,567	561	0	1.8	12
Amerada Hess Cp	13.4	13.4	30.7	295.8q	3.66	-81.9	-81.9	7.3	-2	06-12-90	.60	1.4	-13	10	60	5.1	.84	4.3	2.70	11.6	0	1.3	3,572	80,944	16,649	-3	0.4	12
Am Entprs	.0	.0	.0	-.3t	-.08	NC	NC	NC	10	-50	07-99	.00	.8	0	0	0	-15.0	1.82	-27.3	1.88	-50.0	0	.2	0	3,178	0	0	0.0	07
An Oil & Gas	219.7	219.7	88.1	-14.2q	-1.56	NE	NE	-34.5	-16	03-90	.00	.0	0	0	70	-5.0	1.02	-5.1	3.12	-15.9	70	1.2	67	8,462	3,220	0	1.3	12
An Petrofina	24.7	24.7	16.9	96.6q	6.24	-3.4	-3.4	-34.5	NC	4	05-30-90	3.20	4.1	0	51	42	3.0	1.30	3.9	2.33	9.1	41	1.3	1,213	15,452	458	0	0.0	12
Amoco Cp •	-25.3	13.3	13.3	1610.0t	3.12	-13.9	-22.0	-22.0	-1	4	12-88	2.04	4.0	4	61	58	6.7	.79	5.3	2.23	11.8	41	1.1	26,152	511,528	23,788	+16	1.6	12

(continued)

Oil Refining and Marketing (Continued)

Company	Rev %Qtr	Rev %FY-Date	Rev %12Mo	Earn $Mil	EPS 12Mo	EPS Qtr	EPS%Qtr	EPS%FY-Date	EPS%12Mo	5YrGr	ParGr	Div Date	Div Amt	Div Yld	Div 5YrGr	Payout FY	Payout 5Yr	X-Dvd Date	Profit Mgn	Asset TO	Ret TotAssets	Leverage	Ret Equity	Debt/Eq	Current	MktVal $Mil	Shares Out	Banks-Funds	Insider NetTrad	Short Int	FY End
Ashland Oil	10.9	5.7	4.9	27.0q	.48	NE	-66.5	-72.3	-87.0	NC	-3	03-90	1.00	2.9	5	65	37	05-23-90	.3	2.00	.6	4.00	2.4	94	1.2	1,944	55,556	22,814	+14	2.0	09
Atlantic Rchfld	6.4	6.4	-8.1	1473.0q	8.60	-66.5	-66.5	-18.7	-18.7	NC	9	03-90	5.00	4.3	9	40	70	05-14-90	9.4	.70	6.6	3.41	22.5	81	1.6	19,292	164,187	87,407	-3	2.0	12
British Petro □	-65.9	3.8	3.7	2861.9t	6.47	-29.7	49.8	49.8	49.8	5.1	8	12-89	3.40	5.1	15	53	60	05-21-90	5.9	.28	5.5	2.95	16.2	53	1.0	29,399	442,093	25,210	0	0.8	12
Buckeye Prtnr	-1.0	-1.0	1.9	32.9q	2.72	-29.7	-5.9	-23.7	-5.9	NE	1	03-90	2.60	10.0	0	83	59	05-02-90	20.6	.28	5.7	2.14	12.2	102	2.0	311	12,000	2,252	0	0.0	12
Challenger Intl	2200.0	2200.0	.0	-.8q	-.18	NE	-21	NE	NE	NC	-21	01-90	.00	.0	0	0	NE	01-13-86	-40.0	.27	-10.8	1.90	-20.5	0	1.9	311	4,316	110	0	0.0	10
Charter Co	-21.6	-21.6	13.5	.1q	.01	-46.2	-46.2	-100.0	-100.0	NC	-4	03-90	.05	1.2	0	100	NE	12-05-89	.0	NC	.1	2.42	.1	16	3.2	200	47,042	27,478	0	0.1	12
Chevron Cp	21.9	21.9	19.1	411.0Q	1.15	46.2	46.2	-72.4	-72.4	9	-1	03-90	2.80	4.0	3	394	81	05-01-90	1.2	1.00	1.2	4.90	2.9	53	1.1	24,951	354,538	140,774	+3384	3.7	12
Coastal Corp	3.0	3.0	1.7	185.3q	1.86	7.5	7.5	-1.6	-1.6	8	8	03-90	.40	1.2	8	15	15	05-24-90	2.2	.95	2.1	2.03	10.3	181	1.1	3,411	101,448	64,591	+0	0.7	12
Crown Ctrl A	61.2	61.2	34.3	19.3q	2.11	-45.5	-45.5	-68.5	-68.5	NC	5	03-90	.00	.0	NA	59	17	05-01-90	1.2	2.58	3.1	2.03	6.3	14	1.3	324	9,833	816	0	0.2	12
Crown Ctrl B	NA	NA	NA	NA	NA	NA	NA	NA	NA	NA	NA	00-00	.00	.0	NA	NA	NA	05-01-90	NA	NA	NA	NA	NA	NA	NA	165	5,011	2,044	0	0.0	12
De Shamrock Inc ◇	25.3	25.3	19.2	49.5q	1.75	-80.4	-80.4	-79.3	-39.7	NC	13	03-90	.48	2.1	0	20	29	05-14-90	2.2	2.18	4.8	3.81	18.3	129	1.7	560	24,346	14,239	0	3.6	12
DWG Corp	5.6	5.3	6.8	-4.8n	-.26	2100.0	2100.0	-79.3	-100.0	NC	-14	01-90	.60	6.1	0	0	0	01-29-90	-.4	1.25	-4.1	8.20	-4.1	370	1.4	255	25,800	2,064	-5	2.5	04
Eastex Energy	.5	.5	52.7	-1.1q	-.23	-100.0	-100.0	-100.0	NE	NC	-8	03-90	.00	.0	0	0	0	00-00-00	-.8	3.00	-7.9	3.29	-7.9	17	1.0	7	4,955	192	-5	0.0	02
El Paso Refinery	NA	NA	.5	NA	NA	NE	NE	NE	NA	NA	-5	00-00	.00	.0	NA	NA	NA	00-00-00	NA	NC	NC	NC	NC	NA	NA	169	7,200	1,586	0	NA	12
Enron Corp	79.3	79.3	98.7	237.9q	4.22	11.2	11.2	86.7	66.7	NC	6	03-90	2.48	4.4	0	62	156	05-25-90	2.1	1.24	2.6	5.92	15.4	206	1.0	2,857	50,336	24,637	-20	10.5	12
Enron Oil&Gas	37.8	37.8	351.4	7.5q	.09	NE	NE	NC	NC	-5	-1	07-90	.15	.6	0	0	0	07-10-90	2.4	.05	1.3	2.60	1.3	62	1.4	1,803	75,900	8,707	+7	0.0	12
Exxon Cp	20.1	20.1	11.9	2985.0q	2.34	2.0	2.0	-39.7	-39.7	-5	-5	03-90	2.40	5.0	7	99	59	05-08-90	3.3	1.09	3.6	2.83	10.2	32	1.3	59,844	1,250,000	435,211	+15	4.5	12
Getty Petro ◇	-8.0	-8.0	10.7	15.5q	1.11	-66.6	-66.6	-48.8	-48.8	22	10	04-90	.28	1.6b	22	18	11	06-28-90	1.3	3.85	5.0	2.56	12.8	80	1.4	234	13,027	1,666	+5	1.4	01
High Plains	6.3	6.3	5.2	.2n	-.04	NE	NE	NE	NE	NC	0	03-90	.00	.0	0	0	0	00-00-00	1.0	.70	.7	.00	NS	-3743	1.3	4	2,134	21	0	0.0	06
Holly Cp	20.9	20.9	65.6	20.1n	2.44	-58.5	-58.5	-53.4	-43.0	NC	0	04-90	.40	1.4	6	257	257	06-18-90	4.6	2.76	12.7	.00	NM	7467	1.2	228	8,254	4,762	+0	6.8	07
Howell Corp □	49.0	49.0	31.7	4.5q	.92	-6.7	-6.7	NE	NE	10	10	03-90	.28	2.1	0	0	0	05-17-90	1.4	2.57	3.6	3.89	14.0	134	1.0	65	4,796	942	+3	0.0	12
Huntway Ptnrs	15.3	15.3	15.0	-5.8q	-.53	-100.0	-100.0	-100.0	-100.0	NC	-38	03-90	.54	5.7	0	NE	946	05-09-89	-6.3	.87	-8.7	3.38	-18.6	172	1.0	104	10,931	253	0	0.0	12
Interhome Energy	28.2	28.2	17.1	111.4q	2.81	45.2	45.2	35.7	35.7	NC	4	03-90	2.00	4.8	NA	79	85	05-10-90	13.8	.30	4.2	2.95	12.4	101	.6	1,664	13,617	824	0	0.0	12
Kaneb Pipe	NA	NA	NA	NA	NA	NE	NE	NA	NA	NC	NC	03-90	.00	.0	NA	NA	NA	05-01-90	NA	NA	NA	.00	NA	NA	1.0	231	13,810	184	0	NA	12
Lyondell Petroch	17.4	17.4	16.8	318.0q	3.98	-41.3	-41.3	-43.0	-43.0	NC	0	03-90	1.60	8.2	NA	26	10	05-14-90	5.7	4.40	25.1	.00	NM	7333	1.8	1,560	80,000	27,999	+1	2.9	12
Mobil Corp ◇	6.3	6.3	5.2	1780.0q	4.30	-9.6	-9.6	-11.9	-11.9	11	4	03-90	2.68	4.3	3	58	62	05-07-90	3.2	1.44	4.6	2.37	10.9	33	1.1	25,238	408,718	195,168	+7	3.2	12
Murphy Oil	18.9	18.9	14.8	53.1q	1.71	178.9	178.9	12.5	12.5	NC	3	03-90	1.00	2.5	0	73	23	05-10-90	3.4	.82	2.8	2.68	7.5	43	1.3	1,372	33,887	16,658	-12	2.7	12
N Cdn Oils	48.3	48.3	7.1	24.1f	.47	-16.1	-16.1	-16.1	-16.1	NC	2	12-89	.20	1.3	0	43	898	06-11-90	26.8	.41	2.8	1.50	4.2	24	2.6	553	35,371	3,092	-12	0.2	12
Pennzoil Co	12.9	12.9	-10.1	87.0q	1.93	-36.6	-36.6	-16.1	-16.1	NC	-4	03-90	3.00	4.0	6	124	828	05-24-90	4.1	.41	1.7	3.82	6.5	139	.4	2,763	36,411	20,400	0	0.4	12
Petro Heat Pwr	12.5	12.5	20.8	-3.1q	-.20	7.6	7.6	NE	NE	NC	0	04-90	1.70	14.2	6	NE	828	06-11-90	-.5	2.20	-1.1	.00	NS	-4364	1.1	189	15,760	303	0	4.4	12
Phillips Petrol	1.0	1.0	7.1	50.0q	.21	-88.5	-88.5	-92.9	-92.9	-13	-9	03-90	1.00	3.9	0	198	65	04-30-90	.4	1.00	.4	5.75	2.3	185	1.1	6,282	243,955	88,783	+219	1.7	12
Polar Molecular Cp	25.0	25.0	87.5	-8.9n	-.35	NE	NE	NE	NE	NC	NC	12-89	.00	.0	0	NA	NC	00-00-00	NM	NC	NC	NC	NC	0	2.0	12	17,915	346	0	0.0	NA
Pride Cos □	NA	NA	NA	13.7q	.21	800.0	800.0	13.0	13.0	NC	NC	00-00	.00	.0	-1	182	132	05-09-90	1.6	1.13	1.8	2.50	4.5	32	1.0	66	3,500	NA	0	+1	12
Quaker St Co	8.6	8.6	-3.8	58.0q	.54	-50.0	-50.0	-50.0	-50.0	NC	-4	03-90	.80	6.5	-2	196	103	05-04-90	.5	1.40	.7	2.57	1.8	42	1.0	332	27,125	9,496	+1	0.5	12
Sun Co □	18.1	18.1	16.8	13.7q	1.80	-50.0	-50.0	116.0	116.0	NA	-44	03-90	1.80	4.8	-2	196	103	05-04-90	.5	1.40	1.8	2.57	1.8	42	1.0	3,961	106,693	54,785	0	1.8	12
Tesoro Petrol	18.6	39.0	7.2	-15.6n	-2.10	NE	NE	NE	NE	-13	-13	03-90	.00	.0	0	0	0	08-05-86	-1.8	1.94	-12.6	3.60	-12.6	88	NA	130	14,061	3,701	+13	9.4	05
Tenaco ◇	-7.0	-7.0	-7.8	1286.0q	4.36	-80.5	-80.5	-57.5	-57.5	NC	4	03-90	3.00	5.3	12	111	430	05-04-90	4.1	1.22	14.0	2.80	14.0	51	1.2	14,930	263,670	162,296	+0	0.8	12
Tosco Corp ◇	73.7	73.7	42.3	41.6q	2.27	-16.1	-16.1	27.5	27.5	NC	26	03-90	.60	3.2	0	18	18	06-14-90	2.5	1.76	3.9	8.16	35.9	428	1.4	302	15,978	3,749	+1	9.3	12
Unocal Cp ◇	12.3	12.3	12.3	250.0q	1.07	-10.8	-10.8	-35.9	-35.9	NC	-20	03-90	.70	2.6	0	50	68	07-03-90	2.4	1.13	2.7	4.04	10.9	169	1.4	6,347	233,980	136,993	+0	1.5	12
Valero Energy □	29.3	29.3	31.4	39.8q	.92	-21.4	-21.4	37.3	37.3	NC	5	03-90	.28	1.8	0	15	NE	04-24-90	4.0	.98	3.9	2.00	7.8	43	2.0	566	35,910	16,366	+39	1.3	12

Source: Media General Financial Services, Richmond, VA.

Trends and Forecasts: Health and Medical Services (SIC 80)*

(in billions of dollars except as noted)

Item	1987[1]	1988[2]	1989[2]	1990[3]	Percent change		
					1987-88	1988-89	1989-90
TOTAL EXPENDITURES	496.5	544.2	599.2	661.3	9.6	10.1	10.4
Health services and supplies	475.0	519.8	571.7	632.3	9.4	10.0	10.6
Personal health care	436.5	478.9	529.8	589.3	9.7	10.6	11.2
Hospital care	194.3	211.0	230.1	252.0	8.6	9.1	9.5
Physicians' services	93.6	105.7	119.4	137.3	12.9	13.0	15.0
Dentists' services	28.4	30.8	33.7	36.8	8.5	9.4	9.2
Other professional services	20.8	23.6	26.6	30.0	13.5	12.7	12.8
Consumer nondurables[4]	38.6	41.9	45.8	49.6	8.5	9.3	8.3
Consumer durables	10.8	10.8	12.9	14.1	0.0	19.4	9.3
Nursing home care	39.7	43.9	48.8	54.8	10.6	11.2	12.3
Other health services	10.3	11.2	12.5	14.7	8.7	11.6	17.6
Program administration and net cost of insurance	24.0	25.0	25.0	25.0	4.2	0.0	0.0
Government public health activities	14.5	15.9	16.9	18.0	9.7	6.3	6.5
Research and construction of medical facilities	21.5	24.4	27.5	29.0	13.5	12.7	5.5
Research[5]	13.3	14.9	17.0	18.1	12.0	14.1	6.5
Construction	8.2	9.5	10.5	10.9	15.9	10.5	3.8

*Health Care Financing Administration (HCFA) expects to make major revisions in health accounts. Hence data may not match current HCFA statistics especially for physicians' services and program administration and net cost of insurance.

[1]Preliminary

[2]Estimated

[3]Forecast

[4]Includes only expenditures for prescription drugs, over-the-counter drugs, and medical sundries dispensed through retail channels. Spending for drugs dispensed in hospitals and by physicians is reported within those cost categories.

[5]Research now includes commercial research activities of drug companies.

NOTE: Totals may differ from sum of constituent figures because of rounding.

SOURCE: Bureau of Data Management and Strategy, Office of National Cost Estimates, Office of the Actuary, Health Care Financing Administration. Estimates and forecasts by U.S. Department of Commerce, International Trade Administration.

Source: U.S. Industrial Outlook 1990, U.S. Department of Commerce.

Trends and Forecasts: X-ray Apparatus and Tubes (SIC 3844)

(in millions of dollars except as noted)

Item	1987[1]	1988[2]	1989[3]	1990[4]	Percent Change		
					1987–88	1988–89	1989–90
Industry Data							
Value of shipments[5]	1,656	1,747	1,817	1,829	5.5	4.0	0.7
Value of shipments (1987$)	1,656	1,682	1,737	1,772	1.6	3.3	2.0
Total employment (000)	9.6	9.9	10.1	—	3.1	2.0	—
Production workers (000)	5.7	7.1	7.4	—	24.6	4.2	—
Average hourly earnings ($)	12.51	—	—	—	—	—	—
Product Data							
Value of shipments[6]	1,576	1,663	1,729	1,740	5.5	4.0	0.6
Value of shipments (1987$)	1,576	1,601	1,653	1,686	1.6	3.2	2.0
Trade Data							
Value of imports (ITA)[7]	763	860	795	866	12.7	-7.6	8.9
Value of exports (ITA)[8]	338	410	466	508	21.3	13.7	9.0

[1]Industry and product data are preliminary. Trade data are adjusted to conform to the 1987 SIC.

[2]Estimated, except for exports and imports.

[3]Estimated.

[4]Forecast.

[5]Value of all products and services sold by establishments in the x-ray apparatus and tubes industry.

[6]Value of products classified in the x-ray apparatus and tubes industry produced by all industries.

[7]Import data, c.i.f. valuation, are developed by the chapter author.

[8]Export data are developed by the chapter author.

SOURCE: U.S. Department of Commerce: Bureau of the Census; International Trade Administration (ITA). Estimates and forecasts by ITA.

Source: *U.S. Industrial Outlook 1990*, U.S. Department of Commerce.

Trends and Forecasts: Electromedical Equipment (SIC 3845)

(in millions of dollars except as noted)

Item	1987[1]	1988[2]	1989[3]	1990[4]	Percent Change		
					1987–88	1988–89	1989–90
Industry Data							
Value of shipments[5]	3,453	3,802	4,113	4,443	10.1	8.2	8.0
Value of shipments (1987$)	3,453	3,798	4,089	4,314	10.0	7.7	5.5
Total employment (000)	28.1	29.9	31.4	–	6.4	5.0	–
Production workers (000)	12.7	14.6	16.9	–	15.0	15.8	–
Average hourly earnings ($)	10.34	–	–	–	–	–	–
Product Data							
Value of shipments[6]	3,389	3,731	4,037	4,361	10.1	8.2	8.0
Value of shipments (1987$)	3,389	3,727	4,013	4,234	10.0	7.7	5.5
Trade Data							
Value of imports (ITA)[7]	676	878	837	921	24.0	-0.1	10.0
Value of exports (ITA)[8]	1,274	1,682	1,549	1,671	32.0	-7.9	8.0

[1] Industry and product data are preliminary. Trade data are adjusted to conform to the 1987 SIC.
[2] Estimated, except for exports and imports.
[3] Estimated.
[4] Forecast.
[5] Value of all products and services sold by establishments in the electromedical equipment industry.
[6] Value of products classified in the electromedical equipment industry produced by all industries.
[7] Import data are developed by the chapter author.
[8] Export data are developed by the chapter author.

SOURCE: U.S. Department of Commerce: Bureau of the Census; International Trade Administration (ITA). Estimates and forecasts by ITA.

Source: *U.S. Industrial Outlook 1990*, U.S. Department of Commerce.

Trends and Forecasts: Surgical Appliances and Supplies (SIC 3842)

(in millions of dollars except as noted)

Item	1987[1]	1988[2]	1989[3]	1990[4]	Percent Change		
					1987–88	1988–89	1989–90
Industry Data							
Value of shipments[5]	8,472	9,619	10,485	11,593	13.5	9.0	10.6
Value of shipments (1987$)	8,472	9,360	10,178	11,094	10.5	8.7	9.0
Total employment (000)	78.2	84.8	89.7	–	8.4	5.8	–
Production workers (000)	50.4	55.3	56.9	–	9.7	2.9	–
Average hourly earnings ($)	8.72	–	–	–	–	–	–
Product Data							
Value of shipments[6]	8,004	9,045	9,859	10,900	13.0	9.0	10.6
Value of shipments (1987$)	8,004	8,801	9,570	10,431	10.0	8.7	9.0
Trade Data							
Value of imports (ITA)[7]	338	373	400	420	16.3	1.8	5.0
Value of exports (ITA)[8]	521	668	306	1,042	28.2	35.6	15.0

[1]Industry and product data are preliminary. Trade data are adjusted to conform to the 1987 SIC.

[2]Estimated, except for exports and imports.

[3]Estimated.

[4]Forecast.

[5]Value of all products and services sold by establishments in the surgical appliances and supplies industry.

[6]Value of products classified in the surgical appliances and supplies industry produced by all industries.

[7]Import data are developed by the chapter author.

[8]Export data are developed by the chapter author.

SOURCE: U.S. Department of Commerce: Bureau of the Census; International Trade Administration (ITA). Estimates and forecasts by ITA.

Source: *U.S. Industrial Outlook 1990*, U.S. Department of Commerce.

Trends and Forecasts: Dental Equipment and Supplies (SIC 3843)

(in millions of dollars except as noted)

Item	1987[1]	1988[2]	1989[3]	1990[4]	Percent Change		
					1987–88	1988–89	1989–90
Industry Data							
Value of shipments[5]	1,384	1,460	1,549	1,662	5.5	6.1	7.3
Value of shipments (1987$)	1,384	1,426	1,543	1,637	3.0	8.2	6.1
Total employment (000)	14.1	14.4	15.1	-	2.1	4.9	-
Production workers (000)	8.5	8.9	9.0	-	4.7	1.1	-
Average hourly earnings ($)	9.50	-	-	-	-	-	-
Product Data							
Value of shipments[6]	1,199	1,267	1,343	1,440	5.7	6.0	7.2
Value of shipments (1987$)	1,199	1,239	1,339	1,419	3.3	8.1	6.0
Trade Data							
Value of imports (ITA)[7]	104	112	131	143	7.7	17.0	9.2
Value of exports (ITA)[8]	272	322	277	307	18.4	-14.0	10.8

[1]Industry and product data are preliminary. Trade data are adjusted to conform to the 1987 SIC.

[2]Estimated, except for exports and imports.

[3]Estimated.

[4]Forecast.

[5]Value of all products and services sold by establishments in the dental equipment and supplies industry.

[6]Value of products classified in the dental equipment and supplies industry produced by all industries.

[7]Import data, c.i.f. valuation, are developed by the chapter author.

[8]Export data are developed by the chapter author.

SOURCE: U.S. Department of Commerce: Bureau of the Census; International Trade Administration (ITA). Estimates and forecasts by ITA.

Source: *U.S. Industrial Outlook 1990*, U.S. Department of Commerce.

STOCKS by INDUSTRY

MEDIA GENERAL FINANCIAL SERVICES

Medical Instruments and Supplies

Company	Rev %Chg Last Qtr	Rev %Chg FY to Date	Rev %Chg Last 12 Mos	Rev Last 12 Mos $Mil	EPS Last 12 Mos $	EPS Last Qtr $	Earn %Chg Last Qtr	Earn %Chg FY to Date	Earn %Chg Last 12 Mos	Earn 5-Yr Growth	Earn Par Growth	Earn Date of Report	Div Amt $	Div Yield %	Div 5-Yr Growth	Payout Last FY %	Payout Last 5 Yrs %	Last X-Dvd Date	Profit Margin %	Asset Turnover	Return Total Assets %	Leverage Ratio	Return Equity %	Debt to Equity %	Current Ratio	Mkt Value $Mil	Shares Outstndng 000	Held by Banks/Funds 000	Insider Net Trading 000	Short Int Ratio Days	Fiscal Year Ends Mo
Ind. Group	17.2	10.3	17.1	1,538.5	.67	.57	-100.0	-100.0	-31.3	38	4	--	.42	1.7	1	32	32	--	4.4	1.02	4.5	2.20	9.9	46	2.0	52,443	2,060,488	732,300	-664	1.2	--
Abiomed Inc	71.4	51.7	33.3	-1.9h	-.36	-.17	NE	NE	NE	NE	-17	09-90	.00	.0	0	0	0	00-00-00	-47.5	.32	-15.2	1.11	-16.8	0	10.2	68	6,069	535	0	0.3	03
Acme United Cp	16.0	16.0	2.6	-1.1q	-.34	-.11	1200.8	1200.8	-100.0	NE	-7	03-90	.04	.8	0	31	0	06-09-90	-2.8	1.48	-4.9	1.50	-6.0	35	6.9	17	3,173	1,576	0	4.8	12
ADAC Laboratories	-17.1	-19.8	-2.1	11.5s	.26	-.06	-77.8	-72.2	-23.5	NE	38	08-90	.04	.9	0	0	0	08-12-90	12.9	1.47	19.0	1.71	32.5	1	2.2	61	44,109	18,496	-521	0.0	09
Advanced NMR Systems	.0	.0	.0	-.8h	-.98	-.21	NE	NE	NE	NC	-36	12-89	.00	.0	0	0	0	00-00-00	-40.0	.74	-29.6	1.28	-36.4	0	4.4	12	12,276	449	+9	0.0	12
Aequitron Med	18.2	13.1	13.0	1.0f	.10	.21	NE	NE	NC	NE	13	04-90	.00	.0	0	0	0	00-00-00	3.8	1.84	7.0	1.80	12.8	21	1.8	11	4,681	504	0	0.0	04
American Body Armor &	12.0	12.0	23.0	-.8q	-.30	-.11	NE	NE	NC	NC	-57	03-90	.00	.0	0	0	0	00-00-00	-8.0	1.73	-13.8	4.14	-57.1	29	1.0	7	2,337	24	0	0.0	12
An Electromedic	-20.0	-23.5	-50.0	-.6f	-.61	-.11	NE	NE	NE	NC	0	07-89	.00	.0	0	0	0	00-00-00	-60.0	.68	-37.5	.09	NM	50	1.1	0	3,000	0	0	0.0	07
Am Med Electro	37.5	37.5	11.1	.4q	.19	.10	9.1	.9	-38.3	NC	16	09-90	.00	.0	0	0	0	00-00-00	4.0	1.78	6.8	2.18	14.8	52	2.8	45	4,013	14	0	0.0	12
Amserv Inc	30.0	44.3	44.4	1.5h	.46	.46	73.7	28.7	27.8	NC	66	03-90	.10	.3	0	0	0	12-23-88	11.5	2.83	32.6	1.92	62.5	21	2.9	16	3,114	44	+0	0.0	06
Ballard Med Prods	48.0	47.3	47.0	5.0s	.92	.92	50.0	50.0	50.8	NC	38	03-90	.00	.0	0	0	0	02-09-90	20.0	1.57	31.4	1.17	36.8	0	6.5	145	5,036	751	+0	0.0	09
Bard C R	-1.0	-1.0	.1	53.3q	.97	.88	-55.3	-55.3	-32.6	16	9	09-90	.46	2.6	27	31	22	04-24-90	6.9	1.38	9.5	1.68	16.0	21	2.5	825	54,517	31,818	+5	2.2	12
Bausch&Lomb	13.9	13.9	20.9	117.6q	3.88	.97	15.6	15.6	15.5	18	11	09-90	1.32	1.9	8	30	31	05-25-90	9.3	.88	8.2	2.01	16.5	31	1.8	2,090	30,125	22,093	0	3.5	12
Baxter Intl	7.3	7.3	7.5	-38.0q	-.48	.07	-100.0	-100.0	-100.0	NC	-3	09-90	.64	2.7	11	37	40	06-07-90	-.6	.80	-.4	2.75	-1.1	61	1.8	5,988	249,482	142,252	-43	7.1	12
Beckman Instrmts	-6.8	-6.8	-1.4	39.2q	1.37	.88	-26.3	-26.3	-9.9	19	12	09-90	.28	1.6	19	19	7	05-21-90	5.1	1.27	6.5	2.25	14.6	28	1.8	499	28,507	12,293	0	0.7	12
Becton, Dick	12.5	9.3	6.0	169.5s	4.34	1.08	3.6	3.3	2.1	20	12	09-90	1.08	1.5	12	23	23	06-04-90	9.0	.88	7.5	2.11	15.8	48	1.5	2,688	38,330	25,332	-5	0.6	09
Bio Medicus	52.8	67.4	66.1	4.3f	.56	.56	-3.4	-3.4	-3.4	NC	24	09-90	.00	.0	0	0	0	00-00-00	13.9	1.54	21.4	1.14	24.4	0	8.2	198	7,788	2,530	0	0.0	03
Biomagnetic Tech	NA	NA	NA	NM	NA	NA	NA	NA	NA	NA	NC	06-90	.00	.0	NA	NA	NA	00-00-00	NA	1.36	NA	NC	NA	NA	NA	34	5,532	743	0	NA	NA
Biomet Inc	20.3	19.5	19.1	29.9f	1.08	.34	34.8	38.5	38.5	48	31	05-90	.00	.0	0	0	0	05-09-89	18.5	1.36	25.1	1.22	30.6	0	4.5	811	27,737	13,881	0	0.0	05
Bioplasty Inc	66.7	60.6	75.0	-.2n	.07	.07	50.0	16.7	25.0	NC	13	04-90	.00	.0	0	0	0	09-14-88	2.9	2.55	7.4	1.80	13.3	20	2.6	11	2,764	0	0	0.0	07
Birtcher Cp	226.3	125.5	86.7	-.2n	-.14	-.14	-100.0	-100.0	-100.0	NC	-12	03-90	.00	.0	0	0	0	00-00-00	-1.5	1.87	-2.8	4.21	-11.8	6	4.9	11	2,073	31	0	0.0	08
Cabot Medical	18.2	19.0	15.0	1.5s	.23	.23	20.0	20.0	35.3	NC	16	04-90	.00	.0	0	0	0	00-00-00	6.5	1.75	11.4	1.46	16.3	9	3.4	69	6,886	69	0	0.0	06
Circadian	-15.6	-5.6	-5.5	-5.0n	-1.09	-1.09	NE	NE	NE	NC	-57	09-90	.00	.0	0	0	0	00-00-00	-29.4	1.38	-38.1	1.45	-56.8	0	2.2	5	4,590	835	0	0.0	10
Clin-Therm	-69.2	-61.9	-50.0	-3.2f	-.18	-.18	NE	NE	NE	NC	0	06-89	.00	.0	0	0	0	00-00-00	NM	NC	NC	NC	NM	47	1.2	4	16,864	19	0	0.0	06
Coherent Inc	-9.0	-7.1	11.9	5.9s	.69	.63	-96.2	-70.5	293.8	NC	6	06-90	.00	.0	0	0	0	10-01-84	3.0	1.20	3.6	1.72	6.2	7	2.3	105	9,301	4,429	0	0.0	09
Collagen Cp	23.9	32.7	33.3	3.8n	.43	.43	14.3	40.9	59.3	NC	10	03-90	.00	.0	0	0	0	07-26-86	7.3	.79	5.8	1.74	10.1	42	3.3	180	8,121	2,207	+1	0.0	06

Company																													
Concept Inc	24.0	21.0	17.0	5.2a	.54	7.7	13.0	3.8	42	14	02.90	.00	.0	0	0	02-21-89	9.5	1.11	10.5	1.29	13.5	12	6.5	217	9,608	2,803	+5	0.0	08
Conmed Cp	105.1	105.1	60.0	.1q	.03	150.0	150.0	-88.0	NC	-1	03-90	.00	.0	0	0	00-00-00	.4	1.25	.5	2.00	1.0	51	2.6	23	2,911	145	0	0.0	12
Cooper Cos	-9.0	-18.5	-85.3	-2.7s	-.31	NE	NE	NE	NC	-3	04-90	10	.0	0	2.6	12-28-88	-5.6	.16	-.9	3.00	-2.7	101	4.3	91	23,551	6,803	0	101.6	10
Cordis Cp	19.6	13.5	11.5	5.2n	.38	50.0	NE	NE	NC	10	03-90	.00	.0	0	0	00-00-00	3.4	1.18	4.0	2.50	10.0	71	1.9	256	13,493	9,217	0	0.0	08
Criticare Systs	31.6	24.5	6.6	-.4n	-.05	50.0	-33.3	-100.0	NC	-3	03-90	.00	.0	0	0	00-00-00	-2.5	1.08	-3.2	1.19	-3.2	71	6.1	23	5,827	357	0	0.0	06
Customedix Cp	13.7	4.8	8.1	1.3n	.04	NE	33.3	33.3	NC	12	03-90	.00	.0	0	0	00-00-00	2.5	1.64	4.1	3.02	12.4	134	2.5	10	32,691	1,075	0	0.0	06
Dahlberg	8.4	8.4	6.3	2.8q	.95	122.2	122.2	179.4	NC	16	03-90	.00	.0	0	0	00-00-00	4.2	2.17	9.1	1.79	16.3	15	2.3	42	2,728	562	-6	0.0	12
Datascope Cp	3.9	2.7	.8	10.3n	1.98	43.9	-6.5	-15.0	37	13	03-90	.00	.0	0	0	09-23-86	9.0	1.10	9.9	1.26	12.5	101	4.5	116	5,168	2,674	0	0.2	06
Delmed Inc	.0	.0	14.2	-4.6q	-.11	NC	NC	NE	NC	13	03-90	.00	.0	0	0	00-00-00	-19.2	.92	NC	2.54	44.7	99	2.2	11	45,620	2,237	0	0.0	12
Dento Med	.0	.0	.0	-1.3r	-.09	NE	NE	NE	NC	-18	12-88	.00	.0	0	0	00-00-00	NC	NC	NC	NC	-17.8	0	.0	13	14,929	243	0	0.0	12
Diasonic	23.5	23.5	-22.7	-20.4q	-.28	25.0	25.0	-100.0	NC	-18	03-90	.00	.0	0	0	00-00-00	-9.7	.79	-7.7	2.29	-17.6	23	1.7	271	72,330	27,376	0	0.4	12
Durr Fillauer	16.8	16.8	20.4	15.3q	1.52	-2.8	-2.8	49.0	14	11	05-21-90	.00	15	.0	0	00-00-00	2.1	3.48	7.3	1.88	13.7	37	2.1	244	10,002	5,599	+29	0.0	12
Dynatech Cp	18.8	8.5	8.2	14.7t	1.43	1333.3	-6.5	-6.5	4	10	03-02-84	.00	.0	0	0	00-00-00	3.4	1.65	5.6	1.77	9.9	31	3.1	165	10,302	4,094	0	0.0	03
Electro Catheter	5.3	.0	.0	-.3s	-.08	-50.0	NE	NE	NC	-9	02-90	.00	.0	0	0	00-00-00	-3.8	1.53	-5.8	1.62	-9.4	31	3.6	4	3,787	161	0	0.0	08
Elscint Ltd	.3	.3	-5033.3	6.0q	.13	NE	NE	NE	NC	0	12-89	.00	.0	0	0	00-00-00	4.1	.93	3.8	.00	NS	340	1.0	181	60,383	237	0	0.0	06
EMPI Inc	24.1	24.1	18.1	.6q	.51	120.0	120.0	244.4	NC	16	03-90	.00	.0	0	0	00-00-00	4.6	1.63	7.5	2.11	15.8	55	3.3	11	1,884	49	0	0.0	12
Everest&Jen A	NA	NA	NA	NA	NA	NA	NA	NA	NA	NC	00-00-00	.00	NA	NA	NA	05-52-89	NA	NC	NC	NC	NA	NA	NA	23	5,755	1,126	0	NA	NA
Everest&Jen B	-1.5	-3.8	-3.6	-42.1t	-5.16	-100.0	NA	NA	37	0	05-22-89	.00	0	NE	NE	05-22-89	-22.9	1.23	-28.2	1.88	NM	110	1.3	36	8,162	130	0	0.0	09
Fiberchem	.0	.0	.0	-1.4f	-.33	-100.0	-100.0	NC	NC	-78	12-89	.00	.0	0	0	00-00-00	-3.8	NC	-8.2	1.22	-77.8	78	15.0	9	4,710	12	0	0.0	03
Gamma Biologicals	4.5	22	-5.2	-2.2n	-.48	NC	NC	NC	NC	-18	12-20-85	.00	.0	0	NE	12-20-85	4.1	.82	-10.0	1.77	-17.7	34	2.7	14	4,551	417	+9	0.3	03
Gelman Sci	3.3	4.2	4.2	1.1n	.45	-82.1	-72.9	-40.0	NC	5	04-90	.00	.0	0	0	00-00-00	1.5	1.13	1.7	3.06	5.2	122	2.3	21	2,474	613	+2	0.0	07
Gendex	71.7	58.1	52.6	2.4f	.61	31.3	37.3	37.3	NC	23	03-90	.00	.0	0	0	00-00-00	8.3	2.10	17.4	1.32	22.9	0	4.4	36	2,949	233	+3	0.0	03
Gish Biomedical	25.6	20.2	21.4	1.2n	.68	83.3	42.9	38.8	NC	19	09-42-88	.00	.0	0	0	00-00-00	7.1	2.04	14.5	1.28	18.5	3	5.2	29	1,726	235	+5	0.0	06
Hana Biologics	-28.6	281.0	200.0	5.3n	.57	NE	NE	NE	NC	36	03-90	.00	.0	0	0	00-00-00	29.4	.97	28.6	1.22	34.9	7	5.5	13	6,682	724	0	0.3	06
Hlth-Chem	-4.7	-4.7	7.6	-2.1q	-.21	NE	-100.0	-100.0	NC	-22	12-89	.55	.0	0	NE	12-20-85	-5.0	.70	-3.5	6.37	-22.3	233	1.6	11	7,098	984	0	0.3	12
Hittdyne	5.3	5.3	-3.6	6.3q	.38	NC	NC	NE	NC	8	03-90	.00	.0	0	0	00-00-00	6.0	.90	5.4	1.50	8.1	5	5.5	189	15,410	6,877	+38	0.0	12
Hemacare Cp	30.8	30.8	.0	.2q	.04	-66.7	NA	-66.7	NC	5	03-90	.00	.0	0	0	00-00-00	3.3	1.30	4.3	1.23	5.3	3	4.3	11	3,220	74	-10	0.0	12
Hemodynamics	-50.0	-50.0	9725.0	26.0q	-.87	NE	-100.0	NC	NC	0	09-42-88	.00	.0	0	0	00-00-00	3.3	1.00	3.3	.00	NM	137	2.8	1	3,542	99	0	0.0	12
HnhyGp	.0	.0	.0	-187.0f	-9.44	NC	NC	NC	NC	-16	12-89	.55	.0	0	0	00-00-00	-11.9	.46	-5.5	2.93	-16.1	183	2.0	623	20,938	11,046	-44	0.0	12
Hillenbrand Ind	19.5	19.5	30.3	78.1q	2.10	17.8	17.8	16.0	19	14	04-16-90	.55	25	0	27	00-00-00	6.6	1.17	7.7	2.51	19.3	28	2.3	1,656	37,113	12,477	0	0.3	11
Imatron	-4.5	19.1	16.6	-4.2f	-.14	NE	NE	NE	NC	-53	12-89	.00	.0	0	NE	00-00-00	-30.0	.75	-22.6	2.32	-52.5	26	2.3	21	31,859	1,239	0	0.0	12
Immunomedics Inc	-83.3	-83.3	-33.3	-1.9q	-.09	NE	-66.7	NE	NC	-21	03-90	.00	.0	0	38	00-00-00	-95.0	.19	-17.9	1.16	-20.7	8	12.7	72	23,074	1,863	0	0.0	06
Intersec Inc	-2.7	-2.7	-9.6	-7.1q	-1.17	NE	NE	NE	NC	-59	03-90	.00	.0	0	0	00-00-00	-12.7	1.08	-13.7	4.28	-58.7	140	1.5	22	6,073	1,258	0	0.0	12
Imacare Corp	20.5	20.5	16.7	2.5q	.44	-14.3	-14.3	-52.7	NC	8	03-90	.00	.0	0	0	00-00-00	1.3	1.54	7.8	3.90	7.8	183	3.1	80	5,638	1,040	0	1.5	06
IPCO Corp	-68.9	-26.1	-32.4	-6.2q	-1.23	NE	17.8	16.0	19	-16	10-03-88	.55	.0	0	241	00-00-00	-6.2	.92	-5.7	2.77	-15.8	106	1.9	51	5,061	1,612	0	0.0	12
Johson & John	16.1	16.1	11.1	1009.0q	3.03	-23.2	-23.2	1.0	21	13	05-16-90	1.36	15	-6	39	00-00-00	9.9	1.28	12.7	1.91	24.3	28	2.0	22,564	333,054	161,635	+27	3.8	12
Kirschner Medical	-1.3	-1.3	-1.7	-15.2q	-5.34	-44.4	-44.4	-100.0	NC	13	03-90	.00	.0	0	0	00-00-00	-27.6	.71	-19.5	.00	NM	40	.9	27	2,358	237	0	0.0	12
Laser Indus	1.4	1.4	16.0	-16.7q	-3.58	NE	NE	NE	NC	0	03-90	.00	.0	0	0	00-00-00	-57.6	.64	-36.6	.00	NM	688	1.3	26	4,703	172	0	2.7	12
Lectec Cp	556.3	314.6	266.6	.1n	.05	-100.0	-88.2	-81.5	NC	0	03-90	.00	.0	0	0	00-00-00	.5	2.40	.12	1.25	1.5	18	5.8	14	3,235	49	0	0.0	06
Leeco Diagnostics	17.5	17.5	88.8	-.8q	-.13	NE	-100.0	NE	NC	2	03-90	.00	.0	0	0	00-00-00	-4.7	.70	-3.3	1.45	-4.8	106	3.0	12	5,798	43	0	1.5	06
Life Tech	10.0	10.0	4.5	13.4q	.99	8.3	8.3	15.1	17	13	03-90	.00	.0	0	0	00-00-00	9.7	1.06	10.3	1.28	13.2	5	5.0	239	13,296	2,138	0	0.0	12

(continued)

Medical Instruments and Supplies (Continued)

Company	Rev %Chg Last Qtr	Rev %Chg FY to Date	Rev %Chg Last 12 Mos	Rev Last 12 Mos $Mil	Ern Per Share Last 12 Mos $	Ern Last 12 Mos $Mil	Ern %Chg Last Qtr	Ern %Chg FY to Date	Ern %Chg Last 12 Mos	Ern 5-Yr Growth Rate	Par Growth Rate	Date of Report	Div Current Amt $	Div Yield %	Div 5-Yr Growth Rate	Payout Last FY	Payout Last 5 Yrs	Last X-Divd Date	Profit Margin %	Asset Turn-over	Return on Total Assets %	Leverage Ratio	Return on Equity %	Debt to Equity %	Current Ratio	Market Value $Mil	Latest Shares Outstanding 000	Held by Banks-Funds 000	Insider Net Trading 000	Short Interest Ratio Days	Fiscal Year Ends Mo
Lumex	2.9	2.9	7.3		.52	2.2a	-100.0	-100.0	52.9	-14	5	03-90	.08	1.0	0	12	13	07-16-90	2.5	1.36	3.4	1.65	5.6	19	2.6	33	4,211	930	0	0.0	12
Luther Med Prods	.0	.0	100.0		-.03	-.38	NA	NA	NC	NC	-38	12-89	.00	–	0	0	0	00-00-00	-15.0	1.17	-17.6	2.13	-37.5	NA	1.8	6	13,725	90	-100	0.0	06
Luxtr'ca Group	NA	NA	NA		NA	NA	NA	NA	NA	NA	NC	00-00	.68	2.6	NA	0	0	05-14-90	NA	NC	NA	NC	NA	NA	NA	727	27,550	0	0	NA	NA
Marquest Med	16.5	16.7	15.8		.66	2.8	83.3	83.3	83.3	NC	13	03-90	.00	–	0	0	0	06-30-87	NA	1.42	5.4	2.41	13.0	83	1.8	42	4,167	1,038	0	0.0	03
MDT Cp	-4.7	.6	.9		.04	.2	-100.0	-95.3	-95.3	13	1	03-90	.00	–	NA	NA	58	00-00-00	3.8	1.50	.3	1.67	.5	27	2.3	42	6,167	3,206	0	0.0	03
Medex Inc	22.6	17.2	17.1		.68	2.9n	37.5	5.8	-4.2	14	12	03-90	.09	.60	16	14	12	09-11-89	7.1	1.42	10.1	1.33	13.4	8	3.4	64	4,458	660	0	0.0	06
Medical Action	-7.4	-.5	8.0		.04	.3n	100.0	-71.4	-63.6	NC	6	12-89	.00	–	0	0	0	00-00-00	1.1	2.45	2.7	2.19	5.9	8	1.5	8	5,113	115	0	0.0	03
Medical Dynamics ... ◆	-20.0	-5.9	.0		.09	.1n	NE	NE	NE	NE	3	03-90	.00	–	0	0	0	00-00-00	3.3	.76	2.5	1.20	3.0	0	5.0	4	2,375	26	0	0.0	03
Medical Graphics	.0	.0	.0		-.31	-.5n	-100.0	-100.0	-100.0	NC	-12	03-90	.00	–	0	0	0	00-00-00	-4.5	1.56	-7.0	1.74	-12.2	0	2.1	7	1,986	211	0	0.0	12
Medical Tech Syst	83.3	61.9	50.0		.08	.6f	100.0	100.0	100.0	NC	30	03-90	.00	–	0	0	0	00-00-00	20.0	.73	14.6	2.05	30.0	40	1.3	11	7,642	0	0	0.0	03
Mediq Inc	9.6	9.5	3.4		.36	8.6n	-33.3	-36.4	NE	NE	9	03-90	.12	3.8	27	27	46	06-07-90	2.4	.46	1.1	12.73	14.0	393	NA	52	16,587	1,057	0	8.5	09
Medphone Cp	.0	.0	.0		-.25	-1.5q	NE	NE	NE	NE	0	09-89	.00	–	0	0	0	00-00-00	NC	NC	NC	1.36	NM	0	4.3	8	6,876	108	0	0.0	06
Medstone Internat'l	2.4	2.4	-44.0		-.65	-3.1q	-100.0	-100.0	-100.0	NE	-18	03-90	.00	–	0	0	0	00-00-00	-22.1	.61	-13.5	1.36	-18.3	0	3.4	21	4,655	1,165	+1	0.0	12
Medtronic Inc	19.6	12.8	12.8		4.03	108.7	21.1	10.4	10.4	26	18	04-90	.82	1.0	14	17	17	07-03-90	13.0	1.10	14.3	1.61	23.0	2	1.8	2,248	27,007	18,811	-16	0.7	04
Mentor Cp Minn	19.0	16.9	16.2		.78	8.4f	100.0	47.2	47.2	22	22	03-90	.16	.8	8	5	14	06-29-90	16.8	.73	12.3	2.01	24.7	76	6.2	215	10,633	4,929	+1	0.0	03
Meridian Diag	33.3	23.3	-13.3		.10	.4f	200.0	100.0	233.3	NC	5	03-90	.00	–	0	0	0	00-00-00	5.7	.75	4.3	1.12	4.8	1	8.7	9	4,800	170	0	0.0	09
Mesa Medical	200.0	154.5	200.0		.10	.4f	400.0	150.0	150.0	24	24	10-89	.00	–	0	0	0	00-00-00	13.3	1.20	16.0	1.47	23.5	12	3.0	5	3,928	0	0	0.0	09
Mintech Cp	12.9	29.9	26.3		.71	1.9f	4.2	136.7	136.7	22	22	03-90	.00	–	0	0	0	11-24-89	7.9	1.92	15.2	1.42	21.6	18	3.2	37	2,349	148	-49	0.0	03
Moleculon Inc	433.3	113.0	150.0		-.34	-1.6f	NE	NE	NE	NE	0	11-89	.00	–	0	0	0	00-00-00	-32.0	.16	-5.0	1.50	-7.5	13	2.3	24	10,782	103	0	0.0	11
Monoclonal Antibod ◆	25.0	3.4	.0		-.36	-1.2f	NE	NE	NE	NE	-8	00-00	.00	–	0	0	0	00-00-00	-13.3	1.56	-20.7	.00	NS	NS	4.6	23	3,756	358	+0	0.0	03
Mtn Med Equip ◆	-18.2	-2.5	-2.7		-.28	-.9f	-100.0	NE	-100.0	NE	-7	03-90	.00	–	0	0	0	00-00-00	-2.6	.96	-2.5	2.96	-7.4	61	1.6	21	3,294	725	+12	5.0	03
Nat'l Hlth Enhncmnt	16.7	47.1	50.0		-.20	-.4n	NE	NE	NE	-57	-57	10-89	.00	–	0	0	0	00-00-00	-13.3	2.32	-30.8	1.85	-57.1	14	1.8	1	1,635	0	+9	0.0	01
Nat'l Patent	-2.0	-2.0	5.1		-1.64	-21.8q	-100.0	-100.0	NE	-26	-26	04-90	.00	–	0	NE	10	12-27-88	-8.2	.88	-7.2	3.58	-25.8	143	1.7	76	12,621	2,007	0	2.2	07
Newport Cp	-.7	.0	-1.7		.64	5.2n	-31.8	-32.8	-28.9	NC	-66	04-90	.16	1.8	13	14	10	06-04-90	9.1	.70	6.4	1.16	7.4	0	6.3	72	7,978	4,513	0	0.0	07
N Am Biologicals	30.9	30.9	28.5		.09	1.3q	NC	NC	800.0	14	14	03-90	.00	–	0	0	0	00-00-00	2.1	2.52	5.3	2.55	13.5	44	1.7	21	15,497	374	0	0.0	12
Nova Pharm	41.2	41.2	-13.3		-.51	-13.6q	NE	NE	NE	-33	-33	03-90	.00	–	0	0	0	00-00-00	NM	NC	NC	1.12	-32.6	0	3.4	113	26,690	3,156	0	0.0	12
Novametrix Med	-36.8	-40.3	-31.0		-2.89	-11.0n	-100.0	-100.0	-100.0	-62	-62	01-90	.00	–	0	0	0	00-00-00	-55.0	.52	-28.5	2.17	-61.8	76	2.9	9	3,782	414	0	0.0	12
Noven Pharm	.0	.0	.0		.00	.0n	NE	NE	NE	NC	NC	03-90	.00	–	0	0	0	00-00-00	.0	NC	NC	NC	.0	0	2.2	33	11,382	4	0	0.0	12
OCG Technology	.0	-66.7	.0		-.12	-1.1f	NE	-100.0	NE	NC	NC	06-89	.00	–	0	0	0	00-00-00	NC	NC	NC	1.03	NM	0	1.1	2	9,131	174	0	0.0	06
Oncongene Science	-9.1	8.7	.0		-.26	-2.4s	NE	NE	NE	-12	-12	03-90	.00	–	0	0	0	00-00-00	-48.0	.23	-11.2	1.03	-11.5	0	27.0	18	9,171	365	0	0.0	09
Oncor Inc	.0	.0	.0		-.32	-1.8f	NC	NE	NC	NC	NC	12-89	.00	–	0	0	0	00-00-00	-90.0	.74	-66.7	1.35	-90.0	189	3.3	43	7,020	3	-5	0.0	12
Optek Tech	-11.8	-13.4	5.8		-.38	-1.4s	-100.0	-100.0	-100.0	NC	-10	04-90	.00	–	0	0	0	00-00-00	-2.6	1.15	-3.0	3.37	-10.1	6	4.5	9	3,224	221	0	0.0	10
Orthomet Inc	33.3	47.9	55.5		-.03	-.1n	-37.5	-6.3	25.9	NC	20	03-90	.00	–	0	0	0	00-00-00	-.7	1.00	-.7	1.57	-1.1	2	2.5	29	2,928	175	0	0.0	06
Personal Diag	3.4	-1.8	10.0		.34	1.2a	-100.0	-100.0	-100.0	NC	20	03-90	.00	–	0	0	0	00-00-00	10.9	1.47	16.0	1.27	20.3	2	2.4	21	3,502	59	0	0.0	06
Phametrics Inc	50.0	37.9	33.3		-.10	-.3f	-100.0	-100.0	-100.0	NC	-25	12-89	.00	–	0	0	0	00-00-00	-7.5	1.60	-12.0	2.08	-25.0	8	1.9	3	2,950	0	0	0.0	12

Phoenix Med	2.6	2.6	-21.0	-3.1q	-1.64	-100.0	-100.0	-100.0	NC	-39	03-90	.00	.0	0	0	0	00-00-00	-20.7	85	96	1.9	4	1,966	233	-2	0.0	12
Princeton Diag	11.8	11.8		-.04	-.03	100.0	100.0	100.0	0	0	03-90	.00	.0	0	0	0	00-00-00	.0	NC	4	4.6	7	2,868	5	0	0.0	12
Puritan Bennett	14.8	14.8	11.9	16.1q	1.42	0	0	6.0	NC	15	03-90	.11	.5	2	8	10	04-09-90	6.9	1.42	21	3.0	240	11,304	18,538	+2	0.0	12
Q Med	-17.4	-17.4	-12.5	-1.4q	-.24	NE	NE	NE	NC	0	02-90	.00	.0	0	0	0	05-12-87	-20.0	1.35	0	1.1	10	6,640	603	+74	0.0	11
Quest Med	-25.0	-25.0	-25.0	-.4q	-.08	-100.0	-100.0	-100.0	NC	-2	03-90	.00	.0	0	0	0	00-00-00	-6.7	.34	0	47.0	13	6,201	848		0.0	06
Respironics Inc	53.8	27.5	25.0	1.8n	.54	142.9	62.5	45.9	NC	22	03-90	.00	.0	0	0	0	05-01-90	9.0	2.02	0	4.6	72	3,346	70	-1	0.0	12
St Jude Med	17.5	17.5	23.0	54.7q	.98	-33.3	-33.3	21.0	NC	29	03-90	.00	.0	0	0	0	05-01-90	33.3	.77	6	11.9	1,610	46,678	23,962	0	0.0	12
Sci-Med Life	105.0	105.0	128.5	20.7q	1.53	114.3	114.3	168.4	NC	41	05-90	.00	.0	0	0	0	12-21-89	25.9	1.27	6	6.5	475	13,071	5,347	0	0.0	12
Span Amer Med	22.6	22.6	26.3	1.4q	.40	31.3	31.3	33.3	NC	15	03-90	.04	.8	0	0	0	05-09-90	5.8	1.66	29	2.3	17	3,277	334	0	0.0	09
Spectran Cp	31.3	31.3	50.0	-.2q	-.04	NE	NE	NE	NC	-3	03-90	.00	.0	0	0	0	00-00-00	-2.2	.91	19	3.6	8	4,592	263	0	0.0	12
Staodynam Inc	-4.5	-4.5	11.1	-.3q	.10	-100.0	-100.0	11.1	NC	8	05-90	.00	.0	0	0	0	06-20-89	3.0	1.70	22	2.7	7	2,316	41	0	0.0	02
Stryker Cp	25.4	25.4	26.3	20.4q	.88	28.6	28.6	23.9	NC	18	03-90	.00	.0	0	0	0	06-20-89	8.5	1.58	2	3.5	682	23,652	15,532	0	0.0	12
Summit Tech	37.5	37.5	200.0	-2.3q	-.22	NE	NE	NE	NC	-23	03-90	.00	.0	0	0	0	00-00-00	-38.3	.52	0	7.5	168	9,884	314	0	0.0	12
Sunrise Medical	12.5	11.3	27.9	4.7n	1.05	63.2	53.3	64.1	NC	17	03-90	.08	.0	0	0	0	03-26-90	2.8	1.46	209	1.9	70	4,461	2,011	+2	0.0	06
Sunrise Tech	140.0	140.0	200.0	-.2q	.03	NC	NC	NC	NC	11	03-90	.00	.0	0	0	0	00-00-00	6.7	1.36	11	5.3	29	5,834	5	0	0.0	12
Surgical Laser	26.5	26.5	71.4	1.6q	.34	250.0	250.0	NC	NC	9	03-90	.00	.0	0	0	0	00-00-00	6.7	.91	17	4.7	92	5,331	840	0	0.0	12
Survival Tech	16.7	2.4	-15.0	-.9n	-.33	200.0	200.0	NE	NC	-18	04-90	.00	.0	0	0	0	00-00-00	-5.3	1.34	0	1.1	26	2,857	108	0	8.9	07
Symbion Inc	-33.3	-46.6	-50.0	4.4f	.57	NE	NE	NE	NC	5	12-89	.00	.0	0	0	0	00-00-00	NM	.32	0	1.4	0	7,461	202	0	0.0	12
Tambrands Inc	22.6	22.6	9.4	5.8q	.29	25.9	25.9	-92.2	NC	-13	03-90	2.16	2.6	6	2588	69	06-01-90	.9	1.43	0	2.2	1,871	22,138	18,957	+2	2.8	12
Taunton Tech	100.0	100.0		-4.6f	-1.03	NE	NE	NE	NC	11	12-89	.00	.0	0	0	0	00-00-00	NM	1.56	0	1.3	47	4,500	481	0	0.0	12
Tenco Natl	5.2	5.2	41.1	-.9q	-.17	NE	NE	-100.0	NC	-11	03-90	.00	.0	0	0	0	12-10-85	-3.8	1.03	106	2.9	6	5,192	0	+2	0.3	12
Tenet Info	33.3	33.3		-.1q	-.05	NE	NE	-100.0	NC	-3	03-90	.00	.0	0	0	0	00-00-00	-5.0	.46	17	2.6	19	1,788	0	-9	0.0	06
Themedics	10.0	10.0	-4.0	2.5q	.14	100.0	100.0	55.6	NC	5	11-03-86	.00	.0	0	0	0	11-03-86	10.4	.32	6	11.2	290	17,697	1,511	0	8.9	NA
Thermo Cardiosys	NA	NA	NA	NA	NA	NA	NA	NA	NA	NC	03-90	.00	.0	NA	NA	NA	00-00-00	NA	.90	NA	NA	120	8,625	0	0	NA	NA
Timedyne Inc	-57.0	-61.5	-44.7	-2.6s	-.41	-100.0	-100.0	-100.0	NC	-14	03-90	.00	.0	0	NA	0	00-00-00	-12.4	.90	1	4.2	14	6,617	336	0	0.0	09
US Surgical	33.5	33.5	23.5	32.9q	1.38	25.9	25.9	32.7	NC	24	06-8-90	.50	.50	27	0	31	06-08-90	8.8	1.15	58	2.5	540	11,653	1,344	-87	1.7	12
Unigene Labs	.0	-35.7	.0	-1.5f	-.11	NE	NE	NE	NC	-18	12-89	.00	.0	0	0	0	00-00-00	NM	NC	6	25.0	19	13,394	41	0	0.0	12
Unilab	305.2	496.1		.0*	.00	-100.0	-100.0	NE	NC	12	02-90	.00	.0	0	0	0	00-00-00	NC	NC	34	.5	113	17,161	280	0	0.0	05
Utl Industrial	-10.0	-10.0	-11.3	14.3q	1.09	NE	NE	34.6	NC	6	03-90	.64	.0	8	105	80	07-30-90	5.2	1.12	12	1.2	109	13,066	1,997	0	1.2	12
Vestar Inc	-28.6	-28.6		-7.9q	-1.17	NE	NE	NE	NC	6	03-90	.00	.0	0	0	0	00-00-00	NM	2.39	0	3.6	18	6,424	567	0	0.0	12
Vicon Fiber	.0	.0	33.3	-1.5s	-.52	NE	NE	NE	NC	0	06-88	.00	.0	0	0	0	00-00-00	-12.5	1.36	31	.9	1	3,521	2	0	0.0	12
Vivigen Inc	52.6	52.6	66.6	1.5q	.60	-26.7	-26.7	46.3	NC	28	03-90	.00	.0	0	0	33	00-00-00	15.0	1.02	69	3.9	38	2,433	399	-4	0.0	12
Waters Instrument	-18.2	1.1		-.0n	-.31	-100.0	-75.0	-100.0	NC	8	10-89	.08	.0	0	0	0	03-26-90	.0	NC	5	3.4	5	1,446	72	0	0.0	01
West Co	4.6	4.6	4.3	20.8q	1.26	-5.4	-5.4	0	NC	6	03-90	.40	2.3	20	0	20	07-12-90	6.7	.99	29	2.1	277	16,147	577	0	2.9	12
WmCir	900.0	900.0		-3.9q	-1.46	NE	NE	NE	NC	0	03-90	.00	.0	0	0	0	00-00-00	NM	NC	0	4.8	17	3,257	275	0	0.0	12

Institutional Services

Ind. Group																										
Ind. Group	18.1	19.6	16.0	353.0	.16	-17.7	-7.4	-56.6	NC	-1	---	.20	1.4	1	31	31	---	1.5	1.20	123	1.5	21,162	1,483,433	41,319	- 289	1.2	--
Admar Group Inc	.0	.0	-9.0	.2r	.00	NC	NC	NC	NC	0	04-90	.00	.0	0	0	0	00-00-00	2.0	2.00	22	1.1	5	38,730	292	0	0.0	01
Aguoron Pharm	100.0	84.6	50.0	-6.0n	-2.02	NC	NE	NE	NC	0	03-90	.00	.0	0	0	0	00-00-00	NM	.91	25	3.1	37	4,114	968	0	0.0	06
Am Bionetics	-66.7	-33.3	-25.0	-2.1n	-.14	NE	NE	NE	NC	0	02-90	.00	.0	0	0	6	00-00-00	-70.0	NC	-550	1.2	6	15,412	159	0	0.0	05
American Drug Screen I	200.0	200.0	300.0	-.1q	-.01	NC	NC	NC	NC	-4	03-90	.00	.0	0	0	8	00-00-00	-2.5	1.04	26	1.8	8	8,331	15	0	1.2	12
Am Hlth Svcs	29.8	29.8	58.8	1.2q	.13	200.0	200.0	NE	NC	48	03-90	.00	.0	0	0	0	00-00-00	4.4	.84	868	1.6	18	9,151	339	-10	0.0	12

(continued)

Source: Media General Financial Services, Richmond, VA.

Institutional Services (Continued)

Company	Revenue Pct. Change Last Qtr	Revenue FY to Date	Revenue Last 12 Mos	Revenue Last 12 Mos $Mil	Revenue Last 12 Mos %	Earnings Per Share Last 12 Mos $	Earnings Last Qtr %	Earnings FY to Date %	Earnings Last 12 Mos %	Earnings 5-Year Growth Rate %	Par Growth Rate %	Date of Report	Current Rate Amt $	Current Rate Yield %	5-Year Growth Rate %	Payout Last FY %	Payout Last 5 Yrs. %	Last X-Dvd Date	Pro-fit Mar-gin	Asset Turn-over	Return on Total Assets	Lever-age Ratio	Return on Equity	Debt to Eq-uity %	Curr-ent Ratio	Mar-ket Value $Mil	Latest Shares Out-stndng. 000	Held by Banks-Funds 000	Insider Net Trad-ing 000	Short Int-erest Ratio Days	Fiscal Year Ends Mo
Am Healthcare ▫	1.5	1.5	1.9	-34.2q	-6.45	-99.0	-99.0	-100.0	NC	-92	03-90	.00	0	NA	NA	NA	01-05-90	-7.2	1.19	-8.6	10.69	-91.9	782	1.3	25	15,160	233	0	0.0	12
Am Med Hldg	NA	NA	NA	-3.3q	NA	NA	NA	-100.0	NC	NA	03-90	.00	0	NA	NA	NA	00-00-00	NA	NA	NA	NC	NC	NA	NA	562	72,559	0	0	NA	NA
Am Shared Hosp	60.0	60.0	41.0	6.6q	-1.16	0	0	-100.0	NC	-38	03-90	.00	0	0	0	0	00-00-00	-6.0	.73	-4.4	8.52	-37.5	548	1.3	9	2,814	424	+2	0.4	12
Basic Amer Med	22.6	22.6	16.8	6.6q	.84	55.3	55.3	460.0	NC	25	03-90	.00	0	0	0	0	05-05-87	1.9	1.74	3.3	7.42	24.5	422	1.2	77	7,863	530	+5	0.2	12
Beverly Enterp	-1.8	-1.8	2.6	-94.1q	-1.78	NE	NE	NE	NC	-26	03-90	.00	0	NE	0	NE	12-24-87	-4.5	1.27	-5.7	4.58	-26.1	166	1.2	376	64,060	23,980	0	0.2	12
Bio Tech Gnl	-12.5	-12.5	-25.0	-7.5q	-.99	NE	NE	NE	NC	0	03-90	.00	0	0	0	0	00-00-00	NM	NM	NM	NC	NM	4167	3.6	53	13,992	1,872	0	0.0	12
Biogen Inc	45.7	45.7	39.1	4.8q	.01	0	0	NC	NC	3	03-90	.00	0	0	0	0	00-00-00	15.0	.22	3.3	1.03	3.4	0	19.9	542	22,468	9,346	0	0.0	12
Biospherics Inc	-2.6	-2.6	0	-.5q	-.14	-100.0	-100.0	-100.0	NC	-19	03-90	.00	0	0	0	0	00-00-00	-3.3	2.27	-7.5	2.56	-19.2	65	2.1	18	3,501	118	0	0.0	12
Biotech Rsch Lab	-38.6	-38.6	-11.7	-.4q	.06	-50.0	-50.0	-50.0	NC	3	03-90	.00	0	0	0	0	00-00-00	2.7	.63	1.7	1.76	3.0	46	3.4	24	6,233	1,233	0	0.0	12
Care Plus	26.2	26.2	22.5	2.6q	.46	85.7	85.7	43.8	NC	14	03-90	.00	0	0	0	0	10-13-87	6.8	1.21	8.2	1.68	13.8	32	3.2	96	5,173	1,400	0	0.0	12
Cel Sci	0	0	0	-1.11	-.04	NE	NE	NE	NC	0	09-89	.00	0	0	0	0	00-00-00	NM	NM	NM	NC	NC	0	.2	49	29,927	136	-866	0.0	09
Calgene	33.3	33.3	0	-5.8q	-1.09	NE	NE	NE	NC	-30	03-90	.00	0	0	0	0	00-00-00	NM	NM	NM	NC	-29.6	0	24.6	36	5,410	557	0	0.0	12
Century Medicorp	35.2	35.2	56.2	1.1n	.28	NE	NE	-40.0	NC	28	03-90	.00	0	0	0	0	05-14-90	2.2	2.00	4.4	6.25	27.5	255	1.0	9	4,087	0	0	0.0	06
Cetus Corp	-3.0	-13.5	-2.3	-59.3n	-2.15	NE	NE	NE	NC	-50	03-90	.00	0	0	0	0	00-00-00	NM	NC	NC	1.76	-49.9	117	16.1	591	27,977	5,800	0	0.0	06
Chemex Pharma	-50.0	-50.0	0	-6.6f	-.54	NE	NE	NE	NC	0	12-89	.00	0	0	0	0	00-00-00	NM	NC	NC	1.68	NM	0	2.8	23	13,657	1,480	+162	0.0	12
Commun Psych	-10.3	-13.1	-24.6	79.1s	1.71	-3.2	1.2	14	NC	16	05-90	.36	1.3	23	21	0	06-04-90	27.2	.61	16.6	1.23	20.4	8	4.3	1,240	46,348	30,424	0	8.5	11
Comprehen Cr	-39.2	-29.3	-25.2	-34.4n	-3.39	-100.0	-100.0	-100.0	NC	-43	02-90	.00	0	6	600	44	01-24-89	-21.1	.78	-16.4	2.65	-43.4	91	1.8	27	10,174	1,576	-72	5.5	05
Contl Med Sys	65.5	63.2	62.4	1.9n	.10	63.6	16.7	-78.7	NC	4	03-90	.00	0	6	0	0	00-00-00	.9	1.11	1.0	3.70	3.7	185	1.8	211	14,073	3,675	0	0.0	06
Crop Genetics	0	5.3	0	-6.0n	-1.30	NE	NE	NE	NC	-36	12-89	.00	0	0	0	0	00-00-00	NM	NC	NC	NC	-35.7	0	27.8	37	4,668	964	0	0.0	08
Daxor	150.0	150.0	-25.0	-.5q	-.10	-5.6	-5.6	-100.0	NC	-3	03-90	.00	0	0	0	0	00-00-00	-16.7	.11	-1.9	1.42	-2.7	0	3.2	17	5,310	460	0	11.8	12
DDI Pharm	-27.3	-27.3	25.0	.7q	.15	0	0	114.3	NC	18	03-90	.00	0	0	0	0	00-00-00	14.0	1.14	15.9	1.13	17.9	0	8.6	14	4,983	295	0	0.0	12
Diagnostek	104.7	73.5	72.9	7.2q	.38	71.4	58.3	58.3	NC	24	03-90	.00	0	NA	NA	NA	00-00-00	4.9	3.33	16.3	1.50	24.4	5	2.7	309	18,155	1,751	0	NA	08
Diversicare Cp	-2.7	-2.7	163.3	1.1q	.04	-90.0	-90.0	-60.0	NC	5	02-90	.00	0	0	0	0	08-02-89	1.6	.69	1.1	4.82	5.3	338	1.2	14	11,459	4	0	0.0	12
Employee Benefit •▫	55.8	37.4	36.0	-5.6n	-1.01	-100.0	-100.0	NE	NC	27	02-90	.00	0	0	0	0	00-00-00	-6.7	1.61	-10.8	.00	NM	588	1.0	133	6,341	1,387	-5	23.9	05
Enzo Biochem	170.8	136.8	133.3	-4.8n	-.43	NE	NE	NE	NC	-6	04-90	.06	.0	2	NE	NE	06-30-86	-22.9	.28	-6.4	4.97	-31.8	326	6.7	38	11,359	1,220	-1	0.0	07
Enzon Inc	33.3	16.0	0	-3.2n	-.24	NA	NE	NE	NC	-38	03-90	.00	.0	0	0	0	00-00-00	1.3	.28	-3.6	NC	-37.6	1	2.3	134	12,352	563	0	0.0	06
Epitope Inc	NA	NA	NA	-1.2f	-.36	NA	NA	NA	NC	NC	00-00	.00	.0	NA	NA	NA	00-00-00	NM	NC	NM	NC	NM	NA	.4	60	6,597	476	0	NA	09
Exovir	0	0	0	-.1q	-.01	NE	NE	NE	NC	0	12-89	.00	.0	0	0	0	12-08-89	NC	NC	NC	NC	NC	NA	1.1	5	3,546	181	-5	0.0	12
FHP Cp	100.9	39.9	39.2	29.9m	1.19	34.6	22.9	20.2	NC	27	03-90	.00	.0	0	NE	NE	12-14-89	3.3	2.85	9.4	2.90	27.3	31	1.1	448	24,872	15,675	+5	0.0	06
Forum Grp	68.6	34.3	34.5	-5.3f	-.16	NE	NE	NE	NC	-6	02-90	.06	8.0	2	NE	363	04-10-89	-4.9	.28	-1.0	4.50	-4.5	242	.5	24	32,548	10,105	-1	0.0	08
Geriatric & Med ○ ▫	12.8	13.0	17.5	1.7n	.19	NE	NE	NE	NC	0	03-90	.00	.0	0	NE	NE	01-12-88	1.3	.92	1.2	.00	NS	9417	2.3	36	9,516	626	+10	0.0	05
Greenery Rehab	22.5	21.9	27.5	7.2s	.80	90.0	56.0	37.9	NC	24	03-90	.00	.0	0	0	0	07-22-86	8.2	.85	7.0	3.44	24.1	105	4.9	116	8,918	2,104	0	0.0	09
Heath Concepts	53.6	51.9	55.5	.6s	.24	37.5	31.3	-17.2	NC	20	05-90	.00	.0	0	0	0	06-25-90	4.3	1.60	6.9	2.90	20.0	77	2.0	10	2,443	0	0	1.8	11
Hlth Equity	-4.3	-4.3	5.5	.0q	-.14	NE	NE	NE	NC	0	03-90	1.41	24.0	0	NE	NE	03-90	0	NC	NC	NC	NC	276	NA	21	3,622	1,129	0	1.7	12
Hlth Images	46.2	46.2	45.8	2.4q	.37	33.3	33.3	15.6	NC	15	03-90	.02	.2	6	NE	NE	11-24-88	6.9	.57	3.9	4.00	15.6	216	1.7	73	6,053	+542	0	0.0	12
Hlthcre Intl A •	-26.5	-16.2	-9.1	-189.9n	-25.51	NE	NE	NE	NC	0	03-90	.00	.0	0	NE	0	00-00-00	-57.9	1.24	-71.6	.00	NS	-2	-.1	2	7,615	496	0	0.0	05

Company																														
Healtsth Rehab	94.2	94.2	68.1	9.1q	.84	50.0	50.0	35.5	NC	14	03-90	.00	0	0	0	00-00-00	6.1	.69	4.2	3.29	13.8	201	5.8	243	10,274	7,613	0	13.6	12
Hlthwatch Inc	140.0		-25.0	.5n	.2c	-24.6	-24.6	-76.7	NC	10	03-90	.00	0	0	0	00-00-00	16.7	.51	8.6	1.21	10.4	2	2.8	13	2,34C	11	0	.00	06
HEI Cp	8.6	7.0	6.6	1.8f	.33	200.0	200.0	371.4	0	9	03-90	.00	0	0	0	00-00-00	2.5	1.04	2.6	3.31	8.6	123	2.0	22	4,93C	164	0	.00	08
Hillaven	NA	NA	NA	NA	NA	NA	NA	NA	NC	NC	00-00	.00	NA	NA	NA	00-00-00	NA	NC	NC	NC	NC	NA	NA	168	95,80C	0	NA	NA	NA
HMO Amer	29.8	29.8	32.1	6.3q	.85	-30.3	-30.3	NE	NC	84	03-90	.00	0	0	0	00-00-00	4.3	4.72	20.3	4.14	84.0	NA	1.0	45	6,993	2,178	0	NA	12
Home Intensive Cre	-38.9	-35.9	16.6	-7.4s	-.80	-100.0	-100.0	57.4	-69	12	03-90	.00	0	0	0	08-24-87	-15.1	1.38	-20.8	3.29	-68.5	43	1.2	25	9,127	385	0	.00	09
Horizon Hlthcre	-4.3	-4.7	1.9	.4n	.04	NE	NE	NE	3	8	02-90	.00	0	•	0	00-00-00	4	1.75	.7	3.57	2.5	146	1.0	17	6,69C	475	0	.00	05
Humagn	.0	100.0	.0	-2.0f	-.70	16.7	16.7	18.9	16	13	12-89	.00	0	0	38	00-00-00	NC	NC	NC	NC	NM	1	5.5	1	2,853	39	0	4.9	08
Humana Inc	19.4	18.7	18.8	299.8n	2.96	16.7	21.1	18.9	-63	16	06-90	1.20	.38	42	11	06-26-90	6.4	1.27	.81	2.79	22.6	86	1.3	4,834	98,644	67,567	+8	4.9	12
Imrez Inc	.0	.0	.0	-1.0q	-.09	NE	NE	NE	16	NC	03-90	.00	0	0	0	00-00-00	.0	NC	NC	NC	-62.5	0	2.6	8	6,969	719	0	.00	12
Institute Clin	NA	NA	NA	NA	NA	NA	NA	NA	NC	NC	01-25-89	.00	NA	NA	NE	06-29-90	NA	NC	NC	NC	NA	NA	NA	2	15,465	170	+1	NA	04
Manor Care Inc	9.4	14.9	14.9	26.7t	.69	26.7	26.7	15.0	11	6	05-09-90	.13	24	23	20	06-25-90	3.8	.84	3.2	4.13	13.2	215	1.4	54	38,516	15,443	-26	4.3	12
Marrow Tech	.0	.0	.0	-2.7t	-.24	NC	NC	NC	0	NC	05-90	.13	0	0	0	07-11-89	.4	.84	.0	1.98	-21.2	4	5.0	65	13,702	280	0	.00	06
Medco Containment	38.5	37.8	38.8	-9.4n	-.18	-100.0	-100.0	-100.0	0	4	03-90	.04	2	7	0	04-18-90	-1.0	1.90	-1.9	1.68	-3.2	36	3.2	1,103	47,206	29,756	-57	.00	08
Medco Researca	.0	.0	.0	-1.0f	-.12	NE	NE	NE	-48	NC	08-89	.00	0	0	0	00-00-00	NC	NC	NC	NC	-47.6	0	7.7	107	8,607	2,456	0	.00	08
Medical Care	68.7	68.7	45.0	19.5q	1.07	52.4	52.4	57.4	12	12	03-90	.00	0	0	NE	04-02-90	12.1	.66	8.0	1.46	11.7	25	3.1	649	17,532	11,508	0	.00	12
Medical Imag Crs	80.9	80.9	95.8	4.4q	.58	9.1	9.1	23.4	29	NC	03-90	.00	0	0	0	00-00-00	9.4	.95	8.9	3.21	28.6	158	2.6	95	7,401	2,339	0	.00	12
Medical Mgmt Am	9.1	.0	-25.0	-6.9t	-.42	200.0	200.0	-100.0	-34	NC	04-90	.09	0	0	0	06-28-90	-46.0	.42	-9.4	1.46	-28.4	35	6.7	76	20,967	717	0	10.1	10
Medical Sterilization	20.0	20.0	16.6	-.4Q	-.17	NE	NE	NE	-25	NC	03-90	.00	0	0	0	00-00-00	-5.7	.82	-4.7	5.32	-25.0	75	.9	4	1,636	18	0	.00	12
Medicore Inc	-8.3	-8.3	9.5	-1.1q	-.23	-100.0	-100.0	-100.0	-11	NC	10-24-85	.00	0	0	0	00-00-00	-5.3	1.10	-5.3	2.08	-11.0	11	1.7	5	4,296	206	0	.00	12
MMI Medical	1.0	.3	.0	1.4f	.51	-67.9	-67.9	-50.0	4	6	04-90	.12	24	8	NE	06-29-90	3.7	1.32	4.9	1.67	8.2	15	1.7	13	2,749	428	0	.00	04
Natl Hlth Cp	16.7	16.7	19.3	14.7q	2.12	6.4	6.4	20.5	16	16	06-25-90	1.10	48	57	NE	06-25-90	10.4	.74	7.7	4.32	33.3	261	2.5	102	6,935	548	0	6.7	12
Natl Heritage	30.9	36.9	51.4	-6.5n	-.38	-100.0	-100.0	-100.0	-21	-21	07-11-89	.00	800	800	0	07-11-89	-6.3	1.70	-10.7	1.98	-21.2	57	2.2	17	17,210	882	0	.00	06
Natl Med Ent	7.8	13.4	13.5	177.3n	2.23	16.7	16.7	4.7	11	11	05-14-90	.72	35	36	0	05-14-90	4.4	1.05	4.6	3.50	16.1	152	1.8	3,085	81,445	54,214	0	15.8	05
Neorx Cp	-46.7	-46.7	-12.5	-15.5q	-1.06	NE	NE	NE	0	NC	12-89	.00	0	0	0	00-00-00	NM	NC	NC	NC	NM	237	5.9	29	14,600	2,558	0	.00	09
New Eng Critica	66.0	66.0	72.2	9.3q	.74	38.5	38.5	45.1	14	14	04-02-90	.00	0	0	0	04-02-90	10.0	.76	7.6	1.78	13.5	60	8.4	364	12,170	8,570	0	.00	12
Nichols Institute	35.4	35.4	37.2	5.5q	.46	30.0	30.0	35.3	14	14	04-09-90	.00	0	0	0	04-09-90	3.9	1.56	6.1	2.33	14.2	87	2.5	172	10,757	2,858	+10	2.6	12
NovaCare	45.1	44.3	40.9	10.3n	.73	140.0	140.0	231.8	21	21	06-23-87	.00	0	0	0	06-23-87	11.1	1.27	14.1	1.47	20.7	29	5.0	278	13,323	2,571	0	.00	06
Nu-Med	-16.0	-16.2	-31.7	-16.9n	-1.94	-100.0	-100.0	NE	2	0	04-30-45	.00	0	0	0	04-30-45	-7.3	.63	-4.6	.00	NS	-8573	1.7	32	8,867	721	-30	.00	04
Occupational Med	-11.1	-9.3	-12.5	-.5n	-.22	-100.0	-81.8	-52.2	15	15	00-00-00	.00	0	0	0	00-00-00	7.1	1.21	8.6	1.71	14.7	21	2.4	4	2,520	5	0	.00	06
Occulare Inc	11.9	11.9	38.4	3.6q	.37	0	0	42.3	56	56	09-01-89	.00	0	0	0	09-01-89	20.0	2.10	41.9	1.34	56.3	17	4.7	220	9,244	2,691	0	.00	12
Omnicare Inc	-41.5	-41.5	-49.3	1.1q	.25	-100.0	-40.0	-19.4	1	1	05-24-90	.10	17	17	0	05-24-90	1.4	.86	1.2	1.17	1.4	17	5.5	69	8,933	7,183	0	2.6	12
PacifiCare Hlth	59.2	61.1	59.4	14.5s	1.26	83.3	107.1	103.2	33	33	09-01-89	.00	0	0	0	09-01-89	1.8	4.17	7.5	4.41	33.1	5	1.2	291	11,428	3,248	-30	.00	09
Preferred Hlmcre	220.0	220.0	300.0	-.6q	-.10	NE	NE	NC	-19	-19	00-00-00	.00	0	0	0	00-00-00	-15.0	.85	-12.8	1.47	-18.8	3	2.4	4	4,546	29	0	.00	06
Prime Medical	.0	-.2.9	5.2	-5.8n	-.69	NE	NE	NE	-38	-38	00-00-00	.00	0	0	0	00-00-00	-41.4	.63	-4.6	1.47	-38.2	21	2.4	3	8,442	733	0	.00	06
Pro-Dex	.0	.0	.0	.1n	.06	NE	NE	NE	0	0	00-00-00	.00	0	0	0	00-00-00	5.0	1.06	5.3	.00	NM	500	1.7	1	1,233	0	0	.00	06
Prof Care	-15.9	-19.2	-24.1	1.1s	-.31	NE	-40.0	-26.1	-11	17	00-00-00	.00	0	0	0	00-00-00	-18.5	.52	-11.0	1.65	16.7	12	1.2	17	3,312	256	0	.4	09
Pscor Inc	34.7	33.6	33.3	1.7s	.43	-47.1	-47.1	-25.9	NC	13	00-00-00	.00	0	0	0	00-00-00	4.8	2.03	8.1	1.70	10.4	35	3.2	35	3,873	726	0	.00	12
Ramsay Hlth Cre	33.8	27.1	56.3	5.5n	.37	50.0	50.0	420.0	20	24	00-00-00	.00	0	0	0	10-16-85	3.2	.94	3.0	7.97	23.9	439	.9	40	14,085	1,509	0	.00	09
Readicare Inc	6.5	4.1	5.2	1.7f	.22	NE	NE	311.1	12	12	00-00-00	.00	0	0	0	00-00-00	8.5	1.02	8.7	1.33	11.6	1	1.3	34	7,873	815	0	.00	06
Ren Cp USA	217.4	217.4	162.5	1.0q	.13	NE	NE	NE	6	6	00-00-00	.00	0	0	0	00-00-00	4.8	.65	6.5	1.90	5.9	63	2.7	76	7,995	50	0	.00	06
Replgen Cp	100.0	50.6	44.4	-2.4f	-.31	NE	NE	-46.7	-11	NC	00-00-00	.00	0	0	0	00-00-00	-18.5	.52	-9.7	1.13	-11.0	12	4.1	118	8,395	568	0	.00	09
Safeguard Hlth	-3.2	-3.2	-8.9	2.9q	.82	-18.8	-18.8	-18.8	20	20	00-00-00	.00	0	0	0	00-00-00	4.8	2.90	13.9	1.42	19.7	10	3.1	30	4,492	2,057	0	.00	12
Salick Health Care	36.9	42.1	40.9	3.0s	.52	-44.4	-44.4	57.6	10	11	02-90	.00	0	0	0	02-90	4.8	.85	4.1	2.39	9.8	111	4.6	39	5,517	2,231	0	.00	08
ServiceMaster	12.4	12.4	7.0	68.3q	2.13	6.0	6.0	5.4	21	0	06-28-90	1.82	84	62	0	06-28-90	4.1	2.80	11.5	.00	NM	995	1.7	674	30,648	6,114	-0	.1	12

(continued)

Institutional Services (Continued)

Company	Revenue Pct. Change Last Qtr %	FY to Date %	Last 12 Mos %	Last 12 Mos $Mil	Last 12 Mos $	Earnings Per Share Pct. Change Last Qtr %	FY to Date %	Last 12 Mos %	5-Year Growth Rate %	Par Growth Rate %	Date of Report	Dividends Current Rate Amt $	Yield %	5-Year Growth Rate %	Payout Last FY %	Last 5 Yrs. %	Last X-Dvd Date	Pro-fit Mar-gin	Asset Turn-over	Return on Total Assets	Lever-age Ratio	Return on Equity	Debt to Eq-uity %	Curr-ent Ratio	Mar-ket Value $Mil	Shareholdings Latest Shares Out-stndng. 000	Held by Banks-Funds 000	Insider Net Trad-ing 000	Short Int-erest Ratio Days	Fiscal Year Ends Mo
												r/t x r/a =						r/t x r/a = r/a x r/a x a/e = r/e											
Sierra Hlth	16.4	16.4	.0	3.9q	.68	171.4	171.4	NE	NC	46	03-90	.00	.0	0	0	0	00-00-00	2.7	2.56	6.9	6.65	45.9	99	.8	39	5,767	1,109	-7	0.1	12
Summit Hlth	-.3	-.4	.0	-6.8n	-.22	NE	NE	NE	NC	-10	03-90	.00	.0	0	0	83	06-14-88	-1.8	1.17	-2.1	4.67	-9.8	196	1.7	63	31,250	3,074	0	0.0	06
Surgical Care	46.8	46.8	49.1	7.4q	.65	61.5	61.5	58.5	NC	17	03-90	.07	.3	0	4	2	05-25-90	8.1	.85	6.9	2.84	19.6	101	2.3	233	10,450	3,101	+40	0.0	12
T 2 Medical	48.1	111.1	170.0	11.2s	.95	18.2	41.7	39.7	NC	27	03-90	.00	.0	0	0	0	00-00-00	20.7	.74	15.3	1.75	26.7	54	1.8	337	12,728	2,565	+25	0.0	09
US Hlthcare	39.3	39.3	37.0	35.2q	.74	127.3	127.3	957.1	-8	11	03-90	.36	1.9	0	37	25	06-07-90	3.2	2.66	8.5	2.53	21.5	3	1.1	856	45,948	32,665	0	0.0	12
Untd Medical	10.5	10.5	8.5	2.0q	.83	-94.7	-94.7	-74.8	NC	7	03-90	.05	.5	0	0	0	07-24-90	-5.3	.94	-5.0	1.40	7.0	13	4.2	31	2,850	414	0	0.0	12
Unity Hlthcre	95.0	95.0	100.0	-1.3q	-.24	NE	NE	NE	NC	-68	03-90	.00	.0	0	0	0	10-11-89	-13.0	2.38	-31.0	2.21	-68.4	5	1.4	23	6,687	136	-6	0.0	12
Univ Health	8.5	8.5	6.7	10.1q	.70	26.7	26.7	48.9	-17	6	03-90	.00	.0	0	0	0	00-00-00	1.7	1.12	1.9	3.37	6.4	130	1.0	133	14,143	7,990	0	0.0	12
Vari Care	7.1	8.5	11.6	1.0s	.20	-50.0	-26.7	33.3	NC	12	03-90	.04	1.3	18	17	23	12-12-89	2.1	1.29	2.7	5.44	14.7	356	1.3	16	5,278	235	0	0.0	09
Vencor Inc	41.8	41.8	37.2	.9q	.18	25.0	25.0	NC	NC	6	03-90	.00	.0	0	0	0	00-00-00	1.5	1.73	2.6	2.12	5.5	55	1.8	62	5,725	478	0	0.0	12

Source: Media General Financial Services, Richmond, VA.

U.S. Health Care Expenditures: Amount and Share of GNP

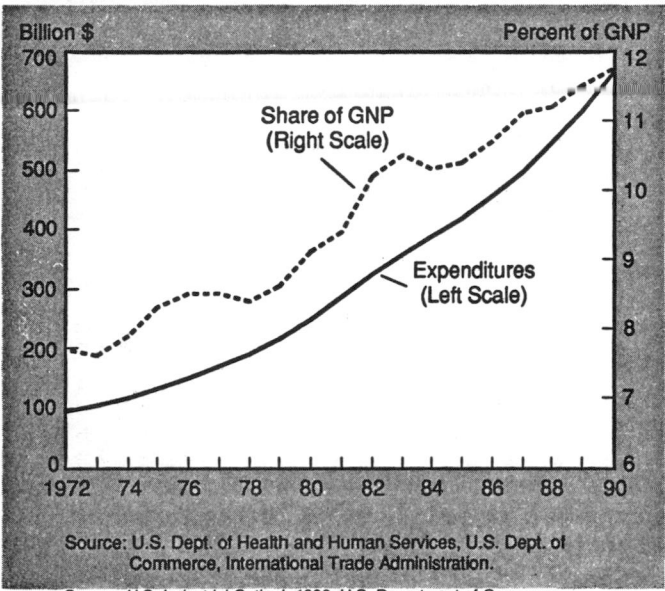

Source: U.S. Dept. of Health and Human Services, U.S. Dept. of Commerce, International Trade Administration.

Source: *U.S. Industrial Outlook 1990,* U.S. Department of Commerce.

Trends and Forecasts: Household Appliances (SIC 363)

(in millions of dollars except as noted)

Item	1987[1]	1988	1989[3]	1990[4]	Percent Change		
					1987-88	1988-89	1989-90
Industry Data							
Value of shipments[5]	16,714	16,941	17,161	—	1.4	1.3	—
Value of shipments (1987$)	16,714	16,935	16,858	16,265	1.3	-0.5	-3.5
Total employment (000)	118	120	119	116	1.7	-0.8	-2.5
Production workers (000)	93.0	95.6	95.5	92.0	2.8	-0.1	-3.7
Average hourly earnings ($)	10.68	10.96	11.09	—	2.6	1.2	—
Product Data							
Value of shipments[6]	15,516	15,717	15,916	—	1.3	1.3	—
Value of shipments (1987$)	15,516	15,715	15,640	15,090	1.3	-0.5	-3.5
Trade Data							
Value of imports (ITA)[7]	2,900	3,128	3,283	—	7.9	5.0	—
Import/new supply ratio[8]	0.157	0.166	0.171	—	5.7	3.0	—
Value of exports (ITA)[9]	1,119	1,546	1,629	—	38.2	5.4	—
Export/shipments ratio	0.072	0.098	0.102	—	36.1	4.1	—

[1]Industry and product data are preliminary. Trade data are adjusted to conform to the 1987 SIC.
[2]Estimated, except for exports and imports.
[3]Estimated.
[4]Forecast.
[5]Value of all products and services sold by establishments in the household appliances industry.
[6]Value of products classified in the household appliances industry produced by all industries.
[7]Import data are developed by the chapter author.
[8]New supply is imports plus corresponding product shipments.
[9]Export data are developed by the chapter author.

SOURCE: U.S. Department of Commerce: Bureau of the Census; International Trade Administration (ITA). Estimates and forecasts by ITA.

Source: *U.S. Industrial Outlook 1990*, U.S. Department of Commerce.

Trends and Forecasts: Household Furniture (SIC 251)
(in millions of dollars except as noted)

Item	1987[1]	1988[2]	1989[3]	1990[4]	Percent Change		
					1987-88	1988-89	1989-90
Industry Data							
Value of shipments[5]	18,526	19,411	19,883	—	4.8	2.4	—
2511 Wood furniture, house	7,929	8,294	8,521	—	4.6	2.7	—
2512 Upholstered furniture, house	5,248	5,518	5,610	—	5.1	1.7	—
2514 Metal furniture, house	2,079	2,161	2,196	—	3.9	1.6	—
2515 Mattresses & bedsprings	2,447	2,600	2,726	—	6.3	4.8	—
Value of shipments (1987$)	18,526	18,665	18,466	18,158	0.8	-1.1	-1.7
2511 Wood furniture, house	7,929	7,929	7,810	7,654	0.0	-1.5	-2.0
2512 Upholstered furniture, house	5,248	5,300	5,247	5,142	1.0	-1.0	-2.0
2514 Metal furniture, house	2,079	2,100	2,058	2,027	1.0	-2.0	-1.5
2515 Mattresses & bedsprings	2,447	2,508	2,533	2,533	2.5	1.0	0.0
Total employment (000)	283	289	289	—	2.1	0.0	—
Production workers (000)	240	245	245	—	2.1	0.0	—
Average hourly earnings ($)	6.99	7.22	7.49	—	3.3	3.7	—
Product Data							
Value of shipments[6]	17,765	18,610	19,063	—	4.8	2.4	—
2511 Wood furniture, house	7,421	7,748	7,937	—	4.4	2.4	—
2512 Upholstered furniture, house	4,895	5,161	5,243	—	5.4	1.6	—
2514 Metal furniture, house	1,893	1,958	2,009	—	3.4	2.6	—
2515 Mattresses & bedsprings	2,706	2,876	3,015	—	6.3	4.8	—
Value of shipments (1987$)	17,765	17,905	17,723	17,434	0.8	-1.0	-1.6
2511 Wood furniture, house	7,421	7,421	7,310	7,164	0.0	-1.5	-2.0
2512 Upholstered furniture, house	4,895	4,944	4,894	4,796	1.0	-1.0	-2.0
2514 Metal furniture, house	1,893	1,912	1,874	1,846	1.0	-2.0	-1.5
2515 Mattresses & bedsprings	2,706	2,773	2,801	2,801	2.5	1.0	0.0
Trade Data							
Value of imports (ITA)[7]	2,889	2,910	2,765	—	0.7	-5.0	—
Import/new supply ratio[8]	0.140	0.135	0.127	—	-3.6	-5.9	—
Value of exports (ITA)[9]	226	313	414	—	38.5	32.3	—
Export/shipments ratio	0.013	0.017	0.022	—	30.8	29.4	—

[1]Industry and product data are preliminary. Trade data are adjusted to conform to the 1987 SIC.
[2]Estimated, except for exports and imports.
[3]Estimated.
[4]Forecast.
[5]Value of all products and services sold by establishments in the household furniture industry.
[6]Value of products classified in the household furniture industry produced by all industries.
[7]Import data are developed by the chapter author.
[8]New supply is imports plus corresponding product shipments.
[9]Export data are developed by the chapter author.
SOURCE: U.S. Department of Commerce: Bureau of the Census; International Trade Administration (ITA). Estimates and forecasts by ITA.

Source: U.S. Industrial Outlook 1990, U.S. Department of Commerce.

MEDIA GENERAL FINANCIAL SERVICES

STOCKS by INDUSTRY

Ratio Analysis identity: = r/l × r/a = r/a × a/e = r/e

Appliances

Company	Rev Last Qtr %	Rev FY to Date %	Rev Last 12 Mos %	Last 12 Mos $Mil	EPS Last 12 Mos $	EPS Chg Last Qtr %	EPS Chg FY to Date %	EPS Chg Last 12 Mos %	EPS 5-Yr Growth %	Par Growth %	Date of Report	Div Amt $	Div Yield %	Div 5-Yr Growth %	Payout Last FY %	Payout Last 5 Yrs %	Last X-Div Date	Profit Margin	Asset Turnover	Return on Total Assets	Leverage Ratio	Return on Equity	Debt to Equity %	Current Ratio	Mkt Value $Mil	Shares Outstndg 000	Held by Banks-Funds 000	Insider Net Trading	Short Int Days	Fiscal Yr Ends Mo
Ind. Group	5.4	6.2	34.1	348.2	1.64	-.21	-8.0	-2.4	-1	6	----	.89	4.2	1	56	50	----	3.4	1.21	4.1	3.12	12.8	73	1.6	4,407	210,322	102,903	+1	2.6	--
Hlth-Mor	15.5	15.5	17.1	1.40	.69	33.3	33.3	30.2	-20	0	02-90	.68	5.8	4	110	91	06-11-90	15.8	1.24	4.2	1.21	5.1	2	3.8	25	2,159	479	0	18.5	12
Juno Lighting	17.4	16.4	23.8	13.1s	2.21	240.0	124.2	82.6	19	3	06-90	.28	1.3	0	12	7	06-08-90	15.8	1.13	17.9	1.21	21.7	7	7.4	199	9,184	5,726	0	0.0	11
Linc Foodsvc	-5.9	-5.9	.0	.60	.18	-85.7	-85.7	-71.9	3	4	03-90	.00	.0	0	0	0	00-00-00	1.3	1.62	2.1	1.57	3.3	28	3.9	19	3,294	728	0	0.0	12
Maytag Co	12.3	12.3	50.6	130.0q	1.23	-11.4	-11.4	-38.2	6	4	03-90	.90	5.2	6	76	58	05-25-90	4.1	1.29	5.3	2.62	13.9	93	2.3	1,820	105,500	35,841	0	1.9	12
Mor-Flo Inds	-.7	-.7	-3.1	-7.80	-3.09	NE	NE	NE	-29	-29	03-90	.01	.2	6	NE	NE	12-13-89	-3.7	1.81	-6.7	4.39	-29.4	164	2.0	13	2,521	89	0	0.0	12
Natl Presto	-15.2	-15.2	.5	28.8q	3.90	1.7	1.7	34.5	11	9	02-90	1.50	3.7	23	94	61	02-26-90	23.2	.51	11.9	1.19	14.2	3	6.9	298	7,330	2,579	-1	0.0	12
Scotsman Inds	.7	.7	.5	6.1q	1.06	NC	NC	20.5	NC	23	06-90	.10	1.2	0	6	NE	06-25-90	3.5	1.23	4.3	5.81	25.0	241	1.9	59	7,079	3,755	0	2.4	12
Scottish Heritable	-20.5	-73.0	30.9	.0*	-2.90	NE	NE	-100.0	NC	7	03-90	.00	.0	2	6	NE	02-06-87	NC	NC	NC	NC	.0	137	1.0	22	3,855	0	+2	0.0	07
Whirlpool Cp	3.9	3.9	30.9	176.0q	2.53	-28.8	-28.8	72.1	-4	7	03-90	1.10	3.9	2	41	45	05-16-90	2.8	1.18	3.3	3.76	12.4	69	1.3	1,952	69,400	53,606	0	1.0	12

Furniture and Home Furnishings

Company	Rev Last Qtr %	Rev FY to Date %	Rev Last 12 Mos %	Last 12 Mos $Mil	EPS Last 12 Mos $	EPS Chg Last Qtr %	EPS Chg FY to Date %	EPS Chg Last 12 Mos %	EPS 5-Yr Growth %	Par Growth %	Date of Report	Div Amt $	Div Yield %	Div 5-Yr Growth %	Payout Last FY %	Payout Last 5 Yrs %	Last X-Div Date	Profit Margin	Asset Turnover	Return on Total Assets	Leverage Ratio	Return on Equity	Debt to Equity %	Current Ratio	Mkt Value $Mil	Shares Outstndg 000	Held by Banks-Funds 000	Insider Net Trading	Short Int Days	Fiscal Yr Ends Mo
Ind. Group	10.9	12.9	15.8	134.1	1.20	-19.9	-34.6	-2.5	5	8	----	.41	2.3	1	29	27	----	3.7	1.65	6.1	1.87	11.4	40	2.8	1,965	110,475	32,825	-1123	2	--
Bassett Furniture	-2.9	-2.9	18.0	9.2q	1.10	-100.0	-100.0	-50.9	0	0	02-90	1.00	2.9	-12	33	45	05-11-90	2.0	1.50	3.0	1.17	3.5	0	6.0	285	8,248	2,626	0	0.0	12
Bush Industries	-6.4	-6.4	2.0	1.7q	.37	-62.5	-82.5	-48.6	7	7	03-90	.00	.0	0	0	0	04-19-88	1.7	1.53	2.6	2.58	6.7	39	1.4	28	4,554	939	0	0.0	09
Cathmtric/Contour	52.0	47.3	42.8	2.9s	.76	-57.9	.0	137.5	26	26	03-90	.00	.0	0	33	14	00-00-00	4.8	2.69	12.9	2.02	26.1	12	2.0	11	3,644	390	-1134	0.0	08
DMI Furniture	-5.5	-3.8	15.1	1.7s	.30	-50.0	-50.0	-30.2	35	7	04-90	.00	.0	0	0	0	00-00-00	5.3	1.89	7.2	.00	NM	5650	2.1	4	2,829	474	0	0.0	08
Falcon Prod	20.0	18.8	15.1	2.0s	.67	85.7	85.7	71.8	35	35	04-90	.00	.0	0	0	0	03-27-90	5.3	2.13	11.3	3.05	34.5	90	2.0	17	2,765	57	0	0.0	10
Flexsteel Ind	-2.0	.9	2.9	6.7n	.95	-32.0	-4.1	-12.0	5	5	03-90	.48	3.8	7	49	38	05-17-90	3.9	2.13	8.3	1.23	10.2	2	4.5	89	7,122	2,226	+1	0.0	06
Huffman Koos	6.7	6.7	-4.7	-1.7q	-.43	NE	NE	NE	-12	-9	04-90	.00	.0	0	0	0	00-00-00	-2.1	2.14	-4.5	2.64	-11.9	28	1.6	8	4,000	372	0	0.0	01
La-Z-Boy	6.3	7.1	7.0	28.3f	1.58	5.1	2.6	2.6	9	6	04-90	.56	3.0	11	35	30	05-14-90	4.8	1.69	8.1	1.80	14.6	36	3.1	329	17,901	3,015	+1	0.0	04
Ladd Furniture	48.6	48.6	31.3	13.6q	.72	-54.8	-54.8	-43.8	6	6	03-90	.28	2.5	18	35	20	04-25-90	2.7	1.30	3.5	2.94	10.3	111	2.2	207	18,788	8,105	+5	0.0	12
Lechter	22.5	22.5	503.7	9.1q	1.36	33.3	33.3	NC	16	16	04-90	.00	.0	0	0	0	00-00-00	5.6	1.80	10.1	1.57	15.9	26	3.9	184	7,154	1,826	0	0.0	01
Leggett Platt	12.6	12.6	18.0	46.8q	2.69	6.0	6.0	17.5	10	11	05-21-90	.84	2.3	21	28	23	05-21-90	4.6	1.76	8.1	2.02	16.6	52	2.6	641	17,323	8,114	+2	2.9	12
Library Bureau	-9.1	-14.9	77.7	.2s	.06	-41.7	-41.7	NC	7	7	00-00-00	.00	.0	0	0	0	00-00-00	4.3	2.00	8.6	2.85	7.4	8	2.3	1	1,256	581	0	0.0	09
Pulaski Furn	2.7	2.8	9.0	6.4s	2.23	10.8	11.1	12.1	12	11	04-90	.47	2.0	12	20	21	05-25-90	4.8	1.44	6.9	2.09	14.4	61	3.5	68	2,840	581	+2	0.0	10
Rowe Furniture	-12.4	-10.6	-9.3	1.3s	.51	-100.0	-53.8	-42.7	-6	4	05-90	.16	3.1b	17	38	25	06-19-90	1.7	1.82	3.1	2.03	6.3	32	2.1	13	2,572	419	+0	0.0	11
Shelby Wms	1.7	1.7	6.9	5.9n	.63	11.1	11.1	10.5	-3	6	03-90	.24	2.8	25	39	26	04-25-90	3.5	1.63	5.7	1.82	10.4	37	3.0	81	9,479	3,481	0	0.0	12

Source: Media General Financial Services, Richmond, VA.

Insurance

Trends and Forecasts: Life Insurance
(in billions of dollars except as noted)

Item	1985	1986	1987	1988	1989[1]	1990[2]	Percent Change Compound Annual 1985-88	Annual 1988-89	1989-90
Premium receipts	155.9	194.1	213.0	229.1	247.4	265.2	13.7	8.0	7.2
New life insurance purchases[3]	1,231.2	1,308.8	1,352.5	1,406.9	1,446.3	1,482.5	4.6	2.8	2.5
Life insurance in force[3]	6,053.1	6,720.3	7,452.5	8,020.2	8,742.0	9,511.3	9.8	9.0	8.8
Total benefits paid	66.5	68.3	71.4	74.1	77.7	81.2	3.7	4.8	4.6
Life insurance assets	825.9	937.6	1,044.5	1,166.9	1,285.9	1,414.5	12.2	10.2	10.0
Employment (SIC 6311)[4]	559.3	578.3	578.1	576.5	575.8	575.0	1.0	-0.1	-0.1

[1]Estimated.
[2]Forecast.
[3]Excludes foreign business.
[4]Employees on payroll only.

SOURCE: American Council of Life Insurance; U.S. Department of Labor, Bureau of Labor Statistics. Estimates and forecasts by the U.S. Department of Commerce, International Trade Administration.

Source: *U.S. Industrial Outlook 1990*, U.S. Department of Commerce.

Trends and Forecasts: Property/Casualty Insurance
(in billions of dollars except as noted)

Item	1985	1986	1987	1988	1989[1]	1990[2]	Percent Change Compound Annual 1985-88	Annual 1988-89	1989-90
Net written premiums	144.2	176.6	193.2	202.0	207.6	216.9	11.9	2.8	4.5
Underwriting gain (loss)	(22.6)	(13.7)	(7.1)	(8.4)	(16.6)	(22.7)	—	—	—
Net investment income	19.5	21.9	24.0	27.7	29.7	32.4	12.4	7.2	9.1
Operating earnings after taxes	(3.3)	6.6	11.0	12.9	8.6	6.4	—	(33.3)	(25.6)
Assets	311.4	374.1	426.7	476.9	522.2	569.2	15.3	9.5	9.0
Policyholders' surplus	75.5	94.3	104.0	118.2	128.8	138.6	16.1	9.0	7.6
Employment (000) (SIC 633)	474.9	499.6	526.2	540.2	547.5	555.7	4.4	1.4	1.5

[1]Estimated.
[2]Forecast.

SOURCE: A. M. Best Company, *Best's Aggregates and Averages*; U.S. Department of Labor, Bureau of Labor Statistics. Estimates and forecasts by U.S. Department of Commerce, International Trade Administration.

Source: *U.S. Industrial Outlook 1990*, U.S. Department of Commerce.

LIFE INSURANCE COMPANY ASSETS, 1986 AND 1988

Type of Asset	1986 Billions of Dollars	1986 Percent of Total	1988 Billions of Dollars	1988 Percent of Total
TOTAL	937.6	100.0	1,166.9	100.0
Corporate securities	432.9	46.2	584.7	50.1
Bonds	342.0	36.5	480.3	41.2
Stocks	90.9	9.7	104.4	8.9
Mortgages	193.8	20.6	232.9	20.0
Policy loans	54.1	5.8	54.2	4.6
Government securities	144.6	15.4	159.8	13.7
Real estate	31.6	3.4	37.4	3.2
Miscellaneous	80.6	8.6	97.9	8.4

SOURCE: The American Council of Life Insurance.

Source: *U.S. Industrial Outlook 1990*, U.S. Department of Commerce.

U.S. LIFE INSURANCE COMPANIES—SUMMARY: 1970 TO 1988

[As of **December 31** or **calendar year**, as applicable. Covers domestic and foreign business of U.S. companies. See also *Historical Statistics, Colonial Times to 1970*, series X 879 and X 890–917]

ITEM	Unit	1970	1980	1981	1982	1983	1984	1985	1986	1987	1988
U.S. companies	Number..	1,780	1,958	1,991	2,060	2,117	2,193	2,261	2,254	2,337	2,395
Sales [1]	Bil. dol...	207	655	1,139	920	1,279	1,390	1,530	1,578	1,656	1,716
Ordinary	Bil. dol...	135	462	700	661	972	1,074	1,187	1,178	1,267	1,287
Group [1]	Bil. dol...	65	190	436	257	306	315	342	400	388	428
Industrial	Bil. dol...	7	4	3	2	2	1	1	(Z)	(Z)	(Z)
Income	**Bil. dol...**	**49.1**	**130.9**	**151.9**	**170.0**	**176.0**	**206.1**	**234.0**	**282.3**	**314.3**	**338.1**
Life insurance premiums	Bil. dol...	21.7	40.8	46.3	50.8	50.3	51.3	60.1	66.2	76.7	73.5
Percent of total	Percent..	44.2	31.2	30.5	29.9	28.6	24.9	25.7	23.5	24.4	21.7
Annuity considerations	Bil. dol...	3.7	22.4	27.6	34.6	30.5	42.8	53.9	83.7	88.7	103.3
Health insurance premiums	Bil. dol...	11.4	29.4	31.8	35.0	38.2	40.7	41.8	44.2	47.6	52.3
Investment and other	Bil. dol...	12.3	38.3	46.2	49.6	57.0	71.3	78.2	88.2	101.3	109.0
Disbursements	**Bil. dol...**	**39.0**	**88.2**	**101.8**	**113.3**	**123.5**	**138.5**	**151.8**	**186.5**	**202.3**	**221.4**
Payments to policyholders [2] [3]	Bil. dol...	25.6	59.0	65.1	71.2	80.9	89.8	95.7	131.4	144.4	156.8
Percent of total	Percent..	65.6	66.9	63.9	62.8	65.5	64.8	63.0	70.5	71.4	70.8
Death payments	Bil. dol...	7.2	12.9	13.6	14.5	16.8	17.6	18.5	19.6	20.7	22.4
Matured endowments	Bil. dol...	1.0	.8	.7	.6	.6	.7	.8	.8	.8	.8
Annuity payments	Bil. dol...	1.7	7.4	9.6	10.3	12.7	18.0	19.7	17.8	20.3	21.9
Policy dividends	Bil. dol...	3.8	8.1	9.3	9.6	10.8	11.4	12.4	12.4	13.0	13.8
Surrender values [3]	Bil. dol...	2.9	6.4	7.1	9.8	12.5	14.5	15.9	49.6	53.7	58.1
Disability benefits	Bil. dol...	.2	.5	.6	.5	.5	.4	.5	.5	.5	.4
Commissions, expenses, etc.[3]	Bil. dol...	12.9	27.8	35.1	40.3	40.7	46.0	53.1	51.4	54.7	61.3
Dividends to stockholders	Bil. dol...	.5	1.4	1.6	1.8	1.9	2.7	3.0	3.7	3.3	3.4
BALANCE SHEET											
Assets	**Bil. dol...**	**207.3**	**479.2**	**525.8**	**588.2**	**654.9**	**723.0**	**825.9**	**937.6**	**1,044.5**	**1,166.9**
Government securities	Bil. dol...	11.1	33.0	39.5	55.5	76.6	99.8	124.6	144.6	151.4	159.8
Corporate securities	Bil. dol...	88.5	227.0	241.5	268.5	297.0	322.5	374.3	432.9	502.2	584.7
Percent of total assets	Percent..	42.7	47.4	45.9	45.7	45.3	44.6	45.3	46.2	48.1	50.1
Bonds	Bil. dol...	73.1	179.6	193.8	212.8	232.1	259.1	296.8	342.0	405.7	480.3
Stocks	Bil. dol...	15.4	47.4	47.7	55.7	64.9	63.4	77.5	90.9	96.5	104.4
Mortgages	Bil. dol...	74.4	131.1	137.7	142.0	151.0	156.7	171.8	193.8	213.5	232.9
Real estate	Bil. dol...	6.3	15.0	18.3	20.6	22.2	25.7	28.8	31.6	34.2	37.4
Policy loans	Bil. dol...	16.1	41.4	48.7	53.0	54.1	54.5	54.4	54.1	53.6	54.2
Other	Bil. dol...	10.9	31.7	40.1	48.6	54.0	63.8	72.0	80.6	89.6	97.9
Interest earned on assets [4]	Percent..	5.30	8.02	8.57	8.91	8.96	9.45	9.63	9.35	9.10	9.03
Liabilities [2] [5]	**Bil. dol...**	**189.9**	**444.8**	**488.4**	**546.7**	**608.5**	**672.6**	**769.1**	**873.4**	**977.1**	**1,091.9**
Policy reserves [2]	**Bil. dol...**	**167.8**	**390.4**	**428.0**	**479.4**	**532.4**	**584.2**	**665.3**	**761.9**	**862.1**	**969.0**
Annuities	Bil. dol...	48.9	181.5	209.1	252.4	296.5	341.7	410.6	488.6	561.7	642.2
Group	Bil. dol...	34.0	140.4	161.0	191.9	221.7	254.6	303.0	355.8	392.5	433.9
Individual [6]	Bil. dol...	14.9	41.0	48.1	60.5	74.8	87.1	107.6	132.8	169.2	208.3
Life insurance	Bil. dol...	115.4	197.9	207.0	213.8	221.0	225.9	235.9	252.0	276.4	299.9
Health insurance	Bil. dol...	3.5	11.0	11.9	13.2	15.0	16.6	18.8	21.3	24.0	26.9
Capital and surplus [2]	Bil. dol...	17.3	34.4	37.4	41.5	46.4	50.4	56.8	64.1	67.4	75.0

Z Less than $500 million.   [1] Includes Servicemen's Group Life Insurance: $16.8 billion in 1970, $44.5 billion in 1981, and $50.8 billion in 1986; as well as Federal Employees' Group Life Insurance: $81.5 billion in 1981 and $10.8 billion in 1986. [2] Includes operations of accident and health departments of life insurance companies. [3] Beginning in 1986, data not comparable to prior years due to change in accounting method.   [4] Net rate.   [5] Includes other obligations not shown separately.   [6] Includes reserves for supplementary contracts with and without life contingencies.

Source: American Council of Life Insurance, Washington, DC, *Life Insurance Fact Book*, biennial, and unpublished data.

Source: *Statistical Abstract of the United States 1990*, U.S. Department of Commerce, Bureau of the Census.

MEDIA GENERAL FINANCIAL SERVICES

STOCKS by INDUSTRY

Life, Accident and Health

Company	Rev Last Qtr %	Rev FY to Date %	Rev Last 12 Mos %	Rev Last 12 Mos $Mil	EPS Last 12 Mos $	EPS Last Qtr $	EPS FY to Date %	EPS Last 12 Mos %	EPS 5-Yr Gr %	Par Gr %	Date of Report	Div Amt $	Div Yield %	Div 5-Yr Gr %	Payout Last FY %	Payout Last 5 Yrs %	Last X-Dvd Date	Profit Margin	Retn Tot Assets	Asset Turnover	Leverage Ratio	Return Equity	Debt to Equity	Curr Ratio	Mkt Value $Mil	Shares Out 000	Held Banks-Funds 000	Insider Net Trade 000	Short Int Days	FY Ends Mo
Ind. Group	-1.7	2.0	-5.5	4,398.0	2.00	.03	-32.9	-39.6	15	3	03-90	.96	3.5	1	32	34	—	3.8	.8	.21	7.75	6.2	29	1.9	58,348	2,092,364	637,748	+398	.9	—
Academy Insur	6.5	6.5	.0	2.6	.03	.03	-50.0	-50.0	NC	3	03-90	.00	.00	0	0	NE	06-24-85	2.4	.7	.29	4.00	2.8	0	NA	77	70,834	3,185	0	0.0	12
Acap Cp	94.7	86.1	87.5	-.9	-.40		NE	NE	NE	-21	12-89	.00	.00	0	0	0	00-00-00	-6.0	-1.1	.18	19.00	-20.9	244	NA	1	3,085	0	0	0.0	12
Accel Int'l Cp	37.9	37.9	22.0	5.2	1.14		54.5	54.5	19	9	03-90	.05	.76	0	17	17	07-02-90	7.2	2.6	.36	3.65	9.5	7	NA	37	4,950	2,332	0	0.0	12
Aegon NV	30.2	30.2	33.9	254.2	7.74		-31.4	-31.4	NC	11	03-90	.98	1.40	17	49	46	05-19-89	3.8	.9	.24	14.44	13.0	239	NA	2,552	36,582	61	-3	2.5	12
Aetna Life Casualty	4.7	4.7	-13.2	646.9	5.78		5.9	-11.1	20	-5	03-90	2.76	5.3	1	49	1	07-23-90	10.0	.7	.22	13.29	9.3	15	NA	5,837	111,716	12,305	-3	0.0	12
Alfa Cp	9.9	9.9	4.2	19.7	.94		-48.4	-48.4	11	7	03-90	.40	4.2	18	32	31	08-09-90	11.2	4.1	.41	3.00	12.3	0	NA	199	20,925	1,347	0	0.0	12
AllCity Insur	2.8	5.9	5.3	6.6	.85		.0	-56.9	NC	25	03-90	.00	.00	0	0	0	00-00-00	5.0	4.8	.43	5.19	24.9	35	NA	42	7,063	48	-0	0.0	12
Alleghany Cp	40.1	40.1	15.8	59.0	9.21		56.9	56.9	NC	10	03-90	.00	.00	0	0	0	03-27-90	2.6	1.5	.58	6.40	9.6	56	NA	569	6,442	3,840	-0	0.0	12
Ambase Cp	-99.9	-99.9	-12.4	70.0	.83		-100.0	-88.9	NC	7	03-90	.00	.00	0	7	14	02-23-90	2.2	.5	.19	13.00	6.5	107	NA	237	33,914	5,260	-26	5.0	12
Am Bankers Insur	14.0	14.0	1.6	14.7	1.03		-42.6	-27.5	13	-5	03-90	.50	6.0	0	41	102	06-04-90	3.2	1.2	.55	7.75	9.3	121	NA	121	14,433	7,549	0	0.0	12
Am Family	2.7	488.9	3.8	78.2	.97		-8.6	-8.6	NC	7	03-90	.32	2.0	14	29	22	05-14-90	3.2	1.2	.38	9.25	11.1	30	NA	1,290	81,272	2,799	0	0.9	12
Am First Okla	-185.7	2.3	.0	.0*	.0*		-100.0	-100.0	NC	2	03-90	.00	.00	0	0	0	12-03-86	NC	NC	NC	NC	NC	131	NA	3	5,484	434	-0	0.0	09
Am Genl Cp	2.3	2.3	6.4	473.9	3.89		16.9	16.9	8	8	03-90	3.20	6.7	11	40	35	05-10-90	11.2	1.5	.13	7.73	11.6	92	NA	5,723	119,224	11,682	-0	0.3	12
Am Guaranty	450.0	450.0	.0	.0	-.01		NE	NE	NC	-5	03-90	.00	.00	0	0	0	00-00-00	NC	NC	NC	NC	NC	0	NA	3	6,113	54	-2	0.0	12
Am Heritage Life	3.9	3.9	-11.6	11.9	2.02		16.7	8.0	6	6	03-90	1.10	5.0b	15	60	47	07-10-90	5.8	1.9	.33	5.74	10.9	0	NA	131	5,971	613	-2	2.7	12
Am Indemnity Fncl	-9.0	-9.0	-2.4	-8.4	-4.34		-100.0	-100.0	NC	-30	03-90	.44	8.4	-15	NE	NE	05-07-90	-10.6	-6.8	.64	4.06	-27.6	8	NA	10	1,924	568	+2	0.0	12
Am Integrity	52.4	52.4	30.5	4.6	.70		-70.0	-70.0	11	11	03-90	.00	.00	9	42	41	00-00-00	6.4	4.3	.72	2.60	11.2	0	NA	41	6,631	770	-6	0.0	12
Am Natl Insur	1.5	1.5	9.0	100.1	3.55		-4.3	1.1	3	3	03-90	1.60	4.7	9	42	41	06-11-90	9.6	2.2	.23	2.82	6.2	2	NA	968	28,267	5,811	0	0.0	12
Am Reliance Grp	16.4	16.4	15.3	6.5	2.56		26.5	48.0	NC	13	03-90	.44	4.3	0	12	7	05-11-90	8.7	4.4	.51	3.45	15.2	9	NA	26	2,549	117	0	0.0	12
Am Travelers	86.0	86.0	78.1	7.8	1.05		100.0	105.9	21	25	03-90	.00	.0	0	0	0	05-11-90	13.7	10.4	.76	2.38	24.8	17	NA	115	7,321	3,166	+3	0.0	12
Amvestors Financial	7.7	7.7	34.4	-5.3	-.38		-53.8	-53.8	18	-20	03-90	.20	5.5	18	NE	113	04-11-90	-4.4	-.4	.09	33.00	-13.2	79	NA	52	14,377	3,038	-7	0.0	12
Aon Cp	-24.4	-15.8	-15.8	232.4	3.54		26.9	26.9	6	9	03-90	1.52	4.1	6	39	42	05-02-90	10.2	2.5	.25	6.56	16.4	31	NA	2,461	65,635	3,955	+23	0.1	12
Argonaut Grp	16.4	16.4	16.9	81.0	8.39		6.5	15.9	NC	14	03-90	1.60	2.1	6	6	2	05-01-90	14.3	4.2	.29	4.07	17.1	0	NA	715	9,343	2,567	+0	0.0	12
Atlantic Amer	-20.6	-41.5	-41.6	-23.8	-2.46		NE	NE	NC	0	12-89	.00	.0	0	0	0	08-16-88	-28.3	-14.1	.50	.00	.00	104	NA	21	9,789	678	+0	0.0	12
BMA Cp	-1.0	-1.0	-9.0	32.5	3.35		741.7	44.4	NC	6	03-90	1.20	3.9	4	49	119	05-16-90	7.0	2.8	.40	3.32	9.3	8	NA	301	9,699	3,407	-5	0.0	12

(continued)

Life, Accident and Health (Continued)

Company	Rev Last Qtr %	Rev FY to Date %	Rev Last 12 Mos %	Rev Last 12 Mos $Mil	EPS Last 12 Mos $	EPS %Last Qtr	EPS %FY to Date	EPS %Last 12 to Date	EPS 5-Yr Growth %	Date of Report	Par Growth %	Div Amt	Div Yield %	Div 5-Yr Growth %	Payout Last FY %	Payout Last 5 Yrs %	Last X-Dvd Date	Profit Margin %	Asset Turnover	Return on Total Assets	Leverage Ratio	Return on Equity %	Debt to Equity %	Current Ratio	Market Value $Mil	Shares Out (000)	Held by Banks-Funds (000)	Insider Net Trading (000)	Short Int Ratio (Days)	FY Ends Mo
Broad Inc ◆	26.6	66.8	220.8	30.6q	.93	20.0	48.1	49.7	NC	03-90	7	.20	1.9	0	26	26	05-08-90	4.4	.09	.4	21.00	8.4	126	NA	354	33,307	17,177	0	0.2	09
Cap Holding ◦◦	6.0	6.0	20.9	268.21q	5.66	-24.1	-24.1	49.7	19	03-90	15	1.08	2.4	6	17	24	08-27-90	10.6	.17	1.8	10.50	18.9	23	NA	2,032	44,908	29,375	2	0.3	12
Celina Fincl A	-30.8	-30.8	-25.0	2.1q	1.23	-100.0	-100.0	.0	NC	03-90	20	.00	.0	0	0	0	00-00-00	17.5	.36	6.3	3.11	19.6	6	NA	2	1,755	96	+0	0.0	12
Cent Res Life	28.9	28.9	26.0	2.4q	.58	-53.8	-53.8	.0	NC	03-90	6	.28	5.6	23	40	32	11-08-90	2.0	2.25	4.5	2.73	12.3	6	NA	20	3,932	378		0.0	12
CIGNA Cp ◦	-14.4	-12.5	-12.5	562.0?	7.00	34.3	23.2	23.2	NC	12-89	6	3.04	6.1	3	42	94	06-06-90	3.6	.28	1.0	10.20	10.2	12	NA	4,092	81,631	64,732	+0	3.0	12
Citizens Inc A	50.0	39.2	30.7	-.41	-.02	NE	23.1	23.1	NC	12-89	-6	.00	.0	0	0	0	00-00-00	-2.4	.48	-.7	8.86	-6.2	0	NA	59	15,169	40	0	0.0	12
CNL Financial	36.6	31.4	33.3	1.2q	.64	-46.7	23.1	23.1	NC	12-89	7	.24	5.3	3	38	46	05-31-90	6.0	.48	2.9	4.10	11.9	0	NA	8	1,866	0	0	0.0	12
Colonial Cos	12.2	12.2	10.4	30.6q	2.02	5.7	5.7	9.2	8	12-89	9	.64	3.0	13	28	28	07-09-90	11.1	.57	6.3	2.10	13.2	1	NA	320	15,082	0	0	0.0	12
Condor Services ◦	6000.0	6000.0	800.0	.89q	.35	-25.0	-25.0	-43.5	9	03-90	30	.00	.0	0	0	0	00-00-00	4.4	1.09	4.8	1.90	9.1	0	NA	2	2,165	264	0	0.3	12
Conseco	23.4	23.4	-12.5	48.9q	7.08	8.7	8.7	69.0	NC	03-90	-19	.20	.8	0	3	2	06-14-90	7.1	1.09	7.1	34.33	30.9	195	NA	138	5,713	2,799	0	0.3	12
Consumers Fncl	-56.9	-56.9	39.0	2.5q	.63	-100.0	-100.0	-30.8	NC	04-06-90	23	.14	3.3	23	16	19	04-06-90	4.4	.36	1.6	7.06	11.3	0	NA	14	3,207	84	+2	0.0	12
Cotton St Lf	9.8	9.8	-9.5	2.8q	1.00	75.0	75.0	.0	NC	03-90	9	.26	4.0	1	26	35	06-11-90	14.7	.21	3.1	3.35	10.4	0	NA	16	2,748	20	+0	0.0	12
Donegal Grp	-3.8	-3.8	13.3	3.9q	1.35	-4.7	-4.7	92.9	NC	06-89	8	.24	2.8	3	15	24	04-23-90	7.6	.68	5.2	3.08	16.0	0	NA	18	2,957	94	0	0.5	06
Durham Cp	-37.9	-37.9	-34.7	15.0q	1.77	190.0	190.0	2.3	NC	03-90	3	.92	3.0	3	58	51	05-16-90	5.6	1.8	.8	3.61	6.5	0	NA	262	8,451	624	0	0.0	12
Empire State	-12.5	-10.0		-.8	-.46	NE	NE	NE	NE	12-89	0	.00	.0	0	0	0	00-00-00	-26.7	.13	-3.6	5.17	-18.6	0	NA	3	1,663		0	0.3	12
Equitable Iowa ◻	NA	NA	NA	NA	NA	NA	NA	NA	NA	00-00	NA	1.20	4.0	NA	NA	NA	05-11-90	NA	NC	NC	NC	NA	NA	NA	37	1,207	53	0	NA	12
Equitable of Iowa	18.6	18.6	18.5	31.3q	4.40	65.0	65.0	31.3	6	06-89	5	1.20	4.0	5	26	38	05-11-90	5.2	.21	1.1	10.55	11.6	20	NA	218	7,194	1,990	+0	0.0	12
FAI Insurance	.0	.0		45.4q	1.02	NC	NC	NC	96	06-89	8	.50	6.7	0	34	34	03-06-90	2.7	.67	1.8	6.28	11.3	123	1.9	340	45,352	87		0.5	06
Fst Capital Hldg ◻	20.5	20.5	30.2	70.1q	1.70	-14.6	-14.6	-8.1	NC	00-00	0	.00	.0	0	0	0	00-00-00	6.9	.10	.7	26.29	18.4	0	NA	216	46,691	30,017	+20	4.8	12
Fst Executive	-58.3	-58.3	-60.8	-831.41	-10.33	-100.0	-100.0	-100.0	NC	12-89	6	.00	.0	0	0	0	00-00-00	-69.6	.06	-4.3	19.26	-82.8	72	NA	313	84,935	29,644	+5	0.0	12
Fla Employers Ins ◻	38.1	41.5	39.1	-2.3	-1.00	NA	NA	-100.0	NA	12-89	13	.24	3.0	0	NE	18	02-12-90	-7.2	1.14	-8.2	2.30	-18.9	0	NA	1	2,255	332	0	0.0	12
Fortune Natl	84.2	88.6	87.5	-.8	-.30	NE	NE	NE	NC	12-89	-16	.00	.0	0	0	0	00-00-00	-5.3	.19	-1.0	16.30	-16.3	220	NA	1	2,617	0	0	0.0	12
Forum Re Group ◦◻	52.0	-16.4	-16.6	-.51	-.09	NE	NE	80.2	NC	12-88	-1	.00	.0	0	0	0	05-01-90	-5.0	.22	-1.1	6.09	-6.7	1	1.1	2	4,984	2	0	0.0	12
Fremont Genl ◻	31.8	14.5	14.4	17.7	2.18	80.2	80.2	-8.4	NC	12-89	11	.80	5.2	8	32	36	06-25-90	3.8	.32	1.2	8.92	10.7	69	NA	126	8,105	3,074	0	0.0	12
Hlth Insur Vt	10.0	10.0	10.0	.4q	.76	-18.2	-18.2	-8.4	NC	03-90	6	.18	2.3	23	23	25	12-11-89	10.0	.36	3.6	2.03	7.3	5	NA	4	560	28	0	0.0	12
Home Beneficial	108.1	108.1	26.5	67.1q	6.47	219.8	219.8	59.0	4	03-90	8	1.32	3.5	8	28	28	05-16-90	28.2	.21	6.0	2.77	16.6	0	NA	388	10,347	2,423	-7	0.0	12
ICH Corp ◻	-37.3	-25.1	-25.1	-342.8	-7.69	-100.0	-100.0	-100.0	NC	12-89	NC	.00	.0	0	NE	NE	05-20-90	-15.9	.25	-4.0	.00	NM	730	NA	234	48,000	9,084	+0	2.8	12
Independent Ins ◻	-1.6	3.3	3.4	29.3q	2.20	-41.9	11.7	11.7	-6	12-89	1	.80	3.9	1	36	35	02-02-90	5.7	.39	2.2	4.05	8.9	8	NA	276	13,316	1,746	0	0.0	12
Integon Cp	.5	.5	-25.9	-7.2q	-.49	-38.5	11.7		NC	03-90	0	.16	2.9	0	40	40	04-29-88	-1.6	-.5	-.9	9.20	-4.6	18	NA	161	29,246	661	0	0.0	12
Intercontinental Lf	-6.3	-6.3	100.0	12.4q	1.24	76.9	76.9	300.0	NC	03-90	42	.00	.0	0	0	0	02-22-90	7.2	.13	.9	47.00	42.3	433	NA	34	4,440	51	-6	0.0	12
Investors Heritage	.0	.0	-44.4	1.6q	1.78	1.7	1.7	1.7	5	12-89	5	.00	.0	0	38	38	00-00-00	3.2	.34	1.2	4.55	5.0	0	NA	31	1,188	14	+0	0.0	12
John Adams Life	-50.0	-50.0	-3.2	.19	.03	NE	NE	45.4	NC	03-90	1	.00	.0	0	0	0	00-00-00	2.0	.10	.2	6.50	1.3	0	NA	4	2,843	223	0	0.0	12
Kansas City Life	1.5	1.5	1.5	25.2q	3.62	7.3	7.3	7.3	1	03-90	6	1.12	3.1	29	33	33	05-01-90	9.3	.14	1.3	6.38	8.3	19	NA	263	7,315	678	0	0.0	12
KauflHW	2.1	2.1	300.0	.89	.43	-84.6	-84.6	28.0	14	03-90	2	.17	2.8	0	29	15	01-16-90	4.0	1.00	4.0	5.73	22.9	6	1.1	11	1,885	31	0	0.0	12
Kent Cent Life	23.6	23.6	-10.2	36.5q	.76	20.8	20.8	28.0	2	03-90	9	.40	3.0	9	15	18	03-09-90	8.0	.22	1.8	6.39	11.5	73	NA	178	13,430	3,992	+2	0.0	12
Laurentin Cap	-6.0	-6.0	-7.3	2.8q	.15	100.0	100.0		3	03-90	0	.00	.0	0	0	0	00-00-00	2.0	.15	.3	9.33	2.8	51	NA	41	16,229	753	0	0.0	12
Lawrence Ins	89.2	14.5	14.2	6.2q	.54	66.7	31.7	31.7	NC	12-89	3	.36	4.0	0	46	24	07-12-90	7.8	.40	3.1	3.23	10.0	0	NA	127	14,121	244	0	0.1	12
Lib Cp	-6.1	-6.1	-9.9	37.2q	4.36	271.4	271.4		11	03-90	10	.92	2.0	0	20	26	06-11-90	10.6	.23	2.4	5.42	13.0	80	NA	390	8,475	2,107	-23	4.4	12
Linc Natl Cp	10.4	10.4	9.9	244.0q	5.47	-52.2	-52.2	38.5	7	03-90	8	2.60	4.7	8	41	45	07-03-90	3.0	.33	1.0	11.10	11.1	17	NA	2,326	42,000	26,005	0	0.5	12

Company									
Manhattan Natl	-32.6	-32.6	-12.3	-3.1q	-.36			8,525	1,57
Mega Group	50.0	79.2	3	.0*	-.02		11,070	0
Mid South Insur	-24.2	-24.2	-15.2	1.1q	.44		2,602	-37
Midland Co	14.2	14.2	10.0	6.9q	2.14		3,250	-77
Milwaukee Insur	17.0	17.0	13.8	.3q	.10		3,075	39
Monarch Cap	-87.6	-87.6	-17.9	-15.6q	-2.74		6,643	4,71
Natl Western Life	32.3	32.3	-43.2	2.0q	.58		3,478	66
Nobel Insur	-18.5	-18.9	-18.5	-10.7f	-2.02		5,278	85
N Am Natl	-64.7	10.3	4.1	2.7q	.87		3,119	242
NWNL Cos	26.5	4.5	-36.7	57.6q	4.46		12,815	8,75
Old Rep Intl	14.5	7.2	7.2	98.2f	4.23		19,992	11,313
Orion Cap Cp	-5.4	-5.4	-1.6	23.9q	3.35		6,496	4,523
Penn Treaty	51.5	51.5	54.5	5.1q	1.85		3,218	75
PHLCORP Inc	-15.3	-9.2	-9.2	26.3f	1.94		13,518	1,64
Pioneer Fincl	75.2	75.2	41.6	17.3q	2.38		6,453	2,310
Pres Life	55.9	55.9	28.0	46.3q	1.25		28,593	5,108
Protective Life	10.8	10.8	5.7	22.5f	1.64		13,657	5,14
Provident Lf Acc	-8.6	-2.9	1.3	147.1n	3.15		46,691	19,391
Re Capital	8.3	8.3	7.2	8.4q	1.22		6,498	3,088
Reliable Life Insur Cl	-1.8	-1.7	-1.8	11.2f	3.97		8,355	197
SAI	-16.7	-11.1	-20.0	-2.4f	-.16		15,272	111
SafeEdc	-12.3	-11.8	-12.5	1.9f	.94		1,998	0
Sothrn Sec Life	23.5	23.5	14.2	.5q	.28		1,845	0
Stamford Cap	16.6	17.0	17.7	-3.0f	-.33		18,020	3324
Tokio Mar&Fire	7.1	7.1	7.1	701.11	2.25		291,116	-343
Torchmark Cp	-2.4	-1.9	-1.8	211.3f	3.88		52,856	21799
Travelers Cp	1.6	1.6	-21.6	418.0q	3.98		102,546	73856
Unicare Fincl	34.8	34.8	41.0	7.8q	1.43		5,454	351
Utd Cos Fincl	8.1	8.1	-30.4	8.1q	2.07		3,888	1388
Utd Home Life	.0	.0	11.1	.5q	.29		1,689	547
Utd Insurance	6.1	6.1	6.1	6.3q	1.88		3,344	529
UniServ	36.6	36.6	63.6	1.5q	.16		8,733	0
Univ Holding	50.0	236.4	-20.0	-.6n	-.20		3,018	15
USLICO Cp	4.5	4.5	-10.0	29.2q	2.68		10,853	3686
USLIFE Cp	3.6	3.6	.0	78.3q	4.54		16,217	10376
Walshire Assnce	25.7	25.7	21.4	2.7q	1.26		2,178	744
Wash Natl Cp	8.6	8.6	-10.8	3.2q	.26		10,821	6355
Westbridge Cap	2.9	2.9	.0	-.2q	-.03		4,148	184

Source: Media General Financial Services, Richmond, VA.

Trends and Forecasts: Sawmills and Planing Mills, General (SIC 2421)
(in millions of dollars except as noted)

Item	1987[1]	1988[2]	1989[3]	1990[4]	Percent Change 1987–88	Percent Change 1988–89	Percent Change 1989–90
Industry Data							
Value of shipments[5]	17,177	17,865	17,829	—	4.0	-0.2	—
Value of shipments (1987$)	17,177	17,345	16,478	16,891	1.0	-5.0	2.5
Total employment (000)	147	147	141	—	0.0	-4.1	—
Production workers (000)	128	128	122	—	0.0	-4.7	—
Average hourly earnings ($)	8.30	8.36	8.41	—	0.7	0.6	—
Product Data							
Value of shipments[6]	16,775	17,454	17,330	—	4.0	-0.7	—
Value of shipments (1987$)	16,775	16,946	16,017	16,384	1.0	-5.5	2.3
Trade Data							
Value of imports[7]	3,312	3,169	3,033	3,057	-4.3	-4.3	0.8
Import/new supply ratio[7]	0.167	0.158	0.151	0.176	-5.4	-4.4	16.6
Value of exports	1,518	2,087	2,377	2,466	37.5	13.9	3.5
Export/shipments ratio	0.092	0.124	0.140	0.146	34.8	12.9	4.3

[1]Industry and product data are preliminary. Trade data are adjusted to conform to the 1987 SIC.

[2]Estimated, except for exports and imports.

[3]Estimated.

[4]Forecast.

[5]Value of all products and services sold by establishments in the sawmills and planing mills, general industry.

[6]Value of products classified in the sawmills and planing mills, general industry produced by all industries.

[7]New supply is imports plus corresponding product shipments.

SOURCE: U.S. Department of Commerce: Bureau of the Census; International Trade Administration (ITA). Estimates and forecasts by ITA.

Source: *U.S. Industrial Outlook 1990*, U.S. Department of Commerce.

MEDIA GENERAL FINANCIAL SERVICES

STOCKS by INDUSTRY

Lumber and Wood Products

Company	Rev Pct Chg Last Qtr %	Rev FY to Date %	Rev Last 12 Mos %	Rev Last 12 Mos $Mil	EPS Last 12 Mos $	EPS Pct Chg Last 12 Mos %	EPS FY to Date %	EPS Last Qtr %	EPS 5-Yr Growth %	EPS Par Growth %	Date of Report	Div Current Rate Amt $	Div Yield %	Div 5-Yr Growth %	Payout Last FY %	Payout Last 5 Yrs %	Last X-Dvd Date	Profit Margin %	Asset Turnover	Return on Total Assets %	Leverage Ratio	Return on Equity %	Debt to Equity %	Current Ratio	Market Value $Mil	Latest Shares Outstanding 000	Held by Reliants-Funds 000	Insider Net Trading 000	Short Interest Ratio Days	Fiscal Year Ends Mo
Ind Group	4.5	5.1	6.5	2,536.8	15.0	101.4	15.0	32.9	38	11	---	1.08	4.2	1	22	31	---	6.0	.87	5.2	2.77	14.4	72	1.9	21,463	839,937	307,296	+21	3.4	
Baltek Cp	-8.2	-8.2	-12.5	2.2a	.90	-47.5	-47.5	-49.7	38	8	03-90	.15	1.9	0	14	8	07-10-90	6.3	1.17	7.4	1.24	9.2	3	3.2	20	2,523	468	0	0.0	12
Bohemia Inc	-3.4	14.4	14.3	17.0q	3.24	45.9	45.9	45.9	NC	16	04-90	.20	1.40	0	6	11	06-05-90	4.9	1.47	7.2	2.35	16.9	69	1.3	78	5,256	2,466	0	0.0	04
Champ Intl	-.3	-.3	.1	388.7q	4.05	-42.9	-52.1	-17.7	NC	8	03-90	1.10	3.6	24	24	21	06-11-90	7.5	.69	5.2	2.08	10.8	56	1.3	2,910	95,394	63,221	0	2.0	12
Etz Lavud Ltd	29.1	72.1	73.0	-1.11	-.68	-100.0	-100.0	-100.0	NC	-7	12-88	.00	.0	0	0	0	09-17-85	-1.2	1.67	-2.0	3.45	-6.9	81	1.8	14	1,744	7	0	0.0	12
Fibreboard Cp	21.0	21.0	22.3	3.8q	.95	-44.0	-44.0	-34.0	NC	-3	03-90	.00	.0	0	0	5	00-00-00	1.7	.88	1.5	1.87	2.8	34	2.1	35	3,883	1,122	0	1.8	12
Georgia Pacific	8.7	8.7	5.5	608.0q	6.95	-28.5	-28.5	28.9	45	17	03-90	1.60	3.9	16	20	26	05-14-90	5.9	1.46	8.6	2.60	22.4	86	2.0	3,585	86,655	55,849	0	0.5	12
IP Timberlands	.0	.0	16.9	127.1q	3.06	1.3	1.3	14.6	NC	0	03-90	2.84	13.8	0	90	99	06-25-90	57.5	1.09	12.9	1.09	14.1	0	4.5	955	46,283	331	0	0.0	12
Kamenstein	1.8	1.8	19.2	1.50	.60	-57.1	-57.1	5.3	NC	16	03-90	.00	.0	0	0	0	00-00-00	4.8	2.69	12.9	1.22	15.8	5	6.8	10	2,413	239	0	0.0	12
La Pacific	1.7	1.7	13.1	188.5q	4.93	-10.4	-10.4	27.4	45	13	03-90	1.00	2.6	5	0	19	05-15-90	9.3	1.00	9.3	1.72	16.0	45	3.6	1,476	38,453	17,309	+0	0.4	12
Macmillan Bloedel	-1.3	-1.3	1.5	177.1q	1.61	-61.4	-61.4	-34.6	NC	8	03-90	.80	5.2	0	41	38	08-20-90	6.3	1.41	8.9	1.79	15.9	38	11.7	1,578	102,650	6,098	0	0.0	12
Morgan Prods	-5.4	-5.4	-5.3	-3.7q	-.43	0	0	-100.0	NC	-5	03-90	.00	.0	0	0	0	00-00-00	-.9	2.67	-2.4	1.88	-4.5	38	2.9	88	8,428	4,321	+5	13.0	12
Plum Creek	NA	NA	NA	NA	NA	-100.0	-100.0	NA	NA	NC	00-00	2.25	8.6	NA	13	0	05-09-99	NA	NC	NA	NC	NA	NA	NA	373	14,203	957	+1	NA	NA
Ply-Gem	23.4	23.4	34.8	6.2q	.54	17.5	17.5	-58.8	4	4	05-90	.12	1.6	5	16	13	05-11-90	1.2	1.67	2.0	2.85	5.7	134	3.6	77	10,474	3,668	0	28.6	12
Pope & Talbot	1.1	1.1	13.3	45.2q	3.84	-1.5	-1.5	36.7	NC	18	03-90	.72	3.0	8	23	22	04-24-90	7.3	1.74	12.7	1.79	22.7	34	1.9	281	11,788	5,912	0	24.2	12
Potlatch Cp	9.9	9.9	11.9	137.8q	4.77	8.7	8.7	8.7	33	12	03-90	1.20	3.0	7	23	29	05-15-90	11.0	.75	8.2	2.02	16.6	55	2.7	1,172	28,845	12,325	0	1.2	12
Rayonier Tmbrld	-5.7	-5.7	-2.1	70.2q	3.72	-3.6	-3.6	3.6	NC	4	03-90	3.15	14.2	0	70	90	05-24-90	75.5	.30	23.0	1.24	28.5	18	7.6	89	4,000	646	0	0.0	12
Repap Enterpr	1.6	1.6	18.2	65.7q	1.28	-69.2	-69.2	-15.8	25	12	03-90	.28	3.9	0	11	11	06-25-90	6.9	.39	3.4	5.52	14.9	216	1.5	354	48,791	1,175	0	0.0	12
Svenska Cellulosa	17.7	17.7	17.6	172.4q	17.55	372.0	375.0	375.6	NC	25	12-89	.19	1.0	8	2	1	05-22-90	4.3	.79	3.4	7.29	24.8	33	1.7	1,695	84,750	35	+8	0.0	12
TJ Intl	9.7	9.7	10.8	14.9q	2.07	-17.9	-17.9	-18.2	26	13	03-90	.42	1.8	18	18	18	06-18-90	4.2	2.05	8.6	1.88	16.2	90	1.9	166	7,009	3,017	0	2.8	12
Weyerhaeuser	-1.7	-1.7	2.2	323.1q	1.47	-12.9	-12.9	-48.2	16	8	03-90	1.20	4.7	7	77	59	04-30-90	3.2	.63	12.1	3.90	7.8	121	1.4	5,221	204,753	11,224	+7	0.0	12
Willamette Inds	7.3	7.3	10.0	193.7q	7.62	6.4	6.4	20.6	28	17	03-90	1.60	3.2	8	19	23	05-21-90	10.1	1.20	12.1	1.78	21.5	43	2.1	1,258	25,417	14,870	0	0.0	12
WTD Inds	20.2	27.9	27.7	-1.5q	-.23	-100.0	-100.0	-100.0	NC	-4	04-90	.00	.0	0	0	0	00-00-00	-.3	2.67	-.8	4.63	-3.7	226	1.7	26	6,225	2,036	0	0.0	04

Source: Media General Financial Services, Richmond, VA.

Trends and Forecasts: Machine Tools (SIC 3541, 3542)
(in millions of dollars except as noted)

Item	1987[1]	1988[2]	1989[3]	1990[4]	Percent Change		
					1987-88	1988-89	1989-90
Industry Data							
Value of shipments[5]	4,658	4,993	6,691	7,026	7.2	34.0	5.0
Value of shipments (1987$)	4,658	4,812	6,186	6,262	3.3	28.6	1.2
Total employment (000)	46.4	48.0	49.0	49.0	3.4	2.1	0.0
Production workers (000)	27.5	28.5	29.2	29.2	3.6	2.5	0.0
Average hourly earnings ($)	13.05	-	-	-	-	-	-
Product Data							
Value of shipments[6]	4,042	4,354	5,835	6,126	7.7	34.0	5.0
Value of shipments (1987$)	4,042	4,199	5,398	5,464	3.9	28.6	1.2
Trade Data							
Value of imports	2,397	2,476	2,915	-	3.3	17.7	-
Import/new supply ratio[7]	0.372	0.363	0.333	-	-2.4	-8.3	-
Value of exports	1,011	1,226	1,513	-	21.3	23.4	-
Export/shipments ratio	0.250	0.282	0.259	-	12.8	-8.2	-

[1]Industry and product data are preliminary. Trade data are adjusted to conform to the 1987 SIC.
[2]Estimated, except for exports and imports.
[3]Estimated.
[4]Forecast.
[5]Value of all products and services sold by establishments in the machine tools industry.
[6]Value of products classified in the machine tools industry produced by all industries.
[7]New supply is imports plus corresponding product shipments.
SOURCE: U.S. Department of Commerce: Bureau of the Census; International Trade Administration (ITA). Estimates and forecasts by ITA.

Source: *U.S. Industrial Outlook 1990*, U.S. Department of Commerce.

MEDIA GENERAL FINANCIAL SERVICES

STOCKS by INDUSTRY

Machine Tools and Accessories

Company	Rev Last Qtr %	Rev FY to Date %	Rev Last 12 Mos %	Rev Last 12 Mos $Mil	EPS Last 12 Mos $	Earn FY to Date %	Earn Last Qtr %	Earn Last 12 Mos %	Earn 5-Yr Growth %	Par Growth Rate	Date of Report	Div Amt $	Div Yield %	Div 5-Yr Growth %	Payout Last FY %	Payout Last 5 Yrs %	Last X-Div Date	Profit Margin %	Asset Turnover	Return on Total Assets %	Leverage Ratio	Return on Equity %	Debt to Equity %	Current Ratio	Market Value $Mil	Shares Out 000	Held by Banks-Funds 000	Insider Net Trading 000	Short Int Ratio Days	Fiscal Yr Ends Mo
Ind. Group	-2.5	-1.4	-2.3	152.8	.83	-15.9	-17.2	-5.1	NC	2	---	.58	3.4		49	66	---	2.6	1.23	3.2	2.03	6.5	30	2.2	3,013	173,721	78,836	+5	1.4	--
Acme-Cleveland Cp	8.7	8.3	9.9	5.6a	.65	-20.8	-100.0	21.9	NE	5	03-90	.40	4.9	0	51	NE	04-30-90	2.8	1.46	4.1	2.10	8.6	14	1.7	51	6,291	3,627	0	.1	09
American Vanguard	-42.2	-42.2	-20.0	.9a	.35	-100.0	-100.0	-44.4	NE	6	03-90	.09	1.2	0	15	6	11-09-89	5.0	.76	3.8	2.08	7.9	30	1.0	17	2,281	2	0	.0	12
Barden Cp	8.0	7.9	9.6	4.3a	.21	-35.0	-43.9	-17.5	3	4	04-90	1.00	3.1b	2	33	38	05-29-90	4.2	1.33	5.6	1.32	7.4	0	3.5	62	1,928	740	0	.0	10
Brenco Inc	13.5	13.5	30.3	3.3a	.34	27.3	27.3	-2.9	NC	3	03-90	.20	2.7	-6	58	246	06-11-90	4.5	1.51	6.8	1.22	8.3	0	5.5	71	9,687	4,577	0	.0	10
Brown & Strpe	8.9	8.9	2.6	4.9a	1.07	25.0	25.0	40.8	NC	4	03-90	.32	2.0	17	38	61	05-14-90	2.6	1.12	2.9	1.93	5.6	22	2.5	73	4,551	1,915	0	.0	12
Cinn Milacron	1.2	1.2	-.6	12.9a	.51	-58.3	-58.3	-51.9	NC	-2	03-90	.72	3.9	0	111	NE	05-14-90	1.5	1.27	1.9	3.06	5.8	75	2.1	444	24,327	14,535	0	15.8	12
Cross Trecker	-4.4	-7.6	-3.9	-38.3a	-3.25	NE	NE	NE	NC	-33	03-90	.00	.0	0	0	0	08-18-86	-8.7	1.23	-10.7	3.10	-33.2	65	1.9	105	12,383	8,893	0	.0	09
Fed Mogul	-2.9	-2.9	-7.9	33.6a	1.25	-5.6	-5.6	-19.9	2	4	03-90	.92	5.2	4	72	62	05-18-90	3.1	1.35	4.2	3.38	14.2	75	1.8	397	22,522	10,994	+4	3.4	12
Gleason Cp	-39.5	-39.5	-35.7	17.9a	3.14	NE	NE	NE	NC	16	03-90	.05	.3	0	0	0	05-07-90	12.8	.76	9.7	1.71	16.6	14	1.8	94	5,726	1,685	0	.0	12
Hein-Werner	-14.3	-14.3	-5.2	2.4a	1.28	-46.8	-46.8	-17.4	13	9	03-90	.25	2.4	8	20	20	12-21-88	2.2	1.59	3.5	3.11	10.9	104	2.7	21	1,947	826	0	1.0	12
Kaydon Cp	15.3	15.3	14.5	23.2q	2.70	6.1	6.1	7.6	31	22	03-90	.40	1.1	0	13	7	09-11-90	14.8	1.02	15.1	1.70	25.6	30	2.6	312	8,481	4,782	0	.0	12
Metallurgical A	44.4	44.4	25.0	-.8q	-.50	-100.0	-57.1	-100.0	NC	-29	03-90	.00	.0	0	0	0	12-26-89	-16.0	1.32	-21.1	1.36	-28.6	0	4.1	11	1,045	9	0	.0	12
Monarch Mach	13.1	13.1	7.6	1.7q	.44	-57.1	-57.1	-20.0	-6	-2	03-90	.80	4.9	0	154	190	05-11-90	1.7	1.18	2.0	1.35	2.7	55	3.5	61	3,745	1,609	0	2.7	12
Newcor	-34.4	-26.8	9.8	.9a	.28	35.4	35.4	-40.4	20	4	04-90	.00	.0	14	0	917	04-16-90	1.0	1.80	1.8	2.44	4.4	23	2.2	26	3,243	413	0	.0	10
Regal-Beloit Co	11.7	11.7	10.2	10.9a	1.09	-17.6	-17.6	-1.8	NC	8	03-90	.52	3.2	0	40	37	06-25-90	6.3	1.56	9.8	1.50	14.7		4.2	162	10,052	4,506	0	3.2	12
Sun Dist	9.3	9.3	12.9	21.1q	1.89	122.2	122.2	54.9	NC	13	03-90	1.10	12.8	0	66	141	06-25-90	3.7	2.19	8.1	3.80	30.8	172	2.4	96	11,100	1,934	0	.0	12
Sun Dist B	NA	NA	NA	NA	NA	NA	NA	NA	NC	NC	00-00	.00	.0	NA	NA	NA	00-00-00	NA	NC	NC	NC	NC	NA	NA	42	11,100	0	0	NA	12
Timken Co	-6.0	-6.0	-6.2	46.7q	1.53	-36.7	-35.7	-46.2	NC	2	03-90	1.00	3.2b	-3	49	363	05-15-90	3.1	.97	3.0	1.47	4.4	5	2.4	949	30,238	7,485	+1	.5	12
Wesco Tech	11.3	-1.7	-4.1	1.7l	.54	-38.6	-38.6	-38.6	NC	10	03-90	.15	2.4	0	15	21	02-23-90	7.4	.85	6.3	2.13	13.4	67	1.2	20	3,064	304	0	.0	08

Source: Media General Financial Services, Richmond, VA.

Trends and Forecasts: Metals and Industrial Minerals Mining (SIC 10, 14)

(in millions of dollars except as noted)

Item	1987	1988[1]	1989[2]	1990[3]	Percent Change		
					1987-88	1988-89	1989-90
Industry Data							
Value of shipments[4]	26,346	29,200	30,590	—	10.8	4.8	—
Value of shipments (1987$)	26,346	28,339	28,485	28,357	7.6	0.5	-0.4
Total employment (000)	154	164	172	—	6.5	4.9	—
Production workers (000)	118	126	132	—	6.8	4.8	—
Average hourly earnings ($)	11.25	11.68	12.03	—	3.8	3.0	—
Trade Data							
Value of imports (BuM)[5]	3,336	4,181	4,125	—	25.3	-1.3	—
Import/new supply ratio[6]	0.112	0.125	0.119	—	11.6	-4.8	—
Value of exports (BuM)[7]	2,648	3,244	2,248	—	22.5	-30.7	—
Export/shipments ratio	0.101	0.111	0.073	—	9.9	-34.2	—

[1]Data are preliminary.
[2]Estimated.
[3]Forecast.
[4]Value of all products and services sold by establishments in the metal and industrial mineral mining industry.
[5]Import data are developed by the chapter author.

[6]New supply is imports plus corresponding product shipments.
[7]Export data are developed by the chapter author.
SOURCE: U.S. Department of the Interior: Bureau of Mines (BuM); U.S. Department of Commerce: Bureau of the Census; U.S. Department of Labor, Bureau of Labor Statistics. Estimates and forecasts by the Bureau of Mines.

Source: *U.S. Industrial Outlook 1990*, U.S. Department of Commerce.

Trends and Forecasts: Steel Mill Products (SIC 3312, 3315, 3316, 3317)
(in millions of dollars except as noted)

Item	1987[1]	1988[2]	1989[3]	1990[4]	Percent Change		
					1987-88	1988-89	1989-90
Industry Data							
Value of shipments[5]	51,488	62,815	62,435	60,375	22.0	-0.6	-3.3
Value of shipments (1987$)	51,488	56,590	54,768	52,500	9.9	-3.2	-4.1
Total employment (000)	251	259	256	249	6.0	-3.0	-3.5
Production workers (000)	194	204	201	194	7.2	-3.4	-3.5
Average hourly earnings ($)	14.91	—	—	—	—	—	—
Product Data							
Value of shipments[6]	50,731	61,936	61,500	59,495	22.1	-0.7	-3.3
Value of shipments (1987$)	50,731	55,798	53,947	51,735	10.0	-3.3	-4.1
Trade Data							
Value of imports	8,540	10,468	8,180	8,500	22.6	-21.9	3.9
Import/new supply ratio[7]	0.149	0.149	0.123	0.132	0.0	-17.4	7.3
Value of exports	978	1,705	2,900	2,650	74.3	-0.1	-8.6
Export/shipments ratio	0.020	0.028	0.048	0.047	40.0	-1.4	-2.1

[1] Industry and product data are preliminary. Trade data are adjusted to conform to the 1987 S C.
[2] Estimated, except for exports and imports.
[3] Estimated.
[4] Forecast.
[5] Value of all products and services sold by establishments in the steel mill products industry.
[6] Value of products classified in the steel mill products industry produced by all industries.
[7] New supply is imports plus corresponding product shipments.
SOURCE: U.S. Department of Commerce: Bureau of the Census: International Trade Administration (ITA). Estimates and forecasts by ITA.

Source: *U.S. Industrial Outlook 1990*, U.S. Department of Commerce.

Trends and Forecasts: Titanium

(in short tons except as noted)

Item	1983	1984	1985	1986	1987	1988	1989[1]	1990[2]	1994[2]
Sponge Metal									
Production	13,966	24,326	23,257	17,402	19,675	24,548	26,400	27,000	25,000
Consumption	16,100	24,713	21,606	19,489	19,812	23,152	27,700	28,000	25,000
Imports for consumption	1,199	2,267	1,717	1,626	1,018	1,504	700	1,000	1,000
Imports as a percent of consumption	7	9	8	8	5	6	3	4	4
Industry stocks (Dec. 31)	3,136	3,147	4,755	3,180	2,504	2,689	2,000	1,500	2,000
Government stocks	32,331	32,470	36,831	36,831	36,831	36,831	36,831	36,831	36,831
Producer price ($/lb)	3.50-4.00	3.50-4.00	3.75-4.00	3.75-4.25	4.00-4.20	4.25-4.75	4.75-5.25	—	—
Scrap Metal									
Consumption	10,467	15,549	14,720	16,487	18,037	19,906	21,100	21,500	21,000
Stocks	12,635	12,489	11,686	11,558	10,115	9,475	9,900	9,000	10,000
Imports	1,572	1,850	2,134	2,374	2,445	4,668	6,300	6,000	4,000
Exports	5,379	4,109	6,760	6,403	5,603	6,602	6,600	5,500	5,500
Ingot									
Production	26,411	39,530	35,387	35,093	37,216	42,831	47,100	48,500	43,000
Consumption	25,495	39,062	35,020	33,801	35,561	39,194	33,300	40,000	34,000
Stocks (Dec. 31)	3,242	4,526	4,000	4,100	4,458	4,335	4,300	4,100	4,400
Mill Products									
Net Shipments	15,933	22,690	23,253	20,842	22,286	24,866	25,950	27,000	25,500
Imports	953	843	1,449	1,345	983	1,167	1,200	2,000	2,000
Exports	2,154	2,849	3,395	3,251	4,704	5,249	5,000	5,000	5,000

[1] Estimated
[2] Forecast

SOURCE: U.S. Department of Commerce: International Trade Administration (ITA); U.S. Bureau of Mines and estimates and forecasts by ITA.

Source: U.S. Industrial Outlook 1990, U.S. Department of Commerce.

Trends and Forecasts: Lead

(in thousands of metric tons except as noted)

Item	1984	1985	1986	1987	1988	1989[1]	1990[2]	1994[2]
Mine Production	335	424	353	318	394	440	490	515
Consumption	1,207	1,148	1,126	1,230	1,231	1,225	1,220	1,280
Total refined production	1,022	1,110	995	1,084	1,129	1,140	1,150	1,200
Primary	389	494	370	374	392	390	390	400
Secondary	633	616	625	710	737	750	760	800
Year end stocks (primary, (secondary, and consumer)	142.2	177.6	104.2	110.2	105.2	115.0	125.0	125.0
Imports for consumption:								
Unwrought[3]	161	132	140	197	153	120	105	130
% of consumption	13.3	11.5	12.4	16.0	12.4	9.8	8.6	10.2
Scrap (lead content)	5	3	3	7	7	11	15	25
Export								
Unwrought	5	25	11	4	6	15	25	50
Scrap (gross weight)	45	60	59	53	82	51	50	40
U.S. producer price (cents per pound)[4]	25.6	19.1	22.0	35.9	37.1	39.5	—	—

[1]Estimated.
[2]Forecast.
[3]Includes base bullion and pigs and bars.
[4]Metals Week average.
SOURCE: U.S. Department of Commerce: International Trade Administration (ITA); U.S. Bureau of Mines. Estimates and forecasts by ITA.

Source: U.S. Industrial Outlook 1990, U.S. Department of Commerce.

STOCKS by INDUSTRY

MEDIA GENERAL FINANCIAL SERVICES

Iron and Steel Furnaces, Mills, Foundrie[s]

Company	Rev % Last Qtr	Rev % FY to Date	Rev % Last 12 Mos	Rev Last 12 Mos $Mil	Earn Last 12 Mos $Mil	EPS Last 12 Mos $	EPS % Last Qtr	EPS % FY to Date	EPS % Last 12 Mos	EPS 5-Yr Gr Rate	Par Gr Rate	Rpt Date	Div Amt	Div Yield	Div 5-Yr Gr	Payout Last FY	Payout Last 5 Yrs	Last X-Dvd Date	Profit Margin	Asset Turnover	Ret on Tot Assets	Leverage Ratio	Ret on Equity	Debt to Equity	Current Ratio	Mkt Value $Mil	Latest Shares Outstndg 000	Held by Banks-Funds 000	Insider Net Trading 000	Short Int Ratio Days	Fiscal Yr Ends Mo
Ind. Group	-6.0	-1.2	-2.4	2,782.3		1.31	-35.4	-16.0	-38.6	5	NC	---	.87	4.0	0	33	33	--:--	5.1	.96	4.9	2.94	14.4	81	1.6	32,381	1,475,266	403,072	+264	2.2	--
Acme Steel Co	5.7	-19.4	-14.3	11.5g		2.14	-85.1	-58.4	-42.5	8	NC	05-90	.48	4.5	4	42	80	06-05-90	2.6	1.54	4.0	1.95	7.8	40	2.4	92	5,524	1,251	+4	0.0	12
Amcast Indust	-10.9	-14.3	-13.4	4.7h		.67	-4.0	-6.0	-39.1	1	NC	03-90	.48		0	42		07-02-90	1.7	1.41	2.4	2.17	5.2	37	1.9	71	6,687	2,803	0	0.0	08
Am Steel & Wire	-8.6	-13.4	-5.0	2.1n		.25	-15.4	NE	-76.6	-78	NC	03-90				NE			1.1	2.09	2.3	2.83	6.5	50	1.3	54	8,371	1,031	0	0.0	06
Ampco-Pitts ◻	-18.1	-12.5	-12.7	9.3i		.97	NE	NE	NE	5	NC	12-89	.30	3.6	0	31	NE	07-10-90	4.2	.86	3.6	2.06	7.4	45	2.0	80	9,578	6,408	+1	0.3	12
Armco Inc ◇	-50.4	-50.4	-41.7	182.0g		1.96	-72.7	-72.7	28.1	15	NC	03-90	.30	5.3	0	13	NE	05-07-90	9.2	.79	7.3	2.56	18.7	44	1.7	663	88,461	47,209	+0	0.3	12
Athlone Indus ■	-21.1	-21.1	-12.3	11.1q		1.74	-57.0	-57.0	-54.5	13	NC	03-90	1.00	7.1b	0	39	NE	04-25-90	4.4	1.20	5.3	5.89	31.2	208	1.7	84	5,960	1,258	0	0.0	12
Bayou Steel	8.0	4.2	13.9	1.8s		.14	-92.9	-86.0	-89.6	3	NC	03-90	.00	.0	0	0	27	--:--	.8	1.38	1.1	2.27	2.5	90	3.9	39	12,685	3,689	0	0.0	08
Bethlehem St	-13.3	-13.3	-8.9	202.3q		2.35	-74.4	-74.4	-50.1	10	NC	03-90	.40	2.5	7	7	NA	05-04-90	4.0	1.05	4.2	2.86	12.0	39	1.7	1,214	75,270	53,363	0	2.0	12
Birmingham St	1.7	1.4	6.9	24.1n		1.96	-40.8	-46.7	-41.3	12	NC	03-90	.50	2.6	13	13	6	05-01-90	5.4	1.48	8.0	2.08	16.6	21	1.3	235	12,231	3,804	0	0.5	08
British Steel	NA	NA	NA	NA		NA	NA	NA	NA	NC	NA	00-00	1.85	7.4	0	188	NA	06-29-90	NA	NC	NA	NC	NA	NA	NA	5,025	200,000	0	0	NA	NA
Broken Hill	-5.1	7.3	-12.2	800.4s		.51	-21.1	-5.6	-78.8	-10	NC	11-89	.82	2.8b	0	66	53	11-03-89	9.7	.55	5.3	3.00	15.9	105	1.3	10,627	360,252	1,672	0	1.2	06
Carpenter Tech	-7.4	-7.1	-4.6	46.5n		5.16	2583.3	119.0	79.2	16	NC	03-90	2.40	4.4	0	66	103	04-30-90	7.7	.90	6.9	2.12	14.6	41	2.3	487	8,936	5,928	+0	0.0	06
CCX Inc	53.8	-50.8	37.7	-4.3n		-1.12	-100.0	-100.0	-100.0	-35	NC	03-90	.00	.0	0	0	0	--:--	-6.9	1.51	-10.4	3.37	-35.0	91	1.8	10	3,913	890	+270	0.0	06
CF I Steel	5.9	5.9	3.8	-9.9q		-1.50	NE	NE	NE	-18	NC	03-90	.00	.0	0	0	0	--:--	-3.3	1.15	-3.8	4.68	-17.8	234	1.5	7	6,615	1,374	-6	0.0	12
Chaparral Steel	-17.1	-10.3	-2.1	29.9n		.93	-68.4	-55.7	-38.8	14	NC	02-90	.20	2.1	6	6	4	05-01-90	7.2	1.11	8.0	2.30	18.4	59	2.3	283	29,939	4,587	0	0.0	05
Copperweld Cp	-.9	-.9	-1.6	14.4q		1.56	-36.3	-36.3	-34.5	11	NC	11-89	.24	2.4	6	21	83	05-09-90	4.9	1.18	5.8	2.47	14.3	53	1.9	148	8,764	1,488	0	0.0	12
CSC Inds	-1.4	-1.4	-24.5	-33.8q		-3.91	NE	NE	NE	NC	NC	03-90	.00	.0	0	0	0	--:--	-19.7	1.29	-25.5	.00	NM	44	.7	9	8,632	1,053	0	0.0	12
Foster L B	5.2	5.2	-6.5	1.8q		.17	66.7	66.7	-76.4	4	NC	03-90	.00	.0	0	89	NE	01-07-66	.7	2.57	1.8	2.11	3.8	10	1.7	57	9,870	4,042	0	0.0	12
Friedman Ind	-11.9	-3.1	-3.7	1.9n		.43	12.5	-31.0	-23.2	6	NC	12-89	.21	4.7b	21	44	203	06-29-90	3.7	2.35	8.7	1.39	12.1	7	4.2	20	4,351	593	0	0.0	06
Geneva Steel A	NA	NA	NA	NA		NA	NA	NA	NA	NC	NC	03-90	.00	.0	NA	NA	NA	00-00	NA	NC	NA	NC	NA	NA	NA	208	17,853	0	0	NA	NA
Inland Steel	-9.9	-9.9	-3.9	89.0q		2.14	-73.2	-73.2	-69.3	2	NC	03-90	1.40	4.4	0	44	42	05-02-90	2.2	1.36	3.0	2.00	6.0	39	2.5	1,114	34,664	27,190	+1	0.6	12
Interlake Cp	-15.2	-15.2	-4.0	-9.5q		-.94	-100.0	-100.0	NC	NC	NC	03-90	.00	.0	0	0	0	00-00	-1.1	1.45	-1.6	.00	NS	-258	1.6	84	10,193	4,273	0	0.7	12
Keystone ◻	10.5	10.5	3300.0	9.5q		2.42	76.7	76.7	NC	37	NC	03-90	.00	.0	0	0	0	00-00	3.1	1.77	5.5	6.80	37.4	84	.8	115	5,475	856	-34	0.0	12
Laclede Steel	-5.9	-5.9	-3.5	7.1q		1.73	-76.8	-76.8	-54.2	5	NC	03-90	.40	2.5	12	18	14	02-03-90	2.4	1.17	2.8	2.21	6.2	45	2.8	64	4,056	828	0	0.0	09
Lindberg Corp ◇	-9.4	-9.4	-6.0	2.7q		.56	-25.0	-25.0	-25.3	6	NC	03-90	.28	5.0	9	46	56	05-04-90	3.5	1.57	5.5	2.11	11.6	40	2.5	27	4,725	872	0	0.0	12
Lukens Inc	6.9	6.9	4.7	45.3q		5.16	51.8	51.8	30.6	19	NC	03-90	1.40	3.6	32	23	24	05-01-90	6.9	1.74	12.0	2.23	26.7	34	2.1	324	8,228	4,791	0	0.0	12

LW Grp	-15.8	-15.8	-9.8	-23.5q	-1.34	NE	NE	NE	.00	0	NC	0	-73	03-90	.00	0	0	00-00-00	.00	-5.5	215	-11.8	.00	NS	446	7	21,181	6,097	0	8.3	12
Margate Ventures ▲ □	-20.7	-20.7	-22.2	-2.4q	-.08	0	0	-100.0	-.08	-73	NC	0	0	00-00-00	.00	NE	NE	00-00-00	.00	-8.6	1.71	-14.7	4.95	-72.7	39	1	20,961	10	0	0.0	12
Natl Intergrp ▲ □	-13.6	-3.3	3.2	26.3n	.76	-90.5	NE	0	.76	4	NC	12-89	03-25-89	NE	NS	3.8	389	21,74E	8,437	0	0.6	03
Natl-Standard	-8.7	-7.6	-3.3	-13.5q	-3.92	NE	NE	NE	-3.92	-20	NC	03-90	02-27-87	.9	1.56	-7.5	2.71	-20.3	68	18	4,465	1,404	0	2.4	08
New Jersey Steel □	-7.3	-10.7	-10.7	5.8	1.01	NE	-63.3	-63.3	1.01	3	NC	11-89	03-26-90	-4.6	1.63	5.6	2.71	6.8	78	5,784	1,597	-8	11
Oregon Steel	30.1	30.1	22.6	23.4q	2.95	50.8	50.8	6.9	2.95	15	NC	05-04-90	.80	2.1	0	0	30	20	05-04-90	00-00-00	9.4	1.52	14.3	1.46	20.9	6	305	7,875	3,372	+0	0.1	12
Petibone Cp	.0	12.2	12.3	4.3q	.67	-47.1	-5.6	-5.6	.67	38	NC	03-90	.80	0	0	30	20	2.9	2.17	6.3	6.10	38.4	193	27	9,131	43	0	0.0	08
Proler Intl	-14.1	-14.1	-16.3	1.3q	.26	-86.1	-93.6	-93.6	.26	-1	NC	04-90	.32	2.6	-3	0	43	34	06-25-90	1.3	.77	1.0	1.30	1.3	70	93	4,714	2,576	0	4.9	01
Quanex Cp	25.8	25.7	16.2	24.6q	1.74	-15.9	-32.2	-26.9	1.74	14	NC	04-90	.40	2.4	0	11	14	06-11-90	4.3	1.42	6.1	3.03	18.5	7	207	12,277	6,621	+0	3.7	10
Roanoke Elec	-9.6	-7.6	-6.1	9.6q	1.81	-42.2	-46.4	-27.9	1.81	12	23	NC	04-90	05-02-90	.48	3.6	-3	0	14	23	6.3	1.29	8.1	2.05	16.6	29	71	5,333	1,710	0	0.0	10
Steel West Va	-13.4	-13.4	-5.1	5.7q	1.09	-8.8	-8.8	-10.7	1.09	56	NC	00-00-00	.00	0	491	185	349	6.2	1.40	8.7	6.43	55.9	18	64	5,000	1,097	0	0.0	11
Talley Ind	.7	.7	8.7	25.7q	2.08	0	0	123.7	2.08	13	NC	06-12-90	.00	6.9	-1	19	43	170	6.1	.39	2.4	7.08	17.0	187	8,797	2,690	+32	25.2	12
Tubos Mexico	123.6	124.0	123.8	160.9n	.85	NE	NE	NE	.85	17	NC	12-88	.50	.0	0	0	0	17	45.2	.27	12.4	1.33	16.5	108	21,000	2,723	0	0.3	12
UNR Inds	10.4	10.4	3.1	46.8q	1.01	66.7	66.7	-81.8	1.01	20	NC	04-90	.00	.0	0	0	33	4	11.9	1.29	15.3	1.30	19.9	207	46,092	1,181	0	0.0	12
USX Cp ◇	5.2	5.2	9.2	845.0q	3.32	-39.4	-46.4	-3.8	3.32	9	NC	04-30-90	1.40	4.2	6	37	153	107	5.8	1.07	4.8	3.29	15.8	8,434	255,563	139,050	+3	2.4	05
Valley Inds	-14.7	-21.1	-20.6	-8.5f	-.94	-100.0	-100.0	-10.7	-.94	9	NC	11-89	.00	.0	0	0	0	123	-11.0	2.65	-29.1	.00	NM	6	9,063	795	0	0.0	11
Weirton Steel □	-14.4	-14.4	-8.9	31.7q	1.51	350.0	350.0	NE	1.51	6	NC	05-25-90	.64	6.8	0	23	0	108	2.5	1.32	3.3	2.94	9.7	187	19,949	4,734	+8	0.2	12
Wheel-Pitts St □ ◆	-10.7	-10.7	-1.0	126.0q	2.270	-9.8	-9.8	-31.4	2.270	0	NC	00-00-00	.00	.0	0	0	0	3	11.3	.75	8.5	.00	NM	40	5,115	300	0	39.3	12
Worthington Ind ○	-9.4	-9.0	-8.9	53.2f	1.33	-12.7	-15.8	-15.8	1.33	9	NC	05-90	.60	2.4	15	30	153	41	15	5.8	1.64	9.5	1.75	16.6	981	40,045	15,360	+3	0.0	05

					Copper Mining																					
Ind. Group	248.9	743.3	727.7	359.7	.92	62.0	188.3	42.7	.92	40	NC	---	2.24	21	0	45	28	---	9.9	.98	9.7	5.33	51.7	230	4,635	372,915	46,580	+60	2.1	--
Ashland Coal	17.8	17.8	25.0	24.7q	1.51	10.5	10.5	-16.1	1.51	17	NC	05-09-90	.32	1.4	0	16	5	7.5	1.03	7.7	2.73	21.0	22	268	11,539	2,643	0	1.8	12
Atlas Consol B	1833.9	1833.9	493.8	21.6q	.06	158.3	158.3	-13.3	.06	63	NC	00-00-00	.00	.0	0	0	0	212	1.5	3.73	5.6	11.29	63.2	115	83,611	436	0	7.9	12
Avery Inc	-100.0	-99.4	-100.0	-14.5f	-1.78	NE	NE	NE	-1.78	0	NC	09-99	.00	.0	0	0	0	-313	NC	NC	NS	NC	NS	11	12,365	582	0	0.0	09
Campbell Rsc	16.5	16.5	6.4	2.8q	.03	0	0	NE	.03	4	NC	05-21-94	.00	.0	0	0	0	18	8.5	.31	2.6	1.50	3.9	49	77,700	2,830	+82	0.1	12
Fire Mc Cop	-4.6	-4.6	5.5	89.5q	1.05	-37.9	-37.9	-5.4	1.05	47	NC	04-09-90	.60	2.0	6	97	52	90	24.6	.88	26	2.88	62.3	1,046	85,380	7,730	0	0.2	12
Magma Copper □	48.1	48.1	18.7	37.5q	1.30	-55.3	-55.3	-29.0	1.30	8	NC	00-00-00	.00	.0	0	0	0	86	5.3	.74	3.9	2.13	8.3	140	27,967	15,245	0	8.4	12
Newmont Mng □	25.2	25.2	35.4	173.9q	2.58	507.1	507.1	14.7	2.58	0	NC	05-17-90	.60	1.4	6	32	27	-483	24.4	.55	13.4	.00	NS	2,938	67,353	17,114	+8	0.0	12
O'Okiep Copp	-65.4	-48.4	-48.1	24.2q	3.46	-26.3	-26.3	-19.0	3.46	16	NC	12-22-88	1.59	16.3	15	33	17	0	59.0	.39	23.1	1.26	29.1	68	7,000	0	0	0.0	12

					Copper Refining																					
Ind. Group	-14.5	-14.5	1.3	410.8	5.26	-38.2	-38.2	-46.8	5.26	8	NC	---	2.24	5.4	0	103	37	---	8.7	.95	8.3	1.77	14.7	27	3,163	76,235	45,495	+0	.8	--
ASARCO Inc	-15.7	-15.7	-2.1	198.4q	4.73	-47.2	-47.2	-14.0	4.73	9	NC	05-04-90	1.60	6.0	0	27	19	23	9.4	.86	8.1	1.70	13.8	1,103	41,616	20,526	+0	0.3	12
Phelps Dodge	-13.5	-13.5	4.2	212.4q	5.90	-34.6	-34.6	-61.1	5.90	8	NC	05-14-90	3.00	5.0	0	169	52	32	8.2	1.04	8.5	1.85	15.7	2,060	34,619	24,969	0	1.3	12

					Aluminum Refining																					
Ind. Group	-2.6	-2.5	3.0	2,041.6	5.40	-41.4	-41.4	-20.0	5.40	12	NC	---	1.34	3.5	2	26	26	---	7.9	.97	7.7	2.12	16.3	28	14,046	371,343	211,189	+0	.4	--
Alcan Alum Ltd	-5.1	-5.1	-1.0	738.0q	3.16	-36.2	-36.2	-26.7	3.16	10	NC	05-14-90	1.12	5.0	13	31	30	23	8.5	.92	7.8	2.05	16.0	5,037	223,879	113,038	0	0.1	12
Alum Co Of Am	.5	.5	5.8	817.5q	9.24	-45.8	-45.8	-14.8	9.24	13	NC	04-30-90	1.60	2.5	13	25	30	32	7.5	.95	7.1	2.21	15.7	5,574	87,435	35,394	-0	0.9	12
Genl Metal	.0	.0	.0	.2q	.19	33.3	33.3	100.0	.19	10	NC	00-00-00	.00	.0	0	0	0	24	10.0	.71	7.1	1.34	9.5	699	0	0.0	06
Renolds Metal	-4.1	-4.1	4.0	485.9q	8.23	-42.5	-42.5	-17.5	8.23	14	NC	06-01-90	1.80	3.1	27	18	21	42	8.0	1.09	8.7	2.08	18.1	3,434	59,330	112,757	+0	0.7	12

(continued)

Lead, Nickel, Tin, Zinc Mining and Ref

Company	Revenue Pct. Change Last Qtr %	FY to Date %	Last 12 Mos %	Last 12 Mos $Mil	Earnings Per Share Last 12 Mos $	Pct Change Last Qtr %	FY to Date %	Last 12 Mos %	5-Year Growth Rate %	Par Growth Rate %	Date of Report	Dividends Current Rate Amt $	Yield %	5-Year Growth Rate %	Payout Last FY %	Last 5 Yrs %	Last X-Dvd Date	Ratio Analysis Pro-ft Mar-gin %	Asset Turn-over	Return on Total Assets	Lever-age Ratio	Return on Equity	Debt to Eq-uity %	Curr-ent Ratio	Shareholdings Mar-ket Value $Mil	Latest Shares Out-stndng 000	Held by Banks-Funds 000	Insider Net Trad-ing 000	Short Int-erest Ratio Days	Fiscal Year Ends Mo
Ind. Group	-30.6	-30.0	-4.9	640.4	2.86	-75.4	-75.4	-38.7	NC	18	---	.71	3.2	0	17	17	---	12.8	.80	10.3	2.38	24.5	53	2.1	4,898	219,520	46,373	+469	2.1	--
Cominco Ltd	-20.0	-20.0	-8.4	140.8q	1.73	-76.4	NA	-33.2	NC	9	03-90	.50	2.2	NA	19	32	06-05-90	10.8	.61	6.6	1.89	12.5	32	2.6	1,779	79,085	2,944	0	0.0	12
Curragh Res	NA	NA	NA	NA	NA	NA	NA	NA	NC	NC	00-00	.00	.0	NA	NA	NA	00-00-00	NA	NC	NA	NC	NA	NA	NA	19	2,500	0	0	NA	NA
Gulf Res & Ch	-17.0	-17.0	2.8	-56.7q	-6.06	-100.0	NA	-100.0	NC	-51	03-90	1.30	16.0	0	0	0	01-07-89	-79.9	.24	-19.4	2.15	-41.7	66	5.5	80	9,798	1,720	+467	14.2	12
Inco Ltd	-34.3	-34.3	-3.7	562.1q	5.31	-73.8	-73.8	-32.1	NC	35	03-90	1.00	3.50	0	16	16	04-25-90	15.8	.97	15.3	2.86	43.6	72	1.8	2,983	104,574	40,899	+2	0.6	12
Stansbury Hldgs	.0	.0	.0	-.40	-.02	NE	NE	.0	NC	-1	09-88	.00	.0	0	0	0	00-00-00	NC	0	NC	NC	NC	0	.0	5	10,949	0	0	0.0	06
Utd Park City	.0	.0	-100.0	-1.6q	-.16	NE	NE	NE	NC	-14	03-90	.00	.0	0	0	0	00-00-00	NC	NC	NC	NC	-14.4	0	.3	11	10,801	629	0	0.0	12
Zenex Cp	6.2	6.2	5.1	-3.8q	-2.11	NE	NE	-100.0	NC	-17	03-90	.00	.0	0	0	85	03-06-90	-9.3	.95	-8.8	1.96	-17.2	35	1.4	10	1,813	181	0	0.0	12

r/t x t/a = r/a = r/e; r/t x t/a x a/e = r/e

Source: Media General Financial Services, Richmond, VA.

Motor Vehicles

Trends and Forecasts: Motor Vehicles and Car Bodies (SIC 3711)
(in millions of dollars except as noted)

Item	1987[1]	1988[2]	1989[3]	1990[4]	Percent Change 1987–88	Percent Change 1988–89	Percent Change 1989–90
Industry Data							
Value of shipments[5]	133,339	—	—	—	—	—	—
Value of shipments (1987$)	133,339	—	—	—	—	—	—
Total employment (000)	285	—	—	—	—	—	—
Production workers (000)	236	—	—	—	—	—	—
Average hourly earnings ($)	17.33	—	—	—	—	—	—
Product Data							
Value of shipments[6]	130,851	—	—	—	—	—	—
Value of shipments (1987$)	130,851	—	—	—	—	—	—
Trade Data							
Value of imports	61,915	61,472	—	—	-0.7	—	—
Import/new supply ratio[7]	0.315	—	—	—	—	—	—
Value of exports	10,349	11,663	—	—	12.7	—	—
Export/shipments ratio	0.079	—	—	—	—	—	—

[1]Industry and product data are preliminary. Trade data are adjusted to conform to the 1987 SIC.
[2]Estimated, except for exports and imports.
[3]Estimated.
[4]Forecast.
[5]Value of all products and services sold by establishments in the motor vehicles and car bodies industry.
[6]Value of products classified in the motor vehicles and car bodies industry produced by all industries.
[7]New supply is imports plus corresponding product shipments.

SOURCE: U.S. Department of Commerce: Bureau of the Census; International Trade Administration (ITA). Estimates and forecasts by ITA.

Source: *U.S. Industrial Outlook 1990*, U.S. Department of Commerce.

Trends and Forecasts: Automotive Parts and Accessories (SIC 3465, 3592, 3647, 3691, 3694, 3714)
(in millions of dollars except as noted)

Item	1987[1]	1988[2]	1989[3]	1990[4]	Percent Change		
					1987–88	1988–89	1989–90
Industry Data							
Value of shipments[5]	91,002	94,814	99,121	103,346	4.2	4.5	4.3
Value of shipments (1987$)	91,002	92,052	93,510	94,813	1.2	1.6	1.4
Total employment (000)	631	639	649	657	1.3	1.6	1.2
Production workers (000)	504	513	521	528	1.8	1.6	1.3
Average hourly earnings ($)	13.99	-	-	-	-	-	-
Product Data							
Value of shipments[6]	87,683	91,429	95,989	99,640	4.3	5.0	3.8
Value of shipments (1987$)	87,683	88,766	90,555	91,413	1.2	2.0	0.9
Trade Data							
Value of imports[7]	16,241	18,912	19,865	19,989	16.4	5.0	0.6
Import/new supply ratio[7]	0.156	0.175	0.175	0.170	12.2	0.0	-2.9
Value of exports	12,102	14,164	15,891	17,062	17.0	12.2	7.4
Export/shipments ratio	0.138	0.158	0.169	0.175	14.5	7.0	3.5

[1]Industry and product data are preliminary. Trade data are adjusted to conform to the 1987 SIC.

[2]Estimated, except for exports and imports.

[3]Estimated.

[4]Forecast.

[5]Value of all products and services sold by establishments in the automotive parts & accessories industry.

[6]Value of products classified in the automotive parts & accessories industry produced by all industries.

[7]New supply is imports plus corresponding product shipments.

SOURCE: U.S. Department of Commerce: Bureau of the Census; International Trade Administration (ITA). Estimates and forecasts by ITA.

Source: *U.S. Industrial Outlook 1990*, U.S. Department of Commerce.

MEDIA GENERAL FINANCIAL SERVICES

STOCKS by INDUSTRY

Company	Rev % Last Qtr	Rev % FY to Date	Rev % Last 12 Mos	Last 12 Mos $Mil	EPS Last 12 Mos $	EPS % Last Qtr	EPS % FY to Date	EPS % Last 12 Mos	EPS 5-Yr Gr %	Par Gr %	Date of Report	Div Amt $	Div Yield %	Div 5-Yr Gr %	Payout Last FY %	Payout Last 5 Yrs %	Last X-Dvd Date	Profit Margin %	Asset Turnover	Return Total Assets	Leverage Ratio	Return Equity	Debt to Eq %	Current Ratio	Market Value $Mil	Latest Shares Outstndg 000	Held by Funds 000	Insider Net Trad 000	Short Int Ratio Days	Fiscal Yr Ends Mo
Auto Manufacturers																														
Ind. Group	-13.3	-12.3	-3.6	7,242.4	3.34	-50.0	-40.4	-37.2	1	5	---	1.69	5.2	2	40	25	---	2.4	.71	1.7	5.59	9.5	184	2.5	72,526	2,249,673	672,420	+159	1.6	--
Amertek Inc	20.9	.0	.0	-6.11	-1.89	-100.0	-100.0	-100.0	NC	-70	12-89	.00		0	0	0	00-00-00	-18.5	2.23	-41.2	1.70	-70.1		2.1	19	44,268	223	0	0.0	--
Athey Prods	-3.8	-3.8	2.5	3.6q	.96	-26.1	-26.1	-4.0	19	11	03-90	.10	1.1	0	0	0	05-09-90	8.8	1.18	10.4	1.18	12.3	2	6.8	34	3,867	781	0	0.0	12
Chrysler Cp	-24.1	-24.1	-13.7	79.0q	.37	-78.7	-78.7	-93.1	-25	-2	03-90	1.20	7.6	32	74	17	06-12-90	.2	1.00	.2	5.50	1.1	235	NA	3,514	223,100	182,233	0	1.2	12
ESI Ind	-15.0	-15.0	-9.9	.40	.10	NE	NE	-9.1	-17	2	03-90	.00	.0	0	0	0	10-09-87	.4	2.00	.8	2.50	2.0	NA	2.0	5	4,750	928	+2	0.0	12
Fiat SPA	NA	NA	NA	NA	NA	NA	NA	NE	NA	NC	00-00	.00	.0	NA	NA	NA	00-00-00	NA	NC	NA	NC	NA	NA	NA	2,260	54,294	55	0	NA	12
Ford Motor Co	-8.8	-8.8	-3.7	2704.2q	5.88	-68.0	-68.0	-47.0	13	6	03-90	3.00	6.9	35	36	23	04-26-90	2.9	.59	1.7	7.00	11.9	365	5.9	20,685	472,800	235,997	+15	2.0	12
Ford Motor Cda	-13.0	-13.0	-5.0	206.3q	20.70	-96.4	-96.4	-37.7	9	12	03-90	4.00	2.8	-6	36	19	03-05-90	1.6	4.19	6.7	2.24	15.0	2	1.3	1,184	8,291	153	0	0.0	12
Gen Motors	-9.6	-9.6	2.4	3381.3q	4.99	-57.0	-57.0	-34.7	0	0	03-90	3.00	6.3	10	47	55	05-11-90	2.8	.71	2.0	4.85	9.7	106	1.8	28,846	605,684	232,985	+137	3.3	12
Honda Motor	-17.4	-7.7	-7.7	517.0q	1.06	800.0	606.7	606.7	-19	6	03-90	.17	.7	35	30	33	03-23-90	2.1	1.43	3.0	2.53	7.6	33	1.2	11,020	473,997	4,894	0	19.1	03
Larizza Inds	-16.2	-16.2	5.3	-33.2q	-2.41	NE	NE	NE	NC	0	03-90	.00	.0	0	NE	NE	00-00-00	-18.7	1.36	-25.4	.00	NS	-50	.5	33	13,805	871	0	0.8	08
Mack Trucks	-20.4	-20.4	-21.8	-220.3q	-7.41	-100.0	-100.0	-100.0	4	-65	03-90	.00	.0	0	0	0	00-00-00	-13.4	1.01	-13.6	4.76	-64.7	95	1.0	156	29,696	10,753	0	0.0	12
Oshkosh Truck	16.9	18.6	22.2	8.66	.97	-44.4	-58.2	-45.2	4	3	03-90	.50	5.1	33	33	12	07-09-90	1.9	2.26	4.3	1.60	6.9	86	2.6	88	9,008	3	+5	0.0	09
Rawson-Koenig Inc	22.6	21.4	8.3	.28	.08	100.0	200.0	166.7	NC	7	03-90	.00	.0	0	0	0	00-00-00	1.5	1.67	2.5	2.84	7.1	54	1.7	1	3,901		0	0.0	09
Spartan Motors	10.1	10.1	8.8	1.1q	.25	-12.5	-12.5	-35.9	34	14	03-90	.05	1.0	0	0	0	06-20-88	3.0	2.13	6.4	2.64	16.9	24	1.8	24	4,614	329	0	0.0	12
Subaru of Amer	-33.3	-29.2	-6.2	12.4s	.24	NE	NE	NE	NC	7	04-90	.00	.0	0	0	111	11-17-87	.8	2.13	1.7	3.88	6.6		1.1	401	48,573	8,603	0	0.0	10
Volkr	.0	.0	.0	-1.9q	-.01	NC	NC	NC	NC	-56	12-89	.00	.0	0	0	0	00-00-00	NC	NC	NC	NC	-55.9	9	5.2	27	171,420		0	0.0	09
Volvo AB ADR	-39.5	-39.5	-14.2	590.8q	16.36	282.4	282.4	119.9	NC	21	03-90	2.18	4.0	0	17	18	04-24-90	4.5	.93	4.2	5.81	24.4	9	1.4	4,229	77,605	243	0	0.0	12
Automotive Parts and Accessories																														
Ind. Group	2.1	4.4	2.0	329.8	.58	-63.1	-100.0	-58.6	0	0	---	.59	3.0	1	64	42	---	1.4	1.21	1.7	3.18	5.4	89	1.8	10,032	502,451	198,021	+8	2.9	--
Allen Group	5.2	5.2	1.1	11.0q	.85	55.6	55.6	-5.6	NC	9	03-90	.00	.0	0	0	NE	10-25-88	3.1	1.13	3.5	2.43	23.0	78	2.6	143	8,366	4,602	-6	0.9	12
Appld Power	9.6	106.5	99.5	19.1n	1.45	-23.5	-23.5	-3.3	NC	20	03-90	.12	.50	0	5	7	05-14-90	4.6	1.11	5.1	4.31	22.0	195	1.8	302	12,724	6,524	-6	0.1	08
Arvin Indus	7.0	7.0	14.6	21.5q	.73	-85.7	-85.7	-24.0	41	NC	05-90	.68	4.1	4	86	42	08-31-90	1.4	1.36	1.9	3.16	6.0	93	1.7	315	18,805	5,842	+0	0.1	12
Audiovox	8.3	8.3	-3.5	-.1q	.00	NE	NE	NE	NC	NC	00-00	.00	.0	0	0	0	00-00-00	.0	NC	NC	NC	-2	50	3.3	34	9,007	623	0	0.4	12
Autdole Cp	-7.8	8.3	16.6	-1.2q	-.24	-100.0	-100.0	-100.0	NC	-3	02-90	.00	.0	0	0	0	02-09-90	-1.0	.60	-.6	4.83	-2.9	341	3.0	26	5,151	557	0	0.8	08

(continued)

Automotive Parts and Accessories (Continued)

Company	Rev %Chg Last Qtr	Rev %Chg FY to Date	Rev %Chg Last 12 Mos	Earn Last 12 Mos $Mil	Earn Last 12 Mos $	EPS %Chg Last Qtr	EPS %Chg FY to Date	EPS %Chg Last 12 Mos	EPS 5-Yr Growth Rate	EPS Par Growth Rate	Earn Date of Report	Div Current Rate Amt	Div Yield	Div 5-Yr Growth Rate	Payout Last FY	Payout Last 5 Yrs	Last X-Dvd Date	Profit Margin	Asset Turnover	Return on Total Assets	Leverage Ratio	Return on Equity	Debt to Equity	Current Ratio	Mkt Value $Mil	Latest Shares Outstanding 000	Held by Banks/Funds 000	Insider Net Trading 000	Short Int Ratio Days	Fiscal Yr Ends Mo
Barnes Group	9.7	9.7	4.8	12.6a	2.02	15.1	15.1	-32.0	1	3	03-90	1.40	4.7	12	72	47	05-24-90	2.4	1.58	3.8	2.95	11.2	87	1.9	179	6,067	2,620	0	0.0	12
Buel Indus	-39.0	-39.0	-12.3	-2.8a	-1.24	31.3	31.3	-100.0	NC	-8	01-90	.20	1.1	11	NE	29	05-15-90	-3.6	1.39	-5.0	1.46	-7.3	4	3.0	41	2,285	515	0	20.0	10
Champ Parts	15.8	15.8	2.4	-1.9a	-.54	NE	NE	NE	NC	-7	03-90	.00	.0	NE	0	46	05-01-90	-1.5	1.47	-2.2	3.14	-6.9	30	1.9	14	3,655	564	0	0.0	12
Code Alarm	68.1	68.1	62.5	2.4a	1.01	125.0	125.0	50.7	NC	13	03-90	.00	.0	NC	0	NE	00-00-00	6.2	1.68	10.4	1.25	13.0	1	4.0	38	2,676	889	+0	0.0	12
Dana Corp	-4.2	-4.2	-3.8	116.3a	2.84	-41.7	-41.7	-30.6	4	5	03-90	1.60	4.3	6	49	47	05-25-90	2.3	.96	2.2	5.18	11.4	149	NA	1,514	40,917	24,700	+0	6.5	12
Defiance Inc	-10.2	-2.0	6.7	1.2n	.21	-100.0	-100.0	-100.0	6	6	03-90	.00	.0	0	0	0	00-00-00	1.9	1.21	2.3	2.70	6.2	67	.9	7	5,911	900	0	0.0	06
Donaldson	12.2	4.9	5.1	19.0n	1.97	57.4	27.1	18.7	12	14	04-90	.44	1.3	2	23	25	05-29-90	4.6	2.02	9.3	1.90	17.7	29	2.3	328	9,679	4,631	+31	0.5	07
Durakon Ind	50.2	50.2	53.1	-15.8n	-2.58	NE	NE	NE	NC	-81	03-90	.00	.0	0	0	0	02-03-86	-10.7	2.45	-26.2	3.09	-81.0	125	2.5	43	6,164	1,716	0	0.0	12
Eaton Corp	-1.7	-1.7	8.5	211.4q	5.67	-18.2	-18.2	-11.0	7	12	03-90	2.00	3.2	22	33	28	05-01-90	5.8	1.19	6.9	2.68	18.5	73	2.1	2,290	36,414	20,442	+3	3.1	12
Echlin Inc	12.1	8.5	7.7	36.9n	.66	-6.3	-18.2	-39.4	7	12	05-90	.70	5.0	13	83	53	06-29-90	2.4	1.50	3.6	1.61	5.8	17	2.8	774	55,793	40,012	+4	3.3	08
Envirosource	12.6	12.6	-37.3	10.6q	-.03	NE	NE	-25.6	10	8	03-90	.00	.0	0	0	0	00-00-00	5.4	.41	2.2	32.14	70.7	1191	.5	55	10,171	3,701	0	0.0	12
Excel Ind	-20.7	-20.7	-5.0	5.8q	.90	-53.8	-53.8	-25.6	23	8	03-90	.40	3.4b	23	34	38	06-29-90	2.2	1.59	4.6	2.70	12.4	88	2.5	75	6,453	1,712	0	0.1	12
Hastings Mfg	.0	.0	2.9	2.0q	4.60	159.6	159.6	389.4	NC	-5	03-90	.60	1.3	-5	18	19	05-14-90	2.9	1.59	4.6	2.07	9.5	55	3.8	19	420	420	0	25.0	12
Internet Cp	-11.6	-11.6	-.7	9.2q	.44	-92.3	-92.3	-47.0	-2	5	03-90	.20	2.8	3	29	20	05-04-90	2.4	1.67	4.0	2.18	8.7	45	2.0	129	17,795	4,300	0	0.0	12
Jason Inc	31.1	31.1	33.7	4.1q	.68	-6.3	-6.3	17.2	NC	25	03-90	.00	.0	0	0	0	05-17-90	3.4	1.68	5.7	4.42	25.2	198	1.8	70	5,616	865	0	0.0	12
Jiffy Lube Intl	-29.8	-22.2	-20.0	-142.8n	-9.45	NE	NE	NE	NC	NC	12-88	.00	.0	NM	NE	0	03-23-87	NM	1.47	NC	2.92	-7.3	3044	.2	25	15,324	987	0	0.0	03
Kysor Ind	2.2	2.2	-3.7	-3.8q	-.74	500.0	500.0	-100.0	NC	-13	03-90	.60	5.3	21	47	46	07-05-90	-1.7	1.47	-2.5	2.92	-7.3	98	2.2	68	6,012	1,913	-2	1.7	12
Magna Intl	13.4	15.0	14.4	-196.5n	-7.07	-100.0	-100.0	-100.0	NC	-50	04-90	.00	.0	0	36	29	02-09-90	-10.8	1.16	-12.5	4.00	-50.0	148	1.1	80	27,819	5,365	0	0.0	07
Modine Mfg	-1.7	2.9	2.8	25.2n	1.68	14.6	14.6	-2.9	5	9	03-90	.68	3.4	16	36	0	05-23-90	5.8	1.50	8.7	1.69	14.7	19	2.4	299	14,773	4,586	-48	0.0	03
Mr Gasket	-1.8	-1.8	-10.9	-1.0q	-.09	NE	NE	NE	NC	NC	03-90	.00	.0	0	0	0	00-00-00	-.9	1.50	-.8	3.63	-2.9	229	5.0	2	10,525	1,417	0	0.0	12
Premier Ind	2.1	5.2	6.3	73.9n	1.26	7.4	16.0	14.5	18	24	02-90	.40	1.5	5	14	21	06-18-90	11.9	2.24	26.6	1.31	34.8	3	4.7	1,521	57,931	11,075	+25	9.1	05
Raytech Cp	14.5	14.5	-3.2	4.1n	.58	-7.1	-7.1	-7.1	NC	0	02-90	.05	2.4	0	0	NE	02-22-88	3.5	1.54	5.4	.00	NS	-163	.6	8	3,879	433	0	0.0	12
Schwitzer Inc	-7.7	-7.7	-13.7	2.3n	.89	-33.3	-33.3	-81.3	9	13	03-90	.00	.0	0	578	96	00-00-00	1.9	1.37	2.6	4.92	12.8	241	1.9	49	7,098	2,479	0	0.1	12
Simpson Indust	-8.6	-6.6	2.1	8.5q	.95	-59.0	-59.0	-31.5	-6	4	03-90	.56	5.4	11	50	44	06-01-90	4.4	1.57	6.9	1.93	13.3	39	2.0	100	9,601	4,920	0	0.0	12
Smith AO A	-13.6	-13.6	-9.6	-5.8q	-1.16	-13.6	-13.6	-100.0	NA	NC	03-90	.80	4.8	16	NE	47	07-25-90	-.6	1.17	-.7	3.14	-2.2	57	1.4	131	7,910	1,117	0	1.9	12
Smith AO B	NA	NA	NA	NA	NA	NA	NA	NA	NA	NC	03-90	.80	4.8	NA	NA	104	07-25-90	NA	NC	NA	NA	NA	NA	NA	58	3,497	2,333	NA	NA	12
Sparton Corp	35.5	9.5	-5.2	-9.8n	-1.25	-100.0	-100.0	-100.0	6	-16	03-90	.00	.0	6	NE	NE	12-11-89	-6.0	1.42	-8.5	1.91	-16.2	2	1.6	31	7,792	2,075	0	14.3	06
SPX Cp	1.3	1.3	3.9	72.9q	5.08	-67.4	-67.4	40.3	NC	29	03-90	1.00	3.4	0	247	114	08-20-90	11.5	1.10	12.7	2.80	35.6	74	2.2	432	14,846	6,627	0	2.7	12
Std Motor Prd	35.8	35.8	16.6	12.5q	.95	-18.5	-18.5	25.0	-6	6	03-90	.32	3.0	21	32	31	05-09-90	2.7	1.15	3.1	2.77	8.6	71	2.1	141	13,116	4,877	0	0.1	12
Std Products	8.9	22.0	20.5	14.3n	1.39	-77.6	-66.0	-54.9	0	0	03-90	.92	3.8	0	30	22	07-09-90	2.2	1.95	4.3	2.12	9.1	48	2.0	246	10,150	4,439	0	5.1	06
Sudbury Inc	-21.7	-6.9	-8.6	-6.9n	-.55	NE	-4.4	-6.2	-13	18	02-90	.00	.0	0	0	0	00-00-00	-1.4	1.43	-2.0	2.84	-13.0	299	1.4	50	12,819	1,204	0	0.0	05
Superior Ind	.0	.0	13.3	16.0q	1.83	18.5	18.5	18.5	26	26	03-90	.28	1.1	14	14	15	06-29-90	6.5	1.12	7.3	2.04	20.7	88	1.8	217	8,751	3,327	+0	1.6	12
Trico Prods	-7.8	-7.8	-2.4	.4q	.16	NE	NE	-95.0	NC	-3	03-90	1.00	2.6	0	1667	NE	06-04-90	.2	1.00	.2	2.50	.5	11	1.2	70	1,847	252	0	0.0	12
Venturian Cp	11.5	11.5	-13.1	-1.1q	-1.25	NE	NE	NE	NC	-7	03-90	.00	.0	0	0	0	03-11-85	-3.3	1.61	-5.3	1.40	-7.4	1	3.7	7	802	216	-0	0.0	12
Wynn's Intl	-1.0	-1.0	-5.3	6.2q	1.58	-46.4	-46.4	-22.9	NC	4	03-90	.60	2.8	0	30	63	05-16-90	2.2	1.50	3.3	2.15	7.1	47	2.4	83	3,868	2,534	0	0.0	12

Source: Media General Financial Services, Richmond, VA.

Trends and Forecasts: Total Retail and Selected Retail Establishments (SIC 52-59)

(in billion of dollars except as noted)

Type of Retailer	1987	1988	1989[1]	1990[2]	Percent Change		
					1987-88	1988-89[1]	1989-90[2]
Total retail sales	1,507	1,613	1,710	1,813	7.0	6.0	6.0
Department stores (SIC 5311)	151	159	168	178	5.3	3.8	6.0
Eating and drinking places (SIC 5812,5813)	147	157	167	179	6.8	6.4	7.2
Apparel and accessory stores (SIC 56)	79	83	88	93	5.1	6.0	5.7
Employment all retailing (000)	18,264	19,298	NA	NA	5.7	NA	NA
Average hourly earnings (dollars)	6.12	6.13	NA	NA	3.2	NA	NA

[1]Estimated.
[2]Forecast.
NA = Not available.

SOURCE: U.S. Department of Commerce: Bureau of the Census and International Trade Administration (ITA). Estimates and forecasts by ITA.

Source: U.S. Industrial Outlook 1990, U.S. Department of Commerce.

Trends and Forecasts: Food Retailing (SIC 54)

(in millions of dollars except where noted)

Item	1987	1988	1989[1]	1990[2]	Percent Change		
					1987-88	1988-89[1]	1989-90[2]
Retail Sales							
All food stores	314,287	331,387	353,921	380,465	5.4	6.8	7.5
All chain food stores	175,286	188,181	201,542	216,859	7.4	7.1	7.6
Grocery stores	296,105	312,119	333,967	359,439	5.4	7.0	7.6
Chain grocery stores	172,051	185,419	198,955	214,672	7.8	7.3	7.9
Meat, fish (seafood) markets	5,678	6,029	6,300	6,603	6.2	4.5	4.8
Retail bakeries	5,049	5,247	5,431	5,747	3.9	3.5	5.8
All other food stores	7,455	7,992	8,223	8,676	7.2	2.9	5.5
Employment and Earnings							
Total employment (000)	2,971	3,089	3,206	—	4.0	3.8	—
Nonsupervisory employment (000)	2,742	2,841	2,934	—	3.6	3.3	—
Average hourly earnings-nonsupervisory($)	6.99	7.00	7.14	—	—	2.0	—

[1]Estimated.
[2]forecast.

SOURCE: U.S. Department of Commerce: Bureau of Census, International Trade Administration (ITA).

Source: U.S. Industrial Outlook 1990, U.S. Department of Commerce.

STOCKS by INDUSTRY

MEDIA GENERAL FINANCIAL SERVICES

Ratio Analysis formula: = r/r x r/a = r/a I a/e = r/e

Company	Rev Qtr %	Rev FYtD %	Rev 12Mo %	Rev 12Mo $Mil	EPS 12Mo $	Earn Qtr %	Earn FY %	Earn FYtD %	Earn 12Mo %	Earn 5Yr %	Par Gr %	Date	Div Amt $	Div Yld %	Div 5Yr %	Payout FY %	Payout 5Yr %	X-Div Date	Prof Marg %	Asset T/O	ROA	Lever	ROE %	Debt/Eq %	Curr Ratio	Mkt Val $Mil	Shares 000	Held B-F 000	Insider Net 000	Short Int Days	Fiscal Mo
Ind. Group	-5.9	4.2	5.2	1,290.1	1.10	-100.0	NE	-100.0	-56.3	-8	-1	---	1.29	3.4	1	43	38	---	1.0	.90	.9	5.89	5.3	136	1.8	41,241	1,084,241	542,120	+2577	3.0	--

Retail Trade - Dept. Stores

Company	Rev Qtr %	Rev FYtD %	Rev 12Mo %	Rev 12Mo $Mil	EPS 12Mo $	Earn Qtr %	Earn FY %	Earn FYtD %	Earn 12Mo %	Earn 5Yr %	Par Gr %	Date	Div Amt $	Div Yld %	Div 5Yr %	Payout FY %	Payout 5Yr %	X-Div Date	Prof Marg %	Asset T/O	ROA	Lever	ROE %	Debt/Eq %	Curr Ratio	Mkt Val $Mil	Shares 000	Held B-F 000	Insider Net 000	Short Int Days	Fiscal Mo
Alexander's Inc	7.1	-1.8	-5.0	-4.8n	-.94	-100.0	NE	-100.0	-100.0	NC	-4	04-90	.00	.00	.	0	NE	00-00-00	-1.1	2.09	-2.3	1.91	-4.4	47	2.2	208	4,976	1,468	0	25.1	08
Ames Dept Stores	-14.0	-14.0	24.4	-638.2q	-17.34	NE	NE	NE	-100.0	NC	0	04-90	.00	.00	.	NE	NE	02-15-90	-13.2	2.27	-30.0	.00	NM	125	1.8	70	37,542	25,141	+0	9.3	01
Campeau Cp	-20.1	20.4	20.4	-1740.0f	-39.59	NE	NE	NE	-100.0	NC	0	01-90	.00	.00	.	NE	NE	05-03-89	-16.7	.73	-122	.00	NM	-3646	.9	71	40,845	285	+0	0.0	01
Carter Hawley ■	-.8	3.3	3.6	2.7h	.06	NE	NE	-82.4	-73.2	NC	0	04-90	.00	.00	.	0	NE	09-11-87	.1	1.00	.1	.00	NS	-452	2.8	162	28,749	8,254	+2389	13.4	08
Crowley Milner	3.7	3.7	3.6	.20	.30	NE	NE	-73.2	-73.2	NC	-3	04-90	1.00	3.8	-2	588	107	04-03-90	1.1	2.00	2.2	2.75	6.1	69	2.0	14	509	144	+43	0.2	01
Dayton Hudson ▫	6.4	6.4	10.7	428.0q	5.58	41.2	41.2	41.2	55.0	13	19	04-90	1.32	1.8	11	21	28	05-14-90	3.1	2.06	6.4	3.81	24.4	143	1.4	5,187	71,300	52,833	-25	0.7	01
Dillard Dept ▫	24.1	24.1	20.9	157.9q	4.57	34.4	34.4	34.4	25.5	18	14	04-90	.00	.00	.	2	4	06-25-90	4.9	1.29	6.3	2.29	14.4	71	2.9	3,081	35,009	15,127	+9	1.5	01
Gottschalks	21.2	21.2	20.5	3.4q	.42	-57.1	-57.1	-57.1	-28.8	NC	7	04-90	.00	.00	.	0	0	04-13-87	1.4	1.43	2.0	3.30	6.6	86	1.6	104	8,023	1,994	0	0.0	01
Hills Dept St	13.8	13.8	21.7	2.3q	.12	NE	NE	-29.4	-29.4	NC	22	04-90	.00	.00	.	0	0	00-00-00	.1	3.00	.3	71.67	21.5	5336	1.0	69	19,151	3,757	0	3.9	02
Interco ◆ ▫	-8.1	-17.7	-17.6	35.2l	-1.22	-100.0	-100.0	-100.0	-100.0	NC	0	02-90	.00	.00	.	0	8402	00-00-00	2.1	.95	2.0	.00	NS	-196	1.6	12	38,692	8,883	0	1.3	02
JG Industries	-16.3	-16.3	-5.5	2.5q	.35	NE	NE	NE	NE	-13	12	04-90	.00	.00	.	0	0	00-00-00	1.0	1.90	1.9	6.32	12.0	165	1.5	10	5,968	114	0	1.0	01
May Dept Strs ◆	-14.7	-14.7	-23.3	515.0q	3.76	28.9	28.9	28.9	2.5	11	13	04-90	1.58	2.9	12	38	39	08-27-90	5.6	1.18	6.6	3.36	22.2	129	2.0	6,886	124,355	77,515	+9	1.2	01
Mays J W ◆ ▫	-79.1	-63.2	-63.0	7.5f	3.45	NE	NE	NE	NE	30	11	07-89	.00	.00	.	0	0	00-00-00	27.8	.89	24.8	1.21	30.1	12	6.6	58	2,178	115	+0	0.9	01
Mercantile Strs	3.2	3.2	2.1	131.7q	3.58	5.5	5.5	5.5	-8.2	9	9	05-90	.97	2.4	14	25	21	05-25-90	5.7	1.49	8.5	1.44	12.2	18	4.6	1,488	36,844	13,860	+0	0.0	01
Nordstrom	8.4	8.4	12.7	105.1q	1.29	-42.9	-42.9	-42.9	-16.8	21	11	04-90	.29	.8	24	20	16	05-24-90	3.9	1.59	6.2	2.31	14.3	60	2.1	2,793	81,536	30,732	+17	0.0	01
Penney, JC	5.7	5.7	6.0	828.0q	6.55	24.7	24.7	24.7	8.6	20	14	04-90	2.64	4.4	14	35	35	07-03-90	5.1	1.27	6.5	3.49	22.7	76	2.2	7,287	120,194	69,667	-256	1.0	01
Proffitt's Inc	16.0	16.0	15.2	.33f	.33	550.0	550.0	550.0	-21.4	-1	6	04-90	.00	.00	.	0	0	00-00-00	5.9	1.17	1.4	4.21	5.9	261	3.7	15	2,747	452	+20	3.0	01
Sears, Roebuck ▫	3.7	3.7	5.4	1346.6q	3.88	-60.0	-60.0	-60.0	45.3	5	10	03-90	2.00	5.5	4	47	52	05-25-90	2.5	.60	1.5	6.60	9.9	74	1.8	12,498	342,402	177,802	+378	3.0	12
Strawbrid & Cloth	9.8	9.8	6.2	32.7q	3.58	100.0	100.0	100.0	21.8	6	10	07-90	1.10	3.4b	0	31	28	07-02-90	3.4	1.56	5.3	2.62	13.9	96	2.6	294	9,037	2,443	+0	0.0	01
Stuarts Dept	17.5	17.5	10.6	-.90	-.15	NE	NE	NE	-100.0	NC	-4	04-90	.00	.00	.	0	0	09-03-86	-.4	3.25	-1.3	2.69	-3.5	74	2.0	9	4,301	481	+2	0.0	01
TJX Companies	10.2	10.2	15.1	73.7q	1.21	-51.2	-51.2	-51.2	NE	20	0	04-90	.46	3.5	0	228	273	08-03-90	3.4	2.29	7.8	4.14	32.3	130	1.5	926	69,883	51,053	0	2.5	01

| **Ind. Group** | 18.8 | 19.1 | 16.2 | 2,554.1 | 1.49 | 18.9 | 18.9 | 19.7 | -6.0 | 18 | 17 | --- | .40 | 1.0 | 2 | 49 | 28 | 03-90 | 2.6 | 4.04 | 10.5 | 2.25 | 23.6 | 44 | 1.7 | 65,065 | 1,708,056 | 839,608 | +317 | 2.9 | -- |

Discount and Variety Stores

Company	Rev Qtr %	Rev FYtD %	Rev 12Mo %	Rev 12Mo $Mil	EPS 12Mo $	Earn Qtr %	Earn FY %	Earn FYtD %	Earn 12Mo %	Earn 5Yr %	Par Gr %	Date	Div Amt $	Div Yld %	Div 5Yr %	Payout FY %	Payout 5Yr %	X-Div Date	Prof Marg %	Asset T/O	ROA	Lever	ROE %	Debt/Eq %	Curr Ratio	Mkt Val $Mil	Shares 000	Held B-F 000	Insider Net 000	Short Int Days	Fiscal Mo
Advanced Mktg	36.1	33.2	32.6	.39f	.39	-100.0	NE	-57.6	-57.6	NC	6	03-90	.00	.00	.	0	0	00-00-00	1.1	3.09	3.4	1.88	6.4	0	2.1	37	5,843	2,896	0	0.0	08
Brendle's Inc	16.7	16.7	9.6	.41f	.41	NE	NE	192.9	192.9	NC	5	04-90	.00	.00	.	0	0	04-90	1.1	2.27	2.5	1.88	4.7	15	1.8	58	8,020	1,708	0	0.0	08
Child World	-1.2	-1.2	1.2	.31f	.31	NE	NE	-69.9	-69.9	NC	2	04-90	.00	.00	.	0	0	04-90	.4	2.25	1.6	1.78	1.6	63	1.5	142	11,397	2,204	0	0.0	08
Consol Store	6.4	6.4	-1.2	-9.6q	-.21	NE	NE	-100.0	-100.0	NC	-7	04-90	.00	.00	.	0	0	06-17-86	-1.6	1.94	-3.1	2.13	-6.6	63	3.0	239	45,520	18,117	0	0.9	08
Costco Wholesale	44.2	42.9	47.7	39.2h	1.18	NE	NE	36.2	57.3	16	16	05-90	.00	.00	.	0	0	00-00-00	1.0	6.30	6.3	2.57	16.2	55	1.1	1,447	33,948	17,308	+38	0.0	09

Company																													
Dollar General Cp	3.0	3.0	.0	13.2q	.72	NE	NE	24.1	-6	04-90	.20	.21	2	29	36	08-23-90	2.1	3.24	6.8	1.60	10.9	22	3.4	176	18.29l	18.29l	0	0.0	01
Family Dollar	15.9	17.4	17.7	26.6n	.96	64.7	27.7	14.3	-2	05-90	.40	.29	22	44	28	06-11-90	3.1	2.65	8.2	1.82	14.9		1.7	378	27.74l	12.007	+1	7.0	08
Home Shop Ntwk	37.9	30.1	25.7	4.8n	.04	NE	725.0	-50.0	NC	05-90	.08	.0	0	0	0	01-20-87	-.5	1.80	.9	3.78	3.4	204	2.2	729	89.75l	11,810		7.4	08
Jamesway Corp	15.6	15.6	10.4	6.0q	.42	NE	NE	-27.6	-13	04-90	.08	.14	11	20	0	07-02-90	.7	2.43	1.7	2.65	4.5	85	2.7	90	15.28l	4,587	-14	0.3	01
K mart Co	16.1	16.1	10.8	329.0q	1.64	6.4	6.4	-57.6	3	04-90	1.72	4.9	15	102	45	05-11-90	1.1	83.18	11.5	.01	26.4	60	1.8	6,989	199.67l	135,901	+10	1.4	01
Lawson Prods	7.4	7.4	5.8	22.8q	1.68	22.6	22.6	20.0	20	06-29-90	.36	1.3	NA	20	17	06-29-90	12.7	1.50	19.1	1.31	25.0	110	4.6	386	13.54l	4,989	+1	0.0	12
Lillian Vernon	1.7	1.7	7.6	10.9q	1.77	9.5	9.5	29.2	NC	05-90	.08		20		0	00-00-00	7.0	1.57	11.0	1.76	19.4	34	3.2	148	6.18l	1,130		7.4	02
Lionel Co	7.5	7.5	3.5	-2.1q	-.14	NE	NE	-100.0	NC	04-90	.08		0		0	00-00-00	-.5	1.80	-.9	2.67	-2.4	82	2.4	37	13.51l	2,451	0	16.8	01
Marcade Grp	70.9	31.2	26.4	7.6n	.11	-14.3	-14.3	NC	-2	10-89	.08	.0	14		0	00-00-00	1.8	2.24	4.7	3.47	16.3	144	2.8	28	24.45l	2,652	0	29.7	01
Michaels Str	16.9	20.2	22.7	4.5n	.43	-70.0	-70.0	-43.8	57	10-89	.08		3		12	10-09	1.6	2.06	11.5	3.48	11.5	183	3.7	61	9.69l	2,374	0	4.0	01
Nichols, SE	-60.6	-60.6	-45.9	-35.9q	-7.61	NE	NE	NE	NC	04-90	.00	.0	NA	NA	0	00-00-00	-20.6	1.34	-27.6	3.03	-83.7	110	2.3	2	4.71E	1,157	+16	1.0	01
Pic 'n Save	26.5	26.5	18.4	31.4q	.88	13.3	13.3	-26.4	1	03-90	.00	.0	722	72	0	06-11-86	6.3	1.63	10.3	1.38	14.2	6	2.0	436	35.967l	27,397	+241	0.2	12
Pier 1 Imports	21.5	21.5	25.5	26.5q	.74	15.8	15.8	2.8	8	05-90	.16	1.4	0	18	16	05-04-90	4.9	1.55	7.6	1.93	14.7	51	2.9	391	35.133l	13,344	-20	1.1	02
Price Co	8.3	8.3	14.9	124.4n	2.40	5.7	5.7	7.6	22	06-90	.16	.0	65	65	19	02-04-86	2.3	4.83	11.1	2.09	23.2	40	1.2	2,073	49.951l	27,846	+0	0.0	08
Rose's Stores	7.9	7.9	5.1	6.4q	.33	-52.2	-52.2	-54.2	-17	04-90	.16	2.3	3	47	28	06-04-90	.4	3.25	1.3	2.38	3.1	29	1.9	138	19.715l	2,257	0	0.0	01
Rose's Stores B	NA	NA	NA	NA	NA	NA	NA	NA	NC	00-00	.16	2.2	NA	NA	NC	06-04-90	NA	NC	NA	NC	NA	-2215	NA	80	11,166	2,815	+16	NA	NA
Service Merch	10.6	10.6	7.5	60.9q	1.19	NE	NE	-29.2	NC	04-90	.00	.0	722	404	0	00-00-00	1.8	2.06	3.7	.00	NS		1.4	425	53.127l	30,930	+241	0.2	01
Sharper Image	-1.1	-1.1	7.7	4.0q	.48	NE	NE	-17.2	58	03-90	.00	.0	0	0	16	00-00-00	1.9	3.00	5.7	2.11	12.0	5	1.5	42	8,227	752	-10	0.0	12
Spiegel Inc	20.2	20.2	18.1	74.9q	1.44	25.0	25.0	25.2	12	03-90	.28	1.1	26		11	03-21-90	4.2	1.26	5.3	3.42	18.1	150	3.2	1,266	51.946l	3,966	+0	0.0	08
Three D Dept #	NA	NA	NA	6.4n	.33	NA	NA	NA	NC		.10	2.2	NA	12	28	04-16-90	NA	NC	5.3	NC	18.1	29	NA	8	1.710l	368	0	0.0	NA
Three D Dp B	5.2	-.5	.0	.4s	.12	-29.2	-29.2	-53.8	-13	01-90	.06	1.3	3	32	26	04-16-90	1.1	1.82	2.0	1.40	2.8	10	3.2	13	2,902	372	0	0.0	07
Toys R Us	23.1	23.1	20.4	327.2q	1.67	21.4	21.4	20.1	24	04-90	.00	.0	0	0	0	05-30-99	6.6	1.61	10.6	1.81	19.2	10	1.2	9,470	196.772l	119,629	+13	3.4	01
Tuesday Morning	14.4	14.4	19.2	3.8q	.96	NE	NE	5.5	11	03-90	.00	.0	0	0	11	05-18-87	3.8	2.03	7.7	1.48	11.4	21	4.8	41	3,938	805	0	0.0	12
Wal-Mart Strs	26.0	26.0	25.1	1131.0q	2.00	28.6	28.6	28.2	25	04-90	.28	.4	31	12	11	06-11-90	4.2	3.29	13.8	2.07	28.5	105	1.7	35,303	565,978l	180,644	-10	2.5	01
Warehouse Club	-1.8	-2.2	-.3	-.8s	-.11	NE	NE	NE	-7	03-90	.00	.0	0	0	0	00-00-00	-.3	4.67	-1.4	4.64	-6.5		1.0	11	7,070	803	0	0.0	09
Wholesale Club	41.8	41.8	42.3	7.1q	1.09	NE	NE	122.4	18	04-90	.00	1.3	3	26	18	00-00-00	1.2	5.50	6.6	2.68	17.7	0	1.6	177	7,743	2,979	+1	0.0	01
Woolworth Cp	10.0	10.0	9.2	331.0q	2.57	3.6	3.6	14.2	17	04-90	1.04	3.2	16	36	35	04-27-90	3.7	2.54	9.4	1.91	18.0	19	1.7	4,244	129.10l	0	+42	1.3	01

Retail Trade - Food Stores

Ind. Group																													
Ind. Group	6.5	8.0	9.2	996.0	.79	17.2	15.3	8.5	18		.35	1.6	1	25	20		1.0	3.60	3.6	8.81	31.7	412	1.2	24,991	1,142,746	359,512	+2164	4.6	
Albertson's Inc	10.8	10.8	8.3	203.4q	1.53	18.2	18.2	19.5	20	04-90	.48	1.3	16	25	25	08-06-90	2.7	4.04	10.9	2.01	21.9	24	1.2	4,814	133.714	55,320	+27	1.0	01
Arden Group Inc	-3.0	-3.0	-.5	12.1q	7.41	13.0	13.0	15.2	18	03-90	2.25	3.6	0	0	1	02-12-90	3.5	2.46	8.6	3.02	26.0	75	2.0	93	1,513	774	0	0.0	01
Atlantic Grp	-12.5	-5.8	-2.7	-.2n	.08	-75.0	-40.0	-20.0	8	02-90	.00	.9	0	0	0	04-00-00	.6	1.83	1.1	1.45	1.6	16	2.1	5	2,592	11	0	0.0	05
Bruno's Inc	10.3	12.2	8.7	56.1n	.70	26.7	25.0	20.7	16	05-07-90	.14	.9	14	20	20	05-07-90	1.4	3.54	8.5	2.27	19.3	45	1.3	1,265	81,585	19,930	0	0.0	06
Casey's Gen Str	12.3	19.4	19.5	8.4l	.73	NE	NE	19.7	9	07-26-90	.03	.3	0	0	0	07-26-90	2.4	3.06	7.4	2.27	18.0	74	1.1	97	11,787	4,815	-75	0.0	04
Circle K Cp	-2.3	10.7	16.7	-46.6n	-1.27	-100.0	-100.0	-100.0	-17	01-90	.00	.0	3	133	35	06-05-89	-1.3	1.85	-2.4	7.21	-17.3	394	1.2	54	43,584	16,622	0	8.5	04
Dairy Mart	NA	NA	NA	NA	NA	NA	NA	NA	NC	00-00	.00	.0	NA	NA	0	02-06-89	NA	NC	NA	NC	NA	36	NA	17	2,184	1,208	+1	NA	12
Dairy Mart Conv	7.2	7.2	4.2	2.2q	.52	NE	NE	20.9	7	03-90	.00	.0	NA	19	7	02-06-89	.4	3.75	1.5	4.73	7.1	210	1.0	18	2,307	252	+3	0.0	01
Delchamps Inc	3.3	4.6	2.7	14.8n	2.08	NE	NE	42.5	16	03-90	.40	1.6	14	20	23	05-03-90	1.6	4.56	7.3	2.64	19.3	48	1.6	178	7,132	1,479	+3	0.6	06
Eagle Food Ctrs	3.2	3.2	5.3	10.6q	.54	NE	NE	9.1	18	03-90	.00	.0	0	20	0	00-00-00	.3	4.33	3.9	4.62	18.0	155	1.3	129	11,500	2,642	+3	0.0	01
FFP Partners	2.7	2.7	9.8	1.1q	.30	NE	NE	500.0	-16	03-90	1.34	28.2	0	750	304	06-15-90	-.5	3.40	4.5	2.65	4.5	109	1.4	17	3,650	82	0	0.3	12
Food Lion A	18.8	18.8	21.3	148.2q	.46	33.3	33.3	24.3	19	03-90	.14	1.0	62	88	19	07-13-90	3.0	3.87	11.6	2.37	27.5	36	1.3	2,211	162,311	13,478	+3	NA	12
Food Lion B	7.2	7.2	4.2	2.2q	.52	NE	NE	40.2	9	03-90	.14	1.0	NA	9	7	02-06-89	.4	3.75	1.5	4.73	7.1	210	1.0	2,239	158,490	10,416	0	0.0	01
Foodarama	3.3	NA	NA	NA	NA	NA	NA	NA	16	03-90	.40	1.6	14	20	23	03-00-00	1.6	4.33	7.3	4.46	5.8	187	1.1	34	1,135	275	+3	3.9	06
Gen Host	4.7	4.7	7.2	1.5q	.08	NE	NE	NE	-3	01-90	.32	4.9	7	NE	48	06-18-90	.3	1.00	.3	3.33	1.0	128	1.7	124	19.006	7,347	+25	0.8	01

(continued)

Retail Trade - Food Stores (Continued)

Company	Rev Last Qtr %	Rev FY to Date %	Rev Last 12 Mos %	Rev Last 12 Mos $Mil	EPS Last 12 Mos $	EPS % Chg Last Qtr	EPS % Chg FY to Date	EPS % Chg Last 12 Mos	5-Year Growth Rate %	Par Growth Rate %	Date of Report	Div Current Amt $	Div Yield %	5-Year Growth Rate %	Payout Last FY %	Payout Last 5 Yrs %	Last X-Dvd Date	Profit Margin %	Asset Turnover	Return on Total Assets	Leverage Ratio	Return on Equity	Debt to Equity %	Current Ratio	Market Value $Mil	Latest Shares Outstndg 000	Held by Banks-Funds 000	Insider Net Trading 000	Short Interest Ratio Days	Fiscal Year Ends Mo
Giant Food A	6.2	6.2	7.8	110.4q	1.84	9.1	9.1	6.4	22	15	05-90	.60	2.2	18	27	28	05-07-90	3.4	3.00	10.2	2.20	22.4	49	1.5	1,677	60,168	15,638	+10	1.1	02
Grt A & P Tea	5.5	10.7	10.7	146.77	3.84	12.5	15.0	15.0	26	12	02-90	.70	1.2	12	17	13	04-06-90	1.3	4.31	5.6	2.70	15.1	52	1.1	2,182	38,201	12,658	0	1.1	02
Hannaford Bros	13.2	13.2	17.4	38.6q	1.97	13.6	13.6	23.1	21	14	03-90	.44	1.2	12	19	22	06-11-90	2.5	3.28	8.2	2.20	18.0	58	1.4	722	19,515	6,172	+21	3.6	12
Ingles Markets ♦	14.3	15.1	16.3	12.9s	.72	-88.2	-50.0	-8.9	NC	7	03-90	.22	2.5	0	25	26	05-21-90	1.3	3.15	4.1	2.54	10.4	79	1.6	159	17,869	1,285	0	0.0	09
Kroger Co	1.5	1.5	-.2	-7.8q	-.12	NE	NE	NE	NC	0	03-90	.82	5.1	0	25	450	08-04-88	.0	NC	NC	NC	NS	-159	1.0	1,316	81,592	25,976	+78	1.7	12
Marsh Supermkt	13.4	10.9	10.8	10.7f	1.38	25.5	25.5	25.5	18	13	03-90	.36	2.1	4	14	25	07-16-90	1.1	4.64	5.1	3.33	17.0	119	1.3	130	7,749	3,971	+3	0.0	03
Mcts Holding	.0	.0	.0	1.4q	.68	NC	NE	NC	26	5	03-90	.00	.0	0	15	15	02-04-86	35.0	.11	4.0	1.23	4.9	1	4.0	23	2,610	586	0	4.9	12
Natl Conv Str □	4.2	-.5	1.7	-.2n	-.01	NE	NE	NE	NC	-10	03-90	.32	5.6	2	NE	639	04-24-90	.0	NC	NC	NC	-3	438	1.0	129	22,409	11,382	0	1.7	06
Penn Traffic	37.1	37.1	89.2	-31.9q	-6.05	NE	NE	NE	NC	-100	04-90	.00	.0	0	0	0	00-00-00	-1.1	3.91	-4.3	23.19	-99.7	1533	1.4	108	5,556	1,932	0	65.3	01
Quality Food Ctr	23.9	23.9	37.0	14.8s	1.54	52.4	52.4	85.5	NC	34	03-90	.00	.0	0	0	0	09-27-89	4.4	5.09	24.4	1.53	34.3	0	1.1	354	9,500	1,463	0	0.0	12
Rser Foods □	.0	-1.1	30.0	4.8n	.57	NE	NE	NC	NC	22	03-90	.00	.0	0	0	0	00-00-00	.4	5.75	23	9.57	22.0	446	1.5	81	7,979	1,571	0	0.6	06
Safeway Inc	3.4	3.4	4.1	8.7q	.10	41.7	41.7	-87.8	NC	0	03-90	.00	.0	0	0	0	00-00-00	.1	2.00	2	.00	NS	-694	.9	973	67,700	0	0	1.5	12
Seaway Food Town	6.8	7.9	.0	.0*	1.67	66.7	51.3	-52.0	40	0	05-90	.36	2.0	0	14	25	07-02-90	NC	2.44	3.9	3.05	0.0	137	1.1	42	2,278	456	0	0.0	06
Smith's Food	22.1	22.1	26.0	28.6q	1.19	10.3	10.3	21.4	NC	9	03-90	.28	.8	0	9	5	05-09-90	1.6	5.09	3.9	3.05	11.9	107	1.1	837	25,272	4,754	0	1.9	12
Sunshine-Jr	8.9	8.9	10.1	.7q	.42	NE	NE	NE	-27	0	03-90	.48	5.9	-19	33	43	03-02-89	.4	3.00	1.2	2.42	2.9	71	.9	14	1,702	543	0	0.0	12
Uni Marts Inc	8.2	15.2	37.0	2.8s	.43	-11.1	-4.5	-8.5	20	8	03-90	.10	1.8	0	18	19	06-25-90	1.2	2.58	3.1	3.48	10.8	148	1.1	36	6,529	830	0	0.0	09
Vons Cons	2.6	2.6	20.0	-3.5q	-.09	NE	NE	NE	-2	0	03-90	.00	.0	0	0	0	00-00-00	-.1	2.00	-2	9.00	-1.8	441	.8	871	38,726	6,256	+2070	6.1	12
Weis Markets	4.1	4.1	3.6	85.1q	1.88	-6.7	-6.7	1.6	10	10	03-90	.60	2.1	20	29	26	05-07-90	6.8	1.91	13.0	1.15	15.0	0	6.0	1,325	45,307	21,163	0	46.1	12
Winn Dixie	6.2	6.7	4.5	151.2n	3.81	15.1	19.6	11.7	6	9	03-90	1.98	2.9	-9	24	53	04-09-90	1.6	6.00	9.6	2.01	19.3	9	1.6	2,717	39,594	8,225	-6	6.6	06

$r/r \times r/a = r/a \times a/e = r/e$

Source: Media General Financial Services, Richmond, VA.

Trends and Forecasts: Textile Mill Products (SIC 22)

(in millions of dollars except as noted)

Item	1987[1]	1988[2]	1989[3]	Percent Change 1987-88	Percent Change 1988-89
Industry Data					
Value of shipments[4]	62,871	65,575	68,985	4.3	5.2
Value of shipments (1987$)	62,871	64,038	65,389	1.9	2.1
Total employment (000)	675	679	687	0.6	1.2
Production workers (000)	578	580	583	0.3	0.5
Average hourly earnings ($)	7.37	7.59	7.84	3.0	3.3
Product Data					
Value of shipments[5]	61,359	63,875	66,941	4.1	4.8
Value of shipments (1987$)	61,359	63,055	65,118	2.8	3.3
Trade Data					
Value of imports	4,699	4,458	4,711	-5.1	5.7
Value of exports	1,891	2,339	2,842	23.7	21.5

[1] Industry and product data are preliminary. Trade data are adjusted to conform to the 1987 SIC.
[2] Estimated, except for exports and imports.
[3] Estimated.
[4] Value of all products and services sold by establishments in the textile mill products industry.
[5] Value of products classified in the textile mill products industry produced by all industries.

SOURCE: U.S. Department of Commerce: Bureau of the Census; International Trade Administration (ITA). Estimates and forecasts by ITA.

Source: *U.S. Industrial Outlook 1990*, U.S. Department of Commerce.

STOCKS by INDUSTRY

MEDIA GENERAL FINANCIAL SERVICES

Weaving Mills

Company	Revenue Pct. Change Last Qtr %	Revenue Pct. Change FY to Date %	Revenue Pct. Change Last 12 Mos %	Revenue Last 12 Mos $Mil	Earnings Per Share Last 12 Mos $	Earnings Per Share Last Qtr $	Earnings Pct. Change Last Qtr %	Earnings Pct. Change FY to Date %	Earnings Pct. Change Last 12 Mos %	Earnings 5-Year Growth Rate %	Earnings Par Growth Rate %	Earnings Date of Report	Div Current Rate Amt $	Div Current Rate Yield %	Div 5-Year Growth Rate %	Div Payout Last FY %	Div Payout Last 5 Yrs %	Div Last X-Dvd Date	Ratio Profit Margin %	Ratio Asset Turn-over	Ratio Return on Total Assets %	Ratio Lever-age Ratio	Ratio Return on Equity %	Ratio Debt to Equity %	Ratio Cur-ent Ratio	Mar-ket Value $Mil	Latest Shares Out-stndg 000	Held by Banks-Funds 000	Insider Net Trad-ing 000	Short Int-erest Ratio Days	Fiscal Year Ends Mo.
Ind. Group	-10.7	-4.0	-3.8	298.5	.57		-11.7	-45.9	-40.0	7	-.9	---	1.13	10.3	3	35	30	----	2.3	1.52	3.5	2.74	9.6	86	2.0	5,607	514,517	30,872	+6	5.7	--
Belding Hem ○	.5	4.9	5.2	5.9f	2.91		-25.3	3.2	3.2	14	10	12-89	.64	2.2	8	19	21	05-25-90	3.7	1.57	5.8	2.24	13.0	61	2.5	57	1,946	377	0	0.0	12
Burke Mills	10.0	14.3	15.0	-.2	-.08		-100.0	-100.0	-100.0	NC	-2	12-89	.00	.0	0	0	0	00-00-00	-.9	1.67	-1.5	1.53	-2.3	26	3.1	3	2,741	270	0	0.0	12
Concord Fabrics	11.3	11.8	25.1	4.5s	1.27		80.0	162.5	162.5	NC	17	02-90	.00	.0	0	0	0	00-00-00	2.4	2.08	6.9	2.48	17.1	57	2.2	23	3,565	141	0	4.7	08
Concord Fab B	NA	NA	NA	NA	NA		NA	NA	NA	NA	NC	00-00	.00	.0	NA	NA	NA	00-00-00	NA	NC	NA	NC	NA	NA	NA	11	1,783	156	0	NA	08
Courtaulds Ltd	-1.7	-1.7	-1.7	252.71	.64		6.7	6.7	6.7	15	-33	03-90	1.26	19.4	32	36	26	06-06-90	5.8	1.91	11.1	3.10	34.4	69	1.3	2,538	390,400	572	0	0.9	03
Crown Crafts	1.6	11.7	12.0	6.6f	.96		-12.0	2.1	2.1	NC	26	03-90	.09	.5	0	11	3	06-13-90	6.5	2.34	15.2	1.92	29.2	38	3.0	114	6,951	1,326	0	17.9	03
CrownAmerica	-10.7	-6.5	-10.8	1.0s	.92		250.0	-26.6	-23.3	6	3	02-90	.50	5.0	3	33	40	04-06-90	1.4	2.43	3.4	1.76	6.0	11	1.9	11	1,053	87	0	0.0	08
Culp Inc	-2.5	-4.1	-3.9	2.3f	.52		162.5	NE	NE	NC	4	04-90	.11	1.2	0	15	13	07-03-90	1.4	1.86	2.6	2.04	5.3	60	3.2	41	4,426	982	+1	0.0	04
Dixie Yarns	-3.5	-3.5	-5.6	9.5q	.94		-57.6	-57.6	-40.9	83	1	03-90	.68	5.0	27	60	33	05-10-90	1.7	1.59	2.7	1.89	5.1	60	3.7	134	9,947	4,028	+5	0.0	12
Fab Indus	1.7	1.7	11.9	10.7q	3.27		1.7	1.7	20.7	5	8	02-90	.80	2.3	16	21	20	12-05-89	6.3	1.35	8.5	1.32	11.2	1	4.4	113	3,283	1,450	0	0.0	11

Ratio Analysis formula: $r/l \times r/a = r/a \times a/e = r/e$

Fieldcrest Cannon	-7.4	-7.4	1.3	20.7q	2.01	-90.0	-90.0	24.1	NC	4	03-90	.80	5.8	3	34	49	06-12-90	1.5	1.60	2.4	3.08	7.4	122	2.8	143	10,394	0	1.7	12
Hancock Fab	11.5	11.5	10.5	26.7q	2.22	90.0	24.4	25.4	NC	23	04-90	.56	1.5	0	17	15	06-25-90	7.5	2.03	15.2	2.05	31.2	42	3.0	443	11,997	-0	0.0	01
Ruddick Corp	11.9	12.6	13.9	23.56	2.38	90.0	36.0	25.9	11	12	03-90	.40	1.4	16	46	28	06-11-90	1.7	3.18	5.4	2.76	14.9	71	1.5	271	9,593	+1	26.9	09
Springs Indus	-2.7	-2.7	1.3	57.2q	3.20	-51.2	-51.2	-1.5	25	6	03-90	1.20	3.7	10	33	34	06-04-90	3.0	1.60	4.8	2.04	9.8	39	2.4	570	17,680	0	2.0	12
Utd Mer Mfrs	-30.6	-28.6	-27.6	-135.7n	-14.32	NE	-100.0	-100.0	NC	0	03-90	.00	.0	0	0	0	00-00-00	-35.1	1.05	-36.9	.00	NM	700	3.7	7	9,191	-1	24.7	06
West Point-P	-48.0	-25.6	-25.6	13.11	.45	-33.3	-84.9	-84.9	-20	-3	09-88	1.20	3.2	-18	71	42	02-15-89	.8	.63	.5	3.40	1.7	126	2.6	1,128	29,797	0	11.8	09
Ind. Group	-6.3	-1.4	5.1	103.7	.96	-33.4	-72.4	-17.4	18	8	---	.24	1.5	1	11	13	---	3.9	1.41	5.5	1.98	10.9	46	2.7	1,797	110,394	L	.9	---

Knitting Mills

Aileen Inc	1.3	-8.5	-7.9	-4.4s	-.34	NE	NE	NE	NC	-24	04-90	.00	.0	0	0	0	00-00-00	-7.6	1.96	-14.9	1.61	-24.0	1	1.6	14	5,110	0	0.8	10
Alba-Wald	-7.3	-7.3	-2.1	1.9q	.98	NE	NE	NE	NC	9	03-90	.00	.0	0	0	0	09-07-84	4.1	1.56	6.4	1.38	8.8	6	3.1	12	1,815	0	0.2	12
Bayly Cp	7.1	.9	-6.2	-5.3s	-2.51	-79.5	NE	NE	11	0	04-90	.00	.0	0	0	NE	09-09-87	-7.1	2.30	-16.3	.00	NS	-394	1.7	3	2,222	-1275	0.0	10
Delta Woodsd	-20.4	-14.2	-6.5	11.6n	.62	-100.0	-92.8	-61.0	NC	5	03-90	.30	3.7	0	12	5	05-17-90	2.3	1.52	3.5	2.60	9.1	70	1.7	151	18,641	0	0.1	06
Guilford Mills	-17.0	-11.1	-6.2	-4.0n	-.43	-54.1	-100.0	-100.0	NC	-5	03-90	.80	4.8	3	15	26	05-07-90	-.7	1.43	-1.0	1.90	-1.9	46	3.3	159	9,599	0	1.4	08
Nantucket Ind	5.5	15.4	14.2	1.6f	.66	25.0	-8.3	-8.3	NC	14	02-90	.00	.0	0	0	0	05-13-86	4.0	1.93	7.7	1.86	14.3	45	4.5	17	2,444	0	0.0	02
Rocky Mtn Under	-54.7	-54.7	-48.7	.4q	.13	-100.0	-100.0	NE	NC	5	03-90	.00	.0	0	0	0	00-00-00	1.9	2.00	3.8	1.32	5.0	5	5.1	4	3,190	0	0.0	12
Russell Cp	8.3	8.3	25.0	66.1q	1.60	9.4	9.4	15.1	18	13	05-01-90	.32	1.2	14	18	17	05-01-90	9.4	.98	9.2	1.78	16.4	51	5.5	1,076	40,427	0	6.3	12
Texfi Ind	12.8	13.7	20.2	9.6s	.82	-72.7	-66.1	-40.1	NC	26	04-90	.00	.0	0	0	0	07-24-87	3.9	2.05	8.0	3.28	26.2	55	1.6	58	7,628	+3	0.4	10
Unifi Inc	-2.9	4.9	13.0	26.2n	1.73	17.9	3.6	47.9	37	22	03-90	.00	.0	0	0	0	08-21-89	6.5	2.15	14.0	1.54	21.6	0	1.8	302	19,355	0	0.0	06

Source: Media General Financial Services, Richmond, VA.

Financial Statement Ratios by Industry

Many quantitative indicators are used to assess the financial strength of an enterprise and the success of its operations. The simplest is to assemble related financial items, such as sales and profits, and express the relationship in the form of a ratio. Using these ratios, various aspects of corporate operations may be compared with the performance of other corporations or groups of corporations of similar size or in a similar industry.

The Quarterly Financial Report's (QFR) ratio formatted income statement and selected balance sheet ratios are expressed as a percent of net sales and total assets, respectively. The operating and financial characteristics of the respective industries and asset size groups are thus reduced to a common denominator to facilitate analysis.

The ratio tables include the following additional basic operating ratios:

1. *Annual rate of profit on stockholders' equity at end of the period.* This ratio is obtained by multiplying income for the quarter before or after domestic taxes [including branch income (loss) and equity in the earnings of nonconsolidated subsidiaries net of foreign taxes] by four, to put it on an annual basis, and then dividing by stockholders' equity at the end of the quarter. It measures the rate of return which accrues to stockholders on their investment.

2. *Annual rate of profit on total assets.* This ratio is obtained by multiplying income, as defined in deriving the rate of profit on stockholders' equity, both before and after taxes, by four and then dividing by total assets at the end of the quarter. This ratio measures the productivity of assets in terms of producing income.

3. *Total current assets to total current liabilities.* This ratio is obtained by dividing total current assets by total current liabilities. It measures the ability to discharge current maturing obligations from existing current assets.

4. *Total cash, U.S. government and other securities to current liabilities.* This ratio is obtained by dividing total cash, U.S. government and other securities by total current liabilities. It measures the ability to discharge current liabilities from liquid assets.

5. *Total stockholders' equity to total debt.*

This ratio is obtained by dividing total stockholders' equity by the total of short-term loans, current installments on long-term debt, and long-term debt due in more than one year. It indicates the extent of leverage financing used.

DESCRIPTION OF THE SAMPLE

The frame from which the major portion of the sample continues to be selected consists of the Internal Revenue Service (IRS) file of those corporate entities which are required to file Form 1120 or 1120S and which also have as their principal industrial activity manufacturing, mining, or wholesale or retail trade. The IRS file is sampled once each year. At the time the sample is selected, the file does not contain those corporate entities whose first income tax return has not been processed. In addition, several months elapse between the selection of this sample and its introduction into the QFR program. To keep the QFR sample of corporations with assets over $50 million as up to date as possible, a separate sample is drawn each calendar quarter from a frame comprising applications for a Federal Social Security Employer's Identification Number filed with the Social Security Administration (SSA) during the previous quarter by new corporations. In processing the composite list of sample companies, a screening technique is used to insure that corporations drawn from the SSA frame could not have been drawn from the IRS frame.

Stratification is used in the sample selection process. In sampling from the IRS frame, stratification by industry and size is employed. In sampling from the SSA frame, stratification is by division and size alone. The measures of size used in the IRS frame are total assets and gross receipts while the measure of size used in the SSA frame is number of employees. From the third quarter 1977, through the fourth quarter 1986 the strata composed of manufacturing firms with assets of less than $250,000 and the strata which contained corporations in the SSA frame are estimated by multivariate techniques. Beginning in the first quarter 1987, the QFR universe of corporations was redefined to exclude these strata. The sampling fractions applied to the other various industry-size strata vary according to both industry and size. They range from approximately one out of 850 to one out of one.

Nearly all corporations whose operations

Source: *Quarterly Financial Report,* Bureau of the Census. The exhibits in this section are from the same publication.

are within the scope of the QFR and which have total assets greater than $50 million are included in the sample. They are permanent sample members with a one out of one sampling fraction. In those industry-size strata for which the sampling fraction is less than one out of one, a replacement scheme is utilized which provides that one eighth of the sample is replaced each quarter. Corporations removed are those that have been in the reporting group longest (usually eight quarters). Therefore, samples of small corporations for adjacent quarters are seven-eighths identical; for quarters ending nine months apart they are five eighths identical, etc.

Industry Contents

TABLE 1—INCOME STATEMENT
FOR CORPORATIONS INCLUDED IN ESIC MAJOR GROUPS 20 AND 21

Item	Food and Kindred Products[1]				
	1Q 1989	2Q 1989	3Q 1989	4Q 1989	1Q 1990
	(percent of net sales)				
INCOME STATEMENT IN RATIO FORMAT					
Net sales, receipts, and operating revenues....................................	100.0	100.0	100.0	100.0	100.0
Less: Depreciation, depletion, and amortization of property, plant, and equipment	2.6	2.4	2.4	2.4	2.6
Less: All other operating costs and expenses	90.5	89.4	89.7	89.1	89.9
Income (or loss) from operations..	6.9	8.2	7.9	8.5	7.5
Net nonoperating income (expense)..	(1.0)	(2.1)	(2.7)	(0.6)	(2.0)
Income (or loss) before income taxes	5.9	6.1	5.3	7.9	5.5
Less: Provision for current and deferred domestic income taxes	1.8	2.1	1.9	2.6	1.8
Income (or loss) after income taxes	4.1	4.0	3.4	5.3	3.7
	(percent)				
OPERATING RATIOS (see explanatory notes)					
Annual rate of profit on stockholders' equity at end of period:					
Before income taxes	22.36	25.41	21.78	32.75	22.16
After income taxes...	15.62	16.53	13.90	22.15	14.76
Annual rate of profit on total assets:					
Before income taxes	7.43	8.23	6.90	10.39	7.01
After income taxes...	5.19	5.35	4.40	7.03	4.67
BALANCE SHEET RATIOS (based on succeeding table)					
Total current assets to total current liabilities..	1.24	1.30	1.22	1.25	1.27
Total cash, U.S. Government and other securities to total current liabilities	0.16	0.17	0.15	0.15	0.15
Total stockholders' equity to total debt..	0.79	0.77	0.74	0.77	0.75

[1]In the first quarter 1990, a number of corporations were reclassified by industry. To provide comparability, data for quarters in 1989 were restated to reflect these reclassifications, as well as respondents' corrections of submitted data subsequent to original publication.
[2]Tobacco industry data have been collapsed into food industry data. Major merger and acquisition activity in recent years resulted in the reclassification of a significant portion of gross receipts and assets from tobacco to food. The remainder, composed of data from highly specialized tobacco manufacturers, is too small to be considered publishable as a separate industry.
[3]Revised to reflect respondents' corrections of submitted data subsequent to original publication.

TABLE 2—BALANCE SHEET
FOR CORPORATIONS INCLUDED IN ESIC MAJOR GROUPS 20 and 21

Item	Food and Kindred Products[1]				
	1Q 1989	2Q 1989	3Q 1989	4Q 1989	1Q 1990
	(percent of total assets)				
SELECTED BALANCE SHEET RATIOS					
Total cash, U.S. Government and other securities....................................	3.7	3.8	3.4	3.4	3.4
Trade accounts and trade notes receivable	9.5	9.8	9.9	9.9	9.5
Inventories...	13.3	12.5	12.7	13.0	13.3
Total current assets...	28.6	28.2	28.2	28.5	28.4
Net property, plant, and equipment	29.8	30.2	30.0	30.1	30.5
Short-term debt including installments on long-term debt.............................	7.9	6.5	7.7	6.6	7.1
Total current liabilities...	23.0	21.7	23.1	22.9	22.4
Long-term debt	34.0	35.8	35.0	34.8	35.0
Total liabilities	66.8	67.6	68.3	68.3	68.4
Stockholders' equity	33.2	32.4	31.7	31.7	31.6

[1]In the first quarter 1990, a number of corporations were reclassified by industry. To provide comparability, data for quarters in 1989 were restated to reflect these reclassifications, as well as respondents' corrections of submitted data subsequent to original publication.
[2]Tobacco industry data have been collapsed into food industry data. Major merger and acquisition activity in recent years resulted in the reclassification of a significant portion of gross receipts and assets from tobacco to food. The remainder, composed of data from highly specialized tobacco manufacturers, is too small to be considered publishable as a separate industry.
[3]Revised to reflect respondents' corrections of submitted data subsequent to original publication.

Food and Kindred Products Assets Under $25 Million					Tobacco Manufactures[2]					Tobacco Manufactures Assets Under $25 Million[2]				
1Q 1989	2Q 1989[3]	3Q 1989	4Q 1989	1Q 1990	1Q 1989	2Q 1989	3Q 1989	4Q 1989	1Q 1990	1Q 1989	2Q 1989	3Q 1989	4Q 1989	1Q 1990
(percent of net sales)					(intentionally blank)					(intentionally blank)				
100.0	100.0	100.0	100.0	100.0										
1.9	1.8	1.7	1.7	1.8										
95.3	95.6	95.6	95.1	95.3										
2.8	2.6	2.7	3.2	2.9										
(0.6)	(0.3)	(0.4)	(0.1)	(0.4)										
2.3	2.3	2.3	3.2	2.5										
0.6	0.5	0.6	0.5	0.5										
1.6	1.8	1.7	2.6	2.0										
(percent)					(intentionally blank)					(intentionally blank)				
15.71	18.41	16.66	23.81	15.49										
11.43	14.45	12.31	19.85	12.22										
7.58	8.23	8.06	11.28	8.29										
5.52	6.46	5.96	9.40	6.54										
1.80	1.72	1.77	1.84	2.12										
0.27	0.25	0.28	0.31	0.44										
1.58	1.36	1.55	1.61	2.09										

Food and Kindred Products Assets Under $25 Million					Tobacco Manufactures[2]					Tobacco Manufactures Assets Under $25 Million[2]				
1Q 1989[3]	2Q 1989[3]	3Q 1989[3]	4Q 1989[3]	1Q 1990	1Q 1989	2Q 1989	3Q 1989	4Q 1989	1Q 1990	1Q 1989	2Q 1989	3Q 1989	4Q 1989	1Q 1990
(percent of total assets)					(intentionally blank)					(intentionally blank)				
8.8	8.4	9.2	10.3	12.4										
23.2	24.8	24.5	26.1	24.1										
21.7	21.8	20.9	20.8	20.5										
57.5	58.7	58.1	60.4	60.3										
36.3	35.1	36.9	35.0	34.3										
12.6	13.2	13.9	11.6	9.4										
32.0	34.1	32.8	32.8	28.5										
18.0	19.7	17.2	18.0	16.3										
51.7	55.3	51.6	52.6	46.5										
48.3	44.7	48.4	47.4	53.5										

TABLE 3—INCOME STATEMENT
FOR CORPORATIONS INCLUDED IN ESIC MAJOR GROUPS 22 AND 26

Item	Textile Mill Products[1]				
	1Q 1989	2Q 1989	3Q 1989	4Q 1989	1Q 1990
	(percent of net sales)				
INCOME STATEMENT IN RATIO FORMAT					
Net sales, receipts, and operating revenues...........................	100.0	100.0	100.0	100.0	100.0
Less: Depreciation, depletion, and amortization of property, plant, and equipment	3.3	3.2	3.3	3.3	3.7
Less: All other operating costs and expenses	90.2	89.5	90.1	91.7	91.3
Income (or loss) from operations...........................	6.5	7.3	6.6	5.0	5.0
Net nonoperating income (expense)...........................	(2.8)	(2.5)	(2.6)	(2.9)	(4.5)
Income (or loss) before income taxes...........................	3.7	4.8	4.0	2.1	0.5
Less: Provision for current and deferred domestic income taxes	1.2	1.5	1.0	1.0	0.8
Income (or loss) after income taxes...........................	2.5	3.3	2.9	1.1	(0.4)
	(percent)				
OPERATING RATIOS (see explanatory notes)					
Annual rate of profit on stockholders' equity at end of period:					
Before income taxes......................................	13.99	20.16	16.73	8.69	1.71
After income taxes......................................	9.50	13.70	12.39	4.60	(1.34)
Annual rate of profit on total assets:					
Before income taxes......................................	5.22	7.30	5.90	3.00	0.61
After income taxes......................................	3.54	4.96	4.37	1.59	(0.48)
BALANCE SHEET RATIOS (based on succeeding table)					
Total current assets to total current liabilities...........................	1.99	1.97	1.98	2.03	2.12
Total cash, U.S. Government and other securities to total current liabilities	0.20	0.18	0.20	0.25	0.25
Total stockholders' equity to total debt...........................	0.90	0.85	0.81	0.78	0.81

[1] In the first quarter 1990, a number of corporations were reclassified by industry. To provide comparability, data for quarters in 1989 were restated to reflect these reclassifications.

TABLE 4—BALANCE SHEET
FOR CORPORATIONS INCLUDED IN ESIC MAJOR GROUPS 22 AND 26

Item	Textile Mill Products[1]				
	1Q 1989	2Q 1989[3]	3Q 1989[3]	4Q 1989	1Q 1990
	(percent of total assets)				
SELECTED BALANCE SHEET RATIOS					
Total cash, U.S. Government and other securities...................................	4.8	4.4	5.0	5.9	5.7
Trade accounts and trade notes receivable	19.5	20.2	20.5	18.7	18.8
Inventories..	22.2	22.1	22.0	21.2	21.9
Total current assets..	49.0	49.3	50.1	48.6	48.5
Net property, plant, and equipment	32.1	33.4	33.2	34.6	35.0
Short-term debt including installments on long-term debt............................	8.9	9.1	9.5	9.1	8.4
Total current liabilities..	24.6	24.9	25.3	23.9	22.9
Long-term debt..	32.4	33.4	34.0	35.2	35.7
Total liabilities	62.7	63.8	64.7	65.4	64.5
Stockholders' equity	37.3	36.2	35.3	34.6	35.5

[1] In the first quarter 1990, a number of corporations were reclassified by industry. To provide comparability, data for quarters in 1989 were restated to reflect these reclassifications.
[2] In the first quarter 1990, a number of corporations were reclassified by industry. To provide comparability, data for quarters in 1989 were restated to reflect these reclassifications, as well as respondents' corrections of submitted data subsequent to original publication.
[3] Revised to reflect respondents' corrections of submitted data subsequent to original publication.

	Textile Mill Products Assets Under $25 Million					Paper and Allied Products[1]					Paper and Allied Products Assets Under $25 Million				
	1Q 1989	2Q 1989	3Q 1989	4Q 1989	1Q 1990	1Q 1989	2Q 1989	3Q 1989	4Q 1989	1Q 1990	1Q 1989	2Q 1989	3Q 1989	4Q 1989	1Q 1990
	(percent of net sales)					(percent of net sales)					(percent of net sales)				
	100.0	100.0	100.0	100.0	100.0	100.0	100.0	100.0	100.0	100.0	100.0	100.0	100.0	100.0	100.0
	2.3	2.5	2.6	2.5	2.6	4.3	4.3	4.4	4.5	4.7	2.5	2.2	2.2	2.2	2.5
	91.2	91.6	91.5	97.1	93.5	83.5	83.9	84.2	85.7	85.9	92.4	92.3	91.9	92.3	92.0
	6.4	6.0	5.9	0.4	3.8	12.1	11.8	11.4	9.7	9.4	5.1	5.5	5.9	5.4	5.5
	(0.7)	(0.5)	(1.3)	(1.7)	(1.0)	(1.1)	(1.1)	(0.9)	(3.6)	(2.0)	(1.0)	(0.6)	(0.9)	(1.4)	(0.8)
	5.7	5.4	4.6	(1.3)	2.9	11.0	10.8	10.4	6.1	7.4	4.0	4.8	5.0	4.0	4.7
	1.0	0.9	0.6	0.5	0.7	3.8	3.8	3.9	2.1	2.5	1.1	1.3	1.1	0.7	0.9
	4.7	4.5	4.1	(1.8)	2.2	7.2	7.0	6.6	4.0	4.9	2.9	3.5	3.9	3.4	3.8
	(percent)					(percent)					(percent)				
	26.97	29.14	25.01	(6.41)	15.11	27.79	27.61	25.68	15.33	17.34	22.78	27.88	23.79	22.15	22.62
	22.14	24.20	21.85	(8.74)	11.35	18.24	17.95	16.19	10.16	11.45	16.45	20.18	18.72	18.47	18.27
	12.85	13.24	10.60	(2.69)	6.29	12.35	12.06	11.22	6.42	7.32	9.55	11.59	11.33	9.52	10.03
	10.55	11.00	9.26	(3.67)	4.72	8.11	7.84	7.08	4.25	4.83	6.90	8.39	8.91	7.94	8.10
	1.91	1.77	1.68	1.66	1.73	1.77	1.78	1.82	1.64	1.62	1.84	1.95	2.01	2.09	2.03
	0.26	0.17	0.18	0.22	0.25	0.15	0.17	0.19	0.15	0.15	0.21	0.28	0.32	0.35	0.35
	1.66	1.46	1.31	1.24	1.35	1.37	1.30	1.29	1.20	1.18	1.10	1.27	1.45	1.28	1.38

	Textile Mill Products Assets Under $25 Million					Paper and Allied Products[2]					Paper and Allied Products Assets Under $25 Million				
	1Q 1989	2Q 1989	3Q 1989	4Q 1989	1Q 1990	1Q 1989	2Q 1989	3Q 1989	4Q 1989	1Q 1990	1Q 1989	2Q 1989	3Q 1989	4Q 1989	1Q 1990
	(percent of total assets)					(percent of total assets)					(percent of total assets)				
	8.8	5.9	6.8	8.0	8.9	2.4	2.6	2.9	2.5	2.4	6.4	8.4	9.1	9.8	9.8
	28.0	28.9	27.1	24.2	25.3	11.5	11.5	11.4	10.7	10.4	26.0	25.5	26.0	24.5	24.2
	24.1	22.5	24.5	24.1	24.3	10.8	10.4	10.1	10.2	9.9	21.4	22.0	19.1	21.5	20.0
	64.6	61.2	62.8	59.1	62.6	28.1	27.9	27.7	26.7	25.9	55.4	58.3	57.0	57.9	56.6
	30.7	34.4	33.2	37.9	34.1	57.6	56.5	56.8	57.6	57.5	38.4	36.1	38.4	37.1	38.8
	12.2	13.1	14.1	13.9	11.1	3.0	3.4	2.9	3.3	3.3	12.1	11.6	10.1	10.9	10.0
	33.9	34.5	37.3	35.6	36.1	15.9	15.7	15.2	16.2	16.0	20.1	20.8	20.4	27.7	27.9
	16.6	18.0	18.1	19.9	19.8	29.5	30.4	31.1	31.7	32.2	26.1	21.1	22.7	22.6	22.2
	52.3	54.6	57.6	58.0	58.4	55.6	56.3	56.3	58.1	57.8	58.1	58.4	52.4	57.0	55.7
	47.7	45.4	42.4	42.0	41.6	44.4	43.7	43.7	41.9	42.2	41.9	41.6	47.6	43.0	44.3

TABLE 5—INCOME STATEMENT
FOR CORPORATIONS INCLUDED IN ESIC MAJOR GROUPS 27 AND 28

Item	Printing and Publishing				
	1Q 1989[2]	2Q 1989[2]	3Q 1989[2]	4Q 1989[2]	1Q 1990
	(percent of net sales)				
INCOME STATEMENT IN RATIO FORMAT					
Net sales, receipts, and operating revenues....................	100.0	100.0	100.0	100.0	100.0
Less: Depreciation, depletion, and amortization of property, plant, and equipment	3.9	3.9	3.9	3.5	3.9
Less: All other operating costs and expenses	87.1	85.9	86.8	87.3	88.7
Income (or loss) from operations.............................	9.0	10.2	9.3	9.2	7.4
Net nonoperating income (expense).................................	(0.6)	(1.3)	(2.1)	3.1	(2.0)
Income (or loss) before income taxes	8.3	8.9	7.2	12.3	5.4
Less: Provision for current and deferred domestic income taxes	3.4	3.4	2.4	4.7	2.4
Income (or loss) after income taxes	5.0	5.4	4.9	7.6	3.0
	(percent)				
OPERATING RATIOS (see explanatory notes)					
Annual rate of profit on stockholders' equity at end of period:					
Before income taxes	22.28	23.63	18.55	32.26	12.17
After income taxes............................	13.29	14.45	12.48	19.91	6.80
Annual rate of profit on total assets:					
Before income taxes	9.03	9.54	7.18	12.45	4.91
After income taxes............................	5.39	5.83	4.83	7.68	2.74
BALANCE SHEET RATIOS (based on succeeding table)					
Total current assets to total current liabilities..	1.65	1.59	1.55	1.68	1.64
Total cash, U.S. Government and other securities to total current liabilities	0.29	0.30	0.26	0.37	0.33
Total stockholders' equity to total debt........................	1.15	1.13	1.02	1.04	1.15

[1]In the first quarter 1990, a number of corporations were reclassified by industry. To provide comparability, data for quarters in 1989 were restated to reflect these reclassifications, as well as respondents' corrections of submitted data subsequent to original publication.
[2]Revised to reflect respondents' corrections of submitted data subsequent to original publication.

TABLE 6—BALANCE SHEET
FOR CORPORATIONS INCLUDED IN ESIC MAJOR GROUPS 27 AND 28

Item	Printing and Publishing				
	1Q 1989[2]	2Q 1989[2]	3Q 1989[2]	4Q 1989[2]	1Q 1990
	(percent of total assets)				
SELECTED BALANCE SHEET RATIOS					
Total cash, U.S. Government and other securities.....................................	5.9	6.2	5.2	7.2	6.2
Trade accounts and trade notes receivable	15.9	15.1	14.8	15.2	13.8
Inventories....................................	7.5	7.3	6.7	6.1	6.3
Total current assets.............................	33.6	33.4	31.1	33.0	30.8
Net property, plant, and equipment	27.3	26.4	24.5	23.7	23.4
Short-term debt including installments on long-term debt................	4.5	5.5	4.9	4.0	3.6
Total current liabilities..............................	20.4	20.9	20.0	19.7	18.7
Long-term debt..................................	30.8	30.3	32.9	33.0	31.6
Total liabilities..................................	59.5	59.6	61.3	61.4	59.7
Stockholders' equity..............................	40.5	40.4	38.7	38.6	40.3

[1]In the first quarter 1990, a number of corporations were reclassified by industry. To provide comparability, data for quarters in 1989 were restated to reflect these reclassifications, as well as respondents' corrections of submitted data subsequent to original publication.
[2]Revised to reflect respondents' corrections of submitted data subsequent to original publication.

	Printing and Publishing Assets Under $25 Million					Chemicals and Allied Products[1]					Chemicals and Allied Products Assets Under $25 Million				
	1Q 1989	2Q 1989	3Q 1989	4Q 1989	1Q 1990	1Q 1989	2Q 1989	3Q 1989	4Q 1989	1Q 1990	1Q 1989	2Q 1989	3Q 1989	4Q 1989	1Q 1990
	(percent of net sales)					(percent of net sales)					(percent of net sales)				
	100.0	100.0	100.0	100.0	100.0	100.0	100.0	100.0	100.0	100.0	100.0	100.0	100.0	100.0	100.0
	3.3	3.2	3.1	3.1	3.3	4.1	4.2	4.5	4.7	4.4	2.1	2.0	2.0	2.2	2.1
	91.5	91.6	91.3	91.4	92.2	84.8	85.9	85.9	89.1	86.9	90.8	88.8	88.6	91.0	92.7
	5.2	5.2	5.6	5.5	4.5	11.1	9.9	9.7	6.2	8.7	7.1	9.2	9.5	6.9	5.2
	(1.1)	(1.1)	(1.2)	(1.2)	(1.1)	3.2	3.5	2.7	2.3	2.7	0.0	0.0	(0.3)	(0.1)	(0.7)
	4.1	4.1	4.4	4.3	3.3	14.2	13.4	12.4	8.5	11.4	7.1	9.2	9.1	6.8	4.5
	1.3	1.2	1.0	1.1	0.9	4.2	4.0	3.3	1.9	3.5	1.7	1.7	1.2	1.8	1.1
	2.8	2.9	3.4	3.2	2.4	10.0	9.5	9.0	6.7	7.9	5.4	7.5	8.0	5.0	3.4
	(percent)					(percent)					(percent)				
	21.87	23.51	23.31	21.40	15.55	32.33	31.26	27.17	18.06	23.65	26.86	36.17	33.90	26.23	16.19
	15.11	16.60	18.14	15.75	11.27	22.78	21.99	19.82	14.12	16.46	20.40	29.47	29.50	19.40	12.34
	8.13	8.67	9.12	9.00	6.73	14.10	13.55	11.83	7.87	10.37	14.43	19.76	19.45	14.20	8.74
	5.62	6.12	7.10	6.62	4.88	9.93	9.54	8.63	6.15	7.22	10.96	16.11	16.92	10.50	6.66
	1.67	1.72	1.71	1.96	1.97	1.49	1.47	1.42	1.35	1.32	2.29	2.22	2.50	2.37	2.32
	0.31	0.31	0.34	0.44	0.46	0.18	0.18	0.17	0.17	0.13	0.37	0.39	0.51	0.39	0.37
	0.95	0.98	1.11	1.24	1.31	1.52	1.48	1.49	1.47	1.47	2.49	2.67	2.82	2.23	2.28

	Printing and Publishing Assets Under $25 Million					Chemicals and Allied Products[1]					Chemicals and Allied Products Assets Under $25 Million				
	1Q 1989	2Q 1989	3Q 1989	4Q 1989	1Q 1990	1Q 1989	2Q 1989	3Q 1989	4Q 1989	1Q 1990	1Q 1989	2Q 1989	3Q 1989	4Q 1989	1Q 1990
	(percent of total assets)					(percent of total assets)					(percent of total assets)				
	10.1	10.2	11.4	13.0	13.1	4.4	4.4	4.2	4.2	3.3	10.7	11.5	13.5	10.7	9.9
	28.5	28.7	28.8	28.5	27.1	14.1	14.3	13.8	13.3	13.5	28.1	27.1	25.6	27.2	26.0
	12.0	12.9	12.8	11.9	11.2	12.9	12.8	12.3	12.2	12.2	23.8	23.1	23.3	23.3	22.8
	54.4	56.0	57.0	57.4	55.7	35.7	35.3	34.4	33.9	33.2	66.6	65.2	66.5	65.1	62.7
	34.8	33.6	32.6	32.7	32.9	33.9	34.0	33.8	34.2	33.8	25.5	25.7	24.6	26.0	27.5
	11.8	11.1	11.0	9.3	8.2	6.6	6.8	7.0	7.6	8.2	7.1	7.5	7.3	7.7	7.5
	32.5	32.6	33.3	29.3	28.2	24.0	24.1	24.2	25.1	25.1	29.1	29.4	26.6	27.5	27.0
	27.3	26.7	24.2	24.8	24.8	22.0	22.5	22.1	22.0	21.6	14.5	13.0	13.1	16.6	16.1
	62.8	63.1	60.9	57.9	56.7	56.4	56.6	56.5	56.4	56.1	46.3	45.4	42.6	45.9	46.0
	37.2	36.9	39.1	42.1	43.3	43.6	43.4	43.5	43.6	43.9	53.7	54.6	57.4	54.1	54.0

TABLE 7—INCOME STATEMENT
FOR CORPORATIONS IN ESIC MAJOR GROUPS 28.1 AND 28.3

Item	Industrial Chemicals and Synthetics[1][2]				
	1Q 1989	2Q 1989	3Q 1989	4Q 1989	1Q 1990
	(percent of net sales)				
INCOME STATEMENT IN RATIO FORMAT					
Net sales, receipts, and operating revenues..............................	100.0	100.0	100.0	100.0	100.0
Less: Depreciation, depletion, and amortization of property, plant, and equipment	5.1	5.2	5.8	6.2	5.9
Less: All other operating costs and expenses	82.6	84.1	84.6	88.0	84.9
Income (or loss) from operations.............................	12.3	10.7	9.6	5.9	9.2
Net nonoperating income (expense).............................	2.9	3.4	2.2	0.2	0.3
Income (or loss) before income taxes...........................	15.2	14.1	11.8	6.1	9.5
Less: Provision for current and deferred domestic income taxes	4.8	4.4	3.3	1.8	3.2
Income (or loss) after income taxes	10.4	9.8	8.6	4.3	6.3
	(percent)				
OPERATING RATIOS (see explanatory notes)					
Annual rate of profit on stockholders' equity at end of period:					
Before income taxes...	34.77	31.79	24.30	11.51	17.96
After income taxes..	23.82	21.96	17.59	8.18	11.94
Annual rate of profit on total assets:					
Before income taxes...	15.18	14.13	10.86	5.22	8.12
After income taxes..	10.40	9.76	7.86	3.71	5.40
BALANCE SHEET RATIOS (based on succeeding table)					
Total current assets to total current liabilities.....................	1.53	1.50	1.44	1.42	1.37
Total cash, U.S. Government and other securities to total current liabilities	0.12	0.14	0.13	0.12	0.10
Total stockholders' equity to total debt............................	1.47	1.55	1.55	1.61	1.57

[1]Included in Chemicals and Allied Products.
[2]In the first quarter 1990, a number of corporations were reclassified by industry. To provide comparability, data for quarters in 1989 were restated to reflect these reclassifications.
[3]In the first quarter 1990, a number of corporations were reclassified by industry. To provide comparability, data for quarters in 1989 were restated to reflect these reclassifications, as well as respondents' corrections of submitted data subsequent to original publication.

TABLE 8—BALANCE SHEET
FOR CORPORATIONS INCLUDED IN ESIC MAJOR GROUPS 28.1 AND 28.3

Item	Industrial Chemicals and Synthetics[1][2]				
	1Q 1989	2Q 1989	3Q 1989	4Q 1989	1Q 1990
	(percent of total assets)				
SELECTED BALANCE SHEET RATIOS					
Total cash, U.S. Government and other securities.....................................	2.8	3.0	3.0	2.5	2.3
Trade accounts and trade notes receivable	15.3	15.5	14.8	13.9	14.3
Inventories..	12.4	12.1	11.8	11.5	11.4
Total current assets.......................................	34.6	33.7	32.7	31.2	31.5
Net property, plant, and equipment	38.1	38.8	38.1	38.6	37.9
Short-term debt including installments on long-term debt....................	6.4	5.9	6.4	5.5	6.7
Total current liabilities.....................................	22.6	22.4	22.6	22.0	22.9
Long-term debt..	23.3	22.8	22.4	22.5	22.0
Total liabilities..	56.3	55.5	55.3	54.7	54.8
Stockholders' equity	43.7	44.5	44.7	45.3	45.2

[1]Included in Chemicals and Allied Products.
[2]In the first quarter 1990, a number of corporations were reclassified by industry. To provide comparability, data for quarters in 1989 were restated to reflect these reclassifications.
[3]In the first quarter 1990, a number of corporations were reclassified by industry. To provide comparability, data for quarters in 1989 were restated to reflect these reclassifications, as well as respondents' corrections of submitted data subsequent to original publication.

Industrial Chemicals and Synthetics Assets Under $25 Million[1]					Drugs[1 s]					Drugs Assets Under $25 Million[1]				
1Q 1989	2Q 1989	3Q 1989	4Q 1989	1Q 1990	1Q 1989	2Q 1989	3Q 1989	4Q 1989	1Q 1990	1Q 1989	2Q 1989	3Q 1989	4Q 1989	1Q 1990
(percent of net sales)					(percent of net sales)					(percent of net sales)				
100.0	100.0	100.0	100.0	100.0	100.0	100.0	100.0	100.0	100.0	100.0	100.0	100.0	100.0	100.0
2.0	2.0	1.9	2.4	2.2	3.3	3.9	3.4	4.2	3.3	2.8	2.8	3.4	2.7	2.1
89.6	86.6	86.1	88.3	90.1	83.1	85.3	85.7	88.0	85.6	86.5	92.5	91.4	85.0	86.4
8.4	11.4	12.0	9.4	7.7	13.6	10.8	10.9	7.8	11.1	10.7	4.7	5.2	12.3	11.4
0.1	0.6	0.5	(1.4)	(0.5)	10.0	10.8	6.9	10.0	8.7	(0.1)	0.5	(1.4)	(1.0)	(0.2)
8.4	12.0	12.5	7.9	7.2	23.6	21.6	17.8	17.9	19.8	10.6	5.2	3.8	11.3	11.2
1.8	2.6	1.8	2.6	1.9	6.7	6.3	4.5	2.8	4.9	1.9	1.6	1.2	1.8	1.8
6.7	9.3	10.7	5.3	5.3	16.9	15.3	13.2	15.1	15.0	8.7	3.6	2.6	9.4	9.6
(percent)					(percent)					(percent)				
31.35	45.02	40.92	29.99	26.55	44.48	40.28	33.47	31.66	34.48	25.10	12.27	8.48	29.12	31.03
24.79	35.11	35.18	20.13	19.43	31.82	28.49	24.93	26.71	26.04	20.56	8.50	5.72	24.36	26.73
17.80	26.78	26.36	17.61	14.69	20.59	19.02	15.32	15.57	17.52	15.97	7.53	4.88	17.09	19.21
14.08	20.88	22.66	11.82	10.75	14.73	13.45	11.41	13.14	13.23	13.09	5.21	3.29	14.30	16.55
2.47	2.22	2.84	2.29	2.25	1.30	1.27	1.21	1.18	1.13	3.29	3.31	3.19	2.87	3.42
0.33	0.43	0.62	0.34	0.41	0.17	0.15	0.14	0.18	0.15	1.05	1.13	1.04	0.95	1.20
3.29	4.65	5.33	3.08	3.52	2.18	2.18	2.01	2.21	2.29	3.34	2.71	2.04	2.45	2.96

Industrial Chemicals and Synthetics Assets Under $25 Million[1]					Drugs[1 s]					Drugs Assets Under $25 Million[1]				
1Q 1989	2Q 1989	3Q 1989	4Q 1989	1Q 1990	1Q 1989	2Q 1989	3Q 1989	4Q 1989	1Q 1990	1Q 1989	2Q 1989	3Q 1989	4Q 1989	1Q 1990
(percent of total assets)					(percent of total assets)					(percent of total assets)				
8.7	12.7	15.2	9.4	12.1	4.4	4.0	3.8	5.5	4.6	20.8	22.1	19.0	21.3	24.0
28.4	28.4	25.0	26.5	27.0	12.1	12.4	12.1	12.6	11.5	20.1	18.2	16.8	16.6	19.0
22.6	20.1	22.6	22.1	21.0	11.7	12.0	11.7	11.3	11.0	20.3	20.7	20.1	20.8	20.1
65.8	65.9	69.1	63.2	65.5	34.4	34.2	34.0	36.1	33.9	65.2	64.7	58.1	64.3	68.1
24.8	25.2	22.6	27.9	27.4	28.3	28.6	28.6	28.4	28.1	28.3	28.8	31.2	26.8	22.7
4.5	5.4	5.4	5.9	4.9	7.2	7.9	9.0	10.3	10.9	4.2	4.9	5.4	6.4	4.8
26.6	29.6	24.3	27.6	29.1	26.5	26.9	28.0	30.7	30.0	19.8	19.6	18.2	22.4	19.9
12.9	7.5	6.6	13.1	11.0	14.2	13.7	13.8	12.0	11.3	14.9	17.7	22.7	17.4	16.1
43.2	40.5	35.6	41.3	44.6	53.7	52.8	54.2	50.8	49.2	36.4	38.6	42.5	41.3	38.1
56.8	59.5	64.4	58.7	55.4	46.3	47.2	45.8	49.2	50.8	63.6	61.4	57.5	58.7	61.9

TABLE 9—INCOME STATEMENT
FOR CORPORATIONS INCLUDED IN ESIC MAJOR GROUPS 29 AND 30

Item	Petroleum and Coal Products[1]				
	1Q 1989[2]	2Q 1989[2]	3Q 1989	4Q 1989[2]	1Q 1990
	(percent of net sales)				
INCOME STATEMENT IN RATIO FORMAT					
Net sales, receipts, and operating revenues....................................	100.0	100.0	100.0	100.0	100.0
Less: Depreciation, depletion, and amortization of property, plant, and equipment	7.5	6.6	6.9	6.9	6.4
Less: All other operating costs and expenses	83.7	85.7	85.7	87.4	87.0
Income (or loss) from operations..	8.7	7.7	7.5	5.7	6.6
Net nonoperating income (expense)..	3.6	0.4	1.9	0.5	1.1
Income (or loss) before income taxes	12.4	8.1	9.4	6.2	7.7
Less: Provision for current and deferred domestic income taxes	3.1	2.7	2.2	(1.5)	1.9
Income (or loss) after income taxes	9.3	5.5	7.2	7.7	5.8
	(percent)				
OPERATING RATIOS (see explanatory notes)					
Annual rate of profit on stockholders' equity at end of period:					
Before income taxes	22.75	17.29	18.67	12.39	15.92
After income taxes..	17.01	11.63	14.36	15.45	11.99
Annual rate of profit on total assets:					
Before income taxes	9.60	7.14	7.85	5.28	6.82
After income taxes..	7.18	4.80	6.03	6.58	5.13
BALANCE SHEET RATIOS (based on succeeding table)					
Total current assets to total current liabilities.......................................	1.03	1.04	1.01	1.00	1.03
Total cash, U.S. Government and other securities to total current liabilities	0.24	0.26	0.21	0.18	0.16
Total stockholders' equity to total debt..	1.64	1.55	1.60	1.65	1.66

[1] In the first quarter 1990, a number of corporations were reclassified by industry. To provide comparability, data for quarters in 1989 were restated to reflect these reclassifications.
[2] Revised to reflect respondents' corrections of submitted data subsequent to original publication.
[3] Revised principally to reflect respondents' corrections of submitted data subsequent to original publication.

TABLE 10—BALANCE SHEET
FOR CORPORATIONS INCLUDED IN ESIC MAJOR GROUPS 29 AND 30

Item	Petroleum and Coal Products[1]				
	1Q 1989[3]	2Q 1989[3]	3Q 1989	4Q 1989[3]	1Q 1990
	(percent of total assets)				
SELECTED BALANCE SHEET RATIOS					
Total cash, U.S. Government and other securities	4.5	5.1	3.9	3.3	2.8
Trade accounts and trade notes receivable	7.7	8.0	8.0	8.6	8.1
Inventories...	5.5	5.8	5.9	5.5	5.9
Total current assets...	19.1	20.4	19.2	18.9	18.3
Net property, plant, and equipment	55.2	54.0	54.9	53.8	54.4
Short-term debt including installments on long-term debt..............................	4.2	5.0	5.0	4.1	3.7
Total current liabilities...	18.6	19.6	19.0	18.8	17.7
Long-term debt..	21.5	21.5	21.2	21.7	22.0
Total liabilities..	57.8	58.7	58.0	57.4	57.2
Stockholders' equity	42.2	41.3	42.0	42.6	42.8

[1] In the first quarter 1990, a number of corporations were reclassified by industry. To provide comparability, data for quarters in 1989 were restated to reflect these reclassifications.
[2] In the first quarter 1990, a number of corporations were reclassified by industry. To provide comparability, data for quarters in 1989 were restated to reflect these reclassifications, as well as respondents' corrections of submitted data subsequent to original publication.
[3] Revised to reflect respondents' corrections of submitted data subsequent to original publication.

Petroleum and Coal Products Assets Under $25 Million					Rubber and Misc. Plastics Products[1]					Rubber and Misc. Plastics Products Assets Under $25 Million				
1Q 1989	2Q 1989	3Q 1989	4Q 1989	1Q 1990	1Q 1989[3]	2Q 1989[3]	3Q 1989[3]	4Q 1989	1Q 1990	1Q 1989[3]	2Q 1989[3]	3Q 1989	4Q 1989	1Q 1990
(percent of net sales)					(percent of net sales)					(percent of net sales)				
100.0	100.0	100.0	100.0	100.0	100.0	100.0	100.0	100.0	100.0	100.0	100.0	100.0	100.0	100.0
2.3	2.1	1.9	2.1	2.5	3.2	3.1	3.3	3.2	3.4	3.0	3.0	3.1	2.9	3.0
98.9	94.5	89.9	94.2	99.6	91.4	90.7	92.1	92.7	91.8	91.6	90.3	91.9	93.0	90.5
(1.3)	3.4	8.2	3.6	(2.1)	5.4	6.2	4.7	4.1	4.8	5.4	6.7	4.9	4.1	6.4
(1.7)	(1.4)	(1.4)	(1.6)	(1.1)	0.5	(1.6)	(0.7)	(1.4)	(1.5)	(0.6)	(1.1)	(1.1)	(1.4)	(1.0)
(3.0)	2.0	6.8	2.0	(3.2)	5.9	4.6	4.0	2.7	3.3	4.8	5.7	3.8	2.7	5.4
0.1	0.8	1.7	0.7	0.9	1.8	1.3	1.2	1.0	1.0	1.1	1.2	0.8	0.7	1.1
(3.1)	1.2	5.1	1.3	(4.2)	4.1	3.3	2.8	1.7	2.3	3.7	4.5	3.0	2.1	4.3
(percent)					(percent)					(percent)				
(22.26)	20.01	58.69	13.95	(13.80)	24.22	19.19	15.95	10.60	12.92	27.56	31.20	20.41	14.50	29.09
(23.06)	12.17	43.67	8.99	(17.86)	16.78	13.84	11.05	6.77	8.99	21.03	24.85	16.18	10.98	23.03
(6.01)	4.97	15.31	4.24	(6.02)	8.72	6.81	5.59	3.96	4.63	10.25	12.35	7.76	6.08	11.48
(6.22)	3.02	11.40	2.73	(7.79)	6.04	4.91	3.88	2.53	3.22	7.82	9.84	6.16	4.61	9.09
1.12	1.14	1.10	1.16	1.53	1.38	1.37	1.39	1.39	1.37	1.63	1.70	1.79	1.74	1.74
0.12	0.10	0.09	0.22	0.40	0.09	0.09	0.10	0.12	0.10	0.17	0.19	0.21	0.22	0.23
0.74	0.58	0.77	0.84	1.78	1.00	0.96	0.93	1.07	0.98	1.01	1.12	0.98	1.23	1.11

Petroleum and Coal Products Assets Under $25 Million					Rubber and Misc. Plastics Products[2]					Rubber and Misc. Plastics Products Assets Under $25 Million				
1Q 1989	2Q 1989	3Q 1989	4Q 1989	1Q 1990	1Q 1989	2Q 1989	3Q 1989	4Q 1989	1Q 1990	1Q 1989	2Q 1989	3Q 1989	4Q 1989	1Q 1990
(percent of total assets)					(percent of total assets)					(percent of total assets)				
6.2	5.5	5.1	11.7	17.0	3.0	3.0	3.2	3.7	3.3	6.4	6.7	6.8	7.2	7.7
31.1	31.8	35.5	26.1	22.4	20.6	20.2	20.1	18.7	19.6	28.0	27.4	27.4	26.6	27.9
17.9	21.6	20.2	19.6	21.8	19.2	19.0	18.1	18.3	18.5	22.6	21.9	19.7	20.8	20.0
59.0	65.1	64.2	61.0	64.3	45.1	44.9	44.1	43.3	43.9	60.3	59.4	57.3	57.6	58.9
36.0	30.4	33.2	36.8	35.3	34.4	34.4	35.8	36.3	36.4	33.8	34.1	36.8	35.9	36.6
20.1	29.9	24.0	22.4	12.6	11.3	12.2	12.1	10.8	11.5	13.2	12.0	11.4	10.9	10.7
52.5	57.0	58.6	52.6	42.1	32.6	32.8	31.8	31.3	02.0	37.0	34.9	31.9	33.1	33.8
16.7	13.3	9.7	14.0	11.8	24.6	24.8	25.8	24.2	25.1	23.8	23.5	27.6	23.1	24.7
73.0	75.1	73.9	69.6	56.4	64.0	64.5	64.9	62.7	64.2	62.8	60.4	62.0	58.1	60.5
27.0	24.9	26.1	30.4	43.6	36.0	35.5	35.1	37.3	35.8	37.2	39.6	38.0	41.9	39.5

TABLE 11—INCOME STATEMENT
FOR CORPORATIONS INCLUDED IN ESIC MAJOR GROUPS 32 AND 33

Item	Stone, Clay, and Glass Products[1]				
	1Q 1989	2Q 1989	3Q 1989	4Q 1989	1Q 1990
	(percent of net sales)				
INCOME STATEMENT IN RATIO FORMAT					
Net sales, receipts, and operating revenues............................	100.0	100.0	100.0	100.0	100.0
Less: Depreciation, depletion, and amortization of property, plant, and equipment..........	5.1	4.4	4.4	4.6	5.1
Less: All other operating costs and expenses.....................................	91.1	85.8	86.3	89.0	91.4
Income (or loss) from operations......................................	3.8	9.8	9.4	6.4	3.5
Net nonoperating income (expense)......................................	(3.9)	(1.9)	(1.6)	(3.4)	(3.0)
Income (or loss) before income taxes....................................	(0.1)	8.0	7.7	3.0	0.5
Less: Provision for current and deferred domestic income taxes...................	0.1	2.4	2.1	1.0	0.5
Income (or loss) after income taxes......................................	(0.2)	5.6	5.6	2.0	0.0
	(percent)				
OPERATING RATIOS (see explanatory notes)					
Annual rate of profit on stockholders' equity at end of period:					
Before income taxes...	(0.39)	25.98	25.35	8.37	1.31
After income taxes..	(0.59)	18.12	18.52	5.63	(0.12)
Annual rate of profit on total assets:					
Before income taxes...	(0.12)	8.19	8.04	2.77	0.43
After income taxes..	(0.19)	5.71	5.87	1.87	(0.04)
BALANCE SHEET RATIOS (based on succeeding table)					
Total current assets to total current liabilities.....................................	1.47	1.56	1.51	1.47	1.49
Total cash, U.S. Government and other securities to total current liabilities...............	0.18	0.16	0.16	0.19	0.14
Total stockholders' equity to total debt...	0.73	0.74	0.76	0.81	0.77

[1] In the first quarter 1990, a number of corporations were reclassified by industry. To provide comparability, data for quarters in 1989 were restated to reflect these reclassifications.
[2] Revised to reflect respondents' corrections of submitted data subsequent to original publication.

TABLE 12—BALANCE SHEET
FOR CORPORATIONS INCLUDED IN ESIC MAJOR GROUPS 32 AND 33

Item	Stone, Clay, and Glass Products[1]				
	1Q 1989	2Q 1989	3Q 1989[3]	4Q 1989[3]	1Q 1990
	(percent of total assets)				
SELECTED BALANCE SHEET RATIOS					
Total cash, U.S. Government and other securities.....................................	3.8	3.4	3.4	3.9	2.9
Trade accounts and trade notes receivable	13.3	14.4	14.5	12.5	13.0
Inventories...	11.1	11.4	10.4	10.5	11.0
Total current assets..	30.8	32.3	31.5	30.9	30.3
Net property, plant, and equipment...	45.3	45.2	44.4	44.5	46.0
Short-term debt including installments on long-term debt.............................	5.8	5.8	5.8	6.2	6.3
Total current liabilities..	21.0	20.8	20.8	21.1	20.4
Long-term debt...	37.3	36.7	36.1	34.6	35.9
Total liabilities...	68.7	68.5	68.3	66.8	67.5
Stockholders' equity..	31.3	31.5	31.7	33.2	32.5

[1] In the first quarter 1990, a number of corporations were reclassified by industry. To provide comparability, data for quarters in 1989 were restated to reflect these reclassifications.
[2] In the first quarter 1990, a number of corporations were reclassified by industry. To provide comparability, data for quarters in 1989 were restated to reflect these reclassifications, as well as respondents' corrections of submitted data subsequent to orignial publication.
[3] Revised to reflect respondents' corrections of submitted data subsequent to original publication.

Stone, Clay, and Glass Products Assets Under $25 Million					Primary Metal Industries[1]					Primary Metal Industries Assets Under $25 Million				
1Q 1988	2Q 1988	3Q 1988	4Q 1988	1Q 1989	1Q 1989	2Q 1989	3Q 1989[2]	4Q 1989	1Q 1990	1Q 1989	2Q 1989	3Q 1989	4Q 1989	1Q 1990
(percent of net sales)					(percent of net sales)					(percent of net sales)				
100.0	100.0	100.0	100.0	100.0	100.0	100.0	100.0	100.0	100.0	100.0	100.0	100.0	100.0	100.0
4.0	3.3	3.0	3.8	4.2	3.3	3.3	3.5	3.7	3.6	2.6	2.6	2.7	2.9	2.6
97.5	88.4	89.8	94.0	95.8	88.6	89.3	89.5	90.7	90.9	90.5	91.2	92.2	95.3	93.3
(1.5)	8.3	7.2	2.2	0.0	8.2	7.4	7.0	5.6	5.5	6.9	6.2	5.1	1.8	4.1
(0.7)	0.6	1.7	0.3	(1.0)	(0.3)	0.3	0.6	(3.3)	(0.2)	(0.8)	(0.9)	(0.2)	(1.8)	(1.3)
(2.2)	8.9	8.9	2.5	(1.0)	7.9	7.7	7.6	2.2	5.3	6.1	5.4	4.8	0.0	2.7
(0.8)	2.8	2.1	0.8	0.3	2.1	2.3	2.1	0.6	1.5	1.2	1.3	1.0	0.9	0.9
(1.3)	6.1	6.8	1.6	(1.3)	5.8	5.4	5.5	1.7	3.8	5.0	4.1	3.8	(0.8)	1.9
(percent)					(percent)					(percent)				
(7.70)	34.71	38.99	8.60	(3.57)	31.85	32.38	29.07	8.20	19.20	29.25	27.08	21.16	0.14	12.39
(4.71)	23.91	29.75	5.66	(4.57)	23.43	22.80	21.03	6.15	13.79	23.71	20.66	16.72	(3.75)	8.48
(3.91)	17.68	19.76	4.49	(1.67)	10.28	10.39	9.26	2.60	6.27	14.76	12.64	10.62	0.07	5.70
(2.39)	12.18	15.07	2.96	(2.13)	7.56	7.31	6.70	1.95	4.50	11.96	9.64	8.40	(1.79)	3.91
1.96	2.01	2.08	2.08	1.82	1.76	1.80	1.74	1.70	1.68	1.86	1.89	1.96	1.90	1.93
0.45	0.40	0.40	0.43	0.28	0.29	0.29	0.28	0.28	0.24	0.27	0.30	0.30	0.34	0.31
1.76	1.76	1.77	1.88	1.41	1.11	1.06	1.05	1.02	1.08	1.93	1.52	1.80	1.53	1.45

Stone, Clay, and Glass Products Assets Under $25 Million					Primary Metal Industries[2]					Primary Metal Industries Assets Under $25 Million				
1Q 1989	2Q 1989	3Q 1989	4Q 1989	1Q 1990	1Q 1989	2Q 1989	3Q 1989	4Q 1989	1Q 1990	1Q 1989	2Q 1989	3Q 1989	4Q 1989	1Q 1990
(percent of total assets)					(percent of total assets)					(percent of total assets)				
12.8	11.7	11.7	12.0	8.8	7.1	7.0	6.6	6.7	5.8	9.0	10.0	9.4	10.9	10.0
24.9	25.4	28.0	24.0	25.3	16.7	16.6	16.0	14.8	15.3	28.9	28.5	28.3	25.2	27.2
15.6	18.4	16.4	17.7	17.9	17.6	17.5	16.8	17.1	17.1	23.3	22.7	20.6	21.7	21.9
55.9	59.0	60.2	58.3	56.8	43.3	43.2	41.7	40.5	40.1	63.2	63.4	61.7	60.4	62.4
38.5	35.5	33.2	34.6	38.2	40.9	41.4	41.9	42.5	42.4	30.6	31.1	30.0	30.3	29.4
0.4	10.6	10.2	10.2	12.5	4.9	4.7	4.5	5.0	4.8	12.5	12.6	11.3	12.2	11.2
28.6	29.3	29.0	28.1	31.1	24.6	24.0	24.0	23.8	23.9	34.0	33.5	31.5	31.8	32.3
19.4	18.4	18.5	17.6	20.6	24.3	25.5	25.8	26.2	25.5	13.6	18.1	16.7	19.1	20.5
49.2	49.1	49.3	47.7	53.3	67.7	67.9	68.2	68.3	67.4	49.5	53.3	49.8	52.3	54.0
50.8	50.9	50.7	52.3	46.7	32.3	32.1	31.8	31.7	32.6	50.5	46.7	50.2	47.7	46.0

TABLE 13—INCOME STATEMENT
FOR CORPORATIONS INCLUDED IN ESIC MAJOR GROUPS 33.1−2 AND 33.5−6

Item	Iron and Steel[1][2]				
	1Q 1989	2Q 1989	3Q 1989	4Q 1989	1Q 1990
	(percent of net sales)				
INCOME STATEMENT IN RATIO FORMAT					
Net sales, receipts, and operating revenues............................	100.0	100.0	100.0	100.0	100.0
Less: Depreciation, depletion, and amortization of property, plant, and equipment	3.3	3.3	3.5	3.5	3.5
Less: All other operating costs and expenses	90.8	91.3	92.2	91.9	92.2
Income (or loss) from operations..................................	5.9	5.5	4.4	4.6	4.3
Net nonoperating income (expense).................................	(1.3)	(0.8)	0.2	(2.3)	(0.9)
Income (or loss) before income taxes.............................	4.5	4.7	4.5	2.3	3.4
Less: Provision for current and deferred domestic income taxes	1.2	1.6	1.3	1.1	1.0
Income (or loss) after income taxes	3.3	3.0	3.2	1.3	2.4
	(percent)				
OPERATING RATIOS (see explanatory notes)					
Annual rate of profit on stockholders' equity at end of period:					
Before income taxes	36.49	34.92	32.31	15.75	22.71
After income taxes.......................................	26.72	22.63	23.03	8.52	15.89
Annual rate of profit on total assets:					
Before income taxes	6.12	6.42	5.64	2.77	4.11
After income taxes.......................................	4.49	4.16	4.02	1.50	2.88
BALANCE SHEET RATIOS (based on succeeding table)					
Total current assets to total current liabilities	1.70	1.81	1.73	1.72	1.72
Total cash, U.S. Government and other securities to total current liabilities	0.33	0.36	0.33	0.38	0.34
Total stockholders' equity to total debt..........................	0.54	0.61	0.56	0.55	0.57

[1] Included in Primary Metal Industries.
[2] In the first quarter 1990, a number of corporations were reclassified by industry. To provide comparability, data for quarters in 1989 were restated to reflect these reclassifications.
[3] Revised to reflect respondents' corrections of submitted data subsequent to original publication.

TABLE 14—BALANCE SHEET
FOR CORPORATIONS INCLUDED IN ESIC MAJOR GROUPS 33.1−2 AND 33.5−6

Item	Iron and Steel[1][2]				
	1Q 1989	2Q 1989	3Q 1989	4Q 1989	1Q 1990
	(percent of total assets)				
SELECTED BALANCE SHEET RATIOS					
Total cash, U.S. Government and other securities	9.0	9.6	8.8	10.1	9.1
Trade accounts and trade notes receivable	16.2	16.1	15.7	14.5	15.4
Inventories..	20.3	19.9	19.5	19.6	19.4
Total current assets......................................	47.2	47.7	46.5	45.8	45.4
Net property, plant, and equipment	42.8	41.8	42.7	42.7	42.8
Short-term debt including installments on long-term debt........................	5.0	4.1	4.4	4.6	4.2
Total current liabilities......................................	27.7	26.4	26.9	26.6	26.5
Long-term debt..	25.7	26.1	27.1	27.6	27.7
Total liabilities	83.2	81.6	82.5	82.4	81.9
Stockholders' equity	16.8	18.4	17.5	17.6	18.1

[1] Included in Primary Metal Industries.
[2] In the first quarter 1990, a number of corporations were reclassified by industry. To provide comparability, data for quarters in 1989 were restated to reflect these reclassifications.
[3] In the first quarter 1990, a number of corporations were reclassified by industry, to provide comparability, data for quarters in 1989 were restated to reflect these reclassifications, as well as respondents' corrections of submitted data subsequent to original publication.

	Iron and Steel Assets Under $25 Million[1]					Nonferrous Metals[1][2]					Nonferrous Metals Assets Under $25 Million[1]				
	1Q 1989	2Q 1989	3Q 1989	4Q 1989	1Q 1990	1Q 1989	2Q 1989	3Q 1989[3]	4Q 1989	1Q 1990	1Q 1989	2Q 1989	3Q 1989	4Q 1989	1Q 1990
	(percent of net sales)					(percent of net sales)					(percent of net sales)				
	100.0	100.0	100.0	100.0	100.0	100.0	100.0	100.0	100.0	100.0	100.0	100.0	100.0	100.0	100.0
	3.1	2.9	3.2	3.1	2.7	3.2	3.3	3.6	3.9	3.8	2.3	2.3	2.4	2.7	2.6
	92.6	91.2	92.0	94.0	92.9	86.5	87.5	87.0	89.6	89.6	89.5	91.2	92.4	96.2	93.6
	4.3	5.9	4.7	2.9	4.4	10.3	9.3	9.4	6.4	6.6	8.2	6.5	5.3	1.0	3.8
	(0.5)	(0.6)	0.0	(0.9)	(0.8)	0.7	1.3	0.9	(4.3)	0.4	(0.9)	(1.1)	(0.4)	(2.3)	(1.7)
	3.8	5.3	4.8	2.0	3.5	11.0	10.6	10.4	2.1	7.0	7.3	5.4	4.9	(1.3)	2.1
	1.3	1.5	1.1	1.3	1.0	2.9	2.9	2.8	0.1	1.9	1.1	1.1	0.9	0.6	0.7
	2.5	3.8	3.6	0.7	2.5	8.1	7.7	7.5	2.0	5.1	6.2	4.2	4.0	(1.9)	1.3
	(percent)					(percent)					(percent)				
	14.93	23.83	17.96	6.80	13.44	30.36	31.43	27.94	5.46	17.93	39.24	29.75	23.74	(7.28)	11.22
	9.83	17.30	13.69	2.51	9.58	22.37	22.86	20.33	5.29	13.03	33.39	23.42	19.17	(10.72)	7.28
	8.08	11.61	9.51	3.80	7.20	13.97	13.98	12.50	2.45	8.24	18.91	13.42	11.45	(2.98)	4.47
	5.32	8.43	7.25	1.40	5.13	10.30	10.17	9.10	2.37	5.99	16.10	10.56	9.24	(4.39)	2.90
	1.98	1.97	2.02	2.21	2.31	1.83	1.79	1.74	1.67	1.63	1.79	1.84	1.91	1.69	1.69
	0.28	0.28	0.33	0.45	0.42	0.25	0.21	0.22	0.17	0.13	0.26	0.31	0.28	0.27	0.24
	2.20	1.67	2.10	2.19	2.19	1.66	1.48	1.54	1.48	1.60	1.79	1.41	1.61	1.14	1.06

	Iron and Steel Assets Under $25 Million[1]					Nonferrous Metals[1][3]					Nonferrous Metals Assets Under $25 Million[1]				
	1Q 1989	2Q 1989	3Q 1989	4Q 1989	1Q 1990	1Q 1989	2Q 1989	3Q 1989	4Q 1989	1Q 1990	1Q 1989	2Q 1989	3Q 1989	4Q 1989	1Q 1990
	(percent of total assets)					(percent of total assets)					(percent of total assets)				
	8.8	9.1	10.2	12.7	11.9	5.4	4.6	4.7	3.6	2.8	9.2	10.7	8.8	9.4	8.5
	28.5	27.9	27.0	23.7	27.4	17.1	17.0	16.2	15.0	15.2	29.2	29.0	29.2	26.5	27.0
	23.0	24.0	22.1	22.3	21.2	15.1	15.2	14.4	14.8	15.0	23.4	21.7	19.5	21.3	22.5
	62.9	63.3	62.5	62.1	64.6	40.0	39.1	37.4	35.6	35.3	63.4	63.4	61.1	59.0	60.7
	30.6	30.3	30.9	31.2	29.4	39.3	41.0	41.2	42.3	42.1	30.6	31.8	29.3	29.6	29.3
	13.6	13.0	11.6	11.5	8.2	4.5	5.1	4.5	5.4	5.3	11.7	12.4	11.1	12.7	13.8
	31.7	32.1	30.9	28.1	28.0	21.8	21.8	21.5	21.3	21.6	35.5	34.5	32.0	34.9	35.9
	11.0	16.2	13.6	14.0	16.4	23.2	24.9	24.6	24.7	23.5	15.2	19.4	18.9	23.2	23.9
	45.9	51.3	47.1	44.2	46.5	54.0	55.5	55.3	55.2	54.1	51.8	54.9	51.8	59.0	60.1
	54.1	48.7	52.9	55.8	53.5	46.0	44.5	44.7	44.8	45.9	48.2	45.1	48.2	41.0	39.9

TABLE 15—INCOME STATEMENT
FOR CORPORATIONS INCLUDED IN ESIC MAJOR GROUPS 34 AND 35

Item	Fabricated Metal Products[1]				
	1Q 1989	2Q 1989	3Q 1989	4Q 1989	1Q 1990
	(percent of net sales)				
INCOME STATEMENT IN RATIO FORMAT					
Net sales, receipts, and operating revenues...............	100.0	100.0	100.0	100.0	100.0
Less: Depreciation, depletion, and amortization of property, plant, and equipment	2.8	2.5	2.7	3.0	2.8
Less: All other operating costs and expenses	89.8	90.1	90.6	92.6	90.4
Income (or loss) from operations.........................	7.3	7.4	6.8	4.4	6.8
Net nonoperating income (expense)........................	(1.2)	(1.3)	(1.2)	(0.7)	(1.5)
Income (or loss) before income taxes....................	6.1	6.1	5.6	3.7	5.4
Less: Provision for current and deferred domestic income taxes	1.7	1.7	1.5	1.5	1.4
Income (or loss) after income taxes	4.4	4.4	4.0	2.2	4.0
	(percent)				
OPERATING RATIOS (see explanatory notes)					
Annual rate of profit on stockholders' equity at end of period:					
Before income taxes	22.06	22.52	19.78	12.81	18.21
After income taxes....................	15.91	16.29	14.36	7.74	13.42
Annual rate of profit on total assets:					
Before income taxes	8.81	9.23	8.06	5.18	7.47
After income taxes....................	6.35	6.67	5.85	3.13	5.51
BALANCE SHEET RATIOS (based on succeeding table)					
Total current assets to total current liabilities..............	1.84	1.89	1.87	1.83	1.86
Total cash, U.S. Government and other securities to total current liabilities	0.23	0.22	0.21	0.22	0.21
Total stockholders' equity to total debt................	1.19	1.29	1.26	1.28	1.29

[1] In the first quarter 1990, a number of corporations were reclassified by industry. To provide comparability, data for quarters in 1989 were restated to reflect these reclassifications, as well as respondents' corrections of submitted data subsequent to original publication.
[2] Revised to reflect respondents' corrections of submitted data subsequent to original publication.

TABLE 16—BALANCE SHEET
FOR CORPORATIONS INCLUDED IN ESIC MAJOR GROUPS 34 AND 35

Item	Fabricated Metal Products[1]				
	1Q 1989	2Q 1989	3Q 1989	4Q 1989	1Q 1990
	(percent of total assets)				
SELECTED BALANCE SHEET RATIOS					
Total cash, U.S. Government and other securities....................................	6.7	6.3	6.0	6.4	5.8
Trade accounts and trade notes receivable	20.9	21.8	21.8	19.9	20.4
Inventories.................................	22.0	23.1	22.6	22.0	21.8
Total current assets...........................	52.8	54.2	53.6	52.3	51.9
Net property, plant, and equipment..................	26.6	27.0	27.0	27.3	27.7
Short-term debt including installments on long-term debt....................	8.2	7.2	7.8	7.3	7.6
Total current liabilities.......................	28.7	28.7	28.7	28.6	27.9
Long-term debt	25.4	24.5	24.5	24.3	24.3
Total liabilities	60.1	59.0	59.3	59.5	59.0
Stockholders' equity	39.9	41.0	40.7	40.5	41.0

[1] In the first quarter 1990, a number of corporations were reclassified by industry. To provide comparability, data for quarters in 1989 were restated to reflect these reclassifications, as well as respondents' corrections of submitted data subsequent to original publication.
[2] Revised to reflect respondents' corrections of submitted data subsequent to original publication.

	Fabricated Metal Products Assets Under $25 Million					Machinery, Except Electrical[1]					Machinery, Except Electrical Assets Under $25 Million				
	1Q 1989[2]	2Q 1989[2]	3Q 1989[2]	4Q 1989[2]	1Q 1990	1Q 1989	2Q 1989	3Q 1989	4Q 1989	1Q 1990	1Q 1989	2Q 1989	3Q 1989	4Q 1989	1Q 1990
	(percent of net sales)					(percent of net sales)					(percent of net sales)				
	100.0	100.0	100.0	100.0	100.0	100.0	100.0	100.0	100.0	100.0	100.0	100.0	100.0	100.0	100.0
	2.5	2.3	2.3	2.4	2.3	4.3	4.0	4.3	4.3	4.5	3.1	3.1	3.0	3.3	3.2
	90.4	90.6	91.0	93.2	90.0	91.4	90.3	91.4	96.0	91.1	91.1	89.5	91.3	94.1	91.2
	7.1	7.1	6.7	4.5	7.7	4.3	5.8	4.3	(0.3)	4.5	5.8	7.4	5.8	2.7	5.6
	(0.7)	(1.0)	(0.9)	(0.9)	(1.0)	1.4	(0.2)	0.8	3.7	0.8	(0.8)	(0.9)	(0.7)	0.8	(0.6)
	6.4	6.1	5.8	3.6	6.8	5.7	5.6	5.1	3.4	5.3	4.9	6.6	5.0	3.4	5.0
	1.5	1.3	1.3	1.0	1.4	1.4	2.0	1.6	(0.4)	1.4	1.5	1.7	1.3	1.0	1.2
	5.0	4.8	4.5	2.5	5.4	4.3	3.6	3.5	3.8	3.9	3.4	4.9	3.7	2.5	3.8
	(percent)					(percent)					(percent)				
	26.43	26.15	24.72	15.39	28.33	10.48	11.40	9.89	6.72	9.86	18.55	23.88	17.88	11.52	17.22
	20.43	20.47	19.35	10.92	22.63	7.90	7.31	6.85	7.56	7.24	12.83	17.74	13.10	8.26	13.14
	12.89	12.59	11.71	7.20	13.44	5.34	5.83	5.06	3.42	5.04	8.47	11.90	8.89	5.65	8.32
	9.96	9.86	9.16	5.11	10.73	4.02	3.74	3.50	3.85	3.70	5.86	8.85	6.52	4.05	6.35
	2.20	2.14	2.10	2.07	2.09	1.59	1.90	1.95	1.85	1.84	1.92	2.10	2.07	2.01	2.05
	0.33	0.29	0.28	0.29	0.28	0.18	0.20	0.21	0.23	0.22	0.30	0.31	0.32	0.33	0.32
	1.67	1.65	1.56	1.56	1.60	2.01	2.12	2.10	2.09	2.09	1.55	1.84	1.85	1.78	1.67

	Fabricated Metal Products Assets Under $25 Million					Machinery, Except Electrical[1]					Machinery, Except Electrical Assets Under $25 Million				
	1Q 1989[2]	2Q 1989[2]	3Q 1989[2]	4Q 1989[2]	1Q 1990	1Q 1989	2Q 1989	3Q 1989	4Q 1989	1Q 1990	1Q 1989	2Q 1989	3Q 1989	4Q 1989	1Q 1990
	(percent of total assets)					(percent of total assets)					(percent of total assets)				
	9.9	8.9	8.9	9.2	9.0	4.8	4.9	4.9	5.6	5.4	10.8	10.4	10.8	11.3	10.5
	27.7	27.7	28.1	26.6	27.8	17.0	17.9	17.7	16.9	16.7	25.6	25.8	25.5	24.7	25.1
	25.7	26.6	25.6	25.6	24.5	17.6	18.0	17.6	17.1	17.1	28.6	29.0	28.1	27.8	27.6
	66.8	66.6	66.4	66.1	65.8	43.0	46.3	46.1	45.3	45.1	68.5	69.5	69.2	67.7	67.6
	26.4	25.6	26.1	26.7	27.3	22.9	23.4	23.3	23.8	24.0	25.5	25.2	24.9	26.3	26.7
	9.9	9.7	11.3	10.7	10.3	8.2	4.8	4.4	4.6	4.9	13.0	11.7	11.5	12.1	12.1
	30.4	31.2	31.7	31.9	31.5	27.1	24.3	23.7	24.5	24.5	35.7	33.1	33.5	33.7	32.9
	19.3	19.5	19.2	19.3	19.3	17.0	19.3	19.8	19.8	19.6	16.5	15.3	15.3	15.5	17.1
	51.2	51.8	52.6	53.2	52.6	49.1	48.8	48.9	49.1	48.9	54.3	50.1	50.3	51.0	51.7
	48.8	48.2	47.4	46.8	47.4	50.9	51.2	51.1	50.9	51.1	45.7	49.9	49.7	49.0	48.3

TABLE 17—INCOME STATEMENT
FOR CORPORATIONS INCLUDED IN ESIC MAJOR GROUPS 36 AND 37

Item	Electrical and Electronic Equipment[1]				
	1Q 1989	2Q 1989[2]	3Q 1989	4Q 1989[2]	1Q 1990
	(percent of net sales)				
INCOME STATEMENT IN RATIO FORMAT					
Net sales, receipts, and operating revenues..........................	100.0	100.0	100.0	100.0	100.0
Less: Depreciation, depletion, and amortization of property, plant, and equipment	3.7	3.8	3.7	3.6	3.8
Less: All other operating costs and expenses	90.4	89.8	90.8	90.8	90.4
Income (or loss) from operations................................	5.9	6.4	5.5	5.6	5.8
Net nonoperating income (expense)................................	0.5	0.1	0.4	0.5	0.2
Income (or loss) before income taxes...........................	6.4	6.5	5.9	6.0	6.0
Less: Provision for current and deferred domestic income taxes	2.0	2.0	1.7	1.7	2.0
Income (or loss) after income taxes	4.4	4.4	4.2	4.4	4.0
	(percent)				
OPERATING RATIOS (see explanatory notes)					
Annual rate of profit on stockholders' equity at end of period:					
Before income taxes	15.59	16.37	14.57	15.48	14.41
After income taxes.	10.70	11.19	10.40	11.15	9.53
Annual rate of profit on total assets:					
Before income taxes	6.89	7.24	6.49	6.85	6.22
After income taxes.......................................	4.73	4.95	4.63	4.93	4.11
BALANCE SHEET RATIOS (based on succeeding table)					
Total current assets to total current liabilities	1.50	1.46	1.48	1.47	1.35
Total cash, U.S. Government and other securities to total current liabilities	0.18	0.17	0.17	0.19	0.17
Total stockholders' equity to total debt.............................	1.88	1.78	1.81	1.79	1.69

[1] In the first quarter 1990, a number of corporations were reclassified by industry. To provide comparability, data for quarters in 1989 were restated to reflect these reclassifications.
[2] Revised to reflect respondents' corrections of submitted data subsequent to original publication.

TABLE 18—BALANCE SHEET
FOR CORPORATIONS INCLUDED IN ESIC MAJOR GROUPS 36 AND 37

Item	Electrical and Electronic Equipment[1]				
	1Q 1989[2]	2Q 1989[2]	3Q 1989	4Q 1989	1Q 1990
	(percent of total assets)				
SELECTED BALANCE SHEET RATIOS					
Total cash, U.S. Government and other securities.....................................	6.0	5.7	5.7	6.4	6.0
Trade accounts and trade notes receivable	18.2	17.9	18.5	18.6	17.7
Inventories..	20.6	20.8	20.8	19.5	19.8
Total current assets.....................................	49.0	48.3	49.0	48.5	48.0
Net property, plant, and equipment	22.7	22.6	22.6	22.6	22.1
Short-term debt including installments on long-term debt........	7.6	8.8	8.7	8.4	10.4
Total current liabilities......................................	32.6	33.0	33.1	33.0	35.4
Long-term debt	15.9	16.0	15.9	16.3	15.1
Total liabilities	55.8	55.8	55.5	55.8	56.9
Stockholders' equity	44.2	44.2	44.5	44.2	43.1

[1] In the first quarter 1990, a number of corporations were reclassified by industry. To provide comparability, data for quarters in 1989 were restated to reflect these reclassifications.
[2] Revised to reflect respondents' corrections of submitted data subsequent to original publication.

Electrical and Electronic Equipment Assets Under $25 Million					Transportation Equipment[1]					Transportation Equipment Assets Under $25 Million				
1Q 1989	2Q 1989	3Q 1989	4Q 1989	1Q 1990	1Q 1989[2]	2Q 1989	3Q 1989	4Q 1989	1Q 1990	1Q 1989	2Q 1989	3Q 1989	4Q 1989	1Q 1990
(percent of net sales)					(percent of net sales)					(percent of net sales)				
100.0	100.0	100.0	100.0	100.0	100.0	100.0	100.0	100.0	100.0	100.0	100.0	100.0	100.0	100.0
2.8	2.5	2.6	2.7	2.5	3.6	3.4	3.8	3.7	4.0	2.2	2.9	2.1	2.2	2.3
93.8	89.8	90.9	93.6	93.2	91.4	92.2	94.4	96.1	93.8	95.5	95.0	96.4	95.6	92.4
3.4	7.6	6.5	3.7	4.2	5.0	4.4	1.8	0.2	2.1	2.3	2.1	1.4	2.2	5.3
(0.6)	(0.8)	0.0	(0.7)	(1.4)	3.1	2.7	1.8	(0.7)	2.0	0.3	(1.1)	(0.9)	(1.4)	(1.8)
2.8	6.8	6.5	3.1	2.8	8.0	7.1	3.5	(0.5)	4.2	2.6	1.0	0.5	0.8	3.5
1.5	1.7	1.5	1.1	0.6	2.1	1.9	0.8	(0.9)	0.9	0.9	1.0	0.5	0.6	0.9
1.3	5.1	5.0	1.9	2.2	5.9	5.2	2.8	0.4	3.3	1.7	0.0	0.0	0.2	2.6
(percent)					(percent)					(percent)				
9.76	24.24	22.29	11.14	10.55	25.20	22.58	9.84	(1.42)	11.70	12.34	5.26	2.66	4.35	19.47
4.57	18.05	17.16	7.05	8.22	18.59	16.63	7.70	1.29	9.16	8.08	0.13	(0.02)	1.13	14.31
4.69	12.30	11.13	5.30	4.91	9.41	8.43	3.71	(0.53)	4.36	5.73	1.95	0.96	1.81	7.18
2.20	9.16	8.57	3.36	3.82	6.94	6.21	2.90	0.48	3.41	3.75	0.05	(0.01)	0.47	5.28
2.19	2.25	2.21	2.15	2.06	1.30	1.29	1.27	1.30	1.25	1.76	1.55	1.61	1.91	1.69
0.42	0.41	0.39	0.39	0.33	0.17	0.16	0.12	0.13	0.11	0.18	0.17	0.18	0.23	0.20
1.84	2.01	1.88	1.65	1.57	2.20	2.12	2.16	2.01	2.05	1.69	1.05	1.04	1.21	1.01

Electrical and Electronic Equipment Assets Under $25 Million					Transportation Equipment[1]					Transportation Equipment Assets Under $25 Million				
1Q 1989	2Q 1989	3Q 1989	4Q 1989	1Q 1990	1Q 1989	2Q 1989[2]	3Q 1989[2]	4Q 1989	1Q 1990	1Q 1989	2Q 1989	3Q 1989	4Q 1989	1Q 1990
(percent of total assets)					(percent of total assets)					(percent of total assets)				
13.9	13.5	12.8	13.1	11.6	6.2	5.9	4.5	4.9	4.2	7.2	7.1	7.8	8.1	8.2
27.5	27.7	27.5	27.4	27.1	18.4	18.1	17.6	18.2	17.5	22.3	20.3	19.5	21.2	24.1
28.4	29.4	30.1	28.4	29.8	21.8	21.5	22.2	21.5	22.2	36.4	32.5	39.2	35.5	33.2
73.2	73.6	73.0	72.7	72.1	49.3	48.5	47.5	47.8	46.7	69.3	64.1	69.1	68.1	68.9
20.3	20.5	21.3	23.3	22.9	24.1	24.4	24.8	25.5	25.3	25.6	31.5	23.0	25.6	27.0
0.3	10.2	11.0	11.5	12.6	2.6	2.9	3.1	3.3	3.2	14.1	15.0	14.5	13.0	15.4
33.4	32.6	33.0	33.8	35.0	37.8	37.5	37.3	36.6	37.2	39.4	41.3	42.8	35.6	40.8
16.8	15.2	15.6	17.4	17.1	14.4	14.8	14.4	15.2	14.9	13.4	20.3	20.2	21.3	21.1
52.0	49.3	50.1	52.4	53.5	62.6	62.6	62.3	62.8	62.7	53.5	62.9	64.2	58.3	63.1
48.0	50.7	49.9	47.6	46.5	37.4	37.4	37.7	37.2	37.3	46.5	37.1	35.8	41.7	36.9

TABLE 19—INCOME STATEMENT
FOR CORPORATIONS INCLUDED IN ESIC MAJOR GROUPS 37.1 AND 37.7

Item	Motor Vehicles and Equipment[1] [2]				
	1Q 1989[3]	2Q 1989	3Q 1989	4Q 1989	1Q 1990
	(percent of net sales)				
INCOME STATEMENT IN RATIO FORMAT					
Net sales, receipts, and operating revenues.	100.0	100.0	100.0	100.0	100.0
Less: Depreciation, depletion, and amortization of property, plant, and equipment	3.7	3.5	4.1	3.9	4.6
Less: All other operating costs and expenses	91.5	92.4	96.3	97.8	95.6
Income (or loss) from operations.	4.9	4.1	(0.4)	(1.8)	(0.2)
Net nonoperating income (expense).	4.1	3.7	3.4	(0.8)	3.5
Income (or loss) before income taxes	9.0	7.8	3.0	(2.6)	3.3
Less: Provision for current and deferred domestic income taxes	2.3	2.0	0.6	(2.1)	0.5
Income (or loss) after income taxes	6.7	5.9	2.4	(0.5)	2.8
	(percent)				
OPERATING RATIOS (see explanatory notes)					
Annual rate of profit on stockholders' equity at end of period:					
Before income taxes	28.02	24.13	7.44	(7.18)	8.40
After income taxes.	20.86	18.08	6.03	(1.32)	7.03
Annual rate of profit on total assets:					
Before income taxes	12.10	10.41	3.27	(3.13)	3.71
After income taxes.	9.01	7.80	2.65	(0.58)	3.11
BALANCE SHEET RATIOS (based on succeeding table)					
Total current assets to total current liabilities	1.43	1.38	1.33	1.46	1.31
Total cash, U.S. Government and other securities to total current liabilities	0.26	0.25	0.18	0.25	0.16
Total stockholders' equity to total debt.	2.41	2.40	2.57	2.32	2.46

[1] Included in Transportation Equipment.
[2] In the first quarter 1990, a number of corporations were reclassified by industry. To provide comparability, data for quarters in 1989 were restated to reflect these reclassifications.
[3] Revised to reflect respondents' corrections of submitted data subsequent to original publication.

TABLE 20—BALANCE SHEET
FOR CORPORATIONS INCLUDED IN ESIC MAJOR GROUPS 37.1 AND 37.7

Item	Motor Vehicles and Equipment[1] [2]				
	1Q 1989	2Q 1989[3]	3Q 1989[3]	4Q 1989	1Q 1990
	(percent of total assets)				
SELECTED BALANCE SHEET RATIOS					
Total cash, U.S. Government and other securities	7.1	6.8	4.7	6.2	4.3
Trade accounts and trade notes receivable	18.7	18.6	17.2	17.8	16.6
Inventories.	9.7	8.9	9.9	8.7	9.2
Total current assets.	38.8	37.8	35.8	36.7	33.9
Net property, plant, and equipment	27.0	27.7	28.4	29.7	29.9
Short-term debt including installments on long-term debt.	2.1	2.3	2.4	2.7	2.7
Total current liabilities.	27.3	27.3	26.8	25.1	25.8
Long-term debt	15.9	15.8	14.6	16.0	15.3
Total liabilities	56.8	56.8	56.0	56.4	55.8
Stockholders' equity	43.2	43.2	44.0	43.6	44.2

[1] Included in Transportation Equipment.
[2] In the first quarter 1990, a number of corporations were reclassified by industry. To provide comparability, data for quarters in 1989 were restated to reflect these reclassifications.
[3] Revised to reflect respondents' corrections of submitted data subsequent to original publication.

Motor Vehicles and Equipment Assets Under $25 Million[1]					Aircraft, Guided Missiles, and Parts[1][2]					Aircraft, Guided Missiles, and Parts Assets Under $25 Million[1]				
1Q 1989	2Q 1989	3Q 1989	4Q 1989	1Q 1990	1Q 1989	2Q 1989	3Q 1989	4Q 1989	1Q 1990	1Q 1989	2Q 1989	3Q 1989	4Q 1989	1Q 1990
(percent of net sales)					(percent of net sales)					(percent of net sales)				
100.0	100.0	100.0	100.0	100.0	100.0	100.0	100.0	100.0	100.0	100.0	100.0	100.0	100.0	100.0
1.3	2.3	1.7	2.1	1.7	3.6	3.3	3.4	3.4	3.2	4.6	4.7	3.7	2.8	3.9
95.4	94.5	98.2	96.8	94.1	90.9	91.7	91.7	93.5	91.3	86.7	88.9	88.1	89.3	86.1
3.3	3.2	0.1	1.1	4.2	5.5	5.0	4.9	3.2	5.4	8.7	6.4	8.2	8.0	10.1
0.4	(1.1)	(0.3)	(0.3)	(0.6)	1.0	(0.3)	(0.4)	(0.2)	0.1	(2.6)	(3.5)	(0.6)	(4.2)	(3.2)
3.6	2.0	(0.2)	0.8	3.6	6.5	4.7	4.5	3.0	5.5	6.1	2.9	7.6	3.7	6.9
0.4	0.9	0.3	0.7	0.6	1.8	1.4	1.1	1.0	1.5	2.6	1.8	2.2	2.5	1.4
3.2	1.1	(0.5)	0.1	3.1	4.7	3.3	3.4	1.9	4.0	3.5	1.1	5.4	1.3	5.5
(percent)					(percent)					(percent)				
18.26	12.06	(0.90)	3.88	23.51	19.86	15.37	14.69	10.20	17.51	16.82	7.79	22.56	15.37	17.56
16.18	6.84	(2.53)	0.27	19.94	14.28	10.69	11.16	6.61	12.73	9.67	3.00	16.00	5.25	14.00
9.34	4.60	(0.36)	1.76	9.16	6.11	4.74	4.54	3.10	5.29	8.09	3.47	9.45	5.44	9.72
8.27	2.61	(1.02)	0.12	7.77	4.39	3.30	3.45	2.01	3.85	4.65	1.34	6.70	1.86	7.75
1.76	1.47	1.55	1.78	1.60	1.23	1.23	1.23	1.20	1.21	2.62	2.32	2.04	2.13	2.39
0.19	0.15	0.18	0.24	0.21	0.09	0.09	0.08	0.05	0.07	0.40	0.28	0.20	0.27	0.24
2.21	1.12	1.27	1.59	1.25	2.13	1.94	1.85	1.77	1.76	1.57	1.32	1.26	0.82	2.05

Motor Vehicles and Equipment Assets Under $25 Million[1]					Aircraft, Guided Missiles, and Parts[1][2]					Aircraft, Guided Missiles, and Parts Assets Under $25 Million[1]				
1Q 1989	2Q 1989	3Q 1989	4Q 1989	1Q 1990	1Q 1989	2Q 1989	3Q 1989	4Q 1989	1Q 1990	1Q 1989	2Q 1989	3Q 1989	4Q 1989	1Q 1990
(percent of total assets)					(percent of total assets)					(percent of total assets)				
7.8	6.6	8.3	9.8	9.5	4.6	4.4	3.8	2.7	3.7	10.6	8.0	6.5	7.4	6.3
23.7	21.5	20.9	21.0	22.6	14.9	14.6	14.9	15.4	15.0	16.3	15.2	16.1	17.4	20.9
38.8	34.2	41.0	40.2	38.4	42.1	41.5	41.2	41.1	41.1	39.2	39.4	39.7	32.0	31.9
72.1	64.0	72.7	74.3	73.7	63.6	62.4	61.9	61.1	61.5	69.0	66.6	65.0	59.4	62.4
20.1	29.9	19.2	20.9	21.7	19.7	19.7	20.0	20.1	19.5	24.0	27.3	22.8	28.7	28.7
15.7	16.5	20.2	17.4	17.0	3.0	3.3	3.8	4.2	3.8	7.3	9.5	8.5	7.9	9.1
40.8	43.5	47.0	41.7	46.2	51.9	50.7	50.2	50.8	50.7	26.4	28.7	31.9	27.8	26.1
7.4	17.7	11.6	11.1	14.0	11.5	12.6	13.0	13.0	13.3	23.5	24.3	24.7	35.0	17.8
48.9	61.9	59.8	54.7	61.0	69.2	69.1	69.1	69.6	69.8	51.9	55.5	58.1	64.6	44.7
51.1	38.1	40.2	45.3	39.0	30.8	30.9	30.9	30.4	30.2	48.1	44.5	41.9	35.4	55.3

TABLE 21—INCOME STATEMENT
FOR CORPORATIONS INCLUDED IN ESIC MAJOR GROUP 38
AND OTHER DURABLE MANUFACTURING INDUSTRIES

Item	Instruments and Related Products[1]				
	1Q 1989	2Q 1989[2]	3Q 1989[2]	4Q 1989[2]	1Q 1990
	(percent of net sales)				
INCOME STATEMENT IN RATIO FORMAT					
Net sales, receipts, and operating revenues....................	100.0	100.0	100.0	100.0	100.0
Less: Depreciation, depletion, and amortization of property, plant, and equipment	4.4	4.4	4.4	4.5	4.5
Less: All other operating costs and expenses	89.0	87.7	89.2	91.6	88.7
Income (or loss) from operations......................	6.7	7.9	6.4	3.8	6.8
Net nonoperating income (expense)...........................	2.1	0.4	2.1	2.2	0.7
Income (or loss) before income taxes	8.7	8.3	8.4	6.1	7.5
Less: Provision for current and deferred domestic income taxes	2.2	2.0	1.9	0.8	1.5
Income (or loss) after income taxes	6.6	6.3	6.6	5.2	5.9
	(percent)				
OPERATING RATIOS (see explanatory notes)					
Annual rate of profit on stockholders' equity at end of period:					
Before income taxes	16.84	17.16	16.90	12.34	14.47
After income taxes..................................	12.64	13.06	13.16	10.61	11.49
Annual rate of profit on total assets:					
Before income taxes	7.78	7.91	7.62	5.60	6.52
After income taxes..................................	5.84	6.02	5.93	4.81	5.18
BALANCE SHEET RATIOS (based on succeeding table)					
Total current assets to total current liabilities.......................................	1.57	1.62	1.62	1.66	1.65
Total cash, U.S. Government and other securities to total current liabilities	0.19	0.17	0.18	0.22	0.21
Total stockholders' equity to total debt..	1.62	1.60	1.51	1.49	1.47

[1] In the first quarter 1990, a number of corporations were reclassified by industry. To provide comparability, data for quarters in 1989 were restated to reflect these reclassifications.
[2] Revised to reflect respondents' corrections of submitted data subsequent to original publication.
[3] Revised.

TABLE 22—BALANCE SHEET
FOR CORPORATIONS INCLUDED IN ESIC MAJOR GROUP 38
AND OTHER DURABLE MANUFACTURING INDUSTRIES

Item	Instruments and Related Products[1]				
	1Q 1989	2Q 1989[3]	3Q 1989[3]	4Q 1989[3]	1Q 1990
	(percent of total assets)				
SELECTED BALANCE SHEET RATIOS					
Total cash, U.S. Government and other securities	4.9	4.2	4.4	5.3	5.2
Trade accounts and trade notes receivable	15.2	15.9	15.8	15.2	15.6
Inventories..	16.4	16.9	16.6	15.4	15.8
Total current assets...	40.1	40.4	40.3	39.4	39.9
Net property, plant, and equipment...........................	24.9	25.6	25.3	25.7	24.7
Short-term debt including installments on long-term debt................	6.4	6.1	6.2	6.6	6.7
Total current liabilities..	25.6	24.9	24.9	23.7	24.2
Long-term debt	22.1	22.6	23.7	23.9	23.9
Total liabilities	53.8	53.9	54.9	54.6	54.9
Stockholders' equity	46.2	46.1	45.1	45.4	45.1

[1] In the first quarter 1990, a number of corporations were reclassified by industry. To provide comparability, data for quarters in 1989 were restated to reflect these reclassifications.
[2] In the first quarter 1990, a number of corporations were reclassified by industry. To provide comparability, data for quarters in 1989 were restated to reflect these reclassifications, as well as respondents' corrections of submitted data subsequent to original publication.
[3] Revised to reflect respondents' corrections of submitted data subsequent to original publication.
[4] Revised.

	Instruments and Related Products Assets Under $25 Million					Other Durable Manufacturing Industries[1]					Other Durable Manufacturing Industries Assets Under $25 Million				
	1Q 1989	2Q 1989	3Q 1989	4Q 1989	1Q 1990	1Q 1989	2Q 1989	3Q 1989	4Q 1989	1Q 1990	1Q 1989	2Q 1989	3Q 1989	4Q 1989	1Q 1990
(percent of net sales)															
	100.0	100.0	100.0	100.0	100.0	100.0	100.0	100.0	100.0	100.0	100.0	100.0	100.0	100.0	100.0
	2.9	3.5	2.9	2.7	2.8	2.9	2.7	2.7	2.9	3.0	2.3	2.1	2.1	2.3	2.2
	91.4	89.6	97.5	97.4	91.5	90.3	89.5	88.8	91.0	91.4	92.9	92.2	90.9	94.8	93.6
	5.8	6.8	(0.4)	(0.1)	5.7	6.8	7.8	8.5	6.1	5.6	4.8	5.7	7.0	2.9	4.2
	(1.2)	(1.2)	(0.6)	(0.6)	(2.0)	(1.7)	(1.7)	(1.2)	(2.5)	(1.6)	(1.1)	(0.7)	(1.1)	(1.4)	(0.7)
	4.5	5.6	(1.0)	(0.7)	3.7	5.1	6.1	7.3	3.6	4.0	3.7	5.0	5.9	1.5	3.5
	2.0	2.8	1.6	1.0	1.5	1.8	1.9	2.1	1.5	1.6	0.9	1.2	1.2	0.7	0.9
	2.5	2.8	(2.6)	(1.7)	2.1	3.4	4.2	5.2	2.1	2.4	2.8	3.8	4.7	0.8	2.6
(percent)															
	20.83	28.56	(4.48)	(2.95)	16.44	19.88	25.45	30.67	14.69	15.93	17.10	24.51	30.71	7.55	16.56
	11.52	14.35	(11.41)	(7.01)	9.64	13.02	17.42	21.72	8.60	9.59	12.91	18.76	24.52	4.19	12.26
	7.52	10.38	(1.65)	(1.14)	5.77	8.19	10.39	12.55	5.91	5.94	7.55	11.01	13.51	3.33	6.96
	4.16	5.21	(4.21)	(2.72)	3.38	5.37	7.11	8.89	3.46	3.58	5.70	8.43	10.79	1.85	5.15
	2.07	2.05	2.19	2.41	2.27	2.03	2.01	1.96	1.94	1.92	1.95	2.12	2.03	1.97	1.89
	0.35	0.32	0.43	0.61	0.59	0.24	0.25	0.25	0.26	0.24	0.20	0.22	0.24	0.26	0.21
	0.95	0.97	0.99	1.06	0.88	1.11	1.11	1.09	1.07	0.89	1.21	1.32	1.20	1.31	1.18

	Instruments and Related Products Assets Under $25 Million					Other Durable Manufacturing Industries[2]					Other Durable Manufacturing Industries Assets Under $25 Million				
	1Q 1989	2Q 1989	3Q 1989	4Q 1989	1Q 1990	1Q 1989	2Q 1989	3Q 1989	4Q 1989	1Q 1990	1Q 1989[4]	2Q 1989[4]	3Q 1989[4]	4Q 1989	1Q 1990
(percent of total assets)															
	12.4	11.4	14.6	18.4	19.7	6.1	6.3	6.8	6.9	6.2	6.6	6.7	7.8	8.7	7.3
	26.6	28.1	25.0	25.5	25.2	19.7	20.3	20.2	18.9	18.2	23.8	24.7	24.2	23.1	23.7
	30.0	30.5	31.4	25.9	28.1	23.0	21.8	21.9	22.5	21.7	31.0	28.7	28.8	31.4	30.4
	72.6	73.4	74.8	73.0	75.3	52.0	51.4	52.3	51.8	50.1	64.7	63.6	65.5	66.9	65.6
	21.1	20.2	20.0	20.0	18.1	34.5	34.0	33.7	33.8	32.5	27.3	27.2	28.2	27.8	25.7
	11.0	11.3	10.0	7.5	9.7	9.3	9.6	10.3	10.2	9.6	15.0	12.7	14.8	14.0	14.0
	35.0	35.9	34.1	30.3	33.1	25.7	25.6	26.7	26.7	26.1	33.2	30.1	32.3	34.0	34.7
	27.1	26.0	27.2	29.2	30.3	27.8	27.4	27.1	27.4	32.1	21.4	21.2	21.7	19.8	21.7
	63.9	63.7	63.1	61.1	64.9	58.8	59.2	59.1	59.7	62.7	55.9	55.1	56.0	55.9	58.0
	36.1	36.3	36.9	38.9	35.1	41.2	40.8	40.9	40.3	37.3	44.1	44.9	44.0	44.1	42.0

TABLE 23—INCOME STATEMENT
FOR CORPORATIONS INCLUDED IN ESIC MAJOR GROUP 20,
ASSETS $25 MILLION AND OVER

Item	Food and Kindred Products[1]				
	1Q 1989	2Q 1989	3Q 1989	4Q 1989	1Q 1990
	(percent of net sales)				
INCOME STATEMENT IN RATIO FORMAT					
Net sales, receipts, and operating revenues	100.0	100.0	100.0	100.0	100.0
Less: Depreciation, depletion, and amortization of property, plant, and equipment	2.8	2.5	2.6	2.5	2.7
Less: All other operating costs and expenses	89.4	88.1	88.5	88.0	89.1
Income (or loss) from operations	7.8	9.3	8.9	9.4	8.2
Net nonoperating income (expense)	(2.0)	(3.9)	(4.2)	(1.8)	(3.3)
Income (or loss) before income taxes	5.8	5.5	4.7	7.6	4.9
Net income (or loss) of foreign branches and equity in earnings (losses) of nonconsolidated subsidiaries (net of foreign taxes)	0.8	1.4	1.1	1.1	1.1
Less: Provision for current and deferred domestic income taxes	2.0	2.5	2.2	2.9	2.0
Income (or loss) after income taxes	4.7	4.4	3.7	5.8	3.9
	(percent)				
OPERATING RATIOS (see explanatory notes)					
Annual rate of profit on stockholders' equity at end of period:					
Before income taxes	23.06	26.14	22.30	33.56	22.82
After income taxes	16.06	16.75	14.06	22.35	15.01
Annual rate of profit on total assets:					
Before income taxes	7.42	8.23	6.83	10.34	6.94
After income taxes	5.17	5.27	4.30	6.89	4.56

[1]In the first quarter 1990, a number of corporations were reclassified by industry. To provide comparability, data for quarters in 1989 were restated to reflect these reclassifications, as well as respondents' corrections of submitted data subsequent to original publication.

TABLE 24—INCOME STATEMENT
FOR CORPORATIONS INCLUDED IN ESIC MAJOR GROUP 22,
ASSETS $25 MILLION AND OVER

Item	Textile Mill Products[1]				
	1Q 1989	2Q 1989	3Q 1989	4Q 1989	1Q 1990
	(percent of net sales)				
INCOME STATEMENT IN RATIO FORMAT					
Net sales, receipts, and operating revenues	100.0	100.0	100.0	100.0	100.0
Less: Depreciation, depletion, and amortization of property, plant, and equipment	3.6	3.5	3.6	3.5	4.1
Less: All other operating costs and expenses	89.9	88.7	89.6	90.0	90.6
Income (or loss) from operations	6.5	7.8	6.8	6.4	5.4
Net nonoperating income (expense)	(3.7)	(3.5)	(3.2)	(3.3)	(5.8)
Income (or loss) before income taxes	2.7	4.3	3.6	3.2	(0.4)
Net income (or loss) of foreign branches and equity in earnings (losses) of nonconsolidated subsidiaries (net of foreign taxes)	0.2	0.2	0.1	0.0	0.1
Less: Provision for current and deferred domestic income taxes	1.2	1.8	1.2	1.2	0.9
Income (or loss) after income taxes	1.7	2.8	2.5	2.0	(1.1)
	(percent)				
OPERATING RATIOS (see explanatory notes)					
Annual rate of profit on stockholders' equity at end of period:					
Before income taxes	10.53	17.59	14.37	12.29	(1.06)
After income taxes	6.13	10.70	9.69	7.79	(3.96)
Annual rate of profit on total assets:					
Before income taxes	3.71	6.02	4.84	4.08	(0.37)
After income taxes	2.16	3.66	3.26	2.58	(1.37)

[1]In the first quarter 1990, a number of corporations were reclassified by industry. To provide comparability, data for quarters in 1989 were restated to reflect these reclassifications.

TABLE 25—INCOME STATEMENT
FOR CORPORATIONS INCLUDED IN ESIC MAJOR GROUP 26,
ASSETS $25 MILLION AND OVER

Item	Paper and Allied Products[1]				
	1Q 1989	2Q 1989	3Q 1989	4Q 1989	1Q 1990
	(percent of net sales)				
INCOME STATEMENT IN RATIO FORMAT					
Net sales, receipts, and operating revenues	100.0	100.0	100.0	100.0	100.0
Less: Depreciation, depletion, and amortization of property, plant, and equipment	4.6	4.7	4.8	4.9	5.0
Less: All other operating costs and expenses	82.1	82.5	83.0	84.6	85.0
Income (or loss) from operations	13.3	12.9	12.2	10.4	10.0
Net nonoperating income (expense)	(1.8)	(2.0)	(1.9)	(5.2)	(3.1)
Income (or loss) before income taxes	11.5	10.9	10.4	5.2	6.8
Net income (or loss) of foreign branches and equity in earnings (losses) of nonconsolidated subsidiaries (net of foreign taxes)	0.7	0.8	0.9	1.2	0.9
Less: Provision for current and deferred domestic income taxes	4.2	4.2	4.3	2.3	2.7
Income (or loss) after income taxes	7.9	7.6	7.0	4.2	5.0
	(percent)				
OPERATING RATIOS (see explanatory notes)					
Annual rate of profit on stockholders' equity at end of period:					
Before income taxes	28.12	27.59	25.82	14.86	16.98
After income taxes	18.36	17.80	16.00	9.58	10.99
Annual rate of profit on total assets:					
Before income taxes	12.55	12.10	11.21	6.21	7.15
After income taxes	8.19	7.80	6.95	4.00	4.63

[1]In the first quarter 1990, a number of corporations were reclassified by industry. To provide comparability, data for quarters in 1989 were restated to reflect these reclassifications.

TABLE 26—INCOME STATEMENT
FOR CORPORATIONS INCLUDED IN ESIC MAJOR GROUP 27,
ASSETS $25 MILLION AND OVER

Item	Printing and Publishing				
	1Q 1989[1]	2Q 1989[1]	3Q 1989[1]	4Q 1989[1]	1Q 1990
	(percent of net sales)				
INCOME STATEMENT IN RATIO FORMAT					
Net sales, receipts, and operating revenues	100.0	100.0	100.0	100.0	100.0
Less: Depreciation, depletion, and amortization of property, plant, and equipment	4.2	4.2	4.2	3.7	4.2
Less: All other operating costs and expenses	84.9	83.2	84.8	85.7	87.1
Income (or loss) from operations	10.9	12.5	10.9	10.7	8.7
Net nonoperating income (expense)	(1.6)	(2.7)	(4.4)	3.6	(3.3)
Income (or loss) before income taxes	9.3	9.9	6.5	14.2	5.4
Net income (or loss) of foreign branches and equity in earnings (losses) of nonconsolidated subsidiaries (net of foreign taxes)	1.2	1.3	1.9	1.4	0.9
Less: Provision for current and deferred domestic income taxes	4.4	4.5	2.9	6.2	3.0
Income (or loss) after income taxes	6.0	6.6	5.5	9.4	3.3
	(percent)				
OPERATING RATIOS (see explanatory notes)					
Annual rate of profit on stockholders' equity at end of period:					
Before income taxes	22.36	23.65	17.74	34.20	11.57
After income taxes	12.94	14.07	11.51	20.65	6.00
Annual rate of profit on total assets:					
Before income taxes	9.22	9.71	6.85	13.00	4.61
After income taxes	5.34	5.78	4.45	7.85	2.39

[1]Revised to reflect respondents' corrections of submitted data subsequent to original publication.

TABLE 27—INCOME STATEMENT
FOR CORPORATIONS INCLUDED IN ESIC MAJOR GROUP 28, ASSETS $25 MILLION AND OVER

Item	Chemicals and Allied Products[1]				
	1Q 1989	2Q 1989	3Q 1989	4Q 1989	1Q 1990
	(percent of net sales)				
INCOME STATEMENT IN RATIO FORMAT					
Net sales, receipts, and operating revenues....................	100.0	100.0	100.0	100.0	100.0
Less: Depreciation, depletion, and amortization of property, plant, and equipment	4.3	4.4	4.7	4.9	4.6
Less: All other operating costs and expenses	84.3	85.6	85.6	88.9	86.4
Income (or loss) from operations.................	11.4	10.0	9.7	6.2	9.0
Net nonoperating income (expense).....................	0.0	1.2	0.0	1.4	0.2
Income (or loss) before income taxes	11.4	11.2	9.7	7.7	9.2
Net income (or loss) of foreign branches and equity in earnings (losses) of nonconsolidated subsidiaries (net of foreign taxes)	3.5	2.7	3.0	1.0	2.8
Less: Provision for current and deferred domestic income taxes	4.5	4.2	3.6	1.9	3.6
Income (or loss) after income taxes	10.5	9.6	9.1	6.8	8.3
	(percent)				
OPERATING RATIOS (see explanatory notes)					
Annual rate of profit on stockholders' equity at end of period:					
Before income taxes	32.63	30.99	26.81	17.68	24.02
After income taxes..................	22.91	21.58	19.30	13.87	16.67
Annual rate of profit on total assets:					
Before income taxes	14.08	13.28	11.52	7.63	10.44
After income taxes..................	9.89	9.25	8.29	5.99	7.24

[1]In the first quarter 1990, a number of corporations were reclassified by industry. To provide comparability, data for quarters in 1989 were restated to reflect these reclassifications, as well as respondents' corrections of submitted data subsequent to original publication.

TABLE 28—INCOME STATEMENT
FOR CORPORATIONS INCLUDED IN ESIC MAJOR GROUP 28.1, ASSETS $25 MILLION AND OVER

Item	Industrial Chemicals and Synthetics[1]				
	1Q 1989	2Q 1989	3Q 1989	4Q 1989	1Q 1990
	(percent of net sales)				
INCOME STATEMENT IN RATIO FORMAT					
Net sales, receipts, and operating revenues....................	100.0	100.0	100.0	100.0	100.0
Less: Depreciation, depletion, and amortization of property, plant, and equipment	5.4	5.4	6.1	6.4	6.1
Less: All other operating costs and expenses	82.0	83.9	84.5	87.9	84.6
Income (or loss) from operations.................	12.6	10.7	9.5	5.6	9.3
Net nonoperating income (expense).....................	0.1	1.0	0.4	(0.4)	(1.7)
Income (or loss) before income taxes	12.7	11.7	9.8	5.2	7.5
Net income (or loss) of foreign branches and equity in earnings (losses) of nonconsolidated subsidiaries (net of foreign taxes)	3.0	2.6	2.0	0.7	2.2
Less: Provision for current and deferred domestic income taxes	5.0	4.5	3.3	1.7	3.2
Income (or loss) after income taxes	10.7	9.8	8.4	4.2	6.4
	(percent)				
OPERATING RATIOS (see explanatory notes)					
Annual rate of profit on stockholders' equity at end of period:					
Before income taxes	34.92	31.19	23.51	10.90	17.71
After income taxes..................	23.78	21.36	16.75	7.79	11.72
Annual rate of profit on total assets:					
Before income taxes	15.09	13.71	10.36	4.90	7.96
After income taxes..................	10.28	9.39	7.38	3.50	5.27

[1]In the first quarter 1990, a number of corporations were reclassified by industry. To provide comparability, data for quarters in 1989 were restated to reflect these reclassifications.

TABLE 29—INCOME STATEMENT
FOR CORPORATIONS INCLUDED IN ESIC MAJOR GROUP 28.3, ASSETS $25 MILLION AND OVER

Item	Drugs[1]				
	1Q 1990	2Q 1990	3Q 1989	4Q 1989	1Q 1990
	(percent of net sales)				
INCOME STATEMENT IN RATIO FORMAT					
Net sales, receipts, and operating revenues....................	100.0	100.0	100.0	100.0	100.0
Less: Depreciation, depletion, and amortization of property, plant, and equipment	3.3	4.0	3.4	4.2	3.4
Less: All other operating costs and expenses	83.0	85.0	85.5	88.1	85.5
Income (or loss) from operations....................	13.7	11.9	11.8	7.7	11.1
Net nonoperating income (expense)........................	3.8	6.9	0.2	8.5	2.8
Income (or loss) before income taxes....................	17.5	18.9	11.3	16.2	13.9
Net income (or loss) of foreign branches and equity in earnings (losses) of					
nonconsolidated subsidiaries (net of foreign taxes)	6.5	4.2	6.9	1.8	6.3
Less: Provision for current and deferred domestic income taxes	6.9	6.5	4.7	2.8	4.9
Income (or loss) after income taxes	17.2	15.7	13.5	15.2	15.1
	(percent)				
OPERATING RATIOS (see explanatory notes)					
Annual rate of profit on stockholders' equity at end of period:					
Before income taxes	45.05	41.02	34.03	31.71	34.56
After income taxes.......................................	32.15	29.03	25.35	26.76	26.03
Annual rate of profit on total assets:					
Before income taxes	20.69	19.25	15.51	15.55	17.49
After income taxes.......................................	14.77	13.62	11.55	13.12	13.17

[1] In the first quarter 1990, a number of corporations were reclassified by industry. To provide comparability, data for quarters in 1989 were restated to reflect these reclassifications, as well as respondents' corrections of submitted data subsequent to original publication.

TABLE 30—INCOME STATEMENT
FOR CORPORATIONS INCLUDED IN ESIC MAJOR GROUP 29, ASSETS $25 MILLION AND OVER

Item	Petroleum and Coal Products[1]				
	1Q 1989[2]	2Q 1989[2]	3Q 1989	4Q 1989[2]	1Q 1990
	(percent of net sales)				
INCOME STATEMENT IN RATIO FORMAT					
Net sales, receipts, and operating revenues.........................	100.0	100.0	100.0	100.0	100.0
Less: Depreciation, depletion, and amortization of property, plant, and equipment	7.6	6.6	6.9	7.0	6.5
Less: All other operating costs and expenses	83.5	85.6	85.6	87.3	86.9
Income (or loss) from operations....................	8.9	7.8	7.4	5.7	6.6
Net nonoperating income (expense)........................	1.9	(1.0)	(0.1)	(0.5)	(1.0)
Income (or loss) before income taxes.....................	10.8	6.8	7.4	5.2	5.6
Net income (or loss) of foreign branches and equity in earnings (losses) of					
nonconsolidated subsidiaries (net of foreign taxes)	1.8	1.4	2.0	1.1	2.1
Less: Provision for current and deferred domestic income taxes	3.1	2.7	2.1	(1.5)	1.9
Income (or loss) after income taxes	9.4	5.5	7.2	7.8	5.8
	(percent)				
OPERATING RATIOS (see explanatory notes)					
Annual rate of profit on stockholders' equity at end of period:					
Before income taxes	22.90	17.28	18.57	12.39	16.01
After income taxes.......................................	17.14	11.63	14.28	15.47	12.08
Annual rate of profit on total assets:					
Before income taxes	9.68	7.15	7.82	5.28	6.85
After income taxes.......................................	7.24	4.81	6.01	6.59	5.17

[1] In the first quarter 1990, a number of corporations were reclassified by industry. To provide comparability, data for quarters in 1989 were restated to reflect these reclassifications.
[2] Revised to reflect respondents' corrections of submitted data subsequent to original publication.

TABLE 31—INCOME STATEMENT
FOR CORPORATIONS INCLUDED IN ESIC MAJOR GROUP 30, ASSETS $25 MILLION AND OVER

Item	Rubber and Miscellaneous Plastics Products[1]				
	1Q 1989	2Q 1989	3Q 1989[2]	4Q 1989	1Q 1990
	(percent of net sales)				
INCOME STATEMENT IN RATIO FORMAT					
Net sales, receipts, and operating revenues..........	100.0	100.0	100.0	100.0	100.0
Less: Depreciation, depletion, and amortization of property, plant, and equipment	3.3	3.2	3.3	3.4	3.7
Less: All other operating costs and expenses	91.4	91.0	92.1	92.5	92.6
Income (or loss) from operations........................	5.3	5.8	4.5	4.1	3.7
Net nonoperating income (expense).....................	0.7	(2.9)	(0.4)	(1.5)	(2.2)
Income (or loss) before income taxes	6.1	2.8	4.2	2.6	1.5
Net income (or loss) of foreign branches and equity in earnings (losses) of nonconsolidated subsidiaries (net of foreign taxes)	0.6	1.0	(0.1)	0.1	0.4
Less: Provision for current and deferred domestic income taxes	2.3	1.3	1.5	1.2	1.0
Income (or loss) after income taxes	4.4	2.5	2.6	1.5	1.0
	(percent)				
OPERATING RATIOS (see explanatory notes)					
Annual rate of profit on stockholders' equity at end of period:					
Before income taxes	22.85	14.25	14.27	9.06	6.48
After income taxes.........................	15.02	9.31	9.12	5.11	3.40
Annual rate of profit on total assets:					
Before income taxes	8.11	4.85	4.86	3.24	2.24
After income taxes.........................	5.33	3.17	3.11	1.83	1.18

[1]In the first quarter 1990, a number of corporations were reclassified by industry. To provide comparability, data for quarters in 1989 were restated to reflect these reclassifications.
[2]Revised to reflect respondents' corrections of submitted data subsequent to original publication.

TABLE 32—INCOME STATEMENT
FOR CORPORATIONS INCLUDED IN ESIC MAJOR GROUP 32, ASSETS $25 MILLION AND OVER

Item	Stone, Clay, and Glass Products[1]				
	1Q 1989	2Q 1989	3Q 1989	4Q 1989	1Q 1990
	(percent of net sales)				
INCOME STATEMENT IN RATIO FORMAT					
Net sales, receipts, and operating revenues..........	100.0	100.0	100.0	100.0	100.0
Less: Depreciation, depletion, and amortization of property, plant, and equipment	5.6	4.8	5.0	4.9	5.5
Less: All other operating costs and expenses	88.5	84.7	84.8	87.2	89.7
Income (or loss) from operations........................	5.9	10.5	10.3	7.9	4.8
Net nonoperating income (expense).....................	(6.2)	(4.3)	(5.0)	(5.5)	(4.2)
Income (or loss) before income taxes	(0.3)	6.2	5.3	2.4	0.7
Net income (or loss) of foreign branches and equity in earnings (losses) of nonconsolidated subsidiaries (net of foreign taxes)	1.0	1.4	1.9	0.8	0.4
Less: Provision for current and deferred domestic income taxes	0.4	2.2	2.1	1.0	0.6
Income (or loss) after income taxes	0.3	5.3	5.1	2.2	0.4
	(percent)				
OPERATING RATIOS (see explanatory notes)					
Annual rate of profit on stockholders' equity at end of period:					
Before income taxes	1.88	23.03	21.43	8.30	2.53
After income taxes.........................	0.69	16.16	15.28	5.62	0.99
Annual rate of profit on total assets:					
Before income taxes	0.53	6.43	6.14	2.50	0.76
After income taxes.........................	0.19	4.51	4.38	1.69	0.30

[1]In the first quarter 1990, a number of corporations were reclassified by industry. To provide comparability, data for quarters in 1989 were restated to reflect these reclassifications.

TABLE 33—INCOME STATEMENT
FOR CORPORATIONS INCLUDED IN ESIC MAJOR GROUP 33, ASSETS $25 MILLION AND OVER

Item	Primary Metal Industries[1]				
	1Q 1989	2Q 1989	3Q 1989[2]	4Q 1989	1Q 1990
	(percent of net sales)				
INCOME STATEMENT IN RATIO FORMAT					
Net sales, receipts, and operating revenues	100.0	100.0	100.0	100.0	100.0
Less: Depreciation, depletion, and amortization of property, plant, and equipment	3.4	3.4	3.6	3.8	3.8
Less: All other operating costs and expenses	88.3	89.0	89.1	90.1	90.5
Income (or loss) from operations	8.3	7.6	7.3	6.1	5.7
Net nonoperating income (expense)	(1.7)	(1.5)	(1.1)	(6.0)	(1.6)
Income (or loss) before income taxes	6.6	6.1	6.2	0.1	4.1
Net income (or loss) of foreign branches and equity in earnings (losses) of nonconsolidated subsidiaries (net of foreign taxes)	1.5	2.0	1.7	2.4	1.6
Less: Provision for current and deferred domestic income taxes	2.2	2.4	2.2	0.5	1.5
Income (or loss) after income taxes	5.9	5.6	5.7	2.0	4.1
	(percent)				
OPERATING RATIOS (see explanatory notes)					
Annual rate of profit on stockholders' equity at end of period:					
Before income taxes	32.17	33.01	30.09	9.14	20.00
After income taxes	23.40	23.05	21.58	7.31	14.41
Annual rate of profit on total assets:					
Before income taxes	9.95	10.21	9.15	2.79	6.31
After income taxes	7.24	7.13	6.56	2.23	4.55

[1]In the first quarter 1990, a number of corporations were reclassified by industry. To provide comparability, data for quarters in 1989 were restated to reflect these reclassifications.
[2]Revised to reflect respondents' corrections of submitted data subsequent to original publication.

TABLE 34—INCOME STATEMENT
FOR CORPORATIONS INCLUDED IN ESIC MAJOR GROUP 33.1—2, ASSETS $25 MILLION AND OVER

Item	Iron and Steel[1]				
	1Q 1989	2Q 1989	3Q 1989	4Q 1989	1Q 1990
	(percent of net sales)				
INCOME STATEMENT IN RATIO FORMAT					
Net sales, receipts, and operating revenues	100.0	100.0	100.0	100.0	100.0
Less: Depreciation, depletion, and amortization of property, plant, and equipment	3.4	3.3	3.5	3.5	3.6
Less: All other operating costs and expenses	90.6	91.3	92.2	91.6	92.1
Income (or loss) from operations	6.0	5.4	4.3	4.8	4.3
Net nonoperating income (expense)	(1.5)	(1.2)	(0.1)	(2.8)	(1.1)
Income (or loss) before income taxes	4.5	4.3	4.2	2.1	3.2
Net income (or loss) of foreign branches and equity in earnings (losses) of nonconsolidated subsidiaries (net of foreign taxes)	0.2	0.3	0.3	0.3	0.2
Less: Provision for current and deferred domestic income taxes	1.2	1.7	1.3	1.1	1.0
Income (or loss) after income taxes	3.4	2.9	3.2	1.3	2.3
	(percent)				
OPERATING RATIOS (see explanatory notes)					
Annual rate of profit on stockholders' equity at end of period:					
Before income taxes	41.22	37.28	35.82	18.10	25.16
After income taxes	30.44	23.76	25.31	10.09	17.56
Annual rate of profit on total assets:					
Before income taxes	6.01	6.06	5.37	2.70	3.88
After income taxes	4.44	3.86	3.79	1.51	2.70

[1]In the first quarter 1990, a number of corporations were reclassified by industry. To provide comparability, data for quarters in 1989 were restated to reflect these reclassifications.

TABLE 35—INCOME STATEMENT
FOR CORPORATIONS INCLUDED IN ESIC MAJOR GROUP 33.5–6, ASSETS $25 MILLION AND OVER

Item	Nonferrous Metals[1]				
	1Q 1989	2Q 1989	3Q 1989[2]	4Q 1989	1Q 1990
	(percent of net sales)				
INCOME STATEMENT IN RATIO FORMAT					
Net sales, receipts, and operating revenues.	100.0	100.0	100.0	100.0	100.0
Less: Depreciation, depletion, and amortization of property, plant, and equipment	3.4	3.4	3.8	4.1	3.9
Less: All other operating costs and expenses	85.9	86.8	86.0	88.5	88.9
Income (or loss) from operations.	10.7	9.7	10.2	7.4	7.1
Net nonoperating income (expense).	(1.8)	(1.8)	(2.0)	(9.2)	(2.2)
Income (or loss) before income taxes.	8.9	7.9	8.2	(1.8)	5.0
Net income (or loss) of foreign branches and equity in earnings (losses) of nonconsolidated subsidiaries (net of foreign taxes)	2.8	3.6	3.1	4.5	2.9
Less: Provision for current and deferred domestic income taxes	3.2	3.2	3.2	0.0	2.1
Income (or loss) after income taxes	8.5	8.3	8.2	2.7	5.7
OPERATING RATIOS (see explanatory notes)	(percent)				
Annual rate of profit on stockholders' equity at end of period:					
Before income taxes	29.55	31.57	28.33	6.38	18.42
After income taxes.	21.36	22.81	20.44	6.45	13.45
Annual rate of profit on total assets:					
Before income taxes	13.55	14.03	12.59	2.88	8.56
After income taxes.	9.79	10.14	9.09	2.91	6.25

[1] In the first quarter 1990, a number of corporations were reclassified by industry. To provide comparability, data for quarters in 1989 were restated to reflect these reclassifications.
[2] Revised to reflect respondents' corrections of submitted data subsequent to original publication.

TABLE 36—INCOME STATEMENT
FOR CORPORATIONS INCLUDED IN ESIC MAJOR GROUP 34, ASSETS $25 MILLION AND OVER

Item	Fabricated Metal Products[1]				
	1Q 1989	2Q 1989	3Q 1989[2]	4Q 1989[2]	1Q 1990
	(percent of net sales)				
INCOME STATEMENT IN RATIO FORMAT					
Net sales, receipts, and operating revenues.	100.0	100.0	100.0	100.0	100.0
Less: Depreciation, depletion, and amortization of property, plant, and equipment	3.1	2.7	2.9	3.5	3.2
Less: All other operating costs and expenses	89.4	89.8	90.2	92.1	90.8
Income (or loss) from operations.	7.6	7.6	6.9	4.4	6.0
Net nonoperating income (expense).	(2.3)	(2.3)	(2.3)	(1.0)	(2.5)
Income (or loss) before income taxes.	5.3	5.3	4.6	3.3	3.5
Net income (or loss) of foreign branches and equity in earnings (losses) of nonconsolidated subsidiaries (net of foreign taxes)	0.6	0.8	0.8	0.5	0.6
Less: Provision for current and deferred domestic income taxes	1.9	2.0	1.8	1.8	1.5
Income (or loss) after income taxes	4.0	4.1	3.6	2.0	2.6
OPERATING RATIOS (see explanatory notes)	(percent)				
Annual rate of profit on stockholders' equity at end of period:					
Before income taxes	19.19	20.18	16.79	11.30	11.90
After income taxes.	12.95	13.58	11.35	5.88	7.67
Annual rate of profit on total assets:					
Before income taxes	6.85	7.54	6.30	4.24	4.50
After income taxes.	4.62	5.08	4.26	2.21	2.90

[1] In the first quarter 1990, a number of corporations were reclassified by industry. To provide comparability, data for quarters in 1989 were restated to reflect these reclassifications.
[2] Revised to reflect respondents' corrections of submitted data subsequent to original publication.

TABLE 37—INCOME STATEMENT
FOR CORPORATIONS INCLUDED IN ESIC MAJOR GROUP 35, ASSETS $25 MILLION AND OVER

Item	Machinery, Except Electrical[1]				
	1Q 1988	2Q 1989	3Q 1989	4Q 1989	1Q 1990
	(percent of net sales)				
INCOME STATEMENT IN RATIO FORMAT					
Net sales, receipts, and operating revenues	100.0	100.0	100.0	100.0	100.0
Less: Depreciation, depletion, and amortization of property, plant, and equipment	4.6	4.2	4.6	4.6	4.8
Less: All other operating costs and expenses	91.4	90.5	91.5	96.4	91.0
Income (or loss) from operations	4.6	5.4	3.9	(1.0)	4.2
Net nonoperating income (expense)	(0.5)	(2.6)	(1.3)	(1.1)	(1.5)
Income (or loss) before income taxes	3.4	2.8	2.7	(2.1)	2.7
Net income (or loss) of foreign branches and equity in earnings (losses) of nonconsolidated subsidiaries (net of foreign taxes)	2.5	2.6	2.4	5.5	2.6
Less: Provision for current and deferred domestic income taxes	1.3	2.0	1.6	(0.7)	1.4
Income (or loss) after income taxes	4.5	3.3	3.5	4.1	3.9
OPERATING RATIOS (see explanatory notes)	(percent)				
Annual rate of profit on stockholders' equity at end of period:					
Before income taxes	9.58	9.85	8.92	6.16	9.92
After income taxes	7.35	6.01	6.09	7.48	6.57
Annual rate of profit on total assets:					
Before income taxes	4.94	5.06	4.58	3.15	4.64
After income taxes	3.79	3.09	3.12	3.83	3.38

[1]In the first quarter 1990, a number of corporations were reclassified by industry. To provide comparability, data for quarters in 1989 were restated to reflect these reclassifications as well as respondents' corrections of submitted data subsequent to original publication.

TABLE 38—INCOME STATEMENT
FOR CORPORATIONS INCLUDED IN ESIC MAJOR GROUP 36, ASSETS $25 MILLION AND OVER

Item	Electrical and Electronic Equipment[1]				
	1Q 1989	2Q 1989[2]	3Q 1989	4Q 1989[2]	1Q 1990
	(percent of net sales)				
INCOME STATEMENT IN RATIO FORMAT					
Net sales, receipts, and operating revenues	100.0	100.0	100.0	100.0	100.0
Less: Depreciation, depletion, and amortization of property, plant, and equipment	3.8	4.0	3.9	3.7	4.0
Less: All other operating costs and expenses	89.9	89.8	90.8	90.4	90.0
Income (or loss) from operations	6.3	6.2	5.4	5.8	6.0
Net nonoperating income (expense)	(1.0)	(0.9)	(1.2)	(1.1)	(1.0)
Income (or loss) before income taxes	5.2	5.3	4.1	4.8	5.1
Net income (or loss) of foreign branches and equity in earnings (losses) of nonconsolidated subsidiaries (net of foreign taxes)	1.7	1.2	1.7	1.6	1.4
Less: Provision for current and deferred domestic income taxes	2.1	2.1	1.7	1.8	2.2
Income (or loss) after income taxes	4.9	4.3	4.1	4.7	4.2
OPERATING RATIOS (see explanatory notes)	(percent)				
Annual rate of profit on stockholders' equity at end of period:					
Before income taxes	16.16	15.55	13.77	15.89	14.78
After income taxes	11.30	10.48	9.70	11.54	9.65
Annual rate of profit on total assets:					
Before income taxes	7.09	6.79	6.06	6.98	5.33
After income taxes	4.96	4.57	4.27	5.07	4.13

[1]In the first quarter 1990, a number of corporations were reclassified by industry. To provide comparability, data for quarters in 1989 were restated to reflect these reclassifications.
[2]Revised to reflect respondents' corrections of submitted data subsequent to original publication.

TABLE 39—INCOME STATEMENT
FOR CORPORATIONS INCLUDED IN ESIC MAJOR GROUP 37,
ASSETS $25 MILLION AND OVER

Item	Transportation Equipment[1]				
	1Q 1989[2]	2Q 1989	3Q 1989	4Q 1989	1Q 1990
	(percent of net sales)				
INCOME STATEMENT IN RATIO FORMAT					
Net sales, receipts, and operating revenues..........................	100.0	100.0	100.0	100.0	100.0
Less: Depreciation, depletion, and amortization of property, plant, and equipment	3.7	3.4	3.8	3.7	4.1
Less: All other operating costs and expenses	91.3	92.1	94.4	96.1	93.9
Income (or loss) from operations...........................	5.1	4.5	1.8	0.2	2.0
Net nonoperating income (expense)........................	(0.3)	(0.4)	(0.5)	(2.6)	(0.8)
Income (or loss) before income taxes	4.8	4.1	1.3	(2.5)	1.2
Net income (or loss) of foreign branches and equity in earnings (losses) of nonconsolidated subsidiaries (net of foreign taxes)	3.4	3.2	2.4	1.9	3.0
Less: Provision for current and deferred domestic income taxes	2.2	1.9	0.8	(0.9)	0.9
Income (or loss) after income taxes	6.1	5.4	2.9	0.4	3.3
	(percent)				
OPERATING RATIOS (see explanatory notes)					
Annual rate of profit on stockholders' equity at end of period:					
Before income taxes	25.49	22.94	9.97	(1.53)	11.55
After income taxes.......................	18.83	16.97	7.85	1.30	9.06
Annual rate of profit on total assets:					
Before income taxes	9.48	8.57	3.76	(0.57)	4.31
After income taxes.......................	7.00	6.34	2.96	0.48	3.38

[1] In the first quarter 1990, a number of corporations were reclassified by industry. To provide comparability, data for quarters in 1989 were restated to reflect these reclassifications.
[2] Revised to reflect respondents' corrections of submitted data subsequent to original publication.

TABLE 40—INCOME STATEMENT
FOR CORPORATIONS INCLUDED IN ESIC MAJOR GROUP 37.1,
ASSETS $25 MILLION AND OVER

Item	Motor Vehicles and Equipment[1]				
	1Q 1989[2]	2Q 1989	3Q 1989	4Q 1989	1Q 1990
	(percent of net sales)				
INCOME STATEMENT IN RATIO FORMAT					
Net sales, receipts, and operating revenues..........................	100.0	100.0	100.0	100.0	100.0
Less: Depreciation, depletion, and amortization of property, plant, and equipment	3.7	3.5	4.2	4.0	4.7
Less: All other operating costs and expenses	91.4	92.3	96.2	97.9	95.6
Income (or loss) from operations...........................	4.9	4.1	(0.4)	(1.8)	(0.3)
Net nonoperating income (expense)........................	(0.3)	(0.3)	0.3	(3.7)	(0.7)
Income (or loss) before income taxes	4.6	3.8	(0.2)	(5.6)	(1.1)
Net income (or loss) of foreign branches and equity in earnings (losses) of nonconsolidated subsidiaries (net of foreign taxes)	4.6	4.2	3.3	2.9	4.3
Less: Provision for current and deferred domestic income taxes	2.3	2.0	0.6	(2.2)	0.6
Income (or loss) after income taxes	6.8	6.0	2.5	(0.5)	2.7
	(percent)				
OPERATING RATIOS (see explanatory notes)					
Annual rate of profit on stockholders' equity at end of period:					
Before income taxes	28.16	24.31	7.56	(7.33)	8.22
After income taxes.......................	20.93	18.25	6.14	(1.34)	6.88
Annual rate of profit on total assets:					
Before income taxes	12.13	10.51	3.33	(3.19)	3.64
After income taxes.......................	9.02	7.89	2.71	(0.58)	3.05

[1] In the first quarter 1990, a number of corporations were reclassified by industry. To provide comparability, data for quarters in 1989 were restated to reflect these reclassifications.
[2] Revised to reflect respondents' corrections of submitted data subsequent to original publication.

TABLE 41—INCOME STATEMENT
FOR CORPORATIONS INCLUDED IN ESIC MAJOR GROUP 37.7, ASSETS $25 MILLION AND OVER

Item	Aircraft, Guided Missiles, and Parts[1]				
	1Q 1989	2Q 1989	3Q 1989	4Q 1989	1Q 1990
	(percent of net sales)				
INCOME STATEMENT IN RATIO FORMAT					
Net sales, receipts, and operating revenues.	100.0	100.0	100.0	100.0	100.0
Less: Depreciation, depletion, and amortization of property, plant, and equipment	3.5	3.3	3.4	3.4	3.2
Less: All other operating costs and expenses	91.0	91.7	91.8	93.5	91.4
Income (or loss) from operations.	5.5	5.0	4.9	3.1	5.4
Net nonoperating income (expense).	(0.1)	(1.3)	(1.6)	(0.7)	(0.9)
Income (or loss) before income taxes	5.4	3.7	3.4	2.4	4.5
Net income (or loss) of foreign branches and equity in earnings (losses) of nonconsolidated subsidiaries (net of foreign taxes)	1.1	1.0	1.1	0.5	1.0
Less: Provision for current and deferred domestic income taxes	1.8	1.5	1.0	1.1	1.5
Income (or loss) after income taxes	4.7	3.3	3.4	1.9	4.0
	(percent)				
OPERATING RATIOS (see explanatory notes)					
Annual rate of profit on stockholders' equity at end of period:					
Before income taxes	19.90	15.48	14.59	10.14	17.51
After income taxes.	14.34	10.80	11.10	6.62	12.71
Annual rate of profit on total assets:					
Before income taxes	6.10	4.76	4.50	3.08	5.25
After income taxes.	4.39	3.32	3.42	2.01	3.82

[1] In the first quarter 1990, a number of corporations were reclassified by industry. To provide comparability, data for quarters in 1989 were restated to reflect these reclassifications.

TABLE 42—INCOME STATEMENT
FOR CORPORATIONS INCLUDED IN ESIC MAJOR GROUP 38, ASSETS $25 MILLION AND OVER

Item	Instruments and Related Products[1]				
	1Q 1989	2Q 1989[2]	3Q 1989[2]	4Q 1989[2]	1Q 1990
	(percent of net sales)				
INCOME STATEMENT IN RATIO FORMAT					
Net sales, receipts, and operating revenues.	100.0	100.0	100.0	100.0	100.0
Less: Depreciation, depletion, and amortization of property, plant, and equipment	4.6	4.6	4.7	4.8	4.8
Less: All other operating costs and expenses	88.6	87.3	87.9	90.6	88.2
Income (or loss) from operations.	6.8	8.1	7.4	4.5	7.0
Net nonoperating income (expense).	(1.0)	(2.9)	(0.8)	(1.6)	(1.2)
Income (or loss) before income taxes	5.8	5.1	6.6	3.0	5.8
Net income (or loss) of foreign branches and equity in earnings (losses) of nonconsolidated subsidiaries (net of foreign taxes)	3.6	3.7	3.3	4.2	2.4
Less: Provision for current and deferred domestic income taxes	2.2	1.8	1.9	0.8	1.5
Income (or loss) after income taxes	7.2	7.0	8.0	6.4	6.6
	(percent)				
OPERATING RATIOS (see explanatory notes)					
Annual rate of profit on stockholders' equity at end of period:					
Before income taxes	16.60	10.40	18.31	13.55	14.33
After income taxes.	12.71	12.98	14.78	12.00	11.62
Annual rate of profit on total assets:					
Before income taxes	7.80	7.70	8.38	6.23	6.59
After income taxes.	5.97	6.09	6.76	5.52	5.35

[1] In the first quarter 1990, a number of corporations were reclassified by industry. To provide comparability, data for quarters in 1989 were restated to reflect these reclassifications.
[2] Revised to reflect respondents' corrections of submitted data subsequent to original publication.

General Business and Economic Indicators

SELECTED BUSINESS STATISTICS   SEASONALLY ADJUSTED WHERE APPLICABLE

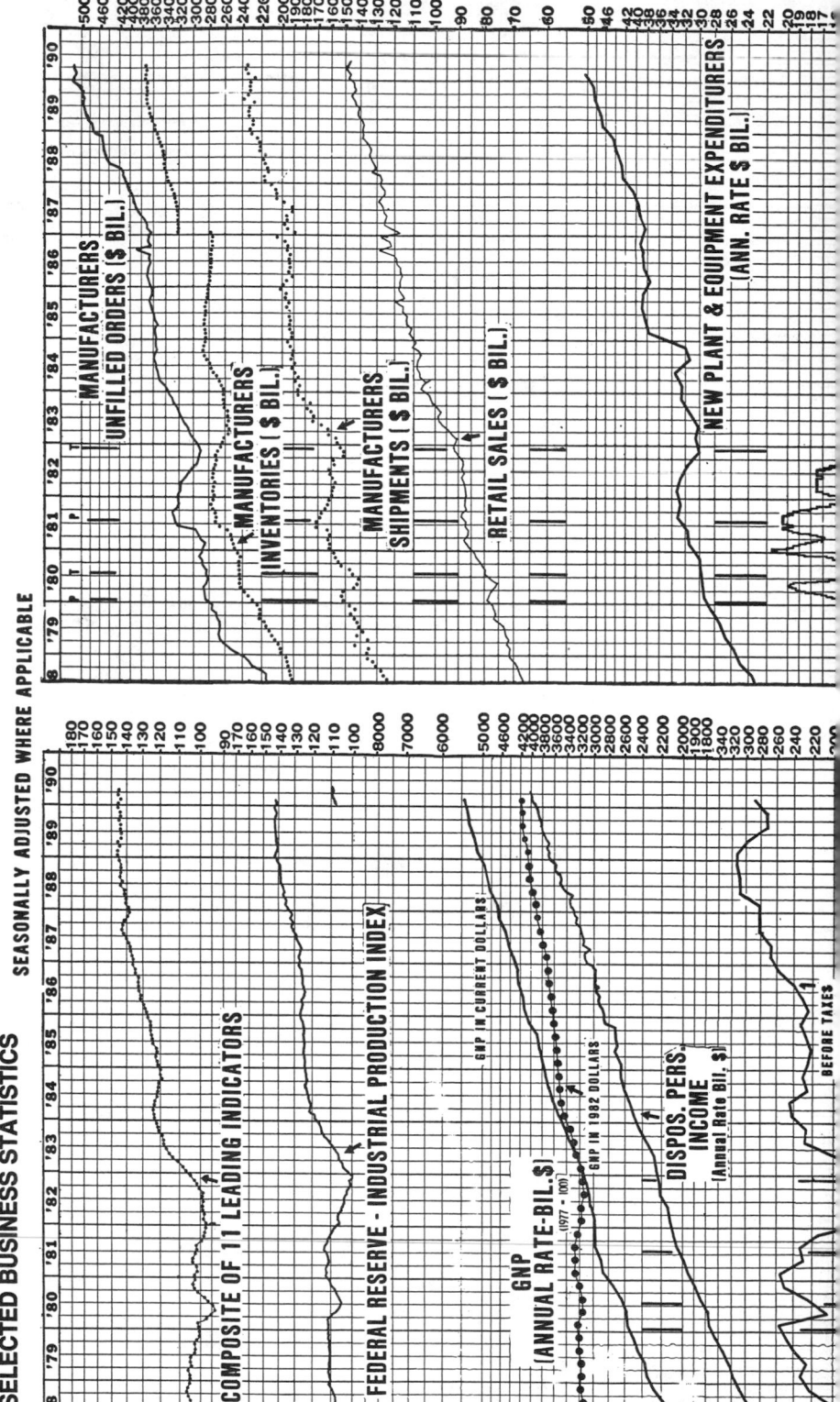

COMPOSITE OF 11 LEADING INDICATORS

FEDERAL RESERVE - INDUSTRIAL PRODUCTION INDEX

GNP IN CURRENT DOLLARS

GNP IN 1982 DOLLARS

GNP (ANNUAL RATE-BIL.$) (1977 - 100)

DISPOS. PERS. INCOME (Annual Rate Bil. $)

BEFORE TAXES

MANUFACTURERS UNFILLED ORDERS ($ BIL.)

MANUFACTURERS INVENTORIES ($ BIL.)

MANUFACTURERS SHIPMENTS ($ BIL.)

RETAIL SALES ($ BIL.)

NEW PLANT & EQUIPMENT EXPENDITURES (ANN. RATE $ BIL.)

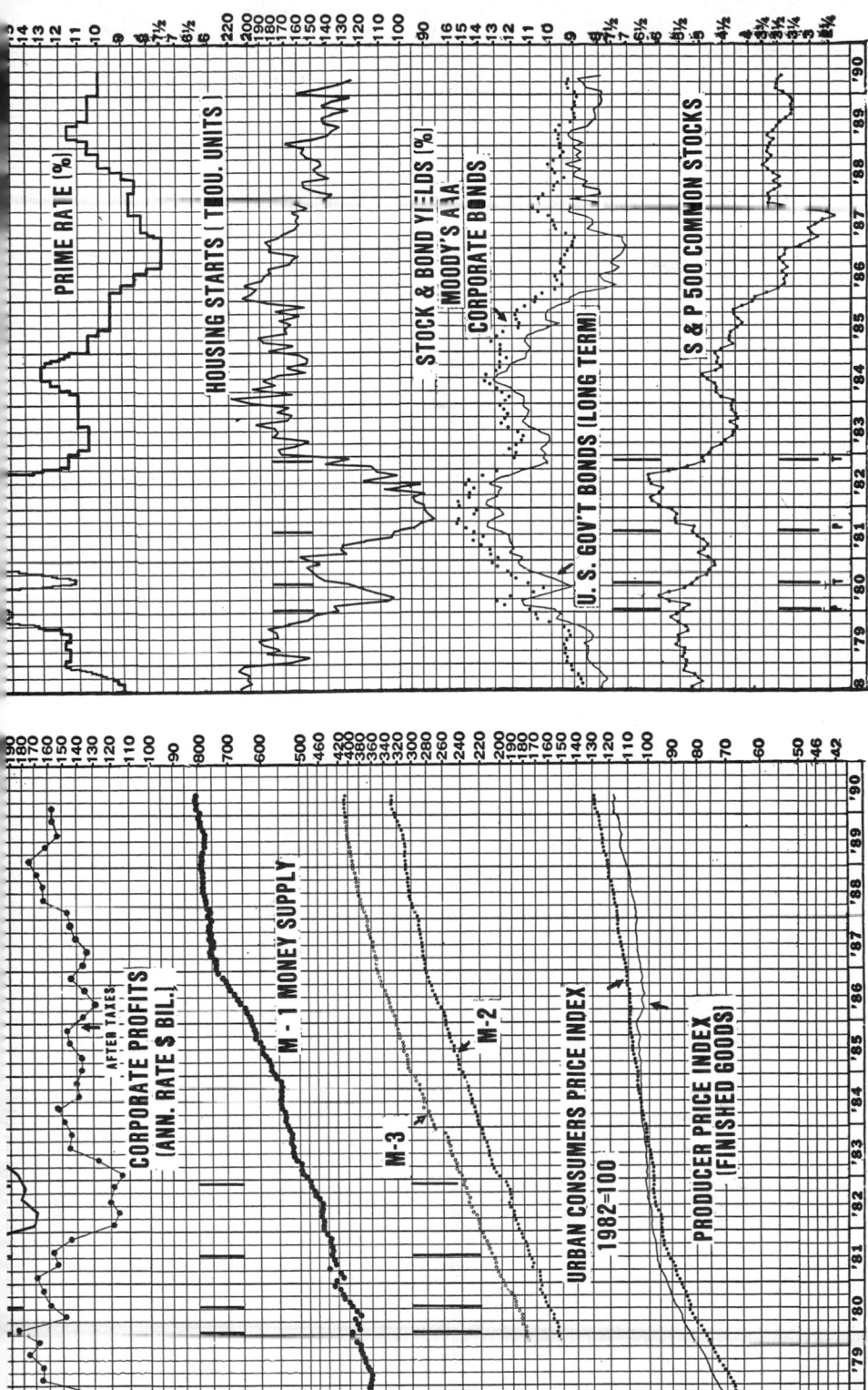

PRIME RATE (%)

HOUSING STARTS (THOU. UNITS)

STOCK & BOND YIELDS (%)

CORPORATE BONDS

MOODY'S AAA

U. S. GOV'T BONDS (LONG TERM)

S & P 500 COMMON STOCKS

CORPORATE PROFITS
AFTER TAXES
(ANN. RATE $ BIL.)

M - 1 MONEY SUPPLY

M-3

M-2

URBAN CONSUMERS PRICE INDEX
1982=100

PRODUCER PRICE INDEX
(FINISHED GOODS)

Source: *5-Trend CYCLI-GRAPHS.* The charts are courtesy of Securities Research Company, a Division of Babson-United Investment Advisors, Inc., Babson-United Building, 101 Prescott St., Wellesley Hills, MA 02181, July quarterly edition, 1990.

163

COMPOSITE INDEXES*

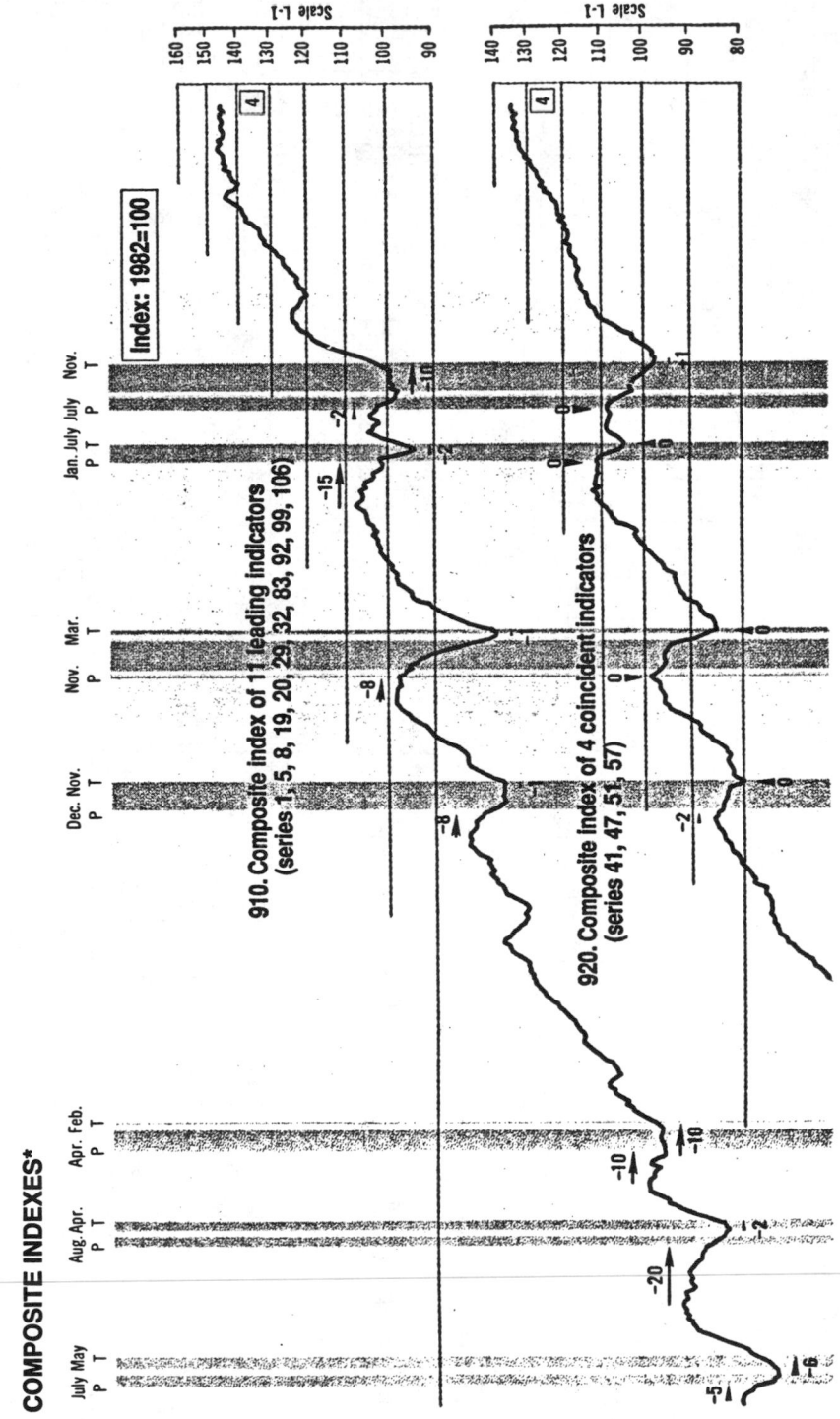

Index: 1982=100

910. Composite index of 11 leading indicators
(series 1, 5, 8, 19, 20, 29, 32, 83, 92, 99, 106)

920. Composite index of 4 coincident indicators
(series 41, 47, 51, 57)

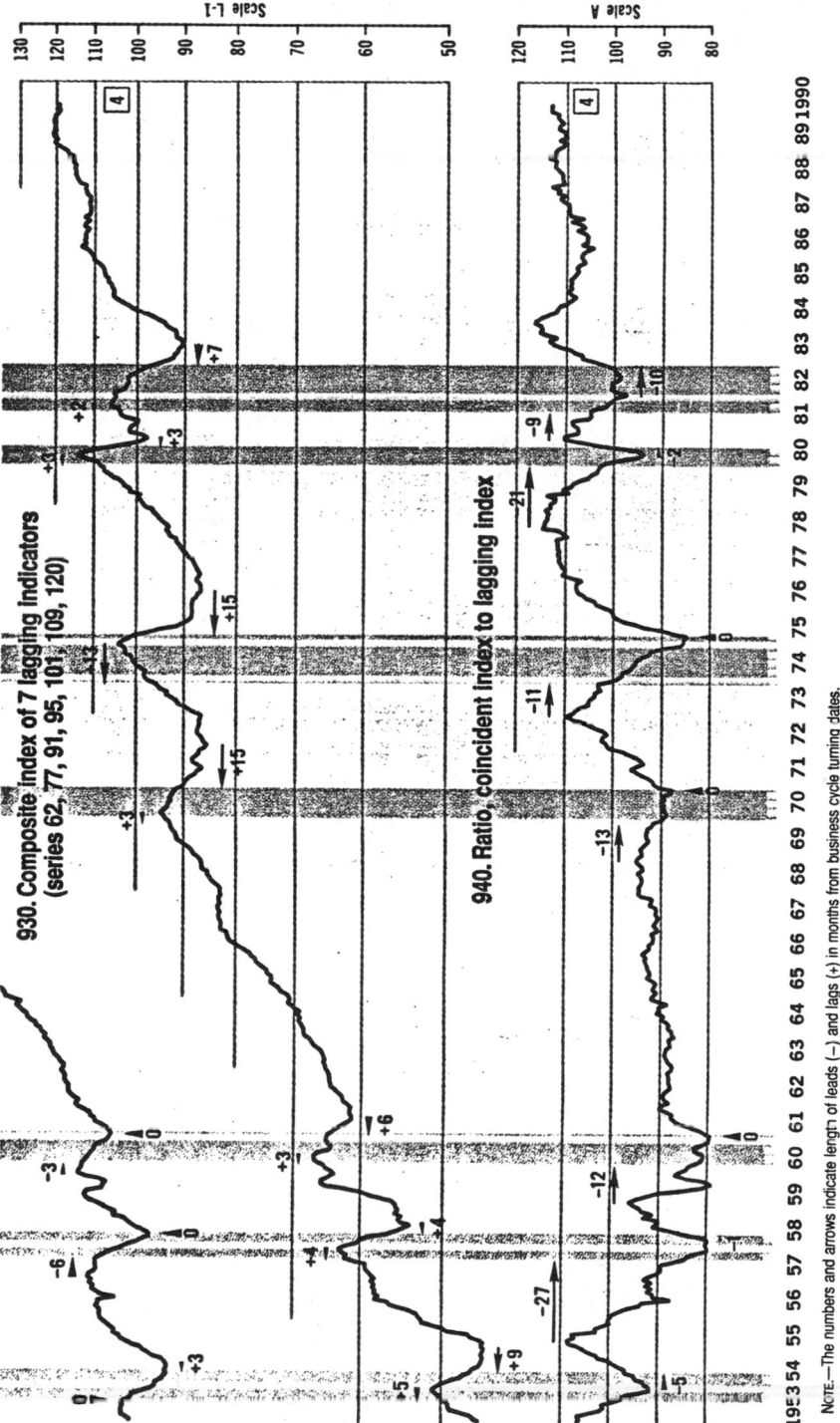

930. Composite index of 7 lagging indicators
(series 62, 77, 91, 95, 101, 109, 120)

940. Ratio, coincident index to lagging index

NOTE.—The numbers and arrows indicate length of leads (−) and lags (+) in months from business cycle turning dates.

* For definitions see page 166.

Source: *Survey of Current Business,* U.S. Department of Commerce, Bureau of Economic Analysis.

Composition of Leading, Coincident, and Lagging Indicators

I. THE ELEVEN LEADING INDICATORS

1. Average weekly hours paid to production or non-supervisory workers in manufacturing.
5. Average weekly claims for Unemployment Insurance (inversely related).
8. New orders for consumer goods and materials in 1982 dollars.
19. Index of 500 common stock prices.
20. Contracts and orders for new plant and equipment in 1982 dollars.
29. Index of new private housing starts.
32. Percentage of purchasing agents in greater Chicago area who experience slower deliveries in current month.
83. Index of consumer expectations.
92. Change in manufacturer's unfilled orders for the durable goods industry.
99. Change in index of 28 sensitive materials prices.
106. Money supply (M2 in 1982 dollars).

II. THE FOUR COINCIDENT INDICATORS

41. Employees on non-agricultural payrolls.
47. Index of industrial production, including all stages in manufacturing, mining, gas and electrical utilities.
51. Personal income less transfer payments in 1982 dollars.
57. Monthly volume of sales in manufacturing, wholesale, and retail in 1982 dollars.

III. THE SEVEN LAGGING INDICATORS

62. Index of labor costs per unit of manufacturing output.
77. Ratio of manufacturing and trade inventories to sales in 1982 dollars.
91. Average duration of unemployment in weeks (inversely related).
95. Ratio of consumer installment credit to personal income.
101. Commercial and industrial loans outstanding in 1982 dollars.
109. Average prime rate charged by banks.
120. Change in consumer price index for services.

Source: *Business Conditions Digest*, U.S. Department of Commerce, Bureau of Economic Analysis.

NATIONAL INCOME

[Billions of dollars; quarterly data at seasonally adjusted annual rates]

| Period | National income | Compensation of employees[1] | Proprietors' income with inventory valuation and capital consumption adjustments | | Rental income of persons with capital consumption adjustment | Corporate profits with inventory valuation and capital consumption adjustments | | | | | | Net interest |
| | | | Farm | Nonfarm | | Total | Profits with inventory valuation adjustment and without capital consumption adjustment | | | | Capital consumption adjustment | |
							Total	Profits before tax	Inventory valuation adjustment			
1982	2,518.4	1,907.0	24.6	150.9	13.6	150.0	159.2	169.6	−10.4	−9.2		272.3
1983	2,719.5	2,020.7	12.4	178.4	13.2	213.7	196.7	207.6	−10.9	17.0		281.0
1984	3,028.6	2,213.9	30.5	204.0	8.5	266.9	234.2	240.0	−5.8	32.7		304.8
1985	3,234.0	2,367.5	30.2	225.6	9.2	282.3	222.6	224.3	−1.7	59.7		319.0
1986	3,412.6	2,511.4	34.7	247.2	11.6	282.1	228.3	221.6	6.7	53.8		325.5
1987	3,665.4	2,690.0	41.6	270.0	13.4	298.7	247.8	266.7	−18.9	50.9		351.7
1988	3,972.6	2,907.6	39.8	288.0	15.7	328.6	281.8	306.8	−25.0	46.8		392.9
1989	4,266.5	3,144.4	46.2	305.9	7.9	301.3	272.0	290.7	−18.7	29.3		460.8
1982: IV	2,548.2	1,931.1	28.5	159.8	15.8	146.1	150.7	164.1	−13.4	−4.5		266.9
1983: IV	2,851.5	2,092.7	19.3	188.6	12.4	248.5	223.4	231.5	−8.1	25.1		290.2
1984: IV	3,096.1	2,272.7	28.1	209.7	5.6	266.9	224.6	226.1	−1.6	42.3		313.1
1985: IV	3,312.8	2,426.7	29.2	235.0	7.8	291.4	228.4	235.0	−6.6	63.0		322.7
1986: IV	3,473.1	2,571.2	37.2	252.0	13.5	275.2	226.1	234.1	−8.0	49.1		324.0
1987: IV	3,799.9	2,778.7	48.4	280.3	14.3	308.2	255.8	276.2	−20.4	52.4		370.0
1988: III	4,005.7	2,935.1	37.7	289.3	16.3	330.9	284.1	314.4	−30.4	46.9		396.4
IV	4,097.4	2,997.2	32.0	296.3	16.1	340.2	298.7	318.8	−20.1	41.5		415.7
1989: I	4,185.2	3,061.7	59.0	300.3	11.8	316.3	279.7	318.0	−38.3	36.6		436.1
II	4,249.6	3,118.2	51.3	304.2	9.8	307.8	275.5	296.0	−20.5	32.3		458.4
III	4,287.3	3,171.9	36.1	307.2	5.4	295.2	268.7	275.0	−6.3	26.5		471.5
IV	4,344.0	3,225.9	38.5	311.8	4.8	285.9	264.0	273.7	−9.7	21.9		477.2
1990: I r	4,438.3	3,285.5	51.9	322.7	8.1	289.7	272.2	283.3	−11.1	17.5		480.4

[1] Includes employer contributions for social insurance.

Source: Economic Indicators, Council of Economic Advisers.

Source: Department of Commerce, Bureau of Economic Analysis.

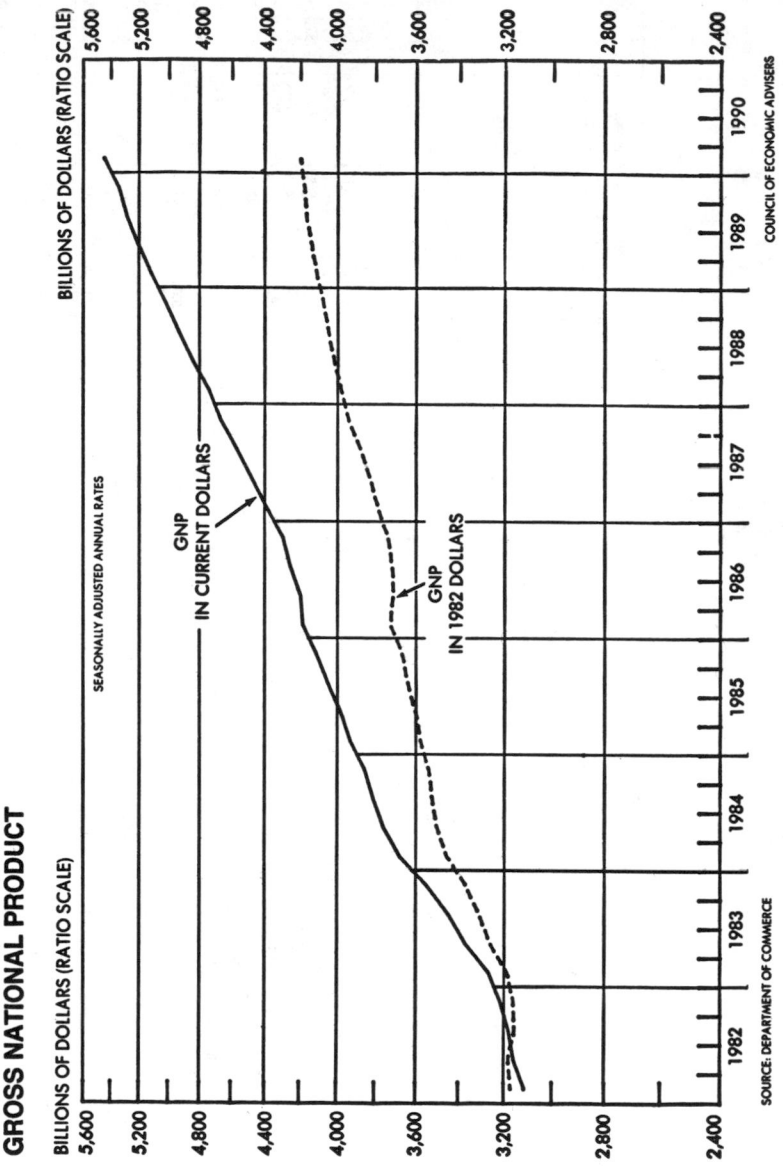

GROSS NATIONAL PRODUCT

BILLIONS OF DOLLARS (RATIO SCALE)

BILLIONS OF DOLLARS (RATIO SCALE)

SEASONALLY ADJUSTED ANNUAL RATES

GNP
IN CURRENT DOLLARS

GNP
IN 1982 DOLLARS

SOURCE: DEPARTMENT OF COMMERCE

COUNCIL OF ECONOMIC ADVISERS

[Billions of current dollars; quarterly data at seasonally adjusted annual rates]

Period	Gross national product	Personal consumption expenditures	Gross private domestic investment	Exports and imports of goods and services				Government purchases of goods and services					Final sales	Gross domestic purchases [1]
				Net exports	Exports	Imports	Total	Total	Federal			State and local		
										National defense	Non-defense			
1980	2,732.0	1,732.6	437.0	32.1	351.0	318.9	530.3	208.1	142.7	65.4	322.2	2,740.3	2,699.8
1981	3,052.6	1,915.1	515.5	33.9	382.8	348.9	588.1	242.2	167.5	74.8	345.9	3,028.6	3,018.7
1982	3,166.0	2,050.7	447.3	26.3	361.9	335.6	641.7	272.7	193.8	78.9	369.0	3,190.5	3,139.7
1983	3,405.7	2,234.5	502.3	-6.1	352.5	358.7	675.0	283.5	214.4	69.1	391.5	3,412.8	3,411.8
1984	3,772.2	2,430.5	664.8	-58.9	383.5	442.4	735.9	310.5	234.3	76.2	425.3	3,704.5	3,831.1
1985	4,014.9	2,629.0	643.1	-78.0	370.9	448.9	820.8	355.2	259.1	96.0	465.6	4,003.6	4,092.8
1986	4,231.6	2,797.4	659.4	-97.4	396.5	493.8	872.2	366.5	277.8	88.7	505.7	4,224.8	4,329.0
1987	4,524.3	3,010.8	699.9	-112.6	448.6	561.2	926.1	381.6	294.8	86.8	544.5	4,495.0	4,636.8
1988	4,880.6	3,235.1	750.3	-73.7	547.7	621.3	968.9	381.3	298.0	83.3	587.6	4,850.0	4,954.3
1989	5,234.0	3,471.1	773.4	-47.1	625.9	673.0	1,036.6	403.2	302.2	101.1	633.4	5,206.9	5,281.1
1982: IV	3,212.5	2,117.0	409.6	14.1	335.9	321.9	671.8	293.2	205.4	87.7	378.7	3,272.4	3,198.5
1983: IV	3,545.8	2,315.8	579.8	-25.8	364.7	390.5	676.1	276.1	221.5	54.6	400.0	3,514.8	3,571.6
1984: IV	3,851.8	2,493.4	661.8	-67.9	385.7	453.6	764.5	326.0	244.1	81.9	438.5	3,806.8	3,919.7
1985: IV	4,107.9	2,700.4	654.1	-103.2	369.2	472.4	856.7	376.6	268.6	108.0	480.1	4,100.7	4,211.2
1986: IV	4,297.3	2,868.5	648.8	-108.9	402.4	511.3	888.9	368.8	280.7	88.1	520.1	4,309.4	4,406.2
1987: IV	4,665.8	3,083.3	749.7	-114.6	482.6	597.2	947.5	388.1	296.8	91.3	559.4	4,602.5	4,780.4
1988: III	4,926.9	3,263.4	771.1	-66.2	556.8	623.0	958.6	367.5	296.1	71.4	591.0	4,882.3	4,993.1
1988: IV	5,017.3	3,324.0	752.8	-70.8	579.7	650.5	1,011.4	406.4	300.5	105.9	604.9	4,998.7	5,088.1
1989: I	5,113.1	3,381.4	769.6	-54.0	605.6	659.6	1,016.0	399.0	298.7	100.4	617.0	5,085.4	5,167.1
1989: II	5,201.7	3,444.1	775.0	-50.6	626.1	676.6	1,033.2	406.0	301.3	104.7	627.2	5,174.3	5,252.3
1989: III	5,281.0	3,508.1	779.1	-45.1	628.5	673.6	1,038.9	402.7	307.8	94.9	636.2	5,253.6	5,326.1
1989: IV	5,340.2	3,550.6	770.1	-38.8	643.5	682.3	1,058.3	405.1	300.9	104.2	653.2	5,314.2	5,379.0
1990: I ʳ	5,433.1	3,629.4	752.9	-32.0	664.7	696.6	1,082.9	413.7	308.6	105.1	669.2	5,444.8	5,465.1

[1] GNP less exports of goods and services plus imports of goods and services.

Source: Economic Indicators, Council of Economic Advisers.

Source: Department of Commerce, Bureau of Economic Analysis.

GROSS NATIONAL PRODUCT IN 1982 DOLLARS

[Billions of 1982 dollars; quarterly data at seasonally adjusted annual rates]

Period	Gross national product	Personal consumption expenditures	Gross private domestic investment Total	Nonresidential fixed	Residential fixed	Change in business inventories	Net exports	Exports	Imports	Total	Government Total	Federal Total	National defense	Non-defense	State and local	Final sales	Gross domestic purchases [1]
1980	3,187.1	2,000.4	509.3	379.2	137.0	-6.9	57.0	388.9	332.0	620.5	246.9	171.2	75.7	373.6	3,194.0	3,130.1
1981	3,248.8	2,024.2	545.5	395.2	126.5	23.9	49.4	392.2	343.4	629.7	259.6	180.3	79.3	370.1	3,225.0	3,199.4
1982	3,166.0	2,050.7	447.3	366.7	105.1	-24.5	26.3	361.9	335.6	641.7	272.7	193.8	78.9	369.0	3,190.5	3,139.7
1983	3,279.1	2,146.0	504.0	361.2	149.3	-6.4	-19.9	348.1	368.1	649.0	275.1	206.9	68.2	373.9	3,285.5	3,299.1
1984	3,501.4	2,249.3	658.4	425.2	170.9	62.3	-84.0	371.8	455.8	677.7	290.8	218.5	72.3	387.0	3,439.1	3,585.4
1985	3,618.7	2,354.8	637.0	453.5	174.4	9.1	-104.3	367.2	471.4	731.2	326.0	237.2	88.8	405.2	3,609.6	3,723.0
1986	3,717.9	2,446.4	639.6	438.4	195.7	5.6	-129.7	397.1	526.9	761.6	334.1	252.1	82.0	427.5	3,712.4	3,847.6
1987	3,853.7	2,513.7	674.0	455.5	194.8	23.7	-115.7	450.9	566.6	781.8	339.6	265.2	74.4	442.1	3,830.0	3,969.4
1988	4,024.4	2,598.4	715.8	493.8	194.1	27.9	-74.9	530.1	605.0	785.1	328.9	261.5	67.4	456.2	3,996.5	4,099.3
1989	4,144.1	2,669.6	720.7	510.3	188.5	21.9	-52.6	589.2	641.8	806.4	337.1	256.5	80.6	469.3	4,122.2	4,196.7
1982: IV	3,159.3	2,078.7	408.8	352.3	115.8	-59.3	11.7	336.0	324.3	660.1	289.5	201.4	88.2	370.6	3,218.6	3,147.6
1983: IV	3,365.1	2,191.9	577.2	390.4	159.9	27.0	-46.2	355.5	401.6	642.2	266.0	211.6	54.4	376.2	3,338.1	3,411.3
1984: IV	3,535.2	2,281.1	655.7	444.4	169.6	41.7	-94.8	376.6	471.4	693.2	300.5	225.3	75.2	392.7	3,493.5	3,630.0
1985: IV	3,662.4	2,386.9	648.0	460.9	179.4	7.7	-125.3	367.4	492.6	752.7	340.6	241.4	99.2	412.1	3,654.7	3,787.6
1986: IV	3,733.6	2,477.8	615.2	435.7	200.3	-20.8	-135.4	406.5	541.9	776.0	342.4	255.8	86.6	433.6	3,754.4	3,869.0
1987: IV	3,935.6	2,532.3	721.1	472.7	191.9	56.6	-109.8	484.1	593.9	792.1	344.9	266.7	78.2	447.2	3,879.0	4,045.5
1988: III	4,042.7	2,608.1	733.6	501.0	195.1	37.5	-74.9	531.9	606.9	775.9	319.8	258.8	61.0	456.1	4,005.2	4,117.6
1988: IV	4,069.4	2,627.7	709.1	492.7	198.1	18.3	-73.8	551.4	625.2	806.4	343.9	261.6	82.3	462.5	4,051.0	4,143.2
1989: I	4,106.8	2,641.0	721.1	501.0	195.6	24.5	-55.0	569.7	624.6	799.7	335.5	254.4	81.1	464.2	4,082.3	4,161.8
II	4,132.5	2,653.7	719.8	511.4	189.3	19.1	-51.2	587.5	638.7	810.3	343.6	255.8	87.8	466.7	4,113.5	4,183.7
III	4,162.9	2,690.1	724.6	517.9	184.8	21.9	-57.1	593.1	650.2	805.3	336.1	260.1	76.0	469.2	4,141.0	4,220.0
IV	4,174.1	2,693.7	717.3	510.8	184.3	22.2	-47.2	606.6	653.8	810.4	333.3	255.7	77.7	477.0	4,151.9	4,221.4
1990: I ʳ	4,193.4	2,704.3	705.4	520.4	188.6	-3.6	-33.6	625.1	658.7	817.3	335.2	254.5	80.7	482.1	4,197.0	4,227.0

[1] GNP less exports of goods and services plus imports of goods and services.

Source: *Economic Indicators*, Council of Economic Advisers.

Source: Department of Commerce, Bureau of Economic Analysis.

PERSONAL CONSUMPTION EXPENDITURES

[Billions of dollars, except as noted; quarterly data at seasonally adjusted annual rates]

Period	Total personal consumption expenditures	Durable goods				Total nondurable goods	Nondurable goods				Services	Retail sales of new passenger cars (millions of units)	
		Total durable goods	Motor vehicles and parts	Furniture and household equipment	Other		Food	Clothing and shoes	Gasoline and oil	Other		Domestics	Imports
1982	2,050.7	252.7	108.9	95.7	48.1	771.0	398.8	124.4	89.1	158.7	1,027.0	5.8	2.2
1983	2,234.5	289.1	130.4	107.1	51.6	816.7	421.9	135.1	90.2	169.5	1,128.7	6.8	2.4
1984	2,430.5	335.5	157.4	118.8	59.3	867.3	448.5	146.7	90.0	182.1	1,227.3	8.0	2.4
1985	2,629.0	372.2	179.1	129.9	63.2	911.2	471.6	156.4	90.6	192.6	1,345.3	8.2	2.8
1986	2,797.4	406.0	196.2	139.7	70.0	942.0	500.0	166.8	73.5	201.7	1,449.5	8.2	3.2
1987	3,010.8	421.0	195.5	149.1	76.5	998.1	529.2	177.2	75.2	216.6	1,591.7	7.1	3.2
1988	3,235.1	455.2	211.6	162.0	81.6	1,052.3	559.7	186.8	76.8	229.0	1,727.3	7.5	3.1
1989	3,471.1	473.2	213.9	173.6	85.8	1,123.4	594.9	200.1	84.0	244.5	1,874.4	7.1	2.8
1982: IV	2,117.0	263.8	115.7	99.1	49.0	786.6	407.0	126.5	89.8	163.4	1,066.5	6.0	2.5
1983: IV	2,315.8	310.0	144.4	112.4	53.2	837.9	430.8	141.1	91.9	174.0	1,167.3	7.4	2.6
1984: IV	2,493.4	346.7	162.3	122.7	61.8	879.6	456.1	149.8	89.0	184.7	1,267.4	7.7	2.6
1985: IV	2,700.4	373.2	173.8	134.7	64.7	932.7	482.5	160.6	91.0	198.5	1,394.5	7.0	3.1
1986: IV	2,868.5	422.0	201.1	143.8	77.1	952.1	511.9	168.7	66.0	205.5	1,494.4	7.7	3.4
1987: IV	3,083.3	424.5	196.3	151.4	76.7	1,015.4	536.8	180.6	76.7	221.3	1,643.3	6.6	3.3
1988: III	3,263.4	452.5	208.4	162.7	81.4	1,066.2	567.8	188.9	78.3	231.2	1,744.7	7.4	3.0
1988: IV	3,324.0	467.4	215.3	166.1	86.0	1,078.4	574.1	193.9	77.6	232.8	1,778.3	7.5	3.0
1989: I	3,381.4	466.4	211.7	172.1	82.6	1,098.3	587.3	195.0	77.9	238.1	1,816.7	7.0	2.8
1989: II	3,444.1	471.0	212.9	173.5	84.6	1,121.5	592.2	198.9	89.5	241.0	1,851.7	7.3	3.0
1989: III	3,508.1	486.1	225.6	173.9	86.7	1,131.4	598.1	202.2	85.2	245.9	1,890.6	7.9	2.9
1989: IV	3,550.6	469.5	205.3	174.8	89.4	1,142.4	601.8	204.3	83.2	253.1	1,938.7	6.2	2.6
1990: I r	3,629.4	489.9	219.0	131.1	89.8	1,168.2	616.5	208.9	85.3	257.5	1,971.3	7.0	2.8

Source: Department of Commerce, Bureau of Economic Analysis.

Source: *Economic Indicators*, Council of Economic Advisers.

CORPORATE PROFITS

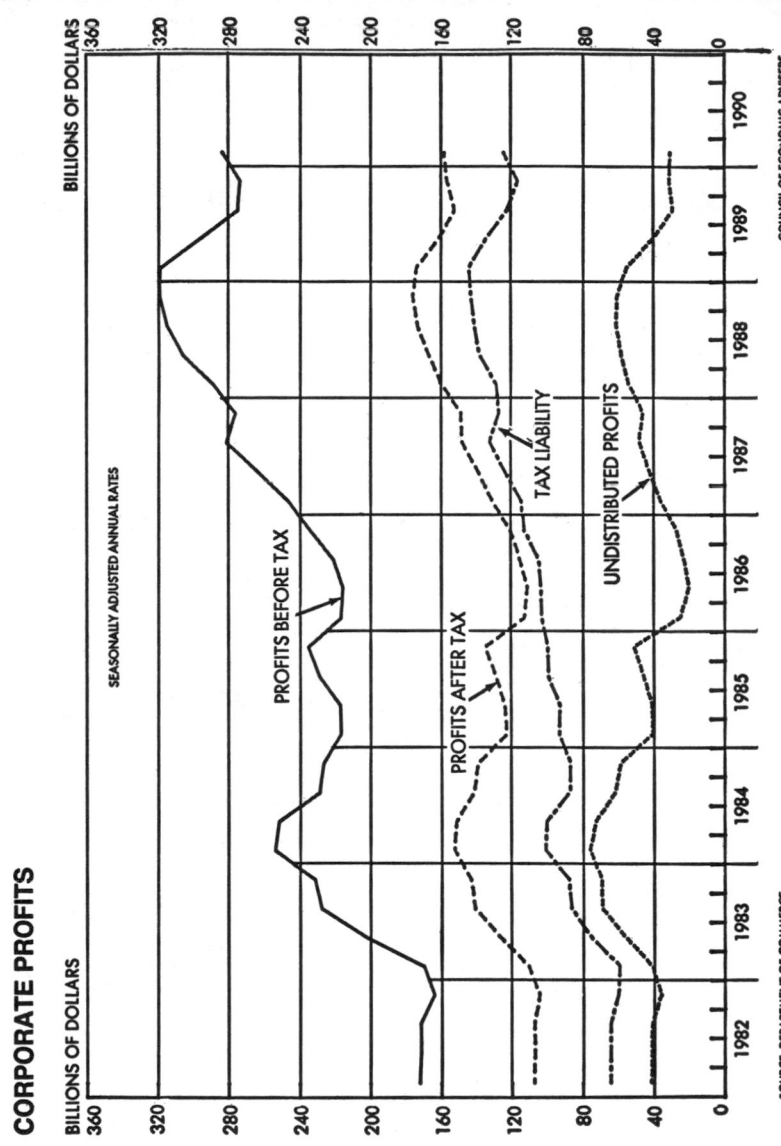

BILLIONS OF DOLLARS

SEASONALLY ADJUSTED ANNUAL RATES

PROFITS BEFORE TAX

PROFITS AFTER TAX

TAX LIABILITY

UNDISTRIBUTED PROFITS

BILLIONS OF DOLLARS

SOURCE: DEPARTMENT OF COMMERCE

COUNCIL OF ECONOMIC ADVISERS

[Billions of dollars; quarterly data at seasonally adjusted annual rates]

Period	Profits (before tax) with inventory valuation adjustment [1]						Profits before tax	Tax liability	Profits after tax			Inventory valuation adjustment
	Total [2]	Domestic industries							Total	Dividends	Undistributed profits	
		Total	Financial	Nonfinancial								
				Total [3]	Manufacturing	Wholesale and retail trade						
1980	194.0	159.6	21.0	138.6	77.1	21.6	237.1	84.8	152.3	54.7	97.6	−43.1
1981	202.3	173.8	16.5	157.3	88.5	32.5	226.5	81.1	145.4	63.6	81.8	−24.2
1982	159.2	131.2	11.8	119.4	58.0	34.6	169.6	63.1	106.5	66.9	39.6	−10.4
1983	196.7	166.6	18.1	148.5	70.1	38.9	207.6	77.2	130.4	71.5	58.9	−10.9
1984	234.2	203.3	13.0	190.3	88.8	51.2	240.0	93.9	146.1	79.0	67.0	−5.8
1985	222.6	191.4	22.8	168.6	79.7	44.1	224.3	96.4	127.8	83.3	44.6	−1.7
1986	228.3	195.2	32.0	163.2	59.5	44.1	221.6	106.3	115.3	91.3	24.0	6.7
1987	247.8	208.7	30.5	178.2	76.6	41.1	266.7	124.7	142.0	98.7	43.3	−18.9
1988	281.8	238.2	29.8	208.4	98.4	40.1	306.8	137.9	168.9	110.4	58.5	−25.0
1989	272.0	224.1	22.2	202.0	86.9	39.1	290.7	129.7	161.0	122.1	38.9	−18.7
1982: IV	150.7	121.6	18.7	102.9	46.8	33.6	164.1	59.8	104.3	68.5	35.8	−13.4
1983: IV	223.4	190.7	15.5	175.2	88.6	43.1	231.5	88.1	143.4	73.9	69.5	−8.1
1984: IV	224.6	193.9	13.6	180.3	79.8	51.8	226.1	87.0	139.2	80.8	58.4	−1.6
1985: IV	228.4	193.6	26.0	167.6	83.8	38.5	235.0	99.8	135.2	84.0	51.2	−6.6
1986: IV	226.1	193.4	28.6	164.8	64.8	41.0	234.1	113.1	121.0	93.6	27.4	−8.0
1987: IV	255.8	211.8	29.9	181.9	84.5	41.2	276.2	127.3	148.9	102.8	46.1	−20.4
1988: III	284.1	239.0	31.6	207.3	95.1	39.2	314.4	141.2	173.2	112.2	61.1	−30.4
1988: IV	298.7	252.2	30.1	222.1	105.5	41.8	318.8	143.2	175.6	115.2	60.4	−20.1
1989: I	279.7	233.1	29.3	203.9	96.5	34.1	318.0	144.4	173.6	118.5	55.1	−38.3
II	275.5	231.8	28.6	203.2	90.3	36.9	296.0	134.9	161.1	120.9	40.2	−20.5
III	268.7	223.0	17.8	205.2	86.6	41.9	275.0	122.6	152.4	123.3	29.1	−6.3
IV	264.0	208.6	13.0	195.6	74.4	43.6	273.7	116.9	156.7	125.6	31.1	−9.7
1990: I '	272.2	220.4	21.5	198.9	80.5	38.4	283.3	124.8	158.5	128.1	30.4	−11.1

[1] See p. 167 for profits with inventory valuation and capital consumption adjustments.
[2] Includes rest of the world, not shown separately.
[3] Includes industries not shown separately.

Source: *Economic Indicators*, Council of Economic Advisers.

Source: Department of Commerce, Bureau of Economic Analysis.

Price Data

Definitions are applicable to the exhibits on pages 175–182.

Price data are gathered by the Bureau of Labor Statistics from retail and primary markets in the United States. Price indexes are given in relation to a base period (1982 = 100 for many Producer Price Indexes or 1982–84 = 100 for many Consumer Price Indexes, unless otherwise noted).

DEFINITIONS

The **Consumer Price Index** (CPI) is a measure of the average change in the prices paid by urban consumers for a fixed market basket of goods and services. The CPI is calculated monthly for two population groups, one consisting only of urban households whose primary source of income is derived from the employment of wage earners and clerical workers, and the other consisting of all urban households. The wage earner index (CPI–W) is a continuation of the historic index that was introduced well over a half-century ago for use in wage negotiations. As new uses were developed for the CPI in recent years, the need for a broader and more representative index became apparent. The all urban consumer index (CPI–U) introduced in 1978 is representative of the 1982–84 buying habits of about 80 percent of the noninstitutional population of the United States at that time, compared with 32 percent represented in the CPI–W. In addition to wage earners and clerical workers, the CPI–U covers professional, managerial, and technical workers, the self-employed, short-term workers, the unemployed, retirees, and others not in the labor force.

The CPI is based on prices of food, clothing, shelter, fuel, drugs, transportation fares, doctor's and dentist's fees, and other goods and services that people buy for day-to-day living. The quantity and quality of these items are kept essentially unchanged between major revisions so that only price changes will

be measured. All taxes directly associated with the purchase and use of items are included in the index.

Data are collected from more than 21,000 retail establishments and 60,000 tenants in 91 urban areas across the country are used to develop the "U.S. city average." Separate estimates for 27 major urban centers are presented in the table on page 182. The areas listed are as indicated in footnote 1 to the table. The area indexes measure only the average change in prices for each area since the base period, and do not indicate differences in the level of prices among cities.

NOTES ON THE DATA

In January 1983, the Bureau changed the way in which homeownership costs are measured for the CPI–U. A rental equivalence method replaced the asset-price approach to homeownership costs for that series. In January 1985, the same change was made in the CPI–W. The central purpose of the change was to separate shelter costs from the investment component of homeownership so that the index would reflect only the cost of shelter services provided by owner-occupied homes. An updated CP–U and CPI–W were introduced with release of the January 1987 data.

Additional Sources of Information

For a discussion of the general method for computing the CPI, see *BLS Handbook of Methods,* Bulletin 2285 (Bureau of Labor Statistics, 1988). The recent change in the measurement of homeownership costs is discussed in Robert Gillingham and Walter Lane, "Changing the treatment of shelter costs for homeowners in the CPI," *Monthly Labor Review,* June 1982, pp. 9–14. An overview of the recently introduced revised CPI, reflecting 1982–84 expenditure patterns, is contained in *The Consumer Price Index: 1987 Revision,* Report 736 (Bureau of Labor Statistics, 1987).

Additional detailed CPI data and regular analyses of consumer price changes are provided in the *CPI Detailed Report,* a monthly publication of the Bureau. Historical data for the overall CPI and for selected groupings may be found in the *Handbook of Labor Statistics,* Bulletin 2344 (Bureau of Labor Statistics, 1989).

Source: *Monthly Labor Review,* U.S. Department of Labor Statistics, Bureau of Labor Statistics.

CONSUMER PRICE INDEXES FOR ALL URBAN CONSUMERS AND FOR URBAN WAGE EARNERS AND CLERICAL WORKERS: U.S. CITY AVERAGE, BY EXPENDITURE CATEGORY AND COMMODITY OR SERVICE GROUP

(1982-84=100, unless otherwise indicated)

Series	Annual average 1988	Annual average 1989	1989 Mar.	Apr.	May	June	July	Aug.	Sept.	Oct.	Nov.	Dec.	1990 Jan.	Feb.	Mar.
CONSUMER PRICE INDEX FOR ALL URBAN CONSUMERS:															
All items	118.3	124.0	122.3	123.1	123.8	124.1	124.4	124.6	125.0	125.6	125.9	126.1	127.4	128.0	128.7
All items (1967=100)	354.3	371.3	366.2	368.8	370.8	371.7	372.7	373.1	374.6	376.2	377.0	377.0	381.5	383.3	385.5
Food and beverages	118.2	124.9	123.3	124.0	124.7	124.9	125.4	125.6	125.9	126.3	126.7	127.2	130.0	130.9	131.2
Food	118.6	125.1	123.5	124.2	124.9	125.0	125.5	125.8	126.1	126.5	126.9	127.4	130.4	131.3	131.5
Food at home	116.6	124.2	122.7	123.5	124.4	124.3	124.8	124.9	125.0	125.4	125.8	126.5	131.0	132.1	131.9
Cereals and bakery products	122.1	132.4	129.7	130.4	131.5	132.1	133.3	134.1	134.6	135.0	135.3	136.1	136.9	137.4	137.6
Meats, poultry, fish, and eggs	114.3	121.3	120.5	120.6	120.7	121.4	121.6	122.3	122.9	122.4	122.8	123.8	126.8	126.7	127.9
Dairy products	108.4	115.6	113.8	114.1	113.8	113.6	114.1	114.5	116.1	118.2	120.2	122.9	125.8	126.9	126.8
Fruits and vegetables	128.1	138.0	135.7	138.0	142.7	140.2	140.1	138.8	136.6	137.1	137.8	136.7	153.7	157.9	153.9
Other foods at home	113.1	119.1	118.1	119.0	118.9	119.2	119.7	119.7	119.7	120.3	119.9	120.1	121.3	121.9	122.2
Sugar and sweets	114.0	119.4	118.0	117.9	118.1	119.2	120.1	120.6	120.8	121.3	120.7	121.1	122.5	122.9	123.0
Fats and oils	113.1	121.2	120.4	121.6	121.6	121.6	121.6	121.7	121.3	121.6	121.0	121.6	123.5	123.4	124.2
Nonalcoholic beverages	107.5	111.3	111.3	111.8	111.5	111.6	112.3	111.2	111.0	111.8	111.2	111.0	112.4	113.3	113.1
Other prepared foods	118.0	125.5	123.7	125.2	125.5	125.5	125.5	126.7	126.7	127.2	127.3	127.6	128.3	128.9	129.6
Food away from home	121.8	127.4	125.7	126.2	126.7	127.1	127.8	128.1	128.8	129.1	129.5	129.8	130.3	131.0	131.8
Alcoholic beverages	118.6	123.5	121.8	122.3	123.1	123.5	124.0	124.5	124.8	125.2	125.5	125.6	126.2	126.9	127.8
Housing	118.5	123.0	121.5	121.6	122.1	122.9	123.9	124.2	124.3	124.4	124.5	124.9	125.9	126.1	126.8
Shelter	127.1	132.8	132.1	132.2	131.8	132.3	133.6	134.1	134.1	134.8	135.2	135.6	136.3	136.6	137.8
Renters' costs (12/82=100)	133.6	138.9	138.6	137.9	137.8	138.7	141.5	141.5	139.4	140.0	140.1	140.1	142.0	143.5	144.8
Rent, residential	127.8	132.8	131.1	131.4	131.7	132.3	133.0	133.5	133.9	134.7	135.2	135.5	135.8	136.0	136.5
Other renters' costs	134.8	140.7	144.7	140.7	139.7	141.5	150.5	148.8	139.1	139.2	138.0	137.2	143.6	149.3	152.7
Homeowners' costs (12/82=100)	131.1	137.3	135.0	135.4	136.2	136.5	137.3	138.1	138.9	139.7	140.3	140.9	141.1	141.0	142.2
Owners' equivalent rent (12/82=100)	131.1	137.4	135.1	135.5	136.3	136.6	137.4	138.0	139.0	139.9	140.5	141.0	141.2	141.1	142.4
Household insurance (12/82=100)	129.0	132.6	131.3	131.4	132.1	132.8	133.1	133.3	133.6	133.7	133.8	134.0	134.1	134.5	134.8
Maintenance and repairs	114.7	118.0	117.1	117.3	117.4	118.3	118.4	118.5	118.6	118.6	119.3	119.5	120.4	120.8	121.2
Maintenance and repair services	117.9	120.6	119.6	119.8	120.2	121.0	121.0	121.3	120.9	121.0	121.7	122.2	123.7	123.7	124.8
Maintenance and repair commodities	110.4	114.6	113.8	114.1	113.8	114.7	115.0	114.8	115.6	115.5	116.2	115.8	116.0	115.9	116.4
Fuel and other utilities	104.4	107.8	105.9	106.2	107.0	109.2	109.7	109.7	109.7	108.0	107.5	108.4	110.8	110.2	109.9
Fuels	98.0	100.9	98.5	98.8	99.6	103.2	103.5	103.7	103.3	101.0	99.9	101.2	104.5	103.1	102.3
Fuel oil, coal, and bottled gas	78.1	81.7	81.5	82.5	81.5	80.2	79.7	78.9	79.3	82.0	83.9	88.7	113.1	95.4	91.5
Gas (piped) and electricity	104.6	107.5	104.8	105.0	106.1	110.5	111.1	111.3	111.0	107.6	106.1	107.0	107.5	108.3	107.9
Other utilities and public services	122.9	127.1	125.9	126.2	127.0	127.1	127.1	127.8	128.1	127.6	127.9	128.2	129.3	130.0	130.0
Household furnishings and operations	109.4	111.2	110.5	110.7	110.8	111.1	111.4	111.4	111.7	111.9	111.9	111.7	112.1	112.8	112.8
Housefurnishings	105.1	105.5	105.1	105.0	104.7	105.1	105.5	105.2	105.7	106.1	106.0	105.5	106.1	106.9	106.9
Housekeeping supplies	114.7	120.9	118.5	119.6	120.9	121.2	121.7	122.5	122.9	122.5	122.5	123.6	123.2	123.5	123.4
Housekeeping services	114.3	117.3	116.9	117.1	117.3	117.4	117.3	117.5	117.5	117.4	117.6	117.6	117.9	118.4	118.7

(continued)

CONSUMER PRICE INDEXES FOR ALL URBAN CONSUMERS AND FOR URBAN WAGE EARNERS AND CLERICAL WORKERS: U.S. CITY AVERAGE, BY EXPENDITURE CATEGORY AND COMMODITY OR SERVICE GROUP (continued)

(1982-84=100, unless otherwise indicated)

Series	Annual average 1988	Annual average 1989	1989 Mar.	Apr.	May	June	July	Aug.	Sept.	Oct.	Nov.	Dec.	1990 Jan.	Feb.	Mar.
Apparel and upkeep	115.4	118.6	119.3	120.9	120.4	117.8	115.0	115.0	120.0	122.7	122.1	119.2	116.7	120.4	125.4
Apparel commodities	113.7	116.7	117.5	119.3	118.6	115.8	112.9	112.8	118.2	121.1	120.4	117.1	114.3	118.3	123.7
Men's and boys' apparel	113.4	117.0	115.9	117.2	117.8	115.9	114.7	114.7	117.7	120.3	121.1	118.8	116.3	117.0	119.3
Women's and girls' apparel	114.9	116.4	119.4	121.5	119.5	114.8	109.6	109.5	119.0	123.1	121.5	116.4	112.0	117.7	126.8
Infants' and toddlers' apparel	116.4	119.1	118.5	123.6	125.4	123.9	117.9	116.7	118.0	118.3	117.2	115.3	112.7	124.3	127.6
Footwear	109.9	114.4	114.1	115.3	114.9	114.0	113.4	112.6	114.1	117.6	116.6	114.7	113.1	114.5	116.9
Other apparel commodities	116.0	122.1	120.4	121.5	121.7	121.6	122.5	124.1	124.5	123.0	123.0	122.8	125.1	130.6	132.7
Apparel services	123.7	129.4	128.5	128.9	129.9	130.0	129.4	129.5	129.7	129.8	130.8	131.3	132.4	132.9	133.8
Transportation	108.7	114.1	111.9	114.6	116.0	115.9	115.4	114.3	113.7	114.5	115.0	115.2	117.2	117.1	116.8
Private transportation	107.6	112.9	110.7	113.6	115.0	114.9	114.3	113.1	112.4	113.3	113.7	113.9	115.9	115.6	115.1
New vehicles	116.5	119.2	119.4	119.2	119.2	118.9	118.5	117.7	117.1	118.5	120.6	121.9	122.4	122.2	121.6
New cars	116.9	119.2	119.6	119.4	119.5	119.1	118.6	117.7	117.0	118.6	120.5	121.8	122.3	121.9	121.3
Used cars	118.0	120.4	120.5	120.7	121.0	121.3	121.1	120.3	119.8	119.7	120.1	119.7	118.9	117.4	116.6
Motor fuel	80.9	88.5	81.5	92.1	96.6	96.0	94.4	91.0	88.8	88.9	87.2	85.8	91.4	90.6	89.3
Gasoline	80.8	88.5	81.3	92.1	96.7	96.2	94.6	91.1	88.8	88.8	87.0	85.5	90.6	90.2	89.1
Maintenance and repair	119.7	124.9	123.5	123.8	124.3	124.5	124.8	125.4	126.2	126.7	126.7	126.9	127.3	127.6	128.8
Other private transportation	127.9	135.8	134.5	134.7	135.6	135.9	135.6	135.7	135.7	137.1	138.2	139.0	140.3	140.8	140.7
Other private transportation commodities	98.9	101.5	100.1	100.8	101.5	101.1	101.3	101.3	102.0	101.9	102.1	102.3	101.9	102.1	102.0
Other private transportation services	133.9	143.2	141.9	142.0	142.9	143.2	143.0	142.9	142.9	144.8	146.0	146.9	148.7	149.3	149.2
Public transportation	123.3	129.5	128.2	128.4	128.9	129.6	129.7	130.1	130.1	130.6	131.3	131.7	134.2	136.7	139.1
Medical care	138.6	149.3	146.1	146.8	147.5	148.5	149.7	150.7	151.7	152.7	153.9	154.4	155.9	157.5	158.7
Medical care commodities	139.9	150.8	147.2	148.4	150.0	151.0	151.4	152.1	153.3	154.1	155.3	156.0	156.9	158.6	159.9
Medical care services	138.3	148.9	145.9	146.4	146.9	147.9	149.3	150.4	151.3	152.3	153.6	154.1	155.7	157.2	158.5
Professional services	137.5	146.4	144.9	144.9	145.2	146.1	147.0	147.5	148.0	148.0	149.3	149.9	151.1	153.2	153.2
Hospital and related services	143.9	160.5	155.8	156.6	157.3	158.5	160.8	162.7	164.3	166.0	167.9	167.9	169.9	171.6	173.0
Entertainment	120.3	126.5	124.7	125.4	125.5	126.2	126.9	127.3	127.8	128.4	128.6	129.1	129.9	130.4	130.9
Entertainment commodities	115.0	119.8	118.5	119.0	119.3	119.5	119.9	120.0	120.5	121.2	121.3	121.6	122.3	122.5	123.1
Entertainment services	127.7	135.4	132.9	134.0	133.9	135.0	136.1	136.7	137.2	137.8	138.2	138.8	139.8	140.5	141.0
Other goods and services	137.0	147.7	144.4	144.7	145.4	146.3	147.3	148.7	151.2	151.8	151.9	152.9	154.0	154.7	155.2
Tobacco products	145.8	164.4	159.2	159.5	161.1	164.2	167.5	168.8	168.2	168.8	168.6	171.9	174.1	175.0	175.1
Personal care	119.4	125.0	123.6	124.1	124.8	124.5	124.8	125.9	124.0	124.4	125.1	127.1	127.6	128.4	129.0
Toilet goods and personal care appliances	118.1	123.2	122.4	122.6	122.7	122.2	122.8	123.8	124.0	124.4	125.1	124.7	125.1	126.0	126.9
Personal care services	120.7	126.8	124.8	125.4	126.8	127.0	126.9	127.3	127.7	128.5	129.0	129.7	130.3	130.9	131.2
Personal and educational expenses	147.9	158.1	154.6	154.9	155.2	155.8	156.3	158.1	162.9	163.5	163.5	164.0	165.1	165.6	166.3
School books and supplies	148.1	158.0	155.1	155.2	155.2	155.6	155.8	156.6	163.0	163.6	163.9	164.0	167.9	169.7	169.9
Personal and educational services	148.0	158.3	154.7	155.1	155.4	156.0	156.5	158.4	163.1	163.7	163.7	164.2	165.1	165.6	166.3

All items	118.3	124.0	122.3	123.1	123.8	124.1	124.4	124.6	125.0	125.6	125.9	126.1	127.4	128.0	128.7
Commodities	111.5	116.7	115.2	116.7	117.5	117.2	117.0	116.7	117.3	118.1	118.3	118.1	119.9	120.6	121.1
Food and beverages	118.2	124.9	123.3	124.0	124.7	124.9	125.4	125.6	125.9	126.3	126.7	127.2	130.0	130.9	131.2
Commodities less food and beverages	107.3	111.6	110.1	112.2	112.9	112.4	111.7	111.1	111.9	113.0	113.0	112.6	113.7	114.2	114.9
Nondurables less food and beverages	105.2	111.2	108.9	112.5	113.6	112.7	111.6	110.9	112.4	113.6	113.1	112.0	113.7	114.5	116.1
Apparel commodities	113.7	116.7	117.5	119.3	118.6	115.8	112.9	112.8	118.2	121.1	120.4	117.1	114.3	118.3	123.7
Nondurables less food, beverages, and apparel	103.2	111.0	106.9	111.5	113.6	113.7	113.6	112.5	112.0	112.4	111.9	112.0	116.0	115.3	114.8
Durables	110.4	112.2	111.9	111.8	111.9	112.1	111.9	111.4	111.3	112.1	113.0	113.5	113.8	113.7	113.4
Services	125.7	131.9	130.0	130.2	130.8	131.6	132.5	133.1	133.4	133.7	134.1	134.6	135.4	136.0	136.9
Rent of shelter (12/82=100)	132.0	138.0	136.3	136.3	136.9	137.4	138.8	139.3	139.3	140.1	140.5	140.9	141.6	142.0	143.3
Household services less rent of shelter (12/82=100)	115.3	118.7	116.9	117.2	118.0	120.1	120.6	120.7	120.7	119.0	118.5	119.0	119.6	120.3	120.5
Transportation services	128.0	135.6	134.3	134.5	135.2	135.6	135.5	135.7	135.9	137.1	138.0	138.6	140.2	141.1	141.9
Medical care services	138.3	148.9	145.9	146.4	146.9	147.9	149.3	150.4	151.3	152.3	153.6	154.1	155.7	157.2	158.5
Other services	132.6	140.9	138.2	138.8	139.2	139.8	140.4	141.5	143.8	144.3	144.6	145.1	146.1	146.6	147.2
Special indexes:															
All items less food	118.3	123.7	122.0	122.9	123.5	123.9	124.2	124.3	124.8	125.4	125.6	125.8	126.7	127.3	128.1
All items less shelter	115.9	121.6	119.9	121.0	121.7	122.0	122.0	122.0	122.6	123.1	123.3	123.5	125.0	125.7	126.2
All items less homeowners' costs (12/82=100)	119.5	125.3	123.7	124.7	125.3	125.6	125.9	125.9	126.3	126.8	127.0	127.1	128.7	129.5	130.1
All items less medical care	117.0	122.4	120.8	121.7	122.3	122.6	122.9	123.0	123.4	124.0	124.2	124.4	125.7	126.2	126.9
Commodities less food	107.7	112.0	110.5	112.5	113.2	112.8	112.1	111.6	112.4	113.4	113.4	113.0	114.1	114.6	115.4
Nondurables less food	105.8	111.7	109.4	112.8	113.9	113.1	112.2	111.5	112.9	114.1	113.6	112.6	114.2	115.0	116.5
Nondurables less food and apparel	104.0	111.3	107.6	111.7	113.6	113.8	113.7	112.8	112.4	112.8	112.4	112.5	116.1	115.5	115.2
Nondurables	111.8	118.2	116.2	118.4	119.3	119.0	118.7	118.4	119.3	120.1	120.0	119.8	122.0	122.9	123.8
Services less rent of shelter (12/82=100)	128.3	135.1	133.0	133.4	134.0	135.2	135.8	136.3	137.0	137.0	137.2	137.8	138.9	139.8	140.3
Services less medical care	124.3	130.1	128.3	128.5	129.1	129.9	130.8	131.3	131.6	131.8	132.1	132.6	133.4	133.9	134.7
Energy	89.3	94.3	89.8	94.9	97.4	99.0	98.5	97.0	95.9	94.6	93.2	93.2	97.6	96.4	95.5
All items less energy	122.3	128.1	126.7	127.1	127.6	127.7	128.2	128.5	129.1	129.9	130.4	130.6	131.5	132.3	133.3
All items less food and energy	123.4	129.0	127.6	128.0	128.3	128.5	129.0	129.3	130.0	130.9	131.3	131.5	132.0	132.8	133.9
Commodities less food and energy	115.8	119.6	119.0	119.6	119.7	119.3	118.8	118.8	120.1	121.2	121.6	121.2	121.0	122.2	123.4
Energy commodities	80.8	87.9	81.7	91.2	95.0	94.4	92.9	89.8	88.0	87.0	86.4	86.4	94.2	91.3	89.8
Services less energy	127.9	134.4	132.7	132.9	133.4	133.9	134.8	135.4	135.8	136.5	137.0	137.5	138.4	138.9	140.0
Purchasing power of the consumer dollar:															
1982-84=$1.00	84.6	80.7	81.8	81.2	80.8	80.6	80.4	80.3	80.0	79.6	79.5	79.3	78.5	78.2	77.7
1967=$1.00	28.2	26.9	27.3	27.1	27.0	26.9	26.8	26.8	26.7	26.6	26.5	26.5	26.2	26.1	25.9

(continued)

CONSUMER PRICE INDEXES FOR ALL URBAN CONSUMERS AND FOR URBAN WAGE EARNERS AND CLERICAL WORKERS: U.S. CITY AVERAGE, BY EXPENDITURE CATEGORY AND COMMODITY OR SERVICE GROUP (continued)

(1982-84=100, unless otherwise indicated)

CONSUMER PRICE INDEX FOR URBAN WAGE EARNERS AND CLERICAL WORKERS:

Series	Annual average		1989										1990		
	1988	1989	Mar.	Apr.	May	June	July	Aug.	Sept.	Oct.	Nov.	Dec.	Jan.	Feb.	Mar.
All items	117.0	122.6	120.8	121.8	122.5	122.8	123.2	123.2	123.6	124.2	124.4	124.6	125.9	126.4	127.1
All items (1967=100)	348.4	365.2	360.0	362.9	364.9	365.9	366.8	367.0	368.3	369.8	370.6	371.1	375.0	376.6	378.5
Food and beverages	117.9	124.6	123.1	123.7	124.4	124.6	125.1	125.3	125.6	126.0	126.4	126.9	129.7	130.6	130.9
Food	117.9	124.8	123.3	123.9	124.6	124.8	125.3	125.5	125.8	126.2	126.6	127.1	130.1	131.1	131.2
Food at home	116.2	123.9	122.4	123.2	124.0	123.9	124.4	124.6	124.6	125.0	125.5	126.2	130.5	131.6	131.5
Cereals and bakery products	122.2	132.4	129.7	130.5	131.5	132.0	133.3	134.1	134.6	135.1	135.3	136.0	136.8	137.4	137.6
Meats, poultry, fish, and eggs	114.1	121.2	120.3	120.4	120.5	121.2	121.5	122.1	122.7	122.2	122.9	123.8	126.7	126.6	127.8
Dairy products	108.1	115.4	113.6	114.0	113.6	113.3	113.8	114.2	115.9	118.0	120.0	122.8	125.7	126.9	126.8
Fruits and vegetables	127.6	137.6	135.4	137.7	142.5	140.0	139.9	138.6	136.1	136.5	137.0	135.8	152.9	157.7	153.3
Other foods at home	113.0	119.0	118.0	118.9	118.8	119.0	119.6	119.6	119.6	120.2	119.8	120.1	121.3	121.8	122.2
Sugar and sweets	113.9	119.5	118.0	118.1	118.4	119.2	120.1	120.6	120.9	121.4	120.7	121.1	122.5	123.0	123.1
Fats and oils	113.0	121.1	120.3	121.5	121.5	121.5	121.5	121.6	121.2	121.5	120.9	121.5	123.4	123.2	124.0
Nonalcoholic beverages	107.7	111.4	111.4	111.9	111.5	111.6	112.2	111.1	111.0	112.0	111.3	111.2	112.7	113.6	113.4
Other prepared foods	117.8	125.3	123.6	125.0	125.0	125.3	125.7	126.5	126.0	127.0	127.1	127.4	128.2	128.7	129.5
Food away from home	121.6	127.3	125.5	126.1	126.5	127.0	127.6	128.0	128.6	129.0	129.4	129.7	130.2	130.9	131.7
Alcoholic beverages	118.3	123.1	121.4	122.0	122.8	123.2	123.6	124.0	124.4	124.7	125.1	125.2	125.9	126.7	127.4
Housing	116.8	121.2	119.6	119.8	120.3	121.1	122.1	122.4	122.5	122.5	122.7	123.1	123.9	124.1	124.7
Shelter	124.3	129.8	128.1	128.3	128.8	129.3	130.5	131.0	131.1	131.8	132.3	132.6	133.2	133.4	134.5
Renters' costs (12/84=100)	119.2	123.9	123.0	122.7	122.8	123.6	123.6	125.9	124.6	125.1	125.3	125.4	126.6	127.5	128.4
Rent, residential	127.5	132.3	130.7	131.0	131.2	131.8	132.5	133.0	133.4	134.2	134.6	135.0	135.3	135.4	136.0
Other renters' costs	135.2	141.5	144.2	140.9	139.9	142.3	153.7	152.0	140.9	140.4	139.1	137.6	141.1	149.8	153.2
Homeowners' costs (12/84=100)	119.5	125.1	123.0	123.4	124.1	124.4	125.2	125.6	126.6	127.3	127.8	128.3	128.5	128.5	129.6
Owners' equivalent rent (12/84=100)	119.5	125.2	123.1	123.5	124.2	124.5	125.2	125.9	126.7	127.4	128.0	128.5	128.6	128.6	129.7
Household insurance (12/84=100)	118.2	121.4	120.1	120.2	120.9	121.5	121.8	122.0	122.4	122.5	122.5	122.7	122.8	123.1	123.3
Maintenance and repairs	114.0	117.6	116.7	116.7	116.9	117.9	117.9	118.0	118.0	118.1	118.9	119.0	120.0	120.7	120.8
Maintenance and repair services	117.7	120.4	119.2	119.3	119.8	121.0	121.2	121.3	120.7	120.9	121.7	122.4	124.1	125.0	125.1
Maintenance and repair commodities	108.3	112.6	112.1	112.1	112.0	112.7	113.2	112.5	113.3	113.4	114.0	113.6	113.8	114.3	114.3
Fuel and other utilities	104.1	107.5	105.7	105.9	106.7	109.0	109.4	109.5	109.3	107.6	107.2	108.0	110.2	109.8	109.6
Fuels	97.7	100.6	98.2	98.5	99.2	103.0	103.4	103.5	103.3	100.6	99.5	100.7	103.8	102.5	101.8
Fuel oil, coal, and bottled gas	77.9	81.4	81.2	82.1	81.2	80.1	79.6	78.8	79.2	81.8	83.6	88.1	112.7	95.2	91.3
Gas (piped) and electricity	104.4	107.3	104.6	104.8	105.8	110.3	110.8	111.0	110.7	107.2	105.8	106.7	107.2	107.9	107.5
Other utilities and public services	122.9	127.4	126.2	126.5	127.2	127.4	127.9	128.0	128.3	127.8	128.2	128.4	129.6	130.4	131.0
Household furnishings and operations	108.9	110.6	110.0	110.1	110.1	110.4	110.8	110.8	111.0	111.2	111.2	111.1	111.5	112.1	112.1
Housefurnishings	104.5	104.8	104.5	104.3	104.0	104.4	104.8	104.6	105.0	105.3	105.2	104.7	105.3	106.1	105.9
Housekeeping supplies	115.1	121.2	118.9	120.0	121.2	121.6	121.6	122.6	122.6	122.7	122.7	123.8	123.5	123.8	123.9
Housekeeping services	115.0	117.4	117.1	117.2	117.4	117.6	117.4	117.6	117.6	117.5	117.7	117.8	118.1	118.7	119.0

Apparel and upkeep	114.9	117.9	118.4	120.0	119.4	116.9	114.4	114.5	119.3	122.0	121.4	118.5	116.1	119.3	124.4
Apparel commodities	113.4	116.1	116.7	118.4	117.7	115.0	112.3	112.4	117.6	120.5	119.8	116.6	114.0	117.3	122.8
Men's and boys' apparel	112.8	116.1	115.1	116.4	116.9	115.0	113.7	113.9	116.9	119.6	120.2	118.0	115.8	116.2	118.3
Women's and girls' apparel	114.5	115.5	118.3	120.2	118.1	113.5	108.7	108.9	118.1	122.0	120.5	115.5	111.3	116.4	125.7
Infants' and toddlers' apparel	118.6	122.5	121.7	126.7	128.3	126.7	121.9	120.4	122.0	122.2	121.0	119.3	116.8	127.1	129.9
Footwear	110.4	114.7	114.1	115.2	115.0	114.1	113.9	113.1	114.5	118.0	117.0	115.4	113.8	115.0	117.4
Other apparel commodities	114.9	120.5	118.5	119.6	119.8	119.8	120.7	122.4	122.5	121.9	122.4	121.5	123.2	127.0	130.5
Apparel services	123.0	128.6	127.7	128.1	128.9	129.0	128.6	128.7	128.8	129.0	130.0	130.6	131.7	132.2	133.2
Transportation	108.3	113.9	111.6	114.5	116.0	116.0	115.4	114.2	113.5	114.3	114.6	114.8	116.8	116.6	116.2
Private transportation	107.5	113.0	110.6	113.7	115.3	115.2	114.6	113.3	112.6	113.3	113.7	113.8	115.8	115.5	114.9
New vehicles	116.2	119.0	119.2	118.9	119.0	118.7	118.3	117.6	117.1	118.4	120.5	122.0	122.4	122.3	121.7
New cars	116.6	119.1	119.4	119.2	119.3	118.9	118.4	117.6	116.9	118.4	120.2	121.7	122.2	121.8	121.2
Used cars	117.9	120.3	120.3	120.5	120.9	121.1	120.9	120.1	119.6	119.5	119.9	119.5	118.7	117.2	116.4
Motor fuel	80.9	88.6	81.5	92.3	96.7	96.1	94.5	91.0	89.0	89.1	87.3	85.6	91.7	90.7	89.4
Gasoline	80.8	88.6	81.4	92.3	96.9	96.3	94.7	91.2	89.0	89.0	87.2	85.6	91.0	90.4	89.2
Maintenance and repair	119.8	124.9	123.5	123.9	124.4	124.6	124.8	123.7	126.2	126.7	126.8	126.9	127.3	127.9	129.0
Other private transportation	125.8	133.7	132.5	132.7	133.5	133.9	133.7	133.7	133.6	134.9	136.0	136.8	138.1	138.5	138.3
Other private transportation commodities	98.6	101.1	99.8	100.4	101.1	101.5	101.0	101.6	101.6	101.5	101.7	101.9	101.4	101.7	101.5
Other private transportation services	131.7	141.0	139.8	139.8	140.7	141.2	141.0	140.8	140.6	142.5	143.8	144.7	146.5	146.9	146.8
Public transportation	122.5	128.2	126.9	127.1	127.5	128.2	129.1	129.1	129.1	129.4	129.7	130.1	132.9	135.4	137.4
Medical care	139.0	149.6	146.5	147.2	147.9	148.8	150.1	151.1	152.1	153.0	154.2	154.7	156.1	157.6	158.8
Medical care commodities	139.0	149.7	146.0	147.4	148.9	149.9	150.3	150.9	152.2	153.1	154.2	154.8	155.7	157.4	158.6
Medical care services	139.0	149.6	146.7	147.2	147.6	148.6	150.0	151.1	152.1	153.0	154.2	154.7	156.2	157.7	158.8
Professional services	137.7	146.7	144.7	145.1	145.5	146.4	147.3	147.8	148.4	149.0	149.6	150.2	151.5	152.6	153.5
Hospital and related services	143.3	159.4	154.8	155.6	156.2	157.3	159.7	161.6	163.3	164.7	166.5	166.8	168.4	170.1	171.3
Entertainment	119.7	125.8	124.1	124.8	124.9	125.5	126.1	126.5	127.0	127.7	127.9	128.4	129.1	129.5	130.0
Entertainment commodities	115.1	119.9	118.7	119.1	119.5	119.7	120.1	120.1	120.6	121.3	121.4	121.7	122.3	122.4	123.0
Entertainment services	127.2	135.1	132.7	133.8	133.6	134.6	135.7	136.4	137.1	137.6	138.0	138.7	139.6	140.4	140.9
Other goods and services	136.5	147.4	144.0	144.4	145.2	146.3	147.5	148.8	150.8	151.4	151.5	152.7	153.9	154.6	155.1
Tobacco products	146.0	164.2	158.9	159.2	160.7	163.8	167.3	168.5	168.0	168.6	168.5	171.8	173.8	174.8	174.8
Personal care	119.3	124.3	123.5	123.9	124.7	124.6	124.6	125.4	125.7	126.3	126.8	126.9	127.3	128.1	128.7
Toilet goods and personal care appliances	118.0	123.3	122.3	122.7	122.4	122.4	122.8	123.8	124.1	124.6	125.1	124.7	124.9	126.0	126.8
Personal care services	120.5	126.6	124.6	125.2	126.7	126.9	126.8	127.1	127.5	128.2	128.7	129.4	130.1	130.5	130.8
Personal and educational expenses	147.4	157.3	153.9	154.3	154.6	155.3	155.7	157.3	161.8	162.5	162.5	163.1	164.2	164.8	165.6
School books and supplies	147.1	156.9	154.0	154.1	154.1	154.5	155.6	155.6	161.7	162.8	162.8	162.9	166.9	165.5	168.7
Personal and educational services	147.7	157.7	154.1	154.6	154.9	155.7	156.1	157.8	162.1	162.7	162.8	163.4	164.3	164.8	165.7
All items	117.0	122.6	120.8	121.8	122.5	122.8	123.2	123.2	123.6	124.2	124.4	124.6	125.9	126.4	127.1
Commodities	111.0	116.3	114.7	116.4	117.1	116.9	116.8	116.4	116.9	117.7	117.8	117.8	119.5	120.1	120.5
Food and beverages	117.9	124.6	123.1	123.7	124.4	124.6	125.1	125.3	125.6	126.0	126.4	126.9	129.7	130.6	130.9
Commodities less food and beverages	106.8	111.2	109.5	111.8	112.6	112.2	111.6	110.9	111.6	112.5	112.5	112.1	113.3	113.6	114.2
Nondurables less food and beverages	104.6	110.9	108.1	112.1	113.4	112.6	111.7	110.8	111.6	113.2	112.6	111.6	113.4	114.0	115.4
Apparel commodities	113.4	116.1	116.7	118.4	117.7	115.0	112.3	112.4	117.6	120.5	119.8	116.6	114.0	117.3	122.8
Nondurables less food, beverages, and apparel	102.9	110.9	106.5	111.6	113.9	114.0	113.9	112.6	112.0	112.3	111.7	111.7	115.7	115.0	114.5
Durables	108.9	110.8	110.6	110.5	110.6	110.7	110.6	110.1	110.0	110.6	111.6	112.0	112.2	112.0	111.6

(continued)

CONSUMER PRICE INDEXES FOR ALL URBAN CONSUMERS AND FOR URBAN WAGE EARNERS AND CLERICAL WORKERS: U.S. CITY AVERAGE, BY EXPENDITURE CATEGORY AND COMMODITY OR SERVICE GROUP (concluded)

(1982-84=100, unless otherwise indicated)

Series	Annual average 1988	Annual average 1989	1989 Mar.	Apr.	May	June	July	Aug.	Sept.	Oct.	Nov.	Dec.	1990 Jan.	Feb.	Mar.
Services	124.7	130.8	128.9	129.1	129.7	130.6	131.5	132.0	132.3	132.6	132.9	133.4	134.2	134.8	135.6
Rent of shelter (12/84=100)	119.4	124.8	123.1	123.2	123.7	124.2	125.4	125.9	126.0	126.7	127.1	127.5	128.0	128.2	129.3
Household services less rent of shelter (12/84=100)	105.9	109.1	107.4	107.6	108.3	110.5	110.9	111.0	111.0	109.3	108.8	109.3	110.0	110.6	110.7
Transportation services	127.1	134.8	133.5	133.7	134.4	134.8	134.8	134.9	135.0	136.3	137.1	137.8	139.4	140.2	140.7
Medical care services	139.0	149.6	146.7	147.2	147.6	148.6	150.0	151.1	152.1	153.0	154.2	154.7	156.2	157.7	158.8
Other services	131.4	139.6	137.0	137.6	137.9	138.6	139.1	140.1	142.3	142.9	143.2	143.8	144.7	145.3	145.9
Special indexes:															
All items less food	116.7	122.0	120.2	121.3	122.0	122.3	122.6	122.6	123.1	123.6	123.8	124.0	124.9	125.3	126.1
All items less shelter	115.2	120.9	119.1	120.4	121.1	121.3	121.4	121.3	121.8	122.3	122.5	122.6	124.2	124.8	125.3
All items less homeowners' costs (12/84=100)	110.4	115.7	114.1	115.2	115.8	116.1	116.3	116.3	116.6	117.1	117.3	117.4	118.8	119.4	119.9
All items less medical care	115.8	121.2	119.5	120.5	121.2	121.5	121.8	121.8	122.2	122.7	122.9	123.1	124.4	124.9	125.5
Commodities less food	107.2	111.6	109.9	112.1	112.9	112.5	112.0	111.4	112.0	112.9	112.9	112.6	113.7	114.0	114.6
Nondurables less food	105.3	111.3	108.7	112.4	113.6	113.0	112.1	111.4	112.5	113.6	113.1	112.2	113.9	114.5	115.8
Nondurables less food and apparel	103.7	111.2	107.2	111.7	113.8	114.0	113.9	112.8	112.3	112.7	112.1	112.2	115.8	115.3	114.9
Nondurables	111.5	118.0	115.8	118.1	119.1	118.8	118.6	118.3	119.1	119.8	119.7	119.5	121.8	122.6	123.4
Services less rent of shelter (12/84=100)	115.6	121.7	119.8	120.1	120.7	121.9	122.3	122.7	123.3	123.3	123.4	123.9	124.9	125.7	126.1
Services less medical care	123.3	129.0	127.2	127.4	128.0	128.9	129.7	130.1	130.4	130.6	130.9	131.4	132.2	132.7	133.4
Energy	88.6	93.9	89.2	94.8	97.4	98.9	98.3	96.6	95.5	94.2	92.8	92.7	97.1	96.0	94.9
All items less energy	121.0	126.7	125.3	125.8	126.2	126.4	126.8	127.1	127.7	128.5	128.9	129.1	130.1	130.8	131.6
All items less food and energy	121.9	127.3	125.9	126.3	126.6	126.8	127.3	127.6	128.3	129.1	129.6	129.7	130.1	130.8	131.8
Commodities less food and energy	114.7	118.6	117.9	118.4	118.5	118.2	117.9	117.9	119.0	120.1	120.5	120.2	119.9	120.8	122.0
Energy commodities	80.9	88.2	81.7	91.6	95.6	94.9	93.5	90.2	88.4	88.7	87.2	86.4	93.9	91.4	89.8
Services less energy	127.0	133.4	131.6	131.9	132.4	132.9	133.8	134.4	134.8	135.5	136.0	136.4	137.3	137.8	138.8
Purchasing power of the consumer dollar:															
1982-84=$1.00	85.5	81.6	82.8	82.1	81.6	81.4	81.2	81.2	80.9	80.5	80.4	80.3	79.4	79.1	78.7
1967=$1.00	28.7	27.4	27.8	27.6	27.4	27.3	27.3	27.2	27.2	27.0	27.0	26.9	26.7	26.6	26.4

Source: *Monthly Labor Review,* U.S. Department of Labor, Bureau of Labor Statistics.

CONSUMER PRICE INDEX—U.S. CITY AVERAGE AND AVAILABLE LOCAL AREA DATA: ALL ITEMS

(1982-84=100, unless otherwise indicated)

Area¹	Pricing schedule²	All Urban Consumers							Urban Wage Earners						
		1989				1990			1989				1990		
		Mar.	Apr.	Nov.	Dec.	Jan.	Feb.	Mar.	Mar.	Apr.	Nov.	Dec.	Jan.	Feb.	Mar.
U.S. city average	M	122.3	123.1	125.9	126.1	127.4	128.0	128.7	120.8	121.8	124.4	124.6	125.9	126.4	127.1
Region and area size³															
Northeast urban	M	126.7	127.4	131.1	131.3	132.9	133.1	134.1	125.4	126.2	129.9	130.1	131.6	131.8	132.8
Size A - More than 1,200,000	M	127.4	128.0	131.6	131.6	133.3	133.6	134.7	125.2	125.9	129.5	129.5	131.0	131.3	132.4
Size B - 500,000 to 1,200,000	M	125.1	126.1	130.7	130.9	132.5	132.8	133.6	123.9	124.9	129.3	129.5	131.1	131.4	132.1
Size C - 50,000 to 500,000	M	125.5	126.2	129.7	130.7	132.0	131.7	132.3	127.8	128.6	132.3	133.1	134.4	134.3	134.7
North Central urban	M	119.8	120.8	123.2	123.2	124.5	124.9	125.5	117.9	118.9	121.2	121.1	122.5	122.8	123.3
Size A - More than 1,200,000	M	121.1	121.9	124.4	124.3	125.7	126.4	126.9	118.4	119.2	121.5	121.5	122.9	123.5	123.9
Size B - 360,000 to 1,200,000	M	119.2	120.6	123.0	123.0	124.2	124.4	124.7	116.8	118.2	120.5	120.4	121.8	121.9	122.2
Size C - 50,000 to 360,000	M	119.9	121.2	123.3	123.2	124.6	124.5	125.3	118.7	120.1	122.0	122.0	123.5	123.3	124.1
Size D - Nonmetropolitan (less than 50,000)	M	115.5	116.3	118.6	118.8	120.0	119.8	120.8	115.1	116.1	118.4	118.6	119.9	119.7	120.6
South urban	M	119.8	120.8	123.2	123.4	124.6	125.4	126.0	119.1	120.3	122.5	122.7	123.9	124.7	125.1
Size A - More than 1,200,000	M	120.5	121.4	124.0	124.0	125.1	126.1	126.7	119.6	120.6	123.0	123.0	124.1	125.0	125.5
Size B - 450,000 to 1,200,000	M	121.0	122.2	124.7	125.1	126.0	126.9	127.3	118.8	120.1	122.4	122.7	123.6	124.4	124.7
Size C - 50,000 to 450,000	M	118.5	119.4	121.6	122.0	123.3	123.9	124.3	119.0	120.0	122.1	122.5	123.8	124.3	124.7
Size D - Nonmetropolitan (less than 50,000)	M	118.0	119.4	121.3	121.4	123.5	124.3	125.0	118.7	120.2	122.0	122.1	124.4	125.0	125.6
West urban	M	123.1	123.8	126.3	126.8	127.8	128.8	129.6	121.7	122.6	124.8	125.3	126.3	127.2	127.9
Size A - More than 1,250,000	M	124.7	125.3	127.8	128.3	129.5	130.6	131.5	121.9	122.7	124.9	125.4	126.6	127.6	128.3
Size C - 50,000 to 330,000	M	120.7	122.1	124.5	125.3	125.4	125.8	126.0	120.1	121.5	123.7	124.4	124.6	125.0	125.2

(continued)

CONSUMER PRICE INDEX—U.S. CITY AVERAGE AND AVAILABLE LOCAL AREA DATA: ALL ITEMS (concluded)

(1982-84=100, unless otherwise indicated)

Area[1]	Pricing schedule[2]	All Urban Consumers							Urban Wage Earners						
		1989				1990			1989				1990		
		Mar.	Apr.	Nov.	Dec.	Jan.	Feb.	Mar.	Mar.	Apr.	Nov.	Dec.	Jan.	Feb.	Mar.
Size classes:															
A (12/86=100)	M	111.2	111.8	114.3	114.4	115.7	116.3	117.1	111.0	111.7	114.1	114.2	115.5	116.1	116.7
B	M	121.5	122.6	125.6	125.9	126.9	127.6	128.1	120.0	121.2	124.0	124.3	125.4	126.0	126.5
C	M	120.5	121.6	124.1	124.5	125.6	125.8	126.3	120.8	122.0	124.3	124.7	125.9	126.1	126.5
D	M	118.4	119.6	121.8	122.0	123.6	123.8	124.8	118.7	119.9	122.1	122.4	124.0	124.1	125.0
Selected local areas															
Chicago, IL-Northwestern IN	M	123.0	123.6	126.7	126.5	128.1	129.2	129.5	119.1	119.8	122.9	122.8	124.4	125.4	125.6
Los Angeles-Long Beach, Anaheim, CA	M	126.2	127.2	130.0	130.6	132.1	133.6	134.5	122.9	124.0	126.4	127.0	128.5	129.8	130.5
New York, NY-Northeastern NJ	M	128.9	129.5	133.2	133.3	135.1	135.3	136.6	126.8	127.5	131.3	131.3	133.0	133.1	134.5
Philadelphia, PA-NJ	M	126.0	126.7	130.1	129.9	131.2	132.2	133.6	125.8	126.7	130.1	130.0	131.0	132.2	133.8
San Francisco-Oakland, CA	M	125.9	125.4	127.2	127.4	128.5	129.2	130.0	124.6	124.8	126.4	126.6	127.6	128.2	129.0
Baltimore, MD	M	122.8	—	126.6	—	127.9	—	129.3	122.3	—	126.0	—	127.2	—	128.6
Boston, MA	M	129.7	—	134.3	—	136.0	—	136.3	129.7	—	134.7	—	136.0	—	136.5
Cleveland, OH	1	121.5	—	123.4	—	125.0	—	127.4	116.2	—	118.0	—	119.5	—	121.5
Miami, FL	1	119.8	—	123.0	—	124.6	—	125.1	118.7	—	121.5	—	123.2	—	123.4
St. Louis, MO-IL	1	119.4	—	123.1	—	125.1	—	127.2	119.1	—	122.6	—	124.6	—	126.5
Washington, DC-MD-VA	1	126.1	—	130.5	—	132.0	—	133.8	125.6	—	129.6	—	131.1	—	132.9
Dallas-Ft. Worth, TX	1	118.7	—	120.5	—	122.2	—	—	118.6	—	120.1	—	121.3	—	—
Detroit, MI	2	—	121.7	—	124.4	—	126.1	—	—	119.0	—	121.4	—	123.2	—
Houston, TX	2	—	113.2	—	115.5	—	118.7	—	—	113.5	—	115.8	—	118.9	—
Pittsburgh, PA	2	—	119.2	—	121.8	—	123.4	—	—	114.7	—	117.1	—	118.6	—

[1] Area is the Consolidated Metropolitan Statistical Area (CMSA), exclusive of farms and military. Area definitions are those established by the Office of Management and Budget in 1983, except for Boston-Lawrence-Salem, MA-NH Area (excludes Monroe County); and Milwaukee, WI Area (includes only the Milwaukee MSA). Definitions do not include revisions made since 1983.

[2] Foods, fuels, and several other items priced every month in all areas; most other goods and services priced as indicated:
M - Every month.
1 - January, March, May, July, September, and November.
2 - February, April, June, August, October, and December.

[3] Regions are defined as the four Census regions.
- Data not available.

NOTE: Local area CPI indexes are byproducts of the national CPI program. Because each local index is a small subset of the national index, it has a smaller sample size and is, therefore, subject to substantially more sampling and other measurement error than the national index. As a result, local area indexes show greater volatility than the national index, although their long-term trends are quite similar. Therefore, the Bureau of Labor Statistics strongly urges users to consider adopting the national average CPI for use in escalator clauses.

Source: *Monthly Labor Review*, U.S. Department of Labor, Bureau of Labor Statistics.

Purchasing Power of the Dollar:
1950 to 1988

[Indexes: PPI, 1982=$1.00; CPI, 1982-84=$1.00. Producer prices prior to 1961, and consumer prices prior to 1964, exclude Alaska and Hawaii. Producer prices based on finished goods index. Obtained by dividing the average price index for the 1982=100, PPI; 1982-84=100, CPI base periods (100.0) by the price index for a given period and expressing the result in dollars and cents. Annual figures are based on average of monthly data]

YEAR	ANNUAL AVERAGE AS MEASURED BY—		YEAR	ANNUAL AVERAGE AS MEASURED BY—		YEAR	ANNUAL AVERAGE AS MEASURED BY—	
	Producer prices	Consumer prices		Producer prices	Consumer prices		Producer prices	Consumer prices
1950	$3.546	$4.151	1963	$2.994	$3.265	1976	$1.645	$1.757
1951	3.247	3.846	1964	2.985	3.220	1977	1.546	1.649
1952	3.268	3.765	1965	2.933	3.166	1978	1.433	1.532
1953	3.300	3.735	1966	2.841	3.080	1979	1.289	1.380
1954	3.289	3.717	1967	2.809	2.993	1980	1.136	1.215
1955	3.279	3.732	1968	2.732	2.873	1981	1.041	1.098
1956	3.195	3.678	1969	2.632	2.726	1982	1.000	1.035
1957	3.077	3.549	1970	2.545	2.574	1983	.984	1.003
1958	3.012	3.457	1971	2.469	2.466	1984	.964	.961
1959	3.021	3.427	1972	2.392	2.391	1985	.955	.928
1960	2.994	3.373	1973	2.193	2.251	1986	.969	.913
1961	2.994	3.340	1974	1.901	2.029	1987	.949	.880
1962	2.985	3.304	1975	1.718	1.859	1988	.926	.846

Source: U.S. Bureau of Labor Statistics. Monthly data in U.S. Bureau of Economic Analysis, *Survey of Current Business*.

Source: *Statistical Abstract of the United States*, 1990, U.S. Department of Commerce.

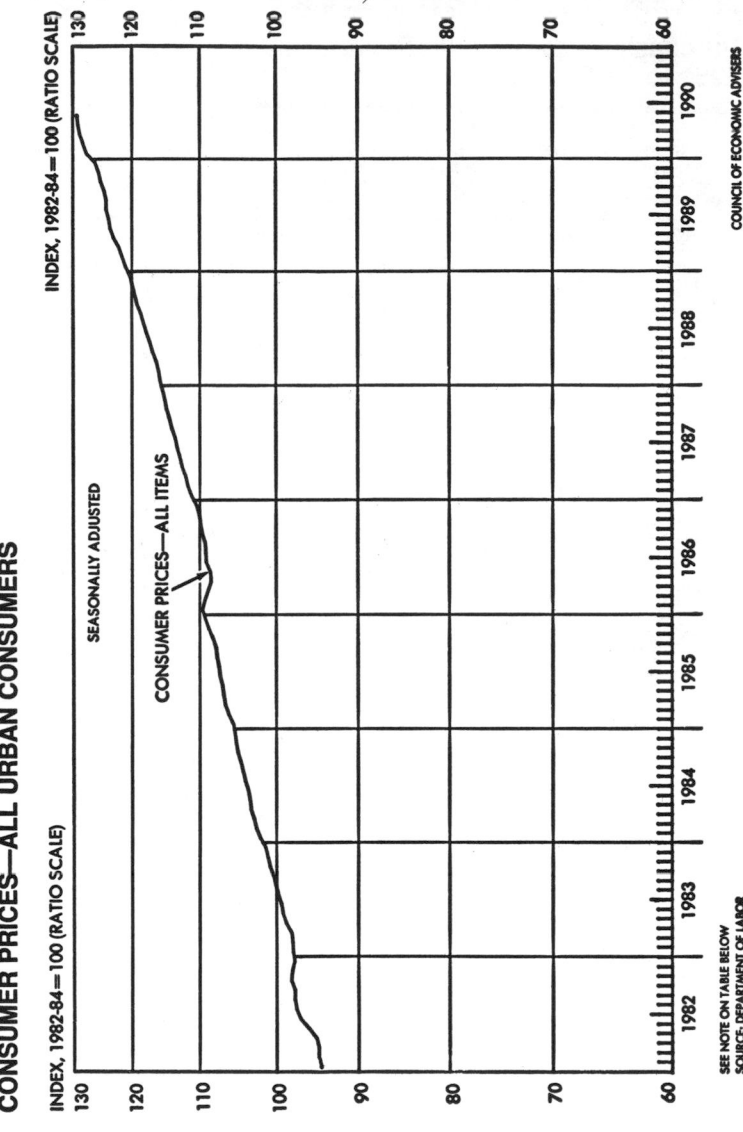

CONSUMER PRICES—ALL URBAN CONSUMERS

INDEX, 1982-84=100 (RATIO SCALE)

INDEX, 1982-84=100 (RATIO SCALE)

SEASONALLY ADJUSTED

CONSUMER PRICES—ALL ITEMS

SEE NOTE ON TABLE BELOW
SOURCE: DEPARTMENT OF LABOR

COUNCIL OF ECONOMIC ADVISERS

[1982-84=100, except as noted; monthly data seasonally adjusted, except as noted]

Period	All items¹ Not seasonally adjusted (NSA)	All items¹ Seasonally adjusted	Food	Housing Total¹	Shelter Total	Renters' costs (Dec. 1982=100)	Homeowners' costs (Dec. 1982=100)	Maintenance and repairs (NSA)	Fuel and other utilities	Apparel and upkeep	Transportation Total¹	New cars	Motor fuel	Medical care	Energy²	All items less food, shelter, and energy
Rel. imp.³	100.0		16.3	42.0	27.9	7.9	19.8	0.2	7.5	6.1	17.1	4.2	3.2	6.2	7.4	48.4
1980	82.4		86.8	81.1	81.0			82.4	75.4	90.9	83.1	88.4	97.4	74.9	86.0	80.6
1981	90.9		93.6	90.4	90.5			90.7	86.4	95.3	93.2	93.7	108.5	82.9	97.7	88.3
1982	96.5		97.4	96.9	96.9			96.4	94.9	97.8	97.0	97.4	102.8	92.5	99.2	95.1
1983	99.6		99.4	99.5	99.1	103.0	102.5	99.9	100.2	100.2	99.3	99.9	99.4	100.6	99.9	100.0
1984	103.9		103.2	104.0	104.0	108.6	107.3	103.7	104.8	102.1	103.7	102.8	97.9	106.8	100.9	105.0
1985	107.6		105.6	107.7	109.8	115.4	113.1	106.5	106.5	105.0	106.4	106.1	98.7	113.5	101.6	109.0
1986	109.6		109.0	110.9	115.8	121.9	119.4	107.9	104.1	105.9	102.3	110.6	77.1	122.0	88.2	112.7
1987	113.6		113.5	114.2	121.3	128.1	124.8	111.8	103.0	110.6	105.4	114.6	80.2	130.1	88.6	117.0
1988	118.3		118.2	118.5	127.1	133.6	131.1	114.7	104.4	115.4	108.7	116.9	80.9	138.6	89.3	121.9
1989	124.0		125.1	123.0	132.8	138.9	137.3	118.0	107.8	118.6	114.1	119.2	88.5	149.3	94.3	127.3
1989:																
May	123.8	123.8	124.9	122.2	131.7	137.4	136.3	117.4	107.5	119.5	115.8	119.5	95.3	147.6	97.0	127.1
June	124.1	124.1	125.2	122.6	132.3	138.0	136.9	118.3	107.3	118.9	115.7	119.3	94.6	148.7	96.4	127.4
July	124.4	124.5	125.6	122.3	133.2	139.6	137.6	118.4	107.8	118.3	115.3	118.8	92.9	149.3	95.9	127.7
Aug	124.6	124.5	125.9	123.5	133.5	139.1	138.2	118.5	107.8	116.9	114.2	118.5	88.4	150.3	93.8	127.8
Sept	125.0	124.8	126.3	123.7	133.7	138.7	138.7	118.6	108.0	118.6	113.9	118.1	87.1	151.3	93.2	128.3
Oct	125.6	125.4	126.8	124.2	134.4	139.8	139.4	118.6	108.1	119.4	114.5	118.8	88.4	153.0	94.1	128.8
Nov	125.9	125.8	127.4	124.7	135.0	140.5	140.0	119.3	108.7	119.4	114.6	119.8	86.8	154.2	93.8	129.3
Dec	126.1	126.3	128.0	125.2	135.6	141.0	140.6	119.5	109.4	119.0	115.0	120.8	86.3	155.1	94.1	129.7
1990:																
Jan	127.4	127.7	130.5	126.1	136.3	142.3	141.0	120.4	111.6	119.0	117.4	121.6	93.4	156.1	98.9	130.4
Feb	128.0	128.3	131.1	126.3	136.6	143.4	141.0	120.8	110.9	122.9	117.7	121.4	93.6	157.3	98.2	131.5
Mar	128.7	128.9	131.5	126.9	137.6	143.8	142.4	121.2	111.0	124.9	117.6	121.2	92.2	158.5	97.4	132.2
Apr	128.9	129.1	131.2	127.0	137.9	143.9	142.8	121.2	110.5	125.0	117.7	120.9	92.5	159.8	97.0	132.6
May	129.2	129.3	131.2	127.2	138.2	143.9	143.2	122.2	110.5	124.6	117.5	120.7	91.2	161.0	96.3	132.9

¹ Includes items not shown separately.
² Household fuels—gas (piped), electricity, fuel oil, etc.—and motor fuel. Motor oil, coolant, etc. also included through 1982.
³ Relative importance, December 1989.

Note.—Data beginning 1983 incorporate a rental equivalence measure for homeownership costs and therefore are not strictly comparable with figures for earlier periods.
Data beginning 1987 and 1988 calculated on a revised basis.
Source: Department of Labor, Bureau of Labor Statistics.

Source: Economic Indicators, Council of Economic Advisers.

SELECTED UNEMPLOYMENT RATES

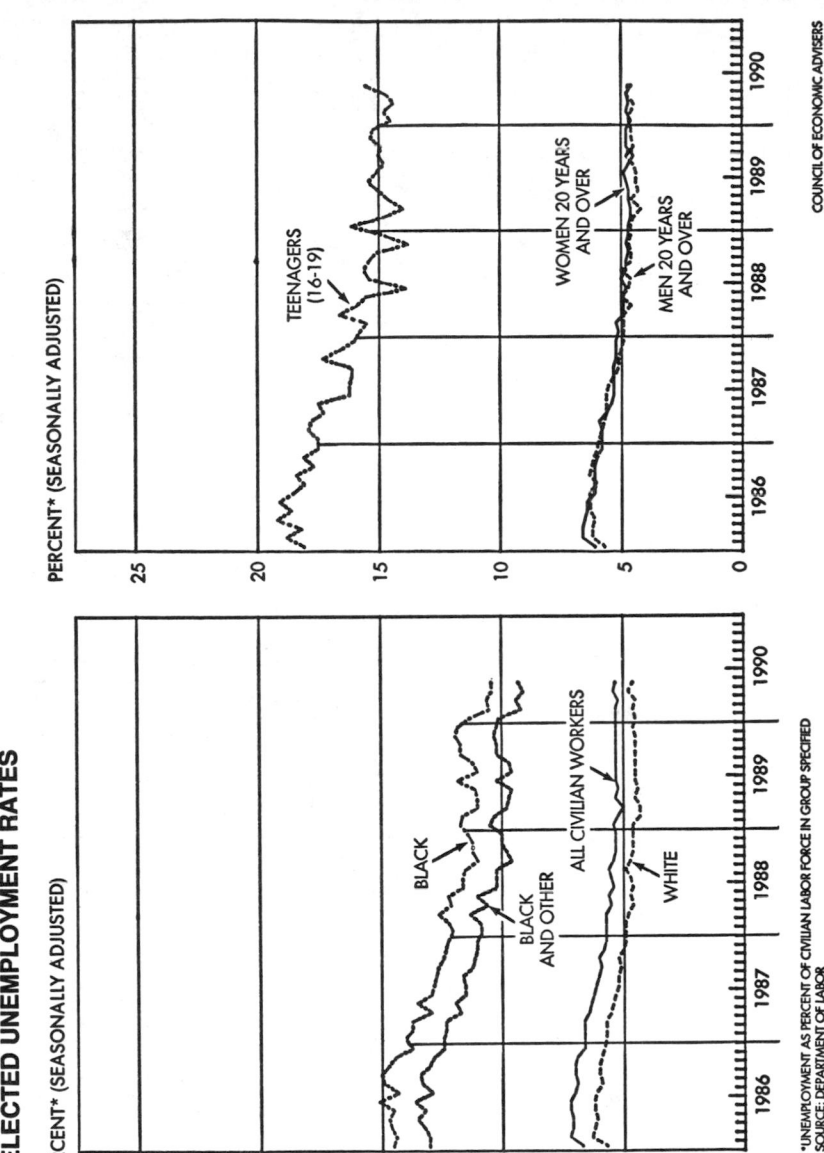

PERCENT* (SEASONALLY ADJUSTED)

PERCENT* (SEASONALLY ADJUSTED)

TEENAGERS (16-19)

WOMEN 20 YEARS AND OVER

MEN 20 YEARS AND OVER

BLACK

BLACK AND OTHER

ALL CIVILIAN WORKERS

WHITE

COUNCIL OF ECONOMIC ADVISERS

*UNEMPLOYMENT AS PERCENT OF CIVILIAN LABOR FORCE IN GROUP SPECIFIED
SOURCE: DEPARTMENT OF LABOR

[Monthly data seasonally adjusted]

Period	Unemployment rate, all workers [1]	All civilian workers	By sex and age			By race			By selected groups					Labor force time lost (percent) [2]
			Men 20 years and over	Women 20 years and over	Both sexes 16–19 years	White	Black and other	Black	Experienced wage and salary workers	Married men, spouse present	Women who maintain families	Full-time workers	Part-time workers	
1981	7.5	7.6	6.3	6.8	19.6	6.7	14.2	15.6	7.3	4.3	10.4	7.3	9.4	8.5
1982	9.5	9.7	8.8	8.3	23.2	8.6	17.3	18.9	9.3	6.5	11.7	9.6	10.5	11.0
1983	9.5	9.6	8.9	8.1	22.4	8.4	17.8	19.5	9.2	6.5	12.2	9.5	10.4	10.9
1984	7.4	7.5	6.6	6.8	18.9	6.5	14.4	15.9	7.1	4.6	10.3	7.2	9.3	8.6
1985	7.1	7.2	6.2	6.6	18.6	6.2	13.7	15.1	6.8	4.3	10.4	6.8	9.3	8.1
1986	6.9	7.0	6.1	6.2	18.3	6.0	13.1	14.5	6.6	4.4	9.8	6.6	9.1	7.9
1987	6.1	6.2	5.4	5.4	16.9	5.3	11.6	13.0	5.8	3.9	9.2	5.8	8.4	7.1
1988	5.4	5.5	4.8	4.9	15.3	4.7	10.4	11.7	5.2	3.3	8.1	5.2	7.6	6.3
1989	5.2	5.3	4.5	4.7	15.0	4.5	10.0	11.4	5.0	3.0	8.1	4.9	7.3	5.9
1989: May	5.1	5.2	4.3	4.7	15.0	4.4	9.6	11.1	4.9	2.9	8.2	4.9	6.9	6.0
June	5.2	5.3	4.4	4.8	15.4	4.5	10.2	11.8	5.0	2.9	7.9	4.9	7.7	6.0
July	5.2	5.3	4.4	4.9	15.1	4.5	9.6	11.0	5.0	3.0	8.5	5.0	7.2	6.0
Aug.	5.2	5.3	4.5	4.7	14.8	4.5	9.7	11.2	5.0	3.1	8.0	4.9	7.1	6.0
Sept.	5.3	5.3	4.8	4.5	15.0	4.5	10.2	11.7	5.0	3.3	7.7	5.0	7.3	6.0
Oct.	5.2	5.3	4.5	4.8	14.9	4.5	10.2	11.7	5.0	3.0	7.8	4.9	7.1	5.9
Nov.	5.3	5.3	4.6	4.8	15.3	4.5	10.3	11.9	5.1	3.1	8.2	5.0	7.4	5.9
Dec.	5.3	5.3	4.6	4.8	15.2	4.6	10.2	11.8	5.0	3.0	8.1	5.0	7.5	6.0
1990: Jan.	5.2	5.3	4.7	4.6	14.5	4.5	10.1	11.3	5.1	3.4	7.5	5.0	7.0	6.0
Feb.	5.2	5.3	4.6	4.8	14.8	4.6	9.2	10.5	5.1	3.0	7.5	4.9	7.4	5.9
Mar.	5.1	5.2	4.5	4.7	14.4	4.5	9.4	10.6	5.0	3.2	8.4	4.9	7.2	5.9
Apr.	5.3	5.4	4.8	4.8	14.7	4.8	9.1	10.4	5.2	3.3	7.5	5.1	7.1	6.2
May	5.3	5.3	4.7	4.6	15.5	4.6	9.3	10.4	5.0	3.3	7.4	4.9	7.4	6.0

[1] Unemployed as percent of total labor force including resident Armed Forces.
[2] Aggregate hours lost by the unemployed and persons on part time for economic reasons as percent of potentially available labor force hours.

Source: Department of Labor, Bureau of Labor Statistics.

Source: Economic Indicators, Council of Economic Advisers.

MONEY STOCK, LIQUID ASSETS, AND DEBT MEASURES

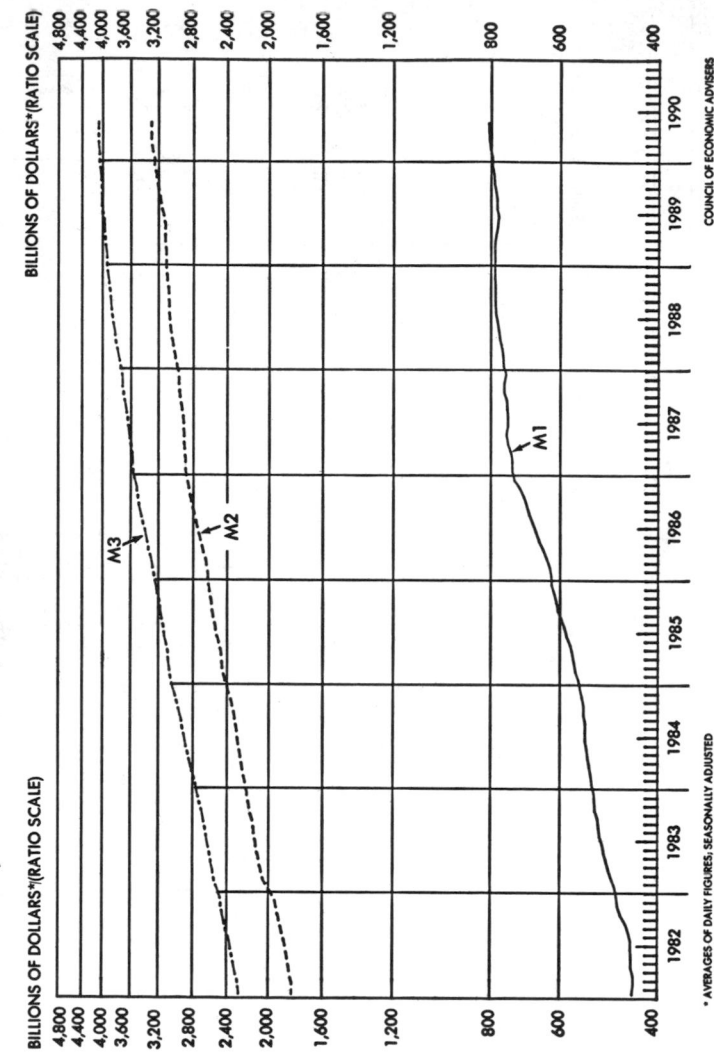

BILLIONS OF DOLLARS*/(RATIO SCALE)

BILLIONS OF DOLLARS*/(RATIO SCALE)

M3

M2

M1

* AVERAGES OF DAILY FIGURES, SEASONALLY ADJUSTED
SOURCE: BOARD OF GOVERNORS OF THE FEDERAL RESERVE SYSTEM

COUNCIL OF ECONOMIC ADVISERS

[Averages of daily figures, except as noted; billions of dollars, seasonally adjusted]

Period	M1 Sum of currency, demand deposits, travelers' checks, and other checkable deposits (OCDs)	M2 M1 plus overnight RPs and Eurodollars, MMMF balances (general purpose and broker/dealer), MMDAs, and savings and small time deposits	M3 M2 plus large time deposits, term RPs, term Eurodollars, and institution-only MMMF balances	L M3 plus other liquid assets	Debt Debt of domestic nonfinancial sectors (monthly average)[1]	Percent change from year or 6 months earlier[2] M1	M2	M3	Debt
1980: Dec.	408.9	1,629.9	1,987.5	2,324.2	3,873.2	6.8	8.9	10.2	9.5
1981: Dec.	436.5	1,793.5	2,234.2	2,596.8	4,260.3	6.7	10.0	12.4	10.0
1982: Dec.	474.5	1,953.1	2,441.9	2,851.6	4,651.3	8.7	8.9	9.3	9.2
1983: Dec.	521.2	2,186.5	2,693.4	3,154.7	5,176.7	9.8	12.0	10.3	11.3
1984: Dec.	552.1	2,371.6	2,982.8	3,524.1	5,924.0	5.9	8.5	10.7	14.4
1985: Dec.	620.1	2,570.6	3,202.1	3,829.5	6,732.8	12.3	8.4	7.4	13.7
1986: Dec.	724.7	2,814.2	3,494.5	4,135.5	7,588.3	16.9	9.5	9.1	12.7
1987: Dec.	750.4	2,913.2	3,678.7	4,338.7	8,307.5	3.5	3.5	5.3	9.5
1988: Dec.	787.5	3,072.4	3,918.4	4,676.0	9,062.0	4.9	5.5	6.5	9.1
1989: Dec.	794.8	3,221.0	4,041.7	r4,867.8	r9,777.6	.9	4.8	3.1	r7.9
1989: May	776.2	3,035.3	3,965.6	4,756.6	r9,358.2	−2.5	1.4	3.2	r7.9
June	773.7	3,101.6	3,984.9	4,778.8	r9,414.9	−3.5	1.9	3.4	r7.8
July	779.1	3,127.0	4,007.2	4,803.8	r9,465.6	−1.7	3.4	4.1	r7.7
Aug	780.4	3,146.7	4,012.0	r4,816.9	r9,529.1	−1.6	4.4	3.8	r7.6
Sept	782.9	3,163.3	4,012.0	r4,822.1	r9,585.2	−.7	4.9	2.8	r7.5
Oct	788.1	3,181.4	4,016.2	r4,830.6	r9,654.8	1.5	6.0	2.6	r7.7
Nov	789.4	3,200.6	4,028.7	r4,845.9	r9,732.4	3.4	7.1	3.2	r8.0
Dec	794.8	3,221.0	4,041.7	r4,867.8	r9,777.6	5.5	7.4	2.9	r7.7
1990: Jan r	794.8	3,229.3	4,044.8	4,869.6	9,827.6	4.0	6.5	1.9	7.6
Feb r	801.4	3,252.4	4,058.9	4,879.5	9,892.8	5.4	6.4	2.3	7.6
Mar r	804.8	3,266.2	4,061.6	4,897.0	9,954.3	5.6	6.3	2.5	7.7
Apr r	807.4	3,271.5	4,064.9	4,897.2	10,004.3	4.9	5.4	2.4	7.2
May p	805.5	3,263.6	4,056.1	....	....	4.1	3.5	1.4	....

[1] Consists of outstanding credit market debt of the U.S. Government, State and local governments, and private nonfinancial sectors; data from flow of funds accounts.

[2] Annual changes are from December to December and monthly changes are from 6 months earlier at a simple annual rate.

Source: *Economic Indicators*, Council of Economic Advisers

Source: Board of Governors of the Federal Reserve System.

Bank Mergers, Consolidations, and Acquisitions

MERGERS, CONSOLIDATIONS, AND ACQUISITIONS OF ASSETS OR ASSUMPTIONS OF LIABILITIES APPROVED BY THE BOARD OF GOVERNORS, 1989

First Western Bank Custer, Custer, South Dakota, *to acquire the* **Hill City South Dakota branch of Rushmore State Bank, Rapid City, South Dakota**

SUMMARY REPORT BY THE ATTORNEY GENERAL (12/16/88)
The proposed transaction would not be significantly adverse to competition.

BASIS FOR APPROVAL BY THE FEDERAL RESERVE (1/20/89)
First Western Bank Custer (Applicant) has assets of $32 million and the Hill City Branch (Branch) has assets of $5.6 million. Applicant and Branch operate in the same banking market.

    The banking factors and considerations relating to the convenience and needs of the community are consistent with approval.

Central Bank, Hollidaysburg, Pennsylvania, *to acquire the* **Pleasant Valley and Logan Valley branches of United States National Bank, Johnstown, Pennsylvania**

SUMMARY REPORT BY THE ATTORNEY GENERAL (1/13/89)
The proposed transaction would not be significantly adverse to competition.

BASIS FOR APPROVAL BY THE FEDERAL RESERVE (2/17/89)
Central Bank (Applicant) has assets of $167 million and the two branches (Branches) have assets of $15.7 million. Applicant and Bank operate in the same banking market.

    The banking factors and considerations relating to the convenience and needs of the community are consistent with approval.

Crestar Bank, Richmond, Virginia, *to merge with* **Colonial American National Bank, Roanoke County, Virginia**

SUMMARY REPORT BY THE ATTORNEY GENERAL (1/13/89)
The proposed transaction would not be significantly adverse to competition.

BASIS FOR APPROVAL BY THE FEDERAL RESERVE (3/14/89)
Crestar Bank (Applicant) has assets of $9.4 billion and Colonial American National Bank (Bank) has assets of $367 million. Applicant and Bank operate in the same banking market.

    The banking factors and considerations relating to the convenience and needs of the community are consistent with approval.

The Bank of Mid Jersey, Bordentown, New Jersey, *to acquire the* **University Plaza branch office of Howard Savings Bank, Livingston, New Jersey**

SUMMARY REPORT BY THE ATTORNEY GENERAL (3/17/89)
The proposed transaction would not be significantly adverse to competition.

BASIS FOR APPROVAL BY THE FEDERAL RESERVE (3/17/89)
The Bank of Mid Jersey (Applicant) has assets of $527.8 million and the University Plaza Branch (Branch) has assets of $5.7 million. Applicant and Branch operate in the same banking market.

    The banking factors and considerations relating to the convenience and needs of the community are consistent with approval.

Kent City State Bank, Kent City, Michigan, *to acquire the* **Sparta, Michigan branch office of PrimeBank Federal Savings Bank, Grand Rapids, Michigan**

SUMMARY REPORT BY THE ATTORNEY GENERAL (3/3/89)
The proposed transaction would not be significantly adverse to competition.

BASIS FOR APPROVAL BY THE FEDERAL RESERVE (3/31/89)
Kent City State Bank (Applicant) has assets of $53.6 million and the Sparta Branch (Branch) has assets of $7.5 million. Applicant and Bank operate in the same banking market.

    The banking factors and considerations relating to the convenience and needs of the community are consistent with approval.

Central Bank of Oklahoma City, Oklahoma City, Oklahoma, *to acquire certain assets and assume liabilities of* **Allied Oklahoma Bank, N.A., Oklahoma City, Oklahoma**

SUMMARY REPORT BY THE ATTORNEY GENERAL
No report received. Request for report on the competitive factors was dispensed with, as authorized by the Bank Merger Act, to permit the Federal Reserve System to act immediately to safeguard the depositors of Allied Oklahoma Bank.

BASIS FOR APPROVAL BY THE FEDERAL RESERVE (4/13/89)

MERGERS, CONSOLIDATIONS, AND ACQUISITIONS OF ASSETS OR ASSUMPTIONS OF LIABILITIES APPROVED BY THE BOARD OF GOVERNORS, 1989 *(continued)*

Central Bank of Oklahoma City (Applicant) has assets of $229.3 million and Allied Oklahoma Bank (Bank) has assets of $ 59.1 million. The OCC has recommended immediate action by the Federal Reserve System to prevent the probable failure of Bank.

Family Bank of Hallandale, Hallandale, Florida, *to merge with* Seminole National Bank, Hollywood, Florida

SUMMARY REPORT BY THE ATTORNEY GENERAL
No report received. Request for report on the competitive factors was dispensed with, as authorized by the Bank Merger Act, to permit the Federal Reserve System to act immediately to safeguard the depositors of the Bank.

BASIS FOR APPROVAL BY THE FEDERAL RESERVE (4/26/89)
Family Bank (Applicant) has assets of $93.3 million and Seminole National Bank (Bank) has assets of $7.3 million. The OCC has recommended immediate action by the Federal Reserve System to prevent the probable failure of Bank.

Bank of Fountain Hills, Fountain Hills, Arizona, *to assume deposit liabilities of* Grand Canyon State Bank, Scottsdale, Arizona

SUMMARY REPORT BY THE ATTORNEY GENERAL
No report received. Request for report on the competitive factors was dispensed with, as authorized by the Bank Merger Act, to permit the Federal Reserve System to act immediately to safeguard the depositors of the Bank.

BASIS FOR APPROVAL BY THE FEDERAL RESERVE (5/22/89)
Bank of Fountain Hills (Applicant) has assets of $6.9 million and Grand Canyon State Bank (Bank) has deposits of $12.3 million. The State has recommended immediate action to prevent the probable failure of the Bank.

Banco De Ponce, Ponce, Puerto Rico, *to acquire the* Prospect Avenue Branch of Banco Central S.A., New York, New York

SUMMARY REPORT BY THE ATTORNEY GENERAL (4/14/89)
The proposed transaction would not be significantly adverse to competition.

BASIS FOR APPROVAL BY THE FEDERAL RESERVE (6/1/89)
Banco De Ponce (Applicant) has assets of $2.9

billion and the Prospect Avenue Branch (Branch) has assets of $3.4 million. Applicant and Bank operate in the same banking market.

The banking factors and considerations relating to the convenience and needs of the community are consistent with approval.

Union Colony Bank, Greeley, Colorado, *to merge with* Northern Bank and Trust, Ft. Collins, Colorado

SUMMARY REPORT BY THE ATTORNEY GENERAL
No report received. Request for report on the competitive factors was dispensed with, as authorized by the Bank Merger Act, to permit the Federal Reserve System to act immediately to safeguard the depositors of Northern Bank and Trust.

BASIS FOR APPROVAL BY THE FEDERAL RESERVE (6/15/89)
Union Colony Bank (Applicant) has assets of $115.6 million and Northern Bank and Trust (Bank) has assets of $6.2 million. The FDIC has recommended immediate action by the Federal Reserve System to prevent the probable failure of Bank.

Liberty Bank South, San Francisco, California, *to acquire certain assets and liabilities of the* Boulder Creek Branch of Pacific Western Bank, San Jose, California

SUMMARY REPORT BY THE ATTORNEY GENERAL (3/3/89)
The proposed transaction would not be significantly adverse to competition.

BASIS FOR APPROVAL BY THE FEDERAL RESERVE (6/16/89)
Liberty Bank (Applicant) has assets of $47 million and the Boulder Creek Branch (Branch) has assets of $14 million. Applicant and Bank do not operate in the same banking market.

The banking factors and considerations relating to the convenience and needs of the community are consistent with approval.

Texas Commerce Bank Rio Grande Valley, Brownsville, Texas, *to merge with* National Bank of Brownsville, Brownsville, Texas

SUMMARY REPORT BY THE ATTORNEY GENERAL
No report received. Request for report on the competitive factors was dispensed with, as authorized by the Bank Merger Act, to permit the Federal Reserve System to act immediately to safeguard the depositors of the National Bank of Brownsville.

(continued)

MERGERS, CONSOLIDATIONS, AND ACQUISITIONS OF ASSETS OR ASSUMPTIONS OF LIABILITIES APPROVED BY THE BOARD OF GOVERNORS, 1989 *(continued)*

BASIS FOR APPROVAL BY THE FEDERAL RESERVE
(7/13/89)
Texas Commerce Bank (Applicant) has assets of
$442.2 million and National Bank of Brownsville
(Bank) has assets of $32.7 million. The Federal
Reserve System has acted immediately to prevent
the probable failure of Bank.

Bank of Fountain Hills, Fountain Hills, Arizona,
to merge with **Fidelity Bank, Scottsdale, Arizona**

SUMMARY REPORT BY THE ATTORNEY GENERAL
No report received. Request for report on the
competitive factors was dispensed with, as authorized by the Bank Merger Act, to permit the Federal
Reserve System to act immediately to safeguard the
depositors of the Fidelity Bank.

BASIS FOR APPROVAL BY THE FEDERAL RESERVE
(7/21/89)
Bank of Fountain Hills (Applicant) has assets of
$11.8 million and Fidelity Bank (Bank) has assets
of $11.5 million. The Federal Reserve System has
acted immediately to prevent the probable failure of
Bank.

BancFirst, Oklahoma City, Oklahoma, *to assume
the liabilities of* **The Liberty State Bank, Tahle-
quah, Oklahoma**

SUMMARY REPORT BY THE ATTORNEY GENERAL
(7/14/89)
The proposed transaction would not be significantly
adverse to competition.

BASIS FOR APPROVAL BY THE FEDERAL RESERVE
(7/27/89)
BancFirst (Applicant) has assets of $657 million
and The Liberty State Bank (Bank) has assets of $41
million. Applicant and Bank do not operate in the
same banking market.
The banking factors and considerations relating
to the convenience and needs of the community are
consistent with approval.

**First Community Bank, Princeton, West Vir-
ginia,** *to merge with* **Cherry River National Bank,
Richwood, West Virginia**

SUMMARY REPORT BY THE ATTORNEY GENERAL
(7/5/89)
The proposed transaction would not be significantly
adverse to competition.

BASIS FOR APPROVAL BY THE FEDERAL RESERVE
(7/28/89)
First Community Bank (Applicant) has assets of

$360.2 million and Cherry River National Bank
(Bank) has assets of $36.8 million. Applicant and
Bank operate in the same banking market.
The banking factors and considerations relating
to the convenience and needs of the community are
consistent with approval.

**First Interstate Bank of California, Los Angeles,
California,** *to merge with* **Bank of Alex Brown,
Sacramento, California**

SUMMARY REPORT BY THE ATTORNEY GENERAL
(5/10/89)
The proposed transaction would not be significantly
adverse to competition.

BASIS FOR APPROVAL BY THE FEDERAL RESERVE
(8/1/89)
First Interstate Bank of California (Applicant) has
assets of $19.6 billion and Bank of Alex Brown
(Bank) has assets of $324 million. Applicant and
Bank operate in the same banking market.
The banking factors and considerations relating
to the convenience and needs of the community are
consistent with approval.

Comerica Bank–Detroit, Detroit, Michigan, *to
merge with* **Dearborn Bank and Trust Company,
Dearborn, Michigan**

SUMMARY REPORT BY THE ATTORNEY GENERAL
(8/11/89)
The proposed transaction would not be significantly
adverse to competition.

BASIS FOR APPROVAL BY THE FEDERAL RESERVE
(9/21/89)
Comerica Bank Detroit (Applicant) has assets of
$9.1 billion and Dearborn Bank and Trust Com-
pany (Bank) has assets of $287.2 million. Applicant
and Bank do not operate in the same banking
market.
The banking factors and considerations relating
to the convenience and needs of the community are
consistent with approval. Manufacturers Hanover
Trust Company, New York, New York, to purchase
certain branches of Goldome, Buffalo, New York

SUMMARY REPORT BY THE ATTORNEY GENERAL
(4/14/89)
The proposed transaction would not be significantly
adverse to competition.

BASIS FOR APPROVAL BY THE FEDERAL RESERVE
(9/26/89)
Manufacturers Hanover Trust Company (Applicant) has assets of $57 billion and the 12 branches

MERGERS, CONSOLIDATIONS, AND ACQUISITIONS OF ASSETS OR ASSUMPTIONS OF LIABILITIES APPROVED BY THE BOARD OF GOVERNORS, 1989 (continued)

(Branches) has assets of $1.2 billion. Applicant and Bank operate in the same banking market.

The banking factors and considerations relating to the convenience and needs of the community are consistent with approval.

Central Savings Bank, Sault Ste. Marie, Michigan, to acquire certain assets and liabilities of the **Main Street Branch of First of America Bank, Northern Michigan, Cheboygan, Michigan**

SUMMARY REPORT BY THE ATTORNEY GENERAL
(9/1/89)
The proposed transaction would not be significantly adverse to competition.

BASIS FOR APPROVAL BY THE FEDERAL RESERVE
(10/3/89)
Central Savings Bank (Applicant) has assets of $68 million and The Main Street Branch (Branch) has assets of $2.2 million. Applicant and Bank do not operate in the same banking market.

The banking factors and considerations relating to the convenience and needs of the community are consistent with approval.

Meridian Bank, Reading, Pennsylvania, to merge with **Hill Financial Savings Association, Red Hill, Pennsylvania**

SUMMARY REPORT BY THE ATTORNEY GENERAL
(9/12/89)
The proposed transaction would not be significantly adverse to competition.

BASIS FOR APPROVAL BY THE FEDERAL RESERVE
(10/13/89)
Meridian Bank (Applicant) has assets of $8.5 billion and Hill Financial Savings Association (Bank) has assets of $2.0 billion. Applicant and Bank operate in the same banking market.

The banking factors and considerations relating to the convenience and needs of the community are consistent with approval.

Heartland Bank, Croton, Ohio, to merge with **Lyndon Guaranty Bank of Ohio, Columbus, Ohio**

SUMMARY REPORT BY THE ATTORNEY GENERAL
(10/4/89)
The proposed transaction would not be significantly adverse to competition.

BASIS FOR APPROVAL BY THE FEDERAL RESERVE
(10/23/89)
Heartland Bank (Applicant) has assets of $36

million and Lyndon Guaranty Bank of Ohio (Bank) has assets of $16 million. Applicant and Bank do not operate in the same banking market.

The banking factors and considerations relating to the convenience and needs of the community are consistent with approval.

CivicBank of Commerce, Oakland, California, to merge with **Meridian National Bank, Concord, California**

SUMMARY REPORT BY THE ATTORNEY GENERAL
(10/18/89)
The proposed transaction would not be significantly adverse to competition.

BASIS FOR APPROVAL BY THE FEDERAL RESERVE
(11/9/89)
CivicBank of Commerce (Applicant) has assets of $232 million and Meridian National Bank (Bank) has assets of $87 million. Applicant and Bank operate in the same banking market.

The banking factors and considerations relating to the convenience and needs of the community are consistent with approval.

Central Bank, Hollidaysburg, Pennsylvania, to merge with **two branches of Landmark Savings Association**

SUMMARY REPORT BY THE ATTORNEY GENERAL
(10/12/89)
The proposed transaction would not be significantly adverse to competition.

BASIS FOR APPROVAL BY THE FEDERAL RESERVE
(12/6/89)
Central Bank (Applicant) has assets of $203.8 million and the two branches (Branches) have assets of $17.0 million. Applicant and Bank operate in the same banking market.

The banking factors and considerations relating to the convenience and needs of the community are consistent with approval.

Rapides Bank and Trust Company in Alexandria, Alexandria, Louisiana, to merge with **First Bank, Pineville, Pineville, Louisiana**

SUMMARY REPORT BY THE ATTORNEY GENERAL
No report received. Request for report on the competitive factors was dispensed with, as authorized by the Bank Merger Act, to permit the Federal Reserve System to act immediately to safeguard the depositors of First Bank.

(continued)

MERGERS, CONSOLIDATIONS, AND ACQUISITIONS OF ASSETS OR ASSUMPTIONS OF LIABILITIES APPROVED BY THE BOARD OF GOVERNORS, 1989 *(continued)*

BASIS FOR APPROVAL BY THE FEDERAL RESERVE (12/8/89)
Rapides Bank and Trust Company (Applicant) has assets of $415.9 million and First Bank (Bank) has assets of $84.6 million. The State has recommended immediate action by the Federal Reserve System to prevent the probable failure of Bank.

Central State Bank, Elkader, Iowa, *to merge with* **First State Savings Bank, McGregor, Iowa**

SUMMARY REPORT BY THE ATTORNEY GENERAL
No report received. Request for report on the competitive factors was dispensed with, as authorized by the Bank Merger Act, to permit the Federal Reserve System to act immediately to safeguard the depositors of First State Savings Bank.

BASIS FOR APPROVAL BY THE FEDERAL RESERVE (12/12/89)
Central State Bank (Applicant) has assets of $44.7 million and First State Savings Bank (Bank) has assets of $7.8 million. The FDIC has recommended

immediate action by the Federal Reserve System to prevent the probable failure of Bank.

Mergers Approved Involving Wholly Owned Subsidiaries of the Same Bank Holding Company

The following transactions involve banks that are subsidiaries of the same bank holding company. In each case, the summary report by the Attorney General indicates that the transaction would not have a significantly adverse effect on competition because the proposed merger is essentially a corporate reorganization. The Board of Governors, the Federal Reserve Bank, or the Secretary of the Board of Governors, whichever approved the application, determined that the competitive effects of the proposed transaction, the financial and managerial resources and prospects of the banks concerned, as well as the convenience and needs of the community to be served were consistent with approval.

Institution [1]	Assets (millions of dollars)	Date of approval
Texas Bank of Denton, Denton, Texas	16	1/9/89
Merger		
Texas Bank of Weatherford, Weatherford, Texas	153	
BancFirst and Trust Company, Oklahoma City, Oklahoma	657	2/10/89
Merger		
American Bank of Commerce, McAlester, Oklahoma	41	
Citizens State Bank, Hugo Oklahoma	26	
City Bank, Muskogee, Oklahoma	34	
Federal Bank and Trust Company, Shawnee, Oklahoma	239	
First Bank & Trust Company, Sand Springs, Oklahoma	50	
First National Bank of Guthrie, Guthrie, Oklahoma	45	
First National Bank in Madill, Madill, Oklahoma	35	
First National Bank of Prague, Prague, Oklahoma	40	
First National Bank of Seminole, Seminole, Oklahoma	40	
First National Bank, Stillwater, Oklahoma	93	
First Oklahoma Bank and Trust Company, Sulphur, Oklahoma	30	
Oklahoma State Bank, Konawa, Oklahoma	22	
Sovran Bank, Memphis Tennessee	303	2/16/89
Merger		
First National Bank, Collierville, Tennessee	54	
Sovran Bank, Chattanooga, Tennessee	213	3/1/89
Merger		
First Bank of Marion County, South Pittsburg, Tennessee	96	

MERGERS, CONSOLIDATIONS AND ACQUISITIONS OF ASSETS OR ASSUMPTIONS OF LIABILITIES APPROVED BY THE BOARD OF GOVERNORS, 1989 *(continued)*

Institution[1]	Assets (millions of dollars)	Date of approval
Macomb County Bank, Richmond, Michigan	54	3/23/89
Merger		
First State Bank of East Detroit, (Clinton Branch), East Detroit, Michigan	6	
Chemical Bank Bay Area, Bay City, Michigan	28	4/17/89
Merger		
Cass City State Bank, Cass City, Michigan	18	
Huron City Bank, Harbor Beach, Michigan	32	
The Peoples State Bank of Caro, Caro, Michigan	37	
Sovran Bank Central South, Nashville, Texas	3,200	4/26/89
Merger		
Sovran Bank Marshall City, N.A., Lewisburg, Tennessee	76	
First of America Bank–Northern Michigan, Cheboygan, Michigan	131	5/25/89
Merger		
First of America–Petoskey, N.A., Petoskey, Michigan	165	
First Bank of Stockton/Warren, Stockton, Illinois	40	5/31/89
Merger		
First National Bank of Freeport, Freeport, Illinois	152	
Mount Carroll National Bank, Mount Carroll, Illinois	29	
First Bank/Dixon, Dixon, Illinois	56	5/31/89
Merger		
Polo National Bank, Polo, Illinois	34	
Lincolnway State Bank, Sterling, Illinois	22	
First Nebraska Bank–Valley, Valley, Nebraska	78	6/8/89
Merger		
First Nebraska Bank–Arcadia, Arcadia, Nebraska	10	
Lake Buchanan State Bank, Buchanan Dam, Texas	12	6/8/89
Merger		
Lake Country National Bank, Burnet, Texas	6	
Pioneer Bank and Trust Company, Belle Fourche, South Dakota	96	6/16/89
Merger		
First State Bank, Buffalo, South Dakota	19	
Bank of New York, New York, New York	23	6/29/89
Merger		
Irving Trust Company, New York, New York	21	
Bank of Long Island, Babylon, New York	294	
Dutchess Bank & Trust Company, Poughkeepsie, New York	299	
Nanuet National Bank, Nanuet, New York	385	
Scarsdale National Bank & Trust Company, Scarsdale, New York	498	

(continued)

MERGERS, CONSOLIDATIONS AND ACQUISITIONS OF ASSETS OR ASSUMPTIONS OF LIABILITIES APPROVED BY THE BOARD OF GOVERNORS, 1989 *(continued)*

Institution [1]	Assets (millions of dollars)	Date of approval
First of America Bank–Northern Michigan, Cheboygan, Michigan ...	131	6/30/89
Merger		
First of America Bank–Grand Travers, N.A., Traverse City, Michigan	165	
Norstar Bank, Hepstead, New York	2520	7/5/89
Merger		
First National Bank of Downsville, Downsville, New York	72	
Crestar Bank, Richmond, Virginia	10,038	7/10/89
Merger		
Mountain National Bank of Clifton Forge, Clifton Forge, Virginia ...	58	
Sovran Bank/Central South, Nashville, Tennessee	3,221	8/23/89
Merger		
Sovran Bank/Eastern, Oak Ridge, Tennessee	199	
Sovran Bank/Hickman County, Centerville, Tennessee	39	
Security Bank and Trust Company, Southgate, Michigan	1,403	8/30/89
Merger		
Trenton Bank and Trust Company, Trenton, Michigan	135	
Indian Head Bank and Trust Company, Portsmouth, New Hampshire.	377	8/31/89
Merger		
Indian Head National Bank, Nashua, New Hampshire	976	
Indian Head Bank North, Littleton, New Hampshire	208	
Dartmouth National Bank, Hanover, New Hampshire	175	
Indian Head National Bank of Keene, Keene, New Hampshire	166	
Fleet Bank of New Hampshire, Nashua, New Hampshire	3	
Victoria Bank & Trust Company, Victor, Texas	613	9/25/89
Merger		
Bank of Commerce Calhoun City, Point Comfort, Texas	9	
Jackson County State Bank, Edna County, Texas	52	
Chemical Bank and Trust Company, Midland, Michigan	447	10/17/89
Merger		
Chemical Bank Bay Area (Saginaw Township Branch), Bay City, Michigan	4	
American Bank of St. Louis, St. Louis, Missouri	117	10/31/89
Merger		
American Bank of St. Louis County, Chesterfield, Missouri	11	
Liberty Bank–Oakland, Troy, Michigan	354	11/8/89
Merger		
Liberty State Bank and Trust, Hamtramck, Michigan	99	
Villa Grove State Bank, Villa Grove, Illinois	24	11/10/89
Merger		
First National Bank of Villa Grove, Villa Grove, Illinois	11	

MERGERS, CONSOLIDATIONS AND ACQUISITIONS OF ASSETS OR ASSUMPTIONS OF LIABILITIES APPROVED BY THE BOARD OF GOVERNORS, 1989 *(continued)*

Institution [1]	Assets (millions of dollars)	Date of approval
First of America Bank–Northern Michigan, Cheboygan, Michigan ...	168	11/14/89
Merger		
Antrim County State Bank, Maoncelona, Michigan	32	
Landmark Bank of Highland, Highland, Illinois	96	12/1/89
Merger		
Landmark Bank of Alton, Alton, Illinois	35	
Landmark Bank of Madison County, Glen Carbon, Illinois	26	
Union Bank/Streator, Streator, Illinois	127	12/15/89
Merger		
Union Bank/Triumph, Triumph, Illinois	18	
Sovran Bank/Central South, Nashville, Tennessee	3,621	12/28/89
Merger		
Sovran Bank/Chattanooga, Chattanooga, Tennessee	218	
Sovran Bank/Greenville, Greenville, Tennessee	131	
Sovran Bank/Memphis, Memphis, Tennessee	388	
Sovran Bank/Tri Cities, Johnson City, Tennessee	95	
Sovran Bank/Union City, Union City, Tennessee	105	

1. Each proposed transaction was to be effected under the charter of the first-named bank. The entries are in chronological order of approval.

Mergers Approved Involving a Nonoperating Institution with an Existing Bank

The following transactions have no significant effect on competition; they merely facilitate the acquisition of the voting shares of a bank (or banks) by a holding company. In such cases, the summary report by the Attorney General indicates that the transaction will merely combine an existing bank with a nonoperating institution; in consequence, and without regard to the acquisition of the surviving bank by the holding company, the merger would have no effect on competition. The Board of Governors, the Federal Reserve Bank, or the Secretary of the Board of Governors, whichever approved the application, determined that the proposal would, in itself, have no adverse competitive effects and that the financial factors and considerations relating to the convenience and needs of the community were consistent with approval.

(continued)

MERGERS, CONSOLIDATIONS, AND ACQUISITIONS OF ASSETS OR ASSUMP-TIONS OF LIABILITIES APPROVED BY THE BOARD OF GOVERNORS, 1989 *(concluded)*

Institution [1]	Assets (millions of dollars) [2]	Date of approval
New Byron Bank, Byron Center, Michigan	. . .	1/19/89
Merger		
Byron Center State Bank, Byron Center, Michigan	118	
1st United Interim Bank, Boca Raton, Florida	. . .	3/7/89
Merger		
First United Bank, Boca Raton, Florida	30	
Citizens Bank of Virginia, Arlington, Virginia	. . .	3/21/89
Merger		
Arlington Bank, Arlington, Virginia...................................	64	
Romney Interim Bank Corporation, ...	. . .	5/23/89
Merger		
Bank of Romney, Romney West Virginia	66	
First Interim Bank of Crestview, Crestview, California	. . .	8/4/89
Merger		
First Bank of Crestview, Crestview, California	42	
CB Interim State Bank, Philadelphia, Pennsylvania	. . .	11/3/89
Merger		
Constitution Bank, Philadelphia, Pennsylvania	117	
Effingham Interim Bank, Inc., Effingham, Illinois	. . .	12/8/89
Merger		
Effingham State Bank, Effingham, Illinois	132	

1. Each proposed transaction was to be effected under the charter of the first-named bank. The entries are in chronological order of approval.

2. Where no assets are listed, the bank is newly organized and not in operation.

Source: *Annual Report 1989,* Board of Governors of the Federal Reserve System.

Government Budget, Receipts, and Deficits: Historical Data[1]

Federal Budget: Procedure and Timetable

Congressional Budget Timetable

CONGRESSIONAL BUDGET ACT
OF 1974: THE NEW BUDGET
PROCESS IN TEN STEPS

1. To give Congress an earlier and better start in reviewing and reshaping the budget, the Executive Branch must submit a "current services budget" by November 10th for the new fiscal year that starts the following October 1st. The current services budget should project the spending required to maintain ongoing programs throughout the following fiscal year at existing commitment levels, or at commitment levels specified by existing legislation based on current economic assumptions. The Joint Economic Committee should review and assess the current services budget and report to Congress by December 31st.

2. The President will continue to submit his new budget to Congress in late January or early February. In addition to the traditional budget totals and breakdowns, the budget document must include a list of existing "tax expenditures"—i.e., estimates of revenues lost to the Treasury through preferential tax treatment—as well as any proposed changes in tax expenditures. The budget must also contain estimates of expenditures for programs for which funds are appropriated one year in advance and five-year budget projections of all federal spending under existing programs.

3. Reports of all standing committees to the House and Senate Budget Committees of the spending plans of those committees on all matters under their jurisdiction, including spending under new legislation, are required by March 15th for the upcoming fiscal year.

4. An annual report of the Congressional Budget Office to the Budget Committees on alternative budget levels and national budget priorities is required on or before April 1st.

5. By April 15th, the Budget Committees must report concurrent resolutions to the House and Senate floors, and Congress will have to clear the initial budget resolution by May 15th. This initial budget resolution sets target totals for appropriations, outlays, taxes, the budget surplus or deficit, and the federal debt. Within these overall targets, the resolution will break down appropriations and outlays by the functional categories used in the President's budget document, as well as by classifications used by the appropriations subcommittees for the 13 appropriations bills. The resolution will include any recommended changes in tax revenues and in the level of the federal debt ceiling.

6. Committees report bills or resolutions authorizing new budget authority by May 15th.

7. The basic appropriations process proceeds within the Appropriations Committees, but is subject to targets of the budget resolution.

8. Scorekeeping reports will be issued periodically by the Congressional Budget Office on the status of budget authority, revenue, outlays and debt legislation, comparing the amounts and changes in such legislation with the First Congressional Budget Resolution.

9. Subject to prior authorization, all appropriations bills have to be cleared by the middle of September—no later than the seventh day after Labor Day. By September 15th, after finishing action on all appropriations and other spending bills, Congress must adopt a second, and final, budget resolution that may either affirm or revise the budget targets set by the initial resolution. This resolution must provide for a final budget reconciliation by changing either one or more of the following: (1) appropriations (both for the upcoming fiscal year or carried over from previous fiscal years) and/or entitlements; (2) revenues; and (3) the public debt. The final resolution will direct the committees that have jurisdiction over these matters to report the necessary legislative changes. The Budget Committees will then combine these changes and report them to the floor in the form of a reconciliation bill.

If Congress has withheld all appropriations and entitlement bills from the President until passage of the final reconciliation bill, then this bill becomes the final budget legislation, subject to Presidential signature (or veto). If, on the other hand, each individual appropriations bill has been signed by the President upon passage by the Congress, the final reconciliation bill—upon signature by the President—supersedes all the previously passed individual bills.

10. The new fiscal year begins on October 1st.

---

[1] See page 222 for notes to Exhibits on pages 204 to 221.

FEDERAL BUDGET: PROCEDURE AND TIMETABLE
Congressional Budget Timetable

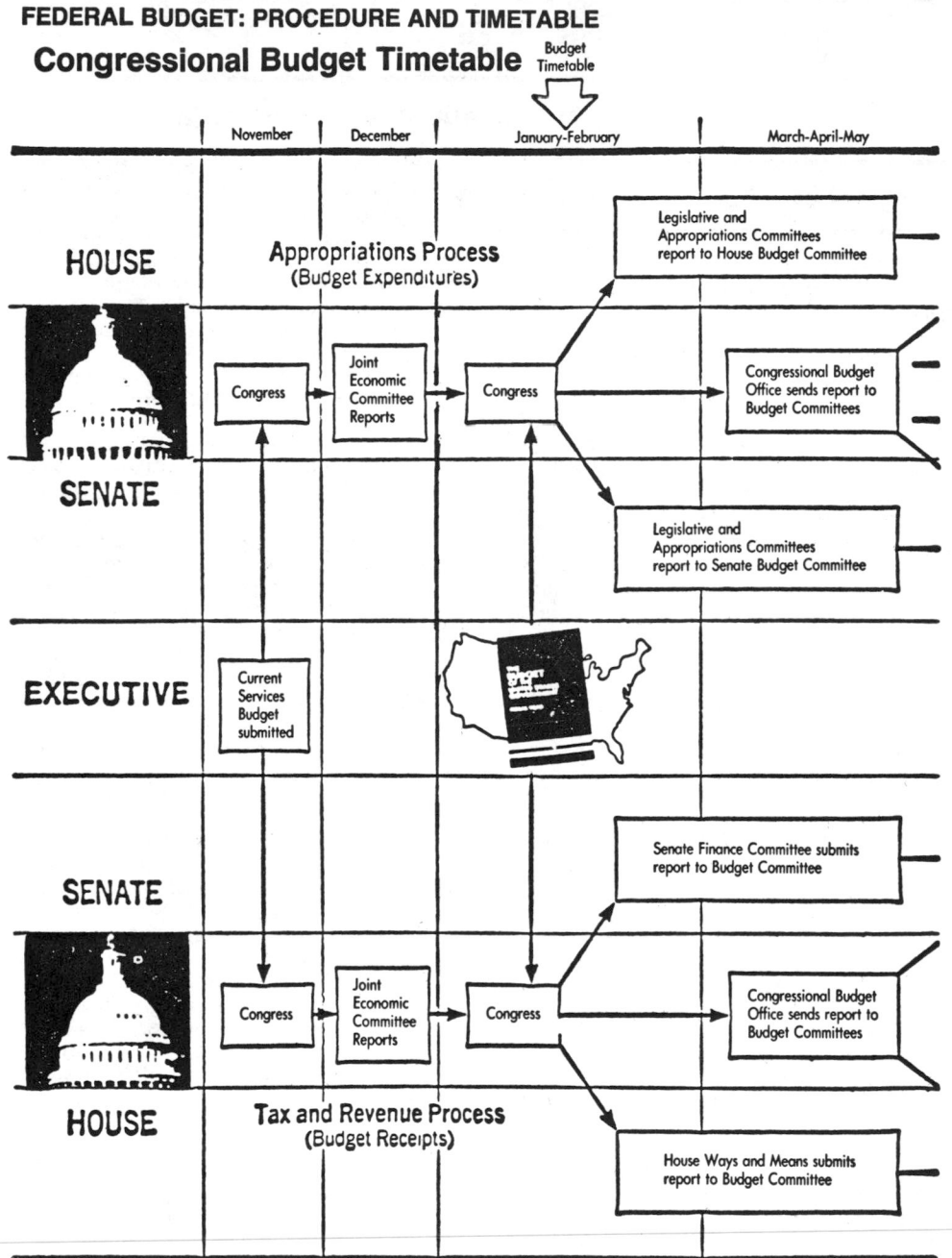

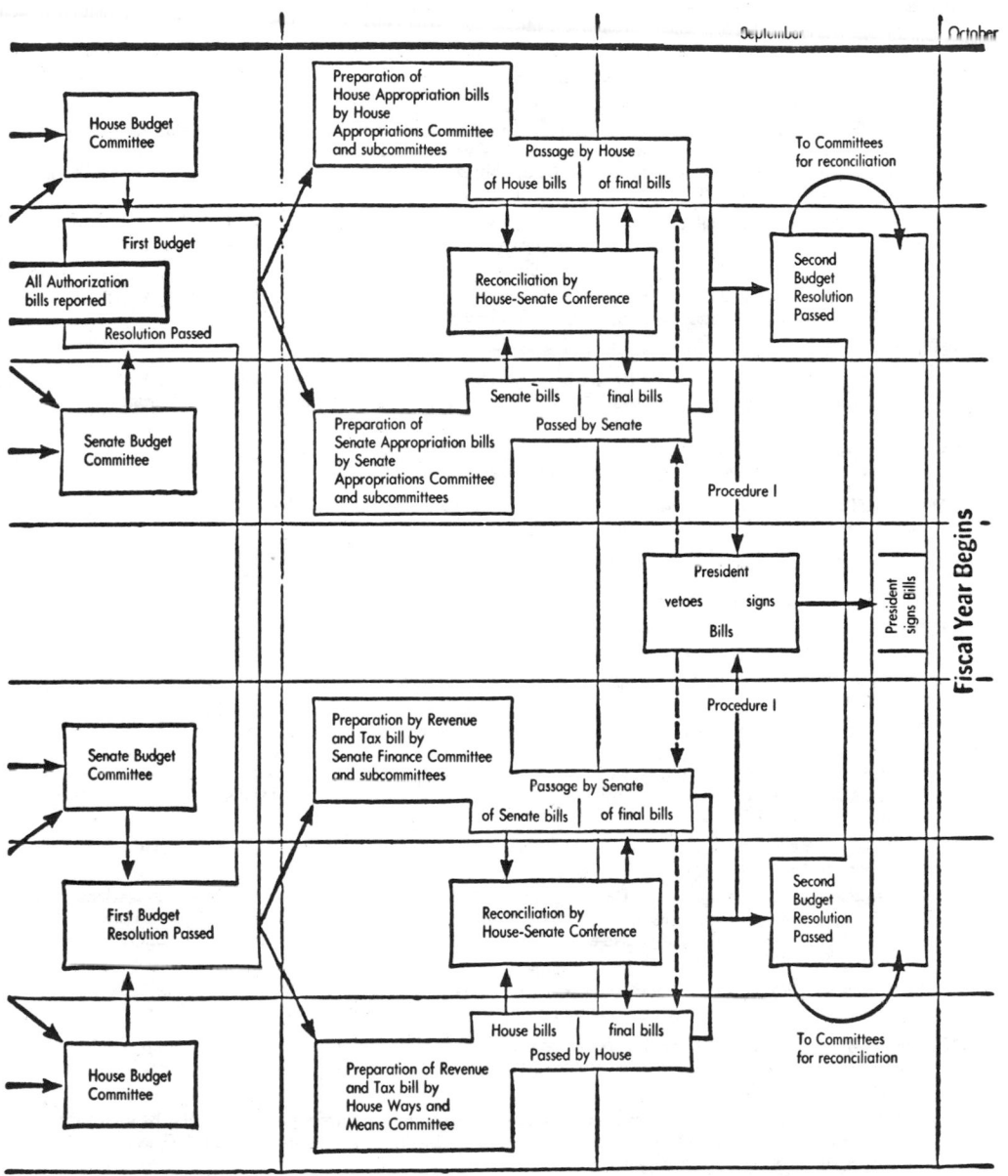

September | October

House Budget Committee

Preparation of House Appropriation bills by House Appropriations Committee and subcommittees

Passage by House of House bills | of final bills

To Committees for reconciliation

First Budget

All Authorization bills reported

Resolution Passed

Reconciliation by House-Senate Conference

Second Budget Resolution Passed

Senate Budget Committee

Preparation of Senate Appropriation bills by Senate Appropriations Committee and subcommittees

Senate bills | final bills

Passed by Senate

Procedure I

President

vetoes   signs

Bills

President signs Bills

Fiscal Year Begins

Procedure I

Senate Budget Committee

Preparation by Revenue and Tax bill by Senate Finance Committee and subcommittees

Passage by Senate of Senate bills | of final bills

First Budget Resolution Passed

Reconciliation by House-Senate Conference

Second Budget Resolution Passed

House bills | final bills

Passed by House

To Committees for reconciliation

House Budget Committee

Preparation of Revenue and Tax bill by House Ways and Means Committee

Source: The Conference Board, "The Federal Budget: Its Impact on the Economy," Michael E. Levy, assisted by Delos R. Smith.

Glossary of Budget Terms[1]

BALANCES, OBLIGATED—Obligated balances are amounts of budgetary resources that have been obligated but not yet spent. (*Cf.* BALANCES, UNOBLIGATED.)

BALANCES, UNOBLIGATED—Unobligated balances are the amounts of budgetary resources that are available by law for obligation beyond the year in which they were provided and that have not yet been obligated or spent. (*Cf.* BALANCES, OBLIGATED.)

BUDGET—The *Budget of the United States Government* (this document) sets forth the President's comprehensive financial plan and indicates his priorities for the Federal Government. The budget document routinely includes the on-budget and off-budget totals and combines them to derive a total for Federal activity. (See ON-BUDGET and OFF-BUDGET.)

BUDGET AUTHORITY (BA)—Budget authority is the primary source of authority granted by law to enter into obligations that will result outlays. Budget authority most commonly is granted in the form of appropriations.

BUDGETARY RESOURCES—Budgetary resources refers generally to all sources of authority granted by law to enter into obligations, including new budget authority, new offsetting collections credited to appropriation and fund accounts, and unobligated balances of those resources.

DEFICIT—A deficit is the amount by which outlays exceed receipts.

FEDERAL FUNDS—Federal funds are the moneys collected and outlayed for the Government other than those designated as trust funds (defined below). Includes general, special, public enterprise, and intragovernmental funds.

FISCAL YEAR—The fiscal year is the Government's accounting period. It begins on October 1st and ends on September 30th, and is designated by the calendar year in which it ends.

GENERAL FUND—The general fund consists of accounts for receipts not earmarked by law for a specific purpose, the proceeds of general borrowing, and the expenditure of those moneys.

INTRAGOVERNMENTAL FUNDS—Intragovernmental funds are accounts for business-type or market-oriented activities conducted primarily within and between Government agencies and financed by offsetting collections that are credited directly to the fund.

OBLIGATIONS—Obligations are binding agreements for immediate or future outlays. Budgetary resources must be available before obligations can be incurred legally.

OFF-BUDGET TOTALS—Off-budget totals reflect the transactions of Government entities that are excluded from the on-budget totals by law.

OFFSETTING COLLECTIONS—Offsetting collections are collections from the public that result from business-type or market-oriented activities and collections from other Government accounts. These collections are deducted from gross disbursements in calculating outlays, rather than counted in receipt totals. Some are credited directly to appropriation or fund accounts; others, called offsetting receipts, are credited to receipts accounts. (*Cf.* RECEIPTS.)

ON-BUDGET—On-budget total reflect the transactions of all Federal Government entities except those excluded from the budget totals by law.

OUTLAYS—Outlays are the measure of Government spending. They are payments to liquidate obligations (other than the repayment of debt), net of refunds and offsetting collections. Outlays generally are recorded on a cash basis, but also include many cash-equivalent transactions and interest accrued on public issues of the public debt.

PUBLIC ENTERPRISE FUNDS—Public enterprise funds are accounts for business or market-oriented activities conducted primarily with the public and financed by collections credited directly to the account.

RECEIPTS—Receipts are collections that result primarily from the Government's exercise of its power to tax or otherwise compel payment. They are compared to outlays in calculating a surplus or deficit. (*Cf.* OFFSETTING COLLECTIONS.)

SEQUESTER—A sequester is a reduction or cancellation of budgetary resources pursuant to the Balanced Budget and Emergency Deficit Control Act of 1985 (also known as the Gramm-Rudman-Hollings Act), as amended, for the purpose of meeting statutory deficit targets.

SPECIAL FUNDS—Special funds are accounts for receipts earmarked for specific purposes and the associated expenditure of those receipts. (*Cf.* TRUST FUNDS.)

SURPLUS—A surplus is the amount by which receipts exceed outlays.

---

[1] These basic terms and other budget terms, concepts, and procedures are described more fully in *The Budget System and Concepts of the United States Government*, a pamphlet available from the Government Printing Office.

SUPPLEMENTAL APPROPRIATION—A supplemental appropriation is one enacted subsequent to a regular annual appropriations act when the need for funds is too urgent to be postponed until the next regular annual appropriations act.

TRUST FUNDS—Trust funds are accounts, designated by law as trust funds, for receipts earmarked for specific purposes and the associated expenditure of those receipts. (*Cf.* SPECIAL FUNDS.)

Source: *Budget of the United States Government, Fiscal 1991,* Executive Office of the President, Office of Management and Budget.

RECEIPTS BY SOURCE AS PERCENTAGES OF GNP: 1934–1995

Fiscal Year	Individual Income Taxes	Corporation Income Taxes	Social Insurance Taxes and Contributions			Excise Taxes	Other	Total Receipts		
			Total	(On-Budget)	(Off-Budget)			Total	(On-Budget)	(Off-Budget)
1934	0.7%	0.6%	*%	(*)%	---	2.2%	1.3%	4.9%	(4.9%)	---
1935	0.8	0.8	*	(*)	---	2.1	1.6	5.2	(5.2)	---
1936	0.9	0.9	0.1	(0.1)	---	2.1	1.1	5.0	(5.0)	---
1937	1.3	1.2	0.7	(0.4)	(0.3)	2.2	0.9	6.2	(5.9)	(0.3)
1938	1.5	1.5	1.7	(1.3)	(0.4)	2.1	0.9	7.6	(7.2)	(0.4)
1939	1.2	1.3	1.8	(1.2)	(0.6)	2.1	0.8	7.1	(6.6)	(0.6)
1940	0.9	1.2	1.9	(1.3)	(0.6)	2.1	0.7	6.8	(6.3)	(0.6)
1941	1.2	1.9	1.7	(1.1)	(0.6)	2.3	0.7	7.7	(7.1)	(0.6)
1942	2.3	3.3	1.7	(1.1)	(0.6)	2.4	0.6	10.3	(9.7)	(0.6)
1943	3.7	5.4	1.7	(1.1)	(0.6)	2.3	0.5	13.7	(13.0)	(0.6)
1944	9.8	7.3	1.7	(1.1)	(0.6)	2.4	0.5	21.7	(21.0)	(0.6)
1945	8.6	7.5	1.6	(1.0)	(0.6)	2.9	0.5	21.3	(20.6)	(0.6)
1946	7.6	5.6	1.5	(0.9)	(0.6)	3.3	0.6	18.5	(17.9)	(0.6)
1947	8.0	3.9	1.5	(0.9)	(0.7)	3.2	0.6	17.2	(16.6)	(0.7)
1948	7.8	3.9	1.5	(0.9)	(0.7)	3.0	0.6	16.8	(16.1)	(0.7)
1949	5.9	4.2	1.4	(0.8)	(0.6)	2.8	0.5	14.9	(14.3)	(0.6)
1950	5.9	3.9	1.6	(0.8)	(0.8)	2.8	0.5	14.8	(14.0)	(0.8)
1951	6.9	4.5	1.8	(0.8)	(1.0)	2.7	0.5	16.4	(15.4)	(1.0)
1952	8.2	6.2	1.9	(0.8)	(1.0)	2.6	0.5	19.3	(18.3)	(1.0)
1953	8.2	5.8	1.9	(0.7)	(1.1)	2.7	0.5	19.0	(17.9)	(1.1)
1954	8.0	5.7	2.0	(0.7)	(1.2)	2.7	0.5	18.9	(17.6)	(1.2)
1955	7.4	4.6	2.0	(0.7)	(1.3)	2.4	0.5	16.9	(15.6)	(1.3)
1956	7.7	5.0	2.2	(0.7)	(1.5)	2.4	0.5	17.8	(16.3)	(1.5)
1957	8.1	4.8	2.3	(0.7)	(1.5)	2.4	0.6	18.2	(16.6)	(1.5)
1958	7.7	4.5	2.5	(0.7)	(1.8)	2.4	0.7	17.7	(15.9)	(1.8)
1959	7.6	3.6	2.4	(0.7)	(1.7)	2.2	0.6	16.5	(14.7)	(1.7)
1960	8.0	4.2	2.9	(0.8)	(2.1)	2.3	0.8	18.3	(16.2)	(2.1)
1961	8.0	4.0	3.2	(0.8)	(2.3)	2.3	0.7	18.2	(15.9)	(2.3)
1962	8.2	3.7	3.1	(0.9)	(2.2)	2.2	0.7	17.9	(15.7)	(2.2)
1963	8.1	3.7	3.4	(1.0)	(2.4)	2.2	0.7	18.1	(15.7)	(2.4)
1964	7.7	3.7	3.5	(0.9)	(2.6)	2.2	0.8	17.9	(15.3)	(2.6)

Year										
1965	7.3	3.8	3.3	(0.8)	(2.5)	2.2	0.9	17.4	(14.9)	(2.5)
1966	7.5	4.1	3.5	(0.9)	(2.6)	1.8	0.9	17.7	(15.1)	(2.6)
1967	7.7	4.3	4.1	(1.0)	(3.1)	1.7	0.9	18.7	(15.7)	(3.1)
1968	8.1	3.4	4.0	(1.1)	(2.9)	1.7	0.9	18.0	(15.1)	(2.9)
1969	9.4	3.9	4.2	(1.1)	(3.1)	1.6	0.9	20.1	(17.0)	(3.1)
1970	9.1	3.3	4.5	(1.1)	(3.4)	1.6	1.0	19.5	(16.1)	(3.4)
1971	8.2	2.5	4.5	(1.1)	(3.4)	1.6	1.0	17.7	(14.3)	(3.4)
1972	8.2	2.8	4.6	(1.1)	(3.5)	1.3	1.1	18.0	(14.5)	(3.5)
1973	8.1	2.8	4.9	(1.3)	(3.6)	1.3	0.9	18.0	(14.4)	(3.6)
1974	8.4	2.7	5.3	(1.5)	(3.8)	1.2	1.0	18.6	(14.8)	(3.8)
1975	8.0	2.7	5.6	(1.5)	(4.1)	1.1	1.0	18.3	(14.2)	(4.1)
1976	7.7	2.4	5.3	(1.4)	(3.9)	1.0	1.0	17.6	(13.6)	(3.9)
TQ	8.6	1.9	5.6	(1.6)	(4.0)	1.0	1.0	18.1	(14.1)	(4.0)
1977	8.2	2.8	5.5	(1.5)	(4.0)	0.9	1.0	18.4	(14.4)	(4.0)
1978	8.3	2.8	5.6	(1.6)	(3.9)	0.8	0.9	18.4	(14.5)	(3.9)
1979	8.9	2.7	5.7	(1.7)	(4.0)	0.8	0.9	18.9	(14.9)	(4.0)
1980	9.1	2.4	5.9	(1.7)	(4.2)	0.9	1.0	19.4	(15.1)	(4.2)
1981	9.6	2.0	6.1	(1.8)	(4.4)	1.4	1.0	20.1	(15.7)	(4.4)
1982	9.5	1.6	6.4	(1.8)	(4.6)	1.2	1.1	19.7	(15.1)	(4.6)
1983	8.7	1.1	6.3	(1.9)	(4.4)	1.1	0.9	18.1	(13.6)	(4.4)
1984	8.1	1.5	6.5	(2.0)	(4.5)	1.0	0.9	18.1	(13.6)	(4.5)
1985	8.5	1.6	6.7	(2.0)	(4.7)	0.9	0.9	18.6	(13.9)	(4.7)
1986	8.3	1.5	6.8	(2.0)	(4.8)	0.8	1.0	18.4	(13.6)	(4.8)
1987	8.9	1.9	6.8	(2.0)	(4.8)	0.7	0.9	19.3	(14.5)	(4.8)
1988	8.4	2.0	7.0	(1.9)	(5.0)	0.7	0.9	19.0	(13.9)	(5.0)
1989	8.7	2.0	7.0	(1.9)	(5.1)	0.7	0.9	19.2	(14.1)	(5.1)
1990 estimate	8.9	2.0	7.0	(1.8)	(5.2)	0.7	0.9	19.6	(14.4)	(5.2)
1991 estimate	9.0	2.2	7.2	(1.8)	(5.3)	0.6	0.9	19.9	(14.5)	(5.3)
1992 estimate	8.9	2.2	7.1	(1.8)	(5.3)	0.6	0.9	19.7	(14.4)	(5.3)
1993 estimate	8.8	2.3	7.1	(1.8)	(5.3)	0.6	0.8	19.6	(14.3)	(5.3)
1994 estimate	8.8	2.2	7.1	(1.7)	(5.4)	0.6	0.8	19.5	(14.1)	(5.4)
1995 estimate	8.7	2.2	7.1	(1.7)	(5.4)	0.6	0.8	19.4	(14.0)	(5.4)

* 0.05 percent or less.

Source: Historical Tables, Budget of the United States Government, Fiscal 1991, Executive Office of the President, Office of Management and Budget.

PERCENTAGE COMPOSITION OF RECEIPTS BY SOURCE: 1934–1995

Fiscal Year	Individual Income Taxes	Corporation Income Taxes	Social Insurance Taxes and Contributions			Excise Taxes	Other	Total Receipts		
			Total	(On-Budget)	(Off-Budget)			Total	(On-Budget)	(Off-Budget)
1934	14.2%	12.3%	1.0%	(1.0)%	-----	45.8%	26.7%	100.0%	(100.0)%	-----
1935	14.6	14.7	0.9	(0.9)	-----	39.9	30.0	100.0	(100.0)	-----
1936	17.2	18.3	1.3	(1.3)	-----	41.6	21.6	100.0	(100.0)	-----
1937	20.3	19.3	10.8	(5.9)	(4.9)	34.8	14.9	100.0	(95.1)	(4.9)
1938	19.1	19.1	22.8	(17.1)	(5.7)	27.6	11.5	100.0	(94.3)	(5.7)
1939	16.3	17.9	25.3	(17.3)	(8.0)	29.7	10.7	100.0	(92.0)	(8.0)
1940	13.6	18.3	27.3	(18.9)	(8.4)	30.2	10.7	100.0	(91.6)	(8.4)
1941	15.1	24.4	22.3	(14.4)	(7.9)	29.3	9.0	100.0	(92.1)	(7.9)
1942	22.3	32.2	16.8	(10.6)	(6.1)	23.2	5.5	100.0	(93.9)	(6.1)
1943	27.1	39.8	12.7	(8.0)	(4.7)	17.1	3.3	100.0	(95.3)	(4.7)
1944	45.0	33.9	7.9	(5.0)	(3.0)	10.9	2.2	100.0	(97.0)	(3.0)
1945	40.7	35.4	7.6	(4.7)	(2.9)	13.9	2.4	100.0	(97.1)	(2.9)
1946	41.0	30.2	7.9	(4.8)	(3.2)	17.8	3.1	100.0	(96.8)	(3.2)
1947	46.6	22.4	8.9	(5.1)	(3.8)	18.7	3.5	100.0	(96.2)	(3.8)
1948	46.5	23.3	9.0	(5.1)	(3.9)	17.7	3.5	100.0	(96.1)	(3.9)
1949	39.5	28.4	9.6	(5.3)	(4.3)	19.0	3.5	100.0	(95.7)	(4.3)
1950	39.9	26.5	11.0	(5.7)	(5.3)	19.1	3.4	100.0	(94.7)	(5.3)
1951	41.9	27.3	11.0	(4.9)	(6.0)	16.8	3.1	100.0	(94.0)	(6.0)
1952	42.2	32.1	9.7	(4.3)	(5.4)	13.4	2.6	100.0	(94.6)	(5.4)
1953	42.8	30.5	9.8	(3.9)	(5.9)	14.2	2.7	100.0	(94.1)	(5.9)
1954	42.4	30.3	10.3	(3.8)	(6.6)	14.3	2.7	100.0	(93.4)	(6.6)
1955	43.9	27.3	12.0	(4.2)	(7.8)	14.0	2.8	100.0	(92.2)	(7.8)
1956	43.2	28.0	12.5	(3.9)	(8.6)	13.3	3.0	100.0	(91.4)	(8.6)
1957	44.5	26.5	12.5	(4.0)	(8.5)	13.2	3.3	100.0	(91.5)	(8.5)
1958	43.6	25.2	14.1	(4.0)	(10.1)	13.4	3.7	100.0	(89.9)	(10.1)
1959	46.3	21.8	14.8	(4.3)	(10.5)	13.3	3.7	100.0	(89.5)	(10.5)
1960	44.0	23.2	15.9	(4.4)	(11.5)	12.6	4.2	100.0	(88.5)	(11.5)
1961	43.8	22.2	17.4	(4.6)	(12.8)	12.6	4.0	100.0	(87.2)	(12.8)
1962	45.7	20.6	17.1	(4.8)	(12.3)	12.6	4.0	100.0	(87.7)	(12.3)
1963	44.7	20.3	18.6	(5.3)	(13.3)	12.4	4.1	100.0	(86.7)	(13.3)
1964	43.2	20.9	19.5	(5.0)	(14.5)	12.2	4.2	100.0	(85.5)	(14.5)

Year									
1965	41.8	21.8	19.0	(4.7)	(14.3)	12.5	4.9	100.0	(85.7)	(14.3)
1966	42.4	23.0	19.5	(4.9)	(14.6)	10.0	5.1	100.0	(85.4)	(14.6)
1967	41.3	22.8	21.9	(5.5)	(16.4)	9.2	4.7	100.0	(83.6)	(16.4)
1968	44.9	18.7	22.2	(5.9)	(16.3)	9.2	5.0	100.0	(83.7)	(16.3)
1969	46.7	19.6	20.9	(5.4)	(15.5)	8.1	4.7	100.0	(84.5)	(15.5)
1970	46.9	17.0	23.0	(5.7)	(17.4)	8.1	4.9	100.0	(82.6)	(17.4)
1971	46.1	14.3	25.3	(6.1)	(19.2)	8.9	5.4	100.0	(80.8)	(19.2)
1972	45.7	15.5	25.4	(6.1)	(19.2)	7.5	6.0	100.0	(80.7)	(19.2)
1973	44.7	15.7	27.3	(7.4)	(20.0)	7.0	5.2	100.0	(80.0)	(20.0)
1974	45.2	14.7	28.5	(8.0)	(20.5)	6.4	5.2	100.0	(79.5)	(20.5)
1975	43.9	14.6	30.3	(7.9)	(22.4)	5.9	5.4	100.0	(77.6)	(22.4)
1976	44.2	13.9	30.5	(8.2)	(22.3)	5.7	5.8	100.0	(77.7)	(22.3)
TQ	47.8	10.4	31.0	(8.9)	(22.2)	5.5	5.3	100.0	(77.8)	(22.2)
1977	44.3	15.4	29.9	(8.3)	(21.6)	4.9	5.3	100.0	(78.4)	(21.6)
1978	45.3	15.0	30.3	(8.9)	(21.4)	4.6	4.8	100.0	(78.6)	(21.4)
1979	47.0	14.2	30.0	(8.8)	(21.2)	4.0	4.8	100.0	(78.8)	(21.2)
1980	47.2	12.5	30.5	(8.6)	(21.9)	4.7	5.1	100.0	(78.1)	(21.9)
1981	47.7	10.2	30.5	(8.8)	(21.7)	6.8	4.8	100.0	(78.3)	(21.7)
1982	48.2	8.0	32.6	(9.4)	(23.2)	5.9	5.3	100.0	(76.8)	(23.2)
1983	48.1	6.2	34.8	(10.3)	(24.5)	5.9	5.0	100.0	(75.5)	(24.5)
1984	44.8	8.5	35.9	(11.0)	(24.9)	5.6	5.2	100.0	(75.1)	(24.9)
1985	45.6	8.4	36.1	(10.8)	(25.4)	4.9	5.0	100.0	(74.6)	(25.4)
1986	45.4	8.2	36.9	(10.9)	(26.0)	4.3	5.2	100.0	(74.0)	(26.0)
1987	46.0	9.8	35.5	(10.5)	(25.0)	3.8	4.9	100.0	(75.0)	(25.0)
1988	44.1	10.4	36.8	(10.2)	(26.6)	3.9	4.8	100.0	(73.4)	(26.6)
1989	45.0	10.5	36.3	(9.7)	(26.6)	3.4	4.8	100.0	(73.4)	(26.6)
1990 estimate	45.6	10.4	35.9	(9.3)	(26.6)	3.4	4.7	100.0	(73.4)	(26.6)
1991 estimate	45.2	11.1	36.0	(9.1)	(26.9)	3.2	4.5	100.0	(73.1)	(26.9)
1992 estimate	45.0	11.3	36.1	(9.0)	(27.1)	3.1	4.4	100.0	(72.9)	(27.1)
1993 estimate	44.7	11.7	36.3	(9.0)	(27.3)	3.1	4.3	100.0	(72.7)	(27.3)
1994 estimate	44.9	11.4	36.5	(9.0)	(27.6)	3.0	4.2	100.0	(72.4)	(27.6)
1995 estimate	45.0	11.4	36.5	(8.9)	(27.6)	2.9	4.2	100.0	(72.4)	(27.6)

Source: Historical Tables, Budget of the United States Government, Fiscal 1991, Executive Office of the President, Office of Management and Budget.

COMPOSITION OF OUTLAYS IN PERCENTAGE TERMS: 1971–1995

Category	1971	1972	1973	1974	1975	1976	TQ	1977	1978	1979	1980	1981	1982
As percentages of GNP													
Total outlays [1]	19.9%	20.0%	19.2%	19.0%	21.8%	21.9%	21.4%	21.2%	21.1%	20.6%	22.1%	22.7%	23.8%
National defense [1]	7.5	6.9	6.0	5.6	5.7	5.3	5.0	5.0	4.8	4.8	5.0	5.3	5.9
Nondefense:													
Payments for individuals	7.6	8.1	8.2	8.5	10.1	10.6	10.1	10.2	9.7	9.5	10.4	10.8	11.4
Direct payments [2]	(6.6)	(6.9)	(7.1)	(7.5)	(9.0)	(9.5)	(9.0)	(9.0)	(8.6)	(8.4)	(9.2)	(9.6)	(10.2)
Grants to State and local governments	(1.0)	(1.2)	(1.1)	(1.0)	(1.1)	(1.2)	(1.1)	(1.1)	(1.1)	(1.1)	(1.2)	(1.2)	(1.2)
All other grants	1.7	1.8	2.2	2.0	2.2	2.3	2.4	2.4	2.5	2.3	2.2	1.9	1.6
Net Interest [2]	1.4	1.3	1.4	1.5	1.5	1.6	1.5	1.5	1.6	1.7	2.0	2.3	2.7
All other [2]	2.7	2.8	2.5	2.6	3.2	3.0	3.3	2.8	3.2	3.0	3.3	3.3	3.0
Undistributed offsetting receipts [2]	-1.0	-.8	-1.0	-1.2	-.9	-.8	-.9	-.8	-.7	-.7	-.7	-.9	-.8
Total nondefense	12.4	13.1	13.2	13.4	16.1	16.6	16.4	16.1	16.3	15.8	17.1	17.4	17.9
Addendum: GNP ($ billions)	1,055.9	1,153.1	1,281.4	1,416.5	1,522.5	1,698.2	448.7	1,933.0	2,171.8	2,447.8	2,670.6	2,986.4	3,139.1
As percentages of outlays													
Total outlays [1]	100.0%	100.0%	100.0%	100.0%	100.0%	100.0%	100.0%	100.0%	100.0%	100.0%	100.0%	100.0%	100.0%
National defense [1]	37.5	34.3	31.2	29.5	26.0	24.1	23.2	23.8	22.8	23.1	22.7	23.2	24.9
Nondefense:													
Payments for individuals	38.3	40.3	42.5	44.6	46.2	48.5	47.3	48.0	46.0	46.3	47.0	47.7	47.8
Direct payments [2]	(33.3)	(34.3)	(37.0)	(39.2)	(41.2)	(43.2)	(42.1)	(42.6)	(40.7)	(40.9)	(41.6)	(42.2)	(42.8)
Grants to State and local governments	(4.9)	(6.0)	(5.6)	(5.4)	(4.9)	(5.3)	(5.2)	(5.4)	(5.3)	(5.3)	(5.4)	(5.4)	(5.1)
All other grants	8.4	8.9	11.4	10.7	10.0	10.6	11.4	11.3	11.7	11.1	10.1	8.5	6.7
Net Interest [2]	7.1	6.7	7.1	8.0	7.0	7.2	7.2	7.3	7.7	8.5	8.9	10.1	11.4
All other [2]	13.5	13.9	13.2	13.5	14.9	13.5	15.3	13.3	15.2	14.5	14.8	14.6	12.7
Undistributed offsetting receipts [2]	-4.8	-4.2	-5.5	-6.2	-4.1	-3.9	-4.4	-3.6	-3.4	-3.5	-3.4	-4.1	-3.5
Total nondefense	62.5	65.7	68.8	70.5	74.0	75.9	76.8	76.2	77.2	76.9	77.3	76.8	75.1

Category	1983	1984	1985	1986	1987	1988	1989	1990 estimate	1991 estimate	1992 estimate	1993 estimate	1994 estimate	1995 estimate
As percentages of GNP													
Total outlays	24.3%	23.1%	23.9%	23.7%	22.7%	22.2%	22.2%	21.8%	20.9%	20.1%	19.5%	19.4%	19.3%
National defense [1]	6.3	6.2	6.4	6.5	6.4	6.1	5.9	5.4	5.1	4.9	4.6	4.4	4.2
Nondefense:													
Payments for individuals	11.9	10.8	10.8	10.7	10.6	10.4	10.4	10.5	10.4	10.3	10.3	10.2	10.2
Direct payments [2]	(10.6)	(9.6)	(9.6)	(9.5)	(9.3)	(9.1)	(9.1)	(9.2)	(9.0)	(8.9)	(8.9)	(8.9)	(8.8)
Grants to State and local governments	(1.3)	(1.2)	(1.2)	(1.3)	(1.3)	(1.3)	(1.3)	(1.4)	(1.4)	(1.4)	(1.4)	(1.4)	(1.4)
All other grants	1.5	1.4	1.5	1.4	1.2	1.1	1.1	1.1	1.1	1.0	0.9	0.9	0.8
Net Interest [2]	2.7	3.0	3.3	3.3	3.1	3.2	3.3	3.2	2.9	2.6	2.3	2.0	1.8
All other [2]	2.9	2.5	2.9	2.5	2.2	2.2	2.3	2.3	2.2	2.0	2.1	2.5	3.0
Undistributed offsetting receipts [2]	-1.0	-.9	-.8	-.8	-.8	-.8	-.7	-.7	-.7	-.7	-.7	-.6	-.6
Total nondefense	18.0	16.9	17.5	17.1	16.3	16.1	16.3	16.4	15.8	15.2	14.9	15.0	15.1
Addendum: GNP ($ billions)	3,321.9	3,687.7	3,952.4	4,180.9	4,430.2	4,792.2	5,151.3	5,488.9	5,892.4	6,329.0	6,770.0	7,213.6	7,659.2
As percentages of outlays													
Total outlays	100.0%	100.0%	100.0%	100.0%	100.0%	100.0%	100.0%	100.0%	100.0%	100.0%	100.0%	100.0%	100.0%
National defense [1]	26.0	26.7	26.7	27.6	28.1	27.3	26.6	24.8	24.6	24.3	23.6	22.6	21.6
Nondefense:													
Payments for individuals	48.9	46.9	45.0	45.4	46.8	46.9	46.7	48.3	49.5	51.2	52.5	52.8	53.0
Direct payments [2]	(43.8)	(41.7)	(39.9)	(40.1)	(41.1)	(41.1)	(41.0)	(42.0)	(42.9)	(44.3)	(45.5)	(45.7)	(45.8)
Grants to State and local governments	(5.2)	(5.2)	(5.1)	(5.3)	(5.6)	(5.7)	(5.8)	(6.2)	(6.5)	(6.8)	(7.0)	(7.1)	(7.2)
All other grants	6.3	6.2	6.1	6.0	5.2	5.1	4.9	4.9	5.1	4.9	4.7	4.5	4.2
Net Interest [2]	11.1	13.0	13.7	13.7	13.8	14.3	14.8	14.7	14.0	12.9	11.9	10.6	9.2
All other [2]	11.9	10.8	12.0	10.6	9.8	10.0	10.3	10.4	10.4	10.2	10.8	12.9	15.3
Undistributed offsetting receipts [2]	-4.2	-3.8	-3.5	-3.3	-3.6	-3.5	-3.3	-3.0	-3.5	-3.4	-3.5	-3.3	-3.4
Total nondefense	74.0	73.3	73.3	72.4	71.9	72.7	73.4	75.2	75.4	75.7	76.4	77.4	78.4

[1] Includes grants to State and local governments
[2] Includes some off-budget amounts; most of the off-budget amounts are direct payments for individuals (social security benefits).

Source: Historical Tables, Budget of the United States Government, Fiscal 1991, Executive Office of the President, Office of Management and Budget.

TOTAL GOVERNMENT EXPENDITURES AS PERCENTAGES OF GNP: 1947-1989

| Fiscal Year | Total Government Expenditures | Federal Government Outlays | | | Addendum: Federal Grants-in-Aid, NIPA Basis | State and Local Government Expenditures From Own Sources Net of Nontax Receipts (NIPA Basis) |
		Total	On-Budget	Off-Budget		
1947	20.1%	15.4%	15.3%	0.1%	(0.7)%	4.6%
1948	17.3	12.0	11.9	0.1	(0.7)	5.3
1949	20.6	14.7	14.6	0.2	(0.8)	5.8
1950	22.7	16.0	15.8	0.2	(0.9)	6.7
1951	20.5	14.4	14.0	0.4	(0.8)	6.1
1952	25.8	19.8	19.3	0.5	(0.7)	6.0
1953	26.8	20.8	20.2	0.6	(0.8)	5.9
1954	25.6	19.2	18.4	0.8	(0.8)	6.4
1955	24.6	17.7	16.7	1.0	(0.8)	6.9
1956	23.8	16.9	15.7	1.2	(0.8)	6.9
1957	24.5	17.4	16.0	1.4	(0.8)	7.1
1958	25.9	18.3	16.6	1.7	(1.0)	7.6
1959	26.8	19.1	17.3	1.9	(1.3)	7.7
1960	25.8	18.2	16.1	2.1	(1.4)	7.6
1961	27.0	18.9	16.6	2.3	(1.3)	8.1
1962	27.2	19.2	16.7	2.4	(1.4)	8.1
1963	27.1	18.9	16.4	2.5	(1.4)	8.2
1964	27.1	18.8	16.3	2.5	(1.6)	8.2
1965	25.9	17.6	15.1	2.5	(1.6)	8.3
1966	26.6	18.2	15.5	2.7	(1.7)	8.4
1967	28.4	19.8	17.2	2.6	(1.9)	8.6
1968	29.9	21.0	18.3	2.6	(2.1)	8.9
1969	29.0	19.8	17.0	2.7	(2.1)	9.2

Year						
1970	29.2	19.8	17.0	2.8	(2.3)	9.4
1971	29.9	19.9	16.8	3.1	(2.5)	10.0
1972	29.8	20.0	16.8	3.2	(2.8)	9.8
1973	28.5	19.2	15.6	3.6	(3.2)	9.3
1974	28.5	19.0	15.3	3.7	(2.9)	9.5
1975	31.8	21.8	17.9	4.0	(3.2)	10.0
1976	31.8	21.9	17.8	4.1	(3.4)	9.9
TQ	31.3	21.4	17.1	4.3	(3.4)	9.9
1977	30.3	21.2	17.0	4.2	(3.4)	9.1
1978	29.9	21.1	17.0	4.1	(3.4)	8.8
1979	29.1	20.6	16.5	4.1	(3.2)	8.5
1980	30.7	22.1	17.8	4.3	(3.2)	8.6
1981	31.0	22.7	18.2	4.5	(3.0)	8.3
1982	32.4	23.8	18.9	4.8	(2.7)	8.6
1983	33.0	24.3	19.9	4.4	(2.6)	8.7
1984	31.4	23.1	18.6	4.5	(2.5)	8.3
1985	32.4	23.9	19.5	4.5	(2.5)	8.5
1986	32.3	23.7	19.3	4.4	(2.6)	8.6
1987	31.8	22.7	18.3	4.4	(2.3)	9.2
1988	31.4	22.2	18.0	4.2	(2.3)	9.2
1989	31.4	22.2	18.1	4.1	(2.3)	9.2

Source: *Historical Tables, Budget of the United States Government, Fiscal 1991*, Executive Office of the President, Office of Management and Budget.

TOTAL GOVERNMENT EXPENDITURES BY MAJOR CATEGORY OF EXPENDITURE AS PERCENTAGES OF GNP: 1947–1989

Fiscal Year	Total Government	Defense and International	Net Interest	Federal Payments For Individuals		Other Federal	State and Local From Own Sources (Except Net Interest)
				Social Security and Medicare	Other		
1947	20.1%	8.3%	1.9%	0.2%	3.9%	1.2%	4.6%
1948	17.3	5.5	1.8	0.2	3.4	1.1	5.3
1949	20.6	7.3	1.7	0.2	3.6	1.9	5.8
1950	22.7	6.9	1.8	0.3	4.8	2.1	6.7
1951	20.5	8.6	1.5	0.5	2.8	1.1	6.1
1952	25.8	14.2	1.4	0.6	2.6	1.0	6.0
1953	26.8	15.0	1.4	0.7	2.3	1.4	5.9
1954	25.6	13.8	1.3	0.9	2.5	0.7	6.4
1955	24.6	11.6	1.3	1.1	2.6	1.1	6.9
1956	23.8	10.7	1.2	1.3	2.4	1.3	6.8
1957	24.5	11.0	1.2	1.5	2.4	1.3	7.1
1958	25.9	11.1	1.3	1.8	2.9	1.3	7.6
1959	26.8	10.8	1.2	2.0	2.8	2.4	7.7
1960	25.8	10.1	1.4	2.2	2.5	2.0	7.5
1961	27.0	10.2	1.3	2.4	3.0	2.1	8.1
1962	27.2	10.4	1.3	2.5	2.7	2.3	8.1
1963	27.1	10.0	1.3	2.6	2.6	2.4	8.1
1964	27.1	9.5	1.3	2.6	2.5	2.9	8.2
1965	25.9	8.3	1.2	2.5	2.4	3.1	8.3
1966	26.6	8.6	1.2	2.7	2.3	3.3	8.4
1967	28.4	9.7	1.2	3.1	2.4	3.4	8.7
1968	29.9	10.3	1.2	3.3	2.5	3.5	9.1
1969	29.0	9.4	1.3	3.6	2.6	2.9	9.4

Year							
1970	29.2	8.7	1.3	3.7	2.9	3.1	9.6
1971	29.9	7.9	1.3	4.0	3.6	3.0	10.1
1972	29.8	7.3	1.2	4.1	3.9	3.3	9.9
1973	28.5	6.3	1.2	4.5	3.7	3.4	9.5
1974	28.5	6.0	1.3	4.6	3.8	3.0	9.8
1975	31.8	6.1	1.2	5.1	5.0	4.1	10.2
1976	31.8	5.7	1.3	5.3	5.3	4.1	10.1
TQ	31.3	5.5	1.4	5.4	4.8	4.2	10.1
1977	30.3	5.4	1.4	5.4	4.8	4.1	9.3
1978	29.9	5.2	1.4	5.4	4.3	4.6	9.0
1979	29.1	5.1	1.3	5.3	4.2	4.3	8.9
1980	30.7	5.5	1.4	5.7	4.7	4.3	9.2
1981	31.0	5.7	1.6	6.0	4.8	3.9	9.0
1982	32.4	6.3	2.0	6.5	4.9	3.4	9.4
1983	33.0	6.7	1.9	6.7	5.2	3.1	9.4
1984	31.4	6.6	2.3	6.4	4.4	2.6	9.1
1985	32.4	6.8	2.5	6.5	4.3	3.1	9.3
1986	32.3	6.9	2.4	6.5	4.3	2.8	9.4
1987	31.8	6.6	2.3	6.4	4.2	2.3	10.0
1988	31.4	6.3	2.3	6.3	4.1	2.4	10.0
1989	31.4	6.1	2.5	6.4	4.2	2.3	10.0

Source: Historical Tables, Budget of the United States Government, Fiscal 1991, Executive Office of the President, Office of Management and Budget.

TOTAL GOVERNMENT EXPENDITURES BY MAJOR CATEGORY OF EXPENDITURE: 1947–1989

(dollar amounts in billions)

Fiscal Year	Total Government	Defense and International	Net Interest	Federal Payments For Individuals		Other Federal	State and Local From Own Sources (Except Net Interest)
				Social Security and Medicare	Other		
1947	44.9	18.6	4.3	0.4	8.6	2.6	10.2
1948	43.0	13.7	4.4	0.5	8.5	2.7	13.1
1949	54.3	19.2	4.6	0.6	9.5	5.0	15.3
1950	60.5	18.4	4.9	0.7	12.9	5.7	17.8
1951	64.7	27.2	4.7	1.5	8.8	3.4	19.1
1952	88.4	48.8	4.7	2.0	8.9	3.4	20.6
1953	97.8	54.9	5.2	2.6	8.3	5.1	21.7
1954	94.5	50.9	4.8	3.3	9.3	2.6	23.6
1955	95.1	45.0	4.9	4.3	10.0	4.3	26.5
1956	99.4	44.9	5.2	5.4	9.8	5.4	28.6
1957	108.0	48.6	5.4	6.5	10.5	5.6	31.4
1958	116.8	50.2	5.7	8.0	12.9	5.7	34.3
1959	129.2	52.2	5.9	9.5	13.2	11.4	36.9
1960	130.5	51.1	7.1	11.4	12.8	10.0	38.2
1961	139.9	52.8	6.8	12.2	15.3	10.7	42.0
1962	151.9	58.0	7.0	14.0	14.9	13.0	45.0
1963	159.3	58.7	7.9	15.5	15.5	13.9	47.9
1964	170.4	59.7	8.2	16.2	16.0	18.4	51.8

Year							
1965	173.9	55.9	8.4	17.1	16.0	20.7	55.9
1966	196.3	63.7	9.0	20.3	16.8	24.4	62.2
1967	226.0	77.0	9.5	24.5	18.7	27.1	69.3
1968	254.1	87.2	10.1	28.4	21.3	30.0	76.9
1969	269.5	87.1	11.7	33.0	24.1	26.7	86.9
1970	288.9	86.0	12.8	36.4	28.3	30.6	94.8
1971	315.5	83.0	13.2	42.6	37.8	31.9	106.9
1972	343.2	84.0	14.2	47.7	45.2	38.4	113.9
1973	365.1	80.8	15.3	57.2	47.3	43.0	121.4
1974	403.9	85.1	17.9	65.7	54.5	42.7	138.2
1975	483.9	93.6	18.9	77.7	75.8	62.0	155.9
1976	540.3	96.1	22.8	89.6	90.5	68.9	172.4
TQ	140.6	24.7	6.1	24.0	21.3	18.9	45.4
1977	585.8	103.6	26.2	104.5	91.8	79.4	180.3
1978	649.2	112.0	29.5	116.7	94.3	100.3	196.4
1979	711.4	123.8	32.0	130.8	102.1	104.2	218.6
1980	820.2	146.7	36.9	151.0	126.5	114.2	244.9
1981	927.2	170.6	49.0	179.1	144.3	115.4	268.7
1982	1,016.5	197.6	61.9	203.1	153.7	106.4	294.0
1983	1,095.7	221.8	63.8	224.0	171.3	101.5	313.4
1984	1,159.3	243.3	83.3	237.0	162.8	97.6	335.3
1985	1,281.6	268.9	98.2	256.1	169.6	122.3	366.6
1986	1,351.2	287.5	101.9	270.7	178.7	117.3	395.0
1987	1,409.9	293.6	101.9	285.0	184.4	102.2	442.8
1988	1,503.2	300.8	112.1	302.5	196.2	112.7	478.8
1989	1,617.8	313.1	127.1	329.1	214.0	117.2	517.2

Source: *Historical Tables, Budget of the United States Government, Fiscal 1991*, Executive Office of the President, Office of Management and Budget.

TOTAL GOVERNMENT SURPLUSES OR DEFICITS (−) IN ABSOLUTE AMOUNTS AND AS PERCENTAGES OF GNP: 1947–1989

(dollar amounts in billions)

Fiscal Year	In Absolute Amounts					As Percentages of GNP		
	Total Government	Federal Government			State and Local (NIPA Basis)	Total Government	Total Federal	State and Local
		Total	On-Budget	Off-Budget				
1947	5.6	4.0	2.9	1.2	1.6	2.5%	1.8%	0.7%
1948	12.4	11.8	10.5	1.2	0.6	5.0	4.8	0.2
1949	0.4	0.6	-.7	1.3	-.2	0.2	0.2	-.1
1950	-4.4	-3.1	-4.7	1.6	-1.3	-1.7	-1.2	-.5
1951	5.6	6.1	4.3	1.8	-.5	1.8	1.9	-.2
1952	-2.0	-1.5	-3.4	1.9	-.4	-.6	-.4	-.1
1953	-6.2	-6.5	-8.3	1.8	0.3	-1.7	-1.8	0.1
1954	-1.4	-1.2	-2.8	1.7	-.3	-.4	-.3	-.1
1955	-4.6	-3.0	-4.1	1.1	-1.6	-1.2	-.8	-.4
1956	3.2	3.9	2.5	1.5	-.8	0.8	0.9	-.2
1957	2.5	3.4	2.6	0.8	-.9	0.6	0.8	-.2
1958	-4.8	-2.8	-3.3	0.5	-2.0	-1.1	-.6	-.4
1959	-14.6	-12.8	-12.1	-.7	-1.8	-3.0	-2.7	-.4
1960	0.7	0.3	0.5	-.2	0.4	0.1	0.1	0.1
1961	-3.6	-3.3	-3.8	0.4	-.3	-.7	-.6	-*
1962	-7.1	-7.1	-5.9	-1.3	*	-1.3	-1.3	*
1963	-4.4	-4.8	-4.0	-.8	0.3	-.8	-.8	0.1
1964	-5.3	-5.9	-6.5	0.6	0.6	-.8	-.9	0.1

Year								
1965	-.7	-1.4	-1.6	0.2	0.8	-.1	-.2	0.1
1966	-3.1	-3.7	-3.1	-.6	0.6	-.4	-.5	0.1
1967	-10.1	-8.6	-12.6	4.0	-1.5	-1.3	-1.1	-.2
1968	-24.7	-25.2	-27.7	2.6	0.4	-2.9	-3.0	0.1
1969	2.9	3.2	-.5	3.7	-.4	0.3	0.3	*
1970	0.8	-2.8	-8.7	5.9	3.7	0.1	-.3	0.4
1971	-23.5	-23.0	-26.1	3.0	-.5	-2.2	-2.2	*
1972	-15.2	-23.4	-26.4	3.1	8.2	-1.3	-2.0	0.7
1973	*	-14.9	-15.4	0.5	14.9	*	-1.2	1.2
1974	4.5	-6.1	-8.0	1.8	10.6	0.3	-.4	0.8
1975	-47.4	-53.2	-55.3	2.0	5.8	-3.1	-3.5	0.4
1976	-66.9	-73.7	-70.5	-3.2	6.8	-3.9	-4.3	0.4
TQ	-16.2	-14.7	-13.3	-1.4	-1.4	-3.6	-3.3	-.3
1977	-29.3	-53.6	-49.7	-3.9	24.4	-1.5	-2.8	1.3
1978	-27.8	-59.2	-54.9	-4.3	31.4	-1.3	-2.7	1.4
1979	-13.7	-40.2	-38.2	-2.0	26.5	-.6	-1.6	1.1
1980	-48.1	-73.8	-72.7	-1.1	25.7	-1.8	-2.8	1.0
1981	-46.5	-78.9	-73.9	-5.0	32.4	-1.6	-2.6	1.1
1982	-93.1	-127.9	-120.0	-7.9	34.8	-3.0	-4.1	1.1
1983	-165.2	-207.8	-208.0	0.2	42.6	-5.0	-6.3	1.3
1984	-122.3	-185.3	-185.6	0.3	63.0	-3.3	-5.0	1.7
1985	-150.4	-212.3	-221.6	9.4	61.8	-3.8	-5.4	1.6
1986	-156.6	-221.2	-237.9	16.7	64.6	-3.7	-5.3	1.5
1987	-95.8	-149.7	-169.3	19.6	53.9	-2.2	-3.4	1.2
1988	-105.0	-155.1	-193.9	38.8	50.0	-2.2	-3.2	1.0
1989	-105.4	-152.0	-204.7	52.8	46.6	-2.0	-2.9	0.9

* If dollars, $50 million or less. If percent, 0.05 percent or less.

Source: Historical Tables, Budget of the United States Government, Fiscal 1991, Executive Office of the President, Office of Management and Budget.

SUMMARY OF RECEIPTS, OUTLAYS, AND SURPLUSES OR DEFICITS (−) IN CURRENT DOLLARS, CONSTANT (FY 1982) DOLLARS, AND AS PERCENTAGES OF GNP: 1940–1995

(dollar amounts in billions)

Fiscal Year	In Current Dollars			In Constant (FY 1982) Dollars			Addendum: Composite Deflator	As Percentages of GNP		
	Receipts	Outlays	Surplus or Deficit (−)	Receipts	Outlays	Surplus or Deficit (−)		Receipts	Outlays	Surplus or Deficit (−)
1940	6.5	9.5	−2.9	57.5	83.2	−25.7	0.1138	6.8%	9.9%	−3.0%
1941	8.7	13.7	−4.9	71.8	112.6	−40.7	0.1213	7.7	12.1	−4.4
1942	14.6	35.1	−20.5	108.5	260.5	−152.0	0.1349	10.3	24.7	−14.4
1943	24.0	78.6	−54.6	162.0	530.1	−368.1	0.1482	13.7	44.7	−31.0
1944	43.7	91.3	−47.6	305.7	638.0	−332.3	0.1431	21.7	45.2	−23.5
1945	45.2	92.7	−47.6	325.8	668.9	−343.1	0.1386	21.3	43.6	−22.4
1946	39.3	55.2	−15.9	295.5	415.3	−119.8	0.1330	18.5	25.9	−7.5
1947	38.5	34.5	4.0	237.6	212.8	24.8	0.1621	17.2	15.4	1.8
1948	41.6	29.8	11.8	220.9	158.2	62.7	0.1881	16.8	12.0	4.8
1949	39.4	38.8	0.6	205.5	202.5	3.0	0.1918	14.9	14.7	0.2
1950	39.4	42.6	−3.1	204.4	220.5	−16.2	0.1930	14.8	16.0	−1.2
1951	51.6	45.5	6.1	284.2	250.6	33.6	0.1816	16.4	14.4	1.3
1952	66.2	67.7	−1.5	341.4	349.3	−7.8	0.1938	19.3	19.8	−.4
1953	69.6	76.1	−6.5	336.1	367.5	−31.4	0.2071	19.0	20.8	−1.8
1954	69.7	70.9	−1.2	325.6	330.9	−5.4	0.2141	18.9	19.2	−.3
1955	65.5	68.4	−3.0	297.5	311.1	−13.6	0.2200	16.9	17.7	−.8
1956	74.6	70.6	3.9	323.3	306.2	17.1	0.2307	17.8	16.9	0.9
1957	80.0	76.6	3.4	333.0	318.8	14.2	0.2402	18.2	17.4	0.8
1958	79.6	82.4	−2.8	311.9	322.8	−10.8	0.2553	17.7	18.3	−.6
1959	79.2	92.1	−12.8	298.5	346.9	−48.4	0.2655	16.5	19.1	−2.7
1960	92.5	92.2	0.3	341.6	340.4	1.1	0.2708	18.3	18.2	0.1
1961	94.4	97.7	−3.3	342.5	354.6	−12.1	0.2756	18.2	18.9	−.6
1962	99.7	106.8	−7.1	358.0	383.7	−25.7	0.2784	17.9	19.2	−1.3
1963	106.6	111.3	−4.8	368.2	384.6	−16.4	0.2894	18.1	18.9	−.8
1964	112.6	118.5	−5.9	382.8	402.9	−20.1	0.2942	17.9	18.8	−.9

1965	116.8	118.2	-1.4	389.9	394.6	-4.7	0.2996	17.4	17.6	-.2
1966	130.8	134.5	-3.7	419.3	431.2	-11.9	0.3120	17.7	18.2	-.5
1967	148.8	157.5	-8.6	461.6	488.4	-26.8	0.3224	18.7	19.8	-1.1
1968	153.0	178.1	-25.2	451.2	525.5	-74.2	0.3390	18.0	21.0	-3.0
1969	186.9	183.6	3.2	519.4	510.4	9.0	0.3598	20.1	19.8	0.3
1970	192.8	195.6	-2.8	502.0	509.4	-7.4	0.3841	19.5	19.8	-.3
1971	187.1	210.2	-23.0	453.6	509.4	-55.8	0.4126	17.7	19.9	-2.2
1972	207.3	230.7	-23.4	474.2	527.6	-53.5	0.4372	18.0	20.0	-2.0
1973	230.8	245.7	-14.9	495.5	527.5	-32.0	0.4658	18.0	19.2	-1.2
1974	263.2	269.4	-6.1	516.6	528.7	-12.0	0.5095	18.6	19.0	-.4
1975	279.1	332.3	-53.2	492.1	586.0	-93.9	0.5671	18.3	21.8	-3.5
1976	298.1	371.8	-73.7	488.9	609.8	-120.9	0.6097	17.6	21.9	-4.3
TQ	81.2	96.0	-14.7	129.0	152.4	-23.4	0.6298	18.1	21.4	-3.3
1977	355.6	409.2	-53.6	541.0	622.6	-81.6	0.6572	18.4	21.2	-2.8
1978	399.6	458.7	-59.2	568.0	652.2	-84.1	0.7034	18.4	21.1	-2.7
1979	463.3	503.5	-40.2	607.5	660.2	-52.7	0.7626	18.9	20.6	-1.6
1980	517.1	590.9	-73.8	611.7	699.1	-87.3	0.8453	19.4	22.1	-2.8
1981	599.3	678.2	-78.9	642.0	726.5	-84.6	0.9335	20.1	22.7	-2.6
1982	617.8	745.7	-127.9	617.8	745.7	-127.9	1.0000	19.7	23.8	-4.1
1983	600.6	808.3	-207.8	575.8	775.0	-199.2	1.0430	18.1	23.3	-6.3
1984	666.5	851.8	-185.3	616.6	788.1	-171.5	1.0808	18.1	23.1	-5.0
1985	734.1	946.3	-212.3	659.1	849.6	-190.6	1.1138	18.6	22.9	-5.4
1986	769.1	990.3	-221.2	674.2	868.0	-193.9	1.1408	18.4	22.7	-5.3
1987	854.1	1,003.8	-149.7	730.1	858.0	-127.9	1.1699	19.3	22.7	-3.4
1988	909.0	1,064.0	-155.1	751.4	879.6	-128.2	1.2097	19.0	22.2	-3.2
1989	990.7	1,142.6	-152.0	786.5	907.1	-120.6	1.2597	19.2	22.2	-2.9
1990 estimate	1,073.5	1,197.2	-123.8	817.9	912.2	-94.3	1.3124	19.6	21.8	-2.3
1991 estimate	1,170.2	1,233.3	-63.1	854.7	900.8	-46.1	1.3692	19.9	20.9	-1.1
1992 estimate	1,246.4	1,271.4	-25.1	874.9	892.5	-17.6	1.4246	19.7	22.1	-.4
1993 estimate	1,327.6	1,321.8	5.7	897.2	893.4	3.9	1.4796	19.6	19.5	0.1
1994 estimate	1,408.6	1,398.0	10.7	919.5	912.6	7.0	1.5319	19.5	19.4	0.1
1995 estimate	1,486.3	1,476.9	9.4	939.8	933.9	5.9	1.5815	19.4	19.3	0.1

Source: *Historical Tables, Budget of the United States Government, Fiscal 1991*, Executive Office of the President, Office of Management and Budget.

SUMMARY OF RECEIPTS, OUTLAYS, AND SURPLUSES OR DEFICITS (—) AS PERCENTAGES OF GNP: 1934–1995

Year	GNP (in billions of dollars)	Total Receipts	Total Outlays	Total Surplus or Deficit (—)	Budget Receipts	Budget Outlays	Budget Surplus or Deficit (—)	Off-Budget Receipts	Off-Budget Outlays	Off-Budget Surplus or Deficit (—)
1934	60.8	4.9%	10.8%	−5.9%	4.9%	10.8%	−5.9%			
1935	69.2	5.2	9.3	−4.1	5.2	9.3	−4.1			
1936	78.0	5.0	10.6	−5.5	5.0	10.6	−5.5			
1937	87.2	6.2	8.7	−2.5	5.9	8.7	−2.8	0.3	*	0.3
1938	88.4	7.6	7.7	−.1	7.2	7.8	−.5	0.4	*	0.4
1939	88.4	7.1	10.3	−3.2	6.6	10.4	−3.8	0.6	*	0.6
1940	95.8	6.8	9.9	−3.0	6.3	9.9	−3.6	0.6	*	0.6
1941	113.0	7.7	12.1	−4.4	7.1	12.1	−5.0	0.6	*	0.6
1942	142.2	10.3	24.7	−14.4	9.7	24.7	−15.0	0.6	*	0.6
1943	175.8	13.7	44.7	−31.0	13.0	44.6	−31.6	0.6	0.1	0.6
1944	202.0	21.7	45.2	−23.5	21.0	45.1	−24.1	0.6	0.1	0.6
1945	212.4	21.3	43.6	−22.4	20.6	43.6	−22.9	0.6	0.1	0.5
1946	212.9	18.5	25.9	−7.5	17.9	25.8	−8.0	0.6	0.1	0.5
1947	223.6	17.2	15.4	1.8	16.6	15.3	1.3	0.7	0.1	0.5
1948	247.8	16.8	12.0	4.8	16.1	11.9	4.3	0.7	0.1	0.5
1949	263.9	14.9	14.7	.2	14.3	14.6	−.3	0.6	0.2	0.5
1950	266.8	14.8	16.0	−1.2	14.0	15.8	−1.8	0.8	0.2	0.6
1951	315.0	16.4	14.4	1.9	15.4	14.0	1.4	1.0	0.4	0.6
1952	342.4	19.3	19.8	−.4	18.3	19.3	−1.0	1.0	0.5	0.5
1953	365.6	19.0	20.8	−1.8	17.9	20.2	−2.3	1.1	0.6	0.5
1954	369.5	18.9	19.2	−.3	17.6	18.4	−.8	1.2	0.8	0.5
1955	386.4	16.9	17.7	−.8	15.6	16.7	−1.1	1.3	1.0	0.3
1956	418.1	17.8	16.9	.9	16.3	15.7	.6	1.5	1.2	0.3
1957	440.5	18.2	17.4	.8	16.6	16.0	.6	1.5	1.4	0.2
1958	450.2	17.7	18.3	−.6	15.9	16.6	−.7	1.8	1.7	0.1
1959	481.5	16.5	19.1	−2.7	14.7	17.3	−2.5	1.7	1.9	−.1
1960	506.7	18.3	18.2	.1	16.2	16.1	.1	2.1	2.1	*
1961	518.2	18.2	18.9	−.6	15.9	16.6	−.7	2.3	2.3	0.1
1962	557.7	17.9	19.2	−1.3	15.7	16.7	−1.1	2.2	2.4	−.2
1963	587.8	18.1	18.9	−.8	15.7	16.4	−.7	2.4	2.5	−.1
1964	629.2	17.9	18.8	−.9	15.3	16.3	−1.0	2.6	2.5	0.1

Fiscal Year	GNP	Total Receipts	Total Outlays	Total Surplus or Deficit (−)	On-budget Receipts	On-budget Outlays	On-budget Surplus or Deficit (−)	Off-budget Receipts	Off-budget Outlays	Off-budget Surplus or Deficit (−)
1965	672.6	17.4	17.6	−.2	14.9	15.1	−.2	2.5	2.5	*
1966	739.0	17.7	18.2	−.5	15.1	15.5	−.4	2.6	2.7	−.1
1967	794.6	18.7	19.8	−1.1	15.7	17.2	−1.6	3.1	2.6	0.5
1968	849.4	18.0	21.0	−3.0	15.1	18.3	−3.3	2.9	2.6	0.3
1969	929.5	20.1	19.8	0.3	17.0	17.0	−.1	3.1	2.7	0.4
1970	990.2	19.5	19.8	−.3	16.1	17.0	−.9	3.4	2.8	0.6
1971	1,055.9	17.7	19.9	−2.2	14.3	16.8	−2.5	3.4	3.1	0.3
1972	1,153.1	18.0	20.0	−2.0	14.5	16.8	−2.3	3.5	3.2	0.3
1973	1,281.4	18.0	19.2	−1.2	14.4	15.6	−1.2	3.6	3.6	*
1974	1,416.5	18.6	19.0	−.4	14.8	15.3	−.6	3.8	3.7	0.1
1975	1,522.5	18.3	21.8	−3.5	14.2	17.9	−3.6	4.1	4.0	0.1
1976	1,698.2	17.6	21.9	−4.3	13.6	17.8	−4.2	3.9	4.1	−.2
TQ	448.7	18.1	21.4	−3.3	14.1	17.1	−3.0	4.0	4.3	−.3
1977	1,933.0	18.4	21.2	−2.8	14.4	17.0	−2.6	4.0	4.2	−.2
1978	2,171.8	18.4	21.1	−2.7	14.5	17.0	−2.5	3.9	4.1	−.2
1979	2,447.8	18.9	20.6	−1.6	14.9	16.5	−1.6	4.0	4.1	−.1
1980	2,670.6	19.4	22.1	−2.8	15.1	17.8	−2.7	4.2	4.3	*
1981	2,986.4	20.1	22.7	−2.6	15.7	18.2	−2.5	4.4	4.5	−.2
1982	3,139.1	19.7	23.8	−4.1	15.1	18.9	−3.8	4.6	4.8	−.3
1983	3,321.9	18.1	24.3	−6.3	13.6	19.9	−6.3	4.4	4.4	*
1984	3,687.7	18.1	23.1	−5.0	13.6	18.6	−5.0	4.5	4.5	*
1985	3,952.4	18.6	23.9	−5.4	13.9	19.5	−5.6	4.7	4.5	0.2
1986	4,180.9	18.4	23.7	−5.3	13.6	19.3	−5.7	4.8	4.4	0.4
1987	4,430.2	19.3	22.7	−3.4	14.5	18.3	−3.8	4.8	4.4	0.4
1988	4,792.2	19.0	22.2	−3.2	13.9	18.0	−4.0	5.0	4.2	0.8
1989	5,151.3	19.2	22.2	−2.9	14.1	18.1	−4.0	5.1	4.1	1.0
1990 estimate	5,488.9	19.6	21.8	−2.3	14.4	17.7	−3.3	5.2	4.1	1.1
1991 estimate	5,892.4	19.9	20.9	−1.1	14.5	16.9	−2.4	5.3	4.0	1.3
1992 estimate	6,329.0	19.7	20.1	−.4	14.4	16.2	−1.9	5.3	3.9	1.5
1993 estimate	6,770.0	19.5	19.5	0.1	14.3	15.8	−1.5	5.3	3.8	1.6
1994 estimate	7,213.6	19.5	19.4	0.1	14.1	15.7	−1.6	5.4	3.7	1.7
1995 estimate	7,659.2	19.4	19.3	0.1	14.0	15.7	−1.7	5.4	3.6	1.8

* 0.05 percent or less.

Note: Fiscal year GNP data for years 1947 to current are those produced by the Bureau of Economic Analysis, Department of Commerce from seasonally unadjusted quarterly data. For years prior to 1947 the Department produces calendar year estimates but not fiscal year or quarterly estimates. For fiscal years prior to 1947 these GNP estimates are the average of the data for the two calendar years; for 1947, they use two quarters of quarterly data and one half of calendar year data.

Source: *Historical Tables, Budget of the United States Government, Fiscal 1991,* Executive Office of the President, Office of Management and Budget.

The Federal Government Dollar
Fiscal Year 1991 Estimate
Where It Comes From...

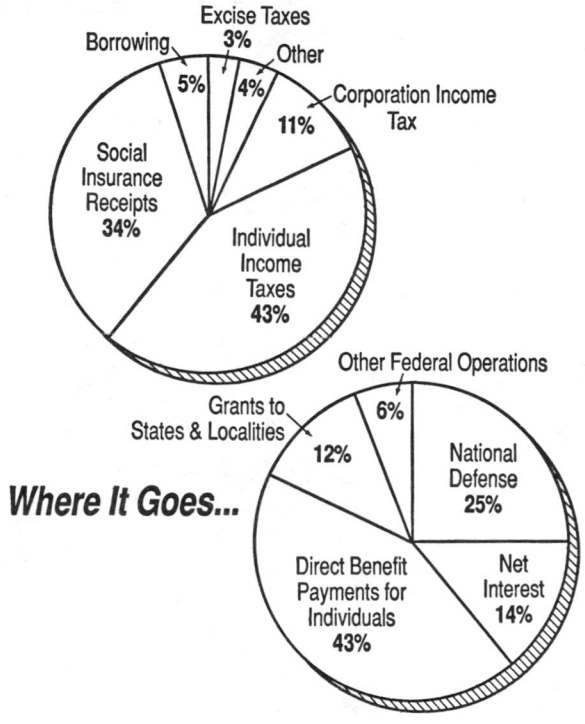

Where It Goes...

Source: *Historical Tables, Budget of the United States Government, Fiscal 1991,* Executive Office of the President, Office of Management and Budget.

NOTES TO HISTORICAL TABLES AND CHARTS

Because of the numerous changes in the way budget data have been presented over time, there are inevitable difficulties in trying to produce comparable data to cover so many years. The general rule underlying all of these tables is to provide data in as meaningful and comparable a fashion as is possible. To the extent feasible, the data are presented on a basis consistent with current budget concepts. When a structural change is made, insofar as possible the data are adjusted for all years. No major structural changes were made in the 1990 Budget. However, an example of the application of this rule comes from the 1989 Budget. Prior to the 1989 Budget, one major function was entitled "general purpose fiscal assistance." The principal component of that function—indeed, the reason that function was of sufficient importance to be a separate major function—was the general revenue sharing program. General revenue sharing started in 1963 and its last significant

outlays were in 1986. With the abolition of general revenue sharing, the general purpose fiscal assistance function has been converted from being a separate major function to being a subfunction in the general government function. The data base incorporates the general purpose fiscal activities as a subfunction of the general government function for all years—not just since the abolition of general revenue sharing.

NOTE ON THE FISCAL YEAR

The Federal fiscal year begins on October 1 and ends on the subsequent September 30. It is designated by the year in which it ends; for example, fiscal year 1987 began October 1, 1986 and ended on September 30, 1987. Prior to fiscal year 1977 the Federal fiscal years began on July 1 and ended on June 30. In calendar year 1976 the July–September period was a separate accounting period (known as the transition quarter or TQ) to bridge the period required to shift to the new fiscal years.

OUTPUT, CAPACITY, AND CAPACITY UTILIZATION[1]

Seasonally adjusted

Output (1987 = 100)

Series	1989 Q2	1989 Q3	1989 Q4	1990 Q1
1 Total industry	108.4	108.1	108.1	108.0
2 Mining	101.1	100.8	100.6	101.6
3 Utilities	106.3	106.2	110.6	105.2
4 Manufacturing	109.3	108.9	108.7	108.9
5 Primary processing	106.4	106.4	106.1	106.0
6 Advanced processing	110.6	110.1	109.9	110.3

Capacity (percent of 1987 output)

Series	1989 Q2	1989 Q3	1989 Q4	1990 Q1
1 Total industry	128.0	128.8	129.5	130.3
2 Mining	117.2	116.7	116.1	115.7
3 Utilities	125.3	125.5	125.7	126.0
4 Manufacturing	129.2	130.2	131.1	132.1
5 Primary processing	122.0	122.7	123.4	124.2
6 Advanced processing	132.6	133.7	134.7	135.8

Utilization rate (percent)

Series	1989 Q2	1989 Q3	1989 Q4	1990 Q1
1 Total industry	84.7	84.0	83.5	82.9
2 Mining	86.2	86.3	86.8	87.8
3 Utilities	84.9	84.5	87.8	83.5
4 Manufacturing	84.5	83.7	82.9	82.4
5 Primary processing	87.3	86.7	85.9	85.4
6 Advanced processing	83.4	82.1	81.7	81.2

Capacity utilization rate (percent)

Series	Previous cycle[2] High	Previous cycle[2] Low	Latest cycle[3] High	Latest cycle[3] Low	1989 Mar.	July	Aug.	Sept.	Oct.	Nov.	Dec.	1990 Jan.	Feb.	Mar.
7 Total industry	89.2	72.6	87.3	71.8	84.5	83.9	84.0	83.9	83.4	83.5	83.7	82.4	82.9	83.3
8 Mining	94.4	88.4	96.6	80.6	83.6	85.6	86.4	87.2	87.3	86.8	86.3	88.5	87.2	87.8
9 Utilities	95.6	82.5	88.3	76.2	85.6	85.0	84.7	84.3	85.5	85.6	92.3	82.5	81.5	86.4
10 Manufacturing	88.9	70.8	87.3	70.0	84.5	83.6	83.8	83.6	82.9	83.0	82.8	82.0	82.6	82.7
11 Primary processing	92.2	68.9	89.7	66.8	87.3	87.2	86.9	86.1	86.6	86.0	85.2	85.6	85.4	85.1
12 Advanced processing	87.5	72.0	86.3	71.4	83.4	82.2	82.4	82.5	81.4	81.8	81.8	80.4	81.5	81.7

1. These data also appear in the Board's G.3 (402) release.
2. Monthly high 1973; monthly low 1975.
3. Monthly highs 1978 through 1980; monthly lows 1982.

Source: *Federal Reserve Bulletin*, Board of Governors of the Federal Reserve System.

INDUSTRIAL PRODUCTION Indexes and Gross Value[1]

Monthly data are seasonally adjusted

Groups	1987 proportion	1989 avg.	1989										1990		
			Mar.[r]	Apr.[r]	May[r]	June[r]	July[r]	Aug.[r]	Sept.[r]	Oct.[r]	Nov.[r]	Dec.[r]	Jan.[r]	Feb.[p]	Mar.[.]
							Index (1977 = 100)								
Major Market															
1 Total index........................	100.00	....	107.7	108.6	108.3	108.4	107.8	108.2	108.2	107.7	108.1	108.6	107.2	108.1	108.8
2 Products..........................	60.79	....	108.3	108.9	108.9	109.1	108.2	108.5	108.8	108.1	108.9	109.7	108.1	109.3	110.0
3 Final products.................	46.05	....	108.7	109.5	109.6	109.8	108.7	109.1	109.6	108.5	109.4	110.3	108.2	109.6	110.4
4 Consumer goods...............	26.02	....	106.9	107.0	106.8	106.3	105.2	105.6	106.3	107.3	107.4	108.3	105.5	107.0	107.8
5 Equipment....................	20.03	....	110.9	112.6	113.1	114.3	113.2	113.6	113.8	110.1	112.0	112.9	111.6	112.9	113.7
6 Intermediate products.............	14.74	....	107.2	107.2	106.6	106.7	106.7	106.4	106.3	106.9	107.3	107.9	107.9	108.5	109.0
7 Materials.........................	39.21	....	106.9	108.0	107.3	107.6	107.3	107.8	107.4	107.1	107.0	106.9	105.8	106.2	107.2
Consumer goods															
8 Durable consumer goods.............	5.58	....	109.0	110.0	109.2	108.4	105.6	105.8	107.6	106.8	105.7	106.8	99.1	107.1	111.0
9 Automotive products.............	2.47	....	110.4	110.2	109.2	106.7	101.1	103.2	104.9	102.9	102.4	104.5	85.2	101.2	109.1
10 Autos and trucks	1.48	....	110.3	109.8	109.6	106.2	97.1	101.1	103.1	99.7	98.4	100.1	66.3	92.1	106.0
11 Autos, consumer	.93	....	105.5	106.2	105.7	100.5	89.3	95.1	102.0	100.7	92.8	92.6	62.1	86.9	100.5
12 Trucks, consumer	.55	....	118.3	115.8	116.2	115.7	110.1	111.3	105.0	98.2	108.0	112.6	73.3	100.8	117.0
13 Auto parts and allied goods........	.99	....	110.4	110.7	108.5	107.4	107.0	106.3	107.4	107.6	108.2	111.2	113.6	114.9	113.7
14 Home goods	3.11	....	108.0	110.0	109.3	109.8	109.2	107.9	109.8	109.8	108.4	108.6	110.1	111.7	112.1
15 Appliances, A/C and TV	.79	....	107.4	108.6	105.9	110.5	107.5	106.5	109.3	107.6	102.0	101.0	108.2	108.4	113.3
16 Carpeting and furniture..........	.91	....	102.3	103.2	104.1	102.1	101.0	98.1	100.9	101.1	100.4	102.0	103.8	104.2	102.6
17 Miscellaneous home goods	1.42	....	112.0	115.1	114.6	114.3	115.4	114.8	115.8	116.6	117.1	117.1	115.2	118.3	117.6
18 Nondurable consumer goods............	20.44	....	106.3	106.2	106.2	105.8	105.1	105.6	106.0	107.4	107.8	108.7	107.3	106.9	107.0
19 Consumer staples...................	17.87	....	106.8	106.8	106.8	106.2	105.6	106.3	106.6	108.2	109.0	110.0	108.2	107.9	108.2
20 Nonfood staples................	8.77	....	109.7	108.8	109.6	109.5	109.2	109.6	109.6	111.0	112.2	113.7	111.0	110.1	111.5
21 Consumer chemical products	3.54	....	108.5	107.8	110.1	109.8	109.6	110.1	107.8	110.3	111.3	110.3	112.7	111.7	111.9
22 Consumer paper products	2.55	....	114.0	112.8	112.7	112.9	113.1	114.1	116.2	117.2	118.1	116.9	116.2	115.6	116.8
23 Consumer energy.............	2.68	....	107.4	106.5	106.1	106.1	105.2	104.7	106.0	106.0	108.0	115.2	103.9	102.6	106.0
24 Consumer fuel	.73	....	103.6	101.8	100.6	103.0	104.5	102.3	103.4	103.1	103.0	105.1	101.7	107.0	102.5
25 Residential utilities	1.96	....	108.8	108.2	108.1	107.2	105.5	105.6	106.9	107.0	109.8	120.7	103.5	101.0	107.3
Equipment															
26 Business and defense equipment	19.28	....	111.8	113.4	114.0	115.0	114.0	114.5	114.7	110.6	112.6	113.4	112.2	113.5	114.1
27 Business equipment.................	13.93	....	117.9	119.6	120.2	121.4	119.9	120.4	120.7	116.0	118.7	119.9	117.9	119.6	120.8
28 Equipment parts................	2.46	....	121.2	127.9	127.6	128.3	123.8	128.4	127.0	112.9	117.0	123.4	111.4	123.7	131.5
29 Defense and space equipment........	5.35	....	96.1	97.1	97.6	98.3	98.7	98.9	98.9	96.6	96.7	96.7	96.4	97.5	96.6
Intermediate products															
30 Construction supplies	6.05	....	105.5	106.3	105.9	106.2	106.5	105.5	105.2	106.3	107.0	107.4	108.0	108.1	108.3
31 Business supplies.....................	8.69	....	108.3	107.8	107.1	107.0	106.8	106.9	107.0	107.3	107.5	108.2	107.9	108.7	109.5
32 General business supplies	7.07	....	108.4	108.0	107.1	107.1	106.6	107.1	107.0	107.0	107.2	107.3	106.6	107.9	109.5
33 Commercial energy products........	1.63	....	108.0	106.8	106.5	106.4	107.6	106.0	106.9	107.6	108.1	115.4	107.7	105.4	....
Materials															
34 Durable goods materials...............	19.35	....	111.1	112.3	111.5	112.1	111.5	112.0	112.0	110.8	110.8	110.4	109.5	110.9	111.2
35 Durable consumer parts...........	4.16	....	110.2	110.8	110.6	110.3	107.7	109.2	108.8	106.9	105.7	102.5	96.5	102.9	104.6
36 Equipment parts.................	7.25	....	113.5	114.9	114.2	115.0	115.0	115.6	115.5	114.4	115.3	115.8	116.5	117.4	117.3
37 Durable materials n.e.c............	7.94	....	109.5	110.7	109.7	110.4	110.4	110.4	110.6	109.5	109.4	109.5	110.1	109.2	109.2
38 Basic metal materials	2.78	....	111.4	114.9	109.9	111.9	113.1	113.0	112.9	111.0	108.6	109.3	109.4	111.0	109.5
39 Nondurable goods materials	9.01	....	104.9	106.0	105.4	105.5	106.7	105.7	104.2	106.1	104.9	104.3	104.4	103.7	103.4
40 Textile, paper, and chemical															
materials	6.86	....	104.5	105.7	104.3	104.8	106.8	105.5	103.6	105.7	103.8	102.4	102.4	102.2	101.7
41 Textile materials.................	1.18	....	99.6	101.9	101.5	103.2	104.9	102.1	99.6	98.6	96.1	95.8	93.5	93.6	92.4
42 Pulp and paper materials	1.87	....	102.5	103.1	102.1	102.4	104.8	103.6	104.1	107.7	104.6	103.7	105.0	103.8	104.4
43 Chemical materials	3.81	....	107.0	108.1	106.1	106.5	108.2	107.3	104.5	106.8	105.8	103.8	103.8	104.0	103.2
44 Miscellaneous nondurable materials ...	2.14	....	106.4	107.0	109.1	107.9	106.8	107.0	106.5	107.5	108.4	110.4	110.8	108.7	108.7
45 Energy materials	10.85	....	100.8	101.9	101.2	101.0	100.1	101.7	101.6	101.3	101.9	102.7	100.3	99.7	102.3
46 Primary energy.....................	7.18	....	97.4	99.8	100.6	100.8	100.0	102.5	100.7	99.8	100.5	99.0	101.5	99.9	101.0
47 Converted fuel materials	3.68	....	107.5	106.0	102.5	101.7	100.4	100.4	103.6	104.2	104.5	110.0	97.8	99.5	104.7

INDUSTRIAL PRODUCTION Indexes and Gross Value[1] (concluded)

Groups	SIC code	1987 proportion	1989 avg.	Mar.[r]	Apr.[r]	May[r]	June[r]	July[r]	Aug.[r]	Sept.[r]	Oct.[r]	Nov.[r]	Dec.[r]	Jan.[r]	Feb.[p]	Mar.[e]
								Index (1977 = 100)								
MAJOR INDUSTRY																
1 Mining and utilities	......	15.56	....	102.7	104.0	103.6	103.3	103.3	103.4	103.7	104.0	104.7	108.0	103.1	101.7	105.1
2 Mining		7.93	....	98.3	101.7	101.1	100.4	100.0	100.7	101.6	100.7	101.2	100.1	102.4	100.8	101.4
3 Utilities		7.63	....	107.2	106.4	106.3	106.3	106.6	106.2	105.9	107.4	108.3	116.1	103.9	102.6	109.0
4 Manufacturing		84.44	....	108.7	109.4	109.2	109.3	108.6	109.1	109.1	108.4	108.9	108.8	108.0	109.2	109.5
5 Nondurable		37.17	....	105.9	106.5	106.4	106.2	106.1	106.2	106.0	107.2	107.3	106.7	107.3	107.5	107.0
6 Durable		47.27	....	110.9	111.6	111.4	111.8	110.6	111.3	111.5	109.4	110.1	110.4	108.6	110.5	111.5
Mining																
7 Metal	10	.32	....	133.3	135.7	136.1	143.3	151.7	144.3	145.4	143.2	145.9	155.5	154.5	152.0	151.0
8 Coal	11.12	1.22	....	105.1	111.1	104.7	100.3	101.1	103.1	109.6	109.9	108.1	103.5	114.1	111.9	111.9
9 Oil and gas extraction	13	5.73	....	93.9	96.7	97.0	96.3	94.9	96.3	95.9	94.3	95.5	94.0	94.9	93.7	94.7
10 Stone and earth minerals	14	.67	....	106.7	111.2	113.0	115.0	116.8	113.3	114.1	118.0	115.8	119.7	121.5	117.4	116.7
Nondurable manufactures																
11 Foods	20	8.76	....	104.5	106.2	105.5	104.2	104.0	104.8	105.4	106.8	107.4	108.0	107.0	107.6	106.8
12 Tobacco products	21	1.02	....	102.8	104.0	101.7	100.4	94.2	95.0	93.3	99.7	98.8	98.5	101.3	102.3	100.0
13 Textile mill products	22	1.84	....	101.7	104.1	103.2	102.4	104.2	101.5	101.5	101.9	99.3	99.8	100.0	101.1	99.6
14 Apparel products	23	2.36	....	104.4	105.1	104.9	105.2	104.4	104.7	104.5	103.9	103.7	102.6	102.4	102.6	101.3
15 Paper and products	26	3.58	....	102.5	103.0	102.1	101.8	104.1	103.0	102.2	105.3	104.1	103.4	103.8	103.7	104.2
16 Printing and publishing	27	6.37	....	108.9	108.6	108.4	108.6	106.6	107.8	109.4	109.3	109.6	109.6	110.5	111.0	110.9
17 Chemicals and products	28	8.60	....	107.5	107.5	108.4	109.1	109.7	109.6	107.5	109.4	109.8	107.6	108.9	109.0	108.4
18 Petroleum products	29	1.32	....	104.1	104.5	104.6	106.6	108.2	107.0	108.7	106.9	109.3	104.3	108.7	109.9	108.0
19 Rubber and plastic products	30	3.02	....	108.5	108.5	109.8	109.0	109.0	109.0	108.5	108.8	109.1	110.1	110.7	108.7	110.4
20 Leather and products	31	.30	....	104.6	105.1	102.8	102.2	103.7	103.2	103.5	102.2	99.4	103.0	104.3	102.9	103.0
Durable manufactures																
21 Lumber and products	24	2.00	....	100.8	102.7	102.3	103.5	102.8	102.4	102.6	103.2	104.8	106.4	105.7	103.6	105.1
22 Furniture and fixtures	25	1.45	....	105.5	105.8	107.9	107.0	104.9	104.5	105.7	105.6	104.4	105.1	105.2	104.6	103.9
23 Clay, glass, and stone products	32	2.46	....	108.4	107.7	108.2	108.0	106.2	107.8	106.5	107.7	108.2	108.6	110.1	109.1	108.9
24 Primary metals	33	3.32	....	108.8	112.7	107.0	108.7	108.8	111.7	109.9	108.6	104.8	102.6	106.7	108.2	104.9
25 Iron and steel	331.2	1.95	....	109.3	115.4	104.8	107.1	107.5	109.8	109.7	109.2	104.1	100.3	107.5	110.4	104.4
26 Fabricated metal products	34	5.38	....	107.4	106.9	107.9	108.3	107.6	106.5	106.0	105.9	106.9	106.3	105.3	105.6	106.2
27 Nonelectrical machinery	35	8.55	....	121.9	121.6	121.8	123.4	121.6	121.8	123.4	119.0	122.9	123.8	123.3	122.8	123.0
28 Electrical machinery	36	8.62	....	109.2	110.1	108.8	109.1	108.6	110.6	110.8	110.2	110.1	110.1	110.0	111.2	111.9
29 Transportation equipment	37	9.80	....	108.7	109.4	109.6	109.0	106.6	107.8	108.0	102.1	102.8	104.4	94.7	103.1	107.9
30 Motor vehicles and parts	371	4.65	....	108.9	108.6	107.8	105.0	99.6	102.7	103.2	99.7	99.0	98.7	76.8	94.3	103.8
31 Aerospace and miscellaneous transportation equipment	372–6.9	5.15	....	108.5	110.1	111.2	112.6	113.0	112.4	112.3	104.3	106.3	109.6	111.0	111.0	111.6
32 Instruments	38	3.26	....	115.2	117.5	118.0	118.3	118.5	116.4	116.2	116.1	115.6	114.8	116.0	116.8	116.6
33 Miscellaneous manufactures	39	1.24	114.9	108.6	112.5	111.0	108.4	114.7	111.0	112.7	115.2	116.9	116.3	114.5	115.8	....
Utilities																
34 Electric	......	6.01	....	108.0	107.1	107.4	107.6	108.5	108.1	107.1	109.7	109.5	116.3	104.9	103.7	110.5
								Gross value (billions of 1982 dollars, annual rates)								
MAJOR MARKET																
35 Products, total	......	1734.82	....	1,890.3	1,894.0	1,894.8	1,894.4	1,869.0	1,883.7	1,894.3	1,878.3	1,896.9	1,905.5	1,860.7	1,903.5	1,922.5
36 Final		1350.87	....	1,479.3	1,485.5	1,485.3	1,485.6	1,459.6	1,475.3	1,486.2	1,465.6	1,482.8	1,492.5	1,444.9	1,487.6	1,501.6
37 Consumer goods		833.36	....	890.2	888.4	885.7	878.5	868.9	870.1	878.8	883.2	889.0	898.6	862.9	891.3	897.7
38 Equipment		517.51	....	589.1	597.1	599.6	607.1	590.8	605.3	607.5	582.4	593.8	594.0	582.0	596.3	604.0
39 Intermediate		383.95	....	411.0	408.5	409.5	408.8	409.3	408.4	408.1	412.7	414.1	413.0	415.8	415.9	420.8

1. These data also appear in the Board's G.12.3 (414) release. For address, see inside front cover.

A major revision of the industrial production index and the capacity utilization rates was released in July 1985. See "A Revision of the Index of Industrial Production" and accompanying tables that contain revised indexes (1977=100) through December 1984 in the *Federal Reserve Bulletin*, vol. 71 (July 1985), pp. 487–501. The revised indexes for January through June 1985 were shown in the September *Bulletin*.

Source: *Federal Reserve Bulletin*, Board of Governors of the Federal Reserve System.

U.S. BUDGET RECEIPTS AND OUTLAYS (millions of dollars)[1]

Millions of dollars

Source or type	Fiscal year 1988	Fiscal year 1989	Calendar year						
			1988		1989		1990		
			H1	H2	H1	H2	Jan.	Feb.	Mar.
RECEIPTS									
1 All sources	908,166	990,691ʳ	475,724	449,320ʳ	527,574	470,329ʳ	99,538ʳ	65,170	64,819
2 Individual income taxes, net	401,181	445,690	207,659	200,300	233,572	218,661	56,044	28,830	13,174
3 Withheld	341,435	361,386	169,300	179,600	174,230	193,296	34,172	32,852	31,323
4 Presidential Election Campaign Fund	33	32	28	4	28	3	0	4	9
5 Nonwithheld	132,199	154,839	101,614	29,880	121,563	33,303	22,389	960	5,455
6 Refunds	72,487	70,567	63,283	9,186	62,251	7,943	517	4,986	23,614
Corporation income taxes									
7 Gross receipts	109,683	117,015	58,002	56,409	61,585	52,269	4,277	2,678	14,477
8 Refunds	15,487	13,723	8,706	7,250	7,259	6,842	1,159	1,447	1,823
9 Social insurance taxes and contributions, net	334,335	359,416	181,058	157,603	200,127	162,574	32,863	29,055	32,961
10 Employment taxes and contributions[2]	305,093	332,859	164,412	144,983	184,569	152,407	31,767	26,473	32,376
11 Self-employment taxes and contributions[3]	17,691	18,405	14,839	3,032	16,371	1,947	1,213	1,500	1,213
12 Unemployment insurance	24,584	22,011	14,363	10,359	13,279	7,909	742	2,230	173
13 Other net receipts[4]	4,659	4,547	2,284	2,262	2,277	2,260	354	352	413
14 Excise taxes	35,540	34,386	16,440	19,299	16,814	16,844	2,624	2,260	2,814
15 Customs deposits	15,411	16,334	7,522	8,107	7,918	8,667	1,440	1,228	1,397
16 Estate and gift taxes	7,594	8,745	3,863	4,054	4,583	4,451	805	664	769
17 Miscellaneous receipts[5]	19,909	22,829ʳ	9,950	10,799ʳ	10,235	13,703ʳ	2,644ʳ	1,902	1,050
OUTLAYS									
18 All types	1,063,318	1,142,680ʳ	512,856	552,727ʳ	565,524	587,303ʳ	91,271ʳ	100,434ʳ	118,155
19 National defense	290,361	303,551	143,080	150,496	148,098	149,613	21,978	24,870	29,516
20 International affairs	10,471	9,596	7,150	2,636	6,605	5,981	1,248	1,144	1,568
21 General science, space, and technology	10,841	12,891	5,361	5,852	6,238	7,091	1,058	1,066	1,244
22 Energy	2,297	3,745	555	1,966	2,221	1,397	40	83	486
23 Natural resources and environment	14,625	16,084	6,776	9,072ʳ	7,022	9,183ʳ	1,129	1,034	1,200
24 Agriculture	17,210	16,948	7,872	6,911	9,619	4,132	1,113	949	1,875
25 Commerce and housing credit	18,828	27,810	5,951	19,836	4,129	22,200	−1,133ʳ	1,886ʳ	7,328
26 Transportation	27,272	27,623	12,700	14,922	13,035	14,982	2,409	2,097	2,103
27 Community and regional development	5,294	5,755	2,765	2,690	1,833	4,879	848	575	797
28 Education, training, employment, and social services	31,938	35,697	15,451	16,152	18,083	18,663	3,496	3,421	3,135
29 Health	44,490	48,391	22,643	23,360	24,078	25,339	4,663	4,459ʳ	4,809
30 Social security and medicare	297,828	317,506	135,322	149,017	162,195	162,322	28,228	28,291ʳ	29,032
31 Income security	129,332	136,765	65,555	64,978	70,937	67,950	12,010	13,609	16,069
32 Veterans benefits and services	29,406	30,066	13,241	15,797	14,891	14,864	1,086	2,608	3,857
33 Administration of justice	8,436	9,396	4,369ʳ	4,361ʳ	4,801	4,963	811	819	738
34 General government	9,518	8,940	4,337	5,137	3,858	4,753	972	484	984
35 General-purpose fiscal assistance	1,816	n.a.	448	0	0	n.a.	n.a.	n.a.	n.a.
36 Net interest[6]	151,748	169,314	76,098	78,317	86,009	87,927	14,281	15,924	15,853
37 Undistributed offsetting receipts[7]	−36,967	−37,212	−17,766	−18,771	−18,131	−18,935	−2,967	−2,884	−2,437

1. Functional details do not add to total outlays for calendar year data because revisions to monthly totals have not been distributed among functions. Fiscal year total for outlays does not correspond to calendar year data because revisions from the *Budget* have not been fully distributed across months.
2. Old-age, disability, and hospital insurance, and railroad retirement accounts.
3. Old-age, disability, and hospital insurance.
4. Federal employee retirement contributions and civil service retirement and disability fund.

5. Deposits of earnings by Federal Reserve Banks and other miscellaneous receipts.
6. Net interest function includes interest received by trust funds.
7. Consists of rents and royalties on the outer continental shelf and U.S. government contributions for employee retirement.

SOURCES. U.S. Department of the Treasury, *Monthly Treasury Statement of Receipts and Outlays of the U.S. Government,* and the U.S. Office of Management and Budget, *Budget of the U.S. Government, Fiscal Year 1990.*

Source: *Federal Reserve Bulletin,* Board of Governors of the Federal Reserve System.

FEDERAL DEBT SUBJECT TO STATUTORY LIMITATION

Billions of dollars

Item	1988				1989				1990
	Mar. 31	June 30	Sept. 30	Dec. 31	Mar. 31	June 30	Sept. 30	Dec. 31	Mar. 31
1 Federal debt outstanding	2,493.2	2,555.1	2,614.6	2,707.3	2,763.6	2,824.0	2,881.1	2,975.5	3,081.9
2 Public debt securities	2,487.6	2,547.7	2,602.2	2,684.4	2,740.9	2,799.9	2,857.4	2,953.0	3,052.0
3 Held by public	1,996.7	2,013.4	2,051.7	2,095.2	2,133.4	2,142.1	2,180.7	2,245.2	n.a.
4 Held by agencies	490.8	534.2	550.4	589.2	607.5	657.8	676.7	707.8	n.a.
5 Agency securities	5.6	7.4	12.4	22.9	22.7	24.0	23.7	22.5	n.a.
6 Held by public	5.1	7.0	12.2	22.6	22.3	23.6	23.5	22.4	n.a.
7 Held by agencies	.6	.5	.2	.3	.4	.5	.1	.1	n.a.
8 Debt subject to statutory limit	2,472.6	2,532.2	2,586.9	2,669.1	2,725.6	2,784.6	2,829.8	2,921.7	2,988.9
9 Public debt securities	2,472.1	2,532.1	2,586.7	2,668.9	2,725.5	2,784.3	2,829.5	2,921.4	2,988.6
10 Other debt[1]	.5	.1	.1	.2	.2	.2	.3	.3	.3
11 MEMO: Statutory debt limit	2,800.0	2,800.0	2,800.0	2,800.0	2,800.0	2,800.0	2,870.0	3,122.7	3,122.7

SOURCES. *Treasury Bulletin* and *Monthly Statement of the Public Debt of the United States.*

1. Includes guaranteed debt of Treasury and other federal agencies, specified participation certificates, notes to international lending organizations, and District of Columbia stadium bonds.

Source: *Economic Indicators*, Council of Economic Advisers.

Largest Companies

The 100 Largest U.S. Industrial Corporations (ranked by sales)

RANK 1989	1988	Company	SALES $ millions	% change from 1988	PROFITS $ millions	Rank	% change from 1988	ASSETS $ millions	Rank	STOCKHOLDER EQUITY $ millions	Rank
1	1	**GENERAL MOTORS** Detroit	126,974.3	4.9	4,224.3	1	(13.0)	173,297.1	1	34,982.5	2
2	2	**FORD MOTOR** Dearborn, Mich.	96,932.6	4.9	3,835.0	3	(27.6)	160,893.3	2	22,727.8	4
3	3	**EXXON** New York	86,656.0*	8.9	3,510.0	5	(33.3)	83,219.0	4	30,244.0	3
4	4	**INT'L BUSINESS MACHINES** Armonk, N.Y.	63,438.0	6.3	3,758.0	4	(35.3)	77,734.0	5	38,509.0	1
5	5	**GENERAL ELECTRIC** Fairfield, Conn.	55,264.0	11.8	3,939.0	2	16.3	128,344.0	3	20,890.0	5
6	6	**MOBIL** New York	50,976.0*	5.8	1,809.0	11	(13.3)	39,080.0	7	16,274.0	6
7	10	**PHILIP MORRIS** New York	39,069.0*	51.1	2,946.0	6	26.1	38,528.0	8	9,571.0	11
8	7	**CHRYSLER** Highland Park, Mich.	36,156.0	1.9	359.0	74	(65.8)	51,038.0	6	7,233.0	15
9	9	**E.I. DU PONT DE NEMOURS** Wilmington, Del.	35,209.0	8.3	2,480.0	8	13.2	34,715.0	10	15,798.0	8
10	8	**TEXACO** White Plains, N.Y.	32,416.0	(3.4)	2,413.0	9	85.0	25,636.0	15	9,180.0	12
11	11	**CHEVRON** San Francisco	29,443.0*	16.9	251.0	107	(85.8)	33,884.0	11	13,980.0	9
12	12	**AMOCO** Chicago	24,214.0*	14.5	1,610.0	13	(22.0)	30,430.0	12	13,684.0	10
13	13	**SHELL OIL** Houston[1]	21,703.0	3.0	1,405.0	15	13.4	27,599.0	14	16,049.0	7
14	15	**PROCTER & GAMBLE** Cincinnati[2]	21,689.0	12.2	1,206.0	17	18.2	16,351.0	24	6,215.0	19
15	19	**BOEING** Seattle	20,276.0	19.5	973.0	21	58.5	13,278.0	30	6,131.0	20
16	14	**OCCIDENTAL PETROLEUM** Los Angeles	20,068.0	3.4	285.0**	88	(5.6)	20,741.0	20	5,899.0	21
17	16	**UNITED TECHNOLOGIES** Hartford[3]	19,765.5	9.3	702.1	35	6.5	14,598.2	27	4,740.3	30
18	18	**EASTMAN KODAK** Rochester, N.Y.	18,398.0	8.0	529.0	45	(62.1)	23,652.0	17	6,642.0	17
19	23	**USX** Pittsburgh	17,755.0*	12.4	965.0	22	27.6	17,500.0	22	5,737.0	22
20	21	**DOW CHEMICAL** Midland, Mich.	17,730.0	6.3	2,487.0	7	3.7	22,166.0	19	7,957.0	14
21	22	**XEROX** Stamford, Conn.	17,635.0	7.3	704.0	34	81.4	30,088.0	13	5,035.0	28
22	17	**ATLANTIC RICHFIELD** Los Angeles	15,905.0	(9.8)	1,953.0	10	23.4	22,261.0	18	6,562.0	18
23	26	**PEPSICO** Purchase, N.Y.	15,419.6	18.5	901.4	26	18.3	15,126.7	26	3,891.1	40
24	20	**RJR NABISCO HOLDINGS** New York[4]	15,224.0¶	(10.2)	(1,149.0)	476	(182.5)	36,412.0	9	1,237.0	133
25	25	**MCDONNELL DOUGLAS** St. Louis	14,995.0	(0.5)	219.0	122	(37.4)	13,397.0	29	3,287.0	49
26	24	**TENNECO** Houston	14,439.0	(8.1)	584.0	42	(29.0)	17,381.0	23	3,277.0	50
27	30	**DIGITAL EQUIPMENT** Maynard, Mass.[2]	12,866.0	12.1	1,072.6	20	(17.8)	10,667.8	37	8,035.7	13
28	27	**WESTINGHOUSE ELECTRIC** Pittsburgh	12,844.0	2.8	922.0	25	12.1	20,314.0	21	4,384.0	33
29	28	**ROCKWELL INTERNATIONAL** El Segundo, Calif.[5]	12,633.1	5.7	734.9	33	(9.5)	8,938.8	46	3,977.6	38
30	31	**PHILLIPS PETROLEUM** Bartlesville, Okla.	12,492.0	10.5	219.0	123	(66.3)	11,256.0	34	2,132.0	75
31	29	**ALLIED-SIGNAL** Morristown, N.J.	12,021.0	0.9	528.0	47	14.0	10,132.0	38	3,412.0	47
32	34	**MINNESOTA MINING & MFG.** St. Paul	11,990.0	13.3	1,244.0	16	7.8	9,776.0	40	5,378.0	24
33	39	**HEWLETT-PACKARD** Palo Alto, Calif.[6,7]	11,899.0	21.0	829.0	29	1.6	10,075.0	39	5,446.0	23
34	36	**SARA LEE** Chicago[2]	11,738.3	12.6	410.5	66	26.3	6,522.7	67	1,914.9	87
35	42	**INTERNATIONAL PAPER** Purchase, N.Y.	11,378.0	19.4	864.0	27	14.6	11,582.0	31	5,147.0	26
36	44	**CONAGRA** Omaha[8]	11,340.4	19.7	197.9	133	27.9	4,278.2	103	949.5	161
37	40	**ALUMINUM CO. OF AMERICA** Pittsburgh	11,161.5	13.9	944.9	23	9.7	11,540.6	32	5,266.9	25
38	35	**CATERPILLAR** Peoria, Ill.	11,126.0	6.6	497.0	50	(19.3)	10,926.0	35	4,474.0	32
39	32	**GOODYEAR TIRE & RUBBER** Akron	11,044.7	2.2	206.8	129	(40.9)	8,460.3	53	2,143.8	74
40	47	**UNOCAL** Los Angeles	10,417.0*	17.7	260.0	101	(45.8)	9,257.0	43	2,300.0	71
41	43	**GEORGIA-PACIFIC** Atlanta	10,171.0	7.0	661.0	38	41.5	7,056.0	61	2,717.0	58
42	37	**WEYERHAEUSER** Tacoma	10,105.6	1.0	341.1	75	(39.6)	15,976.0	25	4,147.6	37
43	38	**UNISYS** Blue Bell, Pa.	10,096.9	2.0	(639.3)	474	(193.9)	10,751.0	36	3,881.8	41
44	41	**GENERAL DYNAMICS** St. Louis	10,053.2	5.3	293.1	84	(22.7)	6,548.6	66	2,125.6	76
45	33	**LOCKHEED** Calabasas, Calif.	9,932.0	(6.9)	2.0	416	(99.7)	6,792.0	63	2,062.0	78
46	48	**SUN** Radnor, Pa.	9,927.0*	15.3	98.0	211	1,300.0	8,699.0	48	3,254.0	51
47	45	**JOHNSON & JOHNSON** New Brunswick, N.J.	9,844.0	9.4	1,082.0	19	11.1	7,919.0	56	4,148.0	36
48	52	**MOTOROLA** Schaumburg, Ill.	9,620.0	16.6	498.0	49	11.9	7,686.0	57	3,803.0	42
49	46	**ANHEUSER-BUSCH** St. Louis	9,481.3*	6.2	767.2	30	7.2	9,025.7	45	3,099.9	52
50	73	**BRISTOL-MYERS SQUIBB** New York[9]	9,422.0	57.8	747.0	32	(9.9)	8,497.0	52	5,084.0	27

The definitions and concepts underlying the figures in this directory are explained on page 232.

MARKET VALUE 3/9/90 $ millions	Rank	PROFITS AS A PERCENT OF SALES %	Rank	ASSETS %	Rank	STOCK-HOLDERS' EQUITY %	Rank	EARNINGS PER SHARE 1989/$	% change from 1988	1979-89 annual growth rate %	Rank	TOTAL RETURN TO INVESTORS 1989 %	Rank	1979-89 annual average %	Rank	INDUSTRY TABLE NUMBER	RANK 1989
27,786.7	6	3.3	317	2.4	370	12.1	277	6.33	(11.7)	2.3	230	8.2	254	12.2	247	17	1
21,803.7	13	4.0	284	2.4	372	16.9	186	8.22	(25.0)	14.3	66	(8.3)	326	25.4	61	17	2
57,968.7	2	4.1	277	4.2	303	11.6	287	2.74	(30.6)	1.2	245	19.5	202	22.0	99	18	3
61,205.5	1	5.9	182	4.8	272	9.8	317	6.47	(34.0)	2.3	231	(19.4)	369	8.2	289	6	4
56,183.5	3	7.1	136	3.1	348	18.9	142	4.36	16.3	10.9	112	48.8	78	22.3	92	7	5
25,123.7	10	3.5	302	4.6	286	11.1	294	4.40	(13.2)	(0.7)	263	44.3	100	15.6	194	18	6
34,605.3	4	7.5	120	7.6	172	30.8	41	3.18	26.8	20.1	23	69.4	29	30.1	28	8	7
4,063.0	79	1.0	399	0.7	409	5.0	375	1.55	(66.7)	–		(22.7)	379	22.6	88	17	8
26,728.0	9	7.0	142	7.1	194	15.7	207	3.53	16.2	5.1	191	44.8	95	17.7	154	5	9
15,665.8	21	7.4	124	9.4	107	26.3	53	9.12	70.5	3.5	222	42.4	105	17.1	164	18	10
24,261.1	12	0.9	404	0.7	408	1.8	394	0.73	(85.9)	(17.9)	322	55.5	51	15.6	195	18	11
27,750.4	7	6.6	155	5.3	255	11.8	283	3.12	(22.0)	2.0	234	51.8	63	16.7	175	18	12
N.A.		6.5	166	5.1	264	8.8	334	N.A.	–	–		–		–		18	13
21,018.3	14	5.6	197	7.4	187	19.4	138	7.12	19.5	7.4	160	66.4	33	19.0	134	23	14
15,624.3	22	4.8	234	7.3	191	15.9	205	4.23	57.8	6.1	178	50.2	74	18.7	141	1	15
7,431.9	39	1.4	387	1.4	399	4.8	379	1.03**	(14.9)	(17.8)	321	27.9	167	10.3	273	8	16
6,599.9	45	3.6	300	4.8	276	14.8	229	5.34	5.7	5.1	193	36.1	132	14.1	219	1	17
12,893.9	25	2.9	337	2.2	376	8.0	347	1.63	(62.2)	(5.1)	284	(4.9)	313	11.8	252	22	18
9,232.9	31	5.4	202	5.5	249	16.8	187	3.53	34.7	–		27.2	172	13.2	232	18	19
18,009.5	18	14.0	26	11.2	62	31.3	38	9.20	8.2	12.3	89	26.3	175	18.3	148	5	20
5,041.8	66	4.0	280	2.3	374	12.9§	263	6.56	87.4	(0.2)	258	3.0	280	5.2	311	22	21
18,861.0	15	12.3	31	8.8	129	29.8	43	11.26	28.2	9.0	135	44.5	98	17.0	170	18	22
15,459.4	23	5.8	185	6.0	233	23.2	81	3.40	17.2	13.6	73	65.1	36	26.7	52	3	23
N.A.		(7.5)	464	(3.2)	444	(92.9)	441	N.A.	–	–		–		–		8	24
2,220.1	130	1.5	385	1.6	393	6.7	363	5.72	(37.3)	1.2	244	(15.7)	353	8.5	287	1	25
8,516.8	34	4.0	279	3.4	339	17.3§	179	4.46	(18.6)	(1.7)	267	34.4	140	12.5	244	11	26
9,337.6	30	8.3	101	10.1	82	13.3	252	8.45	(14.6)	15.2	57	(16.6)	360	9.1	283	6	27
10,703.5	26	7.2	133	4.5	292	21.0	102	6.31	11.5	–		45.6	88	27.4	48	7	28
5,369.4	59	5.8	189	8.2	145	18.5	155	2.87	(5.6)	12.1	92	13.0	228	18.8	140	1	29
6,249.8	50	1.8	375	1.9	383	10.3	307	0.90	(66.9)	(7.3)	295	35.1	135	11.5	256	18	30
5,220.1	62	4.4	256	5.2	260	15.5	212	3.55	14.5	38.8	2	12.8	231	6.7	301	1	31
18,119.3	17	10.4	60	12.7	44	23.1	82	5.60	10.0	7.2	165	33.0	146	17.0	168	22	32
10,670.3	27	7.0	144	8.2	144	15.2	221	3.52	4.8	15.2	58	(10.7)	342	12.9	234	6	33
6,598.4	46	3.5	304	6.3	225	21.4	96	3.50	23.7	14.5	65	64.2	37	32.1	20	8	34
5,557.9	56	7.6	118	7.5	181	16.8	188	7.72	17.5	3.5	221	25.6	179	16.8	172	9	35
3,142.6	97	1.7	376	4.6	287	20.7§	108	2.45	26.3	15.3	56	50.8	72	35.3	12	8	36
5,736.9	54	8.5	95	8.2	146	17.9	164	10.67	9.5	4.1	215	39.6	118	15.0	205	15	37
6,288.0	49	4.5	250	4.5	291	11.1	295	4.90	(19.3)	(1.5)	265	(7.2)	321	3.5	320	11	38
2,052.1	137	1.9	369	2.4	369	9.6	319	3.58	(41.4)	5.9	181	(11.8)	346	18.9	135	21	39
6,962.3	43	2.5	350	2.8	353	11.3	291	1.11	(46.1)	(2.6)	273	60.9	42	13.9	221	18	40
4,149.0	76	6.5	164	9.4	109	24.3	69	7.42	55.9	9.0	134	35.5	134	10.1	275	9	41
5,323.6	60	3.4	314	2.1	378	8.2	337	1.56	(41.8)	(5.3)	285	14.6	221	6.9	297	9	42
2,335.8	122	(6.3)	462	(5.9)	463	(16.5)	426	(4.71)	(231.6)	–		(45.1)	407	(1.1)	336	6	43
1,570.4	170	2.9	335	4.5	295	13.8	245	7.01	(22.4)	7.4	157	(9.9)	338	6.0	306	1	44
2,251.2	126	0.0	422	0.0	422	0.1	405	0.03	(99.7)	(30.8)	332	(1.9)	302	14.7	211	18	45
3,974.3	80	1.0	400	1.1	402	3.0	390	0.92	1,433.3	(16.9)	320	33.1	145	13.8	223	18	46
18,528.7	16	11.0	51	13.7	21	26.1	56	3.25	13.6	13.0	84	42.6	104	19.2	130	19	47
8,303.8	36	5.2	213	6.5	215	13.1	257	3.83	11.7	8.8	141	41.2	113	15.2	203	7	48
10,011.1	28	8.1	107	8.5	139	24.7	65	2.68	9.4	17.6	38	24.8	185	29.4	31	3	49
28,431.9	5	7.9	111	8.8	126	14.7	232	1.43	(50.3)	5.0	197	28.9	161	23.9	74	19	50

(continued)

The 100 Largest U.S. Industrial Corporations (ranked by sales) (concluded)

RANK 1989	1988		SALES $ millions	% change from 1988	PROFITS $ millions	Rank	% change from 1988	ASSETS $ millions	Rank	STOCKHOLDERS EQUITY $ millions	Rank
51	49	COCA-COLA Atlanta	9,170.8	10.0	1,723.8	12	65.0	8,282.5	55	3,485.5	46
52	53	RAYTHEON Lexington, Mass.	8,796.1	7.4	528.8	46	8.0	5,338.3	84	2,426.1	66
53	50	UNION CARBIDE Danbury, Conn.	8,744.0	5.0	573.0	43	(13.4)	8,546.0	50	2,383.0	67
54	54	COASTAL Houston	8,685.6	6.1	170.1	152	8.1	8,773.3	47	1,793.0	94
55	51	MONSANTO St. Louis	8,681.0	4.7	679.0	37	14.9	8,604.0	49	3,941.0	39
56	63	UNILEVER U.S. New York[10],[11]	8,113.8	16.6	139.0	170	4.4	9,379.0	42	2,145.2	73
57	65	ARCHER DANIELS MIDLAND Decatur, Ill.[2]	8,056.5	18.5	424.7	60	20.3	4,728.3	98	3,033.5	54
58	55	ASHLAND OIL Russell, Ky.[5]	8,016.6*	3.4	86.2	228	(61.5)	4,455.7	101	1,140.5	140
59	102	TIME WARNER New York[12]	7,642.0	69.6	(256.0)	472	(188.5)	24,791.0	16	6,756.0	16
60	59	BORDEN New York	7,593.4	4.8	(60.6)	453	(119.4)	4,824.9	94	1,645.4	104
61	61	TEXTRON Providence	7,440.1	4.6	259.2	102	10.6	13,790.4	28	2,547.1	63
62	62	TRW Cleveland	7,408.0	6.1	263.0	99	0.8	5,259.0	85	1,749.0	98
63	64	BAXTER INTERNATIONAL Deerfield, Ill.	7,399.0	7.8	446.0	57	14.9	8,503.0	51	4,246.0	34
64	58	AMERICAN BRANDS Old Greenwich, Conn.	7,264.7*	(2.8)	630.8	39	8.8	11,394.2	33	2,965.9	55
65	60	HONEYWELL Minneapolis	7,241.6¶	1.3	604.1	40	—	5,258.2	86	1,918.2	86
66	87	DEERE Moline, Ill.[6]	7,221.0	34.6	380.2	70	20.5	9,145.4	44	2,780.3	56
67	66	EMERSON ELECTRIC St. Louis[5]	7,071.3	6.3	588.0	41	11.2	5,408.0	82	3,073.4	53
68	81	AMERICAN HOME PRODUCTS New York[13]	6,747.0	22.7	1,102.2	18	18.2	5,681.5	75	1,970.0	84
69	71	RALSTON PURINA St. Louis[5]	6,711.6	8.7	422.5	62	8.9	4,381.7	102	831.7	179
70	74	MERCK Rahway, N.J.	6,698.4	12.8	1,495.4	14	23.9	6,756.7	64	3,520.6	45
71	68	TEXAS INSTRUMENTS Dallas	6,592.2	4.7	291.7	86	(20.4)	4,804.4	95	2,484.9	64
72	56	LTV Dallas	6,362.1	(15.5)	264.9	98	—	6,336.2	68	(4,919.8)	489
73	104	WHIRLPOOL Benton Harbor, Mich.	6,288.6	42.2	187.2	141	98.9	5,353.5	83	1,421.3	119
74	84	NORTH AMERICAN PHILIPS New York[14]	6,202.6	14.4	(178.0)	465	(325.0)	3,879.1	112	1,371.1	123
75	80	REYNOLDS METALS Richmond	6,201.0	11.4	532.7	44	10.5	5,555.6	81	2,684.1	60
76	69	W.R. GRACE New York	6,114.6	(1.4)	253.2	105	8.4	5,619.1	78	1,722.9	100
77	78	HOECHST CELANESE Bridgewater, N.J.[15]	6,016.0	5.9	267.0	96	6.8	6,062.0	71	3,299.0	48
78	72	NCR Dayton	5,956.0	(0.6)	412.0	65	(6.2)	4,500.0	100	1,985.0	83
79	67	HANSON INDUSTRIES NA Iselin, N.J.[5],[16]	5,933.3	(8.6)	760.8	31	153.3	5,811.1	73	2,462.0	65
80	86	PFIZER New York	5,903.7	9.6	681.1	36	(13.9)	8,324.8	54	4,535.8	31
81	92	JAMES RIVER CORP. OF VIRGINIA Richmond[17]	5,901.6	15.8	255.1	104	22.0	5,558.1	80	2,345.8	68
82	89	H.J. HEINZ Pittsburgh[17]	5,831.9	11.2	440.2	58	14.0	4,001.8	108	1,777.2	96
83	79	PPG INDUSTRIES Pittsburgh	5,825.2	3.7	465.2	54	(0.5)	5,645.4	76	2,282.3	72
84	77	MARTIN MARIETTA Bethesda, Md.	5,814.3	1.5	306.9	81	(14.5)	3,504.4	128	1,355.0	124
85	76	GENERAL MILLS Minneapolis[8]	5,798.0	0.4	414.3	63	46.3	2,888.1	152	731.9	200
86	85	KIMBERLY-CLARK Dallas	5,777.1	7.1	423.8	61	11.9	4,923.0	91	2,085.8	77
87	88	QUAKER OATS Chicago[2]	5,724.3	7.4	203.0	131	(20.6)	3,221.9	139	1,137.1	141
88	95	CAMPBELL SOUP Camden, N.J.[18]	5,710.4	17.3	13.1	398	(95.2)	3,932.1	111	1,778.3	95
89	110	AMERADA HESS New York	5,589.0	32.9	476.3	51	283.5	6,867.4	62	2,560.6	61
90	94	ABBOTT LABORATORIES Abbott Park, Ill.	5,453.5	10.5	859.8	28	14.3	4,851.6	93	2,726.4	57
91	99	BAYER USA Pittsburgh[19]	5,424.7	15.0	153.9	161	23.7	4,562.1	99	1,907.5	88
92	93	BASF Parsippany, N.J.[20]	5,421.5	8.4	90.0‡	220	(39.7)	3,594.3	123	1,268.5	130
93	•	LYONDELL PETROCHEMICAL Houston	5,374.0	14.4	374.0	72	(31.1)	1,267.0	259	9.0	460
94	122	STONE CONTAINER Chicago	5,360.7	43.2	285.8	87	(16.4)	6,253.7	70	1,347.6	126
95	82	BETHLEHEM STEEL Bethlehem, Pa.	5,305.9	(3.3)	245.7	111	(39.0)	4,793.3	96	2,002.9	81
96	114	APPLE COMPUTER Cupertino, Calif.[5]	5,284.0	29.8	454.0	55	13.4	2,743.9	155	1,485.7	112
97	91	CHAMPION INTERNATIONAL Stamford, Conn.	5,254.2	2.5	432.4	59	(5.3)	7,530.8	59	3,588.5	44
98	75	NORTHROP Los Angeles	5,200.0	(10.3)	(80.5)	458	(177.3)	3,200.0	140	875.1	173
99	90	DANA Toledo	5,156.7	(0.3)	132.1	177	(18.6)	5,225.4	88	1,019.9	154
100	96	LITTON INDUSTRIES Beverly Hills[18]	5,130.3	5.5	178.3	143	6.7	5,257.7	87	1,267.7	131

- • Indicates that a company was not among the 500 in 1988.
- * Does not include excise tax; see the explanation of "sales" page 232.
- ** Reflects an extraordinary credit of at least 10%; see the explanations of "profits" and "earnings per share" page 232.
- N.A. Not available.
- ‡ Reflects an extraordinary charge of at least 10%; see the explanations of "profits" and "earnings per share" page 232.
- ¶ Includes sales from discontinued operations of at least 10%; see the explanation of "sales" page 232.
- § Dividends paid or mandatory redeemable preferred stock subtracted from profits.
- [1] Owned by Royal Dutch/Shell Group (1988 International (500 rank: 1).
- [2] Figures are for fiscal year ended June 30, 1989.
- [3] Figures include Sheller-Globe (1988 rank: 368), acquired November 9, 1989.
- [4] Name changed from RJR Nabisco.
- [5] Figures are for fiscal year ended September 30, 1989.
- [6] Figures are for fiscal year ended October 31, 1989.
- [7] Figures include Apollo Computer (1988 rank: 423), acquired May 18, 1989.

MARKET VALUE 3/9/90 $ millions	Rank	PROFITS AS A PERCENT OF — SALES %	Rank	ASSETS %	Rank	STOCK-HOLDERS' EQUITY %	Rank	EARNINGS PER SHARE 1989/$	% change from 1988	1979-89 annual growth rate %	Rank	TOTAL RETURN TO INVESTORS 1989 %	Rank	1979-89 annual average %	Rank	INDUSTRY TABLE NUMBER	RANK 1989
24,265.1	11	18.8	7	20.8	10	49.5	18	4.92	72.6	15.8	51	76.9	21	26.8	51	3	51
4,068.4	78	6.0	180	5.5	84	11.8	43	8.01	5.0	9.8	123	6.7	283	10.8	270	7	52
3,132.4	98	6.6	159	6.7	206	24.0	75	4.07	(16.6)	3.7	217	(6.0)	315	15.5	198	5	53
3,343.4	91	2.0	365	1.9	384	9.5§	322	1.81	0.6	–		46.4	84	13.9	222	18	54
7,244.9	41	7.8	112	7.9	163	17.2	182	10.03	21.3	8.2	148	45.5	90	19.8	121	5	55
N.A.		1.7	378	1.5	397	6.5	364	N.A.	–	–		–		–		23	56
5,711.5	55	5.3	210	9.0	119	14.0	241	2.27	22.2	18.3	32	75.2	22	16.1	185	8	57
2,049.2	139	1.1	398	1.9	385	7.6	355	1.55	(61.3)	(14.9)	315	22.4	193	12.7	238	18	58
5,897.8	53	(3.3)	453	(1.0)	428	(3.8)	414	(4.34)	(186.6)	–		13.6	224	22.3	93	20	59
4,660.4	73	(0.8)	428	(1.3)	432	(3.7)	413	(0.41)	(119.4)	–		19.3	203	29.6	30	8	60
2,223.7	129	3.5	305	1.9	388	10.2	310	2.91	9.0	2.6	228	7.8	258	12.0	249	1	61
3,007.8	101	3.6	301	5.0	267	15.0	223	4.31	0.5	3.6	219	23.2	190	14.3	216	7	62
6,212.9	51	6.0	179	5.2	258	10.5	306	1.50	14.5	5.9	182	45.7	87	9.7	277	22	63
6,165.1	52	8.7	87	5.5	248	20.9§	104	6.51	11.5	8.1	150	12.3	234	22.7	86	25	64
3,410.0	90	8.3	100	11.5	58	31.5	37	14.18	–	9.1	133	49.6	76	11.2	260	7	65
5,435.6	58	5.3	211	4.2	306	13.7	247	5.06	12.9	(0.1)	257	31.3	156	8.3	288	11	66
9,007.2	33	8.3	102	10.9	69	19.1	141	2.63	13.9	8.9	140	32.7	147	17.0	169	7	67
15,951.3	20	16.3	14	19.4	11	55.9	14	7.07	10.8	10.9	111	34.5	139	20.4	117	19	68
5,097.3	64	6.3	172	9.6	99	49.2§	19	6.44	14.4	18.4	31	3.4	278	26.6	54	8	69
27,085.4	8	22.3	5	22.1	7	42.5	22	3.78	23.9	16.2	49	37.5	127	23.9	73	19	70
3,015.6	100	4.4	253	6.1	229	11.7	284	3.04	(24.9)	1.9	238	(10.8)	344	3.9	316	7	71
162.9	389	4.2	270	4.2	305	–		2.06	–	(10.2)	301	(50.0)	411	(17.0)	353	15	72
2,299.4	124	3.0	333	3.5	331	13.2	255	2.70	98.5	5.8	185	38.4	124	18.7	143	7	73
N.A.		(2.9)	448	(4.6)	456	(13.0)	424	N.A.	–	–		N.A.		–		7	74
3,233.5	95	8.6	91	9.6	100	19.8	126	9.20	2.1	7.1	167	3.0	281	17.3	160	15	75
2,542.3	119	4.1	272	4.5	293	7.7§	351	2.97	8.0	1.7	239	31.6	152	11.0	267	5	76
N.A.		4.4	252	4.4	298	8.1	342	N.A.	–	–		N.A.		–		5	77
4,853.5	69	6.9	147	9.2	113	20.8	107	5.38	0.9	9.4	130	12.7	232	16.1	186	6	78
N.A.		12.8	30	13.1	36	30.9	40	N.A.	–	–		N.A.		–		5	79
9,960.1	29	11.5	41	8.2	148	15.0	224	4.04	(14.0)	9.5	125	24.2	188	17.2	163	19	80
1,917.5	146	4.3	259	4.6	289	10.9§	300	2.87	21.6	11.5	101	0.9	292	19.5	125	9	81
7,806.0	37	7.5	119	11.0	67	24.8	64	3.34	14.8	15.4	55	54.0	57	31.1	23	8	82
4,402.2	75	8.0	110	8.2	142	20.4	115	4.18	(1.9)	9.4	126	1.9	285	23.7	75	5	83
2,185.0	131	5.3	209	8.8	131	22.7	83	5.82	(13.8)	10.7	114	12.4	233	16.3	179	1	84
5,489.8	57	7.1	135	14.3	25	56.6	13	5.06	55.7	13.2	81	44.0	101	25.4	60	8	85
5,223.6	61	7.3	128	8.6	133	20.3	116	5.26	11.7	4.6	207	31.0	157	27.5	46	9	86
3,613.3	87	3.5	303	6.3	224	17.9	167	2.56	(20.0)	8.0	152	11.0	241	27.5	45	8	87
6,339.1	48	0.2	417	0.3	416	0.7	402	0.10	(95.3)	(20.5)	324	90.2	12	27.9	42	8	88
3,914.7	82	8.5	93	6.9	199	18.6	149	5.87	288.7	(0.3)	260	57.3	45	10.5	271	18	89
14,297.6	24	15.8	16	17.7	14	31.5	36	3.85	15.6	17.9	35	44.6	97	23.6	77	19	90
N.A.		2.8	338	3.4	337	8.1	343	N.A.	–	–		N.A.		–		5	91
N.A.		1.7	382	2.5	368	7.1	357	N.A.	–	–		N.A.		–		5	92
1,430.0	182	7.0	145	29.5	5	4,155.6	1	4.67	–	–		N.A.		–		5	93
1,280.4	195	5.3	205	4.6	290	21.2	99	4.76	(16.3)	24.4	10	(23.4)	381	21.9	102	9	94
1,382.6	186	4.6	241	5.1	263	12.3	274	2.93	(44.9)	(7.4)	296	(19.6)	370	1.6	327	15	95
4,775.2	71	8.6	90	16.5	17	30.6	42	3.53	14.6	–		(11.5)	345			6	96
2,637.7	114	8.2	104	5.7	241	12.0§	278	4.56	(5.0)	(0.3)	259	3.0	282	6.4	305	9	97
805.6	258	(1.5)	435	(2.5)	441	(9.2)	421	(1.71)	(177.0)	–		(33.6)	397	5.9	307	1	98
1,340.4	189	2.6	348	2.5	366	13.0	261	3.24	(18.8)	(0.3)	261	(7.2)	320	12.5	242	17	99
1,751.4	158	3.5	306	3.4	334	14.1	239	7.05	11.4	4.8	202	7.5	261	8.7	285	7	100

[8] Figures are for fiscal year ended May 31, 1989.
[9] Figures include Squibb (1988 rank: 166), acquired October 4, 1989.
[10] Figures include Fabergé (1988 rank: 453), acquired August 3, 1989.
[11] Owned by Unilever (1988 International 500 rank: 11).
[12] Figures include Warner Communications (1988 rank: 109), acquired July 24, 1989.
[13] Figures include A.H. Robins (1988 rank: 346), acquired December 15, 1989.
[14] Owned by Philips' Gloeilampenfabrieken (1988 International 500 rank: 13).
[15] Owned by Hoechst (1988 International 500 rank: 20).
[16] Owned by Hanson (1988 International 500 rank: 62).
[17] Figures are for fiscal year ended April 30, 1989.
[18] Figures are for fiscal year ended July 31, 1989.
[19] Owned by Bayer (1988 International 500 rank: 22).
[20] Owned by BASF (1988 International 500 rank: 19).

Source: Reprinted by permission from the 1990 FORTUNE Directory.

DEFINITIONS AND EXPLANATIONS

Sales All companies on the list must have derived more than 50% of their sales from manufacturing and/or mining. Sales of consolidated subsidiaries are included. Sales from discontinued operations are included when these figures are published. When the sales are at least 10% higher for this reason, there is a symbol (¶) next to the sales figure. All figures are for the year ending December 31, 1989, unless otherwise noted. Sales figures do not include excise taxes collected by the manufacturer, and so the figures for some corporations—most of which sell gasoline, liquor, or tobacco—may be lower than those published by the corporations themselves. If they are at least 5% lower for this reason, there is an asterisk (*) next to the sales figures.

Profits are shown after taxes and after extraordinary credits or charges if any are shown on the income statement. A double asterisk (**) signifies an extraordinary credit reflecting at least 10% of the profits shown, a double dagger (‡) an extraordinary charge of at least 10%. Figures in parentheses indicate a loss. Profit declines over 100% reflect swings from 1988 profits to 1989 losses. Cooperatives provide only "net margin" figures, which are not comparable with the profits figures in these listings, and therefore N.A. is shown in that column.

Assets are those shown at the company's fiscal year-end.

Stockholders' Equity is the sum of capital stock, surplus, and retained earnings at the company's year-end. Redeemable preferred stock is excluded if its redemption is either mandatory or outside the control of the company, except in the case of cooperatives. For purposes of calculating "net income as percent of stockholders' equity," any dividends paid on redeemable preferred stock, if that stock's redemption is either mandatory or outside the control of the company, have been subtracted from the net income figure.

Market Value The figure shown was arrived at by multiplying the number of common shares outstanding (at the latest date available) by the price per common share as of March 9, 1990.

Earnings per Share For all companies, the figures shown are the primary earnings per share that appear on the company's income statement. Per-share earnings for 1988 and 1979 are adjusted for stock splits and stock dividends. They are not restated for mergers, acquisitions, or accounting changes made after 1979. A double asterisk (**) signifies an extraordinary credit reflecting at least 10 percent of the net income shown, a double dagger (‡) an extraordinary charge of at least 10 percent. Results are listed as not available (N.A.) where the companies are cooperatives, joint ventures, or wholly owned subsidiaries of other companies, or if the figures were not published in 1979. The growth rate is the average annual growth, compounded.

Total Return to Investors includes both price appreciation and dividend yield, to an investor in the company's stock. The figures shown assume sales at the end of 1989 of stock owned at the end of 1979 and 1988. It has been assumed that any proceeds from cash dividends, the sale of rights and warrant offerings, and stock received in spin-offs were reinvested at the end of the year in which they were paid. Returns are adjusted for stock splits, stock dividends, recapitalizations, and corporate reorganizations as they occur; however, no effort has been made to reflect the cost of brokerage commissions or of taxes. Results are listed as not available (N.A.) if shares are not publicly traded or traded on only a limited basis. If companies have more than one class of shares outstanding, only the more widely held and actively traded has been considered.

Total-return percentages shown are the returns received by the hypothetical investor described above. The ten-year figures are annual averages, compounded.

Industry Tables See *Fortune,* April 23, 1990 page 371 et. seq.

The World's 100 Biggest Industrial Corporations (ranked by sales)*

1989			SALES $ Millions	PROFITS $ Millions	PROFITS Rank	ASSETS $ Millions	ASSETS Rank	STOCK-HOLDERS' EQUITY $ Millions	EQUITY Rank	EMPLOYEES Number	EMPLOYEES Rank	INDUSTRY TABLE NUMBER
1	GENERAL MOTORS	U.S.	126,974.3	4,224.3	2	173,297.1	1	34,982.5	3	775,100	1	17
2	FORD MOTOR	U.S.	96,932.6	3,835.0	4	160,893.3	2	22,727.8	7	366,641	6	17
3	EXXON	U.S.	86,656.0	3,510.0	7	83,219.0	5	30,244.0	4	104,000	62	18
4	ROYAL DUTCH/SHELL GROUP	BRITAIN/NETHERLANDS	85,527.9	6,482.7	1	91,011.0	4	48,307.5	1	135,000	39	18
5	INT'L BUSINESS MACHINES	U.S.	63,438.0	3,758.0	5	77,734.0	6	38,509.0	2	383,220	4	6
6	TOYOTA MOTOR[1]	JAPAN	60,443.6	2,631.1	12	49,672.8	10	25,761.0	5	91,790	70	17
7	GENERAL ELECTRIC	U.S.	55,264.0	3,939.0	3	128,344.0	3	20,890.0	9	292,000	11	7
8	MOBIL	U.S.	50,976.0	1,809.0	20	39,080.0	15	16,274.0	12	67,900	102	18
9	HITACHI[2]	JAPAN	50,894.0	1,446.7	33	52,253.2	7	17,184.3	11	274,508	13	7
10	BRITISH PETROLEUM	BRITAIN	49,484.4	3,498.8**	8	51,042.4	8	17,412.4	10	119,850	51	18
11	IRI	ITALY	49,077.2	1,177.7	38	N.A.		N.A.		416,200	3	15
12	MATSUSHITA ELECTRIC INDUSTRIAL[2]	JAPAN	43,086.0	1,664.0	26	48,217.9	11	21,590.1	8	193,088	20	7
13	DAIMLER-BENZ	W. GERMANY	40,616.0	3,584.6	6	37,133.5	17	9,710.6	22	368,226	5	17
14	PHILIP MORRIS	U.S.	39,069.0	2,946.0	9	38,528.0	16	9,571.0	23	157,000	31	8
15	FIAT	ITALY	36,740.8	2,410.8	16	46,355.2	12	12,597.5	17	286,294	12	17
16	CHRYSLER	U.S.	36,156.0	359.0	169	51,038.0	9	7,233.0	39	121,947	50	17
17	NISSAN MOTOR[2]	JAPAN	36,078.4	889.7	64	35,713.4	19	12,422.3	18	117,330	52	17
18	UNILEVER	BRITAIN/NETHERLANDS	35,284.4	1,729.7	24	20,804.4	47	4,441.5	88	300,000	10	8
19	E.I. DU PONT DE NEMOURS	U.S.	35,209.0	2,480.0	14	34,715.0	20	15,798.0	13	145,787	35	5
20	SAMSUNG	SOUTH KOREA	35,189.1	515.1	119	28,415.6	32	3,561.8	120	176,947	22	7
21	VOLKSWAGEN	W. GERMANY	34,746.4	523.2	116	33,661.7	23	6,810.2	41	250,616	15	17
22	SIEMENS[3]	W. GERMANY	32,659.6	786.8	71	34,390.5	21	9,531.9	24	365,000	7	7
23	TEXACO	U.S.	32,416.0	2,413.0	15	25,636.0	34	9,180.0	25	37,067	210	18
24	TOSHIBA[2]	JAPAN	29,469.3	930.8	58	31,676.8	25	6,630.7	49	125,000	46	7
25	CHEVRON	U.S.	29,443.0	251.0	235	33,884.0	22	13,980.0	15	54,826	134	18
26	NESTLÉ	SWITZERLAND	29,364.8[4]	1,474.5	31	22,976.0	41	8,565.2	28	196,940	19	8
27	RENAULT[5]	FRANCE	27,456.9	1,457.3	32	21,143.1	46	3,890.9	106	174,573	24	17
28	ENI	ITALY	27,119.3	1,125.9	40	41,479.1	14	10,363.1	21	82,748	81	18
29	PHILIPS' GLOEILAMPENFABRIEKEN	NETHERLANDS	26,992.5	648.1**	93	28,807.4	31	8,848.8	27	304,800	9	7
30	HONDA MOTOR[2]	JAPAN	26,483.4	758.5	74	17,206.1	63	6,789.6	42	71,200	97	17
31	BASF	W. GERMANY	25,317.0[4]	1,071.3	47	20,791.1	48	8,190.1	30	136,900	38	5
32	NEC[2]	JAPAN	24,594.8	502.6**	123	25,204.6	35	5,192.1	69	104,022	60	7
33	HOECHST	W. GERMANY	24,403.0	1,025.6	49	19,737.8	54	6,678.9	46	169,295	26	5
34	AMOCO	U.S.	24,214.0	1,610.0	28	30,430.0	28	13,684.0	16	53,648	138	18
35	PEUGEOT	FRANCE	24,090.5	1,616.1	27	18,584.2	56	6,673.0	47	159,100	30	17
36	BAT INDUSTRIES	BRITAIN	23,528.9	2,123.2	17	18,655.5	55	7,560.7	36	311,917	8	25
37	ELF AQUITAINE[5]	FRANCE	23,501.4	1,132.4	39	33,261.9	24	10,885.0	19	78,179	89	18
38	BAYER	W. GERMANY	23,021.2[4]	1,107.5	42	21,388.6	45	9,154.2	26	170,200	25	5
39	CGE (CIE GÉNÉRALE D'ÉLECTRICITÉ)	FRANCE	22,575.0	774.5	72	31,018.2	27	4,723.6	81	210,300	16	7
40	IMPERIAL CHEMICAL INDUSTRIES	BRITAIN	21,889.4	1,733.0**	23	18,197.0	57	8,095.1	31	133,800	41	5
41	PROCTER & GAMBLE[1]	U.S.	21,689.0	1,206.0	36	16,351.0	68	6,215.0	54	79,300	87	23
42	MITSUBISHI ELECTRIC[2]	JAPAN	21,213.3	415.0	146	20,380.6	50	4,812.8	79	85,723	78	7
43	ASEA BROWN BOVERI	SWITZERLAND	21,209.0	589.0	102	24,156.0	38	3,907.0	104	189,493	21	11
44	NIPPON STEEL[2]	JAPAN	20,767.0	607.9	98	26,143.7	33	5,486.2	62	64,504	109	15
45	BOEING	U.S.	20,276.0	973.0	51	13,278.0	92	6,131.0	55	159,200	29	1
46	OCCIDENTAL PETROLEUM	U.S.	20,068.0	285.0	206	20,741.0	49	5,899.0	57	53,500	140	8
47	DAEWOO	SOUTH KOREA	19,981.4	114.5	360	28,986.2	30	4,645.3	84	91,056	71	7
48	UNITED TECHNOLOGIES[6]	U.S.	19,765.5	702.1	84	14,598.2	80	4,740.3	80	201,400	17	1
49	FUJITSU[2]	JAPAN	18,734.1	541.1	110	19,770.5	53	7,239.4	38	104,503	59	6
50	EASTMAN KODAK	U.S.	18,546.0	529.0	112	23,652.0	39	6,642.0	48	137,750	37	22

The definitions and concepts underlying the figures in this directory are explained on page 235.

* From FORTUNE's Global 500/The World's Biggest Industrial Companies.

** Reflects an extraordinary credit of at least 10%; see the explanations of "profits," page 235.

N.A. Not Available.

‡ Reflects an extraordinary charge of at least 10%; see the explanations of "profits," page 235.

[1] Figures are for fiscal year ended June 30, 1989.

[2] Figures are for fiscal year ended March 31, 1989.

[3] Figures are for fiscal year ended September 30, 1989.

[4] Figure includes some significant subsidiaries owned 50% or less, either fully or on a prorated basis.

[5] Government owned.

The World's 100 Biggest Industrial Corporations (concluded)

1989			SALES $ Millions	PROFITS $ Millions	Rank	ASSETS $ Millions	Rank	STOCK-HOLDERS' EQUITY $ Millions	Rank	EMPLOYEES Number	Rank	INDUSTRY TABLE NUMBER
51	THYSSEN[3]	W. GERMANY	18,298.9[4]	408.0	151	11,154.3	111	2,430.5	178	133,824	40	15
52	USX	U.S.	17,755.0	965.0	52	17,500.0	59	5,737.0	61	53,610	139	18
53	DOW CHEMICAL	U.S.	17,730.0	2,487.0	13	22,166.0	44	7,957.0	33	62,111	116	5
54	XEROX	U.S.	17,635.0	704.0	82	30,088.0	29	5,035.0	74	111,400	54	22
55	TOTAL	FRANCE	16,926.8	346.1	177	15,313.0	74	3,736.6	114	41,200	189	18
56	MITSUBISHI MOTORS[2]	JAPAN	16,839.9	147.4	330	11,276.0	108	1,740.8	248	37,908	205	17
57	SONY[2]	JAPAN	16,680.2	563.8	107	17,811.1	58	6,867.6	40	78,900	88	7
58	PETROBRÁS[5]	BRAZIL	16,359.9	512.6	122	16,065.5	70	8,320.9	29	67,676	103	18
59	ROBERT BOSCH	W. GERMANY	16,263.0[4]	332.8	183	13,142.9	94	3,946.7	102	174,742	23	17
60	ATLANTIC RICHFIELD	U.S.	15,905.0	1,953.0	18	22,261.0	43	6,562.0	50	26,600	283	18
61	USINOR[5]	FRANCE	15,630.1	1,061.0	48	17,121.8	64	3,358.7	130	96,933	66	15
62	MAZDA MOTOR[2]	JAPAN	15,572.5[7]	99.1[7]	372	9,906.2	125	2,599.2	164	28,382	270	17
63	PEPSICO	U.S.	15,419.6	901.4	63	15,126.7	75	3,891.1	105	266,000	14	3
64	INI[5]	SPAIN	15,277.4	702.6[7]	83	31,245.4	26	6,121.7	56	151,423	34	16
65	PEMEX (PETRÓLEOS MEXICANOS)[5]	MEXICO	15,257.8[8]	320.1[8]	188	42,314.4[8]	13	24,200.2[8]	6	164,744[8]	27	18
66	RJR NABISCO HOLDINGS[9]	U.S.	15,224.0	(1,149.0)	497	36,412.0	18	1,237.0	320	48,000	154	8
67	MITSUBISHI HEAVY INDUSTRIES[2]	JAPAN	15,007.1	482.3	126	23,527.1	40	5,815.4	58	55,500	130	11
68	MCDONNELL DOUGLAS	U.S.	14,995.0	219.0	262	13,397.0	89	3,287.0	132	127,926	42	1
69	BRITISH AEROSPACE	BRITAIN	14,895.2	382.0	160	14,814.7	78	3,842.5	109	125,600	45	1
70	VOLVO	SWEDEN	14,637.7	836.9	68	16,245.1	69	5,249.3	68	75,340	93	17
71	NIPPON OIL[2]	JAPAN	14,562.7	216.3	266	13,388.2	90	3,626.6	117	9,669	449	18
72	TENNECO	U.S.	14,439.0	584.0	105	17,381.0	62	3,277.0	133	90,000	73	11
73	GRAND METROPOLITAN[3]	BRITAIN	14,274.6	1,805.9[**]	21	15,450.8	73	4,536.7	85	152,175	33	8
74	BMW (BAYERISCHE MOTOREN WERKE)	W. GERMANY	14,097.7	296.2	197	12,245.5	96	3,152.6	138	66,267	104	17
75	PECHINEY[5]	FRANCE	13,986.8	523.5	115	13,416.5	88	2,486.7	171	70,000	99	15
76	PETRÓLEOS DE VENEZUELA[5]	VENEZUELA	13,677.3	2,718.0	11	8,907.0	144	6,551.7	52	46,940	159	18
77	ELECTROLUX	SWEDEN	13,299.8	355.1	173	10,591.5	118	2,360.1	187	152,913	32	7
78	DIGITAL EQUIPMENT[1]	U.S.	12,866.0	1,072.6	46	10,667.8	117	8,035.7	32	125,800	43	6
79	WESTINGHOUSE ELECTRIC	U.S.	12,844.0	922.0	62	20,314.0	51	4,384.0	90	121,963	49	7
80	ROCKWELL INTERNATIONAL[3]	U.S.	12,633.1	734.9	79	8,938.8	143	3,977.6	101	108,715	56	1
81	CIBA-GEIGY	SWITZERLAND	12,597.9[4]	951.8	54	16,926.0	65	10,536.7	20	92,553	69	5
82	PHILLIPS PETROLEUM	U.S.	12,492.0	219.0	263	11,256.0	109	2,132.0	202	21,800	333	18
83	RUHRKOHLE	W. GERMANY	12,422.1	30.0	447	13,686.7	86	757.9	409	124,838	47	16
84	BRIDGESTONE	JAPAN	12,379.1	68.2	407	11,408.3	103	3,056.4	141	93,193	68	21
85	FERRUZZI FINANZIARIA	ITALY	12,046.9[4]	226.8	252	24,922.7	36	2,513.0	170	44,546	173	8
86	THOMSON[5]	FRANCE	12,027.1	78.0	398	16,863.5	66	1,535.5	274	100,000	65	7
87	ALLIED-SIGNAL	U.S.	12,021.0	528.0	114	10,132.0	122	3,412.0	125	107,100	57	1
88	MINNESOTA MINING & MFG.	U.S.	11,990.0	1,244.0	35	9,776.0	128	5,378.0	66	87,600	76	22
89	HEWLETT-PACKARD[10,11]	U.S.	11,899.0	829.0	70	10,075.0	123	5,446.0	64	95,000	67	6
90	MANNESMANN	W. GERMANY	11,872.5	246.2	241	9,600.4	132	2,721.7	158	125,785	44	11
91	HANSON[3]	BRITAIN	11,833.0	1,861.7[**]	19	17,477.0	60	1,753.3	244	89,000	74	4
92	KUWAIT PETROLEUM[1,5]	KUWAIT	11,796.5	735.2	78	22,725.9	42	14,655.4	14	15,372	396	18
93	SARA LEE[1]	U.S.	11,738.3	410.5	150	6,522.7	202	1,914.9	221	100,000	64	8
94	BTR	BRITAIN	11,544.0	1,082.1	44	9,759.7	129	2,578.4	165	109,501	55	4
95	RHÔNE-POULENC[5]	FRANCE	11,463.1	642.0	95	14,406.3	82	3,684.1	115	86,100	77	5
96	INTERNATIONAL PAPER	U.S.	11,378.0	864.0	66	11,582.0	100	5,147.0	71	63,500	113	9
97	CONAGRA[12]	U.S.	11,340.4	197.9	283	4,278.2	302	949.5	379	48,131	153	8
98	PETROFINA	BELGIUM	11,269.7	554.2	108	10,349.3	120	4,029.9	99	23,600	317	18
99	IDEMITSU KOSAN[2]	JAPAN	11,249.3[8]	13.1[8]	467	9,844.5[8]	126	327.4[8]	474	5,292[8]	482	18
100	ENIMONT	ITALY	11,191.5	522.1	117	14,192.6	83	4,194.9	94	52,656	142	5

[6] Figures include Sheller-Globe, acquired November 9, 1989.

[7] Figure is a FORTUNE estimate.

[8] Figures are unconsolidated.

[9] Name changed from RJR Nabisco.

[10] Figures are for fiscal year ended October 31, 1989.

[11] Figures include Apollo, acquired May 18, 1989.

[12] Figures are for fiscal year ended May 31, 1989.

Source: Reprinted by permission from the *1990 FORTUNE Directory.*

DEFINITIONS AND EXPLANATIONS

Sales All companies on the list must have derived more than 50% of their sales from manufacturing and/or mining. Sales of consolidated subsidiaries are included. All figures are for the year ended December 31, 1989, unless otherwise noted. Sales figures do not include excise taxes collected by manufacturers, and so the figures for some corporations—most of which sell gasoline, liquor, or tobacco—may be lower than those published by the corporations themselves.

Profits Profits are shown after taxes and after extraordinary credits or charges if any appear on the income statement. A double asterisk (**) signifies an extraordinary credit reflecting at least 10% of the profits shown, a double dagger (‡) an extraordinary charge of at least 10%. Figures in parentheses indicate a loss. Profit declines over 100% reflect swings from 1988 profits to 1989 losses. Cooperatives provide only "net margin" figures, which are not comparable with the profits figures in these listings, and therefore N.A. is shown in that column.

Assets Assets shown are those at the company's fiscal year-end.

Stockholders' Equity Stockholders' equity is the sum of capital stock, surplus, and retained earnings at the company's year-end.

Industry Tables Industry table numbers used in the directory indicate the groups in which companies are placed in "The Global 500/The Biggest Companies by Industry," beginning on page 300 of *Fortune*, July 30, 1990. Companies are included in the industry that represents the greatest volume of their industrial sales. Industry groups are based on categories established by the U.S. Office of Management and Budget and issued by the Federal Statistical Policy and Standards Office. The median figures in the tables refer only to results of companies in the 500; no attempt has been made to calculate medians in groups with fewer than four companies.

The 25 Largest Diversified Service Companies (ranked by sales)

RANK BY SALES 1989	1988		(Major Industry)	SALES¹ $Millions	% change from 1988	PROFITS $Millions	Rank	% change from 1988	ASSETS $Millions	Rank	STOCKHOLDERS EQUITY $Millions	Rank
1	1	AMERICAN TELEPHONE & TELEGRAPH New York (Telecomm.)		36,345.0	3.2	2,697.0	1	—	37,687.0	1	12,738.0	1
2	2	FLEMING COS. Oklahoma City (Wholesale)		12,045.3	15.1	80.1	41	22.5	2,689.3	36	741.6	33
3	3	SUPER VALU STORES Eden Prairie, Minn.² (Wholesale)		10,316.1	10.1	135.4	26	21.1	2,305.1	39	778.3	29
4	•	ENRON Houston³ (Wholesale)		9,869.6	72.9	226.3	15	107.7	9,104.8	4	1,785.9	14
5	•	MARRIOTT Bethesda, Md.⁴ (Hotels)		8,382.01	13.7	177.0	20	(23.7)	6,732.0	8	628.0	43
6	6	UNITED TELECOMMUNICATIONS Westwood, Kans. (Telecomm.)		7,549.0	16.3	362.9	10	(28.7)	9,821.3	3	2,076.9	11
7	4	MCKESSON San Francisco⁵ (Wholesale)		7,515.2	3.0	100.6	36	5.9	2,105.8	46	692.2	39
8	5	AMERICAN FINANCIAL Cincinnati (Casualty insurance)		7,285.7	5.6	3.3	74	(96.8)	11,969.1	2	333.0	61
9	13	SYSCO Houston⁶ (Wholesale)		6,851.3	56.3	107.9	35	24.1	1,869.4	49	642.6	41
10	•	PACIFIC ENTERPRISES Los Angeles⁷ (Natural gas)		6,797.0	14.6	211.0	16	(5.0)	7,326.0	5	2,169.0	9
11	6	MCI COMMUNICATIONS Washington (Telecomm.)		6,504.0	26.6	558.0	6	61.3	6,338.0	12	1,995.0	12
12	8	FLUOR Irvine, Calif.⁸ (Eng. & constr.)		6,314.0	23.0	108.5	33	92.4	2,154.3	44	720.4	36
13	28	PARAMOUNT COMM. New York⁸,⁹ (Movies)		5,941.41	94.4	1,465.4	2	280.9	7,065.2	6	3,717.5	2
14	10	HALLIBURTON Dallas (Eng. & constr.)		5,708.5	18.0	135.0	27	44.2	4,263.0	19	2,119.1	10
15	12	ELECTRONIC DATA SYSTEMS Dallas¹⁰ (Computing)		5,466.8	15.2	435.3	9	13.3	3,918.2	26	1,763.6	15
16	9	RYDER SYSTEM Miami (Truck rental)		5,073.4	0.9	46.0‡	56	(76.7)	5,937.5	14	1,486.6	16
17	11	CAPITAL CITIES/ABC New York (Broadcasting)		5,059.6	6.0	485.7	7	25.5	6,359.5	11	3,291.9	3
18	15	WETTERAU Hazelwood, Mo.⁵ (Wholesale)		5,003.0	20.4	43.3	57	12.2	952.1	68	230.0	68
19	21	WALT DISNEY Burbank, Calif.¹¹ (Theme parks)		4,661.7	35.6	703.3	3	34.7	6,657.2	9	3,044.0	5
20	19	WASTE MANAGEMENT Oak Brook, Ill. (Waste)		4,477.7	25.6	562.1	5	21.1	6,405.2	10	2,738.0	6
21	14	DUN & BRADSTREET New York (Info. services)		4,389.1	2.9	586.4	4	17.5	5,184.2	16	2,184.7	8
22	16	HOSPITAL CORP. OF AMERICA Nashville (Hospitals)		4,308.7	4.8	82.6	40	(68.1)	6,879.7	7	564.3	47
23	17	ARA GROUP Philadelphia¹¹ (Food service)		4,243.8	8.3	38.7	60	620.1	1,884.4	48	19.0	94
24	22	HUMANA Louisville, Ky.¹² (Hospitals)		4,148.6	20.8	256.0	14	12.7	3,696.6	29	1,327.0	18
25	18	ALCO STANDARD Valley Forge, Pa.¹¹ (Wholesale)		4,145.9	8.8	170.8	22	55.3	1,478.7	55	594.4	45

N.A. Not available.
• Not on last year's list.
† Average for the year; see the reference to "employee" below.
** Reflects an extraordinary credit of at least 10%; see the explanations of "profits" and "earnings per share" below.
‡ Reflects an extraordinary charge of at least 10%; see the explanations of "profits" and "earnings per share" below.
¶ Includes sales from discontinued operations of at least 10%.
¹ Sales include all operating revenues, other income, and revenues from discontinued operations when they are published. Sales also include consolidated subsidiaries, but they do not include excise taxes. All figures are for the fiscal year ended December 31, 1989, unless otherwise noted. All companies on the list must have derived 50% or more of their revenues from nonmanufacturing and nonmining businesses. Excluded but eligible for the lists that follow are companies deriving more than 50% of revenues solely from banking, life insurance, finance, savings, retail, transportation, or utilities.

DEFINITIONS AND EXPLANATIONS TO THE SERVICE COMPANIES

Assets are those shown at the company's fiscal year-end.

Profits are shown after taxes and after extraordinary credits or charges if any are shown on the income statement. A double asterisk (**) signifies an extraordinary credit reflecting at least 10% of the net income shown, a double dagger (‡) an extraordinary charge of at least 10%. Profit declines over 100% reflect savings from 1988 profits to 1989 losses. Figures in parentheses indicate a loss. Cooperatives provide only "net margin" figures, which are not comparable with the profits in these listings, and therefore N.A. is shown in that column.

Stockholders' equity is the sum of capital stock, surplus, and retained earnings at the company's year-end. Redeemable preferred stock is excluded if its redemption is either mandatory or outside the control of the company, except in the case of cooperatives. For purposes of calculating "net income as percent of stockholders' equity," any dividends paid on redeemable preferred stock, if that stock's redemption is either mandatory or outside the control of the company, have been subtracted from the net income figure.

Employees The figure shown is a year-end total except when it is followed by a dagger (†), in which case it is an average.

Market Value The figure shown was arrived at by multiplying the number of common shares outstanding (at the latest date available) by the price per common share as of April 20, 1990.

Earnings per Share For all companies the figures shown are the primary earnings

MARKET VALUE 4/20/90 $Millions	Rank	NET PROFITS AS PERCENT OF SALES %	Rank	ASSETS %	Rank	STOCK-HOLDERS' EQUITY %	Rank	EARNINGS PER SHARE 1989	% change from 1988	1979-89 annual growth rate %	Rank	TOTAL RETURN TO INVESTORS 1989 %	Rank	1979-89 annual average %	Rank	EMPLOYEES Number	Rank	
43,981.5	1	7.4	18	7.2	21	21.2	17	2.50	—	(11.0)	56	63.4	14	18.9	30	283,500	1	1
961.1	44	0.7	72	3.0	51	10.8	57	2.54	4.5	6.9	31	(11.4)	69	17.0	35	22,800	28	2
1,858.4	31	1.3	65	5.9	28	17.4	31	1.81	20.7	13.4	22	20.8	44	19.7	28	39,711	22	3
2,642.7	22	2.3	51	2.5	60	12.7§	51	4.03	161.7	(0.1)	43	65.7	12	13.7	49	6,296	60	4
2,659.9	21	2.1	55	2.6	56	28.2	8	1.58	(19.0)	15.0	17	6.2	56	26.0	12	229,942	2	5
7,993.3	7	4.8	29	3.7	43	17.3§	32	1.72	(30.5)	2.7	37	66.2	11	23.1	17	41,359	20	6
1,299.7	36	1.3	63	4.8	35	14.5	44	2.28	2.2	1.2	40	19.5	46	16.8	37	14,800	43	7
N.A.		0.0	77	0.0	76	(2.2)§	77	N.A.	—	—		—		—		53,000	12	8
2,767.3	19	1.6	59	5.8	29	16.8	33	1.19	22.7	17.8	11	65.5	13	34.0	5	18,715	37	9
3,017.7	18	3.1	41	2.9	53	9.7	62	3.05	(13.1)	(2.2)	47	45.7	25	18.5	32	43,891	15	10
8,599.7	5	8.6	16	8.8	15	28.0	10	2.09	69.9	43.2	1	94.5	4	39.9	1	19,198	35	11
3,331.6	16	1.7	57	5.0	31	15.1	38	1.35	90.1	(3.9)	49	58.0	16	5.6	61	20,059	30	12
5,466.8	10	24.7	2	20.7	1	39.4§	3	12.21	280.4	20.8	6	26.0	37	24.7	14	11,800	49	13
4,611.0	11	2.4	48	3.2	49	6.4	68	1.27	42.7	(8.9)	55	57.2	17	4.1	63	65,500	9	14
N.A.		8.0	17	11.1	13	24.7	13	N.A.	—	—		—		—		57,000	10	15
1,508.3	34	0.9	69	0.8	70	3.1	72	0.50‡	(79.2)	(7.6)	51	(19.7)	74	13.9	47	42,210	18	16
9,847.5	4	9.6	13	7.6	18	14.8	42	27.25	22.1	19.3	9	55.8	19	28.0	9	19,860	32	17
594.7	53	0.9	70	4.5	38	18.8	27	1.82	15.2	7.8	30	29.6	34	22.5	19	14,319	45	18
15,161.9	3	15.1	5	10.6	14	23.1	14	5.10	34.2	19.2	10	71.1	9	27.6	11	47,000	13	19
16,302.4	2	12.6	7	8.8	16	20.5	20	1.22	38.6	25.2	2	71.0	10	36.1	3	42,640	17	20
8,448.1	6	13.4	6	11.3	10	26.8	11	3.14	17.6	14.7	19	(10.9)	68	19.1	29	71,500	7	21
N.A.		1.9	56	1.2	68	14.6	43	N.A.	—	—		—		—		68,000	8	22
N.A.		0.9	68	2.1	63	203.1	1	N.A.	—	—		—		—		125,000	3	23
3,918.1	14	6.2	22	6.9	23	19.3	25	2.56	11.3	20.1	7	78.6	7	24.0	15	55,100	11	24
1,231.6	37	4.1	34	11.5	8	28.7§	7	3.94	69.1	12.1	23	26.9	36	20.1	27	17,700	39	25

[2] Figures are for fiscal year ended February 28, 1989.
[3] Company was No. 27 on 1988 Utilities list.
[4] Company was No. 14 on 1988 Retailing list.
[5] Figures are for fiscal year ended March 31, 1989.
[6] Figures are for fiscal year ended June 30, 1989.
[7] Company was No. 36 on 1988 Utilities list.
[8] Figures are for fiscal year ended October 31, 1989.
[9] Name changed from Gulf + Western.
[10] Wholly owned by General Motors (No. 1 on the FORTUNE 500 Industrial list).
[11] Figures are for fiscal year ended September 30, 1989.
[12] Figures are for fiscal year ended August 31, 1989.
Source: Reprinted by permission from the 1990 FORTUNE Directory.

per share that appear on the company's income statement. Per-share earnings for 1988 and 1979 are adjusted for stock splits and stock dividends. They are not restated for mergers, acquisitions, or accounting changes made after 1979. A double asterisk (**) signifies an extraordinary credit reflecting at least 10% of the net income shown, a double dagger (‡) an extraordinary charge of at least 10%. Figures in parentheses indicate a loss. Results are listed as not available (N.A.) if the companies are cooperatives, joint ventures, or wholly owned subsidiaries of other companies or if the figures were not published in 1979. The growth rate is the average annual growth, compounded.

Total Return to Investors Total return to investors includes both price appreciation and dividend yield to an investor in the company's stock. The figures shown assume sales at the end of 1989 of stock owned at the end of 1979 and 1988. It has been assumed that any proceeds from cash dividends, the sale of rights and warrant offerings, and stock received in spinoffs were reinvested when they were paid. Returns are adjusted for stock splits, stock dividends, recapitalizations, and corporate reorganizations as they occur; however, no effort has been made to reflect the cost of brokerage commissions or of taxes. Results are listed as not available (N.A.) if shares are not publicly traded or are traded on only a limited basis. If companies have more than one class of shares outstanding, only the more widely held and actively traded has been considered.

Total return percentages shown are the returns received by the hypothetical investor described above. The ten-year figures are annual averages, compounded.

The 25 Largest Life Insurance Companies (ranked by assets)

RANK BY ASSETS 1989	1988		ASSETS[1] $ Millions	% change from 1988	PREMIUM AND ANNUITY INCOME[2] $ Millions	Rank	NET INVESTMENT INCOME $ Millions	Rank	NET GAIN FROM OPERATIONS[3] $ Millions	Mutual Rank	Stock Rank
1	1	PRUDENTIAL OF AMERICA Newark, N.J.*	129,118.1	11.1	21,535.2	1	8,078.1	1	360.0	1	
2	2	METROPOLITAN LIFE New York*	98,740.3	4.8	15,183.1	2	7,380.7	2	183.6	4	
3	3	EQUITABLE LIFE ASSURANCE New York*	52,511.9	4.2	4,620.1	8	2,852.7	6	(28.7)	20	
4	4	AETNA LIFE Hartford[8]	52,022.6	6.4	8,642.6	3	3,551.4	4	353.2		1
5	5	TEACHERS INSURANCE & ANNUITY New York	44,374.1	14.9	3,198.0	12	3,979.3	3	148.6		5
6	6	NEW YORK LIFE New York*	37,302.4	6.1	6,428.1	4	2,948.7	5	116.4	7	
7	7	CONNECTICUT GENERAL LIFE Bloomfield[9]	33,991.2	9.3	2,513.6	19	2,130.1	9	276.9		2
8	8	TRAVELERS Hartford	32,087.5	4.6	5,169.3	7	2,247.6	8	106.1		9
9	9	JOHN HANCOCK MUTUAL LIFE Boston*	30,924.8	9.2	6,017.6	5	2,287.1	7	199.8	2	
10	10	NORTHWESTERN MUTUAL LIFE Milwaukee*	28,500.0	12.4	3,751.9	10	2,130.0	10	188.5	3	
11	11	MASSACHUSETTS MUTUAL LIFE Springfield*	24,842.3	10.9	2,930.4	15	1,866.9	11	123.8	6	
12	12	PRINCIPAL MUTUAL LIFE Des Moines*	24,825.5	12.8	5,495.5	6	1,809.8	12	160.6	5	
13	14	MUTUAL OF NEW YORK New York*	17,181.3	9.0	2,716.6	17	1,115.4	15	12.0	15	
14	13	NEW ENGLAND MUTUAL LIFE Boston*	16,666.7	4.9	2,672.3	18	1,135.2	14	(13.9)	19	
15	33	LINCOLN NATIONAL LIFE Fort Wayne[10,11]	16,161.9	184.2	3,875.3	9	1,029.9	16	71.8		13
16	15	EXECUTIVE LIFE Los Angeles	13,168.2	2.8	637.1	47	1,361.9	13	153.1		4
17	17	IDS LIFE Minneapolis[12]	13,150.2	22.1	1,921.9	23	936.9	18	111.8		8
18	18	MUTUAL BENEFIT LIFE Newark, N.J.*	11,601.3	9.0	2,824.0	16	1,009.3	17	44.4	11	
19	16	CONNECTICUT MUTUAL LIFE Hartford*	11,133.7	2.9	1,610.5	25	815.0	23	53.2	9	
20	21	ALLSTATE LIFE Northbrook, Ill.[13]	10,994.1	24.7	3,107.7	14	936.1	19	183.0		3
21	20	VARIABLE ANNUITY LIFE Houston[14]	10,857.7	18.6	1,290.9	33	878.1	21	55.8		18
22	19	STATE FARM LIFE Bloomington, Ill.	10,839.0	13.0	1,513.8	28	932.3	20	133.7		7
23	22	NATIONWIDE LIFE Columbus, Ohio	10,451.7	20.1	1,548.2	27	628.7	27	22.6		23
24	24	AETNA LIFE & ANNUITY Hartford[8]	9,731.9	22.5	1,609.7	26	555.7	30	59.8		15
25	23	NEW YORK LIFE & ANNUITY Wilmington, Del.	9,567.9	12.6	1,101.8	38	833.5	22	104.9		10

• Not on last year's list.
* Indicates a mutual company.
N.A. Not available.
[1] As of December 31, 1989.
[2] Includes premium income from life, accident, and health policies, annuities, and contributions to deposit administration funds.
[3] After dividends to policyholders and federal income taxes, excluding realized capital gains and losses. Figures in parentheses indicate a loss.
[4] After dividends to policyholders and federal income taxes, including realized capital gains and losses. Figures in parentheses indicate a loss.
[5] Face value of all life policies, including variable life insurance, as of December 31, 1989.
[6] Changes between December 31, 1988, and December 31, 1989.

NET INCOME[4]			% change from 1988	NET INCOME AS PERCENT OF ASSETS		LIFE INSURANCE IN FORCE[5]		INCREASE IN LIFE INSURANCE IN FORCE[6]				EMPLOYEES[7]		
$ Millions	Mutual Rank	Stock Rank		%	Rank	$ Millions	Rank	$ Millions	Rank	%	Rank	Number	Rank	
644.2	1		(26.5)	0.5	28	727,424.3	2	35,926.1	2	5.2	28	69,551	1	1
494.0	2		(40.9)	0.5	27	728,269.9	1	86,931.4	1	13.6	6	46,000	2	2
193.4	7		(21.4)	0.4	35	320,472.7	3	1,729.1	31	0.5	35	23,000	5	3
341.3		2	14.5	0.7	20	282,865.6	4	32,274.3	3	12.9	7	17,377	9	4
406.1		1	(2.7)	0.9	12	24,033.4	34	2,495.0	29	11.6	13	3,495	30	5
212.9	5		(16.8)	0.6	26	256,182.1	5	19,234.9	8	8.1	21	19,438	7	6
288.5		4	(12.6)	0.8	15	147,235.4	12	10,930.7	13	8.0	22	12,896	13	7
121.5	10		(56.0)	0.4	34	181,329.9	9	2,748.2	27	1.5	33	38,000	3	8
231.7	4		25.3	0.7	18	198,180.4	8	13,499.1	11	7.3	23	15,655	11	9
371.6	3		214.2	1.3	6	201,130.2	7	22,348.5	5	12.5	11	8,750	17	10
141.9	9		211.4	0.6	25	105,767.0	14	10,345.2	16	10.8	14	10,226	15	11
209.9	6		104.0	0.8	16	99,804.8	15	10,862.8	14	12.2	12	10,985	14	12
154.2	8		2.1	0.9	13	78,275.1	24	3,549.4	25	4.7	29	4,453	23	13
25.5	17		68.5	0.2	47	76,136.1	25	4,201.8	21	5.8	27	6,235	21	14
125.1		8	273.1	0.8	17	145,862.9	13	3,980.8	22	-		4,312	24	15
5.3		29	(97.9)	0.0	49	60,417.4	28	3,879.2	23	6.9	24	799	44	16
117.3		11	26.6	0.9	14	27,084.3	33	2,276.9	30	9.2	19	6,856	20	17
42.6	13		(49.6)	0.4	36	85,550.8	20	13,708.3	9	19.1	3	4,654	22	18
68.0	11		40.0	0.6	23	61,996.3	27	5,031.5	20	8.8	20	24,240	4	19
198.6		5	-	1.8	5	82,654.0	22	(10,177.3)	50	-		2,393	35	20
52.2	16		-	0.5	29	2.3	49	(0.1)	40	-		1,641	37	21
140.6		7	1.9	1.3	7	156,340.2	10	19,255.7	7	14.0	5	19,505	6	22
26.4		21	74.8	0.3	43	23,656.1	37	1,275.7	32	5.9	26	7,745	19	23
62.5	15		-	0.6	21	34,023.6	30	3,838.0	24	12.7	9	3,229	33	24
123.9		9	77.9	1.3	8	42,339.5	29	(659.7)	44	-		19,438	8	25

[7] Includes home office, field force, and full-time agents.
[8] Wholly owned by Aetna Life & Casualty (F-4).
[9] Wholly owned by Cigna (F-6).
[10] Wholly owned by Lincoln National (F-18).
[11] Figures include Lincoln National Pension (No. 27 on 1988 Life Insurance list), acquired January 1, 1989.
[12] Wholly owned by American Express (F-1).
[13] Wholly owned by Sears Roebuck (R-1).
[14] Wholly owned by American General (F-15).

Source: Reprinted by permission from the *1990 FORTUNE Directory*.

The 25 Largest Commercial Banking Companies (ranked by assets)

RANK BY ASSETS		ASSETS		DEPOSITS		LOANS[2]		PROFITS		
1989	1988	$ Millions	% change from 1988	$ Millions	Rank	$ Millions	Rank	$ Millions	Rank	% change from 1988
1	1	CITICORP New York	230,643.0	11.1	137,922.0	1	155,383.0	1	498.0	4	(73.2)
2	2	CHASE MANHATTAN CORP. New York	107,369.0	10.2	69,073.0	3	73,402.0	2	(665.0)	95	(162.8)
3	3	BANKAMERICA CORP. San Francisco	98,764.0	4.3	81,186.0	2	72,488.0	3	1,103.0**	1	51.9
4	4	J.P. MORGAN & CO. New York	88,964.0	6.0	39,158.0	9	26,030.0	13	(1,275.0)	98	(227.3)
5	5	SECURITY PACIFIC CORP. Los Angeles	83,943.0	7.8	52,630.0	4	60,566.0	4	740.6	2	15.9
6	6	CHEMICAL BANKING CORP. New York	71,513.0	6.2	50,151.0	5	41,876.0	5	(482.2)	93	(164.0)
7	18	NCNB CORP. Charlotte, N.C.[3]	66,190.8	121.8	48,576.3	6	33,943.7	10	447.1	5	77.1
8	7	MANUFACTURERS HANOVER CORP. New York	60,479.0	(9.3)	41,994.0	8	39,145.0	7	(518.0)‡	94	(154.4)
9	8	FIRST INTERSTATE BANCORP Los Angeles	59,051.4	1.5	46,467.7	7	36,767.9	8	(124.5)	88	(196.2)
10	9	BANKERS TRUST NEW YORK CORP. New York	55,658.4	(3.9)	26,220.1	15	18,421.4	24	(979.9)	96	(251.3)
11	10	BANK OF NEW YORK CO. New York	48,856.5	3.1	34,927.1	11	34,629.4	9	50.7	68	(76.2)
12	11	WELLS FARGO & CO. San Francisco	48,736.6	4.5	36,430.3	10	40,988.3	6	601.1	3	17.3
13	12	FIRST CHICAGO CORP. Chicago	47,907.0	7.8	32,935.0	12	28,447.0	11	358.7	9	(30.1)
14	13	PNC FINANCIAL CORP. Pittsburgh	45,660.7	11.9	30,120.2	13	27,490.9	12	377.4	6	(14.7)
15	14	BANK OF BOSTON CORP. Boston	39,177.9	8.6	28,697.4	14	24,215.0	14	70.4	52	(78.1)
16	21	FLEET/NORSTAR FINANCIAL GROUP Providence	33,440.8	15.1	21,676.6	20	21,291.9	19	371.3	7	10.6
17	22	FIRST UNION CORP. Charlotte, N.C.	32,130.6	10.9	21,498.3	21	21,578.6	18	256.2	16	(13.7)
18	16	MELLON BANK CORP. Pittsburgh	31,467.0	1.0	21,344.0	22	18,788.0	22	210.0**	20	—
19	20	SUNTRUST BANKS Atlanta	31,043.6	6.4	24,961.5	18	20,764.5	20	337.3	10	9.3
20	19	FIRST FIDELITY BANCORP Newark, N.J.	30,727.8	3.2	22,872.5	19	19,631.8	21	159.5	24	370.4
21	15	BANK OF NEW ENGLAND CORP. Boston	29,772.7	(7.5)	25,529.6	16	22,288.2	15	(1,113.3)	97	(495.3)
22	17	CONTINENTAL BANK CORP. Chicago	29,549.0	(3.4)	17,176.0	33	15,314.0	30	147.3	26	(53.4)
23	25	BARNETT BANKS Jacksonville, Fla.	29,006.7	12.7	25,055.9	17	22,176.2	16	256.7	15	13.3
24	23	SHAWMUT CORP. Boston	27,885.2	(1.9)	18,765.5	25	18,462.5	23	(128.9)	89	(153.2)
25	24	MARINE MIDLAND BANKS Buffalo[4]	27,066.5	4.2	18,325.6	28	21,720.0	17	13.9**	83	(91.3)

N.A. Not available.

• Not on last year's list.

** Reflects an extraordinary credit of at least 10%; see the explanations of "profits" and "earnings per share" on page 236.

† Average for the year; see the reference to "employees" on page 236.

‡ Reflects an extraordinary charge of at least 10%; see the explanations of "profits" and "earnings per share" on page 236.

§ Dividends paid on mandatory redeemable preferred stock subtracted from profits.

STOCK-HOLDERS' EQUITY		MARKET VALUE 4/20/90		PROFITS AS PERCENT OF ASSETS		STOCK-HOLDERS' EQUITY		EARNINGS PER SHARE				TOTAL RETURN TO INVESTORS 1989		1979-89 annual average		EMPLOYEES		
$ Millions	Rank	$ Millions	Rank	%	Rank	%	Rank	1989/8	% change from 1988	1979-89 annual growth rate %	Rank	%	Rank	%	Rank	Number	Rank	
10,076.0	1	7,590.9	1	0.2	78	4.9§	77	1.16	(78.4)	(6.1)	68	17.7	49	15.9	68	92,000	1	1
4,944.0	3	3,042.9	9	(0.6)	89	(13.5)	91	(7.94)	(168.7)	—		29.8	24	13.6	74	41,610	3	2
5,534.0	2	5,796.6	3	1.1	13	19.9	4	5.19**	36.9	2.4	64	55.3	7	4.2	86	54,779	2	3
4,495.0	5	6,178.2	2	(1.4)	94	(28.4)	93	(7.04)	(230.9)	—		31.7	19	20.0	46	14,207	25	4
4,637.0	4	4,212.2	4	0.9	51	16.0	19	6.26	12.0	9.7	32	18.3	48	19.3	50	41,099	4	5
3,705.0	6	2,720.1	11	(0.7)	91	(13.0)	90	(8.29)	(169.0)	—		3.9	71	14.7	72	29,139	6	6
2,961.5	8	3,758.0	6	0.7	62	15.1	27	4.62	59.3	13.8	9	74.0	1	26.3	7	27,002	7	7
3,381.0	7	2,237.9	14	(0.9)	92	(15.3)	92	(10.21)‡	(155.9)	—		27.7	28	9.9	81	20,034	8	8
2,339.3	14	2,159.0	16	(0.2)	87	(5.3)	87	(3.30)	(225.5)	—		2.2	72	8.9	82	36,000†	5	9
2,385.7	13	2,884.8	10	(1.8)	96	(41.1)	96	(12.10)	(249.6)	—		23.8	37	21.3	39	13,230	29	10
2,764.3	11	2,138.7	17	0.1	81	1.8	81	0.24	(95.7)	(20.4)	73	13.7	53	20.0	45	14,883	23	11
2,860.9	9	3,511.4	7	1.2	5	21.0	2	11.02	19.8	15.0	4	28.2	26	24.9	12	19,500	10	12
2,692.0	12	2,007.5	21	0.7	57	13.3	52	5.10	(37.8)	6.1	52	31.0	20	15.7	69	18,158	13	13
2,829.6	10	3,140.4	8	0.8	53	13.3	51	3.98	(21.8)	8.1	43	9.7	59	20.7	44	17,681	17	14
2,096.6	17	810.3	41	0.2	80	3.4	79	0.80	(82.8)	(6.2)	69	(15.4)	86	17.9	60	18,800	11	15
2,288.7	15	2,177.7	15	1.1	14	16.2	15	3.34	8.8	13.0	14	7.4	65	25.9	8	18,789	12	16
2,076.1	19	1,875.4	23	0.8	54	12.3	58	2.40	(13.0)	7.8	45	(2.7)	76	20.8	42	17,733	16	17
1,549.0	27	930.4	38	0.7	63	12.9§	54	4.01**	—	(2.0)	67	19.6	45	6.3	85	15,300	21	18
2,088.9	18	2,624.4	13	1.1	15	16.1	17	2.61	9.7	11.0	23	19.0	46	18.3	57	20,023	9	19
1,565.0	26	1,078.8	33	0.5	70	10.2	67	2.51	765.5	20.0	2	(7.5)	81	21.2	41	13,500	27	20
457.7	73	251.6	84	(3.7)	98	(243.2)	98	(16.11)	(496.8)	—		(54.5)	89	11.1	78	16,821	18	21
1,680.0	23	720.5	44	0.5	71	8.8	70	2.06	(60.3)	(20.3)	72	(0.5)	73	(12.5)	88	7,560	43	22
1,690.7	22	1,893.0	22	0.9	50	15.2§	25	4.07	8.5	14.1	8	9.6	60	24.4	14	18,109	14	23
1,397.7	31	978.2	37	(0.5)	88	(9.2)	89	(1.77)	(154.0)	—		(8.9)	83	19.0	53	12,019	32	24
1,178.5	36	N.A.		0.1	84	1.2	83	N.A.	—	—		—		—		13,345	28	25

[1] As of December 31, 1989. All companies on the list must have more than 80% of their assets in chartered commercial banking institutions.
[2] Net of unearned discount and loan-loss reserves. Figure includes lease financing.
[3] Figures reflect acquisition of NCNB Texas National Bank (No. 26 on last year's list), August 9, 1989.
[4] A wholly owned subsidiary of Hongkong & Shanghai Banking Corp. (No. 31 among last year's largest International Banks).

Source: Reprinted by permission from the 1990 FORTUNE Directory.

The 50 Largest International Banks*

The top 50** bank holding companies in the world are listed here according to the size of their assets. Also shown are each bank's total deposits, capital and pretax earnings and the bank's ranking (in parentheses) in those categories. For any bank to be ranked in deposits, capital or earnings, the bank must first be among the top 50 in assets. Those cases where bank figures were not available or could not be confirmed for accuracy are indicated by dashes.

Rank 1988	Rank 1989	Name of Bank (Country)	Assets (US$ millions) 1989	Assets (US$ millions) 1988	Deposits (US$ millions) 1989	Capital (US$ millions) 1989	Pretax Earnings (US$ millions) 1989
1	1	Dai-Ichi Kangyo Bank[1] Japan	$389,823	$352,688	$314,796(1)	$11,036(3)	$2,870(3)
2	2	Sumitomo Bank[1] Japan	378,893	334,802	298,209(2)	10,977(4)	3,139(1)
3	3	Fuji Bank[1] Japan	366,759	327,909	285,701(3)	11,283(2)	2,910(2)
4	4	Mitsubishi Bank[1] Japan	353,871	317,903	274,543(4)	10,238(5)	2,642(4)
5	5	Sanwa Bank[1] Japan	350,956	307,528	271,039(5)	9,743(8)	2,479(5)
6	6	Industrial Bank of Japan[1] Japan	269,686	249,604	223,174(6)	9,301(10)	1,463(9)
7	7	Norinchukin Bank[1,2,4] Japan	243,752	231,797	212,340(7)	1,395(137)	464(67)
9	8	Crédit Agricole France	242,075	210,664	192,830(8)	11,806(1)	1,359(10)
12	9	Banque Nationale de Paris France	231,543	197,014	192,338(9)	6,179(20)	918(27)
10	10	Citicorp United States	227,037	207,818	137,922(24)	10,076(6)	1,533(8)
8	11	Tokai Bank[1] Japan	226,800	213,622	176,911(13)	6,511(19)	1,026(20)
11	12	Mitsubishi Trust and Banking Corp.[1,2,4] Japan	214,400	198,306	187,343(10)	6,946(16)	1,300(12)
15	13	Crédit Lyonnais France	210,799	178,931	175,800(14)	6,699(18)	940(26)
13	14	Mitsui Bank[1,3] Japan	207,543	196,205	160,226(17)	5,985(22)	1,300(12)
14	15	Barclays United Kingdom	205,799	189,334	167,402(15)	10,039(7)	1,115(18)
18	16	Deutsche Bank[2,4] West Germany	203,028	171,511	184,762(11)	8,506(11)	2,089(7)
22	17	Bank of Tokyo[1] Japan	199,728	162,640	151,425(19)	4,844(33)	1,225(15)

18	Sumitomo Trust & Banking Co.[1,2,4] Japan	189,798	169,396	179,259(12)	4,937(29)	1,185(16)	19
19	National Westminster Bank United Kingdom	187,371	178,473	156,525(18)	9,592(9)	652(45)	16
20	Mitsui Trust & Banking Co.[1,2] Japan	186,226	173,206	162,431(16)	4,891(32)	994(23)	17
21	Taiyo Kobe Bank[1,2,3,4] Japan	174,966	166,689	140,023(22)	4,784(34)	862(30)	21
22	Long-Term Credit Bank of Japan[1,2,4] Japan	173,624	166,944	148,526(20)	5,077(27)	967(25)	20
23	Société Générale France	164,798	145,741	138,574(23)	4,776(35)	1,013(21)	24
24	Daiwa Bank[1,2,4] Japan	157,334	144,514	135,470(26)	3,227(57)	671(41)	25
25	Yasuda Trust & Banking Co.[1,2,4] Japan	156,674	147,284	132,771(27)	4,579(38)	992(24)	23
26	Centre National des Caisses d'Epargne et de Prévoyance France	150,709	139,461	144,016(21)	7,864(13)	626(49)	26
27	Dresdner Bank West Germany	145,969	129,525	135,952(25)	5,425(25)	799(32)	27
28	Compagnie Financière de Paribas France	138,716	121,654	—	6,970(15)	—	28
29	Hongkong and Shanghai Banking Corp. Hongkong	128,981	109,832	118,634(28)	6,749(17)	—	32
30	Toyko Trust and Banking Co.[1,2,4] Japan	125,149	119,673	106,170(30)	3,234(56)	679(40)	29
31	Nippon Credit Bank[1,2,4] Japan	119,670	110,007	97,455(31)	2,962(63)	564(54)	31
32	Union Bank of Switzerland[2,4] Switzerland	114,142	110,893	97,016(32)	7,963(12)	786(33)	30
33	Commerzbank West Germany	112,466	100,769	106,890(29)	3,886(46)	620(50)	36
34	Deutsche Genossenschaftsbank West Germany	109,581	74,318	57,364(64)	2,661(76)	323(86)	60
35	Istituto Bancario San Paolo di Torino Italy	107,664	81,806	79,615(47)	—	—	52
36	Chase Manhattan Corp. United States	106,347	95,821	69,073(54)	4,944(28)	−469(184)	38
37	Swiss Bank Corp.[2,4] Switzerland	105,356	102,589	91,114(35)	6,168(21)	649(46)	34
38	Kyowa Bank[1,2,4] Japan	104,995	103,155	81,702(43)	2,749(71)	576(53)	33
39	Westdeutsche Landesbank West Germany	104,671	92,760	96,733(33)	2,775(69)	295(97)	41
40	Bank of China[2,4] China	103,738	98,478	80,535(46)	7,718(14)	—	37

(continued)

243

The 50 Largest International Banks (concluded)

Rank 1988	Rank 1989	Name of Bank (Country)	Assets (US$ millions) 1989	1988	Deposits (US$ millions) 1989	Capital (US$ millions) 1989	Pretax Earnings (US$ millions) 1989
43	41	Bayerische Vereinsbank West Germany	102,563	91,620	96,378(34)	2,474(84)	422(72)
45	42	Banca Nazionale del Lavoro[4] Italy	101,212	87,750	83,864(41)	3,917(45)	700(38)
35	43	Midland Bank United Kingdom	100,756	100,830	85,038(38)	4,330(41)	-421(182)
46	44	Saitama Bank[1,2,4] Japan	98,966	86,480	76,517(51)	2,600(79)	501(63)
40	45	BankAmerica Corp. United States	97,231	93,204	81,186(45)	5,534(23)	1,348(11)
50	46	Amsterdam-Rotterdam Bank Netherlands	93,114	83,439	86,996(36)	3,472(51)	500(64)
39	47	Lloyds Bank United Kingdom	92,795	93,783	84,494(40)	3,814(47)	-1,153(187)
42	48	Skoko Chukin Bank[1,2,4] Japan	91,751	91,873	82,580(42)	2,248(93)	123(145)
55	49	Bayerische Landesbank[2] West Germany	91,198	79,984	76,755(50)	1,955(101)	331(84)
49	50	Algemene Bank Nederland Netherlands	90,595	85,053	72,933(53)	3,392(53)	515(61)

*To compile the global banking rankings, *Institutional Investor* first asked more than 300 of the world's leading bank holding companies to report their assets, deposits, capital and pretax earnings in local currencies as of year-end 1988 and year-end 1989. Banks that reported figures for fiscal years are noted in the tables. For the sake of comparability, we then converted the local currencies into U.S. dollars at year-end rates for banks on calendar years. For those not on calendar years, the conversion rates used are those prevailing at the end of each bank's fiscal year. The conversion figures were provided by the money desk of a major U.S. bank.

It should be noted that the banks were asked to report consolidated figures for all other banks in which they have an interest of 50 percent or more. Those that chose not to provide consolidated figures are noted. The banks were also asked if their figures included recent mergers and acquisitions; those that said they did not are also noted. Figures reflect consolidated bank holding company interests only; industrial and other nonbank holdings are not included.

Banks were asked to report their figures published in these tables using the following definitions:

Total assets exclude contra accounts where contra accounts are defined as acceptances, bonds or other securities held for customers; letters of credit; guarantees; and similar instruments.

Capital includes funds supplied by shareholders, such as permanent preferred stock, share capital, retained earnings or undistributed profits and contingent type reserves. It excludes reserves for possible loan losses, subordinated debt and redeemable preferred stock.

Pretax earnings include earnings before taxes and extraordinary items.

** The table reproduced here includes only the top 50 of the top 200 banks in assets listed in the *Institutional Investor*.

[1] As of March 31, 1989, 1988.

[2] Figures do not include all subsidiaries owned 50 percent or more.

[3] Mitsui Bank merged with Taiyo Kobe Bank on April 1, 1990 forming Mitsui Taiyo Kobe Bank.

[4] Not adjusted for all mergers and acquisitions.

Source: *Institutional Investor*, June 1990.

The 100 Largest Brokerage Houses

Rank 1988	1989	Firm	Total Consolidated Capital ($ millions)	Equity Capital ($ millions)	Long Term Debt ($ millions)	"Excess" Net Capital ($ millions)
1	1	Merrill Lynch & Co.[1]	$10,048.4	$3,151.3	$6,897.1	$1,052.8
2	2	Shearson Lehman Hutton	8,966.0	2,200.0	6,766.0	1,140.0
3	3	Salomon Brothers Holding Co.	5,757.0	3,906.0	1,851.0	878.7
4	4	Goldman, Sachs & Co.[2]	4,018.0	2,145.0	1,873.0	684.0
5	5	Morgan Stanley & Co.	2,648.0	2,021.0	627.0	382.7
8	6	Prudential-Bache Securities	1,840.4	959.5	880.9	275.1
7	7	First Boston Corp.	1,783.0	1,056.0	727.0	508.0
9	8	PaineWebber Group	1,523.1	1,001.2	521.9	386.6
11	9	Bear, Stearns & Co.	1,444.0	1,060.0	384.0	277.0
12	10	Dean Witter Reynolds[3]	1,429.0	940.0	489.0	604.0
13	11	Smith Barney, Harris Upham & Co.	927.0	758.0	169.0	184.0
14	12	Donaldson, Lufkin & Jenrette	900.0	289.0	611.0	189.0
15	13	Kidder, Peabody & Co.[4]	728.0	391.0	337.0	161.0
18	14	Shelby Cullom Davis & Co.	550.7	550.7	—	397.1
—	15	BT Securities Corp.	479.0	479.0	—	380.0
17	16	J.P. Morgan Securities	469.0	469.0	—	264.0
20	17	Nomura Securities International	376.0	226.0	150.0	153.0
19	18	Charles Schwab & Co.	344.0	279.0	65.0	77.0
22	19	A.G. Edwards & Sons	304.0	304.0	—	135.0
29	20	UBS Securities	293.0	118.0	175.0	185.5
30	21	Dillon, Read & Co.	251.0	209.0	42.0	44.0
23	22	Deutsche Bank Capital Corp.	249.0	103.0	146.0	52.0
26	23	Oppenheimer & Co.	247.9	182.1	65.8	78.2
25	24	Aubrey G. Lanston & Co.	247.1	247.1	—	106.1
24	25	Spear, Leeds & Kellogg	243.0	158.0	85.0	125.0
27	26	Van Kampen Merritt	238.0	238.0	—	64.0
28	27	Nikko Securities Co. International	232.0	132.0	100.0	167.0
32	28	Daiwa Securities America	218.0	118.0	100.0	138.0
38	29	Allen & Co. Inc.	210.3	206.8	3.5	67.0
34	30	Yamaichi International (America)	188.0	138.0	50.0	140.0
35	31	Gruntal & Co.	179.6	156.4	23.2	46.6
37	32	Wertheim Schroder & Co.	172.3	142.7	29.6	72.2
33	33	Alex. Brown & Sons	148.0	128.0	20.0	84.0
31	34	John Nuveen & Co.	140.0	140.0	—	70.0
43	35	Neuberger & Berman	137.0	137.0	—	92.0
—	36	Sanwa-BGK Securities	135.0	135.0	—	—
40	37	Gruss Partners	134.0	134.0	—	117.0
45	38	Stephens[5]	127.0	127.0	—	43.9
44	39	Prescott, Ball & Turben	124.0	113.0	11.0	17.0
42	40	Edward D. Jones & Co.	123.9	71.1	52.8	67.3
—	41	Manufacturers Hanover Securities	123.4	113.4	10.0	92.1
41	42	Jefferies & Co.	121.0	80.9	40.1	65.8
61	43	Legg Mason Wood Walker/Howard, Weil, Labouisse, Friedrichs	117.0	91.3	25.7	40.1
48	44	M.A. Schapiro & Co.	116.7	116.7	—	86.5
—	45	Discount Corp. of New York	114.0	114.0	—	—
50	46	Fidelity Brokerage Services	112.2	112.2	—	22.4
46	47	Brown Brothers Harriman & Co.	109.9	109.9	—	—
60	48	Raymond James Financial	103.0	75.0	28.0	18.0
—	49	Barclays de Zoete Wedd Securities	101.0	101.0	—	—
47	50	Lazard Frères & Co.	100.0	100.0	—	53.0
54	51	Quick & Reilly Group[6]	97.2	96.8	0.4	52.0
52	52	Cowen & Co.	94.3	82.7	11.6	21.9
51	53	Glickenhaus & Co.	94.0	94.0	—	42.0
55	54	Kloinwort Benson Holdings	93.0	42.7	50.3	17.8
53	55	Interstate/Johnson Lane Corp.	90.2	60.6	29.6	19.0
—	56	Cantor, Fitzgerald & Co.	87.1	87.1	—	23.2
58	57	S.G. Warburg & Co.	83.5	58.5	25.0	28.6

(continued)

The 100 Largest Brokerage Houses *(concluded)*

Rank 1988	1989	Firm	Total Consolidated Capital ($ millions)	Equity Capital ($ millions)	Long Term Debt ($ millions)	"Excess" Net Capital ($ millions)
57	58	Janney Montgomery Scott	81.3	72.3	9.0	34.9
59	59	Advest	75.0	75.0	—	12.0
64	60	Blunt Ellis & Loewi	75.0	50.0	25.0	25.0
65	61	Furman Selz Mager Dietz & Birney	74.7	64.7	10.0	39.8
72	62	Arnhold & S. Bleichroeder	72.0	72.0	—	45.0
62	63	Mabon, Nugent & Co.	69.9	69.9	—	22.2
67	64	Dain Bosworth	68.5	59.4	9.1	19.5
76	65	Tucker Anthony	67.5	66.7	0.8	29.9
73	66	Herzog Heine Geduld	67.0	33.0	34.0	39.0
63	67	Bateman Eichler, Hill Richards	66.0	51.0	15.0	7.3
70	68	J.C. Bradford & Co.	64.5	64.5	—	22.7
66	69	Piper, Jaffray & Hopwood	61.3	61.3	—	20.0
71	70	Keefe, Bruyette & Woods	60.3	50.1	10.2	—
69	71	McDonald & Co. Securities	59.6	38.7	20.9	21.7
77	72	S.D. Securities	56.9	56.9	—	32.2
75	73	Boettcher & Co.	56.0	56.0	—	12.0
80	74	Bernard L. Madoff Investment Securities	55.9	55.9	—	43.3
78	75	Wheat, First Securities	55.8	50.8	5.0	16.6
87	76	Montgomery Securities	55.5	27.1	28.4	28.5
74	77	Weiss, Peck & Greer	55.0	47.0	8.0	15.0
83	78	Robert W. Baird & Co.	51.5	51.5	—	24.9
82	79	Easton & Co.	50.9	50.8	0.1	47.4
79	80	William Blair & Co.	50.0	50.0	—	24.7
83	81	Eaton Vance Distributors[7]	49.8	49.8	—	1.4
81	82	Morgan Keegan & Co.	49.0	49.0	—	14.1
—	83	Miller Tabak Hirsch & Co.	46.0	46.0	—	7.0
56	84	Smith New Court, Carl Marks	46.0	38.2	7.8	22.4
85	85	ABD Securities Corp.	45.0	45.0	—	23.0
—	86	CL GlobalPartners Securities Corp.	45.0	45.0	—	31.0
88	87	Chicago Corp.	43.4	32.4	11.0	5.8
90	88	Eppler, Guerin & Turner	41.0	41.0	—	18.0
67	89	Timber Hill	41.0	36.0	5.0	24.0
86	90	New Japan Securities International[8]	40.9	26.9	14.0	30.5
89	91	McMahan Securities Co.	40.4	31.9	8.5	11.4
—	92	Sanford C. Bernstein & Co.	40.0	40.0	—	17.0
—	93	Printon, Kane Group	39.8	39.8	—	6.2
96	94	Crowell, Weedon & Co.	39.5	37.9	1.6	10.3
91	95	Rothschild Inc.	39.0	39.0	—	19.0
92	96	ScotiaMcLeod (USA)	38.8	38.8	—	14.4
97	97	C.J. Lawrence, Morgan Grenfell	38.0	38.0	—	15.0
94	98	J.J.B. Hilliard, W.L. Lyons	37.7	34.6	3.1	13.5
—	99	Dominick & Dominick	34.5	34.5	—	—
—	100	Kalb, Voorhis & Co.	33.3	33.3	—	27.3

[1] As of 12/29/89.
[2] As of 11/24/89.
[3] Represents U.S. broker-dealer only.
[4] As of 12/25/89.
[5] As of 12/29/89.
[6] As of 11/24/89.
[7] As of 10/31/89. Figures do not include those of parent company, Eaton Vance Management.
[8] As of 3/31/89

Source: *Institutional Investor,* April 1990.

America's Most and Least Admired Corporations*

AT THE TOP AND BOTTOM OF THE 305 COMPANIES

THE MOST ADMIRED

Merck still reigns as America's most admired large corporation. Procter & Gamble, Coca-Cola, and Anheuser-Busch return to the top ten after at least a year away, while Du Pont is the only first-timer.

THE LEAST ADMIRED

California's Gibraltar Financial Corp., the next-to-least- admired in 1988, wins this year's booby prize. New to the bottom ten are Wang Labs, United Merchants & Manufacturers, K-H Corp., and Unisys.

RANK	LAST YEAR	COMPANY	SCORE
1	1	**Merck** Pharmaceuticals	8.90
2	4	**Philip Morris** Tobacco	8.78
3	2	**Rubbermaid** Rubber products	8.42
4	*13	**Procter & Gamble** Soaps, cosmetics	8.37
5	3	**3M** Scientific and photographic equipment	8.21
6	7	**PepsiCo** Beverages	8.16
6	5	**Wal-Mart** Retailing	8.16
8	*13	**Coca-Cola** Beverages	8.15
9	17	**Anheuser-Busch** Beverages	7.96
10	15	**Du Pont** Chemicals	7.93

RANK	LAST YEAR	COMPANY	SCORE
305	304	**Gilbraltar Financial** Savings institutions	2.24
304	289	**Wang Laboratories** Computers (and office equipment)	3.08
303	298	**Control Data** Computers (and office equipment)	3.59
302	302	**Meritor Financial Group** Savings institutions	3.61
301	303	**Texas Air** Transportation	3.72
300	300	**LTV** Metals	3.86
299	—	**National Steel** Metals	4.01
298	295	**United Merchants & Mfrs.** Textiles	4.03
297	292	**K-H** Motor vehicles & parts	4.05
296	260	**Unisys** Computers (and office equipment)	4.18

* P&G and Coca-Cola were tied in score last year.

Source: "Reprinted by permission from FORTUNE Magazine; © 1990 The Time Inc. Magazine Company. All rights reserved."

* HOW IT WAS DONE. Our eighth annual Corporate Reputations Survey covers 305 companies in the 32 industry groups that appeared in last year's FORTUNE 500 and FORTUNE Service 500. We polled more than 8,000 high executives, outside directors, and financial analysts and asked them to rate the ten largest companies in their own industry (a shorter list in some cases) on eight attributes, using a scale of 0 (poor) to 10 (excellent). The attributes were quality of management; quality of products or services; innovativeness; long-term investment value; financial soundness; ability to attract, develop, and keep talented people; community and environmental responsibility; and use of corporate assets.

Companies are assigned to an industry group according to the business that contributed most to their 1988 sales. All of the corporations that appear on FORTUNE's reputations list make public filings of their key financial information.

America's Top 100 Growth Companies

Rank	Company	Growth EPS* 5-yr.	Growth EPS† 12-mo.	Growth Sales* 5-yr.	Latest 12-month Sales	Latest 12-month EPS	Latest 12-month P/E	Return on Capital	Debt as % of Capital	Cash Flow/ Share	Recent Stock Price	Growth‡ Multiple	Market Value
1	Stewart & Stevenson Svcs	255%	2%	22%	$621	$1.94	19	15%	13%	$0.60	$36	0.07	$540
2	Fibreboard	160	102	16	230	1.23	8	3	17	0.90	10	0.05	38
3	Comair Holdings	157	93	26	158	1.60	12	11	22	2.83	19	0.08	156
4	Chemical Fabrics	148	45	10	47	0.96	22	20	14	0.89	21	0.15	95
5	Concord Computing	145	36	36	33	1.17	22	26	6	3.33	26	0.15	85
6	Re Capital	144	22	230	103	1.22	11	7	0	NA	14	0.08	88
7	CSM Systems	135	300	17	9	0.52	10	11	4	1.73	5	0.07	5
8	Fredericks of Hollywood	130	79	15	90	0.68	18	17	1	0.84	12	0.14	70
9	BMC Inds	126	8	15	166	1.03	10	7	77	1.26	10	0.08	54
10	MMI Medical	121	-50	27	38	0.51	9	14	13	2.05	5	0.08	13
11	Union Carbide	121	-39	5	8,676	3.64	5	17	56	5.16	19	0.04	2,759
12	C-COR Electronics	114	6	22	59	1.19	10	27	3	0.76	12	0.09	51
13	DSC Communications	109	65	7	454	0.84	15	8	41	0.43	13	0.14	522
14	Stone Container	104	-35	40	5,656	3.92	4	19	42	1.49	17	0.04	1,041
15	Coast Distribution System	98	-4	35	145	0.86	7	5	65	-2.19	6	0.07	24
16	First Capital Holdings	92	-8	215	1,016	1.70	3	10	48	NA	5	0.03	221
17	Lukens	91	25	12	655	4.66	8	14	22	5.89	38	0.09	311
18	Valmont Inds	89	24	29	815	1.80	11	13	38	3.14	20	0.12	219
19	Reynolds Metals	89	-17	14	6,152	8.23	7	14	29	13.70	57	0.08	3,404
20	Gish Biomedical	86	39	28	17	0.68	26	15	3	0.48	17	0.30	30
21	Oriole Homes	86	-30	14	101	1.82	4	10	46	-5.16	8	0.05	30
22	Dow Chemical	84	-13	14	18,015	8.19	7	21	33	11.75	59	0.09	15,856
23	Chubb	82	15	14	4,052	4.96	9	13	19	NA	45	0.11	3,810
24	CSS Inds	81	2	86	147	2.95	6	25	46	1.75	17	0.07	86
25	Bridgford Foods	81	26	8	79	0.92	21	25	0	0.82	20	0.27	82
26	Danaher	80	15	37	742	1.97	10	14	43	4.57	20	0.13	464
27	Compaq Computer	79	13	59	3,065	3.97	15	23	19	2.74	60	0.19	4,692
28	Seagull Energy	78	21	19	180	1.64	17	5	44	-6.34	27	0.21	192
29	American Fructose	77	46	10	185	2.30	10	10	27	3.52	23	0.13	225
30	Hydro Flame	75	-68	13	29	0.57	8	10	32	0.46	5	0.11	3
31	Autoclave Engineers	73	-3	22	81	1.06	10	13	13	3.06	11	0.14	46
32	Volt Information Sciences	73	-9	5	536	0.49	27	1	52	3.12	13	0.37	78
33	Swift Energy	72	14	50	17	1.51	7	30	0	1.60	11	0.10	52
34	Nike	71	31	16	2,040	5.62	13	28	6	4.43	74	0.19	2,776
35	Federal Paper Board	71	15	14	1,342	4.76	4	14	46	6.86	21	0.06	838
36	Twin Disc	71	-54	10	172	1.53	14	13	0	3.26	22	0.20	62
37	Aluminum Co. of America	70	-15	19	11,149	9.24	7	14	20	17.34	65	0.10	5,669
38	TCBY Enterprises	69	24	68	157	1.14	17	25	18	1.29	19	0.24	502
39	St. Jude Medical	69	40	47	155	1.16	27	27	0	0.99	31	0.39	1,460
40	Capitol Transamerica	69	19	29	27	2.45	6	29	0	2.13	15	0.09	50
41	Hanover Insurance	69	-41	19	1,660	3.13	8	11	0	NA	26	0.12	544
42	Instituform East	67	-20	20	19	0.40	10	17	0	0.62	4	0.15	18
43	K-Tron International	67	-26	16	58	1.08	9	9	60	2.53	10	0.13	28
44	Nature's Sunshine Products	66	10	13	55	0.75	16	27	0	0.97	12	0.25	62

Rank	Company	Score											
45	Presidential Life	66			340	1.61	5	17	34	NA	8	0.07	225
46	Archive	65	24	32	199	1.17	9	18	1	1.96	11	0.14	134
47	General Re	65	13	8	2,769	6.47	13	18	8	NA	83	0.20	7,417
48	Energy Ventures	64	267	70	113	0.44	39	8	26	-0.15	17	0.60	160
49	Freeport McMoRan	64	19	29	1,880	5.24	6	7	81	6.25	33	0.10	1,755
50	Kilearn Properties	63	14	44	19	1.51	3	8	48	2.59	5	0.05	7
51	Oneida	63	-27	12	408	1.12	12	10	35	2.14	13	0.18	130
52	Selas Corp. of America	62	463	10	59	1.69	8	3	27	2.74	14	0.13	30
53	Alberto-Culver	62	17	18	745	1.21	20	13	30	0.65	24	0.32	62
54	Pioneer Standard Electronics	62	-12	11	320	1.06	12	7	58	1.17	13	0.19	68
55	Comshare	62	45	9	98	1.19	18	18	4	2.65	21	0.28	110
56	Consolidated Products	62	17	8	103	1.10	11	12	50	2.30	12	0.17	49
57	Home Depot	61	47	43	2,998	1.05	37	14	37	1.02	38	0.60	4,425
58	International Paper	61	4	25	11,916	7.41	7	12	31	10.86	51	0.11	5,571
59	Terex	60	29	137	954	1.96	11	5	77	-8.00	22	0.18	212
60	Esquire Radio & Electric	60	-22	126	46	2.27	12	7	0	-6.96	27	0.20	13
61	Fedders	60	15	38	373	1.22	13	13	50	-0.86	15	0.21	255
62	Telecredit	60	25	16	167	2.52	20	33	0	2.16	51	0.34	563
63	Stride Rite	60	20	12	485	1.90	14	27	3	2.26	26	0.23	694
64	Baldwin & Lyons	60	4	10	112	2.94	8	13	0	4.05	23	0.13	125
65	DH Technology	59	48	40	44	1.27	11	23	12	1.63	14	0.19	6
66	Incomp Computer Centers	59	21	29	467	0.94	9	10	32	NA	8	0.14	5
67	Walt Disney	59	26	23	5,105	5.49	23	18	22	7.92	126	0.39	17,069
68	Keane	59	21	17	84	0.97	17	20	26	0.24	17	0.29	72
69	Monsanto	58	13	7	8,702	4.88	10	13	27	6.14	49	0.17	6,449
70	Integrated Device Technology	56	-6	44	210	0.66	8	13	19	1.26	6	0.15	139
71	Georgia-Pacific	56	28	11	10,383	6.95	6	13	46	14.67	41	0.11	3,564
72	Varian Associates	56	-41	9	1,347	1.30	22	7	11	NA	28	0.38	530
73	Ardahl	55	-36	26	2,138	1.24	12	12	7	2.58	15	0.23	1,674
74	Crystal Brands	55	50	10	853	3.08	9	5	53	5.55	29	0.17	262
75	Puerto Rican Cement	55	-18	8	80	6.71	7	15	29	6.68	49	0.13	9
76	Franklin Resources	54	21	38	270	2.18	15	35	3	1.95	32	0.27	1,255
77	Hufy	54	191	11	462	1.92	11	10	38	2.69	21	0.20	180
78	TBC	54	11	6	486	1.10	11	22	0	0.49	12	0.20	176
79	Costar	53	32	11	42	0.94	22	6	5	-0.75	21	0.42	70
80	Chambers Development	52	24	77	204	0.56	41	7	46	NA	23	0.79	748
81	Apple Computer	51	26	30	5,472	3.88	11	27	0	4.64	41	0.21	5,162
82	Marshall Inds	51	-15	21	526	2.03	14	12	23	0.58	29	0.28	242
83	Sequa	50	-21	47	2,046	5.34	14	4	57	12.01	73	0.27	714
84	Biomet	50	45	44	155	1.00	27	22	0	0.91	27	0.54	742
85	Dynamics Research	50	-9	12	89	0.71	7	20	0	1.80	5	0.14	25
86	Equitable Iowa	50	41	7	610	4.40	7	9	17	NA	30	0.14	211
87	JWP	49	26	85	1,910	1.99	19	7	53	-1.40	38	0.39	953
88	Software Publishing	49	22	36	117	1.60	15	26	0	1.23	25	0.32	292
89	Berkshire Hathaway	49	-5	31	2,484	390	18	8	17	924	6,925	0.36	7,943
90	First Financial Management	48	29	93	737	2.33	9	8	45	NA	22	0.19	571

(continued)

America's Top 100 Growth Companies (concluded)

Rank	Company	Growth EPS* 5-yr.	Growth EPS† 12-mo.	Growth Sales* 5-yr.	Latest 12-month Sales	Latest 12-month EPS	Latest 12-month P/E	Return on Capital	Debt as % of Capital	Cash Flow/ Share	Recent Stock Price	Growth‡ Multiple	Market Value
91	Zenith National Insurance	48	-6	23	487	2.03	7	15	5	1.27	15	0.15	304
92	Boole & Babbage	47	27	26	86	1.36	15	20	10	2.60	21	0.33	81
93	Odetics	47	75	15	55	0.28	21	2	56	-0.37	6	0.46	26
94	General Binding	47	29	13	292	1.25	15	18	5	NA	19	0.32	252
95	Mark IV Inds	46	15	78	840	1.81	7	3	82	-9.99	14	0.16	200
96	Neutrogena	46	-11	29	205	0.83	25	34	0	1.43	21	0.54	539
97	Stuart Hall	46	-18	14	93	0.53	22	7	51	0.24	12	0.49	43
98	Genentech	45	280	48	430	0.57	48	7	25	1.19	28	1.07	2,308
99	Span-America Medical Systems	45	33	38	24	0.40	11	6	30	0.57	4	0.24	14
100	Helen of Troy	45	-15	31	119	1.98	8	17	2	-0.90	15	0.17	78

* Annualized.

† Trailing 12-month EPS compared with trailing 12-month EPS one year ago.

‡ Price/earnings ratio divided by five-year annual EPS growth rate.

NA—not available, not applicable.

Notes: Sales and market value are in millions. Prices are as of June 25, 1990.

Sources: William O'Neil & Co.; FW.

Source: Reprinted with the permission of Financial World Magazine, 1990.

Largest Certified Public Accounting (CPA) Firms*

Altschuler, Melvoin & Glasser
69 West Washington Street
Chicago, IL 60602
312-236-9500

Arthur Andersen & Company
69 West Washington Street
Chicago, IL 60602
312-346-6262

Baird, Kurtz & Dobson
928 Grand Avenue
Kansas City, MO 64106
816-221-7544

BDO/Seidman & Seidman
15 Columbus Circle
New York, NY 10023
212-765-7500

Cherry, Bekaert & Holland
1 NCNB Plaza
Charlotte, NC 28280
704-377-3741

Clifton, Gunderson & Co.
808 Commercial National Bank Building
Peoria, IL 61602
309-671-4511

Coopers & Lybrand
1251 Avenue of the Americas
New York, NY 10020
212-536-2000

Crowe, Chizek & Co.
330 East Jefferson Boulevard
South Bend, IN 46624
219-232-3992

Deloitte Touche
1114 Avenue of the Americas
New York, NY 10036
219-790-0500

1633 Broadway
New York, NY 10019
212-489-1600

Ernst & Young
277 Park Avenue
New York, NY 10017
212-922-2000

Grant Thornton
605 Third Avenue
New York, NY 10016
212-599-0100

Kenneth Leventhal & Company
2049 Century Park East
Los Angeles, CA 90067
213-277-0880

KPMG Peat, Marwick, Main & Co.
345 Park Avenue
New York, NY 10022
212-758-9700

Laventhol & Horwath
1845 Walnut Street
Philadelphia, PA 19103
215-299-1700

McGladrey & Pullen
640 Capital Square
4th & Locust
Des Moines, IA 50309
515-284-8660

Moss Adams & Co.
2830 Bank of California Center
Seattle, WA 98164
206-223-1820

George S. Olive & Co.
320 North Meridian Street
Indianapolis, IN 46204
317-267-8400

---

* Firms with the largest number of American Institute of Certified Public Accountants (AICPA) members.

Source: American Institute of Certified Public Accountants.

Pannell, Kerr, Forster & Co.
420 Lexington Avenue
New York, NY 10017
212-867-8000

Plante & Moran
26211 Central Park Boulevard
Southfield, MI 48037
313-352-2500

Price Waterhouse & Co.
1251 Avenue of the Americas
New York, NY 10020
212-489-8900

Spicer & Oppenheim
7 World Trade Center
New York, NY 10048
212-422-1000

Capital Sources for Startup Companies and Small Businesses

Sources of Venture Capital

Small Business Investment Companies (SBICs)

The following is an alphabetical listing by state of Small Business Investment Companies (including branch offices). The listed companies received licenses from SBA and their licenses remain outstanding. This list does not include currently licensed SBICs that are in the process of surrendering their licenses or subject to legal proceedings that might terminate their licenses. This publication does not purport to characterize the relative merits, as investment companies or otherwise, of the listed licensees. Inclusion on this list should not be interpreted as approval of a company's operations or as a recommendation by the SBA.

Details on any of the SBICs can be obtained by calling the company directly or from the *Directory of Small Business Investment Companies* available by writing John Edson c/o SBA, 1441 L Street, NW, Washington, DC 20416.

Alabama

First SBIC of
    Alabama
David Delaney, President
16 Midtown Park East
Mobile, AL 36606
(205) 476-0700

Hickory Venture
    Capital Corporation
J. Thomas Noojin, President
699 Gallatin Street, Suite A-2
Huntsville, AL 35801
(205) 539-1931

Source: *Directory of Operating Small Business Investment Companies*, U.S. Small Business Administration, Investment Division.

Note: In addition to the companies listed in this section of the *Almanac*, the *Directory of Small Business Investment Companies* includes SBICs designed to assist small businesses owned by socially or economically disadvantaged persons.

Alaska

Alaska Business
    Investment Corp.
James Cloud, Vice President
301 West Northern Lights Blvd.
Mail: P.O. Box 100600; Anchorage 99510
Anchorage, AK 99510
(907) 278-2071

Arizona

First Interstate
    Equity Corp.
Edmund G. Zito, President
100 West Washington Street
Phoenix, AZ 85003
(602) 271-1392

Northwest Venture
    Partners
(Main Office: Minneapolis, MN)
88777 E. Via de Ventura
Suite 335
Scottsdale, AZ 85258
(602) 483-8940

Norwest Growth Fund,
    Inc.
(Main Office: Minneapolis, MN)
88777 E. Via de Ventura
Suite 335
Scottsdale, AZ 85258
(602) 483-8940

Rocky Mountain Equity
    Corporation
Anthony J. Nicoli, President
4530 Central Avenue
Phoenix, AZ 85012
(602) 274-7534

Valley National
    Investors, Inc.
John M. Holliman III, V.P. & Manager
201 North Central Avenue, Suite 900
Phoenix, AZ 85004
(602) 261-1577

Wilbur Venture
   Capital Corp.
Jerry F. Wilbur, President
4575 South Palo Verde, Suite 305
Tucson, AZ 85714
(602) 747-5999

Arkansas

Small Business
   Inv. Capital, Inc.
Charles E. Toland, President
10003 New Benton Hwy.
Mail: P.O. Box 3627
Little Rock, AR 72203
(501) 455-6599

Southern Ventures, Inc
Jeffrey A. Doose, President & Director
605 Main Street, Suite 202
Arkadelphia, AR 71923
(501) 246-9627

California

AMF Financial, Inc.
William Temple, Vice President
4330 La Jolla Village Drive
Suite 110
San Diego, CA 92122
(619) 546-0167

BNP Venture Capital
   Corporation
Edgerton Scott II, President
3000 Sand Hill Road
Building 1, Suite 125
Menlo Park, CA 94025
(415) 854-1084

Bancorp Venture
   Capital, Inc.
Arthur H. Bernstein, President
11812 San Vicente Boulevard
Los Angeles, CA 90049
(213) 820-7222

BankAmerica Ventures,
   Inc.
Patrick Topolski, President
555 California Street
San Francisco, CA 94104
(415) 953-3001

CFB Venture Capital
   Corporation
Richard J. Roncaglia, Vice President
530 B Street, Third Floor
San Diego, CA 92101
(619) 230-3304

CFB Venture Capital
   Corporation
(Main Office: San Diego, CA)
350 California Street, Mezzanine
San Francisco, CA 94104
(415) 445-0594

Citicorp Venture
   Capital, Ltd.
(Main Office: New York, NY)
2 Embarcadero Place
2200 Geny Road, Suite 203
Palo Alto, CA 94303
(415) 424-8000

City Ventures, Inc.
James Bandler, Vice President
120 S. Spalding Drive, Suite 320
Beverly Hills, CA 90212
(213) 550-5686

Crosspoint Investment
   Corporation
Max Simpson, Pres. & Chief F.O.
1951 Landings Drive
Mountain View, CA 94043
(415) 968-0930

Developers Equity
   Capital Corporation
Larry Sade, Chairman of the Board
1880 Century Park East
Suite 311
Los Angeles, CA 90067
(213) 277-0330

Draper Associates,
   a California LP
Bill Edwards, President
c/o Timothy C. Draper
3000 Sand Hill Road, Bldg. 4, #235
Menlo Park, CA 94025
(415) 854-1712

First Interstate
   Capital, Inc.
Ronald J. Hall, Managing Director
5000 Birch Street, Suite 10100
Newport Beach, CA 92660
(714) 253-4360

First SBIC of
   California
Tim Hay, President
650 Town Center Drive
Seventeenth Floor
Costa Mesa, CA 92626
(714) 556-1964

First SBIC of
   California
(Main Office: Costa Mesa, CA)
5 Palo Alto Square, Suite 938
Palo Alto, CA 94306
(415) 424-8011

First SBIC of
   California
(Main Office: Costa Mesa, CA)
155 North Lake Avenue, Suite 1010
Pasadena, CA 91109
(818) 304-3451

G C & H Partners
James C. Gaither, General Partner
One Maritime Plaza, 20th Floor
San Francisco, CA 94110
(415) 981-5252

Hamco Capital Corp.
William R. Hambrecht, President
One Bush Street, 18th Floor
San Francisco, CA 94104
(415) 576-3635

Imperial Ventures,
   Inc.
H. Wayne Snavely, President
9920 South La Cienega Blvd.
Mail: P.O. Box 92991; L.A. 90009
Inglewood, CA 90301
(213) 417-5888

Jupiter Partners
John M. Bryan, President
600 Montgomery Street
35th Floor
San Francisco, CA 94111
(415) 421-9990

Marwit Capital Corp.
Martin W. Witte, President
180 Newport Center Drive
Suite 200
Newport Beach, CA 92660
(714) 640-6234

Merrill Pickard
   Anderson & Eyre I
Steven L. Merrill, President
Two Palo Alto Square, Suite 425
Palo Alto, CA 94306
(415) 856-8880

Metropolitan Venture
   Company, Inc.
Rudolph J. Lowy, Chairman of the Board
4021 Rosewood Avenue, 3rd Floor
Los Angeles, CA 90004
(213) 666-9882

New West Partners II
Timothy P. Haidinger, Manager
4350 Executive Drive, Suite 206
San Diego, CA 92121
(619) 457-0723

New West Partners II
(Main Office: San Diego, CA)
4600 Campus Drive, Suite 103
Newport Beach, CA 92660
(714) 756-8940

PBC Venture Capital
   Inc.
Henry L. Wheeler, Manager
1408 - 18th Street
Mail: P.O. Box 6008; Bakersfield 93386
Bakersfield, CA 93301
(805) 395-3555

Ritter Partners
William C. Edwards, President
150 Isabella Avenue
Atherton, CA 94025
(415) 854-1555

Round Table Capital
   Corporation
Richard Dumke, President
655 Montgomery Street, Suite 700
San Francisco, CA 94111
(415) 392-7500

San Joaquin Capital
   Corporation
Chester Troudy, President
1415 18th Street, Suite 306
Mail: P.O. Box 2538
Bakersfield, CA 93301
(805) 323-7581

Seaport Ventures, Inc.
Michael Stopler, President
525 B Street, Suite 630
San Diego, CA 92101
(619) 232-4069

Southwest Capital
   Investments, Inc.
Martin J. Roe, President
11812 San Vincente Blvd.
Los Angeles, CA 90049
(213) 820-7222

Union Venture Corp.
Jeffrey Watts, President
445 South Figueroa Street
Los Angeles, CA 90071
(213) 236-4092

VK Capital Company
Franklin Van Kasper, General Partner
50 California Street, Suite 2350
San Francisco, CA 94111
(415) 391-5600

Vista Capital Corp.
Frederick J. Howden, Jr., Chairman
9919 Via Pasar
San Diego, CA 92126
(619) 271-5952

Wells Fargo Capital
   Corporation
Ms. Sandra J. Menichelli, V.P. & G.M.
420 Montgomery Street, 9th Floor
San Francisco, CA 94163
(415) 396-2059

Westamco Investment
   Company
Leonard G. Muskin, President
8929 Wilshire Blvd., Suite 400
Beverly Hills, CA 90211
(213) 652-8288

Colorado

UBD Capital, Inc.
Allan R. Haworth, President
1700 Broadway
Denver, CO 80274
(303) 863-6329

Connecticut

AB SBIC, Inc.
Adam J. Bozzuto, President
275 School House Road
Cheshire, CT 06410
(203) 272-0203

All State Venture
   Capital Corporation
Ceasar N. Anquillare, President
The Bishop House
32 Elm Street, P.O. Box 1629
New Haven, CT 06506
(203) 787-5029

Capital Impact Corp.
Francis J. Waitr, President
10 Middle Street
Bridgeport, CT 06601
(203) 384-5670

Capital Resource Co.
   of Connecticut
I. Martin Fierberg, Managing Partner
699 Bloomfield Avenue
Bloomfield, CT 06002
(203) 243-1114

Dewey Investment Corp.
George E. Mrosek, President
85 Charter Oak Street
Manchester, CT 06040
(203) 649-0654

First Connecticut SBIC
David Engelson, President
177 State Street
Bridgeport, CT 06604
(203) 366-4726

First New England
   Capital, LP
Richard C. Klaffky, President
255 Main Street
Hartford, CT 06106
(203) 728-5200

Marcon Capital Corp.
Martin A. Cohen, President
49 Riverside Avenue
Westport, CT 06880
(203) 226-6893

Northeastern Capital
   Corporation
Joseph V. Ciaburri, Chairman and CEO
209 Church Street
New Haven, CT 06510
(203) 865-4500

Regional Financial
   Enterprises, L.P.
Robert M. Williams, Managing Partner
36 Grove Street
New Canaan, CT 06840
(203) 966-2800

SBIC of Connecticut
   Inc. (The)
Kenneth F. Zarrilli, President
1115 Main Street
Bridgeport, CT 06603
(203) 367-3282

Delaware

BDP Capital Ltd.
Marshall W. Pagon, President
103 Springer Building
3411 Silverside Road
Wilmington, DE 19810
(302) 478-6160

Morgan Investment
   Corporation
William E. Pike, Chairman
902 Market Street
Wilmington, DE 19801
(302) 651-2500

D.C.

Allied Investment
  Corporation
David J. Gladstone, President
1666 K Street, N.W., Suite 901
Washington, DC 20006
(202) 331-1112

American Security
  Capital Corp., Inc.
Richard P. Stifel, President
730 Fifteenth Street, N.W.
Washington, DC 20013
(202) 624-4843

DC Bancorp Venture
  Capital Company
Allan A. Weissburg, President
1801 K Street, N.W.
Washington, DC 20006
(202) 955-6970

Washington Ventures,
  Inc.
Kenneth A. Swain, President
4340 Connecticut Ave., N.W.
Washington, DC 20008
(202) 895-2560

Florida

Allied Investment
  Corporation
(Main Office: Washington, DC)
Executive Office Center, Suite 305
2770 N. Indian River Blvd.
Vero Beach, FL 32960
(407) 778-5556

Gold Coast Capital
  Corporation
William I. Gold, President
3550 Biscayne Blvd., Room 601
Miami, FL 33137
(305) 576-2012

J & D Capital Corp.
Jack Carmel, President
12747 Biscayne Blvd.
North Miami, FL 33181
(305) 893-0303

Mariner Venture
  Capital Corporation
Gary O. Marino, President
2300 W. Glades Road
Suite 440 West Tower
Boca Raton, FL 33431
(407) 394-3066

Market Capital Corp.
E. E. Eads, President
1102 North 28th Street
P.O. Box 22667
Tampa, FL 33630
(813) 247-1357

Quantum Capital
  Partners, Ltd.
Michael E. Chaney, President
2400 East Commercial Boulevard
Suite 814
Fort Lauderdale, FL 33308
(305) 776-1133

Sigma Capital Corp.
Alvin Schwartz, President
1515 N. Federal Highway
Suite 210
Boca Raton, FL 33432
(407) 394-8977

Western Financial
  Capital Corporation
(Main Office: Dallas, TX)
AmeriFirst Bank Building, 2nd Floor S
18301 Biscayne Boulevard
N. Miami Beach, FL 33160
(305) 933-5858

Georgia

Investor's Equity,
  Inc.
I. Walter Fisher, President
2629 First National Bank Tower
Atlanta, GA 30383
(404) 523-3999

North Riverside
  Capital Corporation
Tom Barry, President
50 Technology Park/Atlanta
Norcross, GA 30092
(404) 446-5556

Hawaii

Bancorp Hawaii SBIC
James D. Evans, Jr., President
111 South King Street
Suite 1060
Honolulu, HI 96813
(808) 521-6411

Illinois

ANB Venture
  Corporation
Kurt L. Liljedahl, Exec. Vice-President
33 North LaSalle Street
Chicago, IL 60690
(312) 855-1554

Alpha Capital Venture
Partners, L.P.
Andrew H. Kalnow, General Partner
Three First National Plaza, 14th Floor
Chicago, IL 60602
(312) 372-1556

Business Ventures,
Incorporated
Milton Lefton, President
20 North Wacker Drive, Suite 1741
Chicago, IL 60606
(312) 346-1580

Continental Illinois
Venture Corp.
John L. Hines, President
209 South LaSalle Street
Mail: 231 South LaSalle Street
Chicago, IL 60693
(312) 828-8023

First Capital Corp.
of Chicago
John A. Canning, Jr., President
Three First National Plaza
Suite 1330
Chicago, IL 60670
(312) 732-5400

Frontenac Capital
Corporation
David A. R. Dullum, President
208 South LaSalle Street, Room 1900
Chicago, IL 60604
(312) 368-0047

Heller Equity
Capital Corporation
John M. Goense, President
200 North LaSalle Street
10th Floor
Chicago, IL 60601
(312) 621-7200

Walnut Capital Corp.
Burton W. Kanter, Chairman of the Board
208 South LaSalle Street
Chicago, IL 60604
(312) 346-2033

Indiana

1st Source Capital
Corporation
Eugene L. Cavanaugh, Jr., Vice President
100 North Michigan Street
Mail: P.O. Box 1602; South Bend 46634
South Bend, IN 46601
(219) 236-2180

Circle Ventures, Inc.
Robert Salyers, President
20 N. Meridan Street
Indianapolis, IN 46204
(317) 636-7242

Iowa

MorAmerica Capital
Corporation
David R. Schroder, Vice President
800 American Building
Cedar Rapids, IA 52401
(319) 363-8249

Kansas

Kansas Venture
Capital, Inc.
Larry J. High, Executive Vice President
One Townsite Plaza
Bank IV Tower, Suite 825
Topeka, KS 66603
(913) 233-1368

Kansas Venture
Capital, Inc.
(Main Office: Topeka, KS)
Rex E. Wiggins, President
6700 Antioch, Suite 200
Overland Park, KS 66204
(913) 262-7117

Kansas Venture
Capital, Inc.
(Main Office: Topeka, KS)
Thomas C. Blackburn, Regional V.P.
100 North Main, Suite 806
Wichita, KS 67202
(316) 262-1221

Kentucky

Financial
Opportunities, Inc.
Gary Duerr, Manager
6060 Dutchman's Lane
Mail: PO Box 35710; Louisville, KY 40232
Louisville, KY 40205
(502) 451-3800

Mountain Ventures,
Inc.
Jerry A. Rickett, President
London Bank & Trust Building
400 S. Main Street, Fourth Floor
London, KY 40741
(606) 864-5175

Wilbur Venture
    Capital Corp.
(Main Office: Tucson, AZ)
400 Fincastle Building
3rd & Broadway
Louisville, KY 40202
(502) 585-1214

Louisiana

Capital for
    Terrebonne, Inc.
Hartwell A. Lewis, President
27 Austin Drive
Houma, LA 70360
(504) 868-3930

Premier Venture
    Capital Corporation
G. Lee Griffin, President
451 Florida Street
Baton Rouge, LA 70821
(504) 389-4421

Maine

Maine Capital Corp.
David M. Coit, President
Seventy Center Street
Portland, ME 04101
(207) 772-1001

Maryland

First Maryland
    Capital, Inc.
Joseph A. Kenary, President
107 West Jefferson Street
Rockville, MD 20850
(301) 251-6630

Greater Washington
    Investments, Inc.
Don A. Christensen, President
5454 Wisconsin Avenue
Chevy Chase, MD 20815
(301) 656-0626

Jiffy Lube Capital
    Corporation
Eleanor C. Harding, President
6000 Metro Drive
Mail: PO Box 17223; Baltimore 21203-7223
Baltimore, MD 21215
(301) 764-3234

Massachusetts

Advent Atlantic
    Capital Company, LP
David D. Croll, Managing Partner
75 State Street, Suite 2500
Boston, MA 02109
(617) 345-7200

Advent IV Capital
    Company
David D. Croll, Managing Partner
75 State Street, Suite 2500
Boston, MA 02109
(617) 345-7200

Advent Industrial
    Capital Company, LP
David D. Croll, Managing Partner
75 State Street, Suite 2500
Boston, MA 02109
(617) 345-7200

Advent V Capital
    Company LP
David D. Croll, Managing Partner
75 State Street, Suite 2500
Boston, MA 02109
(617) 345-7200

Atlas II Capital
    Corporation
Joost E. Tjaden, President
101 Federal Street, 4th Floor
Boston, MA 02110
(617) 951-9420

BancBoston Ventures,
    Incorporated
Diana H. Frazier, President
100 Federal Street
Mail: P.O. Box 2016 Stop 01-31-08
Boston, MA 02110
(617) 434-2442

Bever Capital Corp.
Joost E. Tjaden, President
101 Federal Street, 4th Floor
Boston, MA 02110
(617) 951-9420

Boston Hambro Capital
    Company
Edwin Goodman, President of Corp. G.P.
160 State Street, 9th Floor
Boston, MA 02109
(617) 523-7767

Business Achievement
    Corporation
Michael L. Katzeff, President
1172 Beacon Street, Sutie 202
Newton, MA 02161
(617) 965-0550

Chestnut Capital
    International II LP
David D. Croll, Managing Partner
75 State Street, Suite 2500
Boston, MA 02109
(617) 345-7200

Chestnut Street
 Partners, Inc.
David D. Croll, President
75 State Street, Suite 2500
Boston, MA 02109
(617) 345-7220

First Capital Corp.
 of Chicago
(Main Office: Chicago, IL)
One Financial Center
27th Floor
Boston, MA 02111
(617) 542-9185

First United SBIC,
 Inc.
Alfred W. Ferrara, Vice President
135 Will Drive
Canton, MA 02021
(617) 828-6150

LRF Capital,
 Limited Partnership
Joseph J. Freeman, Manager
189 Wells Avenue, Suite 4
Newton, MA 02159
(617) 964-0049

Mezzanine Capital
 Corporation
David D. Croll, President
75 State Street, Suite 2500
Boston, MA 02109
(617) 345-7200

Milk Street Partners,
 Inc.
Richard H. Churchill, Jr., President
75 State Street, Suite 2500
Boston, MA 02109
(617) 345-7224

Monarch-Narragansett
 Ventures, Inc.
George W. Siguler, President
One Financial Plaza, 12th Floor
Springfield, MA 01102
(413) 781-3000

New England Capital
 Corporation
Z. David Patterson, Vice President
One Washington Mall, 7th Floor
Boston, MA 02108
(617) 573-6400

Northeast SBI Corp.
Joseph Mindick, Treasurer
16 Cumberland Street
Boston, MA 02115
(617) 267-3983

Orange Nassau Capital
 Corporation
Joost E. Tjaden, President
101 Federal Street, 4th Floor
Boston, MA 02110
(617) 951-9420

Pioneer Ventures
 Limited Partnership
Christopher W. Lynch, Managing Partner
60 State Street
Boston, MA 02109
(617) 742-7825

Shawmut National
 Capital Corporation
Steven James Lee, President
One Federal Street--30th Floor
Boston, MA 02211
(617) 556-4700

Southern Berkshire
 Investment Corp.
Henry Thornton, President
P.O. Box 669
Sheffield, MA 01257
(413) 229-3106

Stevens Capital
 Corporation
Edward Capuano, President
168 Stevens Street
Fall River, MA 02721
(617) 679-0044

UST Capital Corp.
Walter Dick, President
40 Court Street
Boston, MA 02108
(617) 726-7137

Vadus Capital Corp.
Joost E. Tjaden, President
101 Federal Street, 4th Floor
Boston, MA 02110
(617) 951-9420

Minnesota

FBS SBIC, Limited
 Partnership
John M. Murphy, Jr., Managing Agent
1100 First Bank Place East
Minneapolis, MN 55480
(612) 370-4764

Northland Capital
 Venture Partnership
George G. Barnum, Jr., President
613 Missabe Building
Duluth, MN 55802
(218) 722-0545

Northwest Venture
Partners
Robert F. Zicarelli, Managing G.P.
2800 Piper Jaffray Tower
222 South Ninth Street
Minneapolis, MN 55402
(612) 667-1650

Norwest Equity
Partners IV
Robert Zicarelli, General Partner
2800 Piper Jaffray Tower
Minneapolis, MN 55402
(612) 667-1650

Norwest Growth Fund,
Inc.
Daniel J. Haggerty, President
2800 Piper Jaffray Tower
222 South Ninth Street
Minneapolis, MN 55402
(612) 667-1650

Shared Ventures, Inc.
Howard W. Weiner, President
6550 York Avenue, South
Suite 419
Edina, MN 55435
(612) 925-3411

Missouri

Bankers Capital Corp.
Raymond E. Glasnapp, President
3100 Gillham Road
Kansas City, MO 64109
(816) 531-1600

Capital for
Business, Inc.
James B. Hebenstreit, President
1000 Walnut, 18th Floor
Kansas City, MO 64106
(816) 234-2357

Capital for
Business, Inc.
(Main Office: Kansas City, MO)
11 South Meramec, Suite 804
St. Louis, MO 63105
(314) 854-7427

MBI Venture Capital
Investors, Inc.
Anthony Sommers, President
850 Main Street
Kansas City, MO 64105
(816) 471-1700

MorAmerica Capital
Corporation
(Main Office: Cedar Rapids, IA)
911 Main Street, Suite 2724A
Commerce Tower Building
Kansas City, MO 64105
(816) 842-0114

United Missouri
Capital Corporation
Joe Kessinger, Manager
1010 Grand Avenue
Mail: P.O. Box 419226; K.C., MO 64141
Kansas City, MO 64106
(816) 556-7333

Nebraska

First of Nebraska
Investment Corp.
Dennis O'Neal, Managing Officer
One First National Center
Suite 701
Omaha, NE 68102
(402) 633-3585

United Financial
Resources Corp.
Dennis L. Schulte, Manager
6211 L Street
Mail: P.O. Box 1131
Omaha, NE 68101
(402) 734-1250

New Hampshire

VenCap, Inc.
Richard J. Ash, President
1155 Elm Street
Manchester, NH 03101
(603) 644-6100

New Jersey

Bishop Capital II, LP
Charles J. Irish, General Partner
500 Morris Avenue
Springfield, NJ 07081
(201) 376-0495

Bishop Capital, L.P.
Charles J. Irish, General Partner
500 Morris Avenue
Springfield, NJ 07081
(201) 376-0495

ESLO Capital Corp.
Leo Katz, President
212 Wright Street
Newark, NJ 07114
(201) 242-4488

First Princeton
   Capital Corporation
Michael D. Feinstein, President
Five Garret Mountain Plaza
West Paterson, NJ 07424
(201) 278-8111

Monmouth Capital Corp.
Eugene W. Landy, President
125 Wycoff Road
Midland National Bank Bldg.-P.O. Box 335
Eatontown, NJ 07724
(201) 542-4927

Tappan Zee Capital
   Corporation
Karl Kirschner, President
201 Lower Notch Road
Little Falls, NJ 07424
(201) 256-8280

Unicorn Ventures II,
   L.P.
Frank P. Diassi, General Partner
6 Commerce Drive
Cranford, NJ 07016
(201) 276-7880

Unicorn Ventures, Ltd.
Frank P. Diassi, President
6 Commerce Drive
Cranford, NJ 07016
(201) 276-7880

New Mexico

Albuquerque SBIC
Albert T. Ussery, President
501 Tijeras Avenue, N.W.
P.O. Box 487
Albuquerque, NM 87103
(505) 247-0145

United Mercantile
   Capital Corp.
Joe Justice, General Manager
2400 Louisiana Blvd. NE, Bldg 4, Ste 101
Mail: P.O. Box 37487; Albuquerque 87176
Albuquerque, NM 87110
(505) 883-8201

New York

767 Limited
   Partnership
H. Wertheim and H. Mallement, G.P.
767 Third Avenue
New York, NY 10017
(212) 838-7776

ASEA-Harvest
   Partners II
Harvey Wertheim, General Partner
767 Third Avenue
New York, NY 10017
(212) 838-7776

American Commercial
   Capital Corporation
Gerald J. Grossman, President
310 Madison Avenue, Suite 1304
New York, NY 10017
(212) 986-3305

Amev Capital Corp.
Martin Orland, President
One World Trade Center
Suite 5001
New York, NY 10048
(212) 775-9100

Atalanta Investment
   Company, Inc.
L. Mark Newman, Chairman of the Board
450 Park Avenue
New York, NY 10022
(212) 832-1104

BNY One Capital Corp.
Leonard A. Weiss, President
48 Wall Street
New York, NY 10286
(212) 495-1784

BT Capital Corp.
James G. Hellmuth, Deputy Chairman
280 Park Avenue--10 West
New York, NY 10017
(212) 850-1916

Boston Hambro Capital
   Company
(Main Office: Boston, MA)
17 East 71st Street
New York, NY 10021
(212) 288-9106

Bridger Capital Corp.
Seymour L. Wane, President
645 Madison Avenue, Suite 810
New York, NY 10022
(212) 888-4004

CMNY Capital II, L.P.
Robert G. Davidoff, General Partner
77 Water Street
New York, NY 10005
(212) 437-7078

CMNY Capital L.P.
Robert Davidoff, General Partner
77 Water Street
New York, NY 10005
(212) 437-7078

Chase Manhattan
  Capital Corporation
Gustav H. Koven, President
1 Chase Manhattan Plaza--23rd Floor
New York, NY 10081
(212) 552-6275

Chemical Venture
  Capital Associates
Jeffrey C. Walker, Managing Gen. Partner
885 Third Avenue, Suite 810
New York, NY 10022
(212) 230-2255

Citicorp
  Investments Inc.
David T. King, President
399 Park Avenue
New York, NY 10043
(212) 559-1000

Citicorp Venture
  Capital, Ltd.
William Comfort, Chairman of the Board
399 Park Avenue, 6th Floor
New York, NY 10043
(212) 559-1127

Creditanstalt Capital
  Corporation
Dennis O'Dowd, President
245 Park Avenue
New York, NY 10167
(212) 856-1050

Croyden Capital Corp.
Lawrence D. Gorfinkle, President
45 Rockefeller Plaza, Suite 2165
New York, NY 10111
(212) 974-0184

Diamond Capital Corp.
Steven B. Kravitz, President
805 Third Avenue, Suite 1100
New York, NY 10017
(212) 838-1255

Edwards Capital
  Company
Edward H. Teitlebaum, President
215 Lexington Avenue, Suite 805
New York, NY 10016
(212) 686-2568

Ferranti High
  Technology, Inc.
Sandford R. Simon, President & Director
515 Madison Avenue
New York, NY 10022
(212) 688-9828

Fifty-Third Street
  Ventures, L.P.
Patricia Cloherty & Dan Tessler, G.P.
155 Main Street
Cold Spring, NY 10516
(914) 265-5167

First Wall Street
  SBIC, LP
Alan Farkas, G.P.
44 Wall Street
New York, NY 10005
(212) 495-4890

Franklin Corporation
  SBIC (The)
Norman S. Strobel, President
767 Fifth Avenue
G.M. Building, 23rd Floor
New York, NY 10153
(212) 486-2323

Fundex Capital Corp.
Howard Sommer, President
525 Northern Blvd.
Great Neck, NY 11021
(516) 466-8551

GHW Capital Corp.
Philip Worlitzer, Vice President
501 Madison Avenue
New York, NY 10022
(212) 753-5653

Genesee Funding, Inc.
Stuart Marsh, President & CEO
100 Corporate Woods
Rochester, NY 14623
(716) 272-2332

Hanover Capital Corp.
  (The)
Geoffrey T. Selzer, President
315 East 62nd Street, 6th Floor
New York, NY 10021
(212) 980-9670

Interstate Capital
  Company, Inc.
David Scharf, President
380 Lexington Avenue
New York, NY 10017
(212) 986-7333

Kwiat Capital Corp.
Sheldon F. Kwiat, President
576 Fifth Avenue
New York, NY 10036
(212) 391-2461

M & T Capital Corp.
William Randon, President
One M & T Plaza
Buffalo, NY 14240
(716) 842-5881

MH Capital
 Investors, Inc.
Edward L. Kock III, President
270 Park Avenue
New York, NY 10017
(212) 286-3222

NYBDC Capital Corp.
Robert W. Lazar, President
41 State Street
P.O. Box 738
Albany, NY 12201
(518) 463-2268

NYSTRS/NV Capital,
 Limited Partnership
Raymond A. Lancaster, President
One Norstar Plaza
Albany, NY 12207
(518) 447-4050

NatWest USA Capital
 Corporation
Orville G. Aarons, General Manager
175 Water Street
New York, NY 10038
(212) 602-1200

Norstar Capital Inc.
Raymond A. Lancaster, President
One Norstar Plaza
Albany, NY 12207
(518) 447-4050

Norwood Venture
 Corp.
Mark R. Littell, President
145 West 45th Street, Suite 1211
New York, NY 10036
(212) 869-5075

Onondaga Venture
 Capital Fund, Inc.
Irving W. Schwartz, Exec. V.P.
327 State Tower Building
Syracuse, NY 13202
(315) 478-0157

Paribas Principal
 Incorporated
Steven Alexander, President
727 Seventh Avenue, 33rd Floor
New York, NY 10019
(212) 841-2000

Preferential Capital
 Corporation
Bruce Bayroff, Secretary-Treasurer
380 Lexington Avenue
New York, NY 10017
(212) 661-9030

Pyramid Ventures, Inc.
John Popovitch, Treasurer
280 Park Avenue--10 West
New York, NY 10015
(212) 850-1934

Questech Capital Corp.
John E. Koonce, President
320 Park Avenue, 3rd Floor
New York, NY 10022
(212) 891-7500

R & R Financial Corp.
Imre Rosenthal, President
1451 Broadway
New York, NY 10036
(212) 790-1441

Rand SBIC, Inc.
Donald Ross, President
1300 Rand Building
Buffalo, NY 14203
(716) 853-0802

Realty Growth Capital
 Corporation
Alan Leavit, President
271 Madison Avenue
New York, NY 10016
(212) 983-6880

SLK Capital Corp.
Edward A. Kerbs, President
115 Broadway, 20th Floor
New York, NY 10006
(212) 587-8800

Small Bus. Electronics
 Investment Corp.
Stanley Meisels, President
1220 Peninsula Blvd.
Hewlett, NY 11557
(516) 374-0743

Southern Tier Capital
   Corporation
Harold Gold, Secretary-Treasurer
55 South Main Street
Liberty, NY 12754
(914) 292-3030

Sterling Commercial
   Capital, Inc.
Harvey L. Granat, President
175 Great Neck Road--Suite 404
Great Neck, NY 11021
(516) 482-7374

TLC Funding Corp.
Philip G. Kass, President
660 White Plains Road
Tarrytown, NY 10591
(914) 683-1144

Tappan Zee Capital
   Corporation
(Main Office: Little Falls, NJ)
120 North Main Street
New City, NY 10956
(914) 634-8890

Vega Capital Corp.
Victor Harz, President
720 White Plains Road
Scarsdale, NY 10583
(914) 472-8550

WFG-Harvest Partners,
   Ltd.
Harvey J. Wertheim, General Partner
767 Third Avenue
New York, NY 10017
(212) 838-7776

Winfield Capital Corp.
Stanley M. Pechman, President
237 Mamaroneck Avenue
White Plains, NY 10605
(914) 949-2600

Wood River Capital
   Corporation
Thomas A. Barron, President
667 Madison Avenue, 12th Floor
New York, NY 10021
(212) 750-9420

North Carolina

Falcon Capital Corp.
P.S. Prasad, President
400 West Fifth Street
Greenville, NC 27834
(919) 752-5918

Heritage Capital Corp.
William R. Starnes, President
2095 Two First Union Center
Charlotte, NC 28282
(704) 334-2867

Kitty Hawk Capital,
   Limited Partnership
Walter H. Wilkinson, President
Independence Center, Suite 1640
Charlotte, NC 28246
(704) 333-3777

NCNB SBIC Corporation
Troy S. McCrory, Jr., President
One NCNB Plaza--T05--2
Charlotte, NC 28255
(704) 374-5583

NCNB Venture Company,
   L.P.
S. Epes Robinson, General Partner
One NCNB Plaza, T-39
Charlotte, NC 28255
(704) 374-5723

Ohio

A.T. Capital Corp.
Robert C. Salipante, President
900 Euclid Avenue, T-18
Mail: P.O. Box 5937
Cleveland, OH 44101
(216) 687-4970

Capital Funds Corp.
Carl G. Nelson, Chief Inv. Officer
800 Superior Avenue
Cleveland, OH 44114
(216) 344-5774

Clarion Capital Corp.
Morton A. Cohen, President
Ohio Savings Plaza, Suite 1520
1801 E. 9th Street
Cleveland, OH 44114
(216) 687-1096

First Ohio Capital
   Corporation
David J. McMacken, General Manager
606 Madison Avenue
Mail: P.O. Box 2061; Toledo, OH 43603
Toledo, OH 43604
(419) 259-7146

Gries Investment
   Company
Robert D. Gries, President
1500 Statler Office Tower
Cleveland, OH 44115
(216) 861-1146

JRM Capital Corp.
H.F. Meyer, President
13900 Broadway Avenue
Cleveland, OH 44125
(216) 475-8488

National City Capital
  Corporation
Michael Sherwin, President
629 Euclid Avenue
Cleveland, OH 44114
(216) 575-2491

SeaGate Venture
  Management, Inc.
Charles A. Brown, Vice-President
245 Summit Street, Suite 1403
Toledo, OH 43603
(419) 259-8605

Tamco Investors (SBIC)
  Incorporated
Nathan H. Monus, President
375 Victoria Road
Youngstown, OH 44515
(216) 792-3811

Oklahoma

Alliance Business
  Investment Company
Barry Davis, President
17 East Second Street
One Williams Center, Suite 2000
Tulsa, OK 74172
(918) 584-3581

Western Venture
  Capital Corporation
William B. Baker, Chief Operating Office
4880 South Lewis
Tulsa, OK 74105
(918) 749-7981

Oregon

First Interstate
  Capital, Inc.
(Main Office: Newport Beach, CA)
227.S.W. Pine Street, Suite 200
Portland, OR 97204
(503) 223-4334

Northern Pacific
  Capital Corporation
John J. Tennant, Jr., President
1201 S.W. 12th Avenue, Suite 608
Mail: P.O. Box 1658; Portland, OR 97207
Portland, OR 97205
(503) 241-1255

U.S. Bancorp Capital
  Corporation
Stephen D. Fekety, President
111 S.W. Fifth Avenue
Suite 1570
Portland, OR 97204
(503) 275-5860

Pennsylvania

Enterprise Venture Cap
  Corp of Pennsylvania
Don Cowie, C.E.O.
227 Franklin Street, Suite 215
Johnstown, PA 15901
(814) 535-7597

Erie SBIC
George R. Heaton, President
32 West 8th Street, Suite 615
Erie, PA 16501
(814) 453-7964

Fidelcor Capital
  Corporation
Mark J. DeNiro, President
Witherspoon Building, 6th Floor
123 South Broad Street
Philadelphia, PA 19109
(215) 985-7287

First SBIC of
  California
(Main Office: Costa Mesa, CA)
Daniel A. Dye, Contact
P.O. Box 512
Washington, PA 15301
(412) 223-0707

First Valley Capital
  Corporation
Matthew W. Thomas, President
One Bethlehem Plaza
Bethlehem, PA 18018
(215) 865-8916

Franklin Corporation
  SBIC (The)
(Main Office: New York, NY)
Plymouth Meeting Executive Congress
Suite 461-610 W. Germantown Pike
Plymouth Meeting, PA 19462

Meridian Capital Corp.
Joseph E. Laky, President
Horsham Business Center, Suite 200
455 Business Center Drive
Horsham, PA 19044
(215) 957-7520

Meridian Venture
  Partners
Raymond R. Rafferty, General Partner
The Fidelity Court Building
259 Radnor-Chester Road
Radnor, PA 19087
(215) 293-0210

PNC Capital Corp.
Gary J. Zentner, President
Pittsburgh National Building
Fifth Avenue and Wood Street
Pittsburgh, PA 15222
(412) 762-2248

Rhode Island

Domestic Capital Corp.
Nathaniel B. Baker, President
815 Reservoir Avenue
Cranston, RI 02910
(401) 946-3310

Fleet Venture
  Resources, Inc.
Robert M. Van Degna, President
111 Westminster Street
Providence, RI 02903
(401) 278-6770

Moneta Capital Corp.
Arnold Kilberg, President
285 Governor Street
Providence, RI 02906
(401) 861-4600

Old Stone Capital
  Corporation
Stephen P. Higginbotham, President
One Old Stone Square, 11th Floor
Providence, RI 02903
(401) 278-2559

Wallace Capital
  Corporation
Lloyd W. Granoff, President
170 Westminister Street
Suite 300
Providence, RI 02903
(401) 273-9191

South Carolina

Carolina Venture Cap.
  Corporation
Thomas H. Harvey III, President
38D Bow Circle
Hilton Head Isl., SC 29928
(803) 842-3101

Charleston Capital
  Corporation
Henry Yaschik, President
111 Church Street
P.O. Box 328
Charleston, SC 29402
(803) 723-6464

Floco Investment
  Company, Inc. (The)
William H. Johnson, Sr., President
Highway 52 North
Mail: P.O. Box 919; Lake City, SC 29560
Scranton, SC 29561
(803) 389-2731

Lowcountry Investment
  Corporation
Joseph T. Newton, Jr., President
4444 Daley Street
P.O. Box 10447
Charleston, SC 29411
(803) 554-9880

Reedy River Ventures
John M. Sterling, President
233 N. Main Street, Suite 350
Mail: P.O. Box 17526
Greenville, SC 29606
(803) 232-6198

Tennessee

Financial Resources,
  Incorporated
Milton Picard, Chairman of the Board
2800 Sterick Building
Memphis, TN 38103
(901) 527-9411

Leader Capital Corp.
James E. Pruitt, Jr., President
158 Madison Avenue
P.O. Box 708; Memphis, TN 38101-0708
Memphis, TN 38101
(901) 578-2405

Texas

Alliance Business
  Investment Company
(Main Office: Tulsa, OK)
911 Louisiana
One Shell Plaza, Suite 3990
Houston, TX 77002
(713) 224-8224

Brittany Capital
　　Company
Steve Peden, Partner
1525 Elm Street
2424 LTV Tower
Dallas, TX 75201
(214) 954-1515

Business Capital Corp.
James E. Sowell, Chairman of the Board
4809 Cole Avenue, Suite 250
Dallas, TX 75205
(214) 522-3739

Capital Marketing
　　Corporation
Ray Ballard, Manager
100 Nat Gibbs Drive
P.O. Box 1000
Keller, TX 76248
(817) 656-7309

Capital Southwest
　　Venture Corp.
William R. Thomas, President
12900 Preston Road, Suite 700
Dallas, TX 75230
(214) 233-8242

Central Texas SBI
　　Corporation
David G. Horner, President
P.O. Box 2600
Waco, TX 76702
(817) 753-6461

Charter Venture Group,
　　Incorporated
Winston C. Davis, President
2600 Citadel Plaza Drive, Suite 600
Houston, TX 77008
(713) 863-0704

Citicorp Venture
　　Capital, Ltd.
(Main Office: New York, NY)
717 North Harwood
Suite 2920-LB87
Dallas, TX 75201
(214) 880-9670

Energy Assets, Inc.
Laurence E. Simmons, Exec. V.P.
4900 Republic Bank Center
700 Louisiana
Houston, TX 77002
(713) 236-9999

Enterprise Capital
　　Corporation
Fred Zeidman, President
515 Post Oak Blvd., Suite 310
Houston, TX 77027
(713) 621-9444

FCA Investment Company
Robert S. Baker, Chairman
San Felipe Plaza, Suite 850
5847 San Felipe
Houston, TX 77057
(713) 781-2857

First City, Texas
　　Ventures, Inc.
Mr. J.R. Briansky, Manager
1001 Main Street, 15th Floor
Houston, TX 77002
(713) 658-5421

First Interstate Cap.
　　Corp. of Texas
Richard S. Smith, President
1000 Louisiana, 7th Floor
Mail: P.O. Box 3326; Houston, TX 77253
Houston, TX 77002
(713) 224-6611

Ford Capital, Ltd.
C. Jeff Pan, President
1525 Elm Street
Mail: P.O. Box 2140; Dallas, TX 75221
Dallas, TX 75201
(214) 954-0688

Houston Partners, SBIP
Harvard Hill, President, CGP
Capital Center Penthouse, 8th Floor
401 Louisiana
Houston, TX 77002
(713) 222-8600

MVenture Corp
Wayne Gaylord, President
1717 Main Street, 7th Floor
7th Momentum Place
Dallas, TX 75201
(214) 939-3131

Mapleleaf Capital Ltd.
Edward Fink, President
55 Waugh, Suite 710
Houston, TX 77007
(713) 880-4494

Mid-State Capital
　　Corporation
Smith E. Thomasson, President
510 North Valley Mills Drive
Waco, TX 76710
(817) 772-9220

NCNB Texas Venture
   Group, Incorporated
David Franklin, President
1401 Elm Street, Suite 4764
P.O. Box 831000
Dallas, TX 75283
(214) 508-5050

Neptune Capital
   Corporation
Richard C. Strauss, President
5956 Sherry Lane, Suite 800
Dallas, TX 75225
(214) 739-1414

Omega Capital
   Corporation
Theodric E. Moor, Jr., President
755 South 11th Street, Suite 250
Mail: P.O. Box 2173
Beaumont, TX 77704
(409) 832-0221

Revelation Resources,
   Ltd.
Bob Oliver, Manager
2929 Allen Parkway, Suite 1705
Houston, TX 77019
(713) 526-5623

Rust Capital Limited
Jack A. Morgan, Partner
200 Norwood Tower
114 West 7th Street
Austin, TX 78701
(512) 482-0806

SBI Capital Corp.
William E. Wright, President
6305 Beverly Hill Lane
Mail: P.O. Box 570368; Houston, TX 77257
Houston, TX 77057
(713) 975-1188

San Antonio Venture
   Group, Inc.
Domingo Bueno, President
2300 West Commerce Street
San Antonio, TX 78207
(512) 223-3633

South Texas SBIC
Kenneth L. Vickers, President
120 South Main Street
P.O. Box 1698
Victoria, TX 77902
(512) 573-5151

Southwestern Venture
   Cap. of Texas, Inc.
Phil Engelman, President
1336 East Court Street
P.O. Box 1719
Seguin, TX 78155
(512) 379 0380

Southwestern Venture
   Cap. of Texas, Inc.
(Main Office: Seguin, TX)
1250 N.E. Loop 410, Suite 300
San Antonio, TX 78209
(512) 822-9949

Sunwestern Capital
   Corporation
Thomas W. Wright, President
3 Forest Plaza
12221 Merit Drive, Suite 1300
Dallas, TX 75251
(214) 239-5650

Sunwestern Ventures,
   Ltd.
Thomas W. Wright, President
3 Forest Plaza
12221 Merit Drive, Suite 1300
Dallas, TX 75251
(214) 239-5650

Texas Commerce
   Investment Company
Lee E. Straus, Vice President
Texas Commerce Bank Bldg., 30th Floor
712 Main Street
Houston, TX 77002
(713) 236-4719

UNCO Ventures, Inc.
John Gatti, President
909 Fannin Street, 7th Floor
Houston, TX 77010
(713) 853-2422

Wesbanc Ventures, Ltd.
Stuart Schube, General Partner
520 Post Oak Blvd., Suite 130
Houston, TX 77027
(713) 622-9595

Western Financial
   Capital Corporation
Fredric M. Rosemore, President
17772 Preston Road, Suite 101
Dallas, TX 75252
(214) 380-0044

Vermont

Queneska Capital
  Corporation
Albert W. Coffrin, III, President
123 Church Street
Burlington, VT 05401
(802) 865-1806

Virginia

Crestar Capital
A. Hugh Ewing, III, Managing G.P.
9 South 12th Street--Third Floor
Richmond, VA 23219
(804) 643-7358

Metropolitan Capital
  Corporation
John B. Toomey, President
2550 Huntington Avenue
Alexandria, VA 22303
(703) 960-4698

Sovran Funding Corp.
David A. King, Jr., President
Sovran Center, 6th Floor
One Commercial Plaza; Mail: P.O. Box 600
Norfolk, VA 23510
(804) 441-4041

Tidewater SBI Corp.
Gregory H. Wingfield, President
420 Bank Street
P.O. Box 327
Norfolk, VA 23510
(804) 622-2312

Walnut Capital Corp.
(Main Office: Chicago, IL)
8300 Boone Boulevard, Suite 780
Vienna, VA 22180
(703) 448-3771

Washington

Capital Resource
  Corporation
T. Evans Wyckoff, President
1001 Logan Building
Seattle, WA 98101
(206) 623-6550

Norwest Growth Fund,
  Inc.
(Main Office: Minneapolis, MN)
777 108th Avenue, N.E.
Suite 2460
Bellevue, WA 98004
(503) 223-6622

Seafirst Capital
  Corporation
David R. West, Executive Vice President
Columbia Seafirst Center
701 Fifth Avenue, P.O. Box 34103
Seattle, WA 98124
(206) 358-7441

U.S. Bancorp Capital
  Corporation
(Main Office: Portland, OR)
1415 Fifth Avenue
Seattle, WA 98171
(206) 344-8105

Washington Trust
  Equity Corp.
John M. Snead, President
Washington Trust Financial Center
P.O. Box 2127
Spokane, WA 99210
(509) 455-3821

Wisconsin

Banc One Venture Corp.
H. Wayne Foreman, President
111 East Wisconsin Avenue
Milwaukee, WI 53202
(414) 765-2274

Bando McGlocklin
  Capital Corporation
George Schonath, Chief Executive Officer
13555 Bishops Court, Suite 205
Brookfield, WI 53005
(414) 784-9010

Capital Investments,
  Inc.
Robert L. Banner, Vice President
Commerce Building, Suite 400
744 North Fourth Street
Milwaukee, WI 53203
(414) 273-6560

M & I Ventures Corp.
John T. Byrnes, President
770 North Water Street
Milwaukee, WI 53202
(414) 765-7910

MorAmerica Capital
  Corporation
(Main Office: Cedar Rapids, IA)
600 East Mason Street
Milwaukee, WI 53202
(414) 276-3839

Super Market
   Investors, Inc.
David H. Maass, President
23000 Roundy Drive
Mail: P.O. Box 473; Milwaukee 53202
Pewaukee, WI 53072
(414) 547-7999

Wisconsin Community
   Capital, Inc.
Paul J. Eble, President
1 South Pinckney Street
Suite 500
Madison, WI 53703
(608) 266 3441

Small Business Administration (SBA) Business Loan Program

SBA loans have helped thousands of small companies get started, expand, and prosper. The following is designed to explain SBA's business loan program and to describe where and how to apply for a business loan. By law, an applicant must first seek financing from a bank or other lending institution before using SBA loan assistance. For detailed information on SBA loan assistance contact the nearest SBA office listed on page 274.

SBA Offers Two Basic Types of Business Loans:

1. **Guaranty loans** are made by private lenders, usually banks, and guaranteed up to 90 percent by SBA. Most SBA loans are made under the guaranty program. The maximum guaranty percentage of loans exceeding $155,000 is 85 percent. SBA can guarantee up to $500,000 of a private sector loan.

   There are three principal parties to an SBA guaranty loan: SBA, the small business applicant, and the private lender. The lender plays the central role in the loan delivery system. The small business submits the loan application to the lender, who makes the initial review, and, if approved for submission to SBA, forwards the application and analysis to the local SBA office. If approved by SBA, the lender closes the loan and disburses the funds.

2. **SBA direct loans** have an administrative maximum of $150,000 and are available only to applicants unable to secure an SBA-guaranteed loan. Before applying for an SBA direct loan, an applicant must first seek financing from his/her bank of account, and, in cities of over 200,000, from at least one other lender. Direct loan funds are very limited and, at times, available only to certain types of borrowers (e.g., businesses located in high-unemployment areas, or owned by low-income individuals, handicapped individuals, Vietnam-era Veterans, or disabled Veterans).

How to Apply for a Loan

1. Prepare a current, business balance sheet listing all assets, liabilities, and net worth. New business applicants should prepare an estimated balance sheet as of the day

the business starts. The amount that you and/or others have to invest in the business must be stated.

2. Income (profit and loss) statements should be submitted for the current period and for the most recent three fiscal years, if available. New business applicants should prepare a detailed projection of earnings and expenses at least for the first year of operation (a monthly cashflow is recommended).

3. Prepare a current, personal financial statement of the proprietor, or each partner or stockholder owning 20-percent or more of the corporate stock in the business.

4. List collateral to be offered as security for the loan along with an estimate of the present market value of each item as well as the balance of any existing liens.

5. State the amount of the loan requested and purposes for which it is to be used.

6. Take this material to your lender. If the lender is unable or unwilling to provide the financing directly, the possibility of using the SBA guaranty program should be explored. The lender should be encouraged to contact the nearest SBA field office if additional program information is needed. An SBA direct loan may be possible for credit-worthy applicants who are unable to obtain a guaranty loan, depending on availability of funds. Contact the nearest SBA field office for advice on the possibilities of a direct loan.

Terms of Loans

Working capital loans generally have maturities of five-to-seven years. The maximum maturity is 25 years; however, the longer maturities are used to finance fixed assets such as the purchase or major renovation of business premises. Interest rates in the guaranty program are negotiated between the borrower and the lender subject to SBA maximums. Generally, interest rates for loans with maturities of seven years or more cannot exceed 2¾ percent over New York prime, and loans with maturities of less than seven years cannot exceed 2¼ percent over New York prime. Interest rates on direct loans are based on the cost of money to the Federal Government and are calculated quarterly.

Collateral

SBA requires that sufficient assets be pledged to adequately secure the loan to the

Source: *Business Loans from the SBA*, Small Business Administration Office of Public Communication.

extent that they are available. Personal guaranties are required from all the principal owners and from the chief executive officer of the business, irrespective of his/her ownership interest. Liens on personal assets of the principals also may be required where business assets are considered insufficient to secure the loan.

Eligibility Requirements

To be eligible for SBA loan assistance, the business must be operated for profit and qualify as small under SBA size standard criteria (except for sheltered workshops under the Handicapped Assistance loan program). Loans cannot be made to businesses involved in the creation or distribution of ideas or opinions. These would include such businesses as newspapers, magazines, and academic schools. Other types of ineligible borrowers include businesses engaged in speculation or investment in (rental) real estate.

General Size Standards

For business loans, size standard eligibility is based on the average number of employees for the preceding 12 months or on sales volume averaged over a three-year period.
Manufacturing: Maximum number of employees may range from 500 to 1,500, depending on the type of product manufactured.

Wholesaling: Maximum number of employees may not exceed 100.
Services: Annual receipts may not exceed $3.5 to $14.5 million, depending on the industry.
Retailing: Annual receipts may not exceed $3.5 to $13.5 million, depending on the industry.
Construction: General construction annual receipts may not exceed $9.5 to $17 million, depending on the industry.
Special trade construction: Annual receipts may not exceed $7 million.
Agriculture: Annual receipts may not exceed $0.5 to $3.5 million, depending on the industry.

Credit Requirements

A loan applicant must:

Be of good character.
Demonstrate sufficient management expertise and commitment for a good, successful operation.
Have enough capital so that, with an SBA loan, the business can operate on a sound financial basis. For new businesses, this includes sufficient resources to withstand start-up expenses and the initial operating phase during which losses are likely to occur. SBA generally requires that owners inject one-third to one-half of the total assets needed to launch a new business.
Show that the past earnings record and/or probable future earnings will be sufficient to repay the loan in a timely manner.

Small Business Administration (SBA) Field Offices

Alabama
2121 8th Avenue North
Birmingham, Alabama 35203
205/254-1344

Alaska
8th and C Street
Anchorage, Alaska 99501
907/271-4022

Arizona
2005 North Central Avenue
Phoenix, Arizona 85004
602/261-3732

301 West Congress Street
Federal Bldg., Box 33
Tucson, Arizona 85701
602/792-6715

Arkansas
320 W. Capitol Avenue
Little Rock, Arkansas 72201
501/378-5871

California
2202 Monterey Street
Fresno, California 93721
209/487-5189

350 South Figueroa Street
Los Angeles, California 90071
213/688-2956

660 J Street
Sacramento, California 95814
916/551-1446

880 Front Street
San Diego, California 92188
619/557-7252

*450 Golden Gate Avenue
P.O. Box 36044
San Francisco, California 94102
415/556-7487

211 Main Street
San Francisco, California 94105
415/974-0642

2700 N. Main Street
Santa Ana, California 92701
714/836-2494

Colorado
*999 18th Street
Denver, Colorado 80202
303/844-3984

721 19th Street
Denver, Colorado 80202
303/844-2607

Connecticut
One Hartford Square W.
Hartford, Connecticut 06106
203/240-0700

Delaware
844 King Street
Wilmington, Delaware 19801
302/573-6294

District of Columbia
1111 18th St., N.W.
Washington, D.C. 20036
202/634-4950

Florida
400 West Bay Street
Jacksonville, Florida 32202
904/791-3782

1320 S. Dixie Highway
Coral Gables, Florida 33146
305/350-5521

700 Twiggs Street
Tampa, Florida 33602
813/228-2594

5601 Corporate Way S.
West Palm Beach, Florida 33407
407/689-3922

Georgia
*1375 Peachtree Street, N.E.
Atlanta, Georgia 30367
404/347-4999

1720 Peachtree Road, N.W.
Atlanta, Georgia 30309
404/347-2441

52 North Main Street
Statesboro, Georgia 30458
912/489-8719

Source: Small Business Administration.   * Regional Office

Guam
Pacific News Bldg.
238 O'Hara Street
Agana, Guam 96910
671/472-7277

Hawaii
300 Ala Moana
P.O. Box 2213
Honolulu, Hawaii 96850
808/541-2990

Idaho
1020 Main Street
Boise, Idaho 83702
208/334-1696

Illinois
*230 South Dearborn Street
Chicago, Illinois 60604
312/353-0359

219 South Dearborn Street
Chicago, Illinois 60604
312/353-4528

511 W. Capitol Street
Springfield, Illinois 62704
217/492-4416

Indiana
Minton-Capehart Federal Bldg.
575 North Pennsylvania Street
Indianapolis, Indiana 46209
317/269-7272

Iowa
210 Walnut Street
Des Moines, Iowa 50309
515/284-4422

373 Collins Road, N.E.
Cedar Rapids, Iowa 52402
319/399-2571

Kansas
Main Place Bldg.
110 East Waterman Street
Wichita, Kansas 67202
316/269-6271

Kentucky
600 Martin Luther King, Jr. Plaza
Louisville, Kentucky 40202
502/582-5976

Louisiana
1661 Canal Street
New Orleans, Louisiana 70112
504/589-6685

500 Fannin Street
Federal Bldg. & Courthouse
Shreveport, Louisiana 71101
318/226-5196

Maine
40 Western Avenue
Augusta, Maine 04330
207/622-8378

Maryland
10 N. Calvert Street
Baltimore, Maryland 21204
301/962-4392

Massachusetts
*60 Batterymarch Street
Boston, Massachusetts 02110
617/451-2030

10 Causeway Street
Boston, Massachusetts 02114
617/565-5590

1550 Main Street
Springfield, Massachusetts 01103
413/785-0268

Michigan
477 Michigan Avenue
McNamara Bldg.
Detroit, Michigan 48226
313/226-6075

300 S. Front Street
Marquette, Michigan 49885
906/225-1108

Minnesota
100 North 6th Street
Minneapolis, Minnesota 55403
612/370-2324

Mississippi
One Hancock Plaza
Gulfport, Mississippi 39501
601/863-4449

100 West Capitol Street
New Federal Bldg.
Jackson, Mississippi 39269
601/960-4378

Missouri
*911 Walnut Street
Kansas City, Missouri 64106
816/426-2989

* Regional Office

1103 Grand Avenue
Kansas City, Missouri 64106
816/374-3419

815 Olive Street
St. Louis, Missouri 63101
314/536-6600

620 S. Glenstone Street
Springfield, Missouri 65802
417/864-7670

Montana
2601 First Avenue North
Billings, Montana 59101
406/657-6047

301 South Park Avenue
Helena, Montana 59626
406/449-5381

Nebraska
11145 Mill Valley Road
Omaha, Nebraska 68134
402/221-4691

Nevada
301 East Stewart Street
Las Vegas, Nevada 89125
702/385-6611

50 South Virginia Street
Reno, Nevada 89505
702/784-5268

New Hampshire
55 Pleasant Street
Concord, New Hampshire 03301
603/225-1400

New Jersey
2600 Ephrain Avenue
Camden, New Jersey 08104
609/757-5183

60 Park Place
Newark, New Jersey 07102
201/645-2434

New Mexico
Patio Plaza Building
5000 Marble Ave., N.E.
Albuquerque, N.M. 87100
505/262-6171

New York
*26 Federal Plaza
New York, New York 10278
212/264-7772

445 Broadway
Albany, New York 12207
518/472-6300

111 West Huron Street
Buffalo, New York 14202
716/846-4301

333 East Water Street
Elmira, New York 14901
607/734-8130

35 Pinelawn Road
Melville, New York 11747
516/454-0750

26 Federal Plaza
New York, New York 10278
212/264-4355

100 State Street
Rochester, New York 14614
716/263-6700

100 South Clinton St.
Syracuse, New York 13260
315/423-5383

North Carolina
222 S. Church Street
Charlotte, North Carolina 28202
704/371-6563

North Dakota
657 2nd Avenue
Fargo, North Dakota 58108
701/239-5131

Ohio
1240 East 9th St.
AJC Federal Bldg.
Cleveland, Ohio 44199
216/522-4180

85 Marconi Boulevard
Columbus, Ohio 43215
614/469-6860

550 Main Street
Cincinnati, Ohio 45202
513/684-2814

Oklahoma
200 N.W. 5th Street
Oklahoma City, Oklahoma 73102
405/231-4301

Oregon
1220 S.W. Third Avenue
Portland, Oregon 97204
503/221-2682

———————
* Regional Office

Pennsylvania
*475 Allendale Road
King of Prussia, Pennsylvania 19406
215/962-3700

475 Allendale Road
King of Prussia, Pennsylvania 19406
215/062 0846

100 Chestnut Street
Harrisburg, Pennsylvania 17101
717/782-3840

960 Penn Avenue
Pittsburgh, Pennsylvania 15222
412/644-2780

20 North Pennsylvania Avenue
Wilkes-Barre, Pennsylvania 18701
717/826-6497

Puerto Rico
Federal Building
Carlos Chardon Avenue
Hato Rey, Puerto Rico 00918
809/753-4002

Rhode Island
380 Westminster Mall
Providence, Rhode Island 02903
401/528-4586

South Carolina
1835 Assembly Street
P.O. Box 2786
Columbia, South Carolina 29202
803/765-5376

South Dakota
101 South Main Avenue
Sioux Falls, South Dakota 57102
605/336-2980, Ext. 231

Tennessee
404 James Robertson Parkway
Nashville, Tennessee 37219
615/251-5881

Texas
Federal Building
300 East 8th Street
Austin, Texas 78701
512/482-5288

400 Mann Street
Corpus Christi, Texas 78408
512/888-3331

*8625 King George Drive
Bldg. C
Dallas, Texas 75235
214/767-7643

1100 Commerce Street
Dallas, Texas 75242
214/767-0605

10737 Gateway West
El Paso, Texas 79902
915/541-7586

819 Taylor Street
Ft Worth, Texas 76102
817/334-3613

222 East Van Buren Street
Harlingen, Texas 78550
512/427-8533

2525 Murthworth
Houston, Texas 77054
713/660-4401

1611 10th Street
Lubbock, Texas 79401
806/743-7462

505 East Travis
Marshall, Texas 75670
214/935-5257

7400 Blanco Road
San Antonio, Texas 78216
512/229-4535

Utah
125 South State Street
Salt Lake City, Utah 84138
801/524-3209

Vermont
87 State Street
Montpelier, Vermont 05602
802/828-4474

Virginia
400 North 8th Street
P.O. Box 10126
Richmond, Virginia 23240
804/771-2617

Virgin Islands
Veterans Drive
St. Thomas, Virgin Islands 00801
809/774-8530

4C & 4D Estate Sion Farm
P.O. Box 4010
Christiansted, Virgin Islands 00820
809/773-5380

---

* Regional Office

Washington
*2615 4th Avenue
Seattle, Washington 98121
206/442-5676

915 Second Avenue
Seattle, Washington 98174
206/442-5534

Washington, D.C.
1111 18th Street, N.W.
Washington, D.C. 20036
202/634-4950

U.S. Courthouse
P.O. Box 2167
Spokane, Washington 99210
509/456-3786

West Virginia
168 W. Main
Clarksburg, West Virginia 26301
304/623-5631

550 Eagan Street
Charleston, West Virginia 25301
304/347-5220

Wisconsin
500 South Barstow Street
Eau Claire, Wisconsin 54701
715/834-9012

212 East Washington Avenue
Madison, Wisconsin 53703
608/264-5261

310 West Wisconsin Avenue
Milwaukee, Wisconsin 53203
414/291-3942

Wyoming
100 East B Street
Federal Building
P.O. Box 2839
Casper, Wyoming 82602
307/261-5761

---

* Regional Office

Returns on Various Types of Investments*

R. S. Salomon, Jr.
Caroline H. Davenport
Maria A. Fiore
Susan G. Brand

Conspicuous Consumption as an Art Form

When van Gogh's "Portrait of Dr. Gachet" sold recently for $82.5 million—to a buyer who was prepared to pay $100 million—we couldn't help wondering whether the artist's mental state would have been helped or hurt if the sale had taken place in his lifetime. To an outsider, there *appears* to be a certain element of lunacy in recent auction results. This sentiment is only reinforced by the knowledge that other versions of the two canvases that have changed hands recently at record prices—the van Gogh and Renoir's "Au Moulin de la Galette"—hang in a Paris museum . . . available for all to see but not to own.

An expert could undoubtedly justify the high prices and elaborate on the important distinctions between the different versions of the paintings. On the one hand, $80 million plus or minus seems a hefty price tag for a painting. On the other hand, the value of the advertising generated by such purchases may exceed the prices paid. Moreover, past

* Although the information in this report has been obtained from sources which Salomon Brothers Inc. believes to be reliable, we do not guarantee its accuracy and such information may be incomplete or condensed. All opinions and estimates included in this report constitute our judgment as of this date and are subject to change without notice. This report is for information purposes only and is not intended as an offer or solicitation with respect to the purchase or sale of any security.

Editor's Note: Stock returns are for the S&P 500 and include appreciation plus dividends. Bond returns are for Salomon Brothers Index and include appreciation plus interest.

Source: *Annual Survey of Financial and Tangible Assets*, by R. S. Salomon, Jr., Caroline H. Davenport, Maria A. Fiore and Susan G. Brand. © Salomon Brothers Inc., June 4, 1990.

experience suggests that the prices of collectibles could well move even higher if, as we expect, the financial markets remain healthy.

When we began publishing our annual report on investment returns a dozen years ago, we expected that the assets in the survey would generally fall into two classes of investments—financial and tangible—and that returns from these categories would diverge in response to particular economic and political forces. Our thesis has proved correct for financial assets and for categories of tangibles: real estate and commodities.

The third type of tangible asset, collectibles, does not fit the pattern at all. Wealth creation in any area—the oil markets of the 1970s or the financial markets of the 1980s—finds expression in higher demand for such things as Old Master paintings, Chinese ceramics and coins. The primary appeal of these assets is not that they retain their value when inflation is on the rise—a key reason to buy commodities and real estate—but rather that they are a means of proving to others the financial capability of the buyer, i.e., conspicuous consumption.

What would curtail the boom in the collectibles markets? Just as the *creation* of wealth fuels higher prices for collectibles, so does the *destruction* of wealth impair demand. Only a widespread recession or a depression—events not seen for many years—would cause this to occur.

Everyone has a stake, either personal or professional, in one or more of the investment areas represented in this survey. Thus, understanding the reasons why certain types of assets move in different directions at different times is more than idle speculation. In addition, the implications of choosing one asset over another have significant long-term consequences, as evinced in the 20-year data. The 310 basis-point gap in long-term stock and bond returns, by way of example, translates into roughly the difference between ten times your money and six times your money.

(continued)

Figure 1. Financial and Tangible Assets — Compound Annual Rates of Return

	20 Years	Rank	10 Years	Rank	5 Years	Rank	1 Year	Rank
U.S. Coins	17.3	1	7.3	6	15.0	3	14.6	4
Chinese Ceramics[a]	14.4	2	7.6	5	14.6	4	18.0	2
Stocks[b]	12.7	3	17.3	1	17.7	2	15.4	3
Old Masters[a]	12.7	3	12.3	3	23.9	1	44.5	1
Gold	12.3	4	-4.3	13	3.0	11	0.5	12
Diamonds[c]	10.7	5	6.4	7	11.8	7	5.5	8
Bonds[b]	9.6	6	12.6	2	12.0	5	7.5	7
Oil	9.0	7	-3.8	12	-7.0	14	-0.7	13
3-Mos. Treasury Bills[b]	8.6	8	9.5	4	7.0	8	8.3	6
Housing	7.4	9	4.7	9	5.0	9	2.4	11
U.S. Farmland	6.5	10	-0.6	11	-0.6	12	3.9	10
CPI	6.2	11	4.8	8	3.8	10	4.4	9
Silver	5.4	12	-10.2	14	-4.0	13	-2.9	14
Foreign Exchange	4.4	13	1.5	10	11.9	6	10.5	5

[a] Source: Sotheby's.
[b] Stock returns assume quarterly reinvestment of dividends. Bond returns assume monthly reinvestment.
[c] Source: The Diamond Registry.
CPI Consumer Price Index.
Note: All returns are for the period ended June 1, 1990, based on latest available data.

Stock Market: U.S. and Foreign

Investment Returns on Stocks, Bonds, and Bills

Roger G. Ibbotson* and Laurence B. Siegel**

Our look at history consists of examining the returns of five capital market sectors. We measure total returns (capital gains plus income) on common stocks, long-term corporate bonds, long-term government bonds, U.S. Treasury bills, and rates of inflation on consumer goods. Comparing the returns from the various sectors gives us insights into the returns available from taking risk and the relationships between capital market returns and inflation.

THE RISKS AND REWARDS

We display graphically the rewards and risks available from the U.S. capital markets over the past 64 years. Exhibit 1 shows the growth of an investment in common stocks, long-term government bonds, and Treasury bills as well as the increase in the inflation index over the 64-year period. Each of the series is initiated at $1 at year-end 1925. The vertical scale is logarithmic so that equal distances represent equal percentage changes anywhere along the axis. The graph vividly portrays that despite setbacks such as that of October 1987, common stocks were the big winner over the entire period. If $1 were invested in stocks at year-end 1925 and all dividends reinvested, the dollar investment would have grown to $534.46 by year-end 1989. This phenomenal growth was not without substantial risk, especially during the earlier portion of the period. In contrast, long-term government bonds (with a constant 20-year maturity) exhibited much less risk, but grew to only $17.30.

A virtually riskless strategy (for those with short-term time horizons) has been to buy U.S. Treasury bills. However, Treasury bills have had a marked tendency to track inflation, with the result that their real (inflation adjusted) return is near zero for the entire 1926–1989 period. Note that the tracking is only prevalent over the latter portion of the period. During periods of deflation (such as the late 1920s and early 1930s) the Treasury

bill returns were near zero, but not negative, since no one intentionally buys securities with negative yields. Beginning in the early 1940s, the yields (returns) on Treasury bills were pegged by the government at low rates while high inflation was experienced. The government pegging ended with the U.S. Treasury-Federal Reserve Accord in March 1951.

We summarize the investment returns in Exhibit 2 by presenting the average annual returns over the 1926–1989 period. Common stocks returned a compounded (geometric mean) total return of 10.3 percent per year. The annual compound return from capital appreciation alone was 5.3 percent. After adjusting for inflation, annual compounded total returns were 7.0 percent per year.

The average total return over any single year (arithmetic mean) for stocks was 12.4 percent, with positive returns recorded in more than two-thirds of the years (44 out of 64 years). The risk or degree of return fluctuation is measured by standard deviation as 20.9 percent. The frequency distribution (histogram) counts the number of years the returns fell in each 5 percent return increment. Note the wide variations in common stock returns relative to the other capital market sectors. Annual stock returns ranged from 54.0 percent in 1933 to −43.3 percent in 1931.

A simple example illustrates the difference between geometric and arithmetic means. Suppose $1 were invested in a common stock portfolio that experiences successive annual returns of +50 percent and −50 percent. At the end of the first year, the portfolio is worth $1.50. At the end of the second year, the portfolio is worth $0.75. The annual arithmetic mean is 0 percent, whereas the annual geometric mean (compounded return) is −13.4 percent. Naturally, it is the geometric mean that more directly measures the change in wealth over more than one period. On the other hand, the arithmetic mean is a better representation of typical performance over any single annual period.

The other capital market sectors also had returns commensurate with their risks. Long-term corporate bonds outperformed the default-free, long-term government bonds, which in turn outperformed the essentially riskless U.S. Treasury bills. Over the entire period the riskless U.S. Treasury bills had a

* Professor, Yale School of Management, New Haven, Connecticut.

** Managing Director, Ibbotson Associates, Inc., Chicago, Illinois.

EXHIBIT 1:   WEALTH INDEXES OF INVESTMENTS IN THE U.S. CAPITAL MARKETS, 1926–1989 (assumed initial investment of $1.00 at year-end 1925, includes reinvestment income)

Index

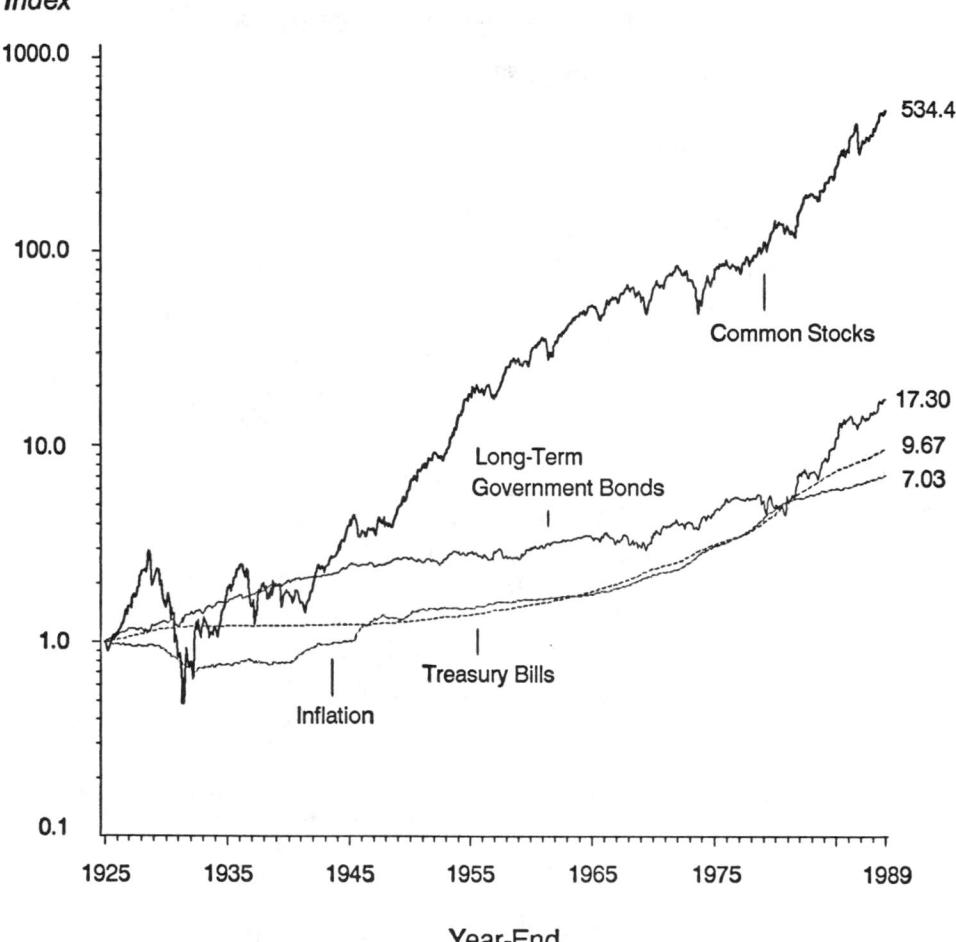

Year-End

Source: *Stocks, Bonds, Bills, and Inflation: 1990 Yearbook*, published by Ibbotson Associates, Inc. [8 S. Michigan Avenue, Suite 700, Chicago, IL. 60603, phone 312-263-3435], 1989.

return almost identical with the inflation rate. Thus, we again note that the real rate of interest (the inflation-adjusted riskless rate) has been on average very near 0 percent historically.

MEASUREMENT OF THE FIVE SERIES

The returns were computed by compounding monthly returns, with no adjustments made for transactions costs or taxes. We describe each of the five total return series which are listed annually in Exhibit 3. The index numbers in Exhibit 3 are dollar values of a $1 investment made on December 31, 1925. They can be converted to yearly returns by taking the ratio of a given year-end index value to the previous year-end value, then subtracting one (1). For example, the return for common stocks for 1989 equals $(534.456 \div 406.455) - 1 = .3149$, or 31.49 percent.

Common Stocks

The total return index is based upon Standard & Poor's (S&P) Composite Index with dividends reinvested monthly. To the extent that the 500 stocks currently included in the S&P Composite Index (prior to March 1957, there were 90 stocks) are representative of

EXHIBIT 2:   BASIC SERIES: TOTAL ANNUAL RETURNS, 1926–1989

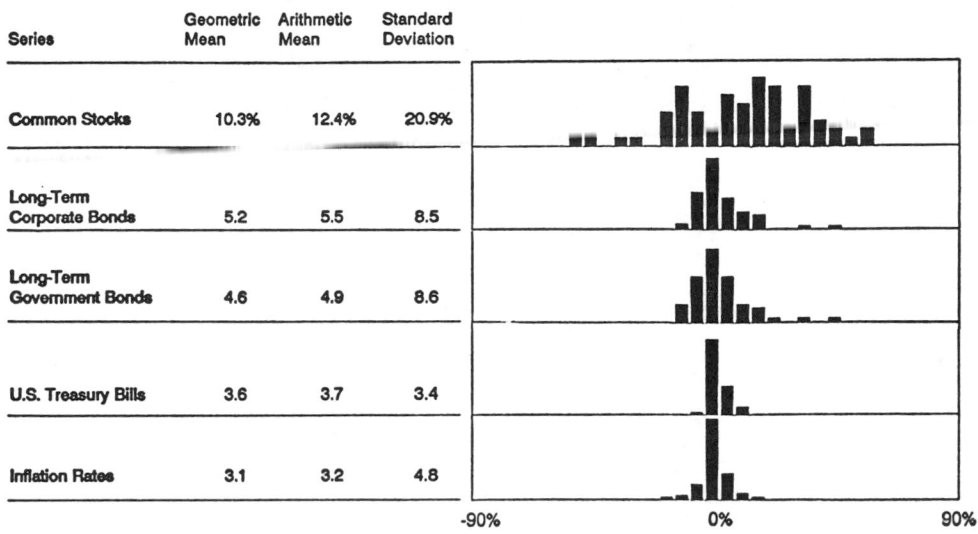

Series	Geometric Mean	Arithmetic Mean	Standard Deviation
Common Stocks	10.3%	12.4%	20.9%
Long-Term Corporate Bonds	5.2	5.5	8.5
Long-Term Government Bonds	4.6	4.9	8.6
U.S. Treasury Bills	3.6	3.7	3.4
Inflation Rates	3.1	3.2	4.8

Source: *Stocks, Bonds, Bills and Inflation: 1990 Yearbook*, Ibbotson Associates, Inc., Chicago, 1990.

EXHIBIT 3:   BASIC SERIES, INDEXES OF YEAR-END CUMULATIVE WEALTH, 1925–1989 (year-end 1925 = 1.000)

Year	Common Stocks Total Returns	Common Stocks Capital Appreciation Only	Long-Term Government Bonds Total Returns	Long-Term Government Bonds Capital Appreciation Only	Long-Term Corporate Bonds Total Returns	U.S. Treasury Bills Total Returns	Consumer Price Index (Inflation)
1925	1.000	1.000	1.000	1.000	1.000	1.000	1.000
1926	1.116	1.057	1.078	1.039	1.074	1.033	.985
1927	1.535	1.384	1.174	1.095	1.154	1.065	.965
1928	2.204	1.908	1.175	1.061	1.186	1.103	.955
1929	2.018	1.681	1.215	1.059	1.225	1.155	.957
1930	1.516	1.202	1.272	1.072	1.323	1.183	.899
1931	.859	.636	1.204	.981	1.299	1.196	.814
1932	.789	.540	1.407	1.108	1.439	1.207	.730
1933	1.214	.792	1.406	1.073	1.588	1.211	.734
1934	1.197	.745	1.547	1.146	1.808	1.213	.749
1935	1.767	1.053	1.624	1.170	1.982	1.215	.771
1936	2.367	1.346	1.746	1.225	2.116	1.217	.780
1937	1.538	.827	1.750	1.194	2.174	1.221	.804
1938	2.016	1.035	1.847	1.228	2.307	1.221	.782
1939	2.008	.979	1.957	1.271	2.399	1.221	.778
1940	1.812	.829	2.076	1.319	2.480	1.221	.786
1941	1.602	.681	2.095	1.305	2.548	1.222	.862
1942	1.927	.766	2.162	1.315	2.614	1.225	.942
1943	2.427	.915	2.207	1.310	2.688	1.229	.972
1944	2.906	1.041	2.270	1.314	2.815	1.233	.993
1945	3.965	1.361	2.513	1.423	2.930	1.237	1.015
1946	3.645	1.199	2.511	1.392	2.980	1.242	1.199
1947	3.853	1.199	2.445	1.027	2.911	1.248	1.307
1948	4.065	1.191	2.528	1.340	3.031	1.258	1.343
1949	4.829	1.313	2.691	1.395	3.132	1.272	1.318

(continued)

EXHIBIT 3: *(concluded)*

Year	Common Stocks		Long-Term Government Bonds		Long-Term Corporate Bonds	U.S. Treasury Bills	
	Total Returns	Capital Appreciation Only	Total Returns	Capital Appreciation Only	Total Returns	Total Returns	Consumer Price Index (Inflation)
1950	6.360	1.600	2.692	1.366	3.198	1.287	1.395
1951	7.888	1.863	2.586	1.281	3.112	1.306	1.477
1952	9.336	2.082	2.616	1.262	3.221	1.328	1.490
1953	9.244	1.944	2.711	1.270	3.331	1.352	1.499
1954	14.108	2.820	2.906	1.325	3.511	1.364	1.492
1955	18.561	3.564	2.868	1.271	3.527	1.385	1.497
1956	19.778	3.658	2.708	1.164	3.287	1.419	1.540
1957	17.646	3.134	2.910	1.208	3.573	1.464	1.587
1958	25.298	4.327	2.733	1.097	3.494	1.486	1.615
1959	28.322	4.694	2.671	1.029	3.460	1.530	1.639
1960	28.455	4.554	3.039	1.124	3.774	1.571	1.663
1961	36.106	5.607	3.068	1.092	3.956	1.604	1.674
1962	32.955	4.945	3.280	1.122	4.270	1.648	1.695
1963	40.468	5.879	3.319	1.092	4.364	1.700	1.723
1964	47.139	6.642	3.436	1.084	4.572	1.760	1.743
1965	53.008	7.244	3.460	1.047	4.552	1.829	1.777
1966	47.674	6.295	3.586	1.036	4.560	1.916	1.836
1967	59.104	7.560	3.257	.895	4.335	1.997	1.892
1968	65.641	8.139	3.248	.846	4.446	2.101	1.981
1969	60.059	7.210	3.083	.754	4.086	2.239	2.102
1970	62.465	7.222	3.457	.791	4.837	2.385	2.218
1971	71.406	8.001	3.914	.843	5.370	2.490	2.292
1972	84.956	9.252	4.136	.840	5.760	2.585	2.371
1973	72.500	7.645	4.090	.775	5.825	2.764	2.579
1974	53.311	5.373	4.268	.748	5.647	2.986	2.894
1975	73.144	7.068	4.661	.754	6.474	3.159	3.097
1976	90.584	8.422	5.441	.815	7.681	3.319	3.246
1977	84.076	7.453	5.405	.750	7.813	3.489	3.466
1978	89.592	7.532	5.342	.682	7.807	3.740	3.778
1979	106.112	8.459	5.277	.615	7.481	4.128	4.281
1980	140.513	10.639	5.069	.530	7.285	4.592	4.812
1981	133.615	9.605	5.162	.475	7.215	5.267	5.242
1982	162.221	11.023	7.245	.589	10.374	5.822	5.445
1983	198.743	12.926	7.294	.530	10.862	6.335	5.652
1984	211.197	13.106	8.420	.542	12.642	6.959	5.875
1985	279.114	16.558	11.027	.639	16.549	7.496	6.097
1986	330.668	18.981	13.722	.735	19.833	7.958	6.166
1987	347.965	19.366	13.352	.657	19.780	8.393	6.438
1988	406.455	21.769	14.643	.659	21.897	8.926	6.722
1989	534.456	27.702	17.296	.716	25.451	9.673	7.035

Source: *Stocks, Bonds, Bills, and Inflation: 1990 Yearbook,* Ibbotson Associates, Inc., Chicago, 1990.

all stocks in the United States, the market value weighting scheme allows the returns of the index to correspond to the aggregate stock market returns in the U.S. economy.

Long-Term Corporate Bonds

We measure the total returns of a corporate bond index with approximately 20 years to maturity. We use Salomon Brothers' High-Grade Long-Term Corporate Bond Index from its beginning in 1969 through 1988. For the period 1946–68 we backdate Salomon Brothers' index using Salomon Brothers' monthly yield data and similar methodology. For the period 1926–45 we compute returns using Standard & Poor's monthly high-grade corporate composite bond yield data, assuming a 4 percent coupon and a 20-year maturity.

Long-Term Government Bonds

To measure the total returns of long-term U.S. government bonds, we use the bond data obtained from the U.S. Government Bond File (constructed by Lawrence Fisher) at the Center for Research in Security Prices

(CRSP) at the University of Chicago. We attempt to maintain a 20-year bond portfolio whose returns do not reflect the potential tax benefits, impaired negotiability, or the special redemption or call privileges frequently characterizing government bond prices and yields.

U.S. Treasury Bills

For the U.S. Treasury bill index, we again use the data in the CRSP U.S. Government Bond File. We measure one-month holding period returns for the shortest-term bills not less than one month in maturity. Since U.S. Treasury bills were not initiated until 1929, we use short-term coupon bonds whenever bill quotes are unavailable.

Consumer Price Index

We utilize the Consumer Price Index for All Urban Consumers (CPI-U), not seasonally adjusted, to measure inflation. The CPI-U, and its predecessor, the CPI (which we use prior to January 1978) is constructed by the Bureau of Labor Statistics, U.S. Department of Labor, Washington, D.C.

The Constant Dollar Dow

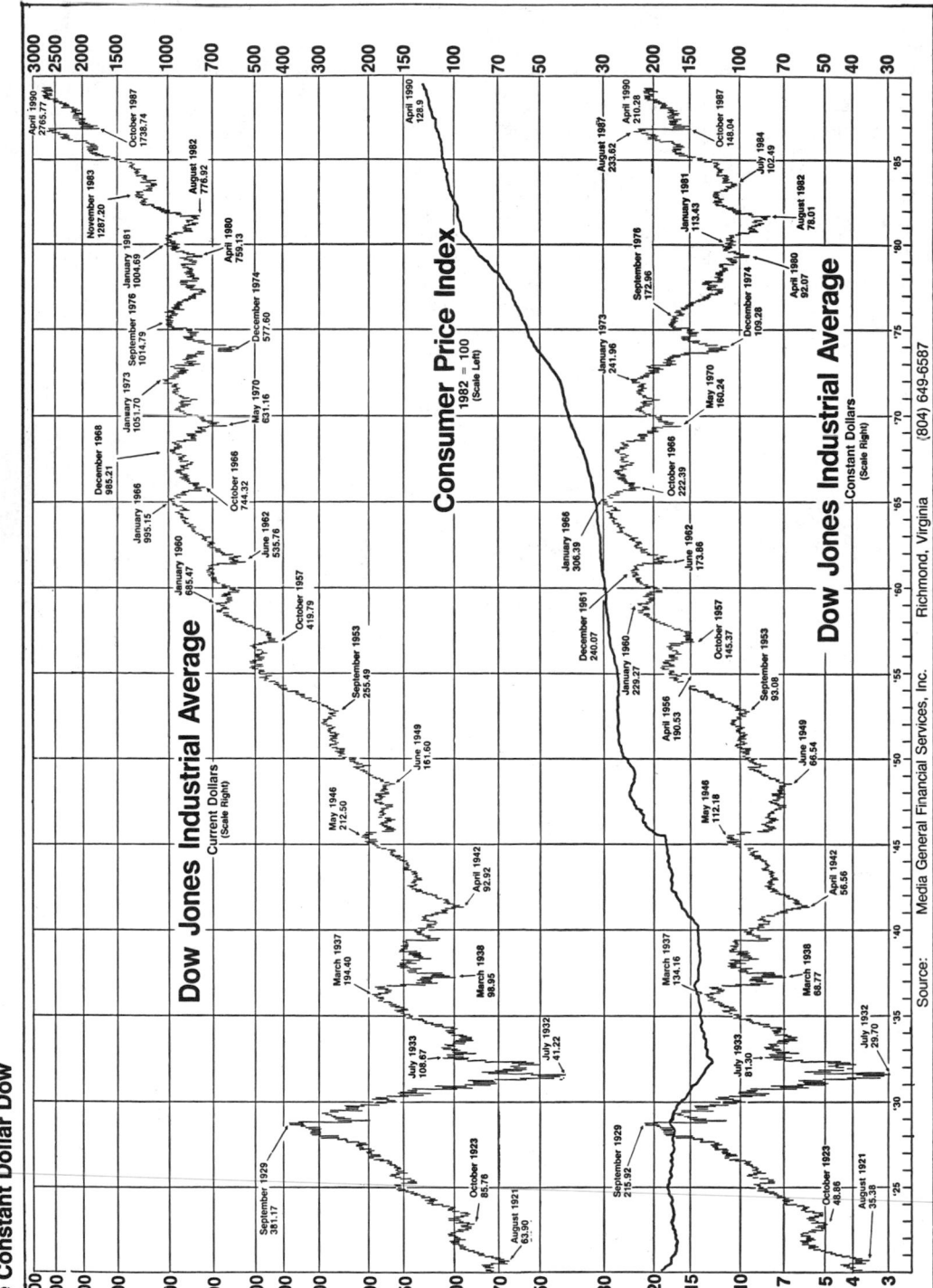

Dow Jones Industrial Average
Current Dollars
(Scale Right)

Consumer Price Index
1982 = 100
(Scale Left)

Dow Jones Industrial Average
Constant Dollars
(Scale Right)

Source: Media General Financial Services, Inc.   Richmond, Virginia   (804) 649-6587

Source: Media General Financial Services, Inc. Richmond, Virginia

Cash Dividends on NYSE Listed Common Stocks

	Common stocks		
	Number of issues listed at year end	Number paying cash dividends during year	Estimated aggregate cash payments (millions)
1929	842	554	$ 2,711
1935	776	387	1,336
1940	829	577	2,099
1041	004	027	2,281
1942	834	648	1,997
1943	845	687	2,063
1944	864	717	2,223
1945	881	746	2,275
1946	933	798	2,669
1947	964	851	3,255
1948	986	883	3,806
1949	1,017	887	4,235
1950	1,039	930	5,404
1951	1,054	961	5,467
1952	1,067	975	5,595
1953	1,069	964	5,874
1954	1,076	968	6,439
1955	1,076	982	7,488
1956	1,077	975	8,341
1957	1,098	991	8,807
1958	1,086	961	8,711
1959	1,092	953	9,337
1960	1,126	981	9,872
1961	1,145	981	10,430
1962	1,168	994	11,203
1963	1,194	1,032	12,096
1964	1,227	1,066	13,555
1965	1,254	1,111	15,302
1966	1,267	1,127	16,151
1967	1,255	1,116	16,866
1968	1,253	1,104	18,124
1969	1,290	1,121	19,404
1970	1,330	1,120	19,781
1971	1,399	1,132	20,256
1972	1,478	1,195	21,490
1973	1,536	1,276	23,627
1974	1,543	1,308	25,662
1975	1,531	1,273	26,901
1976	1,550	1,304	30,608
1977	1,549	1,360	36,270
1978	1,552	1,373	41,151
1979	1,536	1,359	46,937
1980	1,540	1,361	53,072
1981	1,534	1,337	60,628
1982	1,499	1,287	62,224
1983	1,518	1,259	67,102
1984	1,511	1,243	68,215
1985	1,503	1,206	74,237
1986	1,536	1,180	76,161
1987	1,606	1,219	84,377
1988	1,643	1,270	102,190
1989	1,683	1,303	101,778

Source: New York Stock Exchange 1990 *Fact Book.*

NYSE Composite Index, Daily Closings, 1989 (December 31, 1965 = 50)

	Jan.	Feb.	Mar.	Apr.	May	June	July	Aug.	Sept.	Oct.	Nov.	Dec.
1	•	166.47	161.74	•	172.82	179.63	•	191.38	196.37	•	188.84	193.66
2	•	166.35	163.21	•	172.37	181.49	•	191.78	•	194.90	187.64	•
3	154.98	166.50	163.90	166.43	172.35	•	178.51	192.09	•	196.84	187.28	•
4	157.06	•	•	165.95	172.21	•	•	191.64	•	197.98	•	194.07
5	157.49	•	•	166.45	172.14	179.89	179.25	•	195.84	198.05	•	193.19
6	157.96	166.19	165.63	166.02	•	180.93	179.82	•	194.18	198.94	184.77	192.82
7	•	168.02	165.28	166.93	•	182.34	181.56	194.19	193.78	•	185.74	192.38
8	•	167.69	165.45	•	171.26	182.39	•	194.23	193.95	•	187.48	192.92
9	158.15	166.13	165.36	•	170.80	182.37	•	193.20	•	199.34	186.75	•
10	157.85	164.01	164.85	166.89	171.13	•	182.70	193.97	•	199.00	187.90	•
11	158.65	•	•	167.58	171.71	•	183.62	192.27	193.30	197.81	•	192.83
12	159.26	•	•	167.82	175.13	182.14	184.15	•	193.88	196.98	•	194.44
13	159.58	164.15	166.00	166.54	•	180.94	184.31	•	192.29	185.56	188.22	195.01
14	•	163.94	165.93	168.89	•	180.83	185.06	191.37	190.95	•	187.51	193.97
15	•	165.21	166.67	•	176.25	178.97	•	192.08	191.59	•	188.76	193.45
16	159.78	165.51	168.10	•	175.92	179.59	•	192.64	•	189.76	188.75	•
17	159.48	166.45	164.66	169.05	176.98	•	185.37	191.95	•	188.89	189.28	•
18	161.01	•	•	171.13	177.29	•	184.91	192.64	192.43	189.32	•	190.17
19	161.25	•	•	171.70	178.92	179.79	187.10	•	192.46	192.17	•	189.40
20	161.16	•	163.13	171.30	•	179.49	186.11	•	192.45	192.12	188.03	189.54
21	•	166.06	163.80	172.90	•	179.18	187.15	189.97	192.16	•	188.05	190.50
22	•	163.55	163.41	•	179.35	180.05	•	190.11	192.73	•	189.21	191.95
23	160.13	164.09	162.64	•	177.61	182.86	•	191.84	•	190.90	•	•
24	161.99	161.72	•	172.49	177.97	•	186.03	195.29	•	190.05	190.29	•
25	162.33	•	•	171.60	178.05	•	186.10	194.79	191.28	189.52	•	•
26	163.60	•	•	171.75	179.31	182.20	188.14	•	191.47	187.22	•	191.72
27	164.78	161.95	163.32	173.06	•	183.18	190.22	•	191.82	185.60	191.13	192.69
28	•	162.49	163.88	173.13	•	181.87	190.38	195.45	193.55	•	191.34	193.59
29	•		164.25	•	•	178.75	•	194.47	193.97	•	190.25	195.04
30	165.36		164.38	•	178.11	177.90	•	194.91	•	185.59	191.30	•
31	166.63		165.63		178.85		192.41	195.27		188.24		•
High	166.63	168.02	168.10	173.13	179.35	183.18	192.41	195.45	196.37	199.34	191.34	195.04
Low	154.98	161.72	161.74	165.95	170.80	177.90	178.51	189.97	190.95	185.56	184.77	189.40
Avg.	160.40	165.08	164.60	169.38	175.30	180.76	185.15	192.94	193.02	192.49	188.50	192.67

• NYSE closed.

Source: New York Stock Exchange 1990 *Fact Book*.

NYSE Program Trading Participation in NYSE Volume—1989

	Total program trading as % of NYSE volume	Buy programs as % of NYSE volume	Sell programs as % of NYSE volume	Total program trading as % of twice (TTV) NYSE volume
January	8.1%	4.6%	3.4%	4.0%
February	9.9	3.7	6.2	5.0
March	11.1	5.1	6.0	5.6
April	7.6	5.4	2.2	3.8
May	9.2	5.7	3.5	4.6
June	12.3	6.4	5.9	6.1
July	9.4	5.8	3.6	4.7
August	10.3	6.0	4.3	5.2
September	13.8	6.7	7.1	6.9
October	9.7	4.6	5.1	4.9
November	6.4	3.5	3.0	3.2
December	10.8	6.8	4.0	5.4
Year	9.9%	5.4%	4.5%	5.0%

Source: New York Stock Exchange 1990 *Fact Book*.

NYSE Composite Index—Yield and P/E Ratio

End of period	Yield●	Price/ earnings ratio★	End of period	Yield●	Price/ earnings ratio★
1989			**1980**		
December	3.2%	15.0	December	5.4%	13.1
September	3.4	14.2	September	5.7	12.7
June	3.5	13.3	June	6.0	9.8
March	3.9	12.5	March	6.8	9.4
1988			**1979**		
December	3.6	12.7	December	6.2	10.1
September	3.7	13.1	September	6.0	9.9
June	3.4	15.4	June	6.4	9.9
March	3.9	15.4	March	5.7	10.5
1987			**1978**		
December	3.4	15.5	December	5.9	10.3
September	2.9	22.0	September	5.3	10.9
June	2.7	21.1	June	5.5	11.8
March	2.8	20.2	March	6.0	10.7
1986			**1977**		
December	3.4	16.1	December	5.7	11.6
September	3.3	16.6	September	5.5	11.3
June	3.3	16.6	June	5.3	12.7
March	3.5	15.5	March	5.2	12.6
1985			**1976**		
December	3.6	13.5	December	4.6	14.3
September	4.2	10.7	September	4.6	13.4
June	4.2	12.6	June	4.3	14.1
March	4.4	11.3	March	4.2	15.2
1984			**1975**		
December	4.5	10.4	December	4.6	13.8
September	4.5	10.6	September	5.0	13.8
June	4.9	10.1	June	4.3	17.9
March	4.5	11.6	March	5.0	13.3
1983			**1974**		
December	4.4	13.0	December	5.7	7.8
September	4.2	13.9	September	6.2	7.2
June	4.1	13.9	June	4.5	9.7
March	4.9	14.7	March	4.4	10.8
1982			**1973**		
December	5.2	14.7	December	4.1	12.1
September	6.1	12.5	September	3.5	13.6
June	7.0	11.3	June	3.8	12.8
March	7.2	10.3	March	3.4	13.8
1981			**1972**		
December	6.7	11.3	December	3.1	18.5
September	7.1	9.9	September	3.3	17.4
June	6.0	11.9	June	3.4	17.0
March	5.7	12.5	March	3.2	17.0

● Total dollar value of dividend payments during latest 12 months—through June 1983 and indicated dollar value through June 1985—divided by market value at end of period and multiplied by 100. Beginning in July 1985, latest quarterly dividend divided by closing price at end of period.

★ Latest closing price divided by trailing 12 months of earnings.

Source: New York Stock Exchange 1990 *Fact Book*.

Compounded Growth Rates in NYSE Volume (percent)[1]

	'74	'75	'76	'77	'78	'79	'80	'81	'82	'83	'84	'85	'86	'87	'88	Annual average daily volume (thous.)
'74																13,904
'75	33.4															18,551
'76	23.4	14.2														21,186
'77	14.6	6.2	−1.2													20,928
'78	19.7	15.5	16.2	36.6												28,591
'79	18.3	14.8	15.0	24.1	12.8											32,237
'80	21.6	19.3	20.6	28.9	25.3	39.2										44,871
'81	19.0	16.7	17.2	22.3	17.9	20.6	4.4									46,853
'82	21.3	19.6	20.6	25.5	22.8	26.4	20.4	38.8								65,052
'83	22.3	21.0	22.0	26.4	24.4	27.6	23.9	35.0	31.2							85,334
'84	20.7	19.4	20.0	23.4	21.3	23.1	19.4	24.9	18.4	6.9						91,190
'85	20.6	19.4	20.0	22.9	21.1	22.5	19.5	23.5	18.8	13.1	19.7					109,169
'86	21.3	20.3	20.9	23.6	22.1	23.5	21.0	24.7	21.3	18.2	24.4	29.2				141,028
'87	22.2	21.3	22.0	24.6	23.3	24.7	22.8	26.2	23.8	22.0	27.5	31.6	34.0			188,938
'88	19.1	18.1	18.4	20.4	18.9	19.6	17.4	19.3	16.4	13.6	15.4	13.9	7.0	−14.5		161,461
'89	18.0	16.9	17.1	18.8	17.3	17.8	15.6	17.1	14.3	11.7	12.7	11.0	5.5	−6.4	2.5	165,470

[1] To obtain the growth rates, for example, between 1974 and 1989, go down the vertical column under 1974 to the horizontal row opposite 1989 which shows an 18.0% rate. This means that NYSE share volume increased at a yearly rate of 18.0%, compounded annually, between those years.

Source: New York Stock Exchange 1990 *Fact Book*.

NASDAQ Index Performances: 1979–1989

Year	Value	Composite	Industrial	Bank	Other Finance	Insurance	Transportation	Utility
1989	High	485.73 10/09	472.42 10/09	491.16 8/25	567.23 10/09	561.34 12/05	498.20 12/29	788.51 10/09
	Low	378.56 1/03	374.93 1/03	375.38 12/19	457.79 1/03	424.74 1/03	394.62 1/03	500.81 1/03
	Close	454.82	447.99	391.02	505.64	546.01	498.20	737.20
	% Chg.	19.3	18.2	-10.2	10.1	27.2	25.9	47.1
1988	High	396.11 7/05	413.09 7/05	464.91 8/05	477.88 10/10	435.80 10/10	403.68 11/02	501.13 12/30
	Low	331.97 1/12	334.85 1/20	396.44 1/04	410.75 1/13	339.41 1/26	320.91 2/09	349.68 1/12
	Close	381.38	378.95	435.31	459.34	429.14	395.81	501.13
	% Chg.	15.4	11.8	11.4	12.9	22.2	24.0	41.0
1987	High	455.26 8/26	488.92 10/05	526.64 3/20	542.04 3/20	475.78 8/21	436.53 8/21	441.61 8/21
	Low	291.88 10/28	288.30 10/28	366.75 12/07	382.43 12/07	333.66 10/28	276.03 10/28	301.51 10/28
	Close	330.47	338.94	390.66	406.96	351.06	319.21	355.30
	% Chg.	-5.3	-3.0	-5.3	-11.7	-13.1	-8.5	12.4
1986	High	411.16 7/03	414.45 7/03	457.59 7/03	553.42 7/03	467.05 3/19	365.81 6/20	362.86 7/03
	Low	323.01 1/09	326.56 1/09	346.35 1/09	424.52 1/02	381.59 1/09	288.13 1/09	295.97 1/09
	Close	348.83	349.33	412.53	460.64	404.14	348.84	316.09
	% Chg.	7.4	5.8	18.1	8.8	5.8	19.6	4.8
1985	High	325.16 12/16	330.17 12/31	350.08 12/23	423.52 12/16	385.45 12/17	296.91 12/13	303.84 12/20
	Low	245.91 1/02	258.85 1/02	230.23 1/02	298.20 1/02	276.33 1/08	236.20 1/04	234.87 1/02
	Close	324.93	330.17	349.36	423.49	382.07	291.59	301.57
	% Chg.	31.4	26.6	52.0	41.8	35.0	21.9	26.4
1984	High	287.90 1/06	336.16 1/06	229.77 12/31	298.62 12/31	283.91 12/26	290.70 1/09	280.54 1/06
	Low	225.30 7/25	250.18 7/25	192.99 6/01	252.34 5/30	226.87 7/19	194.33 7/25	194.33 7/26
	Close	247.35	260.73	229.77	298.62	283.11	239.29	238.66
	% Chg.	-11.2	-19.4	12.8	7.6	9.9	-14.8	-11.4
1983	High	328.91 6/24	408.42 6/24	203.75 12/30	284.39 9/26	287.34 5/10	293.76 11/30	391.37 6/16
	Low	230.59 1/03	270.55 1/03	155.68 1/12	206.86 1/04	217.33 1/24	194.27 1/04	257.12 10/12
	Close	278.60	323.68	203.75	277.53	257.63	280.80	269.39
	% Chg.	19.9	18.3	30.3	33.7	13.8	43.6	-5.9
1982	High	240.70 12/08	281.64 12/08	160.73 11/12	216.40 12/08	236.76 12/06	205.81 11/05	316.17 12/08
	Low	159.14 8/13	177.70 8/13	127.84 8/13	152.45 8/13	163.78 8/13	145.26 3/16	168.02 3/12
	Close	232.41	273.58	156.37	207.50	226.40	195.48	286.23
	% Chg.	18.7	19.3	9.3	17.8	16.5	16.5	57.6
1981	High	223.47 5/29	283.03 5/29	144.06 12/01	182.10 6/25	204.77 6/15	201.71 6/15	191.18 11/30
	Low	175.03 9/28	204.62 9/25	118.59 1/02	154.61 1/02	166.10 2/13	155.99 1/08	148.69 2/04
	Close	195.84	229.29	143.13	176.20	194.31	167.77	181.67
	% Chg.	-3.2	-12.3	20.9	14.4	16.5	2.2	9.6
1980	High	208.15 11/28	274.70 11/28	118.58 12/24	154.07 12/31	184.71 9/23	179.20 10/10	165.92 11/28
	Low	124.09 3/27	145.03 3/27	91.99 3/27	106.35 3/27	128.74 3/27	100.55 3/27	106.01 3/27
	Close	202.34	261.36	118.39	154.07	166.81	164.19	165.70
	% Chg.	33.9	49.2	9.4	17.7	3.0	39.0	27.1
1979	High	152.29 10/05	175.18 12/31	115.81 8/31	139.50 8/24	166.31 10/05	133.42 10/04	130.41 12/31
	Low	117.84 1/02	126.88 1/02	102.09 1/03	114.18 1/02	126.58 1/02	100.76 1/02	106.27 1/02
	Close	151.14	175.18	108.24	130.92	162.03	118.47	130.41
	% Chg.	28.1	38.1	5.8	14.4	27.3	17.8	23.0

Source: *1990 NASDAQ FACT BOOK*, published by the National Association of Securities Dealers, Inc., 1735 K Street, N.W., Washington, DC. 20006.

50 Most Active NASDAQ/NMS Issues in 1989

Symbol	Company Name	Closing Price	Share Volume
1. MCIC	MCI Communications Corporation	44.000	487,844,000
2. AAPL	Apple Computer, Inc.	35.250	456,200,000
3. INTC	Intel Corporation	34.500	386,356,000
4. SUNW	Sun Microsystems, Inc.	17.250	297,150,000
5. JAGRY	Jaguar plc	13.750	200,334,000
6. SGAT	Seagate Technology, Inc.	15.000	199,583,000
7. TCOMA	Tele-Communications, Inc. Cl A	17.875	185,787,000
8. ORCL	Oracle Systems Corporation	23.375	182,882,000
9. FEXC	First Executive Corporation	9.750	168,594,000
10. LIZC	Liz Claiborne, Inc.	24.000	155,384,000
11. MSFT	Microsoft Corporation	87.000	135,724,000
12. LDMFB	Laidlaw Transportation Ltd. Cl B	22.875	132,939,000
13. LINB	LIN Broadcasting Corporation	120.250	131,009,000
14. LOTS	Lotus Development Corporation	31.000	130,327,000
15. RTRSY	Reuters Holdings PLC	49.625	125,283,000
16. MCRN	Micron Technology, Inc.	9.750	122,689,000
17. MCAWA	McCaw Cellular Comm., Inc. Cl A	38.250	117,132,000
18. COMS	3Com Corporation	13.750	116,817,000
19. BSTN	Boston Technology, Inc.	8.000	115,595,000
20. INGR	Intergraph Corporation	17.250	109,753,000
21. NOVL	Novell, Inc.	31.000	108,962,000
22. CNNR	Conner Peripherals, Inc.	13.125	101,265,000
23. TATE	Ashton-Tate Corporation	12.250	100,713,000
24. NIKE	NIKE, Inc. Cl B	53.250	100,014,000
25. DIGI	DSC Communications Corporation	14.500	99,754,000
26. ENST	Enstar Group, Inc. (The)	3.000	96,954,000
27. VNCP	Valley National Corporation	12.875	94,915,000
28. ADBE	Adobe Systems Incorporated	20.250	94,329,000
29. USHC	U.S. Healthcare, Inc.	13.875	94,098,000
30. MENT	Mentor Graphics Corporation	16.750	83,287,000
31. CHRS	Charming Shoppes, Inc.	10.625	82,201,000
32. AMGN	Amgen Inc.	49.000	79,900,000
33. COMM	Cellular Communications, Inc.	40.125	76,181,000
34. MTTL	Mobile Telecomm. Technologies	8.750	73,300,000
35. QNTM	Quantum Corporation	10.875	72,853,000
36. PCLB	Price Company (The)	46.250	72,621,000
37. CHPS	Chips and Technologies, Inc.	18.000	70,682,000
38. ADAC	ADAC Laboratories	6.125	70,287,000
39. RYAN	Ryan's Family Steak Houses, Inc.	7.625	66,907,000
40. VLID	Valid Logic Systems	4.125	64,493,000
41. ADTLY	ADT Limited ADR	32.000	61,421,000
42. MXTR	Maxtor Corporation	8.750	59,950,000
43. GROS	Grossman's Inc.	5.000	59,148,000
44. JERR	Jerrico, Inc.	23.000	59,120,000
45. PICN	Pic 'N' Save Corporation	13.125	58,112,000
46. NOBE	Nordstrom, Inc.	37.250	57,014,000
47. CTUS	Cetus Corporation	14.250	56,620,000
48. SAFC	SAFECO Corporation	38.625	56,373,000
49. AMAT	Applied Materials, Inc.	28.500	55,520,000
50. NSCO	Network Systems Corporation	8.125	54,832,000

Note: This list includes only securities that had a 1989 closing price of $3 or more.

Source: *1990 NASDAQ FACT BOOK,* published by the National Association of Securities Dealers, Inc., 1735 K Street, N.W., Washington, DC. 20006.

Comparison of Share Volumes: NASDAQ, NYSE, and Amex

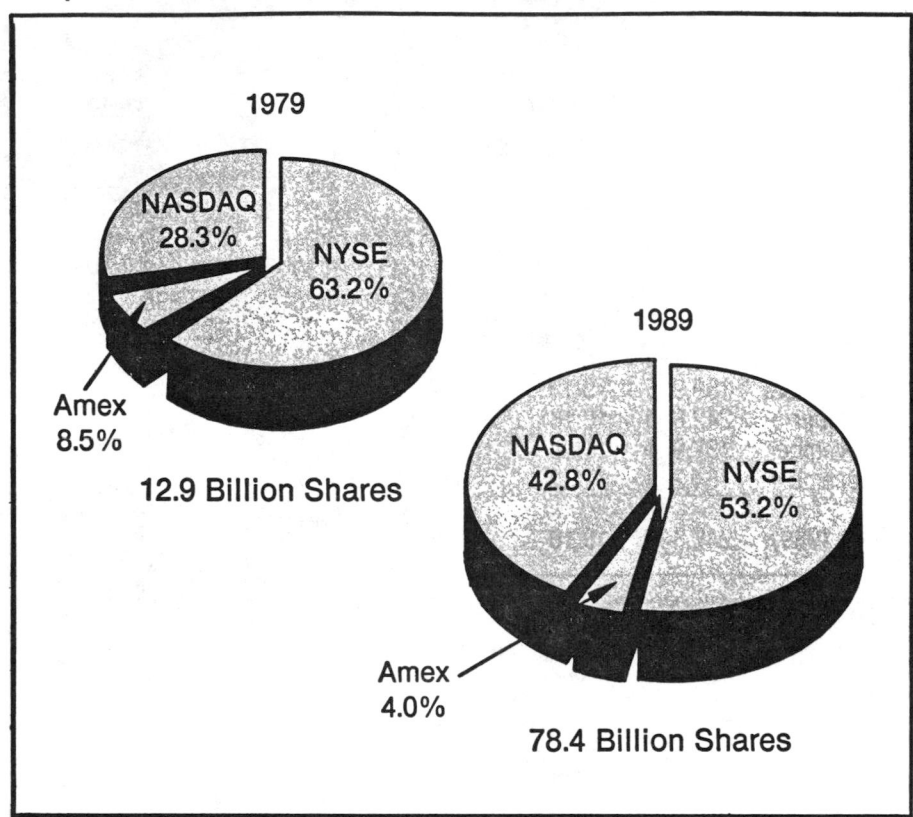

1979

NASDAQ 28.3%

NYSE 63.2%

Amex 8.5%

12.9 Billion Shares

1989

NASDAQ 42.8%

NYSE 53.2%

Amex 4.0%

78.4 Billion Shares

Source: *1990 NASDAQ FACT BOOK*, published by the National Association of Securities Dealers, Inc., 1735 K Street, N.W., Washington, DC. 20006.

Five-Year Comparisons of NASDAQ, NYSE, and Amex

	Companies			Issue			Share Volume (In Millions)		
Year	NASDAQ	NYSE	Amex	NASDAQ	NYSE	Amex	NASDAQ	NYSE	Amex
1989	4,293	1,719	859	4,963	2,241	1,069	33,530	41,699	3,125
1988	4,451	1,681	896	5,144	2,234	1,101	31,070	40,850	2,515
1987	4,706	1,647	869	5,537	2,244	1,077	37,890	47,801	3,506
1986	4,417	1,573	796	5,189	2,257	957	28,737	35,680	2,979
1985	4,136	1,540	783	4,784	2,298	940	20,699	27,511	2,101

Source: *1990 NASDAQ FACT BOOK,* published by the National Association of Securities Dealers, Inc., 1735 K Street, N.W., Washington, DC. 20006.

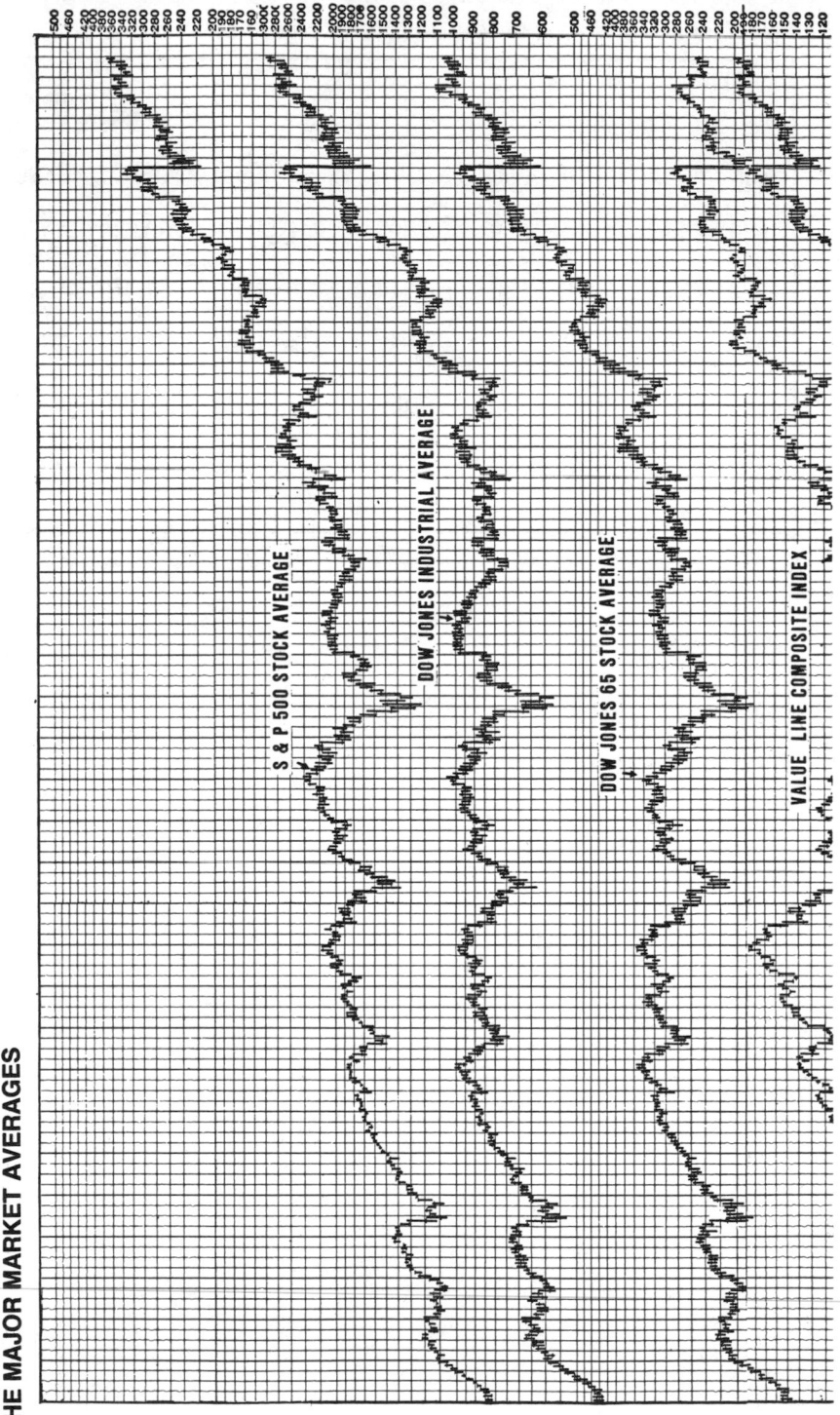

THE MAJOR MARKET AVERAGES

S & P 500 STOCK AVERAGE

DOW JONES INDUSTRIAL AVERAGE

DOW JONES 65 STOCK AVERAGE

VALUE LINE COMPOSITE INDEX

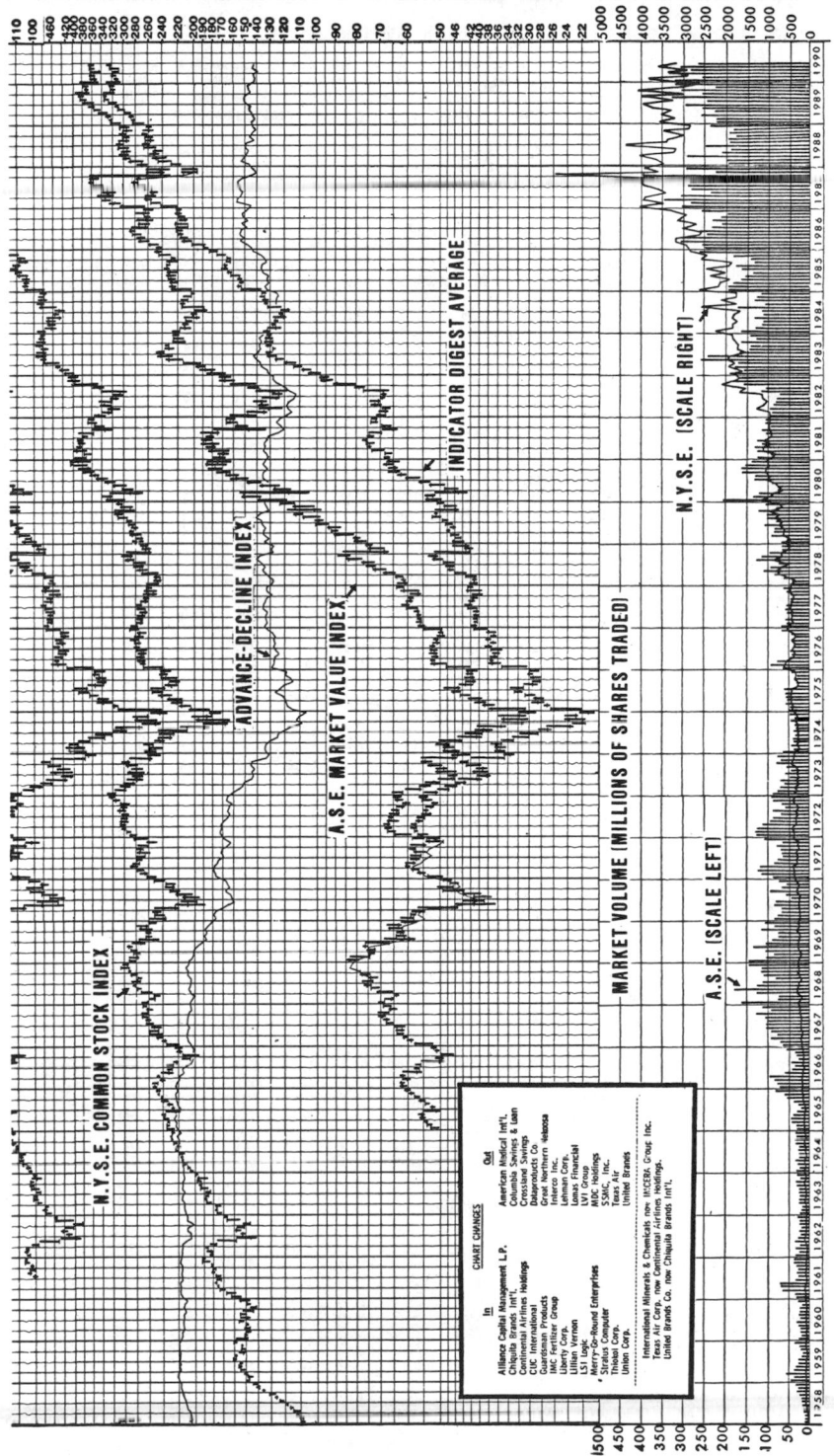

CHART CHANGES

In	Out
Alliance Capital Management L.P.	American Medical Int'L.
Chiquita Brands Int'L.	Columbia Savings & Loan
Continental Airlines Holdings	Crossland Savings
CTC International	Diagaproducts Co.
Guardsman Products	Great Northern Nekoosa
IMC Fertilizer Group	Interco Inc.
Liberty Corp.	Lehman Corp.
Lillian Vernon	Lomas Financial
LSI Logic	LVI Group
Merry-Go-Round Enterprises	MDC Holdings
Stratus Computer	SSMC, Inc.
Thiokol Corp.	Texas Air
Union Corp.	United Brands
International Minerals & Chemicals now IMCERA Group, Inc.	
Texas Air Corp. now Continental Airlines Holdings.	
United Brands Co. now Chiquita Brands Int'L.	

Source: 5-Trend CYCLI-GRAPHS. The charts are courtesy of Securities Research Company, a Division of Babson-United Investment Advisors, Inc., Babson-United Building, 101 Prescott St., Wellesley Hills, MA 02181, July quarterly edition, 1990.

Quarterly Dow Jones Industrial Stock Average

The table below lists the total earnings (losses) of the Dow Jones Industrial Average component stocks of record based on generally accepted accounting principles as reported by the company and adjusted by the Dow Divisor in effect at quarter end and the total dividends of the component stocks based upon the record date and adjusted by the Dow Divisor in effect at quarter end. N.A.-Not available. d-Indicates deficit/negative earnings for the quarter.

Year	Quarter Ended	Clos. Avg.	Qtrly Chg.	% Chg.	Qtrly Earns	12-Mth Earns	P/E Ratio	Qtrly Divs	12-Mth Divs	Divs Yield	Payout Ratio
1990	Mar. 30	2707.21	− 45.99	− 1.67	45.44	205.60	13.2	26.33	106.67	3.94	.5188
1989	Dec. 29	2753.20	+ 60.38	+ 1.69	46.96	221.48	12.4	23.50	103.00	3.74	.4651
	Sept. 29	2692.82	+ 252.76	+ 10.35	56.23	225.48	11.9	28.70	100.29	3.72	.4447
	June 30	2440.06	+ 146.44	+ 6.38	56.97	226.52	10.8	28.14	92.13	3.77	.4067
	Mar. 31	2293.62	+ 125.05	+ 5.77	61.32	229.75	10.0	22.66	84.17	3.67	.3663
1988	Dec. 30	2168.57	+ 55.66	+ 2.63	50.96	215.46	10.1	20.79	79.53	3.67	.3691
	Sept. 30	2112.91	− 28.80	− 1.34	57.27	181.04	11.7	20.54	76.41	3.62	.4221
	June 30	2141.71	+ 153.65	+ 7.73	60.20	168.54	12.7	20.18	73.92	3.45	.4386
	Mar. 31	1988.06	+ 49.23	+ 2.54	47.03	144.45	13.8	18.02	71.85	3.61	.4974
1987	Dec. 31	1938.83	− 657.45	− 25.32	16.54	133.05	14.6	17.67	71.20	3.67	.5351
	Sept. 30	2596.28	+ 177.75	+ 7.34	44.77	137.99	18.8	18.05	70.62	2.72	.5117
	June 30	2418.53	+ 113.84	+ 4.94	36.11	126.23	19.2	18.11	69.36	2.87	.5494
	Mar. 31	2304.64	+ 408.74	+ 21.56	35.63	126.49	18.2	17.37	68.19	2.96	.5391
1986	Dec. 31	1895.95	+ 128.37	+ 7.26	21.48	115.59	16.4	17.09	67.04	3.54	.5800
	Sept. 30	1767.58	− 125.14	− 6.61	33.01	118.80	14.9	16.79	67.14	3.80	.5652
	June 30	1892.72	+ 74.11	+ 4.08	36.37	103.39	18.3	16.94	65.37	3.45	.6323
	Mar. 31	1818.61	+ 271.94	+ 17.58	24.73	96.43	18.9	16.22	63.38	3.49	.6573
1985	Dec. 31	1546.67	+ 218.04	+ 16.41	24.69	96.11	16.1	17.19	62.03	4.01	.6454
	Sept. 30	1328.63	− 6.83	− 0.51	17.60	90.78	14.6	15.02	61.83	4.65	.6811
	June 28	1335.46	+ 68.68	+ 5.14	29.41	102.26	13.1	14.95	61.53	4.61	.6017
	Mar. 29	1266.78	+ 55.21	+ 4.56	24.41	107.87	11.7	14.87	61.56	4.86	.5707
1984	Dec. 31	1211.57	+ 4.86	+ 0.40	19.36	113.58	10.7	16.99	60.63	5.00	.5338
	Sept. 28	1206.71	+ 74.31	+ 6.56	29.08	108.11	11.2	14.72	58.41	4.84	.5403
	June 29	1132.40	− 32.49	− 2.79	35.02	102.07	11.1	14.98	57.67	5.09	.5650
	Mar. 30	1164.89	− 93.75	− 7.45	30.12	87.38	13.3	13.94	56.39	4.84	.6453
1983	Dec. 30	1258.64	+ 25.51	+ 2.07	13.89	72.45	17.4	14.77	56.33	4.47	.7775
	Sept. 30	1233.13	+ 11.17	+ 0.91	23.04	56.12	22.0	13.98	54.59	4.43	.9727
	June 30	1221.96	+ 91.93	+ 8.13	20.33	11.59	105.4	13.70	54.05	4.42	4.6635
	Mar. 31	1130.03	+ 83.49	+ 7.98	15.19	9.52	118.7	13.88	54.10	4.79	5.6828
1982	Dec. 31	1046.54	+ 150.29	+ 16.77	d2.44	9.15	114.4	13.03	54.14	5.17	5.9169
	Sept. 30	896.25	+ 84.32	+ 10.38	d21.49	35.15	25.5	13.44	55.55	6.20	1.5804
	June 30	811.93	− 10.84	− 1.32	18.26	79.90	10.2	13.75	55.84	6.88	.6989
	Mar. 31	822.77	− 52.23	− 5.97	14.82	97.13	8.5	13.92	56.28	6.84	.5794
1981	Dec. 31	875.00	+ 25.02	+ 2.94	23.56	113.71	7.7	14.44	56.22	6.42	.4944
	Sept. 30	849.98	− 126.90	− 12.99	23.26	123.32	6.9	13.73	56.18	6.61	.4539
	June 30	976.88	− 26.99	− 2.69	35.49	128.91	7.6	14.19	55.98	5.73	.4266
	Mar. 31	1003.87	+ 39.88	+ 4.14	31.40	123.60	8.1	13.86	54.99	5.48	.4449
1980	Dec. 31	963.99	+ 31.57	+ 3.39	33.17	121.86	7.9	14.40	54.36	5.64	.4461
	Sept. 30	932.42	+ 64.50	+ 7.43	28.85	111.58	8.4	13.53	53.83	5.77	.4824
	June 30	867.92	+ 82.17	+ 10.46	30.18	116.40	7.5	13.20	52.81	6.08	.4537
	Mar. 31	785.75	− 52.99	− 6.32	29.66	120.77	6.5	13.23	52.10	6.63	.4314
1979	Dec. 31	838.74	− 39.93	− 4.54	22.89	124.46	6.7	13.87	50.98	6.08	.4096
	Sept. 28	878.67	+ 36.69	+ 4.36	33.67	136.26	6.4	12.51	51.45	5.85	.3776
	June 29	841.98	− 20.20	− 2.34	34.55	128.99	6.5	12.49	50.35	5.98	.3903
	Mar. 30	862.18	+ 57.17	+ 7.10	33.35	124.10	6.9	12.11	49.48	5.74	.3987
1978	Dec. 29	805.01	− 60.81	− 7.02	34.69	112.79	7.1	14.34	48.52	6.03	.4302
	Sept. 29	865.82	+ 46.87	+ 5.72	26.40	101.59	8.5	11.41	47.42	5.48	.4668
	June 30	818.95	+ 61.59	+ 8.13	29.66	91.37	9.0	11.62	46.74	5.71	.5115
	Mar. 31	757.36	− 73.81	− 8.88	22.04	89.23	8.5	11.15	46.53	6.14	.5215
1977	Dec. 30	831.17	− 15.94	− 1.88	23.49	89.10	9.3	13.24	45.84	5.51	.5145
	Sept. 30	847.11	− 69.19	− 7.55	16.18	89.86	9.4	10.73	44.73	5.28	.4978
	June 30	916.30	− 2.83	− 0.31	27.52	97.18	9.4	11.41	43.85	4.79	.4512
	Mar. 31	919.13	− 85.52	− 8.51	21.91	95.51	9.6	10.46	42.63	4.64	.4463
1976	Dec. 31	1004.65	+ 14.46	+ 1.46	24.25	96.72	10.4	12.13	41.40	4.12	.4280
	Sept. 30	990.19	− 12.59	− 1.27	23.50	95.81	10.3	9.85	38.90	3.93	.4060
	June 30	1002.78	+ 3.33	+ 0.33	25.85	90.68	11.1	10.19	38.10	3.80	.4202
	Mar. 31	999.45	+ 147.04	+ 17.25	23.12	81.87	12.2	9.23	36.88	3.69	.4505
1975	Dec. 31	852.41	+ 58.53	+ 7.37	23.34	75.66	11.3	9.63	37.46	4.39	.4951
	Sept. 30	793.88	− 85.11	− 10.72	18.37	75.47	10.5	9.05	38.28	4.82	.5072
	June 30	878.99	+ 110.84	+ 12.61	17.04	83.83	10.5	8.97	38.66	4.40	.4612
	Mar. 31	768.15	+ 151.91	+ 24.65	16.91	93.47	8.2	9.81	38.56	5.02	.4125

Stock Market Averages by Industry Group

These definitions apply to pages 300–21.

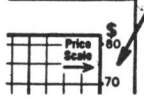

Price Scale — The price ranges are always read from the scale at the right-hand side of each chart. This scale is equal to 15 times the Earnings and Dividend scale at the left, so when the Price Range bars and the Earnings line coincide, it shows the price is at 15 times earnings. When the price is above the earnings line, the ratio of price to earnings is greater than 15 times earnings; when below, it is less.

Monthly Ratio-Cator: The plottings for this line are obtained by dividing the closing price of the stock by the closing price of the Dow-Jones Industrial Average on the same day. The resulting percentage is multiplied by a factor of 4.5 (450) to bring the line closer to the price bars and is read from the right hand scale. The plotting indicates whether the stock has kept pace, outperformed, or lagged behind the general market as represented by the DJIA.

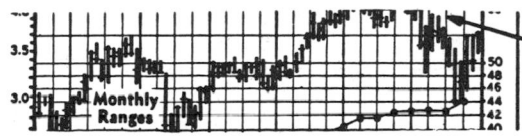

Monthly Price Ranges represented by the solid vertical bars show the highest and lowest point of each month's transactions. Crossbars indicate the month's closing price.

Source: *5-Trend CYCLI-GRAPHS.* The charts are courtesy of Securities Research Company, a Division of Babson-United Investment Advisors, Inc., Babson-United Building, 101 Prescott St., Wellesley Hills, MA 02181, July quarterly edition, 1990.

STOCK MARKET AVERAGES BY INDUSTRY GROUP

PRICES & EARNS. SOURCE: S&P   RATIO-CATOR FACTOR: 7 (700)

AEROSPACE/DEFENSE
1941-1943 = 10

Boeing, General Dynamics, Grumman, Lockheed,
Martin Marietta, McDonnell Douglas, Northrop,
Raytheon, Rockwell Int'l., United Tech.

AUTOMOBILES
1941-1943 = 10

Chrysler, Ford, General Motors

Earns. 12 mos.	
3/31/84	21.44
6/30/84	25.07
9/30/84	25.08
12/31/84	25.09
3/31/85	23.44
6/30/85	21.80
9/30/85	22.32
12/31/85	22.97

Earns. 12 mos.	
3/31/86	22.47
6/30/86	23.05
9/30/86	23.10
12/31/86	20.80
3/31/87	22.33
6/30/87	23.76
9/30/87	25.81
12/31/87	27.89

Earns. 12 mos.	
3/31/88	29.23
6/30/88	31.36
9/30/88	31.73
12/31/88	34.68
3/31/89	36.90

Earns. 12 mos.	
6/30/89	36.19
9/30/89	34.70

AUTO PARTS-AFTER MARKET
1970 = 10

Echlin Mfg., Genuine Parts,
Goodyear, SPX

AIRLINES
1982 = 100

AMR, Delta, NWA, Pan Am, UAL, USAir

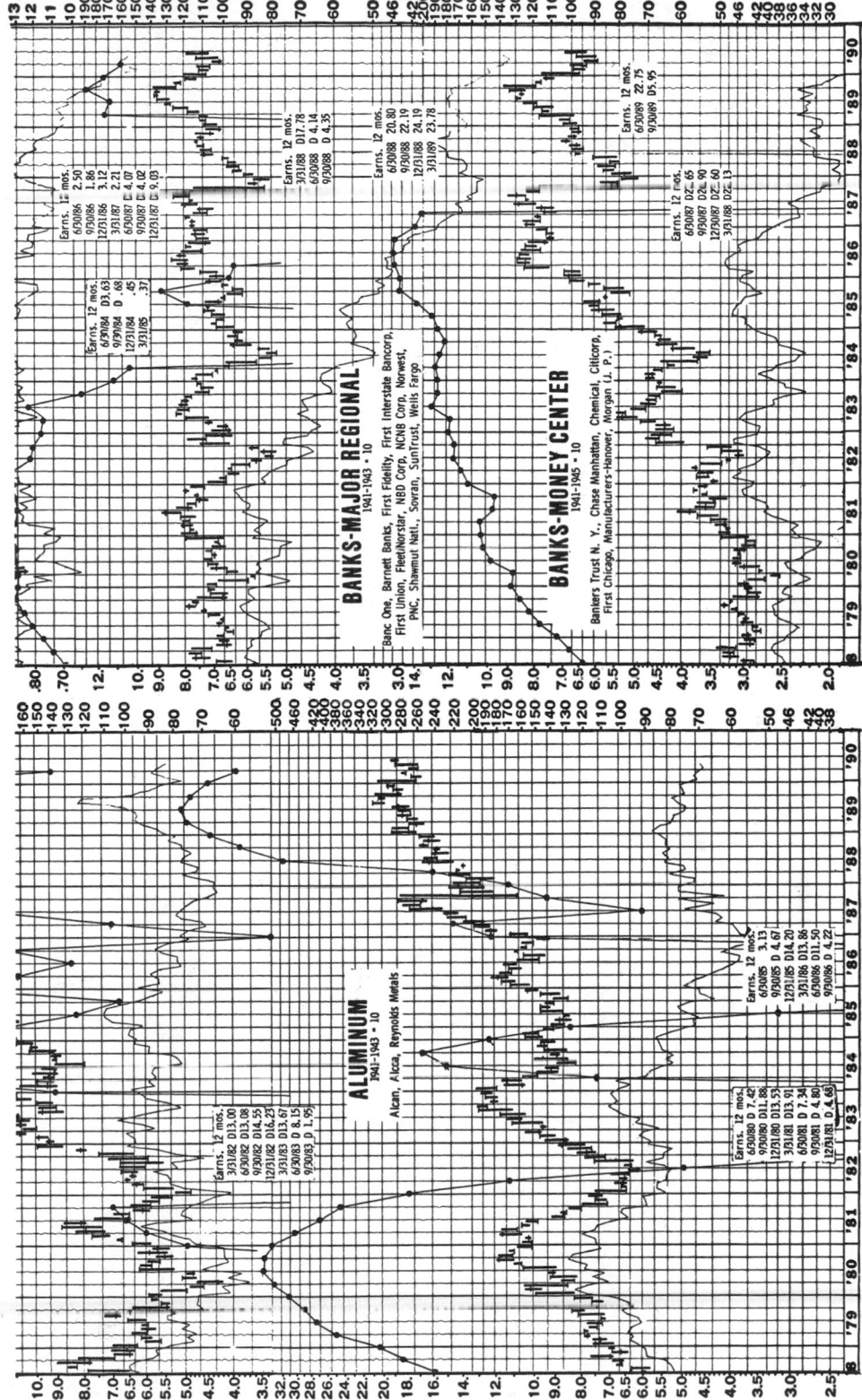

BANKS-MAJOR REGIONAL
1941-1943 • 10

Banc One, Barnett Banks, First Fidelity, First Interstate Bancorp,
First Union, Fleet/Norstar, NBD Corp, NCNB Corp, Norwest,
PNC, Shawmut Natl., Sovran, SunTrust, Wells Fargo

Earns. 12 mos.
6/30/86   2.50
9/30/86   1.86
12/31/86 3.12
3/31/87   2.21
6/30/87   D 4.07
9/30/87   D 4.02
12/31/87 D 9.03

Earns. 12 mos.
6/30/84   D3.63
9/30/84   D .68
12/31/84 .45
3/31/85   .37

Earns. 12 mos.
6/30/88   20.80
9/30/88   22.19
12/31/88 24.19
3/31/89   23.78

BANKS-MONEY CENTER
1941-1945 • 10

Bankers Trust N. Y., Chase Manhattan, Chemical, Citicorp,
First Chicago, Manufacturers-Hanover, Morgan (J. P.)

Earns. 12 mos.
6/30/87   D2.65
9/30/87   D2.90
12/31/87 D2.60
3/31/88   D2.13

Earns. 12 mos.
6/30/88   17.78
3/31/88   D 4.14
9/30/88   D 4.35

Earns. 12 mos.
6/30/89   22.75
9/30/89   D5.95

ALUMINUM
1941-1943 • 10

Alcan, Alcoa, Reynolds Metals

Earns. 12 mos.
3/31/82   D13.00
6/30/82   D3.08
9/30/82   D4.55
12/31/82 D16.23
3/31/83   D13.67
6/30/83   D 8.15
9/30/83   D 1.95

Earns. 12 mos.
6/30/80   D 7.42
9/30/80   D11.88
12/31/80 D13.53
3/31/81   D13.91
6/30/81   D 7.34
9/30/81   D 4.80
12/31/81 D 4.68

Earns. 12 mos.
6/9/85   3.13
9/30/85   D 4.67
12/31/85 D14.20
3/31/86   D13.86
6/30/86   D11.50
9/30/86   D 4.22

STOCK MARKET AVERAGES BY INDUSTRY GROUP (continued)

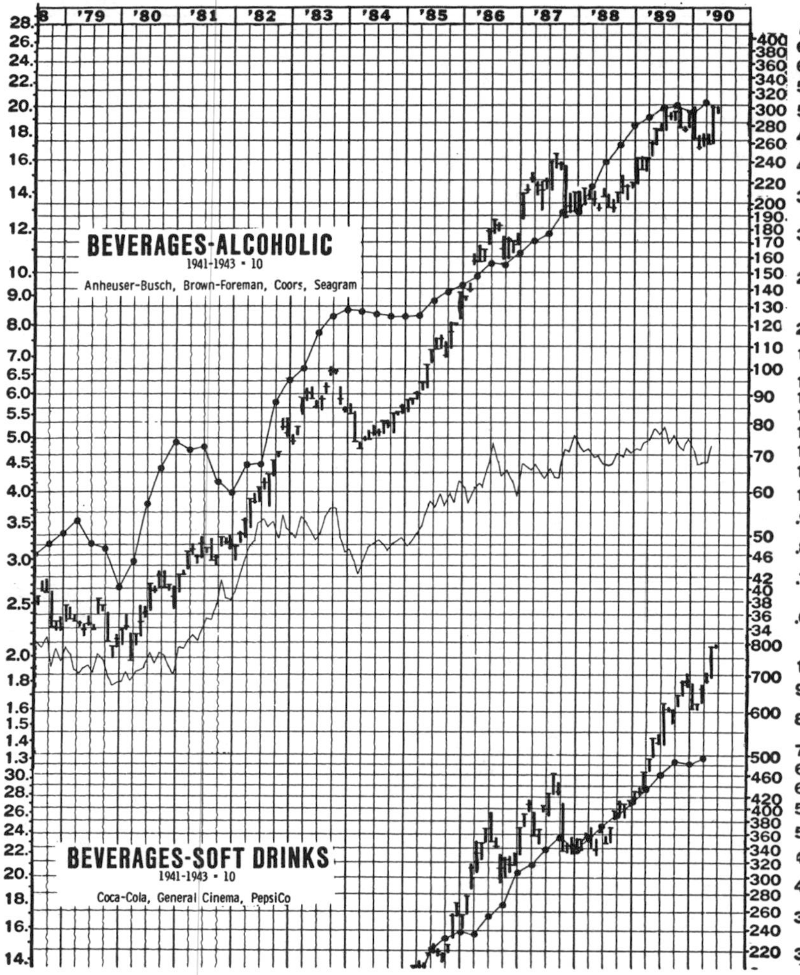

BROKERAGE FIRMS
1978 = 10

Edwards (A. G.), First Boston, Hutton (E. F.) Group,
Merrill Lynch, Paine Webber

BUILDING MATERIALS-COMPOSITE
1941-1943 = 10

Crane, Ideal Basic, Lone Star Inds., Masco,
Owens-Corning, Philips Inds., USG

BEVERAGES-ALCOHOLIC
1941-1943 = 10

Anheuser-Busch, Brown-Foreman, Coors, Seagram

BEVERAGES-SOFT DRINKS
1941-1943 = 10

Coca-Cola, General Cinema, PepsiCo

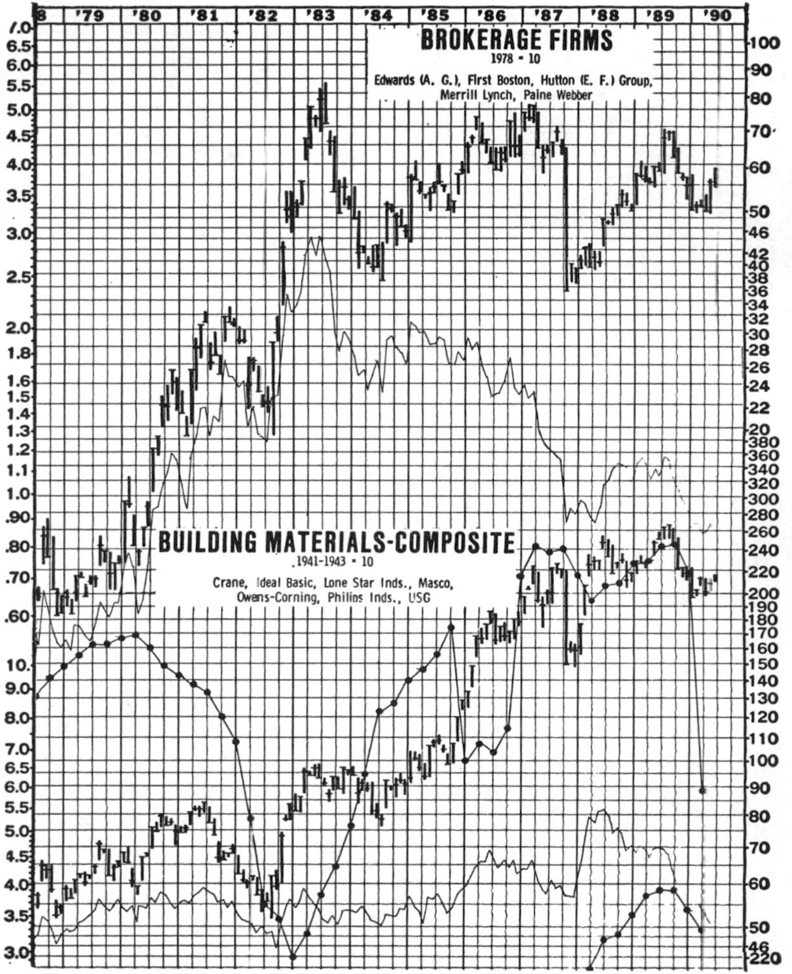

302

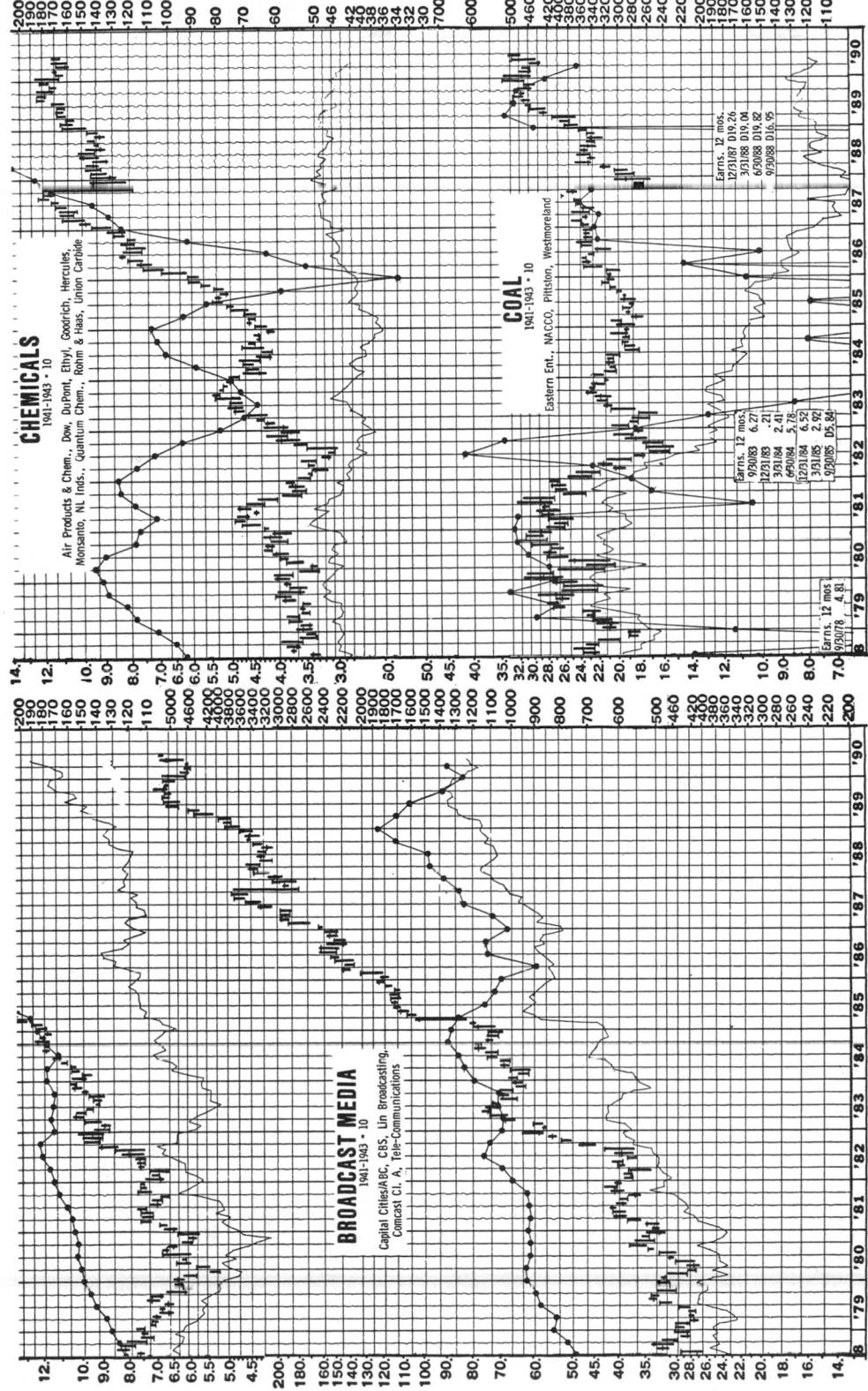

CHEMICALS
1941-1943 = 10

Air Products & Chem., Dow, DuPont, Ethyl, Goodrich, Hercules,
Monsanto, NL Inds., Quantum Chem., Rohm & Haas, Union Carbide

COAL
1941-1943 = 10

Eastern Ent., NACCO, Pittston, Westmoreland

Earns. 12 mos.
12/31/87 D19.26
3/31/88 D19.04
6/30/88 D19.82
9/30/88 D16.95

Earns. 12 mos.
9/30/83   6.27
12/31/83   .21
3/31/84   2.41
6/30/84   5.78
12/31/84   6.52
3/31/85   2.92
9/30/85   D5.84

Earns. 12 mos
9/30/78   4.81

BROADCAST MEDIA
1941-1943 = 10

Capital Cities/ABC, CBS, Lin Broadcasting,
Comcast Cl. A, Tele-Communications

303

STOCK MARKET AVERAGES BY INDUSTRY GROUP (continued)

COMMUNICATIONS EQPT./MFRS.
1941-1943 = 10

Andrew, DSC Communications, General Instrument,
M/A Com, Northern Telecom, Scientific Atlanta

COMPUTER SYSTEMS
1941-1943 = 10

Amdahl, Apple, Compaq, Control Data, Cray Research, Data
General, Datapoint, Digital Equipment, IBM, Intergraph,
NCR, Prime Computer, Tandem, Unisys, Wang Labs. "B"

CONTAINERS-PAPER
1941-1943 = 10

Bemis, Federal, Stone Container, Temple Inland

COSMETICS
1957 = 10

Alberto-Culver, Avon, Gillette,
Intl. Flavors & Fragrances, Noxell

	Earns, 12 mos.	
	6/30/89	165.81
	9/30/89	165.70

	Earns, 12 mos.	
	12/31/88	151.19
	3/31/89	63.69

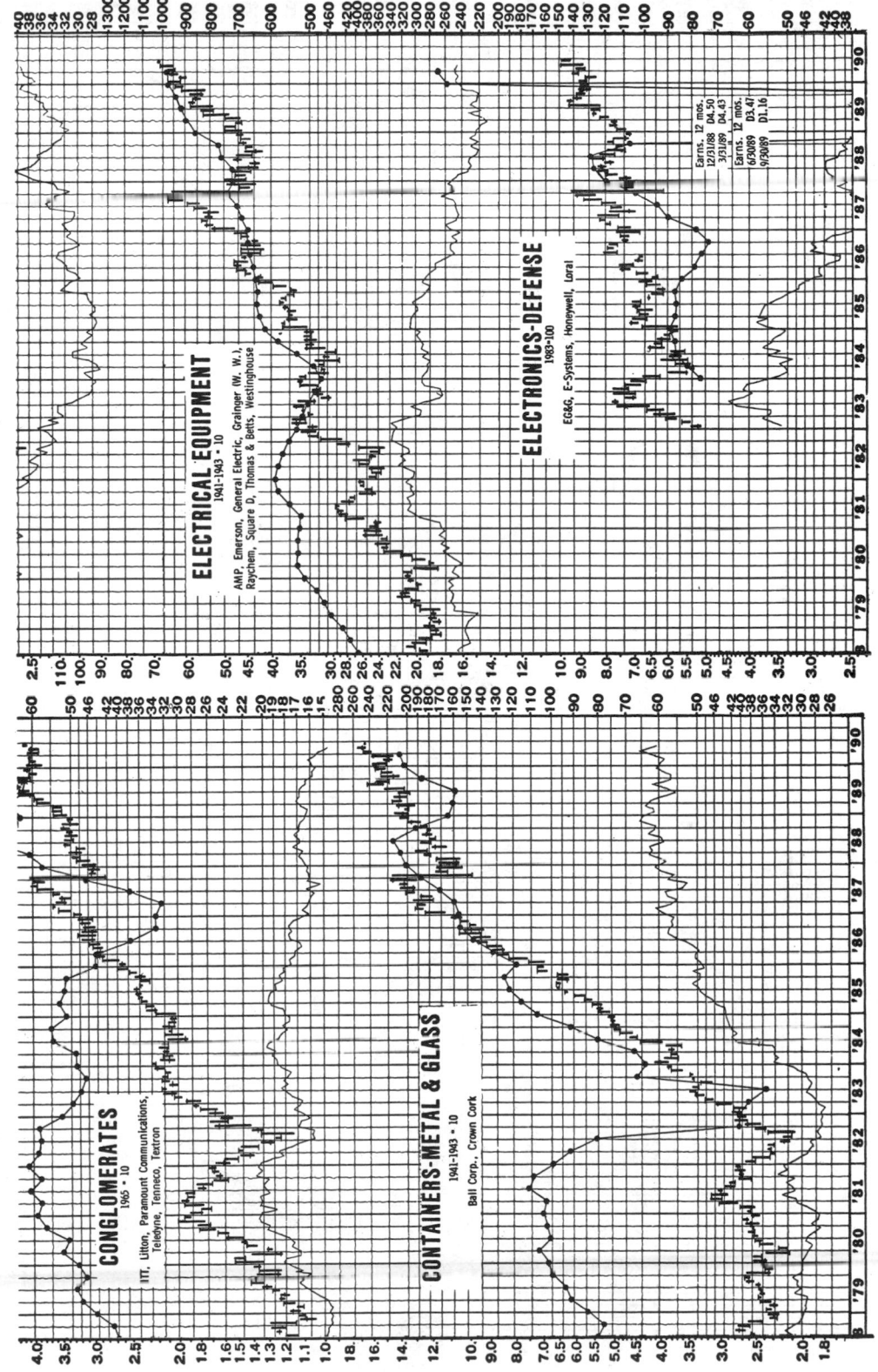

CONGLOMERATES
1965 • 10

ITT, Litton, Paramount Communications,
Teledyne, Tenneco, Textron

CONTAINERS–METAL & GLASS
1941–1943 • 10

Ball Corp., Crown Cork

ELECTRICAL EQUIPMENT
1941–1943 • 10

AMP, Emerson, General Electric, Grainger (W. W.),
Raychem, Square D, Thomas & Betts, Westinghouse

ELECTRONICS–DEFENSE
1983=100

EG&G, E-Systems, Honeywell, Loral

Earns. 12 mos.
12/31/88   D4.50
3/31/89   D4.43
Earns. 12 mos.
6/30/89   D3.47
9/30/89   D1.16

305

STOCK MARKET AVERAGES BY INDUSTRY GROUP (continued)

FOODS-COMPOSITE
1941-1943 = 10

Archer Daniels Midland, Borden, CPC Int'l., Campbell Soup, ConAgra,
Gen. Mills, Gerber Prod., Heinz (H. J.), Hershey Foods, Kellogg,
Quaker Oats, Ralston Purina, Sara Lee, Whitman, Wrigley (Wm.)

GAMING COMPANIES
1978 = 10

Caesars World, Circus Circus, Golden Nugget

ELECTRONICS-INSTRUMENTATION
1970 = 10

Hewlett-Packard, Perkin-Elmer, Tektronix

ELECTRONICS-SEMICONDUCTORS
1970 = 10

Advanced Micro Devices, Intel Corp., Motorola,

	Earns. 12 mos.
9/30/85	.64
12/31/85	.07
3/31/86	D .29
6/30/86	D .34
9/30/86	D .08
12/31/86	D .11
3/31/87	.65

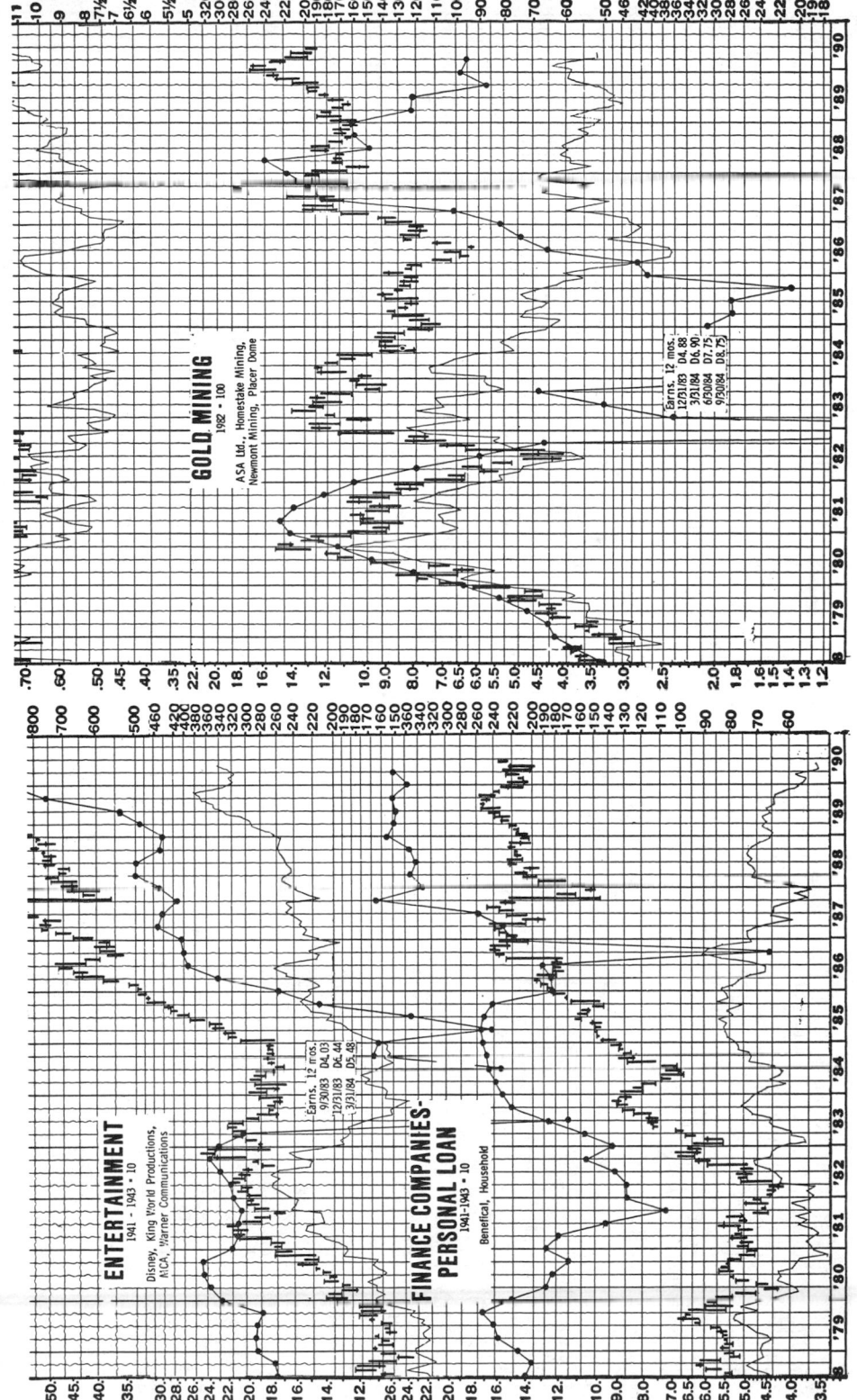

GOLD MINING
1982 = 100

ASA Ltd., Homestake Mining,
Newmont Mining, Placer Dome

Earns. 12 mos.
12/31/83   D4.88
3/31/84   D6.90
6/30/84   D7.75
9/30/84   D8.75

ENTERTAINMENT
1941 - 1943 = 10

Disney, King World Productions,
MCA, Warner Communications

Earns. 12 mos.
9/30/83   D4.03
12/31/83   D6.44
3/31/84   D5.48

**FINANCE COMPANIES-
PERSONAL LOAN**
1941-1943 = 10

Beneficial, Household

STOCK MARKET AVERAGES BY INDUSTRY GROUP (continued)

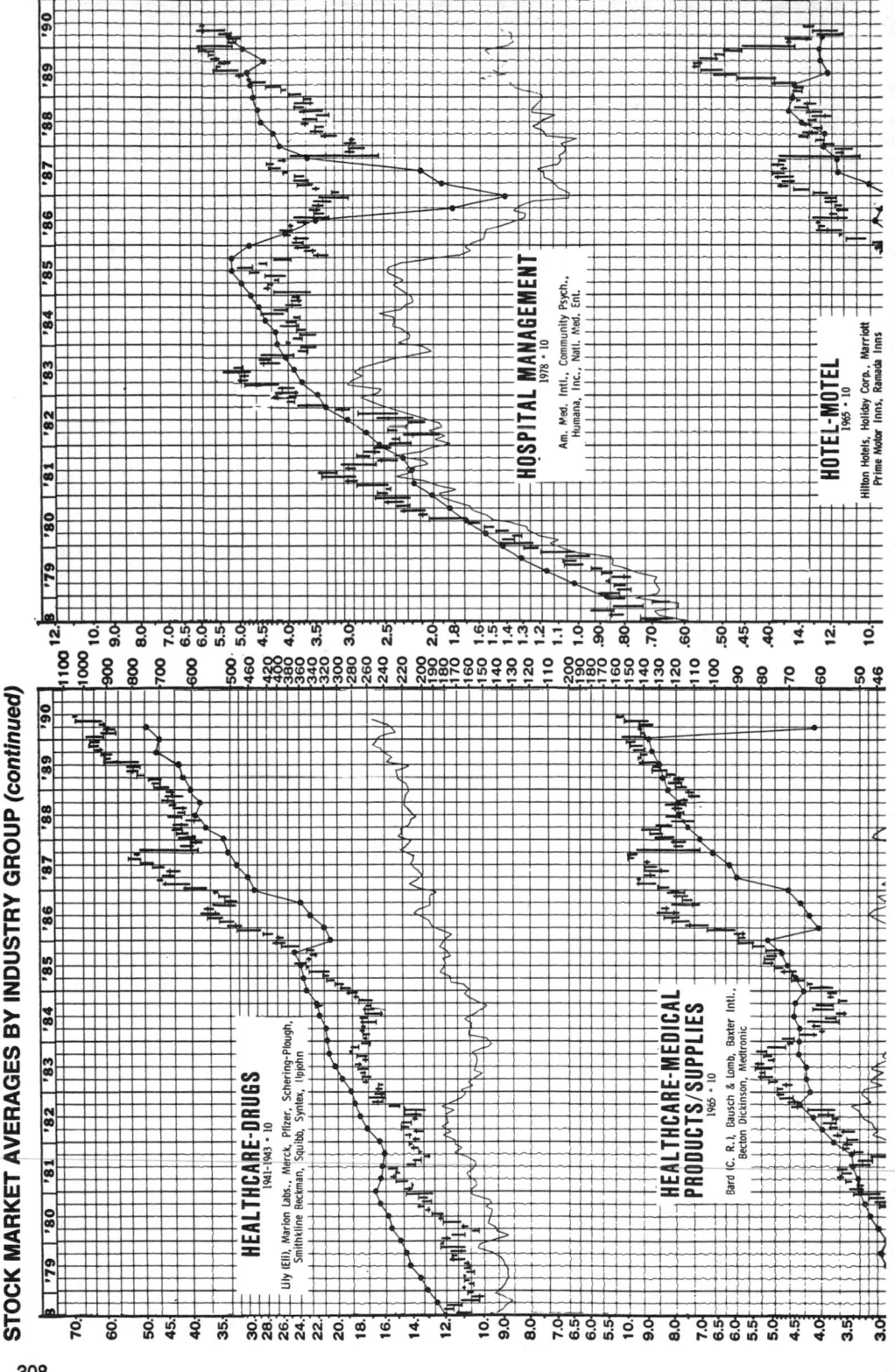

HEALTHCARE-DRUGS
1941-1943 = 10

Lily (Eli), Marion Labs., Merck, Pfizer, Schering-Plough, Smithkline Beckman, Squibb, Syntex, Upjohn

HEALTHCARE-MEDICAL PRODUCTS/SUPPLIES
1965 = 10

Bard (C. R.), Bausch & Lomb, Baxter Intl., Becton Dickinson, Medtronic

HOSPITAL MANAGEMENT
1978 = 10

Am. Med. Intl., Community Psych., Humana, Inc., Natl. Med. Ent.

HOTEL-MOTEL
1965 = 10

Hilton Hotels, Holiday Corp., Marriott Prime Motor Inns, Ramada Inns

308

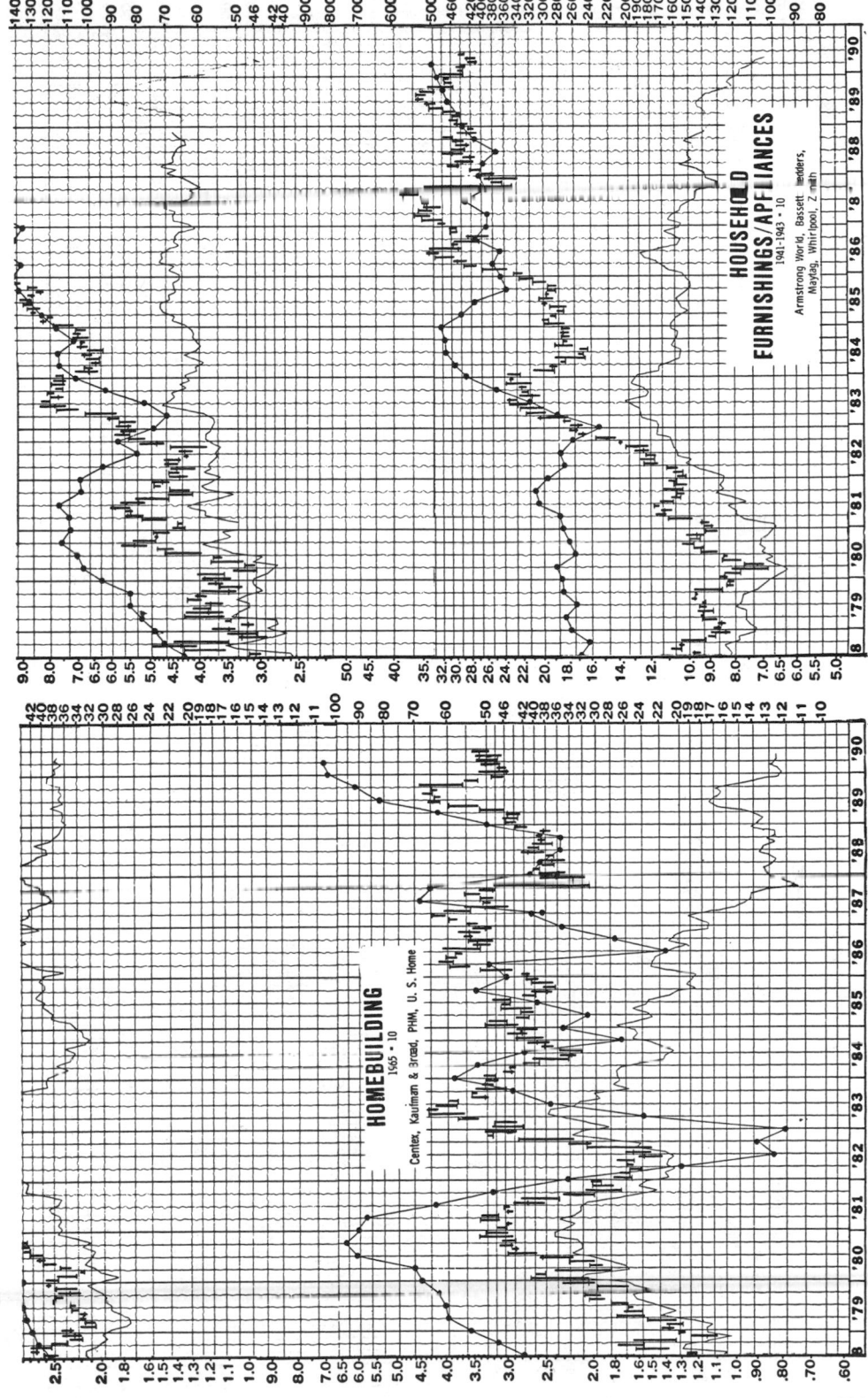

HOUSEHOLD
FURNISHINGS/APPLIANCES
1941-1943 • 10

Armstrong World, Bassett, Fenders,
Maytag, Whirlpool, Z mith

HOMEBUILDING
1965 • 10

Centex, Kaufman & Broad, PHM, U. S. Home

309

STOCK MARKET AVERAGES BY INDUSTRY GROUP *(continued)*

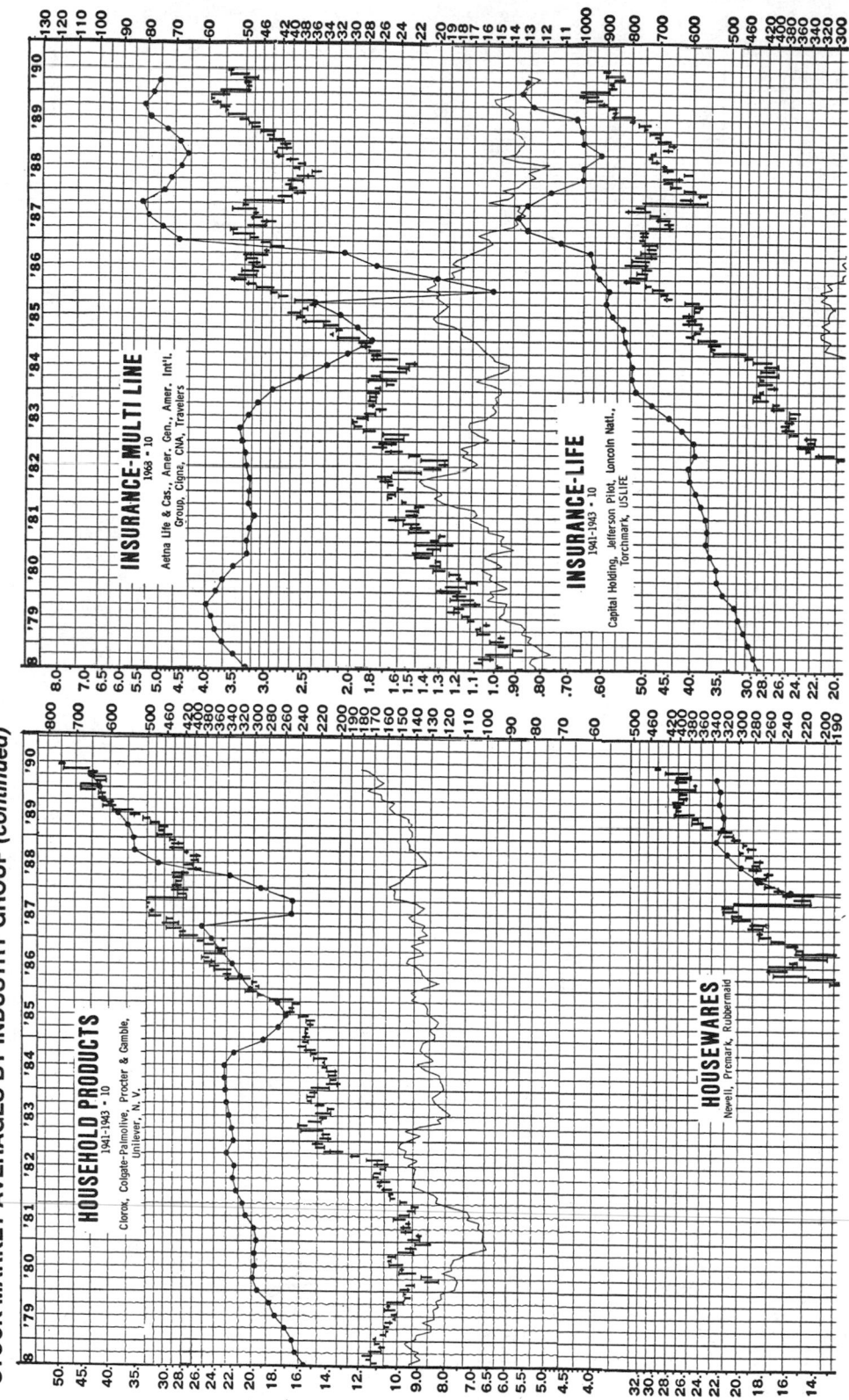

INSURANCE-MULTI LINE
1968 = 10
Aetna Life & Cas., Amer. Gen., Amer. Int'l.
Group, Cigna, CNA, Travelers

INSURANCE-LIFE
1941-1943 = 10
Capital Holding, Jefferson Pilot, Lincoln Natl.,
Torchmark, USLIFE

HOUSEHOLD PRODUCTS
1941-1943 = 10
Clorox, Colgate-Palmolive, Procter & Gamble,
Unilever, N. V.

HOUSEWARES
Newell, Premark, Rubbermaid

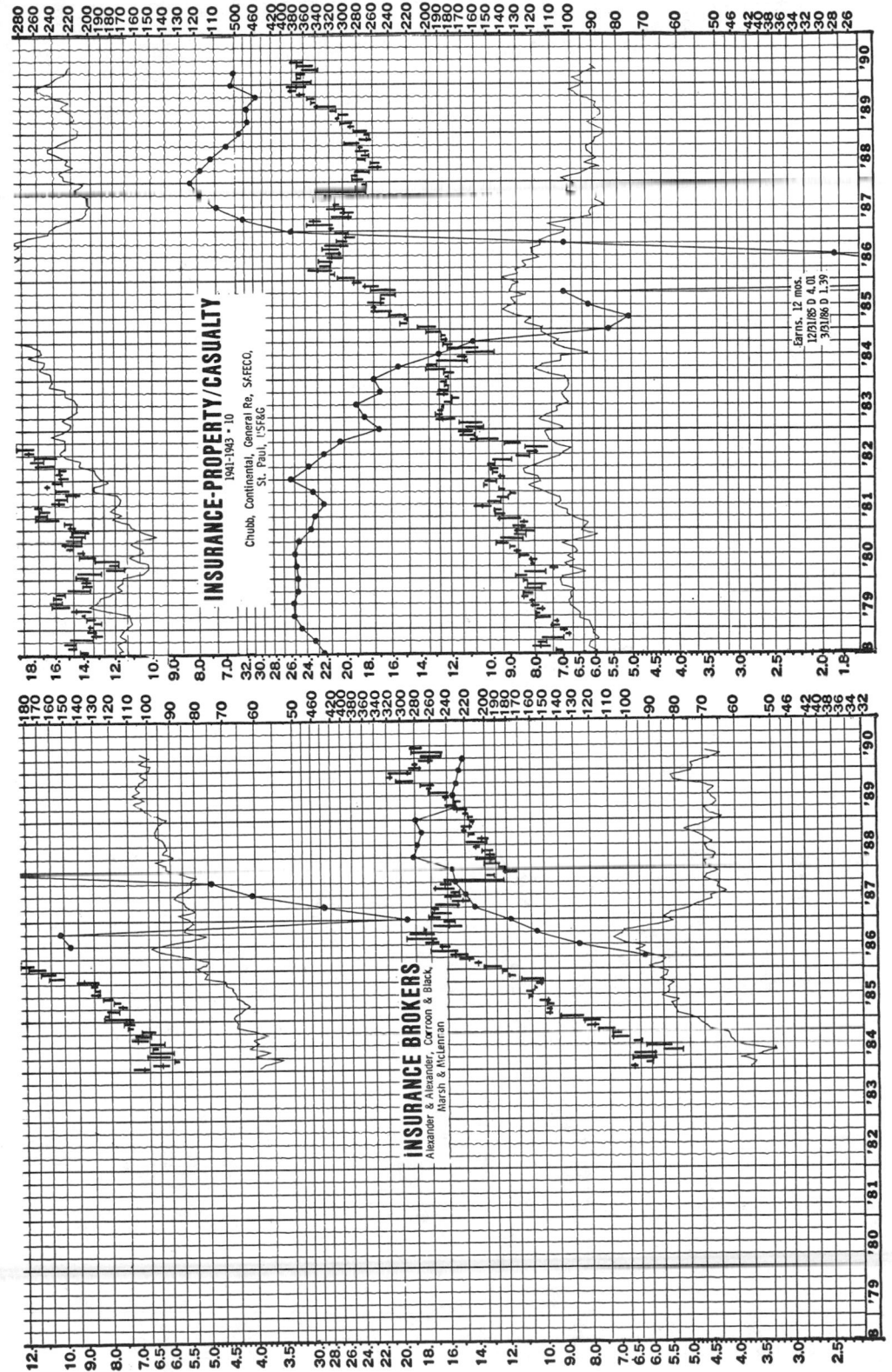

INSURANCE-PROPERTY/CASUALTY

1941-1943 = 10

Chubb, Continental, General Re, SAFECO,
St. Paul, USF&G

Earns. 12 mos.
12/31/85 D 4.01
3/31/86 D 1.39

INSURANCE BROKERS

Alexander & Alexander, Corroon & Black,
Marsh & McLennan

311

STOCK MARKET AVERAGES BY INDUSTRY GROUP (continued)

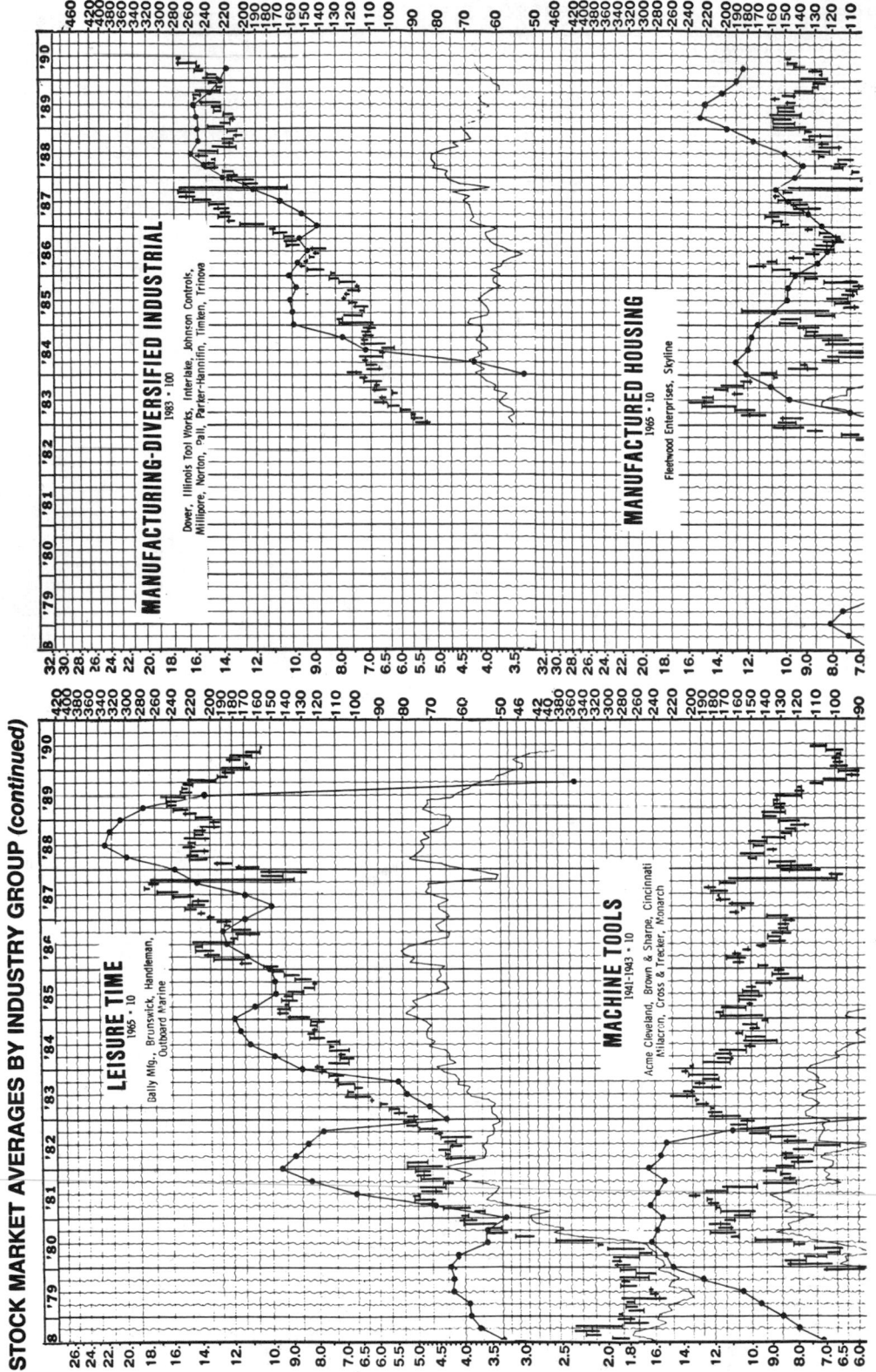

LEISURE TIME
1965 • 10

Bally Mfg., Brunswick, Handleman,
Outboard Marine

MACHINE TOOLS
1941-1943 • 10

Acme Cleveland, Brown & Sharpe, Cincinnati
Milacron, Cross & Trecker, Monarch

MANUFACTURING-DIVERSIFIED INDUSTRIAL
1983 • 100

Dover, Illinois Tool Works, Interlake, Johnson Controls,
Millipore, Norton, Pall, Parker-Hannifin, Timken, Trinova

MANUFACTURED HOUSING
1965 • 10

Fleetwood Enterprises, Skyline

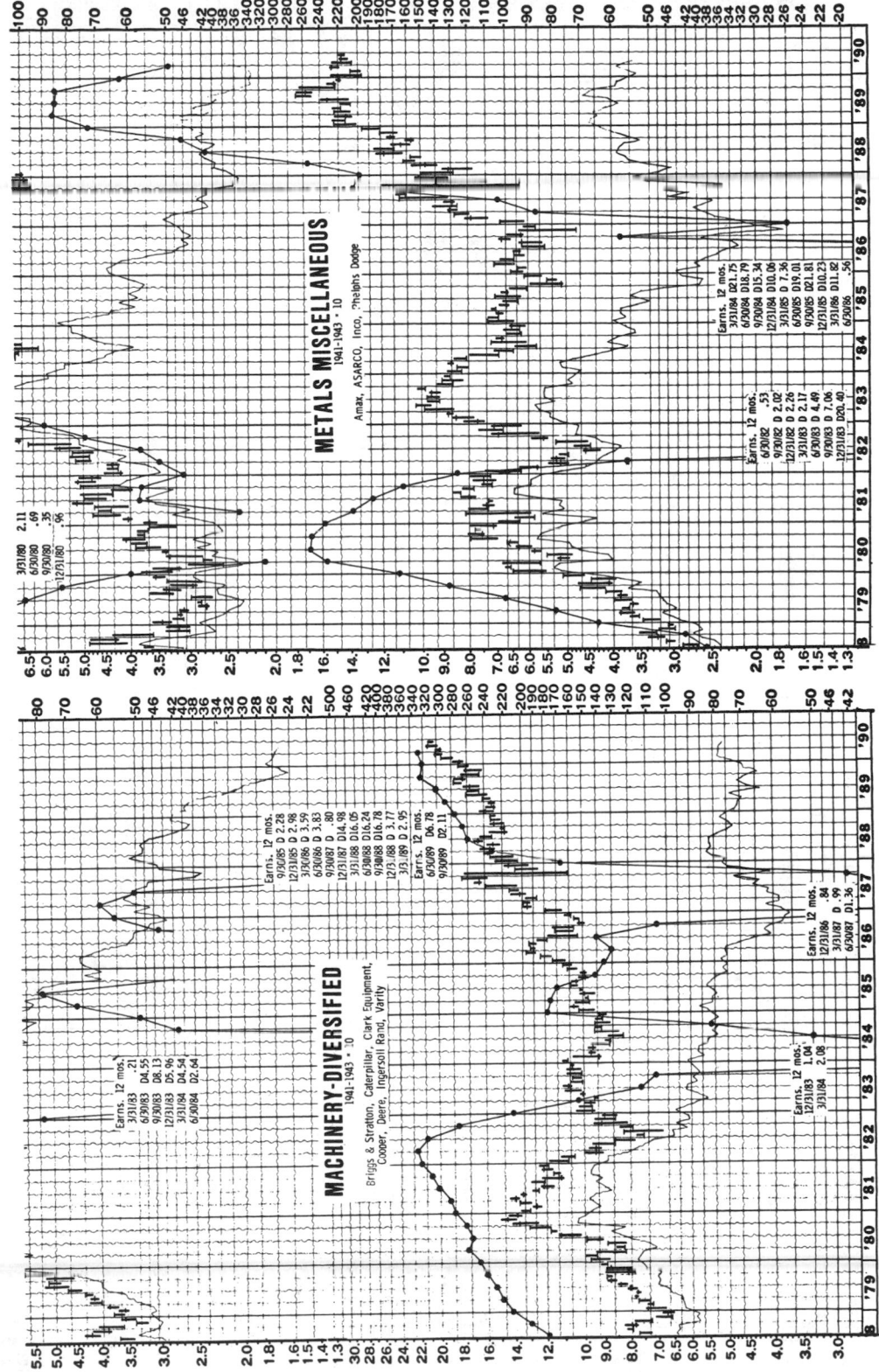

METALS MISCELLANEOUS
1941-1943 · 10

Amax, ASARCO, Inco, Phelps Dodge

3/31/80   2.11
6/30/80   .69
9/30/80   .35
12/31/80   .06

Earns. 12 mos.
6/30/82   .53
9/30/82   D 2.02
12/31/82   D 2.76
3/31/83   D 2.17
6/30/83   D 4.49
9/30/83   D 7.06
12/31/83   D20.40

Earns. 12 mos.
3/31/84   D21.75
6/30/84   D18.79
9/30/84   D15.34
12/31/84   D10.06
3/31/85   D 7.36
6/30/85   D19.01
9/30/85   D21.81
12/31/85   D10.23
3/31/86   D 7.06
6/30/86   .56

MACHINERY-DIVERSIFIED
1941-1943 · 10

Briggs & Stratton, Caterpillar, Clark Equipment,
Cooper, Deere, Ingersoll Rand, Varity

Earns. 12 mos.
3/31/83   .21
6/30/83   D4.55
9/30/83   D8.13
12/31/83   D5.96
3/31/84   D4.54
6/30/84   D2.64

Earns. 12 mos.
12/31/83   1.04
3/31/84   2.08

Earns. 12 mos.
12/31/86   .84
3/31/87   D .99
6/30/87   D1.36

Earns. 12 mos.
9/30/85   D 2.28
12/31/85   D 2.98
3/31/86   D 3.59
6/30/86   D 3.83
9/30/86   D   .80
12/31/86   D14.98
3/31/88   D16.05
6/30/88   D16.24
9/30/88   D16.78
12/31/88   D 3.77
3/31/89   D 2.95

Earns. 12 mos.
6/30/89   D6.78
9/30/89   D2.11

STOCK MARKET AVERAGES BY INDUSTRY GROUP *(continued)*

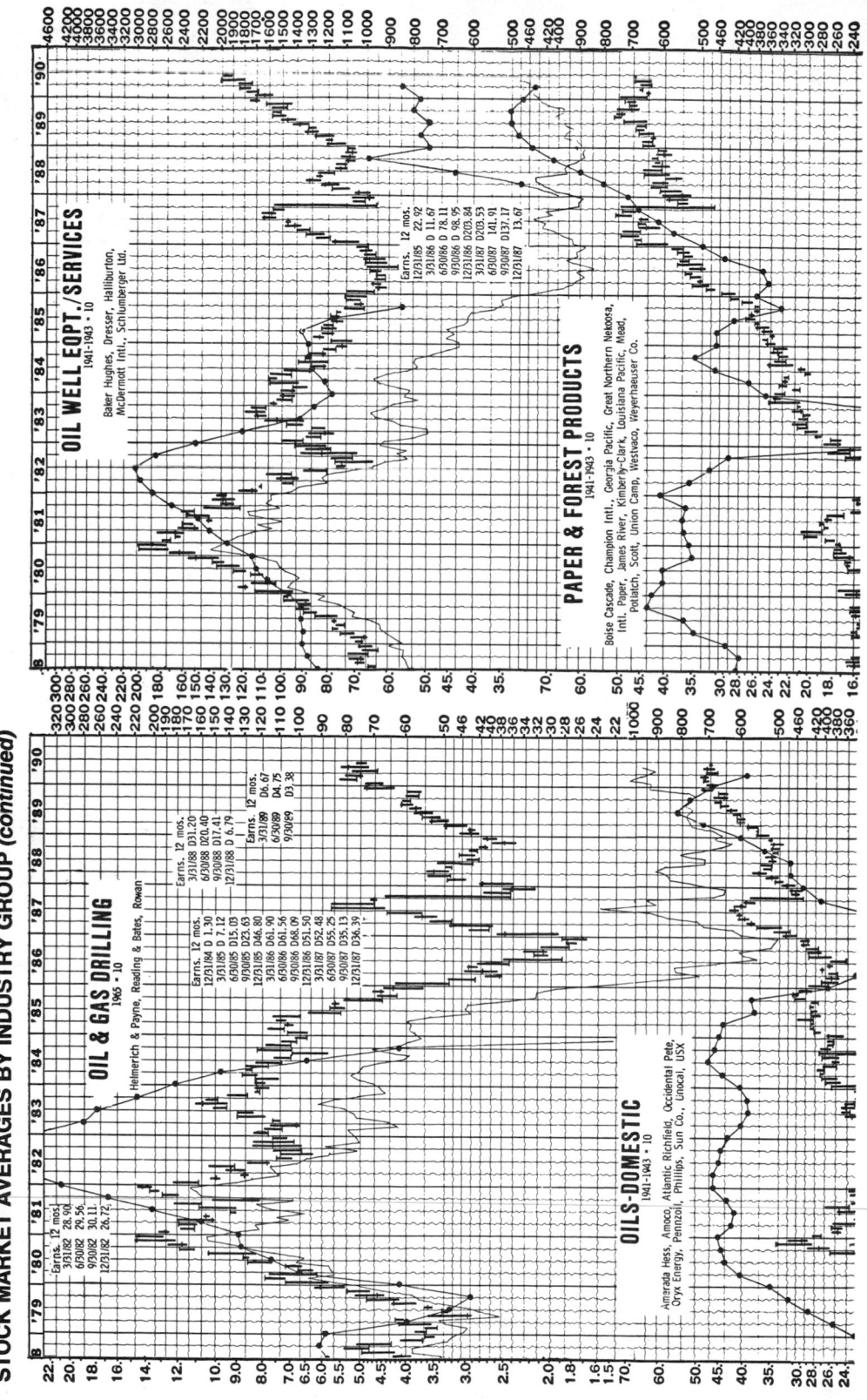

OIL WELL EQPT./SERVICES
1941-1943 = 10

Baker Hughes, Dresser, Halliburton, McDermott Intl., Schlumberger Ltd.

Earns. 12 mos.
12/31/85	22.92
3/31/86	D 11.67
6/30/86	D 78.11
9/30/86	D 98.95
12/31/86	D203.84
3/31/87	D203.53
6/30/87	141.91
9/30/87	D137.17
12/31/87	13.67

PAPER & FOREST PRODUCTS
1941-1943 = 10

Boise Cascade, Champion Intl., Georgia Pacific, Great Northern Nekoosa, Intl. Paper, James River, Kimberly-Clark, Louisiana Pacific, Mead, Potlatch, Scott, Union Camp, Westvaco, Weyerhaeuser Co.

OIL & GAS DRILLING
1965 = 10

Helmerich & Payne, Reading & Bates, Rowan

Earns. 12 mos.
3/31/80	28.90
6/30/82	29.56
9/30/82	30.11
12/31/82	26.72

Earns. 12 mos.
12/31/85	D 7.30
3/31/85	D 7.12
6/30/85	D15.03
9/30/85	D23.63
12/31/85	D46.80
3/31/86	D61.90
6/30/86	D61.56
9/30/86	D68.09
12/31/86	D51.50
3/31/87	D55.25
6/30/87	D35.13
12/31/87	D36.39

Earns. 12 mos.
3/31/88	D31.20
6/30/88	D20.40
9/30/88	D17.41
12/31/88	D 6.79

Earns. 12 mos.
3/31/89	D6.67
6/30/89	D4.75
9/30/89	D3.38

OILS-DOMESTIC
1941-1943 = 10

Amerada Hess, Amoco, Atlantic Richfield, Occidental Pete, Oryx Energy, Pennzoil, Phillips, Sun Co., Unocal, USX

314

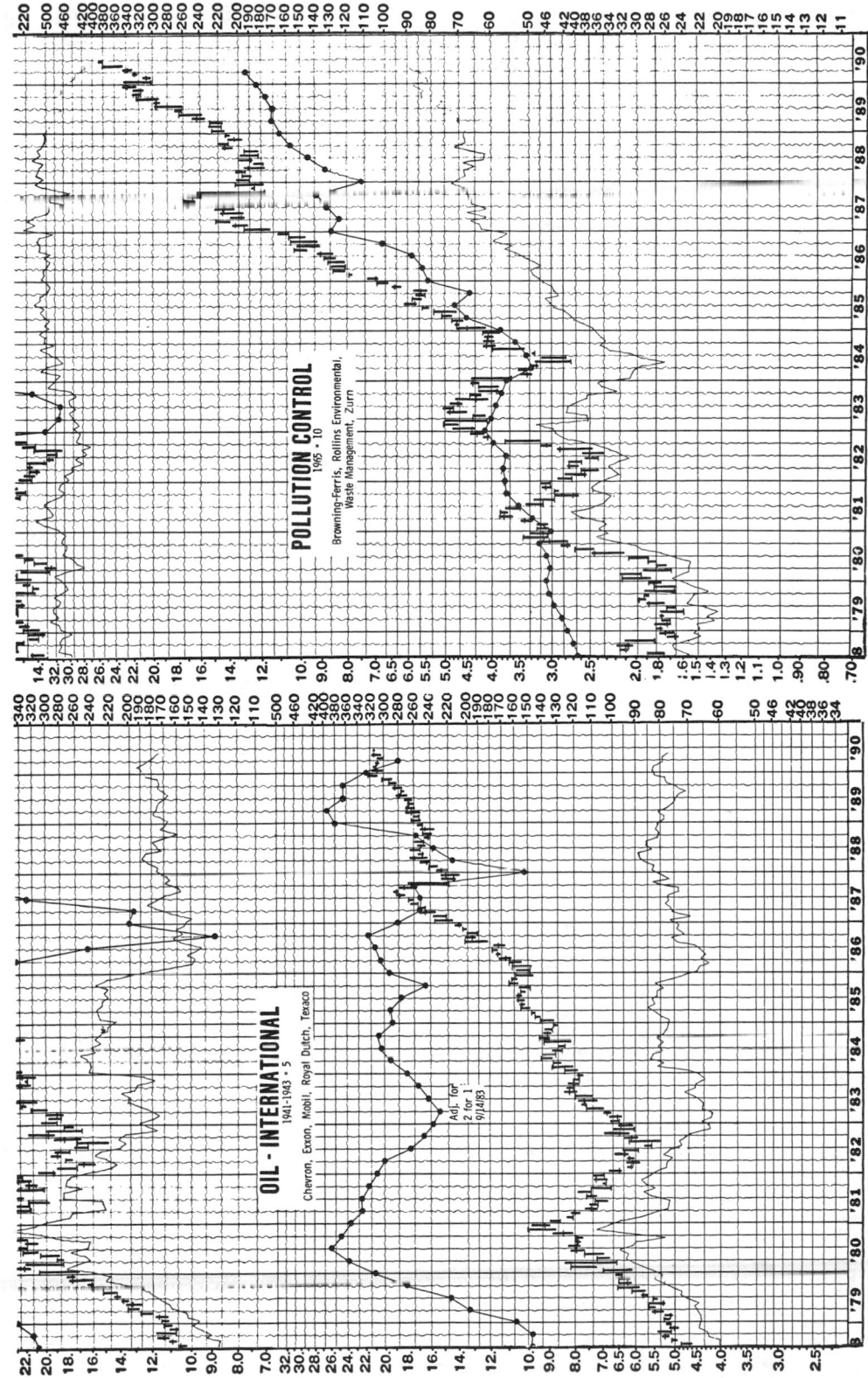

POLLUTION CONTROL
1995 • 10
Browning-Ferris, Rollins Environmental,
Waste Management, Zurn

OIL - INTERNATIONAL
1941-1943 • 5
Chevron, Exxon, Mobil, Royal Dutch, Texaco

Adj. for
2 for 1
9/14/83

STOCK MARKET AVERAGES BY INDUSTRY GROUP (continued)

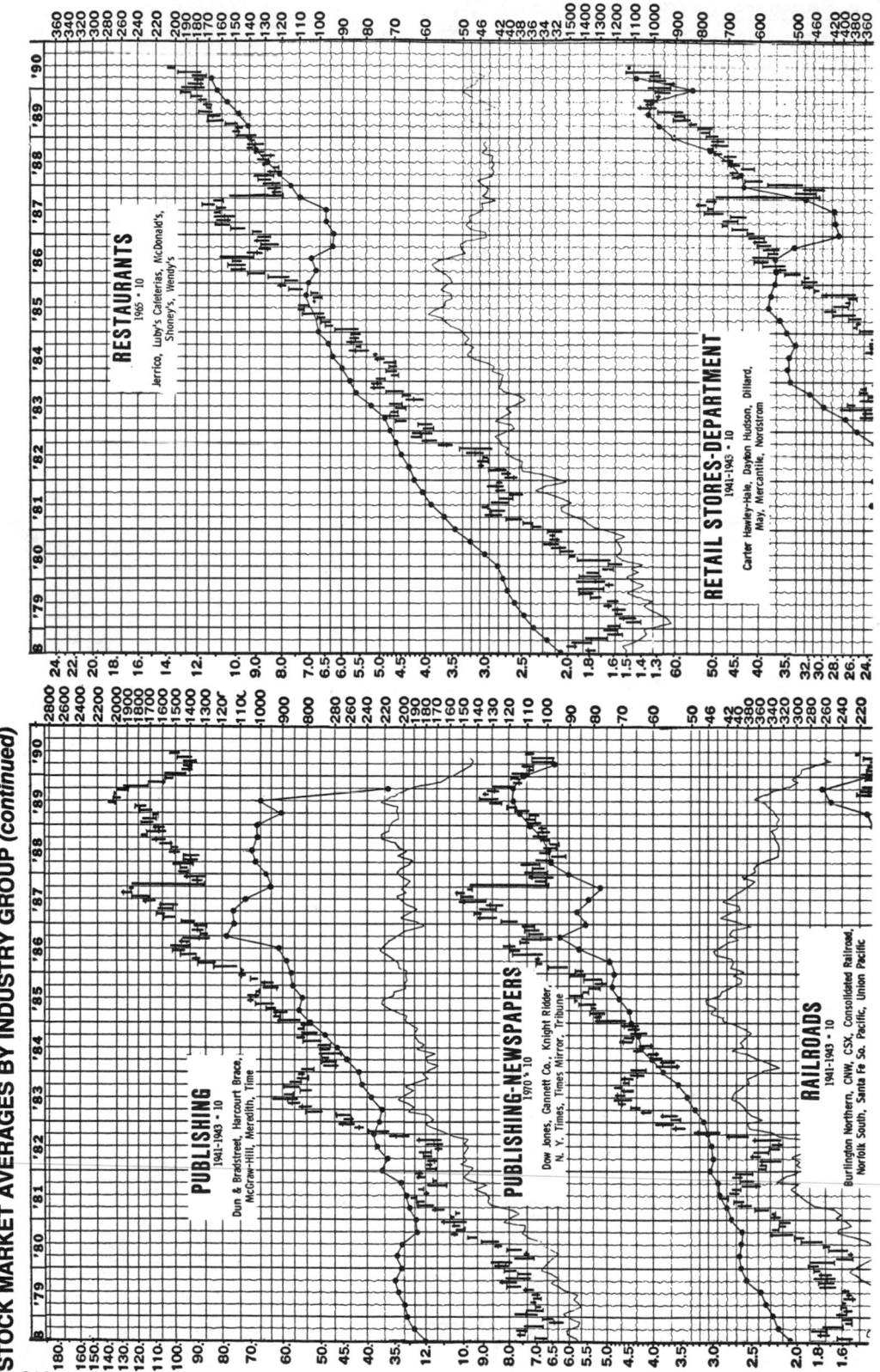

RESTAURANTS
1965 = 10

Jerrico, Luby's Cafeterias, McDonald's,
Shoney's, Wendy's

RETAIL STORES-DEPARTMENT
1941-1943 = 10

Carter Hawley-Hale, Dayton Hudson, Dillard,
May, Mercantile, Nordstrom

PUBLISHING
1941-1943 = 10

Dun & Bradstreet, Harcourt Brace,
McGraw-Hill, Meredith, Time

PUBLISHING-NEWSPAPERS
1970 = 10

Dow Jones, Gannett Co., Knight Ridder,
N. Y. Times, Times Mirror, Tribune

RAILROADS
1941-1943 = 10

Burlington Northern, CNW, CSX, Consolidated Railroad,
Norfolk South, Santa Fe So. Pacific, Union Pacific

316

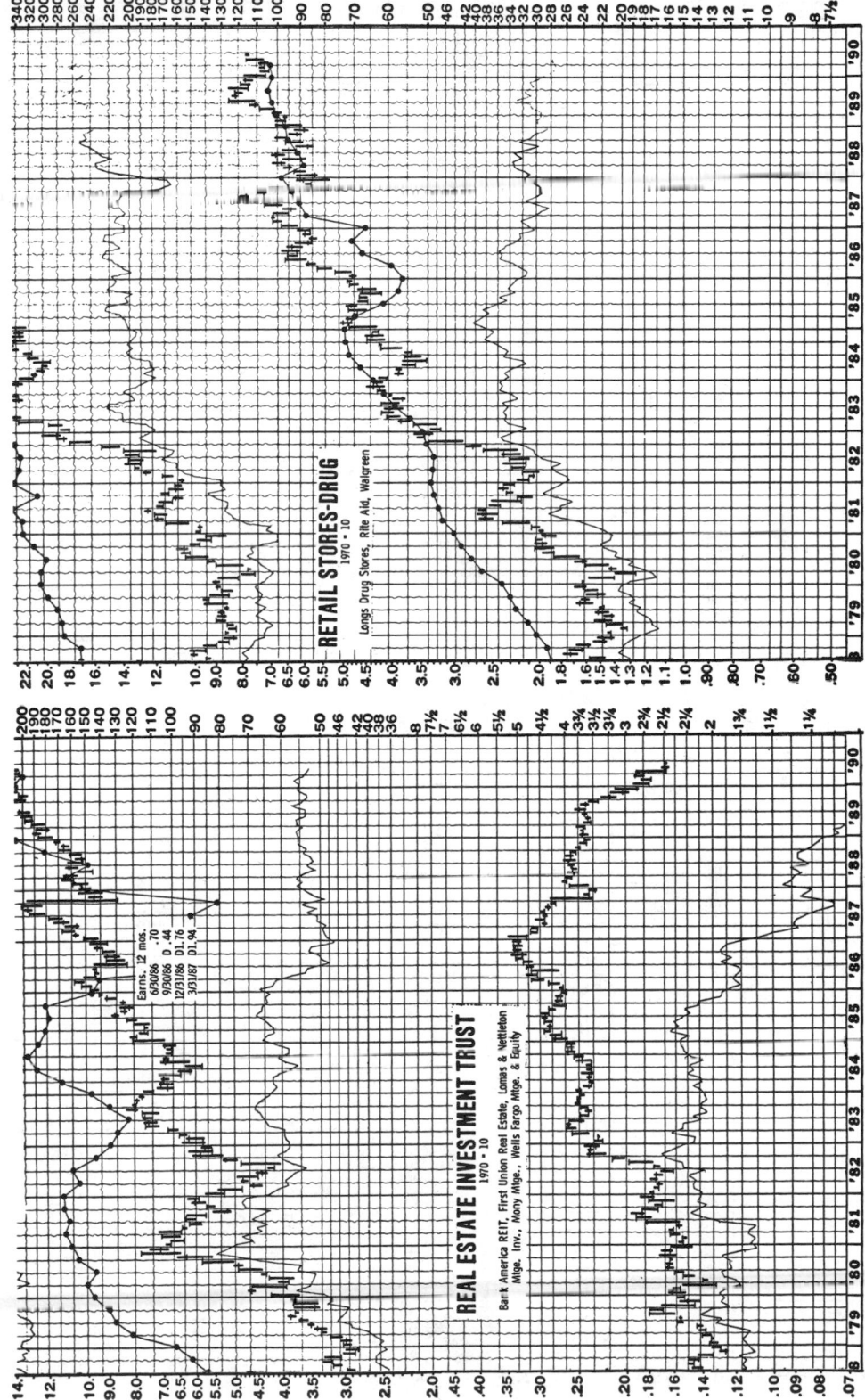

RETAIL STORES-DRUG
1970 - 10

Longs Drug Stores, Rite Aid, Walgreen

REAL ESTATE INVESTMENT TRUST
1970 - 10

Bank America REIT, First Union Real Estate, Lomas & Nettleton
Mtge. Inv., Mony Mtge., Wells Fargo Mtge. & Equity

Earns. 12 mos.
6/30/86   .70
9/30/86   D .44
12/31/86   D1.76
3/31/87   D1.94

317

STOCK MARKET AVERAGES BY INDUSTRY GROUP (continued)

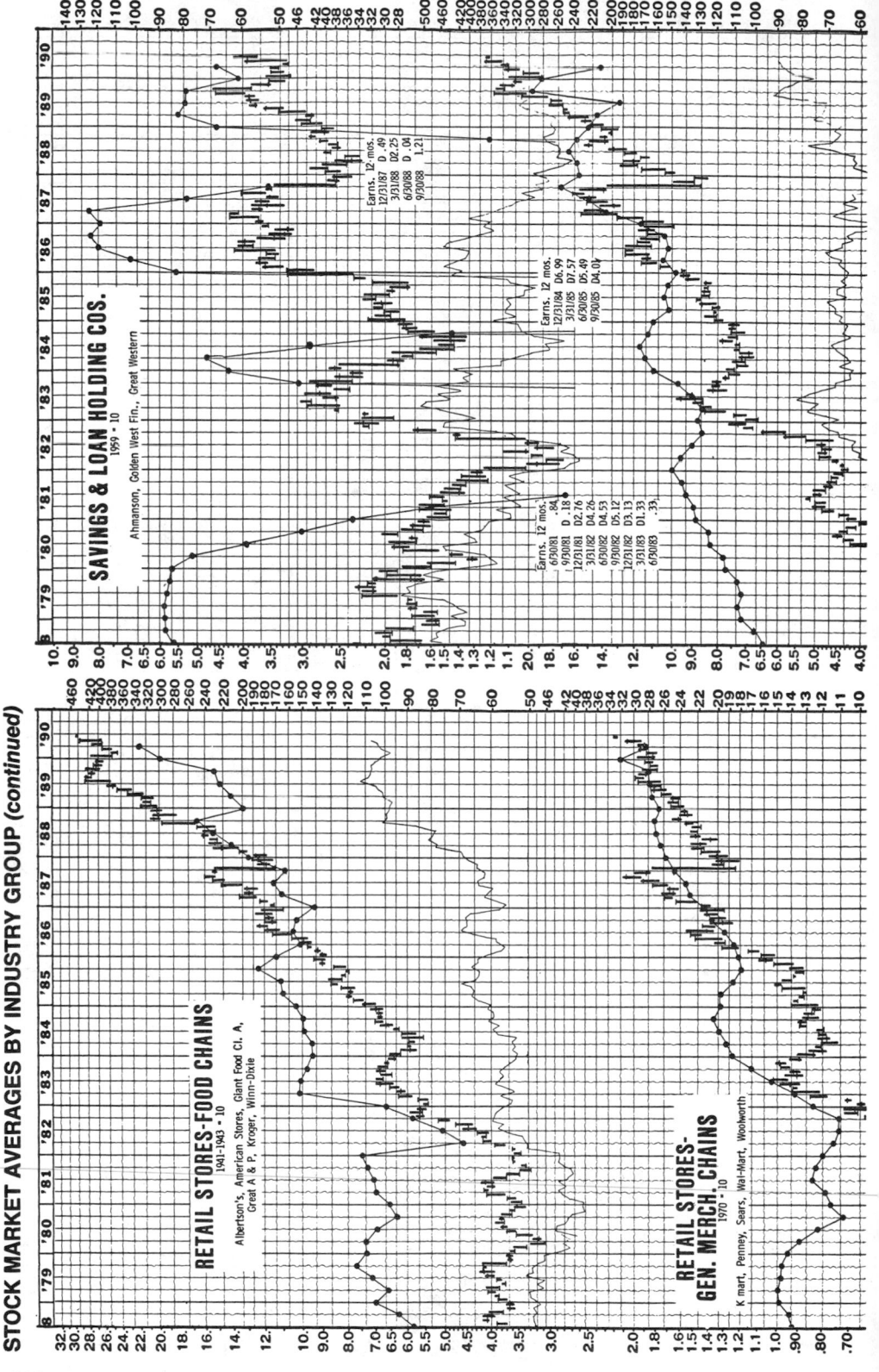

SAVINGS & LOAN HOLDING COS.
1959 · 10

Ahmanson, Golden West Fin., Great Western

Earns. 12 mos.
12/31/87 D .49
3/31/88 D2.25
6/30/88 D .04
9/30/88 1.21

Earns. 12 mos.
12/31/84 D6.99
3/31/85 D7.57
6/30/85 D5.49
9/30/85 D4.0V

Earns. 12 mos.
6/30/81   .84
9/30/81 D .18
12/31/81 D2.76
3/31/82 D4.26
6/30/82 D4.53
9/30/82 D5.12
12/31/82 D3.13
3/31/83 D1.33
6/30/83   .33.

RETAIL STORES-FOOD CHAINS
1941-1943 · 10

Albertson's, American Stores, Giant Food Cl. A,
Great A & P, Kroger, Winn-Dixie

RETAIL STORES-
GEN. MERCH. CHAINS
1970 · 10

K mart, Penney, Sears, Wal-Mart, Woolworth

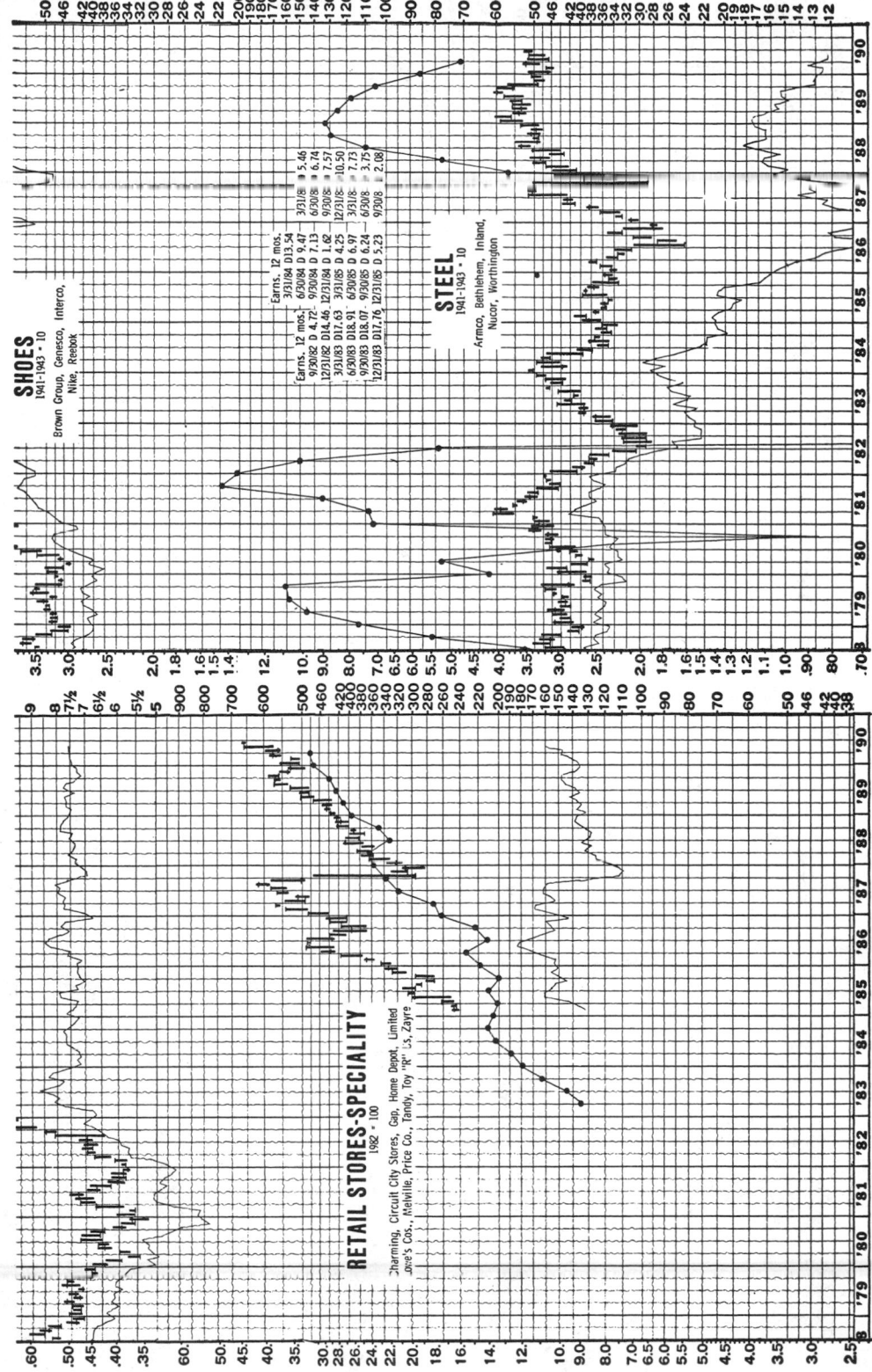

SHOES
1941-1943 · 10

Brown Group, Genesco, Interco,
Nike, Reebok

Earns. 12 mos.	
3/31/84 D13.54	
6/30/84 D 9.47	3/31/8 ▪ 5.46
9/30/84 D 7.13	6/30/8 ▪ 6.74
12/31/84 D 1.62	9/30/8 ▪ 7.57
3/31/85 D 4.25	12/31/8 ▪ 10.50
6/30/85 D 6.97	3/31/8 ▪ 7.73
9/30/85 D 6.24	6/30/8 ▪ 3.75
12/31/85 D 5.23	9/30/8 ▪ 2.08

Earns. 12 mos.	
9/30/82 D 4.72	
12/31/82 D14.46	
3/31/83 D17.63	
6/30/83 D18.91	
9/30/83 D18.07	
12/31/83 D17.76	

STEEL
1941-1943 · 10

Armco, Bethlehem, Inland,
Nucor, Worthington

RETAIL STORES-SPECIALITY
1982 · 100

Charming, Circuit City Stores, Gap, Home Depot, Limited
Love's Cos., Melville, Price Co., Tandy, Toy "R" Us, Zayre

319

STOCK MARKET AVERAGES BY INDUSTRY GROUP *(concluded)*

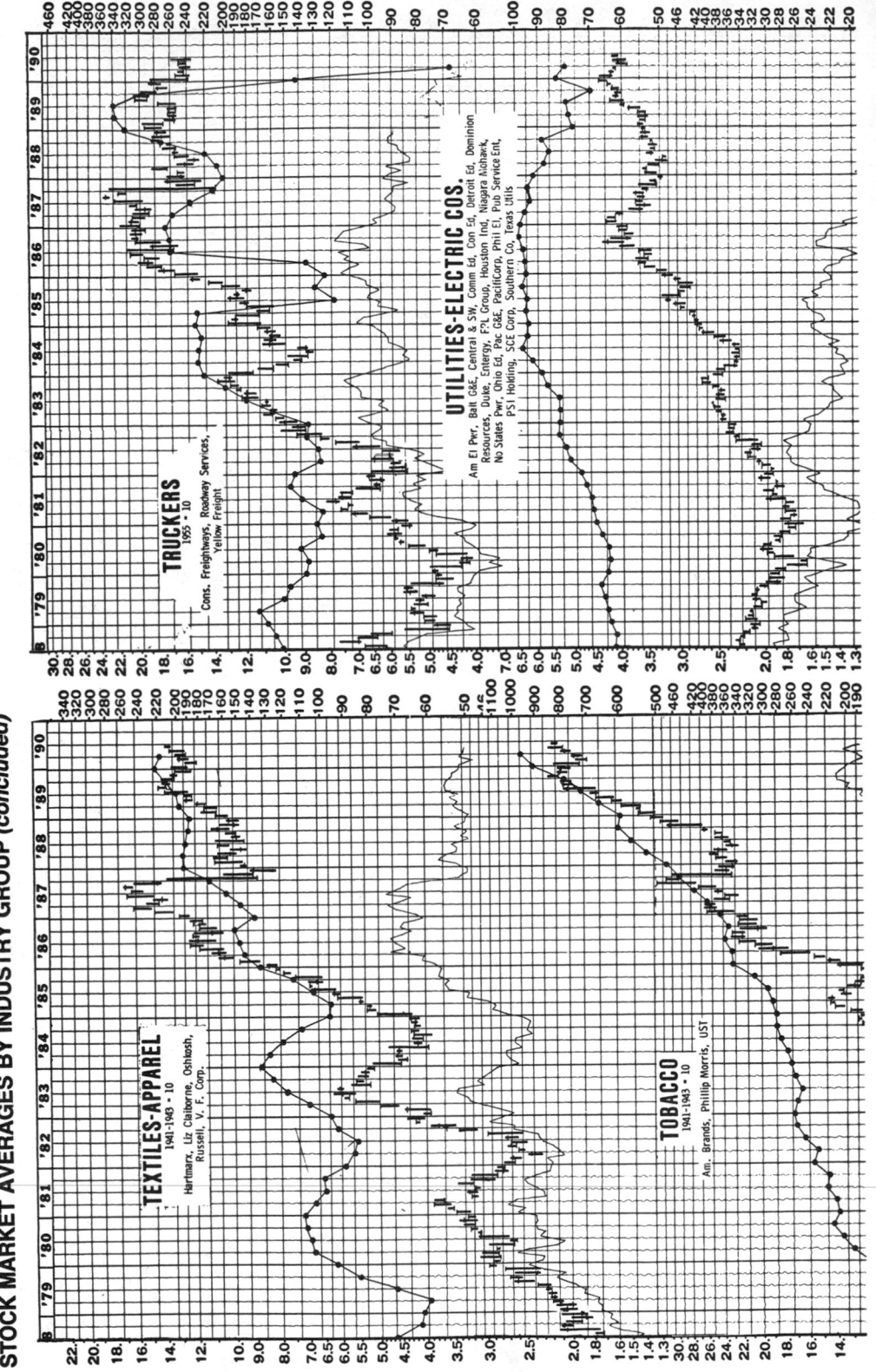

TEXTILES-APPAREL
1941-1943 • 10

Hartmarx, Liz Claiborne, Oshkosh, Russell, V. F. Corp.

TRUCKERS
1955 • 10

Cons. Freightways, Roadway Services, Yellow Freight

TOBACCO
1941-1943 • 10

Am. Brands, Phillip Morris, UST

UTILITIES-ELECTRIC COS.

Am El Pwr, Balt G&E, Central & SW, Comm Ed, Con Ed, Detroit Ed, Dominion Resources, Duke, Entergy, FPL Group, Houston Ind, Niagara Mohawk, No States Pwr, Ohio Ed, Pac G&E, PacifiCorp, Phil El, Pub Service Ent, PSI Holding, SCE Corp, Southern Co, Texas Utils

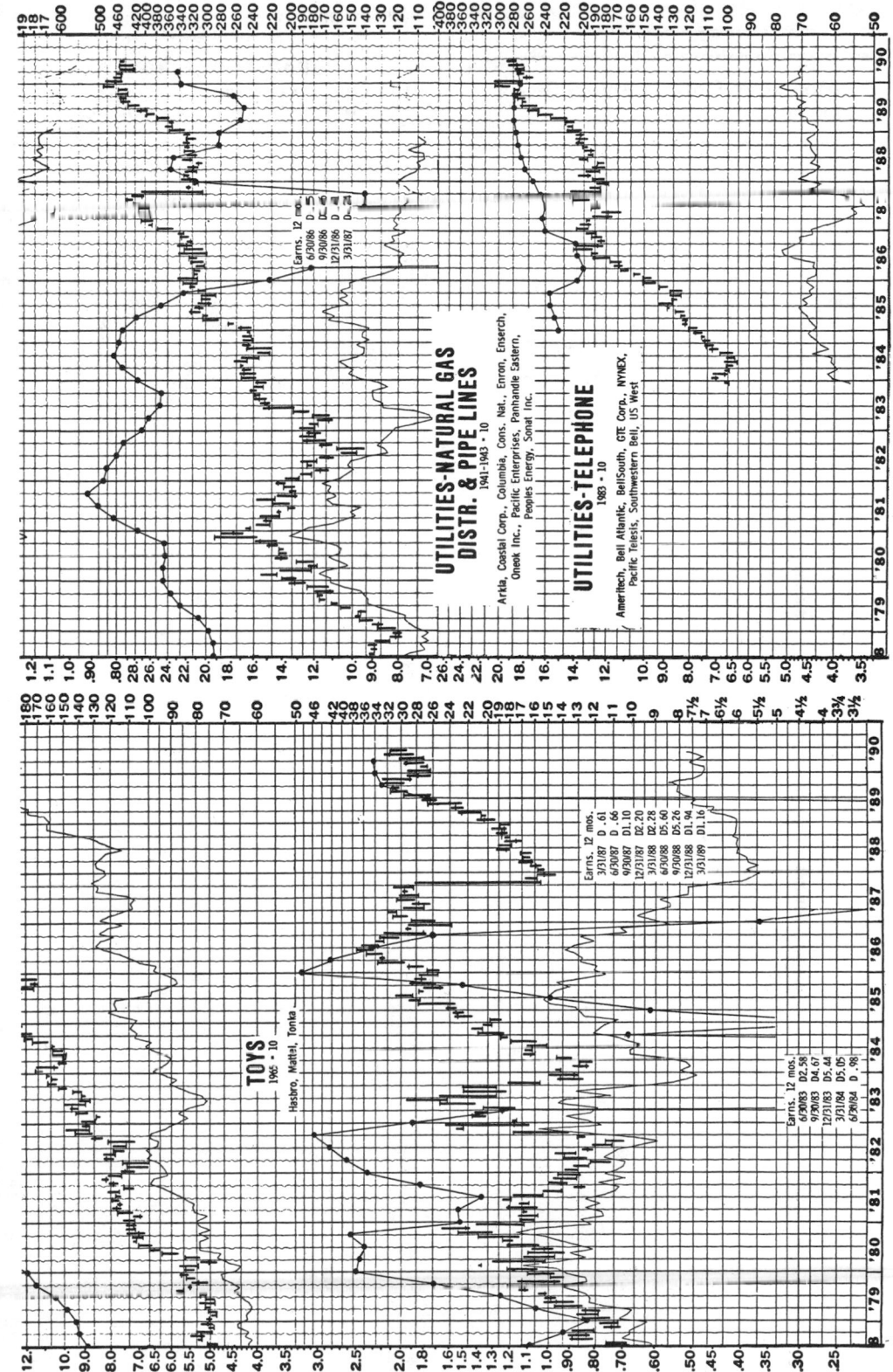

**UTILITIES-NATURAL GAS
DISTR. & PIPE LINES**
1941-1943 · 10

Arkla, Coastal Corp., Columbia, Cons. Nat., Enron, Enserch,
Oneok Inc., Pacific Enterprises, Panhandle Eastern,
Peoples Energy, Sonat Inc.

Earns. 12 mos.
6/30/86   D .5
9/30/86   DL .6
12/31/86   D 6
3/31/87   D 2

UTILITIES-TELEPHONE
1983 · 10

Ameritech, Bell Atlantic, BellSouth, GTE Corp., NYNEX,
Pacific Telesis, Southwestern Bell, US West

TOYS
1965 · 10

Hasbro, Mattel, Tonka

Earns. 12 mos.
3/31/87   D .61
6/30/87   D .66
9/30/87   DL.10
12/31/87   D2.28
3/31/88   D2.20
6/30/88   D5.60
9/30/88   D5.26
12/31/88   D1.94
3/31/89   D1.16

Earns. 12 mos.
6/30/83   D2.58
9/30/83   D4.67
12/31/83   D5.44
3/31/84   D5.05
6/30/84   D .98

Components-Dow Jones 65 Stock Averages

INDUSTRIALS

Allied Sig.	Exxon	Philip Morris
Alum Co	Gen Electric	Primerica
Amer Exp	Gen Motors	Proc Gamb
AT&T	Goodyear	Sears
Beth Steel	IBM	Texaco
Boeing	Int'l Paper	Union Carbide
Chevron	McDonald's	USX Corp.
Coca-Cola	Merck	United Tech
Du Pont	Minn M&M	Westinghouse
Eastman	Navistar	Woolworth

TRANSPORTATION

AMR Corp.	Cons Rail	Santa Fe
Airbrn Freigt	CSX Corp.	Southwest Airl
Alaska Air	Delta Air	UAL Corp.
Amer Pres	Fed Express	Union Pac
Burlington	Norfolk So	USAir
Caro Freight	Pan Am	Xtra Corp.
Cons Freight	Ryder System	

UTILITIES

Am El Power	Cons N Gas	Panhandle
Centerior	Detroit Edis	Peoples En
Colum-Gas	Houston Ind	Phila Elec
Comwlth Edis	Niag Mohawk	Pub Serv E
Cons Edison	Pacific G&E	SCEcorp

FINANCIAL DATA ON DOW JONES INDUSTRIALS

	This Week				History				Earnings			P/E Ratio			Dvds	
	Vol-ume	Close	Price Change	Market Value	Pct. of Total	52-Week		5-Year		Last 12Mos	% Ch	5-Yr. Growth	Today	5-Year Avg		Indic. Amt	Yield
						High	Low	High	Low					High	Low		
	00	$	$	$Mil	%	$	$	$	$	$	%	%				$	%
Dow Jones Ind. ...	1299,229	2961.14	-19.06	630,397.2	100.00	2999.75	2543.24	2999.75	1184.96	189.08	-17.68	18	15.7	17.4	12.6	89.89	3.0
Allied-Signal	10,016	34.13	-1.25	4,914.0	.78	40.38	31.88	49.25	26.00	3.60	12.50	NC	9.5	NC	NC	1.80	5.3
Alum Co Of Am ..	18,880	66.25	-2.50	5,758.8	.91	79.63	59.75	79.63	29.75	7.89	-30.55	NC	8.4	NC	NC	1.60	2.4
Am Express	60,241	30.50	-.12	12,714.3	2.02	39.38	25.50	40.63	17.94	.98	-59.67	5	31.1	18.1	11.4	.92	3.0
Am Tele & Telegr	110,447	37.63	.50	40,975.1	6.50	50.00	36.25	47.38	19.00	2.52	NE	NC	14.9	NC	NC	1.32	3.5
Bethlehem Stl	12,110	15.88	-1.50	1,194.9	.19	23.25	15.13	28.50	4.63	2.35	-50.11	NC	6.8	NC	NC	.40	2.5
Boeing Co	47,895	58.00	-3.12	20,048.3	3.18	61.88	33.09	61.88	12.81	1.96	9.50	-3	29.6	17.0	10.4	1.00	1.7
Chevron Cp	33,272	77.50	3.50	27,476.7	4.36	78.00	53.75	78.00	29.25	1.15	-72.42	-22	67.4	33.0	20.7	2.80	3.6
Coca Cola Co	65,783	47.38	2.50	31,579.7	5.01	48.38	30.63	48.38	9.91	2.64	67.09	23	17.9	17.7	10.9	.80	1.7
Dupont	45,100	40.50	1.00	27,819.4	4.41	42.25	34.88	43.63	15.84	3.40	4.94	16	11.9	13.9	9.2	1.60	4.0
Eastman Kodak ...	65,573	39.75	-.50	12,901.9	2.05	52.00	36.13	70.69	27.38	1.62	-60.77	9	24.5	28.7	20.3	2.00	5.0
Exxon Cp	70,025	48.63	-.12	60,781.3	9.64	51.63	43.13	51.63	22.06	2.34	-39.69	-5	20.8	13.5	9.9	2.40	4.9
Gen Electric	69,010	74.00	-.87	66,388.5	10.53	75.50	52.75	75.50	27.81	4.62	14.36	13	16.0	17.4	12.0	1.88	2.5
Gen Motors	48,128	49.63	.50	30,057.1	4.77	50.50	40.38	50.50	25.00	4.98	-34.73	0	10.0	8.3	5.8	3.00	6.0
Goodyear Tire	12,071	29.00	.00	1,676.4	.27	59.75	27.50	76.50	25.13	1.93	-68.26	5	15.0	17.3	10.9	1.80	6.2
Intl Bus Mach	87,954	117.63	-3.37	67,493.2	10.71	123.13	93.38	175.88	93.38	6.81	-31.83	-8	17.3	18.0	12.7	4.84	4.1
Intl Paper	23,154	55.50	1.50	6,049.5	.96	58.75	47.00	58.75	22.13	7.07	-6.36	51	7.9	14.3	9.5	1.68	3.0
McDonald's Cp	41,593	36.00	-1.00	13,319.8	2.11	38.50	27.88	38.50	11.38	2.00	13.64	15	18.0	18.1	11.5	.34	.9
Merck & Co	44,638	90.00	1.13	35,334.0	5.61	91.13	67.00	91.13	15.03	4.15	21.35	29	21.7	23.8	15.0	1.80	2.0
Minn Mng Mfg	24,203	89.75	-.50	19,984.1	3.17	90.75	67.75	90.75	36.81	5.68	7.17	15	15.8	16.4	11.6	2.92	3.3
Navistar Intl	26,388	3.88	-.37	975.6	.15	5.50	3.25	11.63	3.00	-.10	-100.00	NC	NE	NC	NC	.00	.0
Philip Morris	112,856	50.13	.25	46,542.6	7.38	51.50	36.00	51.50	9.00	3.60	30.91	26	13.9	12.4	7.8	1.38	2.8
Primerica	28,061	33.38	-3.37	3,692.7	.59	37.75	24.75	NC	NC	3.25	-4.97	NC	10.3	NC	NC	.32	1.0
Proct & Gambl ...◊♦	27,401	88.50	-1.62	30,642.2	4.86	91.25	57.88	91.25	24.00	4.20	20.69	16	21.1	25.6	15.5	1.80	2.0
Sears, Roebuck .. □	44,431	34.50	.25	11,812.9	1.87	47.25	33.13	59.50	26.00	3.88	45.32	-1	8.9	14.0	9.3	2.00	5.8
Texaco .... ◊	37,475	60.63	.38	15,985.0	2.54	62.38	49.63	62.38	23.50	4.36	-57.50	NC	13.9	NC	NC	3.00	4.9
Union Carbide	20,686	19.00	-1.50	2,690.0	.43	31.50	18.63	33.25	12.00	3.29	-40.93	NC	5.8	NC	NC	1.00	5.3
Utd Technol	23,625	60.50	1.63	7,326.1	1.16	62.50	48.38	62.50	30.00	5.58	10.28	30	10.8	52.5	36.5	1.80	3.0
USX Cp .... ◊	36,121	34.25	.25	8,754.1	1.39	39.50	31.50	39.50	14.50	3.32	-3.77	NC	10.3	NC	NC	1.40	4.1
Westinghouse	33,415	38.25	.50	11,071.2	1.76	42.31	30.75	39.38	12.69	3.30	10.37	15	11.6	12.8	8.2	1.25	3.3
Woolworth Cp	18,677	34.38	-2.00	4,437.8	.69	36.63	27.06	36.63	9.16	2.57	14.22	17	13.4	13.9	8.0	1.04	3.0
Unweighted Avg. . ♦	43,308	49.83	-.33	21,013.2	3.33	55.43	39.49	60.16	21.90	3.50	-13.08	11	16.7	19.3	12.7	1.66	3.4

Source: Media General Financial Services, Inc., Richmond, Virginia, July 20, 1990

DOW JONES INDUSTRIAL, TRANSPORTATION AND UTILITY AVERAGES

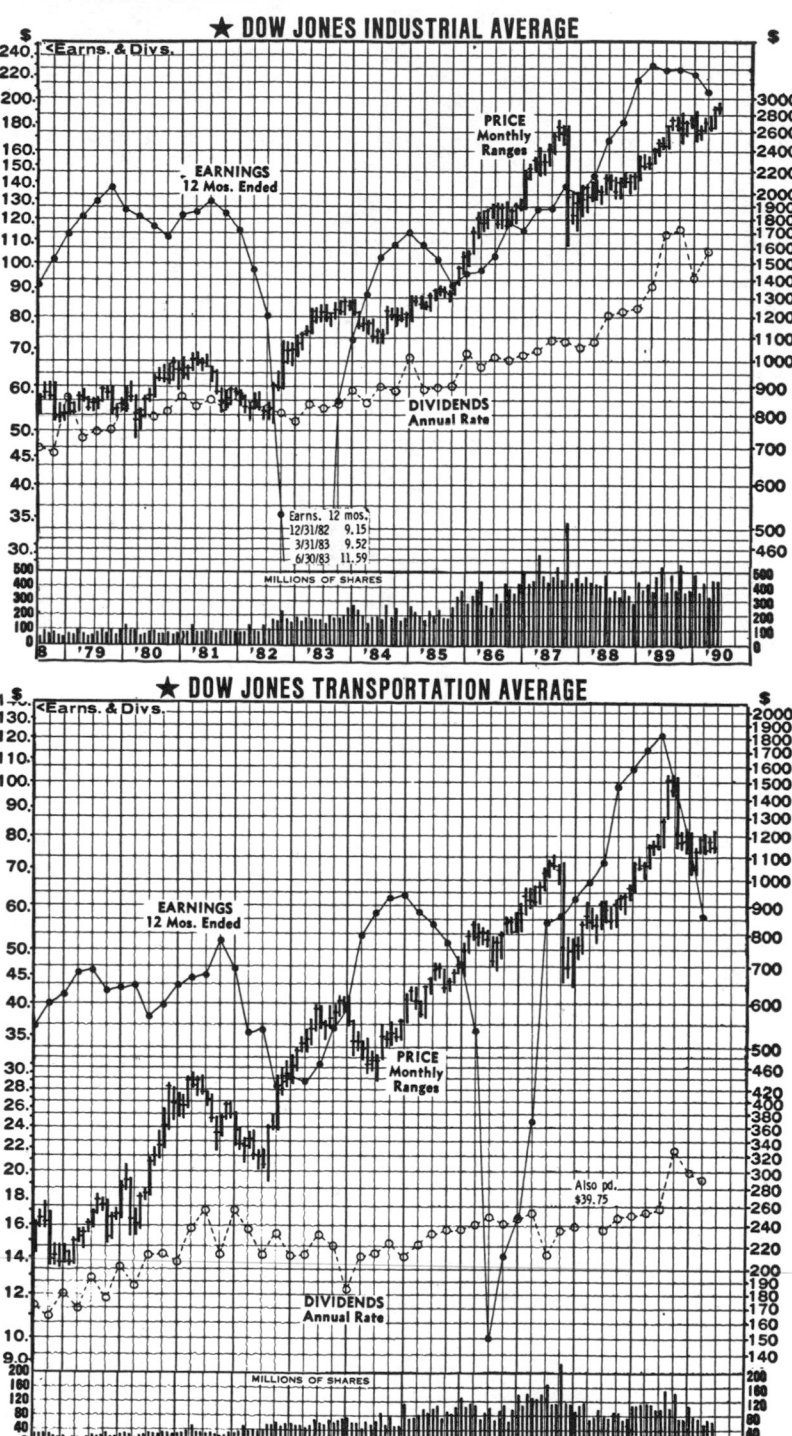

★ DOW JONES INDUSTRIAL AVERAGE

★ DOW JONES TRANSPORTATION AVERAGE

DOW JONES INDUSTRIAL, TRANSPORTATION
AND UTILITY AVERAGES *(concluded)*

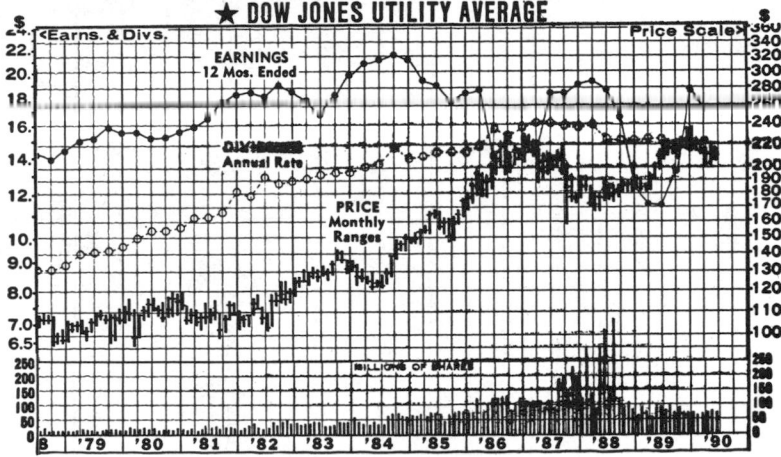

Source: *5-Trend CYCLI-GRAPHS*. The charts are courtesy of Securities Research Company, a Division of Babson-United Investment Advisors, Inc., Babson-United Building, 101 Prescott St., Wellesley Hills, MA 02181, July quarterly edition, 1990.

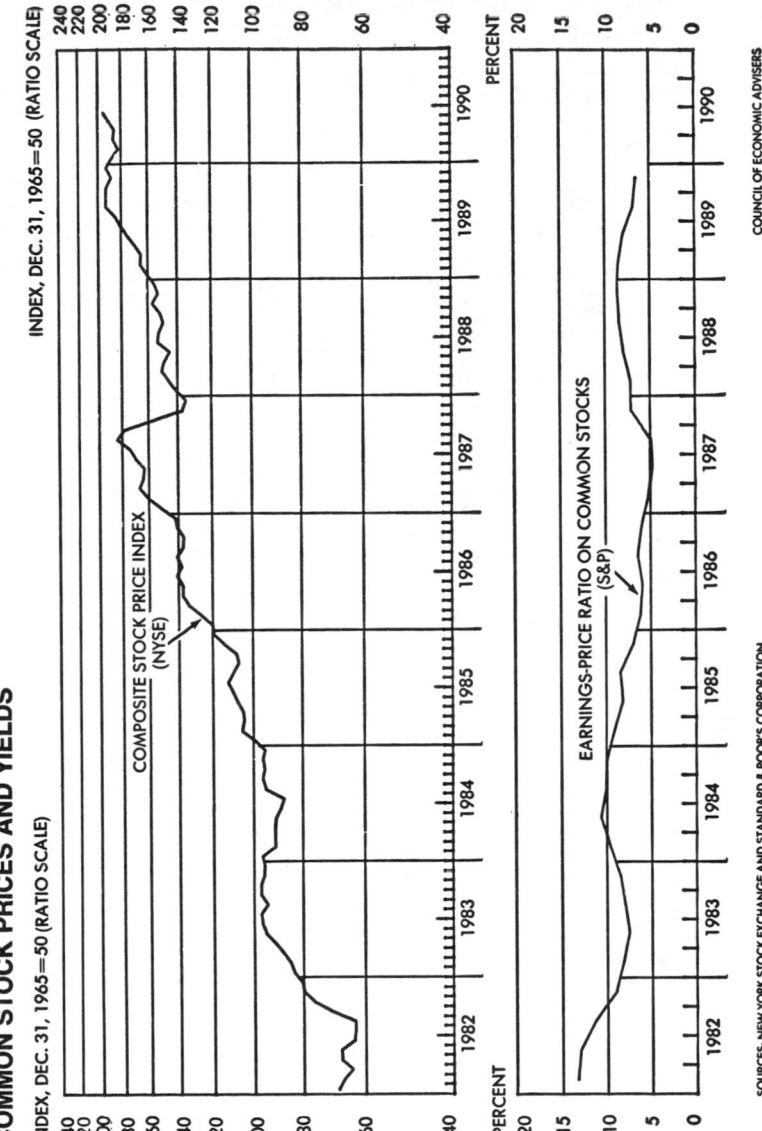

COMMON STOCK PRICES AND YIELDS

INDEX, DEC. 31, 1965=50 (RATIO SCALE)

INDEX, DEC. 31, 1965=50 (RATIO SCALE)

COMPOSITE STOCK PRICE INDEX (NYSE)

PERCENT

EARNINGS-PRICE RATIO ON COMMON STOCKS (S&P)

PERCENT

SOURCES: NEW YORK STOCK EXCHANGE AND STANDARD & POOR'S CORPORATION

COUNCIL OF ECONOMIC ADVISERS

Period	Common stock prices [1] New York Stock Exchange indexes (Dec. 31, 1965=50) [2]					Dow-Jones industrial average [3]	Standard & Poor's composite index (1941-43=10) [4]	Common stock yields (percent) [5]	
	Composite	Industrial	Transportation	Utility	Finance			Dividend-price ratio	Earnings-price ratio
1981	74.02	85.44	72.61	38.91	73.52	932.92	128.05	5.20	11.96
1982	68.93	78.18	60.41	39.75	71.99	884.36	119.71	5.81	11.60
1983	92.63	107.45	89.36	47.00	95.34	1,190.34	160.41	4.40	8.03
1984	92.46	108.01	85.63	46.44	89.28	1,178.48	160.46	4.64	10.02
1985	108.09	123.79	104.11	56.75	114.21	1,328.23	186.84	4.25	8.12
1986	136.00	155.85	119.87	71.36	147.20	1,792.76	236.34	3.49	6.09
1987	161.70	195.31	140.39	74.30	146.48	2,275.99	286.83	3.08	5.48
1988	149.91	180.95	134.12	71.77	127.26	2,060.82	265.79	3.64	8.01
1989	180.02	216.23	175.28	87.43	151.88	2,508.91	322.84	3.45	7.42
1989: June	180.76	216.75	173.47	87.90	154.08	2,494.90	323.73	3.44	7.93
July	185.15	221.74	179.32	90.40	157.78	2,554.03	331.93	3.38	
Aug.	192.94	231.32	197.52	92.91	164.86	2,691.11	346.61	3.28	
Sept.	193.02	230.86	202.02	93.44	165.51	2,693.41	347.33	3.29	6.79
Oct.	192.49	229.40	190.36	94.67	166.55	2,692.01	347.40	3.29	
Nov.	188.50	224.38	174.26	94.95	160.89	2,642.49	340.22	3.39	
Dec.	192.67	230.12	177.25	99.73	155.63	2,728.47	348.57	3.33	6.48
1990: Jan.	187.96	225.79	173.67	95.69	150.11	2,679.24	339.97	3.41	
Feb.	182.55	220.60	166.69	92.15	142.68	2,614.18	330.45	3.54	
Mar.	186.26	226.14	175.08	93.00	143.14	2,700.13	338.47	3.49	
Apr.	185.61	226.86	173.54	91.92	138.57	2,708.26	338.18	3.51	
May r	191.35	234.85	173.53	93.29	142.94	2,793.81	350.25	3.44	
June p	196.68	242.42	177.37	93.65	147.93	2,894.82	360.39	3.36	
Week ended:									
1990: June 2	197.07	242.63	176.00	94.56	148.01	2,881.67	361.48	3.35	
9	198.71	243.71	181.17	95.36	152.26	2,906.31	364.17	3.31	
16	198.38	244.18	180.47	94.70	149.81	2,923.96	363.72	3.32	
23	195.42	241.40	175.92	92.80	145.55	2,885.99	358.07	3.37	
30 p	193.92	240.15	171.86	91.50	143.76	2,861.78	355.03	3.42	

[1] Average of daily closing prices.
[2] Includes all the stocks (more than 1,500) listed on the NYSE.
[3] Includes 30 stocks.
[4] Includes 500 stocks.
[5] Standard & Poor's series. Dividend-price ratios based on Wednesday closing prices. Earnings-price ratios based on prices at end of quarter.

NOTE.—All data relate to stocks listed on the New York Stock Exchange (NYSE).

Sources: New York Stock Exchange, Dow-Jones & Company, Inc., and Standard & Poor's Corporation.

Source: *Economic Indicators*, Council of Economic Advisers.

NEW SECURITY ISSUES U.S. Corporations
Millions of dollars

Type of issue or issuer, or use	1987	1988	1989	1989						1990	
				July	Aug.	Sept.	Oct.	Nov.	Dec.	Jan.	Feb.
1 All issues[1]	392,339	409,925	233,103r	18,094	15,100r	14,704r	24,893r	20,706r	21,584r	15,008r	13,919
2 Bonds[2]	325,838	352,124	201,827r	13,040	13,065r	12,431r	21,213r	16,466r	17,639r	12,730r	11,000
Type of offering											
3 Public, domestic[3]	209,455	201,246	179,069r	11,620	12,249r	11,211r	20,085r	14,383	16,013r	10,678r	10,000
4 Private placement, domestic[3]	92,070	127,700	n.a.	n.a.	n.a.	n.a.	n.a.	n.a.	n.a.	n.a.	n.a.
5 Sold abroad	24,308	23,178	22,758r	1,420	816	1,220r	1,128r	2,083r	1,626r	2,052r	1,000
Industry group											
6 Manufacturing	61,266	70,595	42,366	2,850	2,670	2,247	3,646	3,551	4,193	2,001r	2,355
7 Commercial and miscellaneous	49,773	62,070	15,968	1,354	1,090	1,393	1,830	1,253	347	655r	131
8 Transportation	11,974	10,076	3,586	0	423	30	906	312	1,083	35	0
9 Public utility	23,004	19,318	13,682	1,346	705	1,059	1,748	1,022	1,098	1,018r	1,057
10 Communication	7,340	5,951	3,859	300	358	308	632	812	577	23r	35
11 Real estate and financial	172,474	184,114	122,370r	7,190	7,819r	7,395r	12,452r	9,516r	10,342r	8,999r	7,422
12 Stocks[2]	66,508	57,802	32,225	5,054	2,035	2,273	3,680	4,240	3,945	2,278	2,919
Type											
13 Preferred	10,123	6,544	6,194	920	1,013	519	570	160	626	50	167
14 Common	43,225	35,911	26,030	4,134	1,023	1,754	3,110	4,080	3,319	2,228	2,752
15 Private placement[3]	13,157	15,346	n.a.	n.a.	n.a.	n.a.	n.a.	n.a.	n.a.	n.a.	n.a.
Industry group											
16 Manufacturing	13,880	7,608	5,081	593	393	193	190	378	279	835	431
17 Commercial and miscellaneous	12,888	8,449	4,428	438	343	155	728	498	1,045	248	1,017
18 Transportation	2,439	1,535	532	0	0	0	50	0	0	0	0
19 Public utility	4,322	1,898	2,297	25	137	709	465	211	244	106	582
20 Communication	1,458	515	471	29	20	0	0	0	0	0	0
21 Real estate and financial	31,521	37,798	19,250	3,969	1,020	1,195	2,214	3,153	2,377	1,090	889

1. Figures which represent gross proceeds of issues maturing in more than one year, are principal amount or number of units multiplied by offering price. Excludes secondary offerings, employee stock plans, investment companies other than closed-end, intracorporate transactions, equities sold abroad, and Yankee bonds. Stock data include ownership securities issued by limited partnerships.

2. Monthly data include only public offerings.

3. Data are not available on a monthly basis. Before 1987, annual totals include underwritten issues only.

SOURCES. IDD Information Services, Inc., the Board of Governors of the Federal Reserve System, and before 1989, the U.S. Securities and Exchange Commission.

Source: *Federal Reserve Bulletin*, Board of Governors of the Federal Reserve System.

How to Understand and Analyze Financial Statements*

Fred B. Renwick†

Analyzing financial statements in corporate annual reports can be easy, fun, and rewarding, if you know what to look for. This short essay explains in a nutshell what to look for and how to analyze financial statements.

Only four statements are important to understand and analyze, namely:

- The *balance sheet*, which states the financial condition of the corporation as of one particular date: the date posted at the top of the statement.
- The *income statement*, which shows the amount of earnings for the year currently ending, and conveys information regarding the efficiency and profitability of the business.
- The *statement of retained earnings*, which gives further information regarding one of the lines on the balance sheet, and also shows the division of net income for the year between dividend payout to stockholders and earnings retained and reinvested in the business.
- The *statement of sources and uses of funds*, which gives further information regarding total current assets and total current liabilities as stated on the balance sheet; and shows the net changes during the year in working capital.

Additionally, corporate annual reports usually contain supplementary information which expands upon items in the four basic statements, and includes: (1) a letter or report of independent accountants and auditors addressed to stockholders and directors of the company certifying and validating the figures in the four statements, (2) notes which report material information regarding line items in each statement, (3) segment information which summarizes selected information by industry and geographic segments, (4) restatement pursuant to Financial Accounting Standards Board (FASB) *Statement of Financial Accounting Standards No. 33* to account for effects of inflation and changing prices on items in the four primary statements, and (5) a long-term (5 or 10-year) summary of selected items from the four primary statements. The following section explains each statement in detail, Section II explains how to

analyze the statements, Section III explains notes and supplementary information.

1. FOUR FINANCIAL STATEMENTS: WHAT TO LOOK FOR

BALANCE SHEETS

Exhibit 1 shows a balance sheet for Universal Manufacturing Corporation (UMC), a hypothetical company which produces and distributes goods and services in the health industry. Universal's single line of business is divided into two industry segments: human and animal health products, and environmental health products and services.

Observe the format of Universal's balance sheet, the *report form*, where total assets, $26 million, are itemized first and total financing (total liabilities and stockholders' equity), $26 million, are itemized below the asset section. Some corporations prefer to use the *account form*, where assets are listed on the left side of the form and liabilities and owners' equity sections are listed to the right of the asset section. UMC is using the *report form*.

The balance sheet shows the ownership of total corporate assets as of the date of the statement. For example, the following calculation implies that if UMC's tangible assets were liquidated as of the date posted at the top of the balance sheet, $17.8 million would be available for distribution among the preferred and common stockholders.

Total assets owned by UMC	$26,000,000
Less: Intangibles	200,000
Total tangible assets owned by UMC	$25,800,000
Amount required to pay total liabilities........................	8,000,000
Amount remaining for the stockholders	$17,800,000

Further, the above example illustrates a critical point: the difference between *current market value* (the amount UMC's assets would really bring if sold) versus the *accounting book value* (the $17.8 million). Relationships exist between market and book values, but accounting statements (except for FASB No. 33) are factual reports of *book*, not *market*, values of corporate assets.

The following paragraphs explain each line entry on balance sheets.

Starting at the top of the balance sheet, after the name of the corporation, title, and date of the statement, total assets are itemized, with current assets (total, $13.6 million) always first.

---

* See also the definition of financial terms, page 429.

† Fred B. Renwick is Professor of Finance at the Graduate School of Business Administration, New York University, New York, N.Y.

EXHIBIT 1

UNIVERSAL MANUFACTURING CORPORATION
Balance Sheet
December 31, 1983

Assets	1983	1982
Current assets		
Cash...	$ 350,000	$ 250,000
Marketable securities at cost		
(market value: 1983, $2,980,000; 1982, $1,900,000)	2,850,000	1,830,000
Accounts receivable		
Less: Allowance for bad debt: 1983, $24,000; 1982, $21,000	4,800,000	4,370,000
Inventories..	5,600,000	4,950,000
Total current assets....................................	$13,600,000	$11,400,000
Fixed assets (property, plant, and equipment)		
Land..	$ 734,000	$ 661,000
Building..	5,762,000	5,258,000
Machinery..	11,435,000	10,011,000
Office equipment...	614,000	561,000
	18,545,000	16,491,000
Less: Accumulated depreciation..	6,435,000	5,671,000
Net fixed assets...	12,110,000	10,820,000
Prepayments and deferred charges.......................................	90,000	61,600
Intangibles (goodwill, patent, trademarks)	200,000	200,000
Total assets.....	$26,000,000	$22,481,600

Liabilities	1983	1982
Curent liabilities		
Accounts payable...	$ 2,910,000	$ 2,300,000
Notes payable...	1,420,000	730,000
Accrued expenses payable..	430,000	350,000
Federal income taxes payable.......................................	1,240,000	1,320,000
Total current liabilities.....................................	$ 6,000,000	$ 4,700,000
Long-term liabilities		
First mortgage bonds, 8% interest, due 2003...	$ 2,000,000	$ 2,000,000
Total liabilities...	$ 8,000,000	$ 6,700,000

Stockholders' Equity

	1983	1982
Capital stock		
Preferred stock, 6% cumulative, $100 par value each;		
authorized, issued, and outstanding 13,600 shares	1,360,000	1,360,000
Common stock, 30 cents par value each; authorized, issued,		
and outstanding 760,000 shares	228,000	228,000
Capital surplus	1,112,000	1,112,000
Accumulated retained earnings	15,300,000	13,081,600
Total stockholders' equity	$18,000,000	$15,781,600
Total liabilities and stockholders' equity	$26,000,000	$22,481,600

Current assets consist of:

1. *Cash,* $350,000, which is what you would expect, namely pocket-book currency and coins in the treasurer's office, plus demand deposits at a commercial bank. Cash is synonymous with liquidity,
2. *Marketable securities,* $2.85 million, which usually are cash equivalents or highly liquid securities such as Treasury Bills of the federal government or negotiable certificates of deposit (CDs), or demand notes issued by large corporations,
3. *Accounts receivable,* $4.8 million, which consist of payments due from customers

who purchased UMC's goods and services on credit and have not paid yet but are scheduled to pay within the next few months. Since a small fraction of customers might never pay (because of death, financial disaster, flood, or other catastrophe), an allowance is made, $24,000, pursuant to good accounting practices for bad debts,

4. *Inventories,* $5.6 million, which consist of (a) finished goods in stock and ready for sale or shipment, (b) work and merchandise in process, and (c) supplies and raw materials inventories; and are priced on the balance sheet at the lower of cost or

market on either a first-in-first-out (Fifo) or last-in-first-out (Lifo) basis. Pricing policy is usually stated in a note.

Total current assets, $13.6 million, are the sum of the four aforecited figures and usually are earmarked for use within the coming 12 months. In other words, *current* means within the next 12 months.

Fixed assets (property, plant and equipment) are the permanent tangible capital owned by the business, and are listed *at cost* (original purchase price) next on the balance sheet; and consists of:

1. *Land*, $734,000, or ground upon which buildings or other assets such as forests, air or water rights, and the like are built,
2. *Building*, $5.762 million, which are structures such as offices, warehouses, and the like where business is conducted,
3. *Machinery*, $11.435 million, which are mechanical apparatuses for increasing productivity and economic efficiency,
4. *Office equipment*, $614,000, which is what you would expect, namely desks, typewriters, copiers, and the like.

Accumulated depreciation, $6.435 million, is the total depreciation (deterioration of property, plant, and equipment due to physical wear and tear) accumulated to date for accounting purposes against UMC's assets. It is important to know about three concepts of depreciation, namely: (1) depreciation calculated for tax purposes which is figured pursuant to the Tax Code to benefit from allowable accelerated rates of depreciation, (2) accounting depreciation, which can be either straight-line or accelerated and is usually explained in a note, (3) economic depreciation, which comes from technological obsolescence and deterioration in ability to continue generating future income at current rates due to changes in demand and markets for the goods and services produced by UMC. The balance sheet states only number two, accounting depreciation.

Net fixed assets, $12,110,000, are the sum of the four above figures, minus accounting depreciation; and are used by the business to generate future (beyond the coming 12 months) income.

Prepayments and deferred charges, $90,000, state total amounts paid in advance for assets not yet obtained (such as paid-up premiums on a fire insurance policy covering the next five years, or rental paid on computers for the next three years); and for benefits to be received in future years for expenditures already made (such as for research and development, moving the business to a new location, or expenses incurred in bringing a new product to market).

Intangibles, $200,000, are assets such as goodwill, trademarks, franchises, patents, copyrights, and the like which have no physical existence; yet are valuable in producing business income.

Total assets, $26 million, are current, plus fixed, plus prepayments and deferred charges, plus intangibles; and state the size of the business and are the total property owned by the business.

Look next at the lower part of the balance sheet, which concerns the financing of the business. Financing must come from either borrowing (liabilities) or ownership equity.

Underneath the asset section of the balance sheet (or on the right side if the company uses the account form), total current liabilities, $6 million, always are itemized next, then long-term liabilities, $2 million, then finally stockholders' equity of $18 million.

Total current liabilities consist of bills due and payable by UMC within the next 12 months, all of which fall into one of four categories:

1. *Accounts payable*, $2.91 million, which are bills currently owed and due to creditors,
2. *Notes payable*, $1.42 million, which are current obligations owed to a bank or other short-term lender,
3. *Accrued expenses payable*, $430,000, include wages due employees, fees to attorneys, current pension or retirement obligations, and the like.
4. *Federal income taxes payable*, $1.24 million, is the current tax payable to the Internal Revenue Service, and is sufficiently important to merit a line of its own on the corporate balance sheet.

Long-term liabilities, $2 million for UMC, can include straight debt (like UMC's which pays 8 percent interest and matures in 2003), convertible bonds (bonds which pay interest like straight bonds but are convertible upon demand of the bond owner into a stated number of shares of common stock), or "other" long-term debt (like pollution control and industrial revenue bonds or sinking-fund debentures). UMC has only straight debt outstanding.

Total liabilities, $8 million, are the sum of current and long-term liabilities and constitute the total financing obtained from borrowings.

Stockholders' equity, $18 million consists of:

1. *Capital stock*, $1.588 million, which includes both preferred stock and common

stock but no convertible preferred stock and no warrants or rights to purchase either bonds or common stock,

2. *Capital surplus*, $1.112 million, which is the amount paid in by shareholders over the par or legal value of 30 cents for each common share,

3. *Accumulated retained earnings*, $15.3 million, which are earnings not paid out in dividends but have been retained and reinvested in the business. Further information regarding accumulated retained earnings since inception of the business is set forth below in the *statement of retained earnings*.

Capital stock represents proprietary interest in the company, is represented by stock certificates authorized and issued by the company, and can belong to either of several classes, including:

1. *Preferred stock,* which has preference or takes priority over other shares regarding dividend payout (6 percent in UMC's case), and which can be cumulative, which means that if the company fails to pay dividends for whatever reason for any year, then the 6 percent of $100 or $6 per preferred share accumulates on the books and must be paid before common stockholders can receive future dividends. Total pre-

ferred stock authorized and issued by UMC is $100 per share times 13,600 shares or $1.36 million.

2. *Common stock,* which represents the remaining ownership of the company and is entitled to receive a dividend along with fluctuations in value of the stock. Par value is the legal stated value of each common share; so the par value (30 cents per share times 760,000 shares or $228,000) plus the additional amount or capital surplus ($1.112 million) together state the amount UMC received upon issuing 760,000 shares, namely $1.34 million divided by 760,000 or $1.76 per share.

The bottom line, *total liabilities and stockholders equity,* states the financing of the corporation, and shows where UMC obtained the $26 million to buy the total assets itemized at the top of the balance sheet.

We turn next to income statements.

INCOME STATEMENTS

Exhibit 2 shows UMC's income statement, where the important items to look for, after the name of the company, the title, and date of the statement at the heading, are:

1. *Net sales,* which is where most of the business revenue comes from for most busi-

EXHIBIT 2

UNIVERSAL MANUFACTURING CORPORATION
Consolidated Income Statement
December 31, 1983 and 1982

	1983	1982
Net sales	$23,850,000	$19,810,000
Cost of sales and operating expenses		
Cost of goods sold	8,940,000	7,209,000
Depreciation	800,000	750,000
Selling and administrating expenses	8,232,000	6,814,000
Operating profit	$ 5,878,000	$ 5,037,000
Other income		
Dividends and interest	342,000	183,000
Total income	$ 6,220,000	$ 5,220,000
Less: Interest on bonds	160,000	160,000
Income before provision for federal income tax	$ 6,060,000	$ 5,060,000
Provision for federal income tax	2,240,000	1,980,000
Net profit for year	$ 3,820,000	$ 3,080,000
Common shares outstanding	760,000	760,000
Net earnings per share	$ 4.92	$ 3.95

Statement of Accumulated Retained Earnings

	1983	1982
Balance January 1	$13,081,600	$11,413,200
Net profit for year	3,820,000	3,080,000
Total	$16,901,600	$14,493,200
Less: Dividends paid on		
Preferred stock	81,600	81,600
Common stock	1,520,000	1,330,000
Balance December 31	$15,300,000	$13,081,600

nesses, except rental and leasing companies, $23,850,000.

2. *Net Operating Income* (NOI) or profit before interest and taxes, which states profit from business operations, without regard to financing, $5,878,000.

3. *Total Income* before interest and taxes, which states the return on total capital available to the business during the year, $6,220,000.

4. *Less:* provision for federal income tax, $2,240,000.

5. *Total Income*, after tax but before interest deduction, which states the after-tax profitability of the corporation and is widely used in computing cost of capital for a business enterprise, $3,980,000.

6. *Net income* (NI) or profit for the year, which states earnings after taxes and after all fixed charges. The net profit for the year is available for (a) dividend payout to preferred stockholders, (b) dividend payout to common stockholders, and (c) retention and reinvestment in the business, $3,820,000.

7. *Net earnings per share* (EPS), which equals total earnings available for distribution to common stockholders ($3.82 million minus 6% dividend owed on 13,600 shares of $100 par value preferred stock, or $3,738,400), divided by 760,000 common shares outstanding, $4.92.

$3,820,000 - 0.06(13,600)($100) =
$3,738,400
$3,738,400/760,000 =
$4.92 per share

Cost of sales and operating expenses falls into one of three categories:

1. *Cost of goods sold*, which states the amount of labor, material, and other expenses in producing the items sold, $8,940,000.

2. *Depreciation expense*, which states the amount of capital (producer's durables) consumed in producing the goods and services sold and which must be replaced or restored to its original capacity, $800,000.

3. *Selling and administrating expenses*, which includes office expenses, executives salaries, salespersons salaries, advertising and promotion expenses and the like, $8,232,000.

Operating profit, also called net operating income, $5.878 million, is the income from business operations, and is an important indicator of how efficiently the fixed assets were employed during the year.

Other income, $342,000, is from UMC's marketable securities of $1.83 million at cost as of one year ago.

Total income, $6.22 million, is the sum of operating profit from the business and income from other sources.

Interest on bonds, $160,000, (8 percent of 2 million) is itemized next on the income statement, followed by:

Income after interest, before tax	$6,000,000
Provision for federal income tax	2,240,000
Net profit for the year	3,820,000
Net earnings per share	$4.92

We turn next to statements of accumulated retained earnings.

STATEMENTS OF ACCUMULATED RETAINED EARNINGS

The bottom part of Exhibit 2 contains the accumulated retained earnings statement for UMC, and shows at the beginning of the balance, since the starting date of the business to January 1 of the current year, $13,081,600—to which is added the net profit for the year, $3,820,000, to get total accumulated retained earnings of $16,901,600.

Dividends paid to stockholders are itemized next:

Preferred stock dividend: 6 percent of $1,360,000	$ 81,600
Common stock dividend: $2.00 per share declared times 760,000 shares	1,520,000
Total dividends paid	$1,601,600

Balance, December 31 (15.3 million) equals the difference between the total available ($16,901,600) and total dividends paid. Retained earnings are an important source of finance of corporate capital assets.

We turn next to statements of sources and uses of funds.

STATEMENT OF SOURCE AND APPLICATION OF FUNDS

Exhibit 3 is a statement of source and application or use of funds for UMC. Ordinarily, *funds* imply cash; but in a broader sense, *funds* include cash equivalents and substitutes for cash, such as short-term credit, notes, and account payable and accrued liabilities to meet the short-term financing needs of the business. So *funds* in the broader sense imply net *working capital*, which is the difference between current assets and current liabilities.

Sources of funds in general include transactions which increase the amount of working capital, such as:

1. Net profit from operations.
2. Sale or consumption of noncurrent assets.
3. Long-term borrowing.
4. Issuing additional shares of capital stock.
5. Annual depreciation.

Uses of funds in general include transactions which decrease working capital, such as:

1. Declaring cash dividends.
2. Repaying long-term debt.
3. Buying noncurrent assets.
4. Repurchasing outstanding capital stock.

In the case of UMC and Exhibit 3, funds were provided by net income, $3.82 million, and current depreciation expense, $800,000. Some analysts worry that depreciation is not cash, depreciation is a bookkeeping entry. But the capital was consumed in the process of producing the goods and services sold; so the business pays the cash to itself to ultimately replace the consumed capital. Depreciation expense is a source of funds.

Total funds provided for UMC are $4,-620,000.

Uses of funds are itemized next, where all uses fall into one of four categories:

Dividends on preferred stock .... $ 81,600
Dividends on common stock 1,520,000
Plant and equipment 1,720,300
Sundry assets 398,100
 Total uses or application
  of funds $3,720,000

Increase in working capital, $900,000, is the difference between the total funds pro-

vided, $4.62 million, and the total funds used, $3.72 million.

An *analysis of changes in working capital* for the year is included in the statement of source and application of funds, and gives further information regarding the $900,000 increase in working capital, which is explained by analyzing changes in current assets together with changes in current liabilities.

Changes in current assets total $2.2 million, itemized as follows:

1. *Cash* increased from $250,000 to $350,-000, giving a net change of $100,000,
2. *Marketable securities* increased from $1.83 million to $2.85 million, giving a net change of $1.02 million,
3. *Accounts receivable* increased from $4.37 million to $4.8 million, giving a net change of $430,000,
4. *Inventories* increased from $4.95 million to $5.6 million, giving a net change of $650,000.

Changes in current liabilities total $1.3 million, itemized as follows:

1. *Accounts payable* increased from $2.3 million to $2.91 million, giving a net change of $610,000,
2. *Notes payable* increased from $730,000 to

EXHIBIT 3

UNIVERSAL MANUFACTURING CORPORATION
Statement of Source and Application of Funds
December 31, 1983

		1983
Funds were provided by		
Net income	$3,820,000	
Depreciation	800,000	
Total...............................		$4,620,000
Funds were used for		
Dividends on preferred stock	$ 81,600	
Dividends on common stock...............	1,520,000	
Plant and equipment	1,720,300	
Sundry assets	398,100	
Total...............................		$3,720,000
Increase in Working Capital		$ 900,000
Analysis of changes in working capital—1983		
Changes in current assets		
Cash....................................	$ 100,000	
Marketable securities	1,020,000	
Accounts receivable	430,000	
Inventories	650,000	
Total...............................		$2,200,000
Changes in current liabilities		
Accounts payable	$ 610,000	
Notes payable	690,000	
Accrued expenses payable	80,000	
Federal income tax payable	(80,000)	
Total...............................		$1,300,000

$1.42 million, giving a net change of $690,000,

3. *Accrued expenses payable* increased from $350,000 to $430,000, giving a net change of $80,000,

4. *Federal income taxes payable* decreased from $1.32 million to $1.24 million, giving a net change of ($80,000).

The difference between the changes in current assets ($2.2 million) and changes in current liabilities ($1.3 million) equals the $900,000 increase in working capital.

We turn next to understanding more regarding how to analyze financial statements.

II. ANALYZING FINANCIAL STATEMENTS

The analysis of all four statements consists primarily of calculating ratios; but other methods including the time trend of the ratio, information theory, and flow-of-funds analysis are sometimes used. We shall limit our analysis to using ratios.[1]

In general, financial analysts, investors, creditors, and others look for two kinds of information regarding business enterprises:

1. *Risk*, including financial, business, market, and country or political risks,
2. *Return*, including productivity, efficiency, and profitability of corporate capital investments.

A third factor, *growth rate*, is important too, primarily because high steady growth is usually worth more than low or no growth.

BALANCE SHEET RATIOS

Balance sheet ratios belong to one of the three following categories:

1. *Liquidity and turnover ratios*, which indicate the ability of the corporation to pay current liabilities,
2. *Capitalization*, also called *leverage*, or *debt ratios*, which is the amount of borrowing relative to other factors such as total capitalization, total assets, or total equity,
3. *Net asset ratios*, which indicate the amount of assets backing each class of outstanding securities.

Liquidity ratios are calculated to judge whether the corporation owns sufficient cash and cash-equivalents or substitutes to com-

fortably pay short-term obligations, and include:

1. *Current liquidity*, the ability to pay current liabilities from current assets:

Current ratio:

$$\frac{\text{Current assets}}{\text{Current liabilities}} = \frac{\$13,600,000}{\$6,000,000} = 2.3 \text{ to } 1$$

In total dollar amounts, the numerator in the current ratio, minus the denominator, states *net working capital*, where

Total current assets	$13,600,000
Less: Total current liabilities	6,000,000
Working capital	$ 7,600,000

2. *Quick asset* (sometimes called *acid test*) *ratio:*

$$\frac{\text{Quick assets}}{\text{Current liabilities}} = \frac{\$8,000,000}{\$6,000,000} = 1.33$$

Where quick assets are total current assets minus inventories, because inventories usually are less liquid than either cash, marketable securities, or accounts receivable:

Total current assets	$13,600,000
Less: Inventories	5,600,000
Quick assets	$8,000,000
Less: Total current liabilities	6,000,000
Net quick assets	$2,000,000

3. The *cash plus marketable securities ratio* indicates the firm's ability to pay current liabilities without relying on either inventories or accounts receivable:

$$\frac{\text{Cash plus marketable securities}}{\text{Total current liabilities}} = \frac{\$3,200,000}{\$6,000,000} = 0.53$$

Liquidity and turnover of inventories ratios indicate how close inventories approximate true liquidity through total sales, and are the three following figures:

1. *Inventory as a percent of total current assets:*

$$\frac{\text{Inventory}}{\text{Total current assets}} = \frac{\$5,600,000}{\$13,600,000}$$
$$= 41.18 \text{ percent}$$

2. *Cost of goods sold*, including depreciation and capital consumption, *to average inventory ratio:*

$$\frac{\text{Cost of goods sold plus depreciation}}{\text{Inventory}} = \frac{\$9,740,000}{\$5,600,000} = 1.74$$

3. *Inventory turnover ratio:*

$$\frac{\text{Net sales}}{\text{Inventory}} = \frac{\$23,850,000}{\$5,600,000} = 4.26 \text{ times}$$

---

[1] Comparison of these ratios with those typical of the industry is very helpful. Typical values are given on page 128. More detailed tabulations are provided by Dun & Bradstreet and Robert Morris Associates.

Liquidity of receivables ratios indicate how close accounts receivable approximate true liquidity through total sales, and are the two following figures:

1. Average collection period ratio, which indicates the number of day's sales in accounts receivables:

$$\frac{\text{Receivables} \times \text{Days in year}}{\text{Annual sales}} =$$

$$\frac{\$4,800,000 \times 360}{\$23,850,000} = 72.45$$

2. Accounts receivable turnover ratio:

$$\frac{\text{Annual sales}}{\text{Accounts receivable}} = \frac{\$23,850,000}{\$4,800,000} = 4.97$$

Liquidity and turnover of tangible and fixed asset ratios indicate relationships between total sales and total assets, and are given by the following two figures:

1. Fixed asset turnover ratio:

$$\frac{\text{Sales}}{\text{Net fixed assets}} = \frac{\$23,850,000}{\$12,110,000} = 1.97$$

2. Total asset turnover ratio:

$$\frac{\text{Net sales}}{\text{Average total tangible assets}} = \frac{\$23,850,000}{\$25,800,000}$$
$$= 0.9244$$

Capitalization ratios include:

1. Debt ratio:

$$\frac{\text{Total liabilities}}{\text{Total assets}} = \frac{\$8,000,000}{\$26,000,000}$$
$$= 30.77 \text{ percent}$$

2. Current liabilities as a percent of total liabilities:

$$\frac{\text{Current liabilities}}{\text{Total liabilities}} = \frac{\$6,000,000}{\$8,000,000}$$
$$= 75 \text{ percent}$$

3. Debt-to-net-worth ratio:

$$\frac{\text{Total liabilities}}{\text{Net Worth}} = \frac{\$8,000,000}{\$18,000,000} = 0.4444$$

4. Long-term debt capitalization ratio:

$$\frac{\text{Long-term debt}}{\text{Total capitalization}} = \frac{\$2,000,000}{\$19,800,000}$$
$$= 10.10 \text{ percent}$$

5. Preferred stock ratio:

$$\frac{\text{Preferred stock}}{\text{Total capitalization}} = \frac{\$1,360,000}{\$19,800,000}$$
$$= 6.87 \text{ percent}$$

6. Common stock ratio:

$$\frac{\text{Common stock plus accumulated earnings}}{\text{Total capitalization}} = \frac{\$16,440,000}{\$19,800,000}$$
$$= 83.03 \text{ percent}$$

7. Summary:

Total assets	$26,000,000	
Less: Intangibles	$ 200,000	
Less: Total current liabilities	$ 6,000,000	
Total capitalization	$19,800,000	100.00%
Bonds (long-term debt)	2,000,000	10.10
Preferred stock	1,360,000	6.87
Common stock (including capital surplus and retained earnings)	16,440,000	83.03

8. Long-term debt as a percent of total liabilities:

$$\frac{\text{Long-term debt}}{\text{Total liabilities}} = \frac{\$2,000,000}{\$8,000,000}$$
$$= 25.00 \text{ percent}$$

Net asset value ratios include:

1. Net asset value per $1,000 bond; $9,900 per bond.

$$\frac{\begin{array}{c}\text{Net tangible assets} \\ \text{available to meet} \\ \text{bondholders' claims}\end{array}}{\begin{array}{c}\text{Number of \$1,000} \\ \text{bonds outstanding}\end{array}} = \frac{\$19,800,000}{2,000,000}$$

where the numerator is calculated as follows:

Total assets	$26,000,000
Less: Intangibles	200,000
Total tangible assets	$25,800,000
Less: Current liabilities	6,000,000
Net tangible assets available to meet bondholders' claims	$19,800,000

2. Net asset value per share of preferred stock: $1,308.82

$$\frac{\begin{array}{c}\text{Net assets backing} \\ \text{the preferred stock}\end{array}}{\begin{array}{c}\text{Number of shares} \\ \text{of preferred stock} \\ \text{outstanding}\end{array}} = \frac{\$17,800,000}{13,600}$$

where the numerator is calculated as follows:

Total assets	$26,000,000
Less: Intangibles	200,000
Total tangible assets	$25,800,000
Less: Current liabilities	6,000,000
Less: Long-term liabilities	2,000,000
Net assets backing the preferred stock........................	$17,800,000

3. Net book value per share of common stock: $21.63

$$\frac{\begin{array}{c}\text{Net assets available} \\ \text{for the common stock}\end{array}}{\begin{array}{c}\text{Total number of} \\ \text{shares outstanding}\end{array}} = \frac{\$16,440,000}{760,000}$$
$$= \$21.63$$

where the numerator is calculated as follows:

Total assets	$26,000,000
Less: Intangibles	200,000
Total tangible assets	$25,800,000
Less: Current liabilities	6,000,000
Less: Long-term liabilities	2,000,000
Less preferred stock	1,360,000
Net assets available for the common stock	$16,440,000

Finally, estimate the youngest average plant age by dividing the current (1983) depreciation expense accrual ($800,000 from the Statement of Source and Application of Funds) into accumulated depreciation ($6,435,000 from the Balance Sheet) to get 8.04 years. Because some plants and pieces of equipment may have been fully written off over time, we can say that UMC's Fixed Assets, on average, are over 8 years old.

INCOME STATEMENT RATIOS

Income statement ratios belong to one of the two following categories:

1. *Coverage,* which analyzes financial risk by relating the financial charges of a corporation to its ability to service them.
2. *Productivity* or *capital efficiency ratios,* which relate income to total sales and to investment.

Coverage ratios include:

1. Interest coverage ratio: 38.875

$$\frac{\text{Net operating income before interest and taxes}}{\text{Interest charges on bonds}} = \frac{\$6,220,000}{\$160,000}$$
$$= 38.875$$

2. Cash flow coverage ratio, which indicates the firm's ability to service debt, which is related to both interest and principal payments and is not met out of earnings per se, but out of cash: 19.5 times.

$$\frac{\text{Annual cash flow before interest and taxes}}{\text{Interest on bonds plus principal repayments}/(1-T)} = \frac{\$7,020,000}{\$360,000} = 19.5$$

where:

Net operating income before interest and taxes	$6,220,000
Plus annual depreciation expense	800,000
Annual cash flow before interest and taxes	$7,020,000
Face value 20-year 8% bonds due 2003	$2,000,000
Annual Repayment rate after taxes $2,000,000 divided by 20 years	100,000

Before tax annual bond repayment rate $100,000 divided by 1 minus the effective tax rate, say 50%..........	$200,000
Plus: 8% interest on $2,000,000	100,000
Interest plus principal repayments	$360,000

Since interest payments are made before taxes, the adjustment is necessary to convert principal repayments which are made after taxes to before-tax equivalents.

3. Preferred dividend coverage ratio: 46.81

$$\frac{\text{Income available for paying preferred dividends}}{\text{Total dividends to preferred shareholders}} = \frac{\$3,820,000}{\$81,600} = 46.81$$

4. Earnings per common share: $4.92

$$\frac{\text{Earnings available for distribution to common shareholders}}{\text{Total number of common shares outstanding}} = \frac{\$3,738,400}{760,000} = \$4.92$$

where:

Net profit for the year	$3,820,000
Less: Dividend requirements on preferred stock	81,600
Earnings available for common stock...........................	$3,738,400

5. Primary earnings for the year: $4.94

$$\frac{\text{Earnings for the year}}{\text{Common stock plus stock equivalents}} = \frac{\$3,820,000}{773,500} = \$4.94$$

Assuming the 13,600 preferred shares had been convertible and converted, on a share-for-share basis, into common stock.

13,600 + 760,000 = 773,600 common shares after conversion

6. Fully diluted earnings per share: $4.79

$$\frac{\text{Adjusted earnings}}{\text{Adjusted shares outstanding}} = \frac{\$3,900,000}{813,600}$$
$$= \$4.79$$

where:

Earnings for the year	$3,820,000
Plus: interest on convertible bonds	$ 160,000
Less: income tax applicable to interest deduction	80,000
Adjusted earnings for the year	$3,900,000
Common shares outstanding	760,000
Preferred convertible stock equivalent common shares	13,600
Twenty common shares per $1,000 convertible bond (2,000) outstanding ..	40,000
Adjusted shares outstanding	813,600

7. Summary:

Earnings per share	$4.92
Primary earnings	4.94
Fully diluted earnings	4.79

8. Price-earnings ratio: Approximately 15 times

$$\frac{\text{Market price of stock}}{\text{Earnings per share}} = \frac{\$72.25}{\$4.92} = 14.69$$

Productivity or capital efficiency ratios include:

1. Operating margin of profit: 24.65%.

$$\frac{\text{Operating profit}}{\text{Sales}} = \frac{\$5,878,000}{\$23,850,000} = 24.65\%$$

Previous year:

$$= \frac{\$5,037,000}{\$19,810,000} = 25.43\%$$

2. Operating cost ratio: 75.35%.

	Amount	Ratio
Net sales	$23,850,000	100.00%
Operating costs	17,972,000	75.35
Operating profit	$ 5,878,000	24.65%

3. Net profit ratio: 16.02%.

$$\frac{\text{Net profit for the year}}{\text{Net sales}} = \frac{\$3,820,000}{\$23,850,000}$$
$$= 16.02\%$$

Previous year: 15.55%

$$= \frac{\$3,080,000}{\$19,810,000} = 15.55\%$$

RATIOS FROM STATEMENTS OF ACCUMULATED RETAINED EARNINGS

Retained earnings statements ratios belong to one of the two following categories:

1. Dividend payout ratio.
2. Earnings retention ratio.

The dividend payout ratio for UMC is: 40.66%.

$$\frac{\text{Dividends paid to common stockholders}}{\text{Income available for common stockholders}} = \frac{\$1,520,000}{\$3,738,400}$$
$$= 40.66\%$$

where:

Net profit for the year	$3,820,000
Dividends on preferred stock	81,600
Earnings available for common	$3,738,400

The earnings retention ratio for UMC is: 59.34%.

$$\frac{\text{Earnings retained}}{\text{Earnings available for payout}} = \frac{\$2,218,400}{\$3,738,400} = 59.34\%$$

where:

Net profit for the year	$3,820,000
Less: Dividends paid on preferred stock	$ 81,600
Less: Dividends paid on common stock	1,520,000
Earnings retained	$2,218,400

Summary:

Dividend payout ratio	40.66%
Earnings retention ratio	59.34
Earnings available	100.00%

Dividends per share: $2.00.

$$\frac{\begin{array}{c}\text{Total dividends}\\\text{paid to common}\\\text{shareholders}\end{array}}{\begin{array}{c}\text{Number of}\\\text{common shares}\\\text{outstanding}\end{array}} = \frac{\$1,520,000}{760,000} = \$2.00$$

Balance December 31, $15,300,000.

RATIOS FROM STATEMENTS OF SOURCE AND APPLICATION OF FUNDS

Since an analysis was stated directly on the statement of source and use of funds in Exhibit 3, that part of the analysis is completed; however we still need to calculate profitability ratios which belong to one of the two following categories:

1. Return on assets.
2. Return on equity.

Return on assets ratios include:
Return on total assets: 27.67%.

$$\frac{\text{Total income}}{\text{Last year's total assets}} = \frac{\$6,220,000}{\$22,481,600}$$
$$= 27.67\%$$

After tax return on total assets: 17.70%.

$$\frac{\begin{array}{c}\text{Total income after tax}\\\text{but before interest}\end{array}}{\text{Last year's total assets}} = \frac{\$3,980,000}{\$22,481,600}$$
$$= 17.70\%$$

where:

Total income	$6,220,000
Less: Provision for total taxes	2,240,000
After tax total income	$3,980,000

Return on equity ratio: 25.92%.

$$\frac{\begin{array}{c}\text{Income available for}\\\text{distribution to common}\\\text{stockholders}\end{array}}{\begin{array}{c}\text{Last year's total}\\\text{equity of common}\\\text{stockholders}\end{array}} = \frac{\$3,738,400}{\$14,421,600}$$
$$= 25.92\%$$

where:

Last year's total stockholder
equity $15,781,600
     Less: Preferred stock value 1,360,000
Last year's common stock
equity $14,421,600

We turn next to further discussion of notes and supplemental information.

III. NOTES AND SUPPLEMENTAL INFORMATION

As explained in the introduction, financial statements in corporate annual reports usually are accompanied by:

- A *report of independent accountants and auditors* certifying the statements conform to generally accepted accounting principles and that generally accepted auditing standards and procedures were used.

- *Notes* which further explain details and disclose relevant information regarding line items on all four statements.

- *Segment information*, which summarizes selected items by business, industry, and geographic segment.

- A *restatement* of almost everything in current (in contrast with the traditional historical original purchase) prices, and to account for the effects of inflation on items reported in the standard statements.

- *Long-term record* summarizing selected items over a five- or ten-year time span.

REPORT OF INDEPENDENT ACCOUNTANTS

A typical report of independent accountants is addressed to the stockholders and board of directors of the corporation and will read as follows:

"In our opinion, the accompanying consolidated financial statements, appearing on pages — through —, present fairly the financial position of Universal Manufacturing Corporation and its subsidiary companies at December 31, 1983 and 1982, and the results of their operations and changes in financial position for the years then ended, in conformity with generally accepted accounting principles consistently applied. Also, in our opinion, the five-year comparative consolidated summary of operations presents fairly the financial information included therein. Our examinations of these statements were made in accordance with generally accepted auditing standards and accordingly included such tests of the accounting rec-

ords and such other auditing procedures as we considered necessary in the circumstances."

The report will be signed with the name and address of the accounting firm and dated.

NOTES TO FINANCIAL STATEMENTS

Notes disclose additional information regarding entries in all four primary statements, and usually are considered an integral part of the statements, included in and covered by the auditor's certification. Some corporations include the next three items to be discussed, segment information, effects of inflation, and long-term comparative summary of operations, in the notes. If included in some place other than the notes, then look for whether the statement was excluded from the auditor's audit.

SEGMENT INFORMATION

Notes disclosing geographic area and industry segment information usually summarize selected items such as net sales, operating income, total assets, depreciation and amortization, and capital expenditures for industry segments (business segments or product groups) and foreign operations.

Exhibit 4 shows the segment information for UMC's two segments.

As you can see from Exhibit 4, industry segment number one, Human and Animal Health Products, accounts for 84 percent ($20,044,000 divided by $23,850,000) of total sales, and 92 percent ($5,435,000 divided by $5,878,000) of UMC's operating income; all supported by 83.46 percent ($21,700,000 divided by $26,000,000) of total assets. Eleven percent ($234,100 divided by $2,118,400) of total capital expenditures were made in industry segment number two, Environmental Health Products and Services for the treatment of water and air pollution.

Exhibit 4 also shows, based on the following ratios, that UMC's business is roughly 60 percent domestic United States; 40 percent nondomestic:

Net Sales:

$$\frac{\text{United States}}{\text{Total company}} = \frac{\$14,818,000}{\$23,850,000} = 62.13\%$$

Operating income:

$$\frac{\text{United States}}{\text{Total company}} = \frac{\$3,690,000}{\$5,037,000} = 62.78\%$$

Total assets:

$$\frac{\text{United States}}{\text{Total company}} = \frac{\$16,549,000}{\$26,000,000} = 63.65\%$$

EXHIBIT 4
SEGMENT REPORTING AND FOREIGN OPERATIONS

| | Industry Segments | | | Geographic Segments | | | | |
	Segment No. 1	Segment No. 2	Consolidated	Domestic	Foreign OECD	Foreign Other	Eliminations	Consolidated
1983								
Sales, unaffiliated customers	$20,044,000	$3,806,000	$23,850,000	$12,647,000	$ 9,029,000	$2,175,000		$23,850,000
Sales, intersegment				2,171,000	346,000	21,000	($2,539,000)	
Total sales	$20,044,000	$3,806,000	$23,850,000	$14,818,000	$ 9,375,000	$2,196,000	($2,539,000)	$23,850,000
Pretax operating income	5,435,000	443,000	5,878,000	3,690,000	1,820,000	211,000	157,000	5,878,000
Identifiable assets at December 31	21,700,000	4,300,000	26,000,000	16,549,000	10,168,000	2,353,000	(3,070,000)	26,000,000
Depreciation expense	666,000	134,000	800,000					
Capital spending	1,884,300	234,100	2,118,400					
1982								
Sales, unaffiliated customers	$16,629,000	$3,181,000	$19,810,000	$10,519,000	$ 7,511,000	$1,780,000		$19,810,000
Sales, intersegment				2,614,000	246,000	14,000	($2,878,000)	
Total sales	$16,629,000	$3,181,000	$19,810,000	$13,133,000	$ 7,757,000	$1,794,000	($2,878,000)	$19,810,000
Pretax operating income	4,627,000	410,000	5,037,000	3,512,000	1,449,000	126,000	(50,000)	5,037,000
Identifiable assets at December 31	19,027,000	3,473,000	22,500,000	14,728,000	8,660,000	2,005,000	(2,893,000)	22,500,000
Depreciation expense	611,000	127,000	738,000					
Capital spending	1,751,000	190,000						
1981								
Sales, unaffiliated customers	$14,461,000	$2,779,000	$17,240,000	$ 9,504,000	$ 6,152,000	$1,584,000		$17,240,000
Sales, intersegment				2,677,000	155,000	3,000	($2,835,000)	
Total sales	$14,461,000	$2,779,000	$17,240,000	$12,181,000	$ 6,307,000	$1,587,000	($2,835,000)	$17,240,000
Pretax operating income	4,163,000	378,000	4,541,000	3,552,000	1,234,000	119,000	(364,000)	4,541,000
Identifiable assets at December 31	16,614,000	3,341,000	19,955,000	13,627,000	7,818,000	1,590,000	(3,179,000)	19,955,000
Depreciation expense	551,000	102,000	653,000					
Capital spending	1,969,000	238,000	2,207,000					

SUPPLEMENTAL INFORMATION ON INFLATION ACCOUNTING

Pursuant to Financial Accounting Standards Board (FASB) *Statement of Financial Accounting Standards No. 33*, public enterprises that have either (1) inventories and property, plant, and equipment (before deducting accumulated depreciation) amounting to more than $125 million or (2) total assets amounting to more than $1 billion (after deducting accumulated depreciation) are required to report supplementary information in addition to the primary financial statements. FASB *Standards No. 33* are:

For fiscal years ended on or after December 25, 1979, enterprises are required to report:

a. Income from continuing operations adjusted for the effects of general inflation.
b. The purchasing power gain or loss on net monetary items.

For fiscal years ended on or after December 25, 1979, enterprises are also required to report:

a. Income from continuing operations on a current cost basis.
b. The current cost amounts of inventory and property, plant, and equipment at the end of the fiscal year.
c. Increases or decreases in current cost amounts of inventory and property, plant, and equipment, net of inflation.

Enterprises are required to present a five-year summary of selected financial data, including information on income, sales and other operating revenues, net assets, dividends per common share, and market price per share. In the computation of net assets, only inventory and property, plant, and equipment need be adjusted for the effects of changing prices.

UMC, because of its "small company" asset size, would be exempt from FASB *No. 33*'s reporting requirement. However, Exhibit 5 restates UMC's statement of income from continuing operations, restated for changing prices, for the year ending December 31, 1983; and UMC's five-year comparison of selected data adjusted for changing prices.

A final note on Notes: Feel free to speak with your friendly auditor, or sleuth on your own, regarding additional information which might remain undisclosed and could pertain to:

a. Liabilities arising out of company pension plans (e.g., ERISA).
b. Contractual obligations (e.g., the capitalized value of lease payments).
c. Legal judgments currently enforceable.
d. Contingent liabilities (e.g., pending lawsuits or possible income tax assessment).

TEN-YEAR FINANCIAL SUMMARY

Long-term performance of UMC is summarized and reported on the ten-year financial summary statement, Exhibit 6.

The long-term view is used for detecting trends and changes in trends in important factors such as net sales, total assets, net operating income, earnings per share, and dividends per share. On balance, the trends for UMC look pretty good: upward.

(continued)

EXHIBIT 5

UNIVERSAL MANUFACTURING CORPORATION SCHEDULE OF INCOME FROM CONTINUING OPERATIONS AND OTHER CHANGES IN SHAREHOLDERS' EQUITY ADJUSTED FOR EFFECTS OF CHANGING PRICES
For the Year Ended December 31, 1983

	As Reported (historical cost)	Adjusted for General Inflation (constant 1983 $)	Adjusted for Specific (current) Costs
Income from continuing operations			
Net sales	$23,850,000		
Other income	342,000		
Total revenue from continuing operations	$24,192,000	$24,192,000	$24,192,000
Costs and other deductions			
Depreciation expenses		800,000	1,076,000	1,115,000
Other costs and expenses	17,172,000	17,699,000	17,273,000
Interest expense	160,000	160,000	160,000
Federal and foreign income taxes	2,240,000	2,240,000	2,240,000
Total costs and other deductions	$20,372,000	$21,175,000	$20,788,000
Net income from continuing operations	$ 3,820,000	$ 3,017,000	$ 3,404,000
Purchasing power gain on net monetary liabilities (Net amounts owed)		1,000	1,000
Increase in current cost of inventories and property, plant and equipment during 1983			1,911,000
Less: effect of increase in general price level during 1983			2,788,000
Excess of increase in specific prices over increase in the general price level			($ 877,000)
Net income	$ 3,820,000		
Adjusted net income		$ 3,018,000	
Net change in shareholders' equity from above	$ 3,820,000	$ 3,018,000	$ 2,528,000

Summarized Balance Sheet Adjusted for Changing Prices At December 31, 1983

	As Reported	Adjusted for General Inflation (constant 1983 $)	Adjusted for Specific (current) Costs
Assets			
Inventories	$ 5,600,000	$ 6,175,000	$ 5,670,000
Property, plant and equipment	12,110,000	13,354,000	16,327,000
All other assets	8,290,000	9,141,000	7,506,000
Total assets	$26,000,000	$28,670,000	$29,503,000
Total liabilities	8,000,000	7,600,000	7,600,000
Shareholders' equity	$18,000,000	$21,070,000	$21,903,000

Supplementary financial data Five-Year Comparison of Selected Data Adjusted for Changing Prices

	Years Ended December 31				
	1979	1980	1981	1982	1983
Sales					
As reported	$14,020,000	$15,610,000	$17,240,000	$19,810,000	$23,850,000
1983 constant dollars	19,543,000	20,211,000	20,063,000	20,970,000	23,850,000
Net income					
As reported					$ 3,820,000
1983 constant dollars					3,017,000
Current costs					3,404,000
Earnings per share					
As reported					$4.92
1983 constant dollars					3.86
Current costs					4.37
Common stock dividends declared per share					
As reported	$1.40	$1.43	$1.55	$1.75	$2.00
1983 constant dollars	1.95	1.85	1.80	1.85	2.00
Net assets at year-end					
As reported					$18,000,000
1983 constant dollars					21,070,000
Current costs					21,903,000
Purchasing power gain on net monetary liabilities					1,000
Market price per common share at year-end					
Actual	$69.25	$68.13	$55.50	$67.63	$72.25
1983 constant dollars	90.50	84.95	64.80	72.45	68.50
Average consumer price index*	181.5	195.4	217.4	239.0	253.0

*Hypothetical, for illustrative purposes only.

EXHIBIT 6

TEN-YEAR FINANCIAL SUMMARY
UNIVERSAL MANUFACTURING CORPORATION

	1983	1982	1981	1980	1979	1978	1977	1976	1975	1974
Net sales	$23,850,000	$19,810,000	$17,240,000	$15,610,000	$14,020,000	$12,604,000	$11,040,000	$9,426,000	$E324,000	$7,611,000
Total income before tax	6,060,000	5,060,000	4,535,000	4,164,000	3,783,000	3,619,000	3,195,000	2,747,000	2,521,000	2,286,000
Net profit for the year	3,820,000	3,080,000	2,775,000	2,555,000	2,288,000	2,105,000	1,827,000	1,512,000	1,314,000	1,179,000
Earnings per share	4.92	3.95	3.56	3.28	2.94	2.71	2.36	1.95	1.70	1.53
Dividends per share	2.00	1.75	1.55	1.43	1.40	1.40	1.24	1.12	1.10	1.03
Net working capital	7,600,000	6,700,000	6,300,000	5,500,000	5,023,000	3,596,000	3,424,000	2,964,000	2,604,000	2,261,000
Total assets	26,000,000	22,481,600	19,934,000	17,594,000	15,390,000	12,433,000	9,890,000	8,348,000	7,365,000	6,643,000
Net plant and equipment	12,110,000	10,820,000	9,918,000	8,747,000	6,743,000	4,740,000	3,635,000	3,150,000	2,830,000	2,479,000
Long term debt	2,000,000	2,000,000	2,000,000	2,000,000	2,000,000	2,000,000	2,000,000	1,000,000	1,000,000	1,000,000
Preferred stock	1,360,000	1,360,000	1,360,000	1,360,000	1,360,000	1,360,000	1,360,000	1,360,000	1,360,000	1,360,000
Common stock and surplus	1,340,000	1,340,000	1,340,000	1,340,000	1,340,000	1,340,000	1,340,000	1,340,000	1,340,000	1,340,000
Book value per share	21.63									

A Guide to SEC Corporate Filings

The purpose of the Federal securities laws is to provide disclosure of material financial and other information on companies seeking to raise capital through the public offering of their securities, as well as companies whose securities are already publicly held. This enables investors to evaluate the securities of these companies on an informed and realistic basis.

The Securities Act of 1933 is a *disclosure* statute. It generally requires that, before securities may be offered to the public, a registration statement must be filed with the Commission disclosing prescribed categories of information. Before the sale of securities can begin, the registration statement must become "effective," and investors must be furnished a prospectus containing the most significant information in the registration statement.

The Securities Exchange Act of 1934 deals in large part with securities already outstanding and requires the registration of securities listed on a national securities exchange, as well as Over-the-Counter securities in which there is a substantial public interest. Issuers of registered securities must file annual and other periodic reports designed to provide a public file of current material information. The Exchange Act also requires disclosure of material information to holders of registered securities in solicitations of proxies for the election of directors or approval of corporate action at a stockholder's meeting, or in attempts to acquire control of a company through a tender offer or other planned stock acquisitions. It provides that insiders of companies whose equity securities are registered must report their holdings and transactions in all equity securities of their companies.

Form 10-K

This report provides a comprehensive overview of the registrant. The report must be filed within 90 days after close of company's fiscal year and contains the following items of disclosure:

Items Reported
Part I

1. **Business.** Identifies principal products and services of the company, principal markets and methods of distribution and,

Source: *A Guide to SEC Corporate Filings*, Disclosure, Inc., 5161 River Road, Bethesda, MD 20816. Provided by Disclosure. To order copies of any SEC filings, call 800–638–8241.

if "material," competitive factors, backlog and expectation of fulfillment, availability of raw materials, importance of patents, licenses, and franchises, estimated cost of research, number of employees, and effects of compliance with ecological laws.

If there is more than one line of business, a statement is included for the last three years. The statement includes total sales and net income for each line which during either of the last two fiscal years accounted for 10 percent or more of total sales or pretax income.

2. **Properties.** Location and character of principal plants, mines, and other important properties and if held in fee or leased.
3. **Legal Proceedings.** Brief description of material legal proceedings pending.
4. **Submission of Matters to a Vote of Security Holders.** Information relating to the convening of a meeting of shareholders, whether annual or special, and the matters voted upon.

Part II

5. **Market for the Registrants' Common Stock and Related Security Holder Matters.** Includes principal market in which voting securities are traded with high and low sales prices (in the absence thereof, the range of bid and asked quotations for each quarterly period during the past two years) and the dividends paid during the past two years. In addition to the frequency and amount of dividends paid, this item contains a discussion concerning future dividends.
6. **Selected Financial Data.** These are five-year selected data including net sales and operating revenue; income or loss from continuing operations, both total and per common share; total assets; long-term obligations including redeemable preferred stock; cash dividend declared per common share. The data also includes additional items that could enhance understanding and trends in financial condition and results of operations. Further, the effects of inflation and changing prices should be reflected in the five-year summary.
7. **Management's Discussion and Analysis of Financial Condition and Results of Operations.** Under broad guidelines, this includes: liquidity, capital resources and results of operations; trends that are favorable or unfavorable as well as significant events or uncertainties; causes of any material changes in the financial state-

ments as a whole; limited data concerning subsidiaries; discussion of effects of inflation and changing prices.

8. **Financial Statements and Supplementary Data.** Two-year audited balance sheets as well as three-year audited statements of income and changes in financial condition.

9. **Disagreements on Accounting and Financial Disclosure.**

Part III

10. **Directors and Executive Officers of the Registrant.** Name, office, term of office and specific background data on each.

11. **Remuneration of Directors and Officers.** List of each director and 3 highest paid officers with aggregate annual remuneration exceeding $40,000. Also includes total paid all officers and directors.

12. **Security Ownership of Beneficial Owners and Management.** Identification of owners of 5 percent or more of registrant's stock in addition to listing the amount and percent of each class of stock held by officers and directors.

13. **Certain Relationships and Related Transactions.**

Part IV

14. **Exhibits, Financial Statement Schedules and Reports on Form 8-K.** Complete, audited annual financial information and a list of exhibits filed. Also, any unscheduled material events or corporate changes filed in an 8-K during the year.

Form 10-K
Schedules

I. Investments other than investments in affiliates
II. Receivables from related parties and underwriters, promoters and employees other than affiliates
III. Condensed financial information
IV. Indebtedness of affiliates (not current)
V. Property, plant and equipment
VI. Accumulated depreciation, depletion, and amortization of property, plant and equipment
VII. Guarantees of securities of other issuers
VIII. Valuation and qualifying accounts
IX. Short-term borrowings
X. Supplementary income statement information
XI. Supplementary profit and loss information
XII. Income from dividends (equity in net profit and loss of affiliates)

20-F

Annual Registration/statement filed by certain foreign issuers of securities trading in the United States. The 20-F report must be filed 6 months after close of fiscal year.

Part I

Item 1   Business
Item 2   Description of Property
Item 3   Material Legal Proceedings
Item 4   Control of Registrant
Item 5   Nature of Trading Market
Item 6   Exchange Controls and Other Limitations Affecting Security Holders
Item 7   Taxation
Item 8   Selected Financial Data
Item 9   Management Discussion and Analysis
Item 10   Directors and Officers
Item 11   Compensation
Item 12   Options to Purchase Securities from Registrant or Subsidiaries
Item 13   Interests of Management in Certain Transactions

Part II

Item 14   Description of Securities

Part III

Item 15   Defaults upon Senior Securities
Item 16   Changes in Securities and Changes in Security for Registered Securities

Part IV

Item 17   Financial Statements and Exhibits

10-Q

This is the quarterly financial report filed by most companies, which, although unaudited, provides a continuing view of a company's financial position during the year. The 10-Q report must be filed within 45 days of the close of a fiscal quarter.

Items Reported
Part I

FINANCIAL STATEMENTS

1. Financial Statements
2. Management Discussion
3. A narrative analysis of material changes

In the amount of revenue and expense items in relation to previous quarters, including the effect of any changes in accounting principals.

Part II

1. **Legal Proceedings.** Brief description of material legal proceedings pending; when civil rights or ecological statutes are involved, proceedings must be disclosed.
2. **Changes in Securities.** Material changes in the rights of holders of any class of registered security.
3. **Defaults upon Senior Securities.** Material defaults in the payment if principal, interest, sinking fund or purchase fund installment, dividend, or other material default not cured within 30 days.
4. **Submission of Matters to a Vote of Security Holders.** Information relating to the convening of a meeting of shareholders, whether annual or special, and the matters voted upon, with particular emphasis on the election of directors.
5. **Other Materially Important Events.** Information on any other item of interest to shareholders not already provided for in this form.
6. **Exhibits and Reports on Form 8K.** Any unscheduled material events or corporate changes filed on an 8-K during the prior quarter.

8-K

This is a report of unscheduled material events or corporate changes deemed of importance to the shareholders or to the SEC. Corporate changes must be filed 15 days after the event, except for Other Materially Important Events which has no mandatory filing time.

1. Changes in Control of Registrant.
2. Acquisition or Disposition of Assets.
3. Bankruptcy or Receivership.
4. Changes in Registrant's Certifying Accountant.
5. Other Materially Important Events.
6. Resignations of Registrant's Directors.
7 Financial Statements and Exhibits.

10-C

"Over-the-counter" companies use this form to report changes in name and amount of NASDAQ-listed securities. It is similar in purpose to the 8-K and must be filed 10 days after change.

13-F

A quarterly report of equity holdings required of all institutions with equity assets of $100 million or more. This includes banks, insurance companies, investment companies, investment advisors and large internally managed endowments, foundations and pension funds. This report must be filed 45 days after close of fiscal quarter.

Proxy Statement

A proxy statement provides official notification to designated classes of stockholders of matters to be brought to a vote at a shareholders' meeting. Proxy votes may be solicited for changing the company name, transferring large blocks of stock, electing new officers, or many other matters. Disclosures normally made via a proxy statement may in some cases be made using Form 10-K (Part III).

Registration Statements

Registration statements are of two principal types: (1) "offering" registrations filed under the 1933 Securities Act, and (2) "trading" registrations filed under the 1934 Securities Exchange Act.

"Offering" registrations are used to register securities before they may be offered to investors. Part I of the registration, a preliminary prospectus or "red herring," is promotional in tone; it carries all the sales features that will be contained in the final prospectus. Part II of the registration contains detailed information about marketing agreements, expenses of issuance and distribution, relationship of the company with experts named in the registration, sales to special parties, recent sales of unregistered securities, subsidiaries of registrant, franchises and concessions, indemnification of directors and officers, treatment of proceeds from stock being registered, and financial statements and exhibits.

"Offering" registration statements vary in purpose and content according to the type of organization issuing stock:

S-1   Companies reporting under the 1934 Act for less than 3 years. Permits no incorporation by reference and requires complete disclosure in the prospectus.
S-2   Companies reporting under the

1934 Act for 3 years or more but do not meet the minimum voting stock requirement. Reference of 1934 Act reports permits incorporation and presentation of financial information in the prospectus or in an annual report to shareholders delivered with the prospectus.

S-3 Companies reporting under the 1934 Act for 3 or more years and having at least $150 million of voting stock held by non-affiliates, or as an alternative test, $100 million of voting stock coupled with an annual trading volume of 3 million shares. Allows minimal disclosure in the

Quick Reference Chart to Contents of SEC Filings

REPORT CONTENTS	10-K	20-F	10-Q	8-K	10-C	6-K	Proxy Statements	Prospectus	'34 Act F-10 8-A 8-B	'33 Act "S" Type	ARS	Listing Application
Auditor												
☐ Name												
☐ Opinion												
☐ Changes												
Compensation Plans												
☐ Equity												
☐ Monetary												
Company Information												
☐ Nature of Business												
☐ History												
☐ Organization and Change												
Debt Structure												
Depreciation & Other Schedules												
Dilution Factors												
Directors, Officers, Insiders												
☐ Identification												
☐ Background												
☐ Holdings												
☐ Compensation												
Earnings Per Share												
Financial Information												
☐ Annual Audited												
☐ Interim Audited												
☐ Interim Unaudited												
Foreign Operations												
Labor Contracts												
Legal Agreements												
Legal Counsel												
Loan Agreements												
Plants and Properties												
Portfolio Operations												
☐ Content (Listing of Securities)												
☐ Management												
Product-Line Breakout												
Securities Structure												
Subsidiaries												
Underwriting												
Unregistered Securities												
Block Movements												

TENDER OFFER/ACQUISITION REPORTS	13D	13G	14D-1	14D-9	13E-3	13E-4
Name of Issuer (Subject Company)						
Filing Person (or Company)						
Amount of Shares Owned						
Percent of Class Outstanding						
Financial Statements of Bidder						
Purpose of Tender Offer						
Source and Amount of Funds						
Identity and Background Information						
Persons Retained, Employed or to be Compensated						
Exhibits						

■ *always included* ▨ *frequently included* ▒ *special circumstances*

prospectus and allows maximum incorporation by reference of 1934 Act reports.

S-4 Registration used in certain business combinations or registrations.

N-1A Filed by open-end management investment companies other than separate accounts of insurance companies.

N-2 Filed by closed-end investment companies.

N-5 Registration of small business investment companies.

S-6 Filed by unit investment trusts registered under the Investment Act of 1940 on Form N-8B-2.

S-8 Registration used to register securities to be offered to employees under stock option and various other benefit plans.

S-11 Filed by real estate companies, primarily limited partnerships and investment trusts.

S-18 Short form registration up to $7.5 million.

SE Non-electronically filed exhibits of registrants filing with the EDGAR PILOT PROJECT.

F-1 Registration of securities by foreign private issuers eligible to use form 20-F, for which no other form is prescribed.

F-2 Registration of securities of foreign private issuers meeting certain 1934 Act filing requirements.

F-3 Registration of securities of foreign issuers offered pursuant to certain types of transactions, subject to the 1934 Act filing requirements for the preceding three years.

F-6 Registration of depository shares evidenced by American Depository Receipts (ADRs)

"Trading" registrations are filed to permit trading among investors on a securities exchange or in the over-the-counter market. Registration statements which serve to register securities for trading fall into three categories:

(1) **Form 10** is used by companies during the first two years they are subject to the 1934 Act filing requirements. It is a combination registration statement and annual report with information content similar to that of SEC-required 10-Ks.

(2) **Form 8-A** is used by 1934 Act registrants wishing to register *additional* securities or classes thereof.

(3) **Form 8-B** is used by "successor issuers" (usually companies which have changed their name or state of incorporation) as notification that previously registered securities are to be traded under a new corporate identification.

Prospectus

When the sale of securities as proposed in an "offering" registration statement is approved by the SEC, any changes required by the SEC are incorporated into the prospectus. This document must be made available to investors before the sale of the security is initiated. It also contains the actual offering price, which may have been changed after the registration statement was approved.

Annual Report to Shareholders

The Annual Report is the principal document used by most major companies to communicate directly with shareholders. Since it is not a required, official SEC filing, companies have considerable discretion in determining what types of information this report will contain and how it is to be presented.

In addition to financial information, the Annual Report to Shareholders often provides non-financial details of the business which are not reported elsewhere. These may include marketing plans and forecasts of future programs and plans.

Form 8 (Amendment)

Form 8 is used to amend or supplement any 1934 Act report previously submitted. 1933 Act registration statements are amended by filing an amended registration statement (pre-effective amendment) or by the prospectus itself, as previously noted.

Listing Application

Like the ARS, a listing application is not an official SEC filing. It is filed by the company with the NYSE, AMEX or other stock exchange to document proposed new listings. Usually a Form 8-A registration is filed with the SEC at about the same time.

Tender Offers/Acquisition Reports

13-G

An annual report which must be filed by all reporting persons (primarily institutions) meeting the 5% equity ownership rule within 45 days after the end of each calendar year.

1. Name of issuer
2. Name of person filing
3. 13D-1 or 13D-2 applicability
4. Amount of shares beneficially owned:
   Percent of class outstanding
   Sole or shared power to vote
   Sole or shared power to dispose
5. Ownership of 5% or less of a class of stock
6. Ownership of more than 5% on behalf of another person
7. Identification of subsidiary which acquired the security being reported on by the parent holding company (if applicable)
8. Identification and classification of members of the group (if applicable)
9. Notice of dissolution of the group (if applicable)
10. Certification

13-D

Filing required by 5% (or more) equity owners within ten days of acquisition event.

1. Security and issuer
2. Identity and background of person filing the statement
3. Source and amount of funds or other consideration
4. Purpose of the transaction
5. Interest in securities of the issuer
6. Contracts, arrangements or relationships with respect to securities of the issuer
7. Material to be filed as exhibits which may include but are not limited to:
   a. Letter agreements between the parties
   b. Formal offer to purchase

14D-1

Tender offer filing made with the SEC at time offer is made to holders of equity securities of target company, if acceptance of offer would give the offerer over 5% ownership of the subject securities:

1. Security and subject company
2. Identity and background information
3. Past contacts, transactions or negotiations with subject company
4. Source and amount of funds or other consideration
5. Purpose of the tender offer and plans or proposals of the bidder
6. Interest in securities of the subject company
7. Contracts, arrangements or relationships

with respect to the subject company's securities
8. Persons retained, employed or to be compensated
9. Financial statements of certain bidders
10. Additional information
11. Material to be filed as exhibits which may include but are not limited to:
    a. The actual offer to purchase
    b. The letter to shareholders
    c. The letter of transmittal with notice of guaranteed delivery
    d. The press release
    e. The summary publication in business newspapers or magazines
    f. The summary advertisement to appear in business newspapers or magazines.

14D-9

A solicitation/recommendation statement that must be submitted to equity holders and filed at the SEC by the management of a firm subject to a tender offer within ten days of the making of the tender offer:

1. Security and subject company
2. Tender offer of the bidder
3. Identify and background
4. The solicitation or recommendation
5. Persons retained, employed or to be compensated
6. Recent transactions and intent with respect to securities
7. Certain negotiations and transactions by the subject company
8. Additional information
9. Material to be filed as exhibits

13E-4

Issuer tender offer statement pursuant to the Securities Exchange Act of 1934:

1. Security and issuer
2. Source and amount of funds
3. Purpose of the tender offer and plans or proposals of the issuer or affiliates
4. Interest in securities of the issuer
5. Contracts, arrangements or relationships with respect to the issuer's securities
6. Person retained, employed or to be compensated
7. Financial information
8. Additional information
9. Material to be filed as exhibits which may include but is not limited to the offer to purchase which is being sent to the shareholders to whom the tender offer is being made.

13E-3

Transaction statement pursuant to the Securities Exchange Act of 1934 with respect to a public company or affiliate going private

1. Issuer and class of security subject to the transaction
2. Identity and background of the individuals
3. Past contacts, transactions or negotiations
4. Terms of the transaction
5. Plans or proposals of the issuer or affiliate
6. Source and amount of funds or other considerations
7. Purpose, alternatives, reasons and effects
8. Fairness of the transaction
9. Reports, opinions, appraisals and certain negotiations
10. Interest in securities of the issuer
11. Contracts, arrangements or relationships with respect to the issuer's securities
12. Present intention and recommendation of certain persons with regard to the transaction
13. Other provisions of the transaction
14. Financial information
15. Persons and assets employed, retained or utilized
16. Additional information
17. Material to be filed as exhibits

How to Read the New York Stock Exchange and American Stock Exchange Quotations

(1)	(2)	(3)	(4)	(5)	(6)	(7)	(8)	(9)	(10)	(11)
52 Weeks				Yld	P-E	Sales				Net
High	Low	Stock	Div.	%	Ratio	100s	High	Low	Close	Chg.
					A	A	A			
14¾	9⅛	AAR	.44	4.3	7	26	10½	10¼	10¼	¼
52¼	32¼	ACF	2.76	6.0	10	51	46	45½	46	
27	12⅞	AMF	1.24	5.1	12	1453	24¼	23¾	24⅛ +	¼
24¾	10⅞	AM Intl				51	13⅞	13¾	13¾	
11⅜	6⅜	APL				51	6⅜ d	6¼	6¼	⅛

The composite quotations take into account prices paid for a stock on the New York or American Exchanges, plus those prices paid on regional exchanges, Over-the-Counter (OTC) and elsewhere, as shown in the example from the Wall Street Journal. The stock market quotations are explained below:

(1) The highest price per share paid in the past 52 weeks in terms of ⅛ of a dollar, i.e., 10⅛ means $10.125.
(2) The lowest price paid per share in the last 52 weeks.
(3) The name of the company in abbreviated form.
(4) The regular annual dividend paid. Special or extra dividends are specified by letters given in the footnotes in the Explanatory Notes shown below.
(5) The yield, that is, the annual dividend divided by the current price of the stock expressed in percent. For example, a stock that sells for $20.00 per share and pays a dividend of $2.00 per share has a yield of 10 percent (2/20).
(6) The P/E ratio is the current price of the stock divided by the company's last reported annual earnings per share. The P/E ratio is generally high for companies which are thought to have a relatively large and persistent earning's growth rate. The average P/E ratio for the Dow Jones stocks varied from 7.7 to 10.2 during the last five years.
(7) The number of shares sold on the day reported in 100s of shares.
(8) The highest price paid per share on the day reported.
(9) The lowest price paid per share on the day reported.
(10) The last price paid per share on the day reported.
(11) The change in the closing price from the previous day's closing price.

EXPLANATORY NOTES
(For New York and American Exchange listed issues)

Sales figures are unofficial.

The 52-Week High and Low columns show the highest and the lowest price of the stock in consolidated trading during the preceding 52 weeks plus the current week, but not the current trading day

u—Indicates a new 52-week high. d—Indicates a new 52-week low.

s—Split or stock dividend of 25 percent or more in the past 52 weeks. The high-low range is adjusted from the old stock. Dividend begins with the date of split or stock dividend.

n—New issue in the past 52 weeks. The high-low range begins with the start of trading in the new issue and does not cover the entire 52-week period.

g—Dividend or earnings in Canadian money. Stock trades in U.S. dollars. No yield or PE shown unless stated in U.S. money.

Unless otherwise noted, rates of dividends in the foregoing table are annual disbursements based on the last quarterly or semi-annual declaration. Special or extra dividends or payments not designated as regular are identified in the following footnotes.

a—Also extra or extras. b—Annual rate plus stock dividend. c—Liquidating dividend. e—Declared or paid in preceding 12 months. i—Declared or paid after stock dividend or split up. j—Paid this year, dividend omitted, deferred or no action taken at last dividend meeting, k—Declared or paid this year, an accumulative issue with dividends in arrears. r—Declared or paid in preceding 12 months plus stock dividend. t—Paid in stock in preceding 12 months, estimated cash value on ex-dividend or ex-distribution date.

x—Ex-dividend or ex-rights. v—Ex-dividend and sales in full. z—Sales in full.

wd—When distributed. wi—When issued. ww—With warrants. xw—Without warrants.

vi—In bankruptcy or receivership or being reorganized under the Bankruptcy Act, or securities assumed by such companies.

How to Read Over-the-Counter NASDAQ Listings

The over-the-counter quotations are explained below.

(1) The company's name, usually abbreviated.

(2) Annual regular dividend per share, unless accompanied by a notation which is explained in the OTC Explanatory Notes (below).

(3) Number of shares sold that day in hundreds, i.e., 2 means 200 shares.

(4) Bid price per share at closing time, i.e., the price at which broker-dealer will buy the stock from the investor. Prices do not include mark-up or commission.

(5) Ask price per share at closing time, i.e., the price at which the broker-dealer will sell the stock.*

(6) The change in the closing bid price from the previous day.

(1) (2)	(3)	(4)	(5)	(6)
	Sales			Net
Stock & Div.	100s	Bid	Asked	Chg.
CentVtPS 1.92	8	13⅝	13¾ +	⅛
Centrn CP 2.56	4	23¼	23½	...
Centura Enrg	135	10½	10¾ −	½
CenturyBK .48	573	13	13⅛ −	⅛
CenturyOil Gs	49	7⅜	7⅝	..
Cetus Corptn	231	17⅛	17⅜ +	⅛
CFS Cont .40	18	13⅝	13⅞ +	⅛
CGA Assc Inc	155	10½	11 −	¼
Chalco Ind Inc	2	6	6½ −	¼

* Bid and ask prices are usually quoted in ⅛ (12.5 cents) of a dollar, i.e., 12⅛ means $12.125, 12½ means $12.50, etc. Very inexpensive stocks are quoted at 1/16 (6.25 cents) and 1/32 (3.125 cents) of a dollar.

OTC EXPLANATORY NOTES

z—Sales in full.

a—Annual rate plus cash extra. b—Paid so far in 1981, no regular rate. c—Payment of accumulated dividends. d—Paid in 1980. e—Cash plus stock paid in 1980. f—Cash plus stock paid in 1981. g—Annual rate plus stock dividend. h—Paid in 1981, latest dividend omitted. i—Percent paid in stock in 1980. j—Percent in stock paid in 1981, latest dividend omitted. k—Percent in stock paid in 1981. n—Asked price not applicable. p—Granted temporary exception from Nasdaq qualifications. q—In bankruptcy proceedings. ut—Units. wt—Warrants. x—Ex-dividend, ex-rights or ex-distribution. (z) No representative quote.

The Ex-dividend Explained

The ex-dividend status of a stock is indicated by an x in the newspaper quotation or *xd* on the ticker tape. This is an abbreviation for *without dividend*.

A stock that is purchased during the ex-dividend period will not pay a previously declared dividend to its new owner. The ex-dividend period spans four business days before the so-called record date—the date a dividend issuing corporation uses to tally its shareowners. An ex-dividend stock buyer is not entitled to a dividend because his name is not recorded with the dividend issuing corporation until after the record date.

The New York Stock Exchange requires that the buyer in every transaction be recorded with the issuing corporation on the fifth business day following a trade. A stock buyer, therefore, must purchase his shares at least five business days before the record date in order for the corporation to record his name in time for him to receive his dividend. A purchase one day later disqualifies a buyer from a dividend because the transfer of ownership cannot be completed by the record date. Therefore, on the fourth business day prior to the record date, a stock is sold ex-dividend.

In our example below, the corporation's Board has decided to pay a 50‰ dividend to shareholders of record on Monday, the 10th. A person buying shares up to the close of business on Monday, the 3rd, would be eligible for the dividend because normal settlement (5 business days) will be made on Monday the 10th. On Tuesday, the 4th, however, the stock would begin selling ex-dividend because a stock purchaser as of that date could not settle till after the record date.

On the ex-dividend date, the Exchange specialist will reduce all open buy orders and open sell stop orders by the amount of the dividend. This is done to more equitably reflect the stock's value since purchasers of stock on or after the ex-dividend date are ineligible for a dividend.

EX-DIVIDEND EXPLANATION

Any Month	Date	Calendar Day	Status
	3	Monday	With/Dividend
	4	Tuesday	Ex-Dividend (Without Dividend)
	5	Wednesday	" "
	6	Thursday	" "
	7	Friday	" "
	8	Saturday	Not a trading day
	9	Sunday	Not a trading day
	10	Monday	Record Date/Business Day
	11	Tuesday	Business Day

Source: *Taking The Mystery Out of Ex-Dividend*, The New York Stock Exchange, Inc.

Margin Accounts Explained

Stocks may be purchased by paying the purchase price in full (plus commissions and taxes) or on a margin account. With the margin account, the investors put up part of the purchase price in cash or securities, and the broker lends the remainder. The margin investor must pay the usual commissions as well as interest on the broker's loan. The stocks purchased on margin are held by the broker as collateral on the loan. Dividends are applied to the margin account and help offset the interest payments.

Margin (M) is defined as the market value (V) of the securities less the broker's loan (L), divided by the market value of the securities. The ratio is expressed as a percentage:

$$M = \frac{V - L}{V} \times 100$$

Example: You buy 100 shares of a stock at $20 per share at a total cost (V) of $2,000. You put up $1,200 in cash and borrow (L) $800 from the broker. The margin at the time of purchase is

$$M = \frac{\$2,000 - \$800}{\$2,000} \times 100 = 60\%$$

The margin at the time of purchase is called *initial margin*. The smallest allowed value of initial margin (set by the Federal Reserve) is currently 50%. Thus, with the above stock, if you buy 100 shares at $20 per share on 50% initial margin, you put up $1,000 (.5 × $2,000), and the broker's loan is $1,000.

After the purchase there is a *maintenance margin* (set by the Exchange) below which the margin is not permitted to decrease. The maintenance margin on the New York Stock Exchange is 25%. Some brokers, however, require a higher maintenance margin of about 30%. Thus, if the 100 shares of stocks discussed above decrease in price from $20 to $13 per share, then the margin is

$$M = \left(\frac{\$1,300 - \$1,000}{\$1,300}\right) \times 100 = 23\%$$

The margin of 23% is now below the maintenance margin of 25% set by the Exchange.

The securities are said to be *under margined*, and a call for additional cash (or securities) is issued by the broker in order to bring up the margin to 25%. If the investor does not meet the call for additional cash (margin call) within a specified time, the stocks in the margin account are immediately sold

MARGIN REQUIREMENTS (percent of market value and effective date)

	Mar. 11, 1968	June 8, 1968	May 6, 1970	Dec. 6, 1971	Nov. 24, 1972	Jan. 3, 1974
Margin stocks	70	80	65	55	65	50
Convertible bonds	50	60	50	50	50	50
Short sales.............	70	80	65	55	65	50

Note: Regulations G, T, and U of the Federal Reserve Board of Governors, prescribed in accordance with the Securities Exchange Act of 1934, limit the amount of credit to purchase and carry margin stocks that may be extended on securities as collateral by prescribing a maximum loan value, which is a specified percentage of the market value of the collateral at the time the credit is extended. Margin requirements are the difference between the market value (100 percent) and the maximum loan value. The term "margin stocks" is defined in the corresponding regulation.

Source: *Federal Reserve Bulletin.*

Short Selling Explained

Short selling provides an opportunity to profit from a decline in the price of a stock. If you believe that a stock is due for a substantial decline, you arrange to have your broker borrow the stock from another investor who owns the shares. The borrowed stock is then sold. This cash is held as collateral against the borrowed shares. When (and if) the stock price declines, you purchase the stock at the market price and use it to replace the borrowed shares. The broker arranges the return of your cash collateral less the cost of the repurchased stock. Your profit per share is the price received on the sale of the stock less the purchase price.

There are certain cash outlays and costs associated with the short sale. Generally there is no charge for borrowing the stock, although occasionally stock lenders may charge a premium over the market price. You must deposit $2,000 or the required initial margin, whichever is the greater, at the time the stock is borrowed. Thus, if you borrow 100 shares of a stock priced at $50 per share and the margin required is 50%, you must put up $2,500 (.5 × $50 × 100) in cash or securities. The margin deposit is returned when you close out the short sale. You pay commission when the stock is sold and when it is repurchased. In addition, you must pay the stock lender any dividends which are declared during the period you are short the stock. It is well to remember that if cash is used for the deposit, there is a loss of the interest which you would have obtained if the cash had been invested.

The dividend payments and interest loss can be reduced or eliminated if you short stocks which pay little or no dividends and use interest-bearing securities (such as T-bills or negotiable certificates of deposit) as the margin deposit.

An increase in the price of the stock can result in substantial losses since you may be forced to repurchase at a higher price than you sold. If there are many short sellers seeking to purchase the stock in order to close out their position, prices may be driven to very high levels.

The short sale cannot be executed while the stock price is declining on the exchange. According to the rules of the SEC, the stock must undergo an increase in price prior to the execution of a short sale.

Mutual Fund Reporting Regulations

The new SEC regulations concerning mutual fund reporting practices which went into effect May 1988 require that an easy-to-read table giving all fund charges must appear near the front of all prospectuses. Included must be such items as front end and back end loads, 12b–1 plans to recover marketing and distribution costs, and sales loads imposed on reinvested dividends applied everytime the find reinvest dividends. Typically, fund expense ratios (annual operating expenses to assets) range from .7% to 1%.

Advertisements that contain yields must calculate yields (capital gains plus dividends) on a consistent basis prescribed by the SEC, taking into account any front end sales charges. To put the yield figure into perspective, ads must provide one, five and ten year total return information.

Fund fees are now shown in the newspaper listing by means of the following letters after the fund's name:

r   indicates a back end load or redemption fee

p   indicates a 12b–1 plan is in effect
t   indicates both a back end and a 12b–1 fee
N.L.   indicates there is no front end or back end load

How to Read Mutual Fund Quotations

The following is an example of typical fund quotations as reported in the Wall Street Journal. The mutual fund quotations are explained in the adjacent column.

(1)	(2)	(3)	(4)
	NAV	Offer Price	NAV Chg.
Able Assoc	24.33	N.L.+	.80
Acorn Fnd	28.28	N.L.+	.03
ADV Fund	15.38	N.L.+	.02
Afuture Fd	15.59	N.L.+	.10
AIM funds			
Conv Yld	15.42	16.49+	.09
Edsn Gld	14.59	15.60+	.09
HiYld Sc	8.98	9.60+	.02
Alpha Fnd	17.82	N.L.+	.01
Am Birthrt	12.29	13.43–	.03
American Funds Group			
Am Bal	8.73	9.54	...
Amcap F	6.21	6.79+	.01
Am Mutl	12.46	13.62–	.01

(1) Name of fund in abbreviated form.
(2) NAV means "net asset value" per share of the stock. It is the price at which the fund will buy shares from investors. The NAV is obtained from

$$NAV = \frac{M + C - L}{N}$$

M = market value of all stock in the fund's portfolio at the end of the trading day
C = fund's cash or cash equivalent position
L = fund's liabilities
N = number of shares issued by fund

(3) Offer price is the price per share at which the fund will sell shares to investors. With no load (NL, no sales charge) funds, the offer price and the NAV are the same. With load funds, a sales charge (load) is added to the NAV to arrive at the sales price.
(4) The NAV change is the change in net asset value (at the close of the stock market) from that of the previous day.

Top 50 Performing Mutual Funds for 5 Years

What $10,000 Grew To In 5 Years (1985–1989)**

1	+	Fidelity Overseas Fund	$45,312
2		ML Pacific Fund	42,816
3	*	Trustees' Commingled Fund—Intl	39,218
4	*	Kleinwort Benson Intl Equity Fund	38,239
5		Alliance International Fund	37,958
6	*	T Rowe Price International Stock	36,897
7	*	Twentieth Century Giftrust Investors	36,077
8		GT Pacific Growth Fund	35,840
9	*	Financial Strategic—Pacific Basin	35,517
10		PaineWebber Classic Atlas	35,318
11		Oppenheimer Global Fund	35,036
12		FT International Trust	34,964
13	*	Scudder International Fund	34,194
14	*	Financial Strategic—Health Sciences	33,713
15		Kemper International Fund	33,348
16		First Investors Global Fund	33,221
17		Putnam Intl Equities Fund	33,089
18		Oppenheimer Gold & Spec Minerals	32,700
19		Templeton Foreign Fund	32,458
20	+	Fidelity Select Leisure	31,643
21	+	Fidelity OTC Portfolio	30,574
22		EuroPacific Growth Fund	30,543
23	+	Vanguard Spec Port—Health Care	30,063
24		IDS International Fund	30,000
25	+	Fidelity Select Health Care	29,965
26		American Telecomm Tr Income	29,954
27	+	Fidelity Magellan Fund	29,552
28		Flag Investors Telephone Inc	29,149
29	*	IAI Regional Fund	28,373
30		AIM Weingarten Fund	28,285
31	*	Financial Strategic—Leisure	28,123
32	+	Keystone International Fund	27,552
33		Putnam Voyager Fund	27,522
34	+	Special Situations—Plymouth Class	27,470
35	*	Scudder Capital Growth Fund	27,452
36		Prudential-Bache Global Fund	27,450
37		AIM Constellation Fund	27,279
38		Putnam Health Sciences Trust	27,180
39		Prudential-Bache Utility Fund	27,145
40		New York Venture Fund	27,011
41	*	Federated Growth Trust	26,932
42		New Perspective Fund Inc	26,867
43		United Income Fund	26,819
44		IDS New Dimensions Fund	26,601
45	*	Twentieth Century Growth Investors	26,484
46		Putnam OTC Emerging Growth Fund	26,477
47		United Intl Growth Fund	26,403
48	*	Dodge & Cox Stock Fund	26,365
49	*	One Hundred Fund	26,340
50	+	Hartwell Growth Fund	26,207

Top 50 Performing Mutual Funds for 10 Years

What $10,000 Grew To In 10 Years (1980–1989)**

1	+	Fidelity Magellan Fund	$122,408
2		ML Pacific Fund	104,089
3	*	Loomis Sayles Cap Development (c)	72,422
4	+	Lindner Fund	69,219
5		New England Growth Fund	67,075
6	*	Janus Fund	65,822
7	*	Phoenix Stock Fund Series	65,555
8	+	Lindner Dividend Fund Inc	65,463
9		AIM Weingarten Fund	64,596
10	*	Twentieth Century Select Investors	64,235
11		GT Pacific Growth Fund	64,035
12		Phoenix Growth Fund Series	63,575
13		New York Venture Fund	63,547
14		IDS New Dimensions Fund	63,540
15	*	Windsor Fund (c)	62,481
16		AMEV Growth Fund	62,471
17	*	SteinRoe Special Fund	62,307
18	*	Fidelity Destiny Port I	62,047
19		United Vanguard Fund	61,562
20	*	Vanguard H-Y Stock Fund (c)	61,511
21		Washington Mutual Investors Fund Inc	61,058
22		AMEV Capital Fund	60,499
23	+	SoGen International Fund	60,263
24	*	Sequoia Fund (c)	59,946
25		American Capital Pace Fund	59,755
26		United Intl Growth Fund	59,323
27		United Income Fund	58,599
28		Putnam Intl Equities Fund	58,464
29	+	Fidelity Equity-Income Fund	58,295
30		Alliance Quasar Fund	58,070
31	*	Nicholas Fund	57,528
32		IDS Growth Fund	57,274
33	*	Tudor Fund	56,902
34	*	Ivy Growth Fund	56,816
35	*	AMEV Special Portfolios—Stock	56,697
36		Guardian Park Avenue Fund	56,576
37		Oppenheimer Global Fund	56,160
38	*	Mutual Shares Fund (c)	55,724
39	*	Scudder International Fund	55,692
40	*	Lehman Opportunity Fund	55,527
41	*	Dodge & Cox Stock Fund	55,512
42	*	Neuberger & Berman Manhattan Fund	54,459
43	*	Endowments	54,425
44		United Accumulative Fund	54,373
45		SLH Appreciation Fund	54,331
46	*	Scudder Capital Growth Fund	54,090
47	*	Elfun Trusts	53,458
48		Lehman Capital Fund	53,395
49		Putnam Voyager Fund	53,352
50		Delaware Group Trend Fund	53,134

*   No-load fund, + Low-load fund, (No symbol) Load fund, (c) Fund closed to new investment.
** Does not take into account sales commissions or income taxes that would have to be paid. Includes reinvestment of all dividends and capital gains.

Source: *Donoghue's Mutual Funds Almanac*, 21st edition.

PERFORMANCE OF MUTUAL FUNDS

BARRON'S / LIPPER GAUGE*

Debt and Equity Funds

FUND NAME	OBJECTIVE	TOTAL NET ASSETS (MIL) 6/30/90	NET ASSET VALUE 6/30/90	PERFORMANCE (Return on Initial $10,000 Investment)			DIVIDEND YIELD % 6/30	FEES			PHONE NUMBER		MANAGER	SINCE
				3/31/90-6/30/90	6/30/89-6/30/90	6/30/85-6/30/90		Load	12b-1	Redemption	800	In-State		
AAL FUNDS: CAPITAL GROWTH	Growth	$142.8	$11.66	$10,746.50	$11,694.40	☆	2.1	4.75	0.25	None	553-6319	414-734-7633	Duff & Phelps Group.	'87
AAL FUNDS: INCOME	Fixed Income	103.1	9.51	10,309.00	10,704.80	☆	8.3	4.75	0.25	None	553-6319	414-734-7633	Duff & Phelps Group	'87
AARP GRO TR: CAP GROWTH★	Growth	218.8	29.62	10,418.60	10,147.00	20,628.30	0.6	None	None	None	253-2277	617-482-6169	Steve Aronoff	'89
AARP GRO TR: GROWTH & INC★	Growth & Income	269.3	24.97	10,539.70	10,700.90	18,978.70	4.3	None	None	None	253-2277	617-482-6169	Robert Harvey	'85
AARP INC TR: GNMA & TREAS★	Fixed Income	2,552.6	15.03	10,324.70	10,826.40	15,266.90	8.8	None	None	None	253-2277	617-482-6169	David Glen	'85
AARP INC TR: HI QUAL BOND★	Fixed Income	146.3	14.92	10,322.70	10,628.00	15,119.20	7.9	None	None	None	253-2277	617-482-6169	Samuel Thorne Jr.	'85
ABT GROWTH & INCOME TR	Growth & Income	96.5	9.64	10,167.00	10,552.00	18,952.00	4.1	4.75	0.25	None	441-6580	215-834-3500	Godfrey Birckhead	'84
ABT INV: EMERGING GROWTH	Capital Appreciation	19.5	9.47	10,986.10	11,764.20	17,464.10	0.0	4.75	0.25	None	441-6580	215-834-3500	Harold Ireland	'83
ABT INV: SECURITY INCOME	Balanced	5.3	9.65	10,010.50	9,578.50	12,910.50	5.9	4.75	0.25	None	441-6580	215-834-3500	Timothy O'Neil	'89
ABT INV: US GOVT SEC	Fixed Income	0.9	11.97	10,359.40	10,690.80	☆	9.1	4.75	None	None	441-6580	215-834-3500	Steven Eldredge	'89
ABT UTILITY INCOME FD	Utility	144.0	12.49	10,072.10	11,166.80	17,604.00	6.1	4.75	0.25	None	441-6580	215-834-3500	Phil Cantone	'81
ACORN FUND★	Small-Company Growth	952.8	44.27	10,555.60	11,185.00	21,444.50	1.3	None	None	2.00	922-6769	312-621-0630	Ralph Wanger	'70
ADAM INVESTORS	Capital Appreciation	4.3	14.63	10,749.40	11,753.50	18,222.60	2.7	None	None	None	None	415-461-3850	Gary Kirk	'84
ADDISON CAPITAL	Growth & Income	29.0	18.17	10,502.90	11,169.70	☆	1.1	3.00	0.65	None	526-6397	215-665-6000	Jay Massey	'86
ADTEK FUND	Capital Appreciation	9.1	9.74	10,518.40	10,236.50	12,536.90	3.7	None	None	None	None	414-257-1842	Nick Carver	'88
ADVANCE AMER: EQUITY INC	Equity Income	11.0	10.25	10,228.10	10,249.90	☆	2.5	4.75	0.22	None	634-7966	None	Art Steinmetz	'89
ADVANCE AMER: HIGH YIELD	Fixed Income	5.1	8.79	10,323.10	10,615.20	☆	12.2	4.75	0.22	None	634-7966	None	Art Steinmetz	'89
ADVANCE AMER: US GOVT	Fixed Income	21.9	9.19	10,248.30	10,533.00	☆	8.9	4.75	0.22	None	634-7966	None	Art Steinmetz	'89
ADVANCE CAP: BALANCED	Balanced	13.9	10.29	10,613.70	11,209.70	☆	4.4	None	0.0045	None	None	313-350-8543	John Shoemaker	'87
ADVANCE CAP: BOND	Fixed Income	1.3	9.75	10,297.20	10,678.40	☆	8.0	None	0.0045	None	None	313-350-8543	John Shoemaker	'87
ADVANCE CAP: EQ UNIVERSE	Growth & Income	4.5	10.17	10,815.60	11,527.50	☆	1.9	None	0.0045	None	None	313-350-8543	John Shoemaker	'87
ADVANTAGE: GOVT SEC	Fixed Income	113.0	8.32	10,295.60	10,706.70	☆	8.4	None	0.65	4.00	243-8115	205-525-1421	Margaret Patel	'88
ADVANTAGE: GROWTH	Growth	29.8	14.17	10,509.90	11,343.50	☆	1.2	None	0.95	4.00	243-8115	205-525-1421	Robert Thomas	'88
ADVANTAGE: HIGH YIELD	Fixed Income	13.7	7.82	10,305.70	8,964.20	☆	13.8	None	0.95	4.00	243-8115	205-525-1421	Margaret Patel	'89
ADVANTAGE: INCOME	Mixed Income	51.6	10.45	10,428.60	10,734.10	☆	6.3	None	0.95	4.00	243-8115	205-525-1421	Susann Stauffer	'86
ADVANTAGE: SPECIAL	Capital Appreciation	4.4	13.10	11,322.40	11,855.20	☆	0.0	None	0.95	4.00	243-8115	205-525-1421	Robert Thomas	'88
AFA: NATL AVIATION & TECH	Technology	83.9	11.97	10,442.20	11,261.60	18,367.00	1.3	4.75	None	None	644-0001	212-482-8100	Barry Gordon	'83
AFA: NATL TELECOM & TECH	Technology	39.2	17.73	10,745.50	11,121.90	15,864.80	0.3	4.75	None	None	644-0001	212-482-8100	Barry Gordon	'83
AFFILIATED FUND	Growth & Income	3,469.1	10.32	10,164.50	11,131.90	19,519.40	4.3	7.25	None	None	426-1130	212-848-1800	Jack McCarthy	'72
AFUTURE FUND	Growth	7.3	10.35	10,402.00	10,092.00	10,390.50	0.9	None	None	None	523-7594	None	Donald Goebert	'88
AGE HIGH INCOME	Fixed Income	1,715.4	2.56	10,514.60	9,307.20	13,436.70	16.4	4.00	None	None	342-5236	415-378-2200	Martin Wiskeman	'72
AIM CONVERTIBLE SEC	Convertibles	12.4	10.86	10,967.60	11,604.60	13,260.10	3.2	4.75	0.25	None	347-1919	713-626-1919	J Schodar/L. Sachnowitz	'89
AIM EQUITY: CHARTER FD	Growth & Income	90.1	7.04	11,104.10	12,388.70	21,997.70	3.5	5.50	0.30	None	347-1919	713-626-1919	Julian Lerner	'79
AIM EQUITY: CONSTELLATION	Capital Appreciation	128.9	9.26	11,156.60	13,376.80	26,471.20	0.1	5.50	0.30	None	347-1919	713-626-1919	H. Hutzler/J. Schodar	'76
AIM EQUITY: WEINGARTEN EQ	Growth	684.3	13.27	11,410.10	13,077.50	25,039.40	0.5	5.50	0.30	None	347-1919	713-626-1919	H. Hutzler/J. Schodar	'69

Fund	Objective	Net Assets ($mil)	NAV	Value A	Value B	Value C	%	Phone	Phone (long dist.)	Max Load	12b-1	Manager	Since
AIM GOV FDS: US GOV SEC★	Fixed Income	2.4	9.48	10,374.30	10,467.10	☆	8.4	347-1919	713-626-1919	4.75	0.25	Gary Beauchamp	'88
AIM HIGH YIELD SEC	Fixed Income	46.2	6.44	10,625.00	9,211.40	12,440.70	15.4	347-1919	713-626-1919	4.75	0.15	Gary Crum/Poly Ahrendts	'78
AIM LIMITED MAT TREAS	Fixed Income	74.6	9.78	10,262.10	10,790.50	☆	8.1	347-1919	713-626-1919	1.75	None	G. Crum/G. Beauchamp	'88
AIM SUMMIT FUND	Growth	305.5	8.30	10,935.40	11,979.70	19,319.90	1.9	347-1919	201-547-3600	8.5	None	Julian Lerner	'88
ALGER: GROWTH	Growth	6.9	15.61	11,719.20	13,008.30	☆	0.0	992-3863	201-547-3600	None	1.00	David Alger	'86
ALGER: INCOME & GROWTH	Growth & Income	2.7	12.78	10,526.30	11,717.60	☆	3.2	992-3863	201-547-3600	None	1.00	David Alger	'86
ALGER: SMALL CAPITAL	Small-Company Growth	30.7	16.96	11,291.60	13,486.20	☆	0.0	992-3863	319-366-8400	None	None	John Chapman	'86
ALLEGRO GROWTH	Growth	3.4	12.63	10,136.40	10,573.70	☆	0.0	227-4618	None	5.50	0.30	J. Andrew Richey	'86
ALLIANCE BALANCED SHARES	Balanced	158.1	11.45	10,272.00	9,828.50	17,676.50	3.3	227-4618	None	5.50	0.30	Aiden Hatton Jr.	'85
ALLIANCE BOND: HIGH YLD	Fixed Income	128.1	5.29	10,249.00	7,618.80	10,540.10	17.6	227-4618	None	5.50	0.30		
ALLIANCE BOND: MTY INCO	Fixed Income	68.1	11.39	10,306.20	10,326.30	15,696.30	10.0	227-4618	None	5.50	0.30	Wayne Lyski	'86
ALLIANCE BOND: US GOVT	Fixed Income	509.0	8.14	10,304.00	10,598.80	☆	10.2	227-4618	None	5.50	0.30	Wayne Lyski	'85
ALLIANCE CONVERTIBLE	Convertibles	61.1	9.10	10,127.70	10,161.50	20,414.10	5.2	227-4618	None	5.50	0.30	Arthur Berry	'86
ALLIANCE COUNTERPOINT	Growth & Income	57.4	17.09	10,489.30	10,150.20	20,502.60	1.1	227-4618	None	5.50	0.30	David Handke Jr.	'85
ALLIANCE FUND	Growth	723.8	6.10	10,640.90	11,220.50	☆	1.8	227-4618	None	5.50	0.30	Paul Jenkel	'85
ALLIANCE GLOBAL: CANADIAN	International	25.9	6.53	9,804.80	9,397.20	16,654.60	0.0	227-4618	None	5.50	0.30	Glenn Wellman	'86
ALLIANCE GROWTH & INCOME	Growth & Income	369.1	2.66	10,550.40	11,281.40	20,895.00	3.3	227-4618	None	5.50	0.30	Bruce Calvert	'86
ALLIANCE INTERNATIONAL	International	262.5	17.99	10,526.60	11,698.00	33,599.20	0.2	227-4618	None	5.50	0.30	Glenn Wellman	'81
ALLIANCE MORTGAGE INC	Fixed Income	509.8	8.58	10,342.90	10,812.30	15,301.50	10.6	227-4618	None	5.50	0.30	Paul Zoschke	'84
ALLIANCE QUASAR FD	Small-Company Growth	342.9	21.18	10,521.60	10,251.50	20,473.10	0.0	227-4618	None	5.50	0.30	Frank Burr/Paul Jenkel	'72
ALLIANCE SH-TM MULTI-MKT A	Fixed Income	948.8	9.89	10,361.40	11,508.00	☆	11.0	227-4618	None	3.00	0.30	Robert Sinche	'89
ALLIANCE TECHNOLOGY	Technology	166.2	24.48	11,402.00	12,517.90	20,651.90	0.0	227-4618	None	5.50	0.30	N/A	N/A
ALTURA: GOVT INTMDT BOND	Fixed Income	28.8	9.91	10,360.20	☆	☆	0.0	225-9961	None	None	None	United Bank of Denver	'89
ALTURA: GROWTH PORTFOLIO	Growth & Income	51.4	12.66	10,517.80	11,560.80	☆	3.2	225-9961	None	None	None	United Bank of Denver	'87
ALTURA: INCCME PORTFOLIO	Fixed Income	38.5	9.99	10,287.60	10,867.10	☆	8.9	225-9961	None	None	None	United Bank of Denver	'87
AMA: CLASSIC GROWTH	Growth	28.2	8.84	9,987.90	10,651.80	15,249.30	3.0	523-0084	None	None	0.50	Sec. Coun. Ia/Mackenzie	'87
AMA: GLOBAL GROWTH	Global	108.5	23.16	10,705.30	11,424.10	☆	4.0	523-0084	None	None	0.50	Opp. Cap./Templeton	'87
AMA: GLOBAL INCOME	World Fixed-income	16.7	19.44	10,268.40	10,523.40	☆	6.4	523-0084	None	None	0.50	Patterson/GT Cap.	'87
AMA: GLOBAL SHORT TERM	World Fixed-income	16.9	9.83	10,257.30	10,838.70	☆	7.7	523-0084	None	None	0.50	GT Capital	'89
AMA: GROWTH & INCOME	Growth & Income	9.0	21.16	10,328.30	10,671.50	☆	2.4	523-0084	None	None	0.50	Opp. Cap./Mackenzie	'87
AMA: US GOV' INCOME PLUS	Fixed Income	39.3	8.42	10,217.00	10,706.30	14,538.40	8.5	523-0084	206-734-9900	None	0.50	Oppenheimer Cap.	'87
AMANA: INCOME	Equity Income	4.9	11.80	10,396.60	10,967.00	☆	4.0	728-8762	213-486-9200	None	None	Nicholas Kaiser	'86
AMCAP FUND	Growth	2,162.8	10.66	10,845.60	11,486.60	21,087.50	2.3	421-0180	421-0180	5.75	0.25	Multiple Managers	'67
AMER ADVANTAGE: BALANCED★	Balanced	249.1	11.16	10,319.50	10,694.20	☆	5.7	None	817-967-3509	None	None	AMR Inv. Srv.	'87
AMER ADVANTAGE: EQUITY★	Growth & Income	214.7		10,342.90	10,722.20	☆	4.3	None	817-967-3509	None	None	AMR Inv. Srv.	'87
AMER AADVANTAGE: FIX INC★	Fixed Income	70.8	9.76	10,274.00	10,681.70	☆	9.7	None	817-967-3509	None	None	AMR Inv. Srv.	'87
AMERICAN ASSET YIELD	Equity Income	0.0	0.00	N/A	N/A	☆	N/A	None	801-328-3333	8.5	0.25	K. Eugene Harkins	'87
AMERICAN BALANCED FUND	Balanced	309.9	11.08	10,247.20	10,803.70	18,804.50	5.9	421-0180	213-486-9200	5.75	None	Multiple Managers	'75
AMER CAPITA.: COMSTOCK	Growth	951.6	15.87	10,755.70	11,602.10	18,536.40	3.4	421-5666	None	8.50	None	David Reichelt	'89
AMER CAPITA.: CORP BOND	Fixed Income	203.2	6.41	10,302.00	11,602.60	15,596.20	10.2	421-5666	None	4.75	0.25	Dave Troth	'79
AMER CAPITA.: ENTERPRISE	Growth	601.8	11.85	10,778.80	11,649.00	18,843.10	3.2	421-5666	None	5.75	0.25	Stephen Boyd	'89
AMER CAPITA.: EQUITY INCOME	Equity Income	95.6	4.44	10,470.00	11,233.50	17,963.90	6.0	421-5666	None	5.75	0.25	Jim Gilligan	'90
AMER CAPITA.: FED MORT	Fixed Income	33.0	12.58	10,307.70	11,709.40	☆	9.2	421-5666	None	4.75	0.25	Ladell Graham	'88
AMER CAPITA.: GOVT	Fixed Income	4,108.2	10.00	10,356.10	10,709.40	14,662.40	9.9	421-5666	None	4.75	0.25	Jack Reynoldson	'88
AMER CAPITA.: HARBOR	Convertibles	377.0	13.93	10,434.00	10,819.60	17,113.20	6.0	421-5666	None	5.75	0.25	Jim Behrmann	'84

★AARP FUNDS—Available only to AARP members.

★ACORN FUND—Closed to new investors.

★AIM GOV: US GOV SEC—Closed to new investors.

★AMERICAN AADVANTAGE FUNDS—Open for AMR Corp. pension investments and institutions.

* For explanations and definitions of terms see pages 403-404.

Source: Lipper Analytical Services, Inc. Reprinted by permission of Barron's National Business and Financial Weekly, © Dow Jones & Company, Inc., August 13, 1990.

PERFORMANCE OF MUTUAL FUNDS (continued)

| FUND NAME | OBJECTIVE | TOTAL NET ASSETS (MIL) 6/30/90 | NET ASSET VALUE 6/30/90 | PERFORMANCE (Return on Initial $10,000 Investment) | | | DIVIDEND YIELD % 6/90 | PHONE NUMBER | | FEES | | | MANAGER | SINCE |
				3/31/90- 6/30/90	6/30/89- 6/30/90	6/30/85- 6/30/90		800	In-State	Load	12b-1	Redemption		
AMER CAPITAL HIGH YIELD	Fixed Income	373.8	6.13	10,498.70	8,504.10	11,930.70	16.2	421-5666	None	4.75	0.25	None	Ellis Bigelow	'89
AMER CAPITAL PACE	Growth	2,457.2	12.69	10,650.40	11,368.90	18,403.30	2.8	421-5666	None	5.75	0.25	None	Peter Hidalgo	'88
AMER CAPITAL VENTURE	Capital Appreciation	242.2	16.57	11,128.30	12,489.50	15,946.90	1.5	421-5666	None	5.75	0.25	None	Gary Lewis	'89
AMER GAS INDEX FUND	Natural Resources	91.2	11.08	10,057.40	11,075.70	☆	4.5	343-3355	301-657-1500	None	None	None	Dan Ryczek	'89
AMERICAN GROWTH	Growth	58.6	7.52	10,189.70	11,239.40	14,499.50	4.0	421-9900	714-671-7000	5.75	0.25	None	William Newton	'74
AMERICAN HERITAGE	Capital Appreciation	1.3	1.04	10,196.10	9,285.70	5,581.30	0.0	None	212-474-7308	None	None	None	Heiko Thieme	'90
AMERICAN HIGH-INCOME TR	Fixed Income	144.0	13.08	10,602.80	10,322.80	☆	12.1	421-0180	213-486-9200	4.75	0.25	None	Multiple Managers	'88
AMERICAN INV GROWTH	Growth	73.4	7.86	10,650.40	11,543.60	17,433.40	0.4	243-5353	203-531-5000	8.50	None	None	Warren Greene	'84
AMERICAN INV INCOME	Fixed Income	10.5	5.54	10,035.00	9,105.90	11,208.40	11.6	243-5353	203-531-5000	5.00	None	None	Warren Greene	'75
AMERICAN LEADERS	Growth & Income	149.8	12.29	10,386.50	10,701.30	17,072.40	4.1	356-2805	None	4.50	0.25	None	Peter Anderson	'89
AMERICAN MUTUAL	Growth & Income	3,491.8	20.14	10,223.60	11,093.20	19,801.40	4.8	421-0180	213-486-9200	5.75	0.25	None	Multiple Managers	'50
AMERICAN NATIONAL GROWTH	Growth	106.8	4.33	10,762.70	11,211.90	19,211.50	2.5	231-4639	None	8.50	None	None	Ben Hock	'87
AMERICAN NATIONAL INCOME	Equity Income	73.6	19.62	10,270.00	11,282.70	17,374.80	4.0	231-4639	None	8.50	None	None	James McGlynn	'87
AMERITRUST BALANCED	Balanced	11.0	13.08	10,283.00	10,964.00	☆	0.0	433-7911	800-433-7912	None	None	None	Mike Cobb	'87
AMERITRUST US GOVT	Fixed Income	7.9	12.83	10,313.50	10,682.80	☆	0.0	433-7911	800-433-7912	None	None	None	Paul Lehman	'87
AMEV ADVNTGE: ASSET ALLOC	Flexible	24.1	11.84	10,668.30	11,176.10	☆	5.1	872-2638	612-738-4000	4.50	0.45	None	Stephen Poling	'83
AMEV ADVNTGE: CAP APP	Small-Company Growth	22.5	17.92	11,561.30	13,543.30	☆	0.1	872-2638	612-738-4000	4.50	0.45	None	Stephen Poling	'83
AMEV ADVNTGE: HIGH YLD	Fixed Income	22.1	7.15	10,414.00	8,693.10	☆	16.5	872-2638	612-738-4000	4.50	0.35	None	Dennis Ott	'85
AMEV CAPITAL FD	Growth & Income	158.7	15.93	11,019.80	11,846.40	21,084.40	1.6	872-2638	612-738-4000	8.50	None	None	Stephen Poling	'83
AMEV FIDUCIARY FD	Growth	35.0	26.54	11,104.60	11,928.80	21,802.50	0.6	872-2638	612-738-4000	4.50	0.30	None	Stephen Poling	'83
AMEV GROWTH FD	Capital Appreciation	256.1	21.68	11,061.20	12,336.50	22,076.00	0.2	872-2638	612-738-4000	8.50	None	None	Stephen Poling	'83
AMEV SPECIAL: STOCK	Capital Appreciation	38.6	26.71	11,023.50	12,411.20	21,519.90	0.1	872-2638	612-738-4000	None	None	None	Stephen Poling	'83
AMEV US GOVT FD	Fixed Income	155.0	9.56	10,329.30	10,788.70	16,046.50	9.6	872-2638	612-738-4000	4.50	None	None	Dennis Ott	'85
AMEX: CORPORATE BOND FD	Capital Appreciation	1.4	11.25	10,296.10	10,238.80	☆	8.2	872-1166	None	2.00	None	None	Ray Goodner	'88
AMEX: EQUITY GROWTH FD	Capital Appreciation	3.2	17.28	11,222.90	12,250.50	☆	1.8	872-1166	None	2.00	None	None	Arch Spencer	'88
AMEX: EQUITY VALUE FD	Equity Income	2.1	12.38	10,087.80	10,341.70	☆	3.2	872-1166	None	2.00	None	None	Tom Metcalf	'88
AMEX: INTMDT TERM BOND	Fixed Income	1.6	11.74	10,273.50	10,707.60	☆	7.9	872-1166	None	2.00	None	None	Lorraine Hart	'88
AMEX: INTL EQUITY FUND	International	1.7	15.09	10,778.60	13,461.20	☆	0.0	872-1166	None	2.00	None	None	Jim McAlear	'88
AMEX: US GOVT INCOME FD	Fixed Income	1.6	11.81	10,233.80	10,464.30	☆	7.8	872-1166	None	2.00	None	None	Bill Westhoff	'88
ANALYTIC OPTIONED EQU	Option Income	108.4	13.12	10,312.40	11,076.50	17,183.50	6.8	None	714-833-0294	None	None	None	Chuck Dobson	'78
API TRUST: BALANCED FD	Balanced	3.8	21.06	10,223.30	10,208.90	☆	1.8	868-6060	None	None	1.00	None	David Basten	'88
API TRUST: GROWTH FD	Capital Appreciation	31.0	10.49	10,038.30	10,375.80	17,367.80	0.8	868-6060	None	None	1.00	None	David Basten	'85
API TRUST: PREC RESOURCES	Natural Resources	2.1	7.06	9,778.40	10,663.60	☆	1.2	868-6060	None	None	1.00	None	David Basten	'88
ARCH FD: CAP APPREC	Growth & Income	21.6	12.35	10,882.80	11,612.30	☆	3.4	441-7379	314-425-3882	2.50	None	None	John Blixen	'88
ARCH FD: DVRSD FXD INCO	Fixed Income	10.9	9.74	10,319.30	10,530.70	☆	9.0	441-7379	314-425-3882	2.50	None	None	Dave Bethke	'88
ARCH FD: SHORT GOVT	Fixed Income	6.0	9.97	10,235.80	10,768.80	☆	8.1	441-7379	314-425-3882	2.50	None	None	Dave Bethke	'88
ARMSTRONG ASSOCIATES	Growth	9.8	7.38	10,379.70	10,592.80	15,625.20	3.1	None	214-720-9101	None	None	None	C.K. Lawson	'68
ASO OUTLOOK: BOND FD	Fixed Income	16.4	10.32	10,327.20	10,594.60	☆	7.3	451-8379	None	None	None	None	AmSouth Bank	'88
ASO OUTLOOK: EQUITY FD	Capital Appreciation	14.5	12.18	10,401.70	11,087.00	☆	2.8	451-8379	None	None	None	None	AmSouth Bank	'88
ASO OUTLOOK: LTD MATURITY	Fixed Income	6.0	10.23	10,242.40	10,759.50	☆	7.3	451-8379	None	None	None	None	AmSouth Bank	'88
ASO OUTLOOK: REGIONAL EQU	Capital Appreciation	3.2	12.65	10,678.80	11,714.00	☆	2.1	451-8379	None	None	None	None	AmSouth Bank	'88
ASSOC ADVISERS: BALANCED★	Balanced	2.9	10.41	10,579.30	10,351.80	☆	6.5	638-6441	None	None	None	None	Charles Cain	'88
ASSOC ADVISERS: GROWTH★	Growth	3.1	10.41	10,720.90	10,613.90	☆	0.0	638-6441	None	None	None	None	Charles Cain	'89
ASSOC PLANNERS: INCOME	Equity Income	2.3	10.23	10,339.50	☆	☆	0.0	None	213-553-6740	4.75	None	None	Julian Lerner	'90
ASSOC PLANNERS: INV QUAL BD	Fixed Income	6.4	8.82	10,244.10	10,560.40	☆	7.6	None	213-553-6740	4.75	None	None	Beauchamp/Ahrendts	'88/'90

Fund	Objective							Phone	Phone				Manager	Yr
ASSOC PLANNERS: STOCK	Capital Appreciation	20.1	17.53	10,922.10	12,132.50	22,909.40	1.5	None	213-553-6740	4.75	None	None	Julian Lerner	85
ATLAS: GOV'T &MTGE SEC★	Fixed Income	2.8	9.86	10,346.90	☆	☆	0.0	933-2852	None	3.00	0.25	None	David Welch	90
AVONDALE INV GOV'T SEC	Fixed Income	12.0	9.81	10,313.70	10,645.10	☆	7.7	None	817-761-3777	4.00	None	None	Herbert R. Smith Inc.	86
AVONDALE INV TOT RETURN	Balanced	2.9	21.42	10,394.90	10,810.10	☆	3.6	None	817-761-3777	4.50	0.45	None	Herbert R. Smith Inc.	88
AXE-HOUGHTON FUND B	Balanced	161.2	8.94	10,280.00	10,975.30	18,101.20	6.7	366-0444	914-333-5200	None	0.45	None	Porter Sutro	87
AXE-HOUGHTON INCOME	Fixed Income	63.8	4.99	10,224.40	10,504.10	16,339.50	8.8	366-0444	914-333-5200	None	0.45	None	Robert Manning	87
AXE-HOUGHTON STOCK	Growth	70.3	6.93	10,879.10	11,901.90	15,928.80	0.7	366-0444	914-333-5200	None	0.45	None	John Schroder	84
BABSON BOND PORTFOLIO L	Fixed Income	84.2	1.53	10,290.10	10,642.70	15,834.00	8.9	422-2766	816-471-5200	None	None	None	Ted Martin	84
BABSON BOND PORTFOLIO S	Fixed Income	6.4	9.86	10,292.50	10,691.20	☆	8.4	422-2766	816-471-5200	None	None	None	Ted Martin	88
BABSON ENTERPRISE	Small-Company Growth	96.3	13.43	10,475.80	10,874.60	17,306.60	1.4	422-2766	816-471-5200	None	None	None	Peter Schliemann	85
DAVID L BABSON GROWTH	Growth	259.0	11.18	10,316.50	10,626.60	19,730.10	2.3	422-2766	816-471-5200	None	None	None	David Kirk	85
BABSON-STEWART IVORY	International	10.8	13.18	11,004.50	12,340.60	☆	0.3	422-2766	816-471-5200	None	None	None	Martin Begien	88
BABSON VALUE	Growth & Income	24.8	18.74	10,302.40	10,457.80	19,247.10	2.7	422-2766	816-471-5200	None	None	None	Nick Whitridge	84
BAILARD, BIEHL&KAISER DVR	Global Flexible	99.3	11.23	10,446.90	10,662.40	29,474.00	4.0	882-8383	415-571-6002	None	None	None	David Rahn	86
BAILARD, BIEHL&KAISER INT★	International	84.9	6.57	10,969.30	11,402.70	☆	1.0	882-8383	415-571-6002	None	None	None	Warburg Inv. Mgt. Ltd.	82
BAIRD BLUE CHIP	Growth & Income	33.4	15.20	11,022.50	12,051.70	☆	1.8	792-2473	414-765-3500	5.75	0.45	None	J. Evans/B. Bosworth	87
BAIRD CAP DEVELOPMENT	Growth	23.4	19.67	10,813.60	11,889.10	19,448.40	0.5	792-2473	414-765-3500	5.75	0.45	None	Kellner/Wilson	86
BAKER: EQUITY	Capital Appreciation	0.1	15.48	10,424.20	10,673.70	☆	4.6	937-2257	None	None	1.00	None	Carl Holliday	88
BAKER: US GOVERNMENT	Fixed Income	58.3	15.41	10,185.10	10,580.10	☆	4.2	937-2257	None	None	0.50	None	Doug McQueen	86
BARON ASSET FUND	Small-Company Growth	54.4	14.32	10,324.40	9,782.40	☆	1.0	99B-ARON	212-759-7700	None	0.50	2.00	Ron Baron	87
BARTLETT CAP BASIC VALUE	Growth & Income	109.3	12.67	10,364.60	10,534.20	17,872.90	6.8	543-0863	None	None	None	None	James A. Miller	90
BARTLETT CAP VALUE INTL	International	21.9	10.12	10,398.30	☆	☆	0.0	543-0863	543-0863	None	None	None	Madelynn Matlock	89
BARTLETT CAP FIXED INC	Fixed Income	157.6	9.54	10,291.50	10,646.40	☆	8.4	543-0863	None	None	None	None	Dale Rabiner	86
BASCOM HILL BALANCED	Balanced	14.6	20.56	10,241.20	9,909.30	☆	5.7	767-0300	608-273-2020	None	0.65	None	Frank Burgess	86
BASCOM HILL INVESTORS	Growth & Income	9.0	14.42	10,329.50	9,510.20	15,904.60	5.2	767-0300	608-273-2020	None	None	5.00	Frank Burgess	78
BEACON HILL MUTUAL	Growth	4.0	30.09	11,101.10	11,730.20	17,084.60	0.0	None	617-482-0795	None	None	None	David Stone	64
BELL ATLANTIC BOND★	Fixed Income	4.6	10.17	10,344.00	☆	☆	0.0	527-6644	None	None	None	None	E. P. Rennie	90
BELL ATLANTIC EQUITY★	Growth & Income	11.1	10.77	10,326.00	☆	☆	0.0	527-6644	None	None	None	None	E. P. Rennie	90
BENHAM GOLD EQ INDEX	Gold	79.0	9.93	9,043.70	10,982.90	☆	0.5	None	800-321-8321	None	None	None	Steve Colton	89
BENHAM GOVT TR: GNMA INC	Fixed Income	307.4	9.97	10,350.30	10,835.30	☆	8.9	472-3389	800-321-8321	None	None	None	Randy Merk	87
BENHAM GOVT TR: T NOTE FD	Fixed Income	104.2	9.98	10,305.50	10,685.80	15,075.90	7.6	472-3389	800-321-8321	None	None	None	Jeff Tyler	88
BENHAM TARGET 1990	Fixed Income	17.3	97.48	10,194.50	10,776.00	15,954.80	0.0	472-3389	800-321-8321	None	None	None	Jeff Tyler	88
BENHAM TARGET 1995	Fixed Income	50.4	65.90	10,321.10	10,598.30	11,946.70	0.0	472-3389	800-321-8321	None	None	None	Jeff Tyler	89
BENHAM TARGET 2000	Fixed Income	51.9	44.21	10,382.80	10,049.90	26,049.90	0.0	472-3389	800-321-8321	None	None	None	Jeff Tyler	89
BENHAM TARGET 2005	Fixed Income	37.7	29.39	10,545.40	10,110.10	22,452.20	0.0	472-3389	800-321-8321	None	None	None	Jeff Tyler	89
BENHAM TARGET 2010	Fixed Income	40.6	21.13	10,698.70	9,915.50	23,561.80	0.0	472-3389	800-321-8321	None	None	None	Jeff Tyler	89
BENHAM TARGET 2015	Fixed Income	319.2	15.66	10,682.10	9,601.50	☆	0.0	472-3389	800-321-8321	None	None	None	Jeff Tyler	89
BENHAM TARGET 2020	Fixed Income	50.4	11.11	10,699.00	☆	☆	0.1	472-3389	800-321-8321	None	None	None	Jeff Tyler	90
BERGER ONE HUNDRED	Growth	18.5	8.40	10,852.70	12,821.30	23,492.50	0.0	333-1001	303-837-1020	None	0.30	None	William Berger	73
BERGER ONE HUNDRED & ONE	Growth & Income	3.8	7.17	10,516.40	11,182.30	15,775.00	3.1	333-1001	303-837-1020	None	0.30	None	William Berger	73
S BERNSTEIN: GOVT SH DUR	Fixed Income	171.7	12.55	10,241.90	10,748.30	☆	7.9	None	212-486-8434	None	None	None	Richard Kaye	89
S BERNSTEIN: INT MD T DUR	Fixed Income	245.9	12.54	10,288.40	10,641.40	☆	7.7	None	212-486-8434	None	None	None	Richard Kaye	89
S BERNSTEIN: SH DUR PLUS	Fixed Income	391.3	12.51	10,226.50	10,775.50	☆	8.0	None	212-486-8434	None	None	None	Richard Kaye	89
BERWYN FUND	Growth & Income	14.4	13.30	10,106.40	10,068.60	17,397.40	0.7	None	215-640-4330	None	None	1.00	Robert Killen	84
BERWYN INCOME FUND	Mixed Income	3.9	9.94	10,226.50	10,431.60	☆	7.9	None	215-640-4330	None	None	None	Robert Killen	87

★ASSOCIATED ADVISERS FUNDS—Open only to members of professional organizations.

★ATLAS: GOV'T &MTGE SEC—Fund is waiving 3% load through August; management is absorbing 12b-1 fee.

★BAILARD, BIEHL& KAISER INTL—Limited to clients of Bailard, Biehl & Kaiser.

★BELL ATLANTIC FUNDS—Offered to Bell Atlantic employees.

PERFORMANCE OF MUTUAL FUNDS (continued)

FUND NAME	OBJECTIVE	TOTAL NET ASSETS (MIL.) 6/30/90	NET ASSET VALUE 6/30/90	PERFORMANCE (Return on Initial $10,000 Investment) 3/31/90- 6/30/90	6/30/89- 6/30/90	6/30/85- 6/30/90	DIVIDEND YIELD % 6/90	PHONE NUMBER 800	In-State	FEES Load	12b-1	Redemption	MANAGER	SINCE
BIG E PATHFINDER: GOVT+	Fixed Income	70.2	9.73	10,360.90	10,612.30	☆	7.9	274-2161	716-855-7810	6.25	0.25	None	Gary Bartlett	'88
BLANCHARD PREC METALS	Gold	30.2	6.08	8,710.60	8,745.70	☆	0.5	922-7771	212-779-7979	None	0.85	None	Peter Cavelti	'88
BLANCHARD STR GR: GROWTH	Global Flexible	242.9	10.03	10,346.60	10,795.20	☆	2.4	922-7771	212-779-7979	None	0.85	None	Andre Sharon	'86
BOND FUND OF AMERICA	Fixed Income	1,725.5	12.95	10,368.70	10,525.10	16,386.10	9.9	421-0180	213-486-9200	4.75	0.25	None	Multiple Managers	'74
BOND PORT FOR ENDOWMENTS★	Fixed Income	39.0	17.27	10,347.90	10,719.40	16,384.10	8.6	None	415-421-9360	None	None	None	Multiple Managers	'75
BOSTON CO INV: ASSET ALLOC	Flexible	19.2	13.47	10,393.50	11,171.00	☆	3.3	225-5267	None	None	0.04	None	Edgar Peters	'88
BOSTON CO INV: CASH PLUS	Fixed Income	2.8	11.82	10,227.70	10,789.50	☆	8.0	225-5267	None	None	0.04	None	Roberta Shea	'89
BOSTON CO INV: CONTRARIAN	Growth	2.0	13.40	10,745.80	10,602.50	☆	1.0	225-5267	None	None	0.06	None	J. David Mills	'88
BOSTON CO INV: EQU-INCOME★	Growth & Income	0.1	12.71	9,761.90	10,036.80	☆	4.7	225-5267	None	None	0.45	None	J. David Mills	'89
BOSTON CO INV: INTERNAT'L	International	35.1	13.34	10,545.50	11,468.20	☆	1.4	225-5267	None	None	None	None	Nitin Mehta	'89
BOSTON CO INDEX: BLUE CHIP★	Growth & Income	0.1	8.89	10,000.00	10,069.30	☆	28.1	225-5267	None	None	0.45	None	Richard Wilk	'88
BOSTON CO INDEX: EQU-INDEX★★	Growth & Income	0.1	10.96	10,027.40	11,315.50	☆	7.3	225-5267	None	None	0.45	None	James Rullo	'88
BOSTON CO INDEX: SMALL CAP★	Small-Company Growth	0.1	14.47	9,951.90	10,730.90	☆	1.2	225-5267	None	None	0.45	None	James Rullo	'88
BOSTON CO CAPITAL APPREC	Growth	611.6	27.00	10,299.60	10,773.30	20,607.00	1.8	225-5267	None	None	0.28	None	D. Mills/K. Green	'89/'90
BOSTON CO INTMDT TM GOVT	Fixed Income	15.0	11.77	10,272.80	10,535.60	☆	7.7	225-5267	None	None	0.01	None	Almond Goduti	'90
BOSTON CO MANAGED INCOME	Fixed Income	78.5	10.85	10,270.90	10,312.00	15,752.60	8.6	225-5267	None	None	0.08	None	Arthur Macbride	'89
BOSTON CO SPECIAL GROWTH	Growth	43.5	14.15	10,655.10	9,960.00	16,335.00	1.6	225-5267	None	None	0.04	None	Guy Scott	'90
BRANDYWINE FUND	Growth	287.0	19.39	11,156.50	13,172.00	☆	0.2	338-1579	302-656-6200	None	None	None	Foster Friess	'85
BRUCE FUND	Growth	3.4	113.79	11,227.40	13,039.70	19,685.90	2.4	None	312-236-9160	None	None	None	Robert Bruce	'83
BULL&BEAR CAPITAL GROWTH	Growth	71.5	8.95	11,131.80	11,796.00	16,985.10	0.0	847-4200	212-363-1100	None	1.00	None	Brett Sneed	'88
BULL&BEAR EQUITY-INCOME	Equity Income	10.9	12.16	10,597.10	10,727.10	17,130.80	3.4	847-4200	212-363-1100	None	0.50	None	Robert Radsch	'82
BULL&BEAR FINCL NEWS CMP	Growth	10.1	20.60	10,520.90	11,243.10	☆	2.7	847-4200	212-363-1100	None	0.25	None	Brett Sneed	'89
BULL&BEAR GOLD INVESTORS	Gold	38.9	13.36	9,157.00	10,151.00	14,526.50	1.0	847-4200	212-363-1100	None	0.50	None	Robert Radsch	'82
BULL&BEAR HIGH YIELD	Fixed Income	51.4	8.67	10,616.50	10,053.60	11,184.70	12.5	847-4200	212-363-1100	None	0.50	None	Webb/ Worth	'88
BULL&BEAR OVERSEAS FD	International	1.3	17.84	10,721.20	11,854.10	☆	0.0	847-4200	212-363-1100	None	0.50	None	Robert Radsch	'87
BULL&BEAR SPECIAL EQU	Capital Appreciation	32.4	27.45	12,238.10	14,503.20	☆	0.0	847-4200	212-363-1100	None	0.50	None	Brett Sneed	'86
BULL&BEAR US GOVT SEC	Fixed Income	32.9	13.69	10,328.20	10,642.40	☆	7.8	847-4200	212-363-1100	None	0.50	None	Charles Adams	'88
BURNHAM FUND	Growth & Income	133.4	20.63	10,178.20	10,823.60	19,836.10	5.5	223-4522	212-483-1461	5.00	None	None	Burnham/Fergeson	'89
CA INV TR: US GOVT SEC	Fixed Income	11.8	9.56	10,373.70	10,790.20	☆	8.7	826-8166	415-398-2727	None	None	None	Philip McClanahan	'85
CALAMOS CONV INCOME	Convertibles	14.5	10.70	10,352.40	10,691.60	14,754.00	6.7	323-9943	708-571-7115	None	None	None	John Calamos	'85
CALDWELL FUND	Growth & Income	1.8	13.07	10,541.60	11,182.50	☆	15.7	749-2000	813-485-0654	None	None	None	Roland Caldwell	'88
CALVERT-ARIEL GRO APPREC	Small-Company Growth	17.0	16.58	10,621.40	☆	☆	0.0	368-2748	301-951-4820	4.50	None	None	Eric McKissack	'90
CALVERT-ARIEL GRO: GRO★	Small-Company Growth	247.6	27.81	10,550.10	10,879.00	☆	1.4	368-2748	301-951-4820	4.50	0.17	None	John Rogers	'86
CALVERT FD: CAPITAL VALUE	Growth	9.5	23.53	10,485.70	11,567.60	18,819.40	1.2	368-2748	301-951-4820	4.50	0.50	6.00	Pat Hevner	'88
CALVERT FD: INCOME	Fixed Income	31.1	16.03	10,311.50	10,670.00	16,332.30	8.6	368-2748	301-951-4820	4.50	None	None	Kahn Bros.	'82
CALVERT FD: LTD-TERM GOVT	Fixed Income	4.6	14.41	10,300.70	10,662.90	☆	7.5	368-2748	301-951-4820	2.00	None	None	Calvert Asset Mgmt.	'88
CALVERT FD: US GOVT	Fixed Income	5.2	14.63	10,269.00	10,782.50	☆	8.0	368-2748	301-951-4820	4.50	None	None	Calvert Asset Mgmt.	'86
CALVERT FD: WASH AREA	Growth	16.3	16.06	9,531.20	8,786.60	☆	0.0	368-2748	301-951-4820	4.50	1.25	None	Calvert Asset Mgmt.	'85
CALVERT SOCIAL INV: BOND	Fixed Income	21.6	15.54	10,311.20	10,612.90	☆	8.2	368-2748	301-951-4820	4.50	None	None	Larry Litvak	'87
CALVERT SOCIAL INV: EQTY	Growth	22.2	18.16	10,485.00	11,187.50	☆	1.3	368-2748	301-951-4820	4.50	None	None	Domenic Colasacco	'87
CALVERT SOCIAL INV: GRO	Balanced	250.8	27.44	10,438.00	10,792.60	17,629.00	2.3	368-2748	301-951-4820	4.50	0.20	None	Domenic Colasacco	'82
CAPITAL INCOME BUILDER	Equity Income	221.8	25.15	10,264.70	10,972.50	☆	5.2	421-0180	213-486-9200	5.75	0.25	None	Multiple Managers	'87
CAPITAL WORLD BOND	World Fixed-Income	36.6	13.97	10,471.00	10,709.20	☆	8.5	421-0180	213-486-9200	4.75	0.25	None	Multiple Managers	'87
CAPSTONE: EQUITYGUARD	Capital Appreciation	2.3	7.27	9,868.50	9,556.00	☆	2.2	262-6631	None	4.75	None	None	Paul McEntire	'86
CAPSTONE INTL: EUROPEAN+	European Region	15.3	11.49	10,901.30	12,258.90	☆	0.3	262-6631	None	4.75	None	None	Michael Gillio	'87

Fund	Objective	Assets ($mil)	NAV	1-Yr $10K	5-Yr $10K	10-Yr $10K	Yield	Phone A	Phone B	Load	12b-1	Fee	Manager	Since
CARDINAL FUND	Growth & Income	198.4	11.04	10,371.10	11,019.40	19,323.10	4.7	614-464-6852	848-7734	8.50	None	Ncne	C.A. Peterson	'66
CARDINAL GCVT GUARTD	Fixed Income	116.1	8.71	10,326.90	10,874.50	☆	9.7	614-464-6852	848-7734	4.75	None	Ncne	John Carle	'86
CARILLON INLST: CAPITAL	Flexible	14.6	11.15	10,279.20	10,916.10	☆	5.4	999-1840	999-1840	5.00	None	Ncne	Clucas/Sachdeva	'88
CARNEGIE CAPP: DVD HI INC	Fixed Income	5.8	9.45	10,349.40	☆	☆	0.0	216-781-4440	321-2322	4.50	None	Ncne	Frank Cappiello	'89
CARNEGIE CAPP: EMERG GROWTH	Small-Company Growth	11.5	10.32	10,606.40	☆	☆	0.0	216-781-4440	321-2322	4.50	None	Ncne	Frank Cappiello	'89
CARNEGIE CAPP: GROWTH	Growth	78.1	18.39	10,279.30	11,462.80	20,966.60	1.5	216-781-4440	321-2322	4.50	0.34	None	Frank Cappiello	'84
CARNEGIE CAPP: TOTAL RTN	Flexible	80.5	11.86	9,994.30	10,480.20	15,365.60	5.0	216-781-4440	321-2322	4.50	0.50	None	Frank Cappiello	'85
CARNEGIE GCVT: HI YLD	Fixed Income	42.7	9.22	10,332.40	10,617.90	☆	7.7	216-781-4440	321-2322	4.50	0.31	None	John Shriver	'85
CARNEGIE GCVT: INTERMDT	Fixed Income	3.0	9.54	10,246.20	10,411.90	☆	6.6	216-781-4440	321-2322	2.50	0.16	None	Roy Wallace	'87
CARNEGIE GCVT: LONG	Fixed Income	0.9	8.97	10,341.40	10,335.60	☆	6.4	216-781-4440	321-2322	4.50	None	None	Roy Wallace	'87
CARNEGIE GCVT: SHORT	Fixed Income	3.9	9.83	10,020.70	10,667.50	☆	7.2	216-781-4440	321-2322	2.50	0.11	None	Roy Wallace	'89
CASHMAN FARRELL VALUE	Capital Appreciation	10.4	10.28	10,071.90	9,606.70	☆	2.7	617-482-3060	262-6631	4.75	None	None	Dan Cashman	'86
CENTURY SH-RES TRUST	Financial Services	142.8	18.80	10,352.50	11,541.00	18,164.70	2.7	321-1928	321-1928	None	None	None	Allan Fulkerson	'71
CFS: KALLISTON CV TOT RTN	Convertibles	1.4	11.23	10,646.30	11,043.40	☆	2.3	None	323-9942	4.75	0.50	None	John Calamos	'88
CFS: KALLISTON PREF PLUS	Fixed Income	0.7	9.35	10,328.20	10,042.10	☆	6.3	None	323-9943	2.50	0.50	None	John Calamos	'88
CGM CAPITAL DEVELOP	Growth	208.3	21.43	11,729.60	12,436.00	22,857.90	1.6	617-578-1333	345-4048	None	None	None	Kenneth Heebner	'76
CGM MUTUAL FUND	Balanced	322.7	23.22	11,083.60	11,435.20	21,645.70	3.9	617-578-1333	345-4048	None	None	None	Kenneth Heebner	'76
CHAMPION HI YLD FD-USA	Fixed Income	15.8	11.01	10,369.90	10,596.90	☆	13.0	212-323-0602	327-3069	4.75	0.13	None	Paul Sukow	'87
CHRISTOS FUND	Capital Appreciation	3.2	8.32	9,928.40	8,753.40	☆	2.5	503-686-2744	999-3303	4.00	0.56	None	Thomas Kienlen	'88
CHUBB INV: GOVT SEC	Fixed Income	1.7	10.16	10,562.60	10,765.60	☆	8.5	603-224-1741	258-3648	5.00	0.50	None	Ned Gerstman	'87
CHUBB INV: GROWTH FD	Growth & Income	1.3	13.36	10,503.10	12,218.40	☆	3.0	603-224-1741	258-3648	5.00	0.50	None	Marjorie Raines	'87
CHUBB INV: TOTAL RETURN	Balanced	1.6	12.10	10,477.20	11,800.50	14,547.00	4.0	None	258-3648	5.00	0.50	None	Marjorie Raines	'87
CIGNA: AGGRESSIVE GROWTH	Small-Company Growth	11.5	14.45	11,064.30	11,868.70	☆	0.2	None	572-4462	5.00	0.0025	None	David Shinn	'89
CIGNA: GOVT SEC	Fixed Income	56.7	9.79	10,291.60	10,780.40	☆	8.6	None	572-4462	5.00	0.0025	None	Gary Brown	'87
CIGNA: GROWTH	Growth	186.7	15.13	10,955.80	12,560.10	19,927.20	1.7	None	572-4462	5.00	0.0025	None	David Shinn	'85
CIGNA: HIGH YIELD	Fixed Income	249.9	8.46	10,564.90	9,708.10	15,609.00	14.1	None	572-4462	5.00	0.0025	None	Alan Petersen	'83
CIGNA: INCOME	Fixed Income	222.5	7.52	10,335.00	10,479.90	16,408.50	9.3	None	572-4462	5.00	0.0025	None	Gary Brown	'90
CIGNA: UTILITIES	Utility	66.5	12.86	10,099.50	12,872.80	22,640.10	5.1	None	572-4462	5.00	0.0025	None	James Samuels	'88
CIGNA: VALUE	Growth & Income	90.8	16.61	10,978.20	11,363.60	18,907.60	2.5	None	572-4462	5.00	0.0025	None	James Giblin	'86
CITBANK CIT: BALANCED★	Balanced	188.2	2.25	10,465.10	11,396.40	N/A	0.0	None	248-4472	N/A	N/A	N/A	N/A	N/A
CITBANK CIT: EQUITY★	Growth	161.8	2.53	10,585.80	N/A	N/A	0.0	None	248-4472	N/A	N/A	N/A	N/A	N/A
CITBANK CIT: INCOME★	Fixed Income	57.5	1.98	10,312.50	N/A	N/A	0.0	213-278-5033	248-4472	N/A	N/A	N/A	N/A	N/A
CLIPPER FUND	Growth & Income	151.4	42.53	10,577.00	10,702.70	19,921.30	2.3	None	None	None	None	None	James Gipson	'84
COLONIAL ADV STR GOLD	Gold	61.3	18.05	8,757.90	10,111.90	15,468.80	0.2	None	426-3750	6.75	0.25	None	Daniel Rie	'86
COLONIAL CORP CASH I	Fixed Income	118.0	43.10	10,084.80	9,452.60	19,166.90	9.0	None	426-3750	2.00	0.25	None	John Lennon	'84
COLONIAL CORP CASH II	Fixed Income	71.4	41.29	10,136.20	10,250.50	16,151.10	9.0	None	426-3750	2.00	0.25	None	John Lennon	'84
COLONIAL FUND	Growth & Income	337.8	20.08	10,154.60	10,245.70	13,739.60	4.1	None	426-3750	6.75	0.14	None	Christian Bertelsen	'86
COLONIAL GOVT SEC PLUS	Fixed Income	2,351.0	10.72	10,570.90	10,670.40	12,485.70	8.5	None	426-3750	6.75	0.25	None	Robert Busby	'88
COLONIAL GROWTH SHARES	Growth	137.0	12.39	10,628.70	11,341.70	19,780.10	1.5	None	426-3750	6.75	0.12	None	Daniel Rie	'86
COLONIAL HIGH YIELD	Fixed Income	327.5	5.89	10,493.50	9,560.00	15,745.60	15.1	None	426-3750	4.75	0.25	None	Prescott Crocker	'32
COLONIAL INCOME FUND	Fixed Income	150.8	6.21	10,217.30	10,252.30	21,828.20	10.3	None	426-3750	4.75	0.25	None	Laura Moody	'84
COLONIAL INTL EQ INDEX	International	15.3	18.65	10,645.00	11,557.50	14,786.80	0.0	None	426-3750	4.75	0.25	None	Betsy Palmer	'89
COLONIAL SMALL STK INDEX	Small-Company Growth	43.1	13.55	10,280.50	10,041.90	15,219.50	0.3	None	426-3750	4.75	0.25	None	Paul Samuelson	'86
COLONIAL STRAT: DVSD INC	Income	434.0	6.91	10,351.10	10,411.70	15,352.60	10.3	None	426-3750	6.75	None	None	Jarrod Wilcox	'86
COLONIAL STRAT: INC PLUS	Mixed Income	78.8	8.56	10,529.50	10,145.10	14,132.70	11.7	None	426-3750	6.75	None	None	Carl Ericson	'88

★BOND PORTFOLIO FOR ENDOWMENTS—Limited to tax-exempt institutions.
★BOSTON CO FUNDS—Closed to new investors as of 12/31/89.
★CALVERT-ARIEL GRO: GROWTH—Closed to new investors.
★CITBANK FUNDS—Limited to Citibank IRAs.

®Copyright Lipper Analytical Services, Inc.

PERFORMANCE OF MUTUAL FUNDS (continued)

FUND NAME	OBJECTIVE	TOTAL NET ASSETS (MIL) 6/30/90	NET ASSET VALUE 6/30/90	PERFORMANCE (Return on Initial $10,000 Investment) 3/31/90-6/30/90	6/30/89-6/30/90	6/30/85-6/30/90	DIVIDEND YIELD % 6/90	PHONE NUMBER 800	In-State	FEES Load	12b-1	Redemption	MANAGER	SINCE
COLONIAL US EQUITY INDEX	Growth & Income	38.5	17.41	10,577.00	11,439.30	☆	1.9	426-3750	None	4.75	0.25	None	Steve Lanzendorf	'88
COLONIAL US GOVT TRUST	Fixed Income	85.6	6.99	10,305.00	10,731.80	☆	10.3	426-3750	None	4.75	0.25	None	Leslie Finnemore	'87
COLONIAL VIP: DVSD RETN	Global Flexible	27.4	11.14	10,319.20	10,583.50	☆	3.0	426-3750	None	None	1.25	5.00	Paul Samuelson	'88
COLONIAL VIP: FED SEC	Fixed Income	29.0	9.84	10,278.90	10,699.40	☆	8.2	426-3750	None	None	1.25	5.00	Leslie Finnemore	'88
COLONIAL VIP: GROWTH	Growth	12.2	12.01	10,383.80	10,325.10	☆	0.6	426-3750	None	None	1.25	5.00	Jarrod Wilcox	'88
COLONIAL VIP: HIGH INC	Fixed Income	65.2	8.70	10,413.50	9,914.80	☆	12.1	426-3750	None	None	1.25	5.00	Prescott Crocker	'88
COLONIAL VIP: INFLN HDG	Specialty	5.9	10.97	9,822.10	11,181.50	☆	2.6	426-3750	None	None	1.25	5.00	Lanzendorf/Orr	'88
COLUMBIA: FIXED INCOME	Fixed Income	118.9	12.55	10,348.30	10,722.30	15,821.50	8.3	547-1037	None	None	None	None	Colum. Investment Team	'83
COLUMBIA: GROWTH	Growth	329.1	24.63	10,694.70	11,707.30	19,911.90	2.0	547-1037	None	None	None	None	Colum. Investment Team	'67
COLUMBIA: SPECIAL	Capital Appreciation	142.4	44.80	10,626.20	11,883.20	☆	0.1	547-1037	None	None	None	None	Colum. Investment Team	'85
COLUMBIA: US GOVT GUAR	Fixed Income	17.8	8.25	10,276.00	10,734.10	☆	7.8	547-1037	None	None	None	None	Colum. Investment Team	'86
COMMON SENSE: GOVT	Fixed Income	128.6	10.84	10,345.30	10,543.10	☆	9.0	888-3863	None	6.75	None	None	Jack Reynoldson	'88
COMMON SENSE: GROWTH FD	Growth	988.3	13.53	10,755.20	11,850.20	☆	1.5	888-3863	None	8.50	None	None	Steven Boyd	'89
COMMON SENSE: GRO & INC	Growth & Income	402.3	13.53	10,783.00	11,551.60	☆	2.4	880-3863	None	8.50	None	None	John Gunthorp	'89
COMMONWEALTH INV TR: BAL	Balanced	46.0	2.07	10,575.30	11,275.50	17,580.90	5.4	343-2900	617-482-6500	7.50	None	None	Paul Carlson	'89
COMMONWEALTH INV TR: GRO	Growth	8.2	18.83	10,603.30	11,053.90	18,200.20	3.8	343-2902	617-482-6500	7.50	None	None	Ken Pash	'79
COMPANION FUND	Growth	68.0	12.98	10,955.60	12,375.20	20,088.80	2.2	562-4462	None	None	None	None	David Shinn	'85
COMPASS CAPITAL: EQUITY INC	Equity Income	41.1	10.23	10,320.70	10,829.10	☆	4.1	451-8371	None	4.50	None	None	Midlantic Natl Bank	'89
COMPASS CAPITAL: FIX INC	Fixed Income	78.7	9.90	10,333.10	10,523.20	☆	7.2	451-8371	None	4.50	None	None	Midlantic Natl Bank	'89
COMPASS CAPITAL: GROWTH	Growth	90.3	11.16	10,662.00	11,517.50	☆	2.5	451-8371	None	4.50	None	None	Midlantic Natl Bank	'89
COMPASS CAPITAL: SH/INT	Fixed Income	27.2	9.98	10,270.50	10,680.00	☆	7.5	451-8371	None	4.50	None	None	Midlantic Natl Bank	'89
COMPOSITE BOND & STOCK	Balanced	71.5	10.37	10,303.30	10,311.80	15,829.40	5.8	543-8072	509-353-3400	4.00	0.30	None	Craig Hobbs	'84
COMPOSITE GROWTH FD	Growth & Income	69.6	10.89	10,250.70	10,102.40	16,917.10	4.4	543-8072	509-353-3400	4.00	0.30	None	David Anderson	'87
COMPOSITE INCOME FUND	Fixed Income	69.9	8.24	10,360.90	10,510.20	14,653.60	9.5	543-8072	509-353-3400	4.00	0.15	None	Craig Hobbs	'89
COMPOSITE NRTHWST 50 INX	Growth	45.1	22.98	10,832.80	12,895.20	☆	0.5	543-8072	509-353-3400	4.50	0.25	None	Mark Byl	'86
COMPOSITE US GOVT SEC	Fixed Income	83.6	9.89	10,303.40	10,723.80	15,137.00	8.8	543-8072	509-353-3400	4.00	0.15	None	Alfred Coleman	'89
CONCORD FUND★	Growth	1.2	25.44	10,333.10	9,880.00	11,610.10	1.1	None	617-426-3647	N/A	N/A	N/A	N/A	N/A
CONCORD INC TR: CONVERT	Convertibles	5.5	9.92	10,568.30	10,905.50	☆	7.7	562-0247	201-535-5000	6.50	None	None	Richard Russell	'87
CONCORDE VALUE FUND	Growth & Income	13.8	10.53	10,154.30	9,206.50	☆	3.6	338-1579	214-387-8258	4.50	None	None	Gary B. Wood	'89
CONNECTICUT: GOVT ACCT	Fixed Income	44.3	10.44	10,324.20	10,769.00	☆	8.1	243-2501	203-293-5090	4.50	None	None	Steve Libera	'85
CONNECTICUT: GROWTH ACCT	Growth	39.3	13.31	10,500.70	11,835.10	☆	3.9	293-2501	203-293-5090	6.25	None	None	Peter Antos	'89
CONNECTICUT: INCOME ACCT	Fixed Income	19.3	9.69	10,244.20	10,806.00	☆	9.4	243-2501	203-293-5090	4.50	None	None	Steve Libera	'85
CONNECTICUT: TOT RTN ACCT	Balanced	68.8	12.72	10,410.80	11,226.90	☆	5.9	243-2501	203-293-5090	6.25	None	None	Peter Antos	'89
CONVERTIBLE SEC & INCM	Convertibles	28.7	8.87	10,370.20	9,664.10	☆	9.7	356-2805	412-288-1900	4.50	0.25	None	Durbiano/Madden	'83/'78
COPLEY FUND	Growth & Income	25.4	13.88	10,094.50	10,595.40	15,917.40	0.0	424-8459	508-674-8459	None	None	None	Irving Levine	'78
CORP FD INV ACCUM PROG	Fixed Income	78.6	20.19	10,281.90	10,647.20	15,349.20	8.3	None	609-282-2000	N/A	N/A	N/A	N/A	N/A
COUNSELLORS CAP APPREC	Growth	74.0	11.45	10,585.10	10,983.50	☆	3.3	888-6878	212-878-0600	None	None	None	Andrew Massie	'89
COUNSELLORS EMERGING GR	Small-Company Growth	30.5	13.83	10,697.80	10,449.80	☆	2.9	888-6878	212-878-0600	None	None	None	Elizabeth Dater	'88
COUNSELLORS FIXED INC	Fixed Income	79.2	9.47	10,328.30	10,445.70	☆	9.5	888-6878	212-878-0600	None	None	None	Stuart Goode	'87
COUNSELLORS INTMDT GOVT	Fixed Income	43.2	10.18	10,314.50	10,745.40	☆	7.8	888-6878	212-878-0600	None	None	None	Stuart Goode	'88
COUNSELLORS INTL EQUITY	International	33.5	12.90	10,905.60	12,988.10	☆	1.7	888-6878	212-878-0600	None	None	None	Richard King	'89
COUNTRY CAPITAL GROWTH	Growth	81.5	17.42	10,647.90	11,608.70	19,234.80	5.6	322-3838	309-557-2444	3.00	None	None	Steve Miller	'79
COUNTRY CAPITAL INCOME	Fixed Income	5.7	10.56	10,333.70	10,650.60	15,611.50	7.5	322-3838	309-557-2444	3.00	None	None	John Jacobs	'78
COWEN FUNDS: OPPORTUNITY	Technology	9.4	13.01	11,303.20	13,324.60	☆	0.0	221-5616	212-495-6000	4.85	0.75	None	William Church	'88
COWEN INCOME & GROWTH	Equity Income	43.8	10.82	10,109.60	10,245.50	☆	4.2	221-5616	212-495-6000	4.85	0.75	None	William Rechter	'86

Fund	Objective	Net Assets	NAV	Value 1	Value 2	Value 3	Yield	Phone 1	Phone 2	Load	12b-1	Redemp.	Manager	Year
CROWLEY: GROWTH	Growth	1.5	10.89	10,552.30	☆	☆	0.0	None	302-529-1717	3.00	None	None	Robert Crowley	'90
CROWLEY: INCOME	Fixed Income	1.3	10.41	10,215.90	☆	☆	0.0	None	302-529-1717	3.00	None	None	Robert Crowley	'90
CUMBERLAND GROWTH	Capital Appreciation	1.3	10.61	10,463.50	10,429.90	12,824.00	6.2	257-7013	609-692-6690	None	None	None	Donald Sulam	'85
DEAN WITTER AMER VALUE	Growth	101.4	15.19	10,762.90	11,236.40	19,453.00	1.9	869-3863	212-392-2550	None	1.00	5.00	Anita Kolleeny	'85
DEAN WITTER CAP GR SEC	Growth	192.2	10.98	☆	☆	☆	0.0	869-3863	None	None	0.25	5.00	Paul Vance	'90
DEAN WITTER CONVERT	Convertibles	555.5	8.87	10,021.20	10,214.20	☆	4.9	869-3863	212-392-2550	None	1.00	5.00	Donald Johansen	'89
DEAN WITTER DEV GRO	Small-Company Growth	97.0	12.71	11,328.00	12,698.40	15,406.10	0.4	869-3863	212-392-2550	None	1.00	5.00	Robert Kimtis	'86
DEAN WITTER DIVID GRO	Growth & Income	3,110.6	23.28	10,308.60	11,035.90	20,647.50	3.2	869-3863	212-392-2550	None	1.00	5.00	Paul Vance	'86
DEAN WITTER EURO GROWTH	European Region	230.3	10.13	☆	☆	☆	0.0	869-3863	None	None	1.00	5.00	John Armitage	'90
DEAN WITTER GOVT PLUS	Fixed Income	1,523.5	9.01	10,352.90	10,609.90	☆	7.9	869-3863	212-392-2550	None	0.85	5.00	Rajesh Gupta	'87
DEAN WITTER HIGH YIELD	Fixed Income	771.2	7.22	9,854.80	7,783.80	10,905.10	19.2	869-3863	212-392-2550	5.50	1.00	None	James DiDonato	'89
DEAN WITTER INTMDT INC	Fixed Income	116.1	9.61	10,267.70	10,451.60	☆	9.0	869-3863	212-392-2550	None	0.85	5.00	Rochelle Siegel	'89
DEAN WITTER MGD ASSETS	Flexible	273.1	10.09	10,224.90	10,673.90	☆	6.1	869-3863	212-392-2550	None	1.00	5.00	Vance/Siegel/Page	'88
DEAN WITTER NTRL RES	Natural Resources	159.0	11.45	10,074.90	11,434.90	19,284.50	3.2	869-3863	212-392-2550	None	1.00	5.00	Diane Sobin	'88
DEAN WITTER OPT INC	Option Income	179.3	8.64	10,369.40	10,714.20	14,688.90	8.3	869-3863	212-392-2550	None	1.00	5.00	Kenton Hinchliffe Jr.	'85
DEAN WITTER STRATEGIST	Flexible	179.2	12.00	11,055.70	11,668.80	11,879.70	2.4	869-3863	212-392-2550	None	1.00	5.00	John Connolly	'89
DEAN WITTER TAX ADV	Fixed Income	36.2	7.78	10,227.10	9,765.70	14,648.00	11.7	869-3863	212-392-2550	None	0.50	None	Paula LaCosta	'86
DEAN WITTER US GOVT	Fixed Income	9,887.9	9.36	10,275.30	10,764.10	☆	9.6	869-3863	212-392-2550	None	0.75	5.00	Arthur Forster	'84
DEAN WITTER UTILITIES	Utility	1,267.5	11.47	10,140.50	10,736.00	☆	5.7	869-3863	212-392-2550	None	1.00	5.00	Edward Gaylor	'87
DEAN WITTER VAL ADD: EQ	Growth & Income	147.5	14.21	10,348.30	10,617.00	☆	1.7	869-3863	212-392-2550	None	1.00	5.00	Thomas Connelly	'89
DELAWARE GR WRLDWD INC	World Fixed-Income	431.3	9.77	10,521.50	10,881.30	☆	9.5	869-3863	212-392-2550	None	0.85	5.00	Vin Tran	'89
DELAWARE GR WRLDWD INV	Global	323.2	15.51	10,721.40	11,552.10	23,546.20	1.7	869-3863	212-392-2550	None	1.00	5.00	Thomas Connelly	'83
DELAWARE GR DECATUR I	Equity Income	1,849.8	16.59	10,080.70	10,310.30	19,227.40	6.1	523-1918	215-988-1241	8.50	None	None	Paul Ehrsam	'88
DELAWARE GR DECATUR II	Equity Income	373.9	12.60	10,077.80	10,626.40	☆	4.7	523-1918	215-988-1241	4.75	0.25	None	Marion Dixon	'88
DELAWARE GR DELAWARE FD	Balanced	396.5	18.15	10,726.10	11,336.20	18,280.60	4.3	523-1918	215-988-1241	6.75	None	None	Stanton Feeley	'88
DELAWARE GR DELCAP I	Capital Appreciation	192.1	19.40	10,688.70	11,778.60	☆	0.8	523-1918	215-988-1241	4.75	0.25	None	Edward Antoian	'86
DELAWARE GR DELCHSTR I	Fixed Income	524.0	6.27	10,398.90	9,513.30	15,358.60	14.4	523-1918	215-988-1241	6.75	None	None	J. Michael Pokorny	'81
DELAWARE GR DELCHSTR II	Fixed Income	92.3	6.27	10,391.00	9,484.30	☆	14.1	523-1918	215-988-1241	4.75	0.25	None	J. Michael Pokorny	'81
DELAWARE GR GOVT INCOME	Fixed Income	148.4	8.52	10,319.80	10,715.60	☆	8.8	523-1918	215-988-1241	4.75	0.25	None	Dorothea Dutton	'86
DELAWARE GR TREAS INVSTR	Fixed Income	112.0	9.64	10,353.50	10,811.60	☆	8.5	523-1918	215-988-1241	None	0.25	None	Dorothea Dutton	'86
DELAWARE GR TREND FUND	Capital Appreciation	88.3	9.97	10,968.10	11,432.00	20,538.40	0.5	523-1918	215-988-1241	8.50	None	None	Edward Antoian	'86
DELAWARE GR VALUE FUND	Capital Appreciation	10.3	13.11	10,564.10	10,363.00	☆	1.0	523-1918	215-988-1241	4.75	0.25	None	Edward Trumpbovur	'87
DFA GROUP: CONTL SMALL CO★	European Region	257.1	18.89	10,900.20	14,411.30	☆	1.1	None	213-395-8005	1.50	None	None	Rex Sinquefield	'88
DFA GROUP: 5 YEAR GOVT	Fixed Income	46.0	101.50	10,257.40	10,835.40	☆	7.7	None	213-395-8005	None	None	None	Rex Sinquefield	'87
DFA GROUP: JAPAN SMALL CO★	Pacific Region	165.2	33.94	10,987.40	11,381.40	☆	0.0	None	213-395-8005	1.00	None	None	Rex Sinquefield	'86
DFA GROUP: 1 YEAR FIXED INC	Fixed Income	396.1	101.85	10,255.90	10,899.40	14,822.70	8.4	None	213-395-8005	None	None	None	Edward Antoian	'83
DFA GROUP: UK SMALL CO★	European Region	137.0	23.12	10,854.50	9,968.10	☆	3.2	None	213-395-8005	1.50	None	None	Rex Sinquefield	'86
DFA GROUP: US 9-10 SMALL CO	Small-Company Growth	838.1	7.06	10,428.40	9,883.00	14,666.10	1.1	None	213-395-8005	None	None	None	Rex Sinquefield	'81
DIVIDEND/GROWTH: DIV SRS	Equity Income	2.4	23.43	10,377.00	10,938.00	13,577.70	3.1	638-2042	301-251-1002	None	None	None	David Straus	'80
DIVIDEND/GROWTH: GROW SRS	Growth	32.5	6.54	10,171.00	8,983.50	5,482.00	0.0	638-2042	301-251-1002	None	None	None	Gordon Lamb	'83
DODGE & COX BALANCED	Balanced	62.4	37.10	10,444.00	11,293.70	20,702.10	4.8	None	415-434-0311	None	None	None	Peter Avenali	'65
DODGE & COX INCOME	Fixed Income	41.6	10.48	10,350.30	10,601.90	☆	7.7	None	415-434-0311	None	None	None	Baumgartener/Shapiro	'89
DODGE & COX STOCK	Growth & Income	157.4	43.07	10,444.10	11,554.30	23,202.70	3.0	None	415-434-0311	None	None	None	Joseph Fee	'65
DR FUNDS: BALANCED	Flexible	34.9	10.26	10,384.60	☆	☆	0.0	356-6454	None	None	None	None	Dillon Read Capital	'89
DR FUNDS: EUROPEAN EQUITY	European Region	32.5	10.44	10,620.50	13,531.00	☆	13.7	356-6454	None	None	None	None	Dillon Read Capital	'90
DR FUNDS: EQUITY	Growth & Income	67.2	11.62	10,365.70	10,953.10	☆	3.6	356-6454	None	None	None	None	Dillon Read Capital	'86
DREMAN: BOND PORT	Fixed Income	3.8	10.03	10,241.00	10,841.80	☆	7.8	533-1608	201-332-8228	None	0.15	None	Dreman Value Mgmt. Lp.	'88

★CONCORD FUND—Closed.

★DFA GROUP: CONTINENTAL, JAPAN & U.K. FUNDS—Charges listed under the heading of Load are special fees paid into the funds.

PERFORMANCE OF MUTUAL FUNDS (continued)

NAME CHANGES

FROM	TO
ADVEST ADVANTAGE GOVT	ADVANTAGE: GOVT SEC
ADVEST ADVANTAGE GRO	ADVANTAGE: GROWTH
ADVEST ADVANTAGE HI YLD	ADVANTAGE: HIGH YIELD
ADVEST ADVANTAGE INC	ADVANTAGE: INCOME
ADVEST ADVANTAGE SPEC	ADVANTAGE: SPECIAL
BOSTON CO GNMA	BOSTON CO INT-TERM GOVT
FEDERATED UTILITY	FORTRESS UTILITY
FIDELITY INC: SH-TM GOVT	FIDELITY SPARTAN LTD MAT
FLAG INV TOT RET	TOT RTN TREA: FLAG INV
FRANKLIN INV: ADJ MTGE	FRANKLIN INV: US GOVT SEC
FNL INDEPEN: GOVT SEC	MIDWEST STRT: GOVT SEC
FNL INDEPEN: GROWTH	MIDWEST STRT: GROWTH
FNL INDEPEN: TREAS	MIDWEST STRT: TREAS ALLOC
FNL INDEPEN: UTILITY INC	MIDWEST STRT: UTILITY INC
HARBOR US EQUITIES	HARBOR CAP APP
IVY INSTITUTION	IVY FUND GRO INC
CJ LAWRENCE	TOT RTN TREAS: CJ LAWRENCE
LEHMAN FUNDS	SALOMON BROTHERS FUNDS
MACKAY-SHIELDS: CAP APP	M-S MAINSTAY: CAP APPREC
MACKAY-SHIELDS: CONV	M-S MAINSTAY: CONVTBLE
MACKAY-SHIELDS: GLOBAL	M-S MAINSTAY: GLOBAL

FROM	TO
MACKAY-SHIELDS: GOLD	M-S MAINSTAY: GOLD & MTL.
MACKAY-SHIELDS GOVT +	M-S MAINSTAY: GOVT PLUS
MACKAY-SHIELDS: HI YLD	M-S MAINSTAY: HI YLD
MACKAY-SHIELDS: TOT RET	M-S MAINSTAY: TOT RTN
MACKAY-SHIELDS: VALUE	M-S MAINSTAY: VALUE
WL MORGAN GROWTH	VANGUARD MORGAN GROWTH
NATIONAL AVIATION & TECH	AFA NATIONAL AVIATION
NATIONAL TELECOM & TECH	AFA NATIONAL TELECOM
NEUBERGER & BER GENESIS	N & B GENESIS
NEUBERGER & BER GUARDIAN	N & B GUARDIAN
NEUBERGER & BER LTD MAT BD	N & B LTD MATURITY BOND
NEUBERGER & BER MANHATTAN	N & B MANHATTAN
NEUBERGER & BER MM PLUS	N & B MONEY MARKET PLUS
NEUBERGER & BER PARTNERS	N & B PARTNERS
NEUBERGER & BER SEL SECTOR	N & B SEL SECT ENERGY
PILGRIM FRGN: INTL BOND	FRANKLIN PRT: TX-AD INTL
PILGRIM PREFERRED	PILGRIM SH-TM MULTI MKT
PROVIDEND FD FOR INCOME	AMERICAN CAP EQUITY INCOME
RNC CONVERTIBLE	PROVIDENTMUT CONVERTIBLE
TUDOR FUND	WPG TUDOR FUND

MERGERS

AMER CAP GROWTH	Merged into Amer Cap Enterprise
BIG E PATHFINDER: TOT RET	Merged into PNC Total Return
FEDERATED CORP CASH	Merged into Fortress Utility
FUND SOURCE: BIL INTL GRO	Merged into GT Global International
IMG BOND ACCUMULATION	Merged into Princor Bond Fund
IMG STOCK ACCUMULATION	Merged into Princor Cap Accum
ISI GROWTH	Merged into Providentmut Growth
ISI TRUST	Merged into Providentmut Investment Shs
MACKENZIE GOVT SEC	Merged into Mackenzie Fixed Income
MORISON ASSET ALLOCATION	Merged into Amev Advntge: Asset Alloc
NATIONAL PREMIUM INC	Merged into National Total Income
PROVIDENTMUT INC SHS	Merged into Providentmut US Govt
PROVIDENTMUT SPECIAL	Merged into Providentmut Growth
PROVIDENTMUT VENTURE	Merged into Providentmut Growth
PILGRIM FRGN: GOVT SEC	Merged into Franklin Part: Tx-Adv USG
PILGRIM FRGN: HI INCOME	Merged into Franklin Part: Tx-Adv HY
PUTNAM CORP CASH ARP	Merged into Putnam Corp Cash DSF
RNC INCOME	Merged into Providentmut Total Income
RNC REGENCY	Merged into Providentmut Investmart Shs
RNC SH INT GOVT	Merged into Providentmut US Govt
RNC WESTWIND	Merged into Providentmut Growth
ROCHESTER GROWTH	Merger pending
SEAGATE INTL GOVT	Merged into Emblem Govt
SEAGATE: INTL GRO & INC	Merged into Emblem Intl Gro & Inc
SEAGATE: STOCK FD	Merged into Emblem Relative Value Fund
STEINROE GROWTH & INC	Merged into SteinRoe Prime Equities
ZWEIG SR TR: BLUE CHIP	Merged into Zweig Sr Tr: Priority
ZWEIG SR TR: BOND DEB	Merged into Zweig Sr Tr: Govt Sec
ZWEIG SR TR: CONVERTIBLE	Merged into Zweig Sr Tr: Priority
ZWEIG SR TR: EMERGING GRO	Merged into Zweig Sr Tr: Govt Sec
ZWEIG SR TR: LTD TM GOVT	Merged into Zweig Sr Tr: Govt Sec
ZWEIG SR TR: OPTION INCOME	Merged into Zweig Sr Tr: Priority

NEW FUNDS

ASSOC PLANRS: EQ INCOME	Mar. 5
ATLAS: GOVT & MTGE SEC	Jan. 17
BELL ATLANTIC: BOND	Feb. 5
BELL ATLANTIC: EQUITY	Feb. 5
DEAN WITTER CAP GR SEC	April 2
FIDELITY SEL CNSMR PRD	June 29
FIDELITY SEL DEVLP COMU	June 29
FIDELITY WORLDWIDE	May 30
HELMSMAN: INTL EQUITY	Mar. 30
HERITAGE INC: DIVERSIFIED	Mar. 1
HERITAGE INC: GOVERNMENT	Mar. 1
IDS BLUE CHIP ADVANTAGE	Mar. 5
IDS GLOBAL BOND: GROWTH	May 29
OPPENHEIMER GLBL ENVIRON	Mar. 2
PLYMOUTH EUROPE	April 23
PNC TOTAL RETURN	May 14
T ROWE PRICE INTL: EURO STK	Feb. 28
PUTNAM DIVIDEND GROWTH	Mar. 2
SCHIELD: PROG ENVIRONMENT	Feb. 5
SLH 1990S FUND	Feb. 23
VANGUARD INTL EQ INDEX: EUR	June 18
VANGUARD INTL EQ INDEX: PAC	June 18

LIQUIDATIONS

BOST CO INDEX: BOND INDEX	FIRST INVESTORS QUALIFIED DIV
DFA GRP: 5 YEAR FIXED INC	PRIME: INCOME FD
FDS OF AUSTRALIA: INCOME	SLH CONVERTIBLE SEC FD
FENIMORE INTL: FIXED INCOME	

STOCK SPLITS

AMER CAP PACE	2-for-1 split, 6/8/90
STATE STREET INVESTMENT	5-for-1 split, 5/1/90

FUND NAME	OBJECTIVE	TOTAL NET ASSETS (MIL) 6/30/90	NET ASSET VALUE 6/30/90	PERFORMANCE (Return on Initial $10,000 Investment) 3/31/90- 6/30/90	6/30/89- 6/30/90	6/30/85- 6/30/90	DIVIDEND YIELD % 6/90	PHONE NUMBER 800	In-State	FEES Load	12b-1	Redemption	MANAGER	SINCE
DREMAN: CONTRARIAN PORT	Growth	12.2	11.80	10,655.80	11,255.00	☆	2.5	533-1608	201-332-8228	None	0.25	None	Dreman Value Mgmt. Lp.	'88
DREMAN: HIGH RETURN PORT	Equity Income	4.4	10.20	10,458.50	10,855.80	☆	3.7	533-1608	201-332-8228	None	0.25	None	Dreman Value Mgmt. Lp	'88
DREYFUS A BONDS PLUS	Fixed Income	319.4	13.61	10,344.20	10,426.70	15,836.20	8.6	782-6620	None	None	None	None	N/A	N/A
DREYFUS CAPITAL VALUE	Capital Appreciation	678.5	13.35	9,625.10	9,653.00	☆	0.0	782-6620	None	4.50	0.25	None	Comstock Partners	N/A
DREYFUS CONVERTIBLE SEC	Convertibles	276.7	9.62	10,290.40	11,037.70	20,472.40	4.0	782-6620	None	None	None	None	N/A	N/A
DREYFUS FRGN INV GOVT LP★	Fixed Income	0.3	15.30	10,298.80	10,595.60	☆	7.7	782-6620	None	None	0.25	None	N/A	N/A
DREYFUS FUND	Growth & Income	2,746.5	12.25	10,739.60	11,447.30	19,119.70	4.7	782-6620	None	None	None	None	N/A	N/A
DREYFUS GNMA	Fixed Income	1,528.3	14.44	10,352.60	10,841.90	15,013.10	9.0	782-6620	None	None	0.20	None	N/A	N/A

Fund	Objective	Net Assets	NAV	Value 1	Value 2	Value 3	Yield	Phone	Phone	Max Chg	12b-1	Fee	Manager	Mgr Since
DREYFUS GRO-OPPORTUNITY	Growth	512.3	10.43	10,450.90	10,775.60	20,239.30	4.3	782-6620	None	None	None	None	N/A	N/A
DREYFUS INDEX	Growth & Income	65.5	15.23	10,602.40	11,537.60		3.1	782-6620	None	None	None	None	N/A	N/A
DREYFUS LEVERAGE FUND	Capital Appreciation	473.6	16.44	10,640.80	11,364.90	19,263.20	4.3	782-6620	None	4.50	0.25	None	N/A	N/A
DREYFUS NEW LEADERS	Small-Company Growth	182.8	30.08	10,723.70	11,373.70	21,375.50	1.2	782-6620	None	N/A	0.25	None	N/A	N/A
DREYFUS SHT-INTERM GOVT	Fixed Income	46.8	11.11	10,273.30	10,833.50		9.1	782-6620	None	None	None	None	N/A	N/A
DREYFUS STRAT AGG INV LP	Flexible	80.4	28.85	10,441.50	10,630.10	☆	0.0	782-6620	None	3.00	0.25	None	N/A	N/A
DREYFUS STRATEGIC INCOME	Fixed Income	42.5	12.79	10,342.10	10,441.40	☆	9.1	782-6620	None	4.50	0.25	None	Barbara Kenworthy	N/A
DREYFUS STRATEGIC INVEST	Flexible	112.3	19.14	10,268.20	10,500.80	☆	1.1	782-6620	None	4.50	0.25	None	N/A	N/A
DREYFUS STRAT WORLD INV	Global Flexible	20.7	25.57	10,232.10	11,971.00	☆	0.0	782-6620	None	3.00	0.25	None	N/A	N/A
DREYFUS STRAT WORLD REVS	World Fixed-Income	14.7	13.29	10,015.10	9,595.70		0.0	782-6620	None	3.00	0.25	None	N/A	N/A
DREYFUS THIRD CENTURY	Growth	197.2	7.11	10,756.40	11,960.10	18,885.00	2.5	782-6620	None	None	None	None	N/A	N/A
DREYFUS US GOVT BD LP	Fixed Income	24.3	13.07	10,398.10	10,527.20		8.9	782-6620	None	None	None	None	N/A	N/A
DREYFUS US GOVT INTER LP	Fixed Income	62.3	12.30	10,300.60	10,671.10		9.2	782-6620	None	None	None	None	N/A	N/A
EAGLE GROWTH SHARES	Growth	3.7	11.67	10,570.70	9,895.70	16,714.80	0.5	221-5588	212-425-9655	8.50	None	None	Donald Baxter	'87
EATON VANCE DOLR: CORP INC★	Fixed Income	9.0	8.87	10,199.20	9,314.80	☆	14.6	225-6265	617-482-8260	4.75	0.25	None	Hooker Talcott	'87
EATON VANCE DOLR: US GOVT★	Fixed Income	5.0	10.85	10,242.00	10,600.10	☆	9.2	225-6265	617-482-8260	4.75	0.25	None	Mark Venezia	'87
EATON VANCE EQUITY INC	Equity Income	41.9	10.96	9,981.90	10,569.90		5.4	225-6265	617-482-8260	None	1.25	6	Ed Bragdon	'87
EATON VANCE GOVT OBLIG	Fixed Income	283.8	11.26	10,298.20	10,835.70	15,824.20	9.9	225-6265	617-482-8260	4.75	0.25	None	Mark Venezia	'84
EATON VANCE GROWTH	Growth	91.1	8.62	10,897.60	11,883.20	20,645.10	0.9	225-6265	617-482-8260	4.75	0.25	None	Walker Martin	'87
EATON VANCE HIGH INC	Fixed Income	228.8	7.49	10,472.50	9,369.20		15.2	225-6265	617-482-8260	None	1.25	6	Hooker Talcott	'86
EATON VANCE INC OF BOSTON	Fixed Income	74.0	7.81	10,491.50	9,579.70	15,294.50	14.9	225-6265	617-482-8260	4.75	0.25	None	Hooker Talcott	'86
EATON VANCE INVESTORS	Balanced	205.0	7.19	10,398.10	11,036.70	17,103.70	5.9	225-6265	617-482-8260	4.75	0.25	None	M. Dozier Gardner	'87
EATON VANCE NTRL RES	Natural Resources	4.3	12.08	9,657.60	11,069.10		1.3	225-6265	617-482-8260	None	1.25	6	Landon Clay	'87
EATON VANCE SPL EQUITIES	Growth	59.4	24.20	11,377.50	12,567.80	16,603.70	0.0	225-6265	617-482-8260	4.75	0.25	None	Clifford Krauss	'87
EATON VANCE STOCK FD	Growth & Income	88.4	14.94	10,611.10	11,868.40	20,123.40	3.4	225-6265	617-482-8260	4.75	None	None	Robert Dunbar	'86
EATON VANCE TOTAL RETURN	Growth & Income	479.5	9.05	9,935.00	10,881.50	18,184.70	6.1	225-6265	617-482-8260	4.75	0.25	None	Ed Bragdon	'81
ECLIPSE: BALANCED	Balanced	3.9	15.16	10,026.80	10,358.00	☆	4.8	872-2710	872-2710	None	None	None	Wesley McCain	'89
ECLIPSE: EQUITY FD	Small-Company Growth	200.1	10.91	10,205.30	10,358.60		2.1	872-2710	872-2710	None	None	None	Wesley McCain	'87
EHRENKRANTZ GROWTH	Growth	7.0	5.66	10,719.70	11,418.70	☆	8.8	None	212-344-3799	4.50	None	None	Jeff King/Jack Simon	'87
ELFUN: DIVERS FIED FD★	Balanced	15.8	12.18	10,491.00	11,072.50	☆	4.5	242-0134	203-357-4104	None	None	None	Arthur Bahr	N/A
ELFUN: GLOBAL FUND★	Global	17.5	12.97	11,010.20	12,306.50	☆	0.1	242-0134	203-357-4104	None	None	None	John R. Reinberg	N/A
ELFUN: INCOME FUND★	Fixed Income	96.0	10.87	10,351.10	10,633.70	16,172.90	8.1	242-0134	203-357-4104	None	None	None	Robert MacDougall	N/A
ELFUN: TRUSTS★	Growth	694.4	32.52	10,973.00	11,709.70	22,379.00	3.1	242-0134	203-357-4104	None	None	None	David Carlson	N/A
ELITE GROUP: GROWTH & INC	Growth & Income	5.0	11.88	11,078.00	11,854.10	☆	1.9	423-1068	206-624-5863	None	None	None	Richard McCormick	'87
ELITE GROUP: INCOME	Fixed Income	3.4	9.56	10,295.90	10,611.00		8.9	423-1068	206-624-5863	None	None	None	Richard McCormick	'87
EMBLEM FD: EARN MOMENTUM	Growth	27.4	10.24	10,530.30	☆		0.0	543-6956	None	4.00	None	None	Bruce McCain	'89
EMBLEM FD: OH REGIONAL EQ	Capital Appreciation	19.7	9.61	10,407.50	☆	☆	0.0	543-6956	None	4.00	None	None	Dennis Amato	'89
EMBLEM FD: RELATIVE VALUE	Growth	128.3	10.71	10,690.30	☆		0.0	543-6956	None	4.00	None	None	Larry Babin	'89
EMBLEM FD: SH/INTMDT INC	Fixed Income	31.3	9.97	10,271.70	☆	☆	0.0	543-6956	None	4.00	None	None	Steve Moore	'89
ENDOWMENTS INC★	Growth & Income	40.8	17.16	10,155.20	11,115.60	19,099.30	5.7	None	415-421-9360	None	None	None	Multiple Managers	'75
ENTERPRISE: CAPITAL APPR	Capital Appreciation	13.1	19.20	11,415.00	12,559.30	☆	0.0	432-4320	404-396-8118	4.75	0.45	None	Jeff Miller	'87
ENTERPRISE: GOVT SEC	Fixed Income	31.6	11.80	10,325.20	10,772.80		8.4	432-4320	404-396-8118	4.75	0.45	None	Joe Patterson	'87
ENTERPRISE: GROWTH	Growth	60.5	7.61	10,628.50	11,433.70	20,976.90	0.2	432-4320	404-396-8118	4.75	0.45	None	Ron Canakaris	'72
ENTERPRISE: GRO & INC	Growth & Income	34.7	14.79	10,197.00	10,397.40	☆	3.6	432-4320	404-396-8118	4.75	0.45	None	John Rock	'87
ENTERPRISE: H YLD BOND	Fixed Income	27.8	10.39	10,231.60	9,532.20	☆	12.8	432-4320	404-396-8118	4.75	0.45	None	Jim Caywood	'87

★DREYFUS FOREIGN INVESTING—Designed exclusively for qualifying foreign investors.
★EATON VANCE DOLLAR FUNDS—Designed exclusively for qualifying foreign investors.
★ELFUN FUNDS—Limited to selected General Electric employees.
★ENDOWMENTS INC.—Limited to certain tax-exempt institutions.

PERFORMANCE OF MUTUAL FUNDS (continued)

FUND NAME	OBJECTIVE	TOTAL NET ASSETS (MIL) 6/30/90	NET ASSET VALUE 6/30/90	PERFORMANCE (Return on Initial $10,000 Investment)			DIVIDEND YIELD % 6/90	PHONE NUMBER		FEES			MANAGER	SINCE
				3/31/90-6/30/90	6/30/89-6/30/90	6/30/85-6/30/90		800	In-State	Load	12b-1	Redemption		
ENTERPRISE: INTL GRO	International	10.4	14.50	10,788.70	11,551.90	☆	0.0	432-4320	404-396-8118	None	1.25	5.00	Kathryn Matthews	'87
ENTERPRISE: PREC METALS	Gold	5.5	11.42	9,314.80	10,464.00	☆	2.3	432-4320	404-396-8118	None	1.25	5.00	Bill Curry	'87
EQUITABLE: BALANCED	Balanced	22.3	13.28	10,514.60	10,987.80	☆	1.8	541-2150	212-641-8100	None	1.00	5.00	Judith Taylor	'87
EQUITABLE: GOVT SEC	Fixed Income	20.7	9.76	10,273.80	10,366.10	☆	6.8	541-2150	212-641-8100	None	1.00	5.00	Zane Brown	'87
EQUITABLE: GROWTH	Growth	18.7	15.54	10,401.60	11,196.10	☆	0.0	541-2150	212-641-8100	None	1.00	5.00	Tyler Smith	'87
EQUITEC SIEBEL II: EQU IN	Equity Income	1.3	11.25	10,324.50	10,879.50	☆	3.7	869-8807	415-430-9900	4.75	0.35	None	Ken Siebel	'87
EQUITEC SIEBEL II: GOV IN	Fixed Income	10.7	9.74	10,188.70	☆	☆	0.5	869-8807	415-430-9900	4.75	0.35	None	Edward Sport	'89
EQUITEC SIEBEL: AGGRES GRO	Capital Appreciation	31.9	14.19	10,577.30	11,226.90	☆	0.0	869-8807	415-430-9900	None	0.89	5.00	Ron Sloane	'86
EQUITEC SIEBEL: GLOBAL	Global	4.3	11.90	10,876.20	11,731.70	☆	0.6	869-8807	415-430-9900	None	1.00	5.00	Ken Siebel	'88
EQUITEC SIEBEL: HI YLD	Fixed Income	22.3	7.75	10,003.60	9,923.30	☆	11.9	869-8807	415-430-9900	None	0.90	5.00	Edward Sport	'86
EQUITEC SIEBEL: PRE MTL	Gold	3.4	9.70	9,108.00	10,566.40	☆	0.0	869-8807	415-430-9900	None	1.00	5.00	Gary Kirk	'86
EQUITEC SIEBEL: TOT RET	Growth & Income	125.6	15.43	10,664.30	11,307.50	17,819.20	3.7	869-8807	415-430-9900	None	0.89	5.00	Ken Siebel	'85
EQUITEC SIEBEL: US GOVT	Fixed Income	423.8	8.90	10,194.40	10,749.20	☆	9.8	869-8807	415-430-9900	None	0.98	5.00	Edward Sport	'86
EQUITY PORT: GROWTH	Growth	26.5	17.59	11,290.10	13,148.40	24,955.00	0.4	343-9184	617-570-5511	None	None	None	Bob Stansky	'87
EQUITY PORT: INCOME	Equity Income	368.2	11.17	10,200.50	9,886.10	17,602.10	6.7	343-9184	617-570-5511	None	None	None	Bruce Johnstone	'83
EQUITY STRATEGIES★	Specialty	68.5	27.92	11,013.80	15,154.00	☆	3.9	None	212-888-6685	None	None	None	Martin Whitman	'84
EUROPACIFIC GROWTH	International	805.4	31.33	11,027.30	12,826.90	30,637.30	1.9	421-0180	None	5.75	0.14	None	Multiple Managers	'84
EUROPEAN EMERG COMPANIES	European Region	35.3	13.61	10,716.50	12,552.90	☆	0.2	523-2578	None	4.50	0.0025	None	Bruno Bertocci	'89
EVERGREEN AMER RETIREMNT	Balanced	11.9	10.24	10,241.10	10,498.10	☆	5.7	235-0064	800-252-0064	None	None	None	Irene O'Neill	'88
EVERGREEN FOUNDATION★	Balanced	1.4	10.80	10,803.70	☆	☆	0.0	235-0064	800-252-0064	None	None	None	Stephen Lieber	'90
EVERGREEN FUND	Growth	733.1	12.28	10,678.30	10,215.20	17,675.10	2.9	235-0064	800-252-0064	None	None	None	Stephen Lieber	'71
EVERGREEN GLBL REAL EST	Real Estate	7.3	10.20	10,408.20	10,953.30	☆	1.7	235-0064	800-252-0064	None	None	None	Sam Lieber	'89
EVERGREEN LIMITED MKT★	Small-Company Growth	42.3	18.07	10,573.40	10,892.60	19,565.10	1.8	235-0064	800-252-0064	N/A	N/A	N/A	N/A	N/A
EVERGREEN TOTAL RETURN	Equity Income	1,239.0	18.07	10,045.70	10,141.70	16,254.10	6.0	235-0064	800-252-0064	N/A	N/A	N/A	Nola Falcone	'78
EVERGREEN VALUE TIMING	Capital Appreciation	39.2	12.12	10,279.90	11,126.10	☆	4.2	235-0064	800-252-0064	None	None	None	Ed Nicklin	'86
EXCEL MIDAS GOLD SHARES	Gold	8.6	2.79	9,300.00	10,689.70	☆	0.0	333-9235	619-485-9400	4.50	0.25	None	Jack Hultbron	'89
EXCEL VALUE FUND	Growth	2.7	6.63	10,311.00	10,607.70	17,033.70	3.3	333-9235	619-485-9400	4.50	0.25	None	Gary Sabin	'89
EXECUTIVE INVEST HI YLD	Fixed Income	17.1	7.29	10,467.10	9,507.20	☆	15.1	423-4026	212-208-6000	4.75	0.50	None	N/A	N/A
FAIRMONT FUND	Capital Appreciation	25.9	14.68	9,898.90	9,238.60	11,705.50	1.4	262-9936	502-636-5633	None	None	5.00	Morton H. Sachs	'81
FAM VALUE	Growth & Income	6.6	13.54	10,780.30	10,802.60	☆	0.4	None	518-234-4393	None	None	None	Thomas Putnam	'87
FASCIANO FUND	Small-Company Growth	5.2	14.20	10,790.30	11,291.80	☆	0.8	338-1579	312-444-6050	None	None	None	Michael Fasciano	'87
FBL SERIES: AGG GRO STK	Capital Appreciation	2.3	9.76	10,020.50	9,867.90	☆	10.7	247-4170	515-225-5586	None	0.75	5.00	Roger Grefe	'87
FBL SERIES: BLUE CHIP	Growth & Income	3.1	15.63	10,757.10	11,913.50	☆	1.8	247-4170	515-225-5586	None	0.75	5.00	Roger Grefe	'87
FBL SERIES: GNMA	Fixed Income	2.1	10.06	10,260.90	10,697.50	☆	7.5	247-4170	515-225-5586	None	0.75	5.00	LouAnn Sandburg	'87
FBL SERIES: GRO COM STK	Growth & Income	35.5	11.05	10,137.60	10,998.50	13,938.70	5.6	247-4170	515-225-5586	None	0.75	5.00	Roger Grefe	'86
FBL SERIES: HI QUAL BD	Fixed Income	3.6	9.87	10,292.30	10,634.30	☆	7.5	247-4170	515-225-5586	None	0.75	5.00	LouAnn Sandburg	'87
FBL SERIES: HI YLD BD	Fixed Income	3.4	9.61	10,272.70	10,678.40	☆	10.1	247-4170	515-225-5586	None	0.75	5.00	Bob Rummelhart	'87
FBL SERIES: MANAGED	Flexible	3.6	10.04	10,266.80	10,622.20	☆	6.2	247-4170	515-225-5586	None	0.75	5.00	LouAnn Sandburg	'87
FEDERATED BOND	Fixed Income	44.0	9.06	10,337.90	10,632.20	☆	7.8	245-2423	None	None	None	None	Madden/Durbiano	'85
FEDERATED FLOATING RATE	Fixed Income	67.3	9.13	10,159.70	10,579.60	☆	9.9	245-2423	None	None	None	None	Madden/Durbiano	'86
FEDERATED GNMA TRUST	Fixed Income	1,330.8	10.99	10,353.60	10,833.50	16,182.50	9.1	245-2423	None	None	None	None	Gary Madich	'88
FEDERATED GROWTH TRUST	Growth	179.5	21.20	11,032.60	11,764.20	24,365.90	3.9	245-2423	None	None	None	None	Gregory Melvin	'87
FEDERATED HIGH INCOME	Fixed Income	288.1	9.16	10,608.90	9,558.90	14,186.50	14.8	356-2635	None	4.50	0.25	None	Madden/Durbiano	'83
FEDERATED HIGH YIELD TR	Fixed Income	128.6	8.07	10,469.90	9,551.50	14,675.40	15.4	245-2423	None	None	None	None	Madden/Durbiano	'84
FEDERATED INCOME TRUST	Fixed Income	974.2	10.19	10,300.90	10,909.70	15,367.60	9.1	245-2423	None	None	None	None	Gary Madich	'88

Fund	Objective	Net Assets	NAV	12-mo	36-mo	Yield	Phone	Alt Phone		Load	12b-1	Fee	Manager	Started
FEDERATED INTMDT GOVT	Fixed Income	894.0	9.60	10,316.30	10,737.30	8.2	245-2423		None	None	None	None	Roger Early	'88
FEDERATED SH-IN"MDT GOVT	Fixed Income	1,496.3	9.96	10,272.60	10,791.40	8.2	245-2423		None	None	None	None	Roger Early	'87
FEDERATED STOCK & BOND	Balanced	88.5	15.05	10,275.60	10,586.30	6.2	245-2423		None	None	None	None	David Francis	'85
FEDERATED STOCK TRUST	Growth & Income	446.1	22.79	10,285.10	10,440.20	3.3	245-2423		None	None	None	None	Peter Anderson	'82
FEDERATED US GCVT	Fixed Income	34.1	9.30	10,340.80	10,460.20	7.7	245-2423		None	None	None	None	Roger Early	'87
FENIMORE INTL: EQUITY	International	45.2	14.52	11,008.30	13,057.60	0.0	223-4522	212-232-2888	None	5.00	0.30	None	Fenimore Intl. Mgt. Corp.	'86
FFB EQUITY	Capital Appreciation	2.0	11.78	10,360.60	11,623.90	1.4	626-3863	212-309-8860	None	None	None	None	Franklin Tseng	'89
FIDELITY ADJUSTABLE RATE	Fixed Income	32.3	8.12	10,068.00	10,029.60	10.1	544-6666		None	None	None	None	Donald Taylor	'86
FIDELITY ASSET MANAGER	Flexible	380.0	11.25	10,436.00	10,769.80	3.3	544-6666		None	None	None	None	Bob Beckwitt	'88
FIDELITY BALANCED	Balanced	222.8	11.08	10,236.70	10,768.80	8.9	544-6666		None	2.00	None	None	Robert Haber	'88
FIDELITY BLUE CHIP GRO	Growth	148.9	15.70	11,278.70	12,969.50	0.8	544-6666		None	2.00	None	1.00	Richard O'Rourke	'88
FIDELITY CAPITAL APREC	Capital Appreciation	2,073.5	16.31	10,067.90	10,461.60	1.4	544-6666		None	2.00	None	1.00	Thomas Sweeney	'86
FIDELITY CONTRAFUND	Growth	536.5	18.18	10,971.60	12,488.50	1.3	544-6666		None	3.00	None	None	Jeff Vinik	'88
FIDELITY CONVER"IBLE	Convertibles	70.7	11.73	10,431.50	11,281.40	6.6	544-6666		None	None	None	None	Andrew Midler	'88
FIDELITY DESTINY I	Growth	1,832.7	14.24	10,722.90	11,217.50	2.6	752-2347		None	8.98	None	None	George Vanderheiden	'80
FIDELITY DESTINY II	Growth	221.1	21.11	10,820.10	11,441.60	1.7	752-2347		None	8.98	None	None	George Vanderheiden	'85
FIDELITY DISCIPLIMED EQU	Growth	124.6	14.37	10,723.90	12,058.20	0.9	544-8888		None	3.00	None	None	Brad Lewis	'88
FIDELITY D-MARK PERFORM	World Fixed-Income	6.1	11.53	10,368.70	☆	0.0	544-8888		None	0.40	None	None	Judy Pagliuca	'89
FIDELITY EQUITY-INCOME	Equity Income	4,738.6	25.22	10,202.40	9,944.40	6.8	544-8888		None	2.00	None	None	Bruce Johnstone	'72
FIDELITY EUROPE	European Region	450.2	18.51	10,837.20	13,094.00	1.0	544-8888		None	2.00	None	1.00	Penelope Dobkin	'86
FIDELITY FLEXIBLE BOND	Fixed Income	389.7	6.74	10,344.00	10,629.20	8.8	544-8888		None	None	None	None	Michael Gray	'87
FIDELITY FREEDOM FUND	Capital Appreciation	1,614.3	15.88	10,861.80	12,038.40	2.4	544-8888		None	None	None	None	Stuart Williams	'88
FIDELITY FUND	Growth & Income	1,153.7	18.13	10,404.30	11,313.00	3.6	544-8888		None	None	None	None	Barry Greenfield	'83
FIDELITY GLOBAL BOND	World Fixed-Income	80.3	11.43	10,353.30	11,102.70	4.3	544-8888		None	None	None	None	Judy Pagliuca	'86
FIDELITY GOVT SECURITIES	Fixed Income	484.9	9.41	10,312.50	10,708.50	8.6	544-8888		None	None	None	None	Curt Hollingsworth	'90
FIDELITY GROWTH & INCOME	Growth & Income	1,900.6	17.22	10,413.30	11,094.10	4.3	544-8888		None	2.00	None	None	Beth Terrana	'85
FIDELITY GROWTH COMPANY	Growth	673.3	21.18	11,014.00	12,929.70	0.6	544-8888		None	3.00	None	None	Robert Stansky	'87
FIDELITY HIGH INCOME	Fixed Income	1,192.5	6.88	10,473.50	9,216.90	13.7	544-8888		None	None	None	None	Margaret Eagle	'87
FIDELITY INC: GNMA	Fixed Income	634.3	10.28	10,346.70	10,808.80	8.2	544-8888		None	None	None	None	Jim Wolfson	'87
FIDELITY INC: MORTGAGE	Fixed Income	384.9	10.14	10,349.50	10,833.90	8.1	544-8888		None	None	None	None	Jim Wolfson	'87
FIDELITY INSTL: US EQ INDX	Growth & Income	414.0	13.67	10,624.90	11,617.60	3.3	544-8888		None	None	None	None	Jay Weed	N/A
FIDELITY INTERMED BD	Fixed Income	698.2	9.90	10,291.40	10,656.00	8.5	544-8888		None	None	None	None	Michael Gray	'87
FIDELITY INTL GR 3 INC	International	36.1	14.41	10,958.20	12,110.10	1.1	544-8888		None	1.00	None	1.00	John Hicking	'87
FIDELITY INV TR: CANADA	International	22.5	14.92	10,382.70	10,548.20	0.1	544-8888		None	2.00	None	1.00	George Domolky	'87
FIDELITY LOW-PRICE STK	Small-Company Growth	109.9	10.80	10,671.90	☆	0.0	544-8888		None	None	None	1.50	Joel Tillinghast	'90
FIDELITY MAGELLAN FUND	Growth	14,038.9	60.08	10,560.50	11,701.90	2.3	544-8888		None	3.00	None	None	Morris Smith	'90
FIDELITY NC CASH MGT TRM	Fixed Income	83.0	9.74	10,222.90	10,828.30	8.4	544-8888		None	None	None	None	Judy Pagliuca	'88
FIDELITY OVERSEAS	International	1,108.2	30.23	10,842.90	12,897.00	0.9	544-8888		None	3.00	None	None	George Noble	'84
FIDELITY OTC	Small-Company Growth	728.6	20.69	10,365.70	11,056.40	2.4	544-8888		None	3.00	None	None	Alan Radio	'90
FIDELITY PACIFIC BASIN	Pacific Region	101.4	14.84	11,008.90	10,898.90	0.1	544-8888		None	2.00	None	1.00	John Hicking	'90
FIDELITY POUND PERFORM	World Fixed-Income	2.3	11.93	10,975.20	☆	0.0	544-8888		None	0.40	None	None	Judy Pagliuca	'89
FIDELITY PURITAN	Equity Income	4,864.8	13.20	10,245.00	10,423.50	7.4	544-8888		None	2.00	None	None	Rich Fentin	'87
FIDELITY QUALIFIED DVD	Equity Income	48.9	10.79	9,995.10	10,370.00	8.1	544-8888		None	None	N/A	None-	Alan Berro	'89
FIDELITY REAL ESTATE	Real Estate	45.4	9.11	9,978.70	10,042.80	5.5	544-8888		None	None	None	None	Barry Greenfield	'83
FIDELITY SEL AIR TRANS	Specialty	4.2	11.85	10,331.30	10,348.90	0.0	544-8888		None	2.00	None	1.00	Karen Firestone	'87
FIDELITY SEL AMER GOLD	Gold	198.0	15.50	9,080.30	10,601.90	0.0	544-8888		None	2.00	None	1.00	Malcolm MacNaught	'85
FIDELITY SEL AUTOMATION	Specialty	1.1	11.45	10,303.10	11,431.10	2.2	544-8888		None	2.00	None	1.00	Abigail Johnson	'88

★EQUITY STRATEGIES—Closed to new investors.

★EVERGREEN FOUNDATION—Limited to private charitable foundations.

★EVERGREEN LIMITED MARKET—Closed to new investors.

PERFORMANCE OF MUTUAL FUNDS (continued)

FUND NAME	OBJECTIVE	TOTAL NET ASSETS (MIL) 6/30/90	NET ASSET VALUE 6/30/90	PERFORMANCE (Return on Initial $10,000 Investment) 3/31/90-6/30/90	6/30/89-6/30/90	6/30/85-6/30/90	DIVIDEND YIELD % 6/30/90	PHONE NUMBER 800	In-State	FEES Load	12b-1	Redemption	MANAGER	SINCE
FIDELITY SEL AUTO	Specialty	0.6	12.91	10,720.90	10,566.10	☆	4.6	544-8888	None	2.00	None	1.00	Kevin McCarey	'89
FIDELITY SEL BIO TECH	Health/Biotech.	157.0	18.44	12,357.30	15,636.50	☆	0.0	544-8888	None	2.00	None	1.00	Mike Gordon	'90
FIDELITY SEL BROADCAST	Specialty	7.6	12.65	10,343.40	8,601.00		0.0	544-8888	None	2.00	None	1.00	Fergus Shell	'90
FIDELITY SEL BROKERAGE	Financial Services	3.9	8.71	10,198.50	10,223.10	☆	1.4	544-8888	None	2.00	None	1.00	David Ellison	'88
FIDELITY SEL CAP GOODS	Specialty	2.1	13.23	10,646.60	11,945.20	☆	0.7	544-8888	None	2.00	None	1.00	Abigail Johnson	'88
FIDELITY SEL CHEMICAL	Technology	21.7	24.18	10,704.00	10,917.60	☆	1.0	544-8888	None	2.00	None	1.00	Steve Pesek	'88
FIDELITY SEL COMPUTER	Technology	33.6	14.59	11,197.20	13,108.70	☆	0.0	544-8888	None	2.00	None	1.00	Larry Bowman	'88
FIDELITY SEL CNSMR PRD	Specialty	0.2	10.00	☆	☆	☆	0.0	544-8888	None	2.00	None	1.00	Dave Calabro	'90
FIDELITY SEL DEFENSE	Specialty	1.2	12.71	10,305.50	10,239.50	10,211.20	0.6	544-8888	None	2.00	None	1.00	Jeff Ubben	'89
FIDELITY SEL DVLP COMM	Specialty	0.2	10.00	☆	☆	☆	0.0	544-8888	None	2.00	None	1.00	Jennifer Uhrig	'90
FIDELITY SEL ELEC UTIL	Utility	23.8	10.75	10,103.90	10,827.20	☆	1.9	544-8888	None	2.00	None	1.00	Alan Berro	'86
FIDELITY SEL ELECTRONIC	Technology	43.2	10.61	11,697.90	14,675.00	☆	0.0	544-8888	None	2.00	None	1.00	Harris Leviton	'87
FIDELITY SEL ENERGY	Natural Resources	85.7	16.15	10,008.10	11,788.40	17,797.90	1.3	544-8888	None	2.00	None	1.00	Frank Bracken	'89
FIDELITY SEL ENRGY SER	Natural Resources	79.9	13.51	10,497.30	14,296.30	☆	0.0	544-8888	None	2.00	None	1.00	David Neisser	'89
FIDELITY SEL ENVRNMNT	Specialty	128.4	12.86	11,330.40	12,871.30	☆	0.1	544-8888	None	2.00	None	1.00	Larry Greenberg	'89
FIDELITY SEL FINANCIAL	Financial Services	22.6	29.91	10,201.20	9,401.50	13,765.60	0.3	544-8888	None	2.00	None	1.00	Kevin McCarey	'89
FIDELITY SEL FOOD	Specialty	31.5	25.37	11,179.90	12,526.00	☆	0.2	544-8888	None	2.00	None	1.00	David Calabro	'87
FIDELITY SEL HEALTH	Health/Biotech.	292.1	52.15	11,763.60	13,835.60	23,260.10	0.5	544-8888	None	2.00	None	1.00	Andy Olfit	'90
FIDELITY SEL HOUSING	Specialty	0.7	11.12	10,416.20	10,615.20	☆	1.3	544-8888	None	2.00	None	1.00	Michael Kagan	'89
FIDELITY SEL INDUS MAT	Specialty	2.8	12.71	9,731.40	9,954.30	☆	2.7	544-8888	None	2.00	None	1.00	Steve Pesek	'87
FIDELITY SEL LEISURE	Specialty	50.5	26.65	10,285.60	9,460.90	20,823.40	2.1	544-8888	None	2.00	None	1.00	Karen Firestone	'89
FIDELITY SEL LIFE INS	Financial Services	0.6	11.31	10,580.00	10,714.10	☆	1.1	544-8888	None	2.00	None	1.00	Scott Ofen	'89
FIDELITY SEL MEDICAL	Health/Biotech.	44.9	13.36	12,079.60	13,387.20	☆	0.2	544-8888	None	2.00	None	1.00	Larry Greenberg	'87
FIDELITY SEL PAPER & FRS	Specialty	4.9	11.45	9,736.40	9,867.40	☆	1.3	544-8888	None	2.00	None	1.00	Bob Chon	'90
FIDELITY SEL PREC-MTLS	Gold	184.7	11.99	8,796.80	10,408.60	12,619.10	1.5	544-8888	None	2.00	None	1.00	Malcolm MacNaught	'85
FIDELITY SEL PROP&CAS	Financial Services	2.7	14.92	10,566.60	11,591.40	☆	0.9	544-8888	None	2.00	None	1.00	Steve Pesek	'90
FIDELITY SEL REGL BANK	Financial Services	6.7	10.04	9,691.10	8,935.90	☆	1.0	544-8888	None	2.00	None	1.00	Steve Binder	'87
FIDELITY SEL RESTAURANT	Specialty	2.4	14.68	11,060.90	12,162.20	☆	0.1	544-8888	None	2.00	None	1.00	David Calabro	'87
FIDELITY SEL RETAIL	Specialty	10.5	15.60	11,032.50	12,265.10	☆	0.9	544-8888	None	2.00	None	1.00	Deborah Wheeler	'89
FIDELITY SEL S&L	Financial Services	6.5	9.73	10,576.10	8,855.20	☆	0.4	544-8888	None	2.00	None	1.00	Dave Ellison	'85
FIDELITY SEL SOFTWARE	Technology	16.4	17.95	11,484.30	12,920.50	☆	0.0	544-8888	None	2.00	None	1.00	Tom Sprague	'90
FIDELITY SEL TECH	Technology	92.6	22.87	10,874.90	12,628.40	12,188.10	0.0	544-8888	None	2.00	None	1.00	Larry Bowman	'90
FIDELITY SEL TELECOM	Technology	78.5	25.12	10,194.80	10,982.90	☆	0.4	544-8888	None	2.00	None	1.00	Jennifer Wig	'87
FIDELITY SEL TRANS	Specialty	1.2	12.04	9,866.60	10,577.70	☆	0.0	544-8888	None	2.00	None	1.00	Rick Mace	'89
FIDELITY SEL UTILITIES	Utility	134.0	32.89	10,201.10	11,199.80	19,181.90	1.5	544-8888	None	2.00	None	1.00	Alan Berro	'87
FIDELITY SHORT-TERM BOND	Fixed Income	203.4	9.26	10,262.00	10,771.30	☆	8.3	544-8888	None	N/A	N/A	None	Alan Bembenek	'87
FIDELITY SP SIT: INITIAL★	Capital Appreciation	18.2	18.73	10,005.30	10,628.20	21,631.20	3.8	544-8888	None	N/A	N/A	N/A	Daniel Frank	'83
FIDELITY SP SIT: PLYMOUTH	Capital Appreciation	194.6	18.60	10,000.00	10,588.60	☆	3.0	522-7297	None	4.00	0.65	None	Daniel Frank	'86
FIDELITY SPARTAN GOVT	Fixed Income	331.0	10.36	10,347.00	10,807.50	☆	9.0	544-8888	None	None	None	None	Bob Beckwitt	'88
FIDELITY SPARTAN LTD MAT	Fixed Income	133.8	9.88	10,262.10	10,754.40	19,644.60	8.2	544-8888	None	None	None	None	Curt Hollingsworth	'88
FIDELITY TREND	Growth	837.3	43.82	10,433.30	10,788.90	☆	1.2	544-8888	None	2.00	None	None	Alan Leifer	'87
FIDELITY UTIL INCOME	Utility	180.4	11.59	10,102.80	10,892.30	17,256.20	6.8	544-8888	None	2.00	None	None	Alan Berro	'89
FIDELITY VALUE FUND	Capital Appreciation	118.5	27.75	10,236.10	9,920.40	☆	1.0	544-8888	None	None	None	None	Ernest Wiggins	'86

Fund	Objective	Net Assets ($ mil)	NAV	Value $10K (1)	Value $10K (2)	Value $10K (3)	Yield %	Phone	Phone	Fee	Fee	Fee	Manager	Started
FIDELITY WORLDWIDE	Global	14.8	10.29	☆	☆	☆	0.0	544-8888	None	N/A	N/A	N/A	Judy Pagliuca	N/A
FIDELITY YEN PERFORM	World Fixed-Income	2.4	9.79	10,560.90	10,812.10	14,389.10	0.0	544-8888	None	0.40	None	None	T. Kellner/D. Wilson	'89
FIDUCIARY CAPITAL GROWTH	Small-Company Growth	25.0	18.18	10,644.00	10,648.10	☆	1.1	338-1579	414-226-4555	None	None	None	D. Wilson/T. Kellner	'81
FIDUCIARY INCOME FUND	Fixed Income	0.2	7.09	10,241.90	☆	☆	8.5	338-1579	414-226-4555	None	None	None	D. Wilson/T. Kellner	'85
FIDUCIARY TOTAL RETURN	Growth & Income	3.0	11.03	10,565.10	10,754.50	☆	2.3	338-1579	414-226-4555	None	1.00	1.00	T. Kellner/T. Kellner	'86
FINANCIAL BD: HIGH YIELD	Fixed Income	49.5	6.76	10,401.00	9,852.30	15,424.00	13.3	525-8025	303-779-1233	None	None	None	Bill Veronda	'84
FINANCIAL BD: SELECT INC	Fixed Income	32.6	6.12	10,368.60	10,574.00	15,997.40	9.9	525-8025	303-779-1233	None	None	None	Ron Lout	'90
FINANCIAL BD: LS GOVT	Fixed Income	18.1	6.93	10,327.60	10,520.40	☆	7.9	525-8025	303-779-1233	None	None	None	Ron Lout	'88
FINANCIAL DYNAMICS	Capital Appreciation	72.9	8.27	10,955.80	11,941.50	17,523.90	1.6	525-8085	303-779-1233	None	None	None	Bill Keithler	'89
FINANCIAL INDUST FUND	Growth & Income	414.6	4.99	11,059.80	12,685.80	18,681.40	2.0	525-8085	303-779-1233	None	None	None	Dalton Sim	'87
FINANCIAL INDUST INCOME	Equity Income	572.4	9.39	10,991.80	12,105.10	22,209.10	4.0	525-8085	303-779-1233	None	None	None	John Kaweske	'84
FINANCIAL PORT: ENERGY	Natural Resources	11.7	12.33	9,927.50	11,101.90	18,489.30	2.0	525-8085	303-779-1233	None	None	None	Jerry Mill	'89
FINANCIAL PORT: EUROPEAN	European Region	90.4	12.24	10,841.50	12,515.80	☆	1.1	525-8085	303-779-1233	None	None	None	R. Powe/A. Powell	'87
FINANCIAL PORT: FINANCIAL	Financial Services	1.7	9.25	10,693.60	11,237.00	☆	0.9	525-8085	303-779-1233	None	None	None	Dan Leonard	'89
FINANCIAL PORT: GOLD	Gold	39.6	4.96	8,686.50	10,439.20	11,249.60	0.4	525-8085	303-779-1233	None	None	None	Dan Leonard	'89
FINANCIAL PORT: HEALTH	Health/Biotech.	88.0	24.42	11,894.80	15,541.00	32,045.30	0.4	525-8085	303-779-1233	None	None	None	John Kaweske	'84
FINANCIAL PORT: LEISURE	Specialty	8.9	14.88	10,949.20	11,337.50	24,171.10	1.3	525-8085	303-779-1233	None	None	None	Roger Maurer	'89
FINANCIAL PORT: PACIFIC	Pacific Region	20.3	14.91	10,979.40	11,467.70	30,707.60	0.1	525-8085	303-779-1233	None	None	None	Paul Parsons	'89
FINANCIAL PORT: TECH	Technology	46.2	16.36	11,660.70	14,465.10	23,723.70	0.0	525-8085	303-779-1233	None	None	None	Dan Leonard	'84
FINANCIAL PORT: UTILITIES	Utility	29.2	9.13	10,171.50	10,492.20	☆	3.7	525-8085	303-779-1233	None	None	None	Jerry Mill	'88
FINL HORIZONS GOVT BOND	Fixed Income	1.8	10.15	10,361.00	10,705.30	☆	9.2	533-5622	None	None	6.00	6.00	Randy Baney	'89
FINL HORIZONS GROWTH	Growth	0.6	10.42	10,550.50	9,924.50	☆	2.4	533-5622	None	None	6.00	6.00	John Schaffner	'89
FIRST AUSTRAL A: AS LIQ	World Fixed-Income	5.5	10.00	10,775.20	☆	☆	0.0	522-5465	212-754-6500	3.00	0.50	None	EquitiLink Australia Ltd.	'89
FIRST AUSTRAL A: INCOME	World Fixed-Income	3.1	9.56	10,785.00	☆	☆	0.0	522-5465	212-754-6500	4.75	0.50	None	EquitiLink Australia Ltd.	'89
FIRST AUSTRAL A: INC ENHC	World Fixed-Income	0.8	9.35	10,792.90	☆	☆	0.0	522-5465	212-754-6500	4.75	0.50	None	EquitiLink Australia Ltd.	'89
FIRST AUSTRAL A: PAC RIM	Pacific Region	0.7	8.50	10,107.90	☆	☆	0.0	522-5465	212-754-6500	4.75	0.50	None	EquitiLink Australia Ltd.	'89
FIRST EAGLE FC OF AMER	Capital Appreciation	90.1	12.64	9,921.50	10,669.30	12,322.20	0.8	451-3623	212-943-9200	7.25	1.00	1.00	Kellen/Levy/Cohen	'87
FIRST INV BLUE CHIP	Growth & Income	43.9	13.07	10,873.80	11,588.00	31,652.30	3.4	423-4026	212-208-6000	6.90	None	None	Denise Burns	'89
FIRST INV FD FCR INCOME	Fixed Income	982.3	3.85	10,453.40	8,879.30	☆	15.2	423-4026	212-208-6000	6.90	0.11	None	Nancy Jones	'89
FIRST INV GLOBAL FUND	Global	245.7	5.69	11,334.70	13,934.50	☆	0.0	423-4026	212-208-6000	6.90	0.30	None	Dan Duane	'86
FIRST INV GOVT	Fixed Income	234.6	10.90	10,366.00	10,758.70	14,983.50	8.8	423-4026	212-208-6000	6.90	None	None	Denise Burns	'89
FIRST INV HIGH YIELD	Fixed Income	648.1	4.83	10,485.50	8,831.70	15,346.30	15.1	423-4026	212-208-6000	6.90	0.16	None	George Ganter	'89
FIRST INV SPECIAL BOND	Fixed Income	79.9	10.99	10,618.00	9,648.70	☆	13.3	423-4026	212-208-6000	7.25	None	None	George Ganter	'86
FIRST INV US GOVT PLUS-I	Fixed Income	1.6	11.08	10,562.40	10,053.10	☆	6.6	423-4026	212-208-6000	7.25	None	None	Patricia Poitra	'86
FIRST MUTUAL FUND	Capital Appreciation	14.7	9.30	10,751.40	11,787.40	N/A	0.6	None	212-759-7755	None	None	None	David Como	'82
FIRST PRAIRIE EVRSFD AST	Mixed Income	8.4	11.52	10,370.30	10,988.20	☆	7.3	821-1185	None	4.50	None	None	Arthur Krill	'85
FIRST TRUST AMERICA LP★	Fixed Income	6.6	10.84	10,346.10	10,714.80	☆	7.5	621-4770	800-848-8222	2.50	0.30	0.30	Oppenheimer Management	'90
FIRST TRUST: US GOVT★	Fixed Income	217.1	10.23	10,365.20	10,845.10	☆	8.8	621-4770	800-848-8222	2.50	0.25	0.25	Oppenheimer Management	'90
FLAG INTERNATIONAL	International	51.9	14.00	10,777.50	11,964.00	☆	4.0	767-3524	800-767-3524	4.50	0.25	0.25	Peter Pejacsevich	'86
FLAG INV EMERGING GROWTH	Small-Company Growth	52.8	13.56	10,995.50	10,841.30	☆	7.4	767-3524	800-767-3524	4.50	0.25	0.25	Reid/Hackney	'88
FLAG INV QUALITY GROWTH	Growth	43.3	10.81	10,925.90	☆	☆	0.0	767-3524	800-767-3524	4.50	0.25	0.25	R. Kilebrew/S. Brandaleone	'89
FLAG INV TELEPHONE INC	Equity Income	180.4	10.15	10,032.80	11,324.20	23,470.40	5.3	767-3524	800-767-3524	4.50	0.25	0.25	Bruce Behrens	'84
FLAGSHIP BASIC VALUE	Fixed Income	17.1	31.32	10,179.30	10,257.60	9,840.20	9.7	227-4648	800-354-7447	None	0.40	0.40	Richard Davis	'83
FLEX FUND: BOND	Fixed Income	4.8	18.24	10,188.50	10,810.90	13,761.70	7.8	325-3539	614-766-7000	None	0.20	0.20	Philip Voelker	'87
FLEX FUND: GROWTH	Growth	25.6	10.48	10,145.20	10,154.00	13,487.00	2.7	325-3539	614-766-7000	None	0.20	0.20	Philip Voelker	'89

★FIDELITY SPECIAL SIT: INITIAL—Closed.
★FIRST TRUST AMERICA—Designed exclusively for qualifying foreign investors.
★FIRST TRUST USGOVT—Changed advisers 4/7/90.

PERFORMANCE OF MUTUAL FUNDS (continued)

FUND NAME	OBJECTIVE	TOTAL NET ASSETS ($MIL) 6/30/90	NET ASSET VALUE 6/30/90	PERFORMANCE (Return on Initial $10,000 Investment) 3/31/90-6/30/90	6/30/89-6/30/90	6/30/85-6/30/90	DIVIDEND YIELD % 6/90	PHONE NUMBER 800	In-State	FEES Load	12b-1	Redemption	MANAGER	SINCE
FLEX FUND: MUIRFIELD	Growth	29.9	5.33	10,389.90	11,114.20	☆	13.9	325-3539	614-766-7000	None	0.20	None	Robert Meeder, Sr.	'88
FONTAINE: CAPITAL APPREC	Capital Appreciation	4.9	10.88	10,552.90	☆	☆	0.0	247-1550	301-385-1591	None	None	None	Richard Fontaine	'89
FORTRESS HI QUAL STOCK	Growth & Income	18.2	13.37	10,259.70	10,474.70	☆	3.1	245-5051	412-288-1900	0.50	0.50	0.75	Peter Anderson	'85
FORTRESS TOT PERF TREAS	Fixed Income	21.2	9.67	10,396.30	10,360.10	☆	7.4	245-5051	412-288-1900	1.00	0.25	0.75	Roger Early	'88
FORTRESS UTILITY	Utility	37.5	10.20	10,294.30	11,152.90	☆	6.1	245-5051	412-288-1900	1.00	0.25	0.75	C. H. Wiles	'90
44 WALL STREET FUND	Capital Appreciation	4.8	2.35	10,085.80	8,935.40	6,025.60	0.0	543-2620	212-248-8080	None	None	0.25	Mark Beckerman	'88
44 WALL STREET EQUITY	Capital Appreciation	4.4	5.63	10,503.70	11,237.50	12,853.90	0.0	543-2620	212-248-8080	1.00	None	0.25	Mark Beckerman	'88
FORUM: INVESTORS BOND	Fixed Income	18.3	9.91	10,309.10	☆	☆	0.0	542-0653	207-879-1900	3.75	None	None	John Keffer	'90
FORUM: INVESTORS STOCK	Growth & Income	16.6	9.99	10,359.20	11,973.10	☆	0.0	542-0653	207-879-1900	3.75	None	None	John Keffer	'90
FOUNDERS: BLUE CHIP	Growth & Income	258.2	7.68	11,014.10		21,875.60	2.0	525-2240	303-394-4404	None	0.25	None	Multiple Managers	'38
FOUNDERS: DISCOVERY	Small-Company Growth	4.0	11.78	11,780.00	☆	☆	0.0	525-2440	303-394-4404	None	0.25	None	Multiple Managers	'89
FOUNDERS: EQUITY INCOME	Equity Income	15.0	7.71	10,216.80	10,728.30	16,830.10	4.1	525-2440	303-394-4404	None	0.25	None	Multiple Managers	'63
FOUNDERS: FRONTIER	Small-Company Growth	71.2	19.21	10,865.40	11,523.20	☆	0.2	525-2440	303-394-4404	None	0.25	None	Multiple Managers	'87
FOUNDERS: GOVT SEC	Fixed Income	6.1	9.71	10,227.20	10,346.60	☆	7.6	525-2440	303-394-4404	None	0.25	None	Multiple Managers	'88
FOUNDERS: GROWTH	Growth	112.5	9.44	10,825.70	11,212.30	21,163.30	0.7	525-2440	303-394-4404	None	0.25	None	Multiple Managers	'63
FOUNDERS: SPECIAL	Capital Appreciation	71.3	6.52	10,550.20	10,979.70	19,656.00	2.1	525-2440	303-394-4404	None	None	None	Multiple Managers	'61
FOUNDERS: WORLDWIDE GROWTH	Global	5.3	11.05	10,780.50	☆	☆	0.0	525-2440	303-394-4404	None	0.25	None	Multiple Managers	'89
FPA CAPITAL	Growth	80.6	14.02	10,565.20	11,261.30	22,475.80	1.6	638-3060	213-284-3683	6.50	None	None	Robert Rodriguez	'84
FPA NEW INCOME	Fixed Income	34.7	9.73	10,329.30	10,561.50	16,395.90	8.0	638-3060	213-284-3683	4.50	None	None	Robert Rodriguez	'84
FPA PARAMOUNT★	Growth & Income	219.6	13.16	10,553.30	11,030.20	20,437.60	3.6	638-3060	213-284-3683	6.50	None	None	William Sams	'81
FPA PERENNIAL FUND	Growth & Income	59.1	20.82	10,509.80	11,338.30	18,553.50	3.8	638-3060	213-284-3683	6.50	None	None	Chris Linden	'84
FRANKLIN CUST: DYNATECH	Technology	44.8	16.14	11,278.80	12,744.70	17,954.20	0.8	342-5236	415-570-3000	4.00	None	None	Rupert Johnson	'67
FRANKLIN CUST: GROWTH	Growth	186.4	24.48	10,657.40	11,805.20	22,241.80	1.7	342-5236	415-570-3000	4.00	None	None	Jerry Palmieri	'64
FRANKLIN CUST: INCOME	Income	1,435.8	1.98	10,343.10	10,455.90	15,898.60	11.1	342-5236	415-570-3000	4.00	None	None	Charles Johnson	'56
FRANKLIN CUST: US GOVT	Fixed Income	11,249.6	6.87	10,331.70	10,870.80	15,902.20	10.1	342-5236	415-570-3000	4.00	None	None	Jack Lemein	'84
FRANKLIN CUST: UTILITIES	Utility	777.0	8.06	10,105.30	11,001.50	16,298.50	7.1	342-5236	415-570-3000	4.00	None	None	C. Johnson/G. Johnson	'57
FRANKLIN EQUITY FUND	Growth	419.3	7.17	10,259.10	10,776.10	20,197.40	4.1	342-5236	415-570-3000	4.00	None	None	Hoffman/McClay	'82
FRANKLIN GOLD FUND	Gold	286.8	12.84	9,259.10	11,017.50	18,294.30	3.7	342-5236	415-570-3000	4.00	None	None	Martin Wiskemann	'72
FRANKLIN INV: CONVERTIBLE	Convertibles	20.0	9.65	10,375.20	10,583.20	☆	7.2	342-5236	415-570-3000	4.00	None	None	Ed Jamieson	'87
FRANKLIN INV: GLOBAL INC	World Fixed-Income	18.5	9.51	10,456.80	10,664.70	☆	11.6	342-5236	415-570-3000	4.00	None	None	Ed Jamieson	'88
FRANKLIN INV: SH-INT US	Fixed Income	35.4	10.16	10,276.40	10,767.90	☆	8.5	342-5236	415-570-3000	1.50	None	None	Jack Lemein	'87
FRANKLIN INV: SP EQU INC	Equity Income	10.3	11.66	10,182.20	10,806.50	☆	6.3	342-5236	415-570-3000	4.00	None	None	McEldowney/Felicelli	'88
FRANKLIN INV: US GOVT SEC	Fixed Income	323.8	9.99	10,235.50	11,046.10	☆	10.7	342-5236	415-570-3000	4.00	0.25	None	Jack Lemein	'87
FRANKLIN MGD: CORP CASH	Fixed Income	20.8	20.05	10,174.80	10,350.10	☆	8.6	342-5236	415-570-3000	1.50	0.25	None	Phillip Smith	'88
FRANKLIN MGD: INV GRADE	Fixed Income	17.6	8.42	10,278.20	10,625.70	☆	9.1	342-5236	415-570-3000	4.00	0.25	None	Phillip Smith	'87
FRANKLIN MGD: RISING DVD	Growth & Income	40.6	11.43	10,304.70	10,693.10	☆	3.9	342-5236	415-570-3000	4.00	0.50	None	Bruce Baughman	'87
FRANKLIN OPTION	Option Income	41.0	4.95	10,377.30	10,465.90	16,216.00	3.6	342-5236	415-570-3000	4.00	None	None	Martin Wiskemann	'72
FRANKLIN PRT: TX-AD INTL	World Fixed-Income	3.3	11.14	10,355.80	11,535.30	☆	7.9	342-5236	415-570-3000	4.00	None	None	Lippman/Johnson	'88
FRANKLIN PART: TX-AD HI YLD	Fixed Income	35.5	7.67	10,199.60	9,488.50	☆	15.3	342-5236	415-570-3000	4.00	None	None	Martin Wiskemann	'87
FRANKLIN PART: TX-AD USG	Fixed Income	82.8	10.05	10,306.50	10,846.10	☆	9.4	342-5236	415-570-3000	4.00	None	None	Jack Lemein	'87
FRANKLIN PA: EQUITY PORT★	Capital Appreciation	0.5	12.37	10,165.50	10,736.10	☆	3.8	342-5236	415-570-3000	4.00	None	None	Hoffman/McClay	'86
FRANKLIN PA: HIGH INCOME★	Income	1.0	7.58	10,155.80	9,554.20	☆	14.7	342-5236	415-570-3000	4.00	None	None	Martin Wiskemann	'86
FRANKLIN PA: US GOVT SEC★	Fixed Income	3.9	9.83	10,342.30	10,928.90	☆	10.0	342-5236	415-570-3000	4.00	None	None	Jack Lemein	'86
FREEDOM II: GLOBAL FUND	Global	41.0	11.72	10,752.30	12,165.60	☆	0.0	225-6258	800-392-6037	None	0.75	3.00	Lilia Clemente	'86
FREEDOM II: GLOBAL INC	World Fixed-Income	190.6	9.92	10,448.20	10,749.70	☆	8.6	225-6258	800-392-6037	None	0.75	3.00	Thomas Prapas	'86

Fund	Objective	Assets ($mil)	NAV	$10K 1-Yr	$10K 5-Yr	$10K 10-Yr	Yield %	Phone	800	Load	12b-1	Def.	Manager	Since
FREEDOM III: ENVIRONMNTL	Specialty	61.5	10.23	11,106.50	☆	☆	0.0	225-6258	800-392-6037	4.50	0.50	None	Beckwith/Weld	'89
FREEDOM INV: EQ VALUE	Growth	22.4	11.15	10,305.20	10,583.10		1.7	225-6258	800-392-6037	None	0.75	3.00	J. Schmidt/N. Weld	'90
FREEDOM: GOLD & GOVT	Gold	68.9	14.99	10,104.20	10,677.20	15,522.40	7.2	225-6258	800-392-6037	None	0.75	3.00	A. Arace/T. Urmston	'84/'87
FREEDOM: GOVT INC	Fixed Income	136.2	9.91	10,346.10	10,845.10	☆	8.2	225-6258	800-392-6037	None	0.75	3.00	Thomas Urmston	'88
FREEDOM: REGIONAL BANK	Financial Services	61.7	11.09	10,000.20	9,905.00	☆	1.6	225-6258	800-392-6037	None	0.75	3.00	Jim Schmidt	'85
FT INTERNATIONAL	International	78.4	16.79	10,909.70	12,133.60	32,328.00	1.1	356-2805	None	4.50	0.25	None	David Francis	'84
FUND FOR US GOVT SEC	Fixed Income	1,047.6	8.29	10,311.70	10,759.20	15,340.90	9.3	356-2805	None	4.50	0.25	None	Gary Madich	'88
FUND OF AMERICA	Growth & Income	165.9	11.23	10,546.60	10,815.20	17,873.60	2.4	421-5666	None	5.75	0.25	None	John Gunthorp	'82
FUND OF SOUTH/WEST	Capital Appreciation	16.0	14.56	10,627.70	11,281.80	16,709.50	1.2	262-6631	None	4.75	None	None	Sharon Stone	'87
FUNDAMENTAL INVESTORS	Growth & Income	835.1	16.97	10,452.90	11,556.70	22,818.60	3.5	421-0180	213-486-9200	5.75	0.25	None	Multiple Managers	'78
FUNDTRUST: AGGRESSIVE GR	Capital Appreciation	20.7	14.19	10,558.00	11,198.50	17,605.00	0.5	344-9033	800-638-1896	1.50	0.50	None	Michael Hirsch	'84
FUNDTRUST: GROWTH FUND	Growth	21.8	13.48	10,490.30	10,564.00	16,680.40	1.2	344-9033	800-638-1896	1.50	0.50	None	Michael Hirsch	'84
FUNDTRUST: GROWTH & INC	Growth & Income	30.2	14.26	10,237.20	10,506.00	16,735.70	3.6	344-9033	800-638-1896	1.50	0.50	None	Michael Hirsch	'84
FUNDTRUST: INCOME FUND	Fixed Income	52.2	9.40	10,292.90	10,394.20	13,678.80	7.3	344-9033	800-638-1896	1.50	0.50	None	Michael Hirsch	'88
FUNDTRUST: MGJ TOT RETURN	Flexible	18.9	10.25	10,301.50	10,609.50		6.0	344-9033	800-638-1896	1.50	0.50	None	Michael Hirsch	'88
GABELLI ASSET	Growth	381.2	16.81	10,200.20	9,963.50	☆	3.2	422-3554	212-490-3670	None	0.30	2.00	Mario Gabelli	'86
GABELLI CONVERTIBLE SEC	Convertibles	74.9	10.68	10,208.60	☆	☆	0.9	422-3554	212-490-3670	None	None	None	Mario Gabelli	'89
GABELLI GROWTH	Growth	199.1	17.80	10,639.60	11,749.50	☆	0.0	422-3554	212-490-3670	5.50	0.30	None	Elizabeth Bramwell	'87
GABELLI VALUE FUND	Capital Appreciation	1,039.2	9.36	10,140.80	☆	☆	0.0	422-3554	212-490-3670	4.50	0.25	None	Mario Gabelli	'89
GALAXY: BOND FUND D	Fixed Income	81.0	9.97	10,271.10	10,361.60		7.5	441-7379	302-478-6945	4.50	None	None	Bruce Barton	'88
GALAXY: EQUITY FUND C	Growth & Income	105.6	10.99	10,257.00	10,579.30	☆	3.5	441-7379	302-478-6945	4.50	None	None	Anthony Mordaci	'88
GAM: EUROPE	European Region	11.5	107.12	10,372.80	☆	☆	0.0	356-5740	None	None	0.15	None	Mark Bray	'90
GAM: GLOBAL	Global	22.8	140.13	10,954.50	12,721.40		0.2	356-5740	None	None	1.00	None	John Horseman	'90
GAM: INTERNATIONAL	International	25.9	178.10	11,830.70	12,934.50	35,124.30	0.0	356-5740	None	None	1.00	None	John Horseman	'90
GAM: NORTH AMERICA	Capital Appreciation	0.3	100.13	10,016.00	☆	☆	0.0	356-5740	None	None	0.15	None	Gordon Grender	'90
GAM: PACIFIC BASIN	Pacific Region	11.7	135.64	11,076.30	13,222.50	☆	0.0	356-5740	None	None	1.00	None	Paul Kirkby	'88
JW GANT FUND	Capital Appreciation	1.6	1.87	10,505.60	10,770.50	☆	5.3	354-6339	407-241-3846	6.50	1.00	None	Eric Russell	'85
GATEWAY: GOVT BOND PLUS	Fixed Income	8.6	10.22	10,377.70	10,560.70	☆	7.2	354-6339	513-248-2700	None	None	None	Peter Thayer	'88
GATEWAY: GROWTH PLUS	Growth	12.1	12.16	10,500.90	11,941.30	☆	2.3	354-6339	513-248-2700	None	None	None	Peter Williams	'88
GATEWAY: INDEX PLUS	Growth & Income	48.8	16.25	10,401.10	11,829.80	16,891.50	2.4	354-6339	513-248-2700	None	None	None	Peter Thayer	'77
GEICO QUAL DIVIDEND	Fixed Income	8.1	16.83	10,057.50	9,643.30	☆	19.1	832-6232	301-986-2200	None	0.25	None	Kevin Korycansky	'88
GENERAL AGGRESSIVE GRO	Capital Appreciation	49.4	25.82	10,749.40	11,815.60	☆	1.2	645-6561	None	None	0.20	None	Thomas Frank	'85
GENL ELEC LG TM INTR★	Fixed Income	1,784.9	11.04	10,352.90	10,667.80		8.6	None	203-326-4040	None	None	None	Robert MacDougall	N/A
GENL ELEC S&S PROGRAM★	Growth	1,109.1	36.29	10,601.80	11,485.10		3.6	None	612-332-1212	None	None	None	Arthur Bahr	N/A
GENERAL SECURITIES	Capital Appreciation	19.9	11.94	10,387.90	11,260.90		3.6	331-4923	None	None	None	None	Jack Robinson	'51
GIBRALTAR FUND	Growth & Income	0.7	15.92	11,219.20	11,598.60	17,549.90	2.0	None	215-988-0277	4.50	None	None	S. Grey Dayton Jr.	'89
GINTEL CAPITAL APPREC	Capital Appreciator	34.4	13.79	9,690.80	11,293.20	☆	9.4	243-5808	203-622-6400	None	0.50	None	Robert Gintel	'86
GINTEL ERISA	Growth & Income	89.0	33.78	10,116.80	11,244.00	20,673.10	12.1	243-5808	203-622-6400	None	0.20	None	Robert Gintel	'82
GINTEL FUND	Growth	93.8	77.13	9,879.60	11,665.90	18,915.40	7.6	243-5808	203-622-6400	None	None	None	Robert Gintel	'81
GIT EQUITY: EQ INCOME	Equity Income	2.5	14.53	10,141.20	10,985.10	17,185.50	4.7	336-3063	703-528-6500	None	None	None	John Edwards	'88
GIT EQUITY: SELECT GROWTH	Growth	3.8	18.26	10,734.00	11,411.10	20,609.50	2.8	336-3063	703-528-6500	None	None	None	John Edwards	'88
GIT EQUITY: SPEC GROWTH	Small-Company Growth	43.1	18.34	10,456.00	10,810.30	20,451.10	2.0	336-3063	703-528-6500	None	None	None	Richard Carney	'83
GIT INCOME: GOVERNMENT	Fixed Income	5.9	9.97	10,330.60	10,587.80	15,295.60	7.5	336-3063	703-528-6500	None	None	None	John Edwards	'88
GIT INCOME: MAXIMUM INC	Fixed Income	6.7	7.27	10,422.10	9,942.70	13,348.60	11.8	336-3063	703-528-6500	None	None	None	John Edwards	'88
GLENMEDE: EQUITY FUND★	Growth	7.1	10.07	10,182.30	☆	☆	0.0	N/A	N/A	N/A	N/A	N/A	N/A	N/A

★FPA PARAMOUNT—Closed.
★FRANKLIN PA FUNDS—Designed primarily for Pennsylvania residents.
★GENERAL ELECTRIC FUNDS—Limited to selected General Electric employees.
★GLENMEDE FUNDS—Available to clients of Glenmede Trust Co.

371

PERFORMANCE OF MUTUAL FUNDS (continued)

FUND NAME	OBJECTIVE	TOTAL NET ASSETS (MIL) 6/30/90	NET ASSET VALUE 6/30/90	PERFORMANCE (Return on Initial $10,000 Investment) 3/31/90-6/30/90	6/30/89-6/30/90	6/30/85-6/30/90	DIVIDEND YIELD % 6/90	PHONE NUMBER 800	In-State	FEES Load	12b-1	Redemption	MANAGER	SINCE
GLENMEDE: INTERMDT GOVT★	Fixed Income	187.3	10.23	10,343.90	10,844.40	☆	8.6	N/A	N/A	N/A	N/A	N/A	N/A	N/A
GLENMEDE: INTERNATIONAL★	International	95.9	11.59	10,771.40	11,779.70	☆	3.7	N/A	N/A	N/A	N/A	N/A	N/A	N/A
GMO CORE TR: PELICAN	Growth	80.1	9.99	10,320.40	10,839.90	☆	0.0	None	617-330-7500	None	None	None	Richard Mayo	'89
GNA INVESTORS: US GOVT	Fixed Income	67.1	9.59	10,317.80	10,740.30	☆	8.8	426-5520	800-732-1231	None	0.75	5.00	GNA Capital Mgmt Inc.	'87
GOVERNMENT INC SEC	Fixed Income	1,280.8	9.18	10,313.00		☆	10.2	245-2423	None	1.00	0.25	0.75	Gary Madich	'88
GRADISON GOVT INCOME	Fixed Income	58.3	12.76	10,331.60	10,800.70	☆	8.1	869-5999	None	2.00	0.25	None	Michael Link	'87
GRADISON GR: ESTABLISHED	Growth	139.2	17.45	9,900.00	10,342.30	19,961.80	4.2	869-5999	None	2.00	0.25	None	William Leugers	'83
GRADISON GR: OPPORTUNITY	Small-Company Growth	26.2	14.25	10,187.80	10,716.60	18,006.60	2.5	869-5999	None	2.00	0.25	None	William Leugers	'83
GREENFIELD FUND	Flexible	1.0	12.54	10,308.20	10,841.90	14,125.00	7.9	None	212-986-2600	None	None	1.00	R.F. Nichols	'81
GREENSPRING FUND	Growth	23.1	13.17	9,894.80	10,507.70	18,056.50	5.7	None	301-435-9000	None	None	None	Godack/Carlson	'83
GROWTH FUND OF AMERICA	Growth	2,181.0	21.15	10,628.10	11,227.20	22,193.80	2.8	421-9000	415-421-9360	5.75	0.25	None	Multiple Managers	'73
GROWTH FD OF WASHINGTON	Growth	51.6	12.69	10,055.30	9,578.70	☆	2.2	972-9274	202-842-5300	5.00	0.25	None	Geico Inv. Services Co.	'85
GROWTH INDUSTRY SHARES	Growth	70.9	8.45	10,959.80	12,204.80	18,857.60	1.0	635-2886	312-346-4830	None	None	None	Neal L. Seltzer	'85
GS SHORT-INTMD GOVT	Fixed Income	56.7	9.97	10,249.60	10,771.70	☆	8.8	621-2550	None	None	None	None	Don Mulvihill	'88
GT GLOBAL AMERICA	Growth	67.9	14.84	11,259.50	13,757.60	☆	0.7	824-1580	415-392-6181	4.75	0.35	None	Scott Fearon	'87
GT GLOBAL BOND	World Fixed-Income	40.0	10.62	10,237.90	10,398.00	☆	7.9	824-1580	415-392-6181	4.75	0.35	None	Robert Sterling	'84
GT GLOBAL EUROPE	European Region	1,700.0	11.61	10,393.90	12,964.40	☆	0.0	824-1580	415-392-6181	4.75	0.35	None	Christian Wignall	'85
GT GLOBAL GOVT INCOME	World Fixed-Income	201.2	10.19	10,467.00	10,932.60	☆	11.5	824-1580	415-392-6181	4.75	0.35	None	Dan Gressel	'88
GT GLOBAL HEALTH CARE	Health/Biotech	113.8	13.87	11,378.20	☆	☆	0.0	824-1580	415-392-6181	4.75	0.25	None	Ted Gomoli	'89
GT GLOBAL INTERNATL	International	348.1	9.37	10,445.90	12,613.80	☆	0.2	824-1580	415-392-6181	4.75	0.35	None	Christian Wignall	'87
GT GLOBAL JAPAN	Pacific Region	72.7	16.01	11,314.50	13,692.40	☆	0.7	824-1580	415-392-6181	4.75	0.35	None	Hidekazu Kishimoto	'87
GT GLOBAL PACIFIC	Pacific Region	265.0	12.89	10,777.60	13,044.20	36,973.50	0.5	824-1580	415-392-6181	4.75	0.35	None	Christian Wignall	'87
GT GLOBAL WORLDWIDE	Global	85.2	14.00	10,670.70	12,349.10	☆	0.2	824-1580	415-392-6181	4.75	0.35	None	Christian Wignall	'87
GUARDIAN PARK AVENUE	Growth	249.4	21.08	10,063.60	10,620.60	20,276.00	4.4	221-3253	212-598-8897	4.50	None	None	Chuck Albers	'72
GUARDIAN US GOVT TRUST	Fixed Income	7.8	9.78	10,256.00	10,570.60	☆	7.9	221-3253	212-598-8897	4.50	None	None	Michele Babakian	'89
GW SIERRA: GROWTH & INC	Growth & Income	21.0	10.12	10,344.90	☆	☆	0.0	331-3426	800-221-9876	None	None	3.00	James Rothenberg	'88
GW SIERRA: US GOVT SEC	Fixed Income	31.4	9.93	10,312.80	☆	☆	0.0	331-3426	800-221-9876	None	None	3.00	Peter Hagel	'89
J HANCOCK ASSET ALLOC	Flexible	1,110.2	11.11	10,611.40	10,784.70	16,145.50	4.1	225-5291	617-375-1760	4.50	0.50	None	M. Dicario/A. C. Hodsdon	'88
J HANCOCK GLOBAL	Global	102.9	14.53	10,326.90	10,662.30	20,782.10	9.9	225-5291	617-375-1760	4.50	0.50	None	James Ho/Barry Evans	'88
J HANCOCK GLOBAL	Global		18.29	11,098.30	11,809.40	☆	0.8	225-5291	617-375-1760	4.50	0.50	None	R. Freedman/J. Willis	'85
J HANCOCK GROWTH	Growth	126.2	15.95	11,115.00	11,541.20	20,537.20	1.7	225-5291	617-375-1760	4.50	0.50	None	Multiple Managers	'83
J HANCOCK HI INC: FEDL+	Fixed Income	72.8	9.10	10,215.00	10,636.60	☆	9.3	225-5291	617-375-1760	4.50	0.50	None	Anne Hodsdon	'86
J HANCOCK HI INC: FIX INC	Fixed Income	81.1	7.36	10,291.90	9,205.90	☆	13.9	225-5291	617-375-1760	4.50	0.50	None	Frederick Cavanaugh	'86
J HANCOCK SPEC EQUITY	Small-Company Growth	11.6	6.90	11,075.40	11,531.20	15,193.50	0.3	225-5291	617-375-1760	4.50	0.50	None	Multiple Managers	'85
J HANCOCK US GOVT SEC	Fixed Income	177.8	8.60	10,248.60	10,662.00	15,069.00	9.4	225-5291	617-375-1760	4.50	0.50	None	Anne C. Hodsdon	N/A
J HANCOCK US GUAR MORT	Fixed Income	313.6	9.95	10,309.10	10,798.20	15,329.90	8.9	225-5291	617-375-1760	4.50	0.50	None	Anne C. Hodsdon	'85
J HANCOCK WORLD: PACIFIC	Pacific Region	5.3	11.59	10,613.60	12,218.80	☆	0.0	225-5291	617-375-1760	4.50	0.50	None	John Wills/Sim Yeap	N/A
HARBOR: BOND	Fixed Income	25.0	10.17	10,333.00	10,685.00	☆	8.2	422-1050	419-247-2477	None	None	None	William Gross	'87
HARBOR: CAPITAL APPREC★	Growth	69.9	13.55	11,189.10	11,999.40	☆	1.5	422-1050	419-247-2477	None	None	None	Spiros Segalas	'90
HARBOR: GROWTH	Growth	163.7	13.45	10,768.60	11,143.80	☆	0.8	422-1050	419-247-2477	None	None	None	Bartley Madden	'87
HARBOR: INTERNATIONAL	International	61.5	17.92	10,967.00	12,743.60	☆	0.9	422-1050	419-247-2477	None	None	None	Hakan Castegren	'87
HARBOR: VALUE	Growth & Income	29.4	13.20	10,453.20	11,128.50	☆	4.0	422-1050	419-247-2477	None	None	None	John Strauss	'87
HARTWELL EMERGING FUND	Small-Company Growth	28.8	18.08	11,378.20	13,421.50	26,957.30	0.0	624-363	212-309-8406	4.75	None	None	John Hartwell	'68
HARTWELL GROWTH FUND	Capital Appreciation	18.1	20.90	11,093.40	10,885.40	23,681.60	0.0	624-363	212-309-8406	4.75	None	None	William Miller	'84
HARVEST: GROWTH PORT	Growth	16.1	9.43	10,362.60	9,679.40	☆	6.2	366-2277	704-523-9407	5.75	0.75	None	M.D. Sass	'88

Fund	Objective	Net Assets ($Mil)	NAV	Value $10K A	Value $10K B	Value $10K C	Yield %	Phone 1	Phone 2	Max Load	12b-1	Redemp	Portfolio Manager	Mgr Yr
HARVEST: INCOME PORT	Fixed Income	3.7	9.97	10,319.40	10,646.80	☆	7.9	366-2277	704-523-9407	5.75	None	None	M.D. Sass	'88
HAWAII PACIFIC FUND★	Growth & Income	0.5	9.74	9,959.10	☆	☆	0.0	None	808-521-4831	None	None	None	J.B. Havre Sec	'89
HEARTLAND: US GOVT	Fixed Income	11.7	9.15	10,371.30	10,776.00	☆	8.3	432-7856	414-347-7103	4.50	0.30	None	William Nasgovitz	'87
HEARTLAND: VALUE	Capital Appreciation	27.2	14.76	10,758.00	10,278.60	16,784.30	2.3	432-7856	414-347-7103	4.50	0.30	None	William Nasgovitz	'85
HELMSMAN: D'SCIPLINED EQU	Growth	60.0	10.42	9,953.70	10,345.10	☆	4.5	338-4345	None	4.00	0.35	None	Bank One of Milwaukee	'87
HELMSMAN: GROWTH EQUITY	Growth	31.8	12.14	11,113.70	12,064.70	☆	1.5	338-4345	None	None	0.35	None	Bank One of Milwaukee	'87
HELMSMAN: INCOME EQUITY	Equity Income	37.1	11.06	10,260.10	11,278.50	☆	4.8	338-4345	None	None	0.35	None	Bank One of Milwaukee	'87
HELMSMAN: INCOME PORT	Fixed Income	57.3	9.49	10,281.70	10,637.00	☆	8.3	338-4345	None	None	0.35	None	Bank One of Indianapolis	'87
HELMSMAN: INTL EQUITY	International	12.1	10.58	10,580.00	☆	☆	0.0	338-4345	None	None	0.35	None	Bank One of Columbus	'90
HERITAGE CAPITAL APPREC	Capital Appreciation	66.4	11.99	10,186.90	9,654.90	☆	1.5	421-4184	813-573-8143	4.00	0.50	None	Herb Ehlers	'85
HERITAGE INC: DIVERSIFIED	Fixed Income	8.6	9.88	10,407.90	☆	☆	0.0	421-4184	813-573-8143	4.00	0.35	None	Brown/Ross	'90
HERITAGE INC: GOVERNMENT	Fixed Income	3.4	9.74	10,312.80		☆	0.0	421-4184	813-573-8143	4.00	0.35	None	Ivan Ross	'90
HERITAGE INCOME-GROWTH★	Equity Income	21.6	9.22	10,259.90	9,764.80	☆	5.1	421-4184	813-573-8143	4.00	0.25	None	Lou Kirschbaum	'90
HIGHMARK: BOND FUND	Fixed Income	6.8	10.11	10,307.10	10,589.60	☆	7.5	443-6884	None	None	None	None	Merus Capital Mgmt	'88
HIGHMARK: INCOME EQUITY B	Equity Income	42.6	10.70	10,207.70	10,783.80	☆	4.8	443-6884	None	None	None	None	Merus Capital Mgmt	'89
HIGHMARK: SPL GRO EQUITY B	Small-Company Growth	1.6	10.85	11,116.80	11,874.20	☆	0.5	443-6884	None	None	None	None	Merus Capital Mgmt	'89
HOME: GOVERNMENT SEC FD	Fixed Income	36.7	9.34	10,346.10	10,782.20	☆	9.7	729-3863	212-530-6351	4.75	0.25	None	Richard Seyffarth	'88
HOME: GROWTH & INCOME	Growth & Income	28.2	12.42	10,633.60	11,474.90	☆	3.4	729-3863	212-530-6351	4.75	0.25	None	Donald Gilbert	'88
HOME: HIGH YIELD BOND FD	Fixed Income	23.4	7.82	10,302.30	9,236.70	☆	15.1	729-3863	212-530-6351	4.75	0.25	None	Mark Shapiro	'88
HOME INV GUAR INCOME	Fixed Income	130.0	10.06	10,356.90	10,801.50	14,860.80	8.3	858-8850	None	None	None	5.00	Paul Sullivan	N/A
HT INSIGHT: CONVERTIBLE	Convertibles	13.8	8.80	9,780.20	9,362.10	☆	8.5	441-7379	302-478-6945	4.50	None	None	Michael McCowin	'88
HT INSIGHT: EQUITY	Growth & Income	21.0	11.07	10,250.90	11,170.70	☆	3.8	441-7379	302-478-6945	4.50	None	None	James Depies	'88
HUNTINGTON: CPI+	Global Flexible	18.4	53.41	10,275.60	10,831.40	20,029.50	4.1	354-4111	213-681-3700	3.00	0.45	None	Huntington Advisers	'89
IAI APOLLO FUND	Capital Appreciation	23.8	11.50	10,645.60	11,352.90	15,470.20	1.0	None	612-371-2884	None	None	None	Richard Tschudy	'83
IAI BOND FUND	Fixed Income	88.5	9.84	10,403.60	10,530.10		7.1	None	612-371-2884	None	None	None	Larry Hill	'84
IAI INTERNATIONAL FUND	International	32.8	11.37	10,665.00	11,312.00	☆	2.6	None	612-371-2884	None	None	None	David Tilles	'87
IAI REGIONAL FUND	Growth	190.8	20.00	10,830.70	12,374.80	25,155.30	2.0	None	612-371-2884	None	None	None	Julian Carlin	'80
IAI RESERVE FUND	Fixed Income	89.2	10.09	10,205.70	10,795.30	☆	7.6	None	612-371-2884	None	None	None	Larry Hill	'86
IAI STOCK FUND	Capital Appreciation	80.3	15.16	10,576.00	11,841.80	21,072.60	2.4	None	612-371-2884	None	None	None	Richard Tschudy	'71
IDEX FUND★	Growth	92.7	16.96	11,455.90	12,620.60	25,797.20	0.6	237-3055	800-282-2842	8.50	None	None	Tom Marsico	'86
IDEX FUND II★	Growth	92.3	16.72	11,541.10	12,805.60	☆	0.5	237-3055	800-282-2842	8.50	None	None	Tom Marsico	'86
IDEX FUND 3	Growth	162.9	15.58	11,468.80	12,656.70	☆	0.5	237-3055	800-282-2842	8.50	None	None	Tom Marsico	'87
IDS TOTAL INCOME	Fixed Income	23.3	8.42	10,431.40	9,492.10	☆	11.3	328-8300	612-372-3131	5.00	None	None	Michael McGoldrick	'87
IDS BLUE CHIP ADVANTAGE	Growth & Income	17.3	5.41	10,620.70	☆	☆	0.0	328-8300	612-372-3131	5.00	None	None	Stuart Sedlacek	'90
IDS BOND FUND	Fixed Income	1,779.3	4.49	10,398.40	10,223.80	16,133.90	8.9	328-8300	612-372-3131	5.00	None	None	F. Quirsfeld	'85
IDS DISCOVERY FUND	Small-Company Growth	172.3	9.24	11,092.40	13,063.00	18,610.30	1.5	328-8300	612-372-3131	5.00	0.12	None	Ray Hirsch	'88
IDS EQUITY+	Growth & Income	402.5	9.94	10,726.80	12,041.50	21,606.30	3.0	328-8300	612-372-3131	5.00	0.05	None	Joe Barsky	'83
IDS EXTRA INCOME	Fixed Income	982.4	3.64	10,436.80	8,940.80	13,514.10	12.8	328-8300	612-372-3131	5.00	0.05	None	Jack Utter	'85
IDS FEDERAL INCOME	Fixed Income	234.0	5.34	10,315.20	10,836.90	☆	8.5	328-8300	612-372-3131	5.00	0.06	None	Stu Sedlacek	'86
IDS GLOBAL BOND: BOND	World Fixed-Income	20.0		10,443.30	11,092.50	☆	6.9	328-8300	612-372-3131	5.00	0.07	None	Ray Goodner	'89
IDS GLOBAL BOND: GROWTH	Global	6.1	5.02	☆	☆	☆	0.0	328-8300	612-372-3131	5.00	0.15	None	Multiple Managers	'90
IDS GROWTH FUND	Growth	788.0	24.99	11,644.90	13,123.50	22,092.90	1.0	328-8300	612-372-3131	5.00	0.09	None	G. Fines & Growth Team	'89
IDS INTERNATIONAL	International	237.6	10.06	10,911.10	12,927.30	29,362.00	1.0	328-8300	612-372-3131	5.00	0.05	None	P. Lamaison	'81
IDS MANAGED RETIREMENT	Flexible	796.0	10.33	11,206.60	12,679.00	24,192.00	2.5	328-8300	612-372-3131	5.00	0.10	None	Fines/Schultheis	'85/'87
IDS MUTUAL	Balanced	1,670.6	11.61	10,234.70	10,370.60	18,872.10	7.8	328-8300	612-372-3131	5.00	0.05	None	Labenski/Medcalf	'87/'83

★GLENMEDE FUNDS—Available to clients of Glenmede Trust Co.

★HARBOR CAPITAL APPRECIATION—Changed name and investment objective on 5/1/90.

★HAWAII PACIFIC FUND—Open only to residents of Hawaii, pension funds and institutions.

★HERITAGE INCOME-GROWTH—Changed investment objective on 2/1/90.

★IDEX FUND & IDEXII—Closed.

PERFORMANCE OF MUTUAL FUNDS (continued)

FUND NAME	OBJECTIVE	TOTAL NET ASSETS (MIL) 6/30/90	NET ASSET VALUE 6/30/90	PERFORMANCE (Return on Initial $10,000 Investment) 3/31/90-6/30/90	6/30/89-6/30/90	6/30/85-6/30/90	DIVIDEND YIELD % 6/90	PHONE NUMBER 800	In-State	FEES Load	12b-1	Redemption	MANAGER	SINCE
IDS NEW DIMENSIONS	Growth	915.7	10.95	11,162.10	12,776.50	23,802.10	1.7	328-8300	612-372-3131	5.00	0.07	None	A. Spencer	'87
IDS PAN PACIFIC GRO	Pacific Region	47.1	5.02	11,130.80	12,137.90	☆	0.0	328-8300	612-372-3131	None	1.00	5.00	Wes Wadman	'88
IDS PRECIOUS METALS	Gold	80.8	6.22	8,911.20	9,706.80	16,703.10	1.4	328-8300	612-372-3131	5.00	0.17	None	Doug Groh	'88
IDS PROGRESSIVE	Capital Appreciation	156.5	5.97	9,835.30	9,960.70	16,980.10	5.3	328-8300	612-372-3131	5.00	0.07	None	Markatos/Groh	'83/'89
IDS SELECTIVE	Fixed Income	1,194.2	8.41	10,330.10	10,493.90	16,454.00	8.2	328-8300	612-372-3131	5.00	0.04	None	Ray Goodner	'85
IDS STOCK	Growth & Income	1,371.5	19.31	11,558.30	11,823.00	21,703.30	4.9	328-8300	612-372-3131	5.00	0.04	None	Ted Gemlich	'85
IDS STRATEGY AGGR EQ	Capital Appreciation	317.7	13.79	11,103.10	12,412.20	22,005.10	0.0	328-8300	612-372-3131	None	0.99	5.00	Ray Hirsch	'89
IDS STRATEGY EQUITY	Growth & Income	334.8	8.10	10,310.20	10,754.90	19,663.90	4.5	328-8300	612-372-3131	None	0.84	5.00	Tom Medcalf	'89
IDS STRATEGY INCOME	Fixed Income	242.1	5.56	10,400.90	10,330.40	15,745.10	7.4	328-8300	612-372-3131	None	0.89	5.00	Tom Brakke	'88
IDS STRATEGY SH TM INC	Fixed Income	130.7	1.00	10,171.00	10,744.00	13,578.00	7.2	328-8300	612-373-3131	None	0.89	5.00	Tom Brakke	'89
IDS UTILITIES INCOME	Utility	196.7	5.67	10,169.80	11,058.60	☆	6.7	328-8300	612-372-3131	5.00	0.09	None	Rich Lazarchic	'89
INCOME FUND OF AMERICA	Equity Income	2,093.7	12.26	10,222.00	10,601.90	17,505.20	8.7	421-0180	None	5.75	0.25	None	Multiple Managers	'73
INCOME PORT: LIMITED TERM	Fixed Income	379.3	10.12	10,307.30	10,668.40	15,606.20	9.0	544-6666	None	None	None	None	David Murphy	'89
INCOME PORT: SHORT GOVT	Fixed Income	140.0	9.40	10,266.80	10,807.10	☆	9.1	544-6666	None	None	None	None	Kurt Hollingsworth	'87
INDEPND CAP: OPPORTUNIT	Capital Appreciation	26.1	10.88	10,583.70	☆	☆	0.0	833-4264	215-440-4200	4.50	0.50	None	Robert Mancuso	'90
INDEPND CAP: TOT RTN BOND	Fixed Income	25.0	9.98	10,241.20	☆	☆	0.0	833-4264	215-440-4200	4.50	0.%0	None	Peter Sherman	'90
INDEPND CAP: TOT RTN GRO	Growth & Income	26.5	11.02	10,873.10	☆	☆	0.0	833-4264	215-440-4200	4.50	0.40	None	David Wilson	'90
INSTL INTL: FOREIGN EQU★	International	81.2	11.10	10,839.80	☆	☆	0.0	638-1225	301-625-7700	4.75	None	None	Martin Wade	'89
INTERMEDIATE BD FD AMER	Fixed Income	135.0	13.49	10,291.00	10,640.90	☆	9.3	421-0180	213-486-9200	4.75	0.25	None	Multiple Counselors	'88
INTL CASH: GLOBAL CASH	World Fixed-Income	75.3	13.83	10,360.20	11,200.70	☆	6.9	354-4111	None	2.25	0.55	None	Bankers Trust/London	'86
INTL CASH: HARD CURRENCY	World Fixed-Income	27.3	13.26	10,456.80	☆	☆	0.0	354-4111	None	2.25	0.45	None	Bankers Trust/London	'89
INTL CASH: HI INC CURRENCY	World Fixed-Income	16.8	13.14	10,638.60	☆	☆	0.0	354-4111	None	2.25	0.45	None	Bankers Trust/London	'89
INTL FD FOR INSTITUTIONS	International	17.7	11.50	10,961.10	☆	☆	1.8	221-8120	212-351-5807	8.50	None	None	Simon Fenton	'84
INTERNATIONAL INVESTORS	Gold	701.2	12.83	8,819.50	12,247.90	34,578.40	2.3	221-2220	212-687-5201	8.50	None	None	John VanEck	'55
INVESTMENT CO OF AMERICA	Growth & Income	5,873.9	15.53	10,566.60	11,514.40	22,252.30	3.7	421-0180	213-486-9200	5.75	0.25	None	Multiple Managers	'34
INVEST PORT: DVSFD INC	Fixed Income	279.1	5.35	10,652.60	10,252.60	12,317.40	13.5	621-1048	800-621-1148	None	1.25	5.00	Michael McNamara	'86
INVEST PORT: EQUITY	Growth	338.6	15.71	11,079.00	12,141.80	19,027.60	0.9	621-1048	800-621-1148	None	1.25	5.00	Stephen Lewis	'89
INVEST PORT: GOVERNMENT	Fixed Income	5,189.3	7.20	10,345.60	10,468.90	14,126.80	9.3	621-1048	800-621-1148	None	1.25	5.00	Frank Collecchia	'84
INVEST PORT: HIGH YIELD	Fixed Income	707.0	7.42	10,551.50	9,280.80	14,686.50	13.8	621-1048	800-621-1148	None	1.25	5.00	Kenneth Urbaszewski	'84
INVEST PORT: SH-INT GOV	Fixed Income	51.0	8.36	10,318.10	10,534.70	☆	8.6	621-1048	800-621-1148	None	1.25	5.00	Frank Collecchia	'89
INVEST PORT: TOTL RTN	Balanced	571.9	11.17	11,011.10	11,321.00	☆	4.0	621-1048	800-621-1148	None	1.25	5.00	Beth Kotner	'86
INVMT SRS: CAPITAL GROWTH	Capital Appreciation	7.3	10.54	11,051.70	☆	☆	0.0	245-0242	None	5.75	0.25	None	Greg Melvin	'89
INVMT SRS: HIGH INC SEC	Fixed Income	4.7	8.50	10,716.30	9,830.70	☆	13.7	245-0242	None	5.75	0.25	None	Mark Durbiano	'87
INVMT SRS: HI QUAL STOCK	Growth & Income	6.3	10.65	10,286.90	10,589.30	☆	3.6	245-0242	None	5.75	0.25	None	Peter Anderson	'88
INVMT SRS: US GOVT BOND	Fixed Income	11.1	9.91	10,302.10	10,753.40	☆	9.1	245-0242	None	5.75	0.25	None	Kathy Foody-Malus	'90
INVESTORS INCOME FUND	Fixed Income	19.7	4.89	10,260.70	10,460.90	15,737.20	9.7	262-6631	914-397-2086	4.75	None	None	Edward Jaroski	'87
INVESTORS PREFERENCE INC	Fixed Income	40.0	9.98	10,350.40	10,937.70	☆	9.3	543-8072	805-569-1011	4.00	None	None	Regis Dompka	'87
INVESTORS RESEARCH	Capital Appreciation	67.0	5.83	10,504.50	11,433.80	17,686.20	1.6	None	None	8.50	None	None	Investors Research Co.	'59
ITB: GROWTH OPPORTUNITIES	Growth & Income	62.2	10.99	10,503.80	11,436.50	17,950.60	2.9	888-4823	None	4.25	0.35	None	Charles Glueck	'88
ITB: HIGH INCOME PORT	Fixed Income	8.5	9.68	10,446.80	10,022.30	12,843.40	13.7	888-4823	None	4.25	0.35	None	Charles Glueck	'88
ITB: PREMIUM INCOME FUND	Fixed Income	25.1	12.37	10,382.80	10,886.00	☆	7.6	888-4823	None	2.50	0.35	None	Michael Martino	'89
ITB: WORLD INCOME PORT	World Fixed-Income	4.3	11.90	10,422.80	10,716.60	☆	6.8	888-4823	None	4.25	0.35	None	Nathan Wentworth	'89
IVY FUND: GROWTH WITH INC	Growth	14.9	8.74	11,035.40	11,296.10	21,717.50	10.5	235-3322	None	None	None	None	Michael Peers	'84
IVY GROWTH FUND	Growth	203.0	15.98	10,753.70	11,414.60	☆	2.7	235-3322	None	None	None	None	Michael Peers	'74
IVY INTERNATIONAL	International	80.3	21.38	10,941.70	12,162.30	18,980.20	0.8	235-3322	None	None	None	None	Hakan Castegren	'86

Fund	Objective	Assets	NAV	Value 1	Value 2	Value 3	Yield	Phone	Phone 2	Load	12b-1	Redemp.	Portfolio Manager	Yr
JANUS FLEXIBLE INC	Fixed Income	13.7	8.49	10,438.90	9,514.70	☆	11.4	525-3713	None	None	None	None	Michael McGoldrick	'87
JANUS FUND	Capital Appreciation	1,246.3	15.38	11,242.70	12,350.70	23,430.30	1.1	525-3713	None	None	None	None	James Craig	'83
JANUS TWENTY FUND	Capital Appreciation	205.8	16.54	11,763.90	13,499.50	21,894.60	0.1	525-3713	None	None	None	None	Thomas Marsico	'88
JANUS VENTURE	Small-Company Growth	232.1	38.48	10,956.70	13,159.10	24,820.40	1.1	525-3713	None	None	None	None	James Craig	'85
JAPAN FUND	Pacific Region	379.2	13.01	11,626.50	11,865.80	38,366.50	0.4	535-2726	617-330-5613	None	None	None	Robert Theurkauf	'90
JP GROWTH FUND	Growth	27.8	15.62	10,953.70	12,206.30	18,750.50	2.4	458-4498	None	6.75	None	None	William H. Chenoweth	'88
JP INCOME FUND	Fixed Income	17.9	9.28	10,301.80	10,620.90	16,676.50	8.8	458-4498	None	6.75	None	None	H. Lusby Brown	'87
KAUFMANN FUND	Small-Company Growth	52.5	1.84	11,151.50	12,957.70	☆	0.0	237-0132	212-344-2661	None	1.00	0.0 2	L. Auriana/H. Utch	'86
KEMPER BLUE CHIP FUND	Growth & Income	34.4	11.22	11,162.00	12,271.10	☆	1.2	621-1148	None	4.50	0.50	None	Jim Neel	'90
KEMPER DIVERSIFIED INCM	Fixed Income	238.2	7.09	10,698.10	10,203.30	13,269.60	14.4	621-1148	None	4.50	None	None	Mike McNamara	'89
KEMPER ENHANCED GOVT INC	Fixed Income	75.9	8.21	10,354.00	10,484.60	☆	9.5	621-1148	None	4.50	0.50	0.50	Frank Collecchia	'87
KEMPER GLOEAL INCOME	World Fixed-Income	27.4	9.98	10,763.10	☆	☆	0.0	621-1146	None	4.50	None	None	Gordon Johns	N/A
KEMPER GOLC FUND	Gold	8.4	7.30	8,700.80	9,711.30	21,451.50	0.5	621-1148	None	5.75	None	None	Gordon Wilson	'89
KEMPER GROWTH FUND	Growth	372.5	10.60	11,259.20	12,395.40	15,163.10	1.7	621-1148	None	5.75	0.50	0.50	Ronald Ognar	'89
KEMPER HIGH YIELD	Fixed Income	1,453.6	8.95	10,644.80	9,617.80	☆	14.5	621-1148	None	4.50	None	None	Ken Urbaszewski	'80
KEMPER INCOME & CAP PRES	Fixed Income	414.0	7.97	10,380.70	10,453.30	15,738.40	10.4	621-1148	None	4.50	0.50	None	Harry Resis	'89
KEMPER INTERNATIONAL FD	International	215.2	10.67	10,659.30	12,384.10	32,520.40	0.7	621-1148	None	5.75	None	None	Gordon Wilson	'89
KEMPER RETIREMENT: SRS 1	Balanced	77.0	10.16	10,866.30	☆	☆	0.0	621-1148	None	5.75	None	None	Ron Ognar	'90
KEMPER SUMMIT FUND	Small-Company Growth	269.5	4.66	10,913.30	11,482.00	17,931.80	2.4	621-1148	None	5.75	None	None	Beth Cotner	'87
KEMPER TECHNOLOGY FD	Technology	590.6	11.43	11,060.30	12,783.40	19,915.80	2.5	621-1148	None	4.50	None	None	Ken Knutel	'85
KEMPER TOTAL RETURN	Balanced	914.3	8.71	10,950.70	11,399.60	17,833.00	4.4	621-1148	None	5.75	None	None	Gordon Wilson	'72
KEMPER US GOVT SEC	Fixed Income	4,571.1	8.78	10,315.00	10,647.50	16,169.00	9.9	621-1148	None	4.50	None	None	Pat Beimford	'81
KEY INV: CONVERTIBLE★	Convertibles	20.1	10.52	10,437.90	10,521.90	☆	6.6	N/A	None	N/A	N/A	N/A	N/A	N/A
KEYSTONE AMER EQ INC	Equity Income	24.4	10.95	10,395.10	11,177.70	☆	3.6	343-2898	None	2.00	0.75	2.0 ■	Walter McCormick	'87
KEYSTONE AMER GLBL OPP	Global	1.7	11.52	10,724.10	11,579.10	☆	0.8	343-2898	None	2.00	0.75	2.0 ■	Norman Kurland	'89
KEYSTONE AMER GOVT	Fixed Income	61.9	9.94	10,339.70	10,714.10	☆	7.6	343-2898	None	2.00	0.75	2.0 ■	Christopher Conkey	'88
KEYSTONE AMER GRO STK	Growth	6.6	13.80	11,004.80	11,893.80	☆	0.2	343-2898	None	2.00	0.75	2.0 ■	Donald Dates	'87
KEYSTONE AMER HI YLD	Fixed Income	84.3	7.14	10,322.30	9,021.50	☆	15.3	343-2898	None	2.00	0.75	2.0 ■	Donald Keller	'87
KEYSTONE AMER INV GRD	Fixed Income	24.2	8.55	10,290.10	10,483.00	☆	8.6	343-2898	None	2.00	0.75	2.0 ■	Christopher Conkey	'88
KEYSTONE AMER OMEGA FD	Capital Appreciation	42.8	17.40	10,922.80	12,539.40	22,026.50	1.1	343-2898	None	2.00	0.75	2.0 ■	Maureen Cullinane	'89
KEYSTONE AMER WORLD BD	World Fixed-Income	14.0	9.54	10,464.30	10,557.20	☆	5.8	343-2898	None	2.00	0.75	2.0 ■	C. Walker/J. Minter	'89
KEYSTONE B-1	Fixed Income	454.5	15.40	10,312.30	10,581.30	14,760.60	8.6	343-2898	None	None	1.25	4.0 ■	Barbara McCue	'86
KEYSTONE B-2	Fixed Income	915.3	15.83	10,310.30	9,968.50	14,471.20	11.5	343-2898	None	None	1.25	4.0 ■	Kristine Cloyes	'85
KEYSTONE B-4	Fixed Income	802.2	4.91	10,328.10	8,956.50	11,971.20	17.4	343-2898	None	None	1.25	4.0 ■	Donald Keller	'89
KEYSTONE INTERNATIONAL	International	96.1	6.55	10,702.60	10,110.30	21,975.20	0.0	343-2898	None	None	1.25	4.0 ■	Rosemary Komatsu	'86
KEYSTONE K-1	Mixed Income	826.0	9.10	10,367.50	10,798.90	17,861.40	5.9	343-2898	None	None	1.25	4.0 ■	Walter McCormick	'94
KEYSTONE K-2	Growth	323.4	7.71	10,663.90	11,410.60	19,366.50	2.3	343-2898	None	None	1.25	4.0 ■	Walter McCormick	'89
KEYSTONE PREC METALS	Gold	168.2	15.38	8,778.50	9,533.70	13,780.50	1.8	343-2898	None	None	1.25	4.0 ■	F. Thorne/M. Pirnie	'74/'79
KEYSTONE S-1	Growth & Income	186.1	25.02	10,527.40	11,533.10	18,979.30	3.0	343-2898	None	None	1.25	4.0 ■	Maureen Cullinane	'89
KEYSTONE S-3	Growth	263.7	8.87	10,609.30	11,153.30	18,458.10	2.7	343-2898	None	None	1.25	4.0 ■	Jill Lyndon	'87
KEYSTONE S-4	Small-Company Growth	566.6	6.32	11,146.40	11,852.60	16,327.90	0.8	343-2898	None	None	1.25	4.0 ■	Roland Gillis	'86
KIDDER PEABODY EQU INC★	Equity Income	66.3	21.35	10,768.30	11,704.30	☆	2.5	None	212-510-5351	4.00	0.50	5.0 ■	John Chadwick	'85
KIDDER PEABODY GOV INC★	Fixed Income	101.9	14.47	10,346.10	10,758.90	☆	8.2	None	212-510-5351	4.00	5.00	5.0 ■	David Hartman	'85
KIDDER PEABODY MKTGUARD	Specialty	23.3	14.03	10,130.00	10,568.50	☆	2.7	None	212-510-5351	4.00	None	None	Jonathon Jankus	'87
KIDDER PEABODY SPL GR★	Growth	17.2	20.62	11,115.90	11,519.60	15,507.20	0.0	None	212-510-5351	4.00	0.50	5.0 ■	John Chadwick	'85

★INSTL INTL: FOREIGN EQUITY—Open only to institutional customers. Minimum investment $100,000.
★KEY INV: CONVERTIBLE—Open only to clients of Keystone Financial.
★KIDDER PEABODY EQUITY INCOME, GOVERNMENT INCOME and SPECIAL GROWTH—Shares purchased before 3/1/90 are subject to a 5% redemption fee.

PERFORMANCE OF MUTUAL FUNDS (continued)

FUND NAME	OBJECTIVE	TOTAL NET ASSETS (MIL) 6/30/90	NET ASSET VALUE 6/30/90	PERFORMANCE (Return on Initial $10,000 Investment) 3/31/90-6/30/90	6/30/89-6/30/90	6/30/85-6/30/90	DIVIDEND YIELD % 6/90	PHONE NUMBER 800	In-State	FEES Load	12b-1	Redemption	MANAGER	SINCE
KLEINWORT BENSON: GLO INC	World Fixed-Income	4.8	10.23	10,312.50	10,332.40	☆	0.0	233-9164	212-687-2515	None	0.20	None	Richard Watt	'87
KLEINWORT BENSON: INTL EQ	International	92.8	16.08	11,044.00	12,315.60	36,784.90	1.3	233-9164	212-687-2515	None	0.20	None	John Trott	'80
KOTROZO OPTION INCOME★	Option Income	1.2	8.00	8,782.10	9,133.80	☆	10.2	628-6995	602-949-1369	5.00	None	None	Chuck Dobson	'90
LANDMARK CAPITAL GROWTH	Capital Appreciation	7.9	11.13	10,569.80	10,711.70	☆	0.1	223-4447	212-564-3456	None	None	None	John Hurford	'89
LANDMARK GROWTH & INCOME	Growth & Income	8.6	10.92	10,309.40	10,176.10	☆	4.0	223-4447	212-564-3456	None	None	None	John Hurford	'86
LANDMARK US GOVT INC	Fixed Income	22.4	9.05	10,338.10	10,577.80	☆	7.3	223-4447	212-564-3456	None	None	None	Tom Haley	'88
LAUREL FDS: STOCK	Growth & Income	9.6	14.33	10,832.00	12,163.40	☆	2.0	235-4331	None	None	0.35	None	Burt Mullins	'87
LAZARD SPECIAL EQUITY	Capital Appreciation	113.6	13.83	10,176.60	10,285.00	☆	1.8	N/A	N/A	N/A	N/A	N/A	N/A	N/A
LEGG MASON INC: GOVT INT	Fixed Income	53.9	10.08	10,300.30	10,751.80	☆	7.9	822-5544	None	None	0.50	None	Hildebrandt	'87
LEGG MASON INC: INV GRADE	Fixed Income	16.7	10.04	10,304.60	10,664.30	☆	8.3	822-5544	None	None	0.50	None	Hildebrandt	'87
LEGG MASON SPECIAL INV	Small-Company Growth	79.1	14.55	10,714.30	11,095.50	☆	0.5	822-5544	None	None	1.00	None	William Miller	'85
LEGG MASON TOTAL RETURN	Growth	24.9	10.00	10,070.30	9,916.40	☆	1.7	822-5544	None	None	1.00	None	Ernest Kiehne	'85
LEGG MASON VALUE TRUST	Growth	826.8	29.05	10,327.80	10,480.00	17,096.70	2.3	822-5544	None	None	0.95	None	Kiehne/Miller	'82
LEPERCO-ISTEL FUND	Growth & Income	21.3	13.76	10,392.70	10,516.20	14,940.50	4.5	338-1579	212-698-0749	None	0.001	None	Bruno Desforges	'74
LEXINGTON CORP LEADER	Growth & Income	92.1	11.76	10,331.10	11,407.60	22,683.80	15.5	526-0056	201-845-7300	4.00	None	None	NA-Trust Fund	N/A
LEXINGTON GLOBAL	Global	55.5	12.36	10,823.10	11,533.00	☆	4.7	526-0056	201-845-7300	5.00	None	None	Saesar Bryan	'87
LEXINGTON GNMA INCOME	Fixed Income	97.0	7.79	10,358.60	10,809.50	15,691.40	8.7	526-0056	201-845-7300	None	None	None	Dennis Jamison	'81
LEXINGTON GOLDFUND	Gold	120.6	5.26	9,006.88	10,175.40	16,737.00	1.0	526-0056	201-845-7300	None	None	None	Saesar Bryan	'86
LEXINGTON GROWTH	Growth	27.8	10.92	10,591.70	11,216.30	18,932.30	1.9	526-0056	201-845-7300	None	None	None	Carolyn Croney	'73
LEXINGTON RESEARCH	Growth & Income	120.9	15.98	10,440.00	10,912.90	18,414.30	5.6	526-0056	201-845-7300	None	None	None	James Fargis	'82
LEXINGTON TECH STRATEGY	Capital Appreciation	10.3	11.63	10,477.50	11,155.20	☆	3.3	526-0056	201-845-7300	5.00	None	None	Frank Peluso	'87
LIBERTY ADV: US GOVT	Fixed Income	303.1	9.07	10,325.30	10,840.10	☆	9.5	542-3863	None	4.50	None	None	Alex Fontain	'89
LIBERTY UTILITY FUND	Utility	64.9	9.69	10,325.40	10,935.20	☆	7.7	356-2805	None	4.50	None	None	Henry J. Gailliot	'88
LINDNER DIVIDEND★	Equity Income	152.7	21.83	10,158.70	10,158.60	16,739.70	10.1	None	314-727-5305	None	None	2.00	Eric Ryback	'82
LINDNER FUND	Growth	716.1	19.42	10,204.90	10,789.10	19,464.30	5.2	None	314-727-5305	None	None	2.00	Robert Lange/Eric Ryback	'84
LMH FUND	Growth & Income	27.0	17.88	10,141.80	9,591.90	14,769.50	3.8	422-2564	203-222-1624	None	None	None	Leonard Heine Jr	'83
LOCH NESS OPTION FUND	Option Income	0.6	8.59	10,462.90	10,032.30	☆	4.1	None	407-488-5589	None	None	None	Stephen Ellis	'87
LORD ABBETT BOND-DEB	Fixed Income	594.3	8.68	10,321.70	10,037.20	14,685.90	12.0	426-1130	212-848-1800	4.75	0.25	None	Robert Dow	'82
LORD ABBETT DEVEL GROWTH	Small-Company Growth	140.3	8.61	11,138.40	12,272.70	14,448.50	0.0	426-1130	212-848-1800	6.75	0.25	None	John Gibbons	'89
LORD ABBETT FUNDMNTL VAL	Growth & Income	21.3	12.64	10,360.70	11,545.50	☆	1.7	426-1130	212-848-1800	6.75	0.25	None	Denise Higgins	'88
LORD ABBETT GLBL: EQUITY	Global	36.6	10.83	10,628.10	11,357.00	☆	1.1	426-1130	212-848-1800	6.75	0.25	None	E. Wayne Nordberg	'88
LORD ABBETT GLBL: INCOME	World Fixed-Income	51.1	8.97	10,495.60	11,053.10	☆	10.9	426-1130	212-848-1800	4.75	0.25	None	Robert Dow	'88
LORD ABBETT US GOVT	Fixed Income	1,385.6	2.83	10,379.60	10,716.70	15,743.30	10.6	426-1130	212-848-1800	4.75	0.25	None	Carroll Coward	'86
LORD ABBETT VALUE APPREC	Growth	176.0	10.40	10,286.80	10,852.10	18,212.60	2.8	426-1130	212-848-1800	6.75	0.25	None	Paul Blaney	'83
LUTHERAN BRO FUND	Growth & Income	313.0	17.72	10,951.10	11,565.00	17,247.20	1.8	328-4552	800-752-4208	5.00	None	None	Don Nelson	'87
LUTHERAN BRO HI YLD	Fixed Income	155.1	7.71	10,458.80	9,130.80	☆	14.0	328-4552	800-752-4208	5.00	None	None	Mark Simenstad	'87
LUTHERAN BRO INCOME	Fixed Income	732.5	8.37	10,260.50	10,446.30	15,294.30	9.7	328-4552	800-752-4208	5.00	None	None	Charles Heeren	'86
M-S MAINSTAY: CAP APPREC	Capital Appreciation	40.6	12.57	11,026.30	11,736.90	☆	0.2	522-4202	None	None	1.00	5.00	Mackay-Shlds Mgt Team	'86
M-S MAINSTAY: CONVERTIBLE	Convertibles	20.2	8.61	10,529.10	10,788.20	☆	5.6	522-4202	None	None	1.00	5.00	Mackay-Shlds Mgt Team	'86
M-S MAINSTAY: GLOBAL	Global	20.6	10.43	10,967.40		☆	0.0	522-4202	None	None	1.00	5.00	Gamma Advisors	'87
M-S MAINSTAY: GLD & MIN	Gold	7.3	8.78	9,042.20	10,221.20	☆	0.0	522-4202	None	None	1.00	5.00	Gamma Advisors	'87
M-S MAINSTAY: GOVT PLUS	Fixed Income	474.7	8.71	10,331.10	10,330.40	☆	9.7	522-4202	None	None	1.00	5.00	Mackay-Shlds Mgt Team	'86
M-S MAINSTAY: HI YIELD	Fixed Income	202.4	6.88	10,273.30	9,135.80	☆	15.3	522-4202	None	None	1.00	5.00	Mackay-Shlds Mgt Team	'86
M-S MAINSTAY: TOT RTN	Balanced	46.7	11.81	10,827.60	11,290.60	☆	2.7	522-4202	None	None	1.00	5.00	Mackay-Shlds Mgt Team	'87
M-S MAINSTAY: VALUE	Growth & Income	33.4	11.33	10,295.40	10,642.90	☆	1.5	522-4202	None	None	1.00	5.00	Mackay-Shlds Mgt Team	'86

This page consists of a large mutual‑fund data table (Lipper Analytical Services). Column headers are not printed on this page; the columns below are, left‑to‑right: Fund name, Objective, Net Assets ($mil), NAV, Value A, Value B, Long‑term value, Yield %, Phone (local), Phone (alt), Max Sales Charge, 12b‑1, Redemption Fee, Portfolio Manager, Manager Since.

MACKENZIE CANADA FUND	International	16.3	9.62	9,276.80	9,317.60	☆	2.5	456-5111	407-393-8900	5.00	0.25	None	Alex Christ	'87
MACKENZIE GROWTH & INC	Growth & Income	12.8	10.16	10,147.80	10,257.00	☆	2.9	456-5111	407-393-8900	2.75	1.00	None	Michael Landry	'87
MACKENZIE INC: AMERICAN	Growth	55.0	12.94	10,135.60	10,510.80	☆	1.6	456-5111	407-393-8900	8.50	0.25	None	Alex Christ	'67
MACKENZIE INC: FIXED INC	Fixed Income	70.7	9.84	10,377.00	10,244.00	☆	7.6	456-5111	407-393-8900	4.75	0.25	None	Alex Christ	'67
MACKENZIE N AMER TOT RTN	Flexible	87.2	6.54	10,123.30	10,402.50	☆	5.7	456-5111	407-393-8900	5.00	0.25	None	Leslie Ferris	'87
MADISON BOND FUND	Fixed Income	0.2	20.35	☆	☆	☆	0.0	767-0300	608-274-0300	2.50	0.25	1.00	Frank Burgess	'90
MAIN STREET FDS: ASSET AL	Flexible	1.9	11.46	9,948.00	10,119.90	☆	1.7	548-1225	800-548-1225	4.75	None	None	William Baker	'88
MAIN STREET FDS: GOVT SEC	Fixed Income	5.6	9.42	10,292.60	10,754.10	☆	8.8	548-1225	800-548-1225	4.75	None	None	Art Steinmetz	'88
MAIN STREET FDS: INC & GR	Growth & Income	13.9	12.38	10,239.00	10,906.80	☆	1.5	548-1225	800-548-1225	4.75	None	None	Diane Jarmusz	'89
MARINER MF TF: EQUITY	Capital Appreciation	4.6	11.68	10,327.10	11,092.90	☆	3.1	634-2536	212-503-6826	4.00	0.50	None	Leo Grohowski	'85
MARKETMASTER: MGD BONDS G	Fixed Income	19.3	9.84	10,206.50	10,226.50	☆	0.0	441-7379	None	4.50	None	None	David Hetherington	'89
MARKETMASTER: VALUE F	Growth & Income	20.0	10.44	10,520.90	10,784.80	☆	0.0	441-7379	None	4.50	None	None	Sharon Herrmann	'89
MAS POOLED: CASH PORT★	Fixed Income	22.0	25.04	10,214.10	10,838.10	☆	8.9	332-5577	215-648-6309	None	None	None	Miller, et. al	'87
MAS POOLED: EQUITY★	Growth	579.2	46.95	10,907.30	11,779.50	21,959.80	2.8	332-5577	215-648-6309	None	None	None	Miller, et. al	'84
MAS POOLED: FXED INCOME★	Fixed Income	679.9	28.31	10,406.20	10,500.20	16,679.10	8.6	332-5577	215-648-6309	None	None	None	Miller, et. al	'84
MAS POOLED: GROWTH★	Growth	18.2	26.32	10,947.20	11,782.50	☆	2.0	332-5577	215-648-6309	None	None	None	Miller, et. al	'86
MAS POOLED: HIGH YIELD★	Fixed Income	5.1	20.98	10,592.60	9,258.60	☆	14.6	332-5577	215-648-6309	None	None	None	Miller, et. al	'89
MAS POOLED: INTL EQUITY★	International	148.0	30.20	10,789.40	12,162.30	☆	2.3	332-5577	215-648-6309	None	None	None	Miller, et. al	'88
MAS POOLED: SELECT EQTY★	Growth	70.5	34.81	10,921.30	11,709.90	☆	2.5	332-5577	215-648-6309	None	None	None	Miller, et. al	'88
MAS POOLED: SELECT FIX INC★	Fixed Income	88.9	26.51	10,374.20	10,528.60	☆	8.9	332-5577	215-648-6309	None	None	None	Miller, et. al	'87
MAS POOLED: SELECT VALUE★	Growth & Income	47.5	29.67	10,274.60	10,226.80	☆	4.4	332-5577	215-648-6309	None	None	None	Miller, et. al	'87
MAS POOLED: SMALL CAP★	Small-Company Growth	138.5	24.71	10,492.60	10,784.80	☆	4.6	332-5577	215-648-6309	None	None	None	Miller, et. al	'86
MAS POOLED: VALUE★	Growth	456.7	31.04	10,302.80	10,523.90	19,077.40	4.8	332-5577	215-648-6309	None	None	None	Miller, et. al	'84
MAS CAPITAL DEVELOPMENT	Growth	778.5	10.91	10,561.30	11,033.40	16,773.30	3.1	225-2606	617-954-5000	7.25	None	None	Jeffrey Shames	'87
MAS FINL BOND	Fixed Income	308.0	13.08	10,390.50	10,773.60	16,172.30	9.0	225-2606	617-954-5000	7.25	None	None	Pat Zlotin/G. Kurinsky	'84
MASS FINL DEVELOPMENT	Growth & Income	200.0	11.34	10,376.50	11,265.30	18,885.50	3.3	225-2606	617-954-5000	7.25	None	None	Fredrick Simmons	'88
MASS FINL EMERGING GRO	Small-Company Growth	209.8	17.83	11,033.40	11,453.20	16,709.50	0.0	225-2606	617-954-5000	7.25	None	None	Donald Pitcher	'88
MASS FINL HIGH INC: SRS I	Fixed Income	538.0	4.64	10,329.30	9,022.50	13,314.40	16.3	225-2606	617-954-5000	7.25	None	None	Joan Batchelder	'83
MASS FINL HIGH INC: SRS II	Fixed Income	33.0	7.06	10,397.90	8,932.60	☆	14.3	225-2606	617-954-5000	7.25	None	None	Joan Batchelder	'83
MASS FINL INTL TR-BOND	World Fixed-Income	122.0	12.03	10,433.70	11,362.70	22,321.20	3.9	225-2606	617-954-5000	4.75	0.25	None	Leslie Nanberg	'84
MASS FINL SPECIAL	Capital Appreciation	125.2	8.84	10,411.00	10,637.80	19,913.30	3.7	225-2606	617-954-5000	4.75	0.25	None	J. Shames/B. McAdams	'85
MASS FINL TOTAL RETURN	Balanced	758.8	11.38	10,343.10	11,033.10	20,198.70	5.9	225-2606	617-954-5000	4.75	0.25	None	Richard Dahlberg	'85
MASS INVESTORS GROWTH	Growth	925.4	10.23	11,363.50	11,826.70	20,014.80	0.7	225-2606	617-954-5000	7.25	None	None	Thomas Cashman	'88
MASS INVESTORS TRUST	Growth & Income	1,416.1	14.11	10,867.70	12,260.40	22,561.90	3.2	225-2606	617-954-5000	7.25	None	None	Laurence Leonard	'85
MASSMUTUAL FDS: BAL	Balanced	42.1	11.33	10,371.60	11,069.60	☆	4.4	542-6767	800-854-9100	4.50	0.30	None	Hamline Wilson	'88
MASSMUTUAL FDS: CAP APPR	Small-Company Growth	17.9	13.07	10,420.40	10,597.00	☆	2.2	542-6767	800-854-9100	4.50	0.30	None	George Ulrich	'88
MASSMUTUAL FDS: CORP CASH	Fixed Income	11.3	49.10	10,148.70	10,609.50	15,274.00	6.6	542-6767	800-854-9100	2.50	0.20	None	Robert Long	'88
MASSMUTUAL FDS: GOVT SEC	Fixed Income	29.8	9.82	10,334.90	10,692.70	☆	7.7	542-6767	800-854-9100	4.50	0.30	None	Robert Long	'83
MASSMUTUAL FDS: INV GRADE	Fixed Income	90.5	10.00	10,317.20	10,545.00	☆	9.0	542-6767	800-854-9100	4.50	0.30	None	Robert Long	'88
MASSMUTUAL FDS: VALUE STK	Growth & Income	41.1	12.13	10,408.40	11,205.90	☆	3.2	542-6767	800-854-9100	4.50	0.30	None	David Salerno	'86
MATHERS FUND	Growth	243.6	15.45	10,460.40	11,053.60	21,278.70	5.9	962-3863	708-295-7400	None	None	None	Henry Van der Eb Jr	'70
MAXUS EQUITY	Flexible	1.7	9.83	10,250.30	☆	☆	0.0	None	216-292-3434	None	0.50	None	Richard Barone	'89
MAXUS INCOME	Mixed Income	14.3	10.41	10,153.80	10,389.10	13,966.00	7.0	None	216-292-3434	None	0.50	None	Richard Barone	'85
MEDICAL RESEARCH INV	Health/Biotech	3.8	16.17	11,229.20	13,913.40	☆	0.0	262-6631	800-262-6631	4.75	0.25	4.00	Sam Isaly	'89
MEESCHAERT CAPITAL	Growth	22.1	22.98	10,417.00	11,441.20	15,592.10	8.7	802-748-2400	802-748-2400	None	None	None	Paul Jaspard	'83
MEESCHAERT INTL BOND	World Fixed-Income	23.3	0.00	N/A	N/A	☆	0.0	None	802-748-2400	None	None	4.00	Paul Jaspard	'88
MERGER FUND	Capital Appreciation	11.2	11.75	10,379.90	10,280.40	14,631.10	0.4	343-8959	914-241-3360	None	0.45	None	Frederick W. Green	'89

★KOTROZO OPTION INCOME—The fund merged with Analytic Optioned Equity as of 8/1/90.
★LINDNER DIVIDEND—Redemption fee is charged on shares sold within 60 days of purchase.
★MAS POOLED FUNDS—Designed for certain tax-exempt fiduciary investors.

PERFORMANCE OF MUTUAL FUNDS (continued)

FUND NAME	OBJECTIVE	TOTAL NET ASSETS (MIL) 6/30/90	NET ASSET VALUE 6/30/90	PERFORMANCE (Return on Initial $10,000 Investment)			DIVIDEND YIELD % 6/90	PHONE NUMBER		FEES			MANAGER	SINCE
				3/31/90-6/30/90	6/30/89-6/30/90	6/30/85-6/30/90		800	In-State	Load	12b-1	Redemption		
MERIDIAN FUND	Growth	11.1	17.72	11,750.70	11,978.00	19,185.90	2.7	446-6662	800-445-5553	None	None	None	Richard Aster Jr	'84
MERRILL BASIC VALUE A	Growth & Income	1,556.3	19.32	10,000.00	10,177.10	18,975.60	4.5	637-3863	None	6.50	None	None	Paul Hofman	'77
MERRILL BASIC VALUE B	Growth & Income	922.1	19.12	9,973.90	10,073.00	☆	4.0	637-3863	None	None	1.00	4.00	Paul Hofman	'77
MERRILL CAPITAL A	Growth & Income	945.2	25.00	10,570.80	11,206.70	20,330.20	5.7	637-3863	None	6.50	None	None	Ernest Watts	'83
MERRILL CAPITAL B	Growth & Income	444.7	24.74	10,545.60	11,092.80	☆	5.2	637-3863	None	None	1.00	4.00	Ernest Watts	'83
MERRILL CORP DIV	Fixed Income	64.6	8.78	9,975.00	10,105.20	13,485.60	10.1	637-3863	None	2.00	None	None	Bryan Ison	'84
MERRILL CORP: HI INC A	Fixed Income	541.9	7.04	10,617.60	10,414.90	15,786.80	13.6	637-3863	None	4.00	None	None	V. Lathbury/B. Trosley	'82
MERRILL CORP: HI INC B	Fixed Income	163.5	7.04	10,657.50	10,322.40	☆	12.8	637-3863	None	None	0.75	4.00	V. Lathbury/B. Trosley	'82
MERRILL CORP: HI QUAL A	Fixed Income	313.9	11.07	10,298.30	10,650.10	15,796.90	8.7	637-3863	None	4.00	None	None	Martha Reed	'82
MERRILL CORP: HI QUAL B	Fixed Income	178.1	11.07	10,278.90	10,568.90	☆	7.9	637-3863	None	0.75	None	4.00	Martha Reed	'82
MERRILL CORP: INTMDT TERM	Fixed Income	87.8	10.96	10,296.80	10,736.50	15,566.80	8.8	637-3863	None	2.00	None	None	Martha Reed	'82
MERRILL DEVLOP CAP MKT	International	104.0	11.58	10,772.10	☆	☆	0.0	637-3863	None	4.00	None	2.00	Grace Pineda	'89
MERRILL EQUI-BOND	Balanced	11.3	11.64	10,282.70	10,925.50	16,560.20	4.2	637-3863	None	4.00	None	None	V. Lathbury/B. Vogel	'83
MERRILL EUROFUND A	European Region	82.7	12.15	11,065.60	13,087.00	☆	0.7	637-3863	None	6.50	None	None	A. Albert/A. Holmes	'87
MERRILL EUROFUND B	European Region	528.9	11.93	11,036.10	12,966.70	☆	0.7	637-3863	None	None	1.00	4.00	A. Albert/A. Holmes	'87
MERRILL FEDERAL SEC TR	Fixed Income	2,424.7	9.31	10,340.40	10,926.40	15,897.30	9.1	637-3863	None	4.00	0.17	None	G. Maunz/J. Bevson	'89
MERRILL FD TOMORROW A	Growth	7.4	16.40	10,621.80	10,589.60	☆	2.7	637-3863	None	6.50	None	None	Vincent Dileo	'89
MERRILL FD TOMORROW B	Growth	519.1	16.31	10,597.80	10,478.50	17,531.80	1.6	637-3863	None	None	1.00	4.00	Vincent Dileo	'84
MERRILL GLOBAL ALLOC A	Global	53.3	11.22	10,625.00	11,605.70	☆	6.1	637-3863	None	6.50	None	None	B. Ison/D. Stattman	'89
MERRILL GLOBAL ALLOC B	Global	128.2	11.15	10,598.90	11,493.00	☆	5.3	637-3863	None	None	1.00	4.00	B. Ison/D. Stattman	'89
MERRILL GLOBAL CONV A	World Fixed-Income	0.2	9.31	10,326.30	10,329.30	☆	6.9	637-3863	None	4.00	None	None	Harry Dewdney	'88
MERRILL GLOBAL CONV B	World Fixed-Income	22.8	9.31	10,297.20	10,227.10	☆	5.8	637-3863	None	None	1.00	4.00	Harry Dewdney	'88
MERRILL INSTL INTMDT	Fixed Income	164.2	9.30	10,272.90	10,735.60	☆	8.4	637-3863	None	None	0.15	None	Martha Reed	'86
MERRILL INTL HLDG A	Global	203.9	12.01	10,810.10	11,943.30	23,679.80	7.5	637-3863	None	6.50	None	None	Frederick Ives	'85
MERRILL INTL HLDG B	Global	21.2	11.89	10,789.50	11,829.30	☆	6.9	637-3863	None	None	1.00	4.00	Frederick Ives	'85
MERRILL NATURAL RES A	Natural Resources	5.0	14.85	9,860.60	11,854.90	☆	2.5	637-3863	None	6.50	None	None	Richard Price	'85
MERRILL NATURAL RES B	Natural Resources	404.1	14.78	9,840.20	11,742.50	☆	1.6	637-3863	None	6.50	None	4.00	Richard Price	'85
MERRILL PACIFIC A	Pacific Region	264.2	18.75	11,035.90	11,525.10	32,154.80	0.3	637-3863	None	6.50	None	None	Stephen Silverman	'83
MERRILL PACIFIC B	Pacific Region	62.1	18.52	11,017.30	11,419.20	☆	0.0	637-3863	None	None	1.00	4.00	Stephen Silverman	'83
MERRILL PHOENIX A	Growth & Income	159.1	12.73	10,307.70	10,525.10	20,770.90	4.8	637-3863	None	6.50	None	None	Robert Martorelli	'86
MERRILL PHOENIX B	Growth & Income	98.5	12.63	10,285.00	10,431.10	☆	4.1	637-3863	None	None	1.00	4.00	Robert Martorelli	'86
MERRILL RET BENFT A	Balanced	4.8	11.98	10,265.60	10,818.10	☆	6.4	637-3863	None	6.50	None	None	J. Heymsfeld/J. Rozen	'85
MERRILL RET BENFT B	Balanced	1,428.4	11.93	10,231.60	10,707.60	☆	5.3	637-3863	None	None	1.00	4.00	J. Heymsfeld/J. Rozen	'85
MERRILL RET EQUITY A	Growth & Income	22.5	13.61	10,940.50	11,770.70	☆	1.6	637-3863	None	6.50	None	None	Stephen Johnes	'87
MERRILL RET EQUITY B	Growth & Income	550.6	13.56	10,926.70	11,662.40	☆	0.6	637-3863	None	None	1.00	4.00	Stephen Johnes	'87
MERRILL RET GLBL BD A	World Fixed-Income	12.0	9.67	10,567.00	11,505.60	☆	9.6	637-3863	None	4.00	None	None	David Walter	'86
MERRILL RET GLBL BD B	World Fixed-Income	264.4	9.67	10,546.80	11,417.70	☆	8.8	637-3863	None	None	0.75	4.00	David Walter	'86
MERRILL RET INCOME	Fixed Income	1,646.7	9.40	10,333.90	10,867.10	☆	8.3	637-3863	None	None	0.75	4.00	G. Maunz/J. Rewson	'89
MERRILL SPEC VALUE A	Growth	54.9	11.57	10,184.90	9,370.40	10,700.20	2.0	637-3863	None	6.50	None	None	Dennis Stattman	'89
MERRILL SPEC VALUE B	Growth	1.7	11.47	10,159.40	9,274.50	☆	1.2	637-3863	None	None	1.00	4.00	Dennis Stattman	'89
MERRILL STRTG DVD A	Equity Income	38.8	12.09	10,252.30	10,903.20	☆	5.3	637-3863	None	6.50	None	None	Walter Rodgers	'87
MERRILL STRTG DVD B	Equity Income	346.3	12.05	10,226.80	10,797.30	☆	4.4	637-3863	None	None	1.00	4.00	Walter Rodgers	'87
MERRIMAN: TIMED AST ALLOC	Global Flexible	21.7	10.37	10,402.50	10,784.50	☆	4.5	423-4893	206-285-8877	None	None	None	Paul Merriman	'88

Fund	Objective	Net Assets ($mil)	NAV	$10K Value 1	$10K Value 2	$10K 10-Yr	Yield %	Phone	Toll-Free	Max Load	12b-1	CDSC	Manager	Since
MERRIMAN: TIMED BLUE CHIP	Growth & Income	14.1	10.57	10,501.90	10,665.80	☆	3.9	423-4893	206-285-8877	None	None	None	Paul Merriman	'88
MERRIMAN: TIMED CAP APPREC	Growth	17.9	10.07	10,421.30	10,460.70	☆	4.6	423-4893	206-285-8877	None	None	None	Paul Merriman	'88
MERRIMAN: TIMED GOVT FD	Fixed Income	10.3	13.39	10,252.20	10,426.70	☆	6.0	423-4893	206-285-8877	None	None	None	Paul Merriman	'86
METLIFE CAPITAL APPREC	Capital Appreciation	58.9	11.23	10,510.20	11,733.80	☆	0.2	882-0052	617-348-2000	4.50	0.50	None	Fred Kobrick	'86
METLIFE EQU: ENERGY	Natural Resources	35.3		9,557.40	☆	☆	0.0	882-0052	617-348-2000	4.50	0.50	None	Dan Rice	'90
METLIFE EQUITY INCOME	Equity Income	49.9	9.83	10,206.90	11,128.10	☆	4.7	882-0052	617-348-2000	4.50	0.50	None	Mike Henzi	'90
METLIFE EQU INVESTMENTS	Growth & Income	35.7	12.15	10,906.60	11,653.60	☆	2.4	882-0052	617-348-2000	4.50	0.50	None	Peter Bennet	'89
METLIFE GOVT INCOME	Fixed Income	983.4	11.40	10,370.10	10,685.60	☆	8.5	882-0052	617-348-2000	None	0.25	None	Jack Kallis	'87
METLIFE GOVT SECS	Fixed Income	33.2	6.73	10,374.90	10,654.60	☆	8.2	882-0052	617-348-2000	4.50	0.25	None	Jack Kallis	'87
METLIFE HIGH INCOME	Fixed Income	181.4	5.93	10,437.90	9,417.30	☆	14.8	882-0052	617-348-2000	4.50	0.25	None	Bart Geer	'86
METLIFE MANAGED ASSET	Flexible	64.6	8.02	10,463.50	10,966.40	14,559.20	6.1	882-0052	617-348-2000	4.50	0.25	None	Steve Somes	'88
MFS GOVT GUARANTEED SEC	Fixed Income	326.8	9.20	10,329.60	10,616.00	☆	8.6	225-2606	617-954-5000	4.75	0.35	None	Pat Ziotin/Geoff Kurinsky	'84
MFS GOVT INCOME PLUS	Fixed Income	1,207.0	7.23	10,173.30	10,436.20	☆	6.9	225-2606	617-954-5000	4.75	0.35	None	Pat Ziotin/Steve Nothern	'86
MFS GOVT PREMIUM ACCOUNT	Fixed Income	395.9	9.14	10,135.60	10,436.50	☆	7.0	225-2606	617-954-5000	3.75	0.25	None	Patricia Ziotin	'88
MFS LIFETIME CAP GRO	Capital Appreciation	236.5	12.29	10,527.10	11,509.50	☆	1.6	225-2606	617-954-5000	None	1.00	6.0	Kevin Parke	'88
MFS LIFETIME EMER GRO	Small-Company Growth	100.4	9.18	11,532.70	13,002.80	☆	0.0	225-2606	617-954-5000	None	1.00	6.0	John Ballen	'87
MFS LIFETIME GLOBAL EQ	Global	78.5	13.89	10,506.80	12,384.60	☆	0.0	225-2606	617-954-5000	None	1.00	6.0	N. Langwiser/D. Mannheim	'87
MFS LIFETIME GOLD&PREC	Gold	6.5	5.51	9,122.50	10,054.70	☆	0.0	225-2606	617-954-5000	None	1.00	6.0	Redmond Patriquin	'88
MFS LIFETIME GOVT INC	Fixed Income	3,437.4	7.23	10,215.60	10,414.50	☆	6.4	225-2606	617-954-5000	None	1.00	6.0	Patricia Ziotin	'87
MFS LIFETIME H I INC	Fixed Income	125.8	5.36	10,455.60	8,855.20	☆	13.9	225-2606	617-954-5000	None	1.00	6.0	John Batchelder	'87
MFS LIFETIME INTMDT IN	Fixed Income	95.6	9.12	10,238.40	10,512.00	☆	7.3	225-2606	617-954-5000	None	1.00	6.0	Patricia Ziotin/Les Nanberg	'88
MFS LIFETIME MGD SECTR	Specialty	194.3	11.33	10,894.20	11,228.90	☆	0.0	225-2606	617-954-5000	None	1.00	6.0	Gerry Bennett	'88
MFS LIFETIME CUAL BOND	Fixed Income	24.8	9.62	10,305.40	10,421.60	☆	7.7	225-2606	617-954-5000	None	1.00	6.0	Patricia Ziotin	'88
MFS LIFETIME TOT RTN	Growth & Income	212.2	9.17	10,357.00	10,511.20	☆	5.0	225-2606	617-954-5000	None	1.00	6.0	John Laupheimer Jr.	'87
MFS MANAGED SECTOR TR	Specialty	125.1	14.23	10,086.10	11,292.30	☆	0.6	225-2606	617-954-5000	4.75	0.35	None	George Bennett, Jr.	'88
MIDAMERICA HIGH GROWTH	Capital Appreciation	12.0	3.82	10,268.80	10,320.60	16,194.90	4.5	288-2346	None	5.75	None	None	David Halfpap	'81
MIDAMERICA HIGH YIELD FD	Fixed Income	33.0	9.77	10,383.60	10,705.90	16,787.10	10.7	288-2346	None	5.50	None	None	David Halfpap	'89
MIDAMERICA MUTUAL	Growth	37.2	5.68	10,434.70	10,898.60	17,106.40	3.9	288-2346	None	5.75	None	None	David Halfpap	'81
MIDWEST STRT: INTMDT GOVT	Fixed Income	37.9	9.95	10,276.30	10,521.70	14,303.00	7.6	543-8721	513-629-2000	1.00	0.35	None	William Snider	'87
MIDWEST STRT: GOVT SEC	Fixed Income	36.0	9.87	10,296.50	10,644.70	14,853.80	8.5	543-8721	513-629-2000	4.00	0.25	None	Bill Snider	'86
MIDWEST STRT: GROWTH	Growth	8.9	14.53	10,691.70	11,133.50	16,426.40	1.5	543-8721	513-629-2000	4.75	0.25	None	Thomas Mench	'88
MIDWEST STRT: TREAS ALLOC	Fixed Income	76.0	8.96	10,389.90	10,271.40	☆	6.9	543-8721	513-629-2000	4.00	0.25	None	Thomas Mench	'88
MIDWEST STRT: UTILITY INC	Utility	7.5	9.63	10,028.00	☆	☆	0.0	543-8721	513-629-2000	4.75	0.25	None	Thomas Mench	'89
MILLS VALUE FUND	Growth & Income	12.1	10.77	10,249.10	10,279.50	☆	1.4	441-6580	804-649-2400	4.50	0.30	None	Charles Mills	'88
MIM MUTUAL: BOND INCOME	Fixed Income	5.6	9.02	10,302.20	10,018.10	☆	8.4	233-1240	233-1240	None	0.975	None	Gregory Getts	'86
MIM MUTUAL: STOCK APPREC	Capital Appreciation	4.6	10.44	11,863.60	12,915.80	☆	0.9	233-1240	None	None	0.975	None	Art Bonnel	'87
MIM MUTUAL: STK, CV&OP GRO	Capital Appreciation	7.5	9.83	10,410.00	10,014.20	16,581.50	3.1	233-1240	None	None	0.975	None	Harvey Salkin	'86
MIM MUTUAL: STK, CV&OP INC	Option Income	11.9	10.60	10,307.90	10,428.80	15,643.20	4.0	233-1240	None	None	0.975	None	Harvey Salkin	'86
MIMLIC ASSET ALLOCATION	Flexible	10.3	11.72	10,573.00	11,090.60	☆	6.5	443-3677	612-223-4115	5.00	0.35	None	Thomas Gunderson	'88
MIMLIC FIXED INCOME SEC	Fixed Income	4.4	9.87	10,315.70	10,501.20	☆	8.1	443-3677	612-223-4115	5.00	0.35	None	Fritz Fewerherm	'85
MIMLIC INVESTORS I	Growth & Income	13.4	13.45	10,989.30	11,625.60	☆	2.1	443-3677	612-223-4115	5.00	0.35	None	Jim Tatera	'86
MIMLIC MORTGAGE	Fixed Income	13.9	10.11	10,352.10	10,735.10	☆	8.2	443-3677	612-223-4115	5.00	0.35	None	John Clymer	'85
MONETTA FUND	Growth & Income	5.9	11.82	11,183.00	12,192.30	☆	5.0	666-3882	708-462-9800	None	0.75	None	Robert Bacarella	'75
MONITREND: GOLD FUND	Gold	2.3	17.70	9,882.70	10,850.40	☆	2.3	251-1970	615-298-1000	3.50	0.75	None	Black/Licameli/Liebling	'88
MONITREND: GOVERNMENT FD	Fixed Income	3.9	13.83	10,199.10	10,346.20	☆	6.8	251-1970	615-298-1000	3.50	0.75	None	Black/Licameli/Liebling	'86
MONITREND: SUMMATN INDEX	Growth & Income	4.4	18.89	10,311.10	10,608.90	11,630.60	0.5	251-1970	615-298-1000	3.50	0.75	None	Black/Licameli/Liebling	'88
MONITREND: VALUE FUND	Capital Appreciation	5.8	15.49	10,150.70	9,989.90	☆	2.1	251-1970	615-298-1000	3.50	0.75	None	Black/Licameli/Liebling	'84
MORGAN KEEGAN SOUTHERN	Growth	8.8	11.50	10,360.40	10,377.60	☆	4.1	366-7426	901-524-4100	3.00	0.50	None	Richard McStay	'86
MUTUAL: BEACON	Growth & Income	456.9	24.05	10,282.90	10,413.10	22,648.60	4.3	448-3863	201-912-2100	None	None	None	Michael Price	'83
MUTUAL BENEFIT FUND	Growth & Income	38.3	17.68	10,498.80	10,741.70	22,323.80	2.3	333-4726	401-751-8600	4.75	None	None	J. Stone/M. Mullarkey	'81

FUND NAME	OBJECTIVE	TOTAL NET ASSETS (MIL) 6/30/90	NET ASSET VALUE 6/30/90	PERFORMANCE (Return on Initial $10,000 Investment)			DIVIDEND YIELD % 6/90	PHONE NUMBER		FEES			MANAGER	SINCE
				3/31/90-6/30/90	6/30/89-6/30/90	6/30/85-6/30/90		800	In-State	Load	12b-1	Redemption		
MUTUAL: QUALIFIED★	Growth & Income	1,340.3	21.62	10,218.60	10,076.10	20,810.90	5.8	448-3863	201-912-2100	None	None	None	Michael Price	'83
MUTUAL: SHARES★	Growth & Income	3,110.3	65.61	10,250.80	10,127.40	20,644.60	6.5	448-3863	201-912-2100	None	None	None	Michael Price	'83
MUTUAL OF OMAHA AMERICA	Fixed Income	51.8	10.07	10,333.40	10,633.50	15,216.30	8.2	228-9596	402-397-8555	4.75	0.25	None	Shirley Lang	'68
MUTUAL OF OMAHA GROWTH	Growth	61.7	10.64	11,515.20	13,556.10	23,603.40	0.8	228-9596	402-397-8555	4.75	0.25	None	Gina Simpson	'83
MUTUAL OF OMAHA INCOME	Mixed Income	171.3	9.40	10,357.70	10,871.10	17,045.80	7.8	228-9596	402-397-8555	4.75	0.25	None	Gina Simpson	'83
NATIONAL AGGRESSIVE GRO	Small-Company Growth	70.4	7.56	10,398.90	10,218.60	13,388.60	1.3	356-5555	203-863-5645	7.25	None	None	Mitchell Hauser	'89
NATIONAL BOND	Fixed Income	375.0	1.72	10,463.20	8,514.20	10,535.10	15.7	356-5535	203-863-5645	4.75	None	None	Thomas Ole Dial	'89
NATIONAL FEDERAL SEC TR	Fixed Income	429.5	8.99	10,478.20	10,687.60	13,289.70	8.6	356-5535	203-863-5645	4.75	None	None	John Moore	'87
NATIONAL INDUSTRIES	Growth & Income	32.6	13.54	10,910.60	12,044.40	17,992.80	1.4	None	303-220-8500	None	None	None	Richard Barrett	'84
NATIONAL REAL ESTATE: INC	Specialty	9.3	6.74	9,550.70	8,236.10	☆	14.8	356-5535	203-863-5645	5.75	0.25	None	Martin Cohen	'87
NATIONAL REAL ESTATE: STK	Real Estate	19.0	7.15	9,592.20	9,068.30	12,578.30	7.3	356-5535	203-863-5645	5.75	0.25	None	Martin Cohen	'85
NATIONAL STOCK	Growth & Income	225.9	8.15	10,499.50	11,048.20	19,556.40	3.1	356-5535	203-863-5645	7.25	None	None	William Sadler	'85
NATIONAL STRATEGIC ALLOC	Global Flexible	84.4	11.96	10,372.30	10,963.20	☆	2.6	356-5535	203-863-5645	5.75	0.25	None	Andre Sharon	'87
NATIONAL TOTAL INCOME	Mixed Income	224.2	8.28	10,398.30	10,661.90	19,786.40	5.9	356-5535	203-863-5645	7.25	None	None	John Doney	'87
NATIONAL TOTAL RETURN	Equity Income	265.4	7.33	10,542.90	11,090.40	18,489.80	4.0	356-5535	203-863-5645	7.25	None	None	John Doney	'87
NATIONAL VALUE	Capital Appreciation	2.2	11.45	10,651.20	9,819.90	☆	0.0	654-0001	212-482-8100	4.75	None	None	Barry Gordon	'85
NATIONWIDE BOND	Fixed Income	35.8	9.04	10,300.60	10,630.70	15,212.40	9.8	848-0920	None	7.50	None	None	Mike Groseclose	'80
NATIONWIDE FUND	Growth & Income	507.2	14.18	10,641.20	11,739.10	21,959.50	2.8	848-0920	None	7.50	None	None	Charles Bath	'82
NATIONWIDE GROWTH	Growth	244.7	8.86	10,468.30	10,230.50	18,861.70	3.1	848-0920	None	7.50	None	None	John Schaffner	'78
NAUTILUS FUND	Technology	13.8	14.10	11,463.40	12,679.90	11,913.80	0.0	225-6285	617-482-8260	4.75	None	None	Michael J. Chapman	'88
N & B GENESIS	Small-Company Growth	21.8	5.96	10,419.60	10,084.50	☆	0.3	877-9700	212-850-8300	None	None	2.00	Steven Milman	'88
N & B GUARDIAN	Growth & Income	559.8	39.71	10,493.70	10,839.70	19,030.90	3.2	877-9700	212-850-8300	None	None	None	K. Simons/L. Marx	'82
N & B LTD MATURITY BOND	Fixed Income	117.0	9.91	10,276.30	10,820.50	☆	8.2	877-9700	212-850-8300	None	None	None	T. Havell/T. Giuliano	'86
N & B MANHATTAN	Capital Appreciation	424.8	10.58	10,665.30	11,115.00	20,480.30	1.6	877-9700	212-850-8300	None	None	None	Irwin Lainoff	'79
N & B MONEY MARKET PLUS	Fixed Income	93.7	9.77	10,208.20	10,809.10	☆	8.8	877-9700	212-850-8300	None	None	None	Havell/Giuliano	'86
N & B PARTNERS	Growth	793.8	18.11	10,372.30	10,811.40	19,198.40	4.1	877-9700	212-850-8300	None	None	None	Michael Kassan	'90
N & B SEL SECT ENERGY	Specialty	417.8	18.96	10,417.60	11,224.80	18,094.10	2.5	877-9700	212-850-8300	None	None	None	L. Marx/Simons/Baskir	'89
NEUWIRTH FUND	Small-Company Growth	24.7	11.62	10,338.10	9,714.80	15,957.40	0.5	521-3036	212-504-4000	5.66	None	None	James Engle	'89
NEW ALTERNATIVES FUND	Natural Resources	15.8	27.83	10,626.20	10,896.70	20,671.20	1.7	None	516-466-0808	5.66	None	None	Accrued Equities Inc.	'82
NEW ECONOMY FUND	Growth	921.3	22.56	10,495.40	10,960.00	21,119.00	2.4	421-0180	213-486-9200	5.75	None	None	Multiple Managers	'83
NEW ENG: BOND INCOME	Fixed Income	80.1	11.02	10,301.80	10,626.30	15,467.20	8.2	343-7104	None	4.50	0.25	None	Catherine Bunting	'90
NEW ENG: BALANCED	Balanced	59.0	9.21	10,286.90	9,996.30	16,060.80	6.0	343-7104	None	6.50	0.25	None	Don Shepherd	'89
NEW ENG: GLOBAL GOVT	World Fixed-Income	24.7	11.77	10,443.30	10,903.80	☆	6.0	343-7104	None	4.50	0.25	None	Jeff Hayes/N. Wentworth	'85
NEW ENG: GOVERNMENT SEC	Fixed Income	178.3	11.34	10,291.50	10,404.30	☆	7.8	343-7104	None	4.50	0.25	None	Michael Martino	'82
NEW ENG: GROWTH FUND	Growth	639.9	9.48	11,504.90	12,344.80	21,327.50	1.3	343-7104	None	6.50	0.25	None	Ken Heebner	'72
NEW ENG: RETIREMENT EQU	Growth & Income	145.3	6.53	10,414.70	11,207.30	18,887.70	2.0	343-7104	None	6.50	0.25	None	Ken Heebner	'78
NEW PERSPECTIVE FUND	Global	1,565.7	11.82	10,739.20	12,323.40	26,198.40	2.4	421-0180	213-486-9200	5.75	0.25	None	Multiple Managers	'73
NEW YORK VENTURE	Growth	350.4	9.38	10,586.90	11,587.00	23,145.40	3.8	279-2279	505-983-4335	4.75	0.25	None	Shelby Davis	'69
NEWTON GROWTH FUND	Growth	35.0	23.53	10,537.40	10,959.40	15,999.00	3.7	242-7229	414-347-1141	None	None	None	M&I Inv. Co.	'85
NEWTON INCOME FUND	Fixed Income	19.8	8.02	10,277.60	10,681.20	14,311.60	7.9	242-7229	414-347-1141	None	None	None	M&I Inv. Co	'85
NICHOLAS FUND	Growth	1,519.7	40.16	10,745.40	11,183.70	18,130.40	2.1	None	414-272-6133	None	None	None	A. O. Nicholas	'69
NICHOLAS INCOME	Fixed Income	69.7	3.42	10,175.10	10,203.50	14,740.40	11.3	None	414-272-6133	None	None	None	A. O. Nicholas	'77
NICHOLAS LIMITED EDITION	Small-Company Growth	71.6	13.33	10,802.30	11,422.90	☆	1.1	None	414-272-6133	None	None	None	A. O. Nicholas	'87
NICHOLAS II	Small-Company Growth	426.7	21.01	10,757.80	10,829.00	18,485.50	1.5	None	414-272-6133	None	None	None	A. O. Nicholas	'83
NIKKO JAPAN TILT FD	Pacific Region	8.3	8.38	10,897.30	☆	☆	0.0	None	212-416-5424	2.00	None	1.00	Tetsuzo Nishimura	'89

Fund	Objective	Assets	NAV	$10,000 (1)	$10,000 (2)	$10,000 (3)	Yield	Tel 1	Tel 2	Load	12b-1	Redemp	Manager	Mgr Yr
NODDINGS CONV STRATEGIES	Convertibles	4.3	7.81	10,209.30	10,053.80	13,521.90	8.1	544-7785	312-954-1322	None	None	None	C. Sachs/T. Noddings	'85
NOMURA PACIFIC BASIN	Pacific Region	60.1	16.35	11,895.20	11,573.00	☆	1.1	833-0018	212-208-2604	None	None	None	Haruo Sawada	N/A
NTH AM SEC TR: AGGRESSIVE	Flexible	6.9	6.65	10,280.10	☆	☆	0.0	334-4437	203-698-0068	4.75	0.50	None	M. D. Sass	'86
NTH AM SEC TR: CONSERV	Flexible	11.6	8.81	10,226.40	☆	☆	0.0	334-4437	203-698-0068	4.75	0.50	None	M. D. Sass	'86
NTH AM SEC TR: GROWTH	Capital Appreciation	25.6	10.38	10,157.80	☆	☆	0.0	334-4437	203-698-0068	4.75	0.50	None	M. D. Sass	'86
NTH AM SEC TR: MODERATE	Flexible	44.6	7.51	10,221.20	☆	☆	0.0	334-4437	203-698-0068	4.75	0.50	None	M. D. Sass	'86
NTH AM SEC TR: US GOVT	Fixed Income	46.1	9.53	10,284.00	☆	☆	0.9	334-4437	203-698-0068	4.75	0.50	None	M. D. Sass	'86
NORTHEAST INV GROWTH	Growth	27.2	24.43	10,950.20	12,040.70	21,219.40	0.9	225-6704	None	None	None	None	Ernest Monrad	'69
NORTHEAST INV TRUST	Fixed Income	298.4	9.44	10,291.90	9,450.60	14,166.40	15.4	225-6704	919-972-9922	None	None	None	William A. Oates	'80
NOTTINGHAM FBP CONTRARN	Capital Appreciation	4.2	9.83	10,132.40	☆	☆	0.0	525-FUND	None	None	None	None	Flippin, Bruce & Porter	'89
NOTTINGHAM JAMESTOWN	Growth & Income	8.8	10.69	10,440.80	12,895.90	☆	0.0	525-FUND	919-972-9922	None	None	None	Lowe, Brockenbrough	'89
OBERWEIS EMERGING GROWTH	Small-Company Growth	15.0	15.23	11,555.40	☆	16,655.90	0.0	323-6166	708-897-7100	4.00	0.50	None	Jim Oberweis	'87
OLD DOMINION INVESTORS TR	Equity Income	6.8	20.50	10,047.30	10,250.40	☆	5.9	441-6580	804-539-2396	5.75	0.25	None	Cabell Birdsong	'64
OLYMPIC TR: BALANCED INC	Balanced	9.6	15.13	10,240.60	10,630.70	☆	6.0	346-7301	213-623-7833	None	None	None	Roger DeBard	'85
OLYMPIC TR: EQUITY INC	Equity Income	64.9	12.59	10,000.60	9,958.80	☆	4.7	346-7301	213-623-7833	None	None	None	George Wiley	'87
OLYMPIC TR: SMALL CAPITAL	Small-Company Growth	7.7	20.39	10,714.70	12,048.80	☆	0.9	346-7301	213-623-7833	None	None	None	John Hotchkis	'85
OLYMPUS EQUITY PLUS★	Growth	7.6	10.95	10,873.90	11,485.00	☆	0.7	845-8406	212-309-8480	4.25	0.75	None	Robert Buckles	'89
OLYMPUS PREMIUM INCOME★	Option Income	32.3	7.63	10,231.90	10,687.20	☆	10.1	845-8406	212-309-8480	4.25	0.75	None	Robert Buckles	N/A
OLYMPUS US GOVT PLUS★	Fixed Income	88.2	9.00	10,173.30	10,821.30	☆	8.8	845-8406	212-309-8480	4.25	0.75	None	Robert Schonbrunn	'89
OMNI INVESTMENT	Capital Appreciation	13.2	117.43	9,989.80	10,376.40	21,983.10	2.1	223-9790	312-922-0431	None	None	None	Bob Perkins	'84
OPPENHEIMER ASSET ALLOC	Flexible	84.5	10.37	10,149.70	10,619.10	☆	4.4	525-7048	None	4.75	0.25	None	Baker, et al.	'87
OPPENHEIMER BLUE CHIP	Growth & Income	19.4	15.68	10,115.40	10,986.70	☆	2.7	525-7048	None	4.75	0.25	None	Susan Wilder	'87
OPPENHEIMER DIRECTORS	Capital Appreciation	126.6	21.81	9,931.70	10,316.10	15,668.10	2.7	525-7048	None	8.50	None	None	William Baker	'88
OPPENHEIMER DISCOVERY	Small-Company Growth	61.7	21.68	10,534.50	10,634.90	☆	1.3	525-7048	None	4.75	0.25	None	Donna Calder	'86
OPPENHEIMER EQUITY INCO	Equity Income	1,328.7	9.18	10,207.80	10,906.40	19,507.60	5.4	525-7048	None	8.50	None	None	D. Jarmusz/S. Wilder	'82/'90
OPPENHEIMER FUND	Growth	196.1	9.06	10,088.70	10,603.80	14,950.70	2.6	525-7048	None	8.50	None	None	Susan Wilder	'87
OPPENHEIMER GLO BIO-TECH	Health/Biotech	12.5	14.15	11,627.00	12,993.60	☆	0.0	525-7048	None	4.75	0.25	None	Kenneth Oberman	'88
OPPENHEIMER GLBL ENVIRON	Specialty	33.5	12.81	11,178.00	☆	☆	0.0	525-7048	None	4.75	0.25	None	K. Oberman/D. McKerchar	'90
OPPENHEIMER GLOBAL	Global	809.2	32.95	10,874.60	13,476.30	37,245.00	0.3	525-7048	None	8.50	None	None	Kenneth Oberman	'80
OPPENHEIMER GNMA	Fixed Income	62.9	13.30	10,302.30	10,869.60	☆	9.4	525-7048	None	4.75	0.25	None	Arthur Steinmetz	'86
OPPENHEIMER GLD & SP MIN	Gold	162.9	11.65	9,440.80	10,309.90	26,354.80	2.2	525-7048	None	8.50	None	None	Kenneth Oberman	'88
OPPENHEIMER HIGH YIELD	Fixed Income	651.1	13.60	10,327.90	10,085.00	15,215.90	14.1	525-7048	None	6.75	None	None	Ralph Stellmacher	'87
OPPENHEIMER NINETY-TEN	Capital Appreciation	10.5	12.40	10,136.70	10,279.50	☆	8.8	525-7048	None	7.75	None	None	Robert Doll	'88
OPPENHEIMER PREMIUM INC	Option Income	243.2	19.94	10,500.30	10,471.00	18,216.60	12.0	525-7048	None	8.50	None	None	Charlotte Johnson	'90
OPPENHEIMER REGENCY	Capital Appreciation	125.8	14.08	10,829.60	11,172.30	17,077.40	2.3	525-7048	None	8.50	None	None	Donavon McKerchar	'86
OPPENHEIMEF SPECIAL	Growth	551.4	20.60	10,651.50	11,298.30	17,258.30	3.4	525-7048	None	8.50	None	None	Robert Doll	'87
OPPENHEIMEF STRTEGIC INC	Fixed Income	130.2	13.60	10,584.20	11,309.20	16,982.70	3.0	525-7048	714-957-1217	4.75	0.25	None	A. Steinmetz/D. Negri	'88
OPPENHEIMEF TARGET	Capital Appreciation	63.0	19.43	10,625.70	11,691.30	21,185.30	3.0	525-7048	501-377-2569	8.50	None	None	Robert Doll	'88
OPPENHEIMEF TIME	Capital Appreciation	335.2	16.71	10,542.60	10,912.60	21,391.20	2.9	525-7048	501-377-2569	8.50	None	None	Donna Calder	'87
OPPENHEIMEF TOTAL RETURN	Growth & Income	423.8	6.75	10,387.30	11,223.60	☆	3.9	525-7048	215-643-2510	4.75	0.25	None	D. Jarmusz/J. Wallace	'83/'90
OPPENHEIMEF US GOVT TR	Fixed Income	265.5	9.24	10,286.00	10,636.40	15,021.70	9.5	525-7048	None	4.75	0.25	None	Arthur Steinmetz	'87
ORANGE COUNTY GROWTH FD	Growth & Income	1.0	10.24	10,733.80	9,200.80	☆	5.0	None	714-957-1217	None	None	None	Jeffrey Kilpatrick	'88
OVERLAND EXP: ASSET ALLOC	Capital Appreciation	28.6	10.58	10,285.90	10,287.70	☆	5.8	572-7797	501-377-2569	4.50	0.05	None	Wells Fargo Bank	'88
OVERLAND EXP: US GOV INC	Fixed Income	7.7	10.14	10,414.90	10,542.60	☆	8.9	572-7797	501-377-2569	4.50	0.05	None	Wells Fargo Bank	'88
OVER-THE-COUNTER SEC	Small-Company Growth	291.4	16.01	10,295.80	10,126.00	15,335.20	0.8	523-2578	215-643-2510	4.50	0.25	None	Binkley Shorts	'81
PACIFIC HZN: AGGRESSIVE GRO	Capital Appreciation	99.2	20.93	11,500.00	12,793.40	23,166.10	0.0	332-3863	619-456-9196	4.50	None	None	Henry Alarcon	'90
PACIFIC HZN: CONVERTIBLE	Convertibles	1.1	10.44	10,605.30	11,527.50	☆	4.9	332-3863	619-456-9196	4.50	None	None	Bill Hensel	'87
PACIFIC HZN: GNMA	Fixed Income	3.6	9.65	10,351.90	10,793.50	☆	9.1	332-3863	619-456-9196	4.50	None	None	Jim Miller	'87

★MUTUAL QUALIFIED & MUTUAL SHARES—Closed.
★OLYMPUS FUNDS—Redemption fee applies for shares bought before 1/9/89.

PERFORMANCE OF MUTUAL FUNDS (continued)

FUND NAME	OBJECTIVE	TOTAL NET ASSETS (MIL) 6/30/90	NET ASSET VALUE 6/30/90	PERFORMANCE (Return on Initial $10,000 Investment) 3/31/90-6/30/90	6/30/89-6/30/90	6/30/85-6/30/90	DIVIDEND YIELD % 6/90	PHONE NUMBER 800	In-State	FEES Load	12b-1	Redemption	MANAGER	SINCE
PACIFIC HZN: HIGH YIELD	Fixed Income	12.3	10.06	10,099.00	8,479.10	12,325.50	17.2	332-3863	619-456-9196	4.50	None	None	Tom Nugent	'88
PACIFIC INV INST: GROWTH	Capital Appreciation	4.2	11.39	10,949.40	12,274.40	☆	3.2	443-6915	714-760-4868	None	None	None	Ben Ehlert	'87
PACIFIC INV INST: LOW DUR	Fixed Income	341.8	9.93	10,272.00	10,840.40	☆	8.9	443-6915	714-760-4868	None	None	None	William Gross	'87
PACIFIC INV INST: SH-TM	Fixed Income	16.7	10.00	10,205.20	10,842.60	☆	8.2	443-6915	714-760-4868	None	None	None	William Gross	'87
PACIFIC INV INST: TOT RTN	Fixed Income	758.8	9.89	10,354.90	10,651.20	☆	8.7	443-6915	714-760-4868	None	None	None	William Gross	'87
PAINEWEBBER CLASSIC: ATLAS	Global	219.8	15.86	10,937.90	12,023.80	28,733.40	0.7	544-9300	None	4.50	0.25	None	N. Fachler/E. Harris	'87
PAINEWEBBER CLASSIC: EUROPE	European Region	160.8	10.56	10,977.10	☆	☆	0.0	544-9300	None	4.50	0.25	None	Herve van Caloen	'90
PAINEWEBBER CLASSIC: GROW	Growth	84.7	15.45	10,804.20	11,642.10	20,994.90	0.0	544-9300	None	4.50	0.25	None	Ellen Harris	'85
PAINEWEBBER CLASSIC: GR&IN	Growth & Income	65.3	17.09	11,022.10	11,207.70	18,410.60	2.3	544-9300	None	4.50	0.25	None	Ellen Harris/Whitney Herrill	'83
PAINEWEBBER CLASSIC: RG FN★	Financial Services	50.1	8.68	10,175.10	9,984.70	☆	3.3	544-9300	None	4.50	0.25	None	Karen Levy	'86
PAINEWEBBER CLASSIC: WORLD	Global Flexible	103.1	10.42	10,910.90	11,601.90	15,403.50	5.2	544-9300	None	4.50	0.25	None	Nimrod Fachler	N/A
PAINEWEBBER GNMA	Fixed Income	851.3	9.37	10,351.40	10,865.60	☆	9.0	544-9300	None	4.25	None	None	Stuart Richardson	N/A
PAINEWEBBER HIGH YIELD	Fixed Income	247.5	6.76	10,627.30	9,435.70	12,996.60	15.7	544-9300	None	4.25	None	None	Peter Avelar	'89
PAINEWEBBER INV GRADE	Fixed Income	242.4	9.61	10,306.00	10,761.70	15,795.50	9.2	544-9300	None	4.25	None	None	Stuart Richardson	'84
PAINEWEBBER MASTER: AST AL	Flexible	507.5	9.95	10,263.30	10,573.90	☆	6.0	647-1568	None	None	0.25	5.00	Ellen Harris	'86
PAINEWEBBER MASTER: ENERGY	Specialty	44.7	12.57	10,193.60	11,815.90	☆	0.9	647-1568	None	None	0.25	5.00	W. Furth/N. Fachler	'87
PAINEWEBBER MASTER: GLOBAL	World Fixed-Income	1,110.1	10.76	10,652.40	11,785.00	☆	8.1	647-1568	None	None	0.25	5.00	N. Fachler/S. Waugh	'87
PAINEWEBBER MASTER: GROWTH	Growth	108.7	14.36	10,797.00	10,970.20	☆	0.0	647-1568	None	None	0.25	5.00	Whitney Merrill	'87
PAINEWEBBER MASTER: INCOME	Fixed Income	173.0	8.71	10,471.30	10,365.80	☆	9.7	647-1568	None	None	0.25	5.00	Steven Smith	'88
L ROY PAPP STOCK	Growth	4.5	11.23	11,069.10	☆	☆	0.0	None	602-956-0980	4.50	None	None	L. Roy Papp	'89
PARAGON: INTMDT-TERM BD	Fixed Income	155.7	9.79	10,325.50	☆	☆	0.0	777-5143	504-389-5968	4.50	None	None	Premier Invest Adv	'89
PARAGON: SHORT-TERM GOVT	Fixed Income	86.0	9.93	10,261.30	☆	☆	0.0	777-5143	504-389-5968	4.50	None	None	Premier Invest Adv	'89
PARAGON: VALUE EQUITY INC	Equity Income	81.6	9.81	10,307.60	☆	☆	0.0	777-5143	504-389-5968	4.50	None	None	Premier Invest Adv	'89
PARAGON: VALUE GROWTH	Growth & Income	46.1	10.53	10,754.20	☆	☆	0.0	777-5143	504-389-5968	4.50	None	None	Premier Invest Adv	'89
PARIBAS INSTL: QUANTUS EQ	Growth	4.8	11.32	10,990.30	12,478.40	☆	3.5	446-6960	212-841-3245	4.50	1.00	4.00	Computer-Driven	'84
PARKSTONE: BOND FUND	Fixed Income	316.4	10.00	10,360.20	10,693.80	☆	7.8	451-8377	614-899-4600	4.50	None	None	Securities Counsel Inc.	'85
PARKSTONE: EQUITY FUND	Growth	247.7	12.37	10,753.50	11,942.90	☆	2.2	451-8377	614-899-4600	4.50	None	None	Securities Counsel Inc.	'84
PARKSTONE: HI INC EQUITY	Equity Income	96.3	12.19	10,346.40	11,439.10	☆	4.4	451-8377	614-899-4600	4.50	None	None	Securities Counsel Inc.	'88
PARKSTONE: INTMDT GOVT	Fixed Income	100.2	9.91	10,325.40	10,705.80	☆	8.0	451-8377	614-899-4600	4.50	None	None	Securities Counsel Inc.	'85
PARKSTONE: LTD MAT BOND	Fixed Income	43.7	9.88	10,262.70	10,709.30	☆	8.4	451-8377	614-899-4600	4.50	None	None	Securities Counsel Inc.	'85
PARKSTONE: SMALL CAP VAL	Small-Company Growth	94.5	14.82	11,002.10	12,828.40	☆	0.3	451-8377	614-899-4600	4.50	None	None	Securities Counsel Inc.	'88
PARNASSUS FUND	Growth	26.3	21.32	10,575.40	9,660.80	16,601.60	1.6	999-3505	415-362-3505	3.50	None	None	Jerome Dodson	'85
PASADENA INV: FNDMNTL VAL	Growth	4.7	17.08	11,207.30	12,061.50	☆	3.1	882-2855	818-351-4276	3.00	None	None	Roger Engemann Assoc.	'87
PASADENA INV: GROWTH FD	Growth	51.5	23.40	11,414.60	12,169.00	☆	4.7	882-2855	818-351-4276	3.00	None	None	Roger Engemann Assoc.	'86
PATRIOT CORP CASH	Fixed Income	17.1	46.42	11,090.70	10,362.50	☆	7.3	843-0090	617-426-3310	0.25	0.25	None	Patriot Advisers	'86
PAX WORLD FUND	Balanced	108.3	14.78	10,733.50	11,739.00	17,881.50	4.2	767-1729	603-431-8022	None	0.25	None	Pax World Mgt Corp	'71
PBHG GROWTH	Capital Appreciation	16.9	12.22	11,252.30	12,834.40	☆	0.0	262-6631	713-750-8000	4.75	None	None	Gary Pilgrim	'85
PDC&J PERFORMANCE	Capital Appreciation	9.7	16.22	10,643.00	12,191.90	17,925.30	1.0	None	513-223-0600	None	None	None	J. Johnson/C. Carlson	'83
PDC&J PRESERVATION	Fixed Income	12.2	11.09	10,306.70	10,714.60	14,692.60	7.9	None	513-223-0600	None	None	None	J. Johnson/C. Carlson	'85
PENN SQUARE MUTUAL	Growth & Income	211.8	10.02	10,416.30	11,297.30	19,494.70	3.6	523-8440	215-670-1031	4.75	0.50	None	James E. Jordan Jr.	'89
PENNSYLVANIA MUTUAL	Small-Company Growth	625.1	7.01	10,324.00	10,543.70	18,595.40	3.0	221-4268	212-355-7311	None	None	1.00	Charles Royce	'73
PERMANENT PORTFOLIO	Global Flexible	88.1	15.61	10,129.80	10,182.60	14,634.40	0.0	531-5142	512-453-7558	None	0.25	None	Terry Coxon	'83

Fund	Objective	Assets	NAV	Value 1	Value 2	Value 3	%	Phone A	Phone B	Load	12b-1	Redemp	Manager	Since
PERRITT CAPITAL GROWTH	Small-Company Growth	53.3	10.43	10,430.00	10,085.40	☆	1.6	338-1579	312-649-6940	None	None	None	Gerald W. Perritt	'88
PHILADELPHIA FUND	Growth & Income	100.6	6.03	10,374.70	9,955.60	17,940.30	2.8	221-5588	212-425-9655	None	0.19	None	Donald Baxter	'87
PHILLIPS CAPITAL INV	Growth	3.2	12.06	10,351.90	10,758.60	☆	4.2	N/A	214-380-2448	None	None	1.00	Guy F. Phillips Jr.	'87
PHOENIX: BALANCED	Balanced	489.1	14.53	10,623.60	11,656.10	20,024.90	4.7	243-1574	800-243-4361	6.90	None	None	Patricia Bannan	'86
PHOENIX: CONVERTIBLE	Convertibles	156.1	17.76	10,466.40	11,431.50	18,501.80	5.2	243-1574	800-243-4361	6.90	None	None	Jack Martin	'85
PHOENIX: GROWTH	Growth	756.3	20.03	10,798.10	12,111.00	21,586.90	3.1	243-1574	800-243-4361	6.90	None	None	Robert Chesek	'80
PHOENIX: HIGH QUAL BOND	Fixed Income	20.3	8.94	10,278.70	10,555.70	15,231.30	7.8	243-1574	800-243-4361	4.75	None	None	Curtiss Barrows	'90
PHOENIX: HIGH YIELD	Fixed Income	103.5	7.31	10,334.10	9,515.00	14,267.30	12.2	243-1574	800-243-4361	4.75	None	None	Curtiss Barrows	'85
PHOENIX MULTI: CAP APPREC	Growth	11.1	12.14	11,223.30	☆	☆	0.0	243-1574	800-243-4361	4.75	0.25	None	Robert Chesek	'89
PHOENIX MULTI: INTERNATL	International	15.6	11.56	10,574.50	☆	☆	0.0	243-1574	800-243-4361	4.75	0.25	None	Murray Johnstone	'89
PHOENIX: STOCK	Capital Appreciation	126.6	13.12	10,487.10	11,295.40	18,755.40	2.0	243-1574	800-243-4361	6.90	None	None	Mike Matty	'90
PHOENIX: TOTAL RETURN	Flexible	31.5	14.17	10,556.50	11,271.40	17,181.40	3.8	243-1574	800-243-4361	4.75	0.25	None	Robert Milnamow	'90
PHOENIX: US GOVT SEC	Fixed Income	11.1	9.14	10,320.40	10,679.50	☆	7.8	243-1574	800-243-4361	4.75	None	None	James Wehr	'90
PIERPONT CAP APPREC	Growth	48.8	0.00	N/A	N/A	N/A	0.0	521-5412	213-398-2900	None	None	None	N/A	N/A
PIERPONT EQUITY	Growth & Income	40.1	0.00	N/A	N/A	N/A	0.0	521-5412	213-398-2900	None	None	None	N/A	N/A
PILGRIM CORP INVESTORS	Fixed Income	53.2	13.16	9,648.30	9,373.20	9,186.00	14.4	334-3444	213-551-0833	2.25	0.25	None	Bruce Jensen	'86
PILGRIM GNMA	Fixed Income	122.3	13.79	10,318.00	10,652.00	14,133.90	9.5	334-3444	213-551-0833	4.75	0.25	None	Bruce Jensen	'86
PILGRIM HIGH YIELD	Fixed Income	28.8	5.85	10,457.10	9,633.00	13,644.80	15.0	334-3444	213-551-0833	4.75	0.25	None	Bruce Jensen	'89
PILGRIM MAGNACAP	Growth	224.1	10.74	10,750.80	11,383.80	19,527.80	1.6	334-3444	213-551-0833	4.75	0.30	None	Howard Kornblue	'89
PILGRIM SH-TM MULTI-MKT	Fixed Income	30.5	10.35	8,821.80	6,975.70	☆	26.2	334-3444	213-551-0833	3.50	0.30	None	Bruce Jensen	'90
PINE STREET FUND	Growth & Income	50.2	12.48	10,436.50	11,013.20	17,159.10	4.3	225-8011	212-504-4000	None	None	None	James Engle	'85
PINNACLE FUND	Capital Appreciation	8.1	20.14	11,301.90	12,722.40	22,040.50	1.2	None	317-633-4080	None	None	None	Heartland Cap. Mgmt.	'85
PIONEER BOND FUND	Fixed Income	74.0	8.92	10,310.50	10,623.50	15,281.10	9.0	225-6292	617-742-7825	4.50	None	None	Sherman Russ	'87
PIONEER FUND	Growth & Income	1,570.0	22.58	10,146.20	10,667.50	18,729.30	0.0	225-6292	617-742-7825	8.50	None	None	John Carey	'85
PIONEER II	Growth & Income	4,406.8	18.53	10,171.80	10,729.80	18,841.60	3.3	225-6292	617-742-7825	8.50	None	None	David Tripple	'80
PIONEER THREE	Growth & Income	707.2	15.85	10,144.40	10,470.50	17,696.00	2.8	225-6292	617-742-7825	8.50	None	None	Robert Benson	'88
PIONEER US GOVT TRUST	Fixed Income	12.8	9.92	10,331.60	10,814.50	☆	9.0	225-6292	617-742-7825	4.50	0.25	None	Richard Schlanger	'88
PIPER JAFFRAY: BALANCED	Balanced	15.9	99.00	10,548.50	10,679.00	☆	4.2	333-6000	612-342-6402	4.00	0.30	None	B. Rinkey/T. Elavia/P. Dow	'87
PIPER JAFFRAY: GOVT INC	Fixed Income	75.8	9.11	10,367.30	10,650.90	☆	9.0	333-6000	612-342-6402	4.00	0.30	None	Ben Rinkey	'87
PIPER JAFFRAY: INSTL GOVT	Fixed Income	34.1	10.03	10,373.40	10,910.00	☆	9.0	333-6000	612-342-6402	1.50	0.20	None	W. Brunjten/M. Goldstein	'88
PIPER JAFFRAY: SECTOR	Capital Appreciation	10.8	11.49	11,131.20	13,224.20	☆	2.9	333-6000	612-342-6402	4.00	0.30	None	Ed Nicoski	'87
PIPER JAFFRAY: VALUE	Growth	52.2	13.88	11,056.50	12,607.40	☆	1.3	333-6000	612-342-6402	4.00	0.30	None	John Tauer	'87
PLYMOUTH EUROPE	European Region	9.7	10.84	10,347.50	10,726.60	☆	0.0	522-7297	None	4.75	0.25	None	Penelope Dobkin	N/A
PLYMOUTH GO/ERNMENT	Fixed Income	9.0	9.19	10,883.90	10,767.00	☆	8.1	522-7297	None	4.00	0.65	None	Michael Gray	'87
PLYMOUTH GROWTH OPP	Growth	56.0	16.50	10,469.80	11,267.00	☆	0.3	441-1762	302-791-1111	4.75	0.65	None	George Vanderheiden	'87
PLYMOUTH HIGH YIELD	Fixed Income	15.5	8.95	10,758.60	10,341.60	☆	13.3	522-7297	None	4.75	0.25	None	Margaret Eagle	'87
PLYMOUTH INC & GROWTH	Growth & Income	61.7	11.64	10,279.00	10,728.10	☆	8.9	522-7297	None	4.00	0.65	None	Robert Haber	'87
PLYMOUTH SHORT-TERM BOND	Fixed Income	12.2	9.82	10,245.00	10,767.80	☆	8.6	522-7297	None	4.00	0.15	None	Malcolm MacNaught	'87
PLYMOUTH SR-GLOB NAT RES	Natural Resources	3.8	13.39	10,907.90	12,008.90	☆	0.6	522-7297	None	4.00	0.65	None	Carol Miller	'89
PNC: CAPITAL APPRECIATION	Growth	43.3	10.92	10,302.20	☆	☆	0.0	441-1762	302-791-1111	4.50	0.30	None		'89
PNC: MANAGED INCOME	Fixed Income	36.9	9.81	☆	☆	☆	0.0	441-1762	302-791-1111	4.50	0.30	None	Henry Evans	'89
PNC: TOTAL RETURN	Mixed Income	4.4	10.20	☆	☆	☆	0.0	441-1762	302-791-1111	4.50	0.30	None	Charles Curtis	'90
PNCG ASSET ALLOCATION	Growth & Income	14.0	10.44	10,235.30	10,243.80	☆	0.5	541-9732	503-295-6974	4.50	0.30	None	Crabbe-Huson	'89
PNCG EQUITY	Growth	3.8	10.52	10,354.30	10,462.90	☆	0.1	541-9732	503-295-6974	4.50	0.30	None	Crabbe-Huson	'89
PNCG GROWTH	Growth	3.8	10.60	10,653.30	11,142.80	☆	2.6	541-9732	503-295-6974	4.50	0.30	None	Crabbe-Huson	'87
PNC INCOME FUND	Fixed Income	2.0	10.14	10,223.20	10,593.50	☆	6.6	541-9732	503-295-6974	4.50	0.20	None	Crabbe-Huson	'89
PNCG US GOVT INCOME FUND	Fixed Income	1.9	10.18	10,252.40	10,617.80	☆	6.6	541-9732	503-295-6974	4.50	0.20	None	Crabbe-Huson	'89

*PAINEWBR CLASSIC: RG FN—Converted from closed-end fund 4/1/90.

PERFORMANCE OF MUTUAL FUNDS (continued)

FUND NAME	OBJECTIVE	TOTAL NET ASSETS (MIL.) 6/30/90	NET ASSET VALUE 6/30/90	PERFORMANCE (Return on Initial $10,000 Investment) 3/31/90– 6/30/90	6/30/89– 6/30/90	6/30/85– 6/30/90	DIVIDEND YIELD % 6/90	PHONE NUMBER 800	In-State	FEES Load	12b-1	Redemption	MANAGER	SINCE
PORT DVSD INV: INT FX INC★	Fixed Income	5.6	10.08	10,296.10	10,715.80	★	8.5	221-8120	302-791-1765	None	None	None	Michael S. Hutchinson	'88
PORT DVSD INV: LNG FX INC★	Fixed Income	12.6	9.25	10,313.10	10,608.70	★	8.3	221-8120	302-791-1765	None	None	None	Michael S. Hutchinson	'88
PORT DVSD INV: SHT FX INC★	Fixed Income	5.1	9.94	10,250.50	10,765.80	★	8.4	221-8120	302-791-1765	None	None	None	Michael S. Hutchinson	'88
PORTICO FDS: BOND IMMDEX	Fixed Income	42.0	24.51	10,311.80	★	★	0.0	228-1024	414-287-3808	None	0.07	None	Mary Ellen Stanek	'89
PORTICO FDS: EQUITY INDEX	Growth & Income	35.7	25.43	10,619.90	★	★	0.0	228-1024	414-287-3808	None	0.05	None	Mary Ellen Stanek	'89
PORTICO FDS: INCOME & GRO	Equity Income	62.7	19.74	10,283.00	★	★	0.0	228-1024	414-287-3808	None	0.20	None	Mary Tenwinkel	'89
PORTICO FDS: SH-INTMD INC	Fixed Income	20.7	9.90	10,263.00	★	★	0.0	228-1024	414-287-3808	None	None	None	Mary Ellen Stanek	'89
PORTICO FDS: SPECIAL GRO	Capital Appreciation	44.9	20.89	10,862.40	★	★	0.0	228-1024	414-287-3808	None	0.16	None	Scott Harkness	'89
PREMIER GNMA	Fixed Income	41.4	14.14	10,351.90	10,903.70	★	9.5	242-8671	None	4.50	0.25	None	Barbara Kenworthy	'87
PREMIER INCOME	Fixed Income	3.0	11.10	10,342.70	10,932.70	★	9.4	242-8671	None	4.50	0.25	None	Barbara Kenworthy	'87
T ROWE PRICE CAP APPREC	Capital Appreciation	162.8	11.01	10,213.40	10,845.90	★	3.8	638-5660	301-547-2000	None	None	None	Richard P. Howard	'89
T ROWE PRICE EQUITY INC	Equity Income	1,001.6	13.76	10,132.80	10,081.60	★	5.5	638-5660	301-547-2000	None	None	None	Brian C. Rogers	'85
T ROWE PRICE GNMA	Fixed Income	404.6	9.22	10,353.70	10,810.90	★	9.1	638-5660	301-547-2000	None	None	None	Peter Van Dyke	'87
T ROWE PRICE GROWTH & INC	Growth & Income	557.7	13.00	10,334.20	10,278.20	16,809.30	4.9	638-5660	301-547-2000	None	None	None	Stephen W. Boesel	'87
T ROWE PRICE GROWTH STK	Growth	1,631.3	17.40	10,929.60	11,973.70	20,719.40	1.9	638-5660	301-547-2000	None	None	None	M. David Testa	'84
T ROWE PRICE HIGH YIELD	Fixed Income	692.5	8.17	10,395.00	9,269.10	14,852.50	14.7	638-5660	301-547-2000	None	None	None	Richard S. Swingle	'85
T ROWE PRICE INTL BOND	World Fixed-Income	305.8	9.00	10,624.20	11,040.30	★	8.7	638-5660	301-547-2000	None	None	None	Edward A. Taber III	'86
T ROWE PRICE INTL DISCOV	International	164.1	15.29	11,234.40	14,715.00	★	0.8	638-5660	301-547-2000	None	None	None	Martin G. Wade	'89
T ROWE PRICE INTL: EU STK	European Region	94.9	10.90	10,675.80	★	★	0.0	638-5660	301-547-2000	None	None	None	Martin G. Wade	'90
T ROWE PRICE INTL STOCK	International	1,162.5	10.75	10,814.90	12,566.60	35,495.40	1.4	638-5660	301-547-2000	None	None	None	Martin G. Wade	'85
T ROWE PRICE NEW AMER GR	Growth	140.9	17.69	10,859.40	11,352.20	★	0.0	638-5660	301-547-2000	None	None	None	John H. Laporte	'85
T ROWE PRICE NEW ERA	Natural Resources	783.1	21.27	9,939.30	10,969.20	20,313.60	2.6	638-5660	301-547-2000	None	None	None	George A. Roche	'69
T ROWE PRICE NEW HORIZON	Small-Company Growth	1,051.1	13.41	10,875.90	11,681.00	15,739.00	0.5	638-5660	301-547-2000	None	None	None	John H. Laporte	'87
T ROWE PRICE NEW INCOME	Fixed Income	1,007.6	8.41	10,337.20	10,685.20	15,599.40	8.7	638-5660	301-547-2000	None	None	None	Charles P. Smith	'86
T ROWE PRICE SCI & TECH	Technology	86.4	12.36	11,497.70	14,020.90	★	0.5	638-5660	301-547-2000	None	None	None	John H. Laporte	'88
T ROWE PRICE SH-TERM BD	Fixed Income	208.9	4.92	10,264.80	10,757.90	14,521.80	8.2	638-5660	301-547-2000	None	None	None	Edward A. Taber	'84
T ROWE PRICE SM CAP VAL	Small-Company Growth	32.3	9.96	10,790.90	11,016.10	★	1.3	638-5660	301-547-2000	None	None	None	John A. Powell	'88
T ROWE PRICE TREAS: INTMD	Fixed Income	20.5	4.99	10,317.40	★	★	0.0	638-5660	301-547-2000	None	None	None	Peter Van Dyke	'89
T ROWE PRICE TREAS: LONG	Fixed Income	18.8	9.86	10,371.60	★	★	0.0	638-5660	301-547-2000	None	None	None	Peter Van Dyke	'89
PRIMARY INC: INCOME	Mixed Income	0.8	9.82	10,189.50	★	★	0.0	443-6544	414-271-7870	None	None	None	David Aushwitz	'89
PRIMARY INC: US GOVT	Fixed Income	0.6	9.99	10,338.30	★	★	0.0	443-6544	414-271-7870	None	None	None	David Aushwitz	'89
PRIMARY TREND	Flexible	38.4	11.60	9,957.10	9,859.80	★	2.7	443-6544	414-271-7870	None	None	None	David Aushwitz	'89
PRIMECAP	Growth	310.3	13.91	10,766.30	11,719.20	21,232.50	1.1	662-7447	None	None	None	None	Howard Schow	'84
PRIME VALUE: GOVT INCOME	Fixed Income	5.6	9.75	10,259.20	10,768.10	★	9.9	338-1348	212-363-3300	4.50	None	None	Norwest Bank Minn. N.E.	'88
PRIME VALUE: GROWTH STOCK	Capital Appreciation	0.6	13.65	11,101.10	12,550.30	★	1.4	338-1348	212-363-3300	None	0.05	None	Norwest Bank Minn. N.E.	'88
PRINCIPAL PRES: DIV ACHVR	Growth & Income	12.8	11.80	10,665.40	10,963.60	★	2.1	826-4600	414-334-5521	4.50	None	None	M. & I. Bank	'89
PRINCIPAL PRES: GOVT	Fixed Income	28.8	8.91	10,296.70	10,612.10	★	8.4	826-4600	414-335-5521	4.50	None	None	B.C. Ziegler Co.	'85
PRINCIPAL PRES: S&P 100	Growth & Income	21.5	12.62	10,662.10	11,705.60	★	2.2	826-4600	414-334-5521	4.50	None	None	The Boston Co.	'89
PRINCOR AGGR GROWTH FD	Capital Appreciation	11.2	14.64	10,555.20	10,863.00	★	1.4	247-4123	515-247-5711	5.00	0.25	None	Mike Hamilton	'87
PRINCOR BOND FUND	Fixed Income	22.7	10.26	10,274.20	10,611.00	18,219.10	8.6	247-4123	515-247-5711	5.00	0.25	None	Don Bratteo	'87
PRINCOR CAPITAL ACCUM	Capital Appreciation	136.9	17.89	10,511.20	10,263.70	16,214.80	3.2	247-4123	515-247-5711	5.00	0.25	None	Mike Hamilton	'87
PRINCOR GOVT SEC INCOME	Fixed Income	68.8	10.63	10,370.00	10,806.40	16,201.80	7.9	247-4123	515-247-5711	5.00	0.25	None	Marty Schafer	'85
PRINCOR GROWTH FUND	Growth	35.8	20.83	11,133.10	12,097.20	20,201.80	1.5	247-4123	515-247-5711	5.00	0.25	None	Mike Hamilton	'87

Fund	Objective	Net Assets	NAV				%	Phone	Phone	Load	12b-1	Fee	Manager	Year
PRINCOR HIGH-YIELD FUND	Fixed Income	11.4	8.29	9,893.20	9,396.80	☆	13.2	247-4123	515-247-5711	5.00	0.25	None	Ken Hovey	'87
PRINCOR MANAGED FUND	Flexible	20.7	10.73	10,673.30	10,104.70	☆	4.2	247-4123	515-247-5711	5.00	0.25	None	Mike Hamilton	'87
PRINCOR WORLD FD	Global	17.0	5.39	10,673.30	11,775.50	19,514.60	1.4	247-4123	515-247-5711	5.00	0.25	None	Dan Jaworski	'88
PROVIDENTMUT CONVERTIBLE	Convertibles	8.9	8.93	10,268.20	9,892.50	☆	0.0	441-4490	302-652-3091	4.50	0.25	None	Michael B. Miller	'90
PROVIDENTMUT GROWTH	Growth	154.4	6.74	10,859.50	10,552.10	16,428.30	3.6	441-4490	302-652-3091	6.00	0.25	None	James McCall	'90
PROVIDENTMUT INV SHS	Growth & Income	227.4	8.66	10,517.10	11,295.50	20,353.50	4.5	441-4490	302-652-3091	6.00	0.25	None	Robert Borkowski	'89
PROVIDENTMUT TOTAL RTN	Balanced	70.0	11.95	10,271.90	11,106.40	17,788.10	7.4	441-4490	302-652-3091	6.00	0.25	None	Robert Borkowski	'89
PROVIDENTMUT US GOVT	Fixed Income	55.3	11.66	10,313.20	10,551.20	☆	7.8	441-4490	302-652-3091	6.00	0.25	None	Dina Welch	'89
PROVIDENTMUT VALUE SHS	Growth	12.7	10.53	10,243.30	11,335.70	18,035.90	3.9	441-4490	302-652-3091	6.00	0.25	None	Newbolds Asset Mgt	'89
PROVIDENTMUT WORLD	International	6.7	14.29	10,866.90	11,206.50	23,794.30	0.2	441-4490	302-652-3091	6.00	0.25	None	Michael Miller	'89
PRUDENT SPECULATR: LG CAP	Capital Appreciation	1.0	8.50	10,204.10	9,269.60	☆	0.0	444-4778	None	None	0.25	None	Edwin Bernstein	'89
PRUDENT SPECULATR: LVRGD	Small-Company Growth	8.0	7.57	11,574.90	9,220.50	☆	0.0	444-4778	None	None	0.25	None	Edwin Bernstein	'89
PRU-BACHE EQUITY B	Growth	625.3	11.81	10,270.20	11,506.20	19,918.60	1.6	225-1852	None	None	1.00	5.30	Tom Jackson	'90
PRU-BACHE EQUITY INC B	Equity Income	145.3	10.79	10,255.00	10,444.50	☆	2.9	225-1852	None	None	1.00	5.30	Warren Spitz	'88
PRU-BACHE FLEX/AGGRES B	Flexible	171.5	10.47	10,455.20	10,861.90	☆	3.7	225-1852	None	N/A	N/A	N/A	Multiple Managers	N/A
PRU-BACHE FLEX/CONSER B	Flexible	153.9	10.16	10,416.60	10,956.70	☆	5.1	225-1852	None	N/A	N/A	N/A	Multiple Managers	N/A
PRU-BACHE GLOBAL B	Global	322.3	10.24	10,374.90	10,743.30	22,426.60	2.6	225-1852	None	6.00	1.00	5.30	Peter Lehman	'89
PRU-BACHE GL GENESIS B	Global	41.0	12.90	10,547.80	11,256.80	☆	0.0	225-1852	None	6.00	1.00	5.10	C. Hardiman/C. Wood	'88
PRU-BACHE GL NAT RES B	Natural Resources	44.8	9.96	9,632.50	10,692.50	☆	0.6	225-1852	None	6.00	1.00	5.10	Peter Lehman	'87
PRU-BACHE GNMA B	Fixed Income	219.1	14.58	10,272.70	10,650.60	14,617.50	8.5	225-1852	None	N/A	0.75	5.10	Donna Blair	'89
PRU-BACHE GOVT INTMDT	Fixed Income	343.6	9.68	10,289.10	10,660.70	15,059.00	9.3	225-1852	None	None	0.25	None	Elena Walsh	'86
PRU-BACHE GOVT PLUS B	Fixed Income	3,559.6	9.04	10,366.20	10,585.10	14,779.60	7.2	225-1852	None	None	1.00	5.0	Helen Diktaban	'85
PRU-BACHE GROWTH OPP B	Small-Company Growth	112.3	13.39	10,335.40	10,724.80	17,039.90	1.0	225-1852	None	None	1.00	5.0	Robert Fetch	'84
PRU-BACHE HIGH YIELD B	Fixed Income	2,079.9	7.84	10,309.90	9,239.50	13,603.70	13.8	225-1852	None	None	0.75	5.0	Al Klein	'88
PRU-BACHE INCOMVRTIBLE B	Specialty	513.1	10.54	10,254.20	10,269.10	☆	7.1	225-1852	None	None	1.00	5.0	Theresa Hamacher	'85
PRU-BACHE OPTION GRO B	Capital Appreciation	61.0	8.60	10,128.50	10,852.60	17,955.20	2.5	225-1852	None	None	1.00	5.0	Leigh Goehring	'86
PRU-BACHE RESEARCH B	Growth	324.4	15.37	10,563.30	10,850.70	20,214.60	2.3	225-1852	None	None	0.10	5.0	Stuart Shikiar	'87
PRU-BACHE STRUCTURED MAT	Fixed Income	107.0	11.53	10,289.60	☆	☆	0.0	225-1852	None	3.25	1.00	None	Donna Blair	'89
PRU-BACHE US GOVT B	Fixed Income	178.3	9.18	10,303.20	10,320.90	☆	6.8	225-1852	None	None	1.00	5.0	Donna Blair	'89
PRU-BACHE UTILITY B	Utility	2,432.7	16.28	10,031.40	10,880.10	21,169.70	4.2	225-1852	None	None	1.00	5.0	Warren Spitz	'87
PUTNAM CAP PRESRV/INCO	Fixed Income	52.5	11.39	10,221.10	10,701.50	☆	9.4	225-1581	617-292-1000	4.75	0.25	None	Christopher A. Ray	N/A
PUTNAM CONV INC-GRO TR★	Convertibles	715.7	15.19	10,223.70	10,412.10	15,627.60	6.3	225-1581	617-292-1000	5.75	0.25	None	Anthony I. Kreisel	N/A
PUTNAM CORP-CASH DSP	Equity Income	87.3	38.62	10,003.40	10,325.40	13,265.60	10.9	225-1581	617-292-1000	2.50	0.25	None	John C. Talanian	'87
PUTNAM DIVIDEND GROWTH	Equity Income	8.4	8.78	10,364.90	☆	☆	0.0	225-1581	617-292-1000	5.75	0.25	None	Thomas Reilly	'90
PUTNAM DIVERSIFIED INC	Fixed Income	125.8	11.40	10,469.90	10,480.70	☆	11.1	225-1581	617-292-1000	4.75	0.25	None	Michael Larson	N/A
PUTNAM ENERGY RESOURCES★	Natural Resources	126.7	17.66	10,055.70	11,694.20	18,463.40	3.0	225-1581	617-292-1000	5.75	0.25	None	Ronald C. Clark	N/A
GEORGE PUTNAM FD BOSTON★	Balanced	439.2	13.26	10,338.40	11,153.00	19,382.40	6.0	225-1581	617-292-1000	5.75	0.25	None	Thomas V. Reilly	N/A
PUTNAM GLOBAL GOVT INC	World Fixed-Income	196.5	15.04	10,426.60	11,263.90	☆	9.7	225-1581	617-292-1000	4.75	0.25	None	Gary Kreps	N/A
PUTNAM GNMA PLUS	Fixed Income	865.8	10.03	10,332.70	10,754.20	☆	8.3	225-1581	617-292-1000	4.75	0.25	None	Michael Larson	N/A
PUTNAM GROWTH & INCOME★	Growth & Income	2,138.0	12.24	10,349.00	11,258.70	21,416.10	4.9	225-1581	617-292-1000	5.75	0.25	None	John Maurice	N/A
PUTNAM HEALTH SCIENCE★	Health/Biotech.	347.5	24.32	11,834.50	13,872.60	23,889.40	1.2	225-1581	617-292-1000	5.75	0.25	None	Cheryl D. Alexander	N/A
PUTNAM HIGH INCOME GOVT	Fixed Income	6,742.9	9.64	10,318.20	10,517.20	14,906.50	8.2	225-1581	617-292-1000	6.75	0.35	None	William J. Landes	N/A
PUTNAM HIGH YIELD	Fixed Income	1,739.2	11.39	10,581.50	9,333.80	14,488.50	16.0	225-1581	617-292-1000	6.75	0.35	None	Edward D'Alelio	N/A
PUTNAM HIGH YIELD II	Fixed Income	318.0	8.61	10,633.40	9,094.90	☆	16.0	225-1581	617-292-1000	6.75	0.35	None	Jim Ho	N/A
PUTNAM INCOME	Fixed Income	430.6	6.56	10,244.90	10,475.50	15,561.10	10.2	225-1581	617-292-1000	4.75	0.35	None	John Geissinger	N/A
PUTNAM INFO SCIENCE★	Technology	102.8	21.10	11,175.80	11,630.70	21,107.00	0.5	225-1581	617-292-1000	5.75	0.25	None	Richard M. Frucci	N/A
PUTNAM INTL EQUITIES★	Global	629.5	8.23	10,944.10	12,248.60	28,890.10	1.6	225-1581	617-292-1000	5.75	0.25	None	Anthony Regan	N/A
PUTNAM INVESTORS★	Growth	718.7	8.82	10,647.80	12,102.90	20,028.10	3.1	225-1581	617-292-1000	5.75	0.25	None	Brooke Cobb	'88

★PORT DVSD INV—Open only to institutions.

★PUTNAM FUNDS—12b-1 fee of 0.20% applies to shares purchased before 1/1/90; the fee rises to 0.25% after that date.

PERFORMANCE OF MUTUAL FUNDS (continued)

FUND NAME	OBJECTIVE	TOTAL NET ASSETS (MIL) 6/30/90	NET ASSET VALUE 6/30/90	PERFORMANCE (Return on Initial $10,000 Investment) 3/31/90-6/30/90	6/30/89-6/30/90	6/30/85-6/30/90	DIVIDEND YIELD % 6/90	PHONE NUMBER 800	In-State	FEES Load	12b-1	Redemption	MANAGER	SINCE
PUTNAM OPTION INCOME★	Option Income	781.6	7.64	10,075.20	10,105.40	15,730.80	3.2	225-1581	617-292-1000	6.75	0.25	None	Robert Stephenson	N/A
PUTNAM OPTION INCOME II★	Option Income	930.1	8.67	10,282.30	10,524.80	15,322.50	4.6	225-1581	617-292-1000	6.75	0.25	None	Sumner Abramson	N/A
PUTNAM OTC EMERGING GRO	Small-Company Growth	206.3	8.58	11,000.00	11,879.60	22,800.40	0.0	225-1581	617-292-1000	5.75	0.25	N/A	Richard Jodka	N/A
PUTNAM US GOVT GUAR SEC	Fixed Income	1,529.3	13.62	10,312.40	10,815.10	15,549.10	9.9	225-1581	617-292-1000	4.75	0.35	None	Jaclyn Conrad	N/A
PUTNAM VISTA BASIC VALUE★	Capital Appreciation	263.1	6.54	10,302.50	11,086.50	19,738.40	2.7	225-1581	617-292-1000	5.75	0.25	None	Gerald Zukowski	N/A
PUTNAM VOYAGER★	Capital Appreciation	804.4	8.22	10,815.80	11,393.80	23,044.20	1.1	225-1581	617-292-1000	5.75	0.25	None	Mathew Weatherbie	'83
QUANTUM FUND	Capital Appreciation	0.2	8.39	9,870.60	9,343.00	9,021.20	0.0	None	606-491-4271	6.50	None	None	Stan Foster	'87
QUEST VALUE: ASSET ALLOC	Flexible	6.0	11.93	10,747.70	11,246.10	☆	1.9	544-3147	212-667-6737	5.50	0.50	None	George Long	'89
QUEST VALUE: FIXED INCOME	Fixed Income	0.4	9.75	10,299.00	10,456.40	☆	6.5	544-3147	212-667-6737	5.50	0.40	None	Rob Bluestone	'89
QUEST VALUE: SMALL CAP	Small-Company Growth	2.5	11.20	10,616.10	10,759.80	☆	0.7	544-3147	212-667-6737	5.50	0.50	None	Jeff Whittington	'89
QUEST VALUE: USG HI INC	Fixed Income	55.3	11.35	10,329.60	10,931.40	☆	8.7	544-3147	212-667-6737	5.50	0.30	None	Rob Bluestone	'88
QUEST VALUE: VALUE	Capital Appreciation	69.0	28.46	10,675.20	11,143.30	17,952.50	2.6	544-3147	212-667-6737	5.50	0.50	None	Eileen Rominger	'89
RAINBOW FUND	Capital Appreciation	2.2	5.51	10,998.00	10,317.60	16,306.30	8.0	None	212-509-8532	None	None	None	Furman Anderson & Co	74
RBB: SAFEGUARD BALANCED	Balanced	1.4	11.05	10,457.90	11,139.60	☆	3.8	456-7526	800-456-7526	5.00	0.40	0.35	Bill Wykle	'88
RBB: SAFEGUARD EQ GRO&INC	Growth & Income	1.2	11.46	10,515.30	11,253.60	☆	3.4	456-7526	800-456-7526	5.00	0.40	0.35	Bill Wykle	'88
RBB: SAFEGUARD FIXED INC	Fixed Income	1.2	10.04	10,315.80	10,649.10	☆	9.1	456-7526	800-456-7526	5.00	0.40	0.35	Michael Hutchinson	'88
RCS EMERGING GROWTH	Small-Company Growth	19.0	13.59	11,655.20	14,745.20	☆	0.0	766-FUND	415-781-9700	None	None	3.00	R. C. Czepiel	'87
REA-GRAHAM: BALANCED	Balanced	41.0	13.52	9,970.50	10,264.00	15,182.40	7.1	433-1998	800-433-1998	4.75	0.35	None	J. Rea Jr./J. Rea Sr.	'81/'76
REGIS: DSI DISCIP VALUE	Equity Income	43.5	9.74	10,177.00	☆	☆	0.0	638-7983	None	None	None	None	Dewey Square Inv	'89
REGIS: DSI LTD MAT BOND	Fixed Income	36.1	9.98	10,278.20	11,054.20	☆	0.0	638-7983	None	None	None	None	Dewey Square Inv	'89
REGIS: ICM SMALL COMPANY	Small-Company Growth	23.6	10.90	10,688.00	10,246.00	19,794.60	1.5	221-3079	212-370-1240	None	None	None	Robert McDorman Jr.	'89
REICH & TANG EQUITY	Growth	108.5	14.11	10,219.60			2.5	221-3079	212-370-1240	None	0.40	None	Robert Hoerle	N/A
REICH & TANG GOVT SEC	Fixed Income	10.7	0.00	N/A	N/A	N/A	0.0	221-3079	212-370-1240	None	0.40	None	Robert Hoerle	N/A
RESERVE EQUITY: CONTRARIAN	Growth & Income	3.0	13.50	10,173.70	10,766.40	14,786.20	11.9	421-0261	212-977-9675	4.00	0.25	None	Reserve Management Inc.	'84
RESERVE EQUITY: GROWTH	Growth	1.0	10.44	10,181.50	10,775.30	14,500.70	9.2	421-0261	212-977-9675	4.00	0.25	None	Reserve Management Inc.	'84
RETIREMENT PLAN AM: BOND	Fixed Income	58.1	6.63	10,310.50	10,526.00	14,264.30	9.7	545-2098	None	None	1.25	5.00	Talton Embry	'84
RETIREMENT PLAN AM: EQU	Growth	30.1	22.83	10,643.40	11,865.50	21,658.00	3.3	545-2098	None	None	1.25	5.00	Graham Tanaka	'84
REYNOLDS BLUE CHIP GRO	Growth	10.3	13.02	11,441.10	12,525.20	☆	1.2	338-1579	415-461-7860	4.75	None	None	Frederick Reynolds	'89
RIGHTIME: BLUE CHIP FD	Growth & Income	123.2	27.14	10,218.60	11,488.40	☆	1.7	242-1421	215-887-8111	None	0.90	None	David Rights	'87
RIGHTIME: FUND	Growth & Income	149.4	33.75	10,452.20	11,100.80	☆	1.0	242-1421	215-887-8111	4.75	1.20	None	David Rights	'85
RIGHTIME: GOVT SEC	Fixed Income	51.5	13.42	10,096.10	9,748.60	☆	6.6	242-1421	215-887-8111	None	0.50	None	David Rights	'86
RIGHTIME: GROWTH FUND	Growth	46.0	23.33	9,936.10	10,200.90	☆	0.8	242-1421	215-887-8111	4.75	0.90	None	David Rights	'88
RIGHTIME: SOCIAL AWARENESS	Specialty	6.1	24.92	9,526.00	☆	☆	0.0	242-1421	215-887-8111	4.75	1.20	None	Anthony W. Soslow	'90
ROCHESTER CONVERTIBLE	Convertibles	6.3	8.95	10,352.20	10,369.60	☆	7.0	None	716-442-5500	3.25	0.75	None	Ronald Fielding	'83
ROCHESTER TAX-MGD	Specialty	14.2	8.66	10,509.70	10,196.60	13,081.60	0.0	None	716-442-5500	8.50	0.25	None	Ronald Fielding	'80
ROCKWOOD GROWTH	Capital Appreciation	1.3	12.74	9,688.20	8,413.60	☆	3.7	None	208-522-5593	None	None	None	Ross Farmer	'86
RODNEY SQ BNCHMRK: US TRS	Fixed Income	32.2	8.09	10,263.20	10,451.10	☆	7.2	225-5084	302-791-1086	4.50	0.03	None	Scot Brenner	'87
RODNEY SQ INTL SEC: INTL EQ	International	72.3	13.16	11,021.80	12,190.60	☆	0.6	225-5084	302-791-1086	5.75	None	None	EMF Managers	'87
RODNEY SQ MULTI-MGR: GROWTH	Growth	43.3	13.29	10,720.90	11,333.50	☆	1.1	225-5084	302-791-1086	5.75	0.02	None	3 outside mgt. cos.	'87
RODNEY SQ MULTI-MGR: TOT RTN	Flexible	22.3	11.22	10,552.00	11,100.90	☆	3.0	225-5084	302-791-1086	5.75	0.02	None	3 outside mgt. cos.	'87
RODNEY SQ MULTI-MGR: VALUE	Capital Appreciation	7.6	11.56	10,220.00	10,624.70	☆	2.8	225-5084	302-791-1086	5.75	0.02	None	3 outside mgt. cos.	'87
ROYCE FD: EQUITY INCOME	Equity Income	22.8	4.86	10,041.20	☆	☆	0.0	221-4268	212-355-7311	None	1.00	1.00	C. Royce/T. Ebright	'90

ROYCE FD: INCOME	Fixed Income	4.7	6.92	10,156.00	9,656.50	☆	12.1	221-4268	212-355-7311	None	0.50	1.00	C. Royce/T. Ebright	'87
ROYCE FD: TOTAL RETURN	Equity Income	3.0	4.38	9,799.80	8,991.30	☆	3.7	221-4268	212-355-7311	None	0.50	1.00	C. Royce/T. Ebright	'87
ROYCE FD: VALUE	Small-Company Growth	191.1	8.60	10,274.80	10,376.80	16,992.10	2.0	221-4268	212-355-7311	None	1.00	2.00	C. Royce/T. Ebright	'83
RSSI: ACTIVELY MANAGED BD★	Fixed Income	168.1	18.58	10,322.20	10,526.90	15,292.20	0.0	446-7774	212-503-0160	None	0.10	None	Criterion/Discount Cp.	'83/'85
RSSI: CORE EQUITY★	Growth & Income	161.7	26.24	10,632.10	11,916.40	22,162.20	0.0	446-7774	212-503-0160	None	0.10	None	Rissi Group	'83
RSSI: EMERGING GROWTH EQU★	Small-Company Growth	52.3	20.62	10,858.30	11,249.30	17,298.70	0.0	446-7774	212-503-0160	None	0.10	None	Lieber/Friess Assoc	'82/'90
RSSI: INTMDT-TERM BOND★	Fixed Income	111.6	18.90	10,350.50	10,793.80	15,750.00	0.0	446-7774	212-503-0160	None	0.10	None	Rissi Group	'83
RSSI: INTERNATIONAL EQU★	International	29.1	30.18	10,836.60	10,801.70	28,391.30	0.0	446-7774	212-503-0160	None	0.10	None	Morgan Grenfell Inv. Serv.	'84
RSSI: SHORT-TERM INVEST★	Fixed Income	32.1	15.57	10,196.50	10,827.50	14,297.50	0.0	446-7774	212-503-0160	None	0.10	None	Rissi Group	'88
RSSI: VALUE EQUITY★	Growth	61.0	20.14	10,365.40	10,270.30	17,377.00	0.0	446-7774	212-503-0160	None	0.10	None	Trinity Inv./Dreman Value	'85
RUSHMORE: NOVA	Capital Appreciation	64.0	10.33	10,627.60	☆	☆	0.0	343-3355	301-657-1500	None	None	None	Daniel Ryczek	'89
RUSHMORE: OTC INDEX	Growth	11.0	12.45	10,981.90	10,275.90	☆	0.3	343-3355	301-657-1500	None	None	None	Daniel Ryczek	'85
RUSHMORE: PREC MTL INDEX	Gold	3.2	9.81	8,853.80	☆	☆	0.0	343-3355	301-657-1500	None	None	None	Daniel Ryczek	'89
RUSHMORE: STK MKT INDEX	Growth & Income	51.4	15.19	10,697.40	11,604.30	☆	2.0	343-3355	301-657-1500	None	None	None	Daniel Ryczek	'85
RUSHMORE: USG INT TERM	Fixed Income	5.7	9.62	10,324.20	10,443.10	☆	7.6	343-3355	301-657-1500	None	None	None	Daniel Ryczek	'85
RUSHMORE: USG LONG TERM	Fixed Income	23.6	9.71	10,422.80	10,261.10	☆	7.5	343-3355	301-657-1500	None	None	None	Daniel Ryczek	'85
SAFECO EQUITY FUND	Growth & Income	64.4	10.61	10,631.60	11,778.10	20,971.40	2.0	426-6730	206-545-5530	None	None	None	Doug Johnson	'84
SAFECO GROWTH FUND	Growth	87.9	18.46	11,309.80	11,829.20	18,897.50	1.1	426-6730	206-545-5530	None	None	None	Tom Maguire	'89
SAFECO HIGH-YIELD BOND	Fixed Income	8.9	8.57	10,374.40	10,045.80	☆	12.4	426-6730	206-545-5530	None	None	None	Ron Spaulding	'88
SAFECO INCOME FUND	Equity Income	207.1	15.12	10,090.70	10,291.80	17,232.00	5.5	426-6730	206-545-5530	None	None	None	Arley Hudson	'78
SAFECO INTMDT-TERM BOND	Fixed Income	6.5	9.89	10,266.70	10,649.90	☆	7.8	426-6730	206-545-5530	None	None	None	Ron Spaulding	'88
SAFECO US GOVT	Fixed Income	28.4	9.21	10,300.40	10,745.10	☆	8.2	426-6730	206-545-5530	None	None	None	Paul Stevenson	'88
SALEM: FIXED INCOME	Fixed Income	8.9	9.76	10,226.90	10,609.60	☆	8.1	326-3241	704-374-4343	None	None	None	Tom Ellis	'89
SALEM: GROWTH PORTFOLIO	Growth	104.9	15.66	10,423.30	11,227.50	19,855.30	3.7	326-3241	704-374-4343	None	0.25	None	Edwin Outen	'85
SALOMON BROS CAPITAL	Capital Appreciation	73.5	17.19	10,872.90	11,264.20	17,054.80	0.3	221-5350	212-668-8578	5.00	None	None	Robert Salomon	'90
SALOMON BROS INVESTORS	Growth & Income	378.2	16.53	10,370.40	10,999.90	18,683.50	3.8	221-5350	212-668-8578	5.00	None	None	John Weed	'89
SALOMON BROS OPPORTUNITY	Capital Appreciation	108.3	23.92	10,063.10	9,683.20	17,439.50	3.4	221-5350	212-668-8578	None	None	None	Irving Brilliant	'79
SAM: SMALL-CAP FUND	Small-Company Growth	65.2	11.78	9,889.60	10,257.10	☆	2.0	445-9469	901-761-2474	None	None	None	James Shirclifs	'89
SAM: VALUE TRUST	Growth	148.3	11.88	10,188.70	10,239.70	☆	1.7	445-9469	901-761-2474	None	None	None	Mason Hawkins	'87
SBSF CONVERTIBLE SEC	Convertible	16.3	10.20	10,089.50	10,269.00	☆	7.9	422-7273	212-903-1200	None	None	None	Louis Benzak	'83
SBSF GROWTH FUND	Growth	99.5	16.27	10,523.20	11,607.50	18,701.80	3.1	422-7273	212-903-1200	None	None	None	Louis Benzak	'83
SCHIELD PORT: AGGR GRO	Capital Appreciation	1.5	13.88	11,792.70	11,963.90	☆	0.2	826-8154	303-985-9999	4.00	1.00	None	Marshall L. Schield	'86
SCHIELD PORT: HI YLD	Fixed Income	0.9	7.72	10,079.60	9,038.60	☆	8.9	826-8154	303-985-9999	4.00	0.75	None	Marshall L. Schield	'87
SCHIELD PORT: TIMED ALLOC	Flexible	8.7	8.86	10,045.40	10,067.00	☆	3.1	826-8154	303-985-9999	1.50	1.00	None	Phil Covato	'89
SCHIELD PORT: VALUE	Growth	1.7	10.91	9,990.80	9,489.90	☆	2.0	826-8154	303-985-9999	4.00	1.00	None	Marhsall L. Schield	'86
SCHIELD: PROG ENVIRONMENT	Specialty	1.6	6.49	12,954.10	☆	☆	0.0	826-8154	303-985-9999	4.50	0.95	None	Glenn Cutler	'90
SCHRODER CAP: GLOBAL BOND	World-Fixed Income	5.4	9.82	10,229.20	10,383.00	☆	6.9	344-8332	212-841-3848	None	None	None	Peter Seeley	'88
SCHRODER CAP: INTL EQUITY	International	72.9	19.71	11,160.80	12,626.20	☆	2.2	344-8332	212-841-3848	None	None	None	Mark Smith	'89
SCHRODER CAP: US EQUITY	Growth	22.9	8.37	10,648.90	11,302.50	17,513.70	3.0	344-8332	212-841-3848	None	None	None	Jane Smith	'89
SCI/TECH HOLDINGS A	Technology	152.8	10.37	11,358.20	12,518.70	20,835.20	0.6	637-3863	609-282-2800	6.50	None	None	Merrill Lynch Asset Mgt	'83
SCI/TECH HOLDINGS B	Technology	3.4	10.26	11,337.00	12,393.10	☆	0.1	637-3863	609-282-2800	None	1.00	4.00	Merrill Lynch Asset Mgt	'83
SCM PORTFOLIO FUND	Flexible	0.5	10.17	10,170.00	10,525.80	☆	7.2	N/A	N/A	N/A	N/A	N/A	N/A	N/A
SCUDDER CAPITAL GROWTH	Growth	985.0	19.00	10,474.10	10,056.50	21,354.20	0.8	225-2470	None	None	None	None	Steven Aronoff	'89
SCUDDER DEVELOPMENT	Small-Company Growth	358.0	26.25	11,635.60	12,850.30	17,779.30	0.0	225-2470	None	None	None	None	R. McKay/G. Moran	'88
SCUDDER EQUITY INCOME	Equity Income	21.1	12.17	10,300.30	10,494.90	☆	5.7	225-2470	None	None	None	None	Joanne Howard	'87
SCUDDER FD: LAZARD EQUITY	Capital Appreciation	17.3	12.43	10,299.00	10,809.30	☆	1.1	225-2470	None	None	None	None	Herbert Gullquist	'87
SCUDDER: GLOBAL FD	Global	255.3	20.36	10,489.40	12,000.40	☆	0.5	225-2470	None	None	None	None	William Holzer	'86
SCUDDER GNMA	Fixed Income	250.9	14.40	10,348.00	10,806.70	☆	8.7	225-2470	None	None	None	None	David Glen	'85
SCUDDER GOLD FUND	Gold	16.1	10.21	9,043.40	9,728.50	☆	0.6	225-2470	None	None	None	None	D. Loudon/D. Donald	'88
SCUDDER GROWTH & INCOME	Growth & Income	500.4	13.56	10,572.60	10,689.10	19,169.10	4.9	225-2470	None	None	None	None	R. Harvey/B.Thorndike	'84

★PUTNAM FUNDS—12b-1 fee of 0.20% applies to shares purchased before 1/1/90; the fee rises to 0.25% after that date.

★RSSI FUNDS—Open to certain retirement plans only.

©Copyright Lipper Analytical Services, Inc

PERFORMANCE OF MUTUAL FUNDS (continued)

FUND NAME	OBJECTIVE	TOTAL NET ASSETS (MIL) 6/30/90	NET ASSET VALUE 6/30/90	PERFORMANCE (Return on Initial $10,000 Investment) 3/31/90-6/30/90	PERFORMANCE 6/30/89-6/30/90	PERFORMANCE 6/30/85-6/30/90	DIVIDEND YIELD % 6/90	PHONE NUMBER 800	PHONE NUMBER In-State	FEES Load	FEES 12b-1	Redemption	MANAGER	SINCE
SCUDDER INCOME	Fixed Income	275.0	12.95	10,353.90	10,712.70	15,847.40	8.0	225-2470	None	None	None	None	William Hutchinson	'86
SCUDDER INTERNATIONAL	International	929.5	40.04	11,049.20	12,588.70	32,455.60	1.5	225-2470	None	None	None	None	Nicholas Bratt	'76
SCUDDER INTERNATL BOND	World Fixed-Income	72.7	12.08	11,685.00	11,759.30	☆	9.0	225-2470	None	None	None	None	Turner / Greshin/Haczima	'88
SCUDDER SHORT TERM BOND	Fixed Income	187.1	11.58	10,332.30	10,914.10	15,713.40	8.7	225-2470	None	None	None	None	Tom Poor	'88
SCUDDER ZERO TARGT 1990	Fixed Income	2.7	11.03	10,184.70	10,730.30	☆	7.6	225-2470	None	None	None	None	Ruth Heisler	'88
SCUDDER ZERO TARGT 1995	Fixed Income	8.9	11.62	10,338.10	10,493.70	☆	5.9	225-2470	None	None	None	None	Ruth Heisler	'88
SCUDDER ZERO TARGT 2000	Fixed Income	31.6	12.29	10,424.10	10,212.60	☆	4.2	225-2470	None	None	None	None	Ruth Heisler	'88
SEAFIRST: ASSET ALLOC★	Flexible	24.3	11.70	10,497.50	11,385.80	☆	5.8	323-9919	206-358-6234	None	0.95	None	Gary Beck	'88
SEAFIRST: BLUE CHIP FD★	Growth	26.3	13.83	10,661.90	12,018.10	☆	3.5	323-9919	206-358-6234	None	0.95	None	Donna Jagers	'88
SEAFIRST: BOND FUND★	Fixed Income	5.5	10.23	10,303.00	10,768.90	☆	8.1	323-9919	206-358-6234	None	None	None	Ken Schultz	'88
SECURAL: FIXED INCOME	Fixed Income	2.1	10.06	10,325.30	10,659.10	☆	7.2	426-5975	414-739-3161	4.00	0.50	None	Martin Jones	'87
SECURAL: GOVERNMENT BOND	Fixed Income	1.5	9.94	10,256.30	10,678.70	☆	7.5	426-5975	414-739-3161	4.00	0.50	None	Martin Jones	'87
SECURAL: SPECIAL EQUITY	Capital Appreciation	3.0	12.32	9,777.80	10,250.20	☆	1.8	426-5975	414-739-3161	4.00	0.50	None	Larry Smith	'87
SECURAL: STOCK FUND	Growth & Income	1.2	12.96	10,302.10	11,526.00	☆	0.9	426-5975	414-739-3161	4.00	0.50	None	Jim Doaks	'87
SECURITY ACTION FUND★	Growth	250.9	9.73	11,248.60	11,375.90	17,460.80	1.4	888-2461	913-295-3127	None	None	None	Ron Niecziela	'88
SECURITY EQUITY FUND	Growth	270.2	5.69	10,635.50	11,349.90	21,246.30	6.4	888-2461	913-295-3127	8.50	None	None	Terry Milberger	'81
SECURITY INC: CORP BOND	Fixed Income	56.9	7.37	10,363.00	10,648.90	15,438.40	9.6	888-2461	913-295-3127	4.75	0.25	None	Jane Tedder	'85
SECURITY INC: HIGH YIELD	Fixed Income	6.6	4.49	9,786.50	7,571.90	☆	17.9	888-2461	913-295-3127	4.75	0.25	None	Jane Tedder	'86
SECURITY INC: US GOVT	Fixed Income	4.6	4.84	10,342.50	10,809.20	☆	8.8	888-2461	913-295-3127	4.75	0.25	None	Jane Tedder	'85
SECURITY INVESTMENT FUND	Growth & Income	76.6	7.93	10,062.60	10,348.50	15,327.00	6.3	888-2461	913-295-3127	8.50	None	None	John Cleland	'66
SECURITY OMNI	Capital Appreciation	18.3	2.93	11,400.80	10,464.30	☆	0.0	888-2461	913-295-3127	8.50	None	None	Ron Niecziela	'87
SECURITY ULTRA FUND	Capital Appreciation	58.0	7.58	11,130.70	11,468.10	14,332.10	0.9	888-2461	913-295-3127	8.50	None	None	Ron Niecziela	'87
SEI CASH +: GNMA	Fixed Income	14.0	9.36	10,339.10	10,908.30	☆	9.1	345-1151	215-254-1000	None	0.07	None	SEI Fin. Mgt. Corp.	'87
SEI CASH +: INTMD-TM GOVT	Fixed Income	138.1	9.49	10,279.00	10,714.80	☆	7.8	345-1151	215-254-1000	None	0.09	None	SEI Fin. Mgt. Corp.	'87
SEI CASH +: SHORT-TM GOVT	Fixed Income	43.4	9.66	10,249.60	10,760.70	☆	7.7	345-1151	215-254-1000	None	0.10	None	SEI Fin. Mgt. Corp.	'87
SEI INDEX: BOND	Fixed Income	14.0	9.54	10,321.00	10,680.10	☆	8.5	345-1151	215-254-1000	None	0.05	None	SEI Fin. Mgt. Corp.	'86
SEI INDEX: S & P 500	Growth & Income	183.7	13.13	10,621.80	11,624.30	☆	3.3	345-1151	215-254-1000	None	0.05	None	SEI Fin. Mgt. Corp.	'85
SEI INSTL MGD: BOND	Fixed Income	19.7	9.86	10,385.50	10,382.00	☆	8.1	345-1151	215-254-1000	None	0.27	None	SEI Fin. Mgt. Corp.	'87
SEI INSTL MGD: CAP APPREC	Growth	101.8	13.01	10,901.70	12,278.30	☆	2.8	345-1151	215-254-1000	None	0.27	None	SEI Fin. Mgt. Corp.	'88
SEI INSTL MGD: EQU INCOME	Equity Income	51.7	12.03	10,233.40	10,770.70	☆	5.2	345-1151	215-254-1000	None	0.27	None	SEI Fin. Mgt. Corp.	'88
SEI INSTL MGD: LTD VOLAT	Fixed Income	74.2	9.87	10,292.80	10,646.30	☆	7.7	345-1151	215-254-1000	None	0.27	None	SEI Fin. Mgt. Corp.	'87
SEI INSTL MGD: VALUE	Growth & Income	133.2	11.55	10,652.30	11,166.90	☆	3.4	345-1151	215-254-1000	None	0.27	None	SEI Fin. Mgt. Corp.	'87
SELECTED CAP: GOVT INC	Fixed Income	24.6	9.06	10,305.10	10,527.00	☆	7.9	553-5533	None	None	0.49	None	John Shriver	'83
SELECTED AMERICAN SHARES	Growth & Income	411.6	13.89	10,746.20	10,264.80	19,834.50	3.3	553-5533	None	None	0.35	None	Donald Yacktman	'83
SELECTED SPECIAL SHARES	Growth	59.8	20.99	10,660.20	11,470.20	19,284.90	1.7	553-5533	None	None	0.19	None	Ronald Ball	'87
SELIGMAN CAPITAL	Capital Appreciation	133.0	13.84	11,552.60	12,740.50	18,585.60	0.0	221-2450	212-432-4100	4.75	None	None	Loris Muzzatti	'89
SELIGMAN COMM & INFORMTN	Technology	46.4	11.53	10,816.10	12,537.50	24,683.30	0.0	221-2450	212-432-4100	4.75	None	None	Paul Wick	'90
SELIGMAN COMMON STOCK	Growth & Income	495.4	12.67	10,624.10	11,913.00	20,464.00	3.1	221-2450	212-432-4100	4.75	None	None	Paul Rodriguez	'85
SELIGMAN GROWTH	Growth	555.3	5.29	11,056.70	11,911.60	19,936.60	1.4	221-2450	212-432-4100	4.75	None	None	Suzanne Zak	'89
SELIGMAN HI YLD: BOND	Fixed Income	38.6	6.00	10,343.60	9,767.20	15,037.70	13.8	221-2450	212-432-4100	4.75	0.25	None	D. Charleston	'89
SELIGMAN HI YLD: SEC MTGE	Fixed Income	29.5	6.41	10,280.30	10,428.20	14,579.90	8.8	221-2450	212-432-4100	4.75	0.25	None	James Auchterlonie	'87
SELIGMAN HI YLD: US GOVT	Fixed Income	74.1	6.78	10,287.70	10,392.10	14,997.60	9.1	221-2450	212-432-4100	4.75	0.25	None	James Auchterlonie	'87
SELIGMAN INCOME	Mixed Income	147.6	11.89	10,057.90	10,401.70	15,720.70	8.7	221-2450	212-432-4100	4.75	None	None	Paul Rodriguez	'85
SENTINEL: BALANCED	Balanced	78.1	13.05	10,360.40	10,951.90	17,505.40	6.3	282-3863	802-229-3900	8.50	None	None	Rod Buck	'82
SENTINEL: BOND FUND	Fixed Income	35.2	6.07	10,333.00	10,635.00	15,763.60	8.8	282-3863	802-229-3900	8.50	None	None	Richard Temple	'85

Fund	Objective	Assets ($mil)	NAV	$10K 1yr	$10K 5yr	$10K 10yr	Yield %	Tel (local)	Tel	Max Load	12b-1	Deferred	Manager	Mgr Since
SENTINEL: COMMON STOCK	Growth & Income	597.4	25.43	10,465.60	11,291.80	20,071.50	3.7	282-3863	802-229-3900	8.50	None	None	Chris Martin	'85
SENTINEL: GCVT SEC	Fixed Income	37.0	9.42	10,313.50	10,731.60	☆	8.4	282-3863	802-229-3900	8.50	None	None	William Vautin	'86
SENTINEL: GROWTH	Growth	55.9	15.82	11,213.00	12,311.40	19,738.00	1.1	282-3863	802-229-3900	8.50	None	None	William Hedberg	'87
SENTRY FUND	Growth	51.6	14.01	11,007.60	12,006.90	19,407.80	2.7	533-7827	715-346-7048	8.00	None	None	Keith Ringberg	'77
SEQUOIA FUND ●	Growth	976.5	47.82	10,680.40	11,321.50	19,424.00	4.0	None	212-245-4500	None	None	None	Ruane/Cunniff	'70
SFT: ANTHONY WAYNE TOT RTN	Fixed Income	0.1	10.73	10,697.90	☆	☆	0.0	523-2044	215-337-8422	5.00	0.35	None	Scott Klawans	'89
SFT: ASSET ALLOCATIONS	Flexible	1.5	9.97	10,674.50	10,937.40	☆	0.6	523-2044	215-337-8422	5.00	0.25	None	Roy Jarvis	'89
SFT: ENVIRNMNT'L AWARENESS	Specialty	1.9	15.28	11,497.40	12,743.00	16,569.00	1.4	523-2044	215-337-8422	5.00	0.35	None	Andrew Groshans	'88
SFT: EQUITY SERIES	Capital Appreciation	0.5	11.66	9,991.40	10,401.90	13,621.70	5.1	523-2044	215-337-8422	5.00	0.35	None	Mark Samson	'90
SFT: NEW JERSEY PRIDE	Growth	0.5	10.57	11,010.40	10,936.40	☆	1.9	523-2044	215-337-8422	5.00	0.35	None	Mark Samson	'90
SFT: ODD LOT FUND	Specialty	2.1	24.58	11,443.20	11,698.10	☆	1.1	523-2044	215-337-8422	None	0.50	1.30	Andrew Groshans	'87
SFT: SBA PRIME FUND	Fixed Income	1.7	10.00	10,232.30	10,995.70	☆	9.5	523-2044	215-337-8422	2.50	0.20	None	Andrew Groshans	'88
SFT: SEIDMAN GRO & INC	Growth & Income	0.1	9.55	10,138.00	11,096.40	16,465.60	0.6	523-2044	215-337-8422	5.00	0.35	None	Dan Seidman	'89
SFT: U.S. GOVERNMENT SERIES	Fixed Income	31.3	6.62	10,267.40	9,830.10	☆	10.6	523-2044	215-337-8422	5.00	0.35	None	Andrew Groshans	'85
SHADOW STOCK	Small-Company Growth	24.7	9.01	10,237.70	☆	☆	1.5	422-2766	816-471-5200	None	None	None	Whitridge/Schliemann	'87
SHEFFIELD: INT'MDT TM BOND	Fixed Income	8.7	9.62	☆	☆	☆	0.0	None	404-953-1597	None	0.005	None	Roger Sheffield	'90
SHEFFIELD: TOTAL RETURN	Growth & Income	13.1	10.22	☆	☆	☆	0.0	None	404-953-1597	None	0.005	None	Roger Sheffield	'90
SHERMAN, DEAN FUND	Capital Appreciation	3.3	8.72	10,080.90	10,443.10	14,542.10	0.0	None	512-735-7700	None	None	None	Walter Sherman	'67
SIEBEL CAPITAL PARTNERS	Capital Appreciation	18.9	9.89	10,614.70	11,564.50	21,275.30	8.0	None	415-461-3850	None	None	None	Gary Kirk	'81
SIT "NEW BEGIN" GROWTH	Small-Company Growth	73.5	34.79	10,916.20	12,112.70	☆	1.0	332-5580	612-334-5888	None	None	None	Douglas C. Jones	'81
SIT "NEW BEGIN" INC&GRO	Growth & Income	17.6	22.64	10,785.90	10,793.90	20,342.80	2.3	332-5580	612-334-5888	None	None	None	Peter L. Mitchelson	'81
SIT "NEW BEGIN" INV RESV	Fixed Income	4.7	9.97	10,187.70	10,907.20	14,043.50	7.7	332-5580	612-334-5888	None	None	None	Michael C. Brilley	'85
SIT "NEW BEGIN" US GOVT	Fixed Income	13.1	10.31	10,402.10	10,916.40	☆	7.9	332-5580	612-670-6035	None	None	None	Michael C. Brilley	'87
SKYLINE: BALANCED	Balanced	13.4	10.32	10,320.40	☆	☆	4.6	458-5222	312-670-6035	3.85	0.40	None	Stephen Gaber	'87
SKYLINE: MONTHLY INCOME	Fixed Income	10.8	9.29	10,291.70	10,659.50	☆	10.4	458-5222	312-670-6035	3.85	0.25	None	Thomas Paprocki	'88
SKYLINE: SPECIAL EQUITIES	Small-Company Growth	25.5	12.42	10,498.70	11,499.30	☆	1.0	458-5222	312-670-6035	3.85	0.40	None	William Dutton	'87
SLH AGGRESSIVE GROWTH	Capital Appreciation	107.3	19.71	11,192.50	12,497.30	25,067.80	0.1	451-2010	212-528-2744	5.00	None	None	Richard Freeman	'83
SLH APPRECIATION FUND	Growth	1,120.9	9.05	10,684.80	11,770.90	22,288.30	2.6	451-2010	212-528-2744	5.00	None	None	Harold Williamson	'81
SLH EQ: GROWTH & OPP	Growth	182.9	16.06	10,037.50	9,638.20	☆	2.9	451-2010	212-528-2744	None	1.00	5.0	Irving Brilliant	'86
SLH EQ: INTERNATIONAL	International	58.1	18.22	10,698.80	10,969.90	☆	3.3	451-2010	212-528-2744	None	0.80	5.0	Bernard Rattray	N/A
SLH EQ: SECTOR ANALYSIS	Capital Appreciation	212.8	11.89	10,559.50	11,040.60	☆	3.8	451-2010	212-528-2744	None	1.00	5.0	Elaine Gazarelli	'87
SLH EQ: STRATEGIC INVST	Flexible	217.9	16.30	10,407.50	10,830.70	17,413.30	3.6	451-2010	212-528-2744	None	1.00	5.0	William Carter	'87
SLH FUNDAMENTAL VALUE FD	Growth	81.8	6.60	10,927.20	11,107.50	28,202.10	2.7	451-2010	212-528-2744	5.00	None	None	Kenneth Roberts	'81
SLH GLOBAL OPPOR	Global	77.9	27.68	10,646.20	11,206.10	13,570.30	2.3	451-2010	212-528-2744	5.00	None	None	Mark Tapely	'86
SLH HIGH YIELD	Fixed Income	279.8	13.40	10,335.30	9,194.90	☆	17.0	451-2010	212-528-2744	5.00	None	None	Andrew Brod	N/A
SLH INCOME: CONVERTIBLE	Convertibles	10.9	12.32	9,961.40	9,884.80	☆	7.1	451-2010	212-528-2744	None	0.75	5.0	Norman Mulkowsky	N/A
SLH INCOME: GLOBAL BOND	World Fixed-Income	62.0	16.25	10,401.70	10,803.50	☆	7.0	451-2010	212-528-2744	None	0.75	5.0	Pauline Barrett	'86
SLH INCOME: HIGH INCOME	Fixed Income	321.1	10.59	10,352.50	9,010.90	☆	15.4	451-2010	212-528-2744	None	0.75	5.0	John Bianchi	'87
SLH INCOME: INT'MT TM GOVT	Fixed Income	36.2	11.27	10,179.40	10,765.90	☆	7.4	451-2010	212-528-2744	None	0.75	5.0	James Conroy	N/A
SLH INCOME: MORTGAGE	Fixed Income	644.8	10.80	10,347.00	10,724.80	☆	8.4	451-2010	212-528-2744	None	0.75	5.0	James Conroy	N/A
SLH INCOME: OPTION INC	Option Income	522.0	13.54	10,457.90	11,026.10	17,722.90	7.2	451-2010	212-528-2744	None	0.75	5.0	John Fullerton	'85
SLH INV: DIRECTIONS VAL	Growth	306.9	13.39	10,347.20	11,336.60	☆	1.9	451-2010	212-528-2744	None	1.00	5.0	David Glennon	'85
SLH INV: EUROPEAN	European Region	26.4	14.65	10,859.90	13,021.80	☆	0.5	451-2010	212-528-2744	None	0.98	5.0	Koenraad Foulon	N/A
SLH INV: GLOBAL EQUITY	Global	9.2	12.14	10,772.00	11,344.50	☆	0.9	451-2010	212-528-2744	None	None	5.0	Mark Tapely	'89
SLH INV: GOVT SEC	Fixed Income	1,691.3	9.03	10,345.20	10,645.10	14,617.00	8.3	451-2010	212-528-2744	None	0.75	5.0	James Conroy	'84
SLH INV: GROWTH	Growth	855.8	13.91	10,511.10	11,243.30	17,958.90	5.3	451-2010	212-528-2744	None	1.00	5.0	Steven Knoll	'82
SLH INV: INV GRADE BOND	Fixed Income	440.3	10.63	10,437.30	10,429.80	16,294.80	8.2	451-2010	212-528-2744	None	0.75	5.0	George Mueller	'82

★SEAFIRST FUNDS—Limited to Seafirst Retirement Accounts.
▲SECURITY ACTION—Sold only in a contractual plan. Front-end load equals 50% of first 12 payments.
●SEQUOIA FUND—Closed to new investors.

PERFORMANCE OF MUTUAL FUNDS (continued)

FUND NAME	OBJECTIVE	TOTAL NET ASSETS (MIL) 6/30/90	NET ASSET VALUE 6/30/90	PERFORMANCE (Return on Initial $10,000 Investment) 3/31/90-6/30/90	6/30/89-6/30/90	6/30/85-6/30/90	DIVIDEND YIELD % 6/90	PHONE NUMBER 800	In-State	FEES Load	12b-1	Redemption	MANAGER	SINCE
SLH INV: PACIFIC	Pacific Region	2.2	10.83	10,363.60	9,300.70	☆	4.9	451-2010	212-528-2744	None	1.05	5.00	Margaret Chin	N/A
SLH INV: PRECIOUS METAL	Gold	88.6	12.89	8,932.80	9,659.80	15,392.70	0.4	451-2010	212-528-2744	None	1.00	5.00	Mark Loew	'85
SLH INV: SPECIAL EQUITY	Small-Company Growth	119.5	13.85	10,516.30	10,875.60	14,124.80	3.7	451-2010	212-528-2744	None	1.00	5.00	David Hillson	'82
SLH MANAGED GOVTS FUND	Fixed Income	514.0	12.04	10,344.30	10,860.80	14,802.60	9.1	451-2010	212-528-2744	5.00	None	None	James Conroy	N/A
SLH 1990s FUND	Growth	34.9	9.08	11,421.40	☆	☆	0.0	451-2010	212-528-2744	5.00	None	None	Richard Freeman	N/A
SLH MULTIPLE OPP PORT LP	Global Flexible	201.6	56.28	10,408.70	10,751.70	☆	8.0	451-2010	212-528-2744	5.00	1.00	3.00	Michael Sherman	N/A
SLH PREC MTLS & MINERALS	Gold	26.7	15.07	9,072.80	9,757.30	☆	2.1	451-2010	212-528-2744	5.00	None	None	Herachel Post	N/A
SLH PRIN RTN: ZERO & APPR	Balanced	138.3	10.99	10,608.10	11,262.40	☆	5.7	451-2010	212-528-2744	5.00	None	None	Harold Williamson	'89
SLH SMALL CAP FUND	Small-Company Growth	32.9	16.24	11,340.80	12,017.30	☆	0.0	451-2010	212-528-2744	5.00	None	None	Richard Freeman	'87
SLH SPEC INC: UTILITY	Utility	617.8	12.88	10,146.10	10,707.00	☆	6.9	451-2010	212-528-2744	None	0.75	5.00	Jack Levande	'87
SLH TELECOM: GROWTH	Technology	38.4	8.28	10,324.20	10,197.40	19,563.40	1.8	451-2010	212-528-2744	5.00	None	None	J. David Mills	'84
SLH TELECOM: INCOME★	Specialty	94.8	126.27	10,094.80	11,355.00	22,970.70	4.6	451-2010	212-528-2744	5.00	None	None	J. David Mills	'84
SMITH BARNEY: EQUITY	Growth	83.2	15.86	10,647.40	11,800.20	20,521.90	2.6	544-7835	212-698-5349	5.75	0.25	None	Edmund Keeley	'85
SMITH BARNEY: INC & GR	Growth & Income	587.6	12.16	10,180.50	10,765.50	18,838.20	5.7	544-7835	212-698-5349	5.75	None	None	Bruce Sargent	'72
SMITH BARNEY: INC RETURN	Fixed Income	21.6	9.34	10,262.60	10,817.40	15,412.60	7.1	544-7835	212-698-5349	1.25	None	None	Victor Morris	'85
SMITH BARNEY: MTHLY GOVT	Fixed Income	27.3	12.26	10,372.50	10,865.50	☆	8.1	544-7835	212-698-5349	4.00	None	None	Ellen Bermel	'86
SMITH BARNEY: US GOVT SEC	Fixed Income	336.3	12.96	10,381.40	10,835.30	15,996.00	9.3	544-7835	212-698-5349	4.00	None	None	Ellen Bermel	'84
SMITH BARNEY: ASSET ALLOC	Flexible	0.0	0.00	N/A	N/A	☆	0.0	422-7791	402-476-3000	None	0.80	None	Renaissance	'88
SMITH HAYES: BALANCED	Balanced	0.0	0.00	N/A	N/A	☆	0.0	422-7791	402-476-3000	None	0.80	None	Swanson Cap. Mgt	'88
SMITH HAYES: CONVERTIBLE	Convertibles	0.0	0.00	N/A	N/A	☆	0.0	422-7791	402-476-3000	None	0.80	None	Calamos Ast. Mgt.	'88
SMITH HAYES: DEFENSIVE GR	Growth	0.0	0.00	N/A	N/A	☆	0.0	422-7791	402-476-3000	None	0.60	None	N/A	N/A
SMITH HAYES: GOVT/QUAL BD	Fixed Income	0.0	0.00	N/A	N/A	☆	0.0	422-7791	402-476-3000	None	0.80	None	Bear Stearns	'88
SMITH HAYES: VALUE	Growth	0.0	0.00	N/A	N/A	☆	0.0	422-7791	402-476-3000	None	0.80	None	Kanne Paris Hoban	'88
SOGEN INTERNATIONAL	Growth	194.9	18.32	10,344.40	11,252.10	22,471.70	5.0	334-2143	212-397-8550	3.75	0.25	None	Jean-Marie Eveillard	'79
SOUND SHORE	Growth	38.4	13.94	10,429.90	10,568.00	19,983.40	2.6	None	203-629-1980	None	None	None	T. Gibbs Kane	'85
SOUTHEASTERN GROWTH	Growth	104.8	14.76	10,603.40	10,381.90	15,801.10	1.2	321-0058	804-649-2311	None	1.00	5.00	Theodore Price	'85
SOVEREIGN INVESTORS	Growth & Income	80.1	12.89	10,577.20	11,664.10	19,537.10	4.6	None	215-254-0703	5.00	0.25	None	Cameron/Bailey/Snyder	'51
STATE BOND COMMON STOCK	Growth	39.2	8.53	11,143.00	12,652.70	22,776.60	1.8	328-4735	507-354-2144	4.75	0.25	None	Keith Martins	'72
STATE BOND DIVERSIFIED	Growth & Income	23.9	8.78	10,458.70	11,242.90	20,473.90	4.1	328-4735	507-354-2144	4.75	0.25	None	Keith Martins	'72
STATE BOND PROGRESS	Growth	9.0	12.81	10,482.90	12,547.30	19,896.20	0.9	328-4735	507-354-2144	4.75	0.25	None	Keith Martins	'72
STATE BOND US GOVT SEC	Fixed Income	9.2	4.92	10,361.90	10,844.40	☆	8.3	328-4735	507-354-2144	4.50	None	None	Keith Martins	'72
STATE FARM BALANCED★	Balanced	109.2	23.26	10,848.80	12,112.70	21,740.50	3.9	447-0740	309-766-2029	None	None	None	Rex Bates	'75
STATE FARM GROWTH★	Growth	445.5	18.23	11,024.70	12,684.10	23,152.50	2.2	447-0740	309-766-2029	None	None	None	Rex Bates	'75
STATE FARM INTERIM★	Fixed Income	45.4	10.03	10,288.90	10,753.90	15,136.60	8.1	447-0740	309-766-2029	None	None	None	Rex Bates	'75
STATE STREET INVESTMENT	Growth & Income	585.8	18.32	11,043.70	11,298.70	20,663.60	2.8	882-0052	617-348-2000	4.50	None	None	Peter Bennett	'88
STEADMAN AMER INDUSTRY★	Capital Appreciation	3.9	2.11	10,603.00	9,461.90	7,562.70	0.0	424-8570	202-223-1000	N/A	N/A	N/A	N/A	N/A
STEADMAN ASSOCIATED FD★	Equity Income	12.2	0.80	10,958.90	10,958.90	12,734.90	0.0	424-8570	202-223-1000	N/A	N/A	N/A	N/A	N/A
STEADMAN INVESTMENT★	Growth	4.5	1.37	11,416.70	9,927.50	8,600.60	0.0	424-8570	202-223-1000	N/A	N/A	N/A	N/A	N/A
STEADMAN OCEANOGRAPHIC★	Growth	2.7	4.02	10,777.50	10,748.70	7,556.40	0.0	424-8570	202-223-1000	N/A	N/A	N/A	N/A	N/A
STEINROE EQ: PRIME EQ	Growth & Income	52.6	11.98	10,930.90	11,801.20	☆	2.1	338-2550	None	None	None	None	R. Segall/C. Murphy	'87
STEINROE EQ: STOCK	Growth	242.5	21.54	11,598.30	12,904.00	20,170.30	1.7	338-2550	None	None	None	None	Bruce Dun	'89
STEINROE EQ: TOTAL RETURN	Equity Income	140.4	24.23	10,512.60	10,975.00	16,955.80	4.7	338-2550	None	None	None	None	Bob Christensen	'81
STEINROE GOVT INCOME	Fixed Income	46.8	9.66	10,347.80	10,689.50	☆	7.8	338-2550	None	None	None	None	Mike Kennedy	'88

Fund	Objective	Assets ($mil)	NAV	1-yr	3-yr	5-yr	Yield %	Phone 1	Phone 2	Load A	Load B	Load C	Manager	Year
STEINROE INCOME FUND	Fixed Income	89.1	8.95	10,364.60	10,243.50	☆	10.2	338-2550	None	None	None		Ann Henderson	'90
STEINROE INV: CAPITAL OPP	Capital Appreciation	160.3	21.88	10,233.90	10,827.90	17,608.50	0.5	338-2550	None	None	None		R. Lewison/G. Santella	'89
STEINROE INV: INTL GROWTH	International	19.8	2.50	11,210.80	12,140.70	☆	0.0	338-2550	None	None	None		Touche Rmnt Inv Mgt Ltd	'87
STEINROE INV: SPECIAL	Growth	451.2	19.85	11,776.30	12,117.60	23,589.50	1.9	338-2550	None	None	None		D. Weiss/C. Murphy	'81/'86
STEINROE INTMDT BOND	Fixed Income	161.4	8.38	10,326.80	10,529.60	15,740.20	8.5	338-2550	None	None	None		Mike Kennedy	'88
STRATEGIC GOLD/MINERALS	Gold	2.3	4.14	9,241.10	9,855.60	6,162.50	1.0	527-5027	214-484-1326	8.50	None		Grant Brenna	'86
STRATEGIC INVESTMENTS	Gold	35.1	2.63	7,645.30	8,872.10	5,953.60	5.3	527-5027	214-484-1326	8.50	None		Grant Brenna	'86
STRATEGIC SILVER	Specialty	22.0	4.52	9,243.40	11,863.50	9,385.90	0.0	527-5027	214-484-1326	8.50	None		Grant Brenna	'86
STRATTON GROWTH FUND	Growth & Income	23.3	19.60	9,235.00	10,652.20	16,884.40	3.5	634-5726	215-941-0255	None	None		J. Affleck/J. Stratton	'83
STRATTON MONTHLY DIV	Utility	31.9	24.08	10,139.80	10,156.60	14,469.80	8.5	634-5726	215-941-0255	None	None		G. Heffernan/J. Stratton	'83
STRONG ADVANTAGE	Fixed Income	138.0	9.77	10,220.90	10,656.10	☆	9.4	368-3863	414-359-1400	None	None		R. Strong/W. Corneliuson	'88
STRONG COMMON STOCK★	Capital Appreciation	2.7	10.82	10,783.30	☆	☆	0.0	368-3863	414-359-1400	2.00	None		R. Strong/W. Corneliuson	'90
STRONG DISCOVERY FUND	Capital Appreciation	71.2	13.76	11,049.50	10,301.00	☆	2.3	368-3863	414-359-1400	2.00	None		R. Strong/W. Corneliuson	'88
STRONG GOV'T	Fixed Income	31.1	10.01	11,206.80	10,406.70	☆	7.4	368-3863	414-359-1400	None	None		R. Strong/W. Corneliuson	'86
STRONG INCOME	Fixed Income	125.5	9.50	9,947.10	8,899.20	☆	13.8	368-3863	414-359-1400	None	None		R. Strong/W. Corneliuson	'85
STRONG INVESTMENT	Balanced	230.3	17.69	10,198.50	10,355.10	15,716.50	6.9	368-3863	414-359-1400	1.00	None		R. Strong/W. Corneliuson	'82
STRONG OPPORTUNITY	Capital Appreciation	178.2	18.55	10,422.20	9,687.80	☆	4.8	368-3863	414-359-1400	2.00	None		R. Strong/W. Corneliuson	'86
STRONG SHORT-TERM BOND	Fixed Income	92.0	9.45	10,145.30	10,186.60	☆	9.8	368-3863	414-359-1400	None	None		R. Strong/W. Corneliuson	'87
STRONG TOTAL RETURN	Growth & Income	808.7	16.76	10,485.10	8,963.80	16,878.70	8.4	368-3863	414-359-1400	1.00	None		R. Strong/W. Corneliuson	'82
SUNAMERICA CAP APPREC	Growth	180.1	12.82	10,355.40	9,677.00	17,500.70	1.3	821-5100	212-353-7125	None	1.25	5.0	Harvey Eisen	'85
SUNAMERICA EQ: AGG GROWTH	Small-Company Growth	37.9	16.56	9,981.90	9,925.90	☆	0.0	821-5100	212-353-7125	4.75	0.35		Harvey Eisen	'90
SUNAMERICA EQ: GROWTH	Growth	40.2	16.57	10,460.90	11,489.40	☆	0.7	821-5100	212-353-7125	4.75	0.35		Harvey Eisen	'90
SUNAMERICA NC: CNVRTBLE	Convertible	13.7	9.59	10,270.00	9,771.40	☆	6.7	821-5100	212-353-7125	4.75	0.35		Harvey Eisen	'89
SUNAMERICA NC: GOVT PLUS	Fixed Income	42.8	9.90	10,281.30	10,643.50	☆	11.2	821-5100	212-353-7125	4.75	0.35		Cheryl Fisher	'89
SUNAMERICA INC: HI YIELD	Fixed Income	24.5	8.63	10,651.70	9,380.60	☆	14.4	821-5100	212-353-7125	4.75	0.35		Laurel Kohl	'89
SUNAMERICA INCOME PLUS	Fixed Income	23.1	6.94	10,693.30	9,045.60	☆	14.2	821-5100	212-353-7125	4.75	1.25	5.00	Laurel Kohl	'89
SUNAMERICA MUL-AST: TOTRT	Flexible	32.8	16.08	10,354.20	10,573.80	☆	2.3	821-5100	212-353-7125	4.75	0.35		Harvey Eisen	'87
SURVEYOR FUND	Growth	93.2	11.28	10,551.90	10,170.20	19,645.90	0.0	227-4618	None	5.50	0.30		Frank Burr/Paul Jenkel	'72
TEMPLETON FOREIGN	International	881.0	25.41	10,694.40	13,183.90	32,283.10	2.9	237-0738	None	8.50	None		Templeton Int'l	'82
TEMPLETON GLOBAL FD	Global	893.2	8.30	10,466.60	10,778.00	18,230.50	2.5	237-0738	None	8.50	None		Templeton Int'l	'81
TEMPLETON GROWTH	Global	2,662.2	16.37	10,636.80	11,599.90	21,941.30	3.7	237-0738	None	8.50	None		Templeton Int'l	'54
TEMPLETON INCOME	World Fixed-Income	110.5	9.75	10,445.50	10,827.40	☆	9.9	237-0738	None	4.50	None		Templeton Int'l	'86
TEMPLETON REAL ESTATE TR	Real Estate	11.4	10.05	10,436.10	☆	☆	0.0	237-0738	None	8.50	None		Templeton Int'l	'89
TEMPLETON WORLD	Global	4,581.1	16.12	10,542.80	10,886.60	19,992.50	3.4	237-0738	None	8.50	None		Templeton Int'l	'78
TX COMMERCE RIT: BALANCED★	Balanced	13.3	1.28	10,433.00	10,641.70	☆	0.0	None	713-236-5125	None	None		William Leszinske	'88
TX COMMERCE RIT: EQ GROWTH★★	Growth	3.9	1.46	11,232.70	11,664.00	☆	0.0	None	713-236-5125	None	None		Charles Mehlhouse	'88
TX COMMERCE RIT: EQU INC★	Equity Income	5.2	1.33	10,295.90	10,693.50	☆	0.0	None	713-236-5125	None	None		Robert Heintz	'88
TX COMMERCE RIT: INCOME★	Fixed Income	17.3	1.17	10,318.90	10,401.80	☆	0.0	None	713-236-5125	None	None		Jan Buskop	'88
THOMSON MCKINNON: CNVRT	Convertibles	33.6	9.82	10,235.00	10,111.60	☆	5.1	628-1237	212-482-5894	None	0.90	5.00	David Hoffman	'86
THOMSON MCKINNON: GLOBL	Global	47.1	12.33	10,999.10	11,583.00	☆	0.0	628-1237	212-482-5894	None	0.93	5.00	Smith/Michaelson	'88
THOMSON MCKINNON: GOVT	Fixed Income	479.4	9.19	10,248.30	10,516.80	☆	8.9	628-1237	212-482-5894	None	1.00	5.00	Seth Wohlberg	'88
THOMSON MCKINNON: GRO	Growth	366.4	19.49	11,169.60	12,065.30	24,276.80	0.9	628-1237	212-482-5894	None	0.86	5.00	Irwin Smith	'86
THOMSON MCKINNON: INC	Flexible Income	393.8	8.77	10,303.40	10,283.00	14,496.90	10.9	628-1237	212-482-5894	None	0.93	5.00	David Hoffman	'86
THOMSON MCKINNON: OPPTY	Capital Appreciation	44.2	14.45	10,905.70	11,578.80	19,235.10	0.0	628-1237	212-482-5894	None	0.85	5.00	Don Chiboucas	'86
THOMSON MCKINNON: PR MT	Gold	8.1	8.62	8,672.00	9,451.80	☆	0.0	628-1237	212-482-5894	None	0.99	5.00	John Van Eck	'88

★SLH TELECOM: INCOME—Closed to new investors.

★STATE FARM FUNDS—Open only to State Farm agents and employees.

★STEADMAN FUNDS—Closed.

★STRONG COMMON STOCK—Designed for employee pension and benefits plans.

★TEXAS COMMERCE RIT FUNDS—Limited to retirement accounts established with Texas Commerce Bank and its affiliates.

PERFORMANCE OF MUTUAL FUNDS (continued)

FUND NAME	OBJECTIVE	TOTAL NET ASSETS (MIL) 6/30/90	NET ASSET VALUE 6/30/90	PERFORMANCE (Return on Initial $10,000 Investment) 3/31/90-6/30/90	6/30/89-6/30/90	6/30/85-6/30/90	DIVIDEND YIELD % 6/90	PHONE NUMBER 800	In-State	FEES Load	12b-1	Redemption	MANAGER	SINCE
THOMPSON UNGER & PLUMB	Balanced	11.5	12.28	10,771.90	11,386.60	✩	2.6	None	608-231-1676	None	None	None	Plumb/Unger/Thompson	'87
THORNBURG TR: LTD TERM US	Fixed Income	30.8	11.95	10,279.50	10,809.00	✩	8.5	847-0200	505-984-0200	2.25	0.25	None	Steve Bohlin	'88
THOROUGHBRED BOND	Fixed Income	7.4	9.62	10,268.80	10,742.70	✩	8.6	255-9962	502-581-4492	None	None	None	Elaine Turner	'87
THOROUGHBRED STOCK	Growth & Income	11.5	13.16	10,844.10	12,393.30	✩	2.4	255-9962	502-581-4492	None	0.50	None	Stanley Rourke	'87
TOCQUEVILLE FUND	Capital Appreciation	15.1	11.25	10,504.20	10,878.90	✩	3.2	225-6258	800-392-6037	None	None	None	Francois Sicart	'87
TOT RTN TREA: CJ LAWRENCE	Fixed Income	126.4	10.02	10,360.60	10,461.60	✩	9.2	767-3524	301-727-1700	4.45	0.25	None	Al Medaugh	'88
TOT RTN TREA: FLAG INV	Fixed Income	195.5	10.02	10,360.60	10,461.60	✩	9.2	767-3524	301-727-1700	4.50	0.25	None	Al Medaugh	'88
TOWER: CAPITAL APPREC	Capital Appreciation	68.8	13.16	10,730.00	12,062.30	✩	3.0	999-0124	412-288-6460	4.50	None	None	Hibernia Bank	'88
TOWER: US GOVT INCOME	Fixed Income	28.7	10.13	10,317.70	10,763.90	✩	8.5	999-0124	412-288-6460	4.50	0.25	None	Hibernia Bank	'88
TRANSAM GOVT INCOME TR	Fixed Income	146.3	8.29	10,401.00	10,466.30	✩	10.3	999-3863	None	2.50	0.25	None	Team System	'85
TRANSAM GOVT SEC TRUST	Fixed Income	840.7	7.96	10,397.30	10,482.40	14,010.50	11.1	999-3863	None	4.75	0.25	None	Team System	'84
TRANSAM GROWTH & INCOME	Growth & Income	68.9	10.67	10,750.70	12,008.40	12,438.60	2.6	999-3863	None	4.75	0.25	None	Ed Larsen	'90
TRANSAM INVEST QUAL BOND	Fixed Income	85.6	8.64	10,393.70	10,483.80	15,110.70	10.1	999-3863	None	4.75	0.25	None	Jim Kellerman	'80
TRANSAM LOWRY MKT TIMING	Capital Appreciation	17.4	9.97	10,257.20	11,080.90	12,976.50	2.7	999-3863	None	4.75	0.25	None	Roger Young	'90
TRANSAM PREM LTD TM ACCT	Fixed Income	2.6	9.43	10,208.00	10,796.00	✩	9.0	999-3863	None	2.75	None	None	Team System	'86
TRANSAM SPEC: BLUE CHIP	Growth	11.2	9.94	10,734.30	11,715.60	✩	0.6	999-3863	None	None	0.35	6.00	Ed Larsen	'86
TRANSAM SPEC: CONVERT	Convertible	9.1	10.12	10,532.30	11,240.20	✩	4.5	999-3863	None	None	0.35	6.00	Ed Larsen & Team	'89
TRANSAM SPEC: EMER GROW	Small-Company Growth	16.3	14.77	11,172.50	12,853.60	✩	0.0	999-3863	None	None	0.35	6.00	Ed Larsen & Team	'87
TRANSAM SPEC: GLBL GROW	Global	7.9	12.37	10,673.00	10,747.20	✩	0.0	999-3863	None	4.75	0.35	None	Ed Larsen & Team	'86
TRANSAM SPEC: GOVT INC	Fixed Income	56.1	9.53	10,381.90	10,450.00	✩	10.0	999-3863	None	None	0.35	6.00	Team System	'88
TRANSAM SPEC: HI YIELD	Fixed Income	38.1	7.40	10,544.20	9,550.80	✩	15.2	999-3863	None	None	0.35	6.00	Team System	'87
TRANSAM SPEC: NATRL RES	Natural Resources	6.9	13.04	10,195.50	11,650.20	✩	0.0	999-3863	None	None	0.35	6.00	Team System	'87
TRANSAM SUNBELT GROWTH	Growth	30.9	20.08	10,974.70	11,340.70	✩	6.1	999-3863	None	4.75	0.25	None	Roger Young & Team	'88
TRANSAM TECHNOLOGY	Technology	70.7	25.31	11,669.00	12,973.10	16,733.50	0.5	999-3863	None	4.75	0.25	None	Roger Young & Team	'85
TREASURY FIRST	Fixed Income	4.7	8.66	10,115.70	10,071.50	✩	8.2	234-4111	301-494-8488	None	0.25	None	Kerry Whitmore	'90
TRIFLEX FUND	Balanced	21.4	14.37	10,269.10	10,480.40	15,248.70	5.0	231-4639	800-392-9753	7.50	None	None	Ben Hock	'89
TRIUMPH: EQUITY INCOME	Equity Income	5.1	9.66	9,980.40	✩	✩	0.0	345-3646	None	4.50	None	None	Walter Seibert Jr.	'90
TRIUMPH: TAXABLE INCOME	Mixed Income	5.3	10.06	10,292.80	10,782.10	✩	0.0	345-3646	None	4.50	None	None	Henry Milkewicz	'90
TRUST FED SEC: INTMD GOVT	Fixed Income	14.9	10.05	10,290.60	10,661.50	✩	8.0	221-8120	212-767-3063	None	None	None	Mike Hutchinson	N/A
TRUST FED SEC: LONG GOVT	Fixed Income	5.1	10.07	10,372.30		✩	8.2	221-8120	212-767-3063	None	None	None	Mike Hutchinson	N/A
TRUST FED SEC: SHORT GOVT	Fixed Income	10.0	9.93	10,269.10	10,827.60	✩	7.6	221-8120	212-767-3063	None	None	None	Mike Hutchinson	N/A
TRUSTEES COMMINGLED INTL	International	819.9	32.52	10,850.00	12,572.80	35,602.50	2.5	662-7447	800-662-7447	None	None	None	J. Wagstaff-Callahan	'84
TRUSTEES COMMINGLED US	Growth & Income	120.1	25.72	10,372.40	10,230.90	18,406.30	3.2	662-7447	800-662-7447	None	None	None	J. Wagstaff-Callahan	'80
TWENTIETH CENTURY: BAL	Balanced	60.2	12.37	10,864.00	12,132.40	✩	3.4	345-2021	816-531-5575	None	None	None	Group Managed	'58
TWENTIETH CENTURY: GIFTRUST	Growth	33.4	10.54	11,370.00	13,112.80	28,404.80	0.0	345-2021	816-531-5575	None	None	None	Group Managed	'58
TWENTIETH CENTURY: GROWTH	Capital Appreciation	2,056.7	18.83	11,155.20	12,579.80	24,878.60	0.4	345-2021	816-531-5575	None	None	None	Group Managed	'58
TWENTIETH CENTURY: HERITAGE	Growth	221.4	8.02	10,882.00	11,917.30	✩	0.8	345-2021	816-531-5575	None	None	None	Group Managed	'87
TWENTIETH CENT: LNG TM BD	Fixed Income	72.7	90.45	10,367.50	10,407.00	✩	8.9	345-2021	816-531-5575	None	None	None	Group Managed	'58
TWENTIETH CENTURY: SELECT	Growth	3,298.7	39.09	11,095.70	12,546.40	22,274.20	2.9	345-2021	816-531-5575	None	None	None	Group Managed	'58
TWENTIETH CENTURY: ULTRA INV	Capital Appreciation	397.5	9.47	11,605.40	11,653.60	21,656.70	2.0	345-2021	816-531-5575	None	None	None	Group Managed	'58
TWENTIETH CENTURY: US GOV	Fixed Income	435.3	90.81	10,242.80	10,577.20	14,279.20	8.7	345-2021	816-531-5575	None	None	None	Group Managed	'58
TWENTIETH CENTURY: VISTA INV	Capital Appreciation	493.7	9.29	11,099.20	13,414.70	24,679.60	0.0	345-2021	816-531-5575	None	None	None	Group Managed	'58
TYNDALL-NEWPORT: FAR EAST	Pacific Region	2.9	16.65	10,700.50	11,533.00	25,048.20	0.0	527-9500	None	5.00	None	None	John Mussey	'85
TYNDALL-NEWPORT: GLOBAL	Global	7.8	12.11	10,548.80	11,125.90	12,571.10	0.4	527-9500	None	5.00	None	None	John Mussey	'87
TYNDALL-NEWPORT: TIGER	Pacific Region	8.3	11.80	10,592.50	11,913.00	✩	0.3	527-9500	None	5.00	None	None	John Mussey	'89

Fund	Objective	Net Assets	NAV			Value	Yield %	Phone	Phone	Max Charge			Manager	Since
UNIFIED GRCWTH FUND	Growth	14.2	19.42	10,525.60	10,910.80	15,330.10	2.3	862-7283	317-634-3300	None	None	None	Moran Ast. Mgt.	'90
UNIFIED INCOME FUND	Mixed Income	5.5	10.93	10,238.50	10,672.20	12,881.30	7.4	862-7283	317-634-3300	None	None	None	Laidlaw Holdings	'90
UNIFIED MUTUAL SHARES	Growth & Income	15.6	16.03	10,335.30	10,797.80	16,499.30	4.1	862-7283	317-634-3300	None	None	None	Fiduciary Counsel	'90
UNITED ACCUMULATIVE	Growth	874.3	6.99	10,255.30	11,005.30	19,685.30	4.1	366-5465	816-283-4000	8.50	None	None	Antonio Intagliata	'79
UNITED BOND FUND	Fixed Income	421.8	5.85	10,266.70	10,274.20	16,412.60	9.1	366-5465	816-283-4000	8.50	None	None	Robert Alley	'84
UNITED CON'L INCOME	Balanced	320.1	17.04	10,309.60	11,071.80	17,163.40	5.5	366-5465	816-283-4000	8.50	None	None	Antonio Intagliata	'79
UNITED GOLD & GOVT	Gold	62.6	7.11	9,119.70	9,645.10	☆	2.3	366-5465	816-283-4000	8.50	None	None	John Olsen	'85
UNITED GOVERNMENT	Fixed Income	104.8	4.80	10,302.50	10,613.40	15,391.10	8.5	366-5465	816-283-4000	4.25	None	None	Robert Alley	'88
UNITED HIGH INCOME★	Fixed Income	882.5	8.57	10,441.00	8,605.40	12,532.60	16.4	366-5465	816-283-4000	8.50	None	None	Louis Rieke	'90
UNITED HIGH INCOME II	Fixed Income	277.5	3.71	10,464.70	9,261.40	☆	12.7	366-5465	816-283-4000	8.50	None	None	James Wineland	'90
UNITED INCOME	Equity Income	1,741.6	19.46	10,569.90	11,575.30	24,206.40	3.4	366-5465	816-283-4000	8.50	None	None	Russell Thompson	'79
UNITED INTL GROWTH	International	291.7	6.77	10,575.50	11,433.70	24,071.80	1.9	366-5465	816-283-4000	8.50	None	None	Mark Yockey	'90
UNITED MISSOURI BK BOND	Fixed Income	33.7	10.48	10,271.10	10,810.20	15,343.20	7.5	422-2766	816-471-5200	None	None	None	George Root	'82
UNITED MISSOURI QUAL DVD	Fixed Income	1.6	8.24	10,206.40	10,259.80	☆	7.7	422-2766	816-471-5200	None	None	None	Frank Swyden	'86
UNITED MISSOURI BK STOCK	Growth & Income	48.0	13.69	10,285.00	10,860.80	17,903.30	4.2	422-2766	816-471-5200	None	None	None	David Anderson	'82
UNITED NEW CONCEPTS	Small-Company Growth	65.4	5.79	11,113.20	11,526.70	16,062.80	3.1	366-5465	816-283-4000	8.50	None	None	Mark Seferovich	'89
UNITED RETIREMENT SHARES	Growth & Income	161.3	6.41	10,519.20	11,306.30	18,461.00	4.0	366-5465	816-283-4000	8.50	None	None	James Wineland	'85
UNITED SCIENCE & ENERGY	Technology	263.9	12.27	10,849.80	11,781.90	22,880.20	1.7	366-5465	816-283-4000	8.50	None	None	Abel Garcia	'84
UNITED VANGUARD FUND	Growth	814.3	6.18	10,698.50	11,144.70	20,305.30	3.4	366-5465	816-283-4000	8.50	None	None	Charles Hooper	'87
US BOSTON: BOS FRN G&I	International	24.8	11.75	10,472.40	11,573.50	☆	0.3	None	617-272-6420	None	0.50	1.00	U.S. Boston Inv. Mgt.	'87
US BOSTON: BOS GRO & INC	Growth & Income	36.8	15.34	10,749.80	11,951.50	22,343.90	1.0	None	617-272-6420	None	0.50	1.00	Victor Flores	'85
US GLOBAL RESOURCES	Gold	31.7	0.63	9,264.70	9,552.10	15,037.00	7.7	873-8637	512-523-2453	None	None	None	Edmund Serfaty	'88
US GOLD SHARES	Gold	283.0	3.82	8,347.40	10,551.50	9,781.00	5.0	873-8637	512-523-2453	None	None	None	David Edwards	'87
US GOOD & BAD TIMES	Growth & Income	9.2	16.12	9,867.00	9,959.10	12,645.10	3.1	873-8637	512-523-2453	None	None	None	David Edwards	'87
US GOVT GUARANTEED SEC	Fixed Income	603.0	13.34	10,326.20	10,809.20	☆	9.6	421-0180	213-486-9200	4.75	0.25	None	Multiple Managers	'85
US GNMA	Fixed Income	5.0	9.35	10,306.80	10,668.30	☆	8.3	873-8637	512-523-2453	None	None	None	Allen Parker	'87
US GROWTH FUND	Capital Appreciation	6.5	7.41	10,190.30	10,951.80	14,241.90	1.2	873-8637	512-523-2453	None	None	None	David Edwards	'87
US INCOME FUND	Income	8.0	12.23	10,057.10	10,889.10	16,533.10	3.4	873-8637	512-523-2453	None	None	None	David Edwards	'87
US LOCAP FUND	Small-Company Growth	2.7	6.37	10,511.60	9,891.30	8,394.00	0.0	873-8637	512-523-2453	None	None	None	David Edwards	'87
US NEW PROSPECTOR	Gold	72.4	1.08	8,503.90	9,296.60	☆	0.9	873-8637	512-523-2453	None	None	None	Victor Flores	'90
US REAL ESTATE	Real Estate	6.0	8.37	9,929.50	8,739.00	☆	3.5	873-8637	512-523-2453	None	None	None	Allen Parker	'88
US TREND FUND	Growth	91.2	13.82	10,755.90	11,605.10	19,404.30	2.8	262-6631	None	4.75	None	None	Dan Watson	'88
USAA INV TR: BALANCED★	Balanced	38.3	11.00	10,147.70	10,639.30	☆	4.3	531-8000	512-498-7290	None	None	None	John Saunders Jr	'89
USAA INV TR: CORNERSTONE	Global Flexible	569.9	18.50	10,940.90	10,668.80	19,953.50	3.8	531-8000	512-498-7290	None	None	None	David Peebles	'85
USAA INV TR: GOLD	Gold	141.9	7.39	8,523.60	9,289.50	10,555.30	2.0	531-8000	512-498-7290	None	None	None	David Peebles	'89
USAA INV TR: INTL	International	23.3	12.18	10,665.50	12,151.10	☆	0.2	531-8000	512-498-7290	None	None	None	David Peebles	'88
USAA MUTUAL: AGGR GROWTH	Small-Company Growth	158.2	17.02	10,664.20	11,064.50	15,011.20	1.0	531-8000	512-498-7290	None	None	None	Stuart Wester	'88
USAA MUTUAL: GROWTH	Growth	249.9	14.86	10,539.00	11,495.70	16,952.50	3.1	531-8000	512-498-7290	None	None	None	Bill Fries	'89
USAA MUTUAL: INCOME FD	Fixed Income	417.8	11.37	10,298.40	10,787.70	16,161.90	9.0	531-8000	512-498-7290	None	None	None	John Saunders Jr.	'85
USAA MUTUAL: INCOME STOCK	Equity Income	86.7	11.36	10,216.40	10,817.40	☆	5.1	531-8000	512-498-7290	None	None	None	Harry Miller	'89
UST MASTER: EQUITY	Capital Appreciation	31.2	14.58	10,591.00	11,065.00	20,350.80	2.3	233-1136	None	4.50	None	None	Laird Grant	'89
UST MASTER: NC & GROWTH	Growth & Income	22.9	8.58	9,837.30	9,641.40	☆	5.1	233-1136	None	4.50	None	None	Ted Seibert	'87
UST MASTER: INTERNATIONAL	International	26.2	9.92	10,855.80	12,101.50	☆	1.5	233-1136	None	4.50	None	None	Harry Rowney	'87
UST MASTER: MANAGED INC	Fixed Income	41.1	8.75	10,286.30	10,580.50	☆	7.8	233-1136	None	4.50	None	None	Henry Milkewicz	'86
VALLEY FORGE FUND	Growth	8.0	9.77	10,155.90	10,896.20	14,222.90	6.5	548-1942	215-688-6839	None	None	None	Bernard Klawans	'71
VALUE LINE AGGRS INC	Fixed Income	28.7	6.92	10,240.20	9,925.90	☆	11.8	223-0818	212-687-3965	None	None	None	Joel Goldsmith	'87
VALUE LINE CONVERTIBLE	Convertibles	45.8	11.54	10,559.70	10,795.10	15,930.80	5.4	223-0818	212-687-3965	None	None	None	Allan Lyons	'85
VALUE LINE FUND	Growth & Income	212.0	15.92	10,915.20	12,221.30	20,520.50	2.1	223-0818	212-687-3965	None	None	None	Frank Korth	'90

★UNITED HIGH INCOME—Closed to new investors.

★USAA INV TR BALANCED—55% of assets in tax-exempt bonds.

FUND NAME	OBJECTIVE	TOTAL NET ASSETS (MIL) 6/30/90	NET ASSET VALUE 6/30/90	PERFORMANCE (Return on Initial $10,000 investment) 3/31/90- 6/30/90	6/30/89- 6/30/90	6/30/85- 6/30/90	DIVIDEND YIELD % 6/90	PHONE NUMBER 800	In-State	FEES Load	12b-1	Redemption	MANAGER	SINCE
VALUE LINE INCOME	Equity Income	144.0	6.50	10,425.80	11,068.40	17,084.20	7.1	223-0818	212-687-3965	None	None	None	Lydia Miller	'88
VALUE LINE LVGE GROWTH	Capital Appreciation	260.3	24.49	11,021.60	12,147.40	19,836.30	1.5	223-0818	212-687-3965	None	None	None	David Campbell	'88
VALUE LINE SPECIAL SIT	Growth	119.0	14.47	10,726.50	10,874.80	13,940.60	1.5	223-0818	212-687-3965	None	None	None	Peter Shraga	'87
VALUE LINE US GOVT SEC	Fixed Income	257.0	11.71	10,346.50	10,817.20	15,663.20	8.9	223-0818	212-687-3965	None	None	None	Charles Heebner	'89
VANCE, SANDERS SPECIAL	Growth	56.8	13.93	10,840.50	11,577.90	13,332.20	0.4	225-6265	617-482-8260	4.75	None	None	Albert Toney Jr.	'87
VAN ECK: GOLD/RESOURCES	Gold	194.4	4.19	8,765.70	9,515.20	☆	0.2	221-2220	212-687-5200	6.75	0.25	None	H. Bingham/J. van Eck	'86
VAN ECK: WORLD INCOME	World Fixed-Income	42.8	9.69	10,563.90	11,891.40	☆	9.7	221-2220	212-687-5200	5.75	0.25	None	K. Buescher/D. Tenerson	'87
VAN ECK: WORLD TRENDS	Global	56.6	14.90	10,552.40	11,804.60	11,348.00	1.3	221-2220	212-687-5200	5.75	0.25	None	K. Buescher/D. Tererson	'85
VANGUARD ADJ RATE PREF	Fixed Income	37.6	18.22	10,125.30	10,419.30	☆	8.4	662-7447	None	None	None	None	Earl McEvoy	'83
VANGUARD ASSET ALLOC	Flexible	177.8	11.92	10,498.90	10,988.60	☆	4.3	662-7447	None	None	None	None	William Fouse	'88
VANGUARD BOND MARKET	Fixed Income	170.6	9.26	10,356.00	10,762.60	☆	8.9	662-7447	None	None	None	None	Ian MacKinnon	'88
VANGUARD CONVERTIBLE	Convertibles	55.1	9.56	10,353.30	10,736.40	☆	5.9	662-7447	None	None	None	None	Rohit Desai	'86
VANGUARD EQUITY INCOME	Equity Income	425.4	12.35	10,180.00	10,695.40	☆	5.2	662-7447	None	None	None	None	Roger Newell	'88
VANGUARD EXPLORER	Small-Company Growth	290.2	30.86	11,041.10	10,591.80	13,568.40	1.2	662-7447	None	None	None	None	Wisneski/Granahan	'79/'85
VANGUARD FI: GNMA PORT	Fixed Income	2,317.8	9.59	10,354.90	10,888.10	16,141.90	9.0	662-7447	None	None	None	None	Paul Sullivan	'80
VANGUARD FI: HIGH YIELD	Fixed Income	905.0	7.21	10,424.50	9,898.10	15,404.40	13.3	662-7447	None	None	None	None	Earl McEvoy	'84
VANGUARD FI: INV GRADE	Fixed Income	1,082.0	8.04	10,435.70	10,604.60	16,216.30	9.0	662-7447	None	None	None	None	Paul Sullivan	'76
VANGUARD FI: SHT TERM BD	Fixed Income	668.4	10.36	10,282.30	10,836.10	15,256.50	8.6	662-7447	None	None	None	None	Ian Mackinnon	'82
VANGUARD FI: SHT TERM GOV	Fixed Income	260.2	9.90	10,278.60	10,783.60	☆	8.3	662-7447	None	None	None	None	Ian Mackinnon	'87
VANGUARD FI: US TREAS BD	Fixed Income	528.2	9.51	10,384.60	10,333.90	☆	8.1	662-7447	None	None	None	None	John Neff	'75
VANGUARD HIGH YIELD STK★	Equity Income	110.1	11.37	10,029.80	8,839.50	15,785.90	10.6	662-7447	None	None	None	None	Ian Mackinnon	'87
VANGUARD INDEX: EXTND MKT	Small-Company Growth	184.6	13.62	10,318.20	10,437.40	☆	1.8	662-7447	None	None	None	None	George Sauter	'87
VANGUARD INDEX: 500 PORT	Growth & Income	2,367.8	34.22	10,624.30	11,618.10	21,803.80	3.5	662-7447	None	None	None	None	George Sauter	'87
VANGUARD INTL EQ IDX: EUR	European Region	48.5	10.25	☆	☆	☆	0.0	662-7447	None	None	None	None	George Sauter	'90
VANGUARD INTL EQ IDX: PAC	Pacific Region	14.8	9.94	☆	☆	☆	0.0	662-7447	None	None	None	None	George Sauter	'90
VANGUARD/MORGAN GROWTH	Growth	755.9	12.32	10,731.70	11,604.60	20,712.20	2.3	662-7447	None	None	None	None	Frank Wisneski	'79
VANGUARD PREFERRED STK	Fixed Income	61.1	8.36	10,406.80	10,814.40	16,276.00	8.9	662-7447	None	None	None	None	Earl McEvoy	'82
VANGUARD QUANTITATIVE	Growth & Income	203.7	14.53	10,544.30	11,632.20	☆	3.2	662-7447	None	None	None	None	John Nagorniak	'86
VANGUARD SMALL CAP STK	Small-Company Growth	46.7	11.25	10,568.70	10,100.70	13,745.00	1.2	662-7447	None	None	None	None	Index Fund	'89
VANGUARD SPL: ENERGY	Natural Resources	101.7	15.63	10,142.80	12,154.80	22,048.00	2.4	662-7447	None	None	None	None	Ernst von Metzsch	'84
VANGUARD SPL: GOLD	Gold	161.2	9.79	9,031.40	10,499.10	16,610.00	2.8	662-7447	None	None	None	1.00	David Hutchins	'85
VANGUARD SPL: HEALTH	Health/Biotech.	134.3	25.82	11,231.00	12,968.90	25,957.70	1.8	662-7447	None	None	None	1.00	Edward Owens	'84
VANGUARD SPL: SERVICE	Specialty	22.6	18.49	10,737.50	10,914.30	16,934.60	2.3	662-7447	None	None	None	1.00	Matt Megargel	'84
VANGUARD SPL: TECHNOLOGY	Technology	20.6	13.71	10,933.00	12,274.00	14,429.40	1.1	662-7447	None	None	None	1.00	Perry Traquina	'84
VANGUARD STAR	Balanced	1,076.8	12.09	11,280.60	10,561.10	17,904.40	6.3	662-7447	None	None	None	None	NA	'NA
VANGUARD WORLD: INTL GRO	International	827.8	12.55	11,280.40	12,521.50	35,248.00	1.2	662-7447	None	None	None	None	Richard Foulkes	'81
VANGUARD WORLD: US GRO	Growth	347.2	11.58	11,275.60	13,222.80	19,353.80	1.1	662-7447	None	None	None	None	J. W. Parker Hall III	'87
VANKAMP MERR GRO & INC	Growth & Income	25.9	16.70	10,285.10	10,436.90	☆	3.5	225-2222	312-719-6000	4.90	0.30	None	First Quadrant	'87
VANKAMP MERR HIGH YIELD	Fixed Income	219.9	9.96	10,288.20	8,914.90	☆	16.1	225-2222	312-719-6000	4.90	0.30	None	Kevin Matthews	'87
VANKAMP MERR US GOVT	Fixed Income	3,362.6	15.04	10,546.10	10,870.40	16,265.80	9.8	225-2222	312-719-6000	4.90	0.30	None	Hegel/Doyle	'84
VARIABLE STOCK FUND	Growth	7.7	7.65	10,546.80	11,721.60	16,756.00	0.4	None	413-781-3000	None	None	None	John Lesley III	'87
VENTURE INCOME (+) PLUS	Fixed Income	28.9	5.99	10,353.90	8,974.70	11,760.50	19.9	279-2279	505-983-4335	4.75	0.25	None	Clark Stamper	'90

Fund	Objective	Assets ($mil)	NAV	Value A	Value B	Value C (10-Yr)	Yield	Phone 1	Phone 2	Max Chg	12b-1	Redemp	Manager	Since
VISTA FDS: CAPITAL GRO	Growth	6.5	15.74	10,550.10	11,265.70	☆	3.7	None	622-4273	None	None	None	Paul Frohlich	'89
VISTA FDS: GRO & INC	Growth & Income	23.3	19.97	10,893.30	13,756.40	☆	4.0	None	622-4273	None	None	None	Jim Manley	'87
VISTA FDS: US GOVT INCO	Fixed Income	6.0	10.91	10,319.10	10,606.60	☆	8.1	None	622-4273	None	None	None	Janet Hanlon	'87
VOLLMETRIC FUND	Growth	5.0	13.10	10,147.20	10,414.20	☆	0.7	914-623-7637	541-3863	None	None	None	Gabriel Gibs	'78
VOYAGEUR GRANIT GOVT	Fixed Income	5.7	10.28	10,355.50	10,914.40	☆	8.2	612-341-6728	553-2143	4.75	0.25	None	Jane Wyatt	'89
VOYAGEUR GRANIT GRO STK	Growth	11.8	19.94	11,019.10	12,327.60	☆	0.0	612-341-6728	553-2143	5.75	0.25	None	Rick Leggott	'89
VOYAGEUR US GOVT SEC FD	Fixed Income	8.3	9.77	10,317.80	10,790.10	☆	8.3	None	553-2143	4.75	0.25	None	Paul Zoschky	'88
WADE FUND	Growth	0.5	33.31	10,066.50	11,138.10	14,552.40	2.5	901-682-4613	None	None	None	None	Maury Wade	'73
WALL STREET FUND	Growth	11.1	7.19	10,315.60	10,876.60	17,490.00	0.3	212-319-9400	443-4693	5.50	None	None	Robert Morse	'84
WARBURG INTERNATIONAL FD	International	10.9	7.30	10,928.10	11,457.80	☆	1.1	212-363-3300	None	4.50	None	None	Warburg Inv Mgt Int'l	'85
WASATCH AGGRESSIVE EQU	Small-Company Growth	3.3	13.11	11,195.60	13,391.20	☆	0.0	801-533-0777	345-7460	None	None	None	Samuel Stewart	'86
WASATCH GROWTH	Growth	5.4	13.02	11,005.90	12,552.60	☆	0.9	801-533-0777	345-7460	None	None	None	Samuel Stewart	'86
WASATCH INCOME	Fixed Income	1.7	10.36	10,496.50	10,785.90	☆	6.6	801-533-0777	345-7460	None	None	None	Samuel Stewart	'86
WASHINGTON MUTUAL INV	Growth & Income	5,349.2	14.41	10,246.40	10,896.00	20,932.60	4.3	213-486-9200	421-9900	5.75	0.25	None	Multiple Managers	'52
WAYNE HUMMER GROWTH FUND	Growth	26.6	16.96	10,567.40	11,847.60	19,583.50	1.7	312-431-1700	621-4477	None	None	None	Alan Bird	'83
WEALTH MONITORS	Capital Appreciation	1.4	6.69	9,612.10	9,265.90	☆	0.0	816-941-7990	None	None	0.05	None	Michael Lamb	'86
WEITZ FIXED INCOME	Fixed Income	3.0	10.41	10,261.10	10,773.80	☆	7.2	402-391-1980	None	None	None	None	Wallace Weitz	'88
WEITZ VALUE	Growth & Income	24.3	12.23	10,471.00	10,606.40	☆	3.4	402-391-1980	None	None	None	None	Wallace Weitz	'86
WELLESLEY INCOME	Mixed Income	919.1	16.29	10,280.00	10,827.70	17,772.70	8.0	None	800-662-7447	None	None	None	E. McEvoy/J. Ryan	'82/'86
WELLINGTON FUND	Balanced	2,331.4	17.28	10,301.10	10,668.90	18,908.10	6.0	None	800-662-7447	None	None	None	V. Bajakian/P. Sullivan	'72/'75
WELLS FARGO: ASSET ALLOC★	Flexible	253.5	13.88	10,281.50	10,981.00	☆	0.0	None	None	None	0.95	None	Wells Fargo Inv. Adv.	'87
WELLS FARGO: CORP STOCK★	Growth & Income	171.4	25.20	10,592.70	11,444.10	20,571.40	0.0	None	237-8472	None	0.95	None	Wells Fargo Inv. Adv.	'85
WELLS FARGO: FIXED INCOME★	Fixed Income	17.8	12.49	10,113.40	10,399.70	☆	0.0	None	237-8472	None	0.95	None	Wells Fargo Inv. Adv.	'88
WELLS FARGO: SMALL CO STK★	Small-Company Growth	15.0	13.88	9,625.50	8,840.80	12,315.90	0.0	None	237-8472	None	0.95	None	Wells Fargo Inv. Adv.	'85
WESTCORE: BASIC VALUE	Growth & Income	133.9	19.69	10,123.50	10,234.00	☆	3.6	303-623-2577	237-8472	4.50	None	None	Charles Fish	'88
WESTCORE: BOND PLUS	Fixed Income	77.9	15.16	10,319.30	10,704.50	☆	8.3	303-623-2577	666-0367	4.50	None	None	Phil Diamond	'90
WESTCORE: EQUITY INCOME	Equity Income	16.3	9.87	10,732.40	11,484.50	☆	3.4	303-623-2577	666-0367	4.50	None	None	Larry Luchini	'78
WESTCORE: GNMA	Fixed Income	8.7	15.34	10,315.90	10,794.70	☆	8.5	303-623-2577	666-0367	4.50	None	None	Phil Diamond	'90
WESTCORE: INTMDT-TM BOND	Fixed Income	107.9	9.95	10,289.50	10,649.60	☆	8.5	303-623-2577	666-0367	4.50	None	None	O. James Barr	'89
WESTCORE: LONG-TERM BOND	Fixed Income	18.7	10.16	10,402.70	10,535.10	☆	9.1	303-623-2577	666-0367	4.50	None	None	O. James Barr	'88
WESTCORE: MIDCO GROWTH FD	Small-Company Growth	86.8	11.70	11,149.40	12,096.80	☆	1.5	303-623-2577	666-0367	4.50	None	None	Todger Anderson	'86
WESTCORE: MODERN VAL EQU	Growth	25.8	11.60	10,763.80	11,184.70	☆	3.7	303-623-2577	666-0367	4.50	None	None	Larry Luchini	'88
WESTCORE: SHORT-TERM BOND	Fixed Income	26.6	9.81	10,236.60	10,798.70	☆	8.1	303-623-2577	666-0367	2.00	None	None	Tom Stevens	'88
WESTCORE: SHORT-TERM GOVT	Fixed Income	9.1	15.15	10,342.40	10,824.50	☆	7.8	303-623-2577	666-0367	2.00	None	None	Phil Diamond	'90
WESTON: NEW CENTURY CAP	Flexible	42.6	11.05	10,770.00	11,219.90	☆	3.5	617-235-7055	244-7055	None	0.25	None	Doug Biggar	'89
WESTON: NEW CENTURY I	Mixed Income	20.7	10.69	10,621.80	10,757.00	☆	4.2	617-235-7055	244-7055	None	0.25	None	Doug Biggar	'89
WESTWOOD FUND	Capital Appreciation	55.9	14.09	10,158.60	11,013.50	☆	3.9	412-935-5520	645-6561	4.20	None	None	N/A	N/A
WEXFORD TR: MUHLENKAMP FD	Flexible	1.3	11.39	10,526.60	10,725.50	☆	1.9	None	None	None	None	None	Ronald Muhlenkamp	'88
WILLIAM PENN: QUALITY INC	Fixed Income	1.6	9.53	10,394.50	10,536.40	☆	8.8	800-222-7506	523-8440	4.75	None	None	James Jordan Jr.	'89
WILLIAM PENN: US GOVT	Fixed Income	1.2	10.02	10,403.40	10,754.00	☆	8.0	800-222-7506	523-8440	4.75	None	None	James Jordan Jr.	'89
WINDSOR FUND★	Growth & Income	7,936.6	12.88	10,136.50	9,902.70	19,473.40	5.6	None	662-7447	N/A	N/A	N/A	John Neff	'58
WINDSOR II	Growth & Income	2,510.0	14.29	10,140.80	10,491.80	20,101.50	5.1	None	662-7447	None	None	None	J. Barrow/W. Starke	'85/'87
WINTHROP FOCJS: FIX INC	Fixed Income	9.9	9.56	10,323.60	10,742.00	☆	8.6	212-504-4000	521-3036	None	0.088	4.00	Catherine Jameson	'86
WINTHROP FOCJS: GROWTH	Growth	51.8	10.97	10,489.70	11,448.00	☆	2.1	212-504-4000	521-3036	None	None	4.00	Gary Haubold	'89
WPG FUND	Capital Appreciation	37.1	23.24	10,719.60	11,370.90	19,466.50	1.0	212-908-9582	223-3332	None	None	None	Gerald Levine	'85

★VANGUARD HIGH-YIELD STOCK—Closed to new investors.
★WELLS FARGO FUNDS—Limited to the bank's retirement accounts.
★WINDSOR FUND—Closed.

PERFORMANCE OF MUTUAL FUNDS (continued)

FUND NAME	OBJECTIVE	TOTAL NET ASSETS (MIL) 6/30/90	NET ASSET VALUE 6/30/90	PERFORMANCE (Return on Initial $10,000 Investment) 3/31/90-6/30/90	6/30/89-6/30/90	6/30/85-6/30/90	DIVIDEND YIELD % 6/90	PHONE NUMBER 800	In-State	FEES Load	12b-1	Redemption	MANAGER	SINCE
WPG FUNDS TR: DVD INCOME	Equity Income	8.9	11.09	10,127.90	10,281.70	☆	6.5	223-3332	212-908-9582	None	None	None	Nelson Schaenen	'90
WPG FUNDS TR: GOVT SEC	Fixed Income	105.4	10.04	10,319.90	10,768.70	☆	8.3	223-3332	212-908-9582	None	None	None	David Hoyle	'86
WPG GROWTH	Small-Company Growth	143.2	120.09	10,824.80	11,829.60	☆	0.5	223-3332	212-908-9582	None	None	None	Melville Straus	'86
WPG INTERNATIONAL	International	15.6	10.93	11,244.90	11,121.00	☆	0.0	223-3332	212-908-9582	None	None	None	Peter Kysel	'89
WPG TUDOR FUND	Capital Appreciation	203.0	24.36	10,688.90	11,849.10	20,055.10	0.6	223-3332	212-908-9582	None	None	None	Melville Straus	'73
WRIGHT BD: CURRENT INCOME★	Fixed Income	13.7	9.99	10,366.50	10,855.00	16,405.60	8.6	232-0013	203-333-6666	None	0.20	None	In-house Investmnt Comm.	'87
WRIGHT BD: GOV OBLIGATION★	Fixed Income	55.0	11.84	10,417.00	10,420.50	15,083.60	7.7	232-0013	203-333-6666	None	0.20	None	In-house Investmnt Comm.	'83
WRIGHT BD: NEAR TERM★	Fixed Income	227.3	10.13	10,293.70	10,676.70	16,062.30	8.9	232-0013	203-333-6666	None	0.20	None	In-house Investmnt Comm.	'83
WRIGHT BD: TOTAL RETURN★	Fixed Income	104.9	11.63	10,393.80	10,523.10	☆	7.6	232-0013	203-333-6666	None	0.20	None	In-house Investmnt Comm.	'83
WRIGHT EQ: INTL BLUE CHIP★	International	17.7	10.60	11,136.10	☆	☆	0.0	232-0013	203-333-6666	None	0.20	None	In-house Investmnt Comm.	'89
WRIGHT EQ: JR BLUE CHIP★	Small-Company Growth	76.5	12.96	10,501.20	10,491.80	14,937.30	1.0	232-0013	203-333-6666	None	0.20	None	In-house Investmnt Comm.	'85
WRIGHT EQ: QUAL CORE EQU★	Growth & Income	53.5	11.59	10,768.10	11,159.30	☆	1.7	232-0013	203-333-6666	None	0.20	None	In-house Investmnt Comm.	'85
WRIGHT EQ: SEL BLUE CHIP★	Growth & Income	121.7	15.31	10,732.40	11,057.00	19,042.80	2.0	232-0013	203-333-6666	None	0.20	None	In-house Investmnt Comm.	'83
YAMAICH FDS: GLOBAL FD	Global	81.7	9.18	10,762.00	10,438.30	☆	0.0	257-0228	212-912-6400	4.75	0.40	None	Edward Burke	'89
ZWEIG SR TR: GOVT SEC	Fixed Income	110.9	9.25	10,161.70	10,157.90	13,261.70	8.0	272-2700	212-635-9800	4.75	0.30	None	Bruce Trottier	'88
ZWEIG SR TR: PRIORITY	Capital Appreciation	48.4	10.93	10,780.50	12,057.30	☆	1.7	272-2700	212-635-9800	5.50	0.30	None	Ned Davis	'85
ZWEIG SR TR: STRATEGY	Capital Appreciation	324.6	11.18	10,323.50	☆	☆	0.0	272-2700	212-635-9800	5.50	0.30	None	David Catzen	'89

Benchmarks

Objective	3/31/90-6/30/90	6/30/89-6/30/90	6/30/85-6/30/90
Growth & Income Funds	$10,473.23	$11,065.13	$19,184.20
Fixed-Income Funds	10,318.98	10,410.23	14,933.98
Small-Company Growth Funds	10,751.40	11,282.84	17,241.57
Gold Funds	8,972.61	10,056.91	14,248.05
Global Funds	10,744.82	11,718.61	23,710.40

How a $10,000 investment would have fared in the average fund.

BARRON'S / LIPPER GAUGE

Municipal Bond Funds

Unlike the equity-fund ratings, the municipal-bond fund listings do not show how $10,000 would have grown or declined over specific periods. Although the presentation is different, the information—total return for one quarter, one year and five years—is equivalent.

Short (1-5 Yr) Municipal Bond Funds (SIB)

TNA 6/30/90 (MIL$)	INVESTMENT COMPANY	LOAD	CLOSING NAV 6/30/90	% Chg. 3/31/90 TO 6/30/90	% Chg. 6/30/89 TO 6/30/90	RANK	% Chg. 6/30/85 TO 6/30/90	RANK
227.7	VANGUARD MUNI:LIMITED-TM	NO	10.19	1.99	7.09	1	☆	☆
140.1	FEDERATED SH-INTMDT MUNI	NO	10.14	1.61	6.54	12	31.51	10
722.5	VANGUARD MUNI:SHORT-TM	NO	15.36	1.75	6.54	5	33.15	7
131.4	CALVERT TX-FR RSVS:LTD		10.61	1.74	6.50	3	35.86	4
216.6	LTD TERM MUNI:NATL PORT		12.74	1.87	6.48	3	45.10	1
20.0	FLAGSHIP TX EX:LTD TERM		9.94	1.87	6.45	5	☆	☆
66.8	DREYFUS SH-INT TX EX BD	NO	12.53	1.72	6.35	7	☆	☆
5.2	MUNI FD TEMP:SHORT-TERM	NO	10.03	1.58	6.33	8	☆	☆
74.0	SCUDDER TX FR TGT 1993	NO	10.57	1.69	6.33	8	40.97	2
56.6	FIDELITY SH-TERM TX FREE	NO	9.45	1.25	6.25	16	☆	☆
352.0	MERRILL MUN BD:LTD MAT		9.71	1.67	6.16	11	31.89	9
219.8	T ROWE PRICE TX FR SH-IN	NO	5.08	1.64	5.99	12	32.43	8
19.2	WES'CORE: SH-INTMDT TX-EX		15.07	1.76	5.95	4	N/A	N/A
92.9	AARF INS TX FR-SHORT TM	NO	15.16	1.64	5.82	10	30.14	11
45.8	SCUDDER TX FR TGT 1990	NO	10.44	1.36	5.81	15	34.77	5
17.8	BABSON TX-FR INC:SHORT	NO	10.44	1.45	5.78	14	37.33	3
298.0	USAA TA EX:SHORT-TERM	NO	10.33	1.03	5.65	17	33.82	6
0.0	MUNICIPAL LEASE SEC		N/A	N/A	N/A	N/A	N/A	N/A
20.4	MUNI BOND:LTD TERM PORT		6.33	2.56	7.84	2	☆	☆
24.7	BEN-HAM NATL TX-FR:INT-TM	NO	10.07	2.46	7.03	4	45.16	1
99.0	STEINROE TX-EX:INTMDT	NO	10.54	2.39	6.94	5	☆	☆
5.4	FIRST'PRAIRIE TX EX:INT		11.63	2.00	6.82	3	☆	☆
13.6	N & B MUNI SECURITIES		10.14	2.30	6.75	7	☆	☆
1231.9	VANGUARD MUNI:INTMDT-TM	NO	12.04	2.31	6.73	6	55.79	1
188.5	BEN-AM CA TX FR:INTMDT	NO	10.19	2.14	6.56	11	38.99	7
96.1	FEDERATED INTMDT MUN TR	NO	9.86	1.84	6.37	23	☆	☆
1114.2	DREYFUS INTER TX EX BOND	NO	13.43	1.91	6.35	19	49.12	2
37.8	SCUDDER TX FR TGT 1996	NO	10.82	1.95	6.35	16	☆	☆
5.9	AIM TAX FREE:INTMDT	NO	9.93	1.99	6.32	11	☆	☆
15.9	MIDWEST GR TX FR:INTMDT		10.05	1.78	6.30	26	30.58	12

Municipal Bond Funds

TNA 6/30/90 (MIL$)	INVESTMENT COMPANY	LOAD	CLOSING NAV 6/30/90	% Chg. 3/31/90 TO 6/30/90	% Chg. 6/30/89 TO 6/30/90	RANK	% Chg. 6/30/85 TO 6/30/90	RANK
12.4	MUNI FD CAL:INTERMEDIATE	NO	10.06	1.89	6.23	21	☆	13
8.0	ALPINE:NATL MUNI ASSET	NO	9.69	1.05	6.22	33	☆	14
496.7	USAA TA EX:INTRMDT-TERM	NO	11.88	1.83	6.18	25	46.53	15
36.3	MUNI FD TEMP:INTMDT MUNI	NO	10.09	1.73	6.12	28	33.71	16
11.3	ST CLAIR TX-FR:INTMDT	NO	9.86	1.77	6.03	27	☆	17
0.1	TX-FR INV:INT INSTL SHS		9.93	1.93	6.02	18	☆	18
117.4	FIDELITY TX EX LTD TERM	NO	10.55	1.61	5.93	19	☆	19
20.1	ALPINE:CA MUNI ASSET		9.90	1.93	5.93	29	☆	20
89.8	UST MASTER TX-EX:INTMDT		8.69	1.83	5.84	24	☆	21
48.3	PRU-BACHE MUN:MOD-TM:B		10.20	1.88	5.80	22	☆	22
2.1	MERRILL MUNI SRS:INC:A		9.33	2.50	5.76	21	☆	23
166.0	S BERNSTEIN:DIV MUNI		12.57	1.96	5.68	23	☆	24
23.2	TWENTIETH CENT:TX-EX INT	NO	96.42	1.59	5.58	15	47.80	25
430.8	FIDELITY LTD TERM MUNI	NO	9.21	1.43	5.55	32	☆	26
32.3	ZWEIG TX-FR: LTD TERM		10.23	1.59	5.51	31	40.59	6
118.9	MERRILL MUNI SRS:INC: B		9.33	2.18	5.38	20	☆	28
100.4	PARKSTONE: MUNI BOND FUND	NO	10.03	1.90	4.57	29	☆	29
7.5	FUND FOR T F INV:INTMD		10.14	1.93	4.18	17	37.34	8
0.3	PRU-BACHE MUN:MOD-TM:A	NO	9.82	2.60	☆	1	#	☆
17.9	ALTURA:TX-FR INCOME		10.20	2.00	☆	12	☆	☆
4.2	COMPASS CAPITAL:MUNI BD	NO	10.01	2.22	☆	9	☆	☆

GENERAL MUNICIPAL BOND FUNDS (GM)

TNA 6/30/90 (MIL$)	INVESTMENT COMPANY	LOAD	CLOSING NAV 6/30/90	% Chg. 3/31/90 TO 6/30/90	% Chg. 6/30/89 TO 6/30/90	RANK	% Chg. 6/30/85 TO 6/30/90	RANK
30.1	SIT "NEW BEGIN": TAX-FREE	NO	9.61	1.78	7.53	101	☆	1
123.4	PREMIER TAX EX BOND		13.05	2.50	6.85	25	☆	2
51.0	FLAGSHIP TX EX:ALL-AMER		9.79	2.61	6.70	11	☆	3
19.3	PHOENIX MULTI:TX-EX BOND		10.28	1.87	6.63	6	☆	4
181.7	ALLIANCE MUN INC:NAT		9.57	1.99	6.51	81	☆	5
172.6	MUNI BOND:NATL PORT		12.38	3.09	6.50	6	63.92	12
124.3	STATE FARM MUNICIPAL	NO	7.90	2.37	6.50	39	67.24	4
584.2	STEINROE TX-EX:MGD MUNI	NO	8.71	2.27	6.25	51	☆	8
35.0	UST MASTER TX-EX:LONG		8.94	2.88	6.21	3	☆	9
1294.3	NUVEEN MUNICIPAL BOND		8.79	2.30	6.15	44	63.02	14
185.9	GENERAL TAX EXEMPT BOND	NO	13.93	2.57	6.06	11	56.34	34
54.1	STATE BD TX EXEMPT FUND		10.39	2.15	5.95	66	56.72	32
3758.9	DREYFUS TAX EXEMPT BOND	NO	12.38	2.15	5.94	65	55.12	38
3995.4	FRANKLIN FED TX FREE INC	NO	11.31	2.46	5.93	14	57.99	30
29.3	LIBERTY ADV:TX-FR BOND		9.60	2.54	5.93	19	☆	15
337.3	PAINEWBR TAX EX INC	NO	11.09	2.25	5.93	16	58.21	28
302.0	SAFECO MUNICIPAL BOND	NO	12.79	2.52	5.90	17	64.96	8

*Copyright Lipper Analytical Services, Inc.

PERFORMANCE OF MUTUAL FUNDS (continued)

TNA 6/30/90 (MILS.$)	INVESTMENT COMPANY	LOAD	CLOSING NAV 6/30/90	% Chg 3/31/90 TO 6/30/90	RANK	% Chg 6/30/89 TO 6/30/90	RANK	% Chg 6/30/85 TO 6/30/90	RANK
80.1	EATON VANCE MUNI BOND LP		9.14	2.41	36	5.88	18	63.92	11
321.7	LORD ABBETT TX-FR:NATL		10.92	2.45	32	5.83	19	62.48	16
357.6	MUTUAL OF OMAHA TAX-FREE		11.39	2.58	14	5.80	20	69.27	1
1267.9	USAA TX-EX:HIGH YLD FUND		13.06	2.21	60	5.78	21	57.78	31
5.1	MUNI FD TEMP:LONG	NO	10.20	1.80	98	5.77	22		☆
27.2	KIDDER PEABODY TX-FR:NAT	NO	15.56	2.32	97	5.76	23		☆
21.1	MIDAMERICA TAX EX BOND FD		11.26	2.27	85	5.76	24	52.18	46
94.3	NATIONAL SEC TAX EXEMPT LT		9.95	2.27	85	5.75	25	62.32	17
695.9	VANGUARD MUNI:LONG-TM	NO	10.36	2.46	30	5.69	26	61.36	20
69.5	PRINCIPAL PRES:TAX-EX		8.12	1.28	107	5.68	27	22.77	54
84.8	AAL FUNDS:MUNICIPAL BOND		9.90	2.43	35	5.67	28		☆
277.1	VALUE LINE TX EX:HI YLD		10.18	2.02	78	5.66	29	50.97	47
1434.9	SLH MANAGED MUNI		14.97	2.29	48	5.65	30	61.27	21
363.1	LUTHERAN BOR MUNI BOND		8.17	2.45	33	5.62	31	61.63	19
1715.9	COLONIAL TAX-EXEMPT		12.89	2.11	69	5.59	32	53.91	40
1068.9	FIDELITY MUNICIPAL BOND	NO	8.09	2.45	31	5.57	33	59.13	26
86.0	NATIONWIDE TAX FREE	NO	9.44	2.29	45	5.57	34		☆
105.7	COMPOSITE TAX-EXEMPT BD	NO	7.11	2.54	18	5.55	35	53.07	42
30.0	ADVANCE AMER:TX-FR INC		9.71	2.12	68	5.54	36		☆
1060.5	IDS TAX-EXEMPT BOND		3.93	2.68	7	5.51	37	59.56	24
245.8	AMER CAP MUNI BOND		18.74	2.40	38	5.50	38	53.33	41
152.5	KEYSTONE AMER:TX FR IN R		10.00	1.92	89	5.48	39		☆
20.0	FIRST TR TX-FR:INCOME SR		13.78	2.60	13	5.47	40		☆
33.8	COMMON SENSE:MUNI BOND		12.36	2.22	56	5.44	41		☆
2084.8	KEMPER MUNICIPAL BOND		9.61	2.46	28	5.43	42	62.76	15
31.7	PIONEER MUNICIPAL BOND		9.58	2.36	46	5.42	43		☆
4.8	UNIFIED MUNI:GENERAL		8.61	1.96	86	5.36	44		☆
507.0	FEDERATED TX-FR INCOME	NO	10.51	2.11	71	5.34	45	59.91	23
39.4	AMEV TAX FREE:NATIONAL		9.84	2.04	73	5.32	46		☆
43.1	BENHAM NATL TX-FR:LNG-TM		10.90	2.53	20	5.32	47	48.88	49
36.2	PIPER JAFFRAY:NATL TX-EX		10.09	2.21	59	5.32	48		☆
0.5	SECURAL:MUNICIPAL BOND		10.08	1.64	103	5.31	49		☆
3.8	VISTA FDS:TX FREE INCOME	NO	10.52	2.21	61	5.31	50	56.25	35
697.2	SCUDDER MGD MUNI BOND	NO	8.36	2.01	79	5.29	51		☆
132.4	FREEDOM INV:MGD TAX EX	NO	10.77	2.70	6	5.28	52		☆
11.9	LEAHI TAX FREE INCOME TR		12.48	1.93	87	5.28	53	55.14	37
27.3	PROVIDENTMUT TX-FR BOND		9.03	2.29	47	5.28	54	52.62	45
15.0	CONTRY CAPITAL TX EX BD		8.32	1.88	91	5.24	55	58.86	27
239.0	OPPENHEIMER TAX-FREE:BD		9.32	2.02	77	5.23	56	62.26	18
1026.3	DEAN WITTER TAX EXEMPT		11.09	2.28	49	5.22	57	56.45	33
542.3	TAX EXEMPT BD FD AMERICA		10.97	2.46	29	5.21	58		☆
1.2	MAIN STREET FDS:TX FR IN		10.52	1.84	95	5.20	59		☆
4.7	ARCH TX-EX TR:LG-TM PORT		10.56	2.33	42	5.18	60		☆
379.9	J HANCOCK TAX-EXEMPT RR		10.62	2.22	54	5.17	61	63.22	13
653.0	UNITED MUNICIPAL BOND		6.85	1.45	106	5.14	62	68.93	2
11.5	ZWEIG TX-FR:LONG-TERM	NO	9.29	2.65	9	5.11	63		☆
179.1	FINANCIAL TX-FR INCOME	NO	14.90	1.56	104	5.09	64	68.55	3
10.2	LEXINGTON TAX EXEMPT BD	NO	10.07	1.87	92	5.07	65		☆
20.4	BULL&BEAR TAX-FR INCOME		17.01	1.87	92	5.07	66	59.29	25
258.8	CIGNA:MUNICIPAL BOND		7.69	2.72	5	5.07	67	64.08	10
143.0	NEW ENG:TX EX INCOME FD		7.13	2.24	53	5.07	68	58.10	29
15.0	BOSTON CO TX-FR:BOND	NO	11.44	2.03	74	5.04	69		☆

TNA 6/30/90 (MILS.$)	INVESTMENT COMPANY	LOAD	CLOSING NAV 6/30/90	% Chg 3/31/90 TO 6/30/90	RANK	% Chg 6/30/89 TO 6/30/90	RANK	% Chg 6/30/85 TO 6/30/90	RANK
727.0	AARP INS TX-FR:GEN BOND	NO	16.50	2.31	5	5.24	14	51.20	7
186.3	FIDELITY INSURED TX FR	NO	10.96	2.00	18	5.19	15	61.22	2
647.7	VANKAMP MERR INS TX FREE		17.51	1.29	24	5.19	16	52.98	6
1108.9	FIRST INV INSURED TAX EX		9.92	1.78	6	5.12	17	40.29	10
6.3	WRIGHT BD:INSURED TX FR		10.77	2.39	4	5.11	18		☆
532.4	PRU-BACHE MUN:INSURE;B	NO	10.53	2.19	14	4.99	19		☆
408.6	KIDDER MUNI:INS;B	NO	7.86	2.23	12	4.98	20		☆
305.0	PUTNAM TAX-FR INC:INS	NO	14.10	1.85	19	4.86	21		☆
17.5	PRINCIPAL PRES:INS TX-EX		9.72	1.64	23	4.51	22		☆
21.2	TRANSAM TAX FREE:INCOME		10.07	1.50	23	4.12	23	45.95	9
3.6	PRU-BACHE MUN:INSURE;A		10.53	2.29	7		#		#
17.7	PLYMOUTH HIGH INC MUNI		10.82	2.31	9	9.35	1		☆
200.6	PUTNAM TX-EX:HI INCOME		8.46	1.99	17	7.80	3	68.67	1
310.4	STEINROE TX-EX:HI YLD	NO	11.78	2.62	2	7.64	4		☆
191.2	UNITED MUN HIGH INCOME		4.94	2.40	5	7.22	5		☆
468.3	T ROWE PRICE TX FR HI YD	NO	11.35	2.31	10	6.65	6	65.67	3
224.7	AMER CAP TAX-EX:HI YLD		10.77	1.97	19	6.40	7		☆
1652.8	FRANKLIN TX-FR:HI YD INC		10.51	2.52	3	6.15	8		☆
35.7	CARNEGIE TX EX:NATL HIYD		9.54	1.87	21	6.11	8		☆
1716.4	FIDELITY HI YIELD TX-FR	NO	12.30	1.99	16	6.04	9	59.65	6
81.1	VENTURE MUN (+) PLUS		9.48	1.55	24	6.03	10	49.02	8
87.6	FORTRESS HI YLD MUN FD		10.09	1.91	20	5.84	11		☆
545.8	FIDELITY AGGRESSIVE TX	NO	11.39	1.80	22	5.66	12		☆
665.6	PRU-BACHE MUN:HI YLD;B	NO	10.53	2.06	14	5.60	13		☆
1365.5	MERRILL MUNI:HI YLD;A		10.12	2.33	8	5.53	14		☆
4610.7	IDS HIGH YLD TAX-EXEMPT		4.47	2.36	6	5.39	15	59.58	5
120.5	SCUDDER HIGH YLD TX FREE	NO	11.18	2.37	5	5.32	16	62.33	4
683.3	MFS MGD HIGH YLD MUN		9.34	1.61	23	5.26	17	52.53	8
640.3	VANKAMP MERR TX FR HIGH		16.00	0.66	27	5.24	18	67.05	2
989.2	VANGUARD MUNI:HIGH YIELD	NO	10.10	2.66	1	5.19	19	64.05	4
65.7	PAINEWBR CLASSIC:HI YLD		9.94	2.17	11	5.11	20		☆
34.7	TRANSAM SPEC:HI YLD TX		9.23	1.99	18	4.96	21		☆
40.3	GIT TAX-FREE:HIGH YIELD	NO	10.59	2.35	7	4.77	22	47.61	10
179.4	MERRILL MUNI:HI YLD;B	NO	10.11	2.04	15	4.73	23		☆
641.3	PUTNAM TX-FR INC:HI YD		13.81	1.37	26	3.87	24		☆
46.3	COLONIAL VIP:HIGH MUNI	NO	9.84	2.10	13	3.79	25		☆
1067.7	EATON VANCE HI YLD MUN	NO	9.33	1.40	25	3.57	26		☆
13.7	OLYMPUS TX EX:HI YLD	NO	7.56	0.46	28	1.80	27		☆
1.5	FUNDAMENTAL:HI YLD MUNI		7.54	-0.34	29	-5.47	28		#
8.7	PRU-BACHE MUN:HI YLD;A		10.53	2.15	12		#		#

ARIZONA MUNICIPAL BOND FUNDS (AZ)

TNA 6/30/90 (MILS.$)	INVESTMENT COMPANY	LOAD	CLOSING NAV 6/30/90	% Chg 3/31/90 TO 6/30/90	RANK	% Chg 6/30/89 TO 6/30/90	RANK	% Chg 6/30/85 TO 6/30/90	RANK
273.7	FRANKLIN TX-FR:AZ INC		10.52	2.53	2	5.94	1		☆
18.9	SLH MUNI:AZ		9.56	2.70	1	5.87	2		☆
121.0	TX-FREE TR OF AZ		9.77	2.11	7	5.83	3		☆
61.3	PRU-BACHE MUNI SR:AZ;B	NO	10.99	2.33	5	5.47	4	47.76	1
31.9	FLAGSHIP TX-EX:AZ DOUBLE		9.62	2.22	6	4.90	5		☆
0.4	PRU-BACHE MUNI SR:AZ;A		10.99	2.43	4		#		#
2.8	GIT TAX-FREE:AZ	NO	9.86	2.49	3		☆		#

INVMNT SRS: MUNI BOND

Assets	Fund	NO	NAV	%A	Rk A	%B	Rk B	%C	Rk C
6.3	INVMNT SRS: MUNI BOND		10.71	2.51	22	5.03	70	☆	51
1127.5	T ROWE PRICE TX-FR INC		8.67	2.35	40	5.02	71	47.98	7
20.4	ENTERPRISE:TAX-EX INCOME		12.76	2.22	57	4.91	72	65.04	52
1343.7	PUTNAM TX EX INCOME FUND	NO	8.57	2.51	23	4.80	73	43.78	7
20.7	SECURITY TX EXEMPT FUND		9.50	2.23	55	4.79	74	61.26	22
1395.7	MFS MANAGED MUNI BOND	NO	10.26	2.56	26	4.79	75	☆	☆
24.9	TWENTIETH CENT:TX-EX LNG		9.59	1.89	17	4.77	76	☆	☆
12.9	MACKENZIE IND:NATL MUNI		10.83	2.75	4	4.76	77	☆	☆
3.7	CHUBB INV:TAX EXEMPT FD		7.70	2.61	12	4.68	78	64.49	9
138.6	SELIGMAN TAX-EX:NATL		10.16	2.50	24	4.61	79	☆	☆
26.0	MASSMUTUAL FDS:TX-EX BD	NO	8.63	2.33	41	4.60	80	54.15	81
277	BABSON TX-FR INC:LONG	NO	9.86	1.93	88	4.60	81	☆	☆
3.7	VOYAGEUR GRANIT INS TX		7.90	2.13	67	4.58	82	55.51	36
871.1	KEYSTONE TAX FREE FUND	NO	11.01	2.18	62	4.55	83	☆	☆
44.8	PRINCOR TAX EX BOND		11.35	2.16	63	4.53	84	65.51	50
797.2	ELFUN:TAX-EX INCOME FUND		10.21	2.56	16	4.48	85	48.75	☆
44.9	CALVERT TX-FR RSVS:LONG	NO	7.31	1.78	100	4.37	86	☆	☆
1.2	RBB:SA-EGUARD:TX-FR		10.16	2.67	64	4.33	87	☆	☆
78.8	METLIFE SS TAX-EX:TX-EX	NO	16.84	1.68	8	4.33	88	52.76	44
1.5	FINL HRZNS:MUNI BOND R	NO	11.11	1.84	102	4.32	89	☆	☆
567.5	SLH INCOME:TX EX INC		8.29	1.52	96	4.29	90	☆	☆
8.4	US TAX-FREE FUND		10.05	2.11	105	4.25	91	50.38	48
369.7	MFS LIFETIME MGD MUNI	NO	14.97	2.41	70	4.24	92	☆	☆
26.1	EQUITABLE:TAX EX		10.72	1.84	37	4.19	94	52.95	43
951.0	PRU-BACHE NAT MUN IN:B	NO	12.12	1.97	94	4.17	96	☆	☆
594.4	KEYSTONE TAX EXEMPT TR	NO	11.16	2.06	83	4.14	97	65.73	5
1.7	AMEX:TAX FREE MUNI BOND		11.32	1.99	80	3.96	98	☆	☆
56.0	SEARS TX EX REINVESTMENT	NO	9.17	0.96	72	3.58	99	42.54	53
51.8	THOMSON MCKINNON:TX EX	NO	9.60	2.02	82	2.88	100		
614.0	DEL GR TX-FR:USA		10.08	1.78	108	2.37	101		
21.7	STRONG MUNICIPAL BOND	NO	9.91	2.62	76	2.50	102		
131.4	MACKAY-SHIELDS:TX FR BD	NO	10.06	2.03	99	#	#		
10.4	FUND FOR T F INV:LONG	NO	10.06	#	10	#	#		
1.7	ATLAS:TX FR INCOME		9.91	2.44	75	#	#		
19.1	MGD MUNI FD:CJ LAWRENCE		14.96	3.24	34	#	#		
4.1	PNC:TAX-FREE INCOME		20.00	1.96	1	#	#		
1.1	PRU BACHE NAT MUNI IN:A		6.90	1.96	85	☆	☆		
16.6	TRANSAM TAX FREE:BOND		N/A	N/A	84	N/A	N/A		
3.3	TRIUMPH:TX-FR INCOME		N/A	N/A	N/A	N/A	N/A		
9.9	HOME:NATL TAX-FREE FUND	NO							
0.0	FORUM:TAXSAVER BOND								
0.0	PIERPONT TAX EXEMPT BOND								

INSURED MUNICIPAL BOND FUNDS (MBI)

Assets	Fund	NO	NAV	%A	Rk A	%B	Rk B	%C	Rk C
90.5	SUNAMERICA TX-FR:STRIPES		12.28	1.70	21	7.00	1	☆	☆
133.3	IDS INSURED TAX EXEMPT		4.96	2.44	3	5.75	2	57.29	3
132.4	NUVEEN INS TX-FR BD:NATL		9.49	2.07	17	5.74	3	62.72	4
15.5	FIRST TF TX-FR:INSURED		15.52	2.68	1	5.70	4	57.04	1
131.0	COLONIAL TAX-EX:INSURED		7.62	2.10	16	5.66	5	☆	☆
2019.2	MERRILL MUNI:INS:A		7.86	2.29	6	5.65	6	☆	☆
1124.7	VANGUARD MUNI:INS LG-TM	NO	11.52	2.56	8	5.65	7	55.54	5
26.8	DEL GR TX-FR:USA INSURED		10.64	2.27	10	5.62	8	☆	☆
1.2	FIRST PRAIRIE TX EX:INS		11.77	2.26	9	5.59	10	☆	☆
754.4	FRANKLIN TX-FR:INS		11.24	2.27	15	5.45	11	☆	☆
115.6	ALLIANCE MUN INC:INS NAT	NO	9.43	2.10	11	5.34	12	50.68	8
39.4	AMER CAP TAX-EX:INSURED		10.82	2.25	13	5.31	13	☆	☆
196.8	DREYFUS INS TAX EX BOND	NO	17.45	2.22					

CALIFORNIA MUNICIPAL BOND FUNDS (CA)

Assets	Fund	NO	NAV	%A	Rk A	%B	Rk B	%C	Rk C
106.5	PREMIER CAL TX EX BOND		12.19	2.87	2	7.12	1	☆	☆
48.3	BENHAM CA TX-FR:HIGH YLD		8.72	2.59	5	6.96	2	☆	☆
73.3	OPPENHEIMER CAL TX-EN FD	NO	9.82	2.27	29	6.66	3	☆	☆
12.4	ASSOC PLANRS:CA TAX-FREE		9.49	2.30	25	6.63	4	☆	☆
134.8	ALLIANCE MUN INC:CA		9.65	2.42	15	6.60	5	65.03	1
50.1	SELIGMAN CAL TX EX:HI Y.D		6.32	2.15	33	6.51	6	53.42	8
1091.7	FRANKLIN CAL TX FREE INC		6.96	2.93	1	6.49	7	☆	☆
26.4	LTD TERM MUNI:CA PORT		12.11	1.66	56	6.15	8	☆	☆
78.7	NUVEEN CA TX-FR:SPEC BD		9.79	2.40	17	6.14	9	☆	☆
97.6	OVERLAND EXP:CA TX-FR BD		10.27	2.08	39	6.12	10	☆	☆
86.0	CA INV TR:CA TX-FR INC		11.52	2.59	6	6.08	11	50.11	11
84.2	MUNI BOND:CA PORT		11.53	2.38	18	6.08	12	49.43	13
204.7	PAINEWBR CA TAX-EX INC		10.84	2.28	28	6.06	13	☆	14
104.2	PAC HZN:CA TAX EXEMPT		13.67	2.07	40	6.02	14	☆	☆
74.5	MFS MGD CA MUNI BD TRUST	NO	5.19	1.98	46	5.93	15	56.00	6
106.3	LORD ABBETT TX FR CA		10.35	2.36	22	5.87	16	☆	☆
306.6	FRANKLIN CAL INS TX FREE	NO	11.17	2.51	10	5.86	17	50.28	12
110.0	NATIONAL SEC CAL TAX EX	NO	12.85	2.09	38	5.86	18	57.45	5
28.3	MERRILL CA MUNI:BOND:A		11.23	2.15	32	5.83	19	56.43	4
206.2	COLONIAL CAL TX EX TRUST		6.95	1.80	53	5.73	20	☆	11
1506.2	DREYFUS CAL TAX EX BOND	NO	14.48	2.14	34	5.72	21	50.92	10
50.0	SAFECO CAL TX FR INCOME		11.10	2.47	12	5.72	22	☆	☆
328.0	VANGUARD CA TX-FR:INS LG	NO	15.64	2.22	31	5.69	23	61.41	9
8.7	EQU SIEBEL II:CA TX-EX		10.11	2.78	4	5.59	24	52.31	☆
522.3	FIDELITY CAL INS TX-EX	NO	9.10	2.28	27	5.58	25	52.50	15
10.4	BOSTON CO TX-FR:CA BOND		11.18	1.87	50	5.54	26	☆	7
1782.3	PUTNAM CALIF TAX EX INC	NO	12.06	1.70	55	5.51	27	☆	☆
628.6	DEAN WITTER CAL TX FR	NO	7.85	2.14	36	5.40	28	48.67	3
199.3	SCUDDER CAL TAX FREE	NO	11.97	2.36	21	5.37	29	55.38	☆
13.1	SUNAMERICA TX-FR:CA		10.35	2.44	13	5.37	30	☆	17
677.9	MERRILL CA MUNI:BOND:B		11.41	1.99	45	5.37	31	☆	☆
202.3	BENHAM CA TX-FR:LONG	NO	11.23	2.02	43	5.31	32	60.99	16
63.1	SELIGMAN CA TX-EX:QUAL	NO	10.66	2.36	20	5.29	33	☆	☆
13.4	J HANCOCK TX-EX SRS:CA		6.43	2.53	8	5.19	34	☆	☆
278.8	EATON VANCE CAL MUN TR	NO	10.94	2.30	26	5.15	35	☆	☆
719.2	KEMPER CAL TAX FREE INC		9.85	1.91	49	5.14	36	☆	☆
17.2	MACKENZIE IND:CA MUNI		7.09	2.37	19	5.14	37	44.10	☆
57.0	ALLIANCE MUN INC:INS CA		9.90	1.94	48	5.10	38	☆	☆
7.3	FIRST INV MULTI INS:CA		12.22	1.96	47	5.08	39	48.40	☆
142.2	IDS CAL TAX EXEMPT		10.59	2.01	44	5.02	40	☆	☆
50.6	NUVEEN CA TX-FR:INS BD	NO	4.89	2.06	41	5.00	41	☆	☆
72.1	T ROWE PRICE CA TX FR BD	NO	9.48	1.83	51	4.93	42	☆	☆
92.3	FIDELITY CAL TX FREE INS		9.41	2.25	30	4.88	43	☆	☆
83.1	TAX EXEMPT FUND OF CAL		9.60	1.82	52	4.63	44	☆	☆
58.1	BENHAM CA TX-FR:INSURED		14.19	2.44	14	4.61	45	☆	☆
48.7	VANKAMP MERR CAL INSURED	NO	9.19	2.31	23	4.52	46	☆	☆
178.8	PRU-BACHE CAL MUNI		15.42	1.56	57	4.52	47	☆	☆
26.8	OLYMPUS TX EX:CA		10.78	2.04	42	4.51	48	☆	☆
10.4	FUNDAMENTAL CAL MUNI	NO	7.46	1.41	58	4.16	49	☆	☆
7.9	ATLAS:CA DBL TX FR INC	NO	8.75	1.76	54	4.08	50	☆	☆
1.6	PRU-BACHE MUNI SR:CA-A		9.97	2.49	11	#	#	#	#
39.6	TRANSAM CA TX-EX:INCOME		10.78	2.14	35	#	#	#	#
151.2	FIDELITY SPARTAN CA HIYD	NO	9.80	2.31	24	#	#	#	#
77.6	GENERAL CA MUNI BOND	NO	10.03	2.42	16	#	#	☆	☆
			12.64	2.84	3				

PERFORMANCE OF MUTUAL FUNDS (continued)

TNA 6/30/90 (MIL.$)	INVESTMENT COMPANY	LOAD	CLOSING NAV 6/30/90	% Chg. 3/31/90 TO 6/30/90	RANK	% Chg. 6/30/89 TO 6/30/90	RANK	% Chg. 6/30/85 TO 6/30/90	RANK
93.0	GW SIERRA:CA MUNI INC	NO	10.01	2.11	37	☆	☆	☆	☆
6.0	METLIFE SS TAX-EX:CA		7.28	2.58	7	☆	☆	☆	☆
132.2	USAA TX EX:CA BOND	NO	9.83	2.53	9	☆	☆	☆	☆
	COLORADO MUNICIPAL BOND FUNDS (CO)								
74.6	TX FREE FUND OF CO		9.73	2.00	4	6.24	2	☆	☆
47.7	FRANKLIN TX-FR:CO INC		10.71	2.56	1	6.22	1	☆	☆
43.2	COLO DOUBLE TAX-EXEMPT		9.96	2.12	3	6.18	3	☆	☆
7.4	FLAGSHIP TX EX:CO DOUBLE		9.17	1.91	5	5.38	4	☆	☆
63.7	SELIGMAN TAX-EX:CO	NO	7.07	2.33	2	4.91	5	☆	☆
40.8	HANIFEN,IMHOFF COL BD TX		9.33	1.48	6	4.64	6	49.98	#
	GEORGIA MUNICIPAL BOND FUNDS (GA)								
19.3	FRANKLIN TX-FR:GA INC		10.90	2.47	2	6.56	1	☆	☆
5.6	CARNEGIE TX EX:GA INSURD		9.28	2.66	1	5.94	2	☆	☆
20.3	MFS MGD MULTI-ST MUNI:GA		9.77	2.26	3	5.79	3	☆	☆
18.7	SELIGMAN TAX-EX:GA	NO	7.32	2.22	4	5.10	4	☆	☆
21.2	PRU-BACHE MUNI SR:GA:B		11.23	1.88	7	4.82	5	☆	☆
36.2	FLAGSHIP TX EX:GA DOUBLE		9.69	2.21	5	4.35	6	☆	☆
0.1	PRU-BACHE MUNI SR:GA:A		11.23	1.98	6	#	#	#	#
	MARYLAND MUNICIPAL BOND FUNDS (MD)								
104.0	PREMIER STATE TX EX:MD		11.89	2.80	1	6.81	1	☆	☆
18.7	FRANKLIN TX-FR:MD INC		10.31	2.77	2	5.90	2	☆	☆
96.6	MFS MGD MULTI-ST MUNI:MD		10.85	2.27	4	5.76	3	52.21	1
231.9	T ROWE PRICE TX FR BD	NO	9.44	2.37	3	5.34	4	☆	☆
29.7	TAX EX FUND OF MD		14.04	2.24	5	5.32	5	☆	☆
49.3	PRU-BACHE MUNI SR:MD:B	NO	10.43	1.97	8	5.11	6	43.16	2
0.2	PRU-BACHE MUNI SR:MD:A		10.43	2.07	7	5.10	7	☆	#
	MASSACHUSETTS MUNICIPAL BOND FUNDS (MA)								
48.1	PREMIER STATE TX EX:MA	NO	10.94	2.27	3	5.93	1	52.43	1
713.0	FIDELITY MASS TX F HIYD		11.07	1.89	16	5.92	2	☆	☆
60.3	COLONIAL MASS TX EX TR		7.08	2.33	2	5.54	3	☆	☆
109.1	DREYFUS MASS TAX EX BOND	NO	15.48	2.04	11	5.52	4	45.76	5
217.1	MFS MGD MULTI-ST MUNI:MA		10.58	2.01	12	5.29	5	☆	☆
18.6	NUVEEN TX FR BD:MA		8.83	2.49	1	5.18	6	☆	☆
15.9	BOSTON CO TX-FR:MA BOND	NO	11.09	2.10	9	5.13	7	☆	☆
10.5	FIRST INV MULTI INS:MA		10.80	2.16	8	5.12	8	☆	☆
19.8	SLH MASSACHUSETTS MUNI		11.95	1.90	15	4.90	9	☆	☆
51.4	SCUDDER ST TX FR:MA	NO	12.31	2.26	4	4.75	10	47.12	4
131.1	FRANKLIN TX-FR:MA INSURD		10.68	1.90	14	4.68	11	☆	☆
75.7	PUTNAM MA TAX EX INC	NO	12.01	1.73	17	4.66	12	☆	☆
28.6	IDS MASSACHUSETTS TX EX		4.88	1.66	20	4.19	13	☆	☆
10.3	NUVEEN INS TX-FR BD:MA		9.13	1.68	19	4.19	14	☆	☆
119.0	SELIGMAN TAX-EX:MA		7.53	2.06	10	4.17	15	51.05	2
53.6	ITB:MASS TAX FREE INCOME		15.98	1.72	18	4.16	16	48.89	3

TNA 6/30/90 (MIL.$)	INVESTMENT COMPANY	LOAD	CLOSING NAV 6/30/90	% Chg. 3/31/90 TO 6/30/90	RANK	% Chg. 6/30/89 TO 6/30/90	RANK	% Chg. 6/30/85 TO 6/30/90	RANK
114.6	ALLIANCE MUN INC:NY	NO	8.96	2.04	38	6.39	3	☆	☆
86.2	GENERAL NY MUNI BOND	NO	18.33	2.61	16	6.24	4	41.51	16
4.0	BOSTON CO TX-FR:NY BOND	NO	11.88	1.75	44	5.82	5	☆	☆
94.4	DREYFUS NY INTER TX EX		16.47	1.60	47	5.67	6	☆	☆
28.3	MFS MGD MULTI-ST MUNI:NY		9.80	2.99	1	5.67	7	☆	☆
25.8	PAINEWBR MUNI:CLASSIC NY		9.72	2.64	14	5.61	8	☆	☆
165.9	KEMPER NY TAX FREE INC	NO	10.02	2.73	8	5.53	9	☆	☆
145.8	S BERNSTEIN:NY MUNI		12.59	1.83	41	5.48	10	☆	☆
7.5	MARINER MF TR:NY MGD BD		10.09	2.28	30	5.47	11	☆	☆
2948.4	FRANKLIN NY TAX FREE INC		10.91	2.22	32	5.42	12	58.12	3
37.8	NUVEEN TX FR BD:NY		9.45	2.90	2	5.31	13	☆	☆
182.1	LORD ABBETT TX-FR:NY		10.84	2.60	17	5.28	14	58.01	4
68.2	IDS NEW YORK TAX EXEMPT		4.80	2.72	10	5.23	15	☆	☆
216.4	FIDELITY NY TX-FR:INSURD	NO	10.80	2.00	39	5.21	16	☆	☆
243.0	OPPENHEIMER NY TX EX FD		11.83	2.30	29	5.10	17	53.64	7
19.7	COUNSELLORS NY MUNI BOND	NO	9.56	1.45	48	5.06	18	☆	☆
1684.1	DREYFUS NY TAX EX BOND	NO	14.71	2.15	35	5.06	19	49.31	11
214.3	VANGUARD NY INS TAX FR	NO	9.58	2.40	24	5.05	20	☆	☆
390.0	FIDELITY NY TX-FR:HI YLD		11.65	2.51	20	5.04	21	52.52	8
431.7	SLH NEW YORK MUNI		16.05	2.20	33	5.04	22	56.53	5
54.7	NUVEEN INS TX-FR BD:NY		9.22	1.97	40	5.03	23	☆	☆
27.3	PREMIER NY TX EX BOND		12.92	2.82	5	4.87	24	☆	☆
31.1	MUNI BOND:NY PORT		11.77	2.73	9	4.86	25	☆	☆
25.6	COLONIAL NY TX EX TR		6.61	2.57	19	4.83	26	☆	☆
60.7	EMPIRE BUILDER TX FR BD		16.92	2.66	13	4.79	27	51.54	9
14.6	MACKENZIE IND:NY MUNI		9.55	1.75	45	4.76	28	☆	☆
77.6	LANDMARK NY TX FR INCOME		9.89	2.48	21	4.66	29	☆	☆
8.5	MERRILL MULTI MUN:NY:A	NO	10.83	2.45	22	4.65	30	☆	☆
26.0	BIG E FDS:NY TX-FR INC		10.46	2.36	26	4.48	31	☆	☆
30.8	VALUE LINE NY TX EX TR	NO	9.62	2.35	27	4.47	32	☆	☆
134.7	T ROWE PRICE NY TX FR BD	NO	10.65	2.08	37	4.39	33	45.76	13
50.0	SELIGMAN TAX-EX:NY		9.66	2.58	18	4.36	34	☆	☆
78.7	VISTA FDS:NY TX FR INC		7.64	2.88	3	4.27	35	54.71	6
21.1	DREYFUS NY INS TX EX BD		10.55	2.19	34	4.26	36	☆	☆
82.8	MERRILL MULTI MUN:NY:B		10.60	1.81	42	4.23	37	☆	☆
594.9	J HANCOCK TX-EX SRS:NY		10.83	2.32	28	4.13	38	☆	☆
13.1	FIRST INV NY TAX FREE		10.90	2.69	12	4.04	39	☆	☆
155.4	PUTNAM NY TAX EXEMPT		13.64	1.63	46	4.01	40	48.87	12
1377.6	DEAN WITTER NY TX IN	NO	8.41	2.70	11	4.00	41	68.12	2
153.3	PRU-BACHE MUNI SR:NY:B		11.05	2.11	36	3.97	42	58.90	15
326.9	FUNDAMENTAL NY MUNI		10.77	2.27	31	3.60	43	43.74	14
234.8	OLYMPUS TX EX:NY		1.09	2.61	15	2.87	44	44.80	14
18.5	FIDELITY SPARTAN NY HIYD	NO	7.60	1.18	49	2.21	45	☆	☆
88.9	PRU-BACHE MUNI SR:NY:A		10.01	2.79	7	#	#	☆	☆
0.9	TRIUMPHNY TX-FR INCOME		10.77	2.37	25	#	#	#	#
3.8	METLIFE SS TAX-EX:NY		10.00	1.80	43	#	#	#	#
10.5	PREMIER STAT TX EX:OH		7.16	2.41	23	6.64	1	☆	☆
106.9	NUVEEN TX FR BD:OH		11.81	2.34	2	6.60	2	☆	☆
49.7	CARNEGIE TX EX:OH INSURD		9.49	2.65	1	6.03	3	☆	☆
16.7	NUVEEN TX FR BD:OH		8.88	2.73	4	5.94	4	☆	☆
29.8	SCUDDER ST TX FR:OH	NO	12.05	2.54	5	5.70	5	☆	☆
137.2	SELIGMAN TAX-EX:OH		7.77	2.04	13	5.94	4	59.39	1
5.4	FIRST INV MULTI INS:OH		10.88	2.15	10	5.57	6	☆	☆

Assets	NO	Fund								
53.0	NO	PRU-BACHE MUNI SR:MA:B	10.65	2.12	8	4.01	17	43.03	6	☆
10.2		J HANCOCK TX-EX SR:MA	10.84	1.98	13	3.64	18		#	#
0.2		PRU-BACHE MUNI SR:MA:A	10.65	2.21	6	*	*		*	*
19.9		PUTNAM MA TAX EX INC II	8.53	2.23	5	☆	☆		☆	☆

MICHIGAN MUNICIPAL BOND FUNDS (MI)

Assets	NO	Fund								
8.7		FIRST INV MULTI INS:MI	10.93	2.23	4	5.74	1			☆
454.2		FRANKLIN TX-FR:MI INSURD	11.10	2.63	1	5.52	2	54.34	1	☆
114.6		SELIGMAN TAX-EX:MI	8.10	2.36	2	5.48	3	61.56	2	☆
70.4		PREMIER STATE TX EX:MI	14.12	2.14	6	5.47	4			☆
105.8		FLAGSHIP MI TRIPLE TX EX	10.62	2.06	7	5.33	5			☆
21.0		COLONIAL MICH TX EX TR	6.51	1.88	9	5.05	6			☆
264.2	NO	FIDELITY MICHIGAN TX FR	10.90	1.47	12	4.43	7			☆
41.7		PUTNAM MI TAX EX INC	12.39	1.64	11	4.33	8			☆
50.5	NO	PRU-BACHE MUNI SR:MI:B	10.98	2.22	5	4.21	9	51.81	3	☆
29.2	NO	IDS MICHIGAN TX EXEMPT	4.96	1.64	10	4.16	10			☆
0.5		PRU-BACHE MUNI SR:MI:A	10.98	2.32	3	#	#		#	#
9.5		PUTNAM MI TAX EX INC II	8.45	1.99	8	☆	☆		☆	☆

MINNESOTA MUNICIPAL BOND FUNDS (MN)

Assets	NO	Fund								
54.6		PREMIER STATE TX EX:MN	14.03	2.38	3	6.53	1			☆
22.0		VOYAGEUR MN:INT:MDT TX FR	10.24	1.34	17	6.14	2			☆
2.9		FIRST INV MULTI INS:MN	10.58	2.26	4	6.03	3			☆
21.5		COLONIAL MN TX EX TR	6.87	1.86	12	6.02	4			☆
4.0	NO	PRIME VALU:MN MUNI BD	10.08	1.98	9	5.93	5			☆
12.8		VOYAGEUR MN:INSURED	9.60	1.36	16	5.74	6			☆
181.5		VOYAGEUR MN:TX FR	11.59	1.50	15	5.73	7	54.30	1	☆
16.4		SELIGMAN TAX-EX:MN	9.51	2.26	5	5.60	8	53.80	2	☆
13.5		CARNEGIE TX EX:MN INSURD	11.41	2.01	7	5.55	9			☆
252.3		FRANKLIN TX-FR:MN INSURD	10.13	2.38	1	5.50	10	53.24	3	☆
151.1	NO	STATE BD TX-FR INC:MN	10.40	1.68	13	5.48	11			☆
25.6		FIDELITY MINN TX FR	9.63	2.08	8	5.41	12			☆
61.5		AMEV TAX FREE:MINNESOTA	10.09	1.65	14	5.35	13			☆
181.2		PIPER JAFFRAY:MINN TX-EX	4.95	1.87	11	4.80	14			☆
24.4	NO	IDS MINNESOTA TAX EXEMPT	11.15	1.89	10	4.70	15			☆
30.2	NO	PRU-BACHE MUNI SR:MN:B	12.16	1.14	18	4.35	16	46.83	4	☆
0.1		PRU-BACHE MUNI SR:MN:A	11.15	1.99	6	4.29	17			☆
8.3		PUTNAM MN TAX EX INC II	8.44	1.12	19	☆	☆		☆	☆

NEW JERSEY MUNICIPAL BOND FUNDS (NJ)

Assets	NO	Fund								
300.7	NO	DREYFUS NJ TAX EX BOND	12.31	2.45	5	6.23	1			☆
42.6		SLH NEW JERSEY MUNI	12.02	2.61	3	6.18	2			☆
145.9		FRANKLIN TX-FR:NJ INC	10.66	2.43	7	5.48	3			☆
117.9		PRU-BACHE MUNI SR:NJ:B	10.34	2.51	4	5.45	4			☆
196.2	NO	FIDELITY:NJ TX-FR HI YLD	10.48	2.30	8	5.40	5			☆
189.5	NO	VANGUARD NJ TX-FR:INS LG	10.32	2.70	1	5.37	6			☆
53.6		SELIGMAN TAX-EX:NJ	7.19	2.44	10	5.30	7			☆
25.1		FIRST INV MULTI INS:NJ	11.67	2.26	9	5.01	8		#	#
3.2		PRU-BACHE MUNI SR:NJ:A	10.34	2.61	2	#	#		*	*
34.0		PUTNAM NJ TAX EX INC	8.51	2.27	6	☆	☆		☆	☆

NEW YORK STATE MUNICIPAL BOND FUNDS (NY)

Assets	NO	Fund								
155.6		ROCHESTER FD MUNICIPALS	16.32	2.87	4	8.39	1	73.92	1	☆
8.3		KIDDER PEABODY TX-FR:NY	15.12	2.80	6	6.49	2			☆

(OHIO municipal bond funds, continued)

Assets	NO	Fund								
235.2		FRANKLIN TX-FR:OH INSURD	11.22	2.71	2	5.56	7	53.31	2	☆
16.9		MIDWEST GR TX-FR:OH LONG	10.96	1.90	15	5.53	8	51.95	3	☆
32.3		COLONIAL OHIO TX EX TR	6.81	2.67	3	5.47	9			☆
219.0	NO	FIDELITY OH TX FR HI YLD	10.68	2.07	12	5.30	10			☆
234.5	NO	FLAGSHIP TX EX:OH DOUBLE	10.48	1.96	14	5.28	11	44.65	4	☆
90.9		PRU-BACHE MUNI SR:OH:B	10.86	2.11	11	4.69	12			☆
18.1		CARNEGIE TX EX:OH MUNI	9.08	2.20	8	4.64	13			☆
24.8		IDS OHIO TAX EXEMPT	4.94	2.48	6	4.63	14		#	#
101.6		PRU-BACHE MUNI SR:OH:A	12.25	1.81	16	4.55	15			☆
0.4		PRU-BACHE MUNI SR:OH:A	10.86	2.20	9	#	#			☆
8.5		PUTNAM OH TAX EX INC II	8.40	1.50	17	☆	☆		☆	☆

OREGON MUNICIPAL BOND FUNDS (OR)

Assets	NO	Fund								
19.2	NO	OREGON MUNICIPAL BOND	11.72	1.82	6	5.57	1			☆
32.5	NO	SELIGMAN TAX-EX:OR	7.12	2.68	1	5.37	2	49.29	2	☆
137.7		TX-FREE TR OF OR	9.81	2.18	5	5.25	3			☆
7.2	NO	WESTCORE:OREGON TX-EX FD	15.33	2.19	4	5.15	4			☆
89.8		FRANKLIN TX-FR:OR INC	10.60	2.37	2	5.11	5			☆
192.0		COLUMBIA:MUNI BOND	11.55	2.44	3	5.03	6	54.64	1	☆
11.2	NO	PRU-BACHE MUNI SR:OR:B	11.07	1.65	8	3.64	7	44.59	3	☆
0.1	NO	PRU-BACHE MUNI SR:OR:A	11.07	1.78	7			55.97	1	☆

VIRGINIA MUNICIPAL BOND FUNDS (VA)

Assets	NO	Fund								
252.6		MFS MGD MULTI-ST MUNI:VA	11.01	2.18	4	6.22	1	54.87	1	☆
5.4		FRANKLIN TX-FR:VA INC	10.63	2.48	2	6.06	2			☆
42.5		FLAGSHIP TX EX:VA DOUBLE	9.74	2.51	1	5.83	3			☆
33.2		TAX EX FUND OF VIRGINIA	14.41	2.37	3	5.54	4			☆
24.6	NO	GIT TAX-FREE:VIRGINIA	10.99	1.90	5	5.49	5			☆
82.8	NO	MARKETMASTER:VA MUNI:H	9.99	1.69	6	#	#			☆

ALL OTHER STATES MUNICIPAL BOND FUNDS (OTH)

Assets	NO	Fund								
17.7		OCEAN STATE TX EX FUND	9.95	1.96	8	10.95	1			☆
87.5		PREMIER STATE TX EX:FL	13.70	2.68	4	7.45	2			☆
12.8		FRANKLIN TX-FR:IN	10.83	3.05	1	7.41	3			☆
87.4		DUPREE:KY TX FR INCOME	6.77	1.98	5	7.19	4			☆
84.4		FRANKLIN TX-FR:P RCO INC	10.77	2.45	2	6.87	5			☆
50.1	NO	CHURCHILL TX-FR FD OF KY	9.94	2.03	3	6.68	6	53.19	4	☆
7.2		PREMIER STATE TX EX:TX	18.92	2.04	3	6.59	7	52.08	6	☆
33.5		FIDELITY TEXAS TAX FREE	10.31	2.13	25	6.52	8			☆

PERFORMANCE OF MUTUAL FUNDS (continued)

TNA 6/30/90 (MIL.$)	INVESTMENT COMPANY	LOAD	CLOSING NAV 6/30/90	TOTAL REINVESTMENT % Chg. 3/31/90 TO 6/30/90	RANK	% Chg. 6/30/89 TO 6/30/90	RANK	% Chg. 6/30/85 TO 6/30/90	RANK
1.3	NORTHWEST:ID LTD MAT		4.90	1.54	46	6.50	9		☆
21.2	FRANKLIN TX-FR: LA INC		10.60	2.67	5	6.45	10		☆
1.2	NORTHWEST: ID EXTND MAT		5.04	1.86	43	6.42	11		☆
36.0	FRANKLIN TX-FR: MO INC		10.67	2.73	3	6.31	12		☆
6.7	DUPREE:KY TX FR SHT-MED	NO	4.99	1.44	47	6.30	13		☆
5.4	NO DAKOTA DBL TX EX BOND		9.92	2.38	18	6.29	14		☆
26.6	LORD ABBETT TX-FR: TX		9.46	2.30	20	6.20	15		☆
12.0	FIRST PFC:HAWAII MUNI	NO	10.19	1.83	44	6.17	16		☆
101.6	PREMIER STATE TX EX:CT		11.13	2.19	22	6.16	17		☆
32.8	FRANKLIN TX-FR: NC INC		10.82	2.74	2	6.14	18		☆
56.0	MFS MGD MULTI-ST MUNI:WV		10.76	2.12	27	6.09	19	54.67	3
10.2	UNIFIED MUNI:INDIANA	NO	8.96	2.19	23	6.04	20		☆
113.3	FLAGSHIP TX EX:KY TRIPLE		9.91	2.53	10	5.98	21		☆
19.4	FLAGSHIP MO DOUBLE TX EX		9.81	2.53	9	5.97	22		☆
10.7	FRANKLIN TX-FR:TX INC		10.73	2.57	8	5.97	23		☆
426.3	FRANKLIN TX-FR:FL INC		10.70	2.41	16	5.91	24		☆
2.3	THC FD:MUNI UTIL MO		20.73	1.44	48	5.87	25		☆
44.7	SELIGMAN TAX-EX:LA		7.87	2.44	14	5.82	26		☆
63.5	MFS MGD MULTI-ST MUNI:TN		9.83	1.98	37	5.69	27		☆
30.8	FRANKLIN TX-FR:CT INC		10.36	2.47	11	5.66	28		☆
349.1	HAWAIIAN TX-FR TR		10.79	1.81	45	5.66	29	52.53	5
52.7	SELIGMAN TAX-EX:MO		7.37	2.64	6	5.66	30		☆
30.1	FRANKLIN TX-FR:AL INC		10.72	2.37	19	5.62	31		☆
64.6	MFS MGD MULTI-ST MUNI:SC		11.32	2.12	26	5.53	32	59.43	1
50.0	SELIGMAN TAX-EX:SC		7.47	2.43	15	5.52	33		☆
29.1	TOWER:LA MUNI INCOME		10.12	2.11	28	5.47	34		☆
24.3	SELIGMAN TAX-EX:FL		7.11	2.61	7	5.46	35		☆
196.4	MFS MGD MULTI-ST MUN:NC		11.16	1.91	40	5.42	36	55.54	2
229.9	FIDELITY CT TX FR HI YLD	NO	10.60	1.91	39	5.22	37		☆
10.5	ND TAX FREE FUND	NO	9.21	1.38	49	5.10	38		☆
75.9	FLAGSHIP TX EX:CT DOUBLE		9.66	1.98	36	4.96	39		☆
96.2	FLAGSHIP TX EX:NC TRIPLE		9.49	2.27	21	4.84	40		☆
75.1	FLAGSHIP TX EX:TN DOUBLE		10.12	1.89	42	4.79	41		☆
57.4	PRU-BACHE MUNI SR:NC:B	NO	10.60	1.90	41	4.47	42	46.94	7
13.3	ABT FLORIDA TAX-FREE		10.10	2.04	31	4.09	43		☆
12.5	MFS MGD MULTI-ST MUNI:AL		9.55	2.00	34		#		#
0.1	PRU-BACHE MUNI SR:NC:A		10.61	2.10	29		#		#
13.2	CIGNA:TAX-EXEMPT CT		10.02	2.06	30		#		#
18.0	FLAGSHIP TX EX:LA DOUBLE		9.67	2.40	17		☆		☆
2.8	GIT TAX-FREE:MO	NO	9.84	2.44	13		☆		☆
51.6	PARAGON:LA TAX-FREE		10.02	2.15	24		☆		☆

Source: Lipper Analytical Services, Inc. Reprinted by permission of Barron's National Business and Financial Weekly, © Dow Jones & Company, Inc., August 13, 1990. ALL RIGHTS RESERVED.

How To Read the Gauge

THE MORE, the merrier. That's been the mantra of mutual funds, which have mushroomed from about 840 five years ago to the 1,782 now listed in the *Barron's*/Lipper Gauge. And that's not even counting municipal-bond funds. We include 506 in our supplemental roster of tax-exempt funds starting on page 397; just three years ago, we didn't have such a list, because there weren't even 300 muni funds out there.

The fund explosion has given investors a huge variety to choose from—and made it harder than ever to sort out the good, the bad and the merely mediocre. Indeed, it's tough even for the experts to keep up with the industry's blistering pace. To give you the most up-to-date information available anywhere, Lipper Analytical Services generated the gauge on Aug. 1 and updated some information last week.

There's a lot you can glean from the gauge, but the most important information it provides is every fund's total return, calculated in exactly the same way for each of them. This means that you can accurately compare funds to one other, to average fund performance, and to indexes such as the S&P 500.

What is total return? It measures how much money an investment makes, taking into account both sources of potential gains: dividend payments and share-price appreciation. This is particularly important for bond-fund investors, who all too often fixate on high dividends, only to discover that the drop in their investment's value more than makes up for those lofty payouts, leaving them with a net loss.

Total return also copes with a quirk that makes tracking mutual-fund investments by share price alone impossible: By law, funds must distribute their capital gains to shareholders every year, so that net asset value sometimes declines while the shareholders still make a bundle. Total-return calculations assume that you reinvest all these distributions, as well as regular dividends, in fund shares, as most investors do.

(These factors can make it hard to compare total-return numbers to the figures you see on a brokerage or fund account statement, if you forget to include in your calculations the increase in the number of shares you own—and the price you paid. If you take your distributions in cash, the numbers will look even more different.)

To judge the performance of your mutual funds, current and prospective, begin with the benchmarks on page 396. These tell you how much money you would have had at quarter's end if you'd invested $10,000 in the average fund in five categories: Growth & Income (conservative stocks), Fixed-Income (taxable bonds), Small-Company Growth (aggressive stocks), Gold (mining shares) and Global (U.S. and foreign equities).

Similar information for every fund category that Lipper tracks, as well as the major market indexes, appears on page M40,* expressed in percentage changes. To make this data comparable to the gauge's $10,000 presentation, multiply the percentage number by 100 and add it to (or subtract it from, if it's a loss) $10,000.

As for the individual funds, they appear in alphabetical order, starting on page 356. (The tax-exempt funds are grouped according to their holdings, and are ranked in order of performance over 12 months.)

After a **fund's name**, you may discover a ★, which points you to a footnote at the bottom of the page. These notes may describe an unusual occurrence

that affects performance, or note that the fund is not open to the general public. If the fund you seek doesn't appear, check page 364 for a listing of the quarter's name changes, mergers, and liquidations.

The next column tells you the fund's **objective**; the 26 categories, defined on page 404, indicate a fund's goals and methods. Lipper assigns funds to these groups based on both the language in the prospectus and a review of a fund's practices.

The third column from the left indicates **total net assets** at quarter's end, in millions of dollars. (This is developed by subtracting from a fund's assets all of its liabilities, expenses, advisory fees, etc.)

A fund's size can have a big impact on its performance, so *Barron's* divides large from small funds when determining top and bottom performance. (Large funds began the quarter with assets of $25 million or more.) Small funds can soar or sink with the fortunes of a single holding. Big funds must usually make more correct choices to thrive, but tend to be better cushioned against disasters.

In the following column, you will discover net asset value as of June 30. This figure, reck-

oned by dividing the total net assets by the number of shares outstanding, tells what you would have had to pay for a share (excluding any sales charges).

The next three columns entitled **performance** are most important. They tell you how much you'd get if you invested $10,000 in a fund at the beginning of a period and took it out at the end. Again, they assume that you reinvested any dividends and distributions you received; they do not take into account sales charges or your potential tax liabilities.

These total return figures cover the results for one quarter, one year and five years. A ★ in place of a number in these columns means the fund didn't exist through the entire one-or five-year period, so results aren't available for that timeframe.

Dividend yield tells you the average amount of income dividends a fund has paid in the past 12 months, expressed as a percentage of the NAV. The dividend yield does not reflect any capital-gains distributions; instead, it indicates the income a fund receives—and passes on to shareholders—from dividends or interest payments.

So far all the data discussed

(continued)

*This page number refers to *Barron's National Business and Financial Weekly*, August 13, 1990.

has come from Lipper; what follows was collected from the funds' distributors by *Barron's* staff to make it easier for you to track down any fund that piques your interest. For more information, you can dial up the listing under phone numbers, which includes toll-free 800 numbers where they exist; if the number doesn't work in the fund's home state, use the "in-state" number. ("None" in that column usually means the 800 number works in all states.) Many funds that don't have 800 numbers accept collect calls.

Fees represent the *maximum* amount that a fund will charge for sales and distribution. Loads are one-time, upfront charges; 12b-1s are annual fees. Redemption fees usually decline the longer you remain invested in the fund; again, our table lists the max.

The **fund manager's name and tenure** was supplied by the management companies, often reluctantly and sometimes not at all. Some funds actually are run by a group; where companies have given us their names, we have printed the leader's and/or as many as space permits.

* * *

The definitions of mutual-fund objectives:

Balanced: The fund's goal is preserving principal; it maintains a 60%/40% or so portfolio of stocks and bonds.

Capital Appreciation: The fund tries to achieve maximum capital appreciation through strategies such as high portfolio turnover, leveraging, purchase of unregistered shares or options. It may hold a lot of cash.

Convertibles: The fund invests primarily in convertible bonds and preferred stock.

Equity Income: The fund normally has more than 60% of its assets in equities and seeks high income.

European Region: The fund concentrates on one or more of Europe's stock markets.

Financial Services: The fund holds 65% of its assets in stocks of financial-service companies.

Fixed Income: The fund typically has more than 75% of its assets in fixed-income securities, such as bonds, preferred stocks and money-market instruments.

Flexible: The fund aims for high total return by allocating its portfolio among a wide range of asset classes.

Global: The fund invests at least 25% of its portfolio in non-U.S. securities.

Global Flexible: Similar to flexible; it invests at least 25% of its assets in securities traded outside the U.S.

Gold: The fund has at least 65% of its assets in gold-mining or gold-oriented mining finance shares, gold coins or bullion.

Growth: The fund invests in companies whose long-term earnings it expects to grow faster than those of the stocks in the major market indexes.

Growth & Income: The fund seeks earnings growth as well as dividend income.

Health/Biotech: The fund invests 65% of its portfolio in health-care, medical companies and biotechnology companies.

Income: The fund aims to generate income; it invests less than 75% in fixed-income securities and less than 60% in stocks.

International: The fund invests in securities traded primarily outside the U.S.

Mixed Income: The fund seeks income by investing in stocks, bonds and money-market instruments, but also emphasizes principal preservation.

Natural Resources: The fund usually invests more than 65% of its equity holdings in natural-resource stocks.

Option Income: The fund writes covered options on at least half its portfolio.

Pacific Region: The fund concentrates on stocks trading in one or more of the Pacific Basin markets.

Real Estate: The fund puts 65% of its assets into real-estate company securities.

Small-Company Growth: The fund limits its investment to companies on the basis of their size.

Specialty: The fund's prospectus limits its investments to a specific industry, or it falls outside of other classifications.

Technology: The fund invests 65% of its portfolio in science and technology stocks.

Utility: The fund invests 65% of its equity portfolio in utilities.

World Fixed-Income: The fund may own common and preferred issues, but invests primarily in U.S. and foreign debt.

Selected Mutual Funds Which Invest Abroad

Foreign investments provide a possible opportunity for increased returns and portfolio diversification. Since most investors lack the time, background and information, the only practical way for them to participate is through the purchase of U.S. based mutual funds which invest abroad. A number of these funds are listed below. In general, these mutual funds are divided into three categories: global funds which invest in both U.S. and foreign stocks, international funds which invest in foreign stocks, and regional funds which invest in the equities of a specific country or region. Here we have combined the first two categories.

Global/International Funds	Telephone in State	Out-of-State
Alliance International	(212) 969-1000	(800) 221-5672
Fidelity Overseas	(617) 523-1919	(800) 544-6666
First Investors Global	(212) 208-6000	(800) 423-4026
Kemper International Fund	(312) 781-1121	(800) 621-1148
Keystone International[2]	(617) 338-3395	(800) 343-2898
Merrill/Lynch International Holdings	(609) 282-2800	(800) 637-3863
Merrill Lynch Retirement Global	(800) 637-3863 (NJ)	(800) 637-3863
Prudential Bache Global Genesis	(800) 225-1852	(800) 225-1852
Putnam International Equities	(617) 292-1000	(800) 225-1581
Scudder International[1]	(800) 225-2470 (MA)	(800) 453-3305
Shearson Lehman Spl. Global Bond	(212) 528-2744	(212) 528-2744
Templeton Foreign/Global/ World Funds	(800) 237-0738	(800) 237-0738
T. Rowe Price International[1]	(301) 547-2000	(800) 638-5660
United International Growth	(816) 283-4000 (MO)	(800) 283-4000
Vanguard World Fund International[1]	(800) 662-7447 (PA)	(800) 662-7447

[1] no-load
[2] low-load

Regional Funds	Telephone in State	Out-of-State
Alliance Global Fund Canadian	(800) 227-4618 (NY)	(800) 227-4618
Fidelity Europe[2]	(800) 544-6666	(800) 544-6666
Fidelity Pacific Basin[2]	(800) 544-6666	
GT Global Growth	(415) 392-6181	(800) 824-1580
Merrill Lynch Pacific	(800) 637-3863	(800) 637-3863
Japan Fund (Closed end, NYSE)	(800) 225-2470	(800) 225-2470
Korean Fund	(Closed end, NYSE)	
Mexico Fund	(Closed end, NYSE)	
Nomura Pacific Basin[1]	(212) 208-2604	(800) 833-0018
Taiwan	(Closed end, AMEX)	

[1] no-load
[2] low-load

Selected Mutual Funds Investing in Gold and Precious Metals

Bull & Bear—Gold Investors Ltd[1]
Bull & Bear Service Center, Inc.
11 Hanover Square
New York, NY 10005
Telephone: (800) 847-4200
          (212) 363-1100
Fidelity Select Precious Metals[2]
Fidelity Distributors Corp.
82 Devonshire Street
Boston, MA 02109
Telephone: (800) 544-6666
          (617) 523-1919
Financial Programs—Gold[2]
Financial Programs, Inc.
P.O. Box 2040
Denver, CO 80201
Telephone: (800) 525-8085
          (303) 779-1233 (CO)
Franklin Gold Fund[2]
Franklin Distributors, Inc.
777 Mariner's Island Boulevard
San Mateo, CA 94404
Telephone: (800) 342-5236
          (415) 570-3000
Keystone Precious Metals Holdings[2]
Keystone Distributors, Inc.
99 High Street
Boston MA 02110
Telephone: (800) 633-4900
          (617) 338-3400
Lexington Goldfund[1]
Lexington Management Corp.
P.O. Box 1515
Saddlebrook, NJ 07662
Telephone: (800) 526-0056
          (201) 845-7300

Oppenheimer Gold & Special Minerals
Oppenheimer Fund Management, Inc.
Two World Trade Center
New York, NY 10048
Telephone: (800) 525-7048
          (212) 323-0200
Strategic Gold & Minerals Fund[3]
Strategic Distributors, Inc.
2030 Royal Lane
Dallas, TX 75229
Telephone: (800) 527-5027
          (214) 484-1326
US Gold Shares[1]
United Services Funds, Inc.
P.O. Box 29467
San Antonio, TX 78229
Telephone: (800) 873-8637
          (512) 523-2453
USSA Gold Fund[1]
USSA Investment Management Co.
USSA Building
San Antonio, TX 78288
Telephone: (800) 531-8000
          (512) 498-8000
Vanguard Gold and Precious Metals[2]
Vanguard Group, Inc.
P.O. Box 2600
Valley Forge, PA 19482
Telephone: (800) 662-2739
          (800) 662-7447

---

[1] No-load fund
[2] Low-load fund
[3] Load fund

Foreign Securities Investments

This section provides data on the performance of major foreign securities markets and also listings of foreign stocks traded on the New York and American Exchanges. Over 200 foreign stocks and ADRs are also traded on the Over-The-Counter (OTC) market. A complete listing of foreign OTC stocks is available from the National Association of Securities Dealers, 1735 K Street, Washington, DC 20006.

Foreign securities not traded on the above exchanges may generally be purchased through stock brokers or major foreign banks in the country of interest. Most of these banks, which have U.S. branches in New York and other major cities, provide details concerning opening a foreign brokerage account.

A difficulty associated with foreign stock selection is that of obtaining timely information. The following general information sources may be helpful in this regard.

The Wall Street Journal
The Asian Wall Street Journal
Dow Jones & Company
22 Cortlandt Street
New York, NY 10007

The Asian Wall Street Journal, a weekly, is particularly helpful for the Asian region, including stock market coverage.

Barron's
World Financial Center
200 Liberty Street
New York, NY 10281

The weekly *International Trader* section is of special interest.

Capital International Perspectives
3 Place Des Bergues
1201 Geneva, Switzerland

Capital International Perspectives is a leading monthly publication dealing with international investments.

The Financial Times
Bracken House
10 Cannon Street
London EC4P 4BY, England

The Financial Times provides comprehensive coverage of European businesses and securities markets and is published daily.

Moody's Investor Services, International Manual
Moody's Investor Services
99 Church Street
New York, NY 10007

The International Manual provides financial information on about 3,000 major foreign corporations.

Disclosure
5161 River Road
Bethesda, MD 20816

This service also provides annual reports and filings on foreign firms.

A listing of mutual funds investing in foreign securities is given on page 405.

WORLD STOCK MARKETS (as of end March 1990)

	Market Value	Return in each Currency %				Currency Valuation %				Return in U.S.Dollars %				β
	Billion Dollars	3m	1yr	5yr	σ(A)	3m	1yr	5yr	σ(B)	3m	1yr	5yr	σ(C)	
New York	2907.9	-3.8	15.3	13.5	5.2	0.0	0.0	0.0	0.0	-3.8	15.3	13.5	5.2	0.82
Tokyo	2890.5	-22.7	-9.8	17.4	5.4	-9.2	-16.2	9.6	4.0	-29.8	-24.4	28.6	7.2	1.25
London	764.6	-7.7	3.6	12.9	6.3	2.2	-2.4	5.7	3.5	-5.7	1.1	19.3	7.0	1.15
Toronto	240.6	-8.3	1.7	6.9	4.6	-0.9	1.9	3.1	1.2	-9.2	3.7	10.2	5.1	0.73
Frankfurt	386.9	9.7	45.9	15.3	6.9	-0.1	12.0	12.5	3.7	9.6	63.4	29.7	7.5	0.76
Sydney	120.5	-8.9	5.3	13.1	7.5	-4.7	-8.2	1.4	3.8	-13.2	-3.3	14.7	9.3	0.87
Paris	338.2	-4.4	10.2	19.1	7.0	1.3	12.3	10.4	3.4	-3.2	23.8	31.4	7.6	1.10
Zurich	181.0	-1.8	13.5	12.4	5.6	3.0	11.0	11.5	4.0	1.1	25.9	25.3	5.7	0.75
Hong Kong	82.2	5.7	-0.2	16.8	8.7	-0.2	-0.3	0.0	0.2	5.5	-0.5	16.7	8.7	0.85
Milan	173.6	-0.5	12.4	20.3	7.2	1.4	11.5	9.4	3.3	0.9	25.3	31.6	7.8	0.86
Singapore	68.8	4.9	24.2	12.6	8.1	0.8	3.5	3.1	1.3	5.7	28.6	16.1	8.2	0.77
Total	8154.7									-13.3	-0.3	23.3	4.6	

σ
(A): Standard deviation of monthly returns on each market in each home currency, calculated from the most recent 60 months.
(B): Standard deviation of each currency's value in U.S.$ terms, calculated from the most recent 60 monthly rate of change.
(C): Standard deviation of each market's return in U.S.$ terms, calculated from the most recent 60 monthly returns.
β
Sensitivity of each market's return relative to the world market, calculated from the most recent 60 monthly returns in U.S.$ terms and world market return averaged by weighting each market return with the market value of each month.

Source: *Tokyo Stock Market Quarterly Review*, 1990 Vol. 2. March 31, 1990. A publication of Daiwa Securities Co. Ltd. Available through Daiwa Securities America, Inc. One World Financial Center, New York, NY 10281.

NOTES
Market Value Estimate for the end of March, 1990.
Return in each currency Return solely based upon each market's Stock Price Index (dividends are not included) for the periods ending on the last trading date of the latest quarter. Five-years data are shown in the annual compound rate. Stock price indices referred to are; S & P 500, TOPIX, FT industrial, Toronto composite, Commerzbank general index, Sydney Stock Exchange all ordinaries, CAC industrial, Swiss Bank Corporation general index, Hang Seng Bank index, Banca Commerciale Italiana index, and All Singapore Index.
Currency valuation Rate of change of each currency's value in U.S. dollar terms (NY market) for the corresponding periods. Five-years data are shown in the annual compound rate.
Return in U.S. Dollar Return of each market in U.S. $ terms. Five-years data are shown in the annual compound rate.

PERFORMANCES OF FOREIGN SECURITIES MARKETS

Tokyo Stock Price Index(Japan)

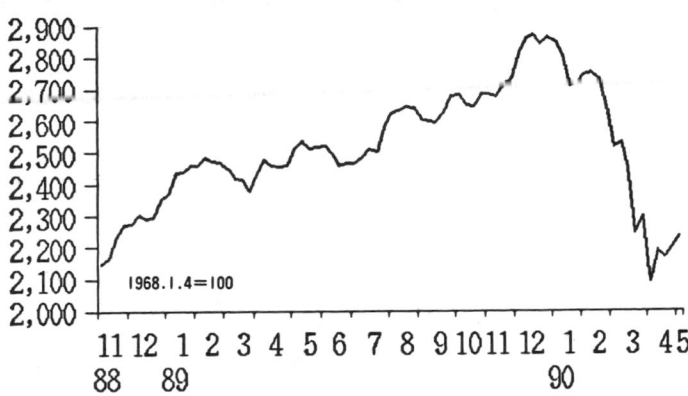

NASDAQ Composite Index(U.S.)

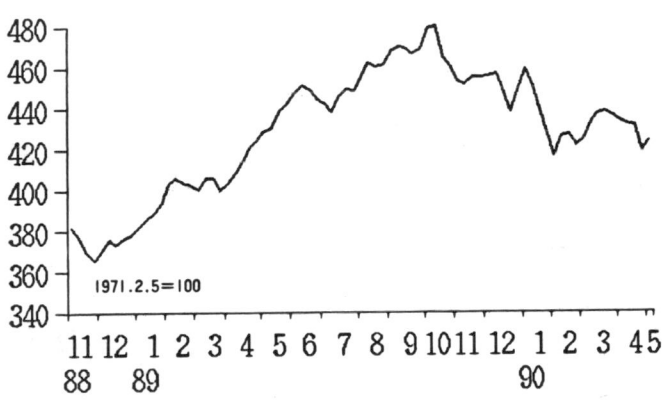

Source: *Investors Guide*, Daiwa Securities Co., Ltd.

(continued)

PERFORMANCES OF FOREIGN SECURITIES MARKETS
(continued)

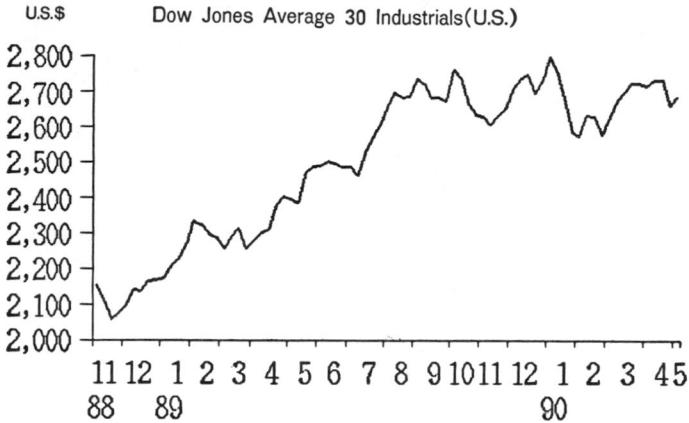

Dow Jones Average 30 Industrials(U.S.)

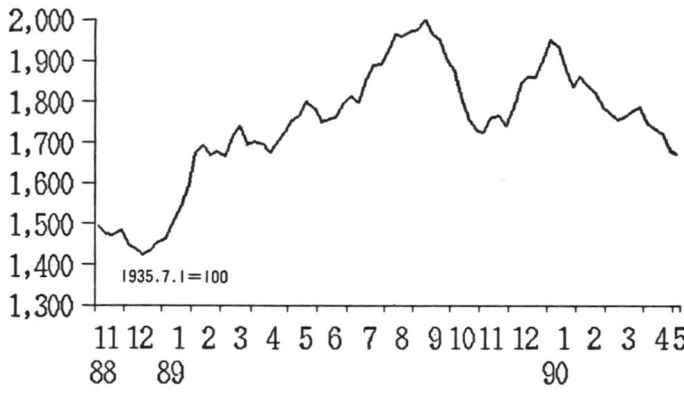

Financial Times Index of Industrial Ordinary Shares(U.K.)

1935.7.1=100

PERFORMANCES OF FOREIGN SECURITIES MARKETS
(continued)

Commerzbank Index(West Germany)

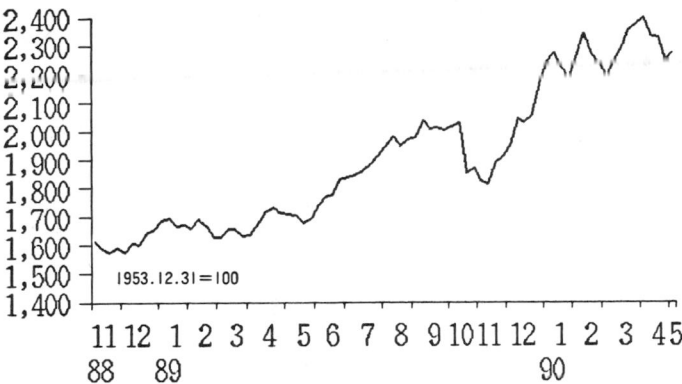

Australia Stock Exchange All Ordinaries Index

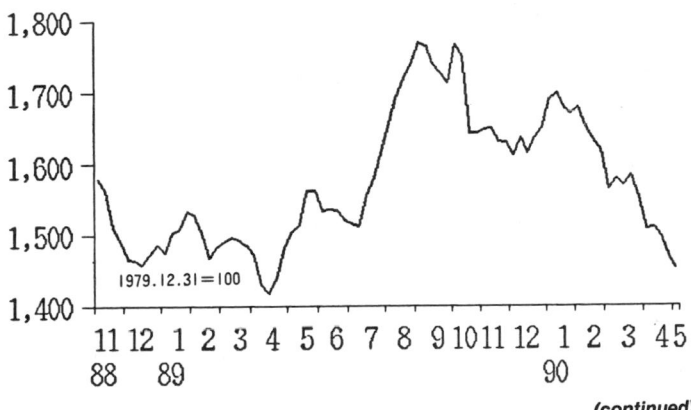

(continued)

PERFORMANCES OF FOREIGN SECURITIES MARKETS
(concluded)

Hang Seng Index(Hong Kong)

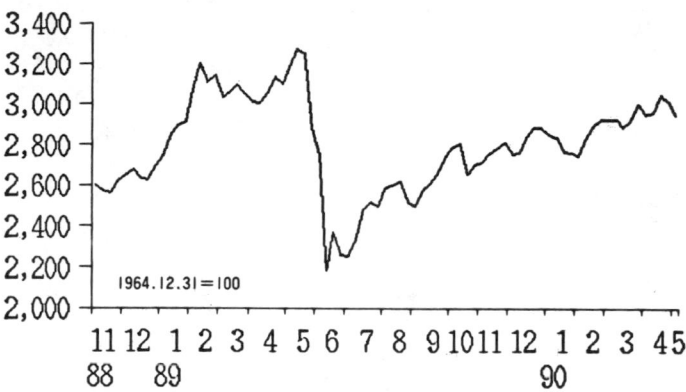

Stock Exchange of Singapore All Singapore Index

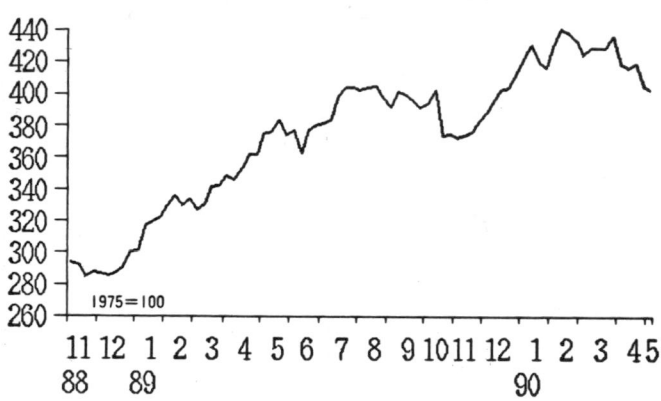

Source: *Investors Guide,* Daiwa Securities Co., Ltd.

Stocks of Foreign Corporate Issuers, December 31, 1989

Country	Company	Industry
Africa	ASA Limited	Closed-end inv. co. - gold mining
Australia	Broken Hill Proprietary Ltd.*	Petroleum; minerals; steel
	Coles Myer Ltd.*	Australian retailer
	FAI Insurances Limited*	Insurance; financial services - Australia
	National Australia Bank Ltd.*	Commercial banking services
	News Corporation Ltd.* (2 issues)	Publishing; broadcasting
	Westpac Banking Corporation* (2 issues)	Commercial banking - Australia
British W.I.	Bond International Gold, Inc.	Gold mining, exploration
	Club Med, Inc.	Hotel, resort operator
Canada	Abitibi-Price Inc.	Newsprint, uncoated papers
	Alcan-Aluminium Ltd.	Aluminum producer
	AMCA International Limited	Industrial prods.; construction services
	American Barrick Resources Corp.	Gold mining
	BCE Inc.	Holding co. - telecommunications services
	Campbell Resources Inc.	Holding co. - diversified natural resources
	Canadian Pacific Limited	Transportation; telecom.; oil; mining
	Cineplex Odeon Corporation	Motion pictures theatres operator
	Domtar Inc.	Pulp, paper, packaging; construction prods.
	Inco Ltd.	Nickel, copper producer
	LAC Minerals Ltd.	Gold mining
	Mitel Corporation	Telecommunications equip. manufacturer
	Moore Corporation Ltd.	Business forms manufacturer
	Northern Telecom Ltd.	Telecommunications equip. manufacturer
	Northgate Exploration Limited	Holding co. - metal producer
	NOVA Corporation of Alberta	Gas transmission; petrochemicals
	Placer Dome Inc.	Gold, silver, copper mining
	Potash Corp. of Saskatchewan Inc.	Potash
	Ranger Oil Limited	Oil & gas exploration, production
	Seagram Co. Ltd.	Distilled spirits producer
	TransCanada PipeLines Ltd.	Natural gas transmission
	Varity Corporation (2 issues)	Farm equipment producer
	Westcoast Energy Inc.	Natural gas distributor
Denmark	Novo-Nordisk A/S*	Industrial enzymes; pharmaceuticals
France	Rhone-Poulenc, S.A.* (3 issues)	Diversified chemicals
Hong Kong	Hong Kong Telecommunications Ltd.*	Telecommunications services, equipment
	Universal Matchbox Group Ltd. Inc.	Designs and manufactures toys
Ireland	Allied Irish Banks PLC*	Merchant banking
Israel	Elscint Ltd.	Diagnostic medical imaging equipment
Italy	Benetton Group S.p.A.*	Casual apparel
	Fiat S.p.A.* (3 issues)	Automobiles; farm equipment
	Montedison S.p.A.* (2 issues)	Diversified chemicals
Japan	Hitachi, Ltd.*	Electronic eq.; machinery; consumer products
	Honda Motor Co., Ltd.*	Motor vehicle manufacturer
	Kubota, Ltd.*	Agricultural equipment; pipe manufacturer
	Kyocera Corp.*	Ceramic products; electronic equipment
	Matsushita Electric Industrial Co., Ltd.*	Consumer electronic manufacturer
	Mitsubishi Bank, Ltd.*	Commercial banking
	Pioneer Electronic Corporation*	Consumer electronic manufacturer
	Sony Corporation*	Consumer electronic manufacturer
	TDK Corporation*	Electronic comp.; magnetic tape producer

(continued)

Stocks of Foreign Corporate Issuers, December 31, 1989 *(concluded)*

Country	Company	Industry
Netherlands	Ausimont N.V.	Chemicals
	KLM Royal Dutch Airlines**	Air transportation
	Philips N.V.**	Electronics, appliances; professional prods.
	Polygram, N.V.**	Recorded music
	Royal Dutch Petroleum Co.**	Holding co. - integrated int'l oil co.
	Unilever N.V.**	Holding co. - branded foods
Netherlands Antilles	Schlumberger Limited	Oilfield services; electronics
Norway	Norsk Hydro a.s.*	Agriculture; oil & gas
Philippines	Benguet Corporation	Mining; industrial construction
Spain	Banco Bilbao Vizcaya, S.A.*	Commercial bank
	Banco Central, S.A.*	Holding company - bank
	Banco de Santander, Sociedad Anonima de Credito*	Banking, financial services
	Empresa Nacional de Electricidad, S.A.*	Electricity producer in Spain
	Repsol, S.A.*	Integrated oil company
	Telefonica de Espana, S.A.*	Telephone service - Spain
United Kingdom	Barclays PLC* (3 issues)	Holding company - bank
	Beazer PLC*	International construction company
	BET Public Limited Company*	Industrial; transport.; construction servs.
	Blue Arrow PLC*	Holding company - employment agency
	British Airways Plc*	Passenger airline
	British Gas PLC*	Natural gas distributor
	British Petroleum Co. p.l.c.*	Holding company - integrated int'l oil co.
	British Steel PLC*	Steel producer
	British Telecommunications PLC*	Telecommunications services & products
	Cable & Wireless Public Limited Co.*	International telecommunications
	Dixons Group plc*	Consumer electronics, appliances retailer
	Glaxo Holdings p.l.c.*	Pharmaceuticals
	Hanson PLC*	Consumer goods; building products
	Huntingdon International Holdings plc*	Research-life sciences; engineering servs.
	Imperial Chemical Industries PLC*	Diversified chemical producer
	National Westminster PLC*	Holding company - bank
	Racal Telecom PLC*	Mobile telecommunications supplier - U.K.
	Royal Bank of Scotland Group PLC*	Banking
	Saatchi & Saatchi Co. PLC*	Advertising; consulting
	"Shell" Transport & Trading Co., Ltd.**	Holding co. - integrated int'l oil co.
	SmithKline Beecham p.l.c.* (2 issues)	Ethical drugs; healthcare products
	Unilever PLC*	Holding co. - branded foods

 *American depository receipts/shares.
**N.Y. shares and/or guilder shares.

Source: New York Stock Exchange *1990 Fact Book.*

TOPIX (Tokyo Stock Price Index)

(Jan.4,1968=100)

Year-end	High		Low	
	Index	Date	Index	Date
1949	12.85	22.06	May 16	11.95	Dec. 14
1950	11.57	13.24	Aug. 21	9.59	July 3
1951	16.94	17.11	Oct. 20	11.58	Jan. 4
1952	33.35	33.55	Nov. 22	17.07	Jan. 8
1953	33.30	42.18	Feb. 4	28.46	Apr. 1
1954	30.27	33.22	Jan. 11	26.79	Nov. 13
1955	39.06	39.06	Dec. 28	30.00	Mar. 28
1956	51.21	52.95	Dec. 6	38.81	Jan. 25
1957	43.40	54.82	Jan. 21	43.18	Dec. 27
1958	60.95	60.95	Dec. 27	43.48	Jan. 4
1959	80.00	90.14	Nov. 30	61.11	Jan. 9
1960	109.18	112.53	Nov. 15	79.46	Jan. 4
1961	101.66	126.59	July 14	90.86	Dec. 19
1962	99.67	111.45	Feb. 14	83.39	Oct. 30
1963	92.87	122.96	May 10	91.21	Dec. 18
1964	90.68	103.77	July 3	87.94	Nov. 11
1965	105.68	105.68	Dec. 28	81.29	July 15
1966	111.41	114.51	Mar. 24	105.21	Jan. 19
1967	100.89	117.60	May 31	99.17	Dec. 11
1968	131.31	142.95	Oct. 2	100.00	Jan. 4
1969	179.30	179.30	Dec. 27	132.62	Jan. 4
1970	148.35	185.70	Apr. 8	147.08	Dec. 9
1971	199.45	209.00	Aug. 14	148.05	Jan. 6
1972	401.70	401.70	Dec. 28	199.93	Jan. 4
1973	306.44	422.48	Jan. 24	284.69	Dec. 18
1974	278.34	342.47	June 5	251.96	Oct. 9
1975	323.43	333.11	July 2	268.24	Jan. 10
1976	383.88	383.88	Dec. 28	326.28	Jan. 5
1977	364.08	390.93	Sept. 29	350.49	Nov. 24
1978	449.55	452.60	Dec. 13	364.04	Jan. 4
1979	459.61	465.24	Sept. 29	435.13	July 13
1980	494.10	497.96	Oct. 20	449.01	Mar. 10
1981	570.31	603.92	Aug. 17	495.79	Jan. 5
1982	593.72	593.72	Dec. 28	511.52	Aug. 17
1983	731.82	731.82	Dec. 28	574.51	Jan. 25
1984	913.37	913.37	Dec. 28	735.45	Jan. 4
1985	1,049.40	1,058.35	July 27	916.93	Jan. 4
1986	1,556.37	1,583.35	Aug. 20	1,025.85	Jan. 21
1987	1,725.83	2,258.56	June 11	1,557.46	Jan. 13
1988	2,357.03	2,357.03	Dec. 28	1,690.44	Jan. 4
1989	2,881.37	2,884.80	Dec. 18	2,364.33	Mar. 27

Source: *Tokyo Stock Exchange Fact Book 1990*, International Department, Tokyo Stock Exchange, Tokyo, Japan.

TOPIX (Tokyo Stock Price Index) (Jan. 4, 1968 = 100)

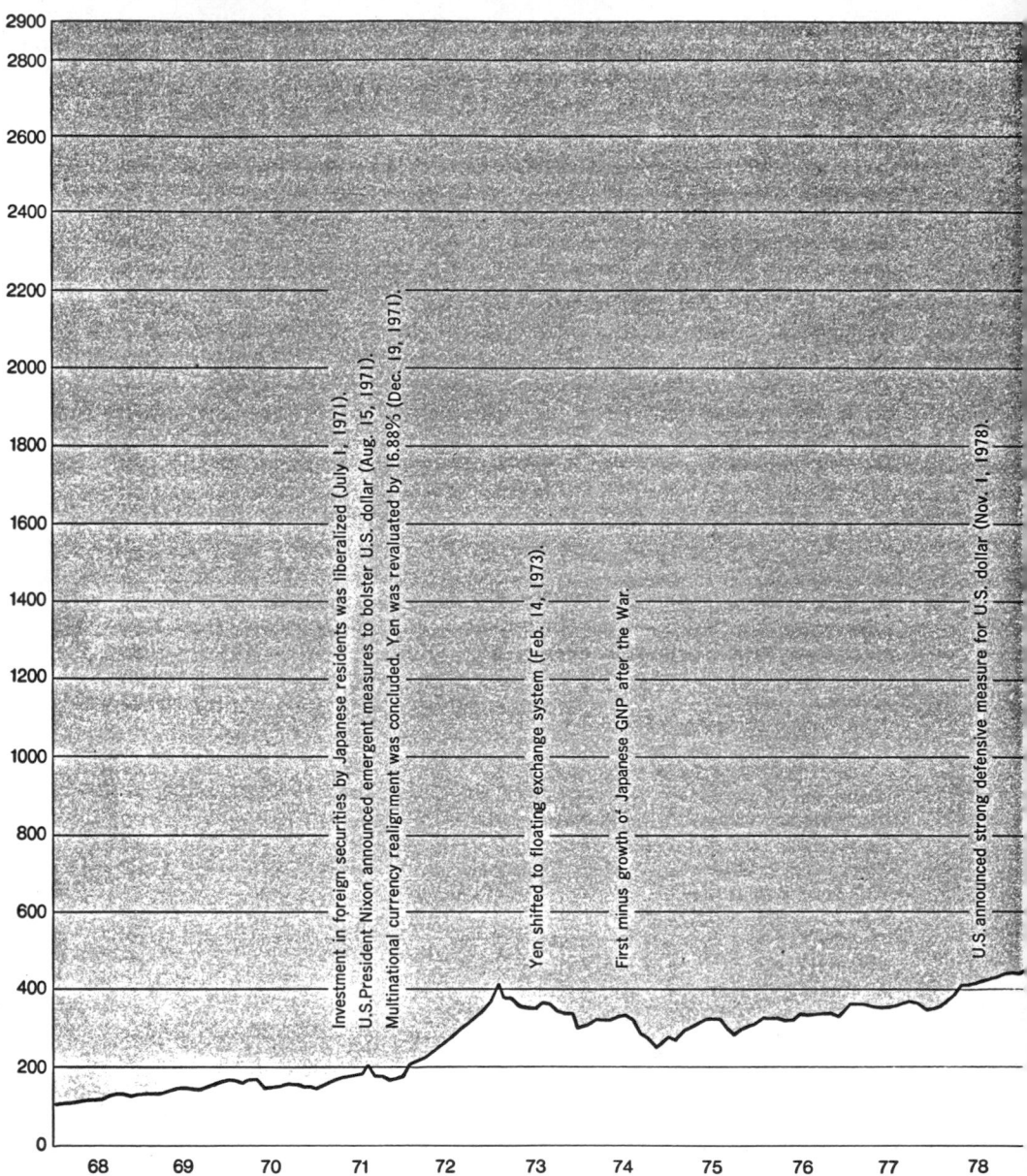

Investment in foreign securities by Japanese residents was liberalized (July 1, 1971).

U.S.President Nixon announced emergent measures to bolster U.S. dollar (Aug. 15, 1971).

Multinational currency realignment was concluded. Yen was revaluated by 16.88% (Dec. 19, 1971).

Yen shifted to floating exchange system (Feb. 14, 1973).

First minus growth of Japanese GNP after the War.

U.S. announced strong defensive measure for U.S. dollar (Nov. 1, 1978).

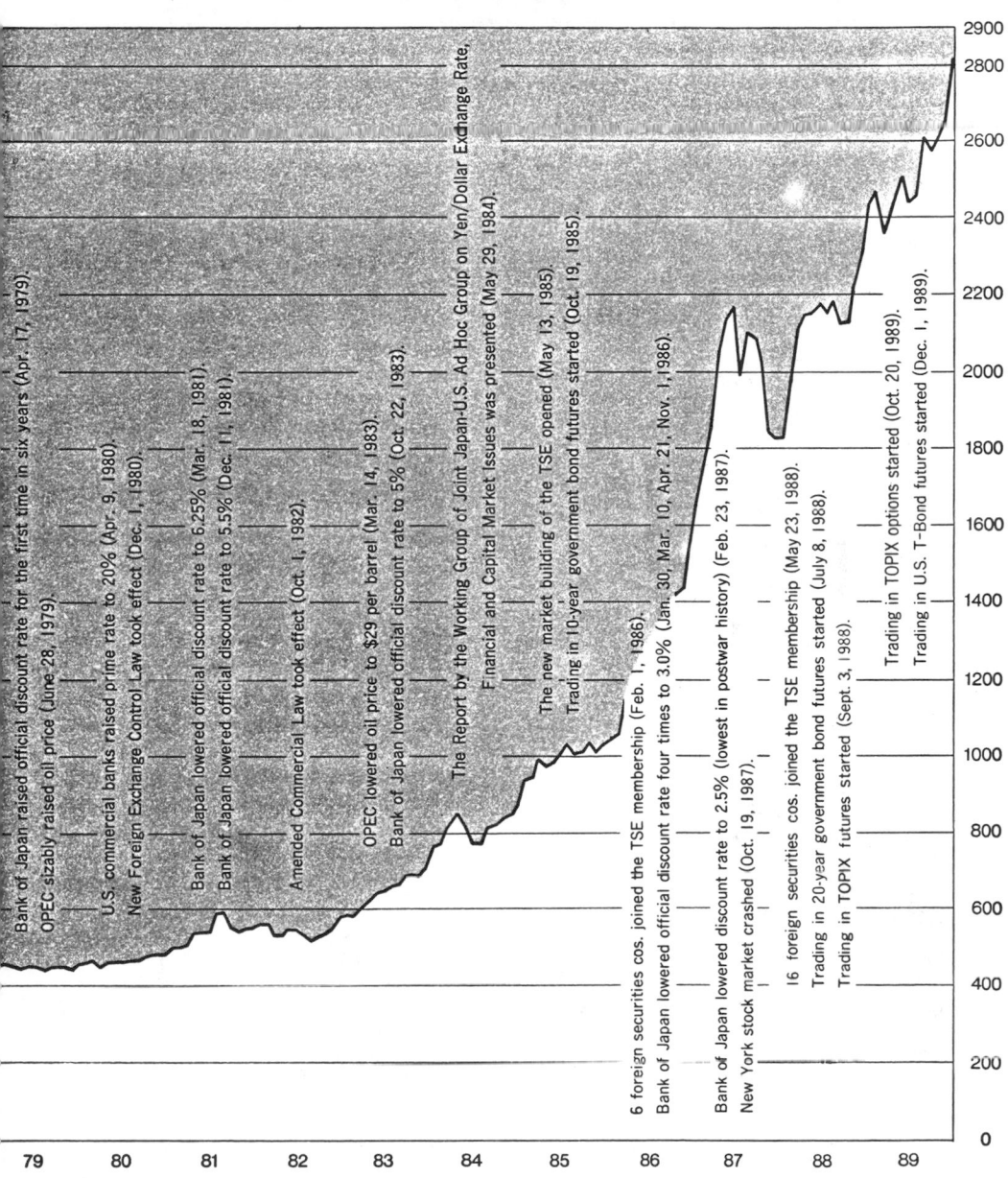

The following event labels appear along the chart:

- Bank of Japan raised official discount rate for the first time in six years (Apr. 17, 1979).
- OPEC sizably raised oil price (June 28, 1979).
- U.S. commercial banks raised prime rate to 20% (Apr. 9, 1980).
- New Foreign Exchange Control Law took effect (Dec. 1, 1980).
- Bank of Japan lowered official discount rate to 6.25% (Mar. 18, 1981).
- Bank of Japan lowered official discount rate to 5.5% (Dec. 11, 1981).
- Amended Commercial Law took effect (Oct. 1, 1982).
- OPEC lowered oil price to $29 per barrel (Mar. 14, 1983).
- Bank of Japan lowered official discount rate to 5% (Oct. 22, 1983).
- The Report by the Working Group of Joint Japan-U.S. Ad Hoc Group on Yen/Dollar Exchange Rate, Financial and Capital Market Issues was presented (May 29, 1984).
- The new market building of the TSE opened (May 13, 1985).
- Trading in 10-year government bond futures started (Oct. 19, 1985).
- 6 foreign securities cos. joined the TSE membership (Feb. 1, 1986).
- Bank of Japan lowered official discount rate four times to 3.0% (Jan. 30, Mar. 10, Apr. 21, Nov. 1, 1986).
- Bank of Japan lowered discount rate to 2.5% (lowest in postwar history) (Feb. 23, 1987).
- New York stock market crashed (Oct. 19, 1987).
- 16 foreign securities cos. joined the TSE membership (May 23, 1988).
- Trading in 20-year government bond futures started (July 8, 1988).
- Trading in TOPIX futures started (Sept. 3, 1988).
- Trading in TOPIX options started (Oct. 20, 1989).
- Trading in U.S. T-Bond futures started (Dec. 1, 1989).

Source: *Tokyo Stock Exchange Fact Book 1990*, International Department, Tokyo Stock Exchange, Tokyo, Japan.

TOPIX (Tokyo Stock Exchange [TOPIX]): Yields and Dividends

	All 1st Section Stocks	1st Section Dividend-Paying Stocks		
	Weighted Average Yields (%)	Average Dividend per Share (¥)	Total Amount of Dividends (¥ mils.)	Simple Average Yields (%)
1949	···	6.09	1,869	6.77
1950	···	6.97	11,525	9.53
1951	···	10.69	28,264	11.91
1952	···	12.88	41,311	9.85
1953	···	11.17	52,414	7.44
1954	···	9.89	60,499	9.44
1955	···	8.70	69,734	7.96
1956	···	8.27	85,109	6.68
1957	···	7.71	113,006	7.14
1958	···	7.14	122,938	6.66
1959	4.68	6.76	138,102	4.54
1960	4.27	6.71	174,225	3.93
1961	4.47	6.63	230,781	3.24
1962	5.82	6.47	307,253	3.86
1963	5.08	6.26	348,900	4.24
1964	6.01	6.26	391,501	5.69
1965	6.01	6.08	409,041	5.92
1966	4.76	5.92	407,890	4.44
1967	4.96	5.97	456,892	4.74
1968	5.00	6.09	506,603	4.36
1969	4.19	6.28	569,413	3.34
1970	4.30	6.55	647,271	3.47
1971	4.01	6.65	710,819	3.41
1972	2.42	6.55	717,714	2.24
1973	2.02	6.75	849,748	2.09
1974	2.55	6.88	912,452	2.53
1975	2.54	6.51	881,019	2.31
1976	2.27	6.25	995,343	1.91
1977	2.16	6.34	1,040,454	1.82
1978	2.00	6.45	1,090,007	1.60
1979	1.87	6.49	1,191,842	1.57
1980	1.79	6.58	1,200,537	1.63
1981	1.65	6.69	1,498,879	1.55
1982	1.80	6.80	1,525,765	1.68
1983	1.55	6.88	1,594,659	1.39
1984	1.24	7.11	1,709,559	1.09
1985	1.05	7.25	1,829,277	0.99
1986	0.83	7.33	1,850,248	0.78
1987	0.56	7.36	2,042,359	0.63
1988	0.52	7.52	2,298,464	0.55
1989	0.46	7.78	2,495,041	0.47

Note: Section 1 is comprised of Japanese stocks.

Source: *Tokyo Stock Exchange Fact Book 1990,* International Department, Tokyo Stock Exchange, Tokyo, Japan.

TOKYO STOCK EXCHANGE (TOPIX): Average Compound Annual Rates of Return on Common Stocks (1st Section)

(%)

To	From									
	1979	1980	1981	1982	1983	1984	1985	1986	1987	1988
1980	8.5									
1981	14.6	21.0								
1982	10.3	11.2	2.1							
1983	13.3	15.0	12.1	23.0						
1984	16.4	18.4	17.6	26.1	29.4					
1985	18.1	20.1	19.9	26.4	28.2	27.0				
1986	21.0	23.2	23.6	29.7	32.0	33.3	40.0			
1987	23.9	26.3	27.1	32.9	35.4	37.5	43.1	46.1		
1988	22.8	24.7	25.3	29.6	31.0	31.4	32.9	29.4	14.6	
1989 (P)	22.6	24.3	24.7	28.3	29.2	29.2	29.7	26.5	17.6	20.7

Source: Japan Securities Research Institute.

Note: The Tokyo Stock Exchange is divided into three sections. Section 1 and 2 are made up of Japanese companies. Section 3, known as the foreign section is comprised of non-Japanese stocks.

Source: *Tokyo Stock Exchange Fact Book 1990,* International Department, Tokyo Stock Exchange, Tokyo, Japan.

TOKYO STOCK EXCHANGE (TOPIX): Average Dividend Yields, All 1st Section Stocks

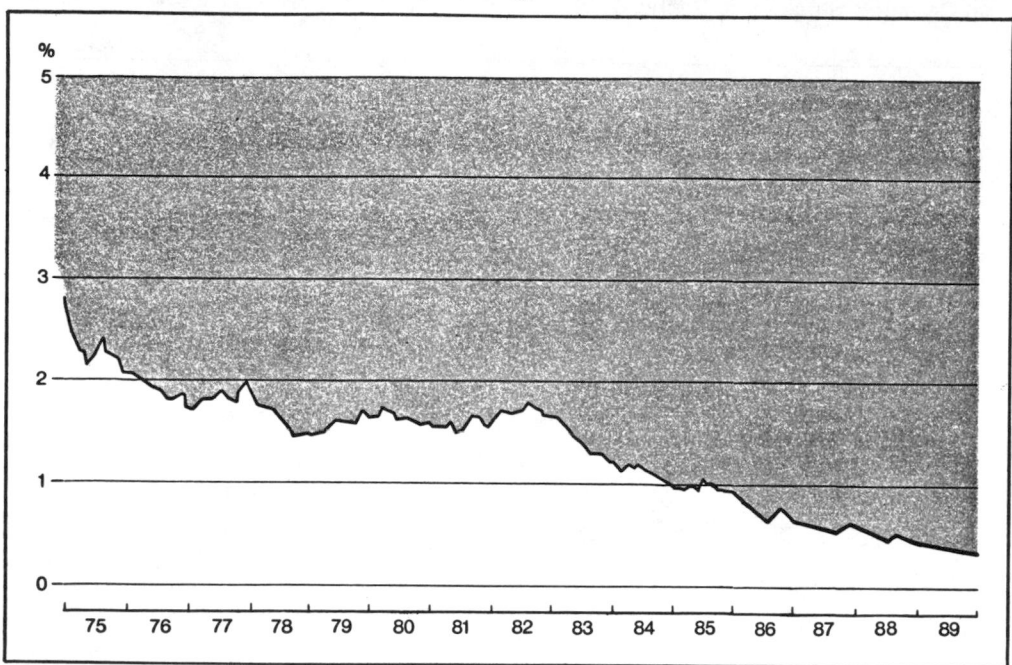

Note: Section 1 is comprised of Japanese stocks.

Source: *Tokyo Stock Exchange Fact Book 1990,* International Department, Tokyo Stock Exchange, Tokyo, Japan.

TOKYO STOCK EXCHANGE (TOPIX): 30 Most Active Stocks (Volume and Value), 1989

		(mils. of shares)			(¥ bils.)
Rank	Stocks	Volume	Rank	Stocks	Value
1	NIPPON STEEL	5,103	1	Mitsubishi Heavy Industries	4,653
2	Sumitomo Metal Industries	4,379	2	NIPPON STEEL	4,478
3	Mitsubishi Heavy Industries	3,968	3	SONY	4,438
4	TOSHIBA	3,333	4	TOSHIBA	4,238
5	NKK	3,278	5	TOKYU	3,857
6	Kobe Steel	3,032	6	Sumitomo Metal Industries	3,730
7	Kawasaki Heavy Industries	2,671	7	TAISEI	3,669
8	Kawasaki Steel	2,389	8	Fujita	3,120
9	TAISEI	2,227	9	NKK	2,967
10	Fujita	1,817	10	Kawasaki Heavy Industries	2,869
11	Mitsubishi Electric	1,810	11	Mitsui Real Estate Development	2,712
12	Mitsui Engineering & Shipbuilding	1,805	12	Fuji Photo Film	2,683
13	Ishikawajima-Harima Heavy Industries	1,789	13	SHIMIZU	2,683
14	Marubeni	1,774	14	SATO KOGYO	2,648
15	TOKYU	1,575	15	Kobe Steel	2,567
16	Hitachi Zosen	1,522	16	OHBAYASHI	2,535
17	Nisshin Steel	1,491	17	KUMAGAI GUMI	2,455
18	OHBAYASHI	1,487	18	Ishikawajima-Harima Heavy Industries	2,277
19	KUMAGAI GUMI	1,479	19	Hitachi	2,275
20	Nippon Yusen	1,472	20	Kawasaki Steel	2,253
21	Sanyo Electric	1,465	21	Nisshin Steel	2,186
22	Hitachi	1,418	22	Nippon Telegraph & Telephone	2,103
23	MITSUBISHI METAL	1,398	23	NIPPON OIL	2,081
24	SATO KOGYO	1,301	24	Tokyo Electric Power	2,068
25	SHIMIZU	1,267	25	Mitsubishi Electric	2,040
26	Mitsui Mining and Smelting	1,257	26	Ebara	1,935
27	NIPPON OIL	1,231	27	KAJIMA	1,925
28	Nishimatsu Construction	1,221	28	FANUC	1,841
29	NISSAN MOTOR	1,211	29	NISSAN MOTOR	1,807
30	Mitsui O.S.K. Lines	1,173	30	Nishimatsu Construction	1,804

Total Trading Volume of the 30 stocks (A)	61,342	A/B	Total Trading Value of the 30 stocks (C)	82,895	C/D
Total Trading Volume of all stocks (B)	222,599	27.6%	Total Trading Value of all stocks (D)	332,617	24.9%

Source: *Tokyo Stock Exchange Fact Book 1990*, International Department, Tokyo Stock Exchange, Tokyo, Japan.

JAPANESE STOCK EXCHANGES: Domestic Companies Listed

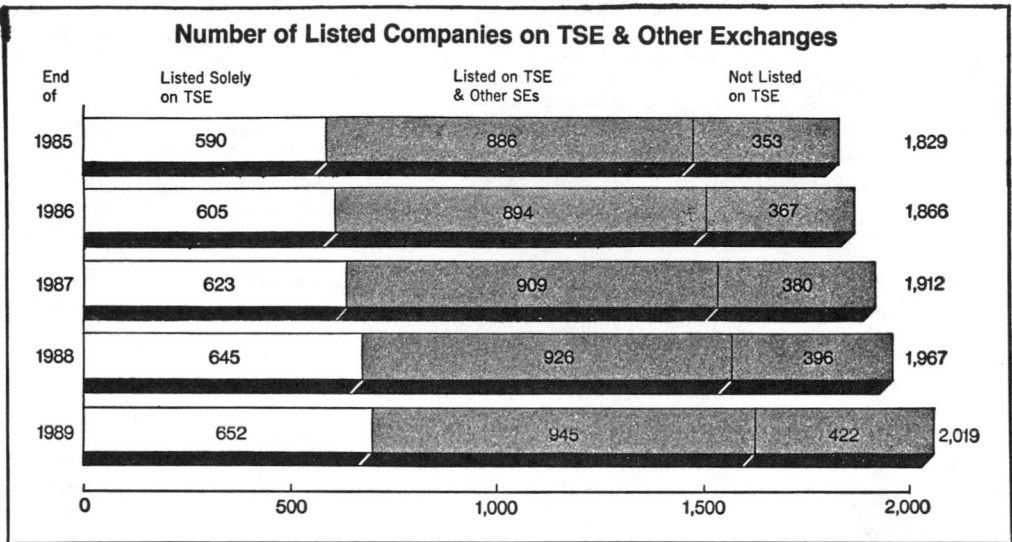

Number of Listed Companies on TSE & Other Exchanges

End of	Listed Solely on TSE	Listed on TSE & Other SEs	Not Listed on TSE	
1985	590	886	353	1,829
1986	605	894	367	1,866
1987	623	909	380	1,912
1988	645	926	396	1,967
1989	652	945	422	2,019

0   500   1,000   1,500   2,000

Source: *Tokyo Stock Exchange Fact Book 1990,* International Department, Tokyo Stock Exchange, Tokyo, Japan.

DOLLAR VOLUME OF EQUITY TRADING IN MAJOR WORLD MARKETS: 1989

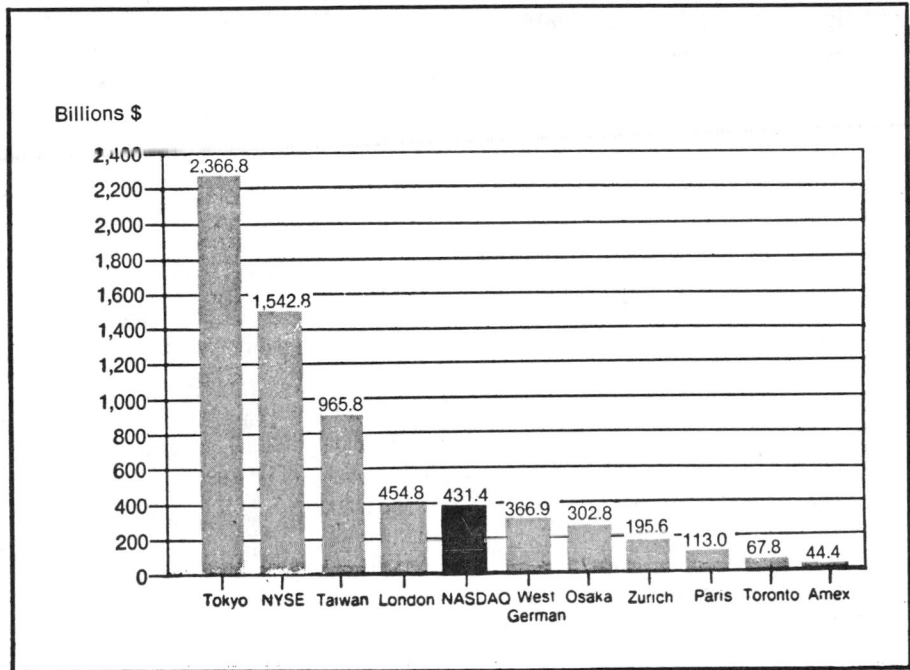

Source: *1990 NASDAQ FACT BOOK*, published by the National Association of Securities Dealers, Inc., 1735 K Street, Washington, DC. 20006.

Securities Markets: Notable Dates

1792 Original brokers' agreement subscribed to by 24 brokers (May 17).
1817 Constitution and the name "New York Stock Exchange Board" adopted (March 8).
1830 Dullest day in history of exchange—31 shares traded (March 16).
1840s Outdoor trading in unlisted securities begins at Wall and Hanover Streets, moves to Wall and Broad, then shifts south along Broad Street.*
1863 Name changed to "New York Stock Exchange" (NYSE) (January 29).
1867 Stock tickers first introduced (November 15).
1868 Membership made salable (October 23).
1869 Exchange required registering of securities by listed companies to prevent their over-issuance (February 1).
NYSE and Open Board of Brokers adopted plan of consolidation (May 8).
Gold speculation resulted in "Black Friday" (September 24).
1871 Continuous markets in stocks established.
1873 NYSE closed September 18–29.
Failure of Jay Cooke & Co. and others (September 18).
Trading hours set at 10 A.M. to 3 P.M.; Saturdays, 10 A.M. to noon (December 1).
1878 First telephones introduced in the exchange (November 13).
1881 Annunciator board installed for paging members (January 29).
1885 Unlisted Securities Department established (March 25).
1886 First million-share day—1,200,000 shares traded (December 15).
1895 Exchange recommended that companies listed or traded publish and distribute to stockholders annual statements showing income and balance sheet (January 23).
Exchange occupied new building with present trading floor at 18 Broad Street (April 23).
Call money loaned as high as 125%, following suspension of payments by

Knickerbocker Trust Company on previous day. This period was generally known as panic of 1907 (October 23).
1908 E. S. Mendels forms New York Curb Agency in first departure from informal trading.*
1910 Unlisted Securities Department abolished (March 31).
1911 Trading rules established with formation of New York Curb Market Association.*
1914 Exchange closed from July 31 through December 11—World War I.
1915 Stock prices quoted in dollars as against percent of par value (October 13).
1919 Separate ticker system installed for bonds (January 2).
1920 Stock Clearing Corporation established (April 26).
1921 New York Curb Market association moves indoors at 86 Trinity Place; name shortened to New York Curb Market and ticker service initiated (June 21).*
1924 Sliding scale of commission rates adopted.
1927 Start of ten-share unit of trading for inactive stocks (January 3).
1929 Stock market crash; 16,410,000 shares traded (October 29).
New York Curb Market modifies its name to New York Curb Exchange.*
1930 Faster ticker—500 characters per minute—installed (September 2).
1931 Exchange building expanded; Telephone Quotation Department formed to send stock quotes to member firm offices.*
1933 Exchange announced formal adoption of rule requiring independent audit of statements of listed companies (January 6).
New York Stock Exchange closed for bank holiday, March 4–14.
Securities Act of 1933 enacted. Its two basic purposes: to provide full disclosure to investors and to prohibit fraud in connection with the sale of securities (May 27).
1934 Enactment of Securities Exchange Act of 1934 (June 6).
1938 First salaried president elected—Wm. McChesney Martin, Jr. (June 30).
1946 Listed stocks outnumber unlisted stocks for first time since the 1934 act imposed restrictions on unlisted trading.*
1952 Trading hours changed: weekdays, 10 A.M. to 3:30 P.M. Closed Saturdays (September 29).
1953 Name of New York Curb Exchange

---

* Refers to American Exchange (AMEX).

† Applies to both the New York Stock Exchange and the American Exchange.

Sources: New York Stock Exchange 1990 *Fact Book*, American Stock Exchange *Data Book* and *The Wall Street Journal*.

changed to American Stock Exchange.*

1958 First member corporation—Woodcock, Hess & Co. (June 4).

Mary C. Roebling becomes first woman governor.*

1962 Committee system of administration replaced by expanded paid staff reporting to president. Specialist system strengthened, surveillance of trading increased, listing and delisting standards introduced, and board restructured to give greater representation to commission and out-of-town brokers.*

1964 New member classification—Registered Trader (August 3).

New ticker—900 characters per minute—put into service (December 1).†

Am-Quote computerized telephone-quotation service was completed as first step in major automation program.*

1965 Fully automated quotation service introduced (March 8).

Electronic Systems Center created (October 15).

First women, Phyllis S. Peterson and Julia Montgomery Walsh, elected to regular membership.*

1966 New NYSE Composite Index inaugurated (July 14).

AMEX Price Change Index System introduced; computer complex installed for ticker, surveillance, and compared-clearance operations.*

1967 First woman member admitted—Muriel F. Siebert (December 28).

1968 Ticker speed increased to maximum 900 characters per minute; transmission begun to six European countries. Trading floor modernized; line capacity for communications doubled. Visitors gallery expanded.*

1969 Central Certificate Service fully activated (February 26).

1970 Public ownership of member firms approved (March 26).

Securities Investor Protection Corporation Act signed (December 30).

1971 New York Stock Exchange Incorporated (February 18).

First negotiated commission rates effective (April 5).

First member organization listed—Merrill Lynch (July 27).

AMEX incorporates and marks 50th anniversary of move indoors; Listed Company Advisory Committee formed, composed of nine chief executives of AMEX-listed companies.

1972 NYSE reorganization, based on Martin Report, approved (January 20).

Board of Directors, with ten public members, replaced Board of Governors (July 13).

Securities Industry Automation Corporation established with AMEX to consolidate facilities of both exchanges (July 17).*

First salaried chairman took office—James J. Needham (August 28).

Board of Governors reorganized to include ten public and ten industry representatives plus full-time salaried chairman as chief executive officer.*

1973 Depository Trust Company succeeded Central Certificate Service (May 11).

Chicago Board of Options Exchange opened with trading in 16 classes of call options (April 26).

AMEX formally adopts affirmative action employment plan; Market Value Index System introduced to replace Price Change Index.

1974 Trading hours extended to 4 P.M. (October 1).

Consolidated tape begun; 15 stocks reported (October 18).

1975 Fixed commission system abolished (April 30).

Full consolidated tape begun (June 16).

AMEX trades call options.

Trading begins in call options and odd lots of U.S. government instruments.*

1976 New data line installed, handling 36,000 characters per minute (January 19).

Specialists began handling odd lots in their stocks (May 24).

Varo, Inc.—first stock traded on both NYSE and AMEX (August 23).

Competition between specialists begun (October 11).

1977 Independent audit committee on listed companies' boards required (January 6).

Competitive Trader category for members approved (January 19).

National Securities Clearing Corporation (NSCC) began merging the clearing operations of the Stock Clearing Corporation of NYSE with American Stock Exchange Clearing Corporation and National Clearing Corporation of the NASD (January 20).

Foreign broker/dealers permitted to obtain membership (February 3).

Full Automated Bond System in effect (July 27).

1978 First 60 million share day in history (63,493,000 shares) (April 17).
Intermarket Trading System (ITS) began.
Registered Competitive Market-Maker category for members approved (May 2).
First 65 million share day in history (66,370,000 shares) (August 3).
Trading in Ginnie Maes inaugurated on the AMEX Commodities Exchange (ACE) (September 12).
AMEX reached an index high of 176.87 (September 13).

1979 Trading began at pilot post on the exchange floor. First stage in a $12-million upgrading of exchange facilities (January 29).
Board of Directors of NYSE approved plan for the creation of the New York Futures Exchange, a wholly owned subsidiary of NYSE. Futures contracts in seven financial instruments will be traded on the NYSE (March 1).
New York Commodities Exchange and NYSE terminated merger talks (March 15).
81,619,000 shares were traded on the NYSE, making it the heaviest trade day in exchange history (October 10).

1980 American Stock Exchange reached an all-time daily stock volume record of 14,980,680 shares sold (January 15).
NYSE volume of 67,752,000 shares traded was second largest volume on record to date (January 16).
NYSE Futures Exchange opened (August 7).
Option seat on the American Stock Exchange sold at an all-time high of $160,000 (December 24).
NYSE index reached an all time high of 81.02 (November 28).

1981 First 90 million share day in the history of the Exchange, 92,881,000 (January 7).
The New York Stock Exchange subsidiary, the New York Futures Exchange, started trading futures in Domestic Bank Certificates of Deposit.

1982 A new AMEX subsidiary, The American Gold Coin Exchange (AGCE), began trading in the Canadian Maple Leaf (January 21).
Trading in NYSE Composite Index Futures began on the New York Futures Exchange (May 6).
Trading started through experimental linkage between ITS operated by

NYSE and six other exchanges and Computer Assisted Execution Service (CAES) operated by NASD, in 30 stocks exempted from exchange off-board trading rules under SEC Rule 19c-3. (May 17).
Record advance of 38.81 points reached in NYSE trading as measured by Dow Jones Industrial Average (August 17).
First 100 million share day (132,-681,120 shares. (August 18).
Trading in Interest Rate Options on U.S. Treasury Bills & Notes started in May on the AMEX.
Trading soared to an all time high of 147,081,070 shares on the NYSE (October 7).
All time options high of 340,550 contracts were traded on the AMEX (October 7).
Dow Jones Industrial Average plunged 36.33 points, the largest one-day loss since the record plunge of 38.33 points on October 28, 1929 (October 25).

1983 Trading in options on NYSE Common Stock Index Futures started on New York Futures Exchange (January 28).
NYSE started trading options on the NYSE Common Stock Index (September 23).
Dow Jones Industrial Average reached an all time high of 1260.77 (September 26).
New shares of common stocks of seven regional telephone companies and shares of the "new" AT&T began trading on a "when issued" basis. Divestiture of AT&T effective January 1, 1984 (November 21).
AMEX stock trading went over the two billion share mark for the first time.
The AMEX list of stock options increased by four index options, two on specific industry groups, one on the AMEX Market Value Index.

1984 Largest NYSE trading day of 159,-999,031 shares traded (January 5).
CBOT (Chicago Board of Trade) began trading a futures contract on the Major Market Index (July 23).*
Trading began in NYSE Double Index Options (July 23).
NYSE volume soared to a record 236,565,110 shares traded (August 3).
NYSE opened on Presidential Election Day for first time ever.
Super DOT 250 (electronic order-

routing system) launched on NYSE (November 16).

1985   For the first time the NYSE index went over 100, closing at 101.12 (January 21).

19,091,950 shares were traded on the AMEX, the highest single day volume ever (February 6).

Ronald Reagan visited the NYSE, the first President to do so while in office (March 28).

Trading in options on gold bullion started on AMEX (April 26).

50 billionth share listed in NYSE (May 30).

NYSE began trading options in three over-the-counter stocks (June 3).

NYSE reached an all time index high of 113.49 (July 17).

Amex and Toronto Stock Exchange linked together as part of the first two-way electronic hookup between primary equity markets in different countries (September 24).

Instinet Corporation and the AMEX reached an agreement enabling European institutional investors to have access to the AMEX options market via Reuter's electronic terminals.

The opening trading time on both the NYSE and AMEX went from 10:00 A.M. to 9:30 A.M. (September 30).

The Dow Jones Industrial Average reached an all-time high of 1368.50 (October 16).

Options traded on two listed stocks on the NYSE (October 21).

Tokyo Stock Exchange admitted its first foreign member firms (December 1).

A daily record of 119,969 contracts traded on the AMEX Major Markets Index Option (December 13).

1986   The Dow Jones Industrial Average for the first time closed above 1600 at 1600.69 (February 6).

The Dow Jones Industrial Average for the first time closed above 1700 at 1713.99. (February 27).

The Dow Jones Industrial Average for the first time closed above 1800 at 1804.24 (March 20).

NYSE began trading the NYSE Beta Index Option (May 22).

NYSE Board of Directors expanded to 24 outside directors: 12 public members and 12 industry members (June 5).

New York Futures Exchange (NYFE) began trading the Commodity Research Bureau (CRB) index futures contract (June 12).

The Dow Jones Industrial Average for the first time closed above 1900 at 1903.54 (July 1).

The Directors of the NYSE voted to abandon the one-share-one-vote rule which gives common shareholders equal voting rights (July 9).

The Dow Jones Industrials nose-dived a record 86.61 points on a record volume of 237,600,000 shares traded (September 11).

$600,000.00 (the highest price ever) was paid for membership in the NYSE (December 1).

1987   The Dow Jones industrials passed the 2000 mark, closing at 2000.25 (January 8).

The Dow Jones Industrials closed above 2300 for the first time, up 33.95 points to 2333.52 (March 20).

The Dow Jones Industrials climbed above 2400 for the first time to close at 2405.54 (April 7).

Foreign currency warrants began trading (June 11).

The Chicago Board of Trade and the Chicago Board Options Exchange agreed to permit members of both exchanges to trade financial futures and options contracts side by side (June 25).

For the first time the Dow Jones Industrials closed over 2500 at 2510.04 (July 16).

AMEX Market Value closed at the all-time high of 365.0 (August 13).

A gain of 15.14 points brought the Dow Jones Industrials above 2700 points for the first time with the market closing at 2700.52 (August 17).

Dow Jones industrial average set a record at 2722.42 (August 25).

New York Futures Exchange began to trade the Russell 2000 and Russell 3000® Stock Index futures contracts (September 10).

A price of $1,150,000 was paid for a member of the NYSE, the highest ever (September 21).

The stock market 'crashed' with the Dow Jones Industrials down 508.00 points or 22% to close at 1738.74 on a record volume of 604.3 shares. Other record declines were: Dow Jones transportations off 164.78; utilities off 29.16; the S & P 500 stock index off 57.86; the AMEX index down 41.05, the NYSE down 30.51, and the NASDAQ composite of over-the-counter stocks off 46.12 (October 19).

A record volume of 608,148,710 shares

traded on the NYSE and 43,432,760 on the AMEX (October 20).

The Dow Jones Industrials rocketed 186.84 points, the highest ever, on a volume of 449,350,000 shares (October 21).

The AMEX Market Value Index registered its largest increase ever, 23.81 (October 21).

1988   343,949,330 shares were traded on the NYSE, making it the highest volume day to date since the 'crash' of 1987 (June 17).

The SEC approved a series of initiatives by the NYSE and the Chicago Mercantile Exchange to coordinate procedures between the equities and futures markets, including coordinated circuit breakers; a joint effort against front-running; inter-exchange communications; and shared audit trail and surveillance information (October 19).

The NYSE opened an office in London to assist European companies in gaining access to the U.S. capital markets and listing on the NYSE (November 7).

1989   Dow Jones industrials established a record high of 2734.64 (August 25).

The Dow Jones industrials plunged 190.58 points to 2569.26 (October 13).

The NYSE launched a new trading vehicle, the Exchange Stock Portfolio, which enables the trading of a standardized basket of stocks in a single execution (October 26).

The NYSE created a blue-ribbon panel to study market volatility and investor confidence (December 7).

The DJIA peaked to a record 2810.12 (December 29).

1990   The Dow Jones industrials closed above 2900 for the first time (June 4).

Investment and Financial Terms

Accelerated Cost Recovery System (ACRS) A system that specifies the allowable depreciation recovery period for different types of assets. The normal recovery period is generally shorter than that allowed before the passage of the 1981 Economic Recovery Tax Act.*

Accruals Recurring continuous short-term liabilities. Examples are accrued wages and accrued interest.

Accrued interest Interest accrued on a bond since the last interest payment was made. The buyer of the bond pays the market price plus accrued interest. Exceptions include bonds that are in default and income bonds. (See: *Flat income bond.*)†

Acquisition The acquiring of control of one corporation by another. In "unfriendly" takeover attempts, the potential buying company may offer a price well above current market values, new securities and other inducements to stockholders. The management of the subject company might ask for a better price or try to join up with a third company. (See: *Merger, Proxy.*)††

Ad valorem tax A tax based on the value (or assessed value) of property.**

Aging of accounts receivable Analyzing accounts by the amount of time they have been on the books.*

American Depository Receipt (ADR) Issued by American banks, an ADR is a certificate which serves as a proxy for a foreign stock deposited in a foreign bank. For all practical purposes, trading an ADR is equivalent to trading the foreign stock. Hundreds of ADRs are traded on U.S. stock exchange.

Amortization Accounting for expenses or charges as applicable rather than as paid. Includes such practices as depreciation, depletion, write-off of intangibles, prepaid expenses, and deferred charges.†

Annual report The formal financial statement issued yearly by a corporation. The annual report shows assets, liabilities, earnings, how the company stood at the close of the business year, how it fared profit-wise during the year and other information of interest to shareowners.†

Arbitrage A technique employed to take advantage of differences in price. If, for example, ABC stock can be bought in New York for $10 a share and sold in London at $10.50, an arbitrageur may simultaneously purchase ABC stock here and sell the same amount in London, making a profit of 50 cents a share, less expenses. Arbitrage may also involve the purchase of rights to subscribe to a security, or the purchase of a convertible security—and the sale at or about the same time of the security obtainable through exercise of the rights or of the security obtainable through conversion.

Arrearage Overdue payment; frequently omitted dividend on preferred stock.

Assessed valuation The valuation placed on property for purposes of taxation.**

Asset-based public offerings Public offerings backed by receivables as collateral. Essentially, a firm factors (sells) its receivables in the securities markets.*

Assets Everything a corporation owns or due to it: Cash, investments, money due it, materials and inventories, which are called current assets; buildings and machinery, which are known as fixed assets; and patents and good will, called intangible assets. (See: *Liabilities.*)†

Asset utilization ratios A group of ratios that measures the speed at which the firm is turning over or utilizing its assets. We measure inventory turnover, fixed asset turnover, total asset turnover, and the average time it takes to collect accounts receivable.*

Assignment The liquidation of assets without going through formal court procedures. In order to affect an assignment, creditors must agree on liquidation values and the relative priority of claims.*

Assignment Notice to an option writer that an option holder has exercised the option and that the writer will now be required to deliver (receive) under the terms of the contract.††

Ask (See: *Bid and asked.*)†

Auction market The system of trading securities through brokers or agents on an exchange such as the New York Stock Exchange. Buyers compete with other buyers

---

* Entries from *Foundations of Financial Management.*
† Entries from *The Language of Investing Glossary.*
** Entries from *Tax-Exempt Securities & the Investor.*
†† Entries from the *Glossary.*
¶ Entries from the Federal Reserve *Glossary.*

Source: *Foundations of Financial Management,* 5th edition by Stanley B. Block and Geoffrey A. Hirt, Irwin, Homewood, IL 1989.

The *Language of Investing Glossary* published by the New York Stock Exchange, Inc.

The *Glossary* published by the New York Stock Exchange.

Tax-Exempt Securities & the Investor published by the Securities Industry Association.

The *Glossary* published by the Board of Governors of the Federal Reserve System.

while sellers compete with other sellers for the most advantageous price.††

Auditor's report Often called the accountant's opinion, it is the statement of the accounting firm's work and its opinion of the corporation's financial statements, especially if they conform to the normal and generally accepted practices of accountancy.††

Automated clearinghouse (ACH) An ACH transfers information between one financial institution and another and from account to account via computer tape. There are approximately 30 regional clearinghouses throughout the United States that claim the membership of over 10,000 financial institutions.*

Average collection period The average amount of time accounts receivable have been on the books. It may be computed by dividing accounts receivable by average daily credit sales.*

Averages Various ways of measuring the trend of securities prices, one of the most popular of which is the Dow-Jones average of 30 industrial stocks listed on the New York Stock Exchange. The prices of the 30 stocks are totaled and then divided by a divisor which is intended to compensate for past stock splits and stock dividends and which is changed from time to time. As a result point changes in the average have only the vaguest relationship to dollar price changes in stocks included in the average. (See: *NYSE composite index.*)††

Balance of payments The term refers to a system of government accounts that catalogs the flow of economic transactions between countries.*

Balance sheet A condensed financial statement showing the nature and amount of a company's assets, liabilities and capital on a given date. In dollar amounts the balance sheet shows what the company owned, what it owed, and the ownership interest in the company of its stockholders. (See: *Assets, Earnings report.*)†

Bankers acceptance Bankers acceptances are negotiable time drafts, or bills of exchange, that have been accepted by a bank which, by accepting, assumes the obligation to pay the holder of the draft the face amount of the instrument on the maturity date specified. They are used primarily to finance the export, import, shipment, or storage of goods.¶

Bankruptcy The market value of a firm's assets are less than its liabilities, and the firm has a negative net worth. The term is also used to describe in-court procedures associated with the reorganization or liquidation of a firm.*

Basis book A book of mathematical tables used to convert yields to equivalent dollar prices.**

Basis point One gradation on a 100-point scale representing one percent; used especially in expressing variations in the yields of bonds. Fixed income yields vary often and slightly within one percent and the basis point scale easily expresses these changes in hundredths of one percent. For example, the difference between 12.83% and 12.88% is 5 basis points.††

Basis price The price expressed in yield or percentage of return on the investment.**

Bear market A declining market. (See: *Bull market.*)†

Bearer bond A bond which does not have the owner's name registered on the books of the issuer and which is payable to the holder. (See: *Coupon bond, Registered bond.*)†

Bearer security A security that has no identification as to owner. It is presumed to be owned, therefore, by the bearer or the person who holds it. Bearer securities are freely and easily negotiable since ownership can be quickly transferred from seller to buyer.**

Beta A measure of the volatility of returns on an individual stock relative to the market. Stocks with a beta of 1.0 are said to have risk equal to that of the market (equal volatility). Stocks with betas greater than 1.0 have more risk than the market, while those with betas of less than 1.0 have less risk than the market.*

Bid and asked Often referred to as a quotation or quote. The bid is the highest price anyone has declared that he wants to pay for a security at a given time, the asked is the lowest price anyone will take at the same time. (See: *Quote.*)†

Blanket inventory liens A secured borrowing arrangement in which the lender has a general claim against the inventory of the borrower.*

Block A large holding or transaction of stock—popularly considered to be 10,000 shares or more.†

Blue chip A company known nationally for the quality and wide acceptance of its products or services, and for its ability to make money and pay dividends.†

Blue-sky laws A popular name for laws various states have enacted to protect the public against securities frauds. The term is believed to have originated when a judge ruled that a particular stock had about the same value as a patch of blue sky.†

Board room A room for registered representatives and customers in a broker's office where opening, high, low, and last prices of leading stocks used to be posted on a board throughout the market day. Today such price displays are normally electronically controlled although most board rooms have replaced the board with the ticker and/or individual quotation machines.†

Bond Basically an IOU or promissory note of a corporation, usually issued in multiples of $1,000 or $5,000, although $100 and $500 denominations are not unknown. A bond is evidence of a debt on which the issuing company usually promises to pay the bondholders a specified amount of interest for a specified length of time, and to repay the loan on the expiration date. In every case a bond represents debt—its holder is a creditor of the corporation and not a part owner as is the shareholder. (See: *Collateral, Convertible security, Debenture, General Mortgage Bond, Income Bond.*)††

Bond ratings Bonds are rated according to risk by Standard & Poor's and Moody's Investor Service. A bond that is rated Aaa by Moody's has the lowest risk, while a bond with a C rating has the highest risk. Coupon rates are greatly influenced by a corporation's bond rating.*

Book A notebook the specialist in a stock uses to keep a record of the buy and sell orders at specified prices, in sequence of receipt, which are left with him by other brokers. (See *Specialist.*)†

Book value (See: *Net worth.*)

Break-even analysis A numerical and graphical technique that is used to determine at what point the firm will break even (revenue = cost). To compute the break-even point, we divide fixed costs by price minus variable cost per unit.*

Broker An agent, who handles the public's orders to buy and sell securities, commodities, or other property. For this service a commission is charged. (See: *Commission broker, Dealer.*)†

Brokers' loans Money borrowed by brokers from banks or other brokers for a variety of uses. It may be used by specialists and to help finance inventories of stock they deal in; by brokerage firms to finance the underwriting of new issues of corporate and municipal securities; to help finance a firm's own investments; and to help finance the purchase of securities for customers who prefer to use the broker's credit when they buy securities. (See: *Margin.*)†

Bull market An advancing market. (See: *Bear market.*)†

Call (1) The right (option) to buy a share of stock at a specified price within a given time period (see options). (2) The redemption of a bond or preferred stock before its normal maturity.

Call feature Used for bonds and some preferred stock. A call allows the corporation to retire securities before maturity by forcing the bondholders to sell bonds back to it at a set price. The call provisions are included in the bond indenture.*

Call premium The premium paid by a corporation to call in a bond issue before the maturity date.*

Callable A bond issue, all or part of which may be redeemed by the issuing corporation under definite conditions before maturity. The term also applies to preferred shares which may be redeemed by the issuing corporation.†

Capital Sources of long-term financing that are available to the business firm.*

Capital asset pricing model A model that relates the risk-return trade offs of individual assets to market returns. A security is presumed to receive a risk-free rate of return plus a premium for risk.*

Capital gain or capital loss Profit or loss from the sale of a capital asset. A capital gain, under current federal income tax laws, may be either short-term (12 months or less) or long-term (more than 12 months). A short-term capital gain is taxed at the reporting individual's full income tax rate. A long-term capital gain is subject to a lower tax. The capital gains provisions of the tax law are complicated. You should consult your tax advisor for specific information.†

Capital lease A long-term, noncancelable lease that has many of the characteristics of debt. Under FASB *Statement No. 13*, the lease obligation must be shown directly on the balance sheet.*

Capital markets Competitive markets for equity securities or debt securities with maturities of more than one year. The best examples of capital market securities are common stock, bonds, and preferred stock.*

Capital rationing Occurs when a corporation has more dollars of capital budgeting projects with positive net present values than it has money to invest in them. Therefore, some projects that should be accepted are excluded because financial capital is rationed.*

Capital stock All shares representing ownership of a business, including preferred and common. (See: *Common stock, Preferred stock.*)†

Capitalization Total amount of the various

securities issued by a corporation. Capitalization may include bonds, debentures, preferred and common stock, and surplus. Bonds and debentures are usually carried on the books of the issuing company in terms of their par or face value. Preferred and common shares may be carried in terms of par or stated value. Stated value may be an arbitrary figure decided upon by the directors or may represent the amount received by the company from the sale of the securities at the time of issuance. (See: *Par.*)†

Carrying costs The cost to hold an asset, usually inventory. For inventory, carrying costs include such items as interest, warehousing costs, insurance, and material-handling expenses.*

Cash budget A series of monthly or quarterly budgets that indicate cash receipts, cash payments, and the borrowing requirements for meeting financial requirements. It is constructed from the pro forma income statement and other supportive schedules.*

Cash flow Reported net income of a corporation *plus* amounts charged off for depreciation, depletion, amortization, extraordinary charges to reserves, which are bookkeeping deductions and not paid out in actual dollars and cents. (See: *Amortization, Depreciation.*)††

Cash sale A transaction on the floor of the Stock Exchange which calls for delivery of the securities the same day. In "regular way" trades, the seller is to deliver on the fifth business day except for bonds, which is the next day.

Certificate The actual piece of paper which is evidence of ownership of stock in a corporation. Watermarked paper is finely engraved with delicate etchings to discourage forgery.††

Certificate of Deposit (CD) A money market instrument issued by banks. The time CD is characterized by its set date of maturity and interest rate and its wide acceptance among investors, companies and institutions as a highly negotiable short-term investment vehicle.††

CFTC The Commodity Futures Trading Commission, created by Congress in 1974 to regulate exchange trading in futures.††

Clientele effect The effect of investor preferences for dividends or capital gains. Investors tend to purchase securities that meet their needs.*

Coefficient of correlation The degree of associated movement between two or more variables. Variables that move in the same direction are said to be positively correlated, while

negatively correlated variables move in opposite directions.*

Coefficient of variation A measure of risk determination that is computed by dividing the standard deviation for a series of numbers by the expected value. Generally, the larger the coefficient of variation, the greater the risk.*

Collateral trust bond A bond secured by collateral deposited with a trustee. The collateral is often the stocks or bonds of companies controlled by the issuing company but may be other securities.†

Combined leverage The total or combined impact of operating and financial leverage.

Commercial paper An unsecured promissory note that large corporations issue to investors. The minimum amount is usually $25,000.*

Commission The broker's basic fee for purchasing or selling securities or property as an agent.†

Commission broker An agent who executes the public's orders for the purchase or sale of securities or commodities.†

Commodities (See: *Futures.*)

Common equity The common stock or ownership capital of the firm. Common equity may be supplied through retained earnings or the sale of new common stock.*

Common stock Securities which represent an ownership interest in a corporation. If the company has also issued preferred stock, both common and preferred have ownership rights. Common stockholders assume the greater risk, but generally exercise the greater control and may gain the greater reward in the form of dividends and capital appreciation. The terms of common stock and capital stock are often used interchangeably when the company has no preferred stock.†

Common stock equivalent Warrants, options, and any convertible securities that pay less than two thirds of the average Aa bond yield at the time of issue.*

Common stockholder Holders of common stock are the owners of the company. Common stockholders elect the members of the board of directors, who in turn help select the top management.*

Compensating balances A bank requirement that business customers maintain a minimum average balance. The required amount is usually computed as a percentage of customer loans outstanding or as a percentage of the future loans to which the bank has committed itself.*

Competitive trader A member of the Exchange who trades in stocks on the Floor for an account in which he has an interest. Also known as a Registered Trader.†

Composition An out-of-court settlement in which creditors agree to accept a fractional settlement on their original claim.*

Compound sum The future value of a single amount or an annuity when compounded at a given interest rate for a specified time period.*

Conglomerate A corporation that has diversified its operations, usually by acquiring enterprises in widely varied industries.†

Consolidated balance sheet A balance sheet showing the financial condition of a corporation and its subsidiaries. (See: *Balance sheet.*)†

Consolidated tape The ticket tape reporting transactions in NYSE listed securities that take place on the NYSE or any of the participating regional stock exchanges and other markets. Similarly, transactions in AMEX-listed securities, and certain other securities listed on regional stock exchanges, are reported and identified on a separate tape.††

Consolidation The combination of two or more firms, generally of equal size and market power, to form an entirely new entity.*

Constant dollar accounting One of two methods of inflation-adjusted accounting that have been approved by the Financial Accounting Standards Board. Financial statements are adjusted to present prices, using the consumer price index. This is shown as supplemental information in the firm's annual report.*

Consumer price index An economic indicator published monthly by the U.S. Commerce Department. It measures the rate of inflation for consumer goods.*

Contribution margin The contribution to fixed costs from each unit of sales. The margin may be computed as price minus variable cost per unit.*

Conversion premium The market price of a convertible bond or preferred stock minus the security's conversion value.*

Conversion price The conversion ratio divided into the par value. The price of the common stock at which the security is convertible. An investor would usually not convert the security into common stock unless the market price were greater than the conversion price.*

Conversion ratio The number of shares of common stock an investor will receive if he exchanges a convertible bond or convertible preferred stock for common stock.*

Conversion value The conversion ratio multiplied by the market price per share of common stock.*

Convertible security A security that may be traded into the company for a different form or type of security. Convertible securities are usually bonds or preferred stock that may be exchanged for common stock.*

Corporate stock repurchase A corporation may repurchase its shares in the market as an alternative to paying a cash dividend. Earnings per share will go up, and if the price-earnings ratio remains the same, the stockholder will receive the same dollar benefit as through a cash dividend. Furthermore, the increase in stock price is a capital gain, whereas the cash dividend would be taxed as ordinary income. A corporation may also justify the repurchase of its stock because it is at a very low price or to maintain constant demand for the shares. Reacquired shares may be used for employee options or as part of a tender offer in a merger or acquisition. Firms may also reacquire part of their shares as a protective device against being taken over as a merger candidate.*

Corporation A form of ownership in which a separate, legal entity is created. A corporation may sue or be sued, engage in contracts and acquire property. It has a continual life and is not dependent on any one stockholder for maintaining its legal existence. A corporation is owned by stockholders who enjoy the privilege of limited liability. There is, however, the potential for double taxation in the corporate form of organization: the first time at the corporate level in the form of profits, and again at the stockholder level in the form of dividends.*

Correlation coefficient Measures the degree of relationship between two variables.*

Correspondent A securities firm, bank, or other financial organization which regularly performs services for another in a place or market to which the other does not have direct access. Securities firms may have correspondents in foreign countries or on exchanges of which they are not members. Correspondents are frequently linked by private wires. Member organizations of the N.Y.S.E. with offices in New York City may also act as correspondents for out-of-town member organizations which do not maintain New York City offices.†

Cost-benefit analysis A study of the incremental costs and benefits that can be derived from a given course of action.*

Cost of capital The cost of alternative sources of financing to the firm. (See: *Weighted average cost of capital.*)*

Cost of goods sold The cost specifically associated with units sold during the time period under study.*

Coupon bond Bond with interest coupons attached. The coupons are clipped as they come due and are presented by the holder for payment of interest. (See: *Bearer bond, Registered bond.*)†

Coupon rate The actual interest rate on the bond, usually payable in semiannual installments. The coupon rate normally stays constant during the life of the bond and indicates what the bondholder's annual dollar income will be.*

Coverage A term usually connected with revenue bonds. It is a ratio of net revenues pledged to principal and interest payments to debt service requirements. It is one of the factors used in evaluating the quality of an issue.**

Covered option An option position that is offset by an equal and opposite position in the underlying security.††

Covering Buying a security previously sold short. (See: *Short sale, Short covering.*)†

Credit terms The repayment provisions that are part of a credit arrangement. An example would be a 2/10, net 30 arrangement in which the customer may deduct 2 percent from the invoice price if payment takes place in the first ten days. Otherwise the full amount is due.*

Cumulative preferred A stock having a provision that if one or more dividends are omitted, the omitted dividends must be paid before dividends may be paid on the company's common stock.†

Cumulative voting A method of voting for corporate directors which enables the shareholder to multiply the number of his shares by the number of directorships being voted on and cast the total for one director or a selected group of directors. A 10-share holder normally casts 10 votes for each of, say 12 nominees to the board of directors. He thus has 120 votes. Under the cumulative voting principle he may do that or he may cast 120 (10 × 12) votes for only one nominee, 60 for two, 40 for three, or any other distribution he chooses. Cumulative voting is required under the corporate laws of some states, is permitted in most others.†

Currency futures contract A futures contract that may be used for hedging or speculation in foreign exchange.*

Current assets Those assets of a company which are reasonably expected to be realized in cash, or sold, or consumed during the normal operating cycle of the business. These include cash, U.S. government bonds, re-

ceivables and money due usually within one year, and inventories.†

Current cost accounting One of two methods of inflation-adjusted accounting approved by the Financial Accounting Standards Board in 1979. Financial statements are adjusted to the present, using current cost data rather than an index. This is shown as supplemental information in the firm's annual report.

Current liabilities Money owed and payable by a company, usually within one year.†

Current return (See: *Yield.*)

Current yield A relation stated as a percent of the annual interest to the actual market price of the bond.**

Day order An order to buy or sell which, if not executed expires at the end of the trading day on which it was entered.†

Dealer An individual or firm in the securities business who buys and sells stocks and bonds as a principal rather than as an agent. The dealer's profit or loss is the difference between the price paid and the price received for the same security. The dealer's confirmation must disclose to the customer that the principal has been acted upon. The same individual or firm may function, at different times, either as broker or dealer. (See: *NASD, Specialist.*)††

Debenture A long-term unsecured corporate bond. Debentures are usually issued by large, prestigious firms having excellent credit ratings in the financial community.*

Debit balance In a customer's margin account that portion of purchase price of stock, bonds, or commodities covered by credit extended by the broker to the margin customer.†

Debt limit The statutory or constitutional maximum debt that a municipality can legally incur.**

Debt service Refers to the payments required for interest and retirement of the principal amount of a debt.**

Debt utilization ratios A group of ratios that indicates to what extent debt is being used and the prudence with which it is being managed. Calculations include debt to total assets, times interest earned, and fixed charge coverage.*

Degree of financial leverage A measure of the impact of debt on the earnings capability of the firm. The percentage change in earnings per share is divided by the percentage change in earnings before interest and taxes at a given level of operation. Other algebraic statements are also used.*

Degree of operating leverage A measure of the impact of fixed costs on the operating earnings of the firm. The percentage change in operating income is divided by the percentage change in volume at a given level of operation. Other algebraic statements are also used.*

Denomination The face amount or par value of a security which the issuer promises to pay on the maturity date. Most municipal bonds are issued with a minimum denomination of $5,000, although a few older issues are available in $1,000 denominations.**

Depletion accounting Natural resources, such as metals, oil and gas, and timber, which conceivably can be reduced to zero over the years, present a special problem in capital management. Depletion is an accounting practice consisting of charges against earnings based upon the amount of the asset taken out of the total reserves in the period for which accounting is made. A bookkeeping entry, it does not represent any cash outlay nor are any funds earmarked for the purpose.†

Depository trust company (DTC) A central securities certificate depository through which members effect security deliveries between each other via computerized bookkeeping entries thereby reducing the physical movement of stock certificates.†

Depreciation Normally, charges against earnings to write off the cost, less salvage value, of an asset over its estimated useful life. It is a bookkeeping entry and does not represent any cash outlay nor are any funds earmarked for the purpose.†

Dilution of earnings This occurs when additional shares of stock are sold without creating an immediate increase in income. The result is a decline in earnings per share until earnings can be generated from the funds raised.*

Director Person elected by shareholders to establish company policies. The directors appoint the president, vice presidents, and all other operating officers. Directors decide, among other matters, if and when dividends shall be paid. (See: *Management, Proxy.*)†

Discount The amount by which a preferred stock or bond may sell below its par value. Also used as a verb to mean "takes into account" as the price of the stock has discounted the expected dividend cut. (See: *Premium.*)†

Discount rate ¹The interest rate at which future sums or annuities are discounted back to the present.*

The interest rate at which eligible depository institutions may borrow funds, usually for short periods, directly from the Federal Reserve Banks. The law requires the board of directors of each Reserve Bank to establish the discount rate every 14 days subject to the approval of the Board of Governors.¶

Discounted loan A loan in which the calculated interest payment is subtracted or discounted in advance. Because this lowers the amount of available funds, the effective interest rate is increased.*

Discretionary account An account in which the customer gives the broker or someone else discretion, which may be complete or within specific limits, either to the purchases, or sale of securities or commodities including selection, timing, amount, and price to be paid or received.†

Diversification Spreading investments among different companies in different fields. Another type of diversification is also offered by the securities of many individual companies because of the wide range of their activities. (See: *Investment trust.*)†

Dividend The payment designed by the board of directors to be distributed pro rata among the shares outstanding. On preferred shares, it is generally a fixed amount. On common shares, the dividend varies with the fortunes of the company and the amount of cash on hand, and may be omitted if business is poor or the directors determine to withhold earnings to invest in plant and equipment. Sometimes a company will pay a dividend out of past earnings even if it is not currently operating at a profit.†

Dividend information content This theory of dividends assumes that dividends provide information about the financial health and economic expectations of the company. If this is true, corporations must actively manage their dividends to provide the market with information.*

Dividend payment date The day on which a stockholder of record will receive his or her dividend.*

Dividend payout The percentage of dividends to earnings after taxes. It can be computed by dividing dividends per share by earnings per share.*

Dividend record date Stockholders owning the stock on the holder-of-record date are entitled to receive a dividend. In order to be listed as an owner on the corporate books, the investor must have bought the stock before it went ex-dividend.*

Dividend reinvestment plans Plans that provide the investor with an opportunity to buy additional shares of stock with the cash dividends paid by the company.*

Dividend valuation model A model for determining the value of a share of stock by taking the present value of an expected stream of future dividends.*

Dividend yield Dividends per share divided by market price per share. Dividend yield indicates the percentage return that a stockholder will receive on dividends alone.*

Dollar bond   A bond that is quoted and traded in dollars rather than in terms of yield.**

Dollar cost averaging   A system of buying securities at regular intervals with a fixed dollar amount. Under this system the investor buys by the dollars' worth rather than by the number of shares. If each investment is of the same number of dollars, payments buy more when the price is low and fewer when it rises. Thus temporary downswings in price benefit the investor if he continues periodic purchases in both good times and bad and the price at which the shares are sold is more than their average cost. (See: *Formula investing*.)†

Double-barrelled bond   A bond secured by the pledge of two or more sources of repayment, e.g., secured by taxes as well as revenues.**

Double exemption   Refers to securities that are exempt from state as well as Federal income taxes.**

Double taxation   Short for *double taxation of dividends*. The federal government taxes corporate profits once as corporate income; any part of the remaining profits distributed as dividends to stockholders may be taxed again as income to the recipient stockholder.†

Dow theory   A theory of market analysis based upon the performance of the Dow-Jones industrial and transportation stock price averages. The theory says that the market is in a basic upward trend if one of these averages advances above a previous important high, accompanied or followed by a similar advance in the other. When the averages both dip below previous important lows, this is regarded as confirmation of a basic downward trend. The theory does not attempt to predict how long either trend will continue, although it is widely misinterpreted as a method of forecasting future action.†

Down tick   (See: *Up tick*.)

Dual trading   Exists when one security, such as General Motors common stock, is traded on more than one stock exchange. This practice is quite common between NYSE-listed companies and regional exchanges.*

Dun & Bradstreet   A credit-rating agency that publishes information on over 3 million business establishments through its *Reference Book*.*

Du Pont System of Ratio Analysis   An analysis of profitability that breaks down return on assets between the profit margin and asset turnover. The second, or modified, version

shows how return on assets is translated into return on equity through the amount of debt that the firm has. Actually return on assets is divided by (1 − debt/assets) to arrive at return on equity.*

Earnings per share   The earnings available to common stockholders divided by the number of common stock shares outstanding.*

Earnings report   A statement—also called an *income statement*—issued by a company showing its earnings or losses over a given period. The earnings report lists the income earned, expenses, and the net result. (See: *Balance sheet*.)†

Economic indicators   Hundreds of indicators exist. Each is a specialized series of data. The data are analyzed for their relationship to economic activity, and the indicator is classified as either a lagging indicator, a leading indicator, or a coincident indicator of economic activity.*

Economical ordering quantity (EOQ)   The most efficient ordering quantity for the firm. The EOQ will allow the firm to minimize the total ordering and carrying costs associated with inventory.*

Efficient frontier   A line drawn through the optimum point selections in a risk-return trade-off diagram. Each point represents the best possible trade-off between risk and return (the highest return at a given risk level or the lowest risk at a given return level).*

Efficient market hypothesis   Hypothesis which suggests that markets adjust very quickly to new information and that it is very difficult for investors to select portfolios of securities that outperform the market.

Electronic funds transfer   A system in which funds are moved between computer terminals without the use of written checks.*

Employment Act of 1946   An act which specifies the four goals that the Federal Reserve Board should strive to achieve: economic growth, stable prices, high employment, and a balance of trade.*

Equipment trust certificate   A type of security, generally issued by a railroad, to pay for new equipment. Title to the equipment, such as a locomotive, is held by a trustee until the notes are paid off. An equipment trust certificate is usually secured by a first claim on the equipment.†

Equity   The net worth of a business, consisting of capital stock, capital (or paid-in) surplus, earned surplus (or retained earnings), and occasionally, certain net worth reserves. *Common equity* is that part of the total net worth belonging to the common stockholders. *Total equity* would include preferred stockholders. The terms *common stock, net worth,* and *common equity* are frequently used interchangeably.†

Eurobonds Bonds payable or denominated in the borrower's currency, but sold outside the country of the borrower, usually by an international syndicate.*

Eurodollar loan A loan from a foreign bank denominated in dollars.*

Eurodollars U.S. dollars held on deposit by foreign banks and loaned out by those banks to anyone seeking dollars.*

Exchange acquisition A method of filling an order to buy a large block of stock on the floor of the exchange. Under certain circumstances, a member-broker can facilitate the purpose of a block by soliciting orders to sell. All orders to sell the security are lumped together and crossed with the buy order in the regular action market. The price to the buyer may be on a net basis or on a commission basis.†

Exchange distribution A method of selling large blocks of stock on the floor of the exchange. Under certain circumstances, a member-broker can facilitate the sale of a block of stock by soliciting and getting other member-brokers to solicit orders to buy. Individual buy orders are lumped together and crossed with the sell order in the regular auction market. A special commission is usually paid by the seller; ordinarily the buyer pays no commission.†

Ex-dividend A synonym for "without dividend." The buyer of a stock selling ex-dividend does not receive the recently declared dividend. Every dividend is payable on a fixed date to all shareholders recorded on the books of the company as of a previous date of record. For example, a dividend may be declared as payable to holders of record on the books of the company on a given Friday. Since five business days are allowed for delivery of stock in a "regular way" transaction on the New York Stock Exchange, the Exchange would declare the stock "ex-dividend" as of the opening of the market on the preceding Monday. That means anyone who bought it on and after Monday would not be entitled to that dividend. When stocks go ex-dividend, the stock tables include the symbol "x" following the name. (See: *Cash sale, Net change, Transfer.*)†

Ex-dividend date Four business days before the holder-of-record date. On the ex-dividend date the purchase of the stock no longer carries with it the right to receive the dividend previously declared.*

Expectations theory of interest rates This theory explains the shape of the term structure relative to expectations for future short-term interest rates. It is thought that long-term rates are an average of the expected short-term rates. Therefore, an upward-sloping yield curve would indicate that short-term rates will rise.*

Expected value A representative value from a probability distribution arrived at by multiplying each outcome by the associated probability and summing up the values.*

Export-Import Bank (Eximbank) An agency of the United States government that facilitates the financing of United States exports through its miscellaneous programs. In its direct loan program, the Eximbank lends money to foreign purchasers of U.S. products—such as aircraft, electrical equipment, heavy machinery, computers, and the like. The Eximbank also purchases eligible medium-term obligations of foreign buyers of U.S. goods at a discount from face value. In this discount program, private banks and other lenders are able to rediscount (sell at a lower price) promissory notes and drafts acquired from foreign customers of U.S. firms.*

Expropriation The action of a country in taking away or modifying the property rights of a corporation or individual.*

Ex-rights The situation in which the purchase of common stock during a rights offering no longer includes rights to purchase additional shares of common stock.*

Extension An out-of-court settlement in which creditors agree to allow the firm more time to meet its financial obligations. A new repayment schedule will be developed, subject to the acceptance of creditors.*

External corporate funds Corporate financing raised through sources outside of the firm. Bonds, common stock, and preferred stock fall in this category.*

External reorganization A reorganization under the formal bankruptcy laws in which a merger partner is found for the distressed firm. Ideally, the firm should be merged with a strong firm in its own industry, although this is not always possible.*

Factoring receivables Selling accounts receivable to a finance company or a bank.*

Federal budget deficit Government expenditures are greater than government tax revenues, and the government must borrow to balance revenues and expenditures. These deficits act as an economic stimulus.*

Federal budget surplus Government tax receipts are greater than government expenditures. A rarity during the last 20 years. These surpluses have a dampening effect on the economy.*

Federal National Mortgage Association A government agency that provides a secondary market in mortgages.*

Federal Reserve discount rate The rate of interest that the Fed charges on loans to the banking system. A monetary tool for management of the money supply.*

Federally sponsored agency securities Securities issued by federal agencies such as the Federal Land Bank and Federal Home Loan Board.*

Field warehousing An inventory financing arrangement in which collateralized inventory is stored on the premises of the borrower but is controlled by an independent warehousing company.*

FIFO A system of writing off inventory into cost of goods sold in which the items purchased first are written off first. Referred to as first-in, first-out.*

Financial Accounting Standards Board A privately supported rulemaking body for the accounting profession.*

Financial capital Common stock, preferred stock, bonds, and retained earnings. Financial capital appears on the corporate balance sheet under long-term liabilities and equity.*

Financial disclosure Presentation of financial information to the investment community.*

Financial futures market A market that allows for the trading of financial instruments related to a future point in time. A purchase or sale takes place in the present, with a reversal necessitated in the future to close out the position. If a purchase (sale) takes place initially, then a sale (purchase) will be necessary in the future. The market provides for futures contracts in Treasury bonds, Treasury bills, certificates of deposits, GNMA certificates, and many other instruments. Financial futures contracts may be executed on the Chicago Board of Trade, the Chicago Mercantile Exchange, the New York Futures Exchange, and other exchanges.*

Financial intermediary A financial institution such as a bank or a life insurance company that directs other people's money into such investments as government and corporate securities.*

Financial lease A long-term noncancelable lease. The financial lease has all the characteristics of long-term debt except that the lease payments are a combination of interest expense and amortization of the cost of the asset.*

Financial leverage A measure of the amount of debt used in the capital structure of the firm.*

Financial sweetener Usually refers to equity options, such as warrants or conversion privileges, attached to a debt security. The sweetener lowers the interest cost to the corporation.*

Fiscal policy The tax policies of the federal government and the spending associated with its tax revenues.*

Fixed costs Costs that remain relatively constant regardless of the volume of operations. Examples are rent, depreciation, property taxes, and executive salaries.*

Float The difference between the corporation's recorded cash balance on its books and the amount credited to the corporation by the bank.*

Floating rate bond The interest payment on the bond changes with market conditions rather than the price of the bond.*

Floating rate preferred stock The quarterly dividend on the preferred stock changes with market conditions. The market price is considerably less volatile than it is with regular preferred stock.*

Floor price Usually equal to the pure bond value. A convertible bond will not sell at less than its pure bond value even when its conversion value is below the pure bond value.*

Flotation cost The distribution cost of selling securities to the public. The cost includes the underwriter's spread and any associated fees.*

Forced conversion Occurs when a company calls a convertible security that has a conversion value greater than the call price. Investors will take the higher of the two values and convert the security to common stock rather than take a lower cash call price.*

Foreign Credit Insurance Association (FCIA) An agency established by a group of 60 U.S. insurance companies. It sells credit export insurance to interested exporters. The FCIA promises to pay for the exported merchandise if the foreign importer defaults on payment.*

Foreign exchange rate The relationship between the value of two or more currencies. For example, the exchange rate between U.S. dollars and French francs is stated as dollars per francs or francs per dollar.*

Foreign exchange risk A form of risk that refers to the possibility of experiencing a drop in revenue or an increase in cost in an international transaction due to a change in foreign exchange rates. Importers, exporters, investors, and multinational firms alike are exposed to this risk.*

Formula investing An investment technique. One formula calls for the shifting of funds from common shares to preferred shares or bonds as the market, on average, rises above a certain predetermined point—and the return of funds to common share investments as the market average declines. (See: *Dollar cost averaging.*)†

Founders' stock Stock owned by the original founders of a company. It often carries special voting rights that allow the founders to maintain voting privileges in excess of their proportionate ownership.*

Fourth market A market of stocks and bonds in which there is direct dealing between financial institutions, such as investment bankers, insurance companies, pension funds, and mutual funds.*

Free and open market A market in which supply and demand are freely expressed in terms of price. Contrasts with a controlled market in which supply, demand, and price may all be regulated.†

Fronting loan A parent company's loan to a foreign subsidiary is channeled through a financial intermediary, usually a large international bank. The bank fronts for the parent in extending the loan to the foreign affiliate.*

Fully diluted earnings per share Equals adjusted earnings after taxes divided by shares outstanding, plus common stock equivalents, plus all convertible securities.*

Fundamental research Analysis of industries and companies based on factors such as sales, assets, earnings, products or services, markets, and management. As supplied to the economy, fundamental research includes consideration of gross national product, interest rates, unemployment, inventories, savings, and so on. (See: *Technical research.*)†

Funded debt Usually long-term, interest-bearing bonds or debentures of a company. Could include long-term bank loans. Does *not* include short-term loans, preferred, or common stock.†

Futures contract A contract to buy or sell a commodity at some specified price in the future.*

General mortgage bond A bond which is secured by a blanket mortgage on the company's property, but which may be outranked by one or more other mortgages.†

General obligation bond A bond secured by the pledge of the issuer's full faith, credit and taxing power.**

Gilt-edged High-grade bond issued by a company which has demonstrated its ability to earn a comfortable profit over a period of years and pay its bondholders their interest without interruption.†

Give up A term with many different meanings. For one, a member of the exchange on the floor may act for a second member by executing an order for him with a third member. The first member tells the third member that he is acting on behalf of the second member and "gives up" the second member's name rather than his own.††

Going private The process by which all publicly owned shares of common stock are repurchased or retired, thereby eliminating listing fees, annual reports, and other expenses involved with publicly owned companies.*

Gold fix The setting of the price of gold by dealers (especially in a twice-daily London meeting at the central bank); the fix is the fundamental worldwide price for setting prices of gold bullion and gold-related contracts and products.††

Golden parachute Highly attractive termination payments made to current management in the event of a takeover of the company.*

Good delivery Certain basic qualifications must be met before a security sold on the exchange may be delivered. The security must be in proper form to comply with the contract of sale and to transfer title to the purchaser.†

Good 'til cancelled order (GTC) or open order An order to buy or sell which remains in effect until it is either executed or cancelled.†

Goodwill An intangible asset that reflects value above that generally recognized in the tangible assets of the firm.*

Government bonds Obligations of the U.S. government, regarded as the highest grade issues in existence.†

Growth stock Stock of a company with a record of growth in earnings at a relatively rapid rate.†

Guaranteed bond A bond which has interest or principal, or both, guaranteed by a company other than the issuer. Usually found in the railroad industry when large roads, leasing sections of trackage owned by small railroads, may guarantee the bonds of the smaller road.†

Guaranteed stock Usually preferred stock on which dividends are guaranteed by another company; under much the same circumstances as a bond is guaranteed.†

Hedge (See: *Arbitrage, Option, Short sale.*)

Hedging The purchase or sale of a derivative security (such as options or futures) in order to reduce or neutralize all or some portion of the risk of holding another security.††

Holding company A corporation which owns the securities of another, in most cases with voting control.†

Hurdle rate The minimum acceptable rate of return in a capital budgeting decision.*

Hypothecation The pledging of securities as collateral—for example, to secure the debit balance in a margin account.†

Inactive stock An issue traded on an exchange or in the over-the-counter market in which there is a relatively low volume of transactions. Volume may be no more than a few hundred shares a week or even less. On the New York Stock Exchange many inactive stocks are traded in 10-share units rather than the customary 100. (See: *Round lot.*)†

In-and-out Purchase and sale of the same security within a short period—a day, a week, even a month. An in-and-out trader is generally more interested in day-to-day price fluctuations than dividends or long-term growth.†

Income bond Generally income bonds promise to repay principal but to pay interest only when earned. In some cases unpaid interest on an income bond may accumulate as a claim against the corporation when the bond becomes due. An income bond may also be issued in lieu of preferred stock.†

Income statement A financial statement that measures the profitability of the firm over a period of time. All expenses are subtracted from sales to arrive at net income.*

Indenture A written agreement under which bonds and debentures are issued, setting forth maturity date, interest rate, and other terms.†

Independent broker Members on the floor of the NYSE who execute orders for other brokers having more business at that time than they can handle themselves, or for firms who do not have their Exchange member on the floor. Formerly known as *two-dollar brokers* from the time when these independent brokers received $2 per hundred shares for executing such orders. Their fees are paid by the commission brokers. (See: *Commission broker.*)†

Index A statistical yardstick expressed in terms of percentages of a base year or years. For instance, the Federal Reserve Board's index of industrial production is based on 1967 as 100. An index is not an average. (See: *Averages.*)†

Industrial revenue bond A security backed by private enterprises that have been financed by a municipal issue.**

Inflation The phenomenon of price increase with the passage of time.*

Inflation premium A premium to compensate the investor for the eroding effect of inflation on the value of the dollar. In the 1980s the inflation premium has been 3 to 4 percent. In the late 1970s it was in excess of 10 percent.*

Installment loan A borrowing arrangement in which a series of equal payments are used to pay off the loan.*

Institutional Investor An organization whose primary purpose is to invest its own assets or those held in trust by it for others. Includes pension funds, investment companies, insurance companies, universities, and banks.†

Interest Payments a borrower pays a lender for the use of his money. A corporation pays interest on its bonds to its bondholders. (See: *Bond, dividend.*)†

Interest factor *(IF)* The tabular value to insert into the various formulas. It is based on the number of periods *(n)* and the interest rate *(i).**

Interest rate parity theory A theory based on the interplay between interest rate differentials and exchange rates. If one country has a higher interest rate than another country after adjustments for inflation, interest rates and foreign exchange rates will adjust until the foreign exchange rates and money market rates reach equilibrium (are properly balanced between the two countries).*

Intermarket Trading System (ITS) An electronic communications network now linking the trading floor of seven registered exchanges to foster competition among them in stocks listed on either the NYSE or AMEX and one or more regional exchanges. Through ITS, any broker or market-maker on the floor of any participating market can reach out to other participants for an execution whenever the nationwide quote shows a better price is available.††

Internal corporate funds Funds generated through the operations of the firm. The principal sources are retained earnings and cash flow added back from depreciation and other noncash deductions.*

Internal financing Funds made available for capital budgeting and working-capital expansion through the normal operations of the firm; internal financing is approximately equal to retained earnings plus depreciation.*

Internal rate of return (IRR) A discounted cash flow method for evaluating capital budgeting projects. The IRR is a discount rate which makes the present value of the cash inflows equal to the present value of the cash outflows.*

Internal reorganization A reorganization under the formal bankruptcy laws. New management may be brought in and a redesign of the capital structure may be implemented.*

International diversification Achieving diversification through many different foreign investments that are influenced by a variety of factors.*

International Finance Corporation (IFC) An affiliate of the World Bank established with the sole purpose of providing partial seed capital for private ventures around the world. Whenever a multinational company has difficulty raising equity capital due to lack of adequate private risk capital, the firm may explore the possibility of selling equity or debt (totaling up to 25 percent) to the International Finance Corporation.*

Intrinsic value The dollar amount of the difference between the exercise price of an option and the current cash value of the underlying security. Intrinsic value and time value are the two components of an option premium, or price.††

Inventory profits Profits generated as a result of an inflationary economy in which old inventory is sold at large profits because of increasing prices. This is particularly prevalent under FIFO accounting.*

Inverted yield curve A downward-sloping yield curve. Short-term rates are higher than long-term rates.*

Investment The use of money for the purpose of making more money, to gain income or increase capital, or both.††

Investment banker A financial organization that specializes in selling primary offerings of securities. Investment bankers can also perform other financial functions, such as advising clients, negotiating mergers and takeovers, and selling secondary offerings.*

Investment company A company or trust which uses its capital to invest in other companies. There are two principal types: the closed-end and the open-end, or mutual fund. Shares in closed-end investment companies, some of which are listed on the New York Stock Exchange, are readily transferable in the open market and are bought and sold like other shares. Capitalization of these companies remains the same unless action is taken to change, which is seldom. Open-end funds sell their own new shares to investors, stand ready to buy back their old shares, and are not listed. Open-end funds are so called because their capitalization is not fixed; they issue more shares as people want them.†

Investment counsel One whose principal business consists of acting as investment adviser and a substantial part of his business consists of rendering investment supervisory services.†

Investment tax credit (ITC) A percentage of the purchase price that may be deducted directly from tax obligations.

IRA Individual Retirement Account. A pension plan with major tax advantages. Any worker can begin an IRA by a cash contribution up to $2,000 annually which is not tax deductible; however, the investment return on which is tax deferred. (See: *Keogh Plan*.)

Issue Any of a company's securities, or the act of distributing such securities.†

Issuer A municipal unit that borrows money through the sale of bonds or notes.**

Keogh Plan Tax advantaged personal retirement program that can be established by a self-employed individual. Currently, annual contributions to a plan can be up to $15,000. Such contributions and reinvestments are not taxed as they accumulate but will be when withdrawn (presumably at retirement when taxable income may be less). (See: *IRA*.)††

Leading indicators The most commonly followed series of economic indicators (a series of the 12 leading indicators). These are used to help forecast economic activity.*

Lease A contractual arrangement between the owner of equipment (lessor) and the user of equipment (lessee) which calls for the lessee to pay the lessor an established lease payment. There are two kinds of leases, financial leases and operating leases.*

Legal list A list of investments selected by various states in which certain institutions and fiduciaries, such as insurance companies and banks, may invest. Legal lists are often restricted to high quality securities meeting certain specifications. (See: *Prudent man rule*.)††

Legal opinion An opinion concerning the legality of a bond issue usually written by a recognized law firm specializing in public borrowings.**

Letter of credit A credit letter normally issued by the importer's bank in which the bank promises to pay out the money for the merchandise when delivered.*

Level production Equal monthly production used to smooth out production schedules and employ manpower and equipment more efficiently and at a lower cost.*

Leverage The effect on a company when the company has bonds, preferred stock, or both outstanding. Example: If the earnings of a company with 1,000,000 common shares increases from $1,000,000 to $1,500,000—earnings per share would go from $1 to $1.50, or an increase of 50 percent. But if earnings of a company that had to pay $500,000 in bond interest increased that much—earnings per common share would jump from 50 cents to $1 a share, or 100 percent.††

Leveraged buy-out Existing management or an outsider makes an offer to "go private" by retiring all the shares of the company. The buying group borrows the necessary money, using the assets of the acquired firm as collateral. The buying group them repurchases all the shares and expects to retire the debt over time with the cash flow from operations or the sale of corporate assets.*

Liabilities All the claims against a corporation. Liabilities include accounts and wages and salaries payable, dividends declared payable, accrued taxes payable, fixed or long-term liabilities such as mortgage bonds, debentures, and bank loans. (See: *Assets, Balance sheet.*)†

LIBOR (See: *London Interbank Offered Rate.*)*

Life cycle curve A curve illustrating the growth phases of a firm. The dividend policy most likely to be employed during each phase is often illustrated.*

LIFO A system of writing off inventory into cost of goods sold in which the items purchased last are written off first. Referred to as last-in, first-out.*

Limit, limited order, or limited price order An order to buy or sell a stated amount of a security at a specified price, or at a better price, if obtainable after the order is represented in the Trading Crowd.†

Limited partnership A special form of partnership to limit liability for most of the partners. Under this arrangement, one or more partners are designated as general partners and have unlimited liability for the debts of the firm, while the other partners are designated as limited partners and are only liable for their initial contribution.*

Limited tax bond A bond secured by a pledge of a tax or group of taxes limited as to rate or amount.**

Liquidation The process of converting securities or other property into cash. The dissolution of a company, with cash remaining after sale of its assets and payment of all indebtedness being distributed to the shareholders.†

Liquidity The ability of the market in a particular security to absorb a reasonable amount of buying or selling at reasonable price changes. Liquidity is one of the most important characteristics of a good market.†

Liquidity ratios A group of ratios that allows one to measure the firm's ability to pay off

short-term obligations as they come due. Primary attention is directed to the current ratio and the quick ratio.*

Listed stock The stock of a company which is traded on a securities exchange. The various stock exchanges have different standards for listing. Some of the guides used by the New York Stock Exchange for an original listing are national interest in the company, a minimum of 1.1-million shares publicly held among not less than 2,000 round-lot stockholders. The publicly held common shares should have a minimum aggregate market value of $18 million. The company should have net income in the latest year of over $2.5-million before federal income tax and $2-million in each of the preceding two years.††

Listing requirements Financial standards that corporations must meet before their common stock can be traded on a stock exchange. Listing requirements are not standard, but are set by each exchange. The requirements for the NYSE are the most stringent.*

Load The portion of the offering price of shares of open-end investment companies in excess of the value of the underlying assets which cover sales commissions and all other costs of distribution. The load is usually incurred only on purchase, there being, in most cases, no charge when the shares are sold (redeemed).†

Lockbox system A procedure used to expedite cash inflows to a business. Customers are requested to forward their checks to a post-office box in their geographic region, and a local bank picks up the checks and processes them for rapid collection. Funds are then wired to the corporate home office for immediate use.*

London Interbank Offered Rate (LIBOR) An interbank rate applicable for large deposits in the London market. It is a bench-mark rate just like the prime interest rate in the United States. Interest rates on Eurodollar loans are determined by adding premiums to this basic rate. Most often LIBOR is lower than the U.S. prime rate.*

Long Signifies ownership of securities: "I am long 100 U.S. Steel" means the speaker owns 100 shares. (See: *Short position, Short sale.*)†

Majority voting All directors must be elected by a vote of more than 50 percent. Minority shareholders are unable to achieve any representation on the board of directors.*

Management The board of directors, elected by the stockholders, and the officers of the corporation, appointed by the board of directors.†

Managing underwriter An investment banker who is responsible for the pricing, prospectus development, and legal work involved in the sale of a new issue of securities.*

Manipulation An illegal operation. Buying or selling a security for the purpose of creating a false or misleading appearance of active trading or for the purpose of raising or depressing the price to induce purchase or sale by others.†

Margin The amount paid by the customer when using a broker's credit to buy or sell a security. Under Federal Reserve regulations, the initial margin required since 1945 has ranged from the current rate 50 percent of the purchase price up to 100 percent. (See: *Brokers' loans, Equity, Margin call.*)††

Margin call A demand upon a customer to put up money or securities with the broker. The call is made when a purchase is made; also if a customer's equity in a margin account declines below a minimum standard set by the exchange or by the firm. (See: *Margin.*)†

Margin requirement A rule that specifies the amount of cash or equity that must be deposited with a brokerage firm or bank, with the balance of funds cligible for borrowing. Margin is set by the Board of Governors of the Federal Reserve Board. For example, margin of 60 percent would mean that a $10,000 purchase would allow the buyer to borrow $4,000 toward the purchase.*

Marginal corporate tax rate The rate that applies to each new dollar of taxable income. For a corporation, the rate in 1986 is 15 percent on the first $25,000, 18 percent on the second $25,000, 30 percent on the third 25,000, 40 percent on the fourth $25,000, and 46 percent on all larger amounts.*

Marginal cost of capital The cost of the last dollar of funds raised. It is assumed that each dollar is financed in proportion to the firm's optimum capital structure.*

Marginal principle of retained earnings The corporation must be able to earn a higher return on its retained earnings than a stockholder would receive after paying taxes on the distributed dividends.*

Market efficiency Markets are considered to be efficient when (1) prices adjust rapidly to new information; (2) there is a continuous market in which each successive trade is made at a price close to the previous price (the faster the price responds to new information and the smaller the differences in price changes, the more efficient the market); and (3) the market can absorb large dollar amounts of securities without destabilizing the prices.*

Market maker (See: *Dealer.*)

Market order An order to buy or sell a stated amount of a security at the most advantageous price obtainable after the order is represented in the trading crowd. (See: *Good 'til cancelled order, Limit order, Stop order.*)††

Market price In the case of a security, market price is usually considered the last reported price at which the stock or bond sold.†

Market risk premium A premium over and above the risk-free rate. It is represented by the difference between the market return (K_m) and the risk-free rate (R_f), and it may be multiplied by the beta coefficient to determine additional risk-adjusted return on a security.*

Market stabilization Intervention in the secondary markets by an investment banker to stabilize the price of a new security offering during the offering period. The purpose of market stabilization is to provide an orderly market for the distribution of the new issue.*

Market value maximization The concept of maximizing the wealth of shareholders. This calls for a recognition not only of earnings per share but also how they will be valued in the marketplace.*

Marketability The measure of the ease with which a security can be sold in the secondary market.**

Maturity The date on which a loan or a bond or debenture comes due and is to be paid off.†

Member corporation A securities brokerage firm, organized as a corporation, with at least one member of the New York Stock Exchange, who is an officer or an employee of the corporation.††

Member firm A securities brokerage firm organized as a partnership and having at least one general partner who is a member of the New York Stock Exchange, Inc. (See: *Member corporation.*)†

Member organization This term includes New York Stock Exchange Member Firm *and* Member Corporation. (See: *Member corporation, Member firm.*)†

Merger The combination of two or more companies in which the resulting firms maintain the identity of the acquiring company.*

Merger arbitrageur A specialist in merger investments who attempts to capitalize on the difference between the value offered and the current market value of the acquisition candidate.*

Merger premium The part of a buy-out or exchange offer which represents a value over and above the market value of the acquired firm.*

Minimum warrant value The market value of the common stock minus the option price of the warrant multiplied by the number of shares of the common stock that each warrant entitles the holder to purchase.*

Monetary policy Management by the Federal Reserve Board of the money supply and the resultant interest rates.*

Money market accounts Accounts at banks, savings and loans, and credit unions in which the depositor receives competitive money market rates on a typical minimum deposit of $1,000. These accounts may generally have three deposits and three withdrawals per month, and are not meant to be transaction accounts, but a place to keep minimum and excess cash balances. These accounts are insured by various appropriate governmental agencies up to $100,000.*

Money market funds A fund in which investors may purchase shares for as little as $500 or $1,000. The fund then reinvests the proceeds in high-yielding $100,000 bank CDs, $25,000–$100,000 commercial paper, and other large-denomination, high-yielding securities. Investors receive their pro rata portion of the interest proceeds daily as a credit to their shares.*

Money markets Competitive markets for securities with maturities of one year or less. The best examples of money market instruments would be Treasury bills, commercial paper, and negotiable certificates of deposit.*

Mortgage agreement A loan which requires real property (plant and equipment) as collateral.*

Mortgage bond A bond secured by a mortgage on a property. The value of the property may or may not equal the value of the bonds issued against it. (See: *Bond, Debenture*.)††

Multinational corporation A firm doing business across its national borders is considered a multinational enterprise. Some definitions require a minimum percentage (often 30 percent or more) of a firm's business activities to be carried on outside its national borders.*

Municipal bond A bond issued by a state or a political subdivision, such as county, city, town, or village. The term also designates bonds issued by state agencies and authorities. In general, interest paid on municipal bonds is exempt from federal income taxes and state and local income taxes within the state of issue.†

Municipal securities Securities issued by state and local government units. The income

from these securities is exempt from federal income taxes.*

Mutual fund (See: *Investment company*.)

Mutually exclusive The selection of one choice precludes the selection of any competitive choice. For example, several machines can do an identical job in capital budgeting. If one machine is selected, the other machines will not be used.*

Naked option An option position that is *not* offset by an equal and opposite position in the underlying security.††

NASD The National Association of Securities Dealers, Inc. An association of brokers and dealers in the over-the-counter securities business.††

NASDAQ An automated information network which provides brokers and dealers with price quotations on securities traded over-the-counter. NASDAQ is an acronym for National Association of Securities Dealers Automated Quotations.†

National Market List The list of the best-known and most widely traded securities in the over-the-counter market.*

National market system A system mandated by the Securities Acts Amendments of 1975. The national market system that is envisioned will include computer processing and computerized competitive prices for all markets trading similar stocks. The exact form of the system is yet to be determined.*

Negotiable Refers to a security, title to which is transferable by delivery. (See: *Good delivery*.)†

Negotiable Order of Withdrawal account An interest earning account on which checks may be drawn. Withdrawals from NOW accounts may be subject to a 14-day or more notice requirement although such is rarely imposed. NOW accounts may be offered by commercial banks, mutual savings banks, and savings and loan associations and may be owned only by individuals and certain non-profit organizations and governmental units.¶

Net asset value Usually used in connection with investment companies to mean net asset value per share. An investment company computes its assets daily, or even twice daily, by totaling the market value of all securities owned. All liabilities are deducted, and the balance divided by the number of shares outstanding. The resulting figure is the net asset value per share. (See: *Assets, Investment company*.)††

Net change The change in the price of a security from the closing price on one day and the closing price on the following day on which the stock is traded. The net change is ordinarily the last figure on the stock price list. The mark + 1⅛ means up $1.125 a share from the last sale on the previous day the stock traded.†

Net debt   Gross debt less sinking fund accumulations and all self-supporting debt.**

Net present value (NPV)   The NPV equals the present value of the cash inflows minus the present value of the cash outflows with the cost of capital used as a discount rate. This method is used to evaluate capital budgeting projects. If the NPV is positive, a project should be accepted.*

Net present value profile   A graphical presentation of the potential net present values of a project at different discount rates. It is very helpful in comparing the characteristics of two or more investments.*

Net trade credit   A measure of the relationship between the firm's accounts receivable and accounts payable. If accounts receivable exceed accounts payable, the firm is a net provider of trade credit; otherwise, it is a net user.*

Net worth, or book value   Stockholders' equity minus preferred stock ownership. Basically, net worth is the common stockholders' interest as represented by common stock par value, capital paid in excess of par, and retained earnings. If you take all the assets of the firm and subtract its liabilities and preferred stock, you arrive at net worth.*

New housing authority bonds   A bond issued by a local public housing authority to finance public housing. It is backed by Federal funds and the solemn pledge of the U.S. Government that payment will be made in full.**

New issue   A stock or bond sold by a corporation for the first time. Proceeds may be issued to retire outstanding securities of the company, for new plant or equipment, or for additional working capital, or to acquire a public ownership interest in the company for private owners.††

New issue market   Market for new issues of municipal bonds and notes.**

New York Futures Exchange (NYFE)   A subsidiary of the New York Stock Exchange devoted to the trading of futures products.††

New York Stock Exchange (NYSE)   The largest organized securities market in the United States, founded in 1792. The Exchange itself does not buy, sell, own, or set the prices of securities traded there. The prices are determined by public supply and demand. The Exchange is a not-for-profit corporation of 1,366 individual members, governed by a Board of Directors consisting of 10 public representatives, 10 Exchange members or allied members and a full-time chairman, executive vice chairman and president.††

Nominal GNP   GNP (gross national product) in current dollars without any adjustments for inflation.*

Nominal yield   A return equal to the coupon rate.*

Noncumulative   A type of preferred stock on which unpaid dividends do not accrue. Omitted dividends are, as a rule, gone forever. (See: *Cumulative preferred.*)††

Nonfinancial corporation   A firm not in the banking or financial services industry. The term would primarily apply to manufacturing, wholesaling, and retail firms.*

Nonlinear break-even analysis   Break-even analysis based on the assumption that cost and revenue relationships to quantity may vary at different levels of operation. Most of our analysis is based on *linear* break-even analysis.*

Normal recovery period   The depreciation recovery period (3, 5, 10, 15 years) under the Accelerated Cost Recovery System of the 1981 Economic Recovery Tax Act.*

Normal yield curve   An upward-sloping yield curve. Long-term interest rates are higher than short-term rates.*

Notes   Short-term unsecured promises to pay specified amounts of money. For municipal notes maturities generally range from six to twelve months.**

NYSE composite index   A composite index covering price movements of all common stocks listed on the "Big Board." It is based on the close of the market December 31, 1965 as 50.00 and is weighted according to the number of shares listed for each issue. The index is computed continuously and printed on the ticker tape each half hour. Point changes in the index are converted to dollars and cents so as to provide a meaningful measure of changes in the average price of listed stocks. The composite index is supplemented by separate indexes for four industry groups: industries, transportation, utilities, and finances. (See: *Averages.*)††

Odd lot   An amount of stock less than the established 100-share unit. (See: *Round lot.*)††

Off-board   This term may refer to transactions over-the-counter in unlisted securities, or to a transaction involving listed shares that is not executed on a national securities exchange.††

Offer   The price at which a person is ready to sell. Opposed to bid, the price at which one is ready to buy. (See: *Bid and asked.*)†

Official statement Document prepared by or for the issuer that gives in detail the security and financial information about the issue.**

Open-end investment company (See: *Investment company.*)

Open interest In options and futures trading, the number of outstanding option contracts, at a given point in time, which have not been exercised and have not yet reached expiration.††

Open-market operations The purchase and sale of government securities in the open market by the Federal Reserve Board for its own account. The most common method for managing the money supply.*

Open order (See: *Good 'til cancelled order.*)

Operating lease A short-term, nonbinding obligation that is easily cancelable.*

Operating leverage A reflection of the extent to which fixed assets and fixed costs are utilized in the business firm.*

Optimum capital structure A capital structure that has the best possible mix of debt, preferred stock, and common equity. The optimum mix should provide the lowest possible cost of capital to the firm.*

Option A right to buy (call) or sell (put) a fixed amount of a given stock at a specified price within a limited period of time. The purchaser hopes that the stock's price will go up (a call) or down (a put) by an amount sufficient to provide a profit when the stock is sold. If the stock price holds steady or moves in the opposite direction, the price paid for the option is lost entirely. There are several other types of options available to the public but these are basically combinations of puts and calls. Individuals may write (sell) as well as purchase options. Options are also traded on stock indexes, futures, and debt instruments.††

Orders good until a specified time A market or limited price order which is to be represented in the Trading Crowd until a specified time, after which such order or the portion thereof not executed is to be treated as cancelled.†

Overbought An opinion as to price levels. May refer to a security which has had a sharp rise or to the market as a whole after a period of vigorous buying, which it may be argued, has left prices "too high."†

Overseas Private Investment Corporation (OPIC) A government agency that sells insurance policies to qualified firms. This agency insures against losses due to inconvertibility into dollars of amounts invested in a foreign country. Policies are also available from OPIC to insure against expropriation and against losses due to war or revolution.*

Oversold The reverse of overbought. A single security or a market which, it is believed, has declined to an unreasonable level.††

Over-the-counter A market for securities made up of securities dealers who may or may not be members of a securities exchange. The over-the-counter market is conducted over the telephone and deals mainly with stocks of companies without sufficient shares, stockholders, or earnings to warrant listing on an exchange. Over-the-counter dealers may act either as principals or as brokers for customers. The over-the-counter market is the principal market for bonds of all types. (See: *NASD, NASDAQ.*)††

Paper profit (LOSS) An unrealized profit or loss on a security still held. Paper profits and losses become realized profits only when the security is sold. (See: *Profit-taking.*)††

Par In the case of a common share, par means a dollar amount assigned to the share by the company's charter. Par value may also be used to compute the dollar amount of the common shares on the balance sheet. Par value has little relationship to the market value of common stock. Many companies issue no-par stock but give a stated per share value on the balance sheet. In the case of preferred stocks, it signifies the dollar value upon which dividends are figured. With bonds, par value is the face amount, usually $1,000.††

Parallel loan A U.S. firm that wishes to lend funds to a foreign affiliate (such as a Dutch affiliate) locates a foreign parent firm (such as a Dutch parent firm) that wishes to loan money to a U.S. affiliate. Avoiding the foreign exchange markets entirely, the U.S. parent lends dollars to the Dutch affiliate in the United States, while the Dutch parent lends guilders to the American affiliate in the Netherlands. At maturity, the two loans would each be repaid to the original lender. Notice that neither loan carries any foreign exchange risk in this arrangement.*

Participating preferred A preferred stock which is entitled to its stated dividend and, also, to additional dividends on a specified basis upon payment of dividends on the common stock.†

Partnership A form of ownership in which two or more partners are involved. Like the sole proprietorship, a partnership arrangement carries unlimited liability for the owners. However, there is only single taxation for the partners, an advantage over the corporate form of ownership.*

Passed dividend Omission of a regular or scheduled dividend.†

Payback A value that indicates the time period required to recoup an initial investment. The payback does not include the time-value-of-money concept.*

Paying agent Place where principal and interest is payable. Usually a designated bank or the treasurer's office of the issuer.**

Penny stocks Low-priced issues often highly speculative, selling at less than $1 a share. Frequently used as a term of disparagement, although a few penny stocks have developed into investment-caliber issues.†

Percent-of-sales method A method of determining future financial needs that is an alternative to the development of pro forma financial statements. We first determine the percentage relationship of various asset and liability accounts to sales, and then we show how that relationship changes as our volume of sales changes.*

Permanent current assets Current assets that will not be reduced or converted to cash within the normal operating cycle of the firm. Though from a strict accounting standpoint the assets should be removed from the current assets category, they generally are not.*

Perpetuity An investment without a maturity date.*

Planning horizon The length of time it takes to conceive, develop, and complete a project and to recover the cost of the project on a discounted cash flow basis.*

Pledging receivables Using accounts receivable as collateral for a loan. The firm usually may borrow 60 to 80 percent of the value of acceptable collateral.*

Point In the case of shares of stock, a point means $1. If ABC shares rises 3 points, each share has risen $3. In the case of bonds a point means $10, since a bond is quoted as a percentage of $1,000. A bond which rises 3 points gains 3 percent of $1,000, or $30 in value. An advance from 87 to 90 would mean an advance in dollar value from $870 to $900. In the case of market averages, the word point means merely that and no more. If, for example, the NYSE Composite Index rises from 90.25 to 91.25, it has risen a point. A point in this average, however, is not equivalent to $1. (See: *Index.*)††

Point-of-sales terminals Computer terminals in retail stores that either allow digital input or use optical scanners. The terminals may be used for inventory control or other purposes.*

Pooling of interests A method of financial recording for mergers in which the financial statements of the firms are combined, subject to minor adjustments, and goodwill is *not* created.*

Portfolio Holdings of securities by an individual or institution. A portfolio may contain bonds, preferred stocks, common stocks and other securities.††

Portfolio effect The impact of a given investment on the overall risk-return composition of the firm. A firm must consider not only the individual investment characteristics of a project, but also how the project relates to the entire portfolio of undertakings.*

Preemptive right The right of current common stockholders to maintain their ownership percentage on new issues of common stock.*

Preferred stock A class of stock with a claim on the company's earnings before payment may be made on the common stock and usually entitled to priority over common stock if the company liquidates. Usually entitled to dividends at a specified rate—when declared by the board of directors and before payment of a dividend on the common stock—depending upon the terms of the issue. (See: *Cumulative preferred, Participating preferred.*)†

Premium The amount by which a bond or preferred stock, may sell above its par value. For options, the price that the buyer pays the writer for an option contract ("option premium") is synonymous with "the price of an option." (See: *Discount.*)††

Present value The current or discounted value of a future sum or annuity. The value is discounted back at a given interest rate for a specified time period.*

Price-earnings ratio A popular way to compare stocks selling at various price levels. The PE ratio is the price of a share of stock divided by earnings per share for a twelve-month period. For example, a stock selling for $50 a share and earning $5 a share is said to be selling at a price-earnings ratio of 10.††

Primary distribution Also called primary offering. The original sale of a company's securities. (See: *Investment banker.*)††

Primary earnings per share Adjusted earnings after taxes divided by shares outstanding plus common stock equivalents.*

Primary market Market for new issues of securities.

Prime rate The lowest interest rate charged by commercial banks to their most creditworthy and largest corporate customers; other interest rates, such as personal, automobile, commercial and financing loans are often pegged to the prime.††

Principal The person for whom a broker

executes an order, or dealers buying or selling for their own accounts. The term *principal* may also refer to a person's capital or to the face amount of a bond.††

Private placement   The sale of securities directly to a financial institution by a corporation. This eliminates the middleman and reduces the cost of issue to the corporation.*

Productivity   The amount of physical output for each unit of productive input.¶

Profitability ratios   A group of ratios that indicates the return on sales, total assets, and invested capital. Specifically, we compute the profit margin (net income to sales), return on assets, and return on equity.*

Profit-taking   Selling stock which has appreciated in value since purchase, in order to realize the profit. The term is often used to explain a downturn in the market following a period of rising prices. (See: *Paper profit*.)††

Pro forma balance sheet   A projection of future asset, liability, and stockholders' equity levels. Notes payable or cash is used as a plug or balancing figure for the statement.*

Pro forma financial statements   A series of projected financial statements. Of major importance are the pro forma income statement, the pro forma balance sheet, and the cash budget.*

Pro forma income statement   A projection of anticipated sales, expenses, and income.*

Prospectus   The official selling circular that must be given to purchasers of new securities registered with the Securities and Exchange Commission. It highlights the much longer Registration Statement filed with the commission.††

Proxy   Written authorization given by a shareholder to someone else to represent him and vote his shares at a shareholders' meeting.††

Proxy statement   Information given to stockholders in conjunction with the solicitation of proxies.††

Prudent man rule   An investment standard. In some states, the law requires that a fiduciary, such as a trustee, may invest the fund's money only in a list of securities designated by the state—the so-called legal list. In other states, the trustee may invest in a security if it is one that would be bought by a prudent man of discretion and intelligence, who is seeking a reasonable income and preservation of capital.††

Public Offering   (See: *Primary distribution*.)

Public placement   The sale of securities to the public through the investment banker-underwriter process. Public placements must

be registered with the Securities and Exchange Commission.*

Public warehousing   An inventory financing arrangement in which inventory, used as collateral, is stored with and controlled by an independent warehousing company.*

Purchase of assets   A method of financial recording for mergers in which the difference between the purchase price and the adjusted book value is recognized as goodwill and amortized over a maximum time period of 40 years.*

Purchasing power parity theory   A theory based on the interplay between inflation and exchange rates. A parity between the purchasing powers of two countries establishes the rate of exchange between the two currencies. Currency exchange rates, therefore, tend to vary inversely with their respective purchasing powers in order to provide the same or similar purchasing power.*

Pure bond value   The value of the convertible bond if its present value is computed at a discount rate equal to interest rates on straight bonds of equal risk, without conversion privileges.*

Quote   The highest bid to buy and the lowest offer to sell a security in a given market at a given time. If you ask your broker for a "quote" on a stock, he may come back with something like "45¼ to 45½." This means that $45.25 is the highest price any buyer wanted to pay at the time the quote was given on the floor of the exchange and that $45.50 was the lowest price which any seller would take at the same time. (See: *Bid and asked*.)††

Rally   A brisk rise following a decline in the general price level of the market, or in an individual stock.†

Ratings   Designations used by investors' services to give relative indications of quality.**

Real capital   Long-term productive assets (plant and equipment).*

Real GNP   GNP (gross national product) in current dollars adjusted for inflation.*

Real rate of return   The rate of return that an investor demands for giving up the current use of his or her funds on a noninflation-adjusted basis. It is payment for forgoing current consumption. Historically, the real rate of return demanded by investors has been of the magnitude of 2 to 3 percent. However, throughout the 1980s the real rate of return has been much higher; that is, 5 to 7 percent.*

Record date   The date on which you must be registered as a shareholder of a company in order to receive a declared dividend or, among other things, to vote on company affairs. (See: *Ex-dividend, Transfer*.)††

Redemption price The price at which a bond may be redeemed before maturity, at the option of the issuing company. Redemption value also applies to the price the company must pay to call in certain types of preferred stock. (See: *Callable*.)†

Red Herring (See: *Prospectus*.)

Refunding The process of retiring an old bond issue before maturity and replacing it with a new issue. Refunding will occur when interest rates have fallen and new bonds may be sold at lower interest rates.*

Registered bond A bond which is registered on the books of the issuing company in the name of the owner. It can be transferred only when endorsed by the registered owner. (See: *Bearer bond, Coupon bond*.)†

Registered representative The man or woman who serves the investor customers of a broker/dealer. In a New York Stock Exchange Member Organization, a Registered Representative must meet the requirements of the exchange as to background and knowledge of the securities business. Also known as an Account Executive or Customer's broker.††

Registrar Usually a trust company or bank charged with the responsibility of keeping a record of the owners of corporation's securities and preventing the issuance of more than the authorized amount. (See: *Transfer*.)††

Registration Before a public offering may be made of new securities by a company, or of outstanding securities by controlling stockholders—through the mails or in interstate commerce—the securities must be registered under the Securities Act of 1933. A statement is filed with the SEC by the issuer. It must disclose pertinent information relating to the company's operations, securities, management and purpose of the public offering.

Before a security may be admitted to dealings on a national securities exchange, it must be registered under the Securities Exchange Act of 1934. The application for registration must be filed with the exchange and the SEC by the company issuing the securities.††

Regional stock exchanges Organized exchanges outside of New York that list securities. Regional exchanges exist in San Francisco, Philadelphia, and a number of other U.S. cities.*

Regulation T The federal regulation governing the amount of credit which may be advanced by brokers and dealers to customers for the purchase of securities. (See: *Margin*.)†

Regulation U The federal regulation governing the amount of credit which may be advanced by a bank to its customers for the purchase of listed stocks. (See: *Margin*.)†

Reinvestment assumption An assumption must be made concerning the rate of return that can be earned on the cash flows generated by capital budgeting projects. The NPV method assumes the rate of reinvestment to be the cost of capital, while the IRR method assumes the rate to be the actual internal rate of return.*

REIT Real Estate Investment Trust, an organization similar to an investment company in some respects but concentrating its holdings in real estate investments. The yield is generally liberal since REIT's are required to distribute as much as 90 percent of their income. (See: *Investment company*.)†

Repatriation of earnings Returning earnings to the multinational parent company in the form of dividends.*

Replacement cost The cost of replacing the existing asset base at current prices as opposed to original cost.*

Replacement cost accounting Financial statements based on the present cost of replacing assets.*

Repurchase agreements When the Federal Reserve makes a repurchase agreement with a government securities dealer, it buys a security for immediate delivery with an agreement to sell the security back at the same price by a specific date (usually within 15 days) and receives interest at a specific rate. This arrangement allows the Federal Reserve to inject reserves into the banking system on a temporary basis to meet a temporary need and to withdraw these reserves as soon as that need has passed.¶

Required rate of return The rate of return that investors demand from an investment (securities) to compensate them for the amount of risk involved.*

Reserve requirements The amount of funds that commercial banks must hold in reserve for each dollar of deposits. Reserve requirements are set by the Federal Reserve Board and are different for savings and checking accounts. Low reserve requirements are stimulating; high reserve requirements are restrictive.*

Residual dividends This theory of dividend payout states that a corporation will retain as much earnings as it may profitably invest. If any income is left after investments, it will pay dividends. This theory assumes that dividends are a passive decision variable.*

Restructuring Redeploying the asset and liability structure of the firm. This can be accomplished through repurchasing shares with cash or borrowed funds, acquiring other firms, or selling off unprofitable or unwanted divisions.*

Revenue bond A bond payable from revenues derived from tolls, charges, or rents paid by users of the facility constructed from the proceeds of the bond issue.**

Rights When a company wants to raise more funds by issuing additional securities, it may give its stockholders the opportunity, ahead of others, to buy the new securities in proportion to the number of shares each owns. The piece of paper evidencing this privilege is called a right. Because the additional stock is usually offered to stockholders below the current market price, rights ordinarily have a market value of their own and are actively traded. In most cases they must be exercised within a relatively short period. Failure to exercise or sell rights may result in actual loss to the holder. (See: *Warrant.*)†

Rights offering A sale of new common stock through a preemptive rights offering. Usually one right will be issued for every share held. A certain number of rights may be used to buy shares of common stock from the company at a set price that is lower than the market price.*

Rights-on The situation in which the purchase of a share of common stock includes a right attached to the stock.*

Risk A measure of uncertainty about the outcome from a given event. The greater the variability of possible outcomes, on both the high side and the low side, the greater the risk.*

Risk-adjusted discount rate A discount rate used in the capital budgeting process that has been adjusted upward or downward from the basic cost of capital to reflect the risk dimension of a given project.*

Risk averse An aversion or dislike for risk. In order to induce most people to take larger risks, there must be increased potential for return.*

Risk-free rate of interest Rate of return on an asset that carries no risk. U.S. Treasury bills are often used to represent this measure, although longer-term government securities have also proved appropriate in some studies.*

Risk premium A premium associated with the special risks of an investment. Of primary interest are two types of risk, business risk and financial risk. Business risk relates to the inability of the firm to maintain its competitive position and sustain stability and growth in earnings. Financial risk relates to the inability of the firm to meet its debt obligations

as they come due. The risk premium will also differ (be greater or less) for different types of investments (bonds, stocks, etc.).*

Risk-return trade-off function (See *Security market line.*)

Round lot A unit of trading or a multiple thereof. On the NYSE the unit of trading is generally 100 shares in stocks and $1,000 or $5,000 par value in the case of bonds. In some inactive stocks, the unit of trading is ten shares. (See: *Odd lot.*)††

Scale order An order to buy (or sell) a security which specifies the total amount to be bought (or sold) and the amount to be bought (or sold) at specified price variations.†

Seat A traditional figure-of-speech for a membership on an exchange.††

SEC The Securities and Exchange Commission, established by Congress to help protect investors. The SEC administers the Securities Act of 1933, the Securities Exchange Act of 1934, the Securities Act Amendments of 1975, the Trust Indenture Act, the Investment Company Act, the Investment Advisers Act, and the Public Utility Holding Company Act.†

Secondary offering The sale of a large block of stock in a publicly traded company, usually by estates, foundations, or large individual stockholders. Secondary offerings must be registered with the SEC and will usually be distributed by investment bankers.*

Secondary trading The buying and selling of publicly owned securities in secondary markets such as the New York Stock Exchange and the over-the-counter markets.*

Secured debt A general category of debt which indicates that the loan was obtained by pledging assets as collateral. Secured debt has many forms and usually offers some protective features to a given class of bondholders.*

Securities Act of 1933 An act that is sometimes referred to as the truth in securities act because it requires detailed financial disclosures before securities may be sold to the public.*

Securities Acts Amendments of 1975 The major feature of this act was to mandate a national securities market. (See: *National market system.*)*

Securities Exchange Act of 1934 Legislation that established the Securities and Exchange Commission (SEC) to supervise and regulate the securities markets.*

Security market line A line or equation that depicts the risk-related return of a security based on a risk-free rate plus a market premium related to the beta coefficient of the security.*

Self-liquidating assets Assets that are converted to cash within the normal operating cycle of the firm. An example is the purchase and sell-off of seasonal inventory.*

Semiannual compounding A compounding period of every six months. For example, a five-year investment in which interest is compounded semiannually would indicate an n value equal to 10 and an i value at one half the annual rate.*

Semivariable costs Costs that are partially fixed but still change somewhat as volume changes. Examples are utilities and "repairs and maintenance."*

Serial bond An issue which matures in part at periodic stated intervals.†

Settlement Conclusion of a securities transaction when a customer pays a broker/dealer for securities purchased or delivers securities sold and receives from the broker the proceeds of a sale. (See: *Cash sale*.)††

Shelf registration A process which permits large companies to file one comprehensive registration statement (under SEC Rule 415), which outlines the firm's plans for future long-term financing. Then, when market conditions appear to be appropriate, the firm can issue the securities without further SEC approval.*

Short covering Buying stock to return stock previously borrowed to make delivery on a short sale.†

Short position Stocks, options, or futures sold short and not covered as of a particular date. On the NYSE, a tabulation is issued once a month listing all issues on the Exchange in which there was a short position of 5,000 or more shares and issues in which the short position had changed by 2,000 or more shares in the preceding month. Short position also means the total amount of stock an individual has sold short and has not covered, as of a particular date.††

Short sale A transaction by a person who believes a security will decline and sells it, though the person does not own any. For instance: You instruct your broker to sell short 100 shares of XYZ. Your broker borrows the stock so delivery of the 100 shares can be made to the buyer. The money value of the shares borrowed is deposited by your broker with the lender. Sooner or later you must cover your short sale by buying the same amount of stock you borrowed for return to the lender. If you are able to buy XYZ at a lower price than you sold it for, your profit is the difference between the two prices— not counting commissions and taxes. But if

you have to pay more for the stock than the price you received, that is the amount of your loss. Stock exchange and federal regulations govern and limit the conditions under which a short sale may be made on a national securities exchange. Sometimes people will sell short a stock they already own in order to protect a paper profit. This is known as selling short against the box.††

Simulation A method of dealing with uncertainty in which future outcomes are anticipated. The model may use random variables for inputs. By programming the computer to randomly select inputs from probability distributions, the outcomes generated by a simulation are distributed about a mean, and instead of generating one return or net present value, a range of outcomes with standard deviations is provided.*

Sinking fund Money regularly set aside by a company to redeem its bonds, debentures or preferred stock from time to time as specified in the indenture or charter.††

SIPC Securities Investor Protection Corporation, which provides funds for use, if necessary, to protect customers' cash and securities which may be on deposit with a SIPC member firm in the event the firm fails and is liquidated under the provisions of the SIPC Act. SIPC is not a government agency. It is a nonprofit membership corporation created, however, by an act of Congress.†

Special bid A method of filling an order to buy a large block of stock on the floor of the New York Stock Exchange. In a special bid, the bidder for the block of stock—a pension fund, for instance, will pay a special commission to the broker who represents him in making the purchase. The seller does not pay a commission. The special bid is made on the floor of the exchange at a fixed price which may not be below the last sale of the security or the current bid in the regular market, whichever is higher. Member firms may sell this stock for customers directly to the buyer's broker during trading hours.†

Special offering Opposite of special bid. A notice is printed on the ticker tape announcing the stock sale at a fixed price usually based on the last transaction in the regular auction market. If there are more buyers than stock, allotments are made. Only the seller pays the commission.†

Special tax bond A bond secured by a special tax, such as a gasoline tax.**

Specialist A member of the New York Stock Exchange, Inc., who has two functions: First, to maintain an orderly market in the securities registered to the specialist. In order to maintain an orderly market, the Exchange expects specialists to buy or sell for the own account, to a reasonable degree, when there is a temporary disparity between supply and demand. Second, the specialist acts as a broker's broker. When a commission broker on the Exchange floor receives a limit order, say, to buy at $50 a stock then selling at $60—he cannot wait at the post where the stock is traded to see if the price reaches the specified level. So he leaves the order with the specialist, who will try to execute it in the market if and when the stock declines to the specified price. At all times the specialist must put his customers' interests above his own. There are about 400 specialists on the NYSE. (See: *Limited order.*)††

Speculation   The employment of funds by a speculator. Safety of principal is a secondary factor. (See: *Investment.*)†

Speculative warrant premium   The market price of the warrant minus the warrant's intrinsic value.*

Speculator   One who is willing to assume a relatively large risk in the hope of gain.††

Spin off   The separation of a subsidiary or division of a corporation from its parent by issuing shares in a new corporate entity. Shareowners in the parent receive shares in the new company in proportion to their original holding and the total value remains approximately the same.††

Split   The division of the outstanding shares of a corporation into a larger number of shares. A 3-for-1 split by a company with 1 million shares outstanding results in 3 million shares outstanding. Each holder of 100 shares before the 3-for-1 split would have 300 shares, although his proportionate equity in the company would remain the same; 100 parts of 1 million are the equivalent of 300 parts of 3 million. Ordinarily splits must be voted by directors and approved by shareholders. (See: *Stock dividend.*)

Spontaneous sources of funds   Funds arising through the normal course of business, such as accounts payable generated from the purchase of goods for resale.*

Standard deviation   A measure of the spread or dispersion of a series of numbers around the expected value. The standard deviation tells us how well the expected value represents a series of values.*

Step-up in conversion   A feature that is sometimes written into the contract which allows the conversion ratio to decline in steps over time. This feature encourages early conversion when the conversion value is greater than the call price.*

Stock ahead   Sometimes an investor who has entered an order to buy or sell a stock at a certain price will see transactions at that price reported on the ticker tape while his own order has not been executed. The reason is that other buy and sell orders at the same price came in to the specialist ahead of his and had priority. (See: *Book, Specialist.*)†

Stock dividend   A dividend paid in securities rather than cash. The dividend may be additional shares of the issuing company, or shares of another company (usually a subsidiary) held by the company.††

Stock Index Futures   Futures contracts based on market indexes, e.g., NYSE Composite Index Futures Contracts.††

Stock split   A division of shares by a ratio set by the board of directors—2 for 1, 3 for 1, 3 for 2, and so on. Stock splits usually indicate that the company's stock has risen in price to a level that the directors feel limits the trading appeal of the stock. The par value is divided by the ratio set, and new shares are issued to the current stockholders of record to increase their shares to the stated level. For example, a two-for-one split would increase your holdings from one share to two shares.*

Stockholder of record   A stockholder whose name is registered on the books of the issuing corporation.†

Stockholder wealth maximization   Maximizing the wealth of the firm's shareholders through achieving the highest possible value for the firm in the marketplace. It is the overriding objective of the firm and should influence all decisions.*

Stockholders' equity   The total ownership position of preferred and common stockholders.*

Stop limit order   A stop order which becomes a limit order after the specified stop price has been reached. (See: *Limit order, Stop order.*)†

Stop order   An order to buy at a price above or sell at a price below the current market. Stop buy orders are generally used to limit loss or protect unrealized profits on a short sale. Stop sell orders are generally used to protect unrealized profits or limit loss on a holding. A stop order becomes a market order when the stock sells at or beyond the specified price and, thus, may not necessarily be executed at that price.†

Stopped stock   A service performed—in most cases by the specialist—for an order given him by a commission broker. Let's say XYZ just sold at $50 a share. Broker A comes along with an order to buy 100 shares at the market. The lowest offer is $50.50. Broker A believes he can do better for his client than $50.50, perhaps might get the stock at $50.25.

But he doesn't want to take a chance that he'll miss the market—that is, the next sale might be $50.50 and the following one even higher. So he asks the specialist if he will stop 100 at ½ ($50.50). The specialist agrees. The specialist guarantees Broker A he will get 100 shares at 50½ if the stock sells at that price. In the meantime, if the specialist or broker A succeeds in executing the order at $50.25, the stop is called off. (See: *Specialist*.)†

Street name Securities held in the name of a broker instead of his customer's name are said to be carried in a *street name*. This occurs when the securities have been bought on margin or when the customer wishes the security to be held by the broker.†

Subchapter S corporation A special corporate form of ownership in which profit is taxed as direct income to the stockholders and thus is only taxed once as would be true of a partnership. The stockholders still receive all the organizational benefits of a corporation, including limited liability. The Subchapter S designation can only apply to corporations with up to 35 stockholders.*

Subdivision Any legal and authorized political entity under a state's jurisdiction (county, city, water district, school district, etc.).**

Subordinated debenture An unsecured bond in which payment to the holder will take place only after designated senior debenture holders are satisfied.*

Swapping Selling one security and buying a similar one almost at the same time to take a loss, usually for tax purposes.††

Switch order or contingent order An order for the purchase (sale) of one stock and the sale (purchase) of another stock at a stipulated price difference.†

Switching Selling one security and buying another.†

Syndicate A group of investment bankers who together underwrite and distribute a new issue of securities or a large block of an outstanding issue.†

Synergy The recognition that the whole may be equal to more than the sum of the parts. The "2 + 2 = 5" effect.

Take-over The acquiring of one corporation by another—usually in a friendly merger but sometimes marked by a "proxy fight." In "unfriendly" take-over attempts, the potential buying company may offer a price well above current market values, new securities, and other inducements to stockholders. The management of the subject company might ask for a better price or fight the take-over or merger with another company. (See: *Proxy*.)†

Tax base The total resources available for taxation.**

Tax-exempt bond Another name for a municipal bond. The interest on a municipal bond is presently exempt from Federal income tax.**

Tax loss carry-forward A loss that can be carried forward for a number of years to offset future taxable income and perhaps be utilized by another firm in a merger or an acquisition.*

Tax shelter A medium or process intended to reduce or eliminate the tax burden of an individual. They range from such conventional ones as tax-exempt municipal securities and interest or dividend exclusion to sophisticated limited partnerships in real estate, cattle raising, equipment leasing, oil drilling, research and development activities and motion picture production.††

Technical insolvency A firm is unable to pay its bills as they come due.*

Technical research Analysis of the market and stocks based on supply and demand. The technician studies price movements, volume, and trends and patterns which are revealed by charting these factors, and attempts to assess the possible effect of current market action on future supply and demand for securities and individual issues. (See: *Fundamental research*.)†

Temporary current assets Current assets that will be reduced or converted to cash within the normal operating cycle of the firm.*

Tender offer A public offer to buy shares from existing stockholders of one public corporation by another company or other organization under specified terms good for a certain time period. Stockholders are asked to "tender" (surrender) their holdings for stated value, usually at a premium above current market price, subject to the tendering of a minimum and maximum number of shares.††

Term issue An issue that has a single maturity.**

Term loan An intermediate-length loan in which credit is generally extended from one to seven years. The loan is usually repaid in monthly or quarterly installments over its life rather than the one single period.*

Term structure of interest rates The relationship between interest rates and maturities for securities of equal risk. Usually government securities are used for the term structure.*

Terms of exchange The buy-out ratio or terms of trade in a merger or an acquisition.*

Thin market A market in which there are

comparatively few bids to buy or offers to sell, or both. The phrase may apply to a single security or to the entire stock market. In a thin market, price fluctuations between transactions are usually larger than when the market is liquid. A thin market in a particular stock may reflect lack of interest in that issue or a limited supply of or demand for stock in the market. (See: *Bid and asked, Liquidity, Offer.*)†

Third market Trading of stock exchange listed securities in the over-the-counter market by non-exchange-member brokers.††

Tight money A term to indicate time periods in which financing may be difficult to find and interest rates may be quite high by normal standards.*

Time order An order which becomes a market or limited price order at a specified time.†

Time value The part of an option premium that is in excess of the intrinsic value.††

Tips Supposedly "inside" information on corporation affairs.†

Trade credit Credit provided by sellers or suppliers in the normal course of business.*

Trader Individuals who buy and sell for their own accounts for short-term profit. Also, an employee of a broker/dealer or financial institution who specializes in handling purchases and sales of securities for the firm and/or its clients. (See: *Investor, Speculator.*)††

Trading market The secondary market for outstanding securities.*

Trading post One of 23 trading locations on the floor of the New York Stock Exchange at which stocks assigned to that location are bought and sold. About 75 stocks are traded at each post.†

Transaction exposure Foreign exchange gains and losses resulting from *actual* international transactions. These may be hedged through the foreign exchange market, the money market, or the currency futures market.*

Transfer This term may refer to two different operations. For one, the delivery of a stock certificate from the seller's broker to the buyer's broker and legal change of ownership, normally accomplished within a few days. For another, to record the change of ownership on the books of the corporation by the transfer agent. When the purchaser's name is recorded, dividends, notices of meetings, proxies, financial reports, and all pertinent literature sent by the issuer to its securities holders are mailed direct to the new owner. (See: *Registrar, Street name.*)††

Transfer agent A transfer agent keeps a record of the name of each registered share-

owner, his or her address, the number of shares owned, and sees that certificates presented for transfer are properly cancelled and new certificates issued in the name of the new owner. (See: *Registrar.*)††

Translation exposure The foreign-located assets and liabilities of a multinational corporation, which are denominated in foreign currency units, and are exposed to losses and gains due to changing exchange rates. This is called accounting, or translation, exposure.*

Treasury bills Short-term U.S. Treasury securities issued in minimum denominations of $10,000 and usually having original maturities of 3, 6, or 12 months. Investors purchase bills at prices lower than the face value of the bills; the return to the investors is the difference between the price paid for the bills and the amount received when the bills are sold or when they mature. Treasury bills are the type of security used most frequently in open market operations.¶

Treasury bonds Long-term U.S. Treasury securities usually having initial maturities of more than 10 years and issued in denominations of $1,000 or more, depending on the specific issue. Bonds pay interest semiannually, with principal payable at maturity.¶

Treasury notes Intermediate-term coupon-bearing U.S. Treasury securities having initial maturities from 1 to 10 years and issued in denominations of $1,000 or more, depending on the maturity of the issue. Notes pay interest semiannually, and the principal is payable at maturity.¶

Treasury stock Stock issued by a company, but later reacquired. It may be held in the company's treasury indefinitely, reissued to the public, or retired. Treasury stock receives no dividends, and has no vote while held by the company.††

Trend analysis An analysis of performance that is made over a number of years in order to ascertain significant patterns.*

Trust receipt An instrument acknowledging that the borrower holds the inventory and proceeds for sale in trust for the lender.*

Two-step buy-out An acquisition plan in which the acquiring company attempts to gain control by offering a very high cash price for 51 percent of the shares of the target company. At the same time the acquiring company announces a second lower price that will be paid, either in cash, stock or bonds, at a subsequent point in time.*

Underwriter (See: *Investment banker.*)

Underwriting The process of selling securities and, at the same time, assuring the seller a specified price. Underwriting is done by investment bankers and represents a form of risk taking.*

Underwriting spread The difference between the price that a selling corporation receives for an issue of securities and the price at which the issue is sold to the public. The spread is the fee that investment bankers and others receive for selling securities.*

Underwriting syndicate A group of investment bankers that is formed to share the risk of a security offering and also to facilitate the distribution of the securities.*

Unlimited tax bond A bond secured by pledge of taxes that are not limited by rate or amount.**

Unlisted A security not listed on a stock exchange. (See: *Over-the-counter*.)†

Unsecured debt A loan which requires no assets as collateral, but allows the bondholder a general claim against the corporation rather than a lien against specific assets.*

Up tick A term used to designate a transaction made at a price higher than the preceding transaction. Also called a *plus-tick*. A *zero-plus* tick is a term used for a transaction at the same price as the preceding trade but higher than the preceding different price.

Conversely, a *down tick*, or *minus* tick, is a term used to designate a transaction made at a price lower than the preceding trade.

A plus sign, or a minus sign, is displayed throughout the day next to the last price of each company's stock traded at each trading post on the floor of the New York Stock Exchange. (See: *Short sale*.)†

Variable annuity A life insurance policy where the annuity premium (a set amount of dollars) is immediately turned into units of a portfolio of stocks. Upon retirement, the policyholder is paid according to accumulated units, the dollar value of which varies according to the performance of the stock portfolio. Its objective is to preserve, through stock investment, the purchasing value of the annuity which otherwise is subject to erosion through inflation.††

Variable costs Costs that move directly with a change in volume. Examples are raw materials, factory labor, and sales commissions.*

Volume The number of shares traded in a security or an entire market during a given period. Volume is usually considered on a daily basis and a daily average is computed for longer periods.†

Voting right The common stockholder's right to vote their stock in the affairs of a company. Preferred stock usually has the right to vote when preferred dividends are in default for a specified period. The right to vote may be delegated by the stockholder to another person. (See: *Cumulative voting, Proxy*.)††

Warrant A certificate giving the holder the right to purchase securities at a stipulated price within a specified time limit or perpetually. Sometimes a warrant is offered with securities as an inducement to buy. (See: *Rights*.)††

Warrant intrinsic value (See: *Minimum warrant value*.)*

Weighted average cost of capital The computed cost of capital determined by multiplying the cost of each item in the optimal capital structure by its weighted representation in the overall capital structure and summing up the results.*

When issued A short form of "when, as, and if issued." The term indicates a conditional transaction in a security authorized for issuance but not as yet actually issued. All "when issued" transactions are on an "if" basis, to be settled if and when the actual security is issued and the exchange or National Association of Securities Dealers rules the transactions are to be settled.†

Wire house A member firm of an exchange maintaining a communications network linking either its own branch offices, offices of correspondent firms, or a combination of such offices.†

Working capital management The financing and management of the current assets of the firm. The financial manager determines the mix between temporary and permanent "current assets" and the nature of the financing arrangement.*

Working control Theoretically, ownership of 51 percent of a company's voting stock is necessary to exercise control. In practice— and this is particularly true in the case of a large corporation—effective control sometimes can be exerted through ownership, individually or by a group acting in concert, of less than 50 percent.†

Yield Also known as return. The dividends or interest paid by a company expressed as a percentage of the current price. A stock with a current market value of $3.20 is said to return 8 percent ($3.20 ÷ $40.00). The current yield on a bond is figured the same way.††

Yield curve A curve that shows interest rates at a specific point in time for all securities having equal risk but different maturity dates. Usually government securities are used to construct such curves. The yield curve is also referred to as the term structure of interest rates.*

Yield to maturity The yield of a bond to maturity takes into account the price discount from or premium over the face amount. It is greater than the current yield when the bond is selling at a discount and less than the current yield when the bond is selling at a premium.†

Zero coupon bonds Bonds which do not convey a coupon (i.e., do not pay interest) but which are offered at a substantial discount from par value and appreciate to their full value (usually $1,000) at maturity. However, under U.S. tax law, the imputed interest is taxed as it accrues. The appeal of Zero coupon bonds is primarily for IRA and other tax sheltered retirement accounts.

Acquisition Takeover Glossary

Asset Play[1] A firm whose underlying assets are worth substantially more (after paying off the firm's liabilities) than the market value of its stock.

Bear hug An unnegotiated offer, in the form of a letter made directly to the board of directors of the target company. The price and terms are sufficiently detailed so that the directors are obliged to make the offer public. The offer states a time limit for a response and may threaten a tender offer or other action if it is not accepted.

Breakup value[1] The sum of the values of the firm's assets if sold off separately.

Crown jewel option[1] The strategem of selling off or spinning off the asset that makes the firm an attractive takeover candidate.

Four-nine position[1] A holding of approximately 4.9% of the outstanding shares of a company. At 5%, the holder must file a form [13d] with the SEC, revealing his position. Thus, a four-nine position is about the largest position that one can quietly hold.

Black knight[1] A potential acquirer that management opposes and would prefer to find an alternative to (i.e. a *white knight*).

Going private[1] The process of buying back the publicly held stock so that what was heretofore a public firm becomes private.

Golden handcuffs[1] Employment agreement that makes the departure of upper level managers very costly to them. For instance, such managers may lose very attractive stock option rights by leaving prior to their normal retirement age.

Golden handshake[1] A provision in a preliminary agreement to be acquired in which the target firm gives the acquiring firm an option to purchase its shares or assets at attractive prices or to receive a substantial bonus if the proposed takeover does not occur.

Golden parachute[1] Extremely generous separation payments for upper level executives that are required to be fulfilled if the firm's control shifts.

Greenmail[1] Incentive payments to dissuade the interest of outsiders who may otherwise seek control of a firm. The payment frequently takes the form of a premium price for the outsiders' shares, coupled with an agreement from them to avoid buying more stock for a set period of time.

The firm bears the cost of the payment. The stock price generally falls after the payment and the removal of the outside threat.

In play[1] The status of being a recognized takeover candidate.

Junk bonds[1] High-risk, high-yield bonds that are often used to finance takeovers.

LBO[1] A leveraged buyout. A purchase of a company financed largely by debt that is backed by the firm's own assets.

Loaded laggard[1] A stock of a company whose assets, particularly its liquid assets, have high values relative to the stock's price.

Lockup agreement[1] An agreement between an acquirer and target that makes the target very unattractive to any other acquirer; similar to a *golden handshake*.

Mezzanine financing Debt financing subordinate to the claims of the senior debt. This financing often has equity participation in the form of stock options, warrants or conversion to cheap stock.

Nibble strategy A takeover approach involving the purchase in the public market of minority stock position in the target company and a subsequent tender offer for the rest of the target stock.

PacMan defense[1] The tactic of seeking to acquire the firm that has targeted your own firm as a takeover prospect.

Poison pill[1] A provision in the corporate by-laws or other governance documents providing for a very disadvantageous result for a potential acquirer should its ownership position be allowed to exceed some preassigned threshold. For example, if anyone acquires more than 20% of Company A's stock, the

[1]Source: From the *AAII Journal*, American Association of *Individual Investors*, 612 North Michigan Avenue, Chicago, IL 60611. Excerpted from Ben Branch "White Knight Rescues Investors From Terminology."

acquirer might then have to sell $100 worth of its own stock to other shareholders at $50.

Raider A hostile outside party that seeks to take over other companies.

Saturday night special A seven day cash tender offer for all of the target firm's stock. It is usually launched on a Saturday on the assumption that the target company will have difficulty mobilizing its key advisors in reaction to the offer.

Scorched earth defense[1] A tactic in which the defending company's management engages in practices that reduce their company's value to such a degree that it is no longer attractive to the potential acquirer. This approach is more often threatened than actually employed.

Senior debt financing The issuance of debt instruments having first claim on a firm's assets (secured debt) or cash flow (unsecured debt).

Shark repellant[1] Anti-takeover provisions such as the poison pill.

Short swing profit[1] A gain made by an insider (including anyone with more than 10% of the stock) who holds stock for less than six months. Such gains must be paid back to the company whose shares were sold.

Standstill agreement[1] A reciprocal understanding between a company's management and an outside party that usually owns a significant minority position. Each party gives up certain rights in exchange for corresponding concessions by the other party. For example, the outside group may agree to limit its stock purchases to keep its ownership percentage below some level (for instance, 20%). In exchange, management may agree to a minority board representation by the outsider.

Swipe An unnegotiated offer to purchase the shares of a target company's stock made after the target's board has announced its intention to sell the company (usually in a leverage buyout to management). The swipe price is higher than that initially proposed by the board of directors.

Tender offer An offer by a firm to buy the stock of another firm (target) by going directly to the stockholders of the target. The offer is often made over the opposition of the management of the target firm.

13d[1] A form that must be filed with the SEC when a single investor or an associated group owns 5% or more of a company's stock. The form reveals the size of the holding and the investor's intentions.

Two-tier offer[1] A takeover device in which a relatively high per share price is paid for controlling interest in a target and a lesser per share price is paid for the remainder.

White knight defense[1] Finding an alternative and presumably more friendly acquirer than the present takeover threat.

White squire defense[1] Finding an important ally to purchase a strong minority position (for example, 25%) of the potential acquisition's stock. Presumably this ally (the "white squire") will oppose and hopefully block the efforts of any hostile firm seeking to acquire the vulnerable firm.

Stock Exchanges

Common Stocks (shares of ownership in a corporation) are traded on several exchanges. The best known are the New York Stock Exchange and the American Stock Exchange, both located in Manhattan's financial district. Generally, the stocks of the largest companies are traded on the New York Stock Exchange, while somewhat smaller companies are traded on the American Exchange. There are also a number of regional exchanges such as the Midwest Exchange in Chicago and the Pacific Exchange in San Francisco. These exchanges trade stocks of local corporations as well as stocks listed on the New York and American Exchanges.

In addition, there is the Over-The Counter-Market (OTC) which, unlike the exchanges previously mentioned, does not have a specific location but consists of a network of brokers and dealers linked by telephone and private wires. Smaller or relatively new companies are traded on the OTC. Trading information for many (but far from all) stocks on the OTC market is collected and displayed on a computerized system, the National Association of Security Dealers Automatic Quote System (NASDAQ).

Large institutional traders (mutual and pension funds, insurance companies, etc.) often trade blocks of stocks directly with one another. This information is collected and displayed on the Instinet System.

Major Stock Exchanges*

UNITED STATES

AMERICAN STOCK EXCHANGE, INC.
86 Trinity Place
New York, New York 10006

BOSTON STOCK EXCHANGE, INC.
One Boston Place
Boston, Massachusetts 02109

THE CINCINNATI STOCK EXCHANGE,
   INC.
205 Dixie Terminal Building
Cincinnati, Ohio 45202

MIDWEST STOCK EXCHANGE, INC.
440 South LaSalle Street
Chicago, Illinois 60603

NEW YORK STOCK EXCHANGE, INC.
11 Wall Street
New York, New York 10005

PACIFIC STOCK EXCHANGE, INC.
618 South Spring Street
Los Angeles, California 90014

301 Pine Street
San Francisco, California 94104

PHILADELPHIA STOCK EXCHANGE,
INC.
1900 Market Street
Philadelphia, Pennsylvania 19103

SPOKANE STOCK EXCHANGE, INC.
206 Radio Central Building
Spokane, Washington 99201

FOREIGN

AUSTRALIA

SYDNEY STOCK EXCHANGE
Tower Building
Australia Square
P.O. Box H67
Sydney, New South Wales 2000

BELGIUM

BRUSSELS STOCK EXCHANGE
Palais de la Bourse
1000 Brussels

---

* See page 521 for a listing of futures and options exchanges.

CANADA

ALBERTA STOCK EXCHANGE
300–5th Avenue S.W.
Calgary, Alberta T2P 3C4

BOURSE DE MONTRÉAL
The Stock Exchange Tower
800 Victoria Square
Montreal, Quebec H4Z 1A9

TORONTO STOCK EXCHANGE
2 First Canadian Place
Toronto, Ontario M5X 1J2

VANCOUVER STOCK EXCHANGE
Stock Exchange Tower
P.O. Box 10333
609 Granville Street
Vancouver, B.C. V7Y 1H1

WINNIPEG STOCK EXCHANGE
303–167 Lombard Avenue
Winnipeg, Manitoba R3B OT6

FRANCE

BOURSE DE PARIS—PARIS STOCK EXCHANGE
Palais de la Bourse
75002 Paris

GERMANY

FRANKFURTER WERTPAPIERBORE—
FRANKFORT EXCHANGE
Borsenplatz 6
6000 Frankfurt am Main 1

HONG KONG

STOCK EXCHANGE OF HONG KONG
One Exchange Square
Hong Kong

JAPAN

TOKYO STOCK EXCHANGE
1–1 Nihonbashi Kayaba-cho-z-chome
Cho-Ku, Tokyo 103

THE NETHERLANDS

AMSTERDAMSE EFFECTENBEURS—
AMSTERDAM STOCK EXCHANGE
Beursplein 5
1012 JW Amsterdam

SWITZERLAND

GENEVA STOCK EXCHANGE
Ruedela Confédération 8
CH-1204 Geneva

ZÜRICH STOCK EXCHANGE
Boersenkommissariat, Bleicherweg 5
CH-8001 Zürich

UNITED KINGDOM

THE INTERNATIONAL STOCK EX-
CHANGE OF THE UNITED KINGDOM
AND THE REPUBLIC OF IRELAND LIM-
ITED
Old Broad Street
London, England EC 2N 1HP

Securities and Exchange Commission

JUDICIARY PLAZA
450 FIFTH STREET, NW
WASHINGTON, DC 20549
PUBLIC AFFAIRS: 202-272-2650
FREEDOM OF INFORMATION ACT:
202-272-7420
FILINGS BY REGISTERED COMPANIES:
202-272-7450

FULL AND FAIR DISCLOSURE

The Securities Act of 1933 requires issuers of securities making public offerings of securities in interstate commerce or through the mails, directly or by others on their behalf, to file registration statements containing financial and other pertinent data about the issuer and the securities being offered. A similar requirement applies to such offerings on behalf of a controlling person of the issuer. Unless a registration statement is in effect with respect to such securities, it is unlawful to sell the securities in interstate commerce or through the mails. (There are certain limited exemptions, such as government securities, nonpublic offerings, and intrastate offerings, as well as offerings not exceeding $1,500,000 in amount, which comply with the commission's Regulation A.) The effectiveness of a registration statement may be refused or suspended after a public hearing, if the statement contains material misstatements or omissions, thus barring sale of the securities until it is appropriately amended. Registration of securities does not imply approval of the issue by the commission or that the commission has found the registration disclosures to be accurate. It does not insure investors against loss in their purchase but serves rather to provide information upon

Source: This material was abstracted from the United States Government Manual.

which investors may make an informed and realistic evaluation of the worth of the securities.

Persons responsible for filing false information with the commission subject themselves to the risk of fine or imprisonment or both; and persons connected with the public offering may be liable in damages to purchasers of the securities if the disclosures in the registration statement and prospectus are materially defective. Also, the above act contains antifraud provisions which apply generally to the sale of securities, whether or not registered (48 Stat. 74; 15 U.S.C. 77a et seq.).

REGULATION OF SECURITIES MARKETS AND PERSONS CONDUCTING A SECURITIES BUSINESS

The Securities Exchange Act of 1934 assigns to the commission board regulatory responsibilities over the securities markets, the self-regulatory organizations within the securities industry, and persons conducting a business in securities. Persons who execute transactions in securities generally are required to register with the Commission as broker-dealers. The Commission is directed to facilitate the establishment of a national market system for securities and a national system for the clearance and settlement of securities transactions. Securities exchanges and certain clearing agencies are required to register with the Commission, and associations of brokers or dealers are permitted to register with the Commission. The securities Exchange Act also provides for the establishment of the Municipal Securities Rulemaking Board to formulate rules for the municipal securities industry. The Commission oversees the self-regulatory activities of the national securities exchanges and associations, registered clearing agencies, and the Municipal Securities Rulemaking Board. In addition, the Commission regulates industry professionals, such as securities brokers and dealers, certain municipal securities professionals, and transfer agents.

The Securities Exchange Act authorizes national securities exchanges, national securities associations, clearing agencies, and the Municipal Securities Rulemaking Board to adopt rules that are designed, among other things to promote just and equitable principles of trade and to protect investors. The Commission is required to approve or disapprove most proposed rules of these self-regulatory organizations and has the power to abrogate or amend existing rules of the national securities exchanges, national securities associations, and the Municipal Securities Rulemaking Board.

In addition, the Commission has broad rulemaking authority over the activities of brokers, dealers, municipal securities dealers, securities information processors, and transfer agents. The Commission may regulate such securities trading practices as short sales and stabilizing transactions. It may regulate the trading of options on national securities exchanges and the activities of members of exchanges who trade on the trading floors and may adopt rules governing broker-dealer sales practices in dealing with investors. The Commission also is authorized to adopt rules concerning the financial responsibility of brokers and dealers and reports to be made by brokers and dealers.

The Securities Exchange Act also empowers the Board of Governors of the Federal Reserve System to prescribe rules relating to the extension of credit by brokers and dealers for securities transactions. Such rules include the establishment of minimum margin requirements with respect to securities registered on national securities exchanges and certain securities traded over-the-counter (48 Stat. 881; U.S.C. 78a et seq.).

The Securities Exchange Act also requires the filing of registration applications and annual and other reports with national securities exchanges and the commission by companies whose securities are listed upon the exchanges, by companies that have assets of $5 million or more and 500 or more shareholders of record, and by companies that distributed securities pursuant to a registration statement declared effective by the commission under the Securities Act of 1933. Such applications and reports must contain financial and other data prescribed by the commission as necessary or appropriate for the protection of investors and to issue fair dealing. In addition, the solicitation of proxies, authorizations, or consents from holders of such registered securities must be made in accordance with rules and regulations prescribed by the commission. These rules provide for disclosures to securities holders of information relevant to the subject matter of the solicitation.

Disclosure of the holdings and transactions by officers, directors, and large (10 percent) holders of equity securities of companies is also required, and any and all persons who acquire more than 5 percent of certain equity securities are required to file detailed information with the commission and any exchange upon which such securities may be traded. Moreover, any person making a tender offer for certain classes of equity securities is required to file reports with the commission if as a result of the tender offer such person would own more than 5 percent of the outstanding shares of the particular class of equity involved. The commission also is authorized to promulgate rules governing the repurchase by a corporate issuer of its own securities.

REGULATION OF MUTUAL FUNDS AND OTHER INVESTMENT COMPANIES

The Investment Company Act of 1940 (15 U.S.C. 80a–64) requires investment companies to register with the Commission and regulates their activities to protect investors. The regulation covers sales and management fees, composition of boards of directors, and capital structure. Additionally, the act prohibits investment companies from engaging in various transactions, including transactions with affiliated persons unless the Commission first determines that such transactions are fair. Under the act, the Commission may institute court action to enjoin the consummation of mergers and other plans for reorganization of investment companies if such plans are unfair to security holders. It also may impose sanctions by administrative proceedings against investment company managements for violations of the act and other federal securities laws, and file court actions to enjoin acts and practices of management officials involving breaches of fiduciary duty involving personal misconduct and to disqualify such officials from office.

REGULATION OF COMPANIES CONTROLLING ELECTRIC OR GAS UTILITIES

The Public Utility Holding Company Act of 1935 (15 U.S.C. 79–6) provides for regulation by the commission of the purchase and sale of securities and assets by companies in electric and gas utility holding company systems, their intra-system transactions and service and management arrangements. It limits holding companies to a single coordinated utility system and requires simplification of complex corporate and capital structures and elimination of unfair distribution of voting power among holders of system securities.

The issuance and sale of securities by holding companies and their subsidiaries, unless exempt (subject to conditions and terms which the commission is empowered to impose) as an issue expressly authorized by the state commission in the state in which the issuer is incorporated, must be found by the commission to meet statutory standards, namely: that the new security is reasonably adapted to the security structure and earning power of the issuer; that the proposed financing is necessary and appropriate to the economical and efficient operation of the company's business; that the consideration received, and fees, commissions, and other remuneration paid, are fair; and that the terms and conditions of the sale are not detrimental to investors, consumers, or the public.

The purchase and sale of utility properties and other assets may not be made in contravention of rules, regulations, or orders of the commission regarding the consideration to be received, maintenance of competitive conditions, fees and commissions, accounts, disclosure of interest, and similar matters. In passing upon proposals for reorganization, merger, or consolidation, the commission must be satisfied that the objectives of the act generally are complied with and that the terms of the proposal are fair and equitable to all classes of security holders affected.

REGULATION OF INVESTMENT COUNSELORS AND ADVISERS

The Investment Advisers Act of 1940 (15 U.S.C. 80b–1–80b–21) provides that persons who, for compensation, engage in the business of advising others with respect to their security transactions must register with the commission. The act prohibits certain types of fee arrangements, makes unlawful practices of investment advisers involving fraud or deceit, and requires, among other things, disclosure of any adverse interests the advisers may have in transactions executed for clients. The act authorizes the commission, by rule, to define fraudulent and deceptive practices and prescribe means to prevent those practices.

REHABILITATION OF FAILING CORPORATIONS

Chapter 11, section 1109(a), of the Bankruptcy Code (11 U.S.C. 1109) provides for Commission participation as a statutory party in corporate reorganization proceedings administered in Federal courts. The principal functions of the Commission are to protect the interests of public investors involved in such cases through efforts to ensure their adequate representation and to participate on legal and policy issues which are of concern to public investors generally.

REPRESENTATION OF DEBT SECURITIES

The interests of purchasers of publicly offered debt securities issued pursuant to trust indentures are safeguarded under the provisions of the Trust Indenture Act of 1939 (15 U.S.C. 77aaa–77bbb). This act, among other things, requires the exclusion from such in-

dentures of certain types of exculpatory clauses and the inclusion of certain protective provisions. The independence of the indenture trustee, who is a representative of the debt holder, is assured by proscribing certain relationships that might conflict with the proper exercise of his duties (53 Stat. 1110, 15 U.S.C. 77aaa–77bbbb).

ENFORCEMENT ACTIVITIES

The commission's enforcement activities are designed to secure compliance with the federal securities laws administered by the commission and the rules and regulations adopted thereunder. These activities include measures to compel obedience to the disclosure requirements of the registration and other provisions of the acts; to prevent fraud and deception in the purchase and sale of securities; to obtain court orders enjoining acts and practices that operate as a fraud upon investors or otherwise violate the laws; to suspend or revoke the registrations of brokers, dealers, investment companies and investment advisers who willfully engage in such acts and practices; to suspend or bar from association persons associated with brokers, dealers, investment companies and investment advisers who have violated any provision of the federal securities laws; and to prosecute persons who have engaged in fraudulent activities, or other willful violations of those laws. In addition, attorneys, accountants, and other professionals who violate the securities laws face possible loss of their privilege to practice before the commission. To this end, private investigations are conducted into complaints or other evidences of securities violations. Evidence thus established of law violations is used in appropriate administrative proceedings to revoke registration or in actions instituted in federal courts to restrain or enjoin such activities. Where the evidence tends to establish fraud or other willful violation of the securities laws, the facts are referred to the Attorney General for criminal prosecution of the offenders. The commission may assist in such prosecutions.

INVESTOR INFORMATION AND PROTECTION

Consumer Activities Publications detailing the Commission's activities, which include material of assistance to the potential investor, are available from the Publications Unit. In addition, the Office of Consumer Affairs and Information Services answers questions from investors, assists investors with specific problems regarding their relations with broker-dealers and companies, and advises the Commission and other offices and divisions regarding problems frequently encountered by investors and possible regulatory solutions to such problems. Phone, 202-272-7440.

Complaints and inquiries may be directed to the home office or to any regional office. Registration statements and other public documents filed with the commission are available for public inspection in the public reference room at the home office. Much of the information also is available in its New York and Chicago regional offices. Copies of the public material may be purchased from the commission's contract copying service at prescribed rates.

Small Business Activities Information on security laws which pertain to small businesses in relation to securities offerings may be obtained from the Commission. Phone, 202-272-2644.

Reading Rooms The Commission maintains a public reference room (phone, 202-272-7450) and also a library (phone, 202-272-2618) where additional information may be obtained.

REGIONAL OFFICES (Securities and Exchange Commission)

Region	Address
1. New York, New Jersey	26 Federal Plaza, New York, NY 10078 Phone: 212-264-1636
2. Maine, Vermont, New Hampshire, Massachusetts, Connecticut, Rhode Island	90 Devonshire Street, Boston, MA 02109 Phone: 617-223-9900
3. Tennessee, North Carolina, South Carolina, Mississippi, Alabama, Georgia, Florida, Louisiana (southeastern portion only)	1375 Peachtree Street NE, Atlanta, GA 30367 Phone: 404-347-4768
4. Minnesota, Wisconsin, Michigan, Iowa, Missouri, Illinois, Indiana, Ohio, Kentucky	219 S. Dearborn Street, Chicago, IL 60604 Phone: 312-353-7390
5. Kansas, Oklahoma, Texas, Arkansas, Louisiana (except southeastern portion)	411 W. 7th Street, Fort Worth, TX 76102 Phone: 817-334-3821
6. North Dakota, South Dakota, Colorado, Kansas, Utah, Wyoming, New Mexico	410 17th Street, Denver, CO 80202 Phone: 303-844-2071
7. California, Nevada, Arizona, Hawaii, Guam	5757 Wilshire Boulevard, Los Angeles, CA 90036 Phone: 213-468-3098
8. Washington, Oregon, Alaska, Montana, Idaho	915 Second Avenue, Seattle, WA 98174 Phone: 206-442-7990
9. Pennsylvania, West Virginia, Virginia, Maryland, Delaware, Washington, D.C.	600 Arch St., Philadelphia, PA 19106 Phone: 215-597-3100

Average Annual Growth Rate in Earnings by Industry, 1979-1988 and 1988-2000, United States

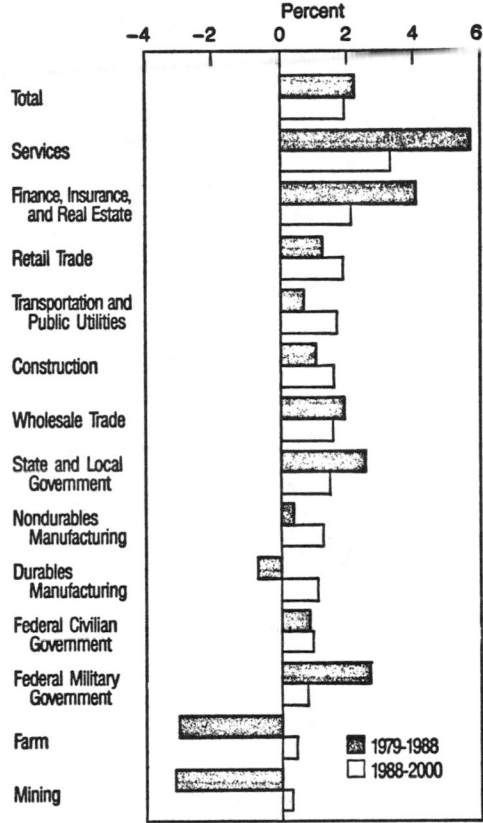

Note.—Industries ranked by average annual growth rate in earnings, 1988-2000.

U.S. Department of Commerce, Bureau of Economic Analysis

Source: *Survey of Current Business*, Bureau of Economic Advisers.

Tracing Obsolete Securities*

The following is a list of some of the available sources of information on tracing obsolete securities. This list should be useful to those who wonder whether their old securities have any value, to researchers, and to collectors. All of the books listed below should be available in large public libraries or in larger business libraries.

To trace a security, you need to know the name of the company, the date of issue and the state in which the company was incorporated; all three pieces of information should appear on the security. Start with volumes appropriate to the issue date of the security and continue through to the present, if necessary. If the security can not be found, contact the department that registers corporations in the state in which the company was incorporated. In most states this will be the office of the Secretary of State. They maintain records of name changes and bankruptcies and can usually answer your inquiry quickly; some charge a nominal fee for the service. Call the department to see what their procedures and costs are. You may need to send a copy of the certificate. Do not send the original certificate.

For an introduction to searching obsolete securities, the best guide, now out-of-print, is:

Cargiulo, Albert F. and Rocco Carlucci.
The Questioned Stock Manual: A Guide to Determining the True Worth of Old and Collectible Securities. New York: McGraw-Hill, 1979, xiv, 193 p.: ill. tables.
Chapters 3 and 4 deal with locating sources of information on securities. Chapter 6 covers the detection and recognition of fraudulent securities and a description of how securities are printed. The appendix contains a table of the top 100 firms, 1917–1977.

For historical data, beginning with colonial times, the Fisher, Scudder, and Smythe manuals are classics. The manuals are still published and the Smythe firm continues to do research into obsolete securities, charging a fee of $25 for each company. They also serve as dealers and appraisers of obsolete securities for collectors. You can contact them at:

R. M. Smythe & Co.
26 Broadway
New York, NY 10004
(212) 943–1880

* Frederick N. Nesta, Director, Library Associates, NY: Director, Marymount Manhattan College Library.

Robert D. Fisher
Manual of Valuable & Worthless Securities: Showing Companies That Have Been Reorganized, Merged, Liquidated or Dissolved, Little Known Companies and Oil Leases. New York: R. M. Smythe, 1926–. 15 v.
First published in 1926 as the *Marvyn Scudder Manual . . .* , the series was taken over by Robert D. Fisher with vol. 5 in 1937. It has been published by the R. M. Smythe firm since 1971 under the editorship of Robert D. Fisher, Jr. With vol. 6 the series limited itself to securities and the date on which they became worthless. The earlier volumes present brief corporate obituaries. Volume 15, 1984, includes a price guide for collectors of obsolete certificates.
Smythe, Roland M.
Valuable Extinct Securities: the Secret of the Obsolete Security Business. Unclaimed Money and How to Collect It, With a List of . . . Extinct Securities of Good Value From the Records of the Four Principal Dealers. . . . New York: R. M. Smythe, 1929. v, 398 p.
By the author and publisher of *Obsolete American Securities and Corporations,* later the *Robert D. Fisher Manual of Valuable and Worthless Securities.* This list of over 1,500 securities gives due and foreclosure dates and the dates of sale or merger.
Smythe, Roland M.
Obsolete American Securities and Corporations. New York: R. M. Smythe, 1911. liv, 1166 p.: ill.
(*Obsolete American Securities and Corporations:* vol. 2). Pages 1–28 discuss Continental and other early U.S. state and foreign notes and bonds. Twenty plates illustrate some of the bonds discussed. Volume 1 was published in 1904.
Valuable Extinct Securities Guide. 1939 ed. New York: R. M. Smythe, Inc., 1938. 127 p. The first edition was published in 1929 and was the sequel to *Obsolete American Securities and Corporations.*

The books below can be consulted to trace more recent corporate reorganizations:

Capital Changes Reporter for Federal Income Tax Purposes. Clark, NJ: Commerce Clearing House (NJ), 1949–. 6 v., looseleaf. Securities distributions, taxability of disbursements, splits, offers, rights, etc.
The National Monthly Stock Summary. Jer-

sey City, NJ: National Quotation Bureau, 1926–.

Summary data from the daily service, supplied either from the service or from dealers' lists. Name, par value, exchange, closing price, bids and offerings. May also include shares outstanding, control, reorganization, dividend or other information. Monthly, with bound cumulative volumes issued twice yearly.

Capital Adjustments, Reorganizations and Exchanges, Stock Dividends. Rights and Splits. Englewood Cliffs, NJ: Prentice-Hall, 1980–. 2 v. in 3, looseleaf.

Current changes, disbursements, etc. Includes notes on taxability. Supplements the bound volumes below.

Capital Adjustments: Stock Dividends, Stock Rights, Reorganizations. Englewood Cliffs, NJ: Prentice-Hall, 1962–.

The earlier volumes cover corporate and government securities from early in the century. Updated by looseleaf supplements. Includes name changes, incorporation dates, mergers.

Bank & Quotation Record. Arlington, MA: National News Services, 1928–.

"A publication of the Commercial and Financial Chronicle." Monthly opening and closing prices, highs, lows, etc. Includes equipment trusts, public utility bonds, Chicago Board Options Exchange, foreign exchange rates for the month, CDs, Federal funds, prime banker acceptance rates, commercial paper statistics. Published continuously for over sixty years, it is a fascinating document of American financial history.

FOREIGN CORPORATIONS

Canada

Canadian Mines Register of Dormant and Defunct Companies: Third Supplement.

Toronto: Northern Miner Press Limited, 1976. 108 p. Originally published in 1960.

Survey of Predecessor and Defunct Companies. 3rd ed. Toronto: The Financial Post Corporation Service Group, 1985. 208 p.

Covers over 12,000 companies and spans over 50 years. Lists name changes, removals, the exchange basis for new shares, along with the addresses and telephone numbers of Canadian Federal and Provincial corporate registry offices.

United Kingdom

The Stock Exchange Official Year-Book. London: Macmillan, 1934–.

Contains substantial information on the London Stock Exchange, foreign securities, municipal securities, regulations and statistics and a directory of International exchanges. The main body lists each company with parent/subsidiary note, background, financial data, stock history, voting, dividends. Includes the *Register of Defunct and Other Companies Removed from the Stock Exchange Official Year-Book,* a listing of over 23,000 companies removed from the Official Year-Book since 1875, along with a list of Commonwealth Government and Provincial stocks redeemed or converted since 1940. The Register was published separately until 1980.

Australia

Register of Companies Removed from the Stock Exchanges Official Lists. Sydney: Stock Exchange Research Pty., 1984? 104 p.

Lists companies that were traded on one or more Australian exchanges. Historical data, with delistings going back to the early 1930s.

Bonds and Money Market Instruments

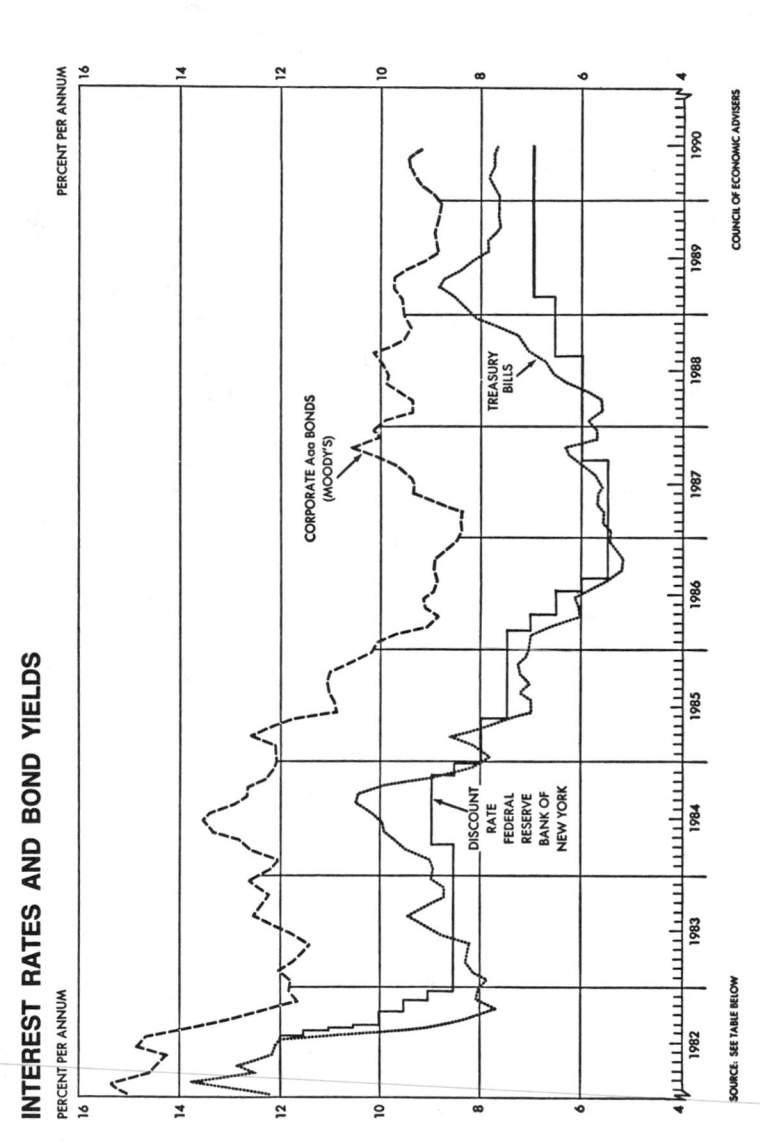

INTEREST RATES AND BOND YIELDS

PERCENT PER ANNUM

PERCENT PER ANNUM

CORPORATE Aaa BONDS (MOODY'S)

TREASURY BILLS

DISCOUNT RATE FEDERAL RESERVE BANK OF NEW YORK

SOURCE: SEE TABLE BELOW

COUNCIL OF ECONOMIC ADVISERS

[Percent per annum]

Period	U.S. Treasury security yields			High-grade municipal bonds (Standard & Poor's) [3]	Corporate Aaa bonds (Moody's) [4]	Prime commercial paper, 6 months [1]	Discount rate (N.Y. F.R. Bank) [5]	Prime rate charged by banks [5]	New-home mortgage yields (FHFB) [6]
	3-month bills (new issues) [1]	Constant maturities [2]							
		3-year	10-year						
1981	14.029	14.44	13.91	11.23	14.17	14.76	13.42	18.87	14.70
1982	10.686	12.92	13.00	11.57	13.79	11.89	11.02	14.86	15.14
1983	8.63	10.45	11.10	9.47	12.04	8.89	8.50	10.79	12.57
1984	9.58	11.89	12.44	10.15	12.71	10.16	8.80	12.04	12.38
1985	7.48	9.64	10.62	9.18	11.37	8.01	7.69	9.93	11.55
1986	5.98	7.06	7.68	7.38	9.02	6.39	6.33	8.33	10.17
1987	5.82	7.68	8.39	7.73	9.38	6.85	5.66	8.21	9.31
1988	6.69	8.26	8.85	7.76	9.71	7.68	6.20	9.32	9.19
1989	8.12	8.55	8.49	7.24	9.26	8.80	6.93	10.87	10.13
1989: June	8.22	8.37	8.28	6.97	9.10	8.80	7.00–7.00	11.50–11.00	10.42
July	7.92	7.83	8.02	6.97	8.93	8.35	7.00–7.00	11.00–10.50	10.48
Aug	7.91	8.13	8.11	7.08	8.96	8.32	7.00–7.00	10.50–10.50	10.22
Sept	7.72	8.26	8.19	7.27	9.01	8.50	7.00–7.00	10.50–10.50	10.24
Oct	7.63	8.02	8.01	7.22	8.92	8.24	7.00–7.00	10.50–10.50	10.11
Nov	7.65	7.80	7.87	7.13	8.89	8.00	7.00–7.00	10.50–10.50	10.09
Dec	7.64	7.77	7.84	7.01	8.86	7.93	7.00–7.00	10.50–10.50	10.07
1990: Jan	7.64	8.13	8.21	7.13	8.99	7.96	7.00–7.00	10.50–10.00	9.91
Feb	7.76	8.39	8.47	7.21	9.22	8.04	7.00–7.00	10.00–10.00	9.88
Mar	7.87	8.63	8.59	7.29	9.37	8.23	7.00–7.00	10.00–10.00	10.03
Apr	7.78	8.78	8.79	7.36	9.46	8.29	7.00–7.00	10.00–10.00	10.17
May r	7.78	8.69	8.76	7.34	9.47	8.23	7.00–7.00	10.00–10.00	10.28
June p	7.74	8.40	8.48	7.22	9.26	8.06	7.00–7.00	10.00–10.00	....
Week ended:									
1990: June 2	7.80	8.50	8.58	7.23	9.38	8.13	7.00–7.00	10.00–10.00	....
9	7.69	8.38	8.46	7.21	9.27	8.06	7.00–7.00	10.00–10.00	....
16	7.73	8.36	8.44	7.18	9.21	8.03	7.00–7.00	10.00–10.00	....
23	7.74	8.44	8.52	7.27	9.26	8.06	7.00–7.00	10.00–10.00	....
30 p	7.78	8.42	8.51	7.23	9.28	8.07	7.00–7.00	10.00–10.00	....

[1] Bank-discount basis.
[2] Yields on the more actively traded issues adjusted to constant maturities by the Treasury Department.
[3] Weekly data are Wednesday figures.
[4] Series excludes public utility issues for January 17, 1984 through October 11, 1984 due to lack of appropriate issues.
[5] Average effective rate for year; opening and closing rate for month and week.
[6] Effective rate in the primary market) on conventional mortgages, reflecting fees and charges as well as contract rate and assumed, on the average, repayment at end of 10 years.

Sources: Department of the Treasury, Board of Governors of the Federal Reserve System, Federal Housing Finance Board, Moody's Investors Service, and Standard & Poor's Corporation.

Source: *Economic Indicators*, Council of Economic Advisers.

PRIME RATE CHARGED BY BANKS on Short-Term Business Loans (percent per year)

Date of change	Rate
1987— Apr. 1	7.75
May 15	8.00
Sept.4	8.25
Oct. 7	8.75
22	9.25
Nov. 5	9.00
1988— Feb. 2	8.75
May 11	8.50
July 14	9.00
Aug. 11	9.50
Nov. 28	10.00
1989— Feb. 10	10.50
24	11.00
June 5	11.50
July 31	11.50
1990— Jan. 8	10.00

Period	Average rate	Period	Average rate	Period	Average rate
1987		1988— Jan.	8.75	1989— July	10.98
1988		Feb.	8.51	Aug.	10.50
1989		Mar.	8.50	Sept.	10.50
1987— Jan.	8.21	Apr.	8.50	Oct.	10.50
Feb.	9.32	May	8.84	Nov.	10.50
Mar.	10.87	June	9.00	Dec.	10.11
Apr.	7.50	July	9.29	1990— Jan.	10.00
May	7.50	Aug.	9.84	Feb.	10.00
June	7.50	Sept.	10.00	Mar.	10.00
July	7.75	Oct.	10.00	Apr.	10.00
Aug.	8.14	Nov.	10.05	May	10.00
Sept.	8.25	Dec.	10.50		
Oct.	8.25	1989— Jan.	10.50		
Nov.	8.25	Feb.	10.93		
Dec.	8.70	Mar.	11.50		
1988— Jan.	9.07	Apr.	11.50		
Feb.	8.78	May	11.50		
Mar.	8.75	June	11.07		

NOTE. These data also appear in the Board's H.15 (519) and G.13 (415) releases.

Source: *Federal Reserve Bulletin*, Board of Governors of the Federal Reserve System.

INTEREST RATES Money and Capital Markets

Averages, percent per year; weekly, monthly and annual figures are averages of business day data unless otherwise noted.

Instrument	1987	1988	1989	1990								
				Jan.	Feb.	Mar.	Apr.	Mar. 30	Apr. 6	Apr. 13	Apr. 20	Apr. 27
MONEY MARKET RATES												
1 Federal funds[1,2]	6.66	7.57	9.21	8.23	8.24	8.28	8.26	8.26	8.33	8.25	8.27	8.24
2 Discount window borrowing[1,2,3]	5.66	6.20	6.93	7.00	7.00	7.00	7.00	7.00	7.00	7.00	7.00	7.00
Commercial paper[4,3]												
3 1-month	6.74	7.58	9.11	8.20	8.22	8.32	8.32	8.35	8.34	8.30	8.30	8.35
4 3-month	6.82	7.66	8.99	8.10	8.14	8.28	8.30	8.30	8.30	8.24	8.27	8.37
5 6-month	6.85	7.68	8.80	7.96	8.04	8.23	8.29	8.27	8.28	8.21	8.24	8.38
Finance paper, directly placed[4,3]												
6 1-month	6.61	7.44	8.99	8.09	8.13	8.23	8.23	8.25	8.25	8.20	8.20	8.27
7 3-month	6.54	7.38	8.72	7.90	7.97	8.04	8.13	8.08	8.09	8.08	8.10	8.20
8 6-month	6.37	7.14	8.16	7.34	7.40	7.49	7.74	7.52	7.61	7.61	7.74	7.96
Bankers acceptances[3,6]												
9 3-month	6.75	7.56	8.87	7.97	8.03	8.15	8.21	8.18	8.17	8.14	8.18	8.30
10 6-month	6.78	7.60	8.67	7.83	7.91	8.11	8.18	8.15	8.14	8.09	8.14	8.32
Certificates of deposit, secondary market[7]												
11 1-month	6.75	7.59	9.11	8.17	8.19	8.30	8.32	8.31	8.31	8.29	8.30	8.38
12 3-month	6.87	7.73	9.09	8.16	8.22	8.35	8.42	8.35	8.37	8.35	8.38	8.53
13 6-month	7.01	7.91	9.08	8.17	8.26	8.48	8.57	8.52	8.54	8.47	8.51	8.72

14	Eurodollar deposits, 3-month	[illegible]	[illegible]	[illegible]	[illegible]	[illegible]	[illegible]	[illegible]	[illegible]	[illegible]	[illegible]	[illegible]	[illegible]
	U.S. Treasury bills[5]												
	Secondary market[9]												
15	3-month	5.78	6.67	8.11	7.64	7.74	7.90	7.77	7.85	7.77	7.78	7.76	7.78
16	6-month	6.03	6.91	8.03	7.55	7.70	7.85	7.84	7.84	7.77	7.78	7.81	7.94
17	1-year	6.33	7.13	7.92	7.38	7.55	7.76	7.80	7.75	7.71	7.70	7.81	7.94
	Auction average[10]												
18	3-month	5.82	6.68	8.12	7.64	7.76	7.87	7.78	7.85	7.83	7.80	7.71	7.78
19	6-month	6.05	6.92	8.04	7.52	7.72	7.83	7.82	7.83	7.81	7.80	7.75	7.91
20	1-year	6.33	7.17	7.91	7.21	7.42	7.76	7.72	n.a.	n.a.	7.72	n.a.	n.a.
	CAPITAL MARKET RATES												
	U.S. Treasury notes and bonds[11]												
	Constant maturities[12]												
21	1-year	6.77	7.65	8.53	7.92	8.11	8.35	8.40	8.34	8.29	8.29	8.41	8.57
22	2-year	7.42	8.10	8.57	8.09	8.37	8.63	8.72	8.61	8.57	8.55	8.75	8.95
23	3-year	7.68	8.26	8.55	8.13	8.39	8.63	8.78	8.63	8.62	8.61	8.80	9.02
24	5-year	7.94	8.47	8.50	8.12	8.42	8.60	8.77	8.57	8.59	8.60	8.79	9.01
25	7-year	8.23	8.71	8.52	8.20	8.48	8.65	8.81	8.62	8.65	8.65	8.84	9.04
26	10-year	8.39	8.85	8.49	8.21	8.47	8.59	8.79	8.56	8.59	8.62	8.83	9.02
27	30-year	8.59	8.96	8.45	8.26	8.50	8.56	8.76	8.53	8.56	8.58	8.80	9.00
	Composite[13]												
28	Over 10 years (long-term)	8.64	8.98	8.58	8.39	8.66	8.74	8.92	8.71	8.74	8.74	8.97	9.15
	State and local notes and bonds												
	Moody's series[14]												
29	Aaa	7.14	7.36	7.00	6.81	7.05	6.98	7.04	7.05	6.83	[illegible]	7.05	7.19
30	Baa	8.17	7.83	7.40	7.35	7.24	7.41	7.43	7.45	7.40	7.50	7.45	7.40
31	*Bond Buyer* series[15]	7.63	7.68	7.23	7.10	7.22	7.29	7.39	7.33	7.33	7.31	7.39	7.51
	Corporate bonds												
	Seasoned issues[16]												
32	All industries	9.91	10.18	9.66	9.43	9.64	9.73	9.82	9.73	9.74	9.73	9.82	9.95
33	Aaa	9.38	9.71	9.26	8.99	9.22	9.37	9.46	9.37	9.38	9.38	9.45	9.59
34	Aa	9.68	9.94	9.46	9.27	9.45	9.51	9.64	9.54	9.55	9.53	9.64	9.77
35	A	9.99	10.24	9.74	9.54	9.75	9.82	9.89	9.80	9.82	9.81	9.89	9.98
36	Baa	10.58	10.83	10.18	9.94	10.14	10.21	10.30	10.20	10.22	[illegible]	10.29	10.45
37	A-rated, recently offered utility bonds[17]	9.96	10.20	9.79	9.63	9.84	9.92	10.09	9.98	9.93	[illegible]	10.25	10.32
	MEMO: Dividend/price ratio[18]												
38	Preferred stocks	8.37	9.23	9.05	8.80	8.90	9.02	9.05	9.00	9.04	9.09	9.02	9.04
39	Common stocks	3.08	3.64	3.45	3.41	3.54	3.49	3.51	3.47	3.48	3.48	3.49	3.59

1. Weekly, monthly and annual figures are averages of all calendar days, where the rate for a weekend or holiday is taken to be the rate prevailing on the preceding business day. The daily rate is the average of the rates on a given day weighted by the volume of transactions at these rates.
2. Weekly figures are averages for statement week ending Wednesday.
3. Rate for the Federal Reserve Bank of New York.
4. Unweighted average of offering rates quoted by at least five dealers (in the case of commercial paper), or finance companies (in the case of finance paper). Before November 1979, maturities for data shown are 30–59 days, 90–119 days, and 120–179 days for commercial paper; and 30–59 days, 90–119 days, and 150–179 days for finance paper.
5. Yields are quoted on a bank-discount basis, rather than in an investment yield basis (which would give a higher figure).
6. Dealer closing offered rates for top-rated banks. Most representative rate (which may be, but need not be, the average of the rates quoted by the dealers).
7. Unweighted average of offered rates quoted by at least five dealers early in the day.
8. Calendar week average. For indication purposes only.
9. Unweighted average of closing bid rates quoted by at least five dealers.
10. Rates are recorded in the week in which bills are issued. Beginning with the Treasury bill auction held on Apr. 18, 1983, bidders were required to state the percentage yield (on a bank discount basis) that they would accept to two decimal places. Thus, average issuing rates in bill auctions will be reported using two rather than three decimal places.
11. Yields are based on closing bid prices quoted by at least five dealers.
12. Yields adjusted to constant maturities by the U.S. Treasury. That is, yields are read from a yield curve at fixed maturities. Based on only recently issued, actively traded securities.
13. Averages (to maturity or call) for all outstanding bonds neither due nor callable in less than 10 years, including one very low yielding "flower" bond.
14. General obligations based on Thursday figures; Moody's Investors Service.
15. General obligations only, with 20 years to maturity, issued by 20 state and local governmental units of mixed quality. Based on figures for Thursday.
16. Daily figures from Moody's Investors Service. Based on yields to maturity on selected long-term bonds.
17. Compilation of the Federal Reserve. This series is an estimate of the yield on recently-offered, A-rated utility bonds with a 30-year maturity and 5 years of call protection. Weekly data are based on Friday quotations.
18. Standard and Poor's corporate series. Preferred stock ratio based on a sample of ten issues: four public utilities, four industrials, one financial, and one transportation. Common stock ratios on the 500 stocks in the price index.

NOTE. These data also appear in the Board's H.15 (519) and G.13 (415) releases. For address, see inside front cover.

Source: *Federal Reserve Bulletin*, Board of Governors of the Federal Reserve System.

NYSE Bond Volume

Annual Bond Volume Growth (billions of dollars)

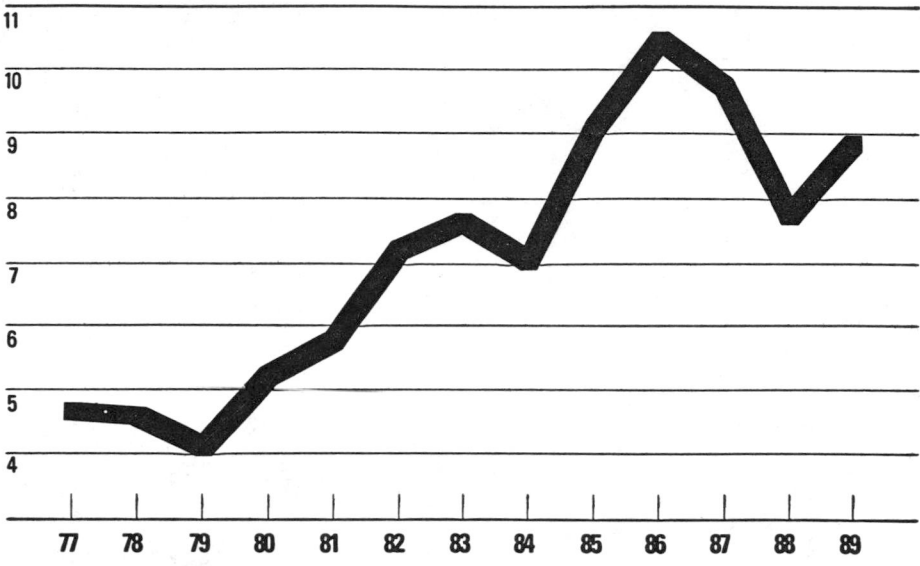

Source: New York Stock Exchange 1990 *Fact Book.*

Reported Bond Volume and Trades on NYSE, 1989 (par value in thousands)

	Par value		No. of trades	Avg. daily trades	Avg. trade size* (No. of bonds)
	For month	Avg. daily			
January	$632,127	$30,101	40,581	1,932	14.2
February	558,876	29,415	36,013	1,895	14.2
March	591,394	26,882	38,796	1,763	14.2
April	553,486	27,674	36,060	1,803	14.4
May	734,367	33,380	42,736	1,943	15.9
June	878,245	39,920	45,406	2,064	18.0
July	712,417	35,621	39,846	1,992	16.9
August	805,747	35,032	45,612	1,983	16.7
September	769,797	38,490	38,377	1,919	19.1
October	925,978	42,090	41,974	1,908	21.1
November	829,834	39,516	43,712	2,082	18.0
December	844,003	42,200	43,807	2,190	18.6
Total	**$8,836,271**	**$35,065**	**492,920**	**1,956**	**16.9**

	Par value	
High Day	$ 80,591	Oct. 16
Low Day	14,434	Jul. 3
High Month	925,978	October
Low Month	553,486	April

*Avg. trade size is adjusted for the volume of two GMAC zero coupon issues trading in units of $10,000.

Source: New York Stock Exchange 1990 *Fact Book.*

Most Active Bonds on NYSE, 1989

Issue	Par Value of Reported Volume (thousands)
RJR Holdings Group exchange debs '07	$622,528
RJR Holdings Capital disc debs '01	447,352
RJR Holdings Corp. zero coupon '09	422,086
General Motors Acceptance zero coupon '15	354,890
General Motors Acceptance zero coupon '12	229,600
Public Service Company of New Hampshire 17½s '04	175,022
International Business Machines CV 7⅞s '04	125,353
Occidental Petroleum deep disc '94	105,694
Pan American World Airways 15s '04	104,397
Southmark Corp. 10⅞s '89	91,760
Southmark Corp. 13¼s '94	82,748
RJR Holdings Capital 13½s '01	70,316
Holiday Inns 10½s '94	63,753
American Telephone & Telegraph 8¾s '00	63,403
Marathon Oil Company 9½s '94	63,113
Pan American World Airways CV 9s '10	62,661
National Gypsum zero coupon '04	59,088
Holiday Inns 11s '99	58,451
RJR Holdings Capital 15s '01	56,678
Pan American World Airways 13½s deep disc '03	55,074
General Motors Acceptance 9¼s '93	50,749
Santa Fe Southern Pacific 16s '03	50,007
Southmark Corp. 11⅞s '93	49,007
Waste Management LYONS '12	45,583
Integrated Resources 13⅛s '95	45,141
USG CORP. 16s '08	40,633
AmBase Corp. 14⅞s '98	37,090
Public Service Company of New Hampshire 15¾s '88	36,229
Southmark Corp. 15¼s '91	34,365
American Telephone & Telegraph 8.8s '05	34,194
Public Service Company of New Hampshire 14⅜s '91	34,098
Integrated Resources 10¾s '96	33,688
Eastman Kodak Co. 8⅝s '16	33,598
LTV Corp. 14s '04	33,536
Public Service Company of New Hampshire 15s '03	33,202
Coleco Industries 11⅛s '01	32,947
Union Carbide Corp. 9¾s '94	32,048
Union Carbide Corp. CV 7½s '12	31,964
Occidental Petroleum 10s '91	31,463
General Motors Acceptance 10⅜s '95	28,205
Occidental Petroleum 10⅞s '96	28,012
American Telephone & Telegraph 8⅝s '26	27,446
Amoco Canada Petroleum 7⅜s '13	27,276
Republic Steel Corp. 12⅛s '03	27,042
Coastal Corp. 8.48s '91	26,516
Golden Nugget Finance 13¼s '95	26,438
IBM Corp. 10¼s '95	25,863
Occidental Petroleum 11¾s '11	25,515
du Pont de Nemours 6s '01	25,266
Southmark Corp. 11½s '91	24,988

Source: New York Stock Exchange 1990 *Fact Book*.

Credit Ratings of Fixed Income and Money Market Securities

KEY TO STANDARD & POOR'S CORPORATE AND MUNICIPAL BOND RATING DEFINITIONS

A Standard & Poor's corporate or municipal debt rating is a current assessment of the creditworthiness of an obligor with respect to a specific debt obligation. This assessment may take into consideration obligors such as guarantors, insurers, or lessees.

The debt rating is not a recommendation to purchase, sell or hold a security, inasmuch as it does not comment as to market price or suitability for a particular investor.

The ratings are based on current information furnished by the issuer or obtained by Standard & Poor's from other sources it considers reliable. Standard & Poor's does not perform an audit in connection with any rating and may, on occasion, rely on unaudited financial information. The ratings may be changed, suspended or withdrawn as a result of changes in, or unavailability of, such information, or for other circumstances.

The ratings are based, in varying degrees, on the following considerations:

I. Likelihood of default—capacity and willingness of the obligor as to the timely payment of interest and repayment of principal in accordance with the terms of the obligation;

II. Nature of and provisions of the obligation;

III. Protection afforded by, and relative position of, the obligation in the event of bankruptcy, reorganization or other arrangement under the laws of bankruptcy and other laws affecting creditor's rights.

AAA

Debt rated **AAA** have the highest rating assigned by Standard & Poor's to a debt obligation. Capacity to pay interest and repay principal is extremely strong.

AA

Debt rated **AA** have a very strong capacity to pay interest and repay principal and differ from the highest rated issues only in a small degree.

A

Debt rated **A** have a strong capacity to pay interest and repay principal although they

Source: From Standard & Poor's Debt Rating Division.

are somewhat more susceptible to the adverse effects of changes in circumstances and economic conditions than debts in higher rated categories.

BBB

Debt rated **BBB** are regarded as having an adequate capacity to pay interest and repay principal. Whereas they normally exhibit adequate protection parameters, adverse economic conditions or changing circumstances are more likely to lead to a weakened capacity to pay interest and repay principal for debts in this category than for debts in higher rated categories.

BB, B, CCC, CC

Debt rated **BB, B, CCC,** and **CC** are regarded, on balance, as predominantly speculative with respect to capacity to pay interest and repay principal in accordance with the terms of the obligation. **BB** indicates the lowest degree of speculation and **CC** the highest degree of speculation. While such debts will likely have some quality and protective characteristics, these are outweighed by large uncertainties or major risk exposures to adverse conditions.

C

The rating **C** is reserved for income bonds on which no interest is being paid.

D

Debt rated **D** are in default, and payment of interest and/or repayment of principal is in arrears.

Plus (+) or minus (−)

The ratings from **AA** to **B** may be modified by the addition of a plus or minus sign to show relative standing within the major rating categories.

Provisional ratings

The letter *p* indicates that the rating is provisional. A provisional rating assumes the successful completion of the project being financed by the debts being rated and indicates that payment of debt service requirements is largely or entirely dependent upon the successful and timely completion of the project. This rating, however, while addressing credit quality subsequent to completion of the project, makes no comment on the likelihood of, or the risk of default upon failure of, such completion. The investor should exercise his own judgment with respect to such likelihood and risk.

L*

The letter "L" indicates that the rating pertains to the principal amount of those bonds where the underlying deposit collateral is fully insured by the Federal Savings & Loan Insurance Corp. or the Federal Deposit Insurance Corp.

NR

Indicates that no rating has been requested, that there is insufficient information on which to base a rating or that S&P does not rate a particular type of obligation as a matter of policy.

Debt Obligations

Debt Obligations of issuers outside the United States and its territories are rated on the same basis as domestic corporate and municipal issues. The ratings measure the creditworthiness of the obligor but do not take into account currency exchange and other uncertainties.

Bond Investment Quality Standards

Under present commercial bank regulations issued by the Comptroller of the Currency, bonds rated in the top four categories (AAA, AA, A, BBB, commonly known as "Investment Grade" ratings) are generally regarded as eligible for bank investment. In addition, the Legal Investment Laws of various states impose certain rating or other standards for obligations eligible for investment by savings banks, trust companies, insurance companies and fiduciaries generally.

KEY TO STANDARD & POOR'S PREFERRED STOCK RATING DEFINITIONS

A Standard & Poor's preferred stock rating is an assessment of the capacity and willingness of an issuer to pay preferred stock dividends and any applicable sinking fund obligations. A preferred stock rating differs from a bond rating inasmuch as it is assigned to an equity issue, which issue is intrinsically different from, and subordinated to, a debt issue. Therefore, to reflect this difference, the preferred stock rating symbol will normally not be higher than the bond rating symbol assigned to, or that would be assigned to, the senior debt of the same issuer.

The preferred stock ratings are based on the following considerations.

* Continuance of the rating is contingent upon S&P's receipt of an executed copy of the escrow agreement or closing documentation confirming investments and the cash flows.

I. Likelihood of payment—capacity and willingness of the issuer to meet the timely payment of preferred stock dividends and any applicable sinking fund requirements in accordance with the terms of the obligation.
II. Nature of, and provisions of, the issue.
III. Relative position of the issue in the event of bankruptcy, reorganization, or other arrangements affecting creditors' rights.

AAA

This is the highest rating that may be assigned by Standard & Poor's to a preferred stock issue and indicates an extremely strong capacity to pay the preferred stock obligations.

AA

A preferred stock issue rated AA also qualifies as a high-quality fixed income security. The capacity to pay preferred stock obligations is very strong, although not as overwhelming as for issues rated AAA.

A

An issue rated A is backed by a sound capacity to pay the preferred stock obligations, although it is somewhat more susceptible to the adverse effects of changes in circumstances and economic conditions.

BBB

An issue rated BBB is regarded as backed by an adequate capacity to pay the preferred stock obligations. Whereas it normally exhibits adequate protection parameters, adverse economic conditions or changing circumstances are more likely to lead to a weakened capacity to make payments for a preferred stock in this category than for issues in the A category.

BB, B, CCC

Preferred stock rated BB, B, and CCC are regarded, on balance, as predominately speculative with respect to the issuer's capacity to pay preferred stock obligations. BB indicates the lowest degree of speculation and CCC the highest degree of speculation. While such issues will likely have some quality and protective characteristics, these are outweighed by large uncertainties or major risk exposures to adverse conditions.

CC

The rating CC is reserved for a preferred stock issue in arrears on dividends or sinking fund payments but that is currently paying.

C

A preferred stock rated C is a non-paying issue.

D

A preferred stock rated **D** is a non-paying issue with the issuer in default on debt instruments.

NR

NR indicates that no rating has been requested, that there is insufficient information on which to base a rating, or that S&P does not rate a particular type of obligation as a matter or policy.

Plus (+) or Minus (−) To provide more detailed indications of preferred stock quality, the ratings from **AA** to **B** may be modified by the addition of a plus or minus sign to show relative standing within the major rating categories.

The preferred stock rating is not a recommendation to purchase or sell a security, inasmuch as market price is not considered in arriving at the rating. Preferred stock *ratings* are wholly unrelated to Standard & Poor's earnings and dividend *rankings* for common stocks.

MUNICIPAL NOTES

A Standard & Poor's role rating reflects the liquidity concerns and market access risks unique to notes. Notes due in 3 years or less will likely receive a long-term debt rating. The following criteria will be used in making that assessment.

—Amortization schedule (the larger the final maturity relative to other maturities the more likely it will be treated as a note).
—Source of Payment (the more dependent the issue is on the market for its refinancing, the more likely it will be treated as a note).

Note rating symbols are as follows:

SP-1 Very strong or strong capacity to pay principal and interest. Those issues determined to possess overwhelming safety characteristics will be given a plus (+) designation.
SP-2 Satisfactory capacity to pay principal and interest.
SP-3 Speculative capacity to pay principal and interest.

TAX-EXEMPT DEMAND BONDS

Standard & Poor's assigns "dual" ratings to all long-term debt issues that have as part of their provisions a demand or double feature.

The first rating addresses the likelihood of repayment of principal and interest as due, and the second rating addresses only the demand feature. The long-term debt rating

symbols are used for bonds to denote the long-term maturity and the commercial paper rating symbols are used to denote the put option (for example, "AAA/A-1+"). For the newer "demand notes," S&P's note rating symbols, combined with the commercial paper symbols, are used (for example, "SP-1+/A-1+").

KEY TO STANDARD & POOR'S COMMERCIAL PAPER RATING DEFINITIONS

A Standard & Poor's Commercial Paper Rating is a current assessment of the likelihood of timely payment of debt having an original maturity of no more than 365 days.

Ratings are graded into four categories, ranging from **A** for the highest quality obligations to **D** for the lowest. The four categories are as follows:

A

Issues assigned this highest rating are regarded as having the greatest capacity for timely payment. Issues in this category are further refined with the designations 1, 2, and 3 to indicate the relative degree of safety.

A-1 This designation indicates that the degree of safety regarding timely payment is very strong.
A-2 Capacity for timely payment on issues with this designation is strong. However, the relative degree of safety is not as overwhelming as for issues designated **A-1**.
A-3 Issues carrying this designation have a satisfactory capacity for timely payment. They are, however, somewhat more vulnerable to the adverse effects of changes in circumstances than obligations carrying the higher designations.

B

Issues rated **B** are regarded as having only an adequate capacity for timely payment. However, such capacity may be damaged by changing conditions for short-term adversities.

C

This rating is assigned to short-term obligations with a doubtful capacity for payment.

D

This rating indicates that the issue is either a default or is expected to be in default upon maturity.

The Commercial Paper Rating is not a recommendation to purchase or sell a security. The ratings are based on current information furnished to Standard & Poor's by the issuer or obtained from other sources it considers reliable. The ratings may be changed, suspended, or withdrawn as a result of changes in, or unavailability of, such information.

KEY TO MOODY'S MUNICIPAL RATINGS*

Aaa

Bonds which are rated **Aaa** are judged to be of the best quality. They carry the smallest degree of investment risk and are generally referred to as "gilt edge." Interest payments are protected by a large or by an exceptionally stable margin and principal is secure. While the various protective elements are likely to change, such changes as can be visualized are most unlikely to impair the fundamentally strong position of such issues.

Aa

Bonds which are rated **Aa** are judged to be of high quality by all standards. Together with the **Aaa** group they comprise what are generally known as high grade bonds. They are rated lower than the best bonds because margins of protection may not be as large as in **Aaa** securities or fluctuation of protective elements may be of greater amplitude or there may be other elements present which make the long term risks appear somewhat larger than in **Aaa** securities.

A

Bonds which are rated **A** possess many favorable instrument attributes and are to be considered as upper medium grade obligations. Factors giving security to principal and interest are considered adequate, but elements may be present which suggest a susceptibility to impairment sometime in the future.

Baa

Bonds which are rated **Baa** are considered as medium grade obligations; i.e., they are neither highly protected nor poorly secured. Interest payments and principal security appear adequate for the present but certain protective elements may be lacking or may be characteristically unreliable over any great length of time. Such bonds lack outstanding investment characteristics and in fact have speculative characteristics as well.

Ba

Bonds which are rated **Ba** are judged to have speculative elements; their future cannot be considered as well assured. Often the protection of interest and principal payments may be very moderate, and thereby not well safeguarded during both good and bad times over the future. Uncertainty of position characterizes bonds in this case.

B

Bonds which are rated **B** generally lack characteristics of the desirable investment. Assurance of interest and principal payments or of maintenance of other terms of the contract over any long period of time may be small.

Caa

Bonds which are rated **Caa** are of poor standing. Such issues may be in default or there may be present elements of danger with respect to principal or interest.

Ca

Bonds which are rated **Ca** represent obligations which are speculative in a high degree. Such issues are often in default-or have other marked shortcomings.

C

Bonds which are rated **C** are the lowest rated class of bonds, and issues so rated can be regarded as having extremely poor prospects of ever attaining any real investment standing.

Con.(—)

Bonds for which the security depends upon the completion of some act or the fulfillment of some condition are rated conditionally. These are bonds secured by (a) earnings of projects under construction, (b) earnings of projects unseasoned in operation experience, (c) rentals which begin when facilities are completed, or (d) payments to which some other limiting condition attaches. Parenthetical rating denotes probable credit stature upon completion of construction or elimination of basis of condition.

KEY TO MOODY'S CORPORATE RATINGS*

Aaa

Bonds which are rated **Aaa** are judged to be of the best quality. They carry the smallest degree of investment risk and are generally referred to as "gilt edge." Interest payments are protected by a large or by an exceptionally

---

*Note: Those bonds in the **Aa, A, Baa, Ba** and **B** groups which Moody's believes possess the strongest investment attributes are designated by the symbols **Aa 1, A 1, Baa 1, Ba 1** and **B 1.**

Source: Moody's Investors Service, Inc.

*Note: Moody's applies numerical modifiers, **1, 2** and **3** in each generic rating classification from **Aa** through **B** in its corporate bond rating system. The modifier **1** indicates that the security ranks in the higher end of its generic rating category; the modifier **2** indicates a mid-range ranking; and the modifier **3** indicates that the issue ranks in the lower end of its generic rating category.

stable margin and principal is secure. While the various protective elements are likely to change, such changes as can be visualized are most unlikely to impair the fundamentally strong position of such issues.

Aa

Bonds which are rated **Aa** are judged to be of high quality by all standards. Together with the **Aaa** group they comprise what are generally known as high grade bonds. They are rated lower than the best bonds because margins of protection may not be as large as in **Aaa** securities or fluctuation of protective elements may be of greater amplitude or there may be other elements present which make the long term risks appear somewhat larger than in **Aaa** securities.

A

Bonds which are rated **A** possess many favorable investment attributes and are to be considered as upper medium grade obligations. Factors giving security to principal and interest are considered adequate but elements may be present which suggest a susceptibility to impairment sometime in the future.

Baa

Bonds which are rated **Baa** are considered as medium grade obligations, i.e., they are neither highly protected nor poorly secured. Interest payments and principal security appear adequate for the present but certain protective elements may be lacking or may be characteristically unreliable over any great length of time. Such bonds lack outstanding investment characteristics and in fact have speculative characteristics as well.

Ba

Bonds which are rated **Ba** are judged to have speculative elements; their future cannot be considered as well assured. Often the protection of interest and principal payments may be very moderate and thereby not well safeguarded during both good and bad times over the future. Uncertainty of position characterizes bonds in this class.

B

Bonds which are rated **B** generally lack characteristics of the desirable investment. Assurance of interest and principal payments or of maintenance of other terms of the contract over any long period of time may be small.

Caa

Bonds which are rated **Caa** are of poor standing. Such issues may be in default or there may be present elements of danger with respect to principal or interest.

Ca

Bonds which are rated **Ca** represent obligations which are speculative in a high degree. Such issues are often in default or have other marked shortcomings.

C

Bonds which are rated **C** are the lowest rated class of bonds and issues so rated can be regarded as having extremely poor prospects of ever attaining any real investment standing.

KEY TO MOODY'S COMMERCIAL PAPER RATINGS

The term "Commercial Paper" as used by Moody's means promissory obligations not having an original maturity in excess of nine months. Moody's makes no representation as to whether such Commercial Paper is by any other definition "Commercial Paper" or is exempt from registration under the Securities Act of 1933, as amended.

Moody's Commercial Paper ratings are opinions of the ability of issuers to repay punctually promissory obligations not having an original maturity in excess of nine months. Moody's makes no representation that such obligations are exempt from registration under the Securities Act of 1933, nor does it represent that any specific note is a valid obligation of a rated issuer or issued in conformity with any applicable law. Moody's employs the following three designations, all judged to be investment grade, to indicate the relative repayment capacity of rated issuers:

Issuers rated **Prime-1** (or related supporting institutions) have a superior capacity for repayment of short-term promissory obligations. Prime-1 repayment capacity will normally be evidenced by the following characteristics:
  -Leading market positions in well established industries.
  -High rates of return on funds employed.
  -Conservative capitalization structures with moderate reliance on debt and ample asset protection.
  -Broad margins in earnings coverage of fixed financial charges and high internal cash generation.
  -Well established access to a range of financial markets and assured sources of alternate liquidity.

Issuers rated **Prime-2** (or related supporting institutions) have a strong capacity for short-term promissory obligations. This will normally be evidenced by many of the characteristics cited above but to a

Source: Moody's Investors Service, Inc.

lesser degree. Earnings trends and coverage ratios, while sound, will be more subject to variation. Capitalization characteristics, while still appropriate, may be more affected by external conditions. Ample alternate liquidity is maintained.

Issuers rated **Prime-3** (or related supporting institutions) have an acceptable capacity for repayment of short-term promissory obligations. The effect of industry characteristics and market composition may be more pronounced. Variability in earnings and profitability may result in changes in the level of debt protection measurements and the requirement for relatively high financial leverage. Adequate liquidity is maintained.

Issuers rated **Not Prime** do not fall within any of the Prime rating categories.

If an issuer represents to Moody's that its Commercial Paper obligations are supported by the credit of another entity or entities, the name or names of such supporting entity or entities are listed within parenthesis beneath the name of the issuer. In assigning ratings to such issuers, Moody's evaluates the financial strength of the indicated affiliated corporations, commercial banks, insurance companies, foreign governments or other entities, but only as one factor in the total rating assessment. Moody's makes no representation and gives no opinion on the legal validity or enforceability of any support arrangement. You are cautioned to review with your counsel any questions regarding particular support arrangements.

KEY TO MOODY'S PREFERRED STOCK RATINGS*

Moody's Rating Policy Review Board Extended its rating services to include quality designations on preferred stocks on October 1, 1973. The decision to rate preferred stocks, which Moody's had done prior to 1935, was prompted by evidence of investor interest. Moody's believes that its rating of preferred stocks is especially appropriate in view of the ever-increasing amount of these securities outstanding, and the fact that continuing inflation and its ramifications have resulted generally in the dilution of some of the protection afforded them as well as other fixed-income securities.

Because of the fundamental differences

*Note: Moody's applies numerical modifiers 1, 2 and 3 in each rating classification from 1 indicates that the security ranks in the higher end of its generic rating category; the modifier 2 indicates a mid-range ranking; and the modifier 3 indicates that the issue ranks in the lower end of its generic rating category.

Source: Moody's Investors Service, Inc.

between preferred stocks and bonds, a variation of our familiar bond rating symbols is being used in the quality ranking of preferred stocks. The symbols, presented below, are designed to avoid comparison with bond quality in absolute terms. It should always be borne in mind that preferred stocks occupy a junior position to bonds within a particular capital structure.

Preferred stock rating symbols and their definitions are as follows:

aaa

An issue which is rated aaa is considered to be a top-quality preferred stock. This rating indicates good asset protection and the least risk of dividend impairment within the universe of preferred stocks.

aa

An issue which is rated aa is considered a high-grade preferred stock. This rating indicates that there is reasonable assurance that earnings and asset protection will remain relatively well maintained in the foreseeable future.

a

An issue which is rated a is considered to be an upper-medium grade preferred stock. While risks are judged to be somewhat greater than in the "aaa" and "aa" classifications, earnings and asset protection are, nevertheless, expected to be maintained at adequate levels.

baa

An issue which is rated baa is considered to be medium grade, neither highly protected nor poorly secured. Earnings and asset protection appear adequate at present but may be questionable over any great length of time.

ba

An issue which is rated ba is considered to have speculative elements and its future cannot be considered well assured. Earnings and asset protection may be very moderate and not well safeguarded during adverse periods. Uncertainty of position characterized preferred stocks in this class.

b

An issue which is rated b generally lacks the characteristics of a desirable investment. Assurance of dividend payments and maintenance of other terms of the issue over any long period of time may be small.

caa

An issue which is rated caa is likely to be in arrears on dividend payments. This rating designation does not purport to indicate the future status of payments.

"ca"

An issue which is rated **"ca"** is speculative in a high degree and is likely to be in arrears on dividends with little likelihood of eventual payment.

"c"

This is the lowest rated class of preferred or preference stock. Issues so rated can be regarded as having extremely poor prospects of ever attaining any real investment standing.

KEY TO SHORT-TERM LOAN RATINGS

MIG 1/VMIG 1

This designation denotes best quality. There is present strong protection by established cash flows, superior liquidity support or demonstrated broadbased access to the market for refinancing.

MIG 2/VMIG 2

This designation denotes high quality. Margins of protection are ample although not so large as in the preceding group.

MIG 3/VMIG 3

This designation denotes favorable quality. All security elements are accounted for but there is lacking the undeniable strength of the preceding grades. Liquidity and cash flow protection may be narrow and market access for refinancing is likely to be less well established.

MIG 4/VMIG 4

This designation denotes adequate quality. Protection commonly regarded as required of an investment security is present and although not distinctly or predominantly speculative, there is specific risk.

Issues or the features associated with **MIG** or **VMIG** ratings are identified by date of issue, date of maturity or maturities or rating expiration date and description to distinguish each rating from other ratings. Each rating designation is unique with no implication as to any other similar issue of the same obligor. **MIG** ratings terminate at the retirement of the obligation while **VMIG** rating expiration will be a function of each issue's specific structural or credit features.

MAJOR MONEY MARKET AND FIXED INCOME SECURITIES

Type	Interest: When Paid	Marketability	Denominations	Maturity
A. *Interest Fully Taxable*				
Corporate Bonds and Notes	S[1]	Very good to poor depending on quality	$1,000	1 to 50 years
Corporate Preferred Stock (Pays dividends as a fixed percentage of face value. Dividends not obligatory, but if declared must be paid before that of the common stock. Dividends fully taxable for individuals, but 85% exempt from federal tax for corporations)	Generally quarterly	Good to poor depending on quality	$100 or less	No maturity
Federal Home Loan Mortgage Corporate Bonds	S	Fair	$25,000	Up to 25 years
Federal Home Loan Mortgage Certificates	S	Fair	$100,000	Up to 3 years
Farmers' Home Administration Notes and Certificates	Annual	Fair	$25,000	1 to 25 years
Federal Housing Administration Debentures (Guaranteed by the U.S. Government)	S	Very good	$50	1 to 40 years
Federal National Mortgage Association Bonds	S	Fair	$25,000	2 to 25 years
Government National Mortgage Modified Pass through Certificates (interest plus some repayment of principal, guaranteed by U.S. Government)	Monthly	Good	$25,000	30 years; average life 12 years
Federal Home Loan Bank Bonds and Notes	S	Good	$10,000	1 to 20 years
Export-Import Bank Debentures and Certificates	S	Good	$5,000	3 to 7 years
International Bank for Reconstruction Development (World Bank), Inter-American Development Bank, Asia Development Bank	S	Fair to poor	$1,000	3 to 25 years
Foreign and Eurodollar Bonds and Notes	May be Annual or S	Poor	$1,000 (amounts vary in foreign currencies)	1 to 30 years
Bankers Acceptances (short-term debt obligations (resulting from international trade and guaranteed by a major bank)	Discounted[2] on a 360-day year basis	Fair	$5,000	1 to 270 days
Commercial Paper (short-term debt issued by a major corporation)	Discounted on a 360-day year basis	No secondary market	$100,000 (occasionally smaller)	1 to 270 days
Negotiable Certificates of Deposit (short-term debt issued by banks and which can be sold on the open market)	Interest paid on maturity; 360-day year basis	Fair	$100,000 (occasionally smaller)	30 days to 1 year
Non-negotiable Certificate of Deposit (savings certificates)	Interest paid on maturity; 360-day year basis	Non-negotiable	$500 $10,000	30 months 6 months
Collateralized Mortgage Obligations (CMO)	S or monthly	Good	$1,000	typically 2 to 20 years
Repurchase Agreements (generally short term loans by large investors, secured by U.S. Government or other high quality issues)[3]	Interest paid on maturity; 360-day year basis	No secondary market	$100,000	1 to 30 days (sometimes more)

(continued)

MAJOR MONEY MARKET AND FIXED INCOME SECURITIES *(concluded)*

Type	Interest: When Paid	Marketability	Denominations	Maturity
Zero Coupon Bonds (Bonds stripped of coupons)	Bonds issued at deep discount. Full yield realized at maturity	Good	$1,000 on maturity	1 to 30 years
B. Interest Exempt from State and Local Income Taxes				
U.S. Treasury Bonds and Notes	S	Very good	$1,000	1 to 20 years
U.S. Treasury Bills	Discounted on a 360-day basis	Very good	$10,000	90 days to 1 year
U.S. Series EE Savings Bonds[4]	Issued at discount, full interest, paid on maturity	No secondary market: available for resale	$50 minimum $10,000 maximum	10 years (can be redeemed before maturity at reduced yields
U.S. Series HH Savings[5] Bonds	S	No secondary market	$10,000 $15,000 maximum	10 years
Federal Land Bank Bonds	S	Good	$1,000	1 to 10 years
Federal Financing Bank Notes and Bonds	S	Good	$1,000	1 to 20 years
Tennessee Valley Authority Notes and Bonds	S	Fair	$1,000	5 to 25 years
Banks for Cooperatives Bonds	Interest: 360-day year basis	Good	$5,000	180 days
Federal Intermediate Credit Bank Bonds	Interest: 360-day year basis	Good	$5,000	270 days
Federal Home Loan Bank Notes and Bonds	Discounted: 360-day year basis	Good	$10,000	30 to 360-day year basis (some more)
Farm Credit Bank Notes and Bonds	Interest: 360-day year basis	Good	$50,000	270 days (some more)
C. Interest Exempt from Federal Income Tax				
State and Local Notes and Bonds (in-State issues, usually exempt from State and local income taxes)	S	Good to fair depending on rating	$5,000	1 to 50 years
Housing Authority Bonds (in-State issues usually exempt from State and local income taxes)	S	Good to fair	$5,000	1 to 40 years

[1] S means semiannually.
[2] A discount means interest paid in advance, thus a 10% discounted security maturing at $10,000 would cost $9,000 to purchase.
[3] Recently some banks have issued repurchase agreements for smaller amounts of money, i.e., several thousands of dollars.
[4] Since November 1982, U.S. Savings Bonds pay variable interest equal to 85% of the 5 year Treasury securities' rate adjusted semi-annually and have a minimum guaranteed rate which is adjustable. The rate applies to bonds held 5 years or more.
[5] Issued in exchange for EE bonds.

U.S. Treasury Bonds, Notes, and Bills: Terms Defined*

U.S. Treasury bonds, notes and bills are interest paying securities representing a debt on the part of the U.S. Government. Treasury bonds have a maturity of over 5 years, while notes mature within 5 to 7 years. Bills are discussed below. Both Treasury bonds and notes are generally issued in minimum denominations of $1,000 and pay interest semiannually. The amount of semiannual interest paid is determined by the coupon rate specified on the bond and is calculated on a 365-day year basis. For a $1,000 face value† bond the interest is given by:

$$\text{semiannual interest} = 1/2\,(\$1,000 \times \text{coupon rate})$$

Bonds may be priced higher (at a premium) or lower (at a discount) than the face value (par) depending on current interest rates. The *current yield* is the rate the investor receives based on the prices actually paid for a bond. The price is given by:

$$\text{current yield} = \frac{\$1,000 \times \text{coupon rate}}{\text{purchase price}}$$

Thus, a $1,000 face value bond with an 8% coupon rate purchased at $850 has a current yield by:

$$\text{current yield} = \frac{\$1,000 \times 8\%}{\$850} = 9.41\%$$

The *yield to maturity* (YTM) is the yield obtained on taking into account the years remaining to maturity, annual interest payments, and the capital gain (or loss) realized at maturity. It is obtained from special tables.

However, the yield to maturity (YTM) may be found approximately from the formula

$$\text{YTM} = \frac{I + A}{B}$$

I = annual interest rate

$$A = \frac{\$1,000 - M}{N}$$

$$B = \frac{\$1,000 + M}{2}$$

where M = current market price of the bond

N = years remaining to maturity

As an example, a bond ($1,000 face value) has a 10% coupon and is currently priced at $1,100 with 10 years remaining to maturity. What is the approximate YTM?

$I = \$1,000 \times .1 = \$100$ interest per year

$$A = \frac{\$1,000 - \$1,100}{10} = \$ - 10$$

$$B = \frac{\$1,000 + \$1,100}{2} = \$1,050$$

$$\text{YTM} = \frac{\$100 - \$10}{\$1,050} = .0857 = 8.57\%$$

U.S. Treasury bills (T-bills) are U.S. Government debt obligations which mature within one year. They are offered by the Federal Reserve Bank with maturities of 90 days (3 month bills) and 182 days (six month bills). Nine-month bills and one-year bills are also available. Treasury bills are sold in a minimum denomination of $10,000. Interest is paid by the discount method based on a 360-day year. With the discount method, interest is, in effect, paid at the time the bill is purchased. Thus a 91-day $10,000 bill (face value) with an 8% discount interest rate would provide the buyer with $202.22 ($10,000 × .08 × 91/360) interest at the time of purchase. This amount is deducted from the face value of the bill at the time of purchase so the buyer actually pays a net amount of $9,797.78 ($10,000 − $202.22). When the bill matures, the buyer receives $10,000 on redemption.

Since T-bills pay interest at the time of purchase (discount basis) on a 360-day year basis, while bonds (and notes) pay interest semiannually on a 365-day year basis, the two rates cannot be compared directly. To compare the two rates, the discount rate must be converted to the so-called *bond equivalent yield*, given by

$$\text{bond equivalent yield} = \frac{365 \times \text{discount rate}}{360 - (\text{discount rate} \times \text{days to maturity})}$$

As an example, a newly issued 91-day note with a discount rate of 12% has a

$$\text{bond equivalent yield} = \frac{365 \times (.12)}{360 - (.12 \times 91)}$$
$$= 12.55\%$$

Interest from U.S. Treasury bonds, notes, and bills are subject to federal income tax, but are exempt from state and local income taxes.

---

* The terms *current yield, yield to maturity,* etc. defined in this section are generally applicable to all fixed incomes.

† Face value is the amount of the bond or note payable upon maturity.

How to Read U.S. Government Bond and Note Quotations

TREASURY BONDS AND NOTES

(1) Rate	(2) Mat.	(3) Date	(4) Bid	(5) Asked	(6) Bid Chg.	(7) Yld.
6¾s,	1981	Jun n ..	99.3	99.7	+ .1	16.51
9⅛s,	1981	Jun n ..	99.12	99.16	+ .2	15.10
9⅜s,	1981	Jul n ...	98.21	98.25	+ .3	16.54
7s,	1981	Aug	97.26	98.10	+ .2	15.19
7⅝s,	1981	Aug n ..	97.30	98.2	+ .6	17.66
8⅜s,	1981	Aug n ..	98.2	98.6	+ .2	17.15
9⅝s,	1981	Aug n ..	98.5	98.9	+ .4	16.53
6¾s,	1981	Sep n ..	96.29	97.1	+ .5	16.10
10⅛s,	1981	Sep n ..	97.28	98	+ .4	16.28
12⅝s,	1981	Oct n...	98.14	98.18	+ .4	16.18
7s,	1981	Nov n ..	96.4	96.8	+ .10	15.86
7¾s,	1981	Nov n ..	96.18	96.22	+ .13	15.55
12⅛s,	1981	Nov n ..	98.1	98.5	+ .3	16.14
7¼s,	1981	Dec n ..	95.12	95.16	+ .10	15.14

Source: Reprinted by permission of *The Wall Street Journal*, Dow Jones & Co., Inc., 1981.

The above exhibit is an example of U.S. Government bond and note quotations as it appears in *The Wall Street Journal.*

(1) Indicates the coupon rate of interest which is designated by *s*. Rates are quoted to ⅛ of a percent. Thus 8⅜ means 8.375%. The semiannual interest payments are calculated, as described elsewhere, using this rate.

(2) Indicates the year of maturity.

(3) Indicates the month (of the above year) in which the bond or note matures. The letter *n* means the security is a note. Otherwise a bond is implied.

(4) The *bid price* per bond or note (the price at which the bond can be sold to the dealer), expressed as a percentage of the face value ($1,000) of the bond. Prices are quoted in terms of 1/32 of a percent. Thus 98.5 means 98 5/32. To find the dollar value of the price, convert 98 5/32 to a decimal (98 5/32 = .98156) and multiply by the face value of the bond to give $981.56 (.98156 × $1,000).

(5) The *ask price* per bond or note (the price at which the dealer will sell the bond). The dollar value is found as indicated above.

(6) The change in the bid price from the closing price of the previous day.

(7) The yield if the bond is held to maturity, based on the ask price.

Some U.S. Treasury bonds can be called back for redemption prior to maturity. These are shown with two dates (under item 2 for example)—*1993–98* indicating that the bonds mature in 1998, but may be called back and redeemed any time after 1993.

Some newspapers (such as *The New York Times*) use a slight modification of the above arrangement, though the various terms have the same meaning as defined above. Thus, a bond maturing in June of 1985 and bearing a 10⅜% coupon is indicated by *May '85 10⅜.*

How to Read U.S. Treasury Bill Quotations

(1) U.S. Treas. Mat. Date	(2) Bills Bid	(3) Asked Discount	(4) Yield
-1981-			
6–18	17.62	17.44	17.69
6–25	17.15	17.03	17.33
7– 2	15.39	15.01	15.31
7– 9	15.18	15.04	15.39
7–16	15.02	14.78	15.17
7–23	14.83	14.67	15.10
7–30	14.72	14.42	14.88
8– 6	14.11	13.89	14.36
8–13	13.94	13.72	14.22
8–20	13.94	13.72	14.26
8–27	13.92	13.70	14.28
9– 3	13.97	13.63	14.24
9–10	13.72	13.64	14.29
9–17	13.52	13.34	14.00
9–24	13.63	13.43	14.14
10– 1	13.74	13.54	14.30

Source: Reprinted by permission of *The Wall Street Journal*, Dow Jones & Co., Inc. 1981.

The above exhibit is an example of Treasury bill quotations as it appears in *The Wall Street Journal.*

(1) The date of maturity, i.e., 6–18 means June 18, 1981.

(2) The bid price at market close quoted as a *discount* rate in percent. This bid price is the price at which the dealer will buy the bill. To convert the discount rate to a dollar price use the formula

$$\text{dollar price} = \$10{,}000 - (\text{discount rate} \times \text{days to maturity} \times .2778)$$

In the above, the discount must be expressed in percent. For example, if the dealer bids 16.18% discount for a bill which will mature in 110 days, the dollar price is given by

$$\text{dollar price} = \$10{,}000 - (16.18 \times 110 \times .2778) = \$9{,}505.57 \text{ per bill}$$

(3) The asked price at market close expressed as a discount rate in percent. The asked price is the price at which the dealer will sell a bill to a buyer. To convert to a dollar price use the above formula.

(4) The bond equivalent yield expressed in percent. This is calculated (as explained elsewhere) from the asked price expressed as a discount rate. This rate is used to compare T-bill yields to that of bonds, notes and certificates of deposit.

Some newspapers (e.g., *The New York Times*) use a somewhat different arrangement, though the meaning of the terms is the same as defined above. Thus, a bill maturing on June 4, 1981, is indicated as such. Also included in some newspapers is the change in bid price expressed as a discount rate.

How to Read Corporate Bond Quotations*

Corporate bonds are debt securities issued by private corporations. They generally have a face value (the amount due on maturity) of $1,000 and a specified interest rate (coupon rate) paid semiannually. Many corporate bonds have a *call* provision which permits the company to recall and redeem the bond after a specified date. Call privileges are usually exercised when interest rates fall sufficiently. Investors, therefore, cannot count on *locking in* high interest rates with corporate bonds. Bond quality designations used by Moody's and Standard & Poor's are given elsewhere in the Almanac (pp. 440–446).

The following is an example of price quotations for bonds traded on The New York Stock Exchange as they appear in *The Wall Street Journal.*

CORPORATION BONDS

VOLUME, $18,990,000

(1) Bonds	(2) Cur YID	(3) Vol	(4) High	(5) Low	(6) Close	(7) Net Chg
AlaP 9s2000	14.	6	63	62	63	2
AlaP 8½s01	15.	10	57½	57½	57¼	. . .
AlaP 8⅞s03	15.	25	60	59½	60	+ ½
AlaP 10⅞05	15.	3	72	72	72	– 2¼
AlaP 10½05	15.	12	70½	70½	70½	– 1
AlaP 12⅝10	16.	7	81¼	81⅛	81⅛	– 1⅝
AlaP 15¼10	16.	111	94⅝	93⅝	94	. . .
AlaP 14¾91	15.	31	97	96½	96½	. . .
AlaP 17⅜11	17.	99	104	103½	103¾	– ¼
Alexn 5½96	cv	34	61¾	61⅝	61¾	+ ¾

(1) Bonds	(2) Cur YID	(3) Vol	(4) High	(5) Low	(6) Close	(7) Net Chg
Allgl 10¾99	15.	2	70½	70½	70½	. . .
AllstF 8⅛87	11.	2	76⅜	76⅜	76⅜	+ 1⅞
AllstF 9⅝86	12.	10	83⅛	83	83	+ 1⅞

Source: Reprinted by permission of *The Wall Street Journal*, Dow Jones and Company, Inc. 1981.

(1) The name of the issue in abbreviated form, followed by the coupon rate of interest in percent (designated by the letter *s*), and the year in which the bond matures. The coupon rate is stated in terms of ⅛ of a percent; 9⅜ means 9.375%.

(2) This is the current yield which is calculated as stated elsewhere. (See U.S. Treasury Bonds, Notes, and Bills, p. 449.)

(3) This item is the number of bonds sold that day.

(4) This is the highest price quoted for the bond sold on that day, expressed as a percentage of face value ($1,000). To convert to dollars, express the price as a decimal and multiply by the face value of the bond. As an example:

$$58\frac{1}{2} = (.5850 \times \$1,000.) = \$585$$

(5) This is the lowest price quoted that day. It is converted into dollars as described above.

(6) This is the price at the close of the market that day.

(7) This is the change in the closing price from that of the previous day. To convert to dollars, express as a decimal and multiply by $1,000. Thus, −1⅞ means a decrease per bond of $18.75 (.01875 × $1,000) from that of the previous day.

* Yield terms are the same as those defined in the section on U.S. Treasury Bonds, Notes and Bills, p. 481.

TAX EXEMPT VERSUS TAXABLE YIELDS

tax bracket	5½%	6%	6½%	7%	7½%	8%	8½%	9%	9½%	10%	10½%	11%
	To equal a tax-free yield of:											
	a taxable investment has to earn:											
28%	7.64%	8.33%	9.03%	9.72%	10.42%	11.11%	11.81%	12.50%	13.19%	13.89%	14.58%	15.28%
30	7.86	8.57	9.29	10.00	10.71	11.43	12.14	12.86	13.57	14.29	15.00	15.71
31	7.97	8.70	9.42	10.14	10.87	11.59	12.32	13.04	13.77	14.49	15.22	15.94
32	8.09	8.82	9.56	10.29	11.03	11.76	12.50	13.24	13.97	14.71	15.44	16.18
34	8.33	9.09	9.85	10.61	11.36	12.12	12.88	13.64	14.39	15.15	15.91	16.67
36	8.59	9.38	10.16	10.94	11.72	12.50	13.28	14.06	14.84	15.63	16.41	17.19
37	8.73	9.52	10.32	11.11	11.90	12.70	13.49	14.29	15.08	15.87	16.67	17.47
39	9.02	9.84	10.66	11.48	12.30	13.11	13.93	14.75	15.57	16.39	17.21	18.03

Tax-Exempt Bonds

Tax exempt (municipal) bonds are issued by state and local governments and are free from federal income tax on interest payments. The bonds are often issued in $5,000 denominations and pay interest semiannually. Capital gains are taxable. In addition, holders of out-of-state bonds may be subject to state and local income taxes of the state in which they reside. For example, a New York City resident holding Los Angeles municipal bonds would be subject to New York State and City income taxes on the interest.

The taxable equivalent yield of a tax exempt bond is obtained by means of the expression

$$\text{taxable equivalent yield} = \frac{\text{tax exempt yield}}{1 - (F + S + L)}$$

where

F is the federal tax bracket of the investor
S is the state tax bracket of the investor
L is the local tax bracket of the investor

Thus, an investor in the 50% federal bracket, 10% state bracket and 3% local bracket who holds a bond with a current yield of 6% which is exempt from all income taxes would enjoy a taxable equivalent yield (TEY) given by

$$\text{TEY} = \frac{6\%}{1 - (.5 + .1 + .03)} = 16.21\%$$

A taxable yield of 16.21% would be necessary to provide the same yield as the 6% current yield on the tax exempt security.

TYPES OF TAX EXEMPT BONDS AND NOTES

General Obligation bonds, also known as GO's, are backed by a pledge of a city's or state's full faith and credit for the prompt repayment of both principal and interest. Most city, county and school district bonds are secured by a pledge of unlimited property taxes. Since general obligation bonds depend on tax resources, they are normally analyzed in terms of the size of the resources being taxed.

Revenue bonds are payable from the earnings of a revenue-producing enterprise such as a sewer, water, gas or electric system, airport, toll bridge, college dormitory, lease payments from property rented to industrial companies, and other income-producing facilities. Revenue bonds are analyzed in terms of their earnings.

Limited and Special Tax bonds are payable from the pledge of the proceeds derived by the issuer from a specific tax such as a property tax levied at a fixed rate, a special assessment, or a tax on gasoline.

Municipal notes are short term obligations maturing from 30 days to a year and are issued in anticipation of revenues coming from the sales of bonds (BANS), taxes (TANS), or other revenues (RANS).

Project notes, issued by local housing and urban renewal agencies, are backed by a U.S. Government guarantee and are also tax exempt.

How to Understand Tax-Exempt Bond Quotations

Generally the prices of municipal bonds are quoted in terms of the yield to maturity (defined elsewhere) rather than in percentage of face value, as with other bonds. The yield to maturity can be converted to a dollar price if the years remaining to maturity and the rate of interest due are known. Certain tables used for this purpose are given in the *Basis Book* (published by the Financial Publishing Company, 82 Brookline Avenue, Boston, Massachusetts). The books list the dollar price (per $1,000 face value of the bond) corresponding to a given coupon rate, yield, and years to maturity.

Some municipal bonds, however, are quoted directly in terms of percentage of face value. Thus, a bid price (the price at which the dealer will buy the bonds from the investor) of 98⅝ for a $5,000 face value bond can be converted to a dollar price by first converting the bid to a decimal expression (.98625) and then multiplying by the face value of the bond. The result in this case is $4,931.25 (.98625 × $5,000). The same calculation applies to the ask price (the price at which the dealer will sell the bond to the investor).

Prices of tax exempt bonds are not quoted in the daily press. They can be obtained by calling municipal bond dealers. Extensive quotations are given in some relatively expensive publications:

The Blue List
Standard & Poor's
25 Broadway
New York, New York 10004
(212) 208-8471

The Daily Bond Buyer
and
The Weekly Bond Buyer
The Bond Buyer
1 State Street Plaza
New York, New York 10004
(212) 943-8200

Bond Week (Formerly Money Manager)
Institutional Investor
488 Madison Avenue
New York, New York 10022
(212) 303-3300

Government National Mortgage Association (GNMA) Modified Pass Through Certificates

A GNMA Mortgage-Backed Security is a government-guaranteed security which is collateralized by a pool of federally-underwritten residential mortgages. The investor receives a monthly check for a proportionate share of the principal and interest on a pool of mortgages whether or not the payments have actually been collected from the borrowers.

The GNMA Mortgage-Backed Security offers the highest yield of any federally-guaranteed security. In addition, the GNMA security offers a very competitive return in comparison to private corporation debt issues. Moreover, the investor receives a monthly return on the GNMA guaranteed investment, rather than semi-annual payments as on most bonds. This monthly payment represents a cash flow available for reinvestment and has the effect of increasing the yield on GNMAs by 10 to 18 basis points (a basis point is 0.1%) when compared to the yield equivalent received on a bond investment with the same "coupon" rate but paying interest semi-annually.

On single-family securities (the most popular form) the maturity is typically 30 years. However, statistical studies have determined that the average life of a single-family security is approximately 12 years, due to prepayments of principal. Nevertheless, some of the mortgages in any pool are likely to remain outstanding for the full 30-year period.

The minimum size of original individual certificates is $25,000 with increments of $5,000 above that amount.

Due to the uncertainties in the maturity of the above mentioned pass-through certificates, collateralized mortgage obligations (CMOs) have been introduced. CMOs are bonds backed by Ginnie Maes, Freddie Macs, and other mortgage instruments providing investors with a wide choice of maturities ranging from 2 to 20 years. Essentially, the monthly payments from the underlying mortgage instruments are initially allocated to the nearest maturity CMO and subsequently to CMO maturities of successively longer duration. CMO interest payments are made semiannually or monthly.

How to Understand Convertible Securities

The term "Convertible Securities" refers to securities that can be exchanged for another type of security, usually the common stock of the company issuing the convertible.

The two basic types of convertible securities are debentures (commonly known as bonds) and preferred stock. These securities have intrinsic value. Bonds represent a debt of the issuing company. Preferred stock represents an ownership interest. Intrinsic value may be enhanced by the convertible feature.

There are other certificates or contracts which are sometimes considered to be convertible securities but which have no intrinsic value based on ownership interest or debt. Their value is derived solely from their ability to be converted into another type of security. To do so requires a payment in addition to the surrender of the security. These are rights, warrants and options. To many investors these securities may offer certain advantages. However, our emphasis here will be on convertible securities—bonds and preferred stock—which have broader application as investment vehicles.

CONVERTIBLE BONDS

Convertible debt securities are almost always issued in the form of debentures. That is, there is no specific collateral pledged by the issuing corporation in the indenture which states the terms under which the security is issued. Rather, the promise to pay interest on stated dates and the principal amount at maturity is backed by the full faith and credit of the corporation. However, even the most sophisticated investors and those in the securities industry commonly refer to this type of security as a convertible bond.

Convertible bonds have been extolled as the ultimate investment medium offering the desirable features of other securities without the normal risks. If this were so, it would not be for long. Demand for such a security would be so great that the price would be driven up to the point where the element of risk would be very evident. Convertible bonds like all other securities have both advantages and disadvantages and the informed investor can measure these against his own objectives.

Here are the three most important characteristics:

1. Convertible bonds pay interest—which, as a general rule yields more than the dividends on common stock of comparable quality and less than the interest on straight (non-convertible) bonds of equivalent quality and maturity.

   The issuing company's obligation to pay this interest comes before dividends on preferred and common stock.

2. Convertible bonds offer appreciable possibilities linked to the earnings and growth of the company. As the common stock rises in value to reflect this growth, the price of the convertible bond should also increase. Conversely, as the common stock declines in value, so should the convertible bond decline.

3. Convertible bonds enjoy some of the stability and relative safety associated with straight bonds and preferred stock. For each outstanding convertible bond, it is possible to estimate an investment value. This is the price below which the convertible bond is not expected to fall, if interest rates remain constant, even if the common stock price falls to such an extent as to render the convertible feature virtually valueless. Investment value is arrived at by estimating a price that would produce a yield comparable to straight bonds of equivalent quality. Investment value, it should be stressed, is only an estimate and subject to change from many influences such as fluctuating interest rates, economic and business conditions, ratings given by investment advisory services and the general well-being of the issuing company.

These characteristics can perhaps best be understood by examining how convertible bonds come into existence and how they behave in various circumstances.

XYZ COMPANY ISSUES CONVERTIBLE BONDS

Let's assume that the XYZ Company wants to raise more capital to expand its business. Interest rates are high and XYZ does not want to pay 12% or more to borrow money in the conventional bond market. XYZ is also reluctant at this time to issue additional common stock as a means of raising additional capital. This could be due to a number of reasons, one of which might be unwillingness to dilute the equity interest of its present stockholders. For example, if there are presently ten million shares outstanding and an additional million are issued, earnings per share will normally be reduced by ten percent at the moment of issue, and the market price of the common stock probably would fall proportionately unless it could support the higher price earnings ratio. (The dilution problem is not quite the same when additional stock is issued to acquire an interest in or control of another company. The acquired company will presumably have its own earnings to contribute to earnings per share.) The XYZ Company is also mindful of the fact that dividends on stock are paid after federal income taxes, whereas interest on debt securities, like bonds, is a deduction before taxes.

Accordingly, the management of the XYZ Company decides to issue convertible bonds. In conjunction with the underwriting firm, the interest is set at 10% and the bonds are priced at par—an even $1,000 per $1,000 face amount bond. Bond prices are commonly stated as a percentage of par which, in this case, would be 100. It is further stipulated that each $1,000 bond can be converted into 25 shares of XYZ common stock. At the time that the bonds are marketed, the common stocks is trading at $32 per share.

DEFINITION OF TERMS

In any discussion of convertible bonds, various terms, related to the above figures, are widely used. Before proceeding, these should be defined.

Market Price Price at which a convertible bond can be bought or sold at a given point in time. Market price is stated as a percentage of par, usually $1,000. 100 means $1,000, 90 means $900, 110 means $1,100, etc.

Conversion Ratio Number of shares of common stock obtainable through conversion of one bond. In the case of XYZ, conversion ratio is 25.

Conversion Price The reciprocal of conversion ratio or the price of the stock when the number of shares obtainable through conversion of one $1,000 bond equals exactly $1,000. Conversion price is $40 when conversion ratio is 25.

Conversion Value Current value of total shares into which a bond can be converted. Conversion value of XYZ $1,000 bond with conversion ratio of 25 shares is $800 when XYZ common stock is trading at $32 per share.

Conversion Premium Percentage difference between conversion value and market value of bond. When conversion value is $800 and market value is $1,000, conversion premium is 25% since difference between conversion and market values ($1,000 − $800 = $200) is 25% of conversion value ($800). This figure represents the judgment of investors, as expressed in the marketplace, with respect to the worth of the three characteristics of convertible securities discussed above. These were yield, appreciation potential and relative safety. With some issues, supply and demand is also a factor in the premium.

Investment Value   Estimated price, usually set by investment advisory services, at which bond would be selling if it had no convertible feature. Investment value is arrived at by estimating the price at which the convertible bond would have to sell to provide a percentage yield comparable to percentage yield on a non-convertible bond of equivalent quality and maturity. Investment value, like market price, is normally stated as a percentage of $1,000. For the XYZ Bonds, investment value will be assumed to be 75 providing a current yield of 13.33%.

Premium Over Investment Value   Percentage difference between estimated investment value and market price of bond. When market price is 100 and investment value is estimated at 75, the difference is 25 which is 33% of 75. Thus, the premium over investment value is 33%. This figure can be considered a measurement of the worth of the conversion privilege as well as an indication of the proportion of the price that is subject to the risks associated with common stock.

To summarize, the position of XYZ Convertible Bonds, and the related stock at the time the bonds are marketed, is as follows:

Market Price of Bond 100	($1,000)
Yield 10%	
Conversion Ratio 25	
Conversion Price $40	$\left(\dfrac{\$1,000}{25}\right)$
Market Price of Stock $32	
Conversion Value $800	(25 × $32)
Conversion Premium . . 25%	$\left(\dfrac{\$1,000 - \$800}{\$800}\right)$
Investment Value. 75	($750)
Premium Over Investment Value 33%	$\left(\dfrac{\$1,000 - \$750}{\$750}\right)$

Obviously, no owners of the bonds would convert them into the common stock at this time, since they would be exchanging $1,000 for $800. However, it is not necessary to convert a convertible bond into stock in order to enjoy its advantages. Bonds are frequently sold many times before they are finally converted into stock and many investors have actively participated in the convertible bond market without ever exercising the conversion privilege. Let's now explore what could happen to the XYZ Convertible Bonds under various circumstances.

IF THE STOCK GOES UP

If the XYZ Company prospers and is considered to have appreciation potential, the price of the common stock should go up. By the same token, the price of the XYZ Convertible Bond should also rise. Let's assume the stock goes up by 25% to $40 per share. Normally, the bond will also go up but not necessarily at the same rate as the stock. There is a good reason for this. As the bond price increases, it acts more like a stock and less like a bond. Investment value is left further behind. The risk increases. Yield diminishes too. Accordingly, even though the appreciation potential of the stock may not have changed, the other factors (greater risk and lower yield) will tend to hold back the price of the bond. Therefore, a rise in the XYZ stock of 25% from $32 to $40 might be reflected in a rise in the bond of 20% from 100 to 120. The most significant figures are now as follows:

Market Price of Bond 120	($1,200)
Current Yield 8.33%	$\left(\dfrac{\$100}{\$1,200}\right)$
Market Price of Stock $40	
Conversion Value $1,000	(25 × $40)
Conversion Premium . . 20%	$\left(\dfrac{\$1,200 - \$1,000}{\$1,000}\right)$
Premium Over Investment Value 60%	$\left(\dfrac{\$1,200 - \$750}{\$750}\right)$

Conversion is still unrealistic. But bondholders who bought at the offering may want to take profits by selling their bonds to other investors who believe the stock will continue to go up but are not quite certain enough in their belief to buy the stock itself. Let's assume now that XYZ common stock goes up to $60 per share, an increase of 87½% since the bonds were issued. What is likely to happen to the XYZ bonds? The bond price may now rise to the level where virtually all of the bond-like characteristics are lost and, from the standpoint of risk, the bond is interchangeable with the stock. If we assume this is so, the bond's conversion value should be approximately the same as its market value and conversion premium will disappear. The picture would now look like this:

Market Price of Bond. . . . 150	($1,500)	
Current Yield 6.67%	$\left(\dfrac{\$100}{\$1,500}\right)$	
Market Price of Stock $60		
Conversion Value $1,500	(25 × $60)	
Conversion Premium 0	$\left(\dfrac{\$1,500 - \$1,500}{\$1,500}\right)$	
Premium Over Investment Value 100%		

Now the owner of the bond will think very seriously about converting. His decision may depend to some extent on the comparative yields of the bond and the stock. Interest on the bond is $100 per year. If the dividend on the stock is less than $4.00 per share, conversion would result in less income. If, on the other hand, the dividend is $4.20 (a yield of 7%) conversion would result in more current income.

In the meantime, while the stock has been rising from $32 to $60 per share, the company has presumably been using the money received from the sale of the convertible bonds to expand its business and improve its earnings. This should have put it in a better position to absorb the dilution that conversion into common stock entails.

When a convertible bond's conversion value and market price become the same, the stock and the bond should move up and down together within a limited range to maintain this relationship. It is virtually impossible for a convertible bond to sell with a negative conversion premium (below its conversion value) for any length of time. If this should happen, professional traders will quickly move in and employ a device known as arbitrage to make a small but rapid profit. They will buy the bonds and simultaneously sell the stock short. Converting the bonds enables them to replace the stock borrowed for the short sale. If, for example, XYZ convertibles are selling at $1,450 while the conversion value is $1,500, the trader can buy ten bonds for $14,500. By selling short 250 shares, he

receives $15,000 for an immediate gross profit of $500. This activity will tend to drive the price of the bond back up to or above conversion value.

IF THE STOCK GOES DOWN

Let us now consider what might happen to the XYZ convertible bonds if the common stock took an opposite course and declined from the price of $32 per share which it was enjoying at the time that the convertible bonds were issued. As the price falls the convertible bond's price will also fall. However, the bond's downside potential is less than that of the stock, since the bond should not decline below its investment value which is the estimated value of the bond when we disregard the conversion feature. We have assumed this to be a price of 75 which is 25% below par. Therefore, while the stock is falling from $32 to an unknown level, the bond should only travel from 100 to 75. This factor serves as a brake on the bond and is the reason why convertible bonds are generally considered to be a more conservative investment than the stock of the same issuing company. In reality, conditions which would cause a stock to decline drastically would probably produce a re-adjustment in the investment value of the convertible bond. Investment value is also subject to adjustment when money rates change.

To see how the convertible bond might be affected by a decline in the common stock of the XYZ Company, let's assume that the market price of the stock sags from its original price of $32 all the way down to $16 per share. It has lost half its value. If we estimated correctly the investment value of the convertible bond, and if other factors are the same, it will be selling in the area of $750. Thus, a drop of 50% in the price of the stock produces a drop of 25% in the price of the bond. The table of values will now be as follows:

Market Price of Bond 75	($750)	
Current Yield 13.33%	$\left(\dfrac{\$100}{\$750}\right)$	
Market Price of Stock $16		
Conversion Value $400	(25 × $16)	
Conversion Premium . . .87½%	$\left(\dfrac{\$750 - \$400}{\$400}\right)$	
Premium Over Investment Value 0		

Thus, we have seen in this example that the price of a convertible bond is controlled primarily by the price of the stock into which it is convertible. However, when the stock goes up, the bond's rise should be held back somewhat as risk increases and yield decreases. Conversely, when the stock goes down, the bond's decline is cushioned as yield increases and investment value is approached. This is an oversimplification which disregards other influences but, hopefully, it provides a basic understanding of how convertible bonds behave. Prices, yields and ratios were chosen in order to illustrate the example and simplify the arithmetic. They are not intended to reflect actual market conditions at any time.

HEDGING

We have seen that convertible bonds offer an investor opportunities to participate in the stock market with somewhat less risk (and less profit potential) than is normally encountered with direct investment in common stocks. This opportunity can be pursued even further by employing hedges. Although extremely complex in practice, the basic principles of hedging are actually quite simple.

Typically, a hedge is established when an investor buys convertible bonds and, at the same time, sells short the stock into which the bond is convertible. If the stock goes up, there should be a profit in the bonds and a loss in the stock. If the stock goes down, there should be a profit in the stock and a loss in the bonds. Obviously, there is no advantage in a hedge unless the profit exceeds the loss and expenses. There is no way to assure a profit but the skillful and judicious use of hedges can greatly reduce the risk of loss and enhance the possibility of profit. An essential feature is the ability to sell stock short without margin when the corresponding convertible security is held.

Convertible hedges are a highly sophisticated investment technique and should not be attempted without a complete understanding of all of their ramifications.

CALLABILITY AND OTHER LIMITATIONS

An important factor to consider with convertible bonds is the call feature. This is the right of the issuing company to redeem the bonds before maturity at a stated price slightly above par. Usually the original purchasers of a bond are given some protection against this privilege of the company through an initial period during which the bond is non-callable. If a bond has been on the market for four years and commands a price of 130, this price may be short lived if the bond

can be called at 105 after five years. When a convertible bond issue listed on the New York Stock Exchange is called for redemption some notice is always given in a newspaper of general circulation to permit the holders to exercise their conversion privilege or sell the bond to someone else who may convert it. Holders of record of registered bonds are notified directly. If, for some reason, the bond is not converted before expiration date for conversion, which may be the same or a few days before the redemption date, it is then worth no more nor less than the call price. It is, therefore, most important for holders of convertible bonds to know what the call features are and to be sure that they will receive information about calls when and if they occur. Obviously, the best way to do this is to hold registered bonds.

Most convertible bonds are convertible into stock at a fixed rate during the entire life of the bond. However, this rate may change because of a stock split, stock dividend, merger or other circumstances. The conversion privilege may expire before the bond matures or it may not be effective until some time after the bond is issued. Sometimes the conversion rate declines at regular intervals. A bond that is convertible into 25 shares of common stock when first issued may become convertible into only 20 shares after five years, 15 shares after ten years, etc. Although the typical convertible bond is exchangeable for the common stock of the issuing company, this is also subject to variation. Conversion may be made into a combination of common and preferred stock. Or a bond of one company may be convertible into the stock of a parent company.

All of these possible limitations should be checked by investors when investigating convertible securities. A member firm of the New York Stock Exchange, Inc. can usually supply the essential information.

MARGIN AND COMMISSION

Two other features of convertible bonds have traditionally appealed to investors—margin requirements and commission rates. Although the current margin requirement for the purchase of common stock or convertible bonds is the same—50%, the convertible bond rate has usually been significantly less. In 1973, for instance, an investor with $6,500 available in cash could have bought $10,000 worth of common stock or $13,000 of convertible bonds. (Margin requirements are subject to change by the Federal Reserve Board).

The commission paid to a member firm broker for the purchase or sale of listed stocks is one of the lowest fees paid for the transfer of property of any kind. However, in most cases, the commission paid for the purchase or sale of bonds is even lower on a given dollar investment.

CONVERTIBLE PREFERRED STOCK

Convertible preferred stock possesses many of the basic characteristics of convertible bonds and will normally perform in approximately the same manner when subject to the same conditions and influences. However, there are also basic differences which should be pointed out.

Convertible preferred stock represents an equity interest and is, therefore, junior to all debt securities including convertible bonds and would not—all else being equal—have as high a degree of relative safety as convertible bonds. However, all else is rarely equal and the convertible preferred stock of Company A could have more relative safety than the convertible bonds of Company B. Convertible preferred stocks do not have maturity dates as do bonds but are usually subject to redemption.

Convertible preferreds, like common stock, require 50% margin currently, and are subject to the same commission structure.

FOREIGN GOVERNMENT BOND YIELDS

by maturity sectors in years, for traded bonds included in the J.P. Morgan Government Bond Index
in percent per annum (semiannual basis), at end of month

	1988	1989	1989				1990						
	Dec	Dec	Sep	Oct	Nov	Dec	Jan	Feb	Mar	Apr	May	Jun	Jul 18
Australia													
1-3	13.78	14.30	15.48	15.49	14.73	14.30	13.61	14.23	14.22	14.42	14.15	14.05	13.75
3-5	13.71	13.57	14.82	14.68	13.99	13.57	13.22	13.86	13.92	14.26	13.96	13.79	13.52
5-7	13.34	13.39	14.38	14.28	13.74	13.39	13.19	13.73	13.83	14.21	13.95	13.81	13.55
7-10	13.08	13.01	13.91	13.79	13.28	13.01	12.89	13.41	13.59	13.91	13.63	13.52	13.31
10+	13.00	12.87	13.65	13.50	13.00	12.87	12.75	13.27	13.44	13.79	13.55	13.39	13.18
Belgium													
<5	7.82	9.74	8.62	9.08	9.69	9.74	10.28	10.55	9.78	9.94	9.62	9.56	9.32
5+	8.00	9.44	8.42	8.80	9.23	9.44	9.98	10.41	9.66	9.85	9.59	9.53	9.30
Canada													
1-3	10.60	10.64	10.34	10.07	10.69	10.64	10.58	11.99	12.48	12.79	12.13	11.79	11.66
3-5	10.38	10.05	10.10	9.91	10.26	10.05	10.21	11.39	11.89	12.40	11.60	11.35	11.20
5-7	10.24	9.76	9.95	9.64	9.92	9.76	10.03	11.00	11.60	12.18	11.37	11.14	11.08
7-10	10.22	9.65	9.83	9.55	9.79	9.65	10.00	10.77	11.30	11.76	11.02	10.86	10.34
10+	10.21	9.51	9.78	9.40	9.61	9.51	9.89	10.49	10.98	11.45	10.68	10.61	10.69
France													
1-3	8.16	10.01	8.94	9.39	9.52	10.01	10.18	10.32	9.93	9.60	9.69	9.62	9.50
3-5	8.32	9.65	8.88	9.20	9.32	9.65	9.93	10.21	9.78	9.61	9.66	9.59	9.48
5-7	8.26	9.32	8.75	8.99	9.13	9.32	9.62	10.00	9.51	9.45	9.50	9.47	9.34
7-10	8.38	9.12	8.64	8.75	8.98	9.12	9.44	9.86	9.37	9.42	9.42	9.38	9.28
10+	8.57	9.14	8.76	8.82	9.03	9.14	9.42	9.81	9.40	9.51	9.56	9.51	9.39
Germany													
<5	5.87	7.57	7.15	7.40	7.66	7.57	8.01	8.74	8.60	8.87	8.76	8.63	8.43
5-7	6.21	7.48	7.07	7.27	7.61	7.48	7.99	8.75	8.62	8.89	8.82	8.71	8.47
7+	6.44	7.33	6.95	7.09	7.39	7.33	7.81	8.67	8.40	8.77	8.70	8.61	8.30

Italy												
1-3	11.40	13.53	13.42	13.60	13.69	13.53	13.63	13.72	13.52	13.35	12.79	12.65	12.70
3+	12.74	13.78	13.37	13.66	13.90	13.78	13.89	13.89	13.79	13.48	13.01	12.90	13.06
Japan												
1-3	3.88	6.04	5.23	5.64	5.91	6.04	6.61	6.87	7.24	7.04	6.59	6.89	7.00
3-5	3.94	5.95	5.15	5.55	5.82	5.95	6.51	6.72	7.07	6.93	6.46	6.80	6.79
5-7	4.04	5.75	4.99	5.33	5.49	5.75	6.48	6.68	7.15	7.04	6.53	6.86	6.87
7-10	4.62	5.56	5.06	5.33	5.39	5.56	6.46	6.76	7.02	7.02	6.60	6.88	6.82
10+	4.94	5.54	5.12	5.33	5.39	5.54	6.25	6.33	6.76	6.72	6.35	6.61	6.65
Netherlands												
1-3	5.99	8.42	7.45	7.79	8.19	8.42	8.54	9.26	8.94	9.06	8.88	8.81	8.63
3-5	6.07	7.91	7.34	7.53	7.88	7.91	8.31	8.95	8.78	8.94	8.84	8.77	8.52
5-7	6.13	7.84	7.27	7.42	7.78	7.84	8.24	8.86	8.66	8.86	8.81	8.72	8.52
7+	6.34	7.71	7.20	7.36	7.66	7.71	8.15	8.70	8.58	8.81	8.78	8.69	8.47
Spain												
1-3	12.78	14.46	13.47	13.63	13.92	14.46	13.97	14.39	14.43	14.26	14.23	14.16	14.05
3+	11.79	13.77	12.93	13.32	13.32	13.77	13.47	13.97	14.04	13.99	13.93	13.92	13.97
United Kingdom												
1-3	11.32	12.38	12.42	11.98	12.52	12.38	12.83	13.30	13.94	14.37	13.17	12.75	12.74
3-5	10.72	11.24	11.34	11.11	11.52	11.24	11.92	12.37	13.09	13.65	12.43	11.98	12.08
5-7	10.58	11.06	11.12	10.97	11.34	11.06	11.71	12.13	12.71	13.36	12.21	11.76	11.88
7-10	10.23	10.59	10.64	10.58	10.88	10.59	11.28	11.76	12.46	13.14	12.12	11.62	11.75
10+	9.79	10.17	10.15	10.15	10.43	10.17	10.79	11.26	11.94	12.53	11.66	11.19	11.30
United States												
1-3	9.14	7.90	8.46	7.92	7.78	7.90	8.30	8.36	8.61	8.93	8.43	8.23	8.11
3-5	9.15	7.92	8.43	7.91	7.81	7.92	8.39	8.49	8.72	9.06	8.58	8.36	8.30
5-7	9.19	7.98	8.40	7.95	7.84	7.98	8.43	8.54	8.71	9.08	8.63	8.44	8.43
7-10	9.18	7.99	8.37	7.97	7.89	7.99	8.45	8.55	8.70	9.07	8.63	8.46	8.51
10+	9.11	8.08	8.38	8.02	7.99	8.08	8.56	8.66	8.78	9.14	8.71	8.52	8.66

Source: *World Financial Markets*, a publication of Morgan Guaranty Trust Company of New York, a subsidiary of J. P. Morgan & Co., Incorporated.

Components—Dow Jones 20 Bond Average

The Dow Jones Bond Averages are a simple arithmetic average compiled daily by using the New York Exchange closing bond prices. A list of the bonds on which these averages are based follows:

10 Public Utilities

Name	Coupon	Maturity
Alabama Pwr	9¾%	2004
Amer T&T	8.8%	2005
Comwlth Ed	8¾%	2005
Cons Ed	7.9%	2001
Cons Pwr	9¾%	2006
Detroit Edison	9%	1999
Mich Bell	7%	2012
Pac G&E	7¾%	2005
Phil Elec	7⅜%	2001
Pub Svc Ind	9.6%	2005

10 Industrials

Name	Coupon	Maturity
BankAm	7⅞%	2003
Beth Steel	6⅞%	1999
Eastman Kodak	8⅝%	2016
Exxon	6%	1997
General Elec	8½%	2004
GM Accept	12%	2005
IBM	9⅜%	2004
Socony	4¼%	1993
Union Carbide	7½%	2012
Weyerhaeusr	5.20%	1991

Components—Barron's Confidence Index

Barron's Confidence Index is the ratio of the average yield to maturity on best grade corporate bonds to the intermediate grade corporate bonds average yield to maturity. A list of the bonds on which the confidence index is based follows:

Best Grade Bonds

Name	Coupon	Maturity
AT&T	8¾%	2000
Anheuser-Busch	8⅝%	2016
Balt G&E	8⅜%	2006
DuPont	8½%	2006
Exxon Pipeline	8¼%	2001
Gen. Elec.	8½%	2004
GMAC	8¼%	2006
IBM	9⅜%	2004
Ill. Bell T	7⅝%	2006
Proc. & G.	8¼%	2005

Intermediate Grade Bonds

Name	Coupon	Maturity
Ala Power	9¾%	2004
Beneficial	9%	2005
Cater Trac	8%	2001
Comwlth Ed	9⅛%	2008
Firestone	9¼%	2004
GTE	9⅜%	1999
Honeywell	9⅜%	2009
Union Carbide	8½%	2005
USX Corp	7¾%	2001
Woolworth	9%	1999

Monetary Aggregates Defined

Money supply data has been revised and expanded to reflect the Federal Reserve's redefinition of the monetary aggregates. The redefinition was prompted by the emergence in recent years of new monetary assets—for example, negotiable order of withdrawal (NOW) accounts and money-market mutual fund shares—and alterations in the basic character of established monetary assets—for example, the growing similarity of and substitution between the deposits of thrift institutions and those of commercial banks.

M1-A has been discontinued with M1-B now designated as "M-1." M-1 is currency in circulation plus all checking accounts including those which pay interest, such as NOW accounts. M-1 excludes deposits due to foreign commercial banks and official institutions.

M-2 as redefined adds to M1-B overnight repurchase agreements (RPs) issued by commercial banks and certain overnight Eurodollars (those issued by Carribbean branches of member banks) held by U.S. nonbank residents, money-market mutual fund shares, and savings and small-denomination time deposits (those issued in denominations of less than $100,000) at all depository institutions. Depository institutions are commercial banks (including U.S. agencies and branches of foreign banks, Edge Act Corporations, and foreign investment companies), mutual savings banks, savings and loan associations, and credit unions.

M-3 as redefined is equal to new M-2 plus large-denomination time deposits (those issued as in denominations of $100,000

or more) at all depository institutions (including negotiable CDs) plus term RPs issued by commercial banks and savings and loan associations.
L, the very broad measure of liquid assets, equals new M-3 plus other liquid assets

consisting of other Eurodollar holdings of U.S. nonbank residents, bankers acceptances, commercial paper, savings bonds, and marketable liquid Treasury obligations.

Federal Reserve Banks

Federal Reserve Bank of

BOSTON	600 Atlantic Avenue, Boston, Massachusetts 02106—(617) 973-3462
NEW YORK	33 Liberty Street (Federal Reserve P.O. Station). New York, New York 10045—(212) 791-5823 (Telephone 24 hours a day, including Saturday & Sunday)
Buffalo Branch	160 Delaware Avenue (P.O. Box 961), Buffalo, New York 14240—(716) 849-5046
PHILADELPHIA	100 North Sixth Street (P.O. Box 90), Philadelphia, Pennsylvania 19105—(215)574-6580
CLEVELAND	1455 East Sixth Street (P.O. Box 6387), Cleveland, Ohio 44101—(216) 241-2800
Cincinnati Branch	150 East Fourth Street (P.O. Box 999), Cincinnati, Ohio 45201—(513) 721-4787 ext 333
Pittsburgh Branch	717 Grant Street (P.O. Box 867), Pittsburgh, Pennsylvania 15230—(412) 261-7864
RICHMOND	701 East Byrd Street (P.O. Box 27622), Richmond, Virginia 23261— (804) 643-1250
Baltimore Branch	502 South Sharp Street, Baltimore, Maryland 21201 (P.O. Box 1378), Baltimore, Maryland 21203—(301) 576-3300
Charlotte Branch	401 South Tyron Street (P.O. Box 300), Charlotte, North Carolina 28230— (704) 373-0200
ATLANTA	104 Marietta Street, N.W., (P.O. Box 1731) Atlanta, Georgia 30301—(404) 586-8657
Birmingham Branch	1801 Fifth Avenue, North (P.O. Box 10447), Birmingham, Alabama 35202—(205) 252-3141 ext. 215
Jacksonville Branch	515 Julia Street, Jacksonville, Florida 32231—(904) 632-4245
Miami Branch	9100 N.W. Thirty-sixth Street Extension, Miami, Florida 33178 (P.O. Box 520847), Miami, Florida 33153—(305) 591-2065
Nashville Branch	301 Eighth Avenue, North, Nashville, Tennessee 37203—(615) 259-4006
New Orleans Branch	525 St. Charles Avenue (P.O. Box 61630), New Orleans, Louisiana 70161 (540) 586-1505 ext. 230, 240, 242
CHICAGO	230 South LaSalle Street (P.O. Box 834), Chicago, Illinois 60690—(312) 786-1110 (Telephone 24 hours a day, including Saturday & Sunday)
Detroit Branch	160 Fort Street, West (P.O. Box 1059), Detroit, Michigan 48231—(313) 961-6880 ext. 372, 373
ST. LOUIS	411 Locust Street (P.O. Box 442), St. Louis, Missouri 63166—(314) 444-8444
Little Rock Branch	325 West Capitol Avenue (P.O. Box 1261), Little Rock, Arkansas 72203—(501) 372-5451 ext. 270
Louisville Branch	410 South Fifth Street (P.O. Box 32710), Louisville, Kentucky 40232 (502) 587-7351 ext. 237, 301
Memphis Branch	200 North Main Street (P.O. Box 407), Memphis, Tennessee 38101—(800) 238-5293 ext. 225
MINNEAPOLIS	250 Marquette Avenue, Minneapolis, Minnesota 55480—(612) 340-2051
Helena Branch	400 North Park Avenue, Helena, Montana 59601—(406) 442-3860
KANSAS CITY	925 Grand Avenue (Federal Reserve Station), Kansas City, Missouri 64198—(816) 881-2783
Denver Branch	1020 16th Street (P.O. Box 5228, Terminal Annex), Denver, Colorado 00217 (303) 292-4020
Oklahoma City Branch	226 Northwest Third Street (P.O. Box 25129), Oklahoma City, Oklahoma 73125—(405) 235-1721 ext. 182
Omaha Branch	102 South Seventeenth Street, Omaha, Nebraska 68102—(402) 341-3610 ext. 242

DALLAS	400 South Akard Street (Station K), Dallas, Texas 75222—(214) 651-6177
El Paso Branch	301 East Main Street (P.O. Box 100), El Paso, Texas 79000—(915) 544-4730 ext. 57
Houston Branch	1701 San Jacinto Street (P.O. Box 2578), Houston, Texas 77001—(713) 659-4433 ext 19, 74, 75, 76
San Antonio Branch	126 East Nueva Street (P.O. Box 1417), San Antonio, Texas 78295—(512) 224-2141 ext 61, 66
SAN FRANCISCO	101 Market Street (P.O. Box 7702), San Francisco, California 94120—(415) 392-6639
Los Angeles Branch	409 West Olympic Boulevard (P.O. Box 2077, Terminal Annex), Los Angeles, California 90051 (213) 683-8563
Portland Branch	915 S.W. Stark Street (P.O. Box 3436), Portland, Oregon 97208—(503) 228-7584
Salt Lake City Branch	120 South State Street (P.O. Box 30780), Salt Lake City, Utah 84130—(801) 355-3131
Seattle Branch	1015 Second Avenue (P.O. Box 3567), Seattle, Washington 98124—(206) 442-1650

TREASURY

General information concerning Treasury Securities and requests for forms:
Bureau of the Public Debt, Dept. F
Washington, D.C. 20226
Telephone: (202) 287-4113

Specific questions concerning Bills:
Bureau of the Public Debt, Dept. X
Washington, D.C. 20226
Telephone: (202) 287-4113

Specific questions concerning registered Notes or Bonds:
Bureau of the Public Debt, Dept. A
Washington, D.C. 20226
Telephone: (202) 287-4113

Options and Futures

What Are Stock Options?

There are two types of stock options—call and put. A call option is the right to buy a specified number of shares of a stock at a given price before a specific date. A put option is the right to sell a specific number of shares of a stock at a given price before a specific date. Options, unlike a futures contract, are a right *not an obligation* to buy or sell stock. The price at which the stock may be bought or sold is referred to as the exercise (or striking) price. The date at which the option expires is the *expiration* date. The term "in-the-money" option refers to either a call option with an exercise price less than that of the market price of the stock, or a put option with an exercise price above the market price of the stock.

Expiration months are set at intervals of three months for the cycles: the January–April–July–October cycle, February–May–August–November cycle, and the March–June–September–December cycle. Options expire at 11:59 P.M. Eastern Standard Time on the Saturday immediately following the third Friday of the expiration month.

The exercise prices are set at 5 point (dollar) intervals for stocks trading below $50, 10 point intervals for stocks trading between $50 to $200, and 20 point intervals for securities trading above $200. Initial exercise prices are set above and below the price of the security. Thus, if a security is priced at 32½ on the New York Stock Exchange at the time new options are opened, the opening exercise prices would be set at 30 and 40. If the price of the security is close to a standard exercise price, three prices are set: at the standard price, as well as above and below the latter.

Standard option contracts are written for 100 shares of stock of the underlying security. The price at which the seller (writer) agrees to sell an option to the buyer is called the *premium*. The premium is quoted *per share* of the underlying stock so that the price per contract is 100 times the quote.

After the option is issued, the premium will fluctuate with the price of the stocks. With call options the premium will increase with an increase in the price of stock. With put options the premium will increase when the stock price declines. The reason should be clear from the following examples. Assume that in January a July call option is written at the exercise price of 50 ($50 per share) on the XYZ Corporation stock. We assume that the stock is selling at $51. The call option writer (seller) asks and receives a premium of $2 ($200 per option contract). After brokerage commission on the sale (say $25 per contract) the option writer nets a profit of $175 per contract. The call option buyer pays $200 for the contract plus the commission or $225. Assume that the stock increases to 60 per share. The option holder (buyer) can, in principle, purchase the stock at 50 (the Exercise price) and sell it at 60 netting a profit on transaction of $10 per share (neglecting commissions). Clearly the call option has acquired increased value which will be reflected in the premium (option price). Let us assume that the premium increases from 2 to 10 ($200 to $1,000 per contract). If the option holder now sells the option, he will make a profit (after commissions) of $750 on a $250 investment ($200 premium and $50 commissions).

Alternatively, the option holder may elect to exercise the option and acquire the shares at 50 (the exercise price). The option writer must then deliver 100 shares of XYZ Corporation at $50 per share.

If the stock price drops below the exercise price and remains so until expiration of the option, the call option buyer can lose his entire investment. Sometimes the loss may be reduced if the option is sold before it matures. The holder then is said to have *closed out* his position.

Similar arguments apply to put options. In this case the option holder benefits if the price of the stock decreases below the exercise price. Assume that the above stock drops to 40. The put holder could, in principle, buy the stock at 40 and sell it at 50 (the exercise price) to the put writer. The put holder would make a profit of $10 per share (neglecting commissions). The put premium would reflect this situation and, as a result, increase.

Instead of selling the option and taking a profit, the put holder may elect to exercise the option and sell 100 shares to the put writer who must purchase these shares at the 50 exercise price.

If the market price of the stock is greater than the exercise price when the put option expires, the holder will lose his investment.

Options are traded on the Chicago Board of Options Exchange, the American Stock Exchange, the Pacific Stock Exchange and the Philadelphia Stock Exchange.

How to Read Option Quotations

(1) Option & NY Close Slb	(2) Strike Price	(3) Calls—Last			(4) Puts—Last		
		Aug	Nov	Feb	Aug	Nov	Feb
94¾	100	2½	7	9½	5⅞	7¾	a
94¾	110	⅝	3⅜	5½	a	16	a
94¾	120	⅛	1⅛	b	a	a	b
94¾	130	1⁄16	b	b	a	b	b
Skylin	15	3⅜	4	a	a	⅝	a
17⅝	20	⅝	1¹¹⁄₁₆	2¼	a	a	a
Southn	10	a	2⅜	2⁷⁄₁₆	b	b	b

Source: Reprinted by permission of *The Wall Street Journal* © Dow Jones and Company, Inc., 1981. All rights reserved.

(1) The name of the company in abbreviated form. Below the company name is the New York or American Exchange closing price of the stock in terms of ⅛ of a dollar.
(2) The striking (exercise) price of the option.
(3) The expiration month of the call option, beneath which is the option's premium (price) per share of stock. Contracts are for 100 shares of stock so that, for example, the price of a contract quoted as 2⅛ ($2.125 per share) is $212.50. Options expire on the Saturday following the third Friday of the expiration month. The premium does not include commissions.
(4) The same as item 3, but for a put option. The letter *a* means the option was not traded that day, and *b* means the option is not offered.

Stock Market Futures*

Standard & Poor's 500 Stock Index futures† combine the unique aspects of the futures market with the opportunities of stock ownership and stock options by helping many investors manage their inherent stock market risks, and at the same time allowing others to participate in broad market moves. S&P 500 Index futures can play an important role

* Although every attempt has been made to insure the accuracy of the information in this section, the Chicago Mercantile Exchange assumes no responsibility for any errors or omissions. All matters pertaining to rules and specifications herein are made subject to and are superseded by official Exchange rules.

† Editor's Note: Futures based on the Value Line (Kansas City Exchange) and the New York Stock Exchange (New York Futures Exchange) indices are also traded. The principles are the same as with the S&P 500 futures.

Source: *Opportunities in Stock Futures*, Index and Option Market, Chicago Mercantile Exchange, 444 West Jackson Street, Chicago, IL 60606.

in an individual's or institution's overall market strategy.

Stock ownership is subject to several risks. Lower earnings reports or changes in industry fundamentals can cause severe declines in individual issues. Or, a promising industry or company might drop because the entire market is heading down. A myriad of decisions go into individual stock selection—but the first question is usually what is the state and direction of the entire market.

The introduction of the Standard & Poor's 500 Stock Index contract allows investors to hedge, and therefore, virtually eliminate their portfolio exposure in a declining market without disturbing their holdings. At the same time, others can purchase or sell the contract according to their expectations of future market activity. This simultaneous ability to hedge the risks of stock ownership and to take advantage of broad market moves creates opportunities for everyone with positions in or opinions about the stock market.

A NEW MARKET FOR TODAY'S INVESTOR

S&P 500 Index futures are traded on the Index and Option Market division of the Chicago Mercantile Exchange. One of the largest commodity exchanges in the world, the CME introduced financial futures trading in 1972 when it formed the International Monetary Market to trade contracts in foreign currencies. Later, the IMM added futures contracts in Gold, 90-Day Treasury Bills, Three-Month Domestic Certificates of Deposit, and Three-Month Eurodollar Time Deposits.

THE S&P 500 INDEX

The Standard & Poor's Stock Price Index has been the standard by which professional portfolio managers and individuals have measured their performance for 65 years. Begun in 1917 as an index based on 200 stocks, the list was expanded to 500 issues in 1957.

Currently, the Index is one of the U.S. Commerce Department's 12 leading economic indicators.

The S&P 500 Index is made up of 400 industrial, 40 public utilities, 20 transportation, and 40 financial companies and represents approximately 80% of the value of all issues traded on the New York Stock Exchange.

The S&P 500 Index is calculated by giving more "weight" to companies with more stock issued and outstanding in the market. Basically, each stock's price is multiplied by its number of shares outstanding. This assures that each stock influences the Index with the same importance that it carries in the actual stock market.

The Index is calculated by multiplying the shares outstanding of each of the 500 stocks by its market price. These amounts are then totaled and compared to a 1941–43 base period.

Calculations are performed continually while the market is open for each of the 500 stocks in the Index. The resulting Index is available minute-by-minute via quote machines throughout the world.

WHAT IS FUTURES TRADING?

The practice of buying or selling goods at prices agreed upon today, but with actual delivery made in the future, dates back to the 12th century. In the United States, organized futures exchanges were active as early as the 1840s. Today, the markets offer futures in grains, meats, lumber, metals, poultry products, currencies and interest-bearing securities.

The ability to contract today at a fixed price for future delivery performs two vital economic functions: risk transfer and price discovery.

For example, suppose a producer of cattle sees that someone is willing to buy his animals for delivery six months hence at a price that insures him an adequate profit. He decides to sell his production, with delivery after the animal matures, at the contracted price. In the process, he has locked in a price that is satisfactory to him and has insulated himself against the risk that the price may fall. In other words, he has transferred the risk of lower prices to someone else. Conversely, the purchaser of his animals has locked in his price and is assured that he will not have to pay a higher price in the future. This transaction could take place directly between the two men, or could be accomplished through futures trading at the CME—without the need for buyer and seller to actually meet. The open public trading system at the CME makes it easy to discover what the market currently considers to be a fair price for future delivery.

If the sale takes place on the Chicago Mercantile Exchange, the Exchange guarantees that both parties adhere to their agreement by placing itself and its resources between them. The Exchange thus becomes the buyer and the seller of the contract. This assures both parties that the contract will be carried out because the Exchange stands behind both parts of the agreement.

When delivery day arrives, the product is delivered to designated delivery points and inspected to make sure it is of the quality stipulated by the contract. The seller receives payment at the agreed price and buyer receives the produce.

Since full payment does not occur until the delivery day, the performance of both parties to the contract requires a good faith deposit or performance bond—known as the margin—when the contract is entered. Margins usually amount to a small percentage of the contract's total face value.

This payment differs from margin for stock purchases in that it is not a partial payment. It serves as a guarantee for both buyer and seller that there are sufficient funds on either side to cover adverse price movements that might otherwise bring the ability to meet contract terms into question.

At the close of business each day, each futures position is revalued at the contract's current closing price. This price is compared to the previous day's close (or if an initial position, the purchase or sale price) and the net gain or loss is calculated. Gains and losses are taken or made from the margin account each day in cash. There are no paper gains or losses in futures trading. If a margin account falls below a specified level, futures traders are required to deposit more money to maintain their positions.

All futures market participants should understand the operation of futures markets and consult with a Registered Commodity Representative before opening a futures trading account.

The S&P 500 Index futures contract is quoted in terms of the actual Index, but carries a face value of 500 times the Index. The contract does not move point-for-point with the actual Index, but it stays close enough to act as an effective proxy for the Index, and by extension, for the stock market as a whole.

If, for example, the futures price is quoted at 108.75, then the face value of the contract would be $54,375 (500 × 108.75). Minimum futures price increments, or movements, are .05 of the Index or $25. So if the futures quote is at 108.75, trades can continue to take place at that level, or move to 108.80 or to 108.70, with each .05 move equal to $25.

Trading opens at 9:00 A.M. and closes at 3:15 P.M. (Chicago time) with contracts trading for settlement in March, June, September and December. The final settlement day is the third Thursday of the contract month. At the close of business on that day all open positions have one final mark-to-market calculation—only on this day the expiration of the contract is marked to the actual closing level of the S&P 500 Index itself. Unlike traditional commodities, there is no physical delivery of the underlying commodity or resulting payment for the commodity in S&P 500 futures.

It is this unique cash settlement feature

of the S&P 500 futures contract that eliminates the prohibitively expensive costs of de-
livering 500 individual issues in varying
amounts. Since there are little or no delivery
costs, investors are assured that there will
be no institutional factors to influence the
futures contract's price. Thus, the price of
the futures contract will reflect the current
expectations about the direction of future
stock prices. The International Monetary
Market division of the CME pioneered this
innovative concept in 1981, when its Eurodollar Time Deposit contract became the first
cash settlement futures contract ever traded.

The S&P 500 futures contract should be
viewed as a complement to equity ownership,
not a substitute for it. Among the many benefits of S&P futures is the hedging ability that
holders of stock can employ to provide an
effective, cost efficient means of protecting
security holdings against temporary market
declines rather than selling and disturbing
stock holdings. In addition, investors find the
futures market equally as liquid for both buyers and sellers. Unlike the stock exchanges,
short sellers do not require an up-tic before
a trade can take place and there are no additional margin requirements.

SITUATIONS & STRATEGIES

Outright positions, either long or short,
spreading and hedging are all uses for S&P
futures. The contract also offers an unusually
large number of hedging strategies when
combined with equity portfolios and options.
The following examples will show some of
these uses in more detail.

LONG POSITION

Situation: An individual sees that interest
rates are declining, the economy is firming
and believes the entire market is under-
valued. He notes that the S&P 500 futures
contract for September delivery is at 108.85
and the actual S&P 500 Index is at 108.70.

It is apparent that most futures market
participants also believe a move up is imminent. As supply and demand factors are bal-

Day	Position	Cost	S&P Future Closing Price	Gain or (Loss) Points × $5 (.01 equals 1 point)		Account Balance	Cumulative Gain or (Loss)
	Long one						
1	contract	108.85	108.90	.05	$ 25	$5,025	$ 25
2	same	108.85	108.60	(.30)	(150)	4,875	(125)
3	same	108.85	108.40	(.20)	(100)	4,775	(225)
4	same	108.85	107.00	(1.40)	(700)	4,075	(925)
5	same	108.85	108.00	1.00	500	4,575	(425)
6	same	108.85	108.70	.70	350	4,925	(75)
7	same	108.85	109.50	.80	400	5,325	325
Sub Total Period one		108.85	109.50	65	$325	$5,325	$325

Period one: Our investor was a little off on his timing and his margin account was debited each day that losses occurred. If his margin balance had fallen to the maintenance minimum ($2,000 per contract) in this example he would have been required to make an additional payment to bring his balance back to the initial margin level ($5.000). As it is, he ended the period with a credit of $325 in cash.

Period two: With minor backing and filling, the trend is up and the S&P futures price closes period two at a level of 115.65.

	Position	Cost	S&P Future Closing Price	Gain or (Loss) Points × $5 (.01 equals 1 point)	Account Balance	Cumulative Gain or (Loss)
Sub Total Period Two	Long one contract	108.85	115.65	6.80	$3,400	$8,400	$3,400

Observations: During the first two weeks our investor's judgment of the market was correct and the S&P futures price advanced 680 index points or 6.25%. This translated into a gain of $3,400 on his initial investment of $5,000 or a gain of 68%.

At this point our investor believes that the market is due for a correction and decides to lock in his profit. He calls his RCR and instructs him to "cover" his September long position. His broker will then enter a sell order. After the close of business, the Exchange Clearing House will match the investor's previous long position and his new short position for a net zero position. All margins will be returned with cash credited to the investor's account with his broker the next day. Brokerage commissions have not been included in this example, but they are usually extremely reasonable and generally are quoted to include *both* the purchase and sale of the contract.

anced in an open marketplace, the intrinsic value of the September contract is established. The market is willing to pay a slight premium (.15) for the futures contract over the actual Index.

He calls his Registered Commodity Representative, enters an order to buy one September S&P 500 futures contract at the market and makes a good faith deposit to his account to guarantee his ability to meet his contractual commitment. For purposes of the following example, a margin account balance of $5,000 will be used. Margin requirements for actual positions vary. Individuals should contact their Registered Commodity Representatives for current information.

SHORT POSITION

If, instead of a rising market our investor believed that tight money would increase interest rates and the economy was weakening, he might have concluded that the S&P 500 Index futures price of 108.85 was an overvaluation and that the price was vulnerable to a decline.

September S&P Index contract to cover his short at the opening.

The opening is down on news that industrial production was weak and his position is covered at 106.55. His gain on his short then amounts to 2.30 at $25 per .05 or $1,150. The money is credited to his account the following day.

REDUCING THE VOLATILITY OF A STOCK PORTFOLIO

One reason for equity ownership is to take advantage of the long-term growth prospects of the company in which stock is purchased. Over time, higher earnings per share might be translated into a higher dividend payout. In the case of a company with a high return on investment and profits that are reinvested in the company's own growth, the expectation is that the growth will be reflected in higher share prices. However carefully constructed and diversified a portfolio may be, it is still subject in varying degrees to the risk that the market will decline. In order to protect principal values in a declining market, inves-

Day	Position	Cost	S&P Future Closing Price	Gain or (Loss) Points × $5 (.01 equals 1 point)		Account Balance	Cumulative Gain or (Loss)
	Short one						
1	contract	108.85	110.05	(1.20)	$ 600	$4,400	($ 600)
2	same	108.85	112.50	(2.45)	(1,225)	3,175	(1,825)
3	same	108.85	112.00	(.50)	(250)	3,425	(1,575)
4	same	108.85	109.50	(2.50)	(1,250)	4,675	(325)
5	same	108.85	108.75	.75	375	5,050	50
6	same	108.85	107.40	1.35	675	5,725	725
7	same	108.85	107.05	.35	175	5,900	900
Sub Total		108.85	107.05	1.80	$ 900	$5,900	$ 900

In our hypothetical example, the short position eventually worked. If the price had gone to a closing level of 114.85, the investor's account balance would have dropped to the maintenance margin level of $2,000 and he would have been required to add additional funds to bring his balance back to $5,000.

He decides to call his Registered Commodity Representative and enter a sell order for one September S&P 500 Stock Index future. Selling is just as easy as buying in an open outcry market. All bids to buy and offers to sell must be made publicly in the trading arena and are subject to immediate acceptance by any member. This differs greatly from stock exchanges where specialists or market makers require an up-tic from the previous sale to transact a short sale.

Let's again assume the initial margin required is $5,000. The above table shows the status of the short position over the course of seven trading days.

Our investor decides at this point that he wants to cover his short position and lock in his profit. The next morning before the opening of trading, he enters an order to buy one

tors have traditionally sold stock to raise cash or shifted to more defensive issues with less volatility. These tactics very often are short-run solutions that disturb carefully tailored long-run objectives. S&P 500 Index futures can be used to add protection against a market downturn and allow an investor to maintain his equity holdings based on the prospects of the companies rather than the direction of the market.

SHORT HEDGE AGAINST A DIVERSIFIED PORTFOLIO

Situation: An investor owns a well-diversified portfolio with a current market value of $110,000. The S&P 500 futures contract is at 108.85. The market appears weak and the investor believes that there is substantial downside risk during the next three months. He decides to short S&P 500 futures to protect his portfolio.

Action: The S&P 500 futures contract at 108.85 represents a contract value of $54,425 (500 × 108.85). In order to protect his portfolio, he sells two contracts ($110,000 divided by $54,425 equals 2.02).

This hypothetical example assumed that the volatility of the portfolio very closely matched that of the market as measured by the S&P 500 futures contract prices. In reality, portfolios may be more or less sensitive to market moves. Statistical regression analysis for individual issues and entire portfolios can be calculated to measure past price volatility relative to the market. Expressed as "beta," it is a statistical measure of past movements which may change in the future. However, it is useful when hedging market risk in portfolios that are more volatile than the market.

tracts to offset the portfolio's greater volatility to the market.

The concept of volatility and hedge ratios also may be applied to industry groupings and individual stocks. However, as the number of individual stock holdings that are being hedged decreases, then the greater is the chance that factors affecting that smaller group will make their prices react differently relative to the market than they have in the past.

ADDITIONAL USES OF THE S&P 500 FUTURES CONTRACT

Spreads: The simultaneous purchase and sale of different contract months to take advantage of perceived price discrepancies is called "spreading." The technique is considered by many to be less volatile than an outright long

Day	Position Short 2 Contracts	Closing Price S&P Contract	Gain or (Loss) Contract Points X $5 X 2 Contracts (.01 equals 1 point)		Value of Stock Portfolio	Portfolio Gain or (Loss)
1	108.85	110.05	(1.20)	($1,200)	$111,213	$1,213
18	108.85	109.50	(.65)	(650)	110,657	657
36	108.85	107.40	1.45	1,450	108,535	(1,465)
54	108.85	106.05	2.80	2,800	107,171	(2,829)
72	108.85	103.10	5.75	5,750	104,190	(5,810)
90	108.85	100.65	8.20	8,200	101,714	(8,286)
Position Closed	108.85	100.65	8.20	$8,200	$101.714	($8,286)

Observations: The market dropped and our investor hedged the cash decline in his portfolio with an offsetting gain in his futures position. Of course, if he were wrong about the direction of the market and it went up, he would have had losses in his futures positions but his stocks may have participated in the advance. The investor throughout this period, did not have to disturb his holdings and continued to receive his dividend payments.

Let us assume that the S&P 500 has a beta of 1.00, (that is, a given percentage move in the market gives rise to the same percentage move in the S&P 500) and our hypothetical portfolio has a beta of 1.50. Our portfolio's past market action relative to moves in the market was 50% greater than a given move in the general market. To compensate for this greater volatility, our hedger would require more S&P contracts to offset a greater decline in the value of his portfolio. Known as a hedge ratio, the dollar value of the portfolio is divided by the dollar value of the S&P 500 futures contract, the resulting figure is multiplied by the beta of the portfolio. Using our investor's portfolio and having calculated a beta of 1.5, we arrive at three contracts instead of two when the beta was 1.00:

$$\frac{\$110,000}{54,425} \times 1.5 = 3.03 \text{ contracts}$$

Thus, our investor would have sold three con-

or short position, and as such, spreads generally carry lower margin requirements.

A characteristic of the futures market is that the closest contract date behaves more like the cash market. (In the S&P 500 futures contract, the cash market is the actual S&P 500 Index.) More distant months or back months have a greater component of their price determined by the expectations of what the price will be in the future.

These changing expectations of price levels of the S&P 500 contract into the future creates spreading opportunities. Options strategists will use the S&P 500 futures contract to reduce market risk when writing uncovered puts and calls. Block traders, investment bankers, stock specialists, options principals and anyone with the risk of stock market volatility, now have a vehicle and a well-capitalized liquid market to buy and sell market risk—the Standard & Poor's 500 Stock Index futures contract.

CONTRACT TERMS SUMMARY

Size	500 times the value of the S&P 500 Index
Delivery	Mark-to-market at closing value of the actual S&P 500 Index on Settlement Date
Hours	9:00 am to 3:15 pm Central Time
Months Traded	March, June, September, December
Clearing House Symbol	SP
Ticker Symbol	SP
Prices	Contract quoted in terms of S&P 500 Index
Minimum Fluctuation in Price	05 ($25)
Limit Move	3.00 ($1,500)
Last Day of Trading	3rd Thursday of Contract Month
Settlement Date	Last Day of Trading

Understanding the Commodities Market

COMMODITY EXCHANGES

A Commodity Exchange is an organized market of buyers and sellers of various types of commodities. It is public to the extent that anyone can trade through member firms. It provides a trading place for commodities, regulates the trading practices of the members, gathers and transmits price information, inspects and governs commodities traded on the Exchange, supervises warehouses that store the commodity, and provides means for settling disputes between members. All transactions must be conducted in a pit on the Exchange floor within certain hours.

FUTURES CONTRACT

A futures contract is a contract between two parties where the buyer agrees to accept delivery at a specified price from the seller of a particular commodity, in a designated month in the future, if it is not liquidated before the contract reaches maturity. A futures contract is not an option; nothing in it is conditional. Each contract calls for a specified amount, and grade of product. For example: *A person buying a February Pork Belly contract at 52.40 in effect is making a legal*

Source: Commodity Educational Services, Division of Commodity Cassettes, Inc., 778 Frontage Road, Northfield, IL 60093.

obligation, now, to accept delivery of 38,000 pounds of frozen Pork Bellies, to be delivered during the month of February, for which the buyer will pay 52.40 per pound.

The average trader does not take delivery of a futures contract, since he normally will close out his position before the futures contract matures. As a matter of fact, a survey conducted by a leading exchange has estimated that less than 3% of the contracts traded are settled by actual delivery.

Editor's Note: The scope of the commodities market has been broadened in recent years to include contracts on financial (debt) instruments (T-bills, bonds, etc.) and composite stock market indices such as Value Line, S&P 500, and the New York Stock Exchange. With the stock market index futures, settlement is made in cash in amount based on the underlying index. Cash, not the securities, is used to offset the long and short positions. The cash value of the contract is defined as the index quotation × 500.

THE HEDGER AND SPECULATOR

A hedger buys or sells a futures contract in order to reduce the risk of loss through price variation. A short hedger sells a futures contract to protect the possible decline in the actual commodity owned by him. A long hedger purchases a futures contract to protect the possible advance in the value of an actual commodity needed to be purchased in the future.

The speculator is an important factor in the volume of future trading today. He, in effect, voluntarily assumes the risk, which the hedger tries to avoid, with the expectations of making a profit. He is somewhat of an insurance underwriter. The largest number of traders on any commodity exchange is the speculator. In order for the hedger to participate, he must have continuous trading interests and activity in the market. This trading activity stems from the role of the speculator, because he involves himself in buying or selling of futures contracts with the idea of making a profit on the advance or decline of prices. The speculator tries to forecast prices in advance of delivery and is willing to buy or sell on this basis. A speculator involves himself in an inescapable risk.

CAN YOU BE A SPECULATOR?

Now, can you be a speculator? Before considering entering into the futures market as a speculator, there are several facts which you should understand about the market and also about yourself. In order to enter into the futures market, you must understand that you are dealing with a margin account. Margins are as low as 5 to 10% of the total value of the futures contract, so you are obtaining a greater leverage on your capital.

Fluctuations in price are rapid, volatile, and wide. It is possible to make a very large profit in a short period of time, but also, it is possible to take a substantial loss. In fact, surveys taken by the Agricultural Department have shown that up to 75% of the individuals speculating in commodity markets have lost money. This does not mean that some of their trades were not profitable, but after a period of time with a given sum of money they ended up being a loser.

Now taking you as an individual, let us see whether you have the characteristics to become a commodity trader. Number one and the most important is that you do not take money that you have set aside for your future, or money you need daily to support your family or yourself. Number two, and almost equally important, is that you must be willing to assume losses and be willing to assume these losses with such a temperament that it is not going to affect your everyday life. Money used in the futures market should be money that has been set aside for strictly risk purposes, and if this money is not risk capital, your methods of trading could be seriously affected, because you cannot afford to be a loser.

Another very important factor is that you must not feel that you are going to take a thousand, two thousand, five or ten thousand dollars and place this with a brokerage firm and not follow the daily happenings of the market. Price fluctuations are fast, and as stated before, wide, so you must not only be in contact with your Account Executive daily, but know and study the technical facts that may be affecting the particular market in which you are speculating.

The individual who makes his first trade by buying a contract on Monday and selling this contract on the following Wednesday, making six hundred dollars on a $1,000 investment, in a period of two days, suddenly says to himself, *"Where has this market been all my life? Why am I working? Why not just concentrate on this market, if every two days or so I can make six hundred dollars?"* This is a fallacy, since this is an individual that is going to destroy himself and most likely his family. The next trade he will feel confident that because of his first profitable trade the market will always go his way even though he is now showing a loss in his position. He still feels that the market will turn around in his direction. If you become married to a particular commodity futures contract and constantly feel that the losses you are taking at the present time will reverse into profits, you are really fighting the market

and in most cases fighting a losing battle. This could lead to disaster. There is a saying that you let your profits ride, but liquidate your losses fast.

In any way that you are uneasy with a position that you are holding, it is better to liquidate it. If, prior to the time of buying or selling a contract, you are not sure that this is the right step to take, do not take it. To protect yourself against this hazard you should pre-decide on every trade and exactly how much you intend to lose.

Another important point is not to involve yourself in too many markets. It is difficult to know all the technical facts and be able to follow numerous markets. In addition, if you are in a winning position, be conservative as to how you add additional contracts or pyramid your position. Being conservative will sometimes cause you to miss certain moves in certain markets and you may feel this to be wrong, but over a long period of time, this conservatism will be profitable to you.

If at this point you feel that you are ready, both financially and mentally to trade commodities, the next step is to begin the actual mechanics of trading a futures contract.

OPENING AN ACCOUNT

The first important factor is to decide which brokerage firm will afford you the best service. To accomplish this, you should do a little research by checking with the various exchanges about different brokerage firms. You should study their advertising, market letters, and other information. These should all be presented in a business-like manner and have no unwarranted claims, such as a guarantee of profit without indicating the possibility of loss.

The brokerage firm must be able to handle orders on all commodity exchanges. Do not pick just any Account Executive in a firm, but one you feel confident to help you make market decisions. Become acquainted with the Account Executive through phone or personal conversations. His knowledge of the factors entering into the market and the understanding of current market trends are important in your final choice.

After making a decision on the brokerage firm and the Account Executive that would be best for you, contact him and have him send you the literature concerning different contracts, and also, any additional information as to his organization. He will then send you the necessary signature cards required by the firm to open an account, and ask you for a deposit of margin money.

You will be trading in regulated commodities, and margin money will be deposited in a segregated fund at the brokerage firm's bank. A segregated account means that the money will only be used for margin and not for expenses of the brokerage firm.

Now you decide to enter into your first trade. Your Account Executive and you decide to enter into a December Live Cattle contract on the Chicago Mercantile Exchange. Your order will be executed as follows: Your Account Executive will place this order with his order desk who will then transmit the order to the floor of the Chicago Mercantile Exchange. There your order will be executed on the trading floor, in the pit. All technical details connected with the transaction will be handled by the brokerage firm.

Upon filling of your order, the filled order will be transmitted back to your Account Executive, who will then contact you, advising you that you have purchased one December Live Cattle contract at a given price. You will also receive a written confirmation on this transaction. You will now show an open position in December Live Cattle on the books of the brokerage firm.

MECHANICS OF A TRADE

Let us go back one step to explain in detail just how your order to buy one December Cattle was handled on the floor of the exchange. All buying and selling in the pit is done by open out-cry, and every price change is reported on the exchange ticker system. Each firm has brokers in the different pits, a pit meaning a trading area for the purpose of buying and selling contracts.

When your order was received on the exchange floor, it was time stamped and given to a runner. This is a person who takes the order from the desk on the exchange floor and gives it to one of the brokers in the December Cattle trading pit. He is then responsible to the brokerage firm to fill that order, if possible, at the stated price. After filling the order, he then has the runner return it to the desk where it is time stamped and transmitted back to the order desk at the brokerage house, and the filled order is reported to you.

MARGIN

Futures trading requires the trader to place margin with his brokerage firm. Initial margin is required and this amount varies with each commodity. The minimum margin is established by each commodity exchange. Additional funds are needed when the equity of your account falls below this level. This is known as a maintenance margin call.

All margin calls must be met immediately. Normally you will be given a reasonable amount of time to comply with this request.

If you do not comply, the firm has the right to liquidate your trades or a sufficient number of trades to restore your account to margin requirements.

The brokerage firm has the right to raise margin requirements to the customer at any time. This is normally done if the price of the commodity is changing sharply or if it is the brokerage firm's opinion that due to the volatility of the market the margin requirement is not sufficient at that particular time.

Most commodity contracts have a minimum fluctuation and also a maximum fluctuation for any one particular day. For example, if you are trading frozen Pork Bellies on the Chicago Mercantile Exchange the fluctuation is considered in points. A point equals three dollars and eighty cents. this means that if you buy a contract at 52.40 and the next price tick is 52.45, you have made a paper profit of five points or nineteen dollars. The maximum fluctuation on a belly contract is 200 points, so your profit or loss cannot exceed in one day more than 200 points from the previous day's settlement. There are exceptions in some commodity contracts, where the spot month has no limit.

Let us assume that you had originally placed in the hands of your brokerage firm two thousand dollars margin money, and that you and your Account Executive decide to purchase a December Live Cattle contract whose initial margin is $1200 with maintenance of $900.00. After the purchase of the contract your account would show initial margin required $1200 dollars with excess funds of eight hundred dollars. At the end of each day the settlement price of December Cattle would be applied to your purchase price and your account would be adjusted to either an increase due to profit or decrease due to loss in your contract.

Further, assume that in a period of two or three days there is a decline in the price of the December Cattle contract and your account now shows a loss of three hundred dollars. Since maintenance margin is only nine hundred dollars on this contract, you will still show an excess of eight hundred dollars over and above maintenance margin. But, in the next four days suppose there is an additional loss of nine hundred dollars. Your account will now need one hundred dollars to maintain the maintenance margin and four hundred dollars additional in order to bring your account up to initial margin. Your Account Executive, or a man from the margin department of the brokerage firm will then contact you, stating that you must place additional money with the firm in order to maintain the December Cattle contract.

At this point, you must decide whether you should continue with the contract, feeling that it may be profitable in the next few days, and thus sending the brokerage firm the required four hundred dollars to maintain your position, or whether to assume your loss and sell the contract.

Let us assume that you decide to sell your December contract at this point and that the selling price causes a loss of four hundred dollars. Added to this loss would be the commission of forty dollars, so your total loss on the transaction would be four hundred forty dollars. A confirmation and purchase and sales statement will be sent to you, showing the original price paid for the contract, the price for which it was sold, the gross loss of four hundred dollars plus the commission of forty dollars making the total loss four hundred forty dollars, and your new ledger balance on deposit with the firm as fifteen hundred sixty dollars.

As shown in our example, commission was charged only when the contract was closed out. A single commission is charged for each round-turn transaction consisting of the creation and liquidation of a single contract.

CONTROLLED, DISCRETIONARY, AND MANAGED ACCOUNTS

There are two methods of trading your account. The first is the professional approach where you and your Account Executive decide on each trade with no discretion being given directly to your Account Executive. This method was illustrated in the discussion about margins. The second method is called a controlled discretionary or managed account. Under this method, you are giving your Account Executive authorization to trade your account at his discretion at any time and as many times that he considers that a trade should be made. The Chicago Mercantile Exchange, and the Board of Trade have rules governing this type of relationship. The following is an excerpt from the C.M.E. rule regarding controlled, discretionary and managed accounts.

REQUIREMENTS

No clearing member shall accept or carry an account over which any individual or organization, other than the person in whose name the account is carried, exercises trading authority or control, hereinafter referred to as controlled accounts, unless:

The account is initiated with a minimum of $5000*, and maintained at a minimum equity of $3,750*, regardless of

---

* Minimums can be changed by each exchange, so consult your Account Executive for current regulations.

lesser applicable margin requirements. In determining equity the accounts or ledger balances and positions in all commodities traded at the clearing member shall be included. Whenever at the close of any business day the equity, calculated with all open positions figured to the settling price, in any such account is below the required minimum, the clearing member shall immediately notify the customer in person, by telephone or telegraph and by written confirmation of such notice mailed directly to the customer, not later than the close of the following business day. Such notice shall advise the customer that unless additional funds are promptly received to restore the customer's controlled account to no less than $5,000*, the clearing member shall liquidate all of the customer's open futures positions at the Exchange.

In the event the call for additional equity is not met within a reasonable time, the customer's entire open position shall be liquidated. No period of time in excess of five business days shall be considered reasonable unless such longer period is approved in writing by an officer or partner of the clearing member upon good cause shown.

REVIEWING YOUR CONFIRMATIONS AND STATEMENTS

An important factor in trading is that you must be sure that no errors occur in your account. For every trade made you should receive a confirmation, and for every close-out a profit and loss statement known as a Purchase-and-Sale, showing the financial results of each transaction closed out in your account. In addition, a monthly statement showing your ledger balance, your open position, the net profit or loss in all contracts liquidated since the date of your last previous statement, and the net unrealized profit and loss on all open contracts figured to the market should be sent to you.

You should carefully review these statements. Upon receiving a confirmation of a trade you should immediately check its accuracy as far as type of commodity, month, trading price and quantity of contracts. If this does not agree with your original order, it should be immediately reported to the main office of your brokerage firm, and any differences should be explained and adjustments should be made.

If you do not receive a confirmation on a trade after it was orally reported to you by your Account Executive, be sure to contact him and the main office so that if an error was made it can be corrected immediately.

You should receive written confirmation when you deposit money with your brokerage firm. If within a few days, you have not received this confirmation, report it immediately to the main office of your brokerage firm.

Never assume that an order has been filled until you receive an oral confirmation from your broker. A ticker or a board that you may be observing can be running several minutes behind and is not the determining factor as to whether your trade was executed or not. Until you receive this oral confirmation, never re-enter an order to buy or sell, against that position.

If you receive a confirmation in the mail showing a trade not belonging to you, immediately notify the main office of your brokerage firm and have them explain why this is on a confirmation with your account number. If it is an error, be sure that it is adjusted immediately and a written confirmation sent to you showing the adjustment of the error. If an error is made and it is profitable to you do not consider this any differently than if it was not profitable. Regardless of whether there is a profit or loss, all errors should be immediately reported to the brokerage firm.

Be sure that when you request funds to be mailed from your account that they are received within a few days from the time of your request. If not, contact the accounting department of the brokerage firm to see what is the cause of the delay.

Never make a check out to an individual. Always make your check out to the brokerage firm.

DAY TRADING

Day trading is where there is a buy and sell made during the trading hours on one particular day. Day trading is not considered to be a sound practice for the new speculator and inexperienced trader. Day trading is something that should be executed only by a sophisticated trader who is in frequent communication with the floor, and even then, on a limited basis.

ORDERS

In order to trade effectively in the commodity market there are several basic types of orders. The most common order is a market order. A market order is one which you authorize your Account Executive to buy or sell at the existing price. This is definitely not a predetermined price, but is executed at a bid or offer at that particular moment.

Example: Buy 5 Feb Pork Bellies at the market.

LIMITED OR PRICE ORDERS AND "OB" DESIGNATION

This type of order to buy or sell commodities at a fixed or "limited" price and the ordinary "market" order are the most common types of orders.

Example: Buy Three Jan Silver 463.10. This limit order instructs the floor broker to buy three contracts of January Silver futures at 463.10. Even with this simple order, however, one presumption is necessary—that the market price prevailing when the order enters the pit is 463.10 or higher. If the price is below 463.10, the broker could challenge on the basis that the client may have meant *"Buy Three Jan Silver 463.10 stop."* Therefore, while it is always assumed that a "limit: order means 'or better,'" if possible, it saves confusion and challenges if the "OB" designation is added to the limit price. This is particularly true on orders near the market, or on pre-opening orders with the limit price based on the previous close, because no one knows whether the opening will be higher or lower than the close, *i.e., Buy Three Jan Silver 463.10 OB.*

STOP ORDERS *(Orders having the effect of market orders)*

Buy Stop Buy stop orders must be written at a price higher than the price prevailing at the time of entry. If the prevailing price for December Wheat is 456 per bushel, a buy stop order must designate a price above 456.

Example: "Buy 20 Dec Wht 456½ Day Stop." The effect of this order is that if December Wheat touches 456½ the order to buy 20 December Wheat becomes a market order. From that point, 456½ on, all the above discussion regarding market orders applies.

Sell Stop Sell stop orders must be written at a price lower than the price prevailing at the time of entry in the trading pit. If the prevailing price of December Wheat is 456 per bushel, a sell stop order must designate a price below 456.

Example: "Sell 20 Dec Wht 455 Day Stop." If this order enters the trading pit with the above price of 456 prevailing, the order to sell 20 December Wheat becomes a market order. From that point 455 on, all the above discussion regarding market orders applies.

Buy stop orders have several specific uses. If you are short a December Wheat at 456, and wish to limit your loss to ½ cent per bushel, the above buy stop order at 456½ would serve this purpose. However, it is important to realize that such *"stop loss"* orders do not actually limit the loss to exactly ½ cent when *"elected"* or *"touched off"* because they become market orders and must be executed at whatever price the market conditions dictate.

Another use is when you are without a position and believe that, because of chart analysis or for other reasons, a buy of December Wheat at 456½ would signal the beginning of an important uptrend in Wheat prices. Thus, the same order to *"Buy 20 Dec Wheat 456½ Day Stop"* would serve this purpose.

Sell stop orders have the same uses in reverse. That is, if you are long 20 December Wheat at 456 and wish to limit this loss to 1 cent per bushel, the above sell stop order at 455 would serve this purpose, within the limitations of the market order possibilities. Similarly, if you are without a position and believe that a sale of December Wheat at 455 would signal a downtrend in wheat prices, and you wish to be short the market, you could use the order to *"Sell 20 December Wheat 455 Day Stop"* for this purpose.

STOP LIMIT ORDERS *(Variations of stop orders)*

Stop limit orders should be used by you when you wish to give the floor broker a limit beyond which he cannot go in executing the order which results when a stop price is *"elected."*

Example: "Buy 20 Dec Wheat 456½ Day Stop Limit." This instructs the broker that when the price of 456½ is reached and *"elects"* this stop order, instead of making it a market order, it becomes a limited order to be executed at 456½ *(or lower)*, but no higher than 456½. Another possibility:

Example: "Buy One February Pork Belly 58.10 Day Stop Limit 58.25 (or any other price above 58.10)." This instructs the broker that when the price of 58.10 *"elects"* the stop order instead of making it a market order, it becomes a limited order to buy at 58.25 *(or lower)*, but no higher as with any limit order.

Stop limit orders are particularly useful to you when you have no position and wish to enter a market via the stop order, but want to put some reasonable limit as to what you will pay. On the other hand, stop limit orders are not useful to you when you have an open position and wish to prevent a loss beyond a certain point. The reason is that by limiting the broker to a certain price after a *"stop loss"* order is elected, **you also run the risk**

that the market may exceed the limit too fast for the broker to execute. This would leave you with your original position because the broker would have to wait for the return to the limit before executing. With a straight stop *(no limit)* order, the broker must execute *"at the market."*

Example: "Buy One February Pork Belly 58.10 Day Stop Limit 58.25." Suppose the market moves to 58.10 but then only 20 February Pork Bellies are offered at that price. Your broker bids for one at 58.10 but another broker in the pit catches the seller's eye first and buys 20 and your broker misses the sale. Your broker then bids 58.20 but the best offer is 58.30. He bids 58.25, but the offer at 58.30 remains unchanged. Then another broker bids for and buys February Pork Bellies at 58.30 and the market moves on up. Your broker is left with no execution to your order unless the market later declines to your limit making a fill possible.

If you did not have a position you might be disappointed, but you would be unhurt financially. However, if you had a position and were trying to limit your loss you would have defeated your purpose with the stop limit order, if you truly wanted *"out"* after the stop was elected.

Stop limit orders on the sell side have exactly the same uses, advantages and disadvantages as discussed above, but in reverse:

Example: "Sell 20 December Wheat 455 Day Stop Limit." This means that when the market declines to 455 per bushel, the broker may sell at 455 *(or higher)*, but no lower.

Another Example: "Sell One February Pork Belly 58.25 Stop Limit 58.10." This instructs the broker to sell a belly after the stop price of 58.25 is reached and *"elects"* the stop order, but no lower than 58.10

M.I.T. ORDERS *(Market-if-touched)*

By adding MIT *(Market-If-Touched)* to a limit order, the limit order will have the effect of a market order when the limit price is reached or touched. This type of order is useful to you, when you have an open position and if a certain limit price is reached.

Example: "Sell One September Sugar 950 MIT." The floor broker is told that if and when the price of September Sugar rises to 9½¢ per pound, he is to sell one contract at the market. At this price of 9½¢ all prior discussion on market orders applies.

Under certain market conditions, not

enough contracts are bid at 9½ cents to fill all offers to sell. Thus, you may see your straight limit price appear on the ticker, but your broker fails to make the sale.

But by adding MIT to the limit price, you will receive an execution, because the order becomes a market order, if the price is touched. However, the price will not necessarily be a good one in your eyes, since it became a market order when touched.

The same reasoning is true on the buy side of MIT orders but in reverse. Assume you are short one contract of September Sugar, with the prevailing price at 9½¢ per pound and you want to cover or liquidate your short at 9¢.

Example: "Buy One September Sugar 9¢ MIT." If and when the price of September sugar declines to 9¢ per pound, the floor broker must buy one contract at the market. Aside from the disadvantages of any market order, the MIT designation on the buy order prevents the disappointment which might arise if a straight limit buy at 9¢ were entered without the MIT added.

SPREAD ORDERS

As explained in the Glossary, a spread is a simultaneous long or short position in the same or related commodity. Thus a spread order would be to buy one month of a certain commodity and sell another month of the same commodity, or buy one month of one commodity and sell the same or another month of a related commodity.

Example: "Buy 5 July Beans Market and Sell 5 May Beans Market" or *"Buy 10 Kansas City Dec Wheat Market and Sell 10 Chicago May Wheat Market."*

Another Example: "Buy 5 May Corn Market and Sell 5 May Wheat Market."

In the example of the related commodity spread, normally the reason you would use such a spread, is that you expect to make a profit out of an expected tightness in the Corn Market, in the hope the corn contract will gain in value faster than wheat.

There may be a situation where you have a position either long or short in a commodity and want to change to a nearer or more distant option of the same commodity. For example you are long 5,000 bushels of May Soybeans on May 20 and want to avoid a delivery notice by moving your position forward into the July option. The basic spread order would be:

"Buy 5 July Beans Market and Sell 5 May Beans Market."

Sometimes you may prefer not to use market orders, in which case you use the difference spread.

Example: "Buy 5 July Beans and Sell 5 May Beans July 2¢ Over." Even though the prices of the two options are not specified, the broker is allowed to execute at any time he can do so with July selling at 2¢ or less above May. Over or under designations are a necessity for clarity to the floor broker. Omitting either is like omitting the price.

All orders, except market orders, can be cancelled, prior to execution. Naturally, a market order is executed immediately upon reaching the pit, so its cancellation is almost impossible.

There are other variations of orders, but for you the new speculator, the types mentioned are sufficient for your trading.

Options on Stock Market Indices, Bond Futures, and Gold Futures

STOCK MARKET INDEX OPTIONS

Stock market index related options are options whose prices are determined by the value of a stock market average such as the Standard and Poor (S&P) 500 Index or the New York Stock Exchange Composite Index, among others. Two types of such options are currently traded; index options and index futures options. The former are settled in cash while the latter are settled by delivery of the appropriate index futures contract.

Both types of options move in the same way in response to the underlying market index, thereby providing investors the opportunity to speculate on the market averages. The buyer of a call index option is betting that the underlying market index value will increase significantly above the strike price (before the option expires) so as to provide a profit when the option is sold. On the other hand, the buyer of a put option is speculating that the market index value will fall sufficiently below the strike price before the option expires so as to provide a profit when the put option is sold. Options writers (sellers), on the other hand, assume an opposite position.

While index futures (page 467) also permit speculation on the market averages, index option tend to be less risky since option *buyers* are not subject to margin calls and losses are limited to the price (premium) paid for the option. However, index option writers (sellers), in return for the premium received, are subject to margin calls and are exposed to losses of indeterminate magnitude. However, writers of call options on index *futures* can protect themselves by holding the underlying futures contract.

Index Options

A number of index options based on the broad market averages are now traded:

S&P 100 Index [Chicago Board of Options Exchange (CBOE)]

S&P 500 Index (Chicago Board of Options Exchange)

Major Market Index [American Exchange (Amex)]

Institutional Index (American Exchange)

NYSE Options Index (New York Stock Exchange)

Value Line Index (Philadelphia Exchange)

National OTC Index (Philadelphia Exchange)

A brief description of some of the more important indices follows.

The S&P 100 Index is a so-called weighted index obtained by multiplying the current price of each of the 100 stocks by the number of shares outstanding and then adding all of the products to obtain the weighted sum. The weighted sum is then multiplied by a scaling factor to provide an index of a convenient magnitude. The S&P 500 Index is calculated similarly except that all of the S&P 500 stocks are included.

The NYSE Index is based on the weighted sum of all of the stocks traded on the New York Exchange while the AMEX Index is based on the weighted sum of all of the issues traded on the American Exchange. The Institutional Index consists of 75 stocks most widely held by institutional investors.

The Major Market Index differs from the above in that it is just the simple (unweighted) sum of 20 blue chip stocks multiplied by a factor of one tenth. This index behaves very similarly to the Dow Jones Index.

Generally index options expire on the Saturday following the third Friday of the expiration month. Hence the last trading day is on the third Friday of the expiration month. The price of an index option contract is $100 times the premium as quoted in the financial press.

Example: The July 120 (an option with a strike price of 120 expiring in July) Major Market Index call option is quoted (Exhibit 1) at 3.00. The cost of an option contract is $300 ($100 × 3).

Option premiums consist of the sum of two components; the intrinsic value and the time value. The intrinsic value of a *call* option

EXHIBIT 1   INDEX OPTIONS QUOTATIONS

CHICAGO BOARD

CBOE 100 INDEX

Strike Price	Calls—Last			Puts—Last		
	June	Sept	Dec	June	Sept	Dec
145	15¼	....	....	1/16	1	....
150	13¾	....	....	⅛	1¾	....
155	9⅛	10	....	7/16	3⅛	....
160	5⅛	9¼	....	17/16	4⅝	8¼
165	2⅛	6½	8⅝	3⅞	7¼	10½
170	11/16	3¾	6	7⅝	12	13½

Total call volume 20846.   Total call open int. 62006.
Total put volume 25167.   Total put open int. 103733.
The index closed at 163.55, +1.91.

AMERICAN EXCHANGE

MAJOR MARKET INDEX

Strike Price	Calls—Last			Puts—Last		
	Jul	Oct	Jan	Jul	Oct	Jan
115	5¾	8⅝	10	1⅞	3¾	5½
120	3	5¾	7	4	5⅞	7½
125	1⅛	3¼	....	7⅜	....	....
130	7/16	2¼	3⅝	....	....	....

Total call volume 2351.   Total call open int. 14572.
Total put volume 5276.   Total put open int. 9593.
The index closed at 118.69, +1.00.

is $100 times the difference obtained by subtracting the strike price from the current value of the index. The intrinsic value of a *put* option is $100 times the difference obtained by subtracting the current value of the index from the strike price. The time value is the money which an option buyer is willing to pay in the expectation that the option will become more valuable (*increase its intrinsic value*) before it expires. Obviously the time value decreases as the time to expiration decreases.

It should be noted that there is a distinction between exercising an index option and selling an index option to close out a position. Exercising an option gives the holder the right to a cash amount equal to the *intrinsic* value of the option. Hence, the time value of the option is lost. When an option is sold to close out a position, the option holder receives a cash amount equal to the *premium* which contains both the intrinsic value and the time value of the option. Thus, in most cases it is more profitable to sell the option. The profit realized (before commissions and taxes) on the *sale* of an option contract is equal to $100 times the difference obtained by subtracting the premium paid when the option was purchased from the premium received when the option was sold.

Example: On May 24 the CBOE 100 Index

was 163.55. In anticipation of a market decline, an investor buys a September 165-put option quoted at 7¼ for a total premium of $725 (7.25 × 100) per option. Assume that on August 10 the puts were selling at a total premium of $850 due to a decline in the CBOE 100 Index to 160.10. If the investor sells the put option he will realize a profit, before commissions and taxes, of $125 (850 − 725). If the market moves in a contrary direction he could lose his entire investment.

Index Futures Options

Index futures options (also called futures options) are the right to buy (call) or sell (put) the underlying index futures contracts (see page 467). Futures options are currently traded on the New York Futures Exchange and the Chicago Mercantile Exchange. The dollar value of the underlying contract for the New York Futures Exchange option is equal to the New York Stock Exchange Composite Index multiplied by 500 while that for the Chicago Mercantile Exchange option is equal to the S&P 500 Index multiplied by 500. Quotations for futures options as they appear in *The Wall Street Journal* are shown in Exhibit 2. The total futures option premium per option is equal to the quoted value multiplied by 500. Gains and losses are calculated in the same way as index options.

The expiration day of the S&P 500 futures option is on the third Thursday of the expiration month while that for the NYSE futures option is the business day prior to the last business day of the expiration month.

Example: On May 24, 1983, the New York Composite Index is 94.39. An investor expects the Index to increase during the next six months and buys a September 96 futures call option at a total premium of $1750 (3.50 × 500), as indicated in Exhibit 2. Assume that by August 10 the Index is at 100 and that the September call premium is quoted at 8.00 corresponding to a total premium per option of $4000 (8.00 × 500). By selling the option at the current value the investor can realize a profit of $2250 (4000 − 1750) before commissions and taxes.

Example: Assume that on May 24, 1983 when the S&P 500 Index is at 163.43, an investor expects a market decline within six months. He purchases a September 155 S&P put option at a total premium per option of $1150 (2.30 × 500), as indicated in the quotations shown in Exhibit 2. Assume that the Index declines to 150 on August 10 and that the quoted put premium is 6.50 corresponding to a total premium per option of $3250 (6.50 × 500). By selling the option at the current value the investor can realize a profit of $2100 (3250 − 1150), before commissions and taxes.

EXHIBIT 2 FUTURES OPTIONS

CHICAGO MERCANTILE EXCHANGE

S&P 500 STOCK INDEX – Price = $500 times premium.

Strike Price	Calls—Settle			Puts—Settle		
	Jun	Sep	Dec	Jun	Sep	Dec
135	....	....	....	.05	....	....
140	23.90	24.25	....	.05	.45	....
145	18.90	20.20	....	.05	.90	....
150	13.95	15.25	....	.10	1.25	....
155	9.20	11.50	....	.30	2.30	4.50
160	4.95	8.60	....	1.05	3.60	....
165	1.90	5.50	8.75	3.00	5.75	7.80
170	.45	3.50	....	6.50	9.50	....
175	.10	1.80	....	11.15	14.00	....

Estimated total vol. 1,440
Calls: Fri. vol. 766; open int. 6,216
Puts: Fri. vol 532; open int. 6,552

N.Y. FUTURES EXCHANGE

NYSE COMPOSITE INDEX – Price = $500 times premium.

Strike Price	Calls—Settle			Puts—Settle		
	Jun	Sep	Dec	Jun	Sep	Dec
84	10.90	11.70	....	.05	.40	.75
86	8.90	10.00	11.00	.05	.70	1.50
88	5.95	8.50	9.70	.05	1.00	1.75
90	5.15	7.00	8.30	.25	1.50	2.30
92	3.35	5.50	7.00	.50	2.00	2.95
94	1.95	4.50	6.00	1.15	3.00	3.75
96	.95	3.50	5.00	2.10	3.90	4.95
98	.40	2.75	3.95	3.50	5.25	6.05
100	.15	1.75	3.25	....	6.25	7.00

Estimated total vol. 1,405
Calls: Fri. vol. 844; open int. 4,836
Puts: Fri. vol. 549; open int. 4,801
S&P 500 Index 163.43
New York Composite Index = 94.39

While a number of the same basic concepts apply to both index options and future options, there are differences between the two because the futures options have underlying index futures contracts which are traded on the open market. This makes possible a number of trading strategies with futures options which are not available with index options; for example, simultaneously buying an index futures contract and writing a corresponding call option. Also, for the reason given above, there is a distinction between selling a futures option, the usual procedure, and exercising the option. When a futures option is exercised, the option is exchanged for a position in the index futures market which may result in a loss in the time value of the option.

Investors planning to trade options should read two free booklets available from any of the options exchanges:

Understanding the Risks and Uses of Options

Listed Options On Stock Indices

Subindex Options

Subindex options are based on an index made up of leading publicly traded companies within a specific industry. These options permit speculation on an industry without the necessity of selecting specific stocks within the industry. As with all stock index options they are settled in cash.

Subindex options currently traded are:

American Stock Exchange (AMEX)
Computer Technology Index Option
Oil and Gas Index Option
Transportation Index Option

Pacific Stock Exchange
Technology Index Option

Philadelphia Stock Exchange
Gold/Silver Index Option

U.S. TREASURY BOND FUTURES OPTIONS

Options on U.S. Treasury Bonds (T-Bonds), traded on the Chicago Board of Trade, are the right to buy (call) or sell (put) a T-Bond futures contract. The T-Bond futures contract underlying the option is for $100,000 of Treasury Bonds, bearing an 8% or equivalent coupon, which do not mature (and are non-callable) for at least 15 years. When long term interest rates decline, the value of the futures contract and the call option increases while the value of a put option decreases. The reverse is true when long term rates increase.

Premiums for T-bond futures *options* are quoted in $\frac{1}{64}$ of 1% (point): Hence each $\frac{1}{64}$ of a point is equal to $15.63 ($100,000 × .01 × $\frac{1}{64}$) per option. Thus a premium quote of 2–16 means 2 $\frac{16}{64}$ or (2 × 64 + 16) × $15.63 or $2250.72 per option. It should be noted that prices of T-bond *futures* are quoted in $\frac{1}{32}$ (of a point) worth $31.25 per futures contract.

As with options trades in general, the profit (before taxes and commissions) is the premium received (per option) when the option is sold minus the premium paid when the option was purchased.

The last trading day for the options is the first Friday, preceded by at least five business days, in the month *prior* to the month in which the underlying futures contract expires. For example, in 1983 a December option stops trading on November 18, 1983.

GOLD FUTURES OPTIONS

The most widely traded gold futures option is on the New York Comex Exchange. The option is the right to buy (call) or sell (put) a gold futures contract for 100 Troy ounces of pure gold. Both the futures contract and the corresponding call option increase or decrease with the price of gold. Put option premiums move in the opposite direction to the price of gold.

Option premiums are in dollars per ounce of gold. Thus a quoted premium of 2.50 corresponds to total premium of $2500 (2.50 × 100) per option.

The profit (before commissions and taxes) to an option buyer is simply the premium received when the option is sold less the premium paid when the option was purchased.

The last trading day for gold futures options is the second Friday in the month *prior* to the expiration date of the underlying gold futures contract. Thus in 1983 a December option expires on Friday November 11, 1983. Example: In August an investor buys a December 400 (an option with a strike price of 400 on a December gold futures contract) Comex call option quoted at 25.00. The total price per option is $2500 (25.00 × 100).

On November 5, the price of gold has increased and the investor sells the option at a quoted premium of 50.00 or $5000.00 (50 × 100) per option. His profit is $2500 (5000 − 2500).

The Commodities Glossary

Acreage allotment The portion of a farmer's total acreage that he can harvest and still qualify for government price supports, low interest crop loans and other programs. It currently applies to specialty crops—tobacco, peanuts and extra long staple cotton—for which complex federal marketing orders have been written to control production closely. Before the 1977 farm bill was passed, the same term also applied more loosely to the portion of a farmer's wheat or feed grain acreage for which government payments would be made. A farmer could harvest 100 acres of wheat, for instance, but he'd receive price support payments only for 70 acres if that was his allotment. The allotment in this sense is called "program acreage" in the new farm bill.

Arbitrage The simultaneous buying and selling of futures contracts to profit from what the trader perceives as a discrepancy in prices. Usually this is done in futures in the same commodity traded on different exchanges, such as cocoa in New York and cocoa in London or silver in New York and silver in Chicago. Some arbitrage occurs between cash markets and futures markets.

Asking price The price offered by one wishing to sell a physical commodity or a futures contract. Sometimes a futures market will close with an asking price when no buyers are around.

Backwardation An expression peculiar to New York markets. It means "nearby" contracts are trading at a higher price, or "premium," to the deferreds. See also *Inverted market.*

Basis A couple of meanings: (1) The difference between the price of the physical commodity (the cash price) and the futures price of that commodity. (2) A geographic reference point for a cash price; for example, the price of a beef carcass is quoted "basic Midwest packing plants."

Bear A trader who thinks prices will decline. "Bearish" is often used to describe news or developments that have, or are expected to have, a downward influence on prices. A bear market is one in which the predominant price trend is down. Some think this term originated with an old axiom about "selling the skin before you've caught the bear."

Bid The price offered by one who wishes to purchase a physical commodity or a futures contract. Sometimes a futures market will close with a bid price when no sellers are around.

Broker An agent who buys and sells futures on behalf of a client for a fee. They work for brokerage firms, some of which have extensive research and analysis departments that occasionally issue trading advice. A few firms have so many customers who follow such advisories that recommendations to buy or sell can influence market prices materially.

Bull A trader who thinks prices will go up. "Bullish" describes developments that have, or are expected to have, an upward influence on prices. A bull market is one in which the predominant price trend is up. Some theorize this term originally related to a bull's habit of tossing its head upward.

Butterfly An unusual sort of spread involving three contract months rather than two. Often used to move profits or losses from one year to the next for tax purposes.

Cash The price at which dealings in the physical commodity take place. Used more sweepingly, it can mean simply the physical commodity itself (as in "cash corn" or "cash lumber"), or refer to a market. For example, the cash hog market is a terminal (or, collectively, all terminals) where live hogs are sold by farmers and bought by meat packers.

Chart A graph of futures prices (and sometimes other statistical trading information) plotted in such a way that the charter believes gives insight into future price movements. Several futures markets regularly are influenced by buying or selling based on traders' price-chart indications.

Clearing house The part of all futures exchanges (usually a separate corporation with its own members, fees, etc.) which clears all trades made on the exchange during the day. It matches the buy transactions with the equal number of sell transactions to provide orderly control over who owns what and who owes what to whom. Although futures traders theoretically trade contracts among themselves, the clearing house technically is in the middle of each transaction—being the buyer to every seller and the seller to every buyer. That's how it keeps track of what is going on.

Close The end of the trading session. On some exchanges, the "close" lasts for several minutes to accommodate customers who have entered buy or sell orders to be consummated "at the close." On those exchanges, the closing price may be a range encompassing the highest and lowest prices of trades consummated at the close. Other exchanges officially use settlement prices as the closing prices.

Source: The *Dow Jones Commodities Handbook,* edited by Dan Ruck, Dow Jones Books, Dow Jones Company, Inc. 1979.

Cold storage Refrigerated warehouses where perishable commodities are stored. In effect, the warehouses are secondary sources of commodities that aren't immediately available from the producers. The Agriculture Department periodically reports the quantities of various commodities stored in warehouses. Futures traders watch these reports to see if the supplies are building or dwindling abnormally fast, which indicates how closely supply and demand are balanced.

Commission The fee charged by a broker for making a trade on behalf of customers.

Contract In the case of futures, an agreement between two parties to make and in turn accept delivery of a specified quantity and quality of a commodity (or whatever is being traded) at a certain place (the delivery point) by a specified time (indicated by the month and year of the contract).

Country Refers to a place relatively close to a farmer where he can sell or deliver his crop or animals. For instance, a country elevator typically is located in a small town and accepts grain from farmers in the immediate vicinity. A country shipping point is a place where farmers in an area combine their marketings for shipment. A country price is the one these elevators, shipping points or whatever pay for the farmers' goods; it's based on the terminal-market prices, less transportation and handling costs.

Covering Buying futures contracts to offset those previously sold. "Short covering" often causes prices to rise even though the overall market trend may be down.

Crop report Estimates issued periodically by the Department of Agriculture on estimated size and condition of major U.S. crops. Similar reports are made on livestock.

Crush The process of reducing the raw, unusable soybean into its two major components, oil and meal. A "crush spread" is a futures spreading position in which a trader attempts to profit from what he believes to be discrepancies in the price relationships between soybeans and the two products. The "crush margin" is the gross profit that a processor makes from selling oil and meal minus the cost of buying the soybeans.

Deferred contracts In futures, those delivery months that are due to expire sometime beyond the next two or three months.

Delivery The tendering of the physical commodity to fulfill a short position in futures. This takes place only during the delivery month and normally takes the form of a warehouse receipt (from an exchange-accredited warehouse, elevator or whatever) that shows where the cash commodity is.

Delivery point The place(s) at which the cash commodity may be delivered to fulfill an expiring futures contract.

Discretionary accounts A futures trading account in which the customer puts up the money but the trading decisions are made at the discretion of the broker or some other person, or maybe a computer. Also known as "managed accounts."

Evening up Liquidating a futures position in advance of a significant crop report or some other scheduled development so as not to be caught on the wrong side of a surprise. In concentrated doses, evening up can cause a bull market to retreat somewhat and a bear market to rebound somewhat.

First notice day The first day of a delivery period when holders of short futures positions can give notice of their intention to deliver the cash commodity to holders of long positions. The number of contracts circulated on first notice day and how they are accepted or not accepted by the longs is often interpreted as an indication of future supply-demand expectations and thus often influence prices of all futures being traded, not just the delivery-month price. This effect also sometimes occurs on subsequent notice days. Rules concerning notices to deliver vary from contract to contract.

F.O.B. Free on Board, meaning that the commodity will be placed aboard the shipping vehicle at no cost to the purchaser, but thereafter the purchaser must bear all shipping costs.

Forward Contract A commercial agreement for the merchandising of commodities in which actual delivery is contemplated but is deferred for purposes of commercial convenience or necessity. Such agreements normally specify the quality and quantity of goods to be delivered at the particular future date. The forward contract may specify the price at which the commodity will be exchanged, or the agreement may stipulate that the price will be determined at some time prior to delivery.

Fundamentalist A trader who bases his buy-sell decisions on supply and demand trends or developments rather than on technical or chart considerations.

Futures Contracts traded on an exchange that call for a cash commodity to be delivered and received at a specified future time, at a specified place and at a specified price. Similar arrangements made directly between buyer and seller are called "forward contracts." They aren't traded on an exchange.

Hedge Using the futures market to reduce the risks of unforeseen price changes that are inherent in buying and selling cash commodities. For example, as an elevator operator buys cash grain from farmer, he can "hedge" his purchases by selling futures contracts; when he sells the cash commodity, he purchases an offsetting number of futures contracts to liquidate his position. If prices rise while he owns the cash grain, he sells the cash grain at a profit and closes out his futures at a loss, which almost always is no greater than his profit in the cash transaction. If prices fall while he owns the cash grain, he sells the cash grain at a loss but recoups all or almost all of the loss by buying back futures contracts at a price correspondingly lower than at which he first sold them. Some users of commodities assure themselves of supplies of their raw materials at a set price by buying futures, which is another form of hedging. When the time comes to acquire inventories, they can either take delivery on their futures contracts or, more likely, simply buy their supplies in the cash market. Futures-contract prices tend to match cash prices at the time the futures expire, so if cash prices have risen the users' higher costs are offset by profits on their futures contracts.

Hedger The Commodity Futures Trading Commission says a hedger in a general sense is someone who uses futures trading as a temporary, risk-reducing substitute for a cash transaction planned later in his main line of business. All other futures traders are classified as speculators. There are more legally specific definitions of hedging and hedgers in such markets as grains, soybeans, potatoes and cotton, where limits are placed on the number of contracts speculators may trade or own. The Commission has broadened these limits to allow hedging in closely related, rather than exactly matching, commodities. A sorghum producer, for instance, can use corn futures as a hedging tool where he couldn't before this rule-broadening. The more general distinction between hedgers and speculators may be important to potential traders. Some may want to use a market like interest rate futures to offset some expected heavy borrowing. The government hasn't set any speculative trading limits in those markets, but lenders or company directors are more apt to back a plan to trade futures for hedging purposes rather than speculation.

Inverted market A futures market where prices for deferred contracts are lower than those for nearby-delivery contracts because of great near-term demand for the cash commodity. Normally, prices of deferred contracts are higher, in part reflecting storage costs.

Last trading day The day when trading in an expiring contract ceases, and traders must either liquidate their positions or prepare to make or accept delivery of the cash commodity. After that, there is no more futures trading for that particular contract month and year.

Life of contract The period of time during which futures trading in a particular contract month and year may take place. This is usually less than a year, but sometimes up to 18 months.

Limit move The maximum that a futures price can rise or fall from the previous session's settlement price. This limit, set by each exchange, varies from commodity to commodity. Some exchanges have variable limits, whereby the limit is expanded automatically if the market moves by the limit for a certain number of consecutive trading sessions. When prices fail to move the expanded limit, or after a specified period of time, the limits revert to normal.

Liquidation Closing out a previous position by taking an opposite position in the same contract. Thus, a previous buyer liquidates by selling, and a previous seller liquidates by buying.

Long A trader who has bought futures, speculating the prices will rise. He is "long" until he liquidates by selling or fulfills his contracts by making delivery.

Margin The amount of "good faith" money that commodity traders must put in order to trade futures. The margins, set by each exchange, usually amount to 5% to 10% of the total value of the commodity contract. The "initial margin" is the amount of money that must be put up to establish a position in a futures market. Exchanges establish this margin, too, but brokerage firms often require even larger amounts to protect their own financial interests. "Maintenance margin" is the money that traders must put up to retain their position in the futures markets.

Margin call A request by a brokerage firm that a customer put up more money. That means the market price has gone against the customer's position and the brokerage firm wants the customer to cover his paper loss, which would become a real loss if the position were liquidated.

Nearby contracts The futures that expire the soonest. Those that expire later are called deferred contracts.

New crop The supply of a commodity that will be available after harvest. The term also is sometimes used in connection with pigs and hogs because the major farrowing periods in the spring and fall are referred to as "crops." There sometimes are substantial price differences between futures contracts related to new-crop supplies and those related to old-crop supplies.

Nominal price An artificial price—usually the midpoint between a bid and an asked price—that gives an indication of the market price level even though no actual transactions may have taken place at that price.

Old crop The supply from previous harvests.

Open The period each session when futures trading commences. Sometimes the open lasts several minutes to accommodate customers who have placed orders to buy or sell contracts "on the open." On these exchanges, opening prices often are reported by the exchange as a range, although these seldom are widely disseminated because of space restrictions in newspapers and periodicals; they are carried on tickers and display panels during that trading day, however.

Open interest Outstanding futures contracts that haven't been liquidated by purchase or sale of offsetting contracts, or by delivery or acceptance of the physical commodity.

Option The right to buy or sell a futures contract over a specified period of time at a set price.

Overbought A term used to express the opinion that prices have risen too high too fast and so will decline as traders liquidate their positions.

Oversold Like "overbought" except the opinion is that prices have fallen too far too fast and so probably will rebound.

Pit The areas on exchange floors where futures trading takes place. Pits usually have three or more levels and can accommodate a large number of traders. On several New York exchanges the trading areas are called rings and consist of open-center, circular tables around which traders sit or stand.

Position A trader's holdings, either long or short. A position limit is the maximum number of contracts a speculator can hold under law; it doesn't apply to bona-fide hedgers, although there really isn't any objective way of telling whether a person in position to hedge actually is hedging or is speculating instead.

Profit taking A trader holding a long position turns paper profits into real ones by selling his contracts. A trader holding a short position takes profits by buying back contracts.

Reaction A decline in prices following a substantial advance.

Recovery An increase in prices following a substantial decline.

Settlement price The single closing price, determined by each exchange's price committee of directors. It is used primarily by the exchange clearing house to determine the need for margin capital to be put up by brokerage-firm members to protect the net position of that firm's total accounts. It's also issued by some exchanges as the official closing price, and it is used to determine the price limits and net price changes on the following trading day. (See also: *Close*.)

Set-aside Acreage withdrawn from crop production for a season and used for soil conservation under a production-control program. Wheat farmers this year must set aside two acreas of land for each 10 acres they plant to wheat in order to get any federal price support or disaster aid. The Agriculture Department has also said corn, sorghum and barley producers similarly may be required to set aside some of their acreage if it appears that surpluses will grow too much otherwise.

Short A trader who has sold futures, speculating that prices will decline. He is "short" until he liquidates by buying back contracts or fulfills his contracts by taking delivery.

Short squeeze A situation in which "short" futures traders are unable to buy the cash commodity to deliver against their positions and so are forced to buy offsetting futures at prices much higher than they'd ordinarily be willing to pay.

Speculation Buying or selling in hopes of making a profit. The word connotes a high degree of risk.

Spot The same as cash commodities. Literally, delivery "on the spot" rather than in the future.

Spreads and straddles Terms for the simultaneous buying of futures in one delivery month and selling of futures in another delivery month (or even the simultaneous buying of futures in one commodity and selling of futures in a different but related commodity). One purpose is to profit from perceived discrepancies in price relationships. Another purpose is to transfer current trading profits to some future time to avoid immediate tax liability.

Stop-loss order An open order given to a brokerage firm to liquidate a position when the market reaches a certain price so as to prevent losses from mounting or profits from eroding. Sometimes market price trends are accelerated when concentrations of stop-loss orders are touched off.

Support price A level below which the government tries to keep the agricultural-commodity prices that farmers receive from falling. They're set basically by Congress when farm legislation is passed and adjusted from time to time by the President or Agriculture Secretary. Subsidy payments, commodity purchases, production controls or commodity-secured loans are among the devices used to make up the difference when market prices dip below the support level. Futures and cash prices often tend to remain near the support level when there are large crop surpluses because lower prices keep commodities off the market and higher ones quickly draw willing sellers.

Switch A trading maneuver in which a trader liquidates his position in one futures delivery and takes the position in another delivery month in expectation that prices will change more rapidly in the second contract than in the first. Thus, a trader might switch out of a position in an October silver futures contract into a position in a December silver futures contract. Warning: Some people use the word "switch" when they mean "spread" or "straddle." Feel free to correct them.

Technical factors Futures prices often are affected by influences related to the market itself, rather than to supply-demand fundamentals of the commodity with which the market is concerned. For example, if a market moves up or down the limit several days in succession there frequently is a subsequent "technical reaction" caused in part by the liquidation of contracts held by traders on the wrong side of the price move.

Terminal Refers to an elevator or livestock market at key distribution points to which commodities are sent from a wide area.

Trading range The amount that futures prices can fluctuate during one trading session—essentially, the price "distance" between limit up and limit down. If, for instance, the soybean futures price can advance or fall by a maximum of 20 cents per bushel in one day, the trading range is double that, or 40 cents per bushel. In one market, cocoa, price movements are restricted to a daily range of six cents a pound.

Visible supply The amount of a commodity that can be accounted for and computed accurately, usually because it is being kept in major known storage places.

Warehouse or elevator receipt The negotiable slip of paper that a short can hand over to fulfill an expiring futures contract's delivery requirement. The receipt shows how much of the commodity is in storage.

Dow Jones Futures and Spot Commodity Indexes

The method for arriving at the Dow Jones Futures and Spot Commodity Indexes differs from some others in the order in which the computations are made. Instead of first weighting each price, then adding them up and finally calculating the percentage or index, this method first turns each price into an index or percentage of its base-year price, then weights each individual index, and finally adds them up. Stated mathematically, the more usual method calculates the percentage relation of one average to another, while the Dow Jones Commodity Index method calculates the average of a set of percentage changes. These two methods do not result in exactly the same figures. However, they are equally valid when used consistently, and the indexes they produce are of the same general magnitude.

The Dow Jones Commodity Index method has two advantages. One is that it saves computation, because the factors or multipliers perform two computations at once. They calculate the individual percentages and weight

them at one stroke. The other advantage is that if you have yesterday's index, you can apply the multipliers to today's individual price changes. Then all you do is add the resulting figures to yesterday's index, or subtract them from it, depending on whether they're up or down. That gives today's index. No need to recalculate the whole thing each day.

As for the weights, they were obtained by the usual mathematical methods. Basically, the weight of each commodity is the percentage of its commercial production value to the total commercial production value of all commodities in the index, in this case for the years 1927–31. In calculating the weights, consideration also was given to the relation between volume of trading in each commodity and its commercial production.

A further refinement was necessary because price changes of the various commodities are quoted in different units. Grain prices change in eighths of a cent, wool prices change in tenths of a cent, and all the other staples in the Dow Jones index move in hundredths of a cent. This adjustment merely required appropriate treatment in each case of the multiplier, so that it would give the

Source: The *Dow Jones Commodities Handbook*, edited by Dan Ruck, Dow Jones Books, Dow Jones & Company, Inc.

right figure for any price change. In the case of grains it meant an adjustment of 20%, since one-tenth is that much smaller than one-eighth. In other cases a mere adjustment of decimal points was sufficient.

The twelve commodities, with the weight of each and the multiplier applied to the price changes of each, are:

	Weight	Multiplier
Wheat	19.5	16
Corn	8	11
Oats	5	13
Rye	4	5
Wool Tops	5.5	4
Cotton	23	10
Cottonseed Oil	4.5	4
Coffee	7	3
Sugar	8.5	27
Cocoa	5	5
Rubber	6	3
Hides	4	3

These are the essentials for calculating the spot index. However, the futures index requires one more set of unusual steps. That's because several times a year an actual quoted "future" disappears. For instance, while early in the year it is possible to buy wheat to be delivered in December, when the month of December actually arrives that "delivery" expires and is no longer quoted.

The result is that futures prices are affected not only by market conditions but also by how close the delivery date looms. Interest charges and other such factors influence them. On July 1, the December delivery is just five months off, but a month later it is only four months away, and a five-month delivery should not, in a precise index, be compared with a four-month delivery.

This problem is overcome by the use of two futures quotations for each commodity. They are combined to produce on each mar-

ket day the calculated price that would apply to a delivery exactly five months off.

On the first day of July, only the December delivery is used, since it is just five months away and thus no adjustment need be made. On the second day, the two quotations used are those for the same December delivery and the one for May of the following year. The quoted price for December is adjusted by one day's proportion of the difference between it and May's quoted price. Since there are 151 days between December and May (except in leap years) the figure for one day's proportion is 1/151 of the price difference between the two. The resulting fraction is added to December's price, or subtracted from it, depending on whether May is quoted above or below December.

The following day 2/151 of the difference are added or subtracted, the third day 3/151 and so on until December 1, on which day only the May contract's price is used. On December 2, the combination used is May and July, and so on around the year.

To facilitate the work of calculating the futures index every hour of each business day and the spot index once a day, tables have been prepared—resembling somewhat tables of logarithms or bond yields—which give the figures arrived at by multiplying the various quotational units of each commodity by its factor or multiplier. For instance, the tables show the proper multiples for one-eighth, one-quarter, three-eighths, etc., when each is multiplied by each grain's factor or multiplier.

The commodity futures index is published once an hour and as of the close of commodity markets each day on the Dow Jones News Service, where also the spot index is published once daily. Both are published likewise in *The Wall Street Journal* (see page 519).

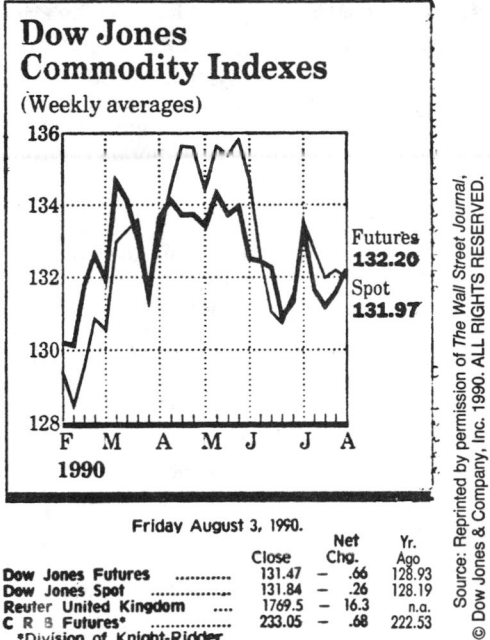

Dow Jones Commodity Indexes
(Weekly averages)

Futures **132.20**
Spot **131.97**

F M A M J J A
1990

Friday August 3, 1990.

		Close	Net Chg.	Yr. Ago
Dow Jones Futures	....	131.47	− .66	128.93
Dow Jones Spot	....	131.84	− .26	128.19
Reuter United Kingdom	....	1769.5	− 16.3	n.a.
C R B Futures*	....	233.05	− .68	222.53

*Division of Knight-Ridder.

Actively Traded Futures and Option Contracts by Exchange[1]

Chicago Board of Trade (CBT)
Futures Contracts Actively Traded

Wheat (5,000 bu)
Corn (5,000 bu)
Soybeans (5,000 bu)
Soybean Oil
Soybean Meal
Silver (1,000 oz)
Silver (5,000 oz)
Gold (kilo)
Gold (100 oz)
GNMA Mrtges, CDR
Corporate Bond Index
T-Bonds
T-Notes (6½-10 yr)
T-Notes (5 yr)
Municipal Bond Index
MMI Maxi
Institutional Index

Option Contracts Actively Traded

T-Bonds
T-Notes
Soybeans
Soybean Oil
Soybean Meal
Corn

Wheat
Silver
Muni Bonds

MidAmerica Commodity Exchange
Futures Contracts Actively Traded

Wheat (1,000 bu)
Corn (1,000 bu)
Oats (1,000 bu)
Soybeans (1,000 bu)
Soybean Meal
Live Cattle (20,000#)
Live Hogs (15,000#)
New York Silver
New York Gold
Platinum
Copper
T-Bonds ($50,000)
T-Bills ($500,000)
British Pound
Swiss Franc
Deutsche Mark
Japanese Yen
Canadian Dollar

Option Contracts Actively Traded

Gold
Soft Red Winter Wheat
Soybeans

---

[1] Addresses of the Exchanges are given on page 521.

Source: *Basic Facts About Commodity Futures Trading*, Commodity Futures Trading Commission.

Chicago Mercantile Exchange (CME)
Futures Contracts Actively Traded

Live Hogs (30,000#)
Pork Bellies (fzn)
Live Cattle (40,000#)
Feeder Cattle
Gold (100 oz)
T-Bills (90-day)
Domestic CD (90-day)
Eurodollar (3-month)
European Currency Unit
British Pound
Canadian Dollar
Deutsche Mark
Japanese Yen
Swiss Franc
French Franc
Australian Dollar
S&P 500 Index
Lumber

Option Contracts Actively Traded

Live Hogs
Live Cattle
Pork Bellies
Feeder Cattle
Lumber
Eurodollar
British Pound
Deutsche Mark
Swiss Franc
Japanese Yen
Canadian Dollar
Australian Dollar
T-Bill
S&P 500 Index

Minneapolis Grain Exchange (MGE)
Futures Contracts Actively Traded

High Fructose Corn Syrup
Oats (5,000 bu)
Wheat (5,000 bu)
White Wheat (5,000 bu)

Option Contracts Actively Traded

Spring Wheat

Commodity Exchange, Inc. (Comex)
Futures Contract Actively Traded

Copper
High Grade Copper
Silver (5,000 oz)
Gold (100 oz)
Aluminum
Moody's Index

Option Contracts Actively Traded

Gold
Silver
High Grade Copper
Copper

Kansas City Board of Trade (KCBT)
Futures Contracts Actively Traded

Wheat (5,000 bu)
Value Line Index
Mini Value Line

Option Contracts Actively Traded

Wheat

Coffee, Sugar & Cocoa Exchange
Futures Contracts Actively Traded

Coffee "C"
Sugar #11
Sugar #14
White Sugar
Cocoa (10 M tons)
CPI-W

Option Contracts Actively Traded

Sugar
Coffee
Cocoa

New York Mercantile Exchange
Futures Contracts Actively Traded

Palladium
Platinum
No. 2 Heating Oil, NY
Unleaded Reg. Gas., NY
Crude Oil
Propane

Option Contracts Actively Traded

Heating Oil
Crude Oil

Chicago Rice and Cotton Exchange (CRCE)
Futures Contracts Actively Traded

Rough Rice
Gold

Philadelphia Board of Trade (PHBT)
Futures Contracts Actively Traded

Swiss Franc
Deutsche Mark
Pound Sterling
Japanese Yen
Canadian Dollar
Australian Dollar
Stock Index, Inc.

Commodity Futures Trading Commission (CFTC)

Federal laws regulating commodity futures trading are enforced by the Commodity Futures Trading Commission. For information on commodity brokers call (202) 254-8630.

Source: U.S. Government Manual and the CFTC.

National Office

Commodity Futures Trading Commission
2033 K Street, NW
Washington, DC 20581
Telephone: (202) 254-6387
Public Information: 8630

Regional Offices

Eastern Region
1 World Trade Center
New York, NY 10048
Telephone: (212) 466-2061

Central Region
233 S. Wacker Drive
Chicago, IL 60606
Telephone: (312) 353-5990

Southwestern Region
4901 Main Street
Kansas City, MO 64112
Telephone: (816) 374-2994

Minneapolis Office
510 Grain Exchange Building
Minneapolis, MN 55415
Telephone: (612) 349-3255

Western Region
10880 Wilshire Boulevard
Los Angeles, CA 90024
Telephone: (213) 209-6783

The Commodity Futures Trading Commission (CFTC), the Federal regulatory agency for futures trading, was established by the Commodity Futures Trading Commission Act of 1974 (88 Stat. 1389; 7 U.S.C. 4a), approved October 23, 1974. The Commission began operation in April 1975, and its authority to regulate futures trading was renewed by Congress in 1978 and in 1982.

The CFTC consists of five Commissioners who are appointed by the President with the advice and consent of the Senate. One Commissioner is designated by the President to serve as Chairman. The Commissioners serve staggered 5-year terms, and by law no more than three Commissioners can belong to the same political party.

FUNCTIONS AND ACTIVITIES

The Commission consists of five major operating components: the divisions of enforcement, economics and education, trading and markets, and the offices of the executive director and the general counsel.

The Commission regulates trading on the 11 U.S. futures exchanges, which offer active futures and options contracts. It also regulates the activities of numerous commodity exchange members, public brokerage houses (futures Commission merchants), Commission-registered futures industry salespeople and associated persons, trading advisers, and commodity pool operators. Some off-exchange transactions involving instruments similar in nature to futures contracts also fall under CFTC jurisdiction.

The Commission's regulatory and enforcement efforts are designed to ensure that the futures trading process is fair and that it protects both the rights of customers and the financial integrity of the marketplace. The CFTC approves the rules under which an exchange proposes to operate and monitors exchange enforcement of those rules. It reviews the terms of proposed futures contracts, and registers companies and individuals who handle customer funds or give trading advice. The Commission also protects the public by enforcing rules that require that customer funds be kept in bank accounts separate from accounts maintained by firms for their own use, and that such customer accounts be marked to present market value at the close of trading each day.

Futures contracts for agricultural commodities were traded in the United States for more than 100 years before futures trading was diversified to include trading in contracts for precious metals, raw materials, foreign currencies, commercial interest rates, and U.S. Government and mortgage securities. Contract diversification has grown in exchange trading volume, a growth not limited to the newer commodities.

Futures and Options Exchanges: Addresses

UNITED STATES

American Stock Exchange (AMEX)
86 Trinity Place
New York, NY 10006
(212) 306-1000

Chicago Board of Trade (CBT)
141 West Jackson Boulevard
Chicago, IL 60604
(312) 435-3500

Chicago Board Options Exchange (CBOE)
400 South LaSalle
Chicago, IL 60605
(312) 786-5600

Chicago Mercantile Exchange (CME) and International Monetary Market (IMM)
30 South Wacker Drive
Chicago, IL 60606
(312) 930-1000

Chicago Rice & Cotton Exchange (CRCE)
141 W. Jackson Boulevard
Chicago, IL 60604
(312) 341-3078

Coffee, Sugar & Cocoa Exchange (CSCE)
4 World Trade Center
New York, NY 10048
(212) 938-2800

Commodity Exchange, Inc. (COMEX)
4 World Trade Center
New York, NY 10048
(212) 938-2900

International Monetary Market [IMM] (see Chicago Merchantile Exchange [CME]

Kansas City Board of Trade (KCBT)
4800 Main Street
Kansas City, MO 64112
(816) 753-7500
(816) 753-1101 (hotline)

Midamerica Commodity Exchange (MCE)
141 West Jackson Boulevard
Chicago, IL 60604
(312) 341-3000

Minneapolis Grain Exchange (MGE)
400 S. Fourth Street
Minneapolis, MN 55415
(612) 338-6212

New York Cotton Exchange & Associates (NYCE)
4 World Trade Center
New York, NY 10048
(212) 938-2650

New York Futures Exchange (NYFE)
20 Broad Street
New York, NY 10005
(212) 623-4949
(800) 221-7722

New York Mercantile Exchange (NYME)
4 World Trade Center
New York, NY 10048
(212) 938-2222

New York Stock Exchange
11 Wall St.
New York, NY 10005
(212) 656-3000
(800) 692-6973 (Out-of-State)

Pacific Stock Exchange
301 Pine St.
San Francisco, CA 94104
(415) 393-4000

Philadelphia Board of Trade
1900 Market St.
Philadelphia, PA 19103
(215) 496-5555

Philadelphia Stock Exchange
1900 Market St.
Philadelphia, PA 19103
(215) 496-5000

Twin Cities Board of Trade
5353 Wayzata Boulevard
Minneapolis, MN 55416
(612) 333-6742

CANADIAN

Montreal Stock Exchange
800 Victoria Square
Montreal, Quebec, Canada H4Z 1A9
(514) 871-2424

Toronto Futures Exchange
2 First Canadian Place
Exchange Tower
Toronto, Ontario, Canada M5X 1J2
(416) 947-4700
(416) 947-4585

Toronto Stock Exchange
2 First Canadian Place
Exchange Tower
Toronto, Ontario, Canada M5X 1J2
(416) 947-4700

Vancouver Stock Exchange
609 Granville
Vancouver, British Columbia
Canada V7Y 1H1
(604) 689-3334

The Winnipeg Commodity Exchange
500 Commodity Exchange Tower
360 Main Street
Winnipeg, Manitoba
Canada R3C 3Z4
(204) 949-0495

SELECTED FOREIGN EXCHANGES

London Commodity Exchange Co. Ltd.
Cereal House, 58 Mark Lane
London, England EC3R 7NE
01-481-2080

The London International Financial Futures Exchange Ltd. (LIFFE)
Royal Exchange
London, England EC3
   01-623-0444

The Hong Kong Futures Exchange Ltd.
Hutchison House, Second Floor
Harcourt Road
Hong Kong
   5-251005

European Options Exchange (EOE)
DAM 21
1012 JS Amsterdam
The Netherlands
   20-26 27 21

Paris Commodity Exchange
Bourse de Commerce
2, rue de Viarmes B.P. 53/01
75040 Paris, Cedex 01 France
1-508-82-50
   (212) 751-9050-New York

The Singapore International Monetary Exchange Ltd.
24 Raffles Place
29-04 Clifford Centre
Singapore 0104

Sydney Futures Exchange Ltd.
13-15 O'Connell St.
Sydney, NSW, Australia 2000
   02-233-7633

Tokyo Stock Exchange
2-1 Nihombashi-Kabuto-cho
Chuo-ku, Tokyo, Japan 103

Tokyo Commodity Exchange for Industry
10-8 Nihonbashi Horidomeche
1 Chome
Chuo-ku, Tokyo, Japan

Futures and Securities Organizations

Futures Industry Association, Inc. (FIA)
1825 I Street, NW
Washington, DC 20006
   (202) 466–5460

National Association of Futures Trading Advisors (NAFTA)
111 East Wacker Drive
Chicago, IL 60601
   (312) 644–6610

National Association of Securities Dealers (NASD)
1735 K Street, NW
Washington, DC 20006
   (202) 728-8233

National Futures Association (NFA)
200 West Madison Street
Chicago, IL 60606
   (312) 781–1300
   (800) 572-9400
   (800) 621-3570

North American Securities Administrators Association, Inc. (NASAA)
425 13th Street, NW
Washington, DC 20004
   (202) 783-2303

FOREIGN

England
Association of Futures Dealers and Brokers (AFBD)
Plantation House
4-16 Mincing Lane
London, England EC 3M 3DX

Association for Futures Investment (AFI)
Sugar Quay
Lower Thames Street
London England EC 3R 6 DU

Japan
Security Dealers Association of Japan
1-5-8 Kayaba-cho
Nihombashi, Chuo-ku
Tokyo, 103 Japan

Switzerland
Swiss Commodities, Futures and Options Association
P.O. Box 260
1 Carrefour de Rive
1211 Geneva 3, Switzerland

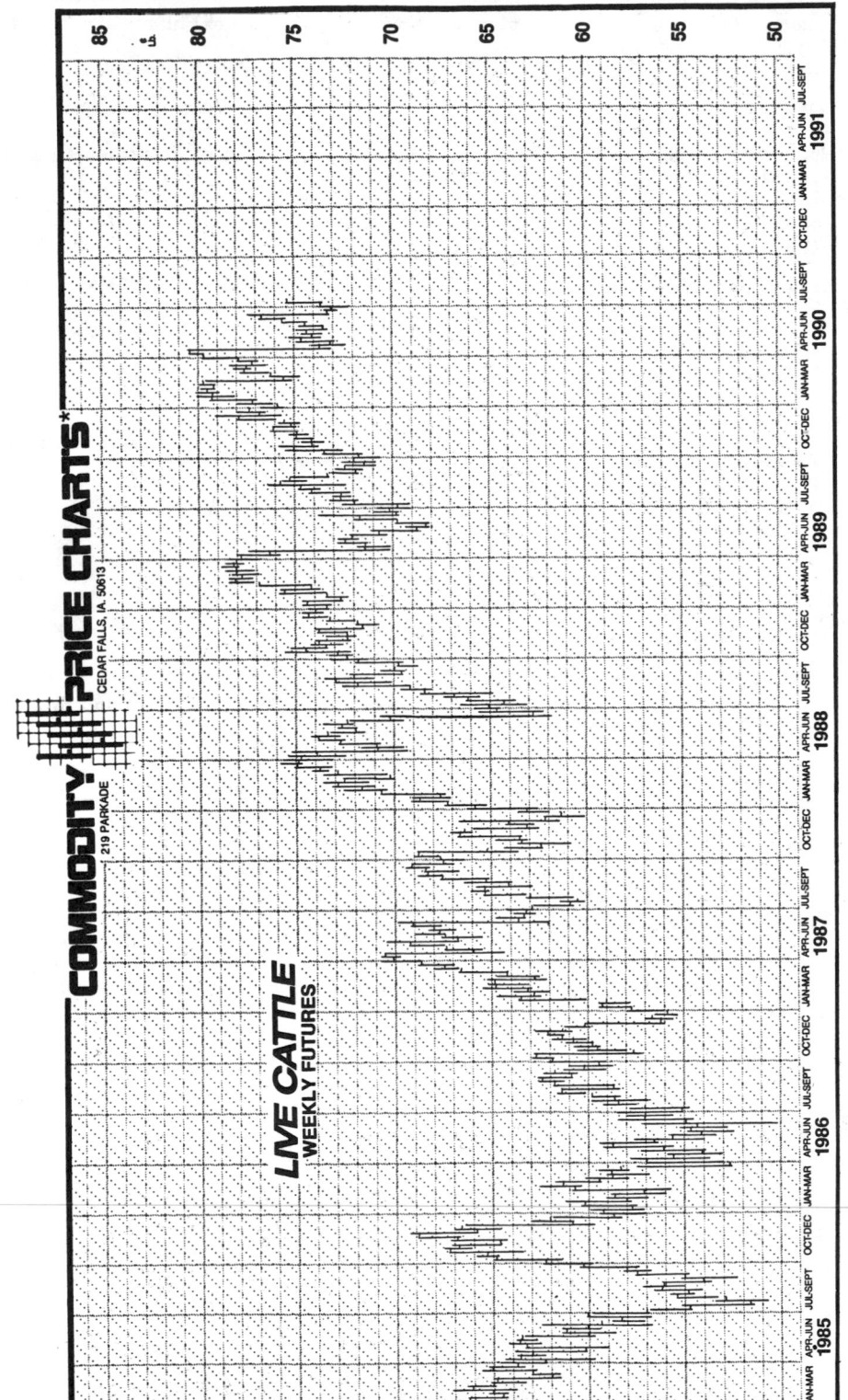

LIVE CATTLE
WEEKLY FUTURES

COMMODITY PRICE CHARTS*
219 PARKADE · CEDAR FALLS, IA. 50613

Source: Reprinted from *Commodity Price Charts*, 219 Parkade, Cedar Falls, Iowa 50613.
* See page 570 for data used in plotting.

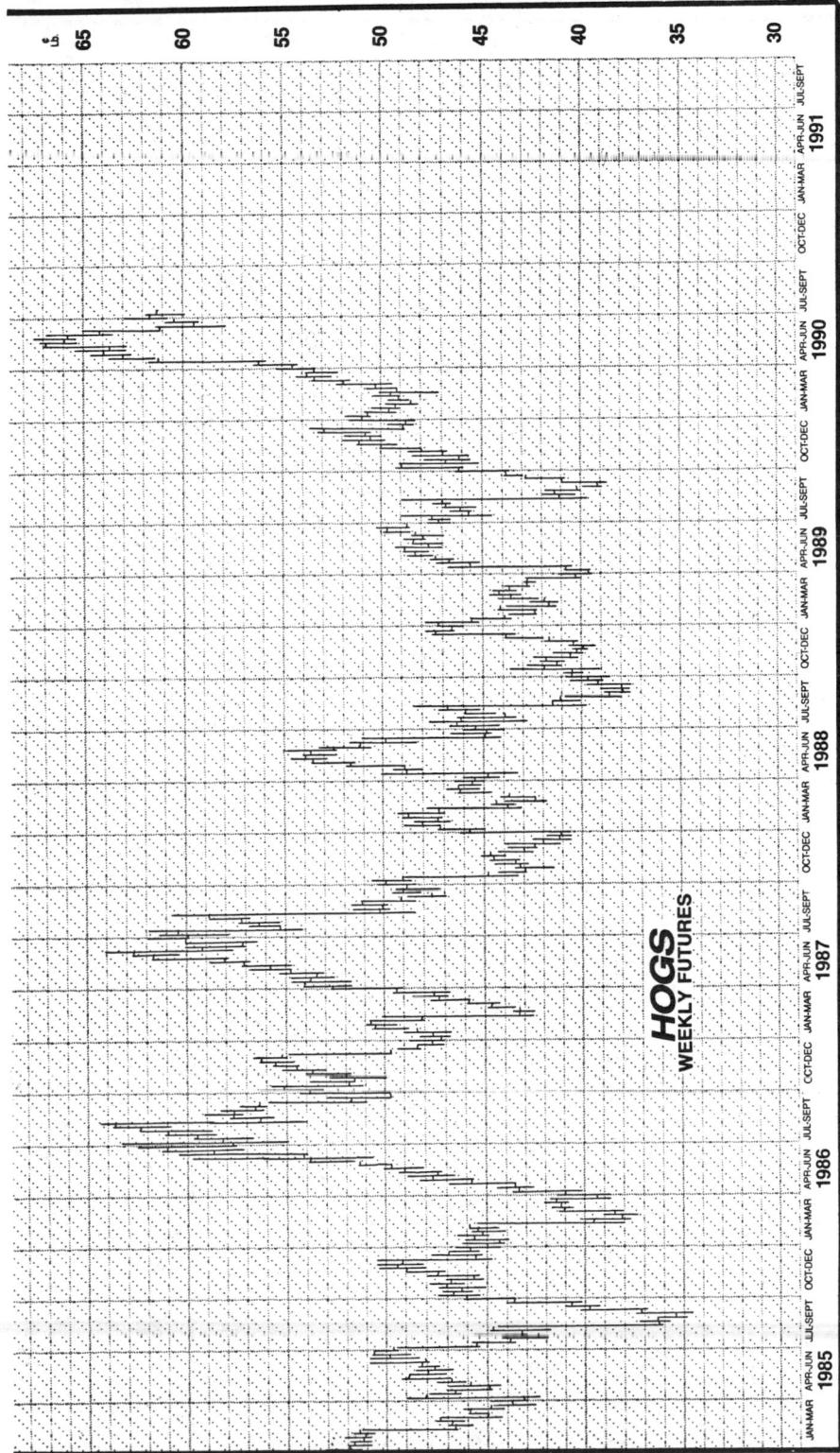

HOGS
WEEKLY FUTURES

Source: Reprinted from *Commodity Price Charts*, 219 Parkade, Cedar Falls, Iowa 50613.

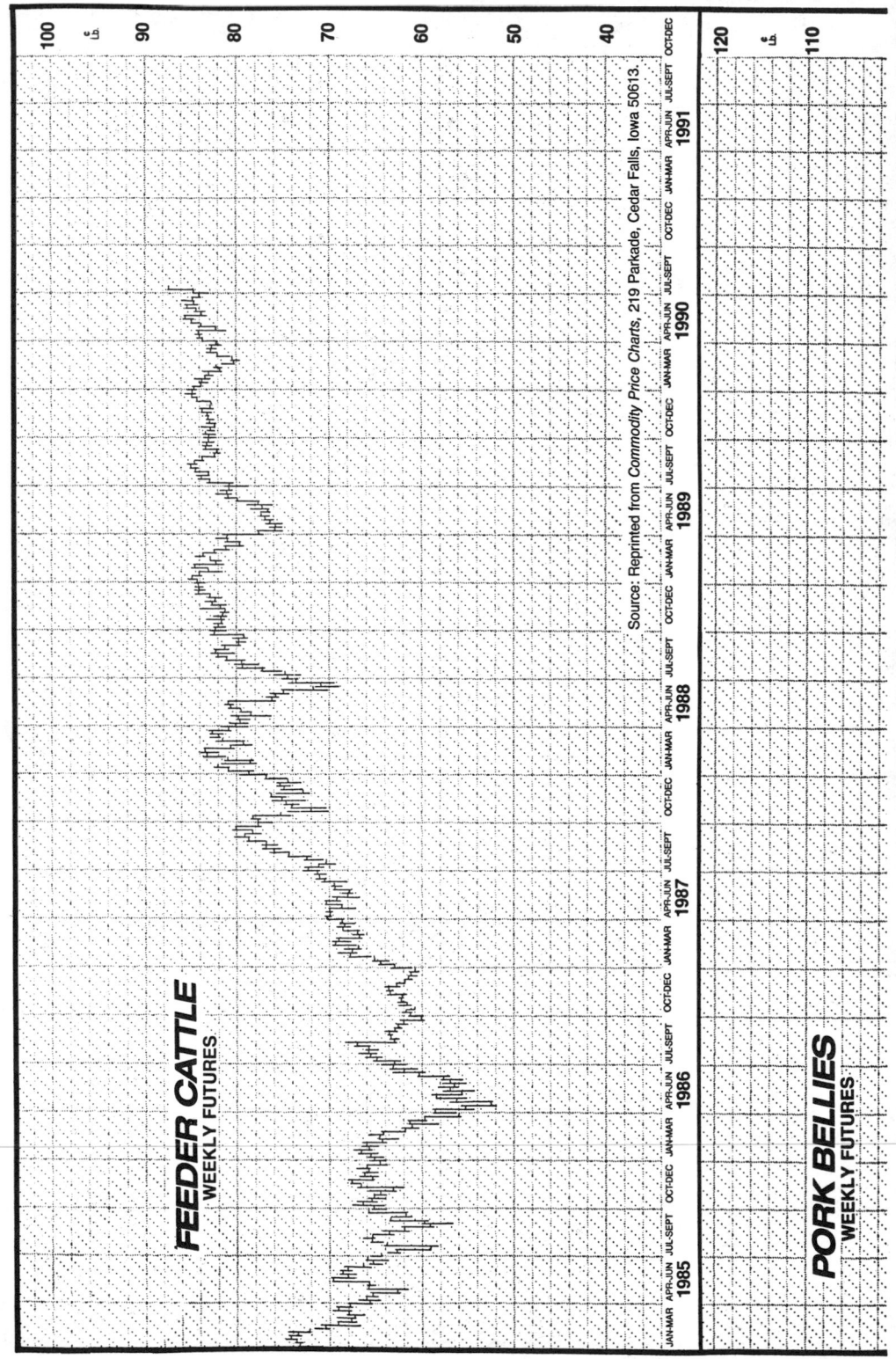

FEEDER CATTLE
WEEKLY FUTURES

PORK BELLIES
WEEKLY FUTURES

Source: Reprinted from Commodity Price Charts, 219 Parkade, Cedar Falls, Iowa 50613.

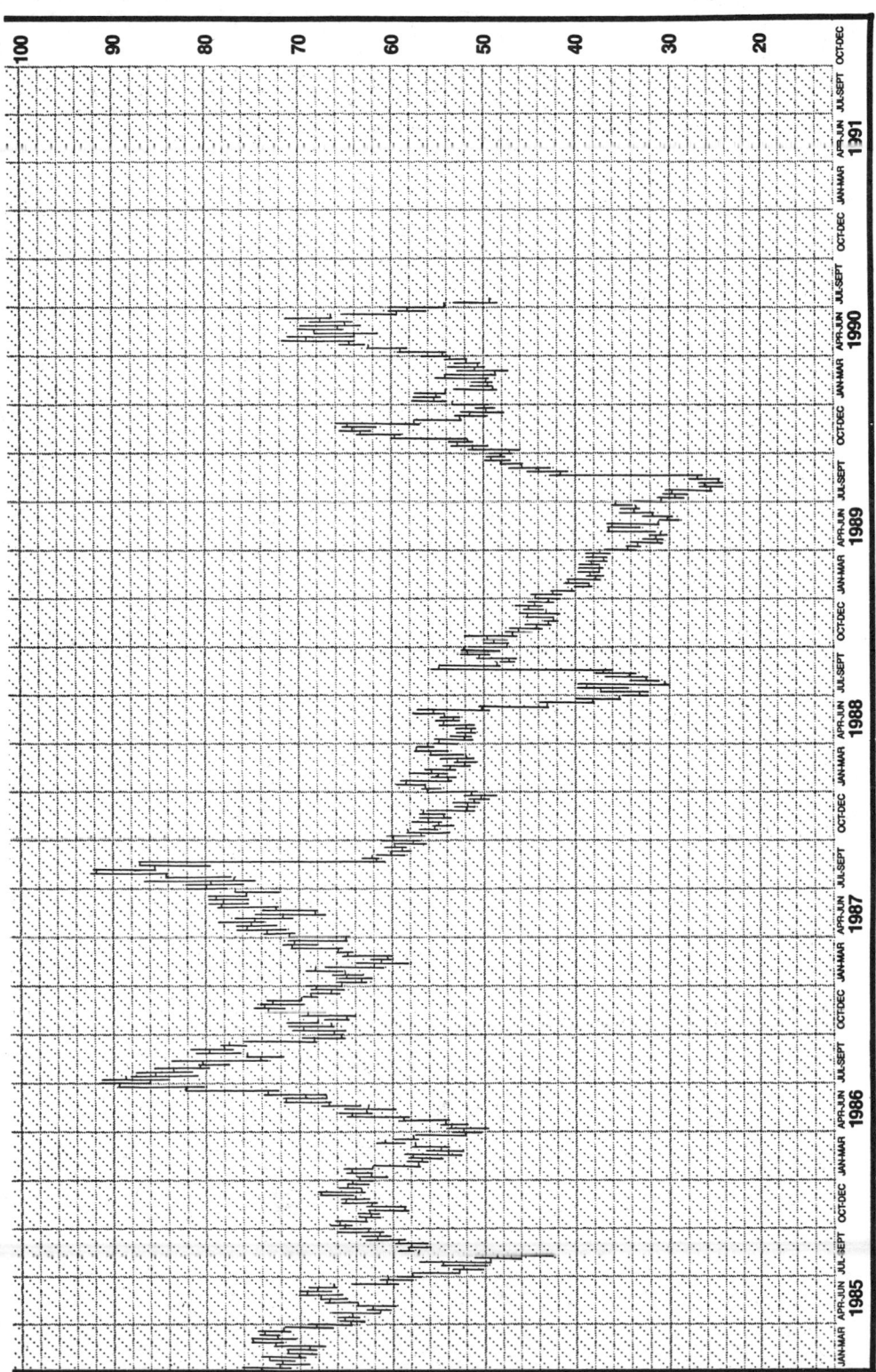

Source: Reprinted from *Commodity Price Charts*, 219 Parkade, Cedar Falls, Iowa 50613.

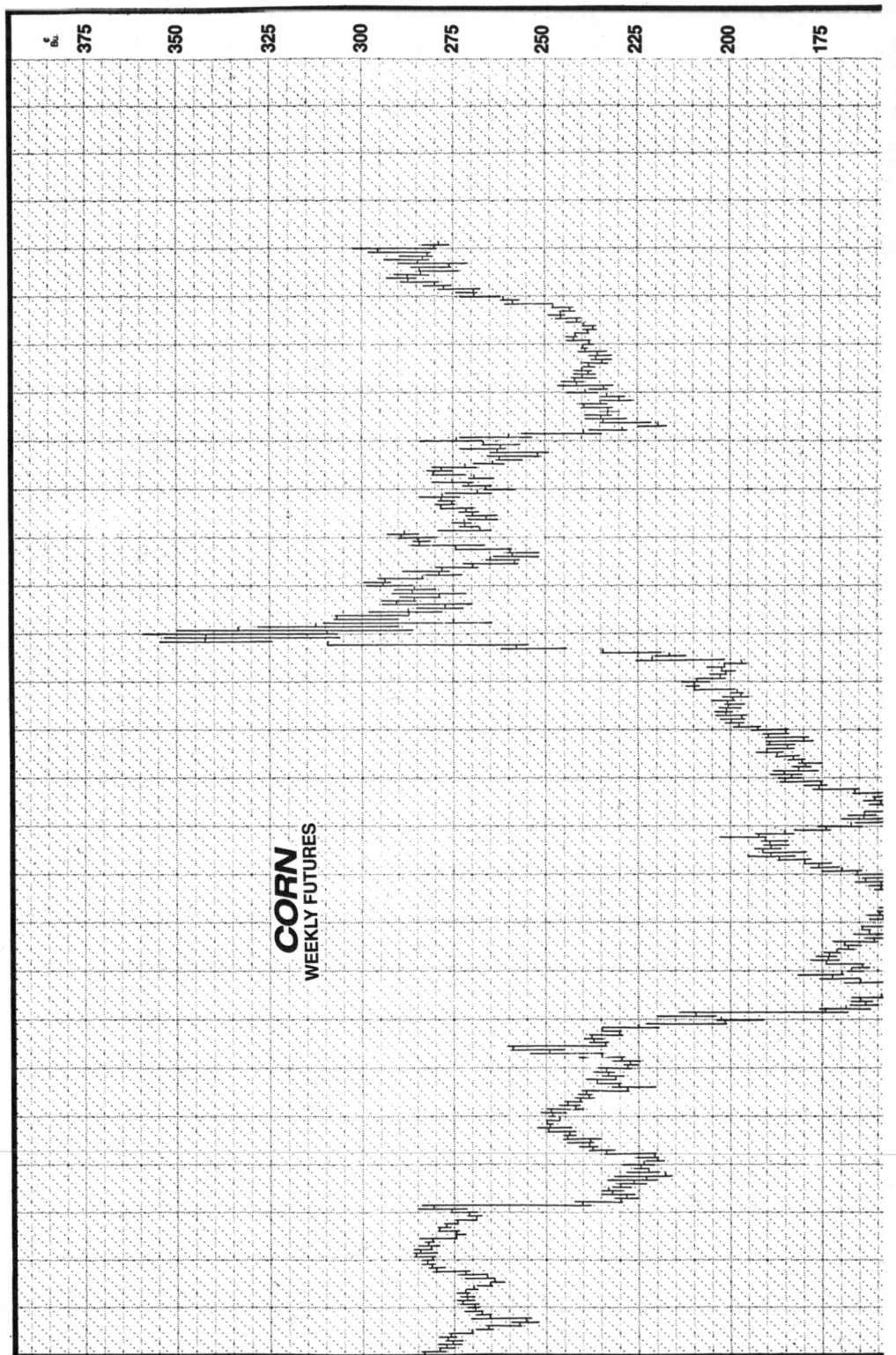

CORN
WEEKLY FUTURES

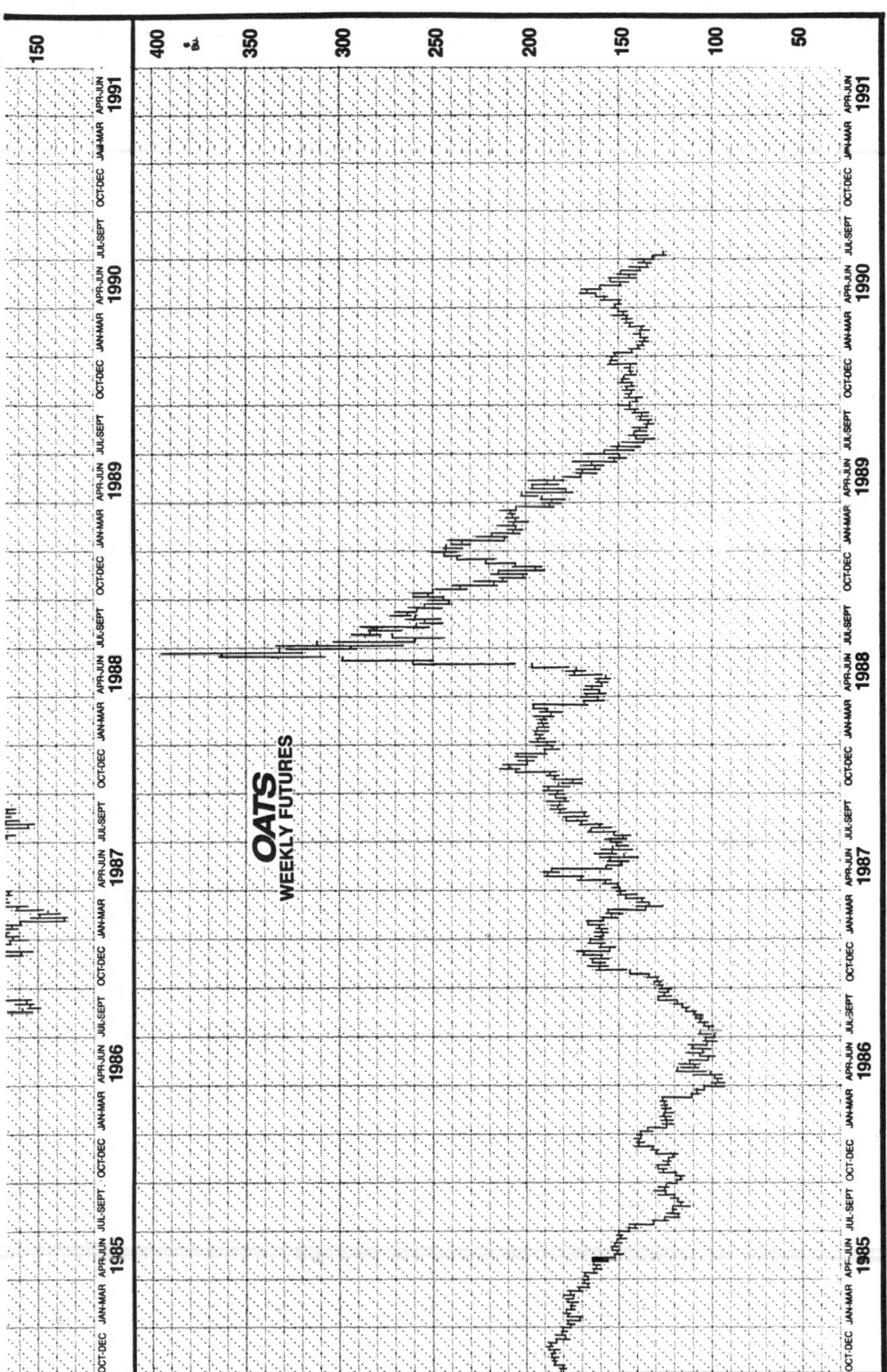

OATS
WEEKLY FUTURES

Source: Reprinted from *Commodity Price Charts*, 219 Parkade, Cedar Falls, Iowa 50613.

¢ Bu.	1300	1250	1200	1150	1100	1050	1000	950	900

SOYBEANS
WEEKLY FUTURES

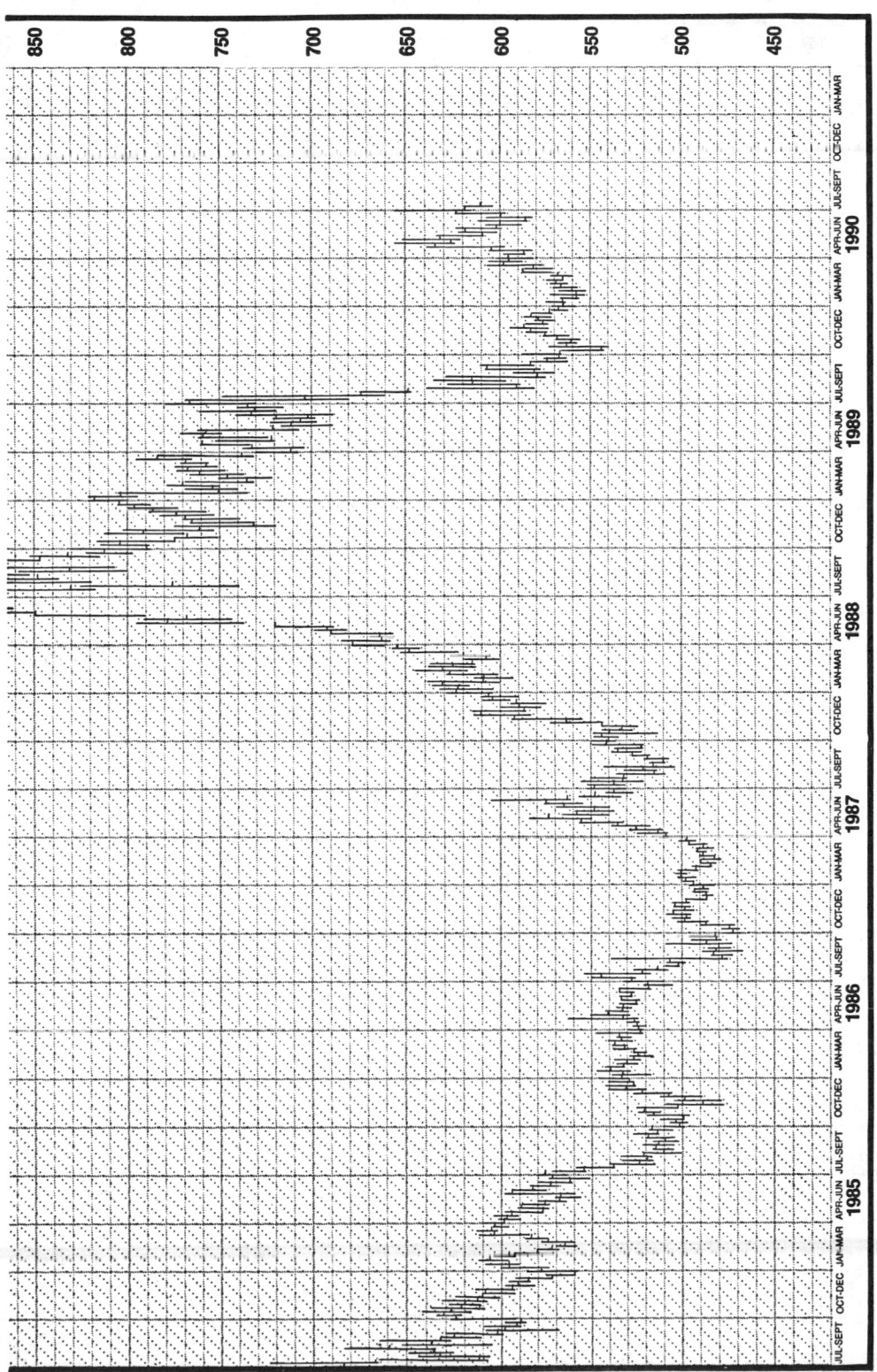

Source: Reprinted from *Commodity Price Charts*, 219 Parkade, Cedar Falls, Iowa 50613.

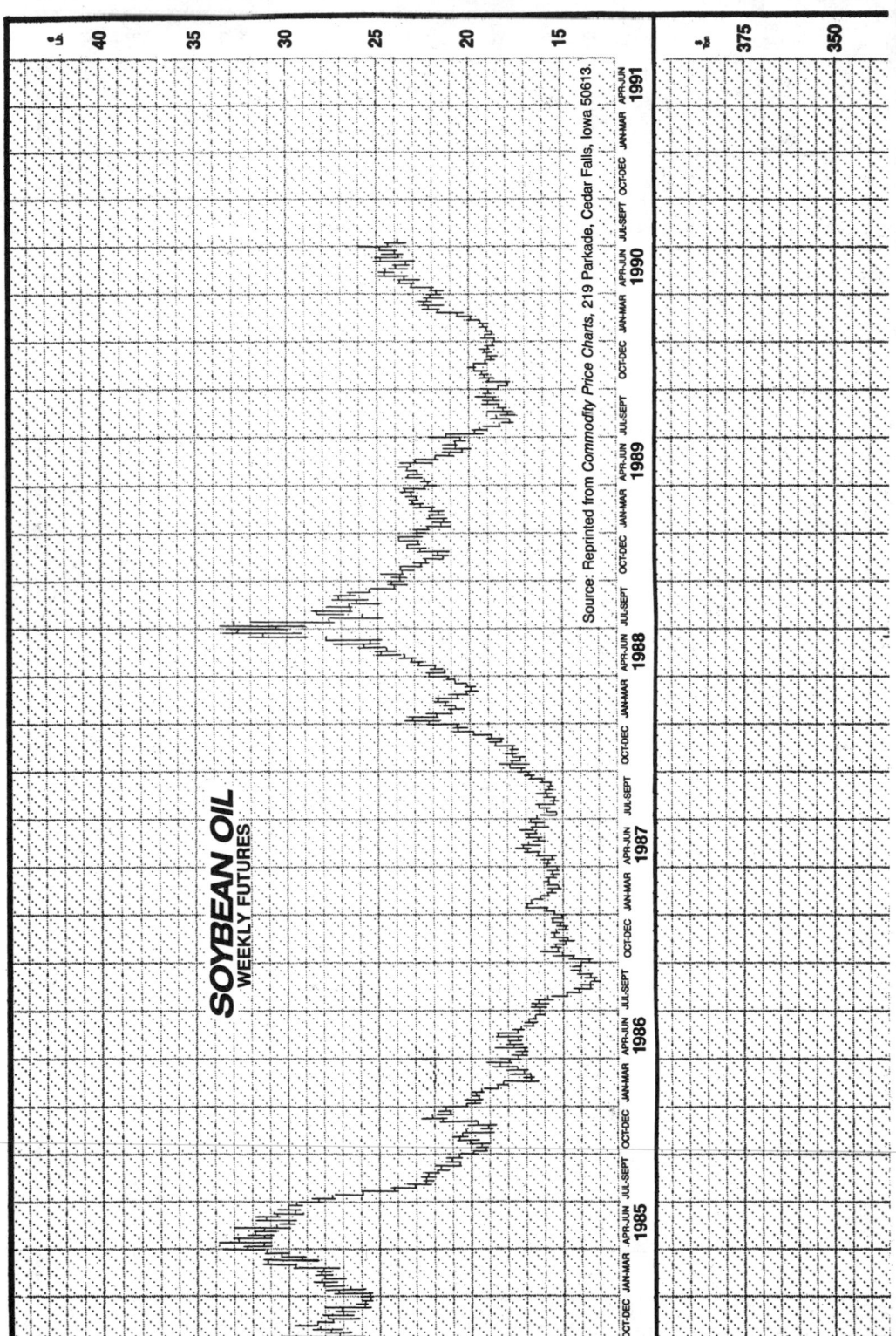

SOYBEAN OIL
WEEKLY FUTURES

Source: Reprinted from *Commodity Price Charts*, 219 Parkade, Cedar Falls, Iowa 50613.

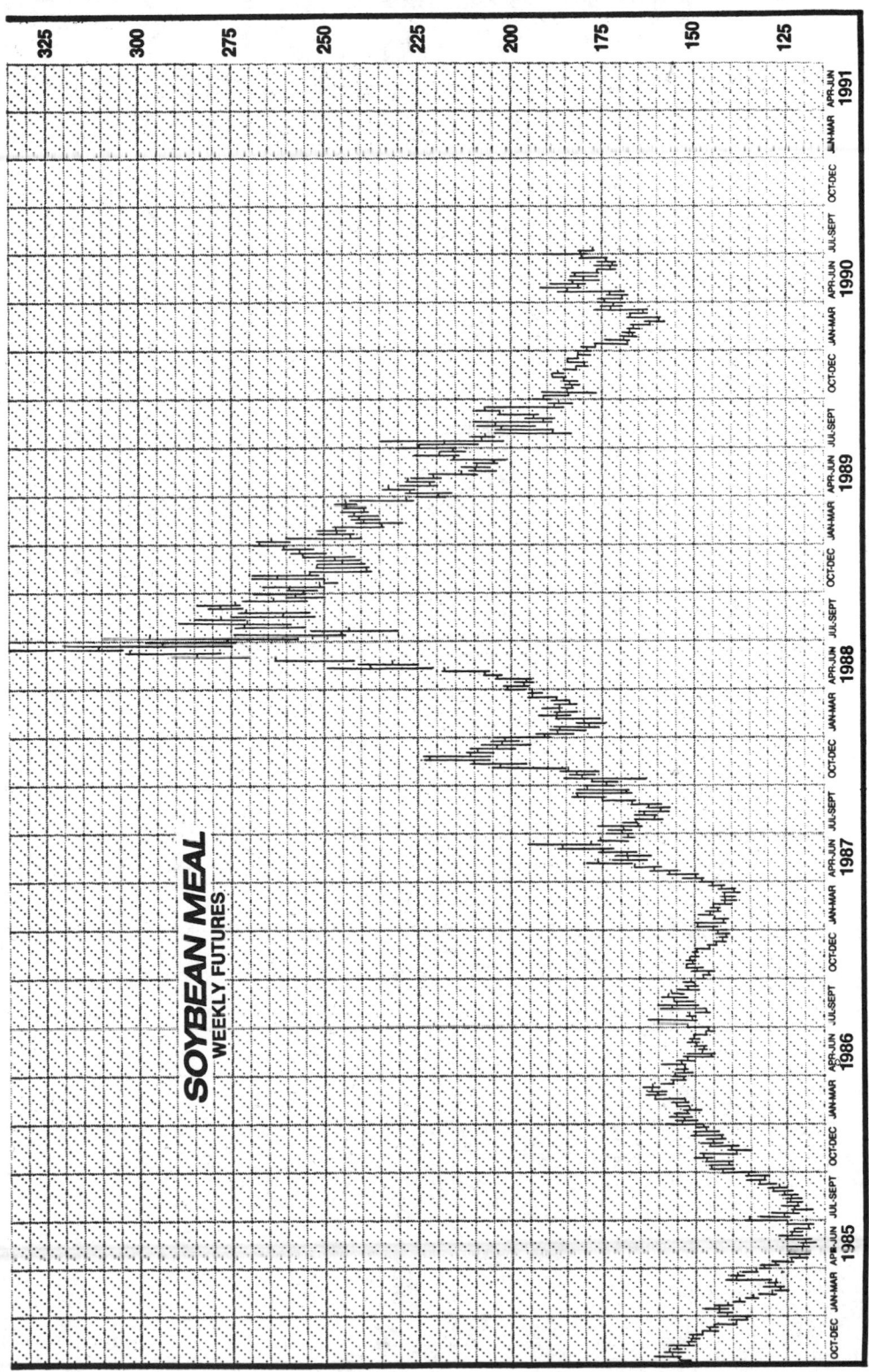

SOYBEAN MEAL
WEEKLY FUTURES

Source: Reprinted from *Commodity Price Charts*, 219 Parkade, Cedar Falls, Iowa 50613.

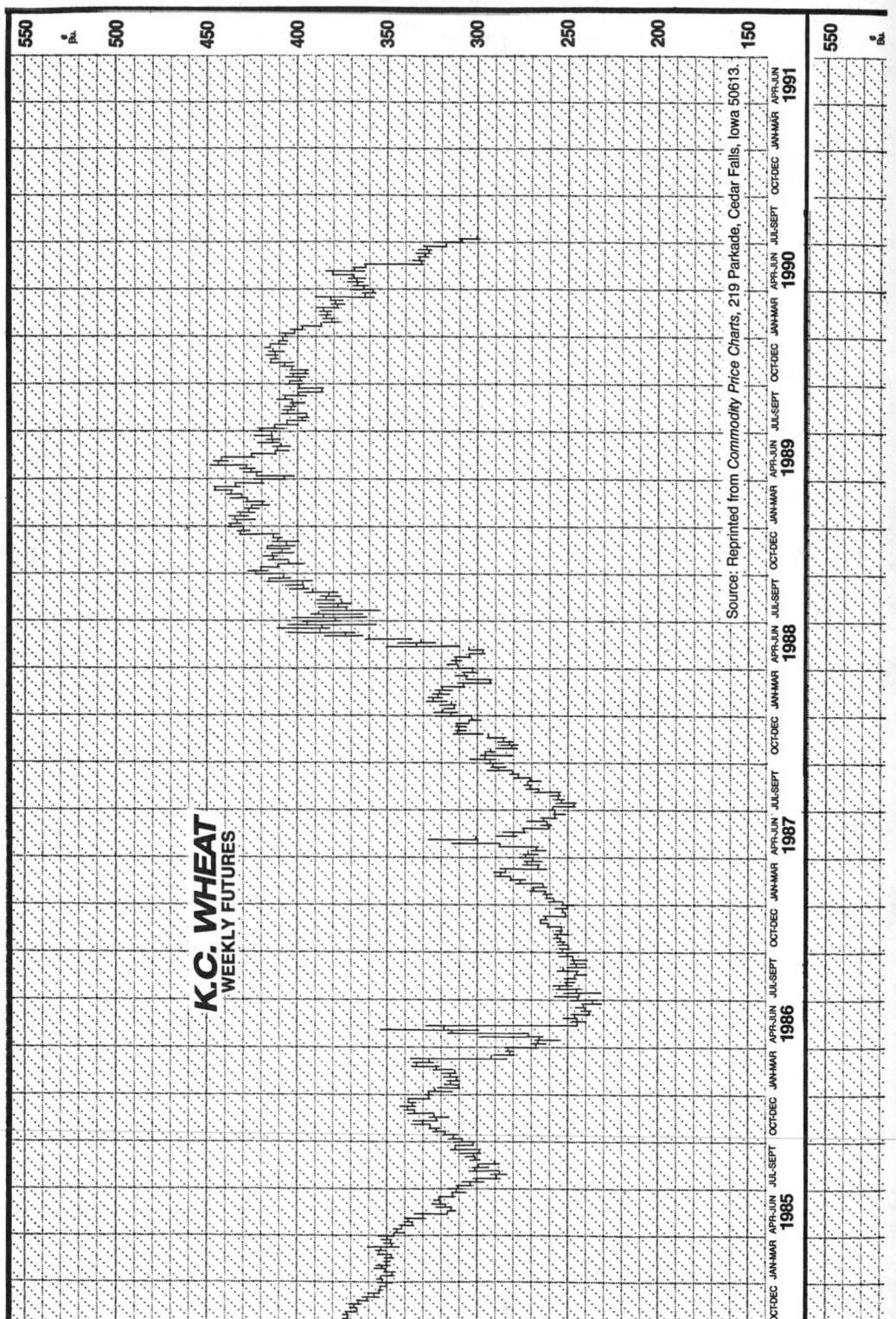

K.C. WHEAT
WEEKLY FUTURES

Source: Reprinted from *Commodity Price Charts*, 219 Parkade, Cedar Falls, Iowa 50613.

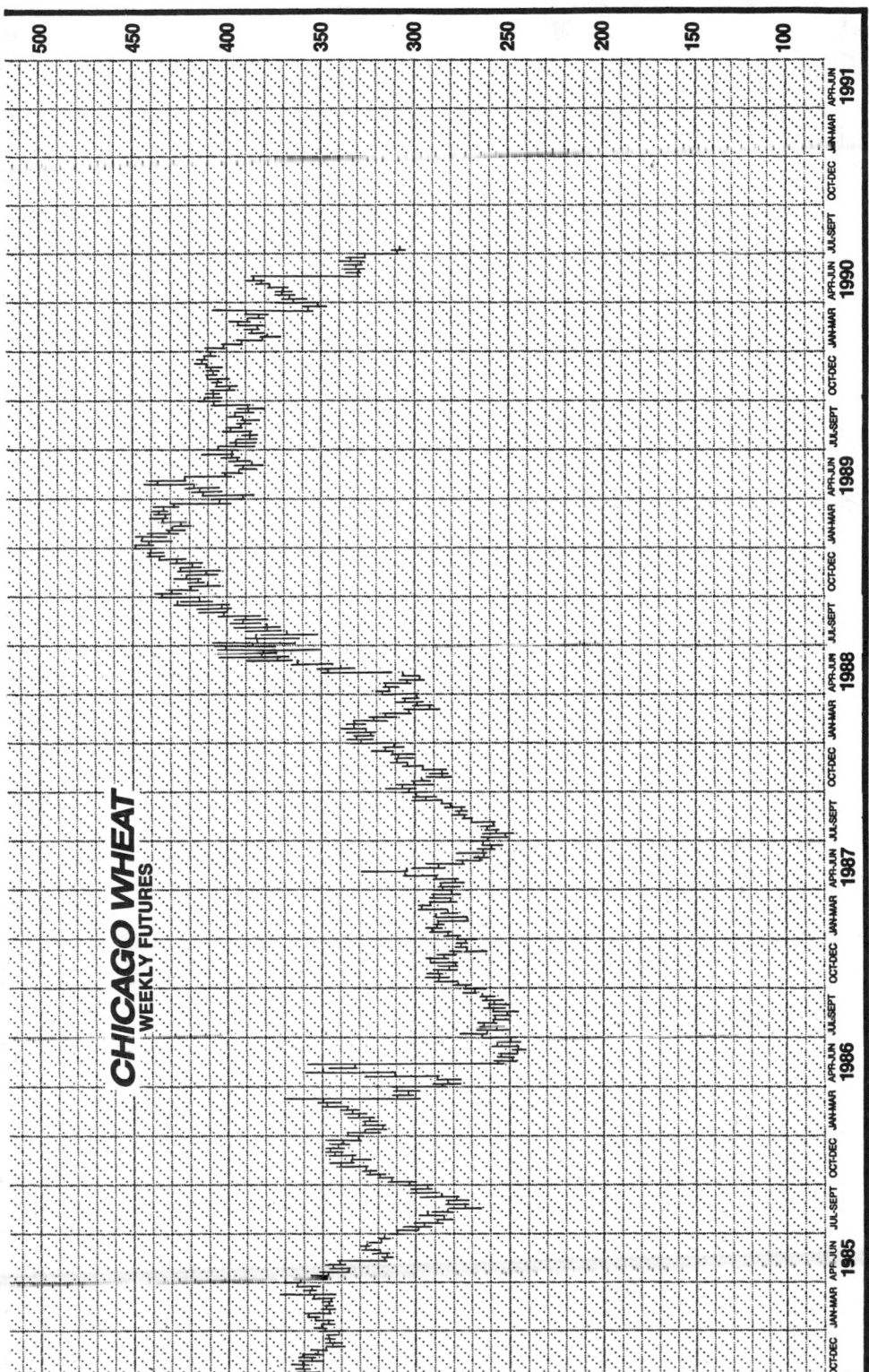

CHICAGO WHEAT
WEEKLY FUTURES

Source: Reprinted from *Commodity Price Charts*, 219 Parkade, Cedar Falls, Iowa 50613.

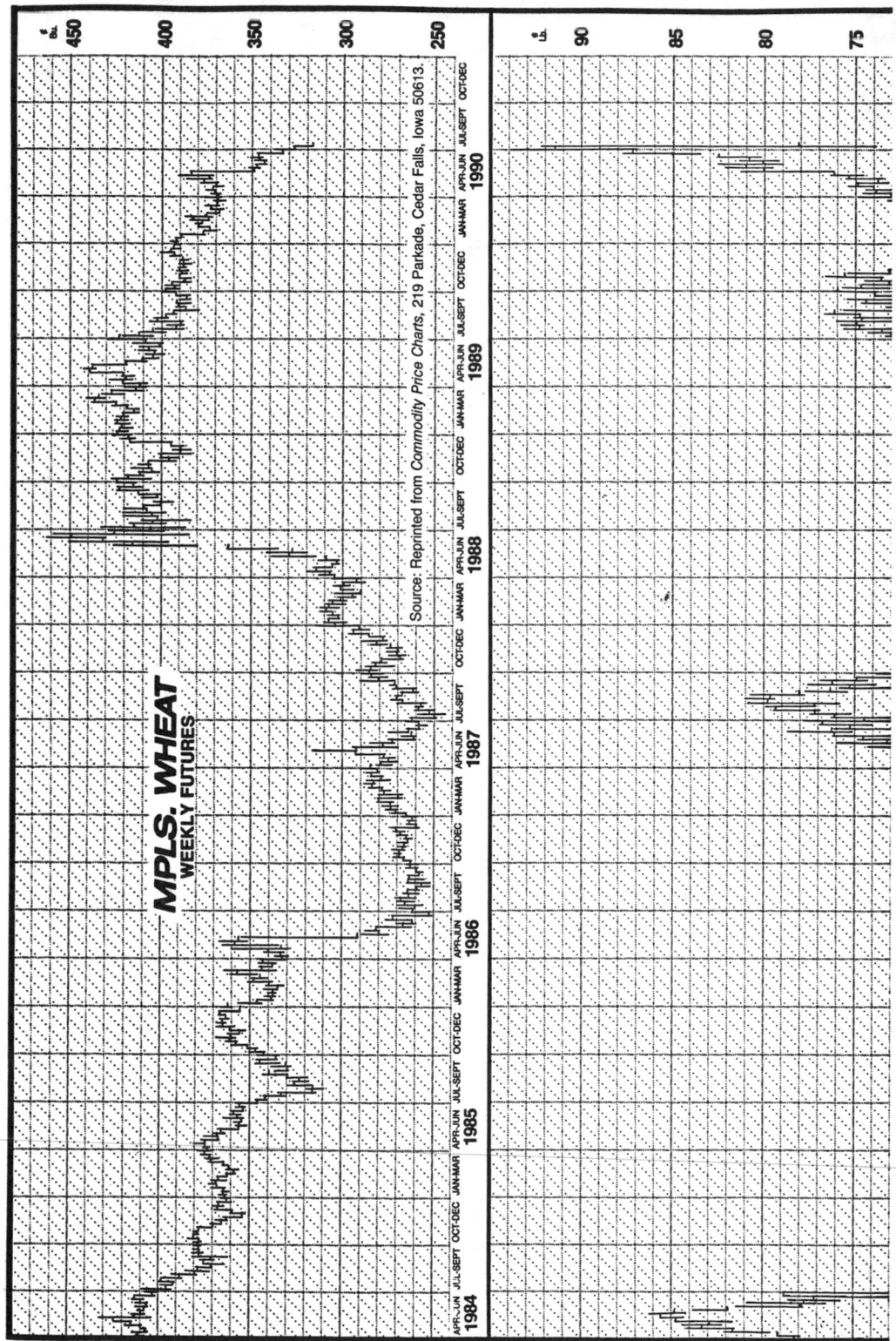

MPLS. WHEAT
WEEKLY FUTURES

Source: Reprinted from *Commodity Price Charts*, 219 Parkade, Cedar Falls, Iowa 50613.

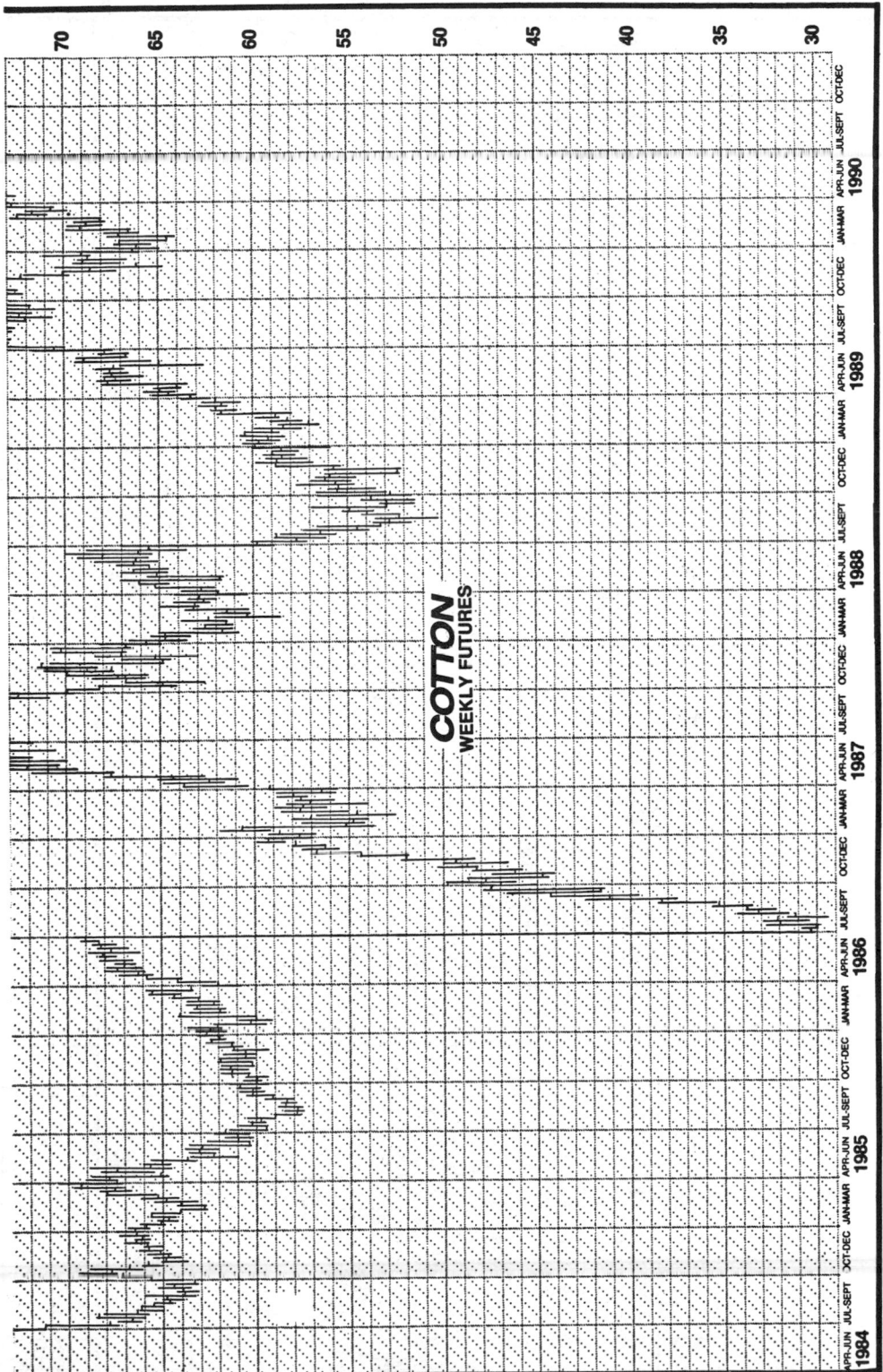

COTTON
WEEKLY FUTURES

Source: Reprinted from *Commodity Price Charts*, 219 Parkade, Cedar Falls, Iowa 50613.

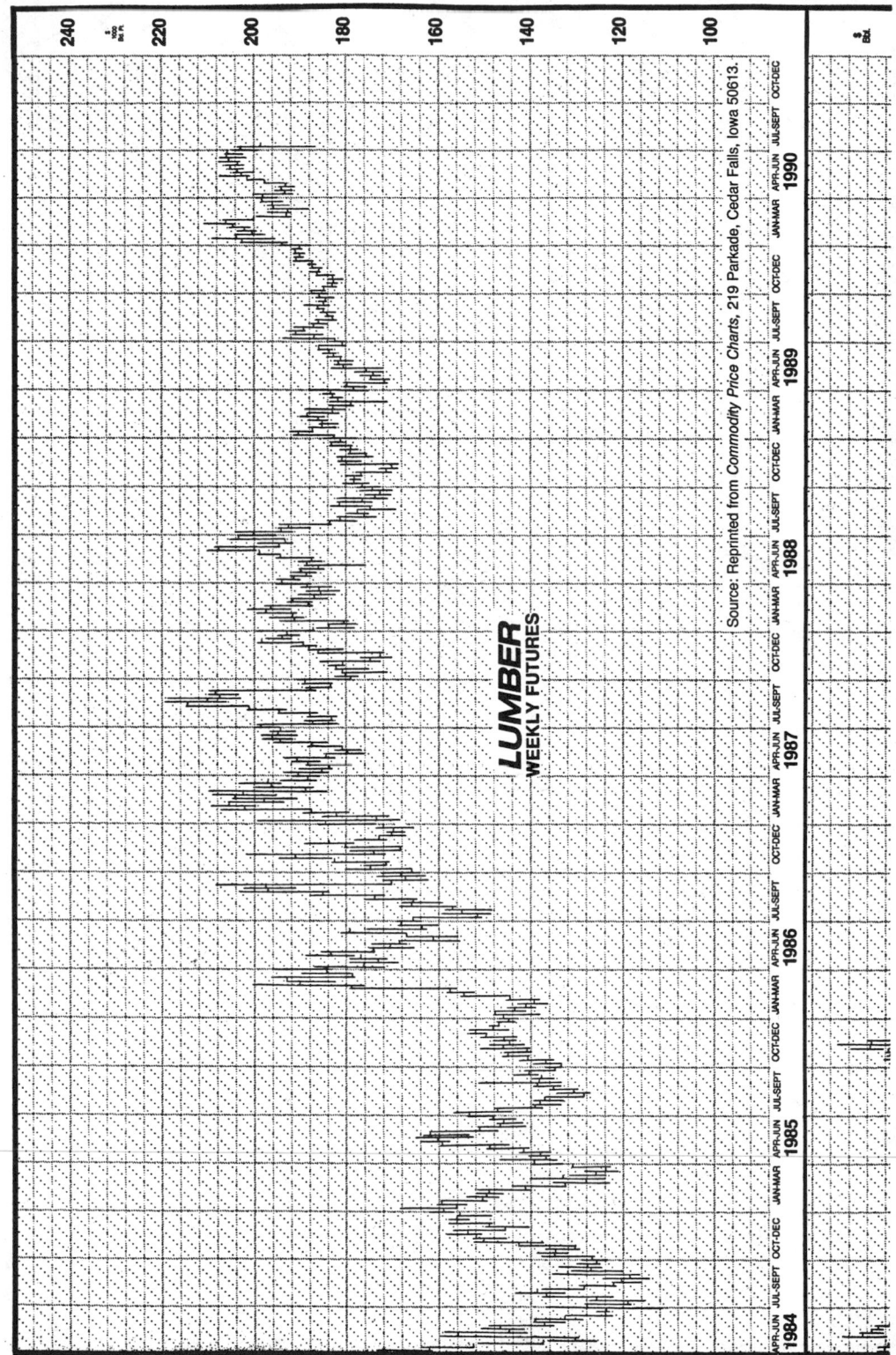

LUMBER
WEEKLY FUTURES

Source: Reprinted from *Commodity Price Charts*, 219 Parkade, Cedar Falls, Iowa 50613.

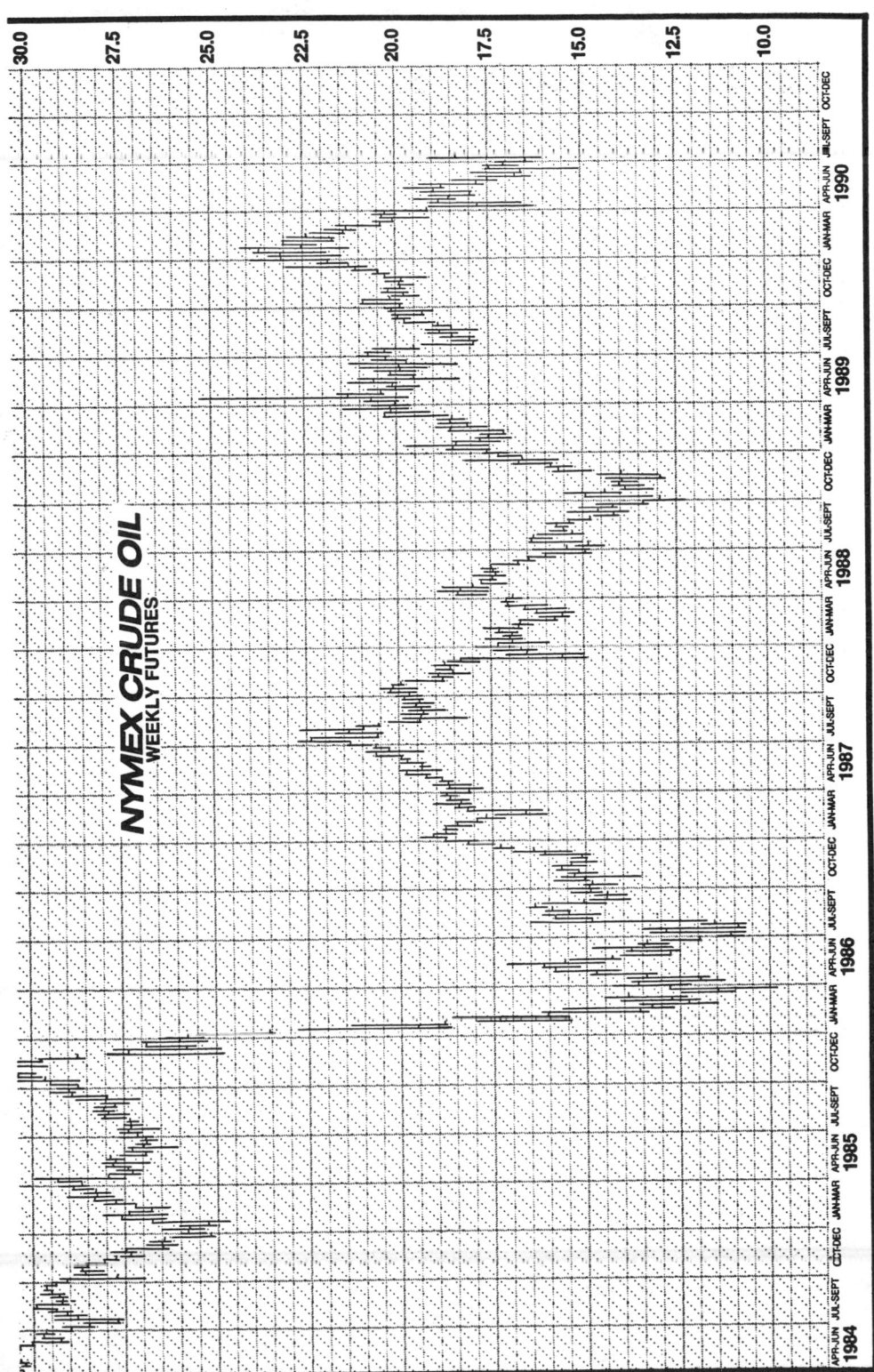

NYMEX CRUDE OIL
WEEKLY FUTURES

Source: Reprinted from *Commodity Price Charts*, 219 Parkade, Cedar Falls, Iowa 50613.

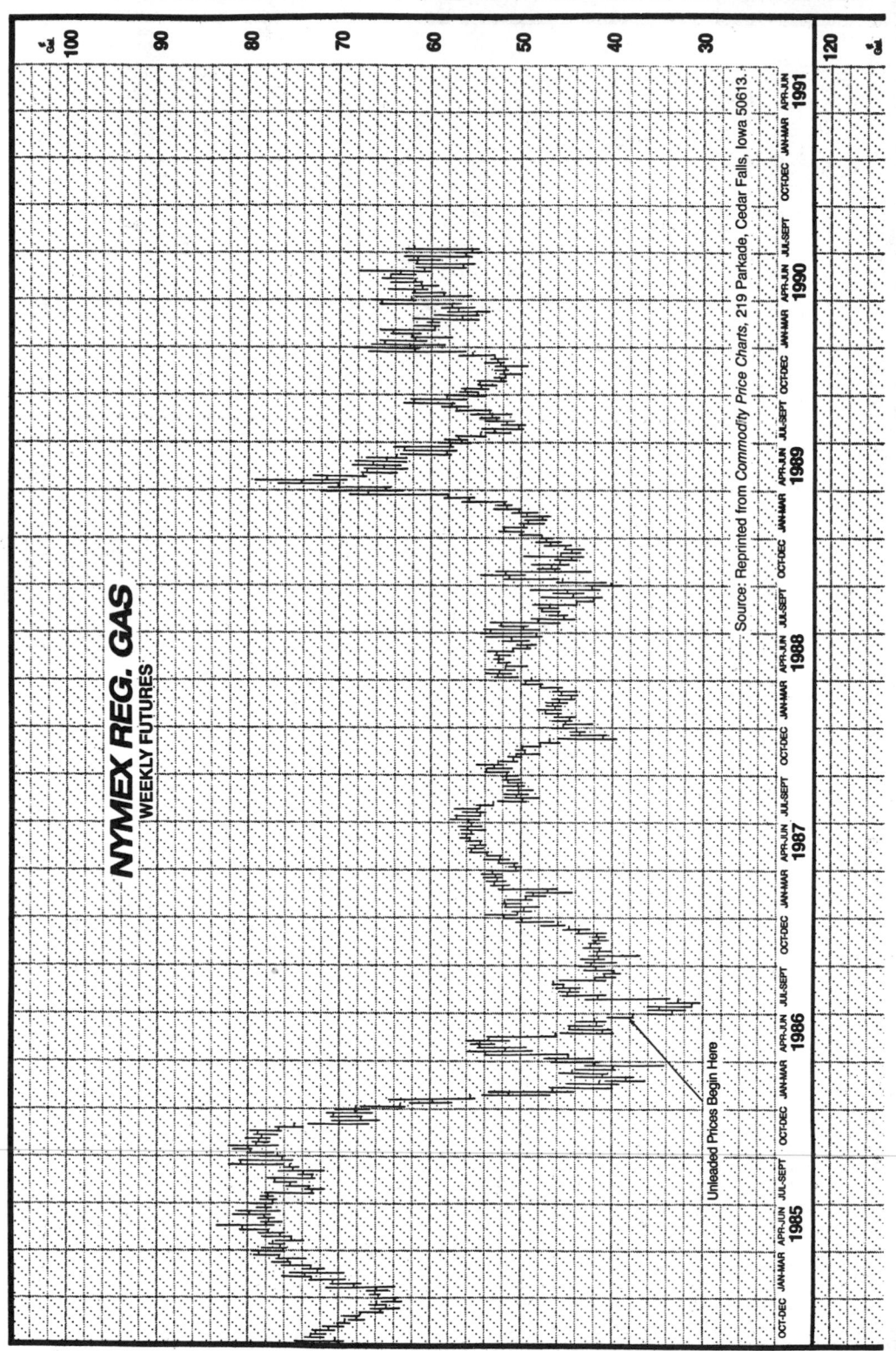

NYMEX REG. GAS
WEEKLY FUTURES

Unleaded Prices Begin Here

Source: Reprinted from *Commodity Price Charts*, 219 Parkade, Cedar Falls, Iowa 50613.

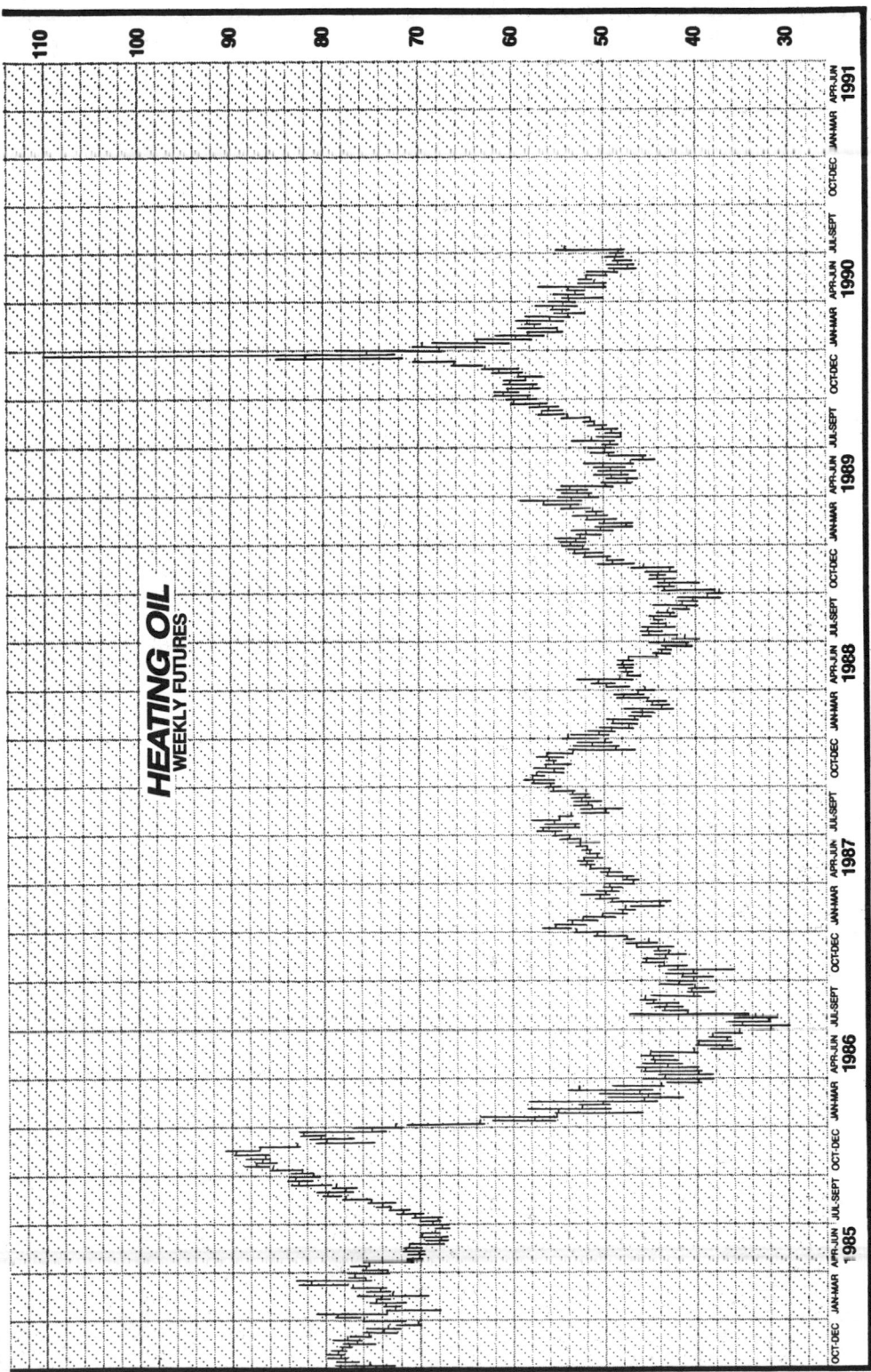

HEATING OIL
WEEKLY FUTURES

Source: Reprinted from Commodity Price Charts, 219 Parkade, Cedar Falls, Iowa 50613.

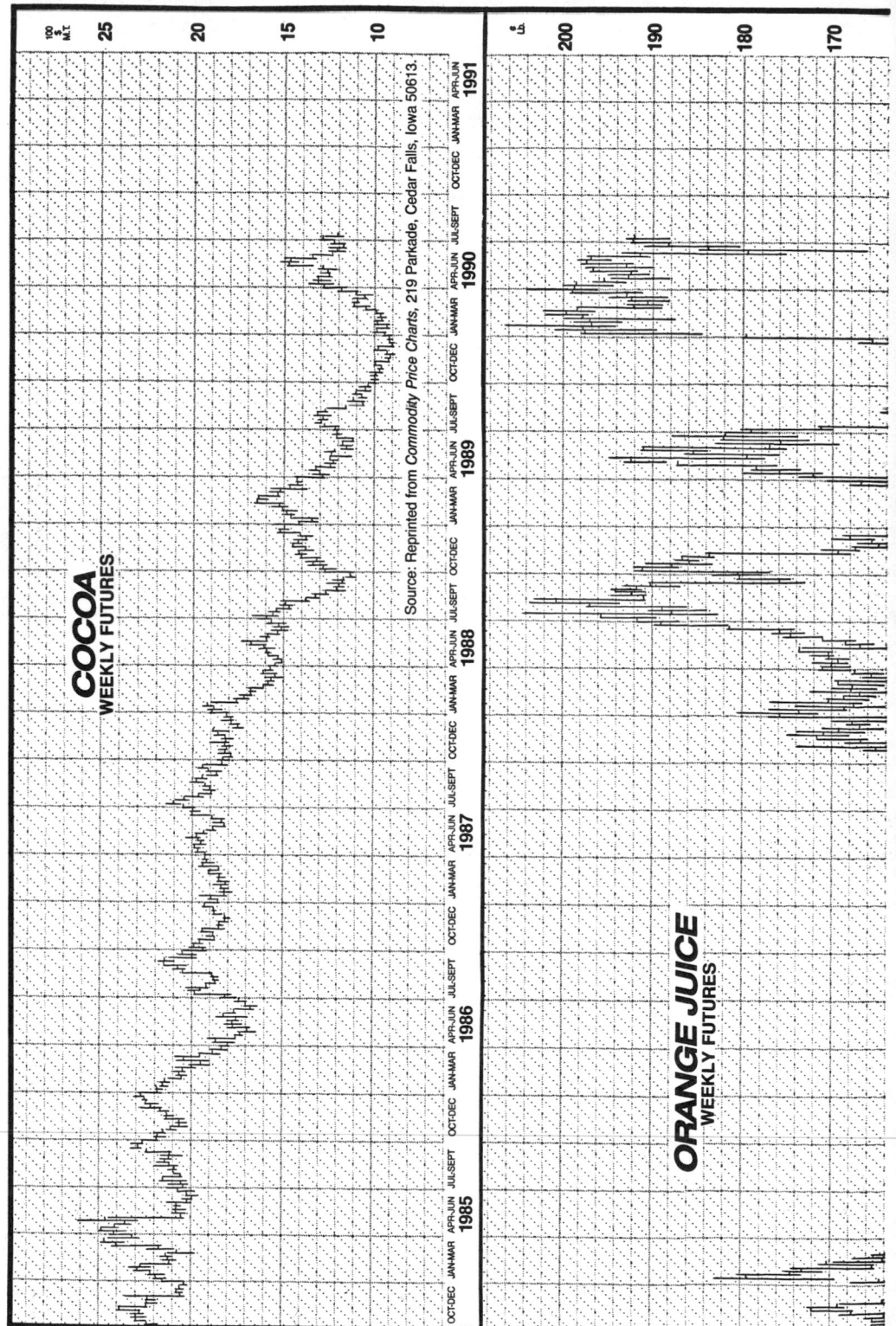

COCOA
WEEKLY FUTURES

ORANGE JUICE
WEEKLY FUTURES

Source: Reprinted from *Commodity Price Charts*, 219 Parkade, Cedar Falls, Iowa 50613.

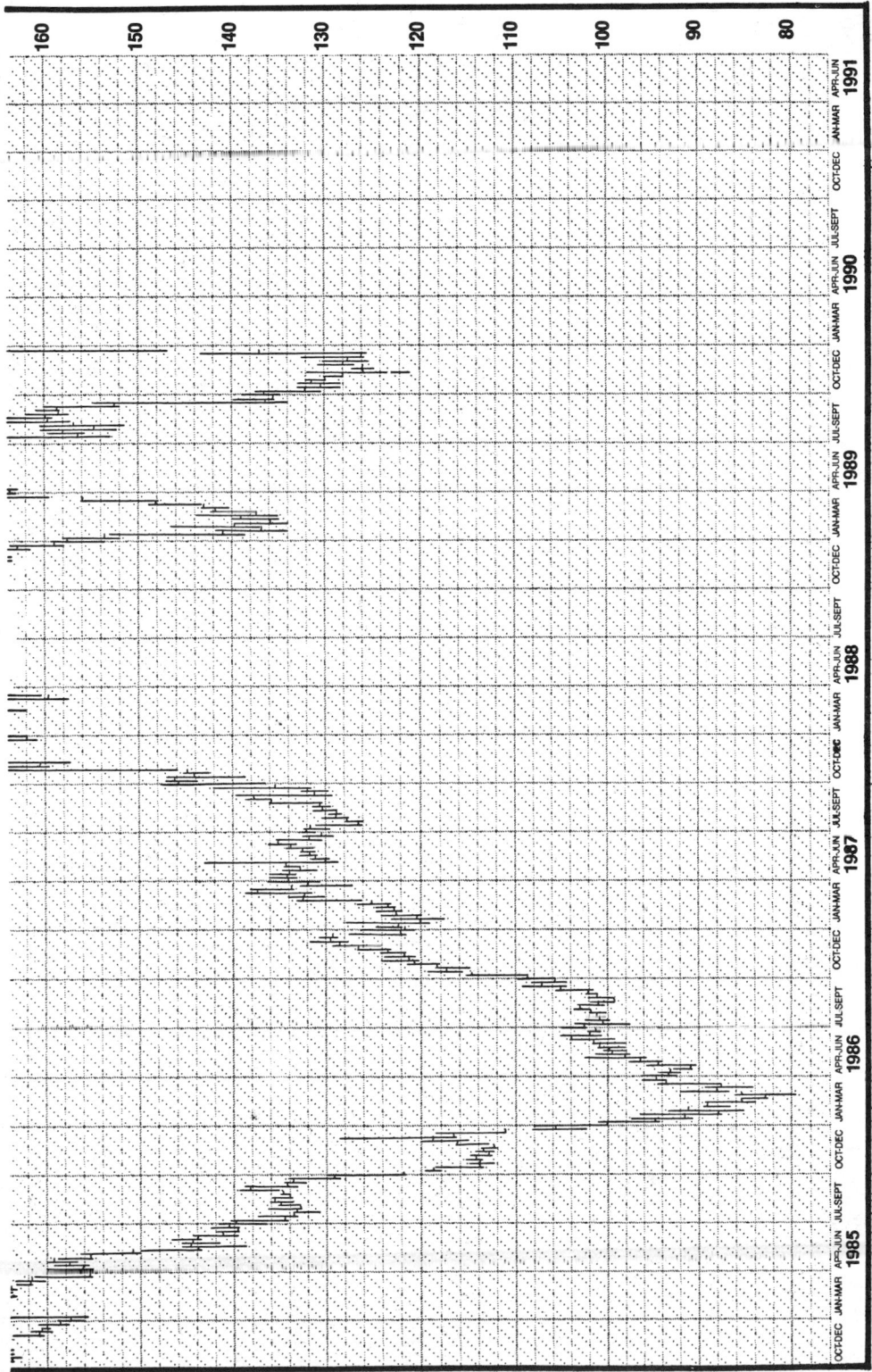

Source: Reprinted from *Commodity Price Charts*, 219 Parkade, Cedar Falls, Iowa 50613.

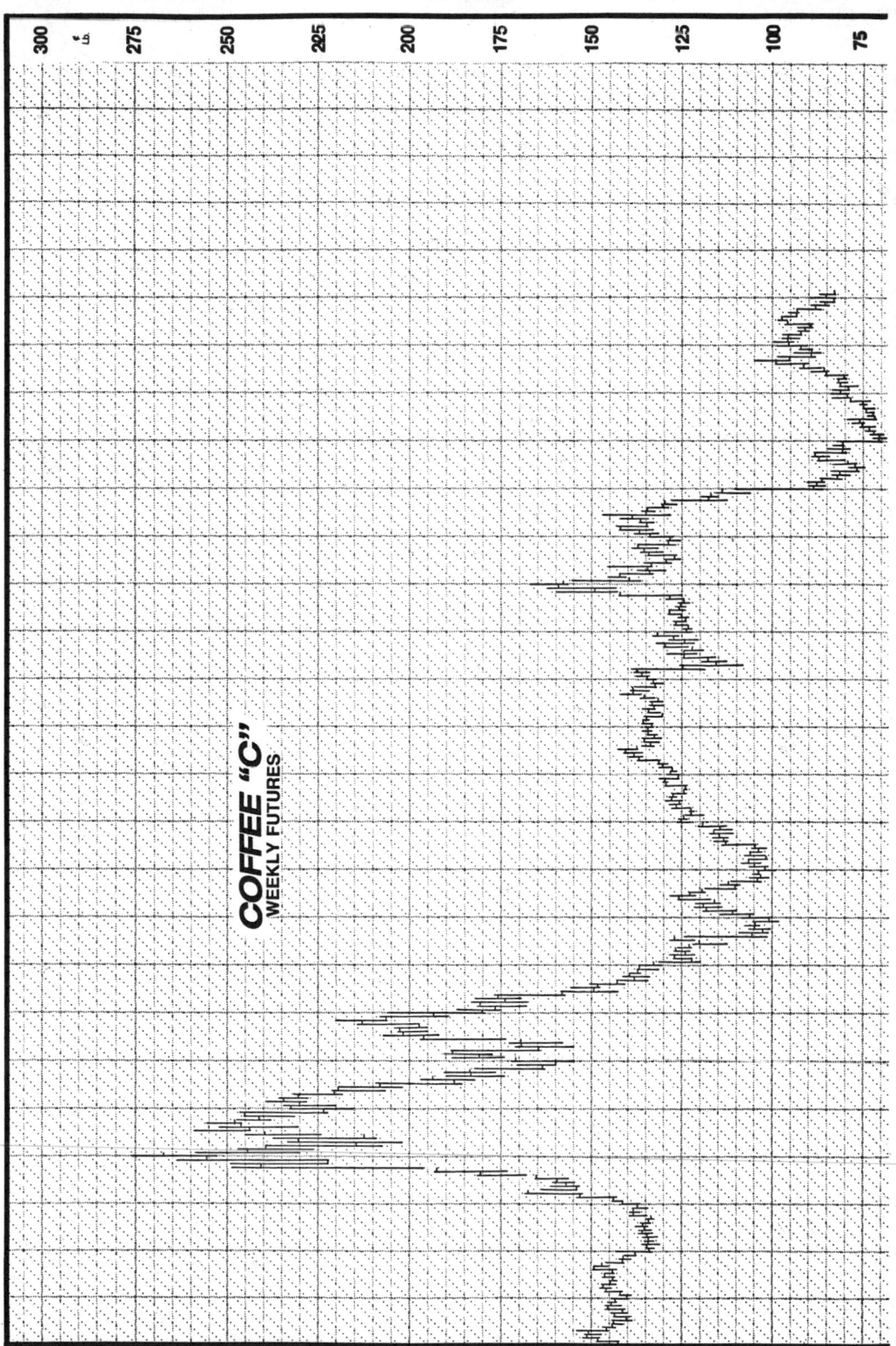

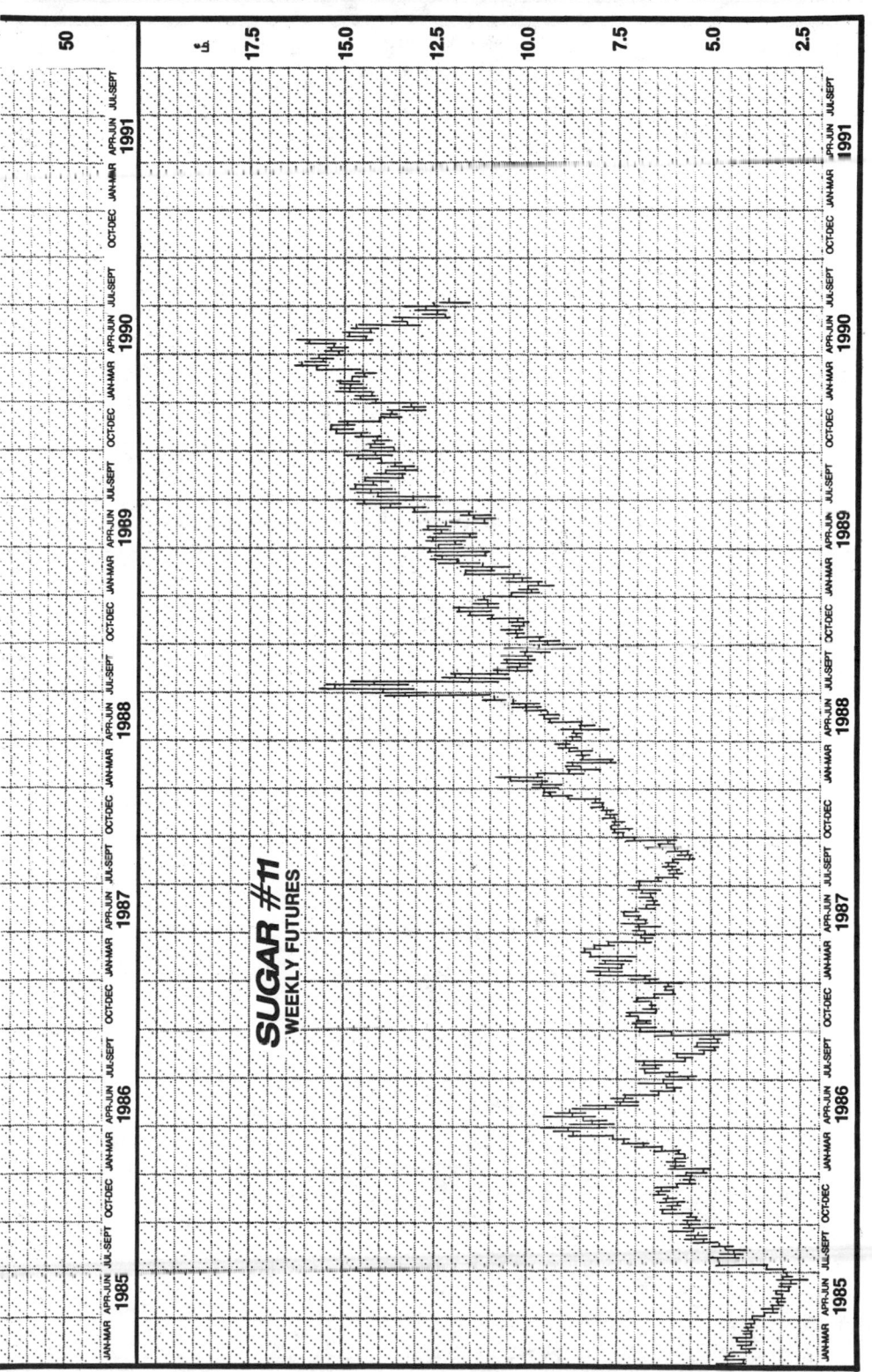

SUGAR #11
WEEKLY FUTURES

Source: Reprinted from *Commodity Price Charts*, 219 Parkade, Cedar Falls, Iowa 50613.

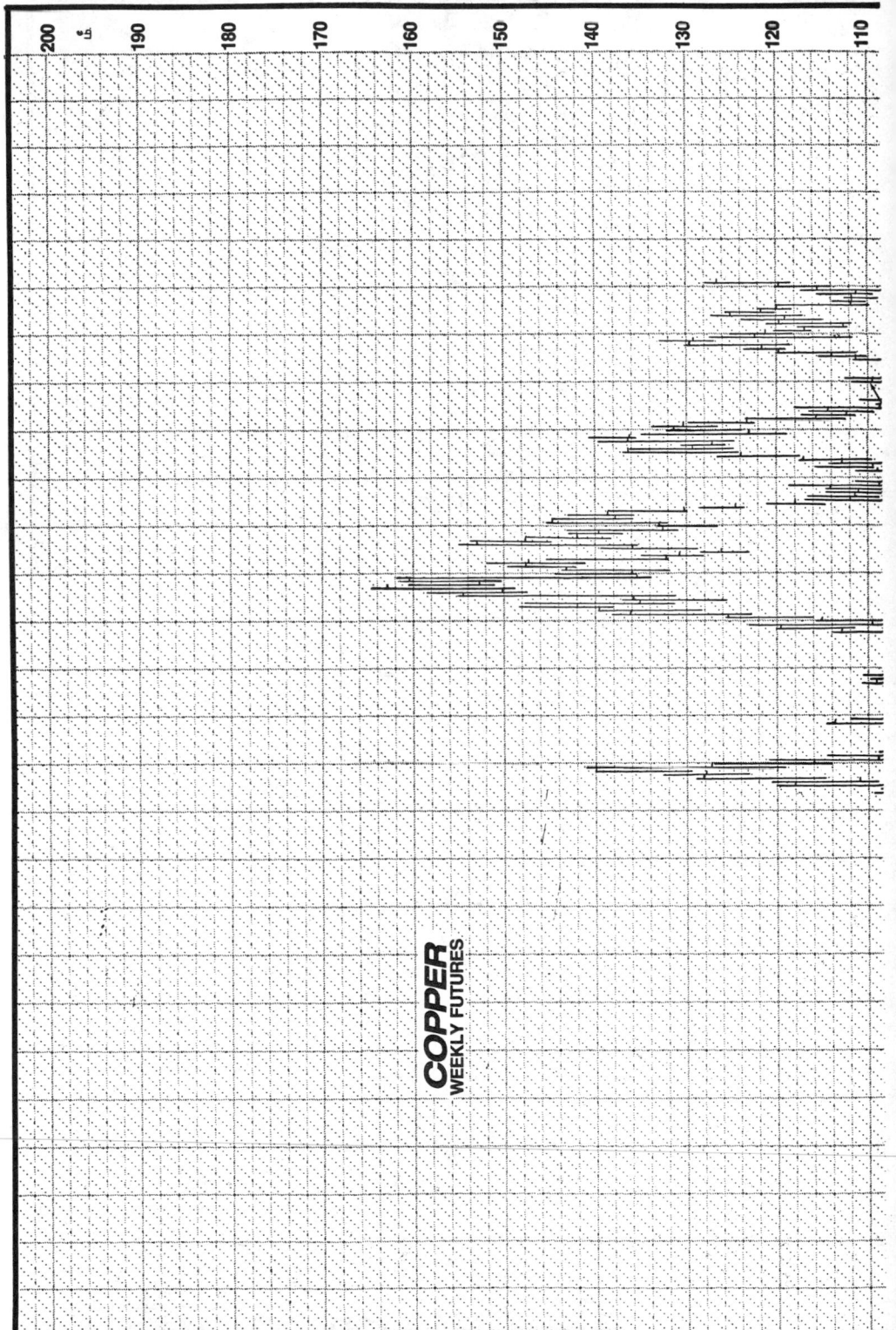

COPPER
WEEKLY FUTURES

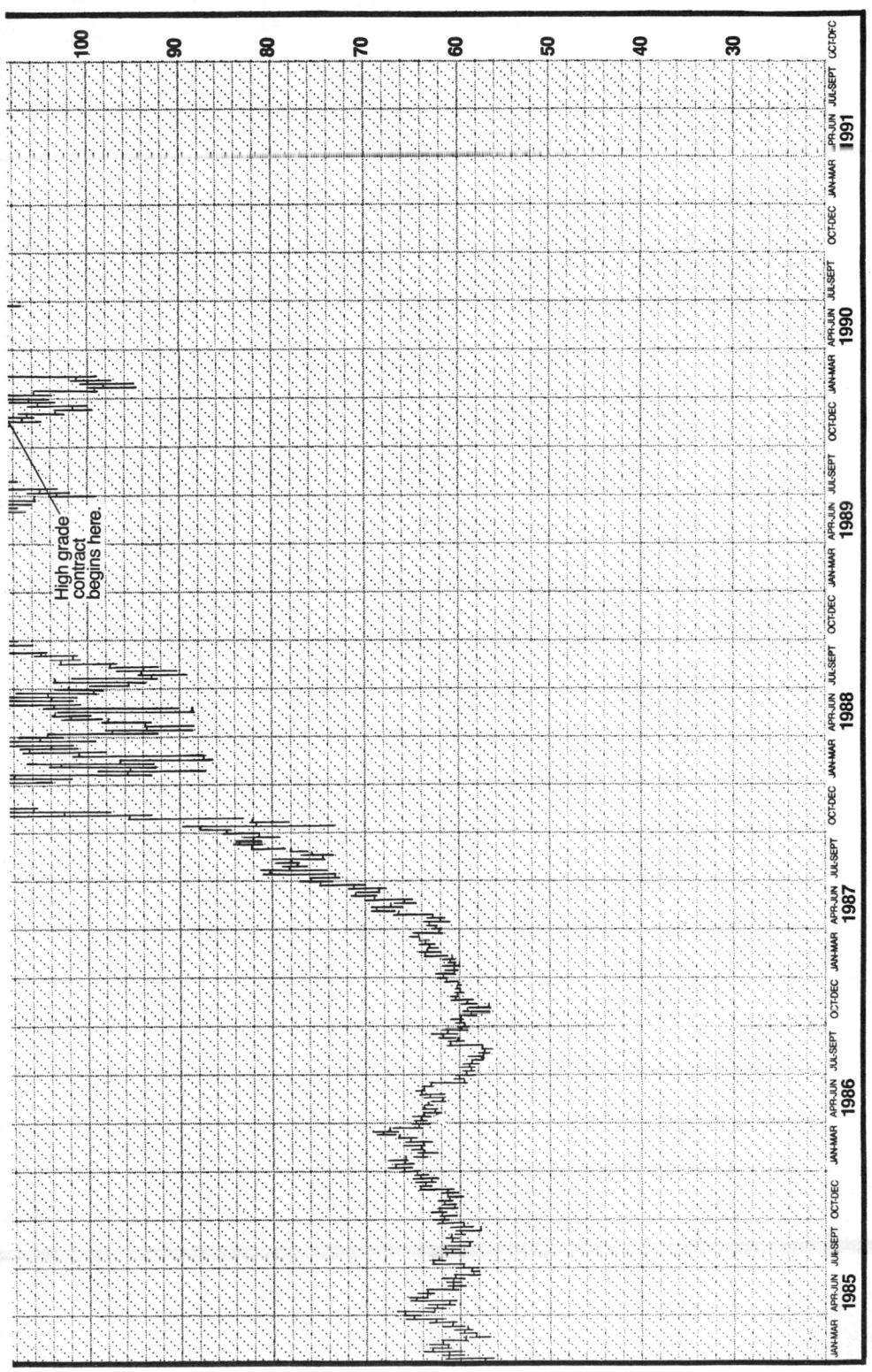

High grade
contract
begins here.

Source: Reprinted from *Commodity Price Charts*, 219 Parkade, Cedar Falls, Iowa 50613.

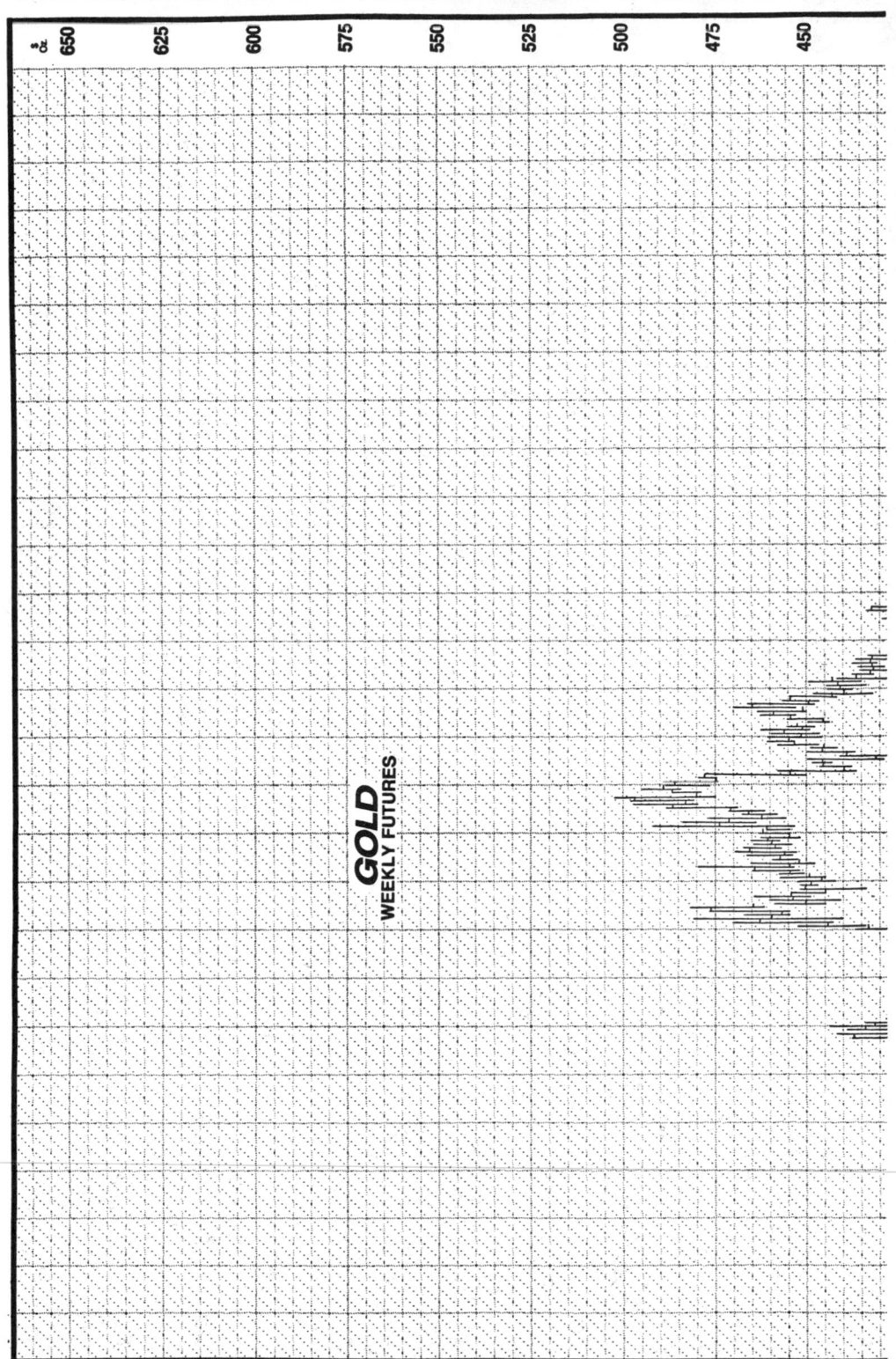

GOLD
WEEKLY FUTURES

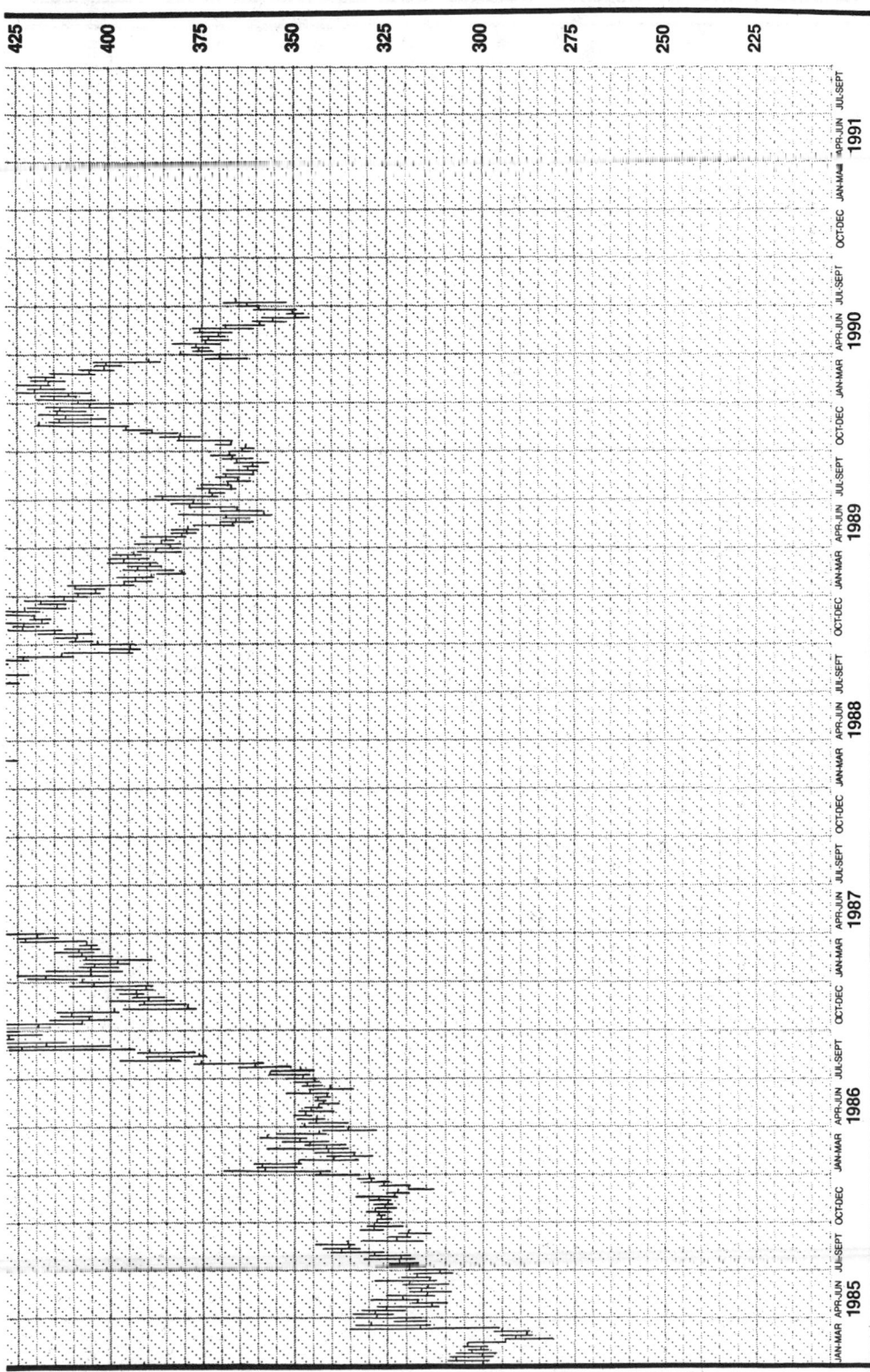

Source: Reprinted from *Commodity Price Charts*, 219 Parkade, Cedar Falls, Iowa 50613.

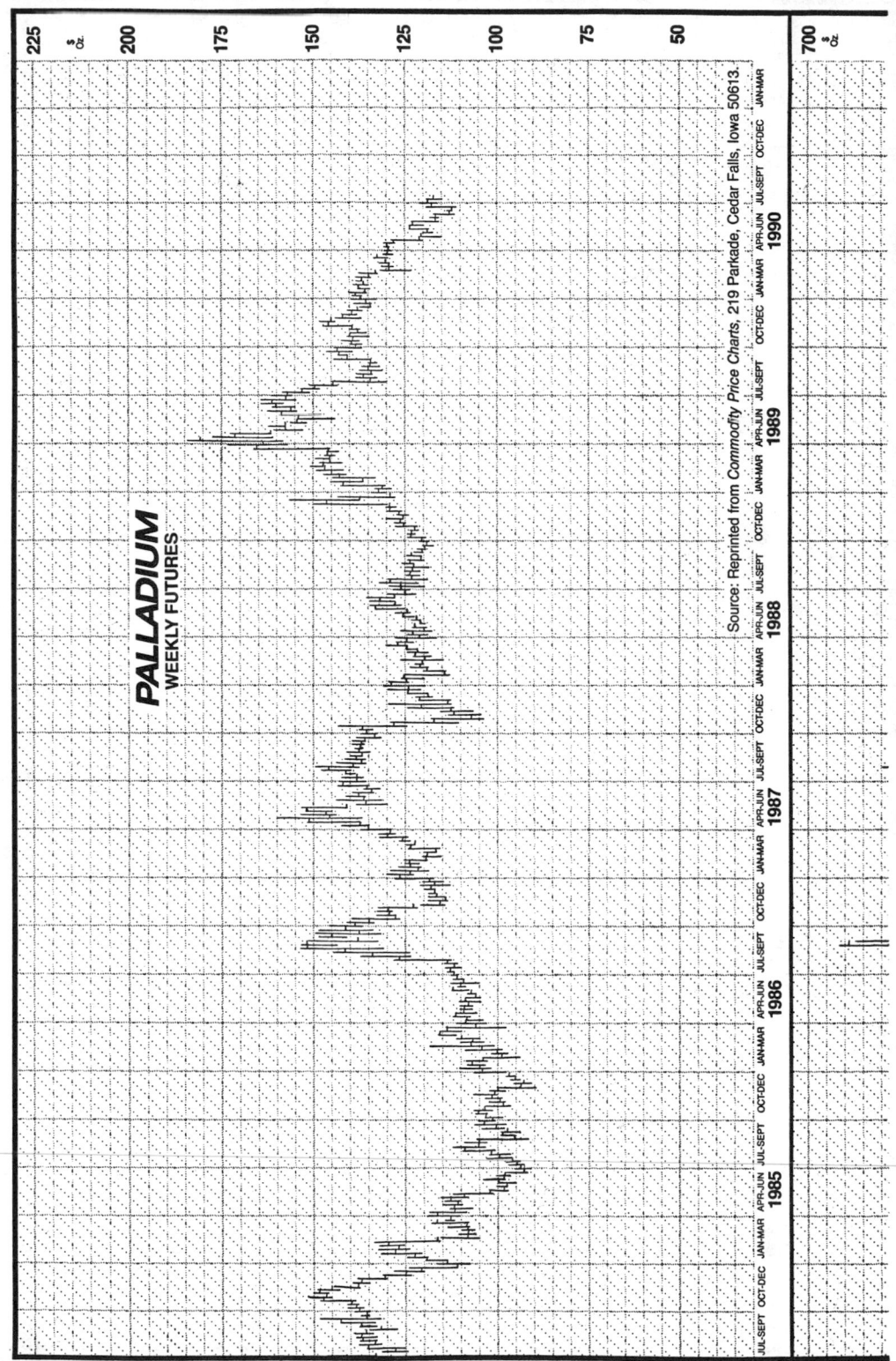

PALLADIUM
WEEKLY FUTURES

Source: Reprinted from *Commodity Price Charts*, 219 Parkade, Cedar Falls, Iowa 50613.

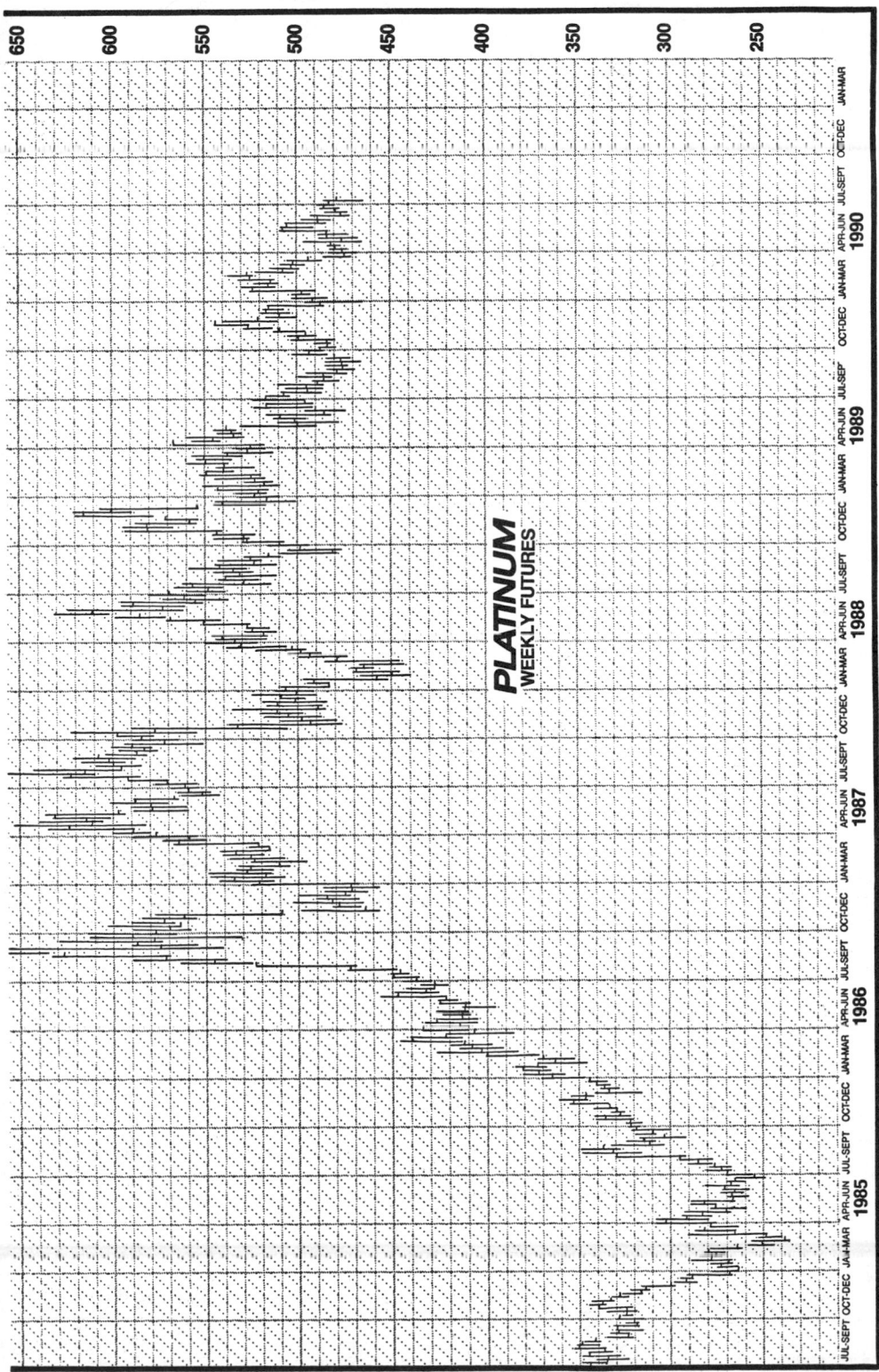

PLATINUM
WEEKLY FUTURES

COMEX SILVER
WEEKLY FUTURES

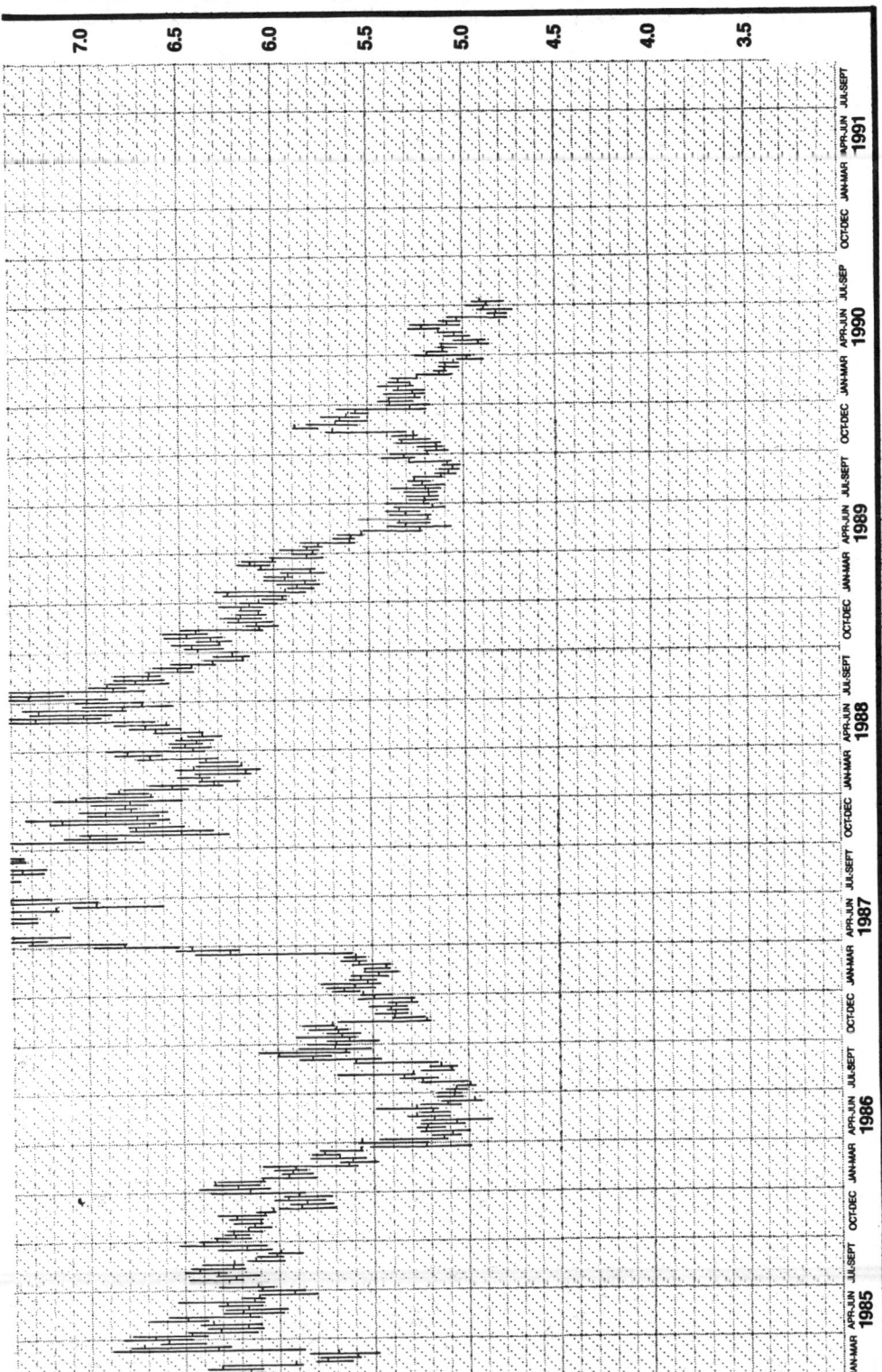

Source: Reprinted from *Commodity Price Charts*, 219 Parkade, Cedar Falls, Iowa 50613.

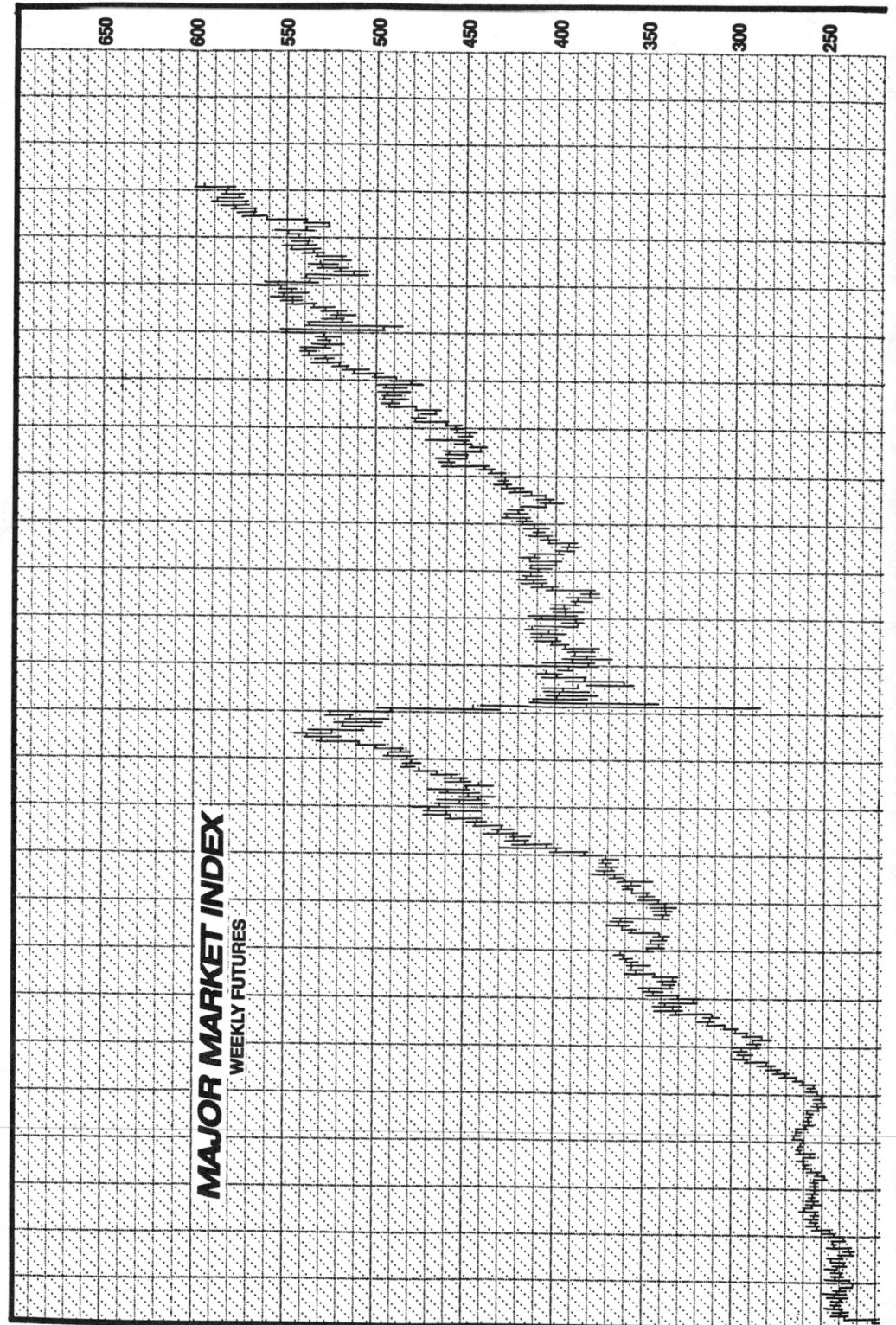

MAJOR MARKET INDEX
WEEKLY FUTURES

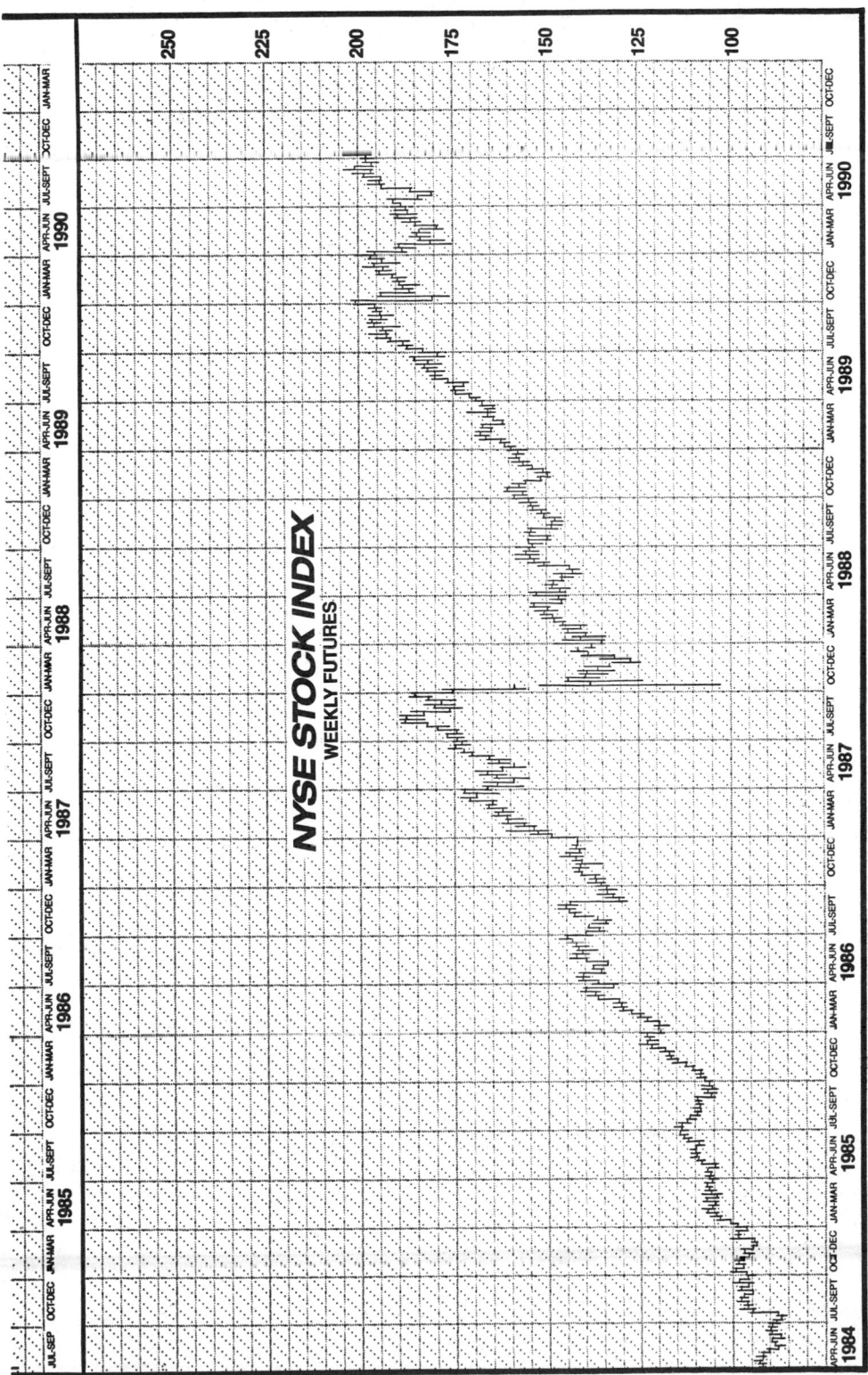

NYSE STOCK INDEX
WEEKLY FUTURES

Source: Reprinted from Commodity Price Charts, 219 Parkade, Cedar Falls, Iowa 50613.

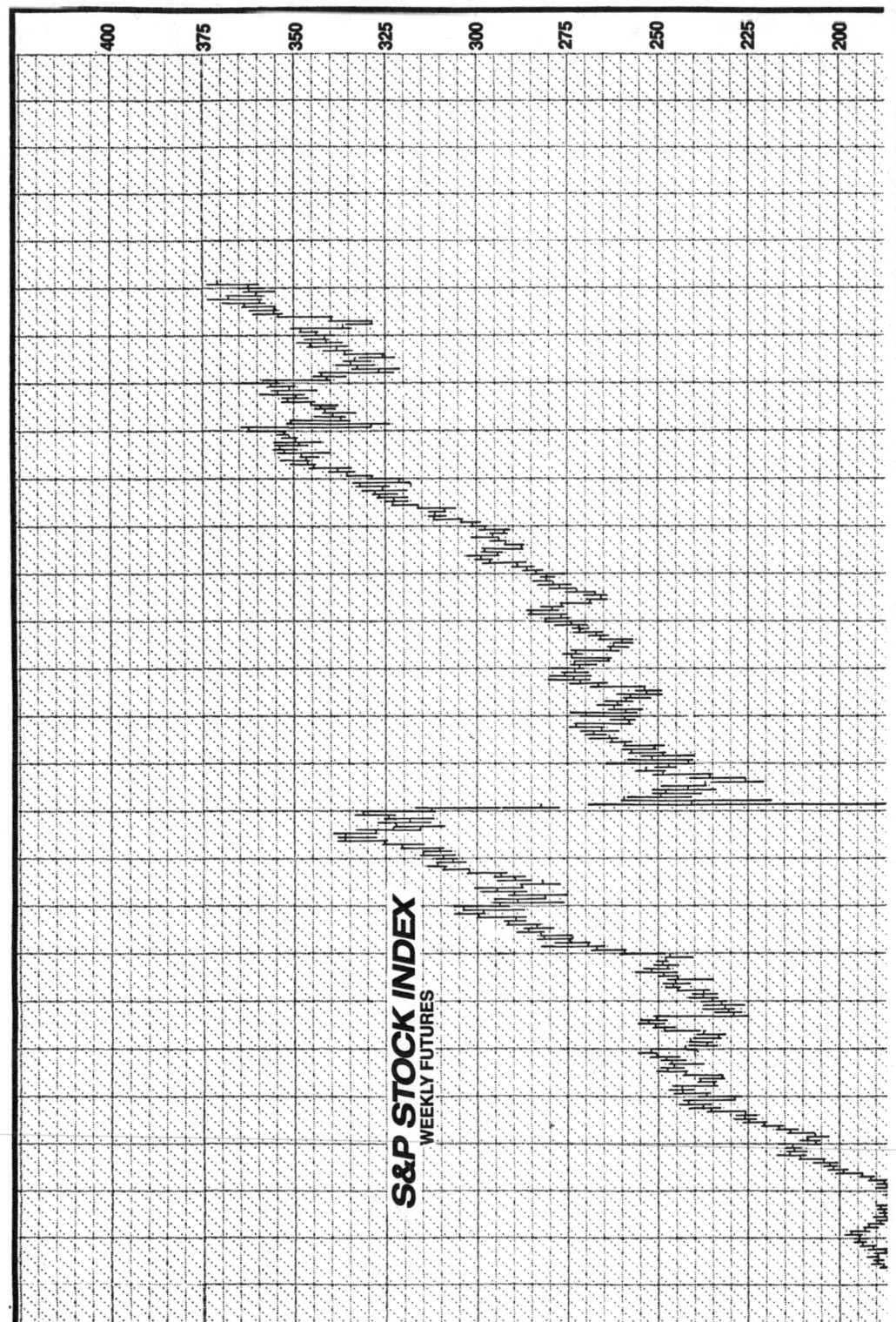

S&P STOCK INDEX
WEEKLY FUTURES

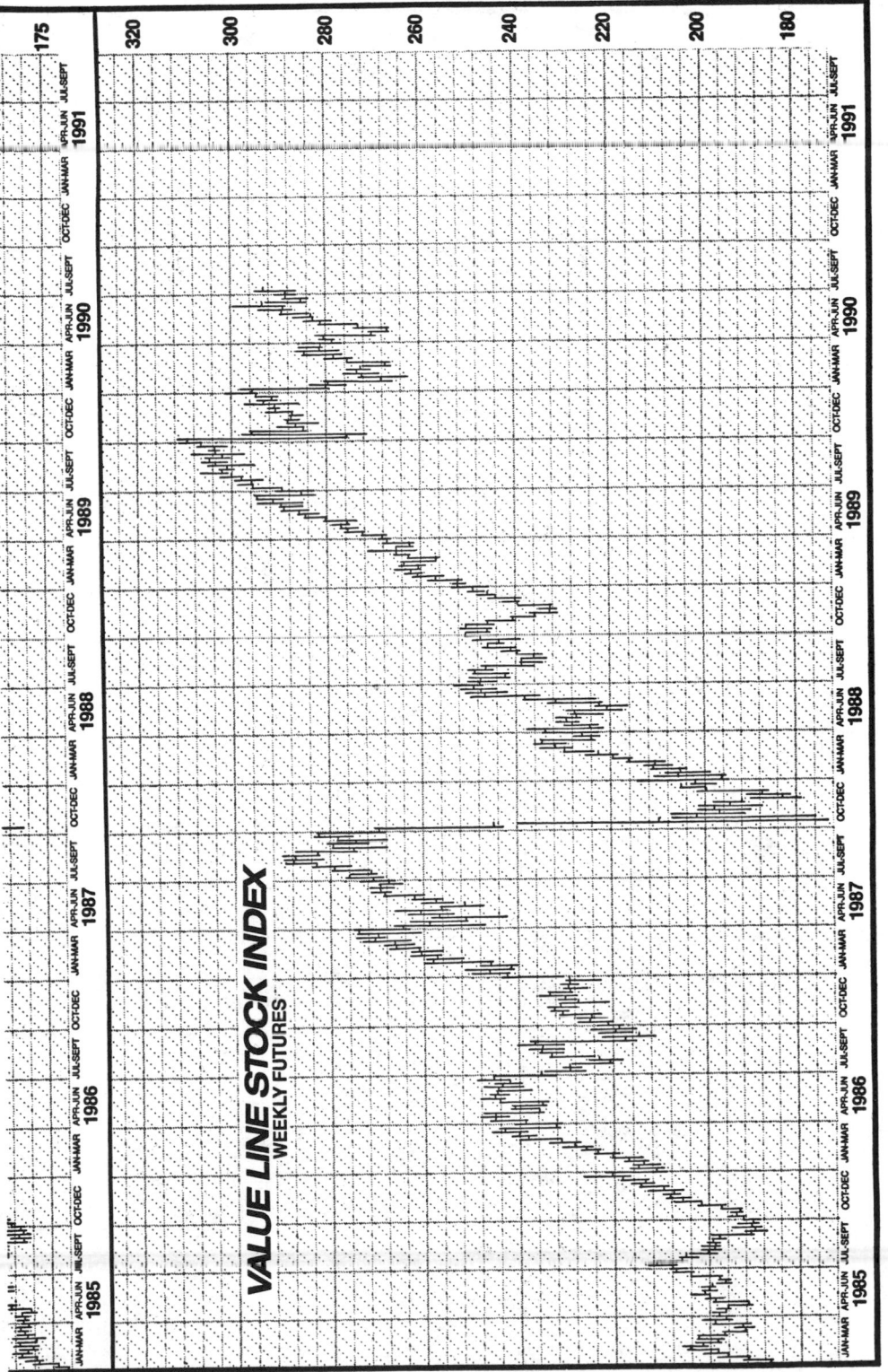

VALUE LINE STOCK INDEX
WEEKLY FUTURES

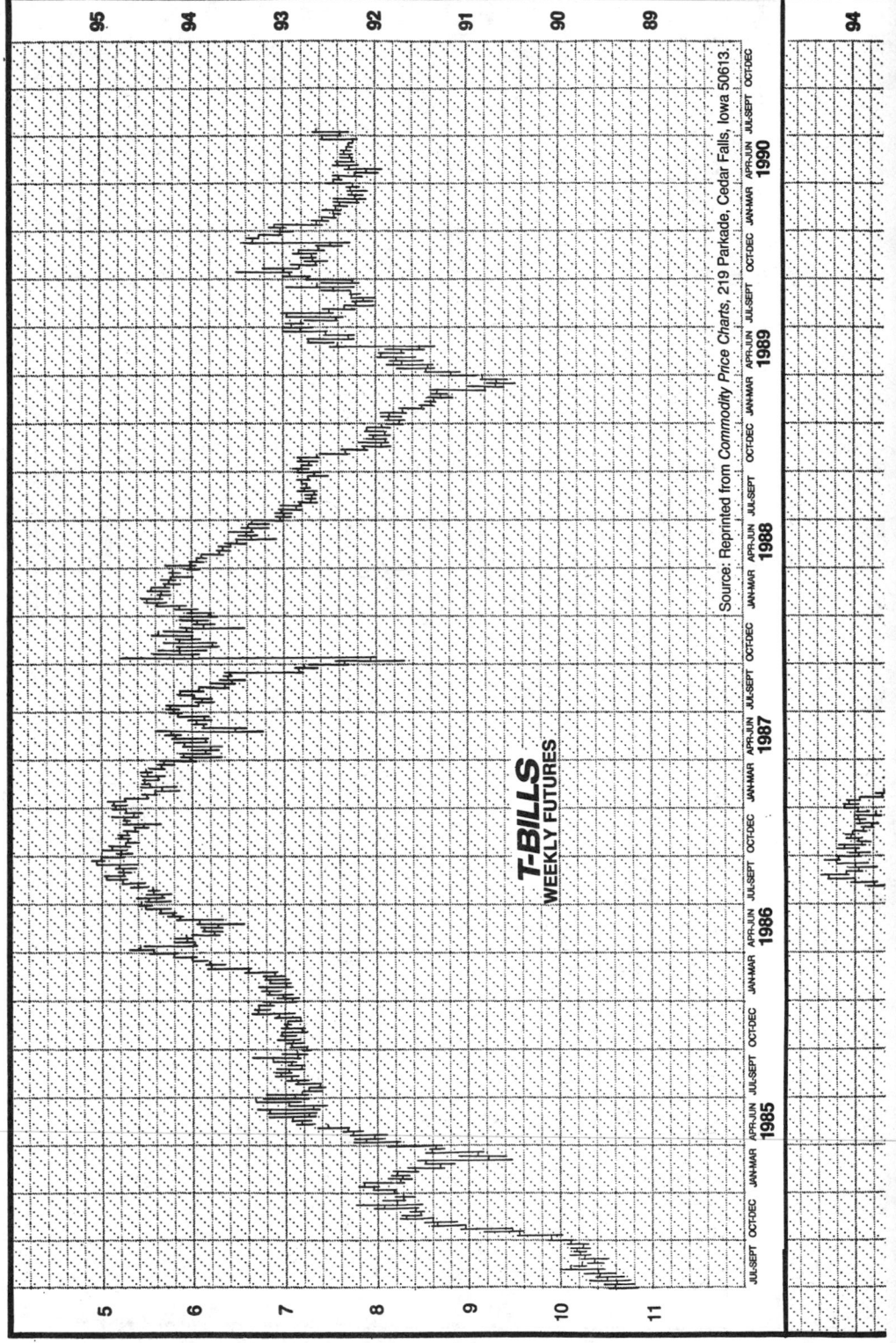

T-BILLS
WEEKLY FUTURES

Source: Reprinted from *Commodity Price Charts*, 219 Parkade, Cedar Falls, Iowa 50613.

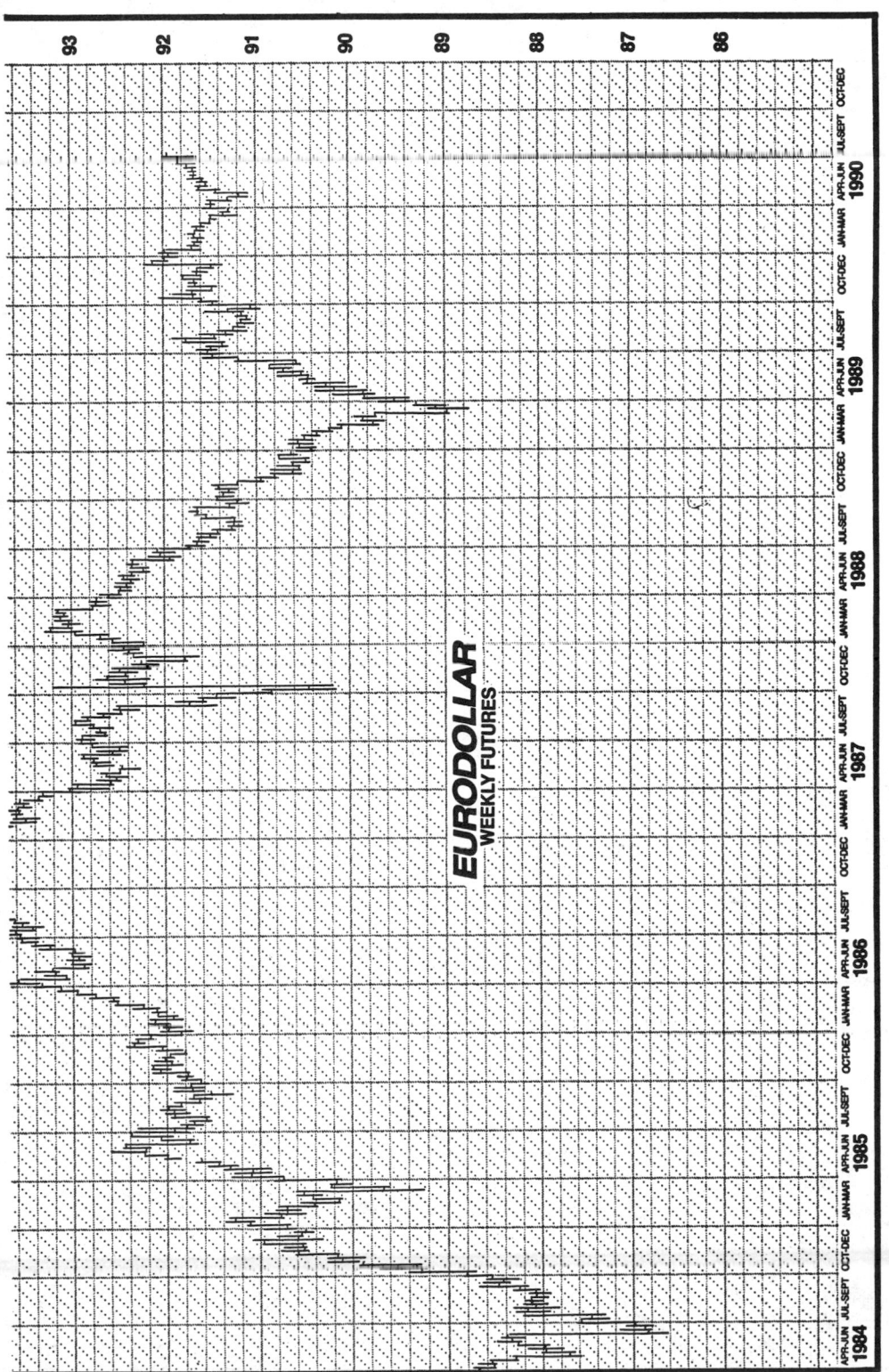

EURODOLLAR
WEEKLY FUTURES

Source: Reprinted from *Commodity Price Charts*, 219 Parkade, Cedar Falls, Iowa 50613.

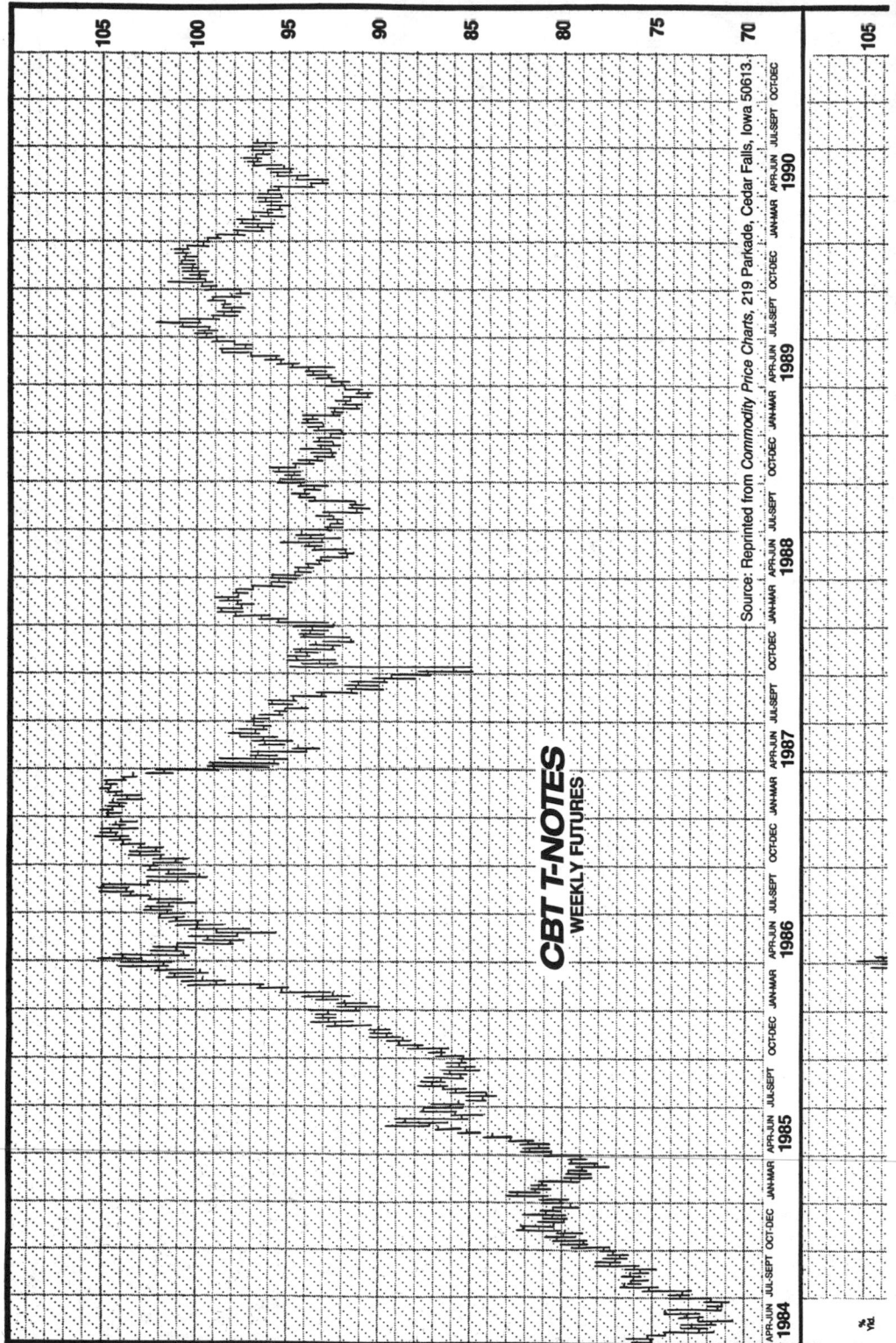

CBT T-NOTES
WEEKLY FUTURES

Source: Reprinted from *Commodity Price Charts*, 219 Parkade, Cedar Falls, Iowa 50613.

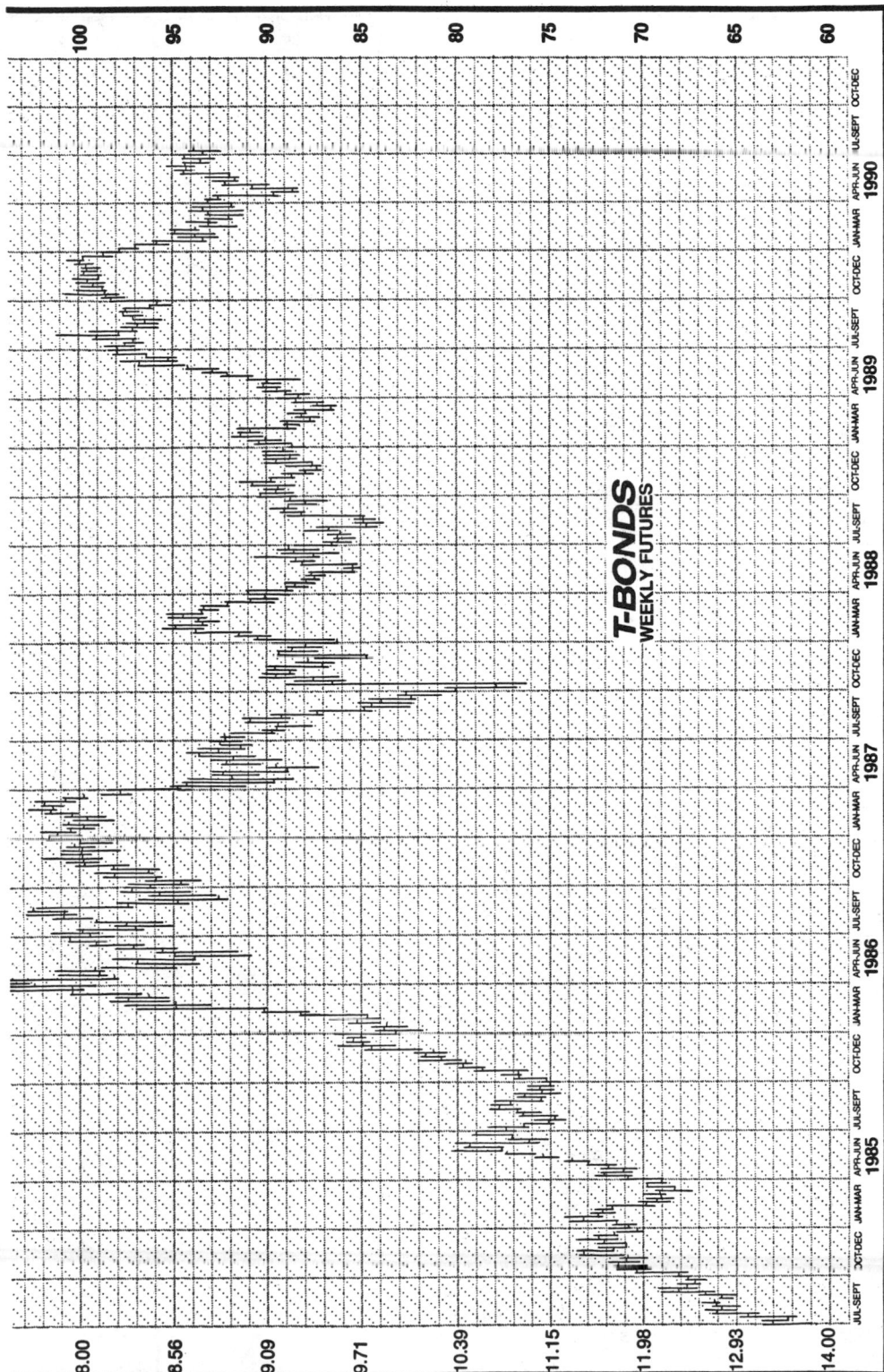

T-BONDS
WEEKLY FUTURES

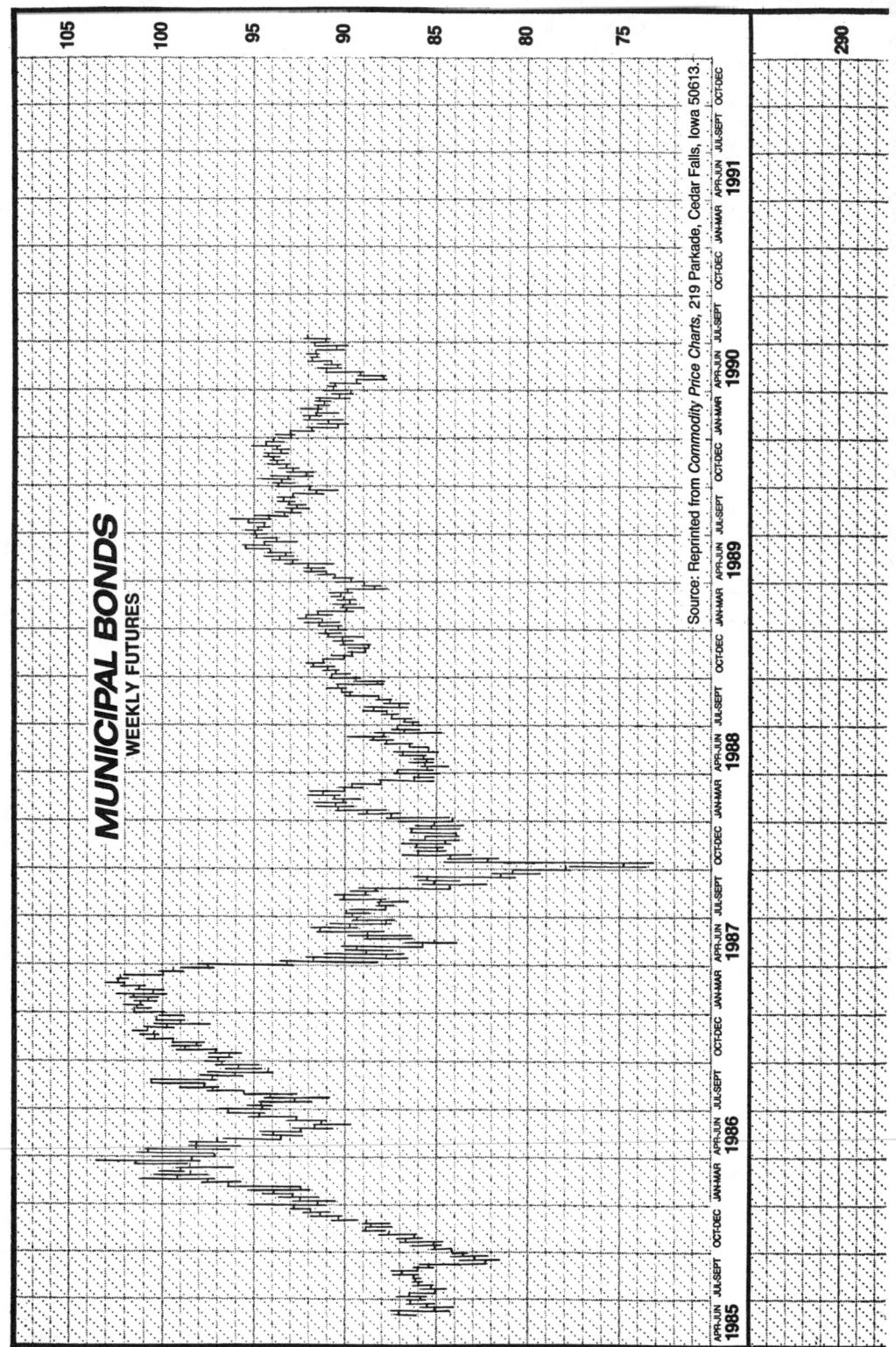

MUNICIPAL BONDS
WEEKLY FUTURES

Source: Reprinted from *Commodity Price Charts*, 219 Parkade, Cedar Falls, Iowa 50613.

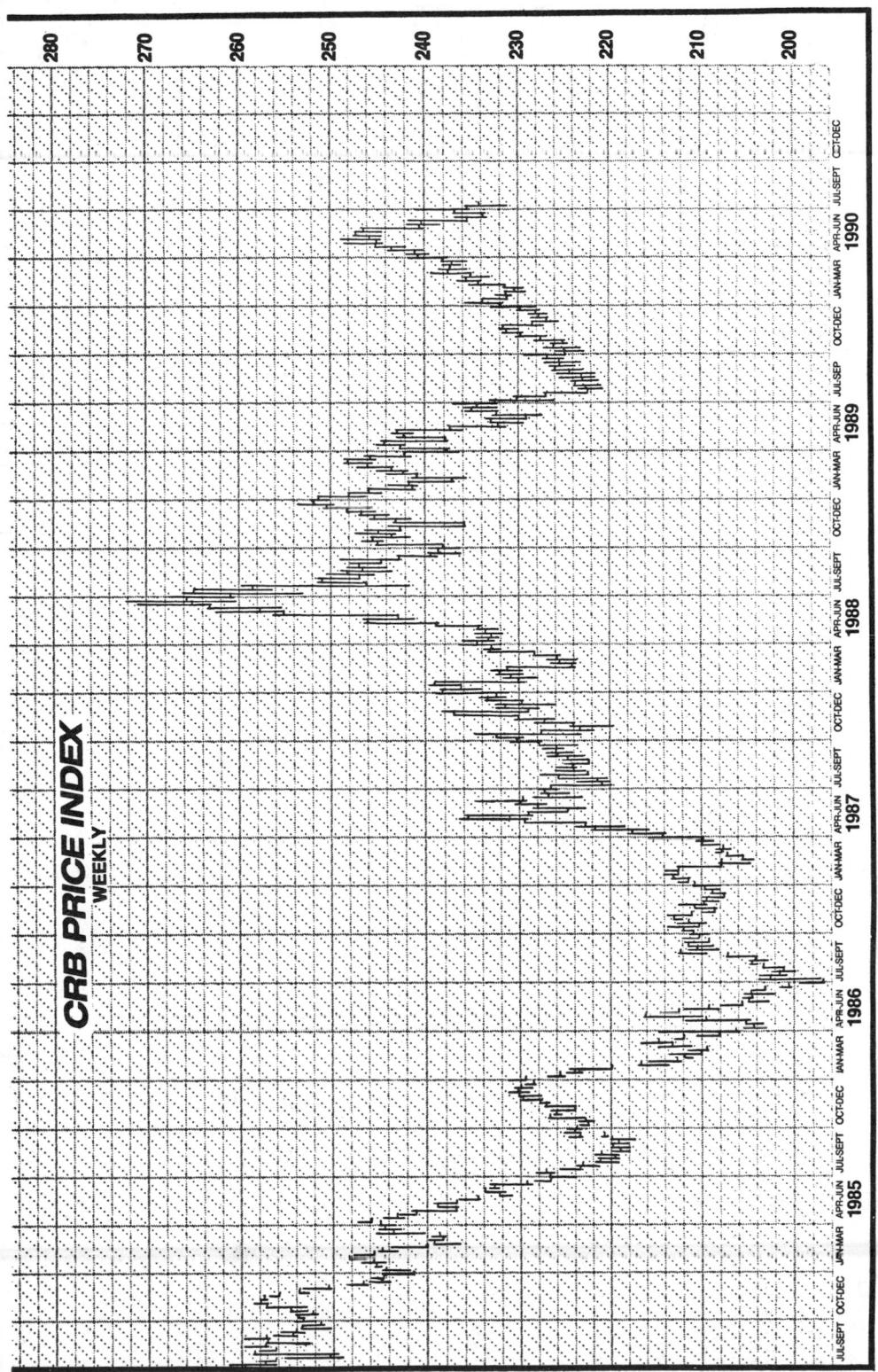

CRB PRICE INDEX
WEEKLY

Source: Reprinted from *Commodity Price Charts*, 219 Parkade, Cedar Falls, Iowa 50613.

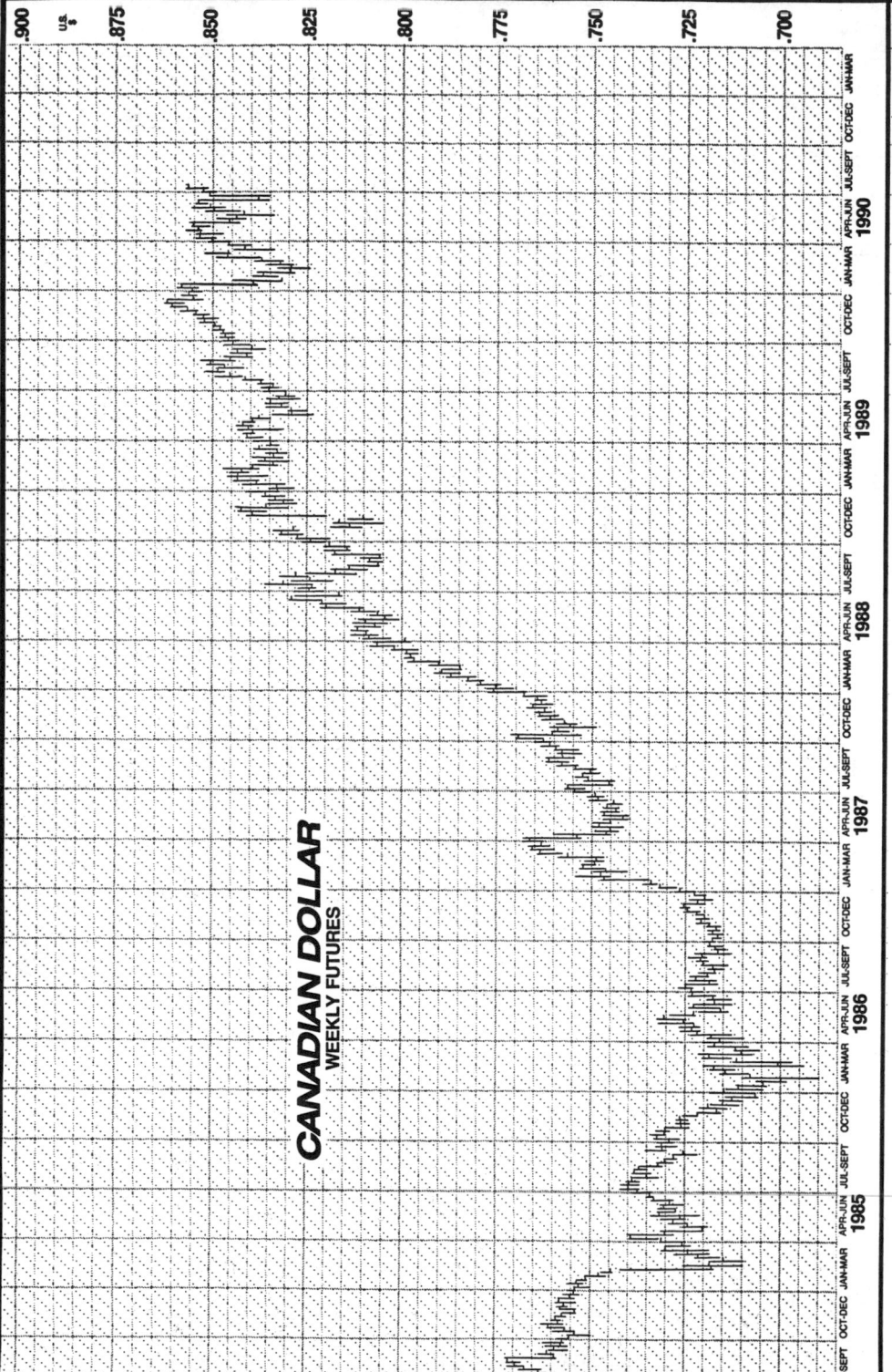

CANADIAN DOLLAR
WEEKLY FUTURES

Source: Reprinted from *Commodity Price Charts*, 219 Parkade, Cedar Falls, Iowa 50613.

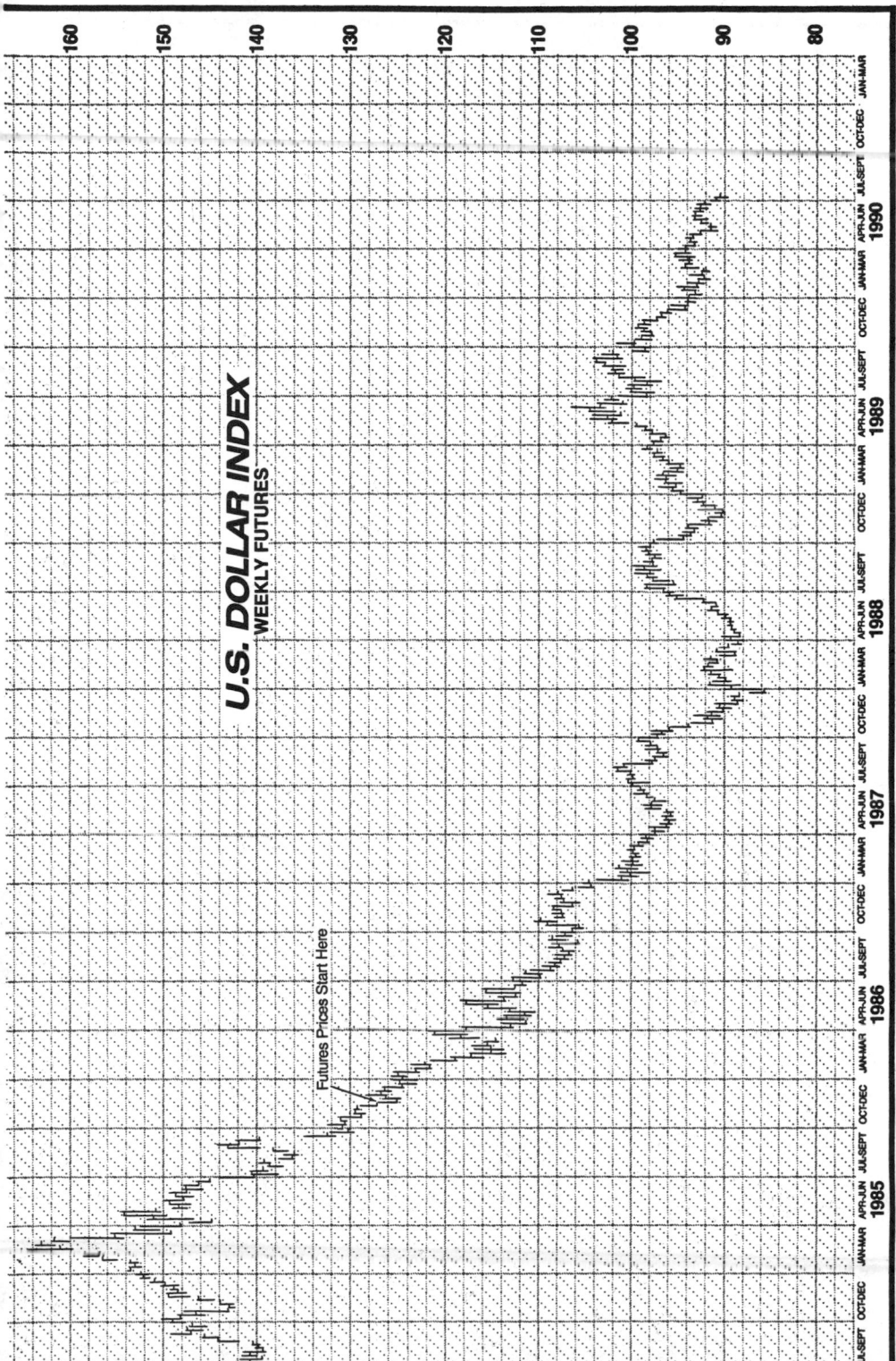

U.S. DOLLAR INDEX
WEEKLY FUTURES

Futures Prices Start Here

Source: Reprinted from *Commodity Price Charts*, 219 Parkade, Cedar Falls, Iowa 50613.

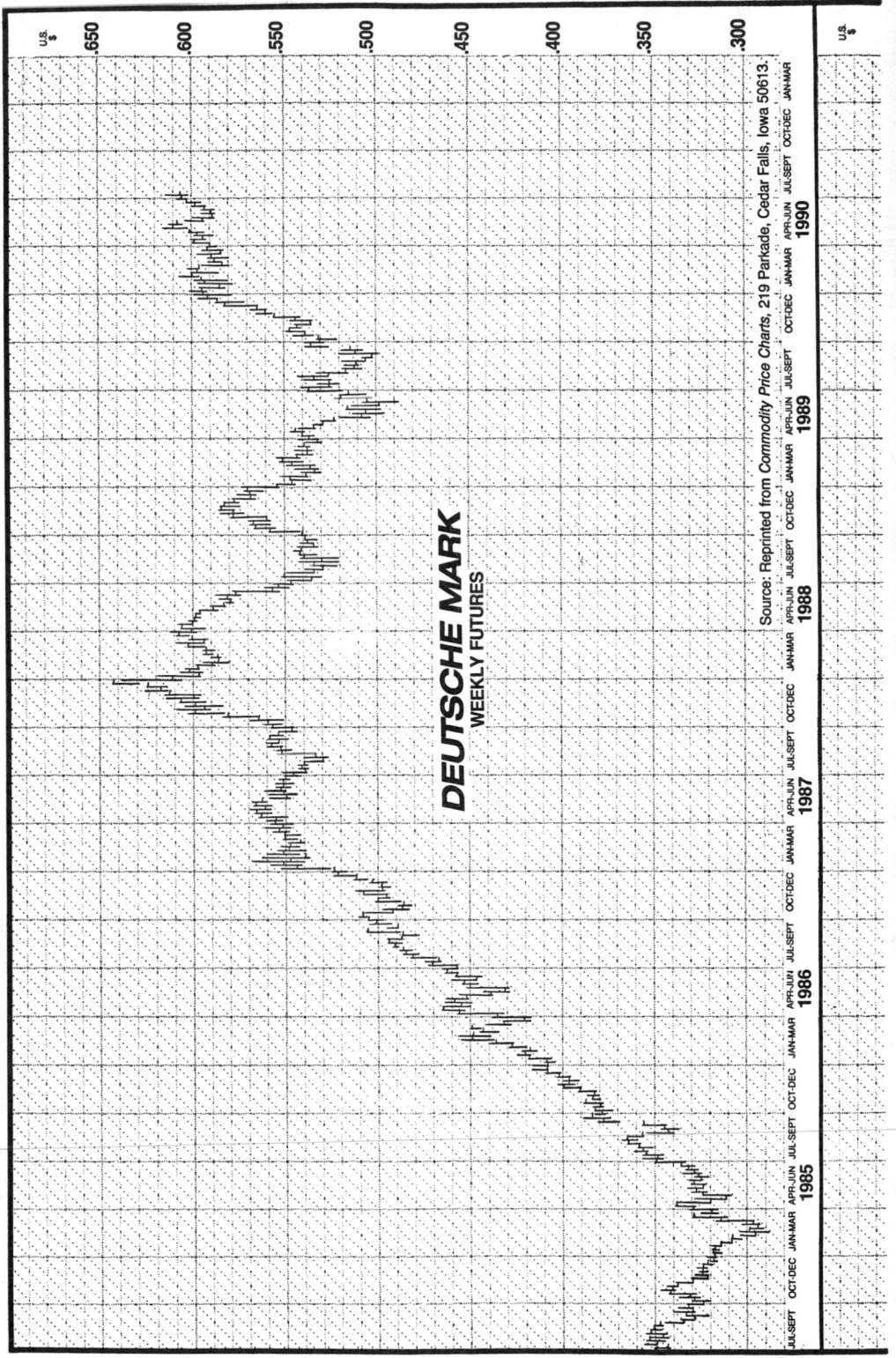

DEUTSCHE MARK
WEEKLY FUTURES

Source: Reprinted from *Commodity Price Charts*, 219 Parkade, Cedar Falls, Iowa 50613.

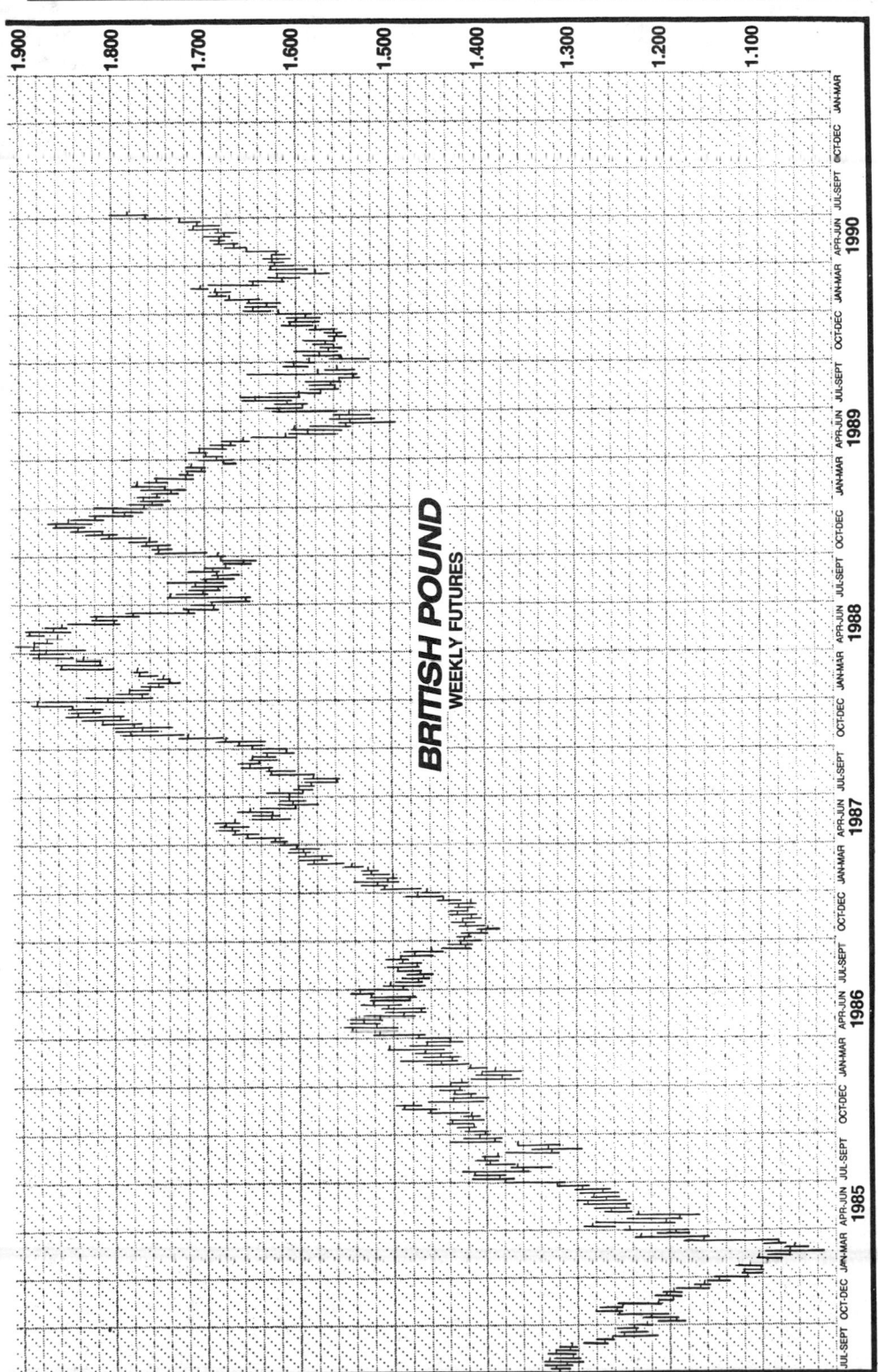

BRITISH POUND
WEEKLY FUTURES

Source: Reprinted from *Commodity Price Charts*, 219 Parkade, Cedar Falls, Iowa 50613.

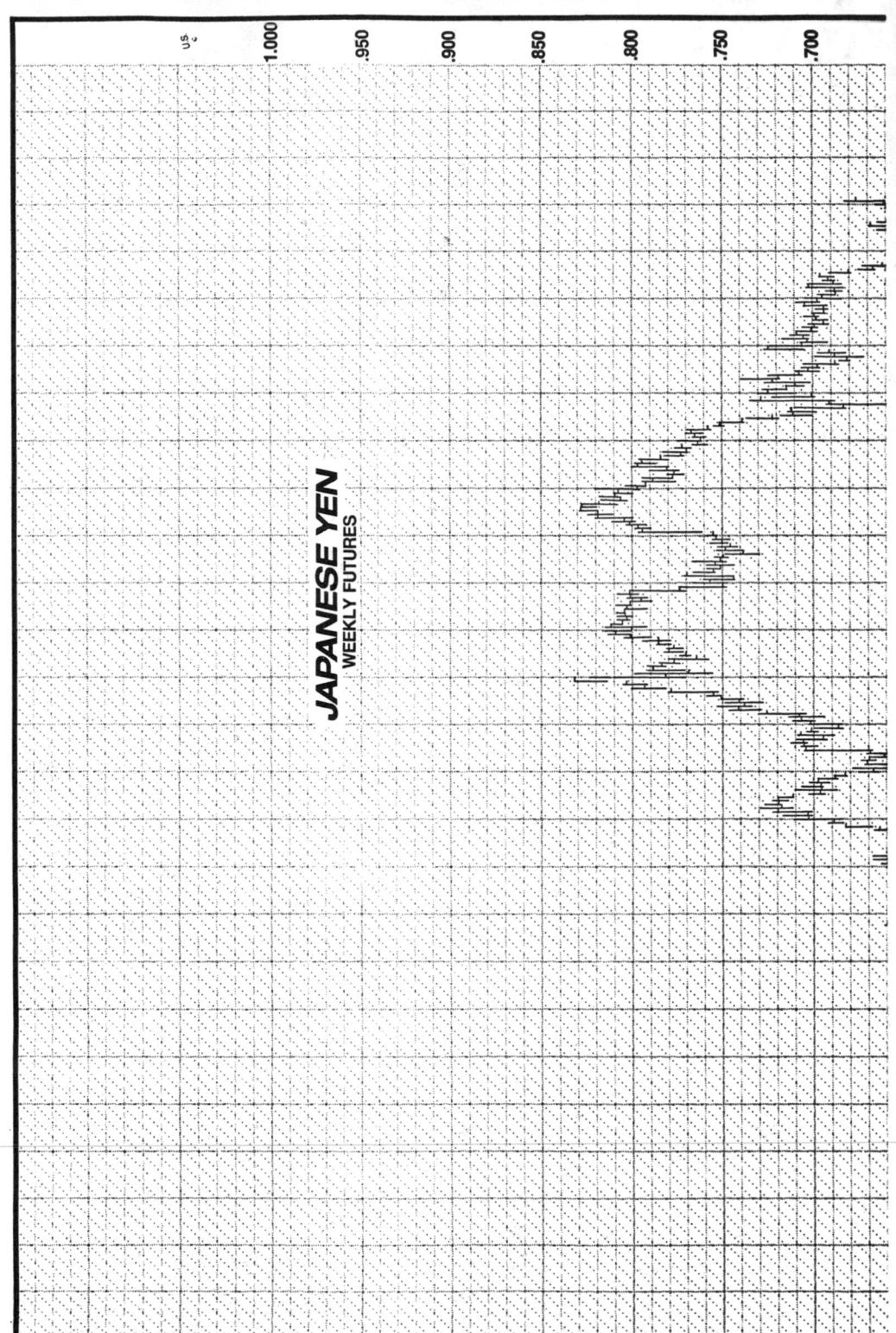

JAPANESE YEN
WEEKLY FUTURES

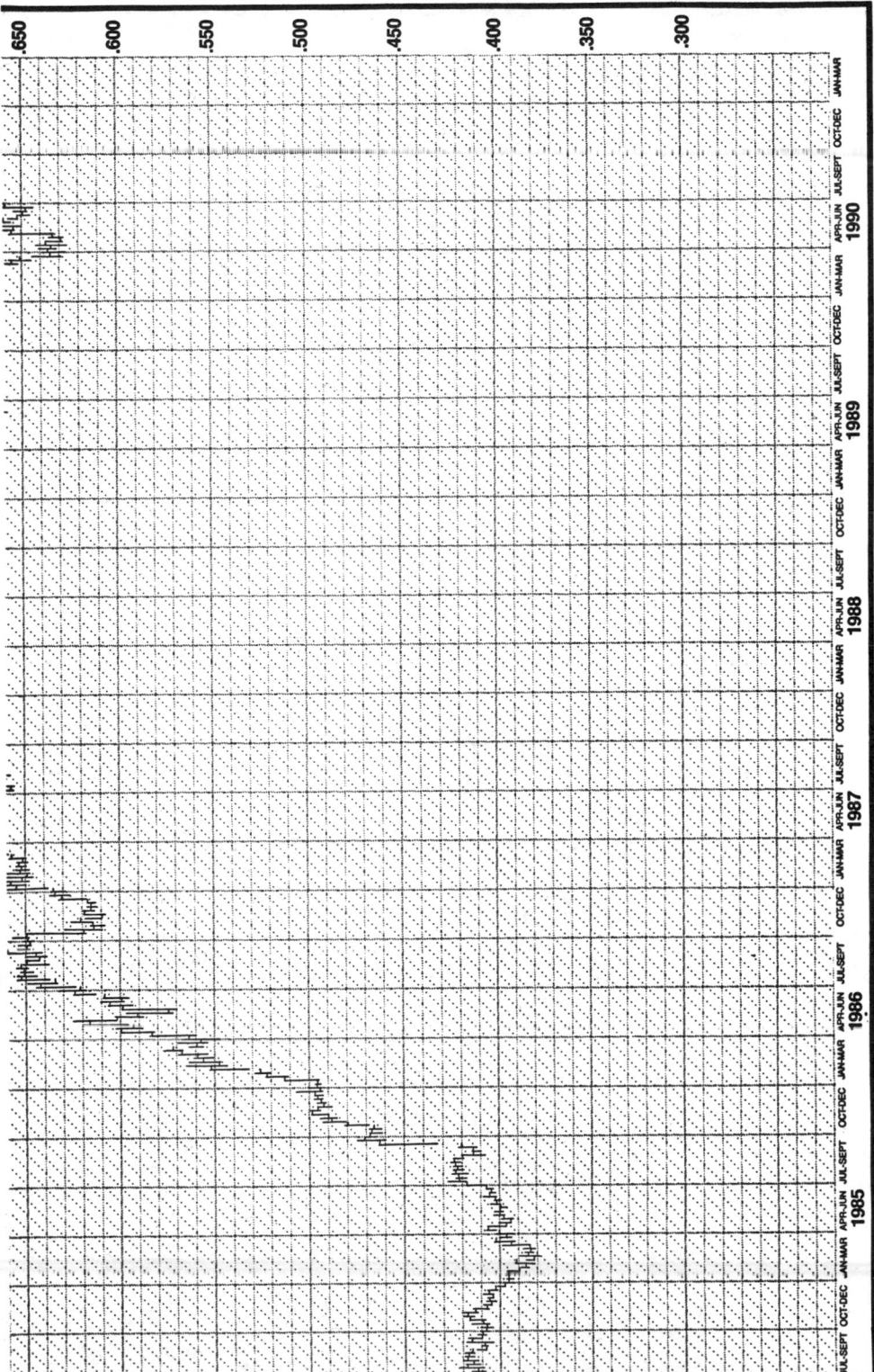

Source: Reprinted from *Commodity Price Charts*, 219 Parkade, Cedar Falls, Iowa 50613.

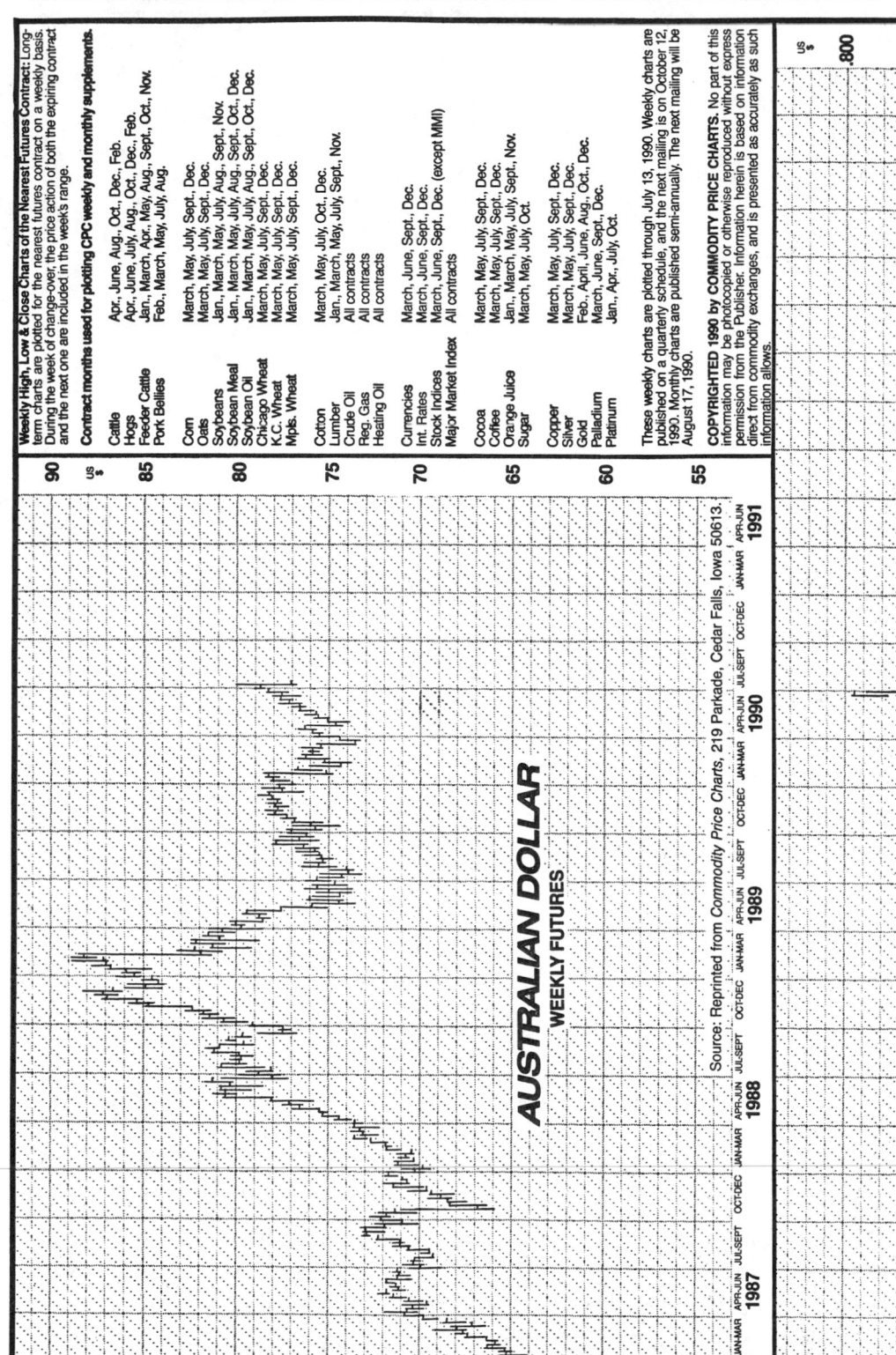

AUSTRALIAN DOLLAR

WEEKLY FUTURES

Weekly High, Low & Close Charts of the Nearest Futures Contract: Long-term charts are plotted for the nearest futures contract on a weekly basis. During the week of change-over, the price action of both the expiring contract and the next one are included in the weeks range.

Contract months used for plotting CPC weekly and monthly supplements.

Cattle	Apr., June, Aug., Oct., Dec., Feb.
Hogs	Apr., June, July, Aug., Oct., Dec., Feb.
Feeder Cattle	Jan., March, Apr., May, Aug., Sept., Oct., Nov.
Pork Bellies	Feb., March, May, July, Aug.
Corn	March, May, July, Sept., Dec.
Oats	March, May, July, Sept., Dec.
Soybeans	Jan., March, May, July, Aug., Sept., Nov.
Soybean Meal	Jan., March, May, July, Aug., Sept., Oct., Dec.
Soybean Oil	Jan., March, May, July, Aug., Sept., Oct., Dec.
Chicago Wheat	March, May, July, Sept., Dec.
K.C. Wheat	March, May, July, Sept., Dec.
Mpls. Wheat	March, May, July, Sept., Dec.
Cotton	March, May, July, Oct., Dec.
Lumber	Jan., March, May, July, Sept., Nov.
Crude Oil	All contracts
Reg. Gas	All contracts
Heating Oil	All contracts
Currencies	March, June, Sept., Dec.
Int. Rates	March, June, Sept., Dec.
Stock Indices	March, June, Sept., Dec. (except MMI)
Major Market Index	All contracts
Cocoa	March, May, July, Sept., Dec.
Coffee	March, May, July, Sept., Dec.
Orange Juice	Jan., March, May, July, Sept., Nov.
Sugar	March, May, July, Oct.
Copper	March, May, July, Sept., Dec.
Silver	March, May, July, Sept., Dec.
Gold	Feb., April, June, Aug., Oct., Dec.
Palladium	March, June, Sept., Dec.
Platinum	Jan., Apr., July, Oct.

These **weekly** charts are plotted through July 13, 1990. Weekly charts are published on a quarterly schedule, and the next mailing is on October 12, 1990. Monthly charts are published semi-annually. The next mailing will be August 17, 1990.

Source: Reprinted from *Commodity Price Charts*, 219 Parkade, Cedar Falls, Iowa 50613.

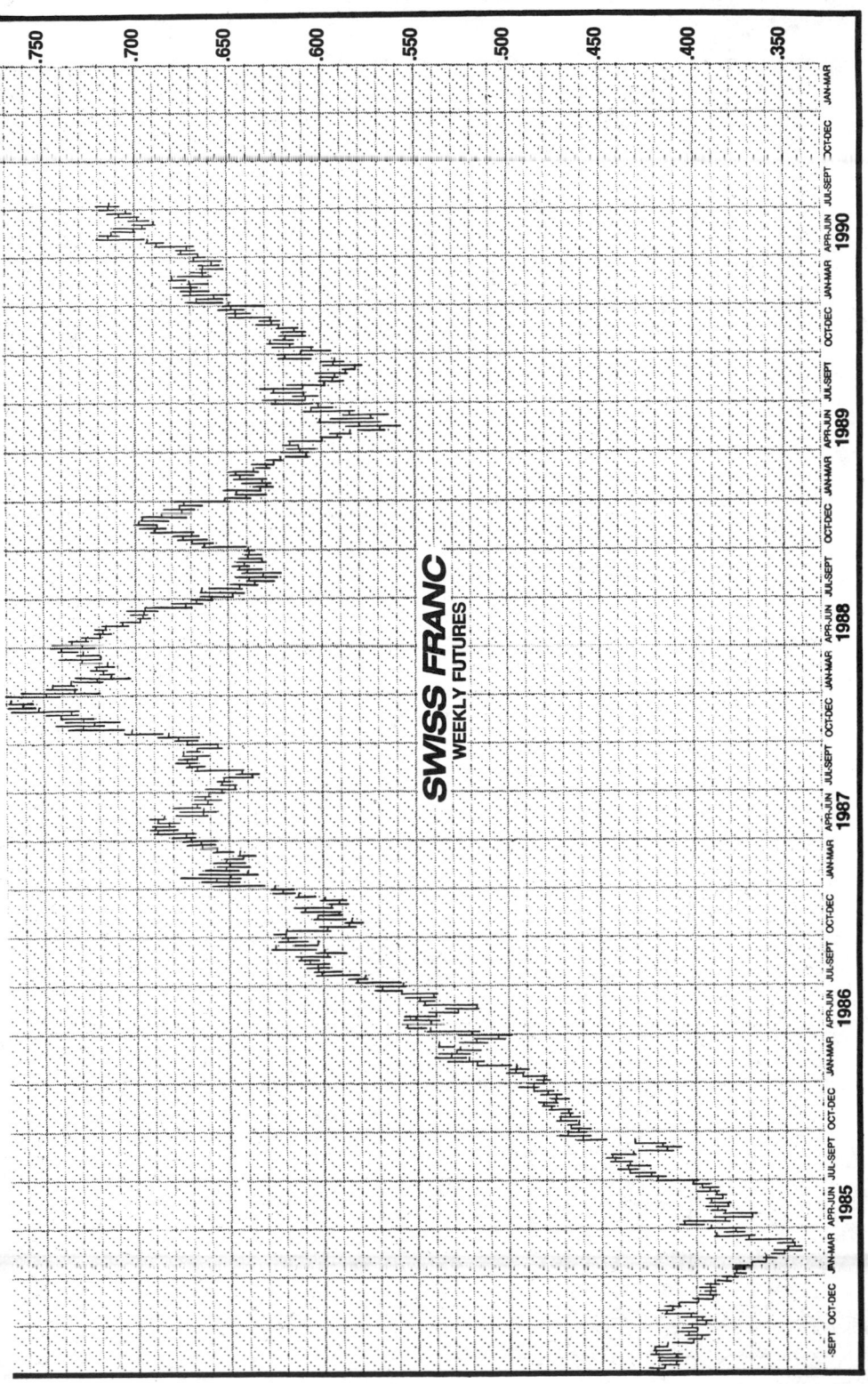

SWISS FRANC
WEEKLY FUTURES

Source: Reprinted from *Commodity Price Charts*, 219 Parkade, Cedar Falls, Iowa 50613.

Taxes

Per Capita Tax Burden by State
Fiscal Years 1989-1991

State	Per Capita Burden			State Rank '90	
	1989	1990	1991	Total Taxes	Per Capita
U.S. Total	$ 3,884	$ 4,170	$ 4,511	—	—
Alabama	2,821	3,037	3,298	25	41
Alaska	4,667	4,891	5,164	46	9
Arizona	3,309	3,483	3,697	24	34
Arkansas	2,655	2,863	3,122	32	48
California	4,331	4,600	4,921	1	11
Colorado	3,660	3,905	4,202	22	22
Connecticut	6,252	6,768	7,358	15	1
Delaware	4,629	4,953	5,344	44	8
Florida	3,908	4,127	4,391	5	19
Georgia	3,424	3,648	3,912	12	29
Hawaii	3,781	4,044	4,354	39	20
Idaho	2,698	2,891	3,137	45	46
Illinois	4,375	4,738	5,166	4	10
Indiana	3,409	3,693	4,032	16	27
Iowa	3,261	3,541	3,886	30	33
Kansas	3,623	3,899	4,236	31	23
Kentucky	2,783	3,008	3,280	26	43
Louisiana	2,725	2,952	3,230	23	44
Maine	3,358	3,607	3,909	42	31
Maryland	4,694	5,046	5,456	13	6
Massachusetts	5,149	5,577	6,076	10	4
Michigan	3,966	4,298	4,695	9	15
Minnesota	3,902	4,200	4,561	20	16
Mississippi	2,276	2,451	2,668	33	51
Missouri	3,544	3,823	4,159	17	24
Montana	2,807	3,024	3,300	47	42
Nebraska	3,277	3,545	3,871	34	32
Nevada	4,159	4,364	4,606	37	13
New Hampshire	4,703	5,014	5,374	35	7
New Jersey	5,780	6,239	6,776	7	2
New Mexico	2,719	2,890	3,105	41	47
New York	4,779	5,178	5,647	2	5
North Carolina	3,237	3,469	3,747	14	35
North Dakota	2,862	3,086	3,366	50	39
Ohio	3,689	3,997	4,366	8	21
Oklahoma	2,959	3,173	3,438	28	38
Oregon	3,423	3,678	3,995	29	28
Pennsylvania	3,873	4,189	4,569	6	17
Rhode Island	4,193	4,517	4,906	40	12
South Carolina	2,843	3,040	3,280	27	40
South Dakota	2,709	2,919	3,179	49	45
Tennessee	3,183	3,424	3,711	21	37
Texas	3,410	3,619	3,870	3	30
Utah	2,568	2,731	2,934	38	50
Vermont	3,511	3,761	4,065	48	26
Virginia	4,052	4,341	4,681	11	14
Washington	3,886	4,146	4,462	18	18
West Virginia	2,541	2,758	3,026	36	49
Wisconsin	3,529	3,803	4,139	19	25
Wyoming	3,189	3,429	3,730	51	36
Dist. of Columbia	5,292	5,770	6,326	43	3

Source: Computations of total and per capita tax burden by state made by Tax Foundation, based on Fiscal Year 1991 Budget of the U.S.

Note: These calculations do not count the federal budget deficit, so, for example, the estimated $124 billion federal budget deficit for 1990 is not included in the 1990 calculation.

Source: Tax Foundation, 470 L'Enfant Plaza, S.W., Washington, DC, 20024.

MAJOR STATE TAXES AND RATES*

State	Income Taxes		General Sales and Use Tax	Gasoline Tax (per gallon)	Cigarette Tax (per pack of 20)	Property Tax
	Corporate	Individual				
Alabama	5% (F)	2 to 5% (F)	4% (a)	11 cents	16.5 cents	X
Arizona	9.3 (F)	3.8 to 7 (F)	5 (a)	17 (b)	15 (b)	X
Arkansas	1 to 6	1 to 7	4 (a)	13.5	21	X
California	9.3 (c)	1 to 9.3 (c)	5 (a, d)	9 (b)	35	X
Colorado	5 to 5.3 (d)	5 (c)	3 (a)	20 (b)	20	X
Connecticut	11.5 (e, f)	1 to 14 (g)	8	22 (b)	40	X
District of Columbia	10 (f)	6 to 9.5	6	18	17	X
Georgia	6	1 to 6	4 (a)	7.5 + 3% of retail	12	X
Hawaii	4.4 to 6.4	2 to 10	4 (a)	19.8 to 27.5	40% of wholesale	
Idaho	8	2 to 8.2	5	18	18	X
Illinois	4.8 (h)	3	6.25 (a)	19	30	X
Indiana	3.4 (i)	3.4	5	15	15.5	X
Iowa	6 to 12 (F, j)	.4 to 9.98 (F,c)	4 (a)	20	31	
Kansas	4.5 (f)	3.65 to 8.75 (k)	4.25 (a)	16 (b)	24	X
Kentucky	3 to 7.25	2 to 6 (F)	6 (a)	15 (l)	3	X
Louisiana	4 to 8 (F)	2 to 6 (F)	4 (a)	20	16	X
Maine	3.5 to 8.93	2 to 8.5	5	17	31 (b)	X
Maryland	7	2 to 5	5	18.5	13	X
Massachusetts	9.5 (m)	5.95 (n)	5	17 (b)	26	X
Michigan	2.35	4.6	4	15	25	X
Minnesota	9.5 (b, c)	6 to 8.5 (o)	6 (a)	20	38	X
Mississippi	3 to 5	3 to 5	6	18 (d)	18	X
Missouri	5 to 6.5 (F, e)	1.5 to 6 (F)	4.225 (a, d)	11	13	X
Nebraska	5.17 to 7.24 (b)	2 to 5.9 (b)	5 (a)	21.9 (l)	27	X
New Jersey	9 (f)	2 to 7	7	10.5	40	X
New Mexico	4.8 to 7.6	1.8 to 8.5	5	16	15	X
New York	9 (c, f)	4 to 7.875 (d, p)	4 (a)	8	39	
North Carolina	7	6 to 7	3 (a)	21.5	2	X
North Dakota	3 to 10.5 (F, c)	2.67 to 12 (F, q)	5	17	30 (d)	X
Ohio	5.1 to 8.9	.743 to 6.9	5 (a)	20	18	X
Oklahoma	6	.5 to 10 (F, k)	4.5 (a)	16	23	
Pennsylvania	8.5	2.1	6 (a)	12	18	X
Rhode Island	9	22.96% of modified Federal income tax	7 (d)	20 (l)	37	X
South Carolina	5	3 to 7 (d)	5 (a)	16	7	X
Tennessee	6	6 (g)	5.5 (a)	20	13	
Utah	5	2.55 to 7.2 (F)	5 (a)	19	23	X
Vermont	5.5 to 8.25	28% of Federal income tax (d)	4	15 (d)	17	X
Virginia	6	2 to 5.75	3.5 (a)	17.5	2.5	X
West Virginia	9.3 (d)	3 to 6.5 (c)	6	15.5	17	X
Wisconsin	7.9	4.9 to 6.93	5 (a)	21.5 (l)	30 (e)	X
Florida	5.5 (c)		6 (a)	4 (r)	33.9	X
Nevada	These 5 states	These 7 states	5.75 (a)	18	35 (d)	X
South Dakota	have no	have no	4 (a)	18	23	
Texas	corporate	individual	6.25 (a)	15	41	
Washington	income tax	income tax	6.5 (a)	22 (b, l)	34 (d)	X
Wyoming			3 (a)	9 (l)	12	X
Alaska	1 to 9.4		These	8	29	X
Delaware	8.7	3.2 to 7.7 (F)	5 states	16 (b)	14 (b)	
Montana	6.75 (f, s)	2 to 11 (F)	have no	20	18	X
New Hampshire	8	5 (g)	general	16	25	X
Oregon	6.6	5 to 9 (F)	sales tax	18 (b)	28	X

(X) Indicates state levies a property tax.
(F) Allows federal income tax as a deduction.

(a) Local taxes are additional.
(b) Future increases scheduled under current law.
(c) Alternative minimum tax is imposed.
(d) Future reductions scheduled under current law.
(e) Alternative methods of calculation may be required.
(f) Corporate surtax is imposed, Connecticut – 20%, District of Columbia – 5%, Kansas – 2.25%, New Jersey – .375%, New York – 15%, Montana – 5%.
(g) In Connecticut, New Hampshire, and Tennessee, rates apply to income from

dividends and interest. Capital gains are taxed at 7% in Connecticut.
(h) Additional 2.5% personal property replacement tax imposed.
(i) A supplemental net income tax is imposed at 4.5%.
(j) Franchise tax is 5% of taxable net income.
(k) In Kansas and Oklahoma, the higher rates apply to taxpayers deducting Federal income tax.
(l) Tax rate is periodically adjusted administratively.
(m) Excise tax is imposed equal to the greater of $456.
(n) Tax of 12% on income derived from interest,

dividends, and capital gains.
(o) Additional tax is imposed on income over specified levels, varying with filing status.
(p) Qualified taxpayers may elect to pay alternative taxes at varying rates.
(q) Optional tax of 14% of taxpayers federal income tax liability.
(r) In addition, Florida imposes a 6.9 cent sales tax on gasoline.
(s) 7% rate for corporations using water's edge apportionment.
Source: Compiled by Tax Foundation from survey of state revenue offices and data reported by Commerce Clearing House through June 15, 1990.

Source: Tax Foundation, 470 L'Enfant Plaza, S.W., Washington, D.C. 20024.

* As of July 15, 1990.

TAX FREEDOM DAY AND 1990 TAX BITE IN 8-HOUR DAY

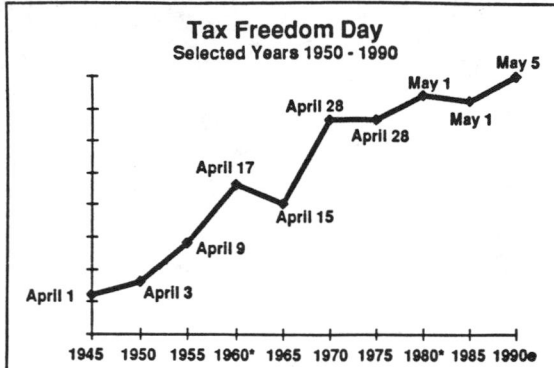

Tax Freedom Day
Selected Years 1950 - 1990

April 1 — April 3 — April 9 — April 17 — April 15 — April 28 — April 28 — May 1 — May 1 — May 5

1945 1950 1955 1960* 1965 1970 1975 1980* 1985 1990e

Tax Freedom Day and Tax Bite in the Eight-Hour Day

Year	Tax Freedom Day		Tax Bite (hrs: min.)		
	Day	Number of Days	Total	Federal	State/Local
1984ª	April 28	119	2:36	1:42	:54
1985	May 1	121	2:38	1:44	:54
1986	May 2	122	2:40	1:44	:56
1987	May 4	124	2:43	1:47	:56
1988*	May 2	123	2:41	1:45	:56
1989	May 3	123	2:42	1:46	:56
1990e	May 5	125	2:45	1:47	:58

* Leap year causes the calendar date of Tax Freedom Day to appear one day earlier.
e Estimates by Tax Foundation.
Source: Tax Foundation

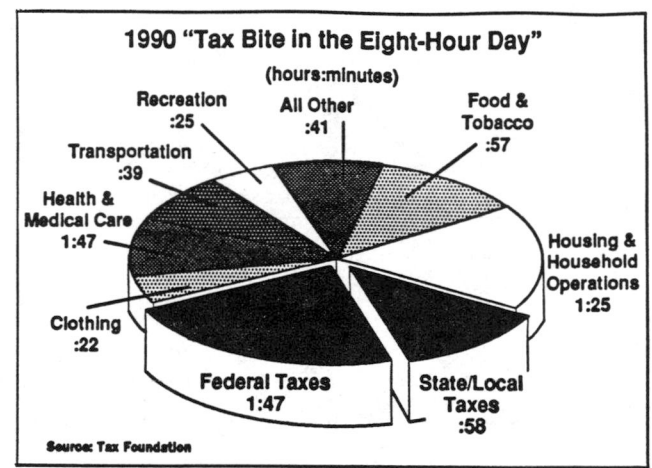

1990 "Tax Bite in the Eight-Hour Day"
(hours:minutes)

Recreation :25
All Other :41
Food & Tobacco :57
Transportation :39
Health & Medical Care 1:47
Clothing :22
Federal Taxes 1:47
State/Local Taxes :58
Housing & Household Operations 1:25

Source: Tax Foundation

Source: Tax Foundation, 470 L'Enfant Plaza, S.W., East Building, Washington, D.C. 20024.

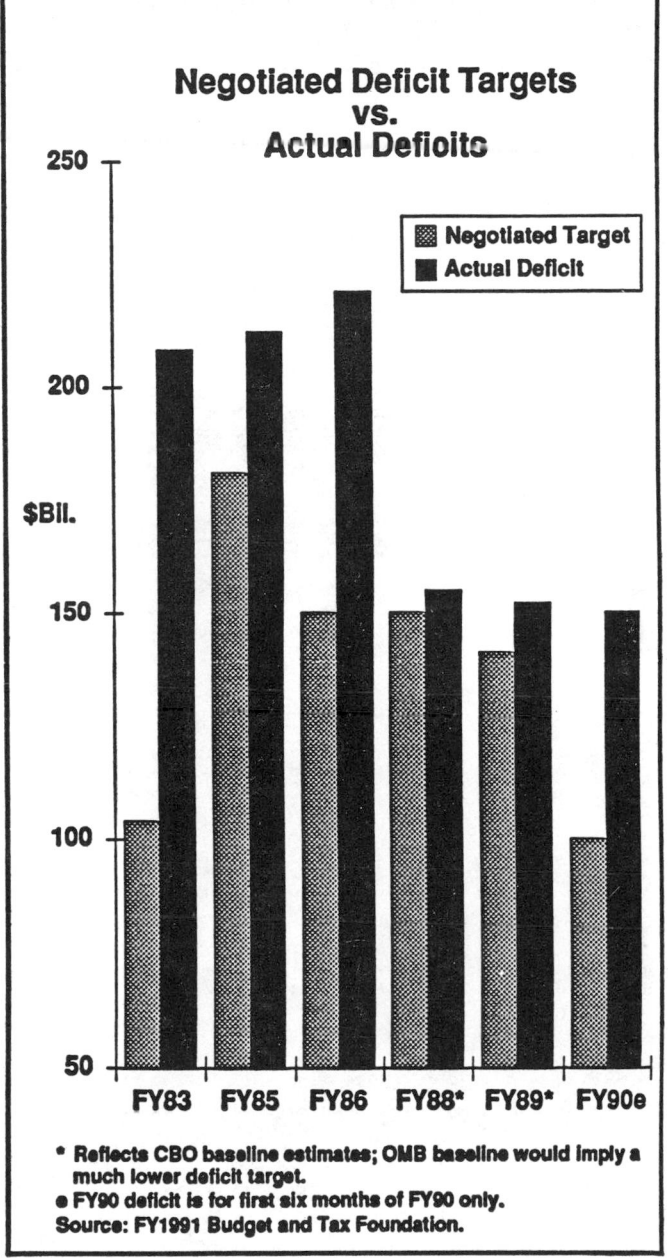

Negotiated Deficit Targets
vs.
Actual Deficits

$Bll.

Legend:
Negotiated Target
Actual Deficit

FY83   FY85   FY86   FY88*   FY89*   FY90e

* Reflects CBO baseline estimates; OMB baseline would imply a
  much lower deficit target.
● FY90 deficit is for first six months of FY90 only.
Source: FY1991 Budget and Tax Foundation.

Source: Tax Foundation, 470 L'Enfant Plaza, S.W., Washington, DC 20024.

PERCENTAGE DISTRIBUTION OF TAX REVENUES IN SELECTED COUNTRIES BY SOURCE (fiscal year 1987)

Country	All Taxes	Taxes on Income and Profits(a)		Social Security Taxes			Taxes on Goods and Services			Property Taxes(d)	Other and Unallocable(e)
		Individual Income	Corporate Profits	Total(b)	Employers' Share	Employees' Share	Total(c)	General Services	Specific		
Australia	100.0%	45.4%	10.3%	-	-	-	29.8%	8.2%	17.6%	9.2%	5.4%
Austria	100.0	22.7	3.3	32.3%	15.9%	13.5%	32.3	20.9	10.2	2.3	7.2
Belgium	100.0	32.7	6.6	33.9	20.3	11.1	24.7	15.7	7.1	2.1	0.0
Canada	100.0	38.7	8.0	13.3	8.5	4.6	28.9	14.1	11.2	9.2	1.3
Denmark	100.0	49.2	4.5	3.7	1.8	1.9	33.9	18.9	13.8	5.1	0.9
Finland	100.0	45.6	3.9	9.0	9.0	-	38.2	24.6	13.1	3.2	0.2
France	100.0	12.7	5.2	43.0	27.2	12.3	29.3	19.5	8.9	4.7	5.0
Germany	100.0	29.0	5.0	37.3	19.1	16.1	25.4	15.7	8.6	3.2	0.0
Greece	100.0	12.3	4.4	22.6	14.2	14.1	46.6	26.9	16.8	2.5	1.1
Ireland	100.0	34.6	3.2	14.0	8.8	5.1	42.5	20.2	20.5	4.4	1.3
Italy	100.0	26.3	10.5	34.3	24.1	6.7	26.4	14.6	10.3	2.6	0.5
Japan	100.0	24.0	22.9	28.6	14.8	10.2	12.9	-	11.1	11.2	0.3
Luxembourg	100.0	25.3	17.1	26.4	14.1	10.8	24.4	13.5	10.3	6.8	0.0
Netherlands	100.0	19.7	7.7	42.7	17.0	18.8	26.0	16.4	7.4	3.6	0.3
New Zealand	100.0	49.9	8.9	-	-	-	32.6	16.7	15.1	7.0	0.9
Norway	100.0	26.4	6.7	23.7	16.3	6.5	40.1	20.8	18.0	2.5	0.7
Portugal	100.0	f	f	28.2	17.8	9.4	49.3	21.0	27.3	2.0	1.0
Spain	100.0	21.3	6.7	36.2	27.4	6.1	30.4	16.9	12.4	3.7	0.2
Sweden	100.0	37.2	4.1	24.2	23.3	-	24.1	13.3	9.8	5.7	4.7
Switzerland	100.0	34.0	6.2	32.1	10.1	10.2	19.1	9.7	8.1	8.5	0.0
Turkey	100.0	24.9	10.7	15.9	9.2	5.9	32.0	23.4	8.2	3.2	13.3
United Kingdom	100.0	26.6	10.6	18.1	9.4	8.3	31.4	16.1	13.6	13.2	0.0
United States	100.0	36.2	8.1	28.8	16.6	11.1	16.7	7.4	7.2	10.2	0.0

(a) Includes taxes on capital gains.

(b) Includes taxes on self-employed.

(c) Includes import duties, profits on public fiscal monopolies, licenses, and other business taxes.

(d) Includes taxes on movable and immovable property, net wealth taxes, and estate and gift taxes.

(e) Includes general and selective taxes on payrolls which are not earmarked for social security purposes, and other taxes not elsewhere classified.

(f) Income and profit taxes are 21.2% of total taxes and are included under other and unallocable, as they are not segregable between individuals and corporations.

Source: Organization for Economic Cooperation and Development.

Source: Tax Foundation, 470 L'Enfant Plaza, S.W., Washington, D.C. 20024.

How the Federal Government Will Spend a Family's Tax Dollar in 1990

Function	Family's Share		Spending (Billions)
	Amount	Percent of Total	
Income Security[b]	$ 4,237	32.75%	$ 418.5
National Defense	3,070	23.73	303.3
Net Interest	1,751	13.54	173.0
Health[c]	1,643	12.70	162.3
Education, Training, Employment, Social Services	415	3.21	41.0
Veterans' Benefits and Services	307	2.37	30.3
Transportation	302	2.33	29.8
Environment and Natural Resources	184	1.42	18.2
International Affairs	184	1.42	18.2
Commerce and Housing Credit	174	1.35	17.2
General Science, Space and Technology	168	1.30	16.6
Agriculture	151	1.17	14.9
Administration of Justice	128	0.99	12.6
General Government	114	0.88	11.3
Community and Regional Development	79	0.61	7.8
Energy	30	0.23	3.0
Total[d]	$ 12,938	100.00%	$ 1,233.3

[a] This example uses a two-earner family earning $45,000 per year with two dependent children.
[b] Primarily social security. Includes federal employee retirement, unemployment compensation, and nutrition assistance. Excludes veteran's income security.
[c] Primarily Medicare and Medicaid. Excludes veteran's health care.
[d] After deducting $44.7 billion in undistributed and offsetting receipts not classified by function.
Source: Tax Foundation computations based on Fiscal Year 1991 U.S. Budget presented January 29, 1990, and 1990 tax laws from U.S. Department of Treasury.

Source: Tax Foundation, 470 L'Enfant Plaza, S.W., East Building, Washington, D.C. 20024.

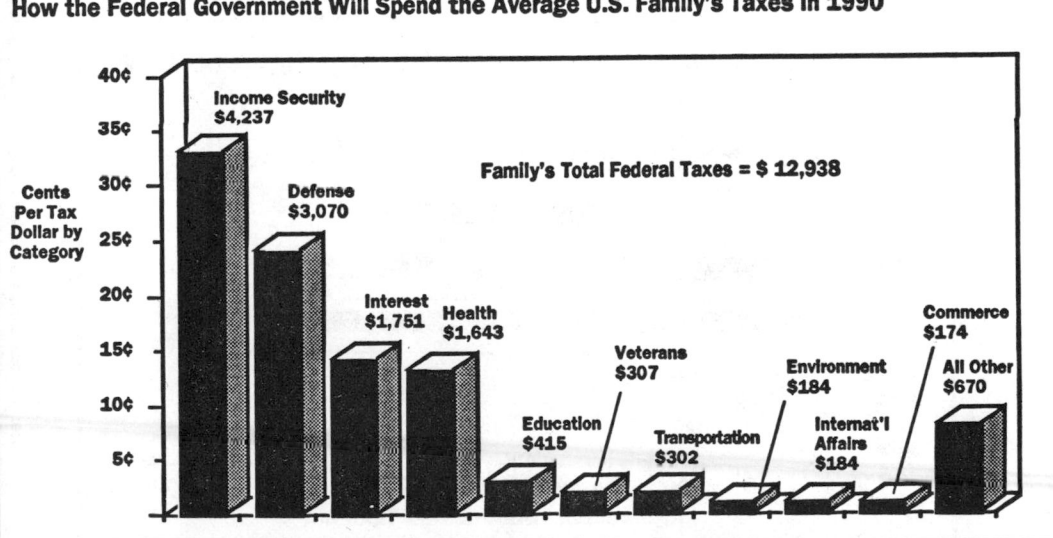

How the Federal Government Will Spend the Average U.S. Family's Taxes in 1990

Source: Tax Foundation, 470 L'Enfant Plaza S.W., East Building, Washington, D.C. 20024.

Federal Income Taxes Paid by High and Low-Income Taxpayers, 1979 and 1988

Adjusted Gross Income Class	Income Level		Percent of Tax Paid		Average Tax	
	1979	1988	1979	1988	1979	1988
Highest 5%	$39,000 or more	$73,757 or more	37.6%	45.9%	$17,407	$34,788
Highest 10%	32,710 or more	58,368 or more	49.5	56.9	11,456	21,573
Highest 25%	21,760 or more	35,609 or more	73.1	77.8	6,769	11,797
Highest 50%	11,870 or more	18,145 or more	93.2	94.5	4,315	7,163
Lowest 50%	11,869 or less	18,144 or less	6.8	5.5	313	416
Lowest 25%	5,565 or less	7,006 or less	0.5	0.6	46	87
Lowest 10%[b]	2,212 or less	2,178 or less	c	c	9	22

[a] Data for 1988 are preliminary.
[b] Includes returns showing no adjusted gross income.
[c] Less than .07 percent.
Source: Tax Foundation computations based on Statistics and Income, Internal Revenue Service, U.S. Department of the Treasury.

Source: Tax Foundation, 470 L'Enfant Plaza, S.W., Washington, D.C. 20024.

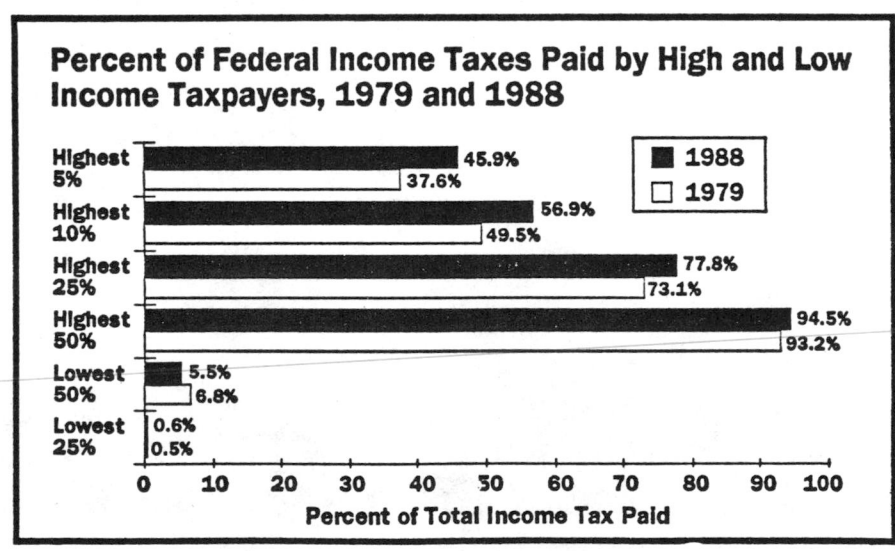

Source: Tax Foundation, 470 L'Enfant Plaza, S.W., Washington, D.C. 20024.

Investing in Gold, Diamonds and Collectibles

Investing in Gold

Gold has been one of the more widely promoted investment vehicles over the last several years. Prices moved from about $140 per ounce in early 1977 to over $800 in early 1980. However, by August 1985 prices declined to $291 an ounce but climbed to over $370.00 by May 1987. Because of such large fluctuations, the metal has stimulated a great deal of speculative interest among many investors.

Investment in gold can be made in a variety of ways:

Gold bullion (bars and wafers) This can be purchased through many stock brokers, bullion currency dealers, and some investment (mutual fund) companies. The purity of gold is indicated by the fineness. Pure gold has a fineness of 1.000 and corresponds to 24 karats.* Each bar is stamped with the fineness as determined by an assay, the refiner's number, a bar identification number and the weight. A bar fineness of .995 or better is acceptable.

Individuals who accept delivery of gold bars and who subsequently wish to resell must have the bar reassayed prior to sale because of the possibility of adulteration with cheaper metals. Because of the latter possibility, individuals should always buy from reputable dealers, and the bar should bear the stamp of well recognized refiners or assayers. Individuals taking physical possession of the metal also have sales taxes, storage, and insurance costs.

The purchaser may arrange to have the dealer (or agent) retain physical possession of the bullion. In this case, evidence of ownership is provided by a *gold deposit certificate* (receipt) issued by the dealer. Since gold certificates are generally nonnegotiable or assignable, there is no loss if it is stolen. The gold deposit certificate method of buying bullion eliminates sales taxes, storage risks (though the dealer will charge a modest storage fee) and the need for assay on resale. It is probably the most convenient way of purchasing gold.

---

*This "karats" is not to be confused with the "carats" that apply to diamonds.

Gold bullion coins Bullion coins are issued in large number by several governments which guarantee their gold content. They have no numismatic value. The best known gold bullion coins are the U.S. Gold One Ounce, South African Krugerrand, Canadian Maple Leaf, Austrian 100 Corona and the Gold Mexican 50 peso. The first three coins have a pure gold content of one ounce. The Austrian Corona has a gold content of .9802 ounce and the Mexican peso 1.2057 ounces. The premium (cost above the gold value) varies from dealer to dealer. For those who do not want to take physical possession, deposit certificates are available for the coins.

One of the largest bullion dealers is Deak International (212-757-0100) headquartered in New York City. Gold coins can also be purchased at banks where there is generally a very low premium over the gold content value.

Gold stocks The stocks of a number of Canadian and U.S. gold mining companies are traded on the New York (N), American (A) and Over-The-Counter (O) exchanges. Of course, with stocks, the investor is not just buying into gold, but also into the many special problems associated with running a company—production costs, quality of the ore, lifetime of the deposit, etc. However, many gold stocks pay dividends, whereas other gold investments do not pay any return during the holding period.

Some listed stocks are given below:

Agnico-Eagle Mines (O)
Campbell Red Lake Mines (N)
Dome Mines (N)
Sunshine Mining (N)
Homestake Mining Company (N)

A publicly-held New York Stock Exchange closed-end gold fund is ASA Limited. Several mutual funds which invest in gold are given in the mutual fund section of the Almanac (page 406).

South African gold mines are traded on the Over-The-Counter Market by means of ADR (American Depository Receipt). ADR is a claim on foreign stocks (South African gold shares, in this case) held by the foreign branches of large U.S.

banks. Holders of ADRs are entitled to dividends which, in the case of South African gold shares, may be substantial. The ADRs of these companies are listed in *The Wall Street Journal*.

Some major South African gold mining companies are:

Blyvooruitzicht
Buffelsfontein
Driefontein
Free Consolidated
Kloof
Orange Free State
President Brand
Randfontein
Western Deep Levels

Mutual funds specializing in gold and precious metals A number of mutual funds (see page 406) specialize in gold and precious metals stocks. These funds provide diversification among a number of issues thereby reducing risk associated with any particular stock.

Options on gold stocks Put and call options are available on Homestake Mining (Chicago Options Exchange) and on ASA Limited (American Options Exchange). These options may be used for leveraged speculation or for hedging existing gold holdings. Holders of call options gain if the gold shares increase, while holders of put options benefit if prices decline.

The Philadelphia Stock Exchange trades a gold/silver option based on an index of seven different stocks in the industry.

Options on gold bullion Put and call options on gold bullion are traded on the International Options Market (IOM) of the Montreal Stock Exchange. IOM options are on 10 ounces of gold. Contract months are Feb/May/Aug/Nov.

Monex (Newport Beach, CA) provides put and call options on 32.15 ounces of gold. The Monex options are not tradeable but can be exercized during the option period. Expiration periods are 30, 60, 90, and 185 days. Mocatta Metals (New York) also offers futures contracts.

Since options are paid in full, they are not subject to margin calls or forced liquidation as is the case with futures contracts. At this time, quotations on bullion options are not available in the daily press.

Gold futures contract Gold futures contracts are obligations to buy or sell 100 ounces of gold on or before a specified date at a specified price. Futures contracts must be exercised if held to maturity, while options contracts need not be exercised if held to maturity. Futures contracts are purchased on margin, and hence, are subject to margin call and possible forced liquidation. They are widely quoted in the financial press, and the market is highly organized.

As with options, futures contracts may be used for leveraged speculation or for hedging. Speculators will buy contracts if they anticipate a price increase or sell contracts in anticipation of a price decrease.

Gold futures are traded on the N.Y. Commodity Exchange, the International Monetary Market of the Chicago Mercantile Exchange, and other markets.

Options on Gold Futures Contracts Options on Gold Futures contracts (the right to buy and sell a gold futures contract rather than the metal) are actively traded on the New York Comex. The futures contract underlying the options is for 100 ounces of gold. Contract months are April/Aug./Dec. Gold futures options premiums are reported daily in the *Wall Street Journal*.

Investing in Diamonds

Diamond prices are very volatile. For example, they have appreciated on the average of about 12.6% over the ten-year period 1969–1979 (compared to a consumer price index of 6.1% during the same period of time). There have been periods (the recession of 1973—1974 and in 1981) when the price of investment quality diamonds slipped as much as 40%. A major factor stabilizing the market is DeBeers, a South African diamond company which handles as much as 80% of the world's diamonds. While the appreciation of diamonds has been impressive, potential buyers should be aware that prices are not quoted in the daily newspapers; therefore, selling the stones at a profit may be difficult. Quotes are available in the *Rappaport Diamond Report*, 15 West 47 Street, New York, NY 10036, (212) 354-0575. Another good source of information on the diamond industry is the Diamond Registry, 30 West 47 Street, New York, NY 10036, (212) 575-0444. The registry publishes a monthly newsletter which includes price ranges, trends, and forecasts as well as other pertinent material.

To locate reputable gem dealers check with the Diamond Registry (address above) or the

American Gem Society
5901 West 3rd Street
Los Angeles, CA 90036-2898
(213) 936-4367

American Diamond Industry Association
71 West 47 Street
New York, NY 10036
(212) 575-0525

Buyers should only deal with reputable firms, and the stones should be certified by an independent laboratory such as the Gemological Institute of America and International Gemological Institute with offices in New York City.

Diamonds are ranked in terms of the 4 C's—carat (one carat equals 1/142 ounces weight), color, clarity, and cut.

Carat For investment purposes the diamond should be more than .5 carat. However, diamonds of more than 2 carats may be difficult to sell.

Color There are six main categories, each with subdivisions:

D,E,F—Colorless
G,H,I,J—Near colorless
K,L,M—Faint yellow
N,O,P,Q,R—Very light yellow
S,T,U,V,W,X,Y,Z—Light yellow
Fancy yellow stone

Color should be in the range from D to H. However, Fancy Yellow Stones often command very high prices because of their scarcity.

Clarity Although bubbles, lines, and specks (inclusions) are natural to diamonds, they may interfere with the passage of light through the diamond. With a 10X magnification, a professional appraiser can grade the diamond according to the ten clarity grades:

FL—Flawless
IF—Internally flawless
VVS-1, VVS-2—Very, very slight inclusions
VS-1, VS-2—Very slight inclusions
SI-1, SI-2—Slight inclusions
I-1, I-2, I-3—Imperfect

Investment grade stones should be in the range FL to VS-2.

Cut There are several types of cuts—oval, marquise, pear shaped, round brilliant and emerald. Round brilliant stones are preferred for investment purposes. Proportions are important, and the preferred values are:

Depth % (total depth divided by girdle diameter): 57% to 63%.
Table (table diameter divided by girdle diameter): 57% to 66%.
Girdle thickness should be neither very thick nor very thin.

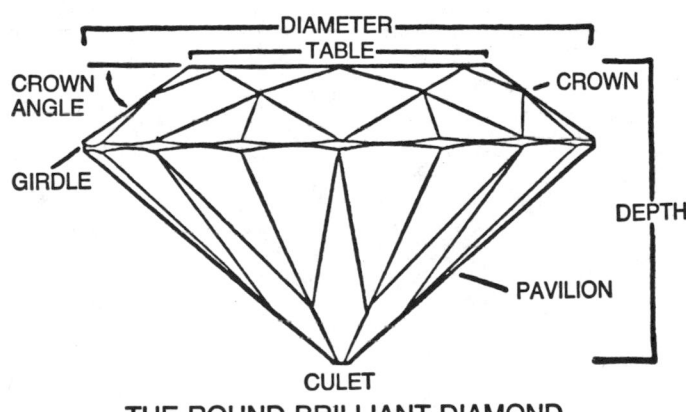

THE ROUND BRILLIANT DIAMOND

Investing in Collectibles

SOTHEBY'S ART INDEX

Index sectors	June 1990	One month ago	One year ago	Two years ago	Five years ago	One month % change	One year % change	Two years % change	Five years % change	Average annual % change
Old Master paintings	812	812	610	373	289	0.0	33.1	117.7	181.0	23.0
19th-century European paintings	679	672	536	347	249	1.0	26.7	95.7	172.7	22.2
Impressionist & Post-impressionist art	1,728	1,779	1,266	1,091	356	-2.9	36.5	58.4	385.4	37.2
Modern paintings (1900–1950)	1,774	1,751	1,264	1,090	336	1.3	40.3	62.8	428.0	39.5
Contemporary art (1945 onward)	1,627	1,627	856	728	470	0.0	90.1	123.5	246.2	28.2
American paintings (1800–pre-WWII)	1,371	1,371	1,371	871	589	0.0	0.0	57.4	132.8	18.4
Continental ceramics	555	555	505	407	284	0.0	9.9	36.4	95.4	14.3
Chinese ceramics	1,010	962	815	684	486	5.0	23.9	47.7	107.8	15.8
English silver	453	453	388	388	298	0.0	16.8	16.8	52.0	8.7
Continental silver	395	395	315	260	178	0.0	25.4	51.9	121.9	17.3
American furniture	510	510	484	469	324	0.0	5.4	8.7	57.4	9.5
French & Continental furniture	500	500	409	355	273	0.0	22.2	40.8	83.2	12.9
English furniture	917	917	822	720	382	0.0	11.6	27.4	140.1	19.1
Aggregate index	1,064	1,067	798	650	332	-0.3	33.3	63.7	220.5	26.2

©Sotheby's 1990

Sotheby's Art Index reflects subjective analyses and opinions of Sotheby's art experts, based on auction sales and other information deemed relevant. Nothing in Sotheby's Art Index is intended or should be relied upon as investment advice or as a prediction or guarantee of future performance or otherwise.

Source: © Sotheby's 1990.

Investing in Real Estate

MEDIAN SALES PRICE OF EXISTING SINGLE-FAMILY HOMES FOR METROPOLITAN AREAS* (not seasonally adjusted in thousands of dollars)

| Metropolitan Area | Years | | | Quarters | | | | 1990 |
| | 1987 | 1988 | 1989 | 1989 | | | | I^r |
				I	II	III	IV	
Akron, OH	$ 57.1	$ 59.9	$ 64.5	$ 56.0	$ 62.9*	$ 66.6	$ 69.7	$ 65.8
Albany/Schenectady/Troy, NY	86.4	92.2	104.9	102.1	104.2	108.6	103.6	102.8
Albuquerque, NM	82.6	80.4	83.0	82.0	84.5	83.5	81.7	82.8
Orange County(Anaheim/Santa Ana MSA), CA**	167.3	206.9	241.6	234.4	245.1	246.1	240.6	243.6
Atlanta, GA	n/a	n/a	84.0	80.3	84.1	85.6	85.0	85.3
Baltimore, MD	81.1	88.7	96.3	92.2	95.1	98.9	97.6	104.2
Baton Rouge, LA	67.8	64.7	63.8	61.1	64.7	63.9	64.3	64.0
Birmingham, AL	71.6	75.7	78.5	77.3	77.8	80.3	78.1	77.5
Boston, MA	177.2	181.2	181.9	176.3	186.2	183.3	180.0	177.3
Buffalo/Niagara Falls, NY	56.7	65.6	72.5	68.7	71.5	74.2	75.7	77.3
Charleston, SC	72.7	73.1	74.5	72.4	75.0	77.1	72.9	74.4
Charlotte, NC	n/a	n/a	88.1	85.2	86.5	89.5	90.5	89.6
Chattanooga, TN	59.0	63.5	65.4	65.6	64.6	64.9	66.7	66.8
Chicago, IL	90.8	98.9	107.0	99.6	105.0	111.4	109.3	112.3
Cincinnati, OH	66.1	69.7	75.8	72.8	76.6	77.8	74.8	77.7
Cleveland, OH	68.1	69.2	75.2	69.4	76.2	77.9	74.2	77.1
Columbia, SC	68.4	69.7	73.9	71.9	73.5	74.9	74.6	74.9
Columbus, OH	68.7	72.6	77.9	73.9	76.7	81.3	77.4	80.2
Corpus Christi, TX	65.9	64.9	64.9	63.2	64.4	66.7	64.5	62.5
Dallas, TX	90.8	90.8	92.4	89.8	92.4	94.7	92.2	89.8
Daytona Beach, FL	60.2	62.6	63.4	59.5	63.0	65.3	65.8	62.4
Dayton/Springfield, OH	59.4	63.3	68.7	64.4	69.0	72.2	67.4	67.1
Denver,CO	88.9	81.8	85.5	80.8	84.2	88.5	86.8	84.5
Des Moines, IA	55.6	55.8	57.5	56.0	57.1	59.2	57.4	61.6
Detroit, MI	65.6	73.1	73.7	70.9	73.1	76.2	73.6	75.5
El Paso, TX	59.2	59.6	63.1	57.2	64.2	65.4	64.2	62.1
Ft.Lauderdale/Hollywood/Pompano Beach, FL	79.6	81.1	83.9	82.1	81.4	83.7	88.9	89.8
Ft. Myers-Cape Coral, FL	59.9	62.7	66.6	66.6	66.1	66.7	66.9	65.1
Ft. Worth, TX	80.0	73.3	79.9	80.9	80.9	80.9	77.1	78.1
Grand Rapids, MI	53.5	57.9	64.2	59.2	65.0	65.6	67.2	67.5
Greenville/Spartanburg, SC	64.2	65.9	68.6	60.8	69.1	71.6	71.0	73.0

(continued)

MEDIAN SALES PRICE OF EXISTING SINGLE-FAMILY HOMES FOR METROPOLITAN AREAS* (not seasonally adjusted in thousands of dollars)

| Metropolitan Area | Years | | | Quarters | | | | 1990 |
	1987	1988	1989	1989 I	II	III	IV	I[r]
Hartford, CT	157.4	167.6	165.9	165.5	165.1	168.5	164.2	157.1
Honolulu, HI	186.0	215.1	267.6	245.0	259.0	275.0	300.0	325.0
Houston, TX	65.9	61.8	66.7	62.9	68.7	70.9	62.6	70.7
Indianapolis, IN	62.5	66.1	71.2	68.0	70.9	72.8	72.2	73.2
Jackson, MS	62.7	n/a	69.0	65.1	69.4	69.1	72.9	65.2
Jacksonville, FL	65.1	67.7	69.3	65.9	67.8	71.8	70.8	70.5
Kalamazoo, MI	49.9	53.2	57.2	56.1	57.6	56.4	58.9	56.4
Kansas City, MO/KS	69.8	70.5	71.6	73.8	72.6	69.1	70.9	73.9
Knoxville, TN	65.4	67.0	71.1	69.8	70.3	73.2	70.5	73.6
Lansing/East Lansing, MI	54.5	56.6	59.8	57.9	59.4	61.5	60.4	59.9
Las Vegas, NV	77.0	78.8	85.7	80.5	86.1	87.3	87.6	88.6
Lexington/Fayette, KY	72.5	73.5	77.0	74.9	78.3	78.2	75.9	76.8
Lincoln, NE	54.8	55.5	57.0	55.0	55.8	58.8	58.1	60.0
Little Rock/N. Little Rock, AR	63.1	63.9	63.7	63.4	62.9	64.3	64.1	n/a
Los Angeles Area, CA**	147.7	179.4	214.1	199.6	218.0	221.8	217.1	211.5
Louisville, KY	51.7	54.5	58.4	57.6	58.4	59.3	58.0	59.3
Madison, WI	69.2	72.0	76.5	74.7	76.8	77.3	76.6	78.7
Melbourne–Titusville–Palm Bay, FL	66.7	68.1	69.9	68.9	70.0	72.6	68.4	70.6
Memphis, TN	75.0	76.3	78.1	77.0	78.0	78.3	79.1	77.9
Miami/Hialeah, FL	81.1	82.9	86.9	83.0	88.1	86.6	89.0	90.0
Milwaukee, WI	70.5	74.5	79.6	76.0	81.2	80.0	79.7	81.8
Minneapolis/St Paul, MN	80.5	85.2	87.2	85.9	87.0	87.8	88.3	87.8
Mobile, AL	55.6	53.0	56.7	55.1	55.4	58.9	56.4	58.7
Montgomery, AL	64.8	64.5	68.8	66.0	69.7	70.0	68.8	66.7
Nashville/Davidson, TN	75.5	77.6	79.9	79.6	79.3	83.0	77.7	80.8
New Haven/Meridan, CT	156.9	169.4	163.4	166.7	156.0	168.4	162.9	153.2
New Orleans, LA	n/a	73.1	70.6	68.4	68.7	72.9	72.2	67.7
NewYork/N. NewJersey/Long Island, NY/NJ/CT	183.5	183.8	183.2	182.7	186.6	183.6	179.3	174.7
Bergen-Passaic, NJ	n/a	n/a	204.5	206.1	212.3	207.6	194.2	191.2
Middlesex-Somerset-Hunterdon, NJ	n/a	n/a	167.0	171.7	169.4	163.5	164.6	163.7
Nassau-Suffolk, NY	168.7	174.4	172.0	173.4	176.9	169.5	168.7	164.9
Oklahoma City, OK	62.3	56.2	53.5	52.3	52.3	55.5	53.9	50.6

Metropolitan Area							
Omaha, NE	$59.0	$59.5	$60.6	$59.3	$58.6	$63.8	$64.8
Orlando, FL	76.2	79.1	79.8	79.1	78.7	83.2	79.9
Peoria, IL	46.5	45.0	46.8	42.0	47.7	48.7	48.0
Philadelphia, PA	97.0	102.4	103.9	96.4	99.9	108.4	95.4
Phoenix, AZ	80.9	80.0	78.8	78.5	82.2	76.8	82.3
Pittsburgh, PA	n/a	63.2	65.8	62.4	65.2	68.1	68.6
Portland, OR	64.2	64.4	70.1	67.1	68.8	71.8	75.3
Providence, RI	121.4	130.6	130.2	128.8	130.9	132.0	127.0
Raleigh/Durham, NC	98.0	97.0	103.6	102.0	99.4	105.7	106.7
Reno, NV	93.8	96.6	102.6	95.6	103.1	103.9	106.4
Richmond, VA	n/a	n/a	n/a	n/a	n/a	83.7	87.9
Riverside/San Bernardino, CA**	96.1	106.7	123.8	116.1	122.2	128.6	130.4
Rochester, NY	72.5	75.7	78.5	76.4	76.8	80.8	79.0
Rockford, IL	56.2	58.3	62.7	59.8	59.8	63.4	66.6
Sacramento, CA**	87.5	95.3	111.1	100.3	107.2	116.2	127.7
Saginaw, MI	42.7	44.3	46.9	46.1	48.0	49.2	46.8
Salt Lake City/Ogden, UT	69.4	67.7	69.4	67.8	69.9	70.3	69.3
San Antonio, TX	70.2	65.0	64.2	61.6	63.0	68.2	62.6
San Diego, CA**	129.2	147.8	181.8	171.4	183.8	186.5	182.3
San Francisco Bay Area, CA**	171.3	212.6	260.2	244.0	266.5	270.0	262.2
Seattle/Tacoma, WA	82.6	88.7	115.0	99.7	109.1	115.9	136.1
Shreveport, LA	n/a	n/a	61.6	57.5	61.5	60.9	62.1
South Bend-Mishawauka, IN	45.4	49.1	52.2	51.1	53.7	51.6	56.3
Spokane, WA	51.2	51.1	52.4	50.2	51.8	52.7	52.0
Springfield, MA	105.2	118.4	127.1	124.4	127.0	131.4	122.0
St. Louis, MO	74.3	78.1	76.9	76.4	75.3	78.3	77.0
Syracuse, NY	68.9	74.6	79.3	76.9	78.9	80.2	78.1
Tampa/St.Petersburg/Clearwater, FL	63.8	65.6	71.9	68.6	71.7	74.0	72.9
Toledo, OH	56.3	58.4	60.8	57.7	62.4	62.3	61.3
Tulsa, OK	65.7	65.0	62.6	60.5	62.6	64.4	62.0
Washington, DC/MD/VA	114.2	132.5	144.4	143.7	140.5	148.3	144.7
W. Palm Beach/Boca Raton/Delray Beach, FL	102.6	99.0	102.6	94.4	96.2	113.5	107.3
Wichita, KS	n/a	60.1	62.0	60.5	61.8	63.7	63.6
Worcester, MA	139.1	147.5	141.5	146.8	138.7	142.8	146.7
Youngstown-Warren, OH	46.6	46.9	48.6	46.9	48.7	50.3	48.8

r Revised
n/a Not Available
* All areas are metropolitan statistical areas (MSA) as defined by the US Office of Management and Budget. They include the named central city and surrounding areas.
** Provided by the California Association of REALTORS®.

Source: National Association of REALTORS®, Economics and Research Division, 777 14th Street, N.W., Washington, D.C. 20005.

MEDIAN SALES PRICE OF APARTMENT CONDOS AND CO-OPS, QUARTERLY (not seasonally adjusted)

Year		United States	Northeast	Midwest	South	West
1984		$65,100	$ 64,700	$55,600	$ 63,300	$ 94,600
1985		67,600	73,600	56,100	62,300	91,100
1986		72,600	84,900	58,700	64,600	90,800
1987		77,800	98,300	61,700	64,100	97,200
1988		83,100	110,600	60,600	64,500	108,900
1989		84,300	110,800	65,600	68,400	110,300
1989	I	$83,900	$108,200	$64,100	$68,300	$114,200
	II	86,200	110,800	65,800	71,700	114,000
	III	84,400	112,500	66,000	68,900	109,900
	IV	82,200	111,300	66,200	64,800	102,700
1990ʳ	I	$83,700	$107,900	$66,100	$68,300	$120,300

r   Revised

Source: National Association of REALTORS®, Economics and Research Division, 777 14th Street, N.W., Washington, D.C. 20005.

HOUSING AFFORDABILITY INDEX FOR METROPOLITAN AREAS

Metropolitan Area*	Years			Quarters				1990
				1989				I^r
	1987	1988	1989	I	II	III	IV	
Baltimore, MD	133.8	129.0	121.9	122.8	113.2	114.0	117.9	113.7
Boston, MA	72.6	74.5	71.8	73.2	67.6	71.2	74.7	74.6
Chicago, IL	116.2	110.1	106.0	107.4	98.8	95.1	99.1	92.4
Cleveland, OH	152.7	154.0	147.6	150.5	133.0	136.8	146.7	142.8
Dallas, TX	132.5	143.2	142.1	142.7	136.5	131.8	137.6	142.5
Denver, CO	127.0	143.8	148.5	153.2	143.1	139.5	140.5	146.6
Detroit, MI	166.5	154.3	150.6	151.5	146.6	147.3	154.9	153.5
Houston, TX	182.5	199.8	194.6	197.1	178.0	179.7	210.5	184.7
Indianapolis, IN	176.4	177.3	169.2	169.7	163.7	161.8	167.6	164.8
Kansas City, MO/KS	149.5	157.2	151.7	146.1	147.9	155.8	154.4	149.1
Los Angeles Area, CA#	72.9	61.2	53.6	53.2	46.1	45.8	48.0	49.6
Miami/Hialeah, FL	108.8	113.4	108.4	109.9	98.9	101.8	100.2	101.2
Milwaukee, WI	162.1	149.3	144.2	142.6	132.9	134.7	141.4	141.8
Minneapolis/St. Paul, MN	164.1	156.7	152.1	158.9	144.9	148.3	154.5	154.8
New York/N. New Jersey/Long Island, NY/NJ/CT	50.4	50.6	50.5	51.5	48.6	49.0	51.2	53.8
Philadelphia, PA	110.3	108.9	108.9	105.6	100.2	105.0	104.7	120.5
Phoenix, AZ	130.6	134.7	131.9	135.1	125.2	134.3	136.5	130.7
Pittsburgh, PA	n/a	144.6	136.5	137.7	130.5	130.6	133.1	133.4
St. Louis, MO	147.3	150.0	144.1	136.8	146.2	141.6	143.4	141.9
San Diego, CA#	83.9	72.2	65.9	65.6	56.7	57.7	58.5	58.2
San Francisco Bay Area, CA#	76.8	69.0	58.0	56.0	48.5	48.8	51.1	51.1
Washington, DC/MD/VA	129.2	119.0	114.0	110.8	106.3	107.7	113.5	116.9

r Revised   * All areas are metropolitan statistical areas (MSA) as defined by the US Office of Management and Budget. They include the named central city and surrounding areas.

Note: The California Association of REALTORS® publishes a housing affordability index for areas within the state which differs significantly from these values because it measures the proportion of households which could theoretically afford to purchase the median price home rather than the ability of a median income family to carry the mortgage. California data is provided for comparision only and is not to replace the currently available measures. The indices are roughly consistent.

Source: National Association of REALTORS®, Economics and Research Division, 777 14th Street, N.W., Washington, D.C. 20005.

METROPOLITAN AREA HOUSING AFFORDABILITY (selected metropolitan areas by major components, first quarter: 1990[r])

Metropolitan Area***	Median-Priced Existing Single-Family Home	Mortgage Rate*	Median Family Income	Qualifying Income**	Composite Afford-ability Index
Baltimore, MD	$104,200	9.76%	$39,108	$34,407	113.7
Boston, MA	182,300	10.11	46,266	62,003	74.6
Chicago, IL	112,300	10.04	36,996	37,971	97.4
Cleveland, OH	77,100	9.94	36,902	28,851	142.8
Dallas, TX	90,400	10.08	43,710	30,669	142.5
Denver, CO	84,500	9.90	41,389	28,236	146.6
Detroit, MI	75,500	10.03	39,152	25,507	153.5
Houston, TX	70,700	10.14	44,523	24,106	184.7
Indianapolis, IN	73,200	10.30	41,691	25,293	164.8
Kansas City, MO/KS	73,900	10.05	37,282	25,008	149.1
Los Angeles Area, CA#	211,500	10.03	35,441	71,453	49.6
Miami/Hialeah, FL	90,200	10.09	30,986	30,627	101.2
Milwaukee, WI	81,800	9.82	38,505	27,149	141.8
Minneapolis/St Paul, MN	87,800	9.84	45,186	29,190	154.8
New York/N. NewJersey/Long Island, NY/NJ/CT	173,700	9.97	31,387	58,387	53.8
Philadelphia, PA	98,400	9.74	39,071	32,436	120.5
Phoenix, AZ	82,300	10.01	36,275	27,757	130.7
Pittsburgh, PA	68,600	9.94	30,679	23,001	133.4
St. Louis, MO	82,600	9.70	38,496	27,135	141.9
San Diego, CA#	182,300	9.73	34,949	60,041	58.2
San Francisco Bay Area, CA#	262,200	9.91	44,815	87,689	51.1
Washington, DC/MD/VA	144,700	9.81	56,095	47,984	116.9

r   Revised   *   Effective rate on loans closed on existing homes - Office of Thrift Supervision

**   Based on current lending requirements of the Federal National Mortgage Association using a 20 percent down payment

*** All areas are metropolitan statistical areas (MSA) as defined by the US Office of Management and Budget. They include the named central city and surrounding areas.

Note: The California Association of REALTORS® publishes a housing affordability index for areas within the state which differs significantly from these values because it measures the proportion of households which could theoretically afford to purchase the median price home rather than the ability of a median income family to carry the mortgage. California data is provided for comparison only and is not to replace the currently available measures. The indices are roughly consistent.

Source: National Association of REALTORS®, Economics and Research Divison, 777 14th Street, N.W., Washington, D.C. 20005.

AVERAGE VALUE PER ACRE OF FARMLAND AND BUILDINGS, BY STATE, 1983–90[1]

State	As of April 1			As of February 1				As of January 1	Percent change 1989-90
	1983	1984	1985	1986	1987	1988	1989	1990	
	Dollars								Percent
Northeast:	1,343	1,391	1,346	1,340	1,491	1,586	1,794	1802	0
Maine	708	713	774	854	885	962	1,029	1029	0
New Hampshire	1,174	1,253	1,439	1,682	1,847	2,112	2,260	2260	0
Vermont	842	862	947	1,060	1,114	1,124	1,203	1203	0
Massachusetts	1,963	2,083	2,377	2,761	3,012	3,553	3,802	3802	0
Rhode Island	2,760	2,770	2,990	3,284	3,389	4,748	5,080	5080	0
Connecticut	2,655	2,723	3,005	3,372	3,557	4,171	4,463	4463	0
New York	817	848	820	843	960	993	1,053	1042	-1
New Jersey	3,140	2,959	2,951	2,997	3,729	3,969	4,644	4737	2
Pennsylvania	1,520	1,596	1,427	1,332	1,540	1,579	1,911	1911	0
Delaware	1,829	1,840	1,596	1,684	1,677	1,765	2,065	2334	13
Maryland	2,121	2,236	2,197	2,023	2,009	2,261	2,487	2512	1
Lake States:	1,160	1,147	952	797	707	788	831	885	6
Michigan	1,223	1,255	1,108	1,012	924	971	1,000	1060	6
Wisconsin	1,113	1,104	944	836	777	826	867	867	0
Minnesota	1,165	1,131	898	694	587	700	749	831	11
Corn Belt:	1,482	1,449	1,108	972	900	1,003	1,107	1129	2
Ohio	1,504	1,500	1,215	1,136	1,097	1,199	1,271	1258	-1
Indiana	1,610	1,647	1,344	1,167	1,061	1,158	1,251	1288	3
Illinois	1,837	1,845	1,381	1,232	1,149	1,262	1,388	1416	2
Iowa	1,684	1,518	1,091	873	786	947	1,108	1130	2
Missouri	856	875	689	648	604	640	678	706	4
Northern Plains:	528	518	412	360	331	368	401	435	8
North Dakota	439	447	373	334	303	319	329	348	6
South Dakota	348	363	289	267	238	269	293	337	15
Nebraska	701	645	485	416	400	457	526	562	7
Kansas	601	597	488	415	373	413	438	473	8
Appalachia:	1,082	1,107	1,035	1,025	1,004	1,037	1,095	1171	7
Virginia	1,125	1,125	1,112	1,179	1,154	1,198	1,354	1597	18
West Virginia	688	698	607	616	633	682	716	652	-9
North Carolina	1,314	1,429	1,331	1,254	1,259	1,263	1,339	1325	-1
Kentucky	1,049	1,034	955	941	878	896	923	1034	12
Tennessee	1,014	1,024	944	935	936	1,001	1,021	1052	3
Southeast:	1,092	1,105	1,068	1,038	1,055	1,130	1,202	1296	8
South Carolina	946	926	898	870	792	871	949	949	0
Georgia	929	921	886	853	889	920	1,003	1053	5
Florida	1,576	1,645	1,599	1,537	1,605	1,790	1,897	2125	12
Alabama	826	824	797	803	786	800	832	882	6
Delta States:	1,038	1,074	1,012	880	757	781	803	808	1
Mississippi	894	950	855	778	685	697	718	754	5
Arkansas	972	964	907	779	724	761	784	776	-1
Louisiana	1,351	1,430	1,407	1,191	921	940	959	940	-2
Southern Plains:	574	632	675	579	532	531	518	508	-2
Oklahoma	699	718	597	520	475	480	523	513	-2
Texas	544	612	694	594	546	544	517	506	-2
Mountain:	314	327	300	267	257	257	261	274	5
Montana	259	276	243	233	200	205	209	243	16
Idaho	814	808	739	631	552	572	601	685	14
Wyoming	193	199	181	159	157	147	143	153	7
Colorado	454	469	437	360	368	369	369	369	0
New Mexico	178	194	185	161	156	180	193	200	4
Arizona	289	311	295	271	299	279	276	268	-3
Utah	560	570	513	476	451	425	425	404	-5
Nevada	249	262	244	219	240	227	234	201	-14
Pacific:	1,356	1,399	1,293	1,201	1,084	1,089	1,140	1208	6
Washington	933	972	943	840	756	739	769	815	6
Oregon	705	719	615	570	541	542	542	602	11
California	1,918	1,981	1,841	1,730	1,554	1,575	1,670	1753	5
48 States	788	801	713	640	599	632	667	693	4
Alaska				445	336	309	250	232	-7

1/ Current dollars. Revised 1984-89 values bench marked to values from the 1987 Census of Agriculture. Details in "Agricultural Resources. Agricultural Land Values and Markets Situation and Outlook Report" published in late June.

Source: *Agriculture Land Values*, Economics Research Service, U.S. Department of Agriculture.

Industrial Real Estate Market: Selected Cities*
Atlanta, Georgia: Industrial

Market Data

Inventory (sf)	Central City	Suburban
Total	18,665,904	182,705,322
Vacant	3,325,322	22,479,091
Vacancy Rates	17.8%	12.3%
Under Construction	18,500	3,617,131
Net Absorption	405,139	7,220,858

Sales Prices ($/sf)	Central City	Suburban
Less than 5,000 sf	30.00-35.00	40.00-45.00
5,000 to 19,999 sf	21.00-30.00	25.00-40.00
20,000 to 39,999 sf	19.00-22.50	22.00-26.00
40,000 to 59,999 sf	16.00-20.00	20.00-24.00
60,000 to 99,999 sf	15.00-17.00	19.00-23.00
More than 100,000 sf	14.00-16.50	18.50-22.00
High Tech/R&D	-	60.00-80.00

Gross Lease Prices ($/sf)	Central City	Suburban
Less than 5,000 sf	3.00-4.00	3.75-5.50
5,000 to 19,999 sf	2.50-3.50	3.00-4.50
20,000 to 39,999 sf	2.25-3.25	2.75-4.25
40,000 to 59,999 sf	2.00-2.60	2.50-3.50
60,000 to 99,999 sf	2.00-2.50	2.25-3.00
More than 100,000 sf	2.00-2.25	2.25-2.75
High Tech/R&D	8.50-10.00	6.00-9.00

Site Prices ($/sf)	Central City	Suburban
Improved Sites		
Less than 2 Acres	-	2.50-3.25
2 to 5 Acres	-	2.25-2.75
5 to 10 Acres	-	1.75-2.50
More than 10 Acres	-	1.50-2.25
Unimproved Sites		
Less than 10 Acres	-	1.25-2.00
10 to 100 Acres	-	1.00-1.75
More than 100 Acres	-	0.75-1.25

Demographics

		Rank
Population:	2,804,063	10
Population Growth Rate:	3.06%	
Unemployment Rate:	5.70%	
Median Household Income:	$36,018	9
Cost of Living Index:	107.1	16

Outlook

Sales Prices
Warehouse/Distribution	Same
Manufacturing	Same
High Tech/R&D	Same

Lease Prices
Warehouse/Distribution	Same
Manufacturing	Same
High Tech/R&D	Up 1-5%

Site Prices	Same

Absorption
Warehouse/Distribution	Down 1-5%
Manufacturing	Same
High Tech/R&D	Same

Construction
Warehouse/Distribution	Down 1-5%
Manufacturing	Same
High Tech/R&D	Down 1-5%
Dollar Volume - Sales	Up 1-5%
Dollar Volume - Leases	Down 1-5%

Prime Source of Financing:
Insurance Companies, Pension Funds

Mortgage Money Supply:
Ample

Construction Costs	
Less than 5,000 sf	-
5,000 to 19,999 sf	25.00
20,000 to 39,999 sf	18.00
40,000 to 59,999 sf	16.00
60,000 to 99,999 sf	14.50
More than 100,000 sf	13.00
High Tech/R&D	30.00

Vacancy Indicators	
Less than 5,000 sf	Balanced Market
5,000 to 19,999 sf	Moderate Oversupply
20,000 to 39,999 sf	Moderate Oversupply
40,000 to 59,999 sf	Moderate Oversupply
60,000 to 99,999 sf	Balanced Market
More than 100,000 sf	Substantial Shortage
High Tech/R&D	Moderate Oversupply

Composition of Absorption	
Warehouse/Distribution	75%
Manufacturing	10%
High Tech/R&D	15%

Rate of Construction	
Warehouse/Distribution	Same
Manufacturing	Same
High Tech/R&D	Down 6-10%

Dollar Volume - Sales	
Warehouse/Distribution	Same
Manufacturing	Same
High Tech/R&D	Down 1-5%

Dollar Volume - Leases	
Warehouse/Distribution	Same
Manufacturing	Same
High Tech/R&D	Up 1-5%

Note - Compared to a year ago

1989 Review

Distribution and service industries are the mainstays of the Atlanta economy, and provide a broad base of support for warehouse facilities. Demand for leased space was moderate, but build-to-suit activity kept construction at 3.6 million sq. ft. even in the face of a 13 percent vacancy rate in the region. Rents were held fairly flat during 1989 as the market remained oversupplied in most size and use categories.

1990 Forecast

Some speculative warehouse space will be built, but brought along in smaller phases. Development activity for R&D facilities should be dormant, according to SIOR's reporters. Land prices and transportation factors are moving new development 25-30 miles from the CBD. In expectation of a slow-growth economy in 1990, developers and industrial users are approaching the year with a cautious outlook.

Sales Prices
Atlanta

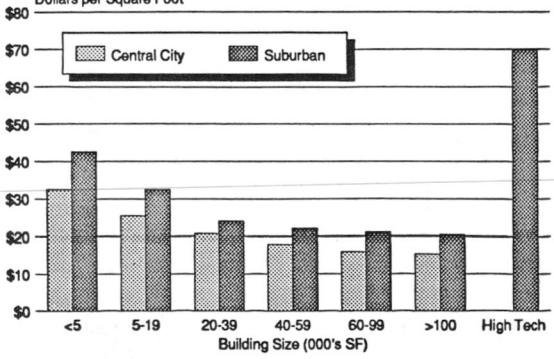

Source: © Copyright *Society of Industrial and Office Realtors®, 1990.* Reprinted with permission from the *1990 Guide to Industrial and Office Real Estate Markets.*

* See Glossary of Terms on page 628.

Chicago, Illinois: Industrial

Central City

Market Data

Inventory (sf)	Central City	Suburban
Total	195,000,000	-
Vacant	11,500,000	-
Vacancy Rates	5.9%	-
Under Construction	200,000	-
Net Absorption	0	-

Sales Prices ($/sf)	Central City	Suburban
Less than 5,000 sf	40.00	-
5,000 to 19,999 sf	35.00	-
20,000 to 39,999 sf	30.00	-
40,000 to 59,999 sf	25.00	-
60,000 to 99,999 sf	22.00	-
More than 100,000 sf	20.00	-
High Tech/R&D	-	-

Net Lease Prices ($/sf)	Central City	Suburban
Less than 5,000 sf	4.50	-
5,000 to 19,999 sf	4.00	-
20,000 to 39,999 sf	3.00	-
40,000 to 59,999 sf	3.00	-
60,000 to 99,999 sf	2.75	-
More than 100,000 sf	2.75	-
High Tech/R&D	-	-

Site Prices ($/sf)	Central City	Suburban
Improved Sites		
Less than 2 Acres	1.50-5.00	-
2 to 5 Acres	1.50-5.00	-
5 to 10 Acres	1.25-4.50	-
More than 10 Acres	1.00-3.50	-
Unimproved Sites		
Less than 10 Acres	-	-
10 to 100 Acres	-	-
More than 100 Acres	-	-

Demographics

		Rank
Population:	6,242,447	4
Population Growth Rate:	0.33%	
Unemployment Rate:	5.50%	
Median Household Income:	$32,453	26
Cost of Living Index:	n/a	n/a

Outlook

Sales Prices
Warehouse/Distribution	Up
Manufacturing	Up
High Tech/R&D	Same

Lease Prices
Warehouse/Distribution	Down
Manufacturing	Down
High Tech/R&D	Down

Site Prices | Down

Absorption
Warehouse/Distribution	Down
Manufacturing	Same
High Tech/R&D	Same

Construction
Warehouse/Distribution	Down 5%
Manufacturing	Same
High Tech/R&D	Same
Dollar Volume - Sales	Same
Dollar Volume - Leases	Down

Prime Source of Financing:
Insurance Companies, Commercial Banks

Mortgage Money Supply:
Moderate

Construction Costs	
Less than 5,000 sf	38.00
5,000 to 19,999 sf	35.00
20,000 to 39,999 sf	30.00
40,000 to 59,999 sf	28.00
60,000 to 99,999 sf	25.00
More than 100,000 sf	25.00
High Tech/R&D	-

Vacancy Indicators	
Less than 5,000 sf	Balanced Market
5,000 to 19,999 sf	Moderate Shortage
20,000 to 39,999 sf	Moderate Oversupply
40,000 to 59,999 sf	Substantial Oversupply
60,000 to 99,999 sf	Balanced Market
More than 100,000 sf	Moderate Oversupply
High Tech/R&D	

Composition of Absorption
Warehouse/Distribution	80%
Manufacturing	15%
High Tech/R&D	5%

Rate of Construction
Warehouse/Distribution	Up 20%
Manufacturing	Same
High Tech/R&D	Same

Dollar Volume - Sales
Warehouse/Distribution	Up
Manufacturing	Same
High Tech/R&D	Same

Dollar Volume - Leases
Warehouse/Distribution	Down 10%
Manufacturing	Same
High Tech/R&D	Same

Note - Compared to a year ago

1989 Review

The City of Chicago industrial market presented a remarkably stable picture during 1989. No net change in occupancy was recorded during the year and, with only token amounts of new construction occurring, vacancy stayed at about six percent. The retail markets in the metropolitan area were thriving, and this kept warehouse demand high. Chicago, as always, benefited from an excellent transportation infrastructure. In supply/demand terms, the central city continued in better balance than the growth markets of the suburbs.

1990 Forecast

Infill and rehabilitation within the City of Chicago is proving successful, according to SIOR's reporters. In contrast to most areas of the nation, this market has long-term viability in its urban industrial stock. The mutually beneficial relationship between core and peripheral industrial markets is testimony to Chicago's strength as a production and shipment center for the nation.

Composition of Absorption
Chicago

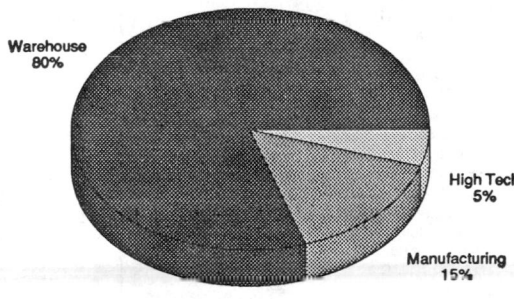

Warehouse 80%

High Tech 5%

Manufacturing 15%

Chicago, Illinois: Industrial

Suburban

Market Data

Inventory (sf)	Central City	Suburban
Total	-	510,000,000
Vacant	-	39,000,000
Vacancy Rates	-	7.6%
Under Construction	-	10,000,000
Net Absorption	-	0

Sales Prices ($/sf)	Central City	Suburban
Less than 5,000 sf	-	55.00
5,000 to 19,999 sf	-	45.00
20,000 to 39,999 sf	-	37.00
40,000 to 59,999 sf	-	35.00
60,000 to 99,999 sf	-	32.00
More than 100,000 sf	-	29.00
High Tech/R&D	-	-

Net Lease Prices ($/sf)	Central City	Suburban
Less than 5,000 sf	-	5.50
5,000 to 19,999 sf	-	4.25
20,000 to 39,999 sf	-	3.75
40,000 to 59,999 sf	-	3.50
60,000 to 99,999 sf	-	3.50
More than 100,000 sf	-	3.25
High Tech/R&D	-	-

Site Prices ($/sf)	Central City	Suburban
Improved Sites		
Less than 2 Acres	-	2.00-5.00
2 to 5 Acres	-	2.00-4.50
5 to 10 Acres	-	1.75-3.75
More than 10 Acres	-	1.50-3.75
Unimproved Sites		
Less than 10 Acres	-	1.65
10 to 100 Acres	-	1.50
More than 100 Acres	-	1.25

Demographics

		Rank
Population:	6,242,447	4
Population Growth Rate:	0.33%	
Unemployment Rate:	5.50%	
Median Household Income:	$32,453	26
Cost of Living Index:	n/a	n/a

Outlook

Sales Prices	
Warehouse/Distribution	Up
Manufacturing	Up
High Tech/R&D	Same
Lease Prices	
Warehouse/Distribution	Down
Manufacturing	Down
High Tech/R&D	Down
Site Prices	Down
Absorption	
Warehouse/Distribution	Down
Manufacturing	Same
High Tech/R&D	Same
Construction	
Warehouse/Distribution	Down 5%
Manufacturing	Same
High Tech/R&D	Same
Dollar Volume - Sales	Same
Dollar Volume - Leases	Down

Prime Source of Financing:
Insurance Companies, Commercial Banks

Mortgage Money Supply:
Moderate

Construction Costs	
Less than 5,000 sf	38.00
5,000 to 19,999 sf	35.00
20,000 to 39,999 sf	30.00
40,000 to 59,999 sf	28.00
60,000 to 99,999 sf	25.00
More than 100,000 sf	25.00
High Tech/R&D	-

Vacancy Indicators	
Less than 5,000 sf	Balanced Market
5,000 to 19,999 sf	Moderate Shortage
20,000 to 39,999 sf	Moderate Oversupply
40,000 to 59,999 sf	Substantial Oversupply
60,000 to 99,999 sf	Balanced Market
More than 100,000 sf	Moderate Oversupply
High Tech/R&D	

Composition of Absorption	
Warehouse/Distribution	80%
Manufacturing	15%
High Tech/R&D	5%
Rate of Construction	
Warehouse/Distribution	Up 20%
Manufacturing	Same
High Tech/R&D	Same
Dollar Volume - Sales	
Warehouse/Distribution	Up
Manufacturing	Same
High Tech/R&D	Same
Dollar Volume - Leases	
Warehouse/Distribution	Down 10%
Manufacturing	Same
High Tech/R&D	Same

Note - Compared to a year ago

1989 Review

This may have been the year when Chicago got caught in the switches. Despite the stability of the overall vacancy picture between 1988 and 1989 (at 7.2 percent for the metro area), absorption dropped from 6.5 million sq. ft. to zero, and the volume of new construction underway surged from seven to 10 million sq. ft. Elements of oversupply appeared in the 20,000 - 60,000 sq. ft. size categories, which had previously had favorable supply/demand relationships. Rents and prices held firm but the production end of the Chicago economy lost share to the distribution sector, a warning signal of a slowing local market.

1990 Forecast

Caution is beginning to pervade the industrial property market, and a small (two percent) retrenchment in rents is anticipated. A pullback in construction should be expected, and would benefit the market. Rents and sales prices for the suburbs should continue to outperform the central city, as the most modern space is being created on the fringes of the metropolitan area.

Construction Costs vs. Sales Prices
Chicago

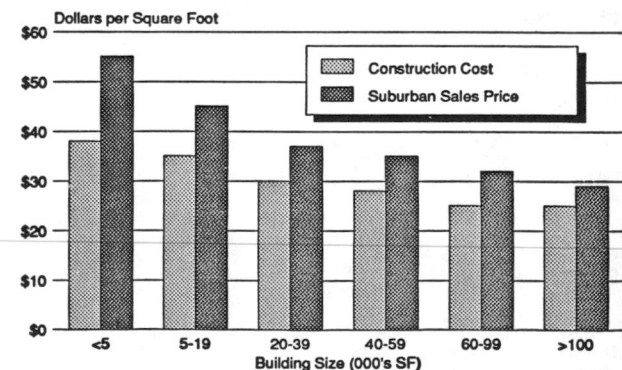

Houston, Texas: Industrial

Houston and Harris County

Market Data

Inventory (sf)

Inventory (sf)	Central City	Suburban
Total	71,000,000	163,000,000
Vacant	8,496,000	22,231,000
Vacancy Rates	12.0%	13.6%
Under Construction	0	750,000
Net Absorption	2,708,000	9,792,000

Sales Prices ($/sf)	Central City	Suburban
Less than 5,000 sf	30.00-40.00	15.00-45.00
5,000 to 19,999 sf	25.00-35.00	20.00-30.00
20,000 to 39,999 sf	20.00-30.00	15.00-35.00
40,000 to 59,999 sf	15.00-30.00	15.00-30.00
60,000 to 99,999 sf	10.00-22.00	15.00-25.00
More than 100,000 sf	10.00-15.00	12.00-25.00
High Tech/R&D	20.00-50.00	15.00-50.00

Gross Lease Prices ($/sf)	Central City	Suburban
Less than 5,000 sf	2.50-4.00	2.50-4.00
5,000 to 19,999 sf	2.20-4.00	2.20-4.00
20,000 to 39,999 sf	2.00-3.25	2.00-3.25
40,000 to 59,999 sf	1.50-3.00	1.85-3.00
60,000 to 99,999 sf	1.25-2.50	1.85-3.00
More than 100,000 sf	1.00-2.50	1.80-3.00
High Tech/R&D	3.50-7.50	3.50-7.50

Site Prices ($/sf)	Central City	Suburban
Improved Sites		
Less than 2 Acres	2.00-6.00	1.00-5.00
2 to 5 Acres	2.00-6.00	1.00-5.00
5 to 10 Acres	1.50-5.00	1.00-4.00
More than 10 Acres	1.00-5.00	1.00-4.00
Unimproved Sites		
Less than 10 Acres	2.00-5.00	0.50-2.50
10 to 100 Acres	0.50-3.00	0.20-2.00
More than 100 Acres	n/a	0.10-1.00

Demographics

		Rank
Population:	3,228,577	8
Population Growth Rate:	1.86%	
Unemployment Rate:	5.70%	
Median Household Income:	$33,251	22
Cost of Living Index:	101.9	26

Outlook

Sales Prices
Warehouse/Distribution	Up 10-20%
Manufacturing	Same
High Tech/R&D	Up 5-10%

Lease Prices
Warehouse/Distribution	Up 10-20%
Manufacturing	Up 5-10%
High Tech/R&D	Up 5-20%

Site Prices Same

Absorption
Warehouse/Distribution	Same
Manufacturing	Same
High Tech/R&D	Up 10-15%

Construction
Warehouse/Distribution	Up 10-20%
Manufacturing	Same
High Tech/R&D	Same

Dollar Volume - Sales Up 10-15%
Dollar Volume - Leases Up 10-15%

Prime Source of Financing:
Insurance Companies, Commercial Banks, Owner Financing

Mortgage Money Supply:
Moderate

Construction Costs

Construction Costs	
Less than 5,000 sf	25.00-35.00
5,000 to 19,999 sf	20.00-30.00
20,000 to 39,999 sf	15.00-25.00
40,000 to 59,999 sf	15.00-23.00
60,000 to 99,999 sf	15.00-22.00
More than 100,000 sf	14.00-22.00
High Tech/R&D	25.00-40.00

Vacancy Indicators

Vacancy Indicators	
Less than 5,000 sf	Moderate Oversupply
5,000 to 19,999 sf	Balanced Market
20,000 to 39,999 sf	Moderate Shortage
40,000 to 59,999 sf	Moderate Shortage
60,000 to 99,999 sf	Substantial Shortage
More than 100,000 sf	Substantial Shortage
High Tech/R&D	Moderate Oversupply

Composition of Absorption

Composition of Absorption	
Warehouse/Distribution	35%
Manufacturing	55%
High Tech/R&D	10%

Rate of Construction
Warehouse/Distribution	Up 10%
Manufacturing	Same
High Tech/R&D	Same

Dollar Volume - Sales
Warehouse/Distribution	Up 10-20%
Manufacturing	Up 10-20%
High Tech/R&D	Same

Dollar Volume - Leases
Warehouse/Distribution	Up 10-20%
Manufacturing	Up 10-20%
High Tech/R&D	Same

Note - Compared to a year ago

1989 Review

Houston's economic recovery took a large step forward in 1989, and the diversification away from energy toward electronics, medical services and port-related trade contributed to the rebound. The inventory of industrial vacancies remains high at more than 30 million sq. ft., but net absorption of 12.5 million sq. ft. last year suggests that the market may be tightening faster than many expected. Already there are reports of spot shortages of large contiguous space. Rental rates and sales prices were still comparatively low, and this prompted renewed interest from out-of-town users and investors.

1990 Forecast

Further gradual improvement in market conditions is foreseen. Lease and sales prices may be stepping upwards smartly, especially in the warehouse/distribution sector. Speculative construction is still some time away, but build-to-suits for corporate users can be anticipated as the year progresses. Houston is once again a market to watch for the national and international real estate community.

Market Inventory
Houston

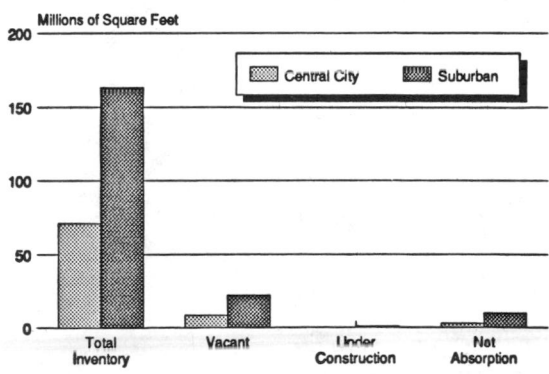

Los Angeles-Central, California: Industrial

Market Data

Inventory (sf)	Central City	Suburban
Total	600,000,000	-
Vacant	48,000,000	-
Vacancy Rates	8.0%	-
Under Construction	5,000,000	-
Net Absorption	n/a	-

Sales Prices ($/sf)	Central City	Suburban
Less than 5,000 sf	90.00	-
5,000 to 19,999 sf	80.00	-
20,000 to 39,999 sf	65.00	-
40,000 to 59,999 sf	60.00	-
60,000 to 99,999 sf	55.00	-
More than 100,000 sf	50.00	-
High Tech/R&D	n/a	-

Net Lease Prices ($/sf)	Central City	Suburban
Less than 5,000 sf	6.60	-
5,000 to 19,999 sf	6.00	-
20,000 to 39,999 sf	4.56	-
40,000 to 59,999 sf	4.20	-
60,000 to 99,999 sf	4.08	-
More than 100,000 sf	3.84	-
High Tech/R&D	n/a	-

Site Prices ($/sf)	Central City	Suburban
Improved Sites		
Less than 2 Acres	13.00	-
2 to 5 Acres	13.00-30.00	-
5 to 10 Acres	13.00-30.00	-
More than 10 Acres	30.00	-
Unimproved Sites		
Less than 10 Acres	10.00	-
10 to 100 Acres	10.00-26.00	-
More than 100 Acres	26.00	-

Demographics

		Rank
Population:	8,804,062	1
Population Growth Rate:	1.83	
Unemployment Rate:	4.80%	
Median Household Income:	$31,276	37
Cost of Living Index:	126.5	6

Outlook

Sales Prices	
Warehouse/Distribution	Same
Manufacturing	Same
High Tech/R&D	Same
Lease Prices	
Warehouse/Distribution	Same
Manufacturing	Same
High Tech/R&D	Same
Site Prices	Up 10-15%
Absorption	
Warehouse/Distribution	Down 15%
Manufacturing	Down 10%
High Tech/R&D	Down 12%
Construction	
Warehouse/Distribution	Down 20%
Manufacturing	Down 20%
High Tech/R&D	Down 30%
Dollar Volume - Sales	Same
Dollar Volume - Leases	Down 15%

Prime Source of Financing:
Insurance Companies, Pension Funds

Mortgage Money Supply:
Ample

Construction Costs	
Less than 5,000 sf	
5,000 to 19,999 sf	33.00
20,000 to 39,999 sf	28.00
40,000 to 59,999 sf	23.00
60,000 to 99,999 sf	19.00
More than 100,000 sf	16.50
High Tech/R&D	

Vacancy Indicators	
Less than 5,000 sf	Moderate Shortage
5,000 to 19,999 sf	Moderate Shortage
20,000 to 39,999 sf	Moderate Oversupply
40,000 to 59,999 sf	Moderate Oversupply
60,000 to 99,999 sf	Moderate Oversupply
More than 100,000 sf	Moderate Oversupply
High Tech/R&D	Balanced Market

Composition of Absorption	
Warehouse/Distribution	55%
Manufacturing	40%
High Tech/R&D	5%
Rate of Construction	
Warehouse/Distribution	Same
Manufacturing	Down 20%
High Tech/R&D	Same
Dollar Volume - Sales	
Warehouse/Distribution	Same
Manufacturing	Down 20%
High Tech/R&D	Down 10%
Dollar Volume - Leases	
Warehouse/Distribution	Down 15%
Manufacturing	Down 25%
High Tech/R&D	Down 10%
Note - Compared to a year ago	

1989 Review

Los Angeles' urban industrial market contains a huge 600 million sq. ft. inventory and, with a vacancy rate of eight percent, ended 1989 in an oversupplied condition. The market is undergoing a rationalization process spurred by high land and building prices and high rents. Demand for leased space dropped in the second half of the year, as sales activity in the upper tier of the market increased. Foreign purchasers were the most prevalent. Balance in the market's absorption of space was good, with a nearly even proportion of distribution and production space being taken in the past year.

1990 Forecast

Softening in the defense sector has lowered expectations for the market in 1990. Layoffs at Hughes Aircraft and Northrop are visible signs of shrinkage in aerospace manufacturing. Non-durables such as apparel and food processing will take up some of the slack, but are not substitute space users by any means. The combination of high land costs, ample existing vacancies, and uncertain demand will hold development to nominal levels in 1990.

Composition of Absorption
Los Angeles-Central

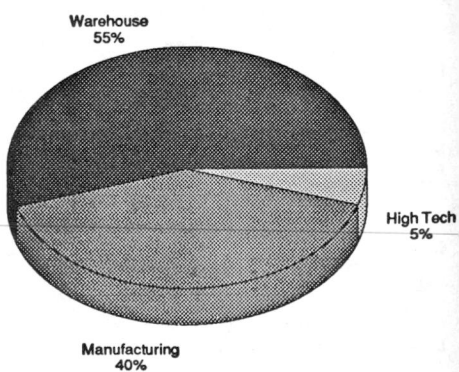

Warehouse 55%

Manufacturing 40%

High Tech 5%

Los Angeles-East, California: Industrial

Santa Fe Springs, Cerritos, La Mirada, and Buena Park

Market Data

Inventory (sf)	Central City	Suburban
Total	71,000,000	-
Vacant	2,800,000	
Vacancy Rates	3.9%	-
Under Construction	1,800,000	-
Net Absorption	2,500,000	-

Sales Prices ($/sf)	Central City	Suburban
Less than 5,000 sf	80.00	-
5,000 to 19,999 sf	75.00	-
20,000 to 39,999 sf	65.00	-
40,000 to 59,999 sf	62.00	-
60,000 to 99,999 sf	58.00	-
More than 100,000 sf	50.00	-
High Tech/R&D	60.00	-

Net Lease Prices ($/sf)	Central City	Suburban
Less than 5,000 sf	6.50	-
5,000 to 19,999 sf	5.90	-
20,000 to 39,999 sf	5.30	-
40,000 to 59,999 sf	5.00	-
60,000 to 99,999 sf	4.25	-
More than 100,000 sf	4.00	-
High Tech/R&D	5.50	-

Site Prices ($/sf)	Central City	Suburban
Improved Sites		
Less than 2 Acres	18.00	-
2 to 5 Acres	15.00	-
5 to 10 Acres	13.00	-
More than 10 Acres	12.00	-
Unimproved Sites		
Less than 10 Acres	11.00	-
10 to 100 Acres	11.00	-
More than 100 Acres	11.00	-

Demographics

		Rank
Population:	8,804,062	1
Population Growth Rate:	1.83	
Unemployment Rate:	4.8%	
Median Household Income:	$31,276	37
Cost of Living Index:	126.5	6

Outlook

Sales Prices	
Warehouse/Distribution	Up 5%
Manufacturing	Up 5%
High Tech/R&D	Same
Lease Prices	
Warehouse/Distribution	Up 5%
Manufacturing	Up 5%
High Tech/R&D	Same
Site Prices	Up 5%
Absorption	
Warehouse/Distribution	Up 5%
Manufacturing	Up 5%
High Tech/R&D	Up 5%
Construction	
Warehouse/Distribution	Up 5%
Manufacturing	Up 5%
High Tech/R&D	Up 5%
Dollar Volume - Sales	Up 5%
Dollar Volume - Leases	Same

Prime Source of Financing:
Insurance Companies

Mortgage Money Supply:
Ample

Construction Costs	
Less than 5,000 sf	35.00
5,000 to 19,999 sf	30.00
20,000 to 39,999 sf	27.00
40,000 to 59,999 sf	25.00
60,000 to 99,999 sf	20.00
More than 100,000 sf	18.00
High Tech/R&D	45.00

Vacancy Indicators	
Less than 5,000 sf	Balanced Market
5,000 to 19,999 sf	Balanced Market
20,000 to 39,999 sf	Balanced Market
40,000 to 59,999 sf	Balanced Market
60,000 to 99,999 sf	Balanced Market
More than 100,000 sf	Balanced Market
High Tech/R&D	Moderate Oversupply

Composition of Absorption	
Warehouse/Distribution	70%
Manufacturing	25%
High Tech/R&D	5%
Rate of Construction	
Warehouse/Distribution	Same
Manufacturing	Same
High Tech/R&D	Same
Dollar Volume - Sales	
Warehouse/Distribution	Up 10%
Manufacturing	Up 10%
High Tech/R&D	Same
Dollar Volume - Leases	
Warehouse/Distribution	Same
Manufacturing	Same
High Tech/R&D	Same

Note - Compared to a year ago

1989 Review

This is the tightest of the L.A. industrial submarkets, with a scant 3.9 percent vacancy rate at the end of 1989. Demand was steady and rents rose only moderately. Absorption was largely weighted toward warehouse/distribution space. Land prices were up sharply this year, reflecting their scarcity. Building quality and amenities were improving under the pressure of competition, and ceiling heights moved toward 30' clear.

1990 Forecast

Steady development of speculative space, at approximately one million sq. ft. over the year, would conform to this market's norm. The population increase in Southern California is the dominant force driving this market, and East Los Angeles is well situated to serve its need for large industrial facilities. SIOR's reporters indicate a prevailing optimism in the local business community, and the outlook for most market measures is up five percent in 1990.

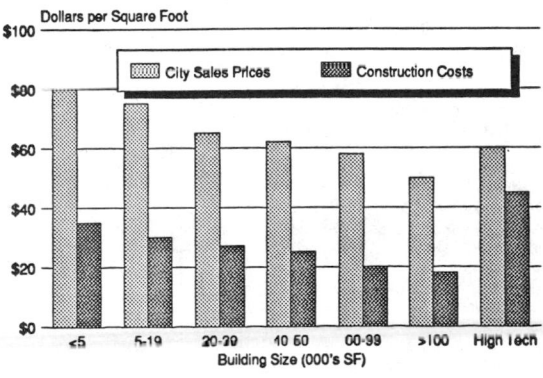

Sales Prices vs. Construction Costs
Los Angeles-East

Los Angeles-Orange County, California: Industrial

Market Data

Inventory (sf)	Central City	Suburban
Total	-	150,085,608
Vacant	-	19,449,883
Vacancy Rates	-	13.0%
Under Construction	-	1,928,600
Net Absorption	-	12,658,634

Sales Prices ($/sf)	Central City	Suburban
Less than 5,000 sf	-	88.00-110.00
5,000 to 19,999 sf	-	75.00-83.00
20,000 to 39,999 sf	-	65.00-74.00
40,000 to 59,999 sf	-	56.00-70.00
60,000 to 99,999 sf	-	55.00-66.00
More than 100,000 sf	-	45.00-56.00
High Tech/R&D	-	85.00-130.00

Net Lease Prices ($/sf)	Central City	Suburban
Less than 5,000 sf	-	6.60-9.00
5,000 to 19,999 sf	-	5.64-6.84
20,000 to 39,999 sf	-	5.04-6.00
40,000 to 59,999 sf	-	4.80-5.76
60,000 to 99,999 sf	-	4.32-4.80
More than 100,000 sf	-	4.20-4.80
High Tech/R&D	-	7.80-14.00

Site Prices ($/sf)	Central City	Suburban
Improved Sites		
Less than 2 Acres	-	16.00-22.00
2 to 5 Acres	-	14.00-20.00
5 to 10 Acres	-	13.00-15.00
More than 10 Acres	-	12.00-14.00
Unimproved Sites		
Less than 10 Acres	-	10.00-12.00
10 to 100 Acres	-	9.50-11.00
More than 100 Acres	-	n/a

Demographics

		Rank
Population:	2,296,839	15
Population Growth Rate:	1.94	
Unemployment Rate:	3.20%	
Median Household Income:	$41,181	5
Cost of Living Index:	132.3	3

Outlook

Sales Prices	
Warehouse/Distribution	Up 5%
Manufacturing	Up 5%
High Tech/R&D	Same
Lease Prices	
Warehouse/Distribution	Up 6-10%
Manufacturing	Up 6-10%
High Tech/R&D	Same
Site Prices	Up 10-15%
Absorption	
Warehouse/Distribution	Same
Manufacturing	Down 1-5%
High Tech/R&D	Up 1-5%
Construction	
Warehouse/Distribution	Down 1-5%
Manufacturing	Down 1-5%
High Tech/R&D	Up 1-5%
Dollar Volume - Sales	Down 1-5%
Dollar Volume - Leases	Down 1-5%

Prime Source of Financing:
Commercial Banks

Mortgage Money Supply:
Ample

Construction Costs	
Less than 5,000 sf	28.00-30.00
5,000 to 19,999 sf	26.00-27.00
20,000 to 39,999 sf	22.00-25.00
40,000 to 59,999 sf	18.00-22.00
60,000 to 99,999 sf	17.00-21.00
More than 100,000 sf	15.00-16.00
High Tech/R&D	35.00-40.00

Vacancy Indicators	
Less than 5,000 sf	Moderate Oversupply
5,000 to 19,999 sf	Moderate Oversupply
20,000 to 39,999 sf	Moderate Oversupply
40,000 to 59,999 sf	Balanced Market
60,000 to 99,999 sf	Balanced Market
More than 100,000 sf	Moderate Shortage
High Tech/R&D	Substantial Oversupply

Composition of Absorption	
Warehouse/Distribution	50%
Manufacturing	10%
High Tech/R&D	40%
Rate of Construction	
Warehouse/Distribution	Down 10%
Manufacturing	Down 10%
High Tech/R&D	Up 10%
Dollar Volume - Sales	
Warehouse/Distribution	Down 10%
Manufacturing	Down 10%
High Tech/R&D	Down 5%
Dollar Volume - Leases	
Warehouse/Distribution	Down 10%
Manufacturing	Down 10%
High Tech/R&D	Down 15%
Note - Compared to a year ago	

1989 Review

The Eighties have been a booming decade for Orange County, and the industrial market ended with a strong year for absorption with 12.7 million sq. ft. Even so, SIOR's local correspondent reported that demand appeared to be down from its 1988 level. Part of the reason may be the high proportion of R&D activity, which is especially vulnerable to the looming downturn in defense. Thus, the dollar volume of leasing activity in the high-tech sector was down 15 percent from the prior year.

1990 Forecast

Population and employment growth are projected to sustain the pace which has made Orange County one of the nation's strongest economies. The shortage of available land will retard the rate of speculative industrial construction. Development opportunities, in fact, are virtually sold in an auction atmosphere. Site prices are expected to see the strongest upward pressure, rising 10 to 15 percent this year. The south part of the county, which is controlled by a few major land holders, will have the largest share of the activity.

Composition of Absorption
Los Angeles-Orange County

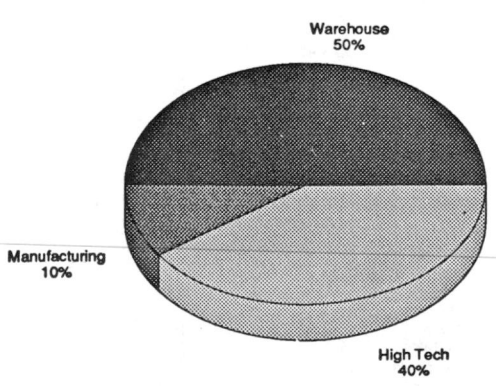

Warehouse 50%

Manufacturing 10%

High Tech 40%

Los Angeles-San Bernardino County, California: Industrial

San Bernardino / Riverside Metropolitan Area

Market Data

Inventory (sf)	Central City	Suburban
Total	35,000,000	-
Vacant	15,000,000	-
Vacancy Rates	42.9%	-
Under Construction	6,000,000	-
Net Absorption	11,000,000	-

Sales Prices ($/sf)	Central City	Suburban
Less than 5,000 sf	55.00	-
5,000 to 19,999 sf	49.00	-
20,000 to 39,999 sf	44.00	-
40,000 to 59,999 sf	38.00	-
60,000 to 99,999 sf	36.00	-
More than 100,000 sf	34.00	-
High Tech/R&D	-	-

Net Lease Prices ($/sf)	Central City	Suburban
Less than 5,000 sf	4.68	-
5,000 to 19,999 sf	4.32	-
20,000 to 39,999 sf	4.20	-
40,000 to 59,999 sf	4.08	-
60,000 to 99,999 sf	3.72	-
More than 100,000 sf	3.48	-
High Tech/R&D	7.80	-

Site Prices ($/sf)	Central City	Suburban
Improved Sites		
Less than 2 Acres	6.50	-
2 to 5 Acres	6.00	-
5 to 10 Acres	5.25	-
More than 10 Acres	4.50	-
Unimproved Sites		
Less than 10 Acres	3.75	-
10 to 100 Acres	3.00	-
More than 100 Acres	2.50	-

Demographics

		Rank
Population:	2,277,982	16
Population Growth Rate:	4.31	
Unemployment Rate:	6.40%	
Median Household Income:	$27,720	65
Cost of Living Index:	106.7	16

Outlook

Sales Prices	
Warehouse/Distribution	Up 5%
Manufacturing	Up 5%
High Tech/R&D	Down 10%
Lease Prices	
Warehouse/Distribution	Up 5%
Manufacturing	Up 5%
High Tech/R&D	Down 10%
Site Prices	Up 10%
Absorption	
Warehouse/Distribution	Up 10%
Manufacturing	Up 5%
High Tech/R&D	Same
Construction	
Warehouse/Distribution	Same
Manufacturing	Up 5%
High Tech/R&D	Same
Dollar Volume - Sales	Up 10%
Dollar Volume - Leases	Up 10%

Prime Source of Financing:
Insurance Companies, Commercial Banks

Mortgage Money Supply:
Ample

Construction Costs	
Less than 5,000 sf	26.00
5,000 to 19,999 sf	24.00
20,000 to 39,999 sf	22.00
40,000 to 59,999 sf	18.00
60,000 to 99,999 sf	16.00
More than 100,000 sf	14.00
High Tech/R&D	-

Vacancy Indicators	
Less than 5,000 sf	Moderate Shortage
5,000 to 19,999 sf	Moderate Oversupply
20,000 to 39,999 sf	Moderate Oversupply
40,000 to 59,999 sf	Substantial Oversupply
60,000 to 99,999 sf	-
More than 100,000 sf	Balanced Market
High Tech/R&D	Substantial Oversupply

Composition of Absorption	
Warehouse/Distribution	80%
Manufacturing	17%
High Tech/R&D	3%
Rate of Construction	
Warehouse/Distribution	Up 10%
Manufacturing	Same
High Tech/R&D	Down 10%
Dollar Volume - Sales	
Warehouse/Distribution	Up 10%
Manufacturing	Up 5%
High Tech/R&D	Down 10%
Dollar Volume - Leases	
Warehouse/Distribution	Up 10%
Manufacturing	Same
High Tech/R&D	Down 10%

Note - Compared to a year ago

1989 Review

Statistics from this market area chart the explosive expansion of the Inland Empire. Although 15 million sq. ft. of vacant inventory exists, this represents little more than a year's supply at 1989's absorption rate. Therefore additional new construction continued to go into the ground. Demand was greatest at the size extremes: for distribution buildings 100,000 sq. ft. or larger, and for facilities smaller than 20,000 sq. ft. When leased, developers find ready buyers for their product with insurance companies the most active purchasers.

1990 Forecast

Another active year for construction is foreseen. Absorption should also be strong, in the eight to 10 million sq. ft. range. Locally affordable housing is shoring up the labor pool and attracting firms from Los Angeles and Orange counties. Lower industrial lease rates and land costs are also part of the Inland Empire's lure. The Ontario International Airport is but one node of industrial park activity. SIOR's reporters note that the market is arriving at the stage of maturity where it is promoting internal expansion needs.

Sales & Lease Price Outlook
Los Angeles-San Bernardino/Riverside

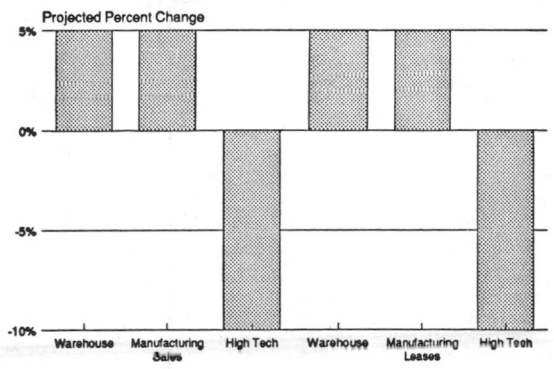

Los Angeles-San Fernando Valley, California: Industrial

Market Data

Inventory (sf)

	Central City	Suburban
Total	135,000,000	35,000,000
Vacant	6,000,000	2,000,000
Vacancy Rates	4.4%	5.7%
Under Construction	2,300,000	1,000,000
Net Absorption	4,200,000	1,900,000

Sales Prices ($/sf)

	Central City	Suburban
Less than 5,000 sf	90.00	80.00
5,000 to 19,999 sf	85.00	77.00
20,000 to 39,999 sf	65.00	60.00
40,000 to 59,999 sf	55.00	48.00
60,000 to 99,999 sf	48.00	43.00
More than 100,000 sf	47.00	45.00
High Tech/R&D	82.00	72.00

Net Lease Prices ($/sf)

	Central City	Suburban
Less than 5,000 sf	9.90	8.90
5,000 to 19,999 sf	9.50	8.50
20,000 to 39,999 sf	7.90	7.25
40,000 to 59,999 sf	6.75	6.25
60,000 to 99,999 sf	7.25	6.60
More than 100,000 sf	6.80	6.25
High Tech/R&D	10.00	8.00

Site Prices ($/sf)

	Central City	Suburban
Improved Sites		
Less than 2 Acres	35.00	15.00
2 to 5 Acres	27.00	12.00
5 to 10 Acres	27.00	11.00
More than 10 Acres	25.00	10.00
Unimproved Sites		
Less than 10 Acres	n/a	5.00-7.00
10 to 100 Acres	n/a	5.00-6.00
More than 100 Acres	n/a	4.00-5.00

Demographics

		Rank
Population:	8,804,062	1
Population Growth Rate:	1.83	
Unemployment Rate:	4.8%	
Median Household Income:	$31,276	37
Cost of Living Index:	126.5	6

Outlook

Sales Prices
Warehouse/Distribution	Up 5%
Manufacturing	Up 5%
High Tech/R&D	Down 10%
Lease Prices	
Warehouse/Distribution	Up 5%
Manufacturing	Up 5%
High Tech/R&D	Down 10%
Site Prices	Up 10%
Absorption	
Warehouse/Distribution	Up 10%
Manufacturing	Up 10%
High Tech/R&D	Down 15%
Construction	
Warehouse/Distribution	Same
Manufacturing	Same
High Tech/R&D	Same
Dollar Volume - Sales	Same
Dollar Volume - Leases	Same

Prime Source of Financing:
Insurance Companies, Commercial Banks

Mortgage Money Supply:
Ample

Construction Costs

Less than 5,000 sf	30.00
5,000 to 19,999 sf	28.50
20,000 to 39,999 sf	26.05
40,000 to 59,999 sf	20.75
60,000 to 99,999 sf	17.95
More than 100,000 sf	15.35
High Tech/R&D	25.00

Vacancy Indicators

Less than 5,000 sf	Moderate Shortage
5,000 to 19,999 sf	Balanced Market
20,000 to 39,999 sf	Balanced Market
40,000 to 59,999 sf	Moderate Oversupply
60,000 to 99,999 sf	Moderate Oversupply
More than 100,000 sf	Balanced Market
High Tech/R&D	Moderate Oversupply

Composition of Absorption
Warehouse/Distribution	55%
Manufacturing	30%
High Tech/R&D	15%
Rate of Construction	
Warehouse/Distribution	Up 52%
Manufacturing	Up 52%
High Tech/R&D	Down 60%
Dollar Volume - Sales	
Warehouse/Distribution	Up 12%
Manufacturing	Up 12%
High Tech/R&D	Down 5%
Dollar Volume - Leases	
Warehouse/Distribution	Up 6%
Manufacturing	Up 8%
High Tech/R&D	Down 10%

Note - Compared to a year ago

1989 Review

With a vacancy of only 4.7 percent in a 170 million sq. ft. market inventory, the San Fernando Valley qualifies as one of the strongest mature industrial markets in the nation. Demand for leased space reportedly slowed during 1989, and the 6.1 million sq. ft. of net absorption represented a turnover rate of only 3.6 percent. Sales of both production and distribution buildings were still brisk, though, with transactions up 12 percent for the year on a dollar-volume basis.

1990 Forecast

A 10 percent rebound in net absorption is expected to lead most market indicators upward during 1990. Less speculative construction is anticipated, as the market corrects its 52 percent rise in development activity in the year just ended. Upward pressure on land values will persist. The R&D sector is the one shadow over this market, affected both by oversupply and by demand retrenchment in the wake of Federal budgetary cuts.

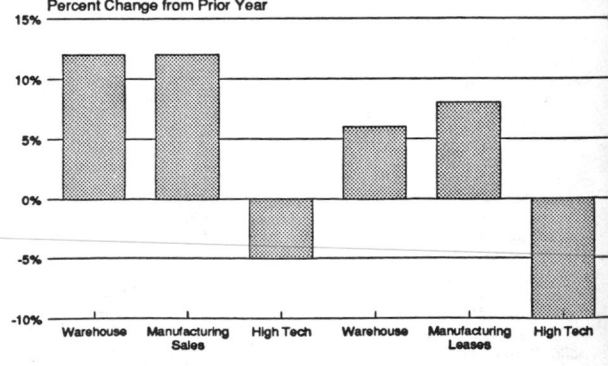

Dollar Volume - Sales & Leases
Los Angeles-San Fernando Valley

Percent Change from Prior Year

Los Angeles-San Gabriel Valley, California: Industrial

San Gabriel Valley and Eastern L.A. County

Market Data

Inventory (sf)	Central City	Suburban
Total	-	42,000,000
Vacant		8,000,000
Vacancy Rates	-	19.0%
Under Construction	-	3,000,000
Net Absorption	-	6,000,000

Sales Prices ($/sf)	Central City	Suburban
Less than 5,000 sf	-	72.00
5,000 to 19,999 sf	-	65.00
20,000 to 39,999 sf	-	60.00
40,000 to 59,999 sf	-	55.00
60,000 to 99,999 sf	-	45.00
More than 100,000 sf	-	43.00
High Tech/R&D	-	n/a

Net Lease Prices ($/sf)	Central City	Suburban
Less than 5,000 sf	-	6.24
5,000 to 19,999 sf	-	5.04
20,000 to 39,999 sf	-	3.84-4.20
40,000 to 59,999 sf	-	3.48-3.72
60,000 to 99,999 sf	-	3.24-3.36
More than 100,000 sf	-	3.24-3.36
High Tech/R&D	-	n/a

Site Prices ($/sf)	Central City	Suburban
Improved Sites		
Less than 2 Acres	-	13.50
2 to 5 Acres	-	12.50
5 to 10 Acres	-	11.50
More than 10 Acres	-	8.50-10.50
Unimproved Sites		
Less than 10 Acres	-	7.50
10 to 100 Acres	-	4.50
More than 100 Acres	-	n/a

Demographics

		Rank
Population:	8,804,062	1
Population Growth Rate:	1.83%	
Unemployment Rate:	4.8%	
Median Household Income:	31,276	37
Cost of Living Index:	126.5	6

Outlook

Sales Prices
Warehouse/Distribution	Up 5%
Manufacturing	Up 5%
High Tech/R&D	Up

Lease Prices
Warehouse/Distribution	Same
Manufacturing	Same
High Tech/R&D	n/a

Site Prices Up 5%

Absorption
Warehouse/Distribution	Same
Manufacturing	Same
High Tech/R&D	n/a

Construction
Warehouse/Distribution	Up 5%
Manufacturing	Up 5%
High Tech/R&D	n/a

Dollar Volume - Sales Same
Dollar Volume - Leases Same

Prime Source of Financing:
Insurance Companies, Commercial Banks

Mortgage Money Supply:
Ample

Construction Costs	
Less than 5,000 sf	35.00
5,000 to 19,999 sf	30.00
20,000 to 39,999 sf	25.00
40,000 to 59,999 sf	19.00-22.00
60,000 to 99,999 sf	18.00
More than 100,000 sf	17.00
High Tech/R&D	n/a

Vacancy Indicators	
Less than 5,000 sf	Moderate Oversupply
5,000 to 19,999 sf	Moderate Oversupply
20,000 to 39,999 sf	Moderate Oversupply
40,000 to 59,999 sf	Balanced Market
60,000 to 99,999 sf	Balanced Market
More than 100,000 sf	Balanced Market
High Tech/R&D	

Composition of Absorption
Warehouse/Distribution	70%
Manufacturing	25%
High Tech/R&D	5%

Rate of Construction
Warehouse/Distribution	Up 10%
Manufacturing	Up 5%
High Tech/R&D	Up

Dollar Volume - Sales
Warehouse/Distribution	Up 20%
Manufacturing	Up 5%
High Tech/R&D	Up

Dollar Volume - Leases
Warehouse/Distribution	Up 10%
Manufacturing	Up 5%
High Tech/R&D	Up

Note - Compared to a year ago

1989 Review

Last year brought excellent transaction volumes in both sales and leasing activity, especially in the large size categories. Net absorption was strong at six million sq. ft., representing a 14 percent turnover rate for this market. Warehouse and distribution functions accounted for 70 percent of the space taken. A 19 percent vacancy rate, however, indicates that the City of Industry found itself with excess capacity as 1989 ended, with problems concentrated in the smaller unit classifications.

1990 Forecast

With the market overextended at the beginning of the year, construction of new properties for lease will be greatly reduced in 1990. The high cost of carrying land will discourage speculation in a softening market. The City of Industry's role as a distribution point for the L.A. basin gives it some protection from the contraction of defense and aerospace manufacturing. Lease rates are expected to remain flat over the year, and sales prices are projected to rise a modest five percent by year-end.

Suburban Market Inventory
Los Angeles-San Gabriel Valley

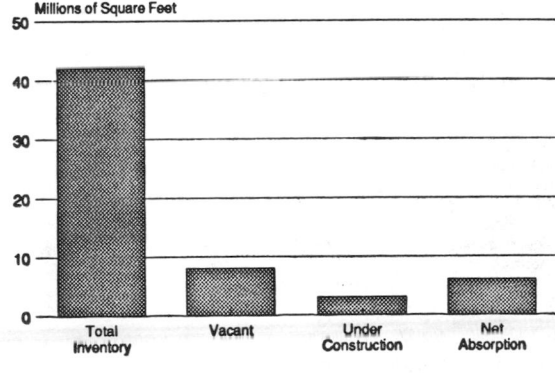

Millions of Square Feet

Los Angeles-South Bay, California: Industrial

Market Data

Inventory (sf)	Central City	Suburban
Total	-	171,008,000
Vacant	-	17,000,000
Vacancy Rates	-	9.9%
Under Construction	-	1,000,000
Net Absorption	-	n/a

Sales Prices ($/sf)	Central City	Suburban
Less than 5,000 sf	-	77.00
5,000 to 19,999 sf	-	77.00
20,000 to 39,999 sf	-	71.00
40,000 to 59,999 sf	-	65.00
60,000 to 99,999 sf	-	54.00
More than 100,000 sf	-	49.00
High Tech/R&D	-	85.00

Gross Lease Prices ($/sf)	Central City	Suburban
Less than 5,000 sf	-	7.50
5,000 to 19,999 sf	-	6.50
20,000 to 39,999 sf	-	5.40
40,000 to 59,999 sf	-	4.85
60,000 to 99,999 sf	-	4.80
More than 100,000 sf	-	4.55
High Tech/R&D	-	10.50

Site Prices ($/sf)	Central City	Suburban
Improved Sites		
Less than 2 Acres	-	20.00-25.00
2 to 5 Acres	-	20.00-25.00
5 to 10 Acres	-	15.00-22.00
More than 10 Acres	-	18.00-20.00
Unimproved Sites		
Less than 10 Acres	-	14.00-18.00
10 to 100 Acres	-	12.00-18.00
More than 100 Acres	-	12.00-18.00

Demographics

		Rank
Population:	8,804,062	1
Population Growth Rate:	1.83%	
Unemployment Rate:	4.8%	
Median Household Income:	31,276	37
Cost of Living Index:	126.5	6

Outlook

Sales Prices	
Warehouse/Distribution	Up 10%
Manufacturing	Up 10%
High Tech/R&D	Up 10%
Lease Prices	
Warehouse/Distribution	Up 5%
Manufacturing	Up 5%
High Tech/R&D	Same
Site Prices	Up 10-15%
Absorption	
Warehouse/Distribution	Same
Manufacturing	Same
High Tech/R&D	Down 10%
Construction	
Warehouse/Distribution	Same
Manufacturing	Same
High Tech/R&D	Same
Dollar Volume - Sales	Up 5-10%
Dollar Volume - Leases	Same

Prime Source of Financing:
Insurance Companies, Savings & Loans

Mortgage Money Supply:
Ample

Construction Costs	
Less than 5,000 sf	37.00
5,000 to 19,999 sf	32.70
20,000 to 39,999 sf	27.90
40,000 to 59,999 sf	22.20
60,000 to 99,999 sf	19.10
More than 100,000 sf	16.45
High Tech/R&D	59.00

Vacancy Indicators	
Less than 5,000 sf	Moderate Oversupply
5,000 to 19,999 sf	Moderate Shortage
20,000 to 39,999 sf	Balanced Market
40,000 to 59,999 sf	Balanced Market
60,000 to 99,999 sf	Balanced Market
More than 100,000 sf	Substantial Oversupply
High Tech/R&D	Moderate Oversupply

Composition of Absorption	
Warehouse/Distribution	85%
Manufacturing	10%
High Tech/R&D	5%
Rate of Construction	
Warehouse/Distribution	Up 25%
Manufacturing	Same
High Tech/R&D	Same
Dollar Volume - Sales	
Warehouse/Distribution	Same
Manufacturing	Same
High Tech/R&D	Same
Dollar Volume - Leases	
Warehouse/Distribution	Down 1-5%
Manufacturing	Same
High Tech/R&D	Same
Note - Compared to a year ago	

1989 Review

Acquisition demand for industrial properties was exceptionally strong in 1989. Most market segments found themselves in a healthy supply/demand equilibrium at year-end, with any oversupply concentrated in the largest and smallest size classes. Vacancy was down a full percentage point to 9.9 percent. Most absorption was concentrated in distribution buildings, but there is a trend toward more service-oriented business uses.

1990 Forecast

Developers are cautious about speculative development. Land is limited and very expensive, and these factors tend to rein in overly ambitious building plans. Site prices could rise as much as 15 percent during 1990. Strong trade volumes through the ports of Los Angeles and San Pedro should continue to support demand in the South Bay market. Investor interest is expected to occasion a capital-driven 10 percent increase in sales prices across the board. The defense-related high-tech sector is anticipating a 10 percent drop in absorption, even holding rents flat for the year.

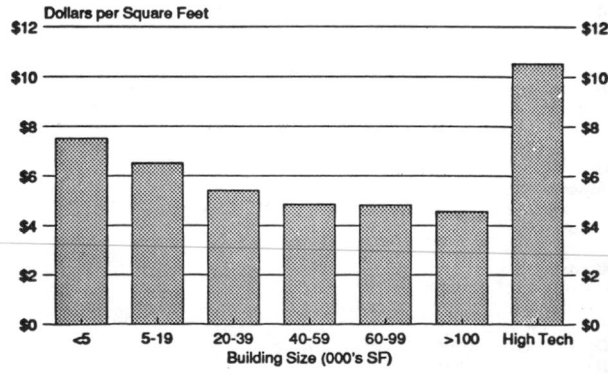

Suburban Gross Lease Prices
Los Angeles-South Bay

Dollars per Square Feet

Building Size (000's SF): <5, 5-19, 20-39, 40-59, 60-99, >100, High Tech

Los Angeles-West, California: Industrial

Market Data

Inventory (sf)	Central City	Suburban
Total	n/a	-
Vacant	n/a	-
Vacancy Rates	n/a	-
Under Construction	n/a	-
Net Absorption	n/a	-

Sales Prices ($/sf)	Central City	Suburban
Less than 5,000 sf	n/a	-
5,000 to 19,999 sf	n/a	-
20,000 to 39,999 sf	n/a	-
40,000 to 59,999 sf	n/a	-
60,000 to 99,999 sf	n/a	-
More than 100,000 sf	n/a	-
High Tech/R&D	n/a	-

Net Lease Prices ($/sf)	Central City	Suburban
Less than 5,000 sf	n/a	-
5,000 to 19,999 sf	n/a	-
20,000 to 39,999 sf	n/a	-
40,000 to 59,999 sf	n/a	-
60,000 to 99,999 sf	n/a	-
More than 100,000 sf	n/a	-
High Tech/R&D	n/a	-

Site Prices ($/sf)	Central City	Suburban
Improved Sites		
Less than 2 Acres	25.00-65.00	-
2 to 5 Acres	25.00-60.00	-
5 to 10 Acres	23.00-50.00	-
More than 10 Acres	23.00-50.00	-
Unimproved Sites		
Less than 10 Acres	23.00-50.00	-
10 to 100 Acres	23.00-50.00	-
More than 100 Acres	n/a	-

Demographics

		Rank
Population:	8,804,062	1
Population Growth Rate:	1.83%	
Unemployment Rate:	4.8%	
Median Household Income:	$31,276	37
Cost of Living Index:	126.5	6

Outlook

Sales Prices
Warehouse/Distribution	Up 6-10%
Manufacturing	Up 6-10%
High Tech/R&D	Up 6-10%

Lease Prices
Warehouse/Distribution	Same
Manufacturing	Same
High Tech/R&D	Same

Site Prices Up 6-10%

Absorption
Warehouse/Distribution	Same
Manufacturing	Same
High Tech/R&D	Same

Construction
Warehouse/Distribution	Down 5-10%
Manufacturing	Down 5-10%
High Tech/R&D	Down 5-10%
Dollar Volume - Sales	Same
Dollar Volume - Leases	Same

Prime Source of Financing:
Insurance Companies, Pension Funds

Mortgage Money Supply:
Ample

Construction Costs	
Less than 5,000 sf	40.00
5,000 to 19,999 sf	35.00-40.00
20,000 to 39,999 sf	30.00-40.00
40,000 to 59,999 sf	25.00-30.00
60,000 to 99,999 sf	20.00-30.00
More than 100,000 sf	25.00
High Tech/R&D	30.00

Vacancy Indicators	
Less than 5,000 sf	Moderate Oversupply
5,000 to 19,999 sf	Moderate Oversupply
20,000 to 39,999 sf	Balanced Market
40,000 to 59,999 sf	Balanced Market
60,000 to 99,999 sf	Balanced Market
More than 100,000 sf	Balanced Market
High Tech/R&D	Moderate Oversupply

Composition of Absorption	
Warehouse/Distribution	35%
Manufacturing	20%
High Tech/R&D	45%

Rate of Construction	
Warehouse/Distribution	Down 5-10%
Manufacturing	Down 5-10%
High Tech/R&D	Down 5-10%

Dollar Volume - Sales	
Warehouse/Distribution	Down 5%
Manufacturing	Down 5%
High Tech/R&D	Down 5%

Dollar Volume - Leases	
Warehouse/Distribution	Down 5%
Manufacturing	Same
High Tech/R&D	Up 5-10%

Note - Compared to a year ago

1989 Review

This market, which has reported inventory shortages in past years, appears to have weakened during 1989. Construction volumes and transaction activity were generally slower than the previous year, and SIOR's local respondent noted that rents stalled in the last six months of 1989. Demand from users for the purchase of their facilities has been strong, and this is raising prices for all buyers.

1990 Forecast

The concentration of high-tech users as a percentage of total absorption should be a warning signal in the coming year. With land sale prices at $30 and up, and the prevalence of redevelopment of existing sites, speculative new construction will be rare. West Los Angeles may be feeling competitive pressures from other submarkets increasing during 1990.

Composition of Absorption
Los Angeles-West

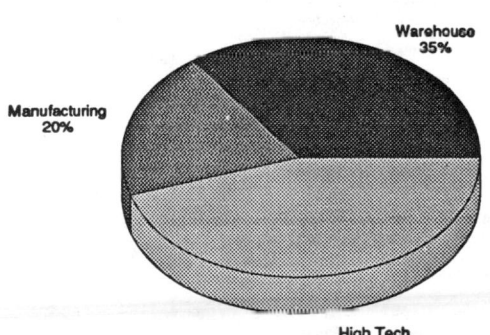

Warehouse 35%

Manufacturing 20%

High Tech 45%

New Jersey-Central: Industrial

Mercer and portions of Middlesex, Monmouth, Morris, Somerset, and Union counties

Market Data

Inventory (sf)	Central City	Suburban
Total	n/a	n/a
Vacant	n/a	n/a
Vacancy Rates	n/a	n/a
Under Construction	n/a	n/a
Net Absorption	n/a	n/a

Sales Prices ($/sf)	Central City	Suburban
Less than 5,000 sf	25.00	45.00
5,000 to 19,999 sf	22.00	40.00
20,000 to 39,999 sf	15.00	38.00
40,000 to 59,999 sf	12.00	38.00
60,000 to 99,999 sf	12.00	32.00
More than 100,000 sf	10.00	30.00
High Tech/R&D	n/a	60.00

Net Lease Prices ($/sf)	Central City	Suburban
Less than 5,000 sf	3.50	6.00
5,000 to 19,999 sf	3.00	5.50
20,000 to 39,999 sf	3.00	5.50
40,000 to 59,999 sf	2.50	5.00
60,000 to 99,999 sf	2.50	4.50
More than 100,000 sf	2.50	4.25
High Tech/R&D	7.50	10.00

Site Prices ($/sf)	Central City	Suburban
Improved Sites		
Less than 2 Acres	2.50	n/a
2 to 5 Acres	n/a	3.00
5 to 10 Acres	n/a	2.50
More than 10 Acres	n/a	2.00
Unimproved Sites		
Less than 10 Acres	n/a	2.00
10 to 100 Acres	n/a	1.50
More than 100 Acres	n/a	1.00

Demographics

		Rank
Population:	n/a	n/a
Population Growth Rate:	n/a	
Unemployment Rate:	n/a	
Median Household Income:	n/a	n/a
Cost of Living Index:	n/a	n/a

Outlook

Sales Prices
Warehouse/Distribution	Same
Manufacturing	Same
High Tech/R&D	Same

Lease Prices
Warehouse/Distribution	Up 5%
Manufacturing	Same
High Tech/R&D	Up 5%

Site Prices Same

Absorption
Warehouse/Distribution	Same
Manufacturing	Same
High Tech/R&D	Same

Construction
Warehouse/Distribution	Same
Manufacturing	Same
High Tech/R&D	Same
Dollar Volume - Sales	Same
Dollar Volume - Leases	Same

Prime Source of Financing:
Commercial Banks

Mortgage Money Supply:
Ample

Construction Costs	
Less than 5,000 sf	n/a
5,000 to 19,999 sf	n/a
20,000 to 39,999 sf	n/a
40,000 to 59,999 sf	n/a
60,000 to 99,999 sf	n/a
More than 100,000 sf	n/a
High Tech/R&D	n/a

Vacancy Indicators	
Less than 5,000 sf	Moderate Shortage
5,000 to 19,999 sf	Moderate Shortage
20,000 to 39,999 sf	Balanced Market
40,000 to 59,999 sf	Balanced Market
60,000 to 99,999 sf	Balanced Market
More than 100,000 sf	Moderate Shortage
High Tech/R&D	Moderate Oversupply

Composition of Absorption	
Warehouse/Distribution	80%
Manufacturing	15%
High Tech/R&D	5%

Rate of Construction	
Warehouse/Distribution	Same
Manufacturing	Same
High Tech/R&D	Same

Dollar Volume - Sales	
Warehouse/Distribution	Same
Manufacturing	Same
High Tech/R&D	Same

Dollar Volume - Leases	
Warehouse/Distribution	Same
Manufacturing	Same
High Tech/R&D	Same

Note - Compared to a year ago

1989 Review

The size and complexity of this market area proved a daunting statistical hurdle for SIOR's local reporters. Qualitatively, the picture emerging is one of a distribution dominated market positioned midway between New York City and Philadelphia, and well-situated to serve the entire Eastern Seaboard. Tight-to-balanced supply demand conditions prevailed, with the exception of the overbuilt high-tech parks. Activity has been steady, but not spectacular during 1989. Mercer County is the market center, with most demand originating from firms already in the area.

1990 Forecast

Central New Jersey appears at least a year away from its next generation of speculative industrial development. Although the statewide economy is expected to be sluggish, this market area will be able to sustain some tightening in 1990, potentially pushing lease rates up by five percent. Foreign investment in the area has been expected for some time, but 1990 shapes up as another year of waiting for off-shore capital.

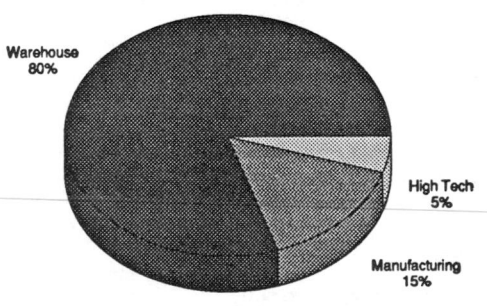

Composition of Absorption
New Jersey-Central

Warehouse 80%

High Tech 5%

Manufacturing 15%

New Jersey-Northern: Industrial

Market Data

Inventory (sf)	Central City	Suburban
Total	100,000,000	1,500,000,000
Vacant	7,000,000	90,000,000
Vacancy Rates	7.0%	6.0%
Under Construction	n/a	n/a
Net Absorption	n/a	n/a

Prime Source of Financing:
Insurance Companies

Mortgage Money Supply:
Moderate

Sales Prices ($/sf)	Central City	Suburban
Less than 5,000 sf	50.00	75.00
5,000 to 19,999 sf	45.00	65.00
20,000 to 39,999 sf	45.00	60.00
40,000 to 59,999 sf	42.00	60.00
60,000 to 99,999 sf	40.00	55.00
More than 100,000 sf	40.00	45.00
High Tech/R&D	n/a	75.00

Construction Costs	
Less than 5,000 sf	45.00
5,000 to 19,999 sf	42.00
20,000 to 39,999 sf	40.00
40,000 to 59,999 sf	35.00
60,000 to 99,999 sf	32.00
More than 100,000 sf	30.00
High Tech/R&D	70.00

Net Lease Prices ($/sf)	Central City	Suburban
Less than 5,000 sf	5.50	7.00
5,000 to 19,999 sf	5.00	6.50
20,000 to 39,999 sf	4.50	6.00
40,000 to 59,999 sf	4.50	5.50
60,000 to 99,999 sf	4.25	5.00
More than 100,000 sf	4.25	4.75
High Tech/R&D	n/a	8.50

Vacancy Indicators	
Less than 5,000 sf	Balanced Market
5,000 to 19,999 sf	Balanced Market
20,000 to 39,999 sf	Moderate Oversupply
40,000 to 59,999 sf	Moderate Oversupply
60,000 to 99,999 sf	Moderate Oversupply
More than 100,000 sf	Moderate Oversupply
High Tech/R&D	Balanced Market

Site Prices ($/sf)	Central City	Suburban
Improved Sites		
Less than 2 Acres	7.00	10.00
2 to 5 Acres	6.00	8.00
5 to 10 Acres	5.00	7.00
More than 10 Acres	n/a	6.00
Unimproved Sites		
Less than 10 Acres	n/a	4.00
10 to 100 Acres	n/a	3.50
More than 100 Acres	n/a	2.50

Composition of Absorption	
Warehouse/Distribution	65%
Manufacturing	30%
High Tech/R&D	5%
Rate of Construction	
Warehouse/Distribution	Up 3%
Manufacturing	Up 3%
High Tech/R&D	Up 3%
Dollar Volume - Sales	
Warehouse/Distribution	Up 5%
Manufacturing	Up 5%
High Tech/R&D	Same
Dollar Volume - Leases	
Warehouse/Distribution	Down 20%
Manufacturing	Down 20%
High Tech/R&D	Same
Note - Compared to a year ago	

Demographics

		Rank
Population:	1,895,623	n/a
Population Growth Rate:	0.10%	
Unemployment Rate:	n/a	
Median Household Income:	$40,118	n/a
Cost of Living Index:	n/a	n/a

Outlook

Sales Prices	
Warehouse/Distribution	Same
Manufacturing	Same
High Tech/R&D	Same
Lease Prices	
Warehouse/Distribution	Same
Manufacturing	Same
High Tech/R&D	Same
Site Prices	Same
Absorption	
Warehouse/Distribution	Same
Manufacturing	Same
High Tech/R&D	Same
Construction	
Warehouse/Distribution	Same
Manufacturing	Same
High Tech/R&D	Same
Dollar Volume - Sales	Same
Dollar Volume - Leases	Same

1989 Review

Some inkling of the size of this market can be gleaned by recognizing that its comparatively low 6.1 percent vacancy rate represents nearly one hundred million sq. ft. of empty space! Real estate demand has been constrained in this area as much by the unavailability of labor and by environmental sensitivities as by any real slackening in the economy. Smaller units were in good balance relative to user requirements, but facilties larger than 20,000 sq. ft. were overbuilt. Some rationale for the abundance of industrial development here can be seen in the sales prices ranging from $45 to $75 per sq. ft.

1990 Forecast

Lack of developable land and enormous site costs will severely restrict construction activity in 1990. Lenders will be more cautious, too, in the wake of the RTC's late 1989 takeover of City Federal Savings. Warehousing will lease more rapidly than manufacturing facilities. The relatively well-balanced R&D market will continue to benefit from sophisticated corporate users like AT&T, Johnson & Johnson and others. Market conditions look generally unchanged for the coming year.

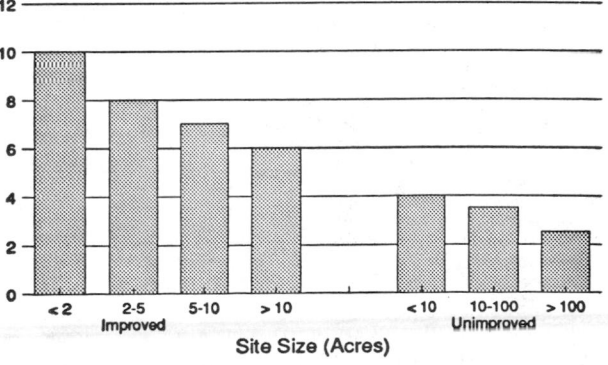

Suburban Site Prices
New Jersey-Northern

Site Size (Acres)

New Jersey-Southern: Industrial

Burlington, Camden, and Gloucester Counties

Market Data

Inventory (sf)	Central City	Suburban
Total	-	22,000,000
Vacant	-	8,000,000
Vacancy Rates	-	36.4%
Under Construction	-	300,000
Net Absorption	-	n/a

Sales Prices ($/sf)	Central City	Suburban
Less than 5,000 sf	-	n/a
5,000 to 19,999 sf	-	n/a
20,000 to 39,999 sf	-	n/a
40,000 to 59,999 sf	-	n/a
60,000 to 99,999 sf	-	n/a
More than 100,000 sf	-	n/a
High Tech/R&D	-	n/a

Net Lease Prices ($/sf)	Central City	Suburban
Less than 5,000 sf	-	4.50
5,000 to 19,999 sf	-	4.00
20,000 to 39,999 sf	-	3.80
40,000 to 59,999 sf	-	3.40
60,000 to 99,999 sf	-	3.25
More than 100,000 sf	-	3.00
High Tech/R&D	-	7.00-10.00

Site Prices ($/sf)	Central City	Suburban
Improved Sites		
Less than 2 Acres	-	1.72
2 to 5 Acres	-	1.72
5 to 10 Acres	-	1.50
More than 10 Acres	-	1.38
Unimproved Sites		
Less than 10 Acres	-	1.15
10 to 100 Acres	-	1.10
More than 100 Acres	-	n/a

Demographics

		Rank
Population:	n/a	n/a
Population Growth Rate:	n/a	
Unemployment Rate:	n/a	
Median Household Income:	n/a	n/a
Cost of Living Index:	n/a	n/a

Outlook

Sales Prices	
Warehouse/Distribution	Up 10%
Manufacturing	Up 10%
High Tech/R&D	Up 10%
Lease Prices	
Warehouse/Distribution	Down 10%
Manufacturing	Down 10%
High Tech/R&D	Down 10%
Site Prices	Same
Absorption	
Warehouse/Distribution	Same
Manufacturing	Same
High Tech/R&D	Same
Construction	
Warehouse/Distribution	Down
Manufacturing	Down
High Tech/R&D	Down
Dollar Volume - Sales	Same
Dollar Volume - Leases	Same

Prime Source of Financing:
Seller

Mortgage Money Supply:

Construction Costs	
Less than 5,000 sf	45.00
5,000 to 19,999 sf	45.00
20,000 to 39,999 sf	40.00
40,000 to 59,999 sf	38.00
60,000 to 99,999 sf	35.00
More than 100,000 sf	27.00
High Tech/R&D	50.00

Vacancy Indicators	
Less than 5,000 sf	Balanced Market
5,000 to 19,999 sf	Balanced Market
20,000 to 39,999 sf	Balanced Market
40,000 to 59,999 sf	Moderate Oversupply
60,000 to 99,999 sf	Moderate Oversupply
More than 100,000 sf	Moderate Shortage
High Tech/R&D	Moderate Oversupply

Composition of Absorption	
Warehouse/Distribution	40%
Manufacturing	20%
High Tech/R&D	40%
Rate of Construction	
Warehouse/Distribution	Same
Manufacturing	Same
High Tech/R&D	Same
Dollar Volume - Sales	
Warehouse/Distribution	Up 10-15%
Manufacturing	Up 10-15%
High Tech/R&D	Up 10-15%
Dollar Volume - Leases	
Warehouse/Distribution	Down 10%
Manufacturing	Down 10%
High Tech/R&D	Down 10%
Note - Compared to a year ago	

1989 Review

Great interest in property for sale, but slightly slower demand for lease space counts as the headline story for the Southern New Jersey suburban industrial market. The basic economy remained good, and clearly less affected by the Northeast slowdown than the remainder of the state. Gloucester County, in particular, continued to move up the growth curve. But even there users found ample vacant space and competitive rents.

1990 Forecast

Trends in rental rates and sales prices are expected to continue on their diverging paths in 1990. Construction will likely pullback marginally, in the face of eight million sq. ft. of vacancies and the slippage in lease prices. The solid local economy gives this market some protection on the downside, and local expansion needs are likely to be supplemented by demand diverted from the higher cost New York-Northern New Jersey markets.

Sales & Lease Price Outlook
New Jersey-Southern

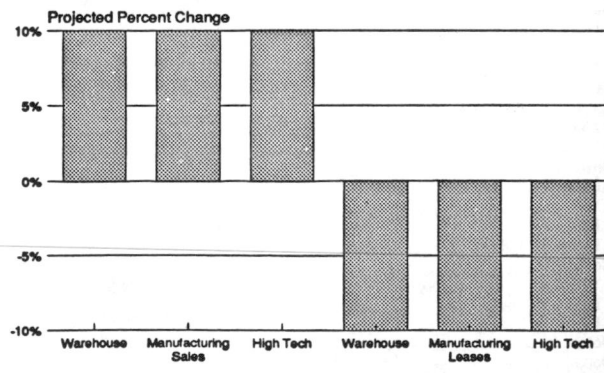

Projected Percent Change

New York City, New York: Industrial

Manhattan

Market Data

Inventory (sf)

Inventory (sf)	Central City	Suburban
Total	n/a	-
Vacant	n/a	-
Vacancy Rates	n/a	-
Under Construction	n/a	-
Net Absorption	n/a	-

Sales Prices ($/sf)	Central City	Suburban
Less than 5,000 sf	50.00-150.00	-
5,000 to 19,999 sf	50.00-150.00	-
20,000 to 39,999 sf	50.00-125.00	-
40,000 to 59,999 sf	50.00-125.00	-
60,000 to 99,999 sf	n/a	-
More than 100,000 sf	n/a	-
High Tech/R&D	n/a	-

Net Lease Prices ($/sf)	Central City	Suburban
Less than 5,000 sf	8.00-20.00	-
5,000 to 19,999 sf	6.50-15.00	-
20,000 to 39,999 sf	6.00-18.00	-
40,000 to 59,999 sf	6.00-18.00	-
60,000 to 99,999 sf	n/a	-
More than 100,000 sf	n/a	-
High Tech/R&D	n/a	-

Site Prices ($/sf)	Central City	Suburban
Improved Sites		
Less than 2 Acres	n/a	-
2 to 5 Acres	n/a	-
5 to 10 Acres	n/a	-
More than 10 Acres	n/a	-
Unimproved Sites		
Less than 10 Acres	n/a	-
10 to 100 Acres	n/a	-
More than 100 Acres	n/a	-

Demographics

		Rank
Population:	8,617,968	2
Population Growth Rate:	0.45%	
Unemployment Rate:	6.20%	
Median Household Income:	$27,043	74
Cost of Living Index:	n/a	n/a

Outlook

Sales Prices
Warehouse/Distribution	Same
Manufacturing	Same
High Tech/R&D	n/a

Lease Prices
Warehouse/Distribution	Down 10%
Manufacturing	Down 10%
High Tech/R&D	Down

Site Prices Up n/a%

Absorption
Warehouse/Distribution	Down 0%
Manufacturing	Down 0%
High Tech/R&D	Down

Construction
Warehouse/Distribution	Down
Manufacturing	Down
High Tech/R&D	Down

Dollar Volume - Sales	n/a
Dollar Volume - Leases	n/a

Prime Source of Financing:
Insurance Companies, Commercial Banks, Owner Financing

Mortgage Money Supply:
Moderate

Construction Costs	
Less than 5,000 sf	n/a
5,000 to 19,999 sf	n/a
20,000 to 39,999 sf	n/a
40,000 to 59,999 sf	n/a
60,000 to 99,999 sf	n/a
More than 100,000 sf	n/a
High Tech/R&D	n/a

Vacancy Indicators	
Less than 5,000 sf	Balanced Market
5,000 to 19,999 sf	Balanced Market
20,000 to 39,999 sf	Moderate Shortage
40,000 to 59,999 sf	Moderate Shortage
60,000 to 99,999 sf	Substantial Shortage
More than 100,000 sf	Substantial Shortage
High Tech/R&D	Substantial Shortage

Composition of Absorption
Warehouse/Distribution	n/a
Manufacturing	n/a
High Tech/R&D	n/a

Rate of Construction
Warehouse/Distribution	n/a
Manufacturing	n/a
High Tech/R&D	n/a

Dollar Volume - Sales
Warehouse/Distribution	Down 15%
Manufacturing	Down 15%
High Tech/R&D	Down

Dollar Volume - Leases
Warehouse/Distribution	Down n/a%
Manufacturing	Down n/a%
High Tech/R&D	Down

Note - Compared to a year ago

1989 Review

There is really a minimal amount of industrial space in Manhattan, much of it consisting of one-story buildings under 10,000 sq. ft. used as taxi fleet garages, or for repair and installation services. Multi-story loft buildings are used for light assembly functions, the printing trade, the garment industry, or as showroom/distribution space. Demand has been small, and most of the market activity is in leasing rather than sales. The stall in the regional economy has kept this unusual urban industrial market flat during 1989.

1990 Forecast

Continued atrophy is the most probable forecast. New facilities are highly unlikely, since market rents for this property type are not consistent with the costs of acquiring or assembling land and today's construction costs. Manufacturing employment in Manhattan has been falling for over 40 years, and will do so again in 1990. Relocation activity from New York to the nearby suburbs will persist as tenants seek the greater efficiency of single-story buildings.

Net Lease Prices
New York City

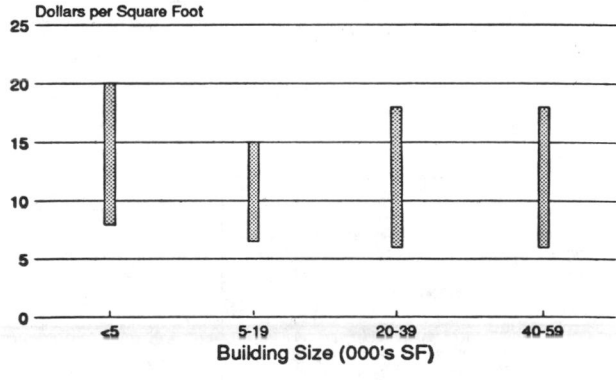

Building Size (000's SF)

New York City-Bronx, New York: Industrial

Market Data

Inventory (sf)	Central City	Suburban
Total	15,000,000	-
Vacant	1,000,000	-
Vacancy Rates	6.7%	-
Under Construction	300,000	-
Net Absorption	1,000,000	-

Prime Source of Financing:
Commercial Banks, Owner Financing

Mortgage Money Supply:
Ample

Sales Prices ($/sf)	Central City	Suburban
Less than 5,000 sf	70.00	-
5,000 to 19,999 sf	70.00	-
20,000 to 39,999 sf	65.00	-
40,000 to 59,999 sf	65.00	-
60,000 to 99,999 sf	60.00	-
More than 100,000 sf	50.00	-
High Tech/R&D	-	-

Construction Costs	
Less than 5,000 sf	60.00
5,000 to 19,999 sf	50.00
20,000 to 39,999 sf	50.00
40,000 to 59,999 sf	50.00
60,000 to 99,999 sf	47.50
More than 100,000 sf	45.00
High Tech/R&D	n/a

Gross Lease Prices ($/sf)	Central City	Suburban
Less than 5,000 sf	7.00	-
5,000 to 19,999 sf	7.00	-
20,000 to 39,999 sf	6.50	-
40,000 to 59,999 sf	6.50	-
60,000 to 99,999 sf	6.00	-
More than 100,000 sf	5.00	-
High Tech/R&D	-	-

Vacancy Indicators	
Less than 5,000 sf	Substantial Shortage
5,000 to 19,999 sf	Balanced Market
20,000 to 39,999 sf	Balanced Market
40,000 to 59,999 sf	Balanced Market
60,000 to 99,999 sf	Moderate Shortage
More than 100,000 sf	Moderate Shortage
High Tech/R&D	Moderate Shortage

Site Prices ($/sf)	Central City	Suburban
Improved Sites		
Less than 2 Acres	n/a	-
2 to 5 Acres	n/a	-
5 to 10 Acres	n/a	-
More than 10 Acres	n/a	-
Unimproved Sites		
Less than 10 Acres	n/a	-
10 to 100 Acres	n/a	-
More than 100 Acres	n/a	-

Composition of Absorption	
Warehouse/Distribution	55%
Manufacturing	40%
High Tech/R&D	5%
Rate of Construction	
Warehouse/Distribution	Same
Manufacturing	Same
High Tech/R&D	Same
Dollar Volume - Sales	
Warehouse/Distribution	Same
Manufacturing	Same
High Tech/R&D	Same
Dollar Volume - Leases	
Warehouse/Distribution	Same
Manufacturing	Same
High Tech/R&D	Same
Note - Compared to a year ago	

Demographics

		Rank
Population:	8,617,968	2
Population Growth Rate:	0.45%	
Unemployment Rate:	6.2%	
Median Household Income:	$27,043	74
Cost of Living Index:	n/a	n/a

Outlook

Sales Prices	
Warehouse/Distribution	Same
Manufacturing	Same
High Tech/R&D	Same
Lease Prices	
Warehouse/Distribution	Same
Manufacturing	Same
High Tech/R&D	Same
Site Prices	n/a
Absorption	
Warehouse/Distribution	Same
Manufacturing	Same
High Tech/R&D	Same
Construction	
Warehouse/Distribution	Same
Manufacturing	Same
High Tech/R&D	Same
Dollar Volume - Sales	Same
Dollar Volume - Leases	Same

1989 Review

The Bronx industrial base consists primarily of older multi-story manufacturing buildings and warehouse/terminal facilities in a broad arc along the Harlem and East Rivers. Like the other industrial areas of the city, its inventory has been shrinking over time. In 1989, most functional properties in the borough were being utilized. There does exist a class of obsolete property sitting idle, but these buildings are simply awaiting their removal through decay or demolition. Rents fall in a tight $5.00 - $7.00 per sq. ft. range.

1990 Forecast

Little incremental change is forecast for the coming year. Some additional demand could emerge in the near future, if the State Department of Transportation will fund a one-half mile rail link allowing passage of full height freight cars. The Bronx is well located for interstate traffic by truck as well, and its location within the densely populated New York metropolitan area could be better exploited.

Construction Costs vs. Sales Prices
New York City-Bronx

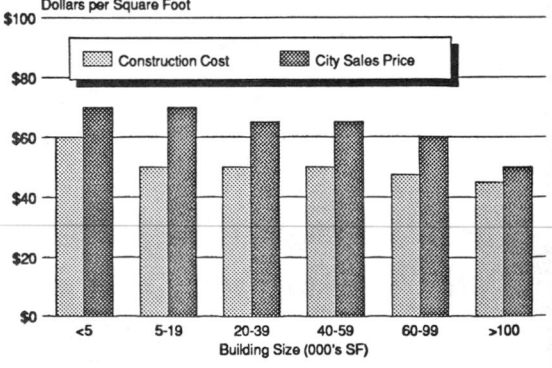

New York City-Brooklyn/Queens, New York: Industrial

Market Data

Inventory (sf)	Central City	Suburban
Total	330,000,000	-
Vacant	49,000,000	-
Vacancy Rates	14.8%	-
Under Construction	n/a	-
Net Absorption	7,000,000	-

Sales Prices ($/sf)	Central City	Suburban
Less than 5,000 sf	90.00-120.00	-
5,000 to 19,999 sf	80.00-100.00	-
20,000 to 39,999 sf	60.00-80.00	-
40,000 to 59,999 sf	40.00-65.00	-
60,000 to 99,999 sf	35.00-60.00	-
More than 100,000 sf	35.00-60.00	-
High Tech/R&D	110.00-130.00	-

Net Lease Prices ($/sf)	Central City	Suburban
Less than 5,000 sf	9.00-10.00	-
5,000 to 19,999 sf	6.50-8.50	-
20,000 to 39,999 sf	6.25-7.75	-
40,000 to 59,999 sf	5.50-6.50	-
60,000 to 99,999 sf	5.00-6.50	-
More than 100,000 sf	3.50-6.00	-
High Tech/R&D	9.00-12.00	-

Site Prices ($/sf)	Central City	Suburban
Improved Sites		
Less than 2 Acres	30.00-60.00	-
2 to 5 Acres	20.00-35.00	-
5 to 10 Acres	15.00-30.00	-
More than 10 Acres	20.00-30.00	-
Unimproved Sites		
Less than 10 Acres	n/a	-
10 to 100 Acres	n/a	-
More than 100 Acres	n/a	-

Demographics

		Rank
Population:	8,617,968	2
Population Growth Rate:	0.45%	
Unemployment Rate:	6.2%	
Median Household Income:	$27,043	74
Cost of Living Index:	n/a	n/a

Outlook

Sales Prices
Warehouse/Distribution	Down 5-10%
Manufacturing	Down 10-15%
High Tech/R&D	Down 10%

Lease Prices
Warehouse/Distribution	Down 5-10%
Manufacturing	Down 10-15%
High Tech/R&D	Down 10%

Site Prices   Same

Absorption
Warehouse/Distribution	Down 10%
Manufacturing	Down 15%
High Tech/R&D	Down 15%

Construction
Warehouse/Distribution	Down 90%
Manufacturing	Down 90%
High Tech/R&D	Down 90%

Dollar Volume - Sales	Same
Dollar Volume - Leases	Same

Prime Source of Financing:
Commercial Banks

Mortgage Money Supply:
Ample

Construction Costs	
Less than 5,000 sf	60.00
5,000 to 19,999 sf	60.00
20,000 to 39,999 sf	55.00
40,000 to 59,999 sf	55.00
60,000 to 99,999 sf	50.00
More than 100,000 sf	45.00-50.00
High Tech/R&D	150.00

Vacancy Indicators	
Less than 5,000 sf	Moderate Shortage
5,000 to 19,999 sf	Balanced Market
20,000 to 39,999 sf	Moderate Oversupply
40,000 to 59,999 sf	Moderate Oversupply
60,000 to 99,999 sf	Moderate Oversupply
More than 100,000 sf	Moderate Oversupply
High Tech/R&D	Balanced Market

Composition of Absorption
Warehouse/Distribution	70%
Manufacturing	25%
High Tech/R&D	5%

Rate of Construction
Warehouse/Distribution	Down
Manufacturing	Down
High Tech/R&D	Down

Dollar Volume - Sales
Warehouse/Distribution	Same
Manufacturing	Same
High Tech/R&D	Down 10%

Dollar Volume - Leases
Warehouse/Distribution	Down 10%
Manufacturing	Down 10%
High Tech/R&D	Down 10%

Note - Compared to a year ago

1989 Review

This two-borough submarket of New York City is large and troubled. With a vacancy rate of nearly 15 percent, existing available inventory stands at 49 million sq. ft. - seven times the level of 1989's net absorption. The dollar volume of leasing activity was down 10 percent from a year ago, and the market surely was not helped by the city's recent trying economy. Manufacturing's share of market activity continued to slip, and warehousing accounted for 70 percent of absorption in 1989.

1990 Forecast

Diminishing expectations mark the outlook for 1990. Most market measures are anticipated to slip between five and 15 percent this year. The forecast for good production facilities is the bleakest. With presumed site prices at a million dollars an acre or more, new development is simply evaporating even in the face of sales prices which are among the highest in the nation. Those looking for bright spots in the gloom will note that, somehow, 281 million sq. ft. of Brooklyn/Queens industrial space remains viably occupied at fairly substantial rents.

Composition of Absorption
New York City-Brooklyn/Queens

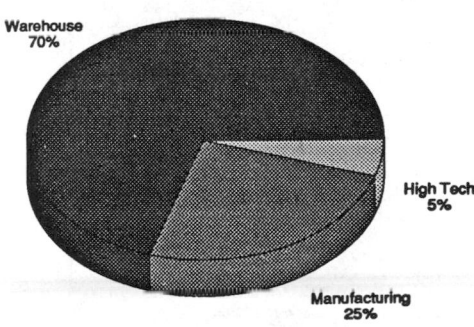

Warehouse 70%

High Tech 5%

Manufacturing 25%

New York-Nassau/Suffolk Counties, New York: Industrial

Market Data

Inventory (sf)	Central City	Suburban
Total	-	231,000,000
Vacant	-	31,000,000
Vacancy Rates	-	13.4%
Under Construction	-	-
Net Absorption	-	7,000,000

Sales Prices ($/sf)	Central City	Suburban
Less than 5,000 sf	-	85.00-100.00
5,000 to 19,999 sf	-	75.00-80.00
20,000 to 39,999 sf	-	55.00-60.00
40,000 to 59,999 sf	-	50.00-60.00
60,000 to 99,999 sf	-	45.00-52.00
More than 100,000 sf	-	45.00-50.00
High Tech/R&D	-	75.00-125.00

Net Lease Prices ($/sf)	Central City	Suburban
Less than 5,000 sf	-	7.50-9.00
5,000 to 19,999 sf	-	6.50-7.50
20,000 to 39,999 sf	-	6.00-7.00
40,000 to 59,999 sf	-	5.00-6.50
60,000 to 99,999 sf	-	5.00-6.50
More than 100,000 sf	-	4.75-6.00
High Tech/R&D	-	7.00-12.00

Site Prices ($/sf)	Central City	Suburban
Improved Sites		
Less than 2 Acres	-	7.00-15.00
2 to 5 Acres	-	5.00-9.00
5 to 10 Acres	-	5.00-9.00
More than 10 Acres	-	4.00-8.00
Unimproved Sites		
Less than 10 Acres	-	n/a
10 to 100 Acres	-	n/a
More than 100 Acres	-	n/a

Demographics

		Rank
Population:	2,643,585	11
Population Growth Rate:	0.16%	
Unemployment Rate:	n/a	
Median Household Income:	$49,412	2
Cost of Living Index:	157.2	1

Outlook

Sales Prices	
Warehouse/Distribution	Down 10%
Manufacturing	Down 10%
High Tech/R&D	Down 15%
Lease Prices	
Warehouse/Distribution	Down 10%
Manufacturing	Down 10%
High Tech/R&D	Down 15%
Site Prices	Same
Absorption	
Warehouse/Distribution	Down 10%
Manufacturing	Down 20%
High Tech/R&D	Down 20%
Construction	
Warehouse/Distribution	Down 90%
Manufacturing	Down 90%
High Tech/R&D	Down 90%
Dollar Volume - Sales	Same
Dollar Volume - Leases	Same

Prime Source of Financing:
Commercial Banks

Mortgage Money Supply:
Ample

Construction Costs	
Less than 5,000 sf	70.00-85.00
5,000 to 19,999 sf	55.00-65.00
20,000 to 39,999 sf	45.00-55.00
40,000 to 59,999 sf	45.00-55.00
60,000 to 99,999 sf	40.00-50.00
More than 100,000 sf	40.00-50.00
High Tech/R&D	75.00-150.00

Vacancy Indicators	
Less than 5,000 sf	Balanced Market
5,000 to 19,999 sf	Balanced Market
20,000 to 39,999 sf	Moderate Oversupply
40,000 to 59,999 sf	Moderate Oversupply
60,000 to 99,999 sf	Substantial Oversupply
More than 100,000 sf	Substantial Oversupply
High Tech/R&D	Moderate Oversupply

Composition of Absorption	
Warehouse/Distribution	50%
Manufacturing	25%
High Tech/R&D	25%
Rate of Construction	
Warehouse/Distribution	Down 75%
Manufacturing	Down 75%
High Tech/R&D	Down 75%
Dollar Volume - Sales	
Warehouse/Distribution	Down 10%
Manufacturing	Down 10%
High Tech/R&D	Down 10%
Dollar Volume - Leases	
Warehouse/Distribution	Down 15%
Manufacturing	Down 15%
High Tech/R&D	Down 15%

Note - Compared to a year ago

1989 Review

Vacancies rose by three million sq. ft., driving the level of available industrial space to 13.4 percent of the market's inventory. Slippage in the manufacturing and high-tech sector was most responsible, with defense-related cutbacks at the core of the problem. Rental rates and sales prices per sq. ft. stayed steady, but transaction volumes were down sharply. Land for industrial development is virtually exhausted in Nassau County, so the market was looking eastward into Suffolk as the 80s ended.

1990 Forecast

Developers are not likely to buck the market heroically (or foolishly) during 1990. In fact, the story of '90 is the 90 percent reduction in the anticipated level of new construction. Weakness is expected to finally impact rental rates and sales prices, which SIOR's Long Island reporter figures will drop by 10 to 15 percent over the year. A metropolitan area market recovery, still two to three years away, is the cure for this market's pervasive ills.

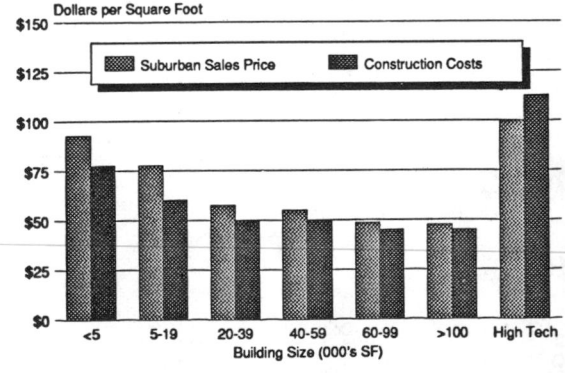

Sales Prices vs. Construction Costs
New York-Nassau/Suffolk Counties

New York-Rockland/Westchester Counties, New York: Industrial

Market Data

Inventory (sf)	Central City	Suburban
Total	-	34,000,000
Vacant	-	1,700,000
Vacancy Rates	-	5.0%
Under Construction	-	300,000
Net Absorption	-	450,000

Sales Prices ($/sf)	Central City	Suburban
Less than 5,000 sf	-	125.00
5,000 to 19,999 sf	-	105.00
20,000 to 39,999 sf	-	90.00
40,000 to 59,999 sf	-	80.00
60,000 to 99,999 sf	-	75.00
More than 100,000 sf	-	70.00
High Tech/R&D	-	120.00

Gross Lease Prices ($/sf)	Central City	Suburban
Less than 5,000 sf	-	11.00
5,000 to 19,999 sf	-	10.00
20,000 to 39,999 sf	-	9.00
40,000 to 59,999 sf	-	8.00
60,000 to 99,999 sf	-	7.50
More than 100,000 sf	-	7.00
High Tech/R&D	-	12.00

Site Prices ($/sf)	Central City	Suburban
Improved Sites		
Less than 2 Acres	-	n/a
2 to 5 Acres	-	n/a
5 to 10 Acres	-	n/a
More than 10 Acres	-	n/a
Unimproved Sites		
Less than 10 Acres	-	5.00-20.00
10 to 100 Acres	-	4.00-12.00
More than 100 Acres	-	n/a

Demographics

		Rank
Population:	8,617,968	2
Population Growth Rate:	0.45%	
Unemployment Rate:	n/a	
Median Household Income:	$27,043	74
Cost of Living Index:	n/a	n/a

Outlook

Sales Prices	
Warehouse/Distribution	Same
Manufacturing	Same
High Tech/R&D	Same
Lease Prices	
Warehouse/Distribution	Same
Manufacturing	Same
High Tech/R&D	Same
Site Prices	Same
Absorption	
Warehouse/Distribution	Same
Manufacturing	Same
High Tech/R&D	Same
Construction	
Warehouse/Distribution	Down 5%
Manufacturing	Down 5%
High Tech/R&D	Down 5%
Dollar Volume - Sales	Down 5%
Dollar Volume - Leases	Down 5%

Prime Source of Financing:
Commercial Banks

Mortgage Money Supply:
Ample

Construction Costs	
Less than 5,000 sf	70.00
5,000 to 19,999 sf	60.00
20,000 to 39,999 sf	55.00
40,000 to 59,999 sf	50.00
60,000 to 99,999 sf	45.00
More than 100,000 sf	42.00
High Tech/R&D	90.00

Vacancy Indicators	
Less than 5,000 sf	Moderate Shortage
5,000 to 19,999 sf	Moderate Shortage
20,000 to 39,999 sf	Moderate Shortage
40,000 to 59,999 sf	Moderate Shortage
60,000 to 99,999 sf	Moderate Shortage
More than 100,000 sf	Moderate Shortage
High Tech/R&D	Moderate Oversupply

Composition of Absorption	
Warehouse/Distribution	75%
Manufacturing	20%
High Tech/R&D	5%
Rate of Construction	
Warehouse/Distribution	Down 5%
Manufacturing	Down 5%
High Tech/R&D	Down 5%
Dollar Volume - Sales	
Warehouse/Distribution	Down 5%
Manufacturing	Down 5%
High Tech/R&D	Down 5%
Dollar Volume - Leases	
Warehouse/Distribution	Down 5%
Manufacturing	Down 5%
High Tech/R&D	Down 5%
Note - Compared to a year ago	

1989 Review

The best performer among the New York metropolitan area markets, Rockland/Westchester ended the 80s with a five percent vacancy rate, and with net absorption running ahead of the pace of new development. There was still considerable demand for industrial purchases, though somewhat less than in 1988. Tenants are slowing their demand for space, too, in the face of the uncertain regional economy. Rents advanced about $0.50 per sq. ft. in 1989 in the face of a moderate shortage of suitable space in all property types, except high-tech.

1990 Forecast

Some speculative construction will continue in Rockland County, which lies west of the Hudson River north of the New Jersey border. Westchester County, though, will see little if any additions to supply. A more sluggish market should be in store in 1990 because of greater caution on the part of users. Stringent governmental involvement in real estate matters makes it more difficult to close deals and to secure occupancy than might be expected. This market, however, is comparatively well able to ride out the current economic downturn.

Suburban Gross Lease Prices
New York-Rockland/Westchester Counties

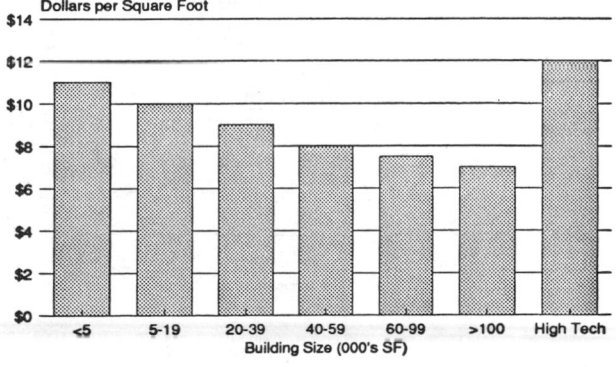

Office Real Estate Market: Selected Cities*
Atlanta, Georgia: Office

Market Data

Inventory (sf)	Class A		Class B	
	CBD	Outside CBD	CBD	Outside CBD
Total	18,161,436	56,390,398	-	-
Vacant	2,834,517	9,840,163	-	-
Vacancy Rate	15.6%	17.5%	-	-
Vacant Sublease	n/a	n/a	-	-
Under Construction	2,801,500	2,164,200	-	-
Substantial Rehab	n/a	n/a	-	-
Net Absorption	457,148	2,722,697	-	-

Rental Rates ($/sf)	Class A		Class B	
	CBD	Outside CBD	CBD	Outside CBD
Lowest	16.00	14.00	15.00	11.00
Highest	27.00	20.00	18.00	16.00
Weighted Average	n/a	n/a	n/a	n/a

Utility Rates: CBD n/a Outside CBD n/a Not Separately Metered	**Parking Ratio:** CBD - 1 per 500 sf Outside CBD - 1 per 250 sf

Standard Work Letter: n/a, typically based on dollars per square foot

Operating Cost Escalation: Base Year

Cumulative Discount Rate: 20%
Landlord Concessions
  Parking
  Rental Abatement
  Lease Assumptions
  Moving Allowance
  Interior Improvements
  Club Memberships

Leasing Activity Profile
Major Activity
  Legal/Accounting
  Finance/Banking
  Government
Minor Activity
  Insurance
  Business Services
  Sales

Demographics

		Rank
Population:	2,804,063	10
Population Growth Rate:	3.06%	
Unemployment Rate:	5.70%	
Median Household Income:	$36,018	9
Cost of living Index:	107.1	16

Outlook

Absorption	Up
Construction	Same
Vacancies	Up 2-5%
Rental Rates	Same
Landlord Concessions	Same

1989 Review

Generalizations can be especially difficult in multi-nodal office markets such as Atlanta's. The city's economic strength comes from its diversification. No one industry dominates the office market consistently. Major submarkets are becoming business centers in their own right, with Perimeter, Buckhead and the Northwest rivalling the traditional CBD as office locations. Vacancy rates in the market were high at 16 to 17 percent, a chronic condition it would appear. The economy appeared to be entering a lull, which slowed construction and allowed the vacancy rate to adjust downward, in the view of SIOR's reporter. The sublease market grew, as cost-conscious tenants tightened their space requirements, and the gap between new construction rents and older space grew wider.

1990 Forecast

Build-to-suit activity is causing development statistics to be stronger than the rent and vacancy data suggest should be the case. The technology/communication sector accounts for much of the demand, with AT&T, IBM and MCI all committing to projects. As a rule, a 30 percent preleasing level is needed to acquire a financing go-ahead in Atlanta. Downtown is expected to see new activity this year as a result of mergers in the fields of banking, accounting and law.

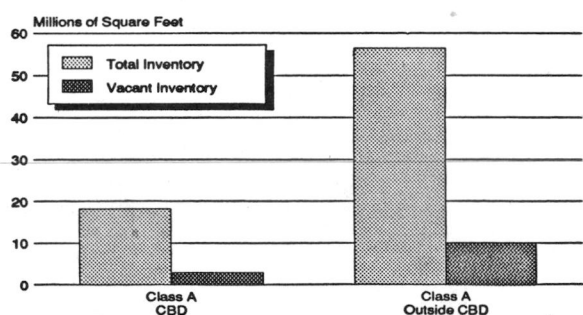

Market Inventory
Atlanta

Millions of Square Feet

Legend:
- Total Inventory
- Vacant Inventory

Class A CBD   Class A Outside CBD

\   * See Glossary of Terms on page 628.

Chicago, Illinois: Office

CBD

Market Data

Inventory (sf)	Class A		Class B	
	CBD	Outside CBD	CBD	Outside CBD
Total	45,583,000	-	44,104,000	-
Vacant	5,077,000	-	6,427,000	-
Vacancy Rate	11.1%	-	14.6%	-
Vacant Sublease	1,694,000	-	n/a	-
Under Construction	5,567,000	-	0	-
Substantial Rehab	0	-	828,000	-
Net Absorption	1,648,000	-	n/a	-

Rental Rates ($/sf)	Class A		Class B	
	CBD	Outside CBD	CBD	Outside CBD
Lowest	28.00	-	20.00	-
Highest	40.00	-	30.00	-
Weighted Average	35.00	-	25.00	-

Utility Rates:	CBD $1.50 per sf Separately Metered	**Parking Ratio:**	CBD - n/a

Standard Work Letter: $16.50 per sf, typically based on $/sf & quantity of materials

Operating Cost Escalation: Base Year & Stop

Cumulative Discount Rate: 20-40%

Landlord Concessions
- Parking
- Rental Abatement
- Lease Assumptions
- Moving Allowance
- Interior Improvements
- Signing Bonuses
- Club Memberships
- Equity

Leasing Activity Profile

Major Activity
- Legal/Accounting
- Business Services
- Sales
- Finance/Banking
- Engineering/Architecture
- Government
- Health Care
- Technology

Minor Activity
- Insurance
- Energy

Demographics

		Rank
Population:	6,242,447	4
Population Growth Rate:	0.33%	
Unemployment Rate:	5.50%	
Median Household Income:	$32,453	26
Cost of living Index:	n/a	n/a

Outlook

Absorption	Same
Construction	Up 10%
Vacancies	Up 5%
Rental Rates	Up 5%
Landlord Concessions	Same

1989 Review

Absorption levels in the Chicago market eased considerably when compared with the outstanding demand registered in the previous few years. The Loop and North Michigan Avenue ended the Eighties in excellent shape, particularly when the high levels of construction for the decade are taken into perspective. Weighted average rents in the core market were toward the high end of the $28 - $40 per sq. ft. range. A lengthy list of landlord concessions, however, suggested that early cash flow on leases may be less than meets the untrained eye. The breadth of the components of demand was impressive, and strong evidence of the diversified economic base of the area. Suburban market conditions were an order of magnitude weaker, with vacancies topping 20 percent.

1990 Forecast

The outlook for 1990 is mixed, in the view of SIOR's Chicago survey respondents. Vacancies are anticipated to move upward on the basis of the presently high level of construction. Also the announcement by Sears that it would relocate 6,000 employees from the Sears Tower to suburban locations could make a major dent in that availability rate. Rental rates, though, are likewise forecast to increase at a five percent rate. In the present environment, new CBD office projects will go forward only when the developer has a lead tenant signed up. On a positive note, few large relocations were undertaken in 1989, but several large deals will be announced during 1990.

Market Inventory
Chicago

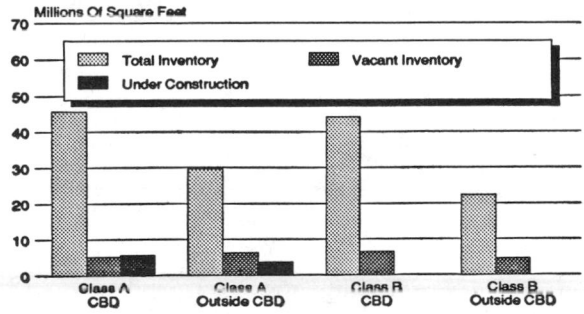

Chicago, Illinois: Office

Outside CBD

Market Data

Inventory (sf)	Class A		Class B	
	CBD	Outside CBD	CBD	Outside CBD
Total	-	29,623,000	-	22,277,000
Vacant	-	6,225,000	-	4,616,000
Vacancy Rate	-	21.0%	-	20.7%
Vacant Sublease	-	1,521,000	-	n/a
Under Construction	-	3,617,000	-	0
Substantial Rehab	-	0	-	0
Net Absorption	-	1,724,000	-	n/a

Rental Rates ($/sf)	Class A		Class B	
	CBD	Outside CBD	CBD	Outside CBD
Lowest	-	20.00	-	15.00
Highest	-	30.00	-	20.00
Weighted Average	-	24.00	-	17.00

Utility Rates: Outside CBD $1.00 per sf Separately Metered	Parking Ratio: OutCBD - 1 per 300 sf
Standard Work Letter: $16.50 per sf, typically based on $/sf & quantity of materials	Operating Cost Escalation: Base Year & Stop

Cumulative Discount Rate: 20-40% Landlord Concessions Parking Rental Abatement Lease Assumptions Moving Allowance Interior Improvements Signing Bonuses Club Memberships Equity	Leasing Activity Profile Major Activity Legal/Accounting Business Services Sales Finance/Banking Engineering/Architecture Government Health Care Technology Minor Activity Insurance Energy

Demographics

		Rank	**Outlook**	
Population:	6,242,447	4	Absorption	Same
Population Growth Rate:	0.33%		Construction	Up 10%
Unemployment Rate:	5.50%		Vacancies	Up 5%
Median Household Income:	$32,453	26	Rental Rates	Up 5%
Cost of living Index:	n/a	n/a	Landlord Concessions	Same

Rental Rates
Chicago

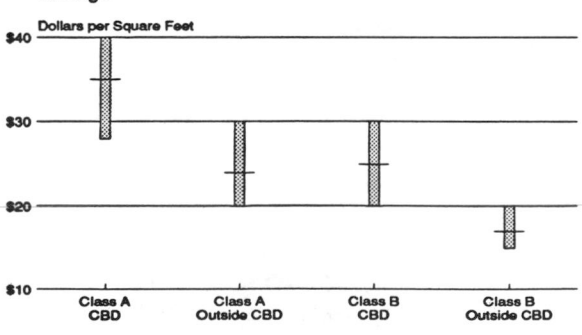

1989 Review

Chicago's suburban markets contained nearly 52 million sq. ft. of office inventory as of 1989, about 37 percent of the metropolitan area's total. Both Class "A" and Class "B" space were in an oversupplied condition, with vacancies measured at 21 percent. This represented a three percentage point rise in availabilities during the year, as absorption during 1989 was only 48 percent of the volume of new construction entering the market. Rents also retreated from the levels reported in last year's *Guide*, as heavy discounting pervaded the market. The size and variety of concessions offered as inducements to prospective tenants was as generous as in any market in the country. Major leasing activity in 1989 came from several financial tenants, health care companies and the rapidly expanding law firms in the Chicago area.

1990 Forecast

Significantly less building will be going into the ground in recognition of the softness of the market and because construction financing requirements will be more stringent. The regional economy has been booming during the late Eighties, but the rate of expansion is cooling down. The Sears relocation is the largest single event affecting the market, bringing 6,000 employees out of the Loop and into the suburbs. The stronger suburban areas appear to be the East-West corridor along I-88 to Naperville and the attractive office market near O'Hare Airport. The Northwest suburbs of Woodfield and Schaumberg have abundant space available and will be very competitive in 1990.

Houston, Texas: Office

Market Data

Inventory (sf)

Inventory (sf)	Class A		Class B	
	CBD	Outside CBD	CBD	Outside CBD
Total	25,043,928	33,133,944	10,399,990	62,795,491
Vacant	3,117,435	5,157,445	2,189,719	16,824,609
Vacancy Rate	12.4%	15.6%	21.1%	26.8%
Vacant Sublease	940,000	322,327	n/a	n/a
Under Construction	0	143,733	0	806,332
Substantial Rehab	n/a	n/a	n/a	n/a
Net Absorption	1,190,262	921,120	n/a	1,317,306

Rental Rates ($/sf)	Class A		Class B	
	CBD	Outside CBD	CBD	Outside CBD
Lowest	10.00	9.50	8.25	7.00
Highest	21.00	18.00	15.50	13.50
Weighted Average	14.08	12.75	10.26	9.90

Utility Rates:	CBD $1.25 per sf	Parking Ratio:	CBD - 1 per 1,500 sf
	Outside CBD $1.00 per sf		Outside CBD - 1 per 300 sf
	Not Separately Metered		

Standard Work Letter: $11.00 per sf, typically based on quantity of materals

Operating Cost Escalation: Base Year

Cumulative Discount Rate: 10-13%

Landlord Concessions
- Parking
- Lease Assumptions
- Moving Allowance
- Interior Improvements
- Club Memberships
- Architectural Allowances

Leasing Activity Profile

Major Activity
- Legal/Accounting
- Insurance
- Business Services
- Finance/Banking
- Engineering/Architecture
- Energy

Minor Activity
- Sales
- Government

Demographics

		Rank
Population:	3,228,577	8
Population Growth Rate:	1.86%	
Unemployment Rate:	5.70%	
Median Household Income:	$33,251	22
Cost of living Index:	101.9	26

Outlook

Absorption	Up 5%
Construction	Up 2.5%
Vacancies	Down 8-10%
Rental Rates	Up 7-9%
Landlord Concessions	Down 5-10%

1989 Review

Additional evidence of the rebounding Houston economy piled up during 1989, and Houston laid claim to the strongest metropolitan area growth in Texas last year. Nearly 3.5 million sq. ft. of net absorption was posted, and the overall vacancy rate ended the year at 20.8 percent, still very high but down substantially from the towering levels of several years ago. Investment interest in Houston office properties intensified during the year, and a major deal for a package of downtown properties was closed at year-end for almost $400 million. No new Class "A" space was under development, as rents were substantially below new construction feasibility levels and good quality properties were on the market for one-third to one-half of their replacement cost. There is an active trade-up market for space, and vacancies in the Class "A" stock have been reduced to 13.5 percent.

1990 Forecast

Houston is expected to take another significant step forward in 1990. The economy is gradually diversifying, but is still closely tied to the energy industry. During the next several years, that linkage should prove a positive influence on the local office market, as a rebound in oil prices and the development of more efficient drilling technologies is improving the outlook for the energy companies. At last year's absorption rate, the resumption of construction activity may only be two or three years away. Some build-to-suit activity will be seen in 1990, and a modest tightening in rents is foreseen this year by SIOR's local observer.

Outlook
Houston

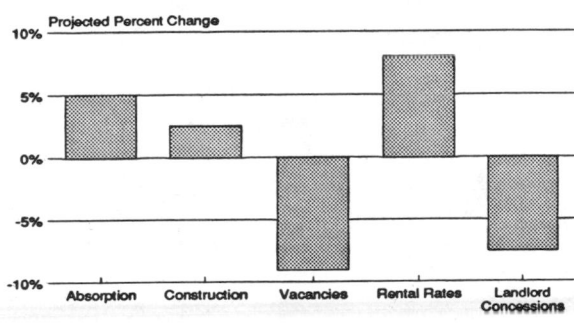

Los Angeles-Central, California: Office

Market Data

1989 Review

Inventory (sf)	Class A		Class B	
	CBD	Outside CBD	CBD	Outside CBD
Total	13,555,860	-	7,257,872	-
Vacant	1,396,721	-	1,408,263	-
Vacancy Rate	10.3%	-	19.4%	-
Vacant Sublease	520,720	-	725,540	-
Under Construction	7,042,528	-	308,000	-
Substantial Rehab	n/a	-	n/a	-
Net Absorption	500,000	-	200,000	-

Rental Rates ($/sf)	Class A		Class B	
	CBD	Outside CBD	CBD	Outside CBD
Lowest	24.00	-	19.00	-
Highest	35.00	-	26.00	-
Weighted Average	29.00	-	23.00	-

Utility Rates:	CBD $1.85 per sf	Parking Ratio:	CBD - 1 per 1,000 sf
	Outside CBD $1.50 per sf		Outside CBD - 1 per 500 sf
	Not Separately Metered		

Standard Work Letter: n/a, typically based on dollars per square foot	Operating Cost Escalation: Base Year

Cumulative Discount Rate: 15-20%	**Leasing Activity Profile**
Landlord Concessions	**Major Activity**
Parking	Legal/Accounting
Rental Abatement	Finance/Banking
Lease Assumptions	Government
Moving Allowance	**Minor Activity**
Interior Improvements	Insurance
	Business Services
	Sales
	Engineering/Architecture
	Energy

Demographics

		Rank
Population:	8,804,062	1
Population Growth Rate:	1.83%	
Unemployment Rate:	4.80%	
Median Household Income:	$31,276	37
Cost of living Index:	126.5	6

Outlook

Absorption	Down 1-5%
Construction	Down 25-50%
Vacancies	Up 1-5%
Rental Rates	Up 1-5%
Landlord Concessions	Same

Outlook
Los Angeles-Central

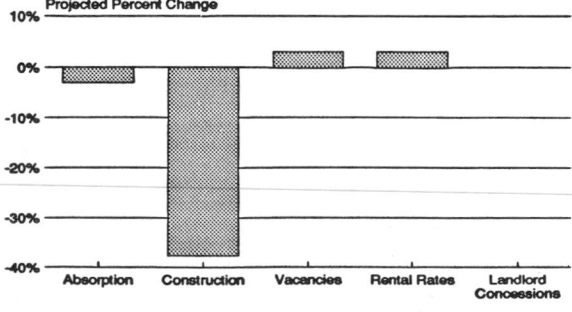

Class "A" office space was in high demand by prestigious law firms, banks, and major accounting firms. Net absorption for 1989 was a solid 700,000 sq. ft. and preleasing for the more than seven million sq. ft. of space under construction has been steady. But large blocks of sublease space are appearing, and signs of concern are starting to appear in the downtown L.A. market. The best buildings saw little in the way of rental increase during 1989, and the Class "B" market has fallen back when this year's SIOR survey is compared to last year. Landlord concessions are five percent higher than twelve months ago. Foreign investors, most visibly the Japanese, have been a major presence in the acquisition and the development of new office space. The Eighties will long be remembered as the decade in which Los Angeles grew a world-class central business district in its historic downtown.

1990 Forecast

Last year's concern is expected to be translated into this year's weakening statistics. Absorption and new construction are anticipated to fall, and vacancies to edge up in 1990. Los Angeles' zoning ordinance was changed several years ago to encourage the concentration of office construction in the downtown area. As a result, a record amount of development is scheduled to enter the market in 1991. Any outlook for the future must account for the fact that seven million sq. ft. of new building is 10 times the rate of last year's absorption. Even Los Angeles is going to be challenged to generate growth enough to warrant such a spectacular amount of inventory additions.

Los Angeles-Orange County, California: Office

Market Data

Inventory (sf)

Inventory (sf)	Class A		Class B	
	CBD	Outside CBD	CBD	Outside CBD
Total	47,855,563	-	-	-
Vacant	10,268,370	-	-	-
Vacancy Rate	21.5%	-	-	-
Vacant Sublease	482,929	-	-	-
Under Construction	3,255,998	-	-	-
Substantial Rehab	n/a	-	-	-
Net Absorption	2,672,236	-	-	-

Rental Rates ($/sf)	Class A		Class B	
	CBD	Outside CBD	CBD	Outside CBD
Lowest	17.00	16.00	17.00	11.00
Highest	27.00	21.00	20.00	15.00
Weighted Average	n/a	n/a	n/a	n/a

Utility Rates:	CBD $1.80 per sf	Parking Ratio:	CBD - 1 per 250 sf
	Outside CBD n/a		Outside CBD - 1 per 250 sf
	Not Separately Metered		

Standard Work Letter: $25.00 per sf, typically based on dollars per square foot

Operating Cost Escalation: Base Year & Stop - Both $6 sq ft

Cumulative Discount Rate: 15-25%
Landlord Concessions
 Parking
 Rental Abatement
 Lease Assumptions
 Moving Allowance
 Interior Improvements
 Cash bonus to broker

Leasing Activity Profile
Major Activity
 Legal/Accounting
 Business Services
 Finance/Banking
Minor Activity
 Insurance
 Sales
 Engineering/Architecture
 Energy

Demographics

		Rank
Population:	2,296,839	15
Population Growth Rate:	1.94%	
Unemployment Rate:	3.20%	
Median Household Income:	$41,181	5
Cost of living Index:	132.3	3

Outlook

Absorption	Same
Construction	Up 5-10%
Vacancies	Same
Rental Rates	Down 5%
Landlord Concessions	Up 1-5%

1989 Review

Leasing activity was off greatly from 1988. The construction of office space for north and central Orange County has virtually stopped to allow demand to catch up. Development continued at a rapid rate near the airport in Irvine and in the southern reaches of the county, even though the present level of demand did not warrant the growth. Hence, Orange County saw a very soft office market during 1989, with occupancy rates below 80 percent and lower effective rents than at any time since 1985. Leasing concession packages reached as much as 25 percent of basic rent over the lease term. A number of Class "A" properties have been placed up for sale as joint venture partners look for ways to realize cash returns on their investments.

1990 Forecast

With SIOR's correspondent predicting a further decline in rental rates and increasing landlord concessions, it is paradoxical that the construction levels are forecast to rise five to 10 percent. Nine major projects are slated for the airport area and more are proposed in the south county markets. Ironically, the slow growth/no growth movements sweeping the state of California are pushing builders to get into the ground quickly before the rules of the game change. Consequently the probability of poorly planned projects exacerbating congestion and environmental problems is rising. Orange County will be a market ripe for investor re-evaluation in 1990 and beyond.

Rental Rates
Los Angeles-Orange County

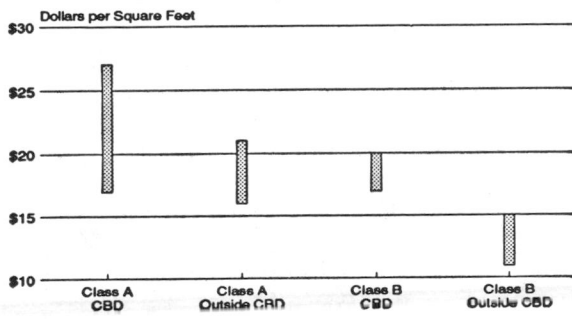

Los Angeles-San Bernardino County, California: Office

Market Data

Inventory (sf)	Class A		Class B	
	CBD	Outside CBD	CBD	Outside CBD
Total	485,321	1,797,046	726,002	3,792,131
Vacant	157,494	411,713	172,284	883,109
Vacancy Rate	32.5%	22.9%	23.7%	23.3%
Vacant Sublease	n/a	n/a	n/a	n/a
Under Construction	54,000	195,000	72,000	44,900
Substantial Rehab	n/a	n/a	n/a	n/a
Net Absorption	52,200	268,400	50,680	202,720

Rental Rates ($/sf)	Class A		Class B	
	CBD	Outside CBD	CBD	Outside CBD
Lowest	15.00	15.00	13.00	12.00
Highest	20.00	24.00	19.00	18.00
Weighted Average	17.00	18.00	16.00	14.00

Utility Rates:	CBD $1.56 per sf	Parking Ratio:	CBD - 1 per 250 sf
	Outside CBD $1.56 per sf		Outside CBD - 1 per 250 sf
	Not Separately Metered		

Standard Work Letter: $18.00 per sf, typically based on dollars per square foot

Operating Cost Escalation: Base Year & Stop - Primarily

Cumulative Discount Rate: 10.4%
Landlord Concessions
  Rental Abatement
  Interior Improvements

Leasing Activity Profile
Major Activity
  Legal/Accounting
  Insurance
  Finance/Banking
  Engineering/Architecture
Minor Activity
  Business Services
  Sales
  Government
  Energy

Demographics

		Rank
Population:	2,277,982	16
Population Growth Rate:	4.31%	
Unemployment Rate:	6.40%	
Median Household Income:	$27,720	65
Cost of living Index:	106.7	16

Outlook

Absorption	Up 10%
Construction	Same
Vacancies	Same
Rental Rates	Same
Landlord Concessions	Up 5%

1989 Review

Leasing activity was once again spirited in the desert counties east of Los Angeles. Relocation of firms from L.A. itself and from Orange County was on the increase, as tenants seek less expensive space, relief from urban congestion, and affordable housing for their workforce. San Bernardino/Riverside registered high vacancy rates, but these were the availabilities of additional inventory being provided to accomodate reasonably predictable future demand. The market is still relatively young and small: total inventory amounts to only 6.8 million sq. ft.. Net absorption for 1989 came to 574,000 sq. ft., which was 57 percent more than the new construction activity reported by SIOR's local researchers. Last year, all in all, was one in which the market assumed greater definition and the lines of future development became more apparent.

1990 Forecast

The new specific development centers around the Ontario Airport and the Haven Avenue corridor. The intersection of Interstate highways 10 and 215 is also a top development node. Market preference is shifting from low-rise structures to mid-rise, identifiably Class "A" buildings. Economic growth in this rapidly evolving metropolitan area is encurging a positive outlook for 1990. Relocation activity and move-up from local users are anticipated to boost absorption by 10 percent during the year. Riverside/San Bernardino will continue to carve out a niche as a lower cost alternative to the large, more established adjacent Southern California markets.

Market Inventory
Los Angeles-San Bernardino County

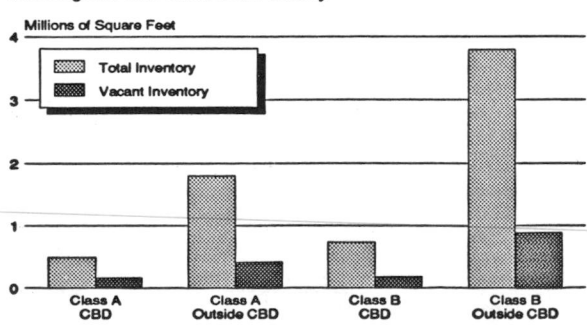

Los Angeles-San Fernando Valley, California: Office

Market Data

Inventory (sf)

Inventory (sf)	Class A		Class B	
	CBD	Outside CBD	CBD	Outside CBD
Total	-	3,500,000	-	1,200,000
Vacant	-	700,000	-	370,000
Vacancy Rate	-	20.0%	-	30.8%
Vacant Sublease	-	40,000	-	n/a
Under Construction	-	620,000	-	440,000
Substantial Rehab	-	100,000	-	n/a
Net Absorption	-	250,000	-	130,000

Rental Rates ($/sf)	Class A		Class B	
	CBD	Outside CBD	CBD	Outside CBD
Lowest	-	25.20	-	18.00
Highest	-	33.00	-	25.20
Weighted Average	-	27.60	-	21.00

Utility Rates:	CBD n/a	Parking Ratio:	CBD - n/a
	Outside CBD $1.20 per sf		Outside CBD - 1 per 300 sf
	Not Separately Metered		

Standard Work Letter: $25.00 per sf

Operating Cost Escalation:
Base Year

Cumulative Discount Rate: 10%

Landlord Concessions
Parking
Rental Abatement
Interior Improvements

Leasing Activity Profile
Major Activity
Legal/Accounting
Insurance
Sales
Minor Activity
Business Services
Finance/Banking
Government

Demographics

		Rank
Population:	8,804,062	1
Population Growth Rate:	1.83%	
Unemployment Rate:	n/a	
Median Household Income:	$31,276	37
Cost of living Index:	n/a	6

Outlook

Absorption	Up 25%
Construction	Down 30%
Vacancies	Down 20%
Rental Rates	Same
Landlord Concessions	Same

1989 Review

Office space demand was very slow for the San Fernando Valley market in 1989. Net absorption was down 40 percent from the average of the prior three years, and amounted to only 380,000 sq. ft.. Over a million sq. ft. of existing space is vacant, and an equivalent volume of new construction is coming to market. The local economy, it must be said, is still one of the soundest in the country. Major law and accounting firms have been focusing their location searches in the west valley area. Larger back office users are moving more to the periphery in search of projects with lower land and building costs. In 1989, the weighted average rent outside the prime area was 24 percent below the prevailing CBD lease rate.

1990 Forecast

A stunning improvement in the fortunes of this market is predicted by SIOR's observers on the scene. Absorption is forecast to rise 25 percent, with a complementary decrease in vacancy. Construction is expected to be sharply lower, as several proposed projects may need to wait until the end of 1990 to secure required government approvals.

Market Inventory
Los Angeles-San Fernando Valley

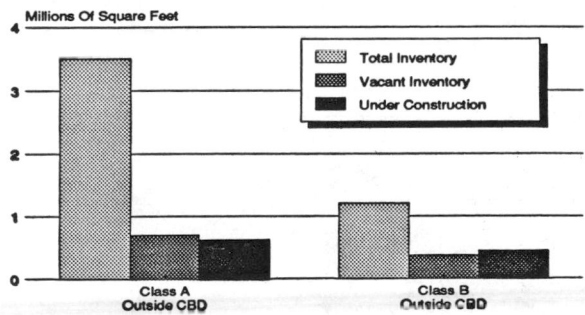

Los Angeles-San Gabriel County, California: Office

Market Data

Inventory (sf)	Class A		Class B	
	CBD	Outside CBD	CBD	Outside CBD
Total	-	3,000,000	-	4,300,000
Vacant	-	700,000	-	600,000
Vacancy Rate	-	23.3%	-	14.0%
Vacant Sublease	-	20,000	-	70,000
Under Construction	-	500,000	-	100,000
Substantial Rehab	-	n/a	-	n/a
Net Absorption	-	400,000	-	300,000

Rental Rates ($/sf)	Class A		Class B	
	CBD	Outside CBD	CBD	Outside CBD
Lowest	-	20.00	-	14.00
Highest	-	24.00	-	18.00
Weighted Average	-	21.00	-	16.00

Utility Rates: CBD n/a Outside CBD $1.44 per sf Not Separately Metered	**Parking Ratio:** CBD - n/a Outside CBD - 1 per 250 sf	
Standard Work Letter: $22.50 per sf, typically based on dollars per square foot	**Operating Cost Escalation:** Base Year & Stop - $5.40-6.00	

Cumulative Discount Rate: 12%
Landlord Concessions
  Rental Abatement
  Interior Improvements

Leasing Activity Profile
Major Activity
  Insurance
  Business Services
  Sales
  Finance/Banking
  Engineering/Architecture
  Government
  Real Estate
Minor Activity
  Legal/Accounting
  Energy

Demographics

		Rank
Population:	8,804,062	1
Population Growth Rate:	1.83%	
Unemployment Rate:	n/a	
Median Household Income:	$31,276	37
Cost of living Index:	n/a	6

Outlook

Absorption	Up 5%
Construction	Same
Vacancies	Same
Rental Rates	Same
Landlord Concessions	Up 5%

Rental Rates
Los Angeles-San Gabriel County

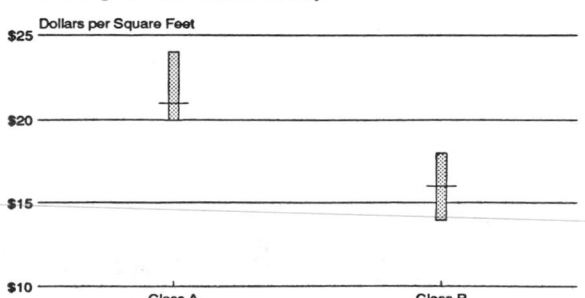

1989 Review

Soft conditions plagued this suburban Los Angeles market once again in 1989. San Gabriel's market niche would appear to be low cost back office space, but the level of rent which characterized the area has not been stimulating the large scale moves necessary to drive its Class "A" vacancy rate below 20 percent. The relatively good affordability of housing here is bolstering the residential base, but as yet the people living in the county are leaving early in the morning and facing a long commute to work. Asian investors have discovered the area, and commerical acquisitions by Chinese and Korean interests were features of the San Gabriel market recently. Construction activity underway nearly matched the amount of net absorption in 1989, leaving this market's condition virtually unchanged from a year ago.

1990 Forecast

The five percent increase in net absorption expected by SIOR's local commentators will not be enough to materially affect the overbuilt situation in San Gabriel County. Vacancies and rental rates are likely to hold steady over the course of the year, with landlords becoming more aggressive discounters in the competition for tenants. The logic of a move from the core markets of L.A. to lower cost alternatives for back office functions seems persuasive, but with so many submarkets ringing the central city the amount of competition is immense. San Gabriel's low housing cost is its hole card, but the game is running long and the stakes are rising.

Los Angeles-South Bay, California: Office

Market Data

Inventory (sf)	Class A		Class B	
	CBD	Outside CBD	CBD	Outside CBD
Total	-	15,449,307	-	12,191,985
Vacant	-	3,290,702	-	1,975,101
Vacancy Rate	-	21.3%	-	16.2%
Vacant Sublease	-	293,536	-	207,263
Under Construction	-	872,628	-	-
Substantial Rehab	-	0	-	-
Net Absorption	-	1,478,515*	-	-

Rental Rates ($/sf)	Class A		Class B	
	CBD	Outside CBD	CBD	Outside CBD
Lowest	-	13.25	-	7.80
Highest	-	34.80	-	29.52
Weighted Average	-	23.52	-	18.36

Utility Rates:	CBD n/a	**Parking Ratio:**	CBD - n/a
	Outside CBD $1.75 per sf		Outside CBD - 1 per 400 sf
	Not Separately Metered		

Standard Work Letter: $25.00 per sf, typically based on dollars per square foot	**Operating Cost Escalation:** Base Year & Stop - $7.50

Cumulative Discount Rate: 15-25% **Landlord Concessions** Parking Rental Abatement Lease Assumptions Moving Allowance Interior Improvements	**Leasing Activity Profile** **Major Activity** Legal/Accounting Business Services Sales Transportation **Minor Activity** Insurance Finance/Banking Government

Demographics

		Rank
Population:	8,804,062	1
Population Growth Rate:	1.83%	
Unemployment Rate:	n/a	
Median Household Income:	$31,276	37
Cost of living Index:	n/a	6

Outlook

Absorption	Up
Construction	Down
Vacancies	Down
Rental Rates	Up
Landlord Concessions	Down

1989 Review

This is a significant component of the Los Angeles metropolitan office market, with 27.5 million sq. ft. of total inventory. It contains a number of distinct submarkets, including the LAX (airport) district, Long Beach and Torrance. Last year LAX and Long Beach posted fine performances, while Torrance lagged considerably behind. LAX, in particular, saw an influx of tenants from the West L.A. markets in search of more economical space. A key reason for the vacancy rate remaining at 19.1 percent in 1989 was the pullback in the aerospace industry, weakening the landlords' hand and prompting ever increasing rental concessions. Corporations were active on their own accounts in 1989. Mattel Toys acquired a 302,000 sq. ft., 14-story office tower for its staff. Toyota Motors also bought an office building to house local operations this past year.

1990 Forecast

Absorption in the coming year is forecast to surpass the 1.5 million sq. ft. of increased occupancy registered in 1989. Tenant demand will likely continue as a mix of services, sales and corporate operations. Defense cutbacks and slashed governmental spending are forces causing serious concern for this market. But the wider mix of tenancies could nonetheless support a decrease in vacancy and higher rents in 1990.

* Net Absorption of Class "A" and "B" space is combined.

Market Inventory
Los Angeles-South Bay

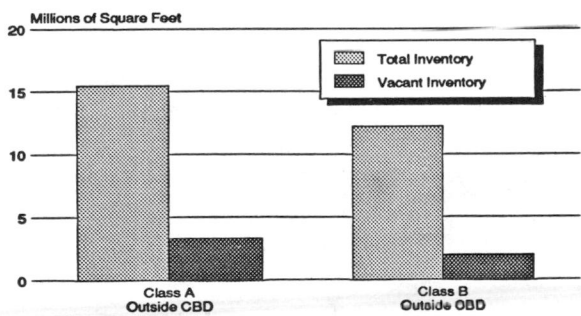

Los Angeles-West, California: Office

Market Data

Inventory (sf)	Class A		Class B	
	CBD	Outside CBD	CBD	Outside CBD
Total	-	31,000,000	-	16,000,000
Vacant	-	3,400,000	-	1,000,000
Vacancy Rate	-	11.0%	-	6.3%
Vacant Sublease	-	1,000,000	-	400,000
Under Construction	-	4,300,000	-	400,000
Substantial Rehab	-	300,000	-	400,000
Net Absorption	-	n/a	-	n/a

Rental Rates ($/sf)	Class A		Class B	
	CBD	Outside CBD	CBD	Outside CBD
Lowest	-	24.10	-	18.25
Highest	-	41.40	-	28.40
Weighted Average	-	32.18	-	23.76

Utility Rates:	CBD n/a	Parking Ratio:	CBD - n/a
	Outside CBD $1.80 per sf		Outside CBD - 1 per 333 sf
	Not Separately Metered		

Standard Work Letter: $29.00 per sf, typically based on dollars per square foot

Operating Cost Escalation: Base Year & Stop - $8.00 sq ft/yr

Cumulative Discount Rate: 10%
Landlord Concessions
  Rental Abatement
  Lease Assumptions
  Interior Improvements

Leasing Activity Profile
Major Activity
  Legal/Accounting
  Entertainment
Minor Activity
  Insurance
  Business Services
  Sales
  Finance/Banking
  Engineering/Architecture
  Government

Demographics

		Rank
Population:	8,804,062	1
Population Growth Rate:	1.83%	
Unemployment Rate:	n/a	
Median Household Income:	$31,276	37
Cost of living Index:	n/a	6

Outlook

Absorption	Down 5%
Construction	Down 10%
Vacancies	Up 5%
Rental Rates	Same
Landlord Concessions	Up 5%

Outlook
Los Angeles-West

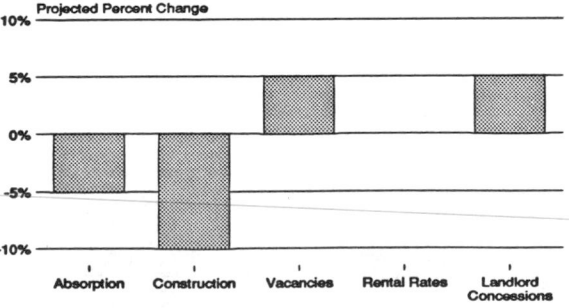

1989 Review

West L.A. was the tightest of all the office markets in the greater Los Angeles area during 1989. Its overall occupancy rate of 90.6 percent was, in fact, one of the strongest in the nation last year. Rents have been rising in response to the increasing scarcity and have broken $40 per sq. ft. for prime buildings. Somewhat anomolously, rents in this submarket exceeded those in downtown L.A. The high cost of space caused some tenants to relocate from the area as leases expired and leasing activity in 1989 was down more than 30 percent from the record year of 1987. The South Bay and San Fernando Valley areas have been the major beneficiaries of moves from West L.A., but even downtown captured some of the relocating firms. In some ways, this is the price of serving as the market leader in the Los Angeles basin.

1990 Forecast

The coming year is expected to be one of adjustment to tough competition for tenants from other locations. Economic activity is strong enough in Southern California to stimulate growth in most services industries, and in the locally important entertainment companies. Banking and defense, however, are expected to be consolidating in 1990. The downzoning of this market will delay the construction of new projects, but is not expected to halt the flow of new projects. Leasing activity this year is forecast to be a notch lower than in 1989.

New Jersey-Central: Office

Mercer, Middlesex, Monmouth, Morris, Somerset, Union, and West Essex Counties

Market Data

Inventory (sf)	Class A CBD	Class A Outside CBD	Class B CBD	Class B Outside CBD
Total	-	85,459,500	-	n/a
Vacant	-	13,755,800	-	n/a
Vacancy Rate	-	16.1%	-	n/a
Vacant Sublease	-	1,470,600	-	-
Under Construction	-	4,667,000	-	-
Substantial Rehab	-	n/a	-	-
Net Absorption	-	3,787,000	-	-

Rental Rates ($/sf)	Class A CBD	Class A Outside CBD	Class B CBD	Class B Outside CBD
Lowest	-	13.00	-	-
Highest	-	28.00	-	-
Weighted Average	-	19.00	-	-

Utility Rates:	CBD n/a	Parking Ratio:	CBD - n/a
	Outside CBD n/a		Outside CBD - 1 per 250 sf
	Not Separately Metered		

Standard Work Letter: $12.00 per sf, typically based on dollars per square foot

Operating Cost Escalation: Base Year

Cumulative Discount Rate: 10-15%

Landlord Concessions
 Rental Abatement
 Lease Assumptions
 Moving Allowance
 Interior Improvements

Leasing Activity Profile
Major Activity
 Business Services
Minor Activity
 Legal/Accounting
 Insurance
 Sales
 Finance/Banking
 Government

Demographics

	Rank	
Population:	n/a	n/a
Population Growth Rate:	n/a	
Unemployment Rate:	n/a	
Median Household Income:	$0	n/a
Cost of living Index:	n/a	n/a

Outlook

Absorption	Up 5%
Construction	Same
Vacancies	Down 3%
Rental Rates	Up 5%
Landlord Concessions	Same

1989 Review

This is a big office market, equivalent to some of the largest cities in the country with over 85 million sq. ft. of total inventory. Flanked by the New York City and Philadelphia metropolitan areas, it is influenced by events in those major urban markets. In 1989, those influences were not especially positive. The financial services slowdown in New York virtually dried up bank and securities firm interest in relocating operations staffs into central New Jersey. The consolidation of pharmaceuticals firms with Philadelphia and New Jersey facilities has put prior expansion plans into limbo. Demand for office space was therefore limited throughout 1989. Absorption of 3.8 million sq. ft. last year was only 81 percent of the new construction being added in the market and a fraction of the 13.8 million sq. ft. of vacancy in central New Jersey.

1990 Forecast

The outlook appears a bit brighter for 1990. Speculative development is reported to be vastly reduced, and a modest improvement in leasing activity would restore the market's tone quickly. Central New Jersey has a wide competitive advantage in rents when compared with New York and Philadelphia, and a utilities cost differential works in its favor as well. Something of a shakeout among smaller developers caught in a financing squeeze will be seen this year, with news of foreclosures and workouts becoming more common. But for the market generally, the end of 1990 should see stronger conditions than those prevailing a year earlier.

Market Inventory
New Jersey-Central

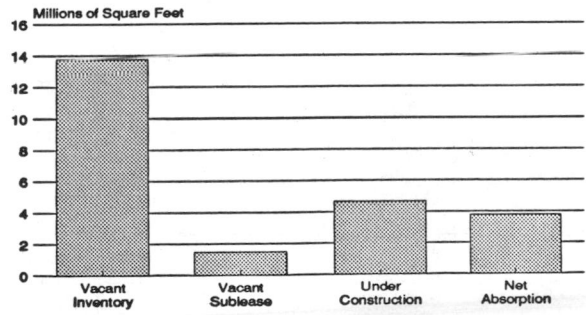

New Jersey-Northern: Office

Market Data

Inventory (sf)	Class A		Class B	
	CBD	Outside CBD	CBD	Outside CBD
Total	121,261,000	-	-	-
Vacant	24,677,000	-	-	-
Vacancy Rate	20.4%	-	-	-
Vacant Sublease	2,129,000	-	-	-
Under Construction	11,950,000	-	-	-
Substantial Rehab	n/a	-	-	-
Net Absorption	5,143,000	-	-	-

Rental Rates ($/sf)	Class A		Class B	
	CBD	Outside CBD	CBD	Outside CBD
Lowest	9.50	-	-	-
Highest	30.00	-	-	-
Weighted Average	21.00	-	-	-

Utility Rates: CBD $2.00 per sf	**Parking Ratio:** CBD - n/a
Outside CBD $1.10 per sf	Outside CBD - 1 per 250 sf
Not Separately Metered	

Standard Work Letter: $19.00 per sf,	**Operating Cost Escalation:**
typically based on dollars per square foot	Base Year

Cumulative Discount Rate: 10-12%	**Leasing Activity Profile**
Landlord Concessions	**Major Activity**
Rental Abatement	Insurance
Interior Improvements	Business Services
	Finance/Banking
	Minor Activity
	Legal/Accounting
	Sales
	Engineering/Architecture

Demographics

		Rank
Population:	1,895,623	n/a
Population Growth Rate:	0.10%	
Unemployment Rate:	n/a	
Median Household Income:	$40,118	n/a
Cost of living Index:	n/a	n/a

Outlook

Absorption	Down 10%
Construction	Down 20%
Vacancies	Down 10%
Rental Rates	Same
Landlord Concessions	Down 6%

1989 Review

In just twenty-five years, the northern New Jersey office market has built more office space than the Wall Street district of Manhattan developed in the past century. The price of this explosive market growth has been a chronically high vacancy rate in all phases of the business cycle. In 1989, the story was as usual. A healthy level of net absorption - 5.1 million sq. ft. of additional occupied space when compared with a year ago - was overwhelmed by nearly 12 million sq. ft. of new projects coming on stream. The result? A vacancy rate still soaring above 20 percent, representing almost 25 million sq. ft. of empty inventory. Demand is generated by the expansion of firms already in this market, but relocations from New York City are important and formed a key portion of leasing gains in 1989.

1990 Forecast

The most important element in the outlook of SIOR's local reporter is the forecast of a 20 percent decline in new construction. This will give the market a chance to regroup and to benefit from the continuing strength of services sector demand. Corporate tenants remain in the driver's seat, even with mergers and acquisitions affecting big firms, and anchor tenants are in a position to command a piece of the developer's equity in exchange for a long-term commitment. Foreign investors are very active here, and their optimism may be a harbinger of brighter times in the near future.

Outlook
New Jersey-Northern

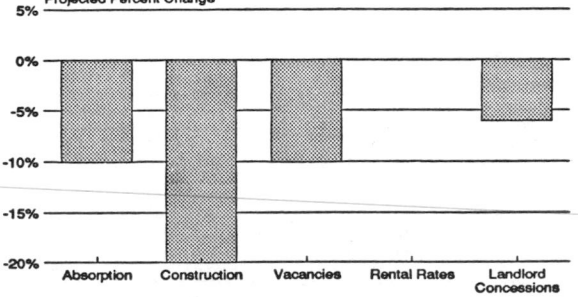

New Jersey-Southern: Office

Camden, Gloucester, and Burlington Counties

Market Data

Inventory (sf)	Class A		Class B	
	CBD	Outside CBD	CBD	Outside CBD
Total	-	20,000,000	-	13,000,000
Vacant	-	3,000,000	-	3,000,000
Vacancy Rate	-	15.0%	-	23.1%
Vacant Sublease	-	n/a	-	n/a
Under Construction	-	250,000	-	n/a
Substantial Rehab	-	n/a	-	n/a
Net Absorption	-	n/a	-	n/a

Rental Rates ($/sf)	Class A		Class B	
	CBD	Outside CBD	CBD	Outside CBD
Lowest	-	17.00	-	13.00
Highest	-	21.00	-	14.00
Weighted Average	-	n/a	-	n/a

Utility Rates:	CBD n/a	Parking Ratio:	CBD - n/a
	Outside CBD $1.50 per sf		Outside CBD - 1 per 250 sf
	Not Separately Metered		

Standard Work Letter: $20.00 per sf

Operating Cost Escalation:
Stop - $3.25-7.00 psf

Cumulative Discount Rate: 10-15%
Landlord Concessions

Leasing Activity Profile

Demographics

	Rank	
Population:	n/a	n/a
Population Growth Rate:	n/a	
Unemployment Rate:	n/a	
Median Household Income:	n/a	n/a
Cost of living Index:	n/a	n/a

Outlook

Absorption	Same
Construction	Same
Vacancies	Same
Rental Rates	Down 10%
Landlord Concessions	Same

1989 Review

This is the smallest of the state's three geographical divisions, at least in terms of its office market inventory measuring a modest 33 million sq. ft.. In effect, southern New Jersey functions as part of the suburban ring surrounding Philadelphia. This office aggregation did not boom to the extent that New York and the adjacent New Jersey market did in the 80s. Correspondingly, it has not been so vulnerable to the slowdown of the northeast regional economy. Marketwide, the vacancy rate in 1989 was 18.2 percent. Office space demand last year was labeled "slow" by SIOR's southern New Jersey researcher, many of the transactions being local and smaller than in previous years. The rental rates reported for 1989 were lower than in last year's *Guide*, and the discount factor for leasing concessions was higher. Clearly, this became a more competitive market as the 80s ended.

1990 Forecast

For the near-term, southern New Jersey will depend upon signs of strength coming first from the larger cities which influence its market area. This is likely to come from the Philadelphia market more than from the New York area to the north or from Wilmington, Delaware to the south. Financing will be tight, and new development slow in 1990. In a specialty market, office condominiums, activity should remain strong with demand for medical and professional users in the $115 - $125 per sq. ft. price range.

Market Inventory
New Jersey-Southern

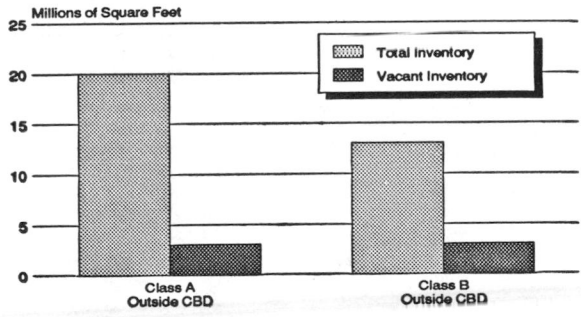

New York City, New York: Office

Manhattan

Market Data

Inventory (sf)

Inventory (sf)	Class A		Class B	
	CBD	Outside CBD	CBD	Outside CBD
Total	243,260,000	-	95,440,000	-
Vacant	32,130,000	-	16,240,000	-
Vacancy Rate	13.2%	-	17.0%	-
Vacant Sublease	8,960,000	-	3,370,000	-
Under Construction	7,200,000	-	n/a	-
Substantial Rehab	n/a	-	n/a	-
Net Absorption	6,200,000	-	-1,560,000	-

Rental Rates ($/sf)	Class A		Class B	
	CBD	Outside CBD	CBD	Outside CBD
Lowest	25.00	-	15.00	-
Highest	75.00	-	35.00	-
Weighted Average	40.70	-	23.43	-

Utility Rates:	CBD $2.50 per sf Outside CBD n/a Not Separately Metered	Parking Ratio:	CBD - n/a Outside CBD - n/a
Standard Work Letter: $25.00 per sf, typically based on dollars per square foot		**Operating Cost Escalation:** Base Year	

Cumulative Discount Rate: 10-15%
Landlord Concessions
  Rental Abatement
  Moving Allowance
  Interior Improvements
		Leasing Activity Profile
		Major Activity
		  Legal/Accounting
		  Finance/Banking
		  Government
		  Printing/Publishing
		Minor Activity
		  Insurance
		  Business Services
		  Engineering/Architecture	

Demographics

		Rank
Population:	8,617,968	2
Population Growth Rate:	0.45%	
Unemployment Rate:	6.20%	
Median Household Income:	$27,043	74
Cost of living Index:	n/a	n/a

Outlook

Absorption	Same
Construction	Up 48%
Vacancies	Up 4%
Rental Rates	Same
Landlord Concessions	Up 2-5%

1989 Review

Manhattan contains, far and away, the largest office market in the nation. Its inventory, Class "A" and Class "B," was 338 million sq. ft.. This market set the pace for the nation during much of the 80s, but it did no better than run in place during 1989. Net absorption for the year was only 5.1 million sq. ft., or 1.5 percent of the inventory. Class "A" absorption of 6.7 million sq. ft. was eroded by rising vacancies in the Class "B" sector. During 1989 the market continually had to cope with large blocks placed on the market by firms merging, consolidating functions or relocating. Still, a high level of leasing was registered - over 20 million sq. ft. of deals were signed with the largest being a law firm lease for 450,000 sq. ft. Throughout the year, though, the psychology of the market became progressively more pessimistic and a booming decade ended with a resounding thud.

1990 Forecast

Retrenchment in the financial sector, one of the key industries for New York, will continue in 1990 and act as a drag on the office market's performance. While the Manhattan economy is highly diversified and less dependent upon Wall Street than commonly supposed, growth in other office using sectors will do no more than offset the contraction of the investment banks in 1990. A weakened fiscal position is pushing city government to look for more property tax revenue. A Manhattan comeback is highly probable, but it will need two to three years to materialize.

Market Inventory
New York City

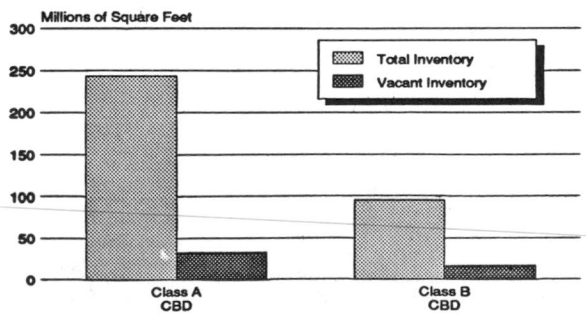

Millions of Square Feet

- Total Inventory
- Vacant Inventory

| Class A CBD | Class B CBD |

New York City-Brooklyn/Queens, New York: Office

Market Data

Inventory (sf)	Class A		Class B	
	CBD	Outside CBD	CBD	Outside CBD
Total	18,000,000	-	-	
Vacant	2,200,000	-	-	-
Vacancy Rate	12.2%	-	-	-
Vacant Sublease	250,000	-	-	-
Under Construction	2,000,000	-	-	-
Substantial Rehab	1,000,000	-	-	-
Net Absorption	1,000,000	-	-	-

Rental Rates ($/sf)	Class A		Class B	
	CBD	Outside CBD	CBD	Outside CBD
Lowest	20.00	15.00	18.00	10.00
Highest	32.00	26.00	26.00	22.00
Weighted Average	25.00	19.00	21.00	14.00

Utility Rates: CBD $2.50 per sf Outside CBD $2.50 per sf Separately Metered	**Parking Ratio:** CBD - 1 per 1,000 sf Outside CBD - 1 per 333 sf
Standard Work Letter: $22.50 per sf, typically based on dollars per square foot	**Operating Cost Escalation:** Base Year
Cumulative Discount Rate: 20% **Landlord Concessions** Parking Rental Abatement Lease Assumptions Interior Improvements Signing Bonuses	**Leasing Activity Profile** **Major Activity** Sales Finance/Banking Engineering/Architecture Government **Minor Activity** Legal/Accounting Insurance Business Services

Demographics

		Rank
Population:	8,617,968	2
Population Growth Rate:	0.45%	
Unemployment Rate:	6.20%	
Median Household Income:	$27,043	74
Cost of living Index:	n/a	n/a

Outlook

Absorption	Same
Construction	Same
Vacancies	Up 10-15%
Rental Rates	Same
Landlord Concessions	Same

1989 Review

Long an office development backwater, and considered to have permanent deficiencies compared with Manhattan and the suburbs surrounding New York City, the two "outer boroughs" of Brooklyn and Queens came into their own in the late 80s and provided some of the City's best office market news during 1989. Citicorp opened a one million sq. ft. tower in the Queens submarket called Long Island City. Brooklyn's multiple building Metrotech project is proceding on schedule, with office buildings for Chase Manhattan Bank and Brooklyn Union Gas Co. commencing development during the year. The large local labor pool already employed by Manhattan firms, plus a generous tax and utility cost abatement package are among the reasons for the Brooklyn/Queens revival.

1990 Forecast

The contraction of the Manhattan financial services economy will negatively affect Brooklyn and Queens this year. A number of announced projects will go nowhere until anchor tenants are signed 25 to 50 percent of their space, and in the meanwhile bank lenders can turn skittish and back out of the deals. Other services industries, such as law, computers and advertising, are holding their own citywide, but cannot substitute for the major tenants needed to sustain development in marginal markets. Brooklyn and Queens will be moving cautiously in 1990, and risk management will be their watchwords.

Market Inventory
New York-Brooklyn/Queens

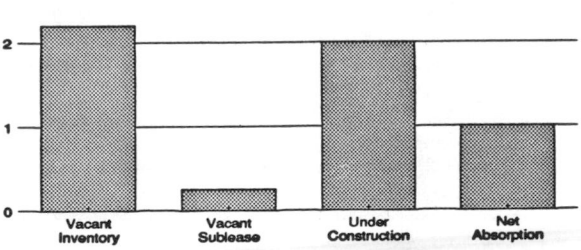

Millions of Square Feet

New York-Nassau/Suffolk Counties, New York: Office

Market Data

Inventory (sf)	Class A		Class B	
	CBD	Outside CBD	CBD	Outside CBD
Total	-	21,449,603	-	8,124,418
Vacant	-	7,821,277	-	1,133,052
Vacancy Rate	-	36.5%	-	13.9%
Vacant Sublease	-	435,175	-	189,380
Under Construction	-	2,072,711	-	276,000
Substantial Rehab	-	n/a	-	n/a
Net Absorption	-	n/a	-	n/a

Rental Rates ($/sf)	Class A		Class B	
	CBD	Outside CBD	CBD	Outside CBD
Lowest	-	12.00	-	9.75
Highest	-	34.00	-	28.00
Weighted Average	-	24.55	-	21.31

Utility Rates:	CBD n/a	Parking Ratio:	CBD - n/a
	Outside CBD $2.00 per sf		Outside CBD - 1 per 250 sf
	Not Separately Metered		

Standard Work Letter: $17.50 per sf, typically based on dollars per square foot	Operating Cost Escalation: Base Year

Cumulative Discount Rate: 10%	Leasing Activity Profile
Landlord Concessions	Major Activity
Rental Abatement	Legal/Accounting
Interior Improvements	Insurance
	Business Services
	Finance/Banking
	Minor Activity
	Sales
	Engineering/Architecture
	Government
	Energy

Demographics   Rank   Outlook

Population:	2,643,585	11	Absorption	Same
Population Growth Rate:	0.16%		Construction	Same
Unemployment Rate:	n/a		Vacancies	Same
Median Household Income:	$49,412	2	Rental Rates	Same
Cost of living Index:	157.2	1	Landlord Concessions	Up

1989 Review

The Long Island suburban markets to the east of New York City were hit with a triple whammy in 1989. The locally important defense and technology sectors pulled back in the face of reduced government funding. The Manhattan economy contracted, withdrawing any beneficial spillover effects from the Nassau/Suffolk market. Environmental and traffic problems forced developers into an involuntary holding pattern. With vacancies in this 30 million sq. ft. market pushing 30 percent, the market ended the Eighties with some serious challenges. The established business centers in Nassau County were relatively strong, and the comparatively low vacancy rates - yet strong rents - noted for the Class "B" inventory reflect this. It is the new speculative construction along the Route 110 corridor and further east into Suffolk County that bore the major risk of the softening market in 1989.

1990 Forecast

The caution flag is up for the coming year. Relocations into the market will be few, and the expansion of local tenants will be slow. During the 90s, Long Island promises to be a solid if low growth market. For the next year or so, though, Nassau/Suffolk offices will be coping with the unpleasant aftereffect of the end of the boom decade of the 80s.

Market Inventory
New York-Nassau/Suffolk Counties

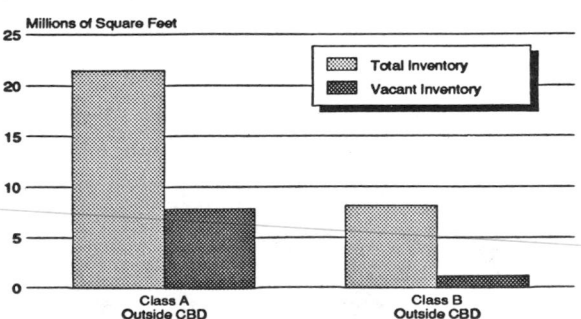

New York-White Plains and Westchester County, New York: Office

Market Data

Inventory (sf)	Class A		Class B	
	CBD	Outside CBD	CBD	Outside CBD
Total	2,180,000	6,800,000	3,800,000	12,000,000
Vacant	381,000	2,173,000	730,000	2,270,000
Vacancy Rate	17.5%	32.0%	19.2%	18.9%
Vacant Sublease	12,000	148,000	44,000	455,000
Under Construction	140,000	240,000	0	50,000
Substantial Rehab	0	0	0	0
Net Absorption	n/a	n/a	n/a	n/a

Rental Rates ($/sf)	Class A		Class B	
	CBD	Outside CBD	CBD	Outside CBD
Lowest	25.00	23.00	15.00	18.00
Highest	30.00	25.00	20.00	22.00
Weighted Average	26.50	23.75	18.00	19.50

Utility Rates: CBD $2.25 per sf
Outside CBD $2.00 per sf
Not Separately Metered

Parking Ratio: CBD - 1 per 500 sf
Outside CBD - 1 per 285 sf

Standard Work Letter: $18.00 per sf, typically based on dollars per square foot

Operating Cost Escalation: Base Year

Cumulative Discount Rate: 15%
Landlord Concessions
Rental Abatement
Lease Assumptions
Moving Allowance
Interior Improvements

Leasing Activity Profile
Major Activity
Insurance
Business Services
Minor Activity
Legal/Accounting
Sales
Finance/Banking
Engineering/Architecture
Government

Demographics

		Rank
Population:	8,617,968	2
Population Growth Rate:	0.45%	
Unemployment Rate:	6.20%	
Median Household Income:	$27,043	74
Cost of living Index:	n/a	n/a

Outlook

Absorption	Same
Construction	Down
Vacancies	Down
Rental Rates	Same
Landlord Concessions	Same

1989 Review

The linkages of the metropolitan area office markets were boldly apparent during the past year. This northern suburban market anchored by the city of White Plains, saw the usual strong demand from small users from within the area, but exceptionally weak demand from large users out of New York City. White Plains and Westchester County posted a 22.4 percent vacancy rate in 1989, well above the national average. Large corporate users already in this market area were on the move northward. IBM relocated major operations to Somers, NY and NYNEX moved staff to Mount Pleasant. These moves threw space in existing facilities back on the market, and backfilling activity was not able to keep up an adequate rate of absorption. This suburban submarket therefore ended the year weaker than it began 1989.

1990 Forecast

Premised on another weak year for Manhattan, White Plains and its suburbs will be marking time in 1990. With the exception of two extremely well-located projects, all new construction is on hold for the coming year. Relocations from Class "B" to Class "A" properties will be a major story for the year. The inventory listed in this year's *Guide* is one indication of change: it is substantially higher than a year ago because it includes former corporate-owned buildings now available to the competitive space market.

Rental Rates
New York-Rockland/Westchester Counties

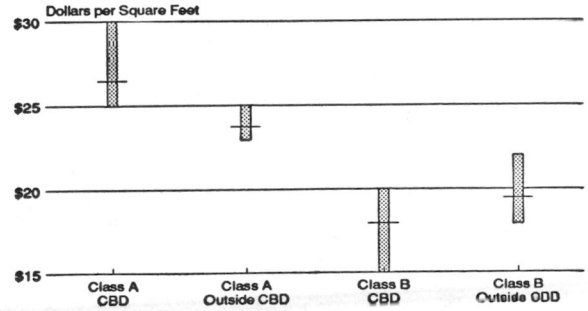

Glossary of Terms

Demographics

Population. The 1989 population projection for the MSA.

Population Growth Rate. The annual percentage change in populations between 1980 and 1989. Figures are based on data from National Planning Data Corporation.

Unemployment Rate. The percent of labor force unemployed in September 1989 as published by the Bureau of Labor Statistics in Employment and Earnings.

Median Household Income. The estimated median household income for 1989 as published by National Planning Data Corporation.

Cost of Living Index. Measures relative price levels for consumer goods and services in participating areas, as published by American Chamber of Commerce Researchers Association (ACCRA).

Demographic Rankings. This ranks local statistics against other U.S. Metropolitan markets.

Industrial Markets

Prime Industrial Building. A prime industrial building is in the top 25 percent of the most desired industrial properties in a given market area. Such buildings are considered to be for general purpose uses such as industrial, research, warehouse and/or manufacturing.

Central City/Suburban. Since the definition of urban and suburban varies widely, it is the responsibility of the individual survey respondent to reflect his or her area's particular characteristics.

Total Inventory. Total square footage (sf) of rentable industrial space, vacant and occupied, ready for tenant finish. Includes owner occupied space.

Vacant Inventory. Total square footage of vacant rentable industrial space, including sublease.

Net Absorption. Net absorption is the net change in occupied space.

Under Construction. Industrial space in construction stages, ground has been broken. Does not include planned projects.

Construction Costs. Construction costs reflect only hard construction costs such as general contractor, overhead, and profit, but exclude architectural and engineering fees, financing fees, and mortgage/brokerage fees for both construction and permanent financing.

Lease Prices. A gross lease is one in which the tenant's rent includes real estate taxes, fire and extended coverage insurance, as well as maintenance of the roof structure and outside walls. A net lease is one in which the tenant assumes the operating expenses of the leased premises.

Improved Sites. Improved sites are in the top 25 percent of overall desirability of the existing inventory. Such sites are in a "ready-to-build" condition and are essentially level and graded and serviced with all necessary utilities. Rail service may or may not be available.

Unimproved Sites. These sites are also in the top 25 percent of overall desirability of the existing inventory and zoned for industrial use. Streets and utilities may not yet be installed, but are reasonably close and available. Rail service may or may not be available.

Prime High-Technology Building. Generally, high-technology (high-tech) buildings are 50 percent or more office, fully air-conditioned, 12-18' clear height, have extensive landscaping and parking, and are architecturally impressive. In some areas of the country where high-tech industries are not prevalent, this building could be used as a showroom or as pure office. These properties are sometimes called "Flex buildings."

Office Markets

CBD. Central Business District space located near the historical urban core, commonly associated with traditional government and financial districts in most cities.

Outside CBD. Outside the CBD includes both suburban area and "urban clusters" with areas of high office space concentrations which often rival nearby CBDs.

Class "A." Excellent locations, high quality tenants, high quality finish, well-maintained, professionally managed, and usually new, or old buildings that are competitive with new buildings.

Class "B." Good location, professionally managed, fairly high quality construction and tenancy. Class "B" buildings generally show very little functional obsolescence and deterioration.

Total Inventory. Total square footage (sf) of rentable space, vacant and occupied, ready for tenant finish. Does not include owner occupied space.

Vacant Inventory. Total square footage of vacant rentable space, including sublease.

Current Construction. Total square footage presently under construction includes any space that will be available for occupancy before the end of 1990.

Substantial Rehabilitation. Repair/replacement of building interior finish and/or systems requiring temporary displacement of tenants.

Net Absorption. Net Absorption refers to the net change in occupied stock.

Rental Rate. Minimum, maximum, and weighted average quoted rental rate for competitive office space in each class, in U.S. dollars per square foot ($/sf).

Weighted Average Rental Rate. Average quoted rental rate weighted by the vacant space available at the rental rate, in each class.

Average Utility Rates. Figures presented are dollars per square foot per year.

Standard Work Letter. Sometimes called a construction rider, this refers to the work that the landlord will do for the tenant, typically to finish out the interior of the space.

Typical Parking Ratio. The ratio refers to the availability of parking spaces per number of square feet leased by a tenant.

Operating Cost Escalation. Operating cost escalation refers to the procedure used to adjust rents over the term of a lease.

Cumulative Discount Rate. The rental rate discount factor is the cumulative effect of landlord lease concessions on gross rental rates. It is expressed as a percentage of base rent.

Miscellaneous Terms

Trophy Property. A broad characterization of the target of institutional and/or offshore investment interest. This is generally used to identify a highly visible property of excellent reputation, in the absolutely highest echelon of its property class. The term is applied almost exclusively to CBD office buildings in the largest markets, to prime hotel properties, and to super-regional shopping centers.

Sea change. A thorough and striking transformation, often for the better. The term has an enduring place in the language thanks to its prominent use by Shakespeare in *The Tempest*.

Maquiladora. The twin plant operation which has grown up along the U.S./Mexico border, in which goods are shipped into Mexico for assembly and finishing work using lower cost labor, and then are distributed through the U.S. market. Import duties are payable only on the imputed value added in the assembly process.

FIRE Sector. An acronym standing for Finance, Insurance and Real Estate, one of the major industry groupings in the Standard Industrial Classification system established by the U.S. Department of Commerce.

Back-filling. A colloquialism referring to the re-leasing of space once occupied by a tenant which has relocated elsewhere.

Source: © Copyright *Society of Industrial and Office Realtors*®, 1990. Reprinted with permission from the *1990 Guide to Industrial and Office Real Estate Markets*.

Glossary of Real Estate and REIT Terms

This glossary of terminology used in conjunction with discussions of real estate investment trusts has been prepared by the Research Department of the National Association of Real Estate Investment Trusts. Credit should be given to Realty Income Trust, a NAREIT member, which produced a glossary of terms upon which NAREIT drew heavily.

Acceleration clause A condition in a loan contract or mortgage note which permits the lender to demand immediate repayment of the entire balance if the contract is breached or conditions for repayment occur, such as sale or demolition.

Accrued interest or rent An amount of interest or rent which has been earned but which may not have been received in the same period as earned. On many short-term first mortgages, accrued interest is not received in cash until permanent financing is obtained.

Acquisition loan See C&D loan.

Advisor A REIT's investment advisor (usually pursuant to a renewable one-year contract) provides analysis of proposed investments, servicing of the portfolio, and other advisory services. Fee limits for advisory services are prescribed by many state securities regulators. Also spelled "adviser."

Amortization The process of retiring debt or recovering a capital investment through scheduled, systematic repayments of principal; that portion of fixed mortgage payment applied to reduction of the principal amount owed.

Anchor tenant An important tenant, usually with an excellent credit rating (also known as a triple-A tenant), which takes a large amount of space in a shopping center or office building and is usually one of the first tenants to commit to lease. The anchor tenant usually is given lower rent because of the desirability of having that tenant at the property, both because of its credit rating and its ability to generate traffic.

Appraisal An opinion by an expert of the value of a property as of a specified date, supported by the presentation and analysis of relevant data. The appraisal may be arrived at by any or all of three methods: the cost approach (cost to reproduce), the market approach (comparison with other similar properties), or the income approach (capitalization of actual or projected income figures).

Assessed value The value of a property which is assigned to it by a taxing authority for purposes of assessing property taxes; often assessed value bears a fixed relationship by local statute to market value.

Asset swaps See swap program.

Assets Anything of value owned by the company. Assets are either financial, as cash or bonds; or physical, as real or personal property. For REIT tax purposes, more than 75% of the trust's assets must be property owned or securities backed by real estate.

Assumption of mortgage When the responsibility for repaying existing indebtedness secured by property is "assumed" by the second purchaser. In most jurisdictions, this relieves the first owner of the original obligations, at least to the extent that can be satisfied by sale of this asset after foreclosure.

Attribution More than 50% of a REIT's shares cannot be held by fewer than six people (otherwise it becomes a personal holding company for tax purposes). When someone has indirect control over someone else's shares (such as a trustee over shares held for the benefit of another) then "control" for personal holding company purposes may be "attributed." This complicated legal topic of "attribution" arises, however, only when the REIT's shares are held by a few.

Audit An examination of the financial status and operations of an enterprise, based mostly on the books of account, and undertaken to assure conformity to generally accepted accounting principles and to secure information for, or to check the accuracy of, the enterprise's balance sheet, income statement, and/or cash flow statement.

Balloon mortgage A mortgage loan which provides for periodic payments, which may include both interest and principal, but which leaves the loan less than fully amortized at maturity, requiring a final large payment which is the "balloon." Usually the term does not apply to an "interest only" loan whose full principal is due upon maturity or upon call during its life.

Bankrupt When liabilities exceed assets, Federal laws enable the entity to dissolve in an orderly fashion (Chapter VII), or permit a court officer to restructure the company into a survivor "going business" (Chapter X), or permit existing management to do the same under court supervision (Chapter XI), or to do so despite the preferred position of secured creditors if real property is the only asset of the business (Chapter XII).

Source: National Association of Real Estate Trusts, 1101 Seventeenth Street, N.W., Washington, D.C. 20036.

Beneficial owner The person who ultimately benefits from ownership of shares or other securities—in contrast to "nominees" (often pseudonyms for control of investment professionals so as to facilitate security transactions without having to track down beneficial owners to participate in each step of the procedures).

Blue sky laws State laws regulating conditions of sale of securities of companies (particularly those just starting out of the "clear blue sky") for the protection of the investing public. National stock exchange rules usually supercede state laws pursuant to a "blue chip" exemption contained in such state laws. The federal securities laws dovetail with state laws and pertain to publicly held companies, primarily as to accounting and disclosure practices.

Bond A debt certificate which (a) represents a loan to a trust, (b) bears interest, and (c) matures on a stated future date. Short term bonds (generally with a maturity of five years or less from the date of issuance) are often called notes. See debentures.

Book value per share Shareholder equity as adjusted to tangible net worth (assets minus liabilities plus paid-in capital) per share outstanding.

Borrower A person or entity who received something of value, ordinarily money, and is obligated to pay it back, as the debtor to the creditor, usually pursuant to a note or "IOU" containing terms and conditions.

Broker A person who is paid to act as an intermediary in connection with a transaction, in contrast to a dealer or principal who buys or sells for his own account. In the REIT world, the term "broker" usually refers to a real estate salesman, although the term is also used for "stockbrokers" too.

Building lien An encumbrance upon the property by the contractor or subcontractors. Also known as a "mechanic's" or "materialman's" lien.

Building permit Written permission by the local municipality (usually through the building inspector or other agent) allowing construction work on a piece of property in accordance with plans which were submitted and conforming to local building codes and regulations.

Business trust An unincorporated business in which assets are given to trustees for management to hold or to sell, as investments. The business trust form was first fully developed in Massachusetts, under common law, and the term "Massachusetts business trust" is sometimes used to describe entities formed in other states. It is a form of business through

a trustee or trustees who hold legal title to the property of the business. Capital contributions are made to the trustees by the beneficiaries whose equitable title and interest in the property of the trust are evidenced by trust certificates, usually called shares of beneficial interest. The earnings of the trust are paid to them, as dividends are paid to stockholders. The beneficiaries generally enjoy limited liability, as the control and management of the trust rests solely with the trustees, but the trust form or organization can be distinguished from a corporation. Early REIT tax laws relied on this distinction to define eligible real estate operations.

Capital gain The amount by which the net proceeds from resale of a capital item exceed the adjusted cost (or "book value") of the asset. If a capital asset is held for more than twelve months before disposition it is taxed on a more favorable basis than a gain after a shorter period of time.

Capitalization rate The rate of return utilized to value a given cash flow, the sum of a Discount Rate and a Capital Recapture Rate. It is applied to any income stream with a finite term over which the invested principal is to be returned to the investor or lender.

Cash flow The revenue remaining after all cash expenses are paid, i.e., non-cash charges such as depreciation are not included in the calculation.
  Cash flow per share. Cash flow divided by the common shares outstanding. Shareholders must make this computation themselves since the SEC has prohibited companies from stating this calculation.
  Net cash flow. Generally determined by net income plus depreciation less principal payments on long-term mortgages.

Cash on cash return The "cash flow" from a property expressed as a percentage of the cash "equity" invested in a property.

Chapter X See bankrupt.

Collateral An item of value, such as real estate or securities, which a borrower pledges as security. A mortgage gives the creditor the right to seize the real estate collateral after non-performance of the debtor.

Commitment A promise to make an investment at some time in the future if certain specified conditions are met. A REIT may charge a fee to the borrower at the time of making the commitment. A REIT's level of commitments minus expected repayments can be regarded as an indication of future funding requirements.
  "Take-out" commitment is one provided by the anticipated long-term lender, usually with complicated terms and conditions that

must be met before the "take-out" becomes effective.

"Gap" commitment is an anticipated short-term loan to cover part of the final "take-out" that the long-term lender refuses to advance until certain conditions are met (like 90% rent-up of an apartment after construction is completed). The amount above the "floor" or basic part of the loan is the "gap," and the gap commitment is issued to enable the construction lender to make a construction loan commitment for the full amount of the take-out loan instead of only for the "floor" amount.

"Standby" commitment is one that the lender and borrower doubt will be used. It exists as reassurance to a short-term construction lender that if, after completion of a building, the borrower cannot find adequate long-term "take-out" financing, the construction lender will be repaid.

Compensating balances Money which is sometimes required by banks to be held in checking accounts by borrowers, as part of their loan agreement.

Condominium A form of fee ownership of whole units or separate portions of multi-unit buildings which facilitates the formal filing, recording and financing of a divided interest in real property. The condominium concept may be used for apartments, offices and other professional uses. See cooperatives.

Conduit tax treatment So long as most (if not all) earnings are passed along by an entity, then federal taxation is avoided at the entity's level. REITs, mutual funds, and certain kinds of holding companies are eligible for "conduit tax treatment" under certain conditions.

Constant The agreed-upon periodic (usually monthly) payment to pay the face interest rate, with any residual amount going to amortize the loan.

Construction and development loan (C&D) A short-term loan for the purpose of constructing a building, shopping center, or other improvement upon real estate, or developing a site in preparation for construction. A C&D loan is normally disbursed in increments (called *draws* or *draw-downs*) as building proceeds, rather than in a single disbursement, and is conditioned upon compliance with a variety of factors. It is usually repaid with the proceeds of the permanent loan. A land loan or purchase and development loan is sometimes made for the purpose of acquiring unimproved vacant land, usually as a future building site and for financing improvements to such land (street, sewers, etc.) as a prerequisite to construction of a building upon the site.

Contingent interest Interest on a loan that is payable only if certain conditions occur, in contrast to interest that becomes an accrued liability (whether or not paid) at a specific time.

Cooperative A form of ownership whereby a structure is owned by a corporation or trust with each individual owner holding stock in the corporation representative of the value of his apartment. Title to the apartment is evidenced by a proprietary lease which often does not qualify as adequate collateral for some lenders.

Cost-to-carry The concept specified by the accounting profession to be used by REITs in computing anticipated interest cost on debt needed to "carry" non-earning or partially-earning assets until they're restored to earning status or sold.

Current liabilities Money owed and due to be paid within one year.

Dealer Someone who buys property with the purpose of selling it at a profit rather than holding it as an investment. A dealer's profits are taxed at the ordinary income rate rather than the capital gains rate regardless of how long the property is held for resale (in contrast to the investor who sells a property after a year and pays at the capital gains rate). A REIT is not permitted to be a dealer unless it is willing to pay a 100% tax on gains from such sales in the year in which it is deemed to be a dealer; sales of foreclosed property do not fall within this definition. See principal.

Debenture An obligation which is secured only by the general credit of the issuing trust, as opposed to being secured by a direct lien on its assets, real estate or otherwise. A debenture is a form of a bond.

Declaration of trust Similar to articles of incorporation for a corporation, this document contains rules for operation of the trust, selection of its governing trustees, etc., and is the keystone of a REIT.

Deed A legal instrument which conveys title from one to another. It must be (a) made between competent parties (b) have legally sound subject matter (c) correctly state what is being conveyed (d) contain good and valuable consideration (e) be properly executed by the parties involved and (f) be delivered to be valid.

Deed in lieu of foreclosure The device by which title to property is conveyed from the mortgagor (borrower) to the mortgagee (lender) as an alternative to foreclosure. While this procedure can transfer effective control more quickly, many lenders eschew it because undiscovered prior liens (from a workman who was never paid but hadn't gotten around to filing his valid, but late, claim for example) remain enforceable in contrast to the more formal foreclosure procedures which wipe out prior claims after due notice.

Deferred maintenance The amount of repairs that should have been made to keep a property in good running condition, but which have been put off. The term contemplates the desirability of immediate expenditures, although it does not necessarily denote inadequate maintenance in the past.

Deficiency dividend The process of paying an "extra" dividend after the close of the fiscal year so as to comply with REIT tax requirements to pay out more than 90% of income. See dividend.

Depreciation The loss in value of a capital asset, due to wear and tear which cannot be compensated for by ordinary repairs, or an allowance made to allow for the fact that the asset may become obsolete before it wears out. The purpose of a depreciation charge is to write off the original cost of an asset by equitably distributing charges against its operation over its useful life, matching "cost" to the period in which it was used to generate earnings. Depreciation is an optional noncash expense recognizable for tax purposes. If the REIT pays out more than its taxable earnings, then it is distributing a "return of capital" or—as is commonly stated in the industry— "paying out depreciation."

Development loans See Construction and development loan.

Dilution The situation which results when an increase occurs in a company's outstanding securities without a corresponding increase in the company's assets and/or income.

Discount rate An interest rate used to convert a future system of payments into a single present value. See capitalization rate.

Dividend or distribution The distribution of cash or stock to shareholders of a company which is made periodically as a means of distributing all or a portion of net income or cash flow. Technically, a dividend can be paid only from net taxable income, so many REITs distribute cash and later characterize their distributions as capital gains or a tax-free return of capital if net taxable income is less than the cash paid out.

Dividend or distribution yield The annual dividend or distribution rate for a security expressed as a percent of its market price. For most REITs, the "annualized" rate is the previous quarter's distribution times four, regardless of how the distribution is characterized.

Draw A request from a borrower to obtain partial payment from the lender pursuant to

a loan commitment. The lender reassures himself that the borrower has completed the required steps (such as putting in the concrete properly) before advancing money. Often, the borrower submits bills from subcontractors, which are then "paid" by the lender after inspecting the subcontractor's work. In such cases, the check is usually made out to the subcontractor but must be signed by the borrower, too, so that the lender ends up only with one borrower. See construction and development loan.

Effective borrowing costs The cost of borrowing after adjustment for compensating balances or fees in lieu of compensating balances, and selling expenses in the case of publicly sold debt.

Encumbrance A legal right or interest in real estate which diminishes its value. Encumbrances can take a number of forms, such as easements, zoning restrictions, mortgages, etc.

Entrepreneur An individual who is responsible for a commercial or real estate activity who takes a certain risk of loss in a transaction for the right to enjoy any profit which may result.

Equity The interest of the shareholders in a company as measured by their paid-in capital and undistributed income. The term is also used to describe (i) the difference between the current market value of a property and the liens or mortgages which encumber it or (ii) the cash which makes up the difference between the mortgage(s) and the construction or sale price.

Equity leveraging The process by which shares are sold at a premium above book value (in anticipation of greater earnings).

Equity participation Usually, the right of an investor to participate to some extent in the increased value of a project by receiving a percentage of the increased income from the project. If a REIT were to participate in a percentage of the net income of a venture (such as the shopping center's owner/lessor), then it could be deemed to be a partner in an active business. Thus, most REIT leases spell out the "equity participation" as a percentage of gross receipts or sales (which is a more stable measure of sales activity, anyway, and one readily identifiable from the lessor's federal income tax statement).

Escrow A deposit of "good faith" money which is entrusted to a third party (often a bank) until fulfillment of certain conditions and agreements, when the escrow may be released or applied as payment for the purchase of property or for services rendered.

Estoppel certificate An instrument used

when a mortgage or lease is assigned to another. The certificate sets forth the exact remaining balance of the lease or mortgage as of a certain date and verifies any promises to tenants that may have been made by the first owner for which the second owner may be held accountable.

Exculpatory clause A clause which relieves one of liability for injuries or damages to another. Exculpatory clauses are placed in REIT documents with the intention of eliminating personal liability of its trustees, shareholders and officers.

Expenses The costs which are charges against current operations or earnings of a building, company or other reporting entity. They may have been "paid out" in cash, or accrued to be paid later, or charged as a bookkeeping procedure to reflect the "using up" of assets (as in depreciation) utilized in the production of income during the period of current operations.

Face value The value which is shown on the face of an instrument such as a bond, debenture or stock certificate. The "face rate" of a debt instrument is often known as its "coupon rate."

Fair market value See Market value.

Fee or fee simple Title to a property which is absolute, good and marketable; ownership without condition.

Fiduciary A relationship of trust and confidence between a person charged with the duty of acting for the benefit of another and the person to whom such duty is owed, as in the case of guardian and ward, trustee and beneficiary, executor and heir.

First mortgage That mortgage which has a prior claim over all other liens against real estate. In some jurisdictions, real estate taxes, mechanics liens, court costs, and other involuntary liens may take priority over such a contractual lien: title companies "clear" properties so as to reassure first mortgage lenders (and owners) of their uncontested position and to guarantee them of that position under certain conditions.

Fiscal year The 12-month period selected as a basis for computing and accounting for a business. A fiscal year need not coincide with the calendar year, except for all REITs initially qualifying for special tax treatment after 1976.

Fixed assets Assets, such as land, buildings and machinery, which cannot be quickly converted into cash. For REITs, most "fixed assets" are real property although some (like furniture in an apartment lobby) may be personal property.

Fixed charges Those interest charges, insurance costs, taxes and other expenses which remain relatively constant regardless of revenue. See net lease.

Floating rate A variable interest rate charged for the use of borrowed money. It is determined by charging a specific percentage above a fluctuating base rate, usually the prime rate as announced by a major commercial bank.

Floor loan A portion or portions of a mortgage loan commitment which is less than the full amount of the commitment and which may be funded upon conditions less stringent than those required for funding the full amount, or the "ceiling" of the loan. For example, the floor loan, equal to perhaps 80% of the full amount of the loan, may be funded upon completion of construction without any occupancy requirements, but substantial occupancy of the building may be required for funding the full amount of the loan, which is referred to as the "ceiling." See commitment, gap.

Foreclosure The legal process of enforcing payment of a debt by taking the properties which secure the debt, once the terms of the obligation are not followed. Upon foreclosure, the entire debt might not be fully discharged by transfer and disposition of the property (as determined by the courts). If so, a "deficiency judgment" may be obtained, at which point the lender is like any other creditor in attempting to get the debtor to pay the deficiency. Collection of the deficiency judgment in major real estate transactions is rare, but it becomes a major factor in negotiations if the borrower decides to return to the real estate business in the future.

Fully diluted earnings The hypothetical earnings per share of a company, computed after giving effect to the number of shares which would be outstanding if all convertible debt and warrants were exercised, and also to any reduction in interest payments resulting from such exercise.

Gap commitment See commitment, gap. Also see floor loan.

General lien A lien against the property of an individual or other entity generally, rather than against specific items of realty or personal property.

Ground lease See sale-leaseback.

Holding company A corporation that owns or controls the operations of various other companies. Many REITs were sponsored by bank or insurance holding companies whose subsidiary companies advise and manage REITs, pursuant to contracts with the REIT's trustees.

Independent contractor A firm hired to actively manage property investments. A tax-qualified REIT must hire an independent contractor to manage and operate its property, so as to distinguish itself as an investor rather than an active manager.

Income property Developed real estate, such as office buildings, shopping centers, apartments, hotels and motels, warehouses and some kinds of agricultural or industrial property, which produce a flow of income—in contrast to non-income generating real estate like raw land which would be bought and held for a speculative profit upon resale or development.

Indenture The legal document prepared in connection with, for example, a bond issue, setting forth the terms of the issue, its specific security, remedies in case of default, etc. It may also be called the "deed of trust."

Indentured trustee A trustee, generally the trust department of a major bank, which represents the interest of bondholders under a publicly offered issue.

Insider A person close to a trust who has intimate knowledge of financial developments before they become public knowledge.

Interest rate The percentage rate which an individual pays for the use of borrowed money for a given period of time.

Intermediate-term loan A loan for a term of three to ten years which is usually not fully amortized at maturity. Often, developers will seek interim loans by which to pay off construction financing, in anticipation of obtaining long-term financing at a later date on more favorable terms, either because long-term rates decline generally or because the project can show an established, stable earnings history.

Interim loan A type of loan which is to be repaid out of the proceeds of another loan. Ordinarily, not self-liquidating (amortized), the lender evaluates the risk of obtaining refinancing as much as the period risk. See C&D loans.

Investment advisor See advisor.

Joint venture The entity which is created when two or more persons or corporate entities join together to carry out a specific business transaction of real estate development. A joint venture is usually of limited duration and usually for a specific property; it can be treated as a partnership for tax purposes. The parties have reciprocal and paralleling rights and obligations.

Junior mortgage loan Any mortgage loan in which the lien and the right of repayment is subordinate to that of another mortgage loan or loans. A "second mortgage" is a junior

mortgage. "Third, fourth," etc. mortgages are always deemed to be secondary.

Land loan See Construction and development loan.

Land-purchase leaseback See sale-leaseback.

Late charge The charge which is levied against a borrower for a payment which was not made in a timely manner.

Lease A contract between the owner of property (lessor) and a tenant (lessee) setting forth the terms, conditions and consideration for the use of the property for a specified period of time at a specified rental. See sale-leaseback and net lease.

Leasehold improvements The cost of improvements or betterments to property leased for a period of years, often paid for by the tenant. Such improvements ordinarily become the property of the lessor (owner) on expiration of the lease; consequently their cost is normally amortized over the life of the lease if the lessor pays for them.

Leverage The process of borrowing upon one's capital base with the expectation of generating a profit above the cost of borrowing.

Liability management The aspect of the management of a company concerned with the planning and procurement of funds for investment through the sale of equity, public debt and bank borrowings. In the REIT industry, the phrase contrasts to "asset management" or the real estate side of the business.

Line of credit Usually, an agreement between a commercial bank and a borrower under which the bank agrees to provide unsecured credit to the borrower upon certain terms and conditions. Normally, the borrower may draw on all or any part of the credit from time to time.

Limited partnership A partnership which limits certain of the partners' (the limited partners) liability to the amount of their investment. At least one partner (the "general partner") is fully liable for the obligations of the partnership and its operations, usually with the limited partners participating as investors only.

Loan loss reserve A reserve set up to offset asset values in anticipation of losses that are reasonably expected. Initially, REITs had insufficient operating experience to anticipate losses in any one class of investments or for a portfolio as a whole, so tax authorities would not permit substantial contributions toward a reserve as an allowable period expense. When difficulties arose, the conversion of short-term loans to longer-term property holdings required some form of recognition of likely losses in the financial statements. A novel procedure for REITs was devised by requiring, for book purposes, computation of additions to the reserve based in part on the probable cost of sustaining the troubled assets over the longer period of time necessary to "cure" the problem. Also known as "allowance for losses."

Loan run-off The rate at which an existing mortgage portfolio will reduce (or "run-off") to zero if no new loans are added to the portfolio.

Loan swaps See asset swaps.

Long-term mortgage Any financing, whether in the form of a first or junior mortgage, the term of which is ten years or more. It is generally fully amortized.

Loss carry forwards The net operating loss (NOL) incurred in prior years, which may be applied for tax purposes against future earnings, thereby reducing taxable income. For REITs (which must pay out most of their taxable income), NOLs can be carried forward eight years; for non-REIT-taxed companies, NOL can be carried forward for only seven years.

Market value The highest price in terms of money which a property will bring in a competitive and open market under all conditions requisite to a fair sale—the buyer and the seller each acting prudently, knowledgeably, and at arm's length. See appraisal.

Moratorium A period in which payments of debts or other performance of a legal obligation is suspended temporarily, usually because of unforeseen circumstances which make timely payment or performance difficult or impossible. This forebearance can be whole or partial.

Mortgage A publicly recorded lien by which the property is pledged as security for the payment of a debt valid even beyond death ("mort" is death in French). In some states a mortgage is an actual conveyance of the property to the creditor until the terms of the mortgage are satisfied. While there is always a "note" secured by a mortgage document, both the note and mortgage instrument are commonly called "the mortgage." For types, see: first, junior, short-term, long-term, wrap-around and construction and development mortgage definitions.

Mortgage banker A non-depository lender who makes loans secured by real estate and then usually packages and sells those loans in large groups to institutional investors, pursuant to a "long-term commitment" he has negotiated with the life insurance company or other institutional investor. Mortgage bankers frequently arrange to service these mortgages for the out-of-town institutions,

collecting regular payments, keeping the lender up to date on the progress of the loan, escrowing payments for taxes and insurance premiums, and, if necessary, administering foreclosure proceedings. Many REITs were sponsored by mortgage bankers.

Mortgage constant The total annual payments of principal and interest (annual debt service) on a mortgage with level-payment amortization schedule, expressed as a percentage of the initial principal amount of the loan.

Mortgagee in possession A lender or one who holds a mortgage who has taken possession of a property in order to protect an interest in the property. Usually, this is done with commercial properties as to which rents, management fees and other disbursements continue even if the mortgage is in default. The possession must be taken with the consent of the mortgagor (or a court, in cases of foreclosure) and the mortgagee must be careful to do only those things to the property that the mortgagor (or court) will agree to accept, should it resume its role as a creditworthy owner.

Net Income The dollar amount that remains after all expenses, including taxes, are deducted from gross income. For regular companies, it is also called after-tax profit, the "bottom line" figure of how a company has performed with its investors' money. For REITs, it is net taxable income which, if fully distributed, is not taxed.

Net lease A lease, sometimes called a net-net (insurance and taxes) or even a net-net-net lease (insurance, taxes, and maintenance) in which the tenant pays all costs, including insurance, taxes, repairs, upkeep and other expenses, and the rental payments are "net" of all these expenses. See lease and fixed charges.

Net worth The remaining asset value of a property company or other entity after deduction of all liabilities against it.

Non-accrual loans See non-earning investments.

Non-earning investments The category of loans or investments which are not earning the originally anticipated rate of return. Some may be characterized as "partially earning." When interest is recorded as earned rather than as received (accrued interest), "non-accrual investments" are those which management expects not to receive interest as originally contemplated. In the vernacular, nonearning investments are "problem loans" or "troubled properties."

Non-qualified REIT A REIT that was formerly qualified, or conducts its affairs as if it is qualified, but that has elected for the tax year in question to be treated like a normal business corporation for tax purposes. Thus, some restraints (primarily against active management and holding property for sale) are lifted, while REIT conduit tax treatment is lost.

Occupancy rate The amount of space or number of apartments or offices or hotel rooms which are rented as compared with the total amount or number available. The rate is usually expressed as a percentage.

Operating expenses Expenses arising out of or relating to business activity such as interest expense, professional fees, salaries, etc.

Operating income Income received directly from business activity in the normal course, as contrasted with capital gains income, or other extraordinary income.

Option A right to buy or lease property at a certain specified price for specified terms. Consideration is typically given for the option, which is exercisable over a limited time span. If the option is not exercised, the consideration is forfeited. A loan to a developer secured by his option to obtain real estate is considered a "qualified" REIT asset.

Origination The process by which a loan is created, including the search for (or receipt of) the initial plans, the analysis and structuring of the proposed financing, and the review and acceptance procedures by which the commitment to make the investment is finally issued.

Overage income Rental income above a guaranteed minimum depending on a particular level of profit or retail sales volume by the tenant, payable under the terms of a lease.

Participations A lender often "participates out" or sells a portion of his loan to another lender while retaining a portion and managing the investment. REITs buy real estate secured participations as well as originating them.

Par value The face value assigned to a security when it is issued. The stated par value of a security generally has nothing to do with its market or book value.

Passivity The state of owning investments but not actively managing them (as a property management firm does for the investor) or engaging in trading the securities (like a broker or dealer). This "passivity" test is implicit behind several of the REIT tax requirements.

Pension funds Money which is accumulated in trust to fund pensions for companies or unions and which is frequently invested in part in real estate. A co-mingled real estate pension fund account is managed, usually under contract to a financial institution, much like a REIT except that its shares are not publicly traded but instead sold to other pension funds.

Permanent financing See long-term loan.

Point An amount which represents 1% of the maximum principal amount of an investment. Used in connection with a discount from, or a share of, a principal amount deducted at the time funds are advanced, it represents additional compensation to the lender.

Portfolio The investments of a company, including investments in mortgages and/or ownership of real property. REIT portfolios usually consist of equity in property, short-term mortgages, long-term mortgages and/or subordinated land sale-lease-backs.

Portfolio turnover The average length of time from the funding of investments until they are paid off or sold.

Preferred shares Stocks which have prior claim on distributions (and/or assets in the event of dissolution) up to a certain definite amount before the shares of beneficial interest are entitled to anything. As a form of ownership, preferred shares stand behind senior subordinated and secured debtholders in dissolution, as well as other creditors.

Prepayment penalty The penalty which is imposed on the borrower for payment of the mortgage before it is due. Often a mortgage contains a clause specifying that there is to be no prepayment penalty, or limits the prepayment penalty to only the first few years of the mortgage term.

Price earning ratio A ratio which consists of the market price divided by current annualized earnings per share. Such a computation is now found in most daily stock listings. For REITs, annualization of quarterly earnings is computed by multiplying the most recent distribution by four, regardless of the distribution's later characterization as a dividend, return-of-capital, or capital gains.

Prime lending rate The rate at which commercial banks will lend money from time to time to their most credit-worthy customers, used as a base for most loans to financial intermediaries such as REITs.

Principal The buyer or seller in a real estate transaction as distinguished from an agent.

Principal The sum of money loaned. The amount of money to be repaid on a loan excluding interest charges.

Prior lien A lien or mortgage ranking ahead of some other lien. A prior lien need not itself be a first mortgage.

Pro forma Projected or hypothetical as opposed to actual as related, for example, to a balance sheet or income statement.

Problem investments See nonearning investments.

Prospectus A document describing an investment opportunity; the detailed description of new securities which must be supplied to prospective interstate purchasers under the Securities Act of 1933.

Provision for loan losses Periodic allocation of funds to loan loss reserves in recognition of a decline in the value of a loan or loans in a trust's portfolio due to a default on the part of the borrowers.

Proxy An authorization given by a registered security holder to vote stock at the annual meeting or at a special meeting of security holders.

Purchase and leaseback See sale-leaseback.

Pyramiding In stock market transactions, this term refers to the practice of borrowing against unrealized "paper" profits in securities to make additional purchases. In corporate finance, it refers to the practice of creating a speculative capital structure by a series of holding companies, whereby a relatively small amount of voting stock in the parent company controls a large corporate system. In real estate, it refers to the practice of financing 100% or more of the value of the property.

Qualified assets Assets which meet tax requirements for special REIT tax treatment, i.e. real property. In any tax year, 75% of a REIT's assets must be invested in real property, either through ownership or by securities secured by real estate. A "partially qualified" asset is one that qualifies under the 90% test of being a passive investment in a security, but not under the 75% real estate test.

Qualified income That portion of income which is classified as interest, rents, or other gain from real property, as spelled out in the REIT tax laws.

Raw land Land which has not been developed or improved.

RCA See revolving credit agreement.

Real estate investment trust (REIT, pronounced "reet") A trust established for the benefit of a group of investors which is managed by one or more trustees who hold title to the assets for the trust and control its acquisitions and investments, at least 75% of which are real estate related. A major advantage of a REIT is that no federal income tax need be paid by the trust if certain qualifications are met. Congress enacted these special tax provisions to encourage an assembly method, which is essentially designed to provide for

investment in real estate what the mutual provided for investment in securities. The REIT provides the small investor with a means of combining his funds with those of others, and protects him from the double taxation that would be levied against an ordinary corporation or trust.

Revolving credit agreement (or "revolver") A formal credit agreement between a group of banks and a REIT, the terms of which are reviewed periodically when it is "rolled over" or "revolved" or refinanced by a similar agreement. For many trusts, "revolvers" have replaced informal lines of credit extended by individual banks to REITs, thereby providing a uniform (and usually restrictive) approach by all creditors, reassuring each bank that others in the RCA would not be paid off preferentially.

Registration statement The forms filed by a company with the Securities and Exchange Commission in connection with an offering of new securities or the listing of outstanding securities on a national exchange.

Reserves for loss See loan loss reserve.

Return of capital A distribution to shareholders in excess of the trust's earnings and profits, usually consisting of either depreciation or repayment of principal from properties or mortgages held by the trust. Each shareholder receiving such a distribution is required to reduce the tax basis of his shares by the amount of such distribution. For financial accounting purposes, what constitutes a return of capital may differ from that determined under Federal income tax requirements.

Return on equity A figure which consists of net income for the period divided by equity and which is normally expressed as a percentage.

Right of first refusal The right or option granted by a seller to a buyer, to have the first opportunity of acquiring a property.

Rights offering The privilege extended to a shareholder of subscribing to additional stock of the same or another class or to bonds, usually at a price below the market and in an amount proportional to the number of shares already held. Rights must be exercised within a time limit and often may be sold if the holder does not wish to purchase additional shares.

Sale-leaseback A common real estate transaction whereby the investor buys property from and simultaneously leases it back to the seller. This enables the previous owner (often a developer) to "cash out" on an older property while retaining control.
    Land   sale-leaseback—this   procedure,

made common by several REITs that specialize in the transaction, affects only the land under income—producing improvements (such as shopping centers, etc.)—leaving the depreciable improvements in the hands of those who might benefit from the tax consequences. Since the improvements were probably financed with the proceeds of a first mortgage which remains in effect, the rights of the new investor are made second, or junior, to those of the first mortgage holder. Hence the common phrase "subordinated land sale-leaseback." In return for accepting a less secure position, the new investor usually obtains an "overage" clause whereby additional rent is paid anytime gross income of the shopping center (or whatever) exceeds a pre-determined floor.

Seasoned issues Securities of large, established companies which have been known to the investment public for a period of years, covering good times and bad.

Second mortgages See junior mortage loan.

Secured mortgages See junior mortgage loan.

Secured debt For REITs, senior mortgage debt secured by specific properties. In case of default on "nonrecourse" debt, the lender may assume property ownership but may not pursue other assets of the lender.

Senior mortgage A mortgage which has first priority.

Senior unsecured debt Funds borrowed under open lines without security. Most bank lines to REITs were unsecured.

Shares of beneficial interest Tradable shares in a REIT. Analogous to common stock in a corporation.

Shareholders' equity Primarily money invested by shareholders through purchase of shares, plus the accumulation of that portion of net income that has been reinvested in the business since the commencement of operations.

Short-term mortgage A loan upon real estate for a term of three years or less, bearing interest payable periodically, with principal usually payable in full at maturity.

Sinking fund An arrangement under which a portion of a bond or preferred stock issue is retired periodically, in advance of its fixed maturity. The company may either purchase a stipulated quantity of the issue itself, or supply funds to a trustee or agent for that purpose. Retirement may be made by call at a fixed price, or by inviting tenders, or by purchase in the open market.

Sponsor The entity which initiated the formation of a REIT and usually acts (often via a subsidiary) as investment advisor to the trust thereafter. The sponsor puts the reputation of its institution on the line for the REIT and usually arranges lines of credit, provides support services and, occasionally, compensating balances.

Spread Difference between percentage return on an investment and cost of funds to support the investment.

Standby commitment See commitment, standby.

Standing loan Usually not amortized, the loan is secured by completed property that has not yet been refinanced with a "permanent" long-term mortgage.

Subordinated debt Debt which is junior to secured and unsecured senior debt, it may be convertible into shares of beneficial interest for REITs. Senior subordinated debt is senior to other subordinated debt.

Subordinated ground lease See sale-leaseback.

Swap program A procedure for reducing debt (by a troubled REIT) by trading an asset to the creditor in return for cancellation of part of a loan to the REIT. Often a cash premium payment is made in addition to reduction of the debt. The premium may then be distributed to the other creditors pro rata. The amount of the cash premium, or the ratio of cash-to-debt reduction to be applied against the value of the asset, is sometimes determined by a sealed-bid "auction" process as set forth in the "revolving credit agreement" between the creditors and the REIT. See RCA.

Syndicate A group of investors who transact business for a limited period of time and sometimes with a single purpose. It is a short-term partnership.

Take-out commitment See commitment.

Tax shelter The various aspects of an investment which offer relief from income taxes or opportunities to claim deductions from taxable income. Although tax shelters are an important facet of real estate investment, they do not have a direct influence on REIT investment choices because qualified trusts are exempt from income taxes.

Usury The charging of interest rates for the use of money higher than what's allowed by local law.

Warrants Stock purchase warrants or options give the holder rights to purchase shares of stock, generally running for a longer period of time than ordinary subscription rights given shareholders. Warrants are often attached to other securities, but they may be issued separately or detached after issuance.

Working capital Determined by subtracting current liabilities from current assets. It represents the amount available to carry on the day-to-day operation of the business.

Work-out When a borrower has problems, the process undertaken by the lender to help the borrower "work out" of the problems becomes known itself as a "work out." The presumption during a "work out" is that the borrower will eventually resume a more normal debtor's position once problems are solved within (presumably) a reasonably short time.

Wrap-around mortgage A type of junior mortgage used to refinance properties on which there is an existing first mortgage loan. The face amount of the wrap-around loan is equivalent to the unpaid balance on the existing mortgage plus cash advanced to the property owner upon funding. Such loans carry a higher interest rate than the existing mortgage. The wrap-around lender assumes the obligation to maintain payments of principal and interest on the existing mortgage so as to enhance his right to make claim from his secondary position.

Yield In the stock market, the rate of annual distribution or dividend expressed as a percentage of price. Current yield is found by dividing the market price into the distribution rate in dollars. In real estate, the term refers to the effective annual amount of income which is being accrued on an investment expressed as a percentage of its value.

Computer Services for Business and Finance

Selected On-Line Business/Financial Data Bases

On-line data bases are collections of computer stored data which are retrievable by remote terminals. The data bases are collected and organized by a so-called *producer*. The latter provides the data base to a *vendor* who distributes the data by means of a telecommunication network to the user. Often a vendor will offer a large number of different data bases. In some instances the producer and vendor are the same.

Using an on-line data base requires: (1) a *terminal* (a typewriter-like device usually equipped with a video display) to receive data and send commands to the vendor's computers, and (2) a *modem* for coupling the terminal to a telephone line. Printouts (hard copy) of the desired information can be obtained with the aid of electronic printers located at the user's terminal or, alternatively, ordered from the vendor.

The user accesses the data base by dialing a telephone number and then typing (on the terminal keyboard) a password provided by the vendor. Searching the data base is done with special commands and procedures peculiar to each base.

The contents of data bases vary. Some provide statistical data only—usually in the form of time series. Other bases provide bibliographic references and, in some instances, abstracts or the full text of articles.

Specifics concerning data base contents, instructions, and prices are available from vendors. Listed below are some major business data bases and vendors. More complete information concerning data bases is available from the sources given below.

ABI Inform
Provides references on all areas of business management with emphasis on "how-to" information.
Producer: Data Courier Inc. (Louisville, KY)
Vendors: BRS, DIALOG, SDC

Accountants Index
Contains reference information on accounting, auditing taxation, management and securities.
Producer: American Institute of Certified Public Accountants (New York, NY)
Vendors: SDC

American Profile
Provides statistical information on U.S. households including population, income, dependents, and also data on types of businesses in an area.
Producer: Donnelley Marketing (Stamford, CT)
Vendors: Business Information Service

Business Credit Service
Provides business credit and financial information.
Producer: TRW, Inc. (Orange, CA)
Vendors: TRW

Canadian Business and Current Affairs
English language business and popular periodicals
Producer: Micromedia Limited (Toronto, Ontario)
Vendor: DIALOG, CISTI

CIS Index
Contains references and abstracts from nearly every publication resulting from Senate and House Committee meetings since 1970.
Producer: Congressional Information Services, Inc. (Washington, DC)
Vendors: Dialog, SDC

Commodities
Contains over 41,000 times series of current commodity prices for the U.S., Canada, U.K., and France.
Producer: Wolff Research (London, U.K.)
Vendor: I. P. Sharp

Compendex (Computerized Engineering Index)
Contains over 1 million citations and abstracts to the world wide engineering literature.
Producer: Engineering Information Inc. (New York)
Vendor: BRS, D-STAR, DIALOG.

CompuServe, Inc.
Provides reference, statistical and full text retrieval of information of personal in-

terest including health, recipes, gardening, financial and investment data including the Compustat and Value Line data bases.

Producer: CompuServe, Inc. (Columbus, OH)

Vendor: CompuServe

Compustat

Provides very extensive financial data on companies.

Producer: Standard And Poor's Compustat Service, Inc. (Englewood, CO)

Vendors: ADP, Business Information Services, CompuServe, Data Resources, Chase Econometrics/Interactive Data Corp.

Disclosure II

Provides extracts of 10K and other reports filed with the Securities and Exchange Commission.

Producer: Disclosure Inc. (Bethesda, Maryland)

Vendors: Business Information Services (Control Data). Dialog, Dow Jones, New York Times Information Services, Mead Data Central.

Dow Jones News/Retrieval Service and Stock Quote Reporters

Contains text of articles appearing in major financial publications including the *Wall Street Journal* and *Barrons*. Quote Service provides quotes on stocks, bonds, mutual funds.

Producer: Dow Jones & Company (New York, NY)

Vendors: BRS, Dow Jones & Company

DRI Capsule/EEI Capsule

Provides over 3700 U.S. social and economic statistical time series such as population, income, money supply data, etc.

Producers: Data Resources, Inc. (Lexington, MA) and Evans Economics Inc. (Washington, DC)

Vendors: Business Information Services, United Telecom Group, I. P. Sharp

Federal Register Abstracts

Provides coverage of federal regulatory agencies as published in the Federal Register.

Producer: Capitol Services (Washington, DC)

Vendors: DIALOG, SDC

GTE Financial System One Quotation Service

Provides current U.S. and Canadian quotations and statistical data on stocks,

bonds, options, commodities and other market data.

Producer: GTE Information Systems (Reston, VA)

Vendor: GTE Information Systems, Inc.

The Information Bank

Provides an extensive current affairs data source consisting of abstracts from numerous English language publications.

Producer: The New York Times Information Service

Vendor: The New York Times Information Service

LEXIS

Contains full text references to a wide range of legal information including court decisions, regulations, government statutes.

Producer: Mead Data Central (New York, NY)

Vendor: Mead Data Central

Media General Financial Services

Provides extensive historical fundamental and technical data and calculations on U.S. publicly owned companies. Also provides data on industries, the financial markets, mutual funds and corporate bonds.

Producer: Media General Financial Services (Richmond, VA)

Vendors: Dow Jones News Retrieval, Dialog, Thomson Financial Networks, Randall—Helms Fiduciary Consultants, Telescan, Lotus One Source (CDROM)

NEXIS

Provides full text business and general news including management, technology, finance, science, politics, religion.

Producer: Mead Data Central (New York, NY)

Vendor: Mead Data Central

PTS Marketing and Advertising Reference Service

Provides citations with abstracts & articles on the marketing and advertising of consumer goods and services.

Producer: Predicast, Inc. (Cleveland, OH)

Vendors: DIALOG, BRS, DATA-STAR

PTS Prompt

Covers world wide business news on new products, market data, etc.

Producer: Predicast, Inc. (Cleveland, OH)

Vendors: ADP, BRS, DIALOG

Quick Quote
Provides current quotations, volume, high-low data for securities of U.S. public corporations.
Producer: CompuServe Inc.
Vendor: CompuServe

Quotron 800
Provides up to the minute quotation and statistics on a broad range of securities such as stocks, bonds, options, commodities.
Producer: Quotron Systems Inc. (Los Angeles, CA)
Vendor: Quotron Systems Inc.

The Source (has been acquired by CompuServe)
Producer: SourceTelecomputing(McLean, VA)
Vendor: Source Telecomputing Corp.

Trinet Company Data Base
Provides data on about 250,000 companies in the U.S.
Producer: Trinet, Inc. (Parsippany, NJ)
Vendors: DRI, DIALOG, Mead Data Central

Value Line II
Provides extensive financial data from the Value Line Investment Survey covering over 1600 major companies.
Producer: Arnold Bernhard & Co. (New York, NY)
Vendors: ADP Service, Chase Econometrics/Interactive Data Corp., CompuServe Data Resources, Inc.

For further information:

Computer Readable Data Bases, Gale Research (835 Penobscot Building, Detroit, MI 48226) A comprehensive data base and CD-ROM directory, revised annually.
Directory ONLINE Data Bases, Cuadra/Elsevier (655 Avenue of the Americas, New York, NY 10010). An annual comprehensive service.

Data Base Vendors

ADP Data Services, Inc.
175 Jackson Plaza
Ann Arbor, MI 48106
313-769-6800

BRS, Inc.
1200 Route 7
Latham, NY 12110
518-783-1161
800-833-4707

Chase Econometrics/Interactive Data Corporation
95 Hayden Avenue
Lexington, MA 02173
617-890-8100

CompuServe, Inc.
5000 Arlington Centre Boulevard
Columbus, OH 43220
614-457-8600
800-848-8990

Data Resources, Inc. (DRI)
1750 K Street NW
Washington, DC 20006
202-663-7720

DIALOG Information Services, Inc.
3460 Hillview Avenue
Palo Alto, CA 94304
415-858-3810
800-334-2564

Dow Jones & Company, Inc.
P.O. Box 300
Princeton, NJ 08540
609-452-2000
800-257-5114

General Electric Information Services Company
401 North Washington Street
Rockville, MD 20850
301-294-5405

GTE Education Services
8505 Freeport Parking
Irving, TX 75063
214-929-3000

Mead Data Central
P.O. Box 933
Dayton, OH 45401
800-227-4908

The New York Times Information Services, Inc.
229 West 43 Street
New York, NY 10036
800-543-6862

Quotron Systems, Inc.
12731 West Jefferson Boulevard
P.O. Box 66914
Los Angeles, CA 90066
213-827-4600

SDC Search Service/Orbit
8000 Westpark Drive
McLean, VA 22102
703-442-0900
800-456-7248

I. P. Sharp Associates
Exchange Tower
Toronto, Ontario, Canada M5X IE3
416-364-5361
800-387-1588

TRW Information Services Division
505 City Parkway West
Orange, CA 92668
714-385-7000

Noteworthy Software of Interest to Investors

The following provides a brief description of moderately priced software products of special interest to investors.

The EQUALIZER (Charles Schwab & Co., 101 Montgomery Street, San Francisco, CA 94104)

To use this software it is necessary to open an account with the discount brokerage firm of Charles Schwab & Co. The EQUALIZER includes the following features:

- access to financial information and data via Dow Jones News Retrieval and Standard and Poor's Marketscope
- price quotes on securities and mutual funds provided by Schwab, Dow Jones, or Warner Communications
- portfolio maintenance and record keeping
- trading capabilities (via Charles Schwab, of course)

This is excellent software for the active investor. The instruction manual which accompanies the software is first class.

QUICKEN 3.0 (Intuit, 66 Willow Place, Menlo Park, CA 04025)

This is a leading program for maintaining records and managing personal finances. QUICKEN permits users to record deposits, monitor investments, keep track of saving, and print out checks as they become due. The software can also be used for small business and bookkeeping.

A 'help' program is provided which facilitates start up. The instruction manual accompanying QUICKEN is excellent. Also available at bookstores are other manuals.

WEALTHBUILDER 1.1. (developed for *Money Magazine* by Reality Technologies, Inc., 3624 Market Street, Philadelphia, PA 19104) is a program intended to guide users on the development of investment strategies to meet their goals (home purchase, college education, retirement, etc.). Given the investor's financial goals, risk tolerance, net worth, and the like, the program provides an allocation of investments among equities, mutual funds, bonds, precious metals, and money market funds.

Information for allocating funds among each type of investment is available (for a price) on quarterly updated disks which contain data provided by Standard & Poor. CompuServe, the online data base, now provides a service for users of WEALTHBUILDERS.

The program is recommended for serious financial planning.

MANAGING YOUR MONEY 6.0 (MECA Ventures, Inc., 355 Riverside Avenue, Westport, CT 06801) is a popular personal financial program providing the following features:

- budget and checkbook program
- a tax estimator
- an estate and insurance planner
- a financial calculator
- a portfolio manager

In addition to the above the program has a built in name filing capability and a word processor.

QUANT IX (Quant Software, 5900 North Port Washington Road, Milwaukee, WI 53217) is an excellent and relatively inexpensive portfolio managtock analyzer with record keeping capability. The software also provides for downloading data from CompuServe and Warner Communications. A unique feature is the availability of six different methods for evaluating stocks.

OPTIONS TOOLS DELUX (Richard Kedrow, 25 Illinois Avenue, Schaumburg, IL 60913). This helpful software provides option investors with the capability of calculating theoretical option values using the Black-Scholes and binomial models, hedge ratios, volatility, breakeven values, and covered call analysis.

Future Employment Opportunities

Every other year, the Bureau of Labor Statistics develops projections of the labor force, economic growth, industry employment, and occupational employment under alternative assumptions. These projections, which usually cover a 10- to 15-year period, provide the framework for the discussion of the job outlook in each of the occupational statements in the *Handbook*. Each of the approximately 250 statements in this edition of the *Occupational Outlook Handbook* identifies the principal factors that affect job prospects and indicates how these factors are expected to affect the occupation in the future. This chapter uses the moderate alternative of each of the projections to provide a framework for the individual job outlook discussions.

Population Trends

Population trends affect employment opportunities in a number of ways. First of all, changes in the size and composition of the population influence the demand for goods and services—a growing and aging population has increased the demand for health services, for example. Equally important, population changes produce corresponding changes in the size and characteristics of the labor force.

The U.S. population is expected to grow more slowly over the next 12 years than it did during the previous 12-year period. However, even slow population growth will increase the demand for goods and services, causing greater demand for workers in many occupations and industries.

The age structure will shift toward relatively fewer children and youth and a growing proportion of middle-aged and older people well into the 21st century. Several things account for this. The decline in the proportion of children and youth reflects low birth rates that have prevailed for the past 20 years and that seem likely to continue; the impending large increase in the middle-aged population reflects the maturing of the "baby boom" generation born after World War II; and the very rapid growth in the number of old people is attributable to high birth rates prior to the Great Depression of the 1930's, together with strides in medical science that have made it possible for most Americans to survive into old age.

Minorities and immigrants will constitute a larger share of the U.S. population in 2000 than they do today. Substantial increases in the number of Hispanics, Asians, and blacks are anticipated, reflecting high birth rates in these population groups as well as net immigration. Substantial inflows of migrants, both documented and undocumented, are expected to continue. The arrival of immigrants from every corner of the world has significant implications for the labor force because immigrants tend to be of working age but of different educational and occupational backgrounds than the U.S. population as a whole.

Population growth varies greatly among geographic regions, which is reflected in differences in the demand for goods and services. Between 1980 and 1988, the population of the Midwest and the Northeast grew by only 1.7 percent and 3 percent, respectively, compared with 12.3 percent in the South and 17.4 percent in the West. These differences reflect the movement of people seeking new jobs or retiring as well as higher birth rates in some areas than in others.

Projections by the Bureau of the Census indicate that the West will continue to be the fastest growing region of the country, increasing about 17 percent between 1988 and the year 2000. In the South, the population is expected to increase about 15 percent. The number of people in the Midwest is expected to remain about the same, while the Northeast is projected to increase slightly, by about 2 percent.

Geographic shifts in the population alter the demand for and the supply of workers in local job markets. Moreover, many areas are dominated by one or two industries, and local job markets may be extremely sensitive to the economic fortunes of those industries. For these and other reasons, local employment opportunities may differ substantially from the projections for the Nation as a whole presented in the *Handbook*.

Labor Force Trends

Population is the single most important factor governing the size and composition of the labor force, which comprises people who are either working or looking for work. The civilian labor force totaled 121.7 million in

Source: *Occupational Outlook Handbook* 1990–1991, U.S. Department of Labor, Bureau of Labor Statistics.

1988 and is expected to reach 141.1 million in the year 2000. This projected increase—16 percent—represents a slowing in both the number added to the labor force and the rate of labor force growth, largely due to slower population growth (chart 1).

American workers will be an increasingly diverse group as we approach the year 2000: White non-Hispanic men will make up a smaller share of the labor force, and women and minority group members will make up a larger share. White non-Hispanics have historically been the largest component of the labor force, but their share has been dropping and is expected to fall to about 74 percent by 2000. Blacks, Hispanics, and Asian and other racial groups will account for roughly 33 percent of labor force entrants between 1988 and 2000.

Women will continue to join the labor force in growing numbers. In the past, much of the growth in the labor force has been due to dramatic increases in participation by women, who are expected to account for slightly over half of all entrants through the year 2000. Not only do most American women of working age hold jobs, they tend to continue working despite competing demands for their time. By 2000, 4 out of 5 women between the ages of 25 and 54 will be in the labor force, which then will be almost evenly divided in terms of its composition by sex. Women were only 41 percent of the labor force as recently as 1976; by 2000, they are expected to account for 47 percent.

The changing age structure of the population will directly affect tomorrow's labor

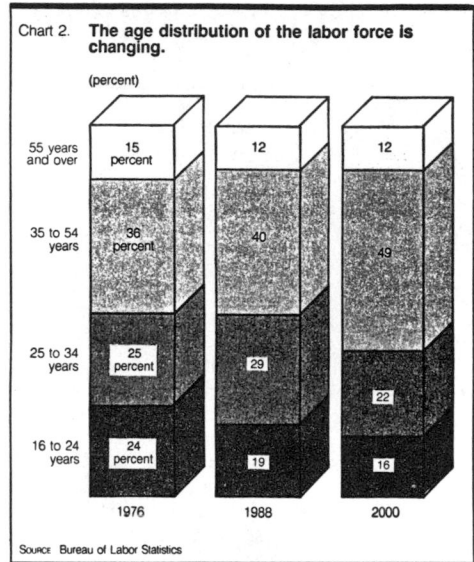

Chart 2. **The age distribution of the labor force is changing.**

(percent)

	1976	1988	2000
55 years and over	15 percent	12	12
35 to 54 years	36 percent	40	49
25 to 34 years	25 percent	29	22
16 to 24 years	24 percent	19	16

Source: Bureau of Labor Statistics

force. As the proportion of young workers declines, the pool of experienced workers will increase (chart 2).

The number of youths (16 to 24 years of age) in the population will drop until the children of the baby-boom generation enter the labor force during the 1990's. Among youths, the teenage labor force (16 to 19 years of age) will decline until 1992, then rise over the rest of the decade for a net increase of 800,000 over the 1988–2000 period. However, because the labor force 22 to 24 years of age is projected to decline until 1998, with only a slight recovery by 2000, the total size of the youth labor force should remain the same over the projection period and account for only 16 percent of the entire labor force at the end of the century, compared to 19 percent in 1988 and 24 percent in 1976. Thus colleges, the Armed Forces, eating and drinking places, and other establishments can expect to see a decrease in the population from which they draw students and young workers throughout most of the 1988–2000 period.

The scenario should be different for prime-age workers (25 to 54 years of age). These workers, many of whom were born during the baby-boom years, should account for 72 percent of the labor force in 2000, up from 69 percent in 1988 and 61 percent in 1976. Even more striking is the growing proportion of workers between the ages of 35 and 54. These workers should account for 49 percent of the labor force by the year 2000, a significant increase from 40 percent in 1988 and 36 percent in 1976. Because workers in their mid-thirties to mid-fifties usually have substantial work experience and tend to be more

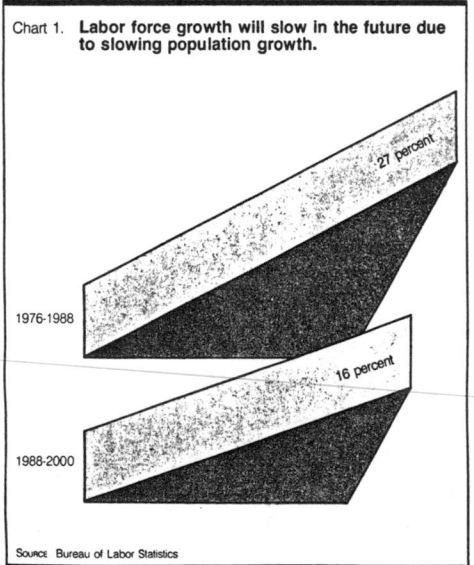

Chart 1. **Labor force growth will slow in the future due to slowing population growth.**

1976-1988

27 percent

1988-2000

16 percent

Source: Bureau of Labor Statistics

stable and reliable than younger workers, this could result in improved productivity and a greater pool of experienced applicants from which employers may choose.

Contrary to popular belief, the number of older workers (55 years and above) is expected to be only slightly higher in 2000 than in 1988 because the labor force participation of those in this age group is not expected to change appreciably. Older workers should make up 12 percent of the work force in 2000, the same as in 1988 and down from 15 percent in 1976.

In recent years, the educational attainment of the labor force has risen dramatically. Between 1976 and 1988, the proportion of the labor force age 18 to 64 with at least 1 year of college increased from 32 to 42 percent, while the proportion with 4 years of college or more increased from 16 to 22 percent (chart 3).

The emphasis on education will continue. Three out of the four fastest growing occupational groups will be the executive, administrative, and managerial; professional specialty; and technicians and related support occupations. These occupations generally require the highest levels of education and skill. In contrast, such factors as office and factory automation, changes in consumer demand, and substitution of imports for domestic products are expected to cause employment to stagnate or decline in many occupations that require little formal education—laborers, assemblers, and machine operators, for example. Opportunities for high school dropouts will be increasingly limited, and workers who cannot read and follow directions may not even be considered for most jobs.

Employment Change

Employment is expected to increase from 118.1 million in 1988 to 136.2 million in 2000, or 15 percent. This is only about half the rate of increase recorded during the previous 12-year period.

The 18.1 million jobs that will be added to the U.S. economy by 2000 will not be evenly distributed across major industry and occupational groups, which means that the structure of employment will change. The following two sections look at projected employment change from both the industry and occupational perspectives.

Industrial Profile

The shift from goods-producing to service-producing employment is very well known and not at all recent. (See chart 4.) By 2000, nearly 4 out of 5 jobs will be in industries that provide services. Expansion of service sector employment is linked to a number of different factors, including changes in consumer tastes and preferences, legal and regulatory changes, advances in science and technology, and changes in the way businesses are organized and managed. Factors responsi-

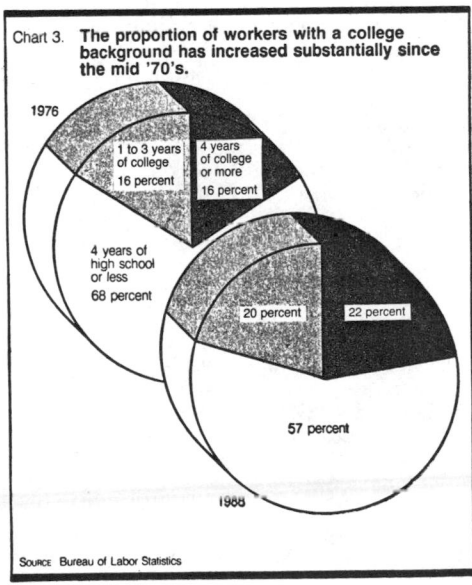

Chart 3. The proportion of workers with a college background has increased substantially since the mid '70's.

1976

1 to 3 years of college 16 percent

4 years of college or more 16 percent

4 years of high school or less 68 percent

20 percent   22 percent

57 percent

1988

Source: Bureau of Labor Statistics

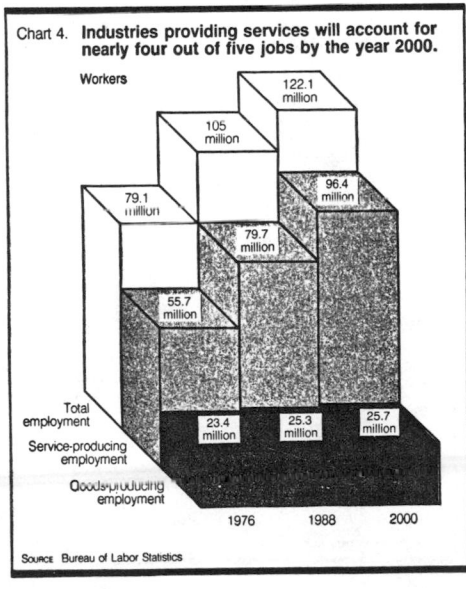

Chart 4. Industries providing services will account for nearly four out of five jobs by the year 2000.

Workers

122.1 million

105 million

79.1 million

96.4 million

79.7 million

55.7 million

Total employment

Service-producing employment

Goods-producing employment

23.4 million   25.3 million   25.7 million

1976   1988   2000

Source: Bureau of Labor Statistics

ble for varying growth prospects in major industry divisions are noted below.

Service-Producing Industries. *Services.* Services is both the largest and the fastest growing industry division within the service-producing sector (chart 5.) This division provided 34.5 million jobs in 1988; employment is expected to rise 28 percent to 44.2 million by 2000, accounting for almost one-half of all new jobs. Jobs will be found in small firms as well as in large corporations, in all levels of government, and in industries as diverse as banking, hospitals, data processing, and management consulting. The two largest industry groups in this division, health services and business services, are projected to continue to grow very fast, and educational services, which has been growing slowly, is projected to have average growth.

Health care will continue to be one of the most important groups of industries in the economy in terms of job creation. Employment in the health services industries is projected to grow from 8.2 to 11.3 million. New technology and a growing and aging population will increase the demand for health services. Because of the rapid expansion of health care employment, 7 of the 10 fastest growing occupations between 1988 and 2000 will be health related. Not all of the health industries will grow at the same rate; outpatient care facilities and offices of "other health practitioners," which includes chiropractors, optometrists, psychologists, and other practitioners will be increasing the fastest. Hospitals, both private and public, will be growing more slowly than all the other health indus-

tries, but faster than the average for all industries. Nonetheless, hospitals will continue to employ the most workers among the health care industries.

Another important industry group that is expected to generate many jobs is business services. These industries employed 5.6 million workers in 1988 and are projected to employ 8.3 million in the year 2000. Personnel supply services, which includes temporary help agencies, is the largest industry in this group and will add the most new jobs. Business services also includes the fastest growing industry in the economy—computer and data processing services. This industry is expected to grow five times faster than the average for all industries, due to a rapidly increasing demand from business firms, government agencies, and individuals. A third industry in business services—research, management, and consulting—is expected to have very rapid growth, although not as rapid as computer and personnel supply services.

Education, in both the private and public sectors, is expected to add 1.2 million jobs to the 8.9 million employed in 1988. The increase reflects rising enrollments projected for elementary and secondary schools. The elementary school age population (ages 5–13) will rise by over 2 million between 1988 and 2000, and the secondary school age (14–17) by 1.3 million. On the other hand, the traditional college age population (18–24) has been declining and is projected to continue to decline for the next decade; however, rising enrollments of older students, women, foreign students, and part-time students have offset the absolute decline in the 18–24 population. Not all the increase in employment in education will be for teachers; teacher aides, counselors, technicians, and administrative staff are also projected to increase.

Retail trade. Nearly 3.8 million jobs will be added to retail trade, which will provide 22.9 million jobs in 2000, up 20 percent from the 1988 level. Eating and drinking places will employ the most workers in the retail trade division and also will be among the fastest growing industries. Substantial increases in retail employment are also anticipated in grocery stores, department stores, and miscellaneous shopping goods stores.

Government. Between 1988 and 2000, government employment, excluding public education and public hospitals, is expected to increase 7 percent, from 9 million to 9.6 million jobs. Most of the growth will be in State and local government; the Federal Government is expected to add only 88,000 jobs.

Finance, insurance, and real estate. Employment is expected to increase 16 percent—adding 1.1 million jobs to the 1988 level of 6.7 million. The fastest growing in-

Chart 5. **Some industries will grow more rapidly than others.**

Percent change in employment, 1988-2000

Source: Bureau of Labor Statistics

dustry within this division is expected to be security and commodity brokers and exchanges, although it will not be growing as fast as in the past.

Wholesale trade. Employment in wholesale trade is expected to rise from 6 million to 6.9 million between 1988 and 2000, an increase of 15 percent.

Transportation, communications, and public utilities. Overall employment in this division is expected to rise 10 percent from the 1988 level of 5.5 million. The three fastest growing industries in this division are arrangement of transportation, freight forwarding, and air carriers, each growing at least three times as fast as the division as a whole. Only modest employment growth is expected in the communications industry. Although output will show an increase, new laborsaving technology will result in very little job growth.

Goods-Producing Industries. Employment in this sector peaked in the late 1970's and has not recovered from the recessionary period of the early 1980's and the trade imbalances that began in the mid-1980's. Although overall employment in goods-producing industries is expected to show little change, growth prospects within the sector vary considerably.

Construction. Construction is expected to add 760,000 jobs between 1988 and 2000. Construction employment is expected to increase by 15 percent, from 5.1 to 5.9 million jobs, in response to economic conditions and demographic trends.

Manufacturing. Manufacturing employment is expected to decline 2 percent from the 1988 level of 19.4 million. The projected loss of manufacturing jobs reflects productivity gains achieved from increased investment in manufacturing technologies as well as a winnowing out of less efficient operations.

The composition of manufacturing employment is expected to shift since most of the jobs that will disappear are production jobs. The number of professional, technical, and managerial positions in manufacturing firms will actually increase.

Mining. Mining employment is expected to remain at about the present level of 700,000. Underlying this projection is the assumption that domestic oil production will drop and oil imports will rise sharply.

Agriculture. Employment in agriculture has been declining for many decades and this trend is expected to continue—the number of jobs is projected to decline 4 percent, from 3.3 million to 3.1 million.

The decline in agricultural jobs reflects a decrease of 225,000 in the number of self-employed workers. Wage and salary positions are projected to increase by 91,000—with especially strong growth in the agricultural services industry.

Occupational Profile

Continued expansion of the service-producing sector conjures up an image of a work force dominated by cashiers, retail sales workers, and waiters. However, although service sector growth will generate millions of clerical, sales, and service jobs, it will also create jobs for financial managers, engineers, nurses, electrical and electronics technicians, and many other managerial, professional, and technical workers. In fact, the fastest growing occupations will be those that require the most educational preparation.

This section furnishes an overview of projected employment in 12 categories or "clusters" of occupations based on the Standard Occupational Classification (SOC). The SOC is used by all Federal agencies that collect occupational employment data, and is the organizational framework for grouping statements in the *Handbook*.

In the discussion that follows, projected employment change is described as faster, slower, or the same as the average for all occupations. (These phrases are explained on page 651.) While occupations that are growing fast generally offer good opportunities, the numerical change in employment also is important because large occupations, such as retail sales worker, may offer many more new jobs than a small, fast-growing occupation, such as paralegal (chart 6).

Technicians and related support occupations. Workers in this group provide technical assistance to engineers, scientists, and other professional workers as well as operate and program technical equipment. Employment in this cluster is expected to increase 32 percent, from 3.9 to 5.1 million, making it the fastest growing in the economy (chart 7). It also contains the fastest growing occupation—paralegals. Employment of paralegals is expected to skyrocket due to increased utilization of these workers in the rapidly expanding legal services industry.

Professional specialty occupations. Employment in this cluster is expected to grow 24 percent, from 14.6 to 18.1 million jobs. Much of this growth is a result of rising demand for engineers; computer specialists; lawyers; health diagnosing and treating occupations; and preschool and elementary and secondary school teachers.

Service occupations. This group includes a wide range of workers in protective services, food and beverage preparation, and cleaning and personal services. These occupa-

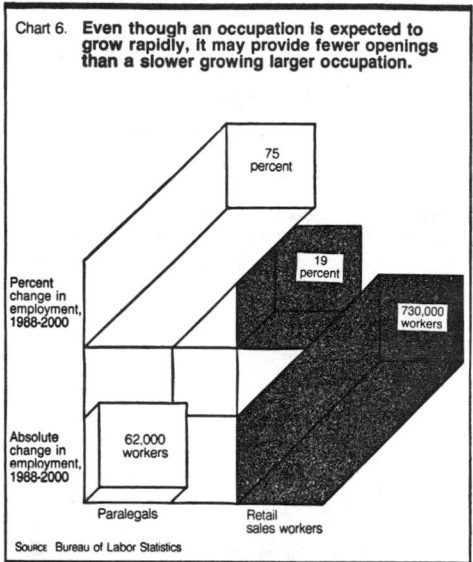

Chart 6. **Even though an occupation is expected to grow rapidly, it may provide fewer openings than a slower growing larger occupation.**

Percent change in employment, 1988-2000

75 percent

19 percent

730,000 workers

Absolute change in employment, 1988-2000

62,000 workers

Paralegals

Retail sales workers

Source: Bureau of Labor Statistics

tions are expected to grow 23 percent, from 18.5 to 22.7 million, because a growing population and economy, combined with higher incomes and increased leisure time, will spur demand for all types of services.

Executive, administrative, and managerial occupations. Employment in this cluster is expected to increase 22 percent, from 12.1 to 14.8 million. Growth will be spurred by the increasing complexity of business operations and by large employment gains in trade and services—industries that employ a higher than average proportion of managers.

Employment in management-related oc-

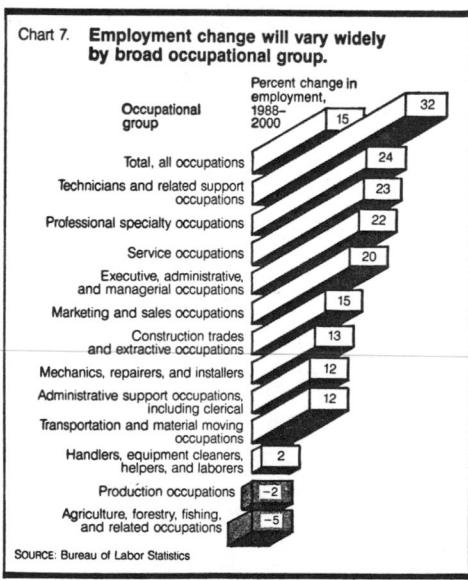

Chart 7. **Employment change will vary widely by broad occupational group.**

Percent change in employment, 1988-2000

Occupational group

Total, all occupations — 15

Technicians and related support occupations — 32

Professional specialty occupations — 24

Service occupations — 23

Executive, administrative, and managerial occupations — 22

Marketing and sales occupations — 20

Construction trades and extractive occupations — 15

Mechanics, repairers, and installers — 13

Administrative support occupations, including clerical — 12

Transportation and material moving occupations — 12

Handlers, equipment cleaners, helpers, and laborers — 2

Production occupations — -2

Agriculture, forestry, fishing, and related occupations — -5

Source: Bureau of Labor Statistics

cupations tends to be tied to industry growth. Thus jobs for employment interviewers are projected to grow much faster than the average, in line with the expected growth in the personnel supply industry.

Hiring requirements in many managerial and administrative jobs are rising. Work experience, specialized training, or graduate study will be increasingly necessary. Familiarity with computers is a "must" in a growing number of firms, due to the widespread use of computerized management information systems.

Marketing and sales occupations. Employment in this large cluster is projected to increase 20 percent, from 13.3 to 15.9 million jobs. Demand for real estate brokers, travel agents, and securities and financial services sales workers is expected to grow much faster than the average due to strong growth in the industries that employ them. Many part- and full-time job openings are expected for retail sales workers and cashiers due to the large size, high turnover, and faster than average employment growth in these occupations. The outlook for higher paying sales jobs, however, will tend to be more competitive.

Construction trades and extractive occupations. Overall employment in this group of occupations is expected to rise from 4.0 to 4.7 million, or 16 percent. Virtually all of the new jobs will be in construction. Employment growth in construction will be spurred by new projects and alterations to existing structures. On the other hand, continued stagnation in the oil and gas industries and low growth in demand for coal, metal, and other materials will result in little change in the employment of extractive workers.

Mechanics, installers, and repairers. These workers adjust, maintain, and repair automobiles, industrial equipment, computers, and many other types of equipment. Overall employment in these occupations is expected to grow 13 percent—from 4.8 to 5.5 million—due to increased use of mechanical and electronic equipment. One of the fastest growing occupations in this group is expected to be automotive body repairers, reflecting the growth in the number of lightweight cars that are prone to collision damage. Telephone installers and repairers, in sharp contrast, are expected to record a decline in employment due to laborsaving advances.

Administrative support occupations, including clerical is the largest major occupational group. Workers in these occupations perform the wide variety of tasks necessary to keep organizations functioning smoothly. The group as a whole is expected to grow 12 percent, from 21.1 to 23.6 million jobs. However, technological advances are projected to decrease the demand for stenographers and typists, word processors, and data entry keyers. Others, such as receptionists and information clerks, will grow much faster than the average, spurred by rapidly expanding industries such as business services. Moreover, because of their large size and substantial turnover, clerical occupations will offer abundant opportunities for qualified jobseekers in the years ahead.

Transportation and material moving occupations. Workers in this cluster operate the equipment used to move people and equipment. Employment in this group is expected to increase 12 percent, from 4.6 to 5.2 million jobs. Employment of busdrivers and truckdrivers will grow as fast as the average, while employment of material moving equipment operators is expected to grow more slowly due to greater use of automated materials handling equipment in factories and warehouses. Railroad transportation workers and water transportation workers are projected to show a decline in employment.

Production occupations. Workers in these occupations set up, install, adjust, operate, and tend machinery and equipment and use handtools and hand-held power tools to fabricate and assemble products. Employment is expected to decline 2 percent, from 12.8 to 12.5 million. More efficient production techniques—such as computer-aided manufacturing and industrial robotics—will eliminate some production worker jobs. Many production occupations are sensitive to fluctuations in the business cycle and competition from imports.

Handlers, equipment cleaners, helpers, and laborers. Workers in this group assist skilled workers and perform routine, unskilled tasks. Employment is expected to increase only about 2 percent, from 4.9 to 5.0 million jobs as routine tasks are automated.

Agriculture, forestry, and fishing occupations. Workers in these occupations cultivate plants, breed and raise animals, and catch fish. Although demand for food, fiber, and wood is expected to increase as the world's population grows, the use of more productive farming and forestry methods and the consolidation of smaller farms are expected to result in a 5 percent decline in employment, from 3.5 to 3.3 million jobs.

Replacement Needs

Most jobs through the year 2000 will become available as a result of replacement needs. Thus, even occupations with little or no employment growth or slower than average employment growth may still offer many job openings.

Replacement openings occur as people leave occupations. Some transfer to other occupations as a step up the career ladder or to change careers. Others stop working in order to return to school, to assume household responsibilities, or to retire.

The number of replacement openings and the proportion of job openings made up by replacement needs varies by occupation. Occupations with the most replacement openings generally are large, with low pay and status, low training requirements, and a high proportion of young and part-time workers. Some examples include cashiers, waiters and waitresses, and childcare workers.

The occupations with relatively few replacement openings, on the other hand, are those with high pay and status, lengthy training requirements, and a high proportion of prime working age, full-time workers. Among these occupations are education administrators, lawyers, and tool and die makers. Workers in these occupations generally have spent several years acquiring training that often is not applicable to other occupations.

Key Phrases in the *Handbook*

Changing employment between 1988 and 2000

If the statement reads . . .	Employment
Grow much faster than the average	Increase 31 percent or more
Grow faster than the average	Increase 20 to 30 percent
Grow about as fast as the average	Increase 11 to 19 percent
Grow more slowly than the average	Increase 4 to 10 percent
Show little change	Increase or decrease 3 percent or less
Decline	Decrease 4 percent or more

Opportunities and competition for jobs

If the statement reads . . .	Job openings compared to jobseekers may be . . .
Excellent opportunities	Much more numerous
Very good opportunities	More numerous
Good or favorable opportunities	About the same
May face competition	Fewer
May face keen competition	Much fewer

Interested in More Detail?

Readers interested in more information about projections and detail on the labor force, economic growth, industry and occupational employment, or methods and assumptions should consult the November 1989 *Monthly Labor Review* or *Outlook 2000*, BLS Bulletin 2352. Information on the limitations inherent in economic projections also can be found in either of these two publications. Additional occupational data as well as statistics on educational and training completions can be found in the 1990 edition of *Occupational Projections and Training Data*, BLS Bulletin 2351.

Displaced workers who lost full-time wage and salary jobs and were reemployed in January 1988, by industry of lost job and characteristics of new job

[Numbers in thousands]

Industry	Total employed, January 1988[2]	Full-time wage and salary job						Part-time job	Self-employed or other full-time job
		Total	Total reporting earnings	Earnings on new job relative to lost job					
				20 percent or more below	Below, but within 20 percent	Equal or above, within 20 percent	20 percent or more above		
Total who lost full-time wage and salary jobs[1]	3,106	2,574	2,368	30.4	13.5	28.0	28.0	302	230
Construction	270	220	205	29.8	11.2	35.6	23.4	20	29
Manufacturing	1,236	1,077	995	28.7	15.9	29.0	26.3	76	82
Durable goods	854	751	687	30.6	15.6	30.6	23.3	48	55
Primary metal industries	91	74	63	50.8	12.7	7.9	28.6	15	3
Steel[3]	67	52	43	48.8	9.3	9.3	32.6	13	2
Other primary metals	24	21	18	61.1	16.7	5.6	16.7	2	1
Fabricated metal products	105	96	97	43.3	7.2	21.6	27.8	3	6
Machinery except electrical	231	200	181	21.0	22.7	35.9	20.4	10	22
Electrical machinery	138	117	110	15.5	14.5	45.5	24.5	10	11
Transportation equipment	125	120	112	41.1	15.2	25.9	17.9	5	—
Automobiles	61	60	52	38.5	11.5	36.5	13.5	2	—
Other transportation equipment	64	60	59	44.1	18.6	16.9	20.3	3	—
Nondurable goods	382	326	307	24.8	16.6	25.7	32.9	28	27
Transportation and public utilities	214	178	156	41.7	7.7	30.1	20.5	26	10
Wholesale and retail trade	591	479	435	34.9	12.6	21.6	30.8	83	29
Finance insurance and real estate	185	146	130	23.1	11.5	27.7	37.7	25	14
Services................................	415	316	292	21.2	13.4	28.8	36.6	59	40
Professional services	204	156	145	22.8	14.5	33.1	29.7	29	19
Other	211	160	149	19.5	12.8	24.8	43.0	30	21
Public administration	18	13	14	0.0	28.6	42.9	28.6	4	1
Other industries	177	144	140	45.0	10.0	24.3	20.7	8	25

[1] Data refer to persons with tenure of 3 years or more who lost or left a job between January 1983 and January 1988 because of plant closings or moves, slack work, or the abolishment of their positions or shifts.

[2] Includes 206,000 persons who did not report earnings on lost job. Also includes a small number who did not report industry.

[3] Includes blast furnaces, steelworks, rolling and finishing mills, and iron and steel foundries.

Source: *Monthly Labor Review*, U.S. Department of Labor, Bureau of Labor Statistics.

Median weekly earnings on lost job and new job for reemployed workers who were displaced between January 1983 and 1988

Industry	Number reemployed (thousands)	Median weekly earnings[1]	
		Lost job	Job held January 1988
Total, workers 20 years and over[2]	3,310	$380	$327
Nonagricultural private wage and salary	3,175	392	328
Mining	148	506	363
Construction	276	438	410
Manufacturing	1,247	385	336
Durable goods	861	415	354
Primary metal industries	91	469	405
Fabricated metal products	105	401	311
Machinery, except electrical	237	466	422
Electrical machinery	140	403	339
Transportation equipment	122	408	348
Nondurable goods	386	314	295
Food and kindred	93	342	289
Apparel and other finished textiles	89	208	214
Transportation and public utilities	214	479	332
Transportation	165	458	309
Wholesale and retail trade	683	293	273
Wholesale trade	184	420	383
Retail trade	498	253	250
Finance, insurance, and real estate	195	405	349
Services	412	319	321
Professional services	181	339	342
Other	231	282	308
Government	98	278	338

[1] Median earnings figures shown are based on data from the 3.1 million persons who reported earnings on their lost job.

[2] Data refer to persons with tenure of 3 years or more who lost or left a job between January 1983 and January 1988 because of plant closings or moves, slack work, or the abolishment of their positions or shifts. Total includes a small number of workers who did not report industry or class of worker.

Source: *Monthly Labor Review*, U.S. Department of Labor, Bureau of Labor Statistics.

U.S. Demographics

PERCENT DISTRIBUTION OF THE POPULATION, BY AGE: 1960 to 2080*

(As of July 1. Includes Armed Forces overseas)

Year	Total	Age (years)									
		Under 5	5-13	14-17	18-24	25-34	35-44	45-64	65 and over	85 and over	100 and over
Estimates											
1960	100.0	11.3	18.2	6.2	8.9	12.7	13.4	20.0	9.2	0.5	-
1965	100.0	10.2	18.4	7.3	10.4	11.6	12.6	20.0	9.5	0.6	-
1970	100.0	8.4	17.9	7.8	12.1	12.3	11.3	20.5	9.8	0.7	-
1975	100.0	7.5	15.7	7.9	13.0	14.6	10.6	20.3	10.5	0.8	-
1980	100.0	7.2	13.7	7.1	13.3	16.5	11.4	19.5	11.3	1.0	-
1985	100.0	7.5	12.6	6.2	12.0	17.7	13.3	18.8	11.9	1.1	-
1987	100.0	7.5	12.6	5.9	11.2	17.8	14.1	18.6	12.2	1.2	-
Projections											
Lowest series:											
1990	100.0	7.2	13.0	5.3	10.4	17.5	15.2	18.8	12.7	1.3	-
1995	100.0	6.4	13.0	5.6	9.3	15.7	16.4	20.5	13.1	1.5	-
2000	100.0	5.7	12.1	5.8	9.5	13.9	16.6	23.3	13.1	1.7	-
2005	100.0	5.4	10.9	5.6	10.0	13.2	15.0	25.7	13.2	1.8	-
2010	100.0	5.2	10.1	5.0	9.7	13.7	13.4	28.9	14.1	2.0	0.1
2020	100.0	4.9	9.6	4.4	8.1	13.5	13.4	27.8	18.2	2.0	0.1
2030	100.0	4.4	9.0	4.4	7.9	11.9	13.6	25.9	22.9	2.4	0.1
2040	100.0	4.3	8.5	4.1	7.7	11.9	12.3	27.3	23.9	3.7	0.1
2050	100.0	4.2	8.4	4.0	7.3	11.7	12.5	26.9	24.9	4.7	0.2
2080	100.0	4.1	8.1	3.9	7.2	11.3	12.3	26.3	26.8	5.3	0.2

Middle series:

Year	Total										
1990	100.0	7.4	12.9	5.3	10.4	17.5	15.1	18.7	12.6	1.3	-
1995	100.0	6.8	13.0	5.6	9.3	15.7	16.3	20.2	13.0	1.5	-
2000	100.0	6.3	12.5	5.7	9.4	13.8	16.4	22.9	13.0	1.7	-
2005	100.0	6.0	11.6	5.6	9.8	13.1	14.9	25.9	13.2	1.9	-
2010	100.0	6.0	11.0	5.2	9.6	13.3	13.2	27.8	13.9	2.2	0.1
2020	100.0	5.8	10.8	4.8	8.5	13.3	12.8	26.4	17.7	2.3	0.1
2030	100.0	5.4	10.4	4.8	8.4	12.1	13.0	24.0	21.8	2.7	0.1
2040	100.0	5.4	10.0	4.7	8.4	12.3	12.1	24.6	22.6	4.1	0.1
2050	100.0	5.3	10.0	4.6	8.1	12.3	12.4	24.4	22.9	5.1	0.3
2080	100.0	5.1	9.7	4.5	8.0	11.9	12.2	24.1	24.5	5.8	0.5

Highest series:

Year	Total										
1990	100.0	7.5	12.9	5.3	10.5	17.5	15.1	18.6	12.6	1.3	-
1995	100.0	7.4	13.1	5.5	9.3	15.7	16.1	20.0	12.9	1.5	-
2000	100.0	7.0	13.0	5.6	9.3	13.8	16.0	22.3	13.0	1.8	-
2005	100.0	6.9	12.5	5.7	9.5	12.9	14.5	25.0	13.2	2.0	0.1
2010	100.0	6.9	12.1	5.4	9.6	12.9	12.7	26.4	13.9	2.3	0.1
2020	100.0	7.0	12.2	5.2	8.9	13.0	11.9	24.4	17.3	2.6	0.2
2030	100.0	6.7	12.1	5.4	9.0	12.3	12.2	21.5	20.8	3.1	0.2
2040	100.0	6.7	11.9	5.3	9.1	12.6	11.6	21.4	21.3	4.6	0.3
2050	100.0	6.7	12.0	5.2	8.9	12.7	11.9	21.3	21.1	5.8	0.6
2080	100.0	6.5	11.6	5.1	8.8	12.3	11.7	21.3	22.7	6.8	1.2

- Represents zero.

*For assumptions concerning lowest, middle, and highest series see publication referenced below.
Source: *Projections of the Population of the United States by Age, Sex, and Race: 1988 to 2080* by Gregory Spencer, U.S. Bureau of the Census, Current Population Reports, Series P-25, No. 1018.

TOTAL POPULATION—ANNUAL PROJECTIONS AND COMPONENTS OF CHANGE, FOR THE UNITED STATES: 1988 to 2080

[Numbers in thousands. Includes Armed Forces overseas]

Calendar year	Rate per 1,000 mid-year population						Population change during calendar year					
	July 1 population	Net change	Natural increase	Births	Deaths	Net immigration	January 1 population	Net change	Natural increase	Births	Deaths	Net immigration
1988	246,048	9.0	6.6	15.3	8.7	2.4	244,938	2,212	1,617	3,758	2,141	595
1989	248,251	8.8	6.4	15.1	8.7	2.4	247,150	2,181	1,596	3,757	2,161	585
1990	250,410	8.5	6.2	14.9	8.7	2.3	249,331	2,126	1,551	3,731	2,180	575
1991	252,502	8.1	5.9	14.6	8.7	2.2	251,456	2,056	1,491	3,690	2,200	565
1992	254,521	7.8	5.6	14.3	8.7	2.2	253,512	1,982	1,427	3,646	2,219	555
1993	256,466	7.4	5.3	14.0	8.7	2.1	255,493	1,908	1,363	3,601	2,238	545
1994	258,338	7.1	5.0	13.8	8.7	2.1	257,402	1,836	1,301	3,558	2,256	535
1995	260,138	6.8	4.8	13.5	8.7	2.0	259,238	1,767	1,242	3,517	2,275	525
1996	261,872	6.5	4.5	13.3	8.8	2.0	261,005	1,702	1,187	3,481	2,293	515
1997	263,543	6.2	4.3	13.1	8.8	1.9	262,707	1,643	1,138	3,449	2,312	505
1998	265,157	6.0	4.1	12.9	8.8	1.9	264,350	1,593	1,093	3,424	2,330	500
1999	266,730	5.8	4.0	12.8	8.8	1.9	265,943	1,555	1,055	3,404	2,349	500
2000	268,266	5.7	3.8	12.6	8.8	1.9	267,498	1,522	1,022	3,389	2,367	500
2001	269,773	5.5	3.7	12.5	8.8	1.9	269,020	1,494	994	3,380	2,386	500
2002	271,254	5.4	3.6	12.4	8.9	1.8	270,514	1,472	972	3,376	2,405	500
2003	272,716	5.3	3.5	12.4	8.9	1.8	271,985	1,455	955	3,379	2,423	500
2004	274,165	5.3	3.4	12.4	8.9	1.8	273,440	1,444	944	3,386	2,442	500
2005	275,604	5.2	3.4	12.3	8.9	1.8	274,884	1,433	933	3,399	2,465	500
2006	277,031	5.1	3.3	12.3	9.0	1.8	276,318	1,418	918	3,414	2,496	500
2007	278,441	5.0	3.2	12.3	9.1	1.8	277,736	1,402	902	3,432	2,530	500
2008	279,835	5.0	3.2	12.3	9.1	1.8	279,138	1,386	886	3,451	2,564	500
2009	281,213	4.9	3.1	12.3	9.2	1.8	280,524	1,370	870	3,469	2,599	500
2010	282,575	4.8	3.0	12.3	9.3	1.8	281,894	1,351	851	3,485	2,634	500
2011	283,916	4.7	2.9	12.3	9.4	1.8	283,245	1,329	829	3,499	2,669	500
2012	285,233	4.6	2.8	12.3	9.5	1.8	284,574	1,303	803	3,508	2,705	500
2013	286,522	4.4	2.7	12.3	9.6	1.7	285,878	1,273	773	3,514	2,741	500
2014	287,778	4.3	2.6	12.2	9.7	1.7	287,150	1,237	737	3,516	2,778	500
2015	288,997	4.1	2.4	12.2	9.7	1.7	288,388	1,197	697	3,513	2,816	500
2016	290,173	4.0	2.2	12.1	9.8	1.7	289,585	1,152	652	3,506	2,854	500
2017	291,302	3.8	2.1	12.0	9.9	1.7	290,737	1,103	603	3,496	2,893	500
2018	292,379	3.6	1.9	11.9	10.0	1.7	291,840	1,049	549	3,482	2,933	500
2019	293,401	3.4	1.7	11.8	10.1	1.7	292,890	993	493	3,466	2,973	500
2020	294,364	3.2	1.5	11.7	10.2	1.7	293,882	933	433	3,448	3,015	500
2021	295,267	3.0	1.3	11.6	10.4	1.7	294,815	872	372	3,429	3,057	500
2022	296,107	2.7	1.0	11.5	10.5	1.7	295,687	809	309	3,410	3,101	500
2023	296,885	2.5	.8	11.4	10.6	1.7	296,496	746	246	3,391	3,145	500

Year												
2024	297,600	2.3	.6	11.3	10.7	1.7	297,242	683	183	3,373	3,190	500
2025	298,252	2.1	.4	11.3	10.8	1.7	297,926	622	122	3,357	3,235	500
2026	298,843	1.9	.2	11.2	11.0	1.7	298,547	561	61	3,343	3,282	500
2027	299,374	1.7	.0	11.1	11.1	1.7	299,109	502	2	3,331	3,329	500
2028	299,848	1.5	-.2	11.1	11.3	1.7	299,611	445	-54	3,322	3,376	500
2029	300,265	1.3	-.4	11.0	11.4	1.7	300,056	391	-108	3,315	3,424	500
2030	300,629	1.3	-.5	11.0	11.5	1.7	300,447	338	-161	3,310	3,472	500
2031	300,942	1.0	-.7	11.0	11.7	1.7	300,785	288	-211	3,307	3,519	500
2032	301,205	.8	-.8	11.0	11.8	1.7	301,073	240	-259	3,306	3,565	500
2033	301,422	.6	-1.0	11.0	12.0	1.7	301,314	195	-304	3,306	3,611	500
2034	301,595	.5	-1.2	11.0	12.1	1.7	301,509	152	-347	3,306	3,655	500
2035	301,725	.4	-1.3	11.0	12.3	1.7	301,660	110	-389	3,308	3,698	500
2036	—	.2	-1.4	11.0	12.4	1.7	301,770	71	-428	3,309	3,738	500
2037	301,815	.1	-1.5	11.0	12.5	1.7	301,841	33	-466	3,310	3,777	500
2038	301,867	.0	-1.7	11.0	12.6	1.7	301,874	-2	-502	3,310	3,813	500
2039	301,861	-.1	-1.8	11.0	12.7	1.7	301,871	-36	-536	3,309	3,847	500
2040	301,807	-.2	-1.9	11.0	12.8	1.7	301,834	-69	-569	3,307	3,877	500
2041	301,721	-.3	-2.0	10.9	12.9	1.7	301,764	-99	-599	3,303	3,904	500
2042	301,606	-.4	-2.1	10.9	13.0	1.7	301,664	-128	-628	3,298	3,927	500
2043	301,463	-.5	-2.2	10.9	13.1	1.7	301,535	-155	-655	3,291	3,947	500
2044	301,294	-.6	-2.3	10.9	13.2	1.7	301,378	-180	-680	3,283	3,964	500
2045	301,100	-.7	-2.3	10.9	13.2	1.7	301,197	-203	-703	3,274	3,978	500
2046	300,885	-.7	-2.4	10.8	13.3	1.7	300,993	-224	-724	3,263	3,988	500
2047	300,651	-.8	-2.5	10.8	13.3	1.7	300,768	-243	-743	3,252	3,995	500
2048	300,398	-.9	-2.5	10.8	13.3	1.7	300,524	-260	-760	3,240	4,000	500
2049	300,130	-.9	-2.6	10.8	13.3	1.7	300,264	-274	-774	3,227	4,002	500
2050	299,849	-1.0	-2.6	10.7	13.3	1.7	299,989	-284	-784	3,215	4,001	500
2051	299,559	-1.0	-2.5	10.7	13.3	1.7	299,704	-292	-792	3,205	3,998	500
2052	299,254	-1.0	-2.7	10.7	13.3	1.7	299,411	-296	-796	3,196	3,993	500
2053	298,955	-1.0	-2.7	10.7	13.3	1.7	299,115	-298	-798	3,188	3,986	500
2054	298,637	-1.0	-2.7	10.6	13.3	1.7	298,816	-297	-797	3,180	3,978	500
2055	298,359	-1.0	-2.7	10.6	13.3	1.7	298,518	-295	-795	3,173	3,969	500
2056	298,076	-1.0	-2.6	10.6	13.3	1.7	298,222	-290	-790	3,167	3,958	500
2057	297,787	-1.0	-2.6	10.6	13.3	1.7	297,931	-284	-784	3,161	3,947	500
2058	297,505	-.9	-2.6	10.6	13.2	1.7	297,646	-278	-778	3,157	3,935	500
2059	297,230	-.9	-2.6	10.6	3.2	1.7	297,367	-270	-770	3,152	3,923	500
2060	296,963	-.9	-2.6	10.6	13.2	1.7	297,097	-262	-762	3,149	3,912	500
2061	296,704	-.9	-2.5	10.6	13.1	1.7	296,834	-254	-754	3,146	3,901	500
2062	296,453	-.8	-2.5	10.6	13.1	1.7	296,579	-246	-746	3,143	3,890	500
2063	296,210	-.8	-2.5	10.6	13.1	1.7	296,331	-239	-739	3,140	3,880	500
2064	295,974	-.8	-2.5	10.6	13.1	1.7	296,092	-232	-732	3,137	3,870	500
2065	295,744	-.8	-2.4	10.6	13.1	1.7	295,859	-226	-726	3,134	3,861	500
2066	295,519	-.8	-2.4	10.6	13.0	1.7	295,631	-222	-722	3,130	3,853	500
2067	295,298	-.7	-2.4	10.6	13.0	1.7	295,409	-219	-719	3,126	3,846	500
2068	295,079	-.7	-2.4	10.6	13.0	1.7	295,189	-217	-717	3,122	3,841	500
2069	294,861	-.7	-2.4	10.6	13.0	1.7	294,970	-217	-717	3,117	3,836	500
2070	294,642	-.7	-2.4	10.6	13.0	1.7	294,752	-219	-719	3,112	3,832	500
2075	293,500	-.8	-2.5	10.5	13.0	1.7	293,618	-239	-739	3,080	3,820	500
2080	292,235	-.9	-2.6	10.4	13.0	1.7	292,366	-267	-767	3,046	3,814	500

Source: Projections of the Population of the United States, by Age, Sex, and Race: 1988 to 2080 by Gregory Spencer, U.S. Bureau of the Census, Current Publication Reports, Series P-25, No. 1018.

POPULATION BY RACE: 1960 to 2080

(Numbers in thousands. As of July 1. Includes Armed Forces overseas. Projection data from middle series)

Year	White	Black	Other races	Average annual percent change from previous date			Percent of total population that is--		
				White	Black	Other races	White	Black	Other races
Estimates:									
1960	160,023	19,006	1,642	(X)	(X)	(X)	88.6	10.6	0.9
1965	171,205	21,064	2,034	1.35	2.06	4.28	88.1	10.8	1.0
1970	179,644	22,801	2,607	0.96	1.58	4.96	87.6	11.1	1.3
1975	187,629	24,778	3,566	0.87	1.66	6.26	86.9	11.5	1.7
1980	195,571	26,903	5,283	0.83	1.65	7.86	85.9	11.8	2.3
1985	203,159	28,994	7,125	0.76	1.50	5.98	84.9	12.1	3.0
1987	206,187	29,856	7,872	0.74	1.46	4.99	84.5	12.2	3.2
Projections:									
1990	210,616	31,148	8,646	0.71	1.41	3.13	84.1	12.4	3.5
1995	216,820	33,199	10,120	0.58	1.28	3.15	83.3	12.8	3.9
2000	221,514	35,129	11,624	0.43	1.13	2.77	82.6	13.1	4.3
2005	225,424	37,003	13,177	0.35	1.04	2.51	81.8	13.4	4.8
2010	228,978	38,833	14,764	0.31	0.97	2.27	81.0	13.7	5.2
2020	234,330	42,128	17,906	0.23	0.81	1.93	79.6	14.3	6.1
2030	235,167	44,596	20,866	0.04	0.57	1.53	78.2	14.8	6.9
2040	231,951	46,239	23,617	-0.14	0.36	1.24	76.9	15.3	7.8
2050	226,611	47,146	26,092	-0.23	0.19	1.00	75.6	15.7	8.7
2080	212,305	47,587	32,343	-0.22	0.03	0.72	72.6	16.3	11.1

X Not applicable.

Source: Current Population Reports, Series P-25, Nos. 519, 917, 1022; table 4; and unpublished data.

Source: Projections of the Population of the United States by Age, Sex, and Race: 1988 to 2080 by Gregory Spencer, U.S. Bureau of the Census, Current Population Reports, Series P-25, No. 1018.

Employee Benefits in Medium and Large Firms

Employee benefits in 1989 focused more than ever before on the care of family members, according to the U.S. Department of Labor's Bureau of Labor Statistics.

The Bureau's latest survey of benefits offered to full-time employees in medium and large firms shows that unpaid maternity leave was available to nearly two-fifths of employees; unpaid paternity leave, to almost one-fifth; reimbursement accounts (to help pay for medical and dependent care expenses), to about one-fourth; and flexible work arrangements, to one-tenth of employees.

The Bureau's 1989 survey of employee benefits in medium and large private firms provides representative data for 32 million full-time employees in the contiguous 48 States and the District of Columbia. Data represent benefit provisions for workers in about 109,000 establishments employing 100 or more employees in private nonfarm industries.

Family Benefits

The care of family members in households where all parents are employed was addressed by employers in a number of ways in 1989. Parental leave plans provide time off for mothers and fathers to care for newborn or newly adopted children. Such plans, as defined in the survey, are separate from other leave benefits, such as short-term disability coverage and paid vacations, which may also be used for parenting purposes. Thirty-seven percent of employees could take unpaid maternity leave, with the maximum leave available averaging 20 weeks. Eighteen percent of employees could take unpaid paternity leave, with the maximum leave available averaging 19 weeks. Paid parental leave was rare.

Five percent of employees were eligible for child care benefits subsidized by their employer. This benefit includes both on-site or near-site child care facilities and reimbursement of employee child care expenses. A more common means of assisting employees with child care expenses was through reimbursement accounts, from which employees pay for a variety of qualified expenses. Child care, elderly or dependent care, and other medical care expenses were the most common items covered by a reimbursement ac-

count. Twenty-three percent of employees were eligible for such accounts in 1989, up from 12 percent in 1988. Reimbursement accounts often are funded solely by employees seeking tax advantages through salary reduction arrangements.

For the first time, the survey included information on flexible work schedules. Eleven percent of workers studied had formal flexible work arrangements, which give employees the opportunity to begin and end work within a range of hours, thereby helping to accommodate family commitments. Limits on the amount of flexibility vary from plan to plan, but generally employees must be at work for a core of hours during mid-day. Fifteen percent of white-collar workers had flexible work schedules available to them, more than double the coverage for blue-collar workers.

Employers also offered a variety of health-related benefits outside the traditional health care plans. Employee assistance programs, which provide counseling and referral services for substance abuse, family, financial, legal, and related problems, were available to 49 percent of workers. Wellness programs, designed to encourage healthier lifestyles, were available to 23 percent of workers. These programs typically include health screenings, smoking cessation classes, and guidance on healthier diets.

For the first time, the survey gathered data on the availability of long-term care insurance. Three percent of employees had long-term care insurance plans available to them in 1989. Such plans are designed to help pay for long-term nursing home care for employees or dependents, including elderly dependents. (Health care plans exclude such coverage from the benefits they provide.) Although these plans are typically wholly employee paid, workers gain because coverage is available through employers at group insurance rates.

Health Care Benefits

Ninety-two percent of full-time employees had medical care benefits (such as hospitalization and care by physicians) fully or partially financed by their employer in 1989. The majority of participants (74 percent) with medical care benefits were in traditional fee-for-service plans. Participation in non-traditional health care plans, such as Health Mainte-

Source: NEWS, Bureau of Labor Statistics, United States Department of Labor, March 30, 1990.

TABLE 1. FULL-TIME EMPLOYEES PARTICIPATING IN SELECTED EMPLOYEE BENEFIT PROGRAMS, MEDIUM AND LARGE FIRMS, UNITED STATES,[1] 1989 (in percent)

Employee Benefit Program	All Employees	Professional and Administrative Employees	Technical and Clerical Employees	Production and Service Employees
Paid:				
Holidays	97	97	96	97
Vacations	97	98	99	95
Personal leave	22	28	30	14
Lunch period	10	4	4	16
Rest period	71	57	69	80
Funeral leave	84	87	86	80
Jury duty leave	90	95	92	87
Military leave	53	61	57	45
Sick leave	68	93	87	44
Maternity leave	3	4	2	3
Paternity leave	1	2	1	1
Unpaid:				
Maternity leave	37	39	37	35
Paternity leave	18	20	17	17
Sickness and accident insurance	43	29	29	58
Long-term disability insurance	45	65	57	27
Medical care	92	93	91	93
Dental care	66	69	66	65
Life insurance	94	95	94	93
Defined benefit pension	63	64	63	63
Defined contribution	48	59	52	40
Retirement[2]	36	43	39	31
Capital accumulation[3]	14	18	14	11
All retirement[4]	81	85	81	80
Flexible benefits plans	9	14	15	3
Reimbursement accounts	23	36	31	11

[1] Survey coverage excludes executives and employees in constant travel status, such as airline pilots, as well as data for Alaska and Hawaii. Except for maternity and paternity leave and reimbursement accounts, benefits paid for entirely by the employee were excluded from the tabulations. Professional-administrative and technical-clerical workers are often discussed jointly as white-collar workers. Production-service workers are often called blue-collar workers.

[2] Includes money purchase pension, profit sharing, savings and thrift, stock bonus, and employee stock ownership plans in which employer contributions must remain in the participant's account until retirement age, death, disability, separation from service, age 59½, or hardship.

[3] Includes plans in which participants may withdraw employer contributions from their accounts without regard to the conditions listed in footnote 2.

[4] Includes defined benefit pension plans and defined contribution retirement plans. Many employees participated in both types of plans.

nance Organizations (HMOs) and Preferred Provider Organizations (PPOs), accounted for 17 percent and 10 percent of medical care participants, respectively. Under PPOs, subscribers are provided health care services at a lower cost if they receive treatment from designated hospitals, physicians, or dentists.

Alcohol and drug abuse treatment coverage was provided to 97 and 96 percent of the medical care participants, respectively. Benefits may be provided for detoxification, rehabilitation services, or both. Detoxification provides supervised medical care to reduce or eliminate the symptoms of chemical dependency. Rehabilitation is designed to al-

ter the behavior of substance abusers, once they are free of acute physical and mental complications. The percent of medical care participants with alcohol and drug abuse treatment coverage reported by the survey increased by 21 and 30 percent, respectively, between 1988 and 1989. (These increases reflect both a greater incidence of these benefits in medical care plans and a refinement of the survey's procedures for tabulating detoxification benefits.)

To reduce health care costs, many plans provide less costly alternatives to hospital care. Three-fourths of the participants with medical care had coverage for home health care, and four-fifths had coverage in extended care facilities. In addition, hospice care, for the terminally ill, was available to approximately two-fifths of medical plan participants.

Other features designed to curb health care expenses included incentives for diagnostic testing prior to hospitalization and a requirement of plan authorization prior to hospital admission. These two features affected just over 40 percent of the medical plan participants. Nearly 60 percent of the participants were in plans that provided coverage for second surgical opinions. Of these participants, the majority were required to obtain a second opinion for selected surgical procedures or have the reimbursement rate reduced.

Dental coverage, generally including preventive and restorative procedures, was available to 66 percent of employees. Thirty-five percent of the medical plan participants had provisions for vision care. Nearly all vision care plan participants had coverage for eye examinations, while 68 percent had coverage for eyeglasses and 66 percent were covered for contact lenses.

Medical coverage for employees was fully paid by the employer for 52 percent of participants, while family coverage was fully paid by the employer for 34 percent of participants. (This is a decrease from 57 and 36 percent, respectively, in 1988.) When employee contributions were required, such contributions averaged $25 per month for individual coverage and $72 per month for family coverage, up from $19 and $60 in 1988. Contributions varied by plan type, with participants in HMOs more often required to contribute than participants in fee-for-service plans.

Defined Benefit Pension Plans

Defined benefit pension plans, which specify a formula for determining an employee's annuity, covered 63 percent of full-time workers in 1989, unchanged from the coverage reported in 1988 when the survey expanded to smaller establishments and more service industries.

The most common type of defined benefit pension plan is the terminal earnings plan, which bases pension payments on an employee's average earnings in the last few years prior to retirement (usually a 5-year period). In 1989, terminal earnings plans covered 64 percent of participants in defined benefit pension plans. The average benefit formula in such plans was approximately 1.5 percent of annual earnings times years of service (for example, 1.5 percent of annual earnings times 30 years of service, or 45 percent of annual earnings). Over half of the participants in these plans were subject to a limit on the years of service that could be applied toward

the pension benefit, commonly 30, 35, or 40 years. In addition, benefits were usually coordinated with Social Security payments.

Earnings-based pension formulas are more common among white-collar workers than blue-collar workers. The latter often have plans calling for dollar amount benefits based on years of service. In 1989, the monthly benefit under dollar amount formulas averaged about $20 times the number of service years (for example, $20 times 25 years, or $500 a month). Unlike earnings-based plans, these plans usually do not limit years of credited service and rarely coordinate benefits with Social Security payments.

Workers earn a vested interest in their accrued pension benefits according to a vesting schedule. In this way, all or a portion of benefits are guaranteed even if a worker ends employment prior to retirement. As a result of the Tax Reform Act of 1986, plan sponsors continued in 1989 the trend toward adopting shorter vesting schedules. Fifty percent of the participants in defined benefit plans satisfied the requirement for 100-percent vesting after 5 years of service, up substantially from 5 percent reported in 1988. Most of the other participants were not fully vested until the completion of 10 years of plan participation.

The purchasing power of a fixed monthly pension benefit can be eroded in periods of even moderate inflation. To compensate for this, some pension plans provide an occasional or ad hoc benefit increase; relatively few provide automatic cost-of-living adjustments. In 1989, 22 percent of participants were in plans that increased regular monthly annuities to current retirees at least once in the last 5 years.

Defined Contribution Plans

Forty-eight percent of employees participated in one or more defined contribution plans in 1989, up from 45 percent in 1988. These plans, which usually specify the employer's contribution but cannot predetermine the employee's actual amount of benefits, include savings and thrift (covering 30 percent of full-time workers), profit-sharing (16 percent), money purchase pension (5 percent), and stock ownership plans (3 percent). Most defined contribution plans require employee contributions; about 30 percent of participants were in plans wholly financed by the employer.

Forty-one percent of the workers covered by the survey participated in 401(k) plans (also known as cash or deferred arrangements), which permit pretax employee contributions. Most of these plans were salary reduction plans, allowing employees to reduce their taxable income by making voluntary contributions that are not taxed until withdrawn from the plan. For example, savings and thrift plans commonly allow participants to make pretax savings, some or all of which are matched by the employer.

Life Insurance

Life insurance benefits were provided to 94 percent of employees in 1989. The cost was paid entirely by the employer for all but 13 percent of covered workers. For 68 percent of the covered workers, the amount of life insurance was based on earnings, typically one or two times annual pay. Most of the remaining participants were provided flat dollar amounts of coverage. Flat dollar amounts were most common among blue-collar workers, with benefits for these workers averaging slightly more than $11,000.

Fifty-two percent of life insurance participants were in plans that reduced life insurance benefits for older employees, normally beginning at ages 65 or 70. Life insurance coverage, typically reduced, continued after retirement for 42 percent of participants. Seventy-one percent of life insurance participants received accidental death and dismemberment insurance, which provides additional benefits in the event of death or disability caused by an accident. For 91 percent of workers with accidental death and dismemberment protection, benefits equaled basic life insurance benefits. The remainder had flat dollar benefit amounts.

Disability Income Benefits

Eighty-nine percent of workers were covered by an income protection plan—either sick leave, sickness and accident insurance, or both—in the event of a short-term illness or injury. Sick leave plans, available to 68 percent of all workers studied, but more frequently to white-collar workers, commonly specified a set number of sick days per year. Workers in such plans with one year of service had an average of 15.4 sick days available; this rose to 27.8 days at 20 years of service.

In 1989, 43 percent of workers surveyed received a sickness and accident insurance plan, and about half of these workers also received sick leave. Sickness and accident insurance, twice as prevalent among blue-collar workers than among white-collar workers, provides either a percentage of pay—commonly 50 percent—or a flat amount per week during a period of disability due to illness or accident. Payments are for a limited period of time, usually 26 weeks.

Forty-five percent of the employees had long-term disability insurance coverage in 1989. Such coverage is intended to replace income lost during an extended or permanent period of disability. The majority of workers with such coverage received between 50 and 60 percent of pre-disability pay during their period of disability.

Nearly all long-term disability insurance participants were in plans that covered disabilities due to mental illness. However, half were in plans that discontinued the benefit after a specified length of time, commonly 24 months, unless the recipient is institutionalized.

Paid Time Off

Time off with pay is available to employees in a variety of forms—from daily rest breaks to annual vacations of several weeks. Most types of paid leave were available to a majority of the employees. The exceptions were paid lunch time, averaging 26 minutes a day, which applied to a tenth of workers; and personal (multipurpose) leave, averaging 3.1 days a year, which covered nearly one-fourth of the workers. The number of paid holidays averaged 9.2 per year; the amount of vacation, which commonly increased with length of service, averaged 9.1 days after 1 year of service, 16.5 days after 10 years, and 20.4 days after 20 years. Paid rest time averaged 26 minutes a day, funeral leave, 3.3 days per occurrence; military leave, 11.9 days a year; and paid time off for jury duty was usually provided as needed.

The European Community

Is Your Business Ready for 1992?

The European Community plans to complete its Internal Market and remove substantially all physical, technical and fiscal barriers to the exchange of goods and services within the Community by 1992. This initiative will radically alter competitive conditions in our largest market. U.S. business should become aware of the opportunities and the risks the E.C.'s program poses for established market access.

For information on the 1992 Internal Market Program, copies of the Single Internal Market regulations, background information on the European Community, or assistance regarding specific opportunities or potential problems, contact:

Single Internal Market: 1992 Information Service
Office of European Community Affairs
U.S. Department of Commerce
Room 3036
14th and Constitution Ave., NW
Washington, D.C. 20230
Charles Ludolph or Mary Saunders, tel. (202) 377-5276

In addition, Trade Development industry experts assigned to this 1992 program are indicated below. Write to the U.S. Department of Commerce, Washington D.C. 20230:

Textiles and Apparel, Michael Hutchinson, Office of Textiles and Apparel, Room 3119, tel. 377-2043

Service Industries, Fred Elliott, Office of Service Industries, Room 1128, tel. 377-3734

Information Technology, Instrumentation and Electronics, Myles Denny-Brown, Office of Telecommunications, Room 1001A, tel. 377-4466

Chemicals, Construction Industry Products, and Basic Industries, Maryanne Smith, Office of Basic Industries, Room 4045, tel. 377-0614

Autos and Consumer Goods, Bruce Miller, Office of Automotive Affairs and Consumer Goods, Room 4324, tel. 377-2762

Construction Projects and Industrial Ma-

chinery, Kay Thompson, Office of the DAS for Capital Goods and International Construction, Room 2001B, tel. 377-2474

Aerospace, Marci Kenney, Office of Aerospace Policy & Analysis, Room 6877, tel. 377-8228

Office of Industrial Trade, Debra L. Miller, Director, Outreach Program to Industry Trade Associations, Room 2800 A, tel. 377-3733

If you want advice or information about any aspect of exporting to the EC, contact your ITA District Office (see page 715) or speak to an ITA European country desk officer: Belgium, Luxembourg—(202) 377-5401, Denmark—(202) 377-3254, France—(202) 377-8008, Federal Republic of Germany—(202) 377-2434, Greece—(202) 377-3945, Ireland—(202) 377-4104, Italy—(202) 377-2177, Netherlands—(202) 377-5401, Portugal—(202) 377-3945, Spain—(202) 377-4508, United Kingdom—(202) 377-3748.

Free brochures can be obtained by writing the Delegation of the Commission of the European Communities, 2100 M St. N.W., Washington, D.C. 20037. EC official publications and studies on the EC 1992 program can be obtained by contacting UNIPUB, 3611-F Assembly Drive, Lanham, Md. 20706-4391, or tel. (301) 459-7666, or (800) 274-4888.

For further information on European standards, the National Institute of Standards and Technology has prepared a more extensive summary of the EC initiatives on standards and other related materials. These can be obtained by contacting: GATT Inquiry Point/Technical Office, Office of Standards Code and Information, National Institute of Standards and Technology, Administration Building, Room A629, Gaithersburg, MD. 20899, tel. (301) 975-4040, and National Center for Standards and Certification Information (NCSCI), National Institute of Standards and Technology, Administration Building, Room A629, Gaithersburg, Md. 20899, tel. (301) 975-4040 (GATT Hotline: (301) 975-4041).

Additional U.S. Government contact points are Michael Brownrigg, U.S. Department of State, Europe/Regional, Political and Economic Affairs, Room 6519, Washington, D.C. 20520, tel. (202) 647-2395; Mark Orr, DAUSTR for Europe and Mediterranean, USTR, 600 17th Street, N.W., Washington, D.C. 20506, tel. (202) 395-3320.

Source: *Business America*, U.S. Department of Commerce, International Trade Administration. January 15, 1990.

Complying With EC Standards, Testing and Certification Requirements for Regulated Products

A Checklist for U.S. Businesses

- Determine If EC-Wide Regulations Cover Your Product*
    1. Check the list of EC 1992 directives available through Commerce's Single Internal Market Information Service [SIMIS: (202) 377-5276]. For a summary of this list, see the following section "1992 at a Glance."
- If An EC-Wide Directive or Regulation Exists Covering Your Product:
    1. Obtain copies of EC Directives that may be applicable from SIMIS or other sources, and see if the "scope" of regulations includes your product.
    2. Read the directive to determine what sort of EC technical requirements exist for your product—also check to see if any European standards are referenced by the directive.
    3. If you have the European standards reference numbers and choose to follow the European standard as a means of demonstrating product conformity to EC requirements, contact the American National Standards Institute [ANSI: (212) 642-4900] to obtain copies of European standards.**
- If No New EC Regulation Exists for Your Product, You May Still Wish to Determine if Other European or National Regulations or Standards Exist That Could Affect It:
    1. Contact the Commerce's National Institute of Standards and Technology, National Center for Standards and Certification Information [NIST/NCSCI: (301) 975-4040, -4038 or -4036] to Determine International Standards or Existing European National Standards for your Product and get Reference Numbers
- If you need further assistance call the Commerce Department's SIMIS, (202) 377-5276, or NIST/NCSCI, (301) 975-4040.

---

* Often your industry trade association will have already gone through these steps and has this information for you. Checking with your trade association first might save you time and expense.

** Many U.S. organizations that are involved in standards development, such as the American Society of Testing and Materials (ASTM), or the American Society of Mechanical Engineers (ASME), can also be good sources of information for European and international requirements.

1992 at a Glance

By 1992, the European Community intends to have implemented 279 regulations to create a single internal market. The following specific changes represent the major part of the 1992 program.

(1) Adopted (2) Mostly Adopted (3) Proposed (4) Proposal Due

In standards, testing and certification Harmonization of standards for:
  Simple pressure vessels (1)
  Toys (1)
  Construction products (1)
  Machine safety (1)
  Agricultural & forestry tractors (1)
  Cosmetics (1)
  Quick frozen foods (1)
  Flavorings (1)
  Food emulsifiers (1)
  Food preservatives (1)
  Jams (1)
  Fruit juices (1)
  Food inspection (1)
  Definition of spirited beverages & aromatised wines (1)
  Coffee extracts & chicory extracts (1)
  Food additives (1)
  Materials & articles in contact with food (1)
  Tower cranes (noise) (1)
  Household appliances (noise) (1)
  Tire pressure gauges (1)
  Hydraulic diggers (noise) (1)
  Detergents (1)
  Lawn mower (noise) (1)
  Radio interferences (1)
  Automobiles, trucks, and motorcycles and their emissions (1)
  Telecommunications (2)
  Earth moving equipment (2)
  Liquid fertilizers & secondary fertilizers (2)
  Medicinal products & medical specialties (3)
  Lifting and loading equipment (3)
  Global Approach to Testing & Certification (3)
  Personal protection equipment (3)
  Measuring instruments (3)
  Medical devices (3)
  Gas appliances (3)
  Extraction solvents (3)
  Infant formula (3)
  Modified starches (3)

New rules for harmonizing packing, labelling and processing requirements
  Ingredients for food & beverages (1)
  Irradiation (1)
  Nutritional labelling (1)

Classification, packaging, & labelling of dangerous preparations (1)
Extraction solvents (3)

Harmonization of regulations for the health industry (including marketing)
Medical specialties (1)
High technology medicines (1)
Pharmaceuticals (2)
Veterinary medicinal products (2)
Implantable electromedical devices (3)
Non implantable, active medical devices (4)
Non active medical devices (4)
In-vitro diagnostics (4)

Changes in government procurement regulations
Coordination of procedures on the award of public works & supply contracts (1)
Extension of E.C. law to telecommunications, utilities, transport (3)
Services (3)

Harmonization of regulation of services
Mutual Funds (1)
Broadcasting (1)
Tourism (1)
Air transport (1)
Electronic payment cards (1)
Information services (2)
Life & nonlife insurance (2)
Banking (2)
Securities (2)
Maritime transport (2)
Road passenger transport (3)
Railways (4)

Liberalization of capital movements
Long-term capital, stocks (1)
Short-term capital (1)

Consumer protection regulations
Misleading definitions of products (1)
Indication of prices (1)

Harmonization of taxation
Value added taxes (3)
Excise taxes on alcohol, tobacco, and other (3)

Harmonization of laws regulating company behavior
Trademarks (2)
Accounting operations across borders (2)
Protection of computer programs (3)
Transaction taxes (3)
Company law (3)
Mergers & acquisitions (2)
Copyrights (3)
Cross-border mergers (3)
Bankruptcy (4)

Harmonization of veterinary & phytosanitary Controls

Harmonization of an extensive list of rules covering items such as:
Antibiotic residues (1)
Bovine animals and meat (1)
Porcine animals and meat (1)
Plant health (1)
Fish & fish products (3)
Live poultry, poultry meat and hatching eggs (3)
Pesticide residues in fruit & vegetables (3)

Elimination and simplification of national transit documents and procedures for intra-EC trade
Introduction of the Single Administrative Document (SAD) (1)
Abolition of customs presentation charges (1)
Elimination of customs formalities & the introduction of common border posts (1)

Harmonization of rules pertaining to the free movement of labor and the professions within the EC
Mutual recognition of higher educational diplomas (1)
Comparability of vocational training qualifications (1)
Specific training in general medical practice (1)
Training of engineers (1)
Activities in the field of pharmacy (1)
Activities related to commercial agents (1)
Income taxation provisions (3)
Elimination of burdensome requirements related to residence permits (4)

European Community Information Sources

EC 1992: A Commerce Department Analysis of European Community Directives (Vol. I) [1989]: Analysis of first 66 of over 300 proposed EC directives implementing a program to permit free movement of products and economic resources within Single Internal Market by the end of 1992.[1]

Europe Now/A Report (Quarterly): Newsletter providing summaries of the latest developments of the EC's 1992 Program).[2]

EC 1992: Growth Markets: Provides information for U.S. firms interested in taking advantage of the expanding opportunities created by the EC's 1992 Internal Market Program.[1]

---

[1] Superintendent of Documents, U.S. Government Printing Office, Washington, DC 20402 (202-783-3238)
[2] Office of European Community Affairs, Room H3036, International Trade Administration, U.S. Department of Commerce, Washington, DC 20230 (202-377-5276)

Business Information Directory

General Reference Sources

The *United States Government Manual* is an annual publication. It describes the organization, purposes, and programs of most government agencies and lists top personnel. Available from the Superintendent of Documents, Government Printing Office, Washington, DC 20402.

Washington Information Directory is an annual publication listing, by topic, organizations and publications which provide information on a wide range of subjects. It also lists congressional committee assignments, regional federal offices, embassies, and state and local officials. Published by the Congressional Quarterly, Inc., 1414 22nd Street NW, Washington, DC 20037.

Statistical Abstract of the United States, published annually by the Bureau of the Census, is the standard summary on the social, political, and economic statistics of the United States. It includes data from both government and private sources. Appendix II gives a comprehensive list of sources. (Available from the Superintendent of Documents, Government Printing Office, Washington, DC 20402.)

Business Information Sources by Lorna M. Daniells ranks among the best general guides to business publications. It contains extensive references to U.S. business and economic data, including statistics, U.S. and foreign investment. Published by the University of California Press, Berkeley, CA.

Who Knows: A Guide to Washington Experts, Washington Researchers, 2612 P Street NW, Washington, DC 20007.

Population information on all aspects of national and world population is provided by the Population Reference Bureau, Inc., 777 14th Street NW, Washington, DC, or call 202–689–8040.

Washington Researchers Publishing provides reports and guidance to information on a fee basis. Write Washington Researchers, 2612 P Street NW, Washington, DC 20007, or call 202–333–3499.

FEDfind which explains how to get services and publications from the U.S. Government is published by ICUC Press, P.O. Box 1447-NR, Springfield, VA 22151.

Standard Rate and Data Service provides information on periodical circulation and advertising rates. Published by Standard Rates and Data Service, Inc., 5201 Old Orchard Road, Skokie, IL 60077–1021.

Encyclopedia of Information Systems and Services. Descriptions of U.S. organizations (and some foreign) that produce, process, store, and use bibliographic and non-bibliographic information. About 1500 data bases covered. Published by Gale Research Co., 835 Penobscot Building, Detroit, MI 48226.

National Directory of Addresses and Telephone Numbers. A national business directory that lists all SEC registered companies, major accounting and law firms, banks, and financial institutions, associations, unions, etc. Included are 50,000 fax numbers. Available from General Information, Inc., 11715 North Creek Parkway South; Bothell, WA 98011.

Encyclopedia of Business Information, a comprehensive single-volume source, is updated periodically. Available from Gale Research Co., 835 Penobscot Building, Detroit, MI 48226.

Business Organizations, Agencies and Publications Directory, lists organizations, agencies and information services that promote, coordinate, and regulate commercial activity in the U.S. Gale Research, 835 Penobscot Building, Detroit, MI 48226.

Business Publications Index and Abstracts is a two volume set listing books, transaction proceedings, etc. with abstracts of each entry. Published by Gale Research Co., 835 Penobscot Building, Detroit, MI 48226.

Professional and trade organizations and publications are a major source of contacts and information. Key directories to these sources are listed below:

Encyclopedia of Associations, published by Gale Research Co., 835 Penobscot Building, Detroit, MI 48226.

The World Guide to Trade Associations gives a comprehensive national and international listing of associations. Published by R. R. Bowker Co., 205 East 42 Street, New York, NY 10017.

Ulrich's International Periodical Directory covers both domestic and foreign periodicals. Published by R. R. Bowker Co., 205 East 42 Street, New York, NY 10017.

Standard Periodical Directory covers U.S. and Canadian periodicals. Published by Oxbridge Communications, Inc., 150 Fifth Avenue, New York, NY 10011.

The Gale Directory of Publications and Broadcast Media, a guide to newspapers, magazines and other periodicals, as well as radio, television and cable companies (formerly *Ayer Directory of Publications* and *IMS Directory of Publications*). (Available from Gale Research Co., 835 Penobscot Building, Detroit, MI 48226.

Trade Directories of the World is published annually (with monthly updates) by Croner Publications, 211–03 Jamaica Avenue, Queens Village, New York 11428.

National Trade and Professional Associations of the United States. A comprehensive listing of professional trade and labor associations, including addresses, membership size, publications by the associations, and convention schedules. An annual published by Columbia Books, 777 14th Street NW, Washington, DC 20005.

Encyclopedia of Banking and Finance, is a comprehensive source on subjects indicated in title. Bankers Publishing Co., 210 South Street, Boston, MA.

Guide to American Directories, published by B. Klein Publications, Inc., P.O. Box 8503, Coral Springs, FL 33065.

Directories in Print, distributed by Gale Research Co., 835 Penobscot Building, Detroit, MI 48226. Contains more than 10,000 detailed entries on directories published in the United States and Canada. Directories outside the U.S. and Canada are listed in *International Directories in Print* and city and state directories are listed in *City and State Directories in Print*.

Directory of Marketing Research Houses and Services is an annual available from the American Marketing Association, 310 Madison Avenue, New York, NY 10017.

The Data Informer directs decision makers to unusual sources of computerized and noncomputerized information on markets, companies, demographics, and technology. Included are little-known commercial databases and free professional bulletin boards, public documents at the federal, state and local governments, reports published by private and non-profit organizations, and free experts in both the public and private sector. *The Data Informer*, published monthly, is available from: *Information USA, Inc.*, P.O. Box 15700, Chevy Chase, MD 20815. 301-657-1200.

BUSINESS AND ECONOMICS INFORMATION

Government publications referred to below may be obtained from the Government Printing Office (GPO), Washington, DC, 20402, unless otherwise indicated.

Census Catalog and Guide is an annual one-step guide to Census Bureau resources. Includes explanations of the censuses and surveys of business, manufacturing, and population, names and phone numbers of over 1,600

sources of assistance—Census Bureau specialists, State and local agencies, and private companies.

Business and economic information is provided by the following key references.

Survey of Current Business is a major publication which is supplemented on a weekly basis with *Current Statistics*. The publication contains articles as well as comprehensive statistics on all aspects of the economy, including data on the GNP, employment, wages, prices, finance, foreign trade, and production by industrial sector. (GPO)

Business Conditions Digest is a monthly with an extensive collection of charts and tables on the national income and products, leading coincident and lagging cyclical indicators, foreign trade, prices, wages, analytical ratios, and international production and stock prices. (GPO)

Economic Indicators is a monthly summary-type publication prepared by the Council of Economic Advisers. It contains charts and tables on natural output, income, spending, employment, unemployment, wages, industrial production, construction, prices, money, credit, federal finance, and international statistics. (GPO)

Federal Reserve Bulletin is a monthly issued by the Federal Reserve System, containing articles and very extensive tabulated data on all aspects of the monetary situation, credit, mortgage markets, interest rates, and stock and bond yields. Available from the Board of Governors, Federal Reserve System, Washington, DC 20551.

Monthly Labor Review. This monthly publication provides articles and statistics on employment, productivity, wages, earnings, prices, wage settlements, and work stoppages. (GPO)

U.S. Industrial Outlook is an annual providing evaluations and projections of all major industrial and commercial segments of the domestic economy. (GPO)

Quarterly Financial Report for Manufacturing, Mining, and Trade Corporations is issued by the Bureau of the Census of the U.S. Department of Commerce. It covers corporate financial statistics including sales, profits, assets, and financial ratios, classified by industry group and size. (GPO)

Current Industrial Reports are a series of over 100 monthly, quarterly, semiannual, and annual reports on major products manufactured in the United States. For subscription, contact the Bureau of the Census, U.S. Department of Commerce, Washington, DC 20233. (GPO)

Annual Survey of Manufacturers. General statistics of manufacturing activity for industry groups, individual industries, states, and geographical regions are provided. (GPO)

County Business Patterns is an annual publication on employment and payrolls, which include a separate paperbound report for each state. (GPO)

Foreign Trade is a Bureau of the Census publication giving monthly reports on U.S. foreign trade. (GPO)

Population: Current Report is a series of monthly and annual reports covering population changes and socioeconomic characteristics of the population. (GPO)

Retail Sales: Current Business Report is a weekly report which provides retail statistics. (GPO)

Wholesale Trade, Sales and Inventories: Current Business Report provides a monthly report on wholesale trade. (GPO)

Key Economic Data Service Package provides access to the Department of Commerce Electronic Bulletin Board. The Bulletin Board includes same day postings of data provided by both the Bureau of Labor Statistics and the Bureau of Economic Analysis. Twice a month there are updates from the Bureau of the Census on the principal indicators, monetary statistics and foreign trade. Also provided is the most current *SIC Manual.* Available from the National Technical Information Service, 5285 Port Royal Road, Springfield, VA 22161.

CORPORATE INFORMATION

The major sources of information on publicly held corporations (as well as government and municipal issues) are: *Moody's Investor Services, Inc.*, owned by Dun & Bradstreet, 99 Church Street, New York, NY 10007, and *Standard & Poor's Corp.*, owned by McGraw-Hill, 25 Broadway, New York, NY 10004.

Standard & Poor's *Corporate Records* and Moody's *Manuals* are large multivolume works published annually and kept up to date with daily (for Standard & Poor's) or semiweekly (for Moody's) reports. The services provide extensive coverage of industrials, public utilities, transportation, banks, and financial companies. Also included are municipal and government issues.

In addition, the above corporations provide computerized data services and magnetic tapes. Compustat tapes, containing major corporate financial data, are available from Investor's Management Services, Inc., Denver, CO, a subsidiary of Standard & Poor's. Time-sharing access to Compustat and other financial data bases is available through Interactive Data Corporation, Waltham, MA.

Media General Financial Services, 301 East Grace Street, Richmond, VA, 23219, maintains a database of corporate and industry information on 5500 companies. It can be accessed via Dow Jones News Retrieval, Dialog, Thomson Financial Networks, Randall-Helms Fiduciary Consultants, Lotus One Source (CD-ROM). Media General Financial Services also provides data on the financial markets, mutual funds and corporate bonds.

The Media General Financial Services proprietary product line also includes direct sales of its data through magnetic tapes, diskettes, custom research applications, specialized screening and report services.

DISCLOSURE II, available from Disclosure, Inc., (5161 River Road, Bethesda, MD 20816) provides an on line data base of corporate information for some 10,000 companies. Disclosure II can be used via the Dow Jones Retrieval Service, New York Times Information Service, Lockheed's DIALOG Information Services, Inc., ADP, CompuServe, among others.

Also available from Disclosure is MICRO/SCAN: Disclosure II, a monthly diskette service which provides information on dividends per share, 4-year growth rate in earnings per share, price/book value, etc. For information call 800–638–8076.

The 10-K and other corporate reports are filed with the Securities and Exchange Commission and are available at local SEC offices, investor relations departments of publicly traded companies, as well as various private services, such as Disclosure Inc. which provides a complete microfiche service. *The SEC News Digest*, formerly published by the government, is now available from Disclosure, Inc. (address above). Included in the *Digest* is a daily listing of 8K reports, a daily Acquisitions of Securities Report, as well as information about what's happening inside the SEC.

Disclosure Inc. has two additional services helpful for researching a corporation. Through the *SEC Watch Service* any report filed by a company with the SEC can be retrieved while corporate information such as prospective supplements and tender offers can be retrieved through the *SEC Research Service.*

Betchel Information Service located at 15740 Shady Grove Road, Gaithersburg, MD 20877 is another SEC document retrieval service. The Index of financial documents is updated several times a day.

Major trade directories include the annual *Thomas Register of American Manufacturers* (published by Thomas Publishing Company, 1 Pennsylvania Plaza, New York, NY 10005) and Dun & Bradstreet's *Reference Book of Manufacturers.*

Thomas Register includes in two volumes an alphabetical listing of manufacturers, giving address, phone number, product, subsidiaries, plant location, and an indication of assets. Dun & Bradstreet's *Reference Book* covers similar information, including sales and credit. Dun & Bradstreet's *Million Dollar Directory* series provides data on U.S. companies whose net worth is $1,000,000 and up, including information on privately held corporations; also published is a companion volume the *Billion Dollar Directory* which tracks America's corporate families.

How to Find Information About Private Companies includes strategies for private company investigation, sources for private company intelligence, and how to find information about private companies. Published by Washington Researchers, 2612 P Street NW, Washington, DC 20007.

The *Corporate Directory*, published by Cambridge Information Group, 7200 Wisconsin Avenue, Bethesda MD 20814 is a two volume compendium of over 9500 public companies. Included is such information as corporate officers, majority stockholders, SIC members, major subsidiaries, P/E ratio, etc.

Monitor Publishing, 104 Fifth Avenue, New York, NY 10011 publishes four directories that list, among other items, names, titles, and addresses of the managers of the listed companies in the U.S. and abroad. The volumes are: *The Corporate 1000* (a quarterly), *The Financial 1000*, *The Over-the-Counter 1000*, and *The International 1000*. Monitor also publishes the *Blue Book of Canadian Business*.

Directory of Wall Street Research, an annual published by Nelson Publishing, 1 Gateway Plaza, Port Chester, NY lists security analysts with a subject specialty, top corporate officers, and brokerage firms researching a given company.

Register of Corporations is published by Standard and Poor's Corp., 345 Hudson Street, New York, NY 10014.

Directory of Corporate Affiliations and International Directory of Corporate Affiliations are references to the structure of major domestic and international corporations. Published by National Register Publishing Company, 3004 Glen View Road, Wilmette, IL 60091.

How to Find Company Intelligence in State Documents provides information filed by companies with the state governments and also business related data collected by the states. Washington Researchers Publishing, 2612 P Street NW, Washington, DC 20007.

How to Find Information About Companies: The Corporate Intelligence Source Book provides information on sources helpful in researching either private or public companies. Available from Washington Researchers Publishing. (See above for the address.)

Ward's Business Directory of U.S. Private and Public Companies 1990. Company profiles on 85,000 private and public U.S. businesses—over 90% of which are privately held. Available from Gale Research, Inc., 835 Penobscot Building, Detroit, MI 48226.

Future earnings projections of listed companies based on surveys by securities analysts are provided by Lynch, Jones, and Ryan, 345 Hudson Street, New York, NY 10013 (212-243-3137).

Zacks Investment Research, Inc., 155 North Wacker Drive, Chicago, IL 60606 also provides future earnings projections.

The Corporate Finance Sourcebook, published by the National Register Publishing Company, Macmillan Directory Division, P.O. Box 609, Wilmette, IL 60091, provides information on sources of capital, financial intermediaries and specialized financial sources.

Information on foreign corporations is provided in *World Trade Data Reports*, distributed by the District Offices of the U.S. Department of Commerce.

TRACKING FEDERAL GOVERNMENT DEVELOPMENTS

Commerce Business Daily (CB). This daily provides information on contract awards and subcontract opportunities, Defense Department awards, and surplus sales. *CB* is available on-line from: United Communications Group, 8701 Georgia Avenue, Silver Springs, MD 20910; DIALOG Information Services, 3460 Hillview Avenue, Palo Alto, CA 94304; or Data Resources, Inc., 2400 Hartwell Avenue, Lexington, ME 02173. Available from the Superintendent of Documents, Government Printing Office, Washington, DC 20402.

Federal Register. This daily provides information on federal agency regulations and other legal documents. Available from the Superintendent of Documents, Government Printing Office, Washington, DC 20402.

CQ Weekly Report. This major service follows every important piece of legislation through both houses of Congress and reports on the political and lobbying pressures being applied. Available from the Congressional Quarterly Service, 1414 22nd Street, Washington, DC 20037.

Daily Report for Executives. A daily series of reports giving Washington developments that affect all aspects of business operations. Available from the Bureau of National Affairs, Inc., 1231 25th Street NW, Washington, DC 20037.

The *Bureau of National Affairs, Inc.* (address above) and the *Commerce Clearing House, Inc.* (4025 West Peterson Avenue, Chicago, IL 60646), publish a large number of valuable weekly loose-leaf reports covering developments in all aspects of law, government regulations, and taxation.

INDEX PUBLICATIONS

Indexes of a wide variety of articles appearing in periodicals, trade presses, and financial services dealing with corporations, industry, and finance are given in the following:

Business Periodicals Index published by H. W. Wilson Co., 950 University Avenue, Bronx, NY.

Funk and Scott Index of Corporations and Industries, published by Predicast, Inc., 11001 Cedar Street, Cleveland, OH 44141.

Major newspaper indexes are:

Wall Street Journal Index published by Dow Jones & Co. Inc., 22 Cortlandt Street, New York, NY 10007 (monthly).

New York Times Index published by the New York Times Company, 229 W. 43rd Street, New York, NY 10036 (semimonthly, cumulates annually).

TRACKING ECONOMIC INDICATORS

Composite Index of Leading Economic Indicators: Each month the Bureau of Economic Analysis compiles this data from the 12 leading economic indicators. This material appears each month in the *Bureau's Survey of Current Business* available by subscription from:

Superintendent of Documents
Government Printing Office
Washington, DC 20402

Index values are available towards the very end of each month by calling: 202-523-0541.

Consumer Price Index (CPI) (changes in cost of goods to customers): For these monthly reports prepared by the Bureau of Labor Statistics write:

Bureau of Labor Statistics
Department of Labor
441 G Street NW
Washington, DC 20212

CPI 24 hour hotline: 202-523-1221.

Producer Price Index (PPI) (measures changes in prices received in primary markets by producers). For monthly reports write:

Bureau of Labor Statistics
Department of Labor
441 G Street NW
Washington, DC 20212

PPI 24 hour hotline: 202-523-1765.

Available from the Bureau of Labor Statistics (BLS) are press releases on *State and Metropolitan Area Unemployment* (issued monthly), the *Employment Cost Index* (issued

quarterly, and the *Employment Situation Study* (released monthly). To subscribe write:

Bureau of Labor Statistics
Department of Labor
411 G Street NW
Washington, DC 20212

BLS hotline: 202-523-1239
Major BLS Statistics:. 523-9658

Unemployment Insurance Claims Weekly may be obtained by calling or by writing:

Employment and Training Administration
Department of Labor
601 D Street, NW
Washington, DC 20213

Releases on the *Money Supply* (Report H-6, issued weekly) and on *Consumer Credit* (Report G-19, issued monthly) may be obtained from the

Publications Services
Federal Reserve Board
Washington, DC 20551
202-452-3244

Personal Consumption Expenditure Deflator is prepared monthly by the Bureau of Economic Analysis of the Department of Commerce. This information appears in a press release *Personal Income and Outlays* and can be obtained in writing from the

Current Business Analysis
Bureau of Economic Analysis
Department of Commerce
Washington, DC 20230

For information call 202-523-0777.

Monthly Trade Report (index of retail sales and accounts receivable) is compiled by the Bureau of the Census and published in *Current Business Reports* as part of what is known as the BR series. Also available are *Current Business Reports Wholesale Trade* and *Current Business Reports Selected Services*. To subscribe contact the Superintendent of Documents (Address given above). For a sample copy call: 301-763-4100.

Value of New Construction Put in Place is a Census Bureau monthly report (part of the C-30 Series) which charts the dollar amount of new construction. It is available on an annual subscription basis from the Superintendent of Documents, Government Printing Office, Washington, DC 20402. For a sample copy call: 301-763-5717.

Joint Economic Committee of Congress Reports

Reports on the economic issues studied by the Joint Economic Committee are available free of charge from:

Joint Economic Committee of Congress
Dirksen Senate Office Building
Washington, DC 20510
202–224–5321

TRACKING CONGRESSIONAL ACTION

Congressional action information can be obtained from several sources. The Legis Office will provide information on whether legislation has been introduced, who sponsored it, and its current status. For House or Senate action, call 202–225–1772.

Cloakrooms of both houses will provide details on what is happening on the floor of the chamber. House cloakrooms: Democrat 202–225–7330; Republican 202–225–7350. Senate cloakrooms: Democrat 202–224–4691; Republican 202–224–6391.

ASSISTANCE FROM U.S. GOVERNMENT AGENCIES

The **Office of Business Liaison (OBL)** serves as the focal point for contact between the Department of Commerce and the business community. Through the *Business Assistance Program* individuals and firms are guided through the entire government complex. Other services include dissemination of information and reports such as *Outlook*. Write Office of Business Liaison, U.S. Department of Commerce, Washington, DC 20230. This office is also a focal point for handling inquiries for domestic business information.

OBL telephone numbers:

Office of the Director . . (202) 377-3942
Outreach Program 1360
Office of Private Sector
  Initiatives 3717
Business Assistance
  Program 3176

Industry experts in the International Trade Administration can provide specifics about an industry.

Country experts in the Department of State provide up to date economic and political information on countries throughout the world, as well as background reports on specific countries. For information contact:

Country Desk Officers
U.S. Department of State
2201 C Street NW
Washington, DC 20520
Telephone: 202–647–4000

Major Bureau of Labor Statistics Indicators are available daily from a recorded message at 202–523–9658.

Economic news and highlights of the day are provided by phone from the Department of Commerce. For economic news call 202–393–4100. For news highlights call 202–393–1847.

The Energy Information Center will provide free information on energy and related matters. Write National Energy Information Center, Forrestal Building, 1000 Independence Avenue SW, Washington, DC 20585. Call 202–586–5000.

Technical and scientific information are provided by the **National Technical Information Service** of the Department of Commerce, 5285 Port Royal, Springfield, VA 22161, which handles requests about government-sponsored research of all kinds. The basic charge to research a subject is $125. For information call 703–487–4600. For orders call 703–487–4650. For rush orders within the local calling area call 703–487–4700. For rush order outside the local calling area call 800–336–4700.

The **Census Bureau** produces detailed statistical information for the U.S. Information is available on population, housing, agriculture, manufacturing, retail trade, service industries, wholesale trade, foreign trade, mining, transportation, construction, and the revenues and expenditures of state and local governments. The Bureau also produces statistical studies of many foreign countries.

Information Sources in the Bureau of the Census

User Services

Product Information .... (301) 763-4100
Guides, Catalogs and Directories 763-1584
Data User Training 763-1510

Government, Commerce and Industry Subjects

Agriculture Data .... (301) 763-1113
Business Data (Retail, Wholesale,
  Services)............................ 763-7564
Construction Statistics 763-7163
Foreign Trade Data.................... 763-5140
  State Exports 763-2725
Government Data 763-7366
Industry Data 763-7800
Manufactures Data 763-7666

Population, Housing and Income Subjects

Housing Data...................... (301) 763-2880
International Statistics.................. 763-4221

Neighborhood Statistics 763-4280
Population Data........................ 763-5020
Special Demographic Studies 763-7720

Government, Commerce and Civic Relations 763-2436

Regional Assistance

Atlanta, Georgia .... (404) 347-2271
Boston, Massachusetts .... (617) 565-7100
Charlotte, North Carolina .... (704) 672-6142
Chicago, Illinois .... (312) 353-6251
Dallas, Texas..................... (214) 767-7488
Denver, Colorado .... (303) 969-7750
Detroit, Michigan .... (313) 354-4654
Kansas City, Kansas .... (913) 236-3728
Los Angeles, California .... (213) 209-6616
New York, New York .... (212) 264-3860
Philadelphia, Pennsylvania .... (215) 597-4920
Seattle, Washington .... (206) 442-7828

For a detailed telephone contact
list .... (301) 763-4100

Source: *Business Services Directory*, U.S. Department of Commerce, Office of Business Liaison.

Information Sources in the U.S. Department of Commerce: Quick Reference List

Aeronautical Chart Sales .... (301) 436-6990
Business Assistance .... (202) 377-3176
Commerce Speakers .... (202) 377-1360
Copyright Information* .... (202) 479-0700
Consumer Affairs .... (202) 377-5001
District Export Councils .... (202) 377-2975
Energy Related Inventions-
  Evaluation .... (301) 975-5500

EXPORT
  Counseling..................... (202) 377-3181
  Export Trading Companies .... (202) 377-5131
  License/Application (STELA) .... (202) 377-2752
Fish Exports/Imports .... (202) 673-5335
Fishery Management Plans.......... (202) 673-5268
Foreign Trade Zones .... (202) 377-2862
Freight Rates** .... (202) 366-2271
Industry/Products Information .... (202) 377-1461
Joint Ventures (National) .... (202) 377-1093
Metric Information .... (202) 377-3036
Minority Owned Business .... (202) 377-2414
Nautical Chart Sales .... (301) 436-6990
NTIS Sales Desk .... (703) 487-4650
Overseas Customer Lists .... (202) 377-3181
Overseas Marketing .... (202) 377-3022
Patent Information .... (703) 557-5168
Productivity Enhancement
  Information .... (202) 377-0940

PROCUREMENT
  Bidder's List.................... (202) 377-3387
  Federal Procurement
    Conferences .... (202) 377-3387

* Handled by the Library of Congress
** Handled by Maritime Commission

MBDA Profile System .... (202) 377-1958
Small Business .... (202) 377-1472
Women Owned Business .... (202) 377-3387

PUBLICATIONS
  "Business America" Magazine ..... (202) 377-3251
  Commerce Business Daily .... (202) 377-0632
  NIST Reference Materials .... (301) 975-2012
  Survey of Current Business .... (202) 523-0777
Quality Award .... (301) 975-2036
Sea Grant Research .... (301) 443-8923

SMALL BUSINESS
  Assistance .... (202) 377-3176
  Procurement/Set Asides .... (202) 377-3387
  Technology .... (202) 377-8111
Standards & Codes for Products ..... (301) 975-4036

STATISTICS
  Business Cycles .... (202) 523-0800
  Capital Investment .... (202) 523-0791
  Gross National Product .... (202) 377-0669
  Foreign Travelers to U.S. .... (202) 377-4028
  Housing Starts................. (301) 763-2880
  Income Data .... (301) 763-5060
  International Investment.......... (202) 523-0659
  International Trade Balance .... (202) 523-0620
  Leading Economic Indicators ...... (202) 523-0777
  Personal Income, Outlays
    and Savings .... (202) 523-0832
  Personal Income by County ...... (202) 523-0966
  Population .... (301) 763-5002
  Price Indexes .... (202) 523-0828
  Regional Projections .... (202) 523-0946
  Retail Trade Data .... (301) 763-5294
  Trade Statistics .... (202) 377-2185

Source: *Business Services Directory*, U.S. Department of Commerce, Office of Business Liaison.

COMMODITIES: SOURCES OF GOVERNMENT INFORMATION*

Information on various commodities may be obtained by calling the following:

Office of Industries
International Trade Commission
Telephone: 292–523–0146

Bureau of Mines
The Bureau uses three basic classifications:
Ferrous Metals
Telephone: 202–634–1010
Nonferrous Metals
Telephone: 202–634–1055
Industrial Minerals
Telephone: 202–634–1202

Crops Branch
Department of Agriculture
Telephone: 202–786–1840

Metals, Minerals and Commodities
Trade Development
Telephone: 202–377–0575

Minerals Industries
Bureau of the Census
Telephone: 202–763–5938

Industry and Commodity Classification
Bureau of the Census
Telephone: 202–763–1935

Federal Agricultural Service: Commodity and Marketing Divisions
Dairy, Livestock and
Poultry . . . . (202) 477-8031
Grain and Feed
Division . . . . . . (202) 477-6219
Horticulture and Tropical
Products . . . . . . (202) 477-6590
Oilseed and Oilseed
Products . . . . . . (202) 447-7037
Tobacco, Cotton and
Seeds . . . . (202) 382-9516
Forest Products . . . . (202) 382-8138

Available through the Government Printing Office (202–783–3238) are the Bureau of the Census Publications, *U.S. Imports, U.S.A. Commodities by Country* and *U.S.*

Exports Schedule 13, Commodities by Country.

DOING BUSINESS WITH THE FEDERAL GOVERNMENT

Publications

Doing Business with the Federal Government contains helpful material for marketing products or services to the Government, i.e., how to make products known, how and where to obtain the necessary forms and papers to get started, and how to bid on Government contracts. It also provides a geographical listing of Business Service Centers that have information about contract opportunities, as well as whom to contact and where to go for the information needed to sell to individual Government agencies. A list of Business Service Centers is given below.

The *Commerce Business Daily* tells, for example, what products and services the Government is buying, which agencies are buying, due dates for bids, how to get complete specifications. Each weekday, the *Commerce Business Daily* gives a complete listing of products and services wanted by the U.S. Government. Each listing includes product or service, along with a short description, name and address of agency, deadline for proposals or bids, phone number to request specifications, and solicitation numbers of product or service needed. Issued Monday through Friday.

The *Federal Acquisition Regulation* (FAR) is the primary source of procurement regulations used by all Federal agencies in their acquisition of supplies and services. It sets forth all the provisions and clauses that are used in Government contracting. Because the clauses in a specific solicitation for bids refer to a numbered provision of FAR rather than providing the full text, the FAR is necessary to understand the solicitation. Subscription service consists of a basic manual and supplementary material for an indeterminate period.

The *United States Government Purchasing and Sales Directory* contains an alphabetical listing of the products and services bought by all military departments and a separate listing for civilian agencies. It also includes an explanation of the ways in which the Small Business Administration can help a business obtain Government prime contracts and subcontracts, data on Government sales of surplus property, and comprehensive descriptions of the scope of the Government market for research and development.

The *Small Business Subcontracting Directory* is designed to aid small business professionals interested in subcontracting opportunities within the Department of Defense

---

* For information on the Department of Agriculture's Foreign Agricultural Service see page 719.

(DOD). The guide is arranged alphabetically by state and includes the name and address of each current DOD prime contractor as well as the product or service being provided to DOD. It also includes the name and telephone number for each DOD Small Business Liaison Officer who knows what the subcontracted products and services are, what the prime contracting firm has purchased in the past, what it is presently purchasing, and what it may be planning to purchase in the future.

The *Federal Register* provides the official version of public regulations issued by the Federal agencies. It also includes announcements of grants and other funding information, as well as data on the availability of Government contracts.

U.S. GENERAL SERVICES ADMINISTRATION: BUSINESS SERVICE CENTERS

The Business Service Centers are a one stop, one point of contact for information on General Services Administration and other Government contract programs. The primary function is to provide advice on doing business with the Federal Government. The Centers provide information, assistance, and counseling and sponsor business clinics, procurement conferences, and business opportunity meetings.

Business representatives interested in selling products and services to the Government should contact the nearest Business Service Center given below.

Mailing Address and Telephone	Area of Service
Business Service Center General Services Administration Tip O'Neill Federal Building 10 Causeway Street Boston, MA 02109 (617) 565–8100	Connecticut, Maine, Massachusetts, New Hampshire, Rhode Island, and Vermont
Business Service Center General Services Administration 26 Federal Plaza New York, NY 10007 (212) 264–1234	New Jersey, New York, Puerto Rico, and Virgin Islands
Business Service Center General Services Administration 7th and D Streets, SW., RM. 1050 Washington, DC 20407 (202) 472–1804	District of Columbia, nearby Maryland, Virginia
Business Service Center General Services Administration 9th and Market Streets Room 5151 Philadelphia, PA 19107 (215) 597–9613	Delaware, Pennsylvania, West Virginia, Maryland, Virginia
Business Service Center General Services Administration Richard B. Russell Federal Building and Court House 75 Spring Street Atlanta, GA 30303 (404) 221–5103	Alabama, Florida, Georgia, Kentucky, Mississippi, North Carolina, South Carolina, and Tennessee
Business Service Center General Services Administration 230 South Dearborn Street Chicago, IL 60604 (312) 353–5383	Illinois, Indiana, Ohio, Michigan, Minnesota, and Wisconsin
Business Service Center General Services Administration 1500 East Bannister Road Kansas City, MO 64131 (816) 926–7203	Iowa, Kansas, Missouri, and Nebraska
Business Service Center General Services Administration 819 Taylor Street Fort Worth, TX 76102 (817) 334–3284	Arkansas, Louisiana, New Mexico, Oklahoma, and Texas

Mailing Address and Telephone	Area of Service
Business Service Center General Services Administration Building 41, Denver Federal Center Denver, CO 80225 (303) 236–7408	Colorado, Montana, North Dakota, South Dakota, Utah, and Wyoming
Business Service Center General Services Administration 525 Market Street San Francisco, CA 94105 (415) 454–9000	California (northern), Hawaii, and Nevada (except Clark County)
Business Service Center General Services Administration 300 North Los Angeles Street Los Angeles, CA 90012 (213) 894–3210	Arizona, Los Angeles, California (southern), and Nevada (Clark County only)
Business Service Center General Services Administration 15th and C Streets, Auburn, WA 98001 (206) 931–7956	Alaska, Idaho, Oregon, and Washington

FEDERAL AND STATE GOVERNMENT ASSISTANCE AVAILABLE TO U.S. BUSINESSES: CENTER FOR THE UTILIZATION OF FEDERAL TECHNOLOGY

Government support of technical innovation is growing rapidly both at the Federal and State levels. A helpful source for information regarding the transfer of Federal technology to the U.S. economy is the **Center for the Utilization of Federal Technology (CUFT)**, which is part of the National Technical Information Service (NTIS) of the U.S. Department of Commerce, (703) 487-4805. One of its major roles is to link U.S. businesses with federally developed technologies and resources having commercial or practical application. By working directly with U.S. Government agencies, CUFT has prepared a number of directories and catalogs to alert companies to these valuable Government resources.

Its most recent directory, *Directory of Federal and State Business Assistance–A Guide for New and Growing Companies*, presents full descriptions to financial, management, innovation, and information programs and services established to help both large and small firms in their day-to-day operations. A listing of state services is given on page 641.

A companion directory, *Directory of Federal Laboratory and Technical Resources–A Guide to Services, Facilities, and Expertise*, provides detailed descriptions of technology-oriented Federal resources. Especially notable are the entries describing the technical information centers offering information assistance in focused technology areas.

Also available are the *Federal Technology Catalogs–Guides to New and Practical Technologies* which annually offer full descriptions to more than 1,200 new technologies and R&D developments. Another annual catalog series, *Catalog of Government Inventions Available for Licensing*. The *Catalog* contains information on licensing and marketing government-owned-inventions, frequently with the benefit of exclusive licensing and/or with the protection of foreign patent rights. To order write the National Technical Information Service, 5285 Port Royal Road, Springfield, VA 22161 or call 703-487-4650.

BUSINESS ASSISTANCE PROGRAM: COMMERCE DEPARTMENT

The Business Assistance program is designed to shorten the time it takes a businessperson to track down information within the labyrinth of government bureaus and agencies. Business Assistance Program staffers can provide information or direct inquiries to the proper authority on such subjects as regulatory changes, government programs, services, policies, and even relevant government publications for the business community. For information call 202–377–3176 or write: Business Assistance Program Business Liason Office, Rm 5898-C, Department of Commerce, Washington, DC 20230.

State Information Guide

Regional Directories

Directory of Central Atlantic States Manufacturers, Manufacturers' News, Inc., 4 E. Huron Street, Chicago, IL 60611; George D. Hall Company, 50 Congress Street, Boston, MA 02109

Directory of New England Manufacturers, The, George D. Hall Company, 50 Congress Street, Boston, MA 02109

Interstate Manufacturers' and Industrial Directory, Bell Directory Publishers, Inc., 1995 Broadway, New York, NY 10023

Midwest Manufacturers' and Industrial Directory, Industrial Directory Publishers, David Whitney Building, Detroit, MI 48226

New England Industrial Service Directory, George D. Hall Company, 50 Congress Street, Boston, MA 02109

New England Manufacturers Directory, Manufacturers' News, Inc., 4 E. Huron Street, Chicago, IL 60611

Southern California Business Directory and Guide, Manufacturers' News, Inc., 4 E. Huron Street, Chicago, IL 60611

State Executive Directory, Carroll Publishing Company, 1058 Thomas Jefferson NW, Washington, DC 20007

State Sales Guides, Dun & Bradstreet, Inc., 99 Church Street, New York, NY 10007

State Business Assistance Publications

Directory of Incentives for Business Investment and Development in the U.S., The Urban Institute Press, available from United Press of America, 4720 Boston Way, Lanhlam, MD 20706. State by state guide to economic business incentives. Included are descriptions of state assistance and financial assistance programs.

Monthly Checklist of State Publications, Superintendent of Documents. Washington, DC 20402. A monthly list of documents and publications received from the States.

The National Directory of State Agencies, Cambridge Information Group, 7200 Wisconsin Avenue, Bethesda, MD 20814-9777. Names, titles, addresses and telephone numbers of state officials.

State Administrative Officials Classified by Function, Council of State Governments, Iron Works Pike, P.O. Box 1190, Lexington, KY 40578. Names, titles, telephone numbers and addresses of state officials and administrators.

Business Assistance Centers by State

These centers offer assistance in business related matters. Such assistance includes information gathering, location of expert help, and guidance on new technologies. Most of these centers also are able to offer other types of assistance, such as market feasibility, or at least link businesses with appropriate contacts.

To find out where a center for a given state is located, contact the Department of Commerce for that state.

State Data Center Program of the Bureau of the Census

Access to the many statistical products available from the Bureau of the Census is provided through the services of the joint federal-state cooperative State Data Center Program. Through the Program, the Bureau furnishes statistical products, training in the data access and use, technical assistance, and consultation to states which, in turn, disseminate the products and provide assistance in their use.

Additional information on the State Data Program and a list of the State Data Centers can be obtained by contacting the User Services staff in any of the Bureau's regional offices or by calling the Data User Services Division of the Bureau of the Census at 301-763-1580.

State Information Offices

Alabama*

STATE CAPITOL, MONTGOMERY, AL 36130
(205) 261-2500

---

* For Small Business Administration offices, see page 274.

INFORMATION OFFICES

Commerce/Economic Development
Alabama Development Office
135 S. Union Street
Montgomery, AL 36130
Department of Economic & Community
Affairs
3465 Norman Bridge Road
Montgomery, AL 36105
Corporate
Secretary of State
State Office Building
Montgomery, AL 36130
Taxation
Department of Revenue
Administrative Building
64 N. Union Street
Montgomery, AL 36130
State Chamber of Commerce
Alabama Chamber of Commerce
468 S. Perry Street
P.O. Box 76
Montgomery, AL 36101
International Commerce
Department of International Trade
Alabama Development Office   ˋ
135 South Union
Montgomery, AL 36130
Banking
State Banking Department
166 Commerce
Montgomery, AL 36130
Securities
Alabama Securities Exchange Commission
166 Commerce Street
Montgomery, AL 36130
Labor and Industrial Relations
Department of Industrial Relations
649 Monroe Street
Montgomery, AL 36130
Alabama Department of Labor
Administrative Building
64 N. Union Street
Montgomery, AL 36130
Insurance
Department of Insurance
135 S. Union Street
Montgomery, AL 36130
Uniform Industrial Code
Alabama Development Office
State Capitol
Montgomery, AL 36130

INDUSTRIAL AND BUSINESS DIRECTORIES

Alabama Directory of Mining and Manufacturing, Alabama Development Office, State Capitol, Montgomery, AL 36130; Manufacturers' News, Inc., 4 E. Huron Street, Chicago, IL 60611
Alabama International Trade Directory, Ala-

bama Development Office, State Capitol, Montgomery, AL 36130
Alabama Metalworking Directory, Alabama Development Office, State Capitol, Montgomery, AL 36130
Birmingham Industrial Directory, Birmingham Chamber of Commerce, 1914 6th Avenue, Birmingham, AL 35200

Alaska

STATE CAPITOL, JUNEAU, AK 99811
(907) 465-2111

INFORMATION OFFICES

Commerce/Economic Development
Department of Commerce & Economic
Development
P.O. Box D
Juneau, AK 99811
Corporate
Department of Commerce & Economic
Development
Corporation Section
P.O. Box D-Corp
Juneau, AK 99811
Taxation
Department of Revenue
P.O. Box S
Juneau, AK 99811-0400
State Chamber of Commerce
Alaska State Chamber of Commerce
310 2nd Street
Juneau, AK 99801
International Commerce
Office of International Trade
3601 C Street
Anchorage, AK 99503
Banking
Division of Banking, Securities and Corporations
Department of Commerce & Economic
Development
P.O. Box D
Juneau, AK 99811
Securities
Division of Banking, Securities and Corporations
Department of Commerce and Economic
Development
P.O. Box D
Juneau, AK 99811
Labor and Industrial Relations
Department of Labor
P.O. Box 21149
Juneau, AK 99802-1149
Insurance
Division of Insurance
Department of Commerce and Economic
Development
P.O. Box D
Juneau, AK 99811

Uniform Industrial Code
Uniform Commercial Code Office
Division of Management
Department of Natural Resources
P.O. Box 107005
Anchorage, AK 99510-7005

INDUSTRIAL AND BUSINESS DIRECTORIES

Alaska Petroleum and Industrial Directory,
409 W. Northern Lights Boulevard, Anchorage, AK 99603

Arizona

STATE CAPITOL, PHOENIX, AZ 85007
(602) 542-4900

INFORMATION OFFICES

Commerce/Economic Development
Department of Commerce
3800 N. Central Avenue
Phoenix, AZ 85012
Corporate
Arizona Corporation Commission
1200 W. Washington Avenue
Phoenix, AZ 85007
Taxation
Department of Revenue
1600 W. Monroe
Phoenix, AZ 85007
State Chamber of Commerce
Arizona State Chamber of Commerce
1221 E. Osborn Road
Phoenix, AZ 85014
Banking
Banking Department
3225 N. Central
Phoenix, AZ 85012
Insurance
Insurance Department
3030 N. 3rd Street
Phoenix, AZ 85012
Securities
Arizona Corporation Commission
1200 W. Washington Avenue
Phoenix, AZ 85007
International Commerce
Department of Commerce
3800 N. Central Avenue
Phoenix, AZ 85012
Labor and Industrial Relations
Industrial Commission
800 W. Washington Street
Phoenix, AZ 85005

INDUSTRIAL AND BUSINESS DIRECTORIES

Arizona Directory of Industries, Manufacturers' News, 4 E. Huron Street, Chicago, IL 60611

Arizona Directory of Manufacturers, Manufacturers' News, Inc., 4 E. Huron Street, Chicago, IL 60611
Arizona USA International Trade Directory, Arizona State Department of Commerce, 3800 N. Central Avenue, Phoenix, AZ 85012
Directory of Arizona Manufacturers, Phoenix Chamber of Commerce, 34 W. Monroe, Phoenix, AZ 85003

Arkansas

STATE CAPITOL, LITTLE ROCK, AR 72201
(501) 682-2345

INFORMATION OFFICES

Commerce/Economic Development
Industrial Development Commission
Big Mac Building
One State Capitol Mall
Little Rock, AR 72201
Corporate
Secretary of State
Corporation Department
State Capitol
Little Rock, AR 72201
Taxation
Division of Revenue Services
Department of Finance and Administration
Joel Y. Ledbetter Building
7th and Wolfe Streets
Little Rock, AR 72201
State Chamber of Commerce
Arkansas State Chamber of Commerce
911 Wallace Building
Little Rock, AR 72201
International Commerce
Industrial Development Commission
Big Mac Building
One State Capitol Mall
Little Rock, AR 72201
Banking
Bank Department
323 Center Street
Little Rock, AR 72201
Securities
Securities Department
Heritage West Building
201 East Markham
Little Rock, AR 72201
Labor and Industrial Relations
Arkansas Department of Labor
1022 High Street
Little Rock, AR 72202
Insurance
Insurance Division
University Towers Building
Little Rock, AR 72204
Ombudsman
State Claims Commission
State Capitol
Little Rock, AR 72201

INDUSTRIAL AND BUSINESS DIRECTORIES

Arkansas Directory of Manufacturers, Manufacturers' News, 4 E. Huron Street, Chicago, IL 60611

Directory of Arkansas Manufacturers, Arkansas Industrial Development Foundation, P.O. Box 1784, Little Rock, AR 72203

State and County Economic Data (annual), University of Arkansas Industrial Research Center, University of Arkansas, Little Rock College of Business Administration, 33rd and University Avenue, Little Rock, AR 72204

California

STATE CAPITOL, SACRAMENTO, CA 95814 (916) 332-9900

INFORMATION OFFICES

Commerce/Economic Development
Department of Commerce
1121 L Street
Sacramento, CA 95814
Corporate
Secretary of State
1230 "J" Street
Sacramento, CA 95814
Taxation
Board of Equalization
1020 N Street
Sacramento, CA 95814
State Chamber of Commerce
California Chamber of Commerce
1027 10th Street
P.O. Box 1736
Sacramento, CA 95814
International Commerce
California State World Trade Commission
1121 L Street
Sacramento, CA 95814
Banking
State Banking Department
11 Pine Street
San Francisco, CA 94111-5613
Securities
Department of Corporations
1107 9th Street
Sacramento, CA 95814
Labor and Industrial Relations
Department of Industrial Relations
525 Golden Gate Avenue
P.O. Box 603
San Francisco, CA 94101
or
1121 L Street
Sacramento, CA 95814
Insurance
Department of Insurance
600 S. Commonwealth Avenue

Los Angeles, CA 90005
or
700 "L" Street
Sacramento, CA 93814

INDUSTRIAL AND BUSINESS DIRECTORIES

California Handbook, Center for California Public Affairs, 226 W. Foothill Boulevard, Claremont, CA 91711

California International Business Directory, Center for International Business, 333 S. Flower Street, Los Angeles, CA 90071

California Manufacturers Register, Time-Mirror Press, 1115 S. Boyle Avenue, Los Angeles, CA 90023; Manufacturers' News, Inc., 4 E. Huron Street, Chicago, IL 60611

California Services Register, Manufacturers' News, Inc., 4 E. Huron Street, Chicago, IL 60611

San Francisco Manufacturers Directory, San Francisco Chamber of Commerce, 333 Pine Street, San Francisco, CA 94577

Southern California Business Directory and Buyers Guide, Los Angeles Chamber of Commerce, 404 S. Bixel Street, Los Angeles, CA 95113; Manufacturers' News, Inc., 4 E. Huron Street, Chicago, IL 60611

Colorado

STATE CAPITOL, DENVER, CO 80203 (303) 866-5000

INFORMATION OFFICES

Commerce/Economic Development
Office of Economic Development
Business Development
1625 Broadway
Denver, CO 80202
Corporate
Secretary of State
Corporation Division
1560 Broadway
Denver, CO 80202
Taxation
Administrative Division
Department of Revenue
1375 Sherman Street
Denver, CO 80203
State Chamber of Commerce
Colorado Association of Commerce and Industry
1860 Lincoln Street
Denver, CO 80295
International Commerce
Office of Economic Development
International Trade Office
1625 Broadway
Denver, CO 80202

Banking
  Division of Banking
  303 W. Colfax Street
  Denver, CO 80204
Securities
  Securities Commission
  Department of Regulatory Agencies
  1525 Sherman Street
  Denver, CO 80203
Labor and Industrial Relations
  Division of Labor
  1313 Sherman Street
  Denver, CO 80203
Insurance
  Division of Insurance
  303 W. Colfax Street
  Denver, CO 80204
Uniform Industrial Code
  Commercial Recordings Division
  1560 Broadway
  Denver, CO 80202

INDUSTRIAL AND BUSINESS DIRECTORIES

Directory of Colorado Manufacturers, Business Research Division, Graduate School of Business Administration, Campus Box 420, University of Colorado, Boulder, CO 80309; Manufacturers' News, Inc., 4 E. Huron Street, Chicago, IL 60611.

Connecticut

STATE CAPITOL, HARTFORD, CT 06106
(203) 566-4200

INFORMATION OFFICES

Commerce/Economic Development
  Department of Economic Development
  865 Brook Street
  Rocky Hill, CT 06067
Corporate
  Secretary of State
  Corporations Division
  30 Trinity Street
  Hartford, CT 06106
Taxation
  Department of Revenue Services
  92 Farmington Avenue
  Hartford, CT 06105
State Chamber of Commerce
  Connecticut Business and Industry Association
  370 Asylum Street
  Hartford, CT 06103
International Commerce
  Department of Economic Development
  865 Brook Street
  Rocky Hill, CT 06067

Banking
  Department of Banking
  44 Capitol Avenue
  Hartford, CT 06106
Securities
  Divisions of Securities & Business Investments
  Department of Banking
  44 Capitol Avenue
  Hartford, CT 06106
Labor and Industrial Relations
  Department of Labor
  200 Folly Brook Boulevard
  Wethersfield, CT 06109
Insurance
  Department of Insurance
  165 Capitol Avenue
  Hartford, CT 06106
Uniform Industrial Code
  Department of Economic Development
  865 Brook Street
  Rocky Hill, CT 06107
Business Ombudsman
  Department of Economic Development
  210 Washington Street
  Hartford, CT 06106

INDUSTRIAL AND BUSINESS DIRECTORIES

Classified Business Directory—State of Connecticut, Connecticut Directory Co., Inc., 322 Main Street, Stamford, CT 06901
Connecticut Classified Business Directory, Connecticut Directory Co., Inc., 322 Main Street, Stamford, CT 06901
Connecticut Service Directory, George D. Hall Co., 50 Congress Street, Boston, MA 02109
Directory of Connecticut Manufacturers, George D. Hall Co., 50 Congress Street, Boston, MA 02109
Directory of Connecticut Manufacturing Establishments, Connecticut Department of Labor, 200 Folly Brook Boulevard, Wethersfield, CT 06109
MacRAE's State Industrial Directory Connecticut/Rhode Island, MacRAE's Industrial Directories, 817 Broadway, New York, NY 10003

Delaware

LEGISLATIVE HALL, DOVER, DE 19901
(302) 736-4101

INFORMATION OFFICES

Commerce/Economic Development
  Delaware Development Office
  99 Kings Highway
  P.O. Box 1401
  Dover, DE 19903

Corporate
  Secretary of State
  Corporations Department
  Townsend Building
  P.O. Box 898
  Dover, DE 19903
Taxation
  Department of Finance
  Division of Revenue
  Carvel State Office Building
  820 N. French Street
  Wilmington, DE 19801
International Commerce
  Delaware Development Office
  99 Kings Highway
  P.O. Box 1401
  Dover, DE 19903
State Chamber of Commerce
  Delaware State Chamber of Commerce,
    Inc.
  One Commerce Center
  Wilmington, DE 19801
Banking
  State Bank Commission
  Department of State
  Thomas Collins Building
  P.O. Box 1401
  Dover, DE 19903
Labor and Industrial Relations
  Division of Industrial Affairs
  Department of Labor
  Carvel State Office Building
  820 N. French Street
  Wilmington, DE 19801
Insurance
  State Insurance Commission
  841 Silver Lake Boulevard
  Rodney Building
  Dover, DE 19901

INDUSTRIAL AND BUSINESS DIRECTORIES

Delaware Directory of Commerce and Industry, Delaware State Chamber of Commerce, One Commerce Center, Wilmington, DE 19801; Manufacturers' News, Inc., 4 E. Huron Street, Chicago, IL 60611

MacRAE's State Industrial Directory Maryland/DC/Delaware, MacRAE's Industrial Directories, 817 Broadway, New York, NY 10003

Florida

STATE CAPITOL, TALLAHASSEE, FL 32399
(904) 488-1234

INFORMATION OFFICES

Commerce/Economic Development
  Department of Commerce
  Collins Building

107 W. Gaines Street
Tallahassee, FL 32399-2001
  Division of Economic Development
  Department of Commerce
  Collins Building
  Tallahassee, FL 32399
Corporate
  Secretary of State
  Division of Corporations
  407 E. Gaines Street
  Tallahassee, FL 32304
Taxation
  Department of Revenue
  Carlton Building
  Tallahassee, FL 32399-0100
State Chamber of Commerce
  Florida State Chamber of Commerce
  P.O. Box 11309
  Tallahassee, FL 32302
International Commerce
  Florida Department of Commerce
  Bureau of International Trade
  Carlton Building
  107 W. Gaines Street
  Tallahassee, FL 32399
Banking
  Florida Department of Banking & Finance
  The Capitol
  Tallahassee, FL 32399
Securities
  Florida Department of Banking & Finance
  Division of Securities
  The Capitol
  Tallahassee, FL 32399
Labor and Industrial Relations
  Florida Department of Labor and Employment Security
  Atkins Building
  1320 Executive Center Drive, East
  Tallahassee, FL 32399
Insurance
  Florida Department of Insurance
  The Capitol
  Tallahassee, FL 32399
Commercial Information Services
  Florida Department of State
  Bureau of Information Services
  407 E. Gaines Street
  Tallahassee, FL 32314
Business Ombudsman
  Florida Department of Commerce
  Bureau of Business and Community Development
  Collins Building
  107 W. Gaines Street
  Tallahassee, FL 32399

INDUSTRIAL AND BUSINESS DIRECTORIES

Florida Manufacturers Register, Manufacturers' News, Inc., 4 E. Huron Street, Chicago, IL 60611

South Florida International Trade and Services Directory 1990
World Trade Center Miami
One World Trade Plaza
80 SW 8th St., Suite 1800
Miami, FL 33130
Directory of International Manufacturing and Commercial Operations In Florida
Florida Department of Commerce
Bureau of International Trade and Development
Collins Building
Tallahassee, FL 32399
Directory of Florida Industries
Florida Chamber of Commerce
Trend Book Division
P.O. Box 611
St Petersburg, FL 33731

Georgia

STATE CAPITOL, ATLANTA, GA 30334
(404) 656-2000

INFORMATION OFFICES

Commerce/Economic Development
Department of Industry, Trade, and Tourism
P.O. Box 1776
285 Peachtree Center Avenue
Atlanta, GA 30301
Corporate
Corporations Division
Secretary of State
2 Martin Luther King Jr. Drive, SE
Atlanta, GA 30334
Taxation
Department of Revenue
270 Washington Street, SW
Atlanta, GA 30334
State Chamber of Commerce
Business Council of Georgia
233 Peachtree Street
Atlanta, GA 30303-2705
International Commerce
Department of Industry, Trade, and Tourism
P.O. Box 1776
285 Peachtree Center Avenue
Atlanta, GA 30303
Banking
Department of Banking and Finance
2990 Brandywine Road
Atlanta, GA 30341
Securities
Securities Division
Secretary of State
2 Martin Luther King Jr. Drive, SE
Atlanta, GA 30334

Labor and Industrial Relations
Department of Labor
148 International Boulevard
Atlanta, GA 30303
Insurance
Office of Commissioner of Insurance
2 Martin Luther King Jr. Drive, SE
Atlanta, GA 30334

INDUSTRIAL AND BUSINESS DIRECTORIES

Georgia Manufacturers Register, Manufacturers' News, Inc., 4 E. Huron Street, Chicago, IL 60611
Georgia Manufacturing Directory, Department of Industry, Trade, and Tourism, P.O. Box 1776, 285 Peachtree Center Avenue, Atlanta, GA 30301
Georgia World Trade Directory, Business Council of Georgia, 233 Peachtree Street, Atlanta, GA 30303
Industrial Sites in Georgia, Georgia Power Company, Box 4545, Atlanta, GA 30303
Georgia International Trade Directory, Department of Industry, Trade, and Tourism, P.O. Box 1776, 285 Peachtree Center Avenue, Atlanta, GA 30301
Georgia Directory of International Services, World Congress Institute, 1 Park Place S, Fulton Federal Building, Atlanta, GA 30303
International Companies with Facilities in Georgia. Department of Industry, Trade, and Tourism, P.O. Box 1776, 285 Peachtree Center Avenue, Atlanta, GA 30301

Hawaii

STATE CAPITOL, HONOLULU, HI 96813
(808) 548-6222

INFORMATION OFFICES

Commerce/Economic Development
Department of Business and Economic Development
250 S. King Street
Honolulu, HI 96813
Department of Commerce and Consumer Affairs
1010 Richards Street
Honolulu, HI 96813
Corporate
Department of Commerce and Consumer Affairs
Business Registration Division
P.O. Box 40
Honolulu, HI 96810
Taxation
Department of Taxation
830 Punchbowl Street
Honolulu, HI 96813

State Chamber of Commerce
Chamber of Commerce of Hawaii
735 Bishop Street
Honolulu, HI 96813
International Commerce
International Services Branch
Department of Business and Economic Development
P.O. Box 2359
Honolulu, HI 96804
Hawaii Foreign-Trade Zone No. 9, Pier 2
521 Ala Moana Blvd.
Honolulu, HI 96804
Banking
Division of Financial Institutions
Department of Commerce and Consumer Affairs
1010 Richards Street
Honolulu, HI 96813
Securities
Division of Financial Institutions
State Department of Commerce and Consumer Affairs
1010 Richards Street
Honolulu, HI 96813
Labor and Industrial Relations
State Department of Labor and Industrial Relations
830 Punchbowl Street
Honolulu, HI 96813
Insurance
Insurance Division
State Department of Commerce and Consumer Affairs
1010 Richards Street
Honolulu, HI 96813
Business Ombudsman
Office of the Ombudsman
465 S. King Street
Honolulu, HI 96813

INDUSTRIAL AND BUSINESS DIRECTORIES

Directory of Manufacturers, State of Hawaii, Chamber of Commerce of Hawaii, Dillingham Building, 735 Bishop Street, Honolulu, HI 96813
Hawaii Business Directory, Hawaii Business Directory, Inc., 1164 Bishop Street, Honolulu, HI 96813

Idaho

STATE CAPITOL, BOISE, ID 83720
(208) 334-2411

INFORMATION OFFICES

Mailing address for all state offices is:
Statehouse
Boise, ID 83720

Commerce/Economic Development
Department of Commerce
700 W. State Street
Boise, ID 83720
Corporate
Secretary of State
State Capitol
Boise, ID 83720
Taxation
Department of Revenue and Taxation
700 W. State Street
Boise, ID 83720
State Chamber of Commerce
Idaho Association of Commerce and Industry
805 West Idaho
Boise, ID 83702
International Commerce
Department of Commerce
700 W. State Street
Boise, ID 83720
Banking
Department of Finance
700 W. State Street
Boise, ID 83720
Securities
Department of Finance
700 W. State Street
Boise, ID 83720
Labor and Industrial Relations
Department of Labor and Industrial Services
277 N. 6th Street
Boise, ID 83720
Insurance
Department of Insurance
500 S. 10th Street
Boise, ID 83720
Uniform Industrial Code
Department of Labor and Industrial Services
277 N. 6th Street
Boise, ID 83720
Business Ombudsman
Department of Commerce
700 W. State Street
Boise, ID 83720

INDUSTRIAL AND BUSINESS DIRECTORIES

Manufacturing Directory of Idaho, Center for Business and Research, University of Idaho, Moscow, ID 83843; Manufacturers' News, Inc., 4 E. Huron Street, Chicago, IL 60611
Idaho Opportunities, Department of Commerce, 700 W. State Street, Boise, ID 83720

Illinois

STATE HOUSE, SPRINGFIELD, IL 62706
(217) 782-2000

INFORMATION OFFICES

Commerce/Economic Development
Department of Commerce and Community Affairs
620 E. Adams Street
Springfield, IL 62701
Corporate
Corporate Division
Centennial Building
Springfield, IL 62756
Taxation
Department of Revenue
101 W. Jefferson Street
Springfield, IL 62708
State Chamber of Commerce
Illinois State Chamber of Commerce
20 N. Wacker Drive
Chicago, IL 60606
International Commerce
Department of Commerce & Community Affairs
State of Illinois Center
100 W. Randolph Street
Chicago, IL 60601
Banking
Department of Financial Institutions
100 W. Randolph Street
Chicago, IL 60601
Securities
Secretary of State
840 S. Spring Street
Springfield, IL 62704
Labor and Industrial Relations
Department of Labor
100 N. 1st, Alzina Building
Springfield, IL 62706
Department of Commerce & Community Affairs
620 E. Adams Street
Springfield, IL 62701
Insurance
Department of Insurance
320 W. Washington Street
Springfield, IL 62767
Uniform Industrial Code
Department of Commerce & Community Affairs
620 E. Adams Street
Springfield, IL 62701
Business Ombudsman
Department of Commerce & Community Affairs
620 E. Adams Street
Springfield, IL 62701

INDUSTRIAL AND BUSINESS DIRECTORIES

Chicago Buyers' Guide, Chicago Association of Commerce and Industry, 130 S. Michigan Avenue, Chicago, IL 60603
Chicago Cook County and Illinois Industrial Directory, Manufacturers' News, Inc., 4 E. Huron Street, Chicago, IL 60611
Chicago Geographic Edition, Manufacturers' News, Inc., 4 E. Huron Street, Chicago, IL 60611
Illinois Industrial Directory, Manufacturers' News, Inc., 4 E. Huron Street, Chicago, IL 60611
Illinois Manufacturers Directory, Manufacturers' News, Inc., 4 E. Huron Street, Chicago, IL 60611
Illinois Services Directory, Manufacturers' News, Inc., 4 E. Huron Street, Chicago, IL 60611
Business Financing Programs, Department of Commerce and Community Affairs, 620 E. Adams, Springfield, IL 62701

Indiana

STATE HOUSE, INDIANAPOLIS, IN 46204
(317) 232-3140

INFORMATION OFFICES

Commerce/Economic Development
Department of Commerce
1 N. Capitol Avenue
Indianapolis, IN 46204
Corporate
Secretary of State
Corporation Division
State House
Indianapolis, IN 46204
Taxation
Department of Revenue
State Office Building
100 N. Senate Avenue
Indianapolis, IN 46204
State Board of Tax Commissioners
201 State Office Building
100 N. Senate Avenue
Indianapolis, IN 46204
State Chamber of Commerce
Indiana State Chamber of Commerce, Inc.
1 N. Capitol Avenue, Ste 200
Indianapolis, IN 46204
International Commerce
International Trade Division
Indiana Department of Commerce
1 N. Capitol Avenue
Indianapolis, IN 46204
Banking
Department of Financial Institutions
State Office Building
100 N. Senate Avenue
Indianapolis, IN 46204
Securities
Secretary of State
Securities Commission
1 N. Capitol Avenue
Indianapolis, IN 46204

Labor and Industrial Relations
Indiana Department of Labor
State Office Building
100 N. Senate Avenue
Indianapolis, IN 46204
Insurance
Indiana Department of Insurance
311 W. Washington Street
Indianapolis, IN 46204
Uniform Industrial Code
Uniform Commercial Code Division
Secretary of State Office
State House
Indianapolis, IN 46204
Business Ombudsman
Business Ombudsman Office
Department of Commerce
1 N. Capitol Avenue
Indianapolis, IN 46204

INDUSTRIAL AND BUSINESS DIRECTORIES

Indiana Manufacturers Directory, Manufacturers' News, Inc., 4 E. Huron Street, Chicago, IL 60611

Iowa

STATE CAPITOL, DES MOINES, IA 50319
(515) 281-5011

INFORMATION OFFICES

Commerce/Economic Development
Department of Economic Development
200 E. Grand
Des Moines, IA 50309
Corporate
Secretary of State
Corporation Division
Hoover Building
Des Moines, IA 50319
Taxation
Department of Revenue
Hoover Building
Des Moines, IA 50319
International Commerce
Department of Economic Development
200 E. Grand
Des Moines, IA 50309
Banking
Department of Commerce
Banking Division
200 E. Grand
Des Moines, IA 50309
Iowa Housing Finance Authority
200 E. Grand
Des Moines, IA 50309
Securities
Department of Commerce
Insurance Division
Securities Bureau

Lucas Building
Des Moines, IA 50319
Labor
Department of Employment Service
Division of Industrial Services
1000 E. Grand
Des Moines, IA 50319
Bureau of Labor
1000 E. Grand
Des Moines, IA 50319
Insurance
Department of Commerce
Insurance Division
Lucas Building
Des Moines, IA 50319

INDUSTRIAL AND BUSINESS DIRECTORIES

Directory of Iowa Manufacturers, Iowa Department of Economic Development, 200 E. Grand, Des Moines, IA 50309
Doing Business in Iowa, Iowa Department of Economic Development, 200 E. Grand, Des Moines, IA 50309
Iowa Manufacturers Register, Manufacturers' News, Inc., 4 E. Huron Street, Chicago, IL 60611

Kansas

STATE HOUSE, TOPEKA, KS 66612
(913) 296-0111

INFORMATION OFFICES

Commerce/Economic Development
Department of Commerce
400 S.W. 8th Street
Topeka, KS 66612
Corporate
Secretary of State
State House
Corporation Department
Topeka, KS 66612
Taxation
Department of Revenue
State Office Building
915 Harrison Street
Topeka, KS 66612
State Chamber of Commerce
Kansas Chamber of Commerce and Industry
500 Bank IV Tower
534 Kansas
Topeka, KS 66603-3460
International Commerce
Department of Commerce
400 S.W. 8th Street
Topeka, KS 66612
Banking
Banking Department
700 Jackson Street
Topeka, KS 66603

Securities
Securities Commissioner of Kansas
900 S.W. Jackson Street
Topeka, KS 66612
Labor and Industrial Relations
Department of Human Resources
401 Topeka
Topeka, KS 66603
Insurance
Insurance Department
420 W. 9th Street
Topeka, KS 66612
Business Ombudsman
Department of Commerce
400 W. 8th Street
Topeka, KS 66612

INDUSTRIAL AND BUSINESS DIRECTORIES

Directory of Kansas Manufacturers and Products, Kansas Department of Commerce, 400 W. 8th Street, Topeka, KS 66603-3957; Manufacturers' News, Inc., 4 E. Huron Street, Chicago, IL 60611, New York, NY 10003
Directory of Manufacturers, Wichita, Kansas, Wichita Area Chamber of Commerce, 350 West Douglas, Wichita, KS 67202
Kansas Fortune 500 Companies, Kansas Department of Commerce, 400 W. 8th Street, Topeka, KS 66603-3957
Kansas Manufacturing Firms in Export, Kansas Department of Commerce, 400 W. 8th Street, Topeka, KS 66603-3957
Kansas Association Directory, Kansas Department of Commerce, 400 W. 8th Street, Topeka, KS 66603-3957

Kentucky

STATE CAPITOL, FRANKFORT, KY 40601
(502) 564-3130

INFORMATION OFFICES

Commerce/Economic Development
Kentucky Economic Development Cabinet
Capital Plaza Office Tower
Frankfort, KY 40601
Corporate
Office of Secretary of State
Corporation Division
Capitol Building
Frankfort, KY 40601
Taxation
Kentucky Revenue Cabinet
Capitol Annex
Frankfort, KY 40601
State Chamber of Commerce
Kentucky Chamber of Commerce
Versailles Road
P.O. Box 817
Frankfort, KY 40602

International Commerce
Kentucky Economic Development Cabinet
Office of International Marketing
Capitol Plaza Tower
Frankfort, KY 40601
Banking
Kentucky Department of Financial Institutions
Division of Banking and Thrift Institutions
911 Leawood Drive
Frankfort, KY 40601-3392
Securities
Kentucky Department of Financial Institutions
Division of Securities
911 Leawood Drive
Frankfort, KY 40601-3392
Labor Industrial Relations
Kentucky Labor Cabinet
The 127 Building
Frankfort, KY 40601
Insurance
Kentucky Department of Insurance
229 West Main Street
P.O. Box 517
Frankfort, KY 40602
Uniform Industrial Code
Kentucky Department of Housing, Buildings, and Construction
The 127 Building
Frankfort, KY 40601
Business Ombudsman
Kentucky Department of Existing Business and Industry
Capitol Plaza Tower
Frankfort, KY 40601

INDUSTRIAL AND BUSINESS DIRECTORIES

Kentucky International Trade Directory, Kentucky Economic Development Cabinet, Capitol Plaza Tower, Frankfort, KY 40601
Kentucky Directory of Manufacturers, Kentucky Economic Development Cabinet, Capitol Plaza Tower, Frankfort, KY 40601; Manufacturers' News, Inc., 4 E. Huron Street, Chicago, IL 60611; Harris Publishing Co., 2057 Aurora Road, Twinsburg, OH 44087-1999

Louisiana

STATE CAPITOL, BATON ROUGE, LA 70804
(504) 342-7015

INFORMATION OFFICES

Commerce/Economic Development
Department of Commerce
P.O. Box 94185
Baton Rouge, LA 70804-9185

Corporate
Secretary of State
Division of Corporation
P.O. Box 94125
Baton Rouge, LA 70804-9125

Taxation
Department of Revenue
P.O. Box 3440
Baton Rouge, LA 70823

State Chamber of Commerce
Louisiana Association of Business and Industry
P.O. Box 80258
Baton Rouge, LA 70898

International Commerce
Department of Commerce
Office of International Trade,
Finance and Development
P.O. Box 94185
Baton Rouge, LA 70804-9185

Banking
Department of Commerce
Office of Financial Institutions
P.O. Box 94095
Baton Rouge, LA 70804

Securities
Louisiana Securities Commission
315 Louisiana State Office Building
325 Loyola Avenue
New Orleans, LA 70112

Labor and Industrial Relations
Department of Labor
P.O. Box 94094
Baton Rouge, LA 70804-9094

Insurance
Office of Insurance Rating Commission
P.O. Box 94157
Baton Rouge, LA 70804

Uniform Industrial Code
Department of Commerce
P.O. Box 94185
Baton Rouge, LA 70804-9185

Department of Employment Security and Training
P.O. Box 94094
Baton Rouge, LA 70804-9094

Business Ombudsman
Department of Commerce
P.O. Box 94185
Baton Rouge, LA 70804-9185

INDUSTRIAL AND BUSINESS DIRECTORIES

Directory of Louisiana Manufacturers, Manufacturers' News, Inc., 4 E. Huron Street, Chicago, IL 60611

Louisiana Directory of Manufacturers, Department of Commerce, 101 France Street, Baton Rouge, LA 70802

Louisiana International Trade Directory, World Trade Center, 2 Canal Street, New Orleans, LA 70130

Maine

STATE HOUSE, AUGUSTA, ME 04333
(207) 289-1110

INFORMATION OFFICES

Commerce/Economic Development
Department of Economic and Community Development
193 State Street
State House Station #59
Augusta, ME 04333

Corporate
Department of State
Division of Corporations
Statehouse Station #101
Augusta, ME 04333

Private Development Associations
Maine Development Foundation
1 Memorial Circle
Augusta, ME 04330

Taxation
Bureau of Taxation
Department of Finance
State House Station #24
Augusta, ME 04333

State Chamber of Commerce
Maine State Chamber of Commerce and Industry
126 Sewall Street
Augusta, ME 04330

International Commerce
Department of Economic and Community Development
193 State Street
State House Station #59
Augusta, ME 04333

Banking
Bureau of Banking
Hallowell Annex
Correspondence to:
State House Station #36
Hallowell, ME 04347

Securities
Bureau of Banking
Securities Division
State House Station #121
Augusta, ME 04333

Labor and Industrial Relations
Department of Labor
20 Union Street
P.O. Box 309
Augusta, ME 04330

Insurance
Bureau of Insurance
Hallowell Annex
Hallowell, ME 04347
Correspondence to:
State House #34
Augusta, ME 04333

INDUSTRIAL AND BUSINESS DIRECTORIES

Maine Marketing Directory, Department of Economic and Community Development, State House Station #59, Augusta, ME 04333

MacRAE's State Industrial Directory Maine/ New Hampshire/Vermont, MacRAE's Industrial Directories, 817 Broadway, New York, NY 10003

Maine Manufacturing Directory, Tower Publishing Company, 34 Diamond Street, Portland, ME 04101

Maryland

STATE HOUSE, ANNAPOLIS, MD 21401
(301) 974-2000

INFORMATION OFFICES

Commerce/Economic Development
Department of Economic and Employment Development
217 E. Redwood Street
Baltimore, MD 21202

Corporate
State Department of Assessments and Taxation
301 W. Preston Street
Baltimore, MD 21201

Taxation
Comptroller of the Treasury
Louis L. Goldstein Treasury Building
P.O. Box 466
Annapolis, MD 21404

State Chamber of Commerce
Maryland Chamber of Commerce
275 West Street
Annapolis, MD 21401

International Commerce
Department of Economic and Employment Development
Office of International Trade
World Trade Center
401 East Pratt Street
Baltimore, MD 21202

Maryland Port Administrator
Office of Port Administration
World Trade Center
401 E. Pratt Street
Baltimore, MD 21202

Banking
State Banking Commission
Department of Licensing and Regulation
34 Market Place
Baltimore, MD 21202

Securities
Division of Securities
Office of the Attorney General
200 St. Paul Place
Baltimore, MD 21202

Labor and Industrial Relations
Division of Labor and Industry
Department of Licensing and Regulation
501 St. Paul Place
Baltimore, MD 21202

Insurance
State Insurance Division
Department of Licensing and Regulation
501 St. Paul Place
Baltimore, MD 21202

Business Ombudsman
Department of Economic and Employment Development
Maryland Business Assistance Center
217 East Redwood Street
Baltimore, MD 21202

INDUSTRIAL AND BUSINESS DIRECTORIES

Directory of Maryland Manufacturers, *Maryland Magazine*, Maryland Department of Economic and Employment Development, 217 East Redwood Street, Baltimore, MD 21202; Manufacturers' News, Inc., 4 E. Huron Street, Chicago, IL 60611

MacRAE's State Industrial Directory Maryland, DC/Delaware, MacRAE's Industrial Directories, 817 Broadway, New York, NY 10003

Maryland High-Tech Directory, *Maryland Magazine*, Maryland Department of Economic Employment and Development, Maryland Business Assistance Center, 211 East Redwood Street, Baltimore, MD 21202

Massachusetts

STATE HOUSE, BOSTON, MA 02133
General Information: (617) 727-2121

INFORMATION OFFICES

Commerce/Economic Development
Governor's Office of Economic Development
Room 109
State House
Boston, MA 02133

Massachusetts Department of Commerce and Development
Division of Economic Development
100 Cambridge Street
Boston, MA 02202

Executive Office of Economic Affairs
2101 McCormack Building
1 Ashburton Place
Boston, MA 02108

Department of Commerce and Development

Leverett Saltonstall Building
100 Cambridge Street
Boston, MA 02202
Corporate
Secretary of State
1 Ashburton Place
Boston, MA 02108
Taxation
Accounting Bureau
Leverett Saltonstall Building
100 Cambridge Street
Boston, MA 02202
International Commerce
Office of International Trade and Invest-
ment
100 Cambridge Street
Boston, MA 02202
Banking
Division of Banks and Loan Agencies
100 Cambridge Street
Boston, MA 02202
Securities
Secretary of State
Securities Division
1 Ashburton Place
Boston, MA 02108
Labor and Industrial Relations
Executive Office of Labor
1 Ashburton Place
Boston, MA 02108

Department of Labor and Industries
Executive Office of Economic Affairs
100 Cambridge Street
Boston, MA 02202
Insurance
Division of Insurance
100 Cambridge Street
Boston, MA 02202

INDUSTRIAL AND BUSINESS DIRECTORIES

Directory of Directors in the City of Boston and Vicinity, Bankers Service Co., 14 Beacon Street, Boston, MA 02108
Directory of Massachusetts Manufacturers, George D. Hall Co., 50 Congress Street, Boston, MA 02109
MacRAE's State Industrial Directory Massachusetts/Rhode Island, MacRAE's Industrial Directories, 817 Broadway, New York, NY 10003
Massachusetts Service Directory, George D. Hall Co., 50 Congress Street, Boston, MA 02109
Massachusetts State Industrial Directory, State Industrial Directories Corp., 2 Penn Plaza, New York, NY 10001

Michigan

STATE CAPITOL, LANSING, MI 48913
(517) 373-1837

INFORMATION OFFICES

Commerce/Economic Development
Department of Commerce
525 W. Ottawa Street
P.O. Box 30225
Lansing, MI 48909
Corporate
Corporation and Securities Bureau
6546 Mercantile Way
Lansing, MI 48909
Taxation
Bureau of Collection
Department of Treasury
Treasury Building
Lansing, MI 48922
State Chamber of Commerce
Michigan State Chamber of Commerce
200 N. Washington Square
Lansing, MI 48933
International Commerce
Manufacturing Development Group
International Development
Department of Commerce
525 W. Ottawa Street
P.O. Box 30225
Lansing, MI 48909
Banking
Financial Institutions Bureau
Department of Commerce
Olds Plaza Building
111 S. Capitol Avenue
P.O. Box 30224
Lansing, MI 48909
Securities
Corporation and Securities Bureau
Department of Commerce
6546 Mercantile Way
P.O. Box 30222
Lansing, MI 48909
Labor and Industrial Relations
Bureau of Labor Relations
Department of Labor
State of Michigan Plaza Building
1200 Sixth Street
Detroit, MI 48226

Department of Labor
Victor Office Center
201 North Washington
P.O. Box 30015
Lansing, MI 48909
Insurance
Insurance Bureau
Department of Licensing and Regulation
611 West Ottawa
North Ottawa Tower
P.O. Box 30220
Lansing, MI 48909

INDUSTRIAL AND BUSINESS DIRECTORIES

Harris Michigan Marketers Industrial Directory, Harris Publishing Company, 2057 Aurora Road, Twinsburg, OH 44139

Michigan Distributors Directory, Manufacturers' News, Inc., 4 E. Huron Street, Chicago, IL 60611

Michigan Manufacturers Directory, Manufacturers' News, Inc., 4 E. Huron Street, Chicago, IL 60611

Minnesota

STATE CAPITOL, ST. PAUL, MN 55155
(612) 296-6013

INFORMATION OFFICES

Commerce/Economic Development
Department of Trade and Economic Development
900 American Center Building
St. Paul, MN 55101
Minnesota Department of Commerce
Metro Square Building
7th and Robert Streets
St. Paul, MN 55101
Corporate
Corporation Division
180 State Office Building
St. Paul, MN 55155
Taxation
Department of Revenue
10 River Park Plaza
St. Paul, MN 55146
State Chamber of Commerce
Minnesota Association of Commerce and Industry
Hanover Building
480 Cedar Street
St. Paul, MN 55101
International Commerce
Minnesota Trade Office
1000 World Trade Center
St. Paul, MN 55101
Banking
Minnesota Department of Commerce
Banking Division
Metro Square Building
7th & Robert Streets
St. Paul, MN 55101
Securities
Minnesota Department of Commerce
Registration Unit
Metro Square Building
7th & Robert Streets
St. Paul, MN 55101
Labor and Industrial Relations
Minnesota Department of Labor and Industry
443 Lafayette Road
St. Paul, MN 55101
Insurance
Minnesota Department of Commerce
Policy Analysis Division
Metro Square Building
7th & Robert Streets
St. Paul, MN 55101

Business Ombudsman
Department of Trade and Economic Development
Small Business Assistance Office
900 American Center Building
St. Paul, MN 55101

INDUSTRIAL AND BUSINESS DIRECTORIES

Minnesota Directory of Manufacturers, Manufacturers' News, Inc., 4 E. Huron Street, Chicago, IL 60611; State Industrial Directories Corp., 2 Penn Plaza, New York, NY 10001

Minnesota Manufacturer's Register, Manufacturers' News, Inc., 4 E. Huron Street, Chicago, IL 60611

Mississippi

NEW CAPITOL, JACKSON, MS 39205
(601) 359-3100

INFORMATION OFFICES

Commerce/Economic Development
Mississippi Department of Economic and Community Development
P.O. Box 849
Jackson, MS 39205
Division of Exports, MDECD
P.O. Box 849
Jackson, MS 39205
Department of Agriculture and Commerce
P.O. Box 1609
Jackson, MS 39215
Corporate
Division of Corporate Development, MDECD
P.O. Box 136
Jackson, MS 39205
Taxation
Tax Commission
102 Woolfolk Building
Jackson, MS 39201
State Chamber of Commerce
P.O. Box 1849
Jackson, MS 39205-1849
Banking
Department of Banking and Consumer Finance
1206 Woolfolk State Office Building
Jackson, MS 39205
Securities
Department of State
Securities Division
P.O. Box 136
Jackson, MS 39205
Labor and Industrial Relations
1520 W. Capitol Street
Jackson, MS 39205

Insurance
Department of Insurance
1804 Sillers Building
Jackson, MS 39205
Business Ombudsman
Mississippi Department of Economic and
Community Development
P O Box 849
Jackson, MS 39205

INDUSTRIAL AND BUSINESS DIRECTORIES

Mississippi International Trade Directory,
Mississippi Marketing Council, Box 849,
Sillers State Office Building, Jackson, MS
39205
Mississippi Manufacturers' Directory, Manufacturers' News, Inc., 4 E. Huron Street,
Chicago, IL 60611; Research Division, Department of Economic and Community Development, P.O. Box 849, Jackson, MS
39205

Missouri

STATE CAPITOL, JEFFERSON CITY, MO 65101
(314) 751-2151

INFORMATION OFFICES

Commerce/Economic Development
Department of Economic Development
Economic Development Programs
P.O. Box 118
Jefferson City, MO 65102
Corporate
Secretary of State
Corporations Division
P.O. Box 778
Jefferson City, MO 65102
Taxation
Department of Revenue
Division of Taxation
Truman State Office Building
P.O. Box 629
Jefferson City, MO 65105
State Chamber of Commerce
Missouri Chamber of Commerce
428 East Capitol Avenue
P.O. Box 149
Jefferson City, MO 65102
International Commerce
International Business Development
Economic Development Program
Truman State Office Building
P.O. Box 118
Jefferson City, MO 65102
Banking
Missouri Division of Finance
Truman State Office Building
P.O. Box 716
Jefferson City, MO 65102

Securities
Office of the Secretary of State
Securities Division
Truman State Office Building
P.O. Box 778
Jefferson City, MO 65102
Labor and Industrial Relations
Missouri Dept. of Labor & Industrial Relations
421 E. Dunklin
Jefferson City, MO 65102
Insurance
Missouri Division of Insurance
Truman State Office Building
P.O. Box 690
Jefferson City, MO 65102
Uniform Industrial Code
Missouri Division of Labor Standards
P.O. Box 449
Jefferson City, MO 65102
Business Ombudsman
Office of the Lieutenant Governor
Missouri State Capitol
P.O. Box 563
Jefferson City, MO 65102

INDUSTRIAL AND BUSINESS DIRECTORY

Contacts Influential: Commerce and Industrial Directory (for Kansas City Area),
Contacts Influential, Inc., 6347 Brookside
Boulevard, Suite 204, Kansas City, MO
64113
*Missouri Directory of Manufacturing and
Mining* (annual), Informative Data Co.,
3546 Watson Road, St. Louis, MO 63139
Missouri Manufacturers' Register, Manufacturers' News, Inc., 4 E. Huron Street, Chicago, IL 60611

Montana

STATE CAPITOL, HELENA, MT 59620
(406) 444-3111

INFORMATION OFFICES

Commerce/Economic Development
Department of Commerce
1424 9th Avenue
Helena, MT 59620
Economic Development and Research
Department of Commerce
1429 9th Avenue
Helena, MT 59620

Census and Economic Information Center
Department of Commerce
1429 9th Avenue
Helena, MT 59620
Corporate
Secretary of State
Corporation Bureau
State Capitol Building
Helena, MT 59620

State Chamber of Commerce
  Montana Chamber of Commerce
  P.O. Box 1730
  Helena, MT 59601
International Commerce
  International Export Officer
  Montana Department of Commerce
  1424 9th Avenue
  Helena, MT 59620
Banking
  Commissioner of Financial Institutions
  Montana Department of Commerce
  1424 9th Avenue
  Helena, MT 59620
Securities
  Securities Division
  State Auditor's Office
  Sam Mitchell Building
  Helena, MT 59620
Labor & Industrial Relations
  Commissioner's Office
  Montana Department of Labor & Industry
  Lockey and Roberts
  Helena, MT 59620
Insurance
  Insurance Division
  State Auditor's Office
  Sam Mitchell Building
  Helena, MT 59620
Uniform Commercial Code
  Secretary of State
  Uniform Commercial Code Bureau
  State Capitol Building
  Capitol Station
  Helena, MT 59620
Business Ombudsman
  Small Business Advocate
  Montana Department of Commerce
  1424 9th Avenue
  Helena, MT 59620

INDUSTRIAL AND BUSINESS DIRECTORIES

Montana Manufacturers and Products Directory, Department of Commerce, 1424 9th Avenue, Helena, MT 59620; Manufacturers' News, Inc., 4 E. Huron Street, Chicago, IL 60611

Montana Business & Industrial Location Guide, Department of Commerce, 1424 9th Avenue, Helena, MT 59620

Nebraska

STATE CAPITOL, LINCOLN, NE 68509
(402) 471-2311

INFORMATION OFFICES

Commerce/Economic Development
  Department of Economic Development
  301 Centennial Mall South
  P.O. Box 94666
  Lincoln, NE 68509-4666
Corporate
  Secretary of State
  Corporation Division
  P.O. Box 94608
  Lincoln, NE 68509-4608
Taxation
  Department of Revenue
  301 Centennial Mall South
  P.O. Box 94818
  Lincoln, NE 68509-4818
State Chamber of Commerce
  Nebraska Chamber of Commerce and Industry
  1320 Lincoln Mall
  P.O. Box 95128
  Lincoln, NE 68501
International Commerce
  Nebraska Department of Economic Development
  Small Business Division
  P.O. Box 94666
  Lincoln, NE 68509-4666
Banking
  Department of Banking and Finance
  301 Centennial Mall South
  P.O. Box 95006
  Lincoln, NE 68509-5006
Securities
  Department of Banking and Finance
  301 Centennial Mall South
  P.O. Box 95006
  Lincoln, NE 68509-5006
Labor and Industrial Relations
  Nebraska Department of Labor
  550 South 16th Street
  P.O. Box 94600
  Lincoln, NE 68509-4600
Insurance
  Department of Insurance
  The Terminal Building
  941 O Street
  Lincoln, NE 68508
Uniform Industrial Code
  Uniform Commercial Code Division
  301 Centennial Mall South
  P.O. Box 95104
  Lincoln, NE 68509-5104
Business Ombudsman
  One-Stop Center
  Department of Economic Development
  P.O. Box 94666
  Lincoln, NE 68509-4666

INDUSTRIAL AND BUSINESS DIRECTORIES

A Directory of Lincoln, Nebraska Manufacturers, Lincoln Chamber of Commerce, 1221 N. Street, Lincoln, NE 68508

Directory of Nebraska Manufacturers and Their Products, Manufacturers' News,

Inc., 4 E. Huron Street, Chicago, IL 60611
Directory of Nebraska Manufacturers and Their Products, Nebraska State Department of Economic Development, P.O. Box 94666, Lincoln, NE 68509-4666

Directory of Manufacturers for the Omaha Metropolitan Area, Omaha Economic Development Council, 1301 Harney, Omaha, NE 68102.

Directory of Major Employers for the Omaha Area, Omaha Economic Development Council, 1301 Harney, Omaha, NE 68102.

Nevada

STATE CAPITOL, CARSON CITY, NV 89710
(702) 885-5000

INFORMATION OFFICES

Commerce/Economic Development
Department of Commerce
Capitol Complex
Carson City, NV 89710
Commission on Economic Development
Capitol Complex
Carson City, NV 89710
Corporate
Secretary of State
Capitol Complex
Carson City, NV 89710
Taxation
Department of Taxation
Capitol Complex
Carson City, NV 89710
State Chamber of Commerce
Nevada Chamber of Commerce Association
P.O. Box 2806
Reno, NV 89505
International Commerce
Capitol Complex
Department of Commerce
Carson City, NV 89710
Banking
Financial Institutions Division
Capitol Complex
Department of Commerce
Carson City, NV 89710
Securities
Secretary of State
Capitol Complex
Carson City, NV 89710
Labor and Industrial Relations
Labor Commission
Capitol Complex
Carson City, NV 89710
Department of Industrial Relations
Carson City, NV 89710
Insurance
Insurance Division
Department of Commerce
Capitol Complex
Carson City, NV 89710

INDUSTRIAL AND BUSINESS DIRECTORIES

Directory of Nevada Mine Operations, Division of Mine Inspection Department of Industrial Relations, 1380 Capitol Complex, Carson City, NV 89710

Nevada Industrial Directory, Gold Hill Publishings Co., Inc., P.O. Drawer F, Virginia City, NV 89440

Nevada Directory of Business, Manufacturers' News, Inc., 4 E. Huron Street, Chicago, IL 60611

New Hampshire

STATE HOUSE, CONCORD, NH 03301
(603) 271-1110

INFORMATION OFFICES

Commerce/Economic Development
Department of Resources and Economic Development
Division of Economic Development
105 Loudon Road, Building #2
Prescott Park
Concord, NH 03301
Corporate
Secretary of State
Corporations Division
State House Annex
Concord, NH 03301
Taxation
Board of Taxation
61 S. Spring Street
Concord, NH 03301
Department of Revenue Administration
61 S. Spring Street
Concord, NH 03301
State Chamber of Commerce
Business and Industry Association of New Hampshire
23 School Street
Concord, NH 03301
International Commerce
Department of Resources & Economic Development
Division of Economic Development
105 Loudon Road, Building #2
Prescott Park—Concord, NH 03301
Banking
Banking Department
State of New Hampshire
45 S. Main Street
Concord, NH 03301
New Hampshire Banking Association
125 N. Main Street
Concord, NH 03301
Securities
Insurance Department, Securities Division
State of New Hampshire
169 Manchester Street
Concord, NH 03301

Labor and Industrial Relations
Department of Employment Security
State of New Hampshire
32 S. Main Street
Concord, NH 03301

Department of Labor
19 Pillsbury Street
Concord, NH 03301

Insurance
Insurance Department
State of New Hampshire
169 Manchester Street
Concord, NH 03301

Standard Industrial Code
Department of Employment Security
State of New Hampshire
32 S. Main Street
Concord, NH 03301

INDUSTRIAL AND BUSINESS DIRECTORIES

Made in New Hampshire, New Hampshire Office of Industrial Development, Department of Resources, Concord, NH 03301

MacRAE's State Industrial Directory Maine/ New Hampshire/Vermont, MacRAE's Industrial Directories, 817 Broadway, New York, NY 10003

New Hampshire Manufacturing Directory, Tower Publishing Company, 34 Diamond Street, Portland, ME 04111

New Jersey

STATE HOUSE, TRENTON, NJ 08625
(609) 292-2121

INFORMATION OFFICES

Commerce/Economic Development
Department of Commerce and Economic Development
CN 820, 20 W. State Street
Trenton, NJ 08625

Division of Travel and Tourism
CN 826, 20 W. State Street
Trenton, NJ 08625

Economic Development Authority
CN 990, Capitol Place One
200 S. Warren Street
Trenton, NJ 08625

Corporate
Secretary of State
Division of Commercial Recreation
820 Bear Tavern Road
W. Trenton, NJ 08625

Taxation
Department of Treasury
Division of Taxation
CN 240, 50 Barrack Street
Trenton, NJ 08625

State Chamber of Commerce
New Jersey State Chamber of Commerce
1 State Street Square
50 W. State Street
Trenton, NJ 08608

International Commerce
Division of International Trade
Gateway 4
100 Mulberry Street
Newark, NJ 07102

Banking
Department of Banking
CN 040, 20 W. State Street
Trenton, NJ 08625

Securities
Bureau of Securities
2 Gateway Center
Newark, NJ 07102

Labor and Labor Relations
Department of Labor and Industry
John Fitch Plaza, CN 110
Trenton, NJ 08625

Insurance
Department of Insurance
20 E. State Street
Trenton, NJ 08625

Business Ombudsman
Department of Public Advocate
CN 850, Justice Complex
25 Market Street
Trenton, NJ 08625

INDUSTRIAL AND BUSINESS DIRECTORIES

New Jersey Manufacturers Directory, George D. Hall Co., 50 Congress Street, Boston, MA 02109

MacRAE's New Jersey State Industrial Directory, MacRAE's Industrial Directories, 817 Broadway, New York, NY 10003

The New Jersey Directory of Manufacturers, Commerce Register®, Inc., 190 Godwin Avenue, Midland Park, NJ 07432

New Mexico

STATE CAPITOL, SANTA FE, NM 87503
(505) 827-3000

INFORMATION OFFICES

Commerce/Economic Development
Economic Development and Tourism
Joseph M. Montoya Building
1100 St. Francis Drive
Santa Fe, NM 87503

Corporate
State Corporation Commission
P.O. Drawer 1269
Santa Fe, NM 87501

Taxation
Taxation and Revenue Department
P.O. Box 630

Manuel Lujan Sr. Building
Santa Fe, NM 87509-0630
State Chamber of Commerce
Association of Commerce and Industry of
New Mexico
4001 Indian School NE
Albuquerque, NM 87110
International Commerce
Trade Division
Economic Development and Tourism De-
partment
Joseph M. Montoya Building
1100 St. Francis Drive
Santa Fe, NM 87503
Banking
Financial Institutions Division
Regulation and Licensing Department
P.O. Box 25101
Santa Fe, NM 87504
Securities
Securities Division
Financial Institutions Division
Regulation and Licensing Department
P.O. Box 25101
Santa Fe, NM 87503
Labor and Industrial
1896 Pacheso Street
Aspen Plaza Building
Santa Fe, NM 87501
Insurance
State Corporation Commission
P.O. Drawer 1269
Santa Fe, NM 87501

INDUSTRIAL AND BUSINESS DIRECTORIES

New Mexico Manufacturing Directory, Manufacturers' News, Inc., 4 E. Huron Street,
Chicago, IL 60611
New Mexico Directory of Manufacturers,
Economic Development Division, New Mexico Economic Development and Tourism
Department, Joseph M. Montoya Building,
1100 St. Francis Drive, Santa Fe, NM
87503

New York

STATE CAPITOL, ALBANY, NY 12224
(518) 474-2121

INFORMATION OFFICES

Commerce/Economic Development
Department of Economic Development
One Commerce Plaza
Albany, NY 12245
Division of Regional Economic Develop-
ment
One Commerce Plaza
Albany, NY 12245

Corporate
Secretary of State
162 Washington Avenue
Albany, NY 12231
Taxation
Department of Taxation and Finance
State Campus Building #9
Albany, NY 12227
State Chamber of Commerce
Business Council of New York State
152 Washington Avenue
Albany, NY 12210
Small Business Advisory Board
Division for Small Business
1515 Broadway
New York, NY 10036
International Commerce
Department of Economic Development
1515 Broadway
New York, NY 10036
Banking
Department of Banking
194 Washington Avenue
New York, NY 12210
Labor and Industrial Relations
Department of Labor
State Campus
Albany, NY 12240
Insurance
Department of Insurance
Empire State Plaza
Agency Building #1
Albany, NY 12257
Business Ombudsman
Department of Economic Development
Division for Small Business
1515 Broadway
New York, NY 10036

INDUSTRIAL AND BUSINESS DIRECTORIES

New York Manufacturers' Directory, George
D. Hall Co., 50 Congress Street, Boston,
MA 02109
*MacRAE's New York State Industrial Direc-
tory*, MacRAE's Industrial Directories, 817
Broadway, New York, NY 10003
The New York State Directory, Cambridge
Information Group, 7200 Wisconsin Ave-
nue, Bethesda, MD 20814-9777
*Directory of Certified Minority and Women-
Owned Business Enterprises*, Minority and
Women's Business Division, New York
State Department of Economic Develop-
ment, 515 Broadway, New York, NY 10036

North Carolina

GENERAL ASSEMBLY LEGISLATIVE BUILDING,
RALEIGH, NC 27601
(919) 733-1110 (government information)
733-7928 (legislators)

INFORMATION OFFICES

Commerce/Economic Development
Department of Economic and Community
Development
430 N. Salisbury Street
Raleigh, NC 27603
Corporate
Secretary of State
Corporation Division
300 N. Salisbury Street
Raleigh, NC 27603
Taxation
Department of Revenue
2 S. Salisbury Street
Raleigh, NC 27602
State Chamber of Commerce
North Carolina Citizens for Business and
Industry
P.O. Box 2508
Raleigh, NC 27602
International Commerce
International Development
Department of Economic and Community
Development
430 N. Salisbury Street
Raleigh, NC 27603
Banking
Banking Commission
Department of Economic and Community
Development
430 N. Salisbury Street
Raleigh, NC 27603
Securities
Secretary of State
Securities Division
300 N. Salisbury Street
Raleigh, NC 27603
Labor and Industrial Relations
Department of Labor
4 W. Edenton Street
Raleigh, NC 27601
Insurance
Department of Insurance
430 N. Salisbury Street
Raleigh, NC 27603
Business Ombudsman
Business Assistance
Department of Economic and Community
Development
430 N. Salisbury Street
Raleigh, NC 27603

INDUSTRIAL AND BUSINESS DIRECTORIES

*Directory of North Carolina Manufacturing
Firms,* North Carolina Department of Eco-
nomic and Community Development, Ra-
leigh, NC 27603; Manufacturers' News,
Inc., 4 E. Huron Street, Chicago, IL 60611
*MacRAE's State Industrial Directory North
Carolina/South Carolina, Virginia,* Mac-
RAE's Industrial Directories, 817 Broad-
way, New York, NY 10003
North Carolina Manufacturers Directory,
George D. Hall Co., 50 Congress Street,
Boston, MA 02109

North Dakota

STATE CAPITOL, BISMARCK, ND 58505
(701) 224-2000

INFORMATION OFFICES

Commerce/Economic Development
Economic Development Commission
604 East Boulevard
Bismarck, ND 58505
Corporate
Corporation Department
Office of the Secretary of State
600 East Boulevard
Bismarck, ND 58505
Taxation
Tax Department
600 East Boulevard
Bismarck, ND 58505
State Chamber of Commerce
Greater North Dakota Association—State
Chamber of Commerce
P.O. Box 2467
Fargo, ND 58102
International Commerce
International Trade Department
Economic Development Commission
604 East Boulevard
Bismarck, ND 58505
Banking
State Banking Commission
600 East Boulevard
Bismarck, ND 58505
Securities
Securities Commissioner
600 East Boulevard
Bismarck, ND 58505
Labor and Industrial Relations
State Commissioner of Labor
600 East Boulevard
Bismarck, ND 58505
Insurance
Insurance Commissioner
604 East Boulevard
Bismarck, ND 58505
Uniform Industrial Code
Secretary of State
604 East Boulevard
Bismarck, ND 58505
Business Ombudsman
Economic Development Commission
604 East Boulevard
Bismarck, ND 58505

INDUSTRIAL AND BUSINESS DIRECTORIES

North Dakota Directory of Manufacturers, Economic Development Commission, 604 East Boulevard, Bismarck, ND 58505; Manufacturers' News, Inc., 4 E. Huron Street, Chicago, IL 60611

Strictly Business, Frontier Directory Co., Inc., 515 E. Main Street, Bismarck, ND 58501

Ohio

STATE HOUSE, COLUMBUS, OH 43215
(614) 466-3455
State Operator: (614) 466-2000

INFORMATION OFFICES

Commerce/Economic Development
Ohio Department of Development
77 S. High Street
P.O. Box 1001
Columbus, OH 43266-0101
Corporate
Secretary of State
Corporation Section
30 E. Broad Street
Columbus, OH 43266-0418
Taxation
Department of Taxation
30 E. Broad Street
Columbus, OH 43266-0420
State Chamber of Commerce
Ohio Chamber of Commerce
35 E. Gay Street
Columbus, OH 43215
International Commerce
Ohio Department of Development
International Trade Division
77 S. High Street
P.O. Box 1001
Columbus, OH 43266-0101
Banking
Ohio Department of Commerce
Division of Banks
77 S. High Street
Columbus, OH 43266-0544
Securities
Ohio Department of Commerce
Division of Securities
77 S. High Street
Columbus, OH 43266-0544
Labor and Industrial Relations
Ohio Department of Industrial Relations
2323 W. Fifth Avenue
P.O. Box 825
Columbus, OH 43266-0567
Insurance
Ohio Department of Insurance
2100 Stella Court
Columbus, OH 43266-0566

Uniform Industrial Code
Industrial Commission of Ohio
Division of Safety and Hygiene
246 N. High Street
Columbus, OH 43266-0589
Business Ombudsman
Ohio Department of Development
Small and Developing Business Division
Minority Business Development Division
77 S. High Street
P.O. Box 1001
Columbus, OH 43266-0101

INDUSTRIAL AND BUSINESS DIRECTORIES

Akron, Ohio Membership Directory and Buyers Guide, Akron Area Chamber of Commerce, P.O. Box 436, Crystal Lake, IL 60014

Directory of Manufacturers in the Toledo Area, Toledo Area Chamber of Commerce, 218 Huron Street, Toledo, OH 43604

Manufacturers Directory, Columbus Area Chamber of Commerce, 37 North High Street, Columbus, OH 43215

Ohio Manufacturers Directory, Manufacturers' News, Inc., 4 E. Huron Street, Chicago, IL 60611

Oklahoma

STATE CAPITOL, OKLAHOMA CITY, OK 73105
(405) 521-1601

INFORMATION OFFICES

Commerce/Economic Development
Department of Commerce
6601 Broadway Extension
Oklahoma City, OK 73116
Corporate
Secretary of State
State Capitol
Oklahoma City, OK 73105
Taxation
Tax Commission
M. C. Connors Building
Oklahoma City, OK 73105
State Chamber of Commerce
Oklahoma State Chamber of Commerce & Industry
4020 North Lincoln
Oklahoma City, OK 73105
International Commerce
International Trade Division
Department of Commerce
6601 Broadway Extension
Oklahoma City, OK 73116
Banking
Oklahoma Banking Department
4100 Lincoln Boulevard
Oklahoma City, OK 73105

Securities
Oklahoma Securities Commission
Will Rogers Building
Oklahoma City, OK 73105

Labor and Industrial Relations
Oklahoma Labor Department
4001 N. Lincoln
Oklahoma City, OK 73105

Insurance
Insurance Commission
1901 N. Walnut Street
P.O. Box 53408
Oklahoma City, OK 73152

Uniform Industrial Code
Universal Commercial Code Division
County Clerk's Office
County Court House
Oklahoma City, OK 73102

INDUSTRIAL AND BUSINESS DIRECTORIES

Oklahoma Directory of Manufacturers and Products, Media/Marketing & Advertising, Department of Commerce, 6601 Broadway Extension, Oklahoma City, OK 73116; Manufacturers' News, Inc., 4 E. Huron Street, Chicago, IL 60611

Oregon

STATE CAPITOL, SALEM, OR 97310
(503) 378-3131

INFORMATION OFFICES

Commerce/Economic Development
Economic Development Department
775 Summer Street N.E.
Salem, OR 97310

Corporate
Corporation Division
Office of Secretary of State
Commerce Building
158 12th Street N.E.
Salem, OR 97310

Taxation
Department of Revenue
Revenue Building
955 Center Street
Salem, OR 97310

International Commerce
International Trade Division
Economic Development Department
One World Trade Center
121 S.W. Salmon
Portland, OR 97201

Banking
Finance Section
Division of Finance and Corporate Securities
Department of Insurance and Finance
21 Labor and Industries Building
Salem, OR 97310

Securities
Corporate Securities Section
Division of Finance and Corporate Securities
Department of Insurance and Finance
21 Labor and Industries Building
Salem, OR 97310

Labor and Industry
Bureau of Labor and Industries
1400 S.W. 5th Avenue
Portland, OR 97201

Insurance
Insurance Division
Department of Insurance and Finance
21 Labor and Industries Building
Salem, OR 97310

Uniform Industrial Code
Building Codes Agency
1535 Edgewater N.W.
Salem, OR 97310

INDUSTRIAL AND BUSINESS DIRECTORIES

Directory of Oregon Manufacturers, Economic Development Department, 595 Cottage Street N.E., Salem, OR 97310; Manufacturers' News, Inc., 4 E. Huron Street, Chicago, IL 60611

Pennsylvania

MAIN CAPITOL BUILDING, HARRISBURG, PA 17120
(717) 787-2121

INFORMATION OFFICES

Department of Commerce
Department of Commerce
Office of the Secretary
Forum Building
Harrisburg, PA 17120

Office of International Development
Department of Commerce
Forum Building
Harrisburg, PA 17120

Office of Program Management
Department of Commerce
Forum Building
Harrisburg, PA 17120

Business Resource Network
Department of Commerce
Forum Building
Harrisburg, PA 17120

Office of Technology Development
Department of Commerce
Forum Building
Harrisburg, PA 17120

Corporate
Department of State
Bureau of Corporations
308 North Office Building
Harrisburg, PA 17120

Taxation
Department of Revenue
P.O. Box 8903
Harrisburg, PA 17105
State Chamber of Commerce
Pennsylvania Chamber of Business and Industry
222 N. Third Street
Harrisburg, PA 17101-1596
Banking
Department of Banking
333 Market Street
Harristown II
Harrisburg, PA 17101-2290
Securities
Securities Commission
East Gate Office Building
1010 N. 7th Street
Harrisburg, PA 17102
Labor and Industrial Relations
Department of Labor & Industry
Labor & Industry Building
7th & Forster Streets
Harrisburg, PA 17120
Insurance
Department of Insurance
1321 Strawberry Square
Harrisburg, PA 17120

INDUSTRIAL AND BUSINESS DIRECTORIES

Harris Pennsylvania Industrial Directory of Pennsylvania, Department of Commerce, Harris Publishing Company, 2057-2 Aurora Road, Twinsburg, OH 44087
MacRAE's State Industrial Directory Pennsylvania, MacRAE's Industrial Directories, 817 Broadway, New York, NY 10003
Pennsylvania Manufacturers Register, Manufacturers' News, Inc., 4 E. Huron Street, Chicago, IL 60611

Rhode Island

STATE HOUSE, PROVIDENCE, RI 02903
(401) 277-2000

INFORMATION OFFICES

Commerce/Economic Development
Department of Economic Development
7 Jackson Walkway
Providence, RI 02903
Taxation
Division of Taxation
Department of Administration
One Capitol Hill
Providence, RI 02908
Corporate
Secretary of State
Corporation Department
100 N. Main Street
Providence, RI 02903

State Chamber of Commerce
Rhode Island Chamber of Commerce
91 Park Street
Providence, RI 02908
International Commerce
Rhode Island Department of Economic Development
European Office
Meir 24
2000 Antwerp
Belgium
Banking
Department of Business Regulation
Banking Division
233 Richmond Street
Providence, RI 02903
Securities
Department of Business Regulation
Banking Division
233 Richmond Street
Providence, RI 02903
Labor and Industrial Relations
Department of Labor
220 Elmwood Avenue
Providence, RI 02907
Insurance
Department of Business Regulation
Insurance Division
233 Richmond Street
Providence, RI 02903
Uniform Industrial Code
Department of Labor
220 Elmwood Avenue
Providence, RI 02907
Business Ombudsman
Business Action Center
Department of Economic Development
7 Jackson Walkway
Providence, RI 02903

INDUSTRIAL AND BUSINESS DIRECTORIES

MacRAE's State Industrial Directory Massachusetts/Rhode Island, MacRAE's Industrial Directories, 817 Broadway, New York, NY 10003
Rhode Island Directory of Manufacturers, Department of Economic Development, 7 Jackson Walkway, Providence, RI 02903; Manufacturers' News, Inc., 4 E. Huron Street, Chicago, IL 60611

South Carolina

STATE HOUSE, COLUMBIA, SC 29211
(803) 734-9818

INFORMATION OFFICES

Commerce/Economic Development
South Carolina State Development Board
P.O. Box 927
1201 Main Street
Columbia, SC 29202

Taxation
  Tax Commission
  P.O. Box 125
  Columbia Mill Building
  Columbia, SC 29201
Corporate
  Secretary of State
  P.O. Box 11350
  Columbia, SC 29211
State Chamber of Commerce
  South Carolina Chamber of Commerce
  1201 Main Street
  Columbia, SC 29202
International Commerce
  South Carolina State Development Board
  1201 Main Street
  P.O. Box 927
  Columbia, SC 29202
Labor and Industrial Relations
  South Carolina Labor Department
  Landmark Center, 3600 Forest Drive
  P.O. Box 11329
  Columbia, SC 29211
Insurance
  South Carolina Department of Insurance
  1612 Marion Street
  P.O. Box 100105
  Columbia, SC 29202-3105
Business Ombudsman
  South Carolina State Development Board
  1201 Main Street
  P.O. Box 927
  Columbia, SC 29202

INDUSTRIAL AND BUSINESS DIRECTORIES

Industrial Directory of South Carolina,
  South Carolina State Development Board,
  P.O. Box 927, 1201 Main Street, Columbia,
  SC 29202
*MacRAE's State Industrial Directory North
  Carolina/South Carolina/Virginia*, Mac-
  RAE's Industrial Directories, 817 Broad-
  way, New York, NY 10003
South Carolina Industrial Directory, Manu-
  facturers' News, Inc., 4 E. Huron Street,
  Chicago, IL 60611

South Dakota

STATE CAPITOL, PIERRE, SD 57501
(605) 773-3011

INFORMATION OFFICES

Commerce/Economic Development
  Governor's Office of Economic Develop-
  ment
  711 Wells Avenue
  Capitol Lake Plaza
  Pierre, SD 57501
  Department of Commerce and Regulation

  910 E. Sioux
  Pierre, SD 57501
Corporate
  Secretary of State
  Corporation Division
  Capitol Building
  Pierre, SD 57501
Taxation
  Department of Revenue
  Kneip Building
  Pierre, SD 57501
State Chamber of Commerce
  Industry & Commerce Association of South
    Dakota
  P.O. Box 190
  Pierre, SD 57501
International Commerce
  Governor's Office of Economic Develop-
    ment
  711 Wells
  Capitol Lake Plaza
  Pierre, SD 57501
Banking
  Department of Commerce and Regulation
  Division of Banking
  105 S. Euclid
  Pierre, SD 57501
Securities
  Department of Commerce and Regulation
  Division of Securities
  910 E. Sioux
  Pierre, SD 57501
Labor and Industrial Relations
  Department of Labor
  Division of Labor and Management
  Kneip Building
  Pierre, SD 57501
Insurance
  Department of Commerce and Regulation
  Division of Insurance
  910 E. Sioux
  Pierre, SD 57501

INDUSTRIAL AND BUSINESS DIRECTORIES

South Dakota Industrial Directory, Manufac-
  turers' News, Inc., 4 E. Huron Street, Chi-
  cago, IL 60611
*South Dakota Manufacturers and Processors
  Directory*, Governor's Office of Economic
  Development, 711 Well Avenue, Capitol
  Lake Plaza, Pierre, SD 57501; Manufactur-
  ers' News, Inc., 4 E. Huron Street, Chi-
  cago, IL 60611
South Dakota Export Directory, Governor's
  Office of Economic Development, 711 Well
  Avenue, Capitol Lake Plaza, Pierre, SD
  57501

Tennessee

STATE CAPITOL, NASHVILLE, TN 37219
(615) 741-2001

INFORMATION OFFICES

Commerce/Economic Development
Department of Economic and Community
Development
Rachel Jackson Building
320 6th Avenue North
Nashville, TN 37219

Corporate
Secretary of State
Records Division
James K. Polk Building
Nashville, TN 37219

Taxation
Department of Revenue
927 Andrew Jackson Building
500 Deaderick Street
Nashville, TN 37242

International Commerce
Department of Economic & Community
Development
International Sales & Marketing
Rachel Jackson Building
320 6th Avenue North
Nashville, TN 37219

Banking
Department of Financial Institutions
John Sevier Building
Nashville, TN 37219

Securities
Department of Commerce & Insurance
Securities Division
500 James Robertson Parkway
Nashville, TN 37219

Labor and Industrial Relations
Department of Labor
501 Union Building
Nashville, TN 37219

Insurance
Department of Commerce & Insurance
Insurance Division
500 James Robertson Parkway
Nashville, TN 37219

Business Ombudsman
Department of Economic & Community
Development
Business & Industry Services Division
Rachel Jackson Building
320 6th Avenue North
Nashville, TN 37219-5308

INDUSTRIAL AND BUSINESS DIRECTORIES

Tennessee Directory of Manufacturers, Manufacturers' News, Inc., 4 E. Huron Street, Chicago, IL 60611

Texas

STATE CAPITOL, AUSTIN, TX 78701
State Information: (512) 463-4630

INFORMATION OFFICES

Commerce/Economic Development
Texas Department of Commerce
P.O. Box 12728
Austin, TX 78711

Corporate
Secretary of State
P.O. Box 12697
1019 Brazos
Austin, TX 78711

Taxation
Comptroller of Public Accounts
104 LBJ State Office Building
Austin, TX 78774

State Chamber of Commerce
Texas State Chamber of Commerce
300 West 15th Street
Austin, TX 78752

Tourism Department
P.O. Box 12008
Austin, TX 78711

Lower Rio Grand Valley Chamber of Commerce
P.O. Box 1499
Weslaco, TX 78596

International Commerce
Business Development Division
Texas Department of Commerce
P.O. Box 12728, Capitol Station
Austin, TX 78711

Banking
Texas Department of Banking
2601 North Lamar
Austin, TX 78705-4294

Securities
State Securities Board
P.O. Box 13167, Capitol Station
1800 San Jacinto St.
Austin, TX 78711-3167

Labor and Industrial Relations
Texas Department of Labor and Standards
P.O. Box 13193, Capitol Station
Austin, TX 78711-3193

Insurance
Texas State Board of Insurance
State Insurance Building
1110 San Jacinto
Austin, TX 78701-1998

Uniform Industrial Code
Uniform Commercial Code Section
Secretary of State's Office
P.O. Box 12887, Capitol Station
Austin, TX 78711

Business Ombudsman
Texas Department of Commerce
P.O. Box 12728
Austin, TX 78711

INDUSTRIAL AND BUSINESS DIRECTORIES

Dallas Business Guide, Dallas Chamber of Commerce, Fidelity Tower, Dallas, TX 75201

Directory of Texas Manufacturers, Bureau
of Business Research, University of Texas,
Austin, TX 78712; State Industrial Directories Corp., 2 Penn Plaza, New York, NY
10001

Fort Worth Directory of Manufacturers, Fort
Worth Area Chamber of Commerce, 700
Throckmorton Street, Fort Worth, TX
76102

Texas Exporter-Importer Directory, Gulf International Trades, Box 52717, Houston,
TX 77052

Texas Manufacturers Register, Manufacturers' News, Inc., 4 E. Huron Street, Chicago, IL 60611

Utah

STATE CAPITOL, SALT LAKE CITY, UT
8414   (801) 538-3000

INFORMATION OFFICES

Commerce/Economic Development
Department of Commerce
160 East 300 South
Salt Lake City, UT 84145

Department of Community and Economic
Development
324 South State
Salt Lake City, UT 84111

Office of Planning & Budget
Data Resources Section
116 Capitol Building
Salt Lake City, UT 84114
Corporate
Division of Corporations
Heber M. Wells Building
160 E. 300 South
Salt Lake City, UT 84145
Taxation
Department of State Tax Commission
Heber M. Wells Building
160 E. 300 South
Salt Lake City, UT 84134
International Commerce
International Business Development
Division of Economic & Business Develop-
ment
324 South State
Salt Lake City, UT 84111
Banking
Financial Institutions
324 S. State
P.O. Box 89
Salt Lake City, UT 84110-0089
Securities
Division of Securities
Heber M. Wells Building
160 E. 300 South
P.O. Box 45802
Salt Lake City, UT 84145-082

Labor and Industrial Relations
Industrial Commission of Utah
Heber M. Wells Building
160 E. 300 South
Salt Lake City, UT 84111
Insurance
Department of Insurance
3110 State Office Building
Salt Lake City, UT 84114
Licensing
Division of Occupational and Professional
Licensing
160 East 300 South
P.O. Box 45802
Salt Lake City, UT 84145-0802
Uniform Industrial Code
Employment Security/Job Service
174 Social Hall Avenue
Salt Lake City, UT 84147

INDUSTRIAL AND BUSINESS DIRECTORIES

Utah Directory of Business and Industry,
Manufacturers' News, Inc., 4 E. Huron
Street, Chicago, IL 60611

Vermont

STATE HOUSE, MONTPELIER, VT 05602
(802) 828-3333 (Action Line)

INFORMATION OFFICES

Commerce/Economic Development
Agency of Development and Community
Affairs
Department of Economic Development
109 State Street
Montpelier, VT 05602
Corporate
Secretary of State
Corporation Department
26 Terrace Street
Montpelier, VT 05602
Taxation
Department of Taxes
Agency of Administration
109 State Street
Montpelier, VT 05602
State Chamber of Commerce
Vermont State Chamber of Commerce
P.O. Box 37
Montpelier, VT 05602
Insurance
Department of Banking and Insurance
120 State Street
Montpelier, VT 05602
Banking
Department of Banking and Insurance
120 State Street
Montpelier, VT 05602

Securities
Department of Banking and Insurance
120 State Street
Montpelier, VT 05602
Labor and Industrial Relations
Department of Labor and Industry
120 State Street
Montpelier, VT 05602
Uniform Commercial Code
Department of Banking and Insurance
120 State Street
Montpelier, VT 05602
Business Ombudsman
Agency Development and Community Affair
Department of Economic Development
109 State Street
Montpelier, VT 05602

INDUSTRIAL AND BUSINESS DIRECTORIES

MacRAE's State Industrial Directory Maine/ New Hampshire/Vermont, MacRAE's Industrial Directories, 817 Broadway, New York, NY 10003
Vermont Directory of Manufacturers, Vermont Agency of Development and Community Affairs, Montpelier, VT 05602
Vermont Business Phone Book, Manufacturers' News, Inc., 4 E. Huron Street, Chicago, IL 60611
Vermont Yearbook, The National Survey, Chester, VT 05143

Virginia

STATE CAPITOL, RICHMOND, VA 23219
(804) 786-0000

INFORMATION OFFICES

Commerce/Economic Development
Department of Economic Development
1000 Washington Building
Richmond, VA 23219
Department of Conservation and Historic Resources
1100 Washington Building
Richmond, VA 23219
Corporate
State Corporation Commission
1220 Bank Street
Richmond, VA 23209
Taxation
Department of Taxation
2200 W. Broad Street
P.O. Box 6-L
Richmond, VA 23282
State Chamber of Commerce
Virginia State Chamber of Commerce
611 E. Franklin Street
Richmond, VA 23219

International Commerce
Department of Economic Development
1000 Washington Building
Richmond, VA 23219
Banking
State Corporation Commission
Bureau of Financial Institutions
701 E. Dyrd Street
P.O. Box 2AE
Richmond, VA 23205
Securities
State Corporation Commission
Division of Securities and Retail Franchising
11 S. 12th Street
Richmond, VA 23219
Labor and Industrial Relations
Department of Labor and Industry
205 N. 4th Street
P.O. Box 12064
Richmond, VA 23241
Insurance
State Corporation Commission
Bureau of Insurance
1220 Bank Street
Richmond, VA 23209
Uniform Industrial Code
Virginia Employment Commission
Research and Analysis Division
703 E. Main Street
Richmond, VA 23211
Business Ombudsman
Department of Agriculture and Consumer Services
Office of Consumer Affairs
1100 Bank Street
Richmond, VA 23219

INDUSTRIAL AND BUSINESS DIRECTORIES

Industrial Directory of Virginia, Chamber of Commerce, 611 E. Franklin Street, Richmond, VA 23219
MacRAE's State Industrial Directory North Carolina/South Carolina/Virginia, MacRAE's Industrial Directories, 817 Broadway, New York, NY 10003
Virginia Industrial Directory, Manufacturers' News, Inc., 4 E. Huron Street, Chicago, IL 60611

Washington

101 GENERAL ADMINISTRATION BUILDING,
OLYMPIA, WA 98504
(206) 753-5630

INFORMATION OFFICES

Commerce/Economic Development
Department of Trade and Economic Development

101 General Administration Building
Olympia, WA 98504
Corporate
Secretary of State
Corporate Division
505 E. Union
Olympia, WA 98504
Taxation
Department of Revenue
412 General Administration Building
Olympia, WA 98504
State Chamber of Commerce
Association of Washington Business
1414 S. Cherry Street
Olympia, WA 98501
International Commerce
Department of Trade & Economic Development
Domestic & International Trade Division
2600 Westin Building
2001 Sixth Avenue
Seattle, WA 98121
Banking
General Administration Building
Banking & Consumer Finance
219 General Administration Building
Olympia, WA 98504
Securities
Department of Licensing Building
Att: Securities Division
7240 Martin Way
Olympia, WA 98506
Labor and Industrial Relations
Department of Labor & Industries
Employment Standards—Apprenticeship
Crime Victims Division
406 Legion Way SE
Olympia, WA 98504
Insurance
Insurance Commissioner's Office
Insurance Building
Olympia, WA 98504
Uniform Commercial Code
Department of Licensing
Business License Services
405 Black Lake Boulevard
Olympia, WA 98504
Business Ombudsman
Department of Trade & Economic Development
Business Assistance Center
919 Lakeridge Way, S.W.
Olympia, WA 98504

INDUSTRIAL AND BUSINESS DIRECTORIES

1988 Directory of Advanced Technology Industries in Washington State, Economic Development Partnership for Washington State, 18000 Pacific Highway South, Seattle, WA 98188
Business Assistance in Washington State,

Washington State International Trade Directory, Department of Trade and Economic Development, 101 General Administration Building, Olympia, WA 98504
Minority Women Business Enterprises, Office of Minority Women Business Enterprises, 406 S. Water Street, Olympia, WA 98504
Washington Manufacturers Register, Times Mirror Press, P.O. Box 7440, Newport Beach, CA 92658
Washington Forest Industry Mill Directory (1984), Department of Natural Resources, 1065 S. Capitol Way, Olympia, WA 98504
Directory of Washington Mining Operations, Department of Natural Resources, Division of Geology, Olympia, WA 98504
Washington Manufacturers Register, Manufacturers' News, Inc., 4 E. Huron Street, Chicago, IL 60611

West Virginia

STATE CAPITOL, CHARLESTON, WV 25305
(304) 348-3456

INFORMATION OFFICES

Commerce/Economic Development
Governor's Office of Community and Industrial Development
1900 Washington Street East
Building I
Charleston, WV 25305
Corporate
Secretary of State
Corporate Division
1900 Washington Street East
Building 1
Charleston, WV 25305
Taxation
Tax Department
1900 Washington Street East
Building 1
Charleston, WV 25305
State Chamber of Commerce
P.O. Box 2789
1101 Kanawha Valley Building
Charleston, WV 25330
International Commerce
Governor's Office of Community and Industrial Development
1900 Washington Street East
Building 6
Charleston, WV 25305
Banking
Department of Banking
1900 Washington Street East
Building 5
Charleston, WV 25305
Securities
Auditor's Office
1900 Washington Street East
Building 1
Charleston, WV 25305

Labor & Industrial Relations

Governor's Office of Community and Industrial Development
1900 Washington Street East
Building 6
Charleston, WV 25305

Insurance

Insurance Department
2100 Washington Street East
Charleston, WV 25305

Uniform Industrial Code

Governor's Office of the Secretary of State
1900 Washington Street East
Building 1
Charleston, WV 25305

Business Ombudsman

Governor's Office of Community and Industrial Development East
Building 6
Charleston, WV 25305

INDUSTRIAL AND BUSINESS DIRECTORIES

West Virginia Manufacturers Directory, Manufacturers' News, Inc., 4 E. Huron Street, Chicago, IL 60611, Harris Publishing, 2057 Aurora Road, Twinsburg, OH 44087

Wisconsin

STATE CAPITOL, MADISON, WI 53702
(608) 266-2211

INFORMATION OFFICES

Commerce/Economic Development
Department of Development
123 W. Washington Avenue
Box 7970
Madison, WI 53707

Corporate
Secretary of State
Corporate Division
301 W. Miffin Street
Box 7848
Madison, WI 53707

Taxation
Department of Revenue
125 S. Webster Avenue
P.O. Box 8933
Madison, WI 53708

State Chamber of Commerce
Wisconsin Association of Manufacturers and Commerce
501 E. Avenue
Box 352
Milwaukee, WI 53201

International Commerce
International Business Services
Department of Development
Box 7970
123 W. Washington Avenue
Madison, WI 53707

Banking

Banking, Office of the Commissioner
131 W. Wilson Avenue
P.O. Box 7876
Madison, WI 53707

Securities

Securities—Office of the Commissioner
111 W. Wilson Avenue
Box 1768
Madison, WI 53701

Labor and Industrial Relations

Department of Industry, Labor, and Human Relations
201 E. Washington Avenue
P.O. Box 7946
Madison, WI 53707

Insurance

Office of the Commissioner of Insurance
123 West Washington Avenue
Box 7873
Madison, WI 53707

Uniform Industrial Code

Department of Industry, Labor and Human Relations
201 E. Washington Avenue
Box 7969
Madison, WI 53707

Business Ombudsman

Small Business Ombudsman
Department of Development
123 W. Washington Avenue
Box 7970
Madison, WI 53707

INDUSTRIAL AND BUSINESS DIRECTORIES

Classified Directory of Wisconsin Manufacturers, Wisconsin Association of Manufacturers and Commerce, 501 E. Washington Avenue, Box 352, Madison, WI 53701; State Industrial Directories Corp., 2 Penn Plaza, New York, NY 10001

Wisconsin Exporters Directory, Wisconsin Department of Development, 123 W. Washington Avenue, Box 7920, Madison, WI 53707

Wisconsin Manufacturers Register, Manufacturers' News, Inc., 4 E. Huron Street, Chicago, IL 60611

Wisconsin Local Development Organizations (annual), Wisconsin Department of Development, 123 W. Washington Avenue, Box 7970, Madison, WI 53707

Wisconsin Services Directory, Wisconsin Association of Manufacturers and Commerce, 501 E. Washington Avenue, Box 352, Madison, WI 53701

Wyoming

STATE CAPITOL, CHEYENNE, WY 82002
(307) 777-7011

INFORMATION OFFICES

Commerce/Economic Development
Economic Development and Stabilization
Board
Herschler Building
Cheyenne, WY 82002
Wyoming Small Business Development
Center
130 N. Ash
Casper, WY 82601
Corporate
Secretary of State
Corporate Division
State Capitol
Cheyenne, WY 82002
Taxation
Department of Revenue and Taxation
Herschler Building
Cheyenne, WY 82002
International Commerce
International Trade Office
State Planning Coordinator
Herschler Building
Cheyenne, WY 82002
Banking
State Examiner
Herschler Building
Cheyenne, WY 82002
Securities
Secretary of State
Securities Division
State Capitol
Cheyenne, WY 82002
Labor and Industrial Relations
Department of Labor and Statistics
Herschler Building
Cheyenne, WY 82002
Insurance
Insurance Commission
Herschler Building
Cheyenne, WY 82002
Uniform Industrial Code
Industrial Siting Administration
Barrett Building
2301 Central
Cheyenne, WY 82002
Industrial Development Division
Economic Planning Development and Stabilization Board
Herschler Building
Cheyenne, WY 82002

INDUSTRIAL AND BUSINESS DIRECTORIES

Wyoming Directory of Manufacturing and Mining, Manufacturers' News, Inc., 4 E. Huron Street, Chicago, IL 60611; Economic Development and Stabilization Board, Herschler Building, Cheyenne, WY 82002

Puerto Rico

CAPITOL, SAN JUAN, PR 00901
(809) 724-6040 (House of Representatives)
(809) 724-2030 (Senate)

INFORMATION OFFICES

Commerce/Economic Development
Puerto Rico Department of Commerce
P.O. Box S 4275
San Juan, PR 00905
Puerto Rico Economic Development Administration
G.P.O. Box 2350
San Juan, PR 00936
Puerto Rico Planning Board
P.O. Box 41119
San Juan, PR 00940
Government Development Bank
P.O. Box 42001
Minillas Station
Santurce, PR 00940
Economic Development Bank
P.O. Box 5009
Hato Rey, PR 00929-5009
Taxation
Puerto Rico Department of Treasury
P.O. Box S-4515
San Juan, PR 00901
Office of Industrial Tax Exemption
P.O. Box 2121
Hato Rey, PR 00918-2121
Chamber of Commerce
Chamber of Commerce of Puerto Rico
P.O. Box 3789
San Juan, PR 00904
Puerto Rico Manufacturers Association
P.O. Box 2410
Hato Rey, PR 00919
Securities
Office of the Commissioner of Financial Institutions
P.O. Box 70324
San Juan, PR 00936
Labor and Industrial Relations
Puerto Rico Labor Relations Board
P.O. Box 4048
San Juan, PR 00905
National Labor Relations Board
Federal Building
Charlos E. Chardon Street
Hato Rey, PR 00918
Insurance
Office of the Insurance Commissioner
P.O. Box 8330, Fdez Juncos Station
Santurce, PR 00910
Puerto Rico Insurance Companies Association, Inc.
P.O. Box 3395
San Juan, PR 00936

Uniform Industrial Code
Department of Labor and Human Resources
505 Muñoz Rivera Avenue
Prudencio Rivera Martínez Building
Hato Rey, PR 00918
Business Ombudsman
Ombudsman Office
1205 Ponce de León Avenue
Banco de San Juan
Santurce, PR 00907-3995
International Commerce
Puerto Rico Department of Commerce
External Trade Promotion Program
P.O. Box S 4275
San Juan, PR 00905

US Department of Commerce
International Trade Administration
Charlos E. Chardon Street
Federal Building
Hato Rey, PR 00918

Puerto Rico Chamber of Commerce
International Trade Division
P.O. Box 3789
San Juan, PR 00904
Banking
Puerto Rico Bankers Association
Banco Popular Center
Hato Rey, PR 00918

INDUSTRIAL AND BUSINESS DIRECTORIES

Puerto Rico Official Industrial and Trade Directory, Witcom Group, Inc., P.O. Box 2310, San Juan, PR 00902

The Businessman's Guide to Puerto Rico, Puerto Rico Almanacs, Inc., P.O. Box 9582, Santurce, Puerto Rico 00908

International Information Sources

Foreign Trade Information

Business people seeking information about foreign commercial opportunities or sources of business contacts have available a number of government and private services that are described in this and subsequent sections. The extensive nature of these services is not always fully appreciated by members of the business community. Some of the most helpful services are provided by the International Trade Administration (ITA) 202-377-3808 of the Department of Commerce, described below. This agency is particularly helpful in establishing initial contacts and in evaluating foreign markets.

Foreign credit information sources are provided at the end of this section.

DEPARTMENT OF COMMERCE

Address: Constitution and 14th Street NW, Washington, DC 20230. Information phone: 202-377-2000.

The central export information source within the Department of Commerce is the **International Trade Administration** (ITA), which promotes the growth of U.S. industry and commerce, both foreign and domestic. Office of Public Affairs: (202) 377-3808. The four units of ITA and the Bureau of Export Administration are discussed below.

- U.S. and Foreign Commercial Service (US&FCS)—the framework within which ITA gathers accurate and timely commercial information, distributes it through a worldwide network of trade specialists, and provides in-depth counseling, assistance, and support to the business community both in the U.S. and abroad (below)

- International Economic Policy (IEP)—the office organized on a country and regional basis which develops and implements policy concerning U.S. international trade, investment, and commercial relations with foreign businesses and governments, and which gives market-specific counsel to American business (page 710).

- Trade Development (TD)—the industry unit responsible for formulating trade policy and promotion activities (page 711).

- Import Administration (IA)—the office responsible for safeguarding the national interest through effective administration of U.S. trade laws (page 712).

- Bureau of Export Administration (BXA)—responsible for export licensing, technology and policy analysis, and foreign availability determinations (page 712).

U.S. and Foreign Commercial Service (US&FCS)

The U.S. and Foreign Commercial Service (US&FCS), the only federal agency with a global network of international trade professionals, is charged with the nuts-and-bolts work of improving the ability of U.S. business to compete overseas. US&FCS collects marketing information at overseas posts and makes it available to U.S. companies at district offices and branch offices.

The US&FCS emphasizes practical advice and information help U.S. exporters in very specific ways. A company can find out which countries have the best market potential for its products and can then find out who to contact overseas.

Through the US&FCS, U.S. firms have direct access to more than 95 percent of the global marketplace for goods and services. Such access can be a big advantage for American firms, particularly small- and medium-sized businesses that lack export departments and overseas representation.

District office trade specialists, drawing from a large commercial data base fed by overseas commercial officers, provide individualized marketing packages for U.S. companies on their specific products and services and offer one-on-one export counseling. Beginners and experienced exporters both are eligible.

The district offices arrange export seminars, conferences, and workshops. To multiply the effects of their efforts, they coordinate activities with state and local governments, trade associations, world trade clubs, banks, local chambers of commerce, small business development centers, and colleges and universities. More than 900 of these organizations are termed "associate offices"; they distribute information to areas where no US&FCS district offices are located. The district offices give U.S. companies direct contact with seasoned exporters through District Export Councils (DECs) comprised of experienced business people.

Commercial officers attached to U.S. embassies and consulates search for sales leads, qualified agents, and distributors; make appointments with key buyers and government officials; and counsel firms frustrated by trade barriers.

Sources: Excerpted from *Business America, Business Services Directory, A Basic Guide to Exporting,* and other U.S. Department of Commerce sources.

The US&FCS has several programs geared toward helping companies make contact with potential agents, distributors, buyers, or joint-venture partners, including:

Agent Distributor Service—This customized search for interested and qualified foreign representatives will identify up to six foreign prospects who have examined a company's product literature and have expressed interest in representing its product. For information contact your local ITA district office (page 715).

Commercial News USA—Published ten times a year, this magazine will promote a company's product or service to more than 100,000 overseas agents, distributors, government officials, and end-users. A black-and-white photo and brief description will highlight a product or service and give a firm an opportunity to search for its best markets worldwide or to focus on a particular region. There is a fee for this service. For information call 1-800-343-4300 Operator 940.

In *Commerce Business Daily*, US&FCS publicizes proposed foreign government procurement actions and foreign trade leads, as well as information on U.S. Government procurement actions. For a sample, write US&FCS, U.S. Department of Commerce, Washington, D.C. 20230. To subscribe, call the Superintendent of Documents, U.S. Government Printing Office, Washington, D.C. 20402.

Commercial Information Management System (CIMS)—This service electronically links US&FCS posts and offices worldwide to provide timely, in-depth data. CIMS creates export information packages customized for special needs, including highly specific market research, trade contact lists and sales leads. Useful for situation and competitive assessment reports. For detailed information on CIMS, including cost, contact CIMS, U.S. & Foreign Commercial Service, U.S. Department of Commerce, Washington, D.C. 20230. Telephone: 202-377-1887

Foreign Buyer Program—Without the expense of traveling overseas, an exporter can meet qualified foreign buyers for his product or service at selected trade shows in the United States. The US&FCS promotes these shows worldwide to attract foreign buyer delegations, manages an International Business Center, counsels U.S. firms, and brings together buyer and seller.

Trade Opportunities Program—This program provides export leads on a daily basis.

TOP leads originate in foreign posts when the U.S. and Foreign Commercial Service (US&FCS) in that country identifies a trade opportunity. The US&FCS then cables the opportunity to the Department of Commerce in Washington, D.C., and it is made available to exporters through Commerce's *Economic Bulletin Board.*

The general public can find TOP listings several places. Anyone can subscribe to the *Economic Bulletin Board* by mail or by calling the National Technical Information Service (NTIS), 5285 Port Royal Road, Springfield, Va. 22161, tel (703) 487-4630. There is a fee both for the *Bulletin Board* and the connect time.

For additional information on the TOP program, contact Commerce's TOP office at (202) 377-8246.

Trade events constitute another major type of US&FCS export assistance. A company can do as little as sending a product catalog overseas or as much as fully participating in trade missions or major international exhibitions. US&FCS programs include:

Catalog and Video-Catalog Shows—A firm can gain market exposure for its product or service without the cost of traveling overseas by participating in a catalog or video-catalog show. The firm provides its product literature or promotional video, and the US&FCS will send an industry expert to display this material to select foreign audiences in several countries.

Custom Statistical Service. Up-to-date marketing data on thousands of individual products and markets can be provided in more than 200 countries. This statistical information is gathered from both U.S. and U.N. sources, using sophisticated and flexible software programs that allow the data to be extracted by dollar value, quantity, unit value, market share percentage, and varying time frames.

Comparison Shopping. Overseas competition is checked out through this personalized product shopping service available in selected markets abroad. US&FCS staff in France, Germany, Italy, and the United Kingdom can conduct on-the-spot surveys to determine key marketing facts about a product and its competition, including sales potential, comparable products, distribution channels, going price, competitive factors, and qualified purchasers.

World Traders Data Reports (WTDRs). Current, made-to-order background checks are prepared on potential trading partners. WTDR will include background information on the foreign firms selected by the client, their standing in the local business community, and overall reliability and suitability as trade contacts.

Trade Fairs—Trade fairs are one of the most popular ways of promoting goods and services overseas because they not only give the seller an opportunity to meet customers face-to-face but also to assess the competition. US&FCS supports U.S. participation in international trade fairs, making it easier for U.S. firms to exhibit and gain international recognition. US&FCS selects certain international trade fairs for special endorsement, called certification. As a result of this cooperation with private show organizers, U.S. exhibitors receive special services designed to enhance their market promotion efforts.

The best way for a U.S. exporter to make use of these services is to visit the closest US&FCS district office.

Matchmakers and Trade Missions—Participating in a trade mission will give an exporter an opportunity to confer directly, on-the-spot, with targeted foreign business and government representatives. US&FCS staff provides complete logistical and promotional support to the missions.

The U.S. Department of Commerce's Matchmaker Trade Delegations are designed to meet the needs and concerns for small businesses trying to get into new markets. Through Matchmakers, U.S. firms are escorted overseas to meet with prospective agents and distributors who are prescreened for interest in the U.S. firms' products or services. The U.S. firms have a first hand opportunity to learn about market requirements and their products' prospects. U.S. embassy staff can provide interpreters, arrange for rental equipment, and will tailor each firm's appointment schedule to the market penetration strategy desired.

For information contact:

Matchmaker Trade Delegations
Export Promotion Services
Room H-2116
U.S. Department of Commerce
Washington, DC 20230
Telephone: (202) 377-4561

Useful US&FCS Telephone Numbers:

Headquarters	(202) 377-5777
Caribbean Basin Business Information Center	377-2527
Domestic Operations	377-4767
Export Promotion Services Office of Commercial Information Management	377-4561
Trade Events	377-1468
Foreign Operations Western Hemisphere and Europe	377-1599
East Asia/Pacific and Africa/Near East	377-2736
Washington Branch office	377-1381

International Economic Policy (IEP)

International Economic Policy (IEP) identifies and analyzes foreign commercial bar-

riers and opportunities, offers a range of counseling services to U.S. businesses, and participates in bilateral and multilateral consultations and negotiations.

IEP is organized by region and country; it has four regional groups: Africa, the Near East, and South Asia; East Asia and the Pacific; Europe; and the Western Hemisphere. IEP's Office of Policy Coordination complements the individual efforts of the regional units by coordinating projects and initiatives affecting countries in more than one region.

The regional groups are staffed by country specialists who counsel U.S. businesses on foreign market conditions, business practices, and government regulations; develop specific information on promising commercial opportunities; identify foreign trade and investment barriers and devise strategies to remove them; and support the efforts of senior U.S. government policymakers to improve U.S. commercial opportunities worldwide. The unit's country specialists publish periodic reports on foreign market conditions and requirements (*Overseas Business Reports* and *Foreign Economic Trends*) and numerous special studies.

Overseas Business Reports (OBR) include current and detailed marketing information, trade outlooks, statistics, regulations, and market profiles. They are available from the Superintendent of Documents, U.S. Government Printing Office, Washington, DC 20402.

Foreign Economic Trends (FET) present current business and economic developments and the latest economic indicators in more than 100 countries. They are prepared on an annual or semiannual basis by the U.S. Foreign Service and U.S. Foreign Commerical Service. Available from the Superintendent of Documents, U.S. Government Printing Office, Washington, D.C. 20402.

Through its Office of Multilateral Affairs, IEP coordinates the Department's involvement in U.S. government efforts to strengthen the world trading system and improve U.S. commercial opportunities through multilateral agencies, such as the General Agreement on Tariffs and Trade (GATT).

The office also develops and coordinates departmental positions on several issue areas affecting multilateral trade policy. These include the U.S. Generalized System of Preferences (GSP) program and Section 301 of the Trade Act of 1974, which provides redress from unfair foreign trade practices.

IEP also works to ensure that foreign governments meet their obligations under existing multilateral agreements, such as the GATT non-tariff codes negotiated during the last major trade round.

Useful IEP Telephone Numbers

Headquarters . . . . (202) 377-3022
GATT Division 377-3681
International Organizations 377-3227
U.S. Trade by Region
Africa 377-2175
Canada 377-3101
Caribbean Basin & Mexico 377-5327
Eastern Europe 377-2645
European Community 377-5276
Israel Information Center 377-4652
Japan 377-4527
Near East 377-4441
Pacific Basin 377-4008
People's Republic of China and
  Hong Kong 377-3583
South America 377-2436
South Asia 377-2954
U.S.S.R. 377-4655
Western Europe 377-5341

Trade Development

Trade Development's analysis, policy development, and export promotion capability are designed to enhance the efforts of businesses of all sizes to increase market share at home and abroad.

Of TD's nine operating units, seven specialize in specific industrial sectors—Science and Electronics, Capital Goods and International Construction, Automotive Affairs and Consumer Goods, Textiles and Apparel, Aerospace, Services, and Basic Industries. An eighth unit is Trade Information and Analysis, which addresses international debt and currency questions and other issues that affect all sectors and coordinates TD policy recommendations on issues that cut across industry sectors. The ninth unit is Trade Adjustment Assistance, which provides technical assistance to firms and industries injured by import competition.

TD industry sector analysts monitor significant developments affecting their industries, especially those relating to efforts by foreign competitors. The Trade Information and Analysis unit follows important trends that affect overall U.S. industry and identify cross-cutting issues that, while of primary concern to one sector, have potential for affecting others.

Each year, TD publishes two major publications. The U.S. Trade Performance and Outlook analyzes the factors that influence the U.S. trade balance. The U.S. Industrial Outlook contains analyses and forecasts of domestic and international trends for more than 350 U.S. manufacturing and service industries.

TD conducts a two-part analytical program. The first measures overall U.S. and foreign competitive performance, using indicators such as productivity and growth rates, and assesses the effectiveness of various measures of competitiveness. The second produces a series of published Competitive Assessments, which include in-depth analyses of individual industries and detailed discussions of their specific position in the international arena.

TRADE PROMOTION

TD helps U.S. businesses in specific export efforts. Analysts identify industries with high export potential and work with the U.S. and Foreign Commercial Service to assist exporters.

Each year, TD organizes dozens of seminars to introduce U.S. producers to export markets. TD recruits companies for trade missions, helps participants in meetings with prospective customers and foreign officials, and assists with trade shows.

TD also organizes "Foreign Buyer" groups to visit U.S. trade shows; administers the Export Trading Company Act program to help companies pool their export efforts, and offers technical assistance to import-injured companies under the Trade Adjustment Assistance program.

Even firms in those U.S. industries unaffected by increased foreign competition need to redouble their efforts to secure their market position. The Trade Development unit can give them some good pointers.

Useful TD Telephone Numbers

Headquarters . . . . (202) 377-1461
Foreign Trade Reference Room 377-2185
Major Projects Reference Room 377-4876
Aerospace 377-8228
Automotive 377-0823
Chemicals and Allied Products 377-0128
Consumer Goods 377-0337
Computer and Business
  Equipment 377-0572
Energy 377-1466
Export Trading Companies 377-5131
Forest Products and Domestic
  Construction 377-0384
General Industrial Machinery 377-5455
Instrumentation 377-5466
Medical Services 377-0550
Major Projects and International
  Construction 377-5225
Metals, Minerals and
  Commodities 377-0575
Micro Electronics &
  Instrumentation 377-2587
Service Industries 377-3575

Special Industrial Machinery ...	(202)	377-0302
Telecommunications		377-4466
Textiles		377-5078
Trade Information Analysis		377-1316
Export Statistics and Trade Data (Foreign)		377-4211
Export Statistics and Trade Data (Domestic)		377-4211

This is a partial listing of industry sectors; for others not listed, call 202-377-1461.

Import Administration (IA)

Import Administration (IA) investigates allegations under the U.S. antidumping (AD) and countervailing duty (CVD) laws that foreign goods are being sold in the United States at less than fair value ("dumped") or being unfairly subsidized by foreign governments. The International Trade Commission, a separate independent agency, conducts a parallel review of injury (or threat of injury) to the domestic industry as a result of these unfairly traded imports. IA also conducts annual reviews of AD and CVD orders, which are imposed to offset findings of injurious dumping and subsidization, to update duty levels, as well as reviews of suspended AD and CVD investigations to monitor compliance with suspension agreements.

In addition, IA implements and enforces four monitoring programs involving bilateral trade agreements with foreign governments for steel, machine tools, semiconductors and softwood lumber. IA oversees the operations of U.S. foreign-trade zones, implements statutory import programs, including the watch quota program for insular possessions and the Florence agreement, and, in conjunction with the U.S. Customs Service, administers quotas covering imports of certain specialty steel products.

Useful IA Telephone Numbers

Office of Assistant Secretary	(202)-377-1780	
Deputy Assistant Secretary for Investigations		377-5497
Investigations		377-5497
Office of Antidumping Investigations		377-1768
Office of Countervailing Investigations		377-2438
Compliance		377-2104
Office of Antidumping Compliance		377-2104
Office of Countervailing Compliance		377-2786
Office of Agreements Compliance		377-3793

Foreign Trade Zones Staff	377-2862
Statutory Import Programs Staff	377-1660

Bureau of Export Administration (BXA)

Public Affairs: 202-377-2721

Established in 1987, the Bureau of Export Administration (BXA) is responsible for export licensing, technology and policy analysis, and foreign availability determinations. These responsibilities include reducing the processing time for granting export licenses, decontrolling those technologies that offer no real threat to U.S. security, and eliminating controls in areas where there is widespread foreign availability.

To reduce unnecessary burdens on U.S. industry through improvements in export control procedures, Commerce has:

- Reduced license processing times by one-half, to 15 days;
- Opened "ELAIN" (Electronic License Application and Information Network), information 202-377-4811 allowing exporters to send applications and receive export licenses from Commerce electronically
- Installed an audio response unit—STELA (System for Tracking Export License Applications)—which automatically handles requests for status checks on export license applications using synthesized voice technology (tel. 202-377-2753);
- Implemented general regulatory changes to reduce the licensing burden on exporters, particularly on exports of certain low level technologies.
- Raised the processing data rate (PDR) levels of computers eligible for export under the distribution license program;
- Reached agreement with countries that are members of the Coordinating Committee for Multilateral Export Controls (COCOM) to improve license processing for the People's Republic of China;
- Reduced paperwork burden by authorizing a 24-month validity period for individual validated licenses; and
- Expanded its export control information program, both in the United States and abroad, through the Exporter Outreach Staff.

The Bureau of Export Administration issues the *Export Administration Regulations* to enforce U.S. export controls. These Regulations contain information on obtaining an export license, documentation requirements, special nuclear controls, reexports, technical data, special commodity and country policies, and other essential guidance on exporting.

SEMINAR PROGRAMS

In its effort to make applying for an export license less intimidating, BXA conducts seminars on export controls and licensing all over the nation as well as overseas.

Learning about export controls and licensing is a must for most U.S. businesses, particularly for high-technology firms most subject to national security controls. The BXA seminars are aimed at providing the knowledge that exporters must have.

Licensing officers and export administration specialists from the Commerce Department teach the courses that are usually co-sponsored by District Export Councils and other not-for-profit trade organizations in conjunction with US&FCS district offices. For information call: 202-377-8731.

The basic program in the BXA seminars focuses on export control fundamentals. Attendees learn about general, special, and individual validated licenses, the Commodity Control List, how to fill out the 622P Application for an export license, and what documentation is needed, depending on commodity and country destination. They receive hands-on instruction in the use of the regulations. In the advanced seminar, attendees receive more in-depth explanations and analyses of the regulations, requirements of supporting documentation, the interagency review process, and distribution license control requirements.

ADDITIONAL BXA PROGRAMS AND SERVICES

To assist the exporter, the following programs are available:

Publication Program: For information on booklets/brochures for the business community call 202-377-8731. Recent publications include: *Export Licensing Information and Assistance* (telephone referral), *Introduction to the Export Administration Regulations*, *The Quick Reference Guide to the Export Administration Regulations*, and an updated copy of the *Denial Orders Currently Affecting Export Privileges*.

Technical Advisory Committees (TACs): The TACs are a voluntary joint industry-government mechanism through which the concerns of various industries can be discussed. For information, call 202-377-2583.

Useful BXA Telephone Numbers

Press and Public Information ... (202) 377-2721

Headquarters 377-5491
Exporter assistance staff 377-4811

ELAIN (Export License Application and Information Network) ... (202) 377-4811 Accepts export license applications ELECTRONICALLY for all freeworld destinations.

Emergency Licensing
   Requests .... (202) 377-4811
Trade Fair Licenses 377-4811
General Regulations
   Information 377-4811
Export Seminar
   Program 377-8731

Major Offices Administering Export Controls:

Office of Export Licensing ..... (202) 377-4811
   Special Licensing Division 377-3287
Office of Technology and Policy
   Analysis 377-4188
   Capital Goods Technical
    Center 377-5695
   Computer Systems Technical
    Center 377-2279
   Telecommunications Technical
    Center 377-0730
   Electronic Components and
    Instrumentation 377-1641
Foreign Availability 377-8074
   Assessments 377-5953
Export Enforcement 377-1561

Major Offices Administering Export Enforcement:

Washington, D.C. .... (202) 377-5282
                           (202) 377-8208

BXA Enforcement Field Offices

California—Los Angeles .... (818) 904-6019
California—San Jose .... (408) 291-4204
Florida—Miami .... (305) 523-1401
Illinois—Chicago .... (312) 353-6640
Massachusetts—Boston .... (617) 565-6030
New York—New York .... (212) 264-1365
Texas—Dallas .... (214) 767-9294
Virginia—Springfield .... (703) 487-4950
Office of Antiboycott
   Compliance .... (202) 377-5914
Office of Export Intelligence .... (202) 377-4255

FOREIGN REQUIREMENTS FOR U.S. PRODUCTS AND SERVICES

U.S. companies wishing to sell abroad must know how to deal with foreign national requirements, standards, testing and certification requirements. The National Center for Standards and Certification Information (NCSCI—within the Commerce Department's National Bureau of Standards) is the government's central repository for standards-related information. For more information about foreign standards and certification systems, write: NCSCI, National Bureau of Standards, Administration Building, A629, Gaithersburg, Md. 20899. The telephone number is (301) 975-4040.

The National Bureau of Standards also maintains a GATT Hotline with a recorded message that reports on the latest notifications of proposed foreign regulations that may affect trade. The hotline number is (301) 975-4041.

Exporters can get information about foreign standards from the non-governmental American National Standards Institute, telephone (212) 354-3300.

SELECTED INTERNATIONAL TRADE ADMINISTRATION PUBLICATIONS AND SERVICES

In addition to the previously mentioned publications there are others to help exporters reach and expand foreign markets. The foremost of these is *Business America*, which is Commerce Department's principal periodical for domestic and international business news and covers a wide range of topics. Subscriptions are available from the Superintendent of Documents, General Printing Office, Washington, DC 20402. Other publications include:

A Basic Guide to Exporting: This publication takes a step-by-step approach to exporting especially designed for firms with little or no export experience. Assessment of export potential is treated first, along with sources of export counseling and education. Other topics include: selecting markets, export strategies, pricing, financing, shipment, methods of payment, export documentation, and government regulations. A glossary of export terms and list of export-assistance groups is provided. Available from the Superintendent of Documents, General Printing Office, Washington, DC 20402.

Expand Overseas Sales With Commerce Department Help describes the various types of assistance available from the Commerce Department for small businesses seeking foreign markets. Available from International Trade Administration.

The U.S. Department of Commerce has discontinued publication of the *Export Promotion Calendar* due to budget cutbacks. However, the same information (e.g., listings of Commerce Department supported trade events in the U.S. and overseas, etc.) that was in the printed publication is now on-line at Department of Commerce District Offices around the country.

Other services available to exporters include the following.

Custom Statistical Service (CSS) is a tailored set of tables of U.S. export or import statistics. The custom service allows an exporter to obtain data for specific products or countries of interest, or for ones which may not appear in the standard ESP country and product rankings. Data can be supplied in other formats such as quantity, unit quantity, unit value and percentages.

New Product Information Service (NPIS)

This program provides worldwide publicity for new U.S. products available for immediate export. Promotional descriptions are published in *Commercial News USA* magazine. Information on selected NPIS products is also broadcast overseas by the U.S. Information Agency's "Voice of America" radio shows. For an application, contact a Trade Specialist at the nearest ITA District Office or write the Director, New Product Information Service, US&FCS, Room 2106, U.S. Department of Commerce, Washington, D.C. 20230.

Industry-Organized Government-Approved (IOGA) Trade Missions

Trade missions of this type are export-oriented events planned and organized by non-federal government groups such as local and state governments, industry trade associations, and chambers of commerce. For information, contact: Export Promotion Services, US&FCS, U.S. Department of Commerce, Washington, D.C. 20230; telephone: 202-377-4231.

DEPARTMENT OF AGRICULTURE: Foreign Agricultural Service

The U.S. Department of Agriculture's (USDA) export promotion efforts are centered in the Foreign Agricultural Service (FAS), but other USDA agencies also offer services to the U.S. exporter of agricultural products. For information on the promotion of U.S. farm products in foreign markets, services of commodity and marketing specialists in Washington, D.C., trade fair exhibits, publications and information services, and financing programs contact the Director of High Value Products Division, FAS, U.S. Department of Agriculture, Washington, D.C. 20250. Telephone: (202) 477-6343.

Department of Commerce International Trade Administration District and Branch Offices

District Offices

Alabama—Birmingham	(205) 731-1331
Alaska—Anchorage	(907) 271-5041
Arizona—Phoenix	(602) 261-3285
Arkansas—Little Rock	(501) 378-5794
*California—Los Angeles	(213) 209-6707
*California—Santa Ana	(714) 836-2461
California—San Diego	(619) 557-5395
California—San Francisco	(415) 556-5860
Colorado—Denver	(303) 844-3246
Connecticut—Hartford	(203) 240-3530
D.C.—Washington	(202) 377-3181
Florida—Miami	(305) 536-5267
*Florida—Clearwater	(813) 461-0011
*Florida—Jacksonville	(904) 791-2796
*Florida—Orlando	(407) 425-1234
*Florida—Tallahassee	(904) 488-6469
Georgia—Atlanta	(404) 347-7000
Georgia—Savannah	(912) 944-4204
Hawaii—Honolulu	(808) 541-1782
*Idaho—Boise	(208) 334-3587
Illinois—Chicago	(312) 353-4450
*Illinois—Palatine	(312) 397-3000
	ext. 2532
Illinois—Rockford	(815) 987-8123
Indiana—Indianapolis	(317) 226-6214
Iowa—Des Moines	(515) 284-4222
*Kansas—Wichita	(316) 269-6160
Kentucky—Louisville	(502) 582-5066
Louisiana—New Orleans	(504) 589-6546
*Maine—Augusta	(207) 622-8249
Maryland—Baltimore	(301) 962-3560
Massachusetts—Boston	(617) 565-8563
Michigan—Detroit	(313) 226-3650
*Michigan—Grand Rapids	(616) 456-2411
Minnesota—Minneapolis	(612) 348-1638
Mississippi—Jackson	(601) 965-4388
Missouri—Kansas City	(816) 426-3141
Missouri—St. Louis	(314) 425-3302
Nebraska—Omaha	(402) 221-3664
Nevada—Reno	(702) 784-5203
*New Jersey—Trenton	(609) 989-2100
*New Mexico—Albuquerque	(505) 766-2386
*New Mexico-Santa Fe	(505) 827-0264
New York—Buffalo	(716) 846-4191
*New York—New York	(212) 264-0634
*New York—Rochester	(716) 263-6480
North Carolina—	
Greensboro	(919) 333-5345
Ohio—Cincinnati	(513) 684-2944
Ohio—Cleveland	(216) 522-4750
Oklahoma—Oklahoma City	(405) 231-5302
*Oklahoma—Tulsa	(918) 581-7650
Oregon—Portland	(503) 221-3001
Pennsylvania—Philadelphia	(215) 962-4980
Pennsylvania—Pittsburgh	(412) 644-2850
*Rhode Island—Providence	(401) 528-5104
	ext. 22
South Carolina—Columbia	(000) 765-5045
South Carolina—Charleston	(803) 724-4361
*Tennessee—Memphis	(901) 521-4137
Tennessee—Nashville	(615) 736-5161
*Texas—Austin	(512) 482-5939

Texas—Dallas	(214) 767-0542
Texas—Houston	(713) 229-2578
Utah—Salt Lake City	(801) 524-5116
Virginia—Richmond	(804) 771-2246
Washington—Seattle	(206) 442-5616
Washington—Spokane	(509) 353-2922
West Virginia—Charleston	(304) 347-5123
Wisconsin—Milwaukee	(414) 291-3473

*Denotes Branch Office

Financing Exports*

Many sources of financial assistance are available to exporters. In addition to your own working capital or bank line of credit, the following are brief descriptions of some important sources of export financing assistance.

COMMERCIAL BANKS

A logical first step in choosing financing is to approach a local commercial bank for advice. If a company finds that its bank does not have an international department, then a good bank can be recommended by several sources:

• The US&FCS District Office.

• Eximbank or The Small Business Administration.

• The company's current bank.

• The company's freight forwarder.

• An experienced exporter referred by the local District Export Council or World Trade Club.

Most of these sources can also discuss financing needs and make helpful suggestions.

If a company is new to exporting or is a small or medium-sized business, it is important to select a bank that not only has an international department, but that also is sincerely interested in serving businesses of similar type or size. Of the many thousands of banks in the United States, several hundred have international departments, about half of which find it profitable to serve small- or medium-sized exporters.

When selecting a bank, the exporter should ask the following questions:

• How big is the bank's international department?

• Does it have foreign branches or correspondent banks? Where are they located?

---

* Source: Excerpted from *A Basic Guide to Exporting*, U.S. Department of Commerce and other sources.

- What are charges for confirming a letter of credit, processing drafts, and collecting payment?
- Can the bank provide buyer credit reports? Free or at what cost?
- Does it have experience with U.S. and State government financing programs that support small business export transactions? If not, is it willing to participate in these programs?
- What other services can it provide (trade leads, etc.)?

TYPES OF BANK FINANCING

The same type of commercial loans that finance domestic activities—including loans for working capital and revolving lines of credit—are available to finance export sales until payment is received. However, most banks do not usually extend credit solely on the basis of an order; thus these loans can tie up assets that must be used as collateral and can use up limited credit lines that may be needed for other transactions.

In many cases, Federal and State small business export finance programs can help reduce the need for collateral and extend the amount of credit available. There are also ways to avoid normal commercial loans altogether by requesting banker's acceptance financing.

If an export transaction is paid by using letters of credit or trade drafts, banker's acceptance financing can be used to provide immediate payment to the exporter. This follows even though the letter of credit or draft calls for payment from the buyer up to 180 days in the future.

When a letter of credit or draft is formally approved for payment (through endorsement by a bank or by the buyer), it is called an "acceptance." This document can either be kept by the exporter until the stated terms of credit have expired and then be presented for payment, or it can usually be sold immediately to a U.S. bank at a discount. In the case of an irrevocable letter of credit, payment is guaranteed by a foreign bank, and the U.S. bank will not require collateral or other proof of ability to pay from the exporter. With a trade draft, such proof may be required since the bank must come to the exporter for repayment if the buyer defaults.

The advantages of banker's acceptance financing, especially when a letter of credit is used, are the following:

- The exporter receives immediate payment in contrast to commerical loans where the cost of goods is financed but profit is not realized until payment is received.

- Less of the exporter's capital and credit line is tied up in financing (none if a letter of credit is used).
- The total interest charges and fees are usually lower—thus costs are lower for both buyer and seller.

As with any type of export financing, it should be noted that finance charges for banker's acceptances may be passed through to the buyer as part of the terms of sale (made clear in the quotation and invoice as part of the price or an added charge). For more information on this type of financing, contact one of the sources of advice listed earlier in this chapter.

FACTORING HOUSES

Certain companies, known as "factoring houses" or simply "factors" will purchase your export receivables (i.e., your invoices to foreign buyers) for a somewhat discounted price, perhaps 2 to 4 percent less than their face value. The actual amount of the discount will depend on the factoring house, the kind of product(s) involved, the customer, and the country. Factors offer two important advantages: (1) They enable you to receive immediate payment for your goods, freeing cash that could otherwise be tied up for months. (2) They relieve you of the burden of collection.

Arrangements with factoring houses are made either with or without "recourse." Arrangements "with recourse" leave you, the exporter, ultimately liable for repaying the factor if the foreign buyer defaults or other problems prevent payment within a reasonable period. Arrangements "without recourse" free you from this responsibility. Naturally, factors that accept export receivables "without recourse" generally require a large discount.

CONFIRMING

Designed to help exporters and importers expand their markets, improve cash flow, and create greater profit leverage, "confirming" is a financial service in which an independent company confirms an export order in the vendor's own country and makes payment for the goods in the currency of that country. This service can pay for and finance on terms the following items: The goods themselves, transportation (ocean or air), inland transportation at both ends, forwarding fees, customs brokerage fees, duties, etc. For the U.S. exporter, this means that the entire export transaction, from factory to end-user, can be fully coordinated and paid for with terms. Though common in Europe, confirming is still in its infancy in the United States. There are, however, U.S. firms that will provide such assistance. For further information, contact: Director, Office of Export Marketing Assistance, International Trade Administration, U.S. Department of Commerce, Washington, D.C. 20230.

FEDERAL GOVERNMENT EXPORT FINANCING PROGRAMS

A bank with a good international department experienced with government export finance programs can often advise an exporter on the different programs available. Most of the programs described below—including State programs—are intended to work through a commercial bank. Banks that participate in these programs are the agents that apply on the exporter's behalf for program benefits. The exporter need not become an expert, yet knowing the existence of these financing opportunities can be quite valuable.

Even if a bank that is currently being used by an exporter has had no experience with government export financing programs, this bank may still be used if it is willing to follow program guidelines. If assistance is needed in locating a bank that uses any of these programs, contact the appropriate Federal or State agency. The descriptions below provide a basic overview. More information can be had from the government agency listed, from banks, and also from the Department of Commerce publication *A Guide to Financing Exports*, available from US&FCS District Offices. The Department of Commerce operates no financing programs but can help exporters

choose among programs that exist: Contact a local US&FCS District Office or the Office of Trade Finance, International Trade Administration, in Washington, DC. Telephone: (202) 377-3277.

EXPORT-IMPORT BANK

Address: 811 Vermont Avenue NW, Washington, DC 20571. Public Affairs Phone: 202–566–8990

Small Business Advisory Hotline Service
800–424–5201

The Export-Import Bank (Eximbank) of the United States offers direct loans for large projects and equipment sales that usually require long-term financing; it guarantees loans made by cooperating U.S. and foreign commercial banks to U.S. exporters and to foreign buyers of U.S. products and services; and, through a private insurance association, the Foreign Credit Insurance Association (FCIA) (see below), it provides insurance to U.S. exporters enabling them to extend credit to their overseas buyers.

In all cases, Eximbank must find a "reasonable assurance of repayment" as a precondition of participating in the transaction. However, because the bank offers loan guarantees and credit insurance, a major effect of using Eximbank programs is to reduce the amount of collateral required to finance a loan and to generally make financing more available than would be the case without its support.

Among Eximbank's array of loan, guarantee, and insurance programs are four that are

EXIMBANK/FCIA
Program Selection Chart

Exports	Appropriate Programs
Short-Term (up to 180 days)	
Consumable	Export Credit Insurance
Small manufactured items	Working Capital Guarantee
Spare Parts	
Raw Materials	
Medium-Term (181 days to 5 years)	
Mining and refining equipment	Export Credit Insurance
Construction equipment	Commercial Bank Guarantees
Agricultural equipment	Small Business Credit Program
General aviation aircraft	Medium-Term Credit
Planning/feasibility studies	Working Capital Guarantee
Long-Term (5 years and longer)	
Power plants	Direct Loans
LPG & gas producing plants	Financial Guarantees
Other major projects	
Commercial jet aircraft or locomotives	
Other heavy capital goods	

especially helpful to small companies and those that are new to exporting:

• Working Capital Guarantee Program.
• Export Credit Insurance.
• Commercial Bank Guarantees.
• Small Business Credit Program.

Details on these programs are available from Eximbank.

Eximbank and FCIA also provide other credit programs for medium and long-term financing. Long-term financing (5 years and longer) is generally for export of capital equipment and large-scale installations. This financing takes the form either of a direct credit to an overseas buyer or a financial guarantee assuring repayment of a private bank credit. Eximbank often blends these two forms of support into a single financing package. The following chart gives a brief guide to the use of different programs. In the chart, exports are divided into three categories, and for each category there are two or more program options.

For complete information on Eximbank programs contact the Export-Import Bank at (202) 566-8990.

Briefing Programs. Eximbank offers briefing programs which are available to the small business community. The program includes group briefings and individual discussions held both within the Bank and around the country. For scheduling information call (202) 566-4490.

Small Business Advisory Service

To encourage small businesses to sell overseas, Eximbank maintains a special office to provide information on the availability and use of export credit insurance, guarantees, direct and intermediary loans extended to finance the sale of U.S. goods and services abroad. Its toll-free number is (800) 424-5201.

FOREIGN CREDIT INSURANCE ASSOCIATION (FCIA)

Address: 40 Rector Street, New York, NY 10006. Phone: 212–306–5000.

The export credit insurance offered by FCIA provides three basic incentives for American exporters when they do offer competitive terms to buyers. It enables them to (1) protect corporate assets as credit is extended; (2) maximize the rate of plant utilization as overseas competition is matched and orders won; and (3) improve corporate liquidity when insured foreign receivables are financed.

FCIA administers the U.S. export credit

insurance program on behalf of its member insurance companies and the Export-Import Bank, an agency of the U.S. Government. The private insurers cover the normal commercial credit risks, primarily the insolvency of or protracted payment default by overseas buyers.

U.S. SMALL BUSINESS ADMINISTRATION [SBA]

Answer desk: 800–368–5855

Through financial assistance programs, the SBA can promote small business participation in international trade by making funds available for export-oriented activities.

Funds may be used to purchase machinery, equipment, facilities, supplies, or materials needed to manufacture or sell products overseas, as well as for working capital. Working capital loans may be used to defray the costs of developing or penetrating foreign markets. Specifically, this can include costs for professional foreign marketing advice and services, foreign business travel, shipping sample merchandise abroad, shopping foreign markets, participating in overseas trade center shows and international fairs, foreign advertising and preparation of promotional materials, and other related purposes.

Small Business Administration (SBA) exporter services, available at no cost to eligible recipients, include the following:

Export Counseling. Export counseling services are furnished to potential and current small business exporters by executives and professional consultants. Members of the Service Corps of Retired Executives (SCORE) and the Active Corps of Executives (ACE), with years of practical experience in international trade, assist small firms in evaluating their export potential and strengthening their domestic operations by identifying financial, managerial or technical problems.

Small Business Institute/Small Business Development Centers. Through the Small Business Institute (SBI), advanced business students from more than 450 colleges and universities provide in-depth, long-term counseling under faculty supervision to small businesses. Additional export counseling and assistance are offered through Small Business Development Centers (SBDCs) which are located within some colleges and universities.

Call Contact Program. A third facet of the SBA counseling service is the Call Contact Program that uses professional management and technical consultants.

Export Training. SBA Field Offices cosponsor export training programs with the Department of Commerce, other federal agencies, and various private sector international-trade organizations.

Legal Advice. Through an arrangement with the Federal Bar Association (FBA), exporters may receive initial assistance, utilizing the Export Legal Assistance Network (ELAN), a cooperative program of the Commerce Department, SBA, and the Federal Bar Association.

For information on the SBA financial assistance programs, policies and requirements, contact the nearest SBA field office (see page 274).

PRIVATE EXPORT FUNDING CORPORATION (PEFCO)

Address: 280 Park Avenue, New York, NY 10017. Telephone: 212–557–3100.

PEFCO, owned mostly by commercial banks, lends only to finance export of goods and services of U.S. manufacture and origin. PEFCO's loans generally have maturities in the medium-term area and all are unconditionally guaranteed by Eximbank as to payment of interest and repayment of principal. PEFCO's funds supplement the financing of U.S. exports available through commercial banks and Eximbank.

Before contacting PEFCO, the potential borrower (a foreign buyer) or the U.S. exporter should obtain an indication from Eximbank that its board will issue a Financial Guarantee for part of the required financing. Exporters or foreign buyers with no experience in using Eximbank or PEFCO funding should first approach an experienced commercial bank; the bank will then determine whether a PEFCO loan would be a reasonable supplement to the funds provided by other sources.

DEPARTMENT OF AGRICULTURE

The Foreign Agricultural Service (FAS) of the U.S. Department of Agriculture provides financial support for U.S. agricultural exports through the Food for Peace program and the Commodity Credit Corporation. Under the Food for Peace program, Title I of the Agricultural Trade Development and Assistance Act of 1954 (Public Law 480, as amended) authorizes U.S. Government financing of sales of U.S. agricultural commodities to friendly countries on concessional credit terms. Sales are made by private business firms usually by bids. FAS administers agreements under this program.

Through the Commodity Credit Corporation (CCC), FAS provides U.S. exporters with short-term, commercial export financing support under two programs: The Export Credit Guarantee Program and the Blended Credit Program.

For additional information contact: General Sales Manager, Export Credits, Foreign Agricultural Service, 14th Street and Independence Ave., S.W., Washington, DC 20250. Telephone: (202) 447-5173.

OVERSEAS PRIVATE INVESTMENT CORPORATION (OPIC)

Address: 1615M 20th Street NW, Washington, DC. 20527. Information phone: 800–424–OPIC; in DC: 202–457–7072.

OPIC, established in 1971, is an independent agency of the U.S. government with the mission of reducing or eliminating private investment risks in the developing countries. OPIC insures U.S. investors against political risks of expropriation, inconvertability of local currency holdings, and damage from war, revolution, or insurrection. The agency offers lenders protection by guaranteeing payment of principal, interest, and loans.

The corporation offers investment information and counseling to business and participates in the cost of locating and developing projects.

AGENCY FOR INTERNATIONAL DEVELOPMENT (AID)

Address: Department of State Building, 320 21st Street, N.W. Washington, D.C. 20523

Office of Business Relations (202) 875-1551

The Agency for International Development administers most of the foreign economic assistance programs for the federal government. AID offers U.S. exporters opportunities to compete in the sales of goods or services supplied to foreign countries under loans and grants made by AID. U.S. exporters can benefit from two AID programs: the Commodity Import Programs and Project Procurements. In both of these programs, AID recipient countries purchase the commodities directly through U.S. suppliers.

TRADE AND DEVELOPMENT PROGRAM (TDP)

Address: Room 304, SA 16 Department of State, Washington, D.C. 20523. Telephone: (703) 875-4357

The Trade and Development Program is an agency of the U.S. Government that primarily funds feasibility studies for both public and private sector projects in developing countries. TDP finances studies in five principal sectors: large scale energy generation and conservation, infrastructure, mineral development, agribusiness, and basic industrial facilities.

A major purpose of TDP funding is to help U.S. engineering and planning firms win major contracts in foreign countries. By encouraging the use of U.S. firms in planning and design of a capital project, TDP participation increases the likelihood that U.S. goods, technology, and services will be procured during project implementation.

STATE AND LOCAL EXPORT FINANCE PROGRAMS

As of January 1, 1985, 15 State governments have authority to operate export financing programs. Some of these programs allow a State development agency to act as a delivery agent for Eximbank programs. Other programs include State funded loan guarantee programs. Exporters should contact the State's economic development agency for more information.

U.S. FOREIGN-TRADE ZONES (FTZs)

Firms involved in certain operations subject to significant customs duties should consider using Foreign Trade Zones (FTZs), which are now available in more than 100 port of entry communities throughout the United States. Among the advantages of using an FTZ are the following:

1. Foreign and domestic merchandise may be moved into an FTZ for storage, exhibition, assembly, manufacture, or other processing free of duties and quotas;
2. Duties are payable and quotas are applied if and when the merchandise enters the U.S. market;
3. Domestic goods entering the FTZ for export are considered exported when they enter the zone.

Information on FTZs is available by calling 202-377-2862.

Export Trading Companies and Export Management Companies

Many export trading companies (ETC's) and export management companies (EMC's) can help finance export sales in addition to acting as export representatives. However, this is true mainly for larger companies. Large ETC's may of course be able to purchase goods for export on-the-spot and thus eliminate the need for financing and other risks. When this is not the case, trading companies in a few instances may provide short-term financing themselves, but more significantly, they are also offering established contacts to make it easier for their exporter clients to obtain credit and credit insurance. Moreover, several trading companies are large enough to arrange countertrade transactions, in which trading and financing would be inseparable.

Export Management Companies

Export management companies (EMCs) will not only act as your export representative but, in some cases, will carry the financing for your export sale, assuring you of immediate payment and removing from your firm any foreign credit risk. EMCs solicit and transact business in the name of the manufacturers they represent for a commission, salary, or retainer plus commission. Many EMCs will also carry the financing for export sales, ensuring immediate payment for the manufacturer's products.

An agreement with an EMC can be an especially advantageous arrangement for smaller firms that do not have the time, personnel, or money to develop foreign markets, but wish nonetheless to establish a corporate and product identity overseas. For a description of services rendered to exporters by EMCs and ETCs (and suggestions for choosing an appropriate firm) request Commerce's pamphlet, *Partners in Trade*. Commerce also publishes a *U.S. Export Management Companies Directory* listing the names, addresses, and industry specialties of more than 1,100 EMCs in the United States. A copy of the first publication may be requested from the Publications Sales Branch, International Trade Administration, U.S. Department of Commerce, Washington, D.C. 20230. The *EMC Directory* can be purchased from: Superintendent of Documents, U.S. Government Printing Office, Washington, D.C. 20402.

Export Trading Companies

The Office of Export Trading Company Affairs (OETCA) promotes the formation of export trading companies and is responsible for administering the antitrust preclearance program set up by the Export Trading Company Act of 1982.

OETCA is also responsible for the Contact Facilitation Service, a clearinghouse for matching U.S. suppliers of exportable goods and services with firms that provide trade facilitation services. To register for this service, contact the nearest Commerce Department District Office. The *Contact Facilitation Service Directory*, giving the names of registered firms and their products and services.

The *Export Trading Company Guidebook*, published by the Department of Commerce, explains the Export Trading Company Act and the Certificate of Review program and offers guidance in setting up and operating various types of export trading companies.

Both of these can be purchased from the Superintendent of Documents, U.S. Government Printing Office, Washington, DC 20402. The *Guidebook* is also available from local Government Printing Office.

For further information contact OETCA at 202-377-5131.

Foreign Sales Corporation (FSC)†

A Foreign Sales Corporation (FSC) is a foreign chartered corporation through which exports can be made. A portion of the foreign income thus generated is exempt from Federal taxation.

In order to qualify as a FSC certain criteria must be met with respect to the management of the FSC and the exports made through it. Among the requirements are:

- The FSC must be incorporated and have its main office in a qualified foreign country or U.S. possession.
- The FSC must not have more than 25 shareholders.
- A statement of election to be treated as a FSC must be filed with the Internal Revenue Service.
- A bank account must be maintained in a foreign bank and accounting records kept in a foreign office.

There are two exceptions for small exporters. (1) Small exporters may use the FSC without meeting some of the export activities test or (2) small exporters may maintain their DISC (Domestic International Sales Corporation) by paying an annual interest charge on the DISC deferred tax liability.

Further information can be obtained by calling 202-377-3277.

Export Assistance from State Governments

State development agencies, departments of commerce, and other departments within State governments often provide valuable assistance to exporters within the State. These groups may provide assistance in marketing, market development, and in arranging for trade shows and trade missions. Information is obtainable from the National Association of State Development Agencies (NASDA), 444 N. Capitol Street, Washington, DC

20001. Telephone: 202–624–5411 and a state Department of Commerce.

Private and Government Information Sources: International Commerce*

ASEAN-U.S. Business Council (U.S. Section)[1]
Phone: (202) 463–5486

Academy of International Business
Tulane University
New Orleans, LA 70118
Phone: (504) 865–5483

Affiliated Advertising Agencies International
World Headquarters
2280 South Xanadu Way
Aurora, CO 80014
Phone: (303) 671–8551

American Arbitration Association
140 West 51st Street
New York, NY 10020
Phone: (212) 484–4000

American Association of Exporters and Importers
30th Floor, 11 West 42nd Street
New York, NY 10036
Phone: (212) 944–2230

American Enterprise Institute for Public Policy Research
1150 17th Street, NW
Washington, DC 20036
Phone: (202) 862–5800

American Importers Association
11 West 42nd Street
New York, NY 10036
Phone: (212) 944–2230

American Institute of Marine Underwriters
14 Wall Street, 21st Floor
New York, NY 10005
Phone: (212) 233–0550

American Management Association
440 1st Street, NW.
Washington, DC 20001
Phone: (202) 347–3092

---

† Source: International Trade Administration, U.S. Department of Commerce.

* Source: *Basic Guide to Exporting,* International Trade Administration, U.S. Department of Commerce and other sources.

[1] Address: Chamber of Commerce of the United States, International Division, 1615 H Street NW, Washington, DC 20062.

American National Metric Council
1010 Vermont Avenue, NW.
Washington, DC 20005
Phone: (202) 628–5757

American Society of International Executives
1777 Walton Road
Blue Bell, PA 19422
Phone: (215) 643–3040

American Society of International Law
2223 Massachusetts Avenue, NW.
Washington, DC 20008
Phone: (202) 265–4313

Bankers Association for Foreign Trade
1600 M Street, NW.
Washington, DC 20036
Phone: (202) 452–0952

Brazil-U.S. Business Council (U.S. Section)[1]
Phone: (202) 463–5485

Brookings Institution (The)
1775 Massachusetts Avenue, NW.
Washington, DC 20036
Phone: (202) 797–6000

Carribbean Central American Action
1211 Connecticut Avenue, NW.
Washington, DC 20036
Phone: (202) 466–7464

Chamber of Commerce of the United States
1615 H Street, NW.
Washington, DC 20062
Phone: (202) 659–6000

Coalition for Employment Through Exports, Inc.
1801 K Street, NW.
Washington, DC 20006
Phone: (202) 296–6107

Committee for Economic Development
1700 K Street, NW
Washington, DC 20006
Phone: (202) 296–5860

Committee on Canada-United States Relations (U.S. Section)[1]
Phone: (202) 463–5488

Conference Board (The)
845 Third Avenue
New York, NY 10022
Phone: (212) 759–0900

Council of the Americas
680 Park Avenue
New York, NY 10021
Phone: (212) 628–3200

Council on Foreign Relations, Inc.
58 East 68th Street
New York, NY 10021
Phone: (212) 734–0400

Customs and International Trade Bar Association
% Barnes, Richardson & Colburn
457 Park Avenue South
New York, NY 10016
Phone: (212) 725–0200

Czechoslovak-U.S. Economic Council (U.S. Section)[1]
Phone: (202) 463–5482

Emergency Committee for American Trade
1211 Connecticut Avenue, Suite 801
Washington, DC 20036
Phone: (202) 659–5147

Foreign Policy Association
205 Lexington Avenue
New York, NY 10016
Phone: (212) 481–8450

Fund for Multi-National Management Education (FMME)
40 East 49 Street
New York, NY 10017
Phone: (212) 758–3007

Hungarian-U.S. Economic Council (U.S. Section)[1]
Phone: (202) 463–5482

Ibero American Chamber of Commerce
733 15th Street, NW.
Washington, DC 20005
Phone: (202) 990–1255

India-U.S. Business Council (U.S. Section)[1]
Phone: (202) 463–5492

International Advertising Association
342 Madison Avenue
New York, NY 10017
Phone: (212) 557–1133

International Bank for Reconstruction and Development
1818 H Street, NW.
Washington, DC 20006
Phone: (202) 477–1234

International Cargo Gear Bureau
17 Battery Place
New York, NY 10004
Phone: (212) 425–2750

International Economic Policy Association
12605 Native Dancer Place
Darnestown, MD
Phone: (301) 990–1255

International Finance Corporation
1818 H Street, NW.
Washington, DC 20433
Phone: (202) 477–1234

**International Insurance Advisory Council
(U.S. Section)[1]**
Phone: (202) 463–5480

International Trade Council
750 13th Street, SE.
Washington, DC 20003
Phone: (202) 546–4770

National Association of Manufacturers
1331 Pennsylvania Avenue, NW.
Washington, DC 20006
Phone: (202) 626–3000

**National Association of State Development
Agencies**
444 North Capitol, NW.
Washington, DC 20001
Phone: (202) 624–5411

**National Committee on International Trade
Documentation (The)**
350 Broadway
New York, NY 10013
Phone: (212) 925–1400

**National Customs Brokers and Forwarders
Association of America**
Five World Trade Center
New York, NY 10048
Phone: (212) 432–0050

National Export Traffic League
234 Fifth Avenue
New York, NY 10001
Phone: (212) 697–5895

National Foreign Trade Council
100 East 42nd Street
New York, NY 10017
Phone: (212) 355–3600

National Industrial Council
1331 Pennsylvania Avenue, NW.
Washington, DC 20006
Phone: (202) 637–3000

Nigeria-U.S. Business Council
1701 K Street, NW.
Washington, DC 20006
Phone: (202) 775–5930

Organization of American States
19th & Constitution Avenue, NW.
Washington, DC 20006
Phone: (202) 458–3000

Overseas Development Council
1717 Massachusetts Avenue, NW.
Suite 501
Washington, DC 20036
Phone: (202) 234–8701

Pan American Development Fund
1889 F Street, NW.
Washington, DC 20006
Phone: (202) 458–3969

Partners of the Americas
1424 K Street, NW.
Washington, DC 20005
Phone: (202) 628–3300

**Philippine-U.S. Economic Council (U.S.
Section)[1]**
Phone: (202) 463–5668

**Polish-U.S. Economic Council (U.S.
Section)[1]**
Phone: (202) 463–5482

Private Export Funding Corporation
280 Park Avenue
New York, NY 10017
Phone: (202) 557–3100

**Romanian-U.S. Economic Council (U.S.
Section)[1]**
Phone: (202) 463–5482

**Trade Relations Council of the United
States, Inc.**
1001 Connecticut Avenue, NW.
Washington, DC 20036
Phone: (202) 785–4185

**Turkish-U.S. Economic Council (U.S.
Section)[1]**
Phone: (202) 463–5482

U.S. China Business Council
1818 N Street, NW.
Washington, DC 20036
Phone: (202) 429–0340

U.S.-Japan Business Council[1]
Phone (202) 463–5489

**The U.S.-U.S.S.R. Trade and Economic
Council**
805 Third Avenue
New York, NY 10022
Phone: (212) 644–4550

The U.S.-Yugoslav Economic Council, Inc.
818 18th Street, NW.
Washington, DC 20005
Phone: (202) 857–0170

The U.S.A.-Republic of China Economic Council
200 Main Street
Crystal Lake, IL 60014
Phone: (815) 459–5875

United States of America Business and Industry Advisory Committee
1212 Avenue of the Americas
New York, NY 10036
Phone: (212) 354–4480

World Trade Institute
1 World Trade Center
New York, NY 10048
Phone: (212) 466–4044

DUN & BRADSTREET

Address: 299 Park Avenue, New York, NY. 10171 Phone: 212–593–6800.

Dun & Bradstreet provides a number of valuable services and publications in the area of international business, i.e., international credit reports on companies, international marketing guides and services, and directories of foreign firms. Dun & Bradstreet's Dun's Marketing Services in Parisipphany, NJ publishes the comprehensive annual, *Exporters Encyclopedia*, with monthly supplements. It details the rules and regulations in over 220 world markets and is arranged alphabetically by country and market area. *Principal International Businesses*, also published by Dun's Marketing Service, is a useful marketing publication providing addresses, lines of business, sales figures, and other information on nearly 50,000 foreign firms.

INTERNATIONAL REPORTS

Address: 200 Park Avenue South, New York, NY 10003 Phone: 888–1508

International Reports publishes reports on sources of worldwide export credit insurance, foreign investment guarantees, and export financing under the title of *Insurance in International Finance*.

It also publishes the monthly *International Commercial Finance Service*, containing extensive information and data on financing and interest rates, surveys of credit ratings, and foreign payment records of individual countries.

BUSINESS INTERNATIONAL

Address: One Dag Hammarskjold Plaza, New York, NY 10017. Phone: 212–750–6300.

Business International publishes a series of weekly reports: *Business International* (a global view of business); *Business Europe;* *Business Latin America; Business Asia; East-* ern Europe Report; *Business China* (People's Republic); *Business International Money Report; Investing, Licensing, Trading Report;* and *Financing Foreign Operations*. It publishes a multivolume series, *Doing Business with Eastern Europe*.

COMMERCE CLEARING HOUSE

Address: 4025 West Peterson Avenue, Chicago, IL 60646. Phone 312–583–8500.

Commerce Clearing House publishes a number of widely used looseleaf series updated on a weekly or monthly basis. In the international field these include: *Euromarket News; Doing Business in Europe; Balance of Payment Reports; Common Market Reports;* and *Income Taxes World Wide*. It also publishes a number of detailed tax and legal guides for specific countries, i.e., Canada, Mexico, Australia, England, and Germany.

U.S. DEPARTMENT OF STATE

Address: New State Building, 2201 C Street, NW, Washington, DC 20520. Information: 202–647–4000.

Selected Publications

To order: Superintendent of Documents, Government Printing Office, Washington, DC 20402
Background Notes of the Countries of the World gives profiles of foreign countries.
Key Officers of Foreign Service Posts lists the addresses and phone numbers of all American embassies and consulates and their key personnel.
Department of State Bulletin is a monthly publication devoted to the latest developments in international politics and trade agreements.
For a list of State Department publications contact the Bureau of Public Affairs, Department of State, Washington, DC 20520.

THE LIBRARY OF CONGRESS

The Library of Congress's international divisions provide overseas free research assistance on social, economic, and political topics. Call:

African and Middle East Division	202–707–5528
Asian Division	5420
European Division	5455
Hispanic Division	5400

Write: Library of Congress, 10 First Street SE, Washington, DC 20540.

UNITED STATES GOVERNMENT INTERNATIONAL TRADE COMMISSION*

Address: 500 E Street SW, Washington, DC 20436. Information phone: 202–252–1000.

Formerly the U.S. Tariff Commission, the name was changed to the U.S. International Trade Commission in 1974.

The commission is given broad powers of investigation relating to the customs laws of the United States and foreign countries, the volume of importation in comparison with domestic production and consumption, the conditions, causes, and effects relating to competition of foreign industries with those of the United States and all other factors affecting competition between articles of the United States and imported articles.

Businesspersons who believe they have been injured by unfair trade methods from abroad may file a complaint with this commission.

Summaries of trade and tariff information may be obtained directly from the commission.

Sources of International Credit Information

International Trade Administration, U.S. Department of Commerce, Washington, DC.

Dun & Bradstreet International, 1 World Trade Center, New York, NY 10048. Phone: 212–524–8200.

Major Commercial Banks

U.S. Department of Agriculture, U.S. Foreign Agriculture Service, Export Credit Sales Program, Washington, DC 20250.

International Organizations

UNITED NATIONS (UN)

Address: New York, NY 10017. Information phone: 212–963–7113.

The UN and its affiliated organizations publish a large number of reports and statistical tables covering all member nations. Publications may be obtained by writing: Sales Section, United Nations Publications, New York, NY 10017. For a catalog of publications call 212–963–8302.

---

* Source: *U.S. Government Organization Manual.*

PUBLICATIONS

Economic Survey of Europe.
Journal of Development Planning.
Guidelines for Contracting for Industrial Projects in Developing Countries.
World Economic Survey.
Annual Bulletin of Exports of Chemical Products.
Annual Bulletin of Coal Statistics for Europe.
Statistics of World Trade in Steel.
Annual Bulletin of Gas Statistics for Europe.
Annual Bulletin of Electric Energy Statistics for Europe.
Economic Bulletin for Europe.
Economic Bulletin for Asia and the Pacific.
Economic Bulletin for Africa.
Economic Bulletin for Latin America.
Quarterly Bulletin of Statistics for Asia and the Pacific.
Statistical Yearbook for Asia and the Pacific.
Demographic Yearbook.
Yearbook of International Trade Statistics Vol. I: Trade by Country; Vol. II: Trade by Commodity.
Monthly Bulletin of Statistics provides monthly statistics on a wide variety of subjects from more than 200 countries and territories together with special tables illustrating important economic developments. Quarterly data for significant world and regional aggregates are also prepared regularly for the bulletin.

Statistical Yearbook is a comprehensive compilation of international statistics relating to: population and manpower; agricultural, mineral, and manufacturing production; construction; energy; trade; transport; communications; consumption; balance of payments; wages and prices; national accounts; finance; development assistance; health; housing; education; science and technology; and culture.

Population and Vital Statistics Reports (quarterly).
Yearbook of National Accounts Statistics.
Yearbook of International Trade Statistics.
Yearbook of Construction Statistics.
Commodity Trade Statistics (quarterly).
World Trade Annual.
The Growth of World Industry: Vol. I General Industrial Statistics; Vol. II Commodities Production Data.

INTERNATIONAL MONETARY FUND (IMF)

Address: 19th and H Streets NW, Washington, DC 20431. Phone: 202–623–7000.

The IMF was organized in 1945 with the purpose of promoting international monetary cooperation and consultation. The fund also seeks to facilitate the expansion of international trade and currency exchange stability. The fund issues Special Drawing Rights (SDR), a form of reserve currency used by central banks for settling balance of payment obligations.

Publications

The IMF issues a broad range of publications (some in conjunction with the World Bank Group) of interest to the business community. A publication catalog is available from: IMF Publications Services 700 19th Street, NW, Washington, DC 20431. Phone: 202–623–7430.

Provisional Oil Statistics (quarterly).

The Annual Report of the Executive Board reviews the funds' activities, policies, organization, and administration and surveys the world economy, with special emphasis on international liquidity, payments problems, exchange rates, and world trade.

Annual Report on Exchange Arrangements and Exchange Restrictions reviews developments in exchange controls and restrictions and other measures that may have direct implications for the balance of payments of member countries.

International Financial Statistics (monthly) reports for most countries of the world current data needed for analyzing problems of international payments and inflation and deflation, i.e., data on exchange rates, international liquidity, money and banking, international trade, prices, production, government finance, interest rates, and other items. Information is presented in country tables for each country and in tables with area and world aggregates. Charts on each country page show recent changes in important series. There is also a yearbook issue.

Balance of Payments Yearbook presents statistics in a standard form, expressed in a common unit of account, for countries that report information to the fund on their balance of payments transactions. In the tables that are designated as "standard presentations," these transactions are classified in terms of objective criteria; in the tables designated as "analytic presentations," they are regrouped to facilitate further analysis and certain cumulative balances are drawn.

Direction of Trade Statistics is published jointly by the International Monetary Fund and the International Bank for Reconstruction and Development. The monthly issues provide the latest available information on each country's direction of trade, with comparative data for the corresponding period of the preceding year. A yearbook is usually published in July.

The *IMF Survey* is a topical report of the fund's activities (including all press releases, texts of communiques and major statements, SDR valuations, and exchange rates) presented in the broader context of developments in national economics and international finance.

ORGANIZATION FOR ECONOMIC COOPERATION AND DEVELOPMENT (OECD)

Address: 2001 L Street NW, Washington, DC, 20036. Phone: 202-785-6323.

The OECD, established in 1961, is an outgrowth of the Organization for European Economic Cooperation, set up under the Marshall Plan in 1948. It consists of 24 developed countries: Canada, United States, Japan, Australia, New Zealand, Austria, Belgium, Denmark, England, Finland, France, West Germany, Greece, Iceland, Italy, Luxembourg, Netherlands, Norway, Portugal, Spain, Sweden, Turkey, Switzerland, and Yugoslavia.

PUBLICATIONS

OECD Observer is intended for people who are interested in and concerned with economic and social planning in the broadest sense and who want to have relevant information in the most succinct form possible. It presents in readable fashion the entire range of OECD's work—in economic affairs, trade, manpower, social affairs, science and education, the environment, financial affairs, and development assistance. (Published bimonthly.)

The *OECD Economic Outlook* is a twice yearly, detailed survey of economic trends and prospects for the immediate future.

OECD Financial Statistics supplies complete, up-to-date, authoritative information on financial markets in European countries, the United States, Canada, and Japan. (Published yearly with bimonthly supplements.)

OECD Economic Surveys is an annual analysis of the economic policy of each OECD country as seen by the others.

Main Economic Indicators, a monthly publication, is an essential source of statistics for the student of the international business cycle.

Indicators of Industrial Activity is a quarterly publication that provides an overall view of short-term economic developments in different industries for all OECD member countries.

Monthly Statistics of Foreign Trade includes a detailed regional analysis of trade of the main country groupings in the OECD area. Series are shown non-adjusted and seasonally adjusted.

Foreign Trade by Commodities is an annual publication with matrix tables showing trade between OECD countries and partner countries of commodity groups defined at 1- and 2-digit levels of the Standard International Trade Classification. Separate volumes are published for exports and imports.

GENERAL AGREEMENT ON TRADE AND TARIFFS (GATT)

Address: Centre William Rappard, 154 Rue de Lausanne, Geneva, Switzerland.

GATT is a multilateral trade treaty (entered into force in 1948) among 83 countries providing for the reduction of tariffs and other trade barriers, standardization of trade procedures, and the resolution of trade disputes. GATT publishes *Compilations of Basic Information on Export Markets; Guide to Sources of Foreign Trade Information; Analytical Bibliography: A Compendium of Sources: International Trade Statistics;* and *World Directory of Industry and Trade Associations.*

Selected Bibliography[1]

A. Market Identification and Assessment

Addresses to AID Missions Overseas, Office of Small and Disadvantaged Business Utilization/Minority Business Center, Agency for International Development, Washington, DC 20523.

AID Commodity Eligibility Listing, Office of Small and Disadvantaged Business Utilization/Minority Resource Center, Agency for International Development, Washington, DC 20523, 1984 revised. Lists groups of commodities, presents the Agency for International Development (AID) commodity eligibility list, gives eligibility requirements for certain commodities and describes commodities that are not eligible for financing by the agency.

AID Regulation 1, Office of Small and Disadvantaged Business Utilization/Minority Resource Center, Agency for International Development, Washington, DC 20523. This tells what transactions are eligible for financing by the Agency for International Development (AID), and the responsibilities of importers, as well as the bid procedures.

AID Financed Export Opportunities, Office of Small and Disadvantaged Business Utilization/Minority Resource Center, Agency for International Development, Washington, DC 20523. Fact sheets also referred to as "Small Business Circulars", they present procurement data about proposed foreign purchases.

American Bulletin of International Technology Transfer, International Advancement, P.O. Box 75537, Los Angeles, CA 90057. Bimonthly. A comprehensive listing of product and service opportunities offered and wanted for licensing and joint ventures agreements in the United States and overseas.

Big Business Blunders: Mistakes in Multinational Marketing, 1982, David A. Ricks, Doug Jones-Irwin, Homewood, IL 60430.

Business America.[2] International Trade Administration, U.S. Department of Commerce. Principle Commerce Department publication for presenting domestic and international business news and news of the application of technology to business and industrial problems.

Catalogo de Publicaciones de la OPS, Pan American Health Organization/World Health Organization, 525 23rd Street, NW., Washington, DC 20037. A free guide of publications, many of which are in English. This catalog is published in Spanish.

Developments in International Trade Policy, International Monetary Fund, Publications Unit, 700 19th Street, NW., Washington, DC 20431. This paper focuses on the main current issues in trade policies of the major trading nations.

Direction of Trade Statistics, International Monetary Fund, Publications Unit, 700 19th Street, NW., Washington, DC 20431. This monthly publication provides data on the country and area distribution of countries' exports and imports as reported by themselves or their partners. A yearbook is published annually which gives seven years of data for 157 countries and two sets of world and area summaries.

Directory of Exporters and Importers, Journal of Commerce, Marshall Street, Phillipsburg, NJ 08865.

Directory of Leading U.S. Export Management Companies, 1984, Bergamo Book Co., 15 Ketchum Street, Westport, CT 06881.

Economic and Social Survey for Asia and the Pacific, UNIPUB, 4611-F Assembly Drive, Lanham, MD 20706–4391. Tel: (800) 521–8110. Analyzes recent economic and social developments in the region in the context of current trends. Examines agriculture, food, industry, transport, public finance, wages and prices, and external trade sectors.

Element of Export Marketing, John Stapleton, 1984, Woodhead-Faulkner, Dover, NH.

EXIM Bank Information Kit, Public Affairs Office, Export-Import Bank of the United States, 811 Vermont Avenue, NW., Washington, DC 20571. Includes the Bank's annual report, which provides information on interest rates and the Foreign Credit Insurance Association.

Export Directory.[3] Describes the principle functions of the Foreign Agricultural Service and lists agricultural attaches.

Export-Import Bank: Financing for American Exports—Support for American Jobs,

Source: Excerpted from *A Basic Guide to Exporting,* International Trade Administration, U.S. Department of Commerce, and other sources.
1. Prices are not given in this section.
2. To order: Superintendent of Documents, General Printing Office, Washington, DC 20402.
3. For information: U.S. Department of Agriculture, Foreign Agricultural Services, Washington, DC 20250. Telephone: 202–477–7937.
4. Contact Local US & FCS District Office.

Export-Import Bank of the United States, 1980.

Export Strategies: Markets and Competition, Nigel Percy, 1982, Allen & Unwin, Winchester, MA 01890.

Exporter's Encyclopedia, annual with semimonthly updates, Dun's Marketing Service, 10 Old Bloomfield Avenue, Mt. Lakes, NJ 07046. Provides a comprehensive, country-by-country coverage of 150 world markets. It contains an examination of each country's communications and transportation facilities, customs and trade regulations, documentation, key contacts, and unusual conditions that may affect operations. Financing and Credit abroad are also examined.

FAS Commodity Report.[3] These reports provide information on foreign agricultural production in 22 commodity areas.

FATUS: Foreign Agricultural Trade of the United States.[3] This report of trends in U.S. agricultural trade by commodity and country and of events affecting this trade is published six times a year with two supplements.

Findex: The Directory of Market Research Reports, Studies and Surveys, FIND/SVP, The Information Clearinghouse, 625 Avenue of the Americas, New York, NY 10016.

Foreign Agriculture.[3] A monthly publication containing information on overseas markets and buying trends, new competitors and products, trade policy developments and overseas promotional activities.

Foreign Agriculture Circulars.[3] Individual circulars report on the supply and demand for commodities around the world. Products covered include: diary, livestock, poultry, grains, coffee, and wood products.

Foreign Commerce Handbook, Chamber of Commerce of the United States, 1615 H Street, NW., Washington, DC 20062. Lists organizations of assistance to U.S. exporters, as well as up-to-date published information on all important phases of international trade and investment.

Foreign Economic Trends (FET), Superintendent of Documents, U.S. Government Printing Office, Washington, DC 20402. Prepared by the U.S. and Foreign Commercial Service. Presents current business and economic developments and the latest economic indications in more than 100 countries. Available from ITA Publications Distribution, Rm. 1617D, U.S. Department of Commerce, Washington, DC 20230.

Foreign Market Entry Strategies, Franklin R. Root, 1982, AMACOM, New York, NY 10020.

Glossary of International Terms, International Trade Institute, Inc., 5055 N. Main Street, Dayton, OH 45415.

A Guide to Export Marketing, International Trade Institute, Inc., 5055 North Main Street, Dayton, OH 45415.

Handbook of International Trade and Development Statistics, UNIPUB, 4611-F Assembly Drive, Lanham, MD 20706-4391. Examines structural trends in developing and developed countries.

Highlights of U.S. Import and Export Trade.[2] Statistical book of U.S. imports and exports.

How to Build an Export Business: An International Marketing Guide for Minority-Owned Businesses.[2]

International Financial Statistics, International Monetary Fund, Publications Unit, 700 19th Street, NW., Washington, DC 20431. Monthly publication is a standard source of international statistics on all aspects of international and domestic finance.

International Marketing, 5th edition, 1983, Philip R. Cateora, Irwin, Homewood, IL 60430.

International Marketing, Raul Kahler, 1983, Southwestern Publishing Co., Cincinnati, OH 45227.

International Marketing, 3rd edition, Vern Terpstra, 1983, Dryden Press, Hinsdale, IL 60521.

International Marketing, Revised Edition, Hans Thorelli & Helmut Becker, eds., 1980, Pergamon Press, Elmsford, NY 10523.

International Marketing, 2nd edition, 1981, L. S. Walsh, International Ideas, Philadelphia, PA 19103.

International Marketing: An Annotated Bibliography, 1983, S. T. Cavusgil & John R. Nevin, eds., American Marketing Association.

International Marketing Handbook, 1985, 3 Vols., Frank S. Bair, ed., Gale Research Co., Detroit, MI 48226.

International Marketing Research, 1983, Susan P. Douglas & C. Samual Craig, Prentice-Hall, Englewood Cliffs, NJ 07632.

International Monetary Fund: Publications Catalog, International Monetary Fund, Publications Unit, 700 19th Street, NW., Washington, DC 20431.

International Trade Operations . . . A Managerial Approach, R. Duane Hall, Unz & Co., 190 Baldwin Ave., Jersey City, NJ 07303.

International Trade Reporter, Bureau of National Affairs, 1231 25th Street NW, Washington, DC 20037.

Local Chambers of Commerce Which Maintain Foreign Trade Services, 1983. International Division, Chamber of Commerce of the United States, 1615 H Street, NW., Washington, DC 20062. A list of chambers of commerce that have programs to aid exporters.

Market Shares Reports, National Technical Information Services, U.S. Department of Commerce, Box 1553, Springfield, VA 22161. These are reports for over 88 countries. They provide basic data needed by exporters to evaluate overall trends in the size of markets for manufacturers.

Marketing Aspects of International Business, 1983, Gerald M. Hampton & Aart Van Gent, Klewer-Nijhoff Publishing, Bingham, MA.

Marketing High-Technology, William L. Shanklin & John K. Ryans, Jr., DC Heath & Co., 125 Spring Street, Lexington, MA 02173.

Marketing in the Third World, Erdener Kaynak, Praeger, New York, NY 10175.

Metric Laws and Practices in International Trade—Handbook for U.S. Exporters, 1982.[2]

Monthly World Crop Production.[3] Report provides estimates on the projection of wheat, rice, coarse grains, oilseeds, and cotton in selected regions and countries around the world.

Multinational Marketing Management, 3rd edition, 1984, Warren J. Keegan, Prentice Hall, Englewood Cliffs, NJ 07632.

OECD Publications, OECD Publications and Information Center, Suite 1207, 1750 Pennsylvania Avenue, NW., Washington, DC 20006–4582.

Outlook for U.S. Agricultural Exports.[3] This report analyzes current developments and forecasts U.S. farm exports in coming months by commodity and region. Country and regional highlights discuss the reasons why sales of major commodities are likely to rise or fall in those areas.

Overseas Business Reports (OBR).[2] Reports include current-marketing information, trade forecasts, statistics, regulations, and marketing profiles. Available from ITA Publications, Rm. 1617D, U.S. Department of Commerce, Washington, DC 20230.

Profitable Export Marketing: A Strategy for U.S. Business, Maria Ortiz-Buonafina, Prentice-Hall, Englewood Cliffs, NJ 07632.

Reference Book for World Traders, Annual, Croner Publications, Inc., 211 Jamaica Avenue, Queens Village, NY 11428. A loose-leaf reference book for traders. Gives information about export documentation, steamship lines and airlines, free trade zones, credit and similar matters.

Source Book . . . The "How to" Guide for Exporters and Importers, Unz & Co., 190 Baldwin Avenue, Jersey City, NJ 07036.

Trade Directories of the World, Annual, Croner Publications, Inc., 211 Jamaica Avenue, Queens Village, NY 11428.

Trends in World Production and Trade, 1982, UNIPUB, P.O. Box 1222, Ann Arbor, MI 48106. 4611-F Assembly Drive, Lanham, MD 20706-4391. Report discusses the structural change in world output, industrial growth patterns since 1960, changes in the pattern of agricultural output, and changes in patterns in trade in goods and services. Product groups and commodity groups are defined according to SITC criteria.

United Nations Publications, United Nations and Information Center, 1889 F Street, NW., Washington, DC 20006.

U.S. Export Sales.[3] A weekly report of agricultural export sales based on reports provided by private exporters.

U.S. Farmers Export Arm.[3] 1980.

Weekly Roundup of World Production and Trade.[3] Provides a summary of the week's important events in agricultural foreign trade and world production.

World Agriculture.[3] Provides production information, data and analyses by commodity and country, along with a review of recent economic conditions and changes in food and trade policies.

World Agriculture Regional Supplements.[3] Provides a look by region at agricultural developments during the previous year and the outlook for the year ahead.

The World Bank Catalog of Publications, World Bank Publications, P.O. Box 37525, Washington, DC 200013.

World Economic Outlook: A Survey by the Staff of the International Monetary Fund, International Monetary Fund, Publications Unit, 700 19th Street, NW., Washington, DC 20431. This yearly report provides a comprehensive picture of the international situation and prospects. Highlights the imbalances that persist in the world economy and their effects on inflation, unemployment, real rates of interest and exchange rates.

World Economic Survey, UNIPUB, 4611-F Assembly Drive, Lanham, MD 20706-4301. Assesses the world economy. It provides an overview of developments in global economics for the past year and provides an outlook for the future.

Yearbook of International Trade Statistics, UNIPUB, 4611-F Assembly Drive, Lanham, MD 20706-4391. Offers international coverage of foreign trade statistics. Tables are provided for overall trade by regions and countries. Vol. I. Trade by Commodity. Vol. II. Commodity Matrix Tables.

B. Selling & Sales Contacts

American Export Register, Thomas Publishing Co., 1 Penn Plaza, 250 N. 34th Street, New York, NY 10010. This book is designed for persons searching for U.S. suppliers, for foreign manufacturers seeking U.S. buyers or representatives for their products. Contains product lists in four languages, an advertiser's index, information about and a list of U.S. Chambers of Commerce abroad, and a list of banks with international services and shipping, financing and insurance information.

Background Notes.[2] Four to twelve page summaries on the economy, people, history, culture and government of about 160 countries.

Commercial News USA (CN), Monthly export promotion magazine circulated only overseas, listing specific products and services of U.S. firms. Applications for participation in the magazine are available from the District Offices of the U.S. and Foreign Commercial Service, U.S. Department of Commerce.

Directory of American Firms Operating in Foreign Countries, 11th Edition, (3 volumes) World Trade Academy Press, 50 E. 42nd Street, New York, NY 10017. Contains the most recent data on some 3000 American companies with more than 22,500 subsidiaries and affiliates in 122 foreign countries. Lists every American firm under the country in which it has subsidiaries or branches, together with their home office branch in the United States. Gives the names and addresses of their subsidiaries or branches, products manufactured or distributed. Foreign operations are grouped by country.

Directory of Foreign Firms Operating in the United States, World Trade Academy Press, 50 E. 42nd Street, New York, NY 10017. Directory is in three parts: (1) foreign firms grouped by country, (2) Alphabetical index of foreign firms, (3) alphabetical index of firms in the U.S.

Export Mailing List Service (EMLS).[4] Targeted mailing lists of prospective overseas customers from the Commerce Department's automated worldwide file of foreign firms. EMLs identify manufacturers, agents, retailers, service firms, government agencies and other one-to-one contacts. Information includes name and address, cable and telephone numbers, name and title of a key official, product/service interests, and additional date.

How to Get the Most from Overseas Exhibitions, International Trade Administration, Publications Distribution, Room 1617D, U.S. Department of Commerce, Washington, DC 20230.

Japan: Business Obstacles and Opportunities, 1983, McKinney & Co., John Wiley, NY.

Management of International Advertising: A Marketing Approach, 1984, Dean M. Peeples & John K. Ryans. Allyn & Bacon, Boston, MA 02159.

Service Industries and Economic Development: Case Studies in Technology Transfer. Praeger Publishers, New York, NY 10175. 1984.

Top Bulletin. Journal of Commerce, 445 Marshall Street, Phillipsburg, NJ 08865. Weekly publication of trade opportunities received each week from overseas embassies and consulates. Also available on computer tape.

World Traders Data Reports (WTDRs).[4] Service provides background reports on individual foreign firms. WTDRs are designed to help U.S. firms evaluate potential foreign customers before making a business commitment.

C. Financing Exports

Chase World Guide for Exporters, Export Credit Reports, Chase Trade Information Corporation, One World Trade Center, Suite 7801, New York, NY 10048. The *Guide,* covering 180 countries, contains current export financing methods, collection experiences and charges, foreign import and exchange regulations and related subjects. Supplementary bulletins keep the guide up to date throughout the year. The *Reports,* issued quarterly, specify credit terms granted for shipment to all the principal world markets. The reports show the credit terms offered by the industry groups as a whole, thereby enabling the reader to determine whether his or her terms are more liberal or conservative than the average for specific commodity groups.

Financing and Insuring Exports: A User's Guide to Eximbank and FCIA Programs, Export-Import Bank of the United States, User's Guide, 811 Vermont Avenue, NW., Washington, DC 20571. A 350 page guide which covers Eximbank's working capital guarantees, credit risk protection (guarantees and insurance), medium-term and long-term lending programs. Includes free updates during calendar year in which the guide is purchased.

A Guide to Checking International Credit, International Trade Institute, Inc., 5055 N. Main Street, Suite 270, Dayton, OH 45415.

A Guide to Financing Exports, U.S. and Foreign Commercial Service, International Trade Administration Publications Distribution, Room 1617D, U.S. Department of Commerce, Washington, DC 20230, 1985. Brochure.

A Guide to Understanding Drafts, International Trade Institute, Inc., 5055 N. Main Street, Dayton, OH 45415.

A Guide to Understanding Letters of Credit, International Trade Institute, Inc., 5055 N. Main Street, Dayton, OH 45415.

A Handbook on Financing U.S. Exports, Machinery and Allied Products Institute, 1200 18th Street, NW., Washington, DC 20036.

Official U.S. and International Financing Institutions: A Guide for Exporters and Investors, International Trade Administration, U.S. Department of Commerce. Available from the Superintendent of Documents, U.S. Government Printing Office, Washington, DC 20402.

Specifics on Commercial Letters of Credit and Bankers Acceptances, James A. Harrington, 1979 UNZ & Co., Division of Scott Printing Corp., 190 Baldwin Avenue, Jersey City, NJ 07036, 1979.

D. Laws and Regulations

Customs Regulations of the United States.[2]

Distribution License, 1985 Office of Export Administration, Room 1620, U.S. Department of Commerce, Washington, DC 20230

Export Administration Regulations.[2] Covers U.S. export control regulations and policies, with instructions, interpretations and explanatory material. Last revised Oct 1, 1984.

Manual for the Handling of Applications for Patents, Designs and Trademarks Throughout the World, Ocrooibureau Los En Stigter B.V., Amsterdam, the Netherlands.

Summary of U.S. Export Regulations, 1985, Office of Export Administration, Room 1620, Department of Commerce, Washington, DC 20230.

E. Shipping and Logistics

Export-Import Traffic Management and Forwarding, 6th edition, 1979. Alfred Murr, Cornell Maritime Press, Box 456, Centerville, MD 21617. Presents the diverse functions and varied services concerned with the entire range of ocean traffic management.

Export Shipping Manual, Indexed, looseleaf reference binder. Detailed current information on shipping and import regulations for all areas of the world. Bureau of National Affairs, 1231 25th Street, NW., Washington, DC 20037.

Guide to Canadian Documentation, International Trade Institute, Inc., 5055 N. Main Street, Dayton, OH 45415.

Guide to Documentary Credit Operations, ICC Publishing Corporation, New York, NY 1985.

Guide to Export Documentation, International Trade Institute, Inc., 5055 N. Main Street, Dayton, OH 45415.

Guide to International Ocean Freight Shipping, International Trade Institute, 5055 N. Main Street, Dayton, OH 45415.

Guide to Selecting the Freight Forwarder, International Trade Institute, Inc., 5055 North Main Street, Suite 270, Dayton, OH 45415.

Journal of Commerce Export Bulletin, 110 Wall Street, New York, NY 10005. A weekly newspaper that reports port and shipping developments. Lists products shipped from New York and ships and cargoes departing from 25 other U.S. ports. A "trade prospects" column lists merchandise offered and merchandise wanted.

Shipping Digest, Geyer-McAllister Publications, Inc., 51 Madison Avenue, New York, NY 10010. A weekly which contains cargo sailing schedules from every U.S. port to every foreign port, as well as international air and sea commerce news.

F. Licensing

Foreign Business Practices . . . Material on Practical Aspects of Exporting,[2] International Licensing and Investment, 1981.

American Bulletin of International Technology Transfer, International Advancement, P.O. Box 75537, Los Angeles, CA 90057, bimonthly. Comprehensive listing of product and service opportunities offered and sought for licensing and joint ventures agreements in the United States and overseas.

International Technology Licensing: Competition, Costs, and Negotiation, 1981, J. Farok Contractor, Lexington Books, Lexington, MA 02173.

Investing, Licensing, and Trading Conditions Abroad, Business International Corporation, base volume with monthly updates.

Sources for Market Research

Product/Industry Data Resources

Foreign Trade Report, FT 410.[2] Monthly FT 410 provides a statistical record of shipments of all merchandise from the United States to foreign countries, including both the quantity and dollar value of exports to each country during the month covered by the report. Also contains cumulative export statistics from the first of the calendar year. Report FT 410 (monthly and cumulative for U.S. Exports, Schedule E Commodity by Country) is available by subscription. The reports may also be available at US&FCS District Offices and many large libraries.

International Market Research (IMR).[4] These reports are in-depth analyses for those who want a more complete picture for one industry in one country. A report includes information such as market size and outlook, end-user analysis, distribution channels, cultural characteristics, business customs and practices, competitive situation, trade barriers, and trade contacts.

Comparison Shopping Service. Service provides a custom-tailored export market research survey on a U.S. client firm's specific product in a single country. The survey covers key marketing factors in the target country, including overall marketability, names of competitors, comparative prices, entry and distribution channels, and names of potential sales representatives or licensees. The survey is conducted on-site by U.S. commercial officers and is available for standard off-the-shelf products (no custom or specialty items) in selected countries.

Market Share Reports. Provides basic data to evaluate overall trends in the size of markets for exporters. Also measures changes in the import demand for specific products and compares the competitive position of U.S. and foreign exporters. Contact the National Technical Information Service, U.S. Department of Commerce, Box 1553, Springfield, VA 22161.

Export Information System (XIS) Data Reports. Available from the U.S. Small Business Administration (SBA) for approximately 1700 product categories, the XIS Data Reports provide to a small business a list of the 25 largest importing markets for its product, the 10 best markets for U.S. exporters of that product, the trends within those markets and the major sources of foreign competition, based on Department of Commerce and United Nations data. There is no charge to small businesses for this service. Contact the local SBA Field Office.

FINDEX: The Directory of Market Research Reports, Studies and Surveys. Publication contains over 10,000 listings of market research reports, studies, and surveys. Contact FIND/SVP The Information Clearinghouse, 625 Avenue of the Americas, New York, NY 10016.

Country Data Resources:

Foreign Economic Trends (FET).[4] FET's present current business and economic developments and the latest economic indicators for more than 100 countries. FET's are prepared either annually or semiannually depending on the country.

Overseas Business Reports (OBR's).[2] Reports provide background statistics and information on specific countries useful to exporters. They present economic and commercial profiles, issue semiannual outlooks for U.S. trade, and publish selected statistical reports on the direction, volume, and nature of U.S. foreign trade with the country.

Background Notes.[2] This series surveys a country's people, geography, economy, government, and foreign policy. Prepared by the Department of State, it includes important national economic and trade information, including major trading partners.

U.S. Agency for International Development's Congressional Presentations. Provide country-by-country data on nations to which the agency will provide funds in the coming year. Also provide detailed information on past funding activities in each individual country. In addition, the publications list projects and their locations that the agency desires to fund in the upcoming year (i.e. a hydroelectric project in Egypt). Since these projects require U.S. goods and services, the *Congressional Presentations* can give U.S. exporters an opportunity to plan ahead by allowing an early look at potential projects. For ordering information, contact the U.S. Agency for International Development (AID), Department of State, Washington, DC 20523. Telephone: (703) 235–1840.

Trade and Development Program's Congressional Presentation. This publication reports the dollar amount spent by the agency by industry in specific countries around the world for the past several years. For ordering information about Trade and Development's *Congressional Presentation*, contact Trade and Development Program, U.S. Department of State, Washington, DC 20523. Telephone: (703) 235–3663.

Exporters Encyclopedia. An extensive handbook on exporting, this publication contains market information on over 150 world markets, which are individually covered. Contact Dun's Marketing Services, 49 Old Bloomfield Avenue, Mt. Lakes, NJ 07046.

Doing Business in Foreign Countries.[2] A series on doing business in most foreign countries, these individual guides are often provided to clients or interested parties by some large or international accounting firms, banks, or other service firms. These publications provide information on specific countries and include demographic and cultural backgrounds, economic climates, restrictions and incentives to trade, duties, documentation requirements, tax structure, and other useful information.

Worldwide Background Data

Statistical Yearbook. This international trade information on products is provided by the United Nations. Information on importing countries and, to help assess competition, exports by country are included. Order by calling 800–521–8110.

World Population. The U.S. Bureau of the Census collects and analyzes worldwide demographic data that can assist exporters in identifying potential markets for their products. Information on each country—total population, fertility, mortality, urban population, growth rate, and life expectancy—is updated every 2 years. Also published are detailed demographic profiles (including analysis of labor force structure, infant mortality, etc.) of individual countries (price and availability varies). *World Population.* Contact the Center for International Research, Room 407, Scuderi Building, U.S. Bureau of the Census, Washington, DC 20233.

International Economic Indicators. These are quarterly reports providing basic data (for years and quarters) on the economies of the United States and seven principal industrial countries. Include statistics on gross national product, industrial production, trade, prices, finance, and labor; they also measure changes in key competitive indicators. Reports can provide an overall view of international trends or a basis for more detailed analyses of the economic situation. Annual subscription is available through: ITA Publications Sales Branch, Room 1617D, U.S. Department of Commerce, Washington, DC 20230.

International Financial Statistics. A monthly publication produced by the International Monetary Fund. It presents statistics on exchange rates, money and banking, production, government finance, interest rates, and other subjects. Available from the International Monetary Fund, Publications Unit, 700 19th Street, NW., Washington, DC 20431. Telephone: (202) 473–7430.

World Bank Atlas. Published by the World Bank, this publication presents population, gross domestic product, and average growth rates for every country. Available from World Bank Publications, P.O. Box 37525, Washington, DC 20013.

Other Publications

Europa Year Book is an annual two-volume work covering a wide range of commercial, economic, and political statistics and information about every country in the world. Volume I deals with international organizations and the countries of Europe, while Volume II covers Africa, the Americas, Asia, and Australia. It is published by Europe Publications, Ltd., 18 Bedford Square, London, England and distributed in North America by Gale Research, Inc., Book Tower, Detroit MI 48227.

Asian Markets: A Guide to Company and Industry Information Sources. In addition to information sources, this volume provides access to country—specific contacts in the U.S. and abroad. Published by Washington Researchers, 2612 P Street, NW, Washington, DC 20007.

Foreign Commerce Handbook provides information on international trade and foreign markets. Included are addresses and phone numbers of organizations involved with foreign trade, a glossary of foreign commercial terms and a bibliography of indexes and periodicals. Available from the Chamber of Commerce of the United States, 1615 H Street NW, Washington, DC 20062.

International Directory of Marketing Research Houses and Services (the "Green Book") is a directory of marketing research organizations in some 50 countries and includes descriptions of services, contact people, phone numbers, and addresses. Available from: American Marketing Association, 420 Lexington Avenue, New York, NY 10170.

Lambert's World Government Directory identifies government officials in 168 countries as well as officials in Inter-Governmental organizations. Published by International Executive Reports, 115 Massachusetts Avenue NW, Washington, DC 20005.

Country Experts in the Federal Government is a guide to U.S. government analysts for almost all countries. Published by Washington Researchers, 2612 P Street, NW, Washington, DC 20007.

International Research Center Directory edited by Anthony F. Kruzas and Kay Gill identifies 15,000 university-related, independent and government research organizations throughout the world. Available from Gale Research Company, Book Tower, Detroit, MI 48226.

Croner's Reference Book for World Traders is a three volume work covering basic data and hard-to-locate information for international traders and market researchers. Available from Croner Publications, 211–05 Jamaica Avenue, Queens Village, New York, 11428.

Incoterms is a booklet providing a set of international rules for interpreting the main terms used in foreign trade contracts. Available from the U.S. Council of the International Chamber of Commerce, Inc. 1212 Avenue of the Americas, New York, NY 10036. Also publishes other useful material.

Revised American Foreign Trade Definitions, is a compilation from the National Council of Importers, the Chamber of Commerce of the U.S., and the National Foreign Trade Council. Available from the National Foreign Trade Council at 100 E. 42nd Street, New York, NY 10017.

European Markets: A Guide to Company and Industry Information Sources is a three volume resource for accessing information on European companies and markets. Available from Washington Researchers, 2612 P Street NW, Washington, DC 20007.

Exporters' Encyclopaedia, Dun's Marketing Service, 49 Old Bloomfield Avenue, Mt. Lakes, NJ 07046. Gives country by country coverage of 150 world markets.

Directory of American Firms Operating in Foreign Countries contains information i.e., addresses, telephone numbers, principal product and/or service on some 3000 American companies with more than 22,500 subsidiaries and affiliates in 122 foreign companies. Three volumes published by World Trade Academy Press, Inc. 50 East 42nd Street, New York, NY 10017.

Directory of Foreign Firms Operating in the United States contains information i.e., addresses, telephone numbers, officers, American firm(s) owned or affiliated with the foreign firm. Three volumes. Published by World Trade Academy Press, Inc. (address above).

International Information Available in the U.S. by Country

This section lists helpful addresses in the United States for those doing business with countries where business practices may present certain problems.

JAPAN

Exporters and importers generally find it essential to use the services of the Japanese trading companies, which offer a wide range of services including negotiation of overseas deals, transportation, storage, finance, and marketing. The largest trading companies are listed below. The small exporter will often do better using smaller trading companies that specialize in one or two types of products. Exporters seeking an appropriate trading company should contact a local JETRO Office (Japan External Trade Office):

Bank of America Tower
725 S. Figuero Street
Los Angeles, CA 90017
Telephone: 213–624–8855

360 Post Street
San Francisco, CA 94108
Telephone: 415–392–1333

245 Peachtree Center Avenue
Atlanta, GA 30303
Telephone: 404–681–0600

401 N. Michigan Avenue
Chicago, IL 60601
Telephone: 312–527–9000

1221 Avenue of the Americas
New York, NY 10020
Telephone: 212–997–0400

One World Trade Center
2100 Stemmons Freeway
Dallas, TX 75258
Telephone: 214–651–0839

One Houston Center
1221 McKinney Street
Houston, TX 77010
Telephone: 713–759–9595

One Tabor Center
1200 17th Street
Denver, CO 80202
Telephone: 303–629–0404

P.O. Box 3356
Marina Station
Mayaguez, PR 00708
Telephone: Mayaquez 832–0861

The Office of Japan of ITA provides counseling for exporters and assistance on specific cases to improve market access. Country desk officers in the Office of Japan can provide general market information, tariffs and trade regulations, economic and trade statistics, information on trade and economic policy issues, and limited industry-specific information. The Japan Desk can direct inquiries for industry-specific information to the proper U.S. agency and should be contacted by U.S. firms that encounter difficulty doing business with Japanese companies because of Japanese regulations. The telephone number is 202–377–4527.

JAPANESE GOVERNMENT REPRESENTATION

The Japanese Government maintains its embassy in the United States at 2520 Massachusetts Avenue, N.W., Washington, DC 20008 (telephone: 202–939–6700). Consulate General Offices are located in the following U.S. cities:

New York, NY	299 Park Ave., 10017	(212) 371–8222
Chicago, IL	625 N. Michigan Ave., 60611	(312) 280–0400
Seattle, WA	3110 Ranier Bank Tower,	
	1301 5th Ave., 98101	(206) 682–9107
Portland, OR	2400 First Interstate Tower,	
	1300 S.W. Fifth Ave., 97201	(503) 227–6694
San Francisco, CA	1601 Post St., 94115	(415) 921–8000
Los Angeles, CA	250 East First St., 94115	(213) 624–8305
Boston, MA	Federal Reserve Plaza,	
	600 Atlantic Ave., 02210	(617) 973–9772
Atlanta, GA	400 Colony Square Bldg.,	
	120 Peachtree St., N.E., 30361	(404) 892–2700
New Orleans, LA	1830 International Trade Mart Bldg.,	
	No. 2 Canal St., 70130	(504) 529–2101
Houston, TX	1612 First City National Bank Bldg.,	
	1000 Louisana St., 77002	(713) 652–2977
Kansas City, MO	2519 Commerce Tower,	
	911 Main St., 64105–2076	(816) 471–0111
Honolulu, HA	1742 Nuuanu Ave., 96817	(808) 536–2226
Anchorage, AK	909 East Ninth Ave., 99501	(907) 279–8428

MAJOR TRADING COMPANIES (NEW YORK OFFICES)

Mitsubishi International Corporation
520 Madison Avenue
New York, NY 10022

Mitsui & Company
200 Park Avenue
New York, NY 10017

Marubeni America Corporation
200 Park Avenue
New York, NY 10066

C. Itoh & Co. (America), Inc.
335 Madison Avenue
New York, NY 10017

Sumitomo Corporation of America
345 Park Avenue
New York, NY 10154

Toyomenka (America), Inc.
One World Trade Center
New York, NY 10048

Kanematsu-Gosho (USA), Inc.
1133 Avenue of the Americas
New York, NY 10036

Nichimen America, Inc.
1185 Avenue of the Americas
New York, NY 10036

Nissho Iwai America
1211 Avenue of the Americas
New York, NY 10036

OTHER ORGANIZATIONS

The Japan Economic Institute (JEI) of America, a research organization supported by the Japanese Ministry of Foreign Affairs maintains a well-organized and comprehensive library and publishes numerous reports on economic and trade issues affecting Japan. Located at 1000 Connecticut Avenue N.W., Washington, DC, 20036 (telephone: 202–296–5633).

The U.S.-Japan Business Council (formerly the Advisory Council on Japan-U.S. Economic Relations) seeks to provide a forum to propose solutions to U.S.-Japan economic problems and facilitate bilateral business relations, sponsors an annual Japan-U.S. Businessmen's Conference with its Japanese counterpart organization, the Japan-U.S. Economic Council. The Council operates under the aegis of the U.S. Chamber located at 1615 H Street, N.W., Washington, DC 20062 (telephone: 202–463–5489).

In addition to its many cultural programs, the Japan Society in New York City sponsors a number of seminars and other activities focusing on political, economic and public affairs issues. For information, contact the Japan Society at 333 East 47th St., New York, NY 10017 (telephone: 212–832–1155). The Asia Society at 725 Park Avenue, New York, NY 10021 (telephone: 212–288–6400) also offers a number of special programs and publications dealing with economic and public affairs issues.

The Manufactured Imports Promotion Organization (MIPRO) of Japan is a non-profit organization supported by MITI and the Japanese business community to foster expansion of Japan's manufactured imports. MIPRO sponsors and supports many exhibitions in its facilities in the World Import Mart in Tokyo, and publishes several helpful pamphlets. Its U.S. office is located at 2000 L St., N.W., Suite 808, Washington, DC 20036 (telephone: 202–659–3729).

PUBLICATIONS ON TRADING WITH JAPAN

Country Market Profiles—Japan contains statistics on exports, information on some seven industries with export potential to Japan, developments in bilateral trade, and much more. This book is available from the Office of Japan, U.S. Department of Commerce, Washington, DC 20030.

Directory of Japanese Technical Resources in the United States provides information to assist U.S. business and industry to take full advantage of technical information emanating from Japan. Included are: translations of Japanese technical documents, commercial services which collect, abstract, translate and disseminate Japanese technical information, U.S. Government agencies, programs, or services involving Japanese technical information, libraries with extensive Japanese holdings, a comparison of technology transfer infrastructures that exist in the U.S. and Japan, and a private sector view on how the Government can work with industry to make Japanese scientific and technical information assessible in the United States. Available from: U.S. Department Commerce, National Technical Information Service, Springfield, VA 22161. Telephone: 703–487–4650.

How to Find Information about Japanese Companies and Industries is an extensive guide to information sources both here and abroad helpful for doing business with Japan. Available from Washington Researchers Publishing, 2612 P Street NW, Washington, DC 20007.

Industrial Grouping in Japan, a guide to the Japanese industrial environment, surveys over 3000 leading companies. Includes information on: major product lines, annual sales, sources of loans, number of employees and degrees of affiliation with their respective groups. This publication also explains origins, structures, and methods of functioning of various groups, together with recent developments. Available from Taylor & Francis, 242 Cherry Street, Philadelphia, PA 19106.

The Overseas Business Report *Marketing in Japan* (DBR 87-02) contains an extensive list of publications on trading with Japan, general economic and business information, and

company-specific information. Included are publications from JETRO, MIPRO and JEI as well as some from the U.S. Department of Commerce. Copies of the report are available from the Superintendent of Documents, U.S. Government Printing Office, Washington, DC and the Publications Sales Branch, Room 1017 U.S. Department of Commerce.

THE PEOPLE'S REPUBLIC OF CHINA (PRC)

For information or advice on contacting the Chinese on commercial matters, call or write to:

U.S. Department of Commerce
International Trade Administration Office
   of PRC and Hong Kong
Washington, DC 20230
Telephone: 202–377–3583/4681

Commercial Office
Embassy of the People's Republic of China
2300 Connecticut Avenue, N.W.
Washington, DC 20008

For free publications on trade with China call 202–328–2520.

Doing Business with China, prepared by the International Trade Administration (Department of Commerce) is available from the:

Superintendent of Documents
Government Printing Office
Washington, D.C. 20402

U.S.-CHINA BUSINESS COUNCIL

Address: 1818 N Street NW, Suite 500. Washington, DC 20220. Phone: 202–429–0340.

The Council, a nonprofit, private organization maintaining close liaison with the U.S. government, serves as a forum for the discussion of trade policy and issues. It also serves as a focal point for business contact and the dissemination of information on marketing in the PRC. The council maintains a business counseling service; it also publishes the *China Business Review* bimonthly. The council facilitates the reciprocal arrangements of trade missions and trade exhibitions in the United States and China.

USSR AND EASTERN EUROPE*

USSR

USSR Affairs Division, International Economic Policy (202–377–4655). This divi-

---

* Source: Excerpted from Department of Commerce Overseas Reports, "Trading with the USSR" and other Department of Commerce sources.

sion collects, analyzes, and disseminates current information on economic, commercial, and other developments in the USSR and estimates their impact on the U.S. business community. The division develops policy guidance in our commercial relationship with the Soviet Union and provides staff support to and representation on the Joint Commercial Commission. It also maintains close contact with the U.S. Commercial Office in Moscow and with USSR commercial officials in the United States in order to initiate and pursue official representations on behalf of the American business community.

Within the U.S. Department of Commerce there are several helpful sources. Among them are:

U.S.S.R. Division: 202–377–4655
Export Administration: 202–377–5497
Export Counseling Center: 202–377–3181

It may be to the company's advantage to touch base with the following USSR commercial organizations in the United States to try to obtain some indication of Soviet interest and to identify contacts in the Soviet Union:

The Trade Representation of the USSR in the U.S.A., 2001 Connecticut Avenue NW, Washington, DC 20008, telephone: 202–232–0975.

The Amtorg Trading Corporation, 1755 Broadway, New York, NY 10019, telephone: 212–956–3010.

Belarus Machinery Inc., 115 East 57 Street, New York, NY 10022, telephone: 212–751–8550.

The staffs of both Amtorg and the Trade Representation include representatives of individual foreign trade organizations (FTOs).

The USSR Consulate General, 2790 Green Street, San Francisco, CA 94123, telephone: 415–922–6642, may have information conveniently available for companies on the West Coast.

U.S.-U.S.S.R. Trade and Economic Council, 805 Third Avenue, New York, NY 10022, telephone: 212–644–4550.

For a list of U.S. business representatives, consultants and trading companies doing business with the U.S.S.R. call 202–377–4655.

EASTERN EUROPE

Commercial transactions with Bulgaria, Czechoslovakia, East Germany, Hungary, Poland, and Romania are similar to those with the USSR. Contracts are negotiated with the appropriate Foreign Trade Organization. For detailed information about trade shows, missions, export licenses, and FTOs, contact the Office of East-West Trade, Department of Commerce in Washington, or the Commerce Department Offices at the district level. Another key source of information is the Eastern Europe Business Information Center (see below).

The Eastern Europe Business Information Center (EEBIC) Room H-6043, U.S. Department of Commerce, Washington, DC 20230. Telephone: 202–377–2645

The Center works with U.S. Government agencies such as the Agency for International Development, the Overseas Private Investment Corporation, the U.S. Trade and Development Program, and the Export-Import Bank.

EEBIC serves as a clearinghouse for information on business conditions in Poland, Hungary, Czechoslovakia, the German Democratic Republic, Romania, Bulgaria, Yugoslavia, and Albania, and on emerging trade and investment opportunities in those countries. It also serves as a source of information on U.S. Government programs supporting private enterprise, trade and investment in Eastern Europe.

A variety of printed materials is available directly from EEBIC, as are directories of data available from other sources. EEBIC information includes publications on export procedures, investment regulations and incentives, industry sectors of prime interest, seminars and conferences, trade promotion events, and information on the programs of other organizations, both in the United States and in Eastern Europe.

BULGARIA

Bulgarian Embassy
1621 22nd Street NW
Washington, DC 20009

Bulgarian Commercial Office
121 E. 62nd Street
New York, NY 10021

CZECHOSLOVAKIA

Czechoslovakian Embassy
3900 Linnean Avenue NW
Washington, DC 20008

Office of the Czechoslovakian Commercial Counselor
292 Madison Avenue
New York, NY 10016

EAST GERMANY
(German Democratic Republic)

Embassy of the German Democratic Republic
1717 Massachusetts Avenue NW
Washington, DC 20036

German Democratic Republic
Commercial Counselor

Commercial Section Branch
820 2nd Avenue
New York, NY 10017
German American Chamber of Commerce
666 Fifth Avenue
New York, NY 10009

HUNGARY

Embassy of Hungary to the United States
3910 Shoemaker Street NW
Washington, DC 20009

Office of the Commercial Counselor of the
Embassy of Hungary
2401 Calvert Street
Washington, DC 20008

Commercial Counselor
Embassy of Hungary
150 East 58 Street
New York, NY 10022

POLAND

Commercial Counselor
Embassy of Poland
2224 Wyoming Avenue, NW
Washington, DC 20008

Polish-U.S. Economic Council
% U.S. Chamber of Commerce
East-West Trade
1615 H Street, NW
Washington, DC 20062

Polish Commercial Counselor's Office
820 2nd Avenue
New York, NY 10009

Polish Chamber of Foreign Trade
44 Montgomery Street
San Francisco, CA 94104

ROMANIA

Romanian Embassy
1607 23rd Street NW
Washington, DC 20008

Romanian Mission to the U.N.
202 E. 38th Street
New York, NY 10016

Economic Counselor
Romanian Commercial Office
573 Third Avenue
New York, NY 10016

NEAR EAST AND NORTH AFRICA*

The Office of the Near East (Telephone:
202–377–4441) within the International Trade
Administration serves as the focal point for
the U.S. Department of Commerce response
to the changing economic situation and signif

icant business opportunities in the Near East
and North Africa. The group assembles, analyzes, and disseminates to the U.S. business
community information on economic conditions and new opportunities in the area, provides counseling for and makes representations on behalf of U.S. exporters, and plans
promotional programs to assist U.S. firms to
take advantage of the expanded commercial
potential.

For information on major projects call
202–377–4332.

ALGERIA

Embassy of Algeria
2118 Kalorama Road NW
Washington, DC 20008

BAHRAIN

Embassy of Bahrain
3502 International Drive NW
Washington, DC 20008

ARAB REPUBLIC OF EGYPT

Embassy of the Arab Republic of Egypt
2310 Decatur Place NW
Washington, DC 20008

Commercial and Economic Office
2232 Connecticut Avenue NW
Washington, DC 20008

Egypt American Chamber of Commerce
1 World Trade Center
New York, NY 10017

Permanent Economic Mission to the U.N.
36 East 67 Street
New York, NY 1010

Consulate of the Arab Republic of Egypt
1110 Second Avenue
New York, NY 10022

Consulate of the Arab Republic of Egypt
3001 Pacific Avenue
San Francisco, CA 94115

IRAQ

Embassy of Iraq
1801 P Street NW
Washington, DC 20036

ISRAEL

Embassy of Israel
3514 International Drive NW
Washington, DC 20008

Israel Consulate General
800 2nd Avenue
New York, NY 10009

Consulates are also located in Atlanta, Boston, Chicago, Houston, Los Angeles,
Philadelphia, and San Francisco

---

* Source: *A Business Guide to the Near East & North
Africa*, International Trade Administration, U.S. Department of Commerce.

Investment Authority
350 Fifth Avenue
New York, NY 10001

Israel Trade Center
174 N. Michigan Avenue
Chicago, IL 60601

Israel Trade Center
350 Fifth Avenue
New York, NY 10001

Israel Supply Mission
350 Fifth Avenue
New York, NY 10001

6380 Wilshire Boulevard
Los Angeles, CA 90048

JORDAN (HASHEMITE KINGDOM OF)

Embassy of Jordan
3504 International Drive, NW
Washington, DC 20008

Jordanian Mission to the U.N.
866 U.N. Plaza
New York, NY 10017

STATE OF KUWAIT

Embassy of Kuwait
2940 Tilden Street NW
Washington, DC 20008

LEBANON

Embassy of Lebanon
2560 28th Street NW
Washington, DC 20008

Consulate General
9 E. 76th Street
New York, NY 10021

Consulate General
1300 Lafayette East
Detroit, Michigan 48207

MOROCCO

Embassy of Morocco
1601 21st Street NW
Washington, DC 20009

Consulate General
437 Fifth Avenue
New York, NY 10016

OMAN

Embassy of the Sultanate of Oman
2342 Massachusetts Avenue NW
Washington, DC 20008

QATAR

Embassy of Qatar
600 New Hampshire Avenue NW
Washington, DC 20037

SAUDI ARABIA

Saudi Arabian Embassy
601 New Hampshire Avenue NW
Washington, DC 20037

Consulate General
866 United Nations Plaza
New York, NY 10017

Consulate
5433 West Heimer
Houston, Texas 77056

SYRIAN ARAB REPUBLIC

Embassy of the Syrian Arab Republic
2215 Wyoming Avenue NW
Washington, DC 20008

TUNISIA

Embassy of Tunisia
1515 Massachusetts Avenue NW
Washington, DC 20005

UNITED ARAB EMIRATES

Embassy of the United Arab Emirates
600 New Hampshire Avenue, NW
Washington, DC 20037

YEMEN ARAB REPUBLIC

Embassy of the Yemen Arab Republic
600 New Hampshire Avenue, NW
Washington, DC 20037

FAST MATCH

A quick, easy way to match your international business requirements to the appropriate Government programs or services designed to satisfy those needs

IF YOU ARE SEEKING
INFORMATION REGARDING ➡

USE ⬇

	Potential Markets	Market Research*	Direct Sales Leads	Agents/Distributors	Licenses	Credit Analysis	Financial Assistance	Risk Insurance	Tax Incentives
Foreign Trade Statistics (FT-410)	•								
Global Market Surveys	•	•							
Foreign Market Reports	•	•							
Market Share Reports	•	•							
Foreign Economic Trends	•	•							
Business America	•	•	•	•	•				
Commercial Exhibitions	**	**	•	•	•				
Overseas Business Reports (OBR)		•							
Overseas Private Investment Corp.		•					•	•	
Commerce Business Daily			•						
New Product Information Service			•	•	•				
Trade Opportunity Program (TOP)			•	•	•				
Industry Trade Lists			•	•	•				
Special Trade Lists			•	•	•				
Export Mailing List Service (EMLS)			•	•	•				
Agent/Distributor Service (ADS)				•					
World Traders Data Reports (WTDR)						•			
Export—Import Bank							•	•	
Foreign Credit Insurance Assoc. (FCIA)								•	
Domestic Int'l. Sales Corp. (DISC)							•		•

* Foreign Trade Outlook Market Profiles; Industry Trends; Distribution and Sales Channels; Transportation Facilities; Local Business Practices and Customs; Investment Criteria; Import Procedures and Trade Regulations; and Industrial Property Rights.

** Research material developed regarding a planned exhibition and released to support promotional activities.

Cost of services may be obtained from Commerce District Offices.

Source: Industry and Trade Administration, U.S. Department of Commerce.

Index